ies NATIONAL CENTER FOR
EDUCATION STATISTICS

Institute of Education Sciences

U.S. Department of Education
NCES 2007-017

Digest of Education Statistics 2006

July 2007

Thomas D. Snyder
National Center for
Education Statistics

Sally A. Dillow
Education Statistics
Services Institute—
American Institutes
for Research

Charlene M. Hoffman
Consultant

U.S. Department of Education
Margaret Spellings
Secretary

Institute of Education Sciences
Grover J. Whitehurst
Director

National Center for Education Statistics
Mark Schneider
Commissioner

The National Center for Education Statistics (NCES) is the primary federal entity for collecting, analyzing, and reporting data related to education in the United States and other nations. It fulfills a congressional mandate to collect, collate, analyze, and report full and complete statistics on the condition of education in the United States; conduct and publish reports and specialized analyses of the meaning and significance of such statistics; assist state and local education agencies in improving their statistical systems; and review and report on education activities in foreign countries.

NCES activities are designed to address high-priority education data needs; provide consistent, reliable, complete, and accurate indicators of education status and trends; and report timely, useful, and high-quality data to the U.S. Department of Education, the Congress, the states, other education policymakers, practitioners, data users, and the general public. Unless specifically noted, all information contained herein is in the public domain.

We strive to make our products available in a variety of formats and in language that is appropriate to a variety of audiences. You, as our customer, are the best judge of our success in communicating information effectively. If you have any comments or suggestions about this or any other NCES product or report, we would like to hear from you. Please direct your comments to

National Center for Education Statistics
Institute of Education Sciences
U.S. Department of Education
1990 K Street NW
Washington, DC 20006-5651

July 2007

The NCES World Wide Web Home Page address is http://nces.ed.gov.
The NCES World Wide Web Electronic Catalog is http://nces.ed.gov/pubsearch.

Suggested Citation

Snyder, T.D., Dillow, S.A., and Hoffman, C.M. (2007). *Digest of Education Statistics 2006* (NCES 2007-017). National Center for Education Statistics, Institute of Education Sciences, U.S. Department of Education. Washington, DC: U.S. Government Printing Office.

For ordering information on this report, write to

U.S. Department of Education
ED Pubs
P.O. Box 1398
Jessup, MD 20794-1398

Call toll free 1-877-4ED-Pubs or order online at http://www.edpubs.org.

Content Contact

Thomas D. Snyder
(202) 502-7452
tom.snyder@ed.gov

For sale by the Superintendent of Documents, U.S. Government Printing Office
Internet: bookstore.gpo.gov   Phone: toll free (866) 512-1800;   DC area (202) 512-1800
Fax: (202) 512-2104 Mail: Stop IDCC, Washington, DC 20402-0001

ISBN 978-0-16-079181-9

FOREWORD

The 2006 edition of the *Digest of Education Statistics* is the 42nd in a series of publications initiated in 1962. The *Digest* has been issued annually except for combined editions for the years 1977–78, 1983–84, and 1985–86. Its primary purpose is to provide a compilation of statistical information covering the broad field of American education from prekindergarten through graduate school. The *Digest* includes a selection of data from many sources, both government and private, and draws especially on the results of surveys and activities carried out by the National Center for Education Statistics (NCES). To qualify for inclusion in the *Digest*, material must be nationwide in scope and of current interest and value. The publication contains information on a variety of subjects in the field of education statistics, including the number of schools and colleges, teachers, enrollments, and graduates, in addition to educational attainment, finances, federal funds for education, libraries, and international comparisons. Supplemental information on population trends, attitudes on education, education characteristics of the labor force, government finances, and economic trends provides background for evaluating education data. Although the *Digest* contains important information on federal education funding, more detailed information on federal activities is available from federal education program offices.

The *Digest* contains seven chapters: All Levels of Education, Elementary and Secondary Education, Postsecondary Education, Federal Programs for Education and Related Activities, Outcomes of Education, International Comparisons of Education, and Libraries and Educational Technology. Preceding these chapters is an Introduction that provides a brief overview of current trends in American education, which supplements the tabular materials in chapters 1 through 7. The *Digest* concludes with three appendixes. The first appendix, Guide to Sources, provides a brief synopsis of the surveys used to generate the *Digest* tables; the second, Definitions, is included to help readers understand terms used in the *Digest*; and the third, Index of Table Numbers, allows readers to quickly locate tables on specific topics.

In addition to updating many of the statistics that have appeared in previous years, this edition contains new material, including

- average base salary for full-time public elementary and secondary school teachers with a bachelor's degree as their highest degree, by years of full-time teaching experience and state (table 73);
- average base salary for full-time public elementary and secondary school teachers with a master's degree as their highest degree, by years of full-time teaching experience and state (table 74);
- averaged freshman graduation rates for public secondary schools, by state (table 101);
- average reading scale scores of 4th- and 8th-graders, by selected student and parent characteristics and school type (table 116);
- average mathematics scale scores of 4th-, 8th-, and 12th-graders, by selected student and parent characteristics and school type (table 127);
- average science scale scores and achievement-level results of 4th-, 8th-, and 12th-graders, by selected student characteristics and percentile (table 128);
- number and percentage of students expelled and suspended from public elementary and secondary schools, by sex, race/ethnicity, and state (tables 148 and 149);
- bachelor's, master's, and doctor's degrees conferred by degree-granting institutions, by field of study (table 257); and
- current postsecondary education and employment status, wages earned, and living arrangements of special education students out of secondary school up to 4 years, by type of disability (table 383).

Updates to tables from the next *Digest of Education Statistics* will appear on the NCES website prior to printing the full edition. The *Digest* can be accessed from http://nces.ed.gov/programs/digest.

Val Plisko
Associate Commissioner
Early Childhood, International, and Crosscutting Studies Division

ACKNOWLEDGMENTS

Many people have contributed in one way or another to the development of the *Digest of Education Statistics 2006*. Thomas D. Snyder was responsible for the overall development and preparation of this edition of the *Digest*, which was prepared under the general direction of Valena Plisko. William Sonnenberg provided statistical computing consultation.

Much of the work for this report was performed by staff of the Education Statistics Services Institute (ESSI), which is funded by NCES and composed of staff from the American Institutes for Research (AIR) and a number of partner organizations. Numerous ESSI staff contributed to this work, which was performed under the management of AIR project leader Sally Dillow. Mary Ann Fox of AIR served as overall manager for ESSI annual reports work, which includes the *Digest* project, and provided statistical consultation and programming support. Also at AIR, Richa Arora played a key role in coordinating the updating and formatting of the *Digest* tables, with other key players in these tasks including Sanyu Kibuka, Charmaine Llagas, and Mary Jo Metzler. Kevin Bianco and Lauren Drake of MacroSys Research and Technology also worked on updating and formatting the tables. Charlene Hoffman, a consultant, did most of the work on chapter 4 as well as the tables on degrees conferred. At AIR, Tom Nachazel, Robin Gurley, and Martin Hahn provided proofreading and editorial support, while Rachel Dinkes, Beth Jacinto, and Jill Walston contributed programming support. Sze-Wei Tang of Quality Information Partners also supplied programming support. At MacroSys Research and Technology, Qingshu Xie provided program-

ming support and Michael Stock desktopped the volume under the supervision of Kalle Culotta. Outside of ESSI, others who provided data for this edition of the *Digest* included Mary Bowler of the Bureau of Labor Statistics, Alison Kennedy of UNESCO Institute for Statistics, and Lynn Newman of SRI International.

This year's edition of the *Digest* has received extensive reviews by many individuals within and outside the U.S. Department of Education. We wish to thank them for their time and expert advice. Marilyn Seastrom, Chief Statistician of the National Center for Education Statistics (NCES), supervised the review of the publication. Duc-Le To of the Institute of Education Sciences reviewed the publication. NCES staff who reviewed portions of the manuscript were Julia Bloom, Stephen Broughman, Kathryn Chandler, Chris Chapman, Steve Gorman, Bernard Greene, Kerry Gruber, Lee Hoffman, Barbara Holton, Frank Johnson, Frank Morgan, Larry Ogle, Jeffrey Owings, Peggy Quinn, Quansheng Shen, Cathy Statham, Bruce Taylor, and John Wirt. Stacey Bielick, Frank Avenilla, and Greg Kienzl of AIR also reviewed the manuscript, as did Sarah Grady of MacroSys Research and Technology. The ESSI technical review team included staff of AIR (Kevin Bromer, Dan McGrath, Stephen Mistler, Alison Slade, Robert Stillwell, Aparna Sundaram, Jed Tank, and Zeyu Xu); Child Trends (Akemi Kinukawa and Siri Warkentien); MacroSys Research and Technology (Matt Adams and Stephen Hocker); the National Institute of Statistical Sciences (Xiaolei Wang); and Quality Information Partners (Alexandra Henning).

Contents

Page

Foreword iii

Acknowledgments v

List of Figures viii

List of Tables ix

Introduction 1

Guide to Tabular Presentation 5

Chapter 1. All Levels of Education 7

Chapter 2. Elementary and Secondary Education 53

Chapter 3. Postsecondary Education 261

Chapter 4. Federal Programs for Education and Related Activities 523

Chapter 5. Outcomes of Education 555

Chapter 6. International Comparisons of Education 579

Chapter 7. Libraries and Educational Technology 613

Appendixes

    A. Guide to Sources 633

    B. Definitions 671

    C. Index of Table Numbers 685

List of Figures

Figure   **Page**

1. The structure of education in the United States   9

2. Enrollment, total expenditures in constant dollars, and expenditures as a percentage of the gross domestic product (GDP), by level of education: 1960–61 through 2004–05   10

3. Percentage of persons 25 years old and over, by highest level of educational attainment: 1940 through 2006   11

4. Percentage of persons 25 through 29 years old, by highest level of educational attainment: 1940 through 2006   11

5. Highest level of education attained by persons 25 years old and over: March 2006   12

6. Enrollment, number of teachers, pupil/teacher ratio, and expenditures in public schools: 1960–61 through 2004–05   57

7. Total and full-day preprimary enrollment of 3- to 5-year-olds: October 1970 through October 2005 . .   58

8. Percentage change in public elementary and secondary enrollment, by state: Fall 1999 to fall 2004 . .   58

9. Percentage of revenue for public elementary and secondary schools, by source of funds: 1970–71 through 2003–04   59

10. Current expenditure per pupil in fall enrollment in public elementary and secondary schools: 1970–71 through 2003–04   59

11. Enrollment, degrees conferred, and expenditures in degree-granting institutions: 1960–61 through 2004–05   264

12. Percentage change in total enrollment in degree-granting institutions, by state: Fall 2000 through fall 2005   265

13. Enrollment in degree-granting institutions, by age: Fall 1970 through fall 2015   265

14. Full-time-equivalent (FTE) students per staff member in public and private degree-granting institutions: 1976 and 2005   266

15. Trends in bachelor's degrees conferred by degree-granting institutions in selected fields of study: 1994–95, 1999–2000, and 2004–05   266

16. Sources of total revenue of public degree-granting institutions: 2003–04   267

17. Sources of total revenue of private not-for-profit degree-granting institutions: 2003–04   267

18. Federal on-budget funds for education, by level or other educational purpose: Selected years, 1965 through 2006   531

19. Percentage of federal on-budget funds for education, by agency: Fiscal year 2006   531

20. Department of Education outlays, by type of recipient: Fiscal year 2006   532

21. Labor force participation rate of persons 20 to 64 years old, by age group and highest level of education: 2005   556

22. Unemployment rates of persons 25 years old and over, by highest level of education: 2005   557

23. Labor force status of 2004–05 high school dropouts and completers not enrolled in college: October 2005   557

24. Median annual income of persons 25 years old and over, by highest level of education and sex: 2005   558

25. Salaries of recent bachelor's degree recipients 1 year after graduation, by field: 1991, 1994, and 2001   558

26. Percentage change in enrollment, by selected areas of the world and level of education: 1990 to 2004   581

27. Bachelor's degree recipients as a percentage of the population of the typical ages of graduation, by country: 2004   581

28. Public direct expenditures for education as a percentage of the gross domestic product (GDP), by country: 2003   582

29. Percentage of all public schools and instructional rooms with internet access: Fall 1994 through fall 2003   614

List of Tables

Chapter 1. All Levels of Education

Enrollment, Teachers, and Schools

Table   **Page**

1. Projected number of participants in educational institutions, by level and control of institution: Fall 2006 13

2. Enrollment in educational institutions, by level and control of institution: Selected years, fall 1980 through fall 2006 13

3. Enrollment in educational institutions, by level and control of institution: Selected years, 1869–70 through fall 2015 14

4. Number of teachers in elementary and secondary schools, and instructional staff in postsecondary degree-granting institutions, by control of institution: Selected years, fall 1970 through fall 2015 . 16

5. Number of educational institutions, by level and control of institution: Selected years, 1980–81 through 2004–05 17

Enrollment Rates

6. Percentage of the population 3 to 34 years old enrolled in school, by sex, race/ethnicity, and age: Selected years, 1980 through 2005 18

7. Percentage of the population 3 to 34 years old enrolled in school, by age group: Selected years, 1940 through 2005 20

Educational Attainment

8. Percentage of persons age 25 and over and 25 to 29, by race/ethnicity, years of school completed, and sex: Selected years, 1910 through 2006 22

9. Number of persons age 18 and over, by highest level of education attained, age, sex, and race/ ethnicity: 2006 24

10. Persons age 18 and over who hold at least a bachelor's degree in specific fields of study, by sex, race/ethnicity, and age: 2001 25

11. Educational attainment of persons 18 years old and over, by state: 2000 and 2005 26

12. Educational attainment of persons 25 years old and over, by race/ethnicity and state: April 1990 and April 2000 27

13. Educational attainment of persons 25 years old and over for the 25 largest states, by sex: 2004 . . 29

14. Educational attainment of persons 25 years old and over for the 15 largest metropolitan areas, by sex: 2002 29

Population

15. Estimates of resident population, by age group: 1970 through 2005 30

16. Estimates of resident population, by race/ethnicity and age group: Selected years, 1980 through 2005 31

17. Estimated total and school-age resident populations, by state: Selected years, 1970 through 2005   32

Characteristics of Families With Children

18. Number and percentage of families, by family status and presence of own children under 18: Selected years, 1970 through 2005 33

19. Characteristics of families with own children under 18, by race/ethnicity and family structure: 2005   34

20. Household income and poverty rates, by state: 1990, 2000, and 2003–2005 35

21. Poverty status of persons, families, and children under age 18, by race/ethnicity: Selected years, 1959 through 2005 37

Opinions on Education

22. Average grade that the public would give the public schools in their community and in the nation at large: 1974 through 2006   40

23. Percentage of elementary and secondary school children whose parents were involved in school activities, by selected child, parent, and school characteristics: 1999 and 2003   41

24. Percentage of kindergartners through fifth-graders whose parents were involved in education-related activities, by selected child, parent, and school characteristics: 1999 and 2003   42

Finances

25. Expenditures of educational institutions related to the gross domestic product, by level of institution: Selected years, 1929–30 through 2005–06   43

26. Expenditures of educational institutions, by level and control of institution: Selected years, 1899–1900 through 2005–06   44

27. Governmental expenditures, by level of government and function: Selected years, 1970–71 through 2003–04   46

28. Direct general expenditures of state and local governments for all functions and for education, by level of education and state: 2003–04   47

29. Direct general expenditures per capita of state and local governments for all functions and for education, by level of education and state: 2003–04   48

30. Gross domestic product, state and local expenditures, personal income, disposable personal income, median family income, and population: Selected years, 1929 through 2005   49

31. Gross domestic product price index, Consumer Price Index, education price indexes, and federal budget composite deflator: Selected years, 1919 to 2005   51

Chapter 2. Elementary and Secondary Education

Enrollment

32. Historical summary of public elementary and secondary school statistics: Selected years, 1869–70 through 2003–04   60

33. Enrollment in public elementary and secondary schools, by state or jurisdiction: Fall 1990 through fall 2006   62

34. Enrollment in public elementary and secondary schools, by level, grade, and state or jurisdiction: Fall 2004   64

35. Enrollment in public elementary and secondary schools, by level, grade, and state or jurisdiction: Fall 2003   66

36. Enrollment in public elementary and secondary schools, by grade: Fall 1990 through fall 2004 . . .   68

37. Number and percentage of homeschooled students ages 5 through 17 with a grade equivalent of kindergarten through 12th grade, by selected child, parent, and household characteristics: 1999 and 2003   69

38. Percentage distribution of all students, homeschooled students, and nonhomeschooled students, ages 5 through 17 with a grade equivalent of kindergarten through 12th grade, by selected child, parent, and household characteristics: 1999 and 2003   70

39. Average daily attendance in public elementary and secondary schools, by state or jurisdiction: Selected years, 1969–70 through 2003–04   71

40. Percentage distribution of enrollment in public elementary and secondary schools, by race/ethnicity and state or jurisdiction: Fall 1994 and fall 2004   72

41. Enrollment of 3-, 4-, and 5-year-old children in preprimary programs, by level of program, control of program, and attendance status: Selected years, 1965 through 2005   74

42. Number of preschool children under 6 years old, percentage in center-based programs, average hours in nonparental care, and percentage in various types of primary care arrangements, by selected child and family characteristics: 2005   75

43. Child care arrangements of 3- to 5-year-old children who are not yet in kindergarten, by age and race/ethnicity: Various years, 1991 through 2005   77

44. Children of prekindergarten through second-grade age, by enrollment status, selected maternal characteristics, and household income: 1995, 2001, and 2005.   78

45. Percentage of 3- to 5-year-olds not yet enrolled in kindergarten who have participated in home literacy activities with a family member, by type of activity and selected child and family characteristics: 1993, 2001, and 2005.   79

46. Percentage distribution of first-time kindergartners, by number of children's books in the home, and number of times each week family members read books to them, by selected child and maternal characteristics: Fall 1998   80

47. Percentage distribution of kindergarten teachers and parents indicating the importance of various factors for kindergarten readiness, by control: Fall 1998   80

48. Children 3 to 21 years old served in federally supported programs for the disabled, by type of disability: Selected years, 1976–77 through 2005–06   81

49. Percentage distribution of students with disabilities 6 to 21 years old receiving education services for the disabled, by educational environment and type of disability: Selected years, fall 1989 through fall 2005   82

50. Number and percentage of children served under Individuals with Disabilities Education Act, Part B, by age group and state or jurisdiction: Selected years, 1990–91 through 2005–06   83

51. Number and percentage of gifted and talented students in public elementary and secondary schools, by sex, race/ethnicity, and state: 2002.   85

52. Enrollment in grades 9 through 12 in public and private schools compared with population 14 to 17 years of age: Selected years, 1889–90 through fall 2006   87

53. Enrollment in foreign language courses compared with enrollment in grades 9 through 12 in public secondary schools: Selected years, fall 1948 through fall 2000   88

54. Number and percentage of schools with students enrolled in distance education courses and enrollment in distance education courses, by instructional level and district characteristics: 2002–03.   89

Private Elementary and Secondary Schools

55. Private elementary and secondary enrollment, teachers, and schools, by orientation of school and selected school characteristics: Fall 2003   90

56. Private elementary and secondary enrollment, number of schools, and average tuition, by school level, orientation, and tuition: 1999–2000 and 2003–04   91

57. Private elementary and secondary school full-time-equivalent staff and student to full-time-equivalent staff ratios, by orientation of school, school level, and type of staff: 2003–04   92

58. Enrollment and instructional staff in Catholic elementary and secondary schools, by level: Selected years, 1919–20 through 2005–06   94

59. Private elementary and secondary schools, enrollment, teachers, and high school graduates, by state: Selected years, 1997 through 2003   95

Teachers and Other Staff

60. Public elementary and secondary pupil/teacher ratios, by enrollment size, type, and level of school: Fall 1987 through fall 2004.   96

61. Public and private elementary and secondary teachers, enrollment, and pupil/teacher ratios: Selected years, fall 1955 through fall 2015   97

62. Public elementary and secondary teachers, by level and state or jurisdiction: Fall 1999 through fall 2004.   98

63. Teachers, enrollment, and pupil/teacher ratios in public elementary and secondary schools, by state or jurisdiction: Fall 1999 through fall 2004.   99

64. Highest degree earned, years of full-time teaching experience, and average class size for teachers in public elementary and secondary schools, by state: 2003–04.   100

65. Highest degree earned and years of full-time teaching experience for teachers in public and private elementary and secondary schools, by selected teacher characteristics: 1999–2000 and 2003–04.. 101

66. Selected characteristics of public school teachers: Selected years, spring 1961 through spring 2001.. 103

67. Percentage of public school teachers of grades 9 through 12, by field of main teaching assignment and selected demographic and educational characteristics: 2003–04..................... 104

68. Teachers' perceptions about serious problems in their schools, by control and level of school: 1993–94, 1999–2000, and 2003–04.. 106

69. Teachers' perceptions about teaching and school conditions, by control and level of school: 1993–94, 1999–2000, and 2003–04.. 107

70. Mobility of public and private elementary and secondary teachers, by selected teacher and school characteristics: Selected years, 1987–88 through 2000–01............................. 108

71. Average base salary for full-time teachers in public elementary and secondary schools, by highest degree earned and years of full-time teaching: Selected years, 1990–91 through 2003–04..... 109

72. Average salaries for full-time teachers in public and private elementary and secondary schools, by selected characteristics: 2003–04.. 111

73. Average base salary for full-time public elementary and secondary school teachers with a bachelor's degree as their highest degree, by years of full-time teaching experience and state: 1993–94, 1999–2000, and 2003–04... 113

74. Average base salary for full-time public elementary and secondary school teachers with a master's degree as their highest degree, by years of full-time teaching experience and state: 1993–94, 1999–2000, and 2003–04... 114

75. Estimated average annual salary of teachers in public elementary and secondary schools: Selected years, 1959–60 through 2004–05... 115

76. Estimated average annual salary of teachers in public elementary and secondary schools, by state or jurisdiction: Selected years, 1969–70 through 2004–05............................. 116

77. Staff employed in public elementary and secondary school systems, by functional area: Selected years, 1949–50 through fall 2004.. 117

78. Staff employed in public elementary and secondary school systems, by type of assignment and state or jurisdiction: Fall 2004.. 118

79. Staff employed in public elementary and secondary school systems, by type of assignment and state or jurisdiction: Fall 2003.. 119

80. Staff and teachers in public elementary and secondary school systems, by state or jurisdiction: Fall 1998 through fall 2004... 120

81. Staff, enrollment, and pupil/staff ratios in public elementary and secondary school systems, by state or jurisdiction: Fall 1997 through fall 2004.. 121

82. Principals in public and private elementary and secondary schools, by selected characteristics: 1993–94, 1999–2000, and 2003–04... 122

Schools and School Districts

83. Number of public school districts and public and private elementary and secondary schools: Selected years, 1869–70 through 2004–05.. 123

84. Number of regular public school districts, by enrollment size of district: Selected years, 1990–91 through 2004–05... 124

85. Number of public elementary and secondary education agencies, by type of agency and state or jurisdiction: 2003–04 and 2004–05... 125

86. Public elementary and secondary students, schools, pupil/teacher ratios, and finances, by type of locale: 2003–04 and 2004–05.. 126

87. Selected statistics on enrollment, teachers, dropouts, and graduates in public school districts enrolling more than 15,000 students, by state: 1990, 2000, 2001–02, 2003–04, and 2004 128

88. Revenues, expenditures, poverty rate, and Title I allocations of public school districts enrolling more than 15,000 students, by state: 2003–04 and fiscal year 2006..................... 139

89. Enrollment, poverty, and federal funds for the 100 largest school districts, by enrollment size: 2003–04 and fiscal year 2006 150

90. Public elementary and secondary schools, by type of school: Selected years, 1967–68 through 2004–05 152

91. Number and percentage distribution of public elementary and secondary schools and enrollment, by type and enrollment size of school: 2004–05 153

92. Average enrollment and percentage distribution of public elementary and secondary schools, by type and size: Selected years, 1982–83 through 2004–05 154

93. Public elementary and secondary school students, by racial/ethnic enrollment concentration of school: Fall 1999 and fall 2004 155

94. Public elementary and secondary schools, by type and state or jurisdiction: 1990–91, 2000–01, and 2004–05 156

95. Public elementary schools, by grade span, average school size, and state or jurisdiction: 2004–05 157

96. Public secondary schools, by grade span, average school size, and state or jurisdiction: 2004–05 158

97. Number and enrollment of traditional public and public charter elementary and secondary schools and percentages of students, teachers, and schools, by selected characteristics: 2003–04 159

98. Percentage of public schools with building deficiencies and renovation plans, by level, enrollment size, metropolitan status, and free lunch eligibility: 1999 161

High School Completers and Dropouts

99. High school graduates, by sex and control of school: Selected years, 1869–70 through 2006–07 . 163

100. Public high school graduates, by state or jurisdiction: Selected years, 1980–81 through 2004–05. 164

101. Averaged freshman graduation rates for public secondary schools, by state: 1990–91 through 2003–04 165

102. Public high school graduates and dropouts, by race/ethnicity and state or jurisdiction: 2001–02 and 2003–04 166

103. General Educational Development (GED) test takers and credentials issued, by age: 1971 through 2004 167

104. Percentage of high school dropouts (status dropouts) among persons 16 through 24 years old, by sex and race/ethnicity: Selected years, 1960 through 2005 168

105. Percentage of high school dropouts (status dropouts) among persons 16 through 24 years old, by income level, and percentage distribution of dropouts, by labor force status and educational attainment: 1970 through 2005 169

106. Number of students with disabilities exiting special education, by basis of exit, age, and type of disability: United States and other jurisdictions, 2003–04 and 2004–05 170

Educational Achievement

107. Percentage of young children born in 2001 demonstrating specific cognitive and motor skills, by child's age at assessment: 2001 through 2003 171

108. Mean reading scale scores and specific reading skills of fall 1998 first-time kindergartners, by time of assessment and selected characteristics: Selected years, fall 1998 through spring 2004 172

109. Mean mathematics and science scale scores and specific mathematics skills of fall 1998 first-time kindergartners, by time of assessment and selected characteristics: Selected years, fall 1998 through spring 2004 173

110. Average reading scale score, by age and selected student and school characteristics: Selected years, 1971 through 2004 174

111. Student scale score in reading, by age and percentile: Selected years, 1971 through 2004...... 176

112. Average reading scale score, by age and amount of time spent on reading and homework: Selected years, 1984 through 2004 177

113. Percentage of students at or above selected reading score levels, by age, sex, and race/ethnicity: Selected years, 1971 through 2004 178

114. Average scale score in reading and percentage of 4th-graders in public schools attaining reading achievement levels, by race/ethnicity and state or jurisdiction: Selected years, 1994 through 2005   180

115. Average scale score in reading and percentage of 8th-graders in public schools attaining reading achievement levels, by locale and state or jurisdiction: Selected years, 1998 through 2005.....   182

116. Average reading scale scores of 4th- and 8th-graders, by selected student and parent characteristics and school type: Various years, 2000 through 2005   184

117. Percentage of students at or above selected writing proficiency levels, by grade level and selected student characteristics: 2002.....   185

118. Percentage of students at or above selected U.S. history proficiency levels, by grade level and selected student characteristics: 2001.....   186

119. Average student scale score in geography and U.S. history, by grade level and selected student characteristics: 2001   187

120. Percentage of students at or above selected geography achievement levels, by grade level and selected student characteristics: 2001.....   188

121. Average scale score in mathematics, by age and selected student and school characteristics: Selected years, 1973 through 2004.....   189

122. Percentage of students at or above selected mathematics proficiency levels, by age, sex, and race/ethnicity: Selected years, 1978 through 2004   190

123. Mathematics performance of 17-year-olds, by highest mathematics course taken, sex, and race/ethnicity: Selected years, 1978 through 2004   192

124. Average scale score in mathematics, percentage attaining mathematics achievement levels, and selected statistics on mathematics education of 4th-graders in public schools, by state or jurisdiction: Selected years, 1992 through 2005   193

125. Average scale score in mathematics and percentage attaining mathematics achievement levels of 8th-graders in public schools, by level of parental education and state or jurisdiction: Selected years, 1990 through 2005   194

126. Selected statistics on mathematics education for public school students, by state or jurisdiction: 2000, 2003, and 2004   196

127. Average mathematics scale scores of 4th-, 8th-, and 12th-graders, by selected student and parent characteristics and school type: 2000, 2003, and 2005.....   198

128. Average science scale scores and percentage of 4th-, 8th-, and 12th-graders attaining science achievement levels, by selected student characteristics and percentile: 1996, 2000, and 2005 ..   199

129. Average scale score in science for 8th-graders in public schools, by selected student characteristics and state or jurisdiction: 1996, 2000, and 2005.....   200

130. Average arts scale score of 8th-grade students, by topic and selected student characteristics: 1997   202

131. SAT score averages of college-bound seniors, by race/ethnicity: Selected years, 1986–87 through 2005–06.....   203

132. SAT score averages of college-bound seniors, by sex: 1966–67 through 2005–06.....   204

133. SAT score averages of college-bound seniors, by selected student characteristics: Selected years, 1995–96 through 2005–06.....   205

134. SAT score averages of college-bound seniors and percent of graduates taking SAT, by state or jurisdiction: Selected years, 1987–88 through 2005–06   207

135. ACT score averages and standard deviations, by sex and race/ethnicity, and percentage of ACT test takers, by selected composite score ranges and planned fields of study: Selected years, 1995 through 2005   208

136. Percentage distribution of elementary and secondary school children, by average grades and selected child and school characteristics: 1996, 1999, and 2003   209

137. Average number of Carnegie units earned by public high school graduates in various subject fields, by selected student characteristics: Selected years, 1982 through 2005   210

138. Average number of Carnegie units earned by public high school graduates in vocational education courses, by selected student characteristics: Selected years, 1982 through 2005   213

139. Percentage of public and private high school graduates taking selected mathematics and science courses in high school, by sex and race/ethnicity: Selected years, 1982 through 2005 216

140. Percentage of public and private high school graduates earning minimum credits in selected combinations of academic courses, by sex and race/ethnicity: Selected years, 1982 through 2005 217

141. Public high schools that offered and students enrolled in dual credit, Advanced Placement, and International Baccalaureate courses, by school characteristics: 2003 218

Student Activities and Behavior

142. Percentage of high school seniors who say they engage in various activities, by selected student and school characteristics: 1992 and 2004 219

143. Percentage of high school sophomores who participate in various school-sponsored extracurricular activities, by selected student characteristics: 1990 and 2002 220

144. Percentage distribution of 4th-graders, by time spent on homework and television viewing each day and selected student and school characteristics: Selected years, 1992 through 2000 221

145. Tenth-graders' attendance patterns, by selected student and school characteristics: 1990 and 2002 222

146. Percentage of schools with various security measures, by control and selected characteristics: 2003–04 223

147. Number and percentage of public schools reporting crime incidents, by school characteristics and seriousness of crime incidents reported: 1999–2000 and 2003–04 224

148. Number and percentage of students expelled from public elementary and secondary schools, by sex, race/ethnicity, and state: 2002 228

149. Number and percentage of students suspended from public elementary and secondary schools, by sex, race/ethnicity, and state: 2002 229

150. Percentage of students in grades 9 through 12 who reported experience with drugs and violence on school property, by race/ethnicity, grade, and sex: Selected years, 1997 through 2005 230

151. Percentage of 12- to 17-year-olds reporting substance abuse during the past 30 days and the past year, by drug used: Selected years, 1982 through 2005 231

152. Percentage of high school seniors reporting drug use, by type of drug and reporting period: Selected years, 1975 through 2005 232

State Regulations

153. Age range for compulsory school attendance, special education services, year-round schools, and kindergarten programs, by state: 1997, 2000, 2002, and 2004 233

154. State requirements for high school graduation, in Carnegie units: 2004 234

155. States that use criterion-referenced assessments aligned to state standards, by subject area and level: 2005–06 237

156. States using minimum-competency testing, by grade levels assessed, expected uses of standards, and state or jurisdiction: 2001–02 238

157. States requiring testing for initial certification of elementary and secondary teachers, by skills or knowledge assessment and state: 2005 and 2006 239

Revenues and Expenditures

158. Revenues for public elementary and secondary schools, by source of funds: Selected years, 1919–20 through 2003–04 240

159. Revenues for public elementary and secondary schools, by source and state or jurisdiction: 2003–04 241

160. Revenues for public elementary and secondary schools, by source and state or jurisdiction: 2002–03 242

161. Summary of expenditures for public elementary and secondary education, by purpose: Selected years, 1919–20 through 2003–04 243

162. Current expenditures for public elementary and secondary education, by state or jurisdiction: Selected years, 1969–70 through 2003–04   244

163. Total expenditures for public elementary and secondary education, by function and state or jurisdiction: 2003–04   246

164. Total expenditures for public elementary and secondary education, by function and state or jurisdiction: 2002–03   248

165. Total expenditures for public elementary and secondary education, by function and subfunction: Selected years, 1990–91 through 2003–04   250

166. Expenditures for instruction in public elementary and secondary schools, by subfunction and state or jurisdiction: 2002–03 and 2003–04   252

167. Total and current expenditures per pupil in public elementary and secondary schools: Selected years, 1919–20 through 2003–04   253

168. Total and current expenditures per pupil in fall enrollment in public elementary and secondary education, by function and state or jurisdiction: 2003–04   254

169. Total and current expenditures per pupil in fall enrollment in public elementary and secondary education, by function and state or jurisdiction: 2002–03   255

170. Current expenditure per pupil in fall enrollment in public elementary and secondary schools, by state or jurisdiction: Selected years, 1969–70 through 2003–04   256

171. Current expenditure per pupil in average daily attendance in public elementary and secondary schools, by state or jurisdiction: Selected years, 1959–60 through 2003–04   258

172. Students transported at public expense and current expenditures for transportation: Selected years, 1929–30 through 2003–04   260

Chapter 3. Postsecondary Education

Enrollment

173. Enrollment, staff, and degrees conferred in postsecondary institutions participating in Title IV programs, by level and control of institution, sex of student, and type of degree: 2004–05 and fall 2005   268

174. Historical summary of faculty, students, degrees, and finances in degree-granting institutions: Selected years, 1869–70 through 2004–05   269

175. Total fall enrollment in degree-granting institutions, by attendance status, sex of student, and control of institution: Selected years, 1947 through 2005   270

176. Total fall enrollment in degree-granting institutions, by control and type of institution: 1963 through 2005   271

177. Total fall enrollment in degree-granting institutions, by attendance status, age, and sex: Selected years, 1970 through 2015   272

178. Total fall enrollment in degree-granting institutions, by level, sex, age, and attendance status of student: 2005   273

179. Total fall enrollment in degree-granting institutions, by control and type of institution, age, and attendance status of student: 2005   274

180. Total fall enrollment in degree-granting institutions, by level of enrollment, sex, attendance status, and type and control of institution: 2005   275

181. Total fall enrollment in degree-granting institutions, by level of enrollment, sex, attendance status, and type and control of institution: 2004   276

182. Total fall enrollment in degree-granting institutions, by attendance status, sex of student, and type and control of institution: Selected years, 1970 through 2005   277

183. Fall enrollment and number of degree-granting institutions, by control and affiliation of institution: Selected years, 1980 through 2005   278

184. Total first-time freshmen fall enrollment in degree-granting institutions, by attendance status, sex of student, and type and control of institution: 1955 through 2005   280

185. Total first-time freshmen fall enrollment in degree-granting institutions, by attendance status, sex, control of institution, and state or jurisdiction: 2000 through 2005 281

186. College enrollment and enrollment rates of recent high school completers, by sex: 1960 through 2005 282

187. College enrollment and enrollment rates of recent high school completers, by race/ethnicity: 1960 through 2005 283

188. Graduation rates of previous year's 12th-graders and college attendance rates of those who graduated, by selected high school characteristics: 1999–2000 and 2003–04 285

189. Enrollment rates of 18- to 24-year-olds in degree-granting institutions, by sex and race/ethnicity: 1967 through 2005 286

190. Total undergraduate fall enrollment in degree-granting institutions, by attendance status, sex of student, and control of institution: 1969 through 2005 287

191. Total graduate fall enrollment in degree-granting institutions, by attendance status, sex of student, and control of institution: 1969 through 2005 288

192. Total first-professional fall enrollment in degree-granting institutions, by attendance status, sex of student, and control of institution: 1969 through 2005 289

193. Total fall enrollment in degree-granting institutions, by state or jurisdiction: Selected years, 1970 through 2005 290

194. Total fall enrollment in public degree-granting institutions, by state or jurisdiction: Selected years, 1970 through 2005 291

195. Total fall enrollment in private degree-granting institutions, by state or jurisdiction: Selected years, 1970 through 2005 292

196. Total fall enrollment in all degree-granting institutions, by attendance status, sex, and state or jurisdiction: 2004 and 2005 293

197. Total fall enrollment in public degree-granting institutions, by attendance status, sex, and state or jurisdiction: 2004 and 2005 294

198. Total fall enrollment in private degree-granting institutions, by attendance status, sex, and state or jurisdiction: 2004 and 2005 295

199. Total fall enrollment in private not-for-profit degree-granting institutions, by attendance status, sex, and state or jurisdiction: 2004 and 2005 296

200. Total fall enrollment in degree-granting institutions, by control and type of institution and state or jurisdiction: 2004 and 2005 297

201. Total fall enrollment in degree-granting institutions, by level of enrollment and state or jurisdiction: 2004 and 2005 298

202. Total fall enrollment in degree-granting institutions, by control, level of enrollment, type of institution, and state or jurisdiction: 2005 299

203. Total fall enrollment in degree-granting institutions, by control, level of enrollment, type of institution, and state or jurisdiction: 2004 300

204. Full-time-equivalent fall enrollment in degree-granting institutions, by control and type of institution: 1969 through 2005 301

205. Full-time-equivalent fall enrollment in degree-granting institutions, by control and type of institution and state or jurisdiction: 2000, 2004, and 2005 302

206. Full-time-equivalent fall enrollment in degree-granting institutions, by control and state or jurisdiction: Selected years, 1980 through 2005 303

207. Residence and migration of all freshmen students in degree-granting institutions, by state or jurisdiction: Fall 2004 304

208. Residence and migration of all freshmen students in degree-granting institutions who graduated from high school in the previous 12 months, by state or jurisdiction: Fall 2004 305

209. Residence and migration of all freshmen students in 4-year degree-granting institutions who graduated from high school in the previous 12 months, by state or jurisdiction: Fall 2004 306

210. Total fall enrollment in degree-granting institutions, by race/ethnicity, sex, attendance status, and level of student: Selected years, 1976 through 2005 307

211. Total fall enrollment in degree-granting institutions, by race/ethnicity of student and type and control of institution: Selected years,1976 through 2005 310

212. Fall enrollment in degree-granting institutions, by race/ethnicity of student and by state or jurisdiction: 2005 312

213. Fall enrollment in degree-granting institutions, by race/ethnicity of student and by state or jurisdiction: 2004 314

214. Total number of institutions and fall enrollment in degree-granting institutions, by type and control of institution and percentage of minority enrollment: 2005 316

215. Number and percentage of students enrolled in postsecondary institutions, by level, disability status, and selected student characteristics: 2003–04 317

216. Enrollment in postsecondary education, by student level, type of institution, age, and major field of study: 2003–04 318

217. Graduate enrollment in science and engineering programs in degree-granting institutions, by field of study: Fall 1991 through fall 2003 320

218. Number of institutions and enrollment in degree-granting institutions, by size, type, and control of institution: Fall 2005 322

219. Enrollment of the 120 largest degree-granting college and university campuses, by selected characteristics and institution: Fall 2005 323

220. Selected statistics for degree-granting institutions enrolling more than 15,000 students in 2005: Selected years, 1990 through 2005 324

221. Enrollment and degrees conferred in degree-granting women's colleges, by selected characteristics and institution: Fall 2005 and 2004–05 334

222. Enrollment and degrees conferred in degree-granting institutions that serve large proportions of Hispanic students, by selected characteristics and institution: Fall 2005 and 2004–05 335

223. Enrollment and degrees conferred in degree-granting tribally controlled institutions, by institution: Fall 2000 through fall 2005, and 2003–04 and 2004–05 345

224. Fall enrollment, degrees conferred, and expenditures in degree-granting historically Black colleges and universities, by institution: 2003, 2003–04, 2004, and 2004–05 346

225. Selected statistics on degree-granting historically Black colleges and universities: Selected years, 1980 through 2005 348

226. Fall enrollment in degree-granting historically Black colleges and universities, by type and control of institution: 1976 through 2004 349

Staff

227. Total and full-time-equivalent staff in degree-granting institutions, by employment status, control of institution, and occupation: Fall 1976, fall 1995, and fall 2005 350

228. Employees in degree-granting institutions, by employment status, sex, control and type of institution, and primary occupation: Fall 2005 351

229. Employees in degree-granting institutions, by race/ethnicity and residency status, sex, employment status, control and type of institution, and primary occupation: Fall 2005 353

230. Number of full-time-equivalent staff and faculty, and full-time-equivalent staff and faculty/student ratios in degree-granting institutions, by control and type of institution and state or jurisdiction: Fall 2005 354

231. Number of instructional faculty in degree-granting institutions, by employment status and control and type of institution: Selected years, fall 1970 through fall 2005 356

232. Full-time instructional faculty in degree-granting institutions, by race/ethnicity and residency status, sex, and academic rank: Fall 2003 and fall 2005 357

233. Percentage distribution of full-time instructional faculty and staff in degree-granting institutions, by type and control of institution, selected instruction activities, and number of classes taught for credit: Fall 2003 358

234. Percentage distribution of part-time instructional faculty and staff in degree-granting institutions, by type and control of institution, selected instruction activities, and number of classes taught for credit: Fall 2003 360

235. Full-time and part-time instructional faculty and staff in degree-granting institutions, by type and control of institution and selected characteristics: Fall 1992, fall 1998, and fall 2003 362

236. Full-time and part-time instructional faculty and staff in degree-granting institutions, by race/ ethnicity, sex, and selected characteristics: Fall 2003 364

237. Full-time and part-time instructional faculty and staff in degree-granting institutions, by field and faculty characteristics: Fall 1992, fall 1998, and fall 2003 366

238. Full-time and part-time instructional faculty and staff in degree-granting institutions, by race/ ethnicity, sex, and program area: Fall 1998 and fall 2003 368

239. Average base salary of full-time instructional faculty and staff in degree-granting institutions, by type and control of institution and field of instruction: Selected years, 1987–88 through 2003–04 370

240. Average salary of full-time instructional faculty on 9-month contracts in degree-granting institutions, by academic rank, control and type of institution, and sex: Selected years, 1970–71 through 2005–06. 371

241. Average salary of full-time instructional faculty on 9-month contracts in degree-granting institutions, by academic rank, sex, and control and type of institution: Selected years, 1980–81 through 2005–06. 374

242. Average salary of full-time instructional faculty on 9-month contracts in degree-granting institutions, by control and type of institution and state or jurisdiction: 2005–06. 375

243. Average salary of full-time instructional faculty on 9-month contracts in degree-granting institutions, by control and type of institution and state or jurisdiction: 2004–05. 376

244. Average salary of full-time instructional faculty on 9-month contracts in 4-year degree-granting institutions, by type and control of institution, rank of faculty, and state or jurisdiction: 2005–06. . 377

245. Average salary of full-time instructional faculty on 9-month contracts in 4-year degree-granting institutions, by type and control of institution, rank of faculty, and state or jurisdiction: 2004–05. . 378

246. Average benefit expenditure for full-time instructional faculty on 9-month contracts in degree-granting institutions, by type of benefit and control of institution: Selected years, 1977–78 through 2005–06. 379

247. Full-time instructional staff with tenure for degree-granting institutions with a tenure system, by academic rank, sex, and control and type of institution: Selected years, 1993–94 through 2005–06. 381

Institutions

248. Degree-granting institutions, by control and type of institution: Selected years, 1949–50 through 2005–06. 382

249. Degree-granting institutions and branches, by type and control of institution and state or jurisdiction: 2005–06 383

250. Degree-granting institutions that have closed their doors, by control and type of institution: 1969–70 through 2005–06. 385

Degrees

251. Degrees conferred by degree-granting institutions, by level of degree and sex of student: Selected years, 1869–70 through 2015–16 386

252. Associate's degrees conferred by degree-granting institutions, by field of study: 1993–94 through 2004–05. 387

253. Associate's degrees and other subbaccalaureate awards conferred by degree-granting institutions, by length of curriculum, sex of student, and field of study: 2004–05 388

254. Bachelor's degrees conferred by degree-granting institutions, by discipline division: Selected years, 1970–71 through 2004–05 389

255. Master's degrees conferred by degree-granting institutions, by discipline division: Selected years, 1970–71 through 2004–05. 390

256. Doctor's degrees conferred by degree-granting institutions, by discipline division: Selected years, 1970–71 through 2004–05. 391

257.   Bachelor's, master's, and doctor's degrees conferred by degree-granting institutions, by field of study and year: Selected years, 1970–71 through 2004–05   392

258.   Bachelor's, master's, and doctor's degrees conferred by degree-granting institutions, by sex of student and field of study: 2004–05   393

259.   Degrees conferred by degree-granting institutions, by control of institution and level of degree: 1969–70 through 2004–05   408

260.   Degrees conferred by degree-granting institutions, by control of institution, level of degree, and discipline division: 2004–05   409

261.   Number of degree-granting institutions conferring degrees, by control, level of degree, and discipline division: 2004–05   410

262.   First-professional degrees conferred by degree-granting institutions in dentistry, medicine, and law, by number of institutions conferring degrees and sex of student: Selected years, 1949–50 through 2004–05   411

263.   First-professional degrees conferred by degree-granting institutions, by sex of student, control of institution, and field of study: Selected years, 1985–86 through 2004–05   412

264.   Associate's degrees conferred by degree-granting institutions, by race/ethnicity and sex of student: Selected years, 1976–77 through 2004–05   413

265.   Associate's degrees conferred by degree-granting institutions, by sex, race/ethnicity, and major field of study: 2004–05   414

266.   Associate's degrees conferred by degree-granting institutions, by sex, race/ethnicity, and major field of study: 2003–04   415

267.   Bachelor's degrees conferred by degree-granting institutions, by race/ethnicity and sex of student: Selected years, 1976–77 through 2004–05   416

268.   Bachelor's degrees conferred by degree-granting institutions, by sex, race/ethnicity, and major field of study: 2004–05   417

269.   Bachelor's degrees conferred by degree-granting institutions, by sex, race/ethnicity, and major field of study: 2003–04   418

270.   Master's degrees conferred by degree-granting institutions, by race/ethnicity and sex of student: Selected years, 1976–77 through 2004–05   419

271.   Master's degrees conferred by degree-granting institutions, by sex, race/ethnicity, and major field of study: 2004–05   420

272.   Master's degrees conferred by degree-granting institutions, by sex, race/ethnicity, and major field of study: 2003–04   421

273.   Doctor's degrees conferred by degree-granting institutions, by race/ethnicity and sex of student: Selected years, 1976–77 through 2004–05   422

274.   Doctor's degrees conferred by degree-granting institutions, by sex, race/ethnicity, and major field of study: 2004–05   423

275.   Doctor's degrees conferred by degree-granting institutions, by sex, race/ethnicity, and major field of study: 2003–04   424

276.   First-professional degrees conferred by degree-granting institutions, by race/ethnicity and sex of student: Selected years, 1976–77 through 2004–05   425

277.   First-professional degrees conferred by degree-granting institutions, by sex, race/ethnicity, and major field of study: 2004–05   426

278.   First-professional degrees conferred by degree-granting institutions, by sex, race/ethnicity, and major field of study: 2003–04   426

279.   Degrees in agriculture and natural resources conferred by degree-granting institutions, by level of degree and sex of student: 1970–71 through 2004–05   427

280.   Degrees in architecture and related services conferred by degree-granting institutions, by level of degree and sex of student: Selected years, 1949–50 through 2004–05   428

281.   Degrees in the biological and biomedical sciences conferred by degree-granting institutions, by level of degree and sex of student: Selected years, 1951–52 through 2004–05   429

282. Degrees in biology, microbiology, and zoology conferred by degree-granting institutions, by level of degree: 1970–71 through 2004–05 430

283. Degrees in business conferred by degree-granting institutions, by level of degree and sex of student: Selected years, 1955–56 through 2004–05 431

284. Degrees in communication, journalism, and related programs and in communications technologies conferred by degree-granting institutions, by level of degree and sex of student: 1970–71 through 2004–05 432

285. Degrees in computer and information sciences conferred by degree-granting institutions, by level of degree and sex of student: 1970–71 through 2004–05 433

286. Degrees in education conferred by degree-granting institutions, by level of degree and sex of student: Selected years, 1949–50 through 2004–05 434

287. Degrees in engineering and engineering technologies conferred by degree-granting institutions, by level of degree and sex of student: Selected years, 1949–50 through 2004–05 435

288. Degrees in chemical, civil, electrical, and mechanical engineering conferred by degree-granting institutions, by level of degree: 1970–71 through 2004–05 436

289. Degrees in English language and literature/letters conferred by degree-granting institutions, by level of degree and sex of student: Selected years, 1949–50 through 2004–05 437

290. Degrees in modern foreign languages and literatures conferred by degree-granting institutions, by level of degree and sex of student: Selected years, 1949–50 through 2004–05 438

291. Degrees in French, German, and Spanish conferred by degree-granting institutions, by level of degree: Selected years, 1949–50 through 2004–05 439

292. Degrees in the health professions and related sciences conferred by degree-granting institutions, by level of degree and sex of student: 1970–71 through 2004–05 440

293. Degrees in mathematics and statistics conferred by degree-granting institutions, by level of degree and sex of student: Selected years, 1949–50 through 2004–05 441

294. Degrees in the physical sciences and science technologies conferred by degree-granting institutions, by level of degree and sex of student: Selected years, 1959–60 through 2004–05 . . 442

295. Degrees in chemistry, geology, and physics conferred by degree-granting institutions, by level of degree: 1970–71 through 2004–05 443

296. Degrees in psychology conferred by degree-granting institutions, by level of degree and sex of student: Selected years, 1949–50 through 2004–05 444

297. Degrees in public administration and social services conferred by degree-granting institutions, by level of degree and sex of student: 1970–71 through 2004–05 445

298. Degrees in the social sciences and history conferred by degree-granting institutions, by level of degree and sex of student: 1970–71 through 2004–05 446

299. Degrees in economics, history, political science and government, and sociology conferred by degree-granting institutions, by level of degree: Selected years, 1949–50 through 2004–05 447

300. Degrees in visual and performing arts conferred by degree-granting institutions, by level of degree and sex of student: 1970–71 through 2004–05 448

301. Statistical profile of persons receiving doctor's degrees, by field of study and selected characteristics: 2003–04 449

302. Statistical profile of persons receiving doctor's degrees in education: Selected years, 1979–80 through 2003–04 450

303. Statistical profile of persons receiving doctor's degrees in engineering: Selected years, 1979–80 through 2003–04 451

304. Statistical profile of persons receiving doctor's degrees in the humanities: Selected years, 1979–80 through 2003–04 452

305. Statistical profile of persons receiving doctor's degrees in the life sciences: Selected years, 1979–80 through 2003–04 453

306. Statistical profile of persons receiving doctor's degrees in the physical sciences: Selected years, 1979–80 through 2003–04 454

307. Statistical profile of persons receiving doctor's degrees in the social sciences and psychology: Selected years, 1979–80 through 2003–04 455

308. Degrees conferred by degree-granting institutions, by control, level of degree, and state or jurisdiction: 2004–05 456

309. Bachelor's and master's degrees conferred by degree-granting institutions, by field of study and state or jurisdiction: 2004–05 457

310. Degrees conferred by degree-granting institutions, by level of degree and state or jurisdiction: 2003–04 and 2004–05 459

311. Doctor's degrees conferred by the 60 institutions conferring the most doctor's degrees: 1995–96 through 2004–05 460

Outcomes

312. Percentage distribution of 1990 high school sophomores, by highest level of education completed through 2000 and selected student characteristics: 1990, 1992, and 2000 461

313. Mean number of semester credits completed by bachelor's degree recipients, by course area and major: 1976, 1984, and 1992–93 462

314. Number and percentage of degree-granting institutions with first-year undergraduates using various selection criteria for admission, by type and control of institution: Selected years, 2000–01 through 2005–06 463

315. Number of applications, admissions, and enrollees; their distribution across institutions accepting various percentages of applications; and SAT and ACT scores of applicants, by type and control of institution: 2004–05 464

316. Percentage of degree-granting institutions offering remedial services, by type and control of institution: 1989–90 through 2005–06 465

317. Percentage distribution of enrollment and completion status of first-time postsecondary students starting during the 1995–96 academic year, by type of institution and other student characteristics: 2001 466

318. Scores on Graduate Record Examination (GRE) general and subject tests: 1965 through 2005 . . 468

Student Charges and Student Financial Assistance

319. Average undergraduate tuition and fees and room and board rates charged for full-time students in degree-granting institutions, by type and control of institution: 1964–65 through 2005–06 470

320. Average undergraduate tuition and fees and room and board rates charged for full-time students in degree-granting institutions, by type and control of institution and state or jurisdiction: 2004–05 and 2005–06 473

321. Average undergraduate tuition and fees and room and board rates of degree-granting institutions, by control and type of institution and percentile of students: 2004–05 and 2005–06 474

322. Average graduate and first-professional tuition and required fees in degree-granting institutions, by first-professional discipline and control of institution: 1987–88 through 2005–06 475

323. Percentage of undergraduates receiving aid, by type and source of aid and selected student characteristics: 2003–04 476

324. Average amount of financial aid awarded to full-time, full-year undergraduates, by type and source of aid and selected student characteristics: 2003–04 477

325. Average amount of financial aid awarded to part-time or part-year undergraduates, by type and source of aid and selected student characteristics: 2003–04 478

326. Amount borrowed, aid status, and sources of aid for full-time and part-time undergraduates, by control and type of institution: 2003–04 479

327. Percentage of full-time, full-year undergraduates receiving aid, by type and source of aid received and control and type of institution: Selected years, 1992–93 through 2003–04 480

328. Percentage of part-time or part-year undergraduates receiving aid, by type and source of aid received and control and type of institution: Selected years, 1992–93 through 2003–04 481

329. Percentage of full-time and part-time undergraduates receiving federal aid, by aid program and control and type of institution: 2003–04   482

330. Amount borrowed, aid status, and sources of aid for full-time, full-year postbaccalaureate students, by level of study and control and type of institution: Selected years, 1992–93 through 2003–04 .   483

331. Amount borrowed, aid status, and sources of aid for part-time or part-year postbaccalaureate students, by level of study and control and type of institution: Selected years, 1992–93 through 2003–04   484

332. Percentage of full-time, full-year postbaccalaureate students receiving aid, by type of aid, level of study, and control and type of institution: Selected years, 1992–93 through 2003–04   485

333. Percentage of part-time or part-year postbaccalaureate students receiving aid, by type of aid, level of study, and control and type of institution: Selected years, 1992–93 through 2003–04   486

334. State awards for need-based undergraduate scholarship and grant programs, by state: Selected years, 1989–90 through 2004–05   487

Revenue

335. Current-fund revenue of degree-granting institutions, by source of funds: Selected years, 1919–20 through 1995–96   489

336. Current-fund revenue of public degree-granting institutions, by source of funds: Selected years, 1980–81 through 2000–01   490

337. Revenues of public degree-granting institutions, by type of institution and source of revenue: 2003–04   491

338. Revenues of public degree-granting institutions, by source of revenue and state or jurisdiction: 2003–04   492

339. Appropriations from state and local governments for public degree-granting institutions, by state or jurisdiction: Selected years, 1990–91 through 2003–04   493

340. Total revenue of private not-for-profit degree-granting institutions, by source of funds and type of institution: 1996–97 through 2003–04   494

341. Total revenue of private not-for-profit degree-granting institutions, by source of funds and type of institution: 2003–04   496

342. Total revenue of private for-profit degree-granting institutions, by source of funds and type of institution: 1997–98 through 2003–04   497

343. Total revenue of private for-profit degree-granting institutions, by source of funds and type of institution: 2002–03 and 2003–04   498

344. Current-fund revenue received from the federal government by the 120 degree-granting institutions receiving the largest amounts, by control and rank order: 2003–04   499

Expenditures

345. Current-fund expenditures and current-fund expenditures per full-time-equivalent student in degree-granting institutions, by type and control of institution: Selected years, 1970–71 through 2000–01   500

346. Current-fund expenditures and educational and general expenditures of degree-granting institutions, by purpose and per student: Selected years, 1929–30 through 1995–96   502

347. Expenses of public degree-granting institutions, by type of expense and type of institution: 2003–04   504

348. Current-fund expenditures of public degree-granting institutions, by purpose: Selected years, 1980–81 through 2000–01   505

349. Current-fund expenditures of public degree-granting institutions, by state or jurisdiction: Selected years, 1980–81 through 2000–01   506

350. Educational and general expenditures of public degree-granting institutions, by state or jurisdiction: Selected years, 1980–81 through 2000–01   507

351. Voluntary support for degree-granting institutions, by source and purpose of support: Selected years, 1959–60 through 2004–05   508

352. Total expenditures of private not-for-profit degree-granting institutions, by purpose and type of institution: 1996–97 through 2003–04 509

353. Total expenditures of private not-for-profit degree-granting institutions, by purpose and type of institution: 2003–04 511

354. Total expenditures of private for-profit degree-granting institutions, by purpose and type of institution: 2002–03 and 2003–04 512

355. Total expenditures of private not-for-profit and for-profit degree-granting institutions, by level and state or jurisdiction: 1997–98 through 2003–04 513

Property

356. Value of property and liabilities of degree-granting institutions: Selected years, 1899–1900 through 1995–96 514

357. Endowment funds of the 120 colleges and universities with the largest amounts, by rank order: 2004 and 2005 515

Adult Education

358. Participants in adult basic and secondary education programs, by type of program and state or jurisdiction: Selected fiscal years, 1990 through 2005 516

359. Participation of employed persons, 17 years old and over, in career-related adult education during the previous 12 months, by selected characteristics of participants: Various years, 1995 through 2005 517

360. Participation of persons, 17 years old and over, in adult education during the previous 12 months, by selected characteristics of participants: Selected years, 1991 through 2005 520

Vocational Education

361. Number of non-degree-granting Title IV institutions offering postsecondary education, by control and state or jurisdiction: Selected years, 2000–01 through 2005–06 522

Chapter 4. Federal Programs for Education and Related Activities

362. Federal support and estimated federal tax expenditures for education, by category: Selected fiscal years, 1965 through 2006 533

363. Federal on-budget funds for education and related programs, by agency: Selected fiscal years, 1970 through 2006 535

364. Federal on-budget funds for education, by level/educational purpose, agency, and program: Selected fiscal years, 1970 through 2006 536

365. Estimated federal support for education, by type of ultimate recipient and agency: Fiscal year 2006   543

366. U.S. Department of Education outlays, by type of recipient and level of education: Selected fiscal years, 1980 to 2006 544

367. U.S. Department of Education appropriations for major programs, by state or jurisdiction: Fiscal year 2005 545

368. Appropriations for Title I, No Child Left Behind Act of 2001, by program and state or jurisdiction: Fiscal years 2005 and 2006 546

369. U.S. Department of Agriculture obligations for child nutrition programs, by state or jurisdiction: Fiscal years 2004 and 2005 547

370. U.S. Department of Health and Human Services allocations for Head Start and enrollment in Head Start, by state or jurisdiction: Fiscal years 2002 through 2005 548

371. Federal science and engineering obligations to colleges and universities, by agency and state or jurisdiction: Fiscal year 2004 550

372.   Federal obligations for research, development, and R&D plant, by performers, fields of science, and category of obligation: Fiscal years 1998 through 2006   551

373.   Federal obligations for research and development and R&D plant, by agency and state or jurisdiction: Fiscal year 2004   553

Chapter 5. Outcomes of Education

Educational Characteristics of the Workforce

374.   Labor force participation rates and employment to population ratios of persons 16 to 64 years old, by highest level of education, age, sex, and race/ethnicity: 2005   559

375.   Unemployment rate of persons 16 years old and over, by age, sex, race/ethnicity, and educational attainment: 2003, 2004, and 2005   560

376.   Occupation of employed persons 25 years old and over, by educational attainment and sex: 2005   561

377.   Median annual income of year-round, full-time workers 25 years old and over, by highest level of educational attainment and sex: 1990 through 2005   562

378.   Distribution of income and median income of persons 25 years old and over, by highest level of educational attainment and sex: 2005   565

379.   Literacy skills of adults, by type of literacy, proficiency levels, and selected characteristics: 1992 and 2003   567

380.   Percentage of 12th-graders working different numbers of hours per week, by selected student characteristics and school locale type: 1992 and 2004   568

Recent High School and College Graduates

381.   College enrollment and labor force status of 2003, 2004, and 2005 high school completers, by sex and race/ethnicity: 2003, 2004, and 2005   569

382.   Labor force status of high school dropouts, by sex and race/ethnicity: Selected years, 1980 through 2005   571

383.   Current postsecondary education and employment status, wages earned, and living arrangements of special education students out of secondary school up to 4 years, by type of disability: 2005 .   572

384.   Full-time employment status of bachelor's degree recipients 1 year after graduation, by field of study: Selected years, 1976 through 2001   572

385.   Percentage distribution of 1999–2000 bachelor's degree recipients 1 year after graduation, by field of study, time to completion, enrollment status, employment status, occupational area, job characteristics, and annual salaries: 2001   573

386.   Enrollment in postbaccalaureate certificate or advanced degree programs and highest degree attained by 1992–93 bachelor's degree recipients, by education characteristics: 2003   574

387.   Average annual salary of bachelor's degree recipients employed full time 1 year after graduation, by field of study: Selected years, 1976 through 2001   575

388.   Percentage of 1988 8th-graders who volunteered in various capacities in a 12-month period ending in 2000, by selected young adult characteristics: 2000   576

389.   Percentage of 18- to 25-year-olds reporting drug use during the past 30 days and the past year, by drug used: Selected years, 1982 through 2005   577

390.   Percentage of 1972 high school seniors, 1992 high school seniors, and 2004 high school seniors who felt that certain life values were "very important," by sex: Selected years, 1972 through 2004   578

391.   Percentage of employed 1988 8th-graders satisfied with various aspects of their job, by educational attainment: 2000   578

Chapter 6. International Comparisons of Education

392. Selected population and finance statistics, school enrollment, and teachers, by major areas of the world: Selected years, 1980 through 2004. 583

393. Selected population and enrollment statistics for countries with populations over 10 million, by continent: Selected years, 1980 through 2004. 584

394. School-age populations as a percentage of total population, by age group and country: Selected years, 1985 through 2002 586

395. Percentage of population enrolled in secondary and postsecondary institutions, by age group and country: Selected years, 1985 through 2003 587

396. Pupils per teacher in public and private elementary and secondary schools, by level of education and country: Selected years, 1985 through 2004 588

397. Average mathematics literacy, reading literacy, science literacy, and problem-solving scores of 15-year-olds, by sex and country: 2003 589

398. Mean scores and percentage distribution of 15-year-olds scoring at each mathematics literacy proficiency level, by country: 2003. 590

399. Average fourth-grade mathematics scores, by content areas, index of time students spend doing mathematics homework in a normal school week, and country: 2003. 591

400. Average eighth-grade mathematics scores, by content areas, index of time students spend doing mathematics homework in a normal school week, and country: 2003. 592

401. Percentage of lesson time spent on various mathematics activities, yearly mathematics instructional time, and mathematics instructional time as a percentage of total instructional time in eighth grade, by country: 2003. 594

402. Average size and scores of eighth-grade mathematics classes and Index of Teachers' Emphasis on Mathematics Homework (EMH), by country: 2003 596

403. Eighth-grade students' perceptions about mathematics and hours spent on leisure activities, by country: 2003. 598

404. Average mathematics scores at the end of secondary school, by sex, average time spent studying mathematics out of school, and country: 1995 599

405. Average fourth-grade science scores in content areas and average time spent teaching science in school, by country: 2003 600

406. Average eighth-grade science scores in content areas and average time spent studying out of school, by country: 2003 601

407. Instructional practices and time spent teaching science in eighth grade, by country: 2003. 603

408. Average science scores at the end of secondary school, by sex, average time spent studying science out of school, and country: 1995. 605

409. Number of bachelor's degree recipients per 100 persons of the typical age of graduation, by sex and country: 2002, 2003, and 2004. 605

410. Percentage of bachelor's degrees awarded in science, by field and country: Selected years, 1985 through 2003. 606

411. Percentage of graduate degrees awarded in science, by field and country: Selected years, 1985 through 2003. 607

412. Public and private education expenditures per student, by level of education and country: 2000 through 2003 608

413. Total public direct expenditures on education as a percentage of the gross domestic product, by level and country: Selected years, 1985 through 2003 610

414. Foreign students enrolled in institutions of higher education in the United States and other jurisdictions, by continent, region, and selected countries of origin: Selected years, 1980–81 through 2004–05 611

Chapter 7. Libraries and Educational Technology

Libraries

415. Selected statistics on school libraries/media centers, by control and level of school: 1999–2000 and 2003–04 615

416. Selected statistics on public school libraries/media centers, by level and enrollment size of school: 2003–04 616

417. Selected statistics on public school libraries/media centers, by state: 2003–04 617

418. Collections, staff, and operating expenditures of degree-granting institution libraries: Selected years, 1976–77 through 2001–02 618

419. Collections, staff, and operating expenditures of the 60 largest college and university libraries: 2001–02 619

420. Selected statistics of public libraries, by population size of legal service area: Fiscal year 2004 . . 620

421. Public libraries, books and serial volumes, library visits, circulation, and reference transactions, by state: Fiscal year 2004 621

Computers and Technology

422. Public schools and instructional rooms with access to the Internet, by selected school characteristics: 1994 through 2003 622

423. Use of the Internet by persons 3 years old and over, by type of use and selected characteristics of students and other users: 2003 625

424. Number and percentage of home computer users, by type of application and selected characteristics: 1997 and 2003 627

425. Number and percentage of student home computer users, by type of application and selected characteristics: 2003 628

426. Student use of computers, by level of enrollment, age, and student and school characteristics: 1993, 1997, and 2003 629

427. Percentage of workers, 18 years old and over, using computers on the job, by type of computer application and selected characteristics: 1993, 1997, and 2003 631

Appendix A. Guide to Sources

A-1. Respondent counts for selected High School and Beyond surveys: 1982, 1984, and 1986 667

A-2. Design effects (DEFF) and root design effects (DEFT) for selected High School and Beyond surveys and subsamples: 1984 and 1986 668

A-3. Respondent counts of full-time workers from the Recent College Graduates survey: Selected years, 1976 to 1991 668

A-4. Sampling errors (95 percent confidence level) for percentages estimated from the Gallup Poll: 1992, 1993, and 1996 through 2006 669

A-5. Sampling errors (95 percent confidence level) for the difference in two percentages estimated from the Gallup Poll: 1992, 1993, and 1996 through 2006. 669

A-6. Maximum differences required for significance (90 percent confidence level) between sample subgroups from the "Status of the American Public School Teacher" survey: 2000–01 669

INTRODUCTION

In the fall of 2006, about 72.7 million persons were enrolled in American schools and colleges (table 1). About 4.5 million persons were employed as elementary and secondary school teachers and as college faculty, in full-time equivalents (FTE). Other professional, administrative, and support staff at educational institutions numbered 5.0 million. All data for 2006 in this Introduction are projected. Some data for other years are projected or estimated as noted.

Elementary/Secondary Education

Enrollment

Enrollment in public elementary and secondary schools rose 24 percent between 1985 and 2006 (table 2). The fastest public school growth occurred in the elementary grades (prekindergarten through grade 8), where enrollment rose 25 percent over this period, from 27.0 million to 33.9 million. Public secondary school enrollment declined 8 percent from 1985 to 1990, but then rose 33 percent from 1990 to 2006, for a net increase of 21 percent. Private school enrollment grew more slowly than public school enrollment from 1985 to 2006, rising 10 percent, from 5.6 million to 6.1 million. As a result, the proportion of students enrolled in private schools declined from 12.4 percent in 1985 to 11.1 percent in 2006. Since the enrollment rates of kindergarten, elementary, and secondary school-age children did not change substantially between 1985 and 2005 (table 7), increases in public and private elementary school enrollment have been driven primarily by increases in the number of children in this age group.

The National Center for Education Statistics (NCES) forecasts record levels of total elementary and secondary enrollment through at least 2015, as the school-age population continues to rise. The projected fall 2006 public school enrollment is expected to be a new record, but new records are expected every year through 2015, the last year for which NCES enrollment projections have been developed (table 3). Public elementary school enrollment (prekindergarten through grade 8) is projected to show a slight decline of 1 percent between 2003 and 2005, and then increase, so that the fall 2015 projected enrollment is 7 percent higher than the 2006 projected enrollment. Public secondary school enrollment (grades 9 through 12) is expected to show a net decline of 2 percent between 2006 and 2015.

Teachers

A projected 3.6 million elementary and secondary school teachers were engaged in classroom instruction in the fall of 2006 (table 4). This number has risen 19 percent since 1996. The 2006 projected number of teachers includes 3.2 million public school teachers and 0.5 million private school teachers.

The number of public school teachers has risen faster than the number of public school students over the past 10 years, resulting in declines in the pupil/teacher ratio (table 61). In the fall of 2006, there were a projected 15.4 public school pupils per teacher, compared with 17.1 public school pupils per teacher 10 years earlier.

The salaries of public school teachers lost purchasing power in the 1970s due to inflation, but increased at a greater rate than inflation in the 1980s, and since 1990–91 the salaries have generally maintained pace with inflation (table 75). The average salary for teachers in 2004–05 was $47,750, about 2 percent higher than in 1994–95, after adjustment for inflation.

Student Performance

Most of the student performance data in the *Digest* are drawn from the National Assessment of Educational Progress (NAEP). NAEP conducts assessments using three basic designs: long-term trend NAEP, national NAEP, and state NAEP. These three basic designs are described in the paragraphs that follow.

NAEP long-term trend assessments provide information on changes in the basic achievement of America's youth since the early 1970s. They are administered nationally and report student performance at ages 9, 13, and 17 in reading and mathematics. Measuring trends of student achievement or change over time requires the precise replication of past procedures. For example, students of specific ages are sampled in order to maintain consistency with the original sample design. Similarly, the long-term trend instrument does not evolve based on changes in curricula or in educational practices.

The main NAEP assessments provide current information for the nation and specific geographic regions. They include students drawn from both public and private schools and report results for student achievement at grades 4, 8, and 12. The main NAEP assessments follow the frameworks developed by the National Assessment Governing Board and use the latest advances in assessment methodology. The NAEP frameworks are designed to reflect changes in educational objectives and curricula. Because the assessment items reflect

curricula associated with specific grade levels, the main
NAEP uses samples of students at those grade levels. The differences in procedures between the main NAEP and the long-
term trend NAEP mean that their results cannot be compared
directly.

Since 1990, NAEP assessments have also been conducted
at the state level. Participating states receive assessment
results that report on the performance of students in that state.
The state assessment is identical in content to the assessment
conducted nationally. However, because the national NAEP
samples prior to 2002 were not designed to support the reporting of accurate and representative state-level results, separate
representative samples of students were selected for each participating jurisdiction/state. From 1990 through 2001, the
national sample was a subset of the combined sample of students assessed in each participating state, plus an additional
sample from the states that did not participate in the state
assessment. Since 2002, a combined sample of public schools
has been selected for both state and national NAEP.

Reading

Overall achievement scores on the NAEP long-term trend
reading assessment for the country's 9-, 13-, and 17-year-old
students are mixed. The average reading scores at ages 9 and
13 were higher in 2004 than in 1971 (table 110). The average
score for 17-year-olds in 2004 was similar to that in 1971.

For Black 9-, 13-, and 17-year-olds, average reading
scores in 2004 were higher than in 1971. At age 9, Black students scored higher on average in 2004 than in any previous
administration year. For Blacks ages 13 and 17, scores
increased between 1971 and 2004 (table 110). For White students, the average scores for 9- and 13-year-olds were also
higher in 2004 than in 1971. Separate data for Hispanics were
not gathered in 1971, but as with the other racial/ethnic
groups, the average reading score for Hispanic students at
age 9 was higher in 2004 than in any other assessment year.
The average score for Hispanic students at age 13 shows an
increase between 1975 and 2004. The scores for 17-year-old
Hispanic students also increased between 1975 and 2004, but
no measurable changes were seen between 1999 and 2004.

The 2005 main NAEP reading assessment of states found
that reading proficiency varied among public school fourth-
graders in the 53 participating jurisdictions (50 states, Department of Defense overseas and domestic schools, and the District of Columbia) (table 114). The U.S. average score was
217. The scores for the participating jurisdictions ranged from
191 in the District of Columbia and 204 in Mississippi to 231
in Massachusetts.

Mathematics

Results from NAEP long-term trend assessments of mathematics proficiency indicate that the scores of 9- and 13-year-
old students were higher in 2004 than in 1973 (table 121). For
White, Black, and Hispanic 9-, 13-, and 17-year-olds, average
mathematics scale scores were higher in 2004 than in 1973.

The 2005 main NAEP assessment of states found that mathematics proficiency varied among public school eighth-graders
in the 53 participating jurisdictions (50 states, Department of
Defense overseas and domestic schools, and the District of
Columbia) (table 125). Overall, 68 percent of these eighth-grade
students performed at or above the *Basic* level in mathematics,
and 29 percent performed at or above the *Proficient* level.

International Comparisons

In 2003, the performance of U.S. 15-year-olds, as measured
by the Program for International Student Assessment (PISA),
in mathematics literacy and problem solving was lower than
the average performance for most Organization for Economic
Cooperation and Development (OECD) countries (table 397).
Along with the scale scores, PISA also used seven proficiency
levels (below level 1 and levels 1 through 6, with level 6 being
the highest level of proficiency) to describe student performance in mathematics literacy (table 398). In mathematics literacy, the United States had greater percentages of students
below level 1 and at levels 1 and 2 than the OECD average percentages. The United States also had a lower percentage of students at levels 4, 5, and 6 than the OECD average percentages.

High School Graduates and Dropouts

The projected number of high school graduates in 2006–07
was 3,232,000 (table 99), including 2,912,000 public school
graduates and 321,000 private school graduates. High school
graduates include only recipients of diplomas, not recipients of
equivalency credentials. The 2006–07 record number of high
school graduates is higher than the former high points in
2005–06, when a projected 3,176,000 students earned diplomas, and in 1976–77, when 3,152,000 students earned diplomas. In 2003–04, an estimated 74.3 percent of public high
school students graduated on time—that is, received a diploma
4 years after beginning their freshman year (table 101). The
number of General Educational Development (GED) credentials issued rose from 332,000 in 1977 to 648,000 in 2001,
before falling to 406,000 in 2004 (table 103). The status dropout rate—that is, the proportion of 16- to 24-year-olds who are
not enrolled in school and have received neither a diploma nor
an equivalency credential—declined over this period, from 14
percent in 1977 to 9 percent in 2005 (table 104).

Educational Technology

There has been widespread introduction of computers into
the schools in recent years. In 2003, the average public school
contained 136 instructional computers (table 422). One
important technological advance that has come to classrooms
following the introduction of computers has been connections
to the Internet. The proportion of instructional rooms with
access to the Internet increased from 51 percent in 1998 to 93
percent in 2003 (figure 29). Nearly all schools had access to
the Internet in 2003 (table 422).

Postsecondary Education

College Enrollment

College enrollment hit a record level of 17.5 million in fall 2005. Another record of 17.6 million is anticipated for fall 2006 (table 3). Enrollment is expected to increase by an additional 13 percent between 2006 and 2015. Despite decreases in the traditional college-age population during the late 1980s and early 1990s, total enrollment increased during the late 1980s and early 1990s (tables 7, 15, 177, and 187). The traditional college-age population (18 to 24 years old) rose 15 percent between 1995 and 2005, which was reflected by an increase in college enrollment. Between 1995 and 2005, the number of full-time students increased by 33 percent compared to a 9 percent increase in part-time students (table 175). During the same time period, the number of men enrolled increased 18 percent, while the number of women enrolled increased 27 percent.

Faculty and Staff

In the fall of 2005, degree-granting institutions—defined as postsecondary institutions that grant an associate's or higher degree and are eligible for Title IV federal financial aid programs—employed 1.3 million faculty members, including 0.7 million full-time and 0.6 million part-time faculty (table 228). About 19 percent of full-time faculty taught 15 or more hours per week, compared with 8 percent of part-time faculty (tables 233 and 234). About 9 percent of full-time faculty taught 150 or more students, compared with 2 percent of part-time faculty.

Postsecondary Degrees

The projections of the number of postsecondary degrees conferred during the 2005–06 school year by degree level show 682,000 associate's degrees; 1,456,000 bachelor's degrees; 584,000 master's degrees; 85,100 first-professional degrees; and 49,500 doctor's degrees (table 251).

Educational Attainment

The U.S. Census Bureau collects annual statistics on the educational attainment of the population. Between 1996 and 2006, the proportion of the adult population 25 years of age and over who had completed high school rose from 82 percent to 85 percent, and the proportion of adults with a bachelor's degree increased from 24 percent to 28 percent (table 8). High school completers include those persons who graduated from high school with a diploma, as well as those who completed high school through equivalency programs. The proportion of young adults (25- to 29-year-olds) who had completed high school in 2006 (86 percent) was about the same as it was in 1996 (87 percent). Also, the proportion of young adults who had completed a bachelor's degree in 2006 (28 percent) was not substantively different from the proportion in 1996 (27 percent).

Education Expenditures

Expenditures for public and private education, from kindergarten through graduate school (excluding postsecondary schools not awarding associate's or higher degrees), are estimated at $922 billion for 2005–06 (table 25). Expenditures of elementary and secondary schools are expected to total $558 billion, while those of degree-granting postsecondary institutions are expected to total $364 billion. Total expenditures for education are expected to amount to 7.4 percent of the gross domestic product in 2005–06, about 0.5 percentage points higher than in 1995–96.

Interpreting Statistics

Readers should be aware of the limitations of statistics. These limitations vary with the exact nature of a particular survey. For example, estimates based on a sample of institutions will differ somewhat from the figures that would have been obtained if a complete census had been taken using the same survey procedures. Standard errors are available for sample survey data appearing in this report. In most cases, standard errors for all items appear in the printed table. In some cases, only standard errors for key items appear in the printed table. Standard errors that do not appear in the tables are available from NCES upon request. Although some of the surveys conducted by NCES are census or universe surveys (which attempt to collect information from all potential respondents), all surveys are subject to design, reporting, and processing errors and errors due to nonresponse. Differences in sampling, data collection procedures, coverage of target population, timing, phrasing of questions, scope of nonresponse, interviewer training, data processing, coding, and so forth mean that the results from the different sources may not be strictly comparable. More information on survey methodologies can be found in the Guide to Sources (appendix A).

Unless otherwise noted, all data in this report are for the 50 states and the District of Columbia. Unless otherwise noted, all financial data are in current dollars, not adjusted for changes in the purchasing power of the dollar. Price indexes for inflation adjustments can be found in table 31.

Common data elements are collected in different ways in different surveys. Since the *Digest* relies on a number of data sources, there are discrepancies in definitions and data across tables in the volume. For example, several different surveys collect data on public school enrollment, and while similar, the estimates are not identical. The definitions of racial/ethnic groups also differ across surveys, particularly with respect to whether Hispanic origin is considered an ethnic group regardless of race, or counted separately as a racial/ethnic group. Individual tables note the definitions used in the given studies.

All statements cited in the text about differences between two or more groups or changes over time were tested for statistical significance and are statistically significant at the .05 level. Various test procedures were used, depending on the nature of the statement tested. The most commonly used test procedures were *t* tests, equivalence tests, and linear trend tests. Equivalence tests were used to determine whether two statistics are substantively equivalent or substantively differ-ent. This was accomplished by using a hypothesis test to determine whether the confidence interval of the difference between sample estimates is substantively significant (i.e., greater or less than a preset substantively important differ-ence). In most cases involving percentages, a difference of 3.0 was used to determine substantive equivalence or differ-

ence. In some comparisons involving only very small per-centages, a lower difference was used. In cases involving only relatively large values, a larger difference was used, such as $1,000 in the case of annual salaries. Linear trend tests were conducted by evaluating the significance of the slope of a simple regression of the data over time, and a t test comparing the end points.

GUIDE TO TABULAR PRESENTATION

This section is intended to assist the reader in following the basic structure of the Digest tables and to provide a legend for some of the common symbols and indexes used throughout the book. Unless otherwise noted, all data are for the 50 states and the District of Columbia.

Table Components

Title   Describes the table content concisely.

Unit indicator   Informs the reader of the measurement unit in the table—"In thousands," "In millions of dollars," etc.

Noted below the title unless several units are used, in which case the unit indicators are generally given in the spanner or individual column heads.

Spanner   Describes a group of two or more columns.

Column head   Describes a specific column.

Stub   Describes a row or a group of rows. Each stub row is followed by a number of dots (leaders).

Field   The area of the table which contains the data elements.

Example of Table Structure

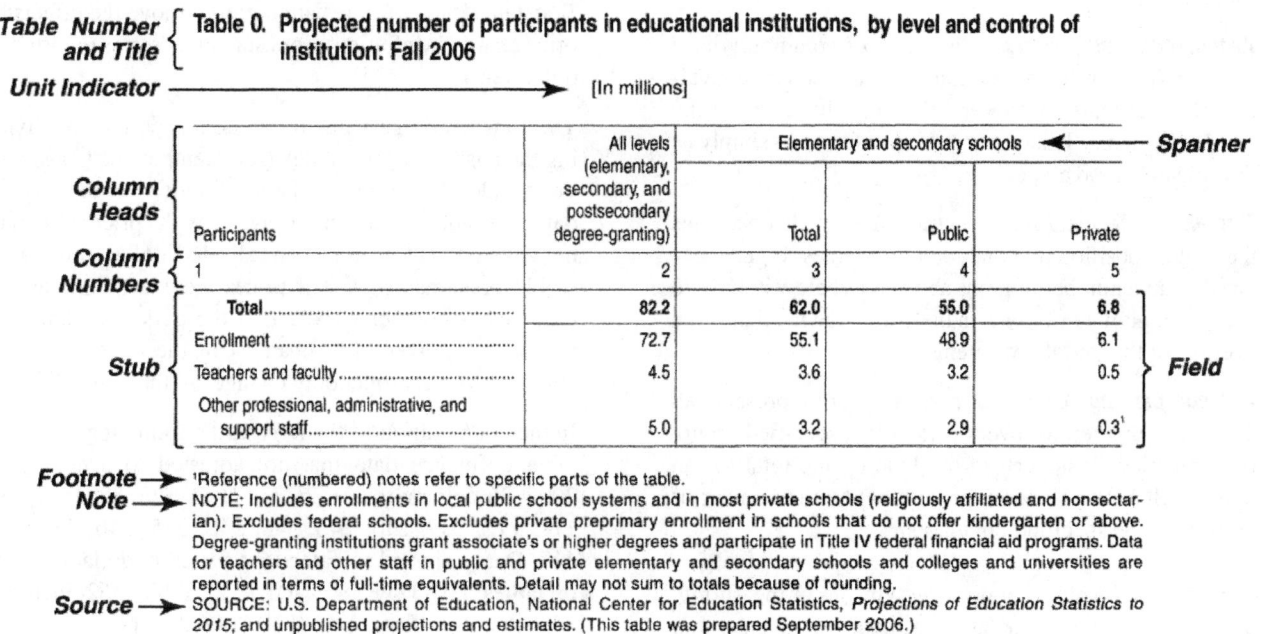

Table Number and Title   Table 0.   Projected number of participants in educational institutions, by level and control of institution: Fall 2006

Unit Indicator → [In millions]

Participants	All levels (elementary, secondary, and postsecondary degree-granting)	Elementary and secondary schools		
		Total	Public	Private
1	2	3	4	5
Total	82.2	62.0	55.0	6.8
Enrollment	72.7	55.1	48.9	6.1
Teachers and faculty	4.5	3.6	3.2	0.5
Other professional, administrative, and support staff	5.0	3.2	2.9	0.3[1]

Footnote → [1]Reference (numbered) notes refer to specific parts of the table.

Note → NOTE: Includes enrollments in local public school systems and in most private schools (religiously affiliated and nonsectarian). Excludes federal schools. Excludes private preprimary enrollment in schools that do not offer kindergarten or above. Degree-granting institutions grant associate's or higher degrees and participate in Title IV federal financial aid programs. Data for teachers and other staff in public and private elementary and secondary schools and colleges and universities are reported in terms of full-time equivalents. Detail may not sum to totals because of rounding.

Source → SOURCE: U.S. Department of Education, National Center for Education Statistics, *Projections of Education Statistics to 2015*; and unpublished projections and estimates. (This table was prepared September 2006.)

Special notes   Symbols used to indicate why data do not appear in designated cell.

— Not available.

† Not applicable.

Rounds to zero.

! Interpret data with caution.

‡ Reporting standards not met.

Footnote   Describes a unique circumstance relating to a specific item within the table.

Note   Furnishes general information that relates to the entire table.

Source   The document or reference from which the data are drawn. This note may also include the organizational unit responsible for preparing the data.

Descriptive Terms

Measures of central tendency   A number that is used to represent the "typical value" of a group of numbers. It is regarded as a measure of "location" or "central tendency" of a group of numbers.

> ***Arithmetic mean (average)***   is the most commonly used average. It is derived by summing the individual item values of a particular group and dividing that sum by the number of items. This value is often referred to simply as the "mean" or "average."

> ***Median***   is the measure of central tendency that occupies the middle position in a rank order of values. It generally has the same number of items above it as below it. If there is an even number of items in the group, the median is the average of the middle two items.

> ***Average per capita,***   or per person, figure represents an average computed for every person in a specified group, or population. It is derived by dividing the total for an item (such as income or expenditures) by the number of persons in the specified population.

Index number   A value that provides a means of measuring, summarizing, and communicating the nature of changes that occur from time to time or from place to place. An index is used to express changes in prices over periods of time, but may also be used to express differences between related subjects at a single point in time.

The *Digest* most often uses the Consumer Price Index to compare purchasing power over time.

To compute a price index, a base year or period is selected. The base-year price is then designated as the base or reference price to which the prices for other years or periods are related.

A method of expressing the price relationship is:

Index number =

$$\frac{\text{Price of a set of one or more items for related year}}{\text{Price of the same set of items for base year}} \times 100$$

When 100 is subtracted from the index number, the result equals the percent change in price from the base year.

Current and constant dollars   are used in a number of tables to express finance data. Unless otherwise noted, all figures are in current dollars, not adjusted for inflation. Constant dollars provide a measure of the impact of inflation on the current dollars.

> ***Current dollar***   figures reflect actual prices or costs prevailing during the specified year(s).

> ***Constant dollar***   figures attempt to remove the effects of price changes (inflation) from statistical series reported in dollar terms.

The constant dollar value for an item is derived by dividing the base-year price index (for example, the Consumer Price Index for 1999) by the price index for the year of data to be adjusted and multiplying by the price of item to be adjusted. The result is an adjusted dollar value as it would presumably exist if prices were the same as the base year—in other words, as if the dollar had constant purchasing power. Any changes in the constant dollar amounts would reflect only changes in the real values.

In the 2006 edition of the *Digest*, the following 19 tables include finance data that are adjusted to school year 2005–06 dollars: tables 26, 32, 71, 75, 76, 82, 167, 170, 171, 172, 239, 240, 246, 340, 342, 345, 346, 352, and 418. Data adjusted to calendar year 2005 dollars appear in tables 20, 377, 387, and 412. Table 362 includes adjustments to fiscal year (FY) 2006 dollars.

NOTE: Tables may not include data for all years implied in table titles. When this is the case, the title will include the term "Selected years."

CHAPTER 1
All Levels of Education

This chapter provides a broad overview of education in the United States. It brings together material from preprimary, elementary, secondary, and postsecondary education, as well as from the general population to present a composite picture of the American educational system. Tables feature data on the total number of persons enrolled in school, the number of teachers, the number of schools, and total expenditures for education at all levels. This chapter also includes statistics on education related topics such as educational attainment, family characteristics, population, and opinions about schools. Economic indicators and price indexes have been added to facilitate analyses.

Figure 1 shows the structure of education in the United States. It presents the three levels of formal education (elementary, secondary, and postsecondary) and gives the approximate age range of persons at the elementary and secondary levels. Students ordinarily spend from 6 to 8 years in the elementary grades, which may be preceded by 1 to 3 years in nursery school and kindergarten. The elementary school program is followed by a 4 to 6 year program in secondary school. Students normally complete the entire program through grade 12 by age 18.

High school graduates who decide to continue their education may enter a technical or vocational institution, a 2-year community or junior college, or a 4-year college or university. A 2-year college normally offers the first 2 years of a standard 4-year college curriculum and a selection of terminal vocational programs. Academic courses completed at a 2-year college are usually transferable for credit at a 4-year college or university. A technical or vocational institution offers postsecondary technical training leading to a specific career.

An associate's degree requires at least 2 years of college-level work, and a bachelor's degree normally requires 4 years of college-level coursework. At least 1 year of coursework beyond the bachelor's is necessary for a master's degree, while a doctor's degree usually requires a minimum of 3 or 4 years beyond the bachelor's.

Professional schools differ widely in admission requirements and program length. Medical students, for example, generally complete a bachelor's program of premedical studies at a college or university before they can enter the 4-year program at a medical school. Law programs normally require 3 years of coursework beyond the bachelor's degree level.

Many of the statistics in this chapter are derived from the statistical activities of the National Center for Education Sta-

tistics (NCES). In addition, substantial contributions have been drawn from the work of other groups, both governmental and nongovernmental, as shown in the source notes of the tables. Information on survey methodologies is contained in Appendix A: Guide to Sources and in the publications cited in the table source notes.

Enrollment and Teachers

Enrollment in elementary and secondary schools grew rapidly during the 1950s and 1960s and reached a peak in 1971 (table 3 and figure 2). This enrollment rise was caused by what is known as the "baby boom," a dramatic increase in births following World War II. From 1971 to 1984, total elementary and secondary school enrollment decreased every year, reflecting the decline in the school-age population over that period. After these years of decline, enrollment in elementary and secondary schools started increasing in fall 1985, and began hitting new record enrollment levels in the mid-1990s.

Public school enrollment in prekindergarten through grade 8 rose from 29.9 million in fall 1990 to 34.2 million in 2003, with a projected enrollment of 33.9 million for fall 2006 (table 3). Public school enrollment in the upper grades rose from 11.3 million in 1990 to 14.6 million in 2004, with a projected enrollment of 15.0 million for 2006. The growing numbers of young pupils who have been filling the elementary schools will cause some increases at the secondary school level through 2007. Between fall 2003 and fall 2005, public elementary enrollment is expected to decrease slightly, and then increase again between 2006 and 2015 (the last year for which NCES has projected school enrollment). Public secondary enrollment is projected to rise through 2007, and then decline until 2014. Overall, school enrollment is projected to set new records every year from 2006 until at least 2015.

The proportion of students in private elementary and secondary schools changed little over the 10 years preceding 2003, remaining between 11 and 12 percent (table 3). The percentage of college students who attended private colleges and universities rose from 22 to 26 percent between 1995 and 2005. In 2006, a projected 6.1 million students were enrolled in private schools at the elementary and secondary levels and 4.3 million students were in private degree-granting institutions.

College enrollment reached 14.5 million in fall 1992 and decreased to 14.3 million in fall 1995 (table 3). Total college enrollment increased between 1995 and 2005, and further increases are expected through 2015.

School enrollment rates among 5- and 6-year-olds, 7- to 13-year-olds, and 14- to 17-year-olds remained relatively steady between 1995 and 2005 (table 7). The proportion of 18- and 19-year-olds enrolled in school rose from 59 to 68 percent between 1995 and 2005, while the proportion of 20- to 24-year-olds enrolled in school rose from 31 to 36 percent.

The percentages of adults 25 years old and over completing high school and pursuing higher education have been rising. In 2006, 85 percent of the population 25 years old and over had completed at least high school and 28 percent had completed a bachelor's or higher degree (table 8 and figure 3). This is higher than in 1996, when 82 percent had completed at least high school and 24 percent had completed a bachelor's or higher degree. In 2006, about 7 percent of persons 25 years old or over held a master's degree as their highest degree, 2 percent held a professional degree (e.g., medicine or law), and 1 percent held a doctor's degree (table 9 and figure 5).

An estimated 3.6 million elementary and secondary school full-time-equivalent teachers were engaged in classroom instruction in the fall of 2006 (table 4). This number has risen about 19 percent since 1996. The number of public school teachers in 2006 was about 3.2 million, and the number in private schools was estimated at 0.5 million.

Expenditures

Expenditures of educational institutions rose to an estimated high of $922 billion in the 2005–06 school year (table 26). Elementary and secondary schools spent about 61 percent of this total, and colleges and universities accounted for the remaining 39 percent. After adjustment for inflation, total expenditures for all educational institutions rose by an estimated 41 percent between 1995–96 and 2005–06. Expenditures for elementary and secondary schools rose by an estimated 36 percent during this period, while total expenditures for colleges and universities rose by 48 percent. In 2005–06, expenditures of educational institutions were an estimated 7.4 percent of the gross domestic product (table 25).

Figure 1.   The structure of education in the United States

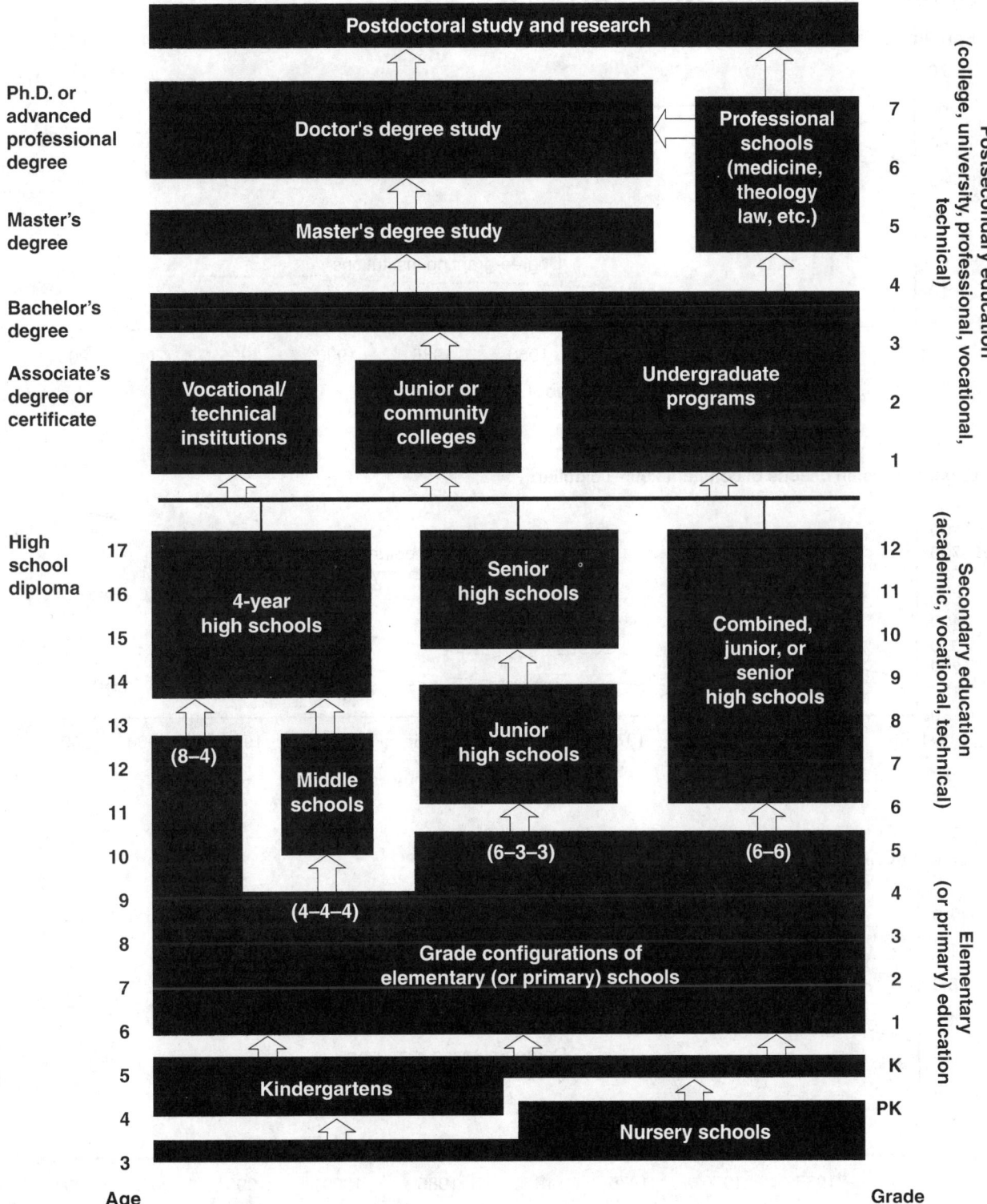

NOTE: Adult education programs, while not separately delineated above, may provide instruction at the adult basic, adult secondary, or postsecondary education levels. Chart reflects typical patterns of progression rather than all possible variations.
SOURCE: U.S. Department of Education, National Center for Education Statistics, Annual Reports Program.

Figure 2.   Enrollment, total expenditures in constant dollars, and expenditures as a percentage of the gross domestic product (GDP), by level of education: 1960–61 through 2004–05

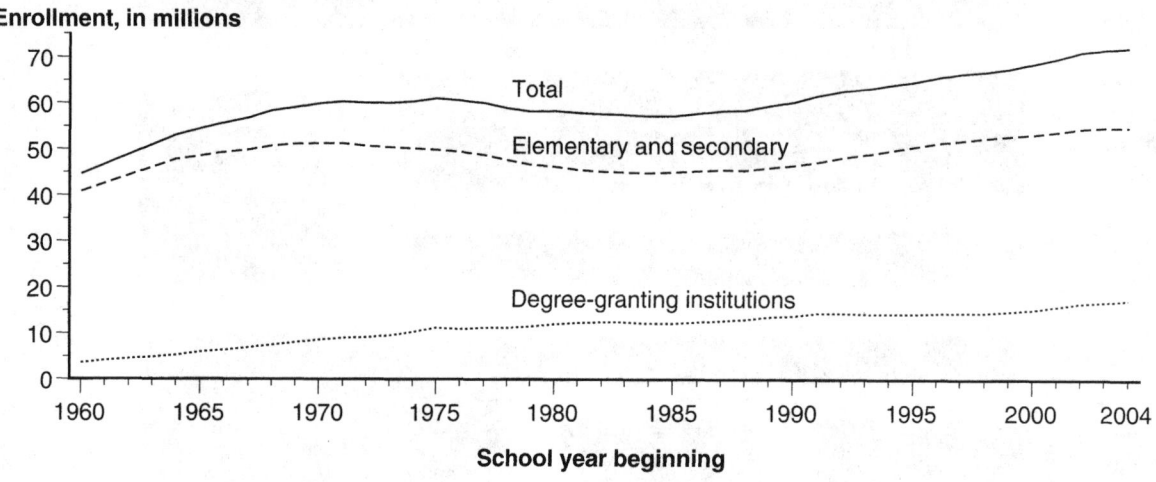

Enrollment, in millions

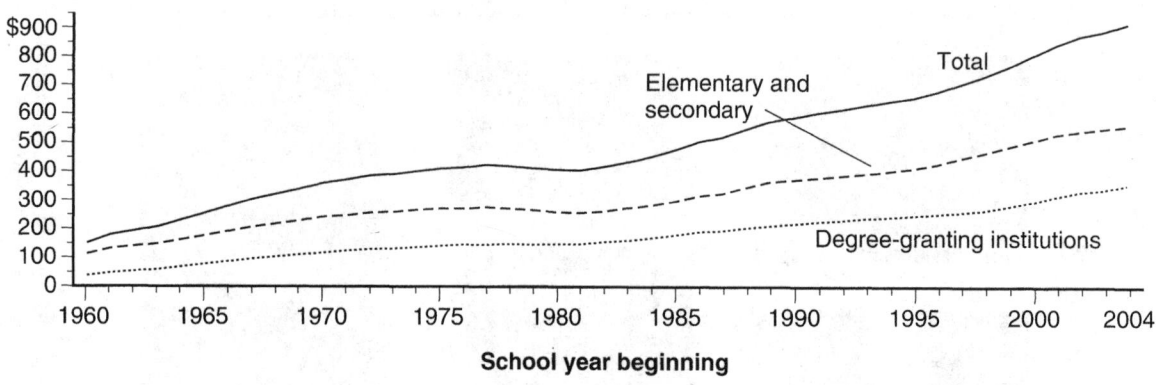

Expenditures, in billions of constant 2005–06 dollars

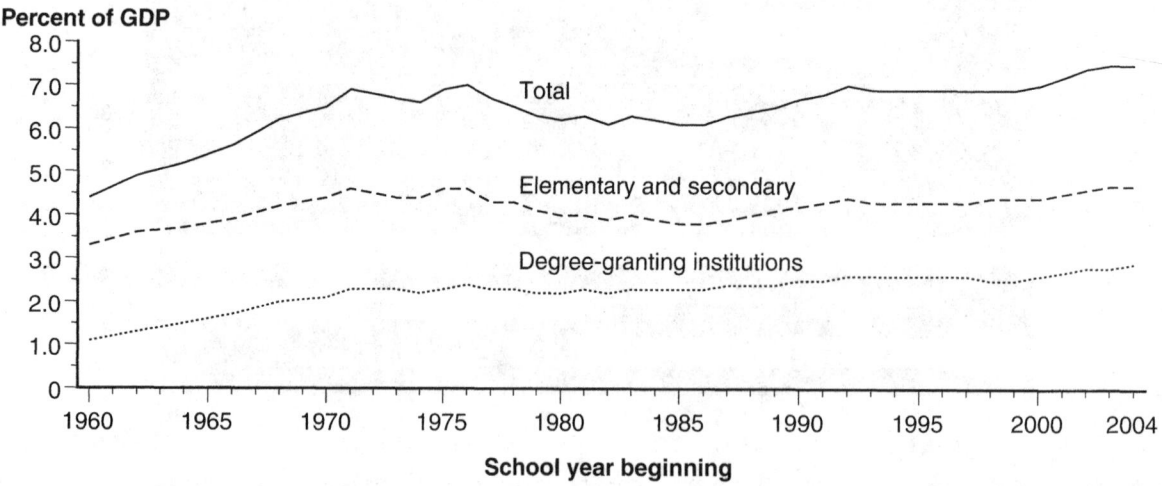

Percent of GDP

NOTE: Expenditure data for school year beginning in 2004 (2004–05) are estimated.
SOURCE: U.S. Department of Education, National Center for Education Statistics, *Statistics of State School Systems*, 1959–60 through 1969–70; *Statistics of Public Elementary and Secondary School Systems*, 1970 through 1980; *Revenues and Expenditures for Public Elementary and Secondary Education*, 1970–71 through 1987–88; Common Core of Data (CCD), "State Nonfiscal Survey of Public Elementary and Secondary Education," 1981–82 through 2004–05; "National Public Education Financial Survey," 1988–89 through 2003–04; *Statistics of Nonpublic Elementary and Secondary Schools*, 1970–71 through 1979–80; Private School Universe Survey (PSS), 1989–90 through 2003–04; *Fall Enrollment in Institutions of Higher Education*, 1959–60 through 1985–86; *Financial Statistics of Institutions of Higher Education*, 1959–60 through 1995–96; 1986–87 through 2004–05 Integrated Postsecondary Education Data System (IPEDS), "Fall Enrollment" surveys, 1986 through 1999, and Spring 2001 through Spring 2005 and Fall 2001 through Fall 2005; and *Projections of Education Statistics to 2015*.

Figure 3. Percentage of persons 25 years old and over, by highest level of educational attainment: 1940 through 2006

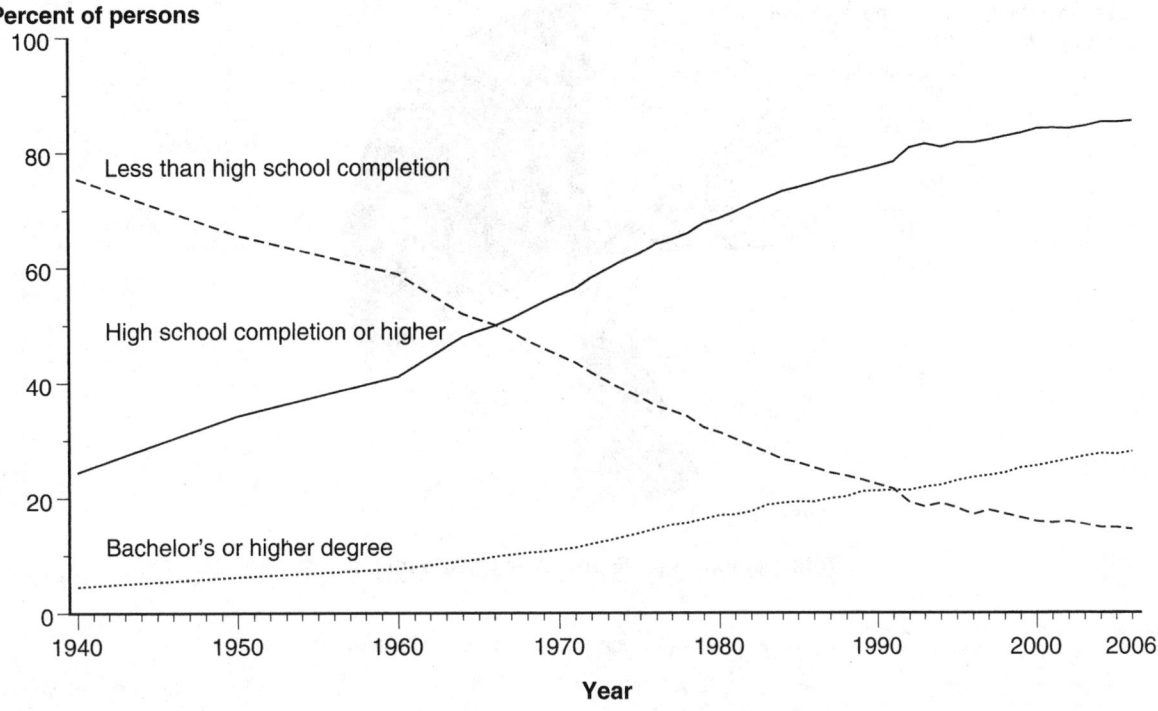

SOURCE: U.S. Department of Commerce, Census Bureau, *U.S. Census of Population, 1960, Volume 1, Part 1*; Current Population Reports, Series P-20; Current Population Survey (CPS), March 1961 through March 2006; and *1960 Census Monograph, Education of the American Population*, by John K. Folger and Charles B. Nam.

Figure 4. Percentage of persons 25 through 29 years old, by highest level of educational attainment: 1940 through 2006

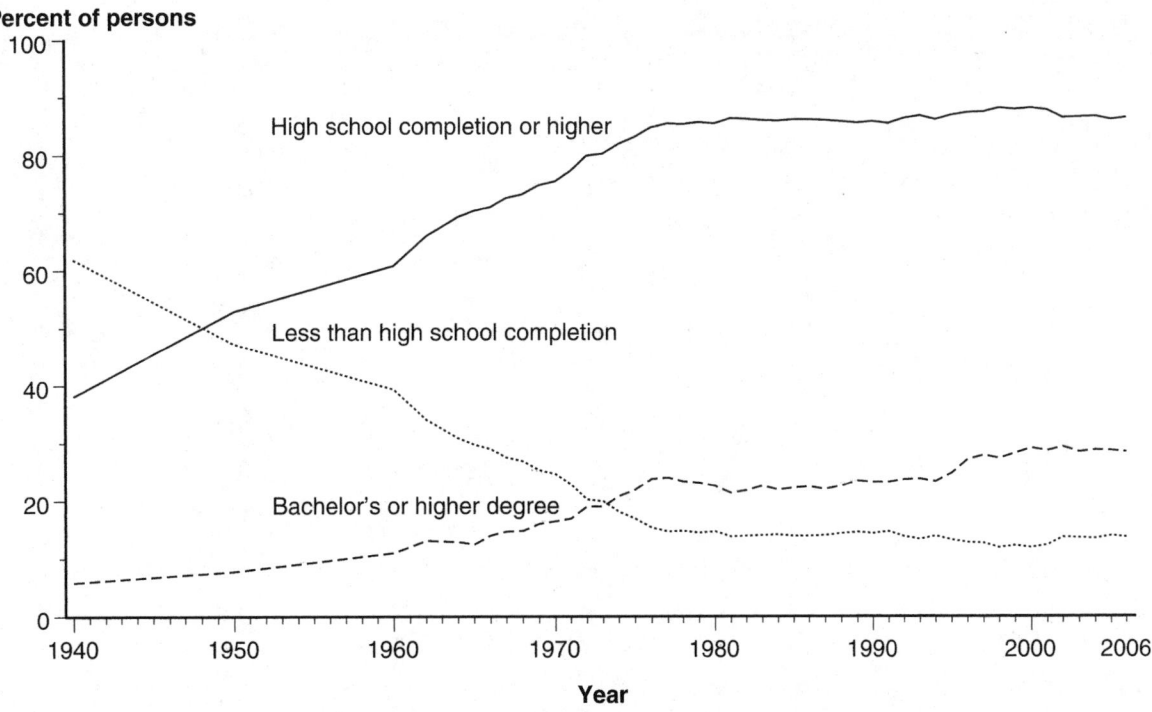

SOURCE: U.S. Department of Commerce, Census Bureau, *U.S. Census of Population, 1960, Volume 1, Part 1*; Current Population Reports, Series P-20; Current Population Survey (CPS), March 1961 through March 2006; and *1960 Census Monograph, Education of the American Population*, by John K. Folger and Charles B. Nam.

Figure 5.   Highest level of education attained by persons 25 years old and over: March 2006

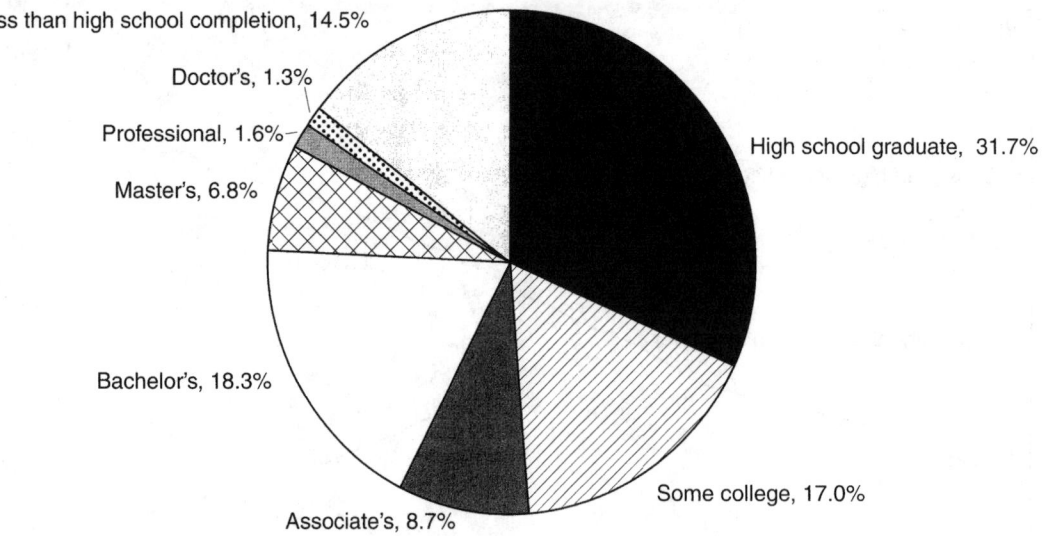

Less than high school completion, 14.5%

Doctor's, 1.3%

Professional, 1.6%

Master's, 6.8%

Bachelor's, 18.3%

Associate's, 8.7%

Some college, 17.0%

High school graduate, 31.7%

Total persons age 25 and over = 191.9 million

NOTE: Detail may not sum to totals because of rounding.
SOURCE: U.S. Department of Commerce, Census Bureau, Current Population Survey (CPS), March 2006, unpublished tabulations.

Table 1. Projected number of participants in educational institutions, by level and control of institution: Fall 2006

[In millions]

Participants	All levels (elementary, secondary, and postsecondary degree-granting)	Elementary and secondary schools			Postsecondary degree-granting institutions		
		Total	Public	Private	Total	Public	Private
1	2	3	4	5	6	7	8
Total................................	82.2	62.0	55.0	6.8	20.3	15.2	5.1
Enrollment	72.7	55.1	48.9	6.1	17.6	13.4	4.3
Teachers and faculty.....................	4.5	3.6	3.2	0.5	0.9	0.6	0.3
Other professional, administrative, and support staff..............................	5.0	3.2	2.9	0.3	1.8	1.2	0.6

NOTE: Includes enrollments in local public school systems and in most private schools (religiously affiliated and nonsectarian). Excludes federal schools. Excludes private prepri-mary enrollment in schools that do not offer kindergarten or above. Degree-granting institu-tions grant associate's or higher degrees and participate in Title IV federal financial aid programs. Data for teachers and other staff in public and private elementary and secondary schools and colleges and universities are reported in terms of full-time equivalents. Detail may not sum to totals because of rounding.
SOURCE: U.S. Department of Education, National Center for Education Statistics, *Projec-tions of Education Statistics to 2015;* and unpublished projections and estimates. (This table was prepared September 2006.)

Table 2. Enrollment in educational institutions, by level and control of institution: Selected years, fall 1980 through fall 2006

[In thousands]

Level of instruction and type of control	Fall 1980	Fall 1985	Fall 1990	Fall 1995	Fall 1996	Fall 1997	Fall 1998	Fall 1999	Fall 2000	Fall 2001	Fall 2002	Fall 2003	Fall 2004[1]	Projected fall 2005	Projected fall 2006
1	2	3	4	5	6	7	8	9	10	11	12	13	14	15	16
All levels....................	58,305	57,226	60,683	65,020	65,911	66,574	67,033	67,667	68,685	69,920	71,015	71,540	72,218	72,260	72,723
Public.............................	50,335	48,901	52,061	55,933	56,732	57,323	57,676	58,167	58,956	59,905	60,935	61,397	61,775	61,732	62,308
Private	7,971	8,325	8,622	9,087	9,180	9,251	9,357	9,500	9,729	10,014	10,080	10,143	10,443	10,528	10,415
Elementary and secondary schools[2]	46,208	44,979	46,864	50,759	51,544	52,071	52,526	52,876	53,373	53,992	54,403	54,639	54,946	54,772	55,075
Public.............................	40,877	39,422	41,217	44,840	45,611	46,127	46,539	46,857	47,204	47,672	48,183	48,540	48,795	48,710	48,948
Private	5,331	5,557	5,648	5,918	5,933[3]	5,944	5,988[3]	6,018	6,169[3]	6,320	6,220[3]	6,099	6,151	6,062	6,127
Prekindergarten to grade 8.....	31,639	31,229	34,392	37,096	37,519	37,832	38,121	38,253	38,594	38,961	39,031	38,990	38,991	38,525	38,658
Public.............................	27,647	27,034	29,878	32,341	32,764	33,073	33,346	33,488	33,688	33,938	34,116	34,202	34,178	33,823	33,906
Private...........................	3,992	4,195	4,514[3]	4,756	4,755[3]	4,759	4,776[3]	4,765	4,906[3]	5,023	4,915[3]	4,788	4,812	4,702	4,752
Grades 9 to 12....................	14,570	13,750	12,472	13,662	14,025	14,239	14,405	14,623	14,779	15,031	15,373	15,649	15,955	16,247	16,417
Public.............................	13,231	12,388	11,338	12,500	12,847	13,054	13,193	13,369	13,515	13,734	14,067	14,338	14,617	14,887	15,042
Private...........................	1,339	1,362	1,134[3]	1,163	1,178[3]	1,185	1,212[3]	1,254	1,264[3]	1,296	1,306[3]	1,311	1,338	1,360	1,375
Postsecondary degree-granting institutions...........	12,097	12,247	13,819	14,262	14,368	14,502	14,507	14,791	15,312	15,928	16,612	16,900	17,272	17,487[4]	17,648
Public.............................	9,457	9,479	10,845	11,092	11,120	11,196	11,138	11,309	11,753	12,233	12,752	12,857	12,980	13,022[4]	13,360
Undergraduate...............	8,442	8,477	9,710	9,904	9,935	10,007	9,950	10,110	10,539	10,986	11,433	11,521	11,651	11,698[4]	11,967
First-professional	114	112	112	115	117	118	121	123	124	128	132	134	136	138[4]	145
Graduate.......................	901	890	1,023	1,074	1,069	1,070	1,067	1,077	1,089	1,119	1,187	1,201	1,194	1,186[4]	1,248
Private	2,640	2,768	2,974	3,169	3,247	3,306	3,369	3,482	3,560	3,695	3,860	4,043	4,292	4,466[4]	4,288
Undergraduate...............	2,033	2,120	2,250	2,328	2,392	2,443	2,487	2,571	2,616	2,730	2,824	2,952	3,130	3,266[4]	3,139
First-professional	163	162	162	183	182	180	182	180	183	181	187	195	199	199[4]	209
Graduate.......................	443	486	563	659	674	683	701	730	761	784	849	896	963	1,001[4]	940

[1]Private elementary and secondary education data are projected.
[2]Includes enrollments in local public school systems and in most private schools (reli-giously affiliated and nonsectarian). Excludes homeschooled children who were not also enrolled in public and private schools. Based on the National Household Education Survey, the homeschooled children numbered approximately 1.1 million in 2003. Private elemen-tary enrollment includes preprimary students in schools offering kindergarten or higher grades.
[3]Estimated.
[4]Actual data.
NOTE: Degree-granting enrollment projections are based on the middle alternative projec-tions published by the National Center for Education Statistics. Data through 1995 are for institutions of higher education, while later data are for degree-granting institutions. Degree-granting institutions grant associate's or higher degrees and participate in Title IV federal financial aid programs. The degree-granting classification is very similar to the ear-lier higher education classification, but it includes more 2-year colleges and excludes a few higher education institutions that did not grant degrees. (See Guide to Sources for details.) Detail may not sum to totals because of rounding. Some data have been revised from pre-viously published figures.
SOURCE: U.S. Department of Education, National Center for Education Statistics, *Statis-tics of Public Elementary and Secondary School Systems, 1980;* Common Core of Data (CCD), "State Nonfiscal Survey of Public Elementary and Secondary Education," 1985–86 through 2004–05; Youth Survey of the National Household Education Surveys Program (Youth-NHES:1999); Private School Universe Survey (PSS), 1995–96 through 2003–04; *Projections of Education Statistics to 2015;* Higher Education General Information Survey (HEGIS), "Fall Enrollment in Institutions of Higher Education" surveys, 1980 and 1985; and 1990 through 2005 Integrated Postsecondary Education Data System (IPEDS), "Fall Enrollment Survey" (IPEDS-EF:90–99), and Spring 2001 through Spring 2006. (This table was prepared September 2006.)

Table 3. Enrollment in educational institutions, by level and control of institution: Selected years, 1869–70 through fall 2015
[In thousands]

Year	Total enrollment, all levels	Elementary and secondary, total	Public elementary and secondary schools			Private elementary and secondary schools[1]			Postsecondary degree-granting institutions[2]		
			Total	Prekindergarten through grade 8	Grades 9 through 12	Total	Prekindergarten through grade 8	Grades 9 through 12	Total	Public	Private
1	2	3	4	5	6	7	8	9	10	11	12
1869–70	—	—	6,872	6,792	80	—	—	—	52	—	—
1879–80	—	—	9,868	9,757	110	—	—	—	116	—	—
1889–90	14,491	14,334	12,723	12,520	203	1,611	1,516	95	157	—	—
1899–1900	17,092	16,855	15,503	14,984	519	1,352	1,241	111	238	—	—
1909–10	19,728	19,372	17,814	16,899	915	1,558	1,441	117	355	—	—
1919–20	23,876	23,278	21,578	19,378	2,200	1,699	1,486	214	598	—	—
1929–30	29,430	28,329	25,678	21,279	4,399	2,651	2,310	341	1,101	—	—
1939–40	29,539	28,045	25,434	18,832	6,601	2,611	2,153	458	1,494	797	698
1949–50	31,151	28,492	25,111	19,387	5,725	3,380	2,708	672	2,659	1,355	1,304
Fall 1959	44,497	40,857	35,182	26,911	8,271	5,675	4,640	1,035	3,640	2,181	1,459
Fall 1969	59,055	51,050	45,550	32,513	13,037	5,500[3]	4,200[3]	1,300[3]	8,005	5,897	2,108
Fall 1970	59,838	51,257	45,894	32,558	13,336	5,363	4,052	1,311	8,581	6,428	2,153
Fall 1971	60,220	51,271	46,071	32,318	13,753	5,200[3]	3,900[3]	1,300[3]	8,949	6,804	2,144
Fall 1972	59,941	50,726	45,726	31,879	13,848	5,000[3]	3,700[3]	1,300[3]	9,215	7,071	2,144
Fall 1973	60,047	50,445	45,445	31,401	14,044	5,000[3]	3,700[3]	1,300[3]	9,602	7,420	2,183
Fall 1974	60,297	50,073	45,073	30,971	14,103	5,000[3]	3,700[3]	1,300[3]	10,224	7,989	2,235
Fall 1975	61,004	49,819	44,819	30,515	14,304	5,000[3]	3,700[3]	1,300[3]	11,185	8,835	2,350
Fall 1976	60,490	49,478	44,311	29,997	14,314	5,167	3,825	1,342	11,012	8,653	2,359
Fall 1977	60,003	48,717	43,577	29,375	14,203	5,140	3,797	1,343	11,286	8,847	2,439
Fall 1978	58,897	47,637	42,551	28,463	14,088	5,086	3,732	1,353	11,260	8,786	2,474
Fall 1979	58,221	46,651	41,651	28,034	13,616	5,000[3]	3,700[3]	1,300[3]	11,570	9,037	2,533
Fall 1980	58,305	46,208	40,877	27,647	13,231	5,331	3,992	1,339	12,097	9,457	2,640
Fall 1981	57,916	45,544	40,044	27,280	12,764	5,500[3]	4,100[3]	1,400[3]	12,372	9,647	2,725
Fall 1982	57,591	45,166	39,566	27,161	12,405	5,600[3]	4,200[3]	1,400[3]	12,426	9,696	2,730
Fall 1983	57,432	44,967	39,252	26,981	12,271	5,715	4,315	1,400	12,465	9,683	2,782
Fall 1984	57,150	44,908	39,208	26,905	12,304	5,700[3]	4,300[3]	1,400[3]	12,242	9,477	2,765
Fall 1985	57,226	44,979	39,422	27,034	12,388	5,557	4,195	1,362	12,247	9,479	2,768
Fall 1986	57,709	45,205	39,753	27,420	12,333	5,452[3]	4,116[3]	1,336[3]	12,504	9,714	2,790
Fall 1987	58,253	45,487	40,008	27,933	12,076	5,479	4,232	1,247	12,767	9,973	2,793
Fall 1988	58,485	45,430	40,189	28,501	11,687	5,242[3]	4,036[3]	1,206[3]	13,055	10,161	2,894
Fall 1989	59,680	46,141	40,543	29,152	11,390	5,599[3]	4,470[3]	1,128[3]	13,539	10,578	2,961
Fall 1990	60,683	46,864	41,217	29,878	11,338	5,648	4,514	1,134	13,819	10,845	2,974
Fall 1991	62,087	47,728	42,047	30,506	11,541	5,681[3]	4,552[3]	1,129[3]	14,359	11,310	3,049
Fall 1992	62,987	48,500	42,823	31,088	11,735	5,677[3]	4,560[3]	1,117[3]	14,487	11,385	3,103
Fall 1993	63,439	49,134	43,465	31,504	11,961	5,669[3]	4,564[3]	1,104[3]	14,305	11,189	3,116
Fall 1994	64,177	49,898	44,111	31,898	12,213	5,787[3]	4,656[3]	1,131[3]	14,279	11,134	3,145
Fall 1995	65,020	50,759	44,840	32,341	12,500	5,918	4,756	1,163	14,262	11,092	3,169
Fall 1996	65,911	51,544	45,611	32,764	12,847	5,933[3]	4,755[3]	1,178[3]	14,368	11,120	3,247
Fall 1997	66,574	52,071	46,127	33,073	13,054	5,944	4,759	1,185	14,502	11,196	3,306
Fall 1998	67,033	52,526	46,539	33,346	13,193	5,988[3]	4,776[3]	1,212[3]	14,507	11,138	3,369
Fall 1999	67,667	52,876	46,857	33,488	13,369	6,018	4,789	1,229	14,791	11,309	3,482
Fall 2000	68,685	53,373	47,204	33,688	13,515	6,169[3]	4,906[3]	1,264[3]	15,312	11,753	3,560
Fall 2001	69,920	53,992	47,672	33,938	13,734	6,320	5,023	1,296	15,928	12,233	3,695
Fall 2002	71,015	54,403	48,183	34,116	14,067	6,220[3]	4,915[3]	1,306[3]	16,612	12,752	3,860
Fall 2003	71,540	54,639	48,540	34,202	14,338	6,099	4,788	1,311	16,900	12,857	4,043
Fall 2004	72,218	54,946	48,795	34,178	14,617	6,151[4]	4,812[4]	1,338[4]	17,272	12,980	4,292
Fall 2005[4]	72,260	54,772	48,710	33,823	14,887	6,062	4,702	1,360	17,487[5]	13,022[5]	4,466[5]
Fall 2006[4]	72,723	55,075	48,948	33,906	15,042	6,127	4,752	1,375	17,648	13,360	4,288
Fall 2007[4]	73,154	55,238	49,091	33,990	15,101	6,147	4,765	1,382	17,916	13,555	4,361
Fall 2008[4]	73,535	55,333	49,167	34,154	15,013	6,166	4,791	1,374	18,202	13,765	4,437
Fall 2009[4]	73,933	55,453	49,267	34,350	14,917	6,186	4,821	1,365	18,480	13,968	4,511

See notes at end of table.

Table 3. Enrollment in educational institutions, by level and control of institution: Selected years, 1869–70 through fall 2015—Continued

[In thousands]

Year	Total enrollment, all levels	Elementary and secondary, total	Public elementary and secondary schools			Private elementary and secondary schools[1]			Postsecondary degree-granting institutions[2]		
			Total	Prekindergarten through grade 8	Grades 9 through 12	Total	Prekindergarten through grade 8	Grades 9 through 12	Total	Public	Private
1	2	3	4	5	6	7	8	9	10	11	12
Fall 2010[4]	74,376	55,630	49,415	34,618	14,797	6,215	4,860	1,355	18,746	14,159	4,587
Fall 2011[4]	74,842	55,886	49,637	34,907	14,730	6,249	4,901	1,348	18,956	14,311	4,645
Fall 2012[4]	75,414	56,232	49,938	35,297	14,641	6,294	4,954	1,341	19,182	14,473	4,709
Fall 2013[4]	76,077	56,638	50,294	35,724	14,569	6,344	5,010	1,334	19,439	14,659	4,780
Fall 2014[4]	76,819	57,137	50,735	36,143	14,593	6,402	5,066	1,335	19,682	14,835	4,847
Fall 2015[4]	77,555	57,681	51,220	36,439	14,780	6,461	5,110	1,351	19,874	14,974	4,900

—Not available.

[1]Beginning in fall 1980, data include estimates for an expanded universe of private schools. Therefore, direct comparisons with earlier years should be avoided.

[2]Data for 1869–70 through 1949–50 include resident degree-credit students enrolled at any time during the academic year. Beginning in 1959, data include all resident and extension students enrolled at the beginning of the fall term.

[3]Estimated.

[4]Projected.

[5]Actual data.

NOTE: Elementary and secondary enrollment includes students in local public school systems and in most private schools (religiously affiliated and nonsectarian), but generally excludes homeschooled children and students in subcollegiate departments of colleges and in federal schools. Based on the National Household Education Survey, the homeschooled children numbered approximately 1.1 million in 2003. Excludes preprimary pupils in private schools that do not offer kindergarten or above. Data through 1995 are for institutions of higher education, while later data are for degree-granting institutions. Degree-granting institutions grant associate's or higher degrees and participate in Title IV federal financial aid programs. The degree-granting classification is very similar to the earlier higher education classification, but it includes more 2-year colleges and excludes a few higher education institutions that did not grant degrees. (See Guide to Sources for details.) Some data have been revised from previously published figures. Detail may not sum to totals because of rounding.

SOURCE: U.S. Department of Education, National Center for Education Statistics, *Annual Report of the Commissioner of Education, 1870 to 1910; Biennial Survey of Education in the United States, 1919–20 through 1949–50; Statistics of Public Elementary and Secondary School Systems, 1959 through 1980;* Common Core of Data (CCD), "State Nonfiscal Survey of Public Elementary and Secondary Education," 1981–82 through 2004–05; Youth Survey of the National Household Education Surveys Program (Youth-NHES:1999); Private School Universe Survey (PSS), 1989–90 through 2003–04; *Projections of Education Statistics to 2015;* Opening (Fall) Enrollment in Higher Education, 1959 through 1962; Higher Education General Information Survey (HEGIS), "Fall Enrollment in Institutions of Higher Education" surveys, 1966 through 1985; and 1986 through 2005 Integrated Postsecondary Education Data System (IPEDS), "Fall Enrollment Survey" (IPEDS-EF:86–99), and Spring 2001 through Spring 2006. (This table was prepared September 2006.)

Table 4. Number of teachers in elementary and secondary schools, and instructional staff in postsecondary degree-granting institutions, by control of institution: Selected years, fall 1970 through fall 2015

[In thousands]

Year	All levels			Elementary and secondary teachers[1]			Degree-granting institutions instructional staff[2]		
	Total	Public	Private	Total	Public	Private	Total	Public	Private
1	2	3	4	5	6	7	8	9	10
1970	2,766	2,373	393	2,292	2,059	233	474	314	160
1975	3,081	2,641	440	2,453	2,198	255 [3]	628	443	185
1980	3,171	2,679	492	2,485	2,184	301	686 [3,4]	495 [3,4]	191 [3,4]
1981	3,145	2,636	509	2,440	2,127	313 [3]	705	509	196
1982	3,168	2,639	529	2,458	2,133	325 [3]	710 [3,4]	506 [3,4]	204 [3,4]
1983	3,200	2,651	549	2,476	2,139	337	724	512	212
1984	3,225	2,673	552	2,508	2,168	340 [3]	717 [3,4]	505 [3,4]	212 [3,4]
1985	3,264	2,709	555	2,549	2,206	343	715 [3,4]	503 [3,4]	212 [3,4]
1986	3,314	2,754	560	2,592	2,244	348 [3]	722 [3,4]	510 [3,4]	212 [3,4]
1987	3,424	2,831	592	2,631	2,279	352 [3]	793	553	240
1988	3,472	2,882	590	2,668	2,323	345 [3]	804 [3]	559 [3]	245 [3]
1989	3,537	2,934	603	2,713	2,357	356 [3]	824	577	247
1990	3,576	2,972	604	2,759	2,398	361 [3]	817 [3]	574 [3]	244 [3]
1991	3,623	3,013	610	2,797	2,432	365 [3]	826	581	245
1992	3,703	3,080	624	2,827	2,459	368 [3]	877 [3]	621 [3]	257 [3]
1993	3,790	3,154	636	2,874	2,504	370 [3]	915	650	265
1994	3,848	3,205	643	2,925	2,552	373 [3]	923 [3]	653 [3]	270 [3]
1995	3,906	3,255	651	2,974	2,598	376 [3]	932	657	275
1996	4,006	3,339	666	3,051	2,667	384 [3]	954 [3]	672 [3]	282 [3]
1997	4,127	3,441	687	3,138	2,746	391	990	695	295
1998	4,230	3,527	703	3,230	2,830	400 [3]	999 [3]	697 [3]	303 [3]
1999	4,347	3,624	723	3,319	2,911	408	1,028	713	315
2000	4,433	3,682	750	3,366	2,941	424 [3]	1,067 [3]	741 [3]	326 [3]
2001	4,554	3,771	783	3,440	3,000	441	1,113	771	342
2002	4,632	3,829	803	3,476	3,034	442 [3]	1,156 [3]	795 [3]	361 [3]
2003	4,664	3,841	823	3,490	3,049	441	1,175	793	382
2004	4,775	3,909	865	3,537	3,091	447 [3]	1,237 [3]	819 [3]	418 [3]
2005[5]	4,883	3,980	903	3,593	3,139	454	1,290	841	449
2006[5]	—	—	—	3,635	3,176	459	—	—	—
2007[5]	—	—	—	3,671	3,207	464	—	—	—
2008[5]	—	—	—	3,705	3,237	468	—	—	—
2009[5]	—	—	—	3,738	3,266	472	—	—	—
2010[5]	—	—	—	3,776	3,299	477	—	—	—
2011[5]	—	—	—	3,820	3,337	483	—	—	—
2012[5]	—	—	—	3,873	3,384	489	—	—	—
2013[5]	—	—	—	3,932	3,435	497	—	—	—
2014[5]	—	—	—	3,997	3,492	505	—	—	—
2015[5]	—	—	—	4,064	3,551	513	—	—	—

—Not available.

[1]Includes teachers in local public school systems and in most private schools (religiously affil-iated and nonsectarian). Teachers are reported in terms of full-time equivalents.

[2]Data through 1995 are for institutions of higher education, while later data are for degree-granting institutions. Degree-granting institutions grant associate's or higher degrees and participate in Title IV federal financial aid programs. The degree-granting classification is very similar to the earlier higher education classification, but it includes more 2-year colleges and excludes a few higher education institutions that did not grant degrees. (See Guide to Sources for details.) Includes full-time and part-time faculty with the rank of instructor or above in colleges, universities, professional schools, and 2-year colleges. Excludes teaching assistants.

[3]Estimated.

[4]Inclusion of institutions is not consistent with surveys for 1987 and later years.

[5]Projected.

NOTE: Detail may not sum to totals because of rounding. Some data have been revised from previously published figures. Headcounts are used to report data for degree-granting institu-tions instructional staff.

SOURCE: U.S. Department of Education, National Center for Education Statistics, *Statistics of Public Elementary and Secondary Day Schools*, 1970 and 1975; Common Core of Data (CCD), "State Nonfiscal Survey of Public Elementary/Secondary Education," 1980 through 2003; *Projections of Education Statistics to 2015*; Higher Education General Information Sur-vey (HEGIS), "Fall Staff" survey, 1970 and 1975; 1987 through 2005 Integrated Postsecond-ary Education Data System (IPEDS), "Fall Staff Survey" (IPEDS-S:87–99), and Winter 2001–02 through Winter 2005–06; U.S. Equal Opportunity Commission, EEO-6, 1981 and 1983; and unpublished data. (This table was prepared October 2006.)

Table 5. Number of educational institutions, by level and control of institution: Selected years, 1980–81 through 2004–05

Level and control of institution	1980–81	1990–91	1993–94	1994–95	1995–96	1996–97	1997–98	1998–99	1999–2000	2000–01	2001–02	2002–03	2003–04	2004–05
1	2	3	4	5	6	7	8	9	10	11	12	13	14	15
All institutions	—	—	—	—	—	—	123,504	—	125,642	—	129,843	—	130,522	—
Elementary and secondary schools	106,746	109,228	111,486	—	114,811	—	116,910	—	119,235	—	123,385	—	124,110	—
Elementary	72,659	74,716	75,591	—	77,909	—	79,362	—	80,661	—	82,655	—	82,955	—
Secondary	24,856	23,602	23,256	—	23,530	—	24,169	—	24,903	—	24,884	—	25,476	—
Combined	5,202	8,847	10,678	—	11,205	—	11,412	—	12,197	—	14,430	—	13,931	—
Other[1]	4,029	2,063	1,962	—	2,167	—	1,967	—	1,474	—	1,416	—	1,749	—
Public schools	85,982	84,538	85,393	86,221	87,125	88,223	89,508	90,874	92,012	93,273	94,112	95,615	95,726	96,513
Elementary	59,326	59,015	60,052	60,808	61,165	61,805	62,739	63,462	64,131	64,601	65,228	65,718	65,758	65,984
Secondary	22,619	21,135	20,705	20,904	20,997	21,307	21,682	22,076	22,365	21,994	22,180	22,599	22,782	23,445
Combined	1,743	2,325	2,674	2,764	2,796	2,980	3,120	3,721	4,042	5,096	5,288	5,552	5,437	5,572
Other[1]	2,294	2,063	1,962	1,745	2,167	2,131	1,967	1,615	1,474	1,582	1,416	1,746	1,749	1,512
Private schools	20,764	24,690	26,093	—	27,686	—	27,402	—	27,223	—	29,273	—	28,384	—
Elementary	13,333	15,701	15,539	—	16,744	—	16,623	—	16,530	—	17,427	—	17,197	—
Secondary	2,237	2,467	2,551	—	2,533	—	2,487	—	2,538	—	2,704	—	2,694	—
Combined	3,459	6,522	8,004	—	8,409	—	8,292	—	8,155	—	9,142	—	8,494	—
Other[1]	1,735	(2)	(2)	—	(2)	—	(2)	—	(2)	—	(2)	—	(2)	—
Postsecondary Title IV institutions	—	—	—	—	—	6,669	6,594	6,431	6,407	6,479	6,458	6,354	6,412	6,383
Public	—	—	—	—	—	2,069	2,163	2,090	2,078	2,084	2,099	2,051	2,047	2,027
Private	—	—	—	—	—	4,600	4,431	4,341	4,329	4,395	4,359	4,303	4,365	4,356
Not-for-profit	—	—	—	—	—	2,027	2,007	1,986	1,936	1,950	1,941	1,921	1,913	1,875
For-profit	—	—	—	—	—	2,573	2,424	2,355	2,393	2,445	2,418	2,382	2,452	2,481
Title IV non-degree-granting institutions	—	—	—	—	—	2,660	2,530	2,383	2,323	2,297	2,261	2,186	2,176	2,167
Public	—	—	—	—	—	367	456	409	396	386	386	339	327	327
Private	—	—	—	—	—	2,293	2,074	1,974	1,927	1,911	1,875	1,847	1,849	1,840
Not-for-profit	—	—	—	—	—	334	300	291	255	255	265	256	249	238
For-profit	—	—	—	—	—	1,959	1,774	1,683	1,672	1,656	1,610	1,591	1,600	1,602
Title IV degree-granting institutions	3,231	3,559	3,632	3,688	3,706	4,009	4,064	4,048	4,084	4,182	4,197	4,168	4,236	4,216
2-year colleges	1,274	1,418	1,442	1,473	1,462	1,742	1,755	1,713	1,721	1,732	1,710	1,702	1,706	1,683
Public	945	972	1,021	1,036	1,047	1,088	1,092	1,069	1,068	1,076	1,085	1,081	1,086	1,061
Private	329	446	421	437	415	654	663	644	653	656	625	621	620	622
Not-for-profit	182	167	181	192	187	184	179	164	150	144	135	127	118	112
For-profit	147	279	240	245	228	470	484	480	503	512	490	494	502	510
4-year colleges	1,957	2,141	2,190	2,215	2,244	2,267	2,309	2,335	2,363	2,450	2,487	2,466	2,530	2,533
Public	552	595	604	605	608	614	615	612	614	622	628	631	634	639
Private	1,405	1,546	1,586	1,610	1,636	1,653	1,694	1,723	1,749	1,828	1,859	1,835	1,896	1,894
Not-for-profit	1,387	1,482	1,506	1,510	1,519	1,509	1,528	1,531	1,531	1,551	1,541	1,538	1,546	1,525
For-profit	18	64	80	100	117	144	166	192	218	277	318	297	350	369

—Not available.

[1]Includes special education, alternative, and other schools not classified by grade span. Because of changes in survey definitions, figures for ""other"" schools are not comparable from year to year.

[2]Included in other private school categories.

NOTE: Postsecondary data through 1994–95 are for institutions of higher education, while later data are for Title IV degree-granting and non-degree-granting institutions. Degree-granting institutions grant associate's or higher degrees and participate in Title IV federal financial aid programs. The degree-granting classification is very similar to the earlier higher education classification, but it includes more 2-year colleges and excludes a few higher education institutions that did not grant degrees. (See Guide to Sources for details.)

SOURCE: U.S. Department of Education, National Center for Education Statistics, Common Core of Data (CCD), "Public Elementary/Secondary School Universe Survey," 1989–90 through 2004–05; *Private Schools in American Education;* Schools and Staffing Survey (SASS), "Public School Questionnaire," 1990–91; Private School Universe Survey (PSS), 1993–94 through 2003–04; Higher Education General Information Survey (HEGIS), "Institutional Characteristics of Colleges and Universities" survey, 1980–81; and 1990–91 through 2004–05 Integrated Postsecondary Education Data System (IPEDS), "Institutional Characteristics Survey" (IPEDS-IC:90–99), and Fall 2001 through Fall 2004. (This table was prepared August 2006.)

Table 6. Percentage of the population 3 to 34 years old enrolled in school, by sex, race/ethnicity, and age: Selected years, 1980 through 2005

Year and age	Total				Male				Female			
	Total	White	Black	Hispanic	Total	White	Black	Hispanic	Total	White	Black	Hispanic
1	2	3	4	5	6	7	8	9	10	11	12	13
1980												
Total, 3 to 34 years	49.7 (0.21)	48.8 (0.24)	54.0 (0.68)	49.8 (1.07)	50.9 (0.30)	50.0 (0.34)	56.2 (0.98)	49.9 (1.53)	48.5 (0.30)	47.7 (0.34)	52.1 (0.94)	49.8 (1.51)
3 and 4 years	36.7 (0.95)	37.4 (1.12)	38.2 (2.83)	28.5 (3.92)	37.8 (1.33)	39.2 (1.58)	36.4 (3.94)	30.1 (5.37)	35.5 (1.34)	35.5 (1.58)	40.0 (4.04)	26.6 (5.71)
5 and 6 years	95.7 (0.40)	95.9 (0.46)	95.5 (1.22)	94.5 (2.13)	95.0 (0.60)	95.4 (0.68)	94.1 (1.95)	94.0 (3.22)	96.4 (0.53)	96.5 (0.61)	97.0 (1.43)	94.9 (2.83)
7 to 9 years	99.1 (0.15)	99.1 (0.17)	99.4 (0.35)	98.4 (0.91)	99.0 (0.22)	99.0 (0.26)	99.5 (0.45)	97.7 (1.57)	99.2 (0.20)	99.2 (0.24)	99.3 (0.54)	99.0 (0.99)
10 to 13 years	99.4 (0.10)	99.4 (0.12)	99.4 (0.31)	99.7 (0.36)	99.4 (0.14)	99.4 (0.16)	99.9 (0.42)	99.4 (0.66)	99.3 (0.15)	99.3 (0.18)	99.3 (0.46)	99.0 (0.25)
14 and 15 years	98.2 (0.22)	98.7 (0.22)	97.9 (0.72)	94.3 (1.87)	98.7 (0.27)	98.9 (0.28)	98.4 (0.88)	96.7 (2.10)	97.7 (0.36)	98.5 (0.34)	97.3 (1.15)	92.1 (2.99)
16 and 17 years	89.0 (0.51)	89.2 (0.57)	90.7 (1.44)	81.8 (3.25)	89.1 (0.71)	89.4 (0.79)	90.7 (2.04)	81.5 (4.70)	88.8 (0.72)	89.0 (0.82)	90.6 (2.05)	82.2 (4.49)
18 and 19 years	46.4 (0.80)	47.0 (0.91)	45.8 (2.56)	37.8 (3.94)	47.0 (1.14)	48.5 (1.29)	42.9 (3.73)	36.9 (5.44)	45.8 (1.11)	45.7 (1.26)	48.3 (3.51)	38.8 (5.71)
20 and 21 years	31.0 (0.74)	33.0 (0.85)	23.3 (2.21)	19.5 (3.29)	32.6 (1.08)	34.8 (1.23)	22.8 (3.29)	21.4 (4.88)	29.5 (1.02)	31.3 (1.18)	23.7 (2.99)	17.6 (4.43)
22 to 24 years	16.3 (0.49)	16.8 (0.56)	13.6 (1.53)	11.7 (2.26)	17.8 (0.73)	18.7 (0.83)	13.4 (2.29)	10.7 (3.14)	14.9 (0.66)	15.0 (0.75)	13.7 (2.05)	12.6 (3.24)
25 to 29 years	9.3 (0.31)	9.4 (0.35)	8.8 (1.04)	6.9 (1.43)	9.8 (0.45)	9.8 (0.50)	10.6 (1.70)	6.8 (2.06)	8.8 (0.42)	9.1 (0.48)	7.5 (1.29)	6.9 (1.99)
30 to 34 years	6.4 (0.27)	6.4 (0.30)	6.9 (1.00)	5.1 (1.35)	5.9 (0.37)	5.6 (0.40)	7.2 (1.55)	6.2 (2.07)	7.0 (0.39)	7.2 (0.45)	6.6 (1.32)	4.1 (1.71)
1990												
Total, 3 to 34 years	50.2 (0.23)	49.8 (0.27)	52.2 (0.71)	47.2 (1.06)	50.9 (0.32)	50.4 (0.38)	54.3 (1.02)	46.8 (1.48)	49.5 (0.32)	49.2 (0.38)	50.3 (0.99)	47.7 (1.52)
3 and 4 years	44.4 (0.99)	47.2 (1.19)	41.8 (2.98)	30.7 (4.08)	43.9 (1.38)	47.9 (1.66)	38.1 (4.14)	28.0 (5.57)	44.9 (1.41)	46.6 (1.70)	45.5 (4.25)	33.6 (5.95)
5 and 6 years	96.5 (0.37)	96.7 (0.43)	96.5 (1.05)	94.9 (1.96)	96.5 (0.51)	96.8 (0.59)	96.2 (1.53)	95.8 (2.48)	96.4 (0.53)	96.7 (0.62)	96.9 (1.43)	93.9 (3.05)
7 to 9 years	99.7 (0.09)	99.7 (0.11)	99.8 (0.19)	99.5 (0.52)	99.7 (0.13)	99.7 (0.16)	99.9 (0.24)	99.5 (0.70)	99.6 (0.14)	99.7 (0.15)	99.8 (0.31)	99.4 (0.79)
10 to 13 years	99.6 (0.09)	99.7 (0.10)	99.9 (0.15)	99.1 (0.64)	99.6 (0.13)	99.6 (0.14)	99.9 (0.19)	99.0 (0.93)	99.7 (0.12)	99.7 (0.13)	99.8 (0.25)	99.1 (0.87)
14 and 15 years	99.0 (0.19)	99.0 (0.23)	99.4 (0.46)	99.0 (0.90)	99.1 (0.25)	99.2 (0.30)	99.7 (0.48)	99.1 (1.11)	98.9 (0.29)	98.8 (0.35)	99.1 (0.79)	98.8 (1.47)
16 and 17 years	92.5 (0.52)	93.5 (0.58)	91.7 (1.59)	85.4 (3.22)	92.6 (0.72)	93.4 (0.82)	93.0 (2.09)	85.5 (4.40)	92.4 (0.74)	93.7 (0.81)	90.5 (2.41)	85.3 (4.74)
18 and 19 years	57.2 (0.94)	59.1 (1.10)	55.0 (2.83)	44.0 (4.36)	58.2 (1.33)	59.7 (1.56)	60.4 (3.99)	40.7 (6.23)	56.3 (1.32)	58.5 (1.57)	49.8 (3.96)	47.2 (6.08)
20 and 21 years	39.7 (0.92)	43.1 (1.10)	28.3 (2.57)	27.2 (3.83)	40.3 (1.32)	44.2 (1.59)	31.0 (3.81)	21.7 (4.95)	39.2 (1.28)	42.0 (1.53)	25.8 (3.45)	33.1 (5.79)
22 to 24 years	21.0 (0.63)	21.9 (0.75)	19.7 (2.01)	9.9 (2.05)	22.3 (0.92)	23.7 (1.11)	19.3 (3.03)	11.2 (2.98)	19.9 (0.86)	20.3 (1.02)	20.0 (2.68)	8.4 (2.77)
25 to 29 years	9.7 (0.33)	10.4 (0.39)	6.1 (0.87)	6.3 (1.29)	9.2 (0.46)	10.0 (0.55)	4.7 (1.14)	4.6 (1.55)	10.2 (0.47)	10.7 (0.56)	7.3 (1.27)	8.1 (2.06)
30 to 34 years	5.8 (0.25)	6.2 (0.30)	4.5 (0.75)	3.6 (0.99)	4.8 (0.33)	5.0 (0.38)	2.3 (0.80)	4.0 (1.45)	6.9 (0.38)	7.4 (0.46)	6.3 (1.19)	3.1 (1.32)
1995												
Total, 3 to 34 years	53.7 (0.21)	53.8 (0.25)	56.3 (0.58)	49.7 (0.65)	54.3 (0.29)	54.2 (0.35)	58.6 (0.83)	49.1 (0.90)	53.2 (0.30)	53.4 (0.36)	54.1 (0.80)	50.3 (0.93)
3 and 4 years	48.7 (0.87)	52.2 (1.09)	47.8 (2.28)	36.9 (2.35)	49.4 (1.22)	51.1 (1.52)	52.4 (3.26)	40.8 (3.33)	48.1 (1.24)	53.5 (1.56)	43.4 (3.17)	32.7 (3.28)
5 and 6 years	96.0 (0.34)	96.6 (0.39)	95.4 (0.96)	93.9 (1.22)	95.3 (0.51)	95.9 (0.60)	94.6 (1.48)	93.6 (1.74)	96.8 (0.44)	97.4 (0.49)	96.3 (1.23)	94.3 (1.71)
7 to 9 years	98.7 (0.17)	98.9 (0.18)	97.7 (0.59)	98.5 (0.55)	98.9 (0.22)	99.0 (0.24)	98.1 (0.74)	98.8 (0.72)	98.5 (0.25)	98.9 (0.27)	97.2 (0.91)	98.2 (0.82)
10 to 13 years	99.1 (0.12)	99.0 (0.15)	99.2 (0.30)	99.2 (0.36)	99.1 (0.17)	99.1 (0.21)	99.5 (0.34)	98.8 (0.58)	99.0 (0.18)	98.9 (0.22)	98.9 (0.50)	99.5 (0.39)
14 and 15 years	98.9 (0.18)	98.8 (0.22)	99.0 (0.46)	98.9 (0.56)	99.0 (0.24)	98.9 (0.30)	99.6 (0.40)	98.4 (0.92)	98.8 (0.27)	98.7 (0.33)	98.3 (0.83)	99.4 (0.58)
16 and 17 years	93.6 (0.42)	94.4 (0.47)	93.0 (1.16)	88.2 (1.82)	94.5 (0.54)	95.0 (0.62)	95.6 (1.30)	88.4 (2.58)	92.6 (0.64)	93.8 (0.72)	90.3 (1.93)	88.0 (2.57)
18 and 19 years	59.4 (0.85)	61.8 (1.03)	57.5 (2.38)	46.1 (2.63)	59.5 (1.21)	61.9 (1.45)	59.2 (3.47)	47.4 (3.62)	59.2 (1.21)	61.8 (1.46)	56.1 (3.26)	44.8 (3.81)
20 and 21 years	44.9 (0.89)	49.7 (1.10)	37.8 (2.47)	27.1 (2.37)	44.7 (1.28)	50.0 (1.56)	36.7 (3.66)	24.8 (3.29)	45.1 (1.25)	49.3 (1.54)	38.7 (3.34)	29.2 (3.39)
22 to 24 years	23.2 (0.60)	24.4 (0.73)	20.0 (1.61)	15.6 (1.52)	22.8 (0.84)	24.1 (1.04)	20.6 (2.41)	14.8 (2.00)	23.6 (0.84)	24.8 (1.04)	19.5 (2.17)	16.6 (2.33)
25 to 29 years	11.6 (0.34)	12.3 (0.42)	10.0 (0.94)	7.1 (0.87)	11.0 (0.48)	12.2 (0.59)	6.3 (1.15)	5.6 (1.09)	12.2 (0.49)	12.3 (0.59)	13.0 (1.41)	8.7 (1.38)
30 to 34 years	5.9 (0.24)	5.7 (0.27)	7.7 (0.80)	4.7 (0.70)	5.4 (0.32)	5.0 (0.37)	6.9 (1.13)	4.5 (0.95)	6.5 (0.35)	6.3 (0.41)	8.3 (1.13)	4.9 (1.02)
2000												
Total, 3 to 34 years	55.9 (0.22)	56.0 (0.27)	59.3 (0.60)	51.3 (0.63)	55.8 (0.31)	55.8 (0.38)	59.7 (0.85)	50.5 (0.88)	56.0 (0.31)	56.1 (0.38)	59.0 (0.83)	52.2 (0.89)
3 and 4 years	52.1 (0.93)	54.6 (1.19)	59.8 (2.51)	35.9 (2.37)	50.8 (1.30)	54.1 (1.66)	58.0 (3.53)	31.9 (3.23)	53.4 (1.33)	55.2 (1.71)	61.8 (3.56)	40.0 (3.44)
5 and 6 years	95.6 (0.38)	95.5 (0.49)	96.7 (0.89)	94.3 (1.13)	95.1 (0.56)	94.5 (0.76)	96.0 (1.38)	95.4 (1.41)	96.1 (0.51)	96.4 (0.63)	97.5 (1.12)	93.1 (1.79)
7 to 9 years	98.1 (0.20)	98.4 (0.24)	97.5 (0.62)	97.5 (0.65)	98.0 (0.29)	98.1 (0.36)	98.2 (0.72)	96.6 (1.09)	98.2 (0.28)	98.6 (0.32)	96.7 (1.01)	98.4 (0.74)
10 to 13 years	98.3 (0.17)	98.5 (0.19)	98.5 (0.42)	97.4 (0.59)	98.3 (0.23)	98.2 (0.30)	98.8 (0.52)	98.4 (0.65)	98.3 (0.24)	98.8 (0.25)	98.1 (0.66)	96.4 (1.01)

See notes at end of table.

Table 6. Percentage of the population 3 to 34 years old enrolled in school, by sex, race/ethnicity, and age: Selected years, 1980 through 2005—Continued

Year and age	Total				Male				Female			
	Total	White	Black	Hispanic	Total	White	Black	Hispanic	Total	White	Black	Hispanic
1	2	3	4	5	6	7	8	9	10	11	12	13
14 and 15 years	98.7 (0.20)	98.9 (0.22)	99.6 (0.30)	96.2 (0.99)	98.7 (0.27)	98.8 (0.33)	99.6 (0.42)	96.9 (1.26)	98.6 (0.29)	99.0 (0.31)	99.6 (0.42)	95.4 (1.54)
16 and 17 years	92.8 (0.45)	94.0 (0.50)	91.7 (1.32)	87.0 (1.77)	92.7 (0.63)	94.7 (0.66)	88.9 (2.10)	85.7 (2.60)	92.9 (0.64)	93.3 (0.76)	94.6 (1.54)	88.3 (2.40)
18 and 19 years	61.2 (0.84)	63.9 (1.02)	57.2 (2.34)	49.5 (2.47)	58.3 (1.19)	61.2 (1.46)	51.5 (3.46)	48.0 (3.41)	64.2 (1.17)	66.7 (1.42)	62.2 (3.15)	51.1 (3.59)
20 and 21 years	44.1 (0.88)	49.2 (1.10)	37.4 (2.38)	26.1 (2.22)	41.0 (1.23)	45.8 (1.54)	31.3 (3.42)	24.2 (3.02)	47.3 (1.26)	52.7 (1.58)	42.3 (3.26)	28.1 (3.26)
22 to 24 years	24.6 (0.63)	24.9 (0.78)	24.0 (1.76)	18.2 (1.64)	23.9 (0.88)	25.0 (1.12)	22.0 (2.46)	15.2 (2.09)	25.3 (0.90)	24.8 (1.09)	25.8 (2.51)	21.6 (2.55)
25 to 29 years	11.4 (0.37)	11.1 (0.45)	14.5 (1.18)	7.4 (0.88)	10.0 (0.50)	10.5 (0.62)	11.6 (1.63)	5.1 (1.06)	12.7 (0.53)	11.8 (0.65)	16.7 (1.66)	9.5 (1.38)
30 to 34 years	6.7 (0.28)	6.1 (0.32)	9.9 (0.97)	5.6 (0.75)	5.6 (0.36)	4.7 (0.41)	8.5 (1.34)	5.7 (1.06)	7.7 (0.41)	7.4 (0.50)	11.2 (1.39)	5.5 (1.05)
2005												
Total, 3 to 34 years	**56.5 (0.21)**	**57.6 (0.27)**	**58.5 (0.60)**	**50.9 (0.56)**	**55.8 (0.30)**	**57.1 (0.39)**	**58.8 (0.87)**	**48.4 (0.77)**	**57.2 (0.30)**	**58.0 (0.39)**	**58.1 (0.84)**	**53.7 (0.81)**
3 and 4 years	53.6 (0.91)	58.5 (1.21)	52.4 (2.51)	43.0 (2.19)	52.8 (1.28)	56.8 (1.69)	54.8 (3.61)	43.0 (3.06)	54.4 (1.30)	60.3 (1.72)	50.1 (3.50)	43.0 (3.12)
5 and 6 years	95.4 (0.39)	95.9 (0.49)	95.9 (1.02)	93.8 (1.12)	94.8 (0.57)	95.4 (0.72)	94.8 (1.58)	92.4 (1.70)	96.1 (0.52)	96.3 (0.67)	97.1 (1.25)	95.3 (1.41)
7 to 9 years	98.6 (0.18)	99.0 (0.20)	98.7 (0.48)	97.4 (0.61)	98.2 (0.29)	98.9 (0.29)	98.0 (0.86)	96.0 (1.05)	99.0 (0.21)	99.5 (0.29)	99.5 (0.43)	98.8 (0.60)
10 to 13 years	98.6 (0.15)	99.0 (0.17)	98.5 (0.42)	97.9 (0.48)	98.4 (0.23)	99.1 (0.23)	97.6 (0.74)	97.2 (0.76)	98.9 (0.19)	98.8 (0.26)	99.5 (0.35)	98.6 (0.57)
14 and 15 years	98.0 (0.24)	98.6 (0.25)	96.1 (0.88)	97.3 (0.74)	97.5 (0.36)	98.4 (0.37)	93.3 (1.61)	97.8 (0.94)	98.4 (0.30)	98.7 (0.34)	98.8 (0.70)	96.7 (1.15)
16 and 17 years	95.1 (0.35)	96.1 (0.40)	93.6 (1.11)	92.6 (1.20)	95.1 (0.50)	95.9 (0.58)	93.6 (1.59)	92.5 (1.70)	95.1 (0.50)	96.3 (0.56)	93.6 (1.55)	92.6 (1.69)
18 and 19 years	67.6 (0.83)	71.6 (1.00)	62.0 (2.43)	54.3 (2.46)	66.5 (1.17)	69.8 (1.43)	66.9 (3.38)	51.8 (3.39)	68.8 (1.18)	73.5 (1.41)	57.4 (3.45)	57.2 (3.56)
20 and 21 years	48.7 (0.84)	54.4 (1.06)	37.9 (2.37)	30.0 (2.07)	45.3 (1.17)	50.5 (1.49)	35.5 (3.29)	25.2 (2.70)	52.3 (1.21)	58.5 (1.50)	40.4 (3.41)	35.3 (3.15)
22 to 24 years	27.3 (0.63)	27.8 (0.81)	28.6 (1.84)	19.5 (1.49)	25.2 (0.87)	26.4 (1.13)	24.0 (2.58)	17.5 (1.95)	29.2 (0.90)	29.1 (1.15)	32.5 (2.59)	21.8 (2.29)
25 to 29 years	11.9 (0.36)	12.5 (0.47)	11.9 (1.06)	7.8 (0.74)	9.6 (0.46)	10.2 (0.61)	9.1 (1.40)	5.6 (0.86)	14.2 (0.54)	14.7 (0.71)	14.2 (1.55)	10.4 (1.25)
30 to 34 years	6.9 (0.28)	6.9 (0.36)	9.8 (1.00)	4.2 (0.57)	5.9 (0.37)	6.5 (0.50)	6.3 (1.21)	2.6 (0.62)	7.9 (0.42)	7.4 (0.52)	12.7 (1.50)	6.1 (1.00)

NOTE: Includes enrollment in any type of graded public, parochial, or other private schools. Includes nursery schools, kindergartens, elementary schools, high schools, colleges, universities, and professional schools. Attendance may be on either a full-time or part-time basis and during the day or night. Enrollments in "special" schools, such as trade schools, business colleges, or correspondence schools, are not included. Beginning in 1995, preprimary enrollment was collected using new pro-

cedures and may not be comparable to figures for earlier years. Total includes persons from other racial/ethnic groups not shown separately. Race categories exclude persons of Hispanic origin. Standard errors appear in parentheses.
SOURCE: U.S. Department of Commerce, Census Bureau, Current Population Survey (CPS), October, selected years, 1980 through 2005, unpublished tabulations. (This table was prepared May 2006.)

Table 7. Percentage of the population 3 to 34 years old enrolled in school, by age group: Selected years, 1940 through 2005

Year	Total, 3 to 34 years	3 and 4 years	5 and 6 years	7 to 13 years	14 to 17 years	18 and 19 years old Total	18 and 19 years old In elementary and secondary	18 and 19 years old In higher education	20 to 24 years old Total	20 to 24 years old 20 and 21 years	20 to 24 years old 22 to 24 years	25 to 29 years	30 to 34 years
1	2	3	4	5	6	7	8	9	10	11	12	13	14
1940	(†)	—	—	95.0 (—)	79.3 (—)	28.9 (—)	(†)	(†)	6.6 (—)	(†)	(†)	(†)	(†)
1945	(†)	—	—	98.1 (—)	78.4 (—)	20.7 (—)	(†)	(†)	3.9 (—)	(†)	(†)	(†)	(†)
1947	(†)	—	73.8 (—)	98.5 (—)	79.3 (—)	24.3 (—)	(†)	(†)	10.2 (—)	(†)	(†)	3.0 (—)	(†)
1948	(†)	—	74.7 (—)	98.1 (—)	81.8 (—)	26.9 (—)	(†)	(†)	9.7 (—)	(†)	(†)	2.6 (—)	(†)
1949	(†)	—	76.2 (—)	98.6 (—)	81.6 (—)	25.3 (—)	(†)	(†)	9.2 (—)	(†)	(†)	3.8 (—)	(†)
1950	(†)	—	74.4 (—)	98.7 (—)	83.7 (—)	29.4 (—)	(†)	(†)	9.0 (—)	(†)	(†)	3.0 (—)	0.9 (—)
1951	(†)	—	73.6 (—)	99.1 (—)	85.2 (—)	26.2 (—)	(†)	(†)	8.6 (—)	(†)	(†)	2.5 (—)	(†)
1952	(†)	—	75.2 (—)	98.8 (—)	85.2 (—)	28.8 (—)	(†)	(†)	9.7 (—)	(†)	(†)	2.6 (—)	1.2 (—)
1953	(†)	—	78.6 (—)	99.4 (—)	85.9 (—)	31.2 (—)	(†)	(†)	11.1 (—)	(†)	(†)	2.9 (—)	1.7 (—)
1954	(†)	—	77.3 (—)	99.4 (—)	87.1 (—)	32.4 (—)	(†)	(†)	11.2 (—)	(†)	(†)	4.1 (—)	1.5 (—)
1955	(†)	—	78.1 (—)	99.2 (—)	86.9 (—)	31.5 (—)	(†)	(†)	11.1 (—)	(†)	(†)	4.2 (—)	1.6 (—)
1956	(†)	—	77.6 (—)	99.3 (—)	88.2 (—)	35.4 (—)	(†)	(†)	12.8 (—)	(†)	(†)	5.1 (—)	1.9 (—)
1957	(†)	—	78.6 (—)	99.5 (—)	89.5 (—)	34.9 (—)	(†)	(†)	14.0 (—)	(†)	(†)	(†)	(†)
1958	(†)	—	80.4 (—)	99.5 (—)	89.2 (—)	37.6 (—)	(†)	(†)	13.4 (—)	(†)	(†)	(†)	(†)
1959	(†)	—	80.0 (—)	99.4 (—)	90.2 (—)	36.8 (—)	(†)	(†)	12.7 (—)	(†)	(†)	(†)	(†)
1960	(†)	—	80.7 (—)	99.5 (—)	90.3 (—)	38.4 (—)	(†)	(†)	13.1 (—)	(†)	(†)	4.9 (—)	2.4 (—)
1961	(†)	—	81.7 (—)	99.3 (—)	91.4 (—)	38.0 (—)	(†)	(†)	13.7 (—)	(†)	(†)	(†)	(†)
1962	(†)	—	82.2 (—)	99.3 (—)	92.0 (—)	41.8 (—)	(†)	(†)	15.6 (—)	(†)	(†)	(†)	(†)
1963	(†)	—	82.7 (—)	99.3 (—)	92.9 (—)	40.9 (—)	(†)	(†)	17.3 (—)	(†)	(†)	(†)	(†)
1964	(†)	—	83.3 (—)	99.0 (—)	93.1 (—)	41.6 (—)	(†)	(†)	16.8 (—)	(†)	(†)	5.2 (—)	2.6 (—)
1965	55.5 (—)	10.6 (—)	84.9 (—)	99.4 (—)	93.2 (—)	46.3 (—)	(†)	(†)	19.0 (—)	27.6 (—)	13.2 (—)	6.1 (—)	3.2 (—)
1966	56.1 (—)	12.5 (—)	85.8 (—)	99.3 (—)	93.7 (—)	47.2 (—)	(†)	(†)	19.9 (—)	29.9 (—)	13.2 (—)	6.5 (—)	2.7 (—)
1967	56.6 (—)	14.2 (—)	87.4 (—)	99.3 (—)	93.7 (—)	47.6 (—)	(†)	(†)	22.0 (—)	33.3 (—)	13.6 (—)	6.6 (—)	4.0 (—)
1968	56.7 (—)	15.7 (—)	87.6 (—)	99.1 (—)	94.2 (—)	50.4 (—)	(†)	(†)	21.4 (—)	31.2 (—)	13.8 (—)	7.0 (—)	3.9 (—)
1969	57.0 (—)	16.1 (—)	88.4 (—)	99.2 (—)	94.0 (—)	50.2 (—)	(†)	(†)	23.0 (—)	34.1 (—)	15.4 (—)	7.9 (—)	4.8 (—)
1970	56.4 (0.22)	20.5 (0.73)	89.5 (0.53)	99.2 (0.08)	94.1 (0.27)	47.7 (0.85)	10.5 (0.52)	37.3 (0.83)	21.5 (0.47)	31.9 (0.85)	14.9 (0.52)	7.5 (0.33)	4.2 (0.27)
1971	56.2 (0.21)	21.2 (0.75)	91.6 (0.49)	99.1 (0.08)	94.5 (0.26)	49.2 (0.84)	11.5 (0.54)	37.7 (0.81)	21.9 (0.46)	32.2 (0.83)	15.4 (0.51)	8.0 (0.33)	4.9 (0.29)
1972	54.9 (0.21)	24.4 (0.80)	91.9 (0.50)	99.2 (0.08)	93.3 (0.28)	46.3 (0.82)	10.4 (0.50)	35.9 (0.79)	21.6 (0.45)	31.4 (0.79)	14.8 (0.50)	8.6 (0.33)	4.6 (0.27)
1973	53.5 (0.21)	24.2 (0.78)	92.5 (0.49)	99.2 (0.08)	92.9 (0.28)	42.9 (0.81)	10.0 (0.49)	32.9 (0.77)	20.8 (0.44)	30.1 (0.78)	14.5 (0.49)	8.5 (0.32)	4.5 (0.26)
1974	53.6 (0.21)	28.8 (0.83)	94.2 (0.43)	99.3 (0.08)	92.9 (0.28)	43.1 (0.80)	9.9 (0.48)	33.2 (0.76)	21.4 (0.44)	30.2 (0.76)	15.1 (0.50)	9.6 (0.33)	5.7 (0.29)
1975	53.7 (0.21)	31.5 (0.87)	94.7 (0.41)	99.3 (0.08)	93.6 (0.27)	46.9 (0.80)	10.2 (0.48)	36.7 (0.77)	22.4 (0.44)	31.2 (0.76)	16.2 (0.51)	10.1 (0.33)	6.6 (0.30)
1976	53.1 (0.21)	31.3 (0.90)	95.5 (0.38)	99.2 (0.09)	93.7 (0.27)	46.2 (0.79)	10.2 (0.48)	36.0 (0.76)	23.3 (0.44)	32.0 (0.75)	17.1 (0.51)	10.0 (0.33)	6.0 (0.28)
1977	52.5 (0.21)	32.0 (0.93)	95.8 (0.38)	99.4 (0.07)	93.7 (0.27)	46.2 (0.80)	10.4 (0.49)	35.7 (0.77)	22.9 (0.44)	31.8 (0.75)	16.5 (0.51)	10.8 (0.34)	6.9 (0.30)
1978	51.2 (0.21)	34.2 (0.94)	95.3 (0.41)	99.1 (0.09)	93.7 (0.27)	45.4 (0.80)	9.8 (0.48)	35.6 (0.77)	21.8 (0.43)	29.5 (0.73)	16.3 (0.50)	9.4 (0.31)	6.4 (0.28)
1979	50.3 (0.21)	35.1 (0.95)	95.8 (0.40)	99.2 (0.09)	93.6 (0.28)	45.0 (0.79)	10.3 (0.48)	34.6 (0.76)	21.7 (0.42)	30.2 (0.74)	15.8 (0.49)	9.6 (0.31)	6.4 (0.28)
1980	49.7 (0.21)	36.7 (0.95)	95.7 (0.40)	99.3 (0.09)	93.4 (0.29)	46.4 (0.80)	10.5 (0.49)	35.9 (0.77)	22.3 (0.43)	31.0 (0.74)	16.3 (0.49)	9.3 (0.30)	6.4 (0.27)
1981	48.9 (0.21)	36.0 (0.92)	94.0 (0.46)	99.2 (0.09)	94.1 (0.27)	49.0 (0.80)	11.5 (0.51)	37.5 (0.78)	22.5 (0.42)	31.6 (0.73)	16.5 (0.48)	9.0 (0.29)	6.9 (0.27)
1982	48.6 (0.22)	36.4 (0.96)	95.0 (0.44)	99.2 (0.10)	94.4 (0.29)	47.8 (0.85)	11.3 (0.54)	36.5 (0.81)	23.5 (0.45)	34.0 (0.79)	16.8 (0.50)	9.6 (0.31)	6.3 (0.27)
1983	48.4 (0.22)	37.5 (0.94)	95.4 (0.42)	99.2 (0.09)	95.0 (0.27)	50.4 (0.86)	12.8 (0.57)	37.6 (0.83)	22.7 (0.44)	32.5 (0.79)	16.6 (0.50)	9.6 (0.31)	6.4 (0.27)
1984	47.9 (0.22)	36.3 (0.92)	94.5 (0.45)	99.2 (0.09)	94.7 (0.28)	50.1 (0.88)	11.5 (0.56)	38.6 (0.86)	23.7 (0.45)	33.9 (0.80)	17.3 (0.51)	9.1 (0.30)	6.3 (0.27)

See notes at end of table.

Table 7. Percentage of the population 3 to 34 years old enrolled in school, by age group: Selected years, 1940 through 2005—Continued

Year	Total, 3 to 34 years	3 and 4 years	5 and 6 years	7 to 13 years	14 to 17 years	18 and 19 years old			20 to 24 years old			25 to 29 years	30 to 34 years
						Total	In elementary and secondary	In higher education	Total	20 and 21 years	22 to 24 years		
1	2	3	4	5	6	7	8	9	10	11	12	13	14
1985	48.3 (0.22)	38.9 (0.94)	96.1 (0.38)	99.2 (0.09)	94.9 (0.27)	51.6 (0.89)	11.2 (0.56)	40.4 (0.88)	24.0 (0.46)	35.3 (0.83)	16.9 (0.51)	9.2 (0.30)	6.1 (0.26)
1986	48.2 (0.22)	38.9 (0.93)	95.3 (0.40)	99.2 (0.10)	94.9 (0.28)	54.6 (0.90)	13.1 (0.61)	41.5 (0.89)	23.6 (0.46)	33.0 (0.83)	17.9 (0.53)	8.8 (0.29)	6.0 (0.25)
1987	48.6 (0.22)	38.3 (0.93)	95.1 (0.41)	99.5 (0.07)	95.0 (0.28)	55.6 (0.89)	13.1 (0.60)	42.5 (0.89)	25.5 (0.48)	38.7 (0.88)	17.5 (0.53)	9.0 (0.30)	5.8 (0.25)
1988	48.7 (0.24)	38.2 (1.01)	96.0 (0.41)	99.7 (0.07)	95.1 (0.30)	55.6 (0.96)	13.9 (0.67)	41.8 (0.95)	26.1 (0.53)	39.1 (0.96)	18.2 (0.60)	8.3 (0.31)	5.9 (0.27)
1989	49.0 (0.22)	39.1 (1.00)	95.2 (0.44)	99.3 (0.09)	95.7 (0.29)	56.0 (0.95)	14.4 (0.68)	41.6 (0.95)	27.0 (0.55)	38.5 (0.97)	19.9 (0.63)	9.3 (0.33)	5.7 (0.26)
1990	50.2 (0.23)	44.4 (0.99)	96.5 (0.37)	99.6 (0.06)	95.8 (0.28)	57.2 (0.94)	14.5 (0.67)	42.7 (0.94)	28.6 (0.54)	39.7 (0.92)	21.0 (0.63)	9.7 (0.33)	5.8 (0.25)
1991	50.7 (0.22)	40.5 (0.96)	95.4 (0.41)	99.6 (0.06)	96.0 (0.27)	59.6 (0.96)	15.6 (0.71)	44.0 (0.97)	30.2 (0.55)	42.0 (0.92)	22.2 (0.64)	10.2 (0.34)	6.2 (0.26)
1992	51.4 (0.22)	39.7 (0.95)	95.5 (0.41)	99.4 (0.08)	96.7 (0.25)	61.4 (0.96)	17.1 (0.74)	44.3 (0.98)	31.6 (0.56)	44.0 (0.95)	23.7 (0.65)	9.8 (0.34)	6.1 (0.26)
1993	51.8 (0.22)	40.4 (0.93)	95.4 (0.41)	99.5 (0.07)	96.5 (0.25)	61.6 (0.95)	17.2 (0.74)	44.4 (0.97)	30.8 (0.56)	42.7 (0.97)	23.6 (0.65)	10.2 (0.35)	5.9 (0.25)
1994	53.3 (0.21)	47.3 (0.87)[†]	96.7 (0.32)	99.4 (0.08)	96.6 (0.22)	60.2 (0.87)	16.2 (0.65)	43.9 (0.88)	32.0 (0.51)	44.9 (0.88)	24.0 (0.59)	10.8 (0.33)	6.7 (0.25)
1995	53.7 (0.21)	48.7 (0.87)[†]	96.0 (0.34)	98.9 (0.10)	96.3 (0.23)	59.4 (0.85)	16.3 (0.64)	43.1 (0.86)	31.5 (0.52)	44.9 (0.89)	23.2 (0.60)	11.6 (0.34)	5.9 (0.24)
1996	54.1 (0.22)	48.3 (0.91)[†]	94.0 (0.43)	97.7 (0.15)	95.4 (0.26)	61.5 (0.87)	16.7 (0.67)	44.9 (0.89)	32.5 (0.55)	44.4 (0.93)	24.8 (0.65)	11.9 (0.36)	6.1 (0.25)
1997	55.6 (0.22)	52.6 (0.92)[†]	96.5 (0.33)	99.1 (0.09)	96.6 (0.22)	61.5 (0.86)	16.7 (0.66)	44.7 (0.88)	34.3 (0.55)	45.9 (0.91)	26.4 (0.66)	11.8 (0.36)	5.7 (0.25)
1998	55.8 (0.22)	52.1 (0.92)[†]	95.6 (0.37)	98.9 (0.10)	96.1 (0.24)	62.2 (0.84)	15.7 (0.63)	46.4 (0.86)	33.0 (0.55)	44.8 (0.91)	24.9 (0.65)	11.9 (0.37)	6.6 (0.27)
1999	56.0 (0.22)	54.2 (0.93)[†]	96.0 (0.36)	98.7 (0.11)	95.8 (0.24)	60.6 (0.84)	16.5 (0.64)	44.1 (0.85)	32.8 (0.54)	45.3 (0.90)	24.5 (0.64)	11.1 (0.36)	6.2 (0.27)
2000	55.9 (0.22)	52.1 (0.93)[†]	95.6 (0.38)	98.2 (0.13)	95.7 (0.25)	61.2 (0.84)	16.5 (0.64)	44.7 (0.85)	32.5 (0.53)	44.1 (0.88)	24.6 (0.63)	11.4 (0.37)	6.7 (0.28)
2001	56.4 (0.22)	52.4 (0.88)[†]	95.3 (0.37)	98.3 (0.12)	95.8 (0.24)	61.1 (0.83)	17.1 (0.64)	44.0 (0.84)	34.1 (0.53)	46.1 (0.87)	25.5 (0.64)	11.8 (0.38)	6.9 (0.28)
2002	56.2 (0.21)	56.3 (0.89)[†]	95.5 (0.37)	98.3 (0.12)	96.4 (0.22)	63.3 (0.83)	18.0 (0.67)	45.3 (0.86)	34.4 (0.52)	47.8 (0.87)	25.6 (0.62)	12.1 (0.37)	6.6 (0.27)
2003	56.2 (0.20)	55.1 (0.85)[†]	94.5 (0.40)	98.3 (0.12)	96.2 (0.21)	64.5 (0.80)	17.9 (0.64)	46.6 (0.84)	35.6 (0.50)	48.3 (0.83)	27.8 (0.59)	11.8 (0.34)	6.8 (0.26)
2004	56.2 (0.20)	54.0 (0.85)[†]	95.4 (0.37)	98.4 (0.12)	96.5 (0.21)	64.4 (0.80)	16.6 (0.62)	47.8 (0.83)	35.2 (0.49)	48.9 (0.82)	26.3 (0.58)	13.0 (0.35)	6.6 (0.26)
2005	56.5 (0.20)	53.6 (0.86)[1]	95.4 (0.37)	98.6 (0.11)	96.5 (0.20)	67.6 (0.79)	18.3 (0.65)	49.3 (0.84)	36.1 (0.49)	48.7 (0.80)	27.3 (0.59)	11.9 (0.34)	6.9 (0.27)

—Not available.
†Not applicable.
[1]Preprimary enrollment collected using new procedures. Data may not be comparable to figures for earlier years.
NOTE: Data for 1940 are for April. Data for all other years are as of October. Includes enrollment in any type of graded public, parochial, or other private schools. Includes nursery schools, kindergartens, elementary schools, high schools, colleges, universities, and professional schools. Attendance may be on either a full-time or part-time basis and during the day or night.

Enrollments in "special" schools, such as trade schools, business colleges, or correspondence schools, are not included.
Standard errors appear in parentheses.
SOURCE: U.S. Department of Commerce, Census Bureau, *Historical Statistics of the United States, Colonial Times to 1970*; *Current Population Reports*, Series P-20, various years; and Current Population Survey, October, 1940 through 2005, unpublished tabulations. (This table was prepared May 2006.)

Table 8. Percentage of persons age 25 and over and 25 to 29, by race/ethnicity, years of school completed, and sex: Selected years, 1910 through 2006

Age and year	Total			White[1]			Black[1]			Hispanic		
	Less than 5 years of elementary school	High school completion or higher[2]	Bachelor's or higher degree[3]	Less than 5 years of elementary school	High school completion or higher[2]	Bachelor's or higher degree[3]	Less than 5 years of elementary school	High school completion or higher[2]	Bachelor's or higher degree[3]	Less than 5 years of elementary school	High school completion or higher[2]	Bachelor's or higher degree[3]
1	2	3	4	5	6	7	8	9	10	11	12	13
Males and females, 25 and over												
1910[4]	23.8 (—)	13.5 (—)	2.7 (—)	— (†)	— (†)	— (†)	— (†)	— (†)	— (†)	— (†)	— (†)	— (†)
1920[4]	22.0 (—)	16.4 (—)	3.3 (—)	— (†)	— (†)	— (†)	— (†)	— (†)	— (†)	— (†)	— (†)	— (†)
1930[4]	17.5 (—)	19.1 (—)	3.9 (—)	— (†)	— (†)	— (†)	— (†)	— (†)	— (†)	— (†)	— (†)	— (†)
April 1940	13.7 (—)	24.5 (—)	4.6 (—)	10.9 (—)	26.1 (—)	4.9 (—)	41.8 (—)	7.7 (—)	1.3 (—)	— (†)	— (†)	— (†)
April 1950	11.1 (—)	34.3 (—)	6.2 (—)	8.9 (—)	36.4 (—)	6.6 (—)	32.6 (—)	13.7 (—)	2.2 (—)	— (†)	— (†)	— (†)
April 1960	8.3 (—)	41.1 (—)	7.7 (—)	6.7 (—)	43.2 (—)	8.1 (—)	23.5 (—)	21.7 (—)	3.5 (—)	— (†)	— (†)	— (†)
March 1970	5.3 (—)	55.2 (—)	11.0 (—)	4.2 (—)	57.4 (—)	11.6 (—)	14.7 (—)	36.1 (—)	6.1 (—)	— (†)	— (†)	— (†)
March 1975	4.2 (—)	62.5 (—)	13.9 (—)	2.6 (—)	65.8 (—)	14.9 (—)	12.3 (—)	42.6 (—)	6.4 (—)	18.2 (—)	38.5 (—)	6.6 (—)
March 1980	3.4 (0.08)	68.6 (0.20)	17.0 (0.16)	1.9 (0.07)	71.9 (0.21)	18.4 (0.18)	9.1 (0.47)	51.4 (0.81)	7.9 (0.44)	15.8 (0.87)	44.5 (1.18)	7.6 (0.63)
March 1985	2.7 (0.07)	73.9 (0.18)	19.4 (0.16)	1.4 (0.05)	77.5 (0.19)	20.8 (0.19)	6.1 (0.36)	59.9 (0.74)	11.1 (0.47)	13.5 (0.68)	47.9 (0.99)	8.5 (0.55)
March 1986	2.7 (0.07)	74.7 (0.18)	19.4 (0.16)	1.4 (0.05)	78.2 (0.19)	20.9 (0.19)	5.3 (0.33)	62.5 (0.72)	10.9 (0.47)	12.9 (0.64)	48.5 (0.96)	8.4 (0.53)
March 1987	2.4 (0.06)	75.6 (0.17)	19.9 (0.16)	1.3 (0.05)	79.0 (0.18)	21.4 (0.19)	4.9 (0.32)	63.6 (0.71)	10.8 (0.46)	11.9 (0.61)	50.9 (0.94)	8.6 (0.53)
March 1988	2.4 (0.06)	76.2 (0.17)	20.3 (0.16)	1.2 (0.05)	79.8 (0.18)	21.8 (0.19)	4.8 (0.31)	63.5 (0.70)	11.2 (0.46)	12.2 (0.60)	51.0 (0.92)	10.0 (0.55)
March 1989	2.5 (0.06)	76.9 (0.17)	21.1 (0.16)	1.2 (0.05)	80.7 (0.18)	22.8 (0.19)	5.2 (0.32)	64.7 (0.69)	11.7 (0.46)	12.2 (0.58)	50.9 (0.89)	9.9 (0.53)
March 1990	2.4 (0.06)	77.6 (0.17)	21.3 (0.16)	1.1 (0.05)	81.4 (0.17)	23.1 (0.19)	5.1 (0.31)	66.2 (0.67)	11.3 (0.45)	12.3 (0.58)	50.8 (0.88)	9.2 (0.51)
March 1991	2.4 (0.06)	78.4 (0.16)	21.4 (0.16)	1.1 (0.05)	82.4 (0.17)	23.3 (0.19)	4.7 (0.30)	66.8 (0.66)	11.5 (0.45)	12.5 (0.57)	51.3 (0.86)	9.7 (0.51)
March 1992	2.1 (0.06)	79.4 (0.16)	21.4 (0.16)	0.9 (0.04)	83.4 (0.16)	23.2 (0.19)	3.9 (0.27)	67.7 (0.65)	11.9 (0.45)	11.8 (0.55)	52.6 (0.85)	9.3 (0.49)
March 1993	2.1 (0.06)	80.2 (0.16)	21.9 (0.16)	0.8 (0.04)	84.1 (0.16)	23.8 (0.19)	3.7 (0.26)	70.5 (0.63)	12.2 (0.45)	11.8 (0.54)	53.1 (0.83)	9.0 (0.48)
March 1994	1.9 (0.05)	80.9 (0.15)	22.2 (0.16)	0.8 (0.04)	84.9 (0.16)	24.3 (0.19)	2.7 (0.22)	73.0 (0.61)	12.9 (0.46)	10.8 (0.48)	53.3 (0.78)	9.1 (0.45)
March 1995	1.8 (0.05)	81.7 (0.15)	23.0 (0.16)	0.7 (0.04)	85.9 (0.16)	25.4 (0.19)	2.5 (0.21)	73.8 (0.61)	13.3 (0.47)	10.6 (0.48)	53.4 (0.78)	9.3 (0.45)
March 1996	1.8 (0.05)	81.7 (0.16)	23.6 (0.17)	0.6 (0.04)	86.0 (0.16)	25.9 (0.20)	2.2 (0.18)	74.6 (0.53)	13.8 (0.42)	10.3 (0.42)	53.1 (0.68)	9.3 (0.40)
March 1997	1.7 (0.05)	82.1 (0.14)	23.9 (0.16)	0.6 (0.03)	86.3 (0.15)	26.2 (0.19)	2.0 (0.17)	75.3 (0.52)	13.3 (0.41)	9.4 (0.32)	54.7 (0.54)	10.3 (0.33)
March 1998	1.6 (0.05)	82.8 (0.14)	24.4 (0.16)	0.6 (0.03)	87.1 (0.14)	26.6 (0.19)	1.7 (0.15)	76.4 (0.50)	14.8 (0.42)	9.3 (0.31)	55.5 (0.53)	11.0 (0.33)
March 1999	1.6 (0.05)	83.4 (0.14)	25.2 (0.16)	0.6 (0.03)	87.7 (0.14)	27.7 (0.19)	1.7 (0.15)	77.4 (0.49)	15.5 (0.43)	9.0 (0.30)	56.1 (0.52)	10.9 (0.33)
March 2000	1.6 (0.05)	84.1 (0.13)	25.6 (0.16)	0.5 (0.03)	88.4 (0.14)	28.1 (0.19)	1.6 (0.15)	78.9 (0.48)	16.6 (0.44)	8.7 (0.29)	57.0 (0.51)	10.6 (0.32)
March 2001	1.6 (0.05)	84.3 (0.13)	26.1 (0.16)	0.5 (0.03)	88.7 (0.13)	28.6 (0.19)	1.3 (0.13)	79.5 (0.47)	16.1 (0.43)	9.3 (0.29)	56.5 (0.50)	11.2 (0.32)
March 2002	1.6 (0.03)	84.1 (0.09)	26.7 (0.11)	0.5 (0.02)	88.7 (0.10)	29.4 (0.14)	1.6 (0.11)	79.2 (0.34)	17.2 (0.31)	8.7 (0.19)	57.0 (0.34)	11.1 (0.21)
March 2003	1.6 (0.03)	84.6 (0.09)	27.2 (0.11)	0.5 (0.02)	89.4 (0.09)	30.0 (0.14)	1.5 (0.10)	80.3 (0.33)	17.4 (0.31)	8.2 (0.18)	57.0 (0.33)	11.4 (0.21)
March 2004	1.5 (0.03)	85.2 (0.09)	27.7 (0.11)	0.4 (0.02)	90.0 (0.09)	30.6 (0.14)	1.3 (0.09)	81.1 (0.32)	17.7 (0.31)	8.1 (0.18)	58.4 (0.32)	12.1 (0.21)
March 2005	1.6 (0.03)	85.2 (0.09)	27.6 (0.11)	0.5 (0.02)	90.1 (0.09)	30.5 (0.14)	1.5 (0.10)	81.5 (0.32)	17.7 (0.31)	7.9 (0.17)	58.5 (0.32)	12.0 (0.21)
March 2006	1.5 (0.03)	85.5 (0.09)	28.0 (0.11)	0.4 (0.02)	90.5 (0.09)	31.0 (0.14)	1.5 (0.10)	81.2 (0.32)	18.6 (0.31)	7.6 (0.17)	59.3 (0.31)	12.4 (0.21)
Males and females, 25 to 29												
1920[4]	— (†)	— (†)	— (†)	12.9 (—)	22.0 (—)	4.5 (—)	44.6 (—)	6.3 (—)	1.2 (—)	— (†)	— (†)	— (†)
April 1940	5.9 (—)	38.1 (—)	5.9 (—)	3.4 (—)	41.2 (—)	6.4 (—)	27.0 (—)	12.3 (—)	1.6 (—)	— (†)	— (†)	— (†)
April 1950	4.6 (—)	52.8 (—)	7.7 (—)	3.3 (—)	56.3 (—)	8.2 (—)	16.1 (—)	23.6 (—)	2.8 (—)	— (†)	— (†)	— (†)
April 1960	2.8 (—)	60.7 (—)	11.0 (—)	2.2 (—)	63.7 (—)	11.8 (—)	7.2 (—)	38.6 (—)	5.4 (—)	— (†)	— (†)	— (†)
March 1970	1.1 (—)	75.4 (—)	16.4 (—)	0.9 (—)	77.8 (—)	17.3 (—)	2.2 (—)	58.4 (—)	10.0 (—)	— (†)	— (†)	— (†)
March 1975	1.0 (—)	83.1 (—)	21.9 (—)	0.6 (—)	86.6 (—)	23.8 (—)	0.5 (—)	71.1 (—)	10.5 (—)	8.0 (—)	53.1 (—)	8.8 (—)
March 1980	0.8 (0.10)	85.4 (0.40)	22.5 (0.47)	0.3 (0.07)	89.2 (0.40)	25.0 (0.55)	0.6 (0.31)	76.7 (1.64)	11.6 (1.24)	6.7 (1.31)	58.0 (2.59)	7.7 (1.39)
March 1985	0.7 (0.09)	86.1 (0.37)	22.2 (0.45)	0.2 (0.06)	89.5 (0.38)	24.4 (0.53)	0.4 (0.23)	80.5 (1.42)	11.6 (1.15)	6.0 (1.05)	60.9 (2.17)	11.1 (1.39)
March 1986	0.9 (0.10)	86.1 (0.37)	22.4 (0.45)	0.4 (0.07)	89.6 (0.37)	25.2 (0.53)	0.5 (0.26)	83.5 (1.32)	11.8 (1.15)	5.6 (0.97)	59.1 (2.07)	9.0 (1.21)
March 1987	0.9 (0.10)	86.0 (0.37)	22.0 (0.44)	0.4 (0.08)	89.4 (0.38)	24.6 (0.53)	0.4 (0.23)	83.4 (1.32)	11.5 (1.13)	4.8 (0.88)	59.8 (2.04)	8.7 (1.17)
March 1988	1.0 (0.11)	85.9 (0.37)	22.7 (0.45)	0.3 (0.07)	89.7 (0.38)	25.1 (0.54)	0.3 (0.21)	80.9 (1.39)	12.0 (1.15)	6.0 (0.96)	62.3 (1.96)	11.3 (1.28)
March 1989	1.0 (0.11)	85.5 (0.38)	23.4 (0.45)	0.3 (0.07)	89.3 (0.38)	26.3 (0.55)	0.5 (0.25)	82.3 (1.35)	12.6 (1.17)	5.4 (0.89)	61.0 (1.92)	10.1 (1.19)
March 1990	1.2 (0.12)	85.7 (0.38)	23.2 (0.46)	0.3 (0.07)	90.1 (0.37)	26.4 (0.55)	1.0 (0.36)	81.7 (1.37)	13.4 (1.20)	7.3 (1.02)	58.2 (1.94)	8.1 (1.07)
March 1991	1.0 (0.11)	85.4 (0.39)	23.2 (0.46)	0.4 (0.08)	89.8 (0.39)	26.7 (0.56)	0.5 (0.26)	81.8 (1.36)	11.0 (1.10)	5.8 (0.93)	56.7 (1.96)	9.2 (1.15)
March 1992	0.9 (0.10)	86.3 (0.38)	23.6 (0.47)	0.3 (0.07)	90.7 (0.38)	27.2 (0.58)	0.8 (0.32)	80.9 (1.41)	11.0 (1.12)	5.2 (0.88)	60.9 (1.93)	9.5 (1.16)
March 1993	0.7 (0.09)	86.7 (0.38)	23.7 (0.48)	0.3 (0.07)	91.2 (0.37)	27.2 (0.59)	0.2 (0.18)	82.6 (1.36)	13.3 (1.22)	4.0 (0.76)	60.9 (1.90)	8.3 (1.08)
March 1994	0.8 (0.10)	86.1 (0.39)	23.3 (0.47)	0.2 (0.07)	91.1 (0.38)	27.1 (0.60)	0.6 (0.28)	84.1 (1.31)	13.6 (1.23)	3.6 (0.66)	60.3 (1.75)	8.0 (0.97)
March 1995	0.9 (0.11)	86.8 (0.39)	24.7 (0.49)	0.3 (0.08)	92.5 (0.36)	28.8 (0.62)	0.2 (0.17)	86.7 (1.23)	15.4 (1.31)	4.9 (0.79)	57.1 (1.80)	8.9 (1.04)

See notes at end of table.

Table 8. Percentage of persons age 25 and over and 25 to 29, by race/ethnicity, years of school completed, and sex: Selected years, 1910 through 2006—Continued

Age and year	Total			White[1]			Black[1]			Hispanic		
	Less than 5 years of elementary school	High school completion or higher[2]	Bachelor's or higher degree[3]	Less than 5 years of elementary school	High school completion or higher[2]	Bachelor's or higher degree[3]	Less than 5 years of elementary school	High school completion or higher[2]	Bachelor's or higher degree[3]	Less than 5 years of elementary school	High school completion or higher[2]	Bachelor's or higher degree[3]
1	2	3	4	5	6	7	8	9	10	11	12	13
March 1996.....	0.8 (0.11)	87.3 (0.40)	27.1 (0.53)	0.2 (0.07)	92.6 (0.38)	31.6 (0.67)	0.4 (0.20)	86.0 (1.14)	14.6 (1.16)	4.3 (0.65)	61.1 (1.58)	10.0 (0.97)
March 1997.....	0.8 (0.10)	87.4 (0.37)	27.8 (0.50)	0.1 (0.05)	92.9 (0.35)	32.6 (0.63)	0.6 (0.25)	86.9 (1.10)	14.2 (1.14)	4.2 (0.51)	61.8 (1.24)	11.0 (0.80)
March 1998.....	0.7 (0.09)	88.1 (0.36)	27.3 (0.50)	0.1 (0.05)	93.6 (0.34)	32.3 (0.64)	0.4 (0.21)	88.2 (1.04)	15.8 (1.18)	3.7 (0.48)	62.8 (1.23)	10.4 (0.78)
March 1999.....	0.6 (0.09)	87.8 (0.37)	28.2 (0.51)	0.1 (0.05)	93.0 (0.35)	33.6 (0.66)	0.2 (0.15)	88.7 (1.03)	15.0 (1.16)	3.2 (0.45)	61.6 (1.26)	8.9 (0.74)
March 2000.....	0.7 (0.09)	88.1 (0.37)	29.1 (0.52)	0.1 (0.04)	94.0 (0.33)	34.0 (0.67)	# (†)	86.8 (1.13)	17.8 (1.28)	3.8 (0.48)	62.8 (1.22)	9.7 (0.75)
March 2001.....	0.8 (0.11)	87.7 (0.38)	28.6 (0.52)	0.2 (0.06)	93.3 (0.36)	33.0 (0.68)	0.1 (0.10)	87.0 (1.11)	17.8 (1.27)	4.7 (0.54)	63.2 (1.23)	11.1 (0.80)
March 2002.....	1.1 (0.08)	86.4 (0.28)	29.3 (0.37)	0.1 (0.04)	93.0 (0.26)	35.9 (0.50)	0.6 (0.19)	87.6 (0.80)	18.0 (0.94)	4.7 (0.34)	62.4 (0.78)	8.9 (0.46)
March 2003.....	1.0 (0.08)	86.5 (0.27)	28.4 (0.36)	0.2 (0.04)	93.7 (0.25)	34.2 (0.49)	0.6 (0.19)	88.5 (0.78)	17.5 (0.93)	4.0 (0.30)	61.7 (0.75)	10.0 (0.47)
March 2004.....	1.1 (0.08)	86.6 (0.27)	28.7 (0.36)	0.3 (0.05)	93.3 (0.26)	34.5 (0.49)	0.3 (0.13)	88.7 (0.76)	17.1 (0.90)	4.1 (0.31)	62.4 (0.75)	10.9 (0.48)
March 2005.....	1.0 (0.08)	86.1 (0.27)	28.6 (0.36)	0.3 (0.05)	92.8 (0.26)	34.1 (0.48)	0.4 (0.15)	86.9 (0.79)	17.5 (0.89)	3.6 (0.28)	63.3 (0.74)	11.2 (0.48)
March 2006.....	0.9 (0.07)	86.4 (0.27)	28.4 (0.35)	0.2 (0.04)	93.4 (0.25)	34.3 (0.48)	0.4 (0.14)	86.3 (0.79)	18.7 (0.90)	3.5 (0.28)	63.2 (0.72)	9.5 (0.44)
Males, 25 and over												
April 1940	15.1 (—)	22.7 (—)	5.5 (—)	12.0 (—)	24.2 (—)	5.9 (—)	46.2 (—)	6.9 (—)	1.4 (—)	— (†)	— (†)	— (†)
April 1950	12.2 (—)	32.6 (—)	7.3 (—)	9.8 (—)	34.6 (—)	7.9 (—)	36.9 (—)	12.6 (—)	2.1 (—)	— (†)	— (†)	— (†)
April 1960	9.4 (—)	39.5 (—)	9.7 (—)	7.4 (—)	41.6 (—)	10.3 (—)	27.7 (—)	20.0 (—)	3.5 (—)	— (†)	— (†)	— (†)
March 1970	5.9 (—)	55.0 (—)	14.1 (—)	4.5 (—)	57.2 (—)	15.0 (—)	17.9 (—)	35.4 (—)	6.8 (—)	— (†)	— (†)	— (†)
March 1980	3.6 (0.12)	69.2 (0.30)	20.9 (0.26)	2.0 (0.10)	72.4 (0.31)	22.8 (0.29)	11.3 (0.78)	51.2 (1.23)	7.7 (0.66)	16.5 (1.30)	44.9 (1.74)	9.2 (1.01)
March 1990	2.7 (0.09)	77.7 (0.24)	24.4 (0.25)	1.3 (0.07)	81.6 (0.25)	26.7 (0.29)	6.4 (0.53)	65.8 (1.03)	11.9 (0.70)	12.9 (0.85)	50.3 (1.27)	9.8 (0.76)
March 1995	2.0 (0.08)	81.7 (0.22)	26.0 (0.25)	0.8 (0.06)	86.0 (0.22)	28.9 (0.29)	3.4 (0.37)	73.5 (0.91)	13.7 (0.71)	10.8 (0.69)	52.9 (1.11)	10.1 (0.67)
March 1996.....	1.9 (0.08)	81.9 (0.23)	26.0 (0.26)	0.7 (0.06)	86.1 (0.23)	28.8 (0.30)	2.9 (0.31)	74.6 (0.80)	12.5 (0.61)	10.1 (0.59)	53.0 (0.97)	10.3 (0.59)
March 1997.....	1.8 (0.07)	82.0 (0.21)	26.2 (0.24)	0.6 (0.05)	86.3 (0.21)	29.0 (0.28)	2.9 (0.30)	73.8 (0.79)	12.5 (0.60)	9.2 (0.44)	54.9 (0.76)	10.6 (0.47)
March 1998.....	1.7 (0.07)	82.8 (0.20)	26.5 (0.24)	0.7 (0.05)	87.1 (0.21)	29.3 (0.28)	2.3 (0.27)	75.4 (0.77)	14.0 (0.62)	9.3 (0.44)	55.7 (0.74)	11.1 (0.47)
March 1999.....	1.6 (0.07)	83.4 (0.20)	27.5 (0.24)	0.6 (0.05)	87.7 (0.20)	30.6 (0.28)	2.0 (0.25)	77.2 (0.74)	14.3 (0.62)	9.0 (0.43)	56.0 (0.75)	10.7 (0.46)
March 2000.....	1.6 (0.07)	84.2 (0.19)	27.8 (0.24)	0.6 (0.05)	88.5 (0.20)	30.8 (0.28)	2.1 (0.25)	79.1 (0.72)	16.4 (0.65)	8.2 (0.40)	56.6 (0.73)	10.7 (0.45)
March 2001.....	1.6 (0.07)	84.4 (0.19)	28.0 (0.24)	0.6 (0.05)	88.6 (0.19)	30.9 (0.28)	1.7 (0.22)	80.6 (0.69)	15.9 (0.64)	9.4 (0.42)	55.6 (0.72)	11.1 (0.45)
March 2002.....	1.7 (0.05)	83.8 (0.14)	28.5 (0.17)	0.5 (0.03)	88.5 (0.14)	31.7 (0.20)	1.9 (0.17)	79.0 (0.51)	16.5 (0.47)	9.0 (0.28)	56.1 (0.48)	11.0 (0.30)
March 2003.....	1.7 (0.05)	84.1 (0.13)	28.9 (0.17)	0.5 (0.03)	89.0 (0.14)	32.3 (0.20)	1.9 (0.17)	79.9 (0.50)	16.8 (0.47)	8.3 (0.26)	56.3 (0.46)	11.2 (0.29)
March 2004.....	1.7 (0.05)	84.8 (0.13)	29.4 (0.17)	0.5 (0.03)	89.9 (0.13)	32.9 (0.20)	1.5 (0.15)	80.8 (0.49)	16.6 (0.46)	8.4 (0.25)	57.3 (0.45)	11.8 (0.30)
March 2005.....	1.7 (0.05)	84.9 (0.13)	28.9 (0.17)	0.5 (0.03)	89.9 (0.13)	32.3 (0.20)	1.7 (0.16)	81.4 (0.48)	16.1 (0.45)	8.0 (0.24)	58.0 (0.44)	11.8 (0.29)
March 2006.....	1.6 (0.05)	85.0 (0.13)	29.2 (0.16)	0.4 (0.03)	90.2 (0.13)	32.8 (0.20)	1.7 (0.16)	80.7 (0.48)	17.5 (0.46)	7.8 (0.23)	58.5 (0.43)	11.9 (0.28)
Females, 25 and over												
April 1940	12.4 (—)	26.3 (—)	3.8 (—)	9.8 (—)	28.1 (—)	4.0 (—)	37.5 (—)	8.4 (—)	1.2 (—)	— (†)	— (†)	— (†)
April 1950	10.0 (—)	36.0 (—)	5.2 (—)	8.1 (—)	38.2 (—)	5.4 (—)	28.6 (—)	14.7 (—)	2.4 (—)	— (†)	— (†)	— (†)
April 1960	7.4 (—)	42.5 (—)	5.8 (—)	6.0 (—)	44.7 (—)	6.0 (—)	19.7 (—)	23.1 (—)	3.6 (—)	— (†)	— (†)	— (†)
March 1970	4.7 (—)	55.4 (—)	8.2 (—)	3.9 (—)	57.7 (—)	8.6 (—)	11.9 (—)	36.6 (—)	5.6 (—)	— (†)	— (†)	— (†)
March 1980	3.2 (0.11)	68.1 (0.28)	13.6 (0.21)	1.8 (0.09)	71.5 (0.30)	14.4 (0.23)	7.4 (0.58)	51.5 (1.10)	8.1 (0.60)	15.3 (1.20)	44.2 (1.66)	6.2 (0.80)
March 1990	2.2 (0.08)	77.5 (0.23)	18.4 (0.22)	1.0 (0.06)	81.3 (0.24)	19.8 (0.25)	4.0 (0.38)	66.5 (0.92)	10.8 (0.60)	11.7 (0.81)	51.3 (1.25)	8.7 (0.70)
March 1995	1.7 (0.07)	81.6 (0.21)	20.2 (0.22)	0.6 (0.05)	85.8 (0.22)	22.1 (0.26)	1.7 (0.24)	74.1 (0.81)	13.0 (0.62)	10.4 (0.67)	53.8 (1.09)	8.4 (0.61)
March 1996.....	1.7 (0.07)	81.6 (0.22)	21.4 (0.23)	0.5 (0.05)	85.9 (0.22)	23.2 (0.27)	1.6 (0.21)	74.6 (0.71)	14.8 (0.58)	10.5 (0.59)	53.3 (0.97)	8.3 (0.53)
March 1997.....	1.6 (0.06)	82.2 (0.20)	21.7 (0.21)	0.5 (0.04)	86.3 (0.20)	23.7 (0.25)	1.3 (0.18)	76.5 (0.68)	14.0 (0.56)	9.5 (0.45)	54.6 (0.76)	10.1 (0.46)
March 1998.....	1.6 (0.06)	82.9 (0.19)	22.4 (0.21)	0.6 (0.04)	87.1 (0.20)	24.1 (0.25)	1.2 (0.17)	77.1 (0.67)	15.4 (0.58)	9.2 (0.44)	55.3 (0.75)	10.9 (0.47)
March 1999.....	1.5 (0.06)	83.3 (0.19)	23.1 (0.22)	0.5 (0.04)	87.6 (0.19)	25.0 (0.26)	1.5 (0.19)	77.5 (0.66)	16.5 (0.59)	9.0 (0.42)	56.3 (0.73)	11.0 (0.46)
March 2000.....	1.5 (0.06)	84.0 (0.19)	23.6 (0.22)	0.4 (0.04)	88.4 (0.19)	25.5 (0.26)	1.1 (0.17)	78.7 (0.64)	16.8 (0.59)	9.3 (0.42)	57.5 (0.71)	10.6 (0.44)
March 2001.....	1.5 (0.06)	84.2 (0.18)	24.3 (0.22)	0.4 (0.04)	88.8 (0.19)	26.5 (0.26)	1.0 (0.16)	78.6 (0.64)	16.3 (0.58)	9.1 (0.41)	57.4 (0.70)	11.3 (0.45)
March 2002.....	1.5 (0.04)	84.4 (0.13)	25.1 (0.15)	0.5 (0.03)	88.9 (0.13)	27.3 (0.19)	1.4 (0.13)	79.4 (0.45)	17.7 (0.42)	8.3 (0.27)	57.9 (0.48)	11.2 (0.31)
March 2003.....	1.5 (0.04)	85.0 (0.13)	25.7 (0.15)	0.4 (0.03)	89.7 (0.13)	27.9 (0.19)	1.2 (0.12)	80.7 (0.44)	18.0 (0.43)	8.1 (0.26)	57.8 (0.46)	11.6 (0.30)
March 2004.....	1.4 (0.04)	85.4 (0.12)	26.1 (0.15)	0.4 (0.02)	90.1 (0.12)	28.4 (0.19)	1.1 (0.12)	81.2 (0.43)	18.5 (0.43)	7.8 (0.25)	59.5 (0.46)	12.3 (0.31)
March 2005.....	1.5 (0.04)	85.4 (0.12)	26.5 (0.15)	0.4 (0.03)	90.3 (0.12)	28.9 (0.19)	1.3 (0.12)	81.5 (0.42)	18.9 (0.43)	7.8 (0.25)	58.9 (0.45)	12.1 (0.30)
March 2006.....	1.5 (0.04)	85.9 (0.12)	26.9 (0.15)	0.4 (0.03)	90.8 (0.12)	29.3 (0.19)	1.3 (0.12)	81.5 (0.42)	19.5 (0.43)	7.4 (0.23)	60.1 (0.44)	12.9 (0.30)

—Not available.
†Not applicable.
#Rounds to zero.
[1]Includes persons of Hispanic origin for years prior to 1980.
[2]Data for years prior to 1993 are for persons with 4 or more years of high school. Data for later years are for high school completers—i.e., those persons who graduated from high school with a diploma, as well as those who completed high school through equivalency programs.
[3]Data for years prior to 1993 are for persons with 4 or more years of college.

[4]Estimates based on Census Bureau retrojection of 1940 census data on education by age.
NOTE: Total includes other racial/ethnic groups not separately shown. Race categories exclude persons of Hispanic origin. Standard errors appear in parentheses.
SOURCE: U.S. Department of Commerce, Census Bureau, U.S. Census of Population, 1960, Volume 1, part 1; Current Population Reports, Series P-20; Current Population Survey, March 1970 through March 2006; and 1960 Census Monograph, Education of the American Population, by John K. Folger and Charles B. Nam. (This table was prepared September 2006.)

Table 9. Number of persons age 18 and over, by highest level of education attained, age, sex, and race/ethnicity: 2006

[In thousands]

Age, sex, and race/ethnicity	Total	Elementary — Less than 7 years	Elementary — 7 or 8 years	High school — 1 to 3 years	High school — 4 years	High school — Completion	(SE)	College — Some college	College — Associate's degree	College — Bachelor's degree	(SE)	College — Master's degree	(SE)	College — Professional degree	College — Doctor's
1	2	3	4	5	6	7		8	9	10		11		12	13
Total, 18 and over	219,849	6,991	5,505	17,728	3,602	69,401	(244.2)	42,412	18,146	37,332	(195.1)	13,184	(122.6)	3,061	2,488
18 and 19 years old	7,572	54	106	2,580	491	2,287	(52.3)	2,012	34	7	(2.9)	#	(†)	2	#
20 to 24 years old	20,393	319	274	1,668	436	6,216	(85.5)	7,789	1,353	2,171	(50.9)	131	(12.6)	10	24
25 years old and over	191,884	6,618	5,124	13,480	2,674	60,898	(234.3)	32,611	16,760	35,153	(190.3)	13,053	(122.0)	3,050	2,464
25 to 29 years old	20,138	562	320	1,529	323	5,768	(82.4)	4,066	1,851	4,429	(72.4)	988	(34.4)	185	117
30 to 34 years old	19,343	569	317	1,243	281	5,534	(80.8)	3,477	1,835	4,187	(70.4)	1,420	(41.3)	281	199
35 to 39 years old	20,771	662	289	1,224	322	6,055	(84.4)	3,506	1,951	4,501	(73.0)	1,594	(43.7)	383	283
40 to 49 years old	44,868	1,179	697	2,647	619	14,421	(127.9)	7,570	4,691	8,874	(101.5)	2,884	(58.6)	773	513
50 to 59 years old	38,106	1,059	708	2,172	423	11,574	(115.3)	6,899	3,607	7,064	(90.9)	3,288	(62.5)	674	640
60 to 64 years old	13,153	423	354	1,005	156	4,511	(73.1)	2,167	1,015	1,945	(48.2)	1,100	(36.3)	217	261
65 years old and over	35,505	2,163	2,438	3,660	551	13,035	(121.9)	4,926	1,811	4,153	(70.2)	1,780	(46.2)	538	451
Males, 18 and over	106,346	3,609	2,715	8,892	1,918	33,895	(187.4)	19,694	7,787	17,945	(141.5)	6,244	(85.6)	1,943	1,704
18 and 19 years old	3,801	42	66	1,431	241	1,135	(36.9)	877	8	1	(1.1)	#	(†)	#	#
20 to 24 years old	10,312	189	159	927	272	3,379	(63.4)	3,816	644	862	(32.2)	39	(6.8)	6	19
25 years old and over	92,233	3,378	2,490	6,534	1,405	29,380	(176.4)	15,001	7,135	17,082	(138.4)	6,205	(85.4)	1,937	1,686
25 to 29 years old	10,185	362	189	846	192	3,166	(61.4)	1,991	865	2,059	(49.6)	381	(21.4)	78	57
30 to 34 years old	9,642	337	163	638	161	3,067	(60.4)	1,647	832	1,941	(48.2)	608	(27.1)	137	110
35 to 39 years old	10,320	394	179	652	204	3,215	(61.8)	1,642	868	2,096	(50.1)	702	(29.1)	200	168
40 to 49 years old	22,103	654	333	1,411	347	7,412	(93.1)	3,539	1,968	4,214	(70.7)	1,398	(40.9)	465	360
50 to 59 years old	18,555	524	361	1,074	207	5,543	(80.8)	3,159	1,592	3,623	(65.6)	1,582	(43.5)	454	437
60 to 64 years old	6,243	212	180	460	71	1,978	(48.6)	998	393	1,040	(35.3)	551	(25.7)	172	189
65 years old and over	15,185	895	1,086	1,454	224	4,999	(76.8)	2,023	616	2,109	(50.2)	983	(34.4)	431	364
Females, 18 and over	113,504	3,382	2,790	8,836	1,684	35,506	(191.1)	22,718	10,359	19,387	(146.6)	6,940	(90.2)	1,119	783
18 and 19 years old	3,771	12	41	1,148	250	1,151	(37.2)	1,135	25	6	(2.6)	#	(†)	2	#
20 to 24 years old	10,082	130	115	742	164	2,837	(58.1)	3,973	709	1,310	(39.6)	93	(10.6)	4	5
25 years old and over	99,651	3,240	2,634	6,946	1,269	31,518	(181.8)	17,610	9,625	18,071	(142.0)	6,848	(89.6)	1,113	778
25 to 29 years old	9,953	200	132	683	130	2,602	(55.7)	2,075	986	2,371	(53.2)	607	(27.0)	107	60
30 to 34 years old	9,701	232	154	605	120	2,467	(54.3)	1,830	1,002	2,246	(51.8)	811	(31.2)	144	89
35 to 39 years old	10,451	269	110	572	118	2,840	(58.2)	1,864	1,083	2,405	(53.6)	892	(32.7)	183	115
40 to 49 years old	22,765	525	364	1,236	273	7,009	(90.6)	4,031	2,722	4,660	(74.2)	1,486	(42.2)	308	153
50 to 59 years old	19,551	535	348	1,098	216	6,031	(84.2)	3,740	2,015	3,441	(64.0)	1,706	(45.2)	220	202
60 to 64 years old	6,910	211	175	545	85	2,533	(55.0)	1,168	622	905	(33.0)	549	(25.7)	44	72
65 years old and over	20,320	1,268	1,352	2,206	327	8,036	(96.8)	2,903	1,194	2,043	(49.4)	797	(30.9)	107	86
White, 18 and over	153,030	1,271	2,966	9,731	1,743	48,988	(217.0)	30,693	13,849	29,045	(175.5)	10,401	(109.6)	2,427	1,916
18 and 19 years old	4,705	7	43	1,553	262	1,424	(41.3)	1,396	14	4	(2.2)	#	(†)	2	#
20 to 24 years old	12,664	29	92	715	179	3,609	(65.5)	5,286	980	1,665	(44.7)	88	(10.3)	2	19
25 years old and over	135,661	1,235	2,831	7,462	1,302	43,955	(208.2)	24,011	12,855	27,376	(171.1)	10,313	(109.1)	2,423	1,898
25 to 29 years old	11,976	35	86	569	96	3,257	(62.2)	2,528	1,297	3,208	(61.8)	677	(28.5)	148	76
30 to 34 years old	11,646	26	103	440	94	3,247	(62.2)	2,206	1,292	2,975	(59.5)	960	(34.0)	179	125
35 to 39 years old	13,343	74	60	507	123	3,788	(67.1)	2,414	1,406	3,345	(63.1)	1,169	(37.5)	270	189
40 to 49 years old	31,199	122	272	1,336	315	10,100	(108.0)	5,397	3,585	6,859	(89.6)	2,246	(51.8)	602	364
50 to 59 years old	28,590	164	338	1,199	229	8,726	(100.7)	5,365	2,926	5,766	(82.4)	2,772	(57.5)	584	522
60 to 64 years old	10,202	104	191	648	76	3,595	(65.4)	1,794	812	1,615	(44.0)	949	(33.8)	191	226
65 years old and over	28,704	709	1,782	2,763	370	11,242	(113.7)	4,307	1,537	3,609	(65.5)	1,539	(42.9)	449	396
Black, 18 and over	24,802	616	542	3,043	648	8,893	(99.2)	5,223	1,762	2,827	(60.2)	987	(36.3)	160	102
18 and 19 years old	1,138	4	15	433	73	362	(22.1)	238	10	2	(1.5)	#	(†)	#	#
20 to 24 years old	2,751	7	15	273	86	1,035	(37.2)	1,016	135	164	(14.9)	15	(4.5)	2	3
25 years old and over	20,913	605	512	2,336	488	7,496	(92.7)	3,969	1,616	2,661	(58.5)	972	(36.0)	158	99
25 to 29 years old	2,564	12	5	275	60	931	(35.3)	631	169	398	(23.2)	70	(9.8)	9	3
30 to 34 years old	2,340	11	21	208	36	848	(33.7)	519	175	355	(21.9)	124	(13.0)	25	17
35 to 39 years old	2,493	25	16	182	46	986	(36.3)	479	204	390	(23.0)	128	(13.2)	25	11
40 to 49 years old	5,335	62	45	471	113	1,958	(50.6)	1,093	516	753	(31.8)	248	(18.3)	47	30
50 to 59 years old	3,970	74	76	448	94	1,419	(43.3)	747	349	494	(25.8)	219	(17.2)	29	19
60 to 64 years old	1,263	58	39	214	33	468	(25.2)	188	88	86	(10.8)	76	(10.2)	8	6
65 years old and over	2,948	363	310	539	105	885	(34.4)	312	115	185	(15.9)	106	(12.0)	17	12
Hispanic, 18 and over	28,366	4,575	1,686	4,145	976	8,250	(75.1)	4,134	1,550	2,197	(43.4)	578	(22.9)	178	97
18 and 19 years old	1,239	43	38	437	119	362	(18.2)	234	5	1	(1.0)	#	(†)	#	#
20 to 24 years old	3,628	278	157	599	144	1,216	(32.8)	926	167	128	(10.8)	12.01	(3.3)	2	#
25 years old and over	23,499	4,254	1,491	3,109	712	6,672	(69.7)	2,974	1,379	2,068	(42.2)	566	(22.6)	176	97
25 to 29 years old	4,088	505	218	632	148	1,290	(33.8)	636	272	326	(17.3)	50.932	(6.8)	6	5
30 to 34 years old	3,763	526	180	540	129	1,157	(32.1)	513	229	364	(18.2)	87.231	(9.0)	32	7
35 to 39 years old	3,409	543	194	478	129	978	(29.6)	418	200	333	(17.4)	97.93	(9.5)	28	10
40 to 49 years old	5,516	920	338	688	160	1,589	(37.3)	703	348	536	(22.0)	148.239	(11.7)	57	29
50 to 59 years old	3,380	684	217	413	62	881	(28.1)	453	191	304	(16.7)	113.907	(10.2)	26	35
60 to 64 years old	1,028	226	97	112	35	280	(16.0)	108	68	68	(7.9)	25.26	(4.8)	7	1
65 years old and over	2,315	850	248	246	51	497	(21.2)	143	71	136	(11.2)	42.981	(6.3)	21	9

†Not applicable.
#Rounds to zero.
NOTE: Total includes other racial/ethnic groups not shown separately. Although cells with fewer than 75,000 weighted persons are subject to relatively wide sampling variation, they are included in the table to permit various types of aggregations. Race categories exclude persons of Hispanic origin. Detail may not sum to totals because of rounding. Standard errors appear in parentheses.
SOURCE: U.S. Department of Commerce, Census Bureau, Current Population Survey (CPS), March 2006, unpublished tabulations. (This table was prepared September 2006.)

Table 10.   Persons age 18 and over who hold at least a bachelor's degree in specific fields of study, by sex, race/ethnicity, and age: 2001

Number (in thousands)

Field of study	Total		Sex				Race/ethnicity									Age					
			Males		Females		White		Black		Hispanic		Asian/Pacific Islander		American Indian/ Alaska Native		18 to 29 years old		30 to 49 years old		50 years old and over	
1	2		3		4		5		6		7		8		9		10		11		12	
Total population, 18 and over (in thousands)	208,762	(680.6)	99,811	(484.3)	108,951	(477.6)	151,898	(779.3)	23,314	(234.3)	23,580	(273.6)	8,097	(252.9)	1,873	(135.5)	44,447	(572.0)	85,830	(721.6)	78,485	(703.0)
Degree holders																						
Total	49,144	(595.5)	24,977	(422.6)	24,166	(419.3)	40,138	(548.5)	3,192	(142.5)	2,189	(145.7)	3,389	(177.9)	235	(49.2)	7,016	(245)	24,666	(444)	17,461	(378.5)
Agriculture/forestry	540	(68.7)	421	(60.6)	‡	(†)	473	(64.3)	‡	(†)	‡	(†)	‡	(†)	‡	(†)	‡	(†)	254	(47.1)	239	(45.7)
Art/architecture	1,450	(112.4)	649	(75.2)	801	(83.5)	1,156	(100.4)	‡	(†)	‡	(†)	‡	(†)	‡	(†)	259	(47.6)	748	(80.8)	443	(62.2)
Business/management	8,976	(275.8)	5,679	(218.3)	3,297	(167.9)	7,254	(248.7)	623	(65.4)	426	(66.1)	633	(80.2)	‡	(†)	1,202	(102.4)	5,102	(209.4)	2,672	(152.2)
Communications	1,164	(100.7)	577	(70.9)	586	(71.5)	945	(90.8)	‡	(†)	‡	(†)	166	(41.4)	‡	(†)	301	(51.3)	706	(78.5)	157	(37.1)
Computer and information sciences	1,249	(104.3)	871	(87.0)	378	(57.4)	895	(88.4)	‡	(†)	‡	(†)	181	(43.2)	‡	(†)	268	(48.4)	828	(85.0)	152	(36.5)
Education	7,102	(246.1)	1,750	(123.0)	5,351	(212.3)	6,160	(229.6)	490	(58.1)	234	(49.1)	559	(75.5)	‡	(†)	663	(76.1)	2,891	(158.2)	3,548	(175.1)
Engineering	3,959	(184.8)	3,558	(174.2)	401	(59.2)	3,085	(163.4)	‡	(†)	173	(42.3)	‡	(†)	‡	(†)	459	(63.3)	2,057	(133.7)	1,443	(112.1)
English/literature	1,527	(115.3)	597	(72.1)	930	(89.9)	1,316	(107.1)	‡	(†)	‡	(†)	‡	(†)	‡	(†)	241	(45.9)	633	(74.3)	654	(75.6)
Foreign languages	448	(62.6)	135	(34.4)	313	(52.3)	344	(54.9)	‡	(†)	‡	(†)	‡	(†)	‡	(†)	‡	(†)	219	(43.7)	189	(40.6)
Health sciences	2,298	(141.3)	482	(64.8)	1,817	(125.3)	1,811	(145.5)	173	(34.8)	‡	(†)	213	(46.9)	‡	(†)	382	(57.8)	1,247	(104.2)	670	(76.5)
Liberal arts/humanities	2,846	(157.0)	1,150	(99.9)	1,695	(121.1)	2,444	(145.6)	146	(31.9)	‡	(†)	142	(38.3)	‡	(†)	400	(59.1)	1,308	(106.7)	1,137	(99.6)
Mathematics/statistics	869	(87.1)	507	(66.5)	362	(56.2)	567	(70.4)	‡	(†)	‡	(†)	149	(39.2)	‡	(†)	‡	(†)	386	(58.1)	363	(56.3)
Natural sciences (biological and physical)	2,910	(158.8)	1,756	(123.2)	1,153	(100.1)	2,260	(140.1)	190	(36.4)	‡	(†)	345	(59.5)	‡	(†)	413	(60.1)	1,426	(111.4)	1,071	(96.6)
Philosophy/religion/theology	628	(74.1)	437	(61.8)	191	(40.9)	533	(68.3)	‡	(†)	‡	(†)	‡	(†)	‡	(†)	‡	(†)	268	(48.4)	255	(47.2)
Pre-professional	596	(72.1)	397	(58.9)	199	(41.7)	448	(62.6)	‡	(†)	‡	(†)	‡	(†)	‡	(†)	‡	(†)	306	(51.7)	216	(43.4)
Psychology	1,903	(128.6)	606	(72.7)	1,297	(106.1)	1,561	(116.6)	157	(33.0)	‡	(†)	‡	(†)	‡	(†)	428	(61.2)	940	(90.6)	535	(68.3)
Social sciences/history	2,436	(145.4)	1,026	(94.4)	1,410	(110.5)	1,981	(131.2)	260	(42.5)	‡	(†)	‡	(†)	‡	(†)	359	(56.0)	1,092	(97.6)	985	(92.7)
Other fields	8,243	(264.6)	4,377	(192.6)	3,866	(181.5)	6,907	(242.8)	417	(53.7)	337	(58.8)	559	(75.5)	‡	(†)	1,253	(104.5)	4,256	(191.5)	2,734	(153.9)

Percentage distribution of degree holders, by field

Field of study	Total		Males		Females		White		Black		Hispanic		Asian/Pacific Islander		American Indian/ Alaska Native		18 to 29		30 to 49		50 and over	
Total	100.0	(†)	100.0	(†)	100.0	(†)	100.0	(†)	100.0	(†)	100.0	(†)	100.0	(†)	100.0	(†)	100.0	(†)	100.0	(†)	100.0	(†)
Agriculture/forestry	1.1	(0.14)	1.7	(0.24)	0.5	(0.13)	1.2	(0.16)	0.7	(0.38)	1.1	(0.73)	0.5	(0.40)	‡	(†)	0.7	(0.29)	1.0	(0.19)	1.4	(0.26)
Art/architecture	3.0	(0.23)	2.6	(0.30)	3.3	(0.34)	2.9	(0.25)	3.3	(0.83)	4.8	(1.47)	2.2	(0.81)	4.4	(4.32)	3.7	(0.67)	3.0	(0.32)	2.5	(0.35)
Business/management	18.3	(0.52)	22.7	(0.78)	13.6	(0.65)	18.1	(0.57)	19.5	(1.86)	19.5	(2.72)	18.7	(2.16)	17.5	(7.98)	17.1	(1.33)	20.7	(0.76)	15.3	(0.81)
Communications	2.4	(0.20)	2.3	(0.28)	2.4	(0.29)	2.4	(0.22)	3.2	(0.82)	3.3	(1.23)	1.2	(0.60)	‡	(†)	4.3	(0.72)	2.9	(0.31)	0.9	(0.21)
Computer and information sciences	2.5	(0.21)	3.5	(0.34)	1.6	(0.24)	2.2	(0.22)	3.9	(0.91)	2.6	(1.10)	4.9	(1.19)	‡	(†)	3.8	(0.68)	3.4	(0.34)	0.9	(0.21)
Education	14.5	(0.47)	7.0	(0.48)	22.1	(0.79)	15.3	(0.53)	15.3	(1.69)	10.7	(2.13)	5.3	(1.24)	16.0	(7.69)	9.5	(1.03)	11.7	(0.61)	20.3	(0.90)
Engineering	8.1	(0.36)	14.2	(0.65)	1.7	(0.24)	7.7	(0.39)	3.6	(0.87)	7.9	(1.86)	16.5	(2.05)	11.4	(6.67)	6.5	(0.87)	8.3	(0.52)	8.3	(0.62)
English/literature	3.1	(0.23)	2.4	(0.29)	3.8	(0.37)	3.3	(0.26)	2.6	(0.75)	3.1	(1.19)	1.7	(0.71)	‡	(†)	3.4	(0.64)	2.6	(0.30)	3.7	(0.43)
Foreign languages	0.9	(0.13)	0.5	(0.14)	1.3	(0.22)	0.9	(0.14)	0.8	(0.42)	1.7	(0.90)	1.0	(0.56)	‡	(†)	0.6	(0.27)	0.9	(0.18)	1.1	(0.23)
Health sciences	4.7	(0.28)	1.9	(0.26)	7.5	(0.50)	4.5	(0.31)	5.4	(1.06)	4.4	(1.41)	6.3	(1.34)	2.1	(2.99)	5.4	(0.80)	5.1	(0.41)	3.8	(0.43)
Liberal arts/humanities	5.8	(0.31)	4.6	(0.39)	7.0	(0.49)	6.1	(0.35)	4.6	(0.98)	4.7	(1.45)	4.2	(1.11)	4.5	(4.37)	5.7	(0.82)	5.3	(0.42)	6.5	(0.55)
Mathematics/statistics	1.8	(0.18)	2.0	(0.26)	1.5	(0.23)	1.4	(0.17)	2.4	(0.72)	2.4	(1.05)	4.4	(1.13)	10.4	(6.41)	1.7	(0.46)	1.6	(0.23)	2.1	(0.32)
Natural sciences (biological and physical)	5.9	(0.31)	7.0	(0.48)	4.8	(0.41)	5.6	(0.34)	6.0	(1.11)	4.9	(1.49)	10.2	(1.67)	2.7	(3.41)	5.9	(0.83)	5.8	(0.44)	6.1	(0.54)
Philosophy/religion/theology	1.3	(0.15)	1.8	(0.25)	0.8	(0.17)	1.3	(0.17)	0.9	(0.45)	1.8	(0.90)	0.8	(0.49)	‡	(†)	1.5	(0.43)	1.1	(0.20)	1.5	(0.27)
Pre-professional	1.2	(0.15)	1.6	(0.23)	0.8	(0.17)	1.1	(0.16)	1.6	(0.59)	2.0	(0.97)	1.5	(0.67)	‡	(†)	1.1	(0.36)	1.2	(0.21)	1.2	(0.25)
Psychology	3.9	(0.26)	2.4	(0.29)	5.4	(0.43)	3.9	(0.29)	4.9	(1.01)	5.0	(1.50)	1.7	(0.72)	7.9	(5.65)	6.1	(0.85)	3.8	(0.36)	3.1	(0.39)
Social sciences/history	5.0	(0.29)	4.1	(0.37)	5.8	(0.45)	4.9	(0.32)	8.1	(1.28)	4.7	(1.45)	2.4	(0.85)	4.7	(4.45)	5.1	(0.78)	4.4	(0.39)	5.6	(0.52)
Other fields	16.8	(0.50)	17.5	(0.71)	16.0	(0.70)	17.2	(0.56)	13.1	(1.58)	15.4	(2.48)	16.5	(2.05)	9.9	(6.26)	17.9	(1.35)	17.3	(0.71)	15.7	(0.81)

†Not applicable.
‡Reporting standards not met.
NOTE: Race categories exclude persons of Hispanic origin. Detail may not sum to totals because of rounding. Standard errors appear in parentheses.

SOURCE: U.S. Department of Commerce, Census Bureau, Survey of Income and Program Participation, 2001, unpublished tabulations. (This table was prepared September 2005.)

Table 11. Educational attainment of persons 18 years old and over, by state: 2000 and 2005

State	Percent of 18- to 24-year-olds who were high school completers[1] 2000	2005	2000 Less than high school completion	High school completion or higher	Bachelor's or higher degree Total	Bachelor's degree	Graduate or professional degree	2005 Less than high school completion	High school completion or higher	Bachelor's or higher degree Total	Bachelor's degree	Graduate or professional degree
1	2	3	4	5	6	7	8	9	10	11	12	13
United States.....	74.7 (0.02)	80.4 (0.16)	19.6	80.4	24.4	15.5	8.9	15.8 (0.03)	84.2 (0.06)	27.2 (0.04)	17.2 (0.03)	10.0 (0.02)
Alabama	72.2 (0.15)	77.6 (1.23)	24.7	75.3	19.0	12.1	6.9	19.7 (0.26)	80.3 (0.49)	21.4 (0.26)	13.5 (0.21)	7.9 (0.16)
Alaska	76.9 (0.40)	76.9 (2.55)	11.7	88.3	24.7	16.1	8.6	9.0 (0.41)	91.0 (1.21)	27.3 (0.68)	17.2 (0.55)	10.1 (0.40)
Arizona	69.2 (0.19)	77.7 (1.19)	19.0	81.0	23.5	15.1	8.4	16.2 (0.24)	83.8 (0.48)	25.6 (0.26)	16.2 (0.22)	9.3 (0.15)
Arkansas	75.4 (0.19)	80.3 (1.49)	24.7	75.3	16.7	11.0	5.7	19.0 (0.29)	81.0 (0.54)	18.9 (0.29)	12.6 (0.24)	6.3 (0.16)
California	70.7 (0.07)	79.6 (0.50)	23.2	76.8	26.6	17.1	9.5	19.9 (0.11)	80.1 (0.20)	29.5 (0.11)	18.9 (0.09)	10.6 (0.07)
Colorado	75.1 (0.15)	80.4 (1.30)	13.1	86.9	32.7	21.6	11.1	11.3 (0.22)	88.7 (0.49)	35.5 (0.29)	23.1 (0.23)	12.3 (0.18)
Connecticut	78.2 (0.21)	84.5 (1.61)	16.0	84.0	31.4	18.1	13.3	12.1 (0.25)	87.9 (0.56)	34.9 (0.35)	20.0 (0.27)	15.0 (0.22)
Delaware	77.6 (0.41)	76.5 (2.94)	17.4	82.6	25.0	15.6	9.4	14.4 (0.50)	85.6 (1.04)	27.6 (0.58)	16.4 (0.42)	11.1 (0.40)
District of Columbia	79.4 (0.40)	83.1 (4.01)	22.2	77.8	39.1	18.1	21.0	16.4 (0.69)	83.6 (1.32)	45.3 (0.97)	20.0 (0.66)	25.2 (0.70)
Florida	71.7 (0.11)	79.4 (0.66)	20.1	79.9	22.3	14.2	8.1	15.4 (0.13)	84.6 (0.26)	25.1 (0.14)	16.3 (0.11)	8.8 (0.08)
Georgia	70.0 (0.15)	75.9 (1.01)	21.4	78.6	24.3	16.0	8.3	17.2 (0.20)	82.8 (0.38)	27.1 (0.23)	17.6 (0.19)	9.5 (0.13)
Hawaii	85.8 (0.25)	91.7 (2.36)	15.4	84.6	26.2	17.8	8.4	11.9 (0.36)	88.1 (0.86)	27.9 (0.49)	18.8 (0.40)	9.1 (0.29)
Idaho	77.3 (0.25)	80.4 (1.93)	15.3	84.7	21.7	14.9	6.8	13.3 (0.37)	86.7 (0.83)	23.3 (0.44)	15.9 (0.36)	7.4 (0.26)
Illinois	76.0 (0.09)	82.1 (0.81)	18.6	81.4	26.1	16.6	9.5	14.3 (0.15)	85.7 (0.29)	29.2 (0.18)	18.3 (0.14)	10.9 (0.11)
Indiana	76.5 (0.15)	78.5 (1.02)	17.9	82.1	19.4	12.2	7.2	14.7 (0.18)	85.3 (0.37)	21.3 (0.20)	13.5 (0.16)	7.7 (0.12)
Iowa	81.4 (0.16)	83.8 (1.43)	13.9	86.1	21.2	14.7	6.5	10.4 (0.19)	89.6 (0.50)	23.8 (0.26)	16.5 (0.22)	7.3 (0.15)
Kansas	78.3 (0.18)	84.2 (1.40)	14.0	86.0	25.8	17.1	8.7	11.3 (0.25)	88.7 (0.59)	28.2 (0.33)	18.6 (0.26)	9.6 (0.20)
Kentucky	74.9 (0.15)	79.1 (1.33)	25.9	74.1	17.1	10.2	6.9	21.0 (0.28)	79.0 (0.46)	19.3 (0.22)	11.5 (0.17)	7.8 (0.15)
Louisiana	72.3 (0.15)	77.7 (1.36)	25.2	74.8	18.7	12.2	6.5	19.5 (0.28)	80.5 (0.52)	20.6 (0.26)	13.4 (0.21)	7.1 (0.16)
Maine	78.9 (0.28)	83.0 (2.21)	14.6	85.4	22.9	15.0	7.9	11.0 (0.30)	89.0 (0.74)	25.6 (0.43)	17.0 (0.36)	8.6 (0.24)
Maryland	79.6 (0.16)	82.9 (1.30)	16.2	83.8	31.4	18.0	13.4	13.0 (0.22)	87.0 (0.46)	34.5 (0.28)	19.3 (0.21)	15.2 (0.18)
Massachusetts	82.2 (0.13)	84.1 (1.32)	15.2	84.8	33.2	19.5	13.7	12.0 (0.19)	88.0 (0.43)	36.9 (0.25)	21.1 (0.19)	15.7 (0.17)
Michigan	76.5 (0.10)	82.7 (0.79)	16.6	83.4	21.8	13.7	8.1	13.0 (0.14)	87.0 (0.32)	24.7 (0.16)	15.1 (0.13)	9.5 (0.10)
Minnesota	79.3 (0.13)	84.0 (1.01)	12.1	87.9	27.4	19.1	8.3	9.1 (0.14)	90.9 (0.38)	30.7 (0.23)	21.0 (0.18)	9.7 (0.14)
Mississippi	71.3 (0.18)	75.1 (1.47)	27.1	72.9	16.9	11.1	5.8	21.5 (0.34)	78.5 (0.59)	18.7 (0.30)	12.2 (0.24)	6.5 (0.18)
Missouri	76.5 (0.13)	80.8 (1.08)	18.7	81.3	21.6	14.0	7.6	15.0 (0.18)	85.0 (0.41)	24.0 (0.22)	15.4 (0.18)	8.6 (0.13)
Montana	78.6 (0.31)	84.6 (2.50)	12.8	87.2	24.4	17.2	7.2	9.3 (0.34)	90.7 (0.91)	26.5 (0.51)	18.4 (0.41)	8.0 (0.30)
Nebraska	80.0 (0.21)	84.0 (1.82)	13.4	86.6	23.7	16.4	7.3	10.5 (0.26)	89.5 (0.63)	27.3 (0.34)	18.8 (0.28)	8.5 (0.20)
Nevada	66.7 (0.32)	74.8 (1.85)	19.3	80.7	18.2	12.1	6.1	17.2 (0.41)	82.8 (0.74)	20.6 (0.36)	14.0 (0.30)	6.6 (0.19)
New Hampshire	77.8 (0.29)	82.4 (2.45)	12.6	87.4	28.7	18.7	10.0	10.1 (0.32)	89.9 (0.79)	31.8 (0.50)	20.1 (0.39)	11.7 (0.31)
New Jersey	76.3 (0.14)	84.2 (1.07)	17.9	82.1	29.8	18.8	11.0	13.7 (0.17)	86.3 (0.34)	34.2 (0.21)	21.7 (0.15)	12.5 (0.14)
New Mexico	70.5 (0.24)	76.9 (1.94)	21.1	78.9	23.5	13.7	9.8	18.0 (0.41)	82.0 (0.72)	25.1 (0.41)	14.2 (0.31)	10.9 (0.27)
New York	76.1 (0.09)	80.9 (0.66)	20.9	79.1	27.4	15.6	11.8	15.7 (0.12)	84.3 (0.25)	31.3 (0.15)	17.9 (0.11)	13.4 (0.10)
North Carolina	74.2 (0.11)	78.0 (0.99)	21.9	78.1	22.5	15.3	7.2	17.7 (0.19)	82.3 (0.35)	25.1 (0.19)	17.1 (0.15)	8.0 (0.11)
North Dakota	84.4 (0.24)	88.1 (2.59)	16.1	83.9	22.0	16.5	5.5	11.8 (0.38)	88.2 (1.05)	25.5 (0.58)	18.7 (0.49)	6.7 (0.32)
Ohio	76.8 (0.09)	81.3 (0.79)	17.0	83.0	21.1	13.7	7.4	13.7 (0.13)	86.3 (0.28)	23.3 (0.15)	14.8 (0.12)	8.5 (0.09)
Oklahoma	74.8 (0.16)	79.2 (1.24)	19.4	80.6	20.3	13.5	6.8	15.7 (0.25)	84.3 (0.51)	22.4 (0.27)	15.2 (0.22)	7.2 (0.15)
Oregon	74.2 (0.17)	80.8 (1.45)	14.9	85.1	25.1	16.4	8.7	12.5 (0.24)	87.5 (0.51)	27.7 (0.27)	17.8 (0.21)	10.0 (0.17)
Pennsylvania	79.8 (0.09)	83.8 (0.80)	18.1	81.9	22.4	14.0	8.4	13.3 (0.12)	86.7 (0.27)	25.7 (0.16)	15.9 (0.12)	9.8 (0.10)
Rhode Island	81.3 (0.32)	82.4 (2.96)	22.0	78.0	25.6	15.9	9.7	16.5 (0.51)	83.5 (1.01)	29.3 (0.59)	17.9 (0.46)	11.5 (0.36)
South Carolina	74.3 (0.18)	78.0 (1.40)	23.7	76.3	20.4	13.5	6.9	18.3 (0.27)	81.7 (0.47)	23.0 (0.26)	15.0 (0.21)	7.9 (0.15)
South Dakota	78.2 (0.33)	81.2 (2.07)	15.4	84.6	21.5	15.5	6.0	11.4 (0.36)	88.6 (0.93)	24.7 (0.54)	17.6 (0.45)	7.0 (0.29)
Tennessee	75.1 (0.16)	80.5 (1.11)	24.1	75.9	19.6	12.8	6.8	18.8 (0.21)	81.2 (0.40)	21.8 (0.21)	14.1 (0.18)	7.6 (0.12)
Texas	68.6 (0.08)	76.5 (0.53)	24.3	75.7	23.2	15.6	7.6	21.2 (0.14)	78.8 (0.23)	25.1 (0.12)	17.0 (0.10)	8.2 (0.07)
Utah	80.3 (0.16)	84.7 (1.57)	12.3	87.7	26.1	17.8	8.3	9.9 (0.28)	90.1 (0.67)	27.9 (0.37)	19.2 (0.31)	8.7 (0.20)
Vermont	83.0 (0.28)	85.6 (3.08)	13.6	86.4	29.4	18.3	11.1	10.5 (0.40)	89.5 (0.99)	32.5 (0.62)	20.2 (0.48)	12.3 (0.40)
Virginia	79.4 (0.13)	82.5 (1.06)	18.5	81.5	29.5	17.9	11.6	14.6 (0.17)	85.4 (0.37)	33.2 (0.22)	19.8 (0.17)	13.4 (0.14)
Washington	75.3 (0.16)	79.5 (1.05)	12.9	87.1	27.7	18.4	9.3	11.2 (0.18)	88.8 (0.40)	30.1 (0.22)	19.6 (0.16)	10.5 (0.15)
West Virginia	78.2 (0.22)	82.0 (1.93)	24.8	75.2	14.8	8.9	5.9	18.8 (0.34)	81.2 (0.69)	16.9 (0.32)	10.2 (0.25)	6.8 (0.20)
Wisconsin	78.9 (0.13)	84.4 (1.01)	14.9	85.1	22.4	15.2	7.2	11.2 (0.15)	88.8 (0.34)	25.0 (0.19)	16.8 (0.15)	8.1 (0.11)
Wyoming	79.0 (0.41)	82.1 (2.77)	12.1	87.9	21.9	14.9	7.0	8.7 (0.46)	91.3 (1.26)	23.2 (0.70)	15.5 (0.55)	7.7 (0.42)

[1]High school completers include diploma recipients and those completing through alternative credentials, such as a GED.
NOTE: Some data have been revised from previously published figures. Detail may not sum to totals because of rounding. Standard errors appear in parentheses.
SOURCE: U.S. Department of Commerce, Census Bureau, Census 2000 Summary File 3, retrieved on October 11, 2006, from http://factfinder.census.gov/servlet/DatasetMainPage Servlet?_ds_name=DEC_2000_SF3_U&_program=DEC&_lang=en; Census Briefs, *Educational Attainment: 2000*; and 2005 American Community Survey, American FactFinder, retrieved on October 10, 2006, from http://factfinder.census.gov/servlet/DatasetMainPage Servlet?_program=ACS&_submenuId=&_lang=en&_ts=. (This table was prepared October 2006.)

Table 12. Educational attainment of persons 25 years old and over, by race/ethnicity and state: April 1990 and April 2000

	Percent with high school completion or higher												Percent with bachelor's degree or higher											
	1990						2000						1990						2000					
State	Total	White[1]	Black[1]	Hispanic[2]	Asian/Pacific Islander[1]	American Indian/Alaska Native[1]	Total	White[1]	Black[1]	Hispanic[2]	Asian/Pacific Islander[1]	American Indian/Alaska Native[1]	Total	White[1]	Black[1]	Hispanic[2]	Asian/Pacific Islander[1]	American Indian/Alaska Native[1]	Total	White[1]	Black[1]	Hispanic[2]	Asian/Pacific Islander[1]	American Indian/Alaska Native[1]
1	2	3	4	5	6	7	8	9	10	11	12	13	14	15	16	17	18	19	20	21	22	23	24	25
United States	75.2	77.9	63.1	49.8	77.5	65.5	80.4	83.6	72.3	52.4	80.4	70.9	20.3	21.5	11.4	9.2	36.6	9.3	24.4	26.1	14.3	10.4	44.1	11.5
Alabama	66.9	70.3	54.6	73.8	78.9	64.9	75.3	78.0	66.9	56.9	81.1	72.4	15.7	17.3	9.3	20.1	43.7	11.6	19.0	21.2	11.5	14.6	48.3	13.0
Alaska	86.6	91.1	88.2	80.4	75.4	63.1	88.3	92.5	88.7	78.3	73.0	71.8	23.0	26.8	14.1	14.6	20.5	4.1	24.7	29.3	14.9	15.3	21.2	6.0
Arizona	78.7	82.4	75.1	51.7	80.2	52.1	81.0	85.4	81.7	52.5	83.4	61.9	20.3	22.2	14.3	6.9	37.5	4.6	23.5	26.0	18.6	8.1	44.5	7.3
Arkansas	66.3	68.6	51.5	59.1	66.4	65.4	75.3	77.5	65.8	41.2	72.9	72.5	13.3	14.1	8.4	11.1	24.6	9.8	16.7	17.8	10.2	7.1	32.6	12.1
California	76.2	81.1	75.6	45.0	77.2	71.4	76.8	83.3	80.5	46.7	80.5	67.5	23.4	25.4	14.8	7.1	34.1	11.1	26.6	29.8	17.2	7.7	41.6	11.4
Colorado	84.4	86.1	80.8	58.3	78.3	73.9	86.9	89.5	84.4	58.1	81.8	76.2	27.0	28.3	17.1	8.6	32.1	12.1	32.7	35.0	20.5	10.4	42.8	14.1
Connecticut	79.2	80.9	67.0	53.5	81.9	68.9	84.0	86.3	73.9	58.5	85.0	67.8	27.2	28.5	12.3	12.1	50.8	12.5	31.4	33.5	13.7	11.3	57.7	15.7
Delaware	77.5	80.3	63.2	60.1	86.1	62.0	82.6	86.0	74.2	57.1	88.1	65.2	21.4	23.0	10.6	16.5	55.9	10.2	25.0	26.7	14.4	13.5	61.8	13.2
District of Columbia	73.1	93.1	63.8	52.6	80.2	66.3	77.8	94.4	70.4	47.8	81.9	71.8	33.3	69.0	15.3	24.0	50.9	17.7	39.1	77.3	17.5	24.8	58.2	28.1
Florida	74.4	77.0	56.4	57.2	77.8	68.2	79.9	82.5	67.0	63.3	80.7	73.5	18.3	19.3	9.8	14.2	33.6	11.5	22.3	23.8	12.4	17.5	40.9	14.9
Georgia	70.9	74.9	58.6	66.2	77.5	71.6	78.6	81.8	72.5	48.5	79.5	73.9	19.3	21.8	11.0	20.5	38.6	12.5	24.3	27.4	15.5	13.6	44.3	18.1
Hawaii	80.1	89.3	94.2	73.9	74.7	84.4	84.6	92.7	92.9	81.5	79.9	91.0	22.9	30.2	15.2	10.3	19.4	17.7	26.2	36.5	21.0	13.3	26.6	21.5
Idaho	79.7	80.9	82.8	43.4	80.3	68.1	84.7	86.6	82.5	44.4	82.0	75.6	17.7	18.0	15.8	6.6	27.6	7.2	21.7	22.3	22.4	6.6	38.3	9.5
Illinois	76.2	79.1	65.2	45.0	83.9	71.4	81.4	85.0	73.0	48.5	86.9	69.5	21.0	22.4	11.4	8.0	49.8	13.4	26.1	27.8	14.7	9.1	58.2	13.3
Indiana	75.6	76.5	65.4	62.6	85.8	65.0	82.1	83.2	74.9	57.9	86.2	73.3	15.6	17.6	9.3	10.8	53.1	8.4	19.4	19.8	12.1	11.3	58.0	10.3
Iowa	80.1	80.3	70.1	64.2	76.4	67.6	86.1	86.9	77.3	52.3	74.3	76.9	16.9	16.7	12.8	13.7	47.3	9.7	21.2	21.3	14.7	11.0	42.9	9.9
Kansas	81.3	82.4	71.0	58.1	73.6	75.4	86.0	87.8	79.7	51.7	74.8	81.3	21.1	21.7	11.6	10.1	39.9	10.8	25.8	26.9	14.9	9.7	40.5	14.9
Kentucky	64.6	64.7	61.7	74.0	77.9	59.8	74.1	74.2	73.2	59.1	86.2	72.5	13.6	13.9	7.7	18.9	44.2	8.0	17.1	17.4	10.7	13.0	53.2	13.9
Louisiana	68.3	74.2	53.1	67.6	68.1	49.1	74.8	80.0	63.1	69.0	67.4	60.5	16.1	18.7	9.1	16.6	31.4	5.5	18.7	21.8	10.9	19.5	35.6	9.2
Maine	78.8	78.9	87.6	83.8	74.3	69.9	85.4	85.5	84.7	57.9	74.6	76.0	18.8	18.8	22.3	23.6	44.9	7.7	22.9	22.9	22.5	21.6	32.6	12.1
Maryland	78.4	80.8	70.6	70.3	84.8	73.4	83.8	86.3	78.9	61.9	85.5	75.5	26.5	28.9	16.1	25.2	50.3	19.7	31.4	34.7	20.3	21.4	55.0	21.2
Massachusetts	80.0	81.2	70.0	52.0	74.1	71.1	84.8	86.8	76.3	57.3	76.2	72.5	27.2	27.7	17.0	13.6	44.9	14.9	33.2	34.3	19.7	14.1	49.8	19.2
Michigan	76.8	78.6	64.9	60.9	83.3	67.8	83.4	85.3	74.1	62.3	85.6	76.4	17.4	18.1	10.1	11.6	54.1	7.6	21.8	22.6	12.8	12.9	61.0	10.3
Minnesota	82.4	82.8	76.2	71.1	69.7	68.2	87.9	89.2	79.0	58.1	71.1	74.5	21.8	21.9	17.5	17.2	33.5	7.7	27.4	27.9	18.7	14.0	36.3	8.8
Mississippi	64.3	71.7	47.3	67.7	68.2	57.4	72.9	78.9	60.4	59.1	72.5	64.0	14.7	17.2	8.8	17.1	35.1	8.1	16.9	20.0	10.1	12.1	35.9	9.1
Missouri	73.9	74.9	65.1	53.9	81.5	65.1	81.3	82.4	73.9	65.7	82.2	74.3	17.8	18.3	11.2	18.0	47.3	11.0	21.6	22.3	13.2	16.1	51.5	12.9
Montana	81.0	81.7	80.9	59.6	78.5	68.1	87.2	87.8	91.2	78.0	85.2	75.5	19.8	20.3	18.4	10.9	32.1	7.9	24.4	25.1	33.2	15.4	41.0	10.5
Nebraska	81.8	82.4	73.2	60.0	80.0	69.0	86.6	88.2	78.6	46.6	77.7	75.9	18.9	19.2	12.4	9.4	39.5	8.8	23.7	24.4	14.1	8.5	42.3	8.8
Nevada	78.8	80.9	70.8	53.7	74.1	69.8	80.7	83.9	78.9	47.3	82.0	75.2	15.3	15.9	9.0	7.0	21.9	8.0	18.2	19.3	12.0	6.4	28.3	8.6
New Hampshire	82.2	82.2	86.1	78.2	82.7	65.9	87.4	87.6	84.4	73.6	84.9	76.5	24.4	24.2	25.7	25.5	26.1	16.0	28.7	28.5	27.8	22.7	54.6	17.0
New Jersey	76.7	78.6	67.0	53.9	86.8	66.9	82.1	84.7	74.5	59.5	88.5	70.4	24.9	25.8	13.6	10.8	57.1	14.8	29.8	31.0	16.2	12.5	62.1	16.4
New Mexico	75.1	78.6	74.7	59.6	80.8	58.2	78.9	83.3	79.4	64.4	83.1	67.1	20.4	23.4	14.2	8.7	38.7	5.8	23.5	28.0	18.8	10.8	44.7	7.7
New York	76.7	78.5	64.7	50.4	72.4	65.2	79.1	84.0	70.6	55.0	73.3	66.4	23.1	25.3	12.6	9.3	38.7	13.4	27.4	30.5	15.8	11.5	41.3	14.4
North Carolina	70.0	73.1	58.1	71.0	77.9	51.5	78.1	81.2	70.7	44.5	79.3	62.7	17.4	19.3	9.5	17.9	39.3	7.9	22.5	25.0	13.1	10.5	43.9	10.4
North Dakota	76.7	76.9	95.9	75.2	83.7	64.3	83.9	84.2	92.6	73.0	84.4	74.8	18.1	18.3	17.1	15.9	37.8	8.3	22.0	22.4	20.5	16.3	48.9	9.7

See notes at end of table.

Table 12. Educational attainment of persons 25 years old and over, by race/ethnicity and state: April 1990 and April 2000—Continued

	Percent with high school completion or higher												Percent with bachelor's degree or higher											
	1990						2000						1990						2000					
State	Total	White[1]	Black[1]	Hispanic[2]	Asian/ Pacific Islander[1]	American Indian/ Alaska Native[1]	Total	White[1]	Black[1]	Hispanic[2]	Asian/ Pacific Islander[1]	American Indian/ Alaska Native[1]	Total	White[1]	Black[1]	Hispanic[2]	Asian/ Pacific Islander[1]	American Indian/ Alaska Native[1]	Total	White[1]	Black[1]	Hispanic[2]	Asian/ Pacific Islander[1]	American Indian/ Alaska Native[1]
1	2	3	4	5	6	7	8	9	10	11	12	13	14	15	16	17	18	19	20	21	22	23	24	25
Ohio	75.7	76.9	64.6	63.3	83.5	65.3	83.0	84.2	73.9	67.1	86.6	73.2	17.0	17.6	9.1	14.2	53.2	8.3	21.1	21.8	11.9	15.2	58.6	12.4
Oklahoma	74.6	75.7	70.1	55.9	76.1	68.1	80.6	82.1	78.5	50.9	77.2	76.5	17.8	18.7	12.0	10.5	34.7	10.8	20.3	21.5	13.7	9.6	37.5	13.2
Oregon	81.5	82.3	75.0	53.0	79.4	71.0	85.1	87.1	79.8	48.8	79.5	77.5	20.6	20.8	9.1	10.1	32.3	8.3	25.1	25.7	17.8	9.6	38.7	12.2
Pennsylvania	74.7	75.9	63.5	52.2	77.1	67.8	81.9	83.4	71.8	56.9	78.4	73.2	17.9	18.5	10.0	11.8	45.2	12.0	22.4	23.1	12.0	12.0	49.2	13.2
Rhode Island	72.0	73.0	65.9	46.8	59.6	64.5	78.0	80.1	71.0	50.4	69.2	68.3	21.3	21.8	12.7	8.9	30.6	8.3	25.6	26.8	16.7	8.6	36.4	14.1
South Carolina	68.3	73.6	53.3	71.8	77.4	62.5	76.3	80.9	64.9	56.4	79.5	64.2	16.6	19.8	7.6	19.8	34.4	10.9	20.4	24.2	9.9	14.1	40.8	11.2
South Dakota	77.1	77.8	82.2	71.3	74.3	62.5	84.6	85.7	84.1	64.9	72.3	70.9	17.2	17.6	24.1	13.4	33.1	6.8	21.5	22.3	19.3	11.7	39.6	8.5
Tennessee	67.1	68.2	59.4	71.5	79.3	63.1	75.9	77.0	70.8	55.4	82.1	74.9	16.0	16.7	10.2	21.9	42.6	10.5	19.6	20.5	12.9	14.1	47.8	14.8
Texas	72.1	76.2	66.1	44.6	79.1	70.9	75.7	79.5	75.8	49.3	80.7	71.5	20.3	22.6	12.0	7.3	41.3	13.9	23.2	25.8	15.3	8.9	47.8	15.7
Utah	85.1	86.2	77.0	61.0	80.7	59.3	87.7	89.9	83.2	56.5	79.9	68.7	22.3	22.7	15.9	9.1	29.4	6.4	26.1	27.1	19.8	9.8	36.4	9.1
Vermont	80.8	80.8	82.9	84.7	87.1	66.8	86.4	86.6	84.2	85.6	78.4	76.9	24.3	24.2	30.5	28.2	52.1	11.1	29.4	29.5	34.8	36.8	46.7	18.1
Virginia	75.2	78.3	60.3	70.5	82.1	70.7	81.5	84.3	71.6	62.9	84.2	78.5	24.5	27.0	11.1	22.4	40.2	14.7	29.5	32.3	15.1	20.7	48.8	19.6
Washington	83.8	85.0	81.2	56.7	77.3	72.3	87.1	89.3	84.0	53.0	80.5	77.4	22.9	23.3	15.4	11.0	30.2	9.1	27.7	28.5	19.4	11.1	36.8	12.4
West Virginia	66.0	66.0	64.7	70.3	88.8	57.9	75.2	75.1	76.6	74.2	90.3	73.5	12.3	12.2	10.9	17.6	63.3	6.5	14.8	14.7	11.5	19.7	63.9	12.8
Wisconsin	78.6	79.6	61.3	54.1	71.5	66.8	85.1	86.6	68.5	54.6	73.2	77.3	17.7	18.1	8.3	10.0	40.4	5.5	22.4	23.0	10.5	11.4	43.0	10.4
Wyoming	83.0	83.9	81.2	59.3	77.5	68.2	87.9	88.8	86.7	66.3	82.4	77.2	18.8	19.3	9.5	4.8	28.6	6.2	21.9	22.6	18.6	7.8	36.3	8.1

[1] Includes persons of Hispanic origin.
[2] Persons of Hispanic origin may be of any race.

SOURCE: U.S. Department of Commerce, Census Bureau, 1990 Decennial Census, *Minority Economic Profiles*; 2000 Decennial Census, Summary File 3; and unpublished tabulations. (This table was prepared June 2003.)

Table 13. Educational attainment of persons 25 years old and over for the 25 largest states, by sex: 2004

State	Number of persons 25 years old and over (in thousands)						Percent with high school completion or higher						Percent with bachelor's or higher degree					
	Total		Males		Females		Total		Male		Female		Total		Male		Female	
1	2		3		4		5		6		7		8		9		10	
United States[1]....	186,877	(225.3)	89,558	(260.6)	97,319	(264.6)	85.2	(0.09)	84.8	(0.13)	85.4	(0.12)	27.7	(0.11)	29.4	(0.17)	26.1	(0.15)
Alabama	2,891	(58.7)	1,353	(40.3)	1,537	(42.9)	82.4	(0.73)	81.9	(1.09)	82.9	(0.97)	22.3	(0.79)	25.2	(1.22)	19.7	(1.03)
Arizona	3,510	(64.6)	1,702	(45.1)	1,808	(46.3)	84.4	(0.79)	84.0	(1.16)	84.8	(1.09)	28.0	(0.97)	29.3	(1.40)	26.7	(1.34)
California	22,096	(155.6)	10,762	(111.4)	11,334	(114.1)	81.3	(0.36)	81.2	(0.55)	81.3	(0.55)	31.7	(0.43)	34.4	(0.67)	29.1	(0.61)
Colorado	2,856	(58.3)	1,401	(41.0)	1,456	(41.8)	88.3	(0.55)	87.8	(0.79)	88.9	(0.73)	35.5	(0.79)	36.0	(1.16)	35.2	(1.16)
Florida..................	11,489	(114.9)	5,481	(80.4)	6,008	(84.1)	85.9	(0.43)	85.6	(0.61)	86.3	(0.55)	26.0	(0.49)	29.3	(0.79)	23.0	(0.67)
Georgia.................	5,525	(80.7)	2,645	(56.2)	2,880	(58.6)	85.2	(0.67)	84.7	(1.03)	85.6	(0.97)	27.6	(0.85)	26.5	(1.28)	28.7	(1.22)
Illinois..................	8,090	(97.1)	3,895	(68.0)	4,196	(70.5)	86.8	(0.43)	87.0	(0.61)	86.7	(0.61)	27.4	(0.55)	28.6	(0.85)	26.3	(0.79)
Indiana.................	4,010	(69.0)	1,921	(47.9)	2,089	(50.0)	87.2	(0.55)	86.6	(0.85)	87.7	(0.79)	21.1	(0.67)	21.5	(0.97)	20.7	(0.91)
Kentucky	2,754	(57.3)	1,317	(39.7)	1,437	(41.5)	81.8	(0.73)	82.3	(1.03)	81.3	(1.03)	21.0	(0.79)	22.6	(1.16)	19.5	(1.03)
Louisiana	2,758	(57.3)	1,296	(39.4)	1,462	(41.9)	78.7	(0.91)	78.1	(1.28)	79.2	(1.22)	22.4	(0.91)	24.5	(1.34)	20.5	(1.22)
Maryland..............	3,609	(65.5)	1,688	(45.0)	1,922	(48.0)	87.4	(0.61)	85.2	(0.97)	89.3	(0.79)	35.2	(0.91)	37.1	(1.34)	33.4	(1.22)
Massachusetts.......	4,344	(71.7)	2,033	(49.3)	2,311	(52.5)	86.9	(0.55)	88.3	(0.79)	85.7	(0.79)	36.7	(0.79)	39.8	(1.16)	34.0	(1.03)
Michigan	6,444	(87.0)	3,040	(60.2)	3,404	(63.6)	87.9	(0.43)	88.4	(0.67)	87.4	(0.61)	24.4	(0.61)	26.4	(0.91)	22.6	(0.79)
Minnesota.............	3,337	(63.0)	1,665	(44.7)	1,672	(44.7)	92.3	(0.43)	91.4	(0.67)	93.2	(0.61)	32.5	(0.79)	32.4	(1.09)	32.6	(1.09)
Missouri	3,698	(66.3)	1,763	(45.9)	1,935	(48.1)	87.9	(0.61)	87.5	(0.85)	88.3	(0.79)	28.1	(0.79)	31.0	(1.22)	25.5	(1.09)
New Jersey............	5,655	(81.6)	2,687	(56.6)	2,969	(59.5)	87.6	(0.49)	87.8	(0.67)	87.3	(0.67)	34.6	(0.67)	37.9	(0.97)	31.7	(0.91)
New York...............	12,508	(119.6)	5,829	(82.8)	6,679	(88.5)	85.4	(0.36)	85.1	(0.55)	85.7	(0.49)	30.6	(0.49)	31.0	(0.73)	30.2	(0.67)
North Carolina	5,313	(79.2)	2,556	(55.2)	2,757	(57.3)	80.9	(0.67)	79.6	(1.03)	82.2	(0.91)	23.4	(0.73)	24.3	(1.09)	22.6	(1.03)
Ohio	7,362	(92.8)	3,474	(64.3)	3,888	(67.9)	88.1	(0.43)	87.9	(0.61)	88.2	(0.61)	24.6	(0.55)	26.7	(0.85)	22.7	(0.79)
Pennsylvania..........	8,272	(98.2)	3,892	(68.0)	4,380	(72.0)	86.5	(0.43)	86.7	(0.61)	86.4	(0.55)	25.3	(0.55)	27.9	(0.79)	22.9	(0.73)
Tennessee	3,972	(68.6)	1,943	(48.2)	2,029	(49.3)	82.9	(0.73)	81.9	(1.09)	83.9	(1.03)	24.3	(0.85)	25.7	(1.28)	23.0	(1.22)
Texas	13,356	(123.4)	6,479	(87.2)	6,877	(89.8)	78.3	(0.49)	78.3	(0.67)	78.3	(0.67)	24.5	(0.49)	26.3	(0.73)	22.8	(0.67)
Virginia.................	4,865	(75.8)	2,373	(53.2)	2,492	(54.5)	88.4	(0.61)	87.1	(0.91)	89.6	(0.79)	33.1	(0.85)	35.5	(1.28)	30.8	(1.22)
Washington............	4,029	(69.1)	1,980	(48.7)	2,049	(49.5)	89.7	(0.61)	89.3	(0.91)	90.2	(0.85)	29.9	(0.91)	32.3	(1.34)	27.5	(1.34)
Wisconsin	3,540	(64.9)	1,721	(45.4)	1,819	(46.7)	88.8	(0.55)	88.2	(0.79)	89.3	(0.73)	25.6	(0.73)	25.6	(1.03)	25.6	(1.03)

[1]Total includes all 50 states.
NOTE: Standard errors appear in parentheses. Detail may not sum to totals because of rounding.

SOURCE: U.S. Department of Commerce, Census Bureau, Current Population Reports, Educational Attainment in the United States, 2004. Retrieved on March 25, 2005, from http://www.census.gov/population/www/socdemo/education/cps2004.html. (This table was prepared April 2005.)

Table 14. Educational attainment of persons 25 years old and over for the 15 largest metropolitan areas, by sex: 2002

Metropolitan area	Number of persons 25 years old and over (in thousands)						Percent high school completion or higher						Percent completed bachelor's or higher degree					
	Total		Males		Females		Total		Male		Female		Total		Male		Female	
1	2		3		4		5		6		7		8		9		10	
Atlanta, GA, MSA	2,736	(57.1)	1,336	(40.0)	1,400	(41.0)	87.7	(0.91)	87.2	(1.40)	88.2	(1.28)	34.9	(1.34)	37.7	(2.01)	32.2	(1.88)
Boston-Worcester-Lawrence, MA/NH/ME/CT,CMSA	4,049	(69.3)	1,956	(48.4)	2,093	(50.0)	87.7	(0.55)	87.9	(0.79)	87.6	(0.79)	36.0	(0.79)	36.9	(1.16)	35.2	(1.16)
Chicago-Gary-Kenosha, IL/IN/WI, CMSA..................	5,723	(82.1)	2,708	(56.8)	3,016	(59.9)	86.1	(0.55)	85.7	(0.79)	86.6	(0.73)	31.7	(0.73)	31.9	(1.09)	31.5	(1.03)
Cleveland-Akron, OH, CMSA	2,144	(50.6)	995	(34.6)	1,149	(37.1)	90.8	(0.73)	91.8	(0.97)	89.9	(1.03)	26.8	(1.09)	30.5	(1.64)	23.6	(1.40)
Dallas-Fort Worth, TX, CMSA	3,391	(63.5)	1,616	(44.0)	1,775	(46.1)	82.1	(0.91)	82.2	(1.34)	82.1	(1.28)	31.1	(1.09)	34.7	(1.64)	27.8	(1.46)
Detroit-Ann Arbor-Flint, MI, CMSA	3,809	(67.2)	1,779	(46.1)	2,029	(49.3)	86.1	(0.61)	85.7	(0.91)	86.5	(0.85)	25.2	(0.79)	26.3	(1.16)	24.3	(1.09)
Houston-Galveston-Brazoria, TX, CMSA	3,043	(60.2)	1,518	(42.7)	1,525	(42.7)	80.0	(1.09)	78.8	(1.58)	81.3	(1.46)	29.0	(1.22)	30.1	(1.76)	28.0	(1.70)
Los Angeles-Riverside-Orange County, CA,CMSA	10,234	(108.7)	4,930	(76.3)	5,304	(79.1)	77.3	(0.55)	78.3	(0.73)	76.4	(0.73)	26.3	(0.55)	29.0	(0.85)	23.7	(0.73)
Miami-Fort Lauderdale, FL, CMSA.............................	2,642	(56.1)	1,286	(39.3)	1,355	(40.3)	81.4	(0.91)	80.3	(1.28)	82.3	(1.22)	27.1	(1.03)	27.9	(1.46)	26.4	(1.40)
New York-Northern New Jersey-Long Island, NY/NJ/CT/PA, CMSA	14,156	(126.8)	6,723	(88.8)	7,433	(93.2)	83.8	(0.36)	84.5	(0.49)	83.2	(0.49)	32.2	(0.43)	34.2	(0.61)	30.4	(0.61)
Philadelphia-Wilmington-Atlantic City, PA/NJ/DE/MD, CMSA	4,274	(71.2)	2,013	(49.1)	2,261	(52.0)	87.0	(0.55)	87.2	(0.79)	86.9	(0.73)	30.5	(0.73)	32.3	(1.09)	28.9	(0.97)
Pittsburgh, PA, MSA	1,672	(44.7)	794	(30.9)	878	(32.5)	90.4	(0.79)	91.3	(1.09)	89.5	(1.16)	30.6	(1.28)	35.9	(1.88)	25.7	(1.64)
St. Louis, MO/IL, MSA	1,680	(44.9)	790	(30.8)	890	(32.7)	87.7	(0.85)	88.6	(1.22)	86.8	(1.22)	30.5	(1.22)	32.9	(1.82)	28.3	(1.64)
San Francisco-Oakland-San Jose, CA, CMSA..............	4,421	(72.3)	2,227	(51.6)	2,193	(51.2)	88.6	(0.73)	88.5	(0.97)	88.6	(0.97)	39.5	(1.09)	41.1	(1.52)	37.8	(1.52)
Washington-Baltimore, DC/MD/VA/WV, CMSA...............	5,157	(78.0)	2,453	(54.1)	2,703	(56.8)	89.3	(0.36)	88.3	(0.61)	90.3	(0.49)	43.1	(0.61)	44.3	(0.91)	42.0	(0.85)

NOTE: CMSA = Consolidated Metropolitan Statistical Area. MSA = Metropolitan Statistical Area. Detail may not sum to totals because of rounding. Standard errors appear in parentheses.

SOURCE: U.S. Department of Commerce, Census Bureau, Current Population Reports, "Educational Attainment in the United States: March 2002." Retrieved June 1, 2003, from http://www.census.gov/population/www/socdemo/education/ppl-169.html. (This table was prepared June 2005.)

Table 15. Estimates of resident population, by age group: 1970 through 2005

[In thousands]

Year	Total, all ages	Total, 3 to 34 years	3 and 4 years	5 and 6 years	7 to 13 years	14 to 17 years	18 and 19 years	20 and 21 years	22 to 24 years	25 to 29 years	30 to 34 years
1	2	3	4	5	6	7	8	9	10	11	12
1970	203,984	108,653	6,962	7,703	28,969	15,921	7,410	6,850	9,728	13,604	11,505
1971	206,827	110,482	6,805	7,344	28,892	16,326	7,644	7,106	10,596	13,927	11,842
1972	209,284	112,287	6,789	7,051	28,628	16,637	7,854	7,447	10,418	15,142	12,321
1973	211,357	113,954	6,938	6,888	28,159	16,864	8,044	7,658	10,615	15,694	13,094
1974	213,342	115,641	7,117	6,864	27,599	17,033	8,196	7,893	10,864	16,428	13,644
1975	215,465	117,006	6,912	7,014	26,904	17,125	8,418	8,089	11,228	17,183	14,131
1976	217,563	118,073	6,437	7,194	26,321	17,117	8,604	8,240	11,554	18,177	14,428
1977	219,760	118,853	6,190	6,978	25,878	17,042	8,613	8,456	11,856	18,180	15,661
1978	222,095	119,414	6,208	6,499	25,593	16,944	8,617	8,628	12,120	18,585	16,218
1979	224,567	120,126	6,252	6,256	25,174	16,610	8,698	8,653	12,443	19,077	16,961
1980	227,225	121,132	6,366	6,291	24,800	16,143	8,718	8,669	12,716	19,686	17,743
1981	229,466	121,999	6,535	6,315	24,396	15,609	8,582	8,759	12,903	20,169	18,731
1982	231,664	121,823	6,658	6,407	24,121	15,057	8,480	8,768	12,914	20,704	18,714
1983	233,792	122,302	6,877	6,572	23,709	14,740	8,290	8,652	12,981	21,414	19,067
1984	235,825	122,254	7,045	6,694	23,367	14,725	7,932	8,567	12,962	21,459	19,503
1985	237,924	122,512	7,134	6,916	22,976	14,888	7,637	8,370	12,895	21,671	20,025
1986	240,133	122,688	7,187	7,086	22,992	14,824	7,483	8,024	12,720	21,893	20,479
1987	242,289	122,672	7,132	7,178	23,325	14,502	7,502	7,742	12,450	21,857	20,984
1988	244,499	122,713	7,176	7,238	23,791	14,023	7,701	7,606	12,048	21,739	21,391
1989	246,819	122,655	7,315	7,184	24,228	13,536	7,898	7,651	11,607	21,560	21,676
1990	249,623	122,787	7,359	7,244	24,785	13,329	7,702	7,886	11,264	21,277	21,939
1991	252,981	123,210	7,444	7,393	25,216	13,491	7,208	8,029	11,205	20,923	22,301
1992	256,514	123,722	7,614	7,447	25,752	13,775	6,949	7,797	11,391	20,503	22,494
1993	259,919	124,371	7,887	7,549	26,212	14,096	6,985	7,333	11,657	20,069	22,584
1994	263,126	124,976	8,089	7,725	26,492	14,637	7,047	7,071	11,585	19,740	22,590
1995	266,278	125,478	8,107	8,000	26,825	15,013	7,182	7,103	11,197	19,680	22,372
1996	269,394	125,924	8,022	8,206	27,168	15,443	7,399	7,161	10,715	19,864	21,945
1997	272,647	126,422	7,915	8,232	27,683	15,769	7,569	7,309	10,601	19,899	21,446
1998	275,854	126,939	7,841	8,152	28,302	15,829	7,892	7,520	10,647	19,804	20,953
1999	279,040	127,446	7,772	8,041	28,763	16,007	8,094	7,683	10,908	19,575	20,603
2000[1]	282,193	128,060	7,729	7,979	29,073	16,122	8,185	7,996	11,131	19,306	20,540
2001[1]	285,108	128,552	7,653	7,912	29,165	16,183	8,170	8,284	11,517	18,937	20,730
2002[1]	287,985	129,168	7,651	7,797	29,174	16,354	8,125	8,326	12,012	18,914	20,815
2003[1]	290,850	129,792	7,717	7,720	29,045	16,504	8,179	8,310	12,458	19,133	20,726
2004[1]	293,657	130,410	7,944	7,713	28,658	16,826	8,272	8,249	12,724	19,555	20,467
2005	296,410	130,685	8,069	7,773	28,314	17,079	8,269	8,298	12,740	20,066	20,077

[1]Revised from previously published figures.
NOTE: Detail may not sum to totals because of rounding. Estimates as of July 1.
SOURCE: U.S. Department of Commerce, Census Bureau, Current Population Reports, Series P-25, Nos. 1000, 1022, 1045, 1057, 1059, 1092, and 1095; and 2000 through 2005 Census Bureau, Population Estimates, retrieved September 14, 2006, from http://www.census.gov/popest/national/asrh/2005_nat_res.html. (This table was prepared September 2006.)

Table 16. Estimates of resident population, by race/ethnicity and age group: Selected years, 1980 through 2005

	Number (in thousands)								Percentage distribution							
Year and age group	Total	White	Black	His-panic	Asian	Pacific Islander	American Indian/ Alaska Native	More than one race	Total	White	Black	His-panic	Asian	Pacific Islander	American Indian/ Alaska Native	More than one race
1	2	3	4	5	6	7	8	9	10	11	12	13	14	15	16	17
Total																
1980	227,225	181,140	26,215	14,869	3,665	(1)	1,336	—	100.0	79.7	11.5	6.5	1.6	(1)	0.6	—
1985	237,924	184,945	27,738	18,368	5,315	(1)	1,558	—	100.0	77.7	11.7	7.7	2.2	(1)	0.7	—
1990	249,623	188,725	29,439	22,573	7,092	(1)	1,793	—	100.0	75.6	11.8	9.0	2.8	(1)	0.7	—
1995	266,278	194,389	32,500	28,158	9,188	(1)	2,044	—	100.0	73.0	12.2	10.6	3.5	(1)	0.8	—
2000[2]	282,193	195,769	34,413	35,648	10,458	369	2,104	3,432	100.0	69.4	12.2	12.6	3.7	0.1	0.7	1.2
2001[2]	285,108	196,319	34,814	37,064	10,868	376	2,130	3,536	100.0	68.9	12.2	13.0	3.8	0.1	0.7	1.2
2002[2]	287,985	196,827	35,201	38,500	11,277	384	2,155	3,642	100.0	68.3	12.2	13.4	3.9	0.1	0.7	1.3
2003[2]	290,850	197,340	35,574	39,935	11,680	391	2,181	3,750	100.0	67.8	12.2	13.7	4.0	0.1	0.7	1.3
2004[2]	293,657	197,843	35,950	41,338	12,061	398	2,207	3,861	100.0	67.4	12.2	14.1	4.1	0.1	0.8	1.3
2005[2]	296,410	198,366	36,325	42,687	12,421	405	2,233	3,974	100.0	66.9	12.3	14.4	4.2	0.1	0.8	1.3
Under 5																
1980	16,451	11,904	2,413	1,677	319	(1)	137	—	100.0	72.4	14.7	10.2	1.9	(1)	0.8	—
1985	17,842	12,683	2,572	1,938	478	(1)	171	—	100.0	71.1	14.4	10.9	2.7	(1)	1.0	—
1990	18,856	12,757	2,825	2,497	593	(1)	184	—	100.0	67.7	15.0	13.2	3.1	(1)	1.0	—
1995	19,627	12,415	3,050	3,245	734	(1)	182	—	100.0	63.3	15.5	16.5	3.7	(1)	0.9	—
2000[2]	19,187	11,268	2,763	3,741	684	29	172	531	100.0	58.7	14.4	19.5	3.6	0.2	0.9	2.8
2001[2]	19,349	11,234	2,796	3,875	709	28	171	536	100.0	58.1	14.4	20.0	3.7	0.1	0.9	2.8
2002[2]	19,537	11,208	2,826	4,029	734	28	171	541	100.0	57.4	14.5	20.6	3.8	0.1	0.9	2.8
2003[2]	19,778	11,212	2,851	4,204	769	28	171	545	100.0	56.7	14.4	21.3	3.9	0.1	0.9	2.8
2004[2]	20,061	11,225	2,892	4,392	805	27	172	547	100.0	56.0	14.4	21.9	4.0	0.1	0.9	2.7
2005[2]	20,304	11,258	2,922	4,532	838	27	173	553	100.0	55.4	14.4	22.3	4.1	0.1	0.9	2.7
5 to 17																
1980	47,232	35,220	6,840	4,005	790	(1)	377	—	100.0	74.6	14.5	8.5	1.7	(1)	0.8	—
1985	44,782	32,099	6,569	4,609	1,111	(1)	393	—	100.0	71.7	14.7	10.3	2.5	(1)	0.9	—
1990	45,359	—	—	—	—	—	—	—	—	—	—	—	—	—	—	—
1995	49,838	—	—	—	—	—	—	—	—	—	—	—	—	—	—	—
2000[2]	53,173	33,016	7,989	8,682	1,825	85	522	1,054	100.0	62.1	15.0	16.3	3.4	0.2	1.0	2.0
2001[2]	53,260	32,801	7,989	8,919	1,860	85	517	1,089	100.0	61.6	15.0	16.7	3.5	0.2	1.0	2.0
2002[2]	53,325	32,552	7,981	9,175	1,895	85	511	1,125	100.0	61.0	15.0	17.2	3.6	0.2	1.0	2.1
2003[2]	53,269	32,210	7,954	9,425	1,928	85	505	1,162	100.0	60.5	14.9	17.7	3.6	0.2	0.9	2.2
2004[2]	53,198	31,877	7,913	9,668	1,954	85	499	1,202	100.0	59.9	14.9	18.2	3.7	0.2	0.9	2.3
2005[2]	53,166	31,561	7,877	9,928	1,983	84	492	1,240	100.0	59.4	14.8	18.7	3.7	0.2	0.9	2.3
18 to 24																
1980	30,103	23,278	3,872	2,284	468	(1)	201	—	100.0	77.3	12.9	7.6	1.6	(1)	0.7	—
1985	28,902	21,375	3,853	2,805	645	(1)	224	—	100.0	74.0	13.3	9.7	2.2	(1)	0.8	—
1990	26,853	—	—	—	—	—	—	—	—	—	—	—	—	—	—	—
1995	25,482	—	—	—	—	—	—	—	—	—	—	—	—	—	—	—
2000[2]	27,311	16,924	3,781	4,780	1,149	50	239	387	100.0	62.0	13.8	17.5	4.2	0.2	0.9	1.4
2001[2]	27,971	17,303	3,889	4,903	1,167	50	249	410	100.0	61.9	13.9	17.5	4.2	0.2	0.9	1.5
2002[2]	28,463	17,581	3,973	4,985	1,184	51	256	432	100.0	61.8	14.0	17.5	4.2	0.2	0.9	1.5
2003[2]	28,947	17,874	4,059	5,047	1,199	51	265	453	100.0	61.7	14.0	17.4	4.1	0.2	0.9	1.6
2004[2]	29,246	18,055	4,113	5,083	1,201	51	271	472	100.0	61.7	14.1	17.4	4.1	0.2	0.9	1.6
2005[2]	29,307	18,089	4,137	5,076	1,192	50	276	487	100.0	61.7	14.1	17.3	4.1	0.2	0.9	1.7
25 and over																
1980	133,438	110,737	13,091	6,903	2,088	(1)	620	—	100.0	83.0	9.8	5.2	1.6	(1)	0.5	—
1985	146,398	118,787	14,744	9,016	3,081	(1)	771	—	100.0	81.1	10.1	6.2	2.1	(1)	0.5	—
1990	158,555	125,653	16,322	11,447	4,190	(1)	944	—	100.0	79.2	10.3	7.2	2.6	(1)	0.6	—
1995	171,332	131,839	18,250	14,519	5,628	(1)	1,096	—	100.0	76.9	10.7	8.5	3.3	(1)	0.6	—
2000[2]	182,522	134,561	19,879	18,445	6,799	205	1,171	1,460	100.0	73.7	10.9	10.1	3.7	0.1	0.6	0.8
2001[2]	184,527	134,981	20,140	19,368	7,133	212	1,193	1,501	100.0	73.1	10.9	10.5	3.9	0.1	0.6	0.8
2002[2]	186,660	135,486	20,420	20,310	7,463	220	1,217	1,544	100.0	72.6	10.9	10.9	4.0	0.1	0.7	0.8
2003[2]	188,856	136,044	20,710	21,258	7,785	228	1,240	1,590	100.0	72.0	11.0	11.3	4.1	0.1	0.7	0.8
2004[2]	191,153	136,687	21,031	22,195	8,100	236	1,265	1,639	100.0	71.5	11.0	11.6	4.2	0.1	0.7	0.9
2005[2]	193,633	137,458	21,389	23,151	8,407	244	1,292	1,693	100.0	71.0	11.0	12.0	4.3	0.1	0.7	0.9

—Not available.
[1]Included under Asian.
[2]Data on persons of more than one race group were collected beginning in 2000. Direct comparability of the data (other than Hispanic) prior to 2000 with the data for 2000 and later years is limited by the extent to which people reporting more than one race in later years had been reported in specific race groups in earlier years.

NOTE: Resident population includes civilian population and armed forces personnel residing within the United States; it excludes armed forces personnel residing overseas. Race categories exclude persons of Hispanic origin. Detail may not sum to totals because of rounding. Some data have been revised from previously published figures. Estimates as of July 1.
SOURCE: U.S. Department of Commerce, Census Bureau, Population Estimates, retrieved September 14, 2006, from http://www.census.gov/popest/national/asrh/2005_nat_res.html. (This table was prepared September 2006.)

Table 17. Estimated total and school-age resident populations, by state: Selected years, 1970 through 2005

[In thousands]

State	Total, all ages								5- to 17-year-olds							
	1970[1]	1980[1]	1990[1]	2000[2]	2002[2]	2003[2]	2004[2]	2005[2]	1970[1]	1980[1]	1990[1]	2000[2]	2002[2]	2003[2]	2004[2]	2005[2]
1	2	3	4	5	6	7	8	9	10	11	12	13	14	15	16	17
United States	203,302	226,546	248,765	282,193	287,985	290,850	293,657	296,410	52,540	47,407	45,178	53,173	53,325	53,269	53,198	53,166
Alabama	3,444	3,894	4,040	4,452	4,480	4,502	4,525	4,558	934	866	774	826	815	807	799	793
Alaska...........................	303	402	550	628	641	649	658	664	88	92	117	143	142	140	139	138
Arizona	1,775	2,718	3,665	5,166	5,438	5,578	5,740	5,939	486	578	686	993	1,058	1,077	1,098	1,121
Arkansas........................	1,923	2,286	2,351	2,679	2,707	2,726	2,750	2,779	498	496	455	499	498	495	491	488
California	19,971	23,668	29,786	34,003	34,988	35,457	35,842	36,132	4,999	4,681	5,344	6,787	6,865	6,908	6,950	7,016
Colorado	2,210	2,890	3,294	4,327	4,498	4,548	4,602	4,665	589	592	607	807	826	833	837	840
Connecticut....................	3,032	3,108	3,287	3,412	3,458	3,486	3,499	3,510	768	638	520	620	625	625	625	624
Delaware........................	548	594	666	786	806	818	830	844	148	125	114	143	143	141	141	141
District of Columbia	757	638	607	571	565	558	554	551	164	109	80	82	77	75	74	75
Florida...........................	6,791	9,746	12,938	16,049	16,678	16,993	17,385	17,790	1,609	1,789	2,011	2,715	2,832	2,872	2,910	2,949
Georgia..........................	4,588	5,463	6,478	8,230	8,582	8,747	8,918	9,073	1,223	1,231	1,230	1,581	1,625	1,640	1,655	1,670
Hawaii...........................	770	965	1,108	1,212	1,234	1,248	1,262	1,275	204	198	196	217	213	211	210	209
Idaho.............................	713	944	1,007	1,300	1,344	1,368	1,395	1,429	200	213	228	271	272	270	269	268
Illinois...........................	11,110	11,427	11,431	12,440	12,587	12,650	12,712	12,763	2,859	2,401	2,095	2,371	2,356	2,352	2,345	2,343
Indiana..........................	5,195	5,490	5,544	6,092	6,155	6,196	6,227	6,272	1,386	1,200	1,056	1,153	1,169	1,170	1,171	1,172
Iowa	2,825	2,914	2,777	2,928	2,934	2,941	2,953	2,966	743	604	525	542	521	510	500	490
Kansas...........................	2,249	2,364	2,478	2,693	2,712	2,724	2,734	2,745	573	468	472	523	511	503	496	486
Kentucky........................	3,221	3,661	3,687	4,049	4,089	4,117	4,142	4,173	844	800	703	728	723	719	715	710
Louisiana........................	3,645	4,206	4,222	4,469	4,475	4,490	4,507	4,524	1,041	969	891	899	867	855	839	825
Maine............................	994	1,125	1,228	1,277	1,297	1,308	1,315	1,322	260	243	223	229	223	219	215	210
Maryland........................	3,924	4,217	4,781	5,312	5,442	5,512	5,561	5,600	1,038	895	803	1,005	1,013	1,016	1,019	1,021
Massachusetts.................	5,689	5,737	6,016	6,362	6,412	6,418	6,407	6,399	1,407	1,153	940	1,101	1,090	1,080	1,071	1,061
Michigan	8,882	9,262	9,295	9,956	10,039	10,078	10,104	10,121	2,450	2,067	1,754	1,923	1,905	1,893	1,883	1,874
Minnesota......................	3,806	4,076	4,376	4,934	5,024	5,062	5,097	5,133	1,051	865	829	955	935	922	908	894
Mississippi......................	2,217	2,521	2,575	2,849	2,866	2,881	2,901	2,921	635	599	550	569	554	548	542	537
Missouri.........................	4,678	4,917	5,117	5,606	5,681	5,719	5,760	5,800	1,183	1,008	944	1,055	1,040	1,028	1,015	1,002
Montana.........................	694	787	799	904	910	918	927	936	197	167	163	174	166	160	156	151
Nebraska........................	1,485	1,570	1,578	1,713	1,727	1,738	1,748	1,759	389	324	309	332	324	318	313	308
Nevada..........................	489	800	1,202	2,018	2,168	2,242	2,333	2,415	127	160	204	371	407	420	433	447
New Hampshire	738	921	1,109	1,241	1,275	1,288	1,299	1,310	189	196	194	234	234	234	232	230
New Jersey.....................	7,171	7,365	7,748	8,434	8,576	8,640	8,685	8,718	1,797	1,528	1,269	1,529	1,555	1,566	1,574	1,580
New Mexico	1,017	1,303	1,515	1,822	1,855	1,879	1,903	1,928	311	303	320	377	370	365	360	355
New York........................	18,241	17,558	17,991	18,999	19,165	19,228	19,281	19,255	4,358	3,552	3,000	3,448	3,365	3,345	3,319	3,297
North Carolina	5,084	5,882	6,632	8,078	8,313	8,422	8,540	8,683	1,323	1,254	1,147	1,432	1,480	1,500	1,517	1,535
North Dakota	618	653	639	641	634	633	636	637	175	136	127	120	112	108	104	100
Ohio..............................	10,657	10,798	10,847	11,364	11,405	11,432	11,450	11,464	2,820	2,307	2,012	2,130	2,093	2,073	2,049	2,027
Oklahoma.......................	2,559	3,025	3,146	3,454	3,487	3,505	3,524	3,548	640	622	609	653	639	629	619	609
Oregon...........................	2,092	2,633	2,842	3,431	3,522	3,563	3,591	3,641	534	525	521	624	628	627	626	624
Pennsylvania...................	11,801	11,864	11,883	12,286	12,324	12,365	12,394	12,430	2,925	2,376	1,996	2,191	2,148	2,135	2,114	2,092
Rhode Island	950	947	1,003	1,051	1,069	1,076	1,080	1,076	225	186	159	184	183	182	182	181
South Carolina.................	2,591	3,122	3,486	4,024	4,103	4,147	4,198	4,255	720	703	662	745	745	745	745	746
South Dakota..................	666	691	696	756	760	765	771	776	187	147	144	151	146	143	140	136
Tennessee	3,926	4,591	4,877	5,703	5,790	5,842	5,893	5,963	1,002	972	882	1,023	1,016	1,012	1,007	1,003
Texas	11,199	14,229	16,986	20,949	21,722	22,099	22,472	22,860	3,002	3,137	3,437	4,277	4,394	4,411	4,429	4,455
Utah	1,059	1,461	1,723	2,243	2,337	2,379	2,421	2,470	312	350	457	509	512	510	509	507
Vermont	445	511	563	610	616	619	621	623	118	109	102	113	108	106	104	101
Virginia..........................	4,651	5,347	6,189	7,104	7,286	7,383	7,481	7,567	1,197	1,114	1,060	1,279	1,300	1,304	1,308	1,312
Washington.....................	3,413	4,132	4,867	5,911	6,066	6,131	6,207	6,288	881	826	893	1,119	1,113	1,107	1,099	1,090
West Virginia...................	1,744	1,950	1,793	1,807	1,805	1,810	1,813	1,817	442	414	337	299	293	288	284	281
Wisconsin	4,418	4,706	4,892	5,374	5,439	5,472	5,504	5,536	1,203	1,011	927	1,023	1,003	986	971	956
Wyoming.........................	332	470	454	494	499	502	506	509	92	101	101	97	92	89	86	83

[1]As of April 1.
[2]Estimates as of July 1.
NOTE: Resident population includes civilian population and armed forces personnel residing within the United States and within each state; it excludes armed forces personnel residing overseas. Some data have been revised from previously published figures. Detail may not sum to totals because of rounding.

SOURCE: U.S. Department of Commerce, Census Bureau, *Current Population Reports*, Series P-25, No. 1095; CPH-L-74 (1990 data); and 2000 through 2005 Census Bureau, Population Estimates, retrieved September 21, 2006, from http://www.census.gov/popest/datasets.html. (This table was prepared September 2006.)

Table 18. Number and percentage of families, by family status and presence of own children under 18: Selected years, 1970 through 2005

Family status	1970		1980		1990		2000		2003		2004		2005		Change, 1970 to 1990	Change, 1990 to 2005
1	2		3		4		5		6		7		8		9	10
	In thousands														Percent change	
All families	**51,456**	**(257.3)**	**59,550**	**(271.4)**	**66,090**	**(307.8)**	**72,025**	**(311.6)**	**75,596**	**(238.1)**	**76,217**	**(238.6)**	**77,010**	**(226.6)**	**28.4**	**16.5**
Married-couple family	44,728	(243.6)	49,112	(252.7)	52,317	(283.3)	55,311	(289.5)	57,320	(217.2)	57,719	(217.7)	58,109	(210.4)	17.0	11.1
Without own children under 18	19,196	(168.7)	24,151	(187.3)	27,780	(218.1)	30,062	(230.5)	31,406	(170.6)	31,926	(171.8)	31,929	(168.8)	44.7	14.9
With own children under 18	25,532	(192.0)	24,961	(190.1)	24,537	(206.4)	25,248	(214.1)	25,914	(156.8)	25,793	(156.4)	26,180	(155.3)	-3.9	6.7
One own child under 18	8,163	(112.5)	9,671	(122.0)	9,583	(133.0)	9,402	(136.2)	9,875	(100.0)	9,763	(99.4)	9,885	(99.6)	17.4	3.2
Two own children under 18	8,045	(111.7)	9,488	(120.9)	9,784	(134.3)	10,274	(142.1)	10,520	(103.1)	10,481	(102.9)	10,676	(103.3)	21.6	9.1
Three or more own children under 18	9,325	(119.9)	5,802	(95.3)	5,170	(98.5)	5,572	(105.9)	5,519	(75.4)	5,548	(75.6)	5,619	(75.9)	-44.6	8.7
Other family, male householder, no spouse present	1,228	(44.2)	1,733	(52.5)	2,884	(73.9)	4,028	(90.4)	4,656	(69.4)	4,716	(69.8)	4,893	(70.9)	134.9	69.7
Without own children under 18	887	(37.6)	1,117	(42.2)	1,731	(57.4)	2,242	(67.7)	2,741	(53.4)	2,786	(53.9)	2,859	(54.5)	95.2	65.2
With own children under 18	341	(23.3)	616	(31.3)	1,153	(46.9)	1,786	(60.5)	1,915	(44.7)	1,931	(44.9)	2,034	(46.0)	238.1	76.4
One own child under 18	179	(16.9)	374	(24.4)	723	(37.2)	1,131	(48.2)	1,174	(35.1)	1,146	(34.6)	1,227	(35.8)	303.9	69.7
Two own children under 18	87	(11.8)	165	(16.2)	307	(24.2)	483	(31.6)	534	(23.7)	550	(24.0)	563	(24.3)	252.9	83.4
Three or more own children under 18	75	(10.9)	77	(11.1)	123	(15.3)	171	(18.8)	208	(14.8)	235	(15.7)	244	(16.0)	64.0	98.4
Other family, female householder, no spouse present	5,500	(92.8)	8,705	(116.0)	10,890	(141.4)	12,687	(156.9)	13,620	(116.6)	13,781	(117.2)	14,009	(117.3)	98.0	28.6
Without own children under 18	2,642	(64.7)	3,261	(71.8)	4,290	(89.9)	5,116	(101.6)	5,481	(75.1)	5,560	(75.7)	5,703	(76.4)	62.4	32.9
With own children under 18	2,858	(67.2)	5,445	(92.3)	6,599	(111.0)	7,571	(122.8)	8,139	(91.1)	8,221	(91.5)	8,305	(91.6)	130.9	25.9
One own child under 18	1,008	(40.1)	2,398	(61.6)	3,225	(78.1)	3,777	(87.6)	4,134	(65.4)	4,055	(64.8)	4,081	(64.9)	219.9	26.5
Two own children under 18	810	(35.9)	1,817	(53.7)	2,173	(64.2)	2,458	(70.9)	2,486	(50.9)	2,665	(52.7)	2,626	(52.2)	168.3	20.8
Three or more own children under 18	1,040	(40.7)	1,230	(44.2)	1,202	(47.9)	1,336	(52.4)	1,519	(39.9)	1,501	(39.6)	1,597	(40.8)	15.6	32.9
	Percentage of all families														Change in percentage points	
All families	**100.0**	**(†)**	**100.0**	**(†)**	**100.0**	**(†)**	**100.0**	**(†)**	**100.0**	**(†)**	**100.0**	**(†)**	**100.0**	**(†)**	**†**	**†**
Married-couple family	86.9	(0.19)	82.5	(0.20)	79.2	(0.22)	76.8	(0.23)	75.8	(0.16)	75.7	(0.16)	75.5	(0.16)	-7.8	-3.7
Without own children under 18	37.3	(0.27)	40.6	(0.25)	42.0	(0.27)	41.7	(0.26)	41.5	(0.18)	41.9	(0.18)	41.5	(0.18)	4.7	-0.6
With own children under 18	49.6	(0.28)	41.9	(0.26)	37.1	(0.26)	35.1	(0.26)	34.3	(0.18)	33.8	(0.18)	34.0	(0.18)	-12.5	-3.1
One own child under 18	15.9	(0.20)	16.2	(0.19)	14.5	(0.19)	13.1	(0.18)	13.1	(0.13)	12.8	(0.12)	12.8	(0.12)	-1.4	-1.7
Two own children under 18	15.6	(0.20)	15.9	(0.19)	14.8	(0.19)	14.3	(0.19)	13.9	(0.13)	13.8	(0.13)	13.9	(0.13)	-0.8	-0.9
Three or more own children under 18	18.1	(0.21)	9.7	(0.15)	7.8	(0.14)	7.7	(0.14)	7.3	(0.10)	7.3	(0.10)	7.3	(0.10)	-10.3	-0.5
Other family, male householder, no spouse present	2.4	(0.09)	2.9	(0.09)	4.4	(0.11)	5.6	(0.12)	6.2	(0.09)	6.2	(0.09)	6.4	(0.09)	2.0	2.0
Without own children under 18	1.7	(0.07)	1.9	(0.07)	2.6	(0.09)	3.1	(0.09)	3.6	(0.07)	3.7	(0.07)	3.7	(0.07)	0.9	1.1
With own children under 18	0.7	(0.05)	1.0	(0.05)	1.7	(0.07)	2.5	(0.08)	2.5	(0.06)	2.5	(0.06)	2.6	(0.06)	1.1	0.9
One own child under 18	0.3	(0.03)	0.6	(0.04)	1.1	(0.06)	1.6	(0.07)	1.6	(0.05)	1.5	(0.05)	1.6	(0.05)	0.7	0.5
Two own children under 18	0.2	(0.02)	0.3	(0.03)	0.5	(0.04)	0.7	(0.04)	0.7	(0.03)	0.7	(0.03)	0.7	(0.03)	0.3	0.3
Three or more own children under 18	0.1	(0.02)	0.1	(0.02)	0.2	(0.02)	0.2	(0.03)	0.3	(0.02)	0.3	(0.02)	0.3	(0.02)	#	0.1
Other family, female householder, no spouse present	10.7	(0.17)	14.6	(0.18)	16.5	(0.20)	17.6	(0.20)	18.0	(0.14)	18.1	(0.14)	18.2	(0.14)	5.8	1.7
Without own children under 18	5.1	(0.12)	5.5	(0.12)	6.5	(0.13)	7.1	(0.14)	7.3	(0.10)	7.3	(0.10)	7.4	(0.10)	1.4	0.9
With own children under 18	5.6	(0.13)	9.1	(0.15)	10.0	(0.16)	10.5	(0.16)	10.8	(0.12)	10.8	(0.12)	10.8	(0.11)	4.4	0.8
One own child under 18	2.0	(0.08)	4.0	(0.10)	4.9	(0.12)	5.2	(0.12)	5.5	(0.08)	5.3	(0.08)	5.3	(0.08)	2.9	0.4
Two own children under 18	1.6	(0.07)	3.1	(0.09)	3.3	(0.10)	3.4	(0.10)	3.3	(0.07)	3.5	(0.07)	3.4	(0.07)	1.7	0.1
Three or more own children under 18	2.0	(0.08)	2.1	(0.07)	1.8	(0.07)	1.9	(0.07)	2.0	(0.05)	2.0	(0.05)	2.1	(0.05)	-0.2	0.3

†Not applicable.
#Rounds to zero.
NOTE: Own children are never-married sons and daughters, including stepchildren and adopted children, of the householder or married couple. Detail may not sum to totals because of rounding. Standard errors appear in parentheses.

SOURCE: U.S. Department of Commerce, Census Bureau, *Current Population Reports*, Series P20, *Household and Family Characteristics: 1995, Children's Living Arrangements and Characteristics: 2002,* and *America's Families and Living Arrangements: 2000, 2003, 2004, and 2005;* Current Population Survey (CPS), Annual Social and Economic Supplement, retrieved July 25, 2006, from http://www.census.gov/population/www/socdemo/hh-fam/cps2005.html. (This table was prepared July 2006.)

Table 19. Characteristics of families with own children under 18, by race/ethnicity and family structure: 2005

[In thousands]

Race/ethnicity and family characteristic	Total families	Families with own children under 18							Families with own children under 6		Families with own children under 3	
		Total	Percent of all families	Percentage distribution	Families with				Total	Percent of all families	Total	Percent of all families
					1 child under 18	2 children under 18	3 children under 18	4 or more under 18				
1	2	3	4	5	6	7	8	9	10	11	12	13
All races[1]	77,010 (226.6)	36,520 (178.2)	47.4 (0.18)	100.0 (†)	15,194 (121.8)	13,865 (116.7)	5,451 (74.7)	2,010 (45.8)	15,971 (124.6)	20.7 (0.15)	9,366 (97.0)	12.2 (0.12)
Married-couple families	58,109 (210.4)	26,180 (155.3)	45.1 (0.21)	71.7 (0.24)	9,885 (99.6)	10,676 (103.3)	4,128 (65.2)	1,491 (39.5)	11,905 (108.7)	20.5 (0.17)	7,166 (85.3)	12.3 (0.14)
Families with male householder, no spouse present	4,893 (70.9)	2,034 (46.0)	41.6 (0.72)	5.6 (0.12)	1,227 (35.8)	563 (24.3)	190 (14.1)	54 (7.5)	835 (29.6)	17.1 (0.55)	504 (23.0)	10.3 (0.45)
Families with female householder, no spouse present	14,009 (117.3)	8,305 (91.6)	59.3 (0.43)	22.7 (0.22)	4,081 (64.9)	2,626 (52.2)	1,132 (34.4)	465 (22.1)	3,232 (57.9)	23.1 (0.37)	1,695 (42.1)	12.1 (0.28)
White	54,383 (206.0)	23,576 (148.4)	43.4 (0.22)	100.0 (†)	10,040 (100.3)	9,267 (96.5)	3,220 (57.8)	1,049 (33.1)	9,823 (99.3)	18.1 (0.17)	5,875 (77.5)	10.8 (0.14)
Married-couple families	44,296 (191.8)	18,235 (132.4)	41.2 (0.24)	77.3 (0.28)	7,015 (84.5)	7,602 (87.8)	2,711 (53.1)	907 (30.8)	7,957 (89.7)	18.0 (0.19)	4,868 (70.7)	11.0 (0.15)
Families with male householder, no spouse present	2,888 (54.7)	1,310 (37.0)	45.4 (0.95)	5.6 (0.15)	819 (29.3)	354 (19.3)	107 (10.6)	30 (5.6)	475 (22.3)	16.4 (0.71)	277 (17.1)	9.6 (0.56)
Families with female householder, no spouse present	7,200 (85.5)	4,030 (64.5)	56.0 (0.60)	17.1 (0.25)	2,205 (47.9)	1,311 (37.0)	402 (20.5)	112 (10.9)	1,392 (38.1)	19.3 (0.48)	730 (27.7)	10.1 (0.36)
Black	8,904 (82.5)	4,833 (64.1)	54.3 (0.52)	100.0 (†)	2,061 (43.3)	1,647 (38.9)	729 (26.1)	397 (19.4)	2,088 (43.5)	23.5 (0.44)	1,112 (32.1)	12.5 (0.34)
Married-couple families	4,180 (60.1)	2,035 (43.0)	48.7 (0.75)	42.1 (0.69)	803 (27.4)	784 (27.1)	291 (16.6)	157 (12.2)	881 (28.7)	21.1 (0.62)	482 (21.3)	11.5 (0.48)
Families with male householder, no spouse present	734 (26.2)	289 (16.5)	39.4 (1.76)	6.0 (0.33)	169 (12.7)	79 (8.7)	27 (5.1)	14 (3.7)	130 (11.1)	17.7 (1.37)	80 (8.7)	10.9 (1.12)
Families with female householder, no spouse present	3,991 (58.9)	2,509 (47.5)	62.9 (0.75)	51.9 (0.70)	1,089 (31.8)	784 (27.1)	411 (19.7)	225 (14.6)	1,076 (31.6)	27.0 (0.69)	550 (22.7)	13.8 (0.53)
Hispanic	9,537 (80.3)	6,001 (68.3)	62.9 (0.48)	100.0 (†)	2,135 (43.6)	2,163 (43.9)	1,229 (33.6)	473 (21.1)	3,090 (51.6)	32.4 (0.47)	1,791 (40.1)	18.8 (0.39)
Married-couple families	6,367 (69.9)	4,172 (58.9)	65.5 (0.58)	69.5 (0.58)	1,327 (34.8)	1,604 (38.1)	891 (28.7)	349 (18.1)	2,244 (44.6)	35.2 (0.58)	1,306 (34.6)	20.5 (0.49)
Families with male householder, no spouse present	930 (29.3)	326 (17.5)	35.1 (1.53)	5.4 (0.29)	175 (12.9)	104 (9.9)	41 (6.2)	6 (2.4)	187 (13.3)	20.1 (1.28)	129 (11.1)	13.9 (1.11)
Families with female householder, no spouse present	2,240 (44.6)	1,503 (37.0)	67.1 (0.97)	25.0 (0.55)	633 (24.3)	455 (20.7)	297 (16.7)	117 (10.5)	659 (24.8)	29.4 (0.94)	356 (18.3)	15.9 (0.75)

†Not applicable.

[1]Race of family is defined as race of head of household. "All races" includes other race/ethnicity groups not separately shown.

NOTE: Own children are never-married sons and daughters, including stepchildren and adopted children, of the householder or married couple. Race categories exclude persons of Hispanic origin. Detail may not sum to totals because of rounding. Standard errors appear in parentheses.

SOURCE: U.S. Department of Commerce, Census Bureau, *American Families and Living Arrangements: 2005*, Current Population Survey (CPS), Annual Social and Economic Supplement, retrieved July 26, 2006, from http://www.census.gov/population/www/socdemo/hh-fam/cps2005.html. (This table was prepared July 2006.)

Table 20. Household income and poverty rates, by state: 1990, 2000, and 2003–2005

State	Median household income, in constant 2005 dollars[1]			Percent of persons below the poverty level			Poverty status of related children 5 through 17 years old[2]					
							1990[3]		2000[4]		2005	
							Number in poverty (in thousands)	Percent in poverty	Number in poverty (in thousands)	Percent in poverty	Number in poverty (in thousands)	Percent in poverty
	1990[3]	2000[4]	2003–2005 (3-year average)	1990[3]	2000[4]	2003–2005 (3-year average)						
1	2	3	4	5	6	7	8	9	10	11	12	13
United States	$45,695	$49,192	$46,037 (131)	13.1	12.4	12.6 (0.12)	7,545 (7.8)	17.0 (0.02)	7,974 (5.8)	15.4 (0.01)	8,498 (176)	16.1 (0.3)
Alabama	35,875	39,986	38,180 (990)	18.3	16.1	16.2 (0.91)	178 (1.2)	23.2 (0.16)	165 (1.2)	20.3 (0.11)	152 (25)	20.3 (3.0)
Alaska	62,953	60,411	55,935 (1,105)	9.0	9.4	9.6 (0.79)	11 (0.3)	9.6 (0.27)	14 (0.3)	10.3 (0.18)	14 (3)	11.1 (2.4)
Arizona	41,870	47,510	44,748 (918)	15.7	13.9	14.4 (0.85)	136 (1.0)	20.3 (0.15)	171 (1.3)	17.8 (0.11)	205 (31)	18.3 (2.6)
Arkansas	32,150	37,698	35,591 (744)	19.1	15.8	15.6 (0.97)	107 (0.9)	23.8 (0.20)	98 (0.6)	20.1 (0.13)	88 (15)	18.1 (2.9)
California	54,424	55,634	51,647 (479)	12.5	14.2	13.2 (0.36)	894 (3.3)	17.2 (0.06)	1,217 (4.6)	18.5 (0.04)	1,181 (76)	16.9 (1.0)
Colorado	45,822	55,294	52,011 (987)	11.7	9.3	10.4 (0.79)	82 (0.8)	13.7 (0.13)	79 (0.7)	10.0 (0.08)	116 (24)	14.3 (2.7)
Connecticut	63,429	63,180	57,369 (1,166)	6.8	7.9	9.2 (0.73)	50 (0.8)	9.8 (0.15)	58 (0.7)	9.6 (0.10)	68 (15)	11.5 (2.5)
Delaware	53,021	55,502	50,970 (946)	8.7	9.2	8.5 (0.73)	12 (0.3)	11.0 (0.27)	15 (0.4)	10.9 (0.22)	15 (4)	11.5 (2.6)
District of Columbia	46,715	47,005	— (†)	16.9	20.2	18.3 (1.16)	18 (0.4)	24.1 (0.59)	24 (0.4)	30.4 (0.44)	32 (5)	39.6 (4.7)
Florida	41,783	45,473	42,079 (524)	12.7	12.5	11.8 (0.43)	344 (2.0)	17.5 (0.10)	434 (2.0)	16.6 (0.07)	416 (43)	14.3 (1.4)
Georgia	44,121	49,706	44,439 (580)	14.7	13.0	13.1 (0.67)	228 (1.6)	18.9 (0.14)	248 (1.4)	16.1 (0.09)	340 (38)	20.5 (2.1)
Hawaii	59,033	58,359	57,572 (1,040)	8.3	10.7	8.8 (0.73)	20 (0.5)	10.5 (0.25)	27 (0.6)	12.9 (0.18)	21 (5)	9.6 (2.2)
Idaho	38,399	44,012	44,994 (883)	13.3	11.8	10.0 (0.79)	32 (0.5)	14.4 (0.23)	33 (0.6)	12.6 (0.14)	32 (7)	11.3 (2.3)
Illinois	49,033	54,576	47,978 (688)	11.9	10.7	12.1 (0.49)	328 (1.6)	15.9 (0.08)	309 (1.5)	13.4 (0.05)	330 (38)	14.3 (1.6)
Indiana	43,781	48,692	43,735 (776)	10.7	9.5	11.4 (0.67)	132 (1.1)	12.8 (0.10)	119 (1.4)	10.6 (0.08)	174 (27)	15.1 (2.2)
Iowa	39,876	46,234	45,086 (922)	11.5	9.1	10.4 (0.79)	65 (0.7)	12.6 (0.14)	50 (0.6)	9.5 (0.09)	57 (13)	12.3 (2.7)
Kansas	41,491	47,587	43,802 (1,013)	11.5	9.9	11.6 (0.85)	59 (0.7)	12.8 (0.15)	53 (0.6)	10.4 (0.10)	73 (15)	15.2 (2.8)
Kentucky	34,259	39,444	37,566 (731)	19.0	15.8	15.6 (0.97)	161 (1.1)	23.2 (0.16)	137 (1.0)	19.4 (0.10)	140 (24)	19.7 (3.1)
Louisiana	33,370	38,148	36,814 (877)	23.6	19.6	17.4 (0.97)	267 (1.6)	30.4 (0.19)	223 (1.1)	25.3 (0.11)	157 (25)	21.8 (3.2)
Maine	42,347	43,623	42,006 (870)	10.8	10.9	11.9 (0.85)	27 (0.4)	12.3 (0.20)	27 (0.5)	12.0 (0.15)	29 (7)	14.6 (3.1)
Maryland	59,879	61,930	58,347 (1,071)	8.3	8.5	9.4 (0.67)	82 (1.0)	10.5 (0.12)	96 (0.9)	9.8 (0.09)	110 (22)	11.3 (2.2)
Massachusetts	56,179	59,158	54,617 (1,075)	8.9	9.3	9.9 (0.61)	112 (1.1)	12.2 (0.12)	122 (1.3)	11.4 (0.08)	116 (22)	10.7 (2.0)
Michigan	47,160	52,323	45,793 (653)	13.1	10.5	12.2 (0.55)	288 (1.5)	16.7 (0.09)	238 (1.1)	12.7 (0.05)	262 (34)	13.9 (1.7)
Minnesota	46,992	55,186	56,084 (846)	10.2	7.9	7.5 (0.61)	93 (0.8)	11.4 (0.10)	81 (0.7)	8.7 (0.06)	86 (19)	9.5 (2.0)
Mississippi	30,613	36,700	34,508 (847)	25.2	19.9	18.3 (1.03)	177 (1.2)	32.6 (0.21)	146 (1.0)	26.0 (0.13)	159 (21)	29.6 (3.4)
Missouri	40,079	44,436	44,324 (712)	13.3	11.7	11.5 (0.73)	150 (1.1)	16.2 (0.12)	148 (1.1)	14.4 (0.08)	149 (26)	14.9 (2.4)
Montana	34,949	38,684	36,200 (695)	16.1	14.6	14.4 (0.97)	29 (0.5)	18.4 (0.30)	29 (0.5)	17.1 (0.20)	26 (5)	16.6 (2.9)
Nebraska	39,553	45,978	46,613 (980)	11.1	9.7	9.6 (0.79)	37 (0.6)	12.0 (0.18)	36 (0.6)	11.1 (0.12)	33 (8)	10.5 (2.4)
Nevada	47,147	52,222	48,314 (1,101)	10.2	10.5	10.8 (0.79)	23 (0.5)	11.7 (0.26)	44 (0.7)	12.3 (0.16)	55 (12)	11.4 (2.4)
New Hampshire	55,232	57,946	58,223 (1,113)	6.4	6.5	5.6 (0.61)	12 (0.3)	6.4 (0.16)	15 (0.3)	6.7 (0.12)	10 (4)	4.6 (1.7)
New Jersey	62,222	64,598	59,989 (1,112)	7.6	8.5	7.8 (0.49)	134 (1.2)	10.8 (0.10)	158 (1.3)	10.5 (0.07)	126 (24)	8.0 (1.5)
New Mexico	36,620	39,984	39,029 (1,074)	20.6	18.4	17.5 (1.09)	83 (0.8)	26.3 (0.25)	87 (0.7)	23.6 (0.17)	89 (14)	24.3 (3.5)
New York	50,117	50,831	46,242 (598)	13.0	14.6	14.6 (0.49)	531 (2.5)	18.1 (0.09)	640 (2.6)	19.1 (0.06)	657 (55)	19.6 (1.5)
North Carolina	40,512	45,900	41,067 (648)	13.0	12.3	14.4 (0.67)	180 (1.2)	16.0 (0.11)	207 (1.2)	14.9 (0.07)	268 (34)	17.3 (2.0)
North Dakota	35,291	40,535	41,869 (810)	14.4	11.9	10.2 (0.79)	20 (0.4)	15.9 (0.30)	15 (0.2)	12.2 (0.17)	11 (3)	10.7 (2.5)
Ohio	43,642	47,976	44,961 (709)	12.5	10.6	11.6 (0.55)	321 (1.6)	16.2 (0.08)	268 (1.5)	12.9 (0.05)	287 (35)	15.0 (1.7)
Oklahoma	35,845	39,125	38,895 (815)	16.7	14.7	13.1 (0.85)	119 (1.0)	19.9 (0.16)	113 (1.0)	17.7 (0.11)	114 (20)	19.4 (3.1)
Oregon	41,429	47,929	43,570 (816)	12.4	11.6	12.1 (0.85)	68 (0.8)	13.4 (0.15)	77 (0.7)	12.8 (0.11)	85 (18)	13.9 (2.8)
Pennsylvania	44,194	46,980	45,814 (630)	11.1	11.0	11.0 (0.49)	284 (1.5)	14.5 (0.08)	292 (1.5)	13.6 (0.05)	307 (36)	15.6 (1.7)
Rhode Island	48,925	49,304	48,823 (1,155)	9.6	11.9	11.7 (0.85)	19 (0.5)	12.3 (0.30)	28 (0.7)	15.6 (0.25)	34 (6)	18.1 (3.1)

See notes at end of table.

Table 20. Household income and poverty rates, by state: 1990, 2000, and 2003–2005—Continued

State	Median household income, in constant 2005 dollars[1]			Percent of persons below the poverty level			Poverty status of related children 5 through 17 years old[2]					
	1990[3]	2000[4]	2003–2005 (3-year average)	1990[3]	2000[4]	2003–2005 (3-year average)	1990[3]		2000[4]		2005	
							Number in poverty (in thousands)	Percent in poverty	Number in poverty (in thousands)	Percent in poverty	Number in poverty (in thousands)	Percent in poverty
1	2	3	4	5	6	7	8	9	10	11	12	13
South Carolina	39,918	43,438	40,350 (799)	15.4	14.1	14.2 (0.91)	131 (1.2)	20.0 (0.19)	130 (1.2)	17.9 (0.12)	132 (24)	19.5 (3.2)
South Dakota	34,212	41,330	42,525 (804)	15.9	13.2	12.7 (0.79)	26 (0.5)	18.7 (0.33)	23 (0.3)	15.5 (0.21)	20 (4)	15.2 (2.6)
Tennessee	37,715	42,592	39,524 (820)	15.7	13.5	15.0 (0.85)	169 (1.2)	19.5 (0.13)	166 (1.2)	16.6 (0.10)	217 (30)	20.9 (2.6)
Texas	41,073	46,771	41,959 (427)	18.1	15.4	16.5 (0.49)	791 (3.1)	23.4 (0.09)	806 (2.6)	19.3 (0.06)	948 (69)	20.6 (1.4)
Utah	44,804	53,564	53,226 (749)	11.4	9.4	9.4 (0.73)	49 (0.7)	10.9 (0.16)	44 (0.6)	8.9 (0.09)	55 (11)	10.8 (2.0)
Vermont	45,293	47,859	48,508 (861)	9.9	9.4	8.0 (0.73)	11 (0.3)	10.7 (0.26)	11 (0.2)	9.9 (0.16)	6 (2)	5.6 (2.0)
Virginia	50,669	54,678	54,301 (930)	10.2	9.6	9.5 (0.61)	129 (1.2)	12.4 (0.12)	142 (1.3)	11.4 (0.08)	150 (25)	11.8 (1.9)
Washington	47,408	53,622	50,885 (847)	10.9	10.6	11.4 (0.73)	111 (0.9)	12.8 (0.10)	132 (1.4)	12.2 (0.09)	160 (27)	14.1 (2.2)
West Virginia	31,615	34,786	35,234 (785)	19.7	17.9	15.6 (0.85)	80 (0.8)	24.0 (0.23)	67 (0.6)	22.9 (0.17)	50 (9)	18.0 (2.9)
Wisconsin	44,761	51,297	47,004 (851)	10.7	8.7	10.8 (0.73)	121 (0.9)	13.3 (0.10)	100 (1.1)	10.0 (0.07)	128 (24)	13.8 (2.4)
Wyoming	41,195	44,387	45,598 (878)	11.9	11.4	10.1 (0.85)	12 (0.3)	12.6 (0.33)	12 (0.3)	12.5 (0.24)	8 (2)	9.4 (2.5)

—Not available.
†Not applicable.
[1] Adjusted by the Consumer Price Index research series using current methods (CPI-U-RS).
[2] Related children in a family include own children and all other children in the household who are related to the householder by birth, marriage, or adoption.
[3] Based on 1989 incomes collected in the 1990 census. Data may differ from figures derived from the Current Population Survey.
[4] Based on 1999 incomes collected in the 2000 census. Data may differ from figures derived from the Current Population Survey.
NOTE: Some data have been revised from previously published figures. Standard errors appear in parentheses.
SOURCE: U.S. Department of Commerce, Census Bureau, 1990 Summary Tape File 3 (STF 3), "Median Household Income in 1989" and "Poverty Status in 1989 by Family Type and Age," retrieved May 12, 2005, from http://factfinder.census.gov/servlet/ DTGeoSearchByListServlet?ds_name=DEC_1990_STF3_&_lang=en&_ts=134048804959; Decennial Census, 1990, *Minority Economic Profiles*, unpublished data; Decennial Census, 2000, *Summary of Social, Economic, and Housing Characteristics*; Census 2000 Summary File 4 (SF 4), "Poverty Status in 1999 of Related Children Under 18 Years by Family Type and Age," retrieved March 28, 2005, from http://factfinder.census.gov/servlet/DTGeoSearchByListServlet?ds_name=DEC_2000_SF4_U&_lang=en&_ts =134049420077; Current Population Reports, Series P-60, *Income, Poverty, and Health Insurance Coverage in the United States: 2005*; "Poverty Status by State: 2005," retrieved September 8, 2006, from http://pubdb3.census.gov/macro/032006/pov/new46_100125_02.htm; and "Income 2005," retrieved September 8, 2006, from http://www.census.gov/hhes/www/income05/statemhi3.html. (This table was prepared September 2006.)

Table 21. Poverty status of persons, families, and children under age 18, by race/ethnicity: Selected years, 1959 through 2005

Year and race/ethnicity	Number below the poverty level (in thousands)						Percent below the poverty level					
	All persons	In all families			In families with female householder, no husband present		All persons	In all families			In families with female householder, no husband present	
		Total	Householder[1]	Related children under 18	Total	Related children under 18		Total	Householder[1]	Related children under 18	Total	Related children under 18
1	2	3	4	5	6	7	8	9	10	11	12	13
All races												
1959	39,490 (641.5)	34,562 (489.5)	8,320 (178.3)	17,208 (289.6)	7,014 (160.3)	4,145 (117.4)	22.4 (0.34)	20.8 (0.17)	18.5 (0.31)	26.9 (0.30)	49.4 (0.71)	72.2 (1.00)
1960	39,851 (644.0)	34,925 (493.6)	8,243 (177.2)	17,288 (290.6)	7,247 (163.6)	4,095 (116.6)	22.2 (0.34)	20.7 (0.17)	18.1 (0.30)	26.5 (0.29)	48.9 (0.69)	68.4 (1.01)
1965	33,185 (595.4)	28,358 (419.2)	6,721 (156.2)	14,388 (255.6)	7,524 (167.4)	4,562 (124.1)	17.3 (0.30)	15.8 (0.14)	13.9 (0.26)	20.7 (0.26)	46.0 (0.66)	64.2 (0.96)
1970	25,420 (431.8)	20,330 (266.6)	5,260 (110.1)	10,235 (166.2)	7,503 (136.5)	4,689 (102.9)	12.6 (0.21)	10.9 (0.10)	10.1 (0.18)	14.9 (0.19)	38.1 (0.48)	53.0 (0.73)
1975	25,877 (435.2)	20,789 (271.0)	5,450 (112.4)	10,882 (173.0)	8,846 (151.3)	5,597 (114.2)	12.3 (0.20)	10.9 (0.10)	9.7 (0.17)	16.8 (0.20)	37.5 (0.43)	52.7 (0.67)
1980	29,272 (460.0)	22,601 (288.2)	6,217 (121.7)	11,114 (175.4)	10,120 (165.0)	5,866 (117.5)	13.0 (0.20)	11.5 (0.10)	10.3 (0.17)	17.9 (0.21)	36.7 (0.40)	50.8 (0.64)
1985	33,064 (513.3)	25,729 (336.0)	7,223 (141.0)	12,483 (200.4)	11,600 (190.8)	6,716 (134.8)	14.0 (0.21)	12.6 (0.11)	11.4 (0.18)	20.1 (0.23)	37.6 (0.40)	53.6 (0.65)
1986	32,370 (508.5)	24,754 (326.3)	7,023 (138.6)	12,257 (197.9)	11,944 (194.6)	6,943 (137.6)	13.6 (0.21)	12.0 (0.10)	10.9 (0.18)	19.8 (0.23)	38.3 (0.40)	54.4 (0.64)
1987	32,221 (507.5)	24,725 (326.0)	7,005 (138.3)	12,275 (198.1)	12,148 (196.8)	7,074 (139.2)	13.4 (0.21)	12.0 (0.10)	10.7 (0.18)	19.7 (0.23)	38.1 (0.40)	54.7 (0.64)
1988	31,745 (504.2)	24,048 (319.3)	6,876 (136.8)	11,935 (194.5)	11,972 (194.9)	6,742 (135.1)	13.0 (0.20)	11.6 (0.10)	10.4 (0.17)	19.0 (0.23)	37.2 (0.39)	50.6 (0.63)
1989	31,528 (548.0)	24,066 (348.2)	6,784 (147.9)	12,001 (212.7)	11,668 (208.8)	6,808 (148.2)	12.8 (0.22)	11.5 (0.11)	10.3 (0.19)	19.0 (0.25)	35.9 (0.42)	51.1 (0.69)
1990	33,585 (534.7)	25,232 (342.5)	7,098 (144.3)	12,715 (209.9)	12,578 (208.4)	7,363 (147.6)	13.5 (0.21)	12.0 (0.11)	10.7 (0.18)	19.9 (0.24)	37.2 (0.40)	53.4 (0.64)
1991	35,708 (549.1)	27,143 (362.1)	7,712 (151.9)	13,658 (220.3)	13,824 (222.2)	8,065 (156.2)	14.2 (0.22)	12.8 (0.11)	11.5 (0.19)	21.1 (0.24)	39.7 (0.39)	55.5 (0.62)
1992	36,880 (556.8)	27,947 (370.3)	7,960 (154.9)	13,876 (222.7)	13,716 (221.0)	8,032 (161.8)	14.8 (0.22)	13.3 (0.11)	11.7 (0.19)	21.1 (0.24)	39.0 (0.39)	54.3 (0.62)
1993	39,265 (571.8)	29,927 (390.5)	8,393 (160.2)	14,961 (234.6)	14,636 (231.0)	8,503 (161.5)	15.1 (0.22)	13.6 (0.11)	12.3 (0.19)	22.0 (0.24)	38.7 (0.38)	53.7 (0.60)
1994	38,059 (564.3)	28,985 (380.9)	8,053 (156.1)	14,610 (230.8)	14,380 (228.3)	8,427 (160.6)	14.5 (0.21)	13.1 (0.11)	11.6 (0.18)	21.2 (0.23)	38.6 (0.38)	52.9 (0.59)
1995	36,425 (553.8)	27,501 (365.8)	7,532 (149.7)	13,999 (224.1)	14,205 (226.3)	8,364 (159.8)	13.8 (0.21)	12.3 (0.10)	10.8 (0.18)	20.2 (0.23)	36.5 (0.37)	50.3 (0.58)
1996	36,529 (572.0)	27,376 (378.5)	7,708 (157.7)	13,764 (230.1)	13,796 (230.4)	7,990 (161.3)	13.7 (0.21)	12.2 (0.11)	11.0 (0.18)	19.8 (0.24)	35.8 (0.38)	49.3 (0.61)
1997	35,574 (565.6)	26,217 (366.2)	7,324 (152.8)	13,422 (226.2)	13,494 (227.0)	7,928 (160.5)	13.3 (0.21)	11.6 (0.11)	10.3 (0.18)	19.2 (0.23)	35.1 (0.38)	49.0 (0.61)
1998	34,476 (558.1)	25,370 (357.2)	7,186 (151.0)	12,845 (219.5)	12,907 (220.3)	7,627 (156.7)	12.7 (0.21)	11.2 (0.10)	10.0 (0.17)	18.3 (0.23)	33.1 (0.37)	46.1 (0.61)
1999	32,258 (543.4)	23,396 (336.1)	6,676 (144.4)	11,510 (204.0)	11,607 (205.1)	6,602 (143.4)	11.8 (0.20)	10.2 (0.10)	9.3 (0.17)	16.3 (0.22)	30.4 (0.37)	41.9 (0.61)
2000	31,054 (534.5)	22,015 (321.2)	6,222 (138.4)	11,018 (198.2)	10,425 (191.2)	6,116 (136.9)	11.3 (0.19)	9.6 (0.10)	8.6 (0.16)	15.6 (0.21)	27.9 (0.36)	39.8 (0.62)
2001	32,907 (548.1)	23,215 (334.2)	6,813 (146.2)	11,175 (200.1)	11,223 (200.6)	6,341 (139.9)	11.7 (0.20)	9.9 (0.10)	9.2 (0.17)	15.8 (0.21)	28.6 (0.36)	39.3 (0.60)
2002	34,570 (399.9)	24,534 (248.6)	7,229 (108.2)	11,646 (146.7)	11,657 (146.8)	6,564 (102.0)	12.1 (0.14)	10.4 (0.07)	9.6 (0.12)	16.3 (0.15)	28.8 (0.25)	39.6 (0.42)
2003	35,861 (407.8)	25,684 (257.3)	7,607 (111.6)	12,340 (152.5)	12,413 (153.1)	7,085 (106.8)	12.5 (0.14)	10.8 (0.07)	10.0 (0.12)	17.2 (0.16)	30.0 (0.25)	41.8 (0.42)
2004	36,997 (413.3)	26,564 (264.0)	7,854 (113.9)	12,460 (153.5)	12,823 (156.5)	7,132 (107.3)	12.7 (0.14)	11.0 (0.07)	10.2 (0.12)	17.3 (0.16)	30.5 (0.25)	41.9 (0.42)
2005	36,950 (413.0)	26,068 (260.3)	7,657 (112.1)	12,335 (152.5)	13,153 (159.2)	7,210 (108.0)	12.6 (0.14)	10.8 (0.07)	9.9 (0.12)	17.1 (0.16)	31.1 (0.25)	42.8 (0.43)
White[2]												
1960	28,309 (555.0)	24,262 (372.2)	6,115 (147.5)	11,229 (216.3)	4,296 (119.8)	2,357 (85.7)	17.8 (0.33)	16.2 (0.16)	14.9 (0.30)	20.0 (0.28)	39.0 (0.50)	44.2 (0.86)
1965	22,496 (500.1)	18,508 (305.1)	4,824 (182.2)	8,595 (182.0)	4,092 (116.5)	2,321 (84.9)	13.3 (0.29)	11.7 (0.14)	11.1 (0.25)	14.4 (0.24)	35.4 (0.78)	59.9 (1.32)
1970	17,484 (363.3)	13,323 (198.0)	3,708 (90.0)	6,138 (120.7)	3,761 (90.7)	2,247 (68.2)	9.9 (0.20)	8.1 (0.09)	8.0 (0.17)	10.5 (0.17)	28.4 (0.54)	52.9 (1.27)
1975	17,770 (366.1)	13,799 (202.8)	3,838 (91.7)	6,748 (127.9)	4,577 (101.5)	2,813 (77.1)	9.7 (0.20)	8.3 (0.09)	7.7 (0.16)	12.5 (0.20)	29.4 (0.50)	43.1 (0.94)
1980	19,699 (384.1)	14,587 (210.7)	4,195 (96.5)	6,817 (128.7)	4,940 (106.1)	2,813 (77.1)	10.2 (0.20)	8.6 (0.09)	8.0 (0.16)	13.4 (0.21)	28.0 (0.46)	41.6 (0.82)
1985	22,860 (435.1)	17,125 (249.2)	4,983 (112.8)	7,838 (148.3)	5,990 (125.8)	3,372 (90.2)	11.4 (0.21)	9.9 (0.10)	9.1 (0.18)	15.6 (0.24)	29.8 (0.47)	45.2 (0.84)
1990	22,326 (445.3)	15,916 (244.9)	4,622 (111.7)	7,696 (151.7)	6,210 (133.0)	3,597 (96.8)	10.7 (0.21)	9.0 (0.10)	8.1 (0.17)	15.1 (0.24)	29.8 (0.48)	45.9 (0.85)
1995	24,423 (463.9)	17,593 (262.9)	4,994 (116.9)	8,474 (161.1)	7,047 (143.7)	4,051 (103.5)	11.2 (0.21)	9.6 (0.10)	8.5 (0.17)	15.5 (0.23)	29.7 (0.45)	42.5 (0.76)
1996	24,650 (481.8)	17,621 (273.3)	5,059 (122.3)	8,488 (167.6)	7,073 (149.6)	4,029 (107.2)	11.2 (0.22)	9.6 (0.11)	8.6 (0.18)	15.5 (0.24)	29.8 (0.46)	43.1 (0.80)
1997	24,396 (479.6)	17,258 (269.3)	4,990 (121.3)	8,441 (167.0)	7,296 (152.5)	4,186 (109.6)	11.0 (0.21)	9.3 (0.11)	8.4 (0.18)	15.4 (0.24)	30.7 (0.47)	44.3 (0.80)

See notes at end of table.

Table 21. Poverty status of persons, families, and children under age 18, by race/ethnicity: Selected years, 1959 through 2005—Continued

Year and race/ethnicity	Number below the poverty level (in thousands) — All persons	In all families — Total	In all families — Householder[1]	In all families — Related children under 18	Female householder, no husband present — Total	Female householder, no husband present — Related children under 18	Percent below the poverty level — All persons	In all families — Total	In all families — Householder[1]	In all families — Related children under 18	Female householder, no husband present — Total	Female householder, no husband present — Related children under 18
1	2	3	4	5	6	7	8	9	10	11	12	13
1998	23,454 (471.2)	16,549 (261.4)	4,829 (119.0)	7,935 (160.6)	6,674 (144.4)	3,875 (104.9)	10.5 (0.21)	8.9 (0.10)	8.0 (0.17)	14.4 (0.23)	27.6 (0.45)	40.0 (0.78)
1999	21,922 (457.5)	15,141 (245.7)	4,377 (112.4)	7,123 (150.2)	5,891 (133.9)	3,266 (95.2)	9.8 (0.20)	8.1 (0.10)	7.3 (0.17)	12.9 (0.22)	24.7 (0.44)	35.5 (0.78)
2000	21,242 (450.9)	14,392 (237.2)	4,151 (109.1)	6,838 (146.5)	5,211 (124.5)	2,955 (90.0)	9.4 (0.20)	7.7 (0.10)	6.9 (0.16)	12.3 (0.22)	22.1 (0.42)	33.0 (0.78)
2001	22,739 (465.2)	15,369 (248.2)	4,579 (115.4)	7,086 (149.8)	5,972 (135.0)	3,291 (95.6)	9.9 (0.20)	8.1 (0.10)	7.4 (0.16)	12.8 (0.22)	24.3 (0.43)	34.7 (0.76)
2002	24,074 (340.8)	16,486 (186.1)	4,954 (86.2)	7,494 (110.6)	6,248 (99.0)	3,462 (70.2)	10.3 (0.14)	8.5 (0.7)	7.9 (0.12)	13.2 (0.16)	24.2 (0.30)	34.7 (0.53)
2003	24,950 (347.2)	17,271 (192.3)	5,171 (88.4)	7,969 (114.9)	6,835 (104.5)	3,797 (74.0)	10.6 (0.15)	8.8 (0.07)	8.1 (0.12)	14.0 (0.16)	25.8 (0.30)	37.0 (0.53)
2004	26,038 (354.0)	18,027 (198.3)	5,428 (91.0)	8,231 (117.3)	7,197 (107.9)	3,984 (76.0)	10.9 (0.15)	9.1 (0.07)	8.5 (0.12)	14.4 (0.16)	26.6 (0.30)	38.1 (0.53)
2005	25,631 (351.5)	17,370 (193.1)	5,195 (88.7)	8,023 (115.4)	7,359 (109.4)	3,985 (76.0)	10.7 (0.15)	8.7 (0.07)	8.1 (0.12)	14.0 (0.16)	27.3 (0.30)	38.7 (0.54)
Black[2]												
1959	9,927 (296.1)	9,112 (202.1)	1,860 (76.8)	5,022 (137.1)	2,416 (88.9)	1,475 (67.6)	55.1 (1.29)	54.9 (0.65)	48.1 (1.35)	65.5 (0.91)	70.6 (1.31)	81.6 (1.53)
1966	8,867 (285.2)	8,090 (186.5)	1,620 (71.2)	4,774 (132.9)	3,160 (103.7)	2,107 (82.3)	41.8 (1.18)	40.9 (0.59)	35.5 (1.19)	50.6 (0.87)	65.3 (1.15)	76.6 (1.36)
1970	7,548 (219.8)	6,683 (134.2)	1,481 (55.3)	3,922 (96.3)	3,656 (92.3)	2,383 (72.0)	33.5 (0.89)	32.2 (0.45)	29.5 (0.88)	41.5 (0.70)	58.7 (0.86)	67.7 (1.08)
1975	7,545 (219.8)	6,533 (132.3)	1,513 (56.0)	3,884 (95.7)	4,168 (99.9)	2,724 (77.7)	31.3 (0.85)	30.1 (0.43)	27.1 (0.82)	41.4 (0.70)	54.3 (0.78)	66.0 (1.01)
1980	8,579 (230.2)	7,190 (140.8)	1,826 (62.1)	3,906 (96.0)	4,984 (111.4)	2,944 (81.3)	32.5 (0.82)	31.1 (0.42)	28.9 (0.78)	42.1 (0.70)	53.4 (0.71)	64.8 (0.97)
1985	8,926 (246.7)	7,504 (153.2)	1,983 (68.7)	4,057 (103.9)	5,342 (123.1)	3,181 (89.9)	31.3 (0.82)	30.5 (0.43)	28.7 (0.79)	43.1 (0.74)	53.2 (0.72)	66.9 (0.99)
1990	9,837 (263.7)	8,160 (167.6)	2,193 (75.2)	4,412 (113.1)	6,005 (137.1)	3,543 (99.1)	31.9 (0.82)	31.0 (0.43)	29.3 (0.79)	44.2 (0.75)	50.6 (0.69)	64.7 (0.97)
1995	9,872 (264.0)	8,189 (168.0)	2,127 (73.9)	4,644 (116.7)	6,553 (145.0)	3,954 (105.9)	29.3 (0.77)	28.5 (0.40)	26.4 (0.74)	41.5 (0.70)	48.2 (0.64)	61.6 (0.91)
1996	9,694 (267.9)	7,993 (161.4)	2,206 (76.7)	4,411 (112.9)	6,123 (137.0)	3,619 (100.9)	28.4 (0.79)	27.6 (0.41)	26.1 (0.75)	39.5 (0.72)	46.4 (0.68)	58.2 (0.98)
1997	9,116 (262.9)	7,386 (153.6)	1,985 (72.5)	4,116 (108.5)	5,654 (130.6)	3,402 (97.4)	26.5 (0.77)	25.5 (0.40)	23.6 (0.72)	36.8 (0.71)	42.8 (0.67)	55.3 (0.99)
1998	9,091 (263.6)	7,259 (152.0)	1,981 (72.4)	4,073 (107.9)	5,629 (130.3)	3,366 (96.8)	26.1 (0.76)	24.7 (0.39)	23.4 (0.72)	36.4 (0.71)	42.8 (0.67)	54.7 (0.99)
1999	8,360 (256.9)	6,688 (144.5)	1,898 (70.7)	3,644 (101.3)	5,179 (124.0)	2,997 (90.7)	23.6 (0.73)	22.7 (0.38)	21.9 (0.69)	32.7 (0.69)	41.0 (0.68)	51.7 (1.03)
2000	7,862 (252.0)	6,108 (136.8)	1,685 (66.4)	3,417 (97.6)	4,697 (117.1)	2,830 (87.9)	22.0 (0.71)	20.7 (0.37)	19.1 (0.65)	30.4 (0.68)	38.6 (0.69)	49.4 (1.03)
2001	8,136 (255.5)	6,389 (140.6)	1,829 (69.3)	3,423 (97.7)	4,694 (117.1)	2,741 (86.4)	22.7 (0.71)	21.4 (0.37)	20.7 (0.67)	30.0 (0.67)	37.4 (0.67)	46.6 (1.02)
2002	8,884 (187.9)	6,985 (105.9)	1,958 (51.3)	3,733 (73.2)	5,145 (88.2)	2,990 (64.7)	23.9 (0.51)	22.5 (0.26)	21.4 (0.48)	31.3 (0.47)	38.0 (0.47)	46.9 (0.70)
2003	9,108 (200.6)	7,162 (107.6)	2,021 (52.2)	3,977 (75.9)	5,312 (89.8)	3,185 (67.0)	24.3 (0.51)	23.1 (0.27)	22.1 (0.48)	33.2 (0.48)	38.9 (0.47)	49.3 (0.69)
2004	9,393 (203.1)	7,482 (110.5)	2,081 (53.0)	3,952 (75.7)	5,464 (91.3)	3,135 (66.4)	24.7 (0.51)	23.8 (0.27)	22.8 (0.49)	32.9 (0.48)	39.6 (0.46)	48.9 (0.70)
2005	9,517 (204.6)	7,459 (110.3)	2,050 (52.6)	3,972 (75.9)	5,524 (91.9)	3,169 (66.8)	24.7 (0.50)	23.6 (0.27)	22.0 (0.48)	33.2 (0.48)	39.2 (0.46)	49.5 (0.70)
Hispanic origin[3]												
1975	2,991 (176.8)	2,755 (90.2)	627 (41.3)	1,619 (67.7)	1,053 (54.0)	694 (43.5)	26.9 (1.41)	26.3 (0.70)	25.1 (1.41)	33.1 (1.09)	57.2 (1.88)	68.4 (2.37)
1980	3,491 (189.8)	3,143 (97.0)	751 (45.3)	1,718 (69.8)	1,319 (60.7)	809 (47.1)	25.7 (1.26)	25.1 (0.63)	23.2 (1.21)	33.0 (1.06)	54.5 (1.65)	65.0 (2.20)
1985	5,236 (202.8)	4,605 (107.7)	1,074 (48.7)	2,512 (76.6)	1,983 (67.4)	1,247 (52.7)	29.0 (1.01)	28.3 (0.51)	25.5 (0.98)	39.6 (0.89)	55.7 (1.21)	72.4 (1.57)
1990	6,006 (222.4)	5,091 (118.2)	1,244 (54.4)	2,750 (83.3)	2,115 (72.2)	1,314 (56.0)	28.1 (0.95)	26.9 (0.48)	25.0 (0.92)	37.7 (0.85)	53.0 (1.19)	68.4 (1.60)
1995	8,574 (256.1)	7,341 (147.3)	1,695 (64.1)	3,938 (101.9)	3,053 (88.3)	1,872 (67.6)	30.3 (0.85)	29.2 (0.43)	27.0 (0.84)	39.3 (0.73)	52.8 (0.99)	65.7 (1.34)
1996	8,697 (250.2)	7,515 (155.3)	1,748 (67.7)	4,090 (108.1)	3,020 (91.1)	1,779 (68.3)	29.4 (0.85)	28.5 (0.43)	26.4 (0.85)	39.9 (0.76)	53.5 (1.04)	67.4 (1.43)
1997	8,308 (246.9)	7,198 (151.2)	1,721 (67.1)	3,865 (104.7)	2,911 (89.3)	1,758 (67.9)	27.1 (0.82)	27.1 (0.41)	24.7 (0.81)	36.4 (0.73)	50.9 (1.03)	62.8 (1.43)
1998	8,070 (248.5)	6,814 (146.2)	1,648 (65.6)	3,670 (101.7)	2,837 (88.0)	1,739 (67.5)	25.6 (0.79)	24.3 (0.40)	22.7 (0.77)	33.6 (0.71)	46.7 (1.00)	59.6 (1.42)
1999	7,439 (243.0)	6,349 (140.1)	1,525 (62.9)	3,382 (97.1)	2,488 (81.9)	1,471 (61.7)	22.8 (0.75)	21.7 (0.38)	20.2 (0.72)	29.9 (0.67)	40.7 (0.98)	52.4 (1.47)
2000	7,153 (240.9)	6,025 (135.7)	1,431 (60.9)	3,173 (93.7)	2,210 (76.8)	1,303 (57.9)	21.2 (0.72)	20.1 (0.36)	18.5 (0.69)	27.3 (0.65)	36.5 (0.97)	48.3 (1.50)

See notes at end of table.

Table 21. Poverty status of persons, families, and children under age 18, by race/ethnicity: Selected years, 1959 through 2005—Continued

Year and race/ethnicity	Number below the poverty level (in thousands)						Percent below the poverty level					
	In all families				In families with female householder, no husband present		In all families				In families with female householder, no husband present	
	All persons	Total	Householder[1]	Related children under 18	Total	Related children under 18	All persons	Total	Householder[1]	Related children under 18	Total	Related children under 18
1	2	3	4	5	6	7	8	9	10	11	12	13
2001	7,997 (251.7)	6,674 (144.4)	1,649 (65.6)	3,433 (97.9)	2,585 (83.6)	1,508 (62.6)	21.4 (0.68)	20.2 (0.35)	19.4 (0.67)	27.4 (0.62)	37.8 (0.92)	49.3 (1.41)
2002	8,555 (186.7)	7,184 (107.8)	1,792 (48.9)	3,653 (72.4)	2,554 (59.3)	1,501 (44.5)	21.8 (0.48)	20.8 (0.24)	19.7 (0.46)	28.2 (0.44)	36.4 (0.64)	47.9 (0.99)
2003	9,051 (192.6)	7,637 (111.9)	1,925 (50.8)	3,982 (76.0)	2,861 (63.1)	1,727 (48.0)	22.5 (0.48)	21.5 (0.24)	20.8 (0.47)	29.5 (0.44)	38.4 (0.63)	50.6 (0.95)
2004	9,132 (193.2)	7,726 (112.7)	1,958 (51.3)	3,989 (76.1)	3,071 (65.6)	1,837 (49.6)	21.9 (0.47)	21.2 (0.24)	20.5 (0.46)	28.6 (0.43)	39.3 (0.62)	51.9 (0.94)
2005	9,368 (196.0)	7,767 (113.1)	1,948 (51.2)	3,977 (75.9)	3,069 (65.6)	1,774 (48.7)	21.8 (0.46)	20.6 (0.23)	19.7 (0.45)	27.7 (0.42)	39.0 (0.61)	50.2 (0.94)
Asian/Pacific Islander[2]												
1990	858 (88.9)	712 (40.7)	— (†)	356 (28.6)	132 (17.3)	— (†)	12.2 (1.21)	11.3 (0.60)	— (†)	17.0 (1.23)	20.7 (2.41)	— (†)
1995	1,411 (112.3)	1,112 (51.3)	— (†)	532 (35.1)	266 (24.7)	— (†)	14.6 (1.11)	13.0 (0.55)	— (†)	18.6 (1.09)	28.9 (2.25)	— (†)
1996	1,454 (118.5)	1,172 (54.9)	— (†)	553 (37.2)	300 (27.3)	— (†)	14.5 (1.13)	13.2 (0.56)	— (†)	19.1 (1.14)	29.5 (2.24)	— (†)
1997	1,468 (119.0)	1,116 (53.5)	244 (24.6)	— (†)	313 (27.9)	— (†)	14.0 (1.09)	12.0 (0.53)	10.2 (0.97)	— (†)	33.6 (2.42)	— (†)
1998	1,360 (114.9)	1,087 (52.8)	270 (25.9)	— (†)	373 (30.5)	— (†)	12.5 (1.02)	11.4 (0.51)	11.0 (0.99)	— (†)	33.2 (2.20)	— (†)
1999	1,163 (106.8)	919 (48.3)	— (†)	— (†)	253 (25.0)	— (†)	10.7 (0.96)	9.6 (0.47)	— (†)	— (†)	23.0 (1.99)	— (†)
2000	1,214 (109.0)	932 (48.7)	235 (24.1)	434 (32.9)	206 (22.6)	128 (17.8)	10.7 (0.94)	9.4 (0.46)	8.8 (0.86)	14.1 (0.98)	19.6 (1.92)	32.3 (3.68)
2001	1,275 (111.5)	873 (47.1)	234 (24.1)	353 (29.6)	198 (22.1)	105 (16.1)	10.2 (0.87)	8.1 (0.41)	7.8 (0.77)	11.1 (0.87)	14.8 (1.52)	26.7 (3.49)
2002	1,161 (76.0)	763 (31.3)	210 (16.2)	302 (19.5)	155 (13.9)	85 (10.3)	10.1 (0.65)	7.7 (0.30)	7.4 (0.55)	11.4 (0.69)	15.2 (1.25)	29.8 (3.02)
2003	1,401 (82.9)	1,017 (36.3)	311 (19.8)	331 (20.4)	242 (17.4)	119 (12.2)	11.8 (0.68)	9.8 (0.33)	10.2 (0.61)	12.1 (0.70)	23.6 (1.48)	37.4 (3.02)
2004	1,209 (77.4)	816 (32.4)	232 (17.1)	269 (18.4)	135 (13.0)	55 (08.3)	9.8 (0.62)	7.6 (0.29)	7.4 (0.52)	9.5 (0.61)	13.2 (1.18)	18.8 (2.55)
2005	1,402 (83.0)	970 (35.4)	289 (19.1)	312 (19.8)	189 (15.4)	68 (09.2)	11.1 (0.64)	8.9 (0.30)	9.0 (0.56)	11.0 (0.66)	17.8 (1.31)	25.6 (2.99)

—Not available.
†Not applicable.
[1]Refers to the person who owns or rents (maintains) the housing unit.
[2]Includes persons of Hispanic origin.
[3]Persons of Hispanic origin may be of any race.

NOTE: Data are from the Current Population Survey and may differ from data shown in other tables obtained from the Decennial Census. Some data have been revised from previously published figures. Standard errors appear in parentheses.
SOURCE: U.S. Department of Commerce, Census Bureau, Current Population Reports, Series P-60, Poverty in the United States, selected years, 1959 through 2002; and Income, Poverty, and Health Insurance Coverage in the United States, 2003 through 2005. Current Population Survey (CPS), Annual Social and Economic Supplement, retrieved September 8, 2006, from http://pubdb3.census.gov/macro/032006/pov/new05_100_01.htm. (This table was prepared September 2006.)

Table 22. Average grade that the public would give the public schools in their community and in the nation at large: 1974 through 2006

Year	All adults		No children in school		Public school parents		Private school parents	
	Nation	Local community	Nation	Local community	Nation	Local community	Nation	Local community
1	2	3	4	5	6	7	8	9
1974	—	2.63	—	2.57	—	2.80	—	2.15
1975	—	2.38	—	2.31	—	2.49	—	1.81
1976	—	2.38	—	2.34	—	2.48	—	2.22
1977	—	2.33	—	2.25	—	2.59	—	2.05
1978	—	2.21	—	2.11	—	2.47	—	1.69
1979	—	2.21	—	2.15	—	2.38	—	1.88
1980	—	2.26	—	—	—	—	—	—
1981	1.94	2.20	—	2.12	—	2.36	—	1.88
1982	2.01	2.24	2.04	2.18	2.01	2.35	2.02	2.20
1983	1.91	2.12	1.92	2.10	1.92	2.31	1.82	1.89
1984	2.09	2.36	2.11	2.30	2.11	2.49	2.04	2.17
1985	2.14	2.39	2.16	2.36	2.20	2.44	1.93	2.00
1986	2.13	2.36	—	2.29	—	2.55	—	2.14
1987	2.18	2.44	2.20	2.38	2.22	2.61	2.03	2.01
1988	2.08	2.35	2.02	2.32	2.13	2.48	2.00	2.13
1989	2.01	2.35	1.99	2.27	2.06	2.56	1.93	2.12
1990	1.99	2.29	1.98	2.27	2.03	2.44	1.85	2.09
1991	2.00	2.36	—	—	—	—	—	—
1992	1.93	2.30	1.92	—	1.94	2.73	1.85	—
1993	1.95	2.41	1.97	2.40	1.97	2.48	1.80	2.11
1994	1.95	2.26	1.95	2.16	1.90	2.55	1.86	1.90
1995	1.97	2.28	1.98	2.25	1.93	2.41	1.81	1.85
1996	1.93	2.30	1.91	2.22	2.00	2.56	1.80	1.86
1997	1.97	2.35	1.99	2.27	2.01	2.56	1.99	1.87
1998	1.93	2.41	1.91	2.36	1.96	2.51	1.81	2.20
1999	2.02	2.44	2.03	2.42	1.97	2.56	—	—
2000	1.98	2.47	1.94	2.44	2.05	2.59	—	—
2001	2.01	2.47	2.00	2.42	2.04	2.66	—	—
2002	2.08	2.44	2.08	2.40	2.06	2.61	—	—
2003	2.11	2.41	2.09	2.32	2.16	2.57	—	—
2004	2.08	2.56	2.15	2.42	2.00	2.58	—	—
2005	2.06	2.45	2.07	2.43	2.11	2.60	—	—
2006	2.03	2.45	2.00	2.41	2.07	2.60	—	—

—Not available.
NOTE: Average based on a scale where A = 4, B = 3, C = 2, D = 1, and F = 0.

SOURCE: Phi Delta Kappa, *Phi Delta Kappan*, "The Annual Gallup Poll of the Public's Attitudes Toward the Public Schools," 1974 through 2006. (This table was prepared August 2006.)

Table 23. Percentage of elementary and secondary school children whose parents were involved in school activities, by selected child, parent, and school characteristics: 1999 and 2003

Child, parent, and school characteristic	Percent of children in 1999 whose parents[1] report that they ...				Percent of children in 2003 whose parents[1] report that they ...				Percentage distribution of children, by parental reports of number of times spent helping with homework per week, 2003[2]				
	Attended a general school meeting	Attended parent-teacher conference	Attended a class event	Volunteered at school	Attended a general school meeting	Attended parent-teacher conference	Attended a class event	Volunteered at school	No help given	Less than once per week	1 to 2 days a week	3 to 4 days a week	5 or more days a week
1	2	3	4	5	6	7	8	9	10	11	12	13	14
Total	78.3 (0.49)	72.8 (0.45)	65.4 (0.44)	36.8 (0.40)	87.7 (0.37)	77.1 (0.42)	69.9 (0.42)	41.8 (0.60)	4.9 (0.23)	24.6 (0.42)	33.9 (0.61)	25.2 (0.50)	11.4 (0.36)
Sex of child													
Male	78.0 (0.62)	74.0 (0.60)	63.4 (0.62)	36.7 (0.65)	87.4 (0.49)	77.7 (0.63)	67.4 (0.75)	41.2 (0.87)	5.4 (0.36)	24.4 (0.58)	32.7 (0.74)	25.5 (0.69)	11.9 (0.49)
Female	78.6 (0.69)	71.5 (0.56)	67.4 (0.59)	37.0 (0.61)	87.9 (0.55)	76.5 (0.63)	72.6 (0.63)	42.4 (0.83)	4.4 (0.31)	24.8 (0.68)	35.1 (0.87)	24.9 (0.66)	10.8 (0.55)
Race/ethnicity of child													
White	80.5 (0.54)	73.6 (0.48)	71.6 (0.53)	42.7 (0.51)	88.7 (0.51)	76.4 (0.62)	74.1 (0.65)	48.4 (0.82)	4.8 (0.34)	29.2 (0.63)	34.0 (0.75)	23.1 (0.60)	8.9 (0.39)
Black	74.5 (1.12)	71.1 (1.23)	53.8 (1.29)	26.2 (1.21)	88.7 (0.85)	78.7 (1.35)	63.3 (1.54)	32.0 (1.65)	4.2 (0.59)	16.2 (1.15)	33.4 (1.48)	29.4 (1.51)	16.7 (1.14)
Hispanic	73.1 (1.18)	71.0 (1.05)	51.5 (1.02)	24.5 (0.90)	82.6 (1.05)	78.1 (1.10)	60.9 (1.36)	27.7 (1.23)	5.8 (0.57)	16.0 (0.89)	35.8 (1.30)	27.5 (1.13)	14.9 (0.91)
Other	76.7 (2.00)	73.2 (1.94)	62.4 (2.01)	30.7 (1.94)	87.5 (1.63)	77.6 (2.25)	68.5 (2.32)	37.2 (2.16)	5.6 (1.06)	22.2 (1.99)	28.4 (1.99)	30.5 (2.67)	13.3 (1.56)
Highest education level of parents													
Less than high school	57.4 (1.77)	60.0 (1.78)	37.8 (1.68)	12.9 (1.05)	69.8 (2.04)	67.8 (2.50)	42.4 (2.42)	15.6 (2.04)	9.4 (1.30)	16.9 (1.85)	40.6 (2.86)	21.0 (1.90)	12.1 (1.66)
High school/GED	72.7 (1.00)	69.7 (0.87)	58.7 (0.93)	26.0 (0.88)	83.8 (0.91)	75.4 (0.93)	62.1 (1.28)	30.3 (1.27)	5.8 (0.55)	21.8 (0.87)	33.8 (0.96)	26.7 (1.00)	11.9 (0.75)
Vocational/technical or some college	78.0 (1.04)	72.8 (0.97)	66.0 (1.05)	35.7 (1.07)	88.5 (0.67)	78.0 (1.02)	69.1 (0.93)	38.8 (1.26)	4.1 (0.41)	24.3 (0.82)	34.1 (1.12)	26.1 (0.87)	11.5 (0.62)
Associate's degree	81.7 (1.14)	75.8 (1.39)	68.7 (1.57)	41.5 (1.53)	88.6 (1.27)	76.6 (1.68)	73.0 (1.76)	39.7 (1.67)	[3] (†)	[3] (†)	[3] (†)	[3] (†)	[3] (†)
Bachelor's degree	87.0 (0.73)	79.6 (0.84)	75.8 (0.93)	49.6 (1.10)	92.0 (0.75)	79.8 (0.89)	80.1 (0.95)	53.9 (1.29)	4.4 (0.54)	27.9 (1.15)	32.8 (1.20)	24.4 (1.03)	10.5 (0.75)
Graduate/professional degree	89.4 (0.70)	76.2 (1.09)	79.2 (0.98)	55.1 (1.21)	94.6 (0.74)	79.4 (0.99)	80.8 (1.09)	61.8 (1.57)	3.9 (0.50)	28.6 (1.11)	32.1 (1.15)	24.1 (1.08)	11.3 (0.91)
Family income													
Less than $5,000	67.0 (2.83)	66.7 (3.14)	47.4 (2.87)	17.6 (2.09)	77.7 (2.84)	72.4 (4.15)	55.6 (3.91)	27.3 (4.09)	3.7 (1.23)	17.0 (3.35)	38.1 (4.10)	25.9 (3.27)	15.2 (2.72)
$5,001 to $10,000	66.8 (2.13)	67.6 (2.25)	50.7 (2.23)	23.3 (1.91)	79.3 (3.26)	75.7 (3.28)	59.9 (3.60)	30.4 (3.35)	5.3 (1.56)	19.2 (2.98)	32.9 (3.14)	29.9 (2.54)	12.8 (1.82)
$10,001 to $15,000	67.1 (1.64)	70.0 (1.62)	49.9 (2.15)	20.4 (1.40)	80.0 (2.41)	75.6 (2.35)	53.4 (2.99)	22.5 (2.44)	5.5 (1.03)	16.5 (2.21)	35.9 (2.63)	27.1 (2.30)	15.1 (1.99)
$15,001 to $20,000	71.1 (1.76)	70.4 (1.52)	55.1 (1.89)	25.3 (1.70)	81.1 (2.60)	74.2 (2.23)	57.5 (2.28)	25.6 (2.84)	5.5 (1.10)	19.2 (1.74)	37.4 (2.63)	22.6 (2.00)	15.4 (2.04)
$20,001 to $25,000	70.6 (1.90)	67.0 (1.62)	53.4 (1.76)	26.2 (1.63)	83.5 (1.64)	79.1 (1.89)	62.4 (1.99)	27.0 (2.39)	7.7 (1.31)	17.0 (1.80)	32.1 (2.26)	30.4 (2.26)	12.8 (1.26)
$25,001 to $30,000	74.3 (1.35)	71.6 (1.31)	59.1 (1.71)	30.9 (1.69)	85.7 (1.46)	75.9 (2.41)	64.2 (2.23)	33.8 (2.86)	4.1 (0.91)	19.1 (1.78)	38.2 (2.95)	25.9 (2.36)	12.8 (1.45)
$30,001 to $35,000	79.0 (1.60)	73.8 (1.72)	67.6 (1.69)	37.9 (1.84)	84.5 (1.59)	76.3 (1.94)	64.7 (2.32)	33.5 (2.51)	6.4 (1.20)	19.9 (1.85)	34.9 (2.14)	27.5 (2.12)	11.2 (1.46)
$35,001 to $40,000	79.4 (1.38)	73.7 (1.38)	68.4 (1.64)	36.1 (1.84)	83.4 (2.50)	74.7 (2.10)	70.9 (2.41)	37.3 (3.50)	3.6 (0.89)	22.8 (2.21)	32.5 (2.32)	27.6 (2.32)	13.4 (1.67)
$40,001 to $50,000	81.6 (1.07)	75.1 (1.13)	72.8 (1.25)	40.1 (1.26)	87.5 (1.18)	79.3 (1.42)	68.5 (2.11)	40.0 (1.89)	4.3 (0.79)	24.7 (1.62)	31.5 (1.75)	28.1 (1.85)	11.4 (1.15)
$50,001 to $75,000	84.6 (0.78)	74.8 (0.91)	72.6 (0.90)	43.8 (1.05)	89.9 (0.79)	76.9 (0.96)	74.5 (1.04)	46.0 (1.27)	5.0 (0.49)	27.2 (1.07)	34.3 (1.11)	23.5 (1.04)	10.0 (0.64)
Over $75,000	88.5 (0.68)	77.3 (0.74)	79.3 (0.80)	54.9 (1.02)	93.9 (0.57)	78.6 (0.89)	79.3 (0.73)	56.8 (1.01)	4.4 (0.41)	30.8 (0.96)	32.4 (0.96)	23.0 (0.80)	9.5 (0.57)
Child attending public schools	76.8 (0.54)	71.4 (0.50)	63.5 (0.48)	33.8 (0.41)	86.7 (0.40)	75.9 (0.45)	68.0 (0.47)	38.5 (0.64)	4.9 (0.24)	24.7 (0.46)	34.2 (0.64)	25.1 (0.51)	11.1 (0.37)
Elementary (kindergarten to grade 8)	81.7 (0.57)	80.9 (0.45)	66.9 (0.55)	38.1 (0.48)	90.9 (0.40)	85.1 (0.42)	71.7 (0.57)	42.8 (0.74)	1.6 (0.17)	16.5 (0.55)	34.7 (0.75)	32.4 (0.67)	14.8 (0.51)
Secondary (grades 9 to 12)	65.8 (0.99)	50.1 (1.10)	55.9 (0.97)	24.0 (0.77)	76.9 (1.06)	54.8 (1.02)	59.4 (1.06)	28.5 (0.98)	12.7 (0.64)	44.2 (0.92)	32.9 (0.97)	7.9 (0.51)	2.4 (0.34)
Child attending private schools	91.4 (0.80)	85.0 (0.95)	81.7 (1.09)	63.8 (1.35)	95.7 (0.61)	86.6 (1.03)	85.6 (1.23)	68.7 (1.57)	4.6 (0.89)	23.7 (1.58)	31.4 (1.54)	26.4 (1.78)	13.9 (1.05)
Elementary (kindergarten to grade 8)	93.0 (0.73)	90.2 (0.81)	84.2 (1.11)	68.8 (1.37)	96.6 (0.69)	91.6 (0.92)	88.4 (1.22)	73.4 (1.90)	1.5 (0.47)	17.5 (1.64)	29.9 (1.68)	33.0 (2.23)	18.1 (1.45)
Secondary (grades 9 to 12)	85.9 (2.09)	66.9 (2.74)	73.0 (2.62)	46.3 (3.23)	93.0 (1.56)	72.2 (2.54)	77.6 (2.93)	55.2 (2.78)	13.4 (2.66)	41.0 (3.23)	35.7 (3.41)	7.8 (1.68)	2.1 (0.78)

†Not applicable.
[1]The respondent was the parent most knowledgeable about the child's education. Responding parents reported on their own and their spouse's, or other household adults', activities.
[2]Excludes children who do not have homework and children who never do homework.
[3]Included under vocational/technical or some college.

NOTE: Includes children enrolled in kindergarten through grade 12. Excludes homeschooled children. Race categories exclude persons of Hispanic origin. Detail may not sum to totals because of rounding. Standard errors appear in parentheses.
SOURCE: U.S. Department of Education, National Center for Education Statistics, *Parent and Family Involvement in Education: 2002–03*; and Parent Survey (Parent:1999) and Parent and Family Involvement in Education Survey (PFI:2003) of the National Household Education Surveys Program, unpublished tabulations. (This table was prepared January 2006.)

Table 24. Percentage of kindergartners through fifth-graders whose parents were involved in education-related activities, by selected child, parent, and school characteristics: 1999 and 2003

Child, parent, and school characteristic	Percent of children in 1999 whose parents report that they did the following things with their children in the past month					Percent of children in 2003 whose parents report that they did the following things with their children in the past month					Percent of children in 1999 whose parents report that they involved their children in the following activities during the past week			Percent of children in 2003 whose parents report that they involved their children in the following activities during the past week		
	Visited a library	Went to a play, concert, or other live show	Visited an art gallery, museum, or historical site	Visited a zoo or aquarium	Attended an event sponsored by a community, religious, or ethnic group[1]	Visited a library	Went to a play, concert, or other live show	Visited an art gallery, museum, or historical site	Visited a zoo or aquarium	Attended an event sponsored by a community, religious, or ethnic group[1]	Told a story	Worked on arts or crafts	Worked on household chores	Told a story	Worked on arts or crafts	Worked on household chores
1	2	3	4	5	6	7	8	9	10	11	12	13	14	15	16	17
Total	48.6 (0.64)	32.1 (0.55)	22.2 (0.67)	14.1 (0.47)	52.8 (0.63)	50.2 (0.80)	35.5 (0.87)	22.2 (0.83)	16.5 (0.69)	62.0 (0.80)	69.4 (0.60)	68.0 (0.60)	93.8 (0.33)	74.9 (0.66)	74.9 (0.70)	97.1 (0.21)
Sex of child																
Male	47.2 (0.91)	30.5 (0.84)	22.3 (0.93)	13.9 (0.70)	50.9 (0.89)	47.3 (1.08)	33.6 (1.09)	23.1 (1.12)	16.3 (0.88)	61.0 (1.08)	69.1 (0.76)	64.2 (0.81)	93.0 (0.41)	73.3 (0.86)	69.7 (0.98)	97.0 (0.33)
Female	50.1 (1.02)	33.7 (0.81)	22.1 (0.89)	14.3 (0.70)	54.8 (0.95)	53.1 (1.11)	37.5 (1.09)	21.2 (1.07)	16.7 (0.87)	63.0 (1.09)	69.7 (0.89)	71.9 (0.90)	94.6 (0.45)	76.6 (0.96)	80.2 (1.01)	97.3 (0.33)
Race/ethnicity of child																
White	48.9 (0.85)	33.9 (0.72)	22.3 (0.76)	12.0 (0.54)	54.6 (0.81)	49.1 (1.03)	37.2 (1.26)	21.2 (1.09)	13.6 (0.85)	64.6 (1.12)	70.9 (0.80)	72.4 (0.73)	96.2 (0.33)	76.0 (0.96)	75.4 (0.89)	98.4 (0.24)
Black	47.8 (1.76)	31.3 (1.60)	21.0 (1.52)	15.7 (1.24)	53.0 (1.40)	52.3 (2.50)	36.7 (2.23)	24.4 (1.97)	18.9 (1.55)	66.3 (2.35)	64.8 (1.73)	58.6 (1.82)	93.9 (0.79)	69.6 (2.00)	68.1 (2.14)	98.9 (0.43)
Hispanic	43.9 (1.65)	24.4 (1.10)	20.6 (1.26)	19.7 (1.02)	45.8 (1.32)	48.2 (1.77)	28.0 (1.53)	20.8 (1.38)	23.7 (1.32)	49.3 (1.75)	66.6 (1.49)	59.4 (1.33)	84.7 (1.19)	74.2 (1.55)	79.6 (1.45)	92.7 (0.86)
Other	61.6 (3.14)	34.9 (3.02)	29.8 (3.16)	18.1 (2.31)	51.7 (3.18)	61.0 (3.80)	37.4 (3.04)	29.9 (2.75)	18.3 (2.76)	62.3 (3.45)	74.0 (2.87)	69.1 (2.47)	92.0 (1.56)	79.9 (3.06)	73.6 (2.52)	93.3 (1.45)
Highest education level of parents																
Less than high school	34.5 (2.33)	17.5 (1.63)	12.1 (1.64)	15.2 (1.65)	36.7 (2.32)	36.1 (3.39)	20.0 (3.10)	9.3 (1.75)	15.3 (2.05)	34.3 (3.06)	61.9 (2.30)	54.4 (2.13)	81.8 (1.97)	67.2 (3.16)	74.8 (3.20)	94.9 (1.22)
High school/GED	40.3 (1.42)	25.9 (1.13)	16.0 (1.04)	12.8 (0.98)	42.6 (1.23)	44.5 (1.64)	28.6 (1.83)	17.8 (1.73)	16.5 (1.18)	50.5 (1.81)	66.5 (1.28)	64.3 (1.27)	92.8 (0.75)	71.3 (1.59)	75.5 (1.32)	97.1 (0.56)
Vocational/technical or some college	47.2 (1.41)	30.2 (1.30)	20.4 (1.21)	11.9 (0.90)	53.7 (1.43)	44.3 (2.04)	32.8 (1.89)	19.1 (1.32)	15.2 (1.29)	62.1 (1.64)	70.2 (1.23)	68.3 (1.18)	96.2 (0.58)	75.9 (1.54)	76.2 (1.51)	97.4 (0.56)
Associate's degree	50.4 (2.12)	35.5 (2.10)	22.0 (1.77)	14.3 (1.42)	53.6 (2.26)	47.4 (3.04)	41.1 (3.24)	22.0 (2.40)	15.4 (2.09)	67.0 (2.85)	70.0 (2.04)	71.9 (1.88)	95.4 (0.92)	76.0 (2.00)	73.6 (2.47)	96.9 (0.73)
Bachelor's degree	57.6 (1.52)	40.0 (1.24)	29.1 (1.37)	15.2 (1.03)	64.6 (1.22)	57.7 (1.74)	40.1 (1.61)	27.6 (1.70)	16.0 (1.32)	71.3 (1.63)	74.2 (1.39)	73.3 (1.10)	96.1 (0.66)	77.3 (1.60)	74.0 (1.48)	97.2 (0.46)
Graduate/professional degree	62.9 (1.53)	43.3 (1.77)	34.7 (1.73)	17.9 (1.33)	65.3 (1.68)	65.2 (2.04)	47.2 (2.53)	31.7 (2.02)	20.7 (1.82)	75.6 (1.55)	71.4 (1.73)	73.3 (1.53)	95.3 (0.79)	78.6 (1.64)	73.9 (1.72)	98.0 (0.46)
Family income																
Less than $5,000	42.7 (4.27)	24.9 (2.73)	16.5 (2.76)	16.6 (2.77)	37.3 (3.55)	38.2 (5.63)	25.7 (4.94)	13.2 (3.10)	18.7 (3.99)	52.9 (4.65)	67.5 (4.39)	55.9 (4.38)	90.9 (2.02)	79.5 (4.52)	78.9 (4.61)	94.3 (1.99)
$5,001 to 10,000	43.8 (2.86)	21.1 (2.34)	17.7 (2.07)	14.5 (1.65)	38.9 (2.62)	42.2 (4.99)	28.5 (4.74)	22.8 (4.79)	23.8 (4.05)	51.6 (4.74)	69.6 (2.30)	58.4 (2.93)	90.0 (1.69)	70.0 (3.88)	75.3 (3.30)	96.3 (1.62)
$10,001 to 15,000	44.8 (2.51)	24.5 (2.32)	18.2 (1.99)	15.3 (2.06)	45.5 (2.83)	49.1 (4.27)	27.3 (3.26)	20.7 (4.22)	20.9 (3.46)	49.1 (4.19)	66.7 (2.62)	61.2 (2.99)	91.9 (1.55)	70.0 (3.62)	74.6 (4.03)	93.8 (1.54)
$15,001 to 20,000	43.0 (3.07)	25.9 (2.37)	13.3 (1.74)	13.7 (1.61)	47.2 (2.78)	44.4 (3.95)	32.9 (3.75)	18.9 (2.83)	17.1 (2.61)	52.1 (4.19)	62.3 (2.29)	64.1 (2.70)	91.4 (1.35)	76.9 (3.45)	76.1 (3.74)	98.0 (0.60)
$20,001 to 25,000	38.9 (2.10)	26.3 (2.05)	18.7 (1.85)	14.7 (1.50)	47.7 (2.53)	48.4 (3.57)	26.0 (3.39)	16.3 (2.22)	16.4 (2.35)	57.8 (3.76)	68.1 (2.34)	63.9 (2.42)	90.5 (1.37)	71.6 (2.86)	80.6 (2.33)	96.0 (1.07)
$25,001 to 30,000	45.3 (2.27)	30.4 (2.35)	20.7 (1.97)	14.4 (1.70)	50.0 (2.30)	51.0 (3.71)	27.1 (3.35)	20.8 (3.12)	15.9 (2.50)	56.7 (3.96)	70.6 (2.32)	68.7 (2.42)	94.6 (0.87)	74.2 (2.86)	71.9 (3.47)	96.6 (1.06)
$30,001 to 35,000	49.2 (2.55)	31.3 (2.66)	21.4 (1.97)	11.9 (1.42)	53.7 (2.48)	44.9 (3.17)	33.2 (3.22)	18.3 (2.72)	17.1 (2.32)	59.7 (3.10)	69.3 (1.85)	66.1 (2.51)	93.2 (1.39)	73.3 (2.88)	78.1 (2.72)	97.9 (0.80)
$35,001 to 40,000	51.9 (2.30)	34.4 (2.60)	23.5 (2.18)	13.2 (1.48)	59.1 (2.45)	45.6 (4.30)	31.4 (3.79)	16.8 (2.99)	11.6 (2.92)	70.7 (3.70)	72.5 (1.94)	71.6 (1.96)	96.2 (0.89)	74.5 (3.68)	75.5 (2.97)	98.3 (0.99)
$40,001 to 50,000	52.1 (2.03)	32.5 (1.71)	22.5 (1.51)	13.1 (1.24)	58.5 (2.01)	52.2 (3.00)	35.8 (2.99)	20.9 (2.41)	14.8 (2.05)	63.1 (2.54)	69.0 (1.82)	72.2 (1.87)	95.7 (0.75)	75.7 (2.20)	71.9 (2.48)	97.0 (0.83)
$50,001 to 75,000	51.5 (1.67)	34.5 (1.47)	23.1 (1.37)	12.2 (0.86)	57.6 (1.72)	50.0 (1.65)	39.0 (1.59)	23.1 (1.42)	14.9 (1.27)	64.5 (1.42)	70.9 (1.43)	72.5 (1.41)	96.3 (0.64)	74.9 (1.53)	75.3 (1.55)	98.1 (0.37)
Over $75,000	55.5 (1.61)	44.5 (1.45)	31.6 (1.75)	15.8 (0.86)	61.9 (1.33)	55.8 (1.69)	42.6 (1.66)	27.3 (1.43)	16.9 (1.31)	67.9 (1.42)	71.4 (1.37)	74.4 (1.31)	95.4 (0.72)	76.8 (1.29)	73.3 (1.32)	97.4 (0.43)
Child attending public schools	47.5 (0.68)	30.4 (0.58)	21.0 (0.70)	13.7 (0.49)	51.2 (0.68)	49.2 (0.87)	34.9 (0.88)	21.2 (0.92)	16.3 (0.71)	60.6 (0.85)	68.8 (0.65)	67.5 (0.66)	93.7 (0.38)	75.0 (0.68)	75.2 (0.72)	97.4 (0.21)
Child attending private schools	56.4 (1.78)	44.3 (1.80)	31.0 (1.55)	17.1 (1.28)	64.8 (1.92)	57.0 (2.31)	40.0 (2.55)	29.0 (2.04)	17.9 (1.85)	72.2 (2.15)	73.7 (1.58)	71.6 (1.64)	94.7 (0.70)	74.2 (2.09)	72.1 (1.94)	95.1 (0.91)

[1] In 1999, one item was used to ask parents if they had attended an event sponsored by a community, ethnic, or religious group. In 2003, attendance at an event sponsored by a religious group was asked about separately from attendance at an event sponsored by a community or ethnic group.

NOTE: The respondent was the parent most knowledgeable about the child's education. The responding parent reported on their own and their spouse's, or other household adults', activities. Excludes homeschooled children. Race categories exclude persons of Hispanic origin. Standard errors appear in parentheses.

SOURCE: U.S. Department of Education, National Center for Education Statistics, Parent Survey (Parent:1999) and Parent and Family Involvement in Education Survey (PFI:2003) of the National Household Education Surveys Program, unpublished tabulations. (This table was prepared June 2005.)

Table 25. Expenditures of educational institutions related to the gross domestic product, by level of institution: Selected years, 1929–30 through 2005–06

Year	Gross domestic product (in billions of current dollars)	School year	Expenditures for education in current dollars					
			All educational institutions		All elementary and secondary schools		All postsecondary degree–granting institutions	
			Amount (in millions)	As a percent of gross domestic product	Amount (in millions)	As a percent of gross domestic product	Amount (in millions)	As a percent of gross domestic product
1	2	3	4	5	6	7	8	9
1929	$103.6	1929–30	—	—	—	—	$632	0.6
1939	92.2	1939–40	—	—	—	—	758	0.8
1949	267.3	1949–50	$8,494	3.2	$6,249	2.3	2,246	0.8
1959	506.6	1959–60	22,314	4.4	16,713	3.3	5,601	1.1
1961	544.7	1961–62	26,828	4.9	19,673	3.6	7,155	1.3
1963	617.7	1963–64	32,003	5.2	22,825	3.7	9,178	1.5
1965	719.1	1965–66	40,558	5.6	28,048	3.9	12,509	1.7
1967	832.6	1967–68	51,558	6.2	35,077	4.2	16,481	2.0
1969	984.6	1969–70	64,227	6.5	43,183	4.4	21,043	2.1
1970	1,038.5	1970–71	71,575	6.9	48,200	4.6	23,375	2.3
1971	1,127.1	1971–72	76,510	6.8	50,950	4.5	25,560	2.3
1972	1,238.3	1972–73	82,908	6.7	54,952	4.4	27,956	2.3
1973	1,382.7	1973–74	91,084	6.6	60,370	4.4	30,714	2.2
1974	1,500.0	1974–75	103,903	6.9	68,846	4.6	35,058	2.3
1975	1,638.3	1975–76	114,004	7.0	75,101	4.6	38,903	2.4
1976	1,825.3	1976–77	121,793	6.7	79,194	4.3	42,600	2.3
1977	2,030.9	1977–78	132,515	6.5	86,544	4.3	45,971	2.3
1978	2,294.7	1978–79	143,733	6.3	93,012	4.1	50,721	2.2
1979	2,563.3	1979–80	160,075	6.2	103,162	4.0	56,914	2.2
1980	2,789.5	1980–81	176,378	6.3	112,325	4.0	64,053	2.3
1981	3,128.4	1981–82	190,825	6.1	120,486	3.9	70,339	2.2
1982	3,255.0	1982–83	204,661	6.3	128,725	4.0	75,936	2.3
1983	3,536.7	1983–84	220,993	6.2	139,000	3.9	81,993	2.3
1984	3,933.2	1984–85	239,351	6.1	149,400	3.8	89,951	2.3
1985	4,220.3	1985–86	259,336	6.1	161,800	3.8	97,536	2.3
1986	4,462.8	1986–87	280,964	6.3	175,200	3.9	105,764	2.4
1987	4,739.5	1987–88	301,786	6.4	187,999	4.0	113,787	2.4
1988	5,103.8	1988–89	333,246	6.5	209,377	4.1	123,868	2.4
1989	5,484.4	1989–90	365,825	6.7	231,170	4.2	134,656	2.5
1990	5,803.1	1990–91	395,318	6.8	249,230	4.3	146,088	2.5
1991	5,995.9	1991–92	417,944	7.0	261,755	4.4	156,189	2.6
1992	6,337.7	1992–93	439,876	6.9	274,635	4.3	165,241	2.6
1993	6,657.4	1993–94	461,157	6.9	287,807	4.3	173,351	2.6
1994	7,072.2	1994–95	485,369	6.9	302,400	4.3	182,969	2.6
1995	7,397.7	1995–96	508,523	6.9	318,046	4.3	190,476	2.6
1996	7,816.9	1996–97	538,854	6.9	338,951	4.3	199,903	2.6
1997	8,304.3	1997–98	570,471	6.9	361,615	4.4	208,856	2.5
1998	8,747.0	1998–99	603,847	6.9	384,638	4.4	219,209	2.5
1999	9,268.4	1999–2000	649,322	7.0	412,538	4.5	236,784	2.6
2000	9,817.0	2000–01	705,017	7.2	444,811	4.5	260,206	2.7
2001	10,128.0	2001–02	752,780	7.4	472,064	4.7	280,715	2.8
2002	10,469.6	2002–03	795,568	7.6	492,807	4.7	302,762	2.9
2003	10,960.8	2003–04	829,913	7.6	513,163	4.7	316,750	2.9
2004	11,712.5	2004–05 [1]	878,300	7.5	536,900	4.6	341,400	2.9
2005	12,455.8	2005–06 [1]	921,800	7.4	558,300	4.5	363,500	2.9

—Not available.
[1]Estimated.
NOTE: Total expenditures for public elementary and secondary schools include current expenditures, interest on school debt, and capital outlay. Data for private elementary and secondary schools are estimated. Expenditures for colleges and universities in 1929–30 and 1939–40 include current-fund expenditures and additions to plant value. Public and private degree-granting institutions data for 1949–50 through 1995–96 are for current-fund expenditures. Data for private degree-granting institutions for 1996–97 and later years are for total expenditures. Data for public degree-granting institutions for 1996–97 through 2000–01 are for current expenditures; data for later years are for total expenditures. Data through 1995–96 are for institutions of higher education, while later data are for degree-granting institutions. Degree-granting institutions grant associate's or higher degrees and participate in Title IV federal financial aid programs. The degree-granting classification is very similar to the earlier higher education classification, but it includes more 2-year colleges and excludes a few higher education institutions that did not grant degrees. (See Guide to Sources for details.) Some data have been revised from previously published figures. Detail may not sum to totals because of rounding.
SOURCE: U.S. Department of Education, National Center for Education Statistics, *Biennial Survey of Education in the United States*, 1919–20 through 1949–50; *Statistics of State School Systems*, 1951–52 through 1969–70; *Revenues and Expenditures for Public Elementary and Secondary Education*, 1970–71 through 1986–87; Common Core of Data (CCD), "National Public Education Financial Survey," 1987–88 through 2003–04; Higher Education General Information Survey (HEGIS), Financial Statistics of Institutions of Higher Education, 1965–66 through 1985–86; 1986–87 through 2003–04 Integrated Postsecondary Education Data System, "Finance Survey" (IPEDS-F:FY87–99), and Spring 2002 through Spring 2005. U.S. Department of Commerce, Bureau of Economic Analysis, unpublished data. (This table was prepared October 2006.)

Table 26. Expenditures of educational institutions, by level and control of institution: Selected years, 1899–1900 through 2005–06
[In millions of dollars]

School year	In current dollars							In constant 2005-06 dollars[1]			
	Total	Elementary and secondary schools			Postsecondary degree-granting institutions			Total	Elementary and secondary schools		Postsecondary degree-granting institutions
		Total	Public	Private[2]	Total	Public	Private		Total	Public	
1	2	3	4	5	6	7	8	9	10	11	12
1899–1900	—	—	$215	—	—	—	—	—	—	—	—
1909–10	—	—	426	—	—	—	—	—	—	—	—
1919–20	—	—	1,036	—	—	—	—	—	—	$10,819	—
1929–30	—	—	2,317	—	$632	$292	$341	—	—	26,934	$7,350
1939–40	—	—	2,344	—	758	392	367	—	—	33,377	10,800
1949–50	$8,494	$6,249	5,838	$411	2,246	1,154	1,092	$71,372	$52,503	49,050	18,869
1951–52	10,332	7,861	7,344	517	2,471	1,305	1,166	78,227	59,518	55,604	18,708
1953–54	12,616	9,733	9,092	641	2,883	1,579	1,304	93,357	72,024	67,281	21,332
1955–56	15,227	11,727	10,955	772	3,499	1,936	1,563	112,709	86,805	81,091	25,904
1957–58	19,035	14,525	13,569	956	4,510	2,535	1,975	132,635	101,211	94,550	31,423
1959–60	22,314	16,713	15,613	1,100	5,601	3,131	2,470	151,118	113,188	105,738	37,930
1961–62	26,828	19,673	18,373	1,300	7,155	3,937	3,218	177,608	130,243	121,636	47,365
1963–64	32,003	22,825	21,325	1,500	9,178	5,073	4,104	206,481	147,266	137,588	59,214
1965–66	40,558	28,048	26,248	1,800	12,509	7,063	5,446	252,934	174,920	163,694	78,015
1967–68	51,558	35,077	32,977	2,100	16,481	10,032	6,449	301,683	205,248	192,960	96,435
1969–70	64,227	43,183	40,683	2,500	21,043	13,250	7,794	338,334	227,483	214,313	110,851
1970–71	71,575	48,200	45,500	2,700	23,375	14,996	8,379	358,537	241,445	227,920	117,092
1971–72	76,510	50,950	48,050	2,900	25,560	16,484	9,075	369,984	246,384	232,360	123,600
1972–73	82,908	54,952	51,852	3,100	27,956	18,204	9,752	385,395	255,444	241,034	129,951
1973–74	91,084	60,370	56,970	3,400	30,714	20,336	10,377	388,739	257,656	243,145	131,083
1974–75	103,903	68,846	64,846	4,000	35,058	23,490	11,568	399,211	264,515	249,147	134,696
1975–76	114,004	75,101	70,601	4,500	38,903	26,184	12,719	409,063	269,473	253,326	139,591
1976–77	121,793	79,194	74,194	5,000	42,600	28,635	13,965	412,934	268,502	251,549	144,432
1977–78	132,515	86,544	80,844	5,700	45,971	30,725	15,246	421,015	274,961	256,852	146,054
1978–79	143,733	93,012	86,712	6,300	50,721	33,733	16,988	417,542	270,198	251,897	147,344
1979–80	160,075	103,162	95,962	7,200	56,914	37,768	19,146	410,311	264,428	245,972	145,883
1980–81	176,378	112,325	104,125	8,200	64,053	42,280	21,773	405,169	258,029	239,192	147,140
1981–82	190,825	120,486	111,186	9,300	70,339	46,219	24,120	403,502	254,768	235,104	148,733
1982–83	204,661	128,725	118,425	10,300	75,936	49,573	26,363	414,935	260,981	240,098	153,954
1983–84	220,993	139,000	127,500	11,500	81,993	53,087	28,907	432,056	271,754	249,270	160,302
1984–85	239,351	149,400	137,000	12,400	89,951	58,315	31,637	450,320	281,084	257,754	169,236
1985–86	259,336	161,800	148,600	13,200	97,536	63,194	34,342	474,243	295,881	271,743	178,362
1986–87	280,964	175,200	160,900	14,300	105,764	67,654	38,110	502,634	313,427	287,845	189,207
1987–88	301,786	187,999	172,699	15,300	113,787	72,641	41,145	518,405	322,942	296,660	195,463
1988–89	333,246	209,377	192,977	16,400	123,868	78,946	44,922	547,175	343,789	316,861	203,386
1989–90	365,825	231,170	212,770	18,400	134,656	85,771	48,885	573,312	362,283	333,447	211,029
1990–91	395,318	249,230	229,430	19,800	146,088	92,961	53,127	587,416	370,339	340,918	217,077
1991–92	417,944	261,755	241,055	20,700	156,189	98,847	57,342	601,756	376,875	347,071	224,881
1992–93	439,876	274,635	252,935	21,700	165,241	104,570	60,671	614,150	383,443	353,145	230,708
1993–94	461,157	287,807	265,307	22,500	173,351	109,310	64,041	627,606	391,686	361,065	235,919
1994–95	485,369	302,400	279,000	23,400	182,969	115,465	67,504	642,150	400,080	369,122	242,070
1995–96	508,523	318,046	293,646	24,400	190,476	119,525	70,952	654,964	409,636	378,209	245,328
1996–97	538,854	338,951	313,151	25,800	199,903	125,978	73,925 [2]	674,778	424,450	392,142	250,328
1997–98	570,471	361,615	334,315	27,300	208,856	132,846	76,010 [2]	701,853	444,897	411,309	256,957
1998–99	603,847	384,638	355,838	28,800	219,209	140,539	78,670	730,273	465,169	430,339	265,104
1999–2000	649,322	412,538	381,838	30,700	236,784	152,325	84,459	763,237	484,912	448,827	278,325
2000–01	705,017	444,811	410,811	34,000	260,206	170,345	89,861	801,251	505,528	466,887	295,724
2001–02	752,780	472,064	435,364	36,700	280,715	183,436	97,280	840,650	527,168	486,184	313,483
2002–03	795,568	492,807	454,907	37,900	302,762	196,891	105,871	869,329	538,497	497,083	330,832
2003–04	829,913	513,163	473,863	39,300	316,750	205,069	111,682	887,443	548,735	506,711	338,707

See notes at end of table.

Table 26. Expenditures of educational institutions, by level and control of institution: Selected years, 1899–1900 through 2005–06—Continued

[In millions of dollars]

	In current dollars							In constant 2005-06 dollars[1]			
		Elementary and secondary schools			Postsecondary degree-granting institutions				Elementary and secondary schools		Postsecond-ary degree-granting institutions
School year	Total	Total	Public	Private[2]	Total	Public	Private	Total	Total	Public	
1	2	3	4	5	6	7	8	9	10	11	12
2004–05[2]	878,300	536,900	495,800	41,100	341,400	218,300	123,100	911,747	557,346	514,681	354,401
2005–06[2]	921,800	558,300	515,600	42,700	363,500	229,900	133,600	921,800	558,300	515,600	363,500

—Not available.

[1]Constant dollars based on the Consumer Price Index, prepared by the Bureau of Labor Statistics, U.S. Department of Labor, adjusted to a school-year basis.

[2]Estimated.

NOTE: Total expenditures for public elementary and secondary schools include current expenditures, interest on school debt, and capital outlay. Expenditures for colleges and universities in 1929–30 and 1939–40 include current-fund expenditures and additions to plant value. Public and private degree-granting institutions data for 1949–50 through 1995–96 are for current-fund expenditures. Data for private degree-granting institutions for 1996–97 and later years are for total expenditures. Data for public degree-granting institutions for 1996–97 through 2000–01 are for current expenditures; data for later years are for total expenditures. Data through 1995–96 are for institutions of higher education, while later data are for degree-granting institutions. Degree-granting institutions grant associate's or higher degrees and participate in Title IV federal financial aid programs. The degree-grant-

ing classification is very similar to the earlier higher education classification, but it includes more 2-year colleges and excludes a few higher education institutions that did not grant degrees. (See Guide to Sources for details.) Some data have been revised from previously published figures. Detail may not sum to totals because of rounding.

SOURCE: U.S. Department of Education, National Center for Education Statistics, *Annual Report of the Commissioner of Education,* 1899–1900 and 1909–10; *Biennial Survey of Education in the United States,* 1919–20 through 1949–50; *Statistics of State School Systems,* 1951–52 through 1969–70; *Revenues and Expenditures for Public Elementary and Secondary Education,* 1970–71 through 1986-87; Common Core of Data (CCD), "National Public Education Financial Survey," 1987–88 through 2003–04; Higher Education General Information Survey (HEGIS), Financial Statistics of Institutions of Higher Education, 1965–66 through 1985–86; 1986–87 through 2003–04 Integrated Postsecondary Education Data System, "Finance Survey," (IPEDS-F:FY87–99), and Spring 2002 through Spring 2005, and unpublished tabulations. (This table was prepared October 2006.)

Table 27. Governmental expenditures, by level of government and function: Selected years, 1970–71 through 2003–04

In millions

Expenditure, by function	All governments[1] (federal, state, and local)				State and local governments[2]									
	1970–71	1980–81	1990–91	1994–95	1970–71	1980–81	1990–91	1994–95	1998–99	1999–2000	2000–01	2001–02	2002–03	2003–04
1	2	3	4	5	6	7	8	9	10	11	12	13	14	15
General expenditures	$301,096	$827,877	$1,804,005	$2,059,334	$150,674	$407,449	$908,108	$1,146,188	$1,398,533	$1,502,768	$1,621,757	$1,732,478	$1,817,513	$1,903,194
Selected federal programs	92,927	200,553	422,728	390,029	†	†	†	†	†	†	†	†	†	†
National defense and international relations	80,910	174,564	366,112	327,231	†	†	†	†	†	†	†	†	†	†
Postal service	8,683	20,466	43,102	49,482	†	†	†	†	†	†	†	†	†	†
Space research and technology	3,334	5,523	13,514	13,514	†	†	†	†	†	†	†	†	†	†
Education and libraries	64,042	158,012	334,333	410,827	60,174	147,649	313,744	383,557	490,100	528,767	571,374	602,954	630,246	664,561
Social services and income maintenance	37,312	127,096	297,854	414,169	30,376	92,555	214,919	303,208	338,964	365,226	396,086	433,685	467,625	501,116
Public welfare	20,446	74,643	167,681	250,356	18,226	54,121	130,402	193,110	215,190	233,350	257,380	281,176	306,463	335,257
Hospitals and health	14,835	47,378	102,817	132,463	11,205	36,101	81,110	105,946	119,361	127,342	134,010	147,065	154,878	159,676
Social insurance administration	2,031	5,075	8,193	9,591	945	2,276	3,250	3,946	4,130	4,178	4,359	5,082	5,267	4,679
Veterans' services	†	†	19,163	21,759	†	57	157	206	283	357	337	361	1,017	1,504
Transportation	23,722	46,578	84,048	99,064	19,819	39,231	75,410	88,938	110,163	118,974	130,422	136,824	142,255	141,959
Public safety	7,685	24,657	88,043	111,785	9,416	31,233	79,932	101,157	128,743	137,809	146,544	156,702	162,279	166,056
Police and fire protection	5,706	16,851	52,738	65,627	7,531	21,283	46,568	58,064	74,629	79,900	84,554	90,456	95,215	98,037
Correction	1,979	7,806	29,297	38,922	1,885	7,393	27,356	35,857	45,598	48,805	52,370	54,615	55,471	56,521
Protective inspection and regulation	†	†	6,008	7,236	†	2,557	6,008	7,236	8,516	9,104	9,620	11,631	11,593	11,498
Environment and housing	22,294	72,391	139,027	150,426	11,832	35,223	76,167	93,221	109,930	117,123	124,203	134,033	141,571	146,895
Natural resources, parks, and recreation	13,740	43,599	74,667	75,133	5,191	13,239	28,505	33,140	41,649	45,272	50,082	52,101	54,573	53,766
Housing and community development	4,467	13,894	33,346	36,721	2,554	7,086	16,648	21,509	25,234	26,590	27,402	31,623	35,275	37,221
Sewerage and sanitation	4,087	14,898	31,014	38,573	4,087	14,898	31,014	38,573	43,047	45,261	46,718	50,309	51,723	55,908
Governmental administration	7,179	22,458	64,181	79,434	6,703	20,001	48,461	60,018	76,699	81,659	85,910	92,779	98,658	100,741
Financial administration	3,612	10,944	27,204	34,824	2,271	7,230	16,995	22,380	27,593	29,300	30,007	32,660	34,911	36,163
General control[3]	3,567	11,514	36,977	44,610	4,432	12,771	31,466	37,638	49,106	52,360	55,903	60,119	63,747	64,579
Interest on general debt	21,688	97,641	247,376	290,195	5,089	17,131	52,234	56,970	67,294	69,814	73,836	75,287	77,277	81,723
Other and unallocable	24,247	78,491	126,416	113,405	7,265	24,426	47,242	59,119	76,640	83,395	93,382	100,215	97,602	100,143

Percentage distribution

Expenditure, by function	All governments[1] (federal, state, and local)				State and local governments[2]									
	1970–71	1980–81	1990–91	1994–95	1970–71	1980–81	1990–91	1994–95	1998–99	1999–2000	2000–01	2001–02	2002–03	2003–04
General expenditures	100.0	100.0	100.0	100.0	100.0	100.0	100.0	100.0	100.0	100.0	100.0	100.0	100.0	100.0
Selected federal programs	30.9	24.2	23.4	18.9	†	†	†	†	†	†	†	†	†	†
National defense and international relations	26.9	21.1	20.3	15.9	†	†	†	†	†	†	†	†	†	†
Postal service	2.9	2.5	2.4	2.4	†	†	†	†	†	†	†	†	†	†
Space research and technology	1.1	0.7	0.7	0.6	†	†	†	†	†	†	†	†	†	†
Education and libraries	21.3	19.1	18.5	19.9	39.9	36.2	34.5	33.5	35.0	35.2	35.2	34.8	34.7	34.9
Social services and income maintenance	12.4	15.4	16.5	20.1	20.2	22.7	23.7	26.5	24.2	24.3	24.4	25.0	25.7	26.3
Public welfare	6.8	9.0	9.3	12.2	12.1	13.3	14.4	16.8	15.4	15.5	15.9	16.2	16.9	17.6
Hospitals and health	4.9	5.7	5.7	6.4	7.4	8.9	8.9	9.2	8.5	8.5	8.3	8.5	8.5	8.4
Social insurance administration	0.7	0.6	0.5	0.5	0.6	0.6	0.4	0.3	0.3	0.3	0.3	0.3	0.3	0.2
Veterans' services	†	†	1.1	1.1	†	#	#	#	#	#	#	#	0.1	0.1
Transportation	7.9	5.6	4.7	4.8	13.2	9.6	8.3	7.8	7.9	7.9	8.0	7.9	7.8	7.5
Public safety	2.6	3.0	4.9	5.4	6.2	7.7	8.8	8.8	9.2	9.2	9.0	9.0	8.9	8.7
Police and fire protection	1.9	2.0	2.9	3.2	5.0	5.2	5.1	5.1	5.3	5.3	5.2	5.2	5.2	5.2
Correction	0.7	0.9	1.6	1.9	1.3	1.8	3.0	3.1	3.3	3.2	3.2	3.2	3.1	3.0
Protective inspection and regulation	†	†	0.3	0.4	†	0.6	0.7	0.6	0.6	0.6	0.6	0.7	0.6	0.6
Environment and housing	7.4	8.7	7.7	7.3	7.9	8.6	8.4	8.1	7.9	7.8	7.7	7.7	7.8	7.7
Natural resources, parks, and recreation	4.6	5.3	4.1	3.6	3.4	3.2	3.1	2.9	3.0	3.0	3.1	3.0	3.0	2.8
Housing and community development	1.5	1.7	1.8	1.8	1.7	1.7	1.8	1.9	1.8	1.8	1.7	1.8	1.9	2.0
Sewerage and sanitation	1.4	1.8	1.7	1.9	2.7	3.7	3.4	3.4	3.1	3.0	2.9	2.9	2.8	2.9
Governmental administration	2.4	2.7	3.6	3.9	4.4	4.9	5.3	5.2	5.5	5.4	5.3	5.4	5.4	5.3
Financial administration	1.2	1.3	1.5	1.7	1.5	1.8	1.9	2.0	2.0	1.9	1.9	1.9	1.9	1.9
General control[3]	1.2	1.4	2.0	2.2	2.9	3.1	3.5	3.3	3.5	3.5	3.4	3.5	3.5	3.4
Interest on general debt	7.2	11.8	13.7	14.1	3.4	4.2	5.8	5.0	4.8	4.6	4.6	4.3	4.3	4.3
Other and unallocable	8.1	9.5	7.0	5.5	4.8	6.0	5.2	5.2	5.5	5.5	5.8	5.8	5.4	5.3

†Not applicable.

#Rounds to zero.

[1]Excludes duplicative intergovernmental transactions.

[2]Excludes monies paid by states to the federal government.

[3]Includes judicial and legal expenditures and expenditures on general and public buildings and other governmental administration.

NOTE: Some data have been revised from previously published figures. Detail may not sum to totals because of rounding.

SOURCE: U.S. Department of Commerce, Census Bureau, Governmental Finances. Retrieved on July 13, 2006, from http://www.census.gov/govs/www/estimate04.html. (This table was prepared July 2006.)

Table 28.   Direct general expenditures of state and local governments for all functions and for education, by level of education and state: 2003–04

[In millions]

State	Total direct general expenditures[1]		Education expenditures							
			Total		Elementary and secondary education				Colleges and universities				Other education[2]
					Total		Current expenditure	Capital outlay			Total		Current expenditure	Capital outlay	
1	2		3		4		5	6			7		8	9	10
United States	$1,903,194	(1,522.6)	$655,361	(131.1)	$452,055	(135.6)	$399,078	$52,977	$173,086	(17.3)	$151,964	$21,121	$30,220
Alabama	27,089	(86.7)	9,437	(37.7)	5,416	(37.9)	4,890	526	3,375	(#)	2,835	540	646
Alaska	8,496	(16.1)	2,299	(22.8)	1,620	(22.7)	1,369	250	581	(#)	463	118	98
Arizona	30,075	(39.1)	10,074	(#)	6,530	(0.7)	5,700	830	3,128	(#)	2,713	415	416
Arkansas	14,577	(115.2)	5,429	(#)	3,418	(#)	3,055	363	1,664	(#)	1,447	216	347
California	260,960	(1,043.8)	84,395	(8.4)	58,948	(11.8)	49,693	9,255	22,054	(#)	19,061	2,992	3,393
Colorado	28,424	(145.0)	9,702	(#)	6,541	(#)	5,682	859	2,878	(#)	2,606	271	284
Connecticut	25,018	(35.0)	8,753	(21.9)	6,587	(21.7)	6,008	579	1,836	(#)	1,583	253	330
Delaware	6,191	(12.4)	2,191	(#)	1,349	(#)	1,190	158	695	(#)	643	52	147
District of Columbia	6,723	(#)	1,369	(#)	1,267	(#)	1,146	122	102	(#)	92	9	#
Florida	100,771	(423.2)	29,396	(#)	21,392	(#)	18,027	3,366	6,757	(#)	5,845	912	1,247
Georgia	50,211	(120.5)	19,239	(#)	13,481	(#)	11,713	1,768	4,479	(#)	3,672	807	1,279
Hawaii	8,673	(0.9)	2,488	(#)	1,675	(#)	1,597	78	770	(#)	768	2	42
Idaho	7,540	(26.4)	2,636	(#)	1,705	(#)	1,522	183	826	(#)	685	141	105
Illinois	79,495	(270.3)	28,621	(#)	19,417	(#)	17,074	2,343	7,655	(#)	6,978	677	1,549
Indiana	35,540	(145.7)	13,616	(32.7)	8,912	(32.1)	7,937	975	3,992	(#)	3,622	370	712
Iowa	18,396	(47.8)	7,020	(#)	4,226	(#)	3,693	533	2,467	(#)	2,197	271	326
Kansas	16,284	(87.9)	6,205	(0.6)	3,695	(0.7)	3,408	287	2,213	(#)	1,956	256	297
Kentucky	23,342	(39.7)	7,748	(#)	4,561	(#)	4,062	499	2,520	(#)	2,232	289	666
Louisiana	27,251	(60.0)	8,616	(#)	5,635	(#)	5,262	373	2,291	(#)	2,102	189	690
Maine	9,282	(37.1)	2,863	(33.8)	2,076	(33.8)	1,851	226	657	(#)	576	80	130
Maryland	34,111	(58.0)	12,519	(#)	8,193	(#)	7,574	619	3,684	(#)	3,315	369	642
Massachusetts	48,446	(72.7)	14,654	(29.3)	10,341	(29.0)	9,784	557	2,707	(#)	2,416	291	1,606
Michigan	67,643	(162.3)	26,974	(#)	18,456	(#)	16,249	2,207	7,939	(#)	6,794	1,145	579
Minnesota	36,637	(249.1)	11,951	(#)	8,259	(#)	7,221	1,038	3,010	(#)	2,740	269	682
Mississippi	17,282	(103.7)	5,611	(#)	3,407	(#)	3,084	323	1,912	(#)	1,729	182	293
Missouri	31,020	(161.3)	10,836	(#)	7,608	(#)	6,869	739	2,724	(#)	2,449	275	504
Montana	5,547	(12.8)	1,935	(#)	1,222	(#)	1,158	64	593	(#)	536	57	120
Nebraska	10,776	(107.8)	4,041	(#)	2,591	(#)	2,295	296	1,307	(#)	1,190	117	143
Nevada	13,619	(100.8)	4,157	(#)	3,059	(#)	2,484	575	995	(#)	845	150	103
New Hampshire	7,549	(12.8)	2,753	(#)	2,059	(#)	1,860	199	613	(#)	554	59	82
New Jersey	61,224	(214.3)	24,712	(14.8)	19,685	(15.7)	17,711	1,974	4,389	(#)	3,766	623	637
New Mexico	12,616	(32.8)	4,657	(#)	2,838	(#)	2,394	444	1,572	(#)	1,449	124	246
New York	175,803	(632.9)	51,655	(10.3)	40,989	(4.1)	37,120	3,869	8,847	(8.8)	7,868	979	1,819
North Carolina	48,490	(116.4)	17,240	(25.9)	10,043	(25.1)	9,104	939	6,745	(6.1)	5,885	860	453
North Dakota	4,157	(11.2)	1,525	(#)	891	(#)	794	97	570	(#)	537	33	65
Ohio	74,445	(230.8)	26,472	(#)	18,742	(#)	16,603	2,140	6,331	(#)	5,539	792	1,398
Oklahoma	18,148	(56.3)	6,921	(#)	4,316	(#)	3,996	320	2,283	(#)	2,079	204	321
Oregon	22,309	(73.6)	7,553	(#)	4,711	(#)	4,225	487	2,622	(#)	2,261	360	220
Pennsylvania	80,339	(241.0)	28,703	(#)	19,811	(#)	17,846	1,965	6,341	(#)	5,750	591	2,550
Rhode Island	7,643	(10.7)	2,441	(4.4)	1,805	(4.3)	1,766	39	494	(#)	461	33	142
South Carolina	25,591	(40.9)	8,999	(#)	5,963	(#)	5,116	847	2,313	(#)	2,076	237	723
South Dakota	4,132	(6.2)	1,422	(#)	964	(#)	862	102	391	(#)	346	45	67
Tennessee	31,581	(173.7)	9,756	(65.4)	6,678	(65.4)	6,080	598	2,675	(#)	2,430	244	403
Texas	124,057	(235.7)	49,707	(5.0)	34,631	(6.9)	29,812	4,819	13,973	(#)	11,881	2,091	1,104
Utah	13,906	(34.8)	5,434	(#)	2,996	(#)	2,517	479	2,231	(#)	2,037	194	207
Vermont	4,398	(8.4)	1,761	(#)	1,155	(#)	1,077	77	519	(#)	465	54	88
Virginia	42,955	(163.2)	16,107	(103.1)	11,192	(103.0)	9,942	1,250	4,311	(#)	3,700	611	604
Washington	42,579	(102.2)	14,228	(#)	8,921	(#)	7,435	1,486	4,384	(#)	3,766	618	924
West Virginia	10,604	(17.0)	3,738	(#)	2,408	(#)	2,227	182	1,029	(#)	903	126	301
Wisconsin	36,714	(135.8)	13,366	(#)	8,722	(0.9)	8,175	547	4,222	(#)	3,734	489	422
Wyoming	4,535	(17.2)	1,437	(#)	946	(#)	819	127	422	(#)	386	36	69

#Rounds to zero.
[1]Includes state and local government expenditures for education services, social services and income maintenance, transportation, public safety, environment and housing, governmental administration, interest on general debt, and other general expenditures.
[2]Includes assistance and subsidies to individuals, private elementary and secondary schools, and colleges and universities, as well as miscellaneous education expenditures.

NOTE: Current expenditure data in this table differ from figures appearing in other tables because of slightly varying definitions used in the Governmental Finances and Common Core of Data surveys. Detail may not sum to totals because of rounding. Standard errors appear in parentheses.
SOURCE: U.S. Department of Commerce, Census Bureau, Governmental Finances. Retrieved on July 13, 2006, from http://www.census.gov/govs/www/estimate04.html. (This table was prepared July 2006.)

Table 29. Direct general expenditures per capita of state and local governments for all functions and for education, by level of education and state: 2003–04

State	Total, all direct general expenditures per capita[1]	Education expenditures							
		Total		Elementary and secondary education		Colleges and universities		Other education[2]	
		Amount per capita	As a percent of all functions	Amount per capita	As a percent of all functions	Amount per capita	As a percent of all functions	Amount per capita	As a percent of all functions
1	2	3	4	5	6	7	8	9	10
United States	$6,481	$2,232	34.4	$1,539	23.8	$589	9.1	$103	1.6
Alabama	5,987	2,086	34.8	1,197	20.0	746	12.5	143	2.4
Alaska	12,912	3,494	27.1	2,461	19.1	884	6.8	149	1.2
Arizona	5,240	1,755	33.5	1,138	21.7	545	10.4	73	1.4
Arkansas	5,301	1,974	37.2	1,243	23.4	605	11.4	126	2.4
California	7,281	2,355	32.3	1,645	22.6	615	8.5	95	1.3
Colorado	6,176	2,108	34.1	1,421	23.0	625	10.1	62	1.0
Connecticut	7,150	2,502	35.0	1,883	26.3	525	7.3	94	1.3
Delaware	7,459	2,640	35.4	1,625	21.8	837	11.2	178	2.4
District of Columbia	12,135	2,471	20.4	2,288	18.9	183	1.5	—	—
Florida	5,796	1,691	29.2	1,230	21.2	389	6.7	72	1.2
Georgia	5,630	2,157	38.3	1,512	26.8	502	8.9	143	2.5
Hawaii	6,872	1,971	28.7	1,327	19.3	610	8.9	33	0.5
Idaho	5,405	1,890	35.0	1,223	22.6	592	11.0	75	1.4
Illinois	6,254	2,251	36.0	1,527	24.4	602	9.6	122	1.9
Indiana	5,707	2,187	38.3	1,431	25.1	641	11.2	114	2.0
Iowa	6,230	2,377	38.2	1,431	23.0	836	13.4	110	1.8
Kansas	5,956	2,269	38.1	1,351	22.7	809	13.6	109	1.8
Kentucky	5,636	1,871	33.2	1,101	19.5	608	10.8	161	2.9
Louisiana	6,046	1,912	31.6	1,250	20.7	508	8.4	153	2.5
Maine	7,058	2,177	30.8	1,579	22.4	499	7.1	99	1.4
Maryland	6,134	2,251	36.7	1,473	24.0	663	10.8	115	1.9
Massachusetts	7,561	2,287	30.2	1,614	21.3	423	5.6	251	3.3
Michigan	6,695	2,670	39.9	1,827	27.3	786	11.7	57	0.9
Minnesota	7,188	2,345	32.6	1,620	22.5	590	8.2	134	1.9
Mississippi	5,957	1,934	32.5	1,174	19.7	659	11.1	101	1.7
Missouri	5,385	1,881	34.9	1,321	24.5	473	8.8	87	1.6
Montana	5,983	2,087	34.9	1,318	22.0	639	10.7	130	2.2
Nebraska	6,165	2,312	37.5	1,482	24.0	747	12.1	82	1.3
Nevada	5,838	1,782	30.5	1,311	22.5	427	7.3	44	0.8
New Hampshire	5,811	2,120	36.5	1,585	27.3	472	8.1	63	1.1
New Jersey	7,049	2,845	40.4	2,267	32.2	505	7.2	73	1.0
New Mexico	6,630	2,447	36.9	1,492	22.5	826	12.5	129	1.9
New York	9,118	2,679	29.4	2,126	23.3	459	5.0	94	1.0
North Carolina	5,678	2,019	35.6	1,176	20.7	790	13.9	53	0.9
North Dakota	6,537	2,398	36.7	1,401	21.4	896	13.7	102	1.6
Ohio	6,502	2,312	35.6	1,637	25.2	553	8.5	122	1.9
Oklahoma	5,150	1,964	38.1	1,225	23.8	648	12.6	91	1.8
Oregon	6,213	2,103	33.9	1,312	21.1	730	11.8	61	1.0
Pennsylvania	6,482	2,316	35.7	1,598	24.7	512	7.9	206	3.2
Rhode Island	7,077	2,260	31.9	1,671	23.6	457	6.5	132	1.9
South Carolina	6,096	2,144	35.2	1,420	23.3	551	9.0	172	2.8
South Dakota	5,360	1,844	34.4	1,251	23.3	507	9.5	87	1.6
Tennessee	5,359	1,656	30.9	1,133	21.1	454	8.5	68	1.3
Texas	5,521	2,212	40.1	1,541	27.9	622	11.3	49	0.9
Utah	5,744	2,245	39.1	1,238	21.5	921	16.0	86	1.5
Vermont	7,082	2,836	40.0	1,859	26.3	835	11.8	141	2.0
Virginia	5,742	2,153	37.5	1,496	26.1	576	10.0	81	1.4
Washington	6,860	2,292	33.4	1,437	21.0	706	10.3	149	2.2
West Virginia	5,849	2,062	35.2	1,328	22.7	567	9.7	166	2.8
Wisconsin	6,670	2,428	36.4	1,585	23.8	767	11.5	77	1.1
Wyoming	8,961	2,840	31.7	1,870	20.9	835	9.3	136	1.5

—Not available.
[1]Includes state and local government expenditures for education services, social services and income maintenance, transportation, public safety, environment and housing, governmental administration, interest on general debt, and other general expenditures.
[2]Includes assistance and subsidies to individuals, private elementary and secondary schools, and colleges and universities, as well as miscellaneous education expenditures.

NOTE: Per capita amounts are based on population figures as of July 2003. Detail may not sum to totals because of rounding.
SOURCE: U.S. Department of Commerce, Census Bureau, Governmental Finances. Retrieved on July 13, 2006, from http://www.census.gov/govs/www/estimate04.html. (This table was prepared July 2006.)

Table 30. Gross domestic product, state and local expenditures, personal income, disposable personal income, median family income, and population: Selected years, 1929 through 2005

Year	Gross domestic product (in billions)		State and local direct general expenditures (in millions)[1]		Personal income (in billions)	Disposable personal income (in billions of chained 2000 dollars)[2]	Disposable personal income per capita		Median family income	Population (in thousands)	
	Current dollars	Chained 2000 dollars[2]	All general expenditures	Education expenditures			Current dollars	Chained 2000 dollars[2]		Midyear data[3]	Resident as of July 1[4]
1	2	3	4	5	6	7	8	9	10	11	12
1929	$103.6	$865.2	—	—	$85.1	$712.7	$684	$5,848	—	121,878	121,767
1939	92.2	950.7	—	—	72.9	774.9	545	5,914	—	131,028	130,880
1940	101.4	1,034.1	$9,229	$2,638	78.5	826.5	581	6,255	—	132,122	132,122
1950	293.8	1,777.3	22,787	7,177	229.0	1,260.0	1,385	8,306	3,319	151,684	152,271
1960	526.4	2,501.8	51,876	18,719	411.5	1,759.7	2,022	9,735	5,620	180,760	180,671
1961	544.7	2,560.0	56,201	20,574	429.0	1,819.2	2,078	9,901	5,735	183,742	183,691
1962	585.6	2,715.2	60,206	22,216	456.7	1,908.2	2,171	10,227	5,956	186,590	186,538
1963	617.7	2,834.0	63,977	23,729	479.6	1,979.1	2,246	10,455	6,249	189,300	189,242
1964	663.6	2,998.6	69,302	26,286	514.6	2,122.8	2,410	11,061	6,569	191,927	191,889
1965	719.1	3,191.1	74,678	28,563	555.7	2,253.3	2,563	11,594	6,957	194,347	194,303
1966	787.8	3,399.1	82,843	33,287	603.9	2,371.9	2,734	12,065	7,532	196,599	196,560
1967	832.6	3,484.6	93,350	37,919	648.3	2,475.9	2,895	12,457	7,933	198,752	198,712
1968	910.0	3,652.7	102,411	41,158	712.0	2,588.0	3,114	12,892	8,632	200,745	200,706
1969	984.6	3,765.4	116,728	47,238	778.5	2,668.7	3,324	13,163	9,433	202,736	202,677
1970	1,038.5	3,771.9	131,332	52,718	838.8	2,781.7	3,587	13,563	9,867	205,089	205,052
1971	1,127.1	3,898.6	150,674	59,413	903.5	2,907.9	3,860	14,001	10,285	207,692	207,661
1972	1,238.3	4,105.0	168,550	65,814	992.7	3,046.5	4,140	14,512	11,116	209,924	209,896
1973	1,382.7	4,341.5	181,357	69,714	1,110.7	3,252.3	4,616	15,345	12,051	211,939	211,909
1974	1,500.0	4,319.6	198,959	75,833	1,222.6	3,228.5	5,010	15,094	12,902	213,898	213,854
1975	1,638.3	4,311.2	230,721	87,858	1,335.0	3,302.6	5,498	15,291	13,719	215,981	215,973
1976	1,825.3	4,540.9	256,731	97,216	1,474.8	3,432.2	5,972	15,738	14,958	218,086	218,035
1977	2,030.9	4,750.5	274,215	102,780	1,633.2	3,552.9	6,517	16,128	16,009	220,289	220,239
1978	2,294.7	5,015.0	296,984	110,758	1,837.7	3,718.8	7,224	16,704	17,640	222,629	222,585
1979	2,563.3	5,173.4	327,517	119,448	2,062.2	3,811.2	7,967	16,931	19,587	225,106	225,055
1980	2,789.5	5,161.7	369,086	133,211	2,307.9	3,857.7	8,822	16,940	21,023	227,726	227,225
1981	3,128.4	5,291.7	407,449	145,784	2,591.3	3,960.0	9,765	17,217	22,388	230,008	229,466
1982	3,255.0	5,189.3	436,733	154,282	2,775.3	4,044.9	10,426	17,418	23,433	232,218	231,664
1983	3,536.7	5,423.8	466,516	163,876	2,960.7	4,177.7	11,131	17,828	24,674	234,333	233,792
1984	3,933.2	5,813.6	505,008	176,108	3,289.5	4,494.1	12,319	19,011	26,433	236,394	235,825
1985	4,220.3	6,053.7	553,899	192,686	3,526.7	4,645.2	13,037	19,476	27,735	238,506	237,924
1986	4,462.8	6,263.6	605,623	210,819	3,722.4	4,791.0	13,649	19,906	29,458	240,683	240,133
1987	4,739.5	6,475.1	657,134	226,619	3,947.4	4,874.5	14,241	20,072	30,970	242,843	242,289
1988	5,103.8	6,742.7	704,921	242,683	4,253.7	5,082.6	15,297	20,740	32,191	245,061	244,499
1989	5,484.4	6,981.4	762,360	263,898	4,587.8	5,224.8	16,257	21,120	34,213	247,387	246,819
1990	5,803.1	7,112.5	834,818	288,148	4,878.6	5,324.2	17,131	21,281	35,353	250,181	249,623
1991	5,995.9	7,100.5	908,108	309,302	5,051.0	5,351.7	17,609	21,109	35,939	253,530	252,981
1992	6,337.7	7,336.6	981,253	324,652	5,362.0	5,536.3	18,494	21,548	36,573	256,922	256,514
1993	6,657.4	7,532.7	1,033,167	342,287	5,558.5	5,594.2	18,872	21,493	36,959	260,282	259,919
1994	7,072.2	7,835.5	1,077,665	353,287	5,842.5	5,746.4	19,555	21,812	38,782	263,455	263,126
1995	7,397.7	8,031.7	1,146,188	378,273	6,152.3	5,905.7	20,287	22,153	40,611	266,588	266,278
1996	7,816.9	8,328.9	1,189,356	398,859	6,520.6	6,080.9	21,091	22,546	42,300	269,714	269,394
1997	8,304.3	8,703.5	1,247,436	419,053	6,915.1	6,295.8	21,940	23,065	44,568	272,958	272,647
1998	8,747.0	9,066.9	1,314,496	450,365	7,423.0	6,663.9	23,161	24,131	46,737	276,154	275,854
1999	9,268.4	9,470.3	1,398,533	483,259	7,802.4	6,861.3	23,968	24,564	48,950	279,328	279,040
2000	9,817.0	9,817.0	1,502,768	521,612	8,429.7	7,194.0	25,472	25,472	50,732	282,429	282,193

See notes at end of table.

Table 30. Gross domestic product, state and local expenditures, personal income, disposable personal income, median family income, and population: Selected years, 1929 through 2005—Continued

Year	Gross domestic product (in billions)		State and local direct general expenditures (in millions)[1]		Personal income (in billions)	Disposable personal income (in billions of chained 2000 dollars)[2]	Disposable personal income per capita		Median family income	Population (in thousands)	
	Current dollars	Chained 2000 dollars[2]	All general expenditures	Education expenditures			Current dollars	Chained 2000 dollars[2]		Midyear data[3]	Resident as of July 1[4]
1	2	3	4	5	6	7	8	9	10	11	12
2001	10,128.0	9,890.7	1,621,757	563,572	8,724.1	7,333.3	26,235	25,697	51,407	285,371	285,108
2002	10,469.6	10,048.8	1,732,478	594,694	8,881.9	7,562.2	27,164	26,235	51,680	288,253	287,985
2003	10,960.8	10,301.0	1,817,513	621,335	9,163.6	7,729.9	28,039	26,553	52,680	291,114	290,850
2004	11,712.5	10,703.5	1,903,194	655,361	9,731.4	8,010.8	29,536	27,254	54,061	293,933	293,657
2005	12,455.8	11,048.6	—	—	10,239.2	8,104.6	30,458	27,318	—	296,677	296,410

—Not available.

[1]Data for years prior to 1963 include expenditures for government fiscal years ending during that particular calendar year. Data for 1963 and later years are the aggregations of expenditures for government fiscal years that ended on June 30 of the stated year. General expenditures exclude expenditures of publicly owned utilities and liquor stores, and of insurance-trust activities. Intergovernmental payments between state and local governments are excluded. Payments to the federal government are included.

[2]Constant dollars based on a chain-price index, which uses the geometric mean of output weights of adjacent time periods compiled over a time series. Chain-price indexes reflect changes in prices, while implicit price deflators reflect both changes in prices and in the composition of output.

[3]Population of the United States including armed forces overseas. Includes Alaska and Hawaii beginning in 1960.

[4]Resident population of the United States. Includes Alaska and Hawaii beginning in 1958. Data for 1990 and later years include revisions based on the 2000 census.

NOTE: Gross domestic product (GDP) data are adjusted by the GDP chained weight price deflator. Personal income data are adjusted by the personal consumption deflator. Some data have been revised from previously published figures.

SOURCE: U.S. Department of Commerce, Census Bureau, Current Population Reports, *Money Income in the United States*, Series P-60, various years, and unpublished data. U.S. Department of Commerce, Bureau of Economic Analysis, National Income and Product Accounts Tables. (This table was prepared September 2006.)

Table 31. Gross domestic product price index, Consumer Price Index, education price indexes, and federal budget composite deflator: Selected years, 1919 to 2005

Calendar year			School year					Federal fiscal year	
Year	Gross domestic product price index	Consumer Price Index[1]	Year	Consumer Price Index[2]	Higher Education Price Index	Research and Development Index	Academic Library Operations Index	Year	Federal budget composite deflator
1	2	3	4	5	6	7	8	9	10
1919	—	17.3	1919–20	19.1	—	—	—	1919	—
1929	11.9	17.1	1929–30	17.1	—	—	—	1929	—
1939	9.7	13.9	1939–40	14.0	—	—	—	1939	—
1949	16.4	23.8	1949–50	23.7	—	—	—	1949	0.1246
1950	16.5	24.1	1950–51	25.1	—	—	—	1950	0.1287
1951	17.6	26.0	1951–52	26.3	—	—	—	1951	0.1279
1952	18.0	26.5	1952–53	26.7	—	—	—	1952	0.1280
1953	18.2	26.7	1953–54	26.9	—	—	—	1953	0.1368
1954	18.4	26.9	1954–55	26.8	—	—	—	1954	0.1409
1955	18.7	26.8	1955–56	26.9	—	—	—	1955	0.1455
1956	19.4	27.2	1956–57	27.7	—	—	—	1956	0.1526
1957	20.0	28.1	1957–58	28.6	—	—	—	1957	0.1601
1958	20.5	28.9	1958–59	29.0	—	—	—	1958	0.1687
1959	20.8	29.1	1959–60	29.4	—	—	—	1959	0.1746
1960	21.0	29.6	1960–61	29.8	25.6	26.7	—	1960	0.1750
1961	21.3	29.9	1961–62	30.1	26.5	27.5	—	1961	0.1795
1962	21.6	30.2	1962–63	30.4	27.6	28.5	—	1962	0.1803
1963	21.8	30.6	1963–64	30.8	28.6	29.5	—	1963	0.1873
1964	22.1	31.0	1964–65	31.2	29.8	30.7	—	1964	0.1900
1965	22.5	31.5	1965–66	31.9	31.3	32.0	—	1965	0.1928
1966	23.2	32.4	1966–67	32.9	32.9	33.8	—	1966	0.1974
1967	23.9	33.4	1967–68	34.0	34.9	35.7	—	1967	0.2026
1968	24.9	34.8	1968–69	35.7	37.1	38.0	—	1968	0.2103
1969	26.2	36.7	1969–70	37.8	39.5	40.3	—	1969	0.2230
1970	27.5	38.8	1970–71	39.7	42.1	42.7	—	1970	0.2363
1971	28.9	40.5	1971–72	41.2	44.3	45.0	—	1971	0.2519
1972	30.2	41.8	1972–73	42.8	46.7	47.1	—	1972	0.2690
1973	31.9	44.4	1973–74	46.6	49.9	50.1	—	1973	0.2833
1974	34.7	49.3	1974–75	51.8	54.3	54.8	—	1974	0.3070
1975	38.0	53.8	1975–76	55.5	57.8	59.0	57.3	1975	0.3384
1976	40.2	56.9	1976–77	58.7	61.5	62.7	61.6	1976	0.3640
1977	42.8	60.6	1977–78	62.6	65.7	66.8	65.8	1977	0.3934
1978	45.8	65.2	1978–79	68.5	70.5	71.7	71.4	1978	0.4195
1979	49.6	72.6	1979–80	77.6	77.5	78.3	78.5	1979	0.4552
1980	54.1	82.4	1980–81	86.6	85.8	86.6	86.1	1980	0.5029
1981	59.1	90.9	1981–82	94.1	93.9	94.0	94.0	1981	0.5562
1982	62.7	96.5	1982–83	98.2	100.0	100.0	100.0	1982	0.5958
1983	65.2	99.6	1983–84	101.8	104.8	104.3	105.1	1983	0.6245
1984	67.7	103.9	1984–85	105.8	110.8	109.8	111.2	1984	0.6555
1985	69.7	107.6	1985–86	108.8	116.3	115.2	117.6	1985	0.6781
1986	71.3	109.6	1986–87	111.2	120.9	120.0	124.2	1986	0.6947
1987	73.2	113.6	1987–88	115.8	126.2	126.8	130.0	1987	0.7143
1988	75.7	118.3	1988–89	121.2	132.8	132.1	138.6	1988	0.7359
1989	78.6	124.0	1989–90	127.0	140.8	139.0	147.4	1989	0.7631
1990	81.6	130.7	1990–91	133.9	148.2	145.8	155.7	1990	0.7882
1991	84.5	136.2	1991–92	138.2	153.5	150.6	163.3	1991	0.8226
1992	86.4	140.3	1992–93	142.5	157.9	155.2	169.8	1992	0.8508
1993	88.4	144.5	1993–94	146.2	163.3	160.1	176.7	1993	0.8725
1994	90.3	148.2	1994–95	150.4	168.1	165.4	183.9	1994	0.8902
1995	92.1	152.4	1995–96	154.5	173.0	170.8	192.6	1995	0.9120
1996	93.9	156.9	1996–97	158.9	178.4	—	—	1996	0.9328
1997	95.4	160.5	1997–98	161.7	184.7	—	—	1997	0.9508
1998	96.5	163.0	1998–99	164.5	189.1	—	—	1998	0.9603
1999	97.9	166.6	1999–2000	169.3	196.9	—	—	1999	0.9748
2000	100.0	172.2	2000–01	175.1	206.5	—	—	2000	1.0000

See notes at end of table.

Table 31. Gross domestic product price index, Consumer Price Index, education price indexes, and federal budget composite deflator: Selected years, 1919 to 2005—Continued

Calendar year			School year					Federal fiscal year	
Year	Gross domestic product price index	Consumer Price Index[1]	Year	Consumer Price Index[2]	Higher Education Price Index	Research and Development Index	Academic Library Operations Index	Year	Federal budget composite deflator
1	2	3	4	5	6	7	8	9	10
2001..........................	102.4	177.1	2001–02.....................	178.2	215.0	—	—	2001	1.0233
2002..........................	104.2	179.9	2002–03.....................	182.1	221.2	—	—	2002	1.0425
2003..........................	106.4	184.0	2003–04.....................	186.1	231.5	—	—	2003	1.0693
2004..........................	109.4	188.9	2004–05.....................	191.7	239.5	—	—	2004	1.0980
2005..........................	112.7	195.3	2005–06.....................	199.0	251.9	—	—	2005	1.1346

—Not available.

[1]Index for urban wage earners and clerical workers through 1977; 1978 and later figures are for all urban consumers.

[2]Consumer Price Index adjusted to a school-year basis (July through June).

NOTE: Some data have been revised from previously published figures.

SOURCE: U.S. Department of Commerce, Bureau of Economic Analysis, unpublished data. U.S. Department of Labor, Bureau of Labor Statistics, Consumer Price Index. U.S. Office of Management and Budget, *Budget of the U.S. Government, Fiscal Year 2007, Historical Tables*. (This table was prepared September 2006.)

CHAPTER 2
Elementary and Secondary Education

This chapter contains a variety of statistics on public and private elementary and secondary education. Data are presented for enrollments, teachers and other school staff, schools, dropouts, achievement, school violence, and revenues and expenditures. These data are derived from surveys conducted by the National Center for Education Statistics (NCES) and other public and private organizations. The information ranges from counts of students and schools to state graduation requirements.

Enrollments

Public elementary and secondary school enrollments increased by 4 percent from 1999 to 2004, but enrollment at the elementary and secondary levels increased at different rates (table 36 and figure 6). Between 1999 and 2004, public elementary enrollment rose by 2 percent, while secondary enrollment increased by 9 percent. Enrollments in private elementary and secondary schools rose by 2 percent between 1999 and 2004 (table 3).

In 2005, about 57 percent of children ages 3 to 5 and not yet enrolled in kindergarten were enrolled in a center-based program (table 43). Some 23 percent of 3- to 5-year-olds who were not yet enrolled in kindergarten received care from relatives and 12 percent received care from nonrelatives. In 2005, 64 percent of 3- to 5-year-olds were enrolled in preprimary education (nursery and kindergarten), the same percentage as in 2000 (table 41 and figure 7). Though participation of young children in preprimary schools did not substantially increase, the proportion of children in full-day programs did. In 2005, about 58 percent of the children enrolled in preprimary education attended preprimary school all day, compared with 53 percent in 2000.

Slowly increasing numbers and proportions of children are being served in programs for those with disabilities. During the 2000–01 school year, 13 percent of students were served in these programs, compared with 14 percent in 2005–06 (table 48). Some of the rise since 2000–01 may be attributed to the increasing proportion of children identified as having other health impairments (limited strength, vitality, or alertness due to chronic or acute health problems such as a heart condition, tuberculosis, rheumatic fever, nephritis, asthma, sickle cell anemia, hemophilia, epilepsy, lead poisoning, leukemia, or diabetes), which rose from 0.6 to 1.2 percent of enrollment; autism, which rose from 0.2 to 0.5

percent of enrollment; and developmental delay, which rose from 0.4 to 0.7 percent of enrollment.

Teachers and Other School Staff

During the 1970s and early 1980s, public school enrollment decreased, while the number of teachers generally increased. As a result, the public school pupil/teacher ratio declined from 22.3 in 1970 to 17.9 in 1985 (table 61 and figure 6).[1] After 1985, the number of pupils per teacher continued to decline, reaching 17.2 in 1989. After a period of relative stability during the late 1980s through the mid-1990s, the ratio declined from 17.3 in 1995 to 16.1 in 1999. Small declines have continued since then, and the public school pupil/teacher ratio was 15.8 in 2004. The estimated pupil/teacher ratio for private schools for 2004 was 13.8.[1] The average class size in 2003–04 was 20.4 pupils for public elementary schools and 24.7 for public secondary schools (table 64).

In 2003–04, 75 percent of public school teachers were women, 41 percent were under 40, and 48 percent had a master's or higher degree (table 65). Compared to public school teachers, a lower proportion of private school teachers (35 percent) had a master's or higher degree. Seventy-six percent of private school teachers were women.

Public school principals tend to be older and have more advanced credentials than public school teachers. In 2003–04, 15 percent of the public school principals were under age 40 and 98 percent of the public school principals had a master's or higher degree (table 82). Principals were less likely than teachers to be women. About 48 percent of public school principals were women, compared to 75 percent of teachers.

The number of nonteaching staff employed by public schools grew during the 1970s, while the number of students declined (tables 77 and 3). Between 1970 and 1980, the proportion of staff who were teachers declined from 60 percent to 52 percent. From 1980 to 2004, the number of teachers and other staff grew at more similar rates (41 and 49 percent, respectively) than in the 1970s. As a result, the proportion of teachers among total staff was 1 percentage point lower in

---

[1] The pupil/teacher ratio includes teachers for students with disabilities and other special teachers, while these teachers are generally excluded from class size calculations. The student count for the pupil/teacher ratio includes all students enrolled in the fall of the school year.

2004 than in 1980, in contrast to the decrease of 8 percentage points during the 1970s. Two staff categories increased staff over 100 percent between 1980 and 2004—instructional aides, which rose 117 percent, and instructional coordinators, which rose 132 percent. Taken together, the proportion of staff with some instructional responsibilities (teachers and instructional aides) increased between 1980 and 2004, from 60 to 63 percent. In 2004, there were 8 pupils per staff member (total staff), compared with 10 pupils per staff member in 1980. In 2003, the number of pupils per staff member at private schools was 7 (table 57).

Schools

During most of the last century, the trend to consolidate small schools brought a large decline in the total number of public schools in the United States. In 1929–30, there were approximately 248,000 public schools, compared with about 97,000 in 2004–05 (table 83). But this number has been increasing in recent years; between 1994–95 and 2004–05, there was an increase of approximately 10,300 schools.

The shift in structure of public school systems toward middle schools (grade spans beginning with 4, 5, or 6 and ending with 6, 7, or 8) since the early 1970s continues (table 90). The number of all elementary schools (beginning in grade 6 or below, with no grade higher than grade 8) rose by 9 percent to 65,984 between 1994–95 and 2004–05, and the subset of middle schools rose by 26 percent during the same time period. Meanwhile, the number of junior high schools (grades 7 and 8 or 7 to 9) declined by 16 percent.

The average number of students in elementary schools was higher in 2004–05 (474) than in 1994–95 (471), but there have been only small fluctuations since 1995–96 (table 92). Secondary schools increased in size fairly consistently between 1994–95 and 2003–04 (with averages of 696 and 722 students, respectively), but then decreased to an average of 713 students in 2004–05. The average size of regular secondary schools, which exclude alternative, special education, and vocational education schools, rose from 759 to 815 students between 1994–95 and 2004–05.

High School Graduates and Dropouts

The projected number of high school graduates in 2006–07 was 3,232,000 (table 99), including 2,912,000 public school graduates and 321,000 private school graduates. The 2006–07 record number of high school graduates is higher than the former high points in 2005–06, when a projected 3,176,000 students earned diplomas, and in 1976–77, when 3,152,000 students earned diplomas. In 2003–04, an estimated 74.3 percent of public high school students graduated on time—that is, received a diploma 4 years after beginning their freshman year (table 101). The number of General Educational Development (GED) credentials issued rose from 332,000 in 1977 to 648,000 in 2001, before falling to 406,000 in 2004 (table 103).

The percentage of dropouts among 16- to 24-year-olds has shown some decreases over the past 20 years (persons who left school but went on to receive a GED credential are not treated as dropouts). This percentage includes all persons in the 16- to 24-year-old age group who are not enrolled in school and who have not completed a high school program, regardless of when they left school. Between 1985 and 2005, the dropout rate declined from 12.6 percent to 9.4 percent (table 104). This measure is based on the civilian noninstitutionalized population, which excludes persons in prisons, persons in the military, and other persons not living in households.

Achievement

Most of the student performance data in the *Digest* are drawn from the National Assessment of Educational Progress (NAEP). The NAEP assessments have been conducted using three basic designs: the national main NAEP, state NAEP, and long-term trend NAEP. The main NAEP reports current information for the nation and specific geographic regions of the country. The assessment program includes students drawn from both public and nonpublic schools and reports results for student achievement at grades 4, 8, and 12. The main NAEP assessments follow the frameworks developed by the National Assessment Governing Board and use the latest advances in assessment methodology. Because the assessment items reflect curricula associated with specific grade levels, the main NAEP uses samples of students at those grade levels.

Since 1990, NAEP assessments have also been conducted at the state level. Participating states receive assessment results that report on the performance of students in that state. In its content, the state assessment is identical to the assessment conducted nationally. However, because the national NAEP samples prior to 2002 were not designed to support the reporting of accurate and representative state-level results, separate representative samples of students were selected for each participating jurisdiction/state. From 1990 through 2001, the national sample was a subset of the combined sample of students assessed in each participating state along with an additional sample from the states that did not participate in the state assessment. Since 2002, a combined sample of public schools has been selected for both state and national NAEP.

NAEP long-term trend assessments are designed to give information on the changes in the basic achievement of America's youth since the early 1970s. They are administered nationally and report student performance at ages 9, 13, and 17 in reading and mathematics. Measuring long-term trends of student achievement requires the precise replication of past procedures. For example, students of specific ages are sampled in order to maintain consistency with the original sample design. Similarly, the long-term trend instrument does not evolve based on changes in curricula or in educational practices. The differences in procedures between the main NAEP and the long-term trend NAEP mean that their results cannot be compared directly.

Long-term trend data have shown improvements in achievement in a number of areas. The average reading score at age 9 was higher in 2004 than in any previous assessment year (table 110). The average score at age 13 was higher in 2004 than in 1971, but not measurably different from the average score in 1999. Between 1999 and 2004, average reading scores at age 17 showed no measurable changes. The average score for 17-year-olds in 2004 was similar to that in 1971.

Significant gaps in performance continue to exist between racial/ethnic subgroups. For Black 9-, 13-, and 17-year-olds, average reading scores in 2004 were higher than in 1971 (table 110). At age 9, Black students scored higher on average in 2004 than in any previous administration year. For White students, the average scores for 9- and 13-year-olds were also higher in 2004 than in 1971. Separate data for Hispanics were not gathered in 1971, but as with the other racial/ethnic groups, the average reading score for Hispanic students at age 9 was higher in 2004 than in any other assessment year. The average score for Hispanic students at age 13 increased between 1975 and 2004. The scores for 17-year-old Hispanic students also increased between 1975 and 2004, but no measurable changes were seen between 1999 and 2004.

All reading score differences show that female students scored higher on average than their male counterparts in 2004. The gender score gap at age 9 decreased from 1971 to 2004. In contrast, there has been no measurable change in the gender score gap at age 13 between 2004 and any previous assessment year. For 17-year-olds, the gender score gap in 2004 was larger than the gaps in 1980 and 1988, but showed no measurable difference from the gaps in other assessment years.

The 2005 main NAEP reading assessment of states found that reading proficiency varied among public school fourth-graders in the 53 participating jurisdictions (the 50 states, the Department of Defense overseas and domestic schools, and the District of Columbia) (table 114). The U.S. average score was 217. The scores for the participating jurisdictions ranged from 191 in the District of Columbia and 204 in Mississippi to 227 in New Hampshire and Vermont and 231 in Massachusetts.

Mathematics achievement results from the long-term trend NAEP indicate a significant improvement for ages 9 and 13 between 1973 and 2004, but not for age 17 (table 121). The average score at age 9 in 2004 (241) was higher than in any previous year—up 9 points from 1999 and 22 points from 1973. The average score at age 13 in 2004 was higher than in any other assessment year. The 5-point increase between 1999 and 2004 resulted in an average score in 2004 that was 15 points higher than the average score in 1973. The average score at age 17 was not measurably different from the average score in 1973 or 1999. The apparent difference in average mathematics scores at age 9 between male and female students in 2004 was not statistically significant. Males had higher average scores than females at ages

13 and 17. The gender score gaps for 13- and 17-year-olds were measurably different between 1973 and 2004.

The 2005 main NAEP assessment of states found that mathematics proficiency varied among public school eighth-graders in the 53 participating jurisdictions (the 50 states, the Department of Defense overseas and domestic schools, and the District of Columbia) (table 125). Overall, 68 percent of these eighth-grade students performed at or above the *Basic* level in mathematics, and 29 percent performed at or above the *Proficient* level. The percentage of students performing at least at the *Basic* level in math ranged from 31 percent in the District of Columbia to 81 percent in North Dakota.

Between 1996 and 2005, the national average 4th-grade science score increased from 147 to 151; there was no measurable change in the 8th-grade score; and the 12th-grade score decreased from 150 to 147 (table 128). Certain subgroups outperformed others in science in 2005. For example, males outperformed females at all three grades. White students scored higher, on average, than Black and Hispanic students at all three grades in 2005. At 4th grade, average scores increased for White, Black, Hispanic, and Asian/Pacific Islander students between 1996 and 2005. At 8th grade, the average score for Black students increased, but no measurable increases occurred for other racial/ethnic groups. At 12th grade, there were no significant measurable changes in average scores for any racial/ethnic group during this period. Asian/Pacific Islander 4th-graders' 2000 results are not included because reporting standards were not met.

The SAT (formerly known as the Scholastic Assessment Test and the Scholastic Aptitude Test) is not designed as an indicator of student achievement, but rather as an aid for predicting how well students will do in college. Between 1995–96 and 2005–06, mathematics SAT scores increased by 10 points, while critical reading scores decreased by 2 points (table 132).

The average number of science and mathematics courses completed by public high school graduates increased between 1982 and 2005. The average number of mathematics courses (Carnegie units) completed in high school rose from 2.6 in 1982 to 3.7 in 2005, and the number of science courses rose from 2.2 to 3.3 (table 137). The average number of courses in vocational areas completed by all high school graduates was lower in 2005 (4.0 units) than in 1982 (4.6 units). As a result of the increased academic course load, the proportion of students completing the 1983 National Commission on Excellence recommendations for college-bound students (4 units of English, 3 units of social studies, 3 units of science, 3 units of mathematics, 2 units of foreign language, and .5 units of computer science) rose from 2 percent in 1982 to 36 percent in 2005 (table 140).

School Violence

In 2003–04, about 89 percent of public schools had a criminal incident, which is defined as a serious violent crime or a less serious crime such as a fight without weapons, theft, or vandalism (table 147). The percentage of schools having a criminal incident in 2003–04 was not measurably different from the percentage of schools having an incident in 1999–2000. In 2003–04, 81 percent of schools reported a violent incident; 46 percent of schools reported a theft/larceny; and 64 percent reported other types of incidents. Overall, there were 4.6 crime incidents reported per 100 students.

Revenues and Expenditures

The state share of revenues for public elementary and secondary schools generally grew from the 1930s through the mid-1980s, while the local share declined at the same time (table 158 and figure 9). However, this pattern changed in the late 1980s, when the local share began to increase at the same time the state share fell. Between 1986–87 and 1993–94, the state share fell from 49.7 percent to 45.2 percent, while the local share rose from 43.9 percent to 47.8 percent. Between 1993–94 and 2000–01, the state share rose to 49.7 percent again, the highest share since 1986–87, but fell every school year afterward until 2003–04, when the state share was 47.1 percent. Between 1993–94 and 2003–04, the federal share of revenues rose to 9.1 percent and the local share fell to 43.9 percent.

After adjustment for inflation, current expenditures per student in fall enrollment in public schools rose during the 1980s, remained stable during the first part of the 1990s, and rose again between 1993–94 and 2003–04 (table 167 and figure 10). There was an increase of 37 percent from 1980–81 to 1990–91; an increase of less than 1 percent from 1990–91 to 1995–96 (which resulted from small decreases at the beginning of this period, followed by small increases after 1992–93); and an increase of 21 percent from 1995–96 to 2003–04. In 2003–04, current expenditures per student in fall enrollment were $8,310 in unadjusted dollars. In 2003–04, 56 percent of students in public schools were transported at public expense at a cost of $640 per pupil, also in unadjusted dollars (table 172).

Figure 6.   Enrollment, number of teachers, pupil/teacher ratio, and expenditures in public schools: 1960–61 through 2004–05

Fall enrollment, in millions

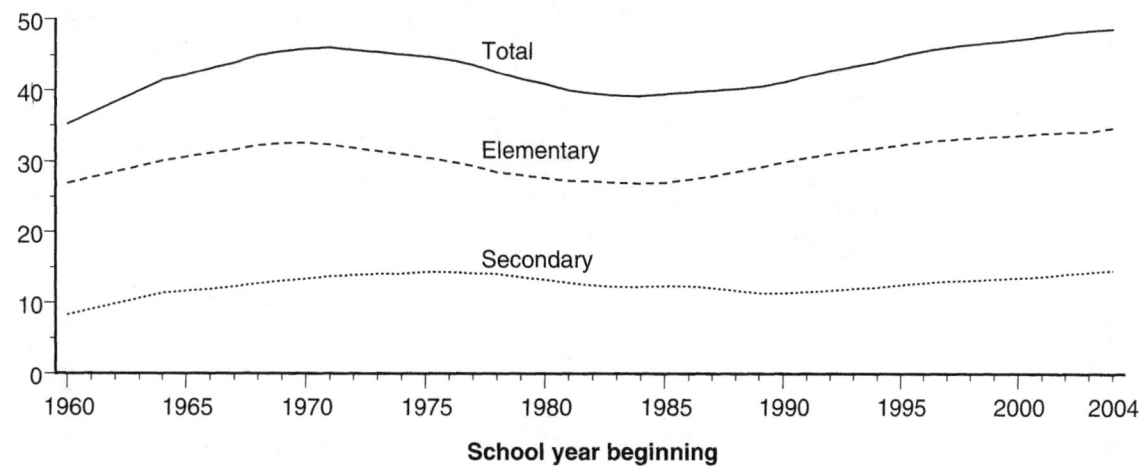

School year beginning

Teachers, in millions   **Pupil/teacher ratio**

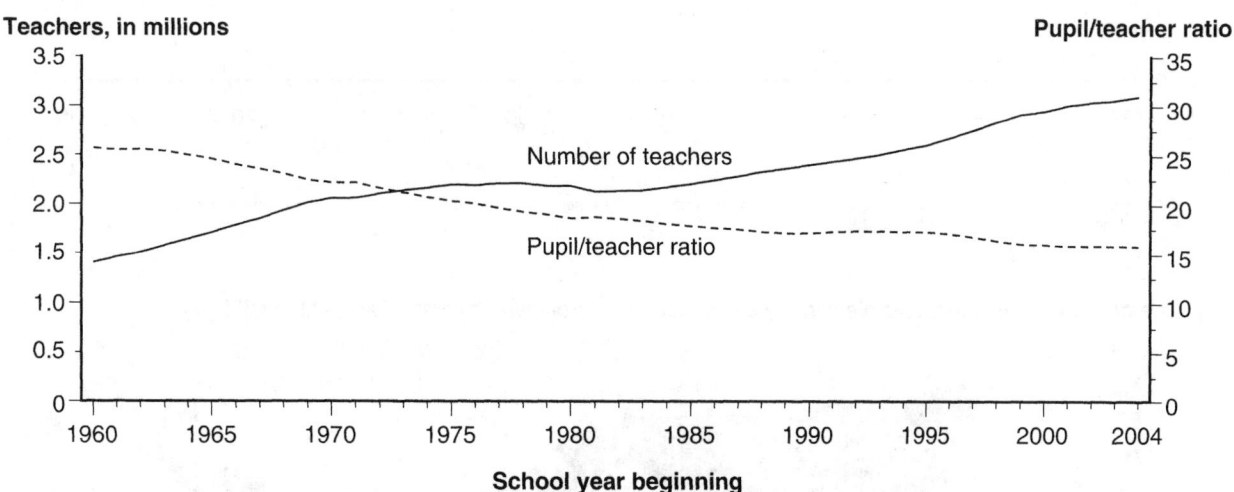

School year beginning

Current expenditures, in billions

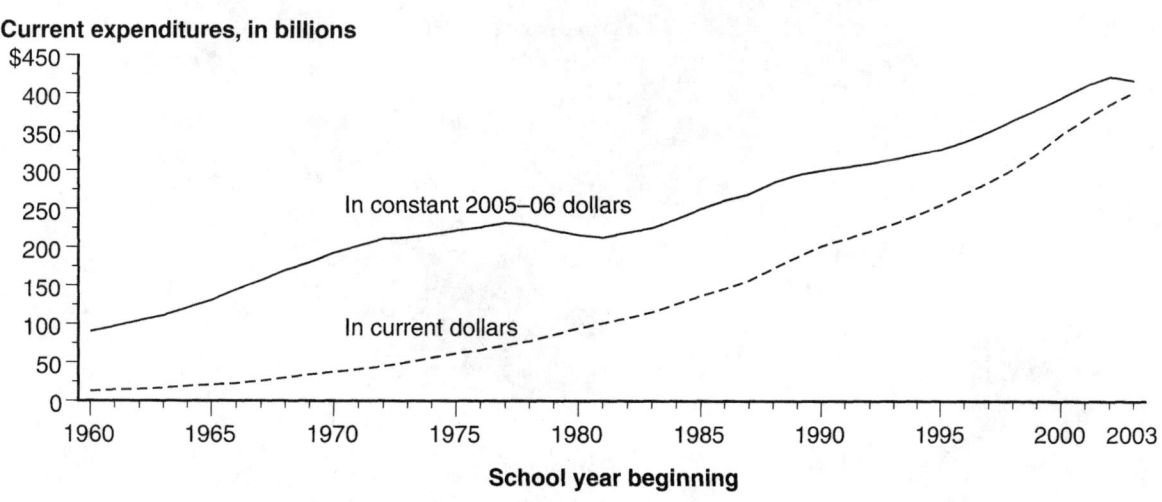

School year beginning

SOURCE: U.S. Department of Education, National Center for Education Statistics, *Statistics of State School Systems*, 1959–60 through 1969–70; *Statistics of Public Elementary and Secondary School Systems*, 1970 through 1980; *Revenues and Expenditures for Public Elementary and Secondary Education*, 1970–71 through 1980–81; and Common Core of Data (CCD), "State Nonfiscal Survey of Public Elementary/Secondary Education," 1981–82 through 2004–05, and "National Public Education Financial Survey," 1989–90 through 2003–04.

Figure 7.   Total and full-day preprimary enrollment of 3- to 5-year-olds: October 1970 through October 2005

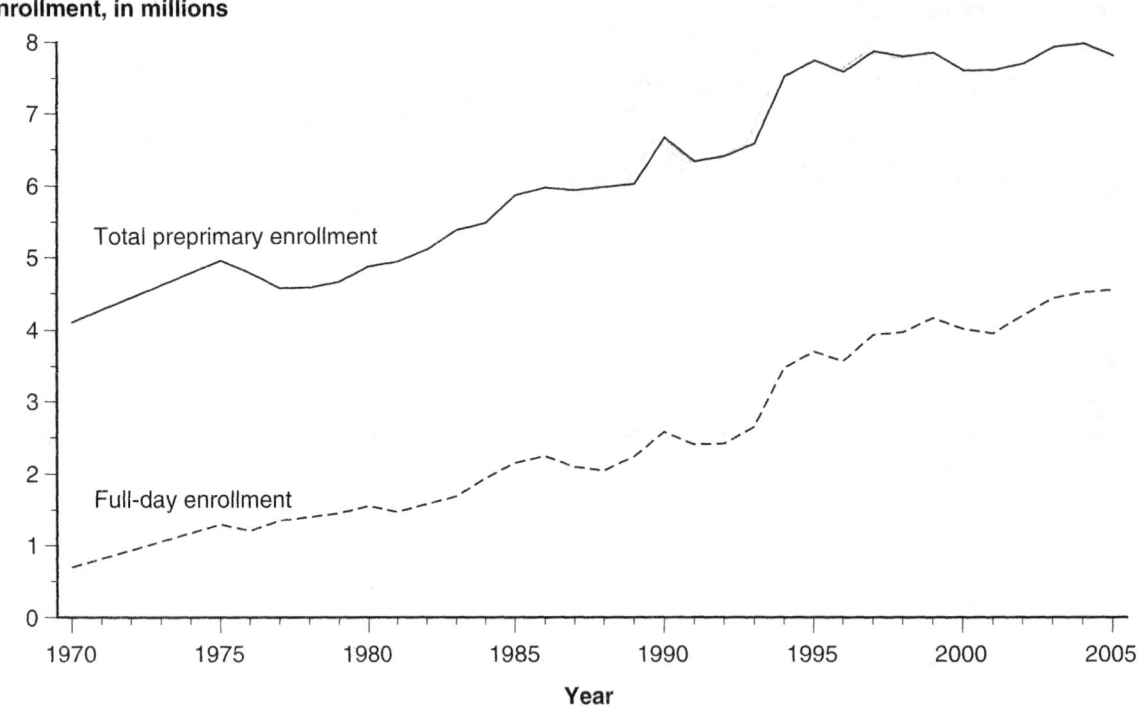

SOURCE: U.S. Department of Education, National Center for Education Statistics, *Preprimary Enrollment*, 1965, 1970, and 1975. U.S. Department of Commerce, Census Bureau, Current Population Survey (CPS), unpublished tabulations.

Figure 8.   Percentage change in public elementary and secondary enrollment, by state: Fall 1999 to fall 2004

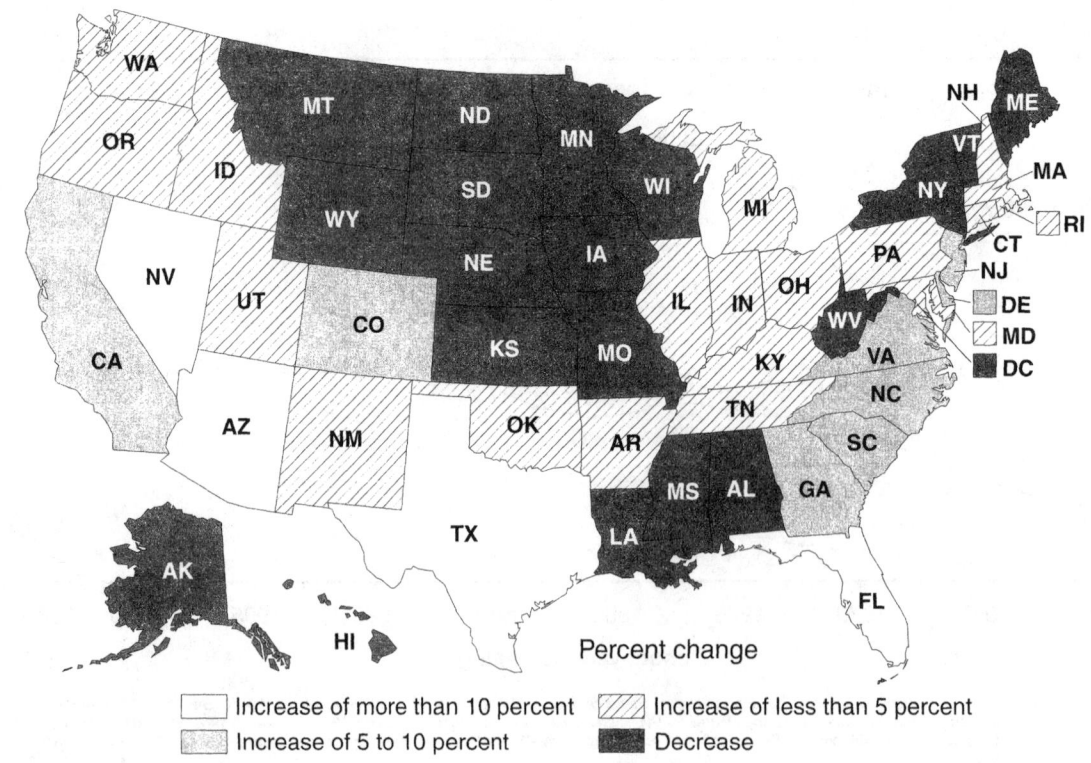

SOURCE: U.S. Department of Education, National Center for Education Statistics, Common Core of Data (CCD), "State Nonfiscal Survey of Public Elementary/Secondary Education," 1999–2000 and 2004–05.

Figure 9.   Percentage of revenue for public elementary and secondary schools, by source of funds: 1970–71 through 2003–04

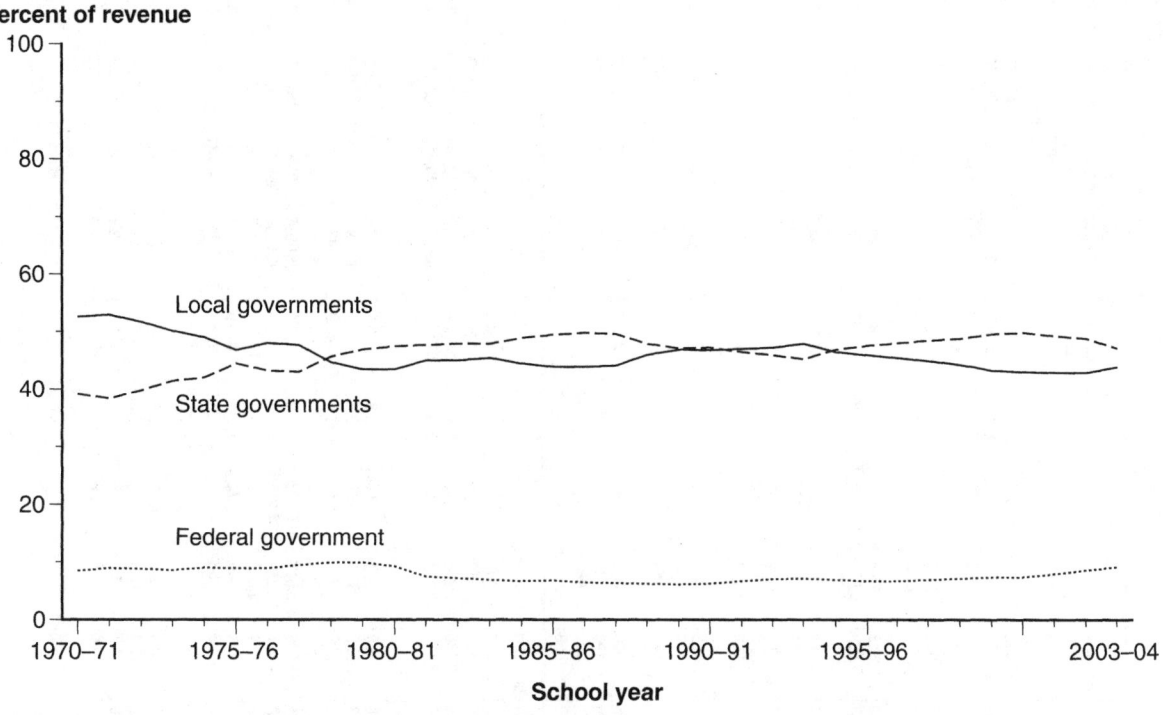

SOURCE: U.S. Department of Education, National Center for Education Statistics, *Revenues and Expenditures for Public Elementary and Secondary Education*, 1970–71 through 1986–87; and Common Core of Data (CCD), "National Public Education Financial Survey," 1987–88 through 2003–04.

Figure 10. Current expenditure per pupil in fall enrollment in public elementary and secondary schools: 1970–71 through 2003–04

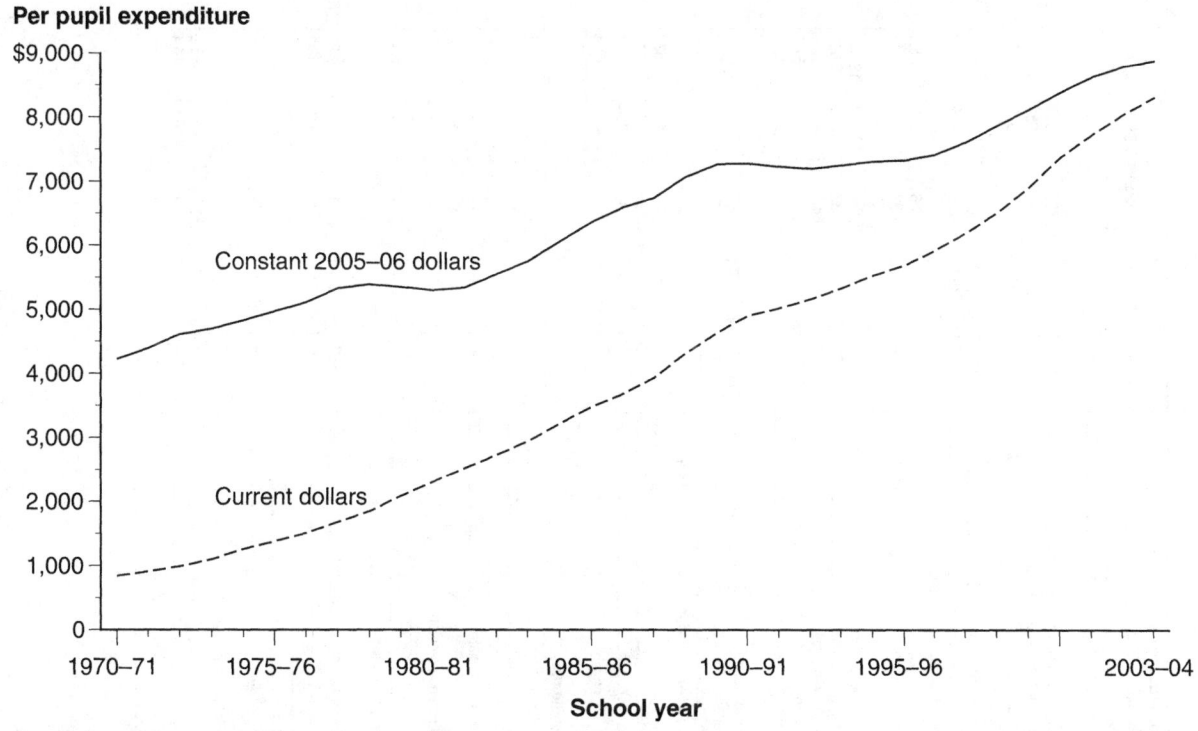

SOURCE: U.S. Department of Education, National Center for Education Statistics, *Revenues and Expenditures for Public Elementary and Secondary Education*, 1970–71 through 1986–87; and Common Core of Data (CCD), "National Public Education Financial Survey," 1987–88 through 2003–04.

Table 32. Historical summary of public elementary and secondary school statistics: Selected years, 1869–70 through 2003–04

Selected characteristic	1869–70	1879–80	1889–90	1899–1900	1909–10	1919–20	1929–30	1939–40	1949–50	1959–60	1969–70	1979–80	1989–90	1999–2000	2001–02	2002–03	2003–04
1	2	3	4	5	6	7	8	9	10	11	12	13	14	15	16	17	18
Population, pupils, and instructional staff																	
Total population (in thousands)[1]	38,558	50,156	62,622	75,995	90,490	104,514	121,878	131,028	149,188	177,830	201,385	224,567	246,819	279,040	285,108	287,985	290,850
5- to 17-year-olds (in thousands)[1]	11,683	15,066	18,473	21,573	24,011	27,571	31,414	30,151	30,223	43,881	52,386	48,041	44,947	52,811	53,260	53,325	53,269
5- to 17-year-olds as a percent of total population	30.3	30.0	29.5	28.4	26.5	26.4	25.8	23.0	20.3	24.7	26.0	21.4	18.2	18.9	18.7	18.5	18.3
Total enrollment in elementary and secondary schools (in thousands)[2]	7,562[3]	9,867	12,723	15,503	17,814	21,578	25,678	25,434	25,112	36,087	45,550	41,651	40,543	46,857	47,672	48,183	48,540
Prekindergarten and grades 1–8 (in thousands)	7,481[3]	9,757	12,520	14,984	16,899	19,378	21,279	18,833	19,387	27,602	32,513	28,034	29,152	33,488	33,938	34,116	34,202
Grades 9–12 (in thousands)	80[3]	110	203	519	915	2,200	4,399	6,601	5,725	8,485	13,037	13,616	11,390	13,369	13,734	14,067	14,338
Enrollment as a percent of total population	19.6[3]	19.7	20.3	20.4	19.7	20.6	21.1	19.4	16.8	20.3	22.6	18.5	16.4	16.8	16.7	16.7	16.7
Enrollment as a percent of 5- to 17-year-olds	64.7[3]	65.5	68.9	71.9	74.2	78.3	81.7	84.4	83.1	82.2	87.0	86.7	90.2	88.7	89.5	90.4	91.1
Percent of total enrollment in high schools (grades 9–12 and postgraduate)	1.1[3]	1.1	1.6	3.3	5.1	10.2	17.1	26.0	22.8	23.5	28.6	32.7	28.1	28.5	28.8	29.2	29.5
High school graduates (in thousands)	—	—	22	62	111	231	592	1,143	1,063	1,627	2,589	2,748	2,320	2,554	2,622	2,720	2,753
Average daily attendance (in thousands)	4,077	6,144	8,154	10,633	12,827	16,150	21,265	22,042	22,284	32,477	41,934	38,289	37,799	43,807	44,605	45,017	45,326
Total number of days attended by pupils enrolled (in millions)	539	801	1,098	1,535	2,011	2,615	3,673	3,858	3,964	5,782	7,501	6,835[4]	—	—	—	—	—
Percent of enrolled pupils attending daily	59.3	62.3	64.1	68.6	72.1	74.8	82.8	86.7	88.7	90.0	90.4	90.1[4]	—	—	—	—	—
Average length of school term, in days	132.2	130.3	134.7	144.3	157.5	161.9	172.7	175.0	177.9	178.0	178.9	178.5[4]	—	—	—	—	—
Average number of days attended per pupil	78.4	81.1	86.3	99.0	113.0	121.2	143.0	151.7	157.9	160.2	161.7	160.8[4]	—	—	—	—	—
Total instructional staff (in thousands)	—	—	—	—	—	678	880	912	963	1,457	2,286	2,406	2,986	3,819	3,989	4,017	4,053
Supervisors (in thousands)	—	—	—	—	—	7	7	5	—	—	—	—	—	—	—	—	—
Principals (in thousands)	—	—	—	—	—	14	31	32	43	64	91	106	126	137	161	164	165
Teachers, librarians, and other nonsupervisory instructional staff (in thousands)[5]	201	287	364	423	523	657	843	875	920	1,393	2,195	2,300	2,860	3,682	3,829	3,853	3,888
Males (in thousands)	78	123	126	127	110	93	140	195	196	404[4]	711[4]	782[4]	—	—	—	—	—
Females (in thousands)	123	164	238	296	413	585	703	681	724	989[4]	1,484[4]	1,518[4]	—	—	—	—	—
Percent male	38.7	42.8	34.5	29.9	21.1	14.1	16.6	22.2	21.3	29.0[4]	32.4[4]	34.0[4]	—	—	—	—	—
Total revenues and expenditures *Amounts in current dollars*																	
Total revenue receipts (in millions)	—	—	$143	$220	$433	$970	$2,089	$2,261	$5,437	$14,747	$40,267	$96,881	$208,548	$372,944	$419,502	$440,112	$462,016
Federal government	—	—	—	—	—	2	7	7	156	652	3,220	9,504	12,701	27,098	33,145	37,516	41,921
State governments	—	—	—	—	—	160	354	684	2,166	5,768	16,063	45,349	98,239	184,613	206,542	214,277	217,383
Local sources, including intermediate	—	—	—	—	—	808	1,728	1,536	3,116	8,327	20,985	42,029	97,608	161,233	179,816	188,318	202,711
Percentage distribution of revenue receipts																	
Federal government	—	—	—	—	—	0.3	0.4	1.8	2.9	4.4	8.0	9.8	6.1	7.3	7.9	8.5	9.1
State governments	—	—	—	—	—	16.5	16.9	30.3	39.8	39.1	39.9	46.8	47.1	49.5	49.2	48.7	47.1
Local sources, including intermediate	—	—	—	—	—	83.2	82.7	68.0	57.3	56.5	52.1	43.4	46.8	43.2	42.9	42.8	43.9
Total expenditures for public schools (in millions)	$63	$78	$141	$215	$426	$1,036	$2,317	$2,344	$5,838	$15,613	$40,683	$95,962	$212,770	$381,838	$435,364	$454,907	$473,863
Current expenditures[6]	—	—	114	180	356	861	1,844	1,942	4,687	12,329[7]	34,218[7]	86,984[7]	188,229[7]	323,889[7]	368,378[7]	387,594[7]	403,376[7]
Capital outlay[8]	—	—	26	35	70	154	371	258	1,014	2,662	4,659	6,506	17,781	43,357	49,961	48,940	50,476
Interest on school debt	—	—	—	—	—	18	93	131	101	490	1,171	1,874	3,776	9,135	10,495	11,499	13,081
Other current expenditures[9]	—	—	—	—	—	3	10	13	36	133	636	598[10]	2,983	5,457	6,531	6,874	6,930
Percentage distribution of total expenditures																	
Current expenditures[6]	—	—	81.3	83.5	83.6	83.1	79.6	82.8	80.3	79.0[7]	84.1[7]	90.6[7]	88.5[7]	84.8[7]	84.7[7]	85.2[7]	85.1[7]
Capital outlay[8]	—	—	18.7	16.5	16.4	14.8	16.0	11.0	17.4	17.0	11.5	6.8	8.4	11.4	11.5	10.8	10.7
Interest on school debt	—	—	—	—	—	1.8	4.0	5.6	1.7	3.1	2.9	2.0	1.8	2.4	2.4	2.5	2.8
Other current expenditures[9]	—	—	—	—	—	0.3	0.4	0.6	0.6	0.8	1.6	0.6[10]	1.4	1.4	1.5	1.5	1.5

See notes at end of table.

Table 32. Historical summary of public elementary and secondary school statistics: Selected years, 1869–70 through 2003–04—Continued

Selected characteristic	1869–70	1879–80	1889–90	1899–1900	1909–10	1919–20	1929–30	1939–40	1949–50	1959–60	1969–70	1979–80	1989–90	1999–2000	2001–02	2002–03	2003–04
1	2	3	4	5	6	7	8	9	10	11	12	13	14	15	16	17	18
Teacher salaries; income and expenditures per pupil and per capita																	
Annual salary of classroom teachers[11]	$189	$195	$252	$325	$485	$871	$1,420	$1,441	$3,010	$4,995	$8,626	$15,970	$31,367	$41,807	$44,660	$45,776	$46,752
Personal income per member of labor force[1]	—	—	—	—	—	—	1,730	1,320	3,379	5,745	9,643	19,647	37,038	55,984	60,696	61,312	62,546
Total school expenditures per capita of total population	1.59	1.56	2.23	2.83	4.71	9.91	19.01	17.89	39	88	202	427	862	1,368	1,527	1,580	1,629
National income per capita[1]	—	—	—	—	—	—	772.90	627.35	1,595	2,563	4,418	10,015	19,555	29,518	31,496	32,048	33,118
Current expenditure per pupil in ADA[6,12,13]	—	—	13.99	16.67	27.85	53.32	86.70	88.09	210	375	816	2,272	4,980	7,394	8,259	8,610	8,899
Total expenditure per pupil in ADA[13,14]	15.55	12.71	17.23	20.21	33.23	64.16	108.49	105.74	260	471	955	2,491	5,550	8,592	9,614	9,952	10,302
National income per pupil in ADA[13]	—	—	—	—	—	—	4,430	3,729	10,680	14,035	21,217	58,740	127,690	188,024	201,320	205,016	212,513
Current expenditure per day per pupil in ADA[6,13,15]	0.12	0.10	0.10	0.12	0.18	0.33	0.50	0.50	1.17	2.11	4.56	12.73	—	—	—	—	—
Total expenditure per day per pupil in ADA[13]	—	—	0.13	0.14	0.21	0.40	0.63	0.60	1.46	2.65	5.34	13.95	—	—	—	—	—
Amounts in constant 2005–06 dollars[16]																	
Annual salary of classroom teachers[11]	—	—	—	—	—	$9,094	$16,508	$20,519	$25,291	$33,828	$45,440	$40,935	$49,158	$49,141	$49,873	$50,020	$49,993
Personal income per member of labor force[1]	—	—	—	—	—	—	20,116	18,795	28,393	38,909	50,796	50,360	58,044	65,806	67,781	66,997	66,882
Total school expenditures per capita of total population	—	—	—	—	—	103	221	255	329	595	1,064	1,095	1,351	1,608	1,705	1,726	1,742
National income per capita[1]	—	—	—	—	—	—	8,985	8,933	13,404	17,358	23,273	25,672	30,646	34,697	35,173	35,019	35,413
Current expenditure per pupil in ADA[6,12,13]	—	—	—	—	—	557	1,008	1,254	1,767	2,541	4,298	5,823	7,804	8,691	9,223	9,408	9,516
Total expenditure per pupil in ADA[13,14]	—	—	—	—	—	670	1,261	1,506	2,188	3,190	5,031	6,384	8,698	10,099	10,736	10,875	11,016
National income per pupil in ADA[13]	—	—	—	—	—	—	51,498	53,101	89,739	95,047	111,766	150,565	200,113	221,010	224,820	224,024	227,244
Current expenditure per day per pupil in ADA[6,13,15]	—	—	—	—	—	3.4	5.8	7.1	9.8	14.3	24.0	32.6	—	—	—	—	—
Total expenditure per day per pupil in ADA[13]	—	—	—	—	—	4.2	7.3	8.5	12.3	17.9	28.1	35.8	—	—	—	—	—

—Not available.

[1] Data on population and labor force are from the Census Bureau, and data on personal income and national income are from the Bureau of Economic Analysis, U.S. Department of Commerce. Population data through 1900 are based on total population. From 1909–10 to 1959–60, population data are total population, including armed forces overseas, as of July 1. Data for later years are for resident population that excludes armed forces overseas.

[2] Data for 1869–70 through 1959–60 are school year enrollment. Data for later years are fall enrollment.

[3] Data for 1870–71.

[4] Estimated by the National Center for Education Statistics.

[5] Prior to 1919–20, data are for the number of different persons employed rather than number of positions.

[6] Prior to 1919–20, includes interest on school debt.

[7] Because of the modification of the scope of "current expenditures for elementary and secondary schools," data for 1959–60 and later years are not entirely comparable with prior years.

[8] Beginning in 1969–70, includes capital outlay by state and local school building authorities.

[9] Includes summer schools, community colleges, and adult education. Beginning in 1959–60, also includes community services, formerly classified with "current expenditures for elementary and secondary schools."

[10] Excludes community colleges and adult education.

[11] Prior to 1959–60, average includes supervisors, principals, teachers, and other nonsupervisory instructional staff. Data for 1959–60 and later years are estimated by the National Education Association.

[12] Excludes current expenditures not allocable to pupil costs.

[13] "ADA" means average daily attendance in elementary and secondary schools.

[14] Expenditure figure is the sum of current expenditures allocable to pupil costs, capital outlay, and interest on school debt.

[15] Per-day rates derived by dividing annual rates by average length of term.

[16] Constant dollars based on the Consumer Price Index, prepared by the Bureau of Labor Statistics, U.S. Department of Labor, adjusted to a school-year basis.

NOTE: Some data have been revised from previously published figures. Beginning in 1959–60, data include Alaska and Hawaii. Detail may not sum to totals because of rounding.

SOURCE: U.S. Department of Education, National Center for Education Statistics, Annual Report of the United States Commissioner of Education, 1869–70 through 1909–10; Biennial Survey of Education in the United States, 1919–20 through 1949–50; Statistics of State School Systems, 1959–60 and 1969–70; Statistics of Public Elementary and Secondary School Systems, 1979–80; Revenues and Expenditures for Public Elementary and Secondary Education, FY 1980; Common Core of Data (CCD), "State Nonfiscal Survey of Public Elementary/Secondary Education," 1989–90 through 2003–04, and "National Public Financial Survey," 1989–90 through 2003–04. Census Bureau, unpublished tabulations. Bureau of Economic Analysis, unpublished tabulations. (This table was prepared March 2007.)

Table 33. Enrollment in public elementary and secondary schools, by state or jurisdiction: Fall 1990 through fall 2006

State or jurisdiction	Fall 1990	Fall 1991	Fall 1992	Fall 1993	Fall 1994	Fall 1995	Fall 1996	Fall 1997	Fall 1998	Fall 1999	Fall 2000	Fall 2001	Fall 2002	Fall 2003 Total	Fall 2003 Prekindergarten to grade 8[1]	Fall 2003 Grades 9 to 12[1]	Fall 2004 Total	Fall 2004 Prekindergarten to grade 8[1]	Fall 2004 Grades 9 to 12[2]	Projected 2005 enrollment	Projected 2006 enrollment
1	2	3	4	5	6	7	8	9	10	11	12	13	14	15	16	17	18	19	20	21	22
United States	41,216,683	42,046,878	42,823,312	43,464,916	44,111,482	44,840,481	45,611,046	46,126,897	46,538,585	46,857,149	47,203,539	47,671,877	48,183,086	48,540,215	34,202,248	14,337,967	48,794,911	34,178,401	14,616,510	48,710,000	48,948,000
Alabama	721,806	722,004	731,634	734,288	736,531	746,149	747,932	749,207	747,980	740,732	739,992	737,190	739,366	731,220	525,313	205,907	730,140	521,757	208,383	735,000	736,000
Alaska	113,903	118,680	122,487	125,948	127,057	127,618	129,919	132,123	135,373	134,391	133,356	134,358	134,364	133,933	93,695	40,238	132,970	91,981	40,989	133,000	132,000
Arizona	639,853	656,980	673,477	709,453	737,424	743,566	799,250	814,113	848,262	852,612	877,696	922,180	937,755	1,012,068	704,327	307,741	1,043,298	722,208	321,090	1,061,000	1,089,000
Arkansas	436,286	438,518	441,490	444,271	447,565	453,257	457,349	456,497	452,256	451,034	449,959	449,805	450,985	454,523	321,509	133,014	463,115	328,188	134,927	457,000	459,000
California	4,950,474	5,107,145	5,254,844	5,327,231	5,407,475	5,536,406	5,686,198	5,803,887	5,926,037	6,038,590	6,140,814	6,247,726	6,353,667	6,413,862	4,540,362	1,873,500	6,441,557	4,507,916	1,933,641	6,428,000	6,451,000
Colorado	574,213	593,030	612,635	625,062	640,521	656,279	673,438	687,167	699,135	708,109	724,508	742,145	751,862	757,693	536,325	221,368	765,976	540,695	225,281	766,000	775,000
Connecticut	469,123	481,050	488,476	496,298	506,824	517,935	527,129	535,164	544,698	553,993	562,179	570,228	570,023	577,203	407,794	169,409	577,390	404,169	173,221	575,000	573,000
Delaware	99,658	102,196	104,321	105,547	106,813	108,461	110,549	111,960	113,262	112,836	114,676	115,560	116,342	117,668	82,898	34,770	119,091	83,599	35,492	120,000	121,000
District of Columbia	80,694	80,618	80,937	80,678	80,450	79,802	78,648	77,111	71,889	77,194	68,925	75,392	76,166	78,057	59,482	18,575	76,714	57,111	19,603	74,000	74,000
Florida	1,861,592	1,932,131	1,981,407	2,040,763	2,111,188	2,176,222	2,242,212	2,294,077	2,337,633	2,381,396	2,434,821	2,500,478	2,539,929	2,587,628	1,832,376	755,252	2,639,336	1,857,798	781,538	2,622,000	2,654,000
Georgia	1,151,687	1,177,569	1,207,186	1,235,304	1,270,948	1,311,126	1,346,761	1,375,980	1,401,291	1,422,762	1,444,937	1,470,634	1,496,012	1,522,611	1,103,181	419,430	1,553,437	1,118,379	435,058	1,556,000	1,585,000
Hawaii	171,708	174,747	177,448	180,410	183,795	187,180	187,653	189,887	188,069	185,860	184,360	184,546	183,829	183,609	130,054	53,555	183,185	128,788	54,397	181,000	182,000
Idaho	220,840	225,680	231,668	236,774	240,448	243,097	245,252	244,403	244,722	245,136	245,117	246,521	248,604	252,120	175,424	76,696	256,084	178,221	77,863	257,000	261,000
Illinois	1,821,407	1,848,166	1,873,567	1,893,078	1,916,172	1,943,623	1,973,040	1,998,289	2,011,530	2,027,600	2,048,792	2,071,391	2,084,187	2,100,961	1,492,730	608,231	2,097,503	1,483,645	613,858	2,100,000	2,107,000
Indiana	954,525	956,988	960,630	965,633	969,022	977,263	982,876	986,836	989,001	988,702	989,267	996,133	1,003,875	1,011,130	716,825	294,305	1,021,348	720,006	301,342	1,025,000	1,030,000
Iowa	483,652	491,363	494,839	498,519	500,440	502,343	502,941	501,054	498,214	497,301	495,080	485,932	482,210	481,226	326,846	154,380	478,319	324,169	154,150	483,000	483,000
Kansas	437,034	445,390	451,536	457,614	460,838	463,008	466,293	468,687	472,353	472,188	470,610	470,205	470,957	470,490	322,575	147,915	469,136	321,259	147,877	464,000	463,000
Kentucky	636,401	646,024	655,041	655,265	657,642	659,821	656,089	669,322	655,687	648,180	665,850	654,363	660,782	663,885	478,258	185,627	674,796	485,801	188,995	664,000	667,000
Louisiana	784,757	794,128	797,985	800,560	797,933	797,366	793,296	776,813	768,734	756,579	743,089	731,328	730,464	727,709	536,390	191,319	724,281	533,751	190,530	721,000	721,000
Maine	215,149	216,400	216,453	216,995	212,601	213,569	213,593	212,579	211,051	209,253	207,037	205,586	204,337	202,084	139,420	62,664	198,820	136,275	62,545	198,000	196,000
Maryland	715,176	736,238	751,850	772,638	790,938	805,544	818,583	830,744	841,671	846,582	852,920	860,640	866,743	869,113	605,905	263,208	865,561	597,417	268,144	870,000	873,000
Massachusetts	834,314	846,155	859,948	877,726	893,727	915,007	933,898	949,006	962,317	971,425	975,150	973,139	982,989	980,459	692,130	288,329	975,574	682,175	293,399	970,000	967,000
Michigan	1,584,431	1,593,561	1,603,610	1,599,377	1,614,784	1,641,456	1,685,714	1,702,717	1,720,287	1,725,639	1,720,626	1,730,669	1,785,160	1,757,604	1,229,121	528,483	1,750,919	1,211,444	539,475	1,754,000	1,751,000
Minnesota	756,374	773,571	793,724	810,233	821,693	835,166	847,204	853,621	856,455	854,034	854,340	851,384	846,891	842,854	564,049	278,805	838,503	558,447	280,056	833,000	832,000
Mississippi	502,417	504,127	506,668	505,907	505,962	506,272	503,967	504,792	502,379	500,716	497,871	493,507	492,645	493,540	360,913	132,627	495,376	361,087	134,289	492,000	494,000
Missouri	816,558	842,965	859,357	866,378	878,541	889,881	900,517	910,613	913,494	914,110	912,744	909,792	906,499	905,941	632,230	273,711	905,449	628,667	276,782	908,000	909,000
Montana	152,974	155,779	160,011	163,009	164,341	165,547	164,627	162,335	159,988	157,556	154,875	151,947	149,995	148,356	100,160	48,196	146,705	98,673	48,032	145,000	144,000
Nebraska	274,081	279,552	282,414	285,097	287,100	289,744	291,967	292,681	291,140	288,261	286,199	285,095	285,402	285,542	195,417	90,125	285,761	194,816	90,945	284,000	285,000
Nevada	201,316	211,810	222,974	235,800	250,747	265,041	282,131	296,621	311,061	325,610	340,706	356,814	369,498	385,401	280,735	104,666	400,083	288,754	111,329	413,000	424,000
New Hampshire	172,785	177,138	181,247	185,360	189,319	194,171	198,308	201,629	204,713	206,783	208,461	206,847	207,671	207,417	142,033	65,384	206,852	140,243	66,609	203,000	201,000
New Jersey	1,089,646	1,109,796	1,130,560	1,151,307	1,174,206	1,197,381	1,227,832	1,250,276	1,268,996	1,289,256	1,313,405	1,341,656	1,367,438	1,380,753	978,589	402,164	1,393,347	975,988	417,359	1,398,000	1,401,000
New Mexico	301,881	308,667	315,668	322,292	327,248	329,640	332,632	331,673	328,753	324,495	320,306	320,260	320,234	323,066	226,032	97,034	326,102	227,900	98,202	319,000	318,000
New York	2,598,337	2,643,993	2,689,686	2,733,813	2,766,208	2,813,230	2,843,131	2,861,823	2,877,143	2,887,776	2,882,188	2,872,132	2,888,233	2,864,775	1,978,673	886,102	2,836,337	1,942,961	893,376	2,821,000	2,804,000
North Carolina	1,086,871	1,097,598	1,114,083	1,133,231	1,156,767	1,183,090	1,210,108	1,236,083	1,254,821	1,275,925	1,293,638	1,315,363	1,335,954	1,360,209	974,019	386,190	1,385,754	985,740	400,014	1,385,000	1,404,000
North Dakota	117,825	118,376	118,734	119,127	119,288	119,100	120,123	118,572	114,927	112,751	109,201	106,047	104,225	102,233	67,870	34,363	100,513	67,122	33,391	98,000	96,000

See notes at end of table.

Table 33. Enrollment in public elementary and secondary schools, by state or jurisdiction: Fall 1990 through fall 2006—Continued

State or jurisdiction	Total													Fall 2003			Fall 2004			Projected 2005 enrollment	Projected 2006 enrollment
	Fall 1990	Fall 1991	Fall 1992	Fall 1993	Fall 1994	Fall 1995	Fall 1996	Fall 1997	Fall 1998	Fall 1999	Fall 2000	Fall 2001	Fall 2002	Total	Prekinder-garten to grade 8[1]	Grades 9 to 12[2]	Total	Prekinder-garten to grade 8[1]	Grades 9 to 12[2]		
1	2	3	4	5	6	7	8	9	10	11	12	13	14	15	16	17	18	19	20	21	22
Ohio	1,771,089	1,783,767	1,795,199	1,807,319	1,814,290	1,836,015	1,844,698	1,847,114	1,842,163	1,836,554	1,835,049	1,830,985	1,838,285	1,845,428	1,278,202	567,226	1,840,032	1,267,088	572,944	1,833,000	1,828,000
Oklahoma	579,087	588,263	597,096	604,076	609,718	616,393	620,695	623,681	628,492	627,032	623,110	622,139	624,548	626,160	450,319	175,841	629,476	452,952	176,524	618,000	618,000
Oregon	472,394	498,614	510,122	516,611	521,945	527,914	537,854	541,346	542,809	545,033	546,231	551,480	554,071	551,273	378,072	173,201	552,322	376,811	175,511	548,000	547,000
Pennsylvania	1,667,834	1,692,797	1,717,613	1,744,082	1,764,946	1,787,533	1,804,256	1,815,151	1,816,414	1,816,716	1,814,311	1,821,627	1,816,747	1,821,146	1,235,624	585,522	1,828,089	1,234,828	593,261	1,803,000	1,793,000
Rhode Island	138,813	142,144	143,798	145,676	147,487	149,799	151,324	153,321	154,785	156,454	157,347	158,046	159,205	159,375	111,209	48,166	156,498	107,040	49,458	159,000	158,000
South Carolina	622,112	627,470	640,464	643,696	648,725	645,586	652,816	659,273	664,600	666,780	677,411	676,198	694,389	699,198	500,743	198,455	703,736	504,264	199,472	702,000	707,000
South Dakota	129,164	131,576	134,573	142,825	143,482	144,685	143,331	142,443	132,495	131,037	128,603	127,542	130,048	125,537	86,015	39,522	122,798	83,891	38,907	123,000	122,000
Tennessee	824,595	833,651	855,231	866,557	881,425	893,770	904,818	893,044	905,454	916,202	909,161	924,899	927,608	936,681	675,276	261,405	941,091	670,880	270,211	947,000	954,000
Texas	3,382,887	3,464,371	3,541,769	3,608,262	3,677,171	3,748,167	3,828,975	3,891,877	3,945,367	3,991,783	4,059,619	4,163,447	4,259,823	4,331,751	3,132,584	1,199,167	4,405,215	3,184,235	1,220,980	4,409,000	4,488,000
Utah	446,652	456,430	463,870	471,365	474,675	477,121	481,812	482,957	481,176	480,255	481,485	484,677	489,262	495,981	348,890	147,091	503,607	355,445	148,162	507,000	514,000
Vermont	95,762	97,137	98,558	102,755	104,533	105,565	106,341	105,984	105,120	104,559	102,049	101,179	99,978	99,103	66,732	32,371	98,352	65,935	32,417	95,000	94,000
Virginia	998,601	1,016,204	1,031,925	1,045,471	1,060,809	1,079,854	1,096,093	1,110,815	1,124,022	1,133,994	1,144,915	1,163,091	1,177,229	1,192,092	837,258	354,834	1,204,739	839,687	365,052	1,208,000	1,220,000
Washington	839,709	869,327	896,475	915,952	938,314	956,572	974,504	991,235	998,053	1,003,714	1,004,770	1,009,200	1,014,798	1,021,349	699,248	322,101	1,020,005	695,405	324,600	1,015,000	1,014,000
West Virginia	322,389	320,249	318,296	314,383	310,511	307,112	304,052	301,419	297,530	291,811	286,367	282,885	282,455	281,215	198,836	82,379	280,129	197,555	82,574	277,000	277,000
Wisconsin	797,621	814,671	829,415	844,001	860,581	870,175	879,259	881,780	879,542	877,753	879,476	879,361	881,231	880,031	589,812	290,219	864,757	577,950	286,807	869,000	867,000
Wyoming	98,226	102,074	100,313	100,899	100,314	99,859	99,058	97,115	95,241	92,105	89,940	88,128	88,116	87,462	59,759	27,703	84,733	57,285	27,448	84,000	83,000
Bureau of Indian Affairs	—	—	—	—	—	—	—	—	—	—	—	—	—	—	—	—	—	—	—	—	—
DoDDS, overseas	—	—	—	—	—	—	80,715	78,254	78,170	108,035 [3]	73,581	73,212	72,889	71,053	56,226	14,827	68,327	53,720	14,607	—	—
DoDDS, domestic	—	—	—	—	—	—	—	—	50,125	49,076	46,938	46,476	46,126	45,828	33,671	12,157	29,151	26,195	2,956	—	—
Other jurisdictions																					
American Samoa	12,463	13,365	13,994	14,484	14,445	14,576	14,766	15,214	15,372	15,477	15,702	15,897	15,984	15,893	11,772	4,121	16,126	11,873	4,253	—	—
Guam	26,391	28,334	30,077	30,920	32,185	32,960	33,393	32,444	32,222	32,951	32,473	31,992	—	31,572	22,551	9,021	30,605	21,686	8,919	—	—
Northern Marianas	6,449	7,096	8,086	8,188	8,429	8,809	9,041	9,246	9,498	9,732	10,004	10,479	11,251	11,244	8,192	3,052	11,601	8,416	3,185	—	—
Puerto Rico	644,734	642,392	637,034	631,460	621,121	627,620	618,861	617,157	613,862	613,019	612,725	604,177	596,502	584,916	418,588	166,328	575,648	408,607	167,041	—	—
Virgin Islands	21,750	22,346	22,887	22,752	23,126	22,737	22,385	22,136	20,976	20,866	19,459	18,780	18,333	17,716	12,738	4,978	16,429	11,650	4,779	—	—

—Not available.

[1]Includes elementary unclassified.
[2]Includes secondary unclassified.
[3]Includes both overseas and domestic schools.

NOTE: DoDDS = Department of Defense dependents schools. Some data have been revised from previously published figures.
SOURCE: U.S. Department of Education, National Center for Education Statistics, Common Core of Data (CCD), "State Non-fiscal Survey of Public Elementary/Secondary Education," 1990–91 through 2004–05, and Projections of Education Statistics to 2015. (This table was prepared September 2006.)

Table 34. Enrollment in public elementary and secondary schools, by level, grade, and state or jurisdiction: Fall 2004

State or jurisdiction	Total, all grades	Prekindergarten through grade 8 and elementary ungraded												Grades 9 through 12 and secondary ungraded					
		Total	Prekindergarten[1]	Kindergarten	Grade 1	Grade 2	Grade 3	Grade 4	Grade 5	Grade 6	Grade 7	Grade 8	Elementary ungraded	Total	Grade 9	Grade 10	Grade 11	Grade 12	Secondary ungraded
1	2	3	4	5	6	7	8	9	10	11	12	13	14	15	16	17	18	19	20
United States	48,794,911[2]	34,178,401	990,421[2]	3,543,554	3,663,005	3,559,854	3,580,462	3,611,638	3,635,181	3,735,281	3,818,427	3,824,670	215,908	14,616,510	4,281,345	3,750,491	3,369,339	3,094,349	120,986
Alabama	730,140	521,757	1,994	56,964	58,567	55,661	54,954	56,182	57,293	59,406	61,450	59,286	0	208,383	64,569	53,604	47,538	42,672	0
Alaska	132,970	91,981	1,760	9,870	9,510	9,773	9,452	9,674	10,048	10,151	10,886	10,857	0	40,989	11,934	10,664	9,625	8,766	0
Arizona	1,043,298	722,208	9,730	80,614	79,773	78,239	78,495	77,110	77,929	77,592	79,811	78,595	4,320	321,090	91,860	82,536	75,259	71,035	400
Arkansas	463,115	328,188	7,688	36,967	36,286	34,795	34,444	33,884	34,457	34,740	36,881	37,369	677	134,927	38,279	35,794	31,928	28,640	286
California	6,441,557[2]	4,507,916	119,410[2]	455,155	477,554	474,856	481,280	488,045	492,895	491,264	492,879	498,806	35,772	1,933,641	549,463	497,197	459,125	409,576	18,280
Colorado	765,976	540,695	21,256	56,968	58,798	56,634	56,470	56,425	56,901	58,298	59,548	59,397	0	225,281	64,446	57,678	52,770	50,387	0
Connecticut	577,390	404,169	12,448	41,886	43,483	42,266	43,083	42,652	43,686	44,457	45,136	45,072	0	173,221	49,177	44,580	41,124	38,340	0
Delaware	119,091	83,599	670	8,279	9,111	8,861	8,783	8,872	9,172	9,491	9,866	10,494	0	35,492	11,249	9,081	7,772	7,390	0
District of Columbia	76,714	57,111	5,432	5,387	5,603	5,275	5,320	5,300	5,579	5,563	5,576	5,189	2,887	19,603	6,285	4,804	3,816	2,820	1,878
Florida	2,639,336	1,857,798	47,995	197,163	201,536	195,370	206,716	197,293	184,067	208,251	209,848	209,559	0	781,538	250,263	202,437	179,028	149,810	0
Georgia	1,553,437	1,118,379	37,791	122,495	120,880	117,310	117,092	116,129	118,762	122,861	122,627	122,432	0	435,058	142,079	113,044	96,063	83,872	0
Hawaii	183,185	128,788	1,288	13,576	14,207	13,899	14,298	14,289	14,548	14,299	13,849	14,422	113	54,397	16,971	13,682	12,845	10,794	105
Idaho	256,084	178,221	2,585	19,603	19,459	19,016	19,356	18,856	19,179	19,552	20,316	20,299	0	77,863	21,344	20,177	18,836	17,506	0
Illinois	2,097,503	1,483,645	68,764	145,797	154,861	152,864	156,370	158,622	160,365	161,487	162,047	162,192	276	613,858	178,240	159,950	142,828	132,658	182
Indiana	1,021,348	720,006	7,967	73,142	80,247	77,902	78,331	78,079	78,326	80,913	82,371	82,728	0	301,342	87,829	78,361	71,836	63,316	0
Iowa	478,319	324,169	6,108	36,713	33,916	33,626	33,588	33,743	34,716	36,141	37,521	38,097	0	154,150	41,196	39,580	36,940	36,434	0
Kansas	469,136	321,259	2,486	34,203	34,534	32,849	33,159	33,503	33,899	34,525	35,752	35,915	10,434	147,877	39,293	36,302	34,349	33,593	4,340
Kentucky	674,796	485,801	37,916	49,027	52,504	47,483	47,483	47,872	48,224	49,542	50,653	51,172	3,925	188,995	56,919	48,559	42,757	39,200	1,560
Louisiana	724,281	533,751	23,467	57,386	58,425	53,697	53,477	61,940	50,171	56,263	58,791	60,194	0	190,530	59,182	48,181	43,133	40,034	0
Maine	198,820	136,275	1,747	13,687	14,184	13,985	14,173	14,439	14,961	15,549	16,700	16,850	0	62,545	16,766	16,056	15,321	14,402	0
Maryland	865,561	597,417	23,380	54,838	60,854	61,152	62,144	63,776	65,688	66,799	69,219	69,567	0	268,144	81,270	68,249	61,193	57,432	0
Massachusetts	975,574	682,175	23,281	68,357	72,840	71,403	71,578	72,818	73,337	74,901	76,829	76,831	0	293,399	84,628	75,478	69,441	63,852	0
Michigan	1,750,919	1,211,444	20,360	131,141	124,663	122,038	122,480	125,319	127,648	132,348	136,430	137,898	31,119	539,475	158,797	135,116	120,228	111,055	14,279
Minnesota	838,503	558,447	11,173	58,657	58,523	58,093	58,048	59,338	60,554	62,870	65,175	66,016	0	280,056	70,751	69,691	67,978	71,636	0
Mississippi	495,376	361,087	2,623	39,547	39,967	37,520	37,004	38,311	38,525	39,603	41,076	39,115	7,796	134,289	40,195	34,245	29,012	25,801	5,036
Missouri	905,449	628,667	13,602	64,328	67,175	65,315	65,343	66,284	67,344	71,141	74,516	73,619	0	276,782	78,748	71,794	64,402	61,838	0
Montana	146,705	98,673	759	10,206	10,481	10,096	10,370	10,440	10,836	11,204	11,977	12,011	293	48,032	13,200	12,039	11,494	11,173	126
Nebraska	285,761	194,816	6,114	21,205	20,572	20,220	20,252	20,429	20,629	21,203	21,925	22,267	0	90,945	25,214	22,734	21,440	21,557	0
Nevada	400,083	288,754	2,894	29,877	32,258	31,338	31,333	31,950	31,439	32,304	32,364	32,472	525	111,329	36,056	30,706	23,167	21,385	15
New Hampshire	206,852	140,243	2,360	10,116	15,269	14,978	15,021	15,501	15,950	16,200	17,017	17,237	594	66,609	18,584	17,233	15,871	14,847	74
New Jersey	1,393,347	975,988	25,211	93,157	101,135	99,019	99,026	100,557	100,892	103,802	104,603	104,437	44,149	417,359	111,479	104,337	95,891	88,378	17,274
New Mexico	326,102	227,900	5,322	24,624	24,670	24,022	23,596	23,880	24,679	25,239	25,657	26,211	0	98,202	30,134	26,387	22,163	19,518	0
New York	2,836,337	1,942,961	39,801	188,633	203,159	198,215	202,014	202,267	208,162	211,816	219,122	218,176	51,596	893,376	262,635	227,717	183,622	166,975	52,427
North Carolina	1,385,754	985,740	12,468	111,753	111,489	105,683	104,054	104,337	106,846	108,064	111,067	109,979	0	400,014	126,414	103,929	90,414	79,257	0
North Dakota	100,513	67,122	1,089	6,643	7,116	6,958	7,044	7,069	7,321	7,726	8,029	8,127	0	33,391	8,547	8,515	8,186	8,143	0
Ohio	1,840,032	1,267,088	26,119	134,215	136,365	131,410	131,752	134,442	137,372	142,538	145,714	147,161	0	572,944	165,656	143,496	136,413	127,379	0
Oklahoma	629,476	452,952	31,803	47,152	50,685	45,295	43,924	44,372	45,177	46,058	47,939	47,270	3,277	176,524	50,035	45,741	41,485	37,938	1,325
Oregon	552,322	376,811	988	38,997	41,319	40,474	41,199	41,298	41,156	42,227	43,751	44,802	600	175,511	46,700	45,148	42,290	41,125	248
Pennsylvania	1,828,089	1,234,828	7,154	124,435	129,233	126,492	129,400	133,418	138,064	143,275	149,056	151,250	3,051	593,261	163,848	153,315	140,618	132,551	2,929
Rhode Island	156,498	107,040	1,633	8,824	11,661	11,408	11,580	11,731	12,273	12,365	12,782	12,783	0	49,458	14,591	12,763	11,571	10,533	0

See notes at end of table.

Table 34. Enrollment in public elementary and secondary schools, by level, grade, and state or jurisdiction: Fall 2004—Continued

State or jurisdiction	Total, all grades	Prekindergarten through grade 8 and elementary ungraded													Grades 9 through 12 and secondary ungraded					
		Total	Prekinder-garten[1]	Kinder-garten	Grade 1	Grade 2	Grade 3	Grade 4	Grade 5	Grade 6	Grade 7	Grade 8	Elementary ungraded	Total	Grade 9	Grade 10	Grade 11	Grade 12	Secondary ungraded
1	2	3	4	5	6	7	8	9	10	11	12	13	14	15	16	17	18	19	20
South Carolina	703,736	504,264	20,961	52,327	53,769	51,359	51,054	51,999	53,043	55,703	57,408	56,641	0	199,472	65,564	53,159	42,013	38,736	0
South Dakota	122,798	83,891	1,173	9,257	8,836	8,778	8,824	8,862	9,166	9,506	9,774	9,715	0	38,907	10,377	9,924	9,217	9,389	0
Tennessee	941,091[2]	670,880	8,132[2]	74,740	74,196	69,321	69,119	70,555	70,671	72,279	74,131	73,233	14,503	270,211	80,890	71,894	61,937	55,490	0
Texas	4,405,215	3,184,235	204,665	333,934	345,674	334,138	326,921	324,389	323,631	328,689	332,980	329,214		1,220,980	386,182	311,905	275,238	247,655	0
Utah	503,607	355,445	9,036	41,088	40,897	39,185	38,265	37,888	36,921	36,672	37,819	37,674	0	148,162	38,069	37,406	37,016	35,671	0
Vermont	98,352	65,935	3,714	6,249	6,452	6,521	6,550	6,807	7,068	7,254	7,474	7,846	0	32,417	8,533	8,237	7,873	7,552	222
Virginia	1,204,739	839,687	18,376	87,223	90,215	87,445	88,264	89,742	91,363	94,345	96,174	96,540	0	365,052	109,375	94,410	83,302	77,965	0
Washington	1,020,005	695,405	11,921	71,219	74,553	73,944	73,227	75,151	75,661	78,244	80,567	80,918	0	324,600	89,802	83,187	77,490	74,121	0
West Virginia	280,129	197,555	7,989	20,942	20,811	19,883	19,896	20,670	20,864	21,499	22,418	22,582	1	82,574	24,199	21,071	18,985	18,319	0
Wisconsin	864,757	577,950	27,444	58,724	58,521	57,807	58,874	59,267	61,493	62,557	66,095	67,168	0	286,807	76,173	71,196	69,928	69,510	0
Wyoming	84,733	57,285	374	6,264	6,209	5,983	6,042	5,862	6,230	6,505	6,831	6,985	0	27,448	7,355	7,202	6,568	6,323	0
Bureau of Indian Affairs																			
DoDDS, overseas	68,327	53,720	2,005	6,283	6,474	6,212	6,085	5,731	5,583	5,493	5,142	4,712	0	14,607	4,527	3,984	3,275	2,821	0
DoDDS, domestic	29,151	26,195	3,009	3,509	3,354	3,062	2,868	2,675	2,419	2,245	1,645	1,409	0	2,956	1,034	729	653	540	0
Other jurisdictions																			
American Samoa	16,126	11,873	1,547	1,016	1,129	1,109	1,080	1,185	1,218	1,258	1,216	1,115	0	4,253	1,140	1,122	1,051	878	62
Guam	30,605	21,686	430	2,203	2,463	2,362	2,463	2,509	2,110	2,439	2,335	2,372	0	8,919	2,815	2,587	1,860	1,657	0
Northern Marianas	11,601	8,416	580	686	921	886	872	851	877	951	880	834	78	3,185	979	857	681	668	0
Puerto Rico	575,648	408,607	199	38,375	45,988	43,084	43,612	44,497	45,012	45,002	46,246	43,212	13,380	167,041	45,140	44,949	37,422	32,917	6,613
Virgin Islands	16,429	11,650	(3)	989	1,088	1,112	1,094	1,315	1,386	1,460	1,747	1,288	171	4,779	1,676	1,145	1,029	929	0

—Not available.
[1] Data include imputations for nonrespondents.
[2] Includes imputations for underreporting.
[3] No prekindergarten pupils reported.

NOTE: DoDDS = Department of Defense dependents schools.
SOURCE: U.S. Department of Education, National Center for Education Statistics, Common Core of Data (CCD), "State Non-fiscal Survey of Public Elementary/Secondary Education," 2004–05. (This table was prepared August 2006.)

Table 35.   Enrollment in public elementary and secondary schools, by level, grade, and state or jurisdiction: Fall 2003

State or jurisdiction	Total, all grades	Prekindergarten through grade 8 and elementary ungraded												Grades 9 through 12 and secondary ungraded					
		Total	Prekindergarten[1]	Kindergarten	Grade 1	Grade 2	Grade 3	Grade 4	Grade 5	Grade 6	Grade 7	Grade 8	Elementary ungraded	Total	Grade 9	Grade 10	Grade 11	Grade 12	Secondary ungraded
1	2	3	4	5	6	7	8	9	10	11	12	13	14	15	16	17	18	19	20
United States	48,540,215[2]	34,202,248	949,649[2]	3,503,280	3,612,509	3,543,781	3,611,041	3,619,089	3,684,539	3,771,934	3,840,514	3,809,431	256,481	14,337,967	4,190,237	3,675,255	3,277,218	3,046,491	148,766
Alabama	731,220	525,313	1,852	56,541	58,064	54,935	56,429	57,323	58,853	59,799	61,854	59,663	0	205,907	62,718	53,695	47,489	42,005	0
Alaska	133,933	93,695	1,883	9,475	9,675	9,501	9,735	10,115	10,169	10,907	11,095	11,140	0	40,238	11,803	10,623	9,161	8,651	0
Arizona	1,012,068	704,327	9,376	76,365	77,612	76,617	75,422	76,207	75,757	77,508	77,943	76,376	5,144	307,741	87,576	79,320	71,561	68,815	469
Arkansas	454,523	321,509	2,573	36,391	35,615	34,242	33,642	34,070	34,265	35,831	37,165	37,004	711	133,014	37,301	35,343	31,228	28,840	302
California	6,413,867[2]	4,540,367	114,939[2]	456,941	481,035	482,626	489,642	493,415	492,523	490,081	500,404	500,143	38,618	1,873,500	528,564	490,214	440,546	395,194	18,982
Colorado	757,693	536,325	19,993	55,913	57,030	56,188	55,840	56,437	57,662	59,013	59,352	58,897	0	221,368	63,312	56,844	52,288	48,924	0
Connecticut	577,203	407,794	11,823	42,310	43,250	43,102	43,124	43,494	44,259	45,245	45,333	45,854	0	169,409	48,643	43,547	39,990	37,229	0
Delaware	117,668	82,898	642	7,904	9,051	8,712	8,898	9,097	9,204	9,439	9,729	10,222	0	34,770	11,009	8,782	7,687	7,292	0
District of Columbia ...	78,057	59,482	5,168	5,659	5,804	5,723	5,611	5,920	6,030	5,834	5,626	5,158	2,949	18,575	5,656	4,585	3,616	2,971	1,747
Florida	2,587,628	1,832,376	49,588	191,986	194,449	188,585	210,301	178,109	199,035	205,864	209,016	205,443	0	755,252	253,565	191,640	165,283	144,764	0
Georgia	1,522,611	1,103,181	36,486	118,849	117,282	113,706	115,849	117,201	118,777	121,716	122,621	120,694	0	419,430	135,091	109,851	93,107	81,381	0
Hawaii	183,609	130,054	1,175	13,779	13,852	14,305	14,291	14,538	14,610	14,444	14,477	14,543	40	53,555	16,459	13,529	12,904	10,627	36
Idaho	252,120	175,424	2,672	18,590	18,805	18,924	18,531	18,710	19,197	19,816	20,088	20,091	0	76,696	20,771	19,963	18,500	17,462	0
Illinois	2,100,961	1,492,730	67,148	146,803	155,142	154,191	161,329	160,246	158,367	163,901	162,933	160,271	2,399	608,231	174,343	155,848	139,504	136,974	1,562
Indiana	1,011,130	716,825	5,561	72,315	79,406	78,267	77,281	77,484	79,582	81,080	83,447	81,494	908	294,305	85,025	76,648	68,227	63,632	773
Iowa	481,226	326,846	6,907	35,295	33,296	33,330	33,326	34,290	35,539	36,701	37,919	38,428	1,815	154,380	40,486	38,451	36,794	36,834	1,815
Kansas	470,490	322,575	2,446	33,677	33,314	32,964	33,436	33,799	34,358	35,440	36,025	36,602	10,514	147,915	38,684	36,652	34,404	33,819	4,356
Kentucky	663,369	478,261	32,034	48,182	51,999	46,957	46,957	47,890	48,640	50,255	51,344	50,186	3,817	185,108	54,730	47,651	42,384	38,834	1,509
Louisiana	727,709	536,390	23,187	56,629	57,028	53,021	55,554	59,928	53,646	58,268	59,116	60,013	0	191,319	58,514	48,397	43,138	41,270	0
Maine	202,084	139,420	1,797	14,021	14,117	14,073	14,350	14,841	15,499	16,510	16,878	17,321	13	62,664	16,891	16,105	15,125	14,538	5
Maryland	869,113	605,905	21,391	55,485	62,341	61,767	63,195	65,119	66,227	69,007	70,013	68,967	2,393	263,208	78,690	66,269	59,670	55,897	2,682
Massachusetts ...	980,459	692,130	22,533	69,704	72,667	71,840	73,614	73,478	74,842	76,945	77,872	78,635	0	288,329	83,759	73,967	68,214	62,389	0
Michigan	1,757,604	1,229,121	21,724	130,527	124,238	122,469	125,417	127,659	130,524	135,570	140,088	139,797	31,108	528,483	153,567	132,565	119,881	108,688	13,782
Minnesota	842,854	564,049	10,876	59,330	58,055	57,610	58,720	60,045	62,175	63,653	65,676	67,909	0	278,805	69,744	68,895	67,558	72,608	0
Mississippi	493,540	360,913	2,208	38,340	39,300	37,396	38,053	38,752	39,468	39,761	41,101	38,231	8,303	132,627	39,536	33,563	28,316	25,918	5,294
Missouri	905,941	632,230	11,215	66,509	65,711	65,061	65,507	66,927	70,059	73,628	74,188	72,806	619	273,711	77,175	70,278	64,387	61,626	245
Montana	148,356	100,160	664	10,147	10,295	10,319	10,416	10,779	11,102	11,839	11,944	12,409	246	48,196	12,915	12,252	11,667	11,258	104
Nebraska	285,542	195,417	5,920	20,719	20,249	20,145	20,279	20,480	21,109	21,531	22,193	22,792	0	90,125	24,374	22,372	21,507	21,872	0
Nevada	385,401	280,735	2,778	28,596	30,595	30,518	31,175	30,653	30,928	31,642	31,884	31,392	574	104,666	34,779	28,685	22,486	18,700	16
New Hampshire ...	207,417	142,033	2,221	9,989	15,364	14,951	15,403	15,810	16,045	16,889	17,166	17,703	492	65,384	18,286	16,715	15,879	14,445	59
New Jersey	1,380,753	978,589	22,746	93,201	99,969	98,078	100,088	99,937	102,102	103,266	104,426	103,603	51,173	402,164	108,480	99,843	90,048	84,539	19,254
New Mexico	323,066	226,032	3,976	23,636	24,165	23,518	23,769	24,382	25,258	25,428	26,043	25,857	0	97,034	29,840	25,622	22,067	19,505	0
New York	2,864,775	1,978,673	41,456	188,638	201,645	201,482	205,635	206,912	210,704	214,819	221,138	219,335	66,909	886,102	257,475	224,166	175,475	163,362	65,624
North Carolina	1,360,209	974,019	11,686	109,336	107,376	103,725	103,063	105,411	105,026	109,682	109,997	108,717	0	386,190	122,508	100,658	87,106	75,918	0
North Dakota	102,233	67,870	752	6,891	7,139	7,053	7,041	7,219	7,603	7,829	8,098	8,245	0	34,363	8,952	8,659	8,439	8,313	0
Ohio	1,845,428	1,278,202	26,151	134,036	134,611	131,269	134,403	136,776	141,935	143,406	148,551	147,064	0	567,226	160,873	144,353	134,007	127,993	0
Oklahoma	626,160	450,319	30,203	46,542	49,434	44,076	44,272	44,829	45,738	47,522	47,511	47,258	2,934	175,841	49,529	45,189	41,333	38,601	1,189
Oregon	551,273	378,072	399	38,785	40,400	40,749	40,864	40,903	41,681	43,168	44,384	44,711	2,028	173,201	46,213	43,984	41,476	40,702	826
Pennsylvania	1,821,146	1,235,624	2,588	118,647	127,988	128,030	131,904	135,765	140,412	145,421	151,157	150,652	3,060	585,522	162,097	150,643	138,685	131,199	2,898
Rhode Island	159,375	111,209	1,473	10,702	11,891	11,745	11,770	12,429	12,362	12,720	13,099	13,018	0	48,166	14,188	12,676	11,345	9,957	0

See notes at end of table.

Table 35. Enrollment in public elementary and secondary schools, by level, grade, and state or jurisdiction: Fall 2003—Continued

State or jurisdiction	Total, all grades	Prekindergarten through grade 8 and elementary ungraded												Grades 9 through 12 and secondary ungraded					
		Total	Prekinder-garten[1]	Kindergarten	Grade 1	Grade 2	Grade 3	Grade 4	Grade 5	Grade 6	Grade 7	Grade 8	Elementary ungraded	Total	Grade 9	Grade 10	Grade 11	Grade 12	Secondary ungraded
1	2	3	4	5	6	7	8	9	10	11	12	13	14	15	16	17	18	19	20
South Carolina	699,198	500,743	20,107	50,985	52,555	50,539	51,634	52,715	54,801	56,563	57,460	53,384	0	198,455	69,415	51,238	39,529	38,273	0
South Dakota	125,537	86,015	2,132	9,201	8,869	8,818	8,762	9,140	9,430	9,825	9,756	10,082	0	39,522	10,375	9,996	9,585	9,566	0
Tennessee	936,682[2]	675,277	16,786[2]	73,202	71,581	68,746	69,911	70,446	71,876	73,218	74,812	72,505	12,194	261,405	79,195	68,430	59,665	54,115	0
Texas	4,331,751	3,132,584	194,150	323,502	338,727	325,943	323,373	321,788	324,047	327,094	329,579	324,381	0	1,199,167	377,912	309,851	267,914	243,490	0
Utah	495,981	348,890	8,598	39,348	38,485	37,380	36,935	36,064	35,566	36,526	36,457	36,386	7,145	147,091	36,028	36,479	35,004	34,629	4,951
Vermont	99,103	66,732	3,027	6,078	6,517	6,558	6,767	7,049	7,239	7,579	7,820	8,098	0	32,371	8,422	8,218	7,837	7,614	280
Virginia	1,192,092	837,258	16,524	86,374	87,674	87,430	88,870	90,729	91,882	95,158	96,661	95,586	370	354,834	107,033	90,009	81,313	76,477	2
Washington	1,021,349	699,248	11,352	70,663	73,989	72,558	74,394	75,108	77,856	80,054	81,000	82,274	0	322,101	88,869	82,120	76,774	74,338	0
West Virginia	281,215	198,836	7,911	20,946	20,446	19,846	20,559	20,753	21,164	22,066	22,885	22,255	5	82,379	23,723	20,659	19,439	18,554	4
Wisconsin	880,031	589,812	26,668	59,372	58,368	58,877	59,196	61,744	62,970	65,762	68,192	68,663	0	290,219	77,798	72,043	70,989	69,389	0
Wyoming	87,462	59,759	2,184	6,224	6,039	5,978	5,842	6,174	6,436	6,711	6,998	7,173	0	27,703	7,346	7,170	6,687	6,500	0
Bureau of Indian Affairs	45,828	33,671	(³)	4,266	3,756	3,432	3,466	3,614	3,685	3,890	3,855	3,707	0	12,157	3,932	3,410	2,509	2,306	0
DoDDS, overseas	71,053	56,226	2,018	6,516	6,610	6,595	6,327	6,126	5,926	5,731	5,347	5,030	0	14,827	4,784	3,945	3,332	2,766	0
DoDDS, domestic	30,603	27,500	3,164	3,623	3,478	3,251	3,037	2,816	2,598	2,386	1,651	1,496	0	3,103	1,044	815	660	584	0
Other jurisdictions																			
American Samoa	15,893	11,772	1,420	1,028	1,140	1,114	1,162	1,215	1,250	1,211	1,125	1,107	0	4,121	1,142	1,037	983	895	64
Guam	31,572	22,551	430	2,343	2,443	2,549	2,569	2,193	2,581	2,472	2,491	2,480	0	9,021	3,122	2,687	1,815	1,397	0
Northern Marianas	11,244	8,192	585	672	897	970	883	841	875	807	808	776	78	3,052	929	802	725	596	0
Puerto Rico	584,916	418,588	232	40,441	45,977	44,647	44,741	46,101	46,175	44,871	46,529	45,866	13,008	166,328	45,479	43,889	37,885	32,824	6,251
Virgin Islands	17,716	12,738	(³)	1,002	1,173	1,091	1,259	1,482	1,549	1,490	1,956	1,388	348	4,978	1,735	1,218	1,081	944	0

[1]Data include imputations for nonrespondents.
[2]Includes imputations for underreporting.
[3]No prekindergarten pupils reported.

NOTE: DoDDS = Department of Defense dependents schools. Some data have been revised from previously published figures.
SOURCE: U.S. Department of Education, National Center for Education Statistics, Common Core of Data (CCD), "State Non-fiscal Survey of Public Elementary/Secondary Education," 2003–04. (This table was prepared June 2006.)

Table 36. Enrollment in public elementary and secondary schools, by grade: Fall 1990 through fall 2004

Grade	Fall 1990	Fall 1991	Fall 1992	Fall 1993	Fall 1994	Fall 1995	Fall 1996	Fall 1997	Fall 1998	Fall 1999	Fall 2000	Fall 2001	Fall 2002	Fall 2003	Fall 2004
1	2	3	4	5	6	7	8	9	10	11	12	13	14	15	16
	Number (in thousands)														
All grades......................	41,217	42,047	42,823	43,465	44,111	44,840	45,611	46,127	46,539	46,857	47,204	47,672	48,183	48,540	48,795
Elementary.............................	29,878	30,506	31,088	31,504	31,898	32,341	32,764	33,073	33,346	33,488	33,688	33,938	34,116	34,202	34,178
Prekindergarten..................	303	375	505	545	603	637	670	695	729	751	776	865	915	950	990
Kindergarten......................	3,306	3,311	3,313	3,377	3,444	3,536	3,532	3,503	3,443	3,397	3,382	3,379	3,434	3,503	3,544
1st grade.........................	3,499	3,556	3,542	3,529	3,593	3,671	3,770	3,755	3,727	3,684	3,636	3,614	3,594	3,613	3,663
2nd grade.........................	3,327	3,360	3,431	3,429	3,440	3,507	3,600	3,689	3,681	3,656	3,634	3,593	3,565	3,544	3,560
3rd grade.........................	3,297	3,334	3,361	3,437	3,439	3,445	3,524	3,597	3,696	3,691	3,676	3,653	3,623	3,611	3,580
4th grade.........................	3,248	3,315	3,342	3,361	3,426	3,431	3,454	3,507	3,592	3,686	3,711	3,695	3,669	3,619	3,612
5th grade.........................	3,197	3,268	3,325	3,350	3,372	3,438	3,453	3,458	3,520	3,604	3,707	3,727	3,711	3,685	3,635
6th grade.........................	3,110	3,239	3,303	3,356	3,381	3,395	3,494	3,492	3,497	3,564	3,663	3,769	3,788	3,772	3,735
7th grade.........................	3,067	3,181	3,299	3,355	3,404	3,422	3,464	3,520	3,530	3,541	3,629	3,720	3,821	3,841	3,818
8th grade.........................	2,979	3,020	3,129	3,249	3,302	3,356	3,403	3,415	3,480	3,497	3,538	3,616	3,709	3,809	3,825
Elementary ungraded	543	545	539	515	494	502	401	442	451	417	336	306	287	256	216
Secondary.............................	11,338	11,541	11,735	11,961	12,213	12,500	12,847	13,054	13,193	13,369	13,515	13,734	14,067	14,338	14,617
9th grade.........................	3,169	3,313	3,352	3,487	3,604	3,704	3,801	3,819	3,856	3,935	3,963	4,012	4,105	4,190	4,281
10th grade.........................	2,896	2,915	3,027	3,050	3,131	3,237	3,323	3,376	3,382	3,415	3,491	3,528	3,584	3,675	3,750
11th grade.........................	2,612	2,645	2,656	2,751	2,748	2,826	2,930	2,972	3,021	3,034	3,083	3,174	3,229	3,277	3,369
12th grade.........................	2,381	2,392	2,431	2,424	2,488	2,487	2,586	2,673	2,722	2,782	2,803	2,863	2,990	3,046	3,094
Secondary ungraded	282	275	269	248	242	245	206	214	212	203	175	157	160	149	121
	Percentage distribution														
All grades......................	100.0	100.0	100.0	100.0	100.0	100.0	100.0	100.0	100.0	100.0	100.0	100.0	100.0	100.0	100.0
Elementary.............................	72.5	72.6	72.6	72.5	72.3	72.1	71.8	71.7	71.7	71.5	71.4	71.2	70.8	70.0	70.0
Prekindergarten..................	0.7	0.9	1.2	1.3	1.4	1.4	1.5	1.5	1.6	1.6	1.6	1.8	1.9	2.0	2.0
Kindergarten......................	8.0	7.9	7.7	7.8	7.8	7.9	7.7	7.6	7.4	7.3	7.2	7.1	7.1	7.3	7.3
1st grade.........................	8.5	8.5	8.3	8.1	8.1	8.2	8.3	8.1	8.0	7.9	7.7	7.6	7.5	7.5	7.5
2nd grade.........................	8.1	8.0	8.0	7.9	7.8	7.8	7.9	8.0	7.9	7.8	7.7	7.5	7.4	7.3	7.3
3rd grade.........................	8.0	7.9	7.8	7.9	7.8	7.7	7.7	7.8	7.9	7.9	7.8	7.7	7.5	7.3	7.3
4th grade.........................	7.9	7.9	7.8	7.7	7.8	7.7	7.6	7.6	7.7	7.9	7.9	7.8	7.6	7.4	7.4
5th grade.........................	7.8	7.8	7.8	7.7	7.6	7.7	7.6	7.5	7.6	7.7	7.9	7.8	7.7	7.4	7.4
6th grade.........................	7.5	7.7	7.7	7.7	7.7	7.6	7.7	7.6	7.5	7.6	7.8	7.9	7.9	7.7	7.7
7th grade.........................	7.4	7.6	7.7	7.7	7.7	7.6	7.6	7.6	7.6	7.6	7.7	7.8	7.9	7.8	7.8
8th grade.........................	7.2	7.2	7.3	7.5	7.5	7.5	7.5	7.4	7.5	7.5	7.5	7.6	7.7	7.8	7.8
Elementary ungraded	1.3	1.3	1.3	1.2	1.1	1.1	0.9	1.0	1.0	0.9	0.7	0.6	0.6	0.4	0.4
Secondary.............................	27.5	27.4	27.4	27.5	27.7	27.9	28.2	28.3	28.3	28.5	28.6	28.8	29.2	30.0	30.0
9th grade.........................	7.7	7.9	7.8	8.0	8.2	8.3	8.3	8.3	8.3	8.4	8.4	8.4	8.5	8.8	8.8
10th grade.........................	7.0	6.9	7.1	7.0	7.1	7.2	7.3	7.3	7.3	7.3	7.4	7.4	7.4	7.7	7.7
11th grade.........................	6.3	6.3	6.2	6.3	6.2	6.3	6.4	6.4	6.5	6.5	6.5	6.7	6.7	6.9	6.9
12th grade.........................	5.8	5.7	5.7	5.6	5.6	5.5	5.7	5.8	5.8	5.9	5.9	6.0	6.2	6.3	6.3
Secondary ungraded	0.7	0.7	0.6	0.6	0.5	0.5	0.5	0.5	0.5	0.4	0.4	0.3	0.3	0.2	0.2

NOTE: Because of changes in reporting practices and imputation of data for nonrespondents since 1992, prekindergarten enrollment data for 1992 and later years are not comparable to prekindergarten enrollment data for prior years. Some data have been revised from previously published figures. Detail may not sum to totals because of rounding.

SOURCE: U.S. Department of Education, National Center for Education Statistics, Common Core of Data (CCD), "State Nonfiscal Survey of Public Elementary/Secondary Education," 1990–91 through 2004–05. (This table was prepared August 2006.)

Table 37.   Number and percentage of homeschooled students ages 5 through 17 with a grade equivalent of kindergarten through 12th grade, by selected child, parent, and household characteristics: 1999 and 2003

Characteristic	1999						2003					
	Number of students[1] (in thousands)		Number homeschooled (in thousands)		Percent homeschooled		Number of students[1] (in thousands)		Number homeschooled (in thousands)		Percent homeschooled	
1	2		3		4		5		6		7	
Total	**50,188**	**(72.7)**	**850**	**(71.1)**	**1.7**	**(0.14)**	**50,707**	**(89.3)**	**1,096**	**(92.3)**	**2.2**	**(0.18)**
Sex of child												
Male	25,515	(233.9)	417	(43.9)	1.6	(0.17)	25,819	(286.8)	569	(61.9)	2.2	(0.24)
Female	24,673	(238.7)	434	(46.1)	1.8	(0.19)	24,888	(277.7)	527	(58.2)	2.1	(0.23)
Race/ethnicity of child												
White	32,474	(168.2)	640	(62.3)	2.0	(0.19)	31,584	(187.2)	843	(77.5)	2.7	(0.25)
Black	8,047	(102.3)	84	(24.8)	1.0	(0.31)	7,985	(45.7)	103	(33.9)	1.3	(0.42)
Hispanic	7,043	(85.5)	77	(17.7)	1.1	(0.25)	8,075	(35.1)	59	(21.1)	0.7	(0.26)
Other	2,623	(114.2)	49	(17.2)	1.9	(0.65)	3,063	(161.1)	91	(31.5)	3.0	(1.02)
Grade equivalent[2]												
Kindergarten through 5th grade	24,428	(20.5)	428	(48.1)	1.8	(0.20)	24,269	(24.7)	472	(55.3)	1.9	(0.23)
Kindergarten	3,790	(20.0)	92	(19.7)	2.4	(0.52)	3,643	(24.7)	98	(23.5)	2.7	(0.64)
Grades 1 through 3	12,692	(6.2)	199	(36.7)	1.6	(0.29)	12,098	(#)	214	(33.3)	1.8	(0.28)
Grades 4 through 5	7,946	(1.3)	136	(22.5)	1.7	(0.28)	8,528	(#)	160	(30.1)	1.9	(0.35)
Grades 6 through 8	11,788	(3.4)	186	(28.0)	1.6	(0.24)	12,472	(6.5)	302	(44.9)	2.4	(0.36)
Grades 9 through 12	13,954	(70.5)	235	(33.2)	1.7	(0.24)	13,958	(81.8)	315	(47.0)	2.3	(0.33)
Number of children in the household												
One child	8,226	(153.8)	120	(20.3)	1.5	(0.24)	8,033	(218.1)	110	(22.3)	1.4	(0.28)
Two children	19,883	(211.4)	207	(27.1)	1.0	(0.14)	20,530	(319.4)	306	(45.1)	1.5	(0.22)
Three or more children	22,078	(241.2)	523	(65.2)	2.4	(0.30)	22,144	(362.8)	679	(80.2)	3.1	(0.36)
Number of parents in the household												
Two parents	33,007	(203.8)	683	(68.3)	2.1	(0.21)	35,936	(315.1)	886	(82.7)	2.5	(0.23)
One parent	15,454	(209.4)	142	(25.0)	0.9	(0.16)	13,260	(319.2)	196	(42.6)	1.5	(0.32)
Nonparental guardians	1,727	(86.0)	25	(14.4)	1.4	(0.82)	1,511	(100.1)	14	(11.1)	0.9	(0.74)
Parent participation in the labor force												
Two parents—both in labor force	22,880	(241.5)	237	(39.8)	1.0	(0.17)	25,108	(373.1)	274	(44.1)	1.1	(0.18)
Two parents—one in labor force	9,628	(194.4)	444	(53.8)	4.6	(0.55)	10,545	(297.2)	594	(73.7)	5.6	(0.67)
One parent in labor force	13,907	(220.0)	98	(21.8)	0.7	(0.16)	12,045	(267.9)	174	(39.8)	1.4	(0.33)
No parent participation in labor force	3,773	(162.3)	71	(18.8)	1.9	(0.48)	3,008	(171.4)	54	(23.7)	1.8	(0.78)
Highest education level of parents												
High school diploma or less	18,334	(217.3)	160	(26.5)	0.9	(0.15)	16,106	(272.3)	269	(51.6)	1.7	(0.32)
Vocational/technical or some college	15,177	(215.2)	287	(37.3)	1.9	(0.25)	16,068	(323.4)	338	(57.7)	2.1	(0.36)
Bachelor's degree	8,269	(182.5)	213	(36.2)	2.6	(0.42)	9,798	(277.3)	274	(47.2)	2.8	(0.48)
Graduate/professional degree	8,407	(207.1)	190	(39.8)	2.3	(0.46)	8,734	(238.1)	215	(44.2)	2.5	(0.51)
Household income												
$25,000 or less	16,776	(116.9)	262	(45.0)	1.6	(0.27)	12,375	(53.6)	283	(56.0)	2.3	(0.45)
$25,001 to $50,000	15,220	(232.7)	278	(36.7)	1.8	(0.24)	13,220	(270.2)	311	(49.9)	2.4	(0.37)
$50,001 to $75,000	8,576	(189.3)	162	(25.5)	1.9	(0.30)	10,961	(282.2)	264	(51.1)	2.4	(0.46)
Over $75,000	9,615	(211.2)	148	(26.5)	1.5	(0.28)	14,150	(261.7)	238	(45.8)	1.7	(0.33)
Urbanicity[3]												
Urban	37,415	(185.2)	575	(51.0)	1.5	(0.15)	40,180	(187.2)	794	(76.6)	2.0	(0.22)
Rural	12,773	(112.6)	275	(39.8)	2.2	(0.31)	10,527	(56.3)	302	(58.0)	2.9	(0.55)
Region												
Northeast	10,220	(103.7)	114	(30.1)	1.1	(0.30)	9,220	(42.6)	168	(53.3)	1.8	(0.58)
South	17,366	(122.5)	355	(48.4)	2.0	(0.28)	17,232	(55.0)	445	(66.7)	2.6	(0.39)
Midwest	12,040	(114.1)	166	(28.6)	1.4	(0.24)	11,949	(61.3)	238	(43.9)	2.0	(0.37)
West	10,560	(97.3)	215	(35.9)	2.0	(0.34)	12,305	(39.8)	245	(42.3)	2.0	(0.34)

#Rounds to zero.
[1]Refers to all students in public and private schools and homeschooled students.
[2]Students whose grade-equivalent was "ungraded" were excluded from the grade analysis. The percentage of students with an "ungraded" grade equivalent was 0.03 percent in 1999 and 0.02 percent in 2003.
[3]Urbanicity is based on a U.S. Census Bureau classification of places. Urban is a place with at least 50,000 people. Rural is a place not classified as urban.

NOTE: The number and percentage of homeschoolers exclude students who were enrolled in school for more than 25 hours a week and students who were homeschooled due to a temporary illness. Race categories exclude persons of Hispanic origin. Standard errors appear in parentheses.
SOURCE: U.S. Department of Education, National Center for Education Statistics, *Homeschooling in the United States: 2003*, Parent Survey (Parent:1999) and Parent and Family Involvement in Education Survey (PFI:2003) of the National Household Education Surveys Program. (This table was prepared September 2006.)

Table 38.   Percentage distribution of all students, homeschooled students, and nonhomeschooled students, ages 5 through 17 with a grade equivalent of kindergarten through 12th grade, by selected child, parent, and household characteristics: 1999 and 2003

Characteristic	1999								2003							
	All students		Homeschooled[1]		Public schooled		Private schooled		All students		Homeschooled[1]		Public schooled		Private schooled	
1	2		3		4		5		6		7		8		9	
Total	100.0	(†)	100.0	(†)	100.0	(†)	100.0	(†)	100.0	(†)	100.0	(†)	100.0	(†)	100.0	(†)
Sex of child																
Male	50.8	(0.47)	49.0	(3.27)	51.1	(0.51)	49.3	(1.32)	50.9	(0.55)	51.9	(3.52)	50.9	(0.59)	50.6	(1.58)
Female	49.2	(0.47)	51.0	(3.27)	48.9	(0.51)	50.7	(1.32)	49.1	(0.55)	48.1	(3.52)	49.1	(0.59)	49.4	(1.58)
Race/ethnicity of child																
White	64.7	(0.32)	75.3	(3.36)	63.1	(0.36)	76.8	(1.06)	62.3	(0.34)	77.0	(3.88)	60.9	(0.40)	70.5	(1.54)
Black	16.0	(0.20)	9.9	(2.80)	16.8	(0.24)	10.0	(0.76)	15.7	(0.08)	9.4	(2.87)	16.3	(0.15)	12.7	(1.14)
Hispanic	14.0	(0.17)	9.1	(2.06)	14.9	(0.19)	7.3	(0.57)	15.9	(0.07)	5.3	(1.92)	16.9	(0.16)	10.5	(0.87)
Other	5.2	(0.23)	5.8	(2.01)	5.2	(0.25)	5.8	(0.68)	6.0	(0.32)	8.3	(2.80)	5.9	(0.35)	6.3	(0.90)
Grade equivalent[2]																
Kindergarten through 5th grade	48.7	(0.07)	50.4	(3.75)	47.8	(0.16)	56.6	(1.26)	47.9	(0.08)	43.3	(3.06)	47.4	(0.21)	52.4	(1.39)
Kindergarten	7.6	(0.04)	10.8	(2.31)	7.0	(0.12)	12.1	(0.94)	7.2	(0.04)	9.0	(2.06)	7.0	(0.10)	8.6	(0.75)
Grades 1 through 3	25.3	(0.04)	23.5	(3.61)	25.1	(0.15)	27.5	(1.16)	23.9	(0.04)	19.7	(2.50)	23.6	(0.17)	26.8	(1.34)
Grades 4 through 5	15.8	(0.02)	16.0	(2.34)	15.7	(0.13)	17.0	(1.08)	16.8	(0.03)	14.7	(2.30)	16.8	(0.14)	17.1	(0.98)
Grades 6 through 8	23.5	(0.04)	21.9	(2.83)	23.7	(0.13)	22.4	(0.97)	24.6	(0.04)	27.8	(3.43)	24.7	(0.16)	23.2	(1.12)
Grades 9 through 12	27.8	(0.10)	27.7	(3.21)	28.6	(0.16)	20.9	(1.06)	27.5	(0.12)	28.9	(3.83)	27.9	(0.22)	24.3	(1.32)
Number of children in the household																
One child	16.4	(0.30)	14.1	(2.53)	16.3	(0.33)	17.8	(0.91)	15.8	(0.43)	10.1	(1.97)	15.8	(0.44)	17.0	(1.20)
Two children	39.6	(0.42)	24.4	(3.06)	39.9	(0.45)	39.6	(1.41)	40.5	(0.63)	28.0	(3.74)	40.6	(0.67)	42.4	(1.47)
Three or more children	44.0	(0.48)	61.6	(3.97)	43.8	(0.53)	42.6	(1.56)	43.7	(0.72)	62.0	(4.35)	43.6	(0.74)	40.6	(1.95)
Number of parents in the household																
Two parents	65.8	(0.41)	80.4	(3.26)	64.4	(0.45)	75.6	(1.36)	70.9	(0.59)	80.8	(3.55)	69.5	(0.66)	80.0	(1.46)
One parent	30.8	(0.41)	16.7	(2.91)	32.0	(0.45)	22.7	(1.33)	26.2	(0.63)	17.9	(3.61)	27.3	(0.71)	18.4	(1.47)
Nonparental guardians	3.4	(0.17)	2.9	(1.70)	3.6	(0.19)	1.7	(0.27)	3.0	(0.20)	1.3	(1.01)	3.2	(0.22)	1.6	(0.40)
Parent participation in the labor force																
Two parents—both in labor force	45.6	(0.48)	27.9	(3.92)	45.5	(0.54)	49.5	(1.56)	49.5	(0.72)	25.0	(3.72)	49.3	(0.72)	56.3	(2.28)
Two parents—one in labor force	19.2	(0.39)	52.2	(4.27)	17.9	(0.40)	25.2	(1.40)	20.8	(0.59)	54.2	(4.73)	19.7	(0.61)	22.9	(1.71)
One parent in labor force	27.7	(0.44)	11.6	(2.53)	28.8	(0.47)	20.4	(1.23)	23.8	(0.53)	15.9	(3.30)	24.7	(0.60)	17.4	(1.42)
No parent participation in labor force	7.5	(0.32)	8.3	(2.21)	7.8	(0.34)	4.9	(0.74)	5.9	(0.34)	4.9	(2.16)	6.3	(0.36)	3.4	(0.62)
Highest education level of parents																
High school diploma or less	36.5	(0.43)	18.9	(2.88)	39.0	(0.46)	17.8	(1.15)	31.8	(0.54)	24.5	(4.24)	34.2	(0.60)	13.1	(1.24)
Vocational/technical or some college	30.2	(0.43)	33.7	(3.85)	31.0	(0.48)	23.2	(1.19)	31.7	(0.62)	30.8	(4.60)	32.6	(0.68)	24.5	(1.35)
Bachelor's degree	16.5	(0.36)	25.1	(3.49)	15.2	(0.33)	26.6	(1.28)	19.3	(0.55)	25.0	(3.92)	17.8	(0.57)	30.9	(1.51)
Graduate/professional degree	16.8	(0.41)	22.3	(4.17)	14.9	(0.40)	32.4	(1.20)	17.2	(0.47)	19.6	(3.67)	15.4	(0.52)	31.5	(1.56)
Household income																
$25,000 or less	33.4	(0.22)	30.9	(4.31)	35.6	(0.25)	14.8	(1.20)	24.4	(0.09)	25.8	(4.32)	26.2	(0.21)	9.4	(1.18)
$25,001 to $50,000	30.3	(0.47)	32.7	(4.00)	30.6	(0.47)	27.5	(1.39)	26.1	(0.53)	28.4	(4.06)	26.9	(0.57)	18.5	(1.29)
$50,001 to $75,000	17.1	(0.38)	19.1	(2.62)	16.8	(0.39)	19.4	(1.21)	21.6	(0.55)	24.1	(4.46)	21.5	(0.59)	22.1	(1.48)
Over $75,000	19.2	(0.42)	17.4	(2.65)	17.0	(0.42)	38.3	(1.40)	27.9	(0.52)	21.7	(3.79)	25.3	(0.60)	50.0	(1.90)
Urbanicity[3]																
Urban	74.5	(0.22)	67.6	(3.81)	73.2	(0.28)	87.2	(1.03)	79.2	(0.10)	72.4	(4.91)	77.9	(0.21)	91.1	(1.19)
Rural	25.5	(0.22)	32.4	(3.81)	26.8	(0.28)	12.8	(1.03)	20.8	(0.10)	27.6	(4.91)	22.1	(0.21)	8.9	(1.19)
Region																
Northeast	20.4	(0.21)	13.4	(3.35)	19.9	(0.26)	25.8	(1.10)	18.2	(0.08)	15.3	(4.51)	17.4	(0.21)	24.8	(1.60)
South	34.6	(0.23)	41.8	(4.36)	34.7	(0.27)	32.2	(1.18)	34.0	(0.10)	40.6	(4.96)	34.8	(0.21)	26.3	(1.41)
Midwest	24.0	(0.23)	19.5	(3.13)	23.8	(0.28)	26.2	(1.27)	23.6	(0.10)	21.8	(3.81)	22.8	(0.31)	30.2	(2.02)
West	21.0	(0.20)	25.3	(3.77)	21.5	(0.25)	15.8	(0.95)	24.3	(0.08)	22.3	(3.77)	25.0	(0.19)	18.7	(1.20)

†Not applicable.
[1] Excludes students who were enrolled in school for more than 25 hours a week and students who were homeschooled due to a temporary illness.
[2] Students whose grade-equivalent was "ungraded" were excluded from the grade analysis. The percentage of students with an "ungraded" grade equivalent was 0.03 percent in 1999 and 0.02 percent in 2003.
[3] Urbanicity is based on a U.S. Census Bureau classification of places. Urban is a place with at least 50,000 people. Rural is a place not classified as urban.

NOTE: Race categories exclude persons of Hispanic origin. Detail may not sum to totals because of rounding. Standard errors appear in parentheses.
SOURCE: U.S. Department of Education, National Center for Education Statistics, *Homeschooling in the United States: 2003*, Parent Survey (Parent:1999) and Parent and Family Involvement in Education Survey (PFI:2003) of the National Household Education Surveys Program. (This table was prepared September 2006.)

Table 39. Average daily attendance in public elementary and secondary schools, by state or jurisdiction: Selected years, 1969–70 through 2003–04

State or jurisdiction	1969–70	1979–80	1989–90	1990–91	1995–96	1999–2000	2000–01	2002–03	2003–04
1	2	3	4	5	6	7	8	9	10
United States	41,934,376	38,288,911	37,799,296	38,426,543	41,501,596	43,806,726	44,075,930	45,017,360	45,325,731
Alabama	777,123	711,432	683,833	682,524	687,076	725,212	719,562	701,235	706,446
Alaska	72,489	79,945	98,213	102,585	115,958	122,412	122,932	123,145	122,341
Arizona	391,526	481,905	557,252	573,140	684,740	782,851	803,453	868,547	878,891
Arkansas	414,158	423,610	403,025	408,145	423,520	422,958	421,625	418,775	425,571
California[1]	4,418,423	4,044,736	4,893,341	5,065,647	5,351,475	5,957,216	6,075,001	6,312,362	6,384,882
Colorado	500,388	513,475	519,419	521,899	608,633	656,700	671,909	709,349	673,285
Connecticut	618,881	507,362	439,524	450,808	495,188	533,779	540,946	557,701	561,530
Delaware	120,819	94,058	89,838	91,052	99,941	106,444	105,681	109,945	108,751
District of Columbia	138,600	91,576	71,468	69,092	71,001	65,371	62,881	61,236	65,625
Florida	1,312,693	1,464,461	1,646,583	1,714,394	1,947,777	2,175,453	2,269,372	2,362,841	2,418,329
Georgia	1,019,427	989,433	1,054,097	1,075,728	1,232,852	1,326,713	1,347,218	1,400,007	1,424,004
Hawaii	168,140	151,563	157,360	160,193	171,977	171,180	171,117	169,797	167,739
Idaho	170,920	189,199	203,987	209,085	228,371	230,828	230,890	234,244	237,095
Illinois	2,084,844	1,770,435	1,587,733	1,618,101	1,750,417	1,789,089	1,805,582	1,855,417	1,862,274
Indiana	1,111,043	983,444	884,568	888,177	909,553	929,281	928,703	942,506	943,735
Iowa	624,403	510,081	450,224	456,614	477,053	471,384	467,404	459,761	457,771
Kansas	470,296	382,019	388,986	397,609	416,674	426,853	425,036	419,285	415,529
Kentucky	647,970	619,868	569,795	569,713	571,934	565,693	564,198	569,538	570,911
Louisiana	776,555	727,601	727,125	720,551	710,925	701,957	684,566	674,949	674,333
Maine	225,146	211,400	195,089	196,229	200,700	194,554	191,963	188,776	187,492
Maryland	785,989	686,336	620,617	637,370	719,433	791,133	797,522	809,398	808,557
Massachusetts	1,056,207	935,960	763,231	770,802	845,270	913,502	920,522	921,201	932,417
Michigan	1,991,235	1,758,427	1,446,996	1,452,700	1,554,358	1,574,894	1,577,260	1,591,900	1,590,555
Minnesota	864,595	748,606	699,001	714,072	786,241	818,819	820,457	813,660	792,896
Mississippi	524,623	454,401	476,048	474,029	470,657	468,746	465,505	461,269	463,470
Missouri	906,132	777,269	729,693	733,680	805,404	836,105	836,411	849,040	851,749
Montana	162,664	144,608	135,406	138,341	148,616	142,313	139,198	133,988	132,356
Nebraska	314,516	270,524	254,754	257,587	270,938	261,767	268,897	269,499	260,352
Nevada	113,421	134,995	173,149	185,755	243,718	305,067	321,679	346,512	364,409
New Hampshire	140,203	154,187	154,915	156,579	187,067	200,283	198,389	200,184	202,352
New Jersey	1,322,124	1,140,111	997,561	1,016,159	1,125,877	1,222,438	1,257,124	1,312,610	1,336,869
New Mexico	259,997	253,453	290,245	291,215	330,851	323,963	319,939	320,189	319,637
New York	3,099,192	2,530,289	2,244,110	2,278,531	2,463,349	2,595,070	2,598,176	2,614,977	2,599,902
North Carolina	1,104,295	1,072,150	1,012,274	1,012,613	1,096,812	1,185,737	1,203,143	1,242,234	1,264,266
North Dakota	141,961	118,986	109,659	109,691	111,870	105,123	103,420	97,879	96,231
Ohio	2,246,282	1,849,283	1,584,735	1,603,025	1,661,014	1,659,903	1,653,316	1,683,337	1,700,533
Oklahoma	560,993	548,065	543,170	548,387	574,538	586,266	580,754	581,767	583,932
Oregon	436,736	418,593	419,771	431,806	462,108	479,321	481,223	487,544	486,073
Pennsylvania	2,169,225	1,808,630	1,524,839	1,542,077	1,651,741	1,684,913	1,683,637	1,694,148	1,701,096
Rhode Island	163,205	139,195	125,934	129,856	137,870	144,422	144,895	144,813	143,792
South Carolina	600,292	569,612	569,029	573,138	605,526	624,456	623,008	629,997	635,750
South Dakota	158,543	124,934	119,823	121,403	127,754	122,252	120,966	118,383	116,651
Tennessee	836,010	806,696	761,766	767,738	819,831	844,878	846,551	850,322	859,522
Texas	2,432,420	2,608,817	3,075,333	3,085,648	3,435,010	3,706,550	3,771,568	3,940,776	4,016,791
Utah	287,405	312,813	408,917	417,609	444,679	448,096	447,450	451,063	456,183
Vermont	97,772	95,045	87,832	88,901	100,166	98,894	97,717	95,868	95,160
Virginia	995,580	955,105	989,197	1,011,513	1,098,862	1,195,123	1,087,591	1,109,459	1,118,446
Washington	764,735	710,929	755,141	781,371	888,142	925,696	927,530	933,702	937,656
West Virginia	372,278	353,264	301,947	300,067	285,548	273,277	264,798	260,365	266,078
Wisconsin	880,609	770,554	711,466	731,088	799,391	825,699	824,002	831,939	826,864
Wyoming	81,293	89,471	91,277	92,506	93,190	86,092	83,243	79,921	78,652
Other jurisdictions									
American Samoa	—	—	11,448	12,272	14,074	15,102	14,818	15,243	15,123
Guam	20,315	—	23,883	25,330	31,998	—	—	—	28,301
Northern Marianas	—	—	6,809	6,062	7,511	8,712	8,968	9,739	10,047
Puerto Rico	—	656,709	597,436	597,418	548,788	540,676	538,738	535,874	534,941
Virgin Islands	—	—	18,924	19,984	19,867	18,676	16,069	16,187	15,878

—Not available.
[1]Data for California for 1990–91 and earlier years are not strictly comparable with those for other states because California's attendance figures included excused absences.
NOTE: Some data have been revised from previously published figures.

SOURCE: U.S. Department of Education, National Center for Education Statistics, *Statistics of State School Systems*, 1969–70; *Revenues and Expenditures for Public Elementary and Secondary Education*, 1979–80; and Common Core of Data (CCD), "National Public Education Financial Survey," 1989–90 through 2003–04. (This table was prepared August 2006.)

Table 40. Percentage distribution of enrollment in public elementary and secondary schools, by race/ethnicity and state or jurisdiction: Fall 1994 and fall 2004

State or jurisdiction	Percentage distribution, fall 1994						Percentage distribution, fall 2004					
	Total	White	Black	Hispanic	Asian/ Pacific Islander	American Indian/ Alaska Native	Total	White	Black	Hispanic	Asian/ Pacific Islander	American Indian/ Alaska Native
1	2	3	4	5	6	7	8	9	10	11	12	13
United States[1]............	100.0	65.6	16.7	13.0	3.6	1.1	100.0	57.9	17.3	19.2	4.5	1.2
Alabama	100.0	62.3	35.8	0.4	0.6	0.8	100.0	59.7	36.1	2.4	1.0	0.8
Alaska................................	100.0	64.7	4.8	2.6	4.1	23.8	100.0	58.3	4.6	4.1	6.7	26.3
Arizona	100.0	58.4	4.3	28.7	1.7	7.0	100.0	48.3	5.0	38.2	2.3	6.2
Arkansas............................	100.0	73.9	23.9	1.1	0.7	0.3	100.0	69.2	23.0	6.0	1.3	0.6
California	100.0	41.4	8.7	37.9	11.2	0.9	100.0	31.9	8.1	47.7	11.5	0.8
Colorado	100.0	73.5	5.4	17.6	2.5	1.0	100.0	63.5	5.9	26.2	3.2	1.2
Connecticut........................	100.0	72.7	13.3	11.4	2.4	0.2	100.0	67.5	13.8	15.0	3.4	0.4
Delaware............................	100.0	65.4	29.1	3.6	1.7	0.2	100.0	56.2	32.3	8.5	2.7	0.3
District of Columbia	100.0	4.0	88.0	6.6	1.3	#	100.0	4.6	84.5	9.5	1.4	0.0
Florida................................	100.0	58.7	25.0	14.4	1.7	0.2	100.0	50.5	24.1	23.0	2.1	0.3
Georgia..............................	100.0	59.1	37.5	1.8	1.5	0.1	100.0	50.5	38.9	7.9	2.7	0.2
Hawaii................................	100.0	23.2	2.7	4.9	68.8	0.4	100.0	20.0	2.4	4.5	72.5	0.6
Idaho..................................	—	—	—	—	—	—	100.0	83.5	1.0	12.4	1.5	1.6
Illinois................................	100.0	64.4	21.0	11.6	3.0	0.1	100.0	57.0	20.7	18.4	3.7	0.2
Indiana...............................	100.0	85.7	11.2	2.2	0.8	0.2	100.0	81.0	12.4	5.2	1.1	0.3
Iowa	100.0	93.1	3.2	1.8	1.5	0.4	100.0	87.4	4.8	5.4	1.9	0.6
Kansas...............................	100.0	83.0	8.4	5.7	1.9	1.0	100.0	75.9	8.7	11.6	2.3	1.4
Kentucky	100.0	89.3	9.7	0.3	0.6	0.1	100.0	86.6	10.5	1.8	0.9	0.2
Louisiana	100.0	51.5	45.7	1.1	1.3	0.5	100.0	48.3	47.7	1.9	1.4	0.7
Maine..................................	100.0	97.5	0.7	0.4	0.8	0.5	100.0	95.5	1.9	0.8	1.3	0.5
Maryland............................	100.0	58.1	34.7	3.1	3.8	0.3	100.0	49.5	38.1	7.0	5.0	0.4
Massachusetts...................	100.0	79.1	8.0	9.0	3.7	0.2	100.0	74.2	8.9	11.8	4.8	0.3
Michigan	100.0	77.4	17.5	2.6	1.5	1.1	100.0	72.7	19.9	4.2	2.2	1.0
Minnesota	100.0	88.1	4.5	1.8	3.7	1.9	100.0	79.3	8.2	5.0	5.5	2.1
Mississippi	100.0	47.8	50.9	0.3	0.5	0.4	100.0	47.0	50.8	1.3	0.8	0.2
Missouri	100.0	82.2	15.8	0.9	1.0	0.2	100.0	77.3	17.9	2.9	1.5	0.4
Montana.............................	100.0	87.7	0.5	1.4	0.8	9.6	100.0	84.5	0.8	2.3	1.1	11.3
Nebraska	100.0	87.8	5.8	3.8	1.2	1.3	100.0	78.5	7.4	10.8	1.7	1.6
Nevada	100.0	69.0	9.3	15.5	4.2	2.0	—	—	—	—	—	—
New Hampshire	100.0	96.8	0.8	1.1	1.0	0.2	100.0	93.8	1.6	2.6	1.8	0.3
New Jersey	100.0	63.0	18.6	13.1	5.2	0.2	100.0	57.1	17.7	17.7	7.2	0.2
New Mexico	100.0	39.9	2.4	46.4	1.0	10.4	100.0	31.9	2.5	53.3	1.2	11.1
New York............................	100.0	57.7	20.2	16.9	4.8	0.4	100.0	53.1	19.9	19.8	6.7	0.5
North Carolina	100.0	65.2	30.5	1.5	1.2	1.5	100.0	57.4	31.6	7.5	2.0	1.5
North Dakota	100.0	90.1	0.8	0.8	0.7	7.6	100.0	87.2	1.2	2.4	0.9	8.3
Ohio....................................	100.0	82.5	15.1	1.4	1.0	0.1	100.0	79.1	17.1	2.3	1.4	0.1
Oklahoma	100.0	70.4	10.4	3.7	1.2	14.3	100.0	60.6	10.8	8.2	1.6	18.7
Oregon...............................	100.0	86.0	2.5	6.3	3.2	1.9	100.0	75.4	3.3	14.5	4.6	2.3
Pennsylvania......................	100.0	80.9	13.9	3.4	1.7	0.1	100.0	75.5	16.0	6.0	2.3	0.1
Rhode Island	100.0	79.9	7.0	9.5	3.2	0.5	100.0	70.9	8.6	16.8	3.2	0.6
South Carolina...................	100.0	56.8	41.7	0.6	0.7	0.2	100.0	54.0	40.8	3.6	1.2	0.3
South Dakota.....................	100.0	84.2	0.8	0.7	0.8	13.6	100.0	84.6	1.6	1.9	1.0	10.9
Tennessee	100.0	75.4	23.0	0.6	0.9	0.1	100.0	70.0	25.1	3.3	1.4	0.2
Texas	100.0	47.1	14.3	36.1	2.3	0.2	100.0	37.7	14.2	44.7	3.0	0.3
Utah	100.0	91.0	0.7	4.8	2.1	1.4	100.0	82.7	1.2	11.6	3.0	1.6
Vermont..............................	100.0	97.5	0.7	0.3	0.9	0.5	100.0	95.8	1.4	0.9	1.5	0.5
Virginia...............................	100.0	67.2	26.2	3.0	3.4	0.2	100.0	60.6	27.1	7.1	4.9	0.3
Washington.........................	100.0	79.1	4.6	7.4	6.3	2.6	100.0	70.7	5.7	12.9	8.0	2.7
West Virginia......................	100.0	95.3	3.9	0.2	0.4	0.1	100.0	93.9	4.8	0.6	0.6	0.1
Wisconsin	100.0	83.7	9.3	3.1	2.6	1.3	100.0	78.3	10.5	6.3	3.4	1.5
Wyoming.............................	100.0	89.4	1.0	6.1	0.8	2.8	100.0	85.6	1.4	8.6	1.0	3.4

See notes at end of table.

Table 40. Percentage distribution of enrollment in public elementary and secondary schools, by race/ethnicity and state or jurisdiction: Fall 1994 and fall 2004—Continued

State or jurisdiction	Percentage distribution, fall 1994						Percentage distribution, fall 2004					
	Total	White	Black	Hispanic	Asian/ Pacific Islander	American Indian/ Alaska Native	Total	White	Black	Hispanic	Asian/ Pacific Islander	American Indian/ Alaska Native
1	2	3	4	5	6	7	8	9	10	11	12	13
Bureau of Indian Affairs	—	—	—	—	—	—	—	—	—	—	—	—
DoDDS, overseas	—	—	—	—	—	—	100.0	54.9	19.8	14.1	10.3	0.8
DoDDS, domestic	—	—	—	—	—	—	100.0	49.9	23.6	21.3	4.2	1.0
Other jurisdictions												
American Samoa	100.0	0.0	0.0	0.0	100.0	0.0	100.0	0.0	0.0	0.0	100.0	0.0
Guam	100.0	8.3	1.8	0.5	89.3	0.1	100.0	1.2	0.3	0.2	98.3	#
Northern Marianas	100.0	1.0	0.0	0.0	98.2	0.8	100.0	0.6	#	0.0	99.4	0.0
Puerto Rico	100.0	0.0	0.0	100.0	0.0	0.0	100.0	0.0	0.0	100.0	0.0	0.0
Virgin Islands	100.0	1.1	85.4	13.1	0.5	#	100.0	1.0	84.7	13.8	0.4	0.2

—Not available.
#Rounds to zero.
[1]Fall 1994 data include estimates for Idaho. Fall 2004 data include estimates for Nevada.
NOTE: Percentage distribution based on students for whom race/ethnicity was reported, which may be less than the total number of students in the state. Race categories exclude persons of Hispanic origin. DoDDS = Department of Defense dependents schools. Detail may not sum to totals because of rounding.
SOURCE: U.S. Department of Education, National Center for Education Statistics, Common Core of Data (CCD), "State Nonfiscal Survey of Public Elementary/Secondary Education," 1994–95 and 2004–05. (This table was prepared August 2006.)

Table 41. Enrollment of 3-, 4-, and 5-year-old children in preprimary programs, by level of program, control of program, and attendance status: Selected years, 1965 through 2005

[In thousands]

Year and age	Total population, 3 to 5 years old		Enrollment by level and control												Enrollment by attendance					
			Total		Percent enrolled		Nursery school				Kindergarten				Full-day		Part-day		Percent full-day	
							Public		Private		Public		Private							
1	2		3		4		5		6		7		8		9		10		11	
Total, 3 to 5 years old																				
1965	12,549	(144.5)	3,407	(87.1)	27.1	(0.69)	127	(19.6)	393	(34.1)	2,291	(75.6)	596	(41.6)	—	(†)	—	(†)	—	(†)
1970	10,949	(109.4)	4,104	(71.5)	37.5	(0.65)	332	(25.3)	762	(37.6)	2,498	(62.0)	511	(31.1)	698	(36.1)	3,405	(34.0)	17.0	(0.83)
1975	10,185	(105.8)	4,955	(71.2)	48.7	(0.70)	570	(32.7)	1,174	(45.5)	2,682	(62.7)	528	(31.6)	1,295	(47.4)	3,659	(43.6)	26.1	(0.88)
1980	9,284	(102.6)	4,878	(68.8)	52.5	(0.74)	628	(34.6)	1,353	(48.6)	2,438	(60.6)	459	(29.9)	1,551	(51.4)	3,327	(46.5)	31.8	(0.95)
1985	10,733	(115.6)	5,865	(77.6)	54.6	(0.72)	846	(42.0)	1,631	(56.0)	2,847	(68.8)	541	(34.1)	2,144	(62.3)	3,722	(55.5)	36.6	(0.95)
1990	11,207	(124.2)	6,659	(82.3)	59.4	(0.73)	1,199	(51.8)	2,180	(66.4)	2,772	(72.3)	509	(34.9)	2,577	(70.6)	4,082	(63.0)	38.7	(0.95)
1995[1]	12,518	(131.5)	7,739	(86.6)	61.8	(0.69)	1,950	(64.6)	2,381	(69.9)	2,800	(74.2)	608	(38.3)	3,689	(81.2)	4,051	(70.0)	47.7	(0.90)
2000[1]	11,858	(133.0)	7,592	(86.3)	64.0	(0.73)	2,146	(69.2)	2,180	(69.7)	2,701	(75.4)	565	(38.3)	4,008	(85.1)	3,584	(71.8)	52.8	(0.95)
2001[1]	11,899	(133.2)	7,602	(86.5)	63.9	(0.73)	2,164	(69.5)	2,201	(69.9)	2,724	(75.7)	512	(36.6)	3,940	(84.8)	3,662	(71.9)	51.8	(0.95)
2002[1]	11,524	(131.2)	7,697	(79.2)	66.8	(0.69)	2,376	(68.0)	2,179	(65.8)	2,621	(70.5)	521	(34.9)	4,191	(80.9)	3,507	(68.4)	54.4	(0.89)
2003[1]	12,204	(134.8)	7,921	(82.6)	64.9	(0.68)	2,512	(70.0)	2,347	(68.2)	2,539	(70.2)	523	(35.0)	4,429	(83.2)	3,492	(69.2)	55.9	(0.87)
2004[1]	12,362	(145.9)	7,969	(83.3)	64.5	(0.67)	2,428	(69.2)	2,243	(67.1)	2,812	(73.0)	484	(33.8)	4,507	(83.8)	3,461	(69.3)	56.6	(0.87)
2005[1]	12,134	(144.6)	7,801	(82.7)	64.3	(0.68)	2,409	(68.8)	2,120	(65.5)	2,804	(72.7)	468	(33.2)	4,548	(83.5)	3,253	(68.2)	58.3	(0.87)
3 years old																				
1965	4,149	(84.9)	203	(24.3)	4.9	(0.59)	41	(11.1)	153	(21.2)	5	(3.9)	4	(3.5)	—	(†)	—	(†)	—	(†)
1970	3,516	(63.2)	454	(28.1)	12.9	(0.80)	110	(14.6)	322	(24.1)	12	(4.9)	10	(4.5)	142	(16.5)	312	(13.9)	31.3	(3.07)
1975	3,177	(60.2)	683	(32.7)	21.5	(1.03)	179	(18.3)	474	(28.3)	11	(4.7)	18	(6.0)	259	(21.8)	423	(17.9)	37.9	(2.62)
1980	3,143	(60.7)	857	(35.7)	27.3	(1.14)	221	(20.5)	604	(31.6)	16	(5.7)	17	(5.9)	321	(24.3)	536	(20.3)	37.5	(2.36)
1985	3,594	(68.2)	1,035	(40.8)	28.8	(1.14)	278	(24.1)	679	(35.3)	52	(10.8)	26	(7.6)	350	(26.7)	685	(22.9)	33.8	(2.21)
1990	3,692	(72.7)	1,205	(45.1)	32.6	(1.22)	347	(28.1)	840	(40.3)	11	(5.4)	7	(4.2)	447	(31.4)	758	(26.6)	37.1	(2.20)
1995[1]	4,148	(77.4)	1,489	(49.2)	35.9	(1.19)	511	(33.7)	947	(43.0)	15	(6.1)	17	(6.5)	754	(39.6)	736	(30.7)	50.6	(2.06)
2000[1]	3,929	(78.2)	1,541	(50.5)	39.2	(1.29)	644	(38.3)	854	(42.7)	27	(8.5)	16	(6.7)	761	(40.9)	779	(32.4)	49.4	(2.10)
2001[1]	3,985	(78.7)	1,538	(50.7)	38.6	(1.27)	599	(37.3)	901	(43.6)	14	(6.2)	23	(7.9)	715	(40.0)	823	(32.3)	46.5	(2.10)
2002[1]	3,831	(77.2)	1,711	(48.2)	44.7	(1.26)	779	(39.0)	864	(40.5)	45	(10.5)	24	(7.6)	937	(41.7)	775	(32.3)	54.7	(1.88)
2003[1]	4,260	(81.3)	1,806	(50.5)	42.4	(1.19)	783	(39.6)	915	(42.0)	83	(14.1)	24	(7.7)	979	(43.0)	826	(33.2)	54.2	(1.84)
2004[1]	4,089	(85.7)	1,583	(48.8)	38.7	(1.19)	674	(37.2)	849	(40.6)	40	(9.9)	20	(7.0)	808	(39.9)	775	(31.2)	51.0	(1.97)
2005[1]	4,151	(86.3)	1,715	(49.7)	41.3	(1.20)	777	(39.4)	869	(41.1)	54	(11.4)	15	(6.0)	901	(41.6)	814	(32.4)	52.5	(1.89)
4 years old																				
1965	4,238	(85.8)	683	(41.8)	16.1	(0.99)	68	(14.3)	213	(24.9)	284	(28.4)	118	(18.7)	—	(†)	—	(†)	—	(†)
1970	3,620	(64.1)	1,007	(38.0)	27.8	(1.05)	176	(18.3)	395	(26.5)	318	(24.0)	117	(15.0)	230	(20.7)	776	(18.8)	22.8	(1.87)
1975	3,499	(63.1)	1,418	(41.0)	40.5	(1.17)	332	(24.5)	644	(32.3)	313	(23.8)	129	(15.7)	411	(26.9)	1,008	(24.1)	29.0	(1.70)
1980	3,072	(60.0)	1,423	(39.5)	46.3	(1.29)	363	(25.6)	701	(33.3)	239	(21.2)	120	(15.4)	467	(28.5)	956	(25.3)	32.8	(1.78)
1985	3,598	(68.2)	1,766	(45.1)	49.1	(1.25)	496	(31.1)	859	(38.5)	276	(24.0)	135	(17.1)	643	(34.6)	1,123	(30.4)	36.4	(1.72)
1990	3,723	(73.0)	2,087	(48.0)	56.1	(1.29)	695	(37.7)	1,144	(44.6)	157	(19.4)	91	(14.9)	716	(38.1)	1,371	(34.4)	34.3	(1.65)
1995[1]	4,145	(77.4)	2,553	(49.9)	61.6	(1.20)	1,054	(44.6)	1,208	(46.8)	207	(22.3)	84	(14.5)	1,104	(45.3)	1,449	(39.9)	43.3	(1.56)
2000[1]	3,940	(78.3)	2,556	(49.5)	64.9	(1.26)	1,144	(47.0)	1,121	(46.8)	227	(24.2)	65	(13.2)	1,182	(47.5)	1,374	(46.1)	46.2	(1.63)
2001[1]	3,927	(78.1)	2,608	(48.9)	66.4	(1.24)	1,202	(47.7)	1,121	(46.7)	236	(24.6)	49	(11.5)	1,255	(48.3)	1,354	(42.1)	48.1	(1.62)
2002[1]	3,851	(77.4)	2,615	(45.4)	67.9	(1.18)	1,198	(45.0)	1,163	(44.6)	174	(20.2)	80	(13.9)	1,259	(45.6)	1,355	(40.0)	48.2	(1.53)
2003[1]	4,076	(79.6)	2,785	(46.5)	68.3	(1.14)	1,324	(46.8)	1,176	(45.3)	184	(20.7)	101	(15.5)	1,400	(47.5)	1,384	(41.3)	50.3	(1.48)
2004[1]	4,339	(88.2)	2,969	(48.0)	68.4	(1.11)	1,462	(48.8)	1,213	(46.3)	208	(22.1)	85	(14.3)	1,484	(48.9)	1,485	(42.7)	50.0	(1.44)
2005[1]	4,028	(85.1)	2,668	(47.0)	66.2	(1.17)	1,295	(46.4)	1,083	(44.1)	215	(22.3)	75	(13.5)	1,332	(46.8)	1,336	(40.5)	49.9	(1.52)
5 years old[2]																				
1965	4,162	(85.1)	2,521	(55.1)	60.6	(1.32)	18	(7.4)	27	(9.1)	2,002	(56.3)	474	(35.8)	—	(†)	—	(†)	—	(†)
1970	3,814	(65.8)	2,643	(40.2)	69.3	(1.05)	45	(9.4)	45	(9.4)	2,168	(43.2)	384	(26.2)	326	(24.4)	2,317	(23.9)	12.3	(0.90)
1975	3,509	(63.2)	2,854	(32.6)	81.3	(0.93)	59	(10.7)	57	(10.6)	2,358	(39.2)	381	(26.0)	625	(32.0)	2,228	(31.2)	21.9	(1.09)
1980	3,069	(60.0)	2,598	(28.6)	84.7	(0.93)	44	(9.4)	48	(9.8)	2,183	(35.9)	322	(24.3)	763	(34.2)	1,835	(33.2)	29.4	(1.28)
1985	3,542	(67.7)	3,065	(30.6)	86.5	(0.86)	73	(12.7)	94	(14.4)	2,519	(40.6)	379	(27.7)	1,151	(41.9)	1,914	(40.3)	37.6	(1.32)
1990	3,792	(73.7)	3,367	(30.8)	88.8	(0.81)	157	(19.4)	196	(21.6)	2,604	(45.2)	411	(30.3)	1,414	(47.2)	1,953	(45.4)	42.0	(1.35)
1995[1]	4,224	(78.1)	3,697	(34.2)	87.5	(0.81)	385	(29.8)	226	(23.3)	2,578	(50.5)	507	(33.7)	1,830	(51.3)	1,867	(48.4)	49.5	(1.31)
2000[1]	3,989	(78.7)	3,495	(34.3)	87.6	(0.86)	359	(29.8)	206	(23.1)	2,447	(50.8)	484	(34.1)	2,065	(52.1)	1,431	(48.0)	59.1	(1.37)
2001[1]	3,987	(78.7)	3,456	(35.4)	86.7	(0.89)	363	(30.0)	179	(21.6)	2,474	(50.6)	440	(32.7)	1,970	(52.1)	1,485	(48.1)	57.0	(1.39)
2002[1]	3,841	(77.3)	3,371	(31.8)	87.8	(0.83)	399	(29.6)	153	(19.0)	2,403	(47.0)	417	(30.2)	1,994	(48.5)	1,377	(44.7)	59.2	(1.33)
2003[1]	3,867	(77.5)	3,331	(33.7)	86.1	(0.87)	404	(29.8)	256	(24.2)	2,272	(47.9)	398	(29.6)	2,050	(48.6)	1,281	(44.0)	61.5	(1.32)
2004[1]	3,934	(84.1)	3,417	(33.2)	86.9	(0.84)	293	(25.8)	181	(20.6)	2,564	(46.8)	380	(29.0)	2,215	(48.7)	1,201	(43.7)	64.8	(1.28)
2005[1]	3,955	(84.3)	3,418	(33.7)	86.4	(0.85)	337	(27.5)	168	(19.9)	2,535	(47.3)	378	(29.0)	2,316	(48.5)	1,102	(42.8)	67.7	(1.25)

—Not available.
†Not applicable.
[1]Data collected using new procedures. May not be comparable with figures prior to 1994.
[2]Enrollment data include only those students in preprimary programs.
NOTE: Data are based on sample surveys of the civilian noninstitutional population. Although cells with fewer than 75,000 children are subject to wide sampling variation, they are included in the table to permit various types of aggregations. Detail may not sum to totals because of rounding. Standard errors appear in parentheses.
SOURCE: U.S. Department of Education, National Center for Education Statistics, *Preprimary Enrollment*, 1965, 1970, and 1975. U.S. Department of Commerce, Census Bureau, Current Population Survey (CPS), October 1980 through October 2005, unpublished tabulations. (This table was prepared May 2006.)

Table 42. Number of preschool children under 6 years old, percentage in center-based programs, average hours in nonparental care, and percentage in various types of primary care arrangements, by selected child and family characteristics: 2005

Child and family characteristic	Number of children, ages 0 to 5 (in thousands)	Percent in center-based programs	Average hours per week in nonparental care[1]	Percentage distribution, by type of primary care arrangement						
				Head Start	Other center-based	Parental care only	Family child care	Sitter	Relative	Multiple arrangements[2]
1	2	3	4	5	6	7	8	9	10	11
Total preschool children[3]	20,665 (9.0)	36.1 (0.60)	29.3 (0.37)	5.1 (0.40)	27.3 (0.49)	39.8 (0.76)	8.3 (0.39)	2.3 (0.24)	15.4 (0.66)	1.7 (0.18)
Age										
Under 1 year	3,519 (#)	12.0 (1.13)	30.9 (0.95)	1.2 (0.57)	10.0 (1.07)	57.7 (1.81)	9.2 (0.90)	3.2 (0.60)	17.2 (1.42)	1.5 (0.47)
1 year old	3,988 (#)	16.9 (1.34)	31.2 (0.81)	0.7 (0.25)	15.0 (1.32)	48.5 (1.89)	11.1 (1.09)	3.4 (0.57)	19.1 (1.52)	2.2 (0.50)
2 years old	4,093 (#)	28.7 (1.84)	29.6 (0.75)	3.5 (0.98)	22.7 (1.66)	44.9 (1.97)	10.7 (1.13)	2.4 (0.49)	14.3 (1.17)	1.5 (0.38)
3 years old	4,070 (93.0)	42.5 (1.67)	28.9 (0.64)	5.3 (0.75)	33.2 (1.64)	34.0 (1.46)	7.6 (0.91)	1.7 (0.38)	16.7 (1.35)	1.5 (0.36)
4 years old	3,873 (92.0)	69.2 (1.36)	27.9 (0.67)	13.2 (1.12)	48.2 (1.29)	20.9 (1.44)	4.0 (0.73)	1.2 (0.50)	10.4 (1.29)	2.2 (0.44)
5 years old	1,123 (67.3)	68.7 (3.51)	26.9 (1.28)	10.4 (2.22)	48.4 (3.33)	21.1 (3.17)	4.6 (1.44)	0.8 (0.44)	13.6 (2.91)	1.1 (0.79)
Race/ethnicity										
White	11,488 (99.2)	37.8 (0.87)	27.1 (0.48)	2.8 (0.35)	30.4 (0.82)	37.7 (0.97)	10.1 (0.59)	3.1 (0.35)	14.1 (0.82)	1.8 (0.26)
Black	2,962 (5.2)	43.8 (2.44)	35.9 (0.85)	13.3 (2.10)	28.8 (2.32)	30.8 (2.67)	6.6 (1.05)	1.0 (0.54)	17.8 (2.76)	1.7 (0.57)
Hispanic	4,283 (4.1)	25.2 (1.28)	28.8 (0.76)	6.2 (0.76)	16.8 (1.01)	50.9 (1.43)	6.4 (0.80)	1.5 (0.32)	16.7 (0.96)	1.4 (0.35)
Other	1,933 (100.2)	37.9 (2.72)	31.8 (0.91)	3.8 (0.94)	29.6 (2.43)	41.5 (2.80)	4.8 (0.76)	1.3 (0.35)	17.1 (2.03)	1.9 (0.68)
Mother's employment status[4]										
Currently employed	11,328 (197.3)	43.8 (0.81)	32.3 (0.40)	5.4 (0.64)	33.1 (0.97)	20.9 (0.97)	13.7 (0.68)	3.0 (0.32)	21.4 (0.92)	2.4 (0.29)
35 or more hours/week	7,038 (185.0)	47.5 (1.15)	37.1 (0.42)	5.7 (0.72)	36.3 (1.14)	14.9 (1.06)	16.6 (0.89)	2.4 (0.32)	22.0 (1.28)	2.1 (0.35)
Less than 35 hours/week	4,290 (156.5)	37.7 (1.52)	22.7 (0.64)	5.1 (0.99)	27.9 (1.43)	30.8 (2.00)	8.9 (0.99)	3.9 (0.64)	20.5 (1.38)	2.9 (0.49)
Looking for work	1,416 (118.3)	22.6 (2.91)	26.0 (1.46)	4.9 (1.11)	17.1 (2.66)	55.0 (4.48)	3.7 (1.03)	1.8 (1.29)	16.7 (5.17)	0.9 (0.65)
Not in labor force	7,238 (173.7)	25.7 (1.03)	16.7 (0.69)	4.2 (0.50)	20.2 (0.91)	67.3 (1.13)	1.3 (0.26)	1.2 (0.22)	5.2 (0.61)	0.7 (0.19)
Mother's highest education[4]										
Less than high school	1,961 (99.4)	18.1 (1.58)	26.0 (1.58)	9.9 (1.33)	8.0 (1.03)	64.8 (2.31)	4.0 (0.89)	# (†)	12.2 (1.70)	1.0 (0.45)
High school/GED	5,590 (182.6)	30.3 (1.49)	29.2 (0.73)	8.0 (0.96)	20.0 (1.25)	45.4 (1.77)	6.3 (0.73)	1.2 (0.42)	17.3 (1.32)	1.8 (0.39)
Vocational/technical or some college	4,122 (145.7)	34.3 (1.80)	30.1 (1.04)	4.5 (0.68)	26.3 (1.59)	39.8 (2.17)	7.9 (0.94)	1.3 (0.42)	18.5 (1.76)	1.5 (0.47)
Associate's degree	1,466 (78.9)	37.1 (2.76)	28.2 (1.04)	3.5 (1.22)	29.9 (2.48)	31.6 (2.90)	15.5 (1.96)	1.4 (0.56)	16.6 (2.27)	1.5 (0.62)
Bachelor's degree	4,593 (123.1)	45.2 (1.55)	27.9 (0.63)	1.9 (0.57)	38.2 (1.39)	33.2 (1.33)	9.9 (0.86)	3.6 (0.58)	11.5 (1.01)	1.8 (0.37)
Graduate/professional degree	2,250 (121.2)	47.1 (1.80)	30.0 (0.75)	1.2 (0.41)	40.3 (1.75)	25.7 (1.89)	11.6 (1.62)	6.5 (0.99)	13.0 (1.69)	1.7 (0.47)
Mother in household										
Yes	19,982 (65.8)	35.7 (0.59)	28.9 (0.38)	4.9 (0.42)	27.3 (0.47)	40.1 (0.78)	8.5 (0.40)	2.3 (0.23)	15.2 (0.67)	1.7 (0.18)
No	683 (63.8)	45.2 (4.17)	38.5 (1.87)	9.9 (2.44)	27.4 (3.62)	30.9 (3.95)	3.5 (1.26)	2.9 (1.76)	22.5 (3.75)	3.0 (1.38)
Household structure[5]										
Two parents	16,275 (114.0)	34.4 (0.70)	27.0 (0.42)	3.4 (0.33)	27.7 (0.58)	43.3 (0.90)	8.6 (0.44)	2.4 (0.24)	12.9 (0.66)	1.7 (0.20)
One parent	4,055 (112.6)	42.2 (1.94)	35.1 (0.77)	11.1 (1.42)	26.3 (1.61)	26.1 (1.68)	7.8 (1.06)	1.6 (0.54)	25.3 (2.28)	1.8 (0.41)
Household income										
$15,000 or less	3,142 (79.3)	29.7 (2.19)	31.4 (1.11)	11.0 (1.61)	16.6 (1.80)	48.2 (2.35)	4.7 (0.90)	1.7 (0.67)	16.9 (2.31)	0.9 (0.35)
$15,001 to $25,000	2,770 (79.2)	29.0 (2.53)	31.0 (1.16)	8.5 (1.02)	19.1 (2.18)	48.9 (2.44)	4.5 (0.70)	1.5 (0.63)	15.9 (1.68)	1.5 (0.57)
$25,001 to $35,000	2,313 (94.5)	30.8 (2.06)	28.7 (1.01)	9.0 (1.52)	19.1 (1.89)	44.2 (2.22)	6.7 (1.39)	0.7 (0.31)	18.4 (1.99)	1.9 (0.52)
$35,001 to $50,000	2,943 (111.8)	28.3 (1.83)	29.5 (1.03)	4.2 (0.91)	21.2 (1.60)	48.5 (2.41)	6.7 (0.97)	0.8 (0.29)	16.7 (1.51)	2.0 (0.58)
More than $50,000	9,498 (112.8)	43.9 (0.95)	28.4 (0.42)	1.5 (0.27)	37.1 (0.88)	30.6 (1.03)	11.5 (0.71)	3.6 (0.38)	13.7 (0.84)	1.9 (0.26)
Poverty status[6]										
Above poverty threshold	15,900 (60.9)	38.4 (0.77)	29.0 (0.37)	3.5 (0.36)	30.6 (0.65)	36.6 (0.87)	9.6 (0.51)	2.5 (0.24)	15.3 (0.72)	1.9 (0.22)
At or below poverty threshold	4,766 (60.7)	28.3 (1.80)	30.2 (0.96)	10.4 (1.15)	16.4 (1.51)	50.5 (1.93)	3.9 (0.63)	1.7 (0.54)	15.9 (1.75)	1.1 (0.29)
Household size										
2 or 3 persons	5,469 (137.6)	38.2 (1.48)	32.5 (0.57)	5.9 (0.90)	28.9 (1.36)	30.6 (1.27)	11.6 (0.94)	2.2 (0.39)	18.5 (1.07)	2.2 (0.41)
4 persons	7,723 (172.4)	39.5 (1.17)	28.4 (0.56)	4.2 (0.56)	31.9 (0.95)	38.1 (1.26)	8.7 (0.65)	2.3 (0.35)	13.3 (1.14)	1.7 (0.33)
5 persons	4,279 (165.9)	34.0 (1.85)	26.8 (0.85)	5.6 (0.84)	24.2 (1.65)	44.3 (2.14)	7.2 (1.01)	3.1 (0.69)	14.4 (1.28)	1.2 (0.31)
6 or more persons	3,194 (138.4)	26.8 (1.90)	27.6 (0.95)	5.4 (0.90)	17.7 (1.70)	53.7 (2.36)	3.3 (0.62)	1.4 (0.35)	16.7 (2.53)	1.8 (0.41)

See notes at end of table.

Table 42. Number of preschool children under 6 years old, percentage in center-based programs, average hours in nonparental care, and percentage in various types of primary care arrangements, by selected child and family characteristics: 2005—Continued

Child and family characteristic	Number of children, ages 0 to 5 (in thousands)	Percent in center-based programs	Average hours per week in nonparental care[1]	Percentage distribution, by type of primary care arrangement						
				Head Start	Other center-based	Parental care only	Family child care	Sitter	Relative	Multiple arrangements[2]
1	2	3	4	5	6	7	8	9	10	11
Mother's home language[4]										
English	16,778 (117.0)	38.1 (0.63)	29.1 (0.41)	4.5 (0.49)	29.5 (0.53)	36.7 (0.86)	9.1 (0.44)	2.5 (0.26)	15.9 (0.77)	1.8 (0.21)
Non-English	3,205 (103.3)	23.5 (1.61)	26.9 (0.97)	7.1 (1.02)	15.9 (1.25)	57.9 (1.76)	5.5 (0.82)	1.0 (0.26)	11.5 (0.99)	1.0 (0.31)
Mother's age at first birth[4]										
Less than 18	1,744 (117.6)	27.7 (2.84)	32.8 (1.40)	10.4 (1.81)	15.4 (2.31)	50.3 (3.11)	4.8 (1.03)	2.0 (1.27)	15.9 (1.91)	1.1 (0.53)
18 or 19	2,529 (135.1)	28.4 (2.14)	30.6 (1.13)	7.6 (1.23)	17.6 (1.90)	46.6 (2.81)	7.1 (1.33)	0.9 (0.34)	19.4 (2.80)	0.8 (0.34)
20 or older	15,709 (140.0)	37.8 (0.68)	28.3 (0.43)	3.9 (0.43)	30.2 (0.65)	37.9 (0.74)	9.1 (0.46)	2.5 (0.24)	14.4 (0.70)	1.9 (0.21)
Urbanicity										
Nonmetropolitan	4,328 (5.4)	32.5 (1.93)	29.7 (0.91)	5.8 (0.82)	22.5 (1.78)	37.5 (2.00)	10.6 (1.04)	1.4 (0.58)	20.0 (1.68)	2.2 (0.48)
Metropolitan	16,337 (7.5)	37.0 (0.58)	29.1 (0.37)	4.9 (0.43)	28.6 (0.54)	40.4 (0.88)	7.7 (0.44)	2.5 (0.27)	14.2 (0.70)	1.6 (0.18)

†Not applicable.
#Rounds to zero.
[1]Mean hours per week per child among preschool children enrolled in any type of nonparental care arrangements. For children with more than one arrangement, the hours of each weekly arrangement were summed to calculate the total amount of time in child care per week.
[2]Children who spend equal hours per week in multiple nonparental care arrangements.
[3]Excludes children who have entered kindergarten.
[4]Excludes data for households with no mother present in household.

[5]Excludes children living apart from their parents.
[6]Poverty status was determined by household income and number of persons in household.
NOTE: A child's "primary arrangement" was defined as the regular nonparental care arrangement or early childhood education program in which the child spent the most time per week. Race categories exclude persons of Hispanic origin. Detail may not sum to totals because of rounding. Standard errors appear in parentheses.
SOURCE: U.S. Department of Education, National Center for Education Statistics, Early Childhood Program Participation Survey of the National Household Education Surveys Program (ECPP-NHES:2005). (This table was prepared October 2006.)

Table 43. Child care arrangements of 3- to 5-year-old children who are not yet in kindergarten, by age and race/ethnicity: Various years, 1991 through 2005

Characteristic	Total		3 years old		4 years old		5 years old		White, non-Hispanic		Black, non-Hispanic		Hispanic		Other	
					Age							Race/ethnicity				
1	2		3		4		5		6		7		8		9	
1991 children																
In thousands	8,402	(40.9)	3,733	(7.1)	3,627	(14.6)	1,042	(38.6)	5,850	(59.9)	1,236	(41.0)	999	(31.3)	317	(34.6)
Percent	100.0	(†)	44.4	(0.21)	43.2	(0.24)	12.4	(0.40)	69.6	(0.67)	14.7	(0.47)	11.9	(0.37)	3.8	(0.41)
Percent in nonparental arrangements																
Relative care	16.9	(0.60)	16.2	(0.72)	18.0	(0.85)	15.6	(1.34)	14.8	(0.66)	24.1	(2.09)	19.6	(2.08)	19.4	(3.87)
Nonrelative care	14.8	(0.56)	14.8	(0.76)	14.7	(0.79)	14.9	(1.81)	17.3	(0.76)	7.9	(1.20)	9.4	(1.27)	12.1	(2.45)
Center-based programs[1]	52.8	(0.89)	42.3	(1.44)	60.4	(1.04)	63.9	(2.12)	54.0	(0.95)	58.3	(2.49)	38.8	(2.20)	52.9	(3.45)
Percent with parental care only	31.0	(0.80)	37.8	(1.19)	26.0	(1.05)	24.3	(2.10)	30.6	(0.87)	24.8	(2.02)	40.7	(2.35)	32.8	(4.03)
1995 children																
In thousands	9,222	(52.9)	4,123	(8.3)	4,061	(12.5)	1,038	(48.3)	6,334	(94.0)	1,389	(56.1)	1,042	(38.8)	457	(39.1)
Percent	100.0	(†)	44.7	(0.25)	44.0	(0.24)	11.3	(0.46)	68.7	(0.94)	15.1	(0.60)	11.3	(0.42)	5.0	(0.42)
Percent in nonparental arrangements																
Relative care	19.4	(0.64)	21.4	(1.23)	18.4	(0.95)	15.2	(2.14)	16.5	(0.84)	28.7	(2.78)	22.8	(2.01)	22.6	(3.75)
Nonrelative care	16.9	(0.84)	18.5	(1.35)	15.3	(1.03)	17.2	(2.19)	19.4	(1.04)	11.3	(1.65)	12.5	(1.64)	10.5	(2.74)
Center-based programs[1]	55.1	(0.97)	40.7	(1.55)	64.8	(1.45)	74.5	(2.35)	56.9	(1.44)	59.8	(3.19)	37.4	(2.15)	56.7	(5.47)
Percent with parental care only	25.9	(1.01)	32.0	(1.95)	22.1	(1.24)	16.2	(1.78)	25.2	(1.39)	19.9	(2.50)	38.4	(2.33)	24.2	(3.59)
1999 children																
In thousands	8,518	(139.7)	3,809	(79.1)	3,703	(79.9)	1,006	(54.2)	5,384	(77.4)	1,214	(59.2)	1,376	(52.3)	545	(38.3)
Percent	100.0	(†)	44.7	(0.93)	43.5	(0.93)	11.8	(0.64)	63.2	(0.91)	14.2	(0.69)	16.2	(0.61)	6.4	(0.45)
Percent in nonparental arrangements																
Relative care	22.8	(0.77)	24.3	(1.28)	22.0	(1.14)	20.2	(2.06)	18.7	(0.90)	33.4	(2.58)	26.5	(1.86)	30.0	(3.97)
Nonrelative care	16.1	(0.67)	16.3	(1.02)	15.9	(1.07)	16.1	(2.08)	19.4	(0.88)	7.4	(1.37)	12.7	(1.29)	10.4	(1.98)
Center-based programs[1]	59.7	(0.63)	45.7	(1.28)	69.6	(1.19)	76.5	(2.40)	60.0	(0.81)	73.2	(2.40)	44.2	(2.19)	66.0	(4.10)
Percent with parental care only	23.1	(0.72)	30.8	(1.42)	17.7	(0.99)	13.5	(1.78)	23.2	(0.91)	13.7	(1.97)	33.4	(2.04)	16.6	(3.50)
2001 children																
In thousands	8,551	(11.0)	3,795	(91.4)	3,861	(89.0)	896	(47.0)	5,313	(68.0)	1,251	(55.1)	1,506	(43.5)	482	(38.3)
Percent	100.0	(†)	44.4	(1.06)	45.1	(1.04)	10.5	(0.55)	62.1	(0.79)	14.6	(0.64)	17.6	(0.51)	5.6	(0.45)
Percent in nonparental arrangements																
Relative care	22.8	(0.89)	23.6	(1.39)	22.5	(1.33)	20.9	(2.66)	19.6	(1.01)	36.7	(3.42)	22.8	(1.89)	22.8	(3.54)
Nonrelative care	14.0	(0.65)	14.7	(1.17)	13.6	(0.95)	13.1	(2.13)	16.5	(0.98)	8.5	(1.65)	11.3	(1.43)	10.8	(2.72)
Center-based programs[1]	56.4	(0.55)	42.8	(1.21)	65.9	(1.25)	73.0	(2.69)	59.1	(0.89)	63.1	(2.93)	39.9	(1.86)	61.8	(4.10)
Percent with parental care only	26.1	(0.67)	33.8	(1.29)	20.4	(1.11)	18.0	(2.49)	25.3	(0.99)	15.1	(2.22)	39.0	(2.03)	23.7	(3.90)
2005 children																
In thousands	9,066	(9.0)	4,070	(93.0)	3,873	(92.0)	1,123	(67.3)	5,177	(80.2)	1,233	(57.1)	1,822	(50.0)	834	(54.3)
Percent	100.0	(†)	44.9	(1.03)	42.7	(1.01)	12.4	(0.74)	57.1	(0.89)	13.6	(0.63)	20.1	(0.56)	9.2	(0.60)
Percent in nonparental arrangements																
Relative care	22.6	(1.02)	24.0	(1.44)	20.8	(1.56)	23.8	(3.17)	21.4	(1.34)	25.0	(3.42)	22.6	(1.79)	26.4	(3.29)
Nonrelative care	11.6	(0.73)	14.4	(1.12)	9.2	(1.03)	9.9	(2.00)	15.0	(1.13)	5.2	(1.31)	8.1	(1.36)	8.1	(1.94)
Center-based programs[1]	57.2	(0.83)	42.5	(1.67)	69.2	(1.36)	68.7	(3.51)	59.1	(1.32)	66.5	(3.41)	43.4	(2.10)	61.5	(3.31)
Percent with parental care only	26.3	(0.92)	33.4	(1.48)	20.6	(1.42)	20.4	(3.15)	24.1	(1.22)	19.5	(2.85)	38.0	(2.10)	24.7	(3.11)

†Not applicable.
[1]Center-based programs include day care centers, nursery schools, prekindergartens, pre-schools, and Head Start programs.
NOTE: Row percents for nonparental and parental care do not add to 100 percent because some children participated in more than one type of nonparental care arrangement. Detail may not sum to totals because of rounding. Standard errors appear in parentheses.

SOURCE: U.S. Department of Education, National Center for Education Statistics, Early Childhood Education Survey, Parent Survey, and Early Childhood Program Participation Survey of the National Household Education Surveys Program (ECE-NHES:1991; Parent-NHES:1999; and ECPP-NHES:1995, 2001, and 2005). (This table was prepared July 2006.)

Table 44. Children of prekindergarten through second-grade age, by enrollment status, selected maternal characteristics, and household income: 1995, 2001, and 2005

Maternal characteristic and household income	3- to 5-year-olds, not enrolled in school (includes homeschooled students)			Enrolled in nursery school or prekindergarten			Enrolled in kindergarten			Enrolled in first grade			Enrolled in second grade		
	1995	2001[1]	2005[1]	1995	2001[1]	2005[1]	1995	2001[1]	2005[1]	1995	2001[2]	2005[1]	1995	2001[2]	2005[1]
1	2	3	4	5	6	7	8	9	10	11	12	13	14	15	16
Total children (in thousands)	4,586 (102.3)	3,990 (3.2)	4,156 (5.0)	4,642 (105.0)	4,586 (#)	4,926 (#)	4,149 (75.6)	3,831 (#)	3,717 (#)	4,025 (76.7)	4,333 (#)	4,118 (#)	3,777 (72.9)	3,934 (#)	3,900 (#)
Percentage distribution															
Mother's highest level of education[3]	100.0 (†)	100.0 (†)	100.0 (†)	100.0 (†)	100.0 (†)	100.0 (†)	100.0 (†)	100.0 (†)	100.0 (†)	100.0 (†)	100.0 (†)	100.0 (†)	100.0 (†)	100.0 (†)	100.0 (†)
Less than high school	16.3 (1.27)	16.4 (1.26)	13.8 (1.24)	6.8 (0.78)	8.0 (1.26)	6.8 (0.76)	13.4 (0.93)	10.7 (1.31)	9.5 (1.16)	12.3 (0.99)	11.7 (1.28)	10.0 (1.20)	15.0 (0.81)	13.5 (1.26)	10.3 (1.21)
High school/GED	41.1 (1.51)	39.7 (1.59)	37.2 (2.18)	30.7 (1.27)	26.1 (1.59)	24.6 (1.34)	36.4 (1.19)	30.3 (1.86)	27.5 (1.92)	34.9 (1.53)	30.3 (2.17)	31.1 (2.13)	35.6 (1.44)	32.8 (2.11)	29.5 (1.77)
Vocational/technical or some college	21.3 (1.34)	19.1 (1.30)	21.2 (1.43)	22.7 (1.01)	24.6 (1.30)	19.2 (1.32)	21.7 (1.00)	23.5 (1.84)	20.7 (1.70)	23.6 (1.29)	24.3 (1.87)	19.9 (1.94)	20.6 (0.94)	22.5 (2.18)	19.8 (1.64)
Associate's degree	7.0 (0.79)	5.9 (0.67)	6.8 (0.82)	8.6 (0.72)	7.7 (0.67)	8.4 (0.71)	7.0 (0.68)	7.6 (1.18)	7.7 (0.96)	7.3 (0.81)	7.5 (1.01)	10.3 (1.22)	7.6 (0.60)	7.5 (0.92)	8.0 (0.99)
Bachelor's degree	11.3 (0.86)	14.0 (1.16)	14.9 (1.20)	22.0 (1.10)	22.5 (1.16)	25.5 (1.13)	15.1 (0.98)	20.8 (1.58)	21.3 (1.42)	15.7 (1.02)	19.5 (1.68)	18.0 (1.23)	15.0 (0.94)	15.8 (1.70)	18.7 (1.46)
Graduate/professional degree	3.0 (0.48)	5.0 (0.63)	6.1 (0.73)	9.1 (0.70)	11.1 (0.63)	15.6 (0.94)	6.3 (0.69)	7.1 (1.02)	13.4 (1.43)	6.3 (0.49)	6.7 (1.04)	10.6 (1.22)	6.2 (0.67)	7.9 (1.28)	13.6 (1.62)
Mother's employment status[3]	100.0 (†)	100.0 (†)	100.0 (†)	100.0 (†)	100.0 (†)	100.0 (†)	100.0 (†)	100.0 (†)	100.0 (†)	100.0 (†)	100.0 (†)	100.0 (†)	100.0 (†)	100.0 (†)	100.0 (†)
Working 35 hours/week or more	33.4 (1.45)	36.7 (1.55)	33.5 (1.92)	38.5 (1.13)	43.7 (1.18)	39.4 (1.42)	35.9 (1.05)	38.9 (1.99)	36.9 (2.25)	38.5 (1.49)	46.1 (2.33)	40.7 (2.35)	40.5 (1.17)	42.3 (2.30)	41.2 (2.19)
Working less than 35 hours/week	17.8 (1.23)	19.2 (1.30)	21.1 (1.50)	23.7 (1.08)	22.8 (1.00)	24.4 (1.36)	20.8 (1.10)	22.6 (1.57)	21.5 (1.62)	20.8 (1.10)	19.7 (1.59)	20.7 (1.42)	21.4 (1.19)	20.1 (1.60)	22.7 (1.72)
Looking for work	6.8 (0.83)	5.7 (0.75)	8.7 (1.37)	5.8 (0.71)	3.9 (0.55)	4.0 (0.59)	5.6 (0.70)	3.9 (0.87)	7.3 (1.06)	5.0 (0.66)	4.1 (0.89)	5.7 (1.07)	5.4 (0.70)	5.1 (1.09)	4.9 (0.82)
Not in labor force	42.0 (1.68)	38.4 (1.48)	36.8 (1.79)	32.0 (1.28)	29.6 (1.27)	32.2 (1.35)	37.7 (1.18)	34.7 (2.16)	34.3 (1.99)	35.6 (1.57)	30.1 (2.05)	32.8 (1.97)	32.7 (1.30)	32.5 (2.22)	31.2 (1.99)
Household income	100.0 (†)	100.0 (†)	100.0 (†)	100.0 (†)	100.0 (†)	100.0 (†)	100.0 (†)	100.0 (†)	100.0 (†)	100.0 (†)	100.0 (†)	100.0 (†)	100.0 (†)	100.0 (†)	100.0 (†)
$10,000 or less	22.7 (1.21)	14.1 (1.07)	10.2 (1.06)	16.1 (1.06)	8.5 (0.81)	7.5 (0.90)	19.4 (1.24)	8.5 (1.22)	8.2 (0.95)	17.4 (1.19)	9.1 (1.18)	7.8 (1.05)	19.5 (1.34)	9.4 (1.07)	7.6 (1.08)
$10,001 to $20,000	15.7 (1.08)	14.5 (1.19)	12.0 (1.14)	10.4 (0.78)	12.7 (0.87)	9.7 (0.75)	12.6 (0.87)	14.1 (1.51)	11.1 (1.05)	13.2 (0.90)	14.0 (1.45)	10.4 (1.15)	11.6 (0.84)	12.4 (1.33)	12.5 (1.39)
$20,001 to $30,000	19.1 (1.12)	15.0 (0.94)	16.9 (1.38)	13.1 (0.81)	11.7 (0.74)	9.9 (1.18)	15.8 (0.76)	16.6 (1.41)	13.0 (1.32)	16.6 (0.91)	16.5 (1.71)	12.3 (1.32)	16.1 (1.05)	14.7 (1.54)	15.4 (1.71)
$30,001 to $40,000	16.2 (1.00)	13.6 (1.07)	15.3 (1.27)	12.4 (0.91)	9.7 (0.79)	9.9 (0.91)	15.1 (1.12)	12.2 (1.29)	11.1 (1.14)	14.1 (0.85)	10.3 (1.16)	10.7 (1.42)	16.1 (0.94)	12.4 (1.33)	10.6 (1.07)
$40,001 to $50,000	11.0 (0.74)	12.0 (1.05)	10.3 (1.12)	11.5 (0.96)	7.5 (0.68)	7.7 (0.64)	11.7 (0.88)	9.1 (1.16)	7.8 (1.07)	11.1 (0.77)	9.7 (1.34)	9.9 (1.14)	11.3 (0.92)	9.2 (1.08)	7.0 (0.87)
$50,001 to $75,000	10.5 (0.69)	18.8 (1.31)	20.0 (1.24)	19.3 (0.93)	21.2 (1.09)	20.8 (0.97)	14.4 (0.82)	20.9 (1.68)	18.4 (1.46)	15.6 (0.84)	18.3 (1.41)	20.4 (1.84)	15.0 (1.00)	19.6 (1.80)	20.3 (1.56)
More than $75,000	4.7 (0.70)	12.1 (0.99)	15.4 (1.30)	17.2 (1.06)	28.7 (1.09)	34.4 (1.13)	11.1 (0.62)	18.6 (1.30)	30.4 (1.54)	22.1 (0.73)	22.1 (1.86)	28.4 (1.56)	10.1 (0.79)	22.3 (1.78)	26.7 (1.83)

†Not applicable.
#Rounds to zero.
[1]Figures exclude children for whom no grade equivalency was available.
[2]Table includes a very small number of older children enrolled in first and second grade and excludes children for whom no grade equivalency was available.

[3]Excludes data for households with no mother present.
NOTE: Detail may not sum to totals because of rounding. Standard errors appear in parentheses.
SOURCE: U.S. Department of Education, National Center for Education Statistics, Early Childhood Program Participation Survey and Before- and After-School Programs and Activities Survey of the National Household Education Surveys Program (ECPP-NHES:1995, 2001, and 2005; and ASPA-NHES:2001 and 2005). (This table was prepared October 2006.)

Table 45. Percentage of 3- to 5-year-olds not yet enrolled in kindergarten who have participated in home literacy activities with a family member, by type of activity and selected child and family characteristics: 1993, 2001, and 2005

Selected child and family characteristic	Children (in thousands)			Percent participating three or more times in the past week														
				Read to by family member			Told a story by family member			Taught letters, words, or numbers			Did arts and crafts			Visited a library[2]		
	1993	2001	2005	1993[1]	2001	2005	1993	2001	2005	1993	2001	2005	1993	2001	2005	1993	2001	2005
1	2	3	4	5	6	7	8	9	10	11	12	13	14	15	16	17	18	19
Total	8,579 (42.0)	8,551 (11.0)	9,066 (9.0)	78 (0.7)	84 (0.8)	86 (0.7)	43 (0.9)	54 (0.9)	54 (1.0)	58 (0.8)	74 (1.0)	77 (0.9)	33 (0.8)	46 (1.0)	43 (1.2)	38 (1.0)	36 (1.1)	42 (1.2)
Age																		
3 years old	3,889 (8.2)	3,795 (91.4)	4,070 (93.0)	79 (1.0)	84 (1.1)	86 (1.2)	46 (1.3)	54 (1.4)	54 (1.9)	57 (1.3)	71 (1.7)	75 (1.2)	34 (1.3)	43 (1.7)	41 (1.8)	34 (1.3)	35 (1.9)	40 (1.7)
4 years old	3,713 (15.7)	3,861 (89.0)	3,873 (92.0)	78 (1.0)	85 (1.2)	85 (1.3)	41 (1.5)	55 (1.4)	53 (1.6)	58 (1.1)	77 (1.3)	77 (1.5)	33 (1.1)	48 (1.5)	44 (1.9)	41 (1.5)	37 (1.4)	44 (2.0)
5 years old	976 (39.4)	896 (47.0)	1,123 (67.3)	76 (2.1)	81 (2.7)	86 (2.2)	36 (2.7)	52 (3.0)	55 (3.4)	58 (2.8)	75 (2.5)	80 (2.3)	33 (2.3)	44 (2.7)	47 (3.5)	38 (2.7)	37 (3.4)	46 (4.0)
Sex																		
Male	4,453 (60.2)	4,292 (79.9)	4,707 (99.2)	77 (1.0)	82 (1.2)	85 (1.2)	43 (1.3)	53 (1.4)	53 (1.8)	58 (1.0)	73 (1.6)	75 (1.4)	31 (1.0)	41 (1.3)	39 (1.6)	38 (1.5)	35 (1.4)	44 (1.6)
Female	4,126 (65.0)	4,260 (79.6)	4,359 (99.6)	79 (1.0)	86 (1.0)	87 (0.9)	43 (1.2)	55 (1.3)	54 (1.6)	58 (1.4)	76 (1.3)	78 (1.2)	36 (1.2)	50 (1.5)	47 (1.6)	38 (1.1)	37 (1.6)	41 (1.7)
Race/ethnicity																		
White	5,902 (63.6)	5,313 (68.0)	5,177 (80.2)	85 (0.7)	89 (0.8)	92 (0.7)	44 (1.0)	58 (1.1)	53 (1.5)	58 (0.9)	75 (1.2)	76 (1.4)	36 (1.0)	49 (1.2)	47 (1.5)	42 (1.3)	39 (1.3)	45 (1.6)
Black	1,271 (44.9)	1,251 (55.1)	1,233 (57.1)	66 (2.4)	77 (2.6)	78 (3.1)	39 (2.7)	51 (2.9)	54 (3.6)	63 (2.7)	78 (3.4)	81 (3.1)	28 (2.4)	34 (3.3)	39 (4.0)	29 (2.6)	31 (2.0)	44 (3.8)
Hispanic	1,026 (34.1)	1,506 (43.5)	1,822 (50.0)	58 (2.4)	71 (1.9)	72 (2.0)	38 (2.2)	42 (2.1)	50 (2.4)	54 (1.9)	68 (2.0)	74 (2.2)	25 (2.1)	42 (2.2)	34 (2.5)	26 (1.6)	30 (2.0)	32 (2.1)
Other	381 (33.5)	482 (38.3)	834 (54.3)	73 (3.8)	87 (2.7)	88 (1.8)	50 (5.3)	60 (4.0)	64 (3.1)	59 (3.9)	78 (3.6)	82 (3.0)	32 (3.3)	46 (3.8)	47 (3.9)	43 (4.6)	38 (4.6)	48 (3.3)
Mother's highest level of education[3]																		
Less than high school	1,036 (50.1)	996 (54.5)	886 (59.4)	60 (2.7)	69 (2.8)	64 (3.3)	37 (3.2)	43 (3.7)	39 (3.5)	56 (2.7)	67 (3.0)	70 (3.0)	25 (2.2)	30 (2.9)	29 (3.2)	22 (2.7)	21 (2.4)	23 (3.2)
High school/GED	3,268 (79.6)	2,712 (89.0)	2,687 (117.9)	75 (1.3)	81 (1.6)	82 (1.6)	41 (1.3)	53 (1.7)	51 (2.4)	56 (1.3)	73 (1.5)	78 (1.9)	30 (1.2)	43 (1.7)	39 (2.3)	30 (1.8)	30 (1.9)	33 (2.5)
Vocational/technical or some college	2,291 (69.1)	1,833 (73.9)	1,782 (81.9)	83 (1.4)	85 (1.8)	88 (1.4)	45 (1.9)	53 (2.5)	56 (2.8)	60 (1.7)	76 (1.8)	78 (2.0)	37 (1.8)	47 (2.3)	45 (2.4)	44 (2.2)	38 (2.2)	47 (3.2)
Associate's degree	332 (25.7)	573 (40.9)	680 (44.1)	84 (3.1)	89 (2.5)	90 (2.3)	44 (4.3)	56 (3.2)	60 (3.6)	63 (3.9)	78 (3.5)	82 (2.8)	39 (4.1)	46 (3.8)	50 (3.5)	38 (4.1)	42 (4.3)	42 (4.1)
Bachelor's degree	912 (42.3)	1,553 (68.4)	1,949 (73.9)	90 (1.6)	93 (1.2)	93 (1.3)	48 (2.4)	58 (2.2)	57 (2.3)	57 (2.2)	78 (1.9)	80 (2.4)	37 (3.0)	53 (2.7)	47 (2.7)	55 (3.5)	46 (2.4)	53 (3.1)
Graduate/professional degree	569 (37.7)	685 (45.7)	879 (50.8)	90 (2.1)	96 (1.1)	94 (1.6)	50 (3.2)	67 (3.6)	63 (2.9)	59 (2.7)	80 (2.8)	75 (2.6)	42 (3.0)	55 (3.8)	48 (3.1)	59 (3.5)	55 (3.8)	58 (3.1)
Mother's employment status[3]																		
Employed	4,486 (77.3)	5,148 (84.2)	5,277 (111.1)	79 (1.0)	86 (1.0)	86 (1.0)	44 (1.0)	54 (1.3)	53 (1.5)	57 (1.2)	73 (1.3)	76 (1.3)	33 (1.1)	45 (1.5)	42 (1.7)	39 (1.2)	36 (1.2)	43 (1.6)
Unemployed	594 (45.0)	396 (36.9)	543 (63.7)	71 (3.4)	77 (5.0)	89 (2.6)	43 (2.9)	56 (5.6)	58 (6.8)	66 (3.7)	73 (5.0)	81 (3.6)	33 (3.9)	38 (5.2)	39 (5.1)	37 (3.7)	37 (4.8)	39 (4.5)
Not in labor force	3,328 (72.9)	2,809 (73.3)	3,043 (96.5)	79 (1.3)	83 (1.4)	85 (1.3)	43 (1.5)	54 (2.0)	55 (2.0)	58 (1.5)	76 (1.7)	76 (1.6)	34 (1.4)	48 (2.0)	45 (1.8)	37 (1.4)	38 (1.9)	43 (1.9)
Family composition of household																		
Two parents	6,226 (78.1)	6,416 (75.1)	7,000 (68.7)	81 (0.7)	87 (0.8)	87 (0.8)	44 (1.0)	55 (1.0)	53 (1.1)	57 (0.9)	74 (1.1)	76 (1.1)	35 (0.9)	48 (1.1)	44 (1.2)	41 (1.2)	38 (1.2)	43 (1.3)
None or one parent	2,353 (66.5)	2,135 (75.1)	2,066 (69.3)	71 (1.7)	76 (2.0)	83 (1.7)	41 (2.0)	51 (2.2)	55 (2.6)	59 (2.1)	73 (2.2)	78 (2.0)	30 (1.9)	39 (2.3)	41 (2.6)	30 (1.7)	30 (2.1)	40 (2.6)
Poverty status[4]																		
Above poverty threshold	6,323 (62.1)	6,620 (61.6)	7,095 (62.9)	82 (0.7)	87 (0.8)	88 (0.8)	44 (0.9)	55 (0.9)	55 (1.1)	57 (0.8)	75 (1.1)	77 (1.1)	36 (0.9)	47 (1.0)	45 (1.4)	41 (1.2)	39 (1.2)	44 (1.3)
At or below poverty threshold	2,256 (56.6)	1,931 (62.1)	1,971 (63.7)	67 (1.6)	74 (2.3)	78 (1.9)	39 (1.8)	51 (2.7)	51 (2.7)	60 (2.0)	72 (2.4)	76 (2.1)	27 (1.9)	40 (2.4)	38 (2.8)	28 (2.0)	27 (2.2)	36 (2.5)

[1] In 1993, respondents were asked about reading frequency in one of two versions. The percentages presented in the table are for all of the respondents who answered three or more times on either version of the questions.
[2] Refers to visiting a library at least once in the past month.
[3] Excludes children who did not have a mother (birth, adoptive, step, or foster) residing in their household and also did not have a female respondent on the telephone.
[4] Poverty status was determined by household income and number of persons in household.

NOTE: Race categories exclude persons of Hispanic origin. Detail may not sum to totals because of rounding. Standard errors appear in parentheses.
SOURCE: U.S. Department of Education, National Center for Education Statistics, School Readiness Survey and Early Childhood Program Participation Survey of the National Household Education Surveys Program (SR-NHES:1993 and ECPP-NHES:2001 and 2005). (This table was prepared October 2006.)

Table 46. Percentage distribution of first-time kindergartners, by number of children's books in the home, and number of times each week family members read books to them, by selected child and maternal characteristics: Fall 1998

Characteristic	Total (in thousands)	Percentage distribution of total	Percentage distribution of first-time kindergartners, by number of children's books in child's home								Percentage distribution of first-time kindergartners, by number of times each week family members read books to child							
			Less than 26		26–50		51–100		101 or more		None		1–2		3–4		More than 4 times	
1	2	3	4		5		6		7		8		9		10		11	
Total.............	3,678	100.0	26	(1.0)	28	(0.5)	29	(0.6)	17	(0.6)	1	(0.1)	19	(0.6)	35	(0.5)	45	(0.6)
Sex																		
Male..............	1,868	50.8	27	(1.1)	28	(0.6)	28	(0.6)	16	(0.7)	1	(0.2)	21	(0.8)	35	(0.6)	43	(0.8)
Female.............	1,811	49.2	25	(1.0)	28	(0.6)	29	(0.8)	17	(0.7)	1	(0.1)	17	(0.6)	35	(0.6)	47	(0.7)
Race/ethnicity																		
White..............	2,118	57.6	9	(0.4)	28	(0.6)	38	(0.6)	25	(0.8)	1	(0.1)	13	(0.5)	37	(0.5)	49	(0.7)
Black..............	570	15.5	50	(1.8)	31	(1.2)	15	(1.0)	4	(0.4)	2	(0.4)	31	(1.2)	33	(1.3)	35	(1.2)
Asian..............	108	2.9	46	(2.7)	26	(1.6)	20	(1.9)	8	(1.2)	1	(0.3)	23	(1.9)	29	(1.8)	47	(2.4)
Hispanic.............	704	19.1	52	(1.5)	27	(0.9)	16	(0.8)	6	(0.5)	3	(0.3)	27	(1.0)	31	(0.9)	39	(0.9)
Native Hawaiian/Pacific Islander.............	21	0.6	34	(3.1)	41	(3.8)	16	(2.3)	9	(3.1)	#	(†)	19	(2.5)	35	(3.0)	45	(2.9)
American Indian/Alaska Native.............	64	1.7	51	(7.8)	22	(2.4)	16	(3.0)	11	(3.3)	3	(0.6)	33	(3.0)	25	(2.7)	40	(2.1)
Other.............	88	2.4	20	(2.4)	36	(3.0)	28	(2.4)	16	(1.7)	#	(†)	15	(1.8)	42	(2.9)	43	(2.7)
Mother's highest level of education[1]																		
Less than high school.....	519	14.1	62	(1.7)	24	(1.2)	10	(0.8)	4	(0.5)	4	(0.5)	34	(1.1)	27	(1.1)	36	(1.1)
High school or equivalent	1,116	30.3	31	(1.4)	32	(0.9)	26	(0.9)	11	(0.5)	1	(0.2)	24	(0.9)	36	(0.8)	39	(0.7)
Some college, including vocational.................	1,153	31.3	17	(0.9)	31	(0.7)	33	(0.8)	19	(0.8)	#	(†)	15	(0.7)	40	(0.8)	45	(0.8)
Bachelor's degree or higher..................	798	21.7	7	(0.6)	22	(1.0)	40	(0.9)	31	(1.0)	#	(†)	7	(0.6)	34	(0.9)	59	(1.0)

†Not applicable.
#Rounds to zero.
[1]Excludes children with no mother present in household.
NOTE: Race categories exclude persons of Hispanic origin. Standard errors appear in parentheses. Detail may not sum to totals because of rounding.

SOURCE: U.S. Department of Education, National Center for Education Statistics, Early Childhood Longitudinal Study, Kindergarten Class of 1998–99 (ECLS-K), fall 1998, unpublished tabulations. (This table was prepared October 2002.)

Table 47. Percentage distribution of kindergarten teachers and parents indicating the importance of various factors for kindergarten readiness, by control: Fall 1998

Teacher and parent perception of student skills	Perception of importance for parents and teachers of public kindergarten children										Perception of importance for parents and teachers of private kindergarten children									
	Not important		Not very important		Somewhat important		Very important		Essential		Not important		Not very important		Somewhat important		Very important		Essential	
1	2		3		4		5		6		7		8		9		10		11	
Kindergarten teachers[1]																				
Can count to 20 or more	12	(0.7)	38	(1.3)	36	(1.2)	11	(0.7)	2	(0.3)	10	(2.0)	37	(3.1)	34	(3.0)	12	(2.0)	6	(2.3)
Knows most of the alphabet..................	9	(0.7)	30	(1.2)	43	(1.2)	14	(0.9)	4	(0.5)	6	(1.4)	26	(2.8)	41	(2.7)	19	(2.6)	8	(2.3)
Takes turns and shares...	#	(†)	1	(0.2)	25	(1.1)	58	(1.4)	16	(1.0)	#	(†)	1	(0.4)	25	(2.5)	58	(3.2)	16	(2.4)
Sits still and pays attention..................	1	(0.2)	4	(0.4)	36	(1.4)	47	(1.3)	13	(0.8)	1	(0.5)	3	(1.1)	35	(3.8)	52	(3.1)	10	(2.7)
Is able to use pencils and paint brushes...........	4	(0.5)	14	(0.9)	47	(1.3)	29	(1.5)	6	(0.5)	5	(1.4)	12	(2.2)	42	(3.1)	32	(3.3)	9	(2.5)
Kindergarten parents[2]																				
Can count to 20 or more	1	(0.1)	6	(0.3)	30	(0.6)	46	(0.7)	17	(0.4)	2	(0.2)	9	(0.6)	33	(1.0)	35	(1.1)	21	(1.0)
Knows most of the alphabet..................	1	(0.1)	4	(0.3)	25	(0.6)	51	(0.8)	19	(0.4)	1	(0.2)	7	(0.6)	29	(1.1)	41	(1.0)	22	(1.0)
Takes turns and shares...	#	(†)	#	(†)	5	(0.2)	63	(0.6)	32	(0.6)	#	(†)	#	(†)	7	(0.5)	55	(1.0)	38	(0.9)
Sits still and pays attention..................	#	(†)	1	(0.1)	14	(0.5)	60	(0.6)	25	(0.5)	#	(†)	2	(0.3)	22	(1.1)	51	(0.9)	25	(0.8)
Is able to use pencils and paint brushes...........	#	(†)	2	(0.2)	23	(0.5)	53	(0.7)	21	(0.4)	#	(†)	3	(0.4)	27	(1.0)	43	(1.1)	26	(0.9)

†Not applicable.
#Rounds to zero.
[1]Estimates pertaining to teachers are based on the responses of a nationally representative sample of kindergarten children's teachers.
[2]Estimates pertaining to parents are based on the responses of a nationally representative sample of kindergarten children's parents.

NOTE: Standard errors appear in parentheses. Detail may not sum to totals because of rounding.
SOURCE: U.S. Department of Education, National Center for Education Statistics, Early Childhood Longitudinal Study, Kindergarten Class of 1998–99 (ECLS-K), fall 1998, unpublished tabulations. (This table was prepared September 2001.)

Table 48. Children 3 to 21 years old served in federally supported programs for the disabled, by type of disability: Selected years, 1976–77 through 2005–06

Type of disability	1976–77	1980–81	1990–91	1994–95	1995–96	1996–97	1997–98	1998–99	1999–2000	2000–01	2001–02	2002–03	2003–04	2004–05	2005–06
1	2	3	4	5	6	7	8	9	10	11	12	13	14	15	16
	Number served (in thousands)														
All disabilities	3,694	4,144	4,710	5,378	5,572	5,737	5,908	6,056	6,195	6,296	6,407	6,523	6,634	6,719	6,713
Specific learning disabilities	796	1,462	2,129	2,489	2,578	2,651	2,727	2,790	2,834	2,868	2,861	2,848	2,831	2,798	2,735
Speech or language impairments	1,302	1,168	985	1,015	1,022	1,045	1,060	1,068	1,080	1,409	1,391	1,412	1,441	1,463	1,468
Mental retardation	961	830	534	555	571	579	589	597	600	624	616	602	593	578	556
Emotional disturbance	283	347	389	427	437	446	454	462	469	481	483	485	489	489	477
Hearing impairments	88	79	58	64	67	68	69	70	71	78	78	78	79	79	79
Orthopedic impairments	87	58	49	60	63	66	67	69	71	83	83	83	77	73	71
Other health impairments[1]	141	98	55	106	133	160	190	220	253	303	350	403	464	521	570
Visual impairments	38	31	23	24	25	25	26	26	26	29	28	29	28	29	29
Multiple disabilities	—	68	96	88	93	98	106	106	111	133	136	138	140	140	141
Deaf-blindness	—	3	1	1	1	1	1	2	2	1	2	2	2	2	2
Autism	—	—	—	22	28	34	42	53	65	94	114	137	163	191	223
Traumatic brain injury	—	—	—	7	9	10	12	13	14	16	22	22	23	24	24
Developmental delay	—	—	—	—	—	—	2	12	19	178	242	283	305	332	339
Preschool disabled[2]	†	†	390	519	544	555	565	568	581	†	†	†	†	†	†
	Percentage distribution of children served														
All disabilities	100.0	100.0	100.0	100.0	100.0	100.0	100.0	100.0	100.0	100.0	100.0	100.0	100.0	100.0	100.0
Specific learning disabilities	21.5	35.3	45.2	46.3	46.3	46.2	46.2	46.1	45.7	45.5	44.7	43.7	42.7	41.6	40.7
Speech or language impairments	35.2	28.2	20.9	18.9	18.3	18.2	17.9	17.6	17.4	22.4	21.7	21.6	21.7	21.8	21.9
Mental retardation	26.0	20.0	11.3	10.3	10.2	10.1	10.0	9.9	9.7	9.9	9.6	9.2	8.9	8.6	8.3
Emotional disturbance	7.7	8.4	8.3	7.9	7.8	7.8	7.7	7.6	7.6	7.6	7.5	7.4	7.4	7.3	7.1
Hearing impairments	2.4	1.9	1.2	1.2	1.2	1.2	1.2	1.2	1.1	1.2	1.2	1.2	1.2	1.2	1.2
Orthopedic impairments	2.4	1.4	1.0	1.1	1.1	1.1	1.1	1.1	1.1	1.3	1.3	1.3	1.2	1.1	1.1
Other health impairments[1]	3.8	2.4	1.2	2.0	2.4	2.8	3.2	3.6	4.1	4.8	5.5	6.2	7.0	7.7	8.5
Visual impairments	1.0	0.7	0.5	0.4	0.4	0.4	0.4	0.4	0.4	0.5	0.4	0.4	0.4	0.4	0.4
Multiple disabilities	—	1.6	2.0	1.6	1.7	1.7	1.8	1.8	1.8	2.1	2.1	2.1	2.1	2.1	2.1
Deaf-blindness	—	0.1	#	#	#	#	#	#	#	#	#	#	#	#	#
Autism	—	—	—	0.4	0.5	0.6	0.7	0.9	1.0	1.5	1.8	2.1	2.5	2.8	3.3
Traumatic brain injury	—	—	—	0.1	0.2	0.2	0.2	0.2	0.2	0.2	0.3	0.3	0.4	0.4	0.4
Developmental delay	—	—	—	—	—	—	0.0	0.2	0.3	2.8	3.8	4.3	4.6	4.9	5.1
Preschool disabled[2]	†	†	8.3	9.7	9.8	9.7	9.6	9.4	9.4	†	†	†	†	†	†
	Number served as a percent of total enrollment[3]														
All disabilities	8.3	10.1	11.4	12.2	12.4	12.6	12.8	13.0	13.2	13.3	13.4	13.5	13.7	13.8	13.8
Specific learning disabilities	1.8	3.6	5.2	5.6	5.8	5.8	5.9	6.0	6.0	6.1	6.0	5.9	5.8	5.7	5.6
Speech or language impairments	2.9	2.9	2.4	2.3	2.3	2.3	2.3	2.3	2.3	3.0	2.9	2.9	3.0	3.0	3.0
Mental retardation	2.2	2.0	1.3	1.3	1.3	1.3	1.3	1.3	1.3	1.3	1.3	1.2	1.2	1.2	1.1
Emotional disturbance	0.6	0.8	0.9	1.0	1.0	1.0	1.0	1.0	1.0	1.0	1.0	1.0	1.0	1.0	1.0
Hearing impairments	0.2	0.2	0.1	0.1	0.1	0.1	0.1	0.2	0.2	0.2	0.2	0.2	0.2	0.2	0.2
Orthopedic impairments	0.2	0.1	0.1	0.1	0.1	0.1	0.1	0.1	0.2	0.2	0.2	0.2	0.2	0.2	0.1
Other health impairments[1]	0.3	0.2	0.1	0.2	0.3	0.4	0.4	0.5	0.5	0.6	0.7	0.8	1.0	1.1	1.2
Visual impairments	0.1	0.1	0.1	0.1	0.1	0.1	0.1	0.1	0.1	0.1	0.1	0.1	0.1	0.1	0.1
Multiple disabilities	—	0.2	0.2	0.2	0.2	0.2	0.2	0.2	0.2	0.3	0.3	0.3	0.3	0.3	0.3
Deaf-blindness	—	#	#	#	#	#	#	#	#	#	#	#	#	#	#
Autism	—	—	—	#	0.1	0.1	0.1	0.1	0.1	0.2	0.2	0.3	0.3	0.4	0.5
Traumatic brain injury	—	—	—	#	#	#	#	#	#	#	#	#	#	#	0.1
Developmental delay	—	—	—	—	—	—	#	#	#	0.4	0.5	0.6	0.6	0.7	0.7
Preschool disabled[2]	†	†	0.9	1.2	1.2	1.2	1.2	1.2	1.2	†	†	†	†	†	†

—Not available.
†Not applicable.
#Rounds to zero.
[1]Other health impairments include having limited strength, vitality, or alertness due to chronic or acute health problems such as a heart condition, tuberculosis, rheumatic fever, nephritis, asthma, sickle cell anemia, hemophilia, epilepsy, lead poisoning, leukemia, or diabetes.
[2]Includes preschool children ages 3–5 served under Chapter 1 and IDEA, Part B. Prior to 1987–88, these students were included in the counts by disability condition. Beginning in 1987–88, states were no longer required to report preschool children (ages 0–5) by disability condition. Beginning in 2002–03, preschool children were again identified by disability condition.
[3]Based on the total enrollment in public schools, prekindergarten through 12th grade.
NOTE: Includes students served under Chapter 1 of the Elementary and Secondary Education Act and under the Individuals with Disabilities Education Act (IDEA), formerly the Education of the Handicapped Act. Prior to October 1994, children and youth with disabilities were served under Chapter 1 as well as IDEA, Part B. In October 1994, funding for children and youth with disabilities was consolidated under IDEA, Part B. Data reported in this table for years prior to 1994–95 include children ages 0–21 served under Chapter 1. Counts are based on reports from the 50 states and the District of Columbia only (i.e., table excludes data for other jurisdictions). Increases since 1987–88 are due in part to new legislation enacted in fall 1986, which added a mandate for public school special education services for 3- to 5-year-old disabled children. Some data have been revised from previously published figures. Detail may not sum to totals because of rounding.
SOURCE: U.S. Department of Education, Office of Special Education and Rehabilitative Services, Annual Report to Congress on the Implementation of the Individuals with Disabilities Education Act, selected years, 1977 through 2005; and Individuals with Disabilities Education Act (IDEA) database, retrieved on September 22, 2006, from http://www.idea_data.org/PartB data.asp. National Center for Education Statistics, Statistics of Public Elementary and Secondary School Systems, 1977; Common Core of Data (CCD), "State Nonfiscal Survey of Public Elementary/Secondary Education," 1981–82 through 2004–05; and Projections of Education Statistics to 2015. (This table was prepared September 2006.)

Table 49. Percentage distribution of students with disabilities 6 to 21 years old receiving education services for the disabled, by educational environment and type of disability: Selected years, fall 1989 through fall 2005

| Type of disability | All environments | Regular school, outside regular class | | | Separate public school facility | Separate private school facility | Public residential facility | Private residential facility | Homebound/ hospital placement |
		Less than 21 percent	21–60 percent	More than 60 percent					
1	2	3	4	5	6	7	8	9	10
All disabled students									
1989............	100.0	31.7	37.5	24.9	3.2	1.3	0.7	0.3	0.6
1990............	100.0	33.1	36.4	25.0	2.9	1.3	0.6	0.3	0.5
1994............	100.0	44.8	28.5	22.4	2.0	1.0	0.5	0.3	0.6
1995............	100.0	45.7	28.5	21.5	2.1	1.0	0.4	0.3	0.5
1996............	100.0	46.1	28.3	21.4	2.0	1.0	0.4	0.3	0.5
1997............	100.0	46.8	28.8	20.4	1.8	1.0	0.4	0.3	0.5
1998............	100.0	46.0	29.9	20.0	1.8	1.1	0.4	0.3	0.5
1999............	100.0	45.9	29.8	20.3	1.9	1.0	0.4	0.3	0.5
2000............	100.0	46.5	29.8	19.5	1.9	1.1	0.4	0.3	0.5
2001............	100.0	48.2	28.5	19.2	1.7	1.2	0.4	0.4	0.4
2002............	100.0	48.2	28.7	19.0	1.7	1.2	0.3	0.4	0.5
2003									
All disabled students............	**100.0**	**49.9**	**27.7**	**18.5**	**1.7**	**1.1**	**0.3**	**0.4**	**0.5**
Specific learning disabilities............	100.0	48.8	37.3	13.0	0.3	0.3	0.1	0.1	0.2
Speech or language impairments............	100.0	88.2	6.8	4.6	0.1	0.2	#	#	0.1
Mental retardation............	100.0	11.7	30.3	51.8	4.4	1.0	0.2	0.3	0.5
Emotional disturbance............	100.0	30.3	22.6	30.2	6.6	5.4	1.1	2.6	1.2
Multiple disabilities............	100.0	12.1	17.2	45.8	12.7	7.6	1.0	1.5	2.2
Hearing impairments............	100.0	45.0	19.1	22.2	4.4	2.5	6.2	0.4	0.2
Orthopedic impairments............	100.0	46.8	20.9	26.2	3.6	0.7	0.1	0.1	1.6
Other health impairments[1]............	100.0	51.1	30.5	15.0	0.8	0.7	0.1	0.2	1.6
Visual impairments............	100.0	54.6	16.9	15.6	3.9	2.0	5.4	0.9	0.6
Autism............	100.0	26.8	17.7	43.9	5.6	4.6	0.1	0.9	0.3
Deaf-blindness............	100.0	22.0	14.0	33.6	8.5	8.0	8.3	4.2	1.4
Traumatic brain injury............	100.0	34.6	30.0	27.1	2.7	3.3	0.3	0.7	1.5
Developmental delay............	100.0	51.2	28.2	18.6	0.6	1.1	0.1	#	0.2
2004									
All disabled students............	**100.0**	**51.9**	**26.5**	**17.6**	**1.8**	**1.2**	**0.3**	**0.3**	**0.4**
Specific learning disabilities............	100.0	51.2	35.8	12.0	0.3	0.4	0.1	0.1	0.2
Speech or language impairments............	100.0	88.3	6.5	4.7	0.1	0.2	#	#	0.1
Mental retardation............	100.0	13.1	29.7	50.8	4.4	1.0	0.3	0.3	0.4
Emotional disturbance............	100.0	32.3	22.0	28.4	7.2	5.8	1.2	2.0	1.2
Multiple disabilities............	100.0	12.8	16.9	45.2	12.7	8.1	0.9	1.3	2.2
Hearing impairments............	100.0	46.9	18.8	20.9	4.3	2.6	5.9	0.4	0.2
Orthopedic impairments............	100.0	48.2	19.5	25.8	4.0	0.8	0.1	0.1	1.5
Other health impairments[1]............	100.0	53.7	29.3	13.6	0.8	0.8	0.1	0.2	1.4
Visual impairments............	100.0	56.1	16.1	15.0	3.7	2.1	5.7	0.8	0.5
Autism............	100.0	29.1	17.8	41.8	5.5	4.7	0.1	0.7	0.3
Deaf-blindness............	100.0	19.4	15.6	35.1	8.5	6.9	7.6	2.9	3.9
Traumatic brain injury............	100.0	37.5	28.4	25.9	2.7	3.1	0.2	0.6	1.5
Developmental delay............	100.0	56.8	25.2	16.7	0.7	0.2	0.1	#	0.2
2005									
All disabled students............	**100.0**	**54.2**	**25.1**	**16.7**	**1.8**	**1.2**	**0.3**	**0.3**	**0.5**
Specific learning disabilities............	100.0	54.5	33.7	10.9	0.3	0.3	0.1	0.1	0.2
Speech or language impairments............	100.0	88.7	6.2	4.6	0.1	0.3	#	#	0.1
Mental retardation............	100.0	14.1	29.1	50.2	4.6	1.0	0.2	0.3	0.5
Emotional disturbance............	100.0	34.7	21.6	26.8	6.9	5.7	1.2	1.8	1.3
Multiple disabilities............	100.0	13.3	16.9	45.1	12.2	8.0	0.9	1.3	2.3
Hearing impairments............	100.0	48.8	18.3	19.5	4.8	2.3	5.8	0.4	0.2
Orthopedic impairments............	100.0	49.5	18.1	25.7	4.1	0.8	0.1	0.1	1.6
Other health impairments[1]............	100.0	56.0	28.0	12.8	0.8	0.8	0.1	0.2	1.3
Visual impairments............	100.0	58.2	15.2	14.2	4.1	1.6	5.4	0.7	0.6
Autism............	100.0	31.4	18.2	39.8	5.1	4.4	0.1	0.6	0.4
Deaf-blindness............	100.0	22.8	15.1	33.6	10.1	7.3	6.6	3.2	1.4
Traumatic brain injury............	100.0	40.0	27.5	24.5	2.8	3.0	0.2	0.5	1.5
Developmental delay............	100.0	59.5	23.4	15.8	0.7	0.3	0.1	#	0.2

#Rounds to zero.

[1]Other health impairments include having limited strength, vitality, or alertness due to chronic or acute health problems such as a heart condition, tuberculosis, rheumatic fever, nephritis, asthma, sickle cell anemia, hemophilia, epilepsy, lead poisoning, leukemia, or diabetes.

NOTE: Data are for the 50 United States, the District of Columbia, and the Bureau of Indian Affairs schools taken on the Child Count date of the last Friday in October or December 1. Data by disabil-

ity status are only reported for 6- to 21-year-old students. Detail may not sum to totals because of rounding.

SOURCE: U.S. Department of Education, Office of Special Education Programs, Individuals with Disabilities Education Act (IDEA) database. Retrieved September 22, 2006, from https://www.ideadata.org/tables29th/ar_2-2.xls. (This table was prepared September 2006.)

Table 50. Number and percentage of children served under Individuals with Disabilities Education Act, Part B, by age group and state or jurisdiction: Selected years, 1990–91 through 2005–06

State or jurisdiction	Ages 3 to 21						Disabled students as a percent of public school enrollment, 2004–05[1]	Percent change, ages 3 to 21, 1990–91 to 2005–06	Ages 3 to 5					
	1990–91	2000–01	2002–03	2003–04	2004–05	2005–06			1990–91	2000–01	2002–03	2003–04	2004–05	2005–06
1	2	3	4	5	6	7	8	9	10	11	12	13	14	15
United States	4,710,089	6,295,816	6,523,428	6,633,902	6,718,619	6,712,605	13.8	42.5	389,751	592,087	638,394	670,406	692,989	698,608
Alabama	94,601	99,828	95,194	93,056	93,402	92,635	12.8	-2.1	7,154	7,554	7,854	7,843	8,270	8,218
Alaska	14,390	17,691	18,116	17,959	18,134	17,997	13.6	25.1	1,458	1,637	1,774	1,968	2,002	2,082
Arizona	56,629	96,442	103,488	112,125	119,841	124,504	11.5	119.9	4,330	9,144	10,606	11,952	13,527	14,062
Arkansas	47,187	62,222	65,610	66,793	68,088	67,314	14.7	42.7	4,626	9,376	10,007	10,670	11,638	10,286
California	468,420	645,287	669,447	675,763	675,417	676,318	10.5	44.4	39,627	57,651	60,265	61,950	63,240	66,653
Colorado	56,336	78,715	81,327	82,447	83,249	83,498	10.9	48.2	4,128	8,202	9,200	9,673	10,307	10,540
Connecticut	63,886	73,886	74,126	73,952	73,028	71,968	12.6	12.7	5,466	7,172	7,722	8,135	7,978	7,881
Delaware	14,208	16,760	17,817	18,417	18,698	18,857	15.7	32.7	1,493	1,652	1,836	2,031	1,975	2,073
District of Columbia	6,290	10,559	12,065	13,242	13,424	11,738	17.5	86.6	411	374	400	301	579	507
Florida	234,509	367,335	390,883	397,758	400,001	398,916	15.2	70.1	14,883	30,660	34,387	35,258	35,124	34,350
Georgia	101,762	171,292	184,142	190,948	195,928	197,596	12.6	94.2	7,098	16,560	18,689	20,260	20,801	20,728
Hawaii	12,705	23,951	23,509	23,266	22,711	21,963	12.4	72.9	809	1,919	2,112	2,284	2,325	2,423
Idaho	21,703	29,174	29,062	29,092	28,880	29,021	11.3	33.7	2,815	3,591	3,684	3,807	3,910	4,043
Illinois	236,060	297,316	311,436	318,111	322,982	323,444	15.4	37.0	22,997	28,787	31,140	32,718	34,519	35,454
Indiana	112,949	156,320	167,584	171,896	175,205	177,826	17.2	57.4	7,243	15,101	17,448	18,439	19,008	19,228
Iowa	59,787	72,461	73,563	73,717	73,637	72,457	15.4	21.2	5,421	5,580	5,773	5,985	6,059	6,118
Kansas	44,785	61,267	63,905	65,139	65,290	65,595	13.9	46.5	3,881	7,728	8,685	9,190	9,179	9,267
Kentucky	78,853	94,572	100,298	103,783	106,916	108,798	15.8	38.0	10,440	16,372	18,637	20,219	20,777	21,317
Louisiana	72,825	97,938	100,942	101,933	102,498	90,453	14.2	24.2	6,703	9,957	10,769	11,386	11,904	10,597
Maine	27,987	35,633	37,139	37,784	37,573	36,522	18.9	30.5	2,895	3,978	4,482	4,647	4,806	4,348
Maryland	88,017	112,077	113,128	113,865	112,404	110,959	13.0	26.1	7,163	10,003	11,510	12,105	12,230	12,148
Massachusetts	149,743	162,216	155,561	159,042	161,993	162,654	16.6	8.6	12,141	14,328	13,955	14,822	14,821	15,195
Michigan	166,511	221,456	231,799	238,292	242,083	243,607	13.8	46.3	14,547	19,937	22,325	23,465	24,058	24,290
Minnesota	79,013	109,880	112,626	114,193	115,491	116,511	13.8	47.5	8,646	11,522	12,370	12,987	12,783	13,402
Mississippi	60,872	62,281	63,807	66,848	68,883	68,099	13.9	11.9	5,642	6,944	7,268	7,994	8,361	8,319
Missouri	101,166	137,381	144,165	143,593	142,872	143,204	15.8	41.6	4,100	11,307	13,966	15,140	15,047	15,268
Montana	16,955	19,313	19,274	19,435	19,515	19,259	13.3	13.6	1,751	1,635	1,728	1,798	1,878	1,925
Nebraska	32,312	42,793	43,891	44,561	45,712	45,239	16.0	40.0	2,512	3,724	4,290	4,445	4,707	4,665
Nevada	18,099	38,160	42,532	45,201	47,015	47,794	11.8	164.1	1,401	3,676	4,401	4,933	5,185	5,492
New Hampshire	19,049	30,077	30,981	31,311	31,675	31,782	15.3	66.8	1,468	2,387	2,570	2,586	2,709	2,902
New Jersey	178,870	221,715	235,515	241,272	245,878	249,385	17.6	39.4	14,741	16,361	17,433	18,545	18,982	19,329
New Mexico	36,000	52,256	51,904	51,814	51,464	50,322	15.8	39.8	2,210	4,970	5,207	5,656	6,207	6,441
New York	307,366	441,333	440,515	442,665	452,312	447,422	15.9	45.6	26,266	51,665	54,328	55,588	60,692	58,297
North Carolina	122,942	173,067	190,806	193,956	193,377	192,820	14.0	56.8	10,516	17,361	19,921	21,018	20,210	20,543
North Dakota	12,294	13,652	13,901	14,044	14,681	13,883	14.6	12.9	1,164	1,247	1,394	1,501	1,531	1,520
Ohio	205,440	237,643	248,127	253,878	260,710	266,447	14.2	29.7	12,487	18,664	19,182	19,659	20,955	22,702
Oklahoma	65,457	85,577	91,226	93,045	95,022	96,601	15.1	47.6	5,163	6,393	7,414	7,769	8,080	8,149
Oregon	54,422	75,204	77,100	76,083	77,094	77,376	14.0	42.2	2,854	6,926	7,370	7,453	7,834	8,167
Pennsylvania	214,254	242,655	262,325	273,259	282,356	288,733	15.4	34.8	17,982	21,477	23,265	24,459	25,438	25,964
Rhode Island	20,646	30,727	32,718	32,223	31,532	30,681	20.1	48.6	1,682	2,614	2,830	2,930	2,935	2,815
South Carolina	77,367	105,922	110,195	111,077	111,509	110,219	15.8	42.5	7,948	11,775	11,927	11,818	11,668	11,603
South Dakota	14,726	16,825	17,441	17,760	17,921	17,631	14.6	19.7	2,105	2,286	2,362	2,540	2,712	2,747
Tennessee	104,853	125,863	125,389	122,627	122,643	120,122	13.0	14.6	7,487	10,699	10,449	11,121	11,713	12,008
Texas	344,529	491,642	496,234	506,771	514,236	507,405	11.7	47.3	24,848	36,442	37,396	40,607	41,564	40,236
Utah	46,606	53,921	56,085	57,745	59,840	60,526	11.9	29.9	3,424	5,785	6,381	6,733	7,221	7,462
Vermont	12,160	13,623	13,722	13,670	13,894	13,917	14.1	14.4	1,097	1,237	1,307	1,378	1,512	1,556
Virginia	112,072	162,212	169,558	172,788	174,417	174,640	14.5	55.8	9,892	14,444	15,691	16,422	16,996	17,480
Washington	83,545	118,851	122,484	123,673	124,067	124,498	12.2	49.0	9,558	11,760	12,445	13,010	13,086	13,429
West Virginia	42,428	50,333	50,443	50,772	50,377	49,677	18.0	17.1	2,923	5,445	5,400	5,604	5,659	5,833

See notes at end of table.

Table 50. Number and percentage of children served under Individuals with Disabilities Education Act, Part B, by age group and state or jurisdiction: Selected years, 1990–91 through 2005–06—Continued

State or jurisdiction	Ages 3 to 21								Ages 3 to 5					
	1990–91	2000–01	2002–03	2003–04	2004–05	2005–06	Disabled students as a percent of public school enrollment, 2004–05[1]	Percent change, ages 3 to 21, 1990–91 to 2005–06	1990–91	2000–01	2002–03	2003–04	2004–05	2005–06
1	2	3	4	5	6	7	8	9	10	11	12	13	14	15
Wisconsin	85,651	125,358	127,031	127,828	129,179	130,076	14.9	51.9	10,934	14,383	14,802	15,393	15,955	16,077
Wyoming	10,852	13,154	13,292	13,430	13,565	13,696	16.0	26.2	1,221	1,695	2,037	2,211	2,332	2,469
Bureau of Indian Affairs	6,997	8,448	8,310	8,343	8,051	7,795	—	11.4	1,092	338	306	344	256	330
Other jurisdictions	**38,986**	**70,670**	**74,964**	**83,948**	**93,716**	**93,256**	—	**139.2**	**3,892**	**8,168**	**8,720**	**9,392**	**8,704**	**5,149**
American Samoa	363	697	969	1,135	1,239	1,211	7.7	233.6	48	48	102	138	98	80
Guam	1,750	2,267	2,406	2,460	2,485	2,480	8.1	41.7	198	205	230	200	172	171
Northern Marianas	411	569	588	669	751	750	6.5	82.5	211	53	52	69	82	70
Palau	—	131	—	—	—	—	—	—	—	10	—	—	—	—
Puerto Rico	35,129	65,504	69,327	77,932	87,485	87,125	15.2	148.0	3,345	7,746	8,159	8,806	8,185	4,677
Virgin Islands	1,333	1,502	1,674	1,752	1,756	1,690	10.7	26.8	90	106	177	179	167	151

—Not available.

[1]Percentage of students who are disabled is based on the enrollment in public schools, prekindergarten through 12th grade.

NOTE: Prior to 1994, children and youth with disabilities were served under the Individuals with Disabilities Education Act (IDEA), Part B, and Chapter 1 of the Elementary and Secondary Education Act. In October 1994, funding for children and youth with disabilities was consolidated under IDEA, Part B. Data reported in this table for years prior to 1994 include children served under Chapter 1. Some data have been revised from previously published figures.

SOURCE: U.S. Department of Education, Office of Special Education and Rehabilitative Services, *Annual Report to Congress on the Implementation of the Individuals with Disabilities Education Act*, selected years, 1992 through 2005, and Individuals with Disabilities Education Act (IDEA) database, retrieved on September 25, 2006, from http://www.idea.data.org/PartB-data.asp. National Center for Education Statistics, Common Core of Data (CCD), "State Nonfiscal Survey of Public Elementary/Secondary Education," 2003–04 and 2004–05. (This table was prepared September 2006.)

Table 51. Number and percentage of gifted and talented students in public elementary and secondary schools, by sex, race/ethnicity, and state: 2002

State	Total	Sex		Race/ethnicity					Gifted and talented as a percentage of total enrollment							
		Male	Female	White	Black	Hispanic	Asian/Pacific Islander	American Indian/Alaska Native	Total	Sex Male	Sex Female	White	Black	Hispanic	Asian/Pacific Islander	American Indian/Alaska Native
1	2	3	4	5	6	7	8	9	10	11	12	13	14	15	16	17
United States	3,002,040 (21,496)	1,462,940 (10,421)	1,539,100 (11,360)	2,179,250 (17,675)	253,140 (2,312)	312,450 (4,432)	229,360 (4,794)	27,840 (1,005)	6.4	6.1	6.7	7.8	3.1	3.7	11.1	4.9
Alabama	32,090 (309)	16,240 (151)	15,850 (160)	26,130 (304)	4,870 (7)	270 (7)	570 (2)	260 (#)	4.5	4.4	4.6	6.0	1.9	2.2	9.1	4.8
Alaska	5,040 (51)	2,590 (22)	2,460 (30)	4,230 (44)	110 (#)	120 (1)	330 (2)	260 (10)	3.9	3.9	3.9	5.5	1.8	2.3	4.2	0.8
Arizona	56,670 (741)	29,000 (349)	27,660 (405)	40,240 (595)	1,490 (26)	9,580 (152)	2,860 (40)	2,510 (345)	6.3	6.2	6.3	8.8	3.5	3.0	14.1	3.8
Arkansas	46,500 (2,252)	21,560 (1,098)	24,940 (1,172)	38,270 (2,140)	620 (318)	620 (53)	600 (29)	90 (8)	10.3	9.3	11.3	12.1	6.4	3.4	13.0	4.6
California	445,870 (11,279)	217,840 (5,288)	228,030 (6,064)	220,770 (7,401)	18,600 (537)	107,430 (2,960)	96,690 (4,430)	2,390 (142)	7.2	6.9	7.6	10.7	3.7	3.8	13.3	4.8
Colorado	50,610 (857)	25,250 (395)	25,360 (470)	39,640 (773)	2,180 (15)	6,230 (82)	2,090 (12)	460 (64)	6.7	6.6	6.9	8.0	5.1	3.5	9.3	5.3
Connecticut	18,990 (1,391)	9,190 ! (723)	9,800 ! (685)	16,030 ! (1,249)	1,180 ! (150)	790 (43)	960 ! (127)	20 ! (6)	3.3	3.1	3.4	4.0	1.4	1.0	5.3	1.6
Delaware[1]	6,140 (†)	2,840 (†)	3,300 (†)	4,640 (†)	940 (†)	180 (†)	370 (†)	10 (†)	5.5	5.0	6.1	7.2	2.7	2.1	13.0	3.7
District of Columbia[1]	— (†)	— (†)	— (†)	— (†)	— (†)	— (†)	— (†)	— (†)	—	—	—	—	—	—	—	—
Florida	111,640 (963)	57,100 (501)	54,540 (464)	73,620 (850)	11,990 (70)	21,130 (80)	4,560 (31)	340 (5)	4.6	4.5	4.6	5.8	2.0	4.0	9.3	5.0
Georgia	113,360 (3,708)	54,090 (1,750)	59,270 (1,962)	87,220 (3,228)	18,630 (526)	1,890 (83)	5,530 (163)	100 (3)	7.9	7.4	8.4	11.8	3.3	2.0	15.5	4.9
Hawaii[2]	11,000 (1,158)	4,640 (523)	6,360 (644)	2,370 (251)	120 (22)	170 (30)	8,300 (956)	40 (6)	6.8	5.5	8.2	8.2	3.2	2.3	6.7	4.4
Idaho	10,180 (740)	5,220 (368)	4,960 (382)	9,560 (712)	50 (6)	370 (44)	200 (20)	40 ! (8)	3.8	3.8	3.8	4.1	2.3	1.3	5.3	1.1
Illinois	136,200 (5,081)	65,020 (2,446)	71,180 (2,693)	105,250 (4,378)	12,780 (702)	9,100 (509)	8,920 (836)	140 (15)	6.7	6.2	7.1	8.7	3.0	2.8	12.6	3.2
Indiana	70,320 (3,760)	32,530 (1,807)	37,790 (1,979)	62,520 (3,537)	4,830 (802)	1,320 (193)	1,570 (174)	90 (19)	7.1	6.4	7.8	7.8	3.5	3.2	15.0	3.8
Iowa	42,140 (1,697)	20,830 (851)	21,310 (877)	38,910 (1,540)	1,140 (114)	820 (69)	1,140 (53)	140 (11)	8.6	8.3	9.0	9.0	5.4	3.8	13.3	4.7
Kansas	14,930 (282)	6,810 (161)	8,110 (147)	13,450 (271)	430 (9)	350 (42)	580 (15)	120 (11)	3.3	3.4	3.1	3.8	1.0	0.8	5.5	1.9
Kentucky	73,470 (2,718)	35,090 ! (1,326)	38,380 ! (1,420)	68,650 (2,544)	3,370 (321)	370 (31)	1,020 (97)	60 (10)	11.7	10.8	12.8	12.6	5.0	4.6	20.0	5.3
Louisiana	25,340 (405)	12,950 (236)	12,390 (171)	17,470 (354)	6,240 (62)	440 (5)	1,070 (2)	120 (1)	3.4	3.4	3.4	4.9	1.8	3.6	11.4	2.5
Maine	7,960 (529)	4,040 (281)	3,920 (255)	7,780 (521)	40 (6)	10 (1)	110 ! (13)	10 (4)	4.0	3.9	4.1	4.1	1.4	0.9	4.6	1.3
Maryland[1]	96,210 (†)	45,820 (†)	50,390 (†)	61,400 (†)	16,020 (†)	6,020 (†)	12,540 (†)	240 (†)	11.3	10.5	12.1	13.9	5.0	12.2	30.8	7.5
Massachusetts	9,000 (1,151)	4,320 (564)	4,680 (596)	7,170 (1,064)	520 (36)	510 (37)	780 (89)	20 (4)	1.1	1.0	1.2	1.2	0.6	0.5	2.0	0.6
Michigan	65,210 (6,849)	31,840 ! (3,572)	33,380 ! (3,329)	54,640 (5,573)	4,720 ! (857)	2,410 ! (867)	3,120 ! (557)	330 ! (60)	3.8	3.6	4.0	4.4	1.4	3.8	8.5	1.6
Minnesota	53,140 (1,346)	26,210 (640)	26,930 (713)	47,150 (1,300)	2,090 (15)	910 (20)	2,670 (35)	320 (10)	6.3	6.1	6.6	6.9	3.5	2.5	6.1	2.1
Mississippi	31,570 (852)	15,220 (363)	16,350 (500)	23,290 (666)	7,620 (269)	220 (19)	410 (49)	30 (2)	6.4	6.0	6.7	10.2	3.0	4.3	11.5	3.7
Missouri	35,120 (706)	18,240 (359)	16,880 (370)	30,910 (683)	2,800 (123)	340 (16)	1,000 (30)	70 (10)	3.9	4.0	3.9	4.4	1.7	1.7	8.9	2.3
Montana	7,240 (304)	3,630 (146)	3,610 (161)	6,700 (286)	20 (2)	70 (4)	90 (5)	360 ! (47)	4.9	4.8	5.0	5.2	2.1	2.3	6.0	2.5
Nebraska	32,740 (780)	16,040 (388)	16,700 (401)	29,250 (750)	1,500 (6)	1,040 (36)	740 (7)	210 ! (66)	11.8	11.2	12.3	13.0	7.8	4.2	16.7	4.0
Nevada[1]	16,040 (†)	8,290 (†)	7,750 (†)	11,330 (†)	1,050 (†)	2,000 (†)	1,540 (†)	120 ! (†)	4.4	4.4	4.4	6.0	2.7	4.4	6.7	1.9
New Hampshire	3,870 (358)	1,920 (171)	1,950 (198)	3,730 (352)	10 (1)	30 (5)	100 (4)	# (†)	1.9	1.8	2.0	1.9	0.5	0.6	2.8	#
New Jersey	103,390 (7,178)	46,850 (3,173)	56,540 (4,332)	76,490 (6,414)	10,100 (938)	7,180 (666)	9,520 (719)	100 (21)	7.6	6.7	8.6	9.8	3.9	3.2	10.5	5.8
New Mexico	12,300 (358)	6,780 (184)	5,510 (181)	7,810 (231)	190 (4)	3,560 (179)	290 (27)	450 (33)	3.8	4.1	3.5	7.3	0.6	2.2	8.1	1.2
New York	66,330 (4,517)	32,280 (2,276)	34,050 (2,265)	53,200 (4,168)	5,300 (260)	3,550 (281)	4,160 (349)	110 (12)	2.3	2.2	2.4	3.4	1.0	0.7	2.2	1.0
North Carolina	135,890 (4,935)	64,790 (2,430)	71,100 (2,523)	113,900 (4,297)	14,250 (563)	2,190 (177)	4,260 (474)	1,290 ! (606)	10.3	9.6	11.1	14.5	3.7	2.6	15.1	5.0
North Dakota	3,380 (78)	1,670 (36)	1,710 (42)	2,590 (48)	80 (1)	60 (#)	90 (2)	560 (58)	3.3	3.2	3.5	2.9	6.4	5.8	11.1	6.5
Ohio	120,710 (5,970)	60,510 (3,080)	60,190 (2,930)	104,300 (5,672)	12,510 (391)	1,010 (107)	2,770 (273)	110 (12)	6.7	6.5	6.9	7.2	4.3	2.4	12.1	4.7
Oklahoma	86,090 (1,835)	44,360 (913)	41,740 (951)	61,670 (1,424)	5,490 (134)	3,400 (152)	2,220 (46)	13,320 (680)	14.0	13.2	14.9	16.0	8.5	7.7	24.5	12.1
Oregon	40,980 (748)	21,620 (424)	19,360 (337)	36,040 (685)	680 (8)	1,240 (98)	2,640 (34)	380 (11)	7.5	7.7	7.4	8.5	4.2	1.8	11.0	3.3
Pennsylvania	78,550 (2,799)	41,330 (1,492)	37,220 (1,342)	67,460 (2,634)	6,610 (274)	1,450 (147)	2,950 (246)	80 (11)	4.5	4.6	4.3	4.9	2.4	1.8	7.9	3.8
Rhode Island	2,710 (274)	1,180 (115)	1,530 (158)	2,220 (270)	170 (6)	190 (7)	110 (#)	10 (1)	1.7	1.5	2.0	2.0	1.3	0.7	2.4	1.7
South Carolina	72,350 (3,454)	34,060 (1,689)	38,290 (1,772)	56,560 (2,859)	13,630 (688)	770 (55)	1,260 (126)	130 (12)	10.6	9.8	11.5	15.6	4.7	4.8	18.0	5.8
South Dakota	3,840 (208)	2,070 (115)	1,770 (93)	3,580 (205)	30 (#)	20 (#)	60 (#)	150 (#)	3.0	3.1	2.8	3.3	1.4	0.7	4.5	1.2
Tennessee	27,090 (913)	12,960 (505)	14,130 (416)	17,410 (878)	8,660 (41)	240 (5)	730 (22)	40 (8)	3.1	2.9	3.4	2.9	4.0	1.1	7.3	2.8
Texas	341,290 (5,210)	164,360 (2,544)	176,930 (2,709)	190,350 (4,034)	27,150 (479)	104,120 (2,997)	18,730 (440)	940 (39)	8.3	7.7	8.8	11.5	4.9	5.8	15.8	7.3
Utah	11,860 (141)	5,830 (64)	6,030 (77)	9,970 (134)	150 (#)	870 (7)	790 (#)	80 (#)	2.5	2.4	2.6	2.5	3.0	1.8	5.8	1.1

See notes at end of table.

Table 51. Number and percentage of gifted and talented students in public elementary and secondary schools, by sex, race/ethnicity, and state: 2002—Continued

State	Sex			Race/ethnicity					Gifted and talented as a percentage of total enrollment							
	Total	Male	Female	White	Black	Hispanic	Asian/ Pacific Islander	American Indian/ Alaska Native	Total	Sex		Race/ethnicity				
										Male	Female	White	Black	Hispanic	Asian/ Pacific Islander	American Indian/ Alaska Native
1	2	3	4	5	6	7	8	9	10	11	12	13	14	15	16	17
Vermont............	1,720 ! (269)	780 ! (119)	940 ! (153)	1,690 ! (265)	10 ! (3)	# (†)	10 ! (4)	# (†)	1.8	1.6	2.0	1.8	1.1	0.3	1.1	0.5
Virginia............	129,770 (3,208)	62,850 (1,582)	66,930 (1,647)	101,860 (2,520)	12,720 (581)	4,060 ! (353)	10,890 (288)	240 (10)	11.0	10.4	11.6	14.0	3.9	5.6	20.9	7.6
Washington.........	47,300 (1,121)	23,030 (620)	24,270 (536)	38,800 (1,008)	1,020 (31)	2,090 (75)	4,890 (123)	500 ! (48)	4.7	4.5	5.0	5.3	1.8	1.9	6.3	2.0
West Virginia......	5,850 (581)	3,210 (316)	2,640 (269)	5,570 (549)	120 (20)	20 ! (4)	130 ! (30)	10 ! (7)	2.1	2.3	2.0	2.1	1.0	1.5	8.4	1.9
Wisconsin..........	79,480 (3,338)	38,140 (1,580)	41,340 (1,797)	73,080 (3,220)	2,010 (59)	1,590 (57)	2,380 (127)	410 ! (118)	9.3	8.7	9.9	10.7	2.3	3.6	8.2	3.1
Wyoming............	2,610 (309)	1,240 (151)	1,360 (160)	2,410 (304)	20 (#)	110 (7)	40 (2)	10 (1)	3.1	2.9	3.4	3.3	1.9	1.7	5.3	0.5

—Not available.
†Not applicable.
#Rounds to zero.
!Interpret data with caution.
[1]State/jurisdiction has 25 or fewer school districts; therefore, data are based on universe count (instead of samples).
[2]State has only one school district, but is sampled within the district.
NOTE: Race categories exclude persons of Hispanic origin. Standard errors appear in parentheses. Detail may not sum to totals because of rounding.
SOURCE: U.S. Department of Education, Office for Civil Rights, OCR Elementary and Secondary School Survey: 2002. (This table was prepared July 2006.)

Table 52. Enrollment in grades 9 through 12 in public and private schools compared with population 14 to 17 years of age: Selected years, 1889–90 through fall 2006

[In thousands]

Year	Enrollment, grades 9 to 12[1]			Population 14 to 17 years of age[2]	Enrollment as a ratio of population 14 to 17 years of age[3]
	All schools	Public schools	Private schools		
1	2	3	4	5	6
1889–90	298	203	95	5,355	5.6
1899–1900	630	519	111	6,152	10.2
1909–10	1,032	915	117	7,220	14.3
1919–20	2,414	2,200	214	7,736	31.2
1929–30	4,741	4,399	341 [4]	9,341	50.7
1939–40	7,059	6,601	458 [5]	9,720	72.6
1949–50	6,397	5,725	672	8,405	76.1
1951–52	6,538	5,882	656	8,516	76.8
1953–54	7,038	6,290	747	8,861	79.4
1955–56	7,696	6,873	823	9,207	83.6
1957–58	8,790	7,860	931	10,139	86.7
Fall 1959	9,306	8,271	1,035	11,155	83.4
Fall 1961	10,489	9,369	1,120	12,046	87.1
Fall 1963	12,170	10,883	1,287	13,492	90.2
Fall 1965	13,010	11,610	1,400	14,146	92.0
Fall 1966	13,294	11,894	1,400	14,398	92.3
Fall 1967	13,650	12,250	1,400	14,727	92.7
Fall 1968	14,118	12,718	1,400	15,170	93.1
Fall 1969	14,337	13,037	1,300 [6]	15,549	92.2
Fall 1970	14,647	13,336	1,311	15,921	92.0
Fall 1971	15,053	13,753	1,300 [6]	16,326	92.2
Fall 1972	15,148	13,848	1,300 [6]	16,637	91.0
Fall 1973	15,344	14,044	1,300 [6]	16,864	91.0
Fall 1974	15,403	14,103	1,300 [6]	17,033	90.4
Fall 1975	15,604	14,304	1,300 [6]	17,125	91.1
Fall 1976	15,656	14,314	1,342	17,117	91.5
Fall 1977	15,546	14,203	1,343	17,042	91.2
Fall 1978	15,441	14,088	1,353	16,944	91.1
Fall 1979	14,916	13,616	1,300 [6]	16,610	89.8
Fall 1980	14,570	13,231	1,339	16,143	90.3
Fall 1981	14,164	12,764	1,400 [6]	15,609	90.7
Fall 1982	13,805	12,405	1,400 [6]	15,057	91.7
Fall 1983	13,671	12,271	1,400	14,740	92.7
Fall 1984	13,704	12,304	1,400 [6]	14,725	93.1
Fall 1985	13,750	12,388	1,362	14,888	92.4
Fall 1986	13,669	12,333	1,336 [6]	14,824	92.2
Fall 1987	13,323	12,076	1,247	14,502	91.9
Fall 1988	12,893	11,687	1,206 [6]	14,023	91.9
Fall 1989	12,519	11,390	1,128 [6]	13,536	92.5
Fall 1990	12,472	11,338	1,134	13,329	93.6
Fall 1991	12,670	11,541	1,129	13,491	93.9
Fall 1992	12,852	11,735	1,117 [6]	13,775	93.3
Fall 1993	13,065	11,961	1,104	14,096	92.7
Fall 1994	13,344	12,213	1,131 [6]	14,637	91.2
Fall 1995	13,662	12,500	1,163	15,013	91.0
Fall 1996	14,025	12,847	1,178 [6]	15,443	90.8
Fall 1997	14,239	13,054	1,185	15,769	90.3
Fall 1998	14,405	13,193	1,212 [6]	15,829	91.0
Fall 1999	14,599	13,369	1,229	16,007	91.2
Fall 2000	14,779	13,515	1,264 [6]	16,122	91.7
Fall 2001	15,031	13,734	1,296	16,183	92.9
Fall 2002	15,373	14,067	1,306 [6]	16,354	94.0
Fall 2003	15,649	14,338	1,311	16,504	94.8
Fall 2004	15,955	14,617	1,338 [6]	16,826	94.8
Fall 2005[7]	16,247	14,887	1,360	17,079	95.1
Fall 2006[7]	16,417	15,042	1,375	—	—

—Not available.

[1]Includes a relatively small number of secondary ungraded students.
[2]Data for 1890 through 1950 are from the decennial censuses of population. Later data are Census Bureau estimates as of July 1 preceding the opening of the school year.
[3]Gross enrollment ratio based on school enrollment of all ages in grades 9 to 12 divided by the 14- to 17-year-old population. Differs from enrollment rates in other tables, which are based on the enrollment of persons in the given age group only.
[4]Data are for 1927–28.
[5]Data are for 1940–41.
[6]Estimated.
[7]Projected.
NOTE: Allocation of ungraded students to secondary levels based on proportions derived from prior years. Includes enrollment in public schools that are a part of state and local school systems and also in most private schools, both religiously affiliated and nonsectarian. Some data have been revised from previously published figures. Detail may not sum to totals because of rounding.
SOURCE: U.S. Department of Education, National Center for Education Statistics, *Annual Report of the Commissioner of Education*, 1890 through 1910; *Biennial Survey of Education in the United States*, 1919–20 through 1949–50; *Statistics of State School Systems*, 1951–52 through 1957–58; *Statistics of Public Elementary and Secondary School Systems*, 1959 through 1980; *Statistics of Nonpublic Elementary and Secondary Schools*, 1959 through 1980; Common Core of Data (CCD), "State Nonfiscal Survey of Public Elementary/Secondary Education," 1981–82 through 2004–05; Private School Universe Survey (PSS), 1987–88 through 2003–04; and *Projections of Education Statistics to 2015*. (This table was prepared September 2006.)

Table 53. Enrollment in foreign language courses compared with enrollment in grades 9 through 12 in public secondary schools: Selected years, fall 1948 through fall 2000

[Number in thousands]

Language	Fall 1948	Fall 1960	Fall 1965	Fall 1968	Fall 1970	Fall 1974	Fall 1976	Fall 1982	Fall 1985	Fall 1990	Fall 1994	Fall 2000	Percent change in enrollment 1976 to 1990	Percent change in enrollment 1990 to 2000
1	2	3	4	5	6	7	8	9	10	11	12	13	14	15
Total enrollment, grades 9 to 12	5,602 [1]	8,589	11,610	12,718	13,336	14,103	14,314	12,405	12,388	11,338	12,213	13,514	-20.8	19.2
All foreign languages[2]														
Number enrolled	1,170	2,522	3,659	3,890	3,779	3,295	3,174	2,910	4,029	4,257	5,002	5,898	34.1	38.6
Percent of all students	20.9	29.4	31.5	30.6	28.3	23.3	22.2	23.3	32.2	37.5	41.0	43.6	—	—
Modern foreign languages														
Number enrolled	741	1,867	3,068	3,518	3,514	3,127	3,023	2,740	3,852	4,093	4,813	5,721	35.4	39.8
Percent of all students	13.2	21.7	26.4	27.7	26.4	22.1	21.1	21.9	31.1	36.1	39.4	42.3	—	—
Spanish														
Number enrolled	443	933	1,427	1,698	1,811	1,678	1,717	1,563	2,334	2,611	3,220	4,058	52.1	55.4
Percent of all students	7.9	10.9	12.3	13.4	13.6	11.9	12.0	12.5	18.8	23.0	26.4	30.0	—	—
French														
Number enrolled	254	744	1,251	1,328	1,231	978	888	858	1,134	1,089	1,106	1,075	22.6	-1.3
Percent of all students	4.5	8.7	10.8	10.4	9.2	6.9	6.2	6.9	9.2	9.6	9.1	8.0	—	—
German														
Number enrolled	43	151	328	423	411	393	353	267	312	295	326	283	-16.2	-4.1
Percent of all students	0.8	1.8	2.8	3.3	3.1	2.8	2.5	2.1	2.5	2.6	2.7	2.1	—	—
Russian														
Number enrolled	—	10	27	24	20	15	11	6	6	16	16	11	46.6	-35.6
Percent of all students	—	0.1	0.2	0.2	0.2	0.1	0.1	#	#	0.1	0.1	0.1	—	—
Italian														
Number enrolled	—	20	25	27	27	40	46	44	47	40	44	64	-11.4	58.7
Percent of all students	—	0.2	0.2	0.2	0.2	0.3	0.3	0.4	0.4	0.4	0.4	0.5	—	—
Japanese[3]														
Number enrolled	—	—	—	—	—	—	—	—	—	25	42	51	—	102.5
Percent of all students	—	—	—	—	—	—	—	—	—	0.2	0.3	0.4	—	—
Other modern foreign languages[4]														
Number enrolled	1	9	9	18	15	23	9	3	18	15	59	179	73.0	1,102.3
Percent of all students	#	0.1	0.1	0.1	0.1	0.2	0.1	#	0.1	0.1	0.5	1.3	—	--
Latin														
Number enrolled	429	655	591	372	265	167	150	170	177	164	189	177	8.9	8.3
Percent of all students	7.7	7.6	5.1	2.9	2.0	1.2	1.1	1.4	1.4	1.4	1.5	1.3	—	—

—Not available.
#Rounds to zero.
[1]Estimated.
[2]Includes enrollment in ancient Greek (not shown separately). Fewer than 1,000 students were enrolled in this language in each of the years shown.
[3]Until 1990, student enrollment in Japanese courses was included in the Other modern foreign languages category.

[4]Includes students enrolled in unspecified modern foreign languages. Since 1990, enrollment in Japanese courses is reported as a separate category.
NOTE: Percent change computed from unrounded numbers.
SOURCE: U.S. Department of Education, National Center for Education Statistics, Common Core of Data (CCD), "State Nonfiscal Survey of Public Elementary/Secondary Education," 1982 through 2000. American Council on the Teaching of Foreign Languages, *Foreign Language Enrollments in U.S. Public Secondary Schools, Fall 2000*. (This table was prepared April 2002.)

Table 54. Number and percentage of schools with students enrolled in distance education courses and enrollment in distance education courses, by instructional level and district characteristics: 2002–03

District characteristic	Number of schools with students enrolled in distance education courses					Percent of schools with students enrolled in distance education courses					Enrollment in distance education courses[1]				
	All instructional levels	Elementary schools	Middle or junior high schools	High schools	Combined or ungraded schools[2]	All instructional levels	Elementary schools	Middle or junior high schools	High schools	Combined or ungraded schools[2]	All instructional levels	Elementary schools	Middle or junior high schools	High schools	Combined or ungraded schools[2]
1	2	3	4	5	6	7	8	9	10	11	12	13	14	15	16
Total	**8,210 (229)**	**130 (42)**	**580 (62)**	**6,250 (198)**	**1,250 (140)**	**9 (0.3)**	**# (†)**	**4 (0.4)**	**38 (1.2)**	**20 (1.8)**	**327,670 (36,233)**	**2,780 ! (1,564)**	**6,280 (1,247)**	**222,090 (26,660)**	**96,530 (26,828)**
District enrollment size															
Less than 2,500	4,520 (175)	40 ! (30)	190 (45)	3,300 (161)	990 (123)	15 (0.6)	# (†)	4 (0.8)	44 (2.1)	29 (2.9)	117,730 (24,742)	80 ! (63)	1,260 (409)	74,160 ! (7,559)	42,240 ! (24,346)
2,500 to 9,999	1,670 (119)	20 (9)	160 (35)	1,360 (100)	130 (39)	6 (0.4)	# (†)	3 (0.8)	31 (2.0)	11 (3.0)	85,640 (7,597)	230 ! (125)	1,750 (639)	44,780 (6,148)	38,880 (3,490)
10,000 or more	2,020 (113)	60 (31)	240 (27)	1,590 (94)	120 (19)	6 (0.3)	# (†)	4 (0.5)	33 (1.9)	8 (1.6)	124,300 (25,922)	2,480 ! (1,563)	3,270 (1,030)	103,150 (24,010)	15,410 ! (11,373)
Metropolitan status															
Urban	960 (110)	50 ! (30)	90 (22)	760 (86)	60 (13)	5 (0.5)	# (†)	3 (0.6)	25 (2.7)	4 (1.3)	103,390 (25,612)	2,390 ! (1,565)	2,120 (996)	63,020 (25,477)	35,860 (1,650)
Suburban	2,980 (168)	30 (17)	280 (41)	2,400 (145)	270 (52)	7 (0.4)	# (†)	4 (0.6)	34 (1.7)	13 (2.4)	123,410 (27,446)	110 ! (64)	2,520 (683)	81,500 (8,967)	39,280 ! (25,200)
Rural	4,260 (162)	40 ! (28)	210 (47)	3,090 (115)	920 (124)	15 (0.6)	# (†)	4 (1.0)	47 (1.7)	32 (2.9)	100,870 (8,232)	270 ! (151)	1,640 (465)	77,570 (7,122)	21,390 (4,196)
Region															
Northeast	820 (88)	30 ! (16)	30 ! (17)	670 (76)	100 (30)	5 (0.5)	# (†)	1 ! (0.6)	25 (2.7)	12 (3.7)	42,070 ! (23,613)	100 ! (62)	190 ! (133)	17,420 (3,715)	24,350 ! (23,364)
Southeast	1,960 (128)	40 ! (26)	220 (34)	1,520 (108)	170 (35)	10 (0.5)	# (†)	6 (0.9)	45 (2.7)	14 (2.3)	59,010 (6,454)	1,390 ! (1,230)	2,530 (725)	50,410 (6,311)	4,680 (1,255)
Central	3,010 (174)	40 ! (28)	150 (34)	2,320 (123)	510 (90)	12 (0.6)	# (†)	3 (0.8)	47 (1.7)	28 (4.6)	108,140 (7,378)	940 ! (590)	1,050 (365)	60,560 (6,597)	45,590 (2,823)
West	2,410 (172)	20 ! (14)	180 (37)	1,750 (141)	460 (82)	8 (0.5)	# (†)	4 (0.7)	31 (2.0)	20 (2.6)	118,450 (27,630)	350 ! (224)	2,510 (996)	93,700 (25,509)	21,900 ! (11,645)
Poverty concentration															
Less than 10 percent	2,260 (144)	30 ! (16)	200 (33)	1,700 (113)	330 (78)	8 (0.5)	# (†)	4 (0.6)	36 (2.0)	29 (5.5)	77,380 (13,761)	570 ! (535)	2,030 (669)	57,320 (8,000)	17,470 ! (11,325)
10 to 19 percent	3,390 (154)	70 ! (39)	240 (34)	2,560 (141)	520 (84)	10 (0.4)	# (†)	4 (0.6)	40 (1.7)	23 (3.2)	97,300 (10,003)	1,450 ! (1,229)	1,710 (395)	77,810 (8,286)	16,330 (4,264)
20 percent or more	2,420 (134)	30 (9)	150 (42)	1,900 (115)	350 (72)	9 (0.5)	# (†)	4 (1.0)	40 (2.0)	16 (3.1)	93,280 (23,194)	760 (338)	2,540 (1,030)	83,100 (23,339)	6,880 (1,783)

†Not applicable.
#Rounds to zero.
!Interpret data with caution.
[1]Enrollment is based on students regularly enrolled in the districts. Enrollments include duplicated counts of students, since districts were instructed to count a student enrolled in each course in which he or she was enrolled.
[2]Combined or ungraded schools are those in which the grades offered in the school span both elementary and secondary grades or that are not divided into grade levels.

NOTE: Percentages are based on unrounded numbers. Percentages are based on the estimated 89,310 public schools in the nation in 2002–03. For the FRSS study sample, there were 3 cases for which district enrollment size was missing and 112 cases for which poverty concentration was missing. Detail may not sum to totals because of rounding or missing data.
SOURCE: U.S. Department of Education, National Center for Education Statistics, Fast Response Survey System (FRSS), "Distance Education Courses for Public Elementary and Secondary School Students: 2002–03." FRSS 84, 2003. (This table was prepared July 2005.)

Table 55. Private elementary and secondary enrollment, teachers, and schools, by orientation of school and selected school characteristics: Fall 2003

Selected school characteristic	Prekindergarten to grade 12 enrollment				Teachers[1]				Schools			
	Total	Catholic	Other religious	Non-sectarian	Total	Catholic	Other religious	Non-sectarian	Total	Catholic	Other religious	Non-sectarian
1	2	3	4	5	6	7	8	9	10	11	12	13
	Number											
Total	6,099,221	2,520,121	2,228,234	1,350,866	440,850	153,038	167,171	120,641	34,681	8,041	15,507	11,133
Level of school												
Elementary	3,569,986	1,810,163	1,051,392	708,431	214,677	101,610	67,572	45,495	23,494	6,661	9,126	7,707
Secondary	845,083	609,601	116,986	118,497	68,344	42,728	11,314	14,301	2,694	1,096	758	840
Combined	1,684,152	100,358	1,059,856	523,939	157,830	8,700	88,285	60,845	8,494	284	5,623	2,587
Type of school												
Coed	5,670,372	2,265,769	2,112,766	1,291,837	403,531	133,753	156,921	112,857	33,295	7,569	15,012	10,714
All female	206,432	119,872	56,275	30,285	18,474	9,649	4,931	3,894	592	254	186	152
All male	222,417	134,480	59,193	28,744	18,844	9,636	5,318	3,890	794	218	309	267
School enrollment												
Less than 50	735,506	18,003	329,748	387,755	48,220	1,549	23,537	23,134	14,911	352	7,403	7,157
50 to 149	936,871	206,563	467,055	263,253	81,722	15,951	39,453	26,318	8,329	1,667	4,323	2,339
150 to 299	1,499,155	758,128	536,653	204,373	106,367	44,815	39,954	21,598	6,327	3,206	2,264	858
300 to 499	1,232,108	691,754	365,841	174,513	84,758	40,867	26,063	17,828	3,000	1,693	884	423
500 to 749	816,250	457,147	249,242	109,862	55,442	26,087	17,885	11,469	1,298	743	381	174
750 or more	879,331	388,526	279,695	211,110	64,342	23,770	20,279	20,294	816	381	252	183
Percent minority students												
None	455,747	47,361	320,788	87,598	34,037	3,286	25,429	5,322	5,805	351	3,919	1,535
1 to 9 percent	2,302,529	1,177,388	831,418	293,724	161,194	70,959	61,531	28,703	9,164	3,537	4,085	1,542
10 to 29 percent	1,745,024	613,362	563,508	568,154	135,974	39,156	43,223	53,595	8,807	1,802	3,385	3,620
30 to 49 percent	555,305	207,895	187,549	159,860	40,060	12,863	13,470	13,727	3,458	644	1,266	1,548
50 percent or more	1,040,616	474,115	324,971	241,530	69,586	26,774	23,517	19,294	7,447	1,707	2,853	2,887
Type of locale												
City	2,591,721	1,160,165	866,824	564,732	185,161	70,124	64,050	50,987	12,096	3,381	4,650	4,065
Suburban	2,439,654	1,032,266	847,598	559,790	167,958	60,662	60,652	46,644	12,533	2,943	4,694	4,896
Town	446,322	213,909	174,965	57,448	34,194	14,246	13,686	6,262	3,367	1,068	1,707	592
Rural	621,525	113,781	338,848	168,896	53,537	8,006	28,783	16,748	6,686	650	4,456	1,580
	Standard errors											
Total	(41,219.4)	(10,580.0)	(19,673.5)	(29,197.4)	(3,107.8)	(613.4)	(1,491.3)	(2,338.2)	(390.1)	(35.3)	(235.8)	(238.7)
Level of school												
Elementary	(26,311.9)	(11,030.3)	(12,563.0)	(14,207.2)	(1,518.5)	(591.0)	(902.7)	(710.7)	(303.3)	(33.5)	(179.6)	(203.8)
Secondary	(24,240.6)	(3,888.4)	(1,536.1)	(23,852.4)	(1,743.7)	(271.9)	(191.0)	(1,709.4)	(43.2)	(5.8)	(30.9)	(30.2)
Combined	(13,205.3)	(194.5)	(11,117.3)	(6,067.0)	(1,699.2)	(19.0)	(875.8)	(1,414.8)	(151.8)	(4.7)	(92.1)	(111.3)
Type of school												
Coed	(40,482.9)	(11,053.5)	(18,654.4)	(29,154.3)	(3,057.7)	(592.4)	(1,434.4)	(2,331.9)	(386.5)	(34.1)	(234.2)	(237.4)
All female	(1,931.8)	(1,892.6)	(0.0)	(387.2)	(179.3)	(175.0)	(0.0)	(38.7)	(9.1)	(4.7)	(0.0)	(7.7)
All male	(6,417.2)	(3,401.2)	(5,430.7)	(347.0)	(374.1)	(208.8)	(309.1)	(29.0)	(33.3)	(6.5)	(25.2)	(20.8)
School enrollment												
Less than 50	(15,260.3)	(356.7)	(8,591.5)	(9,976.6)	(1,188.3)	(46.4)	(790.0)	(705.1)	(327.1)	(13.0)	(190.8)	(215.2)
50 to 149	(8,597.4)	(2,555.3)	(4,931.3)	(5,254.1)	(698.9)	(142.3)	(497.3)	(365.3)	(91.5)	(13.4)	(67.3)	(49.4)
150 to 299	(9,077.3)	(3,759.0)	(8,128.9)	(5,039.9)	(1,421.5)	(144.1)	(775.4)	(1,209.5)	(43.9)	(12.2)	(41.5)	(22.8)
300 to 499	(10,264.3)	(6,167.9)	(5,519.1)	(3,701.5)	(620.8)	(317.3)	(338.9)	(205.1)	(23.5)	(14.0)	(12.1)	(9.3)
500 to 749	(9,265.1)	(6,281.7)	(6,810.4)	(0.0)	(601.2)	(370.2)	(473.7)	(0.0)	(16.0)	(11.6)	(11.1)	(0.0)
750 or more	(25,564.6)	(3,396.7)	(6,873.5)	(23,922.4)	(1,755.6)	(208.1)	(365.6)	(1,688.4)	(13.4)	(3.4)	(6.6)	(10.6)
Percent minority students												
None	(11,956.3)	(169.2)	(10,678.6)	(5,896.4)	(888.0)	(26.5)	(857.6)	(482.7)	(219.6)	(7.4)	(147.3)	(115.4)
1 to 9 percent	(13,616.0)	(8,626.1)	(8,345.9)	(4,416.5)	(1,408.8)	(509.1)	(544.9)	(1,143.8)	(86.7)	(27.7)	(71.3)	(29.5)
10 to 29 percent	(27,413.0)	(3,192.3)	(8,257.0)	(25,313.8)	(1,989.5)	(217.7)	(933.0)	(1,733.1)	(145.7)	(9.5)	(88.3)	(101.7)
30 to 49 percent	(7,300.4)	(0.0)	(6,449.2)	(3,423.9)	(576.5)	(0.0)	(486.0)	(231.8)	(61.5)	(0.0)	(31.3)	(49.7)
50 percent or more	(7,613.8)	(5,105.5)	(2,080.8)	(5,612.7)	(569.2)	(246.4)	(141.9)	(494.9)	(92.1)	(15.7)	(38.9)	(69.1)
Type of locale												
City	(30,993.9)	(6,516.0)	(11,025.5)	(26,043.8)	(2,151.8)	(319.4)	(779.4)	(1,845.7)	(173.6)	(23.6)	(70.4)	(126.3)
Suburban	(23,337.0)	(8,306.6)	(12,817.6)	(10,120.6)	(1,332.9)	(477.8)	(882.3)	(604.1)	(181.3)	(16.9)	(91.4)	(122.0)
Town	(7,669.6)	(2,128.6)	(6,782.3)	(2,879.5)	(1,288.3)	(130.7)	(557.7)	(1,154.0)	(85.6)	(11.6)	(60.8)	(59.1)
Rural	(7,449.7)	(0.0)	(6,159.5)	(3,704.6)	(794.6)	(0.0)	(644.2)	(360.5)	(238.6)	(0.0)	(183.1)	(99.7)

[1]Data reported in full-time equivalents (FTE). Excludes teachers who teach only prekindergarten students.
NOTE: Includes special education, vocational/technical education, and alternative schools. Tabulation includes schools that offer kindergarten or higher grade. Detail may not sum to totals because of rounding. Standard errors appear in parentheses.

SOURCE: U.S. Department of Education, National Center for Education Statistics, Private School Universe Survey (PSS), 2003–2004. (This table was prepared September 2006.)

Table 56. Private elementary and secondary enrollment, number of schools, and average tuition, by school level, orientation, and tuition: 1999–2000 and 2003–04

School orientation and tuition	Kindergarten through 12th-grade enrollment[1]				Schools				Average tuition paid by students[2] (in current dollars)			
	Total	Elementary	Secondary	Combined	Total	Elementary	Secondary	Combined	Total	Elementary	Secondary	Combined
1	2	3	4	5	6	7	8	9	10	11	12	13
1999–2000												
Total	5,262,850 (131,001)	2,920,680 (55,056)	818,920 (34,102)	1,523,240 (88,816)	27,220 (239)	16,560 (278)	2,580 (126)	8,080 (276)	$4,689 (254.3)	$3,267 (128.3)	$6,053 (1,529.3)	$6,779 (798.1)
Catholic	2,548,710 (23,352)	1,810,330 (18,134)	616,190 (25,935)	122,190 (15,613)	7,930 (41)	6,530 (68)	1,100 (56)	300 (28)	3,236 (439.8)	2,451 (109.4)	4,845 (253.7)	6,780 (1,159.7)
Other religious	1,871,850 (86,781)	831,060 (41,035)	115,010 (10,980)	925,780 (66,926)	12,520 (271)	6,610 (231)	720 (76)	5,190 (243)	4,063 (936.7)	3,503 (609.1)	6,536 (787.7)	4,260 (1,240.4)
Nonsectarian	842,290 (61,373)	279,290 (28,987)	87,720 (11,774)	475,270 (43,377)	5,130 (156)	2,780 (153)	590 (90)	1,770 (151)	10,992 (928.4)	7,884 (1,727.8)	14,638 (1,279.2)	12,363 (3,043.5)
2003–04												
Total	5,059,450 (104,287)	2,675,960 (55,714)	832,320 (54,051)	1,551,170 (82,059)	28,380 (262)	17,330 (262)	2,660 (206)	8,400 (217)	$6,600 (144.5)	$5,049 (119.5)	$8,412 (433.4)	$8,302 (289.7)
Less than $2,499	825,410 (33,567)	614,780 (28,503)	† (†)	178,310 (14,033)	8,880 (318)	5,590 (235)	† (†)	2,910 (187)	1,755 (39.5)	1,856 (49.6)	† (†)	1,612 (84.4)
$2,500 to $3,499	1,056,200 (49,470)	779,200 (43,819)	† (†)	265,070 (25,565)	5,910 (281)	4,160 (218)	† (†)	1,700 (157)	3,313 (31.7)	3,358 (40.6)	† (†)	3,190 (42.3)
$3,500 to $5,999	1,561,900 (64,639)	856,260 (44,734)	319,590 (34,338)	386,050 (36,613)	6,890 (301)	4,660 (240)	710 (100)	1,520 (134)	4,992 (54.1)	5,098 (97.4)	4,901 (76.9)	4,831 (71.8)
$6,000 to $9,999	867,100 (70,159)	263,600 (30,526)	314,590 (37,104)	288,910 (43,797)	3,380 (208)	1,920 (165)	720 (105)	750 (94)	8,172 (140.5)	9,604 (270.0)	7,366 (120.3)	7,743 (213.1)
$10,000 or more	748,830 (65,828)	162,120 (18,476)	153,880 (27,201)	432,830 (52,538)	3,300 (196)	1,010 (143)	780 (90)	1,520 (138)	18,110 (407.5)	17,619 (823.9)	19,896 (1,089.0)	17,658 (558.0)
Catholic	2,320,040 (49,156)	1,645,680 (41,231)	584,250 (32,236)	90,110 (14,746)	7,920 (35)	6,530 (50)	1,060 (39)	320 (39)	4,254 (95.9)	3,533 (105.9)	6,046 (130.6)	5,801 (883.0)
Less than $2,499	508,950 (28,976)	478,010 (26,341)	† (†)	† (†)	2,520 (116)	2,370 (113)	† (†)	† (†)	1,803 (49.0)	1,838 (51.8)	† (†)	† (†)
$2,500 to $3,499	635,890 (37,479)	599,610 (36,557)	† (†)	† (†)	2,290 (113)	2,190 (110)	† (†)	† (†)	3,168 (27.7)	3,184 (29.8)	† (†)	† (†)
$3,500 to $5,999	825,850 (44,943)	522,410 (36,627)	284,710 (26,258)	† (†)	2,420 (135)	1,810 (123)	530 (49)	† (†)	4,727 (53.4)	4,615 (68.4)	4,897 (80.4)	† (†)
$6,000 to $9,999	307,270 (34,641)	† (†)	255,650 (31,681)	† (†)	550 (63)	† (†)	410 (46)	† (†)	7,428 (120.7)	† (†)	7,338 (127.4)	† (†)
$10,000 or more	† (†)	† (†)	† (†)	† (†)	† (†)	† (†)	† (†)	† (†)	† (†)	† (†)	† (†)	† (†)
Other religious	1,746,460 (63,090)	714,860 (28,935)	107,980 (33,776)	923,630 (48,379)	13,660 (203)	7,280 (200)	640 (175)	5,740 (182)	5,839 (143.9)	5,398 (161.4)	9,537 (962.6)	5,748 (230.3)
Less than $2,499	258,570 (16,268)	120,700 (10,263)	† (†)	137,010 (12,537)	5,390 (253)	2,830 (192)	† (†)	2,490 (183)	1,891 (66.3)	1,929 (122.6)	† (†)	1,864 (85.5)
$2,500 to $3,499	342,250 (25,879)	171,210 (16,475)	† (†)	169,300 (19,758)	3,180 (237)	1,820 (166)	† (†)	1,350 (139)	3,571 (82.6)	3,946 (133.6)	† (†)	3,194 (62.2)
$3,500 to $5,999	642,470 (45,686)	271,880 (24,925)	34,690 (18,788)	335,890 (35,041)	3,330 (210)	1,870 (139)	180 (82)	1,280 (130)	4,935 (57.4)	5,090 (98.1)	4,936 (224.4)	4,809 (82.3)
$6,000 to $9,999	319,250 (42,256)	101,120 (17,425)	† (†)	190,920 (34,055)	1,060 (116)	540 (73)	† (†)	410 (66)	7,872 (237.0)	8,771 (436.4)	† (†)	7,503 (273.3)
$10,000 or more	183,930 (21,087)	† (†)	† (†)	90,510 (17,086)	700 (76)	† (†)	† (†)	210 (40)	15,237 (586.0)	† (†)	† (†)	16,185 (1,179.3)
Nonsectarian	992,940 (71,519)	315,430 (30,820)	140,080 (27,556)	537,440 (59,332)	6,810 (136)	3,510 (141)	960 (108)	2,340 (144)	13,419 (379.1)	12,169 (468.5)	17,413 (1,987.6)	13,112 (480.4)
Less than $2,499	57,890 (8,890)	† (†)	† (†)	† (†)	990 (127)	† (†)	† (†)	† (†)	719 (309.9)	† (†)	† (†)	† (†)
$2,500 to $3,499	† (†)	† (†)	† (†)	† (†)	† (†)	† (†)	† (†)	† (†)	† (†)	† (†)	† (†)	† (†)
$3,500 to $5,999	93,590 (17,673)	61,960 (9,990)	† (†)	† (†)	1,140 (171)	970 (159)	† (†)	† (†)	7,718 (764.1)	9,209 (882.4)	† (†)	† (†)
$6,000 to $9,999	240,590 (30,450)	131,320 (22,258)	† (†)	† (†)	1,780 (175)	1,270 (148)	† (†)	† (†)	9,519 (293.3)	10,607 (379.7)	† (†)	† (†)
$10,000 or more	522,830 (55,040)	97,690 (16,359)	93,410 (22,905)	331,730 (47,865)	2,460 (172)	730 (129)	460 (77)	1,270 (128)	19,142 (571.0)	18,559 (855.5)	23,415 (1,493.6)	18,111 (618.0)

†Not applicable.
‡Reporting standards not met.
[1]Only includes kindergarten students who attend schools that offer first or higher grade.
[2]Tuition weighted by the number of students enrolled in schools.
NOTE: Excludes schools not offering first or higher grade. Elementary schools have grade 6 or lower and no grade higher than 8. Secondary schools have no grade lower than 7 and higher than 8. Combined schools have grades lower than 7 and higher than 8.

Excludes prekindergarten students. Includes schools reporting tuition of 0. Detail may not sum to totals because of rounding and cell suppression. Standard errors appear in parentheses.

SOURCE: U.S. Department of Education, National Center for Education Statistics, Schools and Staffing Survey (SASS), "Private School Questionnaire," 1999–2000 and 2003–04. (This table was prepared in August 2006.)

Table 57. Private elementary and secondary school full-time-equivalent staff and student to full-time-equivalent staff ratios, by orientation of school, school level, and type of staff: 2003–04

Type of staff	Total				Catholic			
	Total	Elementary[1]	Secondary[2]	Combined[3]	Total	Elementary[1]	Secondary[2]	Combined[3]
1	2	3	4	5	6	7	8	9
Number of schools	28,380 (262)	17,330 (262)	2,660 (206)	8,400 (217)	7,920 (35)	6,530 (50)	1,060 (39)	320 (39)
Enrollment (in thousands)	5,060 (104)	2,680 (56)	830 (54)	1,550 (82)	2,320 (49)	1,650 (41)	580 (32)	90 (15)
Total staff	707,200 (15,342)	325,010 (6,805)	125,520 (8,244)	256,670 (13,136)	240,870 (4,555)	160,690 (3,518)	66,130 (3,172)	14,050 (2,166)
Principals	27,090 (544)	14,490 (325)	2,740 (236)	9,860 (420)	7,750 (119)	6,090 (101)	1,230 (49)	430 (77)
Assistant principals	10,630 (444)	4,260 (196)	2,230 (183)	4,140 (354)	3,570 (163)	1,870 (124)	1,530 (109)	180 (49)
Other managers	19,670 (671)	7,290 (399)	4,740 (345)	7,640 (507)	5,760 (274)	2,430 (197)	2,830 (189)	500 (101)
Instruction coordinators	5,960 (393)	2,090 (182)	1,260 (218)	2,610 (269)	1,550 (211)	780 (138)	680 (146)	90 (30)
Teachers	416,930 (9,490)	197,090 (4,302)	69,200 (4,389)	150,640 (8,081)	149,280 (3,287)	100,360 (2,615)	40,720 (2,018)	8,200 (1,308)
Teacher aides	40,050 (1,667)	22,870 (948)	1,610 (425)	15,570 (1,391)	12,210 (610)	11,020 (507)	270 (57)	920 (405)
Other aides	8,220 (849)	3,930 (462)	‡ (†)	3,990 (737)	2,310 (435)	1,830 (246)	60 (27)	‡ (†)
Guidance counselors	10,200 (479)	2,400 (201)	3,860 (318)	3,950 (330)	4,490 (215)	1,530 (148)	2,650 (169)	320 (64)
Librarians/media specialists	11,060 (370)	5,280 (168)	1,820 (160)	3,970 (300)	4,400 (143)	3,080 (122)	1,080 (63)	240 (50)
Library/media center aides	3,360 (211)	1,590 (126)	700 (115)	1,070 (119)	1,410 (127)	920 (109)	400 (61)	90 (35)
Nurses	7,930 (962)	2,930 (145)	2,560 (899)	2,450 (202)	2,520 (114)	1,920 (105)	400 (60)	200 (49)
Student support staff	19,100 (1,021)	7,600 (776)	3,380 (667)	8,110 (620)	3,940 (247)	2,700 (162)	800 (101)	440 (133)
Secretaries/clerical staff	43,840 (1,307)	18,360 (538)	8,920 (701)	16,570 (1,062)	14,810 (422)	8,790 (247)	5,240 (315)	780 (147)
Food service personnel	26,290 (1,189)	11,110 (444)	6,920 (922)	8,260 (733)	10,430 (417)	6,830 (314)	3,030 (296)	570 (115)
Custodial and maintenance	38,590 (1,263)	16,650 (443)	8,600 (796)	13,340 (1,001)	14,380 (342)	9,570 (298)	4,210 (257)	590 (101)
Other employees[5]	18,290 (2,842)	7,090 (1,831)	6,680 (2,228)	4,520 (598)	2,050 (259)	980 (152)	990 (198)	‡ (†)
Students per full-time-equivalent staff member								
Total staff	7 (0.1)	8 (0.1)	7 (0.3)	6 (0.1)	10 (0.1)	10 (0.1)	9 (0.2)	6 (0.4)
Principals	187 (4.0)	185 (3.9)	304 (18.8)	157 (7.1)	299 (6.8)	270 (6.7)	474 (29.6)	210 (23.5)
Assistant principals	476 (16.5)	628 (29.0)	373 (18.1)	375 (25.0)	649 (24.6)	881 (54.1)	382 (16.9)	514 (128.9)
Other managers	257 (6.2)	367 (17.4)	175 (10.8)	203 (8.1)	403 (17.4)	677 (54.1)	207 (13.8)	180 (18.6)
Instruction coordinators	849 (57.3)	1,281 (115.3)	661 (124.6)	595 (63.4)	1,498 (224.6)	2,115 (480.8)	864 (213.6)	956 (339.4)
Teachers	12 (0.1)	14 (0.2)	12 (0.3)	10 (0.2)	16 (0.2)	16 (0.3)	14 (0.3)	11 (0.6)
Teacher aides	126 (4.9)	117 (4.5)	516 (139.6)	100 (8.6)	190 (9.8)	149 (7.1)	2,134 (416.0)	98 (67.5)
Other aides	616 (71.3)	680 (73.9)	‡ (†)	389 (89.2)	1,002 (203.9)	900 (125.5)	‡ (†)	‡ (†)
Guidance counselors	496 (20.5)	1,115 (92.7)	216 (13.6)	393 (29.9)	517 (23.9)	1,076 (105.9)	221 (7.9)	286 (50.7)
Librarians/media specialists	457 (9.9)	507 (12.7)	458 (28.0)	391 (16.6)	527 (14.5)	534 (16.1)	542 (33.1)	375 (69.7)
Library/media center aides	1,507 (91.8)	1,683 (132.8)	1,191 (238.1)	1,451 (142.2)	1,646 (156.8)	1,794 (226.3)	1,458 (260.7)	981 (392.9)
Nurses	638 (80.2)	913 (41.6)	‡ (†)	634 (52.8)	921 (41.0)	857 (42.6)	1,451 (174.0)	457 (119.8)
Student support staff	265 (14.4)	352 (36.7)	246 (53.1)	191 (14.7)	589 (36.2)	610 (35.8)	733 (84.1)	203 (67.9)
Secretaries/clerical staff	115 (2.4)	146 (3.8)	93 (5.2)	94 (3.2)	157 (3.8)	187 (5.7)	111 (4.6)	116 (10.6)
Food service personnel	192 (8.6)	241 (10.1)	120 (17.6)	188 (13.9)	222 (8.9)	241 (11.7)	193 (15.0)	159 (26.7)
Custodial and maintenance	131 (3.3)	161 (3.7)	97 (7.3)	116 (5.3)	161 (4.3)	172 (4.6)	139 (6.4)	151 (15.2)
Other employees[5]	277 (40.8)	378 (91.0)	125 (58.5)	343 (40.1)	1,131 (151.6)	1,678 (286.2)	592 (150.8)	‡ (†)

See notes at end of table.

Table 57. Private elementary and secondary school full-time-equivalent staff and student to full-time-equivalent staff ratios, by orientation of school, school level, and type of staff: 2003–04—Continued

Type of staff	Other religious orientation				Nonsectarian			
	Total	Elementary[1]	Secondary[2]	Combined[3]	Total	Elementary[1]	Secondary[2]	Combined[3]
1	10	11	12	13	14	15	16	17
Number of schools	13,660 (203)	7,280 (200)	640 (175)	5,740 (182)	6,810 (136)	3,510 (141)	960 (108)	2,340 (144)
Enrollment (in thousands)	1,750 (63)	710 (29)	110 (34)	920 (48)	990 (72)	320 (31)	140 (28)	540 (59)
Total staff	**246,390 (7,622)**	**99,660 (3,678)**	**17,540 (4,199)**	**129,190 (6,449)**	**219,940 (12,237)**	**64,660 (5,231)**	**41,850 (7,112)**	**113,430 (10,239)**
Principals	12,720 (382)	5,360 (194)	650 (189)	6,710 (355)	6,620 (284)	3,030 (200)	860 (128)	2,730 (204)
Assistant principals	3,760 (289)	1,270 (125)	260 (84)	2,230 (254)	3,300 (239)	1,120 (129)	440 (97)	1,730 (207)
Other managers	6,750 (401)	2,530 (213)	610 (230)	3,610 (257)	7,170 (501)	2,330 (313)	1,300 (273)	3,530 (377)
Instruction coordinators	2,080 (232)	660 (90)	130 (56)	1,290 (204)	2,330 (262)	650 (101)	450 (171)	1,230 (162)
Teachers	154,340 (5,000)	62,300 (2,186)	10,550 (2,635)	81,490 (4,099)	113,300 (7,251)	34,430 (2,926)	17,930 (3,161)	60,950 (6,291)
Teacher aides	10,550 (688)	5,950 (461)	‡ (†)	4,480 (544)	17,290 (1,351)	5,890 (643)	1,230 (406)	10,160 (1,127)
Other aides	3,430 (605)	1,340 (276)	‡ (†)	2,070 (511)	2,470 (451)	770 (265)	‡ (†)	1,500 (372)
Guidance counselors	1,950 (181)	290 (45)	280 (107)	1,380 (122)	3,760 (392)	580 (113)	930 (256)	2,250 (305)
Librarians/media specialists	3,770 (204)	1,540 (114)	260 (101)	1,970 (144)	2,890 (252)	660 (96)	480 (115)	1,750 (218)
Library/media center aides	1,160 (111)	510 (69)	130 (54)	520 (75)	790 (130)	160 (32)	‡ (†)	460 (82)
Nurses	1,510 (115)	560 (58)	150 (47)	800 (84)	3,900 (939)	450 (76)	2,000 (901)	1,450 (185)
Student support staff[4]	3,810 (248)	1,910 (184)	260 (99)	1,640 (191)	11,350 (1,005)	2,990 (712)	2,320 (675)	6,030 (575)
Secretaries/clerical staff	15,960 (698)	6,090 (320)	1,200 (341)	8,670 (550)	13,070 (985)	3,480 (350)	2,470 (569)	7,120 (802)
Food service personnel	7,850 (505)	2,830 (209)	720 (205)	4,300 (502)	8,000 (1,015)	1,450 (230)	3,170 (866)	3,390 (505)
Custodial and maintenance	12,410 (513)	4,600 (251)	1,500 (351)	6,320 (446)	11,810 (1,038)	2,480 (247)	2,890 (701)	6,430 (832)
Other employees[5]	4,340 (711)	1,910 (435)	‡ (†)	1,720 (279)	11,890 (2,745)	4,190 (1,676)	4,980 (2,158)	2,720 (551)
Students per full-time-equivalent staff member								
Total staff	7 (0.1)	7 (0.1)	6 (0.6)	7 (0.2)	5 (0.1)	5 (0.3)	3 (0.3)	5 (0.2)
Principals	137 (5.1)	133 (5.0)	166 (23.4)	138 (7.8)	150 (8.9)	104 (10.1)	163 (30.0)	197 (13.2)
Assistant principals	464 (31.2)	563 (62.8)	416 (77.5)	414 (40.5)	301 (16.5)	281 (31.2)	317 (69.4)	310 (28.3)
Other managers	259 (11.6)	283 (20.6)	176 (25.9)	256 (14.6)	139 (7.2)	135 (12.9)	108 (19.6)	152 (10.3)
Instruction coordinators	839 (96.9)	1,081 (138.7)	814 (489.3)	717 (136.7)	427 (46.2)	485 (75.6)	311 (144.5)	438 (66.9)
Teachers	11 (0.2)	11 (0.2)	10 (0.9)	11 (0.2)	9 (0.2)	9 (0.3)	8 (0.5)	9 (0.2)
Teacher aides	166 (12.4)	120 (8.6)	‡ (†)	206 (26.0)	57 (5.1)	54 (6.7)	114 (41.3)	53 (6.9)
Other aides	509 (104.6)	534 (109.4)	‡ (†)	446 (132.9)	401 (89.7)	412 (141.4)	‡ (†)	359 (128.7)
Guidance counselors	898 (61.4)	2,498 (420.6)	388 (50.6)	669 (50.0)	264 (30.8)	540 (136.6)	151 (48.9)	239 (37.1)
Librarians/media specialists	463 (19.1)	465 (26.4)	413 (47.9)	468 (30.9)	343 (15.3)	478 (41.3)	293 (47.9)	306 (16.5)
Library/media center aides	1,508 (143.3)	1,405 (168.3)	‡ (†)	1,791 (289.2)	1,257 (203.1)	1,919 (495.6)	‡ (†)	1,165 (155.1)
Nurses	1,156 (84.9)	1,269 (121.3)	731 (352.8)	1,155 (118.3)	254 (76.2)	703 (127.9)	371 (53.8)	371 (53.8)
Student support staff[4]	458 (29.6)	374 (36.3)	411 (181.8)	565 (56.1)	87 (9.6)	105 (30.4)	60 (21.5)	89 (10.9)
Secretaries/clerical staff	109 (3.1)	117 (4.4)	90 (12.2)	107 (4.0)	76 (4.0)	91 (6.8)	57 (9.5)	75 (4.9)
Food service personnel	222 (14.9)	253 (18.9)	150 (55.0)	215 (24.9)	124 (16.2)	218 (40.6)	44 (11.8)	159 (17.8)
Custodial and maintenance	141 (4.6)	155 (8.1)	72 (15.7)	146 (7.8)	84 (5.4)	127 (11.0)	48 (9.0)	84 (6.3)
Other employees[5]	402 (65.4)	374 (81.4)	‡ (†)	537 (93.3)	83 (20.0)	‡ (†)	‡ (†)	198 (35.9)

†Not applicable.
‡Reporting standards not met.
[1]Includes schools beginning with grade 6 or below and with no grade higher than 8.
[2]Schools with no grade lower than 7.
[3]Schools with grades lower than 7 and higher than 8.
[4]Includes student support services professional staff, such as school psychologists, social workers, occupational therapists, and speech therapists.
[5]Includes health and other noninstructional aides, and other employees not identified by function.
NOTE: Data are based on a sample survey and may not be strictly comparable with data reported elsewhere. Excludes all prekindergarten students from calculations, but includes kindergarten students attending schools that offer first or higher grade. Includes only schools that offer first or higher grade. Standard errors appear in parentheses. Detail may not sum to totals because of rounding.
SOURCE: U.S. Department of Education, National Center for Education Statistics, Schools and Staffing Survey (SASS), "Private School Questionnaire," 2003–04. (This table was prepared August 2006.)

Table 58. Enrollment and instructional staff in Catholic elementary and secondary schools, by level: Selected years, 1919–20 through 2005–06

School year	Number of schools			Enrollment			Instructional staff		
	Total	Elementary	Secondary	Total	Elementary	Secondary	Total	Elementary	Secondary
1	2	3	4	5	6	7	8	9	10
1919–20	8,103	6,551	1,552	1,925,521	1,795,673	129,848	49,516 [1]	41,592 [1]	7,924 [1]
1929–30	10,046	7,923	2,123	2,464,467	2,222,598	241,869	72,552 [1]	58,245 [1]	14,307 [1]
1939–40	10,049	7,944	2,105	2,396,305	2,035,182	361,123	81,057 [1]	60,081 [1]	20,976 [1]
1949–50	10,778	8,589	2,189	3,066,387	2,560,815	505,572	94,295 [1]	66,525 [1]	27,770 [1]
Fall 1960	12,893	10,501	2,392	5,253,791	4,373,422	880,369	151,902 [1]	108,169 [1]	43,733 [1]
1969–70	11,352	9,366	1,986	4,367,000	3,359,000	1,008,000	195,400 [2]	133,200 [2]	62,200 [2]
1970–71	11,350	9,370	1,980	4,363,566	3,355,478	1,008,088	166,208	112,750	53,458
1974–75	10,127	8,437	1,690	3,504,000	2,602,000	902,000	150,179	100,011	50,168
1975–76	9,993	8,340	1,653	3,415,000	2,525,000	890,000	149,276	99,319	49,957
1979–80	9,640	8,100	1,540	3,139,000	2,293,000	846,000	147,294	97,724	49,570
1980–81	9,559	8,043	1,516	3,106,000	2,269,000	837,000	145,777	96,739	49,038
1981–82	9,494	7,996	1,498	3,094,000	2,266,000	828,000	146,172	96,847	49,325
1982–83	9,432	7,950	1,482	3,007,189	2,211,412	795,777	146,460	97,337	49,123
1983–84	9,401	7,937	1,464	2,969,000	2,179,000	790,000	146,913	98,591	48,322
1984–85	9,325	7,876	1,449	2,903,000	2,119,000	784,000	149,888	99,820	50,068
1985–86	9,220	7,790	1,430	2,821,000	2,061,000	760,000	146,594	96,741	49,853
1986–87	9,102	7,693	1,409	2,726,000	1,998,000	728,000	141,930	93,554	48,376
1987–88	8,992	7,601	1,391	2,623,031	1,942,148	680,883	139,887	93,199	46,688
1988–89	8,867	7,505	1,362	2,551,119	1,911,911	639,208	137,700	93,154	44,546
1989–90	8,719	7,395	1,324	2,589,000	1,983,000	606,000	136,900	94,197	42,703
1990–91	8,587	7,291	1,296	2,475,439	1,883,906	591,533	131,198	91,039	40,159
1991–92	8,508	7,239	1,269	2,442,924	1,856,302	586,622	153,334	109,084	44,250
1992–93	8,423	7,174	1,249	2,444,842	1,860,937	583,905	154,816	109,825	44,991
1993–94	8,345	7,114	1,231	2,444,609	1,859,947	584,662	157,201	112,199	45,002
1994–95	8,293	7,055	1,238	2,475,207	1,877,782	597,425	164,219 [3]	117,620 [3]	46,599 [3]
1995–96	8,250	7,022	1,228	2,491,111	1,884,461	606,650	166,759 [3]	118,753 [3]	48,006 [3]
1996–97	8,231	7,005	1,226	2,497,198	1,885,037	612,161	153,276 [3]	107,548 [3]	45,728 [3]
1997–98	8,223	7,004	1,219	2,497,894	1,879,737	618,157	152,259 [3]	105,717 [3]	46,542 [3]
1998–99	8,217	6,990	1,227	2,496,488	1,876,211	620,277	153,081 [3]	105,943 [3]	47,138 [3]
1999–2000	8,144	6,923	1,221	2,653,038	2,013,084	639,954	157,134 [3]	109,404 [3]	47,730 [3]
2000–01	8,146	6,920	1,226	2,647,301	2,004,037	643,264	160,731 [3]	111,937 [3]	48,794 [3]
2001–02	8,114	6,886	1,228	2,616,330	1,971,627	644,703	155,658 [3]	108,485 [3]	47,173 [3]
2002–03	8,000	6,785	1,215	2,553,277	1,906,870	646,407	163,004 [3]	112,884 [3]	50,120 [3]
2003–04	7,955	6,727	1,228	2,484,252	1,842,918	641,334	162,337 [3]	112,303 [3]	50,034 [3]
2004–05	7,799	6,574	1,225	2,420,590	1,793,773	626,817	160,153 [3]	107,764 [3]	52,389 [3]
2005–06	7,589	6,386	1,203	2,363,220	1,726,773	636,447	152,502 [3,4]	103,481 [3,4]	49,021 [3,4]

[1]Includes part-time teachers.
[2]Includes estimates for the nonreporting schools.
[3]Reported in full-time equivalents (FTE).
[4]Excludes the Archdiocese of New Orleans.
NOTE: Data collected by the National Catholic Educational Association and data collected by the National Center for Education Statistics are not directly comparable because survey procedures and definitions differ. Excludes prekindergarten enrollment. Some data have been revised from previously published figures.
SOURCE: National Catholic Educational Association, *A Statistical Report on Catholic Elementary and Secondary Schools for the Years 1967–68 to 1969–70*; *A Report on Catholic Schools*, 1970–71 through 1973–74; *A Statistical Report on U.S. Catholic Schools*, 1974–75 through 1980–81; and *United States Catholic Elementary and Secondary Schools*, 1981–82 through 2005–06. (This table was prepared April 2006.)

Table 59. Private elementary and secondary schools, enrollment, teachers, and high school graduates, by state: Selected years, 1997 through 2003

State	Schools, fall 2003		Enrollment in prekindergarten through grade 12								Teachers,[1] fall 2003		High school graduates, 2002–03	
			Fall 1997		Fall 1999		Fall 2001		Fall 2003					
1	2		3		4		5		6		7		8	
United States	34,681	(390.1)	5,944,320	(18,543)	6,018,280	(30,179)	6,319,650	(40,272)	6,099,220	(41,219)	440,850	(3,108)	295,790	(5,355)
Alabama	590	(103.4)	82,060	(0)	81,040	(0)	92,380	(3,926)	99,580	(12,130)	7,250	(720)	5,980	(1,225)
Alaska....................	97	(28.3)	7,230	(0)	6,980	(0)	7,420	(0)	7,370	(424)	640	(57)	280	(0)
Arizona	616	(208.6)	59,730	(261)	58,740	(2,591)	78,660	(18,218)	75,360	(16,426)	4,840	(907)	2,410	(23)
Arkansas	185	(0.0)	30,410	(0)	29,400	(0)	32,570	(0)	31,300	(0)	2,280	((0))	1,300	(0)
California	4,244	(61.8)	721,210	(2,146)	724,010	(1,403)	757,750	(8,415)	740,460	(8,703)	49,460	(524)	32,000	(594)
Colorado	429	(9.5)	65,410	(0)	65,690	(0)	64,700	(0)	62,080	(476)	4,620	(29)	2,360	(19)
Connecticut............	443	(34.3)	76,740	(785)	80,060	(391)	82,320	(0)	102,960	(25,024)	9,190	(1,814)	10,560	(5,065)
Delaware................	177	(31.8)	36,730	(7,525)	26,940	(0)	31,690	(1,023)	33,020	(2,649)	3,410	(1,306)	1,360	(101)
District of Columbia ...	145	(52.3)	17,480	(0)	17,000	(0)	33,660	(14,373)	23,510	(6,121)	2,410	(527)	1,200	(0)
Florida...................	1,998	(101.8)	329,770	(2,120)	349,180	(4,957)	365,890	(8,301)	398,720	(14,590)	27,720	(998)	16,820	(463)
Georgia..................	895	(169.4)	126,520	(5,983)	137,420	(9,460)	137,060	(4,550)	144,850	(6,527)	11,880	(506)	6,850	(16)
Hawaii	134	(0.0)	35,530	(0)	35,550	(746)	42,980	(220)	39,940	(0)	2,990	(0)	2,740	(0)
Idaho.....................	118	(0.0)	11,140	(0)	12,720	(0)	12,050	(0)	12,570	(0)	910	(0)	510	(0)
Illinois...................	1,618	(37.2)	345,250	(720)	347,750	(700)	357,390	(19,293)	316,430	(1,698)	19,910	(143)	15,090	(63)
Indiana..................	860	(39.3)	122,430	(1,222)	121,960	(0)	129,240	(326)	124,500	(455)	7,900	(39)	4,820	(0)
Iowa......................	278	(21.2)	64,320	(9,269)	54,640	(844)	51,540	(0)	53,850	(4,634)	3,500	(180)	2,620	(0)
Kansas..................	319	(74.6)	45,430	(1,964)	56,840	(12,716)	51,540	(8,341)	47,710	(2,151)	3,350	(223)	2,160	(0)
Kentucky................	465	(63.5)	81,770	(1,078)	89,300	(6,657)	85,230	(3,227)	82,100	(1,525)	5,420	(64)	3,660	(0)
Louisiana	476	(27.8)	153,710	(1,198)	148,020	(0)	159,910	(11,381)	155,780	(3,515)	10,020	(199)	9,010	(42)
Maine....................	237	(82.8)	18,260	((0))	19,820	(261)	20,820	(174)	24,740	(3,629)	2,250	(232)	3,240	(768)
Maryland................	863	(0.0)	154,920	(1,725)	166,570	(1,030)	175,740	(0)	172,360	(0)	13,440	(0)	7,810	(0)
Massachusetts........	1,067	(108.9)	151,300	(0)	154,060	(147)	177,490	(9,836)	164,390	(6,636)	14,360	(258)	10,050	(0)
Michigan................	1,037	(0.0)	211,950	(3,152)	208,470	(4,965)	198,380	(0)	180,080	(0)	11,710	(0)	9,320	(0)
Minnesota..............	627	(43.5)	97,470	(0)	101,360	(0)	112,310	(2,993)	106,010	(3,011)	7,330	(216)	4,750	(189)
Mississippi.............	316	(72.2)	57,150	(416)	67,200	(14,096)	67,380	(10,106)	57,110	(2,981)	4,360	(364)	3,370	(0)
Missouri.................	813	(121.5)	138,460	(6,478)	131,750	(0)	138,140	(4,321)	141,530	(9,966)	9,970	(556)	7,670	(780)
Montana.................	168	(47.7)	9,050	(0)	10,170	(487)	12,930	(1,895)	12,510	(2,091)	1,400	(428)	830	(323)
Nebraska...............	234	(0.0)	43,210	(0)	44,560	(0)	45,590	(618)	41,650	(0)	2,800	(0)	2,360	(0)
Nevada..................	138	(0.0)	15,360	(0)	17,350	(0)	20,370	(385)	23,930	(0)	1,370	(0)	670	(0)
New Hampshire	322	(0.0)	31,670	(1,565)	36,480	(0)	38,650	(0)	33,780	(0)	2,700	(0)	2,240	(0)
New Jersey.............	1,453	(49.4)	248,110	(8,025)	237,540	(2,316)	282,450	(4,182)	269,530	(7,577)	19,270	(459)	11,930	(5)
New Mexico	212	(17.3)	23,580	(84)	28,570	(220)	26,510	(0)	29,310	(3,928)	2,450	(381)	1,240	(0)
New York................	2,228	(64.2)	531,510	(2,416)	542,520	(4,368)	559,670	(1,669)	515,620	(4,071)	39,280	(338)	26,870	(415)
North Carolina	746	(77.8)	105,450	(8,920)	104,370	(1,403)	116,500	(4,112)	126,230	(11,439)	10,570	(800)	5,130	(184)
North Dakota	53	(0.0)	7,970	(0)	7,730	(0)	7,180	(0)	6,840	(0)	540	(0)	460	(0)
Ohio......................	1,174	(53.5)	285,150	(3,088)	280,930	(1,730)	290,370	(7,180)	270,660	(7,094)	17,330	(464)	14,090	(414)
Oklahoma...............	202	(27.4)	39,580	(7,068)	45,660	(7,770)	46,570	(8,723)	34,300	(2,013)	2,580	(87)	1,550	(57)
Oregon...................	412	((0.0))	58,290	(4,441)	61,000	(5,195)	71,500	(15,519)	54,320	(0)	3,620	(0)	2,610	(0)
Pennsylvania...........	2,512	(87.2)	395,940	(5,960)	392,060	(6,679)	374,490	(0)	357,580	(3,364)	24,910	(268)	18,270	(162)
Rhode Island	193	(0.0)	30,310	(0)	29,570	(0)	30,970	(0)	31,960	(0)	2,610	(0)	1,800	(0)
South Carolina........	420	(0.0)	82,390	(7,965)	86,810	(18,537)	70,950	(0)	73,800	(0)	5,250	(0)	2,830	(0)
South Dakota..........	90	(0.0)	10,350	(0)	10,120	(0)	11,740	(0)	11,980	(0)	880	(0)	480	(0)
Tennessee.............	529	(0.0)	91,880	(0)	104,150	(5,281)	98,790	(0)	93,390	(0)	7,920	(0)	5,280	(0)
Texas	1,539	(117.5)	283,120	(7,997)	277,770	(2,338)	314,210	(12,244)	271,380	(2,758)	21,500	(766)	10,600	(267)
Utah	124	(0.0)	18,250	(0)	15,900	(0)	20,040	(0)	19,990	(0)	1,450	(0)	1,030	(0)
Vermont	131	(0.0)	12,230	(398)	15,010	(1,829)	14,090	(0)	12,730	(0)	1,460	(0)	1,260	(0)
Virginia..................	733	(55.7)	115,560	(443)	116,110	(215)	129,470	(0)	131,160	(6,936)	10,480	(474)	5,840	(54)
Washington.............	740	(102.4)	88,160	(1,870)	88,080	(1,493)	91,150	(2,028)	101,130	(7,935)	6,860	(413)	3,750	(0)
West Virginia...........	153	(0.0)	15,260	(0)	16,370	(0)	16,560	(0)	15,300	(0)	1,270	(0)	760	(0)
Wisconsin	1,096	(84.1)	156,330	(0)	154,340	(1,581)	162,220	(9,080)	159,240	(11,743)	10,990	(657)	5,920	(0)
Wyoming.................	38	(0.0)	3,200	(0)	2,640	(0)	2,430	(0)	2,600	(0)	240	(0)	40	(0)

[1]Reported in full-time-equivalents (FTE). Excludes teachers who teach only prekindergarten students.
NOTE: Includes special education, vocational/technical education, and alternative schools. Tabulation includes schools that offer kindergarten or higher grade. Includes enrollment of students in prekindergarten though grade 12 in schools that offer kindergarten or higher grade. Some data have been revised from previously published figures. Detail may not sum to totals because of rounding. Standard errors appear in parentheses.
SOURCE: U.S. Department of Education, National Center for Education Statistics, Private School Universe Survey (PSS), various years, 1997–98 through 2003–2004. (This table was prepared September 2006.)

Table 60. Public elementary and secondary pupil/teacher ratios, by enrollment size, type, and level of school: Fall 1987 through fall 2004

Enrollment size, type, and level of school	1987	1988	1989	1990	1991	1992	1993	1994	1995	1996	1997	1998	1999	2000	2001	2002	2003	2004
1	2	3	4	5	6	7	8	9	10	11	12	13	14	15	16	17	18	19
All schools	**17.9**	**17.9**	**17.9**	**17.4**	**17.6**	**17.7**	**17.8**	**17.7**	**17.8**	**17.6**	**17.2**	**16.9**	**16.6**	**16.4**	**16.3**	**16.2**	**16.4**	**16.2**
Enrollment size of school																		
Under 300	14.6	14.8	14.6	14.0	14.1	14.1	14.3	14.1	14.1	14.0	13.7	13.6	13.3	13.1	12.9	12.8	13.0	12.8
300 to 499	17.6	17.7	17.6	17.0	17.1	17.0	17.3	17.2	17.1	16.9	16.5	16.2	15.8	15.5	15.4	15.3	15.5	15.2
500 to 999	18.5	18.4	18.5	18.0	18.1	18.1	18.2	18.1	18.2	17.9	17.5	17.1	16.8	16.7	16.5	16.5	16.6	16.4
1,000 to 1,499	18.5	18.3	18.5	17.9	18.2	18.6	18.5	18.6	18.7	18.5	18.1	17.7	17.6	17.4	17.4	17.4	17.6	17.3
1,500 or more	19.4	20.1	19.4	19.2	19.6	20.0	19.7	19.9	20.0	20.0	19.7	19.3	19.3	19.1	19.0	18.9	19.2	19.1
Type																		
Regular schools	18.1	18.0	18.1	17.6	17.7	17.8	17.9	17.8	17.9	17.7	17.3	17.0	16.7	16.5	16.4	16.3	16.5	16.3
Alternative	16.0	14.8	16.0	14.2	15.8	16.5	17.4	18.0	16.6	16.6	16.5	16.4	15.8	15.2	14.9	14.9	15.0	14.4
Special education	6.2	6.9	6.2	6.5	6.8	7.0	7.4	6.9	7.2	7.4	7.6	7.3	7.2	7.0	6.4	7.0	7.3	7.4
Vocational	13.0	—	13.0	13.0	12.3	13.0	13.1	12.9	12.7	12.9	12.9	13.1	13.0	12.7	12.7	9.9	10.3	11.5
Level and size																		
Elementary schools	18.6	18.6	18.6	18.1	18.2	18.1	18.2	18.0	18.1	17.8	17.4	17.0	16.7	16.5	16.3	16.2	16.3	16.0
Regular	18.7	18.7	18.7	18.2	18.2	18.1	18.3	18.0	18.1	17.9	17.4	17.0	16.7	16.5	16.3	16.2	16.3	16.0
Under 300	16.6	16.7	16.6	16.0	16.1	15.9	16.0	15.7	15.7	15.6	15.3	15.1	14.6	14.4	14.1	13.9	14.0	13.7
300 to 499	18.3	18.3	18.3	17.6	17.6	17.5	17.7	17.5	17.5	17.2	16.8	16.4	16.1	15.8	15.6	15.5	15.6	15.3
500 to 999	19.4	19.4	19.4	18.8	18.8	18.7	18.8	18.5	18.6	18.3	17.8	17.4	17.1	16.8	16.7	16.7	16.8	16.5
1,000 to 1,499	20.1	20.0	20.1	19.5	19.6	19.7	19.7	19.6	19.7	19.4	18.8	18.4	18.3	18.1	18.0	18.0	18.1	17.7
1,500 or more	19.5	18.9	19.5	19.9	20.9	20.3	21.2	20.4	20.9	21.2	20.7	19.9	20.0	20.5	20.2	20.3	20.8	20.5
Secondary schools	17.2	17.2	17.2	16.6	16.9	17.3	17.3	17.5	17.6	17.5	17.3	17.0	16.8	16.6	16.6	16.7	16.9	16.8
Regular	17.3	17.1	17.3	16.7	17.0	17.4	17.4	17.6	17.7	17.6	17.4	17.1	16.9	16.7	16.7	16.8	17.0	16.9
Under 300	12.4	12.7	12.4	12.3	12.3	12.3	12.6	12.7	12.8	12.7	12.5	12.5	12.0	12.0	11.9	12.0	12.3	12.0
300 to 499	15.5	15.4	15.5	14.9	15.1	15.3	15.5	15.7	15.7	15.5	15.3	15.1	14.6	14.5	14.4	14.4	14.7	14.7
500 to 999	16.8	16.6	16.8	16.1	16.4	16.7	16.7	16.8	16.9	16.7	16.4	16.2	16.0	15.8	15.7	15.8	16.0	15.9
1,000 to 1,499	17.9	17.7	17.9	17.2	17.5	17.9	17.8	17.9	18.0	17.9	17.5	17.2	17.1	16.8	16.8	16.9	17.2	17.0
1,500 or more	19.5	19.5	19.5	19.3	19.6	20.0	19.6	19.9	20.0	20.0	19.7	19.3	19.2	18.9	18.8	18.8	19.0	19.0
Combined schools	15.5	15.9	15.5	14.5	15.0	14.8	15.3	15.1	15.0	14.7	14.4	13.4	13.4	13.7	13.4	13.5	13.8	13.9
Under 300	9.5	9.8	9.5	8.9	9.3	9.3	9.6	9.3	9.0	8.7	8.6	8.9	9.1	9.2	9.1	9.1	9.5	9.2
300 to 499	14.4	15.3	14.4	14.2	14.3	14.4	14.8	14.4	14.7	14.3	14.0	13.6	13.8	13.5	13.1	13.1	14.4	13.4
500 to 999	17.6	17.1	17.6	16.3	16.7	15.6	16.5	16.6	16.6	16.6	16.2	15.5	14.9	15.8	15.6	16.0	15.4	15.8
1,000 to 1,499	19.0	18.5	19.0	17.8	17.9	18.6	18.6	18.3	18.2	18.4	18.0	16.9	16.9	17.5	18.1	17.7	17.5	17.4
1,500 or more	18.8	18.8	18.8	17.7	18.6	18.9	18.8	19.5	19.6	19.3	19.3	18.7	19.2	18.6	18.9	19.1	19.2	18.7
Ungraded	5.9	6.8	5.9	6.4	6.5	6.9	7.1	6.7	6.9	5.9	6.2	5.9	5.3	7.0	6.3	6.8	9.6	8.0

—Not available.
NOTE: Pupil/teacher ratios are based on data reported by types of schools rather than by instructional programs within schools. Only includes schools that reported both enrollment and teacher data. Ratios are based on data reported by schools and may differ from data reported in other tables that reflect aggregate totals reported by states.

SOURCE: U.S. Department of Education, National Center for Education Statistics, Common Core of Data (CCD), "Public Elementary/Secondary School Universe Survey," 1987–88 through 2004–05. (This table was prepared August 2006.)

Table 61. Public and private elementary and secondary teachers, enrollment, and pupil/teacher ratios: Selected years, fall 1955 through fall 2015

Year	Teachers (in thousands)			Enrollment (in thousands)			Pupil/teacher ratio		
	Total	Public	Private	Total	Public	Private	Total	Public	Private
1	2	3	4	5	6	7	8	9	10
1955	1,286	1,141	145 [1]	35,280	30,680	4,600 [1]	27.4	26.9	31.7 [1]
1960	1,600	1,408	192 [1]	42,181	36,281	5,900 [1]	26.4	25.8	30.7 [1]
1965	1,933	1,710	223	48,473	42,173	6,300	25.1	24.7	28.3
1970	2,292	2,059	233	51,257	45,894	5,363	22.4	22.3	23.0
1971	2,293	2,063	230 [1]	51,271	46,071	5,200 [1]	22.4	22.3	22.6 [1]
1972	2,337	2,106	231 [1]	50,726	45,726	5,000 [1]	21.7	21.7	21.6 [1]
1973	2,372	2,136	236 [1]	50,446	45,446	5,000 [1]	21.3	21.3	21.2 [1]
1974	2,410	2,165	245 [1]	50,073	45,073	5,000 [1]	20.8	20.8	20.4 [1]
1975	2,453	2,198	255 [1]	49,819	44,819	5,000 [1]	20.3	20.4	19.6 [1]
1976	2,457	2,189	268	49,478	44,311	5,167	20.1	20.2	19.3
1977	2,488	2,209	279	48,717	43,577	5,140	19.6	19.7	18.4
1978	2,479	2,207	272	47,637	42,551	5,086	19.2	19.3	18.7
1979	2,461	2,185	276 [1]	46,651	41,651	5,000 [1]	19.0	19.1	18.1 [1]
1980	2,485	2,184	301	46,208	40,877	5,331	18.6	18.7	17.7
1981	2,440	2,127	313 [1]	45,544	40,044	5,500 [1]	18.7	18.8	17.6 [1]
1982	2,458	2,133	325 [1]	45,166	39,566	5,600 [1]	18.4	18.6	17.2 [1]
1983	2,476	2,139	337	44,967	39,252	5,715	18.2	18.4	17.0
1984	2,508	2,168	340 [1]	44,908	39,208	5,700 [1]	17.9	18.1	16.8 [1]
1985	2,549	2,206	343	44,979	39,422	5,557	17.6	17.9	16.2
1986	2,592	2,244	348 [1]	45,205	39,753	5,452 [1]	17.4	17.7	15.7 [1]
1987	2,631	2,279	352	45,487	40,008	5,479	17.3	17.6	15.6
1988	2,668	2,323	345	45,430	40,189	5,242 [1]	17.0	17.3	15.2 [1]
1989	2,713	2,357	356	46,141	40,543	5,599	17.0	17.2	15.7
1990	2,759	2,398	361 [1]	46,865	41,217	5,648 [1]	17.0	17.2	15.6 [1]
1991	2,797	2,432	365	47,728	42,047	5,681	17.1	17.3	15.6
1992	2,827	2,459	368 [1]	48,500	42,823	5,677 [1]	17.2	17.4	15.4 [1]
1993	2,874	2,504	370	49,133	43,465	5,668	17.1	17.4	15.3
1994	2,925	2,552	373 [1]	49,898	44,111	5,787 [1]	17.1	17.3	15.5 [1]
1995	2,974	2,598	376	50,759	44,840	5,918	17.1	17.3	15.7
1996	3,051	2,667	384 [1]	51,544	45,611	5,933 [1]	16.9	17.1	15.5 [1]
1997	3,138	2,746	391	52,071	46,127	5,944	16.6	16.8	15.2
1998	3,230	2,830	400 [1]	52,525	46,539	5,988 [1]	16.3	16.4	15.0 [1]
1999	3,319	2,911	408	52,876	46,857	6,018	15.9	16.1	14.7
2000	3,366	2,941	424 [1]	53,373	47,204	6,169 [1]	15.9	16.0	14.5 [1]
2001	3,440	3,000	441	53,992	47,672	6,320	15.7	15.9	14.3
2002	3,476	3,034	442 [1]	54,403	48,183	6,220 [1]	15.7	15.9	14.1 [1]
2003	3,490	3,049	441	54,639	48,540	6,099	15.7	15.9	13.8
2004	3,537	3,091	447 [1]	54,946	48,795	6,151 [1]	15.5	15.8	13.8 [1]
2005[2]	3,593	3,139	454	54,772	48,710	6,062	15.2	15.5	13.4
2006[2]	3,635	3,176	459	55,075	48,948	6,127	15.2	15.4	13.3
2007[2]	3,671	3,207	464	55,238	49,091	6,147	15.0	15.3	13.3
2008[2]	3,705	3,237	468	55,333	49,167	6,166	14.9	15.2	13.2
2009[2]	3,738	3,266	472	55,453	49,267	6,186	14.8	15.1	13.1
2010[2]	3,776	3,299	477	55,630	49,415	6,215	14.7	15.0	13.0
2011[2]	3,820	3,337	483	55,886	49,637	6,249	14.6	14.9	12.9
2012[2]	3,873	3,384	489	56,232	49,938	6,294	14.5	14.8	12.9
2013[2]	3,932	3,435	497	56,638	50,294	6,344	14.4	14.6	12.8
2014[2]	3,997	3,492	505	57,137	50,735	6,402	14.3	14.5	12.7
2015[2]	4,064	3,551	513	57,681	51,220	6,461	14.2	14.4	12.6

[1]Estimated.
[2]Projected.
NOTE: Data for teachers are expressed in full-time equivalents (FTE). Data for private schools include kindergarten and some prekindergarten school teachers and students. The pupil/teacher ratio includes teachers for students with disabilities and other special teachers, while these teachers are generally excluded from class size calculations. Ratios for public schools reflect totals reported by states and differ from totals reported for schools or school districts. Some data have been revised from previously published figures. Detail may not sum to totals because of rounding.
SOURCE: U.S. Department of Education, National Center for Education Statistics, *Statistics of Public Elementary and Secondary Day Schools*, 1955–56 through 1984–85; Common Core of Data (CCD), "State Nonfiscal Survey of Public Elementary/Secondary Education," 1985–86 through 2004–05; Private School Universe Survey (PSS), 1989–90 through 2003–04; *Projections of Education Statistics to 2015*; and unpublished data. (This table was prepared September 2006.)

Table 62. Public elementary and secondary teachers, by level and state or jurisdiction: Fall 1999 through fall 2004

State or jurisdiction	Fall 1999	Fall 2000	Fall 2001	Fall 2002	Fall 2003[1]				Fall 2004			
					Total	Elementary	Secondary	Ungraded	Total	Elementary	Secondary	Ungraded
1	2	3	4	5	6	7	8	9	10	11	12	13
United States	2,910,633 [2]	2,941,461 [2]	2,999,528 [2]	3,034,123 [2]	3,048,652 [2]	1,705,715 [2]	1,101,372 [2]	241,565 [2]	3,090,513 [2]	1,716,961 [2]	1,150,663 [2]	222,889 [2]
Alabama	48,624 [3]	48,194 [3]	46,785 [3]	47,115 [3]	58,070	38,152	19,918	0	51,594	37,330	14,264	0
Alaska..............................	7,838	7,880	8,026	8,080	7,808	5,479	2,329	0	7,756	5,368	2,388	0
Arizona	43,892	44,438	46,015	47,101	47,507	34,048	13,459	0	48,935	34,523	14,412	0
Arkansas..........................	31,362	31,947	33,079	30,330	30,876	13,149	15,499	2,228	31,234	13,561	15,387	2,286
California	287,433 [3]	298,021 [3]	304,203 [3]	307,764 [3]	304,311 [3]	217,470 [3]	78,462	8,379	305,969 [3]	216,293 [3]	81,096	8,580
Colorado	40,772	41,983	44,182	45,401	44,904	22,685	22,219	0	45,165	22,604	22,561	0
Connecticut......................	39,907	41,044	41,773	42,296	42,370	24,830	13,036	4,504	38,808	25,348	12,003	1,457
Delaware..........................	7,318	7,469	7,571	7,698	7,749	3,847	3,902	0	7,856	3,914	3,942	0
District of Columbia	4,812 [3]	4,949	4,951	5,005	5,676	3,396	1,856	424	5,387	2,826	2,286	275
Florida.............................	130,336	132,030	134,684	138,226	144,955	62,787	57,139	25,029	154,864	67,460	60,876	26,528
Georgia	90,638	91,043	92,731	96,044	97,150	56,357	40,793	0	104,987	63,677	41,310	0
Hawaii..............................	10,866	10,927	11,007	10,973	11,129	5,798	5,281	50	11,146	5,805	5,291	50
Idaho...............................	13,641	13,714	13,854	13,896	14,049	7,272	6,777	0	14,269	7,351	6,918	0
Illinois.............................	124,815	127,620	129,600	131,046	127,669	74,957	32,641	20,071	131,047	76,438	33,889	20,720
Indiana............................	58,864	59,226	59,659	59,968	59,924	31,379	25,807	2,738	60,563	31,947	26,352	2,264
Iowa................................	33,480	34,636	34,906	34,573	34,791	19,304	11,353	4,134	34,697	22,503	12,194	0
Kansas............................	32,969	32,742	33,084	32,643	32,589	14,378	14,655	3,556	32,932	14,451	14,831	3,650
Kentucky..........................	41,954	39,589	40,376	40,662	41,246	23,974	9,582	7,690	41,463	23,980	9,608	7,875
Louisiana.........................	50,031	49,915	49,980	50,062	50,495	35,412	15,083	0	49,192	34,367	14,825	0
Maine...............................	16,349	16,559	16,741	16,837	17,621	12,061	5,560	0	16,656	11,196	5,460	0
Maryland..........................	50,995	52,433	53,774	55,382	55,198	32,750	22,448	0	55,101	32,214	22,887	0
Massachusetts..................	77,596	67,432	68,942	74,214	72,062	28,619	31,825	11,618	73,399	29,832	31,370	12,197
Michigan	96,094	97,031	98,849	89,595	97,014	67,852 [4]	22,609 [4]	6,553 [4]	100,634	70,818 [4]	23,637 [4]	6,179 [4]
Minnesota	56,010	53,457	53,081	52,808	51,611	26,048	25,563	0	52,152	26,163	24,333	1,656
Mississippi	30,722	31,006	31,214	31,598	32,591	14,896	13,385	4,310	31,321	14,989	11,833	4,499
Missouri...........................	63,890	64,735	65,240	66,717	65,169	33,556	31,606	7	65,481	33,711	31,770	0
Montana...........................	10,353	10,411	10,408	10,362	10,301	6,869	3,432	0	10,224	6,801	3,423	0
Nebraska	20,766	20,983	21,083	21,043	20,921	12,921	8,000	0	21,077	13,598	7,479	0
Nevada	17,380	18,293	19,276	20,038	20,234	10,059	7,777	2,398	20,950	10,779	7,188	2,983
New Hampshire	14,037	14,341	14,677	14,977	15,112	10,391	4,721	0	15,298	10,497	4,801	0
New Jersey.......................	95,883	99,061	103,611	107,004	109,077	61,331	29,623	18,123	114,875	46,654	68,221	0
New Mexico	19,797	21,042	21,823	21,172	21,569	12,281	4,926	4,362	21,730	12,419	4,913	4,398
New York..........................	202,078	206,961	209,128	210,926	216,116	92,224	90,061	33,831	218,612 [4]	93,036 [4]	91,063 [4]	34,513 [4]
North Carolina	81,914	83,680	85,684	87,677	89,988	53,562	30,946	5,480	92,550	55,206	31,256	6,088
North Dakota	8,150	8,141	8,035	8,078	8,037	4,788	3,249	0	8,070	4,828	3,242	0
Ohio.................................	116,200	118,361	122,115	125,372	121,735	83,290	38,445	0	118,060	80,452	37,608	0
Oklahoma.........................	41,498	41,318	41,632	40,638	39,253	18,269	16,717	4,267	40,416	19,952	16,064	4,400
Oregon.............................	27,803	28,094	28,262	27,126	26,732	11,893	9,795	5,044	27,431	11,689	10,429	5,313
Pennsylvania.....................	114,525	116,963	118,470	118,256	119,889	53,049	50,256	16,584	121,167	52,307	51,750	17,110
Rhode Island	11,041	10,645	11,104	11,196	11,918	8,328 [4]	2,783 [4]	807 [4]	11,898	8,371 [4]	2,796 [4]	731 [4]
South Carolina..................	45,468	45,380	46,616	46,528	45,830	31,957	13,041	832	46,914	32,703	13,431	780
South Dakota....................	9,384	9,397	9,370	9,257	9,245	5,625	2,605	1,015	9,064	5,551	2,533	980
Tennessee	60,702	57,164	58,358	58,652	59,584	42,409	16,168	1,007	60,022	42,571	16,462	989
Texas	267,935	274,826	282,847	288,655	289,481	143,426	112,426	33,629	294,547	146,012	114,796	33,739
Utah................................	21,832	22,008	22,211	22,415	22,147	10,709	8,867	2,571	22,287 [3]	10,813 [3]	9,199	2,275
Vermont	8,474	8,414	8,554	8,542	8,749	3,429	3,554	1,766	8,720	3,367	3,580	1,773
Virginia............................	85,037 [3]	86,977 [3]	89,314	99,919	90,573	39,849	50,724	0	93,732	40,518	53,214	0
Washington.......................	50,368	51,098	52,533	52,953	52,824	26,295	21,569	4,960	53,125	26,120	21,964	5,041
West Virginia.....................	21,082	20,930	20,138	20,119	20,020	9,971	6,729	3,320	19,958	9,909	6,702	3,347
Wisconsin	60,778	60,165	63,310	60,385	58,216	39,256	18,770	190	60,521	40,981	19,424	116
Wyoming	6,940	6,783	6,662	6,799	6,567	3,078	3,401	88	6,657	3,158	3,402	97
Bureau of Indian Affairs	—	—	—	—	—	—	—	—	—	—	—	—
DoDDS, overseas	7,415 [5]	5,105	5,154	4,794	4,728	2,046	1,703	979	4,885	2,008	1,743	1,134
DoDDS, domestic..............	—	2,399	2,486	2,425	2,301	1,113	481	707	2,002	1,055	442	505
Other jurisdictions												
American Samoa	801	820	914	943	988	667	301	20	945	673	252	20
Guam..........................	1,809	1,975	1,918	—	1,760	919	841	0	1,672	880	792	0
Northern Marianas........	488	526	519	545	550	301	242	7	579	313	262	4
Puerto Rico..................	41,349	37,620	42,906	42,369	42,444	23,649	16,322	2,473	43,054	23,970	16,573	2,511
Virgin Islands	1,528	1,511	1,511	1,502	1,512	746	734	32	1,545	753	765	27

—Not available.
[1]Data have been revised from previously published figures.
[2]Includes imputed values for states.
[3]Includes imputations for underreporting of prekindergarten teachers.
[4]Imputed.
[5]Includes domestic schools.

NOTE: Distribution of elementary and secondary teachers determined by reporting units. Teachers reported in full-time equivalents (FTE). DoDDS = Department of Defense dependents schools.
SOURCE: U.S. Department of Education, National Center for Education Statistics, Common Core of Data (CCD), "State Nonfiscal Survey of Public Elementary/Secondary Education," 1999–2000 through 2004–05. (This table was prepared August 2006.)

Table 63. Teachers, enrollment, and pupil/teacher ratios in public elementary and secondary schools, by state or jurisdiction: Fall 1999 through fall 2004

State or jurisdiction	Pupil/ teacher ratio, fall 1999	Pupil/ teacher ratio, fall 2000	Pupil/ teacher ratio, fall 2001	Fall 2002			Fall 2003[1]			Fall 2004		
				Teachers	Enrollment	Pupil/ teacher ratio	Teachers	Enrollment	Pupil/ teacher ratio	Teachers	Enrollment	Pupil/ teacher ratio
1	2	3	4	5	6	7	8	9	10	11	12	13
United States	16.1 [2]	16.0 [2]	15.9 [2]	3,034,123 [2]	48,183,086 [2]	15.9 [2]	3,048,652 [2]	48,540,215 [2]	15.9 [2]	3,090,513 [2]	48,794,911 [2]	15.8 [2]
Alabama	15.2 [3]	15.4 [3]	15.8 [3]	47,115 [3]	739,366 [3]	15.7 [3]	58,070	731,220	12.6	51,594	730,140	14.2
Alaska	17.1	16.9	16.7	8,080	134,364	16.6	7,808	133,933	17.2	7,756	132,970	17.1
Arizona	19.4	19.8	20.0	47,101	937,755	19.9	47,507	1,012,068	21.3	48,935	1,043,298	21.3
Arkansas	14.4	14.1	13.6	30,330	450,985	14.9	30,876	454,523	14.7	31,234	463,115	14.8
California	21.0 [3]	20.6 [3]	20.5 [3]	307,764 [3]	6,353,667 [3]	20.6 [3]	304,311 [3]	6,413,867 [3]	21.1 [3]	305,969 [3]	6,441,557 [3]	21.1 [3]
Colorado	17.4	17.3	16.8	45,401	751,862	16.6	44,904	757,693	16.9	45,165	765,976	17.0
Connecticut	13.9	13.7	13.7	42,296	570,023	13.5	42,370	577,203	13.6	38,808	577,390	14.9
Delaware	15.4	15.4	15.3	7,698	116,342	15.1	7,749	117,668	15.2	7,856	119,091	15.2
District of Columbia	16.0 [3]	13.9	13.9 [4]	5,005	76,166	13.9	5,676	78,057	13.8	5,387	76,714	14.2
Florida	18.3	18.4	18.6	138,226	2,539,929	18.4	144,955	2,587,628	17.9	154,864	2,639,336	17.0
Georgia	15.7	15.9	15.9	96,044	1,496,012	15.6	97,150	1,522,611	15.7	104,987	1,553,437	14.8
Hawaii	17.1	16.9	16.8	10,973	183,829	16.8	11,129	183,609	16.5	11,146	183,185	16.4
Idaho	18.0	17.9	17.8	13,896	248,604	17.9	14,049	252,120	17.9	14,269	256,084	17.9
Illinois	16.2	16.1	16.0	131,046	2,084,187	15.9	127,669	2,100,961	16.5	131,047	2,097,503	16.0
Indiana	16.8	16.7	16.7	59,968	1,003,875	16.7	59,924	1,011,130	16.9	60,563	1,021,348	16.9
Iowa	14.9	14.3	13.9	34,573	482,210	13.9	34,791	481,226	13.8	34,697	478,319	13.8
Kansas	14.3	14.4	14.2	32,643	470,957	14.4	32,589	470,490	14.4	32,932	469,136	14.2
Kentucky	15.4	16.8	16.2	40,662	660,782	16.3	41,246	663,369	16.1	41,463	674,796	16.3
Louisiana	15.1	16.6	16.6	50,062	730,464	16.6	50,495	727,709	16.6	49,192	724,281	16.6
Maine	12.8	12.5	12.3	16,837	204,337	12.1	17,621	202,084	11.5	16,656	198,820	11.9
Maryland	16.6	16.3	16.0	55,382	866,743	15.7	55,198	869,113	15.7	55,101	865,561	15.7
Massachusetts	12.5	14.5	14.1	74,214	982,989	13.2	72,062	980,459	13.6	73,399	975,574	13.3
Michigan	18.0 [3]	17.7 [3]	17.5	89,595	1,785,160	19.9	97,014	1,757,604	18.1	100,634	1,750,919	17.4
Minnesota	15.2	16.0	16.0	52,808	846,891	16.0	51,611	842,854	16.3	52,152	838,503	16.1
Mississippi	16.3	16.1	15.8	31,598	492,645	15.6	32,591	493,540	15.1	31,321	495,376	15.8
Missouri	14.3	14.1	13.9	66,717	906,499	13.6	65,169	905,941	13.9	65,481	905,449	13.8
Montana	15.2	14.9	14.6	10,362	149,995	14.5	10,301	148,356	14.4	10,224	146,705	14.3
Nebraska	13.9	13.6	13.5	21,043	285,402	13.6	20,921	285,542	13.6	21,077	285,761	13.6
Nevada	18.7	18.6	18.5	20,038	369,498	18.4	20,234	385,401	19.0	20,950	400,083	19.1
New Hampshire	14.7	14.5	14.1	14,977	207,671	13.9	15,112	207,417	13.7	15,298	206,852	13.5
New Jersey	13.4	13.3	12.9	107,004	1,367,438	12.8	109,077	1,380,753	12.7	114,875	1,393,347	12.1
New Mexico	16.4	15.2	14.7	21,172	320,234	15.1	21,569	323,066	15.0	21,730	326,102	15.0
New York	14.3	13.9	13.7	210,926	2,888,233	13.7	216,116	2,864,775	13.3	218,612 [5]	2,836,337	13.0
North Carolina	15.6	15.5	15.4	87,677	1,335,954	15.2	89,988	1,360,209	15.1	92,550	1,385,754	15.0
North Dakota	13.8	13.4	13.2	8,078	104,225	12.9	8,037	102,233	12.7	8,070	100,513	12.5
Ohio	15.8	15.5	15.0	125,372	1,838,285	14.7	121,735	1,845,428	15.2	118,060	1,840,032	15.6
Oklahoma	15.1	15.1	14.9	40,638	624,548	15.4	39,253	626,160	16.0	40,416	629,476	15.6
Oregon	19.6	19.4	19.5	27,126	554,071	20.4	26,732	551,273	20.6	27,431	552,322	20.1
Pennsylvania	15.9	15.5	15.4	118,256	1,816,747	15.4	119,889	1,821,146	15.2	121,167	1,828,089	15.1
Rhode Island	14.2	14.8	14.2	11,196	159,205	14.2	11,918	159,375	13.4	11,898	156,498	13.2
South Carolina	14.7	14.9	14.5	46,528	694,389	14.9	45,830	699,198	15.3	46,914	703,736	15.0
South Dakota	14.0	13.7	13.6	9,257	130,048	14.0	9,245	125,537	13.6	9,064	122,798	13.5
Tennessee	15.1 [3]	15.9 [3]	15.8 [3]	58,652	927,608 [3]	15.8 [3]	59,584	936,682 [3]	15.7 [3]	60,022	941,091 [3]	15.7 [3]
Texas	14.9	14.8	14.7	288,655	4,259,823	14.8	289,481	4,331,751	15.0	294,547	4,405,215	15.0
Utah	22.0	21.9	21.8	22,415	489,262	21.8	22,147	495,981	22.4	22,287	503,607	22.6
Vermont	12.3	12.1	11.8	8,542	99,978	11.7	8,749	99,103	11.3	8,720	98,352	11.3
Virginia	13.3 [3]	13.2 [3]	13.0	99,919	1,177,229	11.8	90,573	1,192,092	13.2	93,732	1,204,739	12.9
Washington	19.9	19.7	19.2	52,953	1,014,798	19.2	52,824	1,021,349	19.3	53,125	1,020,005	19.2
West Virginia	13.8	13.7	14.0	20,119	282,455	14.0	20,020	281,215	14.0	19,958	280,129	14.0
Wisconsin	14.4	14.6	13.9	60,385	881,231	14.6	58,216	880,031	15.1	60,521	864,757	14.3
Wyoming	13.3	13.3	13.2	6,799 [3]	88,116	13.0 [3]	6,567	87,462	13.3	6,657	84,733	12.7
Bureau of Indian Affairs ..	—	—	—		46,126		—	45,828		—	—	—
DoDDS, overseas	14.6 [6]	14.4	14.2	4,794	72,889	15.2	4,728	71,053	15.0	4,885	68,327	14.0
DoDDS, domestic	—	14.2	13.2	2,425	32,115	13.2	2,301	30,603	13.3	2,002	29,151	14.6
Other jurisdictions												
American Samoa	19.3	19.1	17.4	943	15,984	17.0	988	15,893	16.1	945	16,126	17.1
Guam	18.2	16.4	16.7	—	—	—	1,760	31,572	17.9	1,672	30,605	18.3
Northern Marianas	19.9	19.0	20.2	545	11,251	20.6	550	11,244	20.4	579	11,601	20.0
Puerto Rico	14.8	16.3	14.1	42,369	596,502	14.1	42,444	584,916	13.8	43,054	575,648	13.4
Virgin Islands	13.7	12.9	12.4	1,502	18,333	12.2	1,512	17,716	11.7	1,545	16,429	10.6

—Not available.
[1]Data have been revised from previously published figures.
[2]Includes imputed values for states.
[3]Includes imputations for underreporting of prekindergarten teachers/enrollment.
[4]Ratio based on enrollment excluding 6,943 charter school students for whom no teacher counts were reported.
[5]Imputed.

[6]Includes both overseas and domestic schools.
NOTE: Teachers reported in full-time equivalents (FTE). DoDDS = Department of Defense dependents schools.
SOURCE: U.S. Department of Education, National Center for Education Statistics, Common Core of Data (CCD), "State Nonfiscal Survey of Public Elementary/Secondary Education," 1999–2000 through 2004–05. (This table was prepared August 2006.)

Table 64. Highest degree earned, years of full-time teaching experience, and average class size for teachers in public elementary and secondary schools, by state: 2003–04

Column groupings: **Percent of teachers, by highest degree earned[1]** (Bachelor's, Master's, Education specialist[3], Doctor's); **Percent of teachers, by years of full-time teaching experience** (Less than 3, 3 to 9, 10 to 20, Over 20); **Average class size[2]** (Elementary, Secondary). Standard errors in parentheses.

State	Total number of teachers (in thousands)	Bachelor's	Master's	Education specialist[3]	Doctor's	Less than 3	3 to 9	10 to 20	Over 20	Elementary	Secondary
(col) 1	2	3	4	5	6	7	8	9	10	11	12
United States	3,250.6 (29.18)	50.8 (0.56)	40.9 (0.56)	6.0 (0.19)	1.2 (0.11)	12.2 (1.23)	32.9 (0.34)	28.4 (0.59)	26.5 (0.77)	20.4 (0.15)	24.7 (0.14)
Alabama	50.9 (2.34)	38.1 (2.08)	50.2 (2.39)	9.4 (1.37)	1.0 (0.35)	12.5 (1.94)	32.8 (2.76)	33.4 (1.88)	21.4 (1.66)	18.4 (0.38)	23.8 (0.66)
Alaska	8.6 (0.40)	58.4 (2.11)	34.3 (1.81)	5.6 (1.19)	1.4 (0.50)	13.0 (1.57)	36.8 (2.25)	31.2 (2.35)	18.9 (1.97)	20.5 (0.35)	23.3 (0.63)
Arizona	56.4 (2.27)	49.7 (2.21)	40.8 (2.07)	7.4 (1.30)	1.0 (0.37)	15.5 (1.73)	38.2 (2.08)	27.2 (1.72)	19.1 (1.84)	23.0 (0.39)	27.0 (0.55)
Arkansas	37.2 (1.80)	60.4 (2.56)	33.8 (2.45)	3.6 (0.62)	1.0 (0.35)	9.5 (2.15)	36.4 (2.58)	31.4 (2.37)	24.4 (1.90)	18.2 (0.64)	18.2 (0.62)
California	284.8 (16.87)	56.0 (1.76)	31.3 (1.65)	10.0 (0.95)	1.8 (0.52)	11.2 (1.45)	36.4 (1.48)	30.3 (1.66)	22.1 (1.79)	21.7 (0.26)	30.5 (0.53)
Colorado	49.1 (1.63)	44.5 (2.18)	47.7 (2.27)	5.4 (1.27)	0.9 (0.42)	12.0 (1.46)	37.4 (2.54)	30.2 (2.37)	20.5 (1.61)	22.1 (0.64)	24.5 (0.65)
Connecticut	45.0 (1.78)	24.5 (2.48)	55.9 (2.83)	16.1 (1.72)	2.2 (0.64)	11.9 (1.25)	29.7 (1.74)	31.0 (2.26)	27.4 (2.41)	19.5 (0.51)	24.5 (0.44)
Delaware	7.9 (0.60)	45.9 (3.20)	49.2 (3.29)	3.7 (1.09)	0.5 (0.36)	11.7 (1.74)	35.0 (3.39)	27.5 (3.15)	25.7 (3.17)	20.1 (0.75)	23.6 (0.82)
District of Columbia	5.4 (0.46)	48.2 (4.25)	41.8 (4.05)	6.2 (1.50)	3.3 (1.29)	15.5 (2.80)	29.8 (3.07)	28.7 (3.96)	26.0 (2.86)	19.0 (0.86)	23.6 (1.26)
Florida	156.8 (8.43)	61.8 (2.20)	32.7 (2.15)	2.4 (0.66)	1.5 (0.45)	14.3 (2.09)	27.9 (1.55)	32.0 (1.96)	25.8 (2.52)	21.2 (0.57)	27.6 (0.64)
Georgia	102.3 (3.08)	46.6 (2.71)	40.5 (2.00)	11.1 (1.81)	1.1 (0.53)	13.2 (2.18)	37.2 (2.01)	27.4 (2.61)	22.3 (1.96)	17.8 (0.59)	25.6 (0.76)
Hawaii	13.6 (0.54)	43.2 (2.43)	26.5 (2.29)	27.5 (2.19)	1.5 (0.59)	16.9 (1.80)	33.0 (2.45)	29.8 (2.27)	20.3 (1.86)	22.3 (0.71)	27.4 (1.93)
Idaho	15.4 (0.76)	71.9 (1.99)	24.9 (1.76)	3.1 (0.61)	0.2 (0.13)	12.3 (1.83)	28.4 (2.32)	36.0 (2.04)	23.3 (1.93)	23.2 (0.33)	24.1 (0.57)
Illinois	139.6 (6.23)	45.7 (2.40)	49.6 (2.89)	3.1 (0.90)	0.8 (0.71)	12.1 (1.67)	32.0 (2.57)	26.8 (2.51)	29.2 (2.87)	22.9 (0.72)	24.1 (0.66)
Indiana	63.0 (3.09)	37.3 (2.54)	56.3 (2.39)	4.3 (1.03)	1.3 (0.71)	11.2 (1.64)	27.1 (2.02)	25.9 (2.38)	35.9 (2.45)	21.3 (0.59)	25.3 (0.64)
Iowa	38.2 (1.03)	65.1 (2.01)	33.0 (1.95)	1.2 (0.50)	‡ (†)	8.4 (1.44)	27.9 (1.68)	27.1 (1.97)	36.7 (2.02)	20.9 (0.88)	23.9 (0.65)
Kansas	37.7 (1.31)	55.0 (2.32)	40.2 (2.28)	3.4 (0.62)	0.9 (0.41)	11.5 (2.00)	27.3 (1.87)	30.7 (1.62)	30.4 (2.10)	19.2 (0.68)	25.2 (0.76)
Kentucky	48.3 (1.80)	28.5 (2.05)	51.6 (2.33)	18.7 (1.90)	0.3 (0.18)	11.6 (1.59)	33.8 (2.03)	32.5 (1.79)	22.1 (1.99)	21.6 (0.57)	23.1 (0.49)
Louisiana	52.5 (1.69)	65.2 (2.43)	24.4 (1.96)	7.3 (1.16)	2.3 (0.65)	9.9 (1.40)	28.2 (2.06)	30.5 (1.99)	31.3 (2.72)	18.7 (0.59)	23.1 (0.58)
Maine	18.9 (0.79)	64.3 (2.34)	30.6 (2.22)	3.1 (0.86)	0.6 (0.27)	7.6 (1.29)	28.3 (1.99)	29.2 (2.20)	34.9 (2.10)	17.1 (0.49)	19.8 (0.54)
Maryland	59.3 (2.84)	42.7 (3.26)	46.6 (2.90)	8.3 (1.27)	1.4 (0.48)	16.0 (2.40)	33.7 (2.69)	22.2 (2.09)	28.1 (3.14)	20.7 (0.66)	25.9 (0.60)
Massachusetts	84.5 (3.81)	37.7 (2.79)	53.6 (2.85)	4.6 (0.97)	2.0 (0.36)	14.4 (1.68)	32.8 (2.29)	23.7 (2.34)	29.1 (2.38)	19.4 (0.48)	21.9 (0.50)
Michigan	100.1 (4.92)	43.3 (2.21)	50.5 (2.50)	4.0 (0.75)	1.0 (0.41)	11.2 (1.68)	35.4 (2.05)	27.3 (2.05)	26.1 (1.69)	21.9 (0.43)	26.5 (0.53)
Minnesota	61.0 (1.03)	49.0 (1.83)	43.6 (1.95)	5.7 (0.79)	0.9 (0.23)	10.4 (1.41)	33.5 (1.80)	28.5 (1.69)	27.6 (1.98)	22.3 (0.50)	26.0 (0.75)
Mississippi	34.4 (1.28)	62.3 (2.32)	30.6 (2.27)	3.9 (0.77)	1.0 (0.51)	16.3 (2.43)	28.0 (1.73)	25.5 (2.11)	30.3 (2.02)	20.4 (0.51)	22.4 (0.77)
Missouri	74.3 (5.34)	47.3 (2.45)	47.4 (2.50)	3.0 (0.77)	0.4 (0.16)	11.9 (1.53)	32.8 (1.90)	29.3 (1.92)	26.0 (2.44)	19.1 (0.51)	22.9 (0.65)
Montana	12.2 (0.76)	66.0 (1.94)	29.5 (1.83)	3.7 (0.75)	0.4 (0.24)	10.7 (1.33)	25.6 (1.86)	31.1 (1.98)	32.7 (2.09)	18.1 (0.81)	19.4 (0.62)
Nebraska	25.9 (1.03)	59.9 (2.49)	37.5 (2.32)	1.2 (0.47)	0.8 (0.38)	9.6 (1.40)	31.2 (1.96)	31.9 (2.07)	27.2 (1.79)	18.1 (0.57)	21.7 (0.68)
Nevada	19.9 (0.91)	43.4 (3.17)	48.9 (3.11)	6.2 (1.26)	0.8 (0.37)	12.0 (2.17)	38.7 (3.24)	35.2 (2.63)	24.0 (2.57)	22.6 (1.00)	29.9 (0.78)
New Hampshire	16.5 (0.64)	56.9 (2.59)	39.4 (2.46)	2.7 (1.04)	0.4 (0.28)	13.7 (2.04)	31.0 (2.29)	27.1 (2.74)	28.2 (2.18)	19.5 (0.53)	22.0 (1.01)
New Jersey	114.0 (4.11)	57.0 (2.59)	34.3 (2.48)	6.1 (1.09)	1.8 (0.48)	13.3 (1.74)	31.9 (2.20)	24.4 (2.07)	30.3 (2.52)	19.3 (0.72)	24.1 (0.94)
New Mexico	21.3 (0.88)	58.1 (2.20)	36.4 (2.28)	4.2 (1.04)	0.4 (0.26)	10.7 (1.96)	37.1 (2.35)	29.7 (1.74)	22.6 (2.19)	18.2 (0.40)	24.3 (0.67)
New York	234.1 (7.62)	21.4 (1.97)	67.2 (2.14)	8.8 (1.03)	2.0 (0.43)	13.1 (1.95)	36.5 (1.80)	27.8 (1.88)	22.6 (1.82)	19.8 (0.56)	23.6 (0.55)
North Carolina	95.6 (3.26)	67.0 (2.08)	27.6 (2.12)	3.1 (0.74)	1.0 (0.41)	13.8 (1.54)	34.9 (2.07)	29.4 (2.43)	21.9 (1.94)	20.3 (0.53)	24.3 (0.73)
North Dakota	9.7 (0.41)	71.7 (1.79)	24.6 (1.64)	2.4 (0.63)	0.4 (0.21)	10.5 (1.65)	21.8 (1.46)	31.4 (1.60)	36.3 (1.82)	17.2 (0.45)	19.5 (0.60)
Ohio	133.5 (4.62)	45.8 (2.12)	49.1 (2.17)	2.8 (0.53)	0.9 (0.36)	9.1 (1.92)	33.1 (1.80)	27.2 (1.90)	30.6 (1.82)	20.3 (0.40)	23.6 (0.42)
Oklahoma	46.0 (1.46)	66.3 (1.51)	30.2 (1.56)	2.7 (0.47)	0.4 (0.22)	8.8 (1.89)	31.1 (1.83)	31.8 (1.80)	28.3 (1.81)	19.9 (0.35)	23.2 (0.58)
Oregon	29.0 (1.48)	41.5 (2.26)	50.5 (2.33)	6.2 (1.17)	1.4 (0.63)	13.8 (2.22)	28.9 (1.99)	34.1 (2.55)	23.1 (2.17)	24.7 (0.54)	28.9 (0.71)
Pennsylvania	125.5 (4.65)	48.6 (1.96)	42.5 (1.93)	6.7 (0.90)	0.5 (0.45)	11.8 (1.55)	32.9 (1.68)	21.5 (1.87)	33.8 (1.97)	20.6 (0.54)	24.9 (0.47)
Rhode Island	13.8 (0.61)	48.0 (3.60)	45.8 (3.44)	4.7 (1.49)	1.1 (0.66)	10.8 (1.90)	35.3 (3.47)	28.2 (2.59)	25.6 (3.81)	19.6 (0.82)	22.4 (0.92)
South Carolina	47.5 (2.02)	42.9 (2.79)	42.0 (2.92)	7.5 (1.12)	0.6 (0.20)	8.5 (1.68)	29.5 (2.07)	31.2 (2.50)	30.8 (2.54)	18.5 (0.73)	23.8 (0.64)
South Dakota	10.8 (0.54)	72.9 (1.62)	24.0 (1.73)	1.7 (0.63)	0.6 (0.26)	9.3 (2.17)	29.1 (2.23)	29.3 (1.94)	32.4 (2.17)	17.8 (0.68)	22.3 (1.06)
Tennessee	64.6 (2.09)	46.1 (2.74)	43.2 (2.51)	8.5 (2.09)	0.6 (0.29)	10.7 (2.41)	29.9 (2.13)	27.5 (2.03)	31.8 (2.32)	19.0 (0.43)	24.5 (0.52)
Texas	291.0 (10.41)	71.9 (1.80)	22.4 (1.78)	3.8 (0.60)	1.0 (0.43)	13.4 (1.70)	33.9 (2.00)	30.7 (1.90)	22.0 (1.56)	18.7 (0.42)	23.3 (0.55)
Utah	23.4 (1.21)	65.2 (1.96)	24.2 (1.68)	7.8 (1.12)	0.7 (0.27)	17.9 (2.05)	30.1 (2.12)	29.5 (2.12)	22.6 (1.72)	24.3 (0.40)	29.0 (1.00)
Vermont	10.0 (0.45)	54.2 (3.21)	41.1 (3.37)	3.1 (1.09)	1.2 (0.57)	10.8 (1.71)	29.7 (2.67)	31.5 (2.80)	27.9 (2.57)	16.0 (0.46)	18.9 (0.89)
Virginia	92.2 (4.41)	58.6 (2.44)	34.1 (2.45)	4.3 (1.13)	1.0 (0.53)	12.7 (1.83)	33.8 (2.00)	24.9 (2.16)	28.6 (1.95)	19.1 (0.54)	22.7 (0.98)
Washington	63.5 (4.32)	42.6 (2.33)	50.7 (2.36)	4.6 (0.97)	1.0 (0.36)	11.7 (1.93)	34.5 (2.16)	27.2 (2.25)	26.7 (2.19)	21.9 (0.52)	26.5 (0.52)
West Virginia	22.9 (1.11)	36.9 (2.35)	53.5 (2.60)	7.2 (1.36)	0.4 (0.15)	7.4 (1.65)	18.6 (1.51)	23.9 (2.10)	50.1 (2.44)	18.8 (0.47)	22.1 (0.47)
Wisconsin	74.8 (3.62)	54.8 (2.72)	40.8 (2.62)	3.7 (0.87)	0.5 (0.22)	13.1 (2.40)	29.7 (1.81)	30.3 (1.93)	26.9 (1.66)	19.5 (0.48)	25.1 (0.74)
Wyoming	7.8 (0.42)	61.4 (3.46)	33.8 (3.11)	2.9 (0.87)	0.6 (0.40)	9.1 (2.88)	25.8 (2.90)	31.3 (3.08)	33.8 (3.34)	18.4 (0.67)	21.5 (0.80)

†Not applicable.

‡Reporting standards not met.

[1]Teachers with less than a bachelor's degree are not shown separately.

[2]Elementary teachers are those who taught self-contained classes at the elementary level, and secondary teachers are those who taught departmentalized classes (e.g., science, art, social science, or other course subjects) at the secondary level. Teachers were classified as elementary or secondary on the basis of the grades they taught, rather than on the level of the school in which they taught.

[3]Includes certificate of advanced graduate studies.

NOTE: Data are based on a head count of all teachers rather than on the number of full-time-equivalent teachers appearing in other tables. Excludes prekindergarten teachers. Standard errors appear in parentheses. Detail may not sum to totals because of rounding, cell suppression, and omitted categories (less than bachelor's).

SOURCE: U.S. Department of Education, National Center for Education Statistics, Schools and Staffing Survey (SASS), "Public Teacher Questionnaire," 2003–04. (This table was prepared July 2006.)

Table 65. Highest degree earned and years of full-time teaching experience for teachers in public and private elementary and secondary schools, by selected teacher characteristics: 1999–2000 and 2003–04

Selected characteristic	Number of teachers, 1999–2000 (in thousands)	Number of teachers, 2003–04 (in thousands)	Percent of teachers, by highest degree earned, 2003–04					Percent of teachers, by years of full-time teaching experience, 2003–04			
			Less than bachelor's	Bachelor's	Master's	Education specialist	Doctor's	Less than 3	3 to 9	10 to 20	Over 20
1	2	3	4	5	6	7	8	9	10	11	12
Public schools											
Total	3,002 (19.4)	3,251 (29.2)	1.1 (0.08)	50.8 (0.56)	40.9 (0.56)	6.0 (0.19)	1.2 (0.11)	12.2 (1.23)	32.9 (0.34)	28.4 (0.59)	26.5 (0.77)
Sex											
Males	754 (10.7)	813 (13.3)	2.6 (0.21)	50.2 (0.90)	40.5 (0.83)	5.1 (0.35)	1.7 (0.26)	12.0 (1.22)	33.9 (0.75)	25.4 (0.74)	28.8 (0.95)
Females	2,248 (16.0)	2,438 (23.5)	0.6 (0.07)	51.0 (0.61)	41.1 (0.61)	6.3 (0.23)	1.0 (0.10)	12.3 (1.26)	32.6 (0.43)	29.5 (0.69)	25.7 (0.84)
Race/ethnicity											
White	2,532 (17.2)[2]	2,702 (30.1)	1.0 (0.08)	49.8 (0.60)	42.3 (0.58)	5.9 (0.22)	1.1 (0.09)	11.5 (1.20)	32.0 (0.36)	29.1 (0.58)	27.4 (0.81)
Black	228 (6.0)[2]	257 (11.0)	1.8 (0.39)	52.3 (1.48)	38.3 (1.69)	5.6 (0.56)	2.0 (0.64)	14.9 (1.56)	35.5 (1.53)	22.1 (1.30)	27.6 (1.78)
Hispanic	169 (6.4)[2]	202 (11.3)	1.3 (0.36)	63.7 (2.14)	26.7 (2.03)	6.9 (1.17)	1.4 (0.51)	16.8 (1.87)	39.5 (1.89)	28.8 (2.26)	15.0 (1.58)
Asian	48 (2.7)[3]	42 (2.5)	0.5 (0.19)	45.5 (3.04)	40.6 (3.23)	10.4 (1.66)	3.1 (1.09)	15.9 (2.26)	41.6 (3.52)	26.0 (2.90)	16.5 (1.71)
Pacific Islander	—	6 (0.8)	‡ (†)	47.7 (†)	39.6 (6.85)	10.7 (3.21)	1.2 (0.84)	17.5 (4.14)	45.9 (6.35)	19.0 (6.33)	17.6 (4.24)
American Indian/Alaska Native	26 (1.9)[2]	17 (1.2)	1.8 (0.55)	52.9 (3.44)	40.8 (3.55)	3.7 (0.95)	0.8 (0.34)	14.4 (3.29)	31.2 (3.25)	30.1 (3.61)	24.3 (3.75)
More than one race	—	24 (2.2)	0.5 (0.32)	49.2 (5.18)	37.3 (4.96)	11.2 (2.70)	1.8 (0.75)	17.0 (3.72)	36.5 (4.77)	25.8 (4.97)	20.7 (3.70)
Age											
Less than 30	509 (9.2)	540 (27.4)	0.5 (0.08)	76.6 (1.22)	21.3 (1.25)	1.6 (0.26)	0.1 (0.04)	41.7 (2.58)	58.3 (2.58)	‡ (†)	† (†)
30 to 39	661 (9.8)	798 (14.5)	0.8 (0.12)	53.4 (0.89)	41.0 (0.88)	4.2 (0.31)	0.6 (0.13)	10.6 (1.16)	55.3 (0.98)	34.2 (1.00)	‡ (†)
40 to 49	953 (10.3)	840 (14.3)	1.5 (0.17)	46.2 (0.77)	44.5 (0.84)	6.2 (0.41)	1.5 (0.25)	6.8 (0.82)	23.5 (0.67)	44.5 (1.03)	25.2 (0.69)
50 to 59	786 (12.6)	942 (26.0)	1.2 (0.14)	40.0 (0.78)	47.8 (0.74)	9.3 (0.46)	1.7 (0.19)	2.8 (0.32)	11.3 (0.53)	26.1 (0.75)	59.8 (1.08)
60 or more	93 (4.0)	131 (4.8)	1.4 (0.27)	35.7 (1.83)	49.4 (2.08)	10.3 (1.18)	3.2 (0.72)	2.1 (0.43)	7.3 (0.95)	25.0 (1.59)	65.5 (1.78)
Level											
Elementary	1,602 (13.5)	1,716 (25.8)	0.4 (0.07)	52.0 (0.75)	40.6 (0.68)	6.2 (0.33)	0.8 (0.15)	11.5 (1.76)	33.5 (0.55)	29.4 (0.83)	25.7 (1.16)
General	1,019 (13.6)	1,130 (25.3)	0.4 (0.08)	55.0 (0.95)	38.1 (0.81)	5.7 (0.44)	0.8 (0.19)	11.1 (1.80)	34.2 (0.75)	29.0 (0.84)	25.8 (1.17)
Arts/music	33 (2.8)	101 (5.3)	0.3 (0.14)	52.8 (2.48)	42.8 (2.45)	3.5 (0.86)	0.7 (0.37)	12.5 (2.54)	28.4 (2.05)	32.7 (2.40)	26.4 (2.78)
English	[4]	70 (5.1)	‡ (†)	40.6 (4.09)	48.7 (4.24)	9.4 (1.60)	1.3 (0.57)	8.5 (2.34)	28.8 (3.47)	34.4 (3.69)	26.3 (3.09)
ESL/bilingual	[4]	25 (3.6)	‡ (†)	51.2 (6.39)	33.1 (5.69)	15.0 (5.02)	‡ (†)	11.5 (4.11)	44.7 (7.64)	31.3 (6.50)	12.5 (3.86)
Health/physical ed.	26 (2.5)	73 (5.0)	‡ (†)	59.5 (3.48)	36.1 (3.32)	3.9 (1.22)	0.4 (0.26)	10.6 (2.49)	25.1 (2.52)	29.8 (2.62)	34.5 (3.46)
Mathematics	[4]	19 (2.3)	‡ (†)	50.1 (6.56)	44.7 (6.16)	4.2 (2.44)	‡ (†)	13.5 (3.30)	29.9 (5.31)	33.2 (5.32)	26.5 (5.31)
Science	[4]	19 (3.0)	‡ (†)	50.4 (7.93)	40.8 (7.92)	7.9 (4.59)	‡ (†)	9.3 (3.30)	27.4 (5.91)	30.2 (8.23)	30.0 (6.65)
Special education	210 (5.8)	240 (20.6)	0.7 (0.31)	41.0 (1.66)	48.9 (1.77)	8.6 (0.86)	0.8 (0.48)	14.2 (1.92)	35.8 (1.49)	27.2 (1.53)	22.7 (1.74)
Other elementary	314 (8.4)	40 (3.5)	0.8 (0.28)	42.9 (4.07)	50.0 (4.27)	6.1 (1.68)	‡ (†)	9.8 (2.43)	34.2 (4.41)	32.1 (4.53)	24.0 (3.83)
Secondary	1,401 (17.7)	1,534 (26.0)	1.8 (0.13)	49.4 (0.64)	41.3 (0.66)	5.8 (0.22)	1.7 (0.12)	13.0 (0.71)	34.4 (0.51)	27.3 (0.58)	24.0 (0.54)
Arts/music	[5]	112 (4.1)	0.7 (0.22)	55.5 (2.01)	37.2 (1.91)	5.1 (0.61)	1.4 (0.39)	12.5 (1.16)	30.5 (1.70)	28.0 (1.62)	29.1 (1.59)
English	235 (5.0)	269 (9.0)	0.3 (0.09)	51.1 (1.40)	40.1 (1.28)	6.8 (0.60)	1.7 (0.34)	14.2 (0.99)	33.6 (1.18)	25.4 (1.15)	27.2 (1.10)
ESL/bilingual	[5]	18 (2.5)	‡ (†)	43.6 (6.06)	49.4 (5.91)	5.4 (1.73)	1.6 (0.80)	18.9 (3.61)	33.6 (5.19)	28.9 (5.96)	18.6 (5.49)
Foreign language	[5]	73 (3.3)	0.4 (0.16)	48.0 (2.13)	43.8 (2.29)	5.5 (0.86)	2.3 (0.64)	13.8 (1.41)	36.2 (1.90)	27.7 (1.70)	22.3 (2.09)
Health/physical ed.	[5]	102 (4.3)	0.5 (0.18)	55.9 (1.83)	38.1 (1.91)	4.7 (0.89)	0.8 (0.20)	9.9 (1.56)	29.6 (1.89)	28.0 (2.20)	31.5 (1.79)
Mathematics	191 (4.3)	213 (5.5)	0.3 (0.11)	51.6 (1.36)	42.0 (1.30)	4.7 (0.58)	1.3 (0.27)	14.2 (1.53)	32.2 (1.31)	28.0 (1.29)	25.5 (1.17)
Science	159 (3.7)	189 (6.8)	0.2 (0.08)	48.4 (1.78)	44.2 (1.77)	4.4 (0.43)	2.8 (0.49)	12.5 (1.02)	34.0 (1.38)	28.3 (1.19)	25.2 (1.13)
Social studies	147 (4.3)	178 (5.7)	0.4 (0.22)	51.1 (1.56)	42.1 (1.40)	4.6 (0.52)	1.7 (0.39)	12.0 (0.92)	34.4 (1.26)	23.4 (1.26)	30.2 (1.28)
Special education	99 (2.3)	174 (7.5)	0.4 (0.13)	42.3 (1.38)	45.1 (1.38)	10.7 (0.94)	1.5 (0.38)	12.1 (1.50)	31.6 (1.25)	29.9 (1.46)	26.4 (1.72)
Vocational/technical	125 (3.2)	169 (5.7)	11.8 (0.99)	44.8 (1.34)	37.6 (1.46)	4.4 (0.52)	1.4 (0.41)	12.6 (1.22)	28.7 (1.34)	28.8 (1.15)	30.0 (1.59)
Other secondary	443 (8.5)	36 (2.1)	7.5 (1.56)	45.6 (2.63)	40.2 (2.71)	5.7 (1.20)	1.0 (0.40)	15.0 (2.41)	32.3 (2.81)	26.7 (2.50)	26.0 (2.61)
Private schools											
Total	449 (10.6)	467 (10.3)	9.2 (4.41)	55.5 (2.90)	29.5 (1.35)	3.6 (0.54)	2.2 (0.26)	24.8 (2.75)	33.0 (1.23)	23.9 (1.19)	18.3 (1.87)
Sex											
Males	107 (3.8)	110 (8.4)	6.5 (1.13)	49.1 (1.49)	36.5 (1.60)	3.8 (0.84)	4.0 (0.99)	25.6 (2.49)	32.3 (1.78)	21.4 (1.85)	20.6 (1.48)
Females	342 (7.7)	357 (14.3)	10.1 (5.69)	57.4 (3.92)	27.3 (1.53)	3.5 (0.54)	1.7 (0.30)	24.6 (3.07)	33.2 (1.54)	24.7 (1.43)	17.6 (2.11)
Race/ethnicity											
White	402 (9.6)[2]	411 (12.0)	8.5 (4.85)	55.5 (2.98)	30.4 (1.63)	3.5 (0.60)	2.1 (0.26)	23.7 (3.38)	33.0 (1.49)	24.2 (1.28)	19.0 (2.15)
Black	17 (1.4)[2]	19 (2.9)	17.9 (5.49)	60.2 (5.17)	16.9 (3.17)	2.9 (1.00)	2.1 (0.98)	29.8 (4.02)	31.2 (7.94)	20.9 (5.01)	18.2 (3.36)
Hispanic	21 (1.5)[2]	23 (3.1)	13.5 (2.34)	55.5 (3.71)	25.9 (3.05)	2.5 (1.59)	2.6 (1.52)	35.2 (3.46)	33.3 (3.63)	22.1 (3.09)	9.4 (2.53)
Age											
Less than 30	87 (3.1)	88 (3.7)	13.5 (1.65)	70.6 (1.87)	14.3 (1.40)	0.8 (0.42)	0.8 (0.37)	55.3 (2.87)	44.5 (2.81)	0.3 (0.14)	‡ (†)
30 to 39	101 (3.2)	103 (5.8)	9.3 (2.85)	57.5 (2.93)	28.1 (3.04)	3.3 (0.53)	1.8 (0.46)	26.3 (3.66)	52.3 (2.44)	21.4 (2.33)	‡ (†)
40 to 49	131 (4.2)	119 (7.1)	9.8 (4.12)	52.8 (3.22)	30.5 (1.92)	3.9 (0.88)	3.1 (0.64)	20.1 (2.16)	30.5 (3.43)	37.1 (1.75)	12.3 (1.59)
50 to 59	106 (3.2)	121 (11.1)	6.3 (11.09)	49.9 (6.72)	36.9 (4.08)	4.4 (0.86)	2.5 (0.50)	10.5 (8.31)	17.7 (2.13)	31.0 (3.77)	40.8 (6.01)
60 or more	25 (1.2)	37 (4.7)	7.0 (7.76)	40.6 (3.30)	41.5 (6.98)	7.5 (2.23)	3.4 (1.10)	9.9 (1.86)	9.8 (6.91)	21.7 (3.54)	58.6 (8.29)

See notes at end of table.

Table 65. Highest degree earned and years of full-time teaching experience for teachers in public and private elementary and secondary schools, by selected teacher characteristics: 1999–2000 and 2003–04—Continued

Selected characteristic	Number of teachers, 1999–2000 (in thousands)	Number of teachers, 2003–04 (in thousands)	Percent of teachers, by highest degree earned, 2003–04					Percent of teachers, by years of full-time teaching experience, 2003–04			
			Less than bachelor's	Bachelor's	Master's	Education specialist[1]	Doctor's	Less than 3	3 to 9	10 to 20	Over 20
1	2	3	4	5	6	7	8	9	10	11	12
Level											
Elementary	261 (5.8)	263 (17.5)	12.0 (6.69)	60.5 (5.01)	23.3 (1.53)	3.2 (0.67)	0.9 (0.22)	25.4 (3.89)	33.2 (1.77)	25.0 (1.80)	16.5 (2.56)
General	168 (4.0)	174 (17.1)	13.0 (9.87)	63.2 (6.93)	20.5 (2.69)	2.5 (0.55)	0.9 (0.26)	19.6 (6.79)	35.4 (3.85)	26.5 (2.76)	18.5 (3.30)
Arts/music	[4] (†)	21 (2.5)	14.7 (2.34)	52.3 (3.30)	27.4 (3.74)	5.5 (1.79)	‡ (†)	49.0 (3.59)	27.9 (3.68)	16.5 (2.58)	6.6 (1.55)
English	[4] (†)	8 (1.1)	3.7 (4.12)	53.4 (5.93)	36.1 (5.31)	3.7 (1.84)	3.2 (1.74)	23.8 (4.36)	27.9 (4.83)	26.9 (4.79)	21.3 (4.29)
Health/physical ed.	[4] (†)	14 (1.8)	11.3 (2.75)	67.6 (6.95)	18.1 (4.54)	1.9 (0.95)	‡ (†)	42.4 (6.89)	25.2 (7.73)	22.6 (6.65)	9.8 (2.36)
Mathematics	[4] (†)	6 (0.7)	4.8 (3.39)	60.3 (6.26)	33.4 (6.21)	‡ (†)	‡ (†)	24.2 (5.49)	31.5 (7.05)	21.9 (4.92)	22.4 (4.55)
Science	[4] (†)	5 (0.8)	‡ (†)	74.2 (7.13)	19.6 (6.90)	4.0 (1.98)	‡ (†)	26.1 (7.54)	28.1 (6.05)	24.0 (6.83)	21.8 (7.19)
Special education	16 (1.6)	12 (2.3)	5.6 (2.55)	52.2 (8.01)	33.3 (11.81)	8.9 (4.04)	‡ (†)	26.1 (8.02)	41.8 (7.02)	22.9 (4.46)	9.3 (3.39)
Other elementary	77 (2.2)	24 (3.5)	13.3 (2.96)	47.8 (6.61)	32.3 (9.54)	4.5 (1.43)	2.0 (1.03)	37.3 (6.33)	25.4 (12.04)	24.0 (4.85)	13.3 (3.14)
Secondary	188 (6.2)	204 (13.4)	5.7 (1.30)	49.0 (1.44)	37.4 (1.43)	4.1 (0.49)	3.9 (0.55)	24.1 (1.62)	32.7 (1.39)	22.5 (1.54)	20.7 (1.10)
Arts/music	[5] (†)	18 (1.9)	7.1 (2.15)	50.3 (4.71)	38.6 (4.67)	3.4 (1.80)	‡ (†)	28.6 (4.14)	33.6 (5.12)	23.7 (4.05)	14.1 (3.24)
English	33 (1.7)	38 (2.8)	4.3 (3.58)	48.6 (2.87)	38.6 (3.19)	5.1 (1.24)	3.3 (1.03)	19.5 (2.11)	30.5 (4.45)	25.0 (3.07)	24.9 (3.01)
Foreign language	[5] (†)	18 (2.1)	4.2 (5.86)	47.7 (5.46)	36.6 (6.02)	4.6 (2.24)	6.9 (2.32)	25.3 (4.07)	34.1 (5.96)	23.9 (4.10)	16.8 (3.43)
Health/physical ed.	33 (1.6)	9 (1.0)	10.4 (3.83)	63.7 (5.46)	24.5 (4.98)	‡ (†)	‡ (†)	32.0 (5.74)	29.7 (5.25)	19.9 (5.64)	18.4 (4.54)
Mathematics	23 (1.3)	31 (3.2)	3.7 (1.51)	49.6 (3.23)	41.8 (2.84)	2.6 (1.44)	2.3 (1.39)	17.3 (2.82)	28.5 (3.01)	24.5 (2.88)	29.7 (3.55)
Science	19 (1.1)	27 (1.8)	1.9 (0.98)	47.4 (3.64)	41.0 (3.57)	3.8 (1.36)	5.9 (1.48)	25.3 (2.96)	35.1 (2.94)	19.0 (2.68)	20.6 (2.56)
Social studies	7 (1.0)	27 (2.4)	3.5 (1.15)	48.3 (3.65)	39.7 (3.69)	2.6 (0.82)	5.8 (1.48)	19.8 (4.74)	35.5 (3.03)	23.4 (3.79)	21.4 (2.79)
Special education	4 (0.6)	7 (1.5)	2.6 (1.30)	52.1 (6.47)	36.4 (7.21)	7.8 (2.79)	‡ (†)	20.7 (4.89)	47.0 (9.66)	20.3 (7.13)	12.0 (4.84)
Vocational/technical	[5] (†)	5 (0.9)	24.9 (8.13)	45.2 (7.34)	20.9 (4.91)	4.7 (2.75)	4.3 (3.63)	39.5 (7.42)	23.1 (5.27)	22.1 (5.55)	15.4 (4.57)
Other secondary	69 (2.6)	24 (2.7)	11.8 (3.39)	45.7 (3.96)	31.5 (3.71)	6.2 (1.69)	4.7 (1.49)	33.7 (3.94)	32.9 (3.82)	18.8 (3.52)	14.6 (2.43)

—Not available.
†Not applicable.
‡Reporting standards not met.
[1]Includes certificate of advanced graduate studies.
[2]Data are only roughly comparable to 2003–04, because the new category of more than one race was introduced in 2003–04.
[3]Includes Pacific Islander.
[4]Included under other elementary.
[5]Included under other secondary.

NOTE: Excludes prekindergarten teachers. Data are based on a head count of full-time and part-time teachers rather than on the number of full-time-equivalent teachers reported in other tables. Detail may not sum to totals because of rounding and cell suppression. Race categories exclude persons of Hispanic origin. Standard errors appear in parentheses.
SOURCE: U.S. Department of Education, National Center for Education Statistics, Schools and Staffing Survey (SASS), "Public Teacher Questionnaire," 1999–2000 and 2003–04; '"Private Teacher Questionnaire," 1999–2000 and 2003–04; and "Charter Teacher Questionnaire," 1999–2000. (This table was prepared September 2006.)

Table 66. Selected characteristics of public school teachers: Selected years, spring 1961 through spring 2001

Selected characteristic	1961	1966	1971	1976	1981	1986	1991	1996	2001
1	2	3	4	5	6	7	8	9	10
Number of teachers (in thousands)	**1,408**	**1,710**	**2,055**	**2,196**	**2,185**	**2,206**	**2,398**	**2,164**	**2,979**
Sex (percent)									
Male	31.3	31.1	34.3	32.9	33.1	31.2	27.9	25.6	21.0
Female	68.7	68.9	65.7	67.1	66.9	68.8	72.1	74.4	79.0
Median age (years)									
All teachers	41	36	35	33	37	41	42	44	46
Males	34	33	33	33	38	42	43	46	47
Females	46	40	37	33	36	41	42	44	45
Marital status (percent)									
Single	22.3	22.0	19.5	20.1	18.5	12.9	11.7	12.4	15.2
Married	68.0	69.1	71.9	71.3	73.0	75.7	75.7	75.9	73.1
Widowed, divorced, or separated	9.7	9.0	8.6	8.6	8.5	11.4	12.6	11.8	11.7
Highest degree held (percent)									
Less than bachelor's	14.6	7.0	2.9	0.9	0.4	0.3	0.6	0.3	0.2
Bachelor's	61.9	69.6	69.6	61.6	50.1	48.3	46.3	43.6	43.1
Master's or specialist degree[1]	23.1	23.2	27.1	37.1	49.3	50.7	52.6	54.5	56.0
Doctor's	0.4	0.1	0.4	0.4	0.3	0.7	0.5	1.7	0.8
College credits earned in last 3 years									
Percent who earned credits	—	—	60.7	63.2	56.1	53.1	50.3	50.2	46.3
Mean number of credits earned[2]	—	—	14	—	9	4	4	—	—
Median years of teaching experience	11	8	8	8	12	15	15	15	14
Teaching for first year (percent)	8.0	9.1	9.1	5.5	2.4	3.1	3.0	2.1	3.1
Average number of pupils per class									
Elementary teachers, not departmentalized	29	28	27	25	25	24	23	24	21
Secondary and departmentalized elementary teachers	27	27	27	25	23	26	26	31	28
Mean number of students taught per day by secondary and departmentalized elementary teachers	—	132	135	127	118	97	93	97	86
Average number of hours in required school day	7.4	7.3	7.3	7.3	7.3	7.3	7.2	7.3	7.4
Average number of hours per week spent on all teaching duties									
All teachers	47	47	47	46	46	49	47	49	50
Elementary teachers	49	47	46	44	44	47	44	47	49
Secondary teachers	46	48	48	48	48	51	50	52	52
Average number of days of classroom teaching in school year	—	181	181	180	180	180	180	180	181
Average number of nonteaching days in school year	—	5	4	5	6	5	5	6	7
Average annual salary as classroom teacher (current dollars)	$5,264 [3]	$6,253	$9,261	$12,005	$17,209	$24,504	$31,790	$35,549	$43,262
Total income, including spouse's (if married) (current dollars)	—	—	15,021	19,957	29,831	43,413	55,491	63,171	77,739
Willingness to teach again (percent)									
Certainly would	49.9	52.6	44.9	37.5	21.8	22.7	28.6	32.1	31.7
Probably would	26.9	25.4	29.5	26.1	24.6	26.3	30.5	30.5	28.7
Chances about even	12.5	12.9	13.0	17.5	17.6	19.8	18.5	17.3	18.4
Probably would not	7.9	7.1	8.9	13.4	24.0	22.0	17.0	15.8	15.7
Certainly would not	2.8	2.0	3.7	5.6	12.0	9.3	5.4	4.3	5.6

—Not available.
[1]Figures for curriculum specialist or professional diploma based on 6 years of college study are not included.
[2]Measured in semester hours.
[3]Includes extra pay for extra duties.

NOTE: Data are based on sample surveys of public school teachers. Data differ from figures appearing in other tables because of varying survey processing procedures and time period coverages. Detail may not sum to totals because of rounding.
SOURCE: National Education Association, *Status of the American Public School Teacher, 2000–01*. (This table was prepared August 2003.)

Table 67. Percentage of public school teachers of grades 9 through 12, by field of main teaching assignment and selected demographic and educational characteristics: 2003–04

Teacher characteristic	Total	Field of main teaching assignment									
		Arts and music	English or language arts	Foreign languages	Health and physical	Mathematics	Natural sciences	Social sciences	Special education	Vocational/technical	All other
1	2	3	4	5	6	7	8	9	10	11	12
Number of teachers (in thousands)	988.1 (19.27)	79.5 (2.92)	143.2 (5.13)	56.7 (2.11)	67.0 (2.85)	127.2 (3.53)	109.5 (4.38)	115.5 (3.42)	113.3 (5.03)	137.1 (4.49)	39.0 (1.92)
Total	**100.0 (0.00)**	**100.0 (0.00)**	**100.0 (0.00)**	**100.0 (0.00)**	**100.0 (0.00)**	**100.0 (0.00)**	**100.0 (0.00)**	**100.0 (0.00)**	**100.0 (0.00)**	**100.0 (0.00)**	**100.0 (0.00)**
Sex											
Male	44.1 (0.46)	45.5 (1.71)	26.1 (1.18)	21.9 (1.82)	63.1 (2.25)	45.1 (1.24)	51.3 (1.40)	65.1 (1.26)	27.9 (1.28)	50.1 (1.31)	47.6 (2.62)
Female	55.9 (0.46)	54.5 (1.71)	73.9 (1.18)	78.1 (1.82)	36.9 (2.25)	54.9 (1.24)	48.7 (1.40)	34.9 (1.26)	72.1 (1.28)	49.9 (1.31)	52.4 (2.62)
Race/ethnicity											
White	84.7 (0.89)	89.1 (1.26)	86.7 (1.10)	72.0 (2.88)	87.9 (1.30)	83.1 (1.48)	85.8 (1.22)	87.1 (1.23)	83.5 (1.69)	85.3 (1.10)	79.1 (1.90)
Black	7.1 (0.40)	5.5 (0.96)	6.9 (0.78)	4.5 (0.98)	6.1 (0.92)	6.8 (0.64)	6.5 (0.66)	5.9 (0.72)	9.4 (1.08)	8.9 (0.91)	9.6 (1.35)
Hispanic	5.4 (0.55)	3.6 (0.87)	3.8 (0.55)	20.8 (2.29)	3.8 (0.89)	6.3 (1.14)	4.0 (0.73)	3.6 (0.76)	4.8 (1.11)	3.9 (0.56)	7.7 (1.61)
Asian	1.3 (0.13)	0.7 (0.25)	1.1 (0.28)	1.5 (0.44)	0.5 (0.16)	2.5 (0.41)	2.0 (0.43)	1.3 (0.35)	0.8 (0.18)	0.4 (0.18)	2.1 (0.63)
Pacific Islander	0.2 (0.04)	‡ (†)	0.1 (0.07)	‡ (†)	0.2 (0.10)	0.1 (0.07)	0.3 (0.14)	0.3 (0.16)	0.3 (0.16)	0.1 (0.07)	‡ (†)
American Indian/Alaska Native	0.6 (0.06)	0.5 (0.12)	0.7 (0.15)	0.2 (0.08)	0.9 (0.34)	0.5 (0.13)	0.4 (0.13)	1.0 (0.35)	0.5 (0.17)	0.8 (0.25)	1.0 (0.30)
More than one race	0.7 (0.06)	0.5 (0.16)	0.7 (0.17)	1.0 (0.31)	0.6 (0.29)	0.7 (0.18)	1.0 (0.20)	0.9 (0.28)	0.7 (0.21)	0.5 (0.13)	0.4 (0.29)
Age											
Under 30 years	15.1 (0.45)	17.3 (1.41)	17.7 (0.93)	15.2 (1.39)	16.2 (1.84)	16.7 (1.00)	15.8 (1.02)	17.4 (1.01)	13.1 (1.15)	9.4 (0.77)	11.8 (1.91)
30 to 39 years	24.5 (0.49)	24.7 (1.56)	24.8 (1.16)	27.5 (1.89)	26.9 (1.60)	27.8 (1.15)	26.6 (1.29)	27.1 (1.37)	22.0 (1.21)	18.8 (0.86)	18.1 (1.95)
40 to 49 years	25.6 (0.41)	26.5 (1.66)	19.6 (1.12)	19.7 (1.70)	28.1 (2.02)	24.4 (1.18)	25.9 (1.45)	21.4 (1.27)	30.6 (1.48)	31.6 (1.17)	30.6 (2.55)
50 to 59 years	29.6 (0.50)	27.1 (1.67)	31.5 (1.18)	32.8 (1.90)	25.5 (1.69)	27.0 (1.24)	25.6 (1.25)	29.8 (1.30)	29.5 (1.48)	34.6 (1.10)	32.2 (2.45)
60 years and over	5.1 (0.19)	4.3 (0.79)	6.4 (0.59)	4.8 (0.72)	3.3 (0.58)	4.2 (0.41)	6.0 (0.74)	4.2 (0.54)	4.8 (0.77)	5.5 (0.54)	7.4 (1.23)
Age at which first began to teach full time or part time											
25 or under	56.0 (0.53)	64.6 (1.67)	56.5 (1.24)	56.2 (2.14)	70.1 (1.98)	61.1 (1.24)	51.4 (1.60)	56.3 (1.54)	53.3 (1.66)	47.5 (1.43)	43.9 (2.35)
26 to 35	28.1 (0.49)	24.2 (1.33)	30.0 (1.21)	26.8 (1.81)	25.2 (1.83)	23.3 (1.18)	32.3 (1.53)	30.9 (1.41)	29.9 (1.48)	28.8 (1.03)	24.6 (1.82)
36 to 45	11.4 (0.30)	9.2 (1.16)	9.8 (0.69)	13.2 (1.62)	3.5 (0.79)	10.6 (0.87)	11.1 (0.94)	9.3 (0.92)	12.1 (0.86)	16.9 (0.92)	20.5 (1.97)
46 to 55	4.1 (0.22)	1.8 (0.52)	3.4 (0.44)	3.4 (0.82)	1.0 (0.47)	4.2 (0.58)	4.6 (0.71)	3.3 (0.52)	4.4 (0.57)	6.2 (0.67)	10.7 (1.50)
56 or over	0.4 (0.06)	0.2 (0.11)	0.3 (0.11)	0.4 (0.22)	‡ (†)	0.9 (0.26)	0.6 (0.27)	0.3 (0.08)	0.3 (0.11)	0.7 (0.22)	0.2 (0.20)
Years of full-time teaching experience											
Less than 3 years	12.6 (0.67)	11.9 (1.18)	14.1 (0.98)	13.2 (1.41)	9.8 (1.47)	12.7 (1.30)	13.1 (0.86)	12.3 (0.79)	12.0 (1.58)	12.6 (1.15)	14.5 (1.67)
3 to 9 years	32.2 (0.43)	32.1 (1.86)	33.0 (1.28)	33.8 (1.68)	26.5 (1.56)	32.6 (1.40)	33.4 (1.29)	35.3 (1.30)	32.7 (1.32)	28.2 (1.05)	36.0 (2.50)
10 to 20 years	27.1 (0.41)	27.2 (1.69)	23.3 (0.98)	29.0 (1.91)	29.3 (1.96)	28.7 (1.44)	28.8 (1.14)	23.0 (1.26)	29.4 (1.64)	27.7 (1.09)	28.4 (1.95)
Over 20 years	28.0 (0.54)	28.8 (1.75)	29.6 (1.10)	24.1 (1.81)	34.3 (1.69)	26.0 (1.21)	24.7 (1.30)	29.5 (1.33)	25.9 (1.58)	31.5 (1.41)	21.2 (2.05)
Highest college degree											
Less than bachelor's degree	2.6 (0.20)	0.8 (0.28)	0.3 (0.09)	0.4 (0.15)	0.7 (0.27)	0.3 (0.08)	0.3 (0.14)	0.6 (0.29)	0.6 (0.21)	14.1 (1.17)	6.7 (1.44)
Bachelor's degree	47.9 (0.60)	55.5 (1.86)	49.3 (1.27)	46.3 (2.00)	54.8 (2.09)	50.8 (1.37)	43.5 (1.38)	50.1 (1.46)	43.0 (1.43)	44.0 (1.08)	41.4 (2.53)
Master's degree	42.0 (0.71)	37.4 (1.72)	41.2 (1.29)	46.0 (2.08)	39.4 (2.17)	43.7 (1.32)	46.8 (1.53)	43.1 (1.38)	43.9 (1.56)	36.4 (1.37)	44.8 (2.40)
Education specialist[1]	5.6 (0.23)	4.7 (0.76)	7.3 (0.77)	5.1 (0.80)	3.9 (0.73)	3.9 (0.48)	5.0 (0.56)	4.2 (0.48)	10.6 (0.97)	4.4 (0.51)	5.7 (1.15)
Doctorate or first professional	2.0 (0.15)	1.6 (0.48)	1.9 (0.35)	2.1 (0.73)	1.2 (0.31)	1.4 (0.27)	4.5 (0.76)	2.1 (0.40)	1.9 (0.42)	1.2 (0.32)	1.4 (0.47)

See notes at end of table.

Table 67. Percentage of public school teachers of grades 9 through 12, by field of main teaching assignment and selected demographic and educational characteristics: 2003–04—Continued

Teacher characteristic	Total	Field of main teaching assignment									
		Arts and music	English or language arts	Foreign languages	Health and physical	Mathematics	Natural sciences	Social sciences	Special education	Vocational/technical	All other
1	2	3	4	5	6	7	8	9	10	11	12
Undergraduate field of study[2]											
Arts and music	8.3 (0.21)	87.7 (0.96)	1.9 (0.26)	2.2 (0.79)	0.4 (0.15)	0.8 (0.18)	0.5 (0.19)	0.9 (0.26)	2.1 (0.37)	1.7 (0.38)	3.0 (0.73)
Education, instruction	8.4 (0.24)	2.5 (0.39)	9.8 (0.70)	6.1 (0.71)	1.9 (0.41)	10.0 (0.70)	6.8 (0.68)	10.7 (0.79)	17.6 (1.00)	3.0 (0.36)	13.0 (1.54)
Education, other	5.1 (0.23)	0.6 (0.32)	1.2 (0.23)	1.2 (0.60)	0.5 (0.25)	0.7 (0.18)	0.4 (0.16)	0.3 (0.09)	38.3 (1.55)	0.6 (0.19)	3.2 (0.66)
English and language arts	13.3 (0.35)	3.8 (0.64)	71.0 (1.15)	7.7 (0.91)	1.1 (0.48)	1.4 (0.35)	0.7 (0.28)	3.4 (0.58)	7.5 (0.77)	1.8 (0.33)	11.6 (1.80)
Foreign languages	4.5 (0.21)	0.1 (0.05)	1.2 (0.25)	65.3 (1.88)	0.2 (0.10)	0.3 (0.12)	0.1 (0.10)	1.3 (0.44)	0.9 (0.54)	0.3 (0.14)	5.4 (1.03)
Health and physical education	9.8 (0.30)	0.8 (0.25)	2.1 (0.37)	2.6 (0.85)	85.6 (1.20)	4.5 (0.55)	6.0 (0.72)	6.5 (0.70)	5.9 (0.71)	2.4 (0.37)	11.3 (1.78)
Mathematics and computer science	8.6 (0.21)	‡ (†)	0.6 (0.20)	1.0 (0.33)	0.3 (0.15)	61.3 (1.29)	1.4 (0.28)	0.5 (0.21)	0.6 (0.19)	0.8 (0.20)	4.0 (0.96)
Natural sciences	10.7 (0.37)	0.3 (0.12)	0.7 (0.26)	1.3 (0.51)	1.7 (0.52)	8.2 (0.66)	77.5 (1.22)	0.9 (0.25)	1.2 (0.21)	2.2 (0.33)	4.7 (1.00)
Social sciences	14.8 (0.31)	1.8 (0.31)	7.3 (0.65)	8.0 (1.18)	4.0 (0.69)	6.4 (0.65)	3.0 (0.42)	71.4 (1.23)	16.8 (1.09)	4.3 (0.51)	21.1 (1.89)
Vocational/technical education	12.7 (0.30)	1.2 (0.31)	2.3 (0.44)	2.4 (0.77)	3.6 (0.73)	5.3 (0.61)	2.5 (0.44)	2.5 (0.39)	6.4 (0.64)	67.7 (1.50)	11.7 (1.28)
Other	3.9 (0.21)	1.2 (0.37)	2.0 (0.41)	2.4 (0.86)	0.8 (0.27)	0.9 (0.24)	1.0 (0.28)	1.7 (0.47)	2.9 (0.62)	15.2 (1.18)	11.0 (1.74)

†Not applicable.
‡Reporting standards not met.
[1]Education specialist degrees or certificates are generally awarded for 1 year's work beyond the master's level.
[2]Data are for bachelor's degrees and major fields of study only.

NOTE: Race categories exclude persons of Hispanic origin. Detail may not sum to totals because of rounding. Standard errors appear in parentheses.
SOURCE: U.S. Department of Education, National Center for Education Statistics, Schools and Staffing Survey (SASS), "Public Teacher Questionnaire," 2003–04. (This table was prepared July 2006.)

Table 68. Teachers' perceptions about serious problems in their schools, by control and level of school: 1993–94, 1999–2000, and 2003–04

Problem area	Public school teachers						Private school teachers					
			2003–04						2003–04			
	1993–94 total	1999–2000 total	Total	Elementary schools	Secondary schools	Combined schools	1993–94 total	1999–2000 total	Total	Elementary schools	Secondary schools	Combined schools
1	2	3	4	5	6	7	8	9	10	11	12	13
Percent of teachers indicating item is a serious problem												
Student tardiness	10.5	10.2 (0.22)	13.8 (0.30)	9.8 (0.39)	23.1 (0.58)	10.8 (0.96)	2.6	2.9 (0.21)	2.9 (0.40)	2.1 (0.45)	5.0 (0.83)	2.8 (0.85)
Student absenteeism	14.4	13.9 (0.26)	13.2 (0.31)	8.3 (0.37)	23.7 (0.59)	12.9 (1.04)	2.2	2.5 (0.22)	1.9 (0.23)	0.9 (0.17)	4.0 (0.75)	2.2 (0.48)
Teacher absenteeism	1.5	2.2 (0.10)	1.1 (0.08)	0.9 (0.12)	1.7 (0.15)	0.7 (0.16)	0.8	0.8 (0.11)	0.3 (0.09)	0.2 (0.07)	0.5 (0.24)	0.3 (0.15)
Students cutting class	5.1	4.7 (0.12)	5.6 (0.23)	1.5 (0.17)	14.5 (0.59)	4.4 (0.55)	0.7	0.8 (0.12)	0.5 (0.11)	0.2 (0.07)	0.9 (0.36)	0.7 (0.28)
Physical conflicts among students	8.2	4.8 (0.19)	— (†)	— (†)	— (†)	— (†)	1.5	1.0 (0.18)	— (†)	— (†)	— (†)	— (†)
Robbery or theft	4.1	2.4 (0.11)	— (†)	— (†)	— (†)	— (†)	0.8	0.9 (0.11)	— (†)	— (†)	— (†)	— (†)
Vandalism of school property	6.7	3.4 (0.15)	— (†)	— (†)	— (†)	— (†)	1.2	0.7 (0.11)	— (†)	— (†)	— (†)	— (†)
Student pregnancy	7.3	3.7 (0.12)	2.4 (0.12)	0.2 (0.06)	7.0 (0.34)	3.6 (0.49)	0.4	0.4 (0.09)	0.1 (0.05)	0.1 (0.04)	0.3 (0.19)	0.1 (0.05)
Student use of alcohol	9.3	7.4 (0.14)	— (†)	— (†)	— (†)	— (†)	3.1	3.1 (0.16)	— (†)	— (†)	— (†)	— (†)
Student drug abuse	5.7	6.0 (0.11)	— (†)	— (†)	— (†)	— (†)	1.3	1.8 (0.14)	— (†)	— (†)	— (†)	— (†)
Student possession of weapons	2.8	0.8 (0.06)	— (†)	— (†)	— (†)	— (†)	0.3	0.3 (0.06)	— (†)	— (†)	— (†)	— (†)
Verbal abuse of teachers	11.1	— (†)	— (†)	— (†)	— (†)	— (†)	2.3	— (†)	— (†)	— (†)	— (†)	— (†)
Student disrespect for teachers	18.5	17.2 (0.34)	— (†)	— (†)	— (†)	— (†)	3.4	3.8 (0.31)	— (†)	— (†)	— (†)	— (†)
Students dropping out	5.8	4.6 (0.11)	3.3 (0.13)	0.3 (0.07)	9.6 (0.41)	4.3 (0.47)	0.6	0.5 (0.10)	0.3 (0.09)	0.2 (0.08)	0.5 (0.26)	0.3 (0.12)
Student apathy	23.6	20.6 (0.30)	16.6 (0.34)	9.9 (0.41)	30.4 (0.56)	19.5 (1.01)	4.5	4.3 (0.29)	3.1 (0.39)	1.4 (0.24)	6.6 (0.95)	3.6 (0.70)
Lack of parental involvement	27.6	23.7 (0.36)	21.6 (0.43)	19.3 (0.59)	26.3 (0.59)	22.7 (1.17)	4.0	3.4 (0.30)	2.5 (0.37)	1.6 (0.27)	3.6 (0.77)	3.2 (0.69)
Poverty	19.5	19.2 (0.43)	21.4 (0.46)	22.4 (0.65)	19.0 (0.57)	22.7 (1.31)	2.7	2.1 (0.21)	2.2 (0.26)	1.8 (0.31)	3.4 (0.78)	2.2 (0.49)
Students come unprepared to learn	28.8	29.5 (0.36)	26.8 (0.46)	23.7 (0.68)	33.5 (0.69)	26.1 (1.39)	4.1	4.9 (0.36)	3.5 (0.30)	2.1 (0.55)	6.8 (0.99)	3.9 (0.70)
Percent of teachers indicating item happens daily												
Physical conflicts among students	—	— (†)	12.1 (0.29)	13.7 (0.43)	9.3 (0.38)	8.2 (0.95)	—	— (†)	2.3 (0.33)	2.6 (0.58)	1.0 (0.35)	2.6 (0.64)
Robbery or theft	—	— (†)	3.7 (0.17)	2.8 (0.22)	5.9 (0.24)	1.9 (0.40)	—	— (†)	0.4 (0.10)	# (†)	1.3 (0.40)	0.4 (0.22)
Vandalism of school property	—	— (†)	3.6 (0.16)	2.5 (0.21)	6.3 (0.33)	2.7 (0.52)	—	— (†)	0.5 (0.11)	0.1 (0.08)	0.8 (0.28)	0.8 (0.24)
Student use of alcohol	—	— (†)	3.1 (0.10)	0.3 (0.07)	9.0 (0.28)	3.5 (0.45)	—	— (†)	0.7 (0.17)	# (†)	3.3 (0.86)	0.5 (0.21)
Student drug abuse	—	— (†)	4.5 (0.14)	0.5 (0.11)	13.0 (0.35)	4.4 (0.51)	—	— (†)	1.1 (0.26)	# (†)	5.2 (1.31)	0.8 (0.36)
Student possession of weapons	—	— (†)	0.5 (0.05)	0.1 (0.05)	1.2 (0.12)	0.3 (0.14)	—	— (†)	# (†)	# (†)	# (†)	0.1 (0.05)
Verbal abuse of teachers	—	— (†)	11.8 (0.31)	9.3 (0.39)	17.1 (0.50)	12.7 (1.10)	—	— (†)	2.4 (0.40)	1.2 (0.29)	4.0 (0.84)	3.3 (0.72)
Student disrespect for teachers	—	— (†)	21.6 (0.45)	18.5 (0.61)	28.3 (0.58)	20.9 (1.08)	—	— (†)	5.1 (0.37)	3.6 (0.56)	6.3 (1.05)	6.5 (1.12)
Racial tension	—	— (†)	2.4 (0.15)	1.8 (0.19)	3.9 (0.22)	1.5 (0.28)	—	— (†)	0.4 (0.08)	0.1 (0.06)	0.9 (0.36)	0.6 (0.20)

—Not available.
†Not applicable.
#Rounds to zero.
NOTE: Standard errors appear in parentheses.

SOURCE: U.S. Department of Education, National Center for Education Statistics, Schools and Staffing Survey (SASS), "Public Teacher Questionnaire," 1993–94, 1999–2000, and 2003–04; "Private Teacher Questionnaire," 1993–94, 1999–2000, and 2003–04; and "Charter Teacher Questionnaire," 1999–2000. (This table was prepared August 2006.)

Table 69. Teachers' perceptions about teaching and school conditions, by control and level of school: 1993–94, 1999–2000, and 2003–04

Percent of teachers somewhat agreeing or strongly agreeing with statement

Statement	Public school teachers						Private school teachers					
	Public total, 1993–94	Public total, 1999–2000	2003–04 Total	2003–04 Elementary schools	2003–04 Secondary schools	2003–04 Combined schools	Private total, 1993–94	Private total, 1999–2000	2003–04 Total	2003–04 Elementary schools	2003–04 Secondary schools	2003–04 Combined schools
1	2	3	4	5	6	7	8	9	10	11	12	13
The school administration's behavior toward the staff is supportive.	79.2 (0.36)	78.8 (0.38)	85.2 (0.33)	85.8 (0.48)	84.1 (0.41)	84.3 (0.98)	88.2 (0.42)	87.3 (0.45)	91.1 (0.74)	91.4 (0.86)	89.6 (1.26)	91.4 (1.12)
My principal enforces school rules for student conduct and backs me up when I need it.	80.8 (0.35)	82.2 (0.33)	87.2 (0.35)	87.8 (0.52)	85.8 (0.44)	87.7 (0.80)	88.4 (0.41)	88.3 (0.39)	92.2 (0.62)	92.0 (0.76)	91.0 (1.17)	92.9 (1.20)
The principal lets staff members know what is expected of them.	85.6 (0.30)	87.7 (0.26)	91.8 (0.23)	92.4 (0.32)	91.0 (0.29)	90.1 (0.61)	88.2 (0.34)	89.8 (0.35)	93.8 (0.55)	93.6 (0.66)	93.4 (0.86)	94.1 (1.03)
Principal talks to me frequently about my instructional practices.	44.3 (0.46)	45.6 (0.43)	— (†)	— (†)	— (†)	—	54.0 (0.64)	50.4 (0.64)	— (†)	— (†)	— (†)	— (†)
In this school, staff members are recognized for a job well done.	67.9 (0.39)	68.3 (0.42)	75.4 (0.38)	77.3 (0.55)	72.1 (0.40)	71.1 (1.28)	81.1 (0.40)	78.9 (0.50)	83.8 (1.09)	83.8 (1.25)	82.9 (1.58)	84.3 (1.91)
Principal knows what kind of school he/she wants and has communicated it to the staff.	80.5 (0.36)	83.2 (0.28)	87.3 (0.30)	88.4 (0.40)	85.3 (0.43)	84.0 (1.07)	88.6 (0.38)	88.4 (0.43)	91.9 (0.68)	91.5 (0.81)	91.2 (0.90)	92.7 (1.21)
Most of my colleagues share my beliefs and values about what the central mission of the school should be.	84.2 (0.22)	84.7 (0.26)	88.1 (0.26)	90.5 (0.38)	83.0 (0.41)	87.4 (0.86)	93.2 (0.37)	92.2 (0.31)	93.8 (0.50)	95.1 (0.55)	91.2 (1.02)	93.3 (1.08)
There is a great deal of cooperative effort among staff.	77.5 (0.31)	78.4 (0.32)	83.2 (0.36)	85.1 (0.56)	79.0 (0.48)	82.8 (1.19)	90.5 (0.29)	89.0 (0.42)	91.1 (0.75)	91.5 (0.84)	88.6 (1.47)	91.8 (1.24)
I receive a great deal of support from parents for the work I do.	52.5 (0.38)	57.9 (0.40)	61.1 (0.50)	63.2 (0.74)	56.7 (0.59)	61.1 (1.38)	84.6 (0.41)	84.0 (0.49)	86.0 (2.39)	88.3 (1.01)	81.5 (2.16)	85.1 (6.59)
I make a conscious effort to coordinate the content of my courses with that of other teachers.	85.0 (0.25)	84.1 (0.24)	86.3 (0.31)	89.1 (0.45)	81.0 (0.40)	82.8 (0.96)	85.2 (0.44)	81.4 (0.55)	84.5 (1.20)	86.8 (1.10)	80.3 (1.54)	83.4 (2.03)
Routine duties and paperwork interfere with my job of teaching.	70.8 (0.38)	71.1 (0.30)	70.8 (0.44)	71.2 (0.64)	70.7 (0.50)	65.9 (1.13)	40.1 (0.65)	44.5 (0.57)	40.8 (2.51)	42.2 (3.64)	44.1 (2.00)	37.5 (3.46)
Level of student misbehavior in this school interferes with my teaching.	44.1 (0.40)	40.8 (0.42)	37.2 (0.53)	35.2 (0.83)	41.5 (0.59)	37.9 (1.48)	22.4 (0.43)	24.1 (0.61)	20.8 (2.55)	21.4 (1.47)	21.0 (1.92)	20.0 (6.60)
Amount of student tardiness and class cutting in this school interferes with my teaching.	27.9 (0.32)	31.5 (0.35)	33.4 (0.45)	27.7 (0.62)	45.7 (0.64)	33.0 (1.32)	16.9 (0.75)	15.0 (0.43)	16.9 (1.01)	15.0 (1.14)	19.9 (1.59)	18.1 (1.93)
Rules for student behavior are consistently enforced by teachers in this school, even for students who are not in their classes.	61.8 (0.42)	62.6 (0.39)	71.1 (0.46)	78.8 (0.60)	54.7 (0.55)	70.5 (1.08)	77.6 (0.50)	75.9 (0.51)	80.9 (1.51)	86.1 (1.12)	69.1 (2.45)	79.5 (2.42)
I am satisfied with my class sizes.	64.9 (0.38)	67.7 (0.36)	69.1 (0.43)	69.7 (0.58)	65.2 (0.52)	83.7 (1.09)	84.4 (0.40)	85.7 (0.45)	87.6 (0.92)	85.4 (1.56)	85.4 (1.74)	91.5 (1.20)
I am satisfied with my teaching salary.	44.9 (0.45)	39.4 (0.36)	45.9 (0.46)	44.2 (0.65)	49.4 (0.60)	46.2 (1.60)	41.6 (0.59)	42.6 (0.73)	50.6 (1.67)	43.7 (2.43)	54.1 (2.09)	57.9 (4.56)
I sometimes feel it is a waste of time to try to do my best as a teacher.	26.8 (0.35)	20.3 (0.29)	16.7 (0.32)	14.6 (0.45)	20.8 (0.43)	18.4 (1.08)	10.2 (0.65)	10.5 (0.38)	8.7 (0.71)	8.5 (1.17)	7.8 (0.78)	9.3 (1.10)
I plan with the librarian/media specialist for the integration of services into my teaching.	66.9 (0.42)	58.6 (0.38)	— (†)	— (†)	— (†)	— (†)	60.6 (0.71)	48.7 (0.74)	— (†)	— (†)	— (†)	— (†)
Necessary materials are available as needed by staff.	73.1 (0.42)	75.0 (0.32)	79.0 (0.42)	79.7 (0.56)	76.9 (0.56)	83.2 (0.87)	85.7 (0.44)	89.0 (0.38)	91.8 (0.71)	91.0 (0.75)	91.5 (1.04)	93.0 (1.40)
I worry about the security of my job because of the performance of my students on state or local tests.	— (†)	28.8 (0.37)	31.2 (0.43)	32.4 (0.55)	28.8 (0.57)	30.8 (1.15)	— (†)	6.7 (0.29)	7.8 (0.65)	9.0 (0.98)	7.9 (0.93)	6.2 (1.14)
I am given the support I need to teach students with special needs.	— (†)	60.9 (0.33)	64.4 (0.46)	64.0 (0.63)	63.7 (0.65)	74.5 (1.37)	— (†)	67.1 (0.58)	71.8 (2.05)	68.6 (2.08)	70.8 (2.01)	76.5 (6.79)
I am generally satisfied with being a teacher at this school.	— (†)	89.7 (0.24)	90.9 (0.28)	91.1 (0.40)	90.4 (0.31)	91.9 (0.75)	— (†)	93.3 (0.26)	95.2 (0.55)	94.8 (0.65)	95.7 (0.88)	95.4 (1.17)

—Not available.
†Not applicable.
NOTE: Standard errors appear in parentheses.

SOURCE: U.S. Department of Education, National Center for Education Statistics, Schools and Staffing Survey (SASS), "Public Teacher Questionnaire," 1993–94, 1999–2000, and 2003–04; "Private Teacher Questionnaire," 1993–94, 1999–2000, and 2003–04; and "Charter Teacher Questionnaire," 1999–2000. (This table was prepared August 2006.)

Table 70. Mobility of public and private elementary and secondary teachers, by selected teacher and school characteristics: Selected years, 1987–88 through 2000–01

Selected characteristic	Percent of public school teachers						Percent of private school teachers					
	Left teaching			1999–2000 to 2000–01			Left teaching			1999–2000 to 2000–01		
	1987–88 to 1988–89	1990–91 to 1991–92	1993–94 to 1994–95	Remained in same school	Changed schools	Left teaching	1987–88 to 1988–89	1990–91 to 1991–92	1993–94 to 1994–95	Remained in same school	Changed schools	Left teaching
1	2	3	4	5	6	7	8	9	10	11	12	13
Total	5.6 (0.30)	5.1 (0.36)	6.6 (0.34)	84.9 (0.58)	7.7 (0.45)	7.4 (0.37)	12.7 (0.85)	12.3 (0.80)	11.9 (0.70)	79.1 (0.83)	8.4 (0.49)	12.5 (0.69)
Sex												
Male	5.1 (0.52)	4.5 (0.60)	5.2 (0.32)	86.7 (0.88)	6.0 (0.69)	7.4 (0.67)	10.2 (1.72)	12.1 (1.91)	13.1 (1.20)	81.1 (1.60)	7.2 (0.79)	11.7 (1.48)
Female	5.8 (0.39)	5.3 (0.48)	7.1 (0.44)	84.3 (0.73)	8.3 (0.52)	7.4 (0.45)	13.4 (0.92)	12.3 (0.84)	11.6 (0.78)	78.5 (0.92)	8.8 (0.57)	12.8 (0.76)
Race/ethnicity												
White, non-Hispanic	5.7 (0.32)	5.1 (0.37)	6.5 (0.36)	85.0 (0.59)	7.6 (0.44)	7.5 (0.45)	12.1 (0.90)	12.0 (0.86)	11.7 (0.69)	79.0 (0.87)	8.7 (0.53)	12.3 (0.73)
Black, non-Hispanic	5.1 (1.84)	6.1 (1.45)	6.6 (1.48)	84.3 (2.36)	8.3 (1.77)	7.4 (1.60)	34.7 (8.35)	19.3 (6.76)	12.6 (4.52)	83.2 (5.44)	2.1 (0.98)	14.8 (5.09)
Hispanic	2.9 (0.84)	4.4 (0.99)	9.1 (2.14)	85.4 (2.12)	7.1 (1.17)	7.5 (1.67)	21.3 (6.46)	13.6 (4.32)	14.6 (4.31)	81.5 (3.41)	8.9 (2.07)	9.6 (2.85)
Asian/Pacific Islander	4.2 (2.77)	7.0 (5.37)	2.4 (0.71)	81.7 (7.70)	16.2 (7.37)	2.1 (0.87)	8.8 (10.39)	12.2 (6.51)	17.5 (8.67)	68.6 (12.71)	7.2 (2.61)	24.2 (12.23)
American Indian/Alaska Native	3.1 (1.70)	1.7 (0.77)	3.5 (1.06)	87.7 (5.51)	4.7 (2.61)	7.6 (3.68)	17.5 (15.61)	16.5 (18.44)	38.5 (20.33)	76.9 (15.48)	2.9 (10.53)	20.2 (12.71)
Age												
Less than 25	4.3 (0.91)	9.1 (2.30)	3.8 (1.05)	76.4 (3.56)	14.4 (2.48)	9.3 (2.20)	19.0 (3.79)	23.8 (4.91)	20.0 (4.19)	58.5 (4.40)	11.5 (2.04)	29.9 (4.24)
25 to 29	9.0 (1.18)	9.0 (1.21)	10.0 (1.25)	74.1 (2.39)	16.2 (2.14)	9.7 (1.39)	17.6 (2.42)	17.8 (2.27)	13.1 (1.35)	67.9 (2.63)	13.6 (1.55)	18.6 (2.07)
30 to 39	5.8 (0.59)	4.2 (0.76)	6.7 (0.94)	84.9 (1.08)	8.6 (0.75)	6.5 (0.88)	12.4 (1.59)	13.7 (1.65)	14.9 (1.54)	77.5 (1.88)	8.8 (1.08)	13.7 (1.52)
40 to 49	2.4 (0.32)	2.0 (0.31)	3.9 (0.54)	88.7 (0.98)	6.7 (0.70)	4.6 (0.62)	10.5 (1.63)	7.7 (1.03)	8.7 (1.02)	83.8 (1.58)	7.7 (0.86)	8.5 (1.34)
50 to 59	5.7 (0.82)	6.7 (0.95)	6.3 (0.77)	88.1 (1.05)	3.8 (0.60)	8.1 (0.80)	11.3 (2.45)	9.6 (1.90)	8.2 (1.53)	88.9 (1.43)	5.2 (1.02)	5.9 (0.90)
60 to 64	23.4 (0.82)	26.8 (4.30)	30.5 (4.78)	72.1 (5.72)	2.2 (1.00)	25.7 (5.44)	16.9 (5.93)	17.8 (4.62)	13.1 (2.74)	71.0 (5.64)	10.9 (4.76)	18.1 (3.72)
65 and over	16.7 (4.90)	40.9 (13.80)	34.1 (7.79)	80.4 (5.83)	3.1 (1.81)	16.6 (5.44)	7.9 (3.16)	20.7 (5.83)	41.9 (8.67)	70.6 (7.60)	# (†)	29.4 (7.60)
Full- and part-time teaching experience												
1 year or less	7.9 (0.96)	7.0 (1.31)	5.7 (0.82)	75.1 (2.56)	14.4 (1.73)	10.5 (1.93)	15.9 (2.73)	22.8 (2.85)	18.2 (2.12)	58.9 (4.37)	12.2 (1.97)	28.9 (3.95)
2 years	7.3 (1.81)	9.5 (1.89)	9.1 (1.51)	77.5 (2.83)	14.0 (2.66)	8.5 (1.94)	18.2 (3.32)	19.5 (3.19)	23.6 (2.72)	70.1 (3.45)	7.3 (1.24)	22.5 (3.24)
3 years	9.3 (1.50)	6.6 (1.24)	9.8 (1.42)	79.6 (2.71)	12.8 (1.98)	7.5 (1.60)	15.4 (3.80)	19.0 (3.35)	12.8 (2.15)	68.0 (3.40)	14.1 (2.49)	17.8 (2.49)
4 to 10 years	6.4 (0.89)	5.3 (0.89)	6.8 (0.94)	82.5 (1.16)	10.3 (1.02)	7.3 (0.72)	14.0 (1.91)	12.4 (1.73)	13.1 (1.51)	76.3 (1.87)	11.1 (1.14)	12.6 (1.37)
11 to 20 years	3.5 (0.42)	2.3 (0.30)	4.9 (0.64)	88.5 (1.08)	6.3 (0.76)	5.2 (0.74)	11.5 (1.73)	6.6 (1.00)	7.1 (0.93)	87.2 (1.36)	5.9 (0.76)	6.9 (1.13)
21 to 25 years	3.5 (0.87)	4.2 (0.87)	4.0 (0.81)	90.7 (1.10)	5.1 (0.88)	4.2 (0.68)	5.2 (2.36)	3.3 (1.40)	6.0 (1.64)	88.0 (1.99)	6.5 (1.41)	5.5 (1.32)
More than 25 years	11.3 (1.63)	11.0 (1.34)	12.0 (1.04)	86.1 (1.37)	2.5 (0.75)	11.4 (1.05)	8.4 (2.03)	15.0 (3.24)	12.7 (2.53)	85.9 (2.08)	4.1 (1.59)	10.0 (1.40)
Level taught												
Elementary	5.5 (0.39)	4.8 (0.45)	6.4 (0.53)	84.8 (0.74)	8.4 (0.57)	6.8 (0.45)	12.5 (0.99)	11.3 (1.02)	11.5 (0.96)	78.4 (0.91)	8.3 (0.46)	13.4 (0.84)
Secondary	5.6 (0.42)	5.5 (0.62)	6.7 (0.53)	85.2 (0.95)	6.2 (0.66)	8.6 (0.71)	12.9 (2.38)	13.3 (1.51)	12.6 (1.51)	82.5 (1.55)	9.0 (1.52)	8.5 (0.90)
School size												
Less than 150	7.3 (1.36)	4.4 (0.69)	6.4 (1.15)	78.1 (4.06)	12.4 (3.03)	9.5 (2.29)	16.6 (1.72)	16.3 (1.87)	14.8 (1.43)	75.4 (2.16)	9.9 (1.39)	14.6 (1.45)
150 to 349	4.8 (0.45)	3.9 (0.53)	7.8 (1.03)	85.1 (1.45)	8.2 (0.90)	6.7 (0.99)	10.9 (1.62)	13.3 (1.42)	12.6 (1.21)	78.0 (1.34)	8.8 (0.71)	13.1 (1.24)
350 to 499	6.1 (0.98)	6.4 (1.03)	5.8 (0.73)	85.1 (1.55)	7.6 (1.07)	7.4 (0.85)	10.7 (2.63)	6.3 (1.47)	12.1 (1.95)	83.2 (1.63)	6.5 (0.98)	10.3 (1.26)
500 to 749	5.6 (0.77)	4.7 (0.68)	7.6 (0.67)	84.7 (1.18)	8.2 (0.77)	7.1 (0.78)	9.6 (2.07)	9.8 (2.11)	7.1 (1.27)	81.9 (2.10)	7.1 (0.96)	11.1 (1.91)
750 or more	5.0 (0.48)	5.4 (0.54)	5.7 (0.57)	85.5 (0.99)	6.8 (0.67)	7.7 (0.74)	12.9 (3.14)	6.7 (2.58)	6.2 (1.18)	81.6 (2.04)	7.6 (1.60)	10.8 (1.64)
Percent minority enrollment												
Less than 5 percent	5.8 (0.60)	4.5 (0.51)	7.1 (0.68)	86.2 (0.95)	7.3 (0.72)	6.5 (0.78)	12.7 (1.27)	12.2 (1.35)	11.2 (0.99)	83.0 (1.35)	9.9 (2.04)	7.1 (0.96)
5 to 19 percent	5.8 (0.74)	5.5 (0.73)	6.0 (0.71)	86.4 (1.02)	6.7 (0.91)	6.9 (0.66)	10.3 (1.37)	12.2 (1.40)	11.1 (1.07)	82.5 (1.42)	9.9 (1.39)	7.6 (1.60)
20 to 49 percent	5.2 (0.64)	5.9 (0.73)	6.2 (0.82)	82.5 (1.45)	8.0 (0.92)	9.5 (1.09)	18.9 (4.18)	12.2 (2.01)	15.6 (2.28)	76.6 (2.73)	8.8 (0.71)	14.6 (1.45)
50 percent or more	5.3 (0.66)	4.9 (0.66)	6.9 (0.72)	83.7 (1.01)	9.0 (0.84)	7.3 (0.68)	13.6 (2.85)	13.1 (2.35)	13.2 (2.15)	78.1 (2.46)	8.8 (0.98)	13.1 (1.24)
Community type												
Central city	4.6 (0.59)	5.2 (0.65)	6.3 (0.64)	84.8 (1.26)	8.1 (1.01)	7.1 (0.65)	13.5 (1.67)	12.7 (1.40)	10.9 (0.75)	79.1 (1.19)	8.8 (0.80)	12.1 (0.96)
Urban fringe/large town	5.6 (0.59)	5.5 (0.75)	6.5 (0.70)	83.7 (0.99)	8.0 (0.66)	8.3 (0.77)	11.5 (1.51)	10.6 (1.21)	12.6 (1.32)	80.6 (1.26)	7.6 (0.81)	11.8 (1.23)
Rural/small town	5.7 (0.52)	4.8 (0.39)	6.8 (0.59)	86.7 (0.78)	7.0 (0.53)	6.3 (0.52)	15.0 (1.78)	13.9 (1.81)	13.6 (1.46)	75.2 (2.77)	9.2 (1.65)	15.5 (1.92)

†Not applicable.
#Rounds to zero.
NOTE: Detail may not sum to totals because of rounding. Standard errors appear in parentheses.

SOURCE: U.S. Department of Education, National Center for Education Statistics, Schools and Staffing Survey (SASS), Characteristics of Stayers, Movers, and Leavers: Results From the Teacher Follow-up Survey 1994–95; Teacher Attrition and Mobility: Results From the Teacher Follow-up Survey: 2000–01; and unpublished tabulations. (This table was prepared October 2005.)

Table 71. Average base salary for full-time teachers in public elementary and secondary schools, by highest degree earned and years of full-time teaching: Selected years, 1990–91 through 2003–04

Years of full-time teaching experience	Number of full-time teachers	Salary (current dollars)					Salary (constant 2005–06 dollars)[3]				
		Highest degree earned					Highest degree earned				
		All teachers[1]	Bachelor's degree	Master's degree	Education specialist[2]	Doctor's degree	All teachers[1]	Bachelor's degree	Master's degree	Education specialist[2]	Doctor's degree
1	2	3	4	5	6	7	8	9	10	11	12
1990–91											
Total	2,336,750 (20,958)	$31,331 (97.1)	$27,736 (102.8)	$34,955 (125.3)	$37,231 (390.5)	$40,065 (816.6)	$46,556 (144.3)	$41,215 (152.8)	$51,941 (186.2)	$55,323 (580.3)	$59,534 (1,213.4)
1 year or less	94,000 (3,014)	22,209 (200.3)	21,512 (207.0)	26,435 (863.3)	26,630 (982.1)	‡ (†)	33,000 (297.7)	31,965 (307.5)	39,281 (1,282.8)	39,570 (1,459.3)	‡ (†)
2 years	86,900 (2,963)	22,119 (162.3)	21,648 (147.4)	25,064 (505.1)	‡ (†)	‡ (†)	32,868 (241.2)	32,168 (219.0)	37,244 (750.5)	‡ (†)	‡ (†)
3 years	80,340 (2,542)	23,010 (177.3)	22,444 (174.2)	25,960 (694.6)	‡ (†)	‡ (†)	34,192 (263.4)	33,350 (258.8)	38,575 (1,032.2)	‡ (†)	‡ (†)
4 years	79,610 (3,271)	23,961 (236.4)	23,150 (245.7)	26,340 (526.0)	29,162 (1,489.3)	‡ (†)	35,605 (351.3)	34,400 (365.1)	39,139 (781.7)	43,332 (2,213.0)	‡ (†)
5 years	83,540 (3,238)	25,084 (201.5)	24,070 (240.5)	27,217 (436.4)	29,870 (2,194.7)	‡ (†)	37,274 (299.5)	35,766 (357.3)	40,443 (648.4)	44,384 (3,261.2)	‡ (†)
6 to 9 years	316,210 (6,805)	26,502 (108.5)	25,013 (135.3)	28,796 (237.4)	30,209 (761.1)	‡ (†)	39,381 (161.3)	37,167 (201.1)	42,788 (352.8)	44,888 (1,130.9)	‡ (†)
10 to 14 years	408,300 (7,843)	29,622 (160.9)	27,319 (171.9)	31,760 (299.5)	33,638 (592.0)	37,904 (1,942.7)	44,017 (239.1)	40,595 (255.4)	47,193 (445.0)	49,984 (879.7)	56,323 (2,886.7)
15 to 19 years	444,930 (7,580)	33,587 (209.0)	30,821 (252.8)	35,243 (248.4)	37,798 (841.9)	40,337 (1,548.3)	49,908 (310.6)	45,798 (375.6)	52,369 (369.1)	56,165 (1,251.0)	59,938 (2,300.7)
20 to 24 years	392,330 (8,038)	36,956 (202.4)	34,054 (274.3)	38,455 (242.6)	39,522 (838.4)	43,736 (1,391.4)	54,914 (300.8)	50,602 (407.7)	57,142 (360.5)	58,727 (1,245.8)	64,989 (2,067.5)
25 to 29 years	219,140 (6,214)	38,104 (305.4)	34,775 (409.2)	39,826 (369.6)	42,462 (1,257.0)	43,112 (2,179.4)	56,620 (453.7)	51,673 (608.0)	59,179 (549.3)	63,095 (1,867.9)	64,062 (3,238.4)
30 to 34 years	100,460 (4,766)	38,528 (379.6)	35,035 (450.8)	40,659 (489.4)	40,905 (1,596.1)	‡ (†)	57,250 (564.0)	52,060 (669.9)	60,416 (727.3)	60,782 (2,371.7)	‡ (†)
35 years or more	30,980 (2,515)	39,154 (888.3)	34,116 (1,258.6)	41,734 (1,115.7)	‡ (†)	‡ (†)	58,180 (1,320.0)	50,694 (1,869.7)	62,015 (1,657.9)	‡ (†)	‡ (†)
1993–94											
Total	2,329,730 (21,660)	$34,189 (90.5)	$30,152 (97.4)	$38,479 (154.4)	$40,680 (419.2)	$41,650 (1,328.9)	$46,529 (123.1)	$41,036 (132.5)	$52,367 (210.2)	$55,363 (570.5)	$56,683 (1,808.5)
1 year or less	105,540 (2,970)	23,637 (140.0)	23,024 (164.0)	26,956 (444.1)	28,470 (1,340.3)	‡ (†)	32,168 (190.5)	31,334 (223.1)	36,685 (604.4)	38,746 (1,824.0)	‡ (†)
2 years	95,880 (3,534)	24,401 (179.6)	23,688 (149.7)	27,202 (421.8)	25,185 (1,178.0)	‡ (†)	33,209 (244.4)	32,238 (203.7)	37,020 (574.1)	34,276 (1,603.2)	‡ (†)
3 years	87,840 (3,416)	25,305 (205.9)	24,286 (198.8)	29,981 (658.1)	28,731 (1,004.2)	‡ (†)	34,438 (280.2)	33,051 (270.5)	40,803 (895.7)	39,101 (1,366.6)	‡ (†)
4 years	98,760 (3,615)	26,320 (242.8)	25,164 (213.7)	30,200 (643.1)	‡ (†)	‡ (†)	35,820 (330.4)	34,247 (290.8)	41,100 (875.2)	‡ (†)	‡ (†)
5 years	90,470 (2,813)	27,136 (215.9)	25,845 (174.9)	30,106 (555.5)	30,639 (671.5)	‡ (†)	36,930 (293.9)	35,174 (238.1)	40,973 (756.0)	41,698 (913.9)	‡ (†)
6 to 9 years	306,960 (6,059)	29,167 (136.2)	27,122 (135.8)	32,241 (289.0)	34,341 (1,051.8)	32,167 (2,297.6)	39,694 (185.4)	36,911 (184.9)	43,879 (393.3)	46,735 (1,431.4)	43,777 (3,126.9)
10 to 14 years	362,360 (6,222)	32,289 (134.4)	29,751 (208.3)	34,733 (225.8)	37,316 (726.9)	39,625 (1,321.5)	43,943 (182.9)	40,489 (283.5)	47,269 (307.3)	50,785 (989.2)	53,927 (1,798.5)
15 to 19 years	372,480 (6,008)	36,107 (182.5)	33,267 (236.8)	38,355 (256.3)	38,647 (575.0)	40,310 (1,248.3)	49,139 (248.4)	45,274 (322.2)	52,199 (348.9)	52,596 (782.6)	54,859 (1,698.9)
20 to 24 years	407,660 (7,928)	39,620 (211.5)	36,536 (267.0)	41,358 (287.5)	43,563 (808.7)	46,126 (2,596.1)	53,921 (287.9)	49,724 (363.4)	56,285 (391.3)	59,287 (1,100.6)	62,775 (3,533.1)
25 to 29 years	264,520 (6,324)	42,833 (258.1)	38,802 (348.8)	45,011 (385.3)	45,977 (867.7)	53,684 (2,007.3)	58,293 (351.2)	52,807 (474.6)	61,257 (524.3)	62,571 (1,180.8)	73,060 (2,731.8)
30 to 34 years	105,460 (3,940)	43,558 (387.0)	39,502 (628.2)	45,434 (417.2)	49,519 (1,687.8)	‡ (†)	59,279 (526.7)	53,759 (855.0)	61,833 (567.7)	67,392 (2,297.0)	‡ (†)
35 years or more	31,790 (1,965)	42,799 (1,082.4)	37,379 (1,228.7)	46,016 (1,643.0)	45,004 (2,085.9)	‡ (†)	58,247 (1,473.1)	50,870 (1,672.2)	62,625 (2,236.0)	61,248 (2,838.8)	‡ (†)
1999–2000											
Total	2,742,210 (20,301)	$39,891 (118.2)	$35,306 (116.1)	$44,704 (173.7)	$47,987 (439.5)	$48,176 (1418.1)	$46,889 (139.0)	$41,499 (136.4)	$52,547 (204.2)	$56,406 (516.5)	$56,628 (1,666.9)
1 year or less	172,710 (5,492)	29,284 (165.6)	28,114 (149.8)	34,007 (446.1)	33,356 (1,009.0)	‡ (†)	34,421 (194.7)	33,046 (176.1)	39,973 (524.4)	39,208 (1,186.0)	‡ (†)
2 years	161,220 (5,678)	29,672 (179.2)	28,797 (165.0)	33,026 (404.2)	‡ (†)	‡ (†)	34,878 (210.6)	33,849 (194.0)	38,820 (475.1)	‡ (†)	‡ (†)
3 years	145,290 (4,630)	30,687 (169.2)	29,652 (198.8)	34,358 (369.6)	34,543 (1,340.6)	‡ (†)	36,071 (198.9)	34,854 (233.6)	40,386 (434.5)	40,603 (1,575.8)	‡ (†)
4 years	133,840 (5,657)	32,382 (257.9)	30,806 (232.5)	35,868 (665.4)	37,125 (1,354.4)	‡ (†)	38,063 (303.2)	36,210 (273.3)	42,160 (782.1)	43,638 (1,592.0)	‡ (†)
5 years	120,490 (4,300)	32,443 (253.3)	31,039 (287.1)	34,884 (392.2)	35,804 (1,915.2)	‡ (†)	38,135 (297.8)	36,484 (337.4)	41,004 (461.0)	42,086 (2,251.3)	‡ (†)
6 to 9 years	385,840 (8,205)	34,963 (167.2)	32,635 (190.5)	37,796 (240.2)	40,173 (836.2)	41,257 (2,301.6)	41,097 (196.6)	38,360 (223.9)	44,427 (282.3)	47,221 (982.9)	48,515 (2,704.6)
10 to 14 years	382,730 (6,298)	34,891 (257.1)	36,160 (190.5)	42,069 (334.5)	44,836 (987.8)	36,501 (2,312.8)	46,238 (302.2)	42,504 (453.8)	49,449 (393.2)	52,702 (1,161.1)	42,905 (2,718.5)
15 to 19 years	321,740 (8,067)	43,397 (224.8)	40,275 (318.1)	45,927 (356.5)	47,266 (916.3)	34,891 (872.2)	51,010 (264.3)	47,341 (373.9)	53,985 (419.0)	55,558 (1,077.0)	41,012 (1,025.2)
20 to 24 years	351,730 (6,993)	45,651 (263.8)	41,259 (278.7)	48,483 (383.2)	49,001 (1,054.8)	33,426 (1,318.8)	53,659 (310.1)	48,497 (327.6)	56,988 (450.4)	57,597 (1,239.8)	39,290 (1,550.2)
25 to 29 years	329,170 (7,167)	48,540 (276.2)	44,752 (333.0)	50,166 (398.5)	54,234 (968.0)	38,152 (2,437.3)	57,055 (324.6)	52,604 (391.5)	58,967 (468.5)	63,749 (1,137.8)	44,845 (2,864.9)
30 to 34 years	185,470 (5,488)	52,155 (345.9)	47,265 (634.0)	54,244 (440.8)	55,994 (1,126.0)	‡ (†)	61,304 (406.6)	55,557 (745.2)	63,761 (518.2)	65,817 (1,323.5)	‡ (†)
35 years or more	51,990 (3,006)	50,619 (672.9)	46,690 (1,359.3)	52,272 (923.3)	56,204 (2,797.3)	‡ (†)	59,499 (791.0)	54,881 (1,597.8)	61,442 (1,085.3)	66,065 (3,288.0)	‡ (†)

See notes at end of table.

Table 71. Average base salary for full-time teachers in public elementary and secondary schools, by highest degree earned and years of full-time teaching: Selected years, 1990–91 through 2003–04—Continued

Years of full-time teaching experience	Number of full-time teachers	Salary (current dollars)					Salary (constant 2005–06 dollars)[3]				
		Highest degree earned					Highest degree earned				
		All teachers[1]	Bachelor's degree	Master's degree	Education specialist[2]	Doctor's degree	All teachers[1]	Bachelor's degree	Master's degree	Education specialist[2]	Doctor's degree
1	2	3	4	5	6	7	8	9	10	11	12
2003–04											
Total	2,948,230 (28,203)	$44,358 (244.8)	$39,196 (299.7)	$49,437 (202.0)	$52,938 (458.1)	$53,745 (1,294.5)	$47,433 (261.7)	$41,913 (320.5)	$52,864 (216.0)	$56,607 (489.9)	$57,471 (1,384.3)
1 year or less	177,920 (17,391)	33,163 (381.3)	31,819 (341.9)	38,604 (731.8)	44,279 (5,029.7)	37,319 (1,690.3)	35,462 (407.7)	34,025 (365.6)	41,280 (782.6)	47,349 (5,378.4)	39,906 (1,807.5)
2 years	153,950 (17,695)	34,057 (284.2)	32,724 (333.9)	37,944 (645.9)	33,959 (1,299.0)	‡ (†)	36,417 (303.9)	34,993 (357.1)	40,574 (690.6)	36,313 (1,389.1)	‡ (†)
3 years	168,140 (9,009)	35,232 (349.1)	33,420 (282.3)	40,228 (682.6)	40,343 (3,172.5)	‡ (†)	37,674 (373.3)	35,737 (301.8)	43,017 (730.0)	43,139 (3,392.4)	‡ (†)
4 years	159,490 (6,723)	36,263 (265.4)	34,560 (279.1)	40,284 (529.5)	38,529 (1,798.6)	‡ (†)	38,777 (283.8)	36,956 (298.5)	43,076 (566.2)	41,200 (1,923.2)	‡ (†)
5 years	153,180 (6,194)	37,369 (403.1)	34,950 (324.5)	40,835 (762.7)	42,810 (1,956.8)	‡ (†)	39,960 (431.0)	37,373 (347.0)	43,666 (815.6)	45,778 (2,092.5)	‡ (†)
6 to 9 years	498,590 (13,859)	40,344 (200.5)	37,075 (208.9)	43,703 (299.6)	45,809 (1,308.4)	44,267 (2,320.6)	43,141 (214.4)	39,645 (223.4)	46,733 (320.3)	48,985 (1,399.1)	47,336 (2,481.4)
10 to 14 years	433,530 (14,595)	44,333 (257.0)	39,734 (267.4)	47,898 (392.8)	50,003 (956.2)	55,035 (3,584.3)	47,406 (274.8)	42,488 (286.0)	51,218 (420.0)	53,469 (1,022.5)	58,850 (3,832.7)
15 to 19 years	343,970 (9,606)	49,200 (356.1)	44,307 (481.7)	52,286 (469.1)	56,255 (1,349.4)	58,353 (3,442.6)	52,611 (380.8)	47,378 (515.1)	55,910 (501.6)	60,154 (1,442.9)	62,398 (3,681.2)
20 to 24 years	285,980 (8,434)	50,808 (362.3)	46,387 (374.5)	53,981 (582.7)	54,900 (998.6)	53,579 (3,530.9)	54,330 (387.4)	49,602 (400.4)	57,723 (623.1)	58,706 (1,067.9)	57,293 (3,775.6)
25 to 29 years	283,460 (11,809)	52,793 (280.7)	48,646 (487.9)	55,000 (411.3)	55,868 (975.3)	65,213 (3,524.3)	56,453 (300.2)	52,018 (521.7)	58,813 (439.9)	59,740 (1,042.9)	69,733 (3,768.7)
30 to 34 years	223,710 (11,435)	56,279 (427.6)	51,315 (606.2)	58,071 (565.8)	62,449 (1,389.0)	60,825 (2,663.7)	60,180 (457.3)	54,872 (648.2)	62,097 (605.0)	66,779 (1,485.2)	65,042 (2,848.4)
35 years or more	66,310 (3,427)	58,224 (754.6)	55,360 (1,296.4)	59,149 (978.2)	61,259 (2,224.2)	‡ (†)	62,260 (806.9)	59,197 (1,386.3)	63,249 (1,046.0)	65,505 (2,378.4)	‡ (†)

†Not applicable.
‡Reporting standards not met.
[1]Includes teachers with levels of education below the bachelor's degree (not shown separately).
[2]Includes certificate of advanced graduate studies.
[3]Constant dollars based on the Consumer Price Index, prepared by the Bureau of Labor Statistics, U.S. Department of Labor, adjusted to a school-year basis.

NOTE: This table includes regular full-time teachers only; it excludes other staff even when they have full-time teaching duties (regular part-time teachers, itinerant teachers, long-term substitutes, administrators, library media specialists, other professional staff, and support staff). Some data have been revised from previously published figures. Detail may not sum to totals because of rounding. Standard errors appear in parentheses.

SOURCE: U.S. Department of Education, National Center for Education Statistics, Schools and Staffing Survey (SASS), "Public Teacher Questionnaire," 1990–91, 1993–94, 1999–2000, and 2003–04; and "Charter Teacher Questionnaire," 1999–2000. (This table was prepared September 2006.)

Table 72. Average salaries for full-time teachers in public and private elementary and secondary schools, by selected characteristics: 2003–04

Selected characteristic	Total earned income	Base salary	Number of full-time teachers (in thousands)	School year supplemental contract[1]		Supplemental contract during summer		Number of teachers with nonschool employment (in thousands)		
				Number of teachers (in thousands)	Supplemental salary	Number of teachers (in thousands)	Supplemental salary	Teaching or tutor	Education related	Not education related
1	2	3	4	5	6	7	8	9	10	11
Public schools										
Total	$47,700 (240)	$44,400 (240)	2,948.2 (28.20)	1,185.9 (19.67)	$2,700 (60)	605.2 (14.05)	$2,500 (60)	120.8 (5.18)	83.7 (4.06)	263.9 (6.67)
Sex										
Males	51,000 (370)	45,000 (330)	750.5 (12.74)	426.6 (10.40)	3,700 (70)	183.0 (7.28)	3,000 (80)	37.1 (2.89)	36.0 (1.96)	120.1 (4.40)
Females	46,600 (240)	44,100 (250)	2,197.7 (22.90)	759.3 (14.53)	2,200 (80)	422.2 (11.16)	2,300 (60)	83.7 (3.86)	47.8 (3.36)	143.7 (4.95)
Race/ethnicity										
White	47,800 (270)	44,500 (280)	2,439.3 (29.86)	994.0 (17.73)	2,800 (70)	467.5 (11.87)	2,400 (60)	104.3 (4.72)	73.0 (3.77)	229.0 (5.70)
Black	46,600 (420)	43,300 (410)	241.2 (9.63)	85.7 (4.46)	2,400 (140)	68.4 (4.93)	3,000 (170)	9.5 (1.04)	5.7 (1.00)	17.0 (1.88)
Hispanic	47,400 (660)	44,000 (600)	187.7 (10.36)	78.5 (6.78)	2,400 (230)	51.2 (5.42)	2,500 (120)	4.1 (0.98)	3.4 (0.81)	11.5 (1.86)
Asian	49,000 (740)	46,800 (770)	38.0 (2.37)	11.3 (1.09)	2,600 (310)	8.5 (1.10)	2,500 (190)	1.3 (0.33)	0.5 (0.11)	2.0 (0.43)
American Indian/Alaska Native	42,600 (1,110)	39,300 (1,020)	15.0 (1.16)	6.5 (0.71)	2,900 (600)	3.8 (0.73)	1,900 (240)	0.4 (0.15)	0.5 (0.29)	1.7 (0.38)
Pacific Islander	46,600 (1,450)	42,800 (1,220)	5.1 (0.68)	2.2 (0.47)	3,000 (780)	1.6 (0.30)	2,400 (280)	0.4 (0.19)	0.2 (0.08)	0.4 (0.12)
More than one race	45,600 (1,570)	42,600 (1,390)	21.9 (2.09)	7.7 (1.16)	2,500 (220)	4.1 (0.95)	2,400 (290)	0.8 (0.31)	0.4 (0.18)	2.2 (0.53)
Age										
Less than 30	37,800 (300)	34,600 (280)	493.2 (21.85)	228.1 (9.75)	2,300 (80)	126.6 (8.42)	2,400 (110)	22.2 (2.44)	12.0 (1.81)	51.4 (4.28)
30 to 39	43,800 (220)	40,300 (220)	724.5 (13.52)	324.8 (9.14)	2,900 (120)	154.7 (6.97)	2,400 (80)	27.6 (2.52)	19.4 (1.57)	65.3 (4.38)
40 to 49	48,700 (250)	45,400 (200)	756.5 (14.12)	294.9 (8.76)	2,900 (170)	145.6 (5.15)	2,500 (80)	32.7 (2.48)	25.7 (1.88)	68.2 (3.44)
50 or more	54,700 (250)	51,500 (230)	973.9 (27.38)	338.1 (11.50)	2,800 (100)	178.3 (8.03)	2,700 (90)	38.3 (2.82)	26.6 (2.94)	78.9 (3.04)
Years of full-time and part-time teaching experience										
1 year or less	36,500 (500)	32,600 (410)	151.6 (15.47)	53.0 (4.81)	1,800 (100)	28.7 (4.42)	3,300 (400)	4.6 (1.02)	3.0 (0.61)	19.0 (2.82)
2 to 4 years	37,800 (240)	34,800 (200)	464.7 (26.82)	197.4 (11.10)	2,300 (90)	115.2 (9.08)	2,400 (80)	17.6 (2.36)	10.7 (1.49)	45.2 (4.03)
5 to 9 years	42,700 (190)	39,400 (160)	641.1 (16.17)	284.3 (10.62)	2,600 (120)	148.4 (7.22)	2,400 (80)	29.7 (3.01)	17.0 (1.55)	64.3 (3.48)
10 to 14 years	47,000 (300)	43,800 (260)	438.6 (14.16)	178.3 (7.17)	2,900 (140)	88.9 (6.03)	2,300 (100)	20.2 (2.58)	11.8 (1.46)	33.3 (2.29)
15 to 19 years	51,900 (410)	48,700 (360)	346.2 (10.03)	133.2 (5.40)	2,800 (210)	56.7 (3.15)	2,500 (140)	13.3 (1.76)	11.2 (1.40)	26.6 (2.01)
20 or more years	56,800 (230)	53,400 (200)	906.0 (26.90)	339.7 (10.80)	3,100 (130)	167.3 (6.99)	2,600 (90)	35.5 (2.31)	30.0 (2.41)	75.5 (3.67)
Level										
Elementary	46,700 (330)	44,400 (330)	1,522.7 (23.56)	461.2 (12.53)	2,100 (120)	304.7 (10.02)	2,200 (70)	52.9 (3.21)	32.7 (3.44)	106.2 (5.70)
Secondary	48,700 (260)	44,300 (250)	1,425.6 (24.05)	724.7 (15.05)	3,100 (70)	300.6 (8.62)	2,800 (70)	67.9 (3.86)	51.0 (2.26)	157.7 (4.79)
Private schools										
Total	$34,700 (1,910)	$31,700 (1,630)	366.5 (11.87)	84.6 (7.07)	$2,400 (130)	74.3 (3.97)	$3,100 (250)	24.5 (2.10)	12.7 (2.01)	37.1 (3.73)
Sex										
Males	40,800 (650)	35,200 (580)	84.6 (6.15)	30.6 (2.45)	2,800 (200)	24.3 (2.25)	3,700 (320)	7.4 (0.92)	4.1 (0.68)	16.0 (1.80)
Females	32,800 (2,260)	30,600 (2,020)	281.9 (13.40)	53.9 (5.23)	2,200 (190)	50.0 (3.49)	2,800 (320)	17.1 (1.59)	8.6 (1.55)	21.2 (3.50)
Race/ethnicity										
White	34,600 (2,140)	31,700 (1,880)	322.1 (11.91)	75.5 (6.49)	2,300 (140)	61.0 (3.77)	3,100 (310)	21.6 (1.95)	11.6 (1.99)	33.4 (3.71)
Black	31,500 (1,240)	27,900 (1,000)	15.7 (2.46)	2.3 (0.48)	2,200 (450)	5.0 (1.14)	3,000 (780)	0.7 (0.25)	0.5 (0.25)	1.3 (0.43)
Hispanic	35,700 (1,660)	32,000 (1,270)	16.6 (2.01)	4.0 (0.79)	3,600 (930)	4.7 (0.87)	3,600 (390)	1.5 (0.39)	0.3 (0.17)	1.5 (0.45)
Asian	37,300 (3,350)	34,500 (2,650)	6.8 (0.84)	1.1 (0.27)	1,900 (490)	2.1 (0.42)	3,200 (860)	0.4 (0.24)	0.2 (0.25)	0.5 (0.20)
American Indian/Alaska Native	35,800 (4,230)	31,900 (3,150)	1.7 (1.94)	0.5 (0.34)	‡ (†)	0.5 (0.55)	‡ (†)	0.1 (0.04)	‡ (†)	0.1 (0.07)
Pacific Islander	‡ (†)	‡ (†)	‡ (†)	‡ (†)	‡ (†)	‡ (†)	‡ (†)	‡ (†)	‡ (†)	‡ (†)
More than one race	38,600 (3,410)	36,900 (3,460)	2.7 (1.20)	1.0 (0.31)	‡ (†)	0.4 (0.20)	‡ (†)	0.1 (0.10)	‡ (†)	0.3 (0.14)

See notes at end of table.

Table 72. Average salaries for full-time teachers in public and private elementary and secondary schools, by selected characteristics: 2003–04—Continued

Selected characteristic	Total earned income		Base salary		Number of full-time teachers (in thousands)		School year supplemental contract[1]				Supplemental contract during summer				Number of teachers with nonschool employment (in thousands)		
							Number of teachers (in thousands)		Supplemental salary		Number of teachers (in thousands)		Supplemental salary		Teaching or tutor	Education related	Not education related
1	2		3		4		5		6		7		8		9	10	11
Age																	
Less than 30	29,100	(640)	25,900	(520)	74.6	(3.20)	20.2	(1.64)	2,300	(250)	19.6	(1.60)	2,700	(180)	6.6 (0.92)	2.7 (0.41)	10.0 (1.19)
30 to 39	33,200	(740)	30,100	(720)	80.3	(5.65)	19.7	(1.76)	2,500	(280)	17.6	(1.95)	3,100	(290)	5.3 (0.99)	2.9 (0.54)	8.7 (2.97)
40 to 49	34,600	(1,770)	31,900	(1,420)	88.4	(4.94)	21.5	(2.82)	2,400	(230)	17.8	(3.94)	3,000	(660)	4.9 (0.66)	2.7 (0.78)	8.4 (1.17)
50 or more	39,000	(4,480)	36,000	(3,990)	123.2	(12.45)	23.1	(2.91)	2,400	(240)	19.4	(2.19)	3,800	(380)	7.7 (1.22)	4.4 (0.87)	10.0 (1.42)
Years of full-time and part-time teaching experience																	
1 year or less	28,100	(1,100)	24,700	(1,040)	24.6	(3.43)	4.7	(0.68)	2,000	(320)	5.6	(0.81)	3,400	(540)	‡ (†)	‡ (†)	3.6 (2.36)
2 to 4 years	29,400	(2,930)	26,100	(2,430)	78.4	(14.11)	18.8	(1.67)	2,000	(310)	18.8	(1.67)	2,900	(220)	5.7 (0.83)	2.5 (0.42)	10.2 (1.19)
5 to 9 years	32,100	(880)	29,500	(780)	77.6	(3.94)	17.7	(2.10)	2,600	(340)	17.0	(1.91)	2,800	(200)	6.4 (1.02)	3.1 (0.70)	7.4 (1.70)
10 to 14 years	34,600	(3,070)	31,800	(2,680)	53.0	(5.17)	13.9	(2.34)	2,400	(280)	10.4	(1.46)	3,400	(450)	3.4 (0.76)	1.9 (0.50)	4.3 (0.84)
15 to 19 years	37,900	(4,030)	35,300	(3,690)	42.6	(3.78)	10.5	(1.61)	2,600	(340)	8.8	(3.73)	3,100	(1,110)	2.2 (0.47)	‡ (†)	3.5 (0.74)
20 or more years	41,700	(920)	38,500	(680)	90.3	(7.21)	19.0	(2.47)	2,700	(300)	13.7	(1.59)	3,600	(480)	6.0 (1.06)	3.2 (0.79)	8.2 (1.17)
Level																	
Elementary	31,400	(2,640)	29,200	(2,380)	209.9	(13.87)	30.1	(3.72)	2,200	(220)	37.0	(3.14)	2,900	(410)	12.3 (1.29)	6.2 (0.98)	17.5 (3.08)
Secondary	39,000	(730)	35,000	(570)	156.5	(9.42)	54.5	(4.01)	2,500	(180)	37.3	(3.37)	3,300	(250)	12.2 (1.35)	6.5 (1.22)	19.7 (1.87)

†Not applicable.
‡Reporting standards not met.
[1]Includes additional compensation for extracurricular instruction or other additional activities, and bonuses and state supplements.
NOTE: This table includes regular full-time teachers only; it excludes other staff even when they have full-time teaching duties (regular part-time teachers, long-term substitutes, itinerant teachers, administrators, library media specialists, other professional staff, and support staff). Race categories exclude persons of Hispanic origin. Standard errors appear in parentheses. Detail may not sum to totals because of rounding, missing values in cells with too few cases to report, and survey item nonresponse.
SOURCE: U.S. Department of Education, National Center for Education Statistics, Schools and Staffing Survey (SASS), "Public Teacher Questionnaire" and "Private Teacher Questionnaire," 2003–04. (This table was prepared July 2006.)

Table 73. Average base salary for full-time public elementary and secondary school teachers with a bachelor's degree as their highest degree, by years of full-time teaching experience and state: 1993–94, 1999–2000, and 2003–04

State	1993–94			1999–2000			2003–04					
	Total	2 or fewer years	Over 20 years	Total	2 or fewer years	Over 20 years	Total	2 or fewer years	3 to 5 years	6 to 10 years	11 to 20 years	Over 20 years
1	2	3	4	5	6	7	8	9	10	11	12	13
United States	$30,150 (97)	$23,330 (98)	$38,090 (205)	$35,310 (116)	$28,450 (109)	$44,130 (230)	$39,200 (300)	$32,230 (290)	$34,240 (151)	$37,330 (204)	$42,540 (265)	$49,130 (327)
Alabama	24,450 (151)	22,220 (209)	26,110 (391)	31,300 (210)	28,280 (142)	33,840 (568)	32,750 (256)	29,640 (291)	30,930 (414)	32,590 (537)	36,180 (613)	37,610 (663)
Alaska	42,620 (308)	32,180 (251)	49,930 (669)	42,170 (269)	34,110 (290)	52,080 (480)	46,160 (720)	37,290 (1,113)	39,820 (638)	44,460 (968)	51,770 (1,019)	58,760 (943)
Arizona	28,050 (347)	22,590 (168)	35,180 (1,127)	30,110 (491)	25,020 (303)	44,110 (1,273)	33,370 (556)	29,510 (408)	30,920 (474)	32,180 (511)	36,150 (870)	44,060 (1,469)
Arkansas	24,970 (199)	20,680 (222)	28,350 (367)	29,810 (345)	25,780 (699)	34,110 (732)	32,710 (328)	26,590 (694)	29,350 (412)	32,110 (472)	35,440 (564)	38,080 (803)
California	37,330 (412)	27,710 (470)	44,920 (424)	31,930 (301)	32,820 (321)	53,250 (656)	51,210 (704)	38,920 (679)	42,830 (666)	49,460 (635)	57,860 (833)	63,110 (1,045)
Colorado	27,590 (391)	21,190 (318)	34,960 (958)	32,180 (428)	25,400 (252)	41,340 (776)	36,140 (699)	30,570 (534)	31,610 (488)	35,260 (875)	41,850 (1,215)	45,480 (2,188)
Connecticut	40,510 (645)	‡ (†)	50,470 (814)	38,530 (883)	32,030 (344)	‡ (†)	48,380 (1,997)	37,800 (820)	40,590 (1,951)	44,360 (3,208)	48,350 (994)	‡ (†)
Delaware	31,400 (375)	‡ (†)	‡ (†)	37,620 (893)	‡ (†)	‡ (†)	41,210 (991)	‡ (†)	35,880 (887)	‡ (†)	56,670 (1,684)	‡ (†)
District of Columbia	37,690 (645)	‡ (†)	‡ (†)	40,980 (593)	‡ (†)	‡ (†)	48,350 (1,290)	‡ (†)	40,850 (1,228)	‡ (†)	‡ (†)	47,040 (843)
Florida	28,970 (229)	23,570 (308)	35,950 (514)	33,650 (407)	27,440 (314)	41,990 (570)	36,460 (624)	31,140 (612)	30,650 (367)	32,250 (345)	38,490 (650)	‡ (†)
Georgia	25,650 (215)	22,100 (441)	29,940 (507)	33,610 (373)	29,410 (287)	38,730 (747)	37,160 (490)	32,220 (424)	34,590 (621)	37,540 (574)	40,840 (808)	45,020 (1,010)
Hawaii	34,060 (460)	24,940 (277)	43,990 (428)	36,710 (533)	27,370 (299)	49,690 (691)	35,430 (887)	32,620 (781)	35,430 (794)	37,430 (759)	42,240 (858)	52,650 (1,779)
Idaho	24,610 (252)	19,080 (281)	30,160 (573)	31,500 (208)	22,880 (245)	38,310 (294)	36,150 (627)	26,060 (579)	28,010 (730)	34,190 (843)	39,390 (757)	45,330 (794)
Illinois	29,480 (277)	23,430 (658)	36,520 (583)	35,250 (563)	28,230 (398)	43,610 (1,139)	38,730 (790)	33,180 (1,047)	32,630 (718)	36,190 (888)	42,290 (2,250)	49,120 (1,797)
Indiana	25,400 (329)	22,770 (194)	‡ (†)	30,760 (296)	27,360 (186)	34,600 (640)	34,600 (606)	30,270 (337)	32,630 (599)	35,700 (643)	43,630 (1,343)	‡ (†)
Iowa	24,950 (319)	19,530 (242)	27,960 (664)	28,910 (279)	23,150 (253)	33,470 (430)	33,600 (696)	26,140 (457)	30,200 (3,349)	31,610 (827)	35,280 (813)	37,580 (840)
Kansas	25,930 (135)	22,850 (229)	29,330 (423)	29,430 (264)	26,110 (261)	33,250 (636)	32,290 (326)	28,500 (447)	29,940 (376)	30,810 (513)	33,770 (631)	36,990 (597)
Kentucky	24,910 (457)	21,620 (243)	‡ (†)	27,720 (358)	24,650 (168)	‡ (†)	31,610 (468)	28,490 (195)	30,030 (466)	33,360 (785)	‡ (†)	‡ (†)
Louisiana	22,520 (159)	18,470 (326)	27,590 (498)	28,020 (476)	24,620 (943)	32,300 (1,002)	32,590 (489)	28,380 (693)	28,450 (513)	31,340 (431)	34,540 (616)	39,200 (646)
Maine	28,550 (330)	20,080 (350)	33,670 (270)	34,690 (775)	27,390 (2,511)	37,570 (531)	36,650 (606)	27,300 (1,078)	28,310 (860)	32,670 (846)	38,590 (794)	43,490 (1,062)
Maryland	33,520 (476)	25,510 (239)	35,180 (456)	37,760 (683)	28,900 (337)	50,340 (597)	42,960 (1,313)	34,100 (381)	36,740 (502)	40,290 (764)	49,250 (3,755)	62,750 (2,717)
Massachusetts	34,340 (309)	24,690 (514)	37,410 (342)	40,410 (464)	29,950 (454)	46,600 (591)	43,930 (964)	35,830 (1,124)	38,620 (700)	44,450 (2,205)	48,570 (1,045)	54,780 (1,331)
Michigan	37,170 (670)	26,700 (947)	45,000 (1,000)	39,950 (838)	30,760 (457)	50,030 (608)	45,230 (682)	35,340 (693)	39,450 (911)	44,540 (1,078)	54,200 (1,107)	55,950 (1,245)
Minnesota	31,010 (419)	23,540 (629)	36,660 (652)	35,270 (685)	28,770 (783)	44,160 (962)	39,030 (566)	31,560 (761)	33,220 (541)	35,560 (469)	43,560 (660)	47,350 (783)
Mississippi	22,640 (106)	19,660 (138)	25,220 (170)	28,000 (186)	24,080 (218)	31,490 (300)	31,890 (425)	27,110 (306)	28,490 (316)	30,440 (659)	33,430 (557)	37,990 (555)
Missouri	23,510 (286)	20,340 (345)	28,110 (821)	28,020 (378)	24,940 (513)	30,550 (525)	31,340 (547)	27,220 (593)	29,540 (542)	31,440 (953)	34,190 (1,312)	36,040 (1,953)
Montana	24,070 (199)	18,720 (156)	29,940 (422)	27,920 (256)	21,080 (252)	34,110 (521)	31,870 (521)	21,870 (382)	25,240 (505)	28,110 (538)	34,620 (685)	38,530 (837)
Nebraska	22,580 (388)	18,760 (361)	25,460 (790)	26,090 (254)	21,940 (215)	28,990 (619)	30,300 (435)	26,790 (590)	27,970 (478)	28,970 (522)	32,590 (803)	33,690 (1,329)
Nevada	29,350 (285)	23,900 (291)	27,480 (755)	34,470 (434)	27,550 (293)	45,270 (895)	35,970 (700)	29,220 (632)	32,020 (420)	36,350 (529)	42,040 (1,042)	46,470 (1,091)
New Hampshire	31,280 (437)	‡ (†)	38,150 (519)	34,210 (542)	25,790 (974)	40,480 (609)	38,800 (644)	28,880 (649)	31,460 (509)	36,260 (878)	42,850 (1,070)	‡ (†)
New Jersey	41,330 (744)	29,730 (479)	52,340 (770)	46,740 (653)	33,810 (290)	61,340 (698)	49,780 (1,049)	38,810 (616)	40,180 (878)	41,420 (614)	51,340 (1,569)	67,380 (1,456)
New Mexico	25,260 (224)	21,680 (280)	31,400 (383)	29,290 (363)	25,700 (321)	38,260 (1,106)	34,310 (470)	28,830 (752)	31,270 (426)	31,780 (439)	36,960 (559)	42,300 (930)
New York	39,650 (1,152)	27,790 (360)	52,140 (698)	41,600 (1,094)	33,250 (654)	55,630 (2,100)	43,650 (1,074)	37,410 (1,058)	37,860 (838)	‡ (†)	36,970 (561)	61,240 (1,827)
North Carolina	26,010 (220)	20,810 (182)	32,520 (273)	31,920 (331)	25,380 (510)	36,560 (500)	33,650 (479)	26,930 (566)	29,020 (633)	32,560 (465)	32,420 (553)	43,830 (730)
North Dakota	22,450 (193)	17,830 (282)	26,060 (512)	25,910 (279)	20,640 (297)	29,730 (461)	30,870 (490)	23,810 (613)	26,600 (669)	28,780 (617)	‡ (†)	33,500 (660)
Ohio	30,370 (399)	22,010 (312)	35,420 (653)	35,120 (583)	25,730 (400)	43,640 (1,019)	41,600 (891)	30,430 (474)	33,460 (626)	39,340 (666)	47,660 (878)	52,220 (1,061)
Oklahoma	24,880 (108)	22,190 (198)	28,500 (325)	27,400 (224)	24,510 (179)	31,770 (566)	31,190 (211)	27,330 (456)	28,650 (276)	29,600 (158)	31,970 (236)	35,700 (260)
Oregon	31,310 (440)	22,440 (470)	36,960 (769)	38,370 (613)	27,350 (418)	44,180 (1,299)	42,430 (865)	‡ (†)	34,170 (1,154)	38,200 (1,628)	45,670 (768)	51,340 (880)
Pennsylvania	37,260 (523)	26,690 (435)	44,790 (634)	42,620 (826)	28,940 (894)	44,710 (932)	49,360 (834)	33,030 (630)	34,870 (963)	41,360 (1,062)	47,890 (1,351)	57,450 (993)
Rhode Island	38,000 (522)	‡ (†)	42,530 (268)	43,900 (357)	‡ (†)	52,310 (259)	‡ (†)	‡ (†)	40,930 (885)	48,890 (1,514)	‡ (†)	58,910 (741)
South Carolina	25,120 (280)	20,440 (151)	30,550 (526)	29,820 (300)	25,220 (175)	37,380 (538)	34,950 (483)	28,610 (1,161)	29,810 (284)	32,810 (423)	38,810 (552)	42,630 (682)
South Dakota	22,000 (186)	18,410 (303)	25,440 (386)	26,000 (230)	23,160 (826)	28,670 (307)	29,360 (301)	24,980 (437)	26,350 (289)	27,700 (536)	30,170 (381)	32,420 (493)
Tennessee	25,650 (291)	21,880 (297)	28,850 (557)	30,830 (378)	27,740 (386)	34,670 (1,188)	34,510 (432)	29,690 (624)	32,110 (922)	32,880 (591)	37,010 (794)	39,100 (756)
Texas	26,950 (295)	21,820 (295)	33,310 (476)	34,770 (386)	29,010 (322)	42,140 (458)	38,140 (278)	33,440 (564)	34,870 (362)	36,140 (315)	39,880 (333)	46,710 (455)
Utah	25,800 (195)	19,170 (223)	31,220 (356)	31,810 (375)	24,530 (271)	39,790 (691)	35,160 (525)	26,140 (259)	29,050 (511)	33,740 (327)	40,820 (753)	45,390 (679)
Vermont	29,750 (494)	24,940 (310)	36,030 (873)	33,470 (733)	25,530 (671)	41,060 (1,235)	39,040 (840)	‡ (†)	31,850 (775)	36,680 (3,075)	39,490 (935)	46,720 (919)
Virginia	29,410 (378)	23,190 (273)	35,160 (584)	34,060 (424)	28,420 (311)	42,370 (1,270)	37,520 (583)	31,990 (556)	33,240 (570)	35,390 (734)	37,840 (767)	45,760 (1,595)
Washington	33,150 (490)	‡ (†)	40,640 (390)	34,040 (359)	26,770 (233)	45,480 (368)	40,040 (916)	31,010 (610)	36,470 (801)	36,470 (563)	45,630 (1,170)	49,840 (1,000)
West Virginia	26,980 (183)	‡ (†)	29,090 (272)	30,040 (246)	‡ (†)	32,630 (284)	32,980 (344)	‡ (†)	32,640 (603)	31,240 (562)	34,030 (500)	35,910 (320)
Wisconsin	31,490 (351)	24,220 (249)	36,130 (773)	35,470 (331)	27,800 (194)	42,710 (696)	37,150 (634)	29,630 (479)	32,650 (658)	35,360 (697)	42,880 (829)	44,200 (1,291)
Wyoming	27,310 (247)	20,900 (137)	32,170 (448)	29,470 (248)	23,760 (266)	34,210 (487)	34,080 (576)	28,270 (1,408)	29,290 (685)	30,850 (724)	36,680 (1,120)	39,190 (1,900)

†Not applicable.

‡Reporting standards not met.

NOTE: This table includes regular full-time teachers only; it excludes other staff even when they have full-time teaching duties (regular part-time teachers, itinerant teachers, long-term substitutes, administrators, library media specialists, other professional staff, and support staff). Standard errors appear in parentheses.

SOURCE: U.S. Department of Education, National Center for Education Statistics, Schools and Staffing Survey (SASS), "Public School Teacher Questionnaire," 1993–94, 1999–2000, and 2003–04; and "Public Charter School Teacher Questionnaire," 1999–2000. (This table was prepared July 2006.)

Table 74. Average base salary for full-time public elementary and secondary school teachers with a master's degree as their highest degree, by years of full-time teaching experience and state: 1993–94, 1999–2000, and 2003–04

State	1993–94			1999–2000			2003–04				
	Total	6 to 10 years	Over 20 years	Total	6 to 10 years	Over 20 years	Total	5 or fewer years	6 to 10 years	11 to 20 years	Over 20 years
1	2	3	4	5	6	7	8	9	10	11	12
United States	$38,480 (154)	$32,600 (243)	$43,690 (242)	$44,700 (174)	$38,350 (237)	$50,760 (262)	$49,440 (202)	$39,790 (373)	$44,410 (281)	$50,770 (291)	$55,960 (303)
Alabama	28,920 (156)	28,160 (262)	29,930 (253)	36,930 (145)	35,790 (298)	38,870 (215)	39,730 (383)	34,140 (547)	38,370 (329)	40,980 (365)	42,870 (779)
Alaska	50,900 (373)	44,950 (826)	54,420 (526)	51,170 (662)	43,940 (576)	58,670 (860)	53,720 (1,005)	43,450 (1,112)	50,560 (1,420)	57,170 (1,064)	60,760 (1,387)
Arizona	35,280 (302)	29,840 (346)	40,670 (458)	38,150 (465)	33,130 (568)	45,050 (691)	41,310 (531)	34,210 (928)	37,850 (477)	43,230 (878)	46,850 (1,268)
Arkansas	29,070 (322)	25,360 (495)	30,890 (592)	34,830 (483)	‡	38,740 (666)	39,480 (639)	33,580 (907)	33,970 (1,210)	38,030 (737)	44,920 (912)
California	43,420 (636)	38,190 (617)	47,760 (439)	50,800 (537)	44,820 (766)	56,960 (572)	59,160 (761)	44,980 (909)	54,150 (819)	62,590 (1,089)	69,990 (999)
Colorado	36,580 (364)	30,050 (381)	41,650 (664)	41,200 (445)	37,350 (766)	47,410 (721)	47,960 (641)	‡	42,330 (1,012)	49,560 (1,098)	55,610 (1,307)
Connecticut	49,310 (416)	43,420 (1,028)	54,360 (386)	50,620 (590)	43,240 (795)	59,920 (604)	57,340 (934)	43,290 (945)	50,720 (810)	61,590 (1,488)	66,970 (743)
Delaware	42,350 (535)	‡	46,460 (480)	48,120 (910)	‡	55,520 (1,366)	54,670 (913)	‡	46,820 (1,061)	57,730 (1,174)	63,070 (1,148)
District of Columbia	45,360 (828)	‡	50,710 (228)	51,040 (472)	‡	54,750 (451)	55,450 (1,568)	43,680 (1,813)	‡	60,080 (1,467)	63,570 (2,537)
Florida	33,150 (487)	28,830 (494)	38,010 (645)	39,330 (476)	32,340 (468)	44,940 (583)	42,120 (784)	33,570 (834)	35,420 (1,016)	41,340 (939)	49,860 (1,027)
Georgia	31,890 (227)	28,930 (453)	36,040 (329)	41,950 (524)	38,130 (581)	47,230 (475)	47,540 (752)	40,490 (1,121)	44,100 (418)	50,200 (1,090)	52,370 (1,322)
Hawaii	36,430 (731)	‡	43,230 (886)	39,280 (524)	‡	42,910 (967)	42,910 (967)	37,550 (1,179)	‡	45,940 (1,377)	‡
Idaho	31,590 (440)	‡	34,140 (654)	42,380 (772)	‡	48,950 (1,559)	44,140 (857)	‡	38,380 (1,648)	45,930 (1,166)	48,580 (1,249)
Illinois	42,400 (588)	34,390 (692)	47,370 (886)	47,470 (953)	41,850 (1,166)	55,180 (1,087)	54,110 (1,253)	42,590 (2,237)	46,450 (1,114)	54,320 (2,228)	61,560 (1,612)
Indiana	38,040 (292)	31,170 (450)	41,560 (279)	45,480 (413)	36,090 (451)	49,420 (362)	45,480 (670)	‡	48,030 (919)	49,090 (1,004)	53,650 (576)
Iowa	32,220 (571)	‡	34,820 (763)	38,010 (494)	33,960 (1,468)	39,340 (714)	41,880 (608)	‡	37,140 (1,001)	42,940 (1,159)	43,880 (900)
Kansas	32,560 (314)	27,710 (339)	35,800 (485)	36,140 (428)	31,990 (622)	38,480 (502)	40,400 (755)	‡	34,940 (963)	40,120 (1,667)	43,700 (912)
Kentucky	31,390 (396)	27,180 (283)	35,140 (359)	36,380 (310)	32,810 (305)	41,260 (481)	40,570 (457)	35,310 (1,064)	37,440 (325)	41,040 (555)	45,610 (913)
Louisiana	27,300 (262)	22,800 (555)	29,500 (361)	33,120 (806)	‡	35,150 (1,051)	38,000 (558)	‡	‡	36,750 (769)	40,860 (828)
Maine	33,060 (499)	28,440 (653)	36,150 (255)	38,770 (458)	‡	42,340 (442)	42,460 (677)	29,830 (991)	36,100 (1,355)	43,780 (753)	47,860 (840)
Maryland	42,340 (406)	36,410 (689)	46,080 (575)	45,930 (1,055)	38,280 (736)	51,740 (900)	51,540 (1,307)	41,540 (1,215)	49,710 (4,001)	51,790 (1,561)	63,410 (1,462)
Massachusetts	39,710 (254)	34,790 (791)	42,330 (247)	47,630 (370)	41,960 (680)	52,390 (334)	53,500 (714)	42,360 (694)	48,280 (823)	56,090 (1,168)	61,270 (670)
Michigan	47,660 (488)	40,280 (1,312)	44,690 (482)	53,050 (651)	46,020 (968)	59,050 (1,034)	59,680 (906)	47,670 (2,452)	53,680 (1,813)	61,720 (1,073)	65,900 (1,194)
Minnesota	40,710 (552)	33,300 (1,049)	44,890 (475)	46,050 (674)	40,420 (1,136)	51,980 (1,175)	49,590 (731)	38,670 (953)	53,490 (621)	51,850 (1,136)	57,090 (1,137)
Mississippi	26,600 (200)	24,200 (382)	28,890 (301)	34,170 (326)	29,040 (271)	38,460 (348)	38,460 (479)	30,810 (1,013)	33,710 (594)	37,660 (629)	44,060 (571)
Missouri	33,180 (625)	27,370 (763)	38,290 (1,002)	37,400 (747)	31,650 (1,028)	44,150 (1,067)	40,880 (761)	34,170 (1,020)	37,090 (1,071)	40,160 (1,011)	46,110 (1,604)
Montana	32,270 (423)	26,250 (684)	35,390 (393)	35,960 (728)	28,230 (508)	41,050 (1,237)	39,650 (885)	‡	‡	40,740 (796)	43,280 (1,218)
Nebraska	30,290 (538)	27,380 (1,109)	32,430 (903)	33,540 (536)	28,580 (667)	37,420 (936)	39,980 (784)	29,930 (1,322)	35,740 (1,248)	38,990 (1,233)	44,380 (1,023)
Nevada	38,570 (353)	‡	42,530 (571)	43,350 (429)	‡	49,500 (575)	45,770 (1,083)	36,130 (904)	44,120 (3,641)	48,050 (1,174)	49,900 (922)
New Hampshire	36,970 (505)	31,540 (889)	40,880 (595)	41,310 (689)	‡	46,210 (660)	45,140 (977)	35,580 (1,185)	‡	49,800 (1,003)	52,340 (636)
New Jersey	50,950 (883)	39,430 (1,132)	58,160 (821)	57,410 (709)	‡	65,640 (670)	60,200 (1,571)	43,310 (799)	45,980 (962)	58,500 (2,452)	76,020 (1,723)
New Mexico	28,400 (281)	25,290 (476)	33,180 (477)	35,570 (539)	30,590 (835)	40,060 (742)	40,100 (810)	33,060 (1,387)	34,170 (572)	40,600 (759)	48,440 (1,013)
New York	47,440 (840)	37,930 (892)	58,710 (1,127)	53,130 (923)	42,590 (884)	66,450 (1,150)	56,650 (746)	45,710 (995)	50,450 (1,119)	61,290 (1,401)	67,470 (1,703)
North Carolina	29,180 (306)	25,350 (343)	33,390 (624)	36,810 (542)	33,780 (725)	41,890 (756)	42,720 (641)	33,670 (1,342)	36,440 (778)	43,620 (1,043)	48,390 (644)
North Dakota	28,520 (730)	‡	31,040 (1,162)	32,920 (559)	‡	35,380 (828)	39,710 (789)	‡	‡	39,620 (1,242)	43,130 (1,234)
Ohio	37,960 (550)	31,420 (1,307)	41,490 (766)	43,420 (585)	35,820 (1,054)	48,710 (836)	50,090 (689)	39,170 (1,098)	43,810 (692)	53,480 (1,108)	55,920 (852)
Oklahoma	28,510 (186)	25,430 (339)	30,460 (286)	31,990 (261)	28,260 (333)	34,280 (458)	34,580 (319)	29,280 (818)	31,370 (329)	33,700 (401)	38,060 (351)
Oregon	36,930 (471)	32,240 (522)	40,940 (714)	42,180 (588)	37,840 (764)	47,990 (1,031)	45,850 (647)	37,040 (770)	41,580 (1,019)	50,150 (672)	54,690 (808)
Pennsylvania	44,830 (816)	36,630 (1,649)	48,550 (875)	50,790 (1,027)	43,650 (1,633)	57,220 (1,154)	54,800 (925)	39,530 (1,277)	46,310 (1,322)	56,640 (2,337)	64,100 (910)
Rhode Island	41,630 (303)	‡	43,200 (261)	48,610 (204)	‡	52,300 (169)	55,110 (909)	‡	49,330 (2,504)	58,990 (1,214)	60,180 (1,080)
South Carolina	31,860 (208)	27,530 (286)	34,620 (234)	38,390 (528)	32,850 (657)	41,660 (960)	42,910 (625)	34,380 (1,594)	43,780 (814)	41,760 (997)	49,410 (679)
South Dakota	28,110 (449)	‡	29,320 (660)	32,800 (443)	‡	35,910 (727)	37,670 (801)	‡	31,200 (971)	40,160 (1,346)	41,740 (1,162)
Tennessee	30,270 (350)	27,710 (409)	32,540 (455)	35,610 (414)	31,750 (533)	38,470 (648)	39,620 (543)	33,590 (747)	36,120 (835)	41,810 (1,182)	42,860 (892)
Texas	31,610 (355)	27,390 (692)	35,650 (529)	40,280 (453)	33,280 (548)	44,820 (764)	43,370 (723)	36,660 (1,126)	37,590 (872)	43,480 (867)	49,650 (881)
Utah	32,590 (277)	‡	35,560 (281)	39,880 (586)	‡	44,960 (1,332)	43,370 (636)	‡	36,950 (1,534)	43,380 (922)	48,730 (598)
Vermont	36,770 (594)	‡	39,190 (730)	37,260 (668)	‡	42,340 (1,073)	44,740 (926)	36,710 (808)	41,140 (1,342)	45,800 (871)	51,090 (1,076)
Virginia	33,740 (579)	33,990 (713)	38,610 (760)	40,230 (668)	35,880 (668)	46,640 (1,263)	43,860 (948)	37,990 (737)	43,230 (829)	43,450 (1,725)	50,370 (1,581)
Washington	38,270 (398)	‡	42,780 (525)	43,160 (364)	36,450 (533)	48,630 (566)	47,970 (500)	34,060 (1,895)	51,300 (668)	51,300 (687)	55,050 (731)
West Virginia	32,130 (195)	28,230 (424)	33,970 (230)	36,590 (226)	‡	38,830 (240)	40,440 (716)	‡	33,580 (956)	40,820 (611)	42,840 (1,081)
Wisconsin	40,920 (486)	35,470 (560)	42,670 (739)	46,420 (512)	39,570 (669)	49,520 (588)	47,750 (713)	35,510 (1,461)	40,870 (†)	48,330 (920)	53,980 (817)
Wyoming	32,490 (371)	‡	34,060 (663)	36,120 (497)	‡	38,480 (810)	41,610 (1,014)	‡	‡	40,480 (1,225)	44,490 (1,557)

†Not applicable.
‡Reporting standards not met.
NOTE: This table includes regular full-time teachers only; it excludes other staff even when they have full-time teaching duties (regular part-time teachers, itinerant teachers, long-term substitutes, administrators, library media specialists, other professional staff, and support staff). Standard errors appear in parentheses.

SOURCE: U.S. Department of Education, National Center for Education Statistics, Schools and Staffing Survey (SASS), "Public School Teacher Questionnaire," 1993–94, 1999–2000, and 2003–04; and "Public Charter School Teacher Questionnaire," 1999–2000. (This table was prepared July 2006.)

Table 75. Estimated average annual salary of teachers in public elementary and secondary schools: Selected years, 1959–60 through 2004–05

	Current dollars					Constant 2005–06 dollars[2]		
School year	All teachers	Elementary teachers	Secondary teachers	Wage and salary accruals per full-time-equivalent (FTE) employee[1]	Ratio of average teachers' salary to accruals per FTE employee	All teachers	Elementary teachers	Secondary teachers
1	2	3	4	5	6	7	8	9
1959–60	$4,995	$4,815	$5,276	$4,749	1.05	$33,828	$32,609	$35,731
1961–62	5,515	5,340	5,775	5,063	1.09	36,511	35,352	38,232
1963–64	5,995	5,805	6,266	5,478	1.09	38,680	37,454	40,428
1965–66	6,485	6,279	6,761	5,934	1.09	42,932	41,569	44,760
1967–68	7,423	7,208	7,692	6,533	1.14	46,293	44,952	47,971
1969–70	8,626	8,412	8,891	7,486	1.15	45,440	44,313	46,836
1970–71	9,268	9,021	9,568	7,998	1.16	46,426	45,188	47,928
1971–72	9,705	9,424	10,031	8,521	1.14	46,931	45,572	48,508
1972–73	10,174	9,893	10,507	9,056	1.12	47,294	45,987	48,842
1973–74	10,770	10,507	11,077	9,667	1.11	45,966	44,843	47,276
1974–75	11,641	11,334	12,000	10,411	1.12	44,726	43,547	46,106
1975–76	12,600	12,280	12,937	11,194	1.13	45,211	44,063	46,420
1976–77	13,354	12,989	13,776	11,971	1.12	45,276	44,038	46,707
1977–78	14,198	13,845	14,602	12,815	1.11	45,109	43,987	46,392
1978–79	15,032	14,681	15,450	13,825	1.09	43,668	42,648	44,882
1979–80	15,970	15,569	16,459	15,088	1.06	40,935	39,907	42,188
1980–81	17,644	17,230	18,142	16,520	1.07	40,531	39,580	41,675
1981–82	19,274	18,853	19,805	17,866	1.08	40,755	39,865	41,878
1982–83	20,695	20,227	21,291	18,950	1.09	41,958	41,009	43,166
1983–84	21,935	21,487	22,554	19,878	1.10	42,884	42,008	44,094
1984–85	23,600	23,200	24,187	20,819	1.13	44,401	43,649	45,506
1985–86	25,199	24,718	25,846	21,732	1.16	46,081	45,201	47,264
1986–87	26,569	26,057	27,244	22,650	1.17	47,531	46,615	48,739
1987–88	28,034	27,519	28,798	23,705	1.18	48,156	47,272	49,469
1988–89	29,564	29,022	30,218	24,655	1.20	48,543	47,653	49,617
1989–90	31,367	30,832	32,049	25,647	1.22	49,158	48,319	50,226
1990–91	33,084	32,490	33,896	26,794	1.23	49,161	48,278	50,367
1991–92	34,063	33,479	34,827	27,999	1.22	49,044	48,203	50,144
1992–93	35,029	34,350	35,880	29,058	1.21	48,907	47,959	50,095
1993–94	35,737	35,233	36,566	29,811	1.20	48,636	47,950	49,764
1994–95	36,675	36,088	37,523	30,606	1.20	48,522	47,745	49,643
1995–96	37,642	37,138	38,397	31,561	1.19	48,482	47,833	49,454
1996–97	38,443	38,039	39,184	32,789	1.17	48,140	47,634	49,068
1997–98	39,350	39,002	39,944	34,346	1.15	48,413	47,984	49,143
1998–99	40,544	40,165	41,203	35,978	1.13	49,033	48,574	49,830
1999–2000	41,807	41,306	42,546	37,800	1.11	49,141	48,553	50,010
2000–01	43,395	42,929	44,013	39,257	1.11	49,318	48,789	50,021
2001–02	44,660	44,192	45,252	40,031	1.12	49,873	49,350	50,534
2002–03	45,776	45,480	46,095	41,004	1.12	50,020	49,697	50,369
2003–04	46,752	46,408	47,120	42,547	1.10	49,993	49,625	50,386
2004–05	47,750	47,487	48,100	—	—	49,568	49,295	49,932

—Not available.
[1]Calendar-year data from the U.S. Department of Commerce have been converted to a school-year basis by averaging the two appropriate calendar years in each case.
[2]Constant dollars based on the Consumer Price Index, prepared by the Bureau of Labor Statistics, U.S. Department of Labor, adjusted to a school-year basis.

NOTE: Some data have been revised from previously published figures.
SOURCE: National Education Association, *Estimates of School Statistics*, 1959–60 through 2004–05; and unpublished tabulations. U.S. Department of Commerce, Bureau of Economic Analysis, National Income and Product Accounts, 1959 through 2004. (This table was prepared September 2006.)

Table 76. Estimated average annual salary of teachers in public elementary and secondary schools, by state or jurisdiction: Selected years, 1969–70 through 2004–05

State	Current dollars							Constant 2005–06 dollars[1]							Percent change, 1989–90 to 2004–05, in constant 2005–06 dollars
	1969–70	1979–80	1989–90	1999–2000	2002–03	2003–04	2004–05	1969–70	1979–80	1989–90	1999–2000	2002–03	2003–04	2004–05	
1	2	3	4	5	6	7	8	9	10	11	12	13	14	15	16
United States...	$8,626	$15,970	$31,367	$41,807	$45,776	$46,752	$47,750	$45,440	$40,935	$49,158	$49,141	$50,020	$49,993	$49,568	0.8
Alabama	6,818	13,060	24,828	36,689	38,246	38,325	38,863	35,916	33,476	38,910	43,126	41,792	40,982	40,343	3.7
Alaska	10,560	27,210	43,153	46,462	49,685	51,736	52,424	55,628	69,746	67,628	54,613	54,292	55,322	54,420	-19.5
Arizona	8,711	15,054	29,402	36,902	40,894	41,843	42,905	45,888	38,587	46,078	43,376	44,685	44,744	44,539	-3.3
Arkansas	6,307	12,299	22,352	33,386	37,753	39,314	40,495	33,224	31,525	35,029	39,243	41,253	42,039	42,037	20.0
California	10,315	18,020	37,998	47,680	56,283	56,444	57,876	54,338	46,190	59,550	56,045	61,501	60,357	60,080	0.9
Colorado	7,761	16,205	30,758	38,163	41,275	43,319	44,161	40,884	41,537	48,203	44,858	45,101	46,322	45,843	-4.9
Connecticut	9,262	16,229	40,461	51,780	54,362	57,337	58,688	48,791	41,599	63,409	60,864	59,402	61,312	60,923	-3.9
Delaware	9,015	16,148	33,377	44,435	50,772	49,366	50,869	47,489	41,391	52,308	52,231	55,479	52,788	52,806	1.0
District of Columbia ..	10,285	22,190	38,402	47,076	50,763	57,009	58,456	54,180	56,878	60,183	55,335	55,469	60,961	60,682	0.8
Florida	8,412	14,149	28,803	36,722	39,465	40,604	41,081	44,313	36,267	45,139	43,164	43,124	43,419	42,645	-5.5
Georgia	7,276	13,853	28,006	41,023	45,533	45,988	46,526	38,329	35,509	43,890	48,220	49,755	49,176	48,298	10.0
Hawaii	9,453	19,920	32,047	40,578	44,464	45,479	44,273	49,797	51,060	50,223	47,697	48,586	48,632	45,959	-8.5
Idaho	6,890	13,611	23,861	35,547	40,148	41,080	42,122	36,295	34,888	37,394	41,783	43,870	43,928	43,726	16.9
Illinois	9,569	17,601	32,794	46,486	51,289	54,230	55,629	50,408	45,116	51,394	54,641	56,044	57,989	57,747	12.4
Indiana	8,833	15,599	30,902	41,850	45,097	45,791	46,851	46,531	39,984	48,429	49,192	49,278	48,965	48,635	0.4
Iowa	8,355	15,203	26,747	35,678	38,921	39,432	40,347	44,013	38,969	41,917	41,937	42,530	42,165	41,883	-0.1
Kansas	7,612	13,690	28,744	34,981	38,123	38,623	39,190	40,099	35,091	45,047	41,118	41,658	41,300	40,682	-9.7
Kentucky	6,953	14,520	26,292	36,380	38,981	40,240	41,002	36,627	37,218	41,204	42,762	42,595	43,029	42,563	3.3
Louisiana	7,028	13,760	24,300	33,109	36,878	37,918	38,880	37,022	35,270	38,082	38,918	40,297	40,546	40,361	6.0
Maine	7,572	13,071	26,881	35,561	38,121	39,864	40,940	39,888	33,504	42,127	41,800	41,655	42,627	42,499	0.9
Maryland	9,383	17,558	36,319	44,048	49,677	50,261	52,331	49,428	45,005	56,918	51,776	54,283	53,745	54,324	-4.6
Massachusetts	8,764	17,253	34,712	46,580	52,043	53,181	54,596	46,167	44,224	54,400	54,752	56,868	56,868	56,675	4.2
Michigan	9,826	19,663	37,072	49,044	54,071	54,412	55,693	51,762	50,401	58,098	57,648	59,084	58,184	57,814	-0.5
Minnesota	8,658	15,912	32,190	39,802	42,833	45,375	46,906	45,609	40,786	50,447	46,785	46,804	48,520	48,692	-3.5
Mississippi	5,798	11,850	24,292	31,857	34,555	35,684	36,590	30,543	30,374	38,070	37,446	37,758	38,158	37,983	-0.2
Missouri	7,799	13,682	27,094	35,656	38,826	38,006	38,971	41,084	35,070	42,461	41,911	42,426	40,641	40,455	-4.7
Montana	7,606	14,537	25,081	32,121	35,754	37,184	38,485	40,067	37,262	39,306	37,756	39,069	39,762	39,951	1.6
Nebraska	7,375	13,516	25,522	33,237	37,896	38,352	39,456	38,850	34,645	39,997	39,068	41,409	41,011	40,959	2.4
Nevada	9,215	16,295	30,590	39,390	41,795	42,254	43,394	48,543	41,768	47,940	46,300	45,670	45,183	45,047	-6.0
New Hampshire	7,771	13,017	28,986	37,734	40,519	42,689	43,941	40,936	33,366	45,426	44,354	44,276	45,648	45,614	0.4
New Jersey	9,130	17,161	35,676	52,015	54,166	55,592	56,600	48,095	43,988	55,911	61,140	59,188	59,446	58,755	5.1
New Mexico	7,796	14,887	24,756	32,554	36,687	38,067	39,328	41,068	38,159	38,797	38,265	40,088	40,706	40,826	5.2
New York	10,336	19,812	38,925	51,020	52,600	55,181	56,200	54,448	50,783	61,002	59,971	57,477	59,006	58,340	-4.4
North Carolina	7,494	14,117	27,883	39,404	43,076	43,211	43,313	39,477	36,185	43,698	46,317	47,070	46,206	44,962	2.9
North Dakota	6,696	13,263	23,016	29,863	33,210	35,441	36,449	35,273	33,996	36,070	35,102	36,289	37,898	37,837	4.9
Ohio	8,300	15,269	31,218	41,436	45,452	47,482	48,692	43,723	39,138	48,924	48,705	49,666	50,773	50,546	3.3
Oklahoma	6,882	13,107	23,070	31,298	34,854	35,061	37,141	36,253	33,596	36,155	36,789	38,085	37,491	38,555	6.6
Oregon	8,818	16,266	30,840	42,336	47,600	49,169	50,790	46,452	41,694	48,332	49,763	52,013	52,577	52,724	9.1
Pennsylvania	8,858	16,515	33,338	48,321	51,800	51,835	52,700	46,662	42,332	52,246	56,798	56,603	55,428	54,707	4.7
Rhode Island	8,776	18,002	36,057	47,041	51,076	52,261	53,473	46,230	46,143	56,508	55,294	55,811	55,884	55,509	-1.8
South Carolina	6,927	13,063	27,217	36,081	41,279	41,162	42,207	36,490	33,484	42,654	42,411	45,106	44,015	43,814	2.7
South Dakota	6,403	12,348	21,300	29,071	32,416	33,236	34,040	33,730	31,651	33,381	34,171	35,421	35,540	35,336	5.9
Tennessee	7,050	13,972	27,052	36,328	39,677	40,318	41,527	37,138	35,814	42,395	42,701	43,356	43,113	43,108	1.7
Texas	7,255	14,132	27,496	37,567	40,001	40,476	41,009	38,218	36,224	43,091	44,158	43,710	43,282	42,571	-1.2
Utah	7,644	14,909	23,686	34,946	38,413	38,976	39,965	40,267	38,215	37,120	41,077	41,974	41,678	41,487	11.8
Vermont	7,968	12,484	29,012	37,758	41,603	42,007	44,535	41,974	31,999	45,467	44,382	45,460	44,919	46,231	1.7
Virginia	8,070	14,060	30,938	38,744	43,152	43,655	44,763	42,511	36,039	48,485	45,541	47,153	46,681	46,468	-4.2
Washington	9,225	18,820	30,457	41,043	44,949	45,434	45,712	48,596	48,240	47,731	48,243	49,116	48,584	47,453	-0.6
West Virginia	7,650	13,710	22,842	35,009	38,508	38,461	38,360	40,299	35,142	35,797	41,151	42,078	41,127	39,821	11.2
Wisconsin	8,963	16,006	31,921	41,153	42,871	42,882	43,466	47,215	41,027	50,026	48,373	46,846	45,855	45,121	-9.8
Wyoming	8,232	16,012	28,141	34,127	37,876	39,532	40,392	43,365	41,043	44,102	40,114	41,388	42,272	41,930	-4.9

[1]Constant dollars based on the Consumer Price Index (CPI), prepared by the Bureau of Labor Statistics, U.S. Department of Labor, adjusted to a school-year basis. The CPI does not account for differences in inflation rates from state to state.

NOTE: Some data have been revised from previously published figures.
SOURCE: National Education Association, *Estimates of School Statistics*, 1969–70 through 2004–05. (This table was prepared September 2006.)

Table 77. Staff employed in public elementary and secondary school systems, by functional area: Selected years, 1949–50 through fall 2004

[In full-time equivalents]

School year	Total	School district administrative staff			Instructional staff						Support staff[1]
		Total	Officials and administrators	Instruction coordinators	Total	Principals and assistant principals	Teachers	Instructional aides	Librarians	Guidance counselors	
1	2	3	4	5	6	7	8	9	10	11	12
1949–50[2]	1,300,031	33,642	23,868	9,774	956,808	43,137	913,671	(3)	(3)	(3)	309,582
1959–60[2]	2,089,283	42,423	28,648	13,775	1,448,931	63,554	1,353,372	(3)	17,363	14,643	597,929
1969–70[2]	3,360,763	65,282	33,745	31,537	2,255,707	90,593	2,016,244	57,418	42,689	48,763	1,039,774
Fall 1980[2]	4,168,286	78,784	58,230	20,554	2,729,023	107,061	2,184,216	325,755	48,018	63,973	1,360,479
Fall 1990	4,494,076	75,868	—	—	3,051,404	127,417	2,398,169	395,959	49,909	79,950	1,366,804
Fall 1991	4,559,359	76,084	—	—	3,103,939	129,304	2,432,243	410,538	49,917	81,937	1,379,336
Fall 1992	4,708,286	78,414	45,712	32,702	3,139,544	121,936	2,458,956	427,279	50,324	81,049	1,490,328
Fall 1993	4,808,080	80,862	47,614	33,248	3,209,381	121,486	2,503,901	450,519	50,511	82,964	1,517,837
Fall 1994	4,904,757	81,867	48,827	33,040	3,280,752	120,017	2,551,875	473,348	50,668	84,844	1,542,138
Fall 1995	4,994,358	82,998	49,315	33,683	3,351,528	120,629	2,598,220	494,289	50,862	87,528	1,559,832
Fall 1996	5,091,205	81,975	48,480	33,495	3,447,580	123,734	2,667,419	516,356	51,464	88,607	1,561,650
Fall 1997	5,266,415	85,267	50,432	34,835	3,572,955	126,129	2,746,157	557,453	52,142	91,074	1,608,193
Fall 1998	5,419,181	88,939	52,975	35,964	3,693,630	129,317	2,830,286	588,108	52,805	93,114	1,636,612
Fall 1999	5,632,004	94,134	55,467	38,667	3,819,057	137,199	2,910,633	621,942	53,659	95,624	1,718,813
Fall 2000	5,709,753	97,270	57,837	39,433	3,876,628	141,792	2,941,461	641,392	54,246	97,737	1,735,855
Fall 2001	5,904,195	109,526	63,517	46,009	3,989,211	160,543	2,999,528	674,741	54,350	100,049	1,805,458
Fall 2002	5,954,661	110,777	62,781	47,996	4,016,963	164,171	3,034,123	663,552	54,205	100,912	1,826,921
Fall 2003	5,953,667	107,483	63,418	44,065	4,052,738	165,233	3,048,652	685,118	54,349	99,387	1,793,445
Fall 2004	6,053,465	111,780	64,092	47,688	4,119,221	165,693	3,090,513	707,028	54,145	101,842	1,822,464
Percentage distribution											
1949–50[2]	100.0	2.6	1.8	0.8	73.6	3.3	70.3	(3)	(3)	(3)	23.8
1959–60[2]	100.0	2.0	1.4	0.7	69.4	3.0	64.8	(3)	0.8	0.7	28.6
1969–70[2]	100.0	1.9	1.0	0.9	67.1	2.7	60.0	1.7	1.3	1.5	30.9
Fall 1980[2]	100.0	1.9	1.4	0.5	65.5	2.6	52.4	7.8	1.2	1.5	32.6
Fall 1990	100.0	1.7	—	—	67.9	2.8	53.4	8.8	1.1	1.8	30.4
Fall 1991	100.0	1.7	—	—	68.1	2.8	53.3	9.0	1.1	1.8	30.3
Fall 1992	100.0	1.7	1.0	0.7	66.7	2.6	52.2	9.1	1.1	1.7	31.7
Fall 1993	100.0	1.7	1.0	0.7	66.7	2.5	52.1	9.4	1.1	1.7	31.6
Fall 1994	100.0	1.7	1.0	0.7	66.9	2.4	52.0	9.7	1.0	1.7	31.4
Fall 1995	100.0	1.7	1.0	0.7	67.1	2.4	52.0	9.9	1.0	1.8	31.2
Fall 1996	100.0	1.6	1.0	0.7	67.7	2.4	52.4	10.1	1.0	1.7	30.7
Fall 1997	100.0	1.6	1.0	0.7	67.8	2.4	52.1	10.6	1.0	1.7	30.5
Fall 1998	100.0	1.6	1.0	0.7	68.2	2.4	52.2	10.9	1.0	1.7	30.2
Fall 1999	100.0	1.7	1.0	0.7	67.8	2.4	51.7	11.0	1.0	1.7	30.5
Fall 2000	100.0	1.7	1.0	0.7	67.9	2.5	51.5	11.2	1.0	1.7	30.4
Fall 2001	100.0	1.9	1.1	0.8	67.6	2.7	50.8	11.4	0.9	1.7	30.6
Fall 2002	100.0	1.9	1.1	0.8	67.5	2.8	51.0	11.1	0.9	1.7	30.7
Fall 2003	100.0	1.8	1.1	0.7	68.1	2.8	51.2	11.5	0.9	1.7	30.1
Fall 2004	100.0	1.8	1.1	0.8	68.0	2.7	51.1	11.7	0.9	1.7	30.1
Pupils per staff member											
1949–50[2]	19.3	746.4	1,052.1	2,569.2	26.2	582.1	27.5	(3)	(3)	(3)	81.1
1959–60[2]	16.8	829.3	1,228.1	2,554.1	24.3	553.6	26.0	(3)	2,026.3	2,402.7	58.8
1969–70[2]	13.6	697.7	1,349.8	1,444.3	20.2	502.8	22.6	793.3	1,067.0	934.1	43.8
Fall 1980[2]	9.8	518.9	702.0	1,988.8	15.0	381.8	18.7	125.5	851.3	639.0	30.0
Fall 1990	9.2	543.3	—	—	13.5	323.5	17.2	104.1	825.8	515.5	30.2
Fall 1991	9.2	552.6	—	—	13.5	325.2	17.3	102.4	842.3	513.2	30.5
Fall 1992	9.1	546.1	936.8	1,309.5	13.6	351.2	17.4	100.2	851.0	528.4	28.7
Fall 1993	9.0	537.5	912.9	1,307.3	13.5	357.8	17.4	96.5	860.5	523.9	28.6
Fall 1994	9.0	538.8	903.4	1,335.1	13.4	367.5	17.3	93.2	870.6	519.9	28.6
Fall 1995	9.0	540.3	909.3	1,331.2	13.4	371.7	17.3	90.7	881.6	512.3	28.7
Fall 1996	9.0	556.4	940.8	1,361.7	13.2	368.6	17.1	88.3	886.3	514.8	29.2
Fall 1997	8.8	541.0	914.6	1,324.2	12.9	365.7	16.8	82.7	884.6	506.5	28.7
Fall 1998	8.6	523.3	878.5	1,294.0	12.6	359.9	16.4	79.1	881.3	499.8	28.4
Fall 1999	8.3	497.8	844.8	1,211.8	12.3	341.5	16.1	75.3	873.2	490.0	27.3
Fall 2000	8.3	485.3	816.1	1,197.1	12.2	332.9	16.0	73.6	870.2	483.0	27.2
Fall 2001	8.1	435.3	750.5	1,036.1	12.0	296.9	15.9	70.7	877.1	476.5	26.4
Fall 2002	8.1	435.0	767.5	1,003.9	12.0	293.5	15.9	72.6	888.9	477.5	26.4
Fall 2003	8.2	451.6	765.4	1,101.6	12.0	293.8	15.9	70.8	893.1	488.4	27.1
Fall 2004	8.1	436.5	761.3	1,023.2	11.8	294.5	15.8	69.0	901.2	479.1	26.8

—Not available.
[1]Includes school district administrative support staff, school and library support staff, student support staff, and other support services staff.
[2]Because of classification revisions, categories other than teachers, principals, librarians, and guidance counselors are only roughly comparable to figures for years after 1980.
[3]Data included in column 8.

NOTE: Data for 1949–50 through 1969–70 are cumulative for the entire school year, rather than counts as of the fall of the year. Some data have been revised from previously published figures. Detail may not sum to totals because of rounding.
SOURCE: U.S. Department of Education, National Center for Education Statistics, *Statistics of State School Systems*, various years; *Statistics of Public Elementary and Secondary Schools*, various years; and Common Core of Data (CCD), "State Nonfiscal Survey of Public Elementary/Secondary Education," 1986–87 through 2004–05. (This table was prepared March 2007.)

Table 78. Staff employed in public elementary and secondary school systems, by type of assignment and state or jurisdiction: Fall 2004

[In full-time equivalents]

State or jurisdiction	Total	School district staff			School staff						Student support staff	Other support services staff
		Officials and administrators	Administrative support staff	Instruction coordinators	Principals and assistant principals	School and library support staff	Teachers	Instructional aides	Guidance counselors	Librarians		
1	2	3	4	5	6	7	8	9	10	11	12	13
United States[1]	6,053,465	64,092	170,618	47,688	165,693	300,244	3,090,513	707,028	101,842	54,145	205,709	1,145,893
Alabama	92,795	1,081	1,907	836	3,487	3,757	51,594	6,458	1,705	1,369	1,764	18,837
Alaska[2]	17,632	445	877	173	707	1,543	7,756	2,200	270	146	452	3,063
Arizona	97,953	418	516	192	2,223	9,269	48,935	13,713	1,351	827	7,202	13,307
Arkansas	66,127	659	1,851	623	1,569	1,573	31,234	7,196	1,264	954	3,760	15,444
California[3]	574,614	2,723	22,907	6,663	13,752	36,101	305,969	68,118	6,508	1,138	15,648	95,087
Colorado	91,337	1,010	2,518	1,425	2,442	5,071	45,165	10,269	1,409	842	3,802	17,384
Connecticut	83,879	1,383	1,727	369	2,258	3,877	38,808	12,689	1,352	789	4,633	15,994
Delaware	14,966	297	333	206	374	489	7,856	1,693	268	132	674	2,644
District of Columbia	12,162	130	686	105	398	414	5,387	1,339	99	41	608	2,955
Florida	311,853	1,892	15,599	677	7,242	16,220	154,864	31,517	5,942	2,800	11,920	63,180
Georgia	209,746	1,982	2,557	1,439	5,169	9,514	104,987	24,535	3,417	2,192	6,043	47,911
Hawaii	20,531	196	261	559	505	1,213	11,146	2,084	657	291	1,278	2,341
Idaho	25,533	115	535	264	716	1,085	14,269	2,736	590	171	523	4,529
Illinois[4,5]	261,237	3,942	6,992	1,059	6,457	13,320	131,047	34,411	3,117	2,176	8,599	50,117
Indiana	133,375	1,045	658	1,720	3,023	8,714	60,563	19,355	1,827	996	2,002	33,472
Iowa	68,450	945	716	482	2,195	4,533	34,697	9,475	1,157	561	2,507	11,182
Kansas	64,114	1,260	850	110	1,717	2,640	32,932	7,108	1,112	924	3,149	12,312
Kentucky	95,920	836	2,402	887	2,208	5,920	41,463	13,634	1,425	1,115	3,057	22,973
Louisiana	101,381	301	2,661	1,446	2,731	3,625	49,192	11,149	3,317	1,259	3,175	22,525
Maine	34,899	610	689	320	947	1,756	16,656	5,974	650	266	1,395	5,636
Maryland	108,296	834	1,070	1,285	3,226	4,640	55,101	9,747	2,230	1,140	3,088	25,935
Massachusetts[6]	137,613	1,603	4,610	908	3,892	6,312	73,399	19,652	2,117	949	6,712	17,459
Michigan	209,831	3,288	1,261	3,338	5,168	15,254	100,634	25,444	2,762	1,429	8,553	42,700
Minnesota	104,367	1,915	2,242	1,450	1,986	4,941	52,152	14,459	1,055	922	10,780	12,465
Mississippi	67,249	984	1,884	703	1,773	2,472	31,321	8,698	1,018	951	2,818	14,627
Missouri	125,868	1,316	8,585	981	3,066	516	65,481	11,575	2,562	1,622	4,521	25,643
Montana[5]	18,762	140	489	188	503	931	10,224	1,917	433	362	70	3,505
Nebraska	40,998	573	799	456	1,014	1,716	21,077	4,720	767	549	1,137	8,190
Nevada	31,260	263	965	546	924	1,705	20,950	3,683	713	343	438	730
New Hampshire	31,408	521	615	201	543	939	15,298	6,429	823	302	629	5,108
New Jersey	213,418	1,488	6,415	2,701	4,013	9,007	114,875	25,878	2,382	1,553	17,298	27,808
New Mexico	46,531	580	1,643	907	1,014	2,277	21,730	5,400	772	296	2,066	9,846
New York	399,089	2,839	26,806	2,172	7,911	7,242	218,612	54,938	6,551	3,329	10,494	58,195
North Carolina	177,308	1,650	3,489	962	4,901	6,611	92,550	28,598	3,514	2,337	5,515	27,181
North Dakota	15,157	478	161	104	388	508	8,070	1,638	277	203	479	2,851
Ohio	239,988	7,991	12,682	601	4,792	19,771	118,060	17,321	3,828	1,642	3,960	49,340
Oklahoma	77,466	528	2,534	472	2,107	3,434	40,416	6,997	1,559	1,016	3,863	14,540
Oregon	56,637	639	1,540	495	1,592	3,778	27,431	9,585	1,221	431	1,934	7,991
Pennsylvania	237,122	1,709	6,772	1,457	4,686	11,425	121,167	34,387	4,409	2,225	11,573	45,189
Rhode Island [2,4,6,7]	23,031	155	343	204	1,991	653	11,898	2,567	2,614	215	549	1,842
South Carolina[8]	65,014	302	2,346	721	3,298	3,762	46,914	2,686	1,736	1,140	1,651	458
South Dakota	18,106	441	332	377	397	542	9,064	3,383	289	148	1,095	2,038
Tennessee	111,891	170	2,565	778	3,420	3,879	60,022	14,181	1,936	1,566	4,099	19,275
Texas	607,364	7,863	3,428	1,518	30,737	34,387	294,547	59,855	10,151	4,893	5,467	154,518
Utah	44,499	375	918	732	1,060	2,561	22,287	6,954	675	262	978	7,697
Vermont	18,899	148	395	296	432	961	8,720	4,339	426	220	819	2,143
Virginia	179,688	1,461	4,570	1,447	4,083	10,626	93,732	17,833	2,579	2,002	3,224	38,131
Washington	111,848	897	1,778	231	2,795	2,646	53,125	10,300	1,981	1,298	2,848	33,949
West Virginia	37,979	437	1,696	354	1,056	433	19,958	3,191	673	387	1,618	8,176
Wisconsin	104,018	926	65	1,395	2,473	4,788	60,521	10,951	1,963	1,292	4,784	14,860
Wyoming	14,256	308	378	153	332	893	6,657	1,946	389	132	458	2,610
Bureau of Indian Affairs	—	—	—	—	—	—	—	—	—	—	—	—
DoDDS, overseas	6,845	42	24	52	259	670	4,885	280	261	152	200	20
DoDDS, domestic	2,865	36	0	28	105	277	2,002	178	94	67	—	78
Other jurisdictions												
American Samoa	1,813	54	59	50	70	157	945	108	44	17	206	103
Guam	3,318	19	185	83	61	260	1,672	687	40	14	62	235
Northern Marianas	1,166	6	65	11	33	58	579	263	18	1	34	98
Puerto Rico	76,865	1,727	88	505	1,498	4,887	43,054	240	1,011	1,095	3,927	18,833
Virgin Islands	2,977	78	129	23	113	84	1,545	322	79	39	85	480

—Not available.
[1]Includes imputations for undercounts in designated states.
[2]Includes imputations for instruction coordinators.
[3]Includes imputations for prekindergarten teachers.
[4]Includes imputations for instructional aides.
[5]Includes imputations for administrative support staff, school and library support staff, and other support services staff.

[6]Includes imputations for library support staff.
[7]Includes imputations for prekindergarten and kindergarten teachers.
[8]Includes imputations for school support staff.
NOTE: DoDDS = Department of Defense dependents schools.
SOURCE: U.S. Department of Education, National Center for Education Statistics, Common Core of Data (CCD), "State Nonfiscal Survey of Public Elementary/Secondary Education," 2004–05. (This table was prepared June 2006.)

Table 79. Staff employed in public elementary and secondary school systems, by type of assignment and state or jurisdiction: Fall 2003

[In full-time equivalents]

State or jurisdiction	Total	School district staff			School staff						Student support staff	Other support services staff
		Officials and administrators	Administrative support staff	Instruction coordinators	Principals and assistant principals	School and library support staff	Teachers	Instructional aides	Guidance counselors	Librarians		
1	2	3	4	5	6	7	8	9	10	11	12	13
United States[1]	5,953,667	63,418	175,443	44,065	165,233	293,469	3,048,652	685,118	99,387	54,349	190,623	1,133,910
Alabama	100,592	1,345	1,276	698	3,452	2,741	58,070	6,240	1,682	1,388	1,479	22,221
Alaska[2]	16,550	413	669	160	675	861	7,808	2,118	274	152	459	2,961
Arizona	96,341	424	520	183	2,240	9,414	47,507	13,438	1,292	802	7,610	12,911
Arkansas	64,693	682	1,797	621	1,552	1,478	30,876	6,623	1,218	934	3,284	15,628
California[3]	572,835	2,766	23,273	6,589	13,340	36,096	304,311	69,201	6,640	1,218	15,076	94,325
Colorado	89,530	974	2,505	963	2,382	4,841	44,904	10,216	1,371	845	3,399	17,130
Connecticut	85,367	1,333	1,771	367	2,193	3,682	42,370	11,567	1,327	789	4,422	15,546
Delaware	14,587	288	327	188	370	498	7,749	1,361	262	129	605	2,810
District of Columbia	10,608	96	76	68	408	369	5,676	1,269	60	40	1,950	596
Florida	295,775	1,819	15,035	696	6,946	15,456	144,955	29,616	5,772	2,710	11,410	61,360
Georgia	200,512	1,913	2,483	1,376	5,063	9,468	97,150	24,111	3,338	2,170	5,888	47,552
Hawaii	21,113	188	306	511	504	1,072	11,129	2,640	648	290	1,296	2,529
Idaho	25,133	116	541	268	726	1,096	14,049	2,637	575	170	531	4,424
Illinois[4,5]	254,119	4,061	7,080	833	6,422	12,537	127,669	33,295	3,049	2,200	8,631	48,342
Indiana	130,532	1,080	623	1,662	2,985	8,520	59,924	18,289	1,804	1,004	2,050	32,591
Iowa	68,137	928	723	472	2,111	4,552	34,791	9,095	1,180	589	2,500	11,196
Kansas	63,778	1,239	916	118	1,709	2,677	32,589	7,085	1,118	923	2,879	12,525
Kentucky	95,926	872	2,492	870	2,211	6,085	41,246	13,620	1,471	1,147	3,066	22,846
Louisiana	102,990	330	2,728	1,387	2,694	3,668	50,495	11,398	3,155	1,233	3,324	22,578
Maine	35,866	625	814	297	967	1,554	17,621	5,952	627	251	1,423	5,735
Maryland	107,529	832	1,099	1,203	3,170	4,065	55,198	9,910	2,233	1,116	3,224	25,479
Massachusetts[6]	134,414	1,751	4,435	1,115	3,666	5,519	72,062	18,272	2,118	946	7,019	17,511
Michigan[7]	206,034	3,304	1,241	3,457	4,937	15,135	97,014	25,170	2,708	1,405	8,325	43,338
Minnesota	103,744	1,030	6,744	467	2,190	3,955	51,611	14,636	1,064	942	6,274	14,831
Mississippi	68,377	986	1,882	671	1,757	2,458	32,591	8,603	1,009	969	2,863	14,588
Missouri	125,783	1,308	8,626	952	3,044	540	65,169	10,906	2,608	1,621	4,493	26,516
Montana	18,656	145	500	182	504	885	10,301	1,870	431	357	67	3,414
Nebraska	40,573	574	823	427	998	1,648	20,921	4,722	757	557	1,122	8,024
Nevada	34,059	263	970	524	1,079	1,575	20,234	2,438	719	324	842	5,091
New Hampshire	30,830	538	643	186	536	915	15,112	6,380	772	296	621	4,831
New Jersey	204,038	1,832	7,434	1,466	4,917	10,659	109,077	24,010	3,673	1,871	11,472	27,627
New Mexico	44,841	858	1,733	724	995	2,141	21,569	5,243	769	298	2,012	8,499
New York	394,178	2,844	26,934	2,083	7,823	7,159	216,116	53,423	6,440	3,318	10,222	57,816
North Carolina	172,193	1,609	3,359	852	4,777	6,393	89,988	27,852	3,444	2,335	5,197	26,387
North Dakota	15,066	436	160	134	395	513	8,037	1,811	278	198	469	2,635
Ohio	242,520	6,214	11,970	500	6,499	16,985	121,735	18,274	3,694	1,669	3,722	51,258
Oklahoma	71,313	710	1,664	248	1,932	4,207	39,253	6,049	1,495	996	2,293	12,466
Oregon	54,272	613	1,704	406	1,539	3,698	26,732	8,466	1,114	461	1,621	7,918
Pennsylvania	233,269	1,667	6,270	1,424	4,630	11,608	119,889	24,897	4,344	2,217	11,071	45,252
Rhode Island [4,7,8]	19,890	164	461	190	555	905	11,918	2,526	380	215	543	2,033
South Carolina[9]	62,888	299	2,356	678	3,224	3,473	45,830	2,311	1,699	1,135	1,520	363
South Dakota	19,039	445	331	380	402	543	9,245	3,337	328	146	1,146	2,736
Tennessee	116,120	1,239	2,662	1,117	5,080	5,325	59,584	14,430	1,918	1,545	4,192	19,028
Texas	596,330	7,833	3,446	1,238	29,621	32,850	289,481	58,741	9,937	4,864	5,312	153,007
Utah	41,545	156	974	711	1,012	2,282	22,147	5,911	683	279	289	7,101
Vermont	18,701	147	385	318	441	895	8,749	4,208	426	226	756	2,150
Virginia	166,578	1,556	3,964	1,525	3,924	8,675	90,573	15,287	2,564	1,986	3,054	33,470
Washington	109,294	915	1,791	546	2,747	5,643	52,824	10,051	1,955	1,309	2,828	28,685
West Virginia	37,957	421	1,735	335	1,044	420	20,020	3,113	660	386	1,645	8,178
Wisconsin	104,531	932	2,827	1,527	2,512	4,863	58,216	10,632	1,910	1,247	4,655	15,210
Wyoming	14,121	305	365	152	333	872	6,567	1,868	394	131	472	2,662
Bureau of Indian Affairs	—	—	—	—	—	—	—	—	—	—	—	—
DoDDS, overseas	7,282	34	23	50	271	706	4,728	280	267	155	411	357
DoDDS, domestic	4,157	28	21	42	108	306	2,301	428	102	69	193	559
Other jurisdictions												
American Samoa	1,771	39	52	45	73	152	988	116	49	6	84	167
Guam	3,466	18	150	104	58	304	1,760	704	54	23	52	239
Northern Marianas	1,155	7	63	12	32	77	550	250	18	1	36	109
Puerto Rico	74,697	1,611	185	312	1,512	4,593	42,444	237	1,009	1,080	3,899	17,815
Virgin Islands	2,896	67	131	19	84	72	1,512	326	81	38	85	481

—Not available.
[1]Includes imputations for undercounts in designated states.
[2]Includes imputations for instruction coordinators.
[3]Includes imputations for prekindergarten teachers.
[4]Includes imputations for instructional aides.
[5]Includes imputations for administrative support staff, school and library support staff, and other support services staff.
[6]Includes imputations for library support staff.

[7]Includes imputations for prekindergarten and kindergarten teachers.
[8]Includes imputations for school administrators, guidance counselors, and librarians.
[9]Includes imputations for administrative support staff and school support staff.
NOTE: Some data have been changed from previously published figures. DoDDS = Department of Defense dependents schools.
SOURCE: U.S. Department of Education, National Center for Education Statistics, Common Core of Data (CCD), "State Nonfiscal Survey of Public Elementary/Secondary Education," 2003–04. (This table was prepared March 2007.)

Table 80. Staff and teachers in public elementary and secondary school systems, by state or jurisdiction: Fall 1998 through fall 2004

State or jurisdiction	Teachers as a percent of staff				Fall 2002			Fall 2003[1]			Fall 2004		
	Fall 1998	Fall 1999	Fall 2000	Fall 2001	All staff	Teachers	Teachers as a percent of staff	All staff	Teachers	Teachers as a percent of staff	All staff	Teachers	Teachers as a percent of staff
1	2	3	4	5	6	7	8	9	10	11	12	13	14
United States[2]	52.2	51.7	51.5	50.8	5,954,661	3,034,123	51.0	5,953,667	3,048,652	51.2	6,053,465	3,090,513	51.1
Alabama	54.5 [3]	54.9 [3]	53.7 [3]	53.1 [3]	88,893 [3]	47,115 [3]	53.0 [3]	100,592	58,070	57.7	92,795	51,594	55.6
Alaska	50.4 [3]	48.7 [3]	49.3 [3]	48.1 [3]	17,101 [3]	8,080	47.2 [3]	16,550 [3]	7,808	47.2 [3]	17,632 [3]	7,756	44.0 [3]
Arizona	49.8 [3]	49.7	49.3	49.0	96,639	47,101	48.7	96,341	47,507	49.3	97,953	48,935	50.0
Arkansas	68.5 [3]	52.5	50.6	49.7	63,815	30,330	47.5	64,693	30,876	47.7	66,127	31,234	47.2
California	54.8 [3]	54.0 [3]	54.1 [3]	53.0 [3]	581,756 [3]	307,764 [3]	52.9 [3]	572,835 [3]	304,311 [3]	53.1 [3]	574,614 [3]	305,969 [3]	53.2 [3]
Colorado	51.8	51.2	50.7	50.4	90,397	45,401	50.2	89,530	44,904	50.2	91,337	45,165	49.4
Connecticut	50.1	50.0	50.0	49.2	86,361	42,296	49.0	85,367	42,370	49.6	83,879	38,808	46.3
Delaware	55.0	54.7	59.2	53.4	14,449	7,698	53.3	14,587	7,749	53.1	14,966	7,856	52.5
District of Columbia	52.7	50.7	46.2	43.5	11,548	5,005	43.3	10,608	5,676	53.5	12,162	5,387	44.3
Florida	48.4	48.0	47.8	47.6	287,091	138,226	48.1	295,775	144,955	49.0	311,853	154,864	49.7
Georgia	49.9	49.3	49.2	48.8	197,944	96,044	48.5	200,512	97,150	48.5	209,746	104,987	50.1
Hawaii	61.3	60.7	59.5	56.6	20,703	10,973	53.0	21,113	11,129	52.7	20,531	11,146	54.3
Idaho	56.3	56.4	56.2	55.9	24,897	13,896	55.8	25,133	14,049	55.9	25,533	14,269	55.9
Illinois	52.0 [3]	51.0 [3]	51.1 [3]	50.7 [3]	257,352 [3]	131,046	50.9 [3]	254,119 [3]	127,669	50.2 [3]	261,237 [3]	131,047	50.2 [3]
Indiana	46.8	47.0	46.7	46.3	126,998	59,968	47.2	130,532	59,924	45.9	133,375	60,563	45.4
Iowa	49.8	50.8	51.1	50.2	67,426	34,573	51.3	68,137	34,791	51.1	68,450	34,697	50.7
Kansas	52.6	51.7	50.9	50.8	63,911	32,643	51.1	63,778	32,589	51.1	64,114	32,932	51.4
Kentucky	44.8	45.0	44.1	42.6	95,839	40,662	42.4	95,926	41,246	43.0	95,920	41,463	43.2
Louisiana	49.4	49.4	49.3	49.2	102,333	50,062	48.9	102,990	50,495	49.0	101,381	49,192	48.5
Maine	50.8	50.3	49.7	49.1	34,586	16,837	48.7	35,866	17,621	49.1	34,899	16,656	47.7
Maryland	53.4	54.5	54.3	54.2	102,642	55,382	54.0	107,529	55,198	51.3	108,296	55,101	50.9
Massachusetts	55.0	56.9	55.1	54.9	143,922	74,214	51.6	134,414 [3]	72,062	53.6 [3]	137,613 [3]	73,399	53.3 [3]
Michigan	44.5	45.6	46.1	46.0	187,093	89,595	47.9	206,034 [3]	97,014 [3]	47.1 [3]	209,831 [3]	100,634 [3]	48.0 [3]
Minnesota	53.6	53.6	51.6 [3]	50.7	105,311 [3]	52,808	50.1 [3]	103,744	51,611	49.7	104,367	52,152	50.0
Mississippi	47.9	48.0	47.9	47.9	66,133	31,598	47.8	68,377	32,591	47.7	67,249	31,321	46.6
Missouri	53.7	54.6	53.2	52.3	128,124	66,717	52.1	125,783	65,169	51.8	125,868	65,481	52.0
Montana	53.8 [3]	51.7 [3]	53.5 [3]	53.4 [3]	18,693 [3]	10,362	55.4 [3]	18,656	10,301	55.2	18,762 [3]	10,224	54.5 [3]
Nebraska	53.2	53.1	52.6	52.0	40,743	21,043	51.6	40,573	20,921	51.6	40,998	21,077	51.4
Nevada	56.3	57.5	58.6	56.7	33,443	20,038	59.9	34,059	20,234	59.4	31,260	20,950	67.0
New Hampshire	52.0	51.7	51.1	50.4	30,087	14,977	49.8	30,830	15,112	49.0	31,408	15,298	48.7
New Jersey	53.9	53.9	53.4	53.6	199,381	107,004	53.7	204,038	109,077	53.5	213,418	114,875	53.8
New Mexico	48.6	45.8	46.8	48.6	43,826	21,172	48.3	44,841	21,569	48.1	46,531	21,730	46.7
New York	52.4	49.4	49.7	49.4	428,045	210,926	49.3	394,178	216,116	54.8	399,089	218,612	54.8
North Carolina	52.0	51.6	51.5	51.6	169,328	87,677	51.8	172,193	89,988	52.3	177,308	92,550	52.2
North Dakota	54.0	53.9	53.9	53.9	15,090	8,078	53.5	15,066	8,037	53.3	15,157	8,070	53.2
Ohio	54.4	53.4	53.1	53.1	242,372	125,372	51.7	242,520	121,735	50.2	239,988	118,060	49.2
Oklahoma	57.8	56.2	55.0	54.5	74,422	40,638	54.6	71,313	39,253	55.0	77,466	40,416	52.2
Oregon	50.5	50.0	50.0	49.3	55,042	27,126	49.3	54,272	26,732	49.3	56,637	27,431	48.4
Pennsylvania	52.9	52.8	52.2	51.7	231,251	118,256	51.1	233,269	119,889	51.4	237,122	121,167	51.1
Rhode Island	62.4	61.6	60.0	59.8	18,303	11,196	61.2	19,890 [3]	11,918 [3]	59.9 [3]	23,031 [3]	11,898 [3]	51.7 [3]
South Carolina	53.6 [3]	53.2 [3]	65.7 [3]	65.3 [3]	63,039 [3]	46,528	73.8 [3]	62,888 [3]	45,830	72.9 [3]	65,014 [3]	46,914	72.2 [3]
South Dakota	56.1	53.8	52.0	50.6	19,031	9,257	48.6	19,039	9,245	48.6	18,106	9,064	50.1
Tennessee	53.8	54.3	52.1	52.1	114,358	58,652	51.3	116,120	59,584 [3]	51.3	111,891	60,022	53.6
Texas	51.3	51.1	50.6	48.6	594,002	288,655	48.6	596,330	289,481	48.5	607,364	294,547	48.5
Utah	54.9	54.3	54.1	54.0	41,588	22,415	53.9	41,545	22,147	53.3	44,499	22,287	50.1
Vermont	48.9	48.7	47.3	47.4	18,384	8,542	46.5	18,701	8,749	46.8	18,899	8,720	46.1
Virginia	55.6 [3]	54.1 [3]	54.1 [3]	54.0	162,994	99,919	61.3	166,578	90,573	54.4	179,688	93,732	52.2
Washington	53.0	52.4	52.3	46.9	112,740	52,953	47.0	109,294	52,824	48.3	111,848	53,125	47.5
West Virginia	54.3	54.5	54.3	53.5	38,132	20,119	52.8	37,957	20,020	52.7	37,979	19,958	52.6
Wisconsin	56.0	55.3	56.3	54.6	113,262	60,385	53.3	104,531	58,216	55.7	104,018	60,521	58.2
Wyoming	48.7	49.8	48.6	48.7	13,841 [3]	6,799 [3]	49.1 [3]	14,121	6,567	46.5	14,256	6,657	46.7
Bureau of Indian Affairs	—	—	—	—	—	—	—	—	—	—	—	—	—
DoDDS, overseas	66.4	64.0 [4]	66.0	65.3	7,045	4,794	68.0	7,282	4,728	64.9	6,845	4,885	71.4
DoDDS, domestic	—	—	59.2	57.5	4,200	2,425	57.7	4,157	2,301	55.4	2,865	2,002	69.9
Other jurisdictions													
American Samoa	50.1	49.7	50.0	54.2	1,735	943	54.4	1,771	988	55.8	1,813	945	52.1
Guam	34.2	49.1	51.5	50.9	—	—	—	3,466	1,760	50.8	3,318	1,672	50.4
Northern Marianas	47.6	51.0	50.2	50.9	1,093	545	49.9	1,155	550	47.6	1,166	579	49.7
Puerto Rico	57.7	57.5	54.4	57.0	74,553	42,369	56.8	74,697	42,444	56.8	76,865	43,054	56.0
Virgin Islands	51.3	51.6	52.1	53.6	3,036	1,502	49.5	2,896	1,512	52.2	2,977	1,545	51.9

—Not available.
[1] Data revised from previously published figures.
[2] U.S. totals include imputations for underreporting and nonreporting states.
[3] Includes imputations for underreporting.
[4] Includes both overseas and domestic schools.

NOTE: DoDDS = Department of Defense dependents schools.
SOURCE: U.S. Department of Education, National Center for Education Statistics, Common Core of Data (CCD), "State Nonfiscal Survey of Public Elementary/Secondary Education," 1998–99 through 2004–05. (This table was prepared March 2007.)

Table 81. Staff, enrollment, and pupil/staff ratios in public elementary and secondary school systems, by state or jurisdiction: Fall 1997 through fall 2004

State or jurisdiction	Pupil/staff ratio					Fall 2002			Fall 2003[1]			Fall 2004		
	Fall 1997	Fall 1998	Fall 1999	Fall 2000	Fall 2001	Staff	Enrollment	Pupil/ staff ratio	Staff	Enrollment	Pupil/ staff ratio	Staff	Enrollment	Pupil/ staff ratio
1	2	3	4	5	6	7	8	9	10	11	12	13	14	15
United States[2]....	8.8	8.6	8.3	8.3	8.1	5,954,661	48,183,086	8.1	5,953,667	48,540,215	8.2	6,053,465	48,794,911	8.1
Alabama..................	8.7[3]	8.5[3]	8.4[3]	8.2[3]	8.4[3]	88,893[3]	739,366[3]	8.3[3]	100,592	731,220	7.3	92,795	730,140	7.9
Alaska.....................	8.8[3]	8.4[3]	8.4[3]	8.3[3]	8.1[3]	17,101[3]	134,364	7.9[3]	16,550[3]	133,933	8.1[3]	17,632[3]	132,970	7.5[3]
Arizona	10.1	10.0[3]	9.7	9.7	9.8	96,639	937,755	9.7	96,341	1,012,068	10.5	97,953	1,043,298	10.7
Arkansas.................	8.9[3]	11.1[3]	7.5	7.1	6.8	63,815	450,985	7.1	64,693	454,523	7.0	66,127	463,115	7.0
California	11.8[3]	11.5[3]	11.3[3]	11.1[3]	10.9[3]	581,756[3]	6,353,667[3]	10.9[3]	572,835[3]	6,413,867[3]	11.2[3]	574,614[3]	6,441,557[3]	11.2[3]
Colorado	9.5	9.2	8.9	8.7	8.5	90,397	751,862	8.3	89,530	757,693	8.5	91,337	765,976	8.4
Connecticut.............	7.3	7.0	6.9	6.8	6.7	86,361	570,023	6.6	85,367	577,203	6.8	83,879	577,390	6.9
Delaware.................	8.9	8.8	8.4	9.1	8.2	14,449	116,342	8.1	14,587	117,668	8.1	14,966	119,091	8.0
District of Columbia	8.8[3]	7.3	8.1	6.4	6.6	11,548	76,166	6.6	10,608	78,057	7.4	12,162	76,714	6.3
Florida....................	9.0	8.9	8.8	8.8	8.8	287,091	2,539,929	8.8	295,775	2,587,628	8.7	311,853	2,639,336	8.5
Georgia..................	8.5[3]	7.9	7.7	7.8	7.7	197,944	1,496,012	7.6	200,512	1,522,611	7.6	209,746	1,553,437	7.4
Hawaii....................	11.1	10.8	10.4	10.0	9.5	20,703	183,829	8.9	21,113	183,609	8.7	20,531	183,185	8.9
Idaho.....................	10.6	10.3	10.1	10.1	10.0	24,897	248,604	10.0	25,133	252,120	10.0	25,533	256,084	10.0
Illinois...................	8.7[3]	8.6[3]	8.3[3]	8.2[3]	8.1[3]	257,352[3]	2,084,187	8.1[3]	254,119[3]	2,100,961	8.3[3]	261,237[3]	2,097,503	8.0[3]
Indiana...................	8.1	8.0	7.9	7.8	7.7	126,998	1,003,875	7.9	130,532	1,011,130	7.7	133,375	1,021,348	7.7
Iowa......................	7.8	7.6	7.5	7.3	7.0	67,426	482,210	7.2	68,137	481,226	7.1	68,450	478,319	7.0
Kansas...................	7.9	7.8	7.4	7.3	7.2	63,911	470,957	7.4	63,778	470,490	7.4	64,114	469,136	7.3
Kentucky................	7.5[3]	7.2	6.9	7.4	6.9	95,839	660,782	6.9	95,926	663,369	6.9	95,920	674,796	7.0
Louisiana	7.9	7.7	7.5	7.3	7.2	102,333	730,464	7.1	102,990	727,709	7.1	101,381	724,281	7.1
Maine.....................	7.0	6.7	6.4	6.2	6.0	34,586	204,337	5.9	35,866	202,084	5.6	34,899	198,820	5.7
Maryland................	9.5	9.0	9.0	8.8	8.7	102,642	866,743	8.4	107,529	869,113	8.1	108,296	865,561	8.0
Massachusetts...........	7.8	7.6	7.1	8.0	7.7	143,922	982,989	6.8	134,414[3]	980,459	7.3[3]	137,613[3]	975,574	7.1[3]
Michigan.................	8.4	8.2[3]	8.2[3]	8.2[3]	8.1	187,093	1,785,160	9.5	206,034[3]	1,757,604	8.5[3]	209,831	1,750,919	8.3
Minnesota...............	8.8	8.4	8.2	8.2[3]	8.1	105,311[3]	846,891	8.0[3]	103,744	842,854	8.1	104,367	838,503	8.0
Mississippi	8.2	7.7	7.8	7.7	7.6	66,133	492,645	7.4	68,377	493,540	7.2	67,249	495,376	7.4
Missouri	8.2	7.9	7.8	7.5	7.3	128,124	906,499	7.1	125,783	905,941	7.2	125,868	905,449	7.2
Montana..................	8.5[3]	8.4[3]	7.9[3]	8.0[3]	7.8[3]	18,693[3]	149,995	8.0[3]	18,656	148,356	8.0	18,762[3]	146,705	7.8[3]
Nebraska	7.7	7.6	7.4	7.2	7.0	40,743	285,402	7.0	40,573	285,542	7.0	40,998	285,761	7.0
Nevada...................	10.7	10.7	10.8	10.9	10.5	33,443	369,498	11.0	34,059	385,401	11.3	31,260	400,083	12.8
New Hampshire	8.1	8.0	7.6	7.4	7.1	30,087	207,671	6.9	30,830	207,417	6.7	31,408	206,852	6.6
New Jersey..............	7.5	7.4	7.2	7.1	6.9	199,381	1,367,438	6.9	204,038	1,380,753	6.8	213,418	1,393,347	6.5
New Mexico	8.2	8.0	7.5	7.1	7.1	43,826	320,234	7.3	44,841	323,066	7.2	46,531	326,102	7.0
New York................	7.6	7.6	7.1	6.9	6.8	428,045	2,888,233	6.7	394,178	2,864,775	7.3	399,089	2,836,337	7.1
North Carolina	8.3[3]	8.2	8.0	8.0	7.9	169,328	1,335,954	7.9	172,193	1,360,209	7.9	177,308	1,385,754	7.8
North Dakota	8.0	7.8	7.5	7.2	7.1	15,090	104,225	6.9	15,066	102,233	6.8	15,157	100,513	6.6
Ohio.......................	9.1	8.8	8.4	8.2	8.0	242,372	1,838,285	7.6	242,520	1,845,428	7.6	239,988	1,840,032	7.7
Oklahoma................	9.0	8.9	8.5	8.3	8.1	74,422	624,548	8.4	71,313	626,160	8.8	77,466	629,476	8.1
Oregon...................	10.2	10.1	9.8	9.7	9.6	55,042	554,071	10.1	54,272	551,273	10.2	56,637	552,322	9.8
Pennsylvania............	8.8	8.7	8.4	8.1	7.9	231,251	1,816,747	7.9	233,269	1,821,146	7.8	237,122	1,828,089	7.7
Rhode Island	8.9	8.7	8.7	8.9	8.5	18,303	159,205	8.7	19,890[3]	159,375	8.0[3]	23,031[3]	156,498	6.8[3]
South Carolina...........	8.3[3]	8.2[3]	7.8[3]	9.8[3]	9.5[3]	63,039[3]	694,389	11.0[3]	62,888[3]	699,198	11.1[3]	65,014[3]	703,736	10.8[3]
South Dakota............	8.5	8.0	7.5	7.1	6.9	19,031	130,048	6.8	19,039	125,537	6.6	18,106	122,798	6.8
Tennessee	8.7[3]	8.2[3]	8.2[3]	8.3[3]	8.3[3]	114,358	927,608[3]	8.1[3]	116,120	936,682[3]	8.1[3]	111,891	941,091[3]	8.4[3]
Texas.....................	7.9	7.8	7.6	7.5	7.1	594,002	4,259,823	7.2	596,330	4,331,751	7.3	607,364	4,405,215	7.3
Utah......................	12.2	12.3	11.9	11.8	11.8	41,588	489,262	11.8	41,545	495,981	11.9	44,499	503,607	11.3
Vermont..................	6.5	6.3	6.0	5.7	5.6	18,384	99,978	5.4	18,701	99,103	5.3	18,899	98,352	5.2
Virginia...................	7.8[3]	7.9[3]	7.2[3]	7.1[3]	7.0	162,994	1,177,229	7.2	166,578	1,192,092	7.2	179,688	1,204,739	6.7
Washington...............	10.7	10.6	10.5	10.3	9.0	112,740	1,014,798	9.0	109,294	1,021,349	9.3	111,848	1,020,005	9.1
West Virginia............	7.8	7.7	7.5	7.4	7.5	38,132	282,455	7.4	37,957	281,215	7.4	37,979	280,129	7.4
Wisconsin	8.6[3]	8.0	8.0	8.2	7.6	113,262	881,231	7.8	104,531	880,031	8.4	104,018	864,757	8.3
Wyoming.................	7.2	6.9	6.6	6.4	6.4	13,841[3]	88,116	6.4[3]	14,121	87,462	6.2	14,256	84,733	5.9
Bureau of Indian Affairs................	—	—	—	—	—	—	46,126	—	—	45,828	—	—	—	—
DoDDS, overseas.......	10.0	10.0	9.3[4]	9.5	9.3	7,045	72,889	10.3	7,282	71,053	9.8	6,845	68,327	10.0
DoDDS, domestic.......	—	—	—	8.4	7.6	4,200	32,115	7.6	4,157	30,603	7.4	2,865	29,151	10.2
Other jurisdictions														
American Samoa	10.1	10.1	9.6	9.6	9.4	1,735	15,984	9.2	1,771	15,893	9.0	1,813	16,126	8.9
Guam.................	11.1	10.5	8.9	8.5	8.5	—	—	—	3,466	31,572	9.1	3,318	30,605	9.2
Northern Marianas..	8.5	9.1	10.2	9.6	10.3	1,093	11,251	10.3	1,155	11,244	9.7	1,166	11,601	9.9
Puerto Rico...........	8.9	8.9	8.5	8.9	8.0	74,553	596,502	8.0	74,697	584,916	7.8	76,865	575,648	7.5
Virgin Islands	7.0	6.9	7.0	6.7	6.7	3,036	18,333	6.0	2,896	17,716	6.1	2,977	16,429	5.5

—Not available.
[1]Data revised from previously published figures.
[2]U.S. totals include imputations for underreporting and nonreporting states.
[3]Includes imputations for underreporting.
[4]Includes both overseas and domestic schools.

NOTE: DoDDS = Department of Defense dependents schools.
SOURCE: U.S. Department of Education, National Center for Education Statistics, Common Core of Data (CCD), "State Nonfiscal Survey of Public Elementary/Secondary Education," 1997–98 through 2004–05. (This table was prepared March 2007.)

Table 82. Principals in public and private elementary and secondary schools, by selected characteristics: 1993–94, 1999–2000, and 2003–04

Characteristic	1993-94[1]	1999-2000[1]	2003-04[1]	Percentage distribution of principals, by highest degree earned, 2003-04				Average years of experience			Average annual salary of principals in current dollars		Average annual salary of principals in constant 2005-06 dollars[2]	
				Bachelor's or less	Master's	Education specialist[3]	Doctor's and first-professional	As a principal, 1993-94	As a principal, 2003-04	Teaching experience, 2003-04	1993-94	2003-04	1993-94	2003-04
1	2	3	4	5	6	7	8	9	10	11	12	13	14	15
Public schools Total	79,620 (235)	83,790 (327)	87,620 (307)	1.9 (0.24)	59.2 (0.71)	30.3 (0.69)	8.6 (0.43)	8.7 (0.10)	7.8 (0.10)	13.5 (0.11)	$54,860 (127)	$75,500 (186)	$74,660 (172)	$80,730 (198)
Sex														
Males	52,110 (613)	47,130 (604)	45,930 (707)	1.6 (0.25)	62.9 (1.04)	27.8 (0.93)	7.7 (0.51)	10.3 (0.16)	9.1 (0.16)	12.2 (0.13)	54,920 (160)	75,630 (290)	74,750 (218)	80,870 (310)
Females	27,500 (542)	36,660 (598)	41,690 (708)	2.2 (0.41)	55.1 (1.23)	33.1 (1.13)	9.7 (0.70)	5.6 (0.12)	6.3 (0.13)	14.9 (0.16)	54,740 (276)	75,360 (334)	74,490 (375)	80,580 (357)
Race/ethnicity														
White	67,080 (540)	68,930 (579)	72,200 (509)	1.8 (0.28)	58.8 (0.74)	30.8 (0.78)	8.6 (0.45)	9.0 (0.12)	8.0 (0.12)	13.5 (0.12)	54,470 (138)	75,080 (221)	74,120 (188)	80,280 (237)
Black	8,020 (351)	9,240 (321)	9,250 (377)	2.0 (0.53)	56.2 (2.32)	30.9 (1.94)	10.9 (1.68)	7.1 (0.21)	6.9 (0.33)	14.3 (0.40)	57,670 (454)	77,360 (665)	78,480 (619)	82,720 (711)
Hispanic	3,270 (258)	4,330 (300)	4,680 (355)	1.5 (0.61)	69.2 (3.85)	24.1 (3.68)	5.2 (1.35)	6.0[4] (0.37)	6.1 (0.43)	11.9 (0.55)	55,860[4] (798)	79,450 (1,369)	76,030 (1,086)	84,960 (1,464)
Asian	620[4] (109)	630[4] (124)	460 (87)	6.8 (2.16)	70.0 (10.11)	20.3 (10.38)	3.0 (1.23)	6.0[4] (0.60)	6.8 (1.17)	13.6 (1.29)	59,450[4] (1,425)	82,640 (1,672)	80,900[4] (1,940)	88,370 (1,788)
American Indian/Alaska Native	630 (67)	660 (60)	600 (80)	4.5 (2.07)	64.4 (5.17)	24.7 (4.67)	6.5 (2.26)	12.6 (0.67)	6.9 (0.63)	12.6 (0.94)	51,120 (1,734)	62,010 (2,127)	69,570 (2,360)	66,310 (2,275)
Pacific Islander	—(†)	—(†)	‡(†)	‡(†)	‡(†)	‡(†)	‡(†)	—(†)	‡(†)	‡(†)	—(†)	‡(†)	—(†)	‡(†)
More than one race	—(†)	—(†)	350 (82)	3.2 (2.30)	48.5 (11.64)	35.6 (10.26)	12.7 (5.94)	—(†)	5.6 (1.12)	13.2 (0.98)	—(†)	75,800 (3,767)	—(†)	81,050 (4,028)
Age														
Under 40	5,940 (273)	8,440 (302)	12,840 (477)	3.5 (0.84)	67.3 (1.98)	26.4 (1.81)	2.9 (0.40)	2.8 (0.13)	2.4 (0.10)	7.6 (0.14)	46,540 (473)	68,820 (544)	63,340 (644)	73,590 (582)
40 to 44	14,570 (496)	10,510 (317)	9,540 (449)	2.4 (0.68)	66.4 (1.85)	26.7 (1.73)	4.5 (0.62)	5.0 (0.12)	4.5 (0.16)	11.0 (0.21)	52,040 (386)	72,310 (662)	70,820 (525)	77,320 (708)
45 to 49	25,430 (429)	19,600 (535)	16,120 (526)	2.2 (0.72)	66.0 (1.81)	29.9 (1.59)	7.9 (0.85)	7.1 (0.13)	6.1 (0.16)	13.4 (0.20)	55,420 (261)	73,280 (527)	75,430 (355)	78,360 (564)
50 to 54	18,870 (539)	27,120 (606)	24,170 (669)	1.3 (0.29)	56.8 (1.47)	31.8 (1.16)	10.1 (1.06)	10.3 (0.18)	8.7 (0.19)	15.2 (0.21)	56,560 (364)	77,050 (437)	76,970 (496)	82,390 (467)
55 or over	14,820 (441)	18,130 (500)	24,960 (679)	1.3 (0.36)	53.9 (1.63)	32.5 (1.60)	12.3 (0.97)	15.1 (0.35)	11.9 (0.23)	15.9 (0.27)	57,830 (495)	80,090 (476)	78,700 (674)	85,640 (509)
Type of school														
Elementary	53,680 (294)	60,110 (253)	61,480 (361)	1.2 (0.22)	59.9 (0.98)	30.5 (0.99)	8.5 (0.57)	8.9 (0.14)	7.9 (0.13)	13.7 (0.13)	54,160 (168)	75,400 (225)	73,710 (229)	80,630 (240)
Secondary	18,260 (161)	20,450 (197)	19,700 (272)	2.9 (0.70)	56.4 (1.30)	30.7 (1.21)	10.0 (0.56)	8.0 (0.12)	7.5 (0.19)	13.1 (0.19)	56,600 (167)	79,370 (442)	77,030 (227)	84,870 (472)
Combined	2,750 (143)	3,230 (146)	6,450 (263)	5.6 (1.05)	60.9 (2.07)	27.9 (1.96)	5.6 (0.86)	7.5 (0.29)	7.4 (0.36)	12.7 (0.35)	52,820 (511)	64,660 (615)	71,890 (695)	69,140 (658)
Location of school														
City[5]	—(†)	—(†)	22,690 (425)	1.7 (0.36)	55.1 (1.70)	31.7 (1.39)	11.4 (1.11)	—(†)	7.3 (0.17)	13.9 (0.23)	—(†)	80,200 (376)	—(†)	85,760 (403)
Suburban[6]	—(†)	—(†)	25,600 (506)	1.0 (0.27)	59.1 (1.30)	28.3 (1.35)	11.5 (0.96)	—(†)	7.9 (0.23)	13.0 (0.20)	—(†)	85,380 (473)	—(†)	91,300 (505)
Town[7]	—(†)	—(†)	13,700 (424)	2.1 (0.77)	62.1 (1.86)	30.7 (1.69)	5.1 (0.64)	—(†)	8.1 (0.28)	13.0 (0.27)	—(†)	68,940 (503)	—(†)	73,720 (538)
Rural[8]	—(†)	—(†)	25,640 (492)	2.8 (0.54)	61.2 (1.32)	30.9 (1.25)	5.1 (0.49)	—(†)	7.9 (0.22)	13.6 (0.18)	—(†)	64,990 (351)	—(†)	69,500 (376)
Private schools Total	25,020 (198)	26,230 (259)	27,690 (677)	33.1 (1.27)	49.5 (1.20)	10.7 (0.61)	6.7 (0.63)	8.8 (0.20)	10.0 (0.24)	14.1 (0.25)	$32,070 (363)	$50,180 (611)	$43,650 (495)	$53,660 (718)
Sex														
Males	11,610 (301)	11,900 (308)	12,110 (552)	29.1 (1.74)	50.6 (1.72)	10.5 (0.95)	9.8 (1.13)	9.0 (0.26)	11.0 (0.35)	13.3 (0.35)	35,600 (565)	55,400 (1,003)	48,440 (768)	59,240 (1,179)
Females	13,410 (283)	14,330 (307)	15,580 (491)	36.2 (1.83)	48.8 (1.80)	10.8 (0.83)	4.3 (0.75)	8.6 (0.27)	9.2 (0.28)	14.7 (0.36)	29,190 (608)	46,260 (843)	39,720 (827)	49,470 (991)
Race/ethnicity														
White	23,130 (270)	23,100 (309)	24,850 (715)	32.3 (1.33)	50.2 (1.26)	11.1 (0.65)	6.4 (0.64)	8.7 (0.22)	10.3 (0.24)	14.4 (0.26)	31,970 (401)	50,590 (603)	43,510 (545)	54,100 (709)
Black	1,060 (124)	1,570 (164)	1,440 (155)	39.6 (6.00)	43.3 (6.40)	7.3 (3.50)	9.7 (4.10)	8.3 (1.04)	7.1 (1.08)	11.9 (1.35)	34,380 (2,476)	44,310 (3,461)	46,790 (3,370)	47,380 (4,069)
Hispanic	520 (91)	830 (135)	820 (116)	33.5 (6.35)	53.0 (6.98)	6.7 (3.27)	6.8 (4.10)	10.1 (1.43)	6.6 (1.29)	10.9 (1.50)	31,350 (1,958)	48,010 (3,940)	42,660 (2,664)	51,340 (4,631)
Age														
Under 40	4,790 (302)	3,750 (223)	4,420 (267)	54.2 (3.41)	39.7 (3.36)	4.9 (1.13)	1.2 (0.59)	3.5 (0.22)	2.9 (0.20)	6.3 (0.37)	26,310 (869)	40,930 (1,582)	35,800 (1,183)	48,110 (1,860)
40 to 44	4,400 (217)	3,450 (212)	3,040 (250)	45.3 (4.75)	43.9 (4.21)	7.2 (2.45)	3.7 (1.59)	5.3 (0.24)	5.4 (0.38)	10.6 (0.57)	30,490 (928)	43,630 (1,719)	41,490 (1,263)	51,280 (2,021)
45 to 49	5,140 (216)	5,210 (261)	4,020 (250)	32.7 (3.49)	53.9 (3.22)	8.7 (1.39)	8.3 (2.16)	8.3 (0.27)	7.6 (0.20)	12.9 (0.51)	34,640 (736)	51,660 (1,467)	47,140 (1,002)	60,720 (1,724)
50 to 54	4,120 (228)	5,840 (291)	5,820 (337)	27.1 (2.46)	53.0 (2.42)	12.3 (1.57)	7.6 (1.23)	9.6 (0.34)	10.1 (0.35)	14.7 (0.49)	37,730 (999)	52,420 (1,568)	51,340 (1,359)	61,620 (1,843)
55 or over	6,550 (244)	7,980 (276)	10,390 (425)	24.1 (1.64)	53.1 (1.81)	14.0 (1.11)	8.7 (1.21)	14.8 (0.40)	15.2 (0.40)	18.6 (0.44)	31,780 (757)	54,000 (1,109)	43,250 (1,030)	63,470 (1,303)
Type of school														
Elementary	13,350 (158)	15,810 (245)	16,750 (327)	33.4 (1.64)	50.0 (1.57)	12.0 (0.81)	4.6 (0.66)	9.4 (0.27)	9.9 (0.30)	14.3 (0.34)	28,780 (444)	47,250 (673)	39,170 (605)	55,540 (791)
Secondary	2,300 (244)	2,630 (133)	2,510 (364)	13.3 (3.27)	62.9 (4.33)	13.0 (2.76)	10.9 (2.56)	7.8 (0.36)	9.3 (0.37)	15.6 (0.68)	43,630 (784)	65,010 (2,593)	59,450 (1,067)	76,420 (3,048)
Combined	6,770 (115)	7,800 (265)	8,430 (281)	38.4 (2.36)	44.7 (2.35)	7.3 (0.93)	9.6 (1.10)	8.0 (0.34)	10.3 (0.39)	13.4 (0.47)	33,630 (1,110)	51,580 (1,516)	45,770 (1,511)	60,630 (1,782)

—Not available.
†Not applicable.
‡Reporting standards not met.
[1]Total differs from data appearing in other tables because of varying survey processing procedures and time period coverages.
[2]Constant dollars based on the Consumer Price Index, prepared by the Bureau of Labor Statistics, U.S. Department of Labor, adjusted to a school-year basis. Excludes principals reporting a salary of $0.
[3]Education specialist degrees or certificates are generally awarded for 1 year's work beyond the master's level. Includes certificate of advanced studies.
[4]Data includes Pacific Islander.
[5]A city consists of a territory inside an urbanized area and inside a principal city.

[6]A suburb is a territory outside a principal city and inside an urbanized area. An urbanized area includes a central place and densely populated surrounding area with at least 50,000 people.
[7]A town is a territory within an urban cluster. An urban cluster is a central place with a densely populated adjacent territory including at least 2,500 people.
[8]A rural area is a Census-defined rural territory that is outside of an urbanized area and urban clusters.
NOTE: Race categories exclude persons of Hispanic origin. Standard errors appear in parentheses.
SOURCE: U.S. Department of Education, National Center for Education Statistics, Schools and Staffing Survey (SASS), "Public School Principal Questionnaire" and "Private School Principal Questionnaire," 1993–94, 1999–2000, and 2003–04. (This table was prepared June 2006.)

Table 83. Number of public school districts and public and private elementary and secondary schools: Selected years, 1869–70 through 2004–05

School year	Regular public school districts[1]	Public schools[2]		Schools with elementary grades		Schools with secondary grades	Private schools[2,3]		Schools with secondary grades
		Total, all schools[4]	Total, schools with reported grade spans[5]	Total	One-teacher		Total[4]	Schools with elementary grades	
1	2	3	4	5	6	7	8	9	10
1869–70	—	116,312	—	—	—	—	—	—	—
1879–80	—	178,122	—	—	—	—	—	—	—
1889–90	—	224,526	—	—	—	—	—	—	—
1899–1900	—	248,279	—	—	—	—	—	—	—
1909–10	—	265,474	—	—	212,448	—	—	—	—
1919–20	—	271,319	—	—	187,948	—	—	—	—
1929–30	—	248,117	—	238,306	148,712	23,930	—	9,275 [6]	3,258 [6]
1939–40	117,108 [7]	226,762	—	—	113,600	—	—	11,306 [6]	3,568 [6]
1949–50	83,718 [7]	—	—	128,225	59,652	24,542	—	10,375 [6]	3,331 [6]
1951–52	71,094 [7]	—	—	123,763	50,742	23,746	—	10,666 [6]	3,322 [6]
1959–60	40,520 [7]	—	—	91,853	20,213	25,784	—	13,574 [6]	4,061 [6]
1961–62	35,676 [7]	107,260	—	81,910	13,333	25,350	18,374	14,762 [6]	4,129 [6]
1963–64	31,705 [7]	104,015	—	77,584	9,895	26,431	—	—	4,451 [6]
1965–66	26,983 [7]	99,813	—	73,216	6,491	26,597	17,849 [6]	15,340 [6]	4,606 [6]
1967–68	22,010 [7]	—	94,197	70,879	4,146	27,011	—	—	—
1970–71	17,995 [7]	—	89,372	65,800	1,815	25,352	—	14,372 [6]	3,770 [6]
1973–74	16,730 [7]	—	88,655	65,070	1,365	25,906	—	—	—
1975–76	16,376 [7]	88,597	87,034	63,242	1,166	25,330	—	—	—
1976–77	16,271 [7]	—	86,501	62,644	1,111	25,378	19,910 [6]	16,385 [6]	5,904 [6]
1978–79	16,014 [7]	—	84,816	61,982	1,056	24,504	19,489 [6]	16,097 [6]	5,766 [6]
1979–80	15,929 [7]	87,004	—	—	—	—	—	—	—
1980–81	15,912 [7]	85,982	83,688	61,069	921	24,362	20,764 [6]	16,792 [6]	5,678 [6]
1982–83	15,824 [7]	84,740	82,039	59,656	798	23,988	—	—	—
1983–84	15,747 [7]	84,178	81,418	59,082	838	23,947	27,694	20,872	7,862
1984–85	—	84,007	81,147	58,827	825	23,916	—	—	—
1985–86	—	—	—	—	—	—	25,616	20,252	7,387
1986–87	15,713	83,455	82,190	60,784	763	23,389	—	—	—
1987–88	15,577	83,248	81,416	59,754	729	23,841	26,807	22,959	8,418
1988–89	15,376	83,165	81,579	60,176	583	23,638	—	—	—
1989–90	15,367	83,425	81,880	60,699	630	23,461	26,712	24,221	10,197
1990–91	15,358	84,538	82,475	61,340	617	23,460	24,690	22,223	8,989
1991–92	15,173	84,578	82,506	61,739	569	23,248	25,998	23,523	9,282
1992–93	15,025	84,497	82,896	62,225	430	23,220	—	—	—
1993–94	14,881	85,393	83,431	62,726	442	23,379	26,093	23,543	10,555
1994–95	14,772	86,221	84,476	63,572	458	23,668	—	—	—
1995–96	14,766	87,125	84,958	63,961	474	23,793	27,686	25,153	10,942
1996–97	14,841	88,223	86,092	64,785	487	24,287	—	—	—
1997–98	14,805	89,508	87,541	65,859	476	24,802	27,402	24,915	10,779
1998–99	14,891	90,874	89,259	67,183	463	25,797	—	—	—
1999–2000	14,928	92,012	90,538	68,173	423	26,407	27,223	24,685	10,693
2000–01	14,859	93,273	91,691	69,697	411	27,090	—	—	—
2001–02	14,559	94,112	92,696	70,516	408	27,468	29,273	26,569	11,846
2002–03	14,465	95,615	93,869	71,270	366	28,151	—	—	—
2003–04	14,383	95,726	93,977	71,195	376	28,219	28,384	25,691	11,188
2004–05	14,205	96,513	95,001	71,556	338	29,017	—	—	—

—Not available.
[1]Includes operating and nonoperating districts.
[2]Schools with both elementary and secondary programs are included under elementary schools and also under secondary schools.
[3]Data for most years prior to 1976–77 are partly estimated.
[4]Includes regular schools and special schools not classified by grade span.
[5]Includes elementary, secondary, and combined elementary/secondary schools.
[6]These data cannot be compared directly with the data for years after 1980–81.
[7]Because of expanded survey coverage, data are not directly comparable with figures after 1983–84.

SOURCE: U.S. Department of Education, National Center for Education Statistics, *Annual Report of the Commissioner of Education*, 1870 through 1910; *Biennial Survey of Education in the United States*, 1919–20 through 1949–50; *Statistics of State School Systems*, 1959–60 through 1967–68; *Statistics of Public Elementary and Secondary School Systems*, 1970–71 through 1980–81; *Statistics of Public and Nonpublic Elementary and Secondary Day Schools*, 1968–69; *Statistics of Nonpublic Elementary and Secondary Schools*, 1970–71; *Private Schools in American Education*; Schools and Staffing Survey (SASS), "Private School Questionnaire," 1987–88 and 1990–91; Private School Universe Survey (PSS), 1989–90 through 2003–2004; and Common Core of Data (CCD), "Local Education Agency Universe Survey" and "Public Elementary/Secondary School Universe Survey," 1982–83 through 2004–05. (This table was prepared August 2006.)

Table 84. Number of regular public school districts, by enrollment size of district: Selected years, 1990–91 through 2004–05

Enrollment size of district	Number of districts											2004–05		
	1990–91	1994–95	1995–96	1996–97	1997–98	1998–99	1999–2000	2000–01	2001–02	2002–03	2003–04	Number of districts	Percent of districts	Percent of students
1	2	3	4	5	6	7	8	9	10	11	12	13	14	15
Total........................	15,358	14,772	14,766	14,841	14,805	14,891	14,928	14,859	14,559	14,465	14,383	14,205	100.0	100.0
25,000 or more	190	207	216	226	230	236	238	240	243	248	256	264	1.9	33.9
10,000 to 24,999............	489	542	553	569	572	574	579	581	573	587	594	588	4.1	18.8
5,000 to 9,999................	937	996	1,013	1,024	1,038	1,026	1,036	1,036	1,067	1,062	1,058	1,059	7.5	15.4
2,500 to 4,999................	1,940	2,013	2,027	2,069	2,079	2,062	2,068	2,060	2,031	2,033	2,031	2,016	14.2	14.9
1,000 to 2,499................	3,542	3,579	3,554	3,536	3,524	3,496	3,457	3,448	3,429	3,411	3,421	3,389	23.9	11.6
600 to 999......................	1,799	1,777	1,777	1,772	1,775	1,790	1,814	1,776	1,744	1,745	1,728	1,737	12.2	2.9
300 to 599......................	2,275	2,113	2,104	2,066	2,044	2,066	2,081	2,107	2,015	1,987	1,981	1,927	13.6	1.8
1 to 299.........................	3,816	3,173	3,123	3,160	3,165	3,245	3,298	3,265	3,127	3,117	2,994	2,890	20.3	0.8
Size not reported	370	372	399	419	378	396	357	346	330	275	320	335	2.4	†

†Not applicable.
NOTE: Size not reported includes school districts reporting enrollment of zero. Regular districts exclude regional education service agencies and supervisory union administrative centers, state-operated agencies, federally operated agencies, and other types of local education agencies, such as independent charter schools. Detail may not sum to totals because of rounding.
SOURCE: U.S. Department of Education, National Center for Education Statistics, Common Core of Data (CCD), "Local Education Agency Universe Survey," 1990–91 through 2004–05. (This table was prepared August 2006.)

Table 85. Number of public elementary and secondary education agencies, by type of agency and state or jurisdiction: 2003–04 and 2004–05

State or jurisdiction	Total agencies		Regular school districts, including supervisory union components[1]		Regional education service agencies and supervisory union administrative centers		State-operated agencies		Federally operated agencies		Other agencies	
	2003–04	2004–05	2003–04	2004–05	2003–04	2004–05	2003–04	2004–05	2003–04	2004–05	2003–04	2004–05
1	2	3	4	5	6	7	8	9	10	11	12	13
United States	**17,468**	**17,618**	**14,383**	**14,205**	**1,445**	**1,447**	**174**	**192**	**0**	**0**	**1,466**	**1,774**
Alabama	133	134	130	131	0	0	3	3	0	0	0	0
Alaska	55	54	53	54	0	0	2	0	0	0	0	0
Arizona	589	593	313	218	10	13	2	2	0	0	264	360
Arkansas	341	291	309	254	15	15	3	3	0	0	14	19
California	1,131	1,129	989	985	130	134	12	10	0	0	0	0
Colorado	200	200	178	178	21	21	1	1	0	0	0	0
Connecticut	195	196	166	166	6	6	7	7	0	0	16	17
Delaware	33	35	19	19	1	1	0	2	0	0	13	13
District of Columbia	38	42	1	1	0	0	0	0	0	0	37	41
Florida	74	74	67	67	0	0	2	2	0	0	5	5
Georgia	198	204	180	180	18	16	0	5	0	0	0	3
Hawaii	1	1	1	1	0	0	0	0	0	0	0	0
Idaho	115	118	114	114	0	0	1	1	0	0	0	3
Illinois	1,101	1,094	887	880	209	209	5	5	0	0	0	0
Indiana	354	359	294	294	29	29	4	4	0	0	27	32
Iowa	382	379	370	367	12	12	0	0	0	0	0	0
Kansas	308	307	302	301	0	0	6	6	0	0	0	0
Kentucky	196	196	176	176	18	18	2	2	0	0	0	0
Louisiana	86	86	68	68	0	0	8	8	0	0	10	10
Maine	328	328	283	283	40	40	4	4	0	0	1	1
Maryland	24	26	24	24	0	0	0	1	0	0	0	1
Massachusetts	487	493	350	350	86	86	1	1	0	0	50	56
Michigan	807	828	553	552	57	57	6	4	0	0	191	215
Minnesota	519	536	348	343	74	60	5	6	0	0	92	127
Mississippi	163	163	152	152	0	0	11	11	0	0	0	0
Missouri	532	532	524	524	0	0	4	4	0	0	4	4
Montana	517	515	438	436	77	77	2	2	0	0	0	0
Nebraska	540	548	518	503	18	41	4	4	0	0	0	0
Nevada	18	18	17	17	0	0	1	1	0	0	0	0
New Hampshire	258	263	178	179	80	81	0	0	0	0	0	3
New Jersey	668	666	598	616	19	0	0	0	0	0	51	50
New Mexico	89	89	89	89	0	0	0	0	0	0	0	0
New York	814	835	726	733	38	38	0	0	0	0	50	64
North Carolina	212	214	117	115	0	0	2	2	0	0	93	97
North Dakota	253	250	213	210	37	37	3	3	0	0	0	0
Ohio	895	982	613	614	109	109	4	4	0	0	169	255
Oklahoma	603	602	541	540	0	0	3	3	0	0	59	59
Oregon	221	220	199	198	20	20	2	2	0	0	0	0
Pennsylvania	722	727	501	501	103	103	15	13	0	0	103	110
Rhode Island	48	49	38	32	0	4	3	12	0	0	7	1
South Carolina	102	102	89	85	13	13	0	4	0	0	0	0
South Dakota	192	188	172	168	17	17	3	3	0	0	0	0
Tennessee	136	136	136	136	0	0	0	0	0	0	0	0
Texas	1,265	1,275	1,040	1,038	20	20	13	16	0	0	192	201
Utah	60	69	40	40	0	0	2	2	0	0	18	27
Vermont	360	363	299	302	60	60	1	1	0	0	0	0
Virginia	226	226	134	134	70	69	22	23	0	0	0	0
Washington	306	306	296	296	10	10	0	0	0	0	0	0
West Virginia	57	57	55	55	0	0	2	2	0	0	0	0
Wisconsin	457	458	437	438	17	17	3	3	0	0	0	0
Wyoming	59	62	48	48	11	14	0	0	0	0	0	0
Bureau of Indian Affairs schools	23	23	0	0	0	0	0	0	23	23	0	0
DoDDS, domestic	7	7	0	0	0	0	0	0	7	7	0	0
DoDDS, overseas	9	9	0	0	0	0	0	0	9	9	0	0
Other jurisdictions												
American Samoa	1	1	1	1	0	0	0	0	0	0	0	0
Guam	1	1	1	1	0	0	0	0	0	0	0	0
Northern Marianas	1	1	1	1	0	0	0	0	0	0	0	0
Puerto Rico	1	1	1	1	0	0	0	0	0	0	0	0
Virgin Islands	1	1	1	1	0	0	0	0	0	0	0	0

[1]Regular school districts include both independent districts and those that are a dependent segment of a local government. Includes nonoperating agencies. Components of supervisory unions operate schools, but share superintendent services with other districts.
NOTE: DoDDS = Department of Defense dependents schools.

SOURCE: U.S. Department of Education, National Center for Education Statistics, Common Core of Data (CCD), "Local Education Agency Universe Survey," 2003–04 and 2004–05. (This table was prepared June 2006.)

Table 86. Public elementary and secondary students, schools, pupil/teacher ratios, and finances, by type of locale: 2003–04 and 2004–05

Selected characteristic	Total	City, large[1]	City, midsize[2]	City, small[3]	Suburban, large[4]	Suburban, midsize[5]	Suburban, small[6]	Town, fringe[7]	Town, distant[8]	Town, remote[9]	Rural, fringe[10]	Rural, distant[11]	Rural, remote[12]
1	2	3	4	5	6	7	8	9	10	11	12	13	14
Enrollment, schools, and pupil/ teacher ratios, fall 2004													
Enrollment (in thousands)	48,582	7,695	3,521	4,115	15,651	1,730	1,042	1,764	2,477	1,892	3,948	3,249	1,497
Percentage distribution of enrollment, by race/ethnicity	100.0	100.0	100.0	100.0	100.0	100.0	100.0	100.0	100.0	100.0	100.0	100.0	100.0
White	57.7	23.1	40.5	54.5	59.5	71.7	72.0	76.8	71.8	69.1	76.7	81.4	77.8
Black	17.1	31.0	28.4	18.1	15.5	9.4	8.9	7.6	12.0	10.9	11.6	9.8	7.5
Hispanic	19.4	38.1	24.6	21.0	18.1	15.0	14.3	13.2	13.3	15.6	9.0	6.0	6.5
Asian/Pacific Islander	4.5	7.0	5.8	5.3	6.4	3.2	3.9	1.3	1.2	1.1	1.4	0.6	0.5
American Indian/Alaska Native	1.2	0.9	0.7	1.0	0.5	0.6	0.8	1.1	1.7	3.2	1.3	2.3	7.7
Schools[13]	96,513	12,361	6,092	7,468	23,857	2,990	1,944	3,736	5,960	5,423	8,229	9,994	8,241
Average school size[14]	521	634	601	570	674	592	556	487	435	368	502	335	186
Pupil/teacher ratio[15]	16.2	17.1	16.6	16.4	16.6	16.7	16.9	16.4	15.6	15.2	15.6	14.7	12.9
Enrollment (percentage distribution)	100.0	15.8	7.2	8.5	32.2	3.6	2.1	3.6	5.1	3.9	8.1	6.7	3.1
Schools (percentage distribution)	100.0	12.8	6.3	7.8	24.8	3.1	2.0	3.9	6.2	5.6	8.5	10.4	8.6
Revenues, 2003–04													
Total revenue (in millions of dollars)	$467,123	$79,827	$33,059	$39,065	$158,051	$15,440	$9,345	$15,764	$21,490	$16,344	$35,039	$28,701	$14,999
Federal	40,319	9,726	3,512	3,727	9,289	1,047	679	1,168	2,114	1,925	2,661	2,546	1,925
Title I	10,182	3,172	937	962	1,941	228	160	285	543	489	476	554	437
Child Nutrition Act	7,933	1,846	702	716	1,816	224	127	248	447	362	577	555	312
Children with disabilities (IDEA)	7,315	1,481	598	674	2,359	244	173	220	319	274	446	357	168
Impact aid	1,140	74	30	114	200	22	16	34	35	115	98	107	297
Bilingual education	208	71	25	24	44	4	3	6	7	4	7	5	8
Indian education	95	9	3	5	6	1	1	2	7	10	6	13	32
Math, science, and professional development	1,386	277	139	149	307	39	29	50	78	85	79	80	75
Safe and drug-free schools	306	72	30	30	69	8	6	9	15	18	18	17	14
Title V, Part A	295	69	22	23	69	8	6	9	16	17	18	21	18
Vocational and technical education	514	118	51	52	121	14	10	14	28	27	32	28	18
Other and unclassified	10,945	2,537	974	977	2,356	256	147	291	621	524	902	811	548
State (in millions of dollars)	215,212	36,388	15,621	18,660	64,406	7,285	4,356	7,922	11,449	8,492	17,062	15,762	7,809
Special education programs	14,051	2,777	1,084	1,117	5,370	467	269	377	520	364	802	599	303
Compensatory and basic skills	4,801	1,271	358	565	1,703	140	74	99	130	69	184	128	81
Bilingual education	608	19	18	34	466	32	5	6	10	5	8	4	2
Gifted and talented	510	34	36	36	308	27	6	6	14	4	24	12	4
Vocational education	765	52	37	60	278	33	18	25	50	42	81	58	31
Other	194,477	32,235	14,089	16,849	56,281	6,585	3,984	7,410	10,725	8,009	15,963	14,961	7,387
Local (in millions of dollars)	211,591	33,713	13,926	16,678	84,357	7,108	4,310	6,673	7,926	5,926	15,316	10,392	5,265
Property tax[16]	132,253	17,924	8,337	10,454	55,526	4,056	2,960	4,468	5,399	4,124	8,883	6,598	3,523
Parent government contribution[16]	35,066	10,088	2,467	2,166	13,121	1,571	423	499	496	195	2,624	1,113	304
Private (fees from individuals)	11,582	1,001	663	958	4,366	441	261	446	600	457	1,106	872	412
Other	32,690	4,700	2,459	3,101	11,343	1,040	666	1,260	1,431	1,150	2,703	1,810	1,026
Total revenue (percentage distribution)	100.0	100.0	100.0	100.0	100.0	100.0	100.0	100.0	100.0	100.0	100.0	100.0	100.0
Federal	8.6	12.2	10.6	9.5	5.9	6.8	7.3	7.4	9.8	11.8	7.6	8.9	12.8
State	46.1	45.6	47.3	47.8	40.7	47.2	46.6	50.3	53.3	52.0	48.7	54.9	52.1
Local	45.3	42.2	42.1	42.7	53.4	46.0	46.1	42.3	36.9	36.3	43.7	36.2	35.1
Expenditures, 2003–04													
Total expenditures (in millions of dollars)	$477,745	$83,304	$33,386	$39,644	$161,523	$15,702	$9,724	$16,292	$22,131	$16,265	$35,588	$29,158	$15,030
Current expenditures for schools	394,227	68,176	27,939	32,871	131,763	12,866	7,839	13,415	18,550	14,030	29,410	24,548	12,820
Instruction	244,165	43,061	17,113	20,385	81,616	7,968	4,814	8,337	11,389	8,623	18,045	15,063	7,751
Support services, students	20,228	3,067	1,519	1,806	7,501	665	402	661	894	697	1,506	1,029	481
Support services, instructional staff	18,367	3,540	1,510	1,625	6,212	577	341	546	803	587	1,231	941	456
Administration	22,532	3,971	1,691	1,890	7,488	756	454	748	1,047	775	1,653	1,367	692
Operation and maintenance	38,211	6,686	2,694	3,183	12,857	1,266	759	1,279	1,785	1,373	2,760	2,295	1,272
Transportation	16,661	2,585	1,003	1,129	5,717	507	342	599	765	540	1,480	1,325	668
Food service	15,305	2,517	1,138	1,309	4,414	508	299	559	864	648	1,269	1,171	608
Other	18,759	2,749	1,270	1,545	5,959	618	428	685	1,003	787	1,466	1,357	892
Other current expenditures	16,192	2,600	1,180	1,379	4,769	568	319	582	886	685	1,363	1,207	653
Interest on school debt	12,136	2,351	723	868	4,391	391	249	458	489	304	1,001	665	245
Capital outlay	52,109	8,858	3,089	4,358	18,664	1,920	1,288	1,814	2,346	1,441	3,898	2,985	1,446

See notes at end of table.

Table 86. Public elementary and secondary students, schools, pupil/teacher ratios, and finances, by type of locale: 2003–04 and 2004–05—Continued

Selected characteristic	Total	City, large[1]	City, midsize[2]	City, small[3]	Suburban, large[4]	Suburban, midsize[5]	Suburban, small[6]	Town, fringe[7]	Town, distant[8]	Town, remote[9]	Rural, fringe[10]	Rural, distant[11]	Rural, remote[12]
1	2	3	4	5	6	7	8	9	10	11	12	13	14
Current expenditures													
(percentage distribution)..............	100.0	100.0	100.0	100.0	100.0	100.0	100.0	100.0	100.0	100.0	100.0	100.0	100.0
Instruction.....................................	61.9	63.2	61.3	62.0	61.9	61.9	61.4	62.1	61.4	61.5	61.4	61.4	60.5
Support services...........................	9.8	9.7	10.8	10.4	10.4	9.7	9.5	9.0	9.2	9.1	9.3	8.0	7.3
Administration..............................	5.7	5.8	6.1	5.7	5.7	5.9	5.8	5.6	5.6	5.5	5.6	5.6	5.4
Operation and maintenance...........	9.7	9.8	9.6	9.7	9.8	9.8	9.7	9.5	9.6	9.8	9.4	9.4	9.9
Transportation..............................	4.2	3.8	3.6	3.4	4.3	3.9	4.4	4.5	4.1	3.9	5.0	5.4	5.2
Food service and other..................	8.6	7.7	8.6	8.7	7.9	8.8	9.3	9.3	10.1	10.2	9.3	10.3	11.7
Current expenditure per student													
(in dollars)................................	$8,187	$8,859	$8,035	$8,035	$8,537	$7,649	$7,525	$7,645	$7,500	$7,407	$7,634	$7,577	$8,438
Instruction expenditure per student													
(in dollars)................................	5,070	5,596	4,922	4,983	5,288	4,737	4,621	4,751	4,605	4,553	4,684	4,649	5,102

[1]Located inside an urbanized area and inside a principal city with a population of at least 250,000.

[2]Located inside an urbanized area and inside a principal city with a population of at least 100,000, but less than 250,000.

[3]Located inside an urbanized area and inside a principal city with a population less than 100,000.

[4]Located inside an urbanized area and outside a principal city with a population of 250,000 or more.

[5]Located inside an urbanized area and outside a principal city with a population of at least 100,000, but less than 250,000.

[6]Located inside an urbanized area and outside a principal city with a population less than 100,000.

[7]Located inside an urban cluster that is 10 miles or less from an urbanized area.

[8]Located inside an urban cluster that is more than 10, but less than or equal to 35 miles from an urbanized area.

[9]Located inside an urban cluster that is more than 35 miles from an urbanized area.

[10]Located outside any urbanized area or urban cluster and is 5 miles or less from an urbanized area or 2 miles or less from an urban cluster.

[11]Located outside any urbanized area or urban cluster and is more than 5 miles and less than or equal to 25 miles from an urbanized area, or more than 2 miles and less than or equal to 10 miles from an urban cluster.

[12]Located outside any urbanized area or urban cluster and more than 25 miles from an urbanized area or more than 10 miles from an urban cluster.

[13]Total includes 218 schools not reported by locale type.

[14]Average for schools reporting enrollment. Enrollment data were available for 93,295 out of 96,513 institutions in 2004–05.

[15]Ratio for schools reporting both full-time-equivalent teachers and fall enrollment data.

[16]Property tax and parent government contributions are determined on the basis of independence or dependence of the local school system and are mutually exclusive.

NOTE: Locale codes for districts with missing values were imputed, where possible. Detail may not sum to totals because of rounding and missing locale codes for some school districts. Race categories exclude persons of Hispanic origin.

SOURCE: U.S. Department of Education, National Center for Education Statistics, Common Core of Data (CCD), "Public Elementary/Secondary School Universe Survey," 2004–05, and "Local Education Agency Universe Survey," 2003–04 and 2004–05; and "National Public Education Financial Survey," 2003–04. (This table was prepared October 2006.)

Table 87. Selected statistics on enrollment, teachers, dropouts, and graduates in public school districts enrolling more than 15,000 students, by state: 1990, 2000, 2001–02, 2003–04, and 2004

Name of district	State	Enrollment, fall 1990	Enrollment, fall 2000	Enrollment, fall 2004	Percentage distribution of enrollment, by race, fall 2004						Number of classroom teachers, fall 2004	Pupil/teacher ratio, fall 2004	Total number of staff, fall 2004	Student/staff ratio, fall 2004	Percent dropouts from grades 9–12, 2001–02[1]					Number of high school graduates, 2003–04[2]	Number of schools, fall 2004
					White	Minority Total	Black	Hispanic	Asian/ Pacific Islander	American Indian/ Alaska Native					Total	Grade 9	Grade 10	Grade 11	Grade 12		
1	2	3	4	5	6	7	8	9	10	11	12	13	14	15	16	17	18	19	20	21	22
Districts with more than 15,000 students	†	**16,907,522**	**20,230,241**	**21,144,745**	**39.9**	**60.1**	**24.8**	**28.1**	**6.5**	**0.7**	—	—	—	—	—	—	—	—	—	—	**30,575**
Baldwin County	AL	17,479	22,656	24,443	80.8	19.2	15.9	2.2	0.6	0.5	1,743	14.0	3,345	7.3	3.1	2.1	3.2	5.2	2.3	1,257	47
Birmingham City	AL	41,536	37,843	31,843	1.1	98.9	97.2	1.5	0.2	#	2,232	14.3	4,113	7.7	2.1	1.9	2.6	2.2	1.8	1,498	81
Huntsville City	AL	23,945	22,832	22,405	50.6	49.4	43.3	3.1	2.4	0.5	1,609	13.9	2,724	8.2	3.1	4.6	2.5	1.7	3.0	1,117	50
Jefferson County	AL	40,664	40,726	39,434	66.0	34.0	31.3	2.0	0.5	0.1	2,570	15.3	4,626	8.5	4.1	2.7	4.7	4.7	4.6	2,080	61
Madison County	AL	13,861	15,675	17,498	77.0	23.0	15.9	1.5	0.9	4.7	1,127	15.5	2,123	8.2	4.9	5.7	5.1	4.5	3.9	925	25
Mobile County	AL	67,203	64,976	63,987	45.4	54.6	50.8	0.8	2.2	0.9	4,228	15.1	7,534	8.5	4.0	4.2	4.1	4.6	3.0	2,972	115
Montgomery County	AL	35,956	33,267	31,985	20.0	80.0	77.0	1.3	1.7	0.1	2,363	13.5	4,533	7.1	4.4	2.0	3.8	7.4	5.1	1,308	63
Shelby County	AL	16,008	20,129	23,336	81.7	18.3	12.0	4.6	1.5	0.2	1,675	13.9	3,159	7.4	2.6	1.3	2.2	3.2	5.1	1,176	35
Tuscaloosa County	AL	14,426	15,666	15,978	73.6	26.4	24.8	1.1	0.5	0.1	992	16.1	1,952	8.2	3.7	3.6	3.6	4.0	3.5	799	30
Anchorage	AK	42,300	49,526	49,545	58.5	41.5	8.7	6.7	11.7	14.4	2,823	17.5	6,718	7.4	8.6	5.4	8.5	9.8	11.3	2,621	94
Amphitheater Unified District	AZ	13,835	16,857	16,703	58.5	41.5	3.7	32.8	3.1	1.8	948	17.6	1,918	8.7	3.4	1.8	2.7	3.6	6.3	1,111	20
Cartwright Elementary District	AZ	14,369	17,746	20,009	8.2	91.8	4.9	85.3	0.7	1.0	1,008	19.8	2,298	8.7	†	†	†	†	†	†	29
Chandler Unified District	AZ	11,038	21,703	29,578	57.7	42.3	6.4	29.3	5.2	1.4	1,454	20.3	2,743	10.8	4.1	4.7	3.7	3.2	4.5	1,312	25
Gilbert Unified District	AZ	10,863	29,188	37,070	75.9	24.1	4.1	15.0	4.2	0.9	2,011	18.4	3,766	9.8	2.5	0.8	2.6	2.7	4.3	†	37
Kyrene Elementary District	AZ	10,487	19,446	18,473	67.8	32.2	7.3	14.3	8.0	2.7	1,032	17.9	1,809	10.2	†	†	†	†	†	†	26
Mesa Unified District	AZ	62,470	73,587	75,471	58.4	41.6	3.9	31.5	2.3	3.9	3,761	20.1	7,788	9.7	3.8	3.4	4.9	3.6	2.8	4,210	91
Paradise Valley Unified District	AZ	26,698	34,882	35,202	73.7	26.3	3.2	19.1	2.9	1.1	1,854	19.0	3,193	11.0	5.9	4.9	4.4	6.4	8.0	2,306	48
Peoria Unified	AZ	20,846	32,608	37,355	68.6	31.4	5.1	22.1	3.1	1.2	1,931	19.3	3,268	11.4	2.4	1.3	3.0	3.2	2.5	—	39
Phoenix Union High	AZ	18,182	22,192	24,776	10.6	89.4	9.8	74.7	1.5	3.5	1,256	19.7	2,605	9.5	11.2	7.4	11.6	12.9	14.6	3,822	14
Scottsdale Unified District	AZ	19,741	26,958	26,356	79.2	20.8	2.4	13.4	3.6	1.5	1,416	18.6	2,622	10.0	1.4	1.2	1.4	1.8	1.3	1,855	33
Deer Valley Unified District	AZ	15,898	27,158	33,318	79.8	20.2	3.1	12.8	3.4	0.8	1,656	20.1	2,966	11.2	6.3	5.5	5.2	6.9	8.0	614	36
Sunnyside Unified District	AZ	13,058	14,518	16,524	6.2	93.8	2.2	87.1	0.5	4.0	899	18.4	1,904	8.7	12.3	13.1	12.1	10.5	12.3	—	22
Tucson Unified District	AZ	56,177	61,869	61,204	34.6	65.4	6.8	51.9	2.6	4.1	3,117	19.6	6,107	10.0	4.7	4.0	5.1	5.7	3.8	3,546	123
Washington Elementary	AZ	22,446	24,723	24,280	45.3	54.7	6.9	41.0	3.1	3.6	1,275	19.0	2,614	9.3	†	†	†	†	†	†	32
Little Rock	AR	25,813	25,502	25,720	24.3	75.7	68.6	5.0	1.8	0.3	1,760	14.6	3,601	7.1	12.1	12.2	11.7	11.5	13.3	1,238	52
Pulaski Co. Spec.	AR	21,495	18,735	18,449	55.1	44.9	41.0	2.5	1.1	0.2	1,144	16.1	2,520	7.3	7.5	7.9	6.4	7.5	8.3	941	36
ABC Unified	CA	20,972	22,303	21,944	10.0	90.0	9.8	39.1	40.8	0.3	981	22.4	1,861	11.8	—	—	—	—	—	1,585	30
Alhambra Unified	CA	20,313	19,776	19,673	6.7	93.3	0.8	40.1	52.3	0.1	875	22.5	1,595	12.3	—	—	—	—	—	1,574	19
Alvord Unified	CA	14,853	17,664	19,964	21.3	78.7	5.5	67.3	5.4	0.5	875	22.8	1,498	13.3	—	—	—	—	—	872	19
Anaheim City	CA	14,972	22,275	21,383	6.8	93.2	1.7	84.7	6.5	0.3	1,029	20.8	1,793	11.9	—	—	—	—	—	—	23
Anaheim Union High	CA	23,086	29,363	32,975	23.0	77.0	3.4	56.9	16.2	0.5	1,290	25.6	2,408	13.7	—	—	—	—	—	3,794	22
Antelope Valley Union High	CA	10,937	19,056	23,900	35.3	64.7	21.3	38.9	3.8	0.6	935	25.6	1,822	13.1	—	—	—	—	—	3,421	13
Antioch Unified	CA	13,045	20,018	21,514	36.2	63.8	20.0	30.5	12.1	1.2	951	22.6	1,428	15.1	—	—	—	—	—	1,333	23
Apple Valley Unified	CA	11,265	13,292	15,166	57.5	42.5	12.0	26.8	3.1	0.6	666	22.8	1,306	11.6	—	—	—	—	—	886	16
Bakersfield City Elementary	CA	24,911	27,674	28,234	15.0	85.0	12.2	70.1	1.6	1.1	1,379	20.5	2,685	10.5	—	—	—	—	—	†	42
Baldwin Park Unified	CA	15,878	17,473	19,187	5.3	94.7	2.1	86.7	5.7	0.2	806	23.8	1,542	12.4	—	—	—	—	—	908	22
Bellflower Unified	CA	9,917	14,935	15,456	21.7	78.3	16.6	51.4	10.1	0.3	689	22.4	1,208	12.8	—	—	—	—	—	842	15
Burbank Unified	CA	12,057	16,170	16,783	49.0	51.0	3.0	38.3	9.5	0.2	778	21.6	1,368	12.3	—	—	—	—	—	1,238	20
Cajon Valley Union Elementary	CA	17,328	19,059	17,348	55.2	44.8	8.6	30.8	4.5	0.9	817	21.2	1,488	11.7	—	—	—	—	—	—	27
Capistrano Unified	CA	26,852	45,074	50,615	72.0	28.0	1.3	19.3	7.1	0.4	2,180	23.2	4,049	12.5	—	—	—	—	—	2,736	57
Chaffey Joint Union High	CA	13,505	19,851	24,416	28.3	71.7	11.4	53.4	6.5	0.4	998	24.5	1,713	14.3	—	—	—	—	—	3,956	11
Chino Valley Unified	CA	23,257	31,763	33,767	34.1	65.9	4.6	47.4	13.7	0.2	1,446	23.3	2,468	13.7	—	—	—	—	—	2,127	35
Chula Vista Elementary	CA	17,604	23,132	26,152	16.3	83.7	4.8	65.3	13.1	0.4	1,375	19.0	2,244	11.7	—	—	—	—	—	†	42
Clovis Unified	CA	23,224	32,717	35,344	58.1	41.9	3.6	22.4	14.7	1.2	1,609	22.0	2,908	12.2	—	—	—	—	—	2,172	40
Coachella Valley Joint Unified	CA	9,091	12,636	15,452	1.5	98.5	0.3	97.6	0.3	0.3	711	21.7	1,410	11.0	—	—	—	—	—	592	19

See notes at end of table.

Table 87. Selected statistics on enrollment, teachers, dropouts, and graduates in public school districts enrolling more than 15,000 students, by state: 1990, 2000, 2001–02, 2003–04, and 2004—Continued

Name of district	State	Enrollment, fall 1990	Enrollment, fall 2000	Enrollment, fall 2004	White	Total	Black	Hispanic	Asian/ Pacific Islander	American Indian/ Alaska Native	Number of classroom teachers, fall 2004	Pupil/ teacher ratio, fall 2004	Total number of staff, fall 2004	Student/ staff ratio, fall 2004	Total	Grade 9	Grade 10	Grade 11	Grade 12	Number of high school graduates, 2003–04[2]	Number of schools, fall 2004
1	2	3	4	5	6	7	8	9	10	11	12	13	14	15	16	17	18	19	20	21	22
Colton Joint Unified	CA	16,415	22,118	24,932	14.1	85.9	8.7	72.7	4.0	0.5	1,140	21.9	1,847	13.5	—	—	—	—	—	1,040	28
Compton Unified	CA	27,585	31,037	31,449	0.4	99.6	27.1	71.4	1.1	#	1,302	24.2	2,581	12.2	—	—	—	—	—	984	40
Conejo Valley Unified	CA	17,209	20,999	22,383	71.2	28.8	1.7	17.7	8.7	0.7	1,002	22.3	1,804	12.4	—	—	—	—	—	1,461	29
Corona-Norco County Unified	CA	23,036	37,487	45,551	40.2	59.8	6.1	46.3	7.0	0.4	2,159	21.1	3,602	12.6	—	—	—	—	—	2,479	44
Covina-Valley Unified	CA	11,666	14,422	15,110	20.4	79.6	5.4	63.8	10.0	0.4	673	21.9	1,309	11.5	—	—	—	—	—	1,028	20
Cupertino Union School	CA	12,227	15,670	16,285	30.4	69.6	1.3	4.7	63.3	0.3	744	21.9	1,216	13.4	—	—	—	—	—	—	24
Desert Sands Unified	CA	16,058	23,500	27,059	30.3	69.7	2.0	65.4	1.9	0.4	1,245	21.7	2,258	12.0	—	—	—	—	—	1,492	28
Downey Unified	CA	15,418	21,474	22,800	13.1	86.9	4.1	76.9	5.5	0.4	985	23.2	1,698	13.4	—	—	—	—	—	1,213	21
East Side Union High	CA	21,973	24,282	25,496	13.3	86.7	4.6	43.9	37.8	0.4	1,149	22.2	2,049	12.4	—	—	—	—	—	4,667	23
Elk Grove Unified	CA	27,246	47,736	58,670	31.9	68.1	19.7	20.4	27.1	1.0	2,769	21.2	4,739	12.4	—	—	—	—	—	3,110	58
Escondido Union Elementary	CA	14,663	19,312	20,239	29.5	70.5	2.9	62.4	4.6	0.5	1,033	19.6	1,752	11.6	—	—	—	—	—	†	23
Fairfield-Suisun Unified	CA	20,227	22,263	23,370	31.5	68.5	23.0	28.2	16.3	1.0	1,138	20.5	1,821	12.8	—	—	—	—	—	1,241	27
Folsom-Cordova Unified	CA	12,656	16,277	18,357	65.5	34.5	8.9	13.8	10.9	1.0	836	22.0	1,488	12.3	—	—	—	—	—	903	32
Fontana Unified	CA	27,043	37,244	42,050	8.7	91.3	8.0	80.6	2.2	0.5	1,909	22.0	3,328	12.6	—	—	—	—	—	1,923	41
Fremont Unified	CA	27,172	31,078	32,036	29.2	70.8	5.9	14.2	50.2	0.5	1,502	21.3	2,297	13.9	—	—	—	—	—	1,966	41
Fresno Unified	CA	71,500	79,007	80,760	16.6	83.4	11.4	55.3	16.1	0.7	3,924	20.6	7,265	11.1	—	—	—	—	—	3,889	104
Fullerton Joint Union High	CA	12,729	15,165	16,742	28.0	72.0	2.1	49.9	19.8	0.2	584	28.7	1,122	14.9	—	—	—	—	—	2,940	8
Garden Grove Unified	CA	37,969	48,742	50,030	15.7	84.3	1.1	52.4	30.5	0.3	2,102	23.8	4,039	12.4	—	—	—	—	—	2,592	67
Glendale Unified	CA	25,459	30,329	28,816	56.8	43.2	1.1	22.7	19.2	0.2	1,331	21.6	2,320	12.4	—	—	—	—	—	2,097	32
Grossmont Union High	CA	18,647	23,639	24,971	61.2	38.8	8.9	23.1	4.7	2.1	1,043	23.9	2,130	11.7	—	—	—	—	—	4,278	19
Hacienda La Puente Unified	CA	23,267	24,646	24,955	7.2	92.8	2.7	73.4	16.3	0.4	1,174	21.3	2,070	12.1	—	—	—	—	—	1,498	39
Hayward Unified	CA	19,122	24,205	23,372	12.2	87.8	15.8	50.5	20.9	0.6	1,137	20.6	1,880	12.4	—	—	—	—	—	1,216	33
Hemet Unified	CA	12,811	17,451	21,276	52.0	48.0	6.5	37.3	3.0	1.2	959	22.2	1,586	13.4	—	—	—	—	—	985	27
Hesperia Unified	CA	13,113	15,360	18,722	45.9	54.1	6.4	45.1	1.8	0.8	761	24.6	1,447	12.9	—	—	—	—	—	893	23
Huntington Beach Union High	CA	14,039	14,359	15,283	49.8	50.2	1.3	18.5	25.0	5.5	589	25.9	1,171	13.0	—	—	—	—	—	2,989	9
Inglewood Unified	CA	16,355	17,295	17,458	0.5	99.5	41.4	57.2	0.8	#	925	18.9	1,581	11.0	—	—	—	—	—	579	20
Jurupa Unified	CA	15,419	19,839	21,222	23.5	76.5	4.2	69.7	2.2	0.4	915	23.2	1,544	13.7	—	—	—	—	—	1,029	24
Kern Union High	CA	20,183	29,333	33,776	37.8	62.2	8.0	49.5	3.9	0.8	1,489	22.7	2,960	11.4	—	—	—	—	—	6,191	23
Lake Elsinore Unified	CA	11,000	17,178	20,203	48.0	52.0	4.9	42.5	3.8	0.9	898	22.5	1,652	12.2	—	—	—	—	—	1,070	22
Lancaster Elementary	CA	11,248	14,433	15,933	26.9	73.1	29.7	39.6	3.2	0.6	752	21.2	1,323	12.0	—	—	—	—	—	†	19
Lodi Unified	CA	23,954	27,339	30,092	34.9	65.1	8.4	33.7	22.3	0.7	1,355	22.2	3,045	9.9	—	—	—	—	—	1,417	49
Long Beach Unified	CA	71,342	93,694	96,319	16.7	83.3	18.2	49.7	15.0	0.3	4,430	21.7	9,888	9.7	—	—	—	—	—	4,785	91
Los Angeles Unified	CA	625,086	721,346	741,367	9.0	91.0	11.7	72.8	6.3	0.3	35,186	21.1	72,983	10.2	—	—	—	—	—	29,621	721
Lynwood Unified	CA	15,469	18,237	19,072	0.2	99.8	8.5	91.0	0.3	#	734	26.0	1,281	14.9	—	—	—	—	—	832	13
Madera Unified	CA	13,728	15,957	17,732	16.3	83.7	3.4	78.6	1.5	0.2	799	22.2	1,585	11.2	—	—	—	—	—	794	20
Manteca Unified	CA	13,356	19,746	23,693	36.1	63.9	9.4	40.5	12.6	1.4	1,029	23.0	1,712	13.8	—	—	—	—	—	1,132	25
Modesto City Elementary	CA	17,405	18,740	18,025	27.7	72.3	4.9	59.6	6.9	1.0	931	19.4	1,576	11.4	—	—	—	—	—	†	27
Modesto City High	CA	10,697	14,547	15,856	43.8	56.2	5.8	39.3	10.0	1.0	628	25.3	1,190	13.3	—	—	—	—	—	3,029	6
Montebello Unified	CA	32,938	34,794	35,999	2.5	97.5	0.4	93.2	3.8	0.1	1,524	23.6	2,820	12.8	—	—	—	—	—	1,691	29
Moreno Valley Unified	CA	29,064	32,730	35,937	18.6	81.4	21.3	54.1	5.5	0.4	1,598	22.5	2,950	12.2	—	—	—	—	—	1,724	35
Mount Diablo Unified	CA	32,840	36,648	36,271	54.9	45.1	5.2	26.7	12.6	0.5	1,792	20.2	2,923	12.4	—	—	—	—	—	2,192	56
Murrieta Valley Unified	CA	3,990	12,065	18,677	62.5	37.5	6.4	21.9	8.6	0.5	807	23.2	1,463	12.8	—	—	—	—	—	940	16
Napa Valley Unified	CA	13,705	16,392	16,974	48.4	51.6	2.0	41.8	6.3	1.5	861	19.7	1,482	11.5	—	—	—	—	—	1,066	36
Newport-Mesa Unified	CA	16,434	21,658	22,487	52.3	47.7	1.3	39.9	6.1	0.3	1,039	21.7	2,047	11.0	—	—	—	—	—	1,214	31
Norwalk-La Mirada Unified	CA	19,179	23,610	23,769	15.5	84.5	4.1	72.0	8.1	0.4	1,067	22.3	2,035	11.7	—	—	—	—	—	1,287	29
Oakland Unified	CA	52,095	54,863	49,214	6.1	93.9	41.7	34.8	17.0	0.4	2,654	18.5	4,596	10.7	—	—	—	—	—	1,592	124
Oceanside Unified	CA	17,034	22,354	22,159	29.7	70.3	9.8	51.6	8.2	0.7	1,103	20.7	1,829	12.1	—	—	—	—	—	974	28
Ontario-Montclair Elementary	CA	21,033	26,407	26,293	8.1	91.9	4.3	84.3	3.0	0.3	1,272	20.7	2,183	12.0	—	—	—	—	—	†	34
Orange Unified	CA	25,224	31,097	31,351	41.4	58.6	1.7	43.5	12.8	0.6	1,534	20.4	2,966	10.6	—	—	—	—	—	1,801	42
Oxnard Elementary	CA	11,212	16,249	16,541	8.1	91.9	2.6	85.3	3.5	0.5	791	20.9	1,334	12.4	—	—	—	—	—	†	21
Oxnard Union High	CA	11,512	14,552	16,032	21.0	79.0	3.7	66.6	7.8	0.8	659	24.3	1,203	13.3	—	—	—	—	—	2,558	9

See notes at end of table.

Table 87. Selected statistics on enrollment, teachers, dropouts, and graduates in public school districts enrolling more than 15,000 students, by state: 1990, 2000, 2001–02, 2003–04, and 2004—Continued

Name of district	State	Enroll-ment, fall 1990	Enroll-ment, fall 2000	Enroll-ment, fall 2004	White	Minority Total	Black	Hispanic	Asian/ Pacific Islander	American Indian/ Alaska Native	Number of classroom teachers, fall 2004	Pupil/ teacher ratio, fall 2004	Total number of staff 2004	Student/ staff ratio, fall 2004	Dropouts Total	Grade 9	Grade 10	Grade 11	Grade 12	Number of high school graduates, 2003–04	Number of schools, fall 2004
1	2	3	4	5	6	7	8	9	10	11	12	13	14	15	16	17	18	19	20	21	22
Pajaro Valley Unified School	CA	16,355	19,864	18,899	19.0	81.0	0.5	78.3	1.9	0.2	872	21.7	1,899	9.9	—	—	—	—	—	955	31
Palm Springs Unified	CA	14,427	20,847	23,217	24.1	75.9	5.1	66.3	3.7	0.8	1,021	22.7	1,775	13.1	—	—	—	—	—	1,019	24
Palmdale Elementary	CA	13,199	20,853	22,704	17.4	82.6	19.7	59.6	2.7	0.6	934	24.3	1,691	13.4	—	—	—	—	—	†	27
Paramount Unified	CA	12,855	16,862	16,823	2.8	97.2	10.9	83.1	2.9	0.3	804	20.9	1,364	12.3	—	—	—	—	—	618	19
Pasadena Unified	CA	21,802	23,559	22,336	15.5	84.5	25.9	54.4	4.1	0.2	1,098	20.3	2,174	10.3	—	—	—	—	—	1,086	33
Placentia-Yorba Linda Unified	CA	21,438	26,046	26,725	56.5	43.5	2.0	31.1	10.1	0.3	1,137	23.5	2,103	12.7	—	—	—	—	—	1,570	31
Pomona Unified	CA	26,918	34,479	34,657	6.8	93.2	7.7	77.8	7.6	0.1	1,506	23.0	2,720	12.7	—	—	—	—	—	1,524	41
Poway Unified	CA	24,662	32,532	32,915	64.2	35.8	3.3	10.0	22.0	0.5	1,458	22.6	2,728	12.1	—	—	—	—	—	2,288	32
Redlands Unified	CA	16,002	19,411	21,135	44.7	55.3	8.0	35.7	10.8	0.7	960	22.0	1,588	13.3	—	—	—	—	—	1,337	21
Rialto Unified	CA	19,794	28,060	30,887	8.3	91.7	21.6	67.4	2.5	0.3	1,334	23.2	2,315	13.3	—	—	—	—	—	1,324	28
West Contra Costa Unified	CA	31,292	34,499	32,719	13.3	86.7	28.0	41.5	17.0	0.2	1,633	20.0	2,873	11.4	—	—	—	—	—	1,815	64
Riverside Unified	CA	31,326	38,124	42,521	36.2	63.8	9.6	48.8	4.9	0.6	1,841	23.1	3,327	12.8	—	—	—	—	—	2,455	47
Rowland Unified	CA	19,143	18,972	17,945	5.2	94.8	3.7	61.5	29.4	0.1	809	22.2	1,588	11.3	—	—	—	—	—	1,080	22
Sacramento City Unified	CA	49,557	52,734	51,420	22.4	77.6	22.3	30.6	23.3	1.4	2,638	19.5	4,995	10.3	—	—	—	—	—	2,369	89
Saddleback Valley Unified	CA	25,130	35,199	34,901	65.7	34.3	2.2	21.2	10.5	0.4	1,477	23.6	2,475	14.1	—	—	—	—	—	2,211	37
San Bernardino City Unified	CA	40,589	52,031	59,105	14.4	85.6	19.0	62.8	2.9	0.9	2,731	21.6	5,064	11.7	—	—	—	—	—	2,138	67
San Diego Unified	CA	121,152	141,804	134,709	25.8	74.2	14.2	42.6	16.9	0.5	7,199	18.7	13,442	10.0	—	—	—	—	—	6,360	202
San Francisco County Unified	CA	61,688	59,979	57,144	9.7	90.3	14.4	22.5	52.8	0.6	3,172	18.0	4,982	11.5	—	—	—	—	—	3,747	119
San Jose Unified	CA	29,630	33,015	31,874	28.8	71.2	3.4	50.7	15.1	2.0	1,656	19.2	2,496	12.8	—	—	—	—	—	1,877	55
San Juan Unified	CA	47,690	50,266	50,089	69.8	30.2	7.6	14.1	6.4	2.1	2,328	21.5	4,670	10.7	—	—	—	—	—	3,826	80
San Marcos Unified	CA	9,108	12,804	15,386	40.8	59.2	3.0	48.4	7.1	0.7	663	23.2	1,212	12.7	—	—	—	—	—	600	16
San Ramon Valley Unified	CA	16,119	20,742	22,857	74.4	25.6	2.0	4.8	18.2	0.5	1,058	21.6	1,901	12.0	—	—	—	—	—	1,496	29
Santa Ana Unified	CA	45,964	60,643	61,693	3.2	96.8	0.8	92.6	3.3	0.1	2,551	24.2	5,059	12.2	—	—	—	—	—	2,903	56
Simi Valley Unified	CA	18,262	21,181	21,533	68.4	31.6	1.5	21.2	7.9	0.9	935	23.0	1,692	12.7	—	—	—	—	—	1,271	29
Stockton City Unified	CA	32,687	37,573	39,268	11.0	89.0	12.9	53.5	18.8	3.7	1,963	20.0	3,723	10.5	—	—	—	—	—	1,411	50
Sweetwater Union High	CA	27,894	35,330	40,888	12.8	87.2	4.8	70.0	11.9	0.5	1,798	22.7	3,534	11.6	—	—	—	—	—	5,034	28
Temecula Valley Unified	CA	7,596	18,980	35,653	62.5	37.5	4.9	21.3	9.8	1.4	1,198	21.4	2,049	12.5	—	—	—	—	—	1,375	27
Torrance Unified	CA	19,645	24,118	25,447	40.4	59.6	4.1	18.8	36.1	0.6	1,159	22.0	2,097	12.1	—	—	—	—	—	1,943	30
Tracy Joint Unified	CA	7,626	13,816	17,011	37.3	62.7	8.5	36.4	16.9	1.0	777	21.9	1,328	12.8	—	—	—	—	—	982	23
Tustin Unified	CA	10,831	16,963	19,736	37.3	62.7	2.9	44.3	15.3	0.3	832	23.7	1,459	13.5	—	—	—	—	—	908	28
Vallejo City Unified	CA	19,049	20,270	18,981	14.4	85.6	34.9	24.9	25.3	0.6	816	23.3	1,552	12.2	—	—	—	—	—	999	29
Ventura Unified	CA	15,383	17,527	17,672	52.7	47.3	2.3	40.3	3.5	1.1	794	22.3	1,416	12.5	—	—	—	—	—	1,046	29
Visalia Unified	CA	21,309	23,989	25,794	36.5	63.5	2.7	53.2	6.5	1.1	1,167	22.1	2,175	11.9	—	—	—	—	—	1,387	34
Vista Unified	CA	18,489	27,651	26,407	39.6	60.4	5.5	48.4	5.9	0.6	1,201	22.0	2,199	12.0	—	—	—	—	—	2,340	30
Walnut Valley Unified	CA	12,613	14,849	15,467	16.9	83.1	3.9	18.7	60.5	0.1	653	23.7	1,081	14.3	—	—	—	—	—	1,411	15
William S. Hart Union High	CA	10,278	17,001	22,226	60.8	39.2	4.4	25.2	9.1	0.5	890	25.0	1,615	13.8	—	—	—	—	—	2,874	17
Irvine Unified	CA	20,735	23,961	25,158	48.0	52.0	2.6	7.7	41.1	0.6	1,114	22.6	1,970	12.8	—	—	—	—	—	1,887	33
Val Verde Unified	CA	—	11,242	15,346	11.4	88.6	19.2	63.6	5.5	0.3	620	24.8	1,128	13.6	—	—	—	—	—	618	16
Academy 20	CO	10,986	17,628	19,825	83.9	16.1	4.2	6.7	4.4	0.8	1,204	16.5	2,369	8.4	—	—	—	—	—	1,321	26
Adams 12 Five Star Schools	CO	20,838	30,079	36,353	63.3	36.7	2.7	27.8	5.1	1.0	1,844	19.7	3,715	9.8	—	—	—	—	—	2,232	50
Adams-Arapahoe	CO	25,897	30,453	32,251	28.4	71.6	21.8	44.8	4.1	0.9	1,750	18.4	3,765	8.6	—	—	—	—	—	1,242	47
Boulder Valley	CO	21,502	27,508	27,926	78.5	21.5	1.6	13.3	5.9	0.7	1,676	16.7	3,572	7.8	—	—	—	—	—	1,894	53
Cherry Creek	CO	29,210	42,320	47,818	68.7	31.3	12.5	11.1	7.2	0.5	2,804	17.1	5,524	8.7	—	—	—	—	—	3,101	50
Colorado Springs	CO	30,009	32,699	31,420	65.6	34.4	10.2	19.9	2.8	1.5	1,897	16.6	3,797	8.3	—	—	—	—	—	2,043	66
Denver County	CO	59,013	70,847	72,410	19.4	80.6	19.0	57.3	3.1	1.2	4,045	17.9	8,318	8.7	—	—	—	—	—	3,205	151
Douglas County	CO	13,125	34,918	44,761	87.1	12.9	1.8	6.5	3.9	0.6	2,460	18.2	5,096	8.8	—	—	—	—	—	2,146	63
Poudre	CO	18,589	24,052	25,000	79.2	20.8	1.9	14.6	3.2	1.1	1,489	16.8	3,009	8.3	—	—	—	—	—	1,563	52
Mesa County Valley	CO	17,024	19,688	20,120	79.9	20.1	1.2	16.6	1.0	1.3	1,154	17.4	2,295	8.8	—	—	—	—	—	1,309	39
Greeley	CO	11,657	15,998	17,978	47.3	52.7	1.2	49.9	1.0	0.6	1,075	16.7	2,070	8.7	—	—	—	—	—	858	31
Jefferson County	CO	76,275	87,703	86,868	77.1	22.9	1.9	16.3	3.6	1.1	4,641	18.7	9,590	9.1	—	—	—	—	—	5,796	167

See notes at end of table.

Table 87. Selected statistics on enrollment, teachers, dropouts, and graduates in public school districts enrolling more than 15,000 students, by state: 1990, 2000, 2001–02, 2003–04, and 2004—Continued

Name of district	State	Enrollment, fall 1990	Enrollment, fall 2000	Enrollment, fall 2004	Percentage distribution of enrollment, by race, fall 2004						Number of classroom teachers, fall 2004	Pupil/ teacher ratio, fall 2004	Total number of staff, fall 2004	Student/ staff ratio, fall 2004	Percent dropouts from grades 9–12, 2001–02[1]					Number of high school graduates, 2003–04[2]	Number of schools, fall 2004
					White	Minority									Total	Grade 9	Grade 10	Grade 11	Grade 12		
						Total	Black	Hispanic	Asian/ Pacific Islander	American Indian/ Alaska Native											
1	2	3	4	5	6	7	8	9	10	11	12	13	14	15	16	17	18	19	20	21	22
Littleton	CO	15,524	16,516	16,245	84.6	15.4	1.9	9.7	3.0	0.7	946	17.2	1,817	8.9	—	—	—	—	—	1,294	25
Saint Vrain Valley	CO	15,070	19,620	22,180	69.5	30.5	1.1	25.6	3.0	0.9	1,222	18.1	2,285	9.7	—	—	—	—	—	1,341	39
Pueblo City	CO	18,364	17,636	17,600	37.0	63.0	2.5	58.4	0.6	1.5	1,096	16.1	2,145	8.2	—	—	—	—	—	965	39
Bridgeport	CT	19,687	22,432	22,264	9.9	90.1	42.9	43.9	3.1	0.1	1,250	17.8	2,767	8.0	10.0	7.3	10.8	14.0	9.2	838	35
Hartford	CT	25,418	22,543	22,296	5.3	94.7	40.4	53.3	0.8	0.2	1,459	15.3	3,279	6.8	6.3	8.7	5.8	5.1	2.2	706	41
New Haven	CT	17,881	19,549	20,499	11.1	88.9	54.6	32.8	1.4	0.1	1,351	15.2	3,184	6.4	5.2	4.7	6.1	5.9	4.0	902	49
Stamford	CT	11,574	14,791	15,077	43.0	57.0	24.0	27.1	5.8	#	1,115	13.5	1,931	7.8	2.7	3.9	1.8	2.7	2.7	929	21
Waterbury	CT	13,323	16,282	17,896	30.6	69.4	26.8	40.3	2.0	0.3	1,213	14.8	2,522	7.1	3.0	3.4	2.8	3.1	2.0	685	30
Christina	DE	17,872	19,882	19,416	44.7	55.3	40.1	10.8	4.1	0.2	1,389	14.0	2,768	7.0	10.5	13.6	10.5	7.8	8.0	879	27
Red Clay Consolidated	DE	14,551	15,827	15,398	49.8	50.2	28.7	17.7	3.7	0.1	929	16.6	1,798	8.6	7.9	10.3	7.0	7.6	5.4	736	28
District of Columbia	DC	80,694	68,925	62,306	5.1	94.9	83.5	9.6	1.7	0.1	4,743	13.1	10,943	5.7	—	—	—	—	—	2,741	174
Alachua County	FL	26,305	29,712	29,259	52.6	47.4	38.8	5.0	3.4	0.2	1,659	17.6	4,098	7.1	6.1	5.4	6.3	5.3	7.9	1,657	69
Bay County	FL	21,827	25,755	27,147	79.4	20.6	15.7	2.5	2.0	0.4	1,599	17.0	3,401	8.0	1.8	1.7	1.6	2.2	1.7	1,294	45
Brevard County	FL	56,503	70,597	74,824	77.4	22.6	14.1	6.4	1.7	0.3	4,468	16.7	8,610	8.7	0.9	1.2	0.8	1.1	0.4	4,346	110
Broward County	FL	161,101	251,129	274,591	34.8	65.2	37.3	24.4	3.1	0.3	15,271	18.0	28,384	9.7	1.6	2.0	1.2	1.4	1.7	13,212	272
Charlotte County	FL	13,030	17,170	17,507	84.4	15.6	8.3	5.6	1.5	0.3	1,005	17.4	2,366	7.4	4.2	2.0	2.7	3.8	8.7	1,154	23
Citrus County	FL	11,697	15,199	15,720	90.2	9.8	4.2	3.9	1.4	0.4	951	16.5	2,160	7.3	4.8	4.9	4.6	4.3	5.2	971	25
Clay County	FL	21,925	28,115	32,605	81.2	18.8	11.2	5.1	2.4	0.2	2,003	16.3	3,924	8.3	2.8	4.1	2.5	2.1	1.7	1,892	34
Collier County	FL	20,850	34,203	42,105	48.8	51.2	11.2	38.7	1.0	0.2	2,479	17.0	5,277	8.0	4.4	4.4	5.3	4.2	3.2	2,152	64
Dade County	FL	292,023	368,625	368,933	10.1	89.9	28.3	60.4	1.1	0.1	20,086	18.4	38,319	9.6	4.8	4.4	3.9	4.0	7.5	17,256	381
Duval County	FL	111,142	125,846	129,486	46.9	53.1	44.4	5.3	3.3	0.2	7,345	17.6	12,647	10.2	6.7	7.8	5.9	5.5	6.6	5,836	182
Escambia County	FL	42,950	45,012	43,953	57.2	42.8	37.1	2.2	2.7	0.8	2,740	16.0	5,589	7.9	2.8	3.1	3.1	2.7	2.2	2,104	78
Hernando County	FL	12,831	17,215	20,666	82.7	17.3	6.8	9.3	1.0	0.3	1,274	16.2	2,775	7.4	2.3	3.1	2.6	1.7	0.9	970	22
Hillsborough County	FL	124,337	164,311	189,469	47.6	52.4	23.4	26.1	2.5	0.3	11,975	15.8	22,911	8.3	2.8	4.2	2.0	2.2	1.6	8,999	257
Indian River County	FL	11,683	14,979	17,099	69.3	30.7	15.8	13.5	1.2	0.2	994	17.2	2,006	8.5	1.8	1.7	1.1	2.3	2.1	924	28
Lake County	FL	21,065	29,293	36,117	69.1	30.9	15.8	13.2	1.5	0.4	2,169	16.7	4,796	7.5	5.5	4.1	5.6	6.4	6.5	1,761	57
Lee County	FL	43,240	58,401	71,210	60.6	39.4	14.5	23.1	1.4	0.4	4,018	17.7	8,222	8.7	9.0	9.4	8.5	7.2	11.0	3,289	98
Leon County	FL	27,241	32,050	32,191	53.6	46.4	41.3	2.6	2.4	0.1	1,878	17.1	4,327	7.4	3.7	4.7	3.4	3.4	2.7	1,848	58
Manatee County	FL	26,207	36,569	41,351	63.5	36.5	16.0	19.2	1.2	0.1	2,407	17.2	5,075	8.1	3.7	2.7	4.0	3.4	6.1	2,048	74
Marion County	FL	29,577	38,562	41,205	67.0	33.0	20.2	11.2	1.2	0.5	2,398	17.2	5,606	7.4	3.5	3.1	3.3	3.6	4.5	2,225	64
Martin County	FL	11,692	16,308	17,917	72.6	27.4	9.5	16.7	1.0	0.3	1,022	17.5	2,010	8.9	0.6	0.6	0.4	0.5	0.9	984	33
Okaloosa County	FL	26,140	30,344	31,756	79.9	20.1	12.4	4.3	2.8	0.5	1,813	17.5	3,708	8.6	3.6	3.0	2.5	3.5	5.8	2,015	55
Orange County	FL	102,672	150,681	173,331	38.7	61.3	28.5	28.5	3.9	0.4	10,183	17.0	21,193	8.2	3.4	3.5	2.7	2.4	4.9	8,274	203
Osceola County	FL	19,514	34,566	47,446	39.2	60.8	10.0	42.0	2.4	0.4	2,485	19.1	5,539	8.6	5.6	5.6	5.8	5.4	5.7	2,134	61
Palm Beach County	FL	105,712	153,871	175,076	45.5	54.5	29.5	22.0	2.4	0.6	10,019	17.5	19,181	9.1	3.1	3.4	3.9	5.4	2.4	8,405	230
Pasco County	FL	33,891	49,704	60,846	83.3	16.7	4.3	10.6	1.5	0.3	3,643	16.7	7,841	7.8	4.2	3.8	4.4	3.8	5.2	2,860	72
Pinellas County	FL	92,976	113,027	113,651	69.4	30.6	19.5	7.4	3.4	0.2	6,768	16.8	14,226	8.0	6.3	7.4	6.4	5.0	5.0	5,681	173
Polk County	FL	64,579	79,477	86,292	59.3	40.7	22.1	17.3	1.2	0.2	5,660	15.2	11,643	7.4	3.6	3.5	3.3	3.3	4.1	4,185	158
Saint Johns County	FL	12,080	20,090	24,403	86.2	13.8	9.0	3.1	1.6	0.1	1,395	17.5	2,814	8.7	2.5	2.3	1.5	3.1	3.4	1,403	38
Saint Lucie County	FL	22,224	29,540	34,912	52.8	47.2	29.2	16.2	1.5	0.3	1,758	19.9	3,846	9.1	1.6	1.7	1.7	1.2	1.8	1,474	47
Santa Rosa County	FL	15,708	22,633	25,038	90.0	10.0	5.3	2.4	1.7	0.6	1,397	17.9	2,399	10.4	2.1	1.3	1.3	2.7	3.7	1,574	37
Sarasota County	FL	26,881	35,533	41,405	78.4	21.6	9.5	10.2	1.7	0.2	2,685	15.4	5,582	7.4	3.6	3.6	3.9	3.3	1.3	2,202	58
Seminole County	FL	48,831	60,869	66,692	66.0	34.0	14.1	16.5	3.2	0.3	3,915	17.0	7,241	9.2	1.5	1.5	1.7	1.5	1.3	3,705	76
Volusia County	FL	48,342	61,517	65,281	70.7	29.3	15.1	12.7	1.3	0.2	4,054	16.1	8,578	7.6	1.9	1.7	2.0	1.9	2.2	3,604	90
Atlanta City	GA	60,714	58,230	51,377	7.5	92.5	88.0	3.9	0.6	#	3,716	13.8	7,019	7.3	8.9	7.7	7.7	10.5	10.8	2,034	98
Bibb County	GA	24,378	24,739	25,148	24.5	75.5	72.8	1.3	1.2	0.2	1,586	15.9	3,391	7.4	10.3	11.7	10.1	9.5	8.3	826	45
Chatham County	GA	34,044	35,344	34,595	28.1	71.9	66.8	3.0	1.8	0.2	2,480	14.0	4,538	7.6	16.8	20.8	15.3	12.1	16.3	1,182	55
Cherokee County	GA	16,086	26,043	31,065	84.6	15.4	5.0	8.8	1.3	0.3	2,082	14.9	3,818	8.1	4.5	2.5	4.1	6.7	5.2	1,428	34

See notes at end of table.

Table 87. Selected statistics on enrollment, teachers, dropouts, and graduates in public school districts enrolling more than 15,000 students, by state: 1990, 2000, 2001–02, 2003–04, and 2004—Continued

Name of district	State	Enrollment, fall 1990	Enrollment, fall 2000	Enrollment, fall 2004	Percentage distribution of enrollment, by race, fall 2004						Number of classroom teachers, fall 2004	Pupil/ teacher ratio, fall 2004	Total number of staff, fall 2004	Student/ staff ratio, fall 2004	Percent dropouts from grades 9–12, 2001–02[1]					Number of high school graduates, 2003–04	Number of schools, fall 2004
					White	Total	Black	Hispanic	Asian/ Pacific Islander	American Indian/ Alaska Native					Total	Grade 9	Grade 10	Grade 11	Grade 12		
1	2	3	4	5	6	7	8	9	10	11	12	13	14	15	16	17	18	19	20	21	22
Clayton County	GA	34,754	46,930	51,405	9.6	90.4	74.6	11.2	4.5	0.1	3,361	15.3	6,999	7.3	8.2	8.4	8.0	7.2	9.3	1,891	59
Cobb County	GA	69,441	95,781	103,935	54.6	45.4	29.3	11.9	4.0	0.2	7,038	14.8	12,868	8.1	3.6	2.1	3.4	4.3	4.8	5,612	106
Columbia County	GA	14,096	18,756	20,570	78.7	21.3	15.2	2.6	3.4	0.1	1,267	16.2	2,646	7.8	4.8	3.6	5.0	5.6	5.2	1,093	27
Coweta County	GA	10,430	16,766	19,685	72.2	27.8	22.6	4.3	0.7	0.1	1,240	15.9	2,638	7.5	5.5	4.3	6.4	6.4	5.3	915	28
DeKalb County	GA	74,108	95,958	99,986	10.6	89.4	78.2	7.7	3.4	0.1	6,620	15.1	13,293	7.5	6.8	7.5	6.6	6.1	6.5	4,499	142
Dougherty County	GA	18,482	16,799	16,894	14.0	86.0	84.6	0.8	0.5	0.1	1,075	15.7	2,397	7.0	8.0	9.7	7.9	8.1	4.5	678	29
Douglas County	GA	14,002	17,489	20,997	54.5	45.5	38.1	5.8	1.4	0.1	1,314	16.0	2,630	8.0	5.7	3.7	7.5	6.7	4.7	966	31
Fayette County	GA	13,105	19,590	21,603	73.0	27.0	19.4	3.9	3.5	0.2	1,483	14.6	2,779	7.8	2.0	2.1	1.6	2.4	1.8	1,475	29
Forsyth County	GA	7,742	17,131	23,612	89.7	10.3	0.9	7.7	1.6	0.1	1,495	15.8	2,890	8.2	2.7	1.5	2.0	3.5	4.6	890	24
Fulton County	GA	41,195	68,583	75,891	42.7	57.3	40.4	9.7	7.2	0.1	5,350	14.2	10,200	7.4	2.5	1.6	2.8	2.6	4.1	3,790	90
Gwinnett County	GA	63,930	110,075	135,392	48.1	51.9	23.6	18.1	10.1	0.1	9,215	14.7	16,744	8.1	3.2	2.8	2.8	3.3	4.0	6,706	107
Hall County	GA	13,738	20,330	23,306	64.2	35.8	5.5	28.9	1.1	0.3	1,531	15.2	2,803	8.3	6.2	1.3	8.2	6.1	12.7	883	33
Henry County	GA	10,929	23,601	32,416	60.8	39.2	32.5	4.1	2.3	0.3	1,999	16.2	3,753	8.6	4.0	1.1	5.1	5.1	7.7	1,315	35
Houston County	GA	16,249	21,529	23,998	60.1	39.9	34.6	3.3	1.9	0.2	1,636	14.7	3,251	7.4	5.8	5.6	7.0	6.0	4.3	1,262	35
Muscogee County	GA	30,038	32,916	33,069	33.3	66.7	61.7	3.3	1.5	0.2	2,207	15.0	4,938	6.7	6.8	6.4	6.9	7.1	6.8	1,388	62
Newton County	GA	8,054	11,734	15,773	53.7	46.3	41.5	3.6	0.9	0.4	1,031	15.3	2,010	7.8	5.0	4.3	6.3	6.3	2.7	452	18
Paulding County	GA	7,604	16,587	21,732	80.7	19.3	15.6	3.1	0.4	0.2	1,402	15.5	2,676	8.1	7.7	3.0	8.6	9.7	13.7	757	25
Richmond County	GA	33,660	35,424	34,141	23.5	76.5	73.1	2.2	1.1	0.1	2,372	14.4	4,879	7.0	5.0	5.4	4.1	4.7	6.0	1,433	58
Hawaii Department of Education	HI	171,309	184,360	183,185	20.1	79.9	2.4	4.5	72.5	0.6	11,146	16.4	20,531	8.9	5.1	2.8	5.4	5.8	7.6	10,324	285
Boise Independent District	ID	23,394	26,598	26,268	86.4	13.6	2.1	7.5	3.5	0.6	1,510	17.4	2,739	9.6	4.0	2.3	3.8	6.2	3.9	1,675	55
Meridian Joint District	ID	14,802	23,854	28,655	91.1	8.9	1.5	4.0	2.5	0.9	1,424	20.1	2,497	11.5	3.5	3.4	2.9	3.9	3.8	1,622	43
City of Chicago	IL	408,714	435,261	426,812	8.8	91.2	49.8	38.0	3.2	0.2	25,260	16.9	30,069	14.2	17.6	22.9	18.2	15.3	8.0	16,745	634
Community Unit 300	IL	11,196	16,711	18,262	65.7	34.3	4.7	25.3	3.9	0.4	926	19.7	1,099	16.6	3.0	3.2	2.4	2.8	3.7	1,127	24
Indian Prairie	IL	7,670	23,173	27,705	72.1	27.9	8.6	5.9	13.2	0.1	1,640	16.9	1,966	14.1	0.9	0.1	0.7	1.2	1.9	1,456	31
Naperville	IL	16,212	18,762	18,729	81.6	18.4	3.1	3.5	11.7	0.1	1,069	17.5	1,301	14.4	0.5	0.0	0.1	0.5	1.4	1,496	21
Peoria	IL	17,378	15,724	15,517	33.7	66.3	59.7	4.1	2.4	0.1	1,064	14.6	1,222	12.7	12.1	11.8	11.9	12.0	12.9	847	43
Plainfield School	IL	3,324	11,986	21,596	73.9	26.1	6.5	15.5	4.0	0.1	1,189	18.2	1,371	15.8	3.0	0.8	1.3	2.9	8.7	922	21
Rockford School	IL	27,255	27,399	28,887	45.2	54.8	31.9	19.6	3.2	0.1	1,593	18.1	1,937	14.9	6.4	8.4	7.2	4.5	3.3	1,264	53
Springfield	IL	15,813	15,387	15,026	58.4	41.6	37.8	1.6	2.0	0.2	943	15.9	1,146	13.1	3.6	0.9	4.0	6.6	3.4	857	36
U-46	IL	27,726	36,767	38,936	46.6	53.4	7.3	38.8	7.1	0.1	2,029	19.2	2,364	16.5	4.7	2.8	6.7	5.6	3.9	2,081	56
Valley View	IL	11,781	13,558	16,847	41.8	58.2	26.0	26.2	5.8	0.1	905	18.6	1,066	15.8	3.8	1.3	2.3	5.2	7.2	790	18
Waukegan	IL	12,116	15,510	16,253	8.8	91.2	20.2	69.0	1.9	0.1	921	17.7	1,098	14.8	11.2	13.6	10.3	10.4	8.2	764	24
Evansville-Vanderburgh	IN	22,918	22,875	22,139	82.2	17.8	15.5	1.3	0.9	0.3	1,413	15.7	2,750	8.1	1.0	0.1	1.3	1.3	1.2	1,412	42
Fort Wayne	IN	31,611	31,843	31,557	61.5	38.5	26.0	9.7	2.3	0.5	1,800	17.5	3,583	8.8	2.9	1.7	3.5	2.6	4.3	1,575	54
Gary	IN	26,620	19,206	16,979	0.9	99.1	97.7	1.1	0.2	0.1	944	18.0	2,484	6.8	0.5	0.6	0.5	0.2	0.5	662	34
Indianapolis Public Schools	IN	48,140	41,008	38,931	30.2	69.8	59.1	10.3	0.4	0.2	2,807	13.9	5,236	7.4	2.2	3.1	1.8	1.6	1.2	997	94
MSD Lawrence Township	IN	11,066	15,692	16,436	56.9	43.1	35.1	6.1	1.6	0.2	919	17.9	2,189	7.5	1.4	1.6	1.1	2.2	0.7	961	20
South Bend	IN	21,425	21,536	21,616	48.4	51.6	37.3	12.8	1.1	0.4	1,314	16.5	3,186	6.8	1.5	1.2	1.7	1.6	1.7	1,102	38
Vigo County	IN	16,982	16,545	16,355	91.5	8.5	6.5	0.7	1.2	0.1	1,025	16.0	1,951	8.4	3.8	2.3	3.4	5.1	4.7	996	29
Cedar Rapids	IA	16,988	17,780	17,307	82.0	18.0	12.6	2.6	2.3	0.6	1,019	17.0	2,145	8.1	2.6	0.1	2.4	3.7	4.4	1,132	34
Davenport	IA	17,841	16,874	15,987	69.1	30.9	19.4	8.0	2.7	0.8	1,101	14.5	1,942	8.2	4.2	2.3	4.6	6.5	3.8	1,006	33
Des Moines Independent	IA	30,514	32,435	32,194	65.4	34.6	16.1	13.2	4.6	0.6	2,290	14.1	4,111	7.8	4.6	5.0	4.0	5.3	3.5	1,630	72
Kansas City	KS	21,948	21,173	20,440	19.2	80.8	46.6	30.4	3.2	0.6	1,482	13.8	2,794	7.3	4.8	3.3	5.2	6.0	5.2	1,050	44
Olathe	KS	14,868	20,703	23,608	82.8	17.2	6.1	6.9	3.7	0.5	1,677	14.1	3,090	7.6	1.8	0.1	1.1	3.0	3.0	1,438	42
Shawnee Mission	KS	30,563	30,765	28,958	81.2	18.8	7.4	7.8	3.1	0.5	1,793	16.2	3,345	8.7	2.0	0.5	2.0	2.5	3.2	2,295	49
Blue Valley	KS	9,432	17,111	19,489	87.9	12.1	3.3	2.0	6.6	0.3	1,262	15.4	2,346	8.3	0.7	0.1	0.4	1.2	1.3	1,339	30
Wichita	KS	46,847	48,228	48,737	47.3	52.7	23.5	21.1	5.3	2.7	3,103	15.7	5,667	8.6	8.7	4.9	8.3	7.9	14.6	2,241	89

See notes at end of table.

Table 87. Selected statistics on enrollment, teachers, dropouts, and graduates in public school districts enrolling more than 15,000 students, by state: 1990, 2000, 2001–02, 2003–04, and 2004—Continued

Name of district	State	Enrollment, fall 1990	Enrollment, fall 2000	Enrollment, fall 2004	White	Total	Black	Hispanic	Asian/ Pacific Islander	American Indian/ Alaska Native	Number of classroom teachers, fall 2004	Pupil/ teacher ratio, fall 2004	Total number of staff, fall 2004	Student/ staff ratio, fall 2004	Total	Grade 9	Grade 10	Grade 11	Grade 12	Number of high school graduates, 2003–04[2]	Number of schools, fall 2004
1	2	3	4	5	6	7	8	9	10	11	12	13	14	15	16	17	18	19	20	21	22
Boone County	KY	9,911	13,445	16,414	93.2	6.8	2.5	2.5	1.6	0.2	931	17.6	1,986	8.3	2.1	1.7	2.2	2.3	2.2	817	18
Fayette County	KY	32,083	33,130	35,004	67.4	32.6	23.4	6.0	3.0	0.2	2,502	14.0	4,927	7.1	5.0	5.1	5.8	4.1	4.9	1,876	62
Jefferson County	KY	91,450	96,860	97,976	59.2	40.8	35.5	3.2	2.0	0.1	5,706	17.2	13,603	7.2	5.9	4.6	6.1	7.2	6.4	5,114	171
Ascension Parish SB	LA	13,001	15,038	16,363	67.5	32.5	28.6	3.1	0.6	0.3	1,063	15.4	2,149	7.6	4.7	3.8	5.3	5.1	4.8	761	23
Bossier Parish SB	LA	17,804	18,797	18,868	64.1	35.9	30.9	3.3	1.4	0.3	1,198	15.7	2,427	7.8	4.6	3.8	4.7	3.8	6.1	1,080	35
Caddo Parish SB	LA	51,375	45,119	43,524	35.3	64.7	62.6	1.0	0.9	0.2	2,885	15.1	6,494	6.7	10.0	7.7	8.5	8.3	17.2	2,287	74
Calcasieu Parish SB	LA	32,917	32,261	32,449	64.0	36.0	34.2	0.9	0.7	0.2	2,231	14.5	4,540	7.1	4.8	3.9	4.8	4.9	5.6	1,690	59
East Baton Rouge Parish SB	LA	61,669	54,246	46,408	19.3	80.7	76.8	1.5	2.4	0.1	3,053	15.2	5,846	7.9	8.5	8.3	9.0	8.2	8.5	2,288	93
Jefferson Parish SB	LA	58,177	50,891	51,403	33.7	66.3	52.0	9.1	4.5	0.7	3,405	15.1	7,011	7.3	9.7	9.8	11.3	9.3	7.6	2,108	86
Lafayette Parish SB	LA	29,403	28,931	29,816	55.5	44.5	41.1	1.7	1.4	0.3	2,126	14.0	4,018	7.4	7.8	7.2	9.1	8.9	5.8	1,632	44
Livingston Parish SB	LA	16,310	19,723	21,397	93.5	6.5	5.3	0.8	0.2	0.2	1,351	15.8	2,692	7.9	1.2	1.3	1.2	1.4	1.0	1,072	39
Orleans Parish SB	LA	82,925	77,610	64,920	3.4	96.6	93.5	1.1	1.9	0.1	3,781	17.2	8,339	7.8	9.1	7.1	9.7	7.5	12.5	3,442	127
Ouachita Parish SB	LA	17,667	17,479	18,328	69.2	30.8	29.2	0.8	0.7	0.1	1,211	15.1	2,664	6.9	7.1	7.7	5.4	7.2	8.2	954	35
Rapides Parish SB	LA	24,765	23,467	22,849	53.4	46.6	43.1	1.5	1.1	0.9	1,567	14.6	3,141	7.3	8.7	7.4	9.4	8.4	10.1	1,242	52
Saint Landry Parish SB	LA	17,213	15,457	15,162	43.1	56.9	56.1	0.3	0.4	0.1	1,049	14.4	2,171	7.0	5.0	4.4	5.4	5.0	5.6	729	38
Saint Tammany Parish SB	LA	27,522	32,392	35,620	78.3	21.7	18.1	2.0	1.3	0.4	2,560	13.9	5,070	7.0	4.0	3.7	3.8	4.9	3.7	1,967	51
Tangipahoa Parish SB	LA	16,724	18,197	18,563	52.6	47.4	45.3	1.5	0.5	0.1	1,070	17.3	2,341	7.9	7.0	6.7	9.3	7.0	4.4	982	37
Terrebonne Parish SB	LA	21,116	19,774	19,135	60.9	39.1	27.9	1.4	1.2	8.6	1,353	14.1	2,592	7.4	8.3	7.9	9.6	6.4	9.8	965	41
Anne Arundel County	MD	65,011	74,491	73,991	71.1	28.9	21.4	4.0	3.2	0.4	4,603	16.1	8,430	8.8	4.4	4.8	4.5	4.7	3.2	4,750	119
Baltimore City	MD	108,663	99,859	88,401	8.7	91.3	88.8	1.6	0.6	0.3	5,351	16.5	10,623	8.3	11.5	10.3	12.7	13.0	10.1	3,643	188
Baltimore County	MD	86,737	106,898	107,701	54.0	46.0	38.1	2.9	4.5	0.5	7,368	14.6	14,004	7.7	3.0	2.5	3.2	3.8	2.5	7,391	168
Calvert County	MD	10,398	16,170	17,451	81.6	18.4	15.6	1.4	1.2	0.3	1,059	16.5	2,094	8.3	3.3	3.1	3.4	3.2	3.7	1,129	27
Carroll County	MD	21,835	27,528	28,792	93.7	6.3	3.0	1.7	1.4	0.3	1,769	16.3	3,232	8.9	2.0	1.3	2.2	2.7	1.9	2,050	45
Cecil County	MD	12,868	15,905	16,535	88.0	12.0	8.4	2.4	0.9	0.3	1,054	15.7	2,040	8.1	3.0	2.5	2.6	3.8	3.5	929	31
Charles County	MD	18,908	23,468	26,026	50.0	50.0	43.3	2.8	2.9	0.9	1,506	17.3	2,840	9.2	3.3	3.2	3.4	3.6	3.0	1,704	34
Frederick County	MD	26,848	36,885	39,489	80.9	19.1	10.3	5.1	3.4	0.3	2,475	16.0	4,786	8.3	1.8	1.3	2.4	1.5	2.2	2,600	61
Harford County	MD	31,500	39,520	40,294	76.8	23.2	17.4	2.8	2.4	0.5	2,378	16.9	4,680	8.6	3.4	2.1	3.4	4.3	4.1	2,681	51
Howard County	MD	29,949	44,946	48,219	63.4	36.6	19.5	4.0	12.8	0.3	3,361	14.3	6,577	7.3	2.0	1.7	2.4	1.8	2.0	3,164	70
Montgomery County	MD	103,757	134,180	139,393	43.3	56.7	22.6	19.4	14.4	0.3	9,135	15.3	18,868	7.4	1.9	1.9	2.4	1.9	2.0	8,982	197
Prince George's County	MD	108,868	133,723	136,095	7.1	92.9	77.1	12.2	3.0	0.6	8,174	16.7	16,691	8.2	3.1	3.7	3.5	2.5	2.5	7,618	205
Saint Mary's County	MD	12,549	15,151	16,567	75.9	24.1	18.9	2.3	2.3	0.6	1,010	16.4	1,850	9.0	3.1	2.2	3.9	2.8	3.8	883	27
Washington County	MD	17,778	19,782	20,807	85.9	14.1	10.1	2.4	1.4	0.2	1,331	15.6	2,506	8.3	3.1	2.1	3.3	4.2	3.1	1,381	46
Boston	MA	60,543	63,024	57,742	14.0	86.0	45.5	31.2	8.9	0.4	4,937	11.7	9,227	6.3	—	—	—	—	—	3,255	136
Brockton	MA	14,529	16,791	16,073	36.1	63.9	48.0	12.3	2.8	0.8	1,128	14.2	2,281	7.0	—	—	—	—	—	725	25
Springfield	MA	24,194	26,526	25,976	19.5	80.5	27.9	49.9	2.5	0.2	2,235	11.6	4,470	5.8	—	—	—	—	—	816	47
Worcester	MA	21,066	25,828	24,514	46.5	53.5	12.6	31.8	8.4	0.7	1,742	14.1	3,387	7.2	—	—	—	—	—	1,117	47
Ann Arbor Public Schools	MI	14,199	16,539	17,156	65.4	34.6	16.2	4.0	14.0	0.5	1,033	16.6	2,015	8.5	—	—	—	—	—	1,111	32
Dearborn City	MI	13,380	17,129	17,659	92.7	7.3	3.7	2.3	0.8	0.5	1,097	16.1	2,135	8.3	—	—	—	—	—	1,087	34
Detroit City	MI	168,116	162,194	141,461	2.8	97.2	90.5	5.5	0.8	0.3	8,034	17.6	19,630	7.2	—	—	—	—	—	4,975	254
Flint City	MI	27,601	22,532	19,760	17.5	82.5	79.1	2.6	0.3	1.0	1,127	17.5	2,521	7.8	—	—	—	—	—	736	40
Grand Rapids Public Schools	MI	26,250	25,625	23,295	26.9	73.1	44.0	26.7	1.4	1.0	1,562	14.9	3,226	7.2	—	—	—	—	—	633	87
Lansing Public Schools	MI	21,350	17,610	16,819	36.5	63.5	41.9	15.6	4.9	1.1	1,113	15.1	2,106	8.0	—	—	—	—	—	691	41
Livonia Public Schools	MI	16,373	18,347	18,133	91.2	8.8	4.4	1.5	2.6	0.2	1,031	17.6	2,053	8.8	—	—	—	—	—	1,377	34
Plymouth-Canton Community Schools	MI	14,955	16,518	18,608	80.9	19.1	5.6	1.9	11.2	0.4	902	20.6	1,679	11.1	—	—	—	—	—	1,077	25
Utica Community Schools	MI	23,960	27,786	29,389	94.0	6.0	2.3	1.1	2.5	0.1	1,521	19.3	3,142	9.4	—	—	—	—	—	1,870	43
Walled Lake Consolidated Schools	MI	9,059	14,438	15,162	87.8	12.2	4.5	1.7	5.5	0.5	837	18.1	1,699	8.9	—	—	—	—	—	953	24
Warren Consolidated Schools	MI	14,336	14,602	16,009	87.6	12.4	6.0	0.8	4.9	0.6	833	19.2	1,541	10.4	—	—	—	—	—	1,070	26

See notes at end of table.

Table 87. Selected statistics on enrollment, teachers, dropouts, and graduates in public school districts enrolling more than 15,000 students, by state: 1990, 2000, 2001–02, 2003–04, and 2004—Continued

Name of district	State	Enrollment, fall 1990	Enrollment, fall 2000	Enrollment, fall 2004	White	Total	Black	Hispanic	Asian/ Pacific Islander	American Indian/ Alaska Native	Number of classroom teachers, fall 2004	Pupil/ teacher ratio, fall 2004	Total number of staff, fall 2004	Student/ staff ratio, fall 2004	Total	Grade 9	Grade 10	Grade 11	Grade 12	Number of high school graduates, 2003–04[2]	Number of schools, fall 2004
1	2	3	4	5	6	7	8	9	10	11	12	13	14	15	16	17	18	19	20	21	22
Anoka-Hennepin	MN	34,524	41,314	41,595	85.3	14.7	5.6	2.3	5.4	1.4	2,373	17.5	4,581	9.1	3.9	0.5	1.5	4.0	9.5	2,687	59
Minneapolis	MN	36,763	48,834	40,510	27.5	72.5	42.4	14.5	11.5	4.1	2,658	15.2	5,747	7.0	12.5	6.9	12.3	13.9	17.6	1,936	135
Osseo	MN	19,483	22,017	21,618	64.3	35.7	18.4	4.1	12.5	0.7	1,205	17.9	2,463	8.8	2.3	6.2	1.7	2.9	4.4	1,402	32
Rochester	MN	13,887	15,929	16,195	75.6	24.4	10.4	5.0	8.7	0.4	950	17.1	1,900	8.5	2.9	1.6	2.2	3.6	4.4	1,245	42
Rosemount-Apple Valley-Eagan	MN	17,029	28,330	28,366	83.6	16.4	6.4	3.4	6.0	0.5	1,690	16.8	3,234	8.8	1.9	0.0	0.6	2.3	4.8	2,076	37
South Washington County	MN	11,260	14,953	15,907	83.2	16.8	5.6	3.8	6.9	0.6	894	17.8	1,693	9.4	2.5	0.0	1.0	2.4	6.6	1,033	24
Saint Paul	MN	32,366	45,115	41,123	28.2	71.8	29.0	12.2	28.7	2.0	2,846	14.5	5,452	7.5	6.6	1.0	3.4	5.7	15.2	2,269	127
DeSoto County	MS	13,470	19,812	25,298	73.1	26.9	21.9	3.7	1.1	0.2	1,381	18.3	2,840	8.9	0.9	1.1	0.8	0.9	0.8	1,055	27
Jackson Public	MS	33,546	31,351	31,611	2.4	97.6	97.0	0.4	0.2	#	1,758	18.0	4,292	7.4	7.0	9.5	5.8	6.3	5.1	1,122	61
Rankin County	MS	12,824	15,013	16,395	76.8	23.2	21.1	1.1	0.9	0.1	1,096	15.0	2,094	7.8	1.6	1.3	1.8	1.8	1.8	807	24
Columbia	MO	12,786	16,178	16,712	70.1	29.9	21.9	2.9	4.8	0.4	1,226	13.6	2,419	6.9	4.5	0.7	3.5	5.7	8.3	1,130	31
Fort Zumwalt	MO	10,110	16,521	18,496	92.2	7.8	4.7	1.6	1.2	0.2	1,095	16.9	2,348	7.9	2.7	1.5	3.3	2.3	4.2	1,177	23
Hazelwood	MO	16,985	18,855	19,315	38.3	61.7	59.7	1.3	0.8	#	1,168	16.5	2,201	8.8	4.6	2.3	6.0	6.4	3.8	1,225	27
Kansas City	MO	34,486	37,298	37,524	13.1	86.9	69.1	15.5	2.0	0.3	2,633	14.3	4,891	7.7	7.6	8.0	10.0	6.8	3.7	1,500	90
Lee's Summit	MO	7,132	14,340	16,334	85.9	14.1	8.9	3.0	2.0	0.2	1,020	16.0	2,213	7.4	2.2	0.8	1.8	3.5	2.8	1,018	23
North Kansas City	MO	15,732	17,258	17,193	78.4	21.6	9.1	8.1	3.4	1.0	1,178	14.6	2,354	7.3	2.9	0.6	2.2	4.4	4.5	1,208	30
Parkway	MO	21,542	20,433	18,994	71.1	28.9	17.1	1.9	9.8	0.1	1,183	16.1	2,512	7.6	1.1	0.4	0.7	1.2	2.1	1,486	28
Rockwood	MO	15,608	21,203	22,531	83.7	16.3	11.2	1.2	3.6	0.2	1,372	16.4	2,985	7.5	1.9	0.8	2.1	3.3	1.3	1,590	31
Springfield	MO	23,631	24,630	24,118	87.9	12.1	6.5	2.7	2.3	0.7	1,460	16.5	2,871	8.4	4.9	1.8	5.2	6.0	6.9	1,621	55
Francis Howell	MO	13,391	19,497	18,336	92.3	7.7	4.5	1.3	1.6	0.2	1,191	15.4	2,011	9.1	2.8	1.5	2.7	3.8	3.5	1,286	23
Saint Louis City	MO	43,284	44,412	39,720	15.0	85.0	81.3	2.0	1.6	0.2	3,246	12.2	5,410	7.3	8.2	8.4	8.2	8.0	7.8	1,640	105
Lincoln	NE	27,986	31,354	32,270	80.8	19.2	8.0	5.8	3.9	1.5	2,272	14.2	4,415	7.3	6.2	0.6	3.9	8.8	11.3	2,015	67
Millard	NE	16,764	19,160	20,371	91.7	8.3	2.3	2.6	3.1	0.3	1,286	15.8	2,303	8.8	1.3	0.3	1.0	1.3	2.7	1,478	34
Omaha	NE	41,699	45,197	46,549	46.0	54.0	31.3	19.6	1.6	1.5	3,130	14.9	6,584	7.1	10.9	12.9	10.6	10.8	8.0	2,514	88
Clark County	NV	121,959	231,655	283,221	—	—	—	—	—	—	14,222	19.9	19,065	14.9	8.1	6.1	5.3	3.2	19.6	9,876	307
Washoe County	NV	38,466	56,268	63,322	—	—	—	—	—	—	3,496	18.1	4,748	13.3	3.4	3.1	2.6	1.7	6.2	2,576	100
Manchester	NH	14,604	17,407	17,737	81.6	18.4	5.7	9.9	2.3	0.5	1,155	15.4	1,945	9.1	6.8	4.0	7.0	7.5	10.0	1,340	22
Camden City	NJ	19,497	17,517	16,385	1.1	98.9	53.8	43.3	1.6	0.1	1,644	10.0	2,628	6.2	14.1	18.4	14.4	13.4	6.2	457	31
Elizabeth	NJ	15,266	19,674	21,124	10.3	89.7	24.6	63.3	1.8	0.0	2,121	10.0	3,266	6.5	5.9	5.7	6.5	5.4	5.8	936	28
Jersey City	NJ	28,585	31,347	30,199	9.1	90.9	35.6	39.3	14.8	1.2	2,953	10.2	4,724	6.4	8.6	12.1	9.2	7.2	3.6	1,542	42
Newark	NJ	48,433	42,150	42,033	7.9	92.1	59.5	31.6	0.8	0.2	3,916	10.7	6,353	6.6	4.2	4.5	4.5	3.8	3.6	1,815	75
Paterson	NJ	22,109	24,629	26,256	5.2	94.8	36.9	55.3	2.5	0.2	2,595	10.1	3,962	6.6	9.3	12.0	11.0	4.8	4.3	937	36
Toms River Regional	NJ	16,002	17,621	17,962	88.0	12.0	3.8	5.3	2.8	0.1	1,187	15.1	1,685	10.7	2.4	0.5	2.1	3.7	3.5	1,339	18
Albuquerque	NM	88,295	85,276	93,341	35.2	64.8	3.9	53.8	2.3	4.8	6,199	15.1	13,062	7.1	7.1	9.0	6.8	6.9	4.6	4,525	157
Las Cruces	NM	19,216	22,185	23,717	26.4	73.6	2.3	69.4	1.0	0.9	1,580	15.0	3,206	7.4	5.5	6.9	5.9	5.5	2.9	1,943	41
Brentwood Union Free	NY	11,749	15,565	16,607	14.0	86.0	20.3	63.7	1.9	0.1	—	—	—	—	3.7	0.1	4.7	5.7	4.9	—	18
Buffalo City	NY	47,235	45,721	41,089	25.7	74.3	58.0	13.5	1.3	1.5	—	—	—	—	7.6	5.4	6.0	7.2	13.4	—	66
New York City	NY	944,113	1,066,516	1,023,674	14.6	85.4	33.1	38.6	13.2	0.4	—	—	—	—	14.2	5.4	23.9	16.9	12.4	—	1,205
Rochester City	NY	32,705	36,294	34,598	13.1	86.9	64.8	20.1	1.7	0.4	—	—	—	—	13.0	12.4	15.0	12.2	11.7	—	64
Sachem Central	NY	15,187	14,948	15,378	89.6	10.4	1.2	5.1	3.9	0.1	—	—	—	—	1.2	0.2	0.3	0.9	3.9	—	18
Syracuse City	NY	22,432	23,015	22,405	34.6	65.4	51.5	9.8	2.9	1.3	—	—	—	—	3.8	2.5	3.9	5.3	4.6	—	34
Yonkers City	NY	18,621	26,201	26,201	18.1	81.9	28.9	46.9	5.9	0.2	—	—	—	—	7.7	9.6	7.8	5.7	5.9	—	39
Cumberland County Schools	NC	44,612	50,850	53,346	39.5	60.5	50.8	6.1	1.7	1.8	3,302	16.2	6,483	8.2	4.3	5.4	5.2	4.0	1.8	3,184	86
Pitt County Schools	NC	17,629	20,040	21,833	41.6	58.4	52.1	4.9	1.3	0.2	1,513	14.4	2,842	7.7	6.7	6.5	7.7	6.9	5.6	988	33

See notes at end of table.

Table 87. Selected statistics on enrollment, teachers, dropouts, and graduates in public school districts enrolling more than 15,000 students, by state: 1990, 2000, 2001–02, 2003–04, and 2004—Continued

Name of district	State	Enrollment, fall 1990	Enrollment, fall 2000	Enrollment, fall 2004	Percentage distribution of enrollment, by race, fall 2004						Number of classroom teachers, fall 2004	Pupil/teacher ratio, fall 2004	Total number of staff, fall 2004	Student/staff ratio, fall 2004	Percent dropouts from grades 9–12, 2001–02[1]					Number of high school graduates, 2003–04[2]	Number of schools, fall 2004
					White	Total	Black	Hispanic	Asian/Pacific Islander	American Indian/Alaska Native					Total	Grade 9	Grade 10	Grade 11	Grade 12		
1	2	3	4	5	6	7	8	9	10	11	12	13	14	15	16	17	18	19	20	21	22
Alamance-Burlington Schools	NC	10,322	20,729	21,882	58.8	41.2	26.5	12.9	1.4	0.3	1,530	14.3	2,721	8.0	5.5	5.5	5.9	4.1	6.8	1,168	33
Buncombe County Schools	NC	22,026	24,708	25,255	84.1	15.9	9.2	5.2	1.0	0.5	1,698	14.9	3,372	7.5	6.4	7.7	5.8	6.6	4.8	1,382	41
Cabarrus County Schools	NC	12,853	19,115	22,477	72.4	27.6	17.5	8.4	1.3	0.4	1,537	14.6	2,720	8.3	5.1	5.3	6.0	4.8	4.0	1,234	28
Catawba County Schools	NC	12,770	16,250	17,061	76.7	23.3	9.0	6.7	7.3	0.3	1,086	15.7	2,028	8.4	4.7	3.5	5.2	6.0	4.3	978	25
Cleveland County Schools	NC	8,131	9,663	17,480	66.6	33.4	30.3	2.1	0.8	0.1	1,257	13.9	2,534	6.9	4.7	5.5	4.9	5.2	2.1	534	28
Davidson County Schools	NC	16,426	19,136	19,624	93.0	7.0	3.2	2.7	0.8	0.3	1,202	16.3	2,260	8.7	5.9	6.1	6.3	6.1	5.2	1,096	29
Durham Public Schools	NC	18,517	29,728	30,955	26.5	73.5	59.2	11.9	2.2	0.2	1,885	16.4	3,766	8.2	6.5	7.7	6.3	7.7	4.6	1,655	45
Forsyth County Schools	NC	37,625	44,769	48,785	48.4	51.6	37.4	12.5	1.4	0.2	3,363	14.5	5,791	8.4	6.3	5.3	5.7	6.3	6.7	2,496	71
Gaston County Schools	NC	29,631	30,603	32,112	71.9	28.1	21.1	5.4	1.5	0.2	1,983	16.2	3,503	9.2	6.4	6.0	5.8	7.6	6.7	1,745	53
Guilford County Schools	NC	24,575	63,417	68,220	44.3	55.7	44.6	6.1	4.4	0.6	4,537	15.0	8,451	8.1	3.9	4.8	3.8	3.7	2.7	3,810	106
Harnett County Schools	NC	11,890	16,338	17,011	56.1	43.9	33.0	9.4	0.4	1.0	1,112	15.3	2,089	8.1	7.9	7.0	8.0	10.1	6.7	831	26
Iredell-Statesville Schools	NC	10,610	17,235	19,503	72.7	27.3	17.8	6.7	2.6	0.2	1,295	15.1	2,348	8.3	6.1	6.1	7.5	5.8	4.6	997	32
Johnston County Schools	NC	14,647	21,334	26,168	65.0	35.0	22.4	11.8	0.4	0.4	1,869	14.0	3,497	7.5	6.5	7.0	6.9	4.9	6.6	1,155	35
Charlotte-Mecklenburg Schools	NC	77,069	103,336	118,765	39.7	60.3	45.1	10.4	4.2	0.6	7,890	15.1	15,442	7.7	5.5	6.8	5.7	3.9	4.4	5,403	138
Nash-Rocky Mount Schools	NC	11,653	18,342	18,566	37.8	62.2	54.6	6.0	1.2	0.4	1,235	15.0	2,343	7.9	6.2	3.8	7.5	8.3	5.2	971	29
New Hanover County Schools	NC	19,090	21,605	23,252	65.1	34.9	29.7	3.5	1.3	0.4	1,534	15.2	3,165	7.3	5.5	4.1	6.3	6.2	6.0	1,287	34
Onslow County Schools	NC	18,605	20,984	22,230	62.8	37.2	29.6	5.3	1.5	0.8	1,404	15.8	2,791	8.0	6.0	4.9	6.3	6.9	6.3	1,215	33
Randolph County Schools	NC	13,572	17,271	18,399	83.8	16.2	6.8	8.2	0.8	0.5	1,142	16.1	2,308	8.0	6.5	7.4	6.6	6.8	4.4	902	28
Robeson County Schools	NC	23,251	23,911	24,557	19.9	80.1	30.3	6.0	0.5	43.3	1,437	17.1	3,171	7.7	9.1	8.5	10.4	9.9	7.1	1,028	41
Rowan-Salisbury Schools	NC	16,403	20,472	20,945	68.7	31.3	23.2	6.4	1.4	0.3	1,357	15.4	2,640	7.9	5.6	5.0	6.4	5.7	5.2	1,174	30
Union County Public Schools	NC	12,864	22,862	28,816	72.6	27.4	17.0	9.1	1.0	0.3	1,836	15.7	3,465	8.3	4.7	4.6	3.8	6.2	4.4	1,443	36
Wake County Schools	NC	64,266	98,950	114,568	56.8	43.2	30.2	8.3	4.5	0.3	7,792	14.7	14,331	8.0	3.7	4.1	3.6	3.4	3.3	6,088	132
Wayne County Public Schools	NC	13,653	19,279	19,465	47.1	52.9	43.3	8.2	1.3	0.2	1,254	15.5	2,507	7.8	4.8	3.9	5.7	5.2	4.6	1,014	31
Akron Public Schools	OH	33,213	31,464	28,067	46.5	53.5	50.5	1.1	1.8	0.1	2,220	12.6	5,676	4.9	5.0	5.1	4.0	6.3	4.7	1,675	63
Cincinnati Public Schools	OH	50,394	46,562	38,283	24.2	75.8	73.7	1.1	0.9	0.1	2,638	14.5	5,399	7.1	8.2	9.1	8.6	7.8	5.5	1,609	84
Cleveland Municipal	OH	68,924	75,684	64,670	17.6	82.4	71.2	10.2	0.7	0.3	3,656	17.7	8,485	7.6	15.1	17.1	13.3	14.9	13.2	2,508	122
Columbus Public Schools	OH	63,956	64,511	60,668	30.8	69.2	62.8	4.1	2.2	0.3	3,669	16.5	8,245	7.4	8.7	8.6	9.6	10.0	6.2	2,724	148
Dayton	OH	28,000	23,522	17,832	26.3	73.7	71.4	1.9	0.4	#	1,094	16.3	2,399	7.4	8.4	9.8	6.4	7.5	8.8	823	38
South-Western	OH	16,605	19,216	21,545	79.7	20.3	12.0	6.2	1.7	0.1	1,267	17.0	2,605	8.3	5.9	6.2	5.2	6.0	6.4	1,079	34
Toledo	OH	40,126	37,738	32,976	44.1	55.9	47.4	7.7	0.7	0.1	2,057	16.0	4,051	8.1	6.7	6.8	7.5	7.0	5.0	1,606	66
Lakota	OH	9,356	14,659	16,980	86.2	13.8	7.0	2.2	4.5	0.1	946	17.9	1,742	9.7	0.9	0.2	1.1	1.8	0.3	1,011	19
Broken Arrow	OK	13,872	14,990	15,054	78.9	21.1	5.4	4.4	1.9	9.4	887	17.0	1,655	9.1	3.9	1.6	2.5	5.6	6.3	923	22
Edmond	OK	13,041	17,084	18,570	80.3	19.7	9.0	3.9	3.3	3.5	938	19.8	1,984	9.4	2.5	2.6	3.1	2.2	2.2	1,295	21
Lawton	OK	17,727	17,338	16,926	49.4	50.6	32.0	10.0	2.1	6.5	1,089	15.5	2,037	8.3	4.8	2.2	7.5	4.8	4.2	934	35
Moore	OK	16,630	18,101	19,392	68.6	31.4	5.8	6.1	4.3	15.2	1,108	17.5	1,922	10.1	3.9	1.2	4.9	5.6	4.4	1,095	27
Oklahoma City	OK	36,038	39,750	40,387	25.7	74.3	33.3	32.6	2.9	5.6	2,381	17.0	4,631	8.7	12.1	14.6	13.9	9.7	6.0	1,447	91
Putnam City	OK	18,071	19,506	19,301	60.0	40.0	21.9	9.9	4.4	3.9	1,179	16.4	2,344	8.2	5.9	9.1	6.3	4.1	2.3	1,166	26
Tulsa	OK	40,732	42,812	41,629	38.4	61.6	35.9	15.5	1.3	9.0	2,616	15.9	6,858	6.1	7.7	7.3	7.3	8.1	8.6	1,749	85
Hillsboro	OR	—	18,315	19,348	63.5	36.5	2.2	26.6	7.2	0.6	867	22.3	1,912	10.1	3.1	1.8	2.7	3.2	5.4	1,086	35
Beaverton	OR	24,874	33,600	36,103	68.0	32.0	3.0	15.2	13.1	0.7	1,840	19.6	3,478	10.4	4.1	2.2	2.6	4.9	7.0	2,183	49
Eugene	OR	17,904	18,432	18,390	81.2	18.8	2.8	7.4	5.9	2.7	826	22.3	1,745	10.5	3.1	1.7	2.3	3.5	5.3	1,402	45
North Clackamas	OR	12,403	14,876	16,546	80.5	19.5	2.1	10.1	6.3	1.0	785	21.1	1,655	10.0	4.0	2.6	2.3	5.4	5.8	883	29
Portland	OR	53,042	53,141	47,649	60.0	40.0	15.4	10.1	10.5	2.1	2,659	17.9	5,048	9.4	10.8	9.8	9.6	11.7	12.5	2,641	105
Salem-Keizer	OR	27,756	35,108	38,195	67.9	32.1	1.4	25.4	3.6	1.7	1,786	21.4	3,957	9.7	7.4	3.0	5.4	6.9	16.0	2,049	68
Allentown City	PA	13,519	16,424	17,521	26.7	73.3	17.1	54.1	1.9	0.2	902	19.4	1,754	10.0	9.3	7.4	9.3	11.4	10.2	788	23
Central Bucks	PA	10,286	17,305	19,586	94.2	5.8	1.5	1.2	3.0	#	997	19.6	2,119	9.2	1.2	0.0	0.5	1.4	3.3	1,210	23
Philadelphia City	PA	190,978	201,190	187,547	14.0	86.0	64.9	15.4	5.5	0.2	9,838	19.1	22,244	8.4	9.8	7.4	10.5	11.9	12.3	10,331	270

See notes at end of table.

Table 87. Selected statistics on enrollment, teachers, dropouts, and graduates in public school districts enrolling more than 15,000 students, by state: 1990, 2000, 2001–02, 2003–04, and 2004—Continued

Name of district	State	Enrollment, fall 1990	Enrollment, fall 2000	Enrollment, fall 2004	White	Minority — Total	Black	Hispanic	Asian/ Pacific Islander	American Indian/ Alaska Native	Number of classroom teachers, fall 2004	Pupil/ teacher ratio, fall 2004	Total number of staff, fall 2004	Student/ staff ratio, fall 2004	Dropouts — Total	Grade 9	Grade 10	Grade 11	Grade 12	Number of high school graduates, 2003–04[2]	Number of schools, fall 2004
1	2	3	4	5	6	7	8	9	10	11	12	13	14	15	16	17	18	19	20	21	22
Pittsburgh	PA	39,896	38,560	34,131	37.0	63.0	60.7	0.7	1.5	0.1	2,688	12.7	5,094	6.7	5.4	3.7	6.0	5.8	7.2	1,945	85
Reading	PA	11,965	15,487	17,413	17.0	83.0	14.4	67.7	0.9	0.1	923	18.9	1,806	9.6	8.7	2.5	9.6	12.2	13.4	616	19
Providence	RI	20,908	26,937	26,741	13.4	86.6	22.0	56.7	7.2	0.7	1,923	13.9	2,612	10.2	8.2	8.0	10.5	7.3	6.1	1,134	58
Aiken County	SC	23,964	25,147	25,299	59.5	40.5	35.9	3.7	0.7	0.2	1,580	16.0	1,832	13.8	3.2	3.6	3.4	3.2	2.1	1,195	39
Beaufort County	SC	12,525	16,721	19,113	46.5	53.5	39.0	13.2	1.1	0.2	1,327	14.4	1,577	12.1	1.7	1.4	2.2	2.1	1.2	792	26
Berkeley County	SC	27,392	26,635	28,387	57.5	42.5	36.1	4.0	2.1	0.3	1,661	17.1	2,045	13.9	4.3	4.0	5.7	3.5	3.8	1,408	35
Charleston County	SC	43,667	44,767	43,812	40.5	59.5	54.6	3.3	1.4	0.2	3,144	13.9	3,711	11.8	3.2	4.4	3.0	2.6	2.0	1,895	79
Dorchester County 02	SC	13,737	16,678	18,863	65.8	34.2	29.0	2.6	2.0	0.6	1,170	16.1	1,378	13.7	3.6	2.4	4.6	4.9	3.0	954	17
Florence County 01	SC	14,736	13,930	15,081	45.1	54.9	52.2	1.2	1.4	0.2	1,001	15.1	1,307	11.5	5.9	5.8	6.4	6.2	5.1	721	20
Greenville County	SC	51,471	59,875	65,265	63.1	36.9	28.0	6.9	1.9	0.2	4,023	16.2	5,139	12.7	2.6	2.6	2.8	2.7	2.3	3,115	90
Horry County	SC	24,085	29,894	33,566	68.6	31.4	25.4	4.3	1.2	0.4	2,844	15.2	2,844	11.8	2.1	2.0	2.4	2.6	1.5	1,579	45
Lexington County 01	SC	11,204	17,285	19,467	86.7	13.3	8.4	2.8	1.6	0.5	1,344	14.5	1,588	12.3	2.4	1.8	2.1	2.6	3.6	1,054	20
Lexington County 05	SC	11,688	15,064	16,532	68.1	31.9	27.8	1.8	2.1	0.2	1,123	14.7	1,428	11.6	1.8	1.5	1.9	1.9	1.7	947	18
Pickens County	SC	14,298	15,938	16,425	87.3	12.7	9.1	2.4	1.0	0.2	1,030	15.9	1,349	12.2	6.3	7.2	6.9	5.1	5.3	763	25
Richland County 01	SC	27,071	27,061	27,068	18.9	81.1	78.3	2.0	0.7	0.1	2,016	13.4	2,468	11.0	3.2	2.8	3.6	3.9	2.5	1,160	50
Richland County 02	SC	12,792	17,409	21,055	35.9	64.1	57.3	3.9	2.8	0.2	1,420	14.8	1,699	12.4	2.6	1.3	2.4	3.9	3.4	1,083	23
York County 03	SC	12,690	14,925	16,445	56.8	43.2	36.4	3.6	1.6	0.2	1,041	15.8	1,252	13.1	1.7	1.1	2.4	2.1	1.2	814	24
Sioux Falls	SD	16,120	19,097	19,900	83.3	16.7	5.6	4.6	2.2	4.3	1,251	15.9	2,254	8.8	4.2	1.6	2.7	5.6	7.8	1,324	44
Hamilton County	TN	22,874	39,915	40,805	—	—	—	—	—	—	2,646	15.4	5,114	8.0	5.8	5.6	5.2	7.2	5.6	1,909	80
Knox County	TN	50,429	51,944	54,247	—	—	—	—	—	—	3,594	15.1	6,576	8.2	3.0	0.1	0.6	3.6	8.6	2,933	87
Memphis City	TN	106,223	113,730	121,028	—	—	—	—	—	—	7,448	16.2	13,190	9.2	8.6	6.9	8.4	9.0	11.5	4,426	192
Montgomery County Schools	TN	17,532	23,339	25,899	—	—	—	—	—	—	1,623	16.0	3,054	8.5	3.3	1.9	2.1	2.7	7.5	1,183	30
Nashville-Davidson County	TN	67,452	67,669	72,807	—	—	—	—	—	—	4,839	15.0	9,351	7.8	7.6	7.9	6.7	8.5	7.0	3,193	130
Rutherford County	TN	18,228	25,356	31,428	—	—	—	—	—	—	1,869	16.8	2,909	10.8	2.2	0.7	1.2	2.3	5.4	1,765	39
Shelby County	TN	37,605	46,972	44,987	—	—	—	—	—	—	2,580	17.4	4,977	9.0	2.1	0.8	1.6	2.8	3.6	2,638	47
Sumner County	TN	19,650	22,347	24,707	—	—	—	—	—	—	1,625	15.2	3,125	7.9	1.4	0.4	1.6	1.3	2.9	1,454	42
Williamson County	TN	11,502	19,545	23,844	—	—	—	—	—	—	1,431	16.7	2,679	8.9	1.7	0.1	0.5	1.3	5.5	1,491	34
Abilene ISD	TX	18,217	18,118	16,930	53.1	46.9	12.9	32.2	1.3	0.4	1,288	13.1	2,673	6.3	4.9	3.6	4.7	5.5	6.4	945	39
Aldine ISD	TX	41,372	52,520	56,375	5.7	94.3	31.7	60.3	2.2	0.1	3,733	15.1	7,973	7.1	5.8	4.3	7.1	6.3	6.0	2,338	66
Alief ISD	TX	29,774	42,151	45,571	5.8	94.2	36.5	44.5	13.0	0.1	3,024	15.1	5,999	7.6	3.3	1.8	5.1	2.8	3.9	2,094	41
Amarillo ISD	TX	27,374	28,908	29,881	47.6	52.4	10.9	38.8	2.4	0.3	2,072	14.4	3,977	7.5	3.1	1.8	3.1	3.6	4.6	1,649	51
Arlington ISD	TX	44,958	58,866	62,267	37.5	62.5	22.7	32.4	6.9	0.5	3,965	15.7	8,239	7.6	2.7	3.7	2.4	2.1	2.0	3,343	77
Austin ISD	TX	65,797	77,816	79,950	29.0	71.0	13.4	54.6	2.8	0.2	5,544	14.4	10,846	7.4	6.0	4.8	6.3	6.4	7.0	3,733	111
Beaumont ISD	TX	18,684	20,696	20,261	21.2	78.8	64.0	11.8	2.8	0.2	1,432	14.2	2,922	6.9	4.4	3.8	5.2	3.8	5.0	1,110	35
Birdville ISD	TX	18,466	21,246	22,333	63.0	37.0	6.1	24.6	5.6	0.7	1,390	16.1	2,001	11.2	1.9	1.8	1.8	2.0	1.8	1,318	33
Brownsville ISD	TX	34,906	40,898	46,846	1.7	98.3	0.1	97.8	0.3	#	2,952	15.9	6,819	6.9	4.1	4.0	5.6	2.8	3.7	2,164	51
Carrollton-Farmers Branch	TX	16,234	24,134	25,860	30.5	69.5	13.2	44.3	11.6	0.5	1,700	15.2	3,158	8.2	2.1	1.3	2.1	2.5	3.1	1,411	40
Clear Creek ISD	TX	22,372	29,875	33,616	65.4	34.6	7.9	16.6	9.8	0.3	1,973	17.0	3,859	8.7	1.8	1.2	1.3	1.9	3.2	1,922	37
Conroe ISD	TX	23,288	34,928	40,432	69.0	31.0	5.5	22.4	2.6	0.4	2,498	16.2	5,106	7.9	1.8	1.9	2.0	1.5	1.6	2,394	47
Corpus Christi ISD	TX	41,881	39,138	39,189	19.0	81.0	5.5	73.6	1.7	0.3	2,389	16.4	5,120	7.7	4.8	4.5	3.9	4.6	6.4	2,228	61
Cypress-Fairbanks ISD	TX	41,196	63,497	79,314	48.7	51.3	11.6	31.0	8.4	0.2	5,128	15.5	10,159	7.8	1.1	0.8	0.9	1.1	1.9	4,578	62
Dallas ISD	TX	135,320	161,548	158,027	5.8	94.2	30.3	62.6	1.1	0.3	10,225	15.5	20,158	7.8	5.1	4.1	6.4	4.5	6.2	7,080	228
Denton ISD	TX	10,690	13,645	16,932	57.5	42.5	11.8	28.0	2.1	0.6	1,219	13.9	2,338	7.2	4.7	3.4	5.3	5.4	5.1	802	25
Ector County ISD	TX	26,993	26,831	26,119	33.8	66.2	5.5	59.3	0.7	0.7	1,684	15.5	3,341	7.8	9.0	5.8	10.5	9.3	11.1	1,354	41
Edinburg CISD	TX	13,685	22,005	26,504	2.4	97.6	0.3	97.0	0.4	#	1,698	15.6	3,801	7.0	3.5	3.5	4.3	3.1	3.0	1,241	37
El Paso ISD	TX	64,092	62,325	63,216	12.9	87.1	4.5	80.9	1.4	0.3	4,417	14.3	8,981	7.0	4.1	2.8	3.8	4.4	6.5	3,412	92
Fort Bend ISD	TX	36,270	53,999	62,853	29.6	70.4	30.6	21.0	18.7	0.3	3,715	16.9	7,757	8.1	2.2	1.4	1.8	1.3	4.9	4,286	61
Fort Worth ISD	TX	69,163	79,661	79,769	16.9	83.1	27.2	54.0	1.7	0.2	4,804	16.6	10,415	7.7	6.5	5.0	7.5	5.8	9.0	3,744	147

See notes at end of table.

Table 87. Selected statistics on enrollment, teachers, dropouts, and graduates in public school districts enrolling more than 15,000 students, by state: 1990, 2000, 2001–02, 2003–04, and 2004—Continued

| Name of district | State | Enrollment, fall 1990 | Enrollment, fall 2000 | Enrollment, fall 2004 | Percentage distribution of enrollment, by race, fall 2004 | | | | | | Number of classroom teachers, fall 2004 | Pupil/teacher ratio, fall 2004 | Total number of staff, fall 2004 | Student/staff ratio, fall 2004 | Percent dropouts from grades 9–12, 2001–02[1] | | | | | Number of high school graduates, 2003–04[2] | Number of schools, fall 2004 |
					White	Total (Minority)	Black	Hispanic	Asian/Pacific Islander	American Indian/Alaska Native					Total	Grade 9	Grade 10	Grade 11	Grade 12		
1	2	3	4	5	6	7	8	9	10	11	12	13	14	15	16	17	18	19	20	21	22
Frisco County ISD	TX	1,310	7,234	16,190	69.7	30.3	8.9	12.9	7.7	0.8	1,123	14.4	2,026	8.0	0.6	0.3	0.6	1.0	0.6	498	24
Galena Park ISD	TX	15,593	18,885	20,805	9.5	90.5	21.0	67.9	1.5	0.1	1,523	13.7	2,944	7.1	3.0	1.3	3.6	3.6	4.3	1,153	23
Garland ISD	TX	37,978	50,312	56,236	37.0	63.0	18.4	36.8	7.2	0.5	3,608	15.6	6,883	8.2	1.7	1.2	1.5	1.8	2.8	3,065	70
Goose Creek CISD	TX	17,654	18,003	19,469	34.1	65.9	17.6	47.0	1.1	0.2	1,228	15.9	2,454	7.9	5.1	2.8	6.8	4.6	7.3	899	25
Grand Prairie ISD	TX	16,482	20,257	22,860	23.3	76.7	15.3	56.8	3.9	0.8	1,448	15.8	2,874	8.0	3.7	2.8	4.5	4.1	3.9	1,061	35
Harlingen CISD	TX	13,805	15,857	17,378	10.2	89.8	0.8	88.3	0.8	#	1,039	16.7	2,414	7.2	4.8	4.0	4.8	5.0	5.9	769	26
Houston ISD	TX	194,435	208,462	208,945	8.9	91.1	29.0	59.0	3.0	0.1	12,009	17.4	24,800	8.4	6.0	4.6	9.0	4.0	8.0	8,520	304
Humble ISD	TX	19,560	24,684	28,159	63.3	36.7	13.3	19.6	3.3	0.5	1,837	15.3	3,693	7.6	1.7	0.2	0.6	3.6	2.6	1,694	31
Hurst-Euless-Bedford ISD	TX	18,733	19,203	19,444	57.5	42.5	12.5	19.6	9.4	0.9	1,273	15.3	2,495	7.8	1.9	1.2	1.8	2.2	2.2	1,285	31
Irving ISD	TX	23,509	29,097	31,917	22.1	77.9	12.1	60.8	4.5	0.4	2,093	15.3	3,938	8.1	3.3	2.5	3.7	4.1	3.3	1,519	39
Judson ISD	TX	13,145	16,603	18,161	27.0	73.0	26.1	43.9	2.6	0.3	1,256	14.5	2,599	7.0	2.9	2.0	2.2	2.9	6.1	1,013	23
Katy ISD	TX	19,507	34,503	44,646	60.6	39.4	7.5	23.8	7.9	0.2	2,914	15.3	5,816	7.7	1.1	1.1	1.5	0.9	1.1	2,642	47
Keller ISD	TX	8,212	17,083	23,756	75.2	24.8	5.6	12.4	6.2	0.5	1,389	17.1	2,511	9.5	2.2	1.0	2.1	2.6	3.8	1,190	28
Killeen ISD	TX	22,131	29,687	33,310	35.4	64.6	40.0	19.4	4.4	0.7	2,457	13.6	5,208	6.4	3.5	2.5	2.2	2.6	7.5	1,553	51
Klein ISD	TX	26,220	32,376	36,964	51.9	48.1	13.9	25.7	8.1	0.4	2,295	16.1	4,743	7.8	2.5	1.6	2.5	2.4	4.3	2,312	36
La Joya ISD	TX	8,523	17,641	23,008	0.3	99.7	0.0	99.6	0.0	#	1,450	15.9	3,243	7.1	7.6	5.4	8.7	7.1	10.8	868	29
Lamar CISD	TX	12,335	15,159	18,574	34.8	65.2	15.2	46.9	2.9	0.2	1,203	15.4	2,544	7.3	3.2	2.6	3.1	3.1	4.6	989	28
Laredo ISD	TX	23,304	22,547	24,825	0.5	99.5	0.1	99.3	0.1	#	1,570	15.8	3,826	6.5	4.6	3.6	4.1	4.4	6.6	1,074	29
Leander ISD	TX	5,419	14,499	19,945	73.0	27.0	5.4	17.7	3.3	0.6	1,353	14.7	2,575	7.7	2.0	0.9	1.8	2.3	3.3	956	26
Lewisville ISD	TX	20,776	39,096	45,527	66.9	33.1	8.5	16.9	7.2	0.5	3,270	13.9	5,516	7.7	1.1	0.8	0.8	1.2	1.8	2,609	59
Lubbock ISD	TX	30,786	29,026	28,741	37.3	62.7	14.8	46.1	1.6	0.2	2,018	14.2	3,802	7.6	3.8	1.2	3.7	4.0	6.6	1,900	58
Mansfield ISD	TX	7,570	14,888	23,069	57.0	43.0	20.8	16.8	4.9	0.5	1,439	16.0	2,786	8.3	2.1	2.0	1.6	2.6	2.7	1,100	28
McAllen ISD	TX	18,432	21,747	24,146	7.6	92.4	0.6	89.8	2.0	0.1	1,580	15.3	3,411	7.1	4.8	5.0	5.5	4.1	4.5	1,281	32
McKinney ISD	TX	4,703	12,000	18,047	66.3	33.7	9.6	21.3	2.3	0.5	1,192	15.1	1,954	9.2	2.7	2.0	3.0	3.5	2.5	811	26
Mesquite ISD	TX	25,920	32,334	34,815	42.1	57.9	22.5	31.1	3.5	0.8	2,212	15.7	4,347	8.0	2.9	1.8	3.3	3.1	3.6	2,102	45
Midland ISD	TX	21,082	20,522	20,716	41.4	58.6	9.8	47.4	0.9	0.4	1,393	14.9	2,710	7.6	5.5	4.1	5.8	6.3	6.3	1,235	36
North East ISD	TX	39,909	50,875	57,599	44.1	55.9	9.3	43.2	3.1	0.3	3,801	15.2	7,467	7.7	1.8	1.3	1.5	1.8	2.7	3,465	65
Northside ISD	TX	50,229	63,739	74,649	29.5	70.5	7.4	60.2	2.7	0.2	4,792	15.6	10,576	7.1	3.0	2.2	2.9	2.7	4.5	4,127	96
Pasadena ISD	TX	37,643	42,577	47,440	17.5	82.5	6.6	72.5	3.3	0.2	3,014	15.7	6,161	7.7	5.4	4.0	4.9	6.5	7.1	2,030	57
Pflugerville ISD	TX	6,482	14,545	17,591	37.6	62.4	22.1	31.8	8.1	0.4	1,082	16.3	1,897	9.3	1.8	0.9	1.4	2.4	2.8	969	23
Pharr-San Juan-Alamo ISD	TX	16,563	22,537	27,338	1.1	98.9	0.2	98.6	0.1	#	1,686	16.2	3,814	7.2	6.1	5.2	6.5	6.1	7.5	1,129	36
Plano ISD	TX	28,398	47,161	52,406	59.7	40.3	9.3	14.1	16.5	0.3	3,761	13.9	6,912	7.6	1.5	0.6	0.7	1.6	3.1	3,074	70
Richardson ISD	TX	32,555	35,138	34,139	38.1	61.9	25.4	27.7	8.4	0.4	2,466	13.8	4,618	7.4	2.0	0.9	1.8	2.4	3.3	1,946	57
Round Rock ISD	TX	19,636	31,536	36,648	58.3	41.7	9.7	22.5	9.1	0.4	2,472	14.8	4,657	7.9	2.1	1.4	1.9	2.3	3.1	2,106	47
San Angelo ISD	TX	16,488	16,092	15,201	42.6	57.4	6.1	49.9	1.1	0.2	957	15.9	1,968	7.7	4.3	3.0	3.8	4.2	6.8	974	27
San Antonio ISD	TX	60,161	57,273	56,639	3.3	96.7	8.8	87.5	0.2	0.1	3,517	16.1	7,919	7.2	7.1	6.2	6.8	6.7	9.5	2,594	106
Socorro ISD	TX	14,350	26,711	34,362	5.0	95.0	1.3	92.9	0.4	0.3	2,015	17.1	4,106	8.4	1.9	1.4	1.7	1.9	3.3	1,719	34
Spring Branch ISD	TX	23,661	31,659	32,343	34.3	65.7	6.1	53.5	5.9	0.1	2,259	14.3	4,798	6.7	3.2	2.9	3.6	2.7	3.9	1,912	48
Spring ISD	TX	18,537	23,034	28,423	27.2	72.8	34.8	32.4	5.4	0.2	1,828	15.5	3,883	7.3	2.9	1.6	3.3	3.1	4.2	1,501	27
Tyler ISD	TX	18,182	16,626	17,591	31.9	68.1	33.9	32.6	1.2	0.3	1,259	14.0	2,478	7.1	4.4	2.8	3.8	5.0	7.0	1,011	29
United ISD	TX	12,553	27,556	33,955	1.9	98.1	0.2	97.5	0.4	#	2,068	16.4	5,048	6.7	1.8	1.6	2.1	1.4	2.4	1,679	39
Waco County ISD	TX	14,304	15,433	15,579	16.2	83.8	36.6	46.7	0.5	0.1	1,055	14.8	2,199	7.1	8.1	7.2	7.4	9.0	10.2	754	34
Weslaco County ISD	TX	10,835	13,407	15,382	2.1	97.9	0.2	97.5	0.3	#	968	15.9	2,242	6.9	5.2	5.2	6.4	5.2	3.4	711	21
Ysleta ISD	TX	49,974	46,394	46,349	6.4	93.6	2.3	90.4	0.4	0.5	3,026	15.3	6,233	7.4	5.6	2.2	4.9	5.5	10.9	2,883	64
Alpine District	UT	38,852	47,117	52,920	89.8	10.2	0.7	6.9	2.0	0.6	2,168	24.4	4,276	12.4	2.1	0.3	0.7	2.5	4.8	3,295	67
Davis District	UT	55,558	59,578	58,953	89.7	10.3	1.4	6.0	2.3	0.6	2,681	22.0	5,525	10.7	2.4	0.3	0.9	2.0	6.1	3,690	96
Granite District	UT	78,554	71,328	68,783	69.6	30.4	1.7	20.7	6.7	1.2	3,125	22.0	6,100	11.3	6.0	3.0	5.0	6.1	10.2	3,916	115
Jordan District	UT	64,991	73,158	75,548	89.6	10.4	0.8	6.6	2.4	0.6	3,013	25.1	5,889	12.8	4.4	2.3	2.9	5.0	7.4	4,922	88
Nebo District	UT	16,393	21,094	24,909	91.2	8.8	0.5	6.4	1.1	0.8	1,025	24.3	2,103	11.8	2.0	0.1	0.8	1.4	6.0	1,364	38
Salt Lake District	UT	24,766	25,367	23,600	49.3	50.7	4.2	34.7	9.8	1.9	1,183	19.9	2,527	9.3	11.2	7.7	8.8	12.5	16.3	1,178	44

See notes at end of table.

Table 87. Selected statistics on enrollment, teachers, dropouts, and graduates in public school districts enrolling more than 15,000 students, by state: 1990, 2000, 2001–02, 2003–04, and 2004—Continued

Name of district	State	Enroll-ment, fall 1990	Enroll-ment, fall 2000	Enroll-ment, fall 2004	Percentage distribution of enrollment, by race, fall 2004						Number of classroom teachers, fall 2004	Pupil/ teacher ratio, fall 2004	Total number of staff, fall 2004	Student/ staff ratio, fall 2004	Percent dropouts from grades 9–12, 2001–02[1]					Number of high school graduates, 2003–04[2]	Number of schools, fall 2004
					White	Minority Total	Black	Hispanic	Asian/ Pacific Islander	American Indian/ Alaska Native					Total	Grade 9	Grade 10	Grade 11	Grade 12		
1	2	3	4	5	6	7	8	9	10	11	12	13	14	15	16	17	18	19	20	21	22
Washington District	UT	13,264	18,374	21,610	87.0	13.0	0.6	8.3	1.9	2.2	981	22.0	1,815	11.9	0.8	0.0	0.1	1.2	2.1	1,357	39
Weber District	UT	25,425	27,783	28,475	89.3	10.7	1.3	7.2	1.7	0.5	1,245	22.9	2,299	12.4	2.2	0.0	0.7	2.6	5.7	1,842	49
Arlington County	VA	14,825	18,870	18,802	43.6	56.4	14.5	31.8	10.1	0.1	1,770	10.6	3,474	5.4	3.0	3.4	1.9	3.9	2.6	1,110	32
Chesapeake City	VA	29,533	37,645	40,265	59.3	40.7	35.5	2.2	2.6	0.3	2,900	13.9	4,898	8.2	2.8	2.5	1.7	2.6	4.6	2,627	46
Chesterfield County	VA	44,480	51,212	56,242	65.6	34.4	26.0	4.8	2.9	0.7	3,922	14.3	6,989	8.0	4.3	5.0	4.5	3.1	4.6	3,695	60
Fairfax County	VA	128,766	156,412	164,765	54.1	45.9	11.2	16.3	18.1	0.3	12,627	13.0	25,440	6.5	2.7	4.5	2.2	3.1	3.7	10,814	204
Hampton City	VA	21,383	23,290	22,938	33.8	66.2	61.4	2.6	1.9	0.4	1,892	12.1	3,218	7.1	3.7	4.5	3.6	2.1	4.4	1,473	37
Hanover County	VA	11,328	16,611	18,529	86.8	13.2	10.1	1.2	1.5	0.4	1,462	12.7	2,692	6.9	0.7	0.2	0.6	0.4	1.8	1,106	21
Henrico County	VA	32,638	41,655	46,711	54.7	45.3	36.8	3.5	4.8	0.3	3,321	14.1	5,947	7.9	2.3	1.4	2.4	2.3	3.6	2,750	68
Loudoun County	VA	14,485	31,804	43,975	70.9	29.1	8.4	10.7	9.7	0.3	3,233	13.6	6,756	6.5	1.1	0.6	1.0	1.2	1.7	2,074	64
Newport News City	VA	28,925	33,008	33,096	34.1	65.9	57.2	5.3	2.7	0.7	2,530	13.1	4,543	7.3	3.0	3.0	3.1	3.1	2.9	1,644	49
Norfolk City	VA	36,541	37,349	36,250	25.3	74.7	69.4	3.1	2.0	0.2	2,596	13.6	4,636	7.8	4.6	6.6	3.3	3.3	2.7	1,422	57
Portsmouth City	VA	18,405	16,473	15,843	25.7	74.3	72.1	1.3	0.7	0.1	1,161	13.6	2,248	7.0	3.3	2.6	6.5	1.6	2.6	706	27
Prince William County	VA	41,888	54,646	66,298	48.9	51.1	23.4	20.6	6.8	0.3	4,417	15.0	11,607	5.7	4.0	3.3	2.9	4.0	6.1	3,529	78
Richmond City	VA	27,021	27,237	25,054	7.1	92.9	89.6	2.6	0.6	0.1	1,965	12.8	4,085	6.1	3.1	6.1	2.9	1.7	0.0	1,101	56
Spotsylvania County	VA	12,227	18,876	22,948	73.8	26.2	18.2	5.3	2.3	0.3	1,710	13.4	3,079	7.5	2.2	2.4	1.5	2.6	2.5	1,652	30
Stafford County	VA	12,555	21,124	25,633	71.4	28.6	20.0	5.6	2.6	0.3	1,783	14.4	3,293	7.8	2.5	2.4	1.8	2.9	2.9	1,537	25
Virginia Beach City	VA	70,266	76,586	75,515	60.1	39.9	28.8	4.8	6.0	0.3	5,626	13.4	10,189	7.4	1.2	2.0	1.4	0.7	0.3	4,599	86
Bellevue	WA	14,748	15,431	15,848	63.5	36.5	2.8	8.8	24.6	0.4	890	17.8	1,805	8.8	2.5	0.6	1.1	2.0	5.7	999	30
Bethel	WA	11,669	16,029	17,804	68.9	31.1	10.6	6.5	10.2	3.8	851	20.9	1,766	10.1	7.1	3.2	7.8	8.0	10.1	1,007	29
Edmonds	WA	18,868	22,067	21,115	71.0	29.0	5.8	7.7	13.9	1.5	1,068	19.8	2,283	9.2	6.9	1.9	3.3	5.6	19.5	1,252	42
Everett	WA	15,343	18,683	17,893	74.3	25.7	4.5	8.1	11.6	1.6	886	20.2	1,746	10.2	11.6	11.8	9.7	7.7	17.6	897	31
Evergreen	WA	14,810	21,650	25,345	80.4	19.6	4.3	6.3	7.9	1.1	1,316	19.3	2,544	10.0	6.3	1.5	3.1	7.5	14.1	1,213	35
Federal Way	WA	18,168	22,623	22,609	55.0	45.0	13.6	6.3	16.8	1.4	1,170	19.3	2,502	9.0	5.9	1.5	7.2	8.7	6.3	1,106	46
Highline	WA	16,208	18,024	17,645	41.5	58.5	14.1	13.2	20.9	2.2	928	19.0	1,938	9.1	10.0	14.0	9.9	7.8	5.7	1,006	43
Issaquah	WA	8,888	14,259	15,558	78.0	22.0	2.2	3.8	15.3	0.7	748	20.8	1,539	10.1	6.6	10.0	5.0	4.0	6.9	1,021	24
Kent	WA	21,027	26,535	27,293	62.7	37.3	10.7	9.1	16.3	1.3	1,364	20.0	2,823	9.7	2.7	3.1	5.0	2.8	2.9	1,533	42
Lake Washington	WA	23,050	23,662	24,189	76.5	23.5	2.8	6.6	13.3	0.7	1,207	20.0	2,301	10.5	1.8	0.3	0.6	0.7	5.3	1,661	51
Northshore	WA	17,511	20,255	20,496	79.7	20.3	2.5	6.6	10.1	1.1	1,002	20.5	2,033	10.1	1.3	0.4	0.5	0.6	3.7	1,511	35
Puyallup	WA	15,100	19,757	20,107	81.1	18.9	4.4	6.1	6.6	1.8	1,013	19.9	1,906	10.5	7.4	4.9	5.3	6.3	13.9	1,227	33
Seattle	WA	43,593	47,575	46,746	41.0	59.0	22.4	11.4	22.9	2.4	2,585	18.1	5,241	8.9	24.4	21.4	21.6	25.3	29.2	2,810	111
Spokane	WA	29,186	31,725	30,945	84.7	15.3	5.0	3.4	2.9	3.9	1,699	18.2	3,550	8.7	3.9	4.9	3.0	3.9	3.8	2,006	65
Tacoma	WA	30,169	34,093	31,948	51.9	48.1	22.6	10.9	12.8	1.9	1,724	18.5	3,560	9.0	5.0	5.7	5.0	4.2	4.7	1,586	63
Vancouver	WA	16,423	21,892	22,317	76.5	23.5	5.3	10.7	5.3	2.2	1,122	19.9	2,447	9.1	10.5	5.2	9.2	12.5	15.6	1,182	39
Kanawha County	WV	34,284	29,250	27,979	86.3	13.7	12.1	0.4	1.2	#	1,938	14.4	3,713	7.5	5.3	5.9	4.7	5.4	5.1	1,683	71
Appleton Area	WI	12,876	14,793	15,060	81.5	18.5	2.6	4.9	10.2	0.8	941	16.0	1,507	10.0	0.8	0.0	0.0	0.4	2.8	—	34
Green Bay Area	WI	18,048	20,104	20,300	67.9	32.1	5.5	13.5	8.1	5.0	1,450	14.0	2,458	8.3	1.6	0.0	0.0	0.7	6.0	—	36
Kenosha	WI	16,219	20,099	21,740	67.9	32.1	14.7	15.3	1.7	0.6	1,516	14.3	2,487	8.7	3.3	2.3	3.4	4.2	3.5	—	40
Madison Metropolitan	WI	23,214	25,087	24,894	57.5	42.5	20.7	11.0	10.1	0.6	1,982	12.6	3,632	6.9	3.0	2.1	2.9	3.6	3.5	—	52
Milwaukee	WI	92,784	97,985	93,654	16.9	83.1	58.6	19.2	4.4	0.9	5,859	16.0	11,180	8.4	9.0	10.7	9.5	8.5	4.9	—	229
Racine	WI	21,904	21,102	21,244	55.2	44.8	26.0	17.2	1.3	0.4	1,302	16.3	2,289	9.3	5.2	1.5	3.6	6.2	11.5	—	35

—Not available.
†Not applicable.
#Rounds to zero.
[1]Alabama, Alaska, Arizona, Florida, Illinois, Maryland, New Jersey, New York, Tennessee, and Vermont reported data on an alternative July through June cycle, rather than the specified October through September cycle.
[2]Includes regular diplomas only.
NOTE: Total enrollment, staff, and teacher data in this table reflect totals reported by school districts and may differ from data derived from summing school-level data to school district aggregates. SB = School board. SC = School corporation. ISD =

Independent school district. Race categories exclude persons of Hispanic origin. Detail may not sum to totals because of rounding.
SOURCE: U.S. Department of Education, National Center for Education Statistics, Common Core of Data (CCD), "Public Elementary/Secondary School Universe Survey," 2004–05; "Local Education Agency Universe Survey," 1990–91, 2000–01, and 2004–05; and "Local Education Agency Universe Survey Dropout and Completion Data File," 2001–02. (This table was prepared October 2006.)

Table 88. Revenues, expenditures, poverty rate, and Title I allocations of public school districts enrolling more than 15,000 students, by state: 2003–04 and fiscal year 2006

Name of district	State	Revenues by source of funds, 2003-04 (in thousands of dollars)				Percentage distribution of revenues, 2003-04				Expenditures, 2003-04 (in thousands of dollars)					Poverty rate of 5- to 17-year-olds, 2004[1]	Current expenditure per pupil,[2] 2003-04	Title I allocations, fiscal year 2006, per poverty child[3]
		Total	Federal	State	Local	Total	Federal	State	Local	Total[4]	Current expenditures Total	Instruction	Capital outlay	Interest on school debt			
1	2	3	4	5	6	7	8	9	10	11	12	13	14	15	16	17	18
Districts with more than 15,000 students	†	$195,675,096	$18,939,549	$90,902,908	$85,832,639	100.0	9.7	46.5	43.9	$201,039,524	$166,755,474	$103,392,188	$23,948,776	$5,413,667	18.5	$7,942	$1,540
Baldwin County	AL	178,731	14,310	83,688	80,733	100.0	8.0	46.8	45.2	184,333	162,575	100,255	15,839	2,541	13.9	6,764	1,170
Birmingham City	AL	269,722	42,328	138,831	88,563	100.0	15.7	51.5	32.8	264,641	243,833	136,666	8,690	5,831	32.9	7,151	1,291
Huntsville City	AL	202,773	18,173	81,592	103,008	100.0	9.0	40.2	50.8	212,688	167,265	101,885	42,326	649	17.7	7,404	1,184
Jefferson County	AL	276,081	21,785	151,061	103,235	100.0	7.9	54.7	37.4	271,159	233,845	146,132	22,758	8,278	9.2	6,049	1,120
Madison County	AL	114,838	8,332	68,585	37,921	100.0	7.3	59.7	33.0	111,964	102,779	62,526	2,886	4,020	10.0	6,038	1,015
Mobile County	AL	459,717	68,643	258,173	132,901	100.0	14.9	56.2	28.9	474,814	416,592	238,977	40,703	13,559	25.5	6,431	1,345
Montgomery County	AL	237,882	33,946	129,372	74,564	100.0	14.3	54.4	31.3	233,658	215,821	124,716	9,542	2,525	25.7	6,630	1,274
Shelby County	AL	181,350	10,912	85,091	85,347	100.0	6.0	46.9	47.1	182,662	157,581	93,809	13,230	7,035	8.4	6,991	994
Tuscaloosa County	AL	113,579	9,868	66,989	36,722	100.0	8.7	59.0	32.3	102,562	96,594	59,867	1,312	2,648	17.6	6,010	1,174
Anchorage	AK	430,337	58,649	233,437	138,251	100.0	13.6	54.2	32.1	559,627	411,794	244,474	126,767	17,547	8.6	8,282	2,491
Amphitheater Unified District	AZ	126,280	11,749	48,834	65,697	100.0	9.3	38.7	52.0	107,023	97,942	53,827	3,415	5,393	15.7	5,806	1,161
Cartwright Elementary District	AZ	138,694	18,099	92,074	28,521	100.0	13.0	66.4	20.6	136,390	108,703	65,050	27,591	92	29.5	5,472	1,197
Chandler Unified District	AZ	206,858	11,373	99,975	95,510	100.0	5.5	48.3	46.2	203,738	154,515	96,019	39,716	8,780	11.7	5,741	1,067
Gilbert Unified District	AZ	241,923	8,987	120,842	112,094	100.0	3.7	50.0	46.3	214,830	182,727	115,118	16,286	13,109	4.8	5,188	628
Kyrene Elementary District	AZ	137,719	6,945	51,639	79,135	100.0	5.0	37.5	57.5	131,923	103,744	66,456	7,285	17,818	5.5	5,584	907
Mesa Unified District	AZ	538,261	42,638	257,708	237,915	100.0	7.9	47.9	44.2	468,828	431,197	269,369	21,821	11,836	13.2	5,719	1,291
Paradise Valley Unified District	AZ	272,118	17,238	92,428	162,452	100.0	6.3	34.0	59.7	251,152	202,185	121,903	19,539	22,525	8.2	5,796	1,021
Peoria Unified	AZ	270,929	13,291	150,838	106,800	100.0	4.9	55.7	39.4	265,019	207,451	125,827	45,246	12,088	7.7	5,650	1,011
Phoenix Union High	AZ	238,116	21,649	42,710	173,757	100.0	9.1	17.9	73.0	212,879	196,104	105,258	7,995	7,780	29.1	8,175	1,283
Scottsdale Unified District	AZ	215,562	9,472	41,014	165,076	100.0	4.4	19.0	76.6	182,216	162,278	102,707	6,287	12,580	6.3	6,110	944
Deer Valley Unified District	AZ	235,433	11,200	112,020	112,213	100.0	4.8	47.6	47.7	248,854	173,320	106,824	65,345	10,189	6.8	5,469	958
Sunnyside Unified District	AZ	110,570	17,331	61,149	32,090	100.0	15.7	55.3	29.0	106,801	100,064	58,243	4,073	2,594	39.1	6,309	1,301
Tucson Unified District	AZ	476,206	57,276	221,843	197,087	100.0	12.0	46.6	41.4	438,681	410,672	221,401	13,217	14,621	21.7	6,683	1,379
Washington Elementary	AZ	204,771	23,567	94,370	86,834	100.0	11.5	46.1	42.4	177,051	147,275	89,592	22,885	3,201	17.3	6,026	1,187
Little Rock	AR	241,816	28,358	101,387	112,071	100.0	11.7	41.9	46.3	269,709	212,787	121,415	41,511	9,241	21.6	8,395	1,321
Pulaski Co. Spec.	AR	151,030	12,993	76,616	61,421	100.0	8.6	50.7	40.7	154,745	140,912	84,725	3,867	2,906	14.2	7,608	1,154
ABC Unified	CA	169,512	13,152	116,164	40,196	100.0	7.8	68.5	23.7	176,473	154,142	97,195	7,293	1,518	13.1	6,935	1,022
Alhambra Unified	CA	202,988	19,232	135,737	48,019	100.0	9.5	66.9	23.7	169,265	144,289	85,779	10,970	720	23.6	7,319	1,179
Alvord Unified	CA	135,000	12,851	80,402	41,747	100.0	9.5	59.6	30.9	137,315	128,100	83,219	6,192	2,785	13.4	6,589	1,147
Anaheim City	CA	177,186	17,548	98,991	60,647	100.0	9.9	55.9	34.2	182,998	148,588	97,503	24,573	2,420	24.2	6,765	1,242
Anaheim Union High	CA	272,965	33,743	144,736	94,486	100.0	12.4	53.0	34.6	292,271	232,430	142,047	32,787	4,674	16.2	7,159	1,224
Antelope Valley Union High	CA	188,480	10,928	129,724	47,828	100.0	5.8	68.8	25.4	213,077	140,116	88,403	68,012	2,428	15.9	6,326	1,192
Antioch Unified	CA	160,746	9,367	81,591	69,788	100.0	5.8	50.8	43.4	150,804	133,518	90,543	15,849	775	10.5	6,173	1,021
Apple Valley Unified	CA	96,035	10,184	59,074	26,777	100.0	10.6	61.5	27.9	94,939	90,839	58,020	2,503	207	23.4	6,276	1,216
Bakersfield City Elementary	CA	232,909	42,563	159,505	30,841	100.0	18.3	68.5	13.2	223,881	217,199	137,231	4,408	1,516	38.0	7,671	1,367
Baldwin Park Unified	CA	147,765	16,766	98,981	32,018	100.0	11.3	67.0	21.7	153,816	127,185	77,837	12,032	1,127	21.9	6,594	1,220
Bellflower Unified	CA	114,151	10,583	72,269	31,299	100.0	9.3	63.3	27.4	122,233	106,982	67,037	9,723	449	19.3	6,892	1,196
Burbank Unified	CA	129,596	7,512	68,877	53,207	100.0	5.8	53.1	41.1	163,272	113,876	76,325	44,935	2,384	15.0	6,673	1,162
Cajon Valley Union Elementary	CA	136,689	14,327	68,680	53,682	100.0	10.5	50.2	39.3	150,027	131,749	86,802	15,961	2,235	16.9	7,291	1,231
Capistrano Unified	CA	346,292	19,426	108,910	217,956	100.0	5.6	31.5	62.9	362,218	328,661	214,898	19,576	2,910	6.1	6,607	1,028
Chaffey Joint Union High	CA	186,643	9,652	112,678	64,313	100.0	5.2	60.4	34.5	189,113	155,604	98,022	18,642	6,026	11.5	6,667	1,077
Chino Valley Unified	CA	231,126	12,823	136,583	81,720	100.0	5.5	59.1	35.4	261,907	208,778	138,978	40,517	6,818	7.9	6,262	1,035
Chula Vista Elementary	CA	225,078	18,360	101,364	105,354	100.0	8.2	45.0	46.8	255,087	190,338	126,536	52,824	6,999	12.2	7,526	1,139
Clovis Unified	CA	301,928	16,463	172,776	112,689	100.0	5.5	57.2	37.3	285,857	238,306	141,465	34,546	7,571	11.1	6,875	1,118
Coachella Valley Joint Unified	CA	140,751	27,201	82,201	31,349	100.0	19.3	58.4	22.3	166,378	117,905	70,169	46,661	722	34.7	8,064	1,362
Colton Joint Unified	CA	171,369	26,396	118,554	36,419	100.0	9.6	69.2	21.3	177,197	157,755	92,959	14,723	1,896	22.2	6,326	1,253
Compton Unified	CA	303,947	36,923	210,505	56,519	100.0	12.1	69.3	18.6	316,471	221,957	135,871	77,780	4,230	36.8	6,832	1,363
Conejo Valley Unified	CA	172,118	6,807	66,701	98,610	100.0	4.0	38.8	57.3	176,677	146,996	97,081	18,756	1,517	5.0	6,609	942
Corona-Norco County Unified	CA	388,687	22,227	201,233	165,227	100.0	5.7	51.8	42.5	436,567	286,253	184,156	92,750	9,558	8.6	6,506	1,155

See notes at end of table.

Table 88. Revenues, expenditures, poverty rate, and Title I allocations of public school districts enrolling more than 15,000 students, by state: 2003–04 and fiscal year 2006—Continued

| Name of district | State | Revenues by source of funds, 2003–04 (in thousands of dollars) | | | | Percentage distribution of revenues, 2003–04 | | | | Expenditures, 2003–04 (in thousands of dollars) | | | | | Poverty rate of 5- to 17-year-olds, 2004[1] | Current expenditure per pupil, 2003–04 | Title I allocations, fiscal year 2006, per poverty child[3] |
| | | Total | Federal | State | Local | Total | Federal | State | Local | Total[4] | Current expenditures Total | Current expenditures Instruction | Capital outlay | Interest on school debt | | | |
1	2	3	4	5	6	7	8	9	10	11	12	13	14	15	16	17	18
Covina-Valley Unified	CA	115,472	8,276	77,494	29,702	100.0	7.2	67.1	25.7	129,000	102,035	60,915	18,152	993	13.3	6,786	973
Cupertino Union School	CA	142,224	3,597	47,706	90,921	100.0	2.5	33.5	63.9	141,906	102,236	67,621	35,523	3,853	6.4	6,371	944
Desert Sands Unified	CA	294,101	22,219	119,856	152,026	100.0	7.6	40.8	51.7	264,136	179,604	113,084	75,301	8,519	17.5	6,876	1,252
Downey Unified	CA	162,394	13,488	102,256	46,650	100.0	8.3	63.0	28.7	178,178	144,686	96,292	27,307	1,840	14.2	6,424	1,096
East Side Union High	CA	240,362	15,924	85,680	138,758	100.0	6.6	35.6	57.7	258,980	196,574	112,620	35,083	10,418	12.2	7,808	1,206
Elk Grove Unified	CA	552,457	36,821	308,655	206,981	100.0	6.7	55.9	37.5	518,361	394,509	255,672	77,362	5,202	13.6	7,094	1,324
Escondido Union Elementary	CA	167,437	14,274	92,759	60,404	100.0	8.5	55.4	36.1	165,672	132,132	84,898	29,490	3,626	15.7	6,553	1,223
Fairfield-Suisun Unified	CA	192,418	12,829	115,803	63,786	100.0	6.7	60.2	33.1	204,607	145,744	89,241	50,408	4,647	11.4	6,271	1,144
Folsom-Cordova Unified	CA	141,225	9,643	61,753	69,829	100.0	6.8	43.7	49.4	147,804	118,069	75,637	25,785	2,713	13.2	6,544	1,320
Fontana Unified	CA	391,951	35,665	308,655	47,631	100.0	9.1	78.7	12.2	354,125	282,425	170,975	67,171	3,375	21.8	6,831	1,308
Fremont Unified	CA	245,173	12,881	117,657	114,635	100.0	5.3	48.0	46.8	258,373	209,948	142,150	20,513	7,549	6.0	6,593	981
Fresno Unified	CA	716,277	113,923	471,149	131,205	100.0	15.9	65.8	18.3	709,717	624,312	373,560	45,360	17,077	36.7	7,669	1,456
Fullerton Joint Union High	CA	144,935	5,379	75,076	64,480	100.0	3.7	51.8	44.5	141,671	101,630	62,258	29,106	1,634	13.5	6,198	954
Garden Grove Unified	CA	365,604	42,243	199,045	124,316	100.0	11.6	54.4	34.0	367,318	352,914	226,751	5,895	145	18.9	7,034	1,524
Glendale Unified	CA	267,603	29,219	156,162	82,222	100.0	10.9	58.4	30.7	281,596	209,584	140,462	57,931	6,463	20.6	7,121	1,423
Grossmont Union High	CA	204,865	11,693	81,322	111,850	100.0	5.7	39.7	54.6	205,777	188,407	114,610	4,932	1,801	9.1	7,704	989
Hacienda La Puente Unified	CA	279,478	22,727	187,732	69,019	100.0	8.1	67.2	24.7	231,111	180,523	106,760	17,614	2,789	15.1	7,080	1,215
Hayward Unified	CA	199,962	19,849	103,161	76,952	100.0	9.9	51.6	38.5	184,929	172,475	109,274	876	1,386	11.2	7,182	1,136
Hemet Unified	CA	161,153	16,922	93,061	51,170	100.0	10.5	57.7	31.8	190,559	130,363	83,131	57,353	2,392	19.1	6,620	1,423
Hesperia Unified	CA	116,193	10,285	74,675	31,233	100.0	8.9	64.3	26.9	108,405	104,206	64,773	3,765	70	16.8	6,111	1,196
Huntington Beach Union High	CA	140,544	11,043	59,011	70,495	100.0	7.9	42.0	50.2	146,377	109,836	63,161	8,740	226	9.5	7,335	944
Inglewood Unified	CA	138,350	18,057	84,982	35,311	100.0	13.1	61.4	25.5	155,296	126,205	75,589	17,220	3,106	28.7	7,023	1,426
Jurupa Unified	CA	150,320	15,955	91,432	42,933	100.0	10.6	60.8	28.6	173,335	139,491	90,496	31,797	1,302	19.7	6,667	1,247
Kern Union High	CA	285,584	27,922	160,309	97,353	100.0	9.8	56.1	34.1	291,552	245,243	131,160	31,340	5,558	20.2	7,579	1,256
Lancaster Elementary	CA	117,844	13,729	76,182	27,933	100.0	11.7	64.6	23.7	124,198	108,636	72,069	12,818	1,324	24.5	6,876	1,219
Lake Elsinore Unified	CA	145,398	13,029	83,589	48,780	100.0	9.0	57.5	33.5	222,303	132,699	83,384	87,708	977	13.0	6,732	1,129
Lodi Unified	CA	255,273	22,417	146,732	86,124	100.0	8.8	57.5	33.7	266,042	200,846	127,685	58,925	2,953	19.5	6,883	1,251
Long Beach Unified	CA	819,059	123,816	517,708	177,535	100.0	15.1	63.2	21.7	820,912	711,945	425,055	51,763	13,521	31.6	7,298	1,424
Los Angeles Unified	CA	7,531,675	995,098	4,834,977	1,701,600	100.0	13.2	64.2	22.6	8,206,329	6,509,341	3,802,228	1,277,590	225,745	30.5	8,714	1,623
Lynwood Unified	CA	253,569	11,570	213,200	28,799	100.0	4.6	84.1	11.4	242,530	124,613	73,453	111,738	621	28.4	6,339	1,241
Madera Unified	CA	159,581	16,345	110,037	33,199	100.0	10.2	69.0	20.8	138,948	119,509	72,134	14,513	1,285	32.3	6,929	1,329
Manteca Unified	CA	160,289	9,598	95,250	55,441	100.0	6.0	59.4	34.6	188,581	135,603	86,327	48,467	2,148	8.8	5,993	1,078
Modesto City Elementary	CA	88,741	4,428	33,902	50,411	100.0	5.0	38.2	56.8	81,250	59,524	33,986	16,158	3,952	29.5	7,746	1,319
Modesto City High	CA	288,855	30,025	174,568	84,262	100.0	10.4	60.4	29.2	270,515	241,731	154,052	16,613	3,139	17.5	7,030	1,162
Montebello Unified	CA	295,118	38,336	185,626	71,156	100.0	13.0	62.9	24.1	288,895	259,842	161,238	12,474	2,283	28.8	7,227	1,326
Moreno Valley Unified	CA	243,733	28,549	167,019	48,165	100.0	11.7	68.5	19.8	250,455	231,689	147,858	15,885	1,617	15.7	6,659	1,269
Mount Diablo Unified	CA	323,098	20,436	159,138	143,524	100.0	6.3	49.3	44.4	352,126	264,709	170,220	75,240	7,508	7.7	7,189	1,126
Murrieta Valley Unified	CA	134,054	3,998	69,728	60,328	100.0	3.0	52.0	45.0	155,300	109,757	70,977	40,270	3,028	3.8	6,279	687
Napa Valley Unified	CA	143,929	9,398	35,764	98,767	100.0	6.5	24.8	68.6	164,397	122,375	81,411	36,312	2,010	10.2	7,189	992
Newport-Mesa Unified	CA	193,228	15,740	41,158	136,330	100.0	8.1	21.3	70.6	233,988	173,590	102,746	50,195	2,804	12.5	7,769	1,026
Norwalk-La Mirada Unified	CA	211,682	18,227	140,483	52,972	100.0	8.6	66.4	25.0	217,578	174,559	106,029	24,088	1,598	13.7	7,243	1,044
Oakland Unified	CA	496,023	76,751	252,241	167,031	100.0	15.5	50.9	33.7	522,597	420,522	251,806	40,794	16,014	27.9	8,338	1,411
Oceanside Unified	CA	178,116	20,984	90,900	66,232	100.0	11.8	51.0	37.2	184,945	160,794	103,765	21,045	2,715	16.4	7,151	1,234
Ontario-Montclair Elementary	CA	204,948	28,078	134,160	42,710	100.0	13.7	65.5	20.8	205,429	191,600	120,152	10,100	2,521	24.6	7,094	1,281
Orange Unified	CA	238,745	16,915	90,424	131,406	100.0	7.1	37.9	55.0	239,743	227,721	146,899	4,407	2,642	10.0	7,109	1,043
Oxnard Elementary	CA	155,938	17,945	96,998	40,995	100.0	11.5	62.2	26.3	138,372	123,072	79,834	8,581	4,209	18.8	7,304	1,208
Oxnard Union High	CA	144,126	8,581	78,402	57,143	100.0	6.0	54.4	39.6	138,836	109,816	66,070	22,796	2,625	12.6	6,974	1,048
Pajaro Valley Unified	CA	203,414	28,875	107,974	66,565	100.0	14.2	53.1	32.7	198,167	162,049	95,192	32,468	568	19.1	8,301	1,230
Palm Springs Unified	CA	193,927	16,751	102,868	74,308	100.0	8.6	53.0	38.3	185,508	155,132	97,819	24,476	5,284	19.4	6,895	1,253
Palmdale Elementary	CA	242,425	34,031	173,163	35,231	100.0	14.0	71.4	14.5	219,417	154,762	98,358	30,425	3,877	23.6	6,807	1,240
Paramount Unified	CA	190,315	17,379	143,759	29,177	100.0	9.1	75.5	15.3	153,395	118,333	70,891	27,654	1,901	26.4	6,955	1,237
Pasadena Unified	CA	227,081	29,613	118,964	78,504	100.0	13.0	52.4	34.6	245,677	194,876	116,193	54,892	9,917	19.0	8,597	1,307
Placentia-Yorba Linda Unified	CA	251,427	11,992	144,446	94,989	100.0	4.8	57.5	37.8	243,998	186,300	116,835	56,564	136	8.3	6,958	993
Pomona Unified	CA	340,776	63,951	197,997	78,828	100.0	18.8	58.1	23.1	343,429	277,128	158,284	18,408	6,798	25.0	7,826	1,316

See notes at end of table.

Table 88. Revenues, expenditures, poverty rate, and Title I allocations of public school districts enrolling more than 15,000 students, by state: 2003–04 and fiscal year 2006—Continued

Name of district	State	Revenues by source of funds, 2003–04 (in thousands of dollars)				Percentage distribution of revenues, 2003–04				Expenditures, 2003–04 (in thousands of dollars)					Poverty rate of 5- to 17-year-olds, 2004[1]	Current expenditure per pupil,[2] 2003–04[1]	Title I allocations, fiscal year 2006, per poverty child[3]
		Total	Federal	State	Local	Total	Federal	State	Local	Total[4]	Current expenditures						
											Total	Instruction	Capital outlay	Interest on school debt			
1	2	3	4	5	6	7	8	9	10	11	12	13	14	15	16	17	18
Poway Unified	CA	303,498	11,202	126,565	165,731	100.0	3.7	41.7	54.6	312,037	240,804	139,904	60,603	9,516	3.9	7,286	684
Redlands Unified	CA	177,743	11,364	112,388	53,991	100.0	6.4	63.2	30.4	179,772	133,281	86,572	39,158	2,147	14.6	6,456	1,222
Rialto Unified	CA	219,642	23,390	151,021	45,231	100.0	10.6	68.8	20.6	245,776	199,639	120,908	43,094	2,079	22.4	6,560	1,268
West Contra Costa Unified	CA	312,344	32,525	155,004	124,815	100.0	10.4	49.6	40.0	376,823	263,336	158,874	96,524	13,553	16.6	6,821	1,310
Riverside Unified	CA	311,053	30,719	192,478	87,856	100.0	9.9	61.9	28.2	318,192	266,751	173,077	39,201	3,645	16.5	6,349	1,286
Rowland Unified	CA	154,267	15,464	105,307	33,496	100.0	10.0	68.3	21.7	175,439	128,815	80,849	39,130	2,280	17.3	7,007	1,219
Sacramento City Unified	CA	464,816	78,317	251,097	135,402	100.0	16.8	54.0	29.1	578,720	442,063	254,304	115,053	11,628	25.6	8,484	1,423
Saddleback Valley Unified	CA	241,691	10,282	99,361	132,048	100.0	4.3	41.1	54.6	269,213	223,225	150,628	36,135	0	4.2	6,315	672
San Bernardino City Unified	CA	493,002	68,822	365,216	58,964	100.0	14.0	74.1	12.0	491,834	418,540	248,759	58,657	2,367	36.5	7,239	1,411
San Diego Unified	CA	1,406,014	158,168	599,294	648,552	100.0	11.2	42.6	46.1	1,564,648	1,147,966	667,131	361,745	50,700	20.0	8,321	1,449
San Francisco County Unified	CA	556,589	71,288	119,762	365,539	100.0	12.8	21.5	65.7	548,893	478,895	257,949	30,498	0	18.7	8,285	1,383
San Jose Unified	CA	307,587	23,758	74,941	208,888	100.0	7.7	24.4	67.9	349,323	266,626	154,824	66,869	12,221	15.0	8,251	1,245
San Juan Unified	CA	433,264	38,876	249,795	144,593	100.0	9.0	57.7	33.4	448,192	393,277	247,684	39,568	4,624	11.4	7,726	1,326
San Marcos Unified	CA	139,528	7,621	43,874	88,033	100.0	5.5	31.4	63.1	159,717	93,667	60,643	61,000	2,414	12.0	6,420	1,059
San Ramon Valley Unified	CA	187,179	3,640	57,528	126,011	100.0	1.9	30.7	67.3	199,219	143,799	93,363	50,621	4,544	1.6	6,540	0
Santa Ana Unified	CA	592,412	77,326	358,686	156,400	100.0	13.1	60.5	26.4	582,080	483,519	304,798	88,188	5,790	24.4	7,690	1,359
Simi Valley Unified	CA	150,805	6,101	83,262	61,442	100.0	4.0	55.2	40.7	160,670	144,022	95,963	8,569	1,209	6.9	6,629	959
Stockton City Unified	CA	370,532	47,471	243,964	79,097	100.0	12.8	65.8	21.3	368,103	309,845	192,223	51,845	2,776	28.3	7,848	1,359
Sweetwater Union High	CA	334,733	25,298	197,228	112,207	100.0	7.6	58.9	33.5	359,733	295,583	181,115	46,203	3,051	14.7	7,535	1,335
Temecula Valley Unified	CA	240,784	6,900	127,944	105,940	100.0	2.9	53.1	44.0	314,876	150,851	103,799	158,167	4,111	4.9	6,420	986
Torrance Unified	CA	237,653	10,442	159,397	67,814	100.0	4.4	67.1	28.5	209,586	168,153	111,512	25,979	1,375	8.0	6,665	969
Tracy Joint Unified	CA	121,661	5,002	60,826	55,833	100.0	4.1	50.0	45.9	105,003	97,556	62,925	5,918	0	6.4	6,073	931
Tustin Unified	CA	181,672	7,437	87,767	86,468	100.0	4.1	48.3	47.6	165,585	120,546	79,114	37,422	2,687	10.6	6,361	965
Vallejo City Unified	CA	170,002	13,987	107,186	48,829	100.0	8.2	63.0	28.7	209,437	157,027	100,516	43,625	5,971	12.1	8,068	1,183
Ventura Unified	CA	146,766	11,616	67,779	67,371	100.0	7.9	46.2	45.9	161,712	125,931	73,601	26,076	3,736	12.0	7,077	1,079
Visalia Unified	CA	200,041	19,714	123,033	57,294	100.0	9.9	61.5	28.6	207,511	173,517	109,317	27,046	1,675	24.7	6,870	1,242
Vista Unified	CA	232,475	17,272	116,199	99,004	100.0	7.4	50.0	42.6	274,625	197,422	132,538	68,065	4,790	12.4	7,315	1,285
Walnut Valley Unified	CA	118,898	3,116	78,692	37,090	100.0	2.6	66.2	31.2	130,730	97,207	60,865	23,727	4,140	8.4	6,288	942
William S. Hart Union High	CA	276,510	5,411	182,928	88,171	100.0	2.0	66.2	31.9	260,275	140,293	84,996	114,204	3,359	5.7	6,642	932
Irvine Unified	CA	176,675	9,621	54,748	112,306	100.0	5.4	31.0	63.6	185,337	173,724	113,230	5,189	3	6.3	6,968	955
Val Verde Unified	CA	192,430	9,594	152,546	30,290	100.0	5.0	79.3	15.7	143,095	92,050	51,577	50,658	387	16.3	6,845	1,182
Academy 20	CO	162,675	7,647	76,273	78,755	100.0	4.7	46.9	48.4	174,168	131,718	79,811	30,266	11,404	3.7	6,902	729
Adams 12 Five Star Schools	CO	294,893	12,106	153,776	129,011	100.0	4.1	52.1	43.7	313,181	230,471	146,149	75,991	2,317	7.9	6,610	1,165
Adams-Arapahoe	CO	262,551	18,532	147,877	96,142	100.0	7.1	56.3	36.6	285,459	224,809	134,981	9,409	10,341	18.0	6,911	1,445
Boulder Valley	CO	250,876	10,371	53,403	187,102	100.0	4.1	21.3	74.6	236,969	214,719	137,205	7,615		6.8	7,723	1,111
Cherry Creek	CO	407,479	13,008	152,365	242,106	100.0	3.2	37.4	59.4	405,690	350,731	221,939	36,037	17,853	6.0	7,527	1,186
Colorado Springs	CO	256,877	17,499	117,660	121,718	100.0	6.8	45.8	47.4	273,664	257,773	143,590	6,277	8,180	15.5	8,096	1,430
Denver County	CO	683,682	69,052	223,617	391,013	100.0	10.1	32.7	57.2	683,127	567,118	299,932	47,972	48,284	22.1	7,866	1,565
Douglas County	CO	361,758	6,424	140,458	214,876	100.0	1.8	38.8	59.4	391,210	311,994	181,365	53,848	25,056	1.8	7,442	0
Poudre	CO	210,022	12,764	76,755	120,503	100.0	6.1	36.5	57.4	246,390	195,355	103,058	33,211	15,479	9.7	7,848	1,167
Mesa County Valley	CO	148,396	12,218	79,170	57,008	100.0	8.2	53.4	38.4	140,494	134,754	80,906	2,619	1,516	13.0	6,682	1,308
Greeley	CO	134,495	11,295	72,475	50,725	100.0	8.4	53.9	37.7	141,269	113,612	70,767	18,350	8,064	15.2	6,456	1,404
Jefferson County	CO	728,636	32,986	311,825	383,825	100.0	4.5	42.8	52.7	772,847	683,352	361,616	46,529	31,069	6.3	7,839	1,375
Littleton	CO	137,895	4,915	62,400	70,580	100.0	3.6	45.3	51.2	149,979	115,769	72,205	26,746	6,346	5.5	7,034	1,096
Saint Vrain Valley	CO	170,537	7,381	73,391	89,765	100.0	4.3	43.0	52.6	218,393	136,735	82,535	68,365	11,344	9.0	6,331	1,123
Pueblo City	CO	138,270	17,424	80,902	39,944	100.0	12.6	58.5	28.9	158,378	129,745	72,052	21,777	5,507	22.8	7,333	1,441
Bridgeport	CT	271,198	35,662	180,682	54,854	100.0	13.1	66.6	20.2	270,582	250,706	167,030	7,382	3,156	21.5	10,982	1,974
Hartford	CT	354,854	41,618	220,357	92,879	100.0	11.7	62.1	26.2	355,318	320,214	207,349	18,475	4,403	34.8	14,183	2,347
New Haven	CT	387,021	49,951	252,787	84,283	100.0	12.9	65.3	21.8	375,551	273,952	169,750	80,240	11,503	28.2	13,392	2,329
Stamford	CT	217,614	7,551	27,294	182,769	100.0	3.5	12.5	84.0	209,674	195,013	125,468	5,060	6,664	7.4	12,740	1,436
Waterbury	CT	206,325	23,593	114,683	68,049	100.0	11.4	55.6	33.0	210,781	201,053	116,390	6,238	485	20.4	11,350	1,944
Christina	DE	237,535	17,363	134,979	85,193	100.0	7.3	56.8	35.9	231,797	214,124	133,999	5,308	1,982	10.9	11,033	2,168
Red Clay Consolidated	DE	209,803	12,254	121,537	76,012	100.0	5.8	57.9	36.2	192,969	167,930	102,437	11,627	913	9.9	10,795	2,065

See notes at end of table.

Table 88. Revenues, expenditures, poverty rate, and Title I allocations of public school districts enrolling more than 15,000 students, by state: 2003–04 and fiscal year 2006—Continued

Name of district	State	Revenues by source of funds, 2003–04 (in thousands of dollars)				Percentage distribution of revenues, 2003–04				Expenditures, 2003–04 (in thousands of dollars)					Poverty rate of 5- to 17-year-olds, 2004[1]	Current expenditure per pupil[2] 2003–04	Title I allocations, fiscal year 2006, per poverty child[3]
		Total	Federal	State	Local	Total	Federal	State	Local	Total[4]	Current expenditures Total	Current expenditures Instruction	Capital outlay	Interest on school debt			
1	2	3	4	5	6	7	8	9	10	11	12	13	14	15	16	17	18
District of Columbia	DC	1,081,501	167,020	0	914,481	100.0	15.4	0.0	84.6	1,087,040	936,196	515,377	128,227	0	29.1	14,381	2,245
Alachua County	FL	236,053	31,984	113,146	90,923	100.0	13.5	47.9	38.5	232,428	203,288	112,054	18,955	6,407	18.1	6,903	1,151
Bay County	FL	211,759	23,532	94,715	93,512	100.0	11.1	44.7	44.2	200,237	172,171	103,470	18,382	4,655	18.5	6,446	1,145
Brevard County	FL	549,521	49,264	282,174	218,083	100.0	9.0	51.3	39.7	552,443	468,986	297,860	71,570	10,655	12.6	6,346	1,217
Broward County	FL	2,231,773	201,622	1,077,893	952,258	100.0	9.0	48.3	42.7	2,297,904	1,839,583	1,079,039	342,719	50,309	16.1	6,742	1,324
Charlotte County	FL	151,485	13,202	37,007	101,276	100.0	8.7	24.4	66.9	137,843	122,439	69,593	11,561	937	14.2	6,691	1,011
Citrus County	FL	123,534	11,810	49,108	62,616	100.0	9.6	39.8	50.7	133,510	109,754	62,767	19,327	289	19.0	7,073	1,114
Clay County	FL	220,780	15,616	138,292	66,872	100.0	7.1	62.6	30.3	217,047	183,665	113,288	29,044	3,416	9.1	5,855	949
Collier County	FL	417,070	36,054	57,574	323,442	100.0	8.6	13.8	77.6	492,198	322,505	185,083	150,993	14,302	14.0	8,031	1,095
Dade County	FL	3,244,666	375,101	1,513,260	1,356,305	100.0	11.6	46.6	41.8	3,131,953	2,713,056	1,626,031	233,933	83,815	24.6	7,297	1,373
Duval County	FL	946,951	100,492	451,760	394,699	100.0	10.6	47.7	41.7	962,314	821,556	499,666	130,339	9,457	16.5	6,341	1,287
Escambia County	FL	337,547	44,223	177,022	116,302	100.0	13.1	52.4	34.5	326,914	285,339	160,269	33,416	4,456	20.5	6,485	1,220
Hernando County	FL	157,601	13,288	75,466	68,847	100.0	8.4	47.9	43.7	144,277	118,189	66,341	19,976	4,896	18.3	6,031	1,132
Hillsborough County	FL	1,579,958	207,334	842,093	530,531	100.0	13.1	53.3	33.6	1,623,469	1,214,654	731,870	287,434	49,307	18.0	6,678	1,315
Indian River County	FL	142,939	11,830	35,750	95,359	100.0	8.3	25.0	66.7	134,040	109,431	62,138	21,304	1,715	14.5	6,578	1,005
Lake County	FL	266,930	21,621	125,129	120,180	100.0	8.1	46.9	45.0	329,508	211,456	123,965	102,301	10,315	15.4	6,221	1,174
Lee County	FL	640,307	53,026	155,622	431,659	100.0	8.3	24.3	67.4	645,480	457,576	250,059	158,454	18,149	14.5	6,884	1,211
Leon County	FL	282,053	28,913	135,342	117,798	100.0	10.3	48.0	41.8	268,580	214,699	117,857	38,543	5,258	15.5	6,669	1,172
Manatee County	FL	347,193	32,133	120,291	194,769	100.0	9.3	34.6	56.1	382,378	272,642	162,366	93,962	9,244	15.0	6,771	1,170
Marion County	FL	308,317	37,436	164,277	106,604	100.0	12.1	53.3	34.6	320,019	268,296	156,993	41,601	4,660	21.2	6,644	1,210
Martin County	FL	167,817	14,193	34,575	119,049	100.0	8.5	20.6	70.9	182,897	122,615	73,206	55,972	457	12.7	6,895	1,001
Okaloosa County	FL	222,170	24,407	111,729	86,034	100.0	11.0	50.3	38.7	213,385	197,433	122,863	13,325	1,507	14.1	6,270	989
Orange County	FL	1,380,847	120,688	570,676	689,483	100.0	8.7	41.3	49.9	1,313,658	1,071,215	625,208	180,591	44,000	16.9	6,453	1,288
Osceola County	FL	345,418	29,275	178,249	137,894	100.0	8.5	51.6	39.9	338,024	267,279	151,292	53,121	12,749	19.2	6,087	1,166
Palm Beach County	FL	1,573,522	120,126	478,565	974,831	100.0	7.6	30.4	62.0	1,819,580	1,248,312	767,419	466,077	72,600	14.4	7,332	1,278
Pasco County	FL	448,929	39,422	262,509	146,998	100.0	8.8	58.5	32.7	416,461	369,692	214,136	34,817	8,190	16.8	6,428	1,213
Pinellas County	FL	920,279	93,248	392,053	434,978	100.0	10.1	42.6	47.3	954,094	773,319	445,852	159,753	2,477	16.3	6,753	1,281
Polk County	FL	644,591	73,278	340,112	231,201	100.0	11.4	52.8	35.9	634,997	574,225	350,942	36,476	14,719	19.5	6,825	1,250
Saint Johns County	FL	192,130	11,041	58,309	122,780	100.0	5.7	30.3	63.9	189,717	160,022	99,306	22,326	3,059	9.8	6,900	946
Saint Lucie County	FL	271,978	28,070	123,848	120,060	100.0	10.3	45.5	44.1	244,287	209,857	120,258	25,874	8,300	18.6	6,398	1,155
Santa Rosa County	FL	171,486	16,709	100,541	54,236	100.0	9.7	58.6	31.6	163,350	144,966	81,824	14,764	1,154	13.0	5,934	1,060
Sarasota County	FL	413,836	25,148	71,304	317,384	100.0	6.1	17.2	76.7	405,348	309,648	185,195	85,139	2,450	11.8	7,832	999
Seminole County	FL	502,201	34,427	245,373	222,401	100.0	6.9	48.9	44.3	477,191	399,519	250,562	63,029	13,076	11.3	6,156	1,165
Volusia County	FL	537,578	48,138	229,671	259,769	100.0	9.0	42.7	48.3	561,034	423,770	255,456	120,944	14,551	16.9	6,612	1,244
Atlanta City	GA	722,138	79,347	158,184	484,607	100.0	11.0	21.9	67.1	753,466	599,307	357,738	154,100	0	37.0	11,502	1,651
Bibb County	GA	223,232	27,408	101,215	94,609	100.0	12.3	45.3	42.4	217,740	183,054	110,424	31,948	2,738	26.4	7,242	1,484
Chatham County	GA	268,435	28,643	114,291	125,501	100.0	10.7	42.6	46.8	280,291	260,156	165,183	11,518	7,067	23.5	7,538	1,501
Cherokee County	GA	291,191	11,788	135,014	144,389	100.0	4.0	46.4	49.6	281,646	215,649	142,404	57,347	7,194	7.8	7,258	1,179
Clayton County	GA	426,744	37,874	211,517	177,353	100.0	8.9	49.6	41.6	432,851	372,027	239,713	59,905	0	18.4	7,359	1,505
Cobb County	GA	945,482	46,631	365,261	533,590	100.0	4.9	38.6	56.4	860,467	787,093	537,707	61,092	8,373	9.1	7,714	1,532
Columbia County	GA	145,619	7,392	79,273	58,954	100.0	5.1	54.4	40.5	140,556	132,007	88,189	6,508	1,911	8.0	6,580	1,075
Coweta County	GA	152,010	9,841	69,634	72,535	100.0	6.5	45.8	47.7	158,849	136,519	89,092	18,301	2,579	11.7	7,172	1,239
DeKalb County	GA	943,522	69,571	361,530	512,421	100.0	7.4	38.3	54.3	928,500	823,036	498,091	102,310	3,154	16.8	8,268	1,637
Dougherty County	GA	149,198	20,276	73,266	55,656	100.0	13.6	49.1	37.3	149,086	133,740	79,926	14,397		30.4	7,940	1,391
Douglas County	GA	169,037	10,043	77,859	81,135	100.0	5.9	46.1	48.0	148,737	137,150	85,651	8,162	3,425	13.8	6,963	1,228
Fayette County	GA	186,859	5,130	83,819	97,910	100.0	2.7	44.9	52.4	191,068	155,278	103,237	28,112	5,293	5.6	7,316	1,094
Forsyth County	GA	210,193	6,403	76,412	127,378	100.0	3.0	36.4	60.6	192,474	157,885	102,590	23,665	10,701	6.4	7,155	1,097
Fulton County	GA	803,163	37,617	228,555	536,991	100.0	4.7	28.5	66.9	859,621	652,440	431,390	192,979	13,451	8.9	8,899	1,460
Gwinnett County	GA	1,503,965	54,277	504,995	944,693	100.0	3.6	33.6	62.8	1,215,701	974,076	626,188	205,598	12,885	10.6	7,550	1,569
Hall County	GA	182,868	13,677	92,914	76,277	100.0	7.5	50.8	41.7	191,996	158,079	102,445	18,403	14,823	13.3	7,015	1,242
Henry County	GA	247,484	9,740	104,952	132,792	100.0	3.9	42.4	53.7	260,689	198,399	132,072	51,531	8,360	8.7	6,648	1,175
Houston County	GA	220,899	17,184	123,492	80,223	100.0	7.8	55.9	36.3	217,518	177,877	117,869	36,200	2,630	15.3	7,603	1,365
Muscogee County	GA	266,774	30,468	154,155	82,151	100.0	11.4	57.8	30.8	280,014	255,594	158,242	22,106	531	23.2	7,732	1,466

See notes at end of table.

Table 88. Revenues, expenditures, poverty rate, and Title I allocations of public school districts enrolling more than 15,000 students, by state: 2003–04 and fiscal year 2006—Continued

Name of district	State	Revenues by source of funds, 2003–04 (in thousands of dollars)				Percentage distribution of revenues, 2003–04				Expenditures, 2003–04 (in thousands of dollars)					Poverty rate of 5- to 17-year-olds, 2004[1]	Current expenditure per pupil,[2] 2003–04	Title I allocations, fiscal year 2006, per poverty child[3]
										Total[4]	Current expenditures						
		Total	Federal	State	Local	Total	Federal	State	Local		Total	Instruction	Capital outlay	Interest on school debt			
1	2	3	4	5	6	7	8	9	10	11	12	13	14	15	16	17	18
Newton County	GA	114,486	9,427	57,885	47,174	100.0	8.2	50.6	41.2	109,094	100,602	67,582	5,833	2,659	16.1	6,838	1,303
Paulding County	GA	159,718	6,767	87,281	65,670	100.0	4.2	54.6	41.1	155,447	135,893	92,264	15,552	2,466	8.5	6,642	1,126
Richmond County	GA	299,903	36,771	145,307	117,825	100.0	12.3	48.5	39.3	266,133	260,100	161,055	0	5,875	24.9	7,561	1,481
Hawaii Department of Education	HI	2,138,137	236,470	1,850,737	50,930	100.0	11.1	86.6	2.4	1,734,591	1,566,793	943,647	116,340	0	12.7	8,533	1,720
Boise Independent District	ID	214,044	14,292	81,591	118,161	100.0	6.7	38.1	55.2	194,394	187,423	117,583	2,900	2,157	12.3	7,151	1,232
Meridian Joint District	ID	163,020	8,466	100,929	53,625	100.0	5.2	61.9	32.9	185,677	138,449	82,371	39,726	7,462	6.3	5,130	1,134
City of Chicago	IL	4,107,617	702,583	1,567,612	1,837,422	100.0	17.1	38.2	44.7	4,224,772	3,629,795	2,292,576	382,735	153,090	28.5	8,356	1,990
Community Unit 300	IL	147,017	7,961	43,394	95,662	100.0	5.4	29.5	65.1	160,694	132,123	80,126	20,102	7,033	6.9	7,269	1,181
Indian Prairie	IL	255,431	6,519	62,217	186,695	100.0	2.6	24.4	73.1	254,346	215,827	143,624	23,184	14,986	2.9	8,060	858
Naperville	IL	192,126	5,379	30,670	156,077	100.0	2.8	16.0	81.2	183,834	172,058	109,248	8,879	0	3.7	9,088	850
Peoria	IL	144,737	22,073	59,398	63,266	100.0	15.3	41.0	43.7	154,721	147,104	84,948	2,401	514	26.0	9,273	1,629
Plainfield School	IL	159,652	2,777	58,239	98,636	100.0	1.7	36.5	61.8	167,441	124,443	80,630	28,021	12,288	1.5	6,562	0
Rockford School	IL	272,050	34,978	95,099	141,973	100.0	12.9	35.0	52.2	271,293	251,904	150,647	4,768	9,970	21.1	8,804	1,596
Springfield	IL	148,632	21,584	42,945	84,103	100.0	14.5	28.9	56.6	142,648	121,977	68,469	5,626	4,096	19.0	8,018	1,538
U-46	IL	385,949	17,980	158,331	209,638	100.0	4.7	41.0	54.3	381,082	302,253	181,327	64,662	11,251	7.7	7,786	1,306
Valley View	IL	165,356	6,661	59,571	99,124	100.0	4.0	36.0	59.9	208,592	120,622	75,846	86,080	1,374	6.9	7,563	1,198
Waukegan	IL	141,547	12,409	63,477	65,661	100.0	8.8	44.8	46.4	143,408	127,585	71,052	1,641	3,431	19.1	7,847	1,473
Evansville-Vanderburgh	IN	221,970	22,656	106,450	92,864	100.0	10.2	48.0	41.8	210,447	185,061	113,662	19,650	2,041	12.9	8,259	1,507
Fort Wayne	IN	312,176	28,545	146,961	136,670	100.0	9.1	47.1	43.8	338,720	312,904	192,051	17,575	793	14.7	9,835	1,673
Gary	IN	202,654	21,075	151,649	29,930	100.0	10.4	74.8	14.8	212,279	193,190	102,428	15,878	1,600	31.8	11,115	1,679
Indianapolis Public Schools	IN	578,789	59,320	294,062	225,407	100.0	10.2	50.8	38.9	493,922	413,722	227,327	38,344	1,946	27.8	10,346	1,902
MSD Lawrence Township	IN	196,796	6,256	82,525	108,015	100.0	3.2	41.9	54.9	174,434	143,577	98,350	16,752	1,336	6.9	8,862	1,238
South Bend	IN	250,906	20,960	118,396	111,550	100.0	8.4	47.2	44.5	280,604	208,127	129,719	55,013	530	17.6	9,516	1,638
Vigo County	IN	142,642	9,739	81,102	51,801	100.0	6.8	56.9	36.3	143,602	119,130	75,283	13,018	1,053	15.5	7,274	1,525
Cedar Rapids	IA	157,923	8,634	72,480	76,809	100.0	5.5	45.9	48.6	153,181	129,551	85,996	13,854	2,208	9.2	7,478	1,353
Davenport	IA	155,262	13,180	70,983	71,099	100.0	8.5	45.7	45.8	145,192	125,110	86,201	13,054	1,884	15.3	7,645	1,434
Des Moines Independent	IA	329,703	27,916	153,603	148,184	100.0	8.5	46.6	44.9	331,919	264,717	170,541	51,903	90	14.9	8,516	1,569
Kansas City	KS	187,629	21,365	105,072	61,192	100.0	11.4	56.0	32.6	175,371	165,045	95,870	5,828	4,498	22.5	7,909	1,704
Olathe	KS	230,870	9,067	89,961	131,842	100.0	3.9	39.0	57.1	188,753	163,405	102,958	11,454	11,731	5.1	7,130	1,388
Shawnee Mission	KS	257,598	11,148	75,590	170,860	100.0	4.3	29.3	66.3	237,437	209,264	136,211	22,032	6,123	4.5	7,120	771
Blue Valley	KS	225,412	3,449	55,171	166,792	100.0	1.5	24.5	74.0	172,048	141,271	84,944	16,886	13,251	2.1	7,414	754
Wichita	KS	452,437	57,466	230,104	164,867	100.0	12.7	50.9	36.4	417,141	373,591	208,004	30,194	12,252	17.6	7,641	1,846
Boone County	KY	113,479	5,732	44,411	63,336	100.0	5.1	39.1	55.8	107,169	91,224	55,274	10,164	5,307	8.1	5,921	1,046
Fayette County	KY	286,988	21,911	112,423	152,654	100.0	7.6	39.2	53.2	293,116	261,805	153,638	21,684	7,401	16.0	7,642	1,388
Jefferson County	KY	842,393	101,812	350,527	390,054	100.0	12.1	41.6	46.3	847,073	802,886	437,782	19,441	17,262	16.8	8,400	1,588
Ascension Parish SB	LA	121,184	10,833	55,082	55,269	100.0	8.9	45.5	45.6	133,303	113,373	72,756	17,130	2,366	14.9	7,171	1,168
Bossier Parish SB	LA	134,807	13,004	69,522	52,281	100.0	9.6	51.6	38.8	128,204	124,539	72,166	2,005	783	18.7	6,635	1,274
Caddo Parish SB	LA	366,072	47,283	183,261	135,528	100.0	12.9	50.1	37.0	358,907	329,823	201,038	25,414	2,432	27.1	7,416	1,414
Calcasieu Parish SB	LA	250,048	28,054	107,932	114,062	100.0	11.2	43.2	45.6	275,664	216,131	125,925	48,151	10,632	21.5	6,723	1,320
East Baton Rouge Parish SB	LA	406,044	53,633	131,003	221,408	100.0	13.2	32.3	54.5	406,480	381,863	209,723	23,088	47	22.4	8,187	1,424
Jefferson Parish SB	LA	423,917	56,892	155,239	211,786	100.0	13.4	36.6	50.0	395,163	358,343	222,047	19,103	12,746	22.1	6,964	1,436
Lafayette Parish SB	LA	221,576	29,280	87,961	104,335	100.0	13.2	39.7	47.1	219,963	206,332	135,426	7,179	4,910	20.8	6,921	1,324
Livingston Parish SB	LA	135,642	11,725	90,863	33,054	100.0	8.6	67.0	24.4	142,085	125,122	78,954	14,917	1,771	15.6	6,032	1,267
Orleans Parish SB	LA	538,644	84,326	237,035	217,283	100.0	15.7	44.0	40.3	531,254	494,182	302,977	19,096	16,589	35.3	7,276	1,550
Ouachita Parish SB	LA	145,699	14,375	81,802	49,522	100.0	9.9	56.1	34.0	150,228	124,926	76,049	18,629	6,153	18.5	6,818	1,254
Rapides Parish SB	LA	172,423	26,069	90,009	56,345	100.0	15.1	52.2	32.7	161,520	161,520	95,339	8,612	3,853	26.6	7,132	1,327
Saint Landry Parish SB	LA	113,353	18,392	65,528	29,433	100.0	16.2	57.8	26.0	114,752	107,176	68,713	4,526	2,600	31.6	7,037	1,299
Saint Tammany Parish SB	LA	297,150	26,094	147,539	123,517	100.0	8.8	49.7	41.6	290,132	266,410	169,379	15,325	6,572	13.7	7,666	1,141
Tangipahoa Parish SB	LA	127,084	21,463	74,799	30,822	100.0	16.9	58.9	24.3	121,451	111,798	70,547	7,212	2,064	29.2	6,055	1,333
Terrebonne Parish SB	LA	135,071	19,295	73,758	42,018	100.0	14.3	54.6	31.1	133,860	130,117	81,638	2,960	141	23.2	6,757	1,302

See notes at end of table.

Table 88. Revenues, expenditures, poverty rate, and Title I allocations of public school districts enrolling more than 15,000 students, by state: 2003–04 and fiscal year 2006—Continued

Name of district	State	Revenues by source of funds, 2003–04 (in thousands of dollars)				Percentage distribution of revenues, 2003–04				Expenditures, 2003–04 (in thousands of dollars)					Poverty rate of 5- to 17-year-olds, 2004[1]	Current expenditure per pupil[2] 2003–04	Title I allocations, fiscal year 2006, per poverty child[3]
		Total	Federal	State	Local	Total	Federal	State	Local	Total[4]	Current expenditures						
											Total	Instruction	Capital outlay	Interest on school debt			
1	2	3	4	5	6	7	8	9	10	11	12	13	14	15	16	17	18
Anne Arundel County	MD	721,559	39,647	230,816	451,096	100.0	5.5	32.0	62.5	722,780	645,296	398,620	51,267	9,440	6.3	8,661	1,541
Baltimore City	MD	965,291	115,355	625,734	224,202	100.0	12.0	64.8	23.2	996,535	868,363	601,279	78,558	834	24.0	9,233	1,982
Baltimore County	MD	1,074,341	67,841	376,910	629,590	100.0	6.3	35.1	58.6	1,032,563	983,521	594,299	14,656	5,666	8.1	9,063	1,820
Calvert County	MD	168,336	8,779	62,726	96,831	100.0	5.2	37.3	57.5	161,183	150,322	94,546	5,268	1,421	6.0	8,628	1,240
Carroll County	MD	277,788	13,414	106,280	158,094	100.0	4.8	38.3	56.9	267,776	238,032	142,758	20,946	2,642	4.6	8,256	878
Cecil County	MD	152,789	9,932	67,601	75,256	100.0	6.5	44.2	49.3	141,793	135,318	83,160	1,535	1,788	9.5	8,214	1,273
Charles County	MD	251,729	13,564	110,676	127,489	100.0	5.4	44.0	50.6	241,277	211,535	123,150	23,180	1,279	8.4	8,260	1,304
Frederick County	MD	407,770	16,004	147,942	243,824	100.0	3.9	36.3	59.8	383,822	329,456	200,062	41,853	7,801	5.5	8,458	1,321
Harford County	MD	359,900	19,843	151,169	188,888	100.0	5.5	42.0	52.5	357,341	324,614	199,653	23,810	1,949	6.5	8,075	1,354
Howard County	MD	537,507	17,975	147,081	372,451	100.0	3.3	27.4	69.3	550,863	478,322	306,615	51,059	7,726	4.4	10,000	884
Montgomery County	MD	1,812,254	74,629	341,638	1,395,987	100.0	4.1	18.9	77.0	1,720,288	1,553,788	994,907	99,762	30,797	7.4	11,162	1,776
Prince George's County	MD	1,397,924	94,939	633,484	669,501	100.0	6.8	45.3	47.9	1,354,565	1,187,040	678,956	102,769	15,448	9.8	8,647	1,807
Saint Mary's County	MD	160,704	13,069	74,536	73,099	100.0	8.1	46.4	45.5	156,822	134,539	78,761	18,454	2,088	9.1	8,274	1,276
Washington County	MD	184,505	13,323	84,234	86,948	100.0	7.2	45.7	47.1	187,117	171,908	106,863	8,873	1,837	11.8	8,453	1,370
Boston	MA	1,077,906	108,651	323,510	645,745	100.0	10.1	30.0	59.9	1,042,803	964,960	589,574	52,967	17,496	22.5	16,043	2,464
Brockton	MA	199,061	18,949	133,732	46,380	100.0	9.5	67.2	23.3	197,897	190,638	118,508	1,277	2,343	17.7	11,586	1,885
Springfield	MA	364,034	44,587	265,827	53,620	100.0	12.2	73.0	14.7	355,755	329,239	215,964	3,266	14,659	25.9	12,599	2,229
Worcester	MA	329,485	40,358	203,761	85,366	100.0	12.2	61.8	25.9	315,785	299,722	207,180	809	7,302	21.9	11,975	1,941
Ann Arbor Public Schools	MI	204,450	4,324	91,493	108,633	100.0	2.1	44.8	53.1	202,382	179,768	102,189	12,571	6,028	8.5	10,764	1,343
Dearborn City	MI	204,177	12,988	107,325	83,864	100.0	6.4	52.6	41.1	248,131	175,533	100,434	60,847	9,707	21.7	9,707	1,646
Detroit City	MI	1,642,402	252,704	1,122,410	267,288	100.0	15.4	68.3	16.3	2,021,123	1,646,167	935,103	280,767	81,455	31.1	10,757	2,203
Flint City	MI	233,888	33,598	154,441	45,849	100.0	14.4	66.0	19.6	233,483	214,712	120,430	4,908	1,091	34.8	10,492	1,869
Grand Rapids Public Schools	MI	254,400	30,346	157,437	66,617	100.0	11.9	61.9	26.2	262,008	251,388	138,629	7,157	553	21.1	10,334	1,757
Lansing Public	MI	176,609	20,414	115,781	40,414	100.0	11.6	65.6	22.9	190,026	181,095	101,205	6,559	1,267	23.8	10,666	1,723
Livonia Public Schools	MI	188,564	2,137	115,783	70,644	100.0	1.1	61.4	37.5	189,413	171,382	97,788	9,528	2,573	2.9	9,325	911
Plymouth-Canton Community Schools	MI	154,733	1,869	100,216	52,648	100.0	1.2	64.8	34.0	155,527	135,527	81,464	8,011	7,359	2.7	7,479	887
Utica Community Schools	MI	264,848	7,447	177,287	80,114	100.0	2.8	66.9	30.2	295,556	248,477	145,468	33,015	6,786	5.3	8,587	1,307
Walled Lake Consolidated Schools	MI	171,322	2,533	98,314	70,475	100.0	1.5	57.4	41.1	160,982	144,527	83,223	2,624	10,557	4.8	9,505	884
Warren Consolidated Schools	MI	173,027	5,480	97,418	70,129	100.0	3.2	56.3	40.5	215,915	147,338	81,961	59,822	7,212	8.6	9,554	1,318
Anoka-Hennepin	MN	392,841	16,390	286,322	90,129	100.0	4.2	72.9	22.9	382,241	322,049	219,003	26,154	10,140	4.7	7,806	1,370
Minneapolis	MN	633,216	68,212	435,811	129,193	100.0	10.8	68.8	20.4	614,401	501,590	329,482	43,637	28,567	24.3	11,558	1,794
Osseo	MN	239,136	10,170	158,608	70,358	100.0	4.3	66.3	29.4	248,342	171,831	116,760	44,763	11,840	3.8	7,919	829
Rochester	MN	160,931	7,275	112,800	40,856	100.0	4.5	70.1	25.4	147,947	125,094	81,658	10,348	4,773	7.9	7,595	1,235
Rosemount-Apple Valley-Eagan	MN	263,390	8,063	188,820	66,507	100.0	3.1	71.7	25.3	252,550	222,234	155,984	16,027	4,823	3.5	7,781	799
South Washington County	MN	155,933	4,085	103,463	48,385	100.0	2.6	66.4	31.0	146,961	113,505	75,718	11,335	9,395	2.8	7,262	849
Saint Paul	MN	558,028	59,682	411,771	86,575	100.0	10.7	73.8	15.5	561,044	464,533	320,703	44,519	15,133	18.9	10,928	1,727
DeSoto County	MS	137,420	8,547	81,103	47,770	100.0	6.2	59.0	34.8	129,979	112,053	68,837	16,197	1,729	11.4	4,734	983
Jackson Public	MS	232,700	34,310	109,885	88,505	100.0	14.7	47.2	38.0	225,201	208,144	118,763	12,640	3,628	34.2	6,579	1,303
Rankin County	MS	109,685	8,556	54,770	46,359	100.0	7.8	49.9	42.3	135,303	90,321	56,062	39,663	4,820	12.4	5,640	920
Columbia	MO	147,197	10,126	44,939	92,132	100.0	6.9	30.5	62.6	147,354	120,755	73,960	13,047	7,477	13.0	7,319	1,172
Fort Zumwalt	MO	133,424	4,462	37,171	91,791	100.0	3.3	27.9	68.8	124,353	109,577	65,107	6,478	6,101	4.0	6,041	706
Hazelwood	MO	148,704	5,603	38,648	104,453	100.0	3.8	26.0	70.2	173,041	129,023	77,269	37,594	4,590	8.3	6,681	1,158
Kansas City	MO	398,493	46,574	145,365	206,554	100.0	11.7	36.5	51.8	393,970	353,656	188,101	30,352	0	30.3	9,237	1,488
Lee's Summit	MO	140,576	3,414	42,750	94,412	100.0	2.4	30.4	67.2	160,857	107,144	67,491	43,655	6,625	4.6	6,755	693
North Kansas City	MO	149,404	7,076	26,191	116,137	100.0	4.7	17.5	77.7	157,500	121,032	75,898	26,135	5,532	7.8	7,118	1,042
Parkway	MO	189,722	4,743	12,363	172,616	100.0	2.5	6.5	91.0	189,005	167,835	96,300	13,661	2,981	3.4	8,573	697
Rockwood	MO	189,307	3,945	22,155	163,207	100.0	2.1	11.7	86.2	202,410	156,381	88,093	32,527	6,298	3.0	6,902	692
Springfield	MO	171,863	15,172	42,693	113,998	100.0	8.8	24.8	66.3	176,609	156,582	92,360	12,563	5,721	17.2	6,448	1,407
Francis Howell	MO	155,845	5,183	44,950	105,712	100.0	3.3	28.8	67.8	168,101	134,313	86,313	19,131	8,007	3.5	7,316	708
Saint Louis City	MO	471,530	59,885	186,394	225,251	100.0	12.7	39.5	47.8	495,017	428,362	220,617	31,354	12,512	29.0	10,492	1,630

See notes at end of table.

Table 88. Revenues, expenditures, poverty rate, and Title I allocations of public school districts enrolling more than 15,000 students, by state: 2003–04 and fiscal year 2006—Continued

Name of district	State	Revenues by source of funds, 2003–04 (in thousands of dollars)				Percentage distribution of revenues, 2003–04				Expenditures, 2003–04 (in thousands of dollars)					Poverty rate of 5- to 17-year-olds, 2004[1]	Current expenditure per pupil,[2] 2003–04	Title I allocations, fiscal year 2006, per poverty child[3]
										Total[4]	Current expenditures						
		Total	Federal	State	Local	Total	Federal	State	Local		Total	Instruction	Capital outlay	Interest on school debt			
1	2	3	4	5	6	7	8	9	10	11	12	13	14	15	16	17	18
Lincoln	NE	301,687	25,600	75,766	200,321	100.0	8.5	25.1	66.4	274,750	247,794	164,098	21,333	5,593	10.2	7,715	1,515
Millard	NE	168,504	6,488	54,922	107,094	100.0	3.9	32.6	63.6	158,018	139,416	88,884	10,757	6,753	3.0	7,004	2,132
Omaha	NE	423,926	51,152	150,592	222,182	100.0	12.1	35.5	52.4	445,152	344,603	202,903	85,939	11,217	15.5	7,486	1,958
Clark County	NV	2,132,656	145,376	555,955	1,431,325	100.0	6.8	26.1	67.1	2,291,888	1,652,435	1,030,190	490,913	139,120	14.3	6,108	1,358
Washoe County	NV	463,123	35,805	134,503	292,815	100.0	7.7	29.0	63.2	465,938	399,325	258,784	44,241	19,474	11.5	6,430	1,207
Manchester	NH	145,700	14,643	75,480	55,577	100.0	10.1	51.8	38.1	137,889	130,348	90,979	2,189	3,282	10.3	7,383	2,726
Camden City	NJ	297,860	33,532	252,414	11,914	100.0	11.3	84.7	4.0	310,443	273,949	165,225	25,341	369	36.8	16,157	2,422
Elizabeth	NJ	354,245	25,311	252,571	76,363	100.0	7.1	71.3	21.6	323,235	310,504	168,327	3,096	304	24.4	14,722	1,876
Jersey City	NJ	607,436	40,229	487,403	79,804	100.0	6.6	80.2	13.1	618,085	539,284	334,319	60,535	6,476	23.0	17,545	2,149
Newark	NJ	970,717	65,314	801,919	103,484	100.0	6.7	82.6	10.7	951,512	810,164	453,993	113,346	1,003	29.3	18,928	2,268
Paterson	NJ	451,068	36,811	372,447	41,810	100.0	8.2	82.6	9.3	454,065	419,373	241,280	6,138	538	25.7	15,857	1,951
Toms River Regional	NJ	192,763	6,954	79,812	105,997	100.0	3.6	41.4	55.0	208,371	183,229	111,423	20,163	2,807	7.7	9,972	1,464
Albuquerque	NM	720,897	92,867	519,921	108,109	100.0	12.9	72.1	15.0	729,651	616,905	364,338	100,230	5,512	18.4	6,814	1,462
Las Cruces	NM	186,540	25,757	139,448	21,335	100.0	13.8	74.8	11.4	184,442	159,548	93,488	19,821	2,756	27.1	6,907	1,299
Brentwood Union Free	NY	225,574	14,073	140,449	71,052	100.0	6.2	62.3	31.5	235,252	217,920	146,165	12,965	2,870	14.7	13,122	1,636
Buffalo City	NY	662,608	103,920	450,612	108,076	100.0	15.7	68.0	16.3	731,899	585,633	401,989	123,420	15,756	36.0	14,253	1,865
New York City	NY	14,723,474	1,711,502	6,158,563	6,853,409	100.0	11.6	41.8	46.5	15,739,985	13,682,193	10,247,313	1,233,517	509,083	29.4	13,131	2,075
Rochester City	NY	557,066	79,201	343,963	133,902	100.0	14.2	61.7	24.0	546,510	471,695	298,022	39,049	6,301	38.6	13,634	1,832
Sachem Central	NY	233,953	5,265	115,306	113,382	100.0	2.3	49.3	48.5	336,364	207,675	143,053	117,338	8,816	4.7	13,505	945
Syracuse City	NY	311,032	45,545	202,858	62,629	100.0	14.6	65.2	20.1	310,602	284,446	198,600	14,677	5,695	32.4	12,696	1,785
Yonkers City	NY	422,792	47,004	247,794	127,994	100.0	11.1	58.6	30.3	424,277	403,648	270,045	7,472	6,418	23.7	15,406	1,773
Cumberland County Schools	NC	368,430	50,843	228,194	89,393	100.0	13.8	61.9	24.3	354,980	335,313	206,972	11,599	5,915	20.1	6,349	1,298
Pitt County Schools	NC	158,037	16,995	97,998	43,044	100.0	10.8	62.0	27.2	151,931	139,764	90,537	7,582	3,529	20.8	6,584	1,206
Alamance-Burlington Schools	NC	141,632	15,538	92,642	33,452	100.0	11.0	65.4	23.6	142,037	135,630	85,997	3,577	2,711	12.9	6,297	1,009
Buncombe County Schools	NC	196,398	17,493	112,887	66,018	100.0	8.9	57.5	33.6	184,179	163,851	103,049	13,971	6,276	14.3	6,599	1,060
Cabarrus County Schools	NC	216,244	11,097	92,191	112,956	100.0	5.1	42.6	52.2	162,705	135,647	85,287	16,699	7,940	10.4	6,227	1,009
Catawba County Schools	NC	121,401	8,200	73,414	39,787	100.0	6.8	60.5	32.8	112,374	102,681	68,852	5,883	3,810	11.0	6,186	958
Cleveland County Schools	NC	73,487	7,328	47,281	18,878	100.0	10.0	64.3	25.7	69,876	63,842	42,253	4,783	753	18.3	6,489	1,175
Davidson County Schools	NC	124,772	8,476	83,396	32,900	100.0	6.8	66.8	26.4	120,729	112,372	71,540	7,074	1,166	9.1	5,781	949
Durham Public Schools	NC	271,648	21,117	140,258	110,273	100.0	7.8	51.6	40.6	274,134	232,784	139,909	28,872	8,792	17.7	7,584	1,224
Forsyth County Schools	NC	413,020	32,133	212,826	168,061	100.0	7.8	51.5	40.7	405,079	333,584	220,729	61,096	10,399	15.7	7,046	1,256
Gaston County Schools	NC	227,828	23,219	133,504	71,105	100.0	10.2	58.6	31.2	208,152	188,365	122,535	15,394	4,387	17.5	6,098	1,218
Guilford County Schools	NC	515,548	47,482	288,287	179,779	100.0	9.2	55.9	34.9	529,713	469,400	281,910	46,945	13,003	17.0	7,125	1,302
Harnett County Schools	NC	117,882	12,392	76,397	29,093	100.0	10.5	64.8	24.7	119,596	101,153	67,140	14,629	3,691	18.1	5,990	1,174
Iredell-Statesville Schools	NC	146,769	9,585	82,419	54,765	100.0	6.5	56.2	37.3	138,616	116,984	73,229	16,065	3,977	11.8	6,141	997
Johnston County Schools	NC	192,065	15,415	113,046	63,604	100.0	8.0	58.9	33.1	207,574	163,171	108,694	32,451	11,950	15.1	6,546	1,179
Charlotte-Mecklenburg Schools	NC	1,067,782	76,490	501,718	489,574	100.0	7.2	47.0	45.8	1,019,823	813,972	492,499	143,451	61,702	14.2	7,149	1,354
Nash-Rocky Mount Schools	NC	132,357	14,937	89,135	28,285	100.0	11.3	67.3	21.4	125,271	117,453	74,772	7,239	512	20.5	6,468	1,191
New Hanover County Schools	NC	180,230	18,243	100,827	61,160	100.0	10.1	55.9	33.9	182,916	162,960	94,071	9,929	9,528	16.3	7,318	1,235
Onslow County Schools	NC	151,084	19,328	97,522	34,234	100.0	12.8	64.5	22.7	146,064	132,566	82,990	10,945	2,395	21.0	6,099	1,201
Randolph County Schools	NC	110,970	8,877	80,191	21,902	100.0	8.0	72.3	19.7	114,442	105,946	69,449	3,631	4,796	11.2	5,853	970
Robeson County Schools	NC	161,023	23,073	115,404	22,546	100.0	14.3	71.7	14.0	159,308	151,822	94,340	7,035	69	28.1	6,311	1,263
Rowan-Salisbury Schools	NC	143,540	14,814	91,227	37,499	100.0	10.3	63.6	26.1	134,124	130,068	83,289	2,142	1,914	14.3	6,252	1,119
Union County Public Schools	NC	204,807	12,637	113,668	78,502	100.0	6.2	55.5	38.3	221,975	166,326	107,227	45,650	8,249	10.5	6,220	1,004
Wake County Schools	NC	970,869	53,908	464,963	451,998	100.0	5.6	47.9	46.6	960,576	737,505	450,064	161,503	56,097	9.5	6,768	1,305
Wayne County Public Schools	NC	128,665	15,977	88,563	24,125	100.0	12.4	68.8	18.8	122,229	118,190	78,324	3,498	541	18.7	6,128	1,182
Akron Public Schools	OH	402,511	34,166	168,918	199,427	100.0	8.5	42.0	49.5	313,461	297,146	180,410	10,950	8	23.6	10,312	1,785
Cincinnati Public Schools	OH	496,899	62,524	171,244	263,131	100.0	12.6	34.5	53.0	543,439	479,107	290,085	46,847	498	25.3	11,867	1,897
Cleveland Municipal	OH	820,215	128,163	446,897	245,155	100.0	15.6	54.5	29.9	821,888	725,795	428,629	68,543	4,884	32.8	10,420	1,973
Columbus Public Schools	OH	694,022	82,466	267,654	343,902	100.0	11.9	38.6	49.6	729,035	682,377	362,869	19,245	11,791	27.3	10,815	1,989

See notes at end of table.

Table 88. Revenues, expenditures, poverty rate, and Title I allocations of public school districts enrolling more than 15,000 students, by state: 2003–04 and fiscal year 2006—Continued

Name of district	State	Revenues by source of funds, 2003–04 (in thousands of dollars)				Percentage distribution of revenues, 2003–04				Expenditures, 2003–04 (in thousands of dollars)					Poverty rate of 5- to 17-year-olds, 2004[1]	Current expenditure per pupil[2] 2003–04	Title I allocations, fiscal year 2006, per poverty child[3]
		Total	Federal	State	Local	Total	Federal	State	Local	Total[4]	Current expenditures						
											Total	Instruction	Capital outlay	Interest on school debt			
1	2	3	4	5	6	7	8	9	10	11	12	13	14	15	16	17	18
Dayton	OH	296,570	35,602	157,418	103,550	100.0	12.0	53.1	34.9	247,437	207,769	101,737	32,480	1,023	27.0	11,236	1,767
South-Western	OH	193,729	13,656	88,885	91,188	100.0	7.0	45.9	47.1	197,853	177,672	101,206	7,974	8,349	11.9	8,369	1,412
Toledo	OH	424,648	44,695	243,597	136,356	100.0	10.5	57.4	32.1	412,917	373,961	219,811	21,406	6,382	23.0	10,844	1,838
Lakota	OH	139,236	3,151	53,216	82,869	100.0	2.3	38.2	59.5	139,171	126,072	72,187	6,747	5,566	4.2	7,707	862
Broken Arrow	OK	94,570	5,388	45,638	43,544	100.0	5.7	48.3	46.0	91,802	81,788	43,723	7,871	1,747	7.3	5,546	929
Edmond	OK	116,141	6,076	45,640	64,425	100.0	5.2	39.3	55.5	118,340	108,209	54,465	7,041	2,580	6.1	5,959	983
Lawton	OK	111,700	20,976	66,383	24,341	100.0	18.8	59.4	21.8	102,408	100,033	55,157	1,514	207	22.8	5,861	1,212
Moore	OK	110,296	8,792	62,905	38,599	100.0	8.0	57.0	35.0	104,012	97,420	57,745	5,421	1,146	9.7	5,142	986
Oklahoma City	OK	280,374	47,534	143,175	89,665	100.0	17.0	51.1	32.0	253,491	240,742	129,952	6,069	5,227	32.7	5,930	1,403
Putnam City	OK	121,947	8,398	58,729	54,820	100.0	6.9	48.2	45.0	112,302	105,793	60,384	5,065	1,298	14.9	5,463	1,181
Tulsa	OK	329,959	48,006	138,835	143,118	100.0	14.5	42.1	43.4	301,359	275,357	144,426	20,518	4,690	26.8	6,513	1,353
Hillsboro	OR	157,084	10,507	81,462	65,115	100.0	6.7	51.9	41.5	143,198	125,372	73,977	9,695	7,874	10.6	6,616	1,261
Beaverton	OR	292,412	15,091	141,012	136,309	100.0	5.2	48.2	46.6	258,779	219,367	130,943	25,678	13,054	9.9	6,209	1,343
Eugene	OR	163,019	14,098	67,892	81,029	100.0	8.6	41.6	49.7	228,803	132,136	81,168	37,460	7,043	13.4	7,152	1,274
North Clackamas	OR	121,261	7,395	66,460	47,406	100.0	6.1	54.8	39.1	123,687	107,387	60,234	5,106	8,947	11.3	6,641	1,219
Portland	OR	505,585	50,455	176,685	278,445	100.0	10.0	34.9	55.1	447,490	424,287	258,535	14,986	7,081	16.0	8,776	1,717
Salem-Keizer	OR	312,207	28,537	187,957	95,713	100.0	9.1	60.2	30.7	381,439	270,121	174,468	9,144	16,499	17.0	7,149	1,644
Allentown City	PA	145,517	14,787	56,102	74,628	100.0	10.2	38.6	51.3	151,356	124,943	84,471	8,507	4,419	27.2	7,365	1,746
Central Bucks	PA	200,032	3,089	32,720	164,223	100.0	1.5	16.4	82.1	259,827	163,593	104,953	72,604	13,604	3.6	8,570	1,042
Philadelphia City	PA	2,111,973	333,586	1,057,020	721,367	100.0	15.8	50.0	34.2	2,421,758	1,622,860	907,007	147,005	134,606	26.5	8,551	2,322
Pittsburgh	PA	560,242	67,333	193,973	298,936	100.0	12.0	34.6	53.4	594,035	424,300	223,816	75,457	18,318	23.8	12,242	2,077
Reading	PA	139,885	24,846	75,653	39,386	100.0	17.8	54.1	28.2	143,935	121,853	79,513	8,914	6,655	35.0	7,378	1,875
Providence	RI	359,829	47,119	207,944	104,766	100.0	13.1	57.8	29.1	331,800	316,686	185,108	3,574	7,432	36.1	11,351	2,004
Aiken County	SC	189,148	19,881	94,433	74,834	100.0	10.5	49.9	39.6	185,909	163,480	103,099	19,923	1,060	18.4	6,453	1,335
Beaufort County	SC	179,924	14,991	46,776	118,157	100.0	8.3	26.0	65.7	205,002	153,211	87,449	38,912	10,670	16.6	8,359	1,286
Berkeley County	SC	214,720	26,169	106,430	82,121	100.0	12.2	49.6	38.2	239,437	182,097	101,713	38,707	16,497	14.8	6,527	1,350
Charleston County	SC	394,804	48,176	142,515	204,113	100.0	12.2	36.1	51.7	465,422	353,960	211,573	95,341	10,322	19.3	8,025	1,450
Dorchester County 02	SC	125,732	8,911	71,415	45,406	100.0	7.1	56.8	36.1	124,891	111,364	69,949	8,624	2,578	12.0	6,140	1,146
Florence County 01	SC	120,916	13,820	57,345	49,751	100.0	11.4	47.4	41.1	108,108	96,840	60,568	5,525	1,450	20.3	6,539	1,283
Greenville County	SC	557,680	41,731	229,308	286,641	100.0	7.5	41.1	51.4	621,286	410,170	242,171	155,965	50,848	15.5	6,384	1,487
Horry County	SC	275,978	23,356	101,366	151,256	100.0	8.5	36.7	54.8	280,100	235,293	140,616	30,271	11,696	20.8	7,435	1,369
Lexington County 01	SC	156,349	7,768	77,331	71,250	100.0	5.0	49.5	45.6	153,503	135,780	82,447	12,503	4,263	10.4	7,109	1,058
Lexington County 05	SC	142,991	7,509	64,630	70,852	100.0	5.3	45.2	49.5	136,298	127,075	73,947	6,853	1,112	7.5	8,010	1,007
Pickens County	SC	122,547	10,114	68,549	43,884	100.0	8.3	55.9	35.8	122,090	103,152	62,808	13,644	3,682	14.0	6,343	1,167
Richland County 01	SC	299,045	27,894	115,105	156,046	100.0	9.3	38.5	52.2	292,238	240,861	141,885	34,335	14,410	24.4	8,924	1,418
Richland County 02	SC	173,781	10,356	75,592	87,833	100.0	6.0	43.5	50.5	210,489	150,428	91,530	52,028	6,276	8.5	7,573	1,051
York County 03	SC	137,753	10,611	66,614	60,528	100.0	7.7	48.4	43.9	154,995	110,870	68,055	37,257	5,373	14.4	6,799	1,151
Sioux Falls	SD	154,712	15,676	43,121	95,915	100.0	10.1	27.9	62.0	155,307	130,911	80,557	18,413	4,345	10.5	6,528	1,632
Hamilton County	TN	283,449	37,907	92,147	153,395	100.0	13.4	32.5	54.1	294,599	282,176	178,050	5,377	4,549	16.9	7,037	1,310
Knox County	TN	363,394	23,229	117,447	222,718	100.0	6.4	32.3	61.3	375,746	341,801	215,250	22,117	10,257	15.1	6,491	1,304
Memphis City	TN	915,781	137,524	327,278	450,979	100.0	15.0	35.7	49.2	950,659	869,868	545,373	68,706	4,643	25.0	7,484	1,409
Montgomery County Schools	TN	149,386	17,021	72,981	59,384	100.0	11.4	48.9	39.8	164,925	144,966	88,234	16,470	3,182	16.7	5,816	1,208
Nashville-Davidson County	TN	593,685	55,910	161,244	376,531	100.0	9.4	27.2	63.4	705,557	570,110	362,960	111,780	19,431	17.7	8,304	1,375
Rutherford County	TN	176,242	12,309	82,028	81,905	100.0	7.0	46.5	46.5	190,911	163,653	113,335	13,197	11,770	8.4	5,542	979
Shelby County	TN	298,026	15,657	127,954	154,415	100.0	5.3	42.9	51.8	351,397	281,441	193,115	54,717	0	5.0	6,013	1,061
Sumner County	TN	150,259	11,956	73,189	65,114	100.0	8.0	48.7	43.3	147,270	143,960	94,691	2,198		11.5	5,998	1,000
Williamson County	TN	156,398	5,490	77,756	93,152	100.0	3.5	36.9	59.6	191,444	150,906	97,951	30,571	8,844	4.0	6,873	649
Abilene ISD	TX	132,962	20,777	63,638	48,547	100.0	15.6	47.9	36.5	133,100	126,623	81,244	4,760	205	22.9	7,433	1,260
Aldine ISD	TX	455,847	57,620	231,323	166,904	100.0	12.6	50.7	36.6	442,759	404,754	248,812	24,007	11,525	24.9	7,190	1,359
Alief ISD	TX	355,949	33,625	174,537	147,787	100.0	9.4	49.0	41.5	360,628	315,211	204,653	28,738	12,278	21.8	6,952	1,324

See notes at end of table.

Table 88. Revenues, expenditures, poverty rate, and Title I allocations of public school districts enrolling more than 15,000 students, by state: 2003–04 and fiscal year 2006—Continued

Name of district	State	Revenues by source of funds, 2003–04 (in thousands of dollars)				Percentage distribution of revenues, 2003–04				Expenditures, 2003–04 (in thousands of dollars)					Poverty rate of 5- to 17-year-olds, 2004[1]	Current expenditure per pupil,[2] 2003–04	Title I allocations, fiscal year 2006, per poverty child[3]
		Total	Federal	State	Local	Total	Federal	State	Local	Total[4]	Current expenditures Total	Current expenditures Instruction	Capital outlay	Interest on school debt			
1	2	3	4	5	6	7	8	9	10	11	12	13	14	15	16	17	18
Amarillo ISD	TX	221,712	25,226	102,212	94,274	100.0	11.4	46.1	42.5	206,839	196,982	124,453	5,497	2,589	22.5	6,671	1,316
Arlington ISD	TX	475,658	37,135	115,429	323,094	100.0	7.8	24.3	67.9	449,796	393,083	254,164	23,855	30,460	14.8	6,294	1,321
Austin ISD	TX	789,887	70,621	72,979	646,287	100.0	8.9	9.2	81.8	801,078	596,977	343,929	17,072	23,591	20.7	7,556	1,391
Beaumont ISD	TX	162,252	22,165	32,798	107,289	100.0	13.7	20.2	66.1	158,490	146,882	87,756	6,514	2,720	25.6	7,085	1,320
Birdville ISD	TX	165,383	11,471	50,300	103,612	100.0	6.9	30.4	62.6	159,893	143,251	92,774	8,886	6,813	8.7	6,365	1,001
Brownsville ISD	TX	395,095	66,909	273,753	54,433	100.0	16.9	69.3	13.8	388,650	333,859	201,239	44,306	5,440	41.5	7,270	1,424
Carrollton-Farmers Branch	TX	264,894	12,210	22,309	230,375	100.0	4.6	8.4	87.0	257,828	179,852	108,401	11,926	14,929	11.0	7,015	1,047
Clear Creek ISD	TX	243,359	9,300	41,535	192,524	100.0	3.8	17.1	79.1	252,566	199,262	126,702	34,060	18,209	4.8	6,073	671
Conroe ISD	TX	294,279	16,363	76,675	201,241	100.0	5.6	26.1	68.4	353,140	248,769	149,693	77,404	25,133	11.8	6,339	1,098
Corpus Christi ISD	TX	309,085	40,194	144,270	124,621	100.0	13.0	46.7	40.3	302,150	275,084	167,881	10,697	10,020	25.8	6,998	1,346
Cypress-Fairbanks ISD	TX	581,678	23,316	183,987	374,375	100.0	4.0	31.6	64.4	630,862	490,374	319,472	88,622	49,486	6.8	6,549	1,088
Dallas ISD	TX	1,344,357	185,142	205,810	953,405	100.0	13.8	15.3	70.9	1,483,942	1,199,194	730,295	222,934	33,429	32.1	7,468	1,471
Denton ISD	TX	143,355	11,239	23,520	108,596	100.0	7.8	16.4	75.8	209,669	116,587	72,359	82,006	10,297	15.9	7,309	1,227
Ector County ISD	TX	182,388	23,536	84,861	73,991	100.0	12.9	46.5	40.6	192,755	162,574	97,632	24,048	4,217	24.9	6,231	1,269
Edinburg CISD	TX	219,638	39,333	128,307	51,998	100.0	17.9	58.4	23.7	243,857	188,422	111,639	43,332	10,030	39.5	7,426	1,370
El Paso ISD	TX	492,139	79,681	256,770	155,688	100.0	16.2	52.2	31.6	514,393	470,365	288,784	32,899	7,727	34.6	7,442	1,465
Fort Bend ISD	TX	459,369	22,699	179,825	256,845	100.0	4.9	39.1	55.9	451,127	401,351	255,126	25,945	22,480	7.5	6,553	1,131
Fort Worth ISD	TX	648,397	78,909	265,303	304,185	100.0	12.2	40.9	46.9	672,072	577,945	327,994	60,461	22,095	27.1	7,194	1,401
Frisco County ISD	TX	127,924	2,616	11,210	114,098	100.0	2.0	8.8	89.2	187,496	93,694	57,482	56,746	20,539	3.5	6,986	670
Galena Park ISD	TX	167,628	17,092	83,484	67,052	100.0	10.2	49.8	40.0	184,550	147,664	88,333	26,030	8,662	20.9	7,219	1,240
Garland ISD	TX	378,731	23,827	164,756	190,148	100.0	6.3	43.5	50.2	404,488	324,754	202,867	57,192	18,780	11.5	5,892	1,099
Goose Creek CISD	TX	157,325	14,248	20,378	122,699	100.0	9.1	13.0	78.0	153,825	134,850	79,244	10,406	6,550	20.3	7,006	1,237
Grand Prairie ISD	TX	169,098	13,644	89,722	65,732	100.0	8.1	53.1	38.9	213,606	148,367	92,086	51,361	11,764	19.6	6,704	1,238
Harlingen CISD	TX	131,327	18,330	74,728	38,269	100.0	14.0	56.9	29.1	145,520	113,066	71,054	25,902	4,345	29.5	6,631	1,249
Houston ISD	TX	1,680,877	237,252	274,127	1,169,498	100.0	14.1	16.3	69.6	1,749,949	1,524,250	903,993	125,926	59,413	28.8	7,207	1,496
Humble ISD	TX	207,083	9,368	74,055	123,660	100.0	4.5	35.8	59.7	222,220	168,673	105,520	42,294	9,962	5.9	6,245	989
Hurst-Euless-Bedford ISD	TX	158,294	8,601	20,884	128,809	100.0	5.4	13.2	81.4	151,470	133,920	83,520	4,408	12,219	9.2	6,858	999
Irving ISD	TX	236,543	21,522	73,019	142,002	100.0	9.1	30.9	60.0	263,962	198,565	127,194	46,918	16,997	16.7	6,354	1,249
Judson ISD	TX	145,117	10,081	68,127	66,909	100.0	6.9	46.9	46.1	182,725	118,245	72,798	56,288	7,455	12.2	6,576	1,049
Katy ISD	TX	340,505	11,884	105,837	222,784	100.0	3.5	31.1	65.4	475,048	279,601	176,079	158,098	36,183	4.5	6,639	684
Keller ISD	TX	151,342	4,494	39,627	107,221	100.0	3.0	26.2	70.8	177,972	125,718	80,311	32,493	19,093	3.7	5,766	696
Killeen ISD	TX	283,824	65,869	160,377	57,578	100.0	23.2	56.5	20.3	317,950	244,366	147,523	62,643	8,222	19.7	7,500	1,295
Klein ISD	TX	267,802	13,037	107,389	147,376	100.0	4.9	40.1	55.0	272,763	225,142	138,238	34,028	12,394	6.1	6,332	1,011
La Joya ISD	TX	179,702	32,134	126,222	21,346	100.0	17.9	70.2	11.9	181,083	163,238	96,752	11,013	5,673	49.6	7,500	1,479
Lamar CISD	TX	143,003	12,815	52,888	77,300	100.0	9.0	37.0	54.1	142,267	127,447	77,397	8,406	5,353	16.9	7,134	1,260
Laredo ISD	TX	221,405	35,824	154,480	31,101	100.0	16.2	69.8	14.0	236,124	185,899	116,781	41,770	7,163	44.5	7,482	1,444
Leander ISD	TX	154,332	6,189	22,500	125,643	100.0	4.0	14.6	81.4	202,503	118,982	70,063	66,448	15,671	5.6	6,537	979
Lewisville ISD	TX	372,976	15,825	45,658	311,493	100.0	4.2	12.2	83.5	414,658	301,253	193,088	78,403	30,530	5.6	6,843	1,045
Lubbock ISD	TX	231,962	37,360	87,852	106,750	100.0	16.1	37.9	46.0	231,131	216,623	135,976	7,787	2,580	23.9	7,465	1,328
Mansfield ISD	TX	162,966	6,625	65,230	91,111	100.0	4.1	40.0	55.9	229,292	131,627	84,760	80,254	16,987	6.6	6,843	964
McAllen ISD	TX	187,825	26,961	92,695	68,169	100.0	14.4	49.4	36.3	181,898	175,829	106,944	1,594	2,038	26.8	7,485	1,255
McKinney ISD	TX	149,033	7,157	21,210	120,666	100.0	4.8	14.2	81.0	167,421	110,577	68,727	40,165	15,274	10.9	6,636	1,059
Mesquite ISD	TX	262,237	15,694	137,570	108,973	100.0	6.0	52.5	41.6	268,549	218,375	134,129	32,035	17,252	11.3	6,346	1,064
Midland ISD	TX	151,945	18,594	53,660	79,701	100.0	12.2	35.3	52.5	160,461	138,261	84,735	16,846	4,264	19.8	6,609	1,253
North East ISD	TX	451,017	28,674	99,149	323,194	100.0	6.4	22.0	71.7	479,264	385,128	242,326	67,236	24,858	11.0	6,841	1,287
Northside ISD	TX	581,114	44,413	222,115	314,586	100.0	7.6	38.2	54.1	685,459	477,122	286,159	163,193	38,564	13.5	6,645	1,339
Pasadena ISD	TX	352,354	28,542	184,967	138,845	100.0	8.1	52.5	39.4	342,663	290,534	178,196	37,274	11,188	18.7	6,297	1,303
Pflugerville ISD	TX	121,816	5,569	27,656	88,591	100.0	4.6	22.7	72.7	128,788	103,680	63,087	11,691	12,749	5.1	6,249	940
Pharr-San Juan-Alamo ISD	TX	223,836	17,346	154,172	34,214	100.0	15.8	68.9	15.3	211,816	194,147	116,217	10,221	5,807	39.5	7,328	1,371
Plano ISD	TX	571,609	5,450	40,578	513,685	100.0	3.0	7.1	89.9	628,283	386,698	252,446	74,470	34,280	5.1	7,455	1,068
Richardson ISD	TX	337,571	18,808	30,257	288,506	100.0	5.6	9.0	85.5	431,188	236,840	145,799	121,748	15,076	13.6	6,858	1,092
Round Rock ISD	TX	308,795	13,803	30,543	264,449	100.0	4.5	9.9	85.6	288,764	248,051	145,812		20,731	5.5	6,977	1,044
San Angelo ISD	TX	104,375	13,631	53,374	37,370	100.0	13.1	51.1	35.8	107,050	96,162	59,822	9,130	1,203	23.0	6,357	1,231
San Antonio ISD	TX	518,758	86,237	279,724	152,797	100.0	16.6	53.9	29.5	583,207	446,064	255,133	98,251	28,682	36.9	7,838	1,416

See notes at end of table.

Table 88. Revenues, expenditures, poverty rate, and Title I allocations of public school districts enrolling more than 15,000 students, by state: 2003–04 and fiscal year 2006—Continued

Name of district	State	Revenues by source of funds, 2003-04 (in thousands of dollars)				Percentage distribution of revenues, 2003-04				Expenditures, 2003-04 (in thousands of dollars)					Poverty rate of 5- to 17-year-olds, 2004[1]	Current expenditure per pupil,[2] 2003-04	Title I allocations, fiscal year 2006, per poverty child[3]
		Total	Federal	State	Local	Total	Federal	State	Local	Total[4]	Current expenditures		Capital outlay	Interest on school debt			
											Total	Instruction					
1	2	3	4	5	6	7	8	9	10	11	12	13	14	15	16	17	18
Socorro ISD	TX	245,867	24,169	165,371	56,327	100.0	9.8	67.3	22.9	230,237	202,677	121,484	13,150	12,509	25.0	6,286	1,272
Spring Branch ISD	TX	277,082	24,796	30,893	221,393	100.0	8.9	11.1	79.9	285,963	239,728	148,243	33,535	7,862	19.2	7,263	1,278
Spring ISD	TX	211,200	11,702	89,728	109,770	100.0	5.5	42.5	52.0	252,367	184,351	114,060	49,257	17,160	9.4	6,887	1,009
Tyler ISD	TX	130,342	18,297	34,641	77,404	100.0	14.0	26.6	59.4	128,620	118,890	75,580	6,589	1,528	23.3	6,835	1,291
United ISD	TX	242,436	29,580	133,154	79,702	100.0	12.2	54.9	32.9	249,146	214,516	128,991	24,470	9,372	29.2	6,649	1,285
Waco County ISD	TX	125,733	20,379	60,705	44,649	100.0	16.2	48.3	35.5	121,939	108,243	61,418	6,203	3,369	35.2	6,908	1,367
Weslaco County ISD	TX	125,945	24,753	83,709	17,483	100.0	19.7	66.5	13.9	120,905	110,354	63,427	6,380	2,346	43.7	7,368	1,423
Ysleta ISD	TX	341,744	55,481	217,554	68,709	100.0	16.2	63.7	20.1	343,793	326,572	199,881	9,826	4,059	31.1	6,998	1,424
Alpine District	UT	278,551	19,131	174,194	85,226	100.0	6.9	62.5	30.6	324,714	229,111	152,445	79,094	12,403	8.5	4,471	1,063
Davis District	UT	344,281	32,004	206,874	105,403	100.0	9.3	60.1	30.6	377,999	293,356	183,703	65,240	8,692	6.6	4,829	1,054
Granite District	UT	393,914	43,542	222,822	127,550	100.0	11.1	56.6	32.4	398,137	336,089	215,169	53,219	0	10.3	4,749	1,257
Jordan District	UT	439,856	30,604	235,837	173,415	100.0	7.0	53.6	39.4	419,246	339,542	211,278	62,741	8,469	5.2	4,542	1,095
Nebo District	UT	139,504	16,124	84,828	38,552	100.0	11.6	60.8	27.6	131,199	110,541	70,132	13,673	4,670	9.5	4,581	979
Salt Lake District	UT	188,353	27,457	72,259	88,637	100.0	14.6	38.4	47.1	205,119	142,305	91,320	42,599	5,084	21.2	5,822	1,232
Washington District	UT	121,658	9,621	63,600	48,437	100.0	7.9	52.3	39.8	134,336	93,692	61,592	33,331	5,566	12.6	4,574	998
Weber District	UT	153,415	10,359	99,174	43,882	100.0	6.8	64.6	28.6	164,173	139,116	93,608	20,433	3,758	6.4	4,934	963
Arlington County	VA	325,607	13,882	37,547	274,178	100.0	4.3	11.5	84.2	344,656	273,452	163,087	43,827	8,687	9.7	14,274	1,296
Chesapeake City	VA	324,872	22,000	159,464	143,408	100.0	6.8	49.1	44.1	329,106	307,495	195,777	10,208	4,424	10.0	7,802	1,288
Chesterfield County	VA	481,820	22,019	189,973	269,828	100.0	4.6	39.4	56.0	419,629	377,056	237,994	27,643	12,449	6.8	6,807	1,262
Fairfax County	VA	1,893,101	72,613	324,199	1,496,289	100.0	3.8	17.1	79.0	1,887,675	1,668,533	1,008,520	162,086	41,922	5.9	10,159	1,627
Hampton City	VA	182,302	16,405	104,168	61,729	100.0	9.0	57.1	33.9	186,770	177,992	105,700	6,833	534	15.3	7,736	1,535
Hanover County	VA	141,335	5,999	54,823	80,513	100.0	4.2	38.8	57.0	143,404	123,173	82,027	13,215	5,795	4.7	6,791	777
Henrico County	VA	359,717	16,769	139,004	203,944	100.0	4.7	38.6	56.7	373,005	308,507	189,007	53,599	8,600	8.3	6,802	1,290
Loudoun County	VA	445,343	11,906	94,355	339,082	100.0	2.7	21.2	76.1	571,864	403,464	258,440	142,294	25,102	3.6	9,901	768
Newport News City	VA	285,012	31,149	140,086	113,777	100.0	10.9	49.2	39.9	273,231	246,994	148,261	12,332	6,494	17.6	7,509	1,534
Norfolk City	VA	319,365	40,947	165,227	113,191	100.0	12.8	51.7	35.4	322,607	292,437	181,684	13,282	101	24.5	7,963	1,668
Portsmouth City	VA	134,301	16,578	79,428	38,295	100.0	12.3	59.1	28.5	133,427	121,960	71,992	7,110	264	21.8	7,371	1,486
Prince William County	VA	612,178	26,399	240,385	345,394	100.0	4.3	39.3	56.4	650,739	511,924	297,824	98,491	18,678	6.8	8,074	1,291
Richmond City	VA	283,466	36,146	100,811	146,509	100.0	12.8	35.6	51.7	282,849	267,655	151,476	7,155	4,583	25.7	10,538	1,611
Spotsylvania County	VA	184,964	8,273	84,006	92,685	100.0	4.5	45.4	50.1	216,688	158,048	98,742	48,525	9,303	6.5	7,160	1,164
Stafford County	VA	201,831	10,156	93,392	98,283	100.0	5.0	46.3	48.7	221,021	172,516	111,357	40,422	7,736	4.9	6,937	1,154
Virginia Beach City	VA	630,291	56,162	289,314	284,815	100.0	8.9	45.9	45.2	669,722	589,852	354,933	50,158	17,495	8.6	7,730	1,539
Bellevue	WA	153,050	6,554	75,116	71,380	100.0	4.3	49.1	46.6	189,687	117,111	70,918	63,406	6,651	6.8	7,263	1,065
Bethel	WA	138,673	9,473	92,966	36,234	100.0	6.8	67.0	26.1	151,965	115,463	66,914	31,032	5,015	10.4	6,637	1,177
Edmonds	WA	171,596	10,655	103,488	57,453	100.0	6.2	60.3	33.5	162,514	148,986	90,206	2,650	9,981	9.9	6,777	1,137
Everett	WA	163,664	9,200	94,849	59,615	100.0	5.6	58.0	36.4	168,042	132,892	79,074	24,284	10,352	13.9	7,141	1,185
Evergreen	WA	207,561	10,954	138,978	57,629	100.0	5.3	67.0	27.8	238,302	168,267	100,144	57,634	11,387	11.7	7,017	1,179
Federal Way	WA	174,118	11,083	114,275	48,760	100.0	6.4	65.6	28.0	171,819	152,376	94,067	13,217	5,564	11.4	6,761	1,177
Highline	WA	162,494	13,668	92,170	56,656	100.0	8.4	56.7	34.9	214,277	135,896	80,484	69,778	7,945	13.8	7,673	1,276
Issaquah	WA	134,066	3,545	71,531	58,990	100.0	2.6	53.4	44.0	142,650	100,183	59,367	29,897	11,007	3.9	6,614	708
Kent	WA	227,890	12,986	128,392	86,512	100.0	5.7	56.3	38.0	241,380	181,450	109,122	47,860	11,452	10.3	6,755	1,191
Lake Washington	WA	214,669	7,793	118,941	87,935	100.0	3.6	55.4	41.0	211,827	162,976	101,320	36,243	10,475	4.9	6,750	1,107
Northshore	WA	187,221	6,517	104,686	76,018	100.0	3.5	55.9	40.6	193,005	147,766	88,880	32,470	12,254	5.1	7,356	1,092
Puyallup	WA	159,235	6,989	105,020	47,226	100.0	4.4	66.0	29.7	154,895	138,844	83,658	9,005	6,316	5.1	6,927	1,133
Seattle	WA	526,366	50,583	250,003	225,780	100.0	9.6	47.5	42.9	484,167	411,881	240,486	68,239	2,899	15.2	8,655	1,520
Spokane	WA	267,975	27,825	165,472	74,678	100.0	10.4	61.7	27.9	273,095	241,438	147,907	16,898	8,697	18.9	7,771	1,436
Tacoma	WA	330,704	33,840	186,750	110,114	100.0	10.2	56.5	33.3	367,379	261,547	152,933	91,445	14,279	18.3	7,783	1,446
Vancouver	WA	193,558	16,531	122,565	54,462	100.0	8.5	63.3	28.1	214,024	159,712	94,387	43,629	9,007	18.3	7,221	1,393
Kanawha County	WV	271,669	28,146	142,428	101,095	100.0	10.4	52.4	37.2	266,933	239,991	149,262	15,820	1,207	21.3	8,478	1,647

See notes at end of table.

Table 88. Revenues, expenditures, poverty rate, and Title I allocations of public school districts enrolling more than 15,000 students, by state: 2003–04 and fiscal year 2006—Continued

Name of district	State	Revenues by source of funds, 2003–04 (in thousands of dollars)				Percentage distribution of revenues, 2003–04				Expenditures, 2003–04 (in thousands of dollars)					Poverty rate of 5- to 17-year-olds, 2004[1]	Current expenditure per pupil,[2] 2003–04[1]	Title I allocations, fiscal year 2006, per poverty child[3]
		Total	Federal	State	Local	Total	Federal	State	Local	Total[4]	Current expenditures						
											Total	Instruction	Capital outlay	Interest on school debt			
1	2	3	4	5	6	7	8	9	10	11	12	13	14	15	16	17	18
Appleton Area	WI	143,143	7,449	81,242	54,452	100.0	5.2	56.8	38.0	141,761	130,256	82,413	4,943	2,493	6.7	8,527	1,342
Green Bay Area	WI	206,985	14,696	118,925	73,364	100.0	7.1	57.5	35.4	200,972	188,082	118,779	6,274	4,909	12.0	9,266	1,459
Kenosha	WI	207,872	14,042	125,824	68,006	100.0	6.8	60.5	32.7	218,175	195,873	125,237	15,087	5,466	11.5	9,142	1,580
Madison Metropolitan	WI	308,006	21,435	77,830	208,741	100.0	7.0	25.3	67.8	314,081	291,544	175,458	7,622	3,595	9.0	11,702	1,540
Milwaukee	WI	1,093,133	167,029	703,725	222,379	100.0	15.3	64.4	20.3	1,165,164	1,010,112	609,401	110,702	9,144	28.1	10,375	2,030
Racine	WI	210,323	15,697	137,107	57,519	100.0	7.5	65.2	27.3	211,453	201,239	127,119	5,892	2,572	13.5	9,379	1,614

†Not applicable.

[1]Poverty is defined based on the number of persons and related children in the family and their income. See http://www.census.gov/hhes/www/poverty/threshld/thresh04.html for information on poverty thresholds for 2004.

[2]Current expenditure per pupil based on fall enrollment collected through the "National Public Education Financial Survey."

[3]Fiscal year 2006 Department of Education funds available for spending by school districts beginning with the 2006–07 school year.

[4]Includes other expenditures not shown separately.

NOTE: Detail may not sum to totals because of rounding. SB = School board. SC = School corporation. ISD = Independent school district.

SOURCE: U.S. Department of Education, National Center for Education Statistics, Common Core of Data (CCD), "National Public Education Financial Survey," 2003–04, and "Local Education Agency Universe Survey," 2004–05; and unpublished Department of Education budget data. (This table was prepared September 2006.)

Table 89. Enrollment, poverty, and federal funds for the 100 largest school districts, by enrollment size: 2003–04 and fiscal year 2006

Name of district	State	Rank order	Enrollment, fall 2004	5- to 17-year-old population, 2004	5- to 17-year-olds in poverty, 2004[1]	Poverty rate of 5- to 17-year-olds, 2004[1]	Total	Federal	Federal as a percent of total	Federal revenue per student[3]	Title I basic and concentration grants	School lunch	Vocational education	Drug-free schools	Eisenhower math and science	Special education	Basic grants	Concentration grants	Targeted grants	Education finance incentive grants[2]
1	2	3	4	5	6	7	8	9	10	11	12	13	14	15	16	17	18	19	20	21
New York City	NY	1	1,023,674	1,349,933	397,230	29.4	$14,723,474	$1,711,502	11.6	$1,643	$740,607	$284,992	—	$8,991	$12,155	266,163	$375,513	$91,656	$196,582	$160,591
Los Angeles Unified	CA	2	741,367	886,436	270,712	30.5	7,531,675	995,098	13.2	1,332	403,719	118,169	$53,708	8,631	11,518	213,233	184,399	45,251	103,094	106,513
City of Chicago	IL	3	426,812	524,587	149,574	28.5	4,107,617	702,583	17.1	1,617	245,901	86,089	—	4,870	8,722	151,207	127,954	31,400	69,879	68,422
Dade County	FL	4	368,933	421,467	103,487	24.6	3,244,666	375,101	11.6	1,009	109,312	69,908	27,529	3,826	7,073	86,287	63,701	15,632	33,923	28,785
Clark County	NV	5	283,221	308,200	44,088	14.3	2,132,656	145,376	6.8	537	34,627	29,782	7,228	1,115	3,007	31,991	28,228	6,927	13,525	11,210
Broward County	FL	6	274,591	312,120	50,166	16.1	2,231,773	201,622	9.0	739	41,218	47,481	12,382	1,728	3,271	44,071	30,932	7,591	15,079	12,795
Houston ISD	TX	7	208,945	241,464	69,489	28.8	1,680,877	237,252	14.1	1,122	78,297	20,215	12,470	1,887	2,919	73,937	46,763	11,476	23,965	21,726
Hillsborough County	FL	8	189,469	203,451	36,548	18.0	1,579,958	207,334	13.1	1,140	32,841	34,424	2,048	1,173	3,014	38,008	22,986	5,641	10,509	8,917
Philadelphia City	PA	9	187,547	267,652	70,931	26.5	2,111,973	333,586	15.8	1,758	137,553	—	—	3,405	5,964	63,557	67,866	16,654	35,035	45,128
Hawaii Depart. of Ed.	HI	10	183,185	209,934	26,720	12.7	2,138,137	236,470	11.1	1,288	35,049	34,359	1,402	861	3,089	43,631	23,123	4,929	8,871	9,049
Palm Beach County	FL	11	175,076	197,615	28,380	14.4	1,573,522	120,126	7.6	706	29,774	29,747	—	39	1,580	28,091	17,562	4,310	7,784	6,605
Orange County	FL	12	173,331	182,369	30,768	16.9	1,380,847	120,688	8.7	727	28,523	31,188	7,430	1,069	2,056	28,014	19,137	4,696	8,539	7,246
Fairfax County	VA	13	164,765	182,279	10,744	5.9	1,893,101	72,613	3.8	442	11,842	25,997	4,230	656	1,671	13,802	8,373	2,055	3,225	3,826
Dallas ISD	TX	14	158,027	187,119	60,014	32.1	1,344,357	185,142	13.8	1,153	60,464	22,521	10,312	1,493	2,285	47,438	40,077	9,835	20,120	18,240
Detroit City	MI	15	141,461	213,379	66,424	31.1	1,642,402	252,704	15.4	1,651		20,721	3,991	2,630	4,381	36,870	40,077	14,659	40,491	40,353
Montgomery County	MD	16	139,393	166,625	12,345	7.4	1,812,254	74,629	4.1	536	14,179	20,721	4,293	633	1,339	12,834	10,940	2,685	4,338	3,966
Prince George's County	MD	17	136,095	161,755	15,813	9.8	1,397,924	94,939	6.8	692	19,511	20,445	3,723	963	1,499	26,836	13,940	3,421	5,776	5,430
Gwinnett County	GA	18	135,392	134,788	14,273	10.6	1,503,965	54,277	3.6	421	—	—	—	—	—	18,466	10,440	2,562	4,263	5,126
San Diego Unified	CA	19	134,709	163,325	32,584	20.0	1,406,014	158,168	11.2	1,146	48,758	21,019	9,189	1,307	1,537	28,049	22,462	5,512	10,077	9,178
Duval County	FL	20	129,486	156,653	25,783	16.5	946,951	100,492	10.6	776	25,475	27,871	6,255	887	1,382	22,770	16,120	3,956	7,093	6,019
Memphis City	TN	21	121,028	121,424	32,825	25.0	915,781	137,524	15.0	1,183	40,316	29,784	—	—	3,439	34,197	20,505	5,032	9,195	11,511
Charlotte-Mecklenburg Schools	NC	22	118,765	140,431	19,995	14.2	1,067,782	76,490	7.2	672	—	—	—	—	—	23,460	12,557	3,082	5,386	6,039
Wake County Schools	NC	23	114,568	130,907	12,401	9.5	970,869	53,908	5.6	495	—	—	—	—	—	12,630	7,746	1,901	3,080	3,453
Pinellas County	FL	24	113,651	136,443	22,224	16.3	920,279	93,248	10.1	814	21,026	29,516	4,958	729	1,719	16,457	13,905	3,412	6,031	5,118
Baltimore County	MD	25	107,701	134,134	10,913	8.1	1,074,341	67,841	6.3	625	16,633	16,939	3,676	602	1,112	12,382	10,007	2,456	3,891	3,511
Cobb County	GA	26	103,935	111,049	10,146	9.1	945,482	46,631	4.9	457	—	—	—	—	—	10,102	7,531	1,848	2,869	3,294
DeKalb County	GA	27	99,986	108,432	18,239	16.8	943,522	69,571	7.4	699	—	—	—	—	—	25,174	13,611	3,340	5,782	7,123
Jefferson County	KY	28	97,976	119,227	19,989	16.8	842,393	101,812	12.1	1,065	—	12,200	—	—	1,290	20,690	14,054	3,449	6,034	8,201
Long Beach Unified	CA	29	96,319	107,134	33,861	31.6	819,059	123,816	15.1	1,269	39,123	—	4,801	924	—	24,092	22,922	5,625	10,298	9,385
Milwaukee	WI	30	93,654	107,181	32,924	28.1	1,093,133	167,029	15.3	1,716	57,633	27,294	—	—	2,081	24,178	29,400	7,215	13,210	17,007
Albuquerque	NM	31	93,341	103,461	19,028	18.4	720,897	92,867	12.9	1,026	18,798	33,104	4,733	754	1,466	15,356	12,830	3,149	5,475	6,362
Baltimore City	MD	32	88,401	114,120	27,430	24.0	965,291	115,355	12.0	1,227	39,360	16,599	8,091	1,131	1,595	23,586	25,595	6,281	11,361	11,119
Jefferson County	CO	33	86,868	97,193	6,093	6.3	728,636	32,986	4.5	378	9,753	10,043	2,549	328	676	5,473	4,599	505	1,562	1,710
Polk County	FL	34	86,292	93,489	18,205	19.5	644,591	73,278	11.4	871	17,265	15,434	4,275	695	1,502	20,183	11,230	2,756	4,750	4,030
Fresno Unified	CA	35	80,760	87,726	32,182	36.7	716,277	113,923	15.9	1,399	48,291	11,986	7,275	1,136	1,686	24,079	22,683	5,425	9,903	8,886
Austin ISD	TX	36	79,950	91,949	19,031	20.7	789,887	70,621	8.9	894	19,424	12,947	4,356	474	874	17,137	12,861	3,156	5,481	4,968
Fort Worth ISD	TX	37	79,769	94,410	25,538	27.1	648,397	78,909	12.2	982	23,373	10,603	—	661	1,140	19,903	17,171	4,214	7,546	6,841
Cypress-Fairbanks ISD	TX	38	79,314	68,706	4,660	6.8	581,678	23,316	4.0	311	2,376	9,538	1,318	220	285	7,272	3,133	—	1,015	920
Fulton County	GA	39	75,891	80,823	7,217	8.9	803,163	37,617	4.7	513	—	—	—	405	—	10,504	5,374	1,319	1,858	1,984
Jordan District	UT	40	75,548	80,668	4,207	5.2	439,856	30,604	7.0	409	2,699	11,554	1,344	341	793	7,299	2,709	0	866	1,031
Virginia Beach City	VA	41	75,515	86,341	7,418	8.6	630,097	56,162	8.9	736	10,201	13,700	2,489	427	1,116	7,644	5,791	1,421	2,005	2,197
Mesa Unified District	AZ	42	75,471	95,390	12,547	13.2	538,261	42,638	7.9	565	10,566	8,503	3,214	339	990	11,457	7,920	1,944	3,164	3,174
Brevard County	FL	43	74,824	83,676	10,579	12.6	549,521	49,264	9.0	667	11,202	17,651	—	558	642	8,785	6,588	1,617	2,525	2,143
Northside ISD	TX	44	74,649	73,903	9,948	13.5	581,114	44,413	7.6	619	9,811	10,865	2,065	312	633	11,921	6,774	1,662	2,564	2,324
Anne Arundel County	MD	45	73,991	87,635	15,511	6.3	721,559	39,647	5.5	532	9,193	11,539	2,071	360	665	4,918	5,112	717	1,713	1,406
Nashville-Davidson County	TN	46	72,807	84,936	18,811	17.7	593,685	55,910	9.4	814	13,832	15,128	—	—	2,025	14,911	9,886	2,426	4,106	4,917
Denver County	CO	47	72,410	76,279	18,811	22.1	683,682	69,052	10.1	958	24,024	11,688	3,929	1,791	1,386	14,237	13,748	3,374	5,853	6,455
Lee County	FL	48	71,210	73,242	11,034	14.5	640,307	53,026	8.3	798	11,297	13,519	—	405	947	12,061	6,818	1,673	2,635	2,236
Granite District	UT	49	68,783	73,242	7,578	10.3	393,914	43,542	11.1	615	8,397	10,623	2,610	596	569	10,271	4,728	1,160	1,640	1,996
Guilford County Schools	NC	50	68,220	76,303	12,961	17.0	515,548	47,482	9.2	721	—	—	—	—	—	14,692	8,055	1,977	3,228	3,620
Seminole County	FL	51	66,692	72,213	8,170	11.3	502,201	34,427	6.9	530	7,251	11,940	2,162	366	670	7,222	5,014	1,230	1,771	1,503
Prince William County	VA	52	66,298	69,068	4,680	6.8	612,178	26,399	4.3	416	5,025	7,416	1,892	232	660	6,082	3,613	0	1,170	1,259
Volusia County	FL	53	65,281	72,709	12,287	16.9	537,578	48,138	9.0	751	13,039	12,472	2,408	547	1,231	10,190	7,719	1,894	3,067	2,603
Greenville County	SC	54	65,265	72,872	11,331	15.5	557,680	41,731	7.5	650	9,787	12,705	2,365	371	1,309	9,976	7,784	1,910	3,044	4,108

See notes at end of table.

Table 89. Enrollment, poverty, and federal funds for the 100 largest school districts, by enrollment size: 2003–04 and fiscal year 2006—Continued

Name of district	State	Rank order	Enrollment, fall 2004	5- to 17-year-old population, 2004	5- to 17-year-olds in poverty, 2004	Poverty rate of 5- to 17-year-olds, 2004[1]	Revenues by source of funds (thousands), 2003–04: Total	Federal	Federal as a percent of total, 2003–04	Federal revenue per student[3]	Selected federal programs (thousands), 2003–04: Title I basic and concentration grants	School lunch	Vocational education	Drug-free schools	Eisenhower math and science	Special education	Title I allocations (thousands), FY 2006[2]: Basic grants	Concentration grants	Targeted grants	Education finance incentive grants
1	2	3	4	5	6	7	8	9	10	11	12	13	14	15	16	17	18	19	20	21
Orleans Parish SB	LA	55	64,920	83,808	29,565	35.3	538,644	84,326	15.7	1,242	36,170	6,215	6,626	645	1,277	20,916	21,702	5,191	9,428	9,514
Cleveland Municipal	OH	56	64,670	92,582	30,413	32.8	820,215	128,163	15.6	1,840	—	13,973	—	980	2,862	23,871	25,830	6,339	11,519	16,320
Mobile County	AL	57	63,987	76,758	19,550	25.5	459,717	68,643	14.9	1,060	25,340	14,465	5,122	583	2,458	17,099	12,241	2,982	5,191	5,876
Washoe County	NV	58	63,322	68,715	7,899	11.5	463,123	35,805	7.7	577	7,610	8,004	1,245	311	699	7,502	5,165	1,267	1,844	1,261
El Paso ISD	TX	59	63,216	64,396	22,296	34.6	492,139	79,681	16.2	1,261	26,164	9,696	7,745	646	1,086	16,629	15,902	3,803	6,737	6,222
Fort Bend ISD	TX	60	62,853	64,815	4,888	7.5	459,369	22,699	4.9	371	3,409	8,495	1,504	225	449	5,296	3,398	—	1,116	1,012
District of Columbia	DC	61	62,306	74,518	21,695	29.1	1,081,501	167,020	15.4	2,566	43,773	12,445	—	2,885	3,829	15,903	23,646	5,803	10,384	8,869
Arlington ISD	TX	62	62,267	69,132	10,214	14.8	475,658	37,135	7.8	595	10,480	7,646	2,072	330	653	11,563	6,853	1,682	2,602	2,358
Santa Ana Unified	CA	63	61,693	66,186	16,169	24.4	592,412	77,326	13.1	1,230	23,027	11,440	5,204	331	726	16,503	10,858	2,664	4,516	3,937
Tucson Unified District	AZ	64	61,204	81,180	17,624	21.7	476,206	57,276	12.0	932	16,862	10,771	4,145	632	1,502	12,645	11,512	2,825	4,885	5,089
Pasco County	FL	65	60,846	63,384	10,621	16.8	448,929	39,422	8.8	685	8,414	9,152	2,538	354	469	10,695	6,595	1,618	2,529	2,146
Columbus Public Schools	OH	66	60,668	75,979	20,722	27.3	694,022	82,466	11.9	1,307	—	9,471	—	499	2,836	16,436	18,099	4,441	7,813	10,871
San Bernardino City Unified	CA	67	59,105	61,169	22,306	36.5	493,002	68,822	14.0	1,190	28,653	8,572	2,693	600	824	17,360	15,227	3,737	6,610	5,911
Davis District	UT	68	58,953	60,441	4,002	6.6	344,281	32,004	9.3	527	3,440	7,873	1,386	183	833	7,182	2,501	—	786	931
Elk Grove Unified	CA	69	58,870	54,577	7,425	13.6	552,457	36,821	6.7	662	10,360	6,714	1,419	243	343	8,323	5,277	1,295	1,842	1,417
Boston	MA	70	57,742	75,711	17,043	22.5	1,077,906	108,651	10.1	1,806	44,815	17,453	—	—	1,439	10,269	19,023	4,550	8,007	10,420
North East ISD	TX	71	57,599	60,871	6,709	11.0	451,017	28,674	6.4	509	5,761	8,930	1,776	223	560	7,776	4,549	1,116	1,557	1,412
San Francisco County Unified	CA	72	57,144	71,073	13,285	18.7	556,589	71,288	12.8	1,233	19,505	9,353	2,236	260	529	11,486	9,202	2,258	3,723	3,190
San Antonio ISD	TX	73	56,639	66,273	24,475	36.9	518,758	86,237	16.6	1,515	28,370	9,067	5,268	684	1,087	24,403	16,649	4,086	7,296	6,614
Aldine ISD	TX	74	56,375	53,839	13,392	24.9	455,847	57,620	12.6	1,024	12,893	8,725	2,708	325	674	19,155	9,035	2,217	3,647	3,306
Chesterfield County	VA	75	56,242	55,965	3,850	6.8	481,820	22,019	4.6	398	3,237	6,629	1,421	206	403	3,134	2,962	0	920	978
Garland ISD	TX	76	56,236	62,758	6,414	10.2	378,731	23,827	6.3	432	5,728	4,915	1,517	203	—	8,607	4,280	1,488	1,454	1,318
Knox County	TN	77	54,247	62,821	9,486	15.1	363,394	23,229	6.4	441	—	6,380	—	—	—	7,572	6,063	1,788	2,274	2,544
Cumberland County Schools	NC	78	53,346	58,020	11,662	20.1	368,430	50,843	13.8	963	2,786	6,624	1,439	210	568	12,868	7,286	0	2,860	3,207
Alpine District	UT	79	52,920	50,918	4,328	8.5	278,551	19,131	6.9	373	2,645	—	1,054	162	488	5,968	2,707	—	865	1,030
Plano ISD	TX	80	52,406	68,902	3,494	5.1	571,609	17,346	3.0	334	—	—	—	—	—	3,445	2,362	—	719	652
Sacramento City Unified	CA	81	51,420	67,396	17,236	25.6	464,816	78,317	16.8	1,503	25,811	8,480	4,890	612	845	13,908	12,030	2,952	5,078	4,467
Clayton County	GA	82	51,405	56,259	10,334	18.4	426,744	37,874	8.9	749	—	—	—	—	—	13,742	7,534	1,849	2,870	3,295
Jefferson Parish SB	LA	83	51,403	79,341	17,545	22.1	423,917	56,892	13.4	1,106	15,082	9,389	4,155	670	914	14,310	12,149	2,922	5,009	5,122
Atlanta City	GA	84	51,377	66,109	24,482	37.0	722,138	79,347	11.0	1,523	—	—	—	—	—	16,914	18,093	4,440	7,931	9,947
Capistrano Unified	CA	85	50,615	58,724	3,590	6.1	346,292	19,426	5.6	391	3,646	6,419	1,062	172	205	2,649	2,411	—	737	545
San Juan Unified	CA	86	50,089	61,852	7,062	11.4	433,264	38,876	9.0	764	10,242	7,265	2,129	338	337	6,173	5,043	1,237	1,745	1,337
Garden Grove Unified	CA	87	50,030	56,688	10,686	18.9	365,604	42,243	11.6	842	14,478	6,681	3,246	516	425	12,023	7,698	3,075	3,002	2,511
Anchorage	AK	88	49,545	56,132	4,837	8.6	430,337	58,649	13.6	1,180	11,121	10,296	4,497	576	1,019	7,228	5,792	678	2,758	2,820
Oakland Unified	CA	89	49,214	71,399	19,922	27.9	496,023	76,751	15.5	1,522	29,039	8,524	4,705	593	752	—	13,673	3,355	5,865	5,209
Forsyth County Schools	NC	90	48,785	56,386	8,826	15.7	413,020	32,133	7.8	679	—	—	—	—	—	9,246	5,492	1,348	2,000	2,243
Wichita	KS	91	48,737	57,095	10,072	17.6	452,437	57,466	12.7	1,175	17,603	6,010	1,011	1,055	—	10,935	8,216	2,016	3,156	5,206
Howard County	MD	92	48,219	53,895	2,376	4.4	537,507	17,975	3.3	376	2,828	6,114	932	171	364	2,030	2,100	0	0	0
Cherry Creek	CO	93	47,818	46,590	2,779	6.0	407,479	13,008	3.2	279	1,551	7,655	2,061	128	152	2,778	2,062	—	590	645
Portland	OR	94	47,649	46,187	9,900	16.0	505,585	50,455	10.0	1,044	17,241	6,325	—	1,195	812	9,512	7,664	1,881	2,913	4,538
Osceola County	FL	95	47,446	42,187	8,115	19.2	345,418	29,275	8.5	667	5,532	4,312	1,798	212	459	8,586	4,988	1,224	1,759	1,492
Pasadena ISD	TX	96	47,440	47,044	8,777	18.7	352,354	28,542	8.1	619	6,803	6,690	4,340	222	657	11,640	5,901	1,448	2,145	1,945
Brownsville ISD	TX	97	46,846	41,415	17,168	41.5	395,095	66,909	16.9	1,457	23,507	8,861	—	471	589	22,367	12,060	2,885	4,943	4,565
Seattle	WA	98	46,746	59,915	9,106	15.2	526,366	50,583	9.6	1,063	14,442	5,126	1,431	—	593	6,862	6,609	1,710	2,456	3,061
Henrico County	VA	99	46,711	49,545	4,124	8.3	359,717	16,769	4.7	370	4,042	—	2,102	210	572	3,195	3,215	—	1,017	1,087
Omaha	NE	100	46,549	58,126	9,005	15.5	423,926	51,152	12.1	1,111	14,400	10,568	—	348	980	10,661	8,056	1,977	3,184	4,416

—Not available

[1]Poverty is defined based on the number of persons and related children in the family and their income. See http://www.census.gov/hhes/www/poverty/threshld/thresh04.html for information on poverty thresholds for 2004.

[2]Fiscal year 2006 Department of Education funds available for spending by school districts in the 2006–07 school year.

[3]Federal revenue per student is based on fall enrollment collected through the "National Public Education Financial Survey."

SOURCE: U.S. Department of Education, National Center for Education Statistics, Common Core of Data (CCD), "National Public Education Financial Survey," 2003–04; "Local Education Agency Universe Survey," 2004–05; and unpublished Department of Education budget data. (This table was prepared October 2006.)

Table 90. Public elementary and secondary schools, by type of school: Selected years, 1967–68 through 2004–05

Year	Total, all public schools	Schools with reported grade spans											Combined elementary/ secondary schools[6]	Other schools[1]
		Total	Elementary schools				Secondary schools						
			Total[2]	Middle schools[3]	One-teacher schools	Other elementary schools	Total[4]	Junior high[5]	3-year or 4-year high schools	5-year or 6-year high schools	Other secondary schools		
1	2	3	4	5	6	7	8	9	10	11	12	13	14
1967–68	—	94,197	67,186	—	4,146	63,040	23,318	7,437	10,751	4,650	480	3,693	—
1970–71	—	89,372	64,020	2,080	1,815	60,125	23,572	7,750	11,265	3,887	670	1,780	—
1972–73	—	88,864	62,942	2,308	1,475	59,159	23,919	7,878	11,550	3,962	529	2,003	—
1974–75	—	87,456	61,759	3,224	1,247	57,288	23,837	7,690	11,480	4,122	545	1,860	—
1975–76	88,597	87,034	61,704	3,916	1,166	56,622	23,792	7,521	11,572	4,113	586	1,538	1,563
1976–77	—	86,501	61,123	4,180	1,111	55,832	23,857	7,434	11,658	4,130	635	1,521	—
1978–79	—	84,816	60,312	5,879	1,056	53,377	22,834	6,282	11,410	4,429	713	1,670	—
1980–81	85,982	83,688	59,326	6,003	921	52,402	22,619	5,890	10,758	4,193	1,778	1,743	2,294
1982–83	84,740	82,039	58,051	6,875	798	50,378	22,383	5,948	11,678	4,067	690	1,605	2,701
1983–84	84,178	81,418	57,471	6,885	838	49,748	22,336	5,936	11,670	4,046	684	1,611	2,760
1984–85	84,007	81,147	57,231	6,893	825	49,513	22,320	5,916	11,671	4,021	712	1,596	2,860
1986–87	83,455	82,190	58,801	7,452	763	50,586	21,406	5,142	11,453	4,197	614	1,983	1,265 [7]
1987–88	83,248	81,416	57,575	7,641	729	49,205	21,662	4,900	11,279	4,048	1,435	2,179	1,832 [7]
1988–89	83,165	81,579	57,941	7,957	583	49,401	21,403	4,687	11,350	3,994	1,372	2,235	1,586 [7]
1989–90	83,425	81,880	58,419	8,272	630	49,517	21,181	4,512	11,492	3,812	1,365	2,280	1,545 [7]
1990–91	84,538	82,475	59,015	8,545	617	49,853	21,135	4,561	11,537	3,723	1,314	2,325	2,063
1991–92	84,578	82,506	59,258	8,829	569	49,860	20,767	4,298	11,528	3,699	1,242	2,481	2,072
1992–93	84,497	82,896	59,676	9,152	430	50,094	20,671	4,115	11,651	3,613	1,292	2,549	1,601
1993–94	85,393	83,431	60,052	9,573	442	50,037	20,705	3,970	11,858	3,595	1,282	2,674	1,962
1994–95	86,221	84,476	60,808	9,954	458	50,396	20,904	3,859	12,058	3,628	1,359	2,764	1,745
1995–96	87,125	84,958	61,165	10,205	474	50,486	20,997	3,743	12,168	3,621	1,465	2,796	2,167
1996–97	88,223	86,092	61,805	10,499	487	50,819	21,307	3,707	12,424	3,614	1,562	2,980	2,131
1997–98	89,508	87,541	62,739	10,944	476	51,319	21,682	3,599	12,734	3,611	1,738	3,120	1,967
1998–99	90,874	89,259	63,462	11,202	463	51,797	22,076	3,607	13,457	3,707	1,305	3,721	1,615
1999–2000	92,012	90,538	64,131	11,521	423	52,187	22,365	3,566	13,914	3,686	1,199	4,042	1,474
2000–01	93,273	91,691	64,601	11,696	411	52,494	21,994	3,318	13,793	3,974	909	5,096	1,582
2001–02	94,112	92,696	65,228	11,983	408	52,837	22,180	3,285	14,070	3,917	908	5,288	1,416
2002–03	95,615	93,869	65,718	12,174	366	53,178	22,599	3,263	14,330	4,017	989	5,552	1,746
2003–04	95,726	93,977	65,758	12,341	376	53,041	22,782	3,251	14,595	3,840	1,096	5,437	1,749
2004–05	96,513	95,001	65,984	12,530	338	53,116	23,445	3,250	14,854	3,945	1,396	5,572	1,512

—Not available.
[1]Includes special education, alternative, and other schools not classified by grade span.
[2]Includes schools beginning with grade 6 or below and with no grade higher than 8.
[3]Includes schools with grade spans beginning with 4, 5, or 6 and ending with 6, 7, or 8.
[4]Includes schools with no grade lower than 7.
[5]Includes schools with grades 7 and 8 or grades 7 through 9.
[6]Includes schools beginning with grade 6 or lower and ending with grade 9 or above.

[7]Because of revision in data collection procedures, figures not comparable to data for other years.
SOURCE: U.S. Department of Education, National Center for Education Statistics, *Statistics of State School Systems*, 1967–68 and 1975–76; *Statistics of Public Elementary and Secondary Day Schools*, 1970–71, 1972–73, 1974–75, and 1976–77 through 1980–81; and Common Core of Data (CCD), "Public Elementary/Secondary School Universe Survey," 1982–83 through 2004–05. (This table was prepared August 2006.)

Table 91. Number and percentage distribution of public elementary and secondary schools and enrollment, by type and enrollment size of school: 2004–05

Enrollment size of school	Number and percentage distribution of schools, by type						Enrollment and percentage distribution, by type of school[1]					
	Total[2]	Elementary[3]	Secondary[4] All schools	Secondary[4] Regular schools[6]	Combined elementary/ secondary[5]	Other[2]	Total[2]	Elementary[3]	Secondary[4] All schools	Secondary[4] Regular schools[6]	Combined elementary/ secondary[5]	Other[2]
1	2	3	4	5	6	7	8	9	10	11	12	13
Number of schools............	96,513	65,984	23,445	19,028	5,572	1,512	48,581,686	31,161,287	15,876,391	15,410,552	1,502,102	41,906
Percent[7]....................	100.00	100.00	100.00	100.00	100.00	100.00	100.00	100.00	100.00	100.00	100.00	100.00
Under 100........................	11.03	6.20	17.81	9.09	41.68	51.19	0.96	0.65	1.08	0.63	5.88	16.18
100 to 199........................	9.69	8.59	11.11	10.35	16.97	24.91	2.78	2.75	2.27	1.86	8.29	24.28
200 to 299........................	11.56	12.85	8.20	8.56	9.80	8.53	5.61	6.87	2.86	2.61	8.07	15.27
300 to 399........................	13.53	15.96	7.82	8.55	7.35	9.56	9.09	11.78	3.81	3.64	8.57	23.33
400 to 499........................	13.20	16.23	6.06	6.80	5.78	3.75	11.37	15.35	3.81	3.74	8.62	11.65
500 to 599........................	10.80	13.06	5.76	6.53	4.23	1.37	11.35	15.05	4.44	4.40	7.72	5.15
600 to 699........................	8.14	9.49	5.36	6.11	3.38	0.00	10.11	12.93	4.87	4.85	7.33	0.00
700 to 799........................	5.56	6.24	4.36	4.99	2.23	0.34	7.96	9.82	4.57	4.58	5.57	1.78
800 to 999........................	6.60	6.68	7.24	8.37	3.08	0.34	11.25	12.47	9.08	9.17	9.17	2.34
1,000 to 1,499..................	5.96	4.08	12.25	14.21	2.96	0.00	13.66	10.02	21.00	21.31	11.91	0.00
1,500 to 1,999..................	2.16	0.49	7.23	8.44	1.57	0.00	7.12	1.74	17.51	17.87	9.06	0.00
2,000 to 2,999..................	1.43	0.10	5.53	6.48	0.64	0.00	6.46	0.51	18.29	18.75	5.08	0.00
3,000 or more	0.33	0.01	1.28	1.50	0.34	0.00	2.27	0.05	6.42	6.59	4.73	0.00
Average enrollment[7]	521	474	713	815	298	143	521	474	713	815	298	143

[1]Totals differ from those reported in other tables because this table represents data reported by schools rather than by states or school districts. Percentage distribution and average enrollment calculations exclude data for schools not reporting enrollment.
[2]Includes special education, alternative, and other schools not classified by grade span.
[3]Includes schools beginning with grade 6 or below and with no grade higher than 8.
[4]Includes schools with no grade lower than 7.
[5]Includes schools beginning with grade 6 or below and ending with grade 9 or above.

[6]Excludes special education schools, vocational schools, and alternative schools.
[7]Data are for schools reporting their enrollment size. Enrollment data were available for 93,295 out of 96,513 institutions in 2004–05.
NOTE: Detail may not sum to totals because of rounding.
SOURCE: U.S. Department of Education, National Center for Education Statistics, Common Core of Data (CCD), "Public Elementary/Secondary School Universe Survey," 2004–05. (This table was prepared August 2006.)

Table 92. Average enrollment and percentage distribution of public elementary and secondary schools, by type and size: Selected years, 1982–83 through 2004–05

Year	Average enrollment in schools, by type						Percentage distribution of schools, by enrollment size							
			Secondary[3]		Combined									
	Total[1]	Elementary[2]	All schools	Regular schools[6]	elementary/ secondary[4]	Other[6]	Under 200	200 to 299	300 to 399	400 to 499	500 to 599	600 to 699	700 to 999	1,000 or more
1	2	3	4	5	6	7	8	9	10	11	12	13	14	15
1982–83........................	478	399	719	—	478	142	21.9	13.8	15.5	13.1	10.2	7.1	10.2	8.3
1983–84........................	480	401	720	—	475	145	21.7	13.7	15.5	13.2	10.2	7.1	10.3	8.3
1984–85........................	482	403	721	—	476	146	21.5	13.6	15.5	13.2	10.3	7.1	10.4	8.4
1987–88........................	490	424	695	711	420	122	20.3	12.9	14.9	13.8	11.1	7.8	11.2	8.0
1988–89........................	494	433	689	697	412	142	20.0	12.5	14.7	13.8	11.4	8.0	11.6	8.0
1989–90........................	493	441	669	689	402	142	19.8	12.2	14.5	13.7	11.5	8.3	12.0	7.9
1990–91........................	497	449	663	684	398	150	19.7	11.9	14.2	13.6	11.7	8.5	12.3	8.1
1991–92........................	507	458	677	717	407	152	19.1	11.7	14.1	13.5	11.8	8.6	12.8	8.5
1992–93........................	513	464	688	733	423	135	18.6	11.6	13.9	13.5	11.9	8.7	13.1	8.7
1993–94........................	518	468	693	748	418	136	18.6	11.5	13.6	13.5	11.7	8.8	13.3	9.0
1994–95........................	520	471	696	759	412	131	18.6	11.4	13.6	13.4	11.8	8.7	13.3	9.2
1995–96........................	525	476	703	771	401	136	18.5	11.2	13.5	13.4	11.8	8.8	13.4	9.4
1996–97........................	527	478	703	777	387	135	18.7	11.3	13.2	13.2	11.8	8.8	13.6	9.5
1997–98........................	525	478	699	779	374	121	19.3	11.2	13.1	13.3	11.6	8.6	13.4	9.6
1998–99........................	524	478	707	786	290	135	19.6	11.2	13.1	13.2	11.5	8.5	13.3	9.6
1999–2000....................	521	477	706	785	282	123	20.0	11.3	13.3	13.2	11.2	8.4	13.1	9.5
2000–01........................	519	477	714	795	274	136	20.4	11.4	13.2	13.3	11.0	8.2	12.9	9.6
2001–02........................	520	477	718	807	270	138	20.5	11.5	13.3	13.1	10.9	8.1	12.7	9.7
2002–03........................	519	476	720	813	265	136	20.7	11.6	13.4	13.0	10.9	8.1	12.4	9.8
2003–04........................	521	476	722	816	269	142	20.7	11.6	13.5	13.2	10.8	8.0	12.3	9.9
2004–05........................	521	474	713	815	298	143	20.7	11.6	13.5	13.2	10.8	8.1	12.2	9.9

—Not available.
[1]Includes elementary, secondary, combined elementary/secondary, and other schools.
[2]Includes schools beginning with grade 6 or below and with no grade higher than 8.
[3]Includes schools with no grade lower than 7.
[4]Includes schools beginning with grade 6 or below and ending with grade 9 or above.
[5]Includes special education, alternative, and other schools not classified by grade span.
[6]Excludes special education schools, vocational schools, and alternative schools.

NOTE: Data reflect reports by schools rather than by states or school districts. Percentage distribution and average enrollment calculations exclude data for schools not reporting enrollment. Enrollment data were available for 93,295 out of 96,513 institutions in 2004–05. Detail may not sum to totals because of rounding.
SOURCE: U.S. Department of Education, National Center for Education Statistics, Common Core of Data (CCD), "Public Elementary/Secondary School Universe Survey," 1982–83 through 2004–05. (This table was prepared August 2006.)

Table 93. Public elementary and secondary school students, by racial/ethnic enrollment concentration of school: Fall 1999 and fall 2004

Racial/ethnic group	Distribution of students in racial/ethnic group, by percent minority in the school							Distribution of students in each racial/ethnic group, by percent of that racial/ethnic group in the school						
	Total	Less than 10 percent minority	10 to 24 percent minority	25 to 49 percent minority	50 to 74 percent minority	75 to 89 percent minority	90 percent or more minority	Total	Less than 10 percent of group	10 to 24 percent of group	25 to 49 percent of group	50 to 74 percent of group	75 to 89 percent of group	90 percent or more of group
1	2	3	4	5	6	7	8	9	10	11	12	13	14	15
Total students enrolled, 1999	45,537,874	13,141,470	8,534,984	8,592,822	5,843,330	3,343,979	6,081,289	†	†	†	†	†	†	†
White	28,137,113	12,594,720	7,102,808	5,451,173	2,234,767	574,416	179,229	28,137,113	178,395	573,557	2,223,628	5,451,594	7,099,379	12,610,560
Minority	17,400,761	546,750	1,432,176	3,141,649	3,608,563	2,769,563	5,902,060	†	†	†	†	†	†	†
Black	7,769,814	181,646	571,543	1,507,985	1,629,443	1,024,102	2,855,095	7,769,814	713,608	1,177,285	1,899,260	1,362,305	848,824	1,768,532
Hispanic	7,232,942	179,141	473,821	1,069,576	1,475,328	1,359,128	2,675,948	7,232,942	715,450	982,483	1,611,509	1,651,005	1,086,227	1,186,268
Asian/Pacific Islander	1,864,825	134,761	286,953	423,818	413,876	341,153	264,264	1,864,825	774,882	506,473	320,623	166,635	81,173	15,039
American Indian/ Alaska Native	533,180	51,202	99,859	140,270	89,916	45,180	106,753	533,180	244,528	83,022	70,232	40,242	15,890	79,266
Total students enrolled, 2004	46,971,679	10,832,525	8,900,363	9,425,184	6,493,471	3,921,711	7,398,425	†	†	†	†	†	†	†
White	27,097,875	10,332,802	7,405,293	5,988,221	2,475,325	669,235	226,999	27,097,875	226,315	667,177	2,465,554	5,986,940	7,404,804	10,347,085
Minority	19,873,804	499,723	1,495,070	3,436,963	4,018,146	3,252,476	7,171,426	†	†	†	†	†	†	†
Black	8,052,258	161,697	537,360	1,471,089	1,676,646	1,106,992	3,098,474	8,052,258	811,199	1,309,815	1,917,491	1,413,833	836,625	1,763,295
Hispanic	9,111,018	176,140	548,255	1,300,672	1,772,646	1,698,307	3,614,998	9,111,018	808,429	1,226,237	1,934,060	2,093,739	1,440,565	1,607,988
Asian/Pacific Islander	2,131,611	117,108	309,113	510,896	462,332	391,647	340,515	2,131,611	871,113	589,382	357,609	197,293	99,068	17,146
American Indian/ Alaska Native	578,917	44,778	100,342	154,306	106,522	55,530	117,439	578,917	266,097	84,477	83,213	44,097	21,992	79,041
Percent of students enrolled, 1999	100.0	28.9	18.7	18.9	12.8	7.3	13.4	†	†	†	†	†	†	†
White	100.0	44.8	25.2	19.4	7.9	2.0	0.6	100.0	0.6	2.0	7.9	19.4	25.2	44.8
Minority	100.0	3.1	8.2	18.1	20.7	15.9	33.9	†	†	†	†	†	†	†
Black	100.0	2.3	7.4	19.4	21.0	13.2	36.7	100.0	9.2	15.2	24.4	17.5	10.9	22.8
Hispanic	100.0	2.5	6.6	14.8	20.4	18.8	37.0	100.0	9.9	13.6	22.3	22.8	15.0	16.4
Asian/Pacific Islander	100.0	7.2	15.4	22.7	22.2	18.3	14.2	100.0	41.6	27.2	17.2	8.9	4.4	0.8
American Indian/ Alaska Native	100.0	9.6	18.7	26.3	16.9	8.5	20.0	100.0	45.9	15.6	13.2	7.5	3.0	14.9
Percent of students enrolled, 2004	100.0	23.1	18.9	20.1	13.8	8.3	15.8	†	†	†	†	†	†	†
White	100.0	38.1	27.3	22.1	9.1	2.5	0.8	100.0	0.8	2.5	9.1	22.1	27.3	38.2
Minority	100.0	2.5	7.5	17.3	20.2	16.4	36.1	†	†	†	†	†	†	†
Black	100.0	2.0	6.7	18.3	20.8	13.7	38.5	100.0	10.1	16.3	23.8	17.6	10.4	21.9
Hispanic	100.0	1.9	6.0	14.3	19.5	18.6	39.7	100.0	8.9	13.5	21.2	23.0	15.8	17.6
Asian/Pacific Islander	100.0	5.5	14.5	24.0	21.7	18.4	16.0	100.0	40.9	27.6	16.8	9.3	4.6	0.8
American Indian/ Alaska Native	100.0	7.7	17.3	26.7	18.4	9.6	20.3	100.0	46.0	14.6	14.4	7.6	3.8	13.7

†Not applicable.
NOTE: Data reflect racial/ethnic data reported by schools. Because some schools do not report complete racial/ethnic data, totals may differ from figures in other tables. Excludes 1999 data for Idaho, and 1999 and 2004 data for Tennessee because racial/ethnic data were not reported. Race categories exclude persons of Hispanic origin. Detail may not sum to totals because of rounding.
SOURCE: U.S. Department of Education, National Center for Education Statistics, Common Core of Data (CCD), "Public Elementary/Secondary School Universe Survey," 1999 and 2004. (This table was prepared August 2006.)

Table 94. Public elementary and secondary schools, by type and state or jurisdiction: 1990–91, 2000–01, and 2004–05

State or jurisdiction	Total, all schools, 1990–91	Total, all schools, 2000–01	Number of schools, 2004–05											
			Total	Elementary[1]	Secondary[2]	Combined elementary/secondary[3]				Other[4]	Alternative[5]	Special education[5]	Charter[5]	One-teacher schools[5]
						Total	Prekindergarten, kindergarten, or 1st grade to grade 12	Other schools ending with grade 12	Other combined schools					
1	2	3	4	5	6	7	8	9	10	11	12	13	14	15
United States	**84,538**	**93,273**	**96,513**	**65,984**	**23,445**	**5,572**	**3,023**	**1,898**	**651**	**1,512**	**6,070**	**1,972**	**3,399**	**338**
Alabama	1,297	1,517	1,549	944	413	192	130	53	9	0	90	35	0	0
Alaska	498	515	506	188	84	234	216	11	7	0	22	4	21	8
Arizona	1,049	1,724	2,047	1,279	563	157	82	46	29	48	72	12	498	10
Arkansas	1,098	1,138	1,158	728	422	8	3	5	0	0	6	4	17	0
California	7,913	8,773	9,473	6,645	2,360	467	352	96	19	1	1,209	131	495	54
Colorado	1,344	1,632	1,693	1,208	409	76	38	34	4	0	74	16	110	5
Connecticut	985	1,248	1,102	820	244	38	14	10	14	0	38	32	14	0
Delaware	173	191	218	139	47	32	26	6	0	0	23	15	13	0
District of Columbia	181	198	215	144	43	13	7	4	2	15	9	14	40	0
Florida	2,516	3,316	3,682	2,420	475	787	380	385	22	0	179	124	319	9
Georgia	1,734	1,946	2,353	1,665	365	42	17	20	5	281	213	52	51	0
Hawaii	235	261	285	207	55	23	18	1	4	0	1	3	27	2
Idaho	582	673	690	415	223	52	32	14	6	0	73	10	20	12
Illinois	4,239	4,342	4,380	3,157	1,001	137	46	63	28	85	165	248	29	0
Indiana	1,915	1,976	2,005	1,449	464	69	27	34	8	23	42	54	28	0
Iowa	1,588	1,534	1,532	1,034	455	43	6	37	0	0	79	10	2	6
Kansas	1,477	1,430	1,400	975	422	2	1	1	0	1	0	0	20	0
Kentucky	1,400	1,526	1,420	1,002	319	99	25	74	0	0	150	10	0	0
Louisiana	1,533	1,530	1,531	1,027	308	184	133	46	5	12	123	37	17	0
Maine	747	714	684	509	155	20	13	7	0	0	0	3	0	5
Maryland	1,220	1,383	1,421	1,083	265	40	25	9	6	33	78	49	1	0
Massachusetts	1,842	1,905	1,878	1,473	348	53	26	17	10	4	27	5	57	1
Michigan	3,313	3,998	4,039	2,727	848	332	239	69	24	132	253	184	247	7
Minnesota	1,590	2,362	2,591	1,263	850	113	24	57	32	365	661	282	129	2
Mississippi	972	1,030	1,049	600	326	114	70	43	1	9	60	0	1	0
Missouri	2,199	2,368	2,363	1,551	654	158	76	79	3	0	81	23	0	1
Montana	900	879	854	491	363	0	0	0	0	0	4	2	0	68
Nebraska	1,506	1,326	1,256	857	334	65	65	0	0	0	0	46	0	74
Nevada	354	511	561	412	136	10	2	5	3	3	34	6	20	1
New Hampshire	439	526	477	379	98	0	0	0	0	0	0	0	3	3
New Jersey	2,272	2,410	2,468	1,892	464	28	2	9	17	84	0	79	50	0
New Mexico	681	765	834	587	224	23	9	7	7	0	59	16	44	0
New York	4,010	4,336	4,624	3,223	1,034	196	88	69	39	171	180	70	61	1
North Carolina	1,955	2,207	2,290	1,786	412	92	34	38	20	0	71	21	97	0
North Dakota	663	579	551	319	198	1	0	1	0	33	0	30	0	2
Ohio	3,731	3,916	3,997	2,727	1,019	214	62	67	85	37	8	15	255	0
Oklahoma	1,880	1,821	1,787	1,201	581	5	0	2	3	0	0	0	12	1
Oregon	1,199	1,273	1,289	854	300	135	70	12	53	0	40	2	57	17
Pennsylvania	3,260	3,252	3,258	2,369	812	68	21	26	21	9	12	12	109	0
Rhode Island	309	328	342	265	72	5	4	1	0	0	8	4	11	0
South Carolina	1,097	1,127	1,145	847	277	21	8	10	3	0	12	10	24	0
South Dakota	802	769	722	434	263	25	9	16	0	0	24	5	0	23
Tennessee	1,543	1,624	1,692	1,257	361	67	32	34	1	7	29	16	7	0
Texas	5,991	7,519	8,070	5,312	2,095	663	329	230	104	0	1,072	3	296	0
Utah	714	793	922	552	327	42	24	11	7	1	109	43	27	3
Vermont	397	393	392	276	70	46	38	8	0	0	2	60	0	3
Virginia	1,811	1,969	2,070	1,485	403	25	14	10	1	157	126	52	5	0
Washington	1,936	2,305	2,246	1,424	586	236	148	55	33	0	273	107	0	6
West Virginia	1,015	840	787	583	185	18	5	10	3	1	25	8	0	0
Wisconsin	2,018	2,182	2,237	1,551	604	82	22	48	12	0	223	8	163	0
Wyoming	415	393	378	249	109	20	11	8	1	0	31	0	2	14
Bureau of Indian Affairs	—	189	189	102	26	60	53	3	4	1	0	0	0	26 [6]
DoDDS, domestic	—	71	68	59	7	2	1	1	0	0	0	0	0	0
DoDDS, overseas	—	156	153	105	38	10	8	2	0	0	0	0	0	0
Other jurisdictions														
American Samoa	30	31	31	24	6	0	0	0	0	1	0	1	0	0
Guam	35	38	36	32	4	0	0	0	0	0	0	0	0	0
Northern Marianas	26	29	32	24	6	0	0	0	0	2	1	0	0	0
Puerto Rico	1,619	1,543	1,523	907	391	191	3	7	181	34	25	28	120	0
Virgin Islands	33	36	34	23	10	1	0	0	1	0	1	0	0	0

—Not available.
[1]Includes schools beginning with grade 6 or below and with no grade higher than 8.
[2]Includes schools with no grade lower than 7.
[3]Includes schools beginning with grade 6 or below and ending with grade 9 or above.
[4]Includes schools not classified by grade span.
[5]Schools are also included under elementary, secondary, combined, or other as appropriate.

[6]Data are for 1998-99.
NOTE: DoDDS = Department of Defense dependents schools.
SOURCE: U.S. Department of Education, National Center for Education Statistics, Common Core of Data (CCD), "Public Elementary/Secondary School Universe Survey," 1990–91, 2000–01, and 2004–05. (This table was prepared August 2006.)

Table 95. Public elementary schools, by grade span, average school size, and state or jurisdiction: 2004–05

State or jurisdiction	Total, all elementary schools	Total, all regular elementary schools[1]	Schools, by grade span						Average number of students per school[2]	
			Prekindergarten, kindergarten, or 1st grade to grades 3 or 4	Prekindergarten, kindergarten, or 1st grade to grade 5	Prekindergarten, kindergarten, or 1st grade to grade 6	Prekindergarten, kindergarten, or 1st grade to grade 8	Grade 4, 5, or 6 to grade 6, 7, or 8	Other grade spans	All elementary schools	Regular elementary schools[1]
1	2	3	4	5	6	7	8	9	10	11
United States	65,984	64,964	4,831	23,495	13,015	5,743	12,530	6,370	474	480
Alabama	944	931	89	306	165	67	214	103	477	479
Alaska	188	187	3	24	108	20	17	16	324	326
Arizona	1,279	1,249	70	238	349	366	173	83	512	517
Arkansas	728	726	126	139	226	5	144	88	390	391
California	6,645	6,461	189	2,287	2,213	766	990	200	603	619
Colorado	1,208	1,205	28	557	270	61	227	65	410	411
Connecticut	820	806	98	299	109	59	146	109	455	461
Delaware	139	137	28	56	7	5	32	11	540	543
District of Columbia	144	142	7	21	78	12	18	8	327	331
Florida	2,420	2,420	23	1,553	157	94	509	84	740	740
Georgia	1,665	1,661	39	993	50	15	415	153	659	660
Hawaii	207	206	1	66	108	5	25	2	550	552
Idaho	415	410	39	113	147	22	68	26	375	377
Illinois	3,157	3,057	309	774	399	700	539	436	444	453
Indiana	1,449	1,433	119	601	340	29	274	86	458	461
Iowa	1,034	1,027	96	345	214	17	226	136	286	288
Kansas	975	975	86	299	241	94	185	70	300	300
Kentucky	1,002	990	49	479	137	96	201	40	439	444
Louisiana	1,027	1,000	90	330	158	88	224	137	460	467
Maine	509	509	60	99	75	101	89	85	249	249
Maryland	1,083	1,060	14	630	134	39	215	51	532	538
Massachusetts	1,473	1,467	200	508	159	98	289	219	434	435
Michigan	2,727	2,711	229	1,005	402	178	525	388	404	405
Minnesota	1,263	1,111	116	331	384	54	206	172	390	436
Mississippi	600	599	81	119	122	42	133	103	519	519
Missouri	1,551	1,540	124	502	328	117	297	183	371	372
Montana	491	488	20	63	221	114	51	22	172	173
Nebraska	857	850	0	0	540	216	77	24	203	204
Nevada	412	403	6	194	104	15	72	21	669	682
New Hampshire	379	379	54	118	40	47	78	42	358	358
New Jersey	1,892	1,884	94	91	186	470	370	681	480	481
New Mexico	587	573	28	230	122	13	131	63	354	361
New York	3,223	3,203	272	1,235	507	128	688	393	563	564
North Carolina	1,786	1,779	67	1,019	55	111	438	96	538	540
North Dakota	319	319	10	42	185	45	23	14	179	179
Ohio	2,727	2,725	372	788	585	165	528	289	408	408
Oklahoma	1,201	1,201	64	340	159	310	219	109	354	354
Oregon	854	838	48	381	154	68	167	36	379	382
Pennsylvania	2,369	2,369	279	835	480	133	445	197	468	468
Rhode Island	265	265	25	119	33	3	47	38	382	382
South Carolina	847	845	51	425	63	25	216	67	568	569
South Dakota	434	434	14	115	98	108	78	21	184	184
Tennessee	1,257	1,251	156	475	108	181	272	65	502	503
Texas	5,312	5,202	596	2,055	751	106	1,196	608	545	554
Utah	552	541	14	104	367	7	39	21	511	520
Vermont	276	243	12	26	112	67	17	42	205	226
Virginia	1,485	1,484	41	841	144	8	305	146	541	541
Washington	1,424	1,360	64	420	525	71	235	109	430	443
West Virginia	583	580	86	217	95	38	108	39	321	323
Wisconsin	1,551	1,480	119	639	205	127	308	153	350	354
Wyoming	249	248	26	49	96	17	41	20	194	195
Bureau of Indian Affairs	102	102	5	4	22	67	3	1	495	495
DoDDS, domestic	59	59	17	16	4	2	12	8	677	677
DoDDS, overseas	105	105	6	24	46	6	18	5	451	451
Other jurisdictions										
American Samoa	24	24	1	0	0	21	1	1	421	421
Guam	32	32	0	24	0	0	7	1	301	301
Northern Marianas	24	24	0	2	10	0	2	10	293	293
Puerto Rico	907	876	49	6	812	4	23	13	393	393
Virgin Islands	23	23	0	1	21	0	1	0	—	—

—Not available.
[1]Excludes special education and alternative schools.
[2]Average for schools reporting enrollment data. Enrollment data were available for 65,691 out of 65,984 regular institutions in 2004–05.

NOTE: Includes schools beginning with grade 6 or below and with no grade higher than 8. Excludes schools not reported by grade level, such as some special education schools for the disabled. DoDDS = Department of Defense dependents schools.
SOURCE: U.S. Department of Education, National Center for Education Statistics, Common Core of Data (CCD), "Public Elementary/Secondary School Universe Survey," 2004–05. (This table was prepared August 2006.)

Table 96. Public secondary schools, by grade span, average school size, and state or jurisdiction: 2004–05

State or jurisdiction	Total, all secondary schools	Total, all regular secondary schools[1]	Schools, by grade span							Vocational schools[2]	Average number of students per school[3]	
			Grades 7 to 8 and 7 to 9	Grades 7 to 12	Grades 8 to 12	Grades 9 to 12	Grades 10 to 12	Other spans ending with grade 12	Other grade spans		All secondary schools	Regular secondary schools[1]
1	2	3	4	5	6	7	8	9	10	11	12	13
United States	23,445	19,028	3,250	3,195	750	14,097	757	351	1,045	1,192	713	815
Alabama	413	310	33	92	6	240	30	4	8	77	674	699
Alaska	84	71	17	20	1	44	2	0	0	2	528	598
Arizona	563	450	82	41	7	411	16	1	5	95	670	721
Arkansas	422	396	56	173	5	114	46	2	26	22	443	447
California	2,360	1,441	347	294	36	1,598	44	21	20	76	948	1,424
Colorado	409	346	62	66	5	262	5	3	6	4	613	694
Connecticut	244	187	35	11	8	162	5	17	6	17	791	951
Delaware	47	34	9	1	27	9	0	0	1	7	991	1,048
District of Columbia	43	36	9	2	0	31	0	0	1	2	445	482
Florida	475	451	16	32	14	393	4	6	10	32	1,487	1,522
Georgia	365	351	16	5	5	329	3	0	7	0	1,194	1,234
Hawaii	55	54	12	8	0	34	0	0	1	0	1,189	1,208
Idaho	223	154	39	48	3	116	13	0	4	10	449	581
Illinois	1,001	798	162	51	14	631	16	34	93	51	703	825
Indiana	464	408	69	92	6	253	3	3	38	29	799	836
Iowa	455	384	49	85	0	304	10	3	4	0	384	441
Kansas	422	422	64	88	3	256	10	1	0	0	411	411
Kentucky	319	253	27	46	6	236	2	1	1	8	662	780
Louisiana	308	273	46	44	180	19	1	1	17	9	689	744
Maine	155	128	17	12	1	123	1	0	1	27	541	541
Maryland	265	201	19	7	5	197	1	6	30	25	1,132	1,325
Massachusetts	348	296	38	34	8	261	0	2	5	39	875	914
Michigan	848	710	105	95	14	564	18	8	44	44	709	792
Minnesota	850	475	75	217	43	291	86	75	63	13	387	647
Mississippi	326	230	33	62	6	186	26	3	10	88	644	644
Missouri	654	581	69	190	2	349	21	11	12	61	553	556
Montana	363	360	187	0	0	174	1	0	1	0	172	173
Nebraska	334	334	32	187	0	112	3	0	0	0	349	349
Nevada	136	112	22	14	9	76	3	6	6	1	917	1,088
New Hampshire	98	98	16	0	1	78	0	1	2	0	726	726
New Jersey	464	403	63	36	5	334	13	1	12	55	1,003	1,097
New Mexico	224	177	39	21	9	126	15	0	14	2	513	618
New York	1,034	925	93	137	17	632	17	4	134	25	912	934
North Carolina	412	377	20	18	5	347	4	3	15	8	1,000	1,069
North Dakota	198	191	13	130	3	38	4	1	9	7	227	227
Ohio	1,019	930	151	138	51	603	12	12	52	90	675	686
Oklahoma	581	581	99	0	0	403	59	3	17	0	347	347
Oregon	300	281	35	49	8	204	0	0	4	0	687	724
Pennsylvania	812	723	102	157	12	453	59	11	18	82	892	903
Rhode Island	72	53	8	1	0	57	4	0	2	10	826	947
South Carolina	277	226	30	13	3	203	15	9	4	39	917	962
South Dakota	263	256	90	0	1	172	0	0	0	3	165	166
Tennessee	361	331	33	25	2	282	12	0	7	23	837	865
Texas	2,095	1,505	360	211	120	1,085	44	43	232	0	669	904
Utah	327	220	96	52	12	75	74	3	15	2	642	915
Vermont	70	56	8	18	0	44	0	0	0	14	626	626
Virginia	403	334	31	6	38	264	4	5	55	48	1,112	1,173
Washington	586	413	102	73	39	321	25	13	13	11	646	845
West Virginia	185	130	16	25	1	123	10	3	7	33	592	683
Wisconsin	604	478	67	60	7	414	12	31	13	1	519	621
Wyoming	109	94	31	8	2	64	4	0	0	0	324	361
Bureau of Indian Affairs	26	26	1	8	0	17	0	0	0	0	699	783
DoDDS, domestic	7	7	2	0	0	5	0	0	0	0	2,230	2,230
DoDDS, overseas	38	38	2	21	0	15	0	0	0	0	470	470
Other jurisdictions												
American Samoa	6	5	0	0	0	6	0	0	0	1	518	518
Guam	4	4	0	0	0	4	0	0	0	0	718	718
Northern Marianas	6	6	1	1	0	4	0	0	0	0	569	574
Puerto Rico	391	367	195	28	0	5	152	0	11	15	793	883
Virgin Islands	10	8	5	0	0	5	0	0	0	1	—	—

—Not available.
[1]Excludes vocational, special education, and alternative schools.
[2]Vocational schools are also included under appropriate grade span.
[3]Average for schools reporting enrollment data. Enrollment data were available for 22,278 out of 23,445 regular institutions in 2004–05.

NOTE: Includes schools with no grade lower than 7. Excludes schools not reported by grade level, such as some special education schools for the disabled. DoDDS = Department of Defense dependents schools.
SOURCE: U.S. Department of Education, National Center for Education Statistics, Common Core of Data (CCD), "Public Elementary/Secondary School Universe Survey," 2004–05. (This table was prepared August 2006.)

Table 97. Number and enrollment of traditional public and public charter elementary and secondary schools and percentages of students, teachers, and schools, by selected characteristics: 2003–04

Selected characteristic	Total elementary and secondary schools			Elementary schools			Secondary schools			Combined elementary/secondary schools		
	Total, all schools	Traditional (non-charter) schools	Public charter schools	Total, all schools	Traditional (non-charter) schools	Public charter schools	Total, all schools	Traditional (non-charter) schools	Public charter schools	Total, all schools	Traditional (non-charter) schools	Public charter schools
1	2	3	4	5	6	7	8	9	10	11	12	13
Number of schools	88,113 (282.8)	85,934 (284.7)	2,179 (41.9)	61,572 (387.9)	60,419 (375.6)	1,152 (88.2)	19,886 (305.4)	19,365 (297.0)	521 (71.1)	6,655 (292.3)	6,150 (275.5)	505 (70.6)
Enrollment (in thousands)	47,316 (497.8)	46,689 (507.2)	627 (42.1)	29,954 (307.7)	29,588 (304.4)	366 (32.6)	15,301 (443.3)	15,186 (443.9)	116 (20.4)	2,060 (124.5)	1,915 (124.1)	145 (22.8)
Percentage distribution of students												
Race/ethnicity												
White	60.3 (0.48)	60.6 (0.49)	43.4 (3.24)	57.8 (0.63)	58.0 (0.63)	42.9 (4.30)	63.4 (1.00)	63.6 (1.00)	34.5 (6.01)	74.2 (1.57)	75.9 (1.55)	51.8 (5.77)
Black	16.8 (0.35)	16.6 (0.35)	29.7 (3.06)	17.7 (0.46)	17.5 (0.47)	31.3 (3.96)	15.7 (0.52)	15.6 (0.52)	28.2 (7.72)	11.6 (1.12)	10.5 (0.97)	26.8 (6.60)
Hispanic	17.7 (0.49)	17.6 (0.49)	21.7 (2.29)	19.6 (0.69)	19.6 (0.70)	20.6 (3.55)	15.0 (0.81)	14.9 (0.82)	32.7 (4.85)	9.0 (1.10)	8.5 (1.18)	15.8 (3.27)
Asian/Pacific Islander	3.9 (0.19)	3.9 (0.19)	3.8 (0.81)	3.8 (0.14)	3.7 (0.14)	4.5 (1.12)	4.6 (0.43)	4.7 (0.43)	1.5 (0.35)	1.6 (0.30)	1.4 (0.31)	4.0 (1.90)
American Indian/Alaska Native	1.3 (0.04)	1.3 (0.04)	1.4 (0.24)	1.2 (0.05)	1.2 (0.05)	0.7 (0.12)	1.2 (0.06)	1.2 (0.06)	3.2 (1.13)	3.6 (0.29)	3.7 (0.32)	1.7 (0.54)
Percentage distribution of teachers												
Race/ethnicity[1]												
White	84.4 (0.33)	84.5 (0.33)	71.1 (2.51)	83.4 (0.44)	83.5 (0.45)	72.4 (3.31)	85.4 (0.48)	85.5 (0.48)	62.4 (5.35)	90.1 (0.69)	91.3 (0.65)	73.2 (3.57)
Black	8.3 (0.22)	8.2 (0.22)	16.4 (2.14)	8.6 (0.28)	8.5 (0.29)	15.5 (2.98)	8.0 (0.37)	7.9 (0.36)	21.4 (4.72)	5.9 (0.57)	5.2 (0.53)	15.3 (3.55)
Hispanic	5.7 (0.28)	5.7 (0.29)	8.8 (1.34)	6.4 (0.42)	6.3 (0.43)	8.8 (2.05)	4.9 (0.30)	4.8 (0.30)	10.7 (2.87)	2.1 (0.27)	1.7 (0.26)	7.7 (1.83)
Asian/Pacific Islander	1.3 (0.05)	1.3 (0.05)	2.6 (0.46)	1.3 (0.06)	1.3 (0.06)	3.0 (0.72)	1.4 (0.10)	1.4 (0.10)	2.3 (0.93)	0.6 (0.12)	0.5 (0.12)	1.7 (0.66)
American Indian/Alaska Native	0.4 (0.02)	0.4 (0.02)	1.2 (0.39)	0.3 (0.02)	0.3 (0.02)	0.3 (0.13)	0.4 (0.03)	0.4 (0.03)	3.1 (1.81)	1.3 (0.18)	1.2 (0.18)	2.1 (0.99)
Years of full-time teaching experience												
Less than 3	12.2 (1.23)	12.0 (1.30)	29.3 (1.67)	12.0 (1.63)	11.8 (1.64)	27.1 (2.27)	12.2 (0.66)	12.0 (0.67)	34.4 (2.90)	15.0 (1.35)	13.8 (1.36)	31.3 (3.80)
3 to 9	32.9 (0.34)	32.8 (0.38)	48.4 (1.89)	33.3 (0.52)	33.1 (0.53)	50.6 (2.97)	32.6 (0.52)	32.5 (0.52)	44.5 (3.22)	31.8 (1.26)	30.8 (1.20)	45.9 (3.77)
10 to 20	28.4 (0.59)	28.8 (0.62)	14.5 (1.58)	29.2 (0.88)	29.4 (0.89)	14.9 (2.43)	27.3 (0.45)	27.4 (0.45)	10.9 (2.96)	28.4 (1.27)	29.3 (1.35)	15.6 (2.53)
More than 20	26.5 (0.77)	26.4 (0.82)	7.7 (1.23)	25.5 (1.06)	25.7 (1.07)	7.4 (2.01)	28.0 (0.59)	28.1 (0.59)	10.2 (2.19)	24.8 (1.17)	26.1 (1.22)	7.3 (1.80)
Percentage distribution of schools												
Size of enrollment												
Less than 300	29.2 (0.70)	28.2 (0.73)	67.9 (2.91)	25.6 (0.89)	25.0 (0.89)	60.3 (4.60)	29.0 (1.42)	27.6 (1.47)	81.4 (4.59)	62.5 (2.07)	61.8 (2.28)	71.4 (5.67)
300 to 599	38.9 (0.76)	39.4 (0.79)	19.2 (2.35)	46.1 (1.08)	46.5 (1.10)	23.7 (3.92)	22.2 (0.94)	22.5 (0.95)	12.0 (3.17)	22.8 (1.82)	23.4 (1.97)	16.4 (3.92)
600 to 999	21.6 (0.62)	21.9 (0.63)	9.9 (1.58)	23.6 (0.82)	23.8 (0.83)	13.4 (2.86)	19.4 (0.87)	19.8 (0.88)	4.4 (3.32)	9.7 (1.22)	9.9 (1.32)	7.3 (3.43)
1,000 or more	10.3 (0.38)	10.5 (0.38)	3.0 (0.75)	4.7 (0.35)	4.8 (0.35)	2.6 (1.04)	29.3 (1.20)	30.0 (1.26)	2.1 (1.35)	4.9 (0.73)	4.9 (0.78)	4.9 (2.05)
Percent minority enrollment												
Less than 10.0	32.1 (0.58)	32.5 (0.59)	14.8 (3.96)	30.0 (0.69)	30.3 (0.71)	13.8 (4.54)	35.6 (1.31)	36.3 (1.31)	11.8 (11.16)	40.7 (2.04)	42.4 (2.12)	20.1 (7.08)
10.0 to 24.9	18.5 (0.65)	18.5 (0.65)	19.7 (3.64)	19.3 (0.85)	19.3 (0.85)	19.5 (4.68)	17.8 (1.22)	17.9 (1.26)	15.9 (4.19)	13.4 (1.86)	12.5 (1.80)	24.2 (7.19)
25.0 to 49.9	17.0 (0.49)	17.0 (0.49)	16.1 (2.69)	17.2 (0.64)	17.2 (0.64)	17.3 (4.10)	17.2 (0.81)	17.3 (0.84)	13.2 (4.30)	14.3 (1.48)	14.1 (1.60)	16.4 (5.54)
50.0 to 74.9	13.1 (0.59)	13.1 (0.60)	12.3 (2.45)	12.4 (0.68)	12.3 (0.69)	13.0 (3.60)	13.7 (1.21)	13.8 (1.22)	11.2 (3.72)	17.6 (2.23)	18.1 (2.35)	11.6 (5.40)
75.0 or more	19.4 (0.57)	18.9 (0.58)	37.1 (3.68)	21.2 (0.76)	20.9 (0.78)	36.4 (4.91)	15.6 (1.09)	14.7 (1.10)	47.9 (8.75)	14.0 (1.34)	12.9 (1.45)	27.7 (7.38)
Percent of students eligible for free or reduced-price lunch												
Less than 15.0	22.0 (0.59)	21.6 (0.60)	38.9 (4.05)	19.4 (0.77)	19.1 (0.80)	33.5 (5.16)	30.7 (1.00)	30.1 (1.02)	55.6 (7.86)	19.9 (2.01)	18.7 (2.07)	33.9 (7.92)
15.0 to 29.9	16.8 (0.59)	17.0 (0.61)	9.7 (2.87)	16.0 (0.76)	16.2 (0.77)	10.1 (4.44)	21.0 (0.86)	21.4 (0.91)	6.7 (4.73)	11.1 (1.29)	11.0 (1.32)	11.7 (4.72)
30.0 to 49.9	22.3 (0.66)	22.4 (0.67)	16.4 (2.84)	22.3 (0.85)	22.4 (0.87)	18.0 (4.16)	21.3 (0.89)	21.5 (0.91)	13.0 (4.80)	25.0 (2.12)	25.7 (2.27)	16.2 (5.47)
50.0 to 74.9	21.0 (0.58)	21.3 (0.60)	12.5 (2.62)	22.3 (0.71)	22.5 (0.72)	13.7 (3.78)	15.4 (1.38)	15.4 (1.41)	12.8 (5.15)	25.9 (2.29)	27.2 (2.45)	9.6 (2.77)
75.0 or more	17.9 (0.65)	17.8 (0.66)	22.5 (3.35)	19.9 (0.68)	19.8 (0.69)	24.7 (4.63)	11.6 (1.50)	11.6 (1.53)	11.8 (5.37)	18.2 (1.79)	17.3 (1.77)	28.6 (8.45)

See notes at end of table.

Table 97. Number and enrollment of traditional public and public charter elementary and secondary schools and percentages of students, teachers, and schools, by selected characteristics: 2003–04—Continued

Selected characteristic	Total elementary and secondary schools			Elementary schools			Secondary schools			Combined elementary/secondary schools		
	Total, all schools	Traditional (non-charter) schools	Public charter schools	Total, all schools	Traditional (non-charter) schools	Public charter schools	Total, all schools	Traditional (non-charter) schools	Public charter schools	Total, all schools	Traditional (non-charter) schools	Public charter schools
1	2	3	4	5	6	7	8	9	10	11	12	13
Percent of schools with selected programs and services												
Programs with special instructional approaches	22.4 (0.65)	21.7 (0.67)	49.0 (3.90)	18.1 (0.74)	17.7 (0.76)	42.3 (5.04)	29.6 (1.62)	28.7 (1.73)	64.3 (7.05)	40.4 (2.69)	39.7 (2.89)	48.4 (8.68)
Talented/gifted program	68.9 (0.67)	69.6 (0.68)	38.9 (4.15)	70.3 (0.86)	71.0 (0.87)	38.4 (6.32)	71.7 (1.47)	72.4 (1.57)	42.8 (7.13)	47.0 (2.53)	47.9 (2.58)	35.9 (7.51)
Immersion in a foreign language program	4.0 (0.40)	4.1 (0.40)	2.5 (1.04)	4.7 (0.55)	4.7 (0.55)	4.2 (1.99)	3.0 (0.41)	3.0 (0.42)	‡ (†)	1.1 (0.29)	1.2 (0.31)	‡ (†)
A program for students with discipline or adjustment problems	31.9 (0.78)	32.3 (0.80)	17.8 (3.71)	26.7 (0.86)	27.0 (0.88)	11.9 (3.30)	46.9 (1.80)	47.5 (1.88)	24.4 (9.84)	35.7 (2.56)	36.6 (2.73)	24.4 (8.55)
Extended day program for students who need academic assistance	46.9 (0.72)	46.8 (0.76)	50.1 (3.98)	49.7 (0.83)	49.7 (0.86)	50.1 (6.11)	41.2 (1.33)	41.0 (1.36)	49.8 (7.22)	37.0 (2.30)	36.0 (2.42)	50.3 (8.26)
Before-school or after-school day care programs	33.1 (0.81)	32.9 (0.83)	40.4 (3.38)	44.1 (1.07)	43.8 (1.08)	61.4 (5.82)	5.4 (0.54)	5.3 (0.55)	8.4 (3.84)	13.8 (1.90)	12.8 (2.02)	25.4 (6.26)
Specialized career academy	6.4 (0.30)	6.4 (0.31)	6.5 (1.48)	0.8 (0.17)	0.8 (0.17)	‡ (†)	22.9 (1.08)	23.1 (1.14)	14.3 (4.10)	9.1 (1.18)	8.8 (1.08)	13.3 (5.95)
Advanced Placement (AP) courses	16.2 (0.40)	16.4 (0.41)	8.8 (1.78)	1.7 (0.32)	1.7 (0.33)	‡ (†)	56.0 (1.28)	57.1 (1.34)	14.5 (3.98)	31.9 (2.00)	32.6 (2.08)	22.8 (5.59)
International Baccalaureate	0.7 (0.11)	0.7 (0.11)	1.1 (0.67)	0.4 (0.13)	0.4 (0.13)	‡ (†)	2.0 (0.25)	2.0 (0.26)	‡ (†)	0.4 (0.21)	‡ (†)	4.4 (2.84)
Distance learning courses	12.2 (0.36)	12.2 (0.36)	8.4 (3.42)	2.6 (0.31)	2.7 (0.32)	‡ (†)	32.1 (1.15)	32.4 (1.12)	21.2 (9.75)	40.3 (2.25)	42.5 (2.52)	14.2 (5.58)
Entire school is for suspended students[2]	3.5 (0.35)	3.4 (0.35)	8.0 (3.12)	0.4 (0.17)	0.5 (0.18)	‡ (†)	7.5 (1.30)	7.0 (1.31)	25.5 (9.54)	20.4 (0.05)	21.4 (0.15)	8.0 (3.92)

†Not applicable.
‡Reporting standards not met.
[1]Based on data reported by schools.
[2]Entire school specifically for students who have been suspended or expelled, who have dropped out, or who have been referred for behavioral or adjustment problems.

NOTE: Race categories exclude persons of Hispanic origin. Detail may not sum to totals because of rounding. Standard errors appear in parentheses.
SOURCE: U.S. Department of Education, National Center for Education Statistics, Schools and Staffing Survey (SASS), "Public School Questionnaire," 2003–04; and "Public Teacher Questionnaire," 2003–04. (This table was prepared June 2006.)

Table 98. Percentage of public schools with building deficiencies and renovation plans, by level, enrollment size, metropolitan status, and free lunch eligibility: 1999

Type of school condition	All public schools	Instructional level[1]		Size of school enrollment			Metropolitan status[2]			Percent of students eligible for free or reduced-price lunch			
		Elementary	Secondary	Less than 300	300 to 599	600 or more	Central city	Urban fringe/ large town	Rural/ small town	Less than 20 percent	20 to 39 percent	40 to 69 percent	70 percent or more
1	2	3	4	5	6	7	8	9	10	11	12	13	14
Estimated number of schools[3]	78,313 (632.0)	59,940 (—)	15,505 (—)	18,095 (—)	31,942 (—)	28,275 (—)	21,294 (—)	27,846 (—)	29,173 (—)	21,216 (—)	20,915 (—)	20,947 (—)	15,234 (—)
Estimated enrollment, in thousands	45,000 (575.3)	— (†)	— (†)	— (†)	— (†)	— (†)	— (†)	— (†)	— (†)	— (†)	— (†)	— (†)	— (†)
Percent of schools with temporary buildings	39 (2.0)	40 (2.5)	37 (2.9)	21 (4.3)	39 (3.1)	50 (2.5)	45 (3.6)	44 (3.1)	29 (2.9)	35 (3.3)	36 (3.0)	42 (3.7)	43 (4.6)
Percent of buildings in less than adequate condition													
Original buildings	19 (1.6)	19 (1.8)	21 (2.3)	22 (3.8)	19 (2.4)	18 (2.0)	20 (2.7)	18 (2.6)	19 (2.5)	20 (3.1)	18 (2.4)	16 (2.5)	25 (4.2)
Permanent additions	16 (1.8)	17 (2.1)	14 (2.5)	16 (3.5)	17 (2.7)	14 (2.4)	18 (3.6)	17 (2.8)	14 (2.5)	8 (2.3)	13 (3.3)	16 (3.2)	30 (5.1)
Temporary buildings	19 (2.2)	18 (2.4)	21 (4.5)	— (†)	22 (3.5)	20 (3.0)	19 (3.8)	18 (3.4)	19 (4.1)	17 (4.4)	16 (3.9)	19 (3.3)	25 (5.3)
Percent of schools with building features rated as less than adequate													
At least one feature less than adequate	50 (1.5)	49 (1.9)	56 (3.0)	55 (4.6)	50 (2.9)	49 (2.3)	56 (3.7)	44 (3.2)	52 (2.6)	45 (3.4)	45 (3.7)	53 (3.3)	63 (4.5)
Roofs	22 (1.7)	22 (1.9)	26 (3.1)	24 (3.8)	22 (2.9)	22 (1.9)	23 (3.2)	19 (2.6)	25 (2.9)	18 (2.9)	21 (2.8)	22 (2.9)	32 (4.6)
Framing, floors, and foundations	14 (1.3)	14 (1.6)	16 (2.2)	19 (3.1)	12 (2.3)	14 (1.8)	12 (2.5)	13 (1.9)	17 (2.5)	14 (2.4)	11 (2.3)	16 (2.3)	17 (3.9)
Exterior walls, finishes, windows, doors	24 (1.5)	23 (1.9)	27 (2.7)	31 (3.9)	21 (2.6)	23 (1.8)	27 (3.1)	21 (2.5)	25 (3.0)	21 (2.6)	21 (2.8)	25 (2.6)	30 (4.4)
Interior finishes, trim	17 (1.4)	17 (1.7)	20 (2.3)	20 (3.2)	16 (2.4)	18 (2.1)	20 (3.2)	16 (2.1)	17 (2.4)	17 (2.5)	14 (2.4)	14 (2.6)	26 (4.2)
Plumbing	25 (1.7)	24 (1.9)	28 (2.7)	28 (4.4)	27 (3.2)	20 (2.1)	28 (3.4)	21 (2.3)	26 (2.5)	23 (3.1)	23 (2.8)	23 (3.4)	32 (4.3)
Heating, ventilation, air conditioning	29 (1.5)	28 (1.8)	34 (2.5)	28 (3.8)	32 (2.9)	26 (1.8)	30 (3.0)	27 (2.5)	31 (2.7)	28 (3.0)	26 (2.7)	29 (2.8)	35 (4.2)
Electric power	22 (1.4)	21 (1.8)	25 (2.6)	23 (3.5)	21 (2.9)	22 (1.8)	26 (2.9)	21 (2.2)	19 (2.4)	18 (2.5)	20 (2.4)	21 (2.6)	30 (4.6)
Electrical lighting	17 (1.5)	17 (1.9)	19 (2.6)	19 (3.2)	17 (2.7)	16 (1.8)	18 (2.7)	15 (2.0)	20 (2.3)	14 (2.1)	15 (2.3)	18 (2.7)	24 (5.2)
Life safety features	20 (1.3)	19 (1.6)	22 (2.8)	26 (4.1)	21 (2.4)	16 (1.7)	21 (2.9)	17 (2.1)	23 (2.3)	16 (2.6)	18 (2.1)	22 (3.3)	27 (3.5)
Percent of schools needing to spend money to bring schools into good overall condition	76 (1.5)	75 (1.7)	79 (2.8)	82 (3.6)	74 (2.3)	74 (2.0)	81 (2.7)	70 (3.1)	78 (2.1)	73 (3.2)	73 (3.2)	77 (2.7)	84 (3.4)
Cost per student for all schools	$2,900 (159)	$2,500 (159)	$3,400 (379)	$3,900 (602)	$3,300 (376)	$2,500 (220)	$2,900 (327)	$2,600 (251)	$3,300 (339)	$2,900 (292)	$2,800 (301)	$3,000 (424)	$2,600 (325)
Cost per student for schools needing to spend money	$3,800 (192)	$3,500 (217)	$4,300 (442)	$4,800 (702)	$4,600 (503)	$3,300 (288)	$3,500 (384)	$3,800 (335)	$4,400 (442)	$4,100 (427)	$3,900 (383)	$3,900 (509)	$3,200 (366)
Percent of schools rating environment factors as unsatisfactory													
At least one factor is unsatisfactory	43 (1.6)	41 (2.1)	48 (2.8)	45 (4.6)	46 (3.0)	39 (2.0)	47 (3.8)	37 (2.9)	47 (2.9)	38 (3.4)	42 (3.2)	41 (3.6)	55 (4.4)
Lighting	12 (1.4)	12 (1.8)	12 (2.0)	12 (2.9)	14 (2.4)	10 (1.4)	14 (2.6)	11 (1.7)	12 (2.2)	8 (2.0)	13 (2.4)	10 (2.2)	19 (4.0)
Heating	17 (1.3)	16 (1.6)	19 (2.5)	16 (3.3)	18 (2.5)	16 (1.6)	18 (2.6)	16 (2.1)	16 (2.2)	17 (2.7)	15 (2.1)	18 (2.7)	18 (3.2)
Ventilation	26 (1.4)	25 (1.7)	31 (2.8)	27 (3.9)	31 (2.8)	21 (2.1)	30 (3.2)	20 (2.8)	29 (2.9)	24 (3.2)	29 (2.8)	24 (2.9)	29 (3.2)
Indoor air quality	18 (1.3)	18 (1.6)	18 (2.4)	19 (3.4)	20 (2.3)	16 (1.7)	22 (3.2)	13 (1.9)	21 (2.4)	14 (2.3)	20 (3.0)	17 (2.6)	24 (3.5)
Acoustics or noise-control	18 (1.1)	17 (1.4)	20 (2.8)	22 (3.8)	19 (2.2)	12 (1.9)	20 (2.6)	17 (2.1)	21 (2.7)	14 (2.3)	18 (2.6)	15 (3.0)	25 (3.8)
Physical security of buildings	20 (1.2)	17 (1.5)	26 (3.1)	21 (3.6)	21 (2.4)	18 (1.7)	14 (2.6)	17 (2.1)	26 (2.7)	17 (2.0)	22 (2.7)	21 (3.0)	17 (3.6)
Average years since original construction	40 (0.8)	40 (1.0)	40 (1.6)	43 (1.7)	42 (1.5)	35 (1.0)	42 (1.2)	37 (1.1)	41 (1.5)	38 (1.6)	38 (1.6)	40 (1.4)	44 (1.7)
Average years since most recent renovation	11 (0.6)	11 (0.6)	11 (0.9)	15 (1.4)	11 (1.0)	9 (0.6)	12 (1.2)	10 (0.8)	12 (0.9)	11 (1.0)	11 (1.0)	11 (1.0)	11 (1.5)
Average functional age[4] of school	16 (0.6)	16 (0.8)	15 (0.8)	20 (1.6)	15 (1.1)	14 (0.8)	17 (1.3)	14 (0.8)	16 (1.1)	14 (1.0)	16 (1.1)	14 (1.1)	19 (1.6)
Distribution, by functional age[4]	100 (†)	100 (†)	100 (†)	100 (†)	100 (†)	100 (†)	100 (†)	100 (†)	100 (†)	100 (†)	100 (†)	100 (†)	100 (†)
Less than 5 years old	32 (1.5)	30 (1.6)	37 (2.7)	25 (4.1)	32 (2.7)	37 (2.4)	30 (3.6)	34 (2.9)	32 (2.9)	32 (3.4)	30 (2.9)	37 (3.8)	30 (4.0)
5 to 14 years old	28 (1.5)	30 (1.9)	24 (2.8)	21 (3.7)	32 (2.7)	28 (2.4)	27 (3.1)	31 (2.7)	26 (2.7)	33 (3.7)	30 (3.0)	24 (3.0)	23 (3.7)
15 to 34 years old	26 (1.4)	25 (1.6)	29 (2.9)	35 (4.1)	23 (2.4)	23 (2.0)	26 (2.8)	23 (2.2)	29 (2.5)	24 (3.1)	25 (2.6)	28 (2.7)	26 (4.0)
35 or more years old	14 (1.4)	15 (1.7)	10 (2.0)	20 (3.6)	13 (2.5)	12 (1.8)	17 (2.9)	12 (1.9)	13 (2.4)	11 (2.2)	15 (2.7)	11 (2.2)	21 (3.9)

See notes at end of table.

Table 98. Percentage of public schools with building deficiencies and renovation plans, by level, enrollment size, metropolitan status, and free lunch eligibility: 1999—Continued

Type of school condition	All public schools	Instructional level[1]		Size of school enrollment			Metropolitan status[2]			Percent of students eligible for free or reduced-price lunch			
		Elementary	Secondary	Less than 300	300 to 599	600 or more	Central city	Urban fringe/ large town	Rural/ small town	Less than 20 percent	20 to 39 percent	40 to 69 percent	70 percent or more
1	2	3	4	5	6	7	8	9	10	11	12	13	14
Percentage distribution of schools, by enrollment capacity	100 (†)	100 (†)	100 (†)	100 (†)	100 (†)	100 (†)	100 (†)	100 (†)	100 (†)	100 (†)	100 (†)	100 (†)	100 (†)
Underenrolled by more than 25 percent	19 (1.5)	17 (1.7)	21 (2.7)	41 (5.0)	15 (2.5)	8 (1.4)	16 (3.0)	12 (2.0)	27 (2.7)	15 (2.4)	19 (3.1)	15 (2.7)	27 (4.0)
Underenrolled by 6 to 25 percent	33 (1.7)	31 (2.1)	43 (3.0)	30 (4.2)	37 (2.8)	31 (3.4)	33 (3.3)	36 (3.0)	30 (3.2)	38 (3.2)	34 (3.2)	33 (4.0)	26 (4.1)
Enrollment within 5 percent of capacity	26 (1.5)	28 (2.0)	17 (1.9)	16 (3.4)	29 (2.6)	30 (2.0)	24 (2.9)	28 (2.8)	26 (2.4)	24 (3.3)	26 (3.0)	29 (3.4)	24 (3.9)
Overcrowded by 6 to 25 percent	14 (1.2)	15 (1.5)	11 (1.9)	10 (2.9)	14 (2.5)	18 (1.6)	15 (1.8)	17 (2.0)	11 (2.4)	16 (2.8)	13 (2.4)	16 (2.6)	12 (2.6)
Overcrowded by more than 25 percent	8 (0.9)	8 (1.1)	8 (1.8)	4 (1.6)	5 (1.2)	14 (1.8)	11 (2.3)	8 (1.6)	6 (1.3)	6 (1.6)	8 (1.8)	7 (2.0)	12 (2.9)
Percent of schools with plans to make building improvements in next 2 years													
At least one major repair, renovation, or replacement planned	51 (1.6)	49 (2.2)	57 (3.1)	45 (4.4)	52 (2.9)	53 (2.4)	55 (3.8)	50 (3.3)	48 (3.2)	52 (3.8)	44 (3.1)	52 (3.4)	56 (3.9)
Major repair or renovation planned	41 (1.8)	39 (2.3)	48 (3.2)	36 (4.2)	40 (3.1)	45 (2.6)	48 (3.6)	40 (3.2)	36 (2.9)	41 (3.5)	36 (3.2)	43 (3.5)	46 (4.1)
Replacement planned	25 (1.2)	23 (1.6)	28 (2.6)	19 (3.2)	26 (2.2)	27 (2.1)	29 (3.2)	24 (2.4)	22 (2.2)	25 (3.4)	21 (2.7)	25 (3.2)	30 (3.7)
Percent of schools with construction projects planned in next 2 years													
Build permanent addition	20 (1.4)	19 (1.7)	23 (2.8)	17 (3.0)	19 (2.4)	24 (1.7)	17 (2.0)	25 (2.4)	17 (2.0)	23 (2.9)	18 (2.5)	21 (3.0)	18 (3.3)
Install new temporary buildings	10 (1.1)	10 (1.3)	13 (1.9)	6 (1.9)	6 (1.4)	18 (2.1)	11 (2.4)	13 (1.7)	7 (1.4)	10 (2.1)	12 (2.3)	10 (2.1)	9 (2.1)

—Not available.
†Not applicable.
[1]Combined elementary/secondary schools are not shown separately, but are included under "All public schools," and under other column variables.
[2]Central city is a large or mid-size central city of a Metropolitan Statistical Area (MSA). Urban fringe/large town includes places that are within an MSA of a central city but not primarily within its central city, as well as towns that are incorporated places not within an MSA and have a population greater than or equal to 25,000. Rural/small town includes places that are defined as rural by the U.S. Bureau of the Census and have a population less than 2,500 and/or a population density of less than 1,000 per square mile, as well as towns that are incorporated places not within an MSA and have a population less than 25,000 but greater than or equal to 2,500.
[3]Excludes special education, vocational, and alternative schools, as well as those schools offering only preprimary education.
[4]Functional age is defined as the age of the school based on the year of the most recent renovation or the year of construction of the main instructional building(s) if no renovation has occurred.
NOTE: Detail may not sum to totals because of rounding. Standard errors appear in parentheses.
SOURCE: U.S. Department of Education, National Center for Education Statistics, Fast Response Survey System (FRSS), "Condition of America's Public School Facilities," 1999, FRSS 73, 1999. (This table was prepared August 2000.)

Table 99. High school graduates, by sex and control of school: Selected years, 1869–70 through 2006–07

| School year | High school graduates (in thousands) | | | | | Averaged freshman graduation rate for public schools[4] |
| | Total[1] | Sex | | Control | | |
		Males	Females	Public[2]	Private[3]	
1	2	3	4	5	6	7
1869–70	16	7	9	—	—	—
1879–80	24	11	13	—	—	—
1889–90	44	19	25	22	22	—
1899–1900	95	38	57	62	33	—
1909–10	156	64	93	111	45	—
1919–20	311	124	188	231	80	—
1929–30	667	300	367	592	75	—
1939–40	1,221	579	643	1,143	78	—
1949–50	1,200	571	629	1,063	136	—
1959–60	1,858	895	963	1,627	231	—
1960–61	1,964	955	1,009	1,725	239	—
1961–62	1,918	938	980	1,678	240	—
1962–63	1,943	956	987	1,710	233	—
1963–64	2,283	1,120	1,163	2,008	275	—
1964–65	2,658	1,311	1,347	2,360	298	—
1965–66	2,665	1,323	1,342	2,367	298	—
1966–67	2,672	1,328	1,344	2,374	298	—
1967–68	2,695	1,338	1,357	2,395	300	—
1968–69	2,822	1,399	1,423	2,522	300	—
1969–70	2,889	1,430	1,459	2,589	300	78.7
1970–71	2,938	1,454	1,484	2,638	300	78.0
1971–72	3,002	1,487	1,515	2,700	302	77.4
1972–73	3,035	1,500	1,535	2,729	306	76.8
1973–74	3,073	1,512	1,561	2,763	310	75.4
1974–75	3,133	1,542	1,591	2,823	310	74.9
1975–76	3,148	1,552	1,596	2,837	311	74.9
1976–77	3,152	1,548	1,604	2,837	315	74.4
1977–78	3,127	1,531	1,596	2,825	302	73.2
1978–79	3,101	1,517	1,584	2,801	300	71.9
1979–80	3,043	1,491	1,552	2,748	295	71.5
1980–81	3,020	1,483	1,537	2,725	295	72.2
1981–82	2,995	1,471	1,524	2,705	290	72.9
1982–83	2,888	1,437	1,451	2,598	290	73.8
1983–84	2,767	—	—	2,495	272	74.5
1984–85	2,677	—	—	2,414	263	74.2
1985–86	2,643	—	—	2,383	260	74.3
1986–87	2,694	—	—	2,429	265	74.3
1987–88	2,773	—	—	2,500	273	74.2
1988–89	2,744	—	—	2,459	285	73.4
1989–90	2,589	—	—	2,320	269	73.6
1990–91	2,493	—	—	2,235	258	73.7
1991–92	2,478	—	—	2,226	252	74.2
1992–93	2,480	—	—	2,233	247	73.8
1993–94	2,464	—	—	2,221	243	73.1
1994–95	2,520	—	—	2,274	246	71.8
1995–96	2,518	—	—	2,273	245	71.0
1996–97	2,612	—	—	2,358	254	71.3
1997–98	2,704	—	—	2,439	265	71.3
1998–99	2,759	—	—	2,486	273	71.1
1999–2000	2,833	—	—	2,554	279	71.7
2000–01	2,848	—	—	2,569	279	71.7
2001–02	2,908	—	—	2,622	286	72.6
2002–03	3,021	—	—	2,720	301	73.9
2003–04[5]	3,057	—	—	2,753	304	74.3
2004–05[6]	3,109	—	—	2,801	307	74.7
2005–06[6]	3,176	—	—	2,861	315	74.6
2006–07[6]	3,232	—	—	2,912	321	74.4

—Not available.

[1]Includes graduates of public and private schools.

[2]Data for 1929–30 and preceding years are from *Statistics of Public High Schools* and exclude graduates from high schools that failed to report to the Office of Education.

[3]For most years, private school data have been estimated based on periodic private school surveys.

[4]The averaged freshman graduation rate provides an estimate of the percentage of high school students who graduate. The rate uses aggregate student enrollment data to estimate the size of an incoming freshman class and aggregate counts of the number of diplomas awarded 4 years later.

[5]Includes estimates for New York and Wisconsin. Without estimates for these two states, the averaged freshman graduation rate for the remaining 48 states and the District of Columbia is 75.0 percent.

[6]Projected.

NOTE: Includes graduates of regular day school programs. Excludes graduates of other programs, when separately reported, and recipients of high school equivalency certificates. Some data have been revised from previously published figures. Detail may not sum to totals because of rounding.

SOURCE: U.S. Department of Education, National Center for Education Statistics, *Annual Report of the Commissioner of Education*, 1870 through 1910; *Biennial Survey of Education in the United States*, 1919–20 through 1949–50; *Statistics of State School Systems*, 1951–52 through 1957–58; *Statistics of Public Elementary and Secondary School Systems*, 1958–59 through 1980–81; *Statistics of Nonpublic Elementary and Secondary Schools*, 1959 through 1980; Common Core of Data (CCD), "State Nonfiscal Survey of Public Elementary/Secondary Education," 1981–82 through 2004–05; Private School Universe Survey (PSS), 1989 through 2003; and *Projections of Education Statistics to 2015*. (This table was prepared March 2007.)

Table 100. Public high school graduates, by state or jurisdiction: Selected years, 1980–81 through 2004–05

State or jurisdiction	1980–81	1985–86	1990–91	1995–96	1999–2000	2000–01[1]	2001–02	2002–03[1]	2003–04	Projected 2004–05 graduates	Percent change, 1990–91 to 2004–05
1	2	3	4	5	6	7	8	9	10	11	12
United States	2,725,285	2,382,616	2,234,893	2,273,109	2,553,844	2,569,200	2,621,534	2,719,947	2,753,438 [1]	2,801,190	25.3
Alabama	44,894	39,620	39,042	35,043	37,819	37,082	35,887	36,741	36,464	36,920	-5.4
Alaska	5,343	5,464	5,458	5,945	6,615	6,812	6,945	7,297	7,236	7,190	31.7
Arizona	28,416	27,533	31,282	30,008	38,304	46,733	47,175	49,986	45,508	62,400	99.5
Arkansas	29,577	26,227	25,668	25,094	27,335	27,100	26,984	27,555	27,181	26,630	3.7
California	242,172	229,026	234,164	259,071	309,866	315,189	325,895	341,097	343,480	355,720	51.9
Colorado	35,897	32,621	31,293	32,608	38,924	39,241	40,760	42,379	44,777	44,070	40.8
Connecticut	38,369	33,571	27,290	26,319	31,562	30,388	32,327	33,667	34,573	35,750	31.0
Delaware	7,349	5,791	5,223	5,609	6,108	6,614	6,482	6,817	6,951	6,830	30.8
District of Columbia[2]	4,848	3,875	3,369	2,696	2,695	2,808	3,090	2,725	3,031	2,900	-13.9
Florida	88,755	83,029	87,419	89,242	106,708	111,112	119,537	127,484	131,418	136,520	56.2
Georgia	62,963	59,082	60,088	56,271	62,563	62,499	65,983	66,890	68,550	71,110	18.3
Hawaii	11,472	9,958	8,974	9,387	10,437	10,102	10,452	10,013	10,324	10,450	16.4
Idaho	12,679	12,059	11,961	14,667	16,170	15,941	15,874	15,858	15,547	16,050	34.2
Illinois	136,795	114,319	103,329	104,626	111,835	110,624	116,657	117,507	124,763	120,950	17.1
Indiana	73,381	59,817	57,892	56,330	57,012	56,172	56,722	57,897	56,008	57,420	-0.8
Iowa	42,635	34,279	28,593	31,689	33,926	33,774	33,789	34,860	34,339	33,160	16.0
Kansas	29,397	25,587	24,414	25,786	29,102	29,360	29,541	29,963	30,155	29,700	21.7
Kentucky	41,714	37,288	35,835	36,641	36,830	36,957	36,337	37,654	37,787	36,850	2.8
Louisiana	46,199	39,965	33,489	36,467	38,430	38,314	37,905	37,610	37,019	35,870	7.1
Maine	15,554	13,006	13,151	11,795	12,211	12,654	12,593	12,947	13,278	13,330	1.4
Maryland	54,050	46,700	39,014	41,785	47,849	49,222	50,881	51,864	52,870	54,180	38.9
Massachusetts	74,831	60,360	50,216	47,993	52,950	54,393	55,272	55,987	58,326	59,140	17.8
Michigan	124,372	101,042	88,234	85,530	97,679	96,515	95,001	100,301	98,823	103,340	17.1
Minnesota	64,166	51,988	46,474	50,481	57,372	56,581	57,440	59,432	59,096	58,380	25.6
Mississippi	28,083	25,134	23,665	23,032	24,232	23,748	23,740	23,810	23,735	23,360	-1.3
Missouri	60,359	49,204	46,928	49,011	52,848	54,138	54,487	56,925	57,983	57,030	21.5
Montana	11,634	9,761	9,013	10,139	10,903	10,628	10,554	10,657	10,500	10,330	14.6
Nebraska	21,411	17,845	16,500	18,014	20,149	19,658	19,910	20,161	20,309	19,710	19.5
Nevada	9,069	8,784	9,370	10,374	14,551	15,127	16,270	16,378	15,201	17,870	90.7
New Hampshire	11,552	10,648	10,059	10,094	11,829	12,294	12,452	13,210	13,309	13,770	36.9
New Jersey	93,168	78,781	67,003	67,704	74,420	76,130	77,664	81,391	83,826	89,310	33.3
New Mexico	17,915	15,468	15,157	15,402	18,031	18,199	18,094	16,923	17,892	17,830	17.6
New York	198,465	162,165	133,562	134,401	141,731	141,884	140,139	143,818	142,526 [3]	149,180	11.7
North Carolina	69,395	65,865	62,792	57,014	62,140	63,288	65,955	69,696	72,126	73,990	17.8
North Dakota	9,924	7,610	7,573	8,027	8,606	8,445	8,114	8,169	7,888	7,600	0.4
Ohio	143,503	119,561	107,484	102,098	111,668	111,281	110,608	115,762	119,029	118,350	10.1
Oklahoma	38,875	34,452	33,007	33,060	37,646	37,458	36,852	36,694	36,799	36,290	9.9
Oregon	28,729	26,286	24,597	26,570	30,151	29,939	31,153	32,587	32,958	32,270	31.2
Pennsylvania	144,645	122,871	104,770	105,981	113,959	114,436	114,943	119,933	123,474	124,660	19.0
Rhode Island	10,719	8,908	7,744	7,689	8,477	8,603	9,006	9,318	9,258	9,900	27.8
South Carolina	38,347	34,500	32,999	30,182	31,617	30,026	31,302	32,482	33,235	32,640	-1.1
South Dakota	10,385	7,870	7,127	8,532	9,278	8,881	8,796	8,999	9,001	8,580	20.4
Tennessee	50,648	43,263	44,847	43,792	41,568	40,642	40,894	44,113	46,096	44,570	-0.6
Texas	171,665	161,150	174,306	171,844	212,925	215,316	225,167	238,111	244,165	240,990	38.3
Utah	19,886	19,774	22,219	26,293	32,501	31,036	30,183	29,527	30,252	29,210	31.5
Vermont	6,424	5,794	5,212	5,867	6,675	6,856	7,083	6,970	7,100	7,160	37.4
Virginia	67,126	63,113	58,441	58,166	65,596	66,067	66,519	72,943	72,042	74,510	27.5
Washington	50,046	45,805	42,514	49,862	57,597	55,081	58,311	60,435	61,274	61,140	43.8
West Virginia	23,580	21,870	21,064	20,335	19,437	18,440	17,128	17,287	17,339	17,040	-19.1
Wisconsin	67,743	58,340	49,340	52,651	58,545	59,341	60,575	63,272	62,784 [3]	63,550	28.8
Wyoming	6,161	5,587	5,728	5,892	6,462	6,071	6,106	5,845	5,833	5,540	-3.3
Bureau of Indian Affairs	—	—	—	—	—	—	—	—	—	—	—
DoDDS, overseas	—	—	—	2,674	2,642	2,621	2,554	2,641	2,766	—	—
DoDDS, domestic	—	—	—	—	560	568	565	590	584	—	—
Other jurisdictions											
American Samoa	—	608	597	719	698	722	823	832	852	—	—
Guam	—	840	1,014	987	1,406	1,371	—	1,502	1,346	—	—
Northern Marianas	—	—	273	325	360	361	416	422	575	—	—
Puerto Rico	—	31,597	29,329	29,499	30,856	30,154	30,278	31,408	30,083	—	—
Virgin Islands	—	1,044	981	937	1,060	966	883	884	816	—	—

—Not available.
[1]Revised from previously published figures.
[2]Beginning in 1985–86, graduates from adult programs are excluded.
[3]Estimated high school graduates from NCES 2006-606rev, *The Averaged Freshman Graduation Rate for Public High Schools From the Common Core of Data: School Years 2002–03 and 2003–04.*

NOTE: Data include graduates of regular day school programs, but exclude graduates of other programs and persons receiving high school equivalency certificates. DoDDS = Department of Defense dependents schools. Detail may not sum to totals because of rounding.
SOURCE: U.S. Department of Education, National Center for Education Statistics, Common Core of Data (CCD), "State Nonfiscal Survey of Public Elementary/Secondary Education," 1981–82 through 2004–05; and *The Averaged Freshman Graduation Rate for Public High Schools From the Common Core of Data: School Years 2002–03 and 2003–04.* (This table was prepared March 2007.)

Table 101. Averaged freshman graduation rates for public secondary schools, by state: 1990–91 through 2003–04

State or jurisdiction	1990–91	1991–92	1992–93	1993–94	1994–95	1995–96	1996–97	1997–98	1998–99	1999–2000	2000–01	2001–02	2002–03	2003–04
1	2	3	4	5	6	7	8	9	10	11	12	13	14	15
United States	**73.7**	**74.2**	**73.8**	**73.1**	**71.8**	**71.0**	**71.3**	**71.3**	**71.1**	**71.7**	**71.7**	**72.6**	**73.9**	**74.3** [1]
Alabama	69.8	70.4	66.1	64.3	64.8	62.7	62.4	64.4	61.3	64.1	63.7	62.1	64.7	65.0
Alaska	74.6	76.0	75.4	73.8	71.2	68.3	67.9	68.9	70.0	66.7	68.0	65.9	68.0	67.2
Arizona	76.7	75.0	75.0	71.7	65.1	60.8	65.3	65.6	62.3	63.6	74.2	74.7	75.9	66.8
Arkansas	76.6	77.8	77.9	76.1	72.7	74.2	70.6	73.9	73.7	74.6	73.9	74.8	76.6	76.8
California	69.6	70.6	69.8	68.6	66.8	67.6	68.8	69.6	71.1	71.7	71.6	72.7	74.1	73.9
Colorado	76.3	77.8	77.8	77.3	76.0	74.8	74.7	73.9	73.4	74.1	73.2	74.7	76.4	78.7
Connecticut	80.2	81.4	81.4	79.9	77.2	76.1	76.7	76.9	76.0	81.9	77.5	79.7	80.9	80.7
Delaware	72.5	74.4	74.5	70.8	68.7	70.4	71.7	74.1	70.4	66.8	71.0	69.5	73.0	72.9
District of Columbia	54.5	56.8	57.9	58.7	54.6	49.7	54.6	53.9	52.0	54.5	60.2	68.4	59.6	68.2
Florida	65.6	69.5	65.8	64.2	63.5	62.3	62.7	62.1	61.4	61.0	61.2	63.4	66.7	66.4
Georgia	70.3	69.5	68.2	66.3	63.5	61.9	62.0	58.2	57.5	59.7	58.7	61.1	60.8	61.2
Hawaii	75.9	77.7	74.9	75.7	74.8	74.5	69.1	68.8	67.5	70.9	68.3	72.1	71.3	72.6
Idaho	79.6	81.6	81.7	79.9	80.2	80.5	80.1	79.7	79.5	79.4	79.6	79.3	81.4	81.5
Illinois	76.6	77.6	77.5	76.3	74.8	75.2	76.1	76.8	76.0	76.3	75.6	77.1	75.9	80.3
Indiana	76.9	78.5	77.8	74.7	73.8	73.6	74.0	73.8	74.3	71.8	72.1	73.1	75.5	73.5
Iowa	84.4	86.4	86.9	86.1	84.5	84.3	84.6	83.9	83.3	83.1	82.8	84.1	85.3	85.8
Kansas	80.8	80.2	80.5	80.2	78.8	77.1	76.9	76.0	76.7	77.1	76.5	77.1	76.9	77.9
Kentucky	72.9	72.8	75.4	79.2	73.8	71.3	71.1	70.2	70.0	69.7	69.8	69.8	71.7	73.0
Louisiana	57.5	56.9	59.4	61.5	62.4	61.7	59.3	61.3	61.1	62.2	63.7	64.4	64.1	69.4
Maine	80.7	83.3	76.4	74.0	73.6	73.7	75.2	78.5	74.7	75.9	76.4	75.6	76.3	77.6
Maryland	77.5	80.3	80.0	78.9	78.2	78.3	76.6	76.2	76.6	77.6	78.7	79.7	79.2	79.5
Massachusetts	79.1	81.3	79.9	79.7	78.1	78.0	78.4	78.3	77.9	78.0	78.9	77.6	75.7	79.3
Michigan	72.1	73.2	72.2	72.4	71.3	71.4	73.5	74.6	73.9	75.3	75.4	72.9	74.0	72.5
Minnesota	90.8	90.0	90.2	88.8	87.7	86.1	78.6	85.0	86.0	84.9	83.6	83.9	84.8	84.7
Mississippi	63.3	63.4	64.6	63.8	62.0	59.7	59.6	59.8	59.2	59.4	59.7	61.2	62.7	62.7
Missouri	76.0	76.7	76.4	76.8	76.0	75.0	74.7	75.2	75.8	76.3	75.5	76.8	78.3	80.4
Montana	84.4	85.0	86.3	85.5	86.5	83.9	83.2	82.2	81.3	80.8	80.0	79.8	81.0	80.4
Nebraska	86.7	88.3	88.3	87.2	86.9	85.6	84.8	85.6	87.3	85.7	83.8	83.9	85.2	87.6
Nevada	77.0	70.6	69.5	68.2	65.8	65.8	73.2	70.6	71.0	69.7	70.0	71.9	72.3	57.4
New Hampshire	78.6	80.4	80.5	80.5	78.4	77.5	77.3	76.7	75.3	76.1	77.8	77.8	78.2	78.7
New Jersey	81.4	82.9	84.1	83.4	82.1	82.8	83.9	76.3	77.5	83.6	85.4	85.8	87.0	86.3
New Mexico	70.1	68.1	68.4	66.9	64.4	63.7	62.5	61.6	63.3	64.7	65.9	67.4	63.1	67.0
New York	66.1	68.0	67.0	66.2	63.7	63.6	65.3	63.4	62.5	61.8	61.5	60.5	60.9	60.9 [2]
North Carolina	71.3	71.5	70.9	69.7	69.1	66.5	65.5	65.6	65.4	65.8	66.5	68.2	70.1	71.4
North Dakota	87.6	88.7	86.6	88.4	87.5	89.5	87.8	86.7	85.6	86.0	85.4	85.0	86.4	86.1
Ohio	77.5	77.7	80.6	81.1	79.9	74.5	76.4	77.0	75.0	75.2	76.5	77.5	79.0	81.3
Oklahoma	76.5	77.6	77.4	77.6	77.4	75.6	74.8	75.1	76.4	75.8	75.8	76.0	76.0	77.0
Oregon	72.7	74.2	75.0	72.9	71.2	68.3	69.1	69.0	68.2	69.6	68.3	71.0	73.7	74.2
Pennsylvania	79.7	81.9	81.9	81.0	80.1	80.0	79.8	79.4	79.1	78.7	79.0	80.2	81.7	82.2
Rhode Island	75.0	77.6	76.3	73.9	74.3	72.7	72.9	72.5	72.2	72.8	73.5	75.7	77.7	75.9
South Carolina	66.6	63.7	65.4	64.3	61.6	60.9	59.6	59.3	59.1	58.6	56.5	57.9	59.7	60.6
South Dakota	83.8	84.8	88.7	90.8	86.9	84.5	84.2	77.7	74.2	77.6	77.4	79.0	83.0	83.7
Tennessee	69.8	71.1	70.0	65.7	66.7	66.6	61.6	58.4	58.5	59.5	59.0	59.6	63.4	66.1
Texas	72.2	67.4	65.8	66.2	66.8	66.1	67.0	69.4	69.2	71.0	70.8	73.5	75.5	76.7
Utah	77.5	79.3	78.8	78.7	77.7	76.9	81.1	80.7	81.6	82.5	81.6	80.5	80.2	83.0
Vermont	79.5	80.7	80.2	83.5	88.9	85.3	83.6	83.9	81.9	81.0	80.2	82.0	83.4	85.4
Virginia	76.2	76.5	77.0	75.7	75.0	76.2	76.6	76.6	76.3	76.9	77.5	76.7	80.6	79.3
Washington	75.7	78.5	77.8	79.5	76.4	75.5	74.0	73.3	73.2	73.7	69.2	72.2	74.2	74.6
West Virginia	76.6	76.0	77.4	77.7	75.7	77.0	76.7	77.4	77.9	76.7	75.9	74.2	75.7	76.9
Wisconsin	85.2	84.9	85.8	84.7	84.0	83.6	83.7	83.1	82.6	82.7	83.3	84.8	85.8	85.8 [2]
Wyoming	81.1	83.5	86.5	84.0	78.8	77.7	78.4	77.1	76.6	76.3	73.4	74.4	73.9	76.0
Other jurisdictions														
American Samoa	85.3	91.7	86.8	83.7	78.7	79.7	79.7	76.6	80.4	71.9	77.0	82.9	81.0	80.2
Guam	48.2	45.8	45.6	45.4	45.2	44.6	45.4	39.5	54.7	52.9	51.7	—	56.3	48.4
Northern Marianas	—	58.7	59.3	78.9	62.9	62.9	68.4	63.4	63.5	61.1	62.7	65.2	65.2	75.3
Puerto Rico	60.9	60.6	60.8	57.1	60.4	60.8	61.5	61.9	63.6	64.7	65.7	66.2	67.8	64.8
Virgin Islands	53.2	58.0	58.2	59.2	59.7	54.2	62.0	58.6	58.6	53.8	57.3	48.7	53.5	—

—Not available.

[1] Includes estimates for New York and Wisconsin. Without estimates for these two states, the averaged freshman graduation rate for the remaining 48 states and the District of Columbia is 75.0 percent.

[2] Estimated high school graduates from NCES 2006-606rev, *The Averaged Freshman Graduation Rate for Public High Schools From the Common Core of Data: School Years 2002–03 and 2003–04.*

NOTE: The averaged freshman graduation rate provides an estimate of the percentage of high school students who graduate. The rate uses aggregate student enrollment data to estimate the size of an incoming freshman class and aggregate counts of the number of diplomas awarded 4 years later.

SOURCE: U.S. Department of Education, National Center for Education Statistics, Common Core of Data (CCD), "State Nonfiscal Survey of Public Elementary/Secondary Education," 1986–87 through 2004–05; and *The Averaged Freshman Graduation Rate for Public High Schools From the Common Core of Data: School Years 2002–03 and 2003–04.* (This table was prepared March 2007.)

Table 102. Public high school graduates and dropouts, by race/ethnicity and state or jurisdiction: 2001–02 and 2003–04

State or other jurisdiction	High school graduates, by race/ethnicity, 2003–04						Percent of 9th- to 12th-graders who dropped out during 2001–02, by race/ethnicity[1]					
	Total	White	Black	Hispanic	Asian/ Pacific Islander	American Indian/ Alaska Native	Total	White	Black	Hispanic	Asian/ Pacific Islander	American Indian/ Alaska Native
1	2	3	4	5	6	7	8	9	10	11	12	13
United States[2,3]	2,747,239	1,850,709	371,585	359,380	137,128	28,436	—	—	—	—	—	—
Alabama	36,464	23,949	11,483	325	368	339	3.7	3.6	3.9	4.5	1.6	2.1
Alaska	7,236	4,972	280	198	461	1,325	8.1	6.2	11.4	8.9	6.7	13.4
Arizona	45,508	25,685	2,204	13,874	1,174	2,571	10.5	6.8	13.4	15.2	3.9	19.0
Arkansas	27,181	20,276	5,596	795	360	154	5.3	4.6	7.0	7.7	4.3	6.9
California	340,069	141,574	25,267	121,418	48,770	3,040	—	—	—	—	—	—
Colorado	44,777	33,385	2,194	7,198	1,597	403	—	—	—	—	—	—
Connecticut	34,573	26,130	3,896	3,319	1,126	102	2.6	1.9	4.0	5.3	2.4	4.9
Delaware	6,951	4,566	1,858	297	210	20	6.2	4.6	9.0	11.6	3.5	5.1
District of Columbia	3,031	114	2,607	239	61	10	—	—	—	—	—	—
Florida	131,418	77,115	26,342	23,925	3,545	491	3.7	3.0	4.9	4.5	1.9	3.6
Georgia	67,789	41,289	22,030	2,122	2,250	98	6.5	5.8	7.6	9.8	3.6	7.5
Hawaii	10,324	1,991	167	465	7,669	32	5.1	5.5	5.5	6.4	4.9	6.6
Idaho	15,547	13,822	79	1,175	289	182	3.9	—	—	—	—	—
Illinois	124,763	86,179	18,341	14,561	5,427	255	6.4	3.7	13.6	10.4	2.6	5.7
Indiana	56,008	49,248	4,342	1,602	696	120	2.3	2.1	3.1	4.0	1.1	2.8
Iowa	34,339	31,718	900	928	672	121	2.4	2.1	6.8	7.1	2.7	6.6
Kansas	29,963	24,938	2,157	1,758	703	407	3.1	2.6	5.3	5.9	2.4	5.4
Kentucky	37,755	33,385	3,387	586	347	50	3.9	3.8	5.3	4.0	1.7	0.0
Louisiana	37,019	20,740	14,782	591	671	235	7.0	5.0	9.5	6.9	5.1	7.3
Maine	13,278	12,822	172	76	137	71	2.8	2.8	4.4	3.7	2.7	5.0
Maryland	52,870	30,541	17,005	2,270	2,919	135	3.9	3.0	5.5	3.7	1.4	4.1
Massachusetts	58,326	46,535	4,584	4,205	2,873	129	—	—	—	—	—	—
Michigan	98,823	81,568	11,737	2,405	2,225	888	—	—	—	—	—	—
Minnesota	59,096	51,688	2,510	1,238	2,861	799	3.8	2.7	9.9	14.5	4.4	14.2
Mississippi	23,716	12,362	11,000	122	212	20	3.9	3.1	4.7	4.1	2.2	2.2
Missouri	57,983	48,118	7,863	947	866	189	3.6	3.2	5.8	5.8	1.6	4.8
Montana	10,500	9,428	36	162	112	762	3.9	3.2	6.7	5.2	2.0	10.3
Nebraska	20,309	17,798	984	1,004	340	183	4.2	3.1	11.3	11.7	3.3	11.9
Nevada	15,216	9,961	1,155	2,659	1,238	203	6.4	5.0	8.9	9.3	5.2	5.6
New Hampshire	13,309	—	—	—	—	—	4.0	3.9	6.5	7.8	3.2	7.5
New Jersey	83,816	53,298	12,768	11,406	6,072	272	2.5	1.5	4.9	4.7	0.9	2.2
New Mexico	17,892	7,205	405	8,123	265	1,894	5.2	3.5	2.6	6.4	3.4	5.8
New York	142,526[4]	—	—	2,291	1,659	—	7.1	3.3	12.9	14.2	5.9	9.4
North Carolina	72,126	47,657	19,685	2,291	1,659	834	5.7	4.9	7.0	9.4	3.7	9.9
North Dakota	7,888	7,253	69	83	66	417	2.0	1.5	2.7	3.4	1.9	8.0
Ohio	118,173	100,613	14,084	1,696	1,648	132	3.1	2.4	7.2	6.6	2.0	7.1
Oklahoma	36,799	24,679	3,386	1,726	727	6,281	4.4	3.8	6.7	9.4	3.2	3.8
Oregon	32,395	26,981	692	2,583	1,565	574	4.6	4.0	9.9	10.5	3.6	0.0
Pennsylvania	123,478	101,989	14,303	4,134	2,952	100	3.3	2.4	7.0	8.9	2.9	3.3
Rhode Island	9,258	7,335	640	950	294	39	4.3	3.3	6.9	8.2	4.6	5.9
South Carolina	33,235	—	—	—	—	—	3.3	3.1	3.7	3.9	1.7	3.1
South Dakota	9,001	8,262	108	98	118	415	2.8	2.0	7.3	6.1	1.9	13.0
Tennessee	46,096	35,364	9,301	642	726	63	3.8	—	—	—	—	—
Texas	244,167	116,499	33,213	85,412	8,304	739	3.8	2.2	4.9	5.5	1.6	4.1
Utah	30,252	26,975	218	1,838	844	377	3.7	3.1	8.8	8.2	5.2	8.1
Vermont	7,092	6,753	89	63	147	40	4.0	3.9	7.3	9.0	2.2	5.9
Virginia	71,754	48,300	16,751	2,956	3,591	156	2.9	2.3	4.0	5.8	2.0	4.1
Washington	61,194	47,582	2,630	4,549	5,163	1,270	7.1	5.6	16.8	12.3	6.6	15.2
West Virginia	17,339	16,462	636	80	149	12	3.7	3.7	3.9	1.8	1.8	8.9
Wisconsin	62,784[4]	—	—	—	—	—	1.9	1.2	8.3	5.6	1.8	4.1
Wyoming	5,833	5,329	33	318	51	102	5.8	5.2	9.9	12.3	2.7	13.0
Bureau of Indian Affairs schools	—	—	—	—	—	—	—	—	—	—	—	—
DoDDS, overseas	2,352	1,333	416	288	299	16	—	—	—	—	—	—
DoDDS, domestic	534	172	103	218	39	2	—	—	—	—	—	—
Other jurisdictions												
American Samoa	852	0	0	0	852	0	1.1	—	—	—	1.1	—
Guam	1,350	22	4	4	1,319	1	—	—	—	—	—	—
Northern Marianas	575	4	0	0	571	0	7.1	0.0	16.7	—	7.2	—
Puerto Rico	30,083	0	0	30,083	0	0	1.2	—	—	1.2	—	—
Virgin Islands	819	5	699	112	2	1	—	—	—	—	—	—

—Not available.

[1] Alabama, Alaska, Arizona, Florida, Illinois, Maryland, New Jersey, New York, Tennessee, Vermont, and Puerto Rico reported data on an alternative July through June cycle, rather than the specified October through September cycle for dropout data.
[2] Includes estimates for nonreporting states, based on 2003 12th-grade enrollment racial/ethnic distribution reported by state.
[3] Data differ slightly from figures reported in other tables due to varying reporting practices for racial/ethnic survey data.

[4] Estimated high school graduates from NCES 2006-606rev, *The Averaged Freshman Graduation Rate for Public High Schools From the Common Core of Data: School Years 2002–03 and 2003–04*.
NOTE: Race categories exclude persons of Hispanic origin.
SOURCE: U.S. Department of Education, National Center for Education Statistics, Common Core of Data (CCD), "State Nonfiscal Survey of Public Elementary/Secondary Education," 2004–05, and "Local Education Agency Universe Survey Dropout and Completion Data File," 2001–02; and unpublished tabulations. (This table was prepared March 2007.)

Table 103. General Educational Development (GED) test takers and credentials issued, by age: 1971 through 2004

Year	Number of test takers (in thousands)[1]	Number completing test battery (in thousands)[2]	Number passing tests (in thousands)[3]	Percentage distribution of credentials issued,[4] by age				
				19 years old or less	20- to 24-year-olds	25- to 29-year-olds	30- to 34-year-olds	35 years old or over
1	2	3	4	5	6	7	8	9
1971[5]	377	—	227	—	—	—	—	—
1972[5]	419	—	245	—	—	—	—	—
1973[5]	423	—	249	—	—	—	—	—
1974	—	—	294	35	27	13	9	17
1975	—	—	340	33	26	14	9	18
1976	—	—	333	31	28	14	10	17
1977	—	—	332	40	24	13	8	14
1978	—	—	381	31	27	13	10	18
1979	—	—	426	37	28	12	13	11
1980	—	—	479	37	27	13	8	15
1981	—	—	489	37	27	13	8	14
1982	—	—	486	37	28	13	8	15
1983	—	—	465	34	29	14	8	15
1984	—	—	427	32	28	15	9	16
1985	—	—	413	32	26	15	10	16
1986	—	—	428	32	26	15	10	17
1987	—	—	444	33	24	15	10	18
1988	—	—	410	35	22	14	10	18
1989	632	541	357	35	24	13	—	—
1990	714	615	410	36	25	13	10	15
1991	755	657	462	33	28	13	10	16
1992	739	639	457	33	28	13	9	17
1993	746	651	469	33	27	13	10	16
1994	774	668	491	36	25	13	9	15
1995	787	682	504	38	25	13	9	15
1996	824	716	488	39	25	13	9	14
1997	785	681	460	43	24	12	8	13
1998	776	673	481	44	24	11	7	13
1999	808	702	498	44	25	11	7	13
2000	811	699	487	45	25	11	7	13
2001	1,016	928	648	41	26	11	8	14
2002	557	467	330	49	25	10	6	11
2003	657	552	387	47	26	10	7	11
2004	666	570	406	46	26	11	6	10

—Not available.
[1]Number of people taking the GED tests (one or more subtests).
[2]Number of people completing the entire GED battery of five tests.
[3]Number of people receiving high school equivalency credentials based on the GED tests.
[4]People who did not report their age were excluded from this calculation. Data for 1988 and prior years are for number of test takers and may not be comparable to data for later years.

[5]Includes other jurisdictions.
NOTE: Data are for United States only and exclude other jurisdictions. Detail may not sum to totals because of rounding. Some data have been revised from previously published figures.
SOURCE: American Council on Education, General Educational Development Testing Service, *Who Took the GED? Statistical Report*, various years; *Who Passed the GED Tests? 2004 Statistical Report*, July 2006. (This table was prepared July 2006.)

Table 104. Percentage of high school dropouts (status dropouts) among persons 16 through 24 years old, by sex and race/ethnicity: Selected years, 1960 through 2005

Year	Total				Male				Female			
	All races[1]	White	Black	Hispanic	All races[1]	White	Black	Hispanic	All races[1]	White	Black	Hispanic
1	2	3	4	5	6	7	8	9	10	11	12	13
1960[2]	27.2 (—)	— (†)	— (†)	— (†)	27.8 (—)	— (†)	— (†)	— (†)	26.7 (—)	— (†)	— (†)	— (†)
1967[3]	17.0 (—)	15.4 (—)	28.6 (—)	— (†)	16.5 (—)	14.7 (—)	30.6 (—)	— (†)	17.3 (—)	16.1 (—)	26.9 (—)	— (†)
1968[3]	16.2 (—)	14.7 (—)	27.4 (—)	— (†)	15.8 (—)	14.4 (—)	27.1 (—)	— (†)	16.5 (—)	15.0 (—)	27.6 (—)	— (†)
1969[3]	15.2 (—)	13.6 (—)	26.7 (—)	— (†)	14.3 (—)	12.6 (—)	26.9 (—)	— (†)	16.0 (—)	14.6 (—)	26.7 (—)	— (†)
1970[3]	15.0 (0.29)	13.2 (0.30)	27.9 (1.22)	— (†)	14.2 (0.42)	12.2 (0.42)	29.4 (1.82)	— (†)	15.7 (0.41)	14.1 (0.42)	26.6 (1.65)	— (†)
1971[3]	14.7 (0.28)	13.4 (0.29)	24.0 (1.14)	— (†)	14.2 (0.41)	12.6 (0.41)	25.5 (1.70)	— (†)	15.2 (0.40)	14.2 (0.42)	22.6 (1.54)	— (†)
1972	14.6 (0.28)	12.3 (0.29)	21.3 (1.07)	34.3 (2.22)	14.1 (0.40)	11.6 (0.40)	22.3 (1.59)	33.7 (3.23)	15.1 (0.39)	12.8 (0.41)	20.5 (1.44)	34.8 (3.05)
1973	14.1 (0.27)	11.6 (0.28)	22.2 (1.06)	33.5 (2.24)	13.7 (0.38)	11.5 (0.39)	21.5 (1.53)	30.4 (3.16)	14.5 (0.38)	11.8 (0.39)	22.8 (1.47)	36.4 (3.16)
1974	14.3 (0.27)	11.9 (0.28)	21.2 (1.05)	33.0 (2.08)	14.2 (0.39)	12.0 (0.40)	20.1 (1.51)	33.8 (2.99)	14.3 (0.38)	11.8 (0.39)	22.1 (1.45)	32.2 (2.90)
1975	13.9 (0.27)	11.4 (0.27)	22.9 (1.06)	29.2 (2.02)	13.3 (0.37)	11.0 (0.38)	23.0 (1.56)	26.7 (2.84)	14.5 (0.38)	11.8 (0.39)	22.9 (1.44)	31.6 (2.86)
1976	14.1 (0.27)	12.0 (0.28)	20.5 (1.00)	31.4 (2.01)	14.1 (0.38)	12.1 (0.39)	21.2 (1.49)	30.3 (2.94)	14.2 (0.37)	11.8 (0.39)	19.9 (1.35)	32.3 (2.76)
1977	14.1 (0.27)	11.9 (0.28)	19.8 (0.99)	33.0 (2.02)	14.5 (0.38)	12.6 (0.40)	19.5 (1.45)	31.6 (2.89)	13.8 (0.37)	11.2 (0.38)	20.0 (1.36)	34.3 (2.83)
1978	14.2 (0.27)	11.9 (0.28)	20.2 (1.00)	33.3 (2.00)	14.6 (0.38)	12.2 (0.40)	22.5 (1.52)	33.6 (2.88)	13.9 (0.37)	11.6 (0.39)	18.3 (1.31)	33.1 (2.78)
1979	14.6 (0.27)	12.0 (0.28)	21.1 (1.01)	33.8 (1.98)	15.0 (0.39)	12.6 (0.40)	22.4 (1.52)	33.0 (2.83)	14.2 (0.37)	11.5 (0.38)	20.0 (1.35)	34.5 (2.77)
1980	14.1 (0.26)	11.4 (0.27)	19.1 (0.97)	35.2 (1.89)	15.1 (0.39)	12.3 (0.40)	20.8 (1.47)	37.2 (2.72)	13.1 (0.36)	10.5 (0.37)	17.7 (1.28)	33.2 (2.61)
1981	13.9 (0.26)	11.3 (0.27)	18.4 (0.93)	33.2 (1.80)	15.1 (0.38)	12.5 (0.40)	19.9 (1.40)	36.0 (2.61)	12.8 (0.35)	10.2 (0.36)	17.1 (1.24)	30.4 (2.48)
1982	13.9 (0.27)	11.4 (0.29)	18.4 (0.97)	31.7 (1.93)	14.5 (0.40)	12.0 (0.42)	21.2 (1.50)	30.5 (2.73)	13.3 (0.38)	10.8 (0.40)	15.9 (1.26)	32.8 (2.71)
1983	13.7 (0.27)	11.1 (0.29)	18.0 (0.97)	31.6 (1.93)	14.9 (0.41)	12.2 (0.43)	19.9 (1.46)	34.3 (2.84)	12.5 (0.37)	10.1 (0.39)	16.2 (1.28)	29.1 (2.61)
1984	13.1 (0.27)	11.0 (0.29)	15.5 (0.91)	29.8 (1.91)	14.0 (0.40)	11.9 (0.43)	16.8 (1.37)	30.6 (2.78)	12.3 (0.37)	10.1 (0.39)	14.3 (1.22)	29.0 (2.63)
1985	12.6 (0.27)	10.4 (0.29)	15.2 (0.92)	27.6 (1.93)	13.4 (0.40)	11.1 (0.42)	16.1 (1.37)	29.9 (2.76)	11.8 (0.37)	9.8 (0.39)	14.3 (1.23)	25.2 (2.68)
1986	12.2 (0.27)	9.7 (0.28)	14.2 (0.90)	30.1 (1.88)	13.1 (0.40)	10.3 (0.42)	15.0 (1.33)	32.8 (2.66)	11.4 (0.37)	9.1 (0.39)	13.5 (1.21)	27.2 (2.63)
1987	12.6 (0.28)	10.4 (0.30)	14.1 (0.90)	28.6 (1.84)	13.2 (0.40)	10.8 (0.43)	15.0 (1.35)	29.1 (2.57)	12.1 (0.38)	10.0 (0.41)	13.3 (1.21)	28.1 (2.64)
1988	12.9 (0.30)	9.6 (0.31)	14.5 (1.00)	35.8 (2.30)	13.5 (0.44)	10.3 (0.46)	15.0 (1.48)	36.0 (3.19)	12.2 (0.42)	8.9 (0.43)	14.0 (1.36)	35.4 (3.31)
1989	12.6 (0.31)	9.4 (0.32)	13.9 (0.98)	33.0 (2.19)	13.6 (0.45)	10.3 (0.47)	14.9 (1.46)	34.4 (3.08)	11.7 (0.42)	8.5 (0.43)	13.0 (1.32)	31.6 (3.11)
1990	12.1 (0.29)	9.0 (0.30)	13.2 (0.94)	32.4 (1.91)	12.3 (0.42)	9.3 (0.44)	11.9 (1.30)	34.3 (2.71)	11.8 (0.41)	8.7 (0.42)	14.4 (1.34)	30.3 (2.70)
1991	12.5 (0.30)	8.9 (0.31)	13.6 (0.95)	35.3 (1.93)	13.0 (0.43)	8.9 (0.44)	13.5 (1.37)	39.2 (2.74)	11.9 (0.41)	8.9 (0.43)	13.7 (1.31)	31.1 (2.70)
1992[4]	11.0 (0.28)	7.7 (0.29)	13.7 (0.95)	29.4 (1.86)	11.3 (0.41)	8.0 (0.42)	12.5 (1.32)	32.1 (2.67)	10.7 (0.39)	7.4 (0.40)	14.8 (1.36)	26.6 (2.56)
1993[4]	11.0 (0.28)	7.9 (0.29)	13.6 (0.94)	27.5 (1.79)	11.2 (0.40)	8.2 (0.42)	12.6 (1.32)	28.1 (2.54)	10.9 (0.40)	7.6 (0.41)	14.4 (1.34)	26.9 (2.52)
1994[4]	11.4 (0.26)	7.7 (0.27)	12.6 (0.75)	30.0 (1.16)	12.3 (0.38)	8.0 (0.38)	14.1 (1.14)	31.6 (1.60)	10.6 (0.36)	7.5 (0.37)	11.3 (0.99)	28.1 (1.66)
1995[4]	12.0 (0.27)	8.6 (0.28)	12.1 (0.74)	30.0 (1.15)	12.2 (0.38)	9.0 (0.40)	11.1 (1.05)	30.0 (1.59)	11.7 (0.37)	8.2 (0.39)	12.9 (1.05)	30.0 (1.66)
1996[4]	11.1 (0.27)	7.3 (0.27)	13.0 (0.80)	29.4 (1.19)	11.4 (0.38)	7.3 (0.38)	13.5 (1.18)	30.3 (1.67)	10.9 (0.38)	7.3 (0.39)	12.5 (1.08)	28.3 (1.69)
1997[4]	11.0 (0.27)	7.6 (0.28)	13.4 (0.80)	25.3 (1.11)	11.9 (0.39)	8.5 (0.41)	13.3 (1.16)	27.0 (1.55)	10.1 (0.36)	6.7 (0.37)	13.5 (1.11)	23.4 (1.59)
1998[4]	11.8 (0.27)	7.7 (0.28)	13.8 (0.81)	29.5 (1.12)	13.3 (0.40)	8.6 (0.41)	15.5 (1.24)	33.5 (1.59)	10.3 (0.36)	6.9 (0.37)	12.2 (1.05)	25.0 (1.56)
1999[4]	11.2 (0.26)	7.3 (0.27)	12.6 (0.77)	28.6 (1.11)	11.9 (0.38)	7.7 (0.39)	12.1 (1.10)	31.0 (1.58)	10.5 (0.36)	6.9 (0.37)	13.0 (1.08)	26.0 (1.54)
2000[4]	10.9 (0.26)	6.9 (0.26)	13.1 (0.78)	27.8 (1.08)	12.0 (0.38)	7.0 (0.37)	15.3 (1.20)	31.8 (1.56)	9.9 (0.35)	6.9 (0.37)	11.1 (1.00)	23.5 (1.48)
2001[4]	10.7 (0.25)	7.3 (0.26)	10.9 (0.71)	27.0 (1.06)	12.2 (0.38)	7.9 (0.39)	13.0 (1.12)	31.6 (1.55)	9.3 (0.34)	6.7 (0.36)	9.0 (0.90)	22.1 (1.42)
2002[4]	10.5 (0.24)	6.5 (0.24)	11.3 (0.70)	25.7 (0.93)	11.8 (0.35)	6.7 (0.35)	12.8 (1.07)	29.6 (1.32)	9.2 (0.32)	6.3 (0.34)	9.9 (0.91)	21.2 (1.27)
2003[4,5]	9.9 (0.23)	6.3 (0.24)	10.9 (0.69)	23.5 (0.90)	11.3 (0.34)	7.1 (0.35)	12.5 (1.05)	26.7 (1.29)	8.4 (0.30)	5.6 (0.32)	9.5 (0.89)	20.1 (1.23)
2004[4,5]	10.3 (0.23)	6.8 (0.24)	11.8 (0.70)	23.8 (0.89)	11.6 (0.34)	7.1 (0.35)	13.5 (1.08)	28.5 (1.30)	9.0 (0.31)	6.4 (0.34)	10.2 (0.92)	18.5 (1.18)
2005[4,5]	9.4 (0.22)	6.0 (0.23)	10.4 (0.66)	22.4 (0.87)	10.8 (0.33)	6.6 (0.34)	12.0 (1.02)	26.4 (1.26)	8.0 (0.29)	5.3 (0.31)	9.0 (0.86)	18.1 (1.16)

—Not available.
†Not applicable.
[1]Includes other racial/ethnic categories not separately shown.
[2]Based on the April 1960 decennial census.
[3]White and Black include persons of Hispanic origin.
[4]Because of changes in data collection procedures, data may not be comparable with figures for years prior to 1992.
[5]White and Black exclude persons identifying themselves as more than one race.
NOTE: "Status" dropouts are 16- to 24-year-olds who are not enrolled in school and who have not completed a high school program regardless of when they left school. People who have received GED credentials are counted as high school completers. All data except for 1960 are based on October counts. Data are based on sample surveys of the civilian noninstitutionalized population, which excludes persons in prisons, persons in the military, and other persons not living in households. Race categories exclude persons of Hispanic origin except where otherwise noted. Standard errors appear in parentheses.
SOURCE: U.S. Department of Commerce, Census Bureau, Current Population Survey (CPS), October 1967 through October 2005, unpublished tabulations. (This table was prepared May 2006.)

Table 105. Percentage of high school dropouts (status dropouts) among persons 16 through 24 years old, by income level, and percentage distribution of dropouts, by labor force status and educational attainment: 1970 through 2005

Year	Dropout rate of 16- to 24-year-olds	Dropout rate of 16- to 24-year-olds, by family income quartile				Percentage distribution of dropouts, by labor force status				Percentage distribution of dropouts, by years of school completed				
		Lowest quartile	Middle low quartile	Middle high quartile	Highest quartile	Total[1]	Employed[2]	Unemployed	Not in labor force	Total[1]	Less than 9	9	10	11 or 12
1	2	3	4	5	6	7	8	9	10	11	12	13	14	15
1970	15.0 (0.27)	28.0 (0.85)	21.2 (0.60)	11.7 (0.46)	5.2 (0.31)	100.0	49.8 (0.98)	10.3 (0.59)	39.9 (0.96)	100.0	28.5 (0.88)	20.6 (0.79)	26.8 (0.87)	24.0 (0.84)
1971	14.7 (0.26)	28.8 (0.83)	20.7 (0.58)	10.9 (0.45)	5.1 (0.30)	100.0	49.5 (0.97)	10.9 (0.60)	39.6 (0.94)	100.0	27.9 (0.87)	21.7 (0.80)	27.8 (0.86)	22.7 (0.81)
1972	14.6 (0.28)	27.6 (0.79)	20.8 (0.58)	10.2 (0.42)	5.4 (0.31)	100.0	51.2 (0.95)	10.2 (0.58)	38.6 (0.93)	100.0	27.5 (0.85)	20.8 (0.77)	29.0 (0.86)	22.7 (0.80)
1973	14.1 (0.27)	28.0 (0.78)	19.6 (0.56)	9.9 (0.41)	4.9 (0.29)	100.0	53.2 (0.96)	9.2 (0.55)	37.5 (0.93)	100.0	26.5 (0.84)	20.9 (0.78)	27.4 (0.85)	25.3 (0.83)
1974	14.3 (0.27)	28.0 (†)	— (†)	— (†)	— (†)	100.0	51.8 (0.94)	12.3 (0.62)	35.9 (0.91)	100.0	25.4 (0.82)	20.1 (0.76)	28.7 (0.85)	25.8 (0.83)
1975	13.9 (0.27)	28.8 (0.76)	18.0 (0.54)	10.2 (0.42)	5.0 (0.28)	100.0	46.0 (0.94)	15.6 (0.69)	38.4 (0.92)	100.0	23.5 (0.80)	21.1 (0.77)	27.5 (0.85)	27.9 (0.85)
1976	14.1 (0.27)	28.1 (0.73)	19.2 (0.55)	10.1 (0.42)	4.9 (0.27)	100.0	48.8 (0.93)	16.0 (0.68)	35.2 (0.89)	100.0	24.3 (0.80)	20.1 (0.75)	27.8 (0.83)	27.8 (0.83)
1977	14.1 (0.27)	28.5 (0.74)	19.0 (0.55)	10.4 (0.42)	4.5 (0.27)	100.0	52.9 (0.94)	13.6 (0.64)	33.6 (0.89)	100.0	24.3 (0.81)	21.7 (0.78)	27.3 (0.84)	26.6 (0.83)
1978	14.2 (0.27)	28.2 (0.74)	18.9 (0.56)	10.5 (0.42)	5.5 (0.29)	100.0	54.3 (0.93)	12.4 (0.61)	33.3 (0.88)	100.0	22.9 (0.78)	20.2 (0.75)	28.2 (0.84)	28.8 (0.84)
1979	14.6 (0.27)	28.1 (0.73)	18.5 (0.55)	11.5 (0.44)	5.6 (0.29)	100.0	54.0 (0.92)	12.7 (0.61)	33.3 (0.87)	100.0	22.6 (0.77)	21.0 (0.75)	28.6 (0.83)	27.8 (0.82)
1980	14.1 (0.26)	27.0 (0.71)	18.1 (0.55)	10.7 (0.43)	5.7 (0.29)	100.0	50.4 (0.93)	17.0 (0.70)	32.6 (0.88)	100.0	23.6 (0.79)	19.7 (0.74)	29.8 (0.85)	27.0 (0.83)
1981	13.9 (0.26)	26.4 (0.70)	17.8 (0.53)	11.1 (0.43)	5.2 (0.28)	100.0	49.8 (0.93)	18.3 (0.72)	31.9 (0.87)	100.0	24.3 (0.80)	18.6 (0.72)	30.2 (0.85)	26.9 (0.82)
1982	13.9 (0.27)	27.2 (0.72)	18.3 (0.58)	10.2 (0.44)	4.4 (0.27)	100.0	45.2 (0.98)	21.1 (0.80)	33.7 (0.93)	100.0	22.9 (0.80)	20.8 (0.80)	28.8 (0.89)	27.6 (0.88)
1983	13.7 (0.27)	26.5 (0.71)	17.8 (0.58)	10.5 (0.46)	4.1 (0.27)	100.0	48.4 (1.00)	18.2 (0.77)	33.4 (0.94)	100.0	23.0 (0.84)	19.3 (0.79)	28.8 (0.91)	28.8 (0.91)
1984	13.1 (0.27)	25.9 (0.70)	16.5 (0.57)	9.9 (0.44)	3.8 (0.26)	100.0	49.7 (1.03)	17.3 (0.78)	32.9 (0.97)	100.0	23.6 (0.88)	21.4 (0.85)	27.5 (0.92)	27.5 (0.92)
1985	12.6 (0.27)	27.1 (0.72)	14.7 (0.55)	8.3 (0.42)	4.0 (0.27)	100.0	50.1 (1.07)	17.5 (0.81)	32.4 (1.00)	100.0	23.9 (0.91)	21.0 (0.87)	27.9 (0.96)	27.2 (0.95)
1986	12.2 (0.27)	25.4 (0.70)	14.8 (0.56)	8.0 (0.41)	3.4 (0.26)	100.0	51.1 (1.09)	16.4 (0.81)	32.5 (1.02)	100.0	25.4 (0.95)	21.5 (0.90)	25.7 (0.95)	27.4 (0.97)
1987	12.6 (0.28)	25.5 (0.71)	16.6 (0.58)	8.0 (0.43)	3.6 (0.26)	100.0	52.4 (1.08)	13.6 (0.74)	34.0 (1.02)	100.0	25.9 (0.94)	20.7 (0.87)	26.0 (0.95)	27.5 (0.96)
1988	12.9 (0.30)	27.2 (0.80)	15.4 (0.64)	8.2 (0.48)	3.4 (0.27)	100.0	52.9 (1.19)	‡ (†)	‡ (†)	100.0	28.9 (1.08)	19.3 (0.94)	25.1 (1.04)	26.8 (1.06)
1989	12.6 (0.31)	25.0 (0.79)	16.2 (0.66)	8.7 (0.49)	3.3 (0.29)	100.0	53.2 (1.22)	13.8 (0.84)	33.0 (1.15)	100.0	29.4 (1.11)	20.8 (0.99)	24.9 (1.06)	25.0 (1.06)
1990	12.1 (0.29)	24.3 (0.76)	15.1 (0.60)	8.7 (0.47)	2.9 (0.26)	100.0	52.5 (1.20)	13.3 (0.81)	34.2 (1.14)	100.0	28.6 (1.08)	20.9 (0.97)	24.4 (1.03)	26.1 (1.05)
1991	12.5 (0.30)	25.9 (0.77)	15.5 (0.61)	7.7 (0.45)	3.0 (0.27)	100.0	47.5 (1.18)	15.8 (0.86)	36.7 (1.14)	100.0	28.6 (1.07)	20.5 (0.96)	26.1 (1.04)	24.9 (1.02)
1992[3]	11.0 (0.28)	23.4 (0.73)	12.9 (0.57)	7.3 (0.45)	2.4 (0.24)	100.0	47.6 (1.26)	15.0 (0.90)	37.4 (1.22)	100.0	21.6 (1.04)	17.5 (0.96)	24.4 (1.09)	36.5 (1.22)
1993[3]	11.0 (0.28)	22.9 (0.72)	12.7 (0.57)	6.6 (0.43)	2.9 (0.27)	100.0	48.7 (1.27)	12.8 (0.85)	38.5 (1.23)	100.0	20.5 (1.02)	16.6 (0.94)	24.1 (1.08)	38.8 (1.23)
1994[3]	11.4 (0.26)	20.7 (0.71)	13.7 (0.59)	8.7 (0.46)	4.9 (0.33)	100.0	49.5 (1.22)	13.0 (0.82)	37.5 (1.18)	100.0	23.9 (1.04)	16.2 (0.90)	20.3 (0.98)	39.6 (1.19)
1995[3]	12.0 (0.27)	23.2 (0.70)	13.8 (0.59)	8.3 (0.47)	3.6 (0.29)	100.0	48.9 (1.19)	14.2 (0.83)	37.0 (1.15)	100.0	22.2 (0.99)	17.0 (0.90)	22.5 (1.00)	38.3 (1.16)
1996[3]	11.1 (0.27)	22.0 (0.72)	13.6 (0.60)	7.0 (0.45)	3.2 (0.28)	100.0	47.3 (1.28)	15.0 (0.91)	37.7 (1.24)	100.0	20.3 (1.03)	17.7 (0.98)	22.6 (1.07)	39.4 (1.25)
1997[3]	11.0 (0.27)	21.8 (0.71)	13.5 (0.59)	6.2 (0.42)	3.4 (0.29)	100.0	53.3 (1.28)	13.2 (0.86)	33.5 (1.21)	100.0	19.9 (1.02)	15.7 (0.93)	22.3 (1.06)	42.1 (1.26)
1998[3]	11.8 (0.27)	22.3 (0.71)	14.9 (0.62)	7.7 (0.45)	3.5 (0.29)	100.0	55.1 (1.22)	10.3 (0.74)	34.6 (1.17)	100.0	21.0 (1.00)	14.9 (0.87)	21.4 (1.01)	42.6 (1.21)
1999[3]	11.2 (0.26)	21.0 (0.70)	14.3 (0.60)	7.4 (0.44)	3.9 (0.30)	100.0	55.6 (1.24)	10.0 (0.75)	34.4 (1.18)	100.0	22.2 (1.03)	16.3 (0.92)	22.5 (1.04)	39.0 (1.21)
2000[3]	10.9 (0.26)	20.7 (0.70)	12.8 (0.56)	8.3 (0.46)	3.5 (0.29)	100.0	56.9 (1.24)	12.3 (0.82)	30.8 (1.16)	100.0	21.5 (1.03)	15.3 (0.90)	23.1 (1.06)	40.0 (1.23)
2001[3]	10.7 (0.25)	19.3 (0.68)	13.4 (0.57)	9.0 (0.47)	3.2 (0.27)	100.0	58.3 (1.24)	14.8 (0.89)	26.9 (1.11)	100.0	18.4 (0.97)	16.8 (0.94)	23.8 (1.07)	40.9 (1.23)
2002[3]	10.5 (0.24)	18.8 (0.62)	12.3 (0.53)	8.4 (0.43)	3.8 (0.28)	100.0	57.4 (1.18)	13.3 (0.81)	29.2 (1.09)	100.0	22.8 (1.00)	17.1 (0.90)	21.3 (0.98)	38.9 (1.17)
2003[3]	9.9 (0.23)	19.5 (0.64)	10.8 (0.49)	7.3 (0.40)	3.4 (0.26)	100.0	53.5 (1.22)	13.7 (0.84)	32.9 (1.15)	100.0	21.2 (1.00)	18.2 (0.94)	20.7 (0.99)	40.0 (1.20)
2004[3]	10.3 (0.23)	18.0 (0.60)	12.7 (0.52)	8.2 (0.43)	3.7 (0.27)	100.0	53.0 (1.19)	14.3 (0.83)	32.7 (1.12)	100.0	21.4 (0.97)	15.9 (0.87)	22.5 (0.99)	40.3 (1.17)
2005[3]	9.4 (0.22)	17.9 (0.60)	11.5 (0.51)	7.1 (0.39)	2.7 (0.23)	100.0	56.9 (1.23)	11.9 (0.80)	31.2 (1.15)	100.0	18.9 (0.97)	16.8 (0.93)	21.4 (1.02)	42.9 (1.23)

—Not available.
†Not applicable.
‡Reporting standards not met.
[1]Standard errors are not applicable.
[2]Includes persons employed, but not currently working.
[3]Data may not be comparable with figures for earlier years because of changes in data collection procedures.

NOTE: "Status" dropouts are 16- to 24-year-olds who are not enrolled in school and who have not completed a high school program, regardless of when they left school. People who have received GED credentials are counted as high school completers. Data are based on sample surveys of the civilian noninstitutionalized population. Some data have been revised from previously published figures. Detail may not sum to totals because of rounding. Standard errors appear in parentheses.
SOURCE: U.S. Department of Commerce, Census Bureau, Current Population Survey (CPS), October 1970 through October 2005, unpublished tabulations. (This table was prepared November 2006.)

Table 106. Number of students with disabilities exiting special education, by basis of exit, age, and type of disability: United States and other jurisdictions, 2003–04 and 2004–05

Age and type of disability	Total exiting special education	Graduated with diploma	Received a certificate of attendance	Reached maximum age[1]	No longer receives special education[2]	Died	Moved, known to continue[2]	Moved, not known to continue	Dropped out[3]
1	2	3	4	5	6	7	8	9	10
				2003–04					
Total, 14 and over	**396,169**	**214,751**	**51,881**	**5,130**	**—**	**1,909**	**—**	**44,079**	**78,419**
Age									
14	9,946	0	52	†	—	284	—	7,149	2,461
15	14,818	0	48	†	—	307	—	8,306	6,157
16	26,985	1,645	615	†	—	366	—	8,812	15,547
17	119,182	73,383	14,178	†	—	357	—	8,737	22,527
18	142,294	94,966	21,039	0	—	266	—	6,112	19,911
19	51,940	32,599	8,158	0	—	156	—	2,774	8,253
20	16,737	7,863	3,832	1,053	—	91	—	1,356	2,542
21	10,851	3,613	3,086	2,676	—	60	—	668	748
22 and over	3,416	682	873	1,401	—	22	—	165	273
Type of disability									
Specific learning disability	237,403	141,418	25,432	889	—	606	—	24,796	44,262
Mental retardation	49,522	18,899	14,642	2,267	—	330	—	4,693	8,691
Emotional disturbance	49,436	18,953	4,077	442	—	177	—	8,957	16,830
Speech or language impairment	9,126	5,579	779	55	—	37	—	1,225	1,451
Multiple disabilities	8,595	4,030	1,702	730	—	297	—	741	1,095
Other health impairment	25,506	15,409	2,651	118	—	253	—	2,598	4,477
Hearing impairment[4]	4,856	3,270	695	64	—	17	—	333	477
Orthopedic impairment	4,117	2,551	623	153	—	118	—	267	405
Visual impairment	1,702	1,236	189	43	—	18	—	79	137
Autism	3,560	1,984	810	287	—	24	—	199	256
Deaf-blindness	133	66	20	17	—	7	—	11	12
Traumatic brain injury	2,213	1,355	261	65	—	25	—	180	327
				2004–05					
Total, 14 through 21[5]	**387,789**	**211,033**	**60,004**	**5,199**	**—**	**1,897**	**—**	**†**	**109,656**
Age									
14	7,086	128	41	†	—	263	—	†	6,654
15	11,645	51	44	†	—	334	—	†	11,216
16	24,563	1,718	632	†	—	393	—	†	21,820
17	124,885	78,786	16,074	†	—	389	—	†	29,636
18	142,116	91,080	24,930	703	—	255	—	†	25,148
19	50,510	28,891	10,600	412	—	141	—	†	10,466
20	16,321	7,344	4,241	1,169	—	74	—	†	3,493
21	10,663	3,035	3,442	2,915	—	48	—	†	1,223
22 and over	—	—	—	—	—	—	—	†	—
Type of disability[5]									
Specific learning disability	233,402	139,171	29,710	1,328	—	591	—	†	62,602
Mental retardation	46,571	16,338	16,544	1,915	—	348	—	†	11,426
Emotional disturbance	47,229	18,947	4,737	591	—	198	—	†	22,756
Speech or language impairment	8,670	5,630	789	37	—	26	—	†	2,188
Multiple disabilities	7,992	3,446	1,972	606	—	287	—	†	1,681
Other health impairment	27,637	17,095	3,331	144	—	252	—	†	6,815
Hearing impairment[4]	4,681	3,260	718	73	—	19	—	†	611
Orthopedic impairment	3,751	2,325	665	108	—	109	—	†	544
Visual impairment	1,799	1,302	243	36	—	14	—	†	204
Autism	3,830	2,129	974	291	—	21	—	†	415
Deaf-blindness	95	51	13	9	—	3	—	†	19
Traumatic brain injury	2,132	1,339	308	61	—	29	—	†	395

—Not available.

†Not applicable.

[1]Students may exit special education services due to maximum age beginning at age 18 depending on state law or practice or order of any court.

[2]Data are not reported for 2003–04 or 2004–05.

[3]"Dropped out" is defined as the total who were enrolled at some point in the reporting year, were not enrolled at the end of the reporting year, and did not exit through any of the other bases described. Beginning in 2004–05, includes students previously categorized as "moved, not known to continue."

[4]Includes deaf and hard of hearing.

[5]Totals for 2004–05 do not include persons over the age of 21.

SOURCE: U.S. Department of Education, Office of Special Education Programs, Individuals with Disabilities Education Act (IDEA) database. Retrieved September 22, 2006, from https://www.ideadata.org/arc_toc6.asp#partbEX and https://www.ideadata.org/arc_toc7.asp#partbCC. (This table was prepared September 2006.)

Table 107. Percentage of young children born in 2001 demonstrating specific cognitive and motor skills, by child's age at assessment: 2001 through 2003

Specific ability	Percentage of children 8 through 10 months								Percentage of children 11 through 13 months								Percentage of children 14 through 22 months	
	Total		8 months		9 months		10 months		Total		11 months		12 months		13 months			
1	2		3		4		5		6		7		8		9		10	
Survey population percentage distribution....	**72.2**	**(0.98)**	**16.1**	**(0.82)**	**34.8**	**(0.71)**	**21.3**	**(0.61)**	**20.9**	**(0.79)**	**10.6**	**(0.49)**	**6.2**	**(0.37)**	**4.1**	**(0.30)**	**6.5**	**(0.50)**
Cognitive abilities																		
Explores objects in play	99.2	(0.03)	98.7	(0.06)	99.2	(0.02)	99.4	(0.03)	99.8	(0.02)	99.7	(0.04)	99.9	(0.01)	100.0	(0.01)	100.0	(0.01)
Explores with purpose	87.8	(0.38)	79.6	(0.75)	88.0	(0.31)	93.8	(0.27)	97.4	(0.14)	96.4	(0.26)	98.8	(0.08)	99.4	(0.05)	99.3	(0.10)
Babbles.................................	46.7	(0.41)	37.9	(0.48)	45.2	(0.33)	55.8	(0.53)	72.1	(0.43)	64.9	(0.57)	76.7	(0.63)	84.1	(0.57)	89.0	(0.62)
Early problem solving	3.4	(0.11)	1.4	(0.08)	2.7	(0.07)	6.0	(0.21)	17.2	(0.46)	11.2	(0.49)	20.1	(0.77)	28.4	(0.98)	46.4	(1.47)
Uses words	0.5	(0.02)	0.2	(0.01)	0.4	(0.01)	1.0	(0.05)	5.0	(0.25)	2.7	(0.23)	5.9	(0.42)	9.9	(0.66)	26.7	(1.42)
Motor abilities																		
Eye-hand coordination..........	90.7	(0.13)	87.7	(0.25)	90.6	(0.16)	93.1	(0.13)	96.4	(0.11)	95.3	(0.16)	97.1	(0.16)	98.2	(0.17)	99.0	(0.09)
Sitting....................................	93.4	(0.13)	90.4	(0.28)	93.4	(0.16)	95.7	(0.13)	98.2	(0.08)	97.4	(0.13)	98.6	(0.12)	99.3	(0.12)	99.6	(0.06)
Prewalking	73.2	(0.40)	63.4	(0.75)	72.9	(0.49)	81.1	(0.43)	91.4	(0.33)	88.1	(0.52)	93.6	(0.47)	96.4	(0.53)	98.2	(0.22)
Independent walking.............	18.5	(0.37)	10.4	(0.44)	16.8	(0.41)	27.4	(0.63)	55.2	(1.06)	42.9	(1.33)	62.2	(1.77)	76.4	(1.93)	89.1	(1.04)
Balance.................................	1.1	(0.04)	0.5	(0.03)	0.9	(0.03)	1.9	(0.10)	10.1	(0.50)	5.0	(0.36)	12.6	(0.95)	19.8	(1.34)	43.1	(1.86)

NOTE: This table is based on a survey that sampled children at or about 9 months of age. Standard errors appear in parentheses.

SOURCE: U.S. Department of Education, National Center for Education Statistics, *Children Born in 2001: First Results From the Base Year of the Early Childhood Longitudinal Study, Birth Cohort*, 2005. (This table was prepared February 2006.)

Table 108. Mean reading scale scores and specific reading skills of fall 1998 first-time kindergartners, by time of assessment and selected characteristics: Selected years, fall 1998 through spring 2004

Selected characteristic	Kindergarten Fall 1998	Kindergarten Spring 1999	First grade Fall 1999	First grade Spring 2000	Third grade, spring 2002	Fifth grade, spring 2004	Score gain, fall 1998 to spring 2004	Deriving meaning from text	Interpreting beyond text	Evaluating nonfiction
	2	3	4	5	6	7	8	9	10	11
Total	30 (0.4)	41 (0.6)	48 (0.7)	72 (0.9)	120 (1.1)	141 (1.0)	111 (0.8)	75 (1.4)	47 (1.2)	8 (0.7)
Sex										
Male	29 (0.5)	41 (0.6)	48 (0.7)	73 (1.0)	119 (1.1)	141 (1.2)	112 (1.0)	76 (1.6)	48 (1.3)	7 (0.8)
Female	30 (0.5)	42 (0.8)	48 (0.9)	72 (1.2)	120 (1.5)	140 (1.3)	110 (1.1)	74 (1.9)	47 (1.5)	8 (0.9)
Race/ethnicity										
White	31 (0.4)	43 (0.7)	49 (0.7)	75 (1.0)	124 (0.9)	145 (0.9)	114 (0.8)	81 (1.2)	53 (1.1)	9 (0.8)
Black	26 (0.7)	38 (1.1)	43 (1.1)	64 (1.7)	107 (2.3)	128 (1.8)	102 (1.7)	58 (2.7)	33 (2.0)	2 (0.4)
Hispanic	29 (1.2)	41 (1.2)	47 (1.4)	69 (1.8)	117 (2.6)	137 (2.2)	108 (1.9)	72 (3.5)	43 (2.3)	4 (0.9)
Asian/Pacific Islander	32 (3.1)	44 (4.6)	52 (5.3)	75 (7.1)	117 (7.8)	143 (4.0)	111 (1.9)	79 (4.4)	49 (5.9)	11 (4.3)
Other	27 (2.2)	38 (2.5)	44 (3.8)	68 (5.4)	109 (9.6)	131 (8.4)	104 (6.2)	61 (12.1)	38 (8.8)	7 (5.3)
Parents' highest level of education[1]										
Less than high school	23 (0.7)	32 (0.9)	38 (1.4)	57 (2.9)	93 (3.1)	117 (3.0)	94 (2.9)	42 (4.7)	24 (2.5)	1 (0.2)
High school	26 (0.4)	38 (0.8)	42 (1.0)	65 (1.4)	112 (2.2)	134 (1.9)	108 (1.7)	67 (2.7)	39 (2.2)	3 (0.6)
Some college	29 (0.4)	41 (0.5)	47 (0.7)	71 (0.9)	120 (1.5)	140 (1.4)	111 (1.3)	75 (2.1)	46 (1.6)	6 (1.0)
Bachelor's or higher	34 (0.7)	47 (1.1)	54 (1.2)	82 (1.6)	130 (1.2)	151 (1.3)	117 (0.8)	88 (1.5)	60 (1.7)	13 (1.6)
Socioeconomic status[1]										
Lowest 20 percent	23 (0.4)	33 (0.7)	38 (0.9)	57 (1.7)	95 (2.4)	119 (1.9)	96 (1.8)	44 (3.1)	25 (1.7)	1 (0.3)
Middle 60 percent	29 (0.4)	41 (0.5)	47 (0.7)	72 (0.8)	120 (1.2)	140 (1.1)	112 (1.0)	76 (1.6)	46 (1.3)	6 (0.6)
Highest 20 percent	35 (0.9)	48 (1.3)	55 (1.5)	82 (2.0)	132 (1.2)	153 (1.6)	118 (1.0)	90 (1.7)	62 (2.2)	16 (2.3)
Number of family risk factors[1,2]										
No risks	32 (0.5)	44 (0.7)	51 (0.8)	77 (1.0)	127 (1.0)	147 (1.0)	115 (0.9)	84 (1.3)	55 (1.3)	10 (1.0)
One risk	27 (0.5)	39 (0.7)	44 (0.8)	68 (1.1)	114 (1.5)	135 (1.2)	109 (1.0)	70 (1.7)	40 (1.4)	4 (0.6)
Two or more risks	25 (0.6)	35 (0.8)	40 (1.0)	59 (1.5)	99 (2.3)	122 (2.2)	97 (1.9)	47 (3.6)	27 (2.0)	2 (0.5)
Kindergarten program type										
Half-day program	30 (0.6)	41 (0.8)	47 (0.8)	73 (1.2)	123 (1.3)	144 (1.1)	114 (1.0)	80 (1.6)	52 (1.2)	9 (0.9)
Full-day program	29 (0.5)	42 (0.8)	48 (1.0)	72 (1.3)	117 (1.7)	138 (1.6)	109 (1.2)	71 (2.2)	44 (1.8)	6 (0.9)
School type across all waves of the study										
Public school all years	29 (0.4)	40 (0.5)	46 (0.6)	71 (0.9)	118 (1.3)	139 (1.2)	110 (1.0)	73 (1.7)	46 (1.4)	7 (0.7)
Private school all years	35 (1.0)	47 (1.3)	56 (1.6)	85 (2.2)	131 (1.9)	153 (1.7)	118 (1.0)	91 (1.7)	62 (2.3)	13 (2.3)
Change in school type during study	32 (1.7)	45 (2.6)	52 (2.5)	77 (3.7)	123 (2.9)	143 (3.3)	111 (2.1)	78 (4.8)	49 (4.2)	9 (3.5)

[1]Status during kindergarten year.
[2]Family risk factors included living below the federal poverty level, primary home language was not English, mother's highest education was less than a high school diploma/GED, and living in a single-parent household. Values range from 0 to 4.
NOTE: Detail may not sum to totals because of rounding. Estimates reflect the sample of children assessed in English in all assessment years. ECLS-K was not administered in 2000–01, when most of the children in the sample were in second grade. Most of the children were in first grade in 1999–2000, but 5 percent were in kindergarten or other grades (e.g., second grade, ungraded classrooms); most were in third grade in 2001–02, but 11 percent were in second grade or other grades (e.g., fourth grade, ungraded classrooms); most were in fifth grade in 2003–04, but 14 percent were in fourth grade or other grades (e.g., sixth grade). Reading scale ranges from 0 to 186. Data were calculated using C1_6FC0 weight and therefore differ from previously published figures. Race categories exclude persons of Hispanic origin. Standard errors appear in parentheses.
SOURCE: U.S. Department of Education, National Center for Education Statistics, Early Childhood Longitudinal Study, Kindergarten Class of 1998–99 (ECLS-K), Longitudinal Kindergarten–Third Grade Public-Use Data File, fall 1998, spring 1999, fall 1999, spring 2000, spring 2002, and Fifth-Grade Restricted-Use Data File. (This table was prepared September 2006.)

Table 109. Mean mathematics and science scale scores and specific mathematics skills of fall 1998 first-time kindergartners, by time of assessment and selected characteristics: Selected years, fall 1998 through spring 2004

Selected characteristic	Mathematics — Mean scale score						Score gain, fall 1998 to spring 2004	Percentage of children with specific skills, fifth grade, spring 2004			Science — Mean scale score		Score gain, spring 2002 to spring 2004
	Kindergarten		First grade		Third grade, spring 2002	Fifth grade, spring 2004		Place value	Rate and measurement	Fractions	Third grade, spring 2002	Fifth grade, spring 2004	
	Fall 1998	Spring 1999	Fall 1999	Spring 2000									
1	2	3	4	5	6	7	8	9	10	11	12	13	14
Total	23 (0.3)	34 (0.4)	41 (0.6)	58 (0.6)	93 (1.0)	114 (1.0)	91 (0.8)	77 (1.7)	46 (1.7)	15 (1.1)	46 (0.6)	58 (0.7)	13 (0.4)
Sex													
Male	24 (0.4)	35 (0.5)	42 (0.8)	60 (0.9)	97 (1.1)	118 (1.1)	94 (1.0)	83 (1.9)	52 (2.0)	20 (1.6)	48 (0.6)	61 (0.7)	13 (0.4)
Female	23 (0.4)	33 (0.6)	40 (0.6)	57 (0.7)	89 (1.3)	110 (1.3)	88 (1.0)	72 (2.1)	40 (2.1)	11 (1.3)	43 (0.9)	55 (0.9)	12 (0.6)
Race/ethnicity													
White	25 (0.3)	36 (0.5)	43 (0.5)	62 (0.7)	98 (0.8)	119 (0.8)	94 (0.7)	84 (1.3)	54 (1.5)	19 (1.3)	49 (0.7)	62 (0.5)	13 (0.5)
Black	19 (0.5)	28 (0.7)	33 (0.8)	49 (1.0)	78 (1.8)	99 (2.2)	80 (1.9)	55 (4.0)	19 (2.0)	3 (0.8)	35 (1.1)	47 (1.3)	12 (0.5)
Hispanic	22 (0.7)	32 (0.9)	39 (0.9)	56 (1.1)	93 (1.7)	112 (2.0)	90 (1.6)	77 (3.0)	42 (3.8)	12 (2.5)	43 (1.2)	56 (1.2)	13 (0.7)
Asian/Pacific Islander	23 (2.2)	32 (3.7)	41 (3.4)	56 (5.4)	88 (8.6)	116 (5.8)	93 (3.8)	75 (11.2)	47 (11.7)	18 (5.8)	43 (5.5)	58 (4.9)	15 (1.4)
Other	21 (2.8)	31 (2.9)	38 (3.9)	54 (3.2)	87 (8.6)	106 (8.1)	86 (5.6)	65 (14.1)	38 (10.1)	13 (5.3)	41 (4.4)	52 (5.3)	12 (1.1)
Parents' highest level of education[1]													
Less than high school	16 (0.6)	24 (1.1)	29 (1.2)	44 (1.8)	71 (2.0)	90 (2.8)	74 (2.4)	40 (4.3)	13 (2.6)	2 (1.0)	34 (1.8)	43 (1.8)	9 (1.4)
High school	21 (0.6)	30 (0.7)	36 (0.9)	53 (1.2)	85 (1.6)	107 (1.7)	86 (1.2)	66 (3.0)	32 (2.4)	6 (1.2)	41 (1.2)	54 (1.2)	13 (0.4)
Some college	22 (0.4)	33 (0.6)	40 (0.7)	58 (0.8)	94 (1.3)	114 (1.2)	92 (1.0)	80 (2.1)	44 (2.3)	12 (1.6)	45 (0.7)	58 (0.8)	13 (0.5)
Bachelor's or higher	28 (0.8)	39 (0.8)	48 (1.0)	66 (1.1)	103 (1.3)	125 (1.3)	96 (1.1)	91 (1.5)	66 (2.6)	29 (2.8)	51 (1.0)	64 (0.8)	13 (0.5)
Socioeconomic status[1]													
Lowest 20 percent	17 (0.5)	25 (0.7)	30 (0.9)	45 (1.2)	73 (1.6)	93 (2.1)	76 (1.7)	44 (3.3)	15 (1.5)	2 (0.7)	33 (1.1)	45 (1.2)	11 (0.8)
Middle 60 percent	23 (0.4)	33 (0.5)	40 (0.6)	58 (0.8)	93 (1.2)	114 (1.1)	91 (0.9)	78 (1.9)	44 (2.2)	12 (1.3)	45 (0.7)	58 (0.7)	13 (0.4)
Highest 20 percent	29 (0.9)	40 (1.0)	47 (1.3)	67 (1.4)	106 (1.2)	127 (1.1)	98 (1.0)	94 (0.8)	70 (2.6)	32 (3.4)	53 (1.0)	66 (0.7)	13 (0.7)
Number of family risk factors[1,2]													
No risks	26 (0.4)	36 (0.5)	44 (0.7)	63 (0.8)	99 (0.9)	120 (0.9)	95 (0.8)	87 (1.4)	58 (1.8)	21 (1.5)	49 (0.7)	62 (0.6)	13 (0.4)
One risk	21 (0.4)	31 (0.7)	38 (0.8)	54 (0.9)	90 (1.4)	108 (1.2)	87 (0.9)	69 (2.2)	32 (2.3)	7 (1.0)	43 (0.8)	56 (0.9)	13 (0.7)
Two or more risks	18 (0.6)	26 (0.6)	31 (0.9)	47 (1.1)	75 (2.1)	96 (2.5)	78 (2.0)	49 (4.1)	19 (2.6)	4 (0.9)	34 (1.2)	45 (1.5)	11 (0.7)
Kindergarten program type													
Half-day program	24 (0.4)	34 (0.5)	41 (0.6)	60 (0.7)	96 (0.9)	118 (0.8)	94 (0.7)	84 (1.3)	52 (1.7)	18 (1.5)	48 (0.7)	61 (0.5)	13 (0.5)
Full-day program	23 (0.6)	34 (0.7)	40 (1.0)	58 (1.1)	91 (1.8)	111 (1.7)	88 (1.3)	72 (2.6)	41 (2.8)	13 (1.5)	44 (1.1)	56 (1.1)	13 (0.4)
School type across all waves of the study													
Public school all years	23 (0.4)	33 (0.5)	40 (0.6)	57 (0.7)	92 (1.3)	113 (1.2)	90 (0.9)	75 (1.9)	44 (1.9)	14 (1.2)	45 (0.8)	57 (0.8)	13 (0.4)
Private school all years	29 (0.9)	40 (1.1)	48 (1.3)	68 (1.6)	101 (1.8)	123 (1.6)	93 (1.0)	90 (2.3)	62 (3.6)	19 (3.1)	49 (1.1)	64 (1.0)	14 (0.5)
Change in school type during study	25 (1.3)	35 (1.7)	44 (2.2)	61 (2.3)	95 (2.9)	118 (2.9)	93 (2.1)	84 (4.0)	52 (5.2)	21 (4.2)	48 (2.1)	60 (1.9)	12 (1.2)

[1] Status during kindergarten year.
[2] Family risk factors included living below the federal poverty level, primary home language was not English, mother's highest education was less than a high school diploma/GED, and living in a single-parent household. Values range from 0 to 4.
NOTE: Detail may not sum to totals because of rounding. Estimates reflect the sample of children assessed in English in all assessment years. ECLS-K was not administered in 2000–01, when most of the children in the sample were in second grade. Most of the children were in first grade in 1999–2000, but 5 percent were in kindergarten or other grades (e.g., second grade, ungraded classrooms); most were in third grade in 2001–02, but 11 percent were in second grade or other grades (e.g. fourth grade, ungraded classrooms); most were in fifth grade in 2003–04, but 14 percent were in fourth grade or other grades (e.g., sixth grade). Mathematics scale ranges from 0 to 153. Data were calculated using C1_6FC0 weight and therefore differ from previously published figures. Race categories exclude persons of Hispanic origin. Standard errors appear in parentheses.
SOURCE: U.S. Department of Education, National Center for Education Statistics, Early Childhood Longitudinal Study, Kindergarten Class of 1998–99 (ECLS-K), Longitudinal Kindergarten–Third Grade Public-Use Data File, fall 1998, spring 1999, fall 1999, spring 2000, and spring 2002, and Fifth-Grade Restricted-Use Data File. (This table was prepared September 2006.)

Table 110. Average reading scale score, by age and selected student and school characteristics: Selected years, 1971 through 2004

Selected student and school characteristic	1971	1975	1980	1984	1988	1990	1992	1994	1996	1999	2004
1	2	3	4	5	6	7	8	9	10	11	12
9-year-olds											
All students	208 (1.0)	210 (0.7)	215 (1.0)	211 (0.8)	212 (1.1)	209 (1.2)	211 (0.9)	211 (1.2)	212 (1.0)	212 (1.3)	219 (1.1)
Sex											
Male	201 (1.1)	204 (0.8)	210 (1.1)	207 (1.0)	207 (1.4)	204 (1.7)	206 (1.3)	207 (1.3)	207 (1.4)	209 (1.6)	216 (1.4)
Female	214 (1.0)	216 (0.8)	220 (1.1)	214 (0.9)	216 (1.3)	215 (1.2)	215 (0.9)	215 (1.4)	218 (1.1)	215 (1.5)	221 (1.0)
Race/ethnicity											
White	214 (0.9)[1]	217 (0.7)	221 (0.8)	218 (0.9)	218 (1.4)	217 (1.3)	218 (1.0)	218 (1.3)	220 (1.2)	221 (1.6)	226 (1.1)
Black	170 (1.7)[1]	181 (1.2)	189 (1.8)	186 (1.3)	189 (2.4)	182 (2.9)	185 (2.2)	185 (2.3)	191 (2.6)	186 (2.3)	200 (2.2)
Hispanic	[2] (†)	183 (2.2)	190 (2.3)	187 (3.0)	194 (3.5)	189 (2.3)	192 (3.1)	186 (3.9)	195 (3.4)	193 (2.7)	205 (1.7)
Region											
Northeast	213 (1.7)	215 (1.3)	221 (2.1)	216 (2.2)	215 (2.6)	217 (2.2)	218 (2.6)	217 (2.9)	220 (1.8)	222 (3.5)	223 (2.5)
Southeast	194 (2.9)	201 (1.2)	210 (2.3)	204 (2.0)	207 (2.1)	197 (3.2)	199 (2.0)	208 (3.0)	206 (2.8)	205 (2.3)	218 (1.8)
Central	215 (1.2)	215 (1.2)	217 (1.4)	215 (1.9)	218 (2.2)	213 (2.0)	216 (1.6)	214 (2.3)	215 (2.6)	215 (3.9)	221 (2.3)
West	205 (2.0)	207 (2.0)	213 (1.8)	209 (2.0)	208 (2.6)	210 (2.8)	209 (2.3)	205 (2.8)	210 (1.9)	206 (1.8)	215 (1.5)
13-year-olds											
All students	255 (0.9)	256 (0.8)	258 (0.9)	257 (0.6)	257 (1.0)	257 (0.8)	260 (1.2)	258 (0.9)	258 (1.0)	259 (1.0)	259 (1.0)
Sex											
Male	250 (1.0)	250 (0.8)	254 (1.1)	253 (0.7)	252 (1.3)	251 (1.1)	254 (1.7)	251 (1.2)	251 (1.2)	254 (1.3)	254 (1.2)
Female	261 (0.9)	262 (0.9)	263 (0.9)	262 (0.7)	263 (1.0)	263 (1.1)	265 (1.2)	266 (1.2)	264 (1.2)	265 (1.2)	264 (1.3)
Race/ethnicity											
White	261 (0.7)[1]	262 (0.7)	264 (0.7)	263 (0.6)	261 (1.1)	262 (0.9)	266 (1.2)	265 (1.1)	266 (1.0)	267 (1.2)	266 (1.0)
Black	222 (1.2)[1]	226 (1.2)	233 (1.5)	236 (1.2)	243 (2.4)	241 (2.2)	238 (2.3)	234 (2.4)	234 (2.6)	238 (2.4)	244 (2.0)
Hispanic	[2] (†)	232 (3.0)	237 (2.0)	240 (2.0)	240 (3.5)	238 (2.3)	239 (3.5)	235 (1.9)	238 (2.9)	244 (2.9)	242 (1.6)
Parents' highest level of education											
Not high school graduate	—	—	239 (1.1)	240 (1.2)	246 (2.1)	241 (1.8)	239 (2.6)	237 (2.4)	239 (2.8)	238 (3.4)	240 (2.7)
Graduated high school	—	—	253 (0.9)	253 (0.8)	253 (1.2)	251 (0.9)	252 (1.7)	251 (1.4)	251 (1.5)	251 (1.8)	251 (1.6)
Some education after high school	— (†)	— (†)	268 (1.0)	266 (1.1)	265 (1.7)	267 (1.7)	265 (2.7)	266 (1.9)	268 (2.3)	269 (2.4)	264 (2.0)
Graduated college	— (†)	— (†)	273 (0.9)	268 (0.9)	265 (1.6)	267 (1.1)	271 (1.5)	269 (1.2)	269 (1.4)	270 (1.2)	270 (1.0)
Region											
Northeast	261 (2.0)	259 (1.8)	260 (1.8)	261 (0.8)	259 (2.4)	259 (1.8)	265 (3.2)	269 (2.0)	259 (2.6)	263 (2.9)	265 (1.9)
Southeast	245 (1.7)	249 (1.5)	253 (1.6)	256 (1.9)	258 (2.2)	256 (2.2)	254 (2.5)	253 (2.5)	251 (3.3)	254 (2.4)	257 (2.3)
Central	260 (1.8)	261 (1.4)	265 (1.4)	258 (1.3)	256 (2.0)	257 (1.5)	263 (3.0)	259 (3.3)	267 (1.8)	261 (1.9)	260 (2.1)
West	254 (1.3)	253 (1.7)	256 (2.0)	254 (1.1)	258 (2.1)	256 (1.6)	258 (1.6)	253 (2.1)	257 (1.7)	259 (2.2)	255 (1.6)

See notes at end of table.

Table 110. Average reading scale score, by age and selected student and school characteristics: Selected years, 1971 through 2004—Continued

Selected student and school characteristic	1971		1975		1980		1984		1988		1990		1992		1994		1996		1999		2004	
1	2		3		4		5		6		7		8		9		10		11		12	
17-year-olds																						
All students	285	(1.2)	286	(0.8)	285	(1.2)	289	(0.8)	290	(1.0)	290	(1.1)	290	(1.1)	288	(1.3)	288	(1.1)	288	(1.3)	285	(1.2)
Sex																						
Male	279	(1.2)	280	(1.0)	282	(1.3)	284	(0.8)	286	(1.5)	284	(1.6)	284	(1.6)	282	(2.2)	281	(1.3)	281	(1.6)	278	(1.5)
Female	291	(1.3)	291	(1.0)	289	(1.2)	294	(0.9)	294	(1.5)	296	(1.2)	296	(1.1)	295	(1.5)	295	(1.2)	295	(1.4)	292	(1.3)
Race/ethnicity																						
White	291	(1.0)[1]	293	(0.6)	293	(0.9)	295	(0.9)	295	(1.2)	297	(1.2)	297	(1.4)	296	(1.5)	295	(1.2)	295	(1.4)	293	(1.1)
Black	239	(1.7)[1]	241	(2.0)	243	(1.8)	264	(1.2)	274	(2.4)	267	(2.3)	261	(2.1)	266	(3.9)	266	(2.7)	264	(1.7)	264	(2.7)
Hispanic	[2]	(†)	252	(3.6)	261	(2.7)	268	(2.9)	271	(4.3)	275	(3.6)	271	(3.7)	263	(4.9)	265	(4.1)	271	(3.9)	264	(2.9)
Parents' highest level of education																						
Not high school graduate	—	(†)	—	(†)	262	(1.5)	269	(1.4)	267	(2.0)	270	(2.8)	271	(3.9)	268	(2.7)	267	(3.2)	265	(3.6)	259	(3.4)
Graduated high school	—	(†)	—	(†)	277	(1.0)	281	(0.8)	282	(1.3)	283	(1.4)	280	(1.6)	276	(1.9)	273	(1.7)	274	(2.1)	274	(1.6)
Some education after high school	—	(†)	—	(†)	295	(1.2)	298	(0.9)	299	(2.2)	295	(1.9)	293	(1.9)	294	(1.6)	295	(2.2)	295	(1.8)	286	(1.9)
Graduated college	—	(†)	—	(†)	301	(1.0)	302	(0.9)	300	(1.4)	302	(1.5)	301	(1.7)	300	(1.7)	299	(1.5)	298	(1.3)	298	(1.3)
Region																						
Northeast	291	(2.8)	289	(1.7)	286	(2.4)	291	(2.5)	295	(2.9)	296	(1.8)	297	(3.2)	297	(4.2)	292	(2.8)	295	(4.0)	290	(2.5)
Southeast	271	(2.4)	277	(1.4)	280	(2.2)	284	(2.1)	286	(2.1)	285	(2.5)	278	(2.9)	283	(2.8)	279	(2.6)	279	(2.4)	281	(2.1)
Central	291	(2.1)	292	(1.4)	287	(2.2)	290	(1.8)	291	(1.9)	294	(2.4)	294	(2.1)	286	(3.7)	293	(2.1)	292	(1.5)	291	(2.2)
West	284	(1.8)	282	(1.9)	287	(2.1)	289	(1.6)	289	(1.8)	287	(2.6)	290	(2.3)	288	(2.8)	287	(2.4)	286	(3.0)	280	(2.5)

—Not available.
†Not applicable.
[1]Data for 1971 include persons of Hispanic origin.
[2]Test scores of Hispanics were not tabulated separately.
NOTE: The NAEP reading scores have been evaluated at certain performance levels. Scale ranges from 0 to 500. Students scoring 150 (or higher) are able to follow brief written directions and carry out simple, discrete reading tasks. Students scoring 200 are able to understand, combine ideas, and make inferences based on short uncomplicated passages about specific or sequentially related information. Students scoring 250 are able to search for specific information, interrelate ideas, and make generalizations about literature, science, and social studies materials. Students scoring 300 are able to find, understand, summarize, and explain relatively complicated literary and informational material. Includes public and private schools. Excludes persons not enrolled in school and those who were unable to be tested due to limited proficiency in English or due to a disability. Race categories exclude persons of Hispanic origin. Some data have been revised from previously published figures. Standard errors appear in parentheses.
SOURCE: U.S. Department of Education, National Center for Education Statistics, National Assessment of Educational Progress (NAEP), *NAEP 2004 Trends in Academic Progress*; and NAEP Data Explorer (http://nces.ed.gov/nationsreportcard/nde/), retrieved January 2006. (This table was prepared February 2006.)

Table 111. Student scale score in reading, by age and percentile: Selected years, 1971 through 2004

Age and percentile	1971	1975	1980	1984	1988	1990	1992	1994	1996	1999			2004		
										Total	Male	Female	Total	Male	Female
1	2	3	4	5	6	7	8	9	10	11	12	13	14	15	16
9-year-olds															
Average	208 (1.0)	210 (0.7)	215 (1.0)	211 (0.9)	212 (1.1)	209 (1.2)	211 (0.9)	211 (1.2)	212 (1.0)	212 (1.3)	209 (1.6)	215 (1.5)	219 (1.1)	216 (1.4)	221 (1.0)
Standard deviation	42 (0.4)	39 (0.3)	38 (0.4)	41 (0.4)	41 (1.0)	45 (0.8)	40 (0.6)	41 (0.8)	39 (0.8)	39 (0.7)	41 (0.9)	38 (0.9)	—	(†)	(†)
Percentile															
5th	135 (2.0)	143 (1.3)	149 (1.6)	141 (1.2)	142 (3.6)	135 (3.2)	141 (1.6)	140 (2.6)	145 (2.4)	143 (1.3)	139 (1.6)	150 (3.1)	—	(†)	(†)
10th	152 (1.6)	159 (1.1)	165 (1.4)	157 (1.2)	157 (2.1)	150 (1.9)	156 (1.5)	156 (2.5)	160 (2.1)	158 (1.4)	153 (2.3)	164 (2.6)	169 (1.7)	(†)	(†)
25th	180 (1.3)	185 (0.8)	191 (1.2)	184 (1.2)	184 (1.8)	179 (1.8)	183 (1.5)	184 (1.9)	186 (1.3)	185 (2.0)	180 (1.8)	189 (1.6)	194 (1.7)	(†)	(†)
50th	209 (1.0)	212 (0.8)	217 (0.9)	213 (1.0)	214 (1.4)	210 (1.5)	214 (0.9)	215 (1.1)	215 (1.2)	215 (1.7)	212 (2.3)	218 (2.7)	221 (1.4)	(†)	(†)
75th	237 (1.0)	237 (0.9)	241 (1.0)	240 (0.9)	240 (1.3)	240 (1.8)	239 (1.2)	240 (1.5)	240 (1.0)	239 (1.4)	237 (2.1)	241 (1.6)	245 (1.3)	(†)	(†)
90th	260 (0.8)	258 (0.8)	262 (1.1)	263 (0.9)	263 (1.7)	266 (1.8)	260 (1.2)	260 (1.6)	260 (1.0)	259 (1.1)	258 (3.0)	260 (2.7)	264 (2.1)	(†)	(†)
95th	274 (0.9)	271 (0.1)	273 (1.6)	277 (1.4)	278 (2.0)	280 (1.3)	272 (1.2)	272 (1.5)	272 (1.3)	272 (2.3)	272 (3.4)	273 (2.0)	—	(†)	(†)
13-year-olds															
Average	255 (0.9)	256 (0.8)	258 (0.9)	257 (0.6)	257 (1.0)	257 (0.8)	260 (1.2)	258 (0.9)	258 (1.0)	259 (1.0)	254 (1.3)	265 (1.2)	259 (1.0)	254 (1.2)	264 (1.3)
Standard deviation	36 (0.4)	36 (0.3)	35 (0.4)	36 (0.3)	35 (0.5)	36 (0.6)	39 (0.8)	40 (0.7)	39 (0.9)	38 (0.8)	39 (1.1)	37 (1.0)	—	(†)	(†)
Percentile															
5th	193 (1.8)	194 (1.1)	199 (1.9)	197 (1.1)	200 (1.7)	196 (1.9)	191 (2.8)	188 (4.9)	189 (2.3)	193 (2.6)	186 (3.6)	203 (3.0)	—	(†)	(†)
10th	208 (1.4)	209 (1.0)	213 (1.5)	210 (0.9)	213 (1.2)	210 (1.8)	208 (1.9)	205 (1.7)	206 (2.1)	209 (1.6)	201 (1.9)	218 (2.4)	210 (1.9)	(†)	(†)
25th	232 (1.2)	233 (1.0)	235 (1.1)	234 (0.8)	234 (1.2)	233 (1.0)	235 (1.8)	233 (1.2)	233 (1.5)	234 (1.1)	227 (2.0)	240 (1.2)	235 (1.3)	(†)	(†)
50th	257 (1.0)	258 (0.9)	260 (0.8)	258 (0.8)	258 (1.2)	257 (0.9)	262 (1.6)	260 (1.1)	261 (0.9)	261 (1.5)	255 (1.4)	266 (1.5)	260 (1.4)	(†)	(†)
75th	280 (0.8)	281 (0.8)	283 (0.8)	282 (0.6)	281 (1.4)	281 (0.8)	287 (1.4)	285 (1.1)	285 (1.6)	286 (1.6)	281 (2.4)	291 (2.6)	285 (1.4)	(†)	(†)
90th	300 (0.9)	300 (1.0)	302 (0.8)	302 (0.8)	302 (1.0)	302 (1.0)	309 (1.8)	307 (1.4)	306 (1.4)	308 (2.4)	302 (2.3)	312 (2.1)	305 (1.2)	(†)	(†)
95th	311 (0.9)	312 (1.0)	314 (0.8)	314 (1.0)	314 (1.3)	314 (1.3)	322 (2.6)	320 (1.4)	319 (1.8)	320 (1.2)	314 (1.7)	325 (2.0)	—	(†)	(†)
17-year-olds															
Average	285 (1.2)	286 (0.8)	285 (1.2)	289 (0.8)	290 (1.0)	290 (1.1)	290 (1.1)	288 (1.3)	288 (1.1)	288 (1.3)	281 (1.6)	295 (1.4)	285 (1.2)	278 (1.5)	292 (1.3)
Standard deviation	46 (0.5)	44 (0.6)	42 (0.6)	40 (0.3)	37 (0.7)	41 (0.7)	43 (0.6)	44 (1.0)	42 (0.8)	42 (0.8)	43 (1.2)	40 (0.8)	—	(†)	(†)
Percentile															
5th	206 (1.5)	209 (3.0)	213 (1.7)	213 (1.3)	226 (1.3)	220 (2.3)	214 (2.9)	211 (3.6)	214 (2.5)	215 (4.5)	207 (3.2)	229 (5.7)	—	(†)	(†)
10th	225 (1.7)	228 (1.7)	231 (1.8)	231 (0.9)	241 (2.2)	237 (3.1)	233 (2.7)	230 (3.1)	232 (1.7)	233 (3.7)	225 (2.3)	244 (1.9)	227 (2.8)	(†)	(†)
25th	256 (1.6)	258 (1.1)	259 (1.2)	262 (1.1)	266 (1.8)	263 (1.3)	263 (1.1)	260 (1.8)	260 (1.1)	261 (2.2)	253 (2.2)	268 (1.6)	258 (1.4)	(†)	(†)
50th	288 (1.4)	288 (0.7)	287 (1.4)	290 (0.9)	291 (1.9)	291 (1.3)	293 (1.2)	290 (1.8)	289 (1.9)	289 (1.8)	283 (1.6)	295 (1.6)	287 (1.5)	(†)	(†)
75th	317 (1.0)	316 (0.7)	315 (1.2)	317 (0.9)	316 (1.4)	319 (1.5)	319 (1.4)	319 (1.8)	316 (1.6)	316 (1.2)	311 (1.9)	322 (1.9)	315 (1.0)	(†)	(†)
90th	342 (1.1)	340 (0.9)	337 (1.4)	340 (0.7)	337 (2.1)	343 (2.1)	343 (1.8)	343 (1.8)	341 (1.7)	341 (2.2)	335 (2.6)	345 (2.9)	338 (1.8)	(†)	(†)
95th	357 (1.5)	354 (0.7)	351 (1.3)	353 (1.0)	349 (1.8)	356 (1.7)	356 (1.9)	358 (1.7)	355 (2.6)	355 (1.7)	350 (6.4)	359 (3.0)	—	(†)	(†)

—Not available.
†Not applicable.
NOTE: The NAEP reading scores have been evaluated at certain performance levels. Scale ranges from 0 to 500. Students scoring 150 (or higher) are able to follow brief written directions and carry out simple, discrete reading tasks. Students scoring 200 are able to understand, combine ideas, and make inferences based on short uncomplicated passages about specific or sequentially related information. Students scoring 250 are able to search for specific information, interrelate ideas, and make generalizations about literature, science, and social studies materials. Students scoring 300 are able to find, understand, summarize, and explain relatively complicated literary and informational material. Includes public and private schools. Excludes persons not enrolled in school and those who were unable to be tested due to limited proficiency in English or due to a disability. Some data have been revised from previously published figures. Standard errors appear in parentheses.
SOURCE: U.S. Department of Education, National Center for Education Statistics, National Assessment of Educational Progress (NAEP), NAEP Data Explorer (http://nces.ed.gov/nationsreportcard/nde/), retrieved July 2005. (This table was prepared February 2006.)

Table 112. Average reading scale score, by age and amount of time spent on reading and homework: Selected years, 1984 through 2004

Time spent on reading and homework	9-year-olds					13-year-olds					17-year-olds				
	1984	1994	1996	1999	2004	1984	1994	1996	1999	2004	1984	1994	1996	1999	2004
1	2	3	4	5	6	7	8	9	10	11	12	13	14	15	16
Average scale score															
Materials read a few times a year or more															
Poems	211 (1.9)	210 (2.9)	215 (2.8)	213 (2.7)	—	260 (1.2)	261 (2.3)	262 (2.5)	263 (1.9)	—	290 (1.5)	293 (2.1)	294 (2.8)	292 (2.6)	—
Plays	211 (2.5)	207 (3.0)	214 (4.1)	211 (3.7)	—	260 (1.3)	263 (2.1)	262 (2.4)	264 (2.3)	—	290 (1.7)	294 (2.4)	293 (2.3)	294 (2.7)	—
Biographies	213 (2.4)	220 (3.4)	220 (3.2)	215 (3.0)	—	261 (1.3)	261 (2.1)	262 (2.3)	263 (2.7)	—	292 (1.4)	293 (2.4)	293 (2.2)	293 (2.8)	—
Science books	212 (1.6)	211 (2.6)	214 (2.0)	213 (2.1)	—	259 (1.2)	260 (2.1)	261 (2.2)	261 (1.7)	—	289 (1.4)	293 (2.4)	290 (2.2)	291 (2.3)	—
Books about other times	211 (1.7)	211 (2.6)	213 (2.3)	213 (2.5)	—	259 (1.1)	260 (2.2)	262 (2.2)	262 (2.1)	—	289 (1.4)	293 (2.3)	292 (2.8)	292 (2.0)	—
Frequency of reading for fun															
Daily	214 (1.1)	215 (2.3)	213 (2.0)	215 (2.4)	220 (1.5)	264 (1.4)	272 (3.2)	269 (3.3)	272 (3.2)	271 (2.8)	297 (1.5)	302 (4.1)	302 (5.2)	301 (4.9)	305 (3.7)
Weekly	212 (1.7)	214 (3.1)	212 (2.6)	215 (2.6)	224 (2.3)	255 (1.4)	255 (3.1)	258 (3.6)	263 (3.2)	261 (2.3)	290 (1.7)	286 (4.5)	293 (4.0)	286 (2.9)	288 (4.3)
Monthly	204 (3.3)	213 (5.8)	210 (5.0)	211 (4.2)	216 (4.6)	255 (2.1)	255 (5.7)	259 (4.6)	260 (3.7)	‡	290 (1.8)	286 (4.5)	290 (5.6)	286 (4.8)	287 (4.7)
Yearly	197 (4.2)	— (†)	— (†)	—	209 (4.6)	252 (3.6)	252 (5.4)	—	253 (4.4)	236 (†)	279 (2.7)	281 (8.2)	285 (5.6)	283 (4.4)	272 (5.0)
Never	198 (2.7)	193 (3.9)	199 (4.3)	195 (3.3)	203 (4.4)	239 (2.5)	237 (5.1)	236 (4.8)	242 (5.3)	236 (3.9)	269 (2.4)	258 (5.2)	270 (5.0)	262 (5.0)	268 (5.8)
Reading of books, newspapers, and magazines															
Yearly/monthly	207 (1.6)	206 (3.8)	208 (3.1)	209 (2.9)	—	244 (1.7)	245 (3.7)	249 (3.4)	252 (2.9)	—	270 (2.0)	279 (4.0)	275 (4.5)	276 (3.8)	—
Weekly	219 (2.5)	216 (3.7)	221 (4.7)	220 (3.5)	—	261 (1.6)	261 (2.6)	262 (3.0)	261 (3.3)	—	288 (1.5)	295 (2.8)	294 (3.2)	292 (2.2)	—
Daily	211 (3.8)	—	— (†)	214 (6.3)	—	269 (2.2)	275 (3.9)	270 (3.4)	271 (4.0)	—	299 (1.9)	296 (4.0)	295 (4.8)	299 (6.5)	—
Time spent on homework															
None	212 (0.9)	213 (2.0)	210 (1.9)	210 (1.9)	217 (2.0)	254 (1.0)	250 (1.7)	254 (1.3)	251 (2.0)	248 (1.7)	276 (0.8)	273 (2.3)	274 (1.9)	275 (2.3)	270 (2.0)
Didn't do assignment	199 (2.1)	200 (4.3)	196 (5.2)	204 (4.4)	204 (4.1)	247 (1.7)	243 (5.6)	249 (3.3)	249 (4.2)	245 (3.4)	287 (1.4)	285 (2.1)	281 (2.2)	282 (3.1)	279 (2.7)
Less than 1 hour	217 (0.8)	212 (1.4)	215 (1.0)	214 (1.4)	221 (1.6)	261 (0.6)	261 (1.3)	258 (1.6)	262 (1.6)	261 (1.6)	290 (0.9)	288 (1.6)	289 (1.5)	291 (3.1)	287 (1.6)
1 to 2 hours	216 (1.4)	214 (3.0)	219 (2.1)	215 (3.2)	221 (2.3)	267 (0.8)	268 (1.7)	266 (1.6)	269 (1.6)	268 (1.6)	296 (0.8)	297 (1.7)	296 (2.1)	296 (2.0)	295 (1.7)
More than 2 hours	201 (1.9)	193 (6.1)	199 (4.5)	197 (3.5)	207 (3.2)	265 (1.2)	270 (2.4)	268 (2.3)	269 (3.0)	272 (2.0)	303 (1.4)	306 (3.1)	307 (3.4)	300 (2.8)	304 (2.4)
Percent															
Materials read a few times a year or more															
Poems	70 (1.5)	62 (2.3)	60 (1.9)	64 (2.4)	—	68 (1.3)	79 (1.4)	80 (1.9)	77 (1.6)	—	76 (1.1)	85 (2.2)	80 (1.8)	85 (2.0)	—
Plays	56 (1.4)	45 (2.2)	42 (2.3)	44 (2.2)	—	59 (1.4)	63 (2.3)	67 (2.1)	61 (1.8)	—	63 (1.0)	70 (2.1)	67 (1.6)	72 (2.0)	—
Biographies	45 (1.5)	47 (2.1)	46 (2.4)	49 (3.0)	—	62 (1.3)	68 (1.7)	65 (2.6)	72 (2.1)	—	59 (1.2)	69 (1.8)	66 (1.7)	84 (1.3)	—
Science books	84 (1.3)	87 (1.8)	83 (2.2)	80 (1.6)	—	90 (0.8)	92 (1.4)	90 (1.9)	89 (1.2)	—	70 (1.1)	84 (1.9)	82 (2.0)	84 (1.3)	—
Books about other times	79 (1.2)	79 (2.0)	78 (1.6)	79 (1.9)	—	83 (0.9)	83 (1.8)	84 (1.8)	84 (1.3)	—	81 (0.9)	82 (2.0)	81 (1.9)	81 (2.0)	—
Frequency of reading for fun															
Total	100	100	100	100	100	100	100	100	100	100	100	100	100	100	100
Daily	53 (1.0)	58 (1.6)	54 (1.9)	54 (1.6)	54 (1.6)	35 (1.0)	32 (1.8)	32 (1.9)	28 (1.7)	30 (2.0)	31 (0.8)	30 (2.6)	23 (1.9)	25 (1.7)	22 (2.0)
Weekly	28 (0.8)	25 (1.5)	27 (1.8)	26 (1.5)	26 (1.2)	32 (0.8)	32 (2.1)	31 (2.1)	36 (1.7)	34 (1.6)	33 (1.1)	31 (1.9)	32 (2.7)	28 (1.7)	30 (1.9)
Monthly	7 (0.6)	5 (0.6)	8 (1.0)	6 (0.6)	7 (0.5)	14 (0.8)	14 (1.7)	15 (1.4)	17 (1.6)	15 (1.2)	15 (1.1)	15 (1.5)	17 (1.6)	19 (1.2)	14 (1.6)
Yearly	3 (0.3)	3 (0.6)	3 (0.5)	4 (0.7)	5 (0.7)	7 (0.5)	10 (1.2)	9 (1.2)	10 (0.7)	9 (0.5)	10 (0.5)	12 (1.5)	12 (1.6)	12 (1.7)	14 (1.5)
Never	9 (0.5)	9 (0.8)	8 (0.8)	10 (0.8)	8 (0.6)	8 (0.6)	12 (1.7)	13 (1.5)	9 (0.8)	13 (1.3)	9 (0.6)	12 (1.4)	16 (2.1)	16 (2.4)	19 (1.8)
Reading of books, newspapers, and magazines															
Total	100	100	100	100	100	100	100	100	100	100	100	100	100	100	100
Yearly/monthly	59 (1.5)	64 (1.8)	67 (2.3)	63 (2.6)	—	30 (1.5)	34 (2.5)	32 (2.6)	32 (2.6)	—	20 (1.0)	22 (1.7)	25 (2.1)	26 (2.1)	—
Weekly	31 (1.5)	27 (1.8)	22 (1.9)	27 (2.4)	—	49 (1.1)	47 (2.5)	47 (2.2)	49 (2.4)	—	53 (1.2)	55 (2.3)	52 (2.6)	52 (2.2)	—
Daily	11 (0.9)	10 (1.3)	10 (1.2)	11 (1.2)	—	21 (1.1)	19 (1.7)	21 (1.7)	19 (1.9)	—	27 (1.3)	23 (1.8)	23 (1.9)	21 (2.1)	—
Time spent on homework															
Total	100	100	100	100	100	100	100	100	100	100	100	100	100	100	100
None	35 (1.3)	32 (2.1)	26 (1.6)	26 (1.6)	21 (1.5)	22 (0.7)	23 (1.4)	22 (1.8)	24 (1.2)	20 (1.3)	22 (0.9)	23 (1.4)	23 (1.4)	26 (1.0)	26 (1.0)
Didn't do assignment	4 (0.3)	4 (0.4)	4 (0.3)	4 (0.3)	3 (0.3)	4 (0.6)	4 (0.6)	5 (0.3)	5 (0.4)	6 (0.4)	11 (0.3)	11 (0.6)	13 (0.6)	13 (0.7)	13 (0.7)
Less than 1 hour	48 (1.7)	48 (1.7)	53 (1.5)	53 (1.4)	59 (1.4)	36 (0.6)	34 (1.0)	37 (1.2)	37 (1.6)	40 (1.0)	27 (0.9)	27 (1.2)	28 (0.9)	28 (1.7)	28 (0.9)
1 to 2 hours	13 (0.4)	11 (0.7)	13 (0.7)	12 (0.7)	13 (0.6)	28 (0.5)	28 (0.7)	27 (1.2)	26 (1.0)	26 (1.0)	26 (0.5)	26 (1.2)	24 (1.0)	23 (2.1)	22 (0.9)
More than 2 hours	6 (0.2)	4 (0.4)	4 (0.3)	5 (0.5)	5 (0.3)	9 (0.3)	9 (0.7)	8 (0.9)	8 (0.8)	9 (0.5)	13 (0.6)	13 (0.9)	11 (0.7)	11 (1.8)	19 (0.6)

—Not available.
†Not applicable.
‡Reporting standards not met.

NOTE: The NAEP reading scores have been evaluated at certain performance levels. Scale ranges from 0 to 500. Students scoring 150 (or higher) are able to follow brief written directions and carry out simple, discrete reading tasks. Students scoring 200 are able to understand, combine ideas, and make inferences based on short uncomplicated passages about specific or sequentially related information. Students scoring 250 are able to search for specific information, interrelate ideas, and make generalizations about literature, science, and social studies materials. Students scoring 300 are able to find, understand, summarize, and explain relatively complicated literary and informational material. Includes public and private schools. Excludes persons not enrolled in school and those who were unable to be tested due to limited proficiency in English or due to a disability. Detail may not sum to totals because of rounding. Standard errors appear in parentheses.

SOURCE: U.S. Department of Education, National Center for Education Statistics, National Assessment of Educational Progress (NAEP), *NAEP Trends in Academic Progress*, 1996 and 1999; and NAEP Data Explorer (http://nces.ed.gov/nationsreportcard/nde/), retrieved July 2005. (This table was prepared February 2006.)

Table 113. Percentage of students at or above selected reading score levels, by age, sex, and race/ethnicity: Selected years, 1971 through 2004

Selected characteristic	1971		1975		1980		1984		1988		1990		1992		1994		1996		1999		2004	
1	2		3		4		5		6		7		8		9		10		11		12	
9-year-olds																						
Total																						
Level 150	91	(0.5)	93	(0.4)	95	(0.4)	92	(0.4)	93	(0.7)	90	(0.9)	92	(0.4)	92	(0.7)	93	(0.6)	93	(0.7)	96	(0.3)
Level 200	59	(1.0)	62	(0.8)	68	(1.0)	62	(0.8)	63	(1.3)	59	(1.3)	62	(1.1)	63	(1.4)	64	(1.3)	64	(1.4)	70	(1.2)
Level 250	16	(0.6)	15	(0.6)	18	(0.8)	17	(0.7)	17	(1.1)	18	(1.0)	16	(0.8)	17	(1.2)	17	(0.8)	16	(1.0)	20	(1.0)
Male																						
Level 150	88	(0.7)	91	(0.5)	93	(0.5)	90	(0.5)	90	(0.9)	88	(1.4)	90	(0.8)	90	(1.0)	92	(0.8)	91	(1.1)	95	(0.6)
Level 200	53	(1.2)	56	(1.0)	63	(1.1)	58	(1.0)	58	(1.8)	54	(1.9)	57	(1.6)	59	(1.5)	58	(2.0)	61	(1.8)	67	(1.7)
Level 250	12	(0.6)	12	(0.6)	15	(0.9)	16	(0.8)	16	(1.4)	16	(1.2)	14	(1.0)	15	(1.2)	14	(1.3)	15	(1.3)	19	(1.3)
Female																						
Level 150	93	(0.5)	95	(0.3)	96	(0.4)	94	(0.5)	95	(1.0)	92	(1.1)	94	(0.6)	94	(0.8)	95	(0.6)	95	(0.8)	97	(0.5)
Level 200	65	(1.1)	68	(0.8)	73	(1.0)	65	(1.0)	67	(1.4)	64	(1.2)	67	(1.2)	67	(1.9)	70	(1.6)	67	(1.6)	74	(1.1)
Level 250	19	(0.8)	18	(0.8)	21	(1.0)	18	(0.8)	19	(1.2)	21	(1.2)	18	(1.1)	18	(1.5)	19	(1.3)	17	(1.3)	21	(1.3)
White																						
Level 150	94 [1]	(0.4)	96	(0.3)	97	(0.2)	95	(0.3)	95	(0.7)	94	(0.9)	96	(0.5)	96	(0.5)	96	(0.6)	97	(0.4)	98	(0.4)
Level 200	65 [1]	(1.0)	69	(0.8)	74	(0.7)	69	(0.9)	68	(1.6)	66	(1.4)	69	(1.2)	70	(1.5)	71	(1.5)	73	(1.6)	78	(1.1)
Level 250	18 [1]	(0.7)	17	(0.7)	21	(0.9)	21	(0.8)	20	(1.5)	23	(1.2)	20	(1.0)	20	(1.5)	20	(1.1)	20	(1.4)	25	(1.2)
Black																						
Level 150	70 [1]	(1.7)	81	(1.1)	85	(1.4)	81	(1.2)	83	(2.4)	77	(2.7)	80	(2.2)	79	(2.4)	84	(1.9)	82	(2.5)	91	(1.2)
Level 200	22 [1]	(1.5)	32	(1.5)	41	(1.9)	37	(1.5)	39	(2.9)	34	(3.4)	37	(2.2)	38	(2.8)	42	(3.2)	36	(3.0)	51	(3.0)
Level 250	2 [1]	(0.5)	2	(0.3)	4	(0.6)	5	(0.5)	6	(1.2)	5	(1.5)	5	(0.8)	4	(1.5)	6	(1.1)	4	(1.1)	8	(1.6)
Hispanic																						
Level 150	[2]	(†)	81	(2.5)	84	(1.8)	82	(3.0)	86	(3.5)	84	(1.8)	83	(2.6)	80	(4.6)	86	(2.4)	87	(3.3)	95	(1.4)
Level 200	[2]	(†)	35	(3.0)	42	(2.6)	40	(2.7)	46	(3.3)	41	(2.7)	43	(3.5)	37	(4.6)	48	(3.8)	44	(3.4)	57	(2.8)
Level 250	[2]	(†)	3	(0.5)	5	(1.4)	4	(0.6)	9	(2.3)	6	(2.0)	7	(2.3)	6	(1.6)	7	(3.2)	6	(1.7)	9	(1.8)
13-year-olds																						
Total																						
Level 150	100	(#)	100	(0.1)	100	(0.1)	100	(#)	100	(0.1)	100	(0.1)	100	(0.3)	99	(0.2)	100	(0.2)	100	(0.2)	—	(†)
Level 200	93	(0.5)	93	(0.4)	95	(0.4)	94	(0.3)	95	(0.6)	94	(0.6)	93	(0.7)	92	(0.6)	92	(0.7)	93	(0.7)	94	(0.6)
Level 250	58	(1.1)	59	(1.0)	61	(1.1)	59	(0.8)	59	(1.3)	59	(1.0)	62	(1.4)	60	(1.2)	60	(1.3)	61	(1.5)	61	(1.3)
Level 300	10	(0.5)	10	(0.5)	11	(0.5)	11	(0.4)	11	(0.8)	11	(0.6)	15	(0.9)	14	(0.8)	14	(1.0)	15	(1.1)	13	(0.9)
Male																						
Level 150	100	(0.1)	100	(0.1)	100	(0.1)	100	(0.1)	100	(0.2)	100	(0.2)	99	(0.4)	99	(0.3)	99	(0.4)	99	(0.3)	—	(†)
Level 200	91	(0.7)	91	(0.5)	93	(0.6)	92	(0.4)	93	(1.0)	91	(0.9)	90	(1.1)	89	(1.1)	89	(1.2)	91	(0.9)	91	(0.8)
Level 250	52	(1.2)	52	(1.1)	56	(1.2)	54	(0.9)	52	(1.9)	52	(1.5)	55	(2.0)	53	(1.9)	53	(1.6)	55	(1.9)	55	(1.5)
Level 300	7	(0.5)	7	(0.4)	9	(0.7)	9	(0.5)	9	(0.9)	8	(0.8)	13	(1.1)	10	(0.7)	10	(1.0)	11	(1.1)	11	(0.9)
Female																						
Level 150	100	(0.1)	100	(0.1)	100	(#)	100	(0.1)	100	(‡)	100	(‡)	100	(‡)	100	(0.2)	100	(‡)	100	(‡)	—	(†)
Level 200	95	(0.4)	96	(0.4)	96	(0.4)	96	(0.3)	97	(0.6)	96	(0.6)	95	(0.7)	95	(0.6)	95	(0.6)	96	(0.7)	96	(0.6)
Level 250	64	(1.1)	65	(1.2)	65	(1.1)	64	(0.8)	65	(1.4)	65	(1.5)	68	(1.4)	68	(1.7)	66	(1.6)	66	(1.9)	67	(1.8)
Level 300	12	(0.6)	13	(0.7)	13	(0.6)	13	(0.6)	13	(0.9)	14	(0.9)	18	(1.1)	18	(1.1)	17	(1.3)	18	(1.7)	15	(1.2)
White																						
Level 150	100 [1]	(#)	100	(#)	100	(‡)	100	(#)	100	(‡)	100	(0.1)	100	(0.1)	100	(0.2)	100	(0.2)	100	(0.1)	—	(†)
Level 200	96 [1]	(0.3)	96	(0.2)	97	(0.2)	96	(0.2)	96	(0.6)	96	(0.6)	96	(0.6)	95	(0.7)	95	(0.5)	96	(0.6)	96	(0.6)
Level 250	64 [1]	(0.9)	65	(0.9)	68	(0.8)	65	(0.8)	64	(1.5)	65	(1.2)	68	(1.4)	68	(1.3)	69	(1.4)	69	(1.7)	69	(1.3)
Level 300	11 [1]	(0.5)	12	(0.5)	14	(0.6)	13	(0.6)	12	(0.9)	13	(0.9)	18	(1.1)	17	(1.0)	17	(1.3)	18	(1.4)	17	(1.2)
Black																						
Level 150	99 [1]	(0.3)	98	(0.3)	99	(0.3)	99	(0.2)	100	(‡)	99	(‡)	99	(‡)	99	(‡)	99	(‡)	99	(‡)	—	(†)
Level 200	74 [1]	(1.7)	77	(1.3)	84	(1.7)	85	(1.2)	91	(2.2)	88	(2.3)	82	(2.7)	81	(2.3)	82	(3.2)	85	(2.3)	89	(2.2)
Level 250	21 [1]	(1.2)	25	(1.6)	30	(2.0)	35	(1.3)	40	(2.3)	42	(3.5)	38	(2.7)	36	(3.5)	34	(3.9)	38	(2.7)	45	(2.8)
Level 300	1 [1]	(0.2)	2	(0.3)	2	(0.5)	3	(0.6)	5	(1.2)	5	(0.8)	6	(1.4)	4	(1.2)	3	(0.9)	5	(1.4)	5	(1.0)
Hispanic																						
Level 150	[2]	(†)	100	(0.3)	100	(‡)	100	(‡)	99	(‡)	99	(0.5)	98	(‡)	99	(‡)	99	(‡)	100	(‡)	—	(†)
Level 200	[2]	(†)	81	(2.3)	87	(2.4)	86	(1.7)	87	(2.6)	86	(2.4)	83	(3.5)	82	(2.7)	85	(3.2)	89	(2.8)	88	(1.8)
Level 250	[2]	(†)	32	(3.6)	35	(2.6)	39	(2.3)	38	(4.4)	37	(2.9)	41	(5.1)	34	(3.9)	38	(3.7)	43	(3.8)	43	(2.0)
Level 300	[2]	(†)	2	(1.0)	2	(0.6)	4	(1.0)	4	(1.9)	4	(1.2)	6	(1.9)	4	(1.8)	5	(1.7)	6	(1.8)	4	(0.8)

See notes at end of table.

Table 113. Percentage of students at or above selected reading score levels, by age, sex, and race/ethnicity: Selected years, 1971 through 2004—Continued

Selected characteristic	1971		1975		1980		1984		1988		1990		1992		1994		1996		1999		2004	
1	2		3		4		5		6		7		8		9		10		11		12	
17-year-olds																						
Total																						
Level 150	100	(0.1)	100	(0.1)	100	(0.1)	100	(#)	100	(‡)	100	(‡)	100	(0.1)	100	(0.1)	100	(‡)	100	(‡)	—	(†)
Level 200	96	(0.3)	96	(0.3)	97	(0.3)	98	(0.1)	99	(0.3)	98	(0.3)	97	(0.4)	97	(0.5)	98	(0.5)	98	(0.4)	—	(†)
Level 250	79	(0.9)	80	(0.7)	81	(0.9)	83	(0.6)	86	(0.8)	84	(1.0)	83	(0.8)	81	(1.0)	82	(0.8)	82	(1.0)	80	(1.0)
Level 300	39	(1.0)	39	(0.8)	38	(1.1)	40	(1.0)	41	(1.5)	41	(1.0)	43	(1.1)	41	(1.2)	39	(1.4)	40	(1.4)	38	(1.2)
Male																						
Level 150	99	(0.1)	99	(0.2)	100	(0.1)	100	(#)	100	(‡)	100	(‡)	100	(0.2)	100	(‡)	100	(‡)	100	(‡)	—	(†)
Level 200	95	(0.4)	95	(0.4)	96	(0.5)	98	(0.2)	99	(0.5)	97	(0.6)	96	(0.7)	96	(0.9)	96	(0.8)	97	(0.6)	—	(†)
Level 250	74	(1.0)	76	(0.8)	78	(1.0)	80	(0.7)	83	(1.4)	80	(1.4)	78	(1.2)	76	(1.5)	77	(1.2)	77	(1.5)	74	(1.4)
Level 300	34	(1.1)	34	(1.0)	35	(1.3)	36	(1.0)	37	(2.3)	36	(1.5)	38	(1.6)	36	(1.9)	34	(1.9)	34	(1.7)	33	(1.5)
Female																						
Level 150	100	(0.1)	100	(0.1)	100	(‡)	100	(‡)	100	(‡)	100	(‡)	100	(‡)	100	(‡)	100	(‡)	100	(‡)	—	(†)
Level 200	97	(0.3)	98	(0.4)	98	(0.3)	99	(0.1)	99	(0.3)	99	(0.3)	98	(0.4)	98	(0.5)	99	(0.5)	99	(0.4)	—	(†)
Level 250	83	(1.0)	84	(0.9)	84	(1.0)	87	(0.6)	88	(1.1)	89	(1.0)	87	(1.1)	86	(1.2)	87	(1.0)	87	(1.0)	86	(1.0)
Level 300	44	(1.2)	44	(0.9)	41	(1.2)	45	(1.1)	44	(2.0)	47	(1.3)	48	(1.5)	46	(1.5)	45	(1.7)	45	(1.8)	42	(1.5)
White																						
Level 150	100 [1]	(#)	100	(#)	100	(‡)	100	(‡)	100	(‡)	100	(‡)	100	(‡)	100	(‡)	100	(‡)	100	(‡)	—	(†)
Level 200	98 [1]	(0.2)	99	(0.1)	99	(0.1)	99	(0.1)	99	(0.3)	99	(0.2)	99	(0.3)	98	(0.4)	99	(0.4)	98	(0.4)	—	(†)
Level 250	84 [1]	(0.7)	86	(0.6)	87	(0.6)	88	(0.5)	89	(0.9)	88	(1.1)	88	(0.9)	86	(1.1)	87	(0.8)	87	(1.3)	86	(1.0)
Level 300	43 [1]	(0.9)	44	(0.8)	43	(1.1)	47	(1.1)	45	(1.6)	48	(1.2)	50	(1.4)	48	(1.4)	46	(1.5)	46	(1.5)	45	(1.4)
Black																						
Level 150	98 [1]	(0.4)	98	(0.8)	99	(0.3)	100	(‡)	100	(‡)	100	(‡)	99	(‡)	99	(‡)	100	(‡)	100	(‡)	—	(†)
Level 200	82 [1]	(1.5)	82	(1.8)	86	(1.7)	96	(0.5)	98	(1.0)	96	(1.3)	92	(1.6)	93	(2.0)	95	(1.9)	95	(1.1)	—	(†)
Level 250	40 [1]	(1.6)	43	(1.6)	44	(2.0)	65	(1.5)	76	(2.4)	69	(2.8)	61	(2.3)	66	(4.1)	68	(4.0)	66	(2.5)	67	(3.0)
Level 300	8 [1]	(0.9)	8	(0.7)	7	(0.8)	16	(1.0)	25	(3.1)	20	(1.8)	17	(2.5)	22	(3.7)	18	(2.2)	17	(1.7)	17	(2.0)
Hispanic																						
Level 150	[2]	(†)	99	(0.4)	100	(‡)	100	(‡)	100	(‡)	100	(‡)	100	(‡)	99	(‡)	100	(‡)	100	(‡)	—	(†)
Level 200	[2]	(†)	89	(2.4)	93	(1.8)	96	(0.7)	96	(2.4)	96	(2.1)	93	(2.3)	91	(3.4)	94	(1.9)	97	(‡)	—	(†)
Level 250	[2]	(†)	53	(4.1)	62	(3.1)	68	(2.4)	71	(4.8)	75	(4.7)	69	(4.0)	63	(4.4)	65	(4.2)	68	(4.3)	64	(3.7)
Level 300	[2]	(†)	13	(2.7)	17	(2.1)	21	(3.0)	23	(3.7)	27	(3.3)	27	(3.2)	20	(3.0)	20	(4.8)	24	(3.8)	20	(2.4)

—Not available.
†Not applicable.
#Rounds to zero.
‡Reporting standards not met.
[1]Data for 1971 include persons of Hispanic origin.
[2]Test scores of Hispanics were not tabulated separately.
NOTE: The NAEP reading scores have been evaluated at certain performance levels. Scale ranges from 0 to 500. Students scoring 150 (or higher) are able to follow brief written directions and carry out simple, discrete reading tasks. Students scoring 200 are able to understand, combine ideas, and make inferences based on short uncomplicated passages about specific or sequentially related information. Students scoring 250 are able to search for specific information, interrelate ideas, and make generalizations about literature, science, and social studies materials. Students scoring 300 are able to find, understand, summarize, and explain relatively complicated literary and informational material. Includes public and private schools. Excludes persons not enrolled in school and those who were unable to be tested due to limited proficiency in English or due to a disability. Race categories exclude persons of Hispanic origin. Standard errors appear in parentheses.
SOURCE: U.S. Department of Education, National Center for Education Statistics, National Assessment of Educational Progress (NAEP), *NAEP 1999 Trends in Academic Progress*; and NAEP Data Explorer (http://nces.ed.gov/nationsreportcard/nde/), retrieved July 2005. (This table was prepared February 2006.)

Table 114. Average scale score in reading and percentage of 4th-graders in public schools attaining reading achievement levels, by race/ethnicity and state or jurisdiction: Selected years, 1994 through 2005

State or jurisdiction	Average scale score					Average scale score by race/ethnicity,[1] 2005					Percent attaining reading achievement levels,[2] 2005			
	1994	1998	2002	2003	2005	White	Black	Hispanic	Asian/Pacific Islander	American Indian/ Alaska Native	Below basic	Basic or above[3]	Proficient or above[4]	Advanced[5]
1	2	3	4	5	6	7	8	9	10	11	12	13	14	15
United States[6]	212 (1.1)	213 (1.2)	217 (0.5)	216 (0.3)	217 (0.2)	228 (0.2)	199 (0.3)	201 (0.5)	227 (0.9)	205 (1.3)	38 (0.3)	63 (0.3)	30 (0.2)	7 (0.1)
Alabama	208 (1.5)	211 (1.9)	207 (1.4)	207 (1.7)	208 (1.2)	220 (1.3)	188 (1.8)	‡ (†)	‡ (†)	‡ (†)	47 (1.3)	53 (1.3)	22 (1.3)	5 (0.6)
Alaska	— (†)	— (†)	— (†)	212 (1.6)	211 (1.4)	225 (1.3)	212 (3.9)	209 (3.6)	206 (4.0)	183 (3.0)	42 (1.5)	58 (1.5)	27 (1.3)	5 (0.5)
Arizona	206 (1.9)	206 (1.4)	205 (1.5)	209 (1.2)	207 (1.6)	224 (1.9)	193 (3.4)	192 (1.7)	224 (5.3)	‡ (†)	48 (1.7)	52 (1.7)	24 (1.7)	6 (0.6)
Arkansas	209 (1.7)	209 (1.6)	213 (1.4)	214 (1.4)	217 (1.1)	225 (1.0)	194 (1.9)	212 (4.2)	‡ (†)	‡ (†)	37 (1.4)	63 (1.4)	30 (1.1)	6 (0.6)
California[7,8]	197 (1.8)	202 (2.5)	206 (2.5)	206 (1.2)	207 (0.7)	225 (1.2)	195 (1.4)	193 (0.8)	223 (1.8)	213 (3.9)	50 (0.9)	50 (0.9)	21 (0.7)	5 (0.4)
Colorado	213 (1.3)	220 (1.4)	— (†)	224 (1.2)	224 (1.1)	232 (1.2)	207 (3.0)	206 (1.6)	231 (3.9)	‡ (†)	31 (1.3)	70 (1.3)	37 (1.6)	8 (0.9)
Connecticut	222 (1.6)	230 (1.6)	229 (1.1)	228 (1.1)	226 (1.0)	234 (1.1)	201 (1.9)	203 (2.2)	236 (4.2)	‡ (†)	29 (1.2)	71 (1.2)	38 (1.2)	12 (1.0)
Delaware	206 (1.1)	207 (1.7)	224 (0.6)	224 (0.7)	226 (0.8)	235 (0.9)	212 (1.1)	216 (2.2)	239 (4.5)	‡ (†)	27 (1.4)	73 (1.4)	34 (1.2)	7 (0.8)
District of Columbia	— (†)	179 (1.2)	191 (0.9)	188 (0.9)	191 (1.0)	252 (3.9)	187 (1.0)	193 (3.4)	‡ (†)	‡ (†)	67 (1.0)	33 (1.0)	11 (0.8)	2 (0.4)
Florida	205 (1.7)	206 (1.4)	214 (1.4)	218 (1.1)	220 (0.9)	228 (1.4)	203 (1.6)	215 (1.6)	230 (4.0)	‡ (†)	35 (1.0)	65 (1.0)	30 (1.2)	7 (0.7)
Georgia	207 (2.4)	209 (1.4)	215 (1.0)	214 (1.3)	214 (1.2)	226 (1.2)	199 (1.5)	203 (4.2)	243 (5.1)	‡ (†)	42 (1.5)	58 (1.5)	26 (1.5)	6 (0.7)
Hawaii	201 (1.7)	200 (1.5)	208 (0.9)	208 (1.4)	210 (1.0)	224 (1.7)	206 (4.8)	211 (4.8)	206 (1.1)	‡ (†)	47 (1.2)	53 (1.2)	23 (1.4)	5 (0.6)
Idaho	— (†)	— (†)	220 (1.1)	218 (1.0)	222 (0.9)	226 (0.8)	‡ (†)	199 (2.8)	‡ (†)	‡ (†)	31 (1.1)	69 (1.1)	33 (1.4)	6 (0.6)
Illinois	— (†)	— (†)	— (†)	216 (1.6)	217 (1.2)	230 (1.1)	194 (2.1)	199 (2.5)	230 (4.8)	‡ (†)	38 (1.3)	62 (1.3)	32 (1.3)	7 (0.7)
Indiana	220 (1.3)	206 (1.4)	222 (1.4)	220 (1.0)	218 (1.1)	223 (1.2)	197 (2.4)	208 (2.9)	‡ (†)	‡ (†)	36 (1.3)	64 (1.3)	30 (1.4)	7 (0.7)
Iowa[7,8]	223 (1.3)	220 (1.6)	223 (1.1)	223 (1.1)	221 (0.9)	224 (0.9)	201 (3.6)	200 (2.9)	224 (5.9)	‡ (†)	33 (1.3)	68 (1.3)	33 (1.2)	7 (0.5)
Kansas[7,8]	— (†)	221 (1.4)	222 (1.4)	220 (1.2)	221 (1.3)	225 (1.3)	196 (2.5)	203 (2.8)	238 (4.9)	‡ (†)	34 (1.5)	66 (1.5)	31 (1.3)	8 (1.0)
Kentucky	212 (1.6)	218 (1.5)	219 (1.1)	219 (1.3)	220 (1.1)	222 (1.1)	203 (2.3)	‡ (†)	‡ (†)	‡ (†)	35 (1.5)	65 (1.5)	31 (1.2)	8 (0.8)
Louisiana	197 (1.3)	200 (1.6)	207 (1.7)	205 (1.4)	209 (1.3)	223 (1.1)	195 (1.7)	204 (3.6)	216 (4.6)	‡ (†)	47 (1.8)	53 (1.8)	20 (1.4)	4 (0.6)
Maine	228 (1.3)	225 (1.4)	225 (1.1)	224 (0.9)	225 (0.9)	225 (1.0)	‡ (†)	‡ (†)	‡ (†)	‡ (†)	29 (1.2)	71 (1.2)	35 (1.3)	9 (0.8)
Maryland	210 (1.5)	212 (1.6)	217 (1.5)	219 (1.4)	220 (1.3)	233 (1.5)	201 (1.5)	210 (2.7)	239 (3.6)	‡ (†)	35 (1.4)	65 (1.4)	32 (1.5)	8 (0.7)
Massachusetts[7]	223 (1.3)	223 (1.4)	234 (1.1)	228 (1.2)	231 (0.9)	237 (0.9)	211 (1.9)	203 (2.4)	234 (4.1)	‡ (†)	22 (1.2)	78 (1.2)	44 (1.4)	12 (0.9)
Michigan	— (†)	216 (1.5)	219 (1.1)	219 (1.2)	218 (1.5)	226 (1.4)	190 (2.7)	‡ (†)	‡ (†)	‡ (†)	37 (1.7)	63 (1.7)	32 (1.4)	7 (0.9)
Minnesota[7,8]	218 (1.4)	219 (1.7)	225 (1.1)	223 (1.1)	225 (1.3)	231 (1.3)	192 (3.8)	204 (3.6)	216 (4.6)	‡ (†)	29 (1.6)	71 (1.6)	38 (1.7)	11 (0.9)
Mississippi	202 (1.6)	203 (1.3)	203 (1.3)	205 (1.3)	204 (1.4)	220 (1.0)	190 (1.6)	‡ (†)	‡ (†)	‡ (†)	52 (1.7)	48 (1.7)	18 (1.4)	3 (0.5)
Missouri	217 (1.5)	216 (1.3)	220 (1.3)	222 (1.2)	221 (0.9)	226 (0.9)	200 (2.6)	210 (4.8)	‡ (†)	‡ (†)	33 (1.2)	67 (1.2)	33 (1.3)	7 (0.8)
Montana[7,8]	222 (1.4)	225 (1.5)	224 (1.8)	223 (1.2)	225 (1.1)	228 (1.1)	‡ (†)	226 (4.5)	‡ (†)	210 (2.0)	29 (1.2)	71 (1.2)	36 (1.4)	8 (0.9)
Nebraska[9]	220 (1.5)	— (†)	222 (1.5)	221 (1.0)	221 (1.2)	228 (1.2)	194 (2.5)	202 (2.5)	‡ (†)	‡ (†)	32 (1.4)	68 (1.4)	34 (1.4)	7 (0.8)
Nevada	218 (1.4)	206 (1.8)	209 (1.2)	207 (1.2)	207 (1.2)	219 (1.5)	192 (2.6)	195 (1.7)	212 (3.4)	‡ (†)	48 (1.5)	52 (1.5)	21 (1.3)	4 (0.6)
New Hampshire[7]	223 (1.5)	226 (1.7)	— (†)	228 (1.0)	227 (0.9)	228 (0.9)	‡ (†)	‡ (†)	‡ (†)	‡ (†)	26 (1.1)	74 (1.1)	39 (1.4)	9 (0.8)
New Jersey	219 (1.2)	— (†)	— (†)	225 (1.2)	223 (1.3)	233 (1.1)	199 (2.4)	206 (2.3)	241 (2.6)	‡ (†)	32 (1.6)	68 (1.6)	37 (1.5)	10 (0.8)
New Mexico	205 (1.7)	205 (1.4)	208 (1.6)	203 (1.5)	207 (1.3)	225 (1.5)	206 (5.3)	199 (1.6)	‡ (†)	190 (2.6)	49 (1.5)	51 (1.5)	21 (1.4)	4 (0.5)
New York[7,8]	212 (1.4)	215 (1.6)	222 (1.5)	222 (1.1)	223 (1.1)	232 (0.9)	207 (1.8)	208 (1.9)	237 (2.9)	‡ (†)	31 (1.5)	69 (1.5)	33 (1.2)	8 (0.6)
North Carolina	214 (1.5)	213 (1.6)	222 (1.0)	221 (1.0)	217 (1.0)	227 (1.2)	201 (1.5)	204 (2.4)	221 (6.2)	‡ (†)	39 (1.5)	62 (1.5)	29 (1.4)	7 (0.6)
North Dakota[8]	225 (1.2)	— (†)	224 (1.0)	222 (0.9)	225 (0.7)	228 (0.7)	‡ (†)	‡ (†)	‡ (†)	199 (2.9)	28 (1.1)	72 (1.1)	36 (1.1)	7 (0.6)

See notes at end of table.

Table 114. Average scale score in reading and percentage of 4th-graders in public schools attaining reading achievement levels, by race/ethnicity and state or jurisdiction: Selected years, 1994 through 2005—Continued

State or jurisdiction	Average scale score					Average scale score by race/ethnicity,[1] 2005					Percent attaining reading achievement levels,[2] 2005			
	1994	1998	2002	2003	2005	White	Black	Hispanic	Asian/Pacific Islander	American Indian/Alaska Native	Below basic	Basic or above[3]	Proficient or above[4]	Advanced[5]
1	2	3	4	5	6	7	8	9	10	11	12	13	14	15
Ohio	— (†)	— (†)	222 (1.3)	222 (1.2)	223 (1.4)	230 (1.3)	197 (1.9)	211 (5.6)	‡ (†)	‡ (†)	31 (1.6)	69 (1.6)	34 (1.6)	8 (0.9)
Oklahoma	— (†)	219 (1.2)	213 (1.2)	214 (1.2)	214 (1.1)	219 (1.3)	197 (2.9)	204 (3.2)	‡ (†)	211 (1.8)	40 (1.6)	60 (1.6)	25 (1.5)	5 (0.7)
Oregon	— (†)	212 (1.8)	220 (1.4)	218 (1.3)	217 (1.4)	223 (1.2)	200 (4.8)	194 (2.2)	221 (4.2)	‡ (†)	38 (1.7)	62 (1.7)	29 (1.5)	7 (0.7)
Pennsylvania[9]	215 (1.6)	— (†)	221 (1.2)	219 (1.3)	223 (1.3)	229 (1.3)	200 (2.5)	203 (4.3)	234 (5.4)	‡ (†)	31 (1.6)	69 (1.6)	36 (1.5)	9 (0.8)
Rhode Island[9]	220 (1.3)	218 (1.4)	220 (1.2)	216 (1.3)	216 (1.2)	224 (1.1)	197 (3.2)	192 (2.5)	219 (6.1)	‡ (†)	38 (1.5)	62 (1.5)	30 (1.3)	7 (0.8)
South Carolina	203 (1.4)	209 (1.4)	214 (1.3)	215 (1.3)	213 (1.3)	225 (1.7)	197 (1.4)	215 (4.4)	‡ (†)	‡ (†)	43 (1.7)	57 (1.7)	26 (1.3)	6 (0.7)
South Dakota	— (†)	— (†)	—	222 (1.2)	222 (0.5)	222 (0.6)	‡ (†)	‡ (†)	‡ (†)	201 (2.3)	30 (1.1)	70 (1.1)	33 (1.3)	6 (0.7)
Tennessee[8,9]	213 (1.7)	212 (1.4)	214 (1.2)	212 (1.6)	214 (1.4)	222 (1.5)	195 (2.5)	199 (4.9)	‡ (†)	‡ (†)	41 (1.7)	59 (1.7)	27 (1.8)	6 (0.8)
Texas	212 (1.9)	214 (1.9)	217 (1.7)	215 (1.0)	219 (0.8)	232 (1.0)	206 (1.7)	210 (1.2)	234 (3.6)	‡ (†)	36 (1.1)	64 (1.1)	29 (0.9)	6 (0.5)
Utah	217 (1.3)	216 (1.2)	222 (1.0)	219 (1.0)	221 (1.1)	226 (1.0)	‡ (†)	199 (2.4)	218 (4.2)	‡ (†)	32 (1.3)	68 (1.3)	34 (1.3)	8 (0.8)
Vermont	— (†)	— (†)	227 (1.1)	226 (0.9)	227 (0.9)	227 (0.9)	‡ (†)	‡ (†)	‡ (†)	‡ (†)	28 (1.3)	72 (1.3)	39 (1.2)	10 (1.0)
Virginia	213 (1.5)	217 (1.2)	225 (1.3)	223 (1.5)	226 (0.8)	233 (1.0)	207 (1.2)	218 (2.2)	239 (2.7)	‡ (†)	28 (1.5)	72 (1.5)	37 (1.4)	8 (0.8)
Washington[8]	213 (1.5)	218 (1.4)	224 (1.2)	221 (1.1)	224 (1.1)	228 (1.1)	212 (2.8)	202 (2.5)	230 (2.6)	‡ (†)	30 (1.4)	70 (1.4)	36 (1.4)	8 (0.9)
West Virginia	213 (1.1)	216 (1.7)	219 (1.2)	219 (1.0)	215 (0.8)	215 (0.8)	202 (3.2)	‡ (†)	‡ (†)	‡ (†)	40 (1.1)	61 (1.1)	26 (1.0)	5 (0.7)
Wisconsin[7,8,9]	224 (1.1)	222 (1.1)	— (†)	221 (0.8)	221 (1.0)	227 (1.0)	194 (2.5)	208 (3.5)	226 (4.5)	‡ (†)	33 (1.3)	67 (1.3)	33 (1.4)	7 (0.7)
Wyoming	221 (1.2)	218 (1.5)	221 (1.0)	222 (0.8)	223 (0.7)	227 (0.8)	199 (†)	204 (3.3)	‡ (†)	‡ (†)	29 (1.2)	71 (1.2)	35 (1.4)	7 (0.6)
Department of Defense dependents schools[10]					226 (0.6)	232 (0.9)	218 (2.0)	219 (1.7)	223 (3.0)	‡ (†)	25 (1.0)	75 (1.0)	36 (1.4)	7 (0.8)
Domestic schools	— (†)	219 (1.6)	225 (0.7)	223 (1.2)	—	—	—	—	—	—	— (†)	— (†)	— (†)	— (†)
Overseas schools	218 (0.9)	221 (1.0)	224 (0.5)	225 (0.6)	—	—	—	—	—	—	— (†)	— (†)	— (†)	— (†)
Other jurisdictions														
Guam	181 (1.2)	— (†)	185 (1.3)	— (†)	—	—	—	—	—	—	— (†)	— (†)	— (†)	— (†)
Virgin Islands	— (†)	174 (2.2)	179 (1.9)	— (†)	—	—	—	—	—	—	— (†)	— (†)	— (†)	— (†)

—Not available.
†Not applicable.
‡Reporting standards not met.
[1]Based on school records.
[2]Achievement levels are in trial status.
[3]The basic level denotes partial mastery of the knowledge and skills that are fundamental for proficient work at the 4th-grade level.
[4]This level represents solid academic performance for 4th-graders. Students reaching this level have demonstrated competency over challenging subject matter.
[5]This level signifies superior performance.
[6]Based on nationally representative sample. Forty-one states and Guam participated in the test in 1994; 44 jurisdictions (state, territory, and Department of Defense schools) participated in 1998; 50 participated in 2002; and 53 participated in 2003 and 2005.

[7]Did not satisfy one or more of the guidelines for school sample participation rates in 1998. Data are subject to appreciable nonresponse bias.
[8]Did not satisfy one or more of the guidelines for school sample participation rates in 2002. Data are subject to appreciable nonresponse bias.
[9]Did not satisfy one or more of the guidelines for school sample participation rates in 1994. Data are subject to appreciable nonresponse bias.
[10]The definition of the nationally representative sample changed in 2005; it now includes all of the Department of Defense schools.
NOTE: The reading data include students for whom accommodations were permitted. Scale ranges from 0 to 500. Race categories exclude persons of Hispanic origin. Standard errors appear in parentheses.
SOURCE: U.S. Department of Education, National Center for Education Statistics, National Assessment of Educational Progress (NAEP), *Reading Report Card for the Nation and the States*, 1994, 1998, 2002, 2003, and 2005; and NAEP Data Explorer (http://nces.ed.gov/nationsreportcard/nde/), retrieved October 2005. (This table was prepared October 2005.)

Table 115. Average scale score in reading and percentage of 8th-graders in public schools attaining reading achievement levels, by locale and state or jurisdiction: Selected years, 1998 through 2005

State or jurisdiction	Average scale score								Percent attaining reading achievement levels, 2005								Average scale score by locale,[1] 2005					
	1998		2002		2003		2005		Below basic		Basic or above[2]		Proficient or above[3]		Advanced[4]		Central city		Urban fringe/large town		Rural/small town	
1	2		3		4		5		6		7		8		9		10		11		12	
United States[5]	261	(0.8)	263	(0.5)	261	(0.2)	260	(0.2)	29	(0.2)	71	(0.2)	29	(0.2)	3	(0.1)	254	(0.4)	264	(0.3)	262	(0.4)
Alabama	255	(1.4)	253	(1.3)	253	(1.5)	252	(1.4)	37	(1.4)	63	(1.4)	22	(1.4)	2	(0.6)	246	(2.8)	260	(3.1)	250	(1.6)
Alaska	—	(†)	—	(†)	256	(1.1)	259	(0.9)	30	(1.3)	70	(1.3)	26	(1.4)	2	(0.3)	‡	(†)	‡	(†)	‡	(†)
Arizona	260	(1.1)	257	(1.3)	255	(1.4)	255	(1.0)	35	(1.3)	65	(1.3)	23	(1.1)	2	(0.3)	253	(1.5)	258	(2.2)	253	(4.5)
Arkansas	256	(1.3)	260	(1.1)	258	(1.3)	258	(1.1)	31	(1.4)	69	(1.4)	26	(1.3)	2	(0.4)	257	(2.8)	261	(2.0)	257	(1.3)
California[6,7,8]	252	(1.6)	250	(1.8)	251	(1.3)	250	(0.6)	40	(0.7)	60	(0.7)	21	(0.6)	2	(0.2)	249	(0.9)	251	(0.9)	257	(3.6)
Colorado	264	(1.0)	—	(†)	268	(1.2)	265	(1.1)	25	(1.3)	75	(1.3)	32	(1.4)	4	(0.5)	260	(2.1)	268	(1.5)	266	(2.0)
Connecticut	270	(1.0)	267	(1.2)	267	(1.1)	264	(1.3)	26	(1.2)	75	(1.2)	34	(1.6)	4	(0.8)	245	(3.0)	270	(1.5)	269	(1.8)
Delaware	254	(1.3)	267	(0.5)	265	(0.7)	266	(0.6)	20	(1.1)	80	(1.1)	30	(0.9)	2	(0.4)	266	(2.4)	265	(0.7)	269	(1.4)
District of Columbia	236	(2.1)	240	(0.9)	239	(0.8)	238	(0.9)	55	(1.2)	45	(1.2)	12	(0.9)	1	(0.3)	238	(0.9)	‡	(†)	‡	(†)
Florida	255	(1.4)	261	(1.6)	257	(1.3)	256	(1.2)	34	(1.4)	66	(1.4)	25	(1.1)	2	(0.3)	252	(2.4)	257	(1.5)	257	(2.6)
Georgia	257	(1.4)	258	(1.0)	258	(1.1)	257	(1.3)	33	(1.5)	67	(1.5)	25	(1.6)	3	(0.5)	245	(2.8)	261	(2.1)	257	(2.1)
Hawaii	249	(1.0)	252	(0.9)	251	(0.9)	249	(0.9)	42	(1.0)	58	(1.0)	18	(1.0)	1	(0.2)	255	(1.6)	249	(1.4)	243	(1.5)
Idaho	—	(†)	266	(1.1)	264	(0.9)	264	(1.1)	24	(1.4)	76	(1.4)	32	(1.2)	2	(0.6)	266	(1.3)	264	(1.4)	263	(2.0)
Illinois	—	(†)	—	(†)	266	(1.0)	264	(1.0)	25	(1.2)	75	(1.2)	31	(1.3)	3	(0.6)	256	(1.9)	268	(1.5)	266	(2.1)
Indiana	—	(†)	265	(1.3)	265	(1.0)	261	(1.1)	27	(1.3)	73	(1.3)	28	(1.5)	2	(0.4)	254	(2.1)	265	(2.0)	263	(1.6)
Iowa	—	(†)	—	(†)	268	(0.8)	267	(0.9)	21	(1.0)	79	(1.0)	34	(1.5)	3	(0.4)	262	(1.5)	272	(2.3)	268	(1.4)
Kansas[6,7,8]	268	(1.4)	269	(1.3)	266	(1.5)	267	(1.0)	22	(1.3)	78	(1.3)	35	(1.4)	3	(0.4)	262	(2.6)	270	(1.7)	267	(1.1)
Kentucky	262	(1.4)	265	(1.0)	266	(1.3)	264	(1.1)	25	(1.5)	75	(1.5)	31	(1.4)	3	(0.5)	271	(2.3)	262	(2.1)	263	(1.6)
Louisiana	252	(1.4)	256	(1.5)	253	(1.6)	253	(1.6)	36	(2.2)	64	(2.2)	20	(1.5)	1	(0.4)	247	(2.8)	255	(2.8)	255	(1.9)
Maine	271	(1.2)	270	(0.9)	268	(1.0)	270	(1.0)	19	(1.0)	81	(1.0)	38	(1.4)	4	(0.6)	269	(2.6)	277	(2.1)	269	(1.1)
Maryland[6,7]	261	(1.8)	263	(1.7)	262	(1.4)	261	(1.2)	31	(1.7)	69	(1.7)	30	(1.4)	4	(0.5)	251	(3.6)	262	(1.5)	266	(2.7)
Massachusetts	269	(1.4)	271	(1.3)	273	(1.0)	274	(1.0)	17	(1.0)	83	(1.0)	44	(1.6)	5	(0.7)	258	(1.4)	280	(1.3)	282	(3.1)
Michigan	—	(†)	265	(1.6)	264	(1.8)	261	(1.2)	27	(1.4)	73	(1.4)	29	(1.6)	2	(0.5)	251	(2.9)	265	(1.4)	266	(2.2)
Minnesota[6,7]	265	(1.4)	—	(†)	268	(1.1)	268	(1.2)	20	(1.2)	80	(1.2)	37	(1.6)	3	(0.5)	264	(3.2)	272	(1.6)	267	(1.6)
Mississippi	251	(1.2)	255	(0.9)	255	(1.4)	251	(1.3)	40	(1.7)	60	(1.7)	19	(1.4)	1	(0.3)	246	(2.9)	254	(2.2)	250	(1.8)
Missouri	262	(1.3)	268	(1.0)	267	(1.0)	265	(1.0)	24	(1.3)	76	(1.3)	31	(1.4)	3	(0.4)	258	(3.0)	267	(1.3)	266	(1.6)
Montana[6,7]	271	(1.3)	270	(1.0)	270	(1.0)	269	(0.7)	19	(1.0)	82	(1.0)	37	(1.2)	3	(0.6)	270	(1.6)	271	(1.8)	268	(0.9)
Nebraska	—	(†)	270	(0.9)	266	(0.9)	268	(0.9)	20	(1.0)	80	(1.0)	35	(1.5)	3	(0.5)	266	(1.6)	268	(1.6)	268	(1.4)
Nevada	258	(1.0)	251	(0.8)	252	(0.8)	253	(1.0)	37	(1.3)	63	(1.3)	22	(0.9)	1	(0.5)	253	(1.4)	251	(1.4)	256	(1.5)
New Hampshire	—	(†)	—	(†)	271	(0.9)	270	(1.2)	20	(1.1)	80	(1.1)	38	(1.6)	4	(0.5)	264	(2.1)	270	(2.0)	272	(1.9)
New Jersey	—	(†)	—	(†)	268	(1.2)	269	(1.2)	20	(1.5)	80	(1.5)	38	(1.7)	4	(0.6)	‡	(†)	270	(1.2)	278	(3.0)
New Mexico	258	(1.2)	254	(1.0)	252	(0.9)	251	(1.0)	38	(1.5)	62	(1.5)	19	(1.1)	1	(0.2)	256	(1.9)	249	(1.9)	248	(1.7)
New York[6,7]	265	(1.5)	264	(1.5)	265	(1.3)	265	(1.0)	25	(0.9)	75	(0.9)	34	(1.3)	3	(0.5)	252	(1.5)	275	(1.4)	272	(1.4)
North Carolina	262	(1.1)	265	(1.1)	262	(1.0)	258	(0.9)	31	(1.3)	69	(1.3)	27	(1.2)	2	(0.4)	257	(1.6)	261	(1.9)	258	(1.5)
North Dakota[7]	—	(†)	268	(0.8)	270	(0.8)	270	(0.6)	17	(1.1)	83	(1.1)	37	(1.3)	3	(0.6)	271	(1.5)	270	(1.8)	270	(0.8)
Ohio	—	(†)	268	(1.6)	267	(1.3)	267	(1.3)	23	(1.4)	78	(1.4)	36	(1.4)	4	(0.7)	248	(3.1)	272	(1.6)	272	(2.2)
Oklahoma	265	(1.2)	262	(0.8)	262	(0.9)	260	(1.1)	28	(1.6)	72	(1.6)	25	(1.4)	1	(0.4)	252	(4.0)	264	(1.3)	259	(1.4)
Oregon[7]	266	(1.5)	268	(1.3)	264	(1.2)	263	(1.1)	26	(1.3)	74	(1.3)	33	(1.5)	3	(0.5)	264	(2.2)	264	(1.7)	261	(1.9)
Pennsylvania	—	(†)	265	(1.0)	264	(1.2)	267	(1.3)	23	(1.6)	77	(1.6)	36	(1.6)	3	(0.6)	247	(3.9)	273	(1.9)	268	(1.4)
Rhode Island	264	(0.9)	262	(0.8)	261	(0.7)	261	(0.7)	29	(1.1)	71	(1.1)	29	(1.0)	3	(0.4)	245	(1.4)	267	(1.0)	275	(1.8)
South Carolina	255	(1.1)	258	(1.1)	258	(1.3)	257	(1.1)	33	(1.3)	67	(1.3)	25	(1.2)	2	(0.4)	259	(2.5)	262	(1.6)	253	(1.5)
South Dakota	—	(†)	—	(†)	270	(0.8)	269	(0.6)	18	(0.8)	82	(0.8)	35	(1.1)	2	(0.3)	267	(1.1)	271	(2.4)	269	(0.7)
Tennessee[7]	258	(1.2)	260	(1.4)	258	(1.2)	259	(0.9)	29	(1.2)	71	(1.2)	26	(1.4)	1	(0.5)	252	(1.7)	264	(2.3)	260	(1.6)
Texas	261	(1.4)	262	(1.4)	259	(1.1)	258	(0.6)	31	(0.8)	69	(0.8)	26	(0.8)	2	(0.3)	256	(1.1)	261	(1.1)	259	(1.6)
Utah	263	(1.0)	263	(1.1)	264	(0.8)	262	(0.8)	27	(0.9)	73	(0.9)	29	(1.2)	2	(0.4)	261	(1.4)	262	(1.0)	264	(3.0)
Vermont	—	(†)	272	(0.9)	271	(0.8)	269	(0.8)	21	(1.0)	79	(1.0)	37	(1.2)	4	(0.4)	‡	(†)	‡	(†)	‡	(†)
Virginia	266	(1.1)	269	(1.0)	268	(1.1)	268	(1.0)	22	(1.2)	78	(1.2)	36	(1.4)	3	(0.5)	260	(1.7)	273	(1.6)	266	(2.1)
Washington[7]	264	(1.2)	268	(1.2)	264	(0.9)	265	(1.3)	25	(1.3)	75	(1.3)	34	(1.5)	3	(0.4)	264	(2.4)	265	(1.5)	265	(2.3)
West Virginia	262	(1.0)	264	(1.0)	260	(1.0)	255	(1.2)	33	(1.5)	67	(1.5)	22	(1.3)	1	(0.3)	261	(2.0)	259	(2.7)	252	(1.3)
Wisconsin[6,7]	265	(1.8)	—	(†)	266	(1.3)	266	(1.1)	23	(1.3)	77	(1.3)	35	(1.4)	3	(0.5)	255	(2.6)	276	(1.6)	266	(1.6)
Wyoming	263	(1.3)	265	(0.7)	267	(0.5)	268	(0.7)	19	(1.0)	81	(1.0)	36	(1.4)	2	(0.4)	267	(1.6)	270	(3.7)	269	(0.8)

See notes at end of table.

Table 115. Average scale score in reading and percentage of 8th-graders in public schools attaining reading achievement levels, by locale and state or jurisdiction: Selected years, 1998 through 2005—Continued

State or jurisdiction	Average scale score				Percent attaining reading achievement levels, 2005				Average scale score by locale,[1] 2005		
	1998	2002	2003	2005	Below basic	Basic or above[2]	Proficient or above[3]	Advanced[4]	Central city	Urban fringe/ large town	Rural/ small town
1	2	3	4	5	6	7	8	9	10	11	12
Department of Defense dependents schools[9]	— (†)	— (†)	— (†)	271 (0.7)	16 (1.2)	84 (1.2)	37 (1.4)	2 (0.5)	‡ (†)	‡ (†)	‡ (†)
Domestic schools........	268 (4.5)	272 (1.0)	269 (1.4)	— (†)	— (†)	— (†)	— (†)	— (†)	‡ (†)	‡ (†)	‡ (†)
Overseas schools	269 (1.0)	273 (0.6)	273 (0.7)	— (†)	— (†)	— (†)	— (†)	— (†)	‡ (†)	‡ (†)	‡ (†)
Other jurisdictions											
American Samoa	— (†)	198 (1.7)	— (†)	— (†)	— (†)	— (†)	— (†)	— (†)	— (†)	— (†)	— (†)
Guam	— (†)	240 (1.2)	— (†)	— (†)	— (†)	— (†)	— (†)	— (†)	— (†)	— (†)	— (†)
Virgin Islands	231 (2.1)	241 (1.3)	— (†)	— (†)	— (†)	— (†)	— (†)	— (†)	— (†)	— (†)	— (†)

—Not available.

†Not applicable.

‡Reporting standards not met.

[1]Central city is a large or mid-size central city of a Metropolitan Statistical Area (MSA). Urban fringe/large town includes places that are within an MSA of a central city but not primarily within its central city, as well as towns that are incorporated places not within an MSA and have a population greater than or equal to 25,000. Rural/small town includes places that are defined as rural by the U.S. Bureau of the Census and have a population less than 2,500 and/or a population density of less than 1,000 per square mile, as well as towns that are incorporated places not within an MSA and have a population less than 25,000 but greater than or equal to 2,500.

[2]The basic level denotes partial mastery of the knowledge and skills that are fundamental for proficient work at the 8th-grade level.

[3]This level represents solid academic performance for 8th-graders. Students reaching this level have demonstrated competency over challenging subject matter.

[4]This level signifies superior performance.

[5]Based on a nationally representative sample. Forty-four jurisdictions (state, District of Columbia, territory, and Department of Defense schools) participated in 1998; 50 participated in 2002; and 53 participated in 2003 and 2005.

[6]Did not satisfy one or more of the guidelines for school sample participation rates in 1998. Data are subject to appreciable nonresponse bias.

[7]Did not satisfy one or more of the guidelines for school sample participation rates in 2002. Data are subject to appreciable nonresponse bias.

[8]Did not satisfy one or more of the guidelines for school sample participation rates in 2003. Data are subject to appreciable nonresponse bias.

[9]The definition of the nationally representative sample changed in 2005; it now includes all of the Department of Defense schools.

NOTE: The reading data include students for whom accommodations were permitted. Scale ranges from 0 to 500. Standard errors appear in parentheses.

SOURCE: U.S. Department of Education, National Center for Education Statistics, National Assessment of Educational Progress (NAEP), *Reading Report Card for the Nation and the States*, 2002, 2003, and 2005; and NAEP Data Explorer (http://nces.ed.gov/nationsreportcard/nde/), retrieved October 2005. (This table was prepared October 2005.)

Table 116. Average reading scale scores of 4th- and 8th-graders, by selected student and parent characteristics and school type: Various years, 2000 through 2005

Year, grade, and school type	All students	Sex of child		Race/ethnicity of child					Highest education level of parents				
		Male	Female	White	Black	Hispanic	Asian/Pacific Islander	American Indian/Alaska Native	Less than high school	Graduated from high school	Some education after high school	Graduated from college	Unknown
1	2	3	4	5	6	7	8	9	10	11	12	13	14
2000													
4th-graders													
Public	211 (1.4)	206 (1.4)	217 (1.6)	223 (1.2)	189 (1.9)	188 (3.1)	223 (5.8)	‡ (†)	—	—	—	—	‡ (†)
Private, total	231 (—)	225 (—)	238 (—)	236 (—)	213! (—)	215 (—)	236! (—)	‡ (†)	—	—	—	—	‡ (†)
Catholic	229 (2.5)	224 (2.9)	233 (2.5)	236 (2.0)	209! (2.5)	211! (5.7)	‡ (†)	‡ (†)	—	—	—	—	‡ (†)
Lutheran	‡ (†)	‡ (†)	‡ (†)	‡ (†)	‡ (†)	‡ (†)	‡ (†)	‡ (†)	—	—	—	—	‡ (†)
Conservative Christian	‡ (†)	‡ (†)	‡ (†)	‡ (†)	‡ (†)	‡ (†)	‡ (†)	‡ (†)	—	—	—	—	‡ (†)
2002													
4th-graders													
Public	217 (0.5)	214 (0.5)	220 (0.5)	227 (0.3)	198 (0.6)	199 (1.4)	223 (1.7)	207 (2.0)	—	—	—	—	‡ (†)
Private, total	234 (—)	231 (—)	237 (—)	239 (—)	212 (—)	223 (—)	231 (—)	‡ (†)	—	—	—	—	‡ (†)
Catholic	234 (1.1)	231 (1.3)	236 (1.2)	239 (0.8)	212 (3.1)	222 (3.1)	229 (4.3)	‡ (†)	—	—	—	—	‡ (†)
Lutheran	236 (1.4)	234 (2.0)	238 (1.8)	238 (1.3)	‡ (†)	‡ (†)	‡ (†)	‡ (†)	—	—	—	—	‡ (†)
Conservative Christian	229 (2.6)	226 (3.4)	233 (2.6)	234 (2.9)	216! (4.3)	‡ (†)	‡ (†)	‡ (†)	—	—	—	—	‡ (†)
8th-graders													
Public	263 (0.5)	258 (0.5)	267 (0.5)	271 (0.5)	244 (0.8)	245 (0.9)	265 (1.8)	252 (2.5)	247 (1.0)	256 (0.5)	267 (0.6)	273 (0.5)	246 (0.8)
Private, total	281 (—)	276 (—)	285 (—)	285 (—)	263 (—)	266 (—)	285 (—)	‡ (†)	264! (—)	270 (—)	279 (—)	285 (—)	265 (—)
Catholic	281 (0.9)	276 (1.3)	285 (1.0)	285 (0.8)	261 (2.5)	271 (2.7)	282 (4.2)	‡ (†)	‡ (†)	272 (2.6)	278 (1.4)	285 (0.9)	266 (3.9)
Lutheran	281 (1.6)	278 (1.8)	284 (2.3)	283 (1.5)	‡ (†)	‡ (†)	‡ (†)	‡ (†)	‡ (†)	271 (3.9)	284 (3.6)	284 (1.6)	‡ (†)
Conservative Christian	‡ (†)	‡ (†)	‡ (†)	‡ (†)	‡ (†)	‡ (†)	‡ (†)	‡ (†)	‡ (†)	‡ (†)	‡ (†)	‡ (†)	‡ (†)
2003													
4th-graders													
Public	216 (0.3)	213 (0.3)	220 (0.3)	227 (0.3)	197 (0.4)	199 (0.6)	225 (1.3)	202 (1.5)	—	—	—	—	‡ (†)
Private, total	235 (—)	232 (—)	237 (—)	239 (—)	210 (—)	220 (—)	236 (—)	‡ (†)	—	—	—	—	‡ (†)
Catholic	235 (1.0)	232 (1.2)	237 (1.2)	240 (0.9)	211 (2.4)	219 (1.9)	231 (3.6)	‡ (†)	—	—	—	—	‡ (†)
Lutheran	232 (1.9)	232 (2.7)	234 (1.9)	236 (1.2)	206! (7.0)	‡ (†)	‡ (†)	‡ (†)	—	—	—	—	‡ (†)
Conservative Christian	‡ (†)	‡ (†)	‡ (†)	‡ (†)	‡ (†)	‡ (†)	‡ (†)	‡ (†)	—	—	—	—	‡ (†)
8th-graders													
Public	261 (0.2)	256 (0.3)	267 (0.3)	270 (0.2)	244 (0.5)	244 (0.7)	268 (1.2)	248 (1.7)	245 (0.6)	253 (0.4)	266 (0.4)	271 (0.3)	242 (0.6)
Private, total	282 (—)	278 (—)	287 (—)	286 (—)	261 (—)	269 (—)	286 (—)	‡ (†)	263 (—)	268 (—)	277 (—)	287 (—)	264 (—)
Catholic	281 (0.9)	277 (1.3)	286 (1.0)	286 (0.8)	260 (2.8)	270 (1.4)	280 (2.8)	‡ (†)	‡ (†)	269 (1.7)	277 (1.5)	285 (0.9)	265 (2.5)
Lutheran	281 (1.6)	275 (2.1)	288 (2.3)	284 (1.5)	260! (4.6)	‡ (†)	‡ (†)	‡ (†)	‡ (†)	271 (4.2)	276 (3.4)	286 (1.6)	‡ (†)
Conservative Christian	276 (1.5)	271 (2.0)	282 (1.9)	280 (1.6)	261 (6.4)	267! (7.1)	‡ (†)	‡ (†)	‡ (†)	263 (3.8)	275 (3.4)	282 (1.7)	258 (6.4)
2005													
4th-graders													
Public	217 (0.2)	214 (0.3)	221 (0.3)	228 (0.2)	199 (0.3)	201 (0.5)	227 (0.9)	205 (1.3)	—	—	—	—	‡ (†)
Private, total	‡ (†)	‡ (†)	‡ (†)	‡ (†)	‡ (†)	‡ (†)	‡ (†)	‡ (†)	—	—	—	—	‡ (†)
Catholic	234 (0.8)	232 (1.1)	236 (1.1)	239 (0.9)	214 (2.4)	222 (2.1)	232 (3.1)	‡ (†)	—	—	—	—	‡ (†)
Lutheran	231 (2.0)	229 (2.9)	234 (2.3)	233 (2.1)	‡ (†)	‡ (†)	‡ (†)	‡ (†)	—	—	—	—	‡ (†)
Conservative Christian	‡ (†)	‡ (†)	‡ (†)	‡ (†)	‡ (†)	‡ (†)	‡ (†)	‡ (†)	—	—	—	—	‡ (†)
8th-graders													
Public	260 (0.2)	255 (0.2)	266 (0.2)	269 (0.2)	242 (0.4)	245 (0.4)	270 (0.8)	251 (1.2)	244 (0.5)	252 (0.3)	265 (0.2)	270 (0.2)	242 (0.4)
Private, total	‡ (†)	‡ (†)	‡ (†)	‡ (†)	‡ (†)	‡ (†)	‡ (†)	‡ (†)	‡ (†)	‡ (†)	‡ (†)	‡ (†)	‡ (†)
Catholic	280 (1.0)	275 (1.3)	284 (1.1)	285 (0.9)	259 (2.7)	268 (1.8)	280 (3.6)	‡ (†)	‡ (†)	269 (2.1)	276 (1.6)	284 (1.0)	258 (2.9)
Lutheran	280 (1.8)	274 (2.7)	285 (2.0)	284 (1.6)	252 (6.0)	‡ (†)	‡ (†)	‡ (†)	‡ (†)	270 (4.5)	275 (5.5)	286 (1.6)	‡ (†)
Conservative Christian	‡ (†)	‡ (†)	‡ (†)	‡ (†)	‡ (†)	‡ (†)	‡ (†)	‡ (†)	‡ (†)	‡ (†)	‡ (†)	‡ (†)	‡ (†)

—Not available.
†Not applicable.
!Interpret data with caution.
‡Reporting standards not met.
NOTE: The NAEP reading scale ranges from 0 to 500. Data for Nonsectarian and Other Religious schools for 2000 and data for Other Private schools for 2002 and 2003 are included in the overall Private data for those years, but not reported separately. Race categories exclude persons of Hispanic origin. Standard errors appear in parentheses.

SOURCE: U.S. Department of Education, National Center for Education Statistics, National Assessment of Educational Progress (NAEP), *Student Achievement in Private Schools: Results From NAEP 2000–2005*; and the NAEP Data Explorer (http://nces.ed.gov/nationsreportcard/nde/), retrieved May 2006. (This table was prepared June 2006.)

Table 117. Percentage of students at or above selected writing proficiency levels, by grade level and selected student characteristics: 2002

Selected student characteristic	Percentage of 4th-graders				Percentage of 8th-graders				Percentage of 12th-graders			
	Below basic	At or above basic	At or above proficient	At advanced	Below basic	At or above basic	At or above proficient	At advanced	Below basic	At or above basic	At or above proficient	At advanced
1	2	3	4	5	6	7	8	9	10	11	12	13
All students	**14** (0.4)	**86** (0.4)	**28** (0.4)	**2** (0.1)	**15** (0.4)	**85** (0.4)	**31** (0.6)	**2** (0.1)	**26** (0.7)	**74** (0.7)	**24** (0.8)	**2** (0.2)
Sex												
Male	19 (0.5)	81 (0.5)	20 (0.5)	1 (0.1)	21 (0.6)	79 (0.6)	21 (0.6)	1 (0.1)	37 (1.0)	63 (1.0)	14 (0.8)	1 (0.1)
Female	9 (0.3)	91 (0.3)	36 (0.6)	3 (0.2)	9 (0.3)	91 (0.3)	42 (0.8)	3 (0.2)	15 (0.7)	85 (0.7)	33 (1.0)	3 (0.3)
Race/ethnicity												
White	9 (0.2)	91 (0.2)	35 (0.4)	3 (0.2)	9 (0.4)	91 (0.4)	39 (0.6)	3 (0.2)	20 (0.7)	80 (0.7)	28 (0.9)	2 (0.3)
Black	21 (0.6)	79 (0.6)	15 (0.7)	1 (0.2)	25 (1.0)	75 (1.0)	13 (0.6)	# (†)	41 (1.8)	59 (1.8)	9 (1.0)	# (†)
Hispanic	22 (1.1)	78 (1.1)	18 (0.7)	1 (0.2)	27 (0.8)	73 (0.8)	17 (0.9)	1 (0.2)	38 (1.5)	62 (1.5)	13 (1.2)	# (†)
Asian/Pacific Islander	7 (0.8)	93 (0.8)	42 (2.0)	4 (0.7)	10 (1.0)	90 (1.0)	42 (2.3)	3 (0.6)	24 (2.5)	76 (2.5)	26 (3.2)	3 (1.0)
American Indian/Alaska Native	20 (1.2)	80 (1.2)	16 (1.0)	1 (0.3)	23 (2.5)	77 (2.5)	18 (2.9)	1 (#)	—	—	— (†)	— (†)
Parents' highest level of education												
Not high school graduate	—	—	— (†)	— (†)	26 (1.3)	74 (1.3)	14 (1.0)	# (†)	43 (2.1)	57 (2.1)	8 (1.4)	# (†)
Graduated high school	—	—	— (†)	— (†)	19 (0.7)	81 (0.7)	20 (0.6)	1 (0.2)	32 (1.2)	68 (1.2)	14 (1.1)	1 (0.2)
Some college	—	—	— (†)	— (†)	11 (0.6)	89 (0.6)	31 (0.8)	1 (0.2)	23 (1.0)	77 (1.0)	22 (1.3)	1 (0.2)
Graduated college	—	—	— (†)	— (†)	9 (0.4)	91 (0.4)	43 (0.8)	4 (0.2)	18 (0.9)	82 (0.9)	32 (1.0)	3 (0.4)
Free/reduced-price lunch eligibility												
Eligible	22 (0.8)	78 (0.8)	15 (0.5)	1 (0.1)	26 (0.6)	74 (0.6)	16 (0.6)	1 (0.1)	40 (1.5)	60 (1.5)	11 (1.0)	1 (0.2)
Not eligible	8 (0.3)	92 (0.3)	36 (0.6)	3 (0.2)	9 (0.4)	91 (0.4)	39 (0.8)	3 (0.2)	23 (0.8)	77 (0.8)	26 (1.0)	2 (0.3)
Information not available	10 (1.1)	90 (1.1)	34 (1.6)	3 (0.3)	11 (0.7)	89 (0.7)	39 (1.7)	4 (0.6)	19 (1.3)	81 (1.3)	29 (1.6)	2 (0.4)

—Not available.
†Not applicable.
#Rounds to zero.
NOTE: Includes public and private schools. Excludes persons unable to be tested due to limited proficiency in English or due to a disability (and the accommodations provided were not sufficient to enable the test to properly reflect the students' writing proficiency). In 2002, the NAEP national samples of 4th- and 8th-graders were obtained by aggregating the samples from each state, rather than by independently selecting national samples for grades 4 and 8. As a consequence, the size of the national samples increased for these grade levels, and smaller differences were found to be statistically significant than would have been detected in previous assessments. Race categories exclude persons of Hispanic origin. Detail may not sum to totals because of rounding. Standard errors appear in parentheses.
SOURCE: U.S. Department of Education, National Center for Education Statistics, National Assessment of Educational Progress (NAEP), 2002 Writing Assessment; and unpublished tabulations, NAEP Data Explorer (http://nces.ed.gov/nationsreportcard/nde/), retrieved August 2003. (This table was prepared August 2003.)

Table 118. Percentage of students at or above selected U.S. history proficiency levels, by grade level and selected student characteristics: 2001

Selected student characteristic	Percentage of 4th-graders				Percentage of 8th-graders				Percentage of 12th-graders			
	Below basic	At or above basic	At or above proficient	At advanced	Below basic	At or above basic	At or above proficient	At advanced	Below basic	At or above basic	At or above proficient	At advanced
1	2	3	4	5	6	7	8	9	10	11	12	13
All students	**33** (1.1)	**67** (1.1)	**18** (1.0)	**2** (0.5)	**36** (0.9)	**64** (0.9)	**17** (0.8)	**2** (0.3)	**57** (1.2)	**43** (1.2)	**11** (0.9)	**1** (0.4)
Sex												
Male	34 (1.3)	66 (1.3)	19 (1.2)	2 (0.7)	35 (1.1)	65 (1.1)	18 (1.0)	2 (0.3)	55 (1.6)	45 (1.6)	12 (1.1)	1 (0.5)
Female	32 (1.4)	68 (1.4)	17 (1.1)	2 (0.4)	37 (1.2)	63 (1.2)	15 (0.8)	1 (0.4)	59 (1.3)	41 (1.3)	10 (0.9)	1 (0.3)
Race/ethnicity												
White	21 (1.3)	79 (1.3)	24 (1.4)	3 (0.7)	25 (1.0)	75 (1.0)	21 (1.1)	2 (0.4)	51 (1.4)	49 (1.4)	13 (1.0)	1 (0.4)
Black	56 (2.1)	44 (2.1)	6 (1.0)	# (0.3)	62 (2.4)	38 (2.4)	4 (0.8)	# (†)	80 (1.5)	20 (1.5)	3 (0.6)	# (†)
Hispanic	58 (3.0)	42 (3.0)	7 (1.1)	1 (0.3)	60 (1.7)	40 (1.7)	5 (0.7)	# (†)	74 (2.4)	26 (2.4)	5 (1.1)	# (†)
Asian/Pacific Islander	29 (3.8)	71 (3.8)	19 (3.2)	3 (1.9)	32 (3.8)	68 (3.8)	20 (3.6)	2 (0.8)	47 (5.1)	53 (5.1)	21 (6.0)	5 (2.3)
American Indian/Alaska Native	47 (6.4)	53 (6.4)	12 (4.6)	4 (†)	50 (7.1)	50 (7.1)	8 (3.5)	1 (†)	66 (7.2)	34 (7.2)	1 (†)	# (†)
Parents' highest level of education												
Not high school graduate	— (†)	— (†)	— (†)	— (†)	59 (3.3)	41 (3.3)	3 (1.8)	# (†)	80 (2.1)	20 (2.1)	2 (0.7)	# (†)
Graduated high school	— (†)	— (†)	— (†)	— (†)	48 (1.7)	52 (1.7)	7 (1.0)	# (†)	74 (1.3)	26 (1.3)	4 (0.8)	# (†)
Some college	— (†)	— (†)	— (†)	— (†)	30 (1.3)	70 (1.3)	14 (1.3)	1 (0.3)	61 (1.3)	39 (1.3)	8 (0.7)	1 (0.2)
Graduated college	— (†)	— (†)	— (†)	— (†)	22 (1.0)	78 (1.0)	27 (1.1)	3 (0.5)	42 (1.5)	58 (1.5)	18 (1.5)	2 (0.8)
Free/reduced-price lunch eligibility												
Eligible	53 (1.7)	47 (1.7)	6 (0.8)	1 (0.2)	59 (1.4)	41 (1.4)	6 (0.7)	# (†)	77 (1.8)	23 (1.8)	3 (0.7)	# (†)
Not eligible	21 (1.7)	79 (1.7)	25 (1.6)	3 (0.8)	27 (1.2)	73 (1.2)	20 (1.2)	2 (0.3)	55 (1.5)	45 (1.5)	11 (1.1)	1 (0.6)
Not available	25 (2.8)	75 (2.8)	24 (2.9)	3 (1.1)	30 (2.4)	70 (2.4)	22 (2.1)	3 (0.6)	47 (2.9)	53 (2.9)	17 (2.3)	2 (0.6)
Region												
Northeast	27 (3.1)	73 (3.1)	23 (2.9)	3 (1.1)	28 (2.2)	72 (2.2)	22 (2.1)	2 (0.8)	55 (3.8)	45 (3.8)	13 (3.2)	2 (—)
Southeast	34 (2.7)	66 (2.7)	16 (2.2)	2 (1.2)	38 (2.3)	62 (2.3)	16 (1.3)	2 (0.4)	61 (2.3)	39 (2.3)	10 (1.3)	1 (0.3)
Central	25 (2.3)	75 (2.3)	24 (2.4)	3 (1.1)	29 (2.2)	71 (2.2)	19 (1.5)	2 (0.5)	54 (2.2)	46 (2.2)	11 (1.3)	1 (0.4)
West	41 (2.5)	59 (2.5)	13 (1.2)	1 (0.4)	45 (1.7)	55 (1.7)	12 (1.3)	1 (0.2)	58 (2.2)	42 (2.2)	11 (1.5)	1 (0.4)

—Not available.
†Not applicable.
#Rounds to zero.
NOTE: Includes public and private schools. Excludes persons unable to be tested due to limited proficiency in English or due to a disability (and the accommodations provided were not sufficient to enable the test to properly reflect the students' history proficiency). Detail may not sum to totals because of rounding. Race categories exclude persons of Hispanic origin. Standard errors appear in parentheses.
SOURCE: U.S. Department of Education, National Center for Education Statistics, National Assessment of Educational Progress (NAEP), *The Nation's Report Card: U.S. History 2001*. (This table was prepared May 2002.)

Table 119. Average student scale score in geography and U.S. history, by grade level and selected student characteristics: 2001

Selected student characteristic	Percentage distribution of 12th-graders in geography		Average geography scores						Percentage distribution of 12th-graders in U.S. history		Average U.S. history scores					
			4th-graders		8th-graders		12th-graders				4th-graders		8th-graders		12th-graders	
1	2		3		4		5		6		7		8		9	
All students	100	(†)	209	(1.0)	262	(0.9)	285	(0.8)	100	(†)	209	(1.0)	262	(0.8)	287	(1.0)
Sex																
Male	48	(0.8)	212	(1.1)	264	(1.0)	287	(0.9)	49	(0.6)	209	(1.1)	264	(0.9)	288	(1.3)
Female	52	(0.8)	207	(1.2)	260	(1.1)	282	(0.8)	51	(0.6)	209	(1.2)	261	(0.9)	286	(0.9)
Race/ethnicity																
White...	70	(0.3)	222	(1.0)	273	(1.0)	291	(0.9)	70	(0.4)	220	(1.1)	271	(0.8)	292	(1.0)
Black...	13	(0.3)	181	(1.8)	234	(1.7)	260	(1.4)	13	(0.2)	188	(1.8)	243	(1.8)	269	(1.5)
Hispanic...	12	(0.2)	184	(2.8)	240	(1.7)	270	(1.5)	12	(0.2)	186	(2.5)	243	(1.5)	274	(1.7)
Asian/Pacific Islander.......................	5	(0.2)	212	(2.7)	266	(2.5)	286	(2.9)	5	(0.2)	213	(2.7)	267	(3.4)	295	(4.6)
American Indian/Alaska Native.........	1	(0.2)	199	(3.6)	261	(5.8)	288	(3.6)	1	(0.2)	197	(6.9)	249	(4.5)	277	(5.5)
Parents' highest level of education																
Not high school graduate	7	(0.4)	—	(†)	241	(1.7)	269	(1.7)	7	(0.4)	—	(†)	243	(2.3)	269	(1.5)
Graduated high school......................	19	(0.7)	—	(†)	253	(1.2)	276	(0.9)	19	(0.6)	—	(†)	253	(1.1)	274	(1.0)
Some college	25	(0.7)	—	(†)	266	(1.0)	284	(0.9)	25	(0.7)	—	(†)	265	(1.0)	286	(0.8)
Graduated college	46	(1.1)	—	(†)	274	(0.9)	293	(1.1)	46	(1.2)	—	(†)	275	(0.8)	298	(1.3)
Free/reduced-price lunch eligibility																
Eligible	16	(1.0)	186	(1.7)	242	(1.4)	269	(1.6)	16	(0.9)	189	(1.6)	245	(1.2)	271	(1.3)
Not eligible	64	(2.2)	221	(1.2)	270	(1.1)	287	(1.0)	64	(2.2)	220	(1.4)	269	(0.9)	289	(1.2)
Not available	21	(2.4)	218	(2.5)	266	(1.8)	289	(1.5)	21	(2.5)	217	(2.8)	268	(2.0)	295	(2.0)
Region																
Northeast...	20	(0.9)	214	(2.8)	266	(2.4)	286	(2.8)	21	(0.9)	215	(2.5)	269	(1.9)	289	(3.4)
Southeast...	21	(1.2)	207	(2.1)	260	(2.0)	281	(1.0)	22	(1.2)	208	(2.6)	261	(2.0)	284	(1.7)
Central	27	(0.6)	219	(1.8)	270	(2.5)	287	(1.3)	26	(0.6)	217	(2.0)	267	(1.7)	289	(1.4)
West...	31	(1.4)	200	(2.5)	255	(1.5)	283	(1.3)	31	(1.5)	200	(2.3)	255	(1.3)	286	(1.6)

—Not available.
†Not applicable.
NOTE: The scores range from 0 to 500 in each test, but the distribution of the scores varies by subject. Therefore, direct score comparisons between the subjects should be avoided. Includes public and private schools. Excludes students unable to be tested due to limited proficiency in English or due to a disability (and the accommodations provided were not sufficient to enable the test to properly reflect the students' proficiency in geography or history). Race catagories exclude persons of Hispanic origin. Detail may not sum to totals because of rounding. Standard errors appear in parentheses.
SOURCE: U.S. Department of Education, National Center for Education Statistics, National Assessment of Educational Progress (NAEP), *The Nation's Report Card: U.S. History 2001*; and *The Nation's Report Card: Geography 2001*. (This table was prepared July 2002.)

Table 120. Percentage of students at or above selected geography achievement levels, by grade level and selected student characteristics: 2001

Selected student characteristic	Percentage of 4th-graders				Percentage of 8th-graders				Percentage of 12th-graders			
	Below basic	At or above basic	At or above proficient	At advanced	Below basic	At or above basic	At or above proficient	At advanced	Below basic	At or above basic	At or above proficient	At advanced
1	2	3	4	5	6	7	8	9	10	11	12	13
All students	26 (1.2)	74 (1.2)	21 (1.0)	2 (0.3)	26 (0.9)	74 (0.9)	30 (1.2)	4 (0.6)	29 (0.9)	71 (0.9)	25 (1.1)	1 (0.3)
Sex												
Male..............	25 (1.3)	75 (1.3)	24 (1.4)	3 (0.5)	25 (1.0)	75 (1.0)	33 (1.5)	5 (0.7)	27 (1.1)	73 (1.1)	28 (1.5)	2 (0.4)
Female............	28 (1.6)	72 (1.6)	18 (1.1)	1 (0.4)	27 (1.2)	73 (1.2)	26 (1.4)	3 (0.6)	30 (1.0)	70 (1.0)	21 (1.0)	1 (0.3)
Race/ethnicity												
White.............	13 (1.3)	87 (1.3)	29 (1.5)	3 (0.5)	14 (0.9)	86 (0.9)	39 (1.7)	5 (0.8)	19 (0.9)	81 (0.9)	31 (1.4)	2 (0.4)
Black.............	56 (2.1)	44 (2.1)	5 (0.9)	# (†)	60 (2.3)	40 (2.3)	6 (0.8)	# (†)	65 (2.3)	35 (2.3)	4 (0.7)	# (†)
Hispanic...........	51 (3.0)	49 (3.0)	6 (1.0)	# (†)	52 (1.9)	48 (1.9)	10 (1.0)	1 (0.2)	48 (2.6)	52 (2.6)	10 (1.4)	# (†)
Asian/Pacific Islander....	23 (3.4)	77 (3.4)	25 (3.0)	1 (0.9)	21 (3.4)	79 (3.4)	32 (3.2)	4 (1.8)	28 (4.3)	72 (4.3)	26 (4.7)	1 (0.7)
Free/reduced-price lunch eligibility												
Eligible...........	49 (2.2)	51 (2.2)	6 (0.9)	# (†)	50 (1.8)	50 (1.8)	11 (1.2)	1 (0.3)	49 (2.3)	51 (2.3)	11 (1.6)	# (†)
Not eligible........	14 (1.1)	86 (1.1)	29 (1.5)	3 (0.6)	17 (0.9)	83 (0.9)	37 (1.7)	5 (0.8)	25 (1.2)	75 (1.2)	26 (1.6)	1 (0.4)
Not available.......	16 (2.5)	84 (2.5)	27 (3.2)	3 (0.8)	21 (2.1)	79 (2.1)	33 (2.5)	4 (0.9)	24 (2.0)	76 (2.0)	31 (2.1)	2 (0.4)
Region												
Northeast..........	22 (3.7)	78 (3.7)	24 (2.2)	3 (0.9)	22 (2.5)	78 (2.5)	34 (3.3)	4 (1.3)	29 (2.3)	71 (2.3)	26 (4.1)	2 (1.1)
Southeast..........	28 (2.5)	72 (2.5)	18 (1.9)	1 (0.6)	27 (2.4)	73 (2.4)	26 (1.6)	3 (0.6)	33 (1.6)	67 (1.6)	21 (1.3)	1 (0.3)
Central............	18 (1.7)	82 (1.7)	30 (2.5)	3 (0.7)	18 (2.3)	82 (2.3)	38 (3.7)	6 (1.3)	24 (1.8)	76 (1.8)	28 (1.9)	1 (0.5)
West..............	34 (2.7)	66 (2.7)	14 (1.7)	1 (0.3)	34 (1.7)	66 (1.7)	23 (1.7)	2 (0.6)	30 (1.9)	70 (1.9)	23 (1.8)	1 (0.4)

†Not applicable.
#Rounds to zero.
NOTE: Includes public and private schools. Excludes students unable to be tested due to limited proficiency in English or due to a disability (and the accommodations provided were not sufficient to enable the test to properly reflect the students' profi-

ciency in geography). Race categories exclude persons of Hispanic origin. Totals include other racial/ethnic groups not shown separately. Detail may not sum to totals because of rounding. Standard errors appear in parentheses.
SOURCE: U.S. Department of Education, National Center for Education Statistics, National Assessment of Educational Progress (NAEP), *The Nation's Report Card: Geography 2001*. (This table was prepared July 2002.)

Table 121. Average scale score in mathematics, by age and selected student and school characteristics: Selected years, 1973 through 2004

Selected student and school characteristic	1973		1978		1982		1986		1990		1992		1994		1996		1999		2004	
1	2		3		4		5		6		7		8		9		10		11	
9-year-olds																				
All students	219	(0.8)	219	(0.8)	219	(1.1)	222	(1.0)	230	(0.8)	230	(0.8)	231	(0.8)	231	(0.8)	232	(0.8)	241	(0.9)
Sex																				
Male	218	(0.7)	217	(0.7)	217	(1.2)	222	(1.1)	229	(0.9)	231	(1.0)	232	(1.0)	233	(1.2)	233	(1.0)	243	(1.1)
Female	220	(1.1)	220	(1.0)	221	(1.2)	222	(1.2)	230	(1.1)	228	(1.0)	230	(0.9)	229	(0.7)	231	(0.9)	240	(1.1)
Race/ethnicity																				
White	225	(1.0)	224	(0.9)	224	(1.1)	227	(1.1)	235	(0.8)	235	(0.8)	237	(1.0)	237	(1.0)	239	(0.9)	247	(0.9)
Black	190	(1.8)	192	(1.1)	195	(1.6)	202	(1.6)	208	(2.2)	208	(2.0)	212	(1.6)	212	(1.4)	211	(1.6)	224	(2.1)
Hispanic	202	(2.4)	203	(2.2)	204	(1.3)	205	(2.1)	214	(2.1)	212	(2.3)	210	(2.3)	215	(1.7)	213	(1.9)	230	(2.0)
Region																				
Northeast	227	(1.9)	227	(1.9)	226	(1.8)	226	(2.7)	236	(2.1)	235	(1.9)	238	(2.2)	236	(2.0)	242	(1.7)	245	(2.0)
Southeast	208	(1.3)	209	(1.2)	210	(2.5)	218	(2.5)	224	(2.4)	221	(1.7)	229	(1.4)	227	(2.0)	226	(2.6)	240	(2.2)
Central	224	(1.5)	224	(1.5)	221	(2.7)	226	(2.3)	231	(1.3)	234	(1.6)	233	(1.8)	233	(2.3)	233	(1.4)	240	(1.5)
West	216	(2.2)	213	(1.3)	219	(1.8)	217	(2.4)	228	(1.8)	229	(2.3)	226	(1.6)	229	(1.3)	228	(1.7)	241	(1.8)
13-year-olds																				
All students	266	(1.1)	264	(1.1)	269	(1.1)	269	(1.2)	270	(0.9)	273	(0.9)	274	(1.0)	274	(0.8)	276	(0.8)	281	(1.0)
Sex																				
Male	265	(1.3)	264	(1.3)	269	(1.4)	270	(1.1)	271	(1.2)	274	(1.1)	276	(1.3)	276	(0.9)	277	(0.9)	283	(1.2)
Female	267	(1.1)	265	(1.1)	268	(1.1)	268	(1.5)	270	(0.9)	272	(1.0)	273	(1.0)	272	(1.0)	274	(1.1)	279	(1.0)
Race/ethnicity																				
White	274	(0.9)	272	(0.8)	274	(1.0)	274	(1.3)	276	(1.1)	279	(0.9)	281	(0.9)	281	(0.9)	283	(0.8)	288	(0.9)
Black	228	(1.9)	230	(1.9)	240	(1.6)	249	(2.3)	249	(2.3)	250	(1.9)	252	(3.5)	252	(1.3)	251	(2.6)	262	(1.6)
Hispanic	239	(2.2)	238	(2.0)	252	(1.7)	254	(2.9)	255	(1.8)	259	(1.8)	256	(1.9)	256	(1.6)	259	(1.7)	265	(2.0)
Parents' highest level of education																				
Not high school graduate	—	(†)	245	(1.2)	251	(1.4)	252	(2.3)	253	(1.8)	256	(1.0)	255	(2.1)	254	(2.4)	256	(2.8)	262	(2.2)
Graduated high school	—	(†)	263	(1.0)	263	(0.8)	263	(1.2)	263	(1.2)	263	(1.2)	266	(1.1)	267	(1.1)	264	(1.1)	271	(1.7)
Some education after high school	—	(†)	273	(1.2)	275	(0.9)	274	(0.8)	277	(1.0)	278	(1.0)	277	(1.6)	277	(1.4)	279	(0.9)	283	(1.0)
Graduated college	—	(†)	284	(1.2)	282	(1.5)	280	(1.4)	280	(1.0)	283	(1.0)	285	(1.2)	283	(1.2)	286	(1.0)	292	(0.9)
Region																				
Northeast	275	(2.4)	273	(2.4)	277	(2.0)	277	(2.2)	275	(2.3)	274	(2.2)	284	(1.5)	275	(2.1)	279	(2.7)	284	(2.1)
Southeast	255	(3.2)	253	(3.3)	258	(2.2)	263	(1.4)	266	(1.9)	271	(2.5)	269	(2.0)	270	(1.8)	270	(2.3)	278	(2.1)
Central	271	(1.8)	269	(1.8)	273	(2.1)	266	(4.5)	272	(2.4)	275	(1.5)	275	(3.4)	280	(1.3)	278	(1.8)	283	(2.2)
West	262	(1.9)	260	(1.9)	266	(2.4)	270	(2.1)	269	(1.6)	272	(1.4)	272	(1.7)	273	(1.9)	276	(1.4)	280	(1.4)
17-year-olds																				
All students	304	(1.1)	300	(1.0)	298	(0.9)	302	(0.9)	305	(0.9)	307	(0.9)	306	(1.0)	307	(1.2)	308	(1.0)	307	(0.8)
Sex																				
Male	309	(1.2)	304	(1.0)	301	(1.0)	305	(1.2)	306	(1.1)	309	(1.1)	309	(1.4)	310	(1.3)	310	(1.4)	308	(1.0)
Female	301	(1.1)	297	(1.0)	296	(1.0)	299	(1.0)	303	(1.1)	305	(1.1)	304	(1.1)	305	(1.4)	307	(1.0)	305	(0.9)
Race/ethnicity																				
White	310	(1.1)	306	(0.9)	304	(0.9)	308	(1.0)	309	(1.0)	312	(0.8)	312	(1.1)	313	(1.4)	315	(1.1)	313	(0.7)
Black	270	(1.3)	268	(1.3)	272	(1.2)	279	(2.1)	289	(2.8)	286	(2.2)	286	(1.8)	286	(1.7)	283	(1.5)	285	(1.6)
Hispanic	277	(2.2)	276	(2.3)	277	(1.8)	283	(2.9)	284	(2.9)	292	(2.6)	291	(3.7)	292	(2.1)	293	(2.5)	289	(1.8)
Parents' highest level of education																				
Not high school graduate	—	(†)	280	(1.2)	279	(1.0)	279	(2.3)	285	(2.2)	285	(2.3)	284	(2.4)	281	(2.4)	289	(1.8)	287	(2.4)
Graduated high school	—	(†)	294	(0.8)	293	(0.8)	293	(1.0)	294	(0.9)	298	(1.7)	295	(1.1)	297	(2.4)	299	(1.6)	295	(1.1)
Some education after high school	—	(†)	305	(0.9)	304	(0.9)	305	(1.2)	308	(1.0)	308	(1.1)	305	(1.3)	307	(1.5)	308	(1.6)	306	(1.1)
Graduated college	—	(†)	317	(1.0)	312	(1.0)	314	(1.4)	316	(1.3)	316	(1.0)	318	(1.4)	317	(1.3)	317	(1.2)	317	(0.9)
Region																				
Northeast	312	(1.8)	307	(1.8)	304	(2.0)	307	(1.9)	304	(2.1)	311	(2.0)	313	(2.9)	309	(3.0)	313	(2.4)	310	(1.4)
Southeast	296	(1.8)	292	(1.7)	292	(2.1)	297	(1.4)	301	(2.3)	301	(1.9)	301	(1.6)	303	(2.1)	300	(1.4)	302	(1.3)
Central	306	(1.8)	305	(1.9)	302	(1.4)	304	(1.9)	311	(2.1)	312	(2.0)	307	(2.2)	314	(2.0)	310	(2.0)	313	(1.0)
West	303	(2.0)	295	(1.8)	294	(1.9)	299	(2.7)	302	(1.5)	303	(2.3)	305	(2.4)	304	(2.3)	310	(2.0)	303	(1.9)

—Not available.
†Not applicable.
NOTE: Excludes persons not enrolled in school and those who were unable to be tested due to limited proficiency in English or due to a disability. Includes public and private schools. A score of 150 implies the knowledge of some basic addition and subtraction facts, and most students at this level can add two-digit numbers without regrouping. They recognize simple situations in which addition and subtraction apply. A score of 200 implies considerable understanding of two-digit numbers and knowledge of some basic multiplication and division facts. A score of 250 implies an initial understanding of the four basic operations. Students at this level can also compare information from graphs and charts and are developing an ability to analyze simple logical relations. A score of 300 implies an ability to compute decimals, simple fractions, and percents. Students at this level can identify geo-metric figures, measure lengths and angles, and calculate areas of rectangles. They are developing the skills to operate with signed numbers, exponents, and square roots. A score of 350 implies an ability to apply a range of reasoning skills to solve multistep problems. Students at this level can solve routine problems involving fractions and percents, recognize properties of basic geometric figures, and work with exponents and square roots. Scale ranges from 0 to 500. Race categories exclude persons of Hispanic origin. Totals include other racial/ethnic groups not shown separately. Some data have been revised from previously published figures. Standard errors appear in parentheses.
SOURCE: U.S. Department of Education, National Center for Education Statistics, National Assessment of Educational Progress (NAEP), *NAEP 2004 Trends in Academic Progress*; and unpublished tabulations, NAEP Data Explorer (http://nces.ed.gov/nationsreportcard/nde/), retrieved July 2005. (This table was prepared July 2005.)

Table 122. Percentage of students at or above selected mathematics proficiency levels, by age, sex, and race/ethnicity: Selected years, 1978 through 2004

Selected characteristic	9-year-olds[1]				13-year-olds[2]				17-year-olds[2]			
	Simple arithmetic facts[3]	Beginning skills and understanding[4]	Numerical operations and beginning problem solving[5]	Moderately complex procedures and reasoning[6]	Beginning skills and understanding[4]	Numerical operations and beginning problem solving[5]	Moderately complex procedures and reasoning[6]	Multistep problem solving and algebra[7]	Beginning skills and understanding[4]	Numerical operations and beginning problem solving[5]	Moderately complex procedures and reasoning[6]	Multistep problem solving and algebra[7]
1	2	3	4	5	6	7	8	9	10	11	12	13
Total												
1978	96.7 (0.3)	70.4 (0.9)	19.6 (0.7)	0.8 (0.1)	94.6 (0.5)	64.9 (1.2)	18.0 (0.7)	1.0 (0.2)	99.8 (0.1)	92.0 (0.5)	51.5 (1.1)	7.3 (0.4)
1982	97.1 (0.3)	71.4 (1.2)	18.8 (1.0)	0.6 (0.1)	97.7 (0.4)	71.4 (1.2)	17.4 (0.9)	0.5 (0.1)	99.9 (†)	93.0 (0.5)	48.5 (1.3)	5.5 (0.4)
1986	97.9 (0.3)	74.1 (1.2)	20.7 (0.9)	0.6 (0.2)	98.6 (0.2)	73.3 (1.6)	15.8 (1.0)	0.4 (0.1)	99.9 (†)	95.6 (0.5)	51.7 (1.4)	6.5 (0.5)
1990	99.1 (0.2)	81.5 (1.0)	27.7 (0.9)	1.2 (0.3)	98.5 (0.2)	74.7 (1.0)	17.3 (1.0)	0.4 (0.1)	100.0 (†)	96.0 (0.5)	56.1 (1.4)	7.2 (0.6)
1992	99.0 (0.2)	81.4 (0.8)	27.8 (0.9)	1.2 (0.3)	98.7 (0.3)	77.9 (1.1)	18.9 (1.4)	0.4 (0.2)	100.0 (†)	96.6 (0.5)	59.1 (1.3)	7.2 (0.6)
1994	99.0 (0.2)	82.0 (0.7)	29.9 (1.1)	1.3 (0.4)	98.5 (0.3)	78.1 (1.1)	21.3 (1.2)	0.6 (0.1)	100.0 (†)	96.5 (0.5)	58.6 (1.4)	7.4 (0.8)
1996	99.1 (0.2)	81.5 (0.8)	29.7 (1.1)	1.6 (0.3)	98.8 (0.2)	78.6 (0.9)	20.6 (1.2)	0.6 (0.1)	100.0 (†)	96.8 (0.4)	60.1 (1.7)	7.4 (0.8)
1999	98.9 (0.2)	82.5 (0.8)	30.9 (1.1)	1.7 (0.3)	98.7 (0.2)	78.8 (1.0)	23.2 (1.0)	0.9 (0.2)	100.0 (†)	96.8 (0.5)	60.7 (1.6)	8.4 (0.8)
2004	99.3 (0.1)	88.6 (0.8)	41.9 (1.2)	— (†)	98.6 (0.2)	83.5 (1.0)	29.0 (1.1)	— (†)	— (†)	96.7 (0.4)	58.6 (1.3)	6.9 (0.6)
Male												
1978	96.2 (0.5)	68.9 (1.0)	19.2 (0.6)	0.7 (0.2)	93.9 (0.5)	63.9 (1.3)	18.4 (0.9)	1.1 (0.2)	99.9 (0.1)	93.0 (0.5)	55.1 (1.2)	9.5 (0.6)
1982	96.5 (0.5)	68.8 (1.3)	18.1 (1.1)	0.6 (0.1)	97.5 (0.6)	71.3 (1.4)	18.9 (1.2)	0.7 (0.2)	100.0 (†)	93.9 (0.6)	51.9 (1.5)	6.9 (0.7)
1986	98.0 (0.5)	74.0 (1.4)	20.9 (1.1)	0.7 (0.3)	98.5 (0.3)	73.8 (1.8)	17.6 (1.1)	0.5 (0.2)	99.9 (†)	96.1 (0.6)	54.6 (1.8)	8.4 (0.9)
1990	99.0 (0.3)	80.6 (1.0)	27.5 (1.0)	1.3 (0.4)	98.2 (0.3)	75.1 (1.8)	19.0 (1.2)	0.5 (0.2)	100.0 (†)	95.8 (0.8)	57.6 (1.4)	8.8 (0.8)
1992	99.0 (0.3)	81.9 (1.0)	29.4 (1.2)	1.4 (0.3)	98.8 (0.4)	78.1 (1.6)	20.7 (1.1)	0.5 (0.2)	100.0 (†)	96.9 (0.6)	60.5 (1.8)	9.1 (0.7)
1994	99.1 (0.2)	82.3 (0.9)	31.5 (1.6)	1.4 (0.4)	98.3 (0.4)	78.9 (1.5)	23.9 (1.6)	0.8 (0.3)	100.0 (†)	97.3 (0.6)	60.2 (2.1)	9.3 (1.0)
1996	99.1 (0.3)	82.5 (1.1)	32.7 (1.7)	2.0 (0.5)	98.7 (0.3)	79.8 (1.4)	23.0 (1.6)	0.8 (0.2)	100.0 (†)	97.0 (0.7)	62.7 (1.8)	9.5 (1.3)
1999	98.8 (0.3)	82.6 (0.9)	32.4 (1.3)	1.9 (0.4)	98.5 (0.3)	79.3 (1.1)	25.4 (1.2)	1.2 (0.2)	100.0 (†)	96.5 (0.8)	63.1 (2.1)	9.8 (1.1)
2004	99.3 (0.2)	89.3 (0.9)	43.5 (1.2)	— (†)	98.3 (0.3)	82.8 (1.2)	32.6 (1.6)	— (†)	— (†)	96.6 (0.6)	60.6 (1.6)	8.8 (1.0)
Female												
1978	97.2 (0.3)	72.0 (1.1)	19.9 (1.0)	0.8 (0.2)	95.2 (0.5)	65.9 (1.2)	17.5 (0.7)	0.9 (0.2)	99.7 (0.1)	91.0 (0.6)	48.2 (1.3)	5.2 (0.7)
1982	97.6 (0.3)	74.0 (1.3)	19.6 (1.1)	0.5 (0.1)	98.0 (0.3)	71.4 (1.3)	15.9 (1.0)	0.4 (0.2)	99.9 (†)	92.1 (0.6)	45.3 (1.4)	4.1 (0.4)
1986	97.8 (0.4)	74.3 (1.3)	20.6 (1.3)	0.6 (0.3)	98.6 (0.2)	72.7 (1.9)	14.1 (1.3)	0.3 (0.1)	100.0 (†)	95.1 (0.7)	48.9 (1.7)	4.7 (0.6)
1990	99.1 (0.3)	82.3 (1.1)	27.9 (1.1)	1.0 (0.3)	98.9 (0.2)	74.4 (1.3)	15.7 (1.0)	0.2 (0.1)	100.0 (†)	96.2 (0.8)	54.7 (1.8)	5.6 (0.8)
1992	99.0 (0.3)	80.9 (1.1)	26.3 (1.5)	1.0 (0.4)	98.6 (0.2)	77.7 (1.1)	17.2 (1.4)	0.3 (†)	100.0 (†)	96.3 (0.8)	57.7 (1.6)	5.2 (0.8)
1994	98.9 (0.3)	81.7 (0.9)	28.3 (1.3)	1.1 (0.4)	98.7 (0.3)	77.3 (1.0)	18.7 (1.4)	0.5 (0.3)	100.0 (†)	96.0 (0.6)	57.2 (1.4)	5.5 (0.8)
1996	99.1 (0.4)	80.7 (1.1)	26.7 (1.1)	1.2 (0.4)	98.8 (0.3)	77.4 (1.1)	18.4 (1.5)	0.5 (0.2)	100.0 (†)	96.7 (0.6)	57.6 (2.2)	5.3 (0.8)
1999	99.0 (0.2)	82.5 (1.2)	29.4 (1.4)	1.6 (0.4)	99.0 (0.3)	78.4 (1.2)	21.0 (1.4)	0.6 (0.3)	100.0 (†)	97.2 (0.4)	58.5 (1.9)	7.1 (1.1)
2004	99.3 (0.2)	87.9 (0.6)	40.3 (1.5)	— (†)	98.8 (0.3)	84.1 (1.1)	25.6 (1.1)	— (†)	— (†)	96.8 (0.5)	56.7 (1.6)	5.1 (0.6)
White												
1978	98.3 (0.2)	76.3 (1.0)	22.9 (0.9)	0.9 (0.2)	97.6 (0.3)	72.9 (0.9)	21.4 (0.7)	1.2 (0.2)	100.0 (†)	95.6 (0.3)	57.6 (1.1)	8.5 (0.5)
1982	98.5 (0.3)	76.8 (1.2)	21.8 (1.1)	0.6 (0.1)	99.1 (0.1)	78.3 (0.9)	20.5 (1.0)	0.6 (0.1)	100.0 (†)	96.2 (0.3)	54.7 (1.4)	6.4 (0.5)
1986	98.8 (0.2)	79.6 (1.3)	24.6 (1.0)	0.8 (0.4)	99.3 (0.3)	78.9 (1.7)	18.6 (1.2)	0.4 (0.1)	100.0 (†)	98.0 (0.4)	59.1 (1.7)	7.9 (0.7)
1990	99.6 (0.1)	86.9 (0.9)	32.7 (1.0)	1.5 (0.4)	99.4 (0.1)	82.0 (1.0)	21.0 (1.2)	0.4 (0.1)	100.0 (†)	97.6 (0.3)	63.2 (1.6)	8.3 (0.7)
1992	99.6 (0.1)	86.9 (0.7)	32.4 (1.0)	1.4 (0.3)	99.6 (0.2)	84.9 (1.1)	22.8 (1.3)	0.4 (0.2)	100.0 (†)	98.3 (0.4)	66.4 (1.4)	8.7 (0.9)
1994	99.6 (0.2)	87.0 (0.8)	35.3 (1.3)	1.5 (0.4)	99.3 (0.2)	85.5 (0.9)	25.6 (1.6)	0.7 (0.3)	100.0 (†)	98.4 (0.4)	67.0 (1.4)	9.4 (1.1)
1996	99.6 (0.1)	86.6 (0.8)	35.7 (1.4)	2.0 (0.4)	99.6 (0.2)	86.4 (1.0)	25.4 (1.5)	0.8 (0.2)	100.0 (†)	98.7 (0.4)	68.7 (2.2)	9.2 (1.0)
1999	99.6 (0.1)	88.6 (0.6)	37.1 (1.4)	2.2 (0.4)	99.4 (0.3)	86.7 (0.9)	29.0 (1.3)	1.2 (0.3)	100.0 (†)	98.7 (0.4)	69.9 (2.0)	10.4 (1.1)
2004	99.7 (0.1)	92.6 (0.6)	49.0 (1.4)	— (†)	99.1 (0.2)	90.5 (0.8)	36.0 (1.3)	— (†)	— (†)	98.4 (0.4)	69.0 (1.3)	8.5 (0.8)
Black												
1978	88.4 (1.0)	42.0 (1.4)	4.1 (0.6)	# (†)	79.7 (1.5)	28.7 (2.1)	2.3 (0.5)	# (†)	98.8 (0.3)	70.7 (1.7)	16.8 (1.6)	# (†)
1982	90.2 (1.0)	46.1 (2.4)	4.4 (0.8)	# (†)	90.2 (1.6)	37.9 (2.5)	2.9 (1.0)	# (†)	99.7 (0.2)	76.4 (1.5)	17.1 (1.5)	# (†)
1986	93.9 (1.4)	53.4 (2.5)	5.6 (0.9)	# (†)	95.4 (0.9)	49.0 (3.7)	4.0 (1.4)	# (†)	100.0 (†)	85.6 (2.5)	20.8 (2.8)	# (†)
1990	96.9 (0.9)	60.0 (2.8)	9.4 (1.7)	# (†)	95.4 (1.1)	48.7 (3.6)	3.9 (1.6)	# (†)	99.9 (†)	92.4 (2.2)	32.8 (4.5)	# (†)
1992	96.6 (1.1)	59.8 (2.8)	9.6 (1.4)	# (†)	95.0 (1.4)	51.0 (2.7)	4.0 (0.7)	# (†)	100.0 (†)	89.6 (2.5)	29.8 (3.9)	2.0 (1.0)
1994	97.4 (1.0)	65.9 (2.6)	11.1 (1.7)	# (†)	95.6 (1.6)	51.0 (3.9)	6.4 (2.4)	# (†)	100.0 (†)	90.6 (1.8)	29.8 (3.4)	0.9 (†)
1996	97.3 (0.8)	65.3 (2.4)	10.0 (1.2)	# (†)	96.2 (1.3)	53.7 (2.6)	4.8 (1.1)	# (†)	100.0 (†)	90.6 (1.3)	31.2 (2.5)	# (†)
1999	96.4 (0.6)	63.3 (2.1)	12.3 (1.5)	# (†)	96.5 (1.1)	50.8 (4.0)	4.4 (1.4)	# (†)	99.9 (†)	88.6 (2.0)	26.6 (2.7)	1.0 (†)
2004	97.6 (0.7)	77.0 (2.4)	23.6 (2.0)	— (†)	97.2 (0.6)	67.2 (2.2)	9.0 (1.1)	— (†)	— (†)	91.7 (1.9)	26.0 (2.6)	0.9 (0.5)

See notes at end of table.

Table 122. Percentage of students at or above selected mathematics proficiency levels, by age, sex, and race/ethnicity: Selected years, 1978 through 2004—Continued

Selected characteristic	9-year-olds[1]				13-year-olds[2]				17-year-olds[2]			
	Simple arithmetic facts[3]	Beginning skills and understanding[4]	Numerical operations and beginning problem solving[5]	Moderately complex procedures and reasoning[6]	Beginning skills and understanding[4]	Numerical operations and beginning problem solving[5]	Moderately complex procedures and reasoning[6]	Multistep problem solving and algebra[7]	Beginning skills and understanding[4]	Numerical operations and beginning problem solving[5]	Moderately complex procedures and reasoning[6]	Multistep problem solving and algebra[7]
1	2	3	4	5	6	7	8	9	10	11	12	13
Hispanic												
1978	93.0 (1.2)	54.2 (2.8)	9.2 (2.5)	# (†)	86.4 (0.9)	36.0 (2.9)	4.0 (1.0)	# (†)	99.3 (0.4)	78.3 (2.3)	23.4 (2.7)	1.4 (0.6)
1982	94.3 (1.2)	55.7 (2.3)	7.8 (1.7)	# (†)	95.9 (0.9)	52.2 (2.5)	6.3 (1.0)	# (†)	99.8 (†)	81.4 (1.9)	21.6 (2.2)	0.7 (0.4)
1986	96.4 (1.3)	57.6 (2.9)	7.3 (2.8)	# (†)	96.9 (1.4)	56.0 (5.0)	5.5 (1.1)	# (†)	99.4 (†)	89.3 (2.5)	26.5 (4.5)	1.1 (‡)
1990	98.0 (0.8)	68.4 (3.0)	11.3 (3.5)	# (†)	96.8 (1.1)	56.7 (3.3)	6.4 (1.7)	# (†)	99.6 (†)	85.8 (4.2)	30.1 (3.1)	1.9 (0.8)
1992	97.2 (1.3)	65.0 (2.9)	11.7 (2.5)	# (†)	98.1 (0.7)	63.3 (2.7)	7.0 (1.2)	# (†)	100.0 (†)	94.1 (2.2)	39.2 (4.9)	1.2 (‡)
1994	97.2 (1.2)	63.5 (3.1)	9.7 (1.8)	# (†)	97.1 (1.3)	59.2 (2.2)	6.4 (1.8)	# (†)	100.0 (†)	91.8 (3.6)	38.3 (5.5)	1.4 (‡)
1996	98.1 (0.7)	67.1 (2.1)	13.8 (2.3)	# (†)	96.2 (0.8)	58.3 (2.3)	6.7 (1.2)	# (†)	99.9 (†)	92.2 (2.2)	40.1 (3.5)	1.8 (‡)
1999	98.1 (0.7)	67.5 (2.5)	10.5 (1.6)	# (†)	97.2 (0.6)	62.9 (2.5)	8.2 (1.4)	# (†)	99.9 (†)	93.6 (2.2)	37.7 (4.1)	3.1 (1.1)
2004	99.6 (0.2)	82.6 (2.4)	26.9 (2.7)	— (†)	97.3 (0.8)	68.4 (3.3)	14.3 (1.8)	— (†)	— (†)	92.1 (2.1)	32.3 (2.1)	1.3 (0.5)

—Not available.
†Not applicable.
#Rounds to zero.
‡Reporting standards not met.
[1]Virtually no students were able to perform multistep problems and algebra.
[2]Virtually all students knew simple arithmetic facts.
[3]Scale score of 150 or above.
[4]Scale score of 200 or above.
[5]Scale score of 250 or above.
[6]Scale score of 300 or above.
[7]Scale score of 350 or above.

NOTE: Excludes persons not enrolled in school and those who were unable to be tested due to limited proficiency in English or due to a disability. Includes public and private schools. Race categories exclude persons of Hispanic origin. Totals include other racial/ethnic groups not shown separately. Standard errors appear in parentheses.

SOURCE: U.S. Department of Education, National Assessment of Educational Progress (NAEP), 1999 NAEP Trends in Academic Progress and NAEP Data Explorer (http://nces.ed.gov/nationsreportcard/nde/), retrieved July 2005. (This table was prepared February 2006.)

Table 123. Mathematics performance of 17-year-olds, by highest mathematics course taken, sex, and race/ethnicity: Selected years, 1978 through 2004

Selected characteristic	Percent of students		Average scale score by highest mathematics course taken										Percent of students at or above score levels							
			All areas		Prealgebra or general mathematics		Algebra I		Geometry		Algebra II		Precalculus or calculus		200		250		300		350	
1	2		3		4		5		6		7		8		9		10		11		12	
1978																					
All students	100	(†)	300	(1.0)	267	(0.8)	286	(0.7)	307	(0.7)	321	(0.7)	334	(1.4)	100	(0.1)	92	(0.5)	52	(1.1)	7	(0.4)
Sex																						
Male......................	49	(0.5)	304	(1.0)	269	(1.0)	289	(0.9)	310	(1.0)	325	(0.8)	337	(2.0)	100	(0.1)	93	(0.5)	55	(1.2)	10	(0.6)
Female...................	51	(0.5)	297	(1.0)	264	(0.9)	284	(1.0)	304	(0.8)	318	(0.9)	329	(1.8)	100	(0.1)	91	(0.6)	48	(1.3)	5	(0.7)
Race/ethnicity																						
White......................	83	(1.3)	306	(0.9)	272	(0.6)	291	(0.6)	310	(0.6)	325	(0.6)	338	(1.1)	100	(‡)	96	(0.3)	58	(1.1)	8	(0.5)
Black.....................	12	(1.1)	268	(1.3)	247	(1.6)	264	(1.5)	281	(1.9)	292	(1.4)	297	(6.5)	99	(0.3)	71	(1.7)	17	(1.6)	#	(†)
Hispanic.................	4	(0.5)	276	(2.3)	256	(2.3)	273	(2.8)	294	(4.4)	303	(2.9)	‡	(†)	99	(0.4)	78	(2.3)	23	(2.7)	1	(0.6)
Other[1]...................	1	(0.1)	313	(3.3)	—	(†)	—	(†)	—	(†)	—	(†)	—	(†)	100	(‡)	94	(2.6)	65	(4.9)	15	(3.2)
1990																					
All students	100	(†)	305	(0.9)	273	(1.1)	288	(1.2)	299	(1.5)	319	(1.0)	344	(2.7)	100	(‡)	96	(0.5)	56	(1.4)	7	(0.6)
Sex																						
Male......................	49	(0.9)	306	(1.1)	274	(1.7)	291	(1.6)	302	(1.6)	323	(1.2)	347	(2.4)	100	(‡)	96	(0.8)	58	(1.4)	9	(0.8)
Female...................	51	(0.9)	303	(1.1)	271	(1.8)	285	(1.8)	296	(1.8)	316	(1.1)	340	(4.0)	100	(‡)	96	(0.8)	55	(1.8)	6	(0.8)
Race/ethnicity																						
White......................	73	(0.5)	309	(1.0)	277	(1.1)	292	(1.6)	304	(1.3)	323	(0.9)	347	(2.8)	100	(‡)	98	(0.3)	63	(1.6)	8	(0.7)
Black.....................	16	(0.3)	289	(2.8)	264	(2.2)	278	(4.0)	285	(3.5)	302	(3.2)	—	(†)	100	(‡)	92	(2.2)	33	(4.5)	2	(1.0)
Hispanic.................	7	(0.4)	284	(2.9)	—	(†)	—	(†)	—	(†)	306	(3.3)	—	(†)	100	(‡)	86	(4.2)	30	(3.1)	2	(0.8)
Other[1]...................	4	(0.5)	312	(5.2)	—	(†)	—	(†)	—	(†)	—	(†)	—	(†)	100	(‡)	98	(‡)	62	(7.0)	16	(4.3)
1994																					
All students	100	(†)	306	(1.0)	272	(1.2)	288	(1.4)	297	(1.7)	316	(1.0)	340	(2.2)	100	(‡)	97	(0.5)	59	(1.4)	7	(0.8)
Sex																						
Male......................	49	(1.3)	309	(1.4)	274	(1.8)	289	(1.6)	301	(2.1)	320	(1.5)	343	(2.6)	100	(‡)	97	(0.6)	60	(2.1)	9	(1.0)
Female...................	51	(1.3)	304	(1.1)	268	(1.9)	286	(1.9)	293	(1.8)	313	(1.1)	337	(2.8)	100	(‡)	96	(0.6)	57	(1.4)	6	(0.9)
Race/ethnicity																						
White......................	73	(0.5)	312	(1.1)	275	(1.4)	292	(1.7)	301	(1.5)	320	(1.0)	344	(2.0)	100	(‡)	98	(0.4)	67	(1.4)	9	(1.1)
Black.....................	15	(0.3)	286	(1.8)	—	(†)	275	(3.3)	283	(3.8)	297	(2.5)	—	(†)	100	(‡)	91	(1.8)	30	(3.4)	#	(†)
Hispanic.................	9	(0.3)	291	(3.7)	—	(†)	—	(†)	—	(†)	304	(4.1)	—	(†)	100	(‡)	92	(3.6)	38	(5.5)	1	(‡)
Other[1]...................	3	(0.3)	313	(4.5)	—	(†)	—	(†)	—	(†)	—	(†)	—	(†)	100	(‡)	97	(‡)	66	(6.6)	12	(3.6)
1996																					
All students	100	(†)	307	(1.2)	269	(1.9)	283	(1.3)	298	(1.3)	316	(1.3)	339	(1.7)	100	(‡)	97	(0.4)	60	(1.7)	7	(0.8)
Sex																						
Male......................	50	(1.2)	310	(1.3)	272	(2.5)	286	(1.5)	302	(1.7)	320	(1.7)	342	(2.3)	100	(‡)	97	(0.7)	63	(1.8)	9	(1.3)
Female...................	50	(1.2)	305	(1.4)	265	(2.2)	278	(2.2)	294	(1.5)	313	(1.4)	335	(2.2)	100	(‡)	97	(0.6)	58	(2.2)	5	(0.8)
Race/ethnicity																						
White......................	71	(0.6)	313	(1.4)	273	(2.3)	287	(2.0)	304	(1.6)	320	(1.4)	342	(1.9)	100	(‡)	99	(0.4)	69	(2.2)	9	(1.0)
Black.....................	15	(0.3)	286	(1.7)	—	(†)	272	(2.4)	280	(3.0)	299	(2.2)	—	(†)	100	(‡)	91	(1.3)	31	(2.5)	1	(‡)
Hispanic.................	9	(0.7)	292	(2.1)	—	(†)	—	(†)	—	(†)	306	(2.8)	—	(†)	100	(‡)	92	(2.2)	40	(3.5)	2	(‡)
Other[1]...................	4	(0.7)	312	(5.7)	—	(†)	—	(†)	—	(†)	—	(†)	—	(†)	100	(‡)	97	(1.2)	64	(7.2)	14	(5.0)
1999																					
All students	100	(†)	308	(1.0)	278	(2.8)	285	(1.7)	298	(1.2)	315	(0.8)	341	(1.4)	100	(‡)	97	(0.5)	61	(1.6)	8	(0.8)
Sex																						
Male......................	48	(1.0)	310	(1.4)	281	(3.2)	288	(2.6)	301	(1.8)	317	(1.3)	343	(1.9)	100	(‡)	96	(0.8)	63	(2.1)	10	(1.1)
Female...................	52	(1.0)	307	(1.0)	274	(3.2)	282	(2.5)	295	(1.3)	314	(1.1)	340	(2.0)	100	(‡)	97	(0.4)	58	(1.9)	7	(1.1)
Race/ethnicity																						
White......................	72	(0.5)	315	(1.1)	282	(3.4)	290	(2.2)	303	(1.5)	320	(0.9)	343	(1.5)	100	(‡)	99	(0.4)	70	(2.0)	10	(1.1)
Black.....................	15	(0.4)	283	(1.5)	—	(†)	267	(2.9)	281	(2.5)	293	(1.4)	—	(†)	100	(‡)	89	(2.0)	27	(2.7)	1	(‡)
Hispanic.................	10	(0.5)	293	(2.5)	—	(†)	—	(†)	—	(†)	308	(3.0)	—	(†)	100	(‡)	94	(2.2)	38	(4.1)	3	(1.1)
Other[1]...................	4	(0.2)	320	(4.0)	—	(†)	—	(†)	—	(†)	—	(†)	—	(†)	100	(‡)	100	(‡)	76	(6.3)	14	(4.1)
2004																					
All students	100	(†)	307	(0.8)	270	(2.6)	282	(1.4)	296	(1.1)	310	(0.7)	336	(1.6)	100	(‡)	97	(0.4)	59	(1.3)	7	(0.6)
Sex																						
Male......................	48	(1.1)	308	(1.0)	273	(3.3)	286	(1.8)	298	(1.6)	313	(1.0)	339	(2.3)	100	(‡)	97	(0.6)	61	(1.6)	9	(1.0)
Female...................	52	(1.1)	305	(0.9)	267	(3.6)	278	(1.8)	293	(1.5)	308	(0.9)	332	(1.3)	100	(‡)	97	(0.5)	57	(1.6)	5	(0.6)
Race/ethnicity																						
White......................	69	(1.5)	313	(0.7)	276	(2.9)	287	(1.3)	302	(1.0)	316	(0.8)	338	(1.4)	100	(‡)	98	(0.4)	69	(1.3)	9	(0.8)
Black.....................	13	(1.1)	285	(1.6)	—	(†)	—	(†)	279	(2.0)	292	(1.5)	—	(†)	100	(‡)	92	(1.9)	26	(2.6)	1	(0.5)
Hispanic.................	14	(1.2)	289	(1.8)	—	(†)	—	(†)	285	(3.5)	293	(2.5)	321	(2.6)	100	(‡)	92	(2.1)	32	(2.1)	1	(0.5)
Other[1]...................	5	(0.5)	320	(2.8)	—	(†)	—	(†)	—	(†)	—	(†)	—	(†)	100	(‡)	99	(‡)	73	(4.2)	16	(3.8)

—Not available.
†Not applicable.
#Rounds to zero.
‡Reporting standards not met.
[1]Includes Asians/Pacific Islanders and American Indians/Alaska Natives.
NOTE: Score level 200 indicates ability to perform simple additive reasoning and problem solving. Score level 250 indicates ability to perform simple multiplicative reasoning and two-step problem solving. Score level 300 indicates ability to perform reasoning and problem solving involving fractions, decimals, percents, elementary geometry, and simple algebra. Score level 350 indicates ability to perform reasoning and problem solving involving geom-

etry, algebra, and beginning statistics and probability. Scale ranges from 0 to 500. Excludes persons not enrolled in school and those who were unable to be tested due to limited proficiency in English or due to a disability. Includes public and private schools. Race categories exclude persons of Hispanic origin. Detail may not sum to totals because of rounding. Standard errors appear in parentheses.
SOURCE: U.S. Department of Education, National Center for Education Statistics, National Assessment of Educational Progress (NAEP), *NAEP Trends in Academic Progress*, 1996 and 1999; and NAEP Data Explorer (http://nces.ed.gov/nations reportcard/nde/), retrieved August 2005. (This table was prepared February 2006.)

Table 124. Average scale score in mathematics, percentage attaining mathematics achievement levels, and selected statistics on mathematics education of 4th-graders in public schools, by state or jurisdiction: Selected years, 1992 through 2005

| State or jurisdiction | Average scale score | | | | Percent of students, 2005 | | | | | Percent of students, 2003 | |
| | 1992 | 2000 | 2003 | 2005 | Below basic | Basic or above[1] | Proficient or above[2] | Advanced[3] | Having 5 or more hours of math instruction each week | Spending 30 minutes or more on math homework each day[4] | Watching 6 hours or more of television each day |
1	2	3	4	5	6	7	8	9	10	11	12
United States[5]	219 (0.8)	224 (1.0)	234 (0.2)	237 (0.2)	21 (0.2)	80 (0.2)	35 (0.2)	5 (0.1)	83 (0.4)	49	21 (0.2)
Alabama	208 (1.6)	217 (1.2)	223 (1.2)	225 (0.9)	34 (1.3)	66 (1.3)	21 (1.1)	2 (0.4)	92 (1.6)	47	22 (1.1)
Alaska	— (†)	— (†)	233 (0.8)	236 (1.0)	23 (1.1)	77 (1.1)	34 (1.7)	5 (0.6)	78 (2.9)	—	— (†)
Arizona	215 (1.1)	219 (1.3)	229 (1.1)	230 (1.1)	30 (1.3)	70 (1.3)	28 (1.6)	3 (0.7)	80 (3.2)	52	19 (1.0)
Arkansas	210 (0.9)	216 (1.1)	229 (0.9)	236 (0.9)	22 (1.2)	78 (1.2)	34 (1.4)	4 (0.5)	91 (1.8)	51	24 (1.0)
California[6]	208 (1.6)	213 (1.6)	227 (0.9)	230 (0.6)	29 (0.7)	71 (0.7)	28 (0.8)	4 (0.4)	87 (1.3)	56	20 (0.7)
Colorado	221 (1.0)	— (†)	235 (1.0)	239 (1.1)	20 (1.4)	81 (1.4)	39 (1.6)	6 (0.8)	88 (1.9)	50	15 (0.8)
Connecticut	227 (1.1)	234 (1.1)	241 (0.8)	242 (0.8)	16 (1.0)	84 (1.0)	43 (1.4)	7 (0.6)	86 (2.2)	42	21 (0.8)
Delaware	218 (0.8)	— (†)	236 (0.5)	240 (0.5)	16 (0.8)	84 (0.8)	36 (1.2)	4 (0.5)	85 (0.4)	49	25 (0.7)
District of Columbia	193 (0.5)	192 (1.1)	205 (0.7)	211 (0.8)	55 (1.2)	45 (1.2)	10 (0.8)	1 (0.3)	86 (0.5)	52	32 (1.0)
Florida	214 (1.5)	— (†)	234 (1.1)	239 (0.7)	18 (0.6)	82 (0.6)	37 (1.1)	5 (0.7)	86 (1.4)	50	26 (1.0)
Georgia	216 (1.2)	219 (1.1)	230 (1.0)	234 (1.0)	24 (1.3)	76 (1.3)	30 (1.5)	4 (0.5)	90 (2.1)	48	23 (1.1)
Hawaii	214 (1.3)	216 (1.0)	227 (1.0)	230 (0.8)	27 (1.1)	73 (1.1)	27 (1.3)	3 (0.4)	78 (3.0)	58	23 (1.1)
Idaho[6]	222 (1.0)	224 (1.4)	235 (0.7)	242 (0.7)	14 (0.8)	86 (0.8)	40 (1.6)	5 (0.6)	77 (2.5)	49	14 (0.6)
Illinois[6]	— (†)	223 (1.9)	233 (1.1)	233 (1.0)	26 (1.2)	74 (1.2)	32 (1.5)	5 (0.8)	69 (2.9)	50	21 (0.9)
Indiana[6]	221 (1.0)	233 (1.1)	238 (0.9)	240 (0.9)	16 (0.9)	84 (0.9)	38 (1.7)	5 (0.6)	78 (2.8)	50	23 (0.9)
Iowa[6]	230 (1.0)	231 (1.2)	238 (0.7)	240 (0.7)	15 (1.0)	85 (1.0)	37 (1.3)	4 (0.4)	72 (3.2)	46	17 (1.0)
Kansas[6]	— (†)	232 (1.6)	242 (1.0)	246 (1.0)	12 (0.7)	88 (0.7)	47 (1.6)	8 (0.8)	92 (1.5)	48	19 (1.1)
Kentucky	215 (1.0)	219 (1.4)	229 (1.1)	232 (0.9)	25 (1.2)	75 (1.2)	26 (1.4)	3 (0.5)	68 (3.3)	49	24 (0.8)
Louisiana	204 (1.5)	218 (1.4)	226 (1.0)	230 (0.9)	26 (1.3)	74 (1.3)	24 (1.3)	2 (0.4)	92 (2.0)	43	24 (1.2)
Maine[6]	232 (1.0)	230 (1.0)	238 (0.7)	241 (0.8)	16 (0.9)	84 (0.9)	39 (1.4)	5 (0.6)	77 (2.8)	46	15 (0.9)
Maryland	217 (1.3)	222 (1.2)	233 (1.3)	238 (1.0)	21 (1.3)	79 (1.3)	38 (1.5)	7 (1.0)	95 (1.2)	42	25 (1.1)
Massachusetts	227 (1.2)	233 (1.2)	242 (0.8)	247 (0.8)	9 (0.7)	91 (0.7)	49 (1.5)	8 (0.7)	89 (1.9)	47	19 (0.7)
Michigan[6]	220 (1.7)	229 (1.6)	236 (0.9)	238 (1.2)	21 (1.5)	79 (1.5)	38 (1.7)	5 (0.7)	73 (3.0)	46	22 (0.9)
Minnesota[6]	228 (0.9)	234 (1.3)	242 (0.9)	246 (1.0)	12 (0.9)	88 (0.9)	47 (1.7)	8 (0.8)	81 (2.7)	48	15 (0.8)
Mississippi	202 (1.1)	211 (1.1)	223 (1.0)	227 (0.9)	31 (1.4)	69 (1.4)	19 (1.2)	1 (0.3)	91 (1.5)	51	24 (1.1)
Missouri	222 (1.2)	228 (1.2)	235 (0.9)	235 (0.9)	21 (1.3)	79 (1.3)	31 (1.3)	3 (0.5)	83 (2.5)	49	21 (1.0)
Montana[6]	— (†)	228 (1.7)	236 (0.8)	241 (0.8)	15 (1.1)	85 (1.1)	38 (1.4)	4 (0.5)	73 (2.0)	49	13 (0.7)
Nebraska	225 (1.2)	225 (1.8)	236 (0.8)	238 (0.9)	20 (1.0)	80 (1.0)	36 (1.3)	5 (0.6)	75 (2.5)	51	19 (1.1)
Nevada	— (†)	220 (1.0)	228 (0.8)	230 (0.8)	28 (1.0)	72 (1.0)	26 (1.2)	3 (0.4)	92 (1.3)	47	19 (0.8)
New Hampshire	230 (1.2)	— (†)	243 (0.9)	246 (0.9)	11 (0.9)	89 (0.9)	47 (1.5)	6 (0.6)	69 (2.9)	45	15 (0.8)
New Jersey	227 (1.5)	— (†)	239 (1.1)	244 (1.1)	14 (1.1)	86 (1.1)	45 (1.7)	8 (0.9)	78 (3.6)	45	20 (1.1)
New Mexico	213 (1.4)	213 (1.5)	223 (1.1)	224 (1.1)	35 (1.5)	65 (1.5)	19 (1.1)	2 (0.4)	76 (2.0)	55	18 (0.8)
New York[6]	218 (1.2)	225 (1.4)	236 (0.9)	238 (0.9)	19 (1.0)	81 (1.0)	36 (1.3)	5 (0.5)	77 (2.2)	47	23 (1.0)
North Carolina	213 (1.1)	230 (1.1)	242 (0.8)	241 (0.9)	17 (1.1)	83 (1.1)	40 (1.4)	7 (0.8)	86 (2.4)	50	20 (0.8)
North Dakota	229 (0.8)	230 (1.2)	238 (0.7)	243 (0.5)	11 (0.8)	89 (0.8)	40 (1.5)	4 (0.6)	63 (0.6)	48	14 (0.7)
Ohio[6]	219 (1.2)	230 (1.5)	238 (1.0)	242 (1.0)	16 (1.2)	84 (1.2)	43 (1.5)	7 (0.7)	79 (2.6)	45	21 (1.0)
Oklahoma	220 (1.0)	224 (1.0)	229 (1.0)	234 (1.0)	21 (1.2)	79 (1.2)	29 (1.5)	2 (0.4)	75 (2.4)	48	21 (1.0)
Oregon[6]	— (†)	224 (1.8)	236 (0.9)	238 (0.8)	20 (0.9)	80 (0.9)	37 (1.3)	6 (0.6)	77 (2.8)	49	16 (0.8)
Pennsylvania	224 (1.3)	— (†)	236 (1.1)	241 (1.2)	18 (1.2)	82 (1.2)	42 (1.6)	6 (0.6)	85 (2.5)	41	23 (1.0)
Rhode Island	215 (1.5)	224 (1.1)	230 (1.0)	233 (0.9)	24 (1.3)	76 (1.3)	31 (1.2)	4 (0.5)	87 (1.8)	44	19 (1.0)
South Carolina	212 (1.1)	220 (1.4)	236 (0.9)	238 (0.9)	19 (1.1)	82 (1.1)	36 (1.5)	5 (0.6)	86 (2.3)	47	25 (0.9)
South Dakota	— (†)	— (†)	237 (0.7)	242 (0.5)	14 (0.8)	86 (0.8)	41 (1.3)	4 (0.4)	71 (0.6)	55	14 (0.8)
Tennessee	211 (1.4)	220 (1.4)	228 (1.0)	232 (1.2)	26 (1.5)	74 (1.5)	28 (1.7)	3 (0.5)	82 (2.3)	50	23 (0.9)
Texas	218 (1.2)	231 (1.1)	237 (0.9)	242 (0.6)	13 (0.6)	87 (0.6)	40 (0.9)	5 (0.4)	92 (1.1)	53	19 (0.9)
Utah	224 (1.0)	227 (1.3)	235 (0.8)	239 (0.8)	17 (1.0)	83 (1.0)	37 (1.5)	4 (0.6)	72 (2.5)	46	15 (0.8)
Vermont[6]	— (†)	232 (1.6)	242 (0.8)	244 (0.9)	13 (0.8)	87 (0.8)	44 (1.1)	6 (0.6)	86 (0.6)	47	14 (0.9)
Virginia	221 (1.3)	230 (1.0)	239 (1.1)	241 (0.9)	17 (1.1)	83 (1.1)	39 (1.5)	6 (0.8)	77 (2.6)	46	23 (1.0)
Washington	— (†)	— (†)	238 (1.0)	242 (0.9)	16 (1.1)	84 (1.1)	42 (1.5)	6 (0.7)	86 (2.1)	51	17 (0.9)
West Virginia	215 (1.1)	223 (1.3)	231 (0.8)	231 (0.7)	25 (1.1)	75 (1.1)	25 (1.3)	2 (0.3)	82 (2.5)	47	22 (0.9)
Wisconsin[6]	229 (1.1)	— (†)	237 (0.9)	241 (0.9)	16 (1.2)	84 (1.2)	40 (1.4)	5 (0.6)	77 (2.7)	49	17 (0.7)
Wyoming	225 (0.9)	229 (1.1)	241 (0.6)	243 (0.6)	13 (0.9)	87 (0.9)	43 (1.4)	5 (0.7)	88 (0.4)	56	15 (0.7)
Department of Defense dependents schools[7]	— (†)	— (†)	— (†)	239 (0.5)	15 (1.0)	85 (1.0)	35 (1.2)	3 (0.4)	74 (0.5)	—	— (†)
Domestic schools	— (†)	228 (1.4)	237 (0.7)	— (†)	— (†)	— (†)	— (†)	— (†)	— (†)	51	21 (1.2)
Overseas schools	— (†)	226 (0.9)	237 (0.5)	— (†)	— (†)	— (†)	— (†)	— (†)	— (†)	52	18 (0.6)
Other jurisdictions											
American Samoa	— (†)	152 (2.5)	— (†)	— (†)	— (†)	— (†)	— (†)	— (†)	— (†)	—	— (†)
Guam	193 (0.8)	184 (1.7)	— (†)	— (†)	— (†)	— (†)	— (†)	— (†)	— (†)	—	— (†)
Virgin Islands	— (†)	181 (1.8)	— (†)	— (†)	— (†)	— (†)	— (†)	— (†)	— (†)	—	— (†)

—Not available.

†Not applicable.

[1]The basic level denotes partial mastery of prerequisite knowledge and skills that are fundamental for proficient work at the 4th-grade level.

[2]This level represents solid academic mastery for 4th-graders. Students reaching this level have demonstrated competency over challenging subject matter, including subject-matter knowledge, application of such knowledge to real-world situations, and analytical skills appropriate to the subject matter.

[3]This level signifies superior performance.

[4]Percentage of students who report spending 30 minutes, 45 minutes, 1 hour, and over 1 hour on mathematics homework each day.

[5]Based on a nationally representative sample. Forty-three jurisdictions (states, the District of Columbia, and Department of Defense schools) participated in the 2000 State Assessment of 4th-graders and met student and school participation criteria for reporting results.

Fifty-three jurisdictions participated in the 2003 and 2005 state assessments and met student and school participation criteria for reporting results.

[6]Did not meet one or more of the guidelines for school sample participation rates in 2000. Data are subject to appreciable nonresponse bias.

[7]The definition of the nationally representative sample changed in 2005; it now includes all of the Department of Defense schools.

NOTE: Excludes students unable to be tested due to limited proficiency in English or due to a disability. Data for 2000, 2003, and 2005 are for situations where student accommodations for the testing were permitted. Scale ranges from 0 to 500. Detail may not sum to totals because of rounding. Standard errors appear in parentheses.

SOURCE: U.S. Department of Education, National Center for Education Statistics, National Assessment of Educational Progress (NAEP), *The Nation's Report Card: Mathematics, 2000; The Nation's Report Card: Mathematics Highlights,* 2003 and 2005; and NAEP Data Explorer (http://nces.ed.gov/nationsreportcard/nde/), retrieved October 2005. (This table was prepared October 2005.)

Table 125. Average scale score in mathematics and percentage attaining mathematics achievement levels of 8th-graders in public schools, by level of parental education and state or jurisdiction: Selected years, 1990 through 2005

State or jurisdiction	Average scale score						Percent attaining mathematics achievement levels, 2005[1]				Average scale score, by highest level of education attained by parents, 2005[2]			
	1990	1992	1996	2000	2003	2005	Below basic	Basic or above[3]	Proficient or above[4]	Advanced[5]	Did not finish high school	Graduated high school	Some education after high school	Graduated college
1	2	3	4	5	6	7	8	9	10	11	12	13	14	15
United States	262 (1.4)	267 (1.0)	271 (1.2)	272 (0.9)	276 (0.3)	278 (0.2)	32 (0.2)	68 (0.2)	29 (0.2)	6 (0.1)	259 (0.5)	267 (0.3)	280 (0.3)	289 (0.3)
Alabama	253 (1.1)	252 (1.7)	257 (2.1)	264 (1.8)	262 (1.5)	262 (1.5)	47 (1.9)	53 (1.9)	15 (1.4)	2 (0.7)	245 (2.8)	254 (1.6)	267 (1.8)	272 (2.1)
Alaska	— (†)	— (†)	278 (1.8)	— (†)	279 (0.9)	279 (0.8)	31 (1.5)	69 (1.5)	29 (1.3)	6 (0.6)	‡ (†)	‡ (†)	‡ (†)	‡ (†)
Arizona[6]	260 (1.3)	265 (1.3)	268 (1.6)	269 (1.8)	271 (1.2)	274 (1.1)	36 (1.5)	64 (1.5)	26 (1.2)	5 (0.4)	255 (1.7)	266 (1.6)	278 (1.9)	290 (1.5)
Arkansas	256 (0.9)	256 (1.2)	262 (1.5)	257 (1.5)	266 (1.2)	272 (1.2)	36 (1.6)	64 (1.6)	22 (1.1)	3 (0.4)	263 (2.5)	264 (1.8)	279 (1.5)	279 (1.7)
California[6]	256 (1.3)	261 (1.7)	263 (1.9)	260 (2.1)	267 (1.2)	269 (0.7)	43 (0.8)	57 (0.8)	22 (0.6)	5 (0.4)	253 (1.2)	258 (1.3)	274 (1.2)	284 (1.0)
Colorado	267 (0.9)	272 (1.0)	276 (1.1)	— (†)	283 (1.1)	281 (1.2)	30 (1.6)	71 (1.6)	32 (1.4)	6 (0.8)	257 (1.9)	266 (2.0)	282 (1.9)	294 (1.1)
Connecticut	270 (1.0)	274 (1.1)	280 (1.1)	281 (1.3)	284 (1.2)	281 (1.4)	30 (1.7)	70 (1.7)	35 (1.4)	8 (0.7)	252 (3.6)	264 (1.8)	280 (1.7)	294 (1.5)
Delaware	261 (0.9)	263 (1.0)	267 (0.9)	— (†)	277 (0.7)	281 (0.6)	28 (1.0)	72 (1.0)	30 (1.0)	5 (0.5)	267 (2.7)	271 (1.7)	284 (1.2)	289 (1.0)
District of Columbia	231 (0.9)	235 (0.9)	233 (1.3)	235 (1.1)	243 (0.8)	245 (0.9)	69 (1.3)	31 (1.3)	7 (0.6)	2 (0.3)	243 (3.6)	238 (1.3)	252 (1.8)	253 (1.3)
Florida	255 (1.2)	260 (1.5)	264 (1.8)	— (†)	271 (1.5)	274 (1.1)	35 (1.3)	65 (1.3)	26 (1.2)	5 (0.7)	260 (2.1)	267 (1.8)	279 (1.6)	282 (1.5)
Georgia	259 (1.3)	259 (1.2)	262 (1.6)	265 (1.2)	270 (1.2)	272 (1.1)	38 (1.3)	62 (1.3)	23 (1.2)	4 (0.5)	252 (2.6)	261 (2.0)	275 (1.9)	284 (1.5)
Hawaii	251 (0.8)	257 (0.9)	262 (1.0)	262 (1.4)	266 (0.8)	266 (0.7)	44 (1.0)	56 (1.0)	18 (0.8)	3 (0.4)	250 (4.4)	255 (1.7)	271 (1.4)	274 (1.3)
Idaho[6]	271 (0.8)	275 (0.7)	— (†)	277 (1.0)	280 (0.9)	281 (0.9)	27 (1.1)	73 (1.1)	30 (1.2)	5 (0.6)	265 (2.3)	270 (1.9)	283 (2.2)	290 (1.0)
Illinois[6]	261 (1.7)	— (†)	— (†)	275 (1.7)	277 (1.1)	278 (1.1)	32 (1.2)	68 (1.2)	29 (1.3)	5 (0.6)	255 (2.0)	266 (1.4)	279 (1.4)	289 (1.4)
Indiana[6]	267 (1.2)	270 (1.1)	276 (1.4)	281 (1.1)	281 (1.1)	282 (1.0)	26 (1.2)	74 (1.2)	30 (1.3)	5 (0.6)	264 (2.5)	274 (1.5)	286 (1.7)	291 (1.5)
Iowa	278 (1.1)	283 (1.0)	284 (1.3)	— (†)	284 (0.8)	284 (0.9)	25 (1.1)	76 (1.1)	34 (1.2)	6 (0.6)	264 (2.6)	272 (1.7)	285 (1.3)	293 (1.0)
Kansas[8]	— (†)	— (†)	— (†)	283 (1.7)	284 (1.3)	284 (1.0)	23 (1.3)	77 (1.3)	34 (1.4)	5 (0.6)	261 (2.7)	273 (1.8)	286 (1.3)	294 (1.3)
Kentucky	257 (1.2)	262 (1.1)	267 (1.1)	270 (1.3)	274 (1.0)	274 (1.5)	36 (1.6)	64 (1.6)	23 (1.4)	3 (0.4)	256 (1.9)	264 (1.4)	277 (1.6)	285 (1.6)
Louisiana	246 (1.2)	250 (1.7)	252 (1.6)	259 (1.5)	266 (1.5)	268 (1.4)	41 (2.1)	59 (2.1)	16 (1.4)	2 (0.4)	260 (2.6)	260 (2.3)	274 (1.6)	275 (1.7)
Maine[6]	— (†)	279 (1.0)	284 (1.1)	281 (1.1)	282 (0.9)	281 (0.8)	26 (1.0)	74 (1.0)	30 (1.1)	5 (0.5)	264 (3.1)	271 (1.7)	284 (1.7)	290 (1.1)
Maryland	261 (1.4)	265 (1.3)	270 (2.1)	272 (1.7)	278 (1.0)	278 (1.1)	34 (1.5)	66 (1.5)	30 (1.3)	7 (0.7)	255 (4.2)	268 (2.2)	277 (1.9)	288 (1.5)
Massachusetts	— (†)	273 (1.0)	278 (1.7)	279 (1.5)	287 (0.9)	292 (0.9)	20 (1.1)	80 (1.1)	43 (1.4)	11 (0.8)	271 (3.2)	278 (1.7)	286 (1.6)	302 (0.9)
Michigan[6]	264 (1.2)	267 (1.4)	277 (1.8)	278 (1.9)	276 (2.0)	277 (1.5)	25 (1.2)	75 (1.2)	29 (1.4)	6 (0.6)	254 (4.0)	265 (2.4)	281 (1.9)	286 (1.9)
Minnesota	275 (0.9)	282 (1.0)	284 (1.3)	287 (1.4)	291 (1.1)	290 (1.2)	21 (1.3)	79 (1.3)	43 (1.6)	11 (0.9)	263 (4.4)	261 (2.5)	291 (1.8)	300 (1.2)
Mississippi	— (†)	246 (1.2)	250 (1.2)	254 (1.1)	261 (1.1)	263 (1.2)	48 (1.7)	52 (1.7)	14 (0.9)	1 (0.3)	254 (2.0)	253 (1.6)	269 (1.8)	269 (1.1)
Missouri	270 (1.1)	271 (1.2)	273 (1.4)	271 (1.5)	279 (1.1)	276 (1.3)	32 (1.4)	68 (1.4)	26 (1.4)	4 (0.6)	263 (3.0)	270 (1.8)	277 (1.9)	285 (1.8)
Montana[6]	280 (0.9)	— (†)	283 (1.3)	285 (1.4)	286 (0.8)	286 (0.7)	21 (1.0)	80 (1.0)	36 (1.1)	6 (0.6)	262 (3.2)	278 (1.7)	288 (1.3)	293 (0.9)
Nebraska	276 (1.0)	278 (1.1)	283 (1.0)	280 (2.2)	282 (0.9)	284 (1.0)	25 (1.2)	75 (1.2)	35 (1.6)	6 (0.6)	263 (3.0)	273 (2.0)	285 (2.0)	293 (1.1)
Nevada	— (†)	— (†)	— (†)	265 (0.8)	268 (0.8)	270 (0.8)	40 (1.1)	60 (1.1)	21 (0.9)	3 (0.5)	257 (3.0)	261 (1.6)	278 (1.8)	281 (1.2)
New Hampshire	273 (0.9)	278 (1.0)	— (†)	— (†)	286 (0.8)	285 (0.8)	23 (0.9)	77 (0.9)	35 (1.6)	7 (0.7)	269 (2.8)	275 (1.4)	283 (2.0)	294 (1.0)
New Jersey	270 (1.1)	272 (1.6)	— (†)	— (†)	281 (1.1)	284 (1.4)	26 (1.4)	74 (1.4)	36 (1.5)	9 (1.0)	266 (3.2)	272 (1.9)	283 (1.8)	294 (1.7)
New Mexico	256 (0.7)	260 (0.9)	262 (1.2)	259 (1.3)	263 (1.0)	263 (0.9)	47 (1.5)	53 (1.5)	14 (1.1)	1 (0.3)	249 (1.8)	254 (1.3)	270 (1.7)	276 (1.4)
New York[6]	261 (1.4)	266 (2.1)	270 (1.7)	271 (2.2)	280 (1.1)	280 (0.9)	30 (1.1)	70 (1.1)	31 (1.3)	6 (0.3)	263 (1.9)	271 (1.3)	285 (1.4)	293 (1.1)
North Carolina	250 (1.1)	258 (1.2)	268 (1.4)	276 (1.3)	281 (1.0)	282 (0.9)	28 (1.2)	72 (1.2)	32 (1.1)	7 (0.8)	265 (3.1)	270 (1.4)	283 (1.5)	294 (1.5)
North Dakota	281 (1.2)	283 (1.1)	284 (0.9)	282 (1.1)	287 (0.8)	287 (0.6)	19 (1.1)	81 (1.1)	35 (1.2)	5 (0.5)	271 (3.7)	274 (1.8)	286 (1.5)	292 (0.8)

See notes at end of table.

Table 125. Average scale score in mathematics and percentage attaining mathematics achievement levels of 8th-graders in public schools, by level of parental education and state or jurisdiction: Selected years, 1990 through 2005—Continued

State or jurisdiction	Average scale score						Percent attaining mathematics achievement levels, 2005[1]				Average scale score, by highest level of education attained by parents, 2005[2]			
	1990	1992	1996	2000	2003	2005	Below basic	Basic or above[3]	Proficient or above[4]	Advanced[5]	Did not finish high school	Graduated high school	Some education after high school	Graduated college
1	2	3	4	5	6	7	8	9	10	11	12	13	14	15
Ohio	264 (1.0)	268 (1.5)	— (†)	281 (1.6)	282 (1.3)	283 (1.1)	26 (1.4)	74 (1.4)	33 (1.4)	7 (0.6)	266 (3.8)	272 (1.6)	283 (1.9)	294 (1.3)
Oklahoma	263 (1.3)	268 (1.1)	— (†)	270 (1.3)	272 (1.1)	271 (1.0)	37 (1.2)	64 (1.2)	21 (1.3)	2 (0.4)	252 (2.1)	262 (2.0)	275 (1.5)	281 (1.5)
Oregon[6]	271 (1.0)	— (—)	276 (1.5)	280 (1.5)	281 (1.3)	282 (1.0)	28 (1.1)	72 (1.1)	34 (1.3)	7 (0.8)	262 (3.2)	270 (1.8)	283 (2.0)	295 (1.3)
Pennsylvania	266 (1.6)	271 (1.5)	— (†)	— (—)	279 (1.1)	281 (1.5)	28 (1.6)	72 (1.6)	31 (1.6)	6 (0.8)	263 (2.9)	269 (1.9)	283 (2.0)	292 (1.5)
Rhode Island	260 (0.6)	266 (0.7)	269 (0.9)	269 (1.3)	272 (0.7)	272 (0.8)	37 (1.1)	64 (1.1)	24 (0.9)	3 (0.5)	255 (2.7)	263 (1.9)	276 (1.6)	284 (1.0)
South Carolina	— (—)	261 (1.0)	261 (1.5)	265 (1.5)	277 (1.3)	281 (0.9)	29 (1.4)	71 (1.4)	30 (0.9)	7 (0.7)	270 (2.8)	273 (1.8)	285 (2.0)	289 (1.2)
South Dakota	— (—)	— (†)	— (—)	— (†)	285 (0.8)	287 (0.6)	20 (0.8)	80 (0.8)	37 (1.0)	7 (0.7)	267 (2.2)	276 (1.7)	287 (1.3)	295 (0.9)
Tennessee	— (—)	259 (1.4)	263 (1.4)	262 (1.4)	268 (1.8)	271 (1.1)	39 (1.6)	61 (1.6)	21 (1.3)	3 (0.4)	259 (2.1)	263 (1.8)	275 (1.9)	279 (1.7)
Texas	258 (1.4)	265 (1.3)	270 (1.4)	273 (1.6)	277 (1.1)	281 (0.6)	28 (0.7)	72 (0.7)	31 (0.8)	6 (0.4)	268 (1.3)	272 (1.2)	286 (1.2)	293 (1.0)
Utah	— (—)	274 (0.7)	277 (1.0)	274 (1.2)	281 (1.0)	279 (0.7)	29 (1.0)	71 (1.0)	30 (1.1)	5 (0.6)	259 (2.8)	262 (1.5)	280 (1.5)	289 (0.9)
Vermont[6]	— (—)	— (†)	279 (1.0)	281 (1.5)	286 (0.8)	287 (0.8)	23 (1.0)	78 (1.0)	38 (1.1)	9 (0.7)	265 (3.8)	275 (1.4)	285 (1.8)	298 (1.1)
Virginia	264 (1.5)	268 (1.2)	270 (1.6)	275 (1.3)	282 (1.3)	284 (1.1)	25 (1.2)	75 (1.2)	33 (1.5)	8 (0.9)	266 (2.2)	271 (1.9)	282 (2.6)	295 (1.3)
Washington	— (—)	— (†)	276 (1.3)	— (—)	281 (0.9)	285 (1.0)	25 (1.2)	75 (1.2)	36 (1.4)	9 (0.8)	264 (3.0)	277 (1.7)	287 (1.5)	295 (1.3)
West Virginia	256 (1.0)	259 (1.0)	265 (1.0)	266 (1.2)	271 (1.2)	269 (1.0)	40 (1.5)	60 (1.5)	18 (1.0)	1 (0.3)	251 (2.4)	263 (1.4)	273 (1.3)	279 (1.4)
Wisconsin	274 (1.3)	278 (1.5)	283 (1.5)	— (—)	284 (1.3)	285 (1.2)	24 (1.4)	76 (1.4)	36 (1.4)	7 (0.7)	264 (3.8)	276 (1.7)	288 (2.0)	293 (1.3)
Wyoming	272 (0.7)	275 (0.9)	275 (0.9)	276 (1.0)	284 (0.7)	282 (0.8)	24 (1.1)	76 (1.1)	29 (1.4)	4 (0.4)	262 (3.6)	274 (1.5)	283 (1.5)	290 (1.1)
Department of Defense dependents schools[7]	— (†)	— (†)	— (†)	— (†)	— (†)	284 (0.7)	24 (0.9)	76 (0.9)	33 (1.6)	5 (0.6)	‡ (†)	273 (2.3)	284 (1.7)	288 (1.0)
Domestic schools	— (†)	— (†)	269 (2.3)	274 (1.8)	282 (1.5)	— (†)	— (†)	— (†)	— (†)	— (†)	‡ (†)	— (†)	— (†)	— (†)
Overseas schools	— (†)	— (†)	275 (0.9)	278 (1.1)	286 (0.7)	— (†)	— (†)	— (†)	— (†)	— (†)	‡ (†)	— (†)	— (†)	— (†)
Other jurisdictions														
American Samoa	— (†)	— (†)	— (†)	192 (5.5)	— (†)	— (†)	— (†)	— (†)	— (†)	— (†)	— (†)	— (†)	— (†)	— (†)
Guam	232 (0.7)	235 (1.0)	239 (1.7)	234 (2.6)	— (†)	— (†)	— (†)	— (†)	— (†)	— (†)	— (†)	— (†)	— (†)	— (†)
Virgin Islands	219 (0.9)	223 (1.1)	— (†)	— (†)	— (†)	— (†)	— (†)	— (†)	— (†)	— (†)	— (†)	— (†)	— (†)	— (†)

—Not available.
†Not applicable.
‡Reporting standards not met.
[1]Achievement levels are in trial status.
[2]Excludes students who responded "I don't know" to the question about educational level of parents.
[3]The basic level denotes partial mastery of prerequisite knowledge and skills that are fundamental for proficient work at the 8th-grade level.
[4]This level represents solid academic performance for 8th-graders. Students reaching this level have demonstrated competency over challenging subject matter, including subject-matter knowledge, application of such knowledge to real-world situations, and analytical skills appropriate to the subject matter.
[5]This level signifies superior performance.
[6]Did not meet one or more of the guidelines for school participation in 2000. Data are subject to appreciable nonresponse bias.
[7]The definition of the national sample changed in 2005; it now includes all of the Department of Defense schools.

NOTE: Excludes persons not enrolled in school and those who were unable to be tested due to limited proficiency in English or due to a disability. Fifty states, the District of Columbia, and Department of Defense school systems participated in the 2005 State Assessment of 8th-graders and met student and school participation criteria for reporting results. Scale ranges from 0 to 500. Data for 2000, 2003, and 2005 are for situations where student accommodations for the testing were permitted. Detail may not sum to totals because of rounding. Standard errors appear in parentheses.

SOURCE: U.S. Department of Education, National Center for Education Statistics, National Assessment of Educational Progress (NAEP), The Nation's Report Card: Mathematics, 2003 and 2005; and NAEP Data Explorer (http://nces.ed.gov/nationsreportcard/nde/), retrieved October 2005. (This table was prepared October 2005.)

Table 126. Selected statistics on mathematics education for public school students, by state or jurisdiction: 2000, 2003, and 2004

State or jurisdiction	Math units required for graduation in 2004	Length of school year (in days)		High school exit exam required for graduation in 2004	Percent of 8th-grade students reporting (2003)							
		2000	2004		3 or more hours of math instruction each week		Spending 30 minutes or more on math homework each day[1]		Positive attitudes toward math[2]		Watching 6 or more hours of television or videotapes each day	
1	2	3	4	5	6		7		8		9	
United States	—	—	—	—	88	(0.7)	57	(—)	72	(—)	15	(0.2)
Alabama	4	175	175	Yes	77	(4.1)	55	(—)	74	(—)	21	(1.1)
Alaska	2	180	180	Yes	92	(2.1)	—	(†)	—	(†)	—	(†)
Arizona	2	175 [3]	175	Yes [4]	86	(3.3)	59	(—)	72	(—)	11	(0.7)
Arkansas	4	178	178	No	86	(3.6)	57	(—)	75	(—)	18	(0.9)
California	2	175	180	Yes [4]	87	(3.4)	70	(—)	67	(—)	14	(0.7)
Colorado	[5]	[6]	170	No	91	(2.9)	63	(—)	68	(—)	9	(0.7)
Connecticut	3	180	180	No	93	(2.3)	56	(—)	73	(—)	15	(0.8)
Delaware	3	[6]	[6]	No	100	(†)	51	(—)	78	(—)	18	(0.8)
District of Columbia	3	180 [7]	180	Yes [4]	92	(0.5)	56	(—)	76	(—)	34	(1.1)
Florida	3	180	180	Yes	79	(4.6)	57	(—)	74	(—)	20	(1.1)
Georgia	4	180 [7]	180	Yes	83	(3.5)	59	(—)	74	(—)	18	(0.9)
Hawaii	3	184	183	No	93	(0.3)	66	(—)	70	(—)	20	(0.8)
Idaho	4 [8]	180	170	Yes [4]	90	(2.1)	56	(—)	70	(—)	9	(0.6)
Illinois	2	180 [9]	185	No	83	(3.6)	62	(—)	73	(—)	15	(0.8)
Indiana	4 [8]	180	180	Yes	87	(3.4)	59	(—)	72	(—)	13	(0.9)
Iowa	[5]	180	180	No	84	(3.6)	56	(—)	75	(—)	10	(0.6)
Kansas	2	186	186	No	83	(4.3)	56	(—)	75	(—)	11	(0.6)
Kentucky	3	175	[6]	No	90	(3.1)	54	(—)	75	(—)	15	(0.8)
Louisiana	3	175	177	Yes	92	(3.0)	50	(—)	78	(—)	23	(1.0)
Maine	2	175	180	No	91	(2.0)	58	(—)	74	(—)	10	(0.7)
Maryland	3	180	180	Yes [4]	83	(4.1)	52	(—)	74	(—)	20	(0.9)
Massachusetts	[5]	180	180	Yes	91	(3.0)	60	(—)	75	(—)	11	(0.6)
Michigan	[5]	180	185	Yes [4]	90	(3.1)	52	(—)	74	(—)	16	(1.0)
Minnesota	3	[10]	[6]	Yes	89	(2.7)	53	(—)	74	(—)	8	(0.6)
Mississippi	3	180	180	Yes	82	(3.5)	50	(—)	78	(—)	23	(1.1)
Missouri	2	174	174	No	91	(2.4)	57	(—)	72	(—)	14	(0.7)
Montana	2	180	180	No	91	(1.3)	58	(—)	75	(—)	9	(0.6)
Nebraska	[5]	[6]	[6]	No	89	(1.4)	59	(—)	74	(—)	10	(0.7)
Nevada	3	180	180	Yes	91	(0.6)	60	(—)	71	(—)	16	(0.7)
New Hampshire	2	180	180	No	92	(1.8)	57	(—)	70	(—)	10	(0.6)
New Jersey	3	180	180	Yes	84	(4.1)	54	(—)	76	(—)	15	(0.7)
New Mexico	3	180	180	Yes	84	(3.1)	61	(—)	72	(—)	13	(0.9)
New York	2	180 [7]	180	Yes	91	(2.7)	51	(—)	74	(—)	17	(0.8)
North Carolina	3	180	180	Yes	81	(3.7)	63	(—)	78	(—)	16	(0.6)
North Dakota	[5]	173	173	No	89	(1.5)	54	(—)	76	(—)	8	(0.6)
Ohio	3	182	182	Yes [4]	91	(3.2)	53	(—)	73	(—)	14	(0.7)
Oklahoma	3	180	180	Yes [4]	84	(3.8)	55	(—)	68	(—)	14	(0.8)
Oregon	2	[6]	[6]	No	88	(3.1)	58	(—)	67	(—)	11	(0.7)
Pennsylvania	[5]	180	180	No	93	(2.6)	46	(—)	75	(—)	14	(0.9)
Rhode Island	2	180	180	No	91	(0.4)	55	(—)	68	(—)	14	(0.8)
South Carolina	4	180	180	Yes [4]	83	(4.0)	55	(—)	77	(—)	19	(0.9)
South Dakota	2	—	170	No	93	(1.0)	60	(—)	76	(—)	8	(0.5)
Tennessee	3	180	180	Yes [4]	85	(3.3)	53	(—)	73	(—)	18	(1.0)
Texas	3	187	180	Yes [4]	92	(2.8)	57	(—)	73	(—)	16	(0.8)
Utah	2	180	180	Yes [4]	95	(1.9)	53	(—)	66	(—)	7	(0.5)

See notes at end of table.

Table 126. Selected statistics on mathematics education for public school students, by state or jurisdiction: 2000, 2003, and 2004—Continued

		Length of school year (in days)			Percent of 8th-grade students reporting (2003)							
State or jurisdiction	Math units required for graduation in 2004	2000	2004	High school exit exam required for graduation in 2004	3 or more hours of math instruction each week		Spending 30 minutes or more on math homework each day[1]		Positive attitudes toward math[2]		Watching 6 or more hours of television or videotapes each day	
1	2	3	4	5	6		7		8		9	
Vermont..................................	5 [11]	175	175	No	78	(2.4)	57	(—)	70	(—)	10	(0.7)
Virginia....................................	3	180	180	Yes	92	(2.7)	55	(—)	74	(—)	17	(1.0)
Washington............................	2	180 [9]	180	Yes [4]	89	(3.5)	59	(—)	70	(—)	12	(0.7)
West Virginia..........................	3	180	180	No	91	(3.0)	47	(—)	75	(—)	15	(1.0)
Wisconsin	2	180	180	No	93	(2.6)	52	(—)	73	(—)	12	(0.9)
Wyoming..................................	3	175	175	No	97	(0.2)	58	(—)	73	(—)	11	(0.6)
Department of Defense dependents schools												
Domestic schools..................	3 [12]	183	—	No [12]	68	(1.3)	63	(—)	79	(—)	17	(1.3)
Overseas schools	3 [12]	183	—	No [12]	91	(0.5)	72	(—)	74	(—)	11	(0.6)

—Not available.
†Not applicable.
[1]Percentage of students who report spending 30 minutes, 45 minutes, 1 hour, and over 1 hour on mathematics homework each day.
[2]Percentage of students agreeing or strongly agreeing with this statement: "Mathematics is useful for solving everyday problems."
[3]1994 data.
[4]Exit exam policy under development or takes effect after 2004.
[5]Local board determines policy.
[6]No statewide policy.
[7]1996 data.

[8]Semester credits.
[9]1998 data.
[10]Varies by district.
[11]Includes math and science courses.
[12]2000 data.
NOTE: Standard errors appear in parentheses.
SOURCE: U.S. Department of Education, National Center for Education Statistics, National Assessment of Educational Progress (NAEP), 2003 Mathematics Assessment; and Council of Chief State School Officers, *Key State Education Policies on PK–12 Education: 2000 and 2004*. (This table was prepared September 2005.)

Table 127. Average mathematics scale scores of 4th-, 8th-, and 12th-graders, by selected student and parent characteristics and school type: 2000, 2003, and 2005

Year, grade, and school type	All students	Sex of child		Race/ethnicity of child					Highest education level of parents				
		Male	Female	White	Black	Hispanic	Asian/ Pacific Islander	American Indian/ Alaska Native	Less than high school	Graduated from high school	Some education after high school	Graduated from college	Unknown
1	2	3	4	5	6	7	8	9	10	11	12	13	14
2000													
4th-graders													
Public	224 (1.0)	225 (1.1)	223 (1.1)	233 (0.9)	203 (1.2)	207 (1.5)	‡ (†)	207! (3.7)	— (†)	— (†)	— (†)	— (†)	— (†)
Private, total[1]	238 (†)	239 (†)	236 (†)	241 (†)	213 (—)	220 (—)	‡ (†)	‡ (†)	— (†)	— (†)	— (†)	— (†)	— (†)
Catholic	237 (1.2)	239 (1.5)	235 (1.1)	241 (0.8)	210 (4.9)	217 (3.4)	‡ (†)	‡ (†)	— (†)	— (†)	— (†)	— (†)	— (†)
Lutheran	241 (—)	243 (—)	239 (—)	242 (—)	‡ (†)	‡ (†)	‡ (†)	‡ (†)	— (†)	— (†)	— (†)	— (†)	— (†)
Conservative Christian	234 (—)	236 (—)	232 (—)	238 (—)	211! (—)	‡ (†)	‡ (†)	‡ (†)	— (†)	— (†)	— (†)	— (†)	— (†)
8th-graders													
Public	272 (0.9)	273 (1.0)	271 (1.0)	283 (0.9)	243 (1.3)	252 (1.4)	288 (3.9)	263! (6.9)	253 (1.4)	260 (1.1)	277 (1.1)	285 (1.2)	253 (1.4)
Private, total[1]	286 (1.5)	288 (†)	285 (†)	291 (†)	258 (—)	273 (—)	300 (—)	‡ (†)	264 (—)	273 (—)	281 (—)	292 (—)	272 (—)
Catholic	284 (1.5)	285 (1.4)	282 (2.0)	289 (1.4)	254 (2.8)	271 (2.5)	296 (2.2)	‡ (†)	‡ (†)	271 (2.3)	279 (2.3)	289 (1.4)	276 (—)
Lutheran	292 (—)	295 (—)	288 (—)	295 (—)	264! (—)	‡ (†)	‡ (†)	‡ (†)	‡ (†)	276 (—)	290! (—)	296 (—)	‡ (†)
Conservative Christian	‡ (†)	‡ (†)	‡ (†)	‡ (†)	‡ (†)	‡ (†)	‡ (†)	‡ (†)	‡ (†)	‡ (†)	‡ (†)	‡ (†)	‡ (†)
12th-graders													
Public	299 (1.1)	301 (1.3)	297 (1.1)	306 (1.2)	272 (2.1)	281 (2.1)	314 (4.4)	293! (5.2)	278 (1.7)	286 (1.3)	298 (1.3)	311 (1.5)	273 (2.6)
Private, total[1]	315 (1.4)	316 (1.6)	314 (1.7)	317 (1.3)	292 (3.5)	300 (3.1)	328 (4.7)	‡ (†)	281 (—)	298 (1.7)	309 (1.7)	321 (1.3)	295 (—)
Catholic	314 (1.4)	315 (1.6)	313 (1.7)	317 (1.3)	290 (2.9)	299 (—)	326! (—)	‡ (†)	‡ (†)	300 (—)	308 (—)	320 (—)	‡ (†)
Lutheran	312 (2.4)	315 (2.9)	310 (2.3)	317 (2.4)	288 (—)	‡ (†)	‡ (†)	‡ (†)	‡ (†)	304 (—)	309 (—)	316 (—)	‡ (†)
Conservative Christian	310 (2.0)	313 (2.8)	307 (1.9)	312 (2.0)	‡ (†)	‡ (†)	‡ (†)	‡ (†)	‡ (†)	294! (—)	309 (—)	315 (—)	‡ (†)
2003													
4th-graders													
Public	234 (0.2)	235 (0.3)	233 (0.2)	243 (0.2)	216 (0.4)	221 (0.4)	246 (1.2)	224 (1.1)	— (†)	— (†)	— (†)	— (†)	— (†)
Private, total[2]	244 (0.7)	247 (0.8)	242 (0.8)	248 (0.7)	221 (1.7)	231 (1.7)	249 (2.6)	‡ (†)	— (†)	— (†)	— (†)	— (†)	— (†)
Catholic	244 (0.8)	246 (0.9)	241 (1.1)	248 (0.7)	222 (2.9)	229 (2.0)	242 (2.8)	‡ (†)	— (†)	— (†)	— (†)	— (†)	— (†)
Lutheran	245 (1.5)	249 (2.0)	242 (1.7)	248 (1.4)	227 (4.0)	‡ (†)	‡ (†)	‡ (†)	— (†)	— (†)	— (†)	— (†)	— (†)
Conservative Christian	‡ (†)	‡ (†)	‡ (†)	‡ (†)	‡ (†)	‡ (†)	‡ (†)	‡ (†)	— (†)	— (†)	— (†)	— (†)	— (†)
8th-graders													
Public	276 (0.3)	277 (0.3)	275 (0.3)	287 (0.3)	252 (0.5)	258 (0.6)	289 (1.3)	265 (1.2)	256 (0.6)	267 (0.4)	280 (0.4)	287 (0.4)	258 (0.5)
Private, total[2]	292 (1.4)	293 (1.3)	290 (1.3)	297 (1.1)	260 (2.4)	274 (2.4)	303 (2.7)	‡ (†)	270 (4.5)	277 (2.0)	285 (1.4)	297 (1.1)	269 (3.1)
Catholic	290 (1.4)	292 (1.7)	288 (1.5)	296 (1.4)	260 (3.0)	272 (2.9)	299 (3.7)	‡ (†)	‡ (†)	276 (2.3)	286 (1.7)	294 (1.5)	270 (3.1)
Lutheran	296 (1.6)	298 (2.1)	295 (1.9)	300 (1.7)	‡ (†)	‡ (†)	‡ (†)	‡ (†)	‡ (†)	288 (4.3)	290 (3.0)	301 (1.8)	‡ (†)
Conservative Christian	286 (2.6)	289 (3.2)	284 (3.4)	293 (2.2)	254 (7.2)	‡ (†)	‡ (†)	‡ (†)	‡ (†)	280 (4.0)	280 (6.5)	291 (2.8)	‡ (†)
2005													
4th-graders													
Public	237 (0.2)	238 (0.2)	236 (0.2)	246 (0.2)	220 (0.3)	225 (0.3)	251 (0.7)	227 (1.0)	— (†)	— (†)	— (†)	— (†)	— (†)
Private, total[2]	‡ (†)	‡ (†)	‡ (†)	‡ (†)	‡ (†)	‡ (†)	‡ (†)	‡ (†)	— (†)	— (†)	— (†)	— (†)	— (†)
Catholic	244 (0.7)	245 (1.0)	242 (0.8)	248 (0.7)	222 (2.0)	233 (2.2)	244 (4.1)	‡ (†)	— (†)	— (†)	— (†)	— (†)	— (†)
Lutheran	246 (1.3)	250 (1.6)	241 (1.8)	249 (1.3)	‡ (†)	‡ (†)	‡ (†)	‡ (†)	— (†)	— (†)	— (†)	— (†)	— (†)
Conservative Christian	‡ (†)	‡ (†)	‡ (†)	‡ (†)	‡ (†)	‡ (†)	‡ (†)	‡ (†)	— (†)	— (†)	— (†)	— (†)	— (†)
8th-graders													
Public	278 (0.2)	278 (0.2)	277 (0.2)	288 (0.2)	254 (0.4)	261 (0.4)	295 (1.0)	266 (1.0)	259 (0.5)	267 (0.3)	280 (0.3)	289 (0.3)	260 (0.4)
Private, total[2]	‡ (†)	‡ (†)	‡ (†)	‡ (†)	‡ (†)	‡ (†)	‡ (†)	‡ (†)	‡ (†)	‡ (†)	‡ (†)	‡ (†)	‡ (†)
Catholic	290 (1.2)	292 (1.3)	288 (1.4)	297 (1.2)	261 (2.6)	276 (2.3)	299 (4.0)	‡ (†)	‡ (†)	276 (2.4)	283 (1.6)	296 (1.3)	269 (3.2)
Lutheran	293 (2.3)	296 (2.4)	291 (2.7)	297 (1.9)	263 (6.6)	‡ (†)	‡ (†)	‡ (†)	‡ (†)	285 (5.8)	289 (4.5)	298 (2.0)	‡ (†)
Conservative Christian	‡ (†)	‡ (†)	‡ (†)	‡ (†)	‡ (†)	‡ (†)	‡ (†)	‡ (†)	‡ (†)	‡ (†)	‡ (†)	‡ (†)	‡ (†)

—Not available.
†Not applicable.
‡Reporting standards not met.
!Interpret data with caution.
[1]The 2000 private school totals include data for two categories of schools (nonsectarian and other religious) that are not shown separately.

[2]The 2003 and 2005 private school totals include data for one school category (other private) that is not shown separately.
NOTE: The NAEP mathematics scale ranges from 0 to 500. Race categories exclude persons of Hispanic origin. Standard errors appear in parentheses.
SOURCE: U.S. Department of Education, National Center for Education Statistics, National Assessment of Educational Progress (NAEP), Student Achievement in Private Schools: Results From NAEP 2000–2005, and the NAEP Data Explorer (http://nces.ed.gov/nationsreportcard/nde/), retrieved August 2006. (This table was prepared August 2006.)

Table 128. Average science scale scores and percentage of 4th-, 8th-, and 12th-graders attaining science achievement levels, by selected student characteristics and percentile: 1996, 2000, and 2005

Selected characteristic, percentile, and achievement level	4th-graders			8th-graders			12th-graders		
	1996[1]	2000	2005	1996[1]	2000	2005	1996[1]	2000	2005
1	2	3	4	5	6	7	8	9	10
All students	**147** (1.1)	**147** (0.9)	**151** (0.3)	**149** (0.8)	**149** (1.0)	**149** (0.3)	**150** (0.7)	**146** (0.9)	**147** (0.6)
Sex									
Male	148 (1.3)	149 (1.1)	153 (0.3)	150 (0.9)	150 (1.1)	150 (0.4)	154 (1.0)	148 (1.1)	149 (0.7)
Female	146 (1.1)	145 (1.0)	149 (0.3)	148 (0.9)	148 (1.1)	147 (0.3)	147 (0.8)	145 (1.0)	145 (0.6)
Race/ethnicity									
White	158 (0.9)	159 (0.7)	162 (0.3)	159 (0.8)	159 (0.8)	160 (0.2)	159 (0.9)	153 (1.2)	156 (0.6)
Black	120 (1.3)	122 (1.0)	129 (0.6)	121 (0.9)	121 (1.4)	124 (0.4)	123 (1.1)	122 (1.7)	120 (0.9)
Hispanic	124 (3.0)	122 (2.3)	133 (0.5)	128 (2.7)	127 (1.4)	129 (0.5)	131 (2.2)	128 (1.7)	128 (1.3)
Asian/Pacific Islander	144 (3.7)	‡ (†)	158 (1.0)	151 (4.2)	153 (2.9)	156 (0.9)	147 (3.3)	149 (3.6)	153 (1.7)
American Indian	129 (11.9)	135 (6.9)	138 (1.9)	148 (3.5)	147 (6.7)	128 (4.0)	144 (7.5)	151 (3.6)	139 (5.3)
Parents' education									
Less than high school	— (†)	— (†)	— (†)	—	—	128 (0.5)	—	—	125 (1.4)
High school diploma or equivalent	— (†)	— (†)	— (†)	—	—	138 (0.5)	—	—	136 (0.9)
Some college	— (†)	— (†)	— (†)	—	—	151 (0.4)	—	—	148 (0.7)
Bachelor's degree or higher	— (†)	— (†)	— (†)	—	—	159 (0.3)	—	—	157 (0.6)
Eligible for free or reduced-price lunch									
Eligible	129 (1.7)	127 (1.3)	135 (0.3)	129 (1.6)	127 (1.1)	130 (0.3)	— (†)	— (†)	— (†)
Not eligible	159 (0.9)	158 (1.1)	162 (0.3)	156 (0.9)	159 (1.0)	159 (0.3)	— (†)	— (†)	— (†)
Information not available	151 (3.9)	160 (1.5)	160 (0.9)	157 (2.3)	155 (1.7)	160 (1.5)	— (†)	— (†)	— (†)
Percentile[2]									
10th	99 (2.1)	99 (1.7)	109 (0.5)	103 (1.5)	101 (1.2)	101 (0.6)	105 (1.4)	101 (1.4)	101 (1.2)
25th	125 (1.6)	125 (1.4)	130 (0.4)	127 (1.2)	126 (1.3)	126 (0.4)	128 (1.1)	124 (1.0)	125 (0.8)
50th	150 (1.2)	150 (0.9)	153 (0.4)	152 (0.7)	152 (0.9)	151 (0.3)	152 (1.2)	148 (1.0)	149 (0.8)
75th	172 (1.0)	172 (0.7)	173 (0.3)	174 (0.8)	175 (0.8)	174 (0.3)	174 (0.8)	170 (1.2)	171 (0.8)
90th	190 (0.8)	190 (1.0)	189 (0.3)	192 (0.8)	194 (1.0)	192 (0.3)	192 (0.9)	189 (1.2)	189 (1.2)
Percentage at achievement level									
Achievement level									
Below basic	37 (1.4)	37 (1.2)	32 (0.4)	40 (1.0)	41 (1.2)	41 (0.4)	43 (1.0)	48 (1.2)	46 (0.8)
At or above basic[3]	63 (1.4)	63 (1.2)	68 (0.4)	60 (1.0)	59 (1.2)	59 (0.4)	57 (1.0)	52 (1.2)	54 (0.8)
At or above proficient[4]	28 (1.0)	27 (0.9)	29 (0.4)	29 (0.9)	30 (1.0)	29 (0.3)	21 (0.8)	18 (0.9)	18 (0.6)
At advanced[5]	3 (0.3)	3 (0.4)	3 (0.1)	3 (0.3)	4 (0.3)	3 (0.1)	3 (0.3)	2 (0.3)	2 (0.2)

—Not available.
†Not applicable.
‡Reporting standards not met.
[1]Testing accommodations (e.g., extended time, small group testing) for children with disabilities and limited-English-proficient students were not permitted on the 1996 science assessment.
[2]The percentile represents a specific point on the percentage distribution of all students ranked by their science score from low to high. For example, 10 percent of students scored at or below the 10th percentile score, while 90 percent of students scored above it.
[3]The basic level denotes partial mastery of the knowledge and skills that are fundamental for proficient work.

[4]The proficient level represents solid academic performance. Students reaching this level have demonstrated competency over challenging subject matter.
[5]The advanced level signifies superior performance.
NOTE: The NAEP science scale ranges from 0 to 500. Race categories exclude persons of Hispanic origin. Standard errors appear in parentheses.
SOURCE: U.S. Department of Education, National Center for Education Statistics, National Assessment of Educational Progress (NAEP), NAEP Data Explorer (http://nces.ed.gov/nationsreportcard/nde/), retrieved November 2006. (This table was prepared November 2006.)

Table 129. Average scale score in science for 8th-graders in public schools, by selected student characteristics and state or jurisdiction: 1996, 2000, and 2005

State or jurisdiction	Average scale score			Sex, 2005		Race/ethnicity, 2005					National School Lunch Program eligibility, 2005	
	1996[1]	2000	2005	Male	Female	White	Black	Hispanic	Asian/ Pacific Islander	American Indian/ Alaska Native	Eligible	Not eligible
1	2	3	4	5	6	7	8	9	10	11	12	13
United States	148 (0.9)	148 (1.1)	147 (0.3)	149 (0.4)	145 (0.4)	159 (0.3)	123 (0.4)	127 (0.5)	155 (0.9)	134 (1.5)	130 (0.3)	158 (0.3)
Alabama	139 (1.6)	143 [3] (1.7)	138 (1.3)	138 (1.6)	137 (1.4)	152 (1.3)	114 (1.5)	‡ (†)	‡ (†)	‡ (†)	123 (1.5)	152 (1.4)
Alaska	153 [2] (1.3)	— (†)	— (†)	— (†)	— (†)	— (†)	— (†)	— (†)	— (†)	‡ (†)	— (†)	— (†)
Arizona	145 [3] (1.6)	145 [3,4] (1.3)	140 (0.9)	141 (1.1)	139 (1.2)	156 (1.0)	125 (3.5)	123 (1.2)	‡ (†)	121 (3.0)	124 (1.2)	152 (1.4)
Arkansas	144 [2] (1.3)	142 (1.2)	144 (1.0)	146 (1.3)	142 (1.1)	155 (0.9)	113 (1.3)	136 (4.0)	‡ (†)	‡ (†)	131 (1.3)	157 (0.9)
California	138 (1.7)	129 [3,4] (1.8)	136 (0.7)	138 (0.8)	135 (0.8)	154 (0.9)	120 (1.5)	122 (0.8)	152 (1.8)	132 (5.2)	121 (0.9)	150 (0.7)
Colorado	155 (0.9)	— (†)	155 (1.3)	158 (1.4)	152 (1.6)	166 (1.1)	133 (3.7)	134 (2.0)	158 (4.4)	‡ (†)	135 (1.9)	164 (1.2)
Connecticut	155 (1.3)	153 (1.6)	152 (1.0)	153 (1.6)	151 (1.1)	163 (0.9)	124 (2.2)	123 (2.7)	163 (3.6)	‡ (†)	127 (1.7)	161 (1.0)
Delaware	142 [3] (0.8)	— (†)	152 (0.6)	154 (0.7)	150 (1.0)	162 (0.6)	134 (1.1)	136 (2.4)	165 (3.4)	‡ (†)	136 (1.0)	158 (0.7)
District of Columbia	113 (0.7)	— (†)	— (†)	— (†)	— (†)	— (†)	— (†)	— (†)	— (†)	— (†)	— (†)	— (†)
Florida	142 (1.6)	— (†)	141 (1.2)	142 (1.2)	140 (1.4)	155 (1.1)	118 (1.5)	131 (2.0)	149 (4.2)	‡ (†)	128 (1.2)	152 (1.2)
Georgia	142 (1.4)	142 (1.6)	144 (1.1)	145 (1.4)	142 (1.2)	159 (1.4)	125 (1.3)	127 (3.6)	163 (5.9)	‡ (†)	127 (1.0)	158 (1.3)
Hawaii	135 (0.7)	130 [3] (1.4)	136 (0.8)	138 (1.4)	135 (0.9)	152 (1.7)	‡ (†)	131 (3.9)	133 (1.0)	‡ (†)	124 (1.2)	146 (0.9)
Idaho	— (†)	158 [4] (1.0)	158 (1.0)	161 (1.4)	154 (1.0)	161 (0.9)	‡ (†)	131 (2.2)	‡ (†)	‡ (†)	147 (1.2)	164 (1.1)
Illinois	— (†)	148 [4] (1.7)	148 (1.1)	150 (1.4)	146 (1.2)	161 (1.2)	120 (1.5)	130 (1.7)	164 (3.7)	‡ (†)	128 (1.2)	161 (1.2)
Indiana	153 (1.4)	154 [3,4] (1.4)	150 (1.3)	154 (1.4)	147 (1.7)	156 (1.3)	119 (2.1)	131 (3.1)	‡ (†)	‡ (†)	135 (2.0)	159 (1.4)
Iowa	158 [2] (1.2)	— (†)	— (†)	— (†)	— (†)	— (†)	— (†)	— (†)	— (†)	— (†)	— (†)	— (†)
Kansas	— (†)	— (†)	— (†)	— (†)	— (†)	— (†)	— (†)	— (†)	— (†)	— (†)	— (†)	— (†)
Kentucky	147 [3] (1.2)	150 [3] (1.2)	153 (0.9)	154 (1.3)	151 (1.0)	155 (0.9)	130 (2.4)	‡ (†)	‡ (†)	‡ (†)	145 (1.4)	159 (1.2)
Louisiana	132 [3] (1.6)	134 [3] (1.5)	138 (1.5)	141 (1.7)	136 (1.6)	153 (1.3)	120 (1.5)	‡ (†)	‡ (†)	‡ (†)	127 (1.4)	153 (1.4)
Maine	163 [3] (1.0)	158 [4] (0.9)	158 (0.7)	159 (1.0)	156 (1.1)	158 (0.8)	‡ (†)	‡ (†)	‡ (†)	‡ (†)	150 (1.2)	161 (0.8)
Maryland	145 [2] (1.5)	146 (1.4)	145 (1.4)	145 (1.7)	144 (1.6)	160 (1.3)	123 (1.8)	132 (6.1)	165 (3.5)	‡ (†)	122 (2.4)	155 (1.3)
Massachusetts	157 [3] (1.4)	158 [3] (1.1)	161 (1.0)	162 (1.2)	160 (1.2)	168 (1.0)	133 (2.2)	133 (2.2)	166 (3.4)	‡ (†)	142 (2.1)	168 (1.2)
Michigan	153 [2] (1.3)	155 [4] (1.8)	155 (1.2)	156 (1.6)	154 (1.4)	163 (1.2)	128 (2.3)	132 (3.8)	‡ (†)	‡ (†)	140 (1.9)	161 (1.3)
Minnesota	159 (1.3)	159 [4] (1.2)	158 (1.1)	161 (1.5)	155 (1.3)	166 (0.9)	120 (2.6)	133 (4.3)	137 (2.7)	‡ (†)	139 (1.5)	166 (1.1)
Mississippi	133 (1.4)	134 (1.2)	132 (1.2)	135 (1.5)	130 (1.3)	150 (1.0)	114 (1.5)	‡ (†)	‡ (†)	‡ (†)	121 (1.3)	151 (1.1)
Missouri	151 (1.2)	154 (1.2)	154 (1.2)	157 (1.3)	151 (1.4)	161 (0.9)	124 (2.8)	150 (4.9)	‡ (†)	‡ (†)	140 (2.1)	162 (1.3)
Montana	162 [2] (1.2)	164 [4] (1.4)	162 (0.8)	162 (1.2)	161 (1.0)	165 (0.7)	‡ (†)	‡ (†)	‡ (†)	135 (2.6)	149 (1.4)	168 (0.7)
Nebraska	157 (1.0)	158 (1.4)	— (†)	— (†)	— (†)	— (†)	— (†)	— (†)	— (†)	— (†)	— (†)	— (†)
Nevada	‡ (†)	141 [3] (1.0)	138 (0.9)	139 (1.1)	138 (1.3)	150 (1.0)	115 (2.4)	122 (1.3)	150 (3.4)	‡ (†)	124 (1.3)	146 (1.0)
New Hampshire	‡ (†)	— (†)	162 (0.9)	163 (1.1)	161 (1.1)	163 0.8	‡ (†)	‡ (†)	‡ (†)	‡ (†)	149 (1.7)	165 (0.9)
New Jersey	‡ (†)	— (†)	153 (1.2)	157 (1.6)	150 (1.3)	165 1.1	131 (2.6)	132 (1.9)	172 (2.4)	‡ (†)	131 (1.9)	162 (1.2)
New Mexico	141 [3] (1.0)	139 (1.5)	138 (0.9)	141 (1.2)	135 (1.3)	157 (1.3)	129 (4.5)	129 (1.1)	‡ (†)	124 (1.5)	129 (1.0)	153 (1.4)
New York	146 [2] (1.6)	145 [4] (2.1)	— (†)	— (†)	— (†)	— (†)	— (†)	— (†)	— (†)	— (†)	— (†)	— (†)
North Carolina	147 (1.2)	145 (1.4)	144 (1.0)	145 (1.3)	143 (1.1)	155 (0.8)	122 (1.6)	132 (3.2)	157 (9.9)	‡ (†)	129 (1.3)	154 (1.0)
North Dakota	162 (0.8)	159 [3] (1.1)	163 (0.6)	165 (0.9)	161 (0.9)	166 (0.6)	‡ (†)	‡ (†)	‡ (†)	137 (3.2)	151 (1.5)	168 (0.6)
Ohio	— (†)	159 (1.5)	155 (1.2)	157 (1.7)	154 (1.3)	162 (1.0)	124 (3.3)	142 (5.6)	‡ (†)	‡ (†)	134 (1.8)	165 (1.0)
Oklahoma	— (†)	149 (1.1)	147 (1.3)	149 (1.4)	144 (1.5)	155 (1.1)	120 (2.7)	132 (3.1)	‡ (†)	139 (2.2)	137 (1.5)	156 (1.2)
Oregon	155 (1.6)	154 [4] (1.3)	153 (1.0)	155 (1.4)	152 (1.3)	159 (0.9)	127 (5.5)	129 (3.1)	154 (4.6)	‡ (†)	141 (1.8)	160 (1.2)
Pennsylvania	— (†)	— (†)	— (†)	— (†)	— (†)	— (†)	— (†)	— (†)	— (†)	— (†)	— (†)	— (†)
Rhode Island	149 [3] (0.8)	148 (0.9)	146 (0.7)	149 (0.9)	144 (0.9)	156 (0.7)	122 (2.2)	115 (1.8)	141 (4.7)	‡ (†)	127 (1.3)	155 (0.8)

See notes at end of table.

Table 129. Average scale score in science for 8th-graders in public schools, by selected student characteristics and state or jurisdiction: 1996, 2000, and 2005—Continued

State or jurisdiction	Average scale score — 1996[1]	Average scale score — 2000	Average scale score — 2005	Sex, 2005 — Male	Sex, 2005 — Female	Race/ethnicity, 2005 — White	Black	Hispanic	Asian/Pacific Islander	American Indian/Alaska Native	National School Lunch Program eligibility, 2005 — Eligible	Not eligible
1	2	3	4	5	6	7	8	9	10	11	12	13
South Carolina	139[2,3] (1.5)	140[3] (1.4)	145 (1.1)	146 (1.5)	144 (1.2)	159 (1.3)	127 (1.4)	130 (5.9)	‡ (†)	‡ (†)	131 (1.2)	158 (1.2)
South Dakota	— (†)	—	161 (0.7)	164 (1.0)	158 (0.9)	165 (0.7)	‡ (†)	‡ (†)	‡ (†)	133 (2.7)	149 (1.3)	168 (0.8)
Tennessee	143 (1.8)	145 (1.5)	145 (1.2)	146 (1.5)	144 (1.4)	153 (1.0)	119 (2.2)	‡ (†)	‡ (†)	‡ (†)	131 (1.5)	156 (1.3)
Texas	145 (1.8)	143 (1.7)	143 (0.8)	145 (1.1)	141 (0.9)	160 (0.9)	125 (1.5)	131 (1.1)	161 (3.8)	‡ (†)	129 (1.0)	156 (1.0)
Utah	156[3] (0.8)	154 (1.0)	154 (0.7)	155 (1.1)	152 (0.9)	158 (0.7)	‡ (†)	130 (2.4)	139 (3.9)	‡ (†)	142 (1.2)	160 (0.9)
Vermont	157[2,3] (1.0)	159[3,4] (1.0)	162 (0.6)	163 (0.9)	161 (0.8)	162 (0.6)	‡ (†)	‡ (†)	‡ (†)	‡ (†)	150 (1.3)	166 (0.6)
Virginia	149[3] (1.6)	151[3] (1.0)	155 (1.1)	157 (1.3)	153 (1.2)	165 (1.1)	133 (1.6)	141 (2.7)	161 (3.0)	‡ (†)	136 (1.4)	163 (1.1)
Washington	150[3] (1.3)	—	154 (0.8)	155 (1.2)	153 (1.0)	160 (0.8)	137 (3.1)	128 (3.2)	149 (2.6)	135 (5.8)	140 (1.4)	161 (0.9)
West Virginia	147 (0.9)	146 (1.1)	147 (0.8)	150 (1.0)	144 (0.9)	148 (0.7)	128 (3.3)	‡ (†)	‡ (†)	‡ (†)	137 (0.9)	156 (0.9)
Wisconsin	160[2] (1.7)	‡ (†)	158 (1.0)	160 (1.3)	156 (1.2)	165 (0.8)	120 (3.1)	133 (3.1)	153 (4.1)	‡ (†)	137 (2.1)	165 (0.9)
Wyoming	158 (0.6)	156[3] (1.0)	159 (0.6)	161 (1.0)	157 (0.9)	161 (0.6)	‡ (†)	145 (2.3)	‡ (†)	145 (4.5)	148 (1.2)	164 (0.7)
Department of Defense dependents schools[5]	155[3] (0.6)	158[3] (0.7)	160 (0.7)	162 (1.1)	158 (1.0)	168 (0.9)	143 (0.7)	160 (1.9)	161 (2.6)	‡ (†)	‡ (†)	‡ (†)
Other jurisdictions												
American Samoa	— (†)	74 (4.2)	—	—	—	— (†)	— (†)	— (†)	— (†)	— (†)	— (†)	— (†)
Guam	120 (1.1)	114 (1.8)	—	—	—	— (†)	— (†)	— (†)	— (†)	— (†)	— (†)	— (†)

—Not available.
†Not applicable.
‡Reporting standards not met.
[1]Accommodations were not permitted for this assessment.
[2]Did not satisfy one or more of the guidelines for school sample participation rates in 1996. Data are subject to appreciable nonresponse bias.
[3]Significantly different from 2005 when only one jurisdiction or the nation is being examined.
[4]Did not satisfy one or more of the guidelines for school sample participation rates in 2000. Data are subject to appreciable nonresponse bias.
[5]Before 2005, Department of Defense domestic and overseas schools were separate jurisdictions in NAEP. Data for 1996 and 2000 were recalculated for comparability.

NOTE: Excludes persons not enrolled in school and those who were unable to be tested due to limited proficiency in English or due to a disability (if sample not tested with accommodations or if the accommodations provided in 2000 and 2005 were not sufficient to enable the test to properly reflect students' science proficiency). Scale ranges from 0 to 300. Race categories exclude persons of Hispanic origin. Standard errors appear in parentheses. Some data have been revised from previously published figures.

SOURCE: U.S. Department of Education, National Center for Education Statistics, National Assessment of Educational Progress (NAEP), NAEP 1996 Science Report Card for the Nation and the States, The Nation's Report Card: Science 2005, and the NAEP Data Explorer (http://nces.ed.gov/nationsreportcard/nde/, retrieved on December 4, 2006). (This table was prepared December 2006.)

Table 130. Average arts scale score of 8th-grade students, by topic and selected student characteristics: 1997

Selected student characteristic	Music						Visual arts				Theatre			
	Average creating score (0 to 100 percent)		Average performing score (0 to 100 percent)		Average responding scale score (0 to 300)		Average creating score (0 to 100 percent)		Average responding scale score (0 to 300)		Average creating/ performing score (0 to 100 percent)		Average responding scale score (0 to 300)	
1	2		3		4		5		6		7		8	
All students	34	(1.1)	34	(1.2)	150	(1.3)	43	(0.7)	150	(1.1)	49	(2.0)	150	(5.7)
Sex														
Male.................................	32	(1.0)	27	(1.4)	140	(1.5)	42	(0.7)	146	(1.5)	46	(2.2)	140	(6.6)
Female...............................	37	(1.6)	40	(1.5)	160	(1.6)	45	(0.9)	154	(1.4)	52	(2.1)	158	(5.6)
Race/ethnicity														
White.................................	36	(1.2)	36	(1.4)	158	(1.4)	46	(0.9)	159	(1.3)	52	(1.9)	159	(4.4)
Black.................................	34	(3.6)	30	(1.9)	130	(2.3)	37	(1.8)	124	(2.0)	39	(2.2)	120	(10.1)
Hispanic.............................	29	(2.7)	24	(3.7)	127	(3.5)	38	(1.3)	128	(2.0)	44	(2.5)	139	(6.2)
Asian/Pacific Islander............	31	(3.8)	‡	(†)	152	(6.2)	45	(1.6)	153	(6.4)	‡	(†)	‡	(†)
Parent's highest level of education														
Not high school graduate	24	(2.5)	21	(2.4)	129	(3.5)	36	(1.4)	125	(2.4)	42	(2.1)	131	(4.4)
Graduated high school..........	29	(2.0)	29	(2.4)	139	(1.3)	41	(1.1)	138	(1.8)	42	(1.9)	130	(8.5)
Some college.......................	35	(1.3)	34	(2.4)	150	(1.8)	44	(0.8)	153	(1.8)	49	(1.8)	153	(5.1)
Graduated college	39	(1.3)	39	(1.5)	159	(1.7)	46	(0.7)	158	(1.4)	52	(2.2)	157	(5.6)
Region														
Northeast............................	39	(2.0)	34	(2.6)	153	(4.0)	45	(1.5)	152	(4.0)	‡	(†)	‡	(†)
Southeast............................	30	(2.7)	33	(2.4)	139	(2.7)	42	(1.0)	143	(3.3)	‡	(†)	‡	(†)
Central	36	(1.4)	33	(2.1)	157	(3.0)	45	(1.8)	157	(3.5)	‡	(†)	‡	(†)
West...................................	33	(2.3)	35	(2.9)	152	(3.0)	43	(1.3)	149	(2.6)	51	(2.1)	157	(5.3)

†Not applicable.
‡Reporting standards not met.
NOTE: Excludes students unable to be tested due to limited proficiency in English or due to a disability (and the accommodations provided were not sufficient to enable the test to properly reflect the students' proficiency in the arts). Creating refers to expressing ideas and feelings in the form of an original work of art; for example, a dance, a piece of music, a dramatic improvisation, or a sculpture. Performing refers to performing an existing work, a process that calls upon the interpretive or recreative skills of the student. Responding refers to observing, describing, analyzing, and evaluating works of art. Includes public and private schools. Race categories exclude persons of Hispanic origin. Totals include other racial/ethnic groups not shown separately. Standard errors appear in parentheses.
SOURCE: U.S. Department of Education, National Center for Education Statistics, National Assessment of Educational Progress (NAEP), *The NAEP 1997 Arts Report Card.* (This table was prepared November 1998.)

Table 131. SAT score averages of college-bound seniors, by race/ethnicity: Selected years, 1986–87 through 2005–06

Race/ethnicity	1986–87	1990–91	1996–97	1999–2000	2000–01	2001–02	2002–03	2003–04	2004–05	2005–06	Score change						
											1986–87 to 1996–97	1996–97 to 2005–06	2000–01 to 2001–02	2001–02 to 2002–03	2002–03 to 2003–04	2003–04 to 2004–05	2004–05 to 2005–06
1	2	3	4	5	6	7	8	9	10	11	12	13	14	15	16	17	18
SAT—Critical reading																	
All students	507	499	505	505	506	504	507	508	508	503	-2	-2	-2	3	1	0	-5
White	524	518	526	528	529	527	529	528	532	527	2	1	-2	2	-1	4	-5
Black.......................	428	427	434	434	433	430	431	430	433	434	6	0	-3	1	-1	3	1
Hispanic or Latino.....	464	458	466	461	460	458	458	457	461	463	458	2	-8	-2	-1	4	2	-5
Mexican American	457	454	451	453	451	446	448	451	453	454	-6	3	-5	2	3	2	1
Puerto Rican............	436	436	454	456	457	455	456	457	460	459	18	5	-2	1	1	3	-1
Asian.......................	479	485	496	499	501	501	508	507	511	510	17	14	0	7	-1	4	-1
American Indian.......	471	470	475	482	481	479	480	483	489	487	4	12	-2	1	3	6	-2
Other.......................	480	486	512	508	503	502	501	494	495	494	32	-18	-1	-1	-7	1	-1
SAT—Mathematics																	
All students	501	500	511	514	514	516	519	518	520	518	10	7	2	3	-1	2	-2
White	514	513	526	530	531	533	534	531	536	536	12	10	2	1	-3	5	0
Black.......................	411	419	423	426	426	427	426	427	431	429	12	6	1	-1	1	4	-2
Hispanic or Latino.....	462	462	468	467	465	464	464	465	469	463	6	-5	-1	0	1	4	-6
Mexican American	455	459	458	460	458	457	457	458	463	465	3	7	-1	0	1	5	2
Puerto Rican............	432	439	447	451	451	451	453	452	457	456	15	9	0	2	-1	5	-1
Asian.......................	541	548	560	565	566	569	575	577	580	578	19	18	3	6	2	3	-2
American Indian.......	463	468	475	481	479	483	482	488	493	494	12	19	4	-1	6	5	1
Other.......................	482	492	514	515	512	514	513	508	513	513	32	-1	2	-1	-5	5	0

NOTE: Data are for seniors who took the SAT any time during their high school years through March of their senior year. If a student took a test more than once, the most recent score was used. Scores from the writing test introduced in March 2005 are not included. The SAT was formerly known as the Scholastic Assessment Test and the Scholastic Aptitude Test. Possible scores on each part of the SAT range from 200 to 800. The critical reading section was formerly known as the verbal section.

SOURCE: College Entrance Examination Board, *College-Bound Seniors: Total Group Profile [National] Report*, selected years, 1986–87 through 2005–06, retrieved August 29, 2006, from http://www.collegeboard.com/about/news_info/cbsenior/yr2006/reports.html. (This table was prepared August 2006.)

Table 132. SAT score averages of college-bound seniors, by sex: 1966–67 through 2005–06

School year	SAT[1]									Scholastic Aptitude Test (old scale)					
	Critical reading score			Mathematics score			Writing score[2]			Verbal score			Mathematics score		
	Total	Male	Female	Total	Male	Female	Total	Male	Female	Total	Male	Female	Total	Male	Female
1	2	3	4	5	6	7	8	9	10	11	12	13	14	15	16
1966–67	543	540	545	516	535	495	†	†	†	466	463	468	492	514	467
1967–68	543	541	543	516	533	497	†	†	†	466	464	466	492	512	470
1968–69	540	536	543	517	534	498	†	†	†	463	459	466	493	513	470
1969–70	537	536	538	512	531	493	†	†	†	460	459	461	488	509	465
1970–71	532	531	534	513	529	494	†	†	†	455	454	457	488	507	466
1971–72	530	531	529	509	527	489	†	†	†	453	454	452	484	505	461
1972–73	523	523	521	506	525	489	†	†	†	445	446	443	481	502	460
1973–74	521	524	520	505	524	488	†	†	†	444	447	442	480	501	459
1974–75	512	515	509	498	518	479	†	†	†	434	437	431	472	495	449
1975–76	509	511	508	497	520	475	†	†	†	431	433	430	472	497	446
1976–77	507	509	505	496	520	474	†	†	†	429	431	427	470	497	445
1977–78	507	511	503	494	517	474	†	†	†	429	433	425	468	494	444
1978–79	505	509	501	493	516	473	†	†	†	427	431	423	467	493	443
1979–80	502	506	498	492	515	473	†	†	†	424	428	420	466	491	443
1980–81	502	508	496	492	516	473	†	†	†	424	430	418	466	492	443
1981–82	504	509	499	493	516	473	†	†	†	426	431	421	467	493	443
1982–83	503	508	498	494	516	474	†	†	†	425	430	420	468	493	445
1983–84	504	511	498	497	518	478	†	†	†	426	433	420	471	495	449
1984–85	509	514	503	500	522	480	†	†	†	431	437	425	475	499	452
1985–86	509	515	504	500	523	479	†	†	†	431	437	426	475	501	451
1986–87	507	512	502	501	523	481	†	†	†	430	435	425	476	500	453
1987–88	505	512	499	501	521	483	†	†	†	428	435	422	476	498	455
1988–89	504	510	498	502	523	482	†	†	†	427	434	421	476	500	454
1989–90	500	505	496	501	521	483	†	†	†	424	429	419	476	499	455
1990–91	499	503	495	500	520	482	†	†	†	422	426	418	474	497	453
1991–92	500	504	496	501	521	484	†	†	†	423	428	419	476	499	456
1992–93	500	504	497	503	524	484	†	†	†	424	428	420	478	502	457
1993–94	499	501	497	504	523	487	†	†	†	423	425	421	479	501	460
1994–95	504	505	502	506	525	490	†	†	†	428	429	426	482	503	463
1995–96	505	507	503	508	527	492	†	†	†	—	—	—	—	—	—
1996–97	505	507	503	511	530	494	†	†	†	—	—	—	—	—	—
1997–98	505	509	502	512	531	496	†	†	†	—	—	—	—	—	—
1998–99	505	509	502	511	531	495	†	†	†	—	—	—	—	—	—
1999–2000	505	507	504	514	533	498	†	†	†	—	—	—	—	—	—
2000–01	506	509	502	514	533	498	†	†	†	—	—	—	—	—	—
2001–02	504	507	502	516	534	500	†	†	†	—	—	—	—	—	—
2002–03	507	512	503	519	537	503	†	†	†	—	—	—	—	—	—
2003–04	508	512	504	518	537	501	†	†	†	—	—	—	—	—	—
2004–05	508	513	505	520	538	504	†	†	†	—	—	—	—	—	—
2005–06	503	505	502	518	536	502	497	491	502	—	—	—	—	—	—

—Not available.
†Not applicable.
[1]Data for 1966–67 to 1985–86 were converted to the recentered scale by using a formula applied to the original mean and standard deviation. For 1986–87 to 1994–95, individual student scores were converted to the recentered scale and then the mean was recomputed. For 1995–96 to 1998–99, nearly all students received scores on the recentered scale; any score on the original scale was converted to the recentered scale prior to recomputing the mean. From 1999–2000 on, all scores have been reported on the recentered scale.
[2]Writing data are based on students who took the SAT writing section, which was introduced in March 2005.

NOTE: Data for 1966–67 through 1970–71 are estimates derived from the test scores of all participants. Data for 1971–72 and later are for seniors who took the SAT any time during their high school years through March of their senior year. If a student took a test more than once, the most recent score was used. The SAT was formerly known as the Scholastic Assessment Test and the Scholastic Aptitude Test. Possible scores on each part of the SAT range from 200 to 800. The critical reading section was formerly known as the verbal section.
SOURCE: College Entrance Examination Board, *College-Bound Seniors: Total Group Profile [National] Report*, selected years, 1986–87 through 2005–06, retrieved August 29, 2006, from http://www.collegeboard.com/about/news_info/cbsenior/yr2006/reports.html. (This table was prepared August 2006.)

Table 133. SAT score averages of college-bound seniors, by selected student characteristics: Selected years, 1995–96 through 2005–06

Selected student characteristic	1995–96 Critical reading score	1995–96 Mathematics score	1995–96 Percentage distribution	1999–2000 Critical reading score	1999–2000 Mathematics score	1999–2000 Percentage distribution	2002–03[1] Critical reading score	2002–03[1] Mathematics score	2003–04 Critical reading score	2003–04 Mathematics score	2003–04 Percentage distribution	2004–05[1] Critical reading score	2004–05[1] Mathematics score	2005–06 Critical reading score	2005–06 Mathematics score	2005–06 Writing score[2]	2005–06 Percentage distribution
	2	3	4	5	6	7	8	9	10	11	12	13	14	15	16	17	18
All students	**505**	**508**	**100**	**505**	**514**	**100**	**507**	**519**	**508**	**518**	**100**	**508**	**520**	**503**	**518**	**497**	**100**
High school rank																	
Top decile	591	606	22	589	608	++	585	607	584	602	29	585	606	580	604	577	31
Second decile	530	539	22	528	543	++	522	539	522	537	24	523	540	516	537	511	25
Second quintile	494	496	28	493	500	++	486	494	486	494	22	488	499	484	498	476	20
Third quintile	455	448	24	455	453	++	449	449	449	451	20	452	455	—	—	—	—
Fourth quintile	429	418	4	425	419	++	420	417	422	421	4	425	424	—	—	—	—
Fifth quintile	411	401	1	408	401	++	410	410	415	418	1	426	430	—	—	—	—
Bottom three quintiles[3]	—	—	—	—	—	—	—	—	—	—	—	—	—	443	449	435	23
High school grade point average																	
A+ (97–100)	617	632	6	610	628	7	607	625	606	620	6	607	625	602	621	599	7
A (93–96)	573	583	14	567	582	16	566	583	567	580	18	570	585	563	582	559	18
A– (90–92)	545	554	15	540	553	17	538	552	537	549	17	541	555	534	552	529	18
B (80–89)	486	485	49	482	486	47	480	485	480	486	47	484	491	479	489	471	46
C (70–79)	432	426	15	428	426	12	425	424	429	431	11	430	432	426	428	414	11
D, E, or F (below 70)	414	408	#	405	406	#	416	430	421	446	#	415	439	406	413	389	#
Intended college major																	
Agriculture/natural resources	491	484	2	490	486	1	484	482	484	483	1	487	486	481	485	469	1
Architecture/environmental design	492	519	3	494	524	2	483	511	479	510	2	495	527	488	528	485	3
Arts: visual/performing	520	497	6	518	502	8	514	500	517	501	8	521	506	516	502	507	9
Biological sciences	546	545	6	544	548	5	543	553	544	552	6	547	558	540	554	532	6
Business and commerce	483	500	13	487	510	14	489	512	486	509	13	491	515	486	511	481	15
Communications	527	497	4	526	505	4	524	506	525	505	4	527	509	522	504	520	4
Computer or information sciences	497	522	3	499	533	6	503	535	504	532	5	508	535	503	534	482	4
Education	487	477	8	483	481	9	482	483	483	482	8	486	488	480	484	478	8
Engineering	525	569	8	523	573	8	525	574	525	573	9	529	579	519	577	506	8
Foreign/classical languages	556	534	#	558	539	1	564	545	570	545	1	575	551	572	549	563	1
General/interdisciplinary	576	553	#	562	545	#	547	539	547	533	#	546	535	542	532	532	#
Health and allied services	500	505	19	497	505	16	489	498	487	495	17	490	501	485	498	483	18
Home economics	458	452	#	462	462	#	462	462	460	461	#	463	466	462	466	461	#
Language and literature	605	545	1	608	552	1	603	550	603	547	2	606	552	597	541	584	2
Library and archival sciences	554	512	#	556	511	#	572	512	567	515	#	577	511	579	509	542	#
Mathematics	552	628	1	551	630	1	545	626	541	621	1	545	626	539	624	537	1
Military sciences	503	505	#	505	512	#	513	516	516	520	1	522	526	510	521	487	1
Philosophy/religion/theology	560	536	#	560	539	1	562	544	560	539	1	561	542	557	537	535	1
Physical sciences	575	595	1	569	592	1	563	588	564	587	1	565	591	557	589	542	2
Public affairs and services	458	448	3	459	454	2	462	458	464	459	2	465	463	462	461	454	3
Social sciences and history	532	509	11	532	513	11	531	514	534	515	3	540	522	539	519	525	9
Technical and vocational	435	441	1	442	452	1	441	450	443	453	1	445	456	437	454	421	1
Undecided	500	507	7	512	521	7	516	528	514	526	6	517	530	512	530	502	3
Degree-level goal																	
Certificate program	434	439	1	439	453	1	441	456	441	456	1	445	463	443	462	435	1
Associate's degree	422	415	2	420	419	2	417	416	417	417	1	420	421	416	420	409	1
Bachelor's degree	476	476	23	478	483	25	475	481	474	479	24	481	487	477	487	469	25
Master's degree	514	518	29	515	526	31	513	524	511	520	29	516	526	512	525	505	30
Doctor's or related degree	548	552	24	547	554	22	542	552	540	547	21	542	552	539	553	532	20
Other	430	438	1	442	454	1	441	453	439	457	1	442	464	439	456	436	1
Undecided	502	503	20	508	514	19	514	523	513	521	23	517	527	515	528	508	22

See notes at end of table.

Table 133. SAT score averages of college-bound seniors, by selected student characteristics: Selected years, 1995–96 through 2005–06—Continued

Selected student characteristic	1995–96			1999–2000			2002–03[1]		2003–04			2004–05[1]		2005–06			
	Critical reading score	Mathematics score	Percentage distribution	Critical reading score	Mathematics score	Percentage distribution	Critical reading score	Mathematics score	Critical reading score	Mathematics score	Percentage distribution	Critical reading score	Mathematics score	Critical reading score	Mathematics score	Writing score[2]	Percentage distribution
1	2	3	4	5	6	7	8	9	10	11	12	13	14	15	16	17	18
Family income[4]																	
Less than $10,000	429	444	4	425	447	‡	420	444	422	450	5	426	458	429	457	427	4
$10,000, but less than $20,000	456	464	8	447	460	‡	437	452	440	457	8	443	463	445	465	440	7
$20,000, but less than $30,000	482	482	10	471	478	‡	460	467	459	467	10	463	474	462	474	454	8
$30,000, but less than $40,000	497	495	12	490	493	‡	480	484	478	482	11	480	487	478	488	470	10
$40,000, but less than $50,000	509	507	10	503	505	‡	495	498	493	496	9	496	500	493	501	483	8
$50,000, but less than $60,000	517	517	9	511	515	‡	504	508	501	504	9	505	509	500	509	490	9
$60,000, but less than $70,000	524	525	7	517	522	‡	511	514	507	510	8	511	515	505	515	496	8
$70,000, but less than $80,000	531	533	6	524	530	‡	518	523	515	518	8	517	522	511	521	502	9
$80,000 to $100,000	541	544	7	536	543	‡	529	536	527	530	12	529	534	523	534	514	13
More than $100,000	560	569	9	558	571	‡	555	568	553	562	20	554	565	549	564	543	24
Highest level of parental education																	
No high school diploma	414	439	4	413	442	4	413	443	415	445	5	419	452	418	445	418	4
High school diploma	475	474	31	472	477	33	470	475	469	474	33	471	479	467	478	460	31
Associate's degree	489	487	7	488	491	9	487	491	486	490	9	489	494	484	493	474	8
Bachelor's degree	525	529	25	525	533	29	525	534	523	531	28	527	536	522	536	514	30
Graduate degree	556	558	23	558	566	25	559	569	558	564	25	561	570	558	571	552	27

—Not available.
#Rounds to zero.
‡Reporting standards not met.
[1]Percentage distribution not reported since this year had less than 80 percent combined unit and item response rate.
[2]Writing data are based on students who took the SAT writing section, which was introduced in March 2005.
[3]In 2005, the College Board reported third, fourth, and fifth quintiles as the bottom three quintiles instead of reporting them separately as in previous years.
[4]Because income categories have not been adjusted for inflation over time, the distribution of students has shifted toward the higher income categories. Differences between specific categories over time should be interpreted with caution.

NOTE: Data are for seniors who took the SAT any time during their high school years through March of their senior year. If a student took a test more than once, the most recent score was used. The SAT was formerly known as the Scholastic Assessment Test and the Scholastic Aptitude Test. Possible scores on each part of the SAT range from 200 to 800. Detail may not sum to totals because of rounding and survey item nonresponse.
SOURCE: College Entrance Examination Board, College-Bound Seniors: Total Group Profile [National] Report, selected years, 1995–96 through 2005–06, retrieved August 29, 2006, from http://www.collegeboard.com/about/news_info/cbsenior/yr2006/reports.html. (This table was prepared August 2006.)

Table 134. SAT score averages of college-bound seniors and percent of graduates taking SAT, by state or jurisdiction: Selected years, 1987–88 through 2005–06

| State or jurisdiction | 1987–88 | | 1995–96 | | 2000–01 | | 2003–04 | | 2004–05 | | 2005–06 | | | Percent of graduates taking SAT, 2004–05[1] | Percent of graduates taking SAT, 2005–06[1] |
	Critical reading	Mathe-matics	Critical reading	Mathe-matics	Critical reading	Mathe-matics	Critical reading	Mathe-matics	Critical reading	Mathe-matics	Critical reading	Mathe-matics	Writing[2]		
1	2	3	4	5	6	7	8	9	10	11	12	13	14	15	16
United States	505	501	505	508	506	514	508	518	508	520	503	518	497	49	48
Alabama	554	540	565	558	559	554	560	553	567	559	565	561	565	10	9
Alaska	518	501	521	513	514	510	518	514	523	519	517	517	493	52	51
Arizona	531	523	525	521	523	525	523	524	526	530	521	528	507	33	32
Arkansas	554	536	566	550	562	550	569	555	563	552	574	568	567	6	5
California	500	508	495	511	498	517	501	519	504	522	501	518	501	50	49
Colorado	537	532	536	538	539	542	554	553	560	560	558	564	548	26	26
Connecticut	513	498	507	504	509	510	515	515	517	517	512	516	511	86	84
Delaware	510	493	508	495	501	499	500	499	503	502	495	500	484	74	73
District of Columbia	479	461	489	473	482	474	489	476	490	478	487	472	482	79	78[3]
Florida	499	495	498	496	498	499	499	499	498	498	496	497	480	65	65
Georgia	480	473	484	477	491	489	494	493	497	496	494	496	487	75	70
Hawaii	484	505	485	510	486	515	487	514	490	516	482	509	472	61	60
Idaho	543	523	543	536	543	542	540	539	544	542	543	545	525	21	19
Illinois	540	540	564	575	576	589	585	597	594	606	591	609	586	10	9
Indiana	490	486	494	494	499	501	501	506	504	508	498	509	486	66	62
Iowa	587	588	590	600	593	603	593	602	596	608	602	613	591	5	4
Kansas	568	557	579	571	577	580	584	585	585	588	582	590	566	9	8
Kentucky	551	535	549	544	550	550	559	557	561	559	562	562	555	12	11
Louisiana	551	533	559	550	564	562	564	561	565	562	570	571	571	8	6
Maine	508	493	504	498	506	500	505	501	509	505	501	501	491	75	73
Maryland	509	501	507	504	508	510	511	515	511	515	503	509	499	71	70
Massachusetts	508	499	507	504	511	515	518	523	520	527	513	524	510	86	85
Michigan	532	533	557	565	561	572	563	573	568	579	568	583	555	10	10
Minnesota	546	549	582	593	580	589	587	593	592	597	591	600	574	11	10
Mississippi	557	539	569	557	566	551	562	547	564	554	556	541	562	4	4
Missouri	547	539	570	569	577	577	587	585	588	588	587	591	582	7	7
Montana	547	547	546	547	539	539	537	539	540	540	538	545	524	31	28
Nebraska	562	561	567	568	562	568	569	576	574	579	576	583	566	8	7
Nevada	517	510	508	507	509	515	507	514	508	513	498	508	481	39	40
New Hampshire	523	511	520	514	520	516	522	521	525	525	520	524	509	81	82
New Jersey	500	495	498	505	499	513	501	514	503	517	496	515	496	86	82
New Mexico	553	543	554	548	551	542	554	543	558	547	557	549	543	13	13
New York	497	495	497	499	495	505	497	510	497	511	493	510	483	92	88
North Carolina	478	470	490	486	493	499	499	507	499	511	495	513	485	74	71
North Dakota	572	569	596	599	592	599	582	601	590	605	610	617	588	4	4
Ohio	529	521	536	535	534	539	538	542	539	543	535	544	521	29	28
Oklahoma	558	542	566	557	567	561	569	566	570	563	576	574	563	7	7
Oregon	517	507	523	521	526	526	527	528	526	528	523	529	503	59	55
Pennsylvania	502	489	498	492	500	499	501	502	501	503	493	500	483	75	74
Rhode Island	508	496	501	491	501	499	503	502	503	505	495	502	490	72	69
South Carolina	477	468	480	474	486	488	491	495	494	499	487	498	480	64	62
South Dakota	585	573	574	566	577	582	594	597	589	589	590	604	578	5	4
Tennessee	560	543	563	552	562	553	567	557	572	563	573	569	572	16	15
Texas	494	490	495	500	493	499	493	499	493	502	491	506	487	54	52
Utah	572	553	583	575	575	570	565	556	566	557	560	557	550	7	7
Vermont	514	499	506	500	511	506	516	512	521	517	513	519	502	67	67
Virginia	507	498	507	496	510	501	515	509	516	514	512	513	500	73	73
Washington	525	517	519	519	527	527	528	531	532	534	527	532	511	55	54
West Virginia	528	519	526	506	527	512	524	514	523	511	519	510	515	20	20
Wisconsin	549	551	577	586	584	596	587	596	592	599	588	600	577	6	6
Wyoming	550	545	544	544	547	545	551	546	544	543	548	555	537	12	10

[1]Participation rate is based on the projection of high school graduates by the Western Interstate Commission for Higher Education (WICHE), and the number of seniors who took the SAT in each state.

[2]Writing data are based on students who took the SAT writing section, which was introduced in March 2005.

[3]Participation rate is based on self-reported 2002 twelfth-grade enrollment from D.C.'s public and nonpublic schools because WICHE estimated fewer graduating seniors than actual SAT test takers.

NOTE: Data are for seniors who took the SAT any time during their high school years through March of their senior year. If a student took a test more than once, the most recent score was used. The SAT was formerly known as the Scholastic Assessment Test and the Scholastic Aptitude Test. Possible scores on each part of the SAT range from 200 to 800.
SOURCE: College Entrance Examination Board, *College-Bound Seniors: Total Group Profile [National] Report*, selected years, 1987–88 through 2005–06, retrieved August 29, 2006, from http://www.collegeboard.com/about/news_info/cbsenior/yr2006/reports.html. (This table was prepared August 2006.)

Table 135. ACT score averages and standard deviations, by sex and race/ethnicity, and percentage of ACT test takers, by selected composite score ranges and planned fields of study: Selected years, 1995 through 2005

Score type and test-taker characteristic	Number										Standard deviation								
	1995	1997	1998	1999	2000	2001	2002	2003	2004	2005	1997	1998	1999	2000	2001	2002	2003	2004	2005
1	2	3	4	5	6	7	8	9	10	11	12	13	14	15	16	17	18	19	20
Total test takers																			
Number (in thousands) ..	945	959	995	1,019	1,065	1,070	1,116	1,175	1,171	1,186	†	†	†	†	†	†	†	†	†
Percentage of graduates .	37.5	36.7	37.7	36.9	37.6	37.6	38.4	38.9	38.2	38.1	†	†	†	†	†	†	†	†	†
										Average test score[1]									
Composite, total	20.8	21.0	21.0	21.0	21.0	21.0	20.8	20.8	20.9	20.9	4.7	4.7	4.7	4.7	4.7	4.8	4.8	4.8	—
Sex																			
Male	21.0	21.1	21.2	21.1	21.2	21.1	20.9	21.0	21.0	21.1	4.9	4.9	4.9	4.9	4.9	5.0	5.0	5.0	5.0
Female	20.7	20.8	20.9	20.9	20.9	20.9	20.7	20.8	20.9	20.9	4.6	4.6	4.6	4.6	4.6	4.7	4.7	4.7	4.7
Race/ethnicity																			
White..................................	—	22.8	22.7	22.7	22.7	21.8	22.6	21.7	21.8	21.9	—	—	—	—	—	—	—	—	—
Black	—	17.9	17.9	17.9	17.8	16.9	17.6	16.9	17.1	17.0	—	—	—	—	—	—	—	—	—
Mexican American	—	19.9	19.6	19.6	19.5	18.5	19.0	18.3	18.4	18.4	—	—	—	—	—	—	—	—	—
Other Hispanic	—	20.1	20.7	20.7	20.5	19.4	20.0	19.0	18.8	18.9	—	—	—	—	—	—	—	—	—
Asian American or Pacific Islander	—	22.5	22.6	22.3	22.4	21.7	22.3	21.8	21.9	22.1	—	—	—	—	—	—	—	—	—
American Indian/Alaska Native	—	20.4	20.4	20.4	20.4	18.8	20.1	18.7	18.8	18.7	—	—	—	—	—	—	—	—	—
Subject area																			
English	20.2	20.3	20.4	20.5	20.5	20.5	20.2	20.3	20.4	20.4	5.4	5.4	5.5	5.5	5.6	5.8	5.8	5.9	—
Male	19.8	19.9	19.9	20.0	20.0	20.0	19.7	19.8	19.9	20.0	5.4	5.4	5.5	5.6	5.6	5.8	5.8	5.9	6.0
Female	20.6	20.7	20.8	20.9	20.9	20.8	20.6	20.7	20.8	20.8	5.4	5.4	5.5	5.5	5.6	5.7	5.8	5.8	5.9
Mathematics	20.2	20.6	20.8	20.7	20.7	20.7	20.6	20.6	20.7	20.7	5.0	5.1	5.0	5.0	5.0	5.0	5.1	5.0	—
Male	20.9	21.3	21.5	21.4	21.4	21.4	21.2	21.2	21.3	21.3	5.2	5.3	5.2	5.2	5.2	5.3	4.8	5.3	5.3
Female	19.7	20.1	20.2	20.2	20.2	20.2	20.1	20.1	20.2	20.2	4.7	4.8	4.7	4.8	4.7	4.8	5.3	4.8	4.8
Reading	21.3	21.3	21.4	21.4	21.4	21.3	21.1	21.2	21.3	21.3	6.1	6.0	6.0	6.1	6.0	6.1	6.1	6.0	—
Male	21.1	21.2	21.1	21.1	21.2	21.1	20.9	21.0	21.1	21.0	6.1	6.2	6.1	6.1	6.1	6.3	5.3	6.1	6.1
Female	21.4	21.5	21.6	21.6	21.5	21.5	21.3	21.4	21.5	21.5	6.0	5.9	5.9	6.0	6.0	6.1	4.8	5.9	6.0
Science reasoning	21.0	21.1	21.1	21.0	21.0	21.0	20.8	20.8	20.9	20.9	4.7	4.6	4.5	4.5	4.6	4.6	4.6	4.6	—
Male	21.6	21.7	21.8	21.5	21.6	21.6	21.3	21.3	21.3	21.4	4.9	4.9	4.8	4.8	4.9	4.9	4.9	4.9	4.9
Female	20.5	20.6	20.6	20.6	20.6	20.6	20.4	20.4	20.5	20.5	4.4	4.3	4.2	4.3	4.3	4.3	4.3	4.3	4.3
										Percent									
Obtaining composite scores of—																			
28 or above	—	10	10	10	10	10	10	10	10	10	—	—	—	—	—	—	—	—	—
17 or below	—	26	25	25	25	25	27	27	26	26	—	—	—	—	—	—	—	—	—
Planned major field of study																			
Business[2]	13	12	12	12	11	11	10	10	9	9	—	—	—	—	—	—	—	—	—
Engineering[3]	8	8	8	8	8	7	7	7	6	6	—	—	—	—	—	—	—	—	—
Social science[4].................	9	9	9	9	9	9	8	8	7	7	—	—	—	—	—	—	—	—	—
Education[5]........................	8	9	9	9	9	8	8	7	7	6	—	—	—	—	—	—	—	—	—

—Not available.
†Not applicable.
[1]Minimum score is 1 and maximum score is 36.
[2]Includes business and management, business and office, and marketing and distribution.
[3]Includes engineering and engineering-related technologies.

[4]Includes social science and philosophy, religion, and theology.
[5]Includes education and teacher education.
NOTE: Race categories exclude persons of Hispanic origin.
SOURCE: ACT, *High School Profile Report*, selected years, 1995 through 2005. (This table was prepared April 2006.)

Table 136. Percentage distribution of elementary and secondary school children, by average grades and selected child and school characteristics: 1996, 1999, and 2003

Distribution of children, by parental reports of average grades in all subjects

Selected characteristic of children and schools	1996				1999				2003			
	Mostly A's	Mostly B's	Mostly C's	Mostly D's or F's	Mostly A's	Mostly B's	Mostly C's	Mostly D's or F's	Mostly A's	Mostly B's	Mostly C's	Mostly D's or F's
1	2	3	4	5	6	7	8	9	10	11	12	13
All students	39.5 (0.53)	37.7 (0.56)	18.5 (0.41)	4.2 (0.22)	40.3 (0.52)	37.7 (0.53)	17.8 (0.42)	4.3 (0.23)	43.6 (0.62)	37.0 (0.58)	15.9 (0.52)	3.6 (0.24)
Sex of child												
Male	32.5 (0.68)	38.3 (0.82)	23.5 (0.63)	5.7 (0.36)	33.7 (0.70)	38.3 (0.73)	21.9 (0.63)	6.2 (0.39)	36.4 (0.72)	38.6 (0.86)	19.8 (0.74)	5.2 (0.40)
Female	46.9 (0.78)	37.2 (0.77)	13.2 (0.60)	2.7 (0.27)	47.0 (0.77)	37.1 (0.76)	13.5 (0.54)	2.4 (0.25)	51.0 (0.84)	35.3 (0.76)	11.9 (0.61)	1.9 (0.24)
Race/ethnicity of child												
White	43.7 (0.66)	36.1 (0.61)	16.5 (0.49)	3.7 (0.27)	44.6 (0.67)	36.1 (0.65)	15.8 (0.50)	3.4 (0.25)	47.8 (0.86)	35.2 (0.75)	14.0 (0.63)	3.1 (0.25)
Black	27.0 (1.40)	41.0 (1.48)	26.2 (1.51)	5.8 (0.67)	27.5 (1.20)	40.3 (1.42)	26.4 (1.22)	5.8 (0.72)	34.5 (1.75)	39.5 (1.65)	20.9 (1.33)	5.0 (0.82)
Hispanic	31.9 (1.40)	43.6 (1.47)	19.6 (1.18)	4.9 (0.70)	33.3 (1.17)	42.7 (1.26)	17.4 (0.98)	6.5 (0.73)	34.9 (1.14)	42.3 (1.24)	18.6 (1.03)	4.2 (0.49)
Other	44.7 (1.80)	33.7 (2.10)	17.1 (1.61)	4.5 (1.12)	45.8 (2.38)	35.8 (2.36)	14.2 (2.03)	4.2 (1.18)	49.3 (2.63)	33.7 (2.32)	14.3 (1.99)	2.7 (0.78)
Highest education level of parents												
Less than high school	29.0 (1.86)	39.0 (1.89)	23.9 (1.66)	8.1 (1.04)	26.3 (1.58)	40.8 (1.82)	22.3 (1.62)	10.5 (1.30)	27.8 (2.17)	41.6 (2.05)	22.7 (2.28)	7.8 (1.46)
High school/GED	30.5 (0.90)	40.5 (1.09)	23.1 (0.91)	5.9 (0.52)	31.6 (0.99)	39.5 (1.06)	23.3 (0.90)	5.6 (0.49)	32.1 (1.20)	41.4 (1.23)	21.7 (1.12)	4.8 (0.57)
Vocational/technical or some college	36.9 (0.99)	40.1 (1.01)	19.1 (0.64)	3.9 (0.43)	38.9 (0.93)	39.0 (0.94)	18.3 (0.75)	3.8 (0.38)	42.0 (1.13)	37.1 (1.19)	16.9 (0.76)	4.0 (0.42)
Bachelor's degree	52.5 (1.40)	32.9 (1.29)	12.7 (1.03)	1.9 (0.34)	51.1 (1.28)	34.9 (1.22)	12.1 (0.85)	1.8 (0.34)	53.2 (1.30)	34.2 (1.29)	10.9 (0.90)	1.7 (0.31)
Graduate/professional degree	58.2 (1.30)	30.9 (1.21)	9.8 (0.86)	1.1 (0.26)	54.8 (1.30)	33.0 (1.23)	10.3 (0.82)	1.9 (0.39)	60.6 (1.67)	30.9 (1.70)	7.5 (0.73)	1.0 (0.24)
Family income												
$5,000 or less	28.9 (2.50)	38.8 (2.39)	23.3 (2.35)	8.9 (1.67)	25.0 (2.59)	42.9 (3.46)	24.4 (2.77)	7.7 (1.77)	31.8 (4.43)	38.9 (4.27)	21.0 (3.53)	8.3 (3.25)
$5,001 to 10,000	26.6 (1.97)	41.9 (2.30)	24.6 (2.33)	6.9 (1.15)	32.1 (2.37)	36.5 (2.35)	24.0 (2.14)	7.4 (1.32)	31.6 (2.90)	40.1 (3.70)	24.9 (2.70)	3.4 (0.98)
$10,001 to 15,000	28.0 (1.98)	39.8 (2.27)	26.0 (1.97)	6.2 (1.10)	30.3 (2.00)	38.9 (2.16)	23.7 (1.92)	7.1 (1.21)	33.5 (3.49)	35.1 (2.85)	23.9 (2.67)	7.5 (1.44)
$15,001 to 20,000	32.7 (2.34)	38.4 (1.99)	21.6 (1.81)	7.3 (1.35)	32.0 (2.03)	40.0 (2.10)	22.3 (1.89)	5.7 (0.94)	34.6 (2.28)	41.1 (2.41)	18.8 (2.00)	5.4 (1.26)
$20,001 to 25,000	34.4 (1.92)	40.8 (2.19)	20.6 (1.77)	4.2 (0.88)	32.8 (1.83)	38.9 (1.88)	21.6 (1.60)	6.7 (1.09)	33.5 (2.51)	42.1 (2.93)	19.8 (1.99)	4.7 (0.96)
$25,001 to 30,000	33.0 (1.88)	42.0 (2.05)	19.8 (1.41)	5.2 (0.76)	37.4 (1.91)	37.4 (1.90)	19.7 (1.54)	5.4 (0.86)	34.5 (2.67)	42.6 (3.13)	17.9 (1.92)	5.0 (1.21)
$30,001 to 35,000	40.0 (1.88)	38.0 (1.66)	18.1 (1.44)	3.9 (0.69)	38.2 (1.88)	38.8 (1.95)	19.2 (1.53)	3.8 (0.75)	35.1 (2.76)	43.1 (2.57)	16.9 (1.84)	5.0 (1.09)
$35,001 to 40,000	40.4 (1.70)	37.3 (1.69)	19.4 (1.22)	2.8 (0.65)	37.5 (1.83)	42.1 (1.89)	17.4 (1.40)	3.0 (0.62)	39.6 (3.20)	37.8 (2.79)	19.1 (1.78)	3.6 (0.93)
$40,001 to 50,000	43.2 (1.49)	36.0 (1.51)	16.8 (1.09)	4.0 (0.57)	45.0 (1.52)	35.1 (1.44)	16.6 (1.14)	3.3 (0.55)	43.9 (2.06)	35.8 (1.95)	15.8 (1.51)	4.4 (0.75)
$50,001 to 75,000	50.2 (1.05)	32.7 (1.04)	14.9 (0.86)	2.2 (0.34)	45.8 (1.20)	36.8 (1.17)	14.5 (0.84)	2.9 (0.41)	48.0 (1.29)	35.0 (1.22)	14.0 (0.81)	3.0 (0.45)
Over $75,000	51.0 (1.58)	36.8 (1.55)	10.9 (0.9)	1.3 (0.31)	51.9 (1.15)	35.4 (1.11)	10.9 (0.72)	1.8 (0.32)	54.0 (1.19)	33.8 (1.18)	11.0 (0.78)	1.2 (0.19)
Child attending public schools	38.2 (0.54)	37.9 (0.56)	19.3 (0.44)	4.6 (0.23)	39.0 (0.55)	37.8 (0.56)	18.5 (0.45)	4.7 (0.26)	41.8 (0.64)	37.5 (0.62)	16.8 (0.57)	3.8 (0.26)
Elementary (kindergarten to grade 8)	43.2 (0.75)	36.6 (0.69)	16.3 (0.55)	3.9 (0.26)	43.5 (0.71)	36.6 (0.71)	15.9 (0.54)	4.1 (0.29)	46.1 (0.80)	35.9 (0.84)	14.6 (0.74)	3.4 (0.32)
Secondary (grades 9 to 12)	29.6 (0.89)	40.2 (1.00)	24.5 (0.89)	5.7 (0.46)	31.8 (0.87)	39.9 (0.92)	22.7 (0.79)	5.6 (0.48)	34.6 (0.96)	40.2 (0.97)	20.6 (0.94)	4.6 (0.46)
Child attending private schools	50.8 (1.64)	36.1 (1.58)	11.8 (0.96)	1.3 (0.40)	51.9 (1.61)	36.1 (1.55)	11.0 (1.09)	1.0 (0.27)	57.6 (1.72)	33.0 (1.68)	8.1 (0.91)	1.0 (0.45)
Elementary (kindergarten to grade 8)	55.7 (2.02)	35.3 (1.90)	7.5 (0.86)	1.4 (0.57)	56.2 (1.88)	34.4 (1.80)	9.0 (1.21)	0.5 (0.21)	61.6 (2.39)	30.3 (2.28)	7.3 (1.03)	0.8 (0.28)
Secondary (grades 9 to 12)	41.5 (2.97)	37.7 (2.40)	20.4 (2.30)	1.0 (0.44)	41.2 (3.09)	40.6 (3.03)	15.9 (2.31)	2.2 (0.79)	48.8 (3.22)	38.9 (2.94)	10.0 (1.77)	2.3 (1.30)

NOTE: Includes children enrolled in kindergarten through grade 12. Excludes children whose programs have no classes with lettered grades. Race categories exclude persons of Hispanic origin. Detail may not sum to totals because of rounding. Standard errors appear in parentheses.

SOURCE: U.S. Department of Education, National Center for Education Statistics, Parent and Family Involvement in Education/Civic Involvement Survey, Parent Survey, and Parent and Family Involvement in Education Survey of The National Household Education Surveys Program (PFI/CI-NHES:1996, Parent-NHES:1999, and PFI-NHES:2003). (This table was prepared July 2005.)

Table 137. Average number of Carnegie units earned by public high school graduates in various subject fields, by selected student characteristics: Selected years, 1982 through 2005

Graduation year and selected student characteristic	Total	English	History/ social studies	Mathematics			Science					Foreign languages	Arts	Vocational education[1]	Personal use[2]	Computer related[3]
				Total	Less than algebra	Algebra or higher	Total	General science	Biology	Chemistry	Physics					
1	2	3	4	5	6	7	8	9	10	11	12	13	14	15	16	17
1982 graduates	**21.58 (0.090)**	**3.93 (0.022)**	**3.16 (0.028)**	**2.63 (0.022)**	**0.90 (0.021)**	**1.74 (0.028)**	**2.20 (0.025)**	**0.73 (0.016)**	**0.94 (0.014)**	**0.34 (0.010)**	**0.17 (0.008)**	**0.99 (0.029)**	**1.47 (0.035)**	**4.62 (0.061)**	**2.58 (0.048)**	**0.12 (0.007)**
Sex																
Male	21.40 (0.108)	3.88 (0.026)	3.16 (0.034)	2.71 (0.030)	0.94 (0.026)	1.77 (0.039)	2.27 (0.031)	0.76 (0.018)	0.91 (0.016)	0.36 (0.014)	0.23 (0.012)	0.80 (0.030)	1.29 (0.044)	4.60 (0.076)	2.69 (0.056)	0.14 (0.012)
Female	21.75 (0.101)	3.98 (0.026)	3.15 (0.029)	2.57 (0.024)	0.86 (0.025)	1.71 (0.032)	2.13 (0.029)	0.71 (0.017)	0.97 (0.017)	0.33 (0.013)	0.12 (0.008)	1.17 (0.036)	1.63 (0.044)	4.64 (0.072)	2.48 (0.049)	0.11 (0.007)
Race/ethnicity																
White	21.69 (0.107)	3.90 (0.025)	3.19 (0.032)	2.68 (0.026)	0.77 (0.023)	1.91 (0.032)	2.27 (0.029)	0.73 (0.017)	0.97 (0.015)	0.38 (0.013)	0.20 (0.010)	1.06 (0.033)	1.53 (0.042)	4.53 (0.071)	2.52 (0.052)	0.13 (0.009)
Black	21.15 (0.169)	4.08 (0.050)	3.08 (0.054)	2.61 (0.043)	1.36 (0.053)	1.25 (0.066)	2.06 (0.049)	0.81 (0.033)	0.90 (0.033)	0.26 (0.023)	0.09 (0.011)	0.72 (0.067)	1.26 (0.063)	4.75 (0.136)	2.60 (0.094)	0.12 (0.016)
Hispanic	21.23 (0.122)	3.94 (0.037)	3.00 (0.037)	2.33 (0.040)	1.21 (0.037)	1.12 (0.047)	1.80 (0.038)	0.75 (0.026)	0.81 (0.025)	0.16 (0.012)	0.07 (0.007)	0.77 (0.042)	1.29 (0.054)	5.22 (0.111)	2.87 (0.081)	0.08 (0.010)
Asian/Pacific Islander	22.46 (0.216)	4.01 (0.091)	3.16 (0.094)	3.15 (0.095)	0.71 (0.083)	2.44 (0.132)	2.64 (0.125)	0.51 (0.061)	1.11 (0.048)	0.61 (0.046)	0.42 (0.048)	1.79 (0.105)	1.31 (0.124)	3.34 (0.226)	3.05 (0.146)	0.22 (0.057)
American Indian/Alaska Native	21.45 (0.330)	3.98 (0.114)	3.25 (0.207)	2.35 (0.129)	1.23 (0.148)	1.12 (0.213)	2.04 (0.090)	0.67 (0.087)	0.84 (0.124)	0.42 (0.087)	0.12 (0.039)	0.48 (0.117)	1.72 (0.338)	4.77 (0.233)	2.84 (0.128)	0.06 (0.024)
Academic track																
Academic[4]	21.75 (0.092)	4.11 (0.026)	3.32 (0.032)	3.04 (0.024)	0.73 (0.027)	2.30 (0.037)	2.65 (0.032)	0.73 (0.018)	1.13 (0.017)	0.53 (0.016)	0.26 (0.012)	1.54 (0.042)	1.91 (0.050)	2.55 (0.042)	2.62 (0.058)	0.10 (0.006)
Vocational[5]	20.21 (0.108)	3.44 (0.035)	2.63 (0.032)	1.80 (0.029)	1.09 (0.036)	0.71 (0.030)	1.32 (0.026)	0.69 (0.023)	0.57 (0.023)	0.04 (0.006)	0.02 (0.006)	0.18 (0.015)	0.59 (0.029)	7.74 (0.082)	2.51 (0.065)	0.12 (0.016)
Both[6]	22.89 (0.196)	4.04 (0.037)	3.33 (0.046)	2.69 (0.041)	1.02 (0.036)	1.67 (0.054)	2.17 (0.037)	0.79 (0.023)	0.94 (0.019)	0.29 (0.018)	0.14 (0.015)	0.75 (0.036)	1.41 (0.055)	6.03 (0.091)	2.47 (0.064)	0.18 (0.020)
Neither[7]	18.73 (0.141)	3.58 (0.054)	2.70 (0.054)	1.73 (0.045)	1.08 (0.055)	0.65 (0.060)	1.33 (0.051)	0.69 (0.037)	0.59 (0.035)	0.03 (0.008)	0.02 (0.007)	0.22 (0.027)	0.85 (0.063)	5.23 (0.137)	3.06 (0.115)	0.05 (0.011)
1987 graduates	**23.00 (0.157)**	**4.12 (0.022)**	**3.32 (0.037)**	**3.01 (0.029)**	**0.86 (0.030)**	**2.14 (0.042)**	**2.55 (0.046)**	**0.76 (0.033)**	**1.10 (0.020)**	**0.47 (0.015)**	**0.21 (0.011)**	**1.35 (0.049)**	**1.44 (0.044)**	**4.55 (0.084)**	**2.67 (0.073)**	**0.47 (0.022)**
Sex																
Male	22.88 (0.162)	4.08 (0.021)	3.29 (0.037)	3.05 (0.029)	0.91 (0.032)	2.14 (0.045)	2.59 (0.049)	0.79 (0.032)	1.05 (0.021)	0.47 (0.016)	0.26 (0.013)	1.16 (0.051)	1.24 (0.046)	4.64 (0.089)	2.83 (0.081)	0.47 (0.023)
Female	23.12 (0.156)	4.15 (0.026)	3.35 (0.041)	2.96 (0.030)	0.82 (0.032)	2.15 (0.045)	2.52 (0.048)	0.74 (0.035)	1.14 (0.022)	0.47 (0.017)	0.17 (0.012)	1.53 (0.051)	1.63 (0.050)	4.47 (0.094)	2.51 (0.069)	0.47 (0.023)
Race/ethnicity																
White	23.11 (0.189)	4.08 (0.028)	3.29 (0.045)	3.01 (0.034)	0.74 (0.031)	2.27 (0.050)	2.61 (0.058)	0.75 (0.040)	1.12 (0.025)	0.50 (0.020)	0.23 (0.012)	1.38 (0.055)	1.50 (0.055)	4.65 (0.107)	2.60 (0.082)	0.49 (0.027)
Black	22.40 (0.251)	4.22 (0.038)	3.34 (0.073)	2.99 (0.060)	1.40 (0.074)	1.59 (0.054)	2.33 (0.060)	0.90 (0.051)	1.01 (0.036)	0.31 (0.021)	0.10 (0.012)	1.08 (0.094)	1.20 (0.064)	4.52 (0.130)	2.73 (0.120)	0.39 (0.032)
Hispanic	22.84 (0.162)	4.30 (0.055)	3.22 (0.061)	2.81 (0.056)	1.30 (0.049)	1.50 (0.039)	2.24 (0.045)	0.78 (0.028)	1.07 (0.028)	0.29 (0.015)	0.10 (0.013)	1.25 (0.071)	1.34 (0.056)	4.49 (0.169)	3.19 (0.096)	0.42 (0.031)
Asian/Pacific Islander	24.47 (0.332)	4.37 (0.076)	3.65 (0.163)	3.71 (0.094)	0.53 (0.072)	3.18 (0.143)	3.14 (0.116)	0.59 (0.048)	1.17 (0.027)	0.87 (0.069)	0.50 (0.045)	2.07 (0.105)	1.18 (0.077)	3.11 (0.221)	3.23 (0.185)	0.58 (0.033)
American Indian/Alaska Native	23.23 (0.153)	4.22 (0.033)	3.18 (0.044)	2.98 (0.113)	1.35 (0.145)	1.63 (0.097)	2.44 (0.104)	0.81 (0.041)	1.22 (0.073)	0.32 (0.035)	0.09 (0.027)	0.75 (0.138)	1.68 (0.112)	4.92 (0.125)	3.06 (0.050)	0.39 (0.058)
Academic track																
Academic[4]	23.20 (0.153)	4.26 (0.029)	3.55 (0.045)	3.33 (0.031)	0.65 (0.034)	2.68 (0.051)	2.97 (0.053)	0.73 (0.031)	1.23 (0.024)	0.68 (0.022)	0.32 (0.014)	1.92 (0.066)	1.87 (0.059)	2.57 (0.071)	2.73 (0.081)	0.38 (0.017)
Vocational[5]	21.07 (0.161)	3.62 (0.032)	2.59 (0.040)	2.00 (0.029)	1.29 (0.051)	0.71 (0.041)	1.48 (0.047)	0.74 (0.053)	0.70 (0.040)	0.03 (0.006)	0.01 (0.003)	0.18 (0.024)	0.47 (0.031)	8.07 (0.155)	2.67 (0.112)	0.39 (0.038)
Both[6]	23.53 (0.179)	4.11 (0.025)	3.29 (0.031)	2.93 (0.026)	0.97 (0.045)	1.96 (0.056)	2.37 (0.051)	0.81 (0.038)	1.07 (0.028)	0.35 (0.016)	0.14 (0.011)	1.01 (0.043)	1.20 (0.054)	6.09 (0.085)	2.53 (0.068)	0.64 (0.034)
Neither[7]	19.56 (0.199)	3.55 (0.050)	2.45 (0.071)	2.11 (0.082)	1.62 (0.100)	0.49 (0.094)	1.47 (0.046)	0.84 (0.075)	0.59 (0.051)	0.03 (0.011)	0.00 (0.004)	0.18 (0.040)	0.76 (0.067)	5.10 (0.233)	3.93 (0.249)	0.17 (0.031)
1990 graduates	**23.53 (0.127)**	**4.19 (0.034)**	**3.47 (0.040)**	**3.15 (0.028)**	**0.90 (0.032)**	**2.25 (0.040)**	**2.75 (0.028)**	**0.85 (0.026)**	**1.14 (0.019)**	**0.53 (0.014)**	**0.23 (0.010)**	**1.54 (0.041)**	**1.55 (0.045)**	**4.19 (0.079)**	**2.68 (0.073)**	**0.54 (0.021)**
Sex																
Male	23.35 (0.133)	4.13 (0.035)	3.45 (0.041)	3.16 (0.028)	0.96 (0.038)	2.20 (0.048)	2.78 (0.033)	0.88 (0.027)	1.11 (0.021)	0.52 (0.017)	0.28 (0.012)	1.33 (0.040)	1.31 (0.047)	4.32 (0.084)	2.87 (0.077)	0.50 (0.020)
Female	23.69 (0.132)	4.25 (0.036)	3.50 (0.041)	3.14 (0.033)	0.85 (0.032)	2.29 (0.039)	2.73 (0.027)	0.83 (0.027)	1.17 (0.019)	0.53 (0.014)	0.19 (0.010)	1.72 (0.045)	1.76 (0.050)	4.08 (0.087)	2.51 (0.072)	0.57 (0.026)
Race/ethnicity																
White	23.54 (0.133)	4.12 (0.036)	3.46 (0.045)	3.13 (0.032)	0.80 (0.033)	2.33 (0.041)	2.80 (0.033)	0.84 (0.022)	1.15 (0.020)	0.55 (0.016)	0.25 (0.011)	1.58 (0.049)	1.61 (0.056)	4.22 (0.085)	2.61 (0.076)	0.52 (0.023)
Black	23.40 (0.255)	4.34 (0.044)	3.49 (0.058)	3.20 (0.064)	1.25 (0.059)	1.95 (0.071)	2.68 (0.061)	0.98 (0.068)	1.11 (0.042)	0.42 (0.024)	0.16 (0.020)	1.20 (0.075)	1.34 (0.052)	4.41 (0.166)	2.74 (0.124)	0.60 (0.055)
Hispanic	23.83 (0.210)	4.51 (0.139)	3.42 (0.071)	3.13 (0.058)	1.30 (0.076)	1.83 (0.090)	2.50 (0.046)	0.83 (0.041)	1.10 (0.034)	0.42 (0.034)	0.14 (0.016)	1.57 (0.060)	1.48 (0.072)	4.12 (0.150)	3.10 (0.103)	0.58 (0.048)
Asian/Pacific Islander	24.07 (0.236)	4.50 (0.117)	3.70 (0.126)	3.52 (0.060)	0.70 (0.121)	2.82 (0.159)	2.97 (0.114)	0.68 (0.080)	1.12 (0.085)	0.74 (0.057)	0.42 (0.047)	2.06 (0.150)	1.29 (0.084)	3.07 (0.337)	2.96 (0.221)	0.54 (0.043)
American Indian/Alaska Native	22.64 (0.267)	4.08 (0.092)	3.34 (0.083)	3.04 (0.152)	1.03 (0.084)	2.01 (0.143)	2.48 (0.175)	0.83 (0.090)	1.09 (0.090)	0.42 (0.072)	0.15 (0.039)	1.15 (0.188)	1.11 (0.126)	4.62 (0.190)	2.81 (0.148)	0.60 (0.130)
Academic track																
Academic[4]	23.53 (0.137)	4.30 (0.044)	3.65 (0.047)	3.37 (0.025)	0.68 (0.031)	2.70 (0.038)	3.06 (0.033)	0.81 (0.033)	1.23 (0.021)	0.70 (0.018)	0.32 (0.012)	2.02 (0.046)	1.93 (0.054)	2.41 (0.048)	2.78 (0.086)	0.42 (0.019)
Vocational[5]	21.73 (0.244)	3.60 (0.063)	2.58 (0.063)	2.07 (0.054)	1.54 (0.080)	0.53 (0.045)	1.62 (0.047)	0.87 (0.031)	0.71 (0.040)	0.03 (0.008)	0.01 (0.004)	0.17 (0.029)	0.42 (0.042)	8.68 (0.179)	2.59 (0.092)	0.46 (0.067)
Both[6]	23.92 (0.128)	4.14 (0.026)	3.38 (0.038)	3.02 (0.031)	1.12 (0.037)	1.90 (0.044)	2.51 (0.031)	0.92 (0.024)	1.09 (0.024)	0.36 (0.015)	0.14 (0.010)	1.07 (0.040)	1.17 (0.049)	6.10 (0.056)	2.53 (0.073)	0.73 (0.034)
Neither[7]	19.81 (0.564)	3.63 (0.153)	2.59 (0.076)	2.01 (0.139)	1.57 (0.176)	0.44 (0.072)	1.47 (0.085)	0.79 (0.080)	0.60 (0.090)	0.04 (0.020)	0.03 (0.018)	0.21 (0.060)	0.79 (0.249)	5.81 (0.529)	3.29 (0.338)	0.36 (0.063)

See notes at end of table.

Table 137. Average number of Carnegie units earned by public high school graduates in various subject fields, by selected student characteristics: Selected years, 1982 through 2005—Continued

Graduation year and selected student characteristic	Total	English	History/ social studies	Mathematics			Science					Foreign languages	Arts	Vocational education[1]	Personal use[2]	Computer related[3]
				Total	Less than algebra	Algebra or higher	Total	General science	Biology	Chemistry	Physics					
1	2	3	4	5	6	7	8	9	10	11	12	13	14	15	16	17
1994 graduates	**24.17** (0.144)	**4.29** (0.028)	**3.55** (0.041)	**3.33** (0.021)	**0.76** (0.029)	**2.57** (0.036)	**3.04** (0.028)	**0.88** (0.024)	**1.26** (0.018)	**0.62** (0.013)	**0.28** (0.011)	**1.71** (0.033)	**1.66** (0.041)	**3.96** (0.068)	**2.63** (0.077)	**0.64** (0.025)
Sex																
Male	23.79 (0.146)	4.26 (0.028)	3.51 (0.041)	3.32 (0.022)	0.85 (0.032)	2.48 (0.038)	3.03 (0.030)	0.91 (0.026)	1.20 (0.020)	0.59 (0.015)	0.32 (0.014)	1.49 (0.034)	1.43 (0.038)	4.13 (0.074)	2.83 (0.081)	0.63 (0.027)
Female	24.11 (0.147)	4.32 (0.030)	3.59 (0.041)	3.34 (0.023)	0.68 (0.029)	2.66 (0.037)	3.06 (0.028)	0.86 (0.024)	1.31 (0.018)	0.64 (0.014)	0.24 (0.010)	1.93 (0.034)	1.87 (0.051)	3.80 (0.074)	2.44 (0.078)	0.65 (0.027)
Race/ethnicity																
White	24.08 (0.183)	4.23 (0.035)	3.56 (0.049)	3.36 (0.030)	0.70 (0.034)	2.66 (0.041)	3.13 (0.032)	0.89 (0.030)	1.29 (0.022)	0.65 (0.014)	0.30 (0.014)	1.76 (0.039)	1.74 (0.049)	3.96 (0.080)	2.61 (0.096)	0.63 (0.028)
Black	23.28 (0.132)	4.36 (0.034)	3.51 (0.039)	3.23 (0.030)	1.09 (0.067)	2.14 (0.079)	2.80 (0.042)	0.92 (0.051)	1.21 (0.036)	0.49 (0.028)	0.17 (0.013)	1.35 (0.052)	1.36 (0.066)	4.29 (0.121)	2.69 (0.101)	0.64 (0.039)
Hispanic	23.71 (0.131)	4.61 (0.075)	3.45 (0.046)	3.28 (0.041)	0.96 (0.030)	2.32 (0.057)	2.69 (0.046)	0.83 (0.058)	1.19 (0.027)	0.49 (0.047)	0.17 (0.021)	1.73 (0.062)	1.51 (0.046)	3.87 (0.124)	2.93 (0.086)	0.76 (0.044)
Asian/Pacific Islander	23.84 (0.256)	4.60 (0.091)	3.66 (0.097)	3.66 (0.082)	0.67 (0.113)	2.98 (0.189)	3.35 (0.131)	0.80 (0.034)	1.22 (0.042)	0.81 (0.062)	0.48 (0.058)	2.09 (0.085)	1.32 (0.121)	3.01 (0.236)	2.78 (0.123)	0.71 (0.034)
American Indian/Alaska Native	23.40 (0.541)	4.27 (0.113)	3.57 (0.201)	3.11 (0.038)	0.94 (0.108)	2.17 (0.125)	2.82 (0.073)	0.91 (0.057)	1.28 (0.069)	0.50 (0.065)	0.13 (0.039)	1.30 (0.150)	2.01 (0.351)	4.27 (0.256)	3.12 (0.355)	0.53 (0.217)
Academic track																
Academic[4]	23.86 (0.133)	4.37 (0.034)	3.69 (0.042)	3.52 (0.022)	0.58 (0.030)	2.94 (0.039)	3.32 (0.031)	0.83 (0.027)	1.34 (0.021)	0.77 (0.017)	0.37 (0.014)	2.14 (0.040)	2.05 (0.054)	2.28 (0.045)	2.71 (0.071)	0.50 (0.022)
Vocational[5]	21.20 (0.252)	3.70 (0.055)	2.49 (0.071)	2.20 (0.052)	1.56 (0.066)	0.64 (0.048)	1.69 (0.064)	0.80 (0.049)	0.83 (0.046)	0.03 (0.006)	0.02 (0.007)	0.14 (0.029)	0.34 (0.036)	8.64 (0.214)	2.41 (0.141)	0.55 (0.055)
Both[6]	24.41 (0.149)	4.23 (0.029)	3.45 (0.039)	3.17 (0.023)	0.96 (0.039)	2.21 (0.045)	2.78 (0.031)	0.96 (0.026)	1.19 (0.021)	0.45 (0.024)	0.17 (0.010)	1.24 (0.037)	1.21 (0.036)	6.01 (0.059)	2.52 (0.095)	0.85 (0.032)
Neither[7]	20.56 (0.476)	3.54 (0.130)	2.24 (0.075)	2.25 (0.073)	1.71 (0.121)	0.54 (0.100)	1.53 (0.078)	0.82 (0.076)	0.63 (0.075)	0.05 (0.024)	0.02 (0.011)	0.19 (0.063)	0.56 (0.105)	6.51 (0.347)	4.47 (0.497)	0.33 (0.063)
1998 graduates	**25.14** (0.162)	**4.25** (0.037)	**3.74** (0.038)	**3.40** (0.024)	**0.67** (0.022)	**2.73** (0.034)	**3.12** (0.026)	**0.89** (0.024)	**1.26** (0.021)	**0.66** (0.015)	**0.31** (0.015)	**1.85** (0.039)	**1.90** (0.079)	**3.99** (0.098)	**2.89** (0.076)	**0.74** (0.033)
Sex																
Male	24.64 (0.162)	4.19 (0.038)	3.68 (0.040)	3.37 (0.024)	0.74 (0.023)	2.64 (0.034)	3.09 (0.028)	0.93 (0.026)	1.20 (0.021)	0.62 (0.014)	0.33 (0.018)	1.62 (0.040)	1.61 (0.072)	4.25 (0.099)	3.12 (0.079)	0.78 (0.032)
Female	25.04 (0.165)	4.31 (0.039)	3.80 (0.036)	3.42 (0.025)	0.62 (0.023)	2.80 (0.035)	3.17 (0.029)	0.87 (0.023)	1.32 (0.023)	0.70 (0.018)	0.28 (0.015)	2.06 (0.041)	2.15 (0.094)	3.77 (0.114)	2.67 (0.080)	0.71 (0.038)
Race/ethnicity																
White	24.87 (0.178)	4.19 (0.049)	3.77 (0.046)	3.40 (0.028)	0.57 (0.022)	2.84 (0.035)	3.18 (0.028)	0.87 (0.027)	1.28 (0.025)	0.69 (0.017)	0.33 (0.019)	1.90 (0.049)	2.00 (0.078)	3.97 (0.114)	2.80 (0.088)	0.73 (0.037)
Black	24.37 (0.250)	4.28 (0.045)	3.69 (0.050)	3.42 (0.042)	0.90 (0.053)	2.53 (0.072)	3.03 (0.064)	0.97 (0.045)	1.24 (0.038)	0.58 (0.025)	0.22 (0.022)	1.58 (0.062)	1.57 (0.152)	4.33 (0.149)	2.94 (0.080)	0.84 (0.064)
Hispanic	24.69 (0.218)	4.51 (0.055)	3.60 (0.051)	3.28 (0.041)	1.05 (0.055)	2.23 (0.061)	2.81 (0.054)	0.97 (0.042)	1.13 (0.026)	0.50 (0.036)	0.20 (0.020)	1.78 (0.055)	1.78 (0.113)	3.97 (0.121)	3.36 (0.121)	0.71 (0.046)
Asian/Pacific Islander	24.67 (0.195)	4.37 (0.068)	3.92 (0.086)	3.62 (0.029)	0.65 (0.134)	2.97 (0.136)	3.43 (0.079)	0.81 (0.041)	1.26 (0.027)	0.83 (0.037)	0.51 (0.036)	2.29 (0.129)	1.52 (0.056)	3.15 (0.222)	2.95 (0.208)	0.67 (0.050)
American Indian/Alaska Native	23.81 (0.350)	4.18 (0.082)	3.67 (0.093)	3.10 (0.081)	0.90 (0.067)	2.20 (0.100)	2.68 (0.081)	0.98 (0.070)	1.07 (0.056)	0.49 (0.038)	0.15 (0.024)	1.45 (0.132)	1.94 (0.146)	4.02 (0.164)	3.40 (0.212)	0.67 (0.059)
Academic track																
Academic[4]	24.61 (0.160)	4.33 (0.034)	3.87 (0.038)	3.54 (0.023)	0.53 (0.024)	3.00 (0.036)	3.34 (0.030)	0.84 (0.028)	1.33 (0.027)	0.78 (0.016)	0.38 (0.020)	2.24 (0.041)	2.41 (0.122)	2.22 (0.061)	2.97 (0.088)	0.52 (0.024)
Vocational[5]	22.10 (0.299)	3.46 (0.092)	2.55 (0.079)	2.17 (0.076)	1.30 (0.073)	0.87 (0.065)	1.69 (0.087)	1.05 (0.088)	0.59 (0.068)	0.03 (0.007)	0.01 (0.005)	0.14 (0.025)	0.47 (0.068)	9.12 (0.239)	3.01 (0.227)	0.81 (0.085)
Both[6]	25.38 (0.190)	4.20 (0.045)	3.66 (0.045)	3.30 (0.030)	0.81 (0.027)	2.49 (0.042)	2.94 (0.038)	0.96 (0.030)	1.20 (0.026)	0.54 (0.022)	0.23 (0.016)	1.45 (0.042)	1.31 (0.048)	6.06 (0.083)	2.73 (0.078)	1.03 (0.048)
Neither[7]	20.39 (0.371)	3.21 (0.146)	2.32 (0.235)	2.19 (0.083)	1.59 (0.137)	0.60 (0.087)	1.58 (0.095)	0.88 (0.089)	0.58 (0.052)	0.04 (0.017)	0.08 (0.031)	0.20 (0.047)	0.55 (0.063)	5.64 (0.598)	5.82 (0.379)	0.51 (0.069)
2000 graduates	**26.05** (0.201)	**4.39** (0.035)	**3.83** (0.033)	**3.56** (0.028)	**0.61** (0.028)	**2.95** (0.038)	**3.20** (0.038)	**0.85** (0.028)	**1.29** (0.028)	**0.69** (0.018)	**0.36** (0.017)	**1.95** (0.044)	**2.03** (0.054)	**4.21** (0.123)	**2.88** (0.065)	**0.83** (0.032)
Sex																
Male	26.23 (0.206)	4.31 (0.034)	3.76 (0.032)	3.53 (0.031)	0.68 (0.032)	2.86 (0.046)	3.16 (0.039)	0.88 (0.028)	1.20 (0.029)	0.65 (0.017)	0.40 (0.018)	1.71 (0.044)	1.75 (0.051)	4.60 (0.154)	3.09 (0.070)	0.93 (0.036)
Female	26.46 (0.203)	4.46 (0.038)	3.89 (0.035)	3.58 (0.028)	0.55 (0.026)	3.03 (0.036)	3.25 (0.040)	0.82 (0.030)	1.36 (0.029)	0.73 (0.020)	0.33 (0.017)	2.18 (0.049)	2.30 (0.065)	3.82 (0.104)	2.69 (0.063)	0.74 (0.034)
Race/ethnicity																
White	26.57 (0.252)	4.32 (0.037)	3.86 (0.037)	3.56 (0.031)	0.58 (0.032)	2.98 (0.043)	3.24 (0.038)	0.84 (0.031)	1.30 (0.034)	0.70 (0.020)	0.38 (0.020)	1.98 (0.053)	2.12 (0.068)	4.34 (0.164)	2.79 (0.075)	0.81 (0.036)
Black	26.28 (0.242)	4.43 (0.078)	3.75 (0.067)	3.54 (0.042)	0.72 (0.062)	2.82 (0.059)	3.13 (0.058)	0.91 (0.043)	1.26 (0.040)	0.65 (0.027)	0.27 (0.020)	1.70 (0.071)	1.95 (0.134)	4.29 (0.173)	2.98 (0.093)	0.85 (0.055)
Hispanic	25.91 (0.323)	4.69 (0.106)	3.77 (0.075)	3.42 (0.074)	0.74 (0.051)	2.68 (0.107)	2.87 (0.112)	0.85 (0.046)	1.19 (0.067)	0.58 (0.055)	0.24 (0.026)	1.90 (0.070)	1.77 (0.063)	3.83 (0.124)	3.21 (0.147)	0.89 (0.056)
Asian/Pacific Islander	26.66 (0.327)	4.57 (0.069)	3.77 (0.051)	3.96 (0.095)	0.35 (0.035)	3.61 (0.106)	3.71 (0.153)	0.71 (0.082)	1.36 (0.060)	0.96 (0.048)	0.65 (0.037)	2.51 (0.083)	1.79 (0.084)	2.82 (0.160)	3.09 (0.184)	0.92 (0.111)
American Indian/Alaska Native	26.03 (0.315)	4.12 (0.064)	3.75 (0.100)	3.29 (0.083)	0.91 (0.164)	2.38 (0.178)	2.88 (0.112)	0.98 (0.037)	1.25 (0.080)	0.45 (0.044)	0.19 (0.042)	1.40 (0.105)	1.99 (0.220)	4.79 (0.429)	2.89 (0.230)	0.96 (0.074)
Academic track																
Academic[4]	25.82 (0.186)	4.47 (0.040)	3.93 (0.043)	3.70 (0.034)	0.49 (0.024)	3.21 (0.042)	3.39 (0.042)	0.81 (0.033)	1.35 (0.033)	0.80 (0.023)	0.42 (0.019)	2.32 (0.050)	2.52 (0.072)	2.28 (0.049)	2.96 (0.075)	0.54 (0.024)
Vocational[5]	24.13 (0.369)	3.33 (0.131)	2.62 (0.121)	2.11 (0.086)	1.28 (0.120)	0.82 (0.100)	1.61 (0.116)	1.05 (0.069)	0.65 (0.091)	0.06 (0.018)	0.05 (0.026)	0.15 (0.042)	0.57 (0.062)	9.56 (0.337)	3.50 (0.249)	1.17 (0.220)
Both[6]	27.16 (0.248)	4.33 (0.035)	3.76 (0.034)	3.45 (0.032)	0.74 (0.040)	2.71 (0.054)	3.04 (0.047)	0.89 (0.031)	1.24 (0.033)	0.59 (0.024)	0.30 (0.024)	1.56 (0.049)	1.47 (0.057)	6.46 (0.170)	2.74 (0.074)	1.20 (0.046)
Neither[7]	22.41 (0.500)	3.50 (0.088)	1.86 (0.142)	2.27 (0.088)	1.76 (0.141)	0.51 (0.101)	1.59 (0.099)	1.04 (0.097)	0.48 (0.082)	0.04 (0.018)	0.02 (0.011)	0.20 (0.056)	0.93 (0.096)	5.52 (0.443)	5.72 (0.506)	0.29 (0.051)

See notes at end of table.

Table 137. Average number of Carnegie units earned by public high school graduates in various subject fields, by selected student characteristics: Selected years, 1982 through 2005—Continued

Graduation year and selected student characteristic	Total	English	History/ social studies	Mathematics			Science					Foreign languages	Arts	Vocational education[1]	Personal use[2]	Computer related[3]
				Total	Less than algebra	Algebra or higher	Total	General science	Biology	Chemistry	Physics					
1	2	3	4	5	6	7	8	9	10	11	12	13	14	15	16	17
2005 graduates......	26.68 (0.100)	4.42 (0.022)	3.98 (0.025)	3.67 (0.016)	0.49 (0.015)	3.19 (0.020)	3.34 (0.019)	0.95 (0.019)	1.28 (0.016)	0.74 (0.010)	0.35 (0.011)	1.97 (0.024)	2.05 (0.035)	4.01 (0.058)	3.23 (0.040)	0.93 (0.021)
Sex																
Male......	26.50 (0.104)	4.36 (0.025)	3.91 (0.028)	3.65 (0.020)	0.54 (0.016)	3.10 (0.024)	3.29 (0.023)	0.97 (0.019)	1.19 (0.016)	0.70 (0.011)	0.39 (0.013)	1.76 (0.026)	1.71 (0.035)	4.35 (0.069)	3.47 (0.043)	1.09 (0.023)
Female......	26.84 (0.103)	4.48 (0.021)	4.05 (0.025)	3.70 (0.016)	0.44 (0.016)	3.26 (0.021)	3.40 (0.020)	0.92 (0.020)	1.37 (0.017)	0.78 (0.011)	0.32 (0.012)	2.16 (0.025)	2.38 (0.045)	3.68 (0.068)	3.00 (0.044)	0.79 (0.024)
Race/ethnicity																
White......	26.87 (0.125)	4.32 (0.029)	4.02 (0.030)	3.69 (0.021)	0.44 (0.017)	3.24 (0.026)	3.43 (0.021)	0.96 (0.022)	1.31 (0.018)	0.76 (0.013)	0.38 (0.012)	2.01 (0.027)	2.17 (0.043)	4.12 (0.075)	3.10 (0.049)	0.90 (0.026)
Black......	26.57 (0.150)	4.54 (0.028)	3.98 (0.045)	3.71 (0.032)	0.63 (0.034)	3.08 (0.047)	3.21 (0.036)	0.99 (0.037)	1.27 (0.025)	0.68 (0.017)	0.27 (0.025)	1.71 (0.040)	1.77 (0.056)	4.11 (0.111)	3.53 (0.076)	1.07 (0.033)
Hispanic......	25.91 (0.142)	4.80 (0.037)	3.75 (0.039)	3.49 (0.032)	0.65 (0.034)	2.83 (0.034)	2.92 (0.035)	0.92 (0.031)	1.11 (0.020)	0.63 (0.022)	0.24 (0.017)	1.88 (0.035)	1.78 (0.054)	3.69 (0.098)	3.62 (0.058)	1.00 (0.040)
Asian/Pacific Islander......	26.32 (0.189)	4.51 (0.057)	3.94 (0.042)	3.90 (0.004)	0.27 (0.025)	3.62 (0.041)	3.63 (0.057)	0.74 (0.060)	1.31 (0.035)	0.97 (0.027)	0.56 (0.032)	2.43 (0.068)	1.80 (0.076)	2.91 (0.144)	3.21 (0.086)	0.94 (0.054)
American Indian/Alaska Native......	26.48 (0.443)	4.44 (0.098)	4.06 (0.129)	3.53 (0.141)	0.69 (0.087)	2.84 (0.182)	3.02 (0.072)	1.04 (0.060)	1.28 (0.063)	0.52 (0.052)	0.17 (0.036)	1.44 (0.105)	2.44 (0.179)	4.20 (0.258)	3.36 (0.291)	0.82 (0.102)
Other......	26.09 (0.374)	4.39 (0.095)	3.87 (0.066)	3.72 (0.087)	0.26 (0.043)	3.46 (0.099)	3.50 (0.083)	0.93 (0.057)	1.35 (0.060)	0.81 (0.049)	0.37 (0.047)	2.31 (0.088)	2.12 (0.232)	2.93 (0.263)	3.26 (0.207)	0.72 (0.119)
Academic track																
Academic[4]......	26.53 (0.092)	4.48 (0.024)	4.09 (0.026)	3.78 (0.017)	0.42 (0.014)	3.36 (0.021)	3.50 (0.021)	0.92 (0.017)	1.35 (0.018)	0.82 (0.010)	0.40 (0.012)	2.20 (0.024)	2.29 (0.043)	2.92 (0.039)	3.27 (0.044)	0.80 (0.018)
Vocational[5]......	24.01 (0.288)	3.56 (0.064)	2.78 (0.051)	2.42 (0.041)	0.96 (0.062)	1.45 (0.074)	1.87 (0.045)	0.90 (0.057)	0.75 (0.037)	0.16 (0.037)	0.05 (0.021)	0.50 (0.052)	1.32 (0.135)	8.16 (0.215)	3.40 (0.148)	0.77 (0.079)
Both[6]......	27.93 (0.132)	4.36 (0.024)	3.90 (0.032)	3.63 (0.021)	0.61 (0.026)	3.02 (0.029)	3.17 (0.027)	1.06 (0.030)	1.19 (0.018)	0.62 (0.015)	0.29 (0.016)	1.51 (0.030)	1.34 (0.032)	7.01 (0.091)	3.00 (0.045)	1.42 (0.046)
Neither[7]......	22.73 (0.213)	4.08 (0.095)	2.92 (0.044)	2.44 (0.045)	0.87 (0.057)	1.57 (0.056)	2.01 (0.033)	0.84 (0.045)	0.85 (0.033)	0.21 (0.037)	0.09 (0.021)	1.02 (0.051)	2.35 (0.125)	3.86 (0.128)	4.05 (0.177)	0.64 (0.033)

[1]Includes general labor market preparation, consumer and homemaking education, agriculture, business, marketing, health, occupational home economics, trade and industry, and technical courses.

[2]Includes general skills, personal health and physical education, religion, military sciences, special education, and other courses not included in other subject fields.

[3]Though shown separately here, computer-related courses are also included in the mathematics and vocational categories.

[4]Includes students who complete at least 12 Carnegie units in academic courses, but less than 3 Carnegie units in any specific labor market preparation field.

[5]Includes students who complete at least 3 Carnegie units in a specific labor market preparation field, but less than 12 Carnegie units in academic courses.

[6]Includes students who complete at least 12 Carnegie units in academic courses and at least 3 Carnegie units in a specific labor market preparation field.

[7]Includes students who complete less than 12 Carnegie units in academic courses and less than 3 Carnegie units in a specific labor market preparation field.

NOTE: The Carnegie unit is a standard of measurement that represents one credit for the completion of a 1-year course. Data differ slightly from figures appearing in other NCES reports because of differences in taxonomies and case exclusion criteria. Race categories exclude persons of Hispanic origin. Detail may not sum to totals because of rounding. Standard errors appear in parentheses.

SOURCE: U.S. Department of Education, National Center for Education Statistics, High School and Beyond Longitudinal Study of 1980 Sophomores (HS&B-So:80/82), "High School Transcript Study"; and 1987, 1990, 1994, 1998, 2000, and 2005 High School Transcript Study (HSTS). (This table was prepared January 2007.)

Table 138. Average number of Carnegie units earned by public high school graduates in vocational education courses, by selected student characteristics: Selected years, 1982 through 2005

Graduation year and selected student characteristic	Total	General labor market preparation	Consumer and homemaking education	Specific labor market preparation								
				Total[1]	Agriculture	Business	Marketing	Health	Occupational home economics	Trade and industrial	Technical/ communications	Other
1	2	3	4	5	6	7	8	9	10	11	12	13
1982 graduates	4.62 (0.061)	0.94 (0.018)	0.68 (0.020)	3.00 (0.052)	0.22 (0.018)	1.03 (0.027)	0.16 (0.011)	0.05 (0.005)	0.11 (0.007)	1.04 (0.035)	0.21 (0.009)	0.10 (0.012)
Sex												
Male	4.60 (0.076)	0.93 (0.026)	0.30 (0.014)	3.36 (0.071)	0.36 (0.033)	0.47 (0.020)	0.14 (0.013)	0.02 (0.004)	0.06 (0.006)	1.96 (0.064)	0.24 (0.014)	0.01 (#)
Female	4.64 (0.072)	0.95 (0.020)	1.03 (0.031)	2.67 (0.056)	0.08 (0.010)	1.55 (0.043)	0.18 (0.015)	0.08 (0.009)	0.15 (0.012)	0.20 (0.016)	0.18 (0.009)	0.18 (0.023)
Race/ethnicity												
White	4.53 (0.071)	0.92 (0.021)	0.63 (0.023)	2.97 (0.059)	0.24 (0.021)	1.06 (0.032)	0.15 (0.012)	0.04 (0.005)	0.10 (0.008)	0.99 (0.038)	0.22 (0.011)	0.09 (0.015)
Black	4.75 (0.136)	0.97 (0.046)	0.90 (0.053)	2.88 (0.130)	0.09 (0.019)	1.00 (0.071)	0.22 (0.031)	0.11 (0.024)	0.14 (0.024)	0.95 (0.091)	0.15 (0.021)	0.12 (0.040)
Hispanic	5.22 (0.111)	1.01 (0.036)	0.85 (0.045)	3.36 (0.106)	0.23 (0.034)	1.00 (0.054)	0.17 (0.020)	0.07 (0.021)	0.13 (0.017)	1.38 (0.094)	0.15 (0.014)	0.12 (0.028)
Asian/Pacific Islander	3.34 (0.226)	1.01 (0.129)	0.30 (0.035)	2.03 (0.157)	0.03 (0.015)	0.58 (0.105)	0.04 (0.023)	0.03 (0.013)	0.06 (0.020)	0.88 (0.095)	0.30 (0.061)	0.02 (0.017)
American Indian/Alaska Native	4.77 (0.233)	0.90 (0.093)	0.47 (0.076)	3.40 (0.257)	0.25 (0.086)	0.74 (0.145)	0.14 (0.045)	0.08 (0.041)	0.06 (0.031)	1.88 (0.441)	0.13 (0.038)	0.03 (0.013)
Academic track												
Academic[2]	2.55 (0.042)	0.84 (0.022)	0.60 (0.025)	1.12 (0.020)	0.04 (0.005)	0.48 (0.017)	0.03 (0.003)	0.02 (0.003)	0.06 (0.006)	0.28 (0.013)	0.17 (0.009)	0.02 (#)
Vocational[3]	7.74 (0.082)	1.02 (0.034)	0.78 (0.036)	5.94 (0.084)	0.58 (0.056)	1.68 (0.075)	0.33 (0.032)	0.08 (0.016)	0.17 (0.018)	2.43 (0.107)	0.21 (0.019)	0.24 (0.048)
Both[4]	6.03 (0.091)	0.86 (0.025)	0.57 (0.033)	4.60 (0.066)	0.29 (0.040)	1.66 (0.059)	0.29 (0.027)	0.09 (0.012)	0.15 (0.016)	1.57 (0.066)	0.29 (0.021)	0.14 (0.028)
Neither[5]	5.23 (0.137)	1.92 (0.130)	1.62 (0.089)	1.68 (0.042)	0.11 (0.030)	0.74 (0.050)	0.09 (0.018)	0.05 (0.024)	0.13 (0.027)	0.37 (0.039)	0.10 (0.016)	0.07 (0.019)
1987 graduates	4.55 (0.084)	0.83 (0.026)	0.61 (0.032)	3.11 (0.060)	0.19 (0.028)	0.96 (0.037)	0.16 (0.014)	0.08 (0.005)	0.11 (0.008)	0.96 (0.036)	0.43 (0.021)	0.11 (0.013)
Sex												
Male	4.64 (0.089)	0.83 (0.035)	0.33 (0.025)	3.47 (0.065)	0.33 (0.047)	0.56 (0.024)	0.13 (0.014)	0.02 (0.003)	0.08 (0.008)	1.73 (0.072)	0.47 (0.023)	0.03 (0.011)
Female	4.47 (0.094)	0.83 (0.023)	0.86 (0.046)	2.77 (0.067)	0.07 (0.012)	1.34 (0.052)	0.19 (0.019)	0.12 (0.010)	0.14 (0.012)	0.23 (0.021)	0.39 (0.022)	0.18 (0.020)
Race/ethnicity												
White	4.65 (0.107)	0.84 (0.030)	0.60 (0.041)	3.20 (0.074)	0.24 (0.039)	0.97 (0.046)	0.16 (0.017)	0.07 (0.005)	0.11 (0.010)	1.00 (0.047)	0.47 (0.026)	0.10 (0.013)
Black	4.52 (0.130)	0.86 (0.026)	0.73 (0.040)	2.92 (0.113)	0.10 (0.016)	1.00 (0.068)	0.17 (0.021)	0.14 (0.027)	0.14 (0.016)	0.76 (0.053)	0.28 (0.032)	0.14 (0.017)
Hispanic	4.49 (0.169)	0.93 (0.069)	0.62 (0.062)	2.95 (0.101)	0.06 (0.020)	0.97 (0.090)	0.16 (0.037)	0.08 (0.020)	0.11 (0.017)	1.00 (0.054)	0.32 (0.020)	0.11 (0.024)
Asian/Pacific Islander	3.11 (0.221)	0.63 (0.064)	0.35 (0.062)	2.13 (0.141)	0.01 (0.006)	0.63 (0.088)	0.13 (0.076)	0.09 (0.020)	0.08 (0.017)	0.47 (0.047)	0.56 (0.065)	0.04 (0.013)
American Indian/Alaska Native	4.92 (0.125)	0.82 (0.048)	0.65 (0.045)	3.45 (0.112)	0.20 (0.036)	1.04 (0.094)	0.08 (0.041)	0.09 (0.021)	0.11 (0.032)	1.32 (0.079)	0.44 (0.062)	0.03 (0.007)
Academic track												
Academic[2]	2.57 (0.071)	0.76 (0.028)	0.57 (0.034)	1.23 (0.027)	0.02 (0.003)	0.45 (0.015)	0.04 (0.005)	0.02 (0.004)	0.04 (0.004)	0.24 (0.011)	0.37 (0.016)	0.02 (0.003)
Vocational[3]	8.07 (0.155)	0.90 (0.038)	0.77 (0.040)	6.39 (0.121)	0.59 (0.087)	1.40 (0.087)	0.38 (0.053)	0.18 (0.037)	0.25 (0.034)	2.60 (0.077)	0.35 (0.047)	0.34 (0.049)
Both[4]	6.09 (0.085)	0.86 (0.039)	0.55 (0.040)	4.69 (0.051)	0.30 (0.057)	1.54 (0.061)	0.27 (0.024)	0.11 (0.011)	0.17 (0.015)	1.43 (0.080)	0.56 (0.029)	0.15 (0.024)
Neither[5]	5.10 (0.233)	1.77 (0.155)	1.72 (0.280)	1.62 (0.052)	0.07 (0.022)	0.60 (0.089)	0.09 (0.036)	0.05 (0.018)	0.11 (0.029)	0.37 (0.064)	0.13 (0.026)	0.10 (0.046)
1990 graduates	4.19 (0.079)	0.73 (0.023)	0.57 (0.026)	2.89 (0.065)	0.20 (0.022)	0.88 (0.035)	0.16 (0.012)	0.04 (0.005)	0.10 (0.009)	0.87 (0.040)	0.41 (0.013)	0.10 (0.010)
Sex												
Male	4.32 (0.084)	0.70 (0.025)	0.33 (0.020)	3.28 (0.074)	0.31 (0.039)	0.57 (0.030)	0.14 (0.014)	0.02 (0.004)	0.07 (0.009)	1.59 (0.064)	0.43 (0.016)	0.02 (0.006)
Female	4.08 (0.087)	0.76 (0.025)	0.79 (0.038)	2.53 (0.073)	0.09 (0.015)	1.16 (0.049)	0.18 (0.014)	0.06 (0.009)	0.13 (0.012)	0.22 (0.026)	0.39 (0.014)	0.17 (0.016)
Race/ethnicity												
White	4.22 (0.085)	0.71 (0.029)	0.55 (0.030)	2.97 (0.075)	0.24 (0.027)	0.85 (0.033)	0.16 (0.014)	0.04 (0.006)	0.09 (0.009)	0.95 (0.047)	0.40 (0.015)	0.09 (0.011)
Black	4.41 (0.166)	0.82 (0.035)	0.80 (0.066)	2.79 (0.135)	0.06 (0.010)	1.05 (0.080)	0.17 (0.023)	0.04 (0.014)	0.15 (0.023)	0.64 (0.059)	0.40 (0.036)	0.16 (0.029)
Hispanic	4.12 (0.150)	0.75 (0.048)	0.53 (0.058)	2.85 (0.126)	0.15 (0.034)	0.93 (0.105)	0.19 (0.026)	0.07 (0.007)	0.11 (0.023)	0.75 (0.061)	0.41 (0.048)	0.18 (0.042)
Asian/Pacific Islander	3.07 (0.337)	0.69 (0.124)	0.31 (0.030)	2.07 (0.201)	0.04 (0.017)	0.65 (0.057)	0.05 (0.013)	0.01 (0.005)	0.03 (0.010)	0.72 (0.178)	0.48 (0.032)	0.03 (0.010)
American Indian/Alaska Native	4.62 (0.190)	0.74 (0.141)	0.72 (0.123)	3.16 (0.157)	0.36 (0.113)	0.95 (0.091)	0.15 (0.056)	0.02 (0.021)	0.07 (0.041)	0.95 (0.193)	0.44 (0.098)	0.02 (0.008)
Academic track												
Academic[2]	2.41 (0.048)	0.67 (0.022)	0.55 (0.030)	1.19 (0.022)	0.03 (0.004)	0.46 (0.019)	0.04 (0.004)	0.01 (0.003)	0.04 (0.005)	0.22 (0.011)	0.34 (0.013)	0.02 (0.003)
Vocational[3]	8.68 (0.179)	1.00 (0.071)	0.74 (0.051)	6.95 (0.171)	0.86 (0.111)	1.22 (0.089)	0.28 (0.056)	0.10 (0.030)	0.26 (0.052)	3.10 (0.231)	0.28 (0.026)	0.30 (0.061)
Both[4]	6.10 (0.056)	0.72 (0.026)	0.57 (0.030)	4.81 (0.048)	0.35 (0.044)	1.47 (0.062)	0.33 (0.027)	0.08 (0.010)	0.16 (0.014)	1.50 (0.060)	0.53 (0.024)	0.19 (0.021)
Neither[5]	5.81 (0.529)	2.81 (0.570)	1.26 (0.232)	1.74 (0.075)	0.10 (0.040)	0.46 (0.054)	0.04 (0.017)	0.04 (0.023)	0.08 (0.032)	0.54 (0.092)	0.32 (0.020)	0.04 (0.020)

See notes at end of table.

Table 138. Average number of Carnegie units earned by public high school graduates in vocational education courses, by selected student characteristics: Selected years, 1982 through 2005—Continued

Graduation year and selected student characteristic	Total	General labor market preparation	Consumer and homemaking education	Specific labor market preparation								
				Total[1]	Agriculture	Business	Marketing	Health	Occupational home economics	Trade and industrial	Technical/ communications	Other
1	2	3	4	5	6	7	8	9	10	11	12	13
1994 graduates	3.96 (0.068)	0.64 (0.021)	0.52 (0.028)	2.79 (0.057)	0.24 (0.023)	0.88 (0.028)	0.18 (0.015)	0.08 (0.007)	0.13 (0.012)	0.70 (0.027)	0.35 (0.017)	0.09 (0.009)
Sex												
Male	4.13 (0.074)	0.70 (0.026)	0.35 (0.026)	3.08 (0.063)	0.37 (0.036)	0.66 (0.023)	0.14 (0.012)	0.03 (0.004)	0.08 (0.008)	1.25 (0.051)	0.36 (0.020)	0.03 (0.005)
Female	3.80 (0.074)	0.58 (0.021)	0.70 (0.035)	2.52 (0.061)	0.11 (0.013)	1.09 (0.039)	0.22 (0.018)	0.12 (0.012)	0.18 (0.017)	0.17 (0.010)	0.34 (0.017)	0.15 (0.015)
Race/ethnicity												
White	3.96 (0.080)	0.63 (0.026)	0.51 (0.028)	2.81 (0.067)	0.27 (0.031)	0.87 (0.031)	0.19 (0.018)	0.08 (0.009)	0.11 (0.012)	0.72 (0.032)	0.35 (0.021)	0.07 (0.010)
Black	4.29 (0.121)	0.72 (0.050)	0.62 (0.036)	2.94 (0.097)	0.13 (0.028)	1.01 (0.050)	0.20 (0.029)	0.11 (0.020)	0.23 (0.023)	0.60 (0.053)	0.29 (0.025)	0.18 (0.023)
Hispanic	3.87 (0.124)	0.64 (0.037)	0.48 (0.027)	2.75 (0.123)	0.13 (0.022)	0.93 (0.064)	0.15 (0.018)	0.07 (0.011)	0.14 (0.026)	0.65 (0.071)	0.36 (0.028)	0.17 (0.024)
Asian/Pacific Islander	3.01 (0.236)	0.51 (0.043)	0.36 (0.057)	2.13 (0.151)	0.14 (0.053)	0.70 (0.046)	0.11 (0.017)	0.06 (0.009)	0.10 (0.028)	0.50 (0.057)	0.46 (0.029)	0.03 (0.009)
American Indian/Alaska Native	4.26 (0.256)	0.80 (0.104)	0.62 (0.091)	2.84 (0.183)	0.36 (0.147)	0.89 (0.197)	0.05 (0.024)	0.15 (0.071)	0.14 (0.044)	0.57 (0.120)	0.44 (0.076)	0.05 (0.043)
Academic track												
Academic[2]	2.28 (0.045)	0.58 (0.022)	0.49 (0.033)	1.21 (0.020)	0.04 (0.003)	0.51 (0.018)	0.05 (0.005)	0.03 (0.004)	0.05 (0.006)	0.20 (0.008)	0.28 (0.015)	0.02 (0.002)
Vocational[3]	8.64 (0.214)	1.00 (0.077)	0.78 (0.083)	6.86 (0.237)	0.90 (0.119)	1.17 (0.124)	0.34 (0.068)	0.08 (0.023)	0.26 (0.053)	2.89 (0.203)	0.26 (0.048)	0.29 (0.077)
Both[4]	6.01 (0.059)	0.66 (0.027)	0.54 (0.031)	4.81 (0.042)	0.48 (0.047)	1.41 (0.042)	0.37 (0.031)	0.16 (0.015)	0.23 (0.022)	1.25 (0.056)	0.46 (0.020)	0.18 (0.018)
Neither[5]	6.51 (0.347)	3.91 (0.432)	1.08 (0.157)	1.52 (0.097)	0.05 (0.015)	0.48 (0.092)	0.08 (0.030)	0.02 (0.015)	0.07 (0.026)	0.46 (0.057)	0.16 (0.047)	0.06 (0.033)
1998 graduates	3.99 (0.098)	0.61 (0.028)	0.51 (0.034)	2.87 (0.074)	0.20 (0.031)	0.70 (0.032)	0.16 (0.014)	0.14 (0.030)	0.16 (0.013)	0.78 (0.042)	0.51 (0.035)	0.07 (0.009)
Sex												
Male	4.25 (0.099)	0.67 (0.028)	0.35 (0.029)	3.23 (0.085)	0.27 (0.039)	0.59 (0.029)	0.15 (0.012)	0.06 (0.019)	0.10 (0.011)	1.37 (0.077)	0.53 (0.039)	0.02 (0.003)
Female	3.77 (0.114)	0.57 (0.032)	0.66 (0.041)	2.54 (0.080)	0.14 (0.026)	0.80 (0.038)	0.18 (0.018)	0.22 (0.041)	0.21 (0.019)	0.23 (0.013)	0.49 (0.035)	0.12 (0.017)
Race/ethnicity												
White	3.97 (0.114)	0.58 (0.031)	0.49 (0.039)	2.90 (0.087)	0.24 (0.039)	0.69 (0.035)	0.15 (0.015)	0.11 (0.016)	0.14 (0.011)	0.83 (0.053)	0.51 (0.042)	0.06 (0.010)
Black	4.33 (0.149)	0.70 (0.037)	0.68 (0.062)	2.95 (0.115)	0.09 (0.015)	0.83 (0.072)	0.24 (0.029)	0.29 (0.098)	0.23 (0.048)	0.56 (0.040)	0.47 (0.040)	0.11 (0.021)
Hispanic	3.97 (0.121)	0.66 (0.048)	0.49 (0.060)	2.82 (0.104)	0.16 (0.043)	0.64 (0.052)	0.18 (0.021)	0.16 (0.070)	0.17 (0.025)	0.75 (0.047)	0.51 (0.058)	0.10 (0.026)
Asian/Pacific Islander	3.15 (0.222)	0.58 (0.107)	0.27 (0.033)	2.30 (0.119)	0.09 (0.033)	0.64 (0.040)	0.13 (0.017)	0.15 (0.082)	0.14 (0.021)	0.57 (0.094)	0.49 (0.047)	0.02 (0.005)
American Indian/Alaska Native	4.02 (0.164)	0.54 (0.063)	0.55 (0.083)	2.92 (0.162)	0.19 (0.041)	0.70 (0.084)	0.14 (0.035)	0.06 (0.035)	0.14 (0.044)	0.98 (0.167)	0.51 (0.081)	0.03 (0.014)
Academic track												
Academic[2]	2.22 (0.061)	0.54 (0.028)	0.49 (0.032)	1.19 (0.027)	0.03 (0.004)	0.41 (0.023)	0.05 (0.006)	0.03 (0.004)	0.07 (0.007)	0.22 (0.010)	0.33 (0.024)	0.02 (0.003)
Vocational[3]	9.12 (0.239)	1.40 (0.180)	0.75 (0.117)	6.97 (0.166)	0.62 (0.123)	0.64 (0.061)	0.29 (0.058)	0.11 (0.032)	0.36 (0.079)	3.36 (0.407)	0.66 (0.091)	0.29 (0.167)
Both[4]	6.06 (0.083)	0.62 (0.032)	0.52 (0.041)	4.92 (0.060)	0.41 (0.067)	1.10 (0.049)	0.31 (0.028)	0.29 (0.067)	0.27 (0.027)	1.39 (0.075)	0.74 (0.050)	0.14 (0.016)
Neither[5]	5.64 (0.598)	2.91 (0.592)	1.20 (0.119)	1.53 (0.144)	0.10 (0.031)	0.43 (0.063)	0.06 (0.024)	0.02 (0.014)	0.07 (0.025)	0.31 (0.080)	0.19 (0.055)	0.06 (0.024)
2000 graduates	4.21 (0.123)	0.69 (0.035)	0.49 (0.023)	3.03 (0.106)	0.25 (0.029)	0.74 (0.040)	0.16 (0.013)	0.13 (0.018)	0.17 (0.016)	0.80 (0.057)	0.61 (0.027)	0.08 (0.009)
Sex												
Male	4.85 (0.154)	0.76 (0.042)	0.33 (0.018)	3.76 (0.135)	0.34 (0.041)	0.65 (0.040)	0.14 (0.013)	0.06 (0.012)	0.12 (0.012)	1.38 (0.098)	0.72 (0.032)	0.02 (0.005)
Female	3.99 (0.104)	0.61 (0.032)	0.64 (0.032)	2.74 (0.086)	0.16 (0.022)	0.83 (0.043)	0.17 (0.015)	0.20 (0.025)	0.23 (0.021)	0.25 (0.020)	0.52 (0.026)	0.13 (0.016)
Race/ethnicity												
White	4.59 (0.164)	0.69 (0.045)	0.49 (0.026)	3.41 (0.137)	0.31 (0.039)	0.73 (0.048)	0.14 (0.015)	0.12 (0.016)	0.18 (0.018)	0.90 (0.077)	0.63 (0.034)	0.07 (0.001)
Black	4.54 (0.173)	0.77 (0.049)	0.67 (0.052)	3.10 (0.125)	0.12 (0.027)	0.88 (0.063)	0.22 (0.034)	0.15 (0.022)	0.16 (0.024)	0.51 (0.043)	0.53 (0.041)	0.16 (0.030)
Hispanic	4.16 (0.124)	0.67 (0.054)	0.37 (0.038)	3.12 (0.148)	0.14 (0.021)	0.75 (0.067)	0.18 (0.032)	0.23 (0.101)	0.19 (0.030)	0.65 (0.051)	0.54 (0.028)	0.07 (0.020)
Asian/Pacific Islander	3.13 (0.160)	0.45 (0.055)	0.25 (0.033)	2.42 (0.146)	0.06 (0.014)	0.50 (0.051)	0.10 (0.031)	0.14 (0.038)	0.09 (0.018)	0.43 (0.054)	0.74 (0.103)	0.02 (0.008)
American Indian/Alaska Native	5.51 (0.429)	0.75 (0.117)	0.68 (0.081)	4.08 (0.394)	0.37 (0.131)	0.72 (0.086)	0.14 (0.037)	0.07 (0.025)	0.23 (0.115)	0.99 (0.235)	0.68 (0.087)	0.07 (0.035)
Academic track												
Academic[2]	2.35 (0.049)	0.61 (0.031)	0.47 (0.021)	1.28 (0.024)	0.03 (0.004)	0.39 (0.021)	0.03 (0.004)	0.03 (0.005)	0.08 (0.009)	0.21 (0.010)	0.38 (0.020)	0.02 (0.003)
Vocational[3]	10.56 (0.337)	1.24 (0.272)	0.59 (0.070)	8.73 (0.365)	0.79 (0.149)	0.63 (0.117)	0.27 (0.064)	0.12 (0.050)	0.35 (0.086)	4.06 (0.438)	0.87 (0.095)	0.14 (0.057)
Both[4]	6.84 (0.170)	0.75 (0.053)	0.50 (0.031)	5.59 (0.132)	0.51 (0.058)	1.20 (0.066)	0.31 (0.025)	0.27 (0.041)	0.29 (0.029)	1.43 (0.115)	0.90 (0.047)	0.15 (0.018)
Neither[5]	5.82 (0.443)	2.83 (0.297)	1.36 (0.331)	1.62 (0.100)	0.05 (0.023)	0.13 (0.032)	0.05 (0.034)	0.04 (0.030)	0.19 (0.053)	0.40 (0.077)	0.32 (0.049)	0.06 (0.023)

See notes at end of table.

Table 138. Average number of Carnegie units earned by public high school graduates in vocational education courses, by selected student characteristics: Selected years, 1982 through 2005—Continued

Graduation year and selected student characteristic	Total	General labor market preparation	Consumer and homemaking education	Specific labor market preparation								
				Total[1]	Agriculture	Business	Marketing	Health	Occupational home economics	Trade and industrial	Technical/ communications	Other
1	2	3	4	5	6	7	8	9	10	11	12	13
2005 graduates	4.01 (0.058)	0.46 (0.021)	0.51 (0.015)	3.03 (0.047)	0.23 (0.014)	0.60 (0.016)	0.15 (0.010)	0.15 (0.010)	0.23 (0.012)	0.69 (0.022)	0.79 (0.020)	0.07 (0.004)
Sex												
Male	4.35 (0.059)	0.52 (0.025)	0.34 (0.015)	3.49 (0.051)	0.32 (0.020)	0.58 (0.017)	0.15 (0.011)	0.06 (0.006)	0.16 (0.009)	1.19 (0.036)	0.90 (0.022)	0.02 (0.003)
Female	3.68 (0.068)	0.41 (0.020)	0.68 (0.020)	2.59 (0.053)	0.15 (0.012)	0.62 (0.018)	0.15 (0.010)	0.23 (0.016)	0.30 (0.017)	0.22 (0.011)	0.68 (0.021)	0.13 (0.007)
Race/ethnicity												
White	4.12 (0.075)	0.46 (0.024)	0.53 (0.019)	3.13 (0.061)	0.29 (0.017)	0.58 (0.018)	0.15 (0.012)	0.13 (0.011)	0.22 (0.014)	0.78 (0.029)	0.80 (0.024)	0.07 (0.005)
Black	4.11 (0.111)	0.50 (0.036)	0.60 (0.033)	3.01 (0.079)	0.10 (0.018)	0.76 (0.036)	0.18 (0.015)	0.24 (0.022)	0.27 (0.029)	0.44 (0.026)	0.81 (0.047)	0.10 (0.012)
Hispanic	3.69 (0.098)	0.45 (0.029)	0.43 (0.026)	2.81 (0.089)	0.14 (0.018)	0.62 (0.033)	0.14 (0.015)	0.15 (0.020)	0.26 (0.029)	0.63 (0.042)	0.69 (0.027)	0.09 (0.010)
Asian/Pacific Islander	2.91 (0.144)	0.33 (0.046)	0.31 (0.029)	2.27 (0.119)	0.06 (0.019)	0.43 (0.038)	0.13 (0.023)	0.10 (0.022)	0.16 (0.019)	0.47 (0.075)	0.83 (0.047)	0.05 (0.010)
American Indian/Alaska Native	4.20 (0.258)	0.67 (0.170)	0.62 (0.081)	2.91 (0.178)	0.45 (0.129)	0.47 (0.074)	0.08 (0.033)	0.10 (0.029)	0.23 (0.045)	0.57 (0.094)	0.78 (0.110)	0.11 (0.048)
Other	2.93 (0.263)	0.32 (0.047)	0.33 (0.044)	2.28 (0.233)	0.13 (0.086)	0.45 (0.098)	0.20 (0.058)	0.05 (0.023)	0.24 (0.070)	0.29 (0.058)	0.83 (0.109)	0.03 (0.016)
Academic track												
Academic[2]	2.92 (0.039)	0.40 (0.021)	0.53 (0.017)	1.99 (0.026)	0.09 (0.005)	0.48 (0.011)	0.09 (0.006)	0.07 (0.005)	0.19 (0.012)	0.31 (0.011)	0.67 (0.016)	0.04 (0.002)
Vocational[3]	8.16 (0.215)	1.07 (0.155)	0.45 (0.044)	6.63 (0.168)	0.93 (0.167)	0.56 (0.066)	0.22 (0.066)	0.20 (0.054)	0.47 (0.081)	3.19 (0.215)	0.56 (0.062)	0.19 (0.073)
Both[4]	7.01 (0.091)	0.56 (0.033)	0.44 (0.019)	6.01 (0.081)	0.61 (0.044)	0.99 (0.038)	0.32 (0.024)	0.40 (0.032)	0.34 (0.029)	1.67 (0.053)	1.20 (0.046)	0.16 (0.013)
Neither[5]	3.86 (0.128)	0.85 (0.084)	0.76 (0.044)	2.24 (0.080)	0.25 (0.044)	0.38 (0.025)	0.14 (0.023)	0.07 (0.013)	0.23 (0.025)	0.49 (0.031)	0.52 (0.032)	0.08 (0.016)

#Rounds to zero.
[1]Includes unclassified courses not shown separately.
[2]Includes students who complete at least 12 Carnegie units in academic courses, but less than 3 Carnegie units in any specific labor market preparation field.
[3]Includes students who complete at least 3 Carnegie units in a specific labor market preparation field, but less than 12 Carnegie units in academic courses.
[4]Includes students who complete at least 12 Carnegie units in academic courses and at least 3 Carnegie units in a specific labor market preparation field.
[5]Includes students who complete less than 12 Carnegie units in academic courses and less than 3 Carnegie units in a specific labor market preparation field.

NOTE: The Carnegie unit is a standard of measurement that represents one credit for the completion of a 1-year course. Data differ slightly from figures appearing in other NCES reports because of differences in taxonomies and case exclusion criteria. Race categories exclude persons of Hispanic origin. Detail may not sum to totals because of rounding. Standard errors appear in parentheses.
SOURCE: U.S. Department of Education, National Center for Education Statistics, High School and Beyond Longitudinal Study of 1980 Sophomores (HS&B-So:80/82), "High School Transcript Study"; and 1987, 1990, 1994, 1998, 2000, and 2005 High School Transcript Study (HSTS). (This table was prepared January 2007.)

Table 139. Percentage of public and private high school graduates taking selected mathematics and science courses in high school, by sex and race/ethnicity: Selected years, 1982 through 2005

Course (Carnegie units)	1982	1987	1990	1994	1998	2000	2005 Total	Sex Male	Sex Female	Race/ethnicity White	Race/ethnicity Black	Race/ethnicity Hispanic	Race/ethnicity Asian/Pacific Islander	Race/ethnicity American Indian/Alaska Native	Race/ethnicity Other
1	2	3	4	5	6	7	8	9	10	11	12	13	14	15	16
Mathematics[1]															
Any mathematics (1.0)	98.5 (0.21)	98.9 (0.24)	99.9 (0.05)	99.8 (0.05)	99.8 (0.06)	99.8 (0.04)	99.9 (0.02)	99.9 (0.03)	100.0 (0.02)	99.9 (0.02)	100.0 (0.02)	99.9 (0.05)	100.0 (#)	100.0 (#)	100.0 (#)
Algebra I (1.0)[2]	55.2 (1.01)	58.8 (1.19)	63.7 (1.54)	65.8 (1.31)	62.8 (1.42)	61.7 (1.66)	62.8 (1.04)	61.5 (1.09)	64.1 (1.13)	60.9 (1.19)	71.8 (1.67)	65.6 (1.73)	58.0 (2.61)	67.9 (4.89)	69.3 (3.49)
Geometry (1.0)	47.1 (0.99)	58.6 (0.97)	63.2 (1.38)	70.0 (1.26)	75.1 (1.06)	78.3 (1.09)	83.3 (0.65)	81.4 (0.71)	85.2 (0.68)	83.4 (0.80)	84.7 (1.03)	80.5 (1.18)	86.1 (1.31)	74.2 (3.20)	89.2 (2.04)
Algebra II (0.5)[3]	39.9 (0.93)	49.0 (1.69)	52.9 (1.32)	61.1 (1.39)	61.7 (1.77)	67.8 (1.43)	70.3 (1.00)	67.1 (1.11)	73.3 (1.02)	71.2 (1.21)	69.2 (1.64)	62.7 (1.54)	78.3 (3.40)	67.5 (3.58)	81.8 (3.43)
Trigonometry (0.5)	8.1 (0.54)	11.5 (1.54)	9.6 (1.07)	11.7 (1.16)	8.9 (1.07)	7.5 (1.31)	8.3 (0.88)	8.1 (0.91)	8.6 (0.91)	9.6 (1.18)	3.9 (0.59)	4.8 (0.83)	9.4 (1.59)	10.4 (4.80)	13.9 (3.18)
Analysis/pre-calculus (0.5)	6.2 (0.46)	12.8 (0.92)	13.3 (0.95)	17.3 (0.86)	23.1 (1.44)	26.7 (1.40)	29.5 (0.98)	28.0 (1.02)	30.8 (1.05)	32.0 (1.18)	17.9 (1.61)	20.5 (1.42)	48.8 (2.85)	15.9 (3.04)	31.6 (5.16)
Statistics/probability (0.5)	1.0 (0.16)	1.1 (0.31)	1.0 (0.21)	2.0 (0.33)	3.7 (0.54)	5.7 (0.86)	7.7 (0.53)	7.7 (0.57)	7.8 (0.55)	8.5 (0.65)	5.8 (0.84)	3.4 (0.48)	13.0 (1.21)	2.8 (0.99)	12.0 (3.04)
Calculus (1.0)	5.0 (0.43)	6.1 (0.49)	6.5 (0.46)	9.3 (0.56)	11.0 (0.85)	11.6 (0.73)	13.6 (0.53)	14.0 (0.63)	13.2 (0.59)	15.3 (0.62)	5.5 (0.53)	6.3 (0.65)	29.8 (1.65)	7.9 (2.59)	16.6 (2.49)
AP calculus (1.0)	1.6 (0.26)	3.4 (0.47)	4.1 (0.44)	7.0 (0.53)	6.7 (0.49)	7.9 (0.58)	9.2 (0.44)	9.8 (0.54)	8.7 (0.44)	10.1 (0.52)	2.9 (0.35)	5.0 (0.51)	24.6 (1.75)	2.8 (1.42)	10.9 (1.78)
Science[1]															
Any science (1.0)	96.4 (0.39)	97.8 (0.32)	99.3 (0.14)	99.5 (0.07)	99.5 (0.09)	99.5 (0.11)	99.6 (0.09)	99.5 (0.11)	99.6 (0.10)	99.7 (0.07)	99.7 (0.12)	99.1 (0.30)	99.3 (0.34)	98.3 (0.73)	100.0 (#)
Biology (1.0)	77.4 (0.87)	86.1 (1.01)	90.9 (0.97)	93.2 (0.97)	92.7 (0.67)	91.2 (1.00)	92.3 (0.63)	90.8 (0.71)	93.7 (0.61)	92.6 (0.72)	93.6 (0.59)	89.1 (1.24)	92.1 (1.83)	92.1 (1.80)	93.9 (2.41)
AP/honors biology (1.0)	10.0 (0.64)	9.4 (0.72)	10.1 (1.02)	11.9 (0.93)	16.2 (1.31)	16.3 (1.46)	16.0 (0.83)	13.9 (0.81)	18.0 (0.94)	17.0 (0.99)	12.0 (1.37)	11.8 (1.38)	24.0 (2.14)	8.3 (1.87)	21.6 (3.61)
Chemistry (1.0)	32.1 (0.84)	44.2 (1.29)	48.9 (1.23)	55.8 (1.04)	60.4 (1.29)	62.0 (1.47)	66.2 (0.92)	62.5 (1.04)	69.7 (0.99)	67.1 (1.04)	63.6 (1.61)	59.2 (2.13)	79.4 (1.60)	49.3 (4.75)	77.8 (3.11)
AP/honors chemistry (1.0)	3.0 (0.33)	3.5 (0.42)	3.5 (0.47)	3.9 (0.53)	4.7 (0.50)	5.8 (0.85)	7.6 (0.53)	7.6 (0.59)	7.6 (0.55)	8.0 (0.58)	4.0 (0.98)	5.7 (0.82)	17.2 (1.41)	4.8 (1.67)	10.5 (2.57)
Physics (1.0)	15.0 (0.62)	20.0 (0.88)	21.5 (0.81)	24.5 (0.87)	28.8 (1.49)	31.4 (1.16)	32.7 (0.92)	34.8 (0.91)	30.8 (1.11)	34.6 (0.88)	25.8 (2.31)	23.3 (1.68)	49.9 (2.42)	18.2 (3.91)	42.7 (4.08)
AP/honors physics (1.0)	1.2 (0.17)	1.8 (0.30)	2.0 (0.38)	2.7 (0.34)	3.0 (0.37)	3.9 (0.61)	5.3 (0.33)	6.6 (0.42)	4.1 (0.34)	5.6 (0.41)	2.5 (0.37)	3.4 (0.50)	14.2 (1.64)	1.5 (0.89)	8.3 (2.24)
Engineering (1.0)	1.2 (0.21)	2.6 (0.63)	4.2 (1.01)	4.5 (0.78)	6.7 (1.75)	3.9 (0.91)	4.3 (0.51)	4.6 (0.59)	4.0 (0.47)	4.4 (0.62)	4.8 (0.87)	3.3 (0.58)	3.7 (1.11)	3.8 (2.15)	4.2 (1.58)
Astronomy (0.5)	1.2 (0.24)	1.0 (0.17)	1.2 (0.31)	1.7 (0.50)	1.9 (0.46)	2.8 (0.59)	2.8 (0.37)	2.9 (0.42)	2.7 (0.34)	3.3 (0.47)	1.4 (0.24)	1.2 (0.25)	3.1 (0.68)	3.5 (1.61)	1.2 (1.19)
Geology/earth science (0.5)	13.6 (1.04)	13.4 (1.66)	24.7 (2.42)	22.9 (2.41)	20.7 (2.34)	17.4 (1.86)	23.1 (1.48)	23.9 (1.51)	22.4 (1.54)	24.0 (1.86)	24.3 (1.88)	19.6 (1.67)	16.2 (2.39)	22.7 (4.39)	23.2 (4.80)
Biology and chemistry (2.0)	29.3 (0.83)	41.4 (1.22)	47.5 (1.23)	53.7 (1.20)	59.0 (1.22)	59.4 (1.49)	64.3 (0.97)	60.3 (1.08)	68.0 (1.03)	65.3 (1.10)	62.0 (1.60)	57.2 (2.29)	75.5 (2.16)	48.0 (4.74)	73.9 (3.97)
Biology, chemistry, and physics (3.0)	11.2 (0.51)	16.5 (0.77)	18.8 (0.70)	21.4 (0.84)	25.4 (1.32)	25.1 (1.09)	27.3 (0.88)	28.2 (0.85)	26.5 (1.10)	29.0 (0.85)	21.3 (2.25)	18.9 (1.63)	42.8 (2.49)	14.1 (3.33)	33.2 (4.02)

#Rounds to zero.

[1]These data only report the percentage of students who earned the indicated credit (0.5 = one semester; 1.0 = one academic year) in each course while in high school and do not count those students who took these courses prior to entering high school.

[2]Excludes pre-algebra.

[3]Includes algebra/trigonometry and algebra/geometry.

NOTE: The Carnegie unit is a standard of measurement that represents one credit for the completion of a 1-year course. Data differ slightly from figures appearing in other NCES reports because of differences in taxonomies and case exclusion criteria.

Some data have been revised from previously published figures. Race categories exclude persons of Hispanic origin. Standard errors appear in parentheses.

SOURCE: U.S. Department of Education, National Center for Education Statistics, High School and Beyond Longitudinal Study of 1980 Sophomores (HS&B-So:80/82), "High School Transcript Study"; and 1987, 1990, 1994, 1998, 2000, and 2005 High School Transcript Study (HSTS). (This table was prepared January 2007.)

Table 140. Percentage of public and private high school graduates earning minimum credits in selected combinations of academic courses, by sex and race/ethnicity: Selected years, 1982 through 2005

Year of graduation and course combination taken[1]	All students		Sex				Race/ethnicity									
			Male		Female		White		Black		Hispanic		Asian/Pacific Islander		American Indian/Alaska Native		Other
1	2		3		4		5		6		7		8		9		10
1982 graduates																	
4 Eng, 3 SS, 3 Sci, 3 Math, .5 Comp, and 2 FL[2]	2.0	(0.22)	2.3	(0.31)	1.8	(0.27)	2.4	(0.28)	0.7	(0.28)	0.6	(0.22)	5.8	(1.72)	1.1	(0.77)	—	(†)
4 Eng, 3 SS, 3 Sci, 3 Math, and 2 FL	9.5	(0.57)	9.1	(0.70)	9.9	(0.71)	10.9	(0.69)	5.2	(1.02)	3.9	(0.57)	17.0	(2.49)	3.3	(1.68)	—	(†)
4 Eng, 3 SS, 3 Sci, 3 Math	14.3	(0.66)	15.2	(0.86)	13.4	(0.79)	15.9	(0.79)	11.0	(1.39)	6.7	(0.79)	21.1	(2.65)	8.1	(3.02)	—	(†)
4 Eng, 3 SS, 2 Sci, 2 Math	31.5	(1.07)	31.7	(1.26)	31.3	(1.22)	32.4	(1.21)	30.8	(2.32)	25.6	(1.76)	32.0	(3.40)	23.6	(5.39)	—	(†)
1987 graduates																	
4 Eng, 3 SS, 3 Sci, 3 Math, .5 Comp, and 2 FL[2]	10.6	(0.73)	11.5	(1.01)	9.8	(0.65)	11.3	(0.97)	6.6	(0.91)	5.5	(1.03)	20.5	(2.57)	2.5	(0.86)	—	(†)
4 Eng, 3 SS, 3 Sci, 3 Math, and 2 FL	18.1	(0.91)	18.0	(1.13)	18.3	(1.01)	19.0	(1.10)	12.7	(1.15)	10.8	(1.70)	35.7	(4.49)	4.9	(1.40)	—	(†)
4 Eng, 3 SS, 3 Sci, 3 Math	24.8	(1.03)	25.9	(1.27)	23.7	(1.07)	26.1	(1.21)	19.6	(1.99)	14.5	(1.69)	39.8	(4.51)	24.3	(3.69)	—	(†)
4 Eng, 3 SS, 2 Sci, 2 Math	48.1	(1.74)	48.0	(2.22)	48.4	(1.56)	48.1	(2.15)	48.3	(2.63)	43.9	(1.92)	57.9	(4.82)	61.8	(5.56)	—	(†)
1990 graduates																	
4 Eng, 3 SS, 3 Sci, 3 Math, .5 Comp, and 2 FL[2]	18.0	(1.06)	17.8	(1.16)	18.2	(1.09)	18.6	(1.21)	15.1	(1.66)	17.8	(2.42)	23.3	(2.23)	7.8	(3.33)	—	(†)
4 Eng, 3 SS, 3 Sci, 3 Math, and 2 FL	29.9	(1.26)	28.8	(1.38)	31.0	(1.36)	31.7	(1.46)	22.9	(2.27)	25.4	(2.41)	42.6	(2.95)	9.9	(3.70)	—	(†)
4 Eng, 3 SS, 3 Sci, 3 Math	38.2	(1.50)	38.5	(1.69)	37.9	(1.54)	39.2	(1.63)	39.0	(3.57)	29.8	(2.51)	47.4	(3.04)	19.2	(4.70)	—	(†)
4 Eng, 3 SS, 2 Sci, 2 Math	65.5	(1.96)	64.3	(2.09)	66.4	(1.98)	64.9	(2.28)	71.3	(3.00)	63.7	(3.01)	69.1	(3.90)	46.3	(6.39)	—	(†)
1994 graduates																	
4 Eng, 3 SS, 3 Sci, 3 Math, .5 Comp, and 2 FL[2]	25.1	(1.05)	23.4	(0.93)	26.8	(1.32)	26.4	(1.19)	19.0	(1.45)	27.1	(3.75)	35.5	(2.84)	12.9	(3.09)	—	(†)
4 Eng, 3 SS, 3 Sci, 3 Math, and 2 FL	39.0	(1.12)	35.0	(1.11)	42.7	(1.33)	41.6	(1.32)	29.6	(1.52)	35.6	(2.94)	50.1	(2.39)	22.5	(4.31)	—	(†)
4 Eng, 3 SS, 3 Sci, 3 Math	49.3	(1.45)	47.0	(1.45)	51.5	(1.58)	52.4	(1.67)	43.7	(2.39)	40.3	(3.25)	54.9	(2.46)	46.0	(3.30)	—	(†)
4 Eng, 3 SS, 2 Sci, 2 Math	73.9	(1.50)	71.2	(1.63)	76.4	(1.46)	75.1	(1.69)	74.5	(2.32)	74.7	(2.61)	72.3	(3.62)	76.3	(3.60)	—	(†)
1998 graduates																	
4 Eng, 3 SS, 3 Sci, 3 Math, .5 Comp, and 2 FL[2]	28.6	(1.72)	27.6	(2.12)	30.1	(1.90)	29.6	(1.99)	27.9	(3.36)	20.4	(2.44)	38.6	(4.61)	16.5	(4.65)	—	(†)
4 Eng, 3 SS, 3 Sci, 3 Math, and 2 FL	44.2	(1.92)	40.5	(2.19)	48.2	(2.05)	46.2	(2.16)	40.0	(3.41)	32.0	(2.94)	57.8	(4.51)	28.3	(4.53)	—	(†)
4 Eng, 3 SS, 3 Sci, 3 Math	55.0	(2.44)	52.9	(2.64)	57.8	(2.48)	56.8	(2.69)	55.6	(4.39)	40.0	(3.28)	66.1	(5.69)	40.0	(4.73)	—	(†)
4 Eng, 3 SS, 2 Sci, 2 Math	74.5	(2.18)	72.8	(2.34)	77.0	(2.14)	74.7	(2.64)	76.0	(3.21)	70.1	(2.57)	79.5	(4.76)	76.4	(5.21)	—	(†)
2000 graduates																	
4 Eng, 3 SS, 3 Sci, 3 Math, .5 Comp, and 2 FL[2]	31.0	(1.53)	28.6	(1.59)	33.2	(1.73)	31.5	(1.55)	28.9	(1.65)	28.4	(5.50)	37.8	(5.45)	16.2	(2.69)	—	(†)
4 Eng, 3 SS, 3 Sci, 3 Math, and 2 FL	46.5	(1.46)	40.3	(1.59)	52.1	(1.60)	47.8	(1.56)	44.2	(2.14)	38.4	(5.05)	56.5	(3.13)	25.6	(3.40)	—	(†)
4 Eng, 3 SS, 3 Sci, 3 Math	57.2	(1.58)	52.9	(1.65)	61.1	(1.70)	58.1	(1.70)	62.4	(2.44)	46.4	(5.46)	61.1	(3.11)	40.9	(5.56)	—	(†)
4 Eng, 3 SS, 2 Sci, 2 Math	77.6	(1.58)	74.2	(1.86)	80.6	(1.44)	77.9	(1.84)	81.2	(2.23)	74.1	(3.24)	74.5	(3.05)	71.2	(4.44)	—	(†)
2005 graduates																	
4 Eng, 3 SS, 3 Sci, 3 Math, .5 Comp, and 2 FL[2]	36.2	(1.00)	34.6	(0.97)	37.7	(1.23)	35.8	(1.22)	39.9	(1.72)	33.0	(1.86)	42.9	(2.34)	24.5	(3.48)	36.8	(5.09)
4 Eng, 3 SS, 3 Sci, 3 Math, and 2 FL	52.1	(1.00)	46.8	(1.16)	57.2	(1.01)	53.3	(1.20)	51.4	(1.88)	41.8	(2.07)	63.6	(2.19)	36.2	(3.40)	65.7	(3.12)
4 Eng, 3 SS, 3 Sci, 3 Math	64.7	(1.07)	61.1	(1.26)	68.0	(0.99)	65.9	(1.32)	69.6	(1.83)	49.8	(2.29)	69.1	(2.20)	59.3	(3.30)	72.4	(3.44)
4 Eng, 3 SS, 2 Sci, 2 Math	81.8	(1.02)	79.2	(1.18)	84.3	(0.97)	81.2	(1.33)	88.7	(0.93)	77.2	(1.33)	83.7	(1.72)	81.0	(3.18)	87.2	(2.71)

—Not available.
†Not applicable.
[1]Eng = English; SS = social studies; Sci = science; Comp = computer science; and FL = foreign language.
[2]The National Commission on Excellence in Education recommended that all college-bound high school students take these courses as a minimum.

NOTE: Data differ slightly from figures appearing in other NCES reports because of differences in taxonomies and case exclusion criteria. Race categories exclude persons of Hispanic origin. Standard errors appear in parentheses.
SOURCE: U.S. Department of Education, National Center for Education Statistics, High School and Beyond Longitudinal Study of 1980 Sophomores (HS&B-So:80/82), "High School Transcript Study"; and 1987, 1990, 1994, 1998, 2000, and 2005 High School Transcript Study (HSTS). (This table was prepared January 2007.)

Table 141. Public high schools that offered and students enrolled in dual credit, Advanced Placement, and International Baccalaureate courses, by school characteristics: 2003

School characteristic	Total number of high schools		Percent of public high schools						Total enrollments of public high school students[1]					
			Offered dual credit courses		Offered Advanced Placement courses		Offered International Baccalaureate courses		Dual credit courses		Advanced Placement courses		International Baccalaureate courses	
1	2		3		4		5		6		7		8	
All public high schools	**16,500**	**(120)**	**71**	**(1.4)**	**67**	**(1.1)**	**2**	**(0.4)**	**1,162,000**	**(53,420)**	**1,795,400**	**(54,930)**	**165,100**	**(32,820)**
Enrollment size														
Less than 500	7,400	(120)	63	(2.5)	40	(2.3)	‡	(†)	185,300	(15,590)	81,100	(8,510)	‡	(†)
500 to 1,199	5,000	(80)	75	(1.7)	82	(1.6)	2	(0.6)	335,100	(24,020)	481,000	(26,970)	24,800	(11,180)
1,200 or more	4,100	(80)	82	(1.8)	97	(0.8)	7	(1.1)	641,600	(47,500)	1,233,300	(47,700)	140,200	(29,740)
School locale														
City	2,700	(110)	65	(3.4)	77	(2.9)	6	(1.3)	246,300	(33,160)	548,400	(32,020)	58,700	(15,920)
Urban fringe	4,100	(130)	74	(1.9)	87	(2.2)	4	(0.9)	458,800	(36,290)	853,200	(41,300)	97,600	(26,990)
Town	2,400	(130)	79	(3.3)	72	(3.8)	1 !	(0.6)	201,700	(20,440)	143,200	(10,970)	8,300 !	(4,770)
Rural	7,200	(220)	70	(2.3)	50	(2.2)	‡	(†)	255,200	(18,150)	250,600	(14,900)	‡	(†)
Region														
Northeast	2,800	(160)	58	(3.5)	84	(2.3)	1	(0.5)	144,800	(20,600)	390,900	(29,210)	7,300 !	(4,880)
Southeast	3,500	(180)	69	(3.4)	69	(2.6)	5	(1.1)	194,000	(19,300)	386,100	(30,540)	65,800	(18,990)
Central	5,200	(190)	80	(2.6)	54	(2.5)	1	(0.4)	333,900	(29,010)	319,300	(22,060)	25,600 !	(14,170)
West	5,100	(230)	71	(2.2)	69	(2.3)	3	(0.9)	489,400	(47,580)	699,100	(48,150)	66,400	(23,380)
Percent minority enrollment[2]														
Less than 6 percent	5,600	(90)	76	(2.5)	58	(2.1)	#	(†)	317,400	(24,840)	267,100	(18,820)	#	(†)
6 to 20 percent	3,800	(80)	78	(2.4)	70	(2.2)	2	(0.6)	380,900	(35,440)	463,800	(21,630)	16,700	(5,470)
21 to 49 percent	3,200	(120)	72	(3.5)	75	(3.0)	5	(1.3)	228,900	(22,890)	528,500	(29,150)	64,300	(19,280)
50 percent or more	3,600	(100)	58	(3.1)	69	(2.5)	4	(1.0)	231,400	(36,220)	497,700	(35,430)	84,100	(26,560)

†Not applicable.
#Rounds to zero.
!Interpret data with caution.
‡Reporting standards not met.
[1]Enrollments may include duplicated counts of students in each type of course, since schools were instructed to count a student enrolled in multiple courses of a particular type for each course in which he or she was enrolled.
[2]Excludes schools not reporting minority enrollment.

NOTE: Data were collected during the 2002–03 12-month school year. Dual credit courses are those in which high school students can earn both high school and postsecondary credits for the same course. Percentages are based on unrounded numbers. Detail may not sum to totals because of rounding or missing data. Standard errors appear in parentheses.
SOURCE: U.S. Department of Education, National Center for Education Statistics, Fast Response Survey System (FRSS), "Dual Credit and Exam-Based Courses," FRSS 85, 2003. (This table was prepared July 2005.)

Table 142. Percentage of high school seniors who say they engage in various activities, by selected student and school characteristics: 1992 and 2004

Activity	Total	Sex		Race/ethnicity					Socioeconomic status[1]			Control of school attended		
		Male	Female	White	Black	Hispanic	Asian/Pacific Islander	American Indian/Alaska Native	Low	Middle	High	Public	Catholic	Other private
1	2	3	4	5	6	7	8	9	10	11	12	13	14	15
1992														
At least once a week														
Use personal computer[2]	23.5 (0.55)	27.5 (0.86)	19.6 (0.67)	23.6 (0.59)	25.0 (2.18)	20.5 (1.49)	26.2 (2.06)	18.3 (3.69)	17.8 (1.14)	23.0 (0.71)	28.3 (1.15)	23.4 (0.58)	24.4 (1.92)	24.1 (2.73)
Work on hobbies	38.1 (0.63)	40.9 (0.95)	35.3 (0.83)	39.3 (0.71)	32.6 (2.19)	36.3 (1.73)	34.9 (2.17)	47.7 (6.11)	35.5 (1.51)	37.5 (0.81)	41.0 (1.24)	37.7 (0.66)	41.0 (2.32)	39.7 (3.49)
Perform community service	10.3 (0.43)	9.5 (0.71)	11.1 (0.49)	10.3 (0.53)	10.1 (1.14)	9.9 (1.04)	13.2 (1.56)	5.3 (2.15)	6.6 (0.57)	8.5 (0.40)	16.1 (1.20)	8.9 (0.41)	16.9 (1.99)	23.9 (3.25)
Driving or riding around	67.7 (0.61)	67.8 (0.92)	67.6 (0.79)	70.0 (0.67)	61.0 (2.30)	61.0 (1.72)	64.9 (2.19)	57.4 (6.03)	66.1 (1.25)	68.8 (0.84)	66.8 (1.21)	67.7 (0.64)	69.7 (2.19)	64.5 (3.43)
Visiting with friends at a local hangout	— (†)	— (†)	— (†)	— (†)	— (†)	— (†)	— (†)	— (†)	— (†)	— (†)	— (†)	— (†)	— (†)	— (†)
Talk on phone with friends	80.3 (0.54)	78.8 (0.83)	81.7 (0.68)	82.6 (0.56)	71.7 (2.30)	75.1 (1.43)	82.3 (1.62)	62.5 (6.24)	75.6 (1.11)	79.4 (0.80)	85.2 (0.93)	79.6 (0.57)	84.5 (2.04)	84.7 (2.50)
Take music, art, or dance class	9.1 (0.33)	6.9 (0.45)	11.4 (0.49)	9.2 (0.38)	8.3 (1.10)	8.7 (1.11)	12.2 (1.27)	9.2 (3.42)	6.2 (0.62)	8.1 (0.42)	13.1 (0.77)	8.9 (0.35)	9.5 (1.19)	12.3 (2.07)
Take sports lessons	6.5 (0.36)	8.4 (0.51)	4.6 (0.41)	6.3 (0.42)	7.0 (0.84)	6.7 (1.14)	8.0 (1.28)	8.2 (2.86)	5.0 (0.58)	6.0 (0.40)	8.5 (0.94)	6.3 (0.35)	8.0 (1.39)	10.2 (2.97)
Play ball or other sports	24.6 (0.56)	35.9 (0.91)	13.2 (0.60)	25.1 (0.64)	22.7 (1.98)	22.7 (1.54)	25.9 (1.99)	25.1 (4.93)	19.1 (0.99)	22.8 (0.68)	31.7 (1.28)	24.0 (0.57)	29.8 (2.33)	27.4 (3.44)
Reading 3 or more hours per week (not for school)	34.8 (0.62)	32.3 (0.91)	37.4 (0.82)	35.4 (0.69)	32.3 (2.31)	34.0 (1.76)	34.7 (2.21)	33.1 (4.74)	30.1 (1.25)	34.8 (0.82)	37.9 (1.26)	34.8 (0.64)	33.9 (2.29)	36.2 (3.54)
Plays video/computer games 3 or more hours per day on weekdays	2.1 (0.16)	3.2 (0.28)	0.9 (0.16)	1.8 (0.16)	3.8 (0.79)	2.0 (0.37)	2.8 (1.03)	1.6 (0.94)	3.0 (0.39)	2.2 (0.26)	1.2 (0.19)	2.2 (0.18)	1.3 (0.39)	0.6 (0.23)
Watches television 3 or more hours per day on weekdays	8.6 (0.35)	8.6 (0.51)	8.7 (0.47)	6.4 (0.34)	22.9 (1.73)	9.0 (1.20)	6.9 (1.16)	8.0 (2.14)	12.9 (0.92)	9.7 (0.51)	4.0 (0.49)	9.0 (0.37)	8.5 (1.42)	3.1 (0.71)
2004														
At least once a week														
Use personal computer at home	85.8 (0.35)	85.6 (0.50)	85.9 (0.48)	90.8 (0.38)	73.9 (1.13)	76.7 (1.06)	94.0 (0.77)	79.0 (3.07)	71.1 (0.90)	87.8 (0.47)	96.3 (0.39)	85.0 (0.37)	96.9 (0.41)	93.9 (0.81)
Work on hobbies	47.2 (0.50)	50.9 (0.71)	43.4 (0.69)	47.8 (0.65)	45.0 (1.29)	45.0 (1.23)	48.5 (1.72)	54.5 (4.93)	44.2 (0.99)	47.3 (0.71)	49.7 (0.97)	47.1 (0.53)	47.3 (1.26)	49.5 (1.61)
Perform community service	18.0 (0.38)	14.9 (0.51)	21.1 (0.57)	17.4 (0.50)	19.5 (1.02)	16.3 (0.92)	25.5 (1.40)	11.8 (2.21)	15.0 (0.71)	16.9 (0.53)	23.1 (0.82)	17.6 (0.41)	23.5 (1.06)	22.4 (1.35)
Driving or riding around	65.5 (0.47)	67.4 (0.66)	63.6 (0.66)	69.9 (0.60)	63.4 (1.23)	52.9 (1.23)	56.3 (1.66)	80.3 (2.73)	58.8 (0.97)	67.2 (0.66)	68.7 (0.82)	65.4 (0.50)	69.2 (1.14)	63.7 (1.56)
Visiting with friends at a local hangout	85.3 (0.35)	88.0 (0.46)	82.4 (0.53)	89.9 (0.40)	79.4 (1.05)	75.7 (1.06)	77.7 (1.40)	83.5 (2.79)	76.5 (0.84)	86.9 (0.48)	90.7 (0.59)	84.8 (0.38)	92.3 (0.64)	89.2 (0.99)
Talk on phone with friends	71.4 (0.45)	65.3 (0.68)	77.7 (0.59)	71.4 (0.60)	78.7 (1.07)	66.1 (1.19)	64.7 (1.62)	75.9 (3.23)	65.3 (0.94)	73.1 (0.64)	74.1 (0.87)	71.1 (0.48)	77.5 (1.04)	72.8 (1.46)
Take music, art, or language class	17.1 (0.37)	13.6 (0.49)	20.6 (0.56)	17.0 (0.49)	18.3 (1.00)	14.9 (0.86)	20.7 (1.28)	18.5 (3.79)	13.2 (0.66)	16.4 (0.52)	22.3 (0.82)	16.8 (0.40)	19.6 (1.00)	22.3 (1.35)
Take sports lessons	12.7 (0.33)	15.5 (0.52)	9.9 (0.41)	12.0 (0.42)	15.1 (0.94)	13.0 (0.82)	13.0 (1.14)	12.4 (1.73)	10.4 (0.62)	12.1 (0.46)	16.2 (0.73)	12.4 (0.36)	18.6 (0.98)	14.6 (1.11)
Play non-school sports	28.3 (0.45)	40.5 (0.70)	15.9 (0.51)	27.2 (0.58)	30.3 (1.19)	29.1 (1.13)	30.8 (1.59)	37.3 (3.84)	26.7 (0.89)	28.3 (0.65)	30.0 (0.90)	28.2 (0.48)	31.5 (1.16)	26.3 (1.43)
Reading 3 or more hours per week (not for school)	33.7 (0.47)	31.5 (0.66)	36.0 (0.67)	33.3 (0.61)	34.6 (1.21)	34.5 (1.18)	32.6 (1.56)	33.6 (4.92)	32.9 (0.94)	32.8 (0.67)	36.3 (0.95)	33.8 (0.50)	29.8 (1.15)	36.2 (1.57)
Plays video/computer games 3 or more hours per day on weekdays	6.3 (0.25)	10.7 (0.44)	1.7 (0.19)	5.6 (0.31)	8.2 (0.75)	6.4 (0.61)	7.0 (1.03)	7.8 (2.73)	7.2 (0.52)	6.7 (0.36)	4.4 (0.41)	6.5 (0.27)	3.9 (0.48)	3.6 (0.63)
Watches television/DVDs 3 or more hours per day on weekdays	30.6 (0.46)	31.9 (0.66)	29.2 (0.64)	24.3 (0.56)	51.9 (1.33)	34.7 (1.18)	26.3 (1.62)	34.4 (3.23)	38.4 (0.96)	31.7 (0.67)	20.7 (0.79)	31.4 (0.49)	24.5 (1.07)	16.8 (1.21)
Hours of homework per week														
Less than 1 hour	13.4 (0.36)	17.4 (0.56)	9.4 (0.43)	14.1 (0.47)	15.4 (0.96)	11.6 (0.83)	6.1 (0.86)	14.3 (3.84)	15.7 (0.77)	14.9 (0.52)	8.7 (0.59)	14.1 (0.39)	5.5 (0.55)	5.3 (0.70)
1 to 3 hours	28.8 (0.47)	30.1 (0.67)	27.5 (0.64)	27.3 (0.59)	33.3 (1.30)	33.9 (1.25)	16.8 (1.28)	30.9 (3.14)	32.6 (0.99)	30.3 (0.68)	22.9 (0.84)	29.7 (0.51)	19.6 (0.99)	16.8 (1.23)
4 to 6 hours	25.1 (0.45)	24.6 (0.64)	25.6 (0.64)	25.9 (0.59)	24.1 (1.19)	22.8 (1.11)	25.5 (1.58)	22.6 (2.96)	24.4 (0.92)	25.1 (0.65)	25.6 (0.87)	25.0 (0.49)	27.4 (1.11)	23.8 (1.38)
7 to 12 hours	21.6 (0.43)	19.8 (0.59)	23.4 (0.61)	22.1 (0.56)	17.6 (1.05)	20.8 (1.06)	28.7 (1.56)	25.3 (4.06)	18.1 (0.83)	20.4 (0.59)	26.7 (0.87)	20.7 (0.46)	29.1 (1.14)	32.6 (1.51)
More than 12 hours	11.1 (0.32)	8.1 (0.39)	14.1 (0.50)	10.6 (0.41)	9.5 (0.84)	10.9 (0.82)	22.9 (1.56)	7.0 (1.67)	9.2 (0.63)	9.3 (0.42)	16.1 (0.71)	10.3 (0.34)	18.5 (0.97)	21.4 (1.29)

—Not available.
†Not applicable.
[1]Socioeconomic status (SES) was measured by a composite score on parental education and occupations, and family income. The "low" SES group is the lowest quartile; the "middle" SES group is the middle two quartiles; and the "high" SES group is the upper quartile.

[2]Question does not specify where computer is used.
NOTE: Race categories exclude persons of Hispanic origin. Standard errors appear in parentheses.
SOURCE: U.S. Department of Education, National Center for Education Statistics, National Education Longitudinal Study of 1988 (NELS:88/92), "Second Follow-up Student Survey, 1992"; and Education Longitudinal Study of 2002 (ELS:2002), "First Follow-up, 2004." (This table was prepared October 2006.)

Table 143. Percentage of high school sophomores who participate in various school-sponsored extracurricular activities, by selected student characteristics: 1990 and 2002

Selected student characteristic	Academic clubs		Sports				Cheerleading and drill team		Hobby clubs		Music (band, orchestra, chorus, or choir)		Vocational clubs	
			Any sport		Interscholastic[1]	Intramural[1]								
	1990	2002	1990	2002	2002	2002	1990	2002	1990	2002	1990	2002	1990	2002
1	2	3	4	5	6	7	8	9	10	11	12	13	14	15
All sophomores	**30.7** (0.62)	**8.4** (0.33)	**52.2** (0.69)	**54.8** (0.63)	**48.8** (0.64)	**33.0** (0.52)	**9.1** (0.43)	**13.7** (0.46)	**7.3** (0.37)	**9.5** (0.34)	**21.5** (0.59)	**21.5** (0.52)	**11.7** (0.54)	**8.3** (0.43)
Sex														
Male	27.4 (0.83)	6.8 (0.38)	63.0 (0.89)	61.0 (0.81)	55.0 (0.80)	38.5 (0.77)	2.1 (0.45)	8.1 (0.52)	7.9 (0.52)	8.1 (0.41)	15.6 (0.63)	16.3 (0.60)	11.0 (0.65)	7.6 (0.53)
Female	34.0 (0.87)	9.9 (0.46)	41.4 (0.89)	48.5 (0.85)	42.5 (0.84)	27.4 (0.64)	15.8 (0.68)	19.2 (0.63)	6.7 (0.50)	10.9 (0.50)	27.3 (0.85)	26.8 (0.71)	12.3 (0.69)	9.1 (0.53)
Race/ethnicity														
White	31.7 (0.72)	8.9 (0.43)	53.5 (0.78)	57.0 (0.79)	52.3 (0.77)	30.9 (0.68)	8.3 (0.38)	13.2 (0.54)	7.5 (0.46)	9.7 (0.47)	22.3 (0.68)	23.9 (0.65)	12.2 (0.64)	9.3 (0.60)
Black	26.2 (1.91)	7.3 (0.67)	51.4 (2.22)	55.0 (1.48)	47.8 (1.51)	39.6 (1.21)	15.7 (2.34)	18.5 (1.16)	5.2 (0.78)	7.8 (0.68)	23.0 (1.77)	21.6 (1.33)	13.7 (1.84)	7.9 (0.81)
Hispanic	27.2 (1.57)	6.1 (0.60)	43.9 (1.82)	48.3 (1.59)	40.0 (1.57)	35.3 (1.41)	8.3 (0.86)	12.3 (0.97)	6.7 (0.67)	8.0 (0.64)	14.8 (1.19)	13.0 (0.91)	7.4 (0.87)	5.4 (0.63)
Asian/Pacific Islander	36.7 (2.24)	14.3 (1.33)	54.9 (2.86)	47.7 (1.87)	38.6 (1.99)	29.5 (1.37)	5.2 (0.98)	9.1 (1.06)	11.8 (1.47)	15.5 (1.41)	20.6 (2.76)	15.5 (1.56)	5.1 (0.81)	5.2 (0.57)
American Indian/Alaska Native	31.9 (4.66)	5.2 (2.15)	44.2 (5.05)	54.6 (5.33)	44.4 (5.45)	40.8 (5.94)	11.3 (3.06)	10.8 (2.90)	8.4 (2.83)	5.3 (2.23)	17.3 (3.66)	12.3 (3.75)	16.9 (3.30)	14.3 (3.61)
Test performance quartile[2]														
Lowest test quartile	22.5 (1.21)	4.4 (0.43)	47.4 (1.42)	47.7 (1.03)	40.5 (1.04)	38.2 (0.93)	9.5 (0.95)	15.0 (0.82)	6.5 (0.59)	6.3 (0.52)	16.0 (0.87)	15.3 (0.78)	17.3 (1.19)	8.9 (0.63)
Second test quartile	29.9 (1.18)	5.1 (0.44)	50.8 (1.22)	52.5 (1.03)	45.1 (1.03)	37.5 (1.00)	8.6 (0.94)	14.4 (0.74)	6.1 (0.58)	7.3 (0.50)	20.5 (1.08)	18.7 (0.78)	13.2 (0.86)	9.5 (0.70)
Third test quartile	30.3 (1.15)	8.1 (0.56)	51.8 (1.22)	56.5 (1.06)	50.6 (1.05)	32.1 (0.97)	9.2 (0.82)	13.7 (0.74)	7.6 (0.65)	10.8 (0.63)	22.1 (1.05)	23.0 (0.88)	11.4 (0.90)	7.6 (0.64)
Highest test quartile	40.0 (1.17)	15.6 (0.80)	59.0 (1.25)	62.3 (1.04)	58.5 (1.05)	24.3 (0.87)	9.0 (0.72)	11.7 (0.73)	8.7 (0.75)	13.4 (0.75)	26.9 (1.05)	28.7 (1.02)	6.7 (0.60)	7.4 (0.67)
Socioeconomic status[3]														
Low	26.3 (1.05)	5.6 (0.46)	42.0 (1.19)	44.9 (1.09)	37.3 (1.12)	32.3 (0.97)	8.2 (0.82)	13.5 (0.73)	5.8 (0.56)	6.7 (0.50)	18.3 (0.93)	15.6 (0.75)	17.1 (1.15)	9.2 (0.76)
Middle	31.5 (0.89)	7.2 (0.38)	52.7 (0.92)	54.9 (0.82)	48.8 (0.82)	34.1 (0.72)	9.6 (0.65)	14.2 (0.60)	7.1 (0.55)	8.8 (0.39)	22.1 (0.77)	21.6 (0.64)	11.4 (0.67)	8.6 (0.50)
High	34.9 (1.16)	13.3 (0.74)	63.2 (1.21)	64.3 (1.05)	59.9 (1.10)	31.3 (0.90)	9.3 (0.65)	12.8 (0.78)	9.4 (0.68)	13.5 (0.79)	24.4 (1.09)	27.1 (1.02)	6.5 (0.54)	7.0 (0.57)
Region														
Northeast	26.9 (1.35)	7.6 (0.85)	55.7 (1.49)	59.3 (1.36)	52.7 (1.42)	34.9 (1.14)	8.0 (0.66)	14.5 (1.26)	11.0 (1.21)	11.2 (0.78)	22.7 (1.33)	20.8 (1.29)	3.5 (0.46)	4.9 (0.63)
Midwest	33.4 (1.27)	6.8 (0.57)	58.3 (1.27)	57.9 (1.36)	52.7 (1.33)	31.2 (1.15)	8.6 (0.63)	13.7 (0.89)	5.4 (0.53)	8.8 (0.77)	26.6 (1.22)	27.5 (1.07)	11.7 (1.17)	8.0 (1.10)
South	32.6 (1.06)	10.8 (0.58)	46.3 (1.16)	52.7 (0.89)	47.3 (0.92)	32.2 (0.77)	11.3 (0.96)	15.4 (0.76)	5.9 (0.53)	9.8 (0.50)	18.8 (0.93)	21.4 (0.85)	18.6 (1.10)	11.5 (0.73)
West	27.5 (1.32)	7.0 (0.66)	51.6 (1.59)	50.9 (1.53)	43.6 (1.53)	34.5 (1.20)	6.8 (0.71)	10.4 (0.88)	8.7 (0.78)	8.5 (0.77)	18.2 (1.30)	15.8 (0.95)	7.2 (0.86)	7.0 (0.80)
Sophomore's school sector														
Public	31.0 (0.65)	8.1 (0.37)	50.8 (0.70)	53.2 (0.67)	47.2 (0.67)	32.7 (0.55)	9.2 (0.46)	13.8 (0.49)	6.7 (0.38)	8.9 (0.35)	22.1 (0.61)	21.2 (0.53)	12.6 (0.60)	8.8 (0.46)
Catholic	28.6 (2.40)	11.3 (0.51)	66.5 (2.76)	73.1 (1.38)	67.7 (1.61)	35.4 (1.50)	7.1 (1.18)	10.7 (1.06)	12.3 (1.53)	17.1 (1.35)	12.6 (1.60)	18.1 (1.82)	2.8 (0.64)	2.2 (0.37)
Other private	29.1 (4.60)	10.5 (0.56)	68.0 (4.46)	73.9 (2.16)	68.3 (2.81)	37.0 (2.64)	9.9 (2.47)	15.5 (1.96)	13.1 (3.50)	14.8 (2.14)	25.7 (5.01)	33.9 (3.61)	5.5 (2.32)	3.8 (1.02)

[1]Interscholastic refers to competition between teams from different schools. Intramural refers to competition between teams or students within the same school. Data on these categories are available only for 2002.
[2]Composite test performance quartile on mathematics, reading, science, and social studies in 1990 and composite test performance quartile on mathematics, reading, and science in 2002.
[3]Socioeconomic status (SES) was measured by a composite score on parental education and occupations, and family income.

NOTE: Race categories exclude persons of Hispanic origin. Standard errors appear in parentheses.
SOURCE: U.S. Department of Education, National Center for Education Statistics, Education Longitudinal Study of 2002 (ELS:2002); and America's High School Sophomores: A Ten Year Comparison, 1980–1990, National Education Longitudinal Study of 1988 (NELS:88/90), "First Follow-up, 1990." (This table was prepared December 2006.)

Table 144. Percentage distribution of 4th-graders, by time spent on homework and television viewing each day and selected student and school characteristics: Selected years, 1992 through 2000

Selected student and school characteristic	Time spent on homework each day					Amount of television watched each day						
	Don't have	Don't do	Half hour or less	One hour	More than one hour	None	One hour or less	Two hours	Three hours	Four hours	Five hours	Six or more hours
1	2	3	4	5	6	7	8	9	10	11	12	13
1992												
All students	16 (1.6)	2 (0.2)	39 (1.2)	28 (0.9)	15 (0.6)	2 (0.2)	17 (0.8)	21 (0.7)	19 (0.6)	13 (0.6)	9 (0.4)	20 (0.7)
Sex												
Male	18 (1.8)	3 (0.4)	39 (1.4)	26 (1.0)	14 (0.8)	2 (0.3)	16 (0.8)	20 (0.9)	18 (0.9)	13 (0.7)	9 (0.7)	21 (0.9)
Female	14 (1.5)	1 (0.3)	39 (1.4)	30 (1.1)	16 (0.8)	2 (0.3)	18 (1.2)	22 (0.9)	19 (0.9)	13 (0.8)	8 (0.6)	18 (0.9)
Race/ethnicity												
White	18 (1.9)	2 (0.3)	38 (1.5)	29 (1.2)	13 (0.6)	2 (0.3)	18 (0.9)	23 (1.0)	21 (0.8)	14 (0.7)	9 (0.6)	13 (0.8)
Black	10 (1.6)	3 (0.6)	45 (2.3)	24 (1.5)	18 (1.4)	2 (0.5)	11 (1.5)	11 (1.0)	12 (1.0)	10 (1.1)	9 (1.2)	44 (1.9)
Hispanic	11 (1.7)	4 (0.5)	39 (2.2)	28 (1.7)	18 (1.9)	2 (0.5)	15 (1.2)	20 (1.6)	14 (1.3)	13 (1.2)	10 (1.0)	27 (1.6)
Asian/Pacific Islander	10 (4.5)	1 (#)	39 (3.4)	28 (4.3)	22 (3.4)	3 (1.3)	26 (3.7)	17 (2.7)	15 (2.8)	11 (1.9)	7 (1.6)	21 (3.2)
American Indian/Alaska Native	17 (5.0)	4 (2.4)	31 (5.7)	18 (4.2)	30 (5.7)	1 (#)	18 (3.8)	13 (3.3)	16 (3.7)	17 (3.3)	11 (3.3)	23 (4.4)
Control of school												
Public	17 (1.7)	2 (0.3)	40 (1.3)	26 (0.9)	14 (0.6)	2 (0.2)	16 (0.8)	21 (0.9)	19 (0.7)	13 (0.7)	9 (0.5)	21 (0.8)
Private	7 (1.8)	1 (0.2)	34 (2.4)	38 (2.2)	21 (1.9)	2 (0.6)	21 (2.3)	24 (1.5)	18 (1.4)	14 (1.1)	9 (1.0)	12 (1.4)
1994												
All students	13 (0.9)	3 (0.3)	39 (1.0)	30 (0.7)	15 (0.6)	2 (0.2)	17 (0.6)	21 (0.6)	17 (0.5)	13 (0.6)	9 (0.4)	21 (0.7)
Sex												
Male	14 (1.0)	5 (0.5)	39 (1.1)	28 (1.0)	15 (0.7)	2 (0.3)	15 (0.8)	19 (0.8)	16 (0.6)	13 (0.7)	10 (0.6)	25 (0.9)
Female	12 (1.1)	2 (0.2)	40 (1.2)	32 (1.0)	15 (0.8)	2 (0.3)	20 (0.9)	23 (0.8)	17 (0.9)	13 (0.8)	8 (0.6)	17 (0.9)
1998												
All students	8 (0.8)	2 (0.2)	43 (1.0)	31 (0.8)	16 (0.6)	3 (0.5)	21 (0.6)	22 (0.7)	19 (0.6)	11 (0.5)	8 (0.4)	16 (0.6)
Sex												
Male	9 (1.0)	3 (0.3)	41 (1.1)	30 (1.0)	16 (0.8)	3 (0.5)	18 (0.9)	22 (0.9)	18 (1.0)	12 (0.7)	8 (0.6)	18 (1.0)
Female	7 (0.7)	1 (0.2)	44 (1.2)	32 (1.0)	16 (0.7)	3 (0.5)	24 (0.8)	22 (0.8)	19 (0.7)	10 (0.6)	7 (0.5)	14 (0.7)
Race/ethnicity												
White, non-Hispanic	9 (0.9)	2 (0.2)	43 (1.2)	32 (1.1)	15 (0.7)	3 (0.7)	23 (0.9)	24 (0.8)	20 (0.8)	12 (0.7)	7 (0.7)	11 (0.8)
Black, non-Hispanic	6 (0.9)	3 (0.5)	45 (1.9)	27 (1.5)	19 (1.5)	2 (0.5)	14 (1.2)	14 (1.1)	14 (1.2)	11 (0.8)	12 (0.9)	34 (1.5)
Hispanic	7 (1.1)	3 (0.5)	42 (1.9)	30 (1.5)	18 (1.2)	3 (0.5)	21 (1.2)	19 (1.0)	18 (1.2)	11 (0.9)	8 (0.8)	19 (1.0)
Asian/Pacific Islander	4 (1.7)	1 (#)	39 (3.1)	36 (2.6)	20 (2.3)	4 (1.1)	26 (2.8)	20 (3.0)	16 (2.5)	10 (2.8)	9 (1.9)	14 (2.4)
American Indian/Alaska Native	8 (2.2)	7 (2.0)	40 (4.9)	27 (2.8)	19 (3.6)	1 (#)	19 (3.6)	19 (2.3)	15 (2.6)	8 (2.1)	12 (3.1)	27 (3.4)
2000												
All students	10 (0.9)	2 (0.2)	43 (0.9)	29 (0.6)	16 (0.7)	2 (0.2)	23 (0.7)	23 (0.6)	17 (0.4)	11 (0.5)	6 (0.4)	18 (0.6)
Sex												
Male	11 (0.9)	3 (0.3)	43 (1.2)	27 (0.8)	16 (0.9)	2 (0.3)	20 (1.1)	21 (0.8)	18 (0.7)	11 (0.6)	7 (0.5)	22 (0.9)
Female	9 (1.0)	1 (0.2)	43 (1.1)	31 (0.9)	16 (0.7)	2 (0.3)	26 (0.9)	24 (0.8)	17 (0.7)	10 (0.6)	6 (0.4)	15 (0.7)
Race/ethnicity												
White, non-Hispanic	11 (1.1)	1 (0.2)	43 (1.2)	30 (0.8)	15 (0.9)	2 (0.3)	25 (0.9)	25 (0.9)	19 (0.6)	11 (0.6)	6 (0.5)	13 (0.7)
Black, non-Hispanic	8 (0.9)	4 (0.8)	45 (1.8)	26 (1.3)	17 (1.0)	2 (0.3)	14 (0.9)	13 (1.0)	13 (0.9)	10 (0.9)	8 (0.6)	42 (1.5)
Hispanic	7 (1.0)	3 (0.5)	43 (1.4)	29 (1.3)	18 (1.3)	2 (0.4)	22 (1.2)	21 (1.2)	16 (1.1)	10 (1.0)	7 (0.6)	22 (1.5)
Asian/Pacific Islander	1 (0.7)	1 (0.7)	42 (3.2)	35 (3.2)	21 (3.4)	6 (1.4)	29 (2.7)	28 (3.1)	15 (2.8)	8 (1.6)	7 (1.7)	8 (1.8)
American Indian/Alaska Native	15 (4.7)	7 (2.2)	42 (5.4)	24 (4.5)	13 (2.6)	1 (#)	20 (3.6)	18 (2.2)	21 (3.8)	11 (3.4)	7 (2.2)	23 (3.4)
Control of school												
Public	10 (1.0)	2 (0.2)	44 (1.0)	29 (0.7)	15 (0.7)	2 (0.2)	22 (0.8)	22 (0.7)	17 (0.5)	11 (0.5)	6 (0.4)	19 (0.7)
Private	8 (1.6)	1 (0.4)	37 (1.6)	34 (1.5)	20 (1.7)	5 (1.0)	25 (1.4)	24 (0.9)	19 (0.8)	10 (0.9)	6 (0.7)	11 (1.3)
Type of location												
Central city	8 (1.0)	3 (0.4)	41 (1.4)	30 (1.1)	18 (1.2)	2 (0.4)	21 (0.9)	21 (1.1)	16 (0.6)	10 (0.8)	7 (0.6)	24 (1.3)
Urban fringe/large town	8 (1.3)	2 (0.3)	44 (1.3)	30 (1.2)	16 (1.1)	3 (0.3)	24 (1.3)	24 (1.0)	18 (0.8)	10 (0.7)	6 (0.6)	15 (1.0)
Rural/small town	15 (2.3)	2 (0.5)	44 (2.0)	27 (1.4)	12 (1.2)	2 (0.4)	22 (1.8)	23 (1.4)	19 (1.0)	13 (1.1)	6 (0.7)	16 (1.5)

#Rounds to zero.
NOTE: Race categories exclude persons of Hispanic origin. Detail may not sum to totals because of rounding. Standard errors appear in parentheses.

SOURCE: U.S. Department of Education, National Center for Education Statistics, National Assessment of Educational Progress (NAEP), 1992 through 2000 Reading Assessments; retrieved October 2001 from the NAEP Data Explorer (http://nces.ed.gov/nationsreportcard/nde/). (This table was prepared November 2001.)

Table 145. Tenth-graders' attendance patterns, by selected student and school characteristics: 1990 and 2002

Attendance pattern	All students	Sex		Race/ethnicity					Socioeconomic status[1]			Control of school attended		
		Male	Female	White	Black	Hispanic	Asian/Pacific Islander	American Indian/Alaska Native	Low	Middle	High	Public	Catholic	Other private
1	2	3	4	5	6	7	8	9	10	11	12	13	14	15
Percentage of 10th-graders in 1990														
Number of days missed in first half of current school year														
None	13.5 (0.44)	16.1 (0.66)	10.7 (0.53)	12.4 (0.48)	19.5 (1.75)	10.4 (0.90)	22.3 (1.74)	10.2 (2.11)	12.3 (0.95)	14.0 (0.61)	15.0 (0.82)	13.4 (0.47)	18.0 (2.16)	15.5 (2.14)
1 or 2 days	21.6 (0.46)	23.0 (0.72)	20.2 (0.59)	21.5 (0.56)	23.7 (1.41)	19.1 (1.17)	27.4 (1.97)	13.5 (4.21)	16.9 (0.75)	22.2 (0.68)	26.0 (0.98)	21.3 (0.46)	26.0 (2.45)	34.0 (3.92)
3 or 4 days	26.1 (0.52)	25.4 (0.71)	26.8 (0.76)	27.3 (0.60)	23.7 (1.51)	23.3 (1.15)	22.7 (2.07)	26.8 (3.39)	22.6 (0.89)	26.4 (0.73)	29.1 (0.99)	26.5 (0.56)	27.3 (2.23)	26.9 (2.93)
5 or more days	38.8 (0.63)	35.5 (0.87)	42.2 (0.84)	38.8 (0.72)	33.2 (1.98)	47.2 (1.71)	27.7 (2.22)	49.4 (3.32)	48.2 (1.18)	37.4 (0.85)	29.9 (1.20)	38.8 (0.65)	28.6 (2.35)	23.6 (3.14)
Number of times late in first half of current school year														
Never	24.7 (0.60)	24.8 (0.80)	24.6 (0.77)	27.4 (0.70)	18.1 (1.33)	17.3 (1.48)	23.0 (1.94)	16.0 (3.20)	24.4 (1.17)	25.0 (0.78)	25.9 (0.95)	24.9 (0.61)	27.5 (2.70)	18.3 (2.76)
1 or 2 days	38.2 (0.62)	38.0 (0.88)	38.4 (0.83)	38.1 (0.69)	40.4 (2.02)	36.7 (1.54)	38.0 (2.22)	35.4 (3.64)	37.5 (1.10)	38.6 (0.84)	38.4 (1.16)	37.8 (0.63)	40.4 (2.26)	44.6 (3.87)
3 or more days	37.1 (0.72)	37.1 (0.96)	37.0 (0.88)	34.5 (0.77)	41.5 (2.16)	46.0 (2.07)	39.0 (2.35)	48.6 (3.51)	38.1 (1.30)	36.4 (0.88)	35.7 (1.23)	37.3 (0.75)	32.1 (2.68)	37.1 (4.07)
Number of times cut classes in first half of current school year														
Never	62.4 (0.71)	60.6 (0.90)	64.2 (0.91)	64.0 (0.80)	63.5 (2.12)	50.5 (1.69)	66.4 (2.36)	48.8 (3.91)	59.0 (1.30)	62.4 (0.91)	65.9 (1.24)	61.0 (0.77)	78.6 (2.36)	70.3 (3.66)
1 or 2 times	22.0 (0.49)	22.3 (0.71)	21.7 (0.67)	21.3 (0.54)	22.5 (1.82)	24.6 (1.44)	20.3 (2.01)	35.1 (3.97)	23.4 (1.09)	21.5 (0.68)	22.2 (1.05)	22.3 (0.52)	16.6 (1.92)	19.9 (3.44)
3 to 6 times	8.4 (0.33)	9.2 (0.45)	7.7 (0.48)	8.1 (0.40)	7.5 (0.81)	12.6 (1.02)	5.7 (0.87)	8.3 (3.25)	9.6 (0.73)	8.2 (0.44)	7.3 (0.56)	8.8 (0.35)	3.2 (0.87)	6.9 (1.28)
More than 6 times	7.2 (0.35)	8.0 (0.49)	6.5 (0.44)	6.5 (0.38)	6.4 (1.03)	12.2 (1.23)	7.6 (1.21)	7.8 (2.04)	8.1 (0.64)	7.9 (0.50)	4.6 (0.43)	7.9 (0.39)	1.6 (0.55)	2.9 (1.03)
Percentage of 10th-graders in 2002														
Number of days missed in first half of current school year														
None	14.3 (0.38)	16.1 (0.51)	12.5 (0.47)	13.0 (0.48)	16.5 (0.84)	14.2 (0.88)	28.3 (1.59)	12.1 (0.14)	13.5 (0.67)	13.9 (0.48)	16.0 (0.79)	14.0 (0.40)	16.1 (1.23)	19.2 (2.22)
1 or 2 days	35.4 (0.52)	36.1 (0.69)	34.8 (0.68)	35.5 (0.66)	38.4 (1.17)	33.5 (1.46)	35.7 (1.58)	25.0 (0.92)	32.8 (0.97)	35.3 (0.72)	38.2 (0.96)	35.0 (0.56)	41.0 (1.62)	39.8 (1.71)
3 to 6 days	33.0 (0.53)	31.9 (0.69)	34.3 (0.69)	34.4 (0.69)	30.7 (1.08)	32.7 (1.01)	24.3 (1.23)	35.5 (1.38)	33.1 (0.87)	32.7 (0.74)	33.8 (0.97)	33.2 (0.56)	33.1 (1.51)	29.9 (2.04)
More than 6 days	17.2 (0.41)	16.0 (0.56)	18.5 (0.59)	17.1 (0.49)	14.3 (0.95)	19.6 (1.09)	11.7 (1.16)	27.4 (0.32)	20.6 (0.90)	18.1 (0.53)	12.0 (0.65)	17.8 (0.44)	9.8 (0.77)	11.1 (1.21)
Number of times late in first half of current school year														
Never	26.0 (0.54)	26.0 (0.73)	26.0 (0.68)	29.8 (0.67)	17.4 (0.86)	20.4 (1.18)	27.4 (1.41)	19.8 (0.65)	24.6 (0.87)	25.8 (0.66)	28.1 (0.94)	25.7 (0.58)	33.3 (1.79)	25.1 (2.28)
1 or 2 days	37.4 (0.54)	36.5 (0.75)	38.4 (0.71)	38.7 (0.66)	36.5 (1.33)	34.9 (1.17)	36.2 (1.52)	35.8 (2.42)	36.9 (0.98)	36.7 (0.72)	39.4 (0.91)	37.3 (0.57)	40.4 (1.32)	38.3 (1.39)
3 or more days	36.5 (0.62)	37.4 (0.82)	35.6 (0.77)	31.5 (0.71)	46.1 (1.48)	44.8 (1.45)	36.4 (1.58)	44.4 (1.89)	38.5 (1.01)	37.5 (0.79)	32.5 (1.05)	37.0 (0.67)	26.3 (1.54)	36.7 (2.11)
Number of times cut classes in first half of current school year														
Never	68.4 (0.70)	68.1 (0.87)	68.8 (0.83)	72.9 (0.75)	64.6 (1.64)	56.3 (1.48)	68.9 (1.76)	70.3 (3.43)	62.4 (1.10)	67.1 (0.86)	77.0 (1.04)	67.1 (0.75)	86.1 (1.39)	80.7 (1.90)
1 or 2 times	18.7 (0.46)	18.8 (0.65)	18.5 (0.58)	16.7 (0.55)	20.2 (1.15)	23.9 (1.01)	17.5 (1.25)	22.2 (3.43)	21.3 (0.79)	19.6 (0.63)	14.2 (0.81)	19.2 (0.49)	11.0 (1.12)	13.7 (1.38)
3 to 6 times	6.8 (0.32)	6.8 (0.40)	6.9 (0.41)	5.7 (0.34)	9.0 (0.76)	9.0 (0.83)	8.2 (1.08)	4.7 (0.29)	7.9 (0.65)	7.1 (0.40)	5.2 (0.47)	7.2 (0.34)	1.8 (0.40)	3.9 (0.57)
More than 6 times	6.1 (0.30)	6.3 (0.40)	5.9 (0.40)	4.7 (0.31)	6.2 (0.67)	10.9 (0.97)	5.3 (0.65)	2.7 (0.32)	8.4 (0.62)	6.2 (0.39)	3.7 (0.38)	6.5 (0.32)	1.0 (0.26)	1.7 (0.47)

[1] Socioeconomic status (SES) was measured by a composite score on parental education and occupations, and family income. The "low" SES group is the lowest quartile; the "middle" SES group is the middle two quartiles; and the "high" SES group is the upper quartile. Data for 2002 for persons reporting more than one race are not shown separately, but are included in totals. NOTE: Race categories exclude persons of Hispanic origin. Detail may not sum to totals because of rounding. Standard errors appear in parentheses.

SOURCE: U.S. Department of Education, National Center for Education Statistics, National Education Longitudinal Study of 1988 (NELS:88/90), "First Follow-up Student Survey, 1990"; and Education Longitudinal Study of 2002, Base Year (ELS:02). (This table was prepared November 2005.)

Table 146. Percentage of schools with various security measures, by control and selected characteristics: 2003–04

Selected school characteristic	Total schools — Number	Total schools — Percentage distribution	Controlled access to school buildings[1]	Controlled access to school grounds[2]	School uniforms	Strict dress code	Daily metal detector checks[3]	Random metal detector checks	Closed lunch[4]	Random sweeps for contraband	Daily presence of police or security	Video surveillance	Violence prevention program
1	2	3	4	5	6	7	8	9	10	11	12	13	14
Public total	87,600 (310)	100.0 (†)	81.5 (0.60)	39.4 (0.83)	13.5 (0.53)	49.3 (0.70)	2.0 (0.21)	5.7 (0.32)	88.0 (0.50)	12.8 (0.48)	24.8 (0.59)	32.5 (0.68)	66.3 (0.73)
School enrollment													
Under 300	25,400 (680)	29.0 (0.77)	74.9 (1.43)	33.3 (1.60)	11.9 (1.02)	44.6 (1.61)	4.1 (0.69)	7.1 (0.89)	83.2 (1.22)	17.6 (1.44)	12.6 (1.29)	25.7 (1.56)	62.6 (1.62)
300 to 499	24,800 (640)	28.4 (0.71)	84.4 (1.04)	36.0 (1.38)	12.3 (1.09)	45.4 (1.38)	0.5 (0.41)	2.8 (0.41)	88.4 (0.95)	8.1 (0.69)	13.4 (0.91)	30.5 (1.34)	66.9 (1.37)
500 to 999	28,200 (560)	32.2 (0.64)	84.7 (0.94)	43.7 (1.31)	15.6 (0.95)	54.4 (1.35)	1.2 (0.18)	4.7 (0.48)	91.9 (0.76)	10.2 (0.61)	29.0 (1.21)	32.8 (1.23)	67.9 (1.32)
1,000 to 1,499	5,500 (260)	6.3 (0.30)	84.9 (1.63)	50.6 (2.91)	18.8 (2.63)	59.4 (2.52)	2.4 (0.58)	12.2 (1.51)	90.6 (1.21)	20.0 (1.50)	67.7 (2.36)	52.2 (2.59)	68.2 (2.02)
1,500 or more	3,600 (210)	4.1 (0.24)	77.9 (2.09)	55.6 (2.64)	8.6 (1.66)	55.6 (2.40)	3.4 (0.61)	14.5 (1.57)	83.7 (2.01)	21.7 (1.88)	90.4 (1.83)	61.5 (2.77)	73.7 (2.09)
Percent of students approved for free or reduced-price school lunch													
Does not participate	3,500 (290)	4.0 (0.33)	69.3 (3.21)	42.1 (3.57)	14.8 (2.59)	41.7 (3.25)	3.1 (0.84)	10.0 (2.22)	64.2 (3.82)	23.1 (2.70)	28.3 (3.39)	37.0 (3.88)	61.5 (3.36)
Less than 15	15,000 (480)	17.1 (0.54)	85.3 (1.42)	31.4 (1.78)	3.1 (0.63)	37.7 (1.76)	† (†)	1.3 (0.27)	85.9 (1.33)	8.9 (0.99)	21.2 (1.31)	32.8 (1.67)	62.8 (2.24)
15 to 29	14,900 (510)	17.0 (0.58)	84.3 (1.28)	37.5 (1.43)	5.0 (0.80)	45.1 (1.86)	0.7 (0.19)	3.1 (0.54)	86.3 (1.29)	10.5 (0.92)	23.8 (1.34)	33.1 (1.59)	61.8 (1.60)
30 to 49	21,600 (590)	24.6 (0.67)	78.8 (1.22)	34.1 (1.53)	7.1 (0.77)	49.9 (1.57)	1.6 (0.37)	4.3 (0.48)	87.7 (1.12)	12.6 (0.64)	23.6 (1.07)	31.2 (1.35)	66.0 (1.54)
50 to 74	17,700 (510)	20.2 (0.58)	81.6 (1.51)	41.9 (1.97)	16.4 (1.36)	53.0 (1.58)	1.9 (0.30)	7.1 (1.06)	91.5 (0.83)	13.1 (1.06)	24.5 (1.59)	32.9 (1.42)	69.3 (1.77)
75 to 100	15,000 (570)	17.1 (0.64)	81.7 (1.58)	53.5 (2.13)	37.8 (1.93)	61.9 (1.96)	5.7 (1.01)	12.4 (1.27)	93.5 (1.06)	16.8 (1.68)	30.3 (1.88)	31.9 (2.03)	72.5 (1.85)
Location of school													
City	22,700 (420)	25.9 (0.49)	84.9 (1.16)	49.0 (1.64)	29.3 (1.48)	56.2 (1.63)	4.8 (0.68)	11.4 (0.83)	91.0 (0.80)	14.4 (0.85)	36.5 (1.09)	34.0 (1.24)	70.4 (1.35)
Suburban	25,600 (510)	29.2 (0.56)	86.4 (0.91)	40.1 (1.55)	11.0 (1.03)	44.2 (1.36)	1.1 (0.25)	3.6 (0.48)	88.0 (0.92)	6.1 (0.49)	26.2 (1.13)	34.7 (1.43)	67.7 (1.60)
Town	13,700 (420)	15.6 (0.48)	79.2 (1.51)	33.3 (1.94)	7.4 (0.96)	49.7 (1.84)	1.0 (0.30)	4.8 (0.73)	83.7 (1.62)	13.8 (1.25)	20.2 (1.39)	31.5 (1.67)	64.9 (2.03)
Rural	25,600 (490)	29.3 (0.55)	74.9 (1.28)	33.6 (1.43)	5.3 (0.82)	48.2 (1.55)	1.0 (0.20)	3.4 (0.36)	87.5 (0.88)	17.6 (1.08)	15.3 (0.81)	29.5 (1.34)	62.1 (1.36)
Level[5]													
Elementary	61,500 (360)	70.2 (0.32)	84.7 (0.65)	39.0 (1.03)	14.7 (0.67)	45.2 (0.94)	0.8 (0.23)	3.4 (0.33)	91.2 (0.62)	5.6 (0.44)	15.5 (0.62)	26.3 (0.77)	68.4 (1.00)
Secondary	19,700 (270)	22.5 (0.32)	75.0 (1.33)	41.4 (1.38)	8.8 (1.11)	59.7 (1.33)	3.7 (0.38)	10.2 (0.64)	80.4 (1.04)	28.2 (1.33)	53.9 (1.61)	51.1 (1.55)	61.3 (1.20)
Combined	6,400 (260)	7.4 (0.30)	70.9 (1.89)	37.2 (2.37)	16.1 (1.40)	57.2 (2.08)	8.8 (1.22)	14.8 (1.72)	80.7 (1.76)	35.0 (2.10)	24.4 (1.83)	34.7 (2.14)	62.3 (2.01)
Private total	27,700 (680)	100.0 (†)	73.5 (1.02)	40.2 (1.08)	55.5 (1.06)	73.7 (1.00)	0.8 (0.21)	0.7 (0.20)	88.4 (0.82)	7.7 (0.61)	5.9 (0.50)	19.4 (0.79)	39.0 (1.07)
School enrollment													
Under 300	22,500 (650)	81.3 (0.67)	72.2 (1.25)	40.3 (1.22)	52.4 (1.22)	71.2 (1.16)	1.0 (0.25)	0.9 (0.24)	88.2 (0.98)	8.0 (0.70)	4.0 (0.55)	15.6 (0.88)	37.4 (1.32)
300 to 499	3,100 (140)	11.3 (0.60)	81.1 (1.95)	39.8 (2.56)	69.3 (2.34)	84.2 (1.92)	‡ (†)	‡ (†)	90.6 (1.63)	5.7 (1.81)	5.5 (1.11)	32.1 (2.44)	48.0 (2.72)
500 to 999	1,800 (120)	6.3 (0.39)	77.8 (3.09)	37.8 (3.30)	71.5 (3.16)	87.2 (2.23)	‡ (†)	‡ (†)	88.3 (2.30)	5.9 (1.44)	22.1 (2.85)	41.3 (3.08)	42.2 (3.23)
1,000 or more	300 (40)	1.1 (0.15)	64.4 (6.81)	50.2 (8.14)	50.1 (6.61)	76.2 (5.48)	‡ (†)	‡ (†)	89.2 (4.06)	16.9 (5.88)	53.2 (7.00)	48.6 (6.59)	48.0 (5.97)
Percent of students approved for free or reduced-price school lunch													
Does not participate	21,100 (570)	76.3 (0.81)	70.3 (1.33)	39.7 (1.21)	51.9 (1.28)	71.5 (1.15)	0.8 (0.26)	0.4 (0.18)	87.4 (0.98)	7.7 (0.68)	6.4 (0.63)	17.8 (0.95)	36.0 (1.23)
Less than 15	3,500 (180)	12.8 (0.61)	85.1 (2.18)	33.7 (2.92)	68.0 (2.72)	84.1 (2.19)	‡ (†)	‡ (†)	91.4 (2.22)	4.1 (1.03)	2.6 (0.87)	23.8 (2.07)	51.8 (3.29)
15 to 29	1,200 (130)	4.3 (0.46)	76.9 (4.48)	41.7 (5.12)	66.5 (4.84)	76.6 (4.77)	‡ (†)	‡ (†)	96.8 (1.69)	4.7 (2.32)	‡ (†)	19.4 (4.12)	41.8 (4.90)
30 or more	1,800 (180)	6.5 (0.58)	86.1 (2.46)	57.1 (4.09)	65.7 (3.56)	76.5 (3.26)	3.1 (1.84)	5.5 (2.19)	89.7 (2.51)	16.8 (3.77)	9.3 (2.60)	29.1 (3.31)	48.0 (3.91)
Level[5]													
Elementary	16,700 (330)	60.5 (1.07)	79.5 (1.19)	44.9 (1.32)	60.6 (1.27)	74.1 (1.32)	0.3 (0.17)	† (†)	90.3 (0.94)	2.4 (0.52)	3.1 (0.50)	19.9 (0.97)	39.2 (1.34)
Secondary	2,500 (360)	9.1 (1.14)	62.9 (3.65)	32.2 (3.80)	44.9 (3.53)	70.0 (3.78)	3.1 (1.87)	2.1 (1.16)	73.4 (3.80)	23.3 (3.75)	16.2 (2.99)	24.4 (3.11)	44.3 (4.00)
Combined	8,400 (280)	30.4 (0.77)	64.8 (2.11)	33.2 (1.96)	48.4 (2.00)	74.0 (1.66)	1.2 (0.49)	1.7 (0.56)	89.3 (1.34)	13.5 (1.33)	8.3 (1.15)	16.9 (1.60)	37.1 (2.05)

†Not applicable.

‡Reporting standards not met.

[1]Access to buildings is controlled during school hours (e.g., by locked or monitored doors).

[2]Access to grounds is controlled during school hours (e.g., by locked or monitored gates).

[3]All students must pass through a metal detector each day.

[4]All or most students are required to stay on school grounds during lunch.

[5]Elementary schools have grade 6 or below, with no grade higher than 8; secondary schools have no grade lower than 7; and combined schools have grades lower than 7 and higher than 8.

NOTE: Detail may not sum to totals because of rounding. Standard errors appear in parentheses.

SOURCE: U.S. Department of Education, National Center for Education Statistics, Schools and Staffing Survey (SASS), "Public School Principal Questionnaire" and "Private School Principal Questionnaire," 2003–04. (This table was prepared July 2006.)

Table 147. Number and percentage of public schools reporting crime incidents, by school characteristics and seriousness of crime incidents reported: 1999–2000 and 2003–04

Type of crime	All public schools, 1999–2000		2003–04														
			All public schools		Instruction level of school						Size of enrollment						
					Elementary		Middle		High		Less than 300		300 to 499		500 to 999		1,000 or more
1	2		3		4		5		6		7		8		9		10
Number of schools (in thousands)	82	(#)	80	(0.2)	49	(0.2)	14	(#)	11	(0.3)	19	(0.2)	24	(0.1)	29	(#)	9	(#)
Percent of schools with incident	86.4	(1.23)	88.5	(0.85)	83.3	(1.43)	96.5	(0.76)	98.6	(0.58)	79.7	(2.43)	88.1	(1.69)	91.3	(1.19)	99.1	(0.53)
Violent incidents[2]	71.4	(1.37)	81.4	(1.05)	74.2	(1.71)	93.6	(1.06)	95.9	(0.93)	68.8	(2.88)	80.2	(2.19)	85.8	(1.33)	97.5	(1.07)
Serious violent incidents[3]	19.7	(0.98)	18.3	(0.99)	13.3	(1.34)	24.4	(1.10)	29.4	(1.71)	15.3	(2.53)	14.8	(1.61)	17.5	(1.35)	36.3	(2.07)
Rape or attempted rape[4]	0.7	(0.10)	0.8	(0.17)	#	(†)	1.0 !	(0.31)	3.4	(0.55)	‡	(†)	0.5 !	(0.21)	0.4 !	(0.14)	3.6	(0.82)
Sexual battery other than rape[5]	2.5	(0.33)	3.0	(0.32)	‡	(†)	6.4	(0.67)	9.2	(0.84)	‡	(†)	0.8 !	(0.28)	3.3	(0.49)	10.6	(0.84)
Physical attack or fight[6] with weapon[7]	5.2	(0.60)	4.0	(0.46)	3.0	(0.63)	4.2	(0.62)	7.9	(0.84)	4.4 !	(1.83)	2.1 !	(0.68)	3.5	(0.57)	9.8	(1.27)
Threat of attack with weapon[7]	11.1	(0.70)	8.6	(0.71)	7.0	(0.93)	11.8	(0.99)	11.6	(1.08)	6.4	(1.84)	6.7	(1.24)	8.9	(0.85)	17.7	(1.68)
Robbery[8] with a weapon[7]	0.5 !	(0.15)	0.6	(0.15)	‡	(†)	0.8 !	(0.27)	1.7	(0.43)	#	(†)	‡	(†)	0.5 !	(0.22)	2.7	(0.72)
Robbery[8] without a weapon[7]	5.3	(0.56)	6.3	(0.60)	4.1	(0.78)	6.6	(0.80)	12.5	(1.23)	5.1	(1.45)	5.4	(1.02)	5.6	(0.81)	13.5	(1.27)
Physical attack or fight without a weapon	63.7	(1.52)	76.7	(1.21)	68.2	(1.94)	91.5	(1.16)	94.5	(1.00)	62.8	(3.05)	73.5	(2.34)	82.5	(1.58)	96.0	(1.24)
Threat of attack without weapon	52.2	(1.47)	53.0	(1.34)	45.4	(1.94)	67.8	(1.60)	71.4	(1.44)	37.6	(3.05)	52.3	(2.52)	56.1	(1.94)	77.0	(1.86)
Theft/larceny[9]	45.6	(1.37)	46.0	(1.29)	29.8	(1.88)	63.3	(1.76)	83.5	(1.27)	40.5	(3.53)	33.8	(2.21)	48.9	(1.73)	80.7	(1.93)
Other incidents[10]	72.7	(1.30)	64.0	(1.27)	50.8	(1.99)	82.9	(1.30)	93.0	(1.04)	50.7	(2.98)	59.6	(2.76)	67.2	(1.62)	93.3	(1.57)
Possess firearm/explosive device[11]	5.5	(0.44)	6.1	(0.49)	3.6	(0.66)	7.9	(0.83)	13.9	(1.41)	2.8 !	(1.11)	3.2	(0.89)	7.2	(0.82)	16.8	(1.78)
Possess knife or sharp object	42.6	(1.28)	15.9	(0.85)	11.1	(1.17)	25.0	(1.10)	29.4	(1.56)	9.5	(2.07)	10.3	(1.66)	18.0	(1.37)	37.8	(1.72)
Distribution of illegal drugs	12.3	(0.50)	12.9	(0.55)	1.5 !	(0.48)	26.6	(1.50)	44.4	(1.78)	3.5 !	(1.14)	6.3	(0.83)	13.8	(0.96)	47.3	(1.73)
Possession or use of alcohol or illegal drugs	26.6	(0.72)	29.3	(0.87)	6.3	(1.00)	55.7	(1.79)	84.7	(1.18)	16.1	(1.96)	19.1	(1.48)	31.0	(1.16)	78.9	(1.31)
Sexual harassment[12]	36.3	(1.26)	—	(†)	—	(†)	—	(†)	—	(†)	—	(†)	—	(†)	—	(†)	—	(†)
Vandalism[13]	51.5	(1.61)	51.4	(1.17)	42.2	(1.81)	65.1	(1.67)	74.5	(1.51)	37.6	(3.06)	47.9	(2.50)	54.3	(1.63)	80.4	(2.09)
Number of incidents (in thousands)	2,259	(117.0)	2,133	(79.4)	752	(53.9)	675	(46.4)	582	(22.2)	189	(22.7)	406	(48.4)	855	(40.7)	683	(23.9)
Violent incidents[2]	1,466	(103.7)	1,553	(73.5)	639	(51.0)	516	(44.7)	320	(17.5)	143	(19.7)	331	(47.2)	656	(37.9)	424	(20.4)
Serious violent incidents[3]	61	(7.0)	55	(4.7)	19	(3.0)	16	(2.2)	17	(2.0)	8	(2.4)	8	(2.1)	19	(2.1)	20	(2.6)
Rape or attempted rape[4]	1	(0.1)	1	(0.2)	#	(†)	#	(†)	1	(0.1)	#	(†)	#	(†)	#	(†)	#	(†)
Sexual battery other than rape[5]	4	(1.1)	5	(0.7)	#	(†)	2	(0.5)	2	(0.5)	#	(†)	#	(†)	2	(0.3)	3	(0.7)
Physical attack or fight[6] with weapon[7]	12	(2.5)	12	(2.3)	5	(1.5)	3 !	(1.0)	3 !	(1.0)	3 !	(1.6)	2 !	(0.8)	3	(0.9)	4	(1.1)
Threat of attack with weapon[7]	21	(1.9)	19	(2.6)	9	(2.1)	5	(1.0)	5	(1.1)	3 !	(1.0)	4 !	(1.8)	7	(2.0)	6	(1.2)
Robbery[8] with a weapon[7]	‡	(†)	1 !	(0.4)	#	(†)	‡	(†)	1 !	(0.2)	#	(†)	#	(†)	‡	(†)	1 !	(0.2)
Robbery[8] without a weapon[7]	20	(3.2)	16	(1.9)	5 !	(1.5)	4	(0.8)	5	(0.6)	2 !	(0.6)	2	(0.5)	6	(1.6)	6	(0.8)
Physical attack or fight without a weapon[7]	807	(59.6)	932	(39.4)	420	(36.4)	297	(14.4)	167	(6.9)	89	(12.6)	181	(17.1)	420	(26.4)	242	(10.7)
Threat of attack without weapon	599	(52.7)	566	(47.4)	199	(18.2)	203	(41.2)	136	(13.0)	45	(7.8)	141	(39.2)	217	(18.0)	163	(14.0)
Theft/larceny[9]	218	(9.2)	200	(7.0)	36	(3.5)	54	(3.2)	94	(4.2)	18	(2.4)	25	(2.3)	68	(4.1)	88	(4.4)
Other incidents[10]	575	(21.3)	380	(9.9)	78	(5.5)	105	(5.0)	168	(5.7)	28	(3.9)	51	(3.1)	131	(4.3)	170	(6.1)
Possess firearm/explosive device[11]	9	(2.2)	7	(0.6)	2	(0.4)	2	(0.3)	3	(0.3)	1 !	(0.2)	1	(0.3)	3	(0.4)	3	(0.4)
Possess knife or sharp object	86	(4.0)	30	(1.5)	9	(1.0)	9	(0.7)	11	(0.8)	2	(0.7)	4	(0.6)	11	(1.0)	13	(0.8)
Distribution of illegal drugs	28	(1.6)	33	(1.7)	1 !	(0.5)	8	(0.5)	21	(1.3)	1 !	(0.6)	2	(0.4)	9	(0.7)	20	(1.4)
Possession or use of alcohol or illegal drugs	114	(4.9)	131	(4.2)	6	(1.4)	30	(1.7)	83	(2.8)	7	(1.3)	13	(1.7)	37	(2.2)	75	(2.7)
Sexual harassment[12]	128	(6.1)	—	(†)	—	(†)	—	(†)	—	(†)	—	(†)	—	(†)	—	(†)	—	(†)
Vandalism[13]	211	(13.6)	179	(6.5)	61	(4.6)	55	(3.8)	51	(3.0)	17	(2.2)	31	(2.1)	72	(3.9)	60	(3.9)

See notes at end of table.

Table 147. Number and percentage of public schools reporting crime incidents, by school characteristics and seriousness of crime incidents reported: 1999–2000 and 2003–04—Continued

Type of crime	All public schools, 1999–2000	2003–04								
		All public schools	Instruction level of school			Size of enrollment			
			Elementary	Middle	High	Less than 300	300 to 499	500 to 999	1,000 or more
1	2	3	4	5	6	7	8	9	10
Number of incidents per 100,000 students	**4,849** (252.4)	**4,568** (165.4)	**3,324** (223.4)	**6,894** (465.1)	**5,004** (175.1)	**4,827** (550.4)	**4,163** (497.5)	**4,365** (202.3)	**5,082** (172.0)
Violent incidents[2]	**3,147** (223.8)	**3,326** (154.8)	**2,821** (214.1)	**5,271** (452.3)	**2,751** (148.1)	**3,644** (486.0)	**3,385** (484.8)	**3,348** (189.5)	**3,157** (150.7)
Serious violent incidents[3]	130 (15.2)	118 (10.0)	84 (13.3)	160 (21.7)	144 (17.0)	208 (61.6)	86 (21.1)	95 (10.6)	149 (18.6)
Rape or attempted rape[4]	1 (0.2)	2 (0.3)	# (†)	2! (0.6)	5 (0.9)	‡ (†)	2! (0.9)	1! (0.3)	3 (0.7)
Sexual battery other than rape[5]	9 (2.4)	12 (1.5)	‡ (†)	24 (5.1)	21 (4.2)	‡ (†)	2! (0.8)	8 (1.3)	24 (4.9)
Physical attack or fight with weapon[6]	26 (5.4)	26 (5.0)	22 (6.4)	35! (10.7)	29! (8.6)	83! (41.2)	16! (7.8)	18 (4.5)	29 (8.3)
Threat of attack with weapon[7]	45 (4.1)	41 (5.5)	38 (9.0)	51 (10.3)	39 (9.9)	67! (23.8)	42! (18.3)	35 (5.6)	41 (8.8)
Robbery[8] with a weapon[7]	‡ (†)	3! (0.9)	‡ (†)	‡ (†)	5! (1.5)	# (†)	‡ (†)	‡ (†)	5! (1.7)
Robbery[8] without a weapon[7]	43 (6.8)	35 (4.0)	22! (6.8)	42 (8.1)	46 (5.3)	48! (16.8)	23 (5.5)	31 (8.0)	45 (6.1)
Physical attack or fight without a weapon	1,732 (128.8)	1,996 (82.1)	1,857 (154.7)	3,032 (141.9)	1,439 (55.4)	2,287 (315.7)	1,853 (174.8)	2,144 (131.6)	1,799 (79.5)
Threat of attack without weapon	1,285 (113.2)	1,212 (101.2)	880 (76.5)	2,079 (420.6)	1,168 (112.0)	1,148 (191.5)	1,446 (402.7)	1,109 (91.2)	1,210 (104.1)
Theft/larceny[9]	**468** (20.2)	**428** (14.7)	**157** (15.2)	**553** (30.7)	**807** (31.0)	**473** (57.5)	**253** (22.9)	**349** (20.9)	**658** (29.9)
Other incidents[10]	**1,234** (44.8)	**814** (19.9)	**346** (22.3)	**1,069** (48.3)	**1,446** (41.5)	**710** (94.0)	**524** (32.3)	**668** (22.1)	**1,267** (45.0)
Possess firearm/explosive device[11]	18 (4.8)	16 (1.3)	10 (1.8)	21 (2.8)	23 (2.7)	14! (5.4)	10 (2.6)	15 (1.9)	24 (2.9)
Possess knife or sharp object	184 (8.7)	65 (3.2)	38 (4.4)	94 (6.8)	92 (6.9)	62 (16.9)	38 (5.9)	56 (5.2)	98 (6.7)
Distribution of illegal drugs	59 (3.5)	70 (3.5)	5! (2.0)	83 (5.5)	178 (10.9)	38! (15.4)	25 (3.8)	45 (3.4)	148 (9.9)
Possession or use of alcohol or illegal drugs	245 (10.4)	281 (8.8)	26 (6.3)	308 (16.9)	717 (22.5)	169 (32.5)	137 (16.9)	188 (10.9)	555 (20.3)
Sexual harassment[12]	274 (13.0)	— (†)	— (†)	— (†)	— (†)	— (†)	— (†)	— (†)	— (†)
Vandalism[13]	453 (28.6)	382 (13.5)	268 (19.2)	564 (37.4)	435 (24.2)	427 (56.1)	315 (22.6)	365 (20.2)	443 (28.1)

See notes at end of table.

Table 147. Number and percentage of public schools reporting crime incidents, by school characteristics and seriousness of crime incidents reported: 1999–2000 and 2003–04—Continued

	2003–04										
	Urbanicity				Percent minority enrollment[1]				Percent of students eligible for free/reduced-price lunch		
Type of crime	City	Urban fringe	Town	Rural	Less than 5	5 to 19	20 to 49	50 or more	0 to 20	21 to 50	50 or more
1	11	12	13	14	15	16	17	18	19	20	21
Number of schools (in thousands)	20 (0.1)	27 (0.2)	10 (0.2)	24 (0.1)	17 (0.9)	20 (1.0)	18 (1.1)	24 (0.8)	19 (0.7)	29 (1.0)	33 (0.9)
Percent of schools with incident	92.1 (1.59)	87.7 (1.61)	92.2 (2.66)	85.0 (2.23)	83.7 (2.43)	88.2 (1.99)	89.2 (1.89)	91.6 (1.55)	84.3 (2.30)	88.5 (1.65)	91.0 (1.35)
Violent incidents[2]	87.7 (1.82)	80.2 (1.83)	86.9 (2.83)	75.4 (2.42)	74.1 (2.79)	76.9 (2.64)	84.5 (2.09)	88.0 (1.56)	71.3 (2.22)	82.0 (1.87)	86.7 (1.65)
Serious violent incidents[3]	21.5 (2.32)	18.5 (1.69)	19.2 (3.10)	15.1 (1.47)	15.6 (2.05)	13.9 (1.61)	19.3 (2.41)	23.6 (1.74)	15.4 (1.97)	16.2 (1.12)	21.8 (2.12)
Rape or attempted rape[4]	1.2 (0.30)	0.7 (0.17)	‡ (†)	‡ (†)	‡ (†)	0.4! (0.16)	0.6! (0.27)	1.1 (0.24)	0.6! (0.19)	1.0! (0.38)	0.8 (0.20)
Sexual battery other than rape[5]	4.8 (0.72)	3.1 (0.50)	2.0 (0.50)	1.8! (0.55)	1.3! (0.44)	1.8 (0.44)	3.7 (0.77)	4.6 (0.75)	2.5 (0.62)	3.5 (0.58)	2.8 (0.48)
Physical attack or fight[6] with weapon[7]	4.8 (0.96)	4.6 (0.90)	5.1! (1.76)	2.1! (0.65)	2.3! (1.09)	2.3! (0.74)	3.0 (0.80)	7.5 (0.99)	2.3 (0.67)	3.0 (0.64)	5.8 (0.93)
Threat of attack with weapon[7]	10.7 (1.87)	9.6 (1.23)	8.1 (1.94)	6.2 (0.92)	7.1 (1.44)	7.6 (1.19)	8.9 (1.66)	10.9 (1.49)	8.5 (1.42)	6.9 (0.89)	10.2 (1.61)
Robbery[8] with a weapon[7]	1.3! (0.40)	0.7! (0.34)	# (†)	‡ (†)	# (†)	‡ (†)	‡ (†)	1.2 (0.30)	0.5! (0.18)	0.6! (0.30)	0.7! (0.21)
Robbery[8] without a weapon[7]	7.8 (1.20)	5.8 (0.98)	5.7 (1.36)	5.8 (1.09)	4.9 (1.15)	4.9 (1.32)	6.5 (1.44)	8.3 (1.06)	4.7 (0.94)	5.0 (0.92)	8.3 (1.22)
Physical attack or fight without a weapon	84.4 (1.99)	75.7 (2.18)	84.0 (2.88)	68.4 (2.77)	66.2 (3.03)	72.5 (2.50)	79.9 (2.57)	85.3 (1.83)	65.2 (2.17)	76.6 (1.94)	83.4 (1.85)
Threat of attack without weapon	57.6 (2.35)	55.0 (2.31)	51.7 (3.47)	47.3 (2.68)	52.5 (3.09)	48.4 (2.86)	56.9 (3.38)	54.0 (2.31)	47.9 (2.18)	53.8 (2.19)	55.2 (2.28)
Theft/larceny[9]	46.6 (2.49)	46.0 (1.66)	45.0 (3.07)	46.0 (2.69)	43.1 (2.69)	45.8 (3.07)	45.3 (3.00)	49.3 (2.43)	46.3 (2.51)	46.6 (2.09)	45.4 (2.24)
Other incidents[10]	68.7 (2.97)	65.2 (2.39)	67.8 (3.26)	57.2 (2.92)	58.3 (3.08)	63.3 (2.67)	64.6 (2.84)	68.0 (2.43)	64.4 (2.75)	65.3 (1.80)	62.6 (2.19)
Possess firearm/explosive device[11]	10.0 (1.48)	5.6 (0.94)	3.8 (0.85)	4.2 (0.83)	1.5 (0.41)	4.7 (0.95)	6.9 (1.33)	10.0 (1.09)	3.9 (0.61)	4.9 (0.66)	8.3 (1.03)
Possess knife or sharp object	22.0 (2.09)	15.7 (1.41)	19.9 (2.49)	9.6 (1.14)	11.2 (1.61)	11.7 (1.55)	17.4 (1.78)	22.1 (1.86)	11.6 (1.29)	15.8 (1.42)	18.6 (1.46)
Distribution of illegal drugs	14.0 (0.93)	14.0 (0.75)	14.1 (1.72)	10.3 (1.07)	11.1 (1.04)	14.7 (1.48)	13.0 (1.23)	12.4 (0.96)	14.1 (0.98)	15.0 (0.96)	10.5 (0.79)
Possession or use of alcohol or illegal drugs	28.8 (1.38)	28.0 (0.89)	35.9 (2.84)	28.6 (1.85)	28.5 (2.23)	28.9 (1.92)	30.1 (1.87)	28.9 (1.55)	31.5 (1.85)	33.3 (1.43)	24.6 (1.70)
Sexual harassment[12]	— (†)	— (†)	— (†)	— (†)	— (†)	— (†)	— (†)	— (†)	— (†)	— (†)	— (†)
Vandalism[13]	56.6 (3.09)	55.8 (2.18)	49.7 (3.79)	42.9 (2.57)	45.1 (3.19)	53.3 (2.65)	51.1 (3.15)	55.0 (2.30)	55.2 (2.55)	51.1 (1.52)	49.5 (2.07)
Number of incidents (in thousands)	671 (36.7)	785 (39.9)	219 (17.0)	459 (58.3)	276 (22.8)	413 (26.0)	489 (30.2)	918 (65.5)	398 (20.7)	741 (35.3)	995 (66.9)
Violent incidents[2]	487 (31.8)	565 (36.5)	159 (13.2)	342 (57.2)	193 (17.9)	279 (19.8)	354 (23.8)	699 (62.5)	248 (17.8)	527 (29.2)	778 (61.8)
Serious violent incidents[3]	20 (3.1)	18 (2.1)	8 (2.2)	8 (1.0)	6 (1.4)	9 (1.8)	11 (1.5)	28 (3.5)	10 (1.6)	17 (2.5)	28 (3.3)
Rape or attempted rape[4]	# (†)	# (†)	# (†)	# (†)	# (†)	# (†)	# (†)	# (†)	# (†)	# (†)	# (†)
Sexual battery other than rape[5]	2 (0.4)	3 (0.6)	# (†)	‡ (†)	‡ (†)	1 (0.3)	1 (0.3)	3 (0.6)	# (†)	2 (0.3)	3 (0.6)
Physical attack or fight[6] with weapon[7]	5 (1.4)	3 (0.6)	3! (1.4)	1! (0.6)	‡ (†)	1! (0.5)	1! (0.5)	7 (1.7)	1! (0.5)	4! (1.4)	7 (1.6)
Threat of attack with weapon[7]	7! (2.2)	8 (1.5)	2! (0.6)	3 (0.5)	2 (0.4)	3 (0.7)	5 (1.1)	9 (2.3)	5 (1.2)	6! (1.8)	9 (2.2)
Robbery[8] with a weapon[7]	1! (0.4)	# (†)	# (†)	# (†)	# (†)	4! (1.5)	1! (0.7)	1! (0.4)	# (†)	1! (0.5)	1! (0.4)
Robbery[8] without a weapon[7]	5 (0.8)	5 (0.9)	3! (1.5)	3 (0.7)	2 (0.4)	4! (1.5)	3 (0.7)	7 (1.1)	3 (0.5)	5 (1.5)	8 (1.1)
Physical attack or fight without a weapon[7]	295 (18.2)	345 (23.0)	93 (7.5)	199 (20.6)	111 (11.7)	175 (15.0)	218 (15.0)	410 (27.4)	146 (10.5)	324 (21.2)	461 (27.7)
Threat of attack without weapon	172 (16.7)	202 (18.6)	58 (7.4)	135! (41.8)	76 (11.5)	95 (7.7)	125 (12.2)	261 (43.2)	92 (11.6)	186 (14.4)	289 (41.8)
Theft/larceny[9]	55 (3.2)	80 (4.8)	20 (2.0)	45 (3.5)	31 (3.0)	51 (4.5)	49 (4.5)	66 (4.7)	57 (3.4)	79 (5.3)	64 (4.0)
Other incidents[10]	129 (7.6)	139 (6.1)	40 (3.5)	72 (4.4)	51 (4.4)	83 (4.9)	85 (5.1)	153 (5.8)	93 (4.3)	135 (†)	152 (†)
Possess firearm/explosive device[11]	3 (0.4)	3 (0.4)	1 (0.1)	1 (0.2)	# (†)	1 (0.3)	2 (0.4)	4 (0.4)	1 (0.2)	2 (0.3)	4 (0.5)
Possess knife or sharp object	12 (1.0)	10 (1.0)	4 (0.6)	3 (0.5)	3 (0.4)	5 (0.6)	8 (0.9)	14 (1.0)	5 (0.7)	10 (0.8)	15 (1.2)
Distribution of illegal drugs	12 (1.1)	11 (1.0)	3 (0.4)	6 (0.7)	4 (0.4)	8 (0.8)	7 (0.6)	13 (1.2)	8 (0.6)	12 (0.8)	13 (1.2)
Possession or use of alcohol or illegal drugs[12]	39 (2.6)	50 (2.2)	15 (1.6)	27 (2.4)	19 (2.5)	33 (2.4)	30 (2.0)	45 (2.3)	39 (2.5)	51 (2.7)	41 (2.9)
Sexual harassment[12]	— (†)	— (†)	— (†)	— (†)	— (†)	— (†)	— (†)	— (†)	— (†)	— (†)	— (†)
Vandalism[13]	62 (5.0)	65 (4.0)	17 (1.9)	34 (3.0)	25 (2.5)	36 (2.4)	38 (3.0)	77 (4.5)	39 (2.1)	59 (3.8)	80 (5.1)

See notes at end of table.

Table 147. Number and percentage of public schools reporting crime incidents, by school characteristics and seriousness of crime incidents reported: 1999–2000 and 2003–04—Continued

Type of crime	2003–04										
	Urbanicity				Percent minority enrollment				Percent of students eligible for free/reduced-price lunch		
	City	Urban fringe	Town	Rural	Less than 5	5 to 19	20 to 49	50 or more	0 to 20	21 to 50	50 or more
1	11	12	13	14	15	16	17	18	19	20	21
Number of incidents per 100,000 students	4,937 (260.9)	4,258 (206.6)	4,415 (299.3)	4,717 (578.8)	3,879 (273.1)	3,654 (203.7)	4,408 (235.6)	5,697 (405.2)	3,055 (145.6)	4,569 (177.7)	5,693 (386.9)
Violent incidents[2]	3,585 (230.2)	3,067 (195.3)	3,213 (246.6)	3,512 (574.6)	2,715 (228.3)	2,468 (158.6)	3,196 (195.6)	4,339 (386.9)	1,904 (133.0)	3,252 (154.3)	4,453 (358.2)
Serious violent incidents[3]	150 (23.1)	99 (11.4)	164 (43.3)	87 (10.2)	87 (19.3)	81 (15.9)	98 (12.5)	175 (21.7)	77 (12.2)	105 (15.1)	161 (18.3)
Rape or attempted rape[4]	2 (0.6)	1 (0.3)	‡ (†)	2! (1.2)	‡ (†)	1! (0.5)	1! (0.5)	2 (0.5)	2! (0.5)	2! (0.8)	2 (0.5)
Sexual battery other than rape[5]	15 (3.1)	14 (3.2)	4 (1.1)	7 (1.8)	4! (1.7)	4 (1.0)	12 (3.0)	20 (4.0)	6 (1.8)	12 (2.3)	15 (3.5)
Physical attack or fight with weapon[7]	37 (10.4)	15 (3.5)	61! (28.2)	14! (5.7)	‡ (†)	13! (4.5)	13! (4.5)	46 (11.0)	11! (4.1)	23! (8.7)	41 (9.2)
Threat of attack with weapon[7]	51! (15.7)	41 (8.1)	37! (11.4)	28 (4.8)	26 (5.8)	30 (6.2)	44 (9.4)	56 (14.4)	36 (9.5)	35 (7.3)	51 (12.5)
Robbery[8] with a weapon[7]	7! (3.1)	1! (0.6)	# (†)	‡ (†)	# (†)	‡ (†)	‡ (†)	6! (2.6)	2! (0.9)	1! (0.6)	5! (2.4)
Robbery[8] without a weapon[7]	37 (5.8)	27 (4.8)	60! (29.7)	34 (6.8)	26 (6.0)	33! (13.3)	28 (5.9)	43 (6.4)	22 (4.0)	32 (9.3)	47 (6.0)
Physical attack or fight without a weapon	2,169 (133.3)	1,873 (123.9)	1,884 (141.3)	2,043 (203.2)	1,564 (156.1)	1,549 (122.0)	1,968 (125.0)	2,542 (166.0)	1,124 (73.5)	2,001 (114.3)	2,640 (166.9)
Threat of attack without weapon	1,266 (120.8)	1,094 (100.2)	1,166 (143.2)	1,382! (425.5)	1,064 (154.8)	839 (66.5)	1,129 (106.5)	1,621 (269.7)	703 (90.5)	1,146 (85.6)	1,652 (238.4)
Theft/larceny[9]	403 (23.8)	434 (24.0)	401 (33.1)	464 (35.2)	442 (36.4)	451 (35.4)	444 (34.4)	410 (28.1)	436 (23.0)	486 (29.5)	368 (22.6)
Other incidents[10]	949 (51.1)	757 (28.5)	800 (60.1)	741 (42.7)	722 (49.4)	735 (41.1)	769 (38.6)	949 (37.4)	715 (28.0)	831 (34.1)	872 (42.9)
Possess firearm/explosive device[11]	23 (3.1)	14 (2.2)	10 (2.7)	13 (2.3)	5 (1.5)	13 (2.5)	16 (3.2)	23 (2.6)	9 (1.3)	15 (2.0)	22 (2.6)
Possess knife or sharp object	88 (6.8)	56 (5.4)	76 (13.2)	42 (5.0)	38 (5.8)	42 (5.3)	70 (8.0)	89 (6.2)	41 (5.5)	62 (5.1)	84 (6.8)
Distribution of illegal drugs	90 (7.6)	61 (5.3)	64 (8.4)	61 (6.8)	51 (5.0)	67 (6.5)	67 (5.7)	79 (7.6)	60 (4.4)	74 (5.1)	73 (6.7)
Possession or use of alcohol or illegal drugs[12]	290 (18.2)	270 (10.9)	307 (26.5)	275 (23.6)	272 (27.9)	296 (21.0)	274 (15.0)	281 (16.4)	302 (17.1)	316 (16.2)	233 (15.4)
Sexual harassment[12]	— (†)	— (†)	— (†)	— (†)	— (†)	— (†)	— (†)	— (†)	— (†)	— (†)	— (†)
Vandalism[13]	457 (35.4)	355 (19.8)	343 (34.8)	349 (30.5)	355 (34.0)	318 (20.0)	341 (25.1)	475 (27.1)	303 (15.5)	363 (20.7)	459 (29.9)

—Not available.
†Not applicable.
#Rounds to zero.
‡Reporting standards not met.
!Interpret data with caution.

[1]Some schools are omitted from these categories because of missing data on their school characteristics. For this reason, the detailed results do not sum to the totals.

[2]Violent incidents include rape, sexual battery other than rape, physical attack or fight with or without a weapon, threat of physical attack with or without a weapon, and robbery with or without a weapon.

[3]Serious violent incidents include rape, sexual battery other than rape, physical attack or fight with a weapon, threat of physical attack with a weapon, and robbery with or without a weapon.

[4]Rape was defined for respondents as "forced sexual intercourse (vaginal, anal, or oral penetration). This includes penetration from a foreign object."

[5]Sexual battery was defined for respondents as an "incident that includes threatened rape, fondling, indecent liberties, child molestation, or sodomy."

[6]Physical attack or fight was defined for respondents as an "actual and intentional touching or striking of another person against his or her will, or the intentional causing of bodily harm to an individual."

[7]Weapon was defined for respondents as "any instrument or object used with the intent to threaten, injure, or kill. Includes look-alikes if they are used to threaten others."

[8]Robbery was defined for respondents as "the taking or attempting to take anything of value that is owned by another person or organization, under confrontational circumstances by force or threat of force or violence and/or by putting the victim in fear."

[9]Theft/larceny (taking things over $10 without personal confrontation) was defined for respondents as "the unlawful taking of another person's property without personal confrontation, threat, violence, or bodily harm. Included are pocket picking, stealing purse or backpack (if left unattended or no force was used to take it from owner), theft from a building, theft from a motor vehicle or motor vehicle parts or accessories, theft of bicycles, theft from vending machines, and all other types of thefts."

[10]Other incidents include possession of a firearm or explosive device, possession of a knife or sharp object, distribution of illegal drugs, possession or use of alcohol or illegal drugs, sexual harassment, or vandalism.

[11]Firearm/explosive device was defined as "any weapon that is designed to (or may readily be converted to) expel a projectile by the action of an explosive. This includes guns, bombs, grenades, mines, rockets, missiles, pipe bombs, or similar devices designed to explode and capable of causing bodily harm or property damage."

[12]Sexual harassment was defined for respondents "as unsolicited, offensive behavior that inappropriately asserts sexuality over another person. The behavior may be verbal or non-verbal."

[13]Vandalism was defined for respondents as "the willful damage or destruction of school property including bombing, arson, graffiti, and other acts that cause property damage. Includes damage caused by computer hacking."

NOTE: Either the school principal or the person most knowledgeable about discipline issues at school completed the SSOCS questionnaire. If the respondent did not provide a value for the total number of specified incidents at the school, the value was imputed to equal the number of specified incidents reported to police. Values associated with violent incidents, serious violent incidents, total incidents, and other incidents were obtained by adding the post-imputed values that comprise each of the preceding composite variables. All public schools include elementary schools, middle schools, high schools, and combined schools. The population counts on SSOCS 2000 and 2004 exclude all schools in outlying U.S. territories; nonregular schools such as special education, vocational, alternative/other, and ungraded schools; and schools with a high grade of kindergarten or lower. "At school/at your school" was defined for respondents as including activities happening in school buildings, on school grounds, on school buses, and at places that are holding school-sponsored events or activities. Respondents were instructed to, unless the survey specified otherwise, only respond for those times that were during normal school hours or when school activities/events were in session. Elementary schools are defined as schools in which the lowest grade is not higher than grade 3 and the highest grade is not higher than grade 8. Middle schools are defined as schools in which the lowest grade is not lower than grade 4 and the highest grade is not higher than grade 9. High schools are defined as schools in which the lowest grade is not lower than grade 9 and the highest grade is not higher than grade 12. Combined schools include all other combinations of grades, including K–12 schools. Detail may not sum to totals because of rounding.

SOURCE: U.S. Department of Education, National Center for Education Statistics, School Survey on Crime and Safety (SSOCS), 2000 and 2004. (This table was prepared February 2007.)

Table 148. Number and percentage of students expelled from public elementary and secondary schools, by sex, race/ethnicity, and state: 2002

State	Total (2)	Students expelled — Sex: Male (3)	Students expelled — Sex: Female (4)	Students expelled — Race/ethnicity: White (5)	Students expelled — Race/ethnicity: Black (6)	Students expelled — Race/ethnicity: Hispanic (7)	% Total (8)	% Sex: Male (9)	% Sex: Female (10)	% Race: White (11)	% Race: Black (12)	% Race: Hispanic (13)
United States	89,131 (1,708.5)	68,183 (1,246.2)	20,948 (505.3)	39,483 (805.8)	28,192 (590.9)	17,697 (764.6)	0.2	0.3	0.1	0.1	0.3	0.2
Alabama	656 (15.6)	503 (13.7)	153 (2.7)	215 (10.0)	433 (12.0)	7 (#)	0.1	0.1	#	#	0.2	0.1
Alaska	332! (85.5)	244! (59.1)	88! (26.5)	111 (1.1)	18 (#)	6 (#)	0.3	0.4	#	0.1	0.3	0.1
Arizona	1,205! (173.1)	905! (114.6)	300! (60.5)	383 (30.1)	146 (43.1)	576! (113.6)	0.1	0.2	0.1	0.1	0.3	0.2
Arkansas	941! (308.1)	727! (220.6)	214! (88.3)	515 (129.7)	404 (181.1)	15 (#)	0.2	0.3	0.1	0.2	0.4	0.3
California	18,682 (1,340.2)	14,932 (972.6)	3,750 (395.6)	5,326 (382.9)	3,111 (325.1)	8,857 (706.6)	0.3	0.5	0.1	0.3	0.6	0.3
Colorado	2,207 (42.7)	1,799 (30.9)	408 (14.5)	1,131 (27.5)	245 (2.8)	755 (26.6)	0.3	0.5	0.1	0.2	0.6	0.4
Connecticut	1,041 (74.2)	774 (60.3)	267 (19.3)	383 (29.3)	388! (56.9)	263 (13.1)	0.2	0.3	0.1	0.1	0.5	0.3
Delaware[1]	109 (†)	85 (†)	24 (†)	58 (†)	49 (†)	3 (†)	0.1	0.1	#	0.1	0.1	#
District of Columbia[1]	174 (†)	120 (†)	54 (†)	2 (†)	169 (†)	3 (†)	0.3	0.4	0.2	0.1	0.3	#
Florida	1,041 (64.5)	791 (44.1)	250 (21.0)	518 (54.5)	407 (25.3)	104 (4.7)	#	0.1	#	#	0.1	#
Georgia	2,768 (395.3)	2,103 (283.8)	665 (112.5)	1,036 (143.2)	1,637! (304.8)	86 (8.0)	0.2	0.3	0.1	0.1	0.3	0.1
Hawaii[2]	193 (21.1)	175 (19.1)	18 (7.8)	36 (4.1)	2! (1.2)	7! (2.4)	0.1	0.2	#	0.1	0.3	0.2
Idaho	295 (27.3)	259 (23.3)	36 (5.1)	218 (22.3)	6! (2.5)	60 (7.1)	0.1	0.2	#	0.1	0.3	0.1
Illinois	2,322 (141.8)	1,804 (107.6)	518 (41.9)	1,037 (94.2)	955 (74.0)	316 (26.9)	0.1	0.2	#	0.1	0.2	0.1
Indiana	6,240 (300.8)	4,553 (221.8)	1,687 (94.2)	4,353 (252.6)	1,576 (149.9)	254! (28.9)	0.6	0.9	0.3	0.5	1.1	0.6
Iowa	746! (181.3)	526! (114.3)	220! (67.4)	523! (158.1)	171 (14.8)	36! (8.1)	0.2	0.2	0.1	0.1	0.8	0.2
Kansas	740 (27.5)	578 (21.1)	162 (9.2)	408 (25.1)	171 (1.4)	125 (4.6)	0.2	0.2	0.1	0.1	0.4	0.3
Kentucky	456! (66.3)	336! (47.6)	120! (22.2)	368! (54.4)	80! (23.8)	5! (2.3)	0.1	0.1	0.1	0.1	0.6	#
Louisiana[1]	5,575 (52.1)	3,878 (26.3)	1,697 (27.3)	1,576 (51.0)	3,877 (26.8)	73! (2.0)	0.8	1.0	0.5	0.4	1.1	0.6
Maine	184 (21.1)	154 (17.2)	30! (6.6)	175 (20.8)	6! (1.9)	1 (0.2)	0.1	0.2	#	0.1	0.2	0.1
Maryland[1]	987 (†)	735 (†)	252 (†)	275 (†)	683 (†)	20 (†)	0.1	0.2	0.1	0.1	0.2	#
Massachusetts	525! (58.8)	403! (41.1)	122! (20.7)	254! (37.8)	154 (7.9)	102! (18.3)	0.1	0.1	#	#	0.2	0.1
Michigan	1,875! (110.9)	1,426! (90.6)	449! (34.0)	1,161! (88.9)	546! (38.3)	116! (17.7)	0.1	0.2	0.1	0.1	0.2	0.2
Minnesota	70! (12.0)	59! (11.5)	11! (2.0)	34! (8.7)	14! (0.9)	6! (1.5)	#	#	#	#	#	#
Mississippi	1,139 (58.8)	872 (46.4)	267 (15.5)	453 (25.6)	662 (41.8)	12 (#)	0.2	0.3	0.1	0.2	0.3	0.2
Missouri	1,203! (383.5)	931! (290.6)	272! (95.8)	845! (337.1)	344! (46.3)	10! (3.2)	0.1	0.2	0.1	0.1	0.2	0.1
Montana	156 (10.7)	122 (8.7)	34! (4.6)	105 (7.9)	1 (1.7)	4 (0.8)	0.1	0.2	#	0.1	0.1	0.1
Nebraska	636 (57.2)	453 (51.1)	183 (5.0)	352 (13.3)	182! (#)	56 (#)	0.2	0.3	0.1	0.2	0.9	0.2
Nevada[1]	781! (129.2)	609! (95.8)	172! (27.3)	286 (25.7)	218! (†)	234! (†)	0.2	0.3	0.1	0.2	0.6	0.2
New Hampshire	100! (27.†)	82! (22.9)	18! (4.3)	89! (4.3)	3 (1.9)	4 (†)	0.1	0.1	#	0.1	0.1	0.1
New Jersey	597 (44.8)	453 (31.9)	144 (18.5)	74! (28.4)	421! (19.7)	100! (20.9)	#	0.1	#	#	0.2	0.1
New Mexico	380! (34.3)	297! (26.1)	83! (8.8)	54! (14.9)	14! (5.3)	103! (14.0)	0.1	0.2	#	0.1	0.2	0.1
New York	1,189! (195.4)	951! (148.6)	238! (51.1)	753! (127.3)	326! (78.4)	98! (21.5)	#	0.1	#	#	#	#
North Carolina	1,338 (111.9)	1,049 (90.5)	289 (25.6)	507 (56.6)	700 (60.8)	75! (16.2)	0.1	0.2	0.1	0.1	0.2	0.1
North Dakota	130! (50.5)	97! (40.0)	33! (10.5)	94! (50.4)	# (†)	3 (#)	0.1	0.1	0.1	0.1	#	0.3
Ohio	6,034 (437.5)	4,215 (291.7)	1,819 (153.2)	3,572 (354.9)	2,256 (163.5)	166! (26.0)	0.3	0.5	0.2	0.2	0.8	0.4
Oklahoma	932! (81.7)	657! (52.6)	275! (33.9)	566! (58.0)	143! (12.5)	49! (5.4)	0.2	0.2	0.1	0.1	0.4	0.1
Oregon	1,495 (57.2)	1,212 (51.1)	283 (8.8)	1,042 (51.5)	81! (3.2)	242 (10.6)	0.3	0.4	0.1	0.2	0.5	0.3
Pennsylvania	1,516 (129.2)	1,130 (95.8)	386 (42.3)	1,052! (99.3)	367! (50.6)	77! (16.3)	0.1	0.1	0.1	0.1	0.3	0.1
Rhode Island	63 (6.4)	54 (6.4)	9 (#)	22! (6.4)	18 (#)	19! (#)	#	0.1	#	#	0.1	0.1
South Carolina	3,884 (196.8)	2,946 (155.7)	938 (45.5)	1,328 (75.4)	2,493 (139.8)	49 (5.7)	0.6	0.8	0.3	0.4	0.9	0.3
South Dakota	79! (8.1)	57! (8.0)	22 (1.4)	54 (6.5)	54! (†)	1 (†)	0.1	0.1	#	0.1	#	0.1
Tennessee	3,674 (93.4)	2,672 (58.8)	1,002 (39.5)	1,591 (90.7)	1,987! (8.7)	60 (2.9)	0.4	0.6	0.2	0.3	0.9	0.3
Texas	7,185 (365.0)	5,651 (284.5)	1,534 (95.7)	1,977 (160.8)	1,252! (99.9)	3,875 (255.3)	0.2	0.3	0.1	0.1	#	0.1
Utah	265 (7.3)	222 (8.6)	43 (2.3)	218 (7.3)	# (†)	31 (#)	0.1	0.1	#	0.1	#	0.1
Vermont	68 (9.1)	55! (7.7)	13! (2.5)	61 (8.6)	# (†)	# (†)	0.1	0.1	#	0.1	#	#
Virginia	1,409! (151.5)	1,176! (142.9)	233! (20.2)	703! (84.8)	608! (84.9)	56! (3.5)	0.1	0.2	#	0.1	0.2	0.1
Washington	3,870 (129.6)	3,105 (110.5)	765 (25.4)	2,380 (113.5)	589! (10.7)	480! (37.6)	0.4	0.6	0.2	0.3	1.0	0.4
West Virginia	291 (33.7)	247! (32.3)	44! (7.1)	273 (32.4)	16! (3.3)	1! (0.8)	0.1	0.2	0.1	0.1	0.3	0.1
Wisconsin	1,262! (76.5)	925! (54.0)	337! (33.2)	867! (66.8)	260! (18.4)	78! (2.8)	0.2	0.2	0.1	0.1	0.3	0.2
Wyoming	95 (4.7)	79 (4.3)	16! (2.0)	68 (3.5)	2 (#)	20! (2.8)	0.1	0.2	0.1	0.1	#	0.3

†Not applicable.
#Rounds to zero.
!Interpret data with caution.
[1]State/jurisdiction has 25 or fewer school districts; therefore, data are based on universe count (instead of samples).
[2]State has only one district, but is sampled within the district.

NOTE: Race categories exclude persons of Hispanic origin. Detail may not sum to totals because of rounding. Standard errors appear in parentheses.
SOURCE: U.S. Department of Education, Office for Civil Rights, OCR Elementary and Secondary School Survey: 2002. (This table was prepared June 2006.)

Table 149. Number and percentage of students suspended from public elementary and secondary schools, by sex, race/ethnicity, and state: 2002

State	Students suspended[1]						Suspended students as a percentage of total enrollment					
	Total	Sex		Race/ethnicity			Total	Sex		Race/ethnicity		
		Male	Female	White	Black	Hispanic		Male	Female	White	Black	Hispanic
1	2	3	4	5	6	7	8	9	10	11	12	13
United States	3,083,810 (18,840.0)	2,165,933 (13,139.2)	917,877 (6,088.5)	1,363,543 (9,887.1)	1,119,969 (10,770.4)	500,347 (5,902.2)	6.6	9.0	4.0	4.9	13.9	6.0
Alabama	63,614 (187.5)	43,911 (156.1)	19,703 (36.1)	24,516 (170.3)	38,360 (#)	375 (46.6)	8.8	11.8	5.7	5.6	14.8	3.1
Alaska	7,289 (149.8)	5,128 (121.0)	2,161 (46.0)	3,217 (93.3)	584 (3.7)	307 (1.3)	5.6	7.6	3.4	4.2	9.2	6.1
Arizona	47,039 (1,383.3)	34,386 (915.3)	12,653 (492.3)	18,954 (791.2)	3,818 (61.2)	17,825 (449.0)	5.2	7.4	2.9	4.2	9.0	5.6
Arkansas	35,350 (1,397.9)	25,483 (989.2)	9,867 (467.5)	17,666 (871.8)	16,686 (1,013.4)	758 (34.4)	7.8	11.0	4.5	5.6	15.3	4.1
California	396,584 (9,797.8)	293,486 (7,192.8)	103,098 (2,781.3)	115,030 (3,539.3)	76,101 (3,378.2)	180,181 (4,771.9)	6.4	9.3	3.4	5.6	15.0	6.4
Colorado	51,435 (482.2)	36,885 (342.0)	14,550 (168.4)	27,114 (320.8)	6,089 (7.3)	16,472 (249.5)	6.9	9.6	4.0	5.5	14.2	9.2
Connecticut	43,986 (1,161.9)	30,080 (782.4)	13,906 (394.2)	15,945 (665.7)	15,998 (884.0)	11,544 (382.9)	7.6	10.1	4.9	4.0	19.1	14.5
Delaware[2]	12,968 (†)	8,560 (†)	4,408 (†)	5,554 (†)	6,576 (†)	720 (†)	11.7	14.9	8.2	8.6	18.9	8.5
District of Columbia[2]	7,292 (†)	4,494 (†)	2,738 (†)	20 (†)	6,888 (†)	316 (†)	11.0	13.7	8.3	0.7	12.5	4.9
Florida	222,573 (1,268.8)	154,587 (897.5)	67,986 (391.2)	86,035 (1,080.4)	99,502 (1,012.4)	35,097 (276.9)	9.1	12.3	5.7	6.8	16.7	6.6
Georgia	121,173 (3,248.1)	84,459 (2,199.4)	36,714 (1,101.4)	38,702 (1,005.0)	75,877 (2,709.2)	5,473 (334.2)	8.4	11.5	5.2	5.2	13.5	5.8
Hawaii[3]	9,644 (1,055.5)	6,967 (747.7)	2,677 (318.7)	1,475 (181.0)	190 (32.5)	310 (41.6)	6.0	8.3	3.5	5.1	4.9	7.3
Idaho	10,096 (562.0)	7,690 (424.0)	2,406 (164.4)	8,140 (486.7)	92 (15.8)	1,522 (125.9)	3.8	5.6	1.9	3.5	4.1	5.5
Illinois	108,141 (4,080.9)	73,746 (2,559.4)	34,395 (1,607.7)	43,608 (1,893.8)	48,413 (3,007.4)	15,025 (1,281.2)	5.3	7.1	3.5	3.6	11.4	4.7
Indiana	85,303 (4,465.7)	60,905 (3,160.6)	24,398 (1,443.0)	54,944 (2,946.4)	26,157 (3,370.2)	3,777 (811.2)	8.6	12.0	5.0	6.9	18.8	9.2
Iowa	17,867 (467.1)	12,974 (359.4)	4,893 (128.4)	13,211 (421.9)	3,405 (33.7)	978 (76.8)	3.7	5.2	2.1	3.0	16.1	4.5
Kansas	25,319 (504.6)	18,098 (384.5)	7,221 (149.7)	14,291 (471.4)	6,860 (99.9)	3,417 (32.9)	5.5	7.7	3.9	4.0	16.3	7.5
Kentucky	40,962 (2,554.4)	29,153 (1,706.2)	11,809 (892.8)	32,210 (1,900.3)	8,342 (964.2)	278 (21.0)	6.6	9.0	3.9	5.9	12.3	3.5
Louisiana	81,395 (938.1)	54,020 (641.5)	27,375 (297.6)	25,579 (418.9)	54,324 (763.4)	699 (9.0)	11.1	14.4	7.6	7.2	15.5	5.7
Maine	10,167 (580.4)	7,358 (400.3)	2,809 (206.1)	9,778 (576.4)	214 (10.8)	51 ! (9.0)	5.1	7.2	2.9	5.1	6.8	3.7
Maryland[2]	58,765 (†)	40,257 (†)	18,508 (†)	25,821 (†)	29,727 (†)	2,186 (†)	6.9	9.2	4.4	3.0	9.3	4.4
Massachusetts	42,184 (2,215.2)	29,267 (1,516.9)	12,917 (735.2)	25,958 (1,366.9)	7,539 (831.9)	7,477 (668.6)	5.1	6.9	3.2	4.3	9.3	7.2
Michigan	119,723 (4,339.9)	83,548 (3,019.6)	36,175 (1,414.4)	75,069 (2,986.1)	37,946 (2,751.4)	4,120 (365.5)	7.0	9.5	4.3	6.0	11.1	6.4
Minnesota	16,335 (548.0)	11,658 (366.4)	4,677 (199.1)	11,552 (430.1)	2,513 (80.7)	916 (85.5)	1.9	2.7	1.1	1.7	4.2	2.5
Mississippi	52,954 (1,473.2)	36,156 (1,049.1)	16,798 (442.4)	14,693 (595.5)	37,760 (1,107.5)	323 ! (78.1)	10.7	14.3	6.9	6.5	14.6	6.4
Missouri	59,002 (1,516.5)	42,214 (1,121.5)	16,788 (452.9)	32,408 (1,105.5)	25,077 (1,248.2)	1,111 (64.5)	6.6	9.2	3.8	4.6	15.4	5.6
Montana	5,556 (271.6)	4,031 (192.6)	1,525 (90.5)	3,753 (139.1)	46 (1.5)	149 (7.4)	3.8	5.3	2.1	2.9	4.5	5.1
Nebraska	9,472 (429.9)	6,577 (235.3)	2,895 ! (201.4)	6,134 (115.1)	1,272 (1.9)	975 (26.7)	3.4	4.6	2.1	2.7	6.6	4.0
Nevada[2]	25,889 (†)	17,235 (†)	8,654 (†)	11,670 (†)	5,239 (†)	7,406 (†)	7.1	9.6	4.9	6.1	13.7	6.9
New Hampshire	10,735 (366.6)	7,419 (264.3)	3,316 (119.0)	9,997 (358.3)	246 (9.8)	383 (4.4)	5.3	7.1	3.3	5.2	8.9	8.3
New Jersey	74,380 (3,880.6)	50,685 (2,463.7)	23,695 (1,538.0)	29,246 (2,222.8)	30,574 (2,270.4)	13,003 (939.7)	5.5	7.3	3.6	3.8	11.9	5.7
New Mexico	19,697 (811.4)	13,969 (601.8)	5,728 (222.4)	5,008 (185.6)	616 (12.0)	10,981 (713.8)	6.2	8.5	3.7	4.7	7.8	6.7
New York	94,932 (3,328.2)	67,544 (2,307.0)	27,388 (1,074.5)	49,576 (2,179.2)	28,802 (1,949.8)	14,314 (588.6)	3.3	4.6	2.0	3.1	5.3	2.6
North Carolina	144,236 (6,376.6)	102,544 (4,433.7)	41,692 (1,984.4)	57,210 (2,595.2)	76,835 (4,216.0)	5,769 (332.8)	11.0	15.2	6.5	7.3	19.7	6.9
North Dakota	2,449 (86.0)	1,782 (62.9)	667 (26.5)	1,568 (54.2)	67 (1.4)	40 (1.1)	2.4	3.4	1.4	1.8	5.5	3.8
Ohio	130,003 (4,692.1)	89,469 (3,259.7)	40,534 (1,497.9)	78,292 (3,368.7)	47,347 (2,188.1)	3,665 (822.0)	7.2	9.7	4.6	5.4	16.3	8.6
Oklahoma	35,078 (1,032.7)	25,177 (762.6)	9,901 (291.2)	17,760 (576.6)	9,958 (394.5)	2,522 (74.2)	5.7	8.0	3.3	4.6	15.5	5.7
Oregon	29,799 (876.1)	22,094 (596.9)	7,705 (313.0)	22,260 (740.9)	1,193 (42.8)	4,413 (279.5)	5.5	7.9	2.9	5.3	7.3	6.4
Pennsylvania	129,649 (5,801.7)	87,621 (3,883.6)	42,028 (1,997.9)	65,358 (3,388.0)	54,035 (3,437.6)	9,010 ! (1,352.0)	7.3	9.7	4.9	4.8	19.6	11.2
Rhode Island	15,777 (505.2)	10,606 (325.7)	5,171 (241.3)	8,350 (465.5)	2,848 (186.4)	3,988 (474.2)	10.1	13.2	6.8	7.5	21.8	15.4
South Carolina	90,123 (2,964.0)	61,152 (2,011.0)	28,971 (979.9)	29,470 (1,042.9)	59,170 (2,308.4)	1,056 (103.0)	13.2	17.6	8.7	8.1	20.3	6.6
South Dakota	2,902 (159.1)	2,077 (98.7)	825 (68.1)	1,868 (66.4)	99 (2.0)	66 (3.3)	5.3	7.2	3.2	1.7	5.3	3.1
Tennessee	69,086 (1,337.0)	46,492 (996.9)	22,594 (366.9)	32,250 (1,211.5)	35,201 (465.3)	1,179 (38.5)	8.0	10.5	5.4	5.3	16.2	5.5
Texas	195,142 (3,038.3)	137,478 (2,124.7)	57,664 (987.4)	46,046 (1,182.0)	56,081 (1,725.6)	90,528 (1,917.8)	4.7	6.5	2.9	2.8	10.1	5.1
Utah	17,435 (146.8)	12,546 (129.3)	4,889 (34.8)	12,263 (123.3)	383 (1.4)	3,686 (36.1)	3.7	5.1	2.1	3.1	7.5	7.5
Vermont	4,687 (213.3)	3,311 (167.7)	1,376 (69.2)	4,556 (210.2)	54 (3.7)	21 (1.0)	4.9	6.7	2.9	4.9	4.7	3.4
Virginia	97,391 (3,622.0)	65,997 (2,404.6)	31,394 (1,258.3)	41,294 (1,292.7)	51,010 (2,891.6)	3,482 (226.9)	8.3	11.0	5.5	5.7	15.7	4.8
Washington	63,875 (1,413.1)	47,337 (1,044.7)	16,538 (486.1)	43,764 (1,254.1)	6,818 (134.9)	8,095 (357.1)	6.4	9.2	3.4	6.0	12.0	7.3
West Virginia	22,789 (1,914.5)	16,958 (1,412.0)	5,831 (516.9)	20,961 (1,707.4)	1,552 (242.9)	127 ! (35.2)	8.3	11.9	4.4	8.1	13.1	8.8
Wisconsin	42,487 (1,100.3)	28,047 (702.9)	14,440 (481.2)	20,909 (848.0)	15,417 (212.1)	3,855 (73.0)	5.0	6.4	3.5	3.1	17.8	8.8
Wyoming	3,142 (187.5)	2,316 (156.1)	826 (36.1)	2,527 (170.3)	68 (#)	377 ! (46.6)	3.7	5.3	2.0	3.5	6.0	5.5

†Not applicable.
#Rounds to zero.
!Interpret data with caution.
[1]Each student is counted only once, regardless of the number of suspensions.
[2]State/jurisdiction has 25 or fewer school districts; therefore, data are based on universe count (instead of samples).
[3]State has only one school district, but is sampled within the district.
NOTE: Race categories exclude persons of Hispanic origin. Detail may not sum to totals because of rounding. Standard errors appear in parentheses.
SOURCE: U.S. Department of Education, Office for Civil Rights, OCR Elementary and Secondary School Survey: 2002. (This table was prepared May 2006.)

Table 150. Percentage of students in grades 9 through 12 who reported experience with drugs and violence on school property, by race/ethnicity, grade, and sex: Selected years, 1997 through 2005

Type of violence or drug-related behavior	1997 total	1999 total	2003 total	2005 Total	2005 Race/ethnicity White	2005 Race/ethnicity Black	2005 Race/ethnicity Hispanic	2005 Grade 9	2005 Grade 10	2005 Grade 11	2005 Grade 12
1	2	3	4	5	6	7	8	9	10	11	12
Felt too unsafe to go to school[1]	4.0 (0.6)	5.2 (1.3)	5.4 (0.41)	6.0 (0.61)	4.4 (0.87)	8.7 (0.97)	10.2 (0.87)	7.7 (0.92)	6.3 (0.71)	4.7 (0.61)	4.9 (0.66)
Male	4.1 (0.8)	4.8 (1.6)	5.5 (0.51)	5.7 (0.56)	3.9 (0.82)	8.2 (1.17)	10.7 (0.92)	7.3 (0.92)	5.3 (0.92)	4.5 (2.40)	5.1 (0.82)
Female	3.9 (0.7)	5.7 (1.5)	5.3 (0.51)	6.3 (0.77)	4.9 (0.97)	9.2 (1.43)	9.7 (1.43)	8.1 (1.22)	7.3 (0.92)	4.9 (0.87)	4.5 (0.71)
Carried a weapon on school property[1,2]	8.5 (1.5)	6.9 (1.2)	6.1 (0.56)	6.5 (0.46)	6.1 (0.66)	5.1 (0.66)	8.2 (0.92)	6.4 (0.77)	6.9 (0.71)	5.9 (0.71)	6.7 (0.66)
Male	12.5 (2.9)	11.0 (2.1)	8.9 (0.77)	10.2 (0.82)	10.1 (1.17)	6.8 (1.22)	13.7 (1.53)	9.8 (1.22)	10.5 (1.22)	9.8 (1.22)	10.8 (1.17)
Female	3.7 (0.7)	2.8 (0.7)	3.1 (0.51)	2.6 (0.31)	2.0 (0.31)	3.3 (0.56)	2.6 (0.51)	2.8 (0.61)	3.0 (0.56)	2.1 (0.46)	2.5 (0.61)
Threatened or injured with a weapon on school property[3]	7.4 (0.9)	7.7 (0.8)	9.2 (0.77)	7.9 (0.36)	7.2 (0.46)	8.1 (0.66)	9.8 (0.87)	10.5 (0.61)	8.8 (0.71)	5.5 (0.41)	5.8 (0.51)
Male	10.2 (1.4)	9.5 (1.6)	11.6 (0.97)	9.7 (0.41)	8.7 (0.56)	10.2 (1.22)	11.9 (1.43)	12.1 (0.97)	11.0 (0.87)	7.1 (0.77)	7.3 (0.82)
Female	4.0 (0.6)	5.8 (1.2)	6.5 (0.61)	6.1 (0.41)	5.7 (0.51)	6.1 (0.82)	7.5 (1.12)	8.8 (0.71)	6.5 (0.77)	3.9 (0.56)	4.2 (0.66)
Engaged in a physical fight on school property[3]	14.8 (1.3)	14.2 (1.3)	12.8 (0.77)	13.6 (0.56)	11.6 (0.66)	16.9 (1.38)	18.3 (1.63)	18.9 (0.92)	14.4 (1.07)	10.4 (0.77)	8.5 (0.71)
Male	20.0 (2.0)	18.5 (1.4)	17.1 (0.92)	18.2 (0.92)	16.2 (1.12)	20.1 (1.84)	24.4 (2.50)	24.0 (1.38)	20.0 (1.73)	14.1 (1.33)	11.8 (1.28)
Female	8.6 (1.5)	9.8 (1.9)	8.0 (0.71)	8.8 (0.51)	6.9 (0.61)	14.0 (1.48)	12.1 (1.38)	13.7 (1.02)	8.4 (1.07)	6.6 (0.66)	5.3 (0.77)
Property stolen or deliberately damaged on school property[3]	32.9 (2.6)	— (†)	29.8 (0.71)	29.8 (0.77)	29.1 (0.92)	29.9 (1.43)	31.9 (1.68)	33.9 (1.02)	29.5 (1.48)	27.0 (1.02)	27.1 (1.22)
Male	36.1 (2.6)	— (†)	33.1 (0.87)	31.4 (0.82)	30.2 (0.87)	31.2 (1.63)	36.1 (2.19)	34.2 (1.38)	30.5 (1.79)	30.6 (1.68)	29.1 (1.38)
Female	29.0 (3.7)	— (†)	26.2 (0.82)	28.0 (1.07)	27.8 (1.48)	28.6 (1.99)	27.3 (1.79)	33.4 (1.63)	28.3 (1.68)	23.5 (1.28)	25.1 (1.58)
Cigarette use on school property[1]	14.6 (1.5)	14.0 (1.9)	8.0 (0.71)	6.8 (0.41)	7.4 (0.56)	3.4 (0.41)	7.2 (0.87)	6.2 (0.61)	6.2 (0.66)	6.8 (0.71)	8.2 (0.97)
Male	15.9 (1.7)	14.8 (2.0)	8.2 (0.66)	7.4 (0.41)	7.9 (0.51)	3.6 (0.61)	8.0 (1.07)	6.3 (0.92)	6.3 (0.87)	7.6 (0.92)	9.5 (0.92)
Female	13.0 (2.2)	13.2 (2.0)	7.6 (0.92)	6.2 (0.61)	6.9 (0.87)	3.3 (0.66)	6.3 (1.12)	6.1 (0.71)	6.2 (0.82)	5.8 (0.97)	6.9 (1.58)
Smokeless tobacco use on school property[4]	5.1 (1.4)	4.2 (1.8)	5.9 (1.53)	5.0 (0.61)	6.3 (0.82)	1.2 (0.31)	3.2 (0.66)	4.5 (0.82)	4.9 (0.77)	5.5 (0.77)	5.2 (0.77)
Male	9.0 (2.5)	8.1 (3.5)	8.5 (1.48)	9.2 (1.12)	11.7 (1.53)	2.2 (0.51)	5.4 (1.12)	7.6 (1.43)	8.9 (1.43)	10.8 (1.43)	10.1 (1.58)
Female	0.4 (0.2)	0.3 (0.2)	3.3 (1.68)	0.8 (0.15)	0.8 (0.20)	0.2 (0.10)	1.0 (0.31)	1.4 (0.36)	0.8 (0.20)	0.4 (0.26)	0.4 (0.20)
Alcohol use on school property[1]	5.6 (0.7)	4.9 (0.7)	5.2 (0.46)	4.3 (0.31)	3.8 (0.41)	3.2 (0.46)	7.7 (1.02)	3.7 (0.46)	4.5 (0.46)	4.0 (0.46)	4.8 (0.56)
Male	7.2 (1.3)	6.1 (1.1)	6.0 (0.61)	5.3 (0.41)	5.0 (0.51)	3.2 (0.61)	9.0 (1.38)	4.6 (0.77)	5.3 (0.61)	5.4 (0.77)	5.9 (0.77)
Female	3.6 (0.7)	3.6 (0.7)	4.2 (0.41)	3.3 (0.31)	2.6 (0.41)	3.3 (0.56)	6.4 (1.07)	2.8 (0.46)	3.7 (0.51)	2.7 (0.61)	3.7 (0.71)
Marijuana use on school property[1]	7.0 (1.0)	7.2 (1.4)	5.8 (0.66)	4.5 (0.31)	3.8 (0.41)	4.9 (0.66)	7.7 (0.77)	5.0 (0.61)	4.6 (0.56)	4.1 (0.51)	4.1 (0.46)
Male	9.0 (1.3)	10.1 (2.6)	7.6 (0.87)	6.0 (0.46)	5.1 (0.61)	5.9 (0.87)	10.4 (1.28)	6.1 (1.02)	5.9 (0.77)	6.1 (0.82)	5.8 (0.82)
Female	4.6 (1.1)	4.4 (0.8)	3.7 (0.46)	3.0 (0.31)	2.4 (0.41)	3.9 (0.82)	5.0 (0.61)	3.9 (0.61)	3.3 (0.66)	2.2 (0.31)	2.3 (0.61)
Offered, sold, or given an illegal drug on school property[3]	31.7 (1.8)	30.2 (2.4)	28.7 (1.94)	25.4 (1.07)	23.6 (1.33)	23.9 (2.19)	33.5 (1.17)	24.0 (1.22)	27.5 (1.68)	24.9 (1.02)	24.9 (1.38)
Male	37.4 (2.3)	34.7 (3.3)	31.9 (2.09)	28.8 (1.22)	26.2 (1.63)	28.7 (2.50)	38.5 (1.84)	26.9 (1.68)	30.6 (2.04)	28.4 (1.73)	29.3 (1.53)
Female	24.7 (2.4)	25.7 (2.4)	25.0 (1.94)	21.8 (1.02)	20.9 (1.22)	19.2 (2.35)	28.5 (1.48)	21.0 (1.43)	24.2 (1.79)	21.3 (1.22)	20.4 (1.73)

—Not available.
†Not applicable.
[1]One or more times during the 30 days preceding the survey.
[2]Such as a gun, knife, or club.
[3]One or more times during the 12 months preceding the survey.
[4]Used chewing tobacco or snuff one or more times during the 30 days preceding the survey.

NOTE: Totals include other racial/ethnic groups not shown separately. Race categories exclude persons of Hispanic origin. Standard errors appear in parentheses.
SOURCE: U.S. Department of Health and Human Services, Centers for Disease Control and Prevention, CDC Surveillance Summaries, MMWR 47(SS-03), 49(SS-05), 53(SS-02), and 55(SS-05). (This table was prepared July 2006.)

Table 151. Percentage of 12- to 17-year-olds reporting substance abuse during the past 30 days and the past year, by drug used: Selected years, 1982 through 2005

Year	Percent reporting substance abuse during the past 30 days						Percent reporting substance abuse during past year				
	Illicit drug use			Alcohol	Cigarettes		Illicit drug use			Alcohol	Cigarettes
	Any[1]	Marijuana	Cocaine				Any[1]	Marijuana	Cocaine		
1	2	3	4	5	6		7	8	9	10	11
1982	— (†)	9.9 (—)	1.9 (—)	34.9 (—)	— (†)		(†)	17.7 (—)	3.7 (—)	46.1 (—)	(†)
1985	13.2 (—)	10.2 (—)	1.5 (—)	41.2 (—)	29.4 (—)		20.7 (—)	16.7 (—)	3.4 (—)	52.7 (—)	29.9 (—)
1988	8.1 (—)	5.4 (—)	1.2 (—)	33.4 (—)	22.7 (—)		14.9 (—)	10.7 (—)	2.5 (—)	45.5 (—)	26.8 (—)
1990	7.1 (—)	4.4 (—)	0.6 (—)	32.5 (—)	22.4 (—)		14.1 (—)	9.6 (—)	1.9 (—)	41.8 (—)	26.2 (—)
1993	5.7 (—)	4.0 (—)	0.4 (—)	23.9 (—)	18.5 (—)		11.9 (—)	8.5 (—)	0.7 (—)	35.9 (—)	22.5 (—)
1994	8.2 (—)	6.0 (—)	0.3 (—)	21.6 (—)	18.9 (—)		15.5 (—)	11.4 (—)	1.1 (—)	36.2 (—)	24.5 (—)
1995	10.9 (—)	8.2 (—)	0.8 (—)	21.1 (—)	20.2 (—)		18.0 (—)	14.2 (—)	1.7 (—)	35.1 (—)	26.6 (—)
1996	9.0 (—)	7.1 (—)	0.6 (—)	18.8 (—)	18.3 (—)		16.7 (—)	13.0 (—)	1.4 (—)	32.7 (—)	24.2 (—)
1997	11.4 (—)	9.4 (—)	1.0 (—)	20.5 (—)	19.9 (—)		18.8 (—)	15.8 (—)	2.2 (—)	34.0 (—)	26.4 (—)
1998	9.9 (—)	8.3 (—)	0.8 (—)	19.1 (—)	18.2 (—)		16.4 (—)	14.1 (—)	1.7 (—)	31.8 (—)	23.8 (—)
1999	9.8 (0.23)	7.2 (0.20)	0.5 (0.06)	16.5 (0.30)	14.9 (0.31)		19.8 (0.32)	14.2 (0.29)	1.6 (0.10)	34.1 (0.41)	23.4 (0.37)
2000	9.7 (0.24)	7.2 (0.21)	0.6 (0.07)	16.4 (0.29)	13.4 (0.28)		18.6 (0.31)	13.4 (0.27)	1.7 (0.12)	33.0 (0.39)	20.8 (0.34)
2001	10.8 (0.26)	8.0 (0.24)	0.4 (0.06)	17.3 (0.33)	13.0 (0.28)		20.8 (0.36)	15.2 (0.32)	1.5 (0.10)	33.9 (0.39)	20.0 (0.35)
2002	11.6 (0.29)	8.2 (0.24)	0.6 (0.07)	17.6 (0.32)	13.0 (0.30)		22.2 (0.38)	15.8 (0.32)	2.1 (0.13)	34.6 (0.42)	20.3 (0.35)
2003	11.2 (0.27)	7.9 (0.24)	0.6 (0.06)	17.7 (0.33)	12.2 (0.29)		21.8 (0.36)	15.0 (0.31)	1.8 (0.11)	34.3 (0.42)	19.0 (0.36)
2004	10.6 (0.27)	7.6 (0.23)	0.5 (0.06)	17.6 (0.32)	11.9 (0.30)		21.0 (0.34)	14.5 (0.31)	1.6 (0.11)	33.9 (0.41)	18.4 (0.35)
2005	9.9 (0.25)	6.8 (0.22)	0.6 (0.06)	16.5 (0.32)	10.8 (0.28)		19.9 (0.35)	13.3 (0.30)	1.7 (0.11)	33.3 (0.41)	17.3 (0.36)

—Not available.
†Not applicable.
[1]Includes other illegal drug use not shown separately.

NOTE: Marijuana includes hashish usage for 1996 and later years. Due to changes in the survey instrument and administration and to improve comparability with new data, estimates for 1982 through 1993 have been adjusted and may differ from those reported in previous years. Data for 1999 have been revised from previously published figures. Data for 1999 and later years were gathered using Computer Assisted Interviewing (CAI) and may not be directly comparable to previous years. Standard errors appear in parentheses.

SOURCE: U.S. Department of Health and Human Services, Substance Abuse and Mental Health Services Administration, *National Household Survey on Drug Abuse: Main Findings*, selected years, 1982 through 2001; and National Survey on Drug Use and Health, 2002 through 2005. (This table was prepared September 2006.)

Table 152. Percentage of high school seniors reporting drug use, by type of drug and reporting period: Selected years, 1975 through 2005

Type of drug	Class of 1975	Class of 1980	Class of 1985	Class of 1990	Class of 1995	Class of 1996	Class of 1997	Class of 1998	Class of 1999	Class of 2000	Class of 2001	Class of 2002	Class of 2003	Class of 2004	Class of 2005
1	2	3	4	5	6	7	8	9	10	11	12	13	14	15	16
Percent reporting having ever used drugs															
Alcohol[1]	90.4 (0.69)	93.2 (0.46)	92.2 (0.48)	89.5 (0.57)	80.7 (0.73)	79.2 (0.77)	81.7 (0.71)	81.4 (0.72)	80.0 (0.78)	80.3 (0.80)	79.7 (0.81)	78.4 (0.83)	76.6 (0.80)	76.8 (0.80)	75.1 (0.81)
Any illicit drug	55.2 (1.68)	65.4 (1.23)	60.6 (1.26)	47.9 (1.33)	48.4 (1.32)	50.8 (1.37)	54.3 (1.31)	54.1 (1.32)	54.7 (1.40)	54.0 (1.44)	53.9 (1.44)	53.0 (1.44)	51.1 (1.35)	51.1 (1.35)	50.4 (1.35)
Marijuana only	19.0 (1.32)	26.7 (1.15)	20.9 (1.05)	18.5 (1.03)	20.3 (1.06)	22.3 (1.14)	24.3 (1.13)	24.7 (1.14)	25.3 (1.22)	25.0 (1.25)	23.2 (1.22)	23.5 (1.22)	23.4 (1.15)	22.4 (1.13)	23.0 (1.14)
Any illicit drug other than marijuana[2]	36.2 (1.33)	38.7 (1.04)	39.7 (1.04)	29.4 (0.99)	28.1 (0.97)	28.5 (1.01)	30.0 (0.99)	29.4 (0.99)	29.4 (1.05)	29.0 (1.08)	30.7 (1.09)	29.5 (1.08)	27.7 (0.99)	28.7 (1.00)	27.4 (0.99)
Use of selected drugs															
Cocaine	9.0 (0.73)	15.7 (0.72)	17.3 (0.74)	9.4 (0.59)	6.0 (0.48)	7.1 (0.53)	8.7 (0.57)	9.3 (0.59)	9.8 (0.63)	8.6 (0.62)	8.2 (0.60)	7.8 (0.59)	7.7 (0.55)	8.1 (0.56)	8.0 (0.56)
Heroin	2.2 (0.21)	1.1 (0.12)	1.2 (0.12)	1.3 (0.13)	1.6 (0.14)	1.8 (0.16)	2.1 (0.16)	2.0 (0.16)	2.0 (0.17)	2.4 (0.19)	1.8 (0.17)	1.7 (0.16)	1.5 (0.14)	1.5 (0.14)	1.5 (0.14)
LSD	11.3 (0.81)	9.3 (0.57)	7.5 (0.52)	8.7 (0.57)	11.7 (0.64)	12.6 (0.69)	13.6 (0.69)	12.6 (0.67)	12.2 (0.70)	11.1 (0.69)	10.9 (0.69)	8.4 (0.61)	5.9 (0.49)	4.6 (0.43)	3.5 (0.38)
Marijuana/hashish	47.3 (1.68)	60.3 (1.27)	54.2 (1.29)	40.7 (1.30)	41.7 (1.30)	44.9 (1.36)	49.6 (1.32)	49.1 (1.33)	49.7 (1.40)	48.8 (1.45)	49.0 (1.45)	47.8 (1.44)	46.1 (1.35)	45.7 (1.35)	44.8 (1.34)
PCP	— (†)	9.6 (0.33)	4.9 (0.24)	2.8 (0.19)	2.7 (0.18)	4.0 (0.23)	3.9 (0.22)	3.9 (0.22)	3.4 (0.22)	3.4 (0.23)	3.5 (0.23)	3.1 (0.22)	2.5 (0.18)	1.6 (0.15)	2.4 (0.18)
Percent reporting use of drugs in the past 12 months															
Alcohol[1]	84.8 (0.84)	87.9 (0.59)	85.6 (0.63)	80.6 (0.73)	73.7 (0.81)	72.5 (0.85)	74.8 (0.80)	74.3 (0.81)	73.8 (0.86)	73.2 (0.89)	73.3 (0.89)	71.5 (0.91)	70.1 (0.86)	70.6 (0.86)	68.6 (0.87)
Any illicit drug	45.0 (1.64)	53.1 (1.26)	46.3 (1.26)	32.5 (1.21)	39.0 (1.26)	40.2 (1.31)	42.4 (1.27)	41.4 (1.28)	42.1 (1.35)	40.9 (1.39)	41.4 (1.39)	41.0 (1.38)	39.3 (1.29)	38.8 (1.29)	38.4 (1.28)
Marijuana only	18.8 (1.29)	22.7 (1.06)	18.9 (0.99)	14.6 (0.91)	19.6 (1.02)	20.4 (1.08)	21.7 (1.06)	21.2 (1.06)	21.4 (1.12)	20.5 (1.14)	19.8 (1.12)	20.1 (1.13)	19.5 (1.05)	18.3 (1.02)	18.8 (1.03)
Any illicit drug other than marijuana[2]	26.2 (1.15)	30.4 (0.92)	27.4 (0.89)	17.9 (0.79)	19.4 (0.81)	19.8 (0.84)	20.7 (0.83)	20.2 (0.82)	20.7 (0.88)	20.4 (0.90)	21.6 (0.92)	20.9 (0.91)	19.8 (0.83)	20.5 (0.85)	19.7 (0.83)
Use of selected drugs															
Cocaine	5.6 (0.52)	12.3 (0.58)	13.1 (0.59)	5.3 (0.40)	4.0 (0.35)	4.9 (0.40)	5.5 (0.41)	5.7 (0.42)	6.2 (0.46)	5.0 (0.43)	4.8 (0.42)	5.0 (0.42)	4.8 (0.39)	5.3 (0.41)	5.1 (0.40)
Heroin	1.0 (0.13)	0.5 (0.07)	0.6 (0.07)	0.5 (0.07)	1.1 (0.10)	1.0 (0.10)	1.2 (0.11)	1.0 (0.10)	1.1 (0.11)	1.5 (0.13)	0.9 (0.10)	1.0 (0.11)	0.8 (0.09)	0.9 (0.10)	0.8 (0.09)
LSD	7.2 (0.59)	6.5 (0.43)	4.4 (0.36)	5.4 (0.41)	8.4 (0.49)	8.8 (0.52)	8.4 (0.49)	7.6 (0.48)	8.1 (0.52)	6.6 (0.49)	6.6 (0.49)	3.5 (0.36)	1.9 (0.25)	2.2 (0.27)	1.8 (0.24)
Marijuana/hashish	40.0 (1.61)	48.8 (1.27)	40.6 (1.24)	27.0 (1.15)	34.7 (1.23)	35.8 (1.28)	38.5 (1.25)	37.5 (1.25)	37.8 (1.33)	36.5 (1.36)	37.0 (1.36)	36.2 (1.35)	34.9 (1.26)	34.3 (1.25)	33.6 (1.24)
PCP	— (†)	4.4 (0.20)	2.9 (0.16)	1.2 (0.11)	1.8 (0.13)	2.6 (0.16)	2.3 (0.15)	2.1 (0.14)	1.8 (0.14)	2.3 (0.16)	1.8 (0.14)	1.1 (0.11)	1.3 (0.11)	0.7 (0.08)	1.3 (0.11)
Percent reporting use of drugs in the past 30 days															
Alcohol[1]	68.2 (1.10)	72.0 (0.81)	65.9 (0.85)	57.1 (0.92)	51.3 (0.92)	50.8 (0.95)	52.7 (0.92)	52.0 (0.92)	51.0 (0.98)	50.0 (1.01)	49.8 (1.01)	48.6 (1.00)	47.5 (0.94)	48.0 (0.94)	47.0 (0.94)
Any illicit drug	30.7 (1.35)	37.2 (1.09)	29.7 (1.03)	17.2 (0.87)	23.8 (0.98)	24.6 (1.03)	26.2 (1.01)	25.6 (1.01)	25.9 (1.07)	24.9 (1.09)	25.7 (1.10)	25.4 (1.09)	24.1 (1.01)	23.4 (1.00)	23.1 (0.99)
Marijuana only	15.3 (1.06)	18.8 (0.88)	14.8 (0.80)	9.2 (0.67)	13.8 (0.79)	15.1 (0.85)	15.5 (0.83)	14.9 (0.82)	15.5 (0.88)	14.5 (0.89)	14.7 (0.89)	14.1 (0.87)	19.5 (0.93)	18.3 (0.91)	12.8 (0.78)
Any illicit drug other than marijuana[2]	15.4 (0.80)	18.4 (0.66)	14.9 (0.60)	8.0 (0.47)	10.0 (0.52)	9.5 (0.53)	10.7 (0.53)	10.7 (0.54)	10.4 (0.56)	10.4 (0.58)	11.0 (0.59)	11.3 (0.60)	10.4 (0.54)	10.8 (0.55)	10.3 (0.54)
Use of selected drugs															
Cocaine	1.9 (0.25)	5.2 (0.31)	6.7 (0.35)	1.9 (0.20)	1.8 (0.19)	2.0 (0.21)	2.3 (0.22)	2.4 (0.22)	2.6 (0.24)	2.1 (0.23)	2.1 (0.23)	2.3 (0.24)	2.1 (0.21)	2.3 (0.22)	2.3 (0.22)
Heroin	0.4 (0.08)	0.2 (0.04)	0.3 (0.05)	0.2 (0.04)	0.6 (0.08)	0.5 (0.07)	0.5 (0.07)	0.5 (0.07)	0.5 (0.07)	0.7 (0.09)	0.4 (0.07)	0.5 (0.08)	0.4 (0.06)	0.5 (0.07)	0.5 (0.07)
LSD	2.3 (0.28)	2.3 (0.21)	1.6 (0.18)	1.9 (0.20)	4.0 (0.28)	2.5 (0.23)	3.1 (0.25)	3.2 (0.26)	2.7 (0.25)	1.6 (0.20)	2.3 (0.24)	0.7 (0.13)	0.6 (0.11)	0.7 (0.12)	0.7 (0.12)
Marijuana/hashish	27.1 (1.30)	33.7 (1.07)	25.7 (0.98)	14.0 (0.80)	21.2 (0.94)	21.9 (0.98)	23.7 (0.98)	22.8 (0.97)	23.1 (1.03)	21.6 (1.04)	22.4 (1.05)	21.5 (1.03)	21.2 (0.96)	19.9 (0.94)	19.8 (0.94)
PCP	— (†)	1.4 (0.11)	1.6 (0.12)	0.4 (0.06)	0.6 (0.08)	1.3 (0.12)	0.7 (0.08)	1.0 (0.10)	0.8 (0.09)	0.9 (0.10)	0.5 (0.08)	0.4 (0.07)	0.6 (0.08)	0.4 (0.06)	0.7 (0.08)

—Not available.
†Not applicable.
[1]Survey question changed in 1993; later data are not comparable to figures for earlier years.
[2]Other illicit drugs include any use of LSD or other hallucinogens, crack or other cocaine, or heroin, or any use of other narcotics, amphetamines, barbiturates, or tranquilizers not under a doctor's orders.

NOTE: Standard errors appear in parentheses. Standard errors were calculated from formulas to perform trend analysis over an interval greater than 1 year (for example, a comparison between 1975 and 1990). A revised questionnaire was used in 1982 and later years to reduce the inappropriate reporting of nonprescription stimulants. This slightly reduced the positive responses for some types of drug abuse.
SOURCE: University of Michigan, Institute for Social Research, Monitoring the Future, selected years, 1975 through 2005. (This table was prepared May 2006.)

Table 153. Age range for compulsory school attendance, special education services, year-round schools, and kindergarten programs, by state: 1997, 2000, 2002, and 2004

State	Compulsory attendance			Compulsory special education services, 1997[1]	Year-round schools, 2004		Kindergarten education, 2004		
	2000	2002	2004		Has policy on year-round schools	Has districts with year-round schools	School districts required to offer		Attendance required
							Half day	Full day	
1	2	3	4	5	6	7	8	9	10
Alabama	7 to 16	7 to 16	7 to 16[2]	6 to 21		X		X	X
Alaska	7 to 16	7 to 16	7 to 16[2]	3 to 22		—	—	—	—
Arizona	6 to 16[3]	6 to 16[3]	6 to 16[3]	3 to 22		—	X		
Arkansas	5 to 17[4]	5 to 17[4]	5 to 17	5 to 21	X	X	X	X	X
California	6 to 18[5]	6 to 18	6 to 18	Birth to 21	X	X	X[6]		
Colorado	—	—	7 to 16	3 to 21		X	—	—	—
Connecticut	7 to 16	7 to 18[2]	7 to 18[2]	Under 21[7]		—	X		
Delaware	5 to 16	5 to 16	5 to 16[8]	3 to 20		X	X		X
District of Columbia	—	5 to 18	5 to 18	—		—			
Florida	6 to 16[9]	6 to 16[9]	6 to 16[8]	—	X	X		X	
Georgia	6 to 16	6 to 16	6 to 16	Under 21[7]		X		X	
Hawaii	6 to 18	6 to 18	6 to 18	Under 20	X	—			
Idaho	7 to 16	7 to 16	7 to 16	3 to 21		X			
Illinois	7 to 16	7 to 16	7 to 17	3 to 21	X	X	X		
Indiana	7 to 16	7 to 16	7 to 16	3 to 22		X	X		
Iowa	6 to 16[10]	6 to 16[10]	6 to 16	Under 21	X	X	X[6]		
Kansas	7 to 18[11]	7 to 18[2]	7 to 18[2]	([12])		—	X		
Kentucky	6 to 16	6 to 16	6 to 16[8]	Under 21		X	X		
Louisiana	7 to 17	7 to 17	7 to 17[8]	3 to 21		X	X		
Maine	7 to 17	7 to 17	7 to 17[13]	5 to 19[14]		X	X		X
Maryland	5 to 16	5 to 16	5 to 16	Under 21	X	X	X		
Massachusetts	6 to 16	6 to 16	6 to 16	3 to 21		—	X[6]		
Michigan	6 to 16	6 to 16	6 to 16	Under 26	X	X	X		
Minnesota	7 to 18[2]	7 to 16	7 to 16	Under 22	X	X		X	
Mississippi	6 to 17	6 to 17	6 to 16	Birth to 20		—	X		
Missouri	7 to 16	7 to 16	7 to 16	Under 21		X	X		
Montana	7 to 16[15]	7 to 16[15]	7 to 16[15]	3 to 18		—	X[6]		
Nebraska	7 to 16	7 to 16	7 to 16	Birth to 21		X	X		
Nevada	7 to 17	7 to 17	7 to 17	Under 22	X	X	—	—	—
New Hampshire	6 to 16	6 to 16	6 to 16	3 to 21		—	X[6]		
New Jersey	6 to 16	6 to 16	6 to 16	5 to 21		X	X		X
New Mexico	5 to 18	5 to 18	5 to 18[16]	([17])	X	X	X[18]	X[18]	
New York	6 to 16[19]	6 to 16	6 to 16	Under 21		—		X	
North Carolina	7 to 16	7 to 16	7 to 16	5 to 20	X	X	—	—	—
North Dakota	7 to 16	7 to 16	7 to 16	3 to 20[20]		—	X[6]		X
Ohio	6 to 18	6 to 18	6 to 18	Under 22		—	X[6]		X
Oklahoma	5 to 18	5 to 18	5 to 18	3 and up[21]	X	X	X[6]		
Oregon	7 to 18	7 to 18	7 to 18[2]	3 to 21		X	X[6]		
Pennsylvania	8 to 17	8 to 17	8 to 17[2]	6 to 21	X	X	—	—	X
Rhode Island	6 to 16	6 to 16	6 to 16	3 to 21		—	X		X
South Carolina	5 to 16	5 to 16	5 to 16	3 to 21		—		X	X
South Dakota	6 to 16	6 to 16	6 to 16	Under 21		—	X[6]		
Tennessee	6 to 17	6 to 17	6 to 17	3 to 21	X	X	X		X
Texas	6 to 18	6 to 18	6 to 18	3 to 21	X	X	X[6]		
Utah	6 to 18	6 to 18	6 to 18	3 to 22		X	X		
Vermont	7 to 16	6 to 16	6 to 16	3 to 21		—	X		
Virginia	5 to 18	5 to 18	5 to 18	2 to 21		X	X[6]		
Washington	8 to 17[2]	8 to 17[8]	8 to 16[8]	3 to 21[22]		X	X		
West Virginia	6 to 16	6 to 16	6 to 16	5 to 21	X	X		X	X
Wisconsin	6 to 18	6 to 18	6 to 18	Under 21		X	X		
Wyoming	6 to 16[3]	6 to 16[3]	7 to 16[3]	3 to 21		X	X		

X State has program.

—Not available.

[1]Most states have provision whereby education is provided up to a certain age or completion of secondary school, whichever comes first.

[2]Eligible for waiver.

[3]Until age 16 or 10th-grade completion.

[4]Must have turned 17 by October 1.

[5]At least 16 and have graduated high school or passed California High School Proficiency Exam (CHSPE) and obtained parental permission.

[6]State requires either half-day or full-day program.

[7]Under 21 or until child graduates from high school.

[8]May exit only with guardian consent.

[9]Compulsory school age for all Manatee County students who turned 16 on or after October 1, 1999, is 18, unless they earned high school diploma prior to reaching 18th birthday.

[10]Must have turned 16 by September 15.

[11]Eligible for waiver at 16.

[12]To be determined by rules and regulations adopted by the state board.

[13]May exit at 15 with guardian consent, if student meets other criteria.

[14]Must be 5 before October 1, and not 20 before start of school year.

[15]Age 16 and completion of eighth grade.

[16]May exit before 18 if exemptions are met.

[17]School-age unless otherwise provided by law.

[18]State requires both half-day and full-day program.

[19]Age 16 and completion of school year.

[20]Must not be 21 by September 1.

[21]Children from birth through age 2 are eligible for additional services. Eligibility for special education services ceases upon completion of a secondary education program; no age limit.

[22]Student may complete school year if 21st birthday occurs while attending school.

NOTE: The Education of the Handicapped Act (EHA) Amendments of 1986 make it mandatory for all states receiving EHA funds to serve all 3- to 18-year-old disabled children.

SOURCE: Council of Chief State School Officers, *Key State Education Policies on PK–12 Education*, 2000, 2002, and 2004; Education Commission of the States, *Clearinghouse Notes*, August 1997; California Department of Education, Safe Schools and Violence Prevention Office, *School Attendance Review Boards, Feb. 2001*; and *School District of Manatee County Policy and Procedure Manual*, retrieved May 4, 2005, from http://www.manatee.k12.fl.us/manatee/policy_procedure/table_noframes.html. (This table was prepared May 2006.)

Table 154. State requirements for high school graduation, in Carnegie units: 2004

State	Total required credits, all courses	Required credits in subject areas									High school exit exam required to graduate	Specific course requirements
		English/ language arts	Social studies	Mathematics	Science	Health	Physical education	Arts	Foreign language	Technology/ life skills		
1	2	3	4	5	6	7	8	9	10	11	12	13
Alabama	24	4	4	4	4	1[1]	(1)	0.5	0	—	Yes	—
Alaska	21	4	3	2	2	1[1]	(1)	—	0	—	Yes	—
Arizona	20	4	2.5	2	2	0	0	1	0	—	Yes[2]	—
Arkansas	21	4	3	4	3	0.5	0.5	0.5	1	—	No	In math: algebra and geometry. In science: biology and physical science. In social studies: world history, U.S. history, and government.
California	13	3	3	2	2	—	2	1[3]	(3)	—	Yes[2]	In math: 2 credits of algebra or higher level courses. In science: biology and physical science. In social studies: 0.5 credit of economics.
Colorado	†[4]	†[4]	†[4]	†[4]	†[4]	0	0	†[4]	0	—	No	—
Connecticut	20	4	3	3	2	—	1	1	—	—	No	—
Delaware	22	4	3	3	3	0.5	1	—	0	4	No	In math and science: Students must meet content standards. In technology/life skills: 3 credits of career pathway and 1 credit of computer literacy.
District of Columbia	23.5	4	3.5	3	3	0.75	0.75	1	2	—	Yes[2]	In math: algebra. In social studies: U.S. history, U.S. government, and DC history and government. Community service hours are also required.
Florida	24/18[5]	4	3	3	3	0.5	0.5	1	2	—	Yes	In math: algebra or the equivalent. In science: 2 to 3 credits of laboratory. In English/language arts: 4 credits of composition and literature.
Georgia	22	4	3	4	3	1	1	—	2	—	Yes	In math: 1 credit each of algebra, geometry, algebra II, and another math. In science: 1 credit each of life, physical, and another science. In social studies: 1 credit of world history, 1 credit of U.S. history, 0.5 credit of government, and 0.5 credit of economics. In English/language arts: 1 credit of American literature.
Hawaii	22	4	4	3	3	0.5	1	—	0	—	No	—
Idaho[6]	42	9	5	4	4	0.5	†[4]	2	†[4]	—	Yes[2]	In science: 2 credits of laboratory. In English/language arts: 1 credit of speech or debate.
Illinois	10.25	3	2	2	1	0.5	—	1	0	—	No	While not a state graduation requirement, daily physical education is required in all 4 years of high school.
Indiana[6]	24	8	4	4	4	1	1	—	†[4]	2	Yes	In science: 4 credits in two out of three specified courses (life, physical, or earth/space science). In social studies: 1 credit in U.S. history and 2 credits in U.S. government. In technology/life skills: 2 credits of computer applications/other.
Iowa	1.5	†[4]	1.5	†[4]	†[4]	†[4]	†[4]	†[4]	†[4]	—	No	In social studies: 1 credit of U.S. history and 0.5 credit of U.S. government. In physical education: 0.125 credit per semester.
Kansas	21	4	3	2	2	0.5	0.5	—	0	—	No	In science: 1 credit of laboratory. In social studies: 1 credit of U.S. history and 0.5 credit each of U.S. government and state history.
Kentucky	22	4	3	3	3	0.5	0.5	1	2[7]	—	No	In math: algebra, geometry, and another math. In science: 1 credit each of life, physical, and earth/space science. In English/language arts: 1 credit each of English I through IV. In technology/life skills: as determined by individual learning plan.
Louisiana	23	4	3	3	3	0.5	1.5	—	0	—	Yes	In science: 1 credit of biology. In social studies: 1 credit of U.S. history, 0.5 credit of civics, and 0.5 credit of enterprise. In English/language arts: 1 credit each of English I through IV.

See notes at end of table.

Table 154. State requirements for high school graduation, in Carnegie units: 2004—Continued

State	Total required credits, all courses	English/ language arts	Social studies	Mathematics	Science	Health	Physical education	Arts	Foreign language	Technology/ life skills	High school exit exam required to graduate	Specific course requirements
1	2	3	4	5	6	7	8	9	10	11	12	13
Maine	16	4	2	2	2	0.5	1	1	2	—	No	—
Maryland	21	4	3	3	3	0.5	0.5	1	2[8]	(8)	Yes[2]	In math: 1 credit each of algebra/data analysis and of geometry. In science: 1 credit of biology and 2 credits of life, physical, or earth science. In social studies: 1 credit of world history, 1 credit of U.S. history, and 1 credit of government.
Massachusetts	†[4]	†[4]	†[4]	†[4]	†[4]	0	0	†[4]	0	—	Yes	—
Michigan	†[4]	†[4]	0.5	†[4]	†[4]	0	0	†[4]	0	—	Yes[2]	—
Minnesota	21.5	4	3.5	3	3	†[4]	†[4]	1	†[4]	1	Yes	In math: 1 credit each of algebra, geometry, and statistics/probability. In science: 1 credit of biology and 1 credit each of 2 electives. In social studies: 3.5 credits of world/U.S. history, government, economics, and geography.
Mississippi	20	4	3	3	3	0.5	(9)	1	0	1	Yes	In math: 1 credit of algebra. In science: 1 credit of biology. In social studies: 1 credit of world history, 1 credit of U.S. history, and 1 credit of U.S. government. In technology/life skills: MS studies, computer applications, and keyboarding.
Missouri	22	3	2	2	2	0	1	1	0	—	No	In social studies: 0.5 credit of American government and civics.
Montana	20	4	2	2	2	1	1	1	0	—	No	—
Nebraska	†[4]	†[4]	†[4]	†[4]	†[4]	0	0	†[4]	0	—	No	—
Nevada	22.5	4	2	3	2	0.5	2	1	0	—	Yes	—
New Hampshire	19.75	4	2.5	2	2	0.25	1	0.5	0	1	No	In science: 1 credit each of biology and physical science. In social studies: 0.5 credit of economics. In technology/life skills: 0.5 credit each of basic business and computer education.
New Jersey	22	4	3	3	3	3.75[1]	(1)	1	1	—	Yes[2]	In social studies: 1 credit of world history and 2 credits of U.S. history.
New Mexico	23	4	3	3	2	0	1	—	0	—	Yes[2]	In math: 1 credit of algebra. In science: 1 credit of one course with a lab. In social studies: 1 credit of world history and geography, 1 credit of U.S. history and geography, 0.5 credit of government, and 0.5 credit of economics. In English/language arts: 1 credit of communication skills.
New York	12	4	4	2	2	0	0	—	0	—	Yes	In math: 1 credit of algebra. In science: 1 credit each of biology, physical, and earth science. In social studies: 1 credit each of world history, U.S. history, and civics and economics.
North Carolina	20	4	3	3	3	1[1]	(1)	†[4]	2[7]	—	Yes	In math: 1 credit of algebra. In science: 1 credit each of biology, physical, and earth science. In social studies: 1 credit each of world history, U.S. history, and civics and economics.
North Dakota	†[4]	†[4]	†[4]	†[4]	†[4]	0	0	†[4]	0	—	No	—
Ohio	21	4	3	3	3	0.5	0.5	†[4]	†[4]	—	Yes[2]	In science: 1 credit each of biology and physical science. In social studies: 0.5 credit each of American history and American government.
Oklahoma	23	4	3	3	3	0	0	2	0	—	Yes[2]	In math: 3 credits of algebra and higher level courses. In science: 1 credit each of biology and of two higher level electives. In social studies: 0.5 to 1 credit of world history, 1 credit of U.S. history, 0.5 to 1 credit of U.S. government, 0.5 credit of Oklahoma history, and 0.5 to 1 credit of geography.
Oregon	22	3	3	2	2	1	1	1	0	—	No	In social studies: history, civics, geography, and economics. In English/language arts: 1 credit of written composition.

See notes at end of table.

Table 154. State requirements for high school graduation, in Carnegie units: 2004—Continued

State	Total required credits, all courses	English/ language arts	Social studies	Mathematics	Science	Health	Physical education	Arts	Foreign language	Technology/ life skills	High school exit exam required to graduate	Specific course requirements
1	2	3	4	5	6	7	8	9	10	11	12	13
Pennsylvania............	†⁴	†⁴	†⁴	†⁴	†⁴	0	0	†⁴	0	—	No	—
Rhode Island............	16	4	2	2	2	(¹⁰)	(¹⁰)	—	0	—	No	In science: lab science (2 credits for college-prep students only).
South Carolina...........	24	4	3	4	3	1¹	(¹)	—	1⁷	—	Yes²	In technology/life skills: computer applications.
South Dakota............	20	4	3	2	2	0	0	0.5	0	—	No	In social studies: U.S. history, U.S. government, and geography. In English/language arts: writing, American literature, and speech.
Tennessee	20	4	3	3	3	1¹	(¹)	—	2	—	Yes²	In math: algebra. In science: biology. In social studies: 1 credit of U.S. history, 0.5 credit of U.S. government, and 0.5 credit of economics.
Texas	24	4	3.5	3	3	0.5	1.5	1	2	1	Yes²	In math: 1 credit each of algebra, geometry, and algebra II. In science: biology, chemistry, physics, and integrated physics. In social studies: 1 credit of world history or world geography, 1 credit of U.S. history from reconstruction, and 0.5 credit each of U.S. government and economics. In English/language arts: 0.5 credit of communications applications. In technology/life skills: 1 credit of technology.
Utah............	24	3	2.5	2	2	0.5	1.5	—	0	—	Yes²	In math: algebra/applied math 1 and geometry/applied math II. In science: biology, chemistry, physics, and earth science. In social studies: 0.5 credit of world civilization, 1 credit of U.S. history, 0.5 credit of U.S. government, and 0.5 credit of geography. In English/language arts: 1 credit each of language arts 9 through 11.
Vermont............	12	4	3	5¹¹	(¹¹)	0	0	1	0	—	No	—
Virginia............	22	4	3	3	3	2¹	(¹)	1	0	—	Yes	In math: 3 credits of algebra or higher level courses. In science: 3 credits in two out of three courses (biology, chemistry, or earth science). In social studies: 1 credit each of world history/geography, U.S. and state history, and U.S. and state government.
Washington............	19	3	2.5	2	2	0	2	1	0	—	Yes²	In math and science: Students must meet content standards. In social studies: 2 credits of U.S. history/government/current affairs and 0.5 credit of state history.
West Virginia............	24	4	4	3	3	1	1	—	0	4	No	In math: algebra and higher level course. In science: coordinated and thematic science in grades 9 and 10. In social studies: world and U.S. studies to 1900 and 20th/21st centuries. In English/language arts: reading and language arts. In technology/life skills: 4 credits in work-based learning and career courses.
Wisconsin............	13	4	3	2	2	0.5	1.5	—	0	—	No	—
Wyoming............	13	4	3	3	3	†⁴	†⁴	†⁴	†⁴	—	No	In social studies: history, American government, and economic institutions.

—Not available.

†Not applicable.

[1]For this state, credits listed under health are for health and physical education combined.

[2]Exit exam policy under development or takes effect after 2004.

[3]For this state, credits listed under arts are for either visual/performing arts or foreign language.

[4]Graduation requirements are determined locally.

[5]Florida offers 3 programs: 4-year, 24-credit; 3-year, 18-credit college-prep; and 3-year, 18-credit career-prep.

[6]Values are based on semester credits.

[7]Credits listed are for college-bound students.

[8]For this state, credits listed under foreign language are for either foreign language or advanced technology.

[9]Unlimited elective credits.

[10]100 minutes/week total of health and physical education.

[11]For this state, credits listed under mathematics are for mathematics and science combined.

NOTE: Local school districts frequently have other graduation requirements in addition to state requirements. The Carnegie unit is a standard of measurement that represents 1 credit for the completion of a 1-year course.

SOURCE: Council of Chief State School Officers, *Key State Education Policies on PK–12 Education: 2004*; and supplemental information from several state education agencies. (This table was prepared June 2006.)

Table 155. States that use criterion-referenced assessments aligned to state standards, by subject area and level: 2005–06

State	Aligned to state standards		Off-the-shelf/ norm-referenced test (NRT)[1]	Criterion-referenced assessments, by subject area and level			
	Custom-developed test (CRT)[2]	Augmented or hybrid test[3]		English/ language arts	Mathematics	Science	Social studies/ history
1	2	3	4	5	6	7	8
Alabama	X		X	ES	ES, MS, HS	ES, MS	MS, HS
Alaska	X		X			ES, MS, HS	
Arizona	X	X	X	ES, MS, HS	ES, MS, HS	ES, MS, HS	ES, MS, HS
Arkansas	X		X	ES, MS	ES, MS, HS	ES, MS, HS	
California	X		X	ES, MS, HS	ES, MS, HS	ES, MS, HS	ES, MS, HS
Colorado	X		X	ES, MS, HS	ES, MS, HS	ES, MS, HS	MS
Connecticut	X				ES, MS, HS	ES, MS, HS	MS
Delaware		X		ES, MS	ES, MS, HS	ES, MS, HS	MS, HS
District of Columbia	X			ES, MS, HS	ES, MS, HS	ES, MS, HS	HS
Florida	X		X	ES, MS, HS	ES, MS, HS	ES, MS, HS	ES, HS
Georgia	X		X	ES, MS, HS	ES, MS, HS	ES, MS, HS	MS, HS
Hawaii		X		ES, MS, HS	ES, MS, HS	ES, MS, HS	MS, HS
Idaho	X			ES, MS, HS	ES, MS, HS	ES, MS, HS	MS
Illinois	X	X		ES, MS, HS	ES, MS, HS	ES, MS, HS	MS, HS
Indiana	X			ES, MS, HS	ES, MS, HS	ES, MS, HS	ES, MS, HS
Iowa			X				
Kansas	X			ES, MS, HS	ES, MS, HS	ES, MS, HS	MS, HS
Kentucky	X	X	X		ES, MS, HS	ES, MS, HS	MS, HS
Louisiana	X	X		ES, MS, HS	ES, MS, HS	ES, MS, HS	MS, HS
Maine	X		X	MS, HS	ES	ES, MS, HS	
Maryland	X	X		ES, MS, HS	ES, MS, HS	ES, MS, HS	MS, HS
Massachusetts	X			ES, HS	ES, MS, HS	ES, MS, HS	ES, MS, HS
Michigan	X			ES, MS	ES, MS, HS	ES, MS, HS	
Minnesota	X			ES, MS, HS	ES, MS, HS	ES, MS, HS	MS, HS
Mississippi	X	X	X	ES, MS	ES, MS, HS	ES, MS	
Missouri		X				ES, MS, HS	MS, HS
Montana	X		X			MS, HS	
Nebraska	X			HS	ES, MS, HS	ES, MS, HS	MS, HS
Nevada	X		X	ES, MS, HS	ES, MS, HS	MS, HS	MS, HS
New Hampshire	X			MS	ES, MS, HS	ES, MS, HS	MS, HS
New Jersey	X			ES, MS, HS	ES, MS, HS	ES, MS, HS	MS, HS
New Mexico	X		X	ES, MS, HS	ES, MS, HS	ES, MS, HS	MS, HS
New York	X			ES, MS, HS	ES, MS, HS	ES, MS, HS	ES, MS, HS
North Carolina	X			ES, MS, HS	ES, MS, HS	ES, MS, HS	HS
North Dakota		X		ES, MS	ES, MS, HS	ES, MS, HS	
Ohio	X			ES, MS, HS	ES, MS, HS	ES, MS, HS	MS, HS
Oklahoma	X			ES, MS, HS	ES, MS, HS	ES, MS, HS	HS
Oregon	X			ES, MS, HS	ES, MS, HS	ES, MS, HS	MS, HS
Pennsylvania	X			ES, MS, HS	ES, MS, HS	ES, MS, HS	ES, MS, HS
Rhode Island	X	X			ES, MS, HS	ES, MS, HS	
South Carolina	X			ES, MS, HS	ES, MS, HS	ES, MS, HS	ES, MS, HS
South Dakota		X	X	ES, MS, HS	ES, MS, HS	ES, MS, HS	ES, HS
Tennessee	X			ES, MS	ES, MS, HS	ES, MS	ES, MS
Texas	X			ES, HS	ES, MS, HS	ES, MS	
Utah	X		X	ES, MS, HS	ES, MS, HS	ES, MS, HS	ES, MS
Vermont	X			ES, MS, HS	ES, MS, HS	ES, MS, HS	
Virginia	X			ES, MS, HS	ES, MS, HS	ES, MS	ES, MS, HS
Washington	X			ES	ES, MS, HS	ES, MS, HS	
West Virginia	X		X	ES, MS, HS	ES, MS, HS	ES, MS, HS	MS, HS
Wisconsin		X		ES, MS, HS	ES, MS, HS		
Wyoming	X				ES, MS, HS		

X State has a test.
[1]Off-the-shelf/norm-referenced tests (NRTs) are commercially developed tests that have not been modified to reflect state content standards.
[2]Custom-developed criterion-referenced tests (CRTs) are explicitly designed to measure state content standards.

[3]Augmented or hybrid tests incorporate elements of both NRTs and CRTs. These tests include NRTs that have been augmented or modified to reflect state standards.
NOTE: ES = elementary school, MS = middle school, and HS = high school.
SOURCE: Quality Counts at 10, A Decade of Standards Based Education, *Education Week*, 25(17), 2006. (This table was prepared September 2006.)

Table 156. States using minimum-competency testing, by grade levels assessed, expected uses of standards, and state or jurisdiction: 2001–02

State or jurisdiction	Grade levels in which students are tested on at least one component	Student diagnosis or placement[1]	Improvement of instruction[1]	Program evaluation[1]	Student promotion[2]	High school exit requirement	School awards or recognition[3]	Public school performance reporting[3]	Accreditation[3]	Other
1	2	3	4	5	6	7	8	9	10	11
Alabama	3–8,10–12	X	X	X		X	X	X		
Alaska	3,4,6–10	X	X	X				X		
Arizona	2–10		X	X				X		
Arkansas	4–12	X	X	X				X		
California	2–12 [4]		X	X	X	X	X	X		(5,6)
Colorado	3–10		X	X				X		
Connecticut	4,6,8,10	X	X	X		X	X	X		
Delaware	2–11	X	X	X	X		X	X		(6)
Florida	3–11		X	X		X	X	X		
Georgia	K–8,11,12	X	X	X		X	X	X		
Hawaii	3,5,8,10		X	X						
Idaho	K–11		X	X				X		
Illinois	3–5,7–11 [4,7]		X	X	X			X		(5)
Indiana	3,6,8,10	X	X	X				X		
Iowa	4,8,11						X	X	X	
Kansas	4–8,10,11	X	X	X				X	X	
Kentucky	3–12		X	X			X	X		
Louisiana	3–11	X	X	X	X	X		X		
Maine	4,8,11 [7]		X	X						
Maryland	3,5–12	X	X	X		X	X	X		
Massachusetts	3–8,10 [7]	X	X	X		X	X	X		(5)
Michigan	4.5,7,8,11	X	X	X				X	X	
Minnesota	3–12	X	X	X		X				
Mississippi	2–12	X	X	X		X				
Missouri	3–5,7–11	X	X	X				X	X	
Montana	4,8,11		X	X						
Nebraska	4,8,11	X	X	X						
Nevada	3-5,8,10–12	X	X	X		X	X	X		
New Hampshire	3,6,10		X	X				X		
New Jersey	4,8,11	X	X	X		X		X	X	(5,8)
New Mexico	K,3–10	X	X	X		X	X	X	X	
New York	4,5,8–12	X	X	X	X	X		X		(5,6)
North Carolina	3–12 [4]	X	X	X	X	X	X	X		
North Dakota	4,8,12	X	X	X	X			X		(6)
Ohio	4,6,9		X	X	X	X	X	X		
Oklahoma	3,5,8,10,11	X	X	X				X	X	
Oregon	3,5,8,10		X	X				X		
Pennsylvania	5,6,8,9,11	X	X	X			X	X		
Rhode Island	3–5,7–11		X	X				X		
South Carolina	1,3–12 [7]	X	X	X		X		X		
South Dakota	2–6,8–11	X	X	X						
Tennessee	3–12	X	X	X		X	X	X		(5,6)
Texas	3–12	X	X	X		X	X	X	X	
Utah	1–12 [4]	X	X	X	X		X	X		
Vermont	2,4,5,8,10,11		X	X				X		
Virginia	3–6,8–12	X	X	X	X	X		X	X	
Washington	2–11 [4,7]	X	X	X				X		
West Virginia	1–12 [7]	X	X	X				X	X	(5,8)
Wisconsin	3,4,8,10	X	X	X				X		
Wyoming	4,8,10–12 [7]		X	X				X	X	
Other jurisdictions										
American Samoa	4,6,8,10,12	X	X	X						
Puerto Rico	—	—	—	—	—	—	—	—	—	—
Virgin Islands	—	—	—	—	—	—	—	—	—	—

X State has program.
—Not available.
[1]Testing program is for instructional purposes.
[2]Testing program is for the purpose of student accountability.
[3]Testing program is for school accountability.
[4]Inclusion is voluntary for students, schools, or school districts for one or more grades.

[5]Endorsed diploma.
[6]Honors diploma.
[7]A sample of students is tested for one or more grades.
[8]High school skills guarantee.
SOURCE: Council of Chief State School Officers, *Annual Survey of State Student Assessment Programs, Fall 2003.* (This table was prepared April 2005.)

Table 157. States requiring testing for initial certification of elementary and secondary teachers, by skills or knowledge assessment and state: 2005 and 2006

State	Assessment for certification, 2005				Assessment for certification, 2006			
	Basic skills exam	Subject-matter exam	Knowledge of teaching exam	Assessment of teaching performance	Basic skills exam	Subject-matter exam	Knowledge of teaching exam	Assessment of teaching performance
1	2	3	4	5	6	7	8	9
Alabama	X	X	X	X	X	X	X	X
Alaska	—	—	—	—	X			
Arizona		X	X			X	X	
Arkansas	X	X	X		X	X	X	X
California	X	—		X	X	—		X
Colorado	—	—	—	—	—	—	—	—
Connecticut	X	(¹)	X	X	X	(¹)	X	X
Delaware	X	X			X	X		
District of Columbia	X	X	—		X	X	—	
Florida	X	X	X		X	X	X	
Georgia	X	X			X	X		
Hawaii	X	X	X	—	X	X	X	—
Idaho		X	X	X		X	X	X
Illinois	X	X	X		X	X	X	
Indiana	X	X		X	X	X		X
Iowa	—	—	—	—	—	—	—	—
Kansas		X	X			X	X	
Kentucky		X	X	X		X	X	X
Louisiana	X	X	X	X	X	X	X	X
Maine	—	—	—	—	—	—	—	—
Maryland	X	X	X	X	X	X	X	X
Massachusetts	X	X		X	X	X		X
Michigan	X	X		X	X	X		X
Minnesota	X	X	X		X	X	X	
Mississippi	—	—	—	—	—	—	—	—
Missouri	X	X		X	X	X		X
Montana								
Nebraska	—	—	—	—	X			
Nevada	—	—	—	—		X	—	—
New Hampshire	X	X			X	X		
New Jersey	—	—	—	—	—	—	—	—
New Mexico	X	X	X	X	X	X	X	X
New York		X	X			X	X	
North Carolina	—	—	—	—	—	—	—	—
North Dakota	—	—	—	—	—	—	—	—
Ohio	—	—	—	—		X	X	X
Oklahoma	—	—	—	—	—	—	—	—
Oregon	—	—	—	—	X	X	—	—
Pennsylvania	X	X	X	X	X	X	X	X
Rhode Island			X	X			X	X
South Carolina		X	X			X	X	
South Dakota	—	—	—		—	—	—	
Tennessee	X	X	X		X	X	X	
Texas	—	—	—		—	—	—	
Utah		X		X		X		X
Vermont	X	X			X	X		
Virginia	X	X	X		X	X	X	
Washington	X	X		X	X	X		X
West Virginia	X	X	X	X	X	X	X	X
Wisconsin	X	X			X	X		
Wyoming	—		—	—	—		—	—

X State requires testing.
—Not available.
¹Subject-matter exams are required for persons seeking Connecticut certification in the following areas: art, biology, business education, chemistry, earth science, elementary education, English, family and consumer sciences, French, general science, German, health education, Italian, mathematics, middle school English, middle school mathematics, middle school science, middle school social studies, music, physical education, physics, Russian, social studies, Spanish, special education, and technology education.

SOURCE: National Association of State Directors of Teacher Education and Certification, *The NASDTEC Manual on the Preparation & Certification of Educational Personnel in the United States & Canada,* 2005 and 2006. (This table was prepared August 2006.)

Table 158. Revenues for public elementary and secondary schools, by source of funds: Selected years, 1919–20 through 2003–04

School year	Total (in thousands)	Federal (in thousands)	Federal revenue per student	State (in thousands)	Local (including intermediate)[1] (in thousands)	Percentage distribution			
						Total	Federal	State	Local (including intermediate)[1]
1	2	3	4	5	6	7	8	9	10
1919–20	$970,121	$2,475	#	$160,085	$807,561	100.0	0.3	16.5	83.2
1929–30	2,088,557	7,334	#	353,670	1,727,553	100.0	0.4	16.9	82.7
1939–40	2,260,527	39,810	$2	684,354	1,536,363	100.0	1.8	30.3	68.0
1941–42	2,416,580	34,305	1	759,993	1,622,281	100.0	1.4	31.4	67.1
1943–44	2,604,322	35,886	2	859,183	1,709,253	100.0	1.4	33.0	65.6
1945–46	3,059,845	41,378	2	1,062,057	1,956,409	100.0	1.4	34.7	63.9
1947–48	4,311,534	120,270	5	1,676,362	2,514,902	100.0	2.8	38.9	58.3
1949–50	5,437,044	155,848	6	2,165,689	3,115,507	100.0	2.9	39.8	57.3
1951–52	6,423,816	227,711	9	2,478,596	3,717,507	100.0	3.5	38.6	57.9
1953–54	7,866,852	355,237	12	2,944,103	4,567,512	100.0	4.5	37.4	58.1
1955–56	9,686,677	441,442	14	3,828,886	5,416,350	100.0	4.6	39.5	55.9
1957–58	12,181,513	486,484	15	4,800,368	6,894,661	100.0	4.0	39.4	56.6
1959–60	14,746,618	651,639	19	5,768,047	8,326,932	100.0	4.4	39.1	56.5
1961–62	17,527,707	760,975	20	6,789,190	9,977,542	100.0	4.3	38.7	56.9
1963–64	20,544,182	896,956	22	8,078,014	11,569,213	100.0	4.4	39.3	56.3
1965–66	25,356,858	1,996,954	47	9,920,219	13,439,686	100.0	7.9	39.1	53.0
1967–68	31,903,064	2,806,469	64	12,275,536	16,821,063	100.0	8.8	38.5	52.7
1969–70	40,266,923	3,219,557	71	16,062,776	20,984,589	100.0	8.0	39.9	52.1
1970–71	44,511,292	3,753,461	82	17,409,086	23,348,745	100.0	8.4	39.1	52.5
1971–72	50,003,645	4,467,969	97	19,133,256	26,402,420	100.0	8.9	38.3	52.8
1972–73	52,117,930	4,525,000	99	20,699,752	26,893,180	100.0	8.7	39.7	51.6
1973–74	58,230,892	4,930,351	108	24,113,409	29,187,132	100.0	8.5	41.4	50.1
1974–75	64,445,239	5,811,595	129	27,060,563	31,573,079	100.0	9.0	42.0	49.0
1975–76	71,206,073	6,318,345	141	31,602,885	33,284,840	100.0	8.9	44.4	46.7
1976–77	75,332,532	6,629,498	150	32,526,018	36,177,019	100.0	8.8	43.2	48.0
1977–78	81,443,160	7,694,194	177	35,013,266	38,735,700	100.0	9.4	43.0	47.6
1978–79	87,994,143	8,600,116	202	40,132,136	39,261,891	100.0	9.8	45.6	44.6
1979–80	96,881,165	9,503,537	228	45,348,814	42,028,813	100.0	9.8	46.8	43.4
1980–81	105,949,087	9,768,262	239	50,182,659	45,998,166	100.0	9.2	47.4	43.4
1981–82	110,191,257	8,186,466	204	52,436,435	49,568,356	100.0	7.4	47.6	45.0
1982–83	117,497,502	8,339,990	211	56,282,157	52,875,354	100.0	7.1	47.9	45.0
1983–84	126,055,419	8,576,547	218	60,232,981	57,245,892	100.0	6.8	47.8	45.4
1984–85	137,294,678	9,105,569	232	67,168,684	61,020,425	100.0	6.6	48.9	44.4
1985–86	149,127,779	9,975,622	253	73,619,575	65,532,582	100.0	6.7	49.4	43.9
1986–87	158,523,693	10,146,013	255	78,830,437	69,547,243	100.0	6.4	49.7	43.9
1987–88	169,561,974	10,716,687	268	84,004,415	74,840,873	100.0	6.3	49.5	44.1
1988–89	192,016,374	11,902,001	296	91,768,911	88,345,462	100.0	6.2	47.8	46.0
1989–90	208,547,573	12,700,784	313	98,238,633	97,608,157	100.0	6.1	47.1	46.8
1990–91	223,340,537	13,776,066	334	105,324,533	104,239,939	100.0	6.2	47.2	46.7
1991–92	234,581,384	15,493,330	368	108,783,449	110,304,605	100.0	6.6	46.4	47.0
1992–93	247,626,168	17,261,252	403	113,403,436	116,961,481	100.0	7.0	45.8	47.2
1993–94	260,159,468	18,341,483	422	117,474,209	124,343,776	100.0	7.1	45.2	47.8
1994–95	273,149,449	18,582,157	421	127,729,576	126,837,717	100.0	6.8	46.8	46.4
1995–96	287,702,844	19,104,019	426	136,670,754	131,928,071	100.0	6.6	47.5	45.9
1996–97	305,065,192	20,081,287	440	146,435,584	138,548,321	100.0	6.6	48.0	45.4
1997–98	325,925,708	22,201,965	481	157,645,372	146,078,370	100.0	6.8	48.4	44.8
1998–99	347,377,993	24,521,817	527	169,298,232	153,557,944	100.0	7.1	48.7	44.2
1999–2000	372,943,802	27,097,866	578	184,613,352	161,232,584	100.0	7.3	49.5	43.2
2000–01	401,356,120	29,100,183	616	199,583,097	172,672,840	100.0	7.3	49.7	43.0
2001–02	419,501,976	33,144,633	695	206,541,793	179,815,551	100.0	7.9	49.2	42.9
2002–03[2]	440,111,653	37,515,909	779	214,277,407	188,318,337	100.0	8.5	48.7	42.8
2003–04	462,015,502	41,921,206	864	217,383,087	202,711,210	100.0	9.1	47.1	43.9

#Rounds to zero.

[1]Includes a relatively small amount from nongovernmental private sources (gifts and tuition and transportation fees from patrons). These sources accounted for 2.3 percent of total revenues in 2003–04.

[2]Revised from previously published figures.

NOTE: Beginning in 1980–81, revenues for state education agencies are excluded. Beginning in 1988–89, data reflect new survey collection procedures and may not be entirely comparable with figures for earlier years. Data are not adjusted for changes in the purchasing power of the dollar due to inflation. Detail may not sum to totals because of rounding.

SOURCE: U.S. Department of Education, National Center for Education Statistics, *Biennial Survey of Education in the United States*, 1919–20 through 1955–56; *Statistics of State School Systems*, 1957–58 through 1969–70; *Revenues and Expenditures for Public Elementary and Secondary Education*, 1970–71 through 1986–87; and Common Core of Data (CCD), "National Public Education Financial Survey," 1987–88 through 2003–04. (This table was prepared August 2006.)

Table 159. Revenues for public elementary and secondary schools, by source and state or jurisdiction: 2003–04

State or jurisdiction	Total (in thousands)	Federal			State		Local and intermediate		Private[1]	
		Amount (in thousands)	Per student	Percent of total	Amount (in thousands)	Percent of total	Amount (in thousands)	Percent of total	Amount (in thousands)	Percent of total
1	2	3	4	5	6	7	8	9	10	11
United States	$462,015,502	$41,921,206	$864	9.1	$217,383,087	47.1	$192,246,280	41.6	$10,464,930	2.3
Alabama	5,373,546	656,858	898	12.2	2,986,962	55.6	1,453,756	27.1	275,970	5.1
Alaska	1,550,365	287,130	2,144	18.5	879,186	56.7	350,328	22.6	33,721	2.2
Arizona	7,641,235	912,542	902	11.9	3,648,871	47.8	2,880,311	37.7	199,510	2.6
Arkansas	3,428,091	436,252	960	12.7	1,826,691	53.3	1,019,125	29.7	146,024	4.3
California	57,598,368	6,293,739	981	10.9	32,021,758	55.6	18,707,743	32.5	575,127	1.0
Colorado	6,545,403	443,466	585	6.8	2,834,721	43.3	2,998,633	45.8	268,584	4.1
Connecticut	7,396,816	379,368	657	5.1	2,686,572	36.3	4,211,508	56.9	119,368	1.6
Delaware	1,296,963	117,055	995	9.0	804,029	62.0	360,220	27.8	15,659	1.2
District of Columbia	1,224,730	186,018	2,383	15.2	†	†	1,027,660	83.9	11,052	0.9
Florida	21,042,496	2,220,113	858	10.6	9,195,242	43.7	8,859,065	42.1	768,075	3.7
Georgia	13,828,817	1,234,022	810	8.9	6,349,957	45.9	6,005,466	43.4	239,372	1.7
Hawaii	2,141,931	236,469	1,288	11.0	1,854,533	86.6	22,356	1.0	28,573	1.3
Idaho	1,752,753	181,466	720	10.4	1,017,686	58.1	524,970	30.0	28,630	1.6
Illinois	20,713,607	1,743,335	830	8.4	6,915,271	33.4	11,621,902	56.1	433,099	2.1
Indiana	10,086,811	683,431	676	6.8	5,139,522	51.0	3,988,684	39.5	275,174	2.7
Iowa	4,256,454	364,467	757	8.6	1,953,414	45.9	1,819,158	42.7	119,415	2.8
Kansas	4,545,376	411,906	875	9.1	2,322,537	51.1	1,702,514	37.5	108,419	2.4
Kentucky	5,077,772	617,504	931	12.2	2,907,751	57.3	1,446,606	28.5	105,911	2.1
Louisiana	5,786,338	782,204	1,075	13.5	2,820,277	48.7	2,123,398	36.7	60,458	1.0
Maine	2,183,576	189,881	940	8.7	921,529	42.2	1,034,522	47.4	37,644	1.7
Maryland	9,004,475	581,031	669	6.5	3,435,060	38.1	4,717,903	52.4	270,482	3.0
Massachusetts	11,716,904	781,255	797	6.7	4,738,773	40.4	6,014,290	51.3	182,587	1.6
Michigan	18,032,874	1,450,861	825	8.0	11,146,466	61.8	5,108,486	28.3	327,061	1.8
Minnesota	8,565,550	527,293	626	6.2	5,956,037	69.5	1,809,388	21.1	272,833	3.2
Mississippi	3,483,210	536,933	1,088	15.4	1,907,470	54.8	935,192	26.8	103,615	3.0
Missouri	7,937,576	684,901	756	8.6	2,720,379	34.3	4,223,395	53.2	308,901	3.9
Montana	1,267,696	194,831	1,313	15.4	565,868	44.6	456,336	36.0	50,661	4.0
Nebraska	2,663,032	239,901	840	9.0	873,661	32.8	1,415,885	53.2	133,584	5.0
Nevada	3,075,673	226,312	587	7.4	910,143	29.6	1,830,833	59.5	108,384	3.5
New Hampshire	2,116,169	120,502	581	5.7	968,753	45.8	980,862	46.4	46,052	2.2
New Jersey	20,476,709	925,100	670	4.5	8,883,028	43.4	10,231,722	50.0	436,859	2.1
New Mexico	2,918,985	514,420	1,592	17.6	2,019,491	69.2	334,733	11.5	50,341	1.7
New York	40,610,043	3,106,451	1,084	7.6	17,561,566	43.2	19,613,074	48.3	328,952	0.8
North Carolina	9,877,454	1,032,439	759	10.5	6,211,941	62.9	2,390,729	24.2	242,345	2.5
North Dakota	877,701	134,751	1,318	15.4	334,525	38.1	365,634	41.7	42,792	4.9
Ohio	18,913,893	1,369,190	742	7.2	8,492,580	44.9	8,401,137	44.4	650,986	3.4
Oklahoma	4,363,285	563,347	900	12.9	2,372,609	54.4	1,213,714	27.8	213,614	4.9
Oregon	5,116,226	467,311	848	9.1	2,658,280	52.0	1,855,117	36.3	135,517	2.6
Pennsylvania	19,966,277	1,649,438	906	8.3	7,144,654	35.8	10,801,474	54.1	370,710	1.9
Rhode Island	1,863,135	138,760	871	7.4	767,153	41.2	933,739	50.1	23,482	1.3
South Carolina	5,978,578	635,833	909	10.6	2,753,882	46.1	2,369,924	39.6	218,938	3.7
South Dakota	1,015,552	159,327	1,269	15.7	348,909	34.4	476,492	46.9	30,825	3.0
Tennessee	6,478,661	696,099	743	10.7	2,776,513	42.9	2,596,773	40.1	409,276	6.3
Texas	35,409,121	3,828,976	884	10.8	13,678,202	38.6	17,106,802	48.3	795,141	2.2
Utah	3,028,885	298,907	603	9.9	1,686,337	55.7	980,590	32.4	63,051	2.1
Vermont	1,208,241	94,542	954	7.8	801,161	66.3	293,516	24.3	19,022	1.6
Virginia	10,921,942	765,357	642	7.0	4,241,321	38.8	5,682,011	52.0	233,252	2.1
Washington	8,910,263	829,554	812	9.3	5,456,536	61.2	2,339,475	26.3	284,698	3.2
West Virginia	2,687,459	308,266	1,096	11.5	1,630,492	60.7	721,660	26.9	27,040	1.0
Wisconsin	9,087,054	587,732	668	6.5	4,747,696	52.2	3,531,642	38.9	219,984	2.4
Wyoming	971,434	94,358	1,079	9.7	507,091	52.2	355,827	36.6	14,159	1.5
Other jurisdictions										
American Samoa	88,949	74,000	4,656	83.2	12,809	14.4	2,043	2.3	97	0.1
Guam	185,620	47,933	1,518	25.8	0	0.0	136,990	73.8	697	0.4
Northern Marianas	64,605	26,180	2,328	40.5	37,230	57.6	1,190	1.8	5	#
Puerto Rico	2,884,128	908,078	1,552	31.5	1,975,579	68.5	12	#	459	#
Virgin Islands	185,139	39,231	2,214	21.2	0	0.0	145,794	78.7	115	0.1

†Not applicable.
#Rounds to zero.
[1]Includes revenues from gifts, and tuition and fees from patrons.
NOTE: Excludes revenues for state education agencies. Detail may not sum to totals because of rounding.

SOURCE: U.S. Department of Education, National Center for Education Statistics, Common Core of Data (CCD), "National Public Education Financial Survey," 2003–04. (This table was prepared June 2006.)

Table 160. Revenues for public elementary and secondary schools, by source and state or jurisdiction: 2002–03

State or jurisdiction	Total (in thousands)	Federal Amount (in thousands)	Federal Per student	Federal Percent of total	State Amount (in thousands)	State Percent of total	Local and intermediate Amount (in thousands)	Local and intermediate Percent of total	Private[1] Amount (in thousands)	Private[1] Percent of total
1	2	3	4	5	6	7	8	9	10	11
United States	$440,111,653	$37,515,909	$779	8.5	$214,277,407	48.7	$178,091,027	40.5	$10,227,310	2.3
Alabama	5,153,795	595,456	805	11.6	2,966,979	57.6	1,326,004	25.7	265,356	5.1
Alaska...............................	1,468,276	260,064	1,936	17.7	834,259	56.8	341,859	23.3	32,093	2.2
Arizona.............................	7,305,663	839,278	895	11.5	3,555,570	48.7	2,724,540	37.3	186,276	2.5
Arkansas...........................	3,266,318	382,871	849	11.7	1,804,362	55.2	940,009	28.8	139,076	4.3
California	57,021,363	5,629,649	886	9.9	33,561,358	58.9	17,264,265	30.3	566,092	1.0
Colorado	6,299,536	409,359	544	6.5	2,715,206	43.1	2,921,298	46.4	253,673	4.0
Connecticut.......................	7,087,302	369,444	648	5.2	2,652,212	37.4	3,955,348	55.8	110,298	1.6
Delaware...........................	1,197,512	102,929	885	8.6	759,290	63.4	320,385	26.8	14,907	1.2
District of Columbia	1,114,021	153,246	2,012	13.8	†	†	952,265	85.5	8,511	0.8
Florida...............................	18,984,106	1,999,264	787	10.5	8,285,654	43.6	7,958,615	41.9	740,573	3.9
Georgia.............................	13,448,966	1,083,873	725	8.1	6,489,049	48.2	5,649,478	42.0	226,566	1.7
Hawaii...............................	2,078,876	170,377	927	8.2	1,873,316	90.1	15,681	0.8	19,502	0.9
Idaho.................................	1,698,503	166,626	670	9.8	1,003,508	59.1	500,910	29.5	27,460	1.6
Illinois...............................	19,154,705	1,618,737	777	8.5	6,327,132	33.0	10,807,708	56.4	401,128	2.1
Indiana..............................	7,926,062	605,523	603	7.6	4,663,625	58.8	2,387,990	30.1	268,924	3.4
Iowa	4,241,508	315,454	654	7.4	1,974,707	46.6	1,734,159	40.9	217,187	5.1
Kansas..............................	4,071,712	370,506	787	9.1	2,326,819	57.1	1,269,069	31.2	105,317	2.6
Kentucky...........................	4,764,253	504,713	764	10.6	2,799,254	58.8	1,358,009	28.5	102,277	2.1
Louisiana	5,549,582	732,835	1,003	13.2	2,723,938	49.1	2,031,773	36.6	61,037	1.1
Maine................................	2,161,238	193,403	946	8.9	927,774	42.9	999,641	46.3	40,420	1.9
Maryland............................	8,668,097	582,440	672	6.7	3,317,559	38.3	4,508,430	52.0	259,667	3.0
Massachusetts...................	11,801,318	705,875	718	6.0	4,827,630	40.9	6,091,947	51.6	175,867	1.5
Michigan	17,954,395	1,407,777	789	7.8	11,358,303	63.3	4,782,850	26.6	405,464	2.3
Minnesota	8,349,227	494,757	584	5.9	6,165,549	73.8	1,426,647	17.1	262,274	3.1
Mississippi	3,263,897	502,816	1,021	15.4	1,754,445	53.8	908,159	27.8	98,476	3.0
Missouri.............................	7,662,199	616,043	680	8.0	2,743,289	35.8	4,005,033	52.3	297,833	3.9
Montana............................	1,204,497	174,685	1,165	14.5	558,114	46.3	422,865	35.1	48,833	4.1
Nebraska...........................	2,550,525	225,769	791	8.9	877,657	34.4	1,319,520	51.7	127,579	5.0
Nevada	2,784,681	196,258	531	7.0	840,435	30.2	1,646,777	59.1	101,210	3.6
New Hampshire	1,957,267	101,904	491	5.2	957,850	48.9	853,865	43.6	43,649	2.2
New Jersey........................	18,905,028	805,498	589	4.3	8,230,289	43.5	9,464,543	50.1	404,698	2.1
New Mexico.......................	2,685,725	402,471	1,257	15.0	1,936,713	72.1	297,040	11.1	49,501	1.8
New York...........................	37,894,517	2,645,471	916	7.0	17,267,655	45.6	17,663,906	46.6	317,484	0.8
North Carolina	9,379,577	899,045	673	9.6	5,975,983	63.7	2,268,536	24.2	236,014	2.5
North Dakota	825,135	126,029	1,209	15.3	303,925	36.8	353,481	42.8	41,700	5.1
Ohio..................................	18,143,062	1,166,816	635	6.4	8,132,703	44.8	8,212,728	45.3	630,815	3.5
Oklahoma..........................	4,161,621	528,646	846	12.7	2,277,241	54.7	1,149,332	27.6	206,402	5.0
Oregon..............................	4,599,717	416,281	751	9.1	2,342,430	50.9	1,711,109	37.2	129,897	2.8
Pennsylvania.....................	18,751,160	1,453,198	800	7.7	6,867,531	36.6	10,076,486	53.7	353,945	1.9
Rhode Island	1,744,838	113,611	714	6.5	733,211	42.0	875,428	50.2	22,588	1.3
South Carolina...................	5,732,697	563,752	812	9.8	2,757,948	48.1	2,200,380	38.4	210,617	3.7
South Dakota	963,997	151,235	1,163	15.7	325,091	33.7	457,932	47.5	29,738	3.1
Tennessee.........................	6,114,870	613,615	662	10.0	2,680,969	43.8	2,419,001	39.6	401,284	6.6
Texas................................	34,605,869	3,417,588	802	9.9	14,146,697	40.9	16,269,993	47.0	771,591	2.2
Utah..................................	2,912,991	269,728	551	9.3	1,643,684	56.4	940,094	32.3	59,486	2.0
Vermont............................	1,149,920	80,022	800	7.0	779,215	67.8	272,841	23.7	17,842	1.6
Virginia..............................	10,283,182	678,459	576	6.6	4,072,761	39.6	5,330,297	51.8	201,665	2.0
Washington........................	8,696,472	779,564	768	9.0	5,373,852	61.8	2,262,619	26.0	280,437	3.2
West Virginia.....................	2,552,446	271,770	962	10.6	1,568,125	61.4	685,820	26.9	26,731	1.0
Wisconsin	8,858,181	536,643	609	6.1	4,727,338	53.4	3,380,439	38.2	213,762	2.4
Wyoming............................	961,248	84,536	959	8.8	489,201	50.9	373,920	38.9	13,590	1.4
Other jurisdictions American Samoa	68,812	53,676	3,358	78.0	12,591	18.3	2,447	3.6	98	0.1
Guam	—	—	—	—	—	—	—	—	—	—
Northern Marianas..........	60,712	23,183	2,060	38.2	37,230	61.3	282	0.5	17	#
Puerto Rico....................	2,619,532	802,703	1,346	30.6	1,816,733	69.4	13	#	82	#
Virgin Islands	177,087	37,119	2,025	21.0	0	0.0	139,757	78.9	212	0.1

—Not available.
†Not applicable.
#Rounds to zero.
[1]Includes revenues from gifts, and tuition and fees from patrons.

NOTE: Excludes revenues for state education agencies. Some data have been revised from previously published figures. Detail may not sum to totals because of rounding.
SOURCE: U.S. Department of Education, National Center for Education Statistics, Common Core of Data (CCD), "National Public Education Financial Survey," 2002–03. (This table was prepared August 2006.)

Table 161. Summary of expenditures for public elementary and secondary education, by purpose: Selected years, 1919–20 through 2003–04

Purpose of expenditures	1919–20	1929–30	1939–40	1949–50	1959–60	1969–70	1979–80	1989–90	1999–2000	2002–03[1]	2003–04
1	2	3	4	5	6	7	8	9	10	11	12
	Amounts in thousands of dollars										
Total expenditures	$1,036,151	$2,316,790	$2,344,049	$5,837,643	$15,613,255	$40,683,429	$95,961,561	$212,769,564	$381,838,155	$454,906,912	$473,862,737
Current expenditures for public elementary and secondary education	861,120	1,843,552	1,941,799	4,687,274	12,329,389	34,217,773	86,984,142	188,229,359	323,888,508	387,593,617	403,376,186
Administration	36,752	78,680	91,571	220,050	528,408	1,606,646	4,263,757	16,346,991 [2]	25,079,298 [2]	29,751,958 [2]	30,864,878 [2]
Instruction	632,556	1,317,727	1,403,285	3,112,340	8,350,738	23,270,158	53,257,937	113,550,405 [2]	199,968,138 [2]	237,731,734 [2]	247,443,145 [2]
Plant operation	115,707	216,072	194,365	427,587	1,085,036	2,537,257	9,744,785	20,261,415 [2]	31,190,295 [2]	36,830,517 [2]	38,720,266 [2]
Plant maintenance	30,432	78,810	73,321	214,164	422,586	974,941	(3)	(3)	(3)	(3)	(3)
Fixed charges	9,286	50,270	50,116	261,469	909,323	3,266,920	11,793,934	—	—	—	—
Other school services[4]	36,387	101,993	129,141	451,663	1,033,297	2,561,856	7,923,729	38,070,548 [2]	67,650,776 [2]	83,279,408 [2]	86,347,897 [2]
Other current expenditures	3,277	9,825	13,367	35,614	132,566	635,803	597,585	2,982,543	5,457,015	6,873,762	6,929,952
Summer schools	(5)	(5)	(5)	(5)	13,263	106,481	24,753	—	—	—	—
Adult education[5]	3,277	9,825	13,367	35,614	26,858	128,778	—	—	—	—	—
Community colleges	(5)	(5)	(5)	(5)	34,492	138,813	—	—	—	—	—
Community services	(4)	(4)	(4)	(4)	57,953	261,731	572,832	—	—	—	—
Capital outlay[6]	153,543	370,878	257,974	1,014,176	2,661,786	4,659,072	6,506,167	17,781,342	43,357,186	48,940,374	50,476,066
Interest on school debt	18,212	92,536	130,909	100,578	489,514	1,170,782	1,873,666	3,776,321	9,135,445	11,499,160	13,080,534
	Percentage distribution										
Total expenditures	100.0	100.0	100.0	100.0	100.0	100.0	100.0	100.0	100.0	100.0	100.0
Current expenditures for public elementary and secondary education	83.1	79.6	82.8	80.3	79.0	84.1	90.6	88.5	84.8	85.2	85.1
Administration	3.5	3.4	3.9	3.8	3.4	3.9	4.4	7.7 [2]	6.6 [2]	6.5 [2]	6.5 [2]
Instruction	61.0	56.9	59.9	53.3	53.5	57.2	55.5	53.4 [2]	52.4 [2]	52.3 [2]	52.2 [2]
Plant operation	11.2	9.3	8.3	7.3	6.9	6.2	10.2	9.5 [2]	8.2 [2]	8.1 [2]	8.2 [2]
Plant maintenance	2.9	3.4	3.1	3.7	2.7	2.4	(3)	(3)	(3)	(3)	(3)
Fixed charges	0.9	2.2	2.1	4.5	5.8	8.0	12.3	—	—	—	—
Other school services[4]	3.5	4.4	5.5	7.7	6.6	6.3	8.3	17.9	17.7	18.3	18.2
Other current expenditures	0.3	0.4	0.6	0.6	0.8	1.6	0.6	1.4	1.4	1.5	1.5
Summer schools	(5)	(5)	(5)	(5)	0.1	0.3	#	—	—	—	—
Adult education[5]	0.3	0.4	0.6	0.6	0.2	0.3	—	—	—	—	—
Community colleges	(5)	(5)	(5)	(5)	0.2	0.3	—	—	—	—	—
Community services	(4)	(4)	(4)	(4)	0.4	0.6	0.6	—	—	—	—
Capital outlay[6]	14.8	16.0	11.0	17.4	17.0	11.5	6.8	8.4	11.4	10.8	10.7
Interest on school debt	1.8	4.0	5.6	1.7	3.1	2.9	2.0	1.8	2.4	2.5	2.8

—Not available.
#Rounds to zero.
[1]Data have been revised from previously published figures.
[2]Data not comparable to figures prior to 1989–90.
[3]Plant operation also includes plant maintenance.
[4]Prior to 1959–60, items included under "other school services" were listed under "auxiliary services," a more comprehensive classification that also included community services.
[5]Prior to 1959–60, data shown for adult education represent combined expenditures for adult education, summer schools, and community colleges.
[6]Prior to 1969–70, excludes capital outlay by state and local school housing authorities.

NOTE: Beginning in 1959–60, includes Alaska and Hawaii. Beginning in 1989–90, state administration expenditures were excluded from both "total" and "current" expenditures. Beginning in 1989–90, extensive changes were made in the data collection procedures. Detail may not sum to totals because of rounding.
SOURCE: U.S. Department of Education, National Center for Education Statistics, *Biennial Survey of Education in the United States*, 1919–20 through 1949–50; *Statistics of State School Systems*, 1959–60 and 1969–70; *Revenues and Expenditures for Public Elementary and Secondary Education*, 1979–80; and Common Core of Data (CCD), "National Public Education Financial Survey," 1989–90 through 2003–04. (This table was prepared August 2006.)

Table 162. Current expenditures for public elementary and secondary education, by state or jurisdiction: Selected years, 1969–70 through 2003–04

[In thousands of dollars]

State or jurisdiction	1969–70	1979–80	1980–81	1989–90	1990–91	1993–94	1994–95	1995–96	1996–97	1997–98	1998–99	1999–2000	2000–01	2001–02	2002–03[1]	2003–04
1	2	3	4	5	6	7	8	9	10	11	12	13	14	15	16	17
United States	$34,217,773	$86,984,142	$94,321,093	$188,229,359	$202,037,752	$231,542,764	$243,877,582	$255,106,683	$270,174,298	$285,485,370	$302,876,294	$323,888,508	$348,360,841	$368,378,006	$387,593,617	$403,376,186
Alabama	422,730	1,146,713	1,393,137	2,275,233	2,475,216	2,809,713	3,026,287	3,240,364	3,436,406	3,633,159	3,880,188	4,176,082	4,354,794	4,444,390	4,657,643	4,812,479
Alaska	81,374	377,947	476,368	828,051	854,499	1,002,515	1,020,675	1,045,022	1,069,379	1,092,750	1,137,610	1,183,499	1,229,036	1,284,854	1,326,226	1,354,846
Arizona	281,941	949,753	1,075,362	2,258,660	2,469,543	2,911,304	3,144,540	3,327,969	3,527,473	3,740,889	3,963,455	4,288,739	4,846,105	5,395,814	5,892,227	6,063,009
Arkansas	235,083	666,949	709,394	1,404,545	1,510,092	1,782,645	1,873,595	1,994,748	2,074,113	2,149,237	2,241,244	2,380,331	2,505,179	2,822,877	2,923,401	3,109,644
California	3,831,595	9,172,158	9,936,642	21,485,782	22,748,218	25,140,639	25,949,033	27,334,639	29,909,168	32,759,492	34,379,878	38,129,479	42,908,787	46,265,544	47,983,402	49,215,866
Colorado	369,218	1,243,049	1,369,883	2,451,833	2,642,850	2,954,793	3,232,976	3,360,529	3,577,211	3,886,872	4,140,699	4,401,010	4,758,173	5,151,003	5,551,506	5,666,191
Connecticut	588,710	1,227,892	1,440,881	3,444,520	3,540,411	3,943,891	4,247,328	4,366,123	4,522,718	4,763,653	5,075,580	5,402,836	5,693,207	6,031,062	6,302,988	6,600,767
Delaware	108,747	269,108	270,439	520,953	543,933	643,915	694,473	726,241	788,715	830,731	872,786	937,630	1,027,224	1,072,875	1,127,745	1,201,631
District of Columbia	141,138	298,448	295,155	639,983	647,901	713,427	666,938	679,106	632,952	647,202	693,712	780,192	830,299	912,432	902,318	1,011,536
Florida	961,273	2,766,468	3,336,657	8,228,531	9,045,710	10,331,896	11,019,735	11,480,359	12,018,676	12,737,325	13,534,374	13,885,988	15,023,514	15,535,864	16,355,123	17,578,884
Georgia	599,371	1,608,028	1,688,714	4,505,962	4,804,225	5,643,843	6,136,689	6,629,646	7,230,405	7,770,241	8,537,177	9,158,624	10,011,343	10,853,496	11,630,576	11,788,616
Hawaii	141,324	351,889	395,038	700,012	827,579	998,143	1,028,729	1,040,682	1,057,069	1,112,351	1,143,713	1,213,695	1,215,968	1,348,381	1,489,092	1,566,792
Idaho	103,107	313,927	352,912	627,794	708,045	859,088	951,350	1,019,594	1,090,597	1,153,778	1,239,755	1,302,817	1,403,190	1,481,803	1,511,862	1,555,006
Illinois	1,896,067	4,579,355	4,773,179	8,125,493	8,932,538	10,076,889	10,640,279	10,727,091	11,720,249	12,473,064	13,602,965	14,462,773	15,634,490	16,480,787	17,271,301	18,081,827
Indiana	809,105	1,851,292	1,898,194	4,074,578	4,379,142	5,064,685	5,243,761	5,493,653	6,055,055	6,234,563	6,697,468	7,110,930	7,548,487	7,704,547	8,088,684	8,524,980
Iowa	527,086	1,186,659	1,337,504	2,004,742	2,136,561	2,527,434	2,622,510	2,753,425	2,885,943	3,005,421	3,110,585	3,264,336	3,430,885	3,565,796	3,652,022	3,669,797
Kansas	362,593	830,133	958,281	1,848,302	1,938,012	2,325,247	2,406,580	2,488,077	2,568,525	2,684,244	2,841,147	2,971,814	3,264,698	3,450,923	3,510,675	3,658,421
Kentucky	353,265	1,054,459	1,096,472	2,134,011	2,480,363	2,952,119	2,988,892	3,171,495	3,382,062	3,489,205	3,696,331	3,837,794	4,047,392	4,268,608	4,401,627	4,551,648
Louisiana	503,217	1,303,902	1,767,692	2,838,283	3,023,690	3,309,018	3,475,926	3,545,832	3,747,508	4,029,139	4,264,981	4,391,189	4,485,878	4,802,565	5,056,583	5,290,964
Maine	155,907	385,492	401,355	1,048,195	1,070,965	1,208,411	1,281,706	1,313,759	1,372,571	1,433,175	1,510,024	1,604,438	1,704,422	1,812,798	1,909,268	1,969,497
Maryland	721,794	1,783,056	1,937,159	3,894,644	4,240,862	4,783,023	5,083,380	5,311,207	5,529,309	5,843,685	6,165,934	6,545,135	7,044,881	7,480,723	7,933,055	8,198,454
Massachusetts	907,341	2,638,734	2,794,762	4,760,390	4,906,828	5,637,337	6,062,303	6,435,458	6,846,610	7,381,784	7,948,502	8,564,039	9,272,387	9,957,292	10,281,820	10,799,765
Michigan	1,799,945	4,642,847	5,196,249	8,025,621	8,545,805	9,816,830	10,440,206	11,137,877	11,686,124	12,003,818	12,785,480	13,994,294	14,243,597	14,975,150	15,674,698	15,983,044
Minnesota	781,243	1,786,768	1,900,322	3,474,398	3,740,820	4,328,093	4,622,930	4,844,879	5,087,353	5,452,571	5,836,186	6,140,442	6,531,198	6,586,559	6,867,403	7,084,005
Mississippi	262,760	756,018	716,878	1,472,710	1,510,552	1,725,386	1,921,480	2,000,321	2,035,675	2,164,592	2,293,188	2,510,376	2,576,457	2,642,116	2,853,531	3,059,569
Missouri	642,030	1,504,988	1,643,258	3,288,738	3,487,786	3,981,614	4,275,217	4,531,192	4,775,931	5,067,720	5,348,366	5,655,531	6,076,169	6,491,885	6,793,957	6,832,454
Montana	127,176	358,118	380,092	641,345	719,963	822,015	844,257	868,892	902,252	929,197	955,695	994,770	1,041,760	1,073,005	1,124,291	1,160,838
Nebraska	231,612	581,615	629,017	1,233,431	1,297,643	1,513,971	1,594,928	1,648,104	1,707,455	1,743,775	1,821,310	1,926,500	2,067,290	2,206,946	2,304,223	2,413,404
Nevada	87,273	281,901	287,752	712,898	864,379	1,099,685	1,186,132	1,296,629	1,434,395	1,570,576	1,738,009	1,875,467	1,978,480	2,169,000	2,251,044	2,470,581
New Hampshire	101,370	295,400	340,518	821,671	890,116	1,007,129	1,053,966	1,114,540	1,173,958	1,241,255	1,316,946	1,418,503	1,518,792	1,641,378	1,781,594	1,900,240
New Jersey	1,343,564	3,638,533	3,648,914	8,119,336	8,897,612	10,448,096	10,776,982	11,208,558	11,771,941	12,056,560	12,874,579	13,327,645	14,773,650	15,822,609	17,185,966	18,416,695
New Mexico	183,736	515,451	560,213	1,020,148	1,134,156	1,323,459	1,441,078	1,517,517	1,557,376	1,659,891	1,788,382	1,890,274	2,022,093	2,204,165	2,281,608	2,446,115
New York	4,111,839	8,760,500	9,259,948	18,090,978	19,514,583	22,059,949	22,989,629	23,522,461	24,237,291	25,332,735	26,885,444	28,433,240	30,884,292	32,218,975	34,546,965	36,205,111
North Carolina	676,193	1,880,862	2,112,417	4,342,826	4,605,384	5,145,416	5,440,426	5,582,994	5,964,939	6,497,648	7,097,882	7,713,293	8,201,901	8,543,290	8,766,968	8,994,620
North Dakota	97,895	228,483	254,197	459,391	460,581	522,377	534,632	557,043	577,498	599,443	625,428	638,946	668,814	711,437	716,007	746,025
Ohio	1,639,805	3,836,576	4,149,858	7,994,379	8,407,428	9,612,678	10,030,956	10,408,022	10,948,074	11,448,722	12,138,937	12,974,575	13,893,495	14,774,065	15,868,494	16,662,985
Oklahoma	339,105	1,055,844	1,193,373	1,905,332	2,107,513	2,680,113	2,763,721	2,804,088	2,990,044	3,138,690	3,332,697	3,382,581	3,750,542	3,875,547	3,804,570	3,853,308
Oregon	403,844	1,126,812	1,292,624	2,297,944	2,453,934	2,852,723	2,948,539	3,056,801	3,184,100	3,474,714	3,706,044	3,896,287	4,112,069	4,214,512	4,150,747	4,199,485
Pennsylvania	1,912,644	4,584,320	4,955,115	9,496,788	10,087,322	11,236,417	11,587,027	12,374,073	12,820,704	13,084,859	13,532,211	14,120,112	14,895,316	15,550,975	16,344,439	17,680,332
Rhode Island	145,443	362,046	395,389	801,908	823,655	990,094	1,050,969	1,094,185	1,151,888	1,215,595	1,283,859	1,393,143	1,465,703	1,533,455	1,647,587	1,765,585

See notes at end of table.

Table 162. Current expenditures for public elementary and secondary education, by state or jurisdiction: Selected years, 1969–70 through 2003–04—Continued

[In thousands of dollars]

State or jurisdiction	1969–70	1979–80	1980–81	1989–90	1990–91	1993–94	1994–95	1995–96	1996–97	1997–98	1998–99	1999–2000	2000–01	2001–02	2002–03[1]	2003–04
1	2	3	4	5	6	7	8	9	10	11	12	13	14	15	16	17
South Carolina	367,689	997,984	1,006,088	2,322,618	2,494,254	2,790,878	2,920,230	3,085,495	3,296,661	3,507,017	3,759,042	4,087,355	4,492,161	4,744,809	4,888,250	5,017,833
South Dakota	109,375	238,332	242,215	447,074	481,304	584,894	612,825	610,640	628,753	665,082	696,785	737,998	796,133	819,296	851,429	887,328
Tennessee	473,226	1,319,303	1,429,938	2,790,808	2,903,209	3,305,579	3,540,682	3,728,486	4,145,380	4,409,338	4,638,924	4,931,734	5,170,379	5,501,029	5,674,773	6,056,657
Texas	1,518,181	4,997,689	5,310,181	12,763,954	13,695,327	16,193,722	17,572,269	18,801,462	20,167,238	21,188,676	22,430,153	25,098,703	26,546,557	28,191,128	30,399,603	30,974,890
Utah	179,981	518,251	587,648	1,130,135	1,235,916	1,511,205	1,618,047	1,719,782	1,822,725	1,916,688	2,025,714	2,102,655	2,250,339	2,374,702	2,366,897	2,475,550
Vermont	78,921	189,811	224,901	546,901	599,018	643,828	665,559	684,864	718,092	749,786	792,664	870,198	934,031	992,149	1,045,213	1,111,029
Virginia	704,677	1,881,519	2,045,412	4,621,071	4,958,213	5,441,384	5,750,318	5,969,608	6,343,768	6,736,863	7,137,419	7,757,598	8,335,805	8,718,554	9,208,329	9,798,239
Washington	699,984	1,825,782	1,791,477	3,550,819	3,906,471	4,892,690	5,138,928	5,394,507	5,587,803	5,987,060	6,098,008	6,399,885	6,782,136	7,103,817	7,359,566	7,549,235
West Virginia	249,404	678,386	754,889	1,316,637	1,473,640	1,663,868	1,758,557	1,806,004	1,847,560	1,905,940	1,986,562	2,086,937	2,157,568	2,219,013	2,349,833	2,415,043
Wisconsin	777,288	1,908,523	2,035,879	3,929,920	4,292,434	5,170,343	5,422,264	5,670,826	5,975,122	6,280,696	6,620,653	6,852,178	7,249,081	7,592,176	7,934,755	8,131,276
Wyoming	69,584	226,067	271,153	509,084	521,549	558,353	577,144	581,817	591,488	603,901	651,622	683,918	704,695	761,830	791,732	814,092
Other jurisdictions																
American Samoa	—	—	—	21,838	24,946	25,161	28,643	30,382	33,780	33,088	35,092	42,395	40,642	46,192	47,566	55,519
Guam	16,652	—	—	101,130	116,406	160,797	161,434	158,303	156,561	168,716	—	—	—	—	—	182,506
Northern Marianas	—	—	—	20,476	26,822	32,824	45,008	44,037	53,140	56,514	50,450	49,832	49,151	46,508	50,843	47,681
Puerto Rico	—	—	713,000	1,045,407	1,142,863	1,360,762	1,501,485	1,667,640	1,740,074	1,981,603	2,024,499	2,086,414	2,257,837	2,152,724	2,541,385	2,425,372
Virgin Islands	—	—	—	128,065	119,950	120,556	122,094	122,286	122,188	131,315	146,474	135,174	125,252	107,343	125,405	128,250

—Not available.

[1]Data have been revised from previously published figures.

NOTE: Beginning in 1980–81, expenditures for state administration are excluded. Data are not adjusted for changes in the purchasing power of the dollar due to inflation. Detail may not sum to totals because of rounding.

SOURCE: U.S. Department of Education, National Center for Education Statistics, *Statistics of State School Systems*, *1969–70; Revenues and Expenditures for Public Elementary and Secondary Education*, 1979–80 and 1980–81; and Common Core of Data (CCD), "National Public Education Financial Survey," 1989–90 through 2003–04. (This table was prepared August 2006.)

Table 163. Total expenditures for public elementary and secondary education, by function and state or jurisdiction: 2003–04

[In thousands of dollars]

| State or jurisdiction | Total | Current expenditures, total | Instruction | Student support services | | | | | | | | Food services | Enterprise operations[3] | Other expenditures[1] | Capital outlay[2] | Interest on school debt |
| | | | | Total | Student support[4] | Instructional staff[4] | General administration | School administration | Operation and maintenance | Student transportation | Other support services | | | | | |
1	2	3	4	5	6	7	8	9	10	11	12	13	14	15	16	17
United States	$473,862,737	$403,376,186	$247,443,145	$139,394,607	$20,839,154	$19,133,353	$8,266,960	$22,597,918	$38,720,266	$16,348,783	$13,488,173	$15,640,225	$898,209	$6,929,952	$50,476,066	$13,080,534
Alabama..........	5,482,123	4,812,479	2,890,905	1,587,264	234,496	202,849	129,974	291,682	427,280	211,086	89,897	334,310	0	104,624	452,859	112,161
Alaska...........	1,652,306	1,354,846	780,675	529,900	89,319	65,434	20,236	78,603	175,131	51,387	49,789	38,686	5,585	10,204	256,100	31,156
Arizona..........	7,115,562	6,063,009	3,639,234	2,146,913	334,075	146,928	100,220	313,988	694,953	218,620	338,130	276,862	0	48,505	785,635	-218,413
Arkansas........	3,616,399	3,109,644	1,887,143	1,053,051	142,810	162,215	102,141	171,074	283,952	110,082	80,777	167,034	2,416	23,849	409,950	72,956
California........	60,424,698	49,215,866	29,869,674	17,463,930	2,201,000	3,163,303	443,884	3,266,852	4,804,008	1,209,449	2,375,434	1,792,338	89,924	996,391	9,126,919	1,085,522
Colorado........	6,874,454	5,666,191	3,243,595	2,224,183	253,380	284,195	79,693	366,760	543,477	171,673	525,006	177,573	20,840	55,189	867,615	285,460
Connecticut....	7,704,868	6,600,767	4,203,232	2,154,599	373,317	227,825	130,583	367,992	591,490	307,094	156,297	186,341	56,595	125,614	842,836	135,650
Delaware........	1,402,691	1,201,631	735,008	410,622	57,673	15,349	13,885	66,824	116,572	68,159	72,160	56,001	0	15,671	164,969	20,420
District of Columbia..	1,177,174	1,011,536	566,099	414,601	64,960	51,803	23,593	51,660	114,268	76,526	31,790	30,835	0	19,785	145,854	0
Florida...........	21,877,780	17,578,884	10,400,072	6,317,391	868,629	1,089,887	200,386	1,041,131	1,881,378	720,116	515,864	861,421	0	433,791	3,361,064	504,042
Georgia..........	13,828,613	11,788,616	7,497,717	3,686,634	544,176	618,595	157,267	709,917	863,301	451,376	342,002	592,649	11,616	62,317	1,812,212	165,468
Hawaii...........	1,771,851	1,566,792	943,647	544,863	173,309	83,599	11,041	99,100	116,130	23,912	37,773	78,282	0	51,458	117,248	36,353
Idaho............	1,782,485	1,555,006	956,401	529,539	86,603	67,323	36,757	87,819	148,207	31,022	31,808	69,012	54	4,227	187,763	35,489
Illinois..........	21,097,122	18,081,827	10,834,897	6,659,281	1,124,763	714,855	631,016	976,563	1,760,055	864,955	587,074	587,649	0	134,066	2,343,375	537,854
Indiana..........	9,862,544	8,524,980	5,153,689	3,019,183	379,084	288,760	167,656	479,011	912,032	470,252	322,387	352,108	0	70,795	896,773	369,996
Iowa.............	4,294,342	3,669,797	2,253,824	1,236,845	229,115	166,605	104,701	202,524	315,736	117,089	101,075	168,549	10,579	31,726	533,010	59,809
Kansas..........	4,070,677	3,658,421	2,175,696	1,313,533	208,943	164,311	131,150	216,250	362,957	144,203	85,719	169,192	0	6,399	272,353	133,504
Kentucky........	4,851,132	4,551,648	2,756,841	1,533,447	199,071	231,711	101,825	264,109	405,287	218,146	113,298	254,020	7,340	65,587	132,745	101,152
Louisiana........	5,819,589	5,290,964	3,196,416	1,774,700	232,567	252,481	125,773	284,399	484,741	274,616	120,122	319,735	114	51,576	371,624	105,425
Maine............	2,214,924	1,969,497	1,319,634	585,968	65,690	63,850	42,007	105,915	189,590	85,388	33,528	63,894	0	22,494	179,062	43,871
Maryland........	8,916,390	8,198,454	5,163,108	2,670,404	291,594	516,828	60,712	479,407	696,951	413,414	211,500	237,160	127,782	23,259	739,948	98,234
Massachusetts..	11,489,116	10,799,765	6,943,985	3,550,997	599,451	548,680	187,736	466,563	986,773	447,122	314,673	304,783	0	170,580	205,442	313,329
Michigan........	19,357,289	15,983,044	9,103,852	6,382,855	1,119,868	775,169	347,056	970,352	1,701,484	673,078	795,848	496,338	0	333,325	2,252,215	788,705
Minnesota.......	8,799,745	7,084,005	4,611,864	2,142,312	224,821	322,339	181,404	303,280	540,596	380,947	188,924	301,103	28,726	323,890	1,036,960	354,890
Mississippi......	3,346,070	3,059,569	1,834,603	1,038,892	138,220	143,948	97,998	171,181	296,190	131,358	59,996	185,806	268	26,759	224,518	35,224
Missouri.........	7,961,108	6,832,454	4,146,110	2,381,846	338,244	304,955	214,186	400,147	661,011	332,207	131,097	304,498	0	153,389	739,948	235,318
Montana.........	1,234,592	1,160,838	709,771	403,094	59,397	44,974	36,147	63,717	117,688	51,180	29,991	46,391	1,582	6,528	55,633	11,593
Nebraska........	2,749,830	2,413,404	1,542,775	703,233	97,847	79,477	83,890	121,888	207,173	63,764	49,193	93,680	73,717	4,205	278,028	54,193
Nevada..........	3,223,659	2,470,581	1,547,312	841,539	94,896	93,946	42,230	169,316	245,160	88,840	107,152	81,730	0	17,721	565,685	169,672
New Hampshire..	2,149,970	1,900,240	1,234,725	607,252	127,383	57,567	63,278	105,122	157,030	82,000	14,870	58,262	0	7,183	199,364	43,183
New Jersey......	20,777,467	18,416,695	10,910,645	6,925,508	1,657,198	616,429	494,240	953,651	1,838,650	992,486	372,854	433,232	147,310	180,167	1,870,292	310,313
New Mexico.....	2,959,048	2,446,115	1,373,197	960,927	242,223	115,301	75,332	146,812	233,447	105,532	42,281	110,608	1,383	26,329	439,834	46,770
New York........	41,539,974	36,205,111	24,770,199	10,588,343	1,238,071	992,695	784,125	1,600,961	3,220,929	1,786,032	965,530	846,568	0	1,529,752	2,773,284	1,031,827
North Carolina..	10,356,368	8,994,620	5,700,768	2,788,838	462,141	303,006	172,837	568,408	720,180	328,975	233,292	505,014	0	45,989	1,004,507	311,253
North Dakota....	856,000	746,025	446,113	241,424	30,092	22,881	35,946	37,219	65,170	33,279	17,036	35,601	22,887	6,078	94,630	9,267
Ohio.............	19,584,115	16,662,985	9,539,582	6,577,735	996,604	1,063,383	466,124	1,034,078	1,540,642	742,637	734,267	544,012	1,655	429,127	2,117,693	374,309
Oklahoma.......	4,180,721	3,853,308	2,186,845	1,400,742	251,383	142,759	114,756	208,608	448,708	122,776	111,751	222,151	43,570	13,407	267,845	46,162
Oregon..........	4,919,701	4,199,485	2,498,569	1,551,644	279,158	157,907	60,678	267,870	352,075	184,348	249,608	147,631	1,641	19,366	486,805	214,045
Pennsylvania....	20,877,878	17,680,332	10,905,967	6,073,053	851,226	668,051	571,780	783,897	1,802,471	837,748	557,880	617,064	84,248	417,619	1,956,395	823,531
Rhode Island....	1,867,732	1,765,585	1,140,209	581,063	141,672	76,747	24,237	87,710	144,900	63,934	41,863	44,313	0	43,544	28,941	29,661
South Carolina..	6,116,477	5,017,833	2,986,340	1,758,809	339,628	322,098	63,987	289,963	448,675	158,466	135,992	251,470	21,214	64,574	833,952	200,117
South Dakota...	1,016,837	887,328	518,064	320,773	48,469	42,534	32,279	44,302	89,759	29,016	34,414	45,583	2,908	2,812	105,775	20,922
Tennessee......	6,830,311	6,056,657	3,880,235	1,851,452	218,594	326,606	116,854	320,727	565,332	209,205	94,135	324,910	0	41,831	557,978	173,844
Texas...........	37,610,640	30,974,890	18,687,758	10,687,740	1,506,362	1,703,258	497,092	1,717,991	3,348,516	827,222	1,087,299	1,599,392	0	287,286	4,811,826	1,536,638
Utah............	3,106,400	2,475,550	1,574,463	752,871	92,731	118,465	29,476	151,437	231,866	78,117	50,779	133,161	15,055	76,158	483,970	70,721

See notes at end of table.

Table 163. Total expenditures for public elementary and secondary education, by function and state or jurisdiction: 2003–04—Continued

[In thousands of dollars]

State or jurisdiction	Total	Total expenditures													Capital outlay[2]	Interest on school debt
		Current expenditures for elementary and secondary programs														
		Current expenditures, total	Instruction	Student support services								Food services	Enterprise operations[3]	Other expenditures[3]		
				Total	Student support[4]	Instructional staff[5]	General administration	School administration	Operation and maintenance	Student transportation	Other support services					
1	2	3	4	5	6	7	8	9	10	11	12	13	14	15	16	17
Vermont	1,206,127	1,111,029	712,137	368,005	80,691	40,338	27,308	76,196	85,690	35,655	22,129	30,306	581	3,156	77,344	14,597
Virginia	11,183,657	9,798,239	6,006,868	3,400,502	474,174	613,090	147,468	574,597	969,698	472,205	149,270	388,250	2,620	65,966	1,125,646	193,805
Washington	9,137,280	7,549,235	4,496,440	2,684,042	468,305	349,688	171,914	446,589	702,648	294,601	250,297	253,112	115,642	41,174	1,219,964	326,907
West Virginia	2,651,865	2,415,043	1,484,554	796,930	81,553	69,296	68,074	130,038	249,043	165,658	33,267	133,502	57	34,073	193,979	8,771
Wisconsin	9,988,217	8,131,276	4,997,142	2,871,673	375,947	398,935	225,276	418,268	775,395	316,365	361,487	262,354	107	198,096	485,456	1,173,389
Wyoming	946,819	814,092	484,484	303,665	48,230	40,326	18,753	45,453	85,872	35,464	29,568	25,749	195	2,339	125,746	4,642
Other jurisdictions																
American Samoa	65,117	55,519	27,476	17,228	2,456	4,690	601	2,293	4,991	652	1,544	10,815	0	3,587	6,011	0
Guam	185,401	182,506	105,211	68,903	20,503	2,911	1,627	9,799	22,074	908	11,079	8,392	0	105	2,265	525
Northern Marianas	48,530	47,681	40,767	4,780	612	310	3,671	0	0	101	87	360	1,773	87	762	0
Puerto Rico	2,582,216	2,425,372	1,779,951	407,169	57,500	47,777	13,612	0	184,527	48,175	55,578	238,252	0	70,166	68,719	17,960
Virgin Islands	147,675	128,250	84,008	40,371	7,175	3,950	6,247	7,328	9,088	4,291	2,292	3,130	741	1,759	17,665	0

[1]Includes expenditures for adult education, community colleges, private school programs funded by local and state education agencies, and community services.

[2]Includes expenditures for property and for buildings and alterations completed by school district staff or contractors.

[3]Includes expenditures for operations funded by sales of products or services (e.g., school bookstore or computer time). Also includes small amounts for direct program support made by state education agencies for local school districts.

[4]Includes expenditures for health, attendance, and speech pathology services.

[5]Includes expenditures for curriculum development, staff training, libraries, and media and computer centers.

NOTE: Excludes expenditures for state education agencies. Detail may not sum to totals because of rounding.

SOURCE: U.S. Department of Education, National Center for Education Statistics, Common Core of Data (CCD), "National Public Education Financial Survey," 2003–04. (This table was prepared June 2006.)

Table 164. Total expenditures for public elementary and secondary education, by function and state or jurisdiction: 2002–03

[In thousands of dollars]

State or jurisdiction	Total	Total expenditures		Current expenditures for elementary and secondary programs				Student support services					Food services	Enterprise operations[3]	Other expenditures[1]	Capital outlay[2]	Interest on school debt
		Current expenditures, total	Instruction	Total	Student support[6]	Instructional staff[4]	General administration[5]	School administration	Operation and maintenance	Student transportation	Other support services					
1	2	3	4	5	6	7	8	9	10	11	12	13	14	15	16	17
United States	**$454,906,912**	**$387,593,617**	**$237,731,734**	**$134,023,019**	**$19,992,229**	**$18,568,413**	**$7,960,378**	**$21,791,580**	**$36,830,517**	**$15,648,821**	**$13,231,082**	**$14,930,942**	**$907,921**	**$6,873,762**	**$48,940,374**	**$11,499,160**
Alabama	5,305,144	4,657,643	2,818,526	1,521,337	222,291	190,115	126,954	285,766	407,103	199,517	89,592	317,780	0	106,661	434,524	106,315
Alaska	1,609,420	1,326,226	771,237	510,329	65,340	84,263	21,054	75,782	169,586	52,234	42,070	38,347	6,314	11,051	247,579	24,565
Arizona	7,051,551	5,892,227	3,530,858	2,083,533	307,957	149,316	96,222	293,770	650,118	201,236	384,914	277,836	0	42,116	851,646	265,562
Arkansas	3,304,710	2,923,401	1,786,323	990,294	130,139	150,834	94,900	164,478	271,264	103,594	75,085	146,727	58	23,798	287,627	69,884
California	56,542,273	47,983,402	29,170,269	17,017,791	2,156,449	3,129,644	433,897	3,271,306	4,573,190	1,151,267	2,302,037	1,727,583	67,759	1,010,545	6,988,779	559,547
Colorado	6,704,415	5,551,506	3,180,392	2,180,040	243,697	269,246	79,469	377,689	514,055	165,272	530,612	171,400	19,674	53,074	825,336	274,499
Connecticut	7,334,520	6,302,988	4,019,659	2,058,828	348,879	217,894	130,653	347,333	567,680	295,902	150,486	169,241	55,261	122,087	768,133	141,313
Delaware	1,342,095	1,127,745	693,970	381,184	53,596	15,143	12,715	62,829	106,170	62,821	67,910	52,592	0	17,846	178,934	17,569
District of Columbia	1,114,681	902,318	473,414	406,079	82,796	91,583	24,368	36,058	100,548	47,649	23,076	22,825	0	16,422	195,941	0
Florida	20,161,939	16,355,123	9,616,720	5,938,232	830,144	1,002,208	184,552	984,370	1,745,187	682,624	509,148	800,171	0	418,707	2,918,212	469,897
Georgia	13,586,716	11,630,576	7,367,694	3,678,590	527,125	624,317	155,117	713,453	852,759	436,957	368,861	573,344	10,949	61,048	1,712,863	182,229
Hawaii	1,657,914	1,489,092	888,473	521,929	162,114	88,294	9,395	96,267	106,427	25,319	34,113	78,689	0	50,252	64,161	54,410
Idaho	1,739,541	1,511,862	924,975	521,688	85,570	70,355	34,710	86,824	144,022	69,454	30,753	65,199	0	4,894	186,889	35,895
Illinois	20,658,276	17,271,301	10,320,227	6,393,248	1,066,937	694,007	609,402	922,117	1,733,174	838,707	528,905	557,826	0	127,354	2,728,064	531,557
Indiana	9,688,103	8,088,684	4,951,003	2,807,529	356,994	264,105	146,868	457,944	874,645	449,178	257,796	330,153	0	63,903	840,802	694,712
Iowa	4,203,671	3,652,022	2,174,018	1,210,993	232,374	164,490	102,444	196,974	306,030	112,323	96,358	161,315	105,695	28,279	459,040	64,330
Kansas	3,910,054	3,510,675	2,078,415	1,269,958	197,924	159,818	124,905	211,301	349,014	138,823	88,173	162,303	0	16,061	250,127	133,191
Kentucky	4,687,217	4,401,627	2,686,505	1,475,797	177,949	217,296	126,747	252,366	370,485	213,682	117,272	239,325	0	53,807	133,703	98,079
Louisiana	5,630,084	5,056,583	3,069,994	1,673,753	214,353	234,756	119,820	273,046	464,025	259,573	108,181	312,751	86	50,551	411,074	111,876
Maine	2,124,554	1,909,268	1,281,073	566,838	64,323	60,128	43,560	102,157	181,045	82,231	33,394	61,357	0	22,294	148,847	44,145
Maryland	8,734,564	7,933,055	4,934,017	2,636,403	308,603	460,560	71,390	519,264	682,697	390,991	202,898	233,590	129,044	22,844	686,976	91,688
Massachusetts	11,084,082	10,281,820	6,542,762	3,426,551	615,326	491,848	188,785	449,711	940,246	430,126	310,508	312,507	0	227,367	272,652	302,243
Michigan	19,291,044	15,674,698	8,929,871	6,264,837	1,070,029	777,470	353,302	1,049,255	1,642,459	644,387	727,934	479,990	0	381,464	2,565,279	669,603
Minnesota	8,720,326	6,867,403	4,404,702	2,147,923	230,704	374,613	178,970	261,993	520,771	372,316	208,556	287,329	27,450	330,091	1,165,500	357,332
Mississippi	3,156,153	2,853,531	1,707,391	968,645	123,997	128,418	94,796	159,968	285,030	122,650	53,786	177,084	411	24,716	210,367	67,539
Missouri	7,953,797	6,793,957	4,142,285	2,358,352	333,196	304,635	208,479	401,895	663,103	321,703	125,342	293,320	0	158,259	767,547	234,034
Montana	1,220,956	1,124,291	690,810	387,437	53,843	43,311	35,445	62,066	113,591	49,078	30,104	44,464	1,579	6,067	78,735	11,863
Nebraska	2,678,767	2,304,223	1,470,002	673,441	96,443	76,788	81,112	118,332	194,619	60,945	45,212	90,224	70,556	4,306	315,737	54,501
Nevada	3,012,227	2,251,044	1,408,570	768,641	83,396	94,306	41,179	154,863	224,695	83,437	86,765	73,834	0	15,529	577,105	168,549
New Hampshire	2,041,865	1,781,594	1,156,573	570,229	117,777	53,942	60,911	100,161	146,442	77,928	13,068	54,792	0	6,285	214,861	39,124
New Jersey	19,168,738	17,185,966	10,152,232	6,504,334	1,555,186	583,395	477,251	891,817	1,697,954	950,926	347,805	399,469	129,932	183,107	1,510,643	289,021
New Mexico	2,734,668	2,281,608	1,266,008	910,138	231,168	105,561	70,742	140,369	220,775	102,564	38,960	104,143	1,319	22,518	393,838	36,704
New York	39,903,445	34,546,965	23,721,563	9,989,057	1,112,897	938,890	726,976	1,430,721	2,972,871	1,697,933	1,108,769	836,345	0	1,442,295	3,176,667	737,518
North Carolina	10,104,266	8,766,968	5,574,861	2,703,000	449,437	307,743	170,143	555,571	684,718	316,768	218,620	489,107	0	46,078	1,010,366	280,854
North Dakota	810,960	716,007	427,511	232,465	28,697	21,916	34,568	35,681	63,604	32,817	15,181	34,039	21,992	6,226	79,894	8,834

See notes at end of table.

Table 164. Total expenditures for public elementary and secondary education, by function and state or jurisdiction: 2002–03—Continued

[In thousands of dollars]

State or jurisdiction	Total	Current expenditures, total	Instruction	Total	Student support[4]	Instructional staff[5]	General administration	School administration	Operation and maintenance	Student transportation	Other support services	Food services	Enterprise operations[3]	Other expenditures[1]	Capital outlay[2]	Interest on school debt
1	2	3	4	5	6	7	8	9	10	11	12	13	14	15	16	17
Ohio	19,000,331	15,868,494	9,110,815	6,232,340	944,733	1,000,770	446,213	965,122	1,475,847	705,157	694,498	523,749	1,591	440,362	2,342,881	348,594
Oklahoma	4,144,802	3,804,570	2,203,126	1,349,256	246,656	122,864	106,363	204,830	421,962	122,324	124,257	208,897	43,292	15,948	272,056	52,228
Oregon	4,976,856	4,150,747	2,458,745	1,550,553	277,037	162,021	60,788	266,887	342,176	182,290	259,355	140,087	1,362	34,179	605,585	186,345
Pennsylvania	19,350,934	16,344,439	10,095,432	5,609,932	792,337	608,640	492,695	723,616	1,672,166	806,993	513,486	573,134	65,940	375,346	1,887,169	743,981
Rhode Island	1,746,150	1,647,587	1,064,304	540,735	131,530	68,751	22,482	84,760	129,039	65,001	39,173	42,548	0	37,659	31,616	29,288
South Carolina	6,028,152	4,888,250	2,915,986	1,711,287	330,343	314,023	62,051	287,430	436,387	151,811	129,242	243,952	17,025	72,231	876,292	191,379
South Dakota	998,417	851,429	498,922	307,100	47,231	43,115	30,069	43,979	82,583	27,710	32,412	43,225	2,182	2,762	122,499	21,727
Tennessee	6,499,907	5,674,773	3,647,986	1,748,705	200,291	308,643	114,908	301,753	539,552	197,764	85,794	278,082	0	42,072	640,826	142,236
Texas	36,903,089	30,399,603	18,347,986	10,516,120	1,477,574	1,722,541	495,247	1,670,719	3,223,281	821,658	1,105,100	1,535,497	0	276,742	4,763,982	1,462,762
Utah	2,991,570	2,366,897	1,518,242	714,894	88,038	111,885	26,655	144,324	218,391	73,833	51,768	126,070	7,691	71,100	464,864	88,710
Vermont	1,110,930	1,045,213	671,163	345,762	74,200	37,993	26,839	71,929	80,908	32,980	20,914	27,531	758	3,710	46,598	15,409
Virginia	10,487,025	9,208,329	5,661,332	3,184,354	442,175	576,194	138,834	545,011	907,832	434,769	139,539	360,124	2,519	63,288	1,069,387	146,022
Washington	8,927,605	7,359,566	4,381,186	2,620,468	513,675	332,723	168,301	350,388	729,430	284,128	241,823	240,634	117,277	42,793	1,201,292	323,954
West Virginia	2,557,190	2,349,833	1,444,689	774,469	81,166	64,886	63,881	131,937	242,176	157,193	33,231	130,662	13	33,080	163,741	10,537
Wisconsin	9,300,201	7,934,755	4,904,809	2,775,318	361,288	412,789	215,391	410,334	706,320	308,661	360,536	254,517	111	182,299	682,823	500,324
Wyoming	911,017	791,732	474,108	292,306	46,318	39,369	17,860	45,069	82,368	33,617	27,705	25,234	83	2,289	110,315	6,681
Other jurisdictions																
American Samoa	54,744	47,566	24,662	14,268	2,037	2,944	617	2,244	4,523	642	1,262	8,637	0	3,201	3,976	0
Guam	—	—	—	—	—	—	—	—	—	—	—	—	—	—	—	—
Northern Marianas	51,249	50,843	43,548	4,922	653	163	3,458	0	0	103	546	2,372	0	1	405	0
Puerto Rico	2,632,580	2,541,385	1,876,195	361,322	51,684	45,300	14,901	0	131,068	56,957	61,412	303,868	0	53,394	19,386	18,415
Virgin Islands	133,034	125,405	81,742	39,754	7,064	3,941	6,089	7,113	8,903	4,389	2,255	3,143	767	1,710	5,920	0

—Not available.

[1]Includes expenditures for adult education, community colleges, private school programs funded by local and state education agencies, and community services.

[2]Includes expenditures for property and for buildings and alterations completed by school district staff or contractors.

[3]Includes expenditures for operations funded by sales of products or services (e.g., school bookstore or computer time). Also includes small amounts for direct program support made by state education agencies for local school districts.

[4]Includes expenditures for health, attendance, and speech pathology services.

[5]Includes expenditures for curriculum development, staff training, libraries, and media and computer centers.

NOTE: Some data have been revised from previously published figures. Excludes expenditures for state education agencies. Detail may not sum to totals because of rounding.

SOURCE: U.S. Department of Education, National Center for Education Statistics, Common Core of Data (CCD). "National Public Education Financial Survey," 2002–03. (This table was prepared August 2006.)

Table 165. Total expenditures for public elementary and secondary education, by function and subfunction: Selected years, 1990–91 through 2003–04

Function and subfunction	Expenditures (in thousands)						Percentage distribution of current expenditures for public schools					
	1990–91	1995–96	1999–2000	2000–01	2002–03[1]	2003–04	1990–91	1995–96	1999–2000	2000–01	2002–03[1]	2003–04
1	2	3	4	5	6	7	8	9	10	11	12	13
Total expenditures............	$229,429,715	$293,646,490	$381,838,155	$410,811,185	$454,906,912	$473,862,737	†	†	†	†	†	†
Current expenditures for public schools	202,037,752	255,106,683	323,888,508	348,360,841	387,593,617	403,376,186	100.00	100.00	100.00	100.00	100.00	100.00
Salaries..............................	132,730,931 [2]	165,806,160	210,158,874	224,305,806	246,349,926	252,179,845	65.70	64.99	64.89	64.39	63.56	62.52
Employee benefits	33,954,456 [2]	44,786,697	53,333,592	57,976,490	68,137,020	74,463,101	16.81	17.56	16.47	16.64	17.58	18.46
Purchased services	16,380,643 [2]	21,579,562	29,051,785	31,778,754	35,325,876	37,502,797	8.11	8.46	8.97	9.12	9.11	9.30
Tuition...............................	1,192,505 [2]	1,590,468	2,231,250	2,458,366	3,298,588	3,327,600	0.59	0.62	0.69	0.71	0.85	0.82
Supplies	14,805,956 [2]	18,756,157	25,896,917	28,262,078	30,528,970	31,904,032	7.33	7.35	8.00	8.11	7.88	7.91
Other.................................	2,973,261 [2]	2,587,639	3,216,089	3,579,347	3,953,237	3,998,812	1.47	1.01	0.99	1.03	1.02	0.99
Instruction	122,223,362	157,473,978	199,968,138	214,333,003	237,731,734	247,443,145	60.50	61.73	61.74	61.53	61.34	61.34
Salaries..........................	90,742,284	114,580,985	145,071,564	154,512,089	168,828,934	172,998,433	44.91	44.91	44.79	44.35	43.56	42.89
Employee benefits.............	22,347,524	30,299,566	36,197,167	39,522,678	45,947,180	50,040,334	11.06	11.88	11.18	11.35	11.85	12.41
Purchased services...........	2,722,639	3,825,111	5,839,673	6,430,708	7,289,623	8,240,541	1.35	1.50	1.80	1.85	1.88	2.04
Tuition.............................	1,192,505	1,590,468	2,231,250	2,458,366	3,298,588	3,327,600	0.59	0.62	0.69	0.71	0.85	0.82
Supplies	4,584,754	6,513,488	9,751,743	10,377,554	11,294,271	11,722,355	2.27	2.55	3.01	2.98	2.91	2.91
Other..............................	633,656	664,360	876,741	1,031,608	1,073,139	1,113,881	0.31	0.26	0.27	0.30	0.28	0.28
Student support[3]	8,926,010	12,266,136	16,046,845	17,292,756	19,992,229	20,839,154	4.42	4.81	4.95	4.96	5.16	5.17
Salaries..........................	6,565,965	8,885,707	11,496,451	12,354,464	14,030,739	14,446,976	3.25	3.48	3.55	3.55	3.62	3.58
Employee benefits.............	1,660,082	2,307,480	2,841,949	3,036,037	3,678,398	4,037,072	0.82	0.90	0.88	0.87	0.95	1.00
Purchased services...........	455,996	687,300	1,180,701	1,328,600	1,646,297	1,708,116	0.23	0.27	0.36	0.38	0.42	0.42
Supplies	191,482	247,262	389,044	421,838	470,505	464,635	0.09	0.10	0.12	0.12	0.12	0.12
Other..............................	52,485	138,387	138,699	151,817	166,291	182,355	0.03	0.05	0.04	0.04	0.04	0.05
Instructional staff services[4]	8,467,142	10,070,241	14,640,411	15,926,856	18,568,413	19,133,353	4.19	3.95	4.52	4.57	4.79	4.74
Salaries..........................	5,560,129	6,418,530	8,971,366	9,790,767	11,312,220	11,522,358	2.75	2.52	2.77	2.81	2.92	2.86
Employee benefits.............	1,408,217	1,719,377	2,169,051	2,356,440	2,909,834	3,160,650	0.70	0.67	0.67	0.68	0.75	0.78
Purchased services...........	622,487	925,403	1,776,849	2,003,598	2,332,965	2,474,224	0.31	0.36	0.55	0.58	0.60	0.61
Supplies	776,863	918,189	1,485,730	1,566,954	1,792,008	1,777,640	0.38	0.36	0.46	0.45	0.46	0.44
Other..............................	99,445	88,743	237,415	209,097	221,387	198,481	0.05	0.03	0.07	0.06	0.06	0.05
General administration..........	5,791,253	5,878,493	6,698,006	7,108,291	7,960,378	8,266,960	2.87	2.30	2.07	2.04	2.05	2.05
Salaries..........................	2,603,562	2,901,172	3,179,793	3,351,554	3,680,522	3,732,878	1.29	1.14	0.98	0.96	0.95	0.93
Employee benefits.............	777,381	828,483	938,113	1,000,698	1,166,775	1,262,867	0.38	0.32	0.29	0.29	0.30	0.31
Purchased services...........	1,482,427	1,626,178	1,941,822	2,099,032	2,384,109	2,505,409	0.73	0.64	0.60	0.60	0.62	0.62
Supplies	172,898	185,831	196,205	206,137	223,696	217,151	0.09	0.07	0.06	0.06	0.06	0.05
Other..............................	754,985	336,828	442,107	450,870	505,276	548,655	0.37	0.13	0.14	0.13	0.13	0.14
School administration............	11,695,344	14,831,159	18,381,292	19,580,890	21,791,580	22,597,918	5.79	5.81	5.68	5.62	5.62	5.60
Salaries..........................	8,935,903	11,156,460	13,923,730	14,817,213	16,206,443	16,626,755	4.42	4.37	4.30	4.25	4.18	4.12
Employee benefits.............	2,257,783	2,963,991	3,455,390	3,689,689	4,341,364	4,710,083	1.12	1.16	1.07	1.06	1.12	1.17
Purchased services...........	247,750	384,908	573,003	611,638	718,442	754,181	0.12	0.15	0.18	0.18	0.19	0.19
Supplies	189,711	256,857	337,651	369,257	416,265	399,456	0.09	0.10	0.10	0.11	0.11	0.10
Other..............................	64,197	68,943	91,519	93,093	109,066	107,443	0.03	0.03	0.03	0.03	0.03	0.03
Operation and maintenance...	21,290,655	25,724,062	31,190,295	34,034,158	36,830,517	38,720,266	10.54	10.08	9.63	9.77	9.50	9.60
Salaries..........................	8,849,559	10,454,854	12,745,457	13,461,242	14,596,762	14,811,538	4.38	4.10	3.94	3.86	3.77	3.67
Employee benefits.............	2,633,075	3,129,632	3,531,423	3,778,520	4,476,354	5,019,476	1.30	1.23	1.09	1.08	1.15	1.24
Purchased services...........	5,721,125	7,698,704	8,866,099	9,642,217	9,866,874	10,462,979	2.83	3.02	2.74	2.77	2.55	2.59
Supplies	3,761,738	4,214,201	5,801,242	6,871,845	7,543,937	8,091,029	1.86	1.65	1.79	1.97	1.95	2.01
Other..............................	325,157	226,670	246,075	280,334	346,590	335,243	0.16	0.09	0.08	0.08	0.09	0.08
Student transportation	8,678,954	10,396,426	13,007,625	14,052,654	15,648,821	16,348,783	4.30	4.08	4.02	4.03	4.04	4.05
Salaries..........................	3,285,127	3,933,969	5,061,209	5,406,092	5,974,787	6,105,136	1.63	1.54	1.56	1.55	1.54	1.51
Employee benefits.............	892,985	1,207,961	1,464,249	1,592,127	1,905,504	2,119,100	0.44	0.47	0.45	0.46	0.49	0.53
Purchased services...........	3,345,232	4,257,805	5,331,435	5,767,462	6,450,377	6,736,969	1.66	1.67	1.65	1.66	1.66	1.67
Supplies	961,447	836,450	1,034,323	1,159,350	1,130,478	1,192,548	0.48	0.33	0.32	0.33	0.29	0.30
Other..............................	194,163	160,239	116,410	127,623	187,675	195,029	0.10	0.06	0.04	0.04	0.05	0.05
Other support services[5]	5,587,837	7,039,408	10,188,917	11,439,134	13,231,082	13,488,173	2.77	2.76	3.15	3.28	3.41	3.34
Salaries..........................	2,900,394	3,450,836	4,930,099	5,521,381	6,234,410	6,344,593	1.44	1.35	1.52	1.58	1.61	1.57
Employee benefits.............	980,859	1,182,229	1,433,054	1,594,540	2,019,058	2,265,788	0.49	0.46	0.44	0.46	0.52	0.56
Purchased services...........	798,922	1,362,961	2,462,775	2,783,176	3,283,907	3,185,502	0.40	0.53	0.76	0.80	0.85	0.79
Supplies	294,527	398,534	573,670	626,889	717,844	766,110	0.15	0.16	0.18	0.18	0.19	0.19
Other..............................	613,135	644,849	789,319	913,148	975,863	926,180	0.30	0.25	0.24	0.26	0.25	0.23
Food services	8,430,490	10,648,844	12,948,807	13,816,635	14,930,942	15,640,225	4.17	4.17	4.00	3.97	3.85	3.88
Salaries..........................	—	3,844,285	4,606,262	4,966,092	5,325,744	5,409,803	†	1.51	1.42	1.43	1.37	1.34
Employee benefits.............	—	1,103,433	1,267,921	1,381,923	1,636,523	1,770,014	†	0.43	0.39	0.40	0.42	0.44
Purchased services...........	—	627,902	897,762	923,091	1,155,396	1,251,525	†	0.25	0.28	0.26	0.30	0.31
Supplies	—	4,916,299	6,041,001	6,420,201	6,641,477	7,006,076	†	1.93	1.87	1.84	1.71	1.74
Other..............................	—	156,924	135,861	125,327	171,801	202,806	†	0.06	0.04	0.04	0.04	0.05
Enterprise operations[6]	946,705	777,937	818,172	776,463	907,921	898,209	0.47	0.30	0.25	0.22	0.23	0.22
Salaries..........................	—	179,360	172,977	124,913	159,366	181,374	†	0.07	0.05	0.04	0.04	0.04
Employee benefits.............	—	44,545	35,276	23,837	56,031	77,717	†	0.02	0.01	0.01	0.01	0.02
Purchased services...........	—	183,288	181,666	189,230	197,885	183,349	†	0.07	0.06	0.05	0.05	0.05
Supplies	—	269,046	286,309	242,052	298,489	267,031	†	0.11	0.09	0.07	0.08	0.07
Other..............................	—	101,697	141,943	196,430	196,150	188,738	†	0.04	0.04	0.06	0.05	0.05

See notes at end of table.

Table 165. Total expenditures for public elementary and secondary education, by function and subfunction: Selected years, 1990–91 through 2003–04—Continued

Function and subfunction	Expenditures (in thousands)						Percentage distribution of current expenditures for public schools					
	1990–91	1995–96	1999–2000	2000–01	2002–03[1]	2003–04	1990–91	1995–96	1999–2000	2000–01	2002–03[1]	2003–04
1	2	3	4	5	6	7	8	9	10	11	12	13
Other current expenditures........	3,295,717	4,724,659	5,457,015	6,063,700	6,873,762	6,929,952	†	†	†	†	†	†
Community services	964,370	1,728,669	2,151,043	2,426,189	2,695,832	2,721,681	†	†	†	†	†	†
Private school programs	527,609	781,148	961,203	1,026,695	1,161,470	1,146,373	†	†	†	†	†	†
Adult education	1,365,523	1,500,438	1,715,332	1,838,265	2,005,813	1,968,046	†	†	†	†	†	†
Community colleges..............	5,356	7,746	265	351	460	210	†	†	†	†	†	†
Other.....................................	432,858	706,657	629,172	772,200	1,010,187	1,093,643	†	†	†	†	†	†
Capital outlay[7]...........................	19,771,478	27,555,667	43,357,186	46,220,704	48,940,374	50,476,066	†	†	†	†	†	†
Interest on school debt	4,324,768	6,259,480	9,135,445	10,165,940	11,499,160	13,080,534	†	†	†	†	†	†

—Not available.
†Not applicable.
[1]Data have been revised from previously published figures.
[2]Includes estimated data for subfunctions of food services and enterprise operations.
[3]Includes expenditures for guidance, health, attendance, and speech pathology services.
[4]Includes expenditures for curriculum development, staff training, libraries, and media and computer centers.
[5]Includes business support services concerned with paying, transporting, exchanging, and maintaining goods and services for local education agencies; central support services, including planning, research, evaluation, information, staff, and data processing services; and other support services.

[6]Includes expenditures for operations funded by sales of products or services (e.g., school bookstore or computer time). Includes very small amounts for direct program support made by state education agencies for local school districts.
[7]Includes expenditures for property, and for buildings and alterations completed by school district staff or contractors.
NOTE: Excludes expenditures for state education agencies. Data are not adjusted for changes in the purchasing power of the dollar due to inflation. Detail may not sum to totals because of rounding.
SOURCE: U.S. Department of Education, National Center for Education Statistics, Common Core of Data (CCD), "National Public Education Financial Survey," 1990–91 through 2003–04. (This table was prepared August 2006.)

Table 166. Expenditures for instruction in public elementary and secondary schools, by subfunction and state or jurisdiction: 2002–03 and 2003–04

[In thousands of current dollars]

State or jurisdiction	2002–03[1]						2003–04					
	Total	Salaries	Employee benefits	Purchased services[2]	Supplies	Tuition and other	Total	Salaries	Employee benefits	Purchased services[2]	Supplies	Tuition and other
1	2	3	4	5	6	7	8	9	10	11	12	13
United States	$237,731,734	$168,828,934	$45,947,180	$7,289,623	$11,294,271	$4,371,726	$247,443,145	$172,998,433	$50,040,334	$8,240,541	$11,722,355	$4,441,482
Alabama......................	2,818,526	1,979,767	530,508	74,940	219,288	14,025	2,890,905	1,987,104	592,821	80,849	215,653	14,478
Alaska........................	771,237	518,112	143,069	45,372	41,992	22,691	780,675	516,985	152,896	46,214	42,841	21,738
Arizona......................	3,530,858	2,506,569	671,154	101,526	163,709	87,900	3,639,234	2,873,806	529,268	65,248	140,699	30,213
Arkansas....................	1,786,323	1,282,075	280,711	50,660	157,189	15,688	1,887,143	1,346,755	303,721	54,973	158,932	22,763
California....................	29,170,269	20,548,956	5,596,635	850,615	1,555,769	618,294	29,869,674	20,763,762	5,887,602	1,037,445	1,517,562	663,303
Colorado....................	3,180,392	2,364,954	443,785	62,450	220,620	88,583	3,243,595	2,379,849	472,336	65,372	228,370	97,667
Connecticut................	4,019,659	2,783,320	743,765	124,293	109,335	258,945	4,203,232	2,880,451	815,593	129,760	109,842	267,586
Delaware....................	693,970	473,465	160,279	13,161	31,708	15,356	735,008	489,724	179,779	16,448	32,464	16,591
District of Columbia	473,414	279,891	87,079	11,831	14,141	80,471	566,099	355,724	40,750	52,243	81,030	36,352
Florida.......................	9,616,720	6,451,460	1,622,841	951,541	479,965	110,913	10,400,072	6,819,679	1,870,176	1,080,269	522,625	107,322
Georgia......................	7,367,694	5,343,778	1,535,410	108,902	368,600	11,003	7,497,717	5,470,730	1,540,039	116,447	359,008	11,493
Hawaii.......................	888,473	628,259	174,755	28,228	44,225	13,007	943,647	640,157	183,571	46,341	59,624	13,954
Idaho.........................	924,975	657,590	195,701	22,616	48,144	924	956,401	673,691	207,801	29,172	44,722	1,015
Illinois.......................	10,320,227	7,507,171	1,925,826	239,329	396,136	251,765	10,834,897	7,716,979	2,248,244	260,021	395,669	213,984
Indiana......................	4,951,003	3,261,483	1,442,278	57,031	178,136	12,075	5,153,689	3,336,402	1,582,628	65,298	158,018	11,343
Iowa..........................	2,174,018	1,582,285	444,273	56,911	71,025	19,523	2,253,824	1,619,777	474,846	58,875	76,949	23,378
Kansas.......................	2,078,415	1,571,521	322,489	57,397	107,427	19,582	2,175,696	1,606,920	360,131	71,034	117,951	19,659
Kentucky....................	2,686,505	2,010,083	494,189	49,081	119,368	13,784	2,756,841	2,046,044	547,238	50,012	101,306	12,240
Louisiana...................	3,069,994	2,207,461	620,927	57,199	164,083	20,324	3,196,416	2,255,865	677,483	51,613	180,569	30,886
Maine........................	1,281,073	808,446	307,685	51,388	40,457	73,096	1,319,634	836,873	313,374	54,553	40,140	74,693
Maryland....................	4,934,017	3,409,666	1,055,203	107,728	142,771	218,649	5,163,108	3,520,283	1,166,435	77,974	168,743	229,672
Massachusetts............	6,542,762	4,590,788	1,451,904	36,314	157,385	306,371	6,943,985	4,677,367	1,691,838	38,254	185,079	351,447
Michigan	8,929,871	5,978,301	2,251,300	338,487	325,071	36,711	9,103,852	6,016,859	2,389,414	345,971	326,269	25,339
Minnesota..................	4,404,702	3,180,600	852,050	156,024	158,353	57,675	4,611,864	3,276,676	911,009	202,624	166,046	55,509
Mississippi.................	1,707,391	1,229,621	317,134	41,021	107,961	11,654	1,834,603	1,318,830	343,149	40,586	120,484	11,555
Missouri.....................	4,142,285	3,020,805	655,388	108,336	308,578	49,178	4,146,110	3,009,494	675,480	125,962	297,569	37,605
Montana.....................	690,810	479,486	131,610	21,893	54,103	3,718	709,771	492,457	135,412	24,157	55,068	2,677
Nebraska	1,470,002	1,062,668	278,989	48,874	49,655	29,816	1,542,775	1,111,676	291,441	57,937	55,386	26,335
Nevada......................	1,408,570	959,395	292,228	23,572	66,601	66,773	1,547,312	1,013,386	333,824	25,882	103,745	70,475
New Hampshire................	1,156,573	770,344	221,417	31,783	36,377	96,652	1,234,725	811,192	251,109	33,476	37,568	101,380
New Jersey.................	10,152,232	6,882,187	2,047,112	242,964	380,087	599,882	10,910,645	7,243,319	2,359,976	273,504	409,816	624,030
New Mexico................	1,266,008	919,979	241,945	26,219	77,540	325	1,373,197	971,261	266,349	31,079	104,359	149
New York....................	23,721,563	16,980,488	4,973,883	893,203	665,614	208,375	24,770,199	17,015,683	5,682,634	1,106,418	745,821	219,644
North Carolina	5,574,861	4,307,889	805,555	117,705	338,096	5,617	5,700,768	4,336,189	914,624	115,412	327,991	6,552
North Dakota	427,511	301,152	87,473	13,572	22,345	2,970	446,113	322,856	85,502	12,275	21,380	4,102
Ohio..........................	9,110,815	6,342,858	1,867,422	269,331	397,876	233,328	9,539,582	6,564,674	2,013,182	300,475	407,777	253,475
Oklahoma..................	2,203,126	1,602,392	404,457	32,428	157,301	6,549	2,186,845	1,602,243	383,188	31,615	163,640	6,160
Oregon......................	2,458,745	1,567,870	645,630	95,924	121,848	27,473	2,498,569	1,585,630	638,438	110,389	138,697	25,416
Pennsylvania..............	10,095,432	7,176,001	1,857,297	480,109	404,584	177,441	10,905,967	7,464,391	2,256,187	569,568	420,285	195,536
Rhode Island..............	1,064,304	739,961	234,364	8,146	23,401	58,432	1,140,209	765,624	272,744	9,676	27,985	64,180
South Carolina............	2,915,986	2,093,030	575,609	70,932	149,800	26,615	2,986,340	2,122,681	587,900	78,606	170,864	26,287
South Dakota..............	498,922	349,991	90,500	21,841	28,890	7,700	518,064	359,038	95,364	22,578	33,658	7,427
Tennessee	3,647,986	2,610,771	587,124	53,374	382,532	14,184	3,880,295	2,744,552	646,689	71,761	403,811	13,482
Texas	18,347,986	14,088,723	2,137,116	535,880	1,398,826	187,441	18,687,758	14,297,667	2,239,499	558,038	1,393,993	198,559
Utah..........................	1,518,242	1,041,674	368,343	27,676	74,741	5,807	1,574,463	1,062,626	397,383	27,063	82,129	5,262
Vermont.....................	671,163	436,793	127,245	35,179	19,998	51,946	712,137	451,815	143,330	39,156	20,245	57,592
Virginia......................	5,661,332	4,218,653	1,065,839	110,321	260,582	5,937	6,006,868	4,434,529	1,147,291	122,041	297,248	5,759
Washington................	4,381,186	3,234,041	699,110	207,742	199,704	40,589	4,496,440	3,276,237	751,556	226,311	200,998	41,338
West Virginia..............	1,444,689	949,554	416,838	22,805	54,824	669	1,484,554	951,657	456,192	24,531	51,628	545
Wisconsin..................	4,904,809	3,212,515	1,360,394	77,351	170,732	83,818	4,997,142	3,232,051	1,424,814	85,269	172,904	82,104
Wyoming....................	474,108	324,091	103,342	18,416	26,777	1,482	484,484	328,213	108,084	19,763	27,197	1,228
Other jurisdictions												
American Samoa	24,662	15,725	3,040	2,858	2,253	785	27,476	17,115	3,309	3,011	2,586	1,455
Guam........................	—	—	—	—	—	—	105,211	79,043	19,201	382	5,609	977
Northern Marianas........	43,548	30,217	7,986	2,505	2,840	0	40,767	30,070	8,066	2,085	540	6
Puerto Rico.................	1,876,195	1,430,330	214,335	6,665	24,985	199,880	1,779,951	1,426,129	221,515	18,347	47,903	66,056
Virgin Islands	81,742	63,994	16,143	164	1,380	60	84,008	65,620	16,795	157	1,387	50

—Not available.
[1]Data have been revised from previously published figures.
[2]Includes purchased professional services of teachers or others who provide instruction for students and travel for instructional staff.

NOTE: Excludes expenditures for state education agencies. Detail may not sum to totals because of rounding.
SOURCE: U.S. Department of Education, National Center for Education Statistics, Common Core of Data (CCD), "National Public Education Financial Survey," 2002–03 and 2003–04. (This table was prepared August 2006.)

Table 167. Total and current expenditures per pupil in public elementary and secondary schools: Selected years, 1919–20 through 2003–04

| | Expenditure per pupil in average daily attendance | | | | Expenditure per pupil in fall enrollment[1] | | | | |
| | Unadjusted dollars | | Constant 2005–06 dollars[2] | | Unadjusted dollars | | Constant 2005–06 dollars[2] | | |
School year	Total expenditure[3]	Current expenditure	Total expenditure[3]	Current expenditure	Total expenditure[3]	Current expenditure	Total expenditure[3]	Current expenditure	Annual percent change in current expenditure
1	2	3	4	5	6	7	8	9	10
1919–20	$64	$53	$668	$557	$48	$40	$500	$417	—
1929–30	108	87	1,261	1,008	90	72	1,044	835	—
1931–32	97	81	1,337	1,119	82	69	1,132	947	—
1933–34	76	67	1,145	1,014	65	57	973	862	—
1935–36	88	74	1,274	1,076	74	63	1,077	910	—
1937–38	100	84	1,385	1,165	86	72	1,189	1,000	—
1939–40	106	88	1,506	1,254	92	76	1,305	1,087	—
1941–42	110	98	1,404	1,255	94	84	1,202	1,074	—
1943–44	125	117	1,424	1,336	105	99	1,200	1,126	—
1945–46	146	136	1,591	1,488	124	116	1,356	1,268	—
1947–48	205	181	1,750	1,550	179	158	1,528	1,353	—
1949–50	260	210	2,188	1,767	231	187	1,941	1,568	—
1951–52	314	246	2,381	1,863	275	215	2,085	1,631	—
1953–54	351	265	2,597	1,960	312	236	2,310	1,743	—
1955–56	387	294	2,865	2,178	354	269	2,619	1,991	—
1957–58	447	341	3,118	2,377	408	311	2,843	2,168	—
1959–60	471	375	3,190	2,541	440	350	2,980	2,373	—
1961–62	517	419	3,424	2,774	485	393	3,212	2,603	—
1963–64	559	460	3,605	2,970	520	428	3,355	2,764	—
1965–66	654	538	4,077	3,353	607	499	3,786	3,113	—
1967–68	786	658	4,602	3,852	732	612	4,281	3,583	—
1969–70	955	816	5,031	4,298	879	751	4,631	3,957	—
1970–71	1,049	911	5,257	4,564	970	842	4,860	4,219	6.6
1971–72	1,128	990	5,454	4,786	1,034	908	5,002	4,389	4.0
1972–73	1,211	1,077	5,627	5,006	1,117	993	5,191	4,618	5.2
1973–74	1,364	1,207	5,821	5,152	1,244	1,101	5,308	4,698	1.7
1974–75	1,545	1,365	5,935	5,243	1,423	1,257	5,468	4,830	2.8
1975–76	1,697	1,504	6,090	5,395	1,563	1,385	5,608	4,968	2.9
1976–77	1,816	1,638	6,158	5,552	1,674	1,509	5,674	5,116	3.0
1977–78	2,002	1,823	6,362	5,791	1,842	1,677	5,851	5,326	4.1
1978–79	2,210	2,020	6,420	5,869	2,029	1,855	5,895	5,390	1.2
1979–80	2,491	2,272	6,384	5,823	2,290	2,088	5,869	5,353	-0.7
1980–81	2,742 [4]	2,502	6,300 [4]	5,747	2,529 [4]	2,307	5,810 [4]	5,301	-1.0
1981–82	2,973 [4]	2,726	6,287 [4]	5,763	2,754 [4]	2,525	5,824 [4]	5,339	0.7
1982–83	3,203 [4]	2,955	6,495 [4]	5,992	2,966 [4]	2,736	6,014 [4]	5,548	3.9
1983–84	3,471 [4]	3,173	6,787 [4]	6,204	3,216 [4]	2,940	6,287 [4]	5,747	3.6
1984–85	3,722 [4]	3,470	7,002 [4]	6,529	3,456 [4]	3,222	6,502 [4]	6,062	5.5
1985–86	4,020 [4]	3,756	7,351 [4]	6,868	3,724 [4]	3,479	6,810 [4]	6,363	5.0
1986–87	4,308 [4]	3,970	7,707 [4]	7,103	3,995 [4]	3,682	7,147 [4]	6,587	3.5
1987–88	4,654 [4]	4,240	7,995 [4]	7,284	4,310 [4]	3,927	7,404 [4]	6,745	2.4
1988–89	5,109	4,645	8,389	7,626	4,738	4,307	7,780	7,072	4.8
1989–90	5,550	4,980	8,698	7,804	5,174	4,643	8,109	7,276	2.9
1990–91	5,885	5,258	8,744	7,813	5,486	4,902	8,153	7,284	0.1
1991–92	6,074	5,421	8,746	7,805	5,629	5,023	8,104	7,232	-0.7
1992–93	6,281	5,584	8,770	7,796	5,804	5,160	8,104	7,204	-0.4
1993–94	6,492	5,767	8,835	7,849	5,996	5,327	8,160	7,250	0.6
1994–95	6,725	5,989	8,897	7,924	6,208	5,529	8,214	7,315	0.9
1995–96	6,962	6,147	8,966	7,917	6,443	5,689	8,299	7,328	0.2
1996–97	7,300	6,393	9,141	8,005	6,764	5,923	8,470	7,418	1.2
1997–98	7,703	6,676	9,477	8,213	7,142	6,189	8,787	7,615	2.7
1998–99	8,118	7,013	9,818	8,482	7,533	6,508	9,111	7,871	3.4
1999–2000	8,592	7,394	10,099	8,691	8,033	6,912	9,442	8,125	3.2
2000–01	9,183	7,904	10,436	8,982	8,575	7,380	9,745	8,387	3.2
2001–02	9,614	8,259	10,736	9,223	8,996	7,727	10,046	8,629	2.9
2002–03	9,952	8,610	10,875	9,408	9,299	8,044	10,161	8,790	1.9
2003–04	10,302	8,899	11,016	9,516	9,620	8,310	10,286	8,886	1.1

—Not available.
[1]Data for 1919–20 to 1953–54 are based on school-year enrollment.
[2]Constant dollars based on the Consumer Price Index, prepared by the Bureau of Labor Statistics, U.S. Department of Labor, adjusted to a school-year basis.
[3]Excludes "Other current expenditures," such as community services, private school programs, adult education, and other programs not allocable to expenditures per student at public schools.
[4]Estimated.
NOTE: Beginning in 1980–81, state administration expenditures are excluded from both "total" and "current" expenditures. Current expenditures include instruction, student support

services, food services, and enterprise operations. Total expenditures include current expenditures, capital outlay, and interest on debt. Beginning in 1988–89, extensive changes were made in the data collection procedures. Some data have been revised from previously published figures.
SOURCE: U.S. Department of Education, National Center for Education Statistics, *Biennial Survey of Education in the United States*, 1919–20 through 1955–56; *Statistics of State School Systems*, 1957–58 through 1969–70; *Revenues and Expenditures for Public Elementary and Secondary Education*, 1970–71 through 1986–87; and Common Core of Data (CCD), "National Public Education Financial Survey," 1987–88 through 2003–04. (This table was prepared August 2006.)

Table 168. Total and current expenditures per pupil in fall enrollment in public elementary and secondary education, by function and state or jurisdiction: 2003–04

									Current expenditures, capital expenditures, and interest on school debt						
State or jurisdiction	Total[1]	Current expenditures												Capital outlay[2]	Interest on school debt
		Total	Instruction	Student services								Food services	Enterprise operations[3]		
				Total	Student support[4]	Instructional staff[5]	General administration	School administration	Operation and maintenance	Student transportation	Other support services				
1	2	3	4	5	6	7	8	9	10	11	12	13	14	15	16
United States	$9,620	$8,310	$5,098	$2,872	$429	$394	$170	$466	$798	$337	$278	$322	$19	$1,040	$269
Alabama	7,354	6,581	3,954	2,171	321	277	178	399	584	289	123	457	0	619	153
Alaska	12,261	10,116	5,829	3,956	667	489	151	587	1,308	384	372	289	42	1,912	233
Arizona	6,983	5,991	3,596	2,121	330	145	99	310	687	216	334	274	0	776	216
Arkansas	7,904	6,842	4,152	2,317	314	357	225	376	625	242	178	367	5	902	161
California	9,266	7,673	4,657	2,723	343	493	69	509	749	189	370	279	14	1,423	169
Colorado	9,000	7,478	4,281	2,935	334	375	105	484	717	227	693	234	28	1,145	377
Connecticut	13,131	11,436	7,282	3,733	647	395	226	638	1,025	532	271	323	98	1,460	235
Delaware	11,788	10,212	6,246	3,490	490	130	118	568	991	579	613	476	0	1,402	174
District of Columbia	14,827	12,959	7,252	5,312	832	664	302	662	1,464	980	407	395	0	1,869	0
Florida	8,287	6,793	4,019	2,441	336	421	77	402	727	278	199	333	0	1,299	195
Georgia	9,041	7,742	4,924	2,421	357	406	103	466	567	296	225	389	8	1,190	109
Hawaii	9,370	8,533	5,139	2,968	944	455	60	540	632	130	206	426	0	639	198
Idaho	7,053	6,168	3,793	2,100	343	267	146	348	588	282	126	274	0	745	141
Illinois	9,978	8,606	5,157	3,170	535	340	300	465	838	412	279	280	0	1,115	256
Indiana	9,684	8,431	5,097	2,986	375	286	166	474	902	465	319	348	0	887	366
Iowa	8,858	7,626	4,684	2,570	476	346	218	421	656	243	210	350	22	1,108	124
Kansas	8,638	7,776	4,624	2,792	444	349	279	460	771	306	182	360	0	579	284
Kentucky	7,214	6,861	4,156	2,312	300	349	153	398	611	329	171	383	11	200	152
Louisiana	7,926	7,271	4,392	2,439	320	347	173	391	666	377	165	439	0	511	145
Maine	10,849	9,746	6,530	2,900	325	316	208	524	938	423	166	316	0	886	217
Maryland	10,232	9,433	5,941	3,073	336	595	70	552	802	476	243	273	147	686	113
Massachusetts	11,544	11,015	7,082	3,622	611	560	191	476	1,006	456	321	311	0	210	320
Michigan	10,824	9,094	5,180	3,632	637	441	197	552	968	383	453	282	0	1,281	449
Minnesota	10,056	8,405	5,472	2,542	267	382	215	360	641	452	224	357	34	1,230	421
Mississippi	6,726	6,199	3,717	2,105	280	292	199	347	600	266	122	376	1	455	71
Missouri	8,618	7,542	4,577	2,629	373	337	236	442	730	367	145	336	0	817	260
Montana	8,278	7,825	4,784	2,717	400	303	244	429	793	345	202	313	11	375	78
Nebraska	9,615	8,452	5,403	2,463	343	278	294	427	726	223	172	328	258	974	190
Nevada	8,318	6,410	4,015	2,184	246	244	110	439	636	231	278	212	0	1,468	440
New Hampshire	10,331	9,161	5,953	2,928	614	278	305	507	757	395	72	281	0	961	208
New Jersey	14,917	13,338	7,902	5,016	1,200	446	358	691	1,332	719	270	314	107	1,355	225
New Mexico	9,078	7,572	4,251	2,974	750	357	233	454	723	327	131	342	4	1,361	145
New York	13,966	12,638	8,646	3,696	432	347	274	559	1,124	623	337	296	0	968	360
North Carolina	7,580	6,613	4,191	2,050	340	223	127	418	529	242	172	371	0	738	229
North Dakota	8,314	7,297	4,364	2,362	294	222	352	364	637	326	167	348	224	926	91
Ohio	10,380	9,029	5,169	3,564	540	576	253	560	835	402	398	295	1	1,148	203
Oklahoma	6,655	6,154	3,492	2,237	401	228	183	333	717	196	178	355	70	428	74
Oregon	8,889	7,618	4,532	2,815	506	286	110	486	639	334	453	268	3	883	388
Pennsylvania	11,235	9,708	5,989	3,335	467	367	314	430	990	460	306	339	46	1,074	452
Rhode Island	11,446	11,078	7,154	3,646	889	482	152	550	909	401	263	278	0	182	186
South Carolina	8,655	7,177	4,271	2,515	486	461	92	415	642	227	194	360	30	1,193	286
South Dakota	8,078	7,068	4,127	2,555	386	339	257	353	715	231	274	363	23	843	167
Tennessee	7,247	6,466	4,143	1,977	233	349	125	342	604	223	100	347	0	596	186
Texas	8,616	7,151	4,314	2,467	348	393	115	397	773	191	251	369	0	1,111	355
Utah	6,110	4,991	3,174	1,518	187	239	59	305	467	158	102	268	30	976	143
Vermont	12,139	11,211	7,186	3,713	814	407	276	769	865	360	223	306	6	780	147
Virginia	9,326	8,219	5,039	2,853	398	514	124	482	813	396	125	326	2	944	163
Washington	8,906	7,391	4,402	2,628	459	342	168	437	688	288	245	248	113	1,194	320
West Virginia	9,309	8,588	5,279	2,834	290	246	242	462	886	589	118	475	0	690	31
Wisconsin	11,125	9,240	5,678	3,263	427	453	256	475	881	359	411	298	0	552	1,333
Wyoming	10,799	9,308	5,539	3,472	551	461	214	520	982	405	338	294	2	1,438	53
Other jurisdictions															
American Samoa	3,872	3,493	1,729	1,084	155	295	38	144	314	41	97	680	0	378	0
Guam	5,869	5,781	3,332	2,182	649	92	52	310	699	29	351	266	0	72	17
Northern Marianas	4,308	4,241	3,626	425	54	28	327	0	0	9	8	32	158	68	0
Puerto Rico	4,295	4,147	3,043	696	98	82	23	0	315	82	95	407	0	117	31
Virgin Islands	8,236	7,239	4,742	2,279	405	223	353	414	513	242	129	177	42	997	0

[1]Excludes "Other current expenditures," such as community services, private school programs, adult education, and other programs not allocable to expenditures per pupil in public schools.
[2]Includes expenditures for property and for buildings and alterations completed by school district staff or contractors.
[3]Includes expenditures for operations funded by sales of products or services (e.g., school bookstore or computer time).
[4]Includes expenditures for health, attendance, and speech pathology services.

[5]Includes expenditures for curriculum development, staff training, libraries, and media and computer centers.
NOTE: Excludes expenditures for state education agencies. "0" indicates none or less than $0.50. Some data have been revised from previously published figures. Detail may not sum to totals because of rounding.
SOURCE: U.S. Department of Education, National Center for Education Statistics, Common Core of Data (CCD), "National Public Education Financial Survey," 2003–04. (This table was prepared August 2006.)

Table 169. Total and current expenditures per pupil in fall enrollment in public elementary and secondary education, by function and state or jurisdiction: 2002–03

State or jurisdiction	Current expenditures, capital expenditures, and interest on school debt														
	Total[1]	Current expenditures											Capital outlay[2]	Interest on school debt
		Total	Instruction	Student services								Food services	Enterprise opera-tions[3]		
				Total	Student support[4]	Instruc-tional staff[5]	General admini-stration	School admini-stration	Operation and mainte-nance	Student transpor-tation	Other support services				
1	2	3	4	5	6	7	8	9	10	11	12	13	14	15	16
United States	$9,299	$8,044	$4,934	$2,782	$415	$385	$165	$452	$764	$325	$275	$310	$19	$1,016	$239
Alabama	7,031	6,300	3,812	2,058	301	257	172	387	551	270	121	430	0	588	144
Alaska	11,896	9,870	5,740	3,798	486	627	157	564	1,262	389	313	285	47	1,843	183
Arizona	7,475	6,283	3,765	2,222	328	159	103	313	693	215	410	296	0	908	283
Arkansas	7,275	6,482	3,961	2,196	289	334	210	365	601	230	166	325	0	638	155
California	8,740	7,552	4,591	2,678	339	493	68	515	720	181	362	272	11	1,100	88
Colorado	8,846	7,384	4,230	2,900	324	358	106	502	684	220	706	228	26	1,098	365
Connecticut	12,653	11,057	7,052	3,612	612	382	229	609	996	519	264	297	97	1,348	248
Delaware	11,382	9,693	5,965	3,276	461	130	109	540	913	540	584	452	0	1,538	151
District of Columbia	14,419	11,847	6,216	5,331	1,087	1,202	320	473	1,320	626	303	300	0	2,573	0
Florida	7,773	6,439	3,786	2,338	327	395	73	388	687	269	200	315	0	1,149	185
Georgia	9,041	7,774	4,925	2,459	352	417	104	477	570	292	247	383	7	1,145	122
Hawaii	8,745	8,100	4,833	2,839	882	480	51	524	579	138	186	428	0	349	296
Idaho	6,978	6,081	3,721	2,098	344	283	140	349	579	279	124	262	0	752	144
Illinois	9,851	8,287	4,952	3,068	512	333	292	442	832	402	254	268	0	1,309	255
Indiana	9,587	8,057	4,932	2,797	356	263	146	456	871	447	257	329	0	838	692
Iowa	8,659	7,574	4,508	2,511	482	341	212	408	635	233	200	335	219	952	133
Kansas	8,268	7,454	4,413	2,697	420	339	265	449	741	295	187	345	0	531	283
Kentucky	7,012	6,661	4,066	2,233	269	329	192	382	561	323	177	362	0	202	148
Louisiana	7,638	6,922	4,203	2,291	293	321	164	374	635	355	148	428	0	563	153
Maine	10,288	9,344	6,269	2,774	315	294	213	500	886	402	163	300	0	728	216
Maryland	10,051	9,153	5,693	3,042	356	531	82	599	788	451	234	270	149	793	106
Massachusetts	11,045	10,460	6,656	3,486	626	500	192	457	957	438	316	318	0	277	307
Michigan	10,593	8,781	5,002	3,509	599	436	198	588	920	361	408	269	0	1,437	375
Minnesota	9,907	8,109	5,201	2,536	272	442	211	309	615	440	246	339	32	1,376	422
Mississippi	6,356	5,792	3,466	1,966	252	261	192	325	579	249	109	359	1	427	137
Missouri	8,600	7,495	4,570	2,602	368	336	230	443	731	355	138	324	0	847	258
Montana	8,100	7,496	4,606	2,583	359	289	236	414	757	327	201	296	11	525	79
Nebraska	9,371	8,074	5,151	2,360	338	269	284	415	682	214	158	316	247	1,106	191
Nevada	8,110	6,092	3,812	2,080	226	255	111	419	608	226	235	200	0	1,562	456
New Hampshire	9,802	8,579	5,569	2,746	567	260	293	482	705	375	63	264	0	1,035	188
New Jersey	13,884	12,568	7,424	4,757	1,137	427	349	652	1,242	695	254	292	95	1,105	211
New Mexico	8,469	7,125	3,953	2,842	722	330	221	438	689	320	122	325	4	1,230	115
New York	13,316	11,961	8,213	3,459	385	325	252	495	1,029	588	384	290	0	1,100	255
North Carolina	7,529	6,562	4,173	2,023	336	230	127	416	513	237	164	366	0	756	210
North Dakota	7,721	6,870	4,102	2,230	275	210	332	342	610	315	146	327	211	767	85
Ohio	10,096	8,632	4,956	3,390	514	544	243	525	803	384	378	285	1	1,274	190
Oklahoma	6,611	6,092	3,528	2,160	395	197	170	328	676	196	199	334	69	436	84
Oregon	8,921	7,491	4,438	2,798	500	292	110	482	618	329	468	253	2	1,093	336
Pennsylvania	10,445	8,997	5,557	3,088	436	335	271	398	920	444	283	315	36	1,039	410
Rhode Island	10,731	10,349	6,685	3,396	826	432	141	532	811	408	246	267	0	199	184
South Carolina	8,577	7,040	4,199	2,464	476	452	89	414	628	219	186	351	25	1,262	276
South Dakota	7,656	6,547	3,836	2,361	363	332	231	338	635	213	249	332	17	942	167
Tennessee	6,962	6,118	3,933	1,885	216	333	124	325	582	213	92	300	0	691	153
Texas	8,598	7,136	4,307	2,469	347	404	116	392	757	193	259	360	0	1,118	343
Utah	5,969	4,838	3,103	1,461	180	229	54	295	446	151	106	258	16	950	181
Vermont	11,075	10,454	6,713	3,458	742	380	268	719	809	330	209	275	8	466	154
Virginia	8,854	7,822	4,809	2,705	376	489	118	463	771	369	119	306	2	908	124
Washington	8,755	7,252	4,317	2,582	506	328	166	345	719	280	238	237	116	1,184	319
West Virginia	8,936	8,319	5,115	2,742	287	230	226	467	857	557	118	463	0	580	37
Wisconsin	10,347	9,004	5,566	3,149	410	468	244	466	802	350	409	289	0	775	568
Wyoming	10,313	8,985	5,381	3,317	526	447	203	511	935	382	314	286	1	1,252	76
Other jurisdictions															
American Samoa	3,225	2,976	1,543	893	127	184	39	140	283	40	79	540	0	249	0
Guam	—	—	—	—	—	—	—	—	—	—	—	—	—	—	—
Northern Marianas	4,555	4,519	3,871	437	58	14	307	0	0	9	48	211	0	36	0
Puerto Rico	4,324	4,260	3,145	606	87	76	25	0	220	95	103	509	0	32	31
Virgin Islands	7,163	6,840	4,459	2,168	385	215	332	388	486	239	123	171	42	323	0

—Not available.

[1]Excludes "Other current expenditures," such as community services, private school programs, adult education, and other programs not allocable to expenditures per pupil in public schools.

[2]Includes expenditures for property and for buildings and alterations completed by school district staff or contractors.

[3]Includes expenditures for operations funded by sales of products or services (e.g., school bookstore or computer time).

[4]Includes expenditures for health, attendance, and speech pathology services.

[5]Includes expenditures for curriculum development, staff training, libraries, and media and computer centers.

NOTE: Excludes expenditures for state education agencies. "0" indicates none or less than $0.50. Some data have been revised from previously published figures. Detail may not sum to totals because of rounding.

SOURCE: U.S. Department of Education, National Center for Education Statistics, Common Core of Data (CCD), "National Public Education Financial Survey," 2002–03. (This table was prepared August 2006.)

Table 170. Current expenditure per pupil in fall enrollment in public elementary and secondary schools, by state or jurisdiction: Selected years, 1969–70 through 2003–04

State or jurisdiction	Unadjusted dollars													
	1969–70	1979–80	1989–90	1990–91	1994–95	1995–96	1996–97	1997–98	1998–99	1999–2000	2000–01	2001–02	2002–03	2003–04
1	2	3	4	5	6	7	8	9	10	11	12	13	14	15
United States	$751	$2,088	$4,643	$4,902	$5,529	$5,689	$5,923	$6,189	$6,508	$6,912	$7,380	$7,727	$8,044	$8,310
Alabama	512	1,520	3,144	3,429	4,109	4,343	4,595	4,849	5,188	5,638	5,885	6,029	6,300	6,581
Alaska..........................	1,059	4,267	7,577	7,502	8,033	8,189	8,231	8,271	8,404	8,806	9,216	9,563	9,870	10,116
Arizona........................	674	1,865	3,717	3,860	4,264	4,476	4,413	4,595	4,672	5,030	5,521	5,851	6,283	5,991
Arkansas......................	511	1,472	3,229	3,461	4,186	4,401	4,535	4,708	4,956	5,277	5,568	6,276	6,482	6,842
California	833	2,227	4,502	4,595	4,799	4,937	5,260	5,644	5,801	6,314	6,987	7,405	7,552	7,673
Colorado......................	686	2,258	4,357	4,603	5,047	5,121	5,312	5,656	5,923	6,215	6,567	6,941	7,384	7,478
Connecticut..................	911	2,167	7,463	7,547	8,380	8,430	8,580	8,901	9,318	9,753	10,127	10,577	11,057	11,436
Delaware......................	833	2,587	5,326	5,458	6,502	6,696	7,135	7,420	7,706	8,310	8,958	9,284	9,693	10,212
District of Columbia	947	2,811	7,872	8,029	8,290	8,510	8,048	8,393	9,650	10,107	12,046	12,102	11,847	12,959
Florida.........................	683	1,834	4,597	4,859	5,220	5,275	5,360	5,552	5,790	5,831	6,170	6,213	6,439	6,793
Georgia........................	539	1,491	4,000	4,171	4,828	5,056	5,369	5,647	6,092	6,437	6,929	7,380	7,774	7,742
Hawaii..........................	792	2,086	4,130	4,820	5,597	5,560	5,633	5,858	6,081	6,530	6,596	7,306	8,100	8,533
Idaho...........................	573	1,548	2,921	3,206	3,957	4,194	4,447	4,721	5,066	5,315	5,725	6,011	6,081	6,168
Illinois..........................	816	2,241	4,521	4,904	5,553	5,519	5,940	6,242	6,762	7,133	7,631	7,956	8,287	8,606
Indiana.........................	661	1,708	4,270	4,588	5,411	5,621	6,161	6,318	6,772	7,192	7,630	7,734	8,057	8,431
Iowa	798	2,164	4,190	4,418	5,240	5,481	5,738	5,998	6,243	6,564	6,930	7,338	7,574	7,626
Kansas.........................	699	1,963	4,290	4,434	5,222	5,374	5,508	5,727	6,015	6,294	6,937	7,339	7,454	7,776
Kentucky	502	1,557	3,384	3,897	4,545	4,807	5,155	5,213	5,637	5,921	6,079	6,523	6,661	6,861
Louisiana	589	1,629	3,625	3,853	4,356	4,447	4,724	5,187	5,548	5,804	6,037	6,567	6,922	7,271
Maine...........................	649	1,692	4,903	4,978	6,029	6,151	6,426	6,742	7,155	7,667	8,232	8,818	9,344	9,746
Maryland.......................	809	2,293	5,573	5,930	6,427	6,593	6,755	7,034	7,326	7,731	8,260	8,692	9,153	9,433
Massachusetts..............	791	2,548	5,766	5,881	6,783	7,033	7,331	7,778	8,260	8,816	9,509	10,232	10,460	11,015
Michigan	841	2,495	5,090	5,394	6,465	6,785	6,932	7,050	7,432	8,110	8,278	8,653	8,781	9,094
Minnesota	855	2,296	4,698	4,946	5,626	5,801	6,005	6,388	6,814	7,190	7,645	7,736	8,109	8,405
Mississippi	457	1,568	2,934	3,007	3,798	3,951	4,039	4,288	4,565	5,014	5,175	5,354	5,792	6,199
Missouri.......................	596	1,724	4,071	4,271	4,866	5,092	5,304	5,565	5,855	6,187	6,657	7,136	7,495	7,542
Montana.......................	728	2,264	4,240	4,706	5,137	5,249	5,481	5,724	5,974	6,314	6,726	7,062	7,496	7,825
Nebraska	700	2,025	4,553	4,735	5,555	5,688	5,848	5,958	6,256	6,683	7,223	7,741	8,074	8,452
Nevada	706	1,908	3,816	4,294	4,730	4,892	5,084	5,295	5,587	5,760	5,807	6,079	6,092	6,410
New Hampshire	666	1,732	4,786	5,152	5,567	5,740	5,920	6,156	6,433	6,860	7,286	7,935	8,579	9,161
New Jersey....................	924	2,825	7,546	8,166	9,178	9,361	9,588	9,643	10,145	10,337	11,248	11,793	12,568	13,338
New Mexico	665	1,870	3,446	3,757	4,404	4,604	4,682	5,005	5,440	5,825	6,313	6,882	7,125	7,572
New York......................	1,194	2,950	7,051	7,510	8,311	8,361	8,525	8,852	9,344	9,846	10,716	11,218	11,961	12,638
North Carolina	570	1,635	4,018	4,237	4,703	4,719	4,929	5,257	5,656	6,045	6,340	6,495	6,562	6,613
North Dakota	662	1,941	3,899	3,909	4,482	4,677	4,808	5,056	5,442	5,667	6,125	6,709	6,870	7,297
Ohio............................	677	1,894	4,531	4,747	5,529	5,669	5,935	6,198	6,590	7,065	7,571	8,069	8,632	9,029
Oklahoma.....................	554	1,810	3,293	3,639	4,533	4,549	4,817	5,033	5,303	5,395	6,019	6,229	6,092	6,154
Oregon.........................	843	2,412	4,864	5,195	5,649	5,790	5,920	6,419	6,828	7,149	7,528	7,642	7,491	7,618
Pennsylvania................	815	2,328	5,737	6,048	6,565	6,922	7,106	7,209	7,450	7,772	8,210	8,537	8,997	9,708
Rhode Island	807	2,340	5,908	5,934	7,126	7,304	7,612	7,928	8,294	8,904	9,315	9,703	10,349	11,078
South Carolina..............	567	1,597	3,769	4,009	4,501	4,779	5,050	5,320	5,656	6,130	6,631	7,017	7,040	7,177
South Dakota	656	1,781	3,511	3,726	4,271	4,220	4,387	4,669	5,259	5,632	6,191	6,424	6,547	7,068
Tennessee	531	1,523	3,405	3,521	4,017	4,172	4,581	4,937	5,123	5,383	5,687	5,948	6,118	6,466
Texas...........................	551	1,740	3,835	4,048	4,779	5,016	5,267	5,444	5,685	6,288	6,539	6,771	7,136	7,151
Utah............................	595	1,556	2,577	2,767	3,409	3,604	3,783	3,969	4,210	4,378	4,674	4,900	4,838	4,991
Vermont........................	790	1,930	5,770	6,255	6,367	6,488	6,753	7,075	7,541	8,323	9,153	9,806	10,454	11,211
Virginia.........................	654	1,824	4,690	4,965	5,421	5,528	5,788	6,065	6,350	6,841	7,281	7,496	7,822	8,219
Washington...................	853	2,387	4,382	4,652	5,477	5,639	5,734	6,040	6,110	6,376	6,750	7,039	7,252	7,391
West Virginia.................	621	1,749	4,020	4,571	5,663	5,881	6,076	6,323	6,677	7,152	7,534	7,844	8,319	8,588
Wisconsin.....................	793	2,225	5,020	5,382	6,301	6,517	6,796	7,123	7,527	7,806	8,243	8,634	9,004	9,240
Wyoming.......................	805	2,369	5,239	5,310	5,753	5,826	5,971	6,218	6,842	7,425	7,835	8,645	8,985	9,308
Other jurisdictions														
American Samoa	—	—	1,781	2,002	1,983	2,084	2,288	2,175	2,283	2,739	2,588	2,906	2,976	3,493
Guam...........................	766	—	3,817	4,411	5,016	4,803	4,688	5,200	—	—	—	—	—	5,781
Northern Marianas...........	—	—	3,356	4,159	5,340	4,999	5,878	6,112	5,312	5,120	4,913	4,438	4,519	4,241
Puerto Rico	—	—	1,605	1,773	2,417	2,657	2,812	3,211	3,298	3,404	3,685	3,563	4,260	4,147
Virgin Islands	—	—	6,043	5,515	5,280	5,378	5,458	5,932	6,983	6,478	6,437	5,716	6,840	7,239

See notes at end of table.

Table 170. Current expenditure per pupil in fall enrollment in public elementary and secondary schools, by state or jurisdiction: Selected years, 1969–70 through 2003–04—Continued

State or jurisdiction	Constant 2005–06 dollars[1]														
	1969–70	1979–80	1989–90	1990–91	1994–95	1995–96	1996–97	1997–98	1998–99	1999–2000	2000–01	2001–02	2002–03	2003–04
1	16	17	18	19	20	21	22	23	24	25	26	27	28	29
United States	$3,957	$5,353	$7,276	$7,284	$7,315	$7,328	$7,418	$7,615	$7,871	$8,125	$8,387	$8,629	$8,790	$8,886
Alabama	2,695	3,897	4,927	5,096	5,436	5,593	5,754	5,966	6,274	6,627	6,688	6,733	6,884	7,038
Alaska.........................	5,580	10,938	11,875	11,147	10,628	10,547	10,307	10,175	10,163	10,351	10,474	10,679	10,786	10,817
Arizona.......................	3,553	4,780	5,826	5,735	5,642	5,765	5,527	5,653	5,651	5,913	6,275	6,534	6,866	6,406
Arkansas.....................	2,691	3,773	5,061	5,143	5,538	5,668	5,679	5,792	5,993	6,203	6,328	7,008	7,083	7,316
California	4,390	5,707	7,056	6,828	6,349	6,359	6,587	6,944	7,016	7,422	7,941	8,270	8,252	8,205
Colorado	3,614	5,788	6,828	6,839	6,678	6,595	6,652	6,959	7,163	7,306	7,464	7,751	8,068	7,997
Connecticut.................	4,798	5,555	11,695	11,214	11,087	10,857	10,744	10,951	11,269	11,463	11,509	11,811	12,083	12,229
Delaware.....................	4,391	6,630	8,347	8,110	8,602	8,624	8,934	9,129	9,319	9,767	10,180	10,368	10,592	10,920
District of Columbia	4,988	7,206	12,336	11,931	10,968	10,961	10,078	10,326	11,670	11,880	13,691	13,515	12,945	13,857
Florida.........................	3,596	4,701	7,205	7,220	6,906	6,795	6,712	6,831	7,002	6,854	7,013	6,938	7,036	7,264
Georgia.......................	2,838	3,822	6,268	6,199	6,388	6,513	6,723	6,948	7,368	7,567	7,874	8,242	8,495	8,279
Hawaii.........................	4,172	5,348	6,472	7,162	7,405	7,161	7,054	7,207	7,355	7,676	7,496	8,159	8,851	9,125
Idaho..........................	3,020	3,969	4,578	4,764	5,235	5,402	5,569	5,808	6,127	6,247	6,506	6,712	6,645	6,595
Illinois.........................	4,297	5,745	7,085	7,287	7,347	7,108	7,439	7,679	8,178	8,384	8,673	8,885	9,055	9,203
Indiana........................	3,483	4,378	6,692	6,817	7,159	7,240	7,715	7,773	8,190	8,454	8,672	8,637	8,805	9,016
Iowa...........................	4,204	5,547	6,566	6,564	6,933	7,060	7,186	7,380	7,551	7,716	7,876	8,195	8,276	8,155
Kansas........................	3,681	5,031	6,723	6,589	6,909	6,921	6,898	7,046	7,274	7,398	7,884	8,196	8,145	8,315
Kentucky	2,644	3,992	5,303	5,791	6,013	6,191	6,455	6,414	6,818	6,960	6,908	7,285	7,279	7,337
Louisiana	3,105	4,175	5,681	5,725	5,763	5,728	5,916	6,381	6,710	6,822	6,861	7,333	7,564	7,775
Maine..........................	3,420	4,337	7,684	7,397	7,976	7,923	8,047	8,295	8,653	9,013	9,356	9,847	10,210	10,422
Maryland	4,263	5,877	8,734	8,811	8,503	8,492	8,459	8,654	8,860	9,088	9,387	9,707	10,001	10,087
Massachusetts.....................	4,165	6,530	9,036	8,739	8,974	9,059	9,180	9,570	9,989	10,363	10,807	11,427	11,430	11,779
Michigan......................	4,433	6,397	7,977	8,015	8,554	8,739	8,681	8,673	8,988	9,532	9,408	9,663	9,595	9,724
Minnesota....................	4,503	5,886	7,363	7,349	7,443	7,472	7,520	7,859	8,241	8,451	8,688	8,639	8,861	8,987
Mississippi	2,406	4,020	4,597	4,468	5,024	5,089	5,058	5,276	5,520	5,893	5,881	5,979	6,329	6,629
Missouri......................	3,139	4,419	6,379	6,347	6,438	6,558	6,641	6,847	7,081	7,272	7,566	7,968	8,190	8,065
Montana......................	3,833	5,802	6,645	6,993	6,797	6,760	6,863	7,042	7,224	7,421	7,645	7,886	8,190	8,367
Nebraska	3,686	5,189	7,135	7,035	7,350	7,326	7,323	7,330	7,566	7,856	8,209	8,645	8,822	9,038
Nevada	3,718	4,891	5,980	6,380	6,258	6,301	6,367	6,514	6,757	6,770	6,600	6,788	6,657	6,855
New Hampshire	3,509	4,440	7,500	7,655	7,365	7,393	7,413	7,574	7,780	8,063	8,280	8,861	9,374	9,797
New Jersey	4,866	7,242	11,826	12,134	12,143	12,057	12,006	11,864	12,270	12,151	12,784	13,170	13,733	14,263
New Mexico	3,503	4,794	5,400	5,583	5,826	5,929	5,863	6,157	6,579	6,847	7,175	7,686	7,785	8,096
New York......................	6,292	7,563	11,050	11,160	10,995	10,769	10,675	10,891	11,301	11,573	12,178	12,527	13,070	13,514
North Carolina	3,004	4,192	6,297	6,296	6,222	6,078	6,173	6,467	6,841	7,106	7,206	7,253	7,171	7,071
North Dakota	3,490	4,976	6,111	5,809	5,930	6,024	6,020	6,220	6,581	6,661	6,961	7,492	7,507	7,803
Ohio.............................	3,564	4,856	7,101	7,054	7,315	7,301	7,432	7,626	7,969	8,304	8,605	9,011	9,433	9,655
Oklahoma....................	2,917	4,639	5,161	5,408	5,997	5,859	6,032	6,192	6,413	6,341	6,841	6,957	6,657	6,580
Oregon........................	4,442	6,183	7,623	7,719	7,474	7,458	7,413	7,897	8,257	8,403	8,556	8,534	8,186	8,146
Pennsylvania...............	4,295	5,968	8,991	8,987	8,686	8,916	8,898	8,869	9,010	9,136	9,331	9,533	9,831	10,381
Rhode Island	4,250	5,999	9,259	8,817	9,428	9,408	9,532	9,754	10,031	10,467	10,587	10,835	11,308	11,846
South Carolina	2,988	4,094	5,907	5,958	5,956	6,156	6,324	6,545	6,840	7,205	7,537	7,836	7,692	7,674
South Dakota	3,456	4,564	5,503	5,537	5,651	5,436	5,493	5,744	6,360	6,620	7,036	7,174	7,154	7,558
Tennessee	2,797	3,904	5,336	5,232	5,315	5,373	5,737	6,075	6,196	6,327	6,463	6,642	6,685	6,914
Texas	2,903	4,459	6,010	6,016	6,322	6,461	6,596	6,698	6,875	7,391	7,432	7,561	7,798	7,646
Utah	3,135	3,989	4,039	4,112	4,510	4,643	4,737	4,883	5,091	5,146	5,312	5,471	5,286	5,337
Vermont......................	4,159	4,948	9,043	9,295	8,424	8,356	8,456	8,704	9,119	9,783	10,402	10,951	11,424	11,988
Virginia........................	3,448	4,676	7,350	7,378	7,172	7,120	7,248	7,462	7,679	8,041	8,275	8,371	8,547	8,789
Washington..................	4,494	6,119	6,868	6,913	7,246	7,263	7,180	7,431	7,389	7,495	7,671	7,861	7,925	7,904
West Virginia................	3,273	4,482	6,300	6,792	7,493	7,574	7,609	7,779	8,075	8,406	8,563	8,760	9,091	9,183
Wisconsin....................	4,178	5,703	7,867	7,997	8,336	8,394	8,510	8,763	9,103	9,176	9,368	9,642	9,839	9,880
Wyoming.....................	4,241	6,073	8,210	7,890	7,612	7,504	7,477	7,651	8,274	8,728	8,905	9,654	9,818	9,953
Other jurisdictions														
American Samoa	—	—	2,792	2,974	2,623	2,685	2,865	2,676	2,761	3,220	2,942	3,245	3,252	3,735
Guam	4,038	—	5,982	6,554	6,636	6,186	5,871	6,398	—	—	—	—	—	6,181
Northern Marianas...........	—	—	5,260	6,180	7,064	6,439	7,360	7,520	6,424	6,019	5,584	4,956	4,938	4,534
Puerto Rico...................	—	—	2,516	2,634	3,198	3,422	3,521	3,950	3,988	4,001	4,188	3,979	4,655	4,434
Virgin Islands	—	—	9,470	8,195	6,985	6,927	6,835	7,298	8,445	7,615	7,315	6,383	7,475	7,741

—Not available.

[1]Constant dollars based on the Consumer Price Index (CPI), prepared by the Bureau of Labor Statistics, U.S. Department of Labor, adjusted to a school-year basis. The CPI does not account for differences in inflation rates from state to state.
NOTE: Expenditures for state administration are excluded in all years except 1969–70 and 1979–80. Beginning in 1989–90, the survey was expanded and coverage of state expendi-tures for public school districts was improved. Some data have been revised from previously published figures.
SOURCE: U.S. Department of Education, National Center for Education Statistics, *Statistics of State School Systems*, 1969–70; *Revenues and Expenditures for Public Elementary and Secondary Schools*, 1979–80; and Common Core of Data (CCD), "National Public Education Financial Survey," 1989–90 through 2003–04. (This table was prepared August 2006.)

Table 171. Current expenditure per pupil in average daily attendance in public elementary and secondary schools, by state or jurisdiction: Selected years, 1959–60 through 2003–04

State or jurisdiction	Unadjusted dollars													
	1959–60	1969–70	1979–80	1989–90	1990–91	1995–96	1996–97	1997–98	1998–99	1999–2000	2000–01	2001–02	2002–03	2003–04
1	2	3	4	5	6	7	8	9	10	11	12	13	14	15
United States	$375	$816	$2,272	$4,980	$5,258	$6,147	$6,393	$6,676	$7,013	$7,394	$7,904	$8,259	$8,610	$8,899
Alabama	241	544	1,612	3,327	3,627	4,716	4,903	5,166	5,512	5,758	6,052	6,327	6,642	6,812
Alaska	546	1,123	4,728	8,431	8,330	9,012	9,097	9,074	9,209	9,668	9,998	10,419	10,770	11,074
Arizona	404	720	1,971	4,053	4,309	4,860	4,940	5,122	5,235	5,478	6,032	6,470	6,784	6,898
Arkansas	225	568	1,574	3,485	3,700	4,710	4,840	4,999	5,193	5,628	5,942	6,676	6,981	7,307
California	424 [2]	867	2,268	4,391	4,491	5,108	5,414	5,795	6,045	6,401	7,063	7,439	7,601	7,708
Colorado	396	738	2,421	4,720	5,064	5,521	5,728	6,099	6,386	6,702	7,082	7,284	7,826	8,416
Connecticut	436	951	2,420	7,837	7,853	8,817	8,901	9,218	9,620	10,122	10,525	11,022	11,302	11,755
Delaware	456	900	2,861	5,799	5,974	7,267	7,804	7,963	8,336	8,809	9,720	9,959	10,257	11,049
District of Columbia	431	1,018	3,259	8,955	9,377	9,565	9,019	9,225	10,611	11,935	13,204	14,557	14,735	15,414
Florida	318	732	1,889	4,997	5,276	5,894	5,986	6,183	6,443	6,383	6,620	6,679	6,922	7,269
Georgia	253	588	1,625	4,275	4,466	5,377	5,708	6,059	6,534	6,903	7,431	7,870	8,308	8,278
Hawaii	325	841	2,322	4,448	5,166	6,051	6,144	6,409	6,648	7,090	7,106	7,919	8,770	9,341
Idaho	290	603	1,659	3,078	3,386	4,465	4,732	5,012	5,379	5,644	6,077	6,391	6,454	6,559
Illinois	438	909	2,587	5,118	5,520	6,128	6,557	7,111	7,676	8,084	8,659	8,967	9,309	9,710
Indiana	369	728	1,882	4,606	4,930	6,040	6,605	6,786	7,249	7,652	8,128	8,268	8,582	9,033
Iowa	368	844	2,326	4,453	4,679	5,772	6,047	6,295	6,548	6,925	7,340	7,714	7,943	8,017
Kansas	348	771	2,173	4,752	4,874	5,971	6,158	6,406	6,708	6,962	7,681	8,342	8,373	8,804
Kentucky	233	545	1,701	3,745	4,354	5,545	5,929	6,125	6,501	6,784	7,174	7,536	7,728	7,973
Louisiana	372	648	1,792	3,903	4,196	4,988	5,201	5,644	6,019	6,256	6,553	7,061	7,492	7,846
Maine	283	692	1,824	5,373	5,458	6,546	6,880	7,238	7,688	8,247	8,879	9,517	10,114	10,504
Maryland	393	918	2,598	6,275	6,654	7,382	7,543	7,812	7,865	8,273	8,833	9,266	9,801	10,140
Massachusetts	409	859	2,819	6,237	6,366	7,613	7,818	8,299	8,750	9,375	10,073	10,808	11,161	11,583
Michigan	415	904	2,640	5,546	5,883	7,166	7,568	7,717	8,142	8,886	9,031	9,428	9,847	10,049
Minnesota	425	904	2,387	4,971	5,239	6,162	6,371	6,795	7,183	7,499	7,960	8,050	8,440	8,934
Mississippi	206	501	1,664	3,094	3,187	4,250	4,312	4,575	4,871	5,356	5,535	5,719	6,186	6,601
Missouri	344	709	1,936	4,507	4,754	5,626	5,823	6,096	6,393	6,764	7,265	7,700	8,002	8,022
Montana	411	782	2,476	4,736	5,204	5,847	6,112	6,448	6,768	6,990	7,484	7,861	8,391	8,771
Nebraska	337	736	2,150	4,842	5,038	6,083	6,472	6,584	6,856	7,360	7,688	8,238	8,550	9,270
Nevada	430	769	2,088	4,117	4,653	5,320	5,541	5,758	5,934	6,148	6,150	6,477	6,496	6,780
New Hampshire	347	723	1,916	5,304	5,685	5,958	6,236	6,487	6,780	7,082	7,656	8,230	8,900	9,391
New Jersey	388	1,016	3,191	8,139	8,756	9,955	10,211	10,233	10,748	10,903	11,752	12,197	13,093	13,776
New Mexico	363	707	2,034	3,515	3,895	4,587	4,674	4,984	5,363	5,835	6,320	6,886	7,126	7,653
New York	562	1,327	3,462	8,062	8,565	9,549	9,658	9,970	10,514	10,957	11,887	12,343	13,211	13,926
North Carolina	237	612	1,754	4,290	4,548	5,090	5,315	5,667	6,088	6,505	6,817	6,970	7,057	7,114
North Dakota	367	690	1,920	4,189	4,199	4,979	5,198	5,353	5,820	6,078	6,467	7,112	7,315	7,752
Ohio	365	730	2,075	5,045	5,245	6,266	6,517	6,808	7,254	7,816	8,403	8,928	9,427	9,799
Oklahoma	311	604	1,926	3,508	3,843	4,881	5,150	5,389	5,684	5,770	6,458	6,672	6,540	6,599
Oregon	448	925	2,692	5,474	5,683	6,615	6,792	7,348	7,787	8,129	8,545	8,725	8,514	8,640
Pennsylvania	409	882	2,535	6,228	6,541	7,492	7,686	7,777	8,026	8,380	8,847	9,196	9,648	10,393
Rhode Island	413	891	2,601	6,368	6,343	7,936	8,307	8,627	9,049	9,646	10,116	10,552	11,377	12,279
South Carolina	220	613	1,752	4,082	4,352	5,096	5,371	5,643	6,003	6,545	7,210	7,549	7,759	7,893
South Dakota	347	690	1,908	3,731	3,965	4,780	4,936	5,281	5,613	6,037	6,581	6,890	7,192	7,607
Tennessee	238	566	1,635	3,664	3,782	4,548	5,011	5,274	5,521	5,837	6,108	6,476	6,674	7,047
Texas	332	624	1,916	4,150	4,438	5,473	5,736	5,910	6,161	6,771	7,039	7,302	7,714	7,711
Utah	322	626	1,657	2,764	2,960	3,867	4,045	4,256	4,478	4,692	5,029	5,294	5,247	5,427
Vermont	344	807	1,997	6,227	6,738	6,837	7,171	7,500	7,984	8,799	9,559	10,229	10,903	11,675
Virginia	274	708	1,970	4,672	4,902	5,433	5,677	5,936	6,129	6,491	7,664	7,928	8,300	8,761
Washington	420	915	2,568	4,702	5,000	6,074	6,182	6,535	6,595	6,914	7,312	7,626	7,882	8,051
West Virginia	258	670	1,920	4,360	4,911	6,325	6,519	6,779	7,189	7,637	8,148	8,451	9,025	9,076
Wisconsin	413	883	2,477	5,524	5,871	7,094	7,398	7,680	8,062	8,299	8,797	9,237	9,538	9,834
Wyoming	450	856	2,527	5,577	5,638	6,243	6,448	6,718	7,393	7,944	8,466	9,321	9,906	10,351
Other jurisdictions														
American Samoa	—	—	—	1,908	2,033	2,159	2,393	2,243	2,354	2,807	2,743	2,983	3,121	3,671
Guam	236	820	—	4,234	4,596	4,947	5,124	5,286	—	—	—	—	—	6,449
Northern Marianas	—	—	—	3,007	4,425	5,863	6,827	7,016	5,973	5,720	5,481	4,934	5,221	4,746
Puerto Rico	106	—	—	1,750	1,913	3,039	3,229	3,648	3,771	3,859	4,191	4,013	4,743	4,534
Virgin Islands	271	—	—	6,767	6,002	6,155	6,274	6,758	7,714	7,238	7,795	6,248	7,747	8,077

See notes at end of table.

Table 171. Current expenditure per pupil in average daily attendance in public elementary and secondary schools, by state or jurisdiction: Selected years, 1959–60 through 2003–04—Continued

State or jurisdiction	Constant 2005–06 dollars[1]													
	1959–60	1969–70	1979–80	1989–90	1990–91	1995–96	1996–97	1997–98	1998–99	1999–2000	2000–01	2001–02	2002–03	2003–04
1	16	17	18	19	20	21	22	23	24	25	26	27	28	29
United States	$2,541	$4,298	$5,823	$7,804	$7,813	$7,917	$8,005	$8,213	$8,482	$8,691	$8,982	$9,223	$9,408	$9,516
Alabama......................	1,633	2,866	4,132	5,214	5,389	6,074	6,140	6,355	6,666	6,769	6,878	7,066	7,258	7,284
Alaska........................	3,700	5,913	12,118	13,213	12,377	11,607	11,392	11,164	11,137	11,364	11,362	11,635	11,768	11,842
Arizona......................	2,733	3,793	5,052	6,352	6,403	6,260	6,186	6,302	6,331	6,439	6,855	7,225	7,413	7,377
Arkansas....................	1,525	2,990	4,036	5,462	5,498	6,066	6,061	6,150	6,280	6,615	6,753	7,456	7,628	7,814
California....................	2,871 [2]	4,568	5,813	6,881	6,673	6,579	6,780	7,130	7,311	7,523	8,027	8,308	8,306	8,243
Colorado.....................	2,683	3,887	6,205	7,398	7,525	7,111	7,172	7,504	7,723	7,877	8,048	8,134	8,552	8,999
Connecticut................	2,953	5,011	6,203	12,282	11,670	11,356	11,146	11,342	11,634	11,898	11,961	12,308	12,350	12,570
Delaware....................	3,086	4,741	7,334	9,088	8,877	9,359	9,772	9,797	10,081	10,354	11,047	11,121	11,208	11,815
District of Columbia	2,920	5,364	8,354	14,034	13,934	12,319	11,294	11,349	12,832	14,029	15,007	16,256	16,101	16,482
Florida........................	2,151	3,858	4,842	7,832	7,840	7,591	7,496	7,607	7,792	7,503	7,524	7,458	7,564	7,773
Georgia......................	1,717	3,097	4,166	6,699	6,636	6,926	7,147	7,454	7,902	8,114	8,445	8,788	9,078	8,852
Hawaii........................	2,198	4,428	5,951	6,972	7,677	7,794	7,693	7,885	8,040	8,334	8,076	8,844	9,583	9,988
Idaho.........................	1,962	3,178	4,253	4,823	5,032	5,750	5,925	6,166	6,505	6,634	6,907	7,137	7,053	7,013
Illinois........................	2,969	4,791	6,630	8,020	8,203	7,893	8,212	8,749	9,283	9,502	9,841	10,014	10,172	10,383
Indiana.......................	2,497	3,835	4,825	7,219	7,326	7,779	8,271	8,349	8,766	8,995	9,237	9,233	9,378	9,659
Iowa..........................	2,490	4,447	5,963	6,978	6,953	7,434	7,573	7,745	7,919	8,140	8,342	8,614	8,680	8,572
Kansas.......................	2,355	4,061	5,570	7,447	7,243	7,691	7,712	7,881	8,112	8,184	8,729	9,316	9,149	9,415
Kentucky....................	1,578	2,872	4,360	5,869	6,469	7,142	7,425	7,535	7,862	7,974	8,153	8,415	8,445	8,525
Louisiana....................	2,519	3,414	4,593	6,117	6,236	6,424	6,513	6,943	7,279	7,353	7,447	7,886	8,186	8,390
Maine.........................	1,915	3,648	4,674	8,420	8,110	8,431	8,615	8,905	9,298	9,694	10,091	10,628	11,052	11,233
Maryland.....................	2,660	4,838	6,659	9,835	9,887	9,508	9,446	9,611	9,512	9,725	10,039	10,348	10,710	10,842
Massachusetts.............	2,769	4,525	7,226	9,775	9,459	9,806	9,790	10,211	10,583	11,020	11,448	12,070	12,196	12,385
Michigan	2,811	4,762	6,768	8,692	8,741	9,229	9,477	9,495	9,847	10,445	10,263	10,529	10,759	10,745
Minnesota...................	2,880	4,760	6,118	7,790	7,784	7,937	7,978	8,360	8,687	8,815	9,047	8,990	9,223	9,554
Mississippi..................	1,394	2,638	4,265	4,848	4,735	5,474	5,400	5,629	5,891	6,295	6,290	6,387	6,760	7,059
Missouri......................	2,329	3,732	4,963	7,063	7,064	7,246	7,292	7,500	7,732	7,951	8,256	8,598	8,744	8,578
Montana.....................	2,782	4,119	6,348	7,423	7,733	7,530	7,653	7,933	8,186	8,216	8,506	8,779	9,169	9,379
Nebraska....................	2,282	3,879	5,511	7,588	7,486	7,835	8,104	8,101	8,291	8,651	8,737	9,199	9,343	9,912
Nevada	2,915	4,053	5,353	6,452	6,915	6,852	6,938	7,084	7,177	7,226	6,990	7,234	7,099	7,250
New Hampshire.................	2,352	3,809	4,911	8,312	8,447	7,674	7,809	7,981	8,199	8,325	8,701	9,191	9,725	10,042
New Jersey..................	2,625	5,353	8,180	12,756	13,011	12,822	12,787	12,590	12,999	12,815	13,356	13,621	14,307	14,731
New Mexico.................	2,456	3,724	5,213	5,508	5,787	5,908	5,852	6,131	6,486	6,858	7,183	7,690	7,786	8,183
New York....................	3,803	6,989	8,875	12,634	12,726	12,299	12,094	12,266	12,716	12,879	13,509	13,784	14,436	14,891
North Carolina	1,607	3,226	4,497	6,723	6,758	6,556	6,656	6,972	7,363	7,646	7,748	7,784	7,712	7,608
North Dakota	2,483	3,633	4,922	6,565	6,239	6,413	6,509	6,586	7,039	7,144	7,350	7,943	7,993	8,290
Ohio..........................	2,472	3,846	5,318	7,906	7,793	8,071	8,160	8,375	8,773	9,188	9,550	9,970	10,301	10,478
Oklahoma...................	2,109	3,184	4,938	5,497	5,711	6,286	6,449	6,630	6,874	6,782	7,340	7,450	7,146	7,056
Oregon.......................	3,036	4,871	6,900	8,579	8,445	8,520	8,506	9,040	9,418	9,555	9,711	9,743	9,303	9,239
Pennsylvania...............	2,773	4,645	6,497	9,760	9,720	9,649	9,624	9,567	9,706	9,851	10,055	10,269	10,542	11,114
Rhode Island	2,800	4,695	6,667	9,979	9,425	10,222	10,402	10,614	10,943	11,339	11,496	11,783	12,432	13,130
South Carolina.................	1,490	3,227	4,491	6,397	6,467	6,563	6,726	6,942	7,260	7,694	8,195	8,431	8,479	8,440
South Dakota.................	2,349	3,634	4,890	5,847	5,891	6,156	6,181	6,497	6,789	7,096	7,480	7,694	7,859	8,134
Tennessee	1,612	2,982	4,192	5,742	5,619	5,858	6,275	6,488	6,677	6,861	6,941	7,232	7,292	7,535
Texas	2,251	3,288	4,910	6,504	6,595	7,050	7,182	7,271	7,451	7,959	7,999	8,155	8,429	8,246
Utah..........................	2,184	3,299	4,247	4,331	4,398	4,981	5,066	5,236	5,415	5,516	5,716	5,912	5,734	5,803
Vermont......................	2,329	4,252	5,119	9,758	10,012	8,806	8,980	9,228	9,656	10,343	10,863	11,423	11,913	12,485
Virginia.......................	1,857	3,729	5,049	7,321	7,284	6,997	7,109	7,303	7,412	7,630	8,711	8,854	9,069	9,368
Washington.................	2,847	4,822	6,583	7,369	7,429	7,823	7,741	8,039	7,976	8,126	8,310	8,516	8,613	8,609
West Virginia...............	1,750	3,529	4,922	6,834	7,297	8,146	8,164	8,341	8,694	8,976	9,260	9,437	9,862	9,706
Wisconsin...................	2,797	4,650	6,349	8,657	8,724	9,137	9,264	9,449	9,750	9,755	9,998	10,315	10,422	10,516
Wyoming....................	3,050	4,509	6,477	8,741	8,378	8,041	8,075	8,265	8,941	9,338	9,621	10,409	10,825	11,068
Other jurisdictions														
American Samoa	—	—	—	2,989	3,020	2,780	2,997	2,760	2,847	3,300	3,117	3,331	3,410	3,926
Guam.........................	1,601	4,318	—	6,636	6,829	6,372	6,416	6,504	—	—	—	—	—	6,896
Northern Marianas.........	—	—	—	4,713	6,575	7,551	8,549	8,632	7,224	6,723	6,229	5,510	5,705	5,075
Puerto Rico	719	—	—	2,742	2,843	3,914	4,044	4,488	4,560	4,536	4,763	4,481	5,182	4,848
Virgin Islands	1,833	—	—	10,606	8,919	7,928	7,857	8,315	9,329	8,508	8,859	6,977	8,466	8,637

—Not available.
[1]Constant dollars based on the Consumer Price Index (CPI), prepared by the Bureau of Labor Statistics, U.S. Department of Labor, adjusted to a school-year basis. The CPI does not account for differences in inflation rates from state to state.
[2]Estimated by the National Center for Education Statistics.
NOTE: State administration expenditures are excluded in all years except 1959–60, 1969–70, and 1979–80. Beginning in 1989–90, extensive changes were made in the data collection procedures. There are discrepancies in average daily attendance reporting practices from state to state. Some data have been revised from previously published figures.
SOURCE: U.S. Department of Education, National Center for Education Statistics, *Statistics of State School Systems*, 1959–60 and 1969–70; *Revenues and Expenditures for Public Elementary and Secondary Education*, 1979–80; and Common Core of Data (CCD), "National Public Education Financial Survey," 1989–90 through 2003–04. (This table was prepared August 2006.)

Table 172. Students transported at public expense and current expenditures for transportation: Selected years, 1929–30 through 2003–04

| School year | Average daily attendance, all students | Students transported at public expense | | Expenditures for transportation (in current dollars) | | Expenditures for transportation (in constant 2005–06 dollars)[1] | |
		Number	Percent of total	Total[2] (in thousands)	Average per student transported	Total[2] (in thousands)	Average per student transported
1	2	3	4	5	6	7	8
1929–30	21,265,000	1,902,826	8.9	$54,823	$29	$637,339	$335
1931–32	22,245,000	2,419,173	10.9	58,078	24	801,627	331
1933–34	22,458,000	2,794,724	12.4	53,908	19	810,094	290
1935–36	22,299,000	3,250,658	14.6	62,653	19	907,251	279
1937–38	22,298,000	3,769,242	16.9	75,637	20	1,050,692	279
1939–40	22,042,000	4,144,161	18.8	83,283	20	1,185,878	286
1941–42	21,031,000	4,503,081	21.4	92,922	21	1,185,912	263
1943–44	19,603,000	4,512,412	23.0	107,754	24	1,230,541	273
1945–46	19,849,000	5,056,966	25.5	129,756	26	1,415,437	280
1947–48	20,910,000	5,854,041	28.0	176,265	30	1,505,379	257
1949–50	22,284,000	6,947,384	31.2	214,504	31	1,802,330	259
1951–52	23,257,000	7,697,130	33.1	268,827	35	2,035,324	264
1953–54	25,643,871	8,411,719	32.8	307,437	37	2,274,933	270
1955–56	27,740,149	9,695,819	35.0	353,972	37	2,620,154	270
1957–58	29,722,275	10,861,689	36.5	416,491	38	2,902,107	267
1959–60	32,477,440	12,225,142	37.6	486,338	40	3,293,652	269
1961–62	34,682,340	13,222,667	38.1	576,361	44	3,815,664	289
1963–64	37,405,058	14,475,778	38.7	673,845	47	4,347,635	300
1965–66	39,154,497	15,536,567	39.7	787,358	51	4,910,303	316
1967–68	40,827,965	17,130,873	42.0	981,006	57	5,740,189	335
1969–70	41,934,376	18,198,577	43.4	1,218,557	67	6,419,142	353
1971–72	42,254,272	19,474,355	46.1	1,507,830	77	7,291,521	374
1973–74	41,438,054	21,347,039	51.5	1,858,141	87	7,930,406	371
1975–76	41,269,720	21,772,483	52.8	2,377,313	109	8,530,172	392
1977–78	40,079,590	21,800,000 [3]	54.4	2,731,041	125 [3]	8,676,821	398 [3]
1979–80	38,288,911	21,713,515	56.7	3,833,145	177	9,825,270	452
1980–81	37,703,744	22,272,000 [3]	59.1	4,408,000 [3]	198 [3]	10,125,907 [3]	455 [3]
1981–82	37,094,652	22,246,000 [3]	60.0	4,793,000 [3]	215 [3]	10,134,831 [3]	456 [3]
1982–83	36,635,868	22,199,000 [3]	60.6	5,000,000 [3]	225 [3]	10,137,137 [3]	457 [3]
1983–84	36,362,978	22,031,000 [3]	60.6	5,284,000 [3]	240 [3]	10,330,544 [3]	469 [3]
1984–85	36,404,261	22,320,000 [3]	61.3	5,722,000 [3]	256 [3]	10,765,477 [3]	482 [3]
1985–86	36,523,103	22,041,000 [3]	60.3	6,123,000 [3]	278 [3]	11,197,037 [3]	508 [3]
1986–87	36,863,867	22,397,000 [3]	60.8	6,551,000 [3]	292 [3]	11,719,513 [3]	523 [3]
1987–88	37,050,707	22,158,000 [3]	59.8	6,888,000 [3]	311 [3]	11,832,124 [3]	534 [3]
1988–89	37,268,072	22,635,000 [3]	60.7	7,550,000 [3]	334 [3]	12,396,772 [3]	548 [3]
1989–90	37,799,296	22,459,000 [3]	59.4	8,030,990	358 [3]	12,585,964	560 [3]
1990–91	38,426,543	22,000,000 [3]	57.3	8,678,954	394 [3]	12,896,365	586 [3]
1991–92	38,960,783	23,165,000 [3]	59.5	8,769,754	379 [3]	12,626,699	545 [3]
1992–93	39,570,462	23,439,000 [3]	59.2	9,252,300	395 [3]	12,917,970	551 [3]
1993–94	40,146,393	23,858,000 [3]	59.4	9,627,155	404 [3]	13,101,943	549 [3]
1994–95	40,720,763	23,693,000 [3]	58.2	9,889,034	417 [3]	13,083,337	552 [3]
1995–96	41,501,596	24,155,000 [3]	58.2	10,396,426	430 [3]	13,390,327	554 [3]
1996–97	42,262,004	24,090,000 [3]	57.0	10,989,809	456 [3]	13,761,951	571 [3]
1997–98	42,765,774	24,342,000 [3]	56.9	11,465,658	471 [3]	14,106,257	580 [3]
1998–99	43,186,715	24,898,000 [3]	57.7	12,224,454	491 [3]	14,783,877	594 [3]
1999–2000	43,806,726	24,951,000 [3]	57.0	13,007,625	521 [3]	15,289,638	613 [3]
2000–01	44,075,930	24,471,000 [3]	55.5	14,052,654	574 [3]	15,970,837	653 [3]
2001–02	44,604,592	24,550,000 [4]	55.0	14,799,365	603 [4]	16,526,866	673 [4]
2002–03	45,017,360	25,168,000 [4]	55.9	15,648,821	622 [4]	17,099,689	679 [4]
2003–04	45,325,731	25,550,000 [4]	56.4	16,348,783	640 [4]	17,482,089	684 [4]

[1]Constant dollars based on the Consumer Price Index, prepared by the Bureau of Labor Statistics, U.S. Department of Labor, adjusted to a school-year basis.
[2]Excludes capital outlay for years through 1979–80, and 1989–90 to the latest year. From 1980–81 to 1988–89 total transportation figures include capital outlay.
[3]Estimate based on data appearing in January issues of *School Bus Fleet.*
[4]Estimate based on data reported by *School Transportation News.*
NOTE: Some data have been revised from previously published figures.

SOURCE: U.S. Department of Education, National Center for Education Statistics, *Statistics of State School Systems*, 1929–30 through 1975–76; *Revenues and Expenditures for Public Elementary and Secondary Education*, 1977–78 and 1979–80; Common Core of Data (CCD), "National Public Education Financial Survey," 1987–88 through 2002–03; Bobit Publishing Co., *School Bus Fleet*, "School Transportation: 2000–2001 School Year"; *School Transportation News*, "K-12 Enrollment/Transportation Data," 2001–02, 2002–03, and 2003–04; and unpublished data. (This table was prepared August 2006.)

CHAPTER 3
Postsecondary Education

Postsecondary education includes an array of diverse educational experiences offered by American colleges and universities. For example, a community college may offer vocational training or the first 2 years of training at the college level. A university typically offers a full undergraduate course of study leading to a bachelor's degree, as well as first-professional and graduate programs leading to advanced degrees. Vocational and technical institutions offer training programs that are designed to prepare students for specific careers. Community groups, religious organizations, libraries, and businesses provide other types of educational opportunities for adults.

This chapter provides an overview of the latest statistics on postsecondary education, which includes academic, vocational, and continuing professional education programs after high school. However, to maintain comparability over time, most of the data in the *Digest* are for degree-granting institutions, which are defined as postsecondary institutions that grant an associate's or higher degree and are eligible for Title IV federal financial aid.[1] Degree-granting institutions include almost all 2- and 4-year colleges and universities; they exclude institutions offering only vocational programs of less than 2 years' duration and continuing education programs. The degree-granting institution classification is very similar to the higher education institution classification that the National Center for Education Statistics (NCES) used prior to 1996–97.[2] This chapter highlights historical data that enable the reader to observe long-range trends in college education in America.

Other chapters provide related information on postsecondary education. Data on price indexes and on the number of degrees held by the general population are shown in chapter 1. Chapter 4 contains tabulations on federal funding for postsecondary education. Information on employment outcomes for college graduates is shown in chapter 5. Chapter 7

contains data on college libraries and use of computers by young adults. Further information on survey methodologies is presented in Appendix A: Guide to Sources and in the publications cited in the table source notes.

Enrollment

Enrollment in degree-granting institutions increased by 16 percent between 1985 and 1995 (table 175 and figure 11). Between 1995 and 2005, enrollment increased at a faster rate (23 percent), from 14.3 million to 17.5 million. Much of the growth between 1995 and 2005 was in female enrollment; the number of women enrolled rose 27 percent, while the number of men rose 18 percent. During the same time period, part-time enrollment rose by 9 percent, compared to an increase of 33 percent in full-time enrollment. Enrollment increases may be affected both by population growth and by rising rates of enrollment. Between 1995 and 2005, the number of 18- to 24-year-olds increased from 25.5 million to 29.3 million (table 16), and the proportion of 18- to 24-year-olds enrolled in college rose from 34 percent to 39 percent (table 189). In addition to the enrollment in accredited 2-year colleges, 4-year colleges, and universities, about 434,000 students attended non-degree-granting, Title IV eligible, postsecondary institutions in fall 2005 (table 173).

The number of young students has been growing more rapidly than the number of older students, but this pattern is expected to shift (table 177 and figure 13). Between 1990 and 2005, the enrollment of students under age 25 increased by 32 percent. Enrollment of persons 25 and over rose by 19 percent during the same period. From 2005 to 2015, NCES projects a rise of 11 percent in enrollments of persons under 25, and a rise of 18 percent in enrollments of persons 25 and over.

Enrollment trends have differed at the undergraduate, graduate, and first-professional levels. Undergraduate enrollment generally increased during the 1970s, but dipped slightly between 1983 and 1985 (table 190). From 1985 to 1992, undergraduate enrollment increased each year, rising 18 percent before declining slightly and stabilizing between 1993 and 1996. Undergraduate enrollment rose 21 percent between 1996 and 2005. Graduate enrollment had been steady at about 1.3 million in the late 1970s and early 1980s, but rose about 59 percent between 1985 and 2005 (table 191). After rising very rapidly during the 1970s, enrollment in first-professional programs stabilized in the 1980s (table 192). First-professional

---

[1] Title IV programs, which are administered by the U.S. Department of Education, provide financial aid to postsecondary students.

[2] Included among degree-granting institutions are some institutions (primarily 2-year colleges) that were not previously designated as higher education institutions. Excluded from degree-granting institutions are a few institutions that were previously designated as higher education institutions even though they did not award an associate's or higher degree. Institutions of higher education were accredited by an agency or association that was recognized by the U.S. Department of Education, or recognized directly by the Secretary of Education. Institutions of higher education offered courses that led to an associate's or higher degree, or were accepted for credit towards a degree.

enrollment began rising again in the 1990s and showed an increase of 13 percent between 1995 and 2005.

Since 1984, the number of women in graduate schools has exceeded the number of men (table 191). Between 1995 and 2005, the number of male full-time graduate students increased by 27 percent, compared to a 65 percent increase for female graduate students. Among part-time graduate students, the number of men increased by 4 percent and the number of women increased by 18 percent.

The proportion of American college students who are minorities has been increasing. In 1976, 15 percent were minorities, compared with 31 percent in 2005 (table 210). Much of the change from 1976 to 2005 can be attributed to rising numbers of Hispanic and Asian or Pacific Islander students. During that time period, the proportion of Asian or Pacific Islander students rose from 2 percent to 6 percent and the Hispanic proportion rose from 3 percent to 11 percent. The proportion of Black students was 9 percent at the beginning of the time period and it fluctuated during the early part of the period before rising to 13 percent in 2005. Nonresident aliens for whom race/ethnicity is not reported made up 3 percent of the total enrollment in 2005.

Despite the sizable numbers of small degree-granting colleges, most students attend the larger colleges and universities. In fall 2005, 40 percent of institutions had fewer than 1,000 students; however, these campuses enrolled 4 percent of college students (table 218). While 12 percent of the campuses enrolled 10,000 or more students, they accounted for 54 percent of total college enrollment.

In 2005, the five colleges with the highest enrollment were University of Phoenix Online Campus, with 117,309 students; Miami-Dade College, with 54,169 students; Arizona State University at the Tempe Campus, with 51,612 students; the University of Minnesota, Twin Cities, with 51,175 students; and Western International University, with 50,663 students (table 219).

Faculty, Staff, and Salaries

Approximately 3.4 million people were employed in colleges and universities in the fall of 2005, including 2.5 million professional and 0.9 million nonprofessional staff (table 228). In the fall of 2005, there were 1.3 million faculty members in degree-granting institutions, including 0.7 million full-time and 0.6 million part-time faculty. The proportion of executive and administrative staff rose from 5 percent in 1976 to 6 percent in 2005 (table 227). The proportion of other non-teaching professional staff rose from 10 percent in 1976 to 19 percent in 2005, while the proportion of nonprofessional staff declined from 42 percent to 27 percent. The student/staff ratio at colleges and universities declined from 5.4 in 1976 to 5.0 in 2005. During the same time period, the student/faculty ratio declined from 16.6 to 15.0.

Colleges differ in their practices of employing part-time and full-time staff. In fall 2005, 48 percent of the employees at public 2-year colleges were employed full-time, compared with 68 percent at public 4-year colleges and 67 per-

cent at private 4-year colleges (table 228). A higher proportion of the faculty at public 4-year colleges were employed full-time (70 percent) than at private 4-year colleges (50 percent) or public 2-year colleges (31 percent).

About 16 percent of U.S. faculty in colleges and universities were minorities in 2005 (based on a total faculty count excluding persons whose race/ethnicity was unknown, but including nonresident aliens who were not identified by race/ethnicity) (table 229). Six percent of the faculty were Black, 6 percent were Asian/Pacific Islander, 4 percent were Hispanic, and 1 percent were American Indian/Alaska Native. Nearly half of college faculty (45 percent) were White males, while 36 percent were White females. About 17 percent of executive, managerial, and administrative staffs were minorities in 2005, compared to about 32 percent of the nonprofessional staff. The proportion of minority staffs at public 4-year colleges (23 percent) was similar to their proportion at private 4-year colleges (21 percent).

The proportion of time that full-time instructional faculty and staff spent teaching averaged 58 percent in 2003 (table 233). For the remaining faculty time, research and scholarship accounted for 20 percent of the time and 22 percent was spent on other activities, e.g., administration, professional growth, etc.

College faculty generally suffered losses in the purchasing power of their salaries from 1972–73 to 1980–81, when average salaries declined 17 percent after adjustment for inflation (table 240). During the 1980s, average salaries rose and recouped most of the losses. Between 1995–96 and 2005–06, there was a further increase in average faculty salaries, resulting in an average of about 3 percent higher than the 1972–73 average, after adjustment for inflation. Average salaries for men in 2005–06 ($71,569) were higher than the average for women ($58,665). Men's and women's salaries have increased at about the same rate (5 and 6 percent, after adjustment for inflation) since 1995–96.

The proportion of faculty with tenure has declined in recent years. About 50 percent of full time instructional faculty had tenure in 2005–06, compared with 56 percent in 1993–94 (table 247). A difference existed between the proportion of men and women with tenure. Fifty-five percent of men compared to 41 percent of women had tenure in 2005–06. About 52 percent of the instructional faculty at public institutions had tenure, compared to 45 percent of faculty at private institutions.

Degrees

During the 2005–06 academic year, 4,276 accredited institutions offered degrees at the associate's degree level or above (table 249). These included 2,582 4-year colleges and universities, and 1,694 2-year colleges. Institutions awarding various degrees in 2004–05 numbered 2,691 for associate's degrees, 2,194 for bachelor's degrees, 1,617 for master's degrees, and 596 for doctor's degrees (table 261).

Growing numbers of people are completing college degrees. Between 1994–95 and 2004–05, the number of associate's, bachelor's, master's, first-professional, and doctor's degrees rose (table 251). Associate's degrees increased 29 percent, bachelor's degrees increased 24 percent, master's degrees increased 45 percent, and doctor's degrees increased 18 percent during this period. The number of first-professional degrees was 15 percent higher in 2004–05 than it was in 1994–95.

Since the mid-1980s, more women than men have earned associate's, bachelor's, and master's degrees (table 251). Also, the number of women receiving all types of degrees has increased at a faster rate than the number for men. Between 1994–95 and 2004–05, the number of bachelor's degrees awarded to men increased by 17 percent, while those awarded to women increased by 30 percent. During the same time period, the number of males earning doctor's degrees stayed about the same, while the number of females earning doctor's degrees rose by 46 percent.

Of the 1,439,000 bachelor's degrees conferred in 2004–05, the largest numbers of degrees were conferred in the fields of business (312,000), social sciences and history (157,000), and education (105,000) (table 254). At the master's degree level, the largest numbers of degrees were in the fields of education (167,000) and business (143,000) (table 255). The fields with the largest number of degrees at the doctor's degree level were education (7,700), engineering (6,500), health professions and related clinical sciences (5,900), biological and biomedical sciences (5,600), and psychology (5,100) (table 256).

In recent years, the numbers of bachelor's degrees conferred have followed patterns that differed significantly by field of study. While the number of degrees increased 24 percent overall between 1994–95 and 2004–05, in some fields such as physical sciences and science technologies and health professions and related clinical sciences, the 2004–05 figures were lower than the 1994–95 figures (table 254). However, there is some evidence that these trends have shifted. The number of bachelor's degrees conferred in the combined fields of engineering and engineering technologies declined 7 percent between 1994–95 and 1999–2000, but then rose 9 percent between 1999–2000 and 2004–05 (table 254 and figure 15). The number of engineering and engineering technologies degrees conferred in 2004–05 was about 1 percent higher than the number conferred in 1994–95. The number of mathematics degrees declined by 15 percent between 1994–95 and 1999–2000, but then rose 26 percent between 1999–2000 and 2004–05. In addition, some technical fields experienced sustained increases in degrees conferred from 1994–95 through 2004–05. After an increase of 53 percent between 1994–95 and 1999–2000, the number of degrees in computer and information sciences grew 43 percent between 1999–2000 and 2004–05. Other fields with sizable numbers of degrees (over 5,000) that showed increases of over 20 percent between 1999–2000 and 2004–05 included visual and performing arts; theological studies/religious vocations; philosophy and religion; communications and journalism; parks, recreation, and leisure studies; security and protective services; social sciences and history; family and consumer/human sciences; area, ethnic, cultural, and gender studies; business; and liberal arts and sciences.

Fifty-eight percent of the students who enrolled in a 4-year college as first-time freshmen in 1995–96 had completed a bachelor's degree by 2001 (table 317). About 7 percent of students had completed a certificate or associate's degree, 14 percent were still enrolled without having received a degree, and 21 percent were no longer working towards a bachelor's degree.

Finances

For the 2005–06 academic year, annual prices for undergraduate tuition, room, and board were estimated to be $10,454 at public colleges and $26,889 at private colleges (table 319). Between 1995–96 and 2005–06, prices for undergraduate tuition, room, and board at public colleges rose by 30 percent, and prices at private colleges rose by 21 percent, after adjustment for inflation (tables 31 and 319).

Trend data show small increases in the current-fund expenditures per student at public 2-year and 4-year colleges and universities in the late 1980s and larger increases during the 1990s (table 345). After an adjustment for inflation at colleges and universities, current fund expenditures per student at public colleges rose about 5 percent between 1985–86 and 1990–91, and another 28 percent between 1990–91 and 2000–01.

At private not-for-profit institutions, total expenditures per full-time-equivalent student rose 14 percent between 1996–97 and 2003–04, after adjustment for inflation (table 352). In 2003–04, total expenditures per full-time-equivalent student were $37,240. At public institutions in 2003–04, the average total expenditure per full-time-equivalent student was $22,202 (table 347).

As of June 30, 2005, the market value of the endowment funds of the 120 colleges and universities with the largest amounts was $235 billion, reflecting an increase of 13 percent compared to 2004 (table 357). The five colleges with the largest endowments in 2005 were Harvard University, Yale University, Stanford University, University of Texas System, and Princeton University.

Figure 11. Enrollment, degrees conferred, and expenditures in degree-granting institutions: 1960–61 through 2004–05

Enrollment, in millions

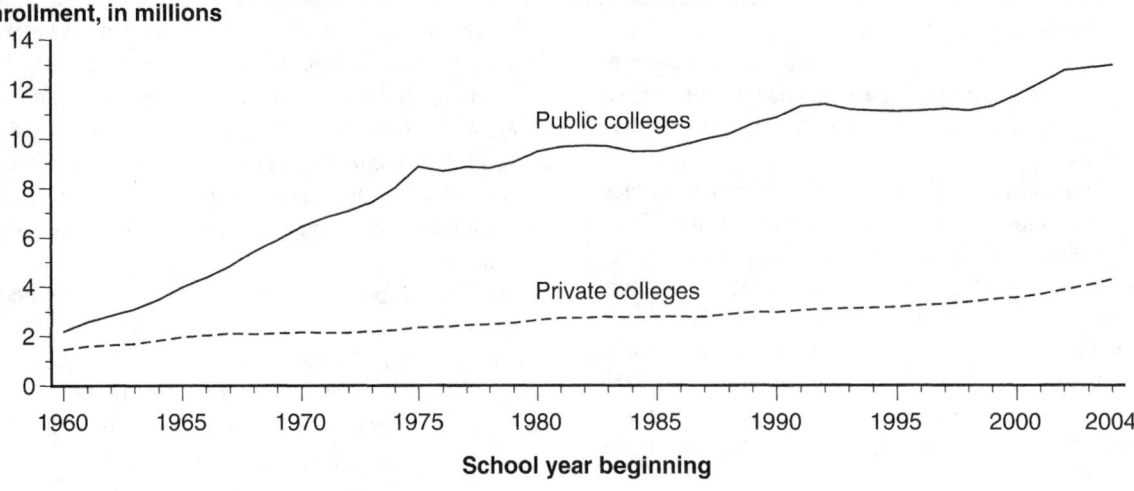

Degrees, in millions

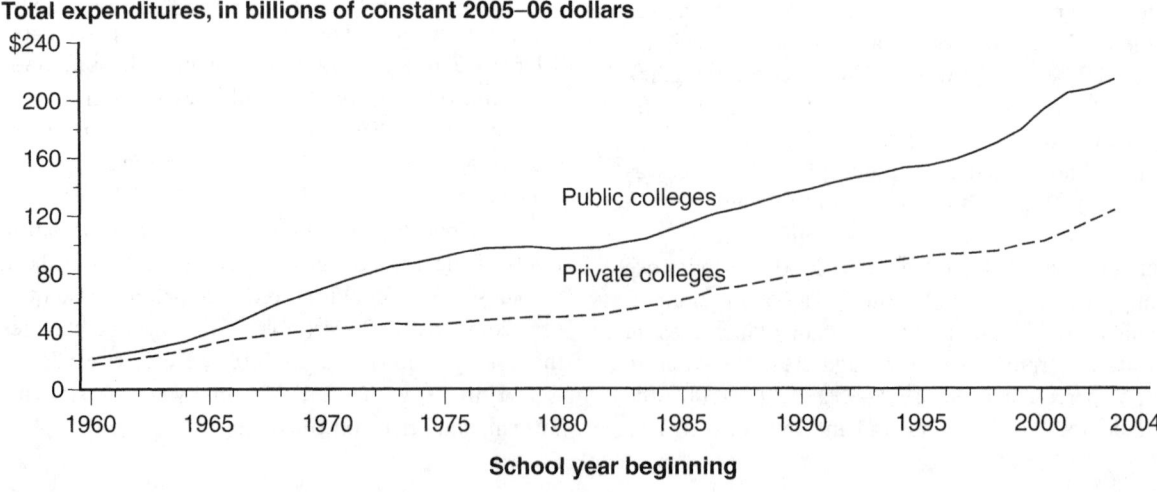

Total expenditures, in billions of constant 2005–06 dollars

SOURCE: U.S. Department of Education, National Center for Education Statistics, *Opening Fall Enrollment in Higher Education*, 1960 through 1965; *Financial Statistics of Higher Education*, 1959–60 through 1964–65; *Earned Degrees Conferred*, 1959–60 through 1965–66; Higher Education General Information Survey (HEGIS), "Fall Enrollment in Institutions of Higher Education," 1966 through 1985, "Degrees and Other Formal Awards Conferred," 1966–67 through 1985–86, and "Financial Statistics of Institutions of Higher Education," 1966–67 through 1985–86; and 1986–87 through 2004–05 Integrated Postsecondary Education Data System, "Fall Enrollment Survey" (IPEDS-EF:86–99), "Completions Survey" (IPEDS-C:87–99), "Finance Survey" (IPEDS-F:FY87–99), Fall 2001 through Fall 2005, and Spring 2001 through Spring 2005.

Figure 12. Percentage change in total enrollment in degree-granting institutions, by state: Fall 2000 through fall 2005

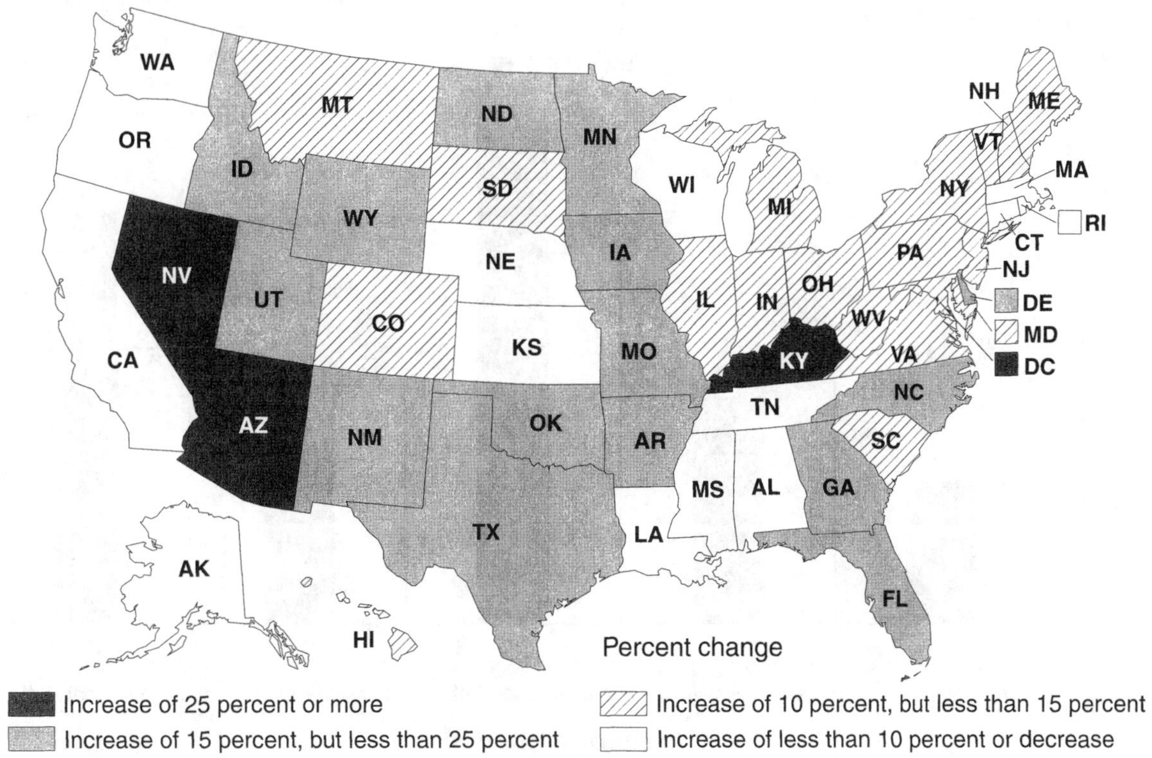

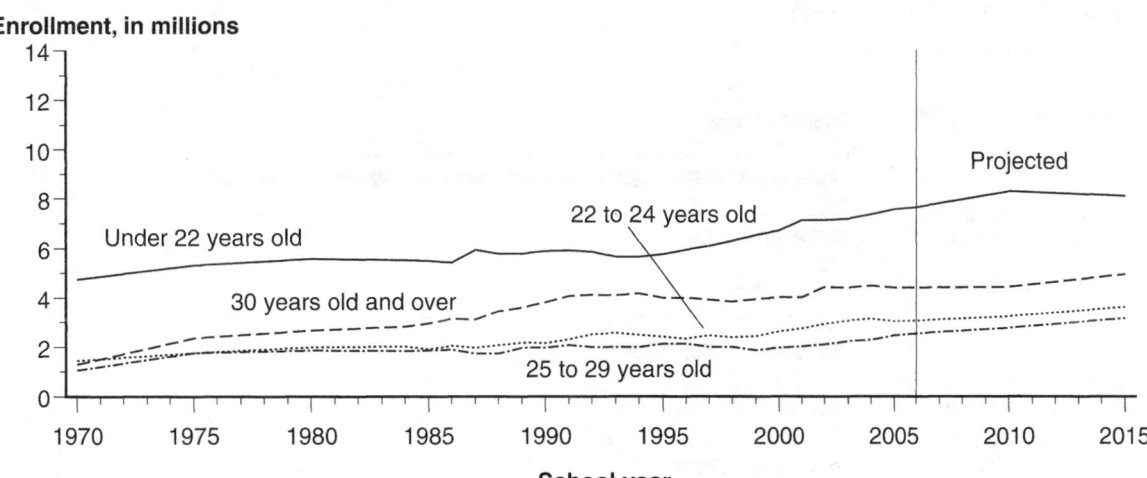

Percent change

■ Increase of 25 percent or more	▨ Increase of 10 percent, but less than 15 percent
▨ Increase of 15 percent, but less than 25 percent	□ Increase of less than 10 percent or decrease

SOURCE: U.S. Department of Education, National Center for Education Statistics, 2000 and 2005 Integrated Postsecondary Education Data System, Spring 2001 and Spring 2006.

Figure 13. Enrollment in degree-granting institutions, by age: Fall 1970 through fall 2015

Enrollment, in millions

SOURCE: U.S. Department of Education, National Center for Education Statistics, Higher Education General Information Survey (HEGIS), "Fall Enrollment in Institutions of Higher Education" surveys, 1970 through 1985; 1986–87 through 2005–06 Integrated Postsecondary Education Data System, "Fall Enrollment Survey" (IPEDS-EF:86–99), and Spring 2001 through Spring 2006; and *Projections of Education Statistics to 2015*.

Figure 14. Full-time-equivalent (FTE) students per staff member in public and private degree-granting institutions: 1976 and 2005

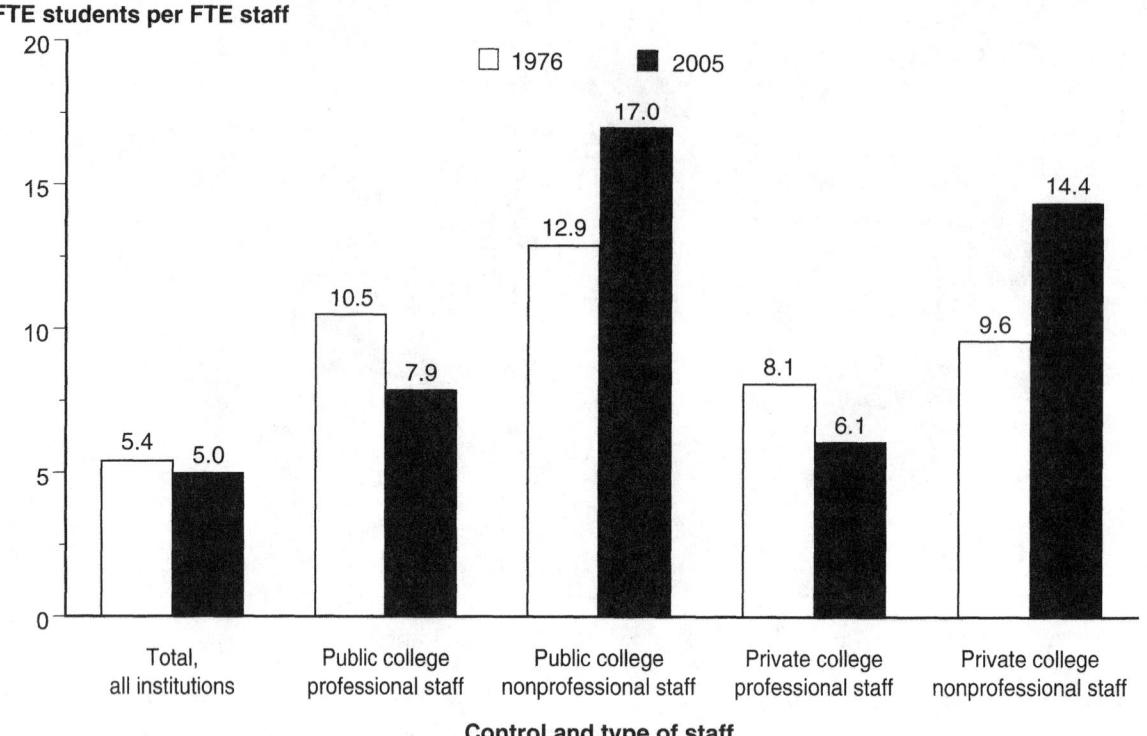

SOURCE: U.S. Department of Education, National Center for Education Statistics, Higher Education General Information Survey (HEGIS), "Staff" survey, 1976, and "Fall Enrollment in Higher Education" survey, 1976; and 2005 Integrated Postsecondary Education Data System, Winter 2005–06 and Spring 2006.

Figure 15. Trends in bachelor's degrees conferred by degree-granting institutions in selected fields of study: 1994–95, 1999–2000, and 2004–05

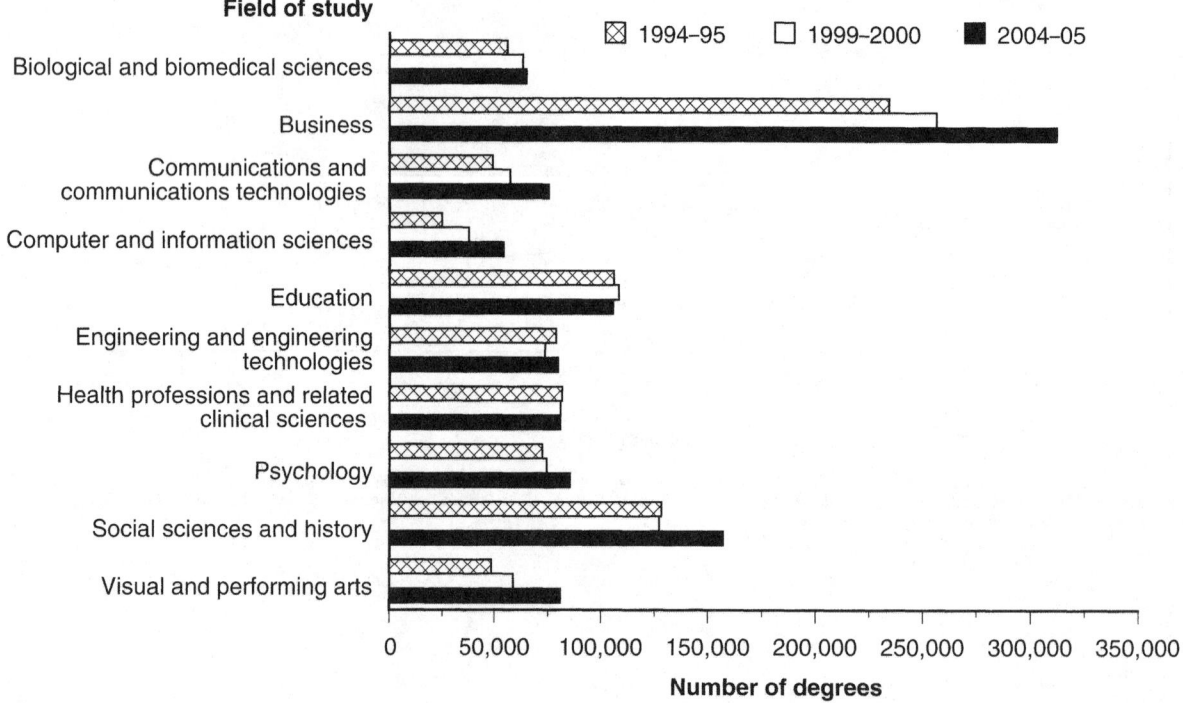

SOURCE: U.S. Department of Education, National Center for Education Statistics, 1994–95, 1999–2000, and 2004–05 Integrated Postsecondary Education Data System, "Completions Survey" (IPEDS-C:95), and Fall 2000 and Fall 2005.

Figure 16. Sources of total revenue of public degree-granting institutions: 2003–04

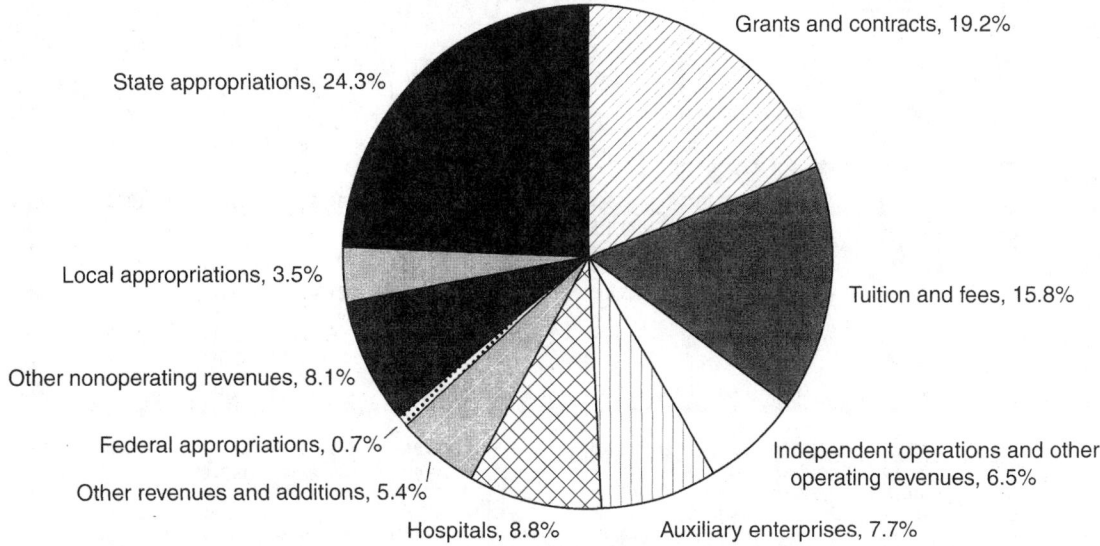

State appropriations, 24.3%

Grants and contracts, 19.2%

Local appropriations, 3.5%

Tuition and fees, 15.8%

Other nonoperating revenues, 8.1%

Federal appropriations, 0.7%

Independent operations and other operating revenues, 6.5%

Other revenues and additions, 5.4%

Hospitals, 8.8%

Auxiliary enterprises, 7.7%

Total revenues = $221.9 billion

NOTE: Detail may not sum to totals because of rounding. Other nonoperating revenues exclude federal, state, and local appropriations.
SOURCE: U.S. Department of Education, National Center for Education Statistics, 2003–04 Integrated Postsecondary Education Data System (IPEDS), Spring 2005.

Figure 17. Sources of total revenue of private not-for-profit degree-granting institutions: 2003–04

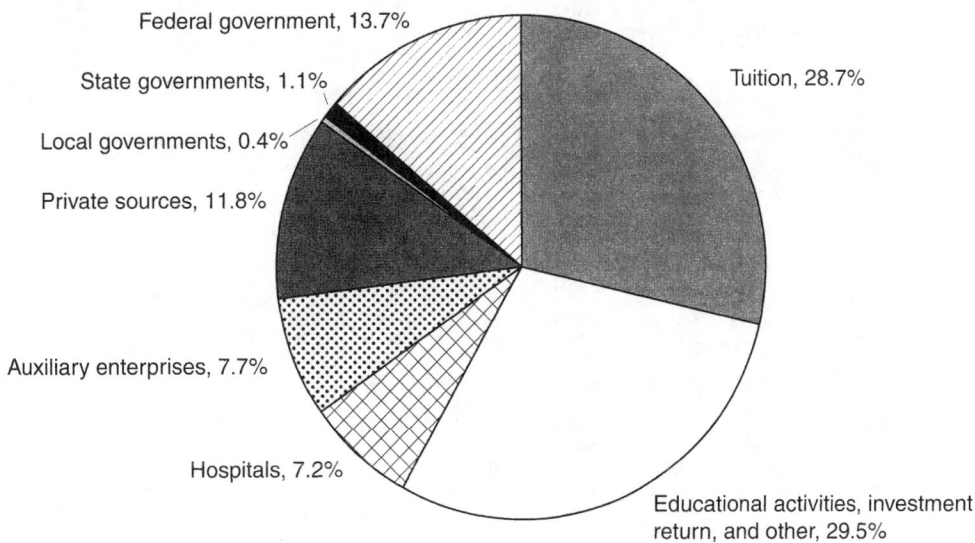

Federal government, 13.7%

Tuition, 28.7%

State governments, 1.1%

Local governments, 0.4%

Private sources, 11.8%

Auxiliary enterprises, 7.7%

Hospitals, 7.2%

Educational activities, investment return, and other, 29.5%

Total revenues = $134.2 billion

NOTE: Detail may not sum to totals because of rounding.
SOURCE: U.S. Department of Education, National Center for Education Statistics, 2003–04 Integrated Postsecondary Education Data System (IPEDS), Spring 2005.

Table 173. Enrollment, staff, and degrees conferred in postsecondary institutions participating in Title IV programs, by level and control of institution, sex of student, and type of degree: 2004–05 and fall 2005

Level of institution, type of degree, sex of student, and type of staff	All Title IV participating institutions[1]	Degree-granting institutions[2]					Non-degree-granting institutions[3]				
		Total	Public	Private			Total	Public	Private		
				Total	Not-for-profit	For-profit			Total	Not-for-profit	For-profit
1	2	3	4	5	6	7	8	9	10	11	12
Enrollment, fall 2005											
Total.........................	17,921,804	17,487,475	13,021,834	4,465,641	3,454,692	1,010,949	434,329	93,343	340,986	29,321	311,665
4-year institutions..........................	10,999,924	10,999,420	6,837,605	4,161,815	3,411,170	750,645	504	36	468	468	0
Males.......................	4,775,697	4,775,557	3,019,831	1,755,726	1,448,647	307,079	140	13	127	127	0
Females.....................	6,224,227	6,223,863	3,817,774	2,406,089	1,962,523	443,566	364	23	341	341	0
2-year institutions..........................	6,613,596	6,488,055	6,184,229	303,826	43,522	260,304	125,541	50,719	74,822	16,456	58,366
Males.......................	2,740,996	2,680,368	2,569,392	110,976	15,652	95,324	60,628	27,081	33,547	4,154	29,393
Females.....................	3,872,600	3,807,687	3,614,837	192,850	27,870	164,980	64,913	23,638	41,275	12,302	28,973
Less-than-2-year institutions...........	308,284	†	†	†	†	†	308,284	42,588	265,696	12,397	253,299
Males.......................	76,370	†	†	†	†	†	76,370	15,490	60,880	4,304	56,576
Females.....................	231,914	†	†	†	†	†	231,914	27,098	204,816	8,093	196,723
Staff, fall 2005											
Total.........................	3,428,811	3,379,087	2,267,687	1,111,400	971,425	139,975	49,724	23,594	26,130	3,618	22,512
Professional staff...........................	2,496,068	2,459,885	1,640,704	819,181	700,202	118,979	36,183	15,841	20,342	2,590	17,752
Administrative.....................	201,571	196,324	101,011	95,313	85,125	10,188	5,247	1,292	3,955	388	3,567
Faculty........................	1,314,506	1,290,426	841,188	449,238	361,523	87,715	24,080	11,114	12,966	1,768	11,198
Faculty assistants..............	317,146	317,141	257,952	59,189	59,061	128	5	2	3	0	3
Other professionals..................	662,845	655,994	440,553	215,441	194,493	20,948	6,851	3,433	3,418	434	2,984
Nonprofessional staff.....................	932,743	919,202	626,983	292,219	271,223	20,996	13,541	7,753	5,788	1,028	4,760
Student/staff ratio.....................	5.2	5.2	5.7	4.0	3.6	7.2	8.7	4.0	13.0	8.1	13.8
Degrees conferred, 2004–05											
Less-than-1-year awards and 1- to 4-year awards	710,873	401,714	307,659	94,055	12,735	81,320	309,159	63,024	246,135	23,233	222,902
4-year institutions.........................	35,145	35,040	13,236	21,804	9,177	12,627	105	0	105	105	0
Males.......................	13,134	13,108	6,071	7,037	3,300	3,737	26	0	26	26	0
Females.....................	22,011	21,932	7,165	14,767	5,877	8,890	79	0	79	79	0
2-year institutions.........................	440,826	366,674	294,423	72,251	3,558	68,693	74,152	33,065	41,087	10,983	30,104
Males.......................	185,679	154,394	131,631	22,763	1,901	20,862	31,285	15,988	15,297	3,153	12,144
Females.....................	255,147	212,280	162,792	49,488	1,657	47,831	42,867	17,077	25,790	7,830	17,960
Less-than-2-year institutions.........	234,902	†	†	†	†	†	234,902	29,959	204,943	12,145	192,798
Males.......................	60,448	†	†	†	†	†	60,448	11,615	48,833	5,211	43,622
Females.....................	174,454	†	†	†	†	†	174,454	18,344	156,110	6,934	149,176
Associate's degrees........................	696,754	696,660	547,519	149,141	45,344	103,797	94	87	7	0	7
4-year institutions.........................	139,550	139,550	55,672	83,878	35,335	48,543	0	0	0	0	0
Males.......................	59,261	59,261	22,282	36,979	12,777	24,202	0	0	0	0	0
Females.....................	80,289	80,289	33,390	46,899	22,558	24,341	0	0	0	0	0
2-year institutions.........................	557,170	557,110	491,847	65,263	10,009	55,254	60	55	5	0	5
Males.......................	208,294	208,275	180,007	28,268	3,836	24,432	19	15	4	0	4
Females.....................	348,876	348,835	311,840	36,995	6,173	30,822	41	40	1	0	1
Less-than-2-year institutions.........	34	†	†	†	†	†	34	32	2	0	2
Males.......................	7	†	†	†	†	†	7	5	2	0	2
Females.....................	27	†	†	†	†	†	27	27	0	0	0
Bachelor's degrees........................	1,439,264	1,439,264	932,443	506,821	457,963	48,858	0	0	0	0	0
Males.......................	613,000	613,000	399,462	213,538	188,220	25,318	0	0	0	0	0
Females.....................	826,264	826,264	532,981	293,283	269,743	23,540	0	0	0	0	0
Master's degrees...........................	574,618	574,618	291,505	283,113	248,031	35,082	0	0	0	0	0
Males.......................	233,590	233,590	117,439	116,151	102,384	13,767	0	0	0	0	0
Females.....................	341,028	341,028	174,066	166,962	145,647	21,315	0	0	0	0	0
First-professional degrees..............	87,289	87,289	35,768	51,521	51,259	262	0	0	0	0	0
Males.......................	43,849	43,849	17,175	26,674	26,540	134	0	0	0	0	0
Females.....................	43,440	43,440	18,593	24,847	24,719	128	0	0	0	0	0
Doctor's degrees...........................	52,631	52,631	31,743	20,888	19,552	1,336	0	0	0	0	0
Males.......................	26,973	26,973	17,024	9,949	9,497	452	0	0	0	0	0
Females.....................	25,658	25,658	14,719	10,939	10,055	884	0	0	0	0	0

†Not applicable.
[1]Includes degree granting and non-degree-granting institutions.
[2]Data are for degree-granting institutions, which grant associate's or higher degrees and participate in Title IV federal financial aid programs.

[3]Data are for institutions that did not offer accredited 4-year or 2-year degree programs, but were participating in Title IV federal financial aid programs. Includes some schools with nonaccredited degree programs.
SOURCE: U.S. Department of Education, National Center for Education Statistics, 2004–05 and fall 2005 Integrated Postsecondary Education Data System (IPEDS), Spring 2006, Winter 2005–06, and Fall 2005. (This table was prepared September 2006.)

Table 174. Historical summary of faculty, students, degrees, and finances in degree-granting institutions: Selected years, 1869–70 through 2004–05

Selected characteristic	1869–70	1879–80	1889–90	1899–1900	1909–10	1919–20	1929–30	1939–40	1949–50	1959–60	1969–70	1979–80	1989–90	1999–2000	2004–05
1	2	3	4	5	6	7	8	9	10	11	12	13	14	15	16
Total institutions[1]	563[3]	811	998	977	951	1,041	1,409	1,708	1,851	2,004	2,525	3,152	3,535	4,084	4,216
Total faculty[2]	5,553[3]	11,522[3]	15,809[3]	23,868	36,480	48,615	82,386	146,929	246,722	380,554	450,000[4]	675,000[4]	824,220[5]	1,027,830[5]	—
Males	4,887[3]	7,328[3]	12,704[3]	19,151	29,132	35,807	60,017	106,328	186,189	296,773	346,000[4]	479,000[4]	577,298[5]	602,469[5]	—
Females	666[3]	4,194[3]	3,105[3]	4,717	7,348	12,808	22,369	40,601	60,533	83,781	104,000[4]	196,000[4]	246,922[5]	425,361[5]	—
Total fall enrollment[6]	52,286[3]	115,817[3]	156,756[3]	237,592	355,213[3]	597,880	1,100,737	1,494,203	2,659,021	3,639,847	8,004,660	11,569,899	13,538,560	14,791,224	17,272,044
Males	41,160[3]	77,972[3]	100,453[3]	152,254	214,648[3]	314,938	619,935	893,250	1,853,068	2,332,617	4,746,201	5,682,877	6,190,015	6,490,646	7,387,262
Females	11,126[3]	37,845[3]	56,303[3]	85,338	140,565[3]	282,942	480,802	600,953	805,953	1,307,230	3,258,459	5,887,022	7,348,545	8,300,578	9,884,782
Earned degrees conferred															
Associate's, total	—	—	—	—	—	—	—	—	—	—	206,023	400,910	455,102	564,933	696,660
Males	—	—	—	—	—	—	—	—	—	—	117,432	183,737	191,195	224,721	267,536
Females	—	—	—	—	—	—	—	—	—	—	88,591	217,173	263,907	340,212	429,124
Bachelor's, total[7]	9,371	12,896	15,539	27,410	37,199	48,622	122,484	186,500	432,058	392,440	792,316	929,417	1,051,344	1,237,875	1,439,264
Males	7,993	10,411	12,857	22,173	28,762	31,980	73,615	109,546	328,841	254,063	451,097	473,611	491,696	530,367	613,000
Females	1,378	2,485	2,682	5,237	8,437	16,642	48,869	76,954	103,217	138,377	341,219	455,806	559,648	707,508	826,264
Master's, total[8]	0	879	1,015	1,583	2,113	4,279	14,969	26,731	58,183	74,435	208,291	298,081	324,301	457,056	574,618
Males	0	868	821	1,280	1,555	2,985	8,925	16,508	41,220	50,898	125,624	150,749	153,653	191,792	233,590
Females	0	11	194	303	558	1,294	6,044	10,223	16,963	23,537	82,667	147,332	170,648	265,264	341,028
First-professional, total[7]	—	—	—	—	—	—	—	—	—	—	34,918	70,131	70,988	80,057	87,289
Males	—	—	—	—	—	—	—	—	—	—	33,077	52,716	43,961	44,239	43,849
Females	—	—	—	—	—	—	—	—	—	—	1,841	17,415	27,027	35,818	43,440
Doctor's, total	1	54	149	382	443	615	2,299	3,290	6,420	9,829	29,866	32,615	38,371	44,808	52,631
Males	1	51	147	359	399	522	1,946	2,861	5,804	8,801	25,890	22,943	24,401	25,028	26,973
Females	0	3	2	23	44	93	353	429	616	1,028	3,976	9,672	13,970	19,780	25,658
Finances *(In thousands of dollars)*															
Current-fund revenue	—	—	—	—	$76,883	$199,922	$554,511	$715,211	$2,374,645	$5,785,537	$21,515,242	$58,519,982	$139,635,477	—	—
Educational and general income	—	—	$21,464	$35,084	67,917	172,929	483,065	571,288	1,833,845	4,688,352	16,486,177	—	—	—	—
Current-fund expenditures	—	—	—	—	—	—	507,142	674,688	2,245,661	5,601,376	21,043,113	56,913,588	134,655,571	—	—
Educational and general expenditures	—	—	—	—	—	—	377,903	521,990	1,706,444	4,685,258	16,845,212	44,542,843	105,585,076	—	—
Value of physical property	—	—	95,426	253,599	457,594	747,333	2,065,049	2,753,780[9]	4,799,964	13,548,548	42,093,580	83,733,387	164,635,000	—	—
Market value of endowment funds	—	—	78,788[10]	194,998[10]	323,661[10]	569,071[10]	1,372,068[10]	1,686,283[10]	2,601,223[10]	5,322,080[10]	11,206,632	20,743,045	67,978,726	—	—

—Not available.
[1]Prior to 1979–80, excludes branch campuses.
[2]Total number of different individuals (not reduced to full-time equivalent). Beginning in 1959–60, data are for the first term of the academic year.
[3]Estimated.
[4]Estimated number of senior instructional staff. Excludes graduate assistants.
[5]Because of revised survey procedures, data may not be directly comparable with figures prior to 1989–90. Estimated number of senior instructional staff. Excludes graduate assistants.
[6]Data for 1869–70 to 1949–50 are for resident degree-credit students who enrolled at any time during the academic year.
[7]From 1869–70 to 1959–60, first-professional degrees are included under bachelor's degrees.
[8]Figures for years prior to 1969–70 are not precisely comparable with later data.
[9]Includes unexpended plant funds.
[10]Book value. Includes other nonexpendable funds.

NOTE: Data through 1989–90 are for institutions of higher education, while later data are for degree-granting institutions. Degree-granting institutions grant associate's or higher degrees and participate in Title IV federal financial aid programs. The degree-granting classification is very similar to the earlier higher education classification, but it includes more 2-year colleges and excludes a few higher education institutions that did not grant degrees. (See Guide to Sources for details.) Detail may not sum to totals because of rounding.
SOURCE: U.S. Department of Education, National Center for Education Statistics, *Biennial Survey of Education in the United States; Education Directory, Colleges and Universities; Faculty and Other Professional Staff in Institutions of Higher Education; Fall Enrollment in Colleges and Universities; Earned Degrees Conferred; Financial Statistics of Institutions of Higher Education;* "Fall Enrollment in Institutions of Higher Education," "Degrees and Other Formal Awards Conferred," and "Financial Statistics of Institutions of Higher Education" surveys; and 1989 through 2005 Integrated Postsecondary Education Data System, "Fall Enrollment Survey" (HEGIS), "Fall Enrollment Survey" (IPEDS-EF:89–99), "Finance Survey" (IPEDS-F:FY90–00), "Completions Survey" (IPEDS-C:90–00), "Institutional Characteristics Survey" (IPEDS-IC:89–99), Winter 2005–06, Spring 2005, and Fall 2005. (This table was prepared September 2006.)

Table 175. Total fall enrollment in degree-granting institutions, by attendance status, sex of student, and control of institution: Selected years, 1947 through 2005

Year	Total enrollment	Attendance status			Sex of student			Control of institution			
		Full-time	Part-time	Percent part-time	Male	Female	Percent female	Public	Private		
									Total	Not-for-profit	For-profit
1	2	3	4	5	6	7	8	9	10	11	12
1947[1]	2,338,226	—	—	—	1,659,249	678,977	29.0	1,152,377	1,185,849	—	—
1948[1]	2,403,396	—	—	—	1,709,367	694,029	28.9	1,185,588	1,217,808	—	—
1949[1]	2,444,900	—	—	—	1,721,572	723,328	29.6	1,207,151	1,237,749	—	—
1950[1]	2,281,298	—	—	—	1,560,392	720,906	31.6	1,139,699	1,141,599	—	—
1951[1]	2,101,962	—	—	—	1,390,740	711,222	33.8	1,037,938	1,064,024	—	—
1952[1]	2,134,242	—	—	—	1,380,357	753,885	35.3	1,101,240	1,033,002	—	—
1953[1]	2,231,054	—	—	—	1,422,598	808,456	36.2	1,185,876	1,045,178	—	—
1954[1]	2,446,693	—	—	—	1,563,382	883,311	36.1	1,353,531	1,093,162	—	—
1955[1]	2,653,034	—	—	—	1,733,184	919,850	34.7	1,476,282	1,176,752	—	—
1956[1]	2,918,212	—	—	—	1,911,458	1,006,754	34.5	1,656,402	1,261,810	—	—
1957	3,323,783	—	—	—	2,170,765	1,153,018	34.7	1,972,673	1,351,110	—	—
1959	3,639,847	2,421,016	1,218,831 [2]	33.5	2,332,617	1,307,230	35.9	2,180,982	1,458,865	—	—
1961	4,145,065	2,785,133	1,359,932 [2]	32.8	2,585,821	1,559,244	37.6	2,561,447	1,583,618	—	—
1963	4,779,609	3,183,833	1,595,776 [2]	33.4	2,961,540	1,818,069	38.0	3,081,279	1,698,330	—	—
1964	5,280,020	3,573,238	1,706,782 [2]	32.3	3,248,713	2,031,307	38.5	3,467,708	1,812,312	—	—
1965	5,920,864	4,095,728	1,825,136 [2]	30.8	3,630,020	2,290,844	38.7	3,969,596	1,951,268	—	—
1966	6,389,872	4,438,606	1,951,266 [2]	30.5	3,856,216	2,533,656	39.7	4,348,917	2,040,955	—	—
1967	6,911,748	4,793,128	2,118,620 [2]	30.7	4,132,800	2,778,948	40.2	4,816,028	2,095,720	—	—
1968	7,513,091	5,210,155	2,302,936	30.7	4,477,649	3,035,442	40.4	5,430,652	2,082,439	—	—
1969	8,004,660	5,498,883	2,505,777	31.3	4,746,201	3,258,459	40.7	5,896,868	2,107,792	—	—
1970	8,580,887	5,816,290	2,764,597	32.2	5,043,642	3,537,245	41.2	6,428,134	2,152,753	—	—
1971	8,948,644	6,077,232	2,871,412	32.1	5,207,004	3,741,640	41.8	6,804,309	2,144,335	—	—
1972	9,214,820	6,072,350	3,142,470	34.1	5,238,718	3,976,102	43.1	7,070,635	2,144,185	—	—
1973	9,602,123	6,189,493	3,412,630	35.5	5,371,052	4,231,071	44.1	7,419,516	2,182,607	—	—
1974	10,223,729	6,370,273	3,853,456	37.7	5,622,429	4,601,300	45.0	7,988,500	2,235,229	—	—
1975	11,184,859	6,841,334	4,343,525	38.8	6,148,997	5,035,862	45.0	8,834,508	2,350,351	—	—
1976	11,012,137	6,717,058	4,295,079	39.0	5,810,828	5,201,309	47.2	8,653,477	2,358,660	2,314,298	44,362
1977	11,285,787	6,792,925	4,492,862	39.8	5,789,016	5,496,771	48.7	8,846,993	2,438,794	2,386,652	52,142
1978	11,260,092	6,667,657	4,592,435	40.8	5,640,998	5,619,094	49.9	8,785,893	2,474,199	2,408,331	65,868
1979	11,569,899	6,794,039	4,775,860	41.3	5,682,877	5,887,022	50.9	9,036,822	2,533,077	2,461,773	71,304
1980	12,096,895	7,097,958	4,998,937	41.3	5,874,374	6,222,521	51.4	9,457,394	2,639,501	2,527,787	111,714[3]
1981	12,371,672	7,181,250	5,190,422	42.0	5,975,056	6,396,616	51.7	9,647,032	2,724,640	2,572,405	152,235[3]
1982	12,425,780	7,220,618	5,205,162	41.9	6,031,384	6,394,396	51.5	9,696,087	2,729,693	2,552,739	176,954[3]
1983	12,464,661	7,261,050	5,203,611	41.7	6,023,725	6,440,936	51.7	9,682,734	2,781,927	2,589,187	192,740
1984	12,241,940	7,098,388	5,143,552	42.0	5,863,574	6,378,366	52.1	9,477,370	2,764,570	2,574,419	190,151
1985	12,247,055	7,075,221	5,171,834	42.2	5,818,450	6,428,605	52.5	9,479,273	2,767,782	2,571,791	195,991
1986	12,503,511	7,119,550	5,383,961	43.1	5,884,515	6,618,996	52.9	9,713,893	2,789,618	2,572,479	217,139[4]
1987	12,766,642	7,231,085	5,535,557	43.4	5,932,056	6,834,586	53.5	9,973,254	2,793,388	2,602,350	191,038[4]
1988	13,055,337	7,436,768	5,618,569	43.0	6,001,896	7,053,441	54.0	10,161,388	2,893,949	2,673,567	220,382
1989	13,538,560	7,660,950	5,877,610	43.4	6,190,015	7,348,545	54.3	10,577,963	2,960,597	2,731,174	229,423
1990	13,818,637	7,820,985	5,997,652	43.4	6,283,909	7,534,728	54.5	10,844,717	2,973,920	2,760,227	213,693
1991	14,358,953	8,115,329	6,243,624	43.5	6,501,844	7,857,109	54.7	11,309,563	3,049,390	2,819,041	230,349
1992	14,487,359	8,162,118	6,325,241	43.7	6,523,989	7,963,370	55.0	11,384,567	3,102,792	2,872,523	230,269
1993	14,304,803	8,127,618	6,177,185	43.2	6,427,450	7,877,353	55.1	11,189,088	3,115,715	2,888,897	226,818
1994	14,278,790	8,137,776	6,141,014	43.0	6,371,898	7,906,892	55.4	11,133,680	3,145,110	2,910,107	235,003
1995	14,261,781	8,128,802	6,132,979	43.0	6,342,539	7,919,242	55.5	11,092,374	3,169,407	2,929,044	240,363
1996	14,367,520	8,302,953	6,064,567	42.2	6,352,825	8,014,695	55.8	11,120,499	3,247,021	2,942,556	304,465
1997	14,502,334	8,438,062	6,064,272	41.8	6,396,028	8,106,306	55.9	11,196,119	3,306,215	2,977,614	328,601
1998	14,506,967	8,563,338	5,943,629	41.0	6,369,265	8,137,702	56.1	11,137,769	3,369,198	3,004,925	364,273
1999[5]	14,791,224	8,786,494	6,004,730	40.6	6,490,646	8,300,578	56.1	11,309,399	3,481,825	3,051,626	430,199
2000	15,312,289	9,009,600	6,302,689	41.2	6,721,769	8,590,520	56.1	11,752,786	3,559,503	3,109,419	450,084
2001	15,927,987	9,447,502	6,480,485	40.7	6,960,815	8,967,172	56.3	12,233,156	3,694,831	3,167,330	527,501
2002	16,611,711	9,946,359	6,665,352	40.1	7,202,116	9,409,595	56.6	12,751,993	3,859,718	3,265,476	594,242
2003	16,900,471	10,311,814	6,588,657	39.0	7,255,551	9,644,920	57.1	12,857,059	4,043,412	3,340,718	702,694
2004	17,272,044	10,610,177	6,661,867	38.6	7,387,262	9,884,782	57.2	12,980,112	4,291,932	3,411,685	880,247
2005	17,487,475	10,797,011	6,690,464	38.3	7,455,925	10,031,550	57.4	13,021,834	4,465,641	3,454,692	1,010,949

—Not available.

[1]Degree-credit enrollment only.

[2]Includes part-time resident students and all extension students.

[3]Large increases are due to the addition of schools accredited by the Accrediting Commission of Career Schools and Colleges of Technology.

[4]Because of imputation techniques, data are not consistent with figures for other years.

[5]Data were imputed using alternative procedures. (See Guide to Sources for details.)

NOTE: Data through 1995 are for institutions of higher education, while later data are for degree-granting institutions. Degree-granting institutions grant associate's or higher degrees and participate in Title IV federal financial aid programs. The degree-granting classification is very similar to the earlier higher education classification, but it includes more 2-year colleges and excludes a few higher education institutions that did not grant degrees. (See Guide to Sources for details.)

SOURCE: U.S. Department of Education, National Center for Education Statistics, *Biennial Survey of Education in the United States*; *Opening Fall Enrollment in Higher Education*, 1963 through 1965; Higher Education General Information Survey (HEGIS), "Fall Enrollment in Colleges and Universities" surveys, 1966 through 1985; and 1986 through 2005 Integrated Postsecondary Education Data System, "Fall Enrollment Survey" (IPEDS-EF:86–99), and Spring 2001 through Spring 2006. (This table was prepared August 2006.)

Table 176. Total fall enrollment in degree-granting institutions, by control and type of institution: 1963 through 2005

| | All institutions | | | | | Public institutions | | | | | Private institutions | | | | |
| | | 4-year | | | | | 4-year | | | | | 4-year | | | |
Year	Total	Total	University	Other 4-year	2-year	Total	Total	University	Other 4-year	2-year	Total	Total	University	Other 4-year	2-year
1	2	3	4	5	6	7	8	9	10	11	12	13	14	15	16
1963[1]	4,779,609	3,929,248	—	—	850,361	3,081,279	2,341,468	—	—	739,811	1,698,330	1,587,780	—	—	110,550
1964[1]	5,280,020	4,291,094	—	—	988,926	3,467,708	2,592,929	—	—	874,779	1,812,312	1,698,165	—	—	114,147
1965[1]	5,920,864	4,747,912	—	—	1,172,952	3,969,596	2,928,332	—	—	1,041,264	1,951,268	1,819,580	—	—	131,688
1966[1]	6,389,872	5,063,902	—	—	1,325,970	4,348,917	3,159,748	—	—	1,189,169	2,040,955	1,904,154	—	—	136,801
1967[1]	6,911,748	5,398,986	—	—	1,512,762	4,816,028	3,443,975	—	—	1,372,053	2,095,720	1,955,011	—	—	140,709
1968[1]	7,513,091	5,720,795	—	—	1,792,296	5,430,652	3,784,178	—	—	1,646,474	2,082,439	1,936,617	—	—	145,822
1969	8,004,660	5,937,127	—	—	2,067,533	5,896,868	3,962,522	—	—	1,934,346	2,107,792	1,974,605	—	—	133,187
1970	8,580,887	6,261,502	—	—	2,319,385	6,428,134	4,232,722	—	—	2,195,412	2,152,753	2,028,780	—	—	123,973
1971	8,948,644	6,369,355	—	—	2,579,289	6,804,309	4,346,990	—	—	2,457,319	2,144,335	2,022,365	—	—	121,970
1972	9,214,820	6,458,634	—	—	2,756,186	7,070,635	4,429,696	—	—	2,640,939	2,144,185	2,028,938	—	—	115,247
1973	9,602,123	6,590,023	—	—	3,012,100	7,419,516	4,529,895	—	—	2,889,621	2,182,607	2,060,128	—	—	122,479
1974	10,223,729	6,819,735	—	—	3,403,994	7,988,500	4,703,018	—	—	3,285,482	2,235,229	2,116,717	—	—	118,512
1975	11,184,859	7,214,740	2,838,266	4,376,474	3,970,119	8,834,508	4,998,142	2,124,221	2,873,921	3,836,366	2,350,351	2,216,598	714,045	1,502,553	133,753
1976	11,012,137	7,128,816	2,780,289	4,348,527	3,883,321	8,653,477	4,901,691	2,079,929	2,821,762	3,751,786	2,358,660	2,227,125	700,360	1,526,765	131,535
1977	11,285,787	7,242,845	2,793,418	4,449,427	4,042,942	8,846,993	4,945,224	2,070,032	2,875,192	3,901,769	2,438,794	2,297,621	723,386	1,574,235	141,173
1978	11,260,092	7,231,625	2,780,729	4,451,222	4,028,467	8,785,893	4,912,203	2,062,295	2,849,908	3,873,690	2,474,199	2,319,422	718,434	1,601,314	154,777
1979	11,569,899	7,353,233	2,839,582	4,513,651	4,216,666	9,036,822	4,980,012	2,099,525	2,880,487	4,056,810	2,533,077	2,373,221	740,057	1,633,164	159,856
1980	12,096,895	7,570,608	2,902,014	4,668,594	4,526,287	9,457,394	5,128,612	2,154,283	2,974,329	4,328,782	2,639,501	2,441,996	747,731	1,694,265	197,505[2]
1981	12,371,672	7,655,461	2,901,344	4,754,117	4,716,211	9,647,032	5,166,324	2,152,474	3,013,850	4,480,708	2,724,640	2,489,137	748,870	1,740,267	235,503[2]
1982	12,425,780	7,654,074	2,883,735	4,770,339	4,771,706	9,696,087	5,176,434	2,152,547	3,023,887	4,519,653	2,729,693	2,477,640	731,188	1,746,452	252,053
1983	12,464,661	7,741,195	2,888,813	4,852,382	4,723,466	9,682,734	5,223,404	2,154,790	3,068,614	4,459,330	2,781,927	2,517,791	734,023	1,783,768	264,136
1984	12,241,940	7,711,167	2,870,329	4,840,838	4,530,773	9,477,370	5,198,273	2,138,621	3,059,652	4,279,097	2,764,570	2,512,894	731,708	1,781,186	251,676
1985	12,247,055	7,715,978	2,870,692	4,845,286	4,531,077	9,479,273	5,209,540	2,141,112	3,068,428	4,269,733	2,767,782	2,506,438	729,580	1,776,858	261,344
1986	12,503,511	7,823,963	2,897,207	4,926,756	4,679,548	9,713,893	5,300,202	2,160,646	3,139,556	4,413,691	2,789,618	2,523,761	736,561	1,787,200	265,857[3]
1987	12,766,642	7,990,420	2,929,327	5,061,093	4,776,222	9,973,254	5,432,200	2,188,008	3,244,192	4,541,054	2,793,388	2,558,220	741,319	1,816,901	235,168[3]
1988	13,055,337	8,180,182	2,978,593	5,201,589	4,875,155	10,161,388	5,545,901	2,229,868	3,316,033	4,615,487	2,893,949	2,634,281	748,725	1,885,556	259,668
1989	13,538,560	8,387,671	3,019,115	5,368,556	5,150,889	10,577,963	5,694,303	2,266,056	3,428,247	4,883,660	2,960,597	2,693,368	753,059	1,940,309	267,229
1990	13,818,637	8,578,554	3,044,670	5,533,884	5,240,083	10,844,717	5,848,242	2,290,464	3,557,778	4,996,475	2,973,920	2,730,312	754,206	1,976,106	243,608
1991	14,358,953	8,707,053	3,065,429	5,641,624	5,651,900	11,309,563	5,904,748	2,301,222	3,603,526	5,404,815	3,049,390	2,802,305	764,207	2,038,098	247,085
1992	14,487,359	8,764,969	3,050,345	5,714,624	5,722,390	11,384,567	5,900,012	2,283,834	3,616,178	5,484,555	3,102,792	2,864,957	766,511	2,098,446	237,835
1993	14,304,803	8,738,936	3,022,728	5,716,208	5,565,867	11,189,088	5,851,760	2,259,692	3,592,068	5,337,328	3,115,715	2,887,176	763,036	2,124,140	228,539
1994	14,278,790	8,749,080	3,009,072	5,740,008	5,529,710	11,133,680	5,825,213	2,244,636	3,580,577	5,308,467	3,145,110	2,923,867	764,436	2,159,431	221,243
1995	14,261,781	8,769,252	2,999,641	5,769,611	5,492,529	11,092,374	5,814,545	2,235,939	3,578,606	5,277,829	3,169,407	2,954,707	763,702	2,191,005	214,700
1996	14,367,520	8,804,193	2,984,965	5,819,228	5,563,327	11,120,499	5,806,036	2,226,529	3,579,507	5,314,463	3,247,021	2,998,157	758,436	2,239,721	248,864
1997	14,502,334	8,896,765	2,995,886	5,900,879	5,605,569	11,196,119	5,835,433	2,231,273	3,604,160	5,360,686	3,306,215	3,061,332	764,613	2,296,719	244,883
1998	14,506,967	9,017,653	3,021,136	5,996,517	5,489,314	11,137,769	5,891,806	2,249,825	3,641,981	5,245,963	3,369,198	3,125,847	771,311	2,354,536	243,351
1999[4]	14,791,224	9,198,525	3,044,369	6,154,156	5,592,699	11,309,399	5,969,950	2,266,494	3,703,456	5,339,449	3,481,825	3,228,575	777,875	2,450,700	253,250
2000	15,312,289	9,363,858	3,061,812	6,302,046	5,948,431	11,752,786	6,055,398	2,280,122	3,775,276	5,697,388	3,559,503	3,308,460	781,690	2,526,770	251,043
2001	15,927,987	9,677,408	3,126,907	6,550,501	6,250,579	12,233,156	6,236,455	2,336,922	3,899,533	5,996,701	3,694,831	3,440,953	789,985	2,650,968	253,878
2002	16,611,711	10,082,332	3,210,271	6,872,061	6,529,379	12,751,993	6,481,613	2,403,149	4,078,464	6,270,380	3,859,718	3,600,719	807,122	2,793,597	258,999
2003	16,900,471	10,407,553	3,242,515	7,165,038	6,492,918	12,857,059	6,649,441	2,419,631	4,229,810	6,207,618	4,043,412	3,758,112	822,884	2,935,228	285,300
2004	17,272,044	10,726,181	3,258,982	7,467,199	6,545,863	12,980,112	6,736,536	2,426,495	4,310,041	6,243,576	4,291,932	3,989,645	832,487	3,157,158	302,287
2005	17,487,475	10,999,420	3,271,620	7,727,800	6,488,055	13,021,834	6,837,605	2,443,682	4,393,923	6,184,229	4,465,641	4,161,815	827,938	3,333,877	303,826

—Not available.
[1]Data for 2-year branch campuses of 4-year institutions are included with the 4-year institutions.
[2]Large increases are due to the addition of schools accredited by the Accrediting Commission of Career Schools and Colleges of Technology.
[3]Because of imputation techniques, data are not consistent with figures for other years.
[4]Data were imputed using alternative procedures. (See Guide to Sources for details.)
NOTE: Data through 1995 are for institutions of higher education, while later data are for degree-granting institutions. Degree-granting institutions grant associate's or higher degrees and participate in Title IV federal financial aid programs. The degree-granting classification is very similar to the earlier higher education classification, but it includes more 2-year colleges and excludes a few higher education institutions that did not grant degrees. (See Guide to Sources for details.)
SOURCE: U.S. Department of Education, National Center for Education Statistics, *Opening Fall Enrollment in Higher Education*, 1965; Higher Education General Information Survey (HEGIS), "Fall Enrollment in Institutions of Higher Education" surveys, 1966 through 1985; and 1986 through 2005 Integrated Postsecondary Education Data System, "Fall Enrollment Survey" (IPEDS-EF:86–99), and Spring 2001 through Spring 2006. (This table was prepared August 2006.)

Table 177. Total fall enrollment in degree-granting institutions, by attendance status, age, and sex: Selected years, 1970 through 2015

[In thousands]

Sex, age, and attendance status	1970	1980	1990	1995	2000	2001	2002	2003	2004	2005	Projected 2006	Projected 2010	Projected 2015
1	2	3	4	5	6	7	8	9	10	11	12	13	14
Males and females	8,581	12,097	13,819	14,262	15,312	15,928	16,612	16,900	17,272	17,487	17,648	18,746	19,874
14 to 17 years old	259	247	177	148	145	133	202	150	200	176	181	187	197
18 and 19 years old	2,600	2,901	2,950	2,894	3,531	3,595	3,571	3,475	3,578	3,660	3,700	3,991	3,853
20 and 21 years old	1,880	2,424	2,761	2,705	3,045	3,408	3,366	3,469	3,651	3,728	3,780	4,107	4,075
22 to 24 years old	1,457	1,989	2,144	2,411	2,617	2,760	2,932	3,480	3,036	3,047	3,049	3,249	3,631
25 to 29 years old	1,074	1,871	1,982	2,120	1,960	2,014	2,102	2,105	2,386	2,456	2,538	2,769	3,164
30 to 34 years old	487	1,243	1,322	1,236	1,265	1,290	1,300	1,368	1,329	1,312	1,294	1,398	1,658
35 years old and over	823	1,421	2,484	2,747	2,749	2,727	3,139	2,852	3,092	3,108	3,105	3,045	3,294
Males	5,044	5,874	6,284	6,343	6,722	6,961	7,202	7,256	7,387	7,456	7,458	7,848	8,162
14 to 17 years old	130	99	87	61	63	54	82	60	78	78	80	81	81
18 and 19 years old	1,349	1,375	1,421	1,338	1,583	1,629	1,616	1,556	1,551	1,585	1,587	1,694	1,646
20 and 21 years old	1,095	1,259	1,368	1,282	1,382	1,591	1,562	1,490	1,743	1,764	1,771	1,902	1,892
22 to 24 years old	964	1,064	1,107	1,153	1,293	1,312	1,342	1,604	1,380	1,376	1,366	1,428	1,558
25 to 29 years old	783	993	940	962	862	905	890	929	1,045	1,066	1,090	1,176	1,289
30 to 34 years old	308	576	537	561	527	510	547	592	518	509	497	531	608
35 years old and over	415	507	824	986	1,012	961	1,164	1,025	1,073	1,078	1,067	1,037	1,088
Females	3,537	6,223	7,535	7,919	8,591	8,967	9,410	9,645	9,885	10,032	10,190	10,897	11,712
14 to 17 years old	129	148	90	87	82	79	121	91	122	97	101	106	117
18 and 19 years old	1,250	1,526	1,529	1,557	1,948	1,966	1,955	1,919	2,027	2,076	2,114	2,297	2,208
20 and 21 years old	786	1,165	1,392	1,424	1,663	1,817	1,804	1,979	1,908	1,964	2,009	2,205	2,183
22 to 24 years old	493	925	1,037	1,258	1,324	1,448	1,590	1,876	1,657	1,671	1,683	1,821	2,073
25 to 29 years old	291	878	1,043	1,159	1,099	1,110	1,212	1,176	1,341	1,390	1,448	1,593	1,875
30 to 34 years old	179	667	784	675	738	780	753	776	812	803	797	867	1,051
35 years old and over	409	914	1,659	1,760	1,736	1,767	1,976	1,827	2,018	2,031	2,038	2,008	2,206
Full-time	5,816	7,098	7,821	8,129	9,010	9,448	9,946	10,312	10,610	10,797	10,935	11,845	12,566
14 to 17 years old	242	223	144	123	125	122	161	120	165	138	142	147	158
18 and 19 years old	2,406	2,669	2,548	2,387	2,932	2,929	2,942	2,949	3,028	3,104	3,142	3,407	3,292
20 and 21 years old	1,647	2,075	2,151	2,109	2,401	2,662	2,759	2,763	2,911	2,981	3,026	3,310	3,290
22 to 24 years old	881	1,121	1,350	1,517	1,653	1,757	1,922	2,141	2,074	2,090	2,096	2,259	2,563
25 to 29 years old	407	577	770	908	878	883	1,013	1,070	1,131	1,172	1,216	1,352	1,618
30 to 34 years old	100	251	387	430	422	494	465	511	490	487	484	535	673
35 years old and over	134	182	471	653	599	602	684	757	812	825	829	836	972
Males	3,505	3,689	3,808	3,807	4,111	4,300	4,501	4,632	4,739	4,803	4,802	5,105	5,287
14 to 17 years old	124	87	71	54	51	43	65	50	63	62	64	64	64
18 and 19 years old	1,265	1,270	1,230	1,091	1,250	1,329	1,327	1,306	1,313	1,342	1,343	1,436	1,401
20 and 21 years old	990	1,109	1,055	999	1,106	1,249	1,275	1,216	1,385	1,404	1,409	1,516	1,517
22 to 24 years old	650	665	742	789	839	854	936	1,040	960	961	952	1,000	1,097
25 to 29 years old	327	360	401	454	415	397	467	502	509	522	533	578	642
30 to 34 years old	72	124	156	183	195	216	183	242	201	198	194	208	242
35 years old and over	75	74	152	238	256	212	247	276	310	313	309	303	324
Females	2,311	3,409	4,013	4,321	4,899	5,148	5,445	5,680	5,871	5,994	6,133	6,740	7,279
14 to 17 years old	117	136	73	69	74	78	96	71	103	75	78	83	94
18 and 19 years old	1,140	1,399	1,318	1,296	1,682	1,600	1,615	1,643	1,716	1,762	1,799	1,970	1,891
20 and 21 years old	657	966	1,096	1,111	1,296	1,413	1,484	1,546	1,526	1,576	1,618	1,794	1,773
22 to 24 years old	231	456	608	729	814	903	985	1,101	1,113	1,129	1,144	1,260	1,466
25 to 29 years old	80	217	369	455	463	486	546	568	622	650	684	773	976
30 to 34 years old	28	127	231	247	227	277	282	270	289	289	290	326	431
35 years old and over	59	108	319	415	343	390	437	481	502	512	520	534	648
Part-time	2,765	4,999	5,998	6,133	6,303	6,480	6,665	6,589	6,662	6,690	6,713	6,901	7,307
14 to 17 years old	17	38	32	25	20	11	41	30	35	38	39	40	40
18 and 19 years old	194	418	402	507	599	666	628	526	549	556	558	585	561
20 and 21 years old	233	441	610	596	644	746	607	707	741	747	754	797	786
22 to 24 years old	576	844	794	894	964	1,003	1,010	1,339	963	957	953	990	1,069
25 to 29 years old	668	1,209	1,213	1,212	1,083	1,132	1,088	1,035	1,255	1,284	1,322	1,418	1,546
30 to 34 years old	388	905	935	805	843	796	835	857	839	825	811	863	985
35 years old and over	689	1,145	2,012	2,093	2,150	2,126	2,456	2,095	2,280	2,283	2,276	2,209	2,322
Males	1,540	2,185	2,476	2,535	2,611	2,661	2,701	2,624	2,648	2,653	2,655	2,743	2,874
14 to 17 years old	5	17	16	7	11	11	17	10	15	16	17	17	16
18 and 19 years old	84	202	191	246	333	300	288	250	239	243	244	258	244
20 and 21 years old	105	201	313	283	276	342	287	274	358	360	362	386	375
22 to 24 years old	314	392	365	365	454	458	405	565	419	415	414	428	461
25 to 29 years old	456	594	539	508	447	508	423	427	536	544	558	598	647
30 to 34 years old	236	397	381	378	332	294	364	350	317	311	304	323	366
35 years old and over	340	382	672	748	757	749	917	748	764	764	758	734	764
Females	1,225	2,814	3,521	3,598	3,692	3,820	3,964	3,965	4,014	4,038	4,057	4,157	4,433
14 to 17 years old	12	20	17	18	9	1	24	20	19	22	23	23	23
18 and 19 years old	110	215	211	261	266	366	340	276	311	314	315	327	316
20 and 21 years old	128	240	297	313	368	404	320	433	382	388	391	411	410
22 to 24 years old	262	452	429	529	510	545	605	774	543	542	540	562	607
25 to 29 years old	212	616	674	704	636	624	666	608	720	739	764	820	899
30 to 34 years old	151	507	554	427	511	502	471	507	523	514	507	540	620
35 years old and over	349	762	1,340	1,345	1,393	1,377	1,539	1,347	1,516	1,519	1,518	1,475	1,557

NOTE: Distributions by age are estimates based on samples of the civilian noninstitutional population from the U.S. Census Bureau's Current Population Survey. Data through 1995 are for institutions of higher education, while later data are for degree-granting institutions. Degree-granting institutions grant associate's or higher degrees and participate in Title IV federal financial aid programs. The degree-granting classification is very similar to the earlier higher education classification, but it includes more 2-year colleges and excludes a few higher education institutions that did not grant degrees. (See Guide to Sources for details.) Some data have been revised from previously published figures. Detail may not sum to totals because of rounding.

SOURCE: U.S. Department of Education, National Center for Education Statistics, Higher Education General Information Survey (HEGIS), "Fall Enrollment in Colleges and Universities" surveys, 1970 and 1980; 1990 through 2005 Integrated Postsecondary Education Data System, "Fall Enrollment Survey" (IPEDS-EF:90–99), and Spring 2001 through Spring 2006; and Projections of Education Statistics to 2015. U.S. Department of Commerce, Census Bureau, Current Population Survey (CPS), October, selected years, 1970 through 2005, unpublished tabulations. (This table was prepared October 2006.)

Table 178. Total fall enrollment in degree-granting institutions, by level, sex, age, and attendance status of student: 2005

Age of student and attendance status	All levels			Undergraduate			First-professional			Graduate		
	Total	Males	Females	Total	Males	Females	Total	Males	Females	Total	Males	Females
1	2	3	4	5	6	7	8	9	10	11	12	13
All students	17,487,475	7,455,925	10,031,550	14,963,964	6,408,871	8,555,093	337,024	169,831	167,193	2,186,487	877,223	1,309,264
Under 18	566,823	233,937	332,886	566,466	233,779	332,687	26	12	14	331	146	185
18 and 19	3,727,670	1,674,704	2,052,966	3,725,669	1,673,882	2,051,787	1,510	613	897	491	209	282
20 and 21	3,508,086	1,573,851	1,934,235	3,480,130	1,563,462	1,916,668	11,724	4,170	7,554	16,232	6,219	10,013
22 to 24	2,912,566	1,332,595	1,579,971	2,422,270	1,141,814	1,280,456	124,496	56,621	67,875	365,800	134,160	231,640
25 to 29	2,410,710	1,030,293	1,380,417	1,619,628	684,946	934,682	130,907	69,591	61,316	660,175	275,756	384,419
30 to 34	1,352,487	549,598	802,889	936,723	354,959	581,764	32,509	19,402	13,107	383,255	175,237	208,018
35 to 39	945,787	355,551	590,236	690,697	242,654	448,043	14,060	8,329	5,731	241,030	104,568	136,462
40 to 49	1,292,761	431,334	861,427	961,765	311,344	650,421	13,364	7,016	6,348	317,632	112,974	204,658
50 to 64	592,741	198,914	393,827	419,326	142,206	277,120	6,115	2,913	3,202	167,300	53,795	113,505
65 and over	71,918	29,213	42,705	65,885	26,362	39,523	260	119	141	5,773	2,732	3,041
Age unknown	105,926	45,935	59,991	75,405	33,463	41,942	2,053	1,045	1,008	28,468	11,427	17,041
Full-time	10,797,011	4,803,388	5,993,623	9,446,430	4,200,863	5,245,567	303,468	151,859	151,609	1,047,113	450,666	596,447
Under 18	156,279	62,847	93,432	156,159	62,792	93,367	23	11	12	97	44	53
18 and 19	3,187,406	1,424,151	1,763,255	3,185,565	1,423,390	1,762,175	1,508	611	897	333	150	183
20 and 21	2,856,016	1,287,060	1,568,956	2,831,119	1,277,679	1,553,440	11,540	4,083	7,457	13,357	5,298	8,059
22 to 24	1,922,734	915,714	1,007,020	1,546,599	763,437	783,162	119,764	54,316	65,448	256,371	97,961	158,410
25 to 29	1,220,032	554,526	665,506	741,124	328,285	412,839	120,564	64,049	56,515	358,344	162,192	196,152
30 to 34	557,219	235,210	322,009	359,286	134,840	224,446	26,717	15,987	10,730	171,216	84,383	86,833
35 to 39	331,983	126,205	205,778	230,997	78,279	152,718	10,144	6,028	4,116	90,842	41,898	48,944
40 to 49	383,582	130,189	253,393	273,414	87,097	186,317	8,064	4,255	3,809	102,104	38,837	63,267
50 to 64	136,105	46,619	89,486	86,835	29,087	57,748	3,259	1,548	1,711	46,011	15,984	30,027
65 and over	5,533	2,611	2,922	4,100	1,920	2,180	132	70	62	1,301	621	680
Age unknown	40,122	18,256	21,866	31,232	14,057	17,175	1,753	901	852	7,137	3,298	3,839
Part-time	6,690,464	2,652,537	4,037,927	5,517,534	2,208,008	3,309,526	33,556	17,972	15,584	1,139,374	426,557	712,817
Under 18	410,544	171,090	239,454	410,307	170,987	239,320	3	1	2	234	102	132
18 and 19	540,264	250,553	289,711	540,104	250,492	289,612	2	2	0	158	59	99
20 and 21	652,070	286,791	365,279	649,011	285,783	363,228	184	87	97	2,875	921	1,954
22 to 24	989,832	416,881	572,951	875,671	378,377	497,294	4,732	2,305	2,427	109,429	36,199	73,230
25 to 29	1,190,678	475,767	714,911	878,504	356,661	521,843	10,343	5,542	4,801	301,831	113,564	188,267
30 to 34	795,268	314,388	480,880	577,437	220,119	357,318	5,792	3,415	2,377	212,039	90,854	121,185
35 to 39	613,804	229,346	384,458	459,700	164,375	295,325	3,916	2,301	1,615	150,188	62,670	87,518
40 to 49	909,179	301,145	608,034	688,351	224,247	464,104	5,300	2,761	2,539	215,528	74,137	141,391
50 to 64	456,636	152,295	304,341	332,491	113,119	219,372	2,856	1,365	1,491	121,289	37,811	83,478
65 and over	66,385	26,602	39,783	61,785	24,442	37,343	128	49	79	4,472	2,111	2,361
Age unknown	65,804	27,679	38,125	44,173	19,406	24,767	300	144	156	21,331	8,129	13,202
	Percentage distribution											
All students	100.0	100.0	100.0	100.0	100.0	100.0	100.0	100.0	100.0	100.0	100.0	100.0
Under 18	3.2	3.1	3.3	3.8	3.6	3.9	#	#	#	#	#	#
18 and 19	21.3	22.5	20.5	24.9	26.1	24.0	0.4	0.4	0.5	#	#	#
20 and 21	20.1	21.1	19.3	23.3	24.4	22.4	3.5	2.5	4.5	0.7	0.7	0.8
22 to 24	16.7	17.9	15.8	16.2	17.8	15.0	36.9	33.3	40.6	16.7	15.3	17.7
25 to 29	13.8	13.8	13.8	10.8	10.7	10.9	38.8	41.0	36.7	30.2	31.4	29.4
30 to 34	7.7	7.4	8.0	6.3	5.5	6.8	9.6	11.4	7.8	17.5	20.0	15.9
35 to 39	5.4	4.8	5.9	4.6	3.8	5.2	4.2	4.9	3.4	11.0	11.9	10.4
40 to 49	7.4	5.8	8.6	6.4	4.9	7.6	4.0	4.1	3.8	14.5	12.9	15.6
50 to 64	3.4	2.7	3.9	2.8	2.2	3.2	1.8	1.7	1.9	7.7	6.1	8.7
65 and over	0.4	0.4	0.4	0.4	0.4	0.5	0.1	0.1	0.1	0.3	0.3	0.2
Age unknown	0.6	0.6	0.6	0.5	0.5	0.5	0.6	0.6	0.6	1.3	1.3	1.3
Full-time	100.0	100.0	100.0	100.0	100.0	100.0	100.0	100.0	100.0	100.0	100.0	100.0
Under 18	1.4	1.3	1.6	1.7	1.5	1.8	#	#	#	#	#	#
18 and 19	29.5	29.6	29.4	33.7	33.9	33.6	0.5	0.4	0.6	#	#	#
20 and 21	26.5	26.8	26.2	30.0	30.4	29.6	3.8	2.7	4.9	1.3	1.2	1.4
22 to 24	17.8	19.1	16.8	16.4	18.2	14.9	39.5	35.8	43.2	24.5	21.7	26.6
25 to 29	11.3	11.5	11.1	7.8	7.8	7.9	39.7	42.2	37.3	34.2	36.0	32.9
30 to 34	5.2	4.9	5.4	3.8	3.2	4.3	8.8	10.5	7.1	16.4	18.7	14.6
35 to 39	3.1	2.6	3.4	2.4	1.9	2.9	3.3	4.0	2.7	8.7	9.3	8.2
40 to 49	3.6	2.7	4.2	2.9	2.1	3.6	2.7	2.8	2.5	9.8	8.6	10.6
50 to 64	1.3	1.0	1.5	0.9	0.7	1.1	1.1	1.0	1.1	4.4	3.5	5.0
65 and over	0.1	0.1	#	#	#	#	#	#	#	0.1	0.1	0.1
Age unknown	0.4	0.4	0.4	0.3	0.3	0.3	0.6	0.6	0.6	0.7	0.7	0.6
Part-time	100.0	100.0	100.0	100.0	100.0	100.0	100.0	100.0	100.0	100.0	100.0	100.0
Under 18	6.1	6.5	5.9	7.4	7.7	7.2	#	#	#	#	#	#
18 and 19	8.1	9.4	7.2	9.8	11.3	8.8	#	#	0.0	#	#	#
20 and 21	9.7	10.8	9.0	11.8	12.9	11.0	0.5	0.5	0.6	0.3	0.2	0.3
22 to 24	14.8	15.7	14.2	15.9	17.1	15.0	14.1	12.8	15.6	9.6	8.5	10.3
25 to 29	17.8	17.9	17.7	15.9	16.2	15.8	30.8	30.8	30.8	26.5	26.6	26.4
30 to 34	11.9	11.9	11.9	10.5	10.0	10.8	17.3	19.0	15.3	18.6	21.3	17.0
35 to 39	9.2	8.6	9.5	8.3	7.4	8.9	11.7	12.8	10.4	13.2	14.7	12.3
40 to 49	13.6	11.4	15.1	12.5	10.2	14.0	15.8	15.4	16.3	18.9	17.4	19.8
50 to 64	6.8	5.7	7.5	6.0	5.1	6.6	8.5	7.6	9.6	10.6	8.9	11.7
65 and over	1.0	1.0	1.0	1.1	1.1	1.1	0.4	0.3	0.5	0.4	0.5	0.3
Age unknown	1.0	1.0	0.9	0.8	0.9	0.7	0.9	0.8	1.0	1.9	1.9	1.9

#Rounds to zero.
NOTE: Degree-granting institutions grant associate's or higher degrees and participate in Title IV federal financial aid programs.

SOURCE: U.S. Department of Education, National Center for Education Statistics, 2005 Integrated Postsecondary Education Data System (IPEDS), Spring 2006. (This table was prepared August 2006.)

Table 179. Total fall enrollment in degree-granting institutions, by control and type of institution, age, and attendance status of student: 2005

Age of student and attendance status	All institutions			Public institutions			Private (not-for-profit and for-profit) institutions			Private not-for-profit institutions only		
	Total	4-year	2-year	Total	4-year	2-year	Total	4-year	2-year	Total	4-year	2-year
1	2	3	4	5	6	7	8	9	10	11	12	13
All students	17,487,475	10,999,420	6,488,055	13,021,834	6,837,605	6,184,229	4,465,641	4,161,815	303,826	3,454,692	3,411,170	43,522
Under 18	566,823	191,533	375,290	500,345	128,219	372,126	66,478	63,314	3,164	60,445	59,337	1,108
18 and 19	3,727,670	2,334,209	1,393,461	2,886,238	1,544,977	1,341,261	841,432	789,232	52,200	751,205	740,808	10,397
20 and 21	3,508,086	2,421,578	1,086,508	2,658,958	1,625,096	1,033,862	849,128	796,482	52,646	740,958	733,662	7,296
22 to 24	2,912,566	2,013,534	899,032	2,242,198	1,395,581	846,617	670,368	617,953	52,415	530,606	524,642	5,964
25 to 29	2,410,710	1,572,796	837,914	1,701,928	919,158	782,770	708,782	653,638	55,144	501,217	495,254	5,963
30 to 34	1,352,487	822,899	529,588	935,432	437,473	497,959	417,055	385,426	31,629	268,359	264,609	3,750
35 to 39	945,787	541,327	404,460	651,699	268,313	383,386	294,088	273,014	21,074	184,772	181,940	2,832
40 to 49	1,292,761	708,032	584,729	905,775	343,391	562,384	386,986	364,641	22,345	251,022	247,232	3,790
50 to 64	592,741	306,794	285,947	434,650	155,726	278,924	158,091	151,068	7,023	109,897	108,554	1,343
65 and over	71,918	16,111	55,807	65,666	10,128	55,538	6,252	5,983	269	4,950	4,868	82
Age unknown	105,926	70,607	35,319	38,945	9,543	29,402	66,981	61,064	5,917	51,261	50,264	997
Full-time	10,797,011	8,150,209	2,646,802	7,408,761	5,021,745	2,387,016	3,388,250	3,128,464	259,786	2,563,732	2,534,793	28,939
Under 18	156,279	92,374	63,905	116,765	55,244	61,521	39,514	37,130	2,384	34,181	33,767	414
18 and 19	3,187,406	2,235,893	951,513	2,369,888	1,467,707	902,181	817,518	768,186	49,332	734,713	725,369	9,344
20 and 21	2,856,016	2,253,466	602,550	2,048,315	1,493,009	555,306	807,701	760,457	47,244	714,373	708,578	5,795
22 to 24	1,922,734	1,574,159	348,575	1,380,262	1,076,897	303,365	542,472	497,262	45,210	427,418	423,394	4,024
25 to 29	1,220,032	948,889	271,143	744,383	519,489	224,894	475,649	429,400	46,249	308,024	304,567	3,457
30 to 34	557,219	410,152	147,067	310,466	188,884	121,582	246,753	221,268	25,485	128,682	126,754	1,928
35 to 39	331,983	236,367	95,616	171,142	92,220	78,922	160,841	144,147	16,694	74,845	73,491	1,354
40 to 49	383,582	270,389	113,193	189,238	93,362	95,876	194,344	177,027	17,317	88,512	86,925	1,587
50 to 64	136,105	96,715	39,390	65,467	31,404	34,063	70,638	65,311	5,327	33,569	33,047	522
65 and over	5,533	3,530	2,003	2,892	1,082	1,810	2,641	2,448	193	1,644	1,611	33
Age unknown	40,122	28,275	11,847	9,943	2,447	7,496	30,179	25,828	4,351	17,771	17,290	481
Part-time	6,690,464	2,849,211	3,841,253	5,613,073	1,815,860	3,797,213	1,077,391	1,033,351	44,040	890,960	876,377	14,583
Under 18	410,544	99,159	311,385	383,580	72,975	310,605	26,964	26,184	780	26,264	25,570	694
18 and 19	540,264	98,316	441,948	516,350	77,270	439,080	23,914	21,046	2,868	16,492	15,439	1,053
20 and 21	652,070	168,112	483,958	610,643	132,087	478,556	41,427	36,025	5,402	26,585	25,084	1,501
22 to 24	989,832	439,375	550,457	861,936	318,684	543,252	127,896	120,691	7,205	103,188	101,248	1,940
25 to 29	1,190,678	623,907	566,771	957,545	399,669	557,876	233,133	224,238	8,895	193,193	190,687	2,506
30 to 34	795,268	412,747	382,521	624,966	248,589	376,377	170,302	164,158	6,144	139,677	137,855	1,822
35 to 39	613,804	304,960	308,844	480,557	176,093	304,464	133,247	128,867	4,380	109,927	108,449	1,478
40 to 49	909,179	437,643	471,536	716,537	250,029	466,508	192,642	187,614	5,028	162,510	160,307	2,203
50 to 64	456,636	210,079	246,557	369,183	124,322	244,861	87,453	85,757	1,696	76,328	75,507	821
65 and over	66,385	12,581	53,804	62,774	9,046	53,728	3,611	3,535	76	3,306	3,257	49
Age unknown	65,804	42,332	23,472	29,002	7,096	21,906	36,802	35,236	1,566	33,490	32,974	516
	Percentage distribution											
All students	100.0	100.0	100.0	100.0	100.0	100.0	100.0	100.0	100.0	100.0	100.0	100.0
Under 18	3.2	1.7	5.8	3.8	1.9	6.0	1.5	1.5	1.0	1.7	1.7	2.5
18 and 19	21.3	21.2	21.5	22.2	22.6	21.7	18.8	19.0	17.2	21.7	21.7	23.9
20 and 21	20.1	22.0	16.7	20.4	23.8	16.7	19.0	19.1	17.3	21.4	21.5	16.8
22 to 24	16.7	18.3	13.9	17.2	20.4	13.7	15.0	14.8	17.3	15.4	15.4	13.7
25 to 29	13.8	14.3	12.9	13.1	13.4	12.7	15.9	15.7	18.1	14.5	14.5	13.7
30 to 34	7.7	7.5	8.2	7.2	6.4	8.1	9.3	9.3	10.4	7.8	7.8	8.6
35 to 39	5.4	4.9	6.2	5.0	3.9	6.2	6.6	6.6	6.9	5.3	5.3	6.5
40 to 49	7.4	6.4	9.0	7.0	5.0	9.1	8.7	8.8	7.4	7.3	7.2	8.7
50 to 64	3.4	2.8	4.4	3.3	2.3	4.5	3.5	3.6	2.3	3.2	3.2	3.1
65 and over	0.4	0.1	0.9	0.5	0.1	0.9	0.1	0.1	0.1	0.1	0.1	0.2
Age unknown	0.6	0.6	0.5	0.3	0.1	0.5	1.5	1.5	1.9	1.5	1.5	2.3
Full-time	100.0	100.0	100.0	100.0	100.0	100.0	100.0	100.0	100.0	100.0	100.0	100.0
Under 18	1.4	1.1	2.4	1.6	1.1	2.6	1.2	1.2	0.9	1.3	1.3	1.4
18 and 19	29.5	27.4	35.9	32.0	29.2	37.8	24.1	24.6	19.0	28.7	28.6	32.3
20 and 21	26.5	27.6	22.8	27.6	29.7	23.3	23.8	24.3	18.2	27.9	28.0	20.0
22 to 24	17.8	19.3	13.2	18.6	21.4	12.7	16.0	15.9	17.4	16.7	16.7	13.9
25 to 29	11.3	11.6	10.2	10.0	10.3	9.4	14.0	13.7	17.8	12.0	12.0	11.9
30 to 34	5.2	5.0	5.6	4.2	3.8	5.1	7.3	7.1	9.8	5.0	5.0	6.7
35 to 39	3.1	2.9	3.6	2.3	1.8	3.3	4.7	4.6	6.4	2.9	2.9	4.7
40 to 49	3.6	3.3	4.3	2.6	1.9	4.0	5.7	5.7	6.7	3.5	3.4	5.5
50 to 64	1.3	1.2	1.5	0.9	0.6	1.4	2.1	2.1	2.1	1.3	1.3	1.8
65 and over	0.1	#	0.1	#	#	0.1	0.1	0.1	0.2	0.1	0.1	0.2
Age unknown	0.4	0.3	0.4	0.1	0.0	0.3	0.9	0.8	1.7	0.7	0.7	1.7
Part-time	100.0	100.0	100.0	100.0	100.0	100.0	100.0	100.0	100.0	100.0	100.0	100.0
Under 18	6.1	3.5	8.1	6.8	4.0	8.2	2.5	2.5	1.8	2.9	2.9	4.8
18 and 19	8.1	3.5	11.5	9.2	4.3	11.6	2.2	2.0	6.5	1.9	1.8	7.2
20 and 21	9.7	5.9	12.6	10.9	7.3	12.6	3.8	3.5	12.3	3.0	2.9	10.3
22 to 24	14.8	15.4	14.3	15.4	17.6	14.3	11.9	11.7	16.4	11.6	11.6	13.3
25 to 29	17.8	21.9	14.8	17.1	22.0	14.7	21.6	21.7	20.2	21.7	21.8	17.2
30 to 34	11.9	14.5	10.0	11.1	13.7	9.9	15.8	15.9	14.0	15.7	15.7	12.5
35 to 39	9.2	10.7	8.0	8.6	9.7	8.0	12.4	12.5	9.9	12.3	12.4	10.1
40 to 49	13.6	15.4	12.3	12.8	13.8	12.3	17.9	18.2	11.4	18.2	18.3	15.1
50 to 64	6.8	7.4	6.4	6.6	6.8	6.4	8.1	8.3	3.9	8.6	8.6	5.6
65 and over	1.0	0.4	1.4	1.1	0.5	1.4	0.3	0.3	0.2	0.4	0.4	0.3
Age unknown	1.0	1.5	0.6	0.5	0.4	0.6	3.4	3.4	3.6	3.8	3.8	3.5

#Rounds to zero.
NOTE: Degree-granting institutions grant associate's or higher degrees and participate in Title IV federal financial aid programs. Detail may not sum to totals because of rounding.

SOURCE: U.S. Department of Education, National Center for Education Statistics, 2005 Integrated Postsecondary Education Data System (IPEDS), Spring 2006. (This table was prepared August 2006.)

Table 180. Total fall enrollment in degree-granting institutions, by level of enrollment, sex, attendance status, and type and control of institution: 2005

Attendance status, and type and control of institution	Total			Undergraduate			First-professional			Graduate		
	Total	Males	Females	Total	Males	Females	Total	Males	Females	Total	Males	Females
1	2	3	4	5	6	7	8	9	10	11	12	13
Total	17,487,475	7,455,925	10,031,550	14,963,964	6,408,871	8,555,093	337,024	169,831	167,193	2,186,487	877,223	1,309,264
Full-time	10,797,011	4,803,388	5,993,623	9,446,430	4,200,863	5,245,567	303,468	151,859	151,609	1,047,113	450,666	596,447
Part-time	6,690,464	2,652,537	4,037,927	5,517,534	2,208,008	3,309,526	33,556	17,972	15,584	1,139,374	426,557	712,817
4-year	10,999,420	4,775,557	6,223,863	8,476,138	3,728,572	4,747,566	337,024	169,831	167,193	2,186,258	877,154	1,309,104
Full-time	8,150,209	3,649,622	4,500,587	6,799,667	3,047,104	3,752,563	303,468	151,859	151,609	1,047,074	450,659	596,415
Part-time	2,849,211	1,125,935	1,723,276	1,676,471	681,468	995,003	33,556	17,972	15,584	1,139,184	426,495	712,689
2-year	6,488,055	2,680,368	3,807,687	6,487,826	2,680,299	3,807,527	†	†	†	229	69	160
Full-time	2,646,802	1,153,766	1,493,036	2,646,763	1,153,759	1,493,004	†	†	†	39	7	32
Part-time	3,841,253	1,526,602	2,314,651	3,841,063	1,526,540	2,314,523	†	†	†	190	62	128
Public	13,021,834	5,589,223	7,432,611	11,697,730	5,046,002	6,651,728	138,207	65,602	72,605	1,185,897	477,619	708,278
Full-time	7,408,761	3,350,485	4,058,276	6,747,911	3,051,732	3,696,179	131,727	62,492	69,235	529,123	236,261	292,862
Part-time	5,613,073	2,238,738	3,374,335	4,949,819	1,994,270	2,955,549	6,480	3,110	3,370	656,774	241,358	415,416
Public 4-year	6,837,605	3,019,831	3,817,774	5,513,730	2,476,679	3,037,051	138,207	65,602	72,605	1,185,668	477,550	708,118
Full-time	5,021,745	2,295,456	2,726,289	4,360,934	1,996,710	2,364,224	131,727	62,492	69,235	529,084	236,254	292,830
Part-time	1,815,860	724,375	1,091,485	1,152,796	479,969	672,827	6,480	3,110	3,370	656,584	241,296	415,288
Public 2-year	6,184,229	2,569,392	3,614,837	6,184,000	2,569,323	3,614,677	†	†	†	229	69	160
Full-time	2,387,016	1,055,029	1,331,987	2,386,977	1,055,022	1,331,955	†	†	†	39	7	32
Part-time	3,797,213	1,514,363	2,282,850	3,797,023	1,514,301	2,282,722	†	†	†	190	62	128
Private	4,465,641	1,866,702	2,598,939	3,266,234	1,362,869	1,903,365	198,817	104,229	94,588	1,000,590	399,604	600,986
Full-time	3,388,250	1,452,903	1,935,347	2,698,519	1,149,131	1,549,388	171,741	89,367	82,374	517,990	214,405	303,585
Part-time	1,077,391	413,799	663,592	567,715	213,738	353,977	27,076	14,862	12,214	482,600	185,199	297,401
Private 4-year	4,161,815	1,755,726	2,406,089	2,962,408	1,251,893	1,710,515	198,817	104,229	94,588	1,000,590	399,604	600,986
Full-time	3,128,464	1,354,166	1,774,298	2,438,733	1,050,394	1,388,339	171,741	89,367	82,374	517,990	214,405	303,585
Part-time	1,033,351	401,560	631,791	523,675	201,499	322,176	27,076	14,862	12,214	482,600	185,199	297,401
Private 2-year	303,826	110,976	192,850	303,826	110,976	192,850	†	†	†	†	†	†
Full-time	259,786	98,737	161,049	259,786	98,737	161,049	†	†	†	†	†	†
Part-time	44,040	12,239	31,801	44,040	12,239	31,801	†	†	†	†	†	†
Not-for-profit	3,454,692	1,464,299	1,990,393	2,418,368	1,017,578	1,400,790	197,289	103,439	93,850	839,035	343,282	495,753
Full-time	2,563,732	1,121,161	1,442,571	1,996,647	860,065	1,136,582	170,560	88,744	81,816	396,525	172,352	224,173
Part-time	890,960	343,138	547,822	421,721	157,513	264,208	26,729	14,695	12,034	442,510	170,930	271,580
Not-for-profit 4-year	3,411,170	1,448,647	1,962,523	2,374,846	1,001,926	1,372,920	197,289	103,439	93,850	839,035	343,282	495,753
Full-time	2,534,793	1,109,075	1,425,718	1,967,708	847,979	1,119,729	170,560	88,744	81,816	396,525	172,352	224,173
Part-time	876,377	339,572	536,805	407,138	153,947	253,191	26,729	14,695	12,034	442,510	170,930	271,580
Not-for-profit 2-year	43,522	15,652	27,870	43,522	15,652	27,870	†	†	†	†	†	†
Full-time	28,939	12,086	16,853	28,939	12,086	16,853	†	†	†	†	†	†
Part-time	14,583	3,566	11,017	14,583	3,566	11,017	†	†	†	†	†	†
For-profit	1,010,949	402,403	608,546	847,866	345,291	502,575	1,528	790	738	161,555	56,322	105,233
Full-time	824,518	331,742	492,776	701,872	289,066	412,806	1,181	623	558	121,465	42,053	79,412
Part-time	186,431	70,661	115,770	145,994	56,225	89,769	347	167	180	40,090	14,269	25,821
For-profit 4-year	750,645	307,079	443,566	587,562	249,967	337,595	1,528	790	738	161,555	56,322	105,233
Full-time	593,671	245,091	348,580	471,025	202,415	268,610	1,181	623	558	121,465	42,053	79,412
Part-time	156,974	61,988	94,986	116,537	47,552	68,985	347	167	180	40,090	14,269	25,821
For-profit 2-year	260,304	95,324	164,980	260,304	95,324	164,980	†	†	†	†	†	†
Full-time	230,847	86,651	144,196	230,847	86,651	144,196	†	†	†	†	†	†
Part-time	29,457	8,673	20,784	29,457	8,673	20,784	†	†	†	†	†	†

†Not applicable.
NOTE: Degree-granting institutions grant associate's or higher degrees and participate in Title IV federal financial aid programs.

SOURCE: U.S. Department of Education, National Center for Education Statistics, 2005 Integrated Postsecondary Education Data System (IPEDS), Spring 2006. (This table was prepared August 2006.)

Table 181. Total fall enrollment in degree-granting institutions, by level of enrollment, sex, attendance status, and type and control of institution: 2004

Attendance status, and type and control of institution	Total			Undergraduate			First-professional			Graduate		
	Total	Males	Females	Total	Males	Females	Total	Males	Females	Total	Males	Females
1	2	3	4	5	6	7	8	9	10	11	12	13
Total	17,272,044	7,387,262	9,884,782	14,780,630	6,340,048	8,440,582	334,529	168,438	166,091	2,156,885	878,776	1,278,109
Full-time	10,610,177	4,739,355	5,870,822	9,284,336	4,140,628	5,143,708	301,543	150,860	150,683	1,024,298	447,867	576,431
Part-time	6,661,867	2,647,907	4,013,960	5,496,294	2,199,420	3,296,874	32,986	17,578	15,408	1,132,587	430,909	701,678
4-year	10,726,181	4,689,666	6,036,515	8,235,060	3,642,541	4,592,519	334,529	168,438	166,091	2,156,592	878,687	1,277,905
Full-time	7,926,639	3,572,783	4,353,856	6,600,847	2,974,074	3,626,773	301,543	150,860	150,683	1,024,249	447,849	576,400
Part-time	2,799,542	1,116,883	1,682,659	1,634,213	668,467	965,746	32,986	17,578	15,408	1,132,343	430,838	701,505
2-year	6,545,863	2,697,596	3,848,267	6,545,570	2,697,507	3,848,063	†	†	†	293	89	204
Full-time	2,683,538	1,166,572	1,516,966	2,683,489	1,166,554	1,516,935	†	†	†	49	18	31
Part-time	3,862,325	1,531,024	2,331,301	3,862,081	1,530,953	2,331,128	†	†	†	244	71	173
Public	12,980,112	5,559,476	7,420,636	11,650,580	5,009,240	6,641,340	135,756	64,636	71,120	1,193,776	485,600	708,176
Full-time	7,369,432	3,325,073	4,044,359	6,711,857	3,025,625	3,686,232	129,423	61,514	67,909	528,152	237,934	290,218
Part-time	5,610,680	2,234,403	3,376,277	4,938,723	1,983,615	2,955,108	6,333	3,122	3,211	665,624	247,666	417,958
Public 4-year	6,736,536	2,976,515	3,760,021	5,407,236	2,426,351	2,980,885	135,756	64,636	71,120	1,193,544	485,528	708,016
Full-time	4,943,811	2,259,946	2,683,865	4,286,257	1,960,503	2,325,754	129,423	61,514	67,909	528,131	237,929	290,202
Part-time	1,792,725	716,569	1,076,156	1,120,979	465,848	655,131	6,333	3,122	3,211	665,413	247,599	417,814
Public 2-year	6,243,576	2,582,961	3,660,615	6,243,344	2,582,889	3,660,455	†	†	†	232	72	160
Full-time	2,425,621	1,065,127	1,360,494	2,425,600	1,065,122	1,360,478	†	†	†	21	5	16
Part-time	3,817,955	1,517,834	2,300,121	3,817,744	1,517,767	2,299,977	†	†	†	211	67	144
Private	4,291,932	1,827,786	2,464,146	3,130,050	1,330,808	1,799,242	198,773	103,802	94,971	963,109	393,176	569,933
Full-time	3,240,745	1,414,282	1,826,463	2,572,479	1,115,003	1,457,476	172,120	89,346	82,774	496,146	209,933	286,213
Part-time	1,051,187	413,504	637,683	557,571	215,805	341,766	26,653	14,456	12,197	466,963	183,243	283,720
Private 4-year	3,989,645	1,713,151	2,276,494	2,827,824	1,216,190	1,611,634	198,773	103,802	94,971	963,048	393,159	569,889
Full-time	2,982,828	1,312,837	1,669,991	2,314,590	1,013,571	1,301,019	172,120	89,346	82,774	496,118	209,920	286,198
Part-time	1,006,817	400,314	606,503	513,234	202,619	310,615	26,653	14,456	12,197	466,930	183,239	283,691
Private 2-year	302,287	114,635	187,652	302,226	114,618	187,608	†	†	†	61	17	44
Full-time	257,917	101,445	156,472	257,889	101,432	156,457	†	†	†	28	13	15
Part-time	44,370	13,190	31,180	44,337	13,186	31,151	†	†	†	33	4	29
Not-for-profit	3,411,685	1,449,223	1,962,462	2,389,366	1,005,076	1,384,290	197,447	103,120	94,327	824,872	341,027	483,845
Full-time	2,522,993	1,104,447	1,418,546	1,964,727	845,735	1,118,992	171,166	88,845	82,321	387,100	169,867	217,233
Part-time	888,692	344,776	543,916	424,639	159,341	265,298	26,281	14,275	12,006	437,772	171,160	266,612
Not-for-profit 4-year	3,369,435	1,433,491	1,935,944	2,347,116	989,344	1,357,772	197,447	103,120	94,327	824,872	341,027	483,845
Full-time	2,494,090	1,092,100	1,401,990	1,935,824	833,388	1,102,436	171,166	88,845	82,321	387,100	169,867	217,233
Part-time	875,345	341,391	533,954	411,292	155,956	255,336	26,281	14,275	12,006	437,772	171,160	266,612
Not-for-profit 2-year	42,250	15,732	26,518	42,250	15,732	26,518	†	†	†	†	†	†
Full-time	28,903	12,347	16,556	28,903	12,347	16,556	†	†	†	†	†	†
Part-time	13,347	3,385	9,962	13,347	3,385	9,962	†	†	†	†	†	†
For-profit	880,247	378,563	501,684	740,684	325,732	414,952	1,326	682	644	138,237	52,149	86,088
Full-time	717,752	309,835	407,917	607,752	269,268	338,484	954	501	453	109,046	40,066	68,980
Part-time	162,495	68,728	93,767	132,932	56,464	76,468	372	181	191	29,191	12,083	17,108
For-profit 4-year	620,210	279,660	340,550	480,708	226,846	253,862	1,326	682	644	138,176	52,132	86,044
Full-time	488,738	220,737	268,001	378,766	180,183	198,583	954	501	453	109,018	40,053	68,965
Part-time	131,472	58,923	72,549	101,942	46,663	55,279	372	181	191	29,158	12,079	17,079
For-profit 2-year	260,037	98,903	161,134	259,976	98,886	161,090	†	†	†	61	17	44
Full-time	229,014	89,098	139,916	228,986	89,085	139,901	†	†	†	28	13	15
Part-time	31,023	9,805	21,218	30,990	9,801	21,189	†	†	†	33	4	29

†Not applicable.
NOTE: Degree-granting institutions grant associate's or higher degrees and participate in Title IV federal financial aid programs.

SOURCE: U.S. Department of Education, National Center for Education Statistics, 2004 Integrated Postsecondary Education Data System (IPEDS), Spring 2005. (This table was prepared September 2005.)

Table 182. Total fall enrollment in degree-granting institutions, by attendance status, sex of student, and type and control of institution: Selected years, 1970 through 2005

Attendance status and sex of student, type and control of institution	1970	1975	1980[1]	1985	1990	1995	2000	2001	2002	2003	2004	2005
1	2	3	4	5	6	7	8	9	10	11	12	13
Total	8,580,887	11,184,859	12,096,895	12,247,055	13,818,637	14,261,781	15,312,289	15,927,987	16,611,711	16,900,471	17,272,044	17,487,475
Full-time	5,816,290	6,841,334	7,097,958	7,075,221	7,820,985	8,128,802	9,009,600	9,447,502	9,946,359	10,311,814	10,610,177	10,797,011
Males	3,504,095	3,926,753	3,689,244	3,607,720	3,807,752	3,807,392	4,111,093	4,299,890	4,501,098	4,631,735	4,739,355	4,803,388
Females	2,312,195	2,914,581	3,408,714	3,467,501	4,013,233	4,321,410	4,898,507	5,147,612	5,445,261	5,680,079	5,870,822	5,993,623
Part-time	2,764,597	4,343,525	4,998,937	5,171,834	5,997,652	6,132,979	6,302,689	6,480,485	6,665,352	6,588,657	6,661,867	6,690,464
Males	1,539,547	2,222,244	2,185,130	2,210,730	2,476,157	2,535,147	2,610,676	2,660,925	2,701,018	2,623,816	2,647,907	2,652,537
Females	1,225,050	2,121,281	2,813,807	2,961,104	3,521,495	3,597,832	3,692,013	3,819,560	3,964,334	3,964,841	4,013,960	4,037,927
4-year	6,261,502	7,214,740	7,570,608	7,715,978	8,578,554	8,769,252	9,363,858	9,677,408	10,082,332	10,407,553	10,726,181	10,999,420
Full-time	4,587,379	5,080,256	5,344,163	5,384,614	5,937,023	6,151,755	6,792,551	7,073,011	7,390,323	7,666,319	7,926,639	8,150,209
Males	2,732,796	2,891,192	2,809,528	2,781,412	2,926,360	2,929,177	3,115,252	3,233,608	3,365,427	3,471,317	3,572,783	3,649,622
Females	1,854,583	2,189,064	2,534,635	2,603,202	3,010,663	3,222,578	3,677,299	3,839,403	4,024,896	4,195,002	4,353,856	4,500,587
Part-time	1,674,123	2,134,484	2,226,445	2,331,364	2,641,531	2,617,497	2,571,307	2,604,397	2,692,009	2,741,234	2,799,542	2,849,211
Males	936,189	1,092,461	1,017,813	1,034,804	1,124,780	1,084,753	1,047,917	1,052,007	1,083,223	1,094,828	1,116,883	1,125,935
Females	737,934	1,042,023	1,208,632	1,296,560	1,516,751	1,532,744	1,523,390	1,552,390	1,608,786	1,646,406	1,682,659	1,723,276
Public 4-year	4,232,722	4,998,142	5,128,612	5,209,540	5,848,242	5,814,545	6,055,398	6,236,455	6,481,613	6,649,441	6,736,536	6,837,605
Full-time	3,086,491	3,469,821	3,592,193	3,623,341	4,033,654	4,084,711	4,371,218	4,532,209	4,724,056	4,864,068	4,943,811	5,021,745
Males	1,813,584	1,947,823	1,873,397	1,863,689	1,982,369	1,951,140	2,008,618	2,082,146	2,166,759	2,224,942	2,259,946	2,295,456
Females	1,272,907	1,521,998	1,718,796	1,759,652	2,051,285	2,133,571	2,362,600	2,450,063	2,557,297	2,639,126	2,683,865	2,726,289
Part-time	1,146,231	1,528,321	1,536,419	1,586,199	1,814,588	1,729,834	1,684,180	1,704,246	1,757,557	1,785,373	1,792,725	1,815,860
Males	609,422	760,469	685,051	693,115	764,248	720,402	683,100	687,436	706,041	712,799	716,569	724,375
Females	536,809	767,852	851,368	893,084	1,050,340	1,009,432	1,001,080	1,016,810	1,051,516	1,072,574	1,076,156	1,091,485
Private 4-year	2,028,780	2,216,598	2,441,996	2,506,438	2,730,312	2,954,707	3,308,460	3,440,953	3,600,719	3,758,112	3,989,645	4,161,815
Full-time	1,500,888	1,610,435	1,751,970	1,761,273	1,903,369	2,067,044	2,421,333	2,540,802	2,666,267	2,802,251	2,982,828	3,128,464
Males	919,212	943,369	936,131	917,723	943,991	978,037	1,106,634	1,151,462	1,198,668	1,246,375	1,312,837	1,354,166
Females	581,676	667,066	815,839	843,550	959,378	1,089,007	1,314,699	1,389,340	1,467,599	1,555,876	1,669,991	1,774,298
Part-time	527,892	606,163	690,026	745,165	826,943	887,663	887,127	900,151	934,452	955,861	1,006,817	1,033,351
Males	326,767	331,992	332,762	341,689	360,532	364,351	364,817	364,571	377,182	382,029	400,314	401,560
Females	201,125	274,171	357,264	403,476	466,411	523,312	522,310	535,580	557,270	573,832	606,503	631,791
Not-for-profit 4-year	—	—	2,413,693	2,463,000	2,671,069	2,853,890	3,050,575	3,119,781	3,218,389	3,296,882	3,369,435	3,411,170
Full-time	—	—	1,733,014	1,727,707	1,859,124	1,989,457	2,226,028	2,285,510	2,364,851	2,441,235	2,494,090	2,534,793
Males	—	—	921,253	894,080	915,100	931,956	996,113	1,015,634	1,045,439	1,073,715	1,092,100	1,109,075
Females	—	—	811,761	833,627	944,024	1,057,501	1,229,915	1,269,876	1,319,412	1,367,520	1,401,990	1,425,718
Part-time	—	—	680,679	735,293	811,945	864,433	824,547	834,271	853,538	855,647	875,345	876,377
Males	—	—	327,986	336,168	352,106	351,874	332,814	331,645	337,765	335,891	341,391	339,572
Females	—	—	352,693	399,125	459,839	512,559	491,733	502,626	515,773	519,756	533,954	536,805
2-year	2,319,385	3,970,119	4,526,287	4,531,077	5,240,083	5,492,529	5,948,431	6,250,579	6,529,379	6,492,918	6,545,863	6,488,055
Full-time	1,228,911	1,761,078	1,753,795	1,690,607	1,883,962	1,977,047	2,217,049	2,374,491	2,556,036	2,645,495	2,683,538	2,646,802
Males	771,299	1,035,561	879,716	826,308	881,392	878,215	995,841	1,066,282	1,135,671	1,160,418	1,166,572	1,153,766
Females	457,612	725,517	874,079	864,299	1,002,570	1,098,832	1,221,208	1,308,209	1,420,365	1,485,077	1,516,966	1,493,036
Part-time	1,090,474	2,209,041	2,772,492	2,840,470	3,356,121	3,515,482	3,731,382	3,876,088	3,973,343	3,847,423	3,862,325	3,841,253
Males	603,358	1,129,783	1,167,317	1,175,926	1,351,377	1,450,394	1,562,759	1,608,918	1,617,795	1,528,988	1,531,024	1,526,602
Females	487,116	1,079,258	1,605,175	1,664,544	2,004,744	2,065,088	2,168,623	2,267,170	2,355,548	2,318,435	2,331,301	2,314,651
Public 2-year	2,195,412	3,836,366	4,328,782	4,269,733	4,996,475	5,277,829	5,697,388	5,996,701	6,270,380	6,207,618	6,243,576	6,184,229
Full-time	1,129,165	1,662,621	1,595,493	1,496,905	1,716,843	1,840,590	2,000,008	2,155,496	2,333,312	2,400,981	2,425,621	2,387,016
Males	720,440	988,701	811,491	742,673	810,664	818,605	891,282	961,588	1,034,547	1,057,761	1,065,127	1,055,029
Females	408,725	673,920	783,622	754,232	906,179	1,021,985	1,108,726	1,193,908	1,298,765	1,343,220	1,360,494	1,331,987
Part-time	1,066,247	2,173,745	2,733,289	2,772,828	3,279,632	3,437,239	3,697,380	3,841,205	3,937,068	3,806,637	3,817,955	3,797,213
Males	589,439	1,107,680	1,152,268	1,138,011	1,317,730	1,417,488	1,549,407	1,596,441	1,604,673	1,516,066	1,517,834	1,514,363
Females	476,808	1,066,065	1,581,021	1,634,817	1,961,902	2,019,751	2,147,973	2,244,764	2,332,395	2,290,571	2,300,121	2,282,850
Private 2-year	123,973	133,753	197,505	261,344	243,608	214,700	251,043	253,878	258,999	285,300	302,287	303,826
Full-time	99,746	98,457	158,302	193,702	167,119	136,457	217,041	218,995	222,724	244,514	257,917	259,786
Males	50,859	46,860	67,845	83,635	70,728	59,610	104,559	104,694	101,124	102,657	101,445	98,737
Females	48,887	51,597	90,457	110,067	96,391	76,847	112,482	114,301	121,600	141,857	156,472	161,049
Part-time	24,227	35,296	39,203	67,642	76,489	78,243	34,002	34,883	36,275	40,786	44,370	44,040
Males	13,919	22,103	15,049	37,915	33,647	32,906	13,352	12,477	13,122	12,922	13,190	12,239
Females	10,308	13,193	24,154	29,727	42,842	45,337	20,650	22,406	23,153	27,864	31,180	31,801
Not-for-profit 2-year	—	—	114,094	108,791	89,158	75,154	58,844	47,549	47,087	43,836	42,250	43,522
Full-time	—	—	83,009	76,547	62,003	54,033	46,670	36,750	35,511	32,171	28,903	28,939
Males	—	—	34,968	30,878	25,946	23,265	21,950	17,965	16,677	14,371	12,347	12,086
Females	—	—	48,041	45,669	36,057	30,768	24,720	18,785	18,834	17,800	16,556	16,853
Part-time	—	—	31,085	32,244	27,155	21,121	12,174	10,799	11,576	11,665	13,347	14,583
Males	—	—	11,445	10,786	7,970	6,080	4,499	3,540	3,547	3,236	3,385	3,566
Females	—	—	19,640	21,458	19,185	15,041	7,675	7,259	8,029	8,429	9,962	11,017

—Not available.

[1]Large increase in private 2-year institutions in 1980 is due to the addition of schools accredited by the Accrediting Commission of Career Schools and Colleges of Technology.
NOTE: Data through 1995 are for institutions of higher education, while later data are for degree-granting institutions. Degree-granting institutions grant associate's or higher degrees and participate in Title IV federal financial aid programs. The degree-granting classification is very similar to the earlier higher education classification, but it includes more 2-year colleges and excludes a few higher education institutions that did not grant degrees. (See Guide to Sources for details.)
SOURCE: U.S. Department of Education, National Center for Education Statistics, Higher Education General Information Survey (HEGIS), "Fall Enrollment in Colleges and Universities" surveys, 1970 through 1985; and 1990 through 2005 Integrated Postsecondary Education Data System, "Fall Enrollment Survey" (IPEDS-EF:90–99), and Spring 2001 through Spring 2006. (This table was prepared August 2006.)

Table 183. Fall enrollment and number of degree-granting institutions, by control and affiliation of institution: Selected years, 1980 through 2005

Control and affiliation[1]	Total enrollment						Enrollment, fall 2005					Number of institutions[2]				
	Fall 1980	Fall 1990	Fall 1995	Fall 2000	Fall 2003	Fall 2004	Total	Full-time Males	Full-time Females	Part-time Males	Part-time Females	Fall 1980	Fall 1990	Fall 2000	Fall 2004	Fall 2005
1	2	3	4	5	6	7	8	9	10	11	12	13	14	15	16	17
All institutions	12,096,895	13,818,637	14,261,781	15,312,289	16,900,471	17,272,044	17,487,475	4,803,388	5,993,623	2,652,537	4,037,927	3,226	3,501	4,056	4,194	4,253
Public institutions	9,457,394	10,844,717	11,092,374	11,752,786	12,857,059	12,980,112	13,021,834	3,350,485	4,058,276	2,238,738	3,374,335	1,493	1,548	1,676	1,694	1,675
Federal	50,989	50,669	90,046	16,917	20,636	20,090	20,197	13,760	4,591	474	1,372	12	17	12	13	13
State	(²)	7,181,380	7,842,782	9,548,090	10,486,958	10,643,035	10,691,230	2,924,101	3,550,032	1,682,563	2,534,534	(²)	978	1,355	1,368	1,352
Local	(²)	3,508,941	3,023,723	2,078,090	2,177,133	2,128,924	2,123,212	365,193	445,348	524,751	787,920	(²)	523	277	266	265
Other public	9,406,405	103,727	135,823	109,689	172,332	188,063	187,195	47,431	58,305	30,950	50,509	1,481	30	32	47	45
Private institutions	2,639,501	2,973,920	3,169,407	3,559,503	4,043,412	4,291,932	4,465,641	1,452,903	1,935,347	413,799	663,592	1,733	1,953	2,380	2,500	2,578
Independent not-for-profit	1,521,614	1,474,818	1,511,151	1,577,242	1,708,135	1,758,209	1,783,462	596,407	714,159	190,124	282,772	795	709	729	747	753
For-profit	111,714	213,693	240,363	450,084	702,694	880,247	1,010,949	331,742	492,776	70,661	115,770	164	322	724	865	933
Religiously affiliated	1,006,173	1,285,409	1,417,893	1,532,177	1,632,583	1,653,476	1,671,230	524,754	728,412	153,014	265,050	774	922	927	888	892
Advent Christian Church	143	—	—	—	—	—	—	—	—	—	—	1	—	—	—	—
African Methodist Episcopal Zion Church	1,091	88	—	34	1,312	1,343	1,269	661	514	53	41	3	1	6	3	3
African Methodist Episcopal	4,541	3,220	3,503	5,980	4,026	3,788	3,475	1,659	1,677	62	77	6	5	6	5	5
American Baptist	6,131	10,800	11,394	15,410	16,073	14,545	14,358	3,848	5,346	1,626	3,538	11	15	17	17	16
American Evangelical Lutheran Church	—	—	779	743	1,413	1,414	1,435	619	709	44	63	—	—	1	1	1
American Lutheran and Lutheran Church in America	3,092	—	1,304	1,460	—	—	—	—	—	—	—	3	—	1	—	—
American Lutheran	21,608	—	10,459	—	—	—	—	—	—	—	—	13	—	—	—	—
Assemblies of God Church	7,814	8,307	9,652	14,272	13,321	13,826	14,095	5,140	6,759	1,035	1,161	10	11	14	14	14
Baptist	38,231	99,510	105,802	107,610	120,198	120,898	126,649	42,075	57,251	11,486	15,837	33	69	68	70	73
Brethren Church	3,925	958	1,456	2,088	8,762	8,437	8,003	2,243	2,854	1,052	1,854	3	3	3	3	3
Brethren in Christ Church	1,301	2,239	2,416	2,797	20,900	21,776	22,045	7,254	9,474	2,024	3,293	1	1	1	12	12
Christian and Missionary Alliance Church	1,705	2,519	3,723	5,278	5,866	5,974	6,320	1,998	2,806	585	931	3	4	4	4	4
Christian Church (Disciples of Christ)	14,913	30,397	33,029	35,984	41,436	43,139	44,923	11,815	18,956	5,549	8,603	12	18	16	17	17
Christian Churches and Churches of Christ	1,342	2,263	3,494	7,277	9,078	9,529	9,686	3,972	4,042	908	764	7	8	18	19	19
Christian Methodist Episcopal	2,486	2,174	2,598	1,502	3,647	3,517	3,778	1,751	1,824	78	125	4	4	1	3	3
Christian Reformed Church	5,408	4,488	4,205	5,999	5,963	5,774	5,757	2,592	2,806	172	187	3	4	3	3	3
Church of Christ (Scientist)	2,773	2,557	4,320	—	—	—	—	—	—	—	—	6	8	—	—	—
Church of God of Prophecy	—	249	—	—	—	—	—	—	—	—	—	—	1	—	—	—
Church of God	6,082	5,627	4,410	12,540	13,743	13,669	14,030	4,515	6,243	1,447	1,825	9	9	7	7	7
Church of New Jerusalem	170	—	—	—	—	—	—	—	—	—	—	1	—	—	—	—
Church of the Brethren	8,482	4,463	2,812	4,187	4,660	5,293	5,382	2,071	2,845	182	284	6	5	4	5	5
Church of the Nazarene	11,716	10,779	14,466	16,661	19,657	19,957	20,418	6,612	9,205	1,682	2,919	10	9	12	10	10
Churches of Christ	9,343	14,611	22,807	30,140	32,226	32,766	33,072	11,282	13,653	3,344	4,793	9	19	19	20	20
Cumberland Presbyterian	594	746	799	1,112	1,610	1,625	1,710	581	665	186	278	2	2	2	2	2
Evangelical Congregational Church	80	88	65	148	153	156	170	19	3	91	57	1	1	1	1	1
Evangelical Covenant Church of America	1,401	1,035	1,745	2,387	2,531	2,563	2,684	691	1,161	238	594	1	1	1	1	1
Evangelical Free Church of America	833	2,355	3,778	4,022	2,846	2,972	3,063	880	772	932	479	1	1	—	2	2
Evangelical Lutheran Church	743	49,210	39,089	49,085	53,330	54,138	54,726	20,912	27,720	2,233	3,861	1	33	34	35	35
Free Methodist	5,543	5,902	8,696	7,323	8,921	8,929	9,250	2,564	4,703	589	1,394	3	3	3	4	4
Free Will Baptist Church	1,132	1,177	1,467	2,378	2,955	3,244	3,519	1,003	1,453	504	559	4	3	4	4	4

See notes at end of table.

Table 183. Fall enrollment and number of degree-granting institutions, by control and affiliation of institution: Selected years, 1980 through 2005—Continued

Control and affiliation[1]	Total enrollment						Enrollment, fall 2005					Number of institutions[2]				
	Fall 1980	Fall 1990	Fall 1995	Fall 2000	Fall 2003	Fall 2004	Total	Full-time Males	Full-time Females	Part-time Males	Part-time Females	Fall 1980	Fall 1990	Fall 2000	Fall 2004	Fall 2005
1	2	3	4	5	6	7	8	9	10	11	12	13	14	15	16	17
Friends United Meeting	1,109	—	—	—	—	—	—	—	—	—	—	1	—	—	—	—
Friends General Conference	5,157	5,844	6,600	10,898	12,009	12,681	13,387	4,324	6,123	1,116	1,824	5	6	8	7	7
General Conference Mennonite Church	820	1,243	1,046	1,059	—	—	—	—	—	—	—	2	2	1	—	—
Greek Orthodox	204	148	168	132	252	255	184	133	44	7	0	2	2	1	1	1
Interdenominational	1,254	11,103	5,571	9,788	21,603	22,120	22,493	7,053	8,419	3,163	3,858	4	17	14	22	23
Jewish	5,738	12,217	11,481	14,182	7,608	7,777	7,847	5,896	1,108	286	557	24	63	62	32	33
Latter-Day Saints	39,172	42,274	40,086	44,680	48,105	49,636	50,840	21,662	22,312	3,370	3,496	4	4	4	4	4
Lutheran Church—Missouri Synod	11,727	13,827	11,315	18,866	21,189	22,748	19,686	5,822	7,641	2,065	4,158	15	14	13	13	12
Lutheran Church in America	23,877	5,796	4,321	4,322	4,500	4,441	8,243	3,304	4,192	257	490	20	5	2	2	3
Mennonite Brethren Church	1,344	1,864	2,269	2,390	2,889	2,813	2,751	702	1,080	336	633	3	3	3	3	3
Mennonite Church	4,008	2,859	3,502	3,553	3,922	4,112	4,186	1,534	2,068	213	371	6	5	5	6	6
Missionary Church Inc.	487	699	1,352	1,647	1,848	1,988	1,959	524	853	190	392	1	1	1	1	1
Moravian Church	2,434	2,511	2,804	2,939	3,193	3,363	3,116	669	1,633	162	652	2	2	2	3	2
Multiple Protestant denominations	5,526	211	164	4,690	4,686	5,092	5,159	1,325	1,472	1,429	933	8	1	7	6	7
North American Baptist	155	—	186	124	136	105	107	38	25	22	22	1	—	1	1	1
Pentecostal Holiness Church	767	566	1,002	976	977	1,013	1,105	429	462	103	111	3	3	2	2	3
Presbyterian U.S.A. and United Presbyterian	47,144	77,700	70,357	78,950	82,350	81,207	82,141	29,910	41,190	3,513	7,528	57	70	64	60	60
Presbyterian Church in America	—	1,877	3,809	4,499	4,371	4,370	2,953	1,066	812	740	335	—	1	5	4	3
Protestant Episcopal	5,396	4,559	4,603	5,479	4,953	5,360	4,970	2,090	2,461	207	212	12	9	12	11	11
Protestant, other	4,072	38,136	60,386	30,116	19,107	11,244	11,589	3,729	4,368	1,663	1,829	11	44	34	20	20
Reformed Church in America	2,713	5,525	5,582	6,002	6,321	6,424	6,311	2,443	3,460	195	213	4	4	5	5	5
Reformed Episcopal Church	67	—	—	—	—	—	—	—	—	—	—	1	—	—	—	—
Reformed Presbyterian Church	2,014	1,556	1,771	2,355	3,143	3,180	3,090	1,151	1,397	286	256	4	2	2	3	3
Reorganized Latter-Day Saints Church	4,274	4,793	11,063	3,390	—	—	—	—	—	—	—	2	1	2	—	—
Roman Catholic	422,842	530,585	594,464	636,336	684,294	695,069	694,517	190,351	291,992	70,956	141,218	229	239	239	243	241
Russian Orthodox	47	38	32	106	89	103	104	72	12	14	6	1	1	1	1	1
Seventh-Day Adventists	19,168	15,771	17,519	19,223	651	722	803	110	365	43	285	11	11	13	1	1
Southern Baptist	85,281	49,493	46,042	54,275	38,313	41,762	38,710	10,507	14,243	5,720	8,240	54	29	32	21	21
Nondenominational[3]	—	6,758	18,729	23,573	32,257	25,465	26,340	7,138	8,745	5,133	5,324	—	14	16	17	16
Unitarian Universalist	87	82	126	132	188	197	200	47	75	20	58	2	2	2	2	2
United Brethren Church	545	601	721	938	969	959	1,005	380	457	82	86	1	1	1	1	1
United Church of Christ	14,169	20,175	24,013	23,709	23,661	28,499	28,651	9,119	12,827	2,092	4,613	16	18	18	20	20
United Methodist	127,099	148,851	148,091	171,109	180,177	185,853	191,468	67,401	89,944	12,481	21,642	91	96	100	99	99
Wesleyan Church	3,583	5,311	7,734	11,128	15,059	16,778	18,043	6,019	10,446	542	1,036	5	4	4	6	6
Wisconsin Evangelical Lutheran Synod	808	931	1,165	1,660	1,726	1,641	1,571	647	816	59	49	1	3	2	2	2
Other religiously affiliated	462	5,743	11,551	2,534	7,410	7,227	7,884	2,402	3,929	447	1,106	1	9	4	7	10

—Not available.

[1]Religious affiliation as reported by institution.

[2]Counts of institutions in this table may be lower than reported in other tables, because counts in this table include only institutions reporting separate enrollment data.

[3]Included under "Other public."

NOTE: Data through 1995 are for institutions of higher education, while later data are for degree-granting institutions. Degree-granting institutions grant associate's or higher degrees and participate in Title IV federal financial aid programs. The degree-granting classification is very similar to the earlier higher education classification, but it includes more 2-year colleges and excludes a few higher education institutions that did not grant degrees. (See Guide to Sources for details.)

SOURCE: U.S. Department of Education, National Center for Education Statistics, Higher Education General Information Survey (HEGIS), "Fall Enrollment in Institutions of Higher Education" and "Institutional Characteristics" surveys, 1980; and 1990 through 2005 Integrated Postsecondary Education Data System, "Fall Enrollment Survey" (IPEDS-EF:90-95), "Institutional Characteristics Survey" (IPEDS-IC:90-95), and Spring 2003 through Spring 2006. (This table was prepared August 2006.)

Table 184. Total first-time freshmen fall enrollment in degree-granting institutions, by attendance status, sex of student, and type and control of institution: 1955 through 2005

[In thousands]

Year	Total, all freshmen	Full-time	Part-time	Males			Females			4-year		2-year	
				Total	Full-time	Part-time	Total	Full-time	Part-time	Public	Private	Public	Private
1	2	3	4	5	6	7	8	9	10	11	12	13	14
1955[1]	670	—	—	416	—	—	254	—	—	283[2]	247[2]	117[2]	23[2]
1956[1]	718	—	—	443	—	—	275	—	—	293[2]	262[2]	137[2]	25[2]
1957[1]	724	—	—	442	—	—	282	—	—	294[2]	263[2]	141[2]	27[2]
1958[1]	775	—	—	465	—	—	310	—	—	328[2]	272[2]	146[2]	29[2]
1959[1]	822	—	—	488	—	—	334	—	—	348[2]	292[2]	153[2]	28[2]
1960[1]	923	—	—	540	—	—	384	—	—	396[2]	313[2]	182[2]	32[2]
1961[1]	1,018	—	—	592	—	—	426	—	—	438[2]	336[2]	210[2]	34[2]
1962[1]	1,031	—	—	598	—	—	432	—	—	445[2]	325[2]	225[2]	36[2]
1963[1]	1,046	—	—	604	—	—	442	—	—	—	—	—	—
1964[1]	1,225	—	—	702	—	—	523	—	—	539[2]	363[2]	275[2]	47[2]
1965[1]	1,442	—	—	829	—	—	613	—	—	642[2]	399[2]	348[2]	53[2]
1966	1,554	—	—	890	—	—	665	—	—	626[2]	383[2]	478[2]	67[2]
1967	1,641	1,336	305	931	761	170	710	574	136	645[2]	368[2]	561[2]	67[2]
1968	1,893	1,471	422	1,082	847	235	810	624	187	725[2]	378[2]	718[2]	72[2]
1969	1,967	1,525	442	1,118	876	242	849	649	200	737[2]	393[2]	776[2]	61[2]
1970	2,063	1,587	476	1,152	896	256	911	691	221	754[2]	397[2]	854[2]	58[2]
1971	2,119	1,606	513	1,171	896	275	949	710	238	738[2]	386[2]	937[2]	58[2]
1972	2,153	1,574	579	1,158	858	299	995	716	279	680	381	1,037	55
1973	2,226	1,607	619	1,182	867	315	1,044	740	304	699	379	1,089	59
1974	2,366	1,673	692	1,244	896	348	1,122	777	345	746	386	1,176	58
1975	2,515	1,763	752	1,328	942	386	1,187	821	366	772	395	1,284	64
1976	2,347	1,662	685	1,170	855	316	1,177	808	369	717	414	1,153	63
1977	2,394	1,681	714	1,156	840	316	1,239	841	398	737	405	1,186	67
1978	2,390	1,651	739	1,142	817	324	1,248	834	414	737	407	1,174	73
1979	2,503	1,707	796	1,180	840	340	1,323	866	457	760	415	1,254	74
1980	2,588	1,750	838	1,219	862	357	1,369	887	481	765	418	1,314	91
1981	2,595	1,738	858	1,218	852	366	1,378	886	492	754	419	1,318	104
1982	2,505	1,689	817	1,199	837	362	1,306	851	455	731	404	1,254	116
1983	2,444	1,678	766	1,159	825	334	1,285	853	431	728	404	1,190	122
1984	2,357	1,613	744	1,112	786	326	1,245	827	418	714	403	1,130	110
1985	2,292	1,602	690	1,076	775	301	1,216	827	389	717	399	1,060	116
1986	2,219	1,589	630	1,047	769	278	1,173	821	352	720	392	991	117[3]
1987	2,246	1,627	620	1,047	779	267	1,200	847	352	758	405	980	104
1988	2,379	1,699	680	1,100	807	293	1,279	892	387	783	426	1,049	121
1989	2,341	1,657	684	1,095	791	303	1,246	865	381	762	414	1,049	116[3]
1990	2,257	1,617	640	1,045	771	274	1,211	846	366	727	400	1,041	88
1991	2,278	1,653	625	1,068	798	270	1,209	855	355	718	393	1,070	97
1992	2,184	1,604	580	1,013	760	253	1,171	843	328	697	408	993	85
1993	2,161	1,608	552	1,008	762	245	1,153	846	307	702	411	974	74
1994	2,133	1,603	530	985	751	233	1,149	852	297	709	406	952	66
1995	2,169	1,647	522	1,001	767	234	1,168	880	288	732	419	955	63
1996	2,274	1,740	534	1,047	806	241	1,228	934	294	741	427	990	116
1997	2,219	1,734	486	1,026	806	220	1,193	927	266	755	442	924	98
1998[1]	2,213	1,775	437	1,023	826	197	1,190	950	240	793	461	858	100
1999[4]	2,352	1,845	507	1,092	863	228	1,260	982	278	819	474	952	107
2000	2,428	1,918	509	1,124	894	230	1,304	1,024	280	842	499	952	135
2001	2,497	1,989	508	1,153	926	226	1,344	1,063	281	867	508	989	134
2002	2,571	2,053	518	1,171	946	225	1,400	1,107	293	886	518	1,037	129
2003	2,605	2,107	497	1,181	967	214	1,423	1,140	283	919	542	1,013	131
2004	2,630	2,148	483	1,190	982	209	1,440	1,166	274	925	562	1,009	133
2005	2,657	2,190	467	1,200	996	204	1,457	1,194	263	954	607	977	119

—Not available.

[1]Excludes first-time freshmen in occupational programs not creditable towards a bachelor's degree.
[2]Data for 2-year branches of 4-year college systems are aggregated with the 4-year institutions.
[3]Because of imputation techniques, data are not consistent with figures for other years.
[4]Data were imputed using alternative procedures. (See Guide to Sources for details.)
NOTE: Data for 1955 through 1995 are for institutions of higher education. Data for 1996 and later years are for degree-granting institutions. Institutions of higher education were accredited by an agency or association that was recognized by the U.S. Department of Education, or recognized directly by the Secretary of Education. The new degree-granting classification is very

similar to the earlier higher education classification, except that it includes some additional institutions, primarily 2-year colleges, and excludes a few higher education institutions that did not award associate's or higher degrees. Alaska and Hawaii are included in all years. Detail may not sum to totals because of rounding. (See Guide to Sources for details.)
SOURCE: U.S. Department of Education, National Center for Education Statistics, *Biennial Survey of Education in the United States; Opening Fall Enrollment in Higher Education*, 1963 through 1965; Higher Education General Information Survey (HEGIS), "Fall Enrollment in Colleges and Universities" surveys, 1966 through 1985; and 1986 through 2005 Integrated Postsecondary Education Data System, "Fall Enrollment Survey" (IPEDS-EF:86–99), and Spring 2001 through Spring 2006. (This table was prepared August 2006.)

Table 185. Total first-time freshmen fall enrollment in degree-granting institutions, by attendance status, sex, control of institution, and state or jurisdiction: 2000 through 2005

State or jurisdiction	Total, fall 2000	Total, fall 2001	Total, fall 2002	Total, fall 2003	Total, fall 2004	Fall 2005 Total	Full-time Total	Full-time Males	Full-time Females	Part-time Total	Part-time Males	Part-time Females	Public institutions	Private institutions
1	2	3	4	5	6	7	8	9	10	11	12	13	14	15
United States	2,427,551	2,497,078	2,570,611	2,604,714	2,630,243	2,657,338	2,189,884	995,610	1,194,274	467,454	204,445	263,009	1,931,127	726,211
Alabama	43,411	43,674	43,065	42,813	42,737	42,461	37,160	17,103	20,057	5,301	2,486	2,815	36,826	5,635
Alaska	2,432	2,585	2,661	2,753	2,760	2,899	2,306	1,049	1,257	593	216	377	2,774	125
Arizona	46,646	42,725	46,879	46,363	50,521	76,987	65,948	23,582	42,366	11,039	5,242	5,797	33,784	43,203
Arkansas	22,695	22,030	23,021	24,538	24,110	24,480	21,707	9,808	11,899	2,773	1,223	1,550	21,312	3,168
California	246,128	264,689	274,436	247,337	259,869	266,989	194,142	86,588	107,554	72,847	34,303	38,544	213,218	53,771
Colorado	43,201	42,834	44,525	46,184	45,341	47,330	38,564	18,352	20,212	8,766	3,859	4,907	31,937	15,393
Connecticut	24,212	24,688	26,408	26,531	27,295	27,520	23,819	10,667	13,152	3,701	1,418	2,283	17,078	10,442
Delaware	7,636	8,509	9,299	8,766	8,253	8,763	7,458	3,183	4,275	1,305	474	831	7,480	1,283
District of Columbia	9,150	10,825	10,462	10,231	11,350	11,334	8,532	3,482	5,050	2,802	864	1,938	1,135	10,199
Florida	109,931	121,508	125,322	130,930	138,561	136,694	105,001	45,937	59,064	31,693	13,688	18,005	100,948	35,746
Georgia	67,616	67,134	75,130	82,614	83,314	74,267	61,025	26,861	34,164	13,242	5,378	7,864	60,144	14,123
Hawaii	8,931	9,560	9,211	9,088	8,492	8,466	6,555	2,900	3,655	1,911	861	1,050	6,754	1,712
Idaho	10,669	11,498	12,950	11,379	11,801	12,549	11,090	4,617	6,473	1,459	655	804	8,731	3,818
Illinois	107,592	107,995	110,013	115,479	103,212	111,724	92,426	41,914	50,512	19,298	8,743	10,555	70,634	41,090
Indiana	59,320	65,582	62,691	62,478	61,520	61,915	53,975	25,526	28,449	7,940	3,560	4,380	43,248	18,667
Iowa	39,564	41,141	43,860	41,835	43,352	41,242	30,361	14,825	15,536	10,881	4,268	6,613	28,372	12,870
Kansas	31,424	32,670	29,271	29,685	28,393	29,173	23,720	12,043	11,677	5,453	2,519	2,934	26,089	3,084
Kentucky	34,140	36,579	37,998	38,390	39,485	37,766	32,782	13,898	18,884	4,984	1,855	3,129	27,845	9,921
Louisiana	45,383	47,167	43,149	46,474	43,572	32,018	28,971	12,087	16,884	3,047	1,255	1,792	28,428	3,590
Maine	9,231	9,768	10,287	10,721	10,760	11,181	9,926	4,735	5,191	1,255	452	803	7,609	3,572
Maryland	35,552	38,548	40,346	42,335	45,815	44,288	33,706	15,115	18,591	10,582	4,316	6,266	36,123	8,165
Massachusetts	66,044	66,774	67,654	68,507	70,869	70,873	63,416	28,957	34,459	7,457	2,789	4,668	33,580	37,293
Michigan	84,998	89,327	88,325	88,578	88,078	93,221	72,321	33,355	38,966	20,900	9,016	11,884	75,832	17,389
Minnesota	63,893	64,361	64,246	62,456	61,042	57,822	48,490	23,605	24,885	9,332	3,942	5,390	43,320	14,502
Mississippi	30,356	32,406	37,841	34,373	33,646	33,665	28,959	12,407	16,552	4,706	1,786	2,920	31,546	2,119
Missouri	48,639	48,446	49,730	51,106	51,431	52,678	46,021	20,409	25,612	6,657	2,813	3,844	35,954	16,724
Montana	7,771	7,786	7,868	8,538	8,484	8,654	7,667	3,875	3,792	987	409	578	7,767	887
Nebraska	19,027	19,280	19,928	20,670	18,855	19,015	16,729	8,053	8,676	2,286	1,006	1,280	14,622	4,393
Nevada	10,490	11,052	10,236	9,969	13,995	15,117	10,237	4,461	5,776	4,880	2,182	2,698	13,012	2,105
New Hampshire	13,143	12,553	12,408	12,832	12,420	12,692	11,409	5,279	6,130	1,283	468	815	7,335	5,357
New Jersey	52,233	53,797	55,624	56,108	57,564	58,396	49,390	23,529	25,861	9,006	3,738	5,268	48,482	9,914
New Mexico	15,261	15,785	15,834	16,655	16,827	16,653	13,713	6,141	7,572	2,940	1,307	1,633	15,275	1,378
New York	168,181	167,849	171,246	178,289	180,253	181,328	170,401	78,619	91,782	10,927	4,479	6,448	101,741	79,587
North Carolina	69,343	74,731	78,576	76,675	81,444	79,628	63,577	28,337	35,240	16,051	6,727	9,324	63,800	15,828
North Dakota	8,929	9,332	9,149	10,154	9,477	8,296	7,898	4,201	3,697	398	170	228	7,175	1,121
Ohio	98,823	95,580	100,076	104,137	104,334	102,800	89,006	40,501	48,505	13,794	6,797	6,997	72,439	30,361
Oklahoma	35,094	36,552	34,659	37,583	34,948	35,318	28,881	13,361	15,520	6,437	2,757	3,680	29,257	6,061
Oregon	26,946	27,119	27,112	27,262	28,402	28,944	21,809	9,881	11,928	7,135	3,366	3,769	22,841	6,103
Pennsylvania	125,578	127,255	131,518	131,582	132,339	132,758	117,137	55,464	61,673	15,621	5,916	9,705	72,007	60,751
Rhode Island	13,789	14,421	14,819	15,070	15,388	15,277	14,106	6,536	7,570	1,171	435	736	6,423	8,854
South Carolina	32,353	34,503	37,589	37,649	37,868	38,469	33,406	14,710	18,696	5,063	1,974	3,089	31,719	6,750
South Dakota	8,597	8,588	9,124	9,577	9,076	8,780	7,839	3,828	4,011	941	352	589	7,085	1,695
Tennessee	43,327	43,411	44,876	45,897	47,991	49,076	44,782	19,488	25,294	4,294	1,742	2,552	31,836	17,240
Texas	181,813	178,185	188,647	206,164	205,221	202,388	141,013	65,081	75,932	61,375	28,169	33,206	174,482	27,906
Utah	24,953	28,211	28,866	27,783	26,787	28,501	21,869	9,992	11,877	6,632	3,517	3,115	20,594	7,907
Vermont	6,810	6,941	6,583	6,341	6,343	7,684	6,946	3,594	3,352	738	242	496	4,553	3,131
Virginia	52,661	51,416	56,031	60,296	66,621	68,005	57,868	25,139	32,729	10,137	4,297	5,840	48,796	19,209
Washington	36,287	38,417	36,549	38,942	37,393	38,367	33,104	15,712	17,392	5,263	2,358	2,905	30,938	7,429
West Virginia	15,659	16,136	16,826	17,858	16,602	16,675	15,526	7,293	8,233	1,149	481	668	14,072	2,603
Wisconsin	53,662	55,800	57,559	56,201	55,331	55,326	46,912	21,980	24,932	8,414	3,330	5,084	45,794	9,532
Wyoming	4,209	5,310	6,230	6,326	6,519	6,661	6,053	4,065	1,988	608	245	363	4,156	2,505
U.S. Service Schools	3,818	4,045	3,898	4,212	4,182	4,225	4,225	3,485	740	0	0	0	4,225	†
Other jurisdictions	39,609	38,182	40,931	43,535	43,506	41,800	38,571	16,678	21,893	3,229	1,433	1,796	16,028	25,772
American Samoa	297	440	477	536	575	597	298	123	175	299	118	181	597	0
Federated States of Micronesia	786	1,002	952	1,102	1,389	761	632	337	295	129	72	57	761	0
Guam	770	729	756	749	724	1,117	714	298	416	403	155	248	1,044	73
Marshall Islands	199	220	224	133	179	12	11	5	6	1	1	0	12	0
Northern Marianas	333	178	241	307	255	199	174	65	109	25	19	6	199	0
Palau	147	147	103	110	115	105	99	61	38	6	3	3	105	0
Puerto Rico	36,773	34,908	37,547	39,967	39,471	38,648	36,335	15,698	20,637	2,313	1,054	1,259	12,949	25,699
Virgin Islands	304	558	631	631	798	361	308	91	217	53	11	42	361	0

†Not applicable.
NOTE: Degree-granting institutions grant associate's or higher degrees and participate in Title IV federal financial aid programs.

SOURCE: U.S. Department of Education, National Center for Education Statistics, 2000 through 2005 Integrated Postsecondary Education Data System, Spring 2001 through Spring 2006. (This table was prepared August 2006.)

Table 186. College enrollment and enrollment rates of recent high school completers, by sex: 1960 through 2005

[Numbers in thousands]

Year	Number of high school completers[1]						Enrolled in college[2]									
	Total		Males		Females		Total				Males				Females	
							Number		Percent		Number		Percent		Number	
1	2		3		4		5		6		7		8		9		10
1960	1,679	(43.8)	756	(31.8)	923	(29.6)	758	(40.9)	45.1	(2.13)	408	(29.5)	54.0	(3.18)	350	(28.2)	37.9	(2.80)
1961	1,763	(46.0)	790	(33.2)	973	(31.3)	847	(42.9)	48.0	(2.09)	445	(30.8)	56.3	(3.10)	402	(29.9)	41.3	(2.77)
1962	1,838	(43.6)	872	(31.5)	966	(30.0)	900	(43.2)	49.0	(2.05)	480	(31.1)	55.0	(2.96)	420	(30.0)	43.5	(2.80)
1963	1,741	(44.2)	794	(32.1)	947	(30.0)	784	(41.5)	45.0	(2.09)	415	(29.8)	52.3	(3.11)	369	(28.8)	39.0	(2.78)
1964	2,145	(43.0)	997	(31.9)	1,148	(28.5)	1,037	(45.6)	48.3	(1.89)	570	(32.9)	57.2	(2.75)	467	(31.4)	40.7	(2.54)
1965	2,659	(47.7)	1,254	(35.1)	1,405	(32.0)	1,354	(51.4)	50.9	(1.70)	718	(36.7)	57.3	(2.45)	636	(35.8)	45.3	(2.33)
1966	2,612	(45.0)	1,207	(33.8)	1,405	(29.0)	1,309	(50.2)	50.1	(1.72)	709	(36.0)	58.7	(2.49)	600	(34.8)	42.7	(2.32)
1967	2,525	(37.9)	1,142	(28.4)	1,383	(24.3)	1,311	(40.9)	51.9	(1.42)	658	(28.9)	57.6	(2.09)	653	(28.9)	47.2	(1.92)
1968	2,606	(37.3)	1,184	(28.2)	1,422	(23.8)	1,444	(41.7)	55.4	(1.39)	748	(29.6)	63.2	(2.00)	696	(29.3)	48.9	(1.89)
1969	2,842	(36.0)	1,352	(26.8)	1,490	(23.7)	1,516	(42.5)	53.3	(1.34)	812	(30.3)	60.1	(1.90)	704	(29.7)	47.2	(1.85)
1970	2,758	(37.4)	1,343	(26.1)	1,415	(26.8)	1,427	(42.2)	51.7	(1.36)	741	(29.7)	55.2	(1.94)	686	(29.8)	48.5	(1.90)
1971	2,875	(38.0)	1,371	(26.6)	1,504	(27.1)	1,538	(43.2)	53.5	(1.33)	790	(30.3)	57.6	(1.90)	749	(30.8)	49.8	(1.84)
1972	2,964	(37.8)	1,423	(27.0)	1,542	(26.4)	1,459	(43.1)	49.2	(1.31)	750	(30.4)	52.7	(1.89)	709	(30.5)	46.0	(1.81)
1973	3,058	(37.1)	1,460	(27.6)	1,599	(24.6)	1,424	(43.0)	46.6	(1.29)	730	(30.6)	50.0	(1.87)	694	(30.2)	43.4	(1.77)
1974	3,101	(38.6)	1,491	(27.8)	1,611	(26.8)	1,475	(43.7)	47.6	(1.28)	736	(30.8)	49.4	(1.85)	740	(31.1)	45.9	(1.77)
1975	3,185	(38.6)	1,513	(27.3)	1,672	(27.2)	1,615	(44.8)	50.7	(1.26)	796	(31.2)	52.6	(1.83)	818	(32.1)	49.0	(1.75)
1976	2,986	(39.8)	1,451	(28.9)	1,535	(27.3)	1,458	(43.6)	48.8	(1.31)	685	(30.4)	47.2	(1.87)	773	(31.2)	50.3	(1.82)
1977	3,141	(40.7)	1,483	(29.7)	1,659	(27.7)	1,590	(45.4)	50.6	(1.29)	773	(31.8)	52.1	(1.87)	817	(32.4)	49.3	(1.77)
1978	3,163	(39.7)	1,485	(29.3)	1,677	(26.7)	1,585	(45.2)	50.1	(1.28)	759	(31.6)	51.1	(1.87)	827	(32.4)	49.3	(1.76)
1979	3,160	(40.0)	1,475	(29.2)	1,685	(27.2)	1,559	(45.1)	49.3	(1.28)	744	(31.4)	50.4	(1.88)	815	(32.4)	48.4	(1.76)
1980	3,088	(39.4)	1,498	(28.4)	1,589	(27.3)	1,523	(44.6)	49.3	(1.30)	700	(30.9)	46.7	(1.86)	823	(32.0)	51.8	(1.81)
1981	3,056	(42.2)	1,491	(30.4)	1,565	(29.1)	1,648	(45.8)	53.9	(1.30)	817	(32.4)	54.8	(1.86)	831	(32.4)	53.1	(1.82)
1982	3,100	(40.4)	1,509	(29.0)	1,592	(28.2)	1,569	(46.9)	50.6	(1.36)	741	(32.7)	49.1	(1.95)	828	(33.6)	52.0	(1.90)
1983	2,963	(41.6)	1,389	(30.4)	1,573	(28.2)	1,562	(46.7)	52.7	(1.39)	721	(32.3)	51.9	(2.03)	841	(33.6)	53.4	(1.91)
1984	3,012	(36.5)	1,429	(28.7)	1,584	(21.9)	1,663	(46.0)	55.2	(1.37)	801	(32.7)	56.0	(1.99)	862	(32.3)	54.5	(1.90)
1985	2,668	(40.1)	1,287	(28.7)	1,381	(27.9)	1,540	(45.1)	57.7	(1.45)	755	(31.6)	58.6	(2.08)	785	(32.1)	56.8	(2.02)
1986	2,786	(38.6)	1,332	(28.5)	1,454	(26.0)	1,498	(45.0)	53.8	(1.43)	743	(31.7)	55.8	(2.06)	755	(31.9)	51.9	(1.99)
1987	2,647	(40.9)	1,278	(29.8)	1,369	(28.0)	1,503	(45.1)	56.8	(1.46)	746	(31.9)	58.3	(2.09)	757	(31.9)	55.3	(2.04)
1988	2,673	(47.0)	1,334	(34.1)	1,339	(32.3)	1,575	(50.3)	58.9	(1.57)	761	(35.6)	57.1	(2.24)	814	(35.4)	60.7	(2.20)
1989	2,450	(46.5)	1,204	(32.9)	1,246	(32.8)	1,460	(48.7)	59.6	(1.64)	693	(34.0)	57.6	(2.35)	767	(34.8)	61.6	(2.27)
1990	2,362	(43.0)	1,173	(30.6)	1,189	(30.2)	1,420	(45.9)	60.1	(1.60)	680	(32.2)	58.0	(2.29)	740	(32.6)	62.2	(2.24)
1991	2,276	(41.0)	1,140	(29.0)	1,136	(29.0)	1,423	(44.8)	62.5	(1.62)	660	(31.4)	57.9	(2.33)	763	(31.9)	67.1	(2.22)
1992	2,397	(40.4)	1,216	(29.1)	1,180	(28.1)	1,483	(45.4)	61.9	(1.58)	729	(32.3)	60.0	(2.24)	754	(31.8)	63.8	(2.23)
1993	2,342	(41.4)	1,120	(30.6)	1,223	(27.7)	1,467	(45.4)	62.6	(1.59)	670	(31.9)	59.9	(2.33)	797	(32.1)	65.2	(2.17)
1994	2,517	(38.1)	1,244	(27.9)	1,273	(25.9)	1,559	(43.0)	61.9	(1.43)	754	(30.6)	60.6	(2.05)	805	(30.2)	63.2	(1.99)
1995	2,599	(40.9)	1,238	(29.9)	1,361	(27.7)	1,610	(44.5)	61.9	(1.41)	775	(31.3)	62.6	(2.03)	835	(31.5)	61.3	(1.95)
1996	2,660	(40.5)	1,297	(29.5)	1,363	(27.7)	1,729	(46.1)	65.0	(1.42)	779	(32.4)	60.1	(2.09)	950	(32.5)	69.7	(1.92)
1997	2,769	(41.8)	1,354	(31.0)	1,415	(27.9)	1,856	(47.3)	67.0	(1.38)	860	(33.6)	63.6	(2.01)	995	(32.9)	70.3	(1.87)
1998	2,810	(43.9)	1,452	(31.0)	1,358	(31.0)	1,844	(48.3)	65.6	(1.38)	906	(34.4)	62.4	(1.96)	938	(33.9)	69.1	(1.93)
1999	2,897	(41.5)	1,474	(29.9)	1,423	(28.8)	1,822	(47.8)	62.9	(1.38)	905	(34.1)	61.4	(1.95)	917	(33.4)	64.4	(1.95)
2000	2,756	(45.3)	1,251	(33.6)	1,505	(29.7)	1,745	(48.4)	63.3	(1.41)	749	(33.4)	59.9	(2.13)	996	(34.4)	66.2	(1.88)
2001	2,549	(46.5)	1,277	(33.7)	1,273	(32.0)	1,574	(47.5)	61.8	(1.48)	767	(33.7)	60.1	(2.11)	808	(33.3)	63.5	(2.08)
2002	2,796	(42.7)	1,412	(31.3)	1,384	(29.0)	1,824	(46.1)	65.2	(1.31)	877	(33.0)	62.1	(1.88)	947	(32.1)	68.4	(1.82)
2003	2,677	(42.2)	1,306	(29.9)	1,372	(29.7)	1,711	(45.2)	63.9	(1.35)	799	(31.5)	61.2	(1.97)	913	(32.3)	66.5	(1.86)
2004	2,752	(40.0)	1,327	(29.1)	1,425	(27.3)	1,835	(44.9)	66.7	(1.31)	815	(31.5)	61.4	(1.95)	1,020	(31.6)	71.5	(1.74)
2005	2,675	(40.8)	1,262	(31.5)	1,414	(24.9)	1,834	(44.8)	68.6	(1.31)	839	(32.2)	66.5	(1.94)	995	(30.6)	70.4	(1.77)

[1]Individuals ages 16 to 24 who graduated from high school or completed a GED during the preceding 12 months.
[2]Enrollment in college as of October of each year for individuals ages 16 to 24 who completed high school during the preceding 12 months.
NOTE: Data are based on sample surveys of the civilian population. High school completion data in this table differ from figures appearing in other tables because of varying survey procedures and coverage. High school completers include GED recipients. Some data have been revised from previously published figures. Standard errors appear in parentheses. Detail may not sum to totals because of rounding.
SOURCE: American College Testing Program, unpublished tabulations, derived from statistics collected by the Census Bureau, 1960 through 1969. U.S. Department of Commerce, Census Bureau, Current Population Survey (CPS), October 1970 through October 2005, unpublished tabulations. (This table was prepared May 2006.)

Table 187. College enrollment and enrollment rates of recent high school completers, by race/ethnicity: 1960 through 2005
[Numbers in thousands]

Year	Number of high school completers[1]				Enrolled in college[2]								
	Total	White	Black[3]	Hispanic[3]	Total		White		Black[3]		Hispanic[3]		
					Number	Percent	Number	Percent	Number	Percent	Number	Percent Annual	3-year moving average
1	2	3	4	5	6	7	8	9	10	11	12	13	14
1960	1,679 (43.8)	1,565 (44.7)	— (†)	— (†)	758 (40.9)	45.1 (2.13)	717 (40.2)	45.8 (2.21)	— (†)	— (†)	— (†)	— (†)	— (†)
1961	1,763 (46.0)	1,612 (46.9)	— (†)	— (†)	847 (42.9)	48.0 (2.09)	798 (42.2)	49.5 (2.19)	— (†)	— (†)	— (†)	— (†)	— (†)
1962	1,838 (43.6)	1,660 (45.2)	— (†)	— (†)	900 (43.2)	49.0 (2.05)	840 (42.4)	50.6 (2.15)	— (†)	— (†)	— (†)	— (†)	— (†)
1963	1,741 (44.2)	1,615 (45.2)	— (†)	— (†)	784 (41.5)	45.0 (2.09)	736 (40.7)	45.6 (2.17)	— (†)	— (†)	— (†)	— (†)	— (†)
1964	2,145 (43.0)	1,964 (45.4)	— (†)	— (†)	1,037 (45.6)	48.3 (1.89)	967 (44.8)	49.2 (1.98)	— (†)	— (†)	— (†)	— (†)	— (†)
1965	2,659 (47.7)	2,417 (50.6)	— (†)	— (†)	1,354 (51.4)	50.9 (1.70)	1,249 (50.4)	51.7 (1.78)	— (†)	— (†)	— (†)	— (†)	— (†)
1966	2,612 (45.0)	2,403 (48.0)	— (†)	— (†)	1,309 (50.2)	50.1 (1.72)	1,243 (49.6)	51.7 (1.79)	— (†)	— (†)	— (†)	— (†)	— (†)
1967	2,525 (37.9)	2,267 (40.3)	— (†)	— (†)	1,311 (40.9)	51.9 (1.42)	1,202 (40.1)	53.0 (1.50)	— (†)	— (†)	— (†)	— (†)	— (†)
1968	2,606 (37.3)	2,303 (40.4)	— (†)	— (†)	1,444 (41.7)	55.4 (1.39)	1,304 (40.9)	56.6 (1.47)	— (†)	— (†)	— (†)	— (†)	— (†)
1969	2,842 (36.0)	2,538 (39.8)	— (†)	— (†)	1,516 (42.5)	53.3 (1.34)	1,402 (42.0)	55.2 (1.41)	— (†)	— (†)	— (†)	— (†)	— (†)
1970	2,758 (37.4)	2,461 (40.7)	— (†)	— (†)	1,427 (42.2)	51.7 (1.36)	1,280 (41.2)	52.0 (1.44)	— (†)	— (†)	— (†)	— (†)	— (†)
1971	2,875 (38.0)	2,596 (41.1)	— (†)	— (†)	1,538 (43.2)	53.5 (1.33)	1,402 (42.5)	54.0 (1.40)	— (†)	— (†)	— (†)	— (†)	— (†)
1972	2,964 (37.8)	2,520 (31.2)	316 (18.3)	101 (14.2)	1,459 (43.0)	49.2 (1.31)	1,252 (39.0)	49.7 (1.42)	141 (16.7)	44.6 (4.62)	46 (11.7)	45.0 (9.74)	— (†)
1973	3,058 (37.1)	2,590 (30.8)	324 (18.5)	119 (13.7)	1,424 (43.0)	46.6 (1.29)	1,238 (39.2)	47.8 (1.40)	105 (15.2)	32.5 (4.30)	64 (13.0)	54.1 (9.01)	48.7 (5.33)
1974	3,101 (38.6)	2,620 (31.4)	325 (19.0)	121 (15.2)	1,475 (43.7)	47.6 (1.28)	1,236 (39.4)	47.2 (1.39)	154 (17.4)	47.2 (4.58)	57 (12.9)	46.9 (8.94)	33.7 (6.01)
1975	3,185 (38.6)	2,701 (31.9)	302 (15.4)	132 (15.8)	1,615 (44.8)	50.7 (1.26)	1,381 (40.5)	51.1 (1.37)	126 (13.6)	41.7 (3.97)	77 (14.5)	58.0 (8.44)	36.9 (5.63)
1976	2,986 (39.8)	2,492 (33.1)	290 (15.8)	152 (16.2)	1,458 (43.6)	48.8 (1.31)	1,217 (39.1)	48.8 (1.43)	129 (13.8)	44.4 (4.08)	80 (14.8)	52.7 (7.97)	53.8 (4.68)
1977	3,141 (40.7)	2,618 (34.0)	325 (19.3)	155 (16.0)	1,590 (45.4)	50.6 (1.29)	1,331 (40.8)	50.8 (1.41)	161 (17.9)	49.5 (4.65)	79 (14.8)	50.8 (7.96)	48.5 (4.72)
1978	3,163 (39.7)	2,615 (33.7)	345 (18.4)	135 (15.3)	1,585 (45.2)	50.1 (1.28)	1,321 (40.6)	50.5 (1.41)	160 (17.7)	46.4 (4.51)	56 (13.0)	42.0 (8.44)	45.9 (4.69)
1979	3,160 (40.0)	2,629 (32.7)	319 (19.7)	155 (16.1)	1,559 (45.1)	49.3 (1.28)	1,313 (40.5)	49.9 (1.41)	149 (17.5)	46.7 (4.69)	70 (14.3)	45.0 (7.92)	46.4 (4.83)
1980	3,088 (39.4)	2,554 (30.9)	350 (19.7)	130 (17.1)	1,523 (44.6)	49.3 (1.30)	1,273 (39.6)	49.8 (1.43)	149 (17.7)	42.7 (4.44)	68 (14.4)	52.3 (8.70)	49.8 (4.78)
1981	3,056 (42.2)	2,490 (34.1)	349 (20.5)	146 (17.6)	1,648 (45.8)	53.9 (1.30)	1,367 (40.5)	54.9 (1.44)	149 (17.8)	42.7 (4.44)	76 (15.1)	52.1 (8.19)	49.2 (4.68)
1982	3,100 (40.4)	2,474 (32.9)	382 (19.6)	173 (18.2)	1,569 (46.9)	50.6 (1.36)	1,303 (41.5)	52.7 (1.52)	137 (17.9)	35.8 (4.33)	75 (15.8)	43.2 (7.96)	49.8 (4.94)
1983	2,963 (41.6)	2,363 (33.1)	390 (21.1)	138 (17.8)	1,562 (46.7)	52.7 (1.39)	1,301 (40.9)	55.0 (1.55)	149 (18.7)	38.2 (4.34)	75 (15.7)	54.2 (8.96)	47.3 (4.73)
1984	3,012 (36.5)	2,331 (29.1)	433 (18.5)	187 (17.0)	1,663 (46.0)	55.2 (1.37)	1,375 (39.9)	59.0 (1.54)	172 (19.4)	39.8 (4.15)	83 (16.2)	44.3 (7.67)	49.9 (4.89)
1985	2,668 (40.1)	2,104 (32.3)	332 (19.3)	141 (19.7)	1,540 (45.1)	57.7 (1.45)	1,264 (39.2)	60.1 (1.62)	140 (17.8)	42.2 (4.78)	72 (17.0)	51.0 (9.76)	46.5 (5.19)
1986	2,786 (38.6)	2,146 (30.3)	378 (18.4)	169 (21.7)	1,498 (45.0)	53.8 (1.43)	1,219 (38.8)	56.8 (1.62)	140 (17.9)	36.9 (4.38)	74 (17.7)	44.0 (8.85)	42.9 (5.21)
1987	2,647 (40.9)	2,040 (32.4)	333 (20.6)	176 (20.9)	1,503 (45.1)	56.8 (1.46)	1,195 (38.7)	58.6 (1.65)	174 (19.3)	52.2 (4.82)	59 (16.1)	33.5 (8.25)	44.9 (5.04)
1988	2,673 (47.0)	2,013 (37.9)	378 (22.3)	179 (26.6)	1,575 (50.3)	58.9 (1.57)	1,230 (42.9)	61.1 (1.79)	168 (21.1)	44.4 (4.91)	102 (23.6)	57.1 (10.14)	48.6 (5.99)
1989	2,450 (46.5)	1,889 (37.3)	332 (21.3)	168 (26.5)	1,460 (48.7)	59.6 (1.64)	1,147 (41.7)	60.7 (1.85)	177 (20.9)	53.4 (5.27)	93 (22.9)	55.1 (10.51)	51.6 (6.33)
1990	2,362 (43.0)	1,819 (32.2)	331 (21.9)	121 (21.8)	1,420 (45.9)	60.1 (1.60)	1,147 (38.5)	63.0 (1.80)	155 (19.7)	46.8 (5.08)	52 (16.0)	42.7 (10.82)	51.7 (5.70)
1991	2,276 (41.0)	1,727 (30.3)	310 (20.2)	154 (23.5)	1,423 (44.8)	62.5 (1.62)	1,129 (37.2)	65.4 (1.82)	144 (18.8)	46.4 (5.25)	88 (19.9)	57.2 (9.58)	51.6 (5.52)
1992	2,397 (40.4)	1,724 (30.9)	354 (21.4)	198 (23.0)	1,483 (45.4)	61.9 (1.58)	1,109 (37.4)	64.3 (1.84)	171 (20.2)	48.2 (4.92)	109 (21.0)	55.0 (8.50)	58.1 (5.04)
1993	2,342 (41.4)	1,719 (32.6)	304 (20.4)	201 (23.1)	1,467 (45.4)	62.6 (1.59)	1,082 (37.9)	62.9 (1.85)	169 (19.6)	55.6 (5.28)	125 (21.9)	62.2 (8.22)	55.4 (4.97)
1994	2,517 (38.1)	1,915 (27.0)	316 (17.9)	178 (17.3)	1,559 (43.0)	61.9 (1.43)	1,236 (35.5)	64.5 (1.61)	161 (16.7)	50.8 (4.42)	87 (14.0)	49.1 (6.28)	55.0 (3.23)

See notes at end of table.

Table 187. College enrollment and enrollment rates of recent high school completers, by race/ethnicity: 1960 through 2005—Continued

[Numbers in thousands]

Year	Number of high school completers[1]				Enrolled in college[2]									
	Total	White	Black[3]	Hispanic[3]	Total		White		Black[3]		Hispanic[3]			
					Number	Percent	Number	Percent	Number	Percent	Number	Percent (Annual)	Percent (3-year moving average)	
1	2	3	4	5	6	7	8	9	10	11	12	13	14
1995	2,599 (40.9)	1,861 (30.1)	349 (19.2)	288 (19.4)	1,610 (44.5)	61.9 (1.41)	1,197 (36.1)	64.3 (1.64)	179 (17.6)	51.2 (4.20)	155 (17.6)	53.7 (4.92)	51.2 (3.18)
1996	2,660 (40.5)	1,875 (30.8)	406 (17.3)	227 (18.9)	1,729 (46.1)	65.0 (1.42)	1,264 (37.5)	67.4 (1.67)	227 (19.0)	56.0 (4.03)	115 (16.3)	50.8 (5.79)	56.7 (2.97)
1997	2,769 (41.8)	1,909 (31.8)	384 (19.2)	336 (19.0)	1,856 (47.3)	67.0 (1.38)	1,301 (38.1)	68.2 (1.64)	225 (19.4)	58.5 (4.12)	220 (19.7)	65.6 (4.53)	54.6 (2.94)
1998	2,810 (43.9)	1,980 (33.0)	386 (20.2)	314 (20.8)	1,844 (48.3)	65.6 (1.38)	1,357 (39.0)	68.5 (1.61)	239 (20.0)	61.9 (4.05)	149 (18.3)	47.4 (4.92)	51.8 (2.79)
1999	2,897 (41.5)	1,978 (31.8)	436 (15.2)	329 (20.9)	1,822 (47.8)	62.9 (1.38)	1,311 (38.6)	66.3 (1.64)	257 (19.1)	58.9 (3.86)	139 (18.0)	42.3 (4.76)	47.5 (2.84)
2000	2,756 (45.3)	1,938 (32.9)	393 (20.0)	300 (22.4)	1,745 (48.4)	63.3 (1.41)	1,272 (38.8)	65.7 (1.66)	216 (19.5)	54.9 (4.11)	159 (19.2)	52.9 (5.03)	49.0 (2.96)
2001	2,549 (46.5)	1,834 (34.8)	381 (20.3)	241 (21.1)	1,574 (47.5)	61.8 (1.48)	1,178 (38.7)	64.3 (1.72)	210 (19.4)	55.0 (4.17)	124 (17.4)	51.7 (5.63)	52.7 (2.93)
2002	2,796 (42.7)	1,903 (31.3)	382 (19.1)	344 (21.6)	1,824 (46.1)	65.2 (1.31)	1,314 (36.5)	69.1 (1.55)	227 (18.7)	59.4 (3.90)	184 (19.2)	53.6 (4.46)	54.6 (2.75)
2003[4]	2,677 (42.2)	1,832 (30.8)	327 (18.4)	314 (20.9)	1,711 (45.2)	63.9 (1.35)	1,213 (35.9)	66.2 (1.61)	188 (17.4)	57.5 (4.25)	184 (18.9)	58.6 (4.61)	58.0 (2.66)
2004[4]	2,752 (40.0)	1,854 (30.9)	398 (15.5)	286 (19.9)	1,835 (44.9)	66.7 (1.31)	1,276 (36.1)	68.8 (1.57)	249 (17.9)	62.5 (3.77)	177 (18.4)	61.8 (4.76)	58.1 (2.60)
2005[4]	2,675 (40.8)	1,799 (30.5)	345 (16.6)	390 (20.6)	1,834 (44.8)	68.6 (1.31)	1,317 (35.4)	73.2 (1.52)	192 (17.1)	55.7 (4.15)	211 (19.7)	54.0 (4.18)	— (†)

—Not available.
†Not applicable.
[1]Individuals ages 16 to 24 who graduated from high school or completed a GED during the preceding 12 months.
[2]Enrollment in college as of October of each year for individuals ages 16 to 24 who completed high school during the preceding 12 months.
[3]Due to the small sample size, data are subject to relatively large sampling errors.
[4]White and Black data exclude persons identifying themselves as multiracial.

NOTE: High school completion data in this table differ from figures appearing in other tables because of varying survey procedures and coverage. High school completers include GED recipients. Moving averages are used to produce more stable estimates. Race categories exclude persons of Hispanic origin. Standard errors appear in parentheses.
SOURCE: American College Testing Program, unpublished tabulations, derived from statistics collected by the Census Bureau, 1960 through 1969. U.S. Department of Commerce, Census Bureau, Current Population Survey (CPS), October 1970 through October 2005, unpublished tabulations. (This table was prepared May 2006.)

Table 188. Graduation rates of previous year's 12th-graders and college attendance rates of those who graduated, by selected high school characteristics: 1999–2000 and 2003–04

Selected high school characteristic	For 1998–99 school year		College attendance rate of 1998–99 graduates in 1999–2000			For 2002–03 school year		College attendance rate of 2002–03 graduates in 2003–04		
	Number of high schools with 12th-graders	Graduation rate of 12th-graders[1]	Total	4-year institutions	2-year institutions	Number of high schools with 12th-graders	Graduation rate of 12th-graders[1]	Total	4-year institutions	2-year institutions
1	2	3	4	5	6	7	8	9	10	11
Public high schools	**20,000 (230)**	**91.4 (0.32)**	**66.8 (0.41)**	**42.9 (0.47)**	**24.0 (0.30)**	**22,500 (400)**	**89.8 (0.50)**	**72.3 (0.39)**	**44.1 (0.62)**	**28.2 (0.59)**
Percent minority students										
Less than 5 percent	6,400 (170)	94.9 (0.28)	65.5 (0.75)	45.8 (0.74)	19.7 (0.43)	6,100 (220)	92.7 (1.41)	70.4 (0.84)	45.6 (0.89)	24.8 (0.60)
5 to 19 percent	4,800 (180)	93.6 (0.34)	68.4 (0.80)	45.9 (0.89)	22.5 (0.53)	5,200 (270)	92.0 (1.12)	75.4 (0.71)	50.1 (1.05)	25.4 (0.74)
20 to 49 percent	4,000 (170)	91.3 (0.45)	67.0 (0.93)	41.8 (0.88)	25.2 (0.70)	4,700 (180)	90.8 (0.68)	72.1 (0.80)	43.7 (1.09)	28.4 (1.07)
50 percent or more	4,800 (150)	86.7 (1.00)	66.1 (0.82)	38.2 (1.01)	27.9 (0.79)	6,500 (280)	85.5 (1.01)	71.0 (1.09)	38.3 (1.35)	32.7 (1.21)
Community type										
Central city	3,600 (150)	87.9 (0.80)	69.3 (0.86)	43.8 (1.00)	25.5 (0.80)	4,400 (260)	85.9 (1.08)	73.3 (1.00)	45.6 (1.41)	27.7 (1.14)
Urban fringe/large town	7,900 (170)	92.6 (0.36)	68.8 (0.70)	44.3 (0.66)	24.5 (0.43)	9,400 (300)	90.9 (0.78)	74.5 (0.46)	45.5 (0.89)	29.0 (0.84)
Rural/small town	8,500 (180)	93.0 (0.44)	59.3 (0.54)	38.3 (0.52)	21.0 (0.40)	8,700 (290)	92.7 (0.43)	65.0 (0.59)	38.1 (0.68)	26.9 (0.54)
Private high schools	**7,600 (240)**	**99.1 (0.11)**	**89.5 (0.62)**	**76.5 (0.87)**	**13.0 (0.48)**	**8,200 (260)**	**98.2 (0.27)**	**92.8 (0.63)**	**79.5 (1.12)**	**13.3 (0.73)**
Percent minority students										
Less than 5 percent	2,700 (150)	98.5 (0.41)	86.4 (0.99)	71.5 (1.52)	14.9 (1.08)	2,500 (180)	97.2 (0.87)	89.0 (1.77)	73.8 (2.86)	15.3 (1.60)
5 to 19 percent	2,500 (130)	99.4 (0.08)	91.5 (0.91)	81.3 (1.13)	10.2 (0.58)	2,900 (170)	99.0 (0.18)	94.1 (0.70)	82.6 (1.58)	11.5 (1.18)
20 to 49 percent	1,400 (100)	99.0 (0.15)	92.7 (0.89)	79.0 (1.55)	13.6 (1.47)	1,700 (140)	97.6 (0.43)	94.7 (1.06)	83.4 (1.94)	11.3 (1.45)
50 percent or more	1,000 (110)	99.0 (0.29)	84.0 (3.08)	66.6 (4.69)	17.4 (2.10)	1,100 (140)	97.9 (0.48)	92.4 (1.67)	73.2 (2.91)	19.2 (2.34)
Community type										
Central city	2,900 (150)	99.0 (0.20)	90.7 (0.79)	78.0 (1.30)	12.6 (0.76)	2,500 (180)	97.9 (0.53)	94.0 (1.01)	81.9 (1.70)	12.1 (1.05)
Urban fringe/large town	2,900 (150)	99.3 (0.09)	90.1 (0.86)	76.9 (1.31)	13.1 (0.82)	4,000 (220)	98.3 (0.26)	92.5 (0.72)	79.2 (1.27)	13.3 (1.03)
Rural/small town	1,800 (140)	98.5 (0.33)	80.5 (2.40)	66.3 (2.63)	14.2 (1.48)	1,700 (150)	98.5 (0.34)	89.5 (1.87)	71.3 (3.82)	18.2 (2.81)

[1]Includes only students who were enrolled in 12th grade in fall of the school year and graduated with a diploma by the end of the following summer.

NOTE: Data are based on a sample survey and may not be strictly comparable with data reported elsewhere. Includes all schools, including combined schools, with students enrolled in the 12th grade. Some data have been revised from previously published figures. Detail may not sum to totals because of rounding. Standard errors appear in parentheses.

SOURCE: U.S. Department of Education, National Center for Education Statistics, Schools and Staffing Survey (SASS), "Public School Questionnaire," 1999–2000 and 2003–04, "Private School Questionnaire," 1999–2000 and 2003–04, and "Charter School Questionnaire," 1999–2000. (This table was prepared August 2006.)

Table 189. Enrollment rates of 18- to 24-year-olds in degree-granting institutions, by sex and race/ethnicity: 1967 through 2005

	Enrollment as a percent of all 18- to 24-year-olds						Enrollment as a percent of all 18- to 24-year-old high school completers[1]					
		Sex		Race/ethnicity				Sex		Race/ethnicity		
Year	Total	Male	Female	White	Black	Hispanic	Total	Male	Female	White	Black	Hispanic
1	2	3	4	5	6	7	8	9	10	11	12	13
1967[2]	25.5 (0.44)	33.1 (0.71)	19.2 (0.54)	26.9 (0.48)	13.0 (1.16)	— (†)	33.7 (0.55)	44.7 (0.87)	25.1 (0.67)	34.5 (0.58)	23.3 (1.96)	— (†)
1968[2]	26.1 (0.44)	34.1 (0.70)	19.5 (0.53)	27.5 (0.48)	14.5 (1.18)	— (†)	34.2 (0.54)	45.9 (0.86)	25.0 (0.66)	34.9 (0.57)	25.2 (1.92)	— (†)
1969[2]	27.3 (0.44)	35.2 (0.69)	20.9 (0.54)	28.7 (0.47)	16.0 (1.20)	— (†)	35.0 (0.53)	45.6 (0.82)	26.4 (0.65)	35.6 (0.56)	27.2 (1.90)	— (†)
1970[2]	25.7 (0.42)	32.1 (0.65)	20.3 (0.52)	27.1 (0.45)	15.5 (1.15)	— (†)	32.6 (0.50)	41.0 (0.78)	25.5 (0.63)	33.2 (0.53)	26.0 (1.81)	— (†)
1971[2]	26.2 (0.41)	32.5 (0.63)	20.8 (0.52)	27.2 (0.44)	18.2 (1.19)	— (†)	33.2 (0.49)	41.5 (0.76)	26.0 (0.63)	33.5 (0.52)	29.2 (1.78)	— (†)
1972	25.5 (0.37)	30.2 (0.56)	21.2 (0.47)	27.2 (0.41)	18.3 (1.18)	13.4 (1.83)	31.9 (0.44)	38.2 (0.66)	26.3 (0.57)	32.6 (0.48)	27.2 (1.65)	25.8 (3.27)
1973	24.0 (0.35)	27.7 (0.54)	20.5 (0.46)	25.5 (0.40)	15.9 (1.09)	16.1 (2.02)	29.7 (0.42)	34.6 (0.63)	25.3 (0.55)	30.2 (0.46)	23.8 (1.55)	29.1 (3.36)
1974	24.6 (0.35)	27.7 (0.53)	21.7 (0.47)	25.8 (0.40)	17.6 (1.14)	18.0 (1.95)	30.5 (0.42)	34.7 (0.63)	26.7 (0.56)	30.5 (0.46)	26.2 (1.60)	32.3 (3.17)
1975	26.3 (0.36)	29.0 (0.53)	23.7 (0.48)	27.4 (0.40)	20.4 (1.18)	20.4 (2.09)	32.5 (0.42)	36.2 (0.63)	29.2 (0.57)	32.3 (0.46)	31.5 (1.69)	35.5 (3.27)
1976	26.7 (0.35)	28.2 (0.52)	25.2 (0.48)	27.6 (0.40)	22.5 (1.20)	20.0 (2.00)	33.1 (0.42)	35.6 (0.62)	30.9 (0.57)	32.8 (0.46)	33.4 (1.66)	35.9 (3.22)
1977	26.1 (0.38)	28.1 (0.56)	24.3 (0.52)	27.2 (0.43)	21.1 (1.18)	17.2 (1.87)	32.5 (0.46)	35.6 (0.68)	29.7 (0.61)	32.3 (0.50)	31.3 (1.63)	31.5 (3.11)
1978	25.3 (0.38)	27.1 (0.55)	23.6 (0.51)	26.5 (0.43)	20.1 (1.15)	15.2 (1.74)	31.4 (0.45)	34.1 (0.66)	28.8 (0.60)	31.3 (0.49)	29.6 (1.59)	27.2 (2.89)
1979	25.0 (0.37)	25.9 (0.54)	24.2 (0.52)	26.3 (0.43)	19.8 (1.13)	16.7 (1.77)	31.2 (0.45)	32.9 (0.66)	29.6 (0.61)	31.3 (0.49)	29.4 (1.58)	30.2 (2.93)
1980	25.7 (0.38)	26.4 (0.54)	25.0 (0.52)	27.3 (0.43)	19.4 (1.12)	16.1 (1.64)	31.8 (0.45)	33.5 (0.66)	30.3 (0.61)	32.1 (0.49)	27.6 (1.51)	29.9 (2.80)
1981	26.1 (0.37)	27.1 (0.54)	25.2 (0.51)	27.7 (0.43)	19.9 (1.09)	16.6 (1.63)	32.4 (0.44)	34.7 (0.65)	30.4 (0.60)	32.7 (0.49)	28.0 (1.46)	29.9 (2.69)
1982	26.6 (0.39)	27.2 (0.57)	26.0 (0.55)	28.1 (0.46)	19.9 (1.14)	16.8 (1.77)	33.0 (0.47)	34.5 (0.68)	31.6 (0.64)	33.3 (0.52)	28.1 (1.52)	29.2 (2.83)
1983	26.2 (0.39)	27.3 (0.57)	25.1 (0.54)	27.9 (0.46)	19.2 (1.12)	17.3 (1.77)	32.5 (0.47)	35.0 (0.69)	30.3 (0.63)	33.0 (0.52)	27.0 (1.50)	31.5 (2.94)
1984	27.1 (0.40)	28.6 (0.58)	25.6 (0.55)	28.9 (0.47)	20.3 (1.15)	17.9 (1.80)	33.2 (0.47)	36.0 (0.70)	30.6 (0.64)	33.9 (0.53)	27.2 (1.47)	29.9 (2.77)
1985	27.8 (0.41)	28.4 (0.60)	27.2 (0.57)	30.0 (0.49)	19.6 (1.16)	16.9 (1.84)	33.7 (0.48)	35.3 (0.70)	32.3 (0.65)	34.9 (0.55)	26.0 (1.47)	26.8 (2.75)
1986	27.9 (0.42)	28.2 (0.60)	27.6 (0.58)	29.7 (0.50)	21.9 (1.21)	17.6 (1.76)	34.0 (0.49)	35.3 (0.71)	32.8 (0.67)	34.5 (0.56)	28.6 (1.52)	29.4 (2.72)
1987	29.6 (0.43)	30.6 (0.62)	28.7 (0.59)	31.9 (0.51)	22.8 (1.25)	17.5 (1.73)	36.2 (0.50)	38.3 (0.73)	34.4 (0.68)	37.3 (0.58)	29.5 (1.54)	28.4 (2.61)
1988	30.3 (0.47)	30.2 (0.68)	30.4 (0.66)	33.2 (0.57)	21.2 (1.33)	17.0 (2.00)	37.2 (0.55)	38.3 (0.81)	36.3 (0.75)	38.6 (0.63)	28.1 (1.69)	30.8 (3.31)
1989	30.9 (0.48)	30.2 (0.68)	31.6 (0.67)	34.2 (0.58)	23.4 (1.38)	16.1 (1.90)	38.1 (0.56)	38.3 (0.81)	37.9 (0.77)	39.8 (0.65)	30.7 (1.72)	28.7 (3.12)
1990	32.0 (0.47)	32.3 (0.68)	31.8 (0.66)	35.1 (0.57)	25.4 (1.37)	15.8 (1.67)	39.1 (0.54)	40.0 (0.79)	38.3 (0.75)	40.4 (0.63)	32.7 (1.68)	28.7 (2.79)
1991	33.3 (0.48)	32.8 (0.68)	33.6 (0.67)	36.8 (0.58)	23.5 (1.34)	17.9 (1.72)	41.0 (0.55)	41.5 (0.80)	40.5 (0.77)	42.4 (0.64)	31.2 (1.68)	34.3 (2.94)
1992	34.4 (0.49)	32.7 (0.68)	36.0 (0.69)	37.3 (0.59)	25.2 (1.37)	21.3 (1.87)	41.7 (0.56)	40.7 (0.80)	42.7 (0.77)	42.6 (0.64)	33.5 (1.71)	36.8 (2.90)
1993	34.0 (0.49)	33.6 (0.69)	34.4 (0.68)	36.8 (0.59)	24.5 (1.35)	21.7 (1.88)	41.3 (0.56)	41.7 (0.80)	40.9 (0.77)	42.3 (0.65)	32.4 (1.69)	35.5 (2.79)
1994	34.6 (0.42)	33.1 (0.59)	36.0 (0.60)	38.1 (0.53)	27.7 (1.17)	18.8 (1.10)	42.3 (0.49)	41.6 (0.70)	43.0 (0.68)	43.7 (0.57)	35.6 (1.42)	33.1 (1.76)
1995	34.3 (0.44)	33.1 (0.63)	35.5 (0.63)	37.9 (0.55)	27.5 (1.18)	20.7 (1.13)	42.3 (0.51)	41.7 (0.73)	43.0 (0.72)	44.0 (0.61)	35.4 (1.43)	35.2 (1.74)
1996	35.5 (0.47)	34.1 (0.66)	37.0 (0.67)	39.5 (0.59)	27.4 (1.23)	20.1 (1.18)	43.4 (0.54)	42.5 (0.77)	44.3 (0.75)	45.1 (0.64)	35.9 (1.51)	34.5 (1.83)
1997	36.8 (0.47)	35.0 (0.66)	38.7 (0.67)	40.6 (0.59)	29.8 (1.25)	22.4 (1.21)	45.2 (0.54)	44.0 (0.77)	46.3 (0.75)	46.6 (0.64)	39.5 (1.54)	36.0 (1.77)
1998	36.5 (0.46)	34.5 (0.65)	38.6 (0.66)	40.6 (0.59)	29.8 (1.24)	20.4 (1.11)	45.2 (0.53)	44.3 (0.77)	46.1 (0.74)	46.9 (0.64)	40.0 (1.54)	33.9 (1.68)
1999	35.6 (0.46)	34.1 (0.64)	37.0 (0.65)	39.4 (0.58)	30.4 (1.24)	18.7 (1.08)	43.7 (0.52)	42.9 (0.75)	44.4 (0.73)	45.3 (0.63)	39.2 (1.50)	31.6 (1.68)
2000	35.5 (0.45)	32.6 (0.62)	38.4 (0.65)	38.7 (0.57)	30.5 (1.21)	21.7 (1.12)	43.2 (0.52)	40.8 (0.73)	45.6 (0.72)	44.1 (0.62)	39.3 (1.46)	36.2 (1.69)
2001	36.3 (0.45)	33.6 (0.63)	39.0 (0.64)	39.5 (0.57)	31.4 (1.22)	21.7 (1.10)	44.3 (0.51)	42.4 (0.73)	46.1 (0.72)	45.4 (0.62)	40.2 (1.45)	34.8 (1.61)
2002	36.7 (0.43)	33.7 (0.59)	39.7 (0.61)	40.9 (0.55)	31.9 (1.18)	19.9 (0.94)	44.7 (0.48)	42.5 (0.69)	46.7 (0.68)	46.7 (0.59)	40.2 (1.39)	31.6 (1.38)
2003[3]	37.8 (0.43)	34.3 (0.59)	41.3 (0.61)	41.6 (0.55)	32.3 (1.20)	23.5 (1.02)	45.7 (0.48)	42.8 (0.69)	48.3 (0.67)	47.2 (0.59)	41.4 (1.43)	35.8 (1.42)
2004[3]	38.0 (0.42)	34.7 (0.59)	41.2 (0.61)	41.7 (0.55)	31.8 (1.18)	24.7 (1.02)	45.8 (0.48)	43.0 (0.68)	48.4 (0.67)	47.4 (0.59)	40.8 (1.41)	37.3 (1.40)
2005[3]	38.9 (0.43)	35.3 (0.59)	42.5 (0.61)	42.8 (0.55)	33.1 (1.18)	24.8 (1.02)	46.8 (0.48)	44.3 (0.68)	49.1 (0.67)	48.6 (0.59)	41.4 (1.39)	37.4 (1.41)

—Not available.
†Not applicable.
[1]Includes students who were enrolled in college, but did not report high school completion.
[2]White and Black data include persons of Hispanic origin.
[3]White and Black data exclude persons identifying themselves as multiracial.
NOTE: Data are based on sample surveys of the civilian noninstitutional population. Percents based on 18- to 24-year-old high school completers for 1992 and later years use a slightly different definition of completion and may not be precisely comparable with figures for other years. All college students are counted as high school completers. Totals include other racial/ethnic groups not separately shown. Race categories exclude persons of Hispanic origin except where otherwise noted. Standard errors appear in parentheses.
SOURCE: U.S. Department of Commerce, Census Bureau, Current Population Survey (CPS), October 1967 through October 2005, unpublished tabulations. (This table was prepared May 2006.)

Table 190. Total undergraduate fall enrollment in degree-granting institutions, by attendance status, sex of student, and control of institution: 1969 through 2005

[In thousands]

						Males		Females		Males		Females	
Year	Total	Full-time	Part-time	Males	Females	Full-time	Part-time	Full-time	Part-time	Public	Private	Public	Private
1	2	3	4	5	6	7	8	9	10	11	12	13	14
1969	6,884	4,991	1,893	4,008	2,876	2,952	1,056	2,039	837	2,997	1,011	2,162	714
1970	7,376	5,280	2,096	4,254	3,122	3,097	1,157	2,183	939	3,241	1,013	2,387	735
1971	7,743	5,512	2,231	4,418	3,325	3,201	1,217	2,311	1,014	3,427	991	2,580	745
1972	7,941	5,488	2,453	4,429	3,512	3,121	1,308	2,367	1,145	3,467	962	2,756	756
1973	8,261	5,580	2,681	4,538	3,723	3,135	1,403	2,445	1,278	3,579	959	2,943	780
1974	8,798	5,726	3,072	4,765	4,033	3,191	1,574	2,535	1,498	3,799	966	3,232	801
1975	9,679	6,169	3,510	5,257	4,422	3,459	1,798	2,710	1,712	4,245	1,012	3,581	841
1976	9,429	6,030	3,399	4,902	4,527	3,242	1,660	2,788	1,739	3,949	953	3,668	859
1977	9,717	6,094	3,623	4,897	4,820	3,188	1,709	2,906	1,914	3,937	960	3,906	914
1978	9,691	5,967	3,724	4,766	4,925	3,072	1,694	2,895	2,030	3,812	954	3,974	951
1979	9,998	6,080	3,919	4,821	5,178	3,087	1,734	2,993	2,185	3,865	956	4,181	995
1980	10,475	6,362	4,113	5,000	5,475	3,227	1,773	3,135	2,340	4,014	985	4,427	1,048
1981	10,755	6,449	4,306	5,109	5,646	3,261	1,848	3,188	2,458	4,090	1,018	4,558	1,088
1982	10,825	6,484	4,341	5,170	5,655	3,299	1,871	3,184	2,470	4,140	1,031	4,573	1,081
1983	10,846	6,514	4,332	5,158	5,688	3,304	1,854	3,210	2,478	4,117	1,042	4,580	1,107
1984	10,618	6,348	4,270	5,007	5,611	3,195	1,812	3,153	2,459	3,990	1,017	4,504	1,107
1985	10,597	6,320	4,277	4,962	5,635	3,156	1,806	3,163	2,471	3,953	1,010	4,525	1,110
1986	10,798	6,352	4,446	5,018	5,780	3,146	1,871	3,206	2,575	4,002	1,015	4,658	1,122
1987	11,046	6,463	4,584	5,068	5,978	3,164	1,905	3,299	2,679	4,076	992	4,842	1,136
1988	11,317	6,642	4,674	5,138	6,179	3,206	1,931	3,436	2,743	4,113	1,024	4,990	1,189
1989	11,743	6,841	4,902	5,311	6,432	3,279	2,032	3,562	2,869	4,272	1,039	5,216	1,216
1990	11,959	6,976	4,983	5,380	6,579	3,337	2,043	3,639	2,940	4,353	1,027	5,357	1,223
1991	12,439	7,221	5,218	5,571	6,868	3,436	2,135	3,786	3,082	4,531	1,040	5,617	1,251
1992	12,538	7,244	5,293	5,583	6,955	3,425	2,158	3,820	3,135	4,537	1,046	5,679	1,275
1993	12,324	7,179	5,144	5,484	6,840	3,382	2,102	3,797	3,043	4,447	1,036	5,565	1,276
1994	12,263	7,169	5,094	5,422	6,840	3,342	2,081	3,827	3,013	4,394	1,028	5,551	1,290
1995	12,232	7,145	5,086	5,401	6,831	3,297	2,105	3,849	2,982	4,380	1,021	5,524	1,307
1996	12,327	7,299	5,028	5,421	6,906	3,339	2,082	3,960	2,947	4,383	1,038	5,553	1,354
1997	12,451	7,419	5,032	5,469	6,982	3,380	2,089	4,039	2,943	4,408	1,060	5,599	1,383
1998	12,437	7,539	4,898	5,446	6,991	3,428	2,018	4,111	2,880	4,361	1,085	5,589	1,402
1999[1]	12,681	7,735	4,946	5,559	7,122	3,516	2,044	4,219	2,903	4,431	1,128	5,679	1,443
2000	13,155	7,923	5,232	5,778	7,377	3,588	2,190	4,335	3,042	4,622	1,156	5,917	1,460
2001	13,716	8,328	5,388	6,004	7,711	3,769	2,236	4,559	3,152	4,804	1,200	6,182	1,529
2002	14,257	8,734	5,523	6,192	8,065	3,934	2,258	4,800	3,265	4,960	1,232	6,473	1,592
2003	14,474	9,035	5,439	6,224	8,250	4,044	2,180	4,991	3,259	4,956	1,269	6,566	1,684
2004	14,781	9,284	5,496	6,340	8,441	4,141	2,199	5,144	3,297	5,009	1,331	6,641	1,799
2005	14,964	9,446	5,518	6,409	8,555	4,201	2,208	5,246	3,310	5,046	1,363	6,652	1,903

[1]Data for 1999 were imputed using alternative procedures. (See Guide to Sources for details.) NOTE: Data include unclassified undergraduate students. Data through 1995 are for institutions of higher education, while later data are for degree-granting institutions. Degree-granting institutions grant associate's or higher degrees and participate in Title IV federal financial aid programs. The degree-granting classification is very similar to the earlier higher education classification, but it includes more 2-year colleges and excludes

a few higher education institutions that did not grant degrees. (See Guide to Sources for details.) Detail may not sum to totals because of rounding.
SOURCE: U.S. Department of Education, National Center for Education Statistics, Higher Education General Information Survey (HEGIS), "Fall Enrollment in Colleges and Universities" surveys, 1969 through 1985; and 1986 through 2005 Integrated Postsecondary Education Data System, "Fall Enrollment Survey" (IPEDS-EF:86–99), and Spring 2001 through Spring 2006. (This table was prepared August 2006.)

Table 191. Total graduate fall enrollment in degree-granting institutions, by attendance status, sex of student, and control of institution: 1969 through 2005

[In thousands]

						Males		Females		Males		Females	
Year	Total	Full-time	Part-time	Males	Females	Full-time	Part-time	Full-time	Part-time	Public	Private	Public	Private
1	2	3	4	5	6	7	8	9	10	11	12	13	14
1969	955	363	593	590	366	252	338	111	255	393	197	273	93
1970	1,031	379	651	630	400	264	366	115	285	423	207	301	99
1971	1,012	388	621	615	394	269	346	119	275	415	200	296	100
1972	1,066	394	671	626	439	268	358	126	313	427	199	330	109
1973	1,123	410	715	648	477	273	375	137	340	442	206	358	119
1974	1,190	427	762	663	526	276	387	151	375	454	209	398	128
1975	1,263	453	810	700	563	290	410	163	400	481	219	425	138
1976	1,333	463	870	714	619	287	427	176	443	477	237	454	165
1977	1,319	473	845	700	617	289	411	184	434	458	243	443	174
1978	1,312	468	844	682	630	280	402	188	442	441	241	453	177
1979	1,309	476	833	669	640	280	389	196	444	427	242	457	182
1980	1,343	485	860	675	670	281	394	204	466	426	247	474	195
1981	1,343	484	859	674	669	277	397	207	462	419	255	468	201
1982	1,322	485	838	670	653	280	390	205	447	417	253	453	200
1983	1,340	497	843	677	663	286	391	211	452	418	259	454	209
1984	1,345	501	844	672	673	286	386	215	459	411	261	459	215
1985	1,376	509	867	677	700	289	388	220	479	414	263	477	223
1986	1,435	522	913	693	742	294	399	228	514	433	260	508	234
1987	1,452	527	925	693	759	294	400	233	525	429	264	516	243
1988	1,472	553	919	697	774	304	393	249	526	429	268	520	254
1989	1,522	572	949	710	811	309	401	263	548	437	273	541	271
1990	1,586	599	987	737	849	321	416	278	571	456	281	567	282
1991	1,639	642	997	761	878	341	419	300	578	471	290	580	299
1992	1,669	666	1,003	772	896	351	421	314	582	474	298	584	313
1993	1,688	688	1,000	771	917	355	416	334	584	473	298	590	327
1994	1,721	706	1,016	776	946	359	417	347	598	472	304	603	343
1995	1,732	717	1,015	768	965	356	412	361	604	464	304	610	355
1996	1,742	737	1,005	759	983	358	401	379	604	456	303	613	370
1997	1,753	752	1,001	758	996	360	398	393	603	452	306	618	377
1998	1,768	754	1,014	754	1,013	355	399	398	615	444	310	623	390
1999[1]	1,807	781	1,026	766	1,041	363	403	418	623	446	320	630	411
2000	1,850	813	1,037	780	1,071	377	402	436	635	447	332	642	428
2001	1,904	843	1,061	796	1,108	388	408	455	653	460	336	659	449
2002	2,036	926	1,109	847	1,189	421	425	505	684	487	360	700	489
2003	2,098	981	1,117	865	1,233	439	426	542	691	491	374	710	523
2004	2,157	1,024	1,133	879	1,278	448	431	576	702	486	393	708	570
2005	2,186	1,047	1,139	877	1,309	451	427	596	713	478	400	708	601

[1]Data for 1999 were imputed using alternative procedures. (See Guide to Sources for details.)
NOTE: Data include unclassified graduate students. Data through 1995 are for institutions of higher education, while later data are for degree-granting institutions. Degree-granting institutions grant associate's or higher degrees and participate in Title IV federal financial aid programs. The degree-granting classification is very similar to the earlier higher education classification, but it includes more 2-year colleges and excludes a few higher education institu-tions that did not grant degrees. (See Guide to Sources for details.) Detail may not sum to totals because of rounding.
SOURCE: U.S. Department of Education, National Center for Education Statistics, Higher Education General Information Survey (HEGIS), "Fall Enrollment in Colleges and Universities" surveys, 1969 through 1985; and 1986 through 2005 Integrated Postsecondary Education Data System, "Fall Enrollment Survey" (IPEDS-EF:86–99), and Spring 2001 through Spring 2006. (This table was prepared August 2006.)

Table 192. Total first-professional fall enrollment in degree-granting institutions, by attendance status, sex of student, and control of institution: 1969 through 2005

Year	Total	Full-time	Part-time	Males	Females	Males Full-time	Males Part-time	Females Full-time	Females Part-time	Males Public	Males Private	Females Public	Females Private
1	2	3	4	5	6	7	8	9	10	11	12	13	14
1969	164,737	143,081	21,656	148,926	15,811	131,368	17,558	11,713	4,098	64,241	84,685	8,354	7,457
1970	173,411	157,384	16,027	158,649	14,762	144,270	14,379	13,114	1,648	68,956	89,693	6,501	8,261
1971	192,668	176,224	16,444	174,058	18,610	159,386	14,672	16,838	1,772	98,233	75,825	9,430	9,180
1972	206,659	190,039	16,620	183,443	23,216	168,990	14,453	21,049	2,167	79,723	103,720	10,842	12,374
1973	218,990	201,663	17,327	186,297	32,693	171,731	14,566	29,932	2,761	81,811	104,486	16,138	16,555
1974	235,452	216,329	19,123	194,079	41,373	178,926	15,153	37,403	3,970	84,271	109,808	20,085	21,288
1975	242,267	219,886	22,381	192,100	50,167	177,117	14,983	42,769	7,398	79,240	112,860	23,557	26,610
1976	244,292	220,124	24,168	189,810	54,482	171,967	17,843	48,157	6,325	77,873	111,937	23,468	31,014
1977	251,357	226,318	25,039	191,451	59,906	173,165	18,286	53,153	6,753	78,189	113,262	24,901	35,005
1978	256,904	232,540	24,364	192,221	64,683	174,906	17,315	57,634	7,049	77,748	114,473	26,839	37,844
1979	263,404	238,949	24,455	193,363	70,041	176,394	16,969	62,555	7,486	77,122	116,241	29,026	41,015
1980	277,767	251,359	26,408	199,344	78,423	181,448	17,896	69,911	8,512	81,022	118,322	33,415	45,008
1981	274,595	248,328	26,267	192,936	81,659	175,414	17,522	72,914	8,745	77,562	115,374	34,177	47,482
1982	278,425	252,108	26,317	191,200	87,225	173,941	17,259	78,167	9,058	76,273	114,927	37,183	50,042
1983	278,529	249,636	28,893	188,096	90,433	169,071	19,025	80,565	9,868	74,938	113,158	38,484	51,949
1984	278,598	249,708	28,890	184,949	93,649	166,286	18,663	83,422	10,227	73,722	111,227	40,186	53,463
1985	274,200	246,619	27,581	179,792	94,408	162,368	17,424	84,251	10,157	71,373	108,419	40,435	53,973
1986	270,401	245,647	24,754	173,851	96,550	158,557	15,294	87,090	9,460	70,326	103,525	41,699	54,851
1987	268,332	241,807	26,525	170,129	98,203	153,668	16,461	88,139	10,064	68,089	102,040	41,947	56,256
1988	267,109	241,228	25,881	166,912	100,197	151,045	15,867	90,183	10,014	66,196	100,716	42,743	57,454
1989	274,451	247,812	26,639	168,773	105,678	152,511	16,262	95,301	10,377	67,548	101,225	45,090	60,588
1990	273,366	245,854	27,512	166,798	106,568	149,805	16,993	96,049	10,519	66,071	100,727	45,674	60,894
1991	280,531	252,012	28,519	169,875	110,656	152,356	17,519	99,656	11,000	64,821	105,054	46,661	63,995
1992	280,922	252,138	28,784	168,620	112,302	151,025	17,595	101,113	11,189	63,511	105,109	47,178	65,124
1993	292,431	259,764	32,667	172,788	119,643	153,873	18,915	105,891	13,752	63,973	108,815	49,681	69,962
1994	294,713	263,311	31,402	173,956	120,757	155,018	18,938	108,293	12,464	63,844	110,112	50,153	70,604
1995	297,592	266,414	31,178	173,897	123,695	155,056	18,841	111,358	12,337	63,594	110,303	51,478	72,217
1996	298,312	267,209	31,103	172,742	125,570	154,107	18,635	113,102	12,468	63,742	109,000	52,923	72,647
1997	298,258	267,218	31,040	169,627	128,631	151,325	18,302	115,893	12,738	63,667	105,960	54,582	74,049
1998	302,473	271,049	31,424	168,846	133,627	150,361	18,485	120,688	12,939	63,800	105,046	56,898	76,729
1999[1]	303,190	270,581	32,609	165,134	138,056	146,613	18,521	123,968	14,088	63,762	101,372	59,123	78,933
2000	306,625	273,571	33,054	163,885	142,740	145,397	18,488	128,174	14,566	63,137	100,748	60,977	81,763
2001	308,647	276,792	31,855	160,666	147,981	143,536	17,130	133,256	14,725	63,566	97,100	64,240	83,741
2002	318,982	285,916	33,066	162,881	156,101	145,482	17,399	140,434	15,667	64,665	98,216	67,629	88,472
2003	329,076	296,364	32,712	166,227	162,849	148,874	17,353	147,490	15,359	64,497	101,730	69,864	92,985
2004	334,529	301,543	32,986	168,438	166,091	150,860	17,578	150,683	15,408	64,636	103,802	71,120	94,971
2005	337,024	303,468	33,556	169,831	167,193	151,859	17,972	151,609	15,584	65,602	104,229	72,605	94,588

[1]Data for 1999 were imputed using alternative procedures. (See Guide to Sources for details.)
NOTE: Data through 1995 are for institutions of higher education, while later data are for degree-granting institutions. Degree-granting institutions grant associate's or higher degrees and participate in Title IV federal financial aid programs. The degree-granting classification is very similar to the earlier higher education classification, but it includes more 2-year colleges and excludes a few higher education institutions that did not grant degrees. (See Guide to Sources for details.)

SOURCE: U.S. Department of Education, National Center for Education Statistics, Higher Education General Information Survey (HEGIS), "Fall Enrollment in Colleges and Universities" surveys, 1969 through 1985; and 1996 through 2005 Integrated Postsecondary Education Data System, "Fall Enrollment Survey" (IPEDS-EF:86–99), and Spring 2001 through Spring 2006. (This table was prepared August 2006.)

Table 193. Total fall enrollment in degree-granting institutions, by state or jurisdiction: Selected years, 1970 through 2005

State or jurisdiction	Fall 1970	Fall 1980	Fall 1990	Fall 1999[1]	Fall 2000	Fall 2001	Fall 2002	Fall 2003	Fall 2004	Fall 2005	Percent change, 2000 to 2005
1	2	3	4	5	6	7	8	9	10	11	12
United States	8,580,887	12,096,895	13,818,637	14,791,224	15,312,289	15,927,987	16,611,711	16,900,471	17,272,044	17,487,475	14.2
Alabama	103,936	164,306	218,589	223,144	233,962	236,146	246,414	253,846	255,826	256,389	9.6
Alaska	9,471	21,296	29,833	26,948	27,953	27,756	29,546	31,035	30,869	30,231	8.1
Arizona	109,619	202,716	264,148	326,159	342,490	366,485	401,605	430,661	490,925	545,597	59.3
Arkansas	52,039	77,607	90,425	115,092	115,172	122,282	127,372	133,950	138,399	143,272	24.4
California	1,257,245	1,790,993	1,808,740	2,017,483	2,256,708	2,380,090	2,474,024	2,338,846	2,374,045	2,399,833	6.3
Colorado	123,395	162,916	227,131	261,744	263,872	269,292	282,343	289,243	300,914	302,672	14.7
Connecticut	124,700	159,632	168,604	156,907	161,243	165,027	170,606	170,976	172,775	174,675	8.3
Delaware	25,260	32,939	42,004	46,613	43,897	47,104	49,228	49,595	49,804	51,612	17.6
District of Columbia	77,158	86,675	79,551	72,118	72,689	87,252	91,014	95,297	99,988	104,897	44.3
Florida	235,525	411,891	588,086	684,745	707,684	753,554	792,079	839,735	866,665	872,662	23.3
Georgia	126,511	184,159	251,786	311,812	346,204	376,098	397,604	411,061	434,283	426,650	23.2
Hawaii	36,562	47,181	56,436	62,578	60,182	62,079	65,368	67,390	67,225	67,083	11.5
Idaho	34,567	43,018	51,881	64,661	65,594	69,674	72,072	75,370	76,311	77,708	18.5
Illinois	452,146	644,245	729,246	733,182	743,918	748,444	776,622	796,774	801,401	832,967	12.0
Indiana	192,668	247,253	284,832	304,725	314,334	338,715	342,064	350,091	356,801	361,253	14.9
Iowa	108,902	140,449	170,515	186,780	188,974	194,822	202,546	213,958	217,646	227,722	20.5
Kansas	102,485	136,605	163,733	176,737	179,968	184,943	188,049	190,291	191,590	191,752	6.5
Kentucky	98,591	143,066	177,852	181,626	188,341	214,839	225,489	235,743	240,097	244,969	30.1
Louisiana	120,728	160,058	186,840	221,348	223,800	228,871	232,140	244,455	246,301	197,713	-11.7
Maine	34,134	43,264	57,186	57,822	58,473	61,127	63,308	64,222	65,415	65,551	12.1
Maryland	149,607	225,526	259,700	268,820	273,745	288,224	300,269	307,543	312,493	314,151	14.8
Massachusetts	303,809	418,415	417,833	419,695	421,142	425,071	431,224	436,068	439,245	443,316	5.3
Michigan	392,726	520,131	569,803	558,998	567,631	585,998	605,835	615,765	620,980	626,751	10.4
Minnesota	160,788	206,691	253,789	282,756	293,445	308,233	323,791	337,780	349,021	361,701	23.3
Mississippi	73,967	102,364	122,883	133,170	137,389	137,882	147,077	148,584	152,115	150,457	9.5
Missouri	183,930	234,421	289,899	317,480	321,348	331,580	348,146	359,680	365,204	374,775	16.5
Montana	30,062	35,177	35,876	43,114	42,240	44,932	45,111	47,240	47,173	47,850	13.3
Nebraska	66,915	89,488	112,831	110,806	112,117	113,817	116,737	119,511	121,053	121,236	8.1
Nevada	13,669	40,455	61,728	89,711	87,893	93,368	95,671	100,995	105,961	110,705	26.0
New Hampshire	29,400	46,794	59,510	63,366	61,718	65,031	68,523	69,608	70,163	69,893	13.2
New Jersey	216,121	321,610	324,286	330,537	335,945	346,507	361,733	372,632	380,374	379,758	13.0
New Mexico	44,461	58,283	85,500	111,896	110,739	112,861	120,997	126,852	131,577	131,337	18.6
New York	806,479	992,237	1,048,286	1,020,991	1,043,395	1,057,794	1,107,201	1,126,087	1,141,525	1,152,081	10.4
North Carolina	171,925	287,537	352,138	395,907	404,652	427,784	447,335	464,430	472,709	484,392	19.7
North Dakota	31,495	34,069	37,878	40,348	40,248	42,843	45,800	48,402	49,533	49,389	22.7
Ohio	376,267	489,145	557,690	548,545	549,553	569,223	587,996	603,378	614,234	616,350	12.2
Oklahoma	110,155	160,295	173,221	179,055	178,016	189,785	198,423	207,781	207,625	208,053	16.9
Oregon	122,177	157,458	165,741	175,635	183,065	191,378	204,565	198,701	199,985	200,033	9.3
Pennsylvania	411,044	507,716	604,060	605,283	609,521	630,299	654,826	675,574	688,780	692,340	13.6
Rhode Island	45,898	66,869	78,273	74,821	75,450	77,235	77,417	79,085	80,377	81,382	7.9
South Carolina	69,518	132,476	159,302	183,626	185,931	191,590	202,007	207,601	208,910	210,444	13.2
South Dakota	30,639	32,761	34,208	42,147	43,221	45,534	47,751	48,967	48,708	48,768	12.8
Tennessee	135,103	204,581	226,238	252,915	263,910	258,534	261,899	267,969	278,055	283,070	7.3
Texas	442,225	701,391	901,437	990,587	1,033,973	1,076,678	1,152,369	1,188,727	1,229,197	1,240,707	20.0
Utah	81,687	93,987	121,303	161,591	163,776	177,045	178,932	185,772	194,324	200,691	22.5
Vermont	22,209	30,628	36,398	36,728	35,489	36,351	36,537	37,831	38,639	39,915	12.5
Virginia	151,915	280,504	353,442	377,970	381,893	389,853	404,966	414,881	425,181	439,166	15.0
Washington	183,544	303,603	263,384	306,723	320,840	325,132	338,820	345,469	343,524	348,482	8.6
West Virginia	63,153	81,973	84,790	88,657	87,888	91,319	93,723	97,005	97,884	99,547	13.3
Wisconsin	202,058	269,086	299,774	304,776	307,179	315,850	329,443	329,691	331,506	335,258	9.1
Wyoming	15,220	21,147	31,326	29,002	30,004	31,095	32,605	33,695	33,955	35,334	17.8
U.S. Service Schools[2]	17,079	49,808	48,692	13,344	13,475	14,561	14,420	14,628	14,754	15,265	13.3
Other jurisdictions	67,237	137,749	164,618	185,244	194,633	201,642	211,204	217,655	220,920	223,165	14.7
American Samoa	0	976	1,219	1,172	297	1,178	1,367	1,537	1,550	1,579	431.6
Federated States of Micronesia	0	224	975	1,506	1,576	2,243	2,173	2,558	2,608	2,283	44.9
Guam	2,719	3,217	4,741	5,727	5,215	4,869	5,157	4,710	4,642	6,064	16.3
Marshall Islands	0	0	0	616	328	220	224	601	623	604	84.1
Northern Marianas	0	0	661	1,080	1,078	982	1,299	1,237	1,101	967	-10.3
Palau	0	0	491	569	581	579	668	727	651	651	12.0
Puerto Rico	63,073	131,184	154,065	171,832	183,290	188,430	197,781	203,745	207,180	208,625	13.8
Virgin Islands	1,445	2,148	2,466	2,742	2,268	3,141	2,535	2,540	2,565	2,392	5.5

[1]Data were imputed using alternative procedures. (See Guide to Sources for details.)
[2]Data for 1999 and later years reflect substantial changes in survey coverage.
NOTE: Data through 1990 are for institutions of higher education, while later data are for degree-granting institutions. Degree-granting institutions grant associate's or higher degrees and partici-pate in Title IV federal financial aid programs. The degree-granting classification is very similar to the earlier higher education classification, but it includes more 2-year colleges and excludes a few higher education institutions that did not grant degrees. (See Guide to Sources for details.)

SOURCE: U.S. Department of Education, National Center for Education Statistics, Higher Education General Information Survey (HEGIS), "Fall Enrollment in Colleges and Universities" surveys, 1970 and 1980; and 1990 through 2005 Integrated Postsecondary Education Data System, "Fall Enrollment Survey" (IPEDS-EF:90–99), and Spring 2001 through Spring 2006. (This table was prepared August 2006.)

Table 194. Total fall enrollment in public degree-granting institutions, by state or jurisdiction: Selected years, 1970 through 2005

State or jurisdiction	Fall 1970	Fall 1980	Fall 1990	Fall 1999[1]	Fall 2000	Fall 2001	Fall 2002	Fall 2003	Fall 2004	Fall 2005	Percent change, 2000 to 2005
1	2	3	4	5	6	7	8	9	10	11	12
United States	6,428,134	9,457,394	10,844,717	11,309,399	11,752,786	12,233,156	12,751,993	12,857,059	12,980,112	13,021,834	10.8
Alabama	87,884	143,674	195,939	197,173	207,435	208,385	217,883	225,347	226,989	228,153	10.0
Alaska	8,563	20,561	27,792	25,687	26,559	26,550	28,314	29,821	29,515	28,866	8.7
Arizona	107,315	194,034	248,213	276,268	284,522	294,174	307,496	310,679	317,974	320,865	12.8
Arkansas	43,599	66,068	78,645	103,326	101,775	108,950	113,509	119,920	123,973	128,117	25.9
California	1,123,529	1,599,838	1,594,710	1,692,607	1,927,771	2,043,182	2,121,106	1,978,831	1,987,283	2,008,155	4.2
Colorado	108,562	145,598	200,653	219,436	217,897	222,815	233,740	236,883	239,308	234,509	7.6
Connecticut	73,391	97,788	109,556	96,834	101,027	104,066	108,522	108,815	110,354	111,705	10.6
Delaware	21,151	28,325	34,252	36,895	34,194	36,510	37,344	37,621	38,243	38,682	13.1
District of Columbia	12,194	13,900	11,990	5,349	5,499	5,589	5,603	5,424	5,388	5,595	1.7
Florida	189,450	334,349	489,081	540,967	556,912	588,921	617,754	643,784	649,857	648,999	16.5
Georgia	101,900	140,158	196,413	237,411	271,755	298,215	317,180	330,052	335,979	342,012	25.9
Hawaii	32,963	43,269	45,728	46,479	44,579	45,994	48,163	50,316	50,569	50,157	12.5
Idaho	27,072	34,491	41,315	52,615	53,751	56,673	57,996	60,481	60,695	60,303	12.2
Illinois	315,634	491,274	551,333	533,522	534,155	534,280	554,093	566,137	563,593	555,149	3.9
Indiana	136,739	189,224	223,953	230,810	240,023	259,258	258,627	262,957	266,916	267,298	11.4
Iowa	68,390	97,454	117,834	133,753	135,008	140,227	145,798	149,195	149,776	148,907	10.3
Kansas	88,215	121,987	149,117	157,088	159,976	164,173	167,741	169,384	170,149	170,319	6.5
Kentucky	77,240	114,884	147,095	146,558	151,973	178,349	188,518	196,474	197,991	201,579	32.6
Louisiana	101,127	136,703	158,290	188,573	189,213	194,790	197,547	207,923	208,218	181,043	-4.3
Maine	25,405	31,878	41,500	40,349	40,662	42,425	44,850	46,714	47,284	47,519	16.9
Maryland	118,988	195,051	220,783	220,809	223,797	236,795	246,792	252,026	256,582	256,073	14.4
Massachusetts	116,127	183,765	186,035	181,514	183,248	186,891	187,874	189,334	187,873	188,295	2.8
Michigan	339,625	454,147	487,359	461,825	467,861	482,154	495,676	501,821	500,873	505,586	8.1
Minnesota	130,567	162,379	199,211	207,474	218,617	225,941	235,513	240,714	241,245	240,853	10.2
Mississippi	64,968	90,661	109,038	121,369	125,355	125,656	134,130	134,318	137,543	135,896	8.4
Missouri	132,540	165,179	200,093	199,324	201,509	206,721	214,022	216,777	214,561	217,722	8.0
Montana	27,287	31,178	31,865	38,336	37,387	39,368	40,615	42,444	42,289	42,997	15.0
Nebraska	51,454	73,509	94,614	88,386	88,531	89,639	92,111	93,432	93,195	93,181	5.3
Nevada	13,576	40,280	61,242	85,270	83,120	86,790	89,547	94,205	96,773	100,043	20.4
New Hampshire	15,979	24,119	32,163	34,927	35,870	37,224	40,958	41,324	40,642	41,007	14.3
New Jersey	145,373	247,028	261,601	263,752	266,921	275,655	289,275	298,906	305,034	304,315	14.0
New Mexico	40,795	55,077	83,403	103,125	101,450	103,758	111,667	117,245	121,339	120,976	19.2
New York	449,437	563,251	616,884	566,306	583,417	584,607	610,756	613,895	623,192	626,222	7.3
North Carolina	123,761	228,154	285,405	321,311	329,422	350,684	367,861	383,720	389,143	396,755	20.4
North Dakota	30,192	31,709	34,690	35,940	36,014	38,560	41,134	43,383	43,275	42,808	18,9
Ohio	281,099	381,765	427,613	411,541	411,161	425,265	441,738	450,369	454,377	453,001	10.2
Oklahoma	91,438	137,188	151,073	155,361	153,699	163,336	171,369	178,612	179,281	179,225	16.6
Oregon	108,483	140,102	144,427	148,177	154,756	162,645	173,698	166,129	165,375	163,752	5.8
Pennsylvania	232,982	292,499	343,478	336,930	339,229	353,950	370,386	381,254	384,525	380,271	12.1
Rhode Island	25,527	35,052	42,350	38,650	38,458	39,149	38,867	39,937	39,920	40,008	4.0
South Carolina	47,101	107,683	131,134	153,496	155,519	158,661	167,563	171,893	172,386	174,686	12.3
South Dakota	23,936	24,328	26,596	34,197	34,857	37,310	37,760	38,179	37,598	37,548	7.7
Tennessee	98,897	156,835	175,049	193,646	202,530	194,696	194,202	196,088	199,904	200,394	-1.1
Texas	365,522	613,552	802,314	862,271	896,534	935,826	1,006,549	1,036,008	1,071,926	1,081,335	20.6
Utah	49,588	59,598	86,108	120,558	123,046	133,790	135,778	140,282	145,182	148,960	21.1
Vermont	12,536	17,984	20,910	20,580	20,021	20,480	21,238	22,607	22,980	24,090	20.3
Virginia	123,279	246,500	291,286	311,536	313,780	326,758	337,286	341,948	343,391	349,195	11.3
Washington	162,718	276,028	227,632	263,415	273,928	277,023	293,007	298,079	293,145	296,756	8.3
West Virginia	51,363	71,228	74,108	76,777	76,136	78,304	79,741	82,273	83,274	85,148	11.8
Wisconsin	170,374	235,179	253,529	249,608	249,737	257,888	268,010	266,805	266,884	268,928	7.7
Wyoming	15,220	21,121	30,623	27,944	28,715	29,545	30,666	31,666	31,597	32.611	13.6
U.S. Service Schools[2]	17,079	49,808	48,692	13,344	13,475	14,561	14,420	14,628	14,754	15,265	13.3
Other jurisdictions	46,680	60,692	66,244	83,919	84,464	85,535	86,484	85,468	83,831	82,341	-2.5
American Samoa	0	976	1,219	1,172	297	1,178	1,367	1,537	1,550	1,579	431.6
Federated States of Micronesia	0	224	975	1,506	1,576	2,243	2,173	2,558	2,608	2,283	44.9
Guam	2,719	3,217	4,741	5,727	5,215	4,869	5,038	4,546	4,470	5,875	12.7
Marshall Islands	0	0	0	616	328	220	224	601	623	604	84.1
Northern Marianas	0	0	661	1,080	1,078	982	1,299	1,237	1,101	967	-10.3
Palau	0	0	491	569	581	579	668	727	651	651	12.0
Puerto Rico	42,516	54,127	55,691	70,507	73,121	73,173	73,180	71,722	70,263	67,990	-7.0
Virgin Islands	1,445	2,148	2,466	2,742	2,268	2,291	2,535	2,540	2,565	2,392	5.5

[1]Data were imputed using alternative procedures. (See Guide to Sources for details.)
[2]Data for 1999 and later years reflect substantial changes in survey coverage.
NOTE: Data through 1990 are for institutions of higher education, while later data are for degree-granting institutions. Degree-granting institutions grant associate's or higher degrees and participate in Title IV federal financial aid programs. The degree-granting classification is very similar to the earlier higher education classification, but it includes more 2-year colleges and excludes a few higher education institutions that did not grant degrees. (See Guide to Sources for details.)

SOURCE: U.S. Department of Education, National Center for Education Statistics, Higher Education General Information Survey (HEGIS), "Fall Enrollment in Colleges and Universities" surveys, 1970 and 1980; and 1990 through 2005 Integrated Postsecondary Education Data System, "Fall Enrollment Survey" (IPEDS-EF:90–99), and Spring 2001 through Spring 2006. (This table was prepared August 2006.)

Table 195. Total fall enrollment in private degree-granting institutions, by state or jurisdiction: Selected years, 1970 through 2005

State or jurisdiction	Fall 1970	Fall 1980	Fall 1990	Fall 1999[1]	Fall 2000	Fall 2001	Fall 2002	Fall 2003	Fall 2004	Fall 2005	Percent change, 2000 to 2005
1	2	3	4	5	6	7	8	9	10	11	12
United States	2,152,753	2,639,501	2,973,920	3,481,825	3,559,503	3,694,831	3,859,718	4,043,412	4,291,932	4,465,641	25.5
Alabama	16,052	20,632	22,650	25,971	26,527	27,761	28,531	28,499	28,837	28,236	6.4
Alaska	908	735	2,041	1,261	1,394	1,206	1,232	1,214	1,354	1,365	-2.1
Arizona	2,304	8,682	15,935	49,891	57,968	72,311	94,109	119,982	172,951	224,732	287.7
Arkansas	8,440	11,539	11,780	11,766	13,397	13,332	13,863	14,030	14,426	15,155	13.1
California	133,716	191,155	214,030	324,876	328,937	336,908	352,918	360,015	386,762	391,678	19.1
Colorado	14,833	17,318	26,478	42,308	45,975	46,477	48,603	52,360	61,606	68,163	48.3
Connecticut	51,309	61,844	59,048	60,073	60,216	60,961	62,084	62,161	62,421	62,970	4.6
Delaware	4,109	4,614	7,752	9,718	9,703	10,594	11,884	11,974	11,561	12,930	33.3
District of Columbia	64,964	72,775	67,561	66,769	67,190	81,663	85,411	89,873	94,600	99,302	47.8
Florida	46,075	77,542	99,005	143,778	150,772	164,633	174,325	195,951	216,808	223,663	48.3
Georgia	24,611	44,001	55,373	74,401	74,449	77,883	80,424	81,009	98,304	84,638	13.7
Hawaii	3,599	3,912	10,708	16,099	15,603	16,085	17,205	17,074	16,656	16,926	8.5
Idaho	7,495	8,527	10,566	12,046	11,843	13,001	14,076	14,889	15,616	17,405	47.0
Illinois	136,512	152,971	177,913	199,660	209,763	214,164	222,529	230,637	237,808	277,818	32.4
Indiana	55,929	58,029	60,879	73,915	74,311	79,457	83,437	87,134	89,885	93,955	26.4
Iowa	40,512	42,995	52,681	53,027	53,966	54,595	56,748	64,763	67,870	78,815	46.0
Kansas	14,270	14,618	14,616	19,649	19,992	20,770	20,308	20,907	21,441	21,433	7.2
Kentucky	21,351	28,182	30,757	35,068	36,368	36,490	36,971	39,269	42,106	43,390	19.3
Louisiana	19,601	23,355	28,550	32,775	34,587	34,081	34,593	36,532	38,083	16,670	-51.8
Maine	8,729	11,386	15,686	17,473	17,811	18,702	18,458	17,508	18,131	18,032	1.2
Maryland	30,619	30,475	38,917	48,011	49,948	51,429	53,477	55,517	55,911	58,078	16.3
Massachusetts	187,682	234,650	231,798	238,181	237,894	238,180	243,350	246,734	251,372	255,021	7.2
Michigan	53,101	65,984	82,444	97,173	99,770	103,844	110,159	113,944	120,107	121,165	21.4
Minnesota	30,221	44,312	54,578	75,282	74,828	82,292	88,278	97,066	107,776	120,848	61.5
Mississippi	8,999	11,703	13,845	11,801	12,034	12,226	12,947	14,266	14,572	14,561	21.0
Missouri	51,390	69,242	89,806	118,156	119,839	124,859	134,124	142,903	150,643	156,723	30.8
Montana	2,775	3,999	4,011	4,778	4,853	5,564	4,496	4,796	4,884	4,853	0.0
Nebraska	15,461	15,979	18,217	22,420	23,586	24,178	24,626	26,079	27,858	28,055	18.9
Nevada	93	175	486	4,441	4,773	6,578	6,124	6,790	9,188	10,662	123.4
New Hampshire	13,421	22,675	27,347	28,439	25,848	27,807	27,565	28,284	29,521	28,886	11.8
New Jersey	70,748	74,582	62,685	66,785	69,024	70,852	72,458	73,726	75,340	75,443	9.3
New Mexico	3,666	3,206	2,097	8,771	9,289	9,103	9,330	9,607	10,238	10,361	11.5
New York	357,042	428,986	431,402	454,685	459,978	473,187	496,514	512,192	518,333	525,859	14.3
North Carolina	48,164	59,383	66,733	74,596	75,230	77,100	79,474	80,710	83,566	87,637	16.5
North Dakota	1,303	2,360	3,188	4,408	4,234	4,283	4,666	5,019	6,258	6,581	55.4
Ohio	95,168	107,380	130,077	137,004	138,392	143,958	146,258	153,009	159,857	163,349	18.0
Oklahoma	18,717	23,107	22,148	23,694	24,317	26,449	27,054	29,169	28,344	28,828	18.6
Oregon	13,694	17,356	21,314	27,458	28,309	28,733	30,867	32,572	34,610	36,281	28.2
Pennsylvania	178,062	215,217	260,582	268,353	270,292	276,349	284,440	294,320	304,255	312,069	15.5
Rhode Island	20,371	31,817	35,923	36,171	36,992	38,086	38,550	39,148	40,457	41,374	11.8
South Carolina	22,417	24,793	28,168	30,130	30,412	32,929	34,444	35,708	36,524	35,758	17.6
South Dakota	6,703	8,433	7,612	7,950	8,364	8,224	9,991	10,788	11,110	11,220	34.1
Tennessee	36,206	47,746	51,189	59,269	61,380	63,838	67,697	71,881	78,151	82,676	34.7
Texas	76,703	87,839	99,123	128,316	137,439	140,852	145,820	152,719	157,271	159,372	16.0
Utah	32,099	34,389	35,195	41,033	40,730	43,255	43,154	45,490	49,142	51,731	27.0
Vermont	9,673	12,644	15,488	16,148	15,468	15,871	15,299	15,224	15,659	15,825	2.3
Virginia	28,636	34,004	62,156	66,434	68,113	63,095	67,680	72,933	81,790	89,971	32.1
Washington	20,826	27,575	35,752	43,308	46,912	48,109	45,813	47,390	50,379	51,726	10.3
West Virginia	11,790	10,745	10,682	11,880	11,752	13,015	13,982	14,732	14,610	14,399	22.5
Wisconsin	31,684	33,907	46,245	55,168	57,442	57,962	61,433	62,886	64,622	66,330	15.5
Wyoming	0	26	703	1,058	1,289	1,550	1,939	2,029	2,358	2,723	111.2
Other jurisdictions	20,557	77,057	98,374	101,325	110,169	116,107	124,720	132,187	137,089	140,824	27.8
American Samoa	0	0	0	0	0	0	0	0	0	0	†
Federated States of Micronesia	0	0	0	0	0	0	0	0	0	0	†
Guam	0	0	0	0	0	0	119	164	172	189	†
Marshall Islands	0	0	0	0	0	0	0	0	0	0	†
Northern Marianas	0	0	0	0	0	0	0	0	0	0	†
Palau	0	0	0	0	0	0	0	0	0	0	†
Puerto Rico	20,557	77,057	98,374	101,325	110,169	115,257	124,601	132,023	136,917	140,635	27.7
Virgin Islands	0	0	0	0	0	850	0	0	0	0	†

†Not applicable.
[1]Data were imputed using alternative procedures. (See Guide to Sources for details.)
NOTE: Data through 1990 are for institutions of higher education, while later data are for degree-granting institutions. Degree-granting institutions grant associate's or higher degrees and participate in Title IV federal financial aid programs. The degree-granting classification is very similar to the earlier higher education classification, but it includes more 2-year colleges and excludes a few higher education institutions that did not grant degrees. (See Guide to Sources for details.)

SOURCE: U.S. Department of Education, National Center for Education Statistics, Higher Education General Information Survey (HEGIS), "Fall Enrollment in Colleges and Universities" surveys, 1970 and 1980; and 1990 through 2005 Integrated Postsecondary Education Data System, "Fall Enrollment Survey" (IPEDS-EF:90–99), and Spring 2001 through Spring 2006. (This table was prepared August 2006.)

Table 196. Total fall enrollment in all degree-granting institutions, by attendance status, sex, and state or jurisdiction: 2004 and 2005

State or jurisdiction	Total	Fall 2004 Full-time Males	Full-time Females	Part-time Males	Part-time Females	Total	Fall 2005 Full-time Males	Full-time Females	Part-time Males	Part-time Females
1	2	3	4	5	6	7	8	9	10	11
United States	17,272,044	4,739,355	5,870,822	2,647,907	4,013,960	17,487,475	4,803,388	5,993,623	2,652,537	4,037,927
Alabama	255,826	74,392	98,345	32,392	50,697	256,389	73,011	97,047	33,448	52,883
Alaska	30,869	5,746	7,384	6,393	11,346	30,231	5,783	7,261	6,094	11,093
Arizona	490,925	133,969	169,730	76,537	110,689	545,597	145,697	207,474	77,511	114,915
Arkansas	138,399	38,407	53,404	17,085	29,503	143,272	39,654	54,229	18,343	31,046
California	2,374,045	534,469	669,926	508,808	660,842	2,399,833	542,176	679,567	515,013	663,077
Colorado	300,914	82,202	93,690	50,320	74,702	302,672	83,152	96,823	49,096	73,601
Connecticut	172,775	48,488	60,198	23,456	40,633	174,675	49,549	61,624	22,764	40,738
Delaware	49,804	13,520	18,416	6,188	11,680	51,612	13,913	19,126	6,476	12,097
District of Columbia	99,988	25,616	35,493	15,322	23,557	104,897	25,805	36,227	16,655	26,210
Florida	866,665	209,498	274,647	150,186	232,334	872,662	212,355	282,656	146,656	230,995
Georgia	434,283	124,187	167,539	51,488	91,069	426,650	119,710	162,697	52,204	92,039
Hawaii	67,225	16,716	23,607	10,738	16,164	67,083	16,667	23,225	10,919	16,272
Idaho	76,311	24,838	27,925	9,578	13,970	77,708	24,793	28,364	9,848	14,703
Illinois	801,401	204,219	245,392	139,236	212,554	832,967	219,365	267,014	137,446	209,142
Indiana	356,801	114,572	131,827	45,406	64,996	361,253	116,230	134,604	45,364	65,055
Iowa	217,646	67,279	78,144	27,716	44,507	227,722	68,344	80,951	29,436	48,991
Kansas	191,590	53,593	59,703	31,054	47,240	191,752	53,832	59,415	31,372	47,133
Kentucky	240,097	65,056	87,840	36,995	50,206	244,969	64,284	88,379	40,874	51,432
Louisiana	246,301	74,073	105,109	23,625	43,494	197,713	60,519	86,134	18,422	32,638
Maine	65,415	18,041	22,030	8,130	17,214	65,551	18,322	22,367	8,107	16,755
Maryland	312,493	72,210	93,404	54,938	91,941	314,151	73,877	95,040	53,669	91,565
Massachusetts	439,245	134,644	164,786	51,649	88,166	443,316	137,526	167,817	50,202	87,771
Michigan	620,980	161,695	197,831	102,243	159,211	626,751	164,820	199,653	102,314	159,964
Minnesota	349,021	99,282	125,724	49,794	74,221	361,701	100,227	128,471	51,918	81,085
Mississippi	152,115	46,663	69,760	11,997	23,695	150,457	46,358	69,104	11,232	23,763
Missouri	365,204	97,658	122,578	57,498	87,470	374,445	99,431	126,375	58,664	89,975
Montana	47,173	16,954	19,002	4,288	6,929	47,850	16,875	18,785	4,643	7,547
Nebraska	121,053	36,743	42,829	17,038	24,443	121,236	37,187	42,701	17,132	24,216
Nevada	105,961	21,577	28,652	24,080	31,652	110,705	23,214	30,164	25,117	32,210
New Hampshire	70,163	21,157	25,682	8,187	15,137	69,893	21,540	26,106	7,740	14,507
New Jersey	380,374	103,233	122,613	59,205	95,323	379,758	105,101	123,299	57,986	93,372
New Mexico	131,577	29,655	39,117	23,983	38,822	131,337	29,352	39,563	23,988	38,434
New York	1,141,525	352,558	446,836	125,270	216,861	1,152,081	357,281	453,230	124,854	216,716
North Carolina	472,709	126,963	172,686	62,503	110,557	484,392	131,161	177,862	62,405	112,964
North Dakota	49,533	19,107	18,771	4,802	6,853	49,389	18,562	18,832	5,009	6,986
Ohio	614,234	184,876	226,639	79,000	123,719	616,350	187,336	230,097	77,315	121,602
Oklahoma	207,625	62,690	73,461	28,415	43,059	208,053	61,510	73,696	28,378	44,469
Oregon	199,985	55,996	66,195	33,087	44,707	200,033	55,268	65,691	33,383	45,691
Pennsylvania	688,780	229,746	264,945	70,172	123,917	692,340	232,614	269,765	67,850	122,111
Rhode Island	80,377	26,415	31,016	8,123	14,823	81,382	27,002	31,904	8,037	14,439
South Carolina	208,910	59,459	81,173	22,118	46,160	210,444	60,370	81,955	21,575	46,544
South Dakota	48,708	15,441	17,479	5,518	10,270	48,768	15,560	17,177	5,512	10,519
Tennessee	278,055	87,349	113,876	28,681	48,149	283,070	88,230	116,131	29,094	49,615
Texas	1,229,197	310,783	375,882	222,925	319,607	1,240,707	313,684	381,292	222,342	323,389
Utah	194,324	61,725	56,982	37,499	38,118	200,691	62,751	59,320	39,134	39,486
Vermont	38,639	13,391	14,412	3,531	7,305	39,915	14,161	14,772	3,468	7,514
Virginia	425,181	114,236	142,856	66,439	101,650	439,166	118,351	150,181	67,327	103,307
Washington	343,524	97,336	116,923	52,967	76,298	348,482	97,592	118,426	54,445	78,019
West Virginia	97,884	33,388	39,681	9,118	15,697	99,547	33,780	40,272	9,489	16,006
Wisconsin	331,506	95,172	116,782	47,249	72,303	335,258	96,589	118,639	46,404	73,626
Wyoming	33,955	10,163	9,355	4,937	9,500	35,334	10,396	9,375	5,863	9,700
U.S. Service Schools	14,754	12,209	2,545	0	0	15,265	12,521	2,744	0	0
Other jurisdictions	220,920	65,959	102,561	20,024	32,376	223,165	66,463	102,684	20,737	33,281
American Samoa	1,550	303	446	270	531	1,579	290	475	310	504
Federated States of Micronesia	2,608	956	992	339	321	2,283	791	762	375	355
Guam	4,642	978	1,503	886	1,275	6,064	1,085	1,644	1,184	2,151
Marshall Islands	623	284	214	69	56	604	254	219	67	64
Northern Marianas	1,101	307	509	99	186	967	260	482	88	137
Palau	651	205	224	72	150	651	212	219	67	153
Puerto Rico	207,180	62,611	97,730	18,009	28,830	208,625	63,240	97,951	18,428	29,006
Virgin Islands	2,565	315	943	280	1,027	2,392	331	932	218	911

NOTE: Degree-granting institutions grant associate's or higher degrees and participate in Title IV federal financial aid programs.

SOURCE: U.S. Department of Education, National Center for Education Statistics, 2004 and 2005 Integrated Postsecondary Education Data System (IPEDS), Spring 2005 and Spring 2006. (This table was prepared August 2006.)

Table 197. Total fall enrollment in public degree-granting institutions, by attendance status, sex, and state or jurisdiction: 2004 and 2005

State or jurisdiction	Fall 2004					Fall 2005				
		Full-time		Part-time			Full-time		Part-time	
	Total	Males	Females	Males	Females	Total	Males	Females	Males	Females
1	2	3	4	5	6	7	8	9	10	11
United States	12,980,112	3,325,073	4,044,359	2,234,403	3,376,277	13,021,834	3,350,485	4,058,276	2,238,738	3,374,335
Alabama	226,989	64,224	84,879	30,405	47,481	228,153	62,860	83,551	31,665	50,077
Alaska	29,515	5,469	6,927	6,155	10,964	28,866	5,531	6,829	5,872	10,634
Arizona	317,974	64,896	76,680	72,177	104,221	320,865	64,483	76,722	73,119	106,541
Arkansas	123,973	32,729	46,801	16,388	28,055	128,117	34,002	47,396	17,506	29,213
California	1,987,283	403,771	505,546	467,917	610,049	2,008,155	411,841	510,396	475,100	610,818
Colorado	239,308	61,997	69,780	42,441	65,090	234,509	61,238	69,071	40,588	63,612
Connecticut	110,354	27,351	33,552	18,083	31,368	111,705	28,158	34,549	17,571	31,427
Delaware	38,243	11,120	14,909	4,289	7,925	38,682	11,155	15,117	4,358	8,052
District of Columbia	5,388	919	1,302	1,024	2,143	5,595	905	1,377	1,069	2,244
Florida	649,857	141,662	188,098	122,270	197,827	648,999	143,833	191,635	118,594	194,937
Georgia	335,979	89,679	117,610	46,159	82,531	342,012	91,393	120,265	47,018	83,336
Hawaii	50,569	12,436	16,253	8,495	13,385	50,157	12,392	15,638	8,645	13,482
Idaho	60,695	18,301	20,316	8,912	13,166	60,303	17,933	19,850	8,963	13,557
Illinois	563,593	131,649	151,928	111,569	168,447	555,149	132,315	150,582	108,988	163,264
Indiana	266,916	81,620	90,713	39,649	54,934	267,298	82,048	91,174	39,547	54,529
Iowa	149,776	47,051	50,581	21,580	30,564	148,907	46,620	49,458	22,002	30,827
Kansas	170,149	46,788	51,533	28,668	43,160	170,319	46,988	51,209	28,992	43,130
Kentucky	197,991	51,993	68,767	33,572	43,659	201,579	51,892	68,773	36,850	44,064
Louisiana	208,218	62,560	85,827	21,067	38,764	181,043	56,570	76,081	17,649	30,743
Maine	47,284	12,515	14,749	6,594	13,426	47,519	12,712	14,734	6,748	13,325
Maryland	256,582	57,801	73,268	46,468	79,045	256,073	58,801	73,872	45,175	78,225
Massachusetts	187,873	47,591	56,791	29,739	53,752	188,295	48,702	58,062	28,910	52,621
Michigan	500,873	131,888	154,965	85,102	128,918	505,586	134,903	156,891	84,999	128,793
Minnesota	241,245	70,043	78,842	37,755	54,605	240,853	69,756	77,948	38,053	55,096
Mississippi	137,543	42,502	61,807	11,277	21,957	135,896	41,987	61,441	10,548	21,920
Missouri	214,561	58,369	71,978	31,196	53,018	217,722	59,306	72,933	31,956	53,527
Montana	42,289	15,371	16,674	3,922	6,322	42,997	15,290	16,570	4,283	6,854
Nebraska	93,195	27,407	29,661	15,139	20,988	93,181	27,738	29,873	15,116	20,454
Nevada	96,773	18,099	23,428	23,789	31,457	100,043	19,112	24,258	24,841	31,832
New Hampshire	40,642	11,257	13,663	5,747	9,975	41,007	11,649	13,940	5,569	9,849
New Jersey	305,034	77,858	96,465	49,587	81,124	304,315	79,713	96,592	48,385	79,625
New Mexico	121,339	26,215	34,150	23,275	37,699	120,976	26,023	34,258	23,323	37,372
New York	623,192	179,130	221,469	81,916	140,677	626,222	181,802	223,026	81,916	139,478
North Carolina	389,143	96,711	132,623	57,746	102,063	396,755	99,205	135,553	57,674	104,323
North Dakota	43,275	17,088	15,630	4,505	6,052	42,808	16,545	15,470	4,686	6,107
Ohio	454,377	131,826	158,484	64,946	99,121	453,001	133,533	158,752	63,639	97,077
Oklahoma	179,281	51,090	61,398	26,301	40,492	179,225	50,140	60,979	26,236	41,870
Oregon	165,375	43,938	50,041	30,386	41,010	163,752	43,121	48,893	30,418	41,320
Pennsylvania	384,525	125,111	139,991	42,974	76,449	380,271	125,517	139,428	41,224	74,102
Rhode Island	39,920	9,290	13,091	5,612	11,927	40,008	9,271	13,444	5,603	11,690
South Carolina	172,386	47,422	63,474	19,889	41,601	174,686	48,413	64,478	19,609	42,186
South Dakota	37,598	12,916	13,057	3,956	7,669	37,548	12,996	12,894	3,953	7,705
Tennessee	199,904	57,983	76,414	24,282	41,225	200,394	58,276	76,438	24,165	41,515
Texas	1,071,926	257,727	311,866	204,248	298,085	1,081,335	259,954	315,314	204,267	301,800
Utah	145,182	42,231	36,788	32,645	33,518	148,960	40,934	36,636	35,703	35,687
Vermont	22,980	6,662	8,043	2,572	5,703	24,090	7,218	8,363	2,497	6,012
Virginia	343,391	86,649	105,164	59,870	91,708	349,195	88,693	107,294	60,538	92,670
Washington	293,145	80,662	94,273	48,131	70,079	296,756	79,941	94,634	50,152	72,029
West Virginia	83,274	28,673	32,150	8,377	14,074	85,148	29,101	32,819	8,719	14,509
Wisconsin	266,884	76,787	90,092	40,700	59,305	268,928	77,667	90,812	39,874	60,575
Wyoming	31,597	7,837	9,323	4,937	9,500	32,611	7,788	9,260	5,863	9,700
U.S. Service Schools	14,754	12,209	2,545	0	0	15,265	12,521	2,744	0	0
Other jurisdictions	83,831	25,681	40,549	6,423	11,178	82,341	24,984	39,115	6,735	11,507
American Samoa	1,550	303	446	270	531	1,579	290	475	310	504
Federated States of Micronesia	2,608	956	992	339	321	2,283	791	762	375	355
Guam	4,470	936	1,442	851	1,241	5,875	1,029	1,567	1,158	2,121
Marshall Islands	623	284	214	69	56	604	254	219	67	64
Northern Marianas	1,101	307	509	99	186	967	260	482	88	137
Palau	651	205	224	72	150	651	212	219	67	153
Puerto Rico	70,263	22,375	35,779	4,443	7,666	67,990	21,817	34,459	4,452	7,262
Virgin Islands	2,565	315	943	280	1,027	2,392	331	932	218	911

NOTE: Degree-granting institutions grant associate's or higher degrees and participate in Title IV federal financial aid programs.

SOURCE: U.S. Department of Education, National Center for Education Statistics, 2004 and 2005 Integrated Postsecondary Education Data System (IPEDS), Spring 2005 and Spring 2006. (This table was prepared August 2006.)

Table 198. Total fall enrollment in private degree-granting institutions, by attendance status, sex, and state or jurisdiction: 2004 and 2005

State or jurisdiction	Fall 2004					Fall 2005				
		Full-time		Part-time			Full-time		Part-time	
	Total	Males	Females	Males	Females	Total	Males	Females	Males	Females
1	2	3	4	5	6	7	8	9	10	11
United States	4,291,932	1,414,282	1,826,463	413,504	637,683	4,465,641	1,452,903	1,935,347	413,799	663,592
Alabama	28,837	10,168	13,466	1,987	3,216	28,236	10,151	13,496	1,783	2,806
Alaska	1,354	277	457	238	382	1,365	252	432	222	459
Arizona	172,951	69,073	93,050	4,360	6,468	224,732	81,214	130,752	4,392	8,374
Arkansas	14,426	5,678	6,603	697	1,448	15,155	5,652	6,833	837	1,833
California	386,762	130,698	164,380	40,891	50,793	391,678	130,335	169,171	39,913	52,259
Colorado	61,606	20,205	23,910	7,879	9,612	68,163	21,914	27,752	8,508	9,989
Connecticut	62,421	21,137	26,646	5,373	9,265	62,970	21,391	27,075	5,193	9,311
Delaware	11,561	2,400	3,507	1,899	3,755	12,930	2,758	4,009	2,118	4,045
District of Columbia	94,600	24,697	34,191	14,298	21,414	99,302	24,900	34,850	15,586	23,966
Florida	216,808	67,836	86,549	27,916	34,507	223,663	68,522	91,021	28,062	36,058
Georgia	98,304	34,508	49,929	5,329	8,538	84,638	28,317	42,432	5,186	8,703
Hawaii	16,656	4,280	7,354	2,243	2,779	16,926	4,275	7,587	2,274	2,790
Idaho	15,616	6,537	7,609	666	804	17,405	6,860	8,514	885	1,146
Illinois	237,808	72,570	93,464	27,667	44,107	277,818	87,050	116,432	28,458	45,878
Indiana	89,885	32,952	41,114	5,757	10,062	93,955	34,182	43,430	5,817	10,526
Iowa	67,870	20,228	27,563	6,136	13,943	78,815	21,724	31,493	7,434	18,164
Kansas	21,441	6,805	8,170	2,386	4,080	21,433	6,844	8,206	2,380	4,003
Kentucky	42,106	13,063	19,073	3,423	6,547	43,390	12,392	19,606	4,024	7,368
Louisiana	38,083	11,513	19,282	2,558	4,730	16,670	3,949	10,053	773	1,895
Maine	18,131	5,526	7,281	1,536	3,788	18,032	5,610	7,633	1,359	3,430
Maryland	55,911	14,409	20,136	8,470	12,896	58,078	15,076	21,168	8,494	13,340
Massachusetts	251,372	87,053	107,995	21,910	34,414	255,021	88,824	109,755	21,292	35,150
Michigan	120,107	29,807	42,866	17,141	30,293	121,165	29,917	42,762	17,315	31,171
Minnesota	107,776	29,239	46,882	12,039	19,616	120,848	30,471	50,523	13,865	25,989
Mississippi	14,572	4,161	7,953	720	1,738	14,561	4,371	7,663	684	1,843
Missouri	150,643	39,289	50,600	26,302	34,452	156,723	40,125	53,442	26,708	36,448
Montana	4,884	1,583	2,328	366	607	4,853	1,585	2,215	360	693
Nebraska	27,858	9,336	13,168	1,899	3,455	28,055	9,449	12,828	2,016	3,762
Nevada	9,188	3,478	5,224	291	195	10,662	4,102	5,906	276	378
New Hampshire	29,521	9,900	12,019	2,440	5,162	28,886	9,891	12,166	2,171	4,658
New Jersey	75,340	25,375	26,148	9,618	14,199	75,443	25,388	26,707	9,601	13,747
New Mexico	10,238	3,440	4,967	708	1,123	10,361	3,329	5,305	665	1,062
New York	518,333	173,428	225,367	43,354	76,184	525,859	175,479	230,204	42,938	77,238
North Carolina	83,566	30,252	40,063	4,757	8,494	87,637	31,956	42,309	4,731	8,641
North Dakota	6,258	2,019	3,141	297	801	6,581	2,017	3,362	323	879
Ohio	159,857	53,050	68,155	14,054	24,598	163,349	53,803	71,345	13,676	24,525
Oklahoma	28,344	11,600	12,063	2,114	2,567	28,828	11,370	12,717	2,142	2,599
Oregon	34,610	12,058	16,154	2,701	3,697	36,281	12,147	16,798	2,965	4,371
Pennsylvania	304,255	104,635	124,954	27,198	47,468	312,069	107,097	130,337	26,626	48,009
Rhode Island	40,457	17,125	17,925	2,511	2,896	41,374	17,731	18,460	2,434	2,749
South Carolina	36,524	12,037	17,699	2,229	4,559	35,758	11,957	17,477	1,966	4,358
South Dakota	11,110	2,525	4,422	1,562	2,601	11,220	2,564	4,283	1,559	2,814
Tennessee	78,151	29,366	37,462	4,399	6,924	82,676	29,954	39,693	4,929	8,100
Texas	157,271	53,056	64,016	18,677	21,522	159,372	53,730	65,978	18,075	21,589
Utah	49,142	19,494	20,194	4,854	4,600	51,731	21,817	22,684	3,431	3,799
Vermont	15,659	6,729	6,369	959	1,602	15,825	6,943	6,409	971	1,502
Virginia	81,790	27,587	37,692	6,569	9,942	89,971	29,658	42,887	6,789	10,637
Washington	50,379	16,674	22,650	4,836	6,219	51,726	17,651	23,792	4,293	5,990
West Virginia	14,610	4,715	7,531	741	1,623	14,399	4,679	7,453	770	1,497
Wisconsin	64,622	18,385	26,690	6,549	12,998	66,330	18,922	27,827	6,530	13,051
Wyoming	2,358	2,326	32	0	0	2,723	2,608	115	0	0
Other jurisdictions	137,089	40,278	62,012	13,601	21,198	140,824	41,479	63,569	14,002	21,774
American Samoa	0	0	0	0	0	0	0	0	0	0
Federated States of Micronesia	0	0	0	0	0	0	0	0	0	0
Guam	172	42	61	35	34	189	56	77	26	30
Marshall Islands	0	0	0	0	0	0	0	0	0	0
Northern Marianas	0	0	0	0	0	0	0	0	0	0
Palau	0	0	0	0	0	0	0	0	0	0
Puerto Rico	136,917	40,236	61,951	13,566	21,164	140,635	41,423	63,492	13,976	21,744
Virgin Islands	0	0	0	0	0	0	0	0	0	0

NOTE: Degree-granting institutions grant associate's or higher degrees and participate in Title IV federal financial aid programs.

SOURCE: U.S. Department of Education, National Center for Education Statistics, 2004 and 2005 Integrated Postsecondary Education Data System (IPEDS), Spring 2005 and Spring 2006. (This table was prepared August 2006.)

Table 199. Total fall enrollment in private not-for-profit degree-granting institutions, by attendance status, sex, and state or jurisdiction: 2004 and 2005

State or jurisdiction	Fall 2004					Fall 2005				
	Total	Full-time		Part-time		Total	Full-time		Part-time	
		Males	Females	Males	Females		Males	Females	Males	Females
1	2	3	4	5	6	7	8	9	10	11
United States	3,411,685	1,104,447	1,418,546	344,776	543,916	3,454,692	1,121,161	1,442,571	343,138	547,822
Alabama	23,181	8,281	11,277	1,491	2,132	23,076	8,382	11,047	1,462	2,185
Alaska	952	183	381	122	266	941	188	345	112	296
Arizona	9,981	3,502	3,787	1,090	1,602	9,684	3,303	3,872	1,101	1,408
Arkansas	13,377	5,204	6,107	635	1,431	13,781	5,121	6,055	787	1,818
California	273,906	85,196	111,626	33,225	43,859	277,096	85,794	113,418	33,139	44,745
Colorado	30,231	8,693	10,876	4,435	6,227	31,096	8,722	11,459	4,546	6,369
Connecticut	60,271	20,527	25,737	5,167	8,840	59,995	20,621	26,077	4,789	8,508
Delaware	11,561	2,400	3,507	1,899	3,755	12,930	2,758	4,009	2,118	4,045
District of Columbia	70,687	22,035	30,753	7,434	10,465	71,695	22,348	31,171	7,763	10,413
Florida	142,340	42,871	52,739	21,751	24,979	146,782	44,242	54,785	22,423	25,332
Georgia	61,190	20,987	31,004	3,363	5,836	62,149	21,389	31,467	3,394	5,899
Hawaii	13,963	3,468	5,607	2,212	2,676	14,294	3,522	5,838	2,244	2,690
Idaho	14,071	5,851	6,927	520	773	15,661	6,159	7,575	806	1,121
Illinois	202,733	62,984	81,881	21,414	36,454	209,775	64,804	84,179	22,730	38,062
Indiana	77,232	28,674	34,847	4,837	8,874	78,761	29,372	35,997	4,661	8,731
Iowa	54,094	18,801	24,415	3,810	7,068	54,591	19,133	24,954	3,583	6,921
Kansas	20,351	6,441	7,502	2,360	4,048	20,152	6,468	7,403	2,352	3,929
Kentucky	28,645	9,225	12,809	2,378	4,233	29,360	9,419	13,172	2,533	4,236
Louisiana	30,249	9,171	14,359	2,190	4,529	9,829	2,334	5,295	515	1,685
Maine	17,170	5,374	6,720	1,472	3,604	17,069	5,460	7,016	1,324	3,269
Maryland	50,625	12,655	17,344	8,033	12,593	52,156	13,189	17,864	8,132	12,971
Massachusetts	246,710	84,927	106,222	21,541	34,020	250,752	86,736	108,097	20,977	34,942
Michigan	111,565	26,278	38,732	16,637	29,918	112,951	26,590	38,487	16,962	30,912
Minnesota	66,786	21,508	29,517	5,735	10,026	68,859	21,875	30,038	6,174	10,772
Mississippi	12,688	3,780	6,616	652	1,640	12,732	3,998	6,389	649	1,696
Missouri	134,829	34,113	42,412	25,008	33,296	138,762	34,237	43,485	25,630	35,410
Montana	4,884	1,583	2,328	366	607	4,853	1,585	2,215	360	693
Nebraska	25,468	8,557	11,711	1,799	3,401	25,920	8,697	11,707	1,910	3,606
Nevada	505	210	227	31	37	644	202	267	58	117
New Hampshire	24,823	8,657	9,882	2,127	4,157	24,352	8,816	10,187	1,802	3,547
New Jersey	69,370	23,216	23,549	8,945	13,660	70,032	23,654	24,003	9,096	13,279
New Mexico	3,614	875	1,482	421	836	3,489	869	1,458	389	773
New York	471,654	157,503	200,054	41,172	72,925	477,333	159,748	204,239	40,353	72,993
North Carolina	80,539	29,383	38,416	4,610	8,130	83,473	30,722	40,053	4,556	8,142
North Dakota	5,536	1,916	2,829	238	553	5,682	1,924	2,974	250	534
Ohio	136,247	45,846	56,294	12,105	22,002	137,437	46,442	57,217	11,981	21,797
Oklahoma	22,095	8,211	9,213	2,112	2,559	22,142	8,254	9,187	2,136	2,565
Oregon	27,035	8,703	12,473	2,405	3,454	28,097	9,013	12,837	2,513	3,734
Pennsylvania	262,148	87,187	108,194	23,993	42,774	268,039	89,782	112,143	23,349	42,765
Rhode Island	39,907	16,979	17,521	2,511	2,896	40,828	17,598	18,047	2,434	2,749
South Carolina	34,589	11,380	16,896	2,091	4,222	33,701	11,184	16,627	1,836	4,054
South Dakota	7,879	1,937	3,366	796	1,780	7,891	2,019	3,346	761	1,765
Tennessee	62,656	22,988	30,292	3,575	5,801	65,177	23,272	30,948	4,105	6,852
Texas	122,989	40,516	48,296	15,559	18,618	125,111	41,437	49,492	15,456	18,726
Utah	40,963	15,949	17,035	4,337	3,642	42,472	17,958	18,972	2,883	2,659
Vermont	15,322	6,519	6,242	959	1,602	15,302	6,599	6,230	971	1,502
Virginia	61,153	20,076	28,549	4,814	7,714	63,818	21,048	29,459	5,247	8,064
Washington	40,855	12,587	19,190	3,739	5,339	41,623	13,355	19,976	3,315	4,977
West Virginia	12,125	4,105	5,752	709	1,559	11,365	3,903	5,662	541	1,259
Wisconsin	59,941	16,435	25,051	5,951	12,504	60,982	16,916	25,831	5,930	12,305
Wyoming	0	0	0	0	0	0	0	0	0	0
Other jurisdictions	118,833	33,582	53,666	12,395	19,190	121,568	34,118	54,734	12,780	19,936
American Samoa	0	0	0	0	0	0	0	0	0	0
Federated States of Micronesia	0	0	0	0	0	0	0	0	0	0
Guam	172	42	61	35	34	189	56	77	26	30
Marshall Islands	0	0	0	0	0	0	0	0	0	0
Northern Marianas	0	0	0	0	0	0	0	0	0	0
Palau	0	0	0	0	0	0	0	0	0	0
Puerto Rico	118,661	33,540	53,605	12,360	19,156	121,379	34,062	54,657	12,754	19,906
Virgin Islands	0	0	0	0	0	0	0	0	0	0

NOTE: Degree-granting institutions grant associate's or higher degrees and participate in Title IV federal financial aid programs.

SOURCE: U.S. Department of Education, National Center for Education Statistics, 2004 and 2005 Integrated Postsecondary Education Data System (IPEDS), Spring 2005 and Spring 2006. (This table was prepared August 2006.)

Table 200. Total fall enrollment in degree-granting institutions, by control and type of institution and state or jurisdiction: 2004 and 2005

State or jurisdiction	2004						2005					
			Private 4-year		Private 2-year				Private 4-year		Private 2-year	
	Public 4-year	Public 2-year	Total	Not-for-profit	Total	Not-for-profit	Public 4-year	Public 2-year	Total	Not-for-profit	Total	Not-for-profit
1	2	3	4	5	6	7	8	9	10	11	12	13
United States	6,736,536	6,243,576	3,989,645	3,369,435	302,287	42,250	6,837,605	6,184,229	4,161,815	3,411,170	303,826	43,522
Alabama..........................	148,293	78,696	28,194	22,987	643	194	149,752	78,401	27,526	22,820	710	256
Alaska.............................	28,329	1,186	1,354	952	0	0	27,765	1,101	1,365	941	0	0
Arizona	116,571	201,403	156,757	9,812	16,194	169	120,020	200,845	211,287	9,414	13,445	270
Arkansas........................	77,857	46,116	13,913	13,174	513	203	80,346	47,771	14,528	13,610	627	171
California	600,027	1,387,256	346,512	267,085	40,250	6,821	609,397	1,398,758	353,786	270,300	37,892	6,796
Colorado	154,592	84,716	52,353	30,009	9,253	222	154,706	79,803	58,930	30,876	9,233	220
Connecticut....................	64,611	45,743	59,867	58,924	2,554	1,347	65,478	46,227	60,387	58,362	2,583	1,633
Delaware........................	24,508	13,735	11,385	11,385	176	176	24,704	13,978	12,751	12,751	179	179
District of Columbia	5,388	0	94,600	70,687	0	0	5,595	0	99,302	71,695	0	0
Florida............................	365,574	284,283	197,509	140,109	19,299	2,231	371,553	277,446	203,001	144,774	20,662	2,008
Georgia..........................	196,056	139,923	95,174	60,036	3,130	1,154	197,418	144,594	79,669	61,108	4,969	1,041
Hawaii	24,671	25,898	15,485	13,095	1,171	868	27,827	22,330	15,749	13,459	1,177	835
Idaho..............................	48,283	12,412	15,292	14,071	324	0	48,289	12,014	16,893	15,661	512	0
Illinois............................	200,467	363,126	231,722	201,863	6,086	870	202,325	352,824	272,200	208,830	5,618	945
Indiana...........................	198,408	68,508	80,489	76,573	9,396	659	207,329	59,969	83,019	78,110	10,936	651
Iowa	67,749	82,027	66,713	53,058	1,157	1,036	66,789	82,118	77,321	53,547	1,494	1,044
Kansas...........................	95,505	74,644	19,728	19,294	1,713	1,057	96,057	74,262	19,757	19,201	1,676	951
Kentucky........................	116,719	81,272	34,307	28,645	7,799	0	116,910	84,669	38,597	29,360	4,793	0
Louisiana.......................	157,859	50,359	33,742	30,249	4,341	0	147,529	33,514	12,733	9,829	3,937	0
Maine..............................	35,070	12,214	17,055	17,055	1,076	115	35,084	12,435	16,945	16,945	1,087	124
Maryland.........................	137,633	118,949	52,854	50,625	3,057	0	136,827	119,246	54,417	52,156	3,661	0
Massachusetts................	102,385	85,488	246,891	244,905	4,481	1,805	104,086	84,209	251,730	248,679	3,291	2,073
Michigan.........................	289,699	211,174	116,980	111,220	3,127	345	290,001	215,585	118,378	112,647	2,787	304
Minnesota.......................	130,229	111,016	102,844	65,368	4,932	1,418	130,529	110,324	115,510	67,395	5,338	1,464
Mississippi.....................	69,323	68,220	12,688	12,688	1,884	0	69,598	66,298	12,732	12,732	1,829	0
Missouri..........................	128,320	86,241	142,955	133,811	7,688	1,018	130,980	86,742	148,291	137,509	8,432	1,253
Montana..........................	33,722	8,567	4,323	4,323	561	561	33,863	9,134	4,368	4,368	485	485
Nebraska........................	52,552	40,643	27,163	25,314	695	154	52,961	40,220	27,447	25,811	608	109
Nevada	80,702	16,071	6,365	505	2,823	0	83,672	16,371	7,734	644	2,928	0
New Hampshire	27,254	13,388	27,531	24,235	1,990	588	27,257	13,750	27,470	24,030	1,416	322
New Jersey	152,991	152,043	73,752	69,244	1,588	126	152,430	151,885	74,200	69,891	1,243	141
New Mexico	57,087	64,252	10,044	3,614	194	0	56,839	64,137	9,840	3,489	521	0
New York........................	350,748	272,444	485,184	465,592	33,149	6,062	354,914	271,308	493,245	471,407	32,614	5,926
North Carolina	189,615	199,528	80,844	79,968	2,722	571	196,248	200,507	86,091	82,740	1,546	733
North Dakota	33,769	9,506	5,000	5,000	1,258	536	33,603	9,205	4,797	4,797	1,784	885
Ohio................................	272,773	181,604	140,834	134,792	19,023	1,455	279,039	173,962	142,155	135,827	21,194	1,610
Oklahoma.......................	113,343	65,938	25,605	22,095	2,739	0	113,608	65,617	26,181	22,142	2,647	0
Oregon............................	82,515	82,860	32,063	26,768	2,547	267	83,239	80,513	33,436	27,891	2,845	206
Pennsylvania..................	256,360	128,165	270,144	257,287	34,111	4,861	256,194	124,077	277,146	262,396	34,923	5,643
Rhode Island	23,627	16,293	39,907	39,907	550	0	23,966	16,042	40,828	40,828	546	0
South Carolina................	93,504	78,882	34,526	33,713	1,998	876	95,803	78,883	33,819	32,833	1,939	868
South Dakota..................	32,216	5,382	10,605	7,374	505	505	32,063	5,485	10,682	7,353	538	538
Tennessee	124,405	75,499	67,731	62,072	10,420	584	125,565	74,829	71,549	64,612	11,127	565
Texas	505,120	566,806	136,669	121,894	20,602	1,095	537,844	543,491	139,782	124,022	19,590	1,089
Utah................................	110,533	34,649	45,528	39,715	3,614	1,248	113,164	35,796	47,712	41,237	4,019	1,235
Vermont..........................	17,361	5,619	15,131	14,932	528	390	18,575	5,515	15,147	14,885	678	417
Virginia...........................	189,665	153,726	77,504	60,997	4,286	156	194,228	154,967	82,535	63,818	7,436	0
Washington.....................	105,366	187,779	49,709	40,855	670	0	106,333	190,423	50,874	41,623	852	0
West Virginia..................	67,586	15,688	12,125	12,125	2,485	0	67,341	17,807	12,193	11,365	2,206	0
Wisconsin.......................	151,635	115,249	63,995	59,434	627	507	153,571	115,357	65,665	60,450	665	532
Wyoming.........................	13,207	18,390	0	0	2,358	0	13,126	19,485	115	0	2,608	0
U.S. Service Schools............	14,754	0	†	†	†	†	15,265	0	†	†	†	†
Other jurisdictions	74,673	9,158	124,357	115,571	12,732	3,262	72,126	10,215	126,693	117,615	14,131	3,953
American Samoa.................	0	1,550	0	0	0	0	0	1,579	0	0	0	0
Federated States of												
Micronesia.....................	0	2,608	0	0	0	0	0	2,283	0	0	0	0
Guam.................................	2,923	1,547	172	172	0	0	3,034	2,841	189	189	0	0
Marshall Islands.................	0	623	0	0	0	0	0	604	0	0	0	0
Northern Marianas	1,101	0	0	0	0	0	967	0	0	0	0	0
Palau.................................	0	651	0	0	0	0	0	651	0	0	0	0
Puerto Rico.........................	68,084	2,179	124,185	115,399	12,732	3,262	65,733	2,257	126,504	117,426	14,131	3,953
Virgin Islands.....................	2,565	0	0	0	0	0	2,392	0	0	0	0	0

†Not applicable.
NOTE: Degree-granting institutions grant associate's or higher degrees and participate in Title IV federal financial aid programs.

SOURCE: U.S. Department of Education, National Center for Education Statistics, 2004 and 2005 Integrated Postsecondary Education Data System (IPEDS), Spring 2005 and Spring 2006. (This table was prepared August 2006.)

Table 201. Total fall enrollment in degree-granting institutions, by level of enrollment and state or jurisdiction: 2004 and 2005

State or jurisdiction	Fall 2004				Fall 2005			
	Total	Undergraduate	First-professional	Graduate	Total	Undergraduate	First-professional	Graduate
1	2	3	4	5	6	7	8	9
United States	17,272,044	14,780,630	334,529	2,156,885	17,487,475	14,963,964	337,024	2,186,487
Alabama	255,826	218,372	4,436	33,018	256,389	219,253	4,403	32,733
Alaska	30,869	28,563	0	2,306	30,231	27,903	0	2,328
Arizona	490,925	410,416	3,178	77,331	545,597	456,881	3,330	85,386
Arkansas	138,399	125,636	1,836	10,927	143,272	129,484	1,879	11,909
California	2,374,045	2,107,426	33,845	232,774	2,399,833	2,135,461	33,817	230,555
Colorado	300,914	248,396	4,169	48,349	302,672	249,616	4,246	48,810
Connecticut	172,775	139,071	3,524	30,180	174,675	141,332	3,409	29,934
Delaware	49,804	41,907	1,167	6,730	51,612	43,382	1,072	7,158
District of Columbia	99,988	59,930	9,790	30,268	104,897	62,888	9,992	32,017
Florida	866,665	761,390	14,804	90,471	872,662	764,577	15,733	92,352
Georgia	434,283	377,266	7,998	49,019	426,650	372,269	8,381	46,000
Hawaii	67,225	58,025	604	8,596	67,083	57,843	645	8,595
Idaho	76,311	68,613	582	7,116	77,708	70,335	563	6,810
Illinois	801,401	667,249	17,859	116,293	832,967	692,401	18,021	122,545
Indiana	356,801	308,358	6,469	41,974	361,253	312,058	6,590	42,605
Iowa	217,646	193,908	7,124	16,614	227,722	203,453	7,067	17,202
Kansas	191,590	168,160	2,501	20,929	191,752	168,065	2,479	21,208
Kentucky	240,097	210,589	4,647	24,861	244,969	215,536	4,546	24,887
Louisiana	246,301	211,901	6,399	28,001	197,713	172,908	4,413	20,392
Maine	65,415	57,394	825	7,196	65,551	57,622	820	7,109
Maryland	312,493	252,340	4,322	55,831	314,151	252,964	4,383	56,804
Massachusetts	439,245	328,335	16,091	94,819	443,316	331,242	15,657	96,417
Michigan	620,980	529,083	12,583	79,314	626,751	536,745	13,244	76,762
Minnesota	349,021	280,739	7,819	60,463	361,701	283,616	7,852	70,233
Mississippi	152,115	135,449	2,525	14,141	150,457	133,642	2,588	14,227
Missouri	365,204	296,969	11,559	56,676	374,445	304,992	11,908	57,545
Montana	47,173	42,743	472	3,958	47,850	43,403	527	3,920
Nebraska	121,053	103,765	3,618	13,670	121,236	103,581	3,646	14,009
Nevada	105,961	95,563	923	9,475	110,705	99,548	988	10,169
New Hampshire	70,163	59,199	726	10,238	69,893	59,081	736	10,076
New Jersey	380,374	321,494	6,184	52,696	379,758	321,118	6,069	52,571
New Mexico	131,577	114,794	981	15,802	131,337	115,048	1,018	15,271
New York	1,141,525	914,620	30,479	196,426	1,152,081	921,458	30,741	199,882
North Carolina	472,709	417,786	7,610	47,313	484,392	426,106	7,926	50,360
North Dakota	49,533	44,774	432	4,327	49,389	44,153	803	4,433
Ohio	614,234	526,569	13,231	74,434	616,350	529,891	13,252	73,207
Oklahoma	207,625	182,767	4,519	20,339	208,053	183,568	4,570	19,915
Oregon	199,985	174,619	4,777	20,589	200,033	174,100	4,559	21,374
Pennsylvania	688,780	571,322	19,053	98,405	692,340	574,319	19,299	98,722
Rhode Island	80,377	69,674	1,515	9,188	81,382	70,518	1,512	9,352
South Carolina	208,910	184,413	3,392	21,105	210,444	185,252	3,384	21,808
South Dakota	48,708	43,202	626	4,880	48,768	43,206	626	4,936
Tennessee	278,055	239,918	5,913	32,224	283,070	243,912	5,921	33,237
Texas	1,229,197	1,082,667	20,367	126,163	1,240,707	1,093,491	20,420	126,796
Utah	194,324	176,909	1,443	15,972	200,691	182,892	1,439	16,360
Vermont	38,639	33,313	957	4,369	39,915	34,161	969	4,785
Virginia	425,181	360,484	9,039	55,658	439,166	373,041	9,821	56,304
Washington	343,524	310,944	4,867	27,713	348,482	315,154	4,870	28,458
West Virginia	97,884	85,388	1,928	10,568	99,547	86,803	1,997	10,747
Wisconsin	331,506	293,127	4,389	33,990	335,258	296,743	4,456	34,059
Wyoming	33,955	30,337	432	3,186	35,334	31,684	437	3,213
U.S. Service Schools	14,754	14,754	0	0	15,265	15,265	0	0
Other jurisdictions	220,920	193,506	3,775	23,639	223,165	193,766	3,871	25,528
American Samoa	1,550	1,550	0	0	1,579	1,579	0	0
Federated States of Micronesia	2,608	2,608	0	0	2,283	2,283	0	0
Guam	4,642	4,417	0	225	6,064	5,850	0	214
Marshall Islands	623	623	0	0	604	604	0	0
Northern Marianas	1,101	1,101	0	0	967	967	0	0
Palau	651	651	0	0	651	651	0	0
Puerto Rico	207,180	180,204	3,775	23,201	208,625	179,647	3,871	25,107
Virgin Islands	2,565	2,352	0	213	2,392	2,185	0	207

NOTE: Degree-granting institutions grant associate's or higher degrees and participate in Title IV federal financial aid programs.

SOURCE: U.S. Department of Education, National Center for Education Statistics, 2004 and 2005 Integrated Postsecondary Education Data System (IPEDS), Spring 2005 and Spring 2006. (This table was prepared August 2006.)

Table 202. Total fall enrollment in degree-granting institutions, by control, level of enrollment, type of institution, and state or jurisdiction: 2005

State or jurisdiction	Public					Private				
	Undergraduate			First-professional	Graduate	Undergraduate			First-professional	Graduate
	Total	4-year	2-year			Total	4-year	2-year		
1	2	3	4	5	6	7	8	9	10	11
United States	11,697,730	5,513,730	6,184,000	138,207	1,185,897	3,266,234	2,962,408	303,826	198,817	1,000,590
Alabama	194,753	116,352	78,401	2,696	30,704	24,500	23,790	710	1,707	2,029
Alaska	26,759	25,658	1,101	0	2,107	1,144	1,144	0	0	221
Arizona	294,515	93,670	200,845	1,972	24,378	162,366	148,921	13,445	1,358	61,008
Arkansas	116,375	68,604	47,771	1,879	9,863	13,109	12,482	627	0	2,046
California	1,891,784	493,026	1,398,758	8,134	108,237	243,677	205,785	37,892	25,683	122,318
Colorado	199,952	120,149	79,803	2,613	31,944	49,664	40,431	9,233	1,633	16,866
Connecticut	96,581	50,354	46,227	1,378	13,746	44,751	42,168	2,583	2,031	16,188
Delaware	34,966	20,988	13,978	0	3,716	8,416	8,237	179	1,072	3,442
District of Columbia	5,169	5,169	0	232	194	57,719	57,719	0	9,760	31,823
Florida	593,134	315,688	277,446	6,452	49,413	171,443	150,781	20,662	9,281	42,939
Georgia	307,511	162,917	144,594	3,251	31,250	64,758	59,789	4,969	5,130	14,750
Hawaii	43,657	21,327	22,330	640	5,860	14,186	13,009	1,177	5	2,735
Idaho	53,520	41,506	12,014	563	6,220	16,815	16,303	512	0	590
Illinois	504,353	151,529	352,824	4,576	46,220	188,048	182,430	5,618	13,445	76,325
Indiana	232,315	172,346	59,969	4,439	30,544	79,743	68,807	10,936	2,151	12,061
Iowa	134,144	52,026	82,118	2,472	12,291	69,309	67,815	1,494	4,595	4,911
Kansas	150,341	76,079	74,262	2,389	17,589	17,724	16,048	1,676	90	3,619
Kentucky	178,596	93,927	84,669	3,389	19,594	36,940	32,147	4,793	1,157	5,293
Louisiana	158,291	124,777	33,514	3,452	19,300	14,617	10,680	3,937	961	1,092
Maine	42,875	30,440	12,435	259	4,385	14,747	13,660	1,087	561	2,724
Maryland	219,934	100,688	119,246	3,585	32,554	33,030	29,369	3,661	798	24,250
Massachusetts	165,005	80,796	84,209	412	22,878	166,237	162,946	3,291	15,245	73,539
Michigan	438,567	222,982	215,585	6,747	60,272	98,178	95,391	2,787	6,497	16,490
Minnesota	215,971	105,647	110,324	3,769	21,113	67,645	62,307	5,338	4,083	49,120
Mississippi	121,884	55,586	66,298	1,998	12,014	11,758	9,929	1,829	590	2,213
Missouri	194,674	107,932	86,742	2,770	20,278	110,318	101,886	8,432	9,138	37,267
Montana	38,700	29,566	9,134	527	3,770	4,703	4,218	485	0	150
Nebraska	81,386	41,166	40,220	1,316	10,479	22,195	21,587	608	2,330	3,530
Nevada	90,622	74,251	16,371	988	8,433	8,926	5,998	2,928	0	1,736
New Hampshire	36,552	22,802	13,750	0	4,455	22,529	21,113	1,416	736	5,621
New Jersey	269,626	117,741	151,885	3,989	30,700	51,492	50,249	1,243	2,080	21,871
New Mexico	106,582	42,445	64,137	1,018	13,376	8,466	7,945	521	0	1,895
New York	557,715	286,407	271,308	4,704	63,803	363,743	331,129	32,614	26,037	136,079
North Carolina	355,536	155,029	200,507	3,401	37,818	70,570	69,024	1,546	4,525	12,542
North Dakota	38,133	28,928	9,205	803	3,872	6,020	4,236	1,784	0	561
Ohio	397,856	224,123	173,733	8,280	46,865	132,035	110,841	21,194	4,972	26,342
Oklahoma	159,797	94,180	65,617	2,945	16,483	23,771	21,124	2,647	1,625	3,432
Oregon	146,894	66,381	80,513	1,775	15,083	27,206	24,361	2,845	2,784	6,291
Pennsylvania	335,932	211,855	124,077	6,058	38,281	238,387	203,464	34,923	13,241	60,441
Rhode Island	35,065	19,023	16,042	553	4,390	35,453	34,907	546	959	4,962
South Carolina	154,204	75,321	78,883	2,573	17,909	31,048	29,109	1,939	811	3,899
South Dakota	32,969	27,484	5,485	569	4,010	10,237	9,699	538	57	926
Tennessee	176,759	101,930	74,829	2,840	20,795	67,153	56,026	11,127	3,081	12,442
Texas	968,697	425,206	543,491	11,951	100,687	124,794	105,204	19,590	8,469	26,109
Utah	137,825	102,029	35,796	978	10,157	45,067	41,048	4,019	461	6,203
Vermont	21,505	15,990	5,515	406	2,179	12,656	11,978	678	563	2,606
Virginia	299,557	144,590	154,967	4,957	44,681	73,484	66,048	7,436	4,864	11,623
Washington	276,873	86,450	190,423	2,577	17,306	38,281	37,429	852	2,293	11,152
West Virginia	73,609	55,802	17,807	1,997	9,542	13,194	10,988	2,206	0	1,205
Wisconsin	245,450	130,093	115,357	2,498	20,980	51,293	50,628	665	1,958	13,079
Wyoming	28,995	9,510	19,485	437	3,179	2,689	81	2,608	0	34
U.S. Service Schools	15,265	15,265	0	0	0	†	†	†	†	†
Other jurisdictions	74,874	64,659	10,215	1,514	5,953	118,892	104,761	14,131	2,357	19,575
American Samoa	1,579	0	1,579	0	0	0	0	0	0	0
Federated States of Micronesia	2,283	0	2,283	0	0	0	0	0	0	0
Guam	5,661	2,820	2,841	0	214	189	189	0	0	0
Marshall Islands	604	0	604	0	0	0	0	0	0	0
Northern Marianas	967	967	0	0	0	0	0	0	0	0
Palau	651	0	651	0	0	0	0	0	0	0
Puerto Rico	60,944	58,687	2,257	1,514	5,532	118,703	104,572	14,131	2,357	19,575
Virgin Islands	2,185	2,185	0	0	207	0	0	0	0	0

†Not applicable.
NOTE: Degree-granting institutions grant associate's or higher degrees and participate in Title IV federal financial aid programs.

SOURCE: U.S. Department of Education, National Center for Education Statistics, 2005 Integrated Postsecondary Education Data System (IPEDS), Spring 2006. (This table was prepared August 2006.)

Table 203. Total fall enrollment in degree-granting institutions, by control, level of enrollment, type of institution, and state or jurisdiction: 2004

State or jurisdiction	Public					Private				
	Undergraduate			First-professional	Graduate	Undergraduate			First-professional	Graduate
	Total	4-year	2-year			Total	4-year	2-year		
1	2	3	4	5	6	7	8	9	10	11
United States	11,650,580	5,407,236	6,243,344	135,756	1,193,776	3,130,050	2,827,824	302,226	198,773	963,109
Alabama	193,216	114,520	78,696	2,724	31,049	25,156	24,513	643	1,712	1,969
Alaska	27,426	26,240	1,186	0	2,089	1,137	1,137	0	0	217
Arizona	291,925	90,522	201,403	1,886	24,163	118,491	102,297	16,194	1,292	53,168
Arkansas	112,831	66,715	46,116	1,836	9,306	12,805	12,292	513	0	1,621
California	1,867,795	480,539	1,387,256	8,166	111,322	239,631	199,381	40,250	25,679	121,452
Colorado	204,664	119,948	84,716	2,543	32,101	43,732	34,479	9,253	1,626	16,248
Connecticut	95,164	49,421	45,743	1,375	13,815	43,907	41,353	2,554	2,149	16,365
Delaware	34,652	20,917	13,735	0	3,591	7,255	7,079	176	1,167	3,139
District of Columbia	4,966	4,966	0	220	202	54,964	54,964	0	9,570	30,066
Florida	594,951	310,668	284,283	5,895	49,011	166,439	147,140	19,299	8,909	41,460
Georgia	300,565	160,642	139,923	3,205	32,209	76,701	73,571	3,130	4,793	16,810
Hawaii	44,165	18,267	25,898	599	5,805	13,860	12,689	1,171	5	2,791
Idaho	53,543	41,131	12,412	582	6,570	15,070	14,746	324	0	546
Illinois	512,481	149,355	363,126	4,485	46,627	154,768	148,682	6,086	13,374	69,666
Indiana	231,786	163,278	68,508	4,364	30,766	76,572	67,176	9,396	2,105	11,208
Iowa	134,782	52,755	82,027	2,533	12,461	59,126	57,969	1,157	4,591	4,153
Kansas	150,448	75,804	74,644	2,426	17,275	17,712	15,999	1,713	75	3,654
Kentucky	174,578	93,306	81,272	3,305	20,108	36,011	28,212	7,799	1,342	4,753
Louisiana	182,196	131,837	50,359	3,272	22,750	29,705	25,364	4,341	3,127	5,251
Maine	42,616	30,402	12,214	281	4,387	14,778	13,702	1,076	544	2,809
Maryland	220,717	101,768	118,949	3,548	32,317	31,623	28,566	3,057	774	23,514
Massachusetts	164,618	79,130	85,488	419	22,836	163,717	159,236	4,481	15,672	71,983
Michigan	432,644	221,470	211,174	6,541	61,688	96,439	93,312	3,127	6,042	17,626
Minnesota	216,269	105,253	111,016	3,883	21,093	64,470	59,538	4,932	3,936	39,370
Mississippi	123,481	55,261	68,220	1,977	12,085	11,968	10,084	1,884	548	2,056
Missouri	192,033	105,792	86,241	2,728	19,800	104,936	97,248	7,688	8,831	36,876
Montana	37,994	29,427	8,567	472	3,823	4,749	4,188	561	0	135
Nebraska	81,453	40,810	40,643	1,316	10,426	22,312	21,617	695	2,302	3,244
Nevada	87,793	71,722	16,071	923	8,057	7,770	4,947	2,823	0	1,418
New Hampshire	36,330	22,942	13,388	0	4,312	22,869	20,879	1,990	726	5,926
New Jersey	269,844	117,801	152,043	3,971	31,219	51,650	50,062	1,588	2,213	21,477
New Mexico	106,518	42,266	64,252	981	13,840	8,276	8,082	194	0	1,962
New York	554,263	281,819	272,444	4,712	64,217	360,357	327,208	33,149	25,767	132,209
North Carolina	349,563	150,035	199,528	3,364	36,216	68,223	65,501	2,722	4,246	11,097
North Dakota	39,046	29,540	9,506	432	3,797	5,728	4,470	1,258	0	530
Ohio	398,523	217,151	181,372	8,197	47,657	128,046	109,023	19,023	5,034	26,777
Oklahoma	159,672	93,734	65,938	2,863	16,746	23,095	20,356	2,739	1,656	3,593
Oregon	148,676	65,816	82,860	1,713	14,986	25,943	23,396	2,547	3,064	5,603
Pennsylvania	339,451	211,286	128,165	6,066	39,008	231,871	197,760	34,111	12,987	59,397
Rhode Island	34,974	18,681	16,293	549	4,397	34,700	34,150	550	966	4,791
South Carolina	152,621	73,739	78,882	2,504	17,261	31,792	29,794	1,998	888	3,844
South Dakota	33,055	27,673	5,382	567	3,976	10,147	9,642	505	59	904
Tennessee	176,682	101,183	75,499	2,790	20,432	63,236	52,877	10,359	3,123	11,792
Texas	958,530	391,724	566,806	11,960	101,436	124,137	103,535	20,602	8,407	24,727
Utah	134,434	99,785	34,649	974	9,774	42,475	38,861	3,614	469	6,198
Vermont	20,808	15,189	5,619	402	1,770	12,505	11,977	528	555	2,599
Virginia	294,112	140,386	153,726	4,859	44,420	66,372	62,086	4,286	4,180	11,238
Washington	273,579	85,800	187,779	2,539	17,027	37,365	36,695	670	2,328	10,686
West Virginia	72,018	56,330	15,688	1,928	9,328	13,370	10,885	2,485	0	1,240
Wisconsin	243,396	128,147	115,249	2,449	21,039	49,731	49,104	627	1,940	12,951
Wyoming	27,979	9,589	18,390	432	3,186	2,358	0	2,358	0	0
U.S. Service Schools	14,754	14,754	0	0	0	†	†	†	†	†
Other jurisdictions	76,404	67,246	9,158	1,500	5,927	117,102	104,370	12,732	2,275	17,712
American Samoa	1,550	0	1,550	0	0	0	0	0	0	0
Federated States of Micronesia	2,608	0	2,608	0	0	0	0	0	0	0
Guam	4,245	2,698	1,547	0	225	172	172	0	0	0
Marshall Islands	623	0	623	0	0	0	0	0	0	0
Northern Marianas	1,101	1,101	0	0	0	0	0	0	0	0
Palau	651	0	651	0	0	0	0	0	0	0
Puerto Rico	63,274	61,095	2,179	1,500	5,489	116,930	104,198	12,732	2,275	17,712
Virgin Islands	2,352	2,352	0	0	213	0	0	0	0	0

†Not applicable.
NOTE: Degree-granting institutions grant associate's or higher degrees and participate in Title IV federal financial aid programs.

SOURCE: U.S. Department of Education, National Center for Education Statistics, 2004 Integrated Postsecondary Education Data System (IPEDS), Spring 2005. (This table was prepared September 2005.)

Table 204. Full-time-equivalent fall enrollment in degree-granting institutions, by control and type of institution: 1969 through 2005

Year	All institutions			Public institutions			Private institutions		
	Total	4-year	2-year	Total	4-year	2-year	Total	4-year	2-year
1	2	3	4	5	6	7	8	9	10
1969	6,334,139	4,899,526	1,434,612	4,577,985	3,259,676	1,318,309	1,756,153	1,639,850	116,303
1970	6,737,817	5,145,410	1,592,404	4,953,149	3,468,572	1,484,577	1,784,665	1,676,838	107,827
1971	7,148,575	5,357,708	1,790,867	5,344,356	3,660,624	1,683,732	1,804,219	1,697,084	107,135
1972	7,253,712	5,406,792	1,846,921	5,452,851	3,706,238	1,746,613	1,800,862	1,700,554	100,308
1973	7,453,467	5,439,226	2,014,241	5,629,568	3,721,035	1,908,533	1,823,899	1,718,191	105,708
1974	7,805,454	5,606,248	2,199,206	5,944,799	3,847,542	2,097,257	1,860,655	1,758,706	101,949
1975	8,479,688	5,900,403	2,579,285	6,522,310	4,056,500	2,465,810	1,957,378	1,843,903	113,475
1976	8,312,502	5,848,001	2,464,501	6,349,903	3,998,450	2,351,453	1,962,599	1,849,551	113,048
1977	8,415,339	5,935,076	2,480,263	6,396,476	4,039,071	2,357,405	2,018,863	1,896,005	122,858
1978	8,348,482	5,932,357	2,416,125	6,279,199	3,996,126	2,283,073	2,069,283	1,936,231	133,052
1979	8,487,317	6,016,072	2,471,245	6,392,617	4,059,304	2,333,313	2,094,700	1,956,768	137,932
1980	8,819,013	6,161,372	2,657,641	6,642,294	4,158,267	2,484,027	2,176,719	2,003,105	173,614[1]
1981	9,014,521	6,249,847	2,764,674	6,781,300	4,208,506	2,572,794	2,233,221	2,041,341	191,880[1]
1982	9,091,648	6,248,923	2,842,725	6,850,589	4,220,648	2,629,941	2,241,059	2,028,275	212,784
1983	9,166,398	6,325,222	2,841,176	6,881,479	4,265,807	2,615,672	2,284,919	2,059,415	225,504
1984	8,951,695	6,292,711	2,658,984	6,684,664	4,237,895	2,446,769	2,267,031	2,054,816	212,215
1985	8,943,433	6,294,339	2,649,094	6,667,781	4,239,622	2,428,159	2,275,652	2,054,717	220,935
1986	9,064,165	6,360,325	2,703,842	6,778,045	4,295,494	2,482,551	2,286,122	2,064,831	221,291[2]
1987	9,229,736	6,486,504	2,743,230	6,937,690	4,395,728	2,541,961	2,292,045	2,090,776	201,269[2]
1988	9,464,271	6,664,146	2,800,125	7,096,905	4,505,774	2,591,131	2,367,366	2,158,372	208,994
1989	9,780,881	6,813,602	2,967,279	7,371,590	4,619,828	2,751,762	2,409,291	2,193,774	215,517
1990	9,983,436	6,968,008	3,015,428	7,557,982	4,740,049	2,817,933	2,425,454	2,227,959	197,495
1991	10,360,606	7,081,454	3,279,152	7,862,845	4,795,704	3,067,141	2,497,761	2,285,750	212,011
1992	10,436,776	7,129,379	3,307,397	7,911,701	4,797,884	3,113,817	2,525,075	2,331,495	193,580
1993	10,351,415	7,120,921	3,230,494	7,812,394	4,765,983	3,046,411	2,539,021	2,354,938	184,083
1994	10,348,072	7,137,341	3,210,731	7,784,396	4,749,524	3,034,872	2,563,676	2,387,817	175,859
1995	10,334,956	7,172,844	3,162,112	7,751,815	4,757,223	2,994,592	2,583,141	2,415,621	167,520
1996	10,481,886	7,234,541	3,247,345	7,794,895	4,767,117	3,027,778	2,686,991	2,467,424	219,567
1997	10,615,028	7,338,794	3,276,234	7,869,764	4,813,849	3,055,915	2,745,264	2,524,945	220,319
1998	10,698,775	7,467,828	3,230,947	7,880,135	4,868,857	3,011,278	2,818,640	2,598,971	219,669
1999[3]	10,943,609	7,638,976	3,304,633	8,020,074	4,944,554	3,075,520	2,923,535	2,694,422	229,113
2000	11,267,025	7,795,139	3,471,886	8,266,932	5,025,588	3,241,344	3,000,093	2,769,551	230,542
2001	11,765,945	8,087,980	3,677,965	8,639,154	5,194,035	3,445,119	3,126,791	2,893,945	232,846
2002	12,331,319	8,439,064	3,892,255	9,061,411	5,406,283	3,655,128	3,269,908	3,032,781	237,127
2003	12,674,309	8,734,596	3,939,713	9,236,579	5,557,573	3,679,006	3,437,730	3,177,023	260,707
2004	13,000,994	9,018,024	3,982,970	9,348,081	5,640,650	3,707,431	3,652,913	3,377,374	275,539
2005	13,200,790	9,261,634	3,939,156	9,390,216	5,728,327	3,661,889	3,810,574	3,533,307	277,267

[1]Large increases are due to the addition of schools accredited by the Accrediting Commission of Career Schools and Colleges of Technology in 1980 and 1981.
[2]Because of imputation techniques, data are not consistent with figures for other years.
[3]Data were imputed using alternative procedures. (See Guide to Sources for details.)
NOTE: Data through 1995 are for institutions of higher education, while later data are for degree-granting institutions. Degree-granting institutions grant associate's or higher degrees and participate in Title IV federal financial aid programs. The degree-granting classification is very similar to the earlier higher education classification, but it includes more 2-year colleges and excludes a few higher education institutions that did not grant degrees. (See Guide to Sources for details.)
SOURCE: U.S. Department of Education, National Center for Education Statistics, Higher Education General Information Survey (HEGIS), "Fall Enrollment in Colleges and Universities" surveys, 1969 through 1985; and 1996 through 2005 Integrated Postsecondary Education Data System, "Fall Enrollment Survey" (IPEDS-EF:96–99), and Spring 2001 through Spring 2006. (This table was prepared August 2006.)

Table 205. Full-time-equivalent fall enrollment in degree-granting institutions, by control and type of institution and state or jurisdiction: 2000, 2004, and 2005

	Public						Private					
	4-year			2-year			4-year			2-year		
State or jurisdiction	2000	2004	2005	2000	2004	2005	2000	2004	2005	2000	2004	2005
1	2	3	4	5	6	7	8	9	10	11	12	13
United States	5,025,588	5,640,650	5,728,327	3,241,344	3,707,431	3,661,889	2,769,551	3,377,374	3,533,307	230,542	275,539	277,267
Alabama...........................	111,322	122,374	122,089	48,545	55,083	54,149	23,518	25,078	24,777	646	615	682
Alaska.............................	16,335	18,722	18,444	473	462	464	672	976	950	307	0	0
Arizona...........................	87,301	98,786	101,763	85,778	103,510	101,330	43,188	151,318	204,596	9,129	15,006	12,315
Arkansas..........................	57,897	65,611	67,440	21,519	29,949	30,820	10,995	12,645	12,931	1,475	466	587
California.........................	476,027	527,193	537,136	707,558	750,326	756,014	250,026	293,184	299,701	34,875	38,017	36,155
Colorado..........................	109,844	123,837	123,746	41,322	46,476	44,001	30,615	42,508	48,212	6,336	8,440	8,679
Connecticut.......................	46,826	52,651	53,737	20,934	25,851	26,403	48,714	51,787	52,654	1,480	1,703	1,468
Delaware..........................	20,427	22,251	22,467	6,939	8,089	8,175	6,549	8,014	9,059	142	160	165
District of Columbia	3,364	3,493	3,615	0	0	0	56,196	72,947	75,302	0	0	0
Florida.............................	190,472	281,779	288,146	173,433	163,945	161,069	107,473	159,920	164,325	15,440	18,858	20,271
Georgia...........................	136,069	162,653	165,257	66,571	90,958	93,177	62,132	86,917	71,354	3,935	2,996	4,885
Hawaii............................	17,015	20,544	22,587	14,996	15,816	13,324	11,649	12,595	12,833	1,669	1,004	1,011
Idaho..............................	34,125	38,514	38,426	6,807	8,447	7,863	2,500	14,398	15,658	8,921	324	512
Illinois............................	164,592	171,933	174,262	186,533	207,711	202,067	164,273	189,254	228,174	4,689	4,805	4,302
Indiana............................	155,982	166,088	173,220	28,131	40,949	34,737	61,851	71,585	74,106	5,034	8,698	9,931
Iowa...............................	61,763	60,801	60,039	44,717	54,865	54,279	43,869	54,657	61,945	2,156	1,005	1,325
Kansas............................	74,307	79,389	79,530	39,457	44,373	44,234	15,014	15,998	16,028	1,061	1,503	1,519
Kentucky..........................	86,080	98,023	98,519	32,239	50,292	50,916	25,793	29,467	32,508	5,283	6,631	4,006
Louisiana	126,372	136,199	127,570	27,130	34,192	23,174	27,203	29,499	11,324	2,956	4,173	3,738
Maine	24,678	26,895	26,946	4,797	7,916	8,062	12,954	14,013	14,205	955	871	906
Maryland..........................	94,929	107,705	107,870	57,367	67,965	68,582	35,969	40,131	41,391	622	2,654	3,271
Massachusetts....................	78,452	81,667	83,859	47,972	52,297	51,788	198,476	213,830	218,514	3,084	3,363	2,229
Michigan..........................	223,981	242,058	244,054	101,794	120,501	123,231	75,020	89,118	89,727	1,224	2,547	2,412
Minnesota.........................	95,345	107,880	107,648	65,167	73,952	73,317	54,476	84,147	91,830	8,244	4,350	4,665
Mississippi........................	56,107	61,002	61,350	47,245	55,114	53,618	9,677	11,292	11,300	775	1,784	1,719
Missouri...........................	99,187	105,253	107,799	46,793	55,422	55,186	84,889	106,336	110,262	6,292	7,312	8,009
Montana...........................	28,278	29,659	29,744	3,900	6,194	6,228	3,336	3,775	3,771	491	519	443
Nebraska..........................	44,374	44,766	45,346	20,812	25,012	24,784	18,750	23,968	23,983	2,057	649	570
Nevada............................	27,631	54,998	57,119	20,468	7,792	8,065	2,519	6,113	7,425	1,959	2,778	2,839
New Hampshire	21,064	23,262	23,682	5,442	7,250	7,348	20,646	23,289	23,540	1,078	1,591	1,178
New Jersey........................	111,449	121,377	121,784	79,367	99,531	100,103	51,557	59,299	60,042	3,074	1,525	1,174
New Mexico	39,779	45,489	45,356	29,541	36,272	36,232	6,799	8,930	8,787	1,296	194	521
New York	269,664	286,399	291,025	168,911	194,276	193,460	366,833	415,504	423,483	20,670	29,923	29,085
North Carolina	140,203	164,141	170,110	96,999	120,789	120,991	67,622	73,030	77,971	981	2,478	1,539
North Dakota......................	24,728	29,512	29,236	6,515	7,123	6,785	3,697	4,577	4,472	290	1,014	1,381
Ohio...............................	215,993	236,762	242,020	92,749	111,748	107,524	107,773	119,015	120,727	9,565	17,321	19,365
Oklahoma..........................	79,786	95,194	94,992	34,997	41,307	40,640	21,723	22,790	23,339	327	2,733	2,628
Oregon............................	59,588	69,258	69,555	46,099	49,886	47,788	23,928	28,252	29,290	1,090	2,510	2,565
Pennsylvania......................	211,132	229,068	229,883	58,759	78,279	75,863	202,341	227,752	234,653	27,497	30,978	31,891
Rhode Island	17,967	19,340	19,653	8,650	9,277	9,215	33,022	36,627	37,676	0	550	546
South Carolina	74,309	81,982	84,069	41,804	50,414	50,418	25,929	30,604	30,142	1,301	1,813	1,784
South Dakota......................	23,881	25,778	25,541	4,193	4,699	4,873	6,688	8,286	8,284	114	293	279
Tennessee.........................	99,636	107,077	108,494	53,146	50,759	49,705	52,015	61,759	64,564	4,303	9,530	10,198
Texas..............................	358,523	419,597	439,659	268,057	325,959	314,319	101,852	114,037	117,380	12,580	18,896	17,974
Utah...............................	71,982	83,226	84,056	16,454	20,890	20,574	35,110	40,735	44,420	2,076	2,655	2,913
Vermont	13,581	15,173	16,156	1,845	2,508	2,490	13,313	13,633	13,718	360	461	595
Virginia............................	147,370	160,904	164,960	72,913	83,857	84,570	51,517	67,708	72,292	5,470	4,047	7,127
Washington........................	83,899	94,707	95,677	114,754	120,901	120,908	34,489	43,109	44,776	3,467	546	694
West Virginia......................	58,171	58,082	58,546	3,969	11,123	11,934	8,891	10,742	10,895	1,931	2,428	2,123
Wisconsin.........................	130,661	136,212	138,334	56,195	65,565	65,178	45,510	52,226	53,896	546	464	485
Wyoming...........................	9,665	10,632	10,546	10,588	11,559	11,914	0	0	115	1,289	2,358	2,608
U.S. Service Schools	13,475	14,754	15,265	0	0	0	†	†	†	†	†	†
Other jurisdictions	66,376	65,963	63,840	7,200	7,091	7,250	83,619	104,124	105,927	8,844	11,800	13,127
American Samoa...................	0	0	0	214	1,018	1,038	0	0	0	0	0	0
Federated States of Micronesia........	0	0	0	1,308	2,169	1,798	0	0	0	0	0	0
Guam..............................	2,802	2,313	2,465	777	828	1,289	0	130	155	0	0	0
Marshall Islands...................	0	0	0	166	540	517	0	0	0	0	0	0
Northern Marianas	0	931	833	707	0	0	0	0	0	0	0	0
Palau..............................	0	0	0	450	504	505	0	0	0	0	0	0
Puerto Rico........................	61,987	60,941	58,830	3,578	2,032	2,103	83,619	103,994	105,772	8,844	11,800	13,127
Virgin Islands......................	1,587	1,778	1,712	0	0	0	0	0	0	0	0	0

†Not applicable.
NOTE: Degree-granting institutions grant associate's or higher degrees and participate in Title IV federal financial aid programs.

SOURCE: U.S. Department of Education, National Center for Education Statistics, 2000 through 2005 Integrated Postsecondary Education Data System (IPEDS), Spring 2001 through Spring 2006. (This table was prepared August 2006.)

Table 206. Full-time-equivalent fall enrollment in degree-granting institutions, by control and state or jurisdiction: Selected years,1980 through 2005

State or jurisdiction	Total					Public			Private		
	1980	1990	2000	2004	2005	1990	2000	2005	1990	2000	2005
1	2	3	4	5	6	7	8	9	10	11	12
United States	8,819,013	9,983,436	11,267,025	13,000,994	13,200,790	7,557,982	8,266,932	9,390,216	2,425,454	3,000,093	3,810,574
Alabama	138,910	174,610	184,031	203,150	201,697	154,343	159,867	176,238	20,267	24,164	25,459
Alaska	10,073	18,496	17,787	20,160	19,858	17,087	16,808	18,908	1,409	979	950
Arizona	127,114	167,617	225,396	368,620	420,004	153,500	173,079	203,093	14,117	52,317	216,911
Arkansas	64,307	74,449	91,886	108,671	111,778	63,472	79,416	98,260	10,977	12,470	13,518
California	1,099,559	1,156,288	1,468,486	1,608,720	1,629,006	979,663	1,183,585	1,293,150	176,625	284,901	335,856
Colorado	123,589	159,032	188,117	221,261	224,638	138,350	151,166	167,747	20,682	36,951	56,891
Connecticut	112,612	115,791	117,954	131,992	134,262	70,870	67,760	80,140	44,921	50,194	54,122
Delaware	26,284	31,612	34,057	38,514	39,866	26,059	27,366	30,642	5,553	6,691	9,224
District of Columbia	62,126	61,549	59,560	76,440	78,917	7,294	3,364	3,615	54,255	56,196	75,302
Florida	290,647	383,385	486,818	624,502	633,811	302,579	363,905	449,215	80,806	122,913	184,596
Georgia	152,369	198,549	268,707	343,524	334,673	149,115	202,640	258,434	49,434	66,067	76,239
Hawaii	35,859	41,097	45,329	49,959	49,755	32,496	32,011	35,911	8,601	13,318	13,844
Idaho	33,938	41,275	52,353	61,683	62,459	31,408	40,932	46,289	9,867	11,421	16,170
Illinois	432,365	493,364	520,087	573,703	608,805	353,247	351,125	376,329	140,117	168,962	232,476
Indiana	193,445	222,835	250,998	287,320	291,994	168,984	184,113	207,957	53,851	66,885	84,037
Iowa	120,083	138,565	152,505	171,328	177,588	95,772	106,480	114,318	42,793	46,025	63,270
Kansas	101,147	118,969	129,839	141,263	141,311	106,570	113,764	123,764	12,399	16,075	17,547
Kentucky	113,709	137,651	149,395	184,413	185,949	111,858	118,319	149,435	25,793	31,076	36,514
Louisiana	132,780	154,132	183,661	204,063	165,806	129,357	153,502	150,744	24,775	30,159	15,062
Maine	34,471	42,021	43,384	49,695	50,119	29,876	29,475	35,008	12,145	13,909	15,111
Maryland	149,202	169,972	188,887	218,455	221,114	141,950	152,296	176,452	28,022	36,591	44,662
Massachusetts	315,937	320,299	327,984	351,157	356,390	130,962	126,424	135,647	189,337	201,560	220,743
Michigan	366,058	389,814	402,019	454,224	459,424	326,952	325,775	367,285	62,862	76,244	92,139
Minnesota	162,559	190,608	223,232	270,329	277,460	143,424	160,512	180,965	47,184	62,720	96,495
Mississippi	85,621	103,957	113,804	129,192	127,987	92,269	103,352	114,968	11,688	10,452	13,019
Missouri	180,156	210,104	237,161	274,323	281,256	142,953	145,980	162,985	67,151	91,181	118,271
Montana	29,428	29,905	36,005	40,147	40,186	26,835	32,178	35,972	3,070	3,827	4,214
Nebraska	68,505	80,989	85,993	94,395	94,683	65,739	65,186	70,130	15,250	20,807	24,553
Nevada	22,467	33,814	52,577	71,681	75,448	33,392	48,099	65,184	422	4,478	10,264
New Hampshire	39,456	45,762	48,230	55,392	55,748	24,948	26,506	31,030	20,814	21,724	24,718
New Jersey	218,838	221,468	245,447	281,732	283,103	174,324	190,816	221,887	47,144	54,631	61,216
New Mexico	43,722	59,517	77,415	90,885	90,896	57,870	69,320	81,588	1,647	8,095	9,308
New York	760,305	798,696	826,078	926,102	937,053	446,379	438,575	484,485	352,317	387,503	452,568
North Carolina	235,266	269,025	305,805	360,438	370,611	208,321	237,202	291,101	60,704	68,603	79,510
North Dakota	30,188	33,118	35,230	42,226	41,874	30,276	31,243	36,021	2,842	3,987	5,853
Ohio	369,342	420,499	426,080	484,846	489,636	317,837	308,742	349,544	102,662	117,338	140,092
Oklahoma	115,701	128,203	136,833	162,024	161,599	108,933	114,783	135,632	19,270	22,050	25,967
Oregon	110,649	120,176	130,705	149,906	149,198	101,424	105,687	117,343	18,752	25,018	31,855
Pennsylvania	404,192	464,179	499,729	566,077	572,290	261,305	269,891	305,746	202,874	229,838	266,544
Rhode Island	50,628	60,168	59,639	65,794	67,090	28,804	26,617	28,868	31,364	33,022	38,222
South Carolina	109,346	127,225	143,343	164,813	166,413	101,918	116,113	134,487	25,307	27,230	31,926
South Dakota	27,873	28,256	34,876	39,056	38,977	22,128	28,074	30,414	6,128	6,802	8,563
Tennessee	161,058	175,961	209,100	229,125	232,961	130,184	152,782	158,199	45,777	56,318	74,762
Texas	527,724	637,742	741,012	878,489	889,332	553,436	626,580	753,978	84,306	114,432	135,354
Utah	78,199	94,012	125,622	147,506	151,963	63,495	88,436	104,630	30,517	37,186	47,333
Vermont	25,572	29,072	29,099	31,775	32,959	16,048	15,426	18,646	13,024	13,673	14,313
Virginia	199,549	251,708	277,270	316,516	328,949	202,285	220,283	249,530	49,423	56,987	79,419
Washington	194,440	189,521	236,609	259,263	262,055	160,889	198,653	216,585	28,632	37,956	45,470
West Virginia	60,394	68,235	72,962	82,375	83,498	59,229	62,140	70,480	9,006	10,822	13,018
Wisconsin	206,790	229,975	232,912	254,467	257,893	192,107	186,856	203,512	37,868	46,056	54,381
Wyoming	14,725	21,888	21,542	24,549	25,183	21,185	20,253	22,460	703	1,289	2,723
U.S. Service Schools[1]	49,736	48,281	13,475	14,754	15,265	48,281	13,475	15,265	†	†	†
Other jurisdictions	117,637	140,954	166,039	190,144	190,144	55,908	73,576	71,090	85,046	92,463	119,054
American Samoa	824	952	214	1,018	1,038	952	214	1,038	0	0	0
Federated States of Micronesia	195	549	1,308	2,169	1,798	549	1,308	1,798	0	0	0
Guam	2,115	2,956	3,579	3,271	3,909	2,956	3,579	3,754	0	0	155
Marshall Islands	0	0	166	540	517	0	166	517	0	0	0
Northern Marianas	0	376	707	931	833	376	707	833	0	0	0
Palau	0	423	450	504	505	423	450	505	0	0	0
Puerto Rico	113,285	134,193	158,028	178,767	179,832	49,147	65,565	60,933	85,046	92,463	118,899
Virgin Islands	1,218	1,505	1,587	1,778	1,712	1,505	1,587	1,712	0	0	0

†Not applicable.
[1]Data for 2000 and later years reflect substantial change in survey coverage.
NOTE: Data through 1990 are for institutions of higher education, while later data are for degree-granting institutions. Degree-granting institutions grant associate's or higher degrees and participate in Title IV federal financial aid programs. The degree-granting classification is very similar to the earlier higher education classification, but it includes more 2-year colleges and excludes a few higher education institutions that did not grant degrees. (See Guide to Sources for details.)
SOURCE: U.S. Department of Education, National Center for Education Statistics, Higher Education General Information Survey (HEGIS), "Fall Enrollment in Colleges and Universities" 1980 survey; and 1990 through 2005 Integrated Postsecondary Education Data System, "Fall Enrollment Survey" (IPEDS-EF:90), and Spring 2001 through Spring 2006. (This table was prepared August 2006.)

Table 207. Residence and migration of all freshmen students in degree-granting institutions, by state or jurisdiction: Fall 2004

State or jurisdiction	Total freshman enrollment in institutions located in the state	State residents enrolled in institutions		Ratio of in-state students		Migration of students		
		In any state[1]	In their home state	To freshman enrollment (col. 4/col. 2)	To residents enrolled in any state (col. 4/col. 3)	Out of state (col. 3 - col. 4)	Into state[2] (col. 2 - col. 4)	Net (col. 8 - col. 7)
1	2	3	4	5	6	7	8	9
United States	2,630,243	2,575,811	2,133,727	0.81	0.83	442,084	496,516	54,432
Alabama	42,737	37,769	34,074	0.80	0.90	3,695	8,663	4,968
Alaska	2,760	4,313	2,430	0.88	0.56	1,883	330	-1,553
Arizona	50,521	40,036	35,972	0.71	0.90	4,064	14,549	10,485
Arkansas	24,110	22,715	20,162	0.84	0.89	2,553	3,948	1,395
California	259,869	253,474	230,354	0.89	0.91	23,120	29,515	6,395
Colorado	45,341	44,616	37,398	0.82	0.84	7,218	7,943	725
Connecticut	27,295	32,649	18,771	0.69	0.57	13,878	8,524	-5,354
Delaware	8,253	6,827	4,846	0.59	0.71	1,981	3,407	1,426
District of Columbia	11,350	3,912	1,055	0.09	0.27	2,857	10,295	7,438
Florida	138,561	120,899	109,133	0.79	0.90	11,766	29,428	17,662
Georgia	83,314	80,377	69,428	0.83	0.86	10,949	13,886	2,937
Hawaii	8,492	8,832	6,057	0.71	0.69	2,775	2,435	-340
Idaho	11,801	11,339	8,525	0.72	0.75	2,814	3,276	462
Illinois	103,212	114,285	90,951	0.88	0.80	23,334	12,261	-11,073
Indiana	61,520	54,805	47,980	0.78	0.88	6,825	13,540	6,715
Iowa	43,352	35,152	31,128	0.72	0.89	4,024	12,224	8,200
Kansas	28,393	26,673	22,970	0.81	0.86	3,703	5,423	1,720
Kentucky	39,485	34,718	30,891	0.78	0.89	3,827	8,594	4,767
Louisiana	43,572	40,910	37,168	0.85	0.91	3,742	6,404	2,662
Maine	10,760	11,860	7,846	0.73	0.66	4,014	2,914	-1,100
Maryland	45,815	53,336	36,575	0.80	0.69	16,761	9,240	-7,521
Massachusetts	70,869	61,944	44,207	0.62	0.71	17,737	26,662	8,925
Michigan	88,078	88,279	79,810	0.91	0.90	8,469	8,268	-201
Minnesota	61,042	62,798	50,355	0.82	0.80	12,443	10,687	-1,756
Mississippi	33,646	30,686	28,659	0.85	0.93	2,027	4,987	2,960
Missouri	51,431	49,183	41,537	0.81	0.84	7,646	9,894	2,248
Montana	8,484	8,593	6,428	0.76	0.75	2,165	2,056	-109
Nebraska	18,855	18,728	15,480	0.82	0.83	3,248	3,375	127
Nevada	13,995	14,332	12,013	0.86	0.84	2,319	1,982	-337
New Hampshire	12,420	11,828	6,495	0.52	0.55	5,333	5,925	592
New Jersey	57,564	84,556	53,103	0.92	0.63	31,453	4,461	-26,992
New Mexico	16,827	16,950	13,913	0.83	0.82	3,037	2,914	-123
New York	180,253	176,350	146,818	0.81	0.83	29,532	33,435	3,903
North Carolina	81,444	71,834	65,215	0.80	0.91	6,619	16,229	9,610
North Dakota	9,477	7,711	5,504	0.58	0.71	2,207	3,973	1,766
Ohio	104,334	105,975	90,920	0.87	0.86	15,055	13,414	-1,641
Oklahoma	34,948	31,937	28,856	0.83	0.90	3,081	6,092	3,011
Oregon	28,402	27,076	22,338	0.79	0.83	4,738	6,064	1,326
Pennsylvania	132,339	119,658	101,314	0.77	0.85	18,344	31,025	12,681
Rhode Island	15,388	9,209	6,246	0.41	0.68	2,963	9,142	6,179
South Carolina	37,868	34,340	30,641	0.81	0.89	3,699	7,227	3,528
South Dakota	9,076	8,920	6,687	0.74	0.75	2,233	2,389	156
Tennessee	47,991	45,448	38,202	0.80	0.84	7,246	9,789	2,543
Texas	205,221	208,106	189,462	0.92	0.91	18,644	15,759	-2,885
Utah	26,787	20,301	18,722	0.70	0.92	1,579	8,065	6,486
Vermont	6,343	4,750	2,013	0.32	0.42	2,737	4,330	1,593
Virginia	66,621	61,956	50,453	0.76	0.81	11,503	16,168	4,665
Washington	37,393	40,604	32,291	0.86	0.80	8,313	5,102	-3,211
West Virginia	16,602	13,989	12,026	0.72	0.86	1,963	4,576	2,613
Wisconsin	55,331	56,165	46,809	0.85	0.83	9,356	8,522	-834
Wyoming	6,519	4,606	3,231	0.50	0.70	1,375	3,288	1,913
U.S. Service Schools	4,182	†	265 [3]	†	†	-265	3,917	4,182
State unknown[4]	†	39,502	†	†	†	39,502	†	-39,502
Other jurisdictions	43,506	44,225	41,186	0.95	0.93	3,039	2,320	-719
American Samoa	575	692	575	1.00	0.83	117	0	-117
Federated States of Micronesia	1,389	1,538	1,387	1.00	0.90	151	2	-149
Guam	724	397	254	0.35	0.64	143	470	327
Marshall Islands	179	276	169	0.94	0.61	107	10	-97
Northern Marianas	255	231	197	0.77	0.85	34	58	24
Palau	115	1,253	74	0.64	0.06	1,179	41	-1,138
Puerto Rico	39,471	38,936	38,192	0.97	0.98	744	1,279	535
Virgin Islands	798	902	338	0.42	0.37	564	460	-104
Foreign countries	†	36,006	†	†	†	36,006	†	-36,006
Residence unknown	†	17,707	†	†	†	17,707	†	-17,707

†Not applicable.
[1]Students residing in a particular state when admitted to an institution anywhere—either in their home state or another state.
[2]Includes students coming to U.S. colleges from foreign countries and other jurisdictions.
[3]Students whose residence is in the same state as the service school.
[4]Institution unable to determine student's home state.

NOTE: Includes all first-time postsecondary students enrolled at reporting institutions. Degree-granting institutions grant associate's or higher degrees and participate in Title IV federal financial aid programs.
SOURCE: U.S. Department of Education, National Center for Education Statistics, Integrated Postsecondary Education Data System (IPEDS), Spring 2005. (This table was prepared September 2005.)

Table 208. Residence and migration of all freshmen students in degree-granting institutions who graduated from high school in the previous 12 months, by state or jurisdiction: Fall 2004

State or jurisdiction	Total freshman enrollment in institutions located in the state	State residents enrolled in institutions		Ratio of in-state students		Migration of students		
		In any state[1]	In their home state	To freshman enrollment (col. 4/col. 2)	To residents enrolled in any state (col. 4/col. 3)	Out of state (col. 3 - col. 4)	Into state[2] (col. 2 - col. 4)	Net (col. 8 - col. 7)
1	2	3	4	5	6	7	8	9
United States	1,731,100	1,709,495	1,385,121	0.80	0.81	324,374	345,979	21,605
Alabama	28,470	24,887	22,425	0.79	0.90	2,462	6,045	3,583
Alaska........................	2,284	3,379	2,024	0.89	0.60	1,355	260	-1,095
Arizona.......................	26,810	22,830	20,032	0.75	0.88	2,798	6,778	3,980
Arkansas....................	17,577	15,934	14,343	0.82	0.90	1,591	3,234	1,643
California	160,721	164,013	146,618	0.91	0.89	17,395	14,103	-3,292
Colorado	27,307	27,296	21,619	0.79	0.79	5,677	5,688	11
Connecticut................	22,664	25,152	14,504	0.64	0.58	10,648	8,160	-2,488
Delaware....................	5,973	4,488	2,941	0.49	0.66	1,547	3,032	1,485
District of Columbia	8,788	2,488	611	0.07	0.25	1,877	8,177	6,300
Florida........................	90,202	79,246	70,729	0.78	0.89	8,517	19,473	10,956
Georgia......................	49,168	48,381	40,174	0.82	0.83	8,207	8,994	787
Hawaii........................	5,955	6,755	4,540	0.76	0.67	2,215	1,415	-800
Idaho	8,220	7,614	5,616	0.68	0.74	1,998	2,604	606
Illinois........................	66,544	77,215	58,151	0.87	0.75	19,064	8,393	-10,671
Indiana.......................	41,617	36,019	31,275	0.75	0.87	4,744	10,342	5,598
Iowa	26,283	22,781	19,566	0.74	0.86	3,215	6,717	3,502
Kansas.......................	21,582	19,821	17,129	0.79	0.86	2,692	4,453	1,761
Kentucky....................	24,295	21,693	19,349	0.80	0.89	2,344	4,946	2,602
Louisiana	28,341	25,174	22,680	0.80	0.90	2,494	5,661	3,167
Maine.........................	6,874	7,965	4,974	0.72	0.62	2,991	1,900	-1,091
Maryland	27,931	35,774	22,508	0.81	0.63	13,266	5,423	-7,843
Massachusetts...................	48,481	43,803	29,869	0.62	0.68	13,934	18,612	4,678
Michigan	63,791	63,706	57,300	0.90	0.90	6,406	6,491	85
Minnesota	38,880	41,619	30,930	0.80	0.74	10,689	7,950	-2,739
Mississippi	17,977	16,297	15,114	0.84	0.93	1,183	2,863	1,680
Missouri	36,026	34,419	28,448	0.79	0.83	5,971	7,578	1,607
Montana	6,398	6,362	4,663	0.73	0.73	1,699	1,735	36
Nebraska....................	13,473	13,557	10,885	0.81	0.80	2,672	2,588	-84
Nevada	8,373	8,744	7,132	0.85	0.82	1,612	1,241	-371
New Hampshire	8,947	8,737	4,781	0.53	0.55	3,956	4,166	210
New Jersey	38,104	60,694	34,841	0.91	0.57	25,853	3,263	-22,590
New Mexico	11,574	11,762	9,908	0.86	0.84	1,854	1,666	-188
New York....................	120,947	123,062	99,455	0.82	0.81	23,607	21,492	-2,115
North Carolina	57,466	49,635	45,212	0.79	0.91	4,423	12,254	7,831
North Dakota	7,448	5,661	4,196	0.56	0.74	1,465	3,252	1,787
Ohio...........................	68,976	70,236	58,900	0.85	0.84	11,336	10,076	-1,260
Oklahoma	22,287	20,265	18,037	0.81	0.89	2,228	4,250	2,022
Oregon.......................	16,575	16,225	12,431	0.75	0.77	3,794	4,144	350
Pennsylvania....................	96,885	84,159	69,840	0.72	0.83	14,319	27,045	12,726
Rhode Island	9,432	6,229	4,011	0.43	0.64	2,218	5,421	3,203
South Carolina	27,581	24,049	21,517	0.78	0.89	2,532	6,064	3,532
South Dakota	6,670	6,541	4,722	0.71	0.72	1,819	1,948	129
Tennessee	25,751	24,498	19,221	0.75	0.78	5,277	6,530	1,253
Texas.........................	126,009	132,198	117,899	0.94	0.89	14,299	8,110	-6,189
Utah...........................	16,131	12,083	10,953	0.68	0.91	1,130	5,178	4,048
Vermont	5,417	3,679	1,592	0.29	0.43	2,087	3,825	1,738
Virginia.......................	48,458	44,937	36,272	0.75	0.81	8,665	12,186	3,521
Washington................	26,861	28,237	22,368	0.83	0.79	5,869	4,493	-1,376
West Virginia..............	12,382	9,681	8,472	0.68	0.88	1,209	3,910	2,701
Wisconsin	39,465	39,168	31,821	0.81	0.81	7,347	7,644	297
Wyoming	4,562	3,461	2,395	0.52	0.69	1,066	2,167	1,101
U.S. Service Schools	2,167	†	128 [3]	†	†	-128	2,039	2,167
State unknown[4]............	†	16,886	†	†	†	16,886	†	-16,886
Other jurisdictions	26,282	27,338	25,815	0.98	0.94	1,523	467	-1,056
American Samoa..............	446	526	446	1.00	0.85	80	0	-80
Federated States of Micronesia	1,362	1,388	1,360	1.00	0.98	28	2	-26
Guam..........................	26	115	5	0.19	0.04	110	21	-89
Marshall Islands................	†	34	†	†	†	34	0	-34
Northern Marianas	129	124	108	0.84	0.87	16	21	5
Palau..........................	†	377	†	†	†	377	0	-377
Puerto Rico.................	24,106	24,209	23,692	0.98	0.98	517	414	-103
Virgin Islands..................	213	565	204	0.96	0.36	361	9	-352
Foreign countries..............	†	20,549	†	†	†	20,549	†	-20,549

†Not applicable.
[1]Students residing in a particular state when admitted to an institution anywhere—either in their home state or another state.
[2]Includes students coming to U.S. colleges from foreign countries and other jurisdictions.
[3]Students whose residence is in the same state as the service school.
[4]Institution unable to determine student's home state.

NOTE: Includes all first-time postsecondary students enrolled at reporting institutions. Degree-granting institutions grant associate's or higher degrees and participate in Title IV federal financial aid programs.
SOURCE: U.S. Department of Education, National Center for Education Statistics, Integrated Postsecondary Education Data System (IPEDS), Spring 2005. (This table was prepared September 2005.)

Table 209. Residence and migration of all freshmen students in 4-year degree-granting institutions who graduated from high school in the previous 12 months, by state or jurisdiction: Fall 2004

State or jurisdiction	Total freshman enrollment in institutions located in the state	State residents enrolled in institutions		Ratio of in-state students		Migration of students		
		In any state[1]	In their home state	To freshman enrollment (col. 4/col. 2)	To residents enrolled in any state (col. 4/col. 3)	Out of state (col. 3 - col. 4)	Into state[2] (col. 2 - col. 4)	Net (col. 8 - col. 7)
1	2	3	4	5	6	7	8	9
United States	1,194,609	1,170,859	882,801	0.74	0.75	288,058	311,808	23,750
Alabama	18,445	15,169	12,989	0.70	0.86	2,180	5,456	3,276
Alaska........................	2,258	3,252	1,999	0.89	0.61	1,253	259	-994
Arizona	16,651	13,649	11,137	0.67	0.82	2,512	5,514	3,002
Arkansas....................	13,092	11,252	10,004	0.76	0.89	1,248	3,088	1,840
California	90,284	97,287	80,880	0.90	0.83	16,407	9,404	-7,003
Colorado	21,091	20,912	15,728	0.75	0.75	5,184	5,363	179
Connecticut.................	17,223	19,554	9,105	0.53	0.47	10,449	8,118	-2,331
Delaware....................	4,689	3,261	1,791	0.38	0.55	1,470	2,898	1,428
District of Columbia	8,788	2,221	611	0.07	0.28	1,610	8,177	6,567
Florida........................	58,981	54,413	46,498	0.79	0.85	7,915	12,483	4,568
Georgia	33,607	33,301	25,616	0.76	0.77	7,685	7,991	306
Hawaii........................	3,144	4,007	1,858	0.59	0.46	2,149	1,286	-863
Idaho..........................	6,616	5,889	4,214	0.64	0.72	1,675	2,402	727
Illinois........................	43,452	53,659	35,407	0.81	0.66	18,252	8,045	-10,207
Indiana.......................	36,068	30,369	26,126	0.72	0.86	4,243	9,942	5,699
Iowa...........................	16,559	13,537	10,651	0.64	0.79	2,886	5,908	3,022
Kansas.......................	13,715	12,947	10,453	0.76	0.81	2,494	3,262	768
Kentucky.....................	18,233	15,775	13,645	0.75	0.86	2,130	4,588	2,458
Louisiana	25,556	21,905	19,933	0.78	0.91	1,972	5,623	3,651
Maine.........................	5,191	6,228	3,336	0.64	0.54	2,892	1,855	-1,037
Maryland.....................	14,360	22,416	9,608	0.67	0.43	12,808	4,752	-8,056
Massachusetts.............	37,678	32,998	19,466	0.52	0.59	13,532	18,212	4,680
Michigan	45,236	44,931	38,990	0.86	0.87	5,941	6,246	305
Minnesota	24,305	27,578	17,492	0.72	0.63	10,086	6,813	-3,273
Mississippi	6,428	5,300	4,210	0.65	0.79	1,090	2,218	1,128
Missouri	25,047	23,189	17,960	0.72	0.77	5,229	7,087	1,858
Montana......................	5,359	5,019	3,688	0.69	0.73	1,331	1,671	340
Nebraska	10,072	9,905	7,668	0.76	0.77	2,237	2,404	167
Nevada	6,925	7,199	5,697	0.82	0.79	1,502	1,228	-274
New Hampshire	6,961	6,702	3,023	0.43	0.45	3,679	3,938	259
New Jersey..................	21,383	43,570	18,311	0.86	0.42	25,259	3,072	-22,187
New Mexico	6,706	7,206	5,605	0.84	0.78	1,601	1,101	-500
New York.....................	84,111	86,688	63,704	0.76	0.73	22,984	20,407	-2,577
North Carolina	40,159	32,634	28,474	0.71	0.87	4,160	11,685	7,525
North Dakota	5,764	3,906	2,830	0.49	0.72	1,076	2,934	1,858
Ohio...........................	54,572	55,622	45,030	0.83	0.81	10,592	9,542	-1,050
Oklahoma....................	15,907	13,849	11,976	0.75	0.86	1,873	3,931	2,058
Oregon	11,479	11,381	7,867	0.69	0.69	3,514	3,612	98
Pennsylvania................	78,048	65,883	52,341	0.67	0.79	13,542	25,707	12,165
Rhode Island	7,539	4,365	2,270	0.30	0.52	2,095	5,269	3,174
South Carolina.............	19,211	15,680	13,378	0.70	0.85	2,302	5,833	3,531
South Dakota...............	5,435	5,169	3,675	0.68	0.71	1,494	1,760	266
Tennessee	18,702	17,376	12,408	0.66	0.71	4,968	6,294	1,326
Texas.........................	70,071	77,747	64,119	0.92	0.82	13,628	5,952	-7,676
Utah...........................	14,186	10,187	9,256	0.65	0.91	931	4,930	3,999
Vermont......................	5,350	3,536	1,585	0.30	0.45	1,951	3,765	1,814
Virginia.......................	36,891	33,203	25,005	0.68	0.75	8,198	11,886	3,688
Washington..................	18,706	19,756	14,411	0.77	0.73	5,345	4,295	-1,050
West Virginia...............	10,480	7,906	6,908	0.66	0.87	998	3,572	2,574
Wisconsin	30,307	29,533	22,879	0.75	0.77	6,654	7,428	774
Wyoming	1,421	1,838	858	0.60	0.47	980	563	-417
U.S. Service Schools..........	2,167	†	128[3]	†	†	-128	2,039	2,167
State unknown[4]...............	†	0	†	†	†	0	†	0
Other jurisdictions	21,783	22,722	21,684	1.00	0.95	1,038	99	-939
American Samoa...............	†	57	†	†	†	57	0	-57
Federated States of Micronesia	†	27	†	†	†	27	0	-27
Guam.........................	21	109	1	0.05	0.01	108	20	-88
Marshall Islands.................	†	3	†	†	†	3	0	-3
Northern Marianas	129	123	108	0.84	0.88	15	21	6
Palau..........................	†	12	†	†	†	12	0	-12
Puerto Rico..................	21,420	21,836	21,371	1.00	0.98	465	49	-416
Virgin Islands.................	213	555	204	0.96	0.37	351	9	-342
Foreign countries...............	†	18,144	†	†	†	18,144	†	-18,144

†Not applicable.
[1]Students residing in a particular state when admitted to an institution anywhere—either in their home state or another state.
[2]Includes students coming to U.S. colleges from foreign countries and other jurisdictions.
[3]Students whose residence is in the same state as the service school.
[4]Institution unable to determine student's home state.

NOTE: Includes all first-time postsecondary students enrolled at reporting institutions. Degree-granting institutions grant associate's or higher degrees and participate in Title IV federal financial aid programs.
SOURCE: U.S. Department of Education, National Center for Education Statistics, Integrated Postsecondary Education Data System (IPEDS), Spring 2005. (This table was prepared September 2005.)

Table 210. Total fall enrollment in degree-granting institutions, by race/ethnicity, sex, attendance status, and level of student: Selected years,1976 through 2005

Race/ethnicity, sex, attendance status, and level of student	Fall enrollment (in thousands)								Percentage distribution of students							
	1976	1980	1990	2000	2002	2003	2004	2005	1976	1980	1990	2000	2002	2003	2004	2005
1	2	3	4	5	6	7	8	9	10	11	12	13	14	15	16	17
All students, total	**10,985.6**	**12,086.8**	**13,818.6**	**15,312.3**	**16,611.7**	**16,900.5**	**17,272.0**	**17,487.5**	**100.0**	**100.0**	**100.0**	**100.0**	**100.0**	**100.0**	**100.0**	**100.0**
White	9,076.1	9,833.0	10,722.5	10,462.1	11,140.2	11,275.4	11,422.8	11,495.4	82.6	81.4	77.6	68.3	67.1	66.7	66.1	65.7
Total minority	1,690.8	1,948.8	2,704.7	4,321.5	4,880.5	5,033.2	5,259.1	5,407.2	15.4	16.1	19.6	28.2	29.4	29.8	30.4	30.9
Black	1,033.0	1,106.8	1,247.0	1,730.3	1,978.7	2,068.9	2,164.7	2,214.6	9.4	9.2	9.0	11.3	11.9	12.2	12.5	12.7
Hispanic	383.8	471.7	782.4	1,461.8	1,661.7	1,716.0	1,809.6	1,882.0	3.5	3.9	5.7	9.5	10.0	10.2	10.5	10.8
Asian/Pacific Islander	197.8	286.4	572.4	978.2	1,074.2	1,075.7	1,108.7	1,134.4	1.8	2.4	4.1	6.4	6.5	6.4	6.4	6.5
American Indian/Alaska Native	76.1	83.9	102.8	151.2	165.9	172.7	176.1	176.3	0.7	0.7	0.7	1.0	1.0	1.0	1.0	1.0
Nonresident alien	218.7	305.0	391.5	528.7	590.9	591.8	590.2	584.8	2.0	2.5	2.8	3.5	3.6	3.5	3.4	3.3
Male	5,794.4	5,868.1	6,283.9	6,721.8	7,202.1	7,255.6	7,387.3	7,455.9	100.0	100.0	100.0	100.0	100.0	100.0	100.0	100.0
White	4,813.7	4,772.9	4,861.0	4,634.6	4,897.9	4,927.9	4,988.0	5,007.2	83.1	81.3	77.4	68.9	68.0	67.9	67.5	67.2
Total minority	826.5	884.4	1,176.6	1,789.8	1,977.2	2,005.0	2,083.7	2,139.2	14.3	15.1	18.7	26.6	27.5	27.6	28.2	28.7
Black	469.9	463.7	484.7	635.3	708.6	730.6	758.4	774.1	8.1	7.9	7.7	9.5	9.8	10.1	10.3	10.4
Hispanic	209.7	231.6	353.9	627.1	699.0	709.1	745.1	774.6	3.6	3.9	5.6	9.3	9.7	9.8	10.1	10.4
Asian/Pacific Islander	108.4	151.3	294.9	465.9	503.9	498.1	511.6	522.0	1.9	2.6	4.7	6.9	7.0	6.9	6.9	7.0
American Indian/Alaska Native	38.5	37.8	43.1	61.4	65.7	67.1	68.6	68.4	0.7	0.6	0.7	0.9	0.9	0.9	0.9	0.9
Nonresident alien	154.1	210.8	246.3	297.3	327.0	322.7	315.6	309.5	2.7	3.6	3.9	4.4	4.5	4.4	4.3	4.2
Female	5,191.2	6,218.7	7,534.7	8,590.5	9,409.6	9,644.9	9,884.8	10,031.6	100.0	100.0	100.0	100.0	100.0	100.0	100.0	100.0
White	4,262.4	5,060.1	5,861.5	5,827.5	6,242.3	6,347.5	6,434.8	6,488.2	82.1	81.4	77.8	67.8	66.3	65.8	65.1	64.7
Total minority	864.2	1,064.4	1,528.1	2,531.7	2,903.3	3,028.2	3,175.4	3,268.0	16.6	17.1	20.3	29.5	30.9	31.4	32.1	32.6
Black	563.1	643.0	762.3	1,095.0	1,270.2	1,338.2	1,406.3	1,440.4	10.8	10.3	10.1	12.7	13.5	13.9	14.2	14.4
Hispanic	174.1	240.1	428.5	834.7	962.7	1,006.9	1,064.5	1,107.3	3.4	3.9	5.7	9.7	10.2	10.4	10.8	11.0
Asian/Pacific Islander	89.4	135.2	277.5	512.3	570.2	577.6	597.1	612.4	1.7	2.2	3.7	6.0	6.1	6.0	6.0	6.1
American Indian/Alaska Native	37.6	46.1	59.7	89.7	100.2	105.6	107.5	107.9	0.7	0.7	0.8	1.0	1.1	1.1	1.1	1.1
Nonresident alien	64.6	94.2	145.2	231.4	263.9	269.2	274.6	275.3	1.2	1.5	1.9	2.7	2.8	2.8	2.8	2.7
Full-time	6,703.6	7,088.9	7,821.0	9,009.6	9,946.4	10,311.8	10,610.2	10,797.0	100.0	100.0	100.0	100.0	100.0	100.0	100.0	100.0
White	5,512.6	5,717.0	6,016.5	6,231.1	6,764.2	6,976.0	7,129.1	7,220.5	82.2	80.6	76.9	69.2	68.0	67.7	67.2	66.9
Total minority	1,030.9	1,137.5	1,514.9	2,368.5	2,721.8	2,870.1	3,015.4	3,117.1	15.4	16.0	19.4	26.3	27.4	27.8	28.4	28.9
Black	659.2	685.6	718.3	982.6	1,144.2	1,216.9	1,282.8	1,321.7	9.8	9.7	9.2	10.9	11.5	11.8	12.1	12.2
Hispanic	211.1	247.0	394.7	710.3	825.1	881.5	936.6	979.7	3.1	3.5	5.0	7.9	8.3	8.5	8.8	9.1
Asian/Pacific Islander	117.7	162.0	347.4	591.2	657.4	670.4	691.4	710.1	1.8	2.3	4.4	6.6	6.6	6.5	6.5	6.6
American Indian/Alaska Native	43.0	43.0	54.4	84.4	95.1	101.3	104.6	105.6	0.6	0.6	0.7	0.9	1.0	1.0	1.0	1.0
Nonresident alien	160.0	234.4	289.6	410.0	460.4	465.8	465.6	459.4	2.4	3.3	3.7	4.6	4.6	4.5	4.4	4.3
Part-time	4,282.1	4,997.9	5,997.7	6,302.7	6,665.4	6,588.7	6,661.9	6,690.5	100.0	100.0	100.0	100.0	100.0	100.0	100.0	100.0
White	3,563.5	4,116.0	4,706.0	4,231.0	4,376.0	4,299.5	4,293.6	4,274.9	83.2	82.4	78.5	67.1	65.7	65.3	64.5	63.9
Total minority	659.9	811.3	1,189.8	1,953.0	2,158.7	2,163.1	2,243.7	2,290.1	15.4	16.2	19.8	31.0	32.4	32.8	33.7	34.2
Black	373.8	421.2	528.7	747.7	834.6	852.0	881.8	892.9	8.7	8.4	8.8	11.9	12.5	12.9	13.2	13.3
Hispanic	172.7	224.8	387.7	751.5	836.6	834.5	873.0	902.2	4.0	4.5	6.5	11.9	12.6	12.7	13.1	13.5
Asian/Pacific Islander	80.2	124.4	225.1	387.1	416.8	405.3	417.3	424.3	1.9	2.5	3.8	6.1	6.3	6.2	6.3	6.3
American Indian/Alaska Native	33.1	40.9	48.4	66.8	70.8	71.3	71.6	70.7	0.8	0.8	0.8	1.1	1.1	1.1	1.1	1.1
Nonresident alien	58.7	70.6	101.8	118.7	130.6	126.1	124.6	125.5	1.4	1.4	1.7	1.9	2.0	1.9	1.9	1.9

See notes at end of table.

Table 210. Total fall enrollment in degree-granting institutions, by race/ethnicity, sex, attendance status, and level of student: Selected years, 1976 through 2005—Continued

Race/ethnicity, sex, attendance status, and level of student	Fall enrollment (in thousands)								Percentage distribution of students							
	1976	1980	1990	2000	2002	2003	2004	2005	1976	1980	1990	2000	2002	2003	2004	2005
1	2	3	4	5	6	7	8	9	10	11	12	13	14	15	16	17
Undergraduate, total	**9,419.0**	**10,469.1**	**11,959.1**	**13,155.4**	**14,257.1**	**14,473.9**	**14,780.6**	**14,964.0**	**100.0**	**100.0**	**100.0**	**100.0**	**100.0**	**100.0**	**100.0**	**100.0**
White	7,740.5	8,480.7	9,272.6	8,983.5	9,564.9	9,662.5	9,771.3	9,828.6	82.2	81.0	77.5	68.3	67.1	66.8	66.1	65.7
Total minority	1,535.3	1,778.5	2,467.7	3,884.0	4,376.2	4,498.3	4,695.5	4,820.7	16.3	17.0	20.6	29.5	30.7	31.1	31.8	32.2
Black	943.4	1,018.8	1,147.2	1,548.9	1,763.8	1,838.2	1,918.5	1,955.4	10.0	9.7	9.6	11.8	12.4	12.7	13.0	13.1
Hispanic	352.9	433.1	724.6	1,351.0	1,533.3	1,579.6	1,666.9	1,733.6	3.7	4.1	6.1	10.3	10.8	10.9	11.3	11.6
Asian/Pacific Islander	169.3	248.7	500.5	845.5	927.4	922.7	949.9	971.4	1.8	2.4	4.2	6.4	6.5	6.4	6.4	6.5
American Indian/Alaska Native	69.7	77.9	95.5	138.5	151.7	157.8	160.3	160.4	0.7	0.7	0.8	1.1	1.1	1.1	1.1	1.1
Nonresident alien	143.2	209.9	218.7	288.0	316.0	313.0	313.8	314.7	1.5	2.0	1.8	2.2	2.2	2.2	2.1	2.1
Male	4,896.8	4,997.4	5,379.8	5,778.3	6,192.4	6,224.4	6,340.0	6,408.9	100.0	100.0	100.0	100.0	100.0	100.0	100.0	100.0
White	4,052.2	4,054.9	4,184.4	4,010.1	4,245.6	4,262.0	4,309.9	4,330.4	82.8	81.1	77.8	69.4	68.6	68.5	68.0	67.6
Total minority	748.2	802.7	1,069.3	1,618.0	1,787.1	1,806.5	1,877.0	1,926.6	15.3	16.1	19.9	28.0	28.9	29.0	29.6	30.1
Black	430.7	428.2	448.0	577.0	642.2	660.4	684.7	697.5	8.8	8.6	8.3	10.0	10.4	10.6	10.8	10.9
Hispanic	191.7	211.2	326.9	582.6	649.2	656.6	690.5	718.5	3.9	4.2	6.1	10.1	10.5	10.5	10.9	11.2
Asian/Pacific Islander	91.1	128.5	254.5	401.9	435.4	427.9	439.1	448.1	1.9	2.6	4.7	7.0	7.0	6.9	6.9	7.0
American Indian/Alaska Native	34.8	34.8	39.9	56.4	60.3	61.5	62.7	62.5	0.7	0.7	0.7	1.0	1.0	1.0	1.0	1.0
Nonresident alien	96.4	139.8	126.1	150.2	159.7	155.9	153.1	151.8	2.0	2.8	2.3	2.6	2.6	2.5	2.4	2.4
Female	4,522.1	5,471.7	6,579.3	7,377.1	8,064.7	8,249.5	8,440.6	8,555.1	100.0	100.0	100.0	100.0	100.0	100.0	100.0	100.0
White	3,688.3	4,425.8	5,088.2	4,973.3	5,319.3	5,400.5	5,461.4	5,498.2	81.6	80.9	77.3	67.4	66.0	65.5	64.7	64.3
Total minority	787.0	975.8	1,398.5	2,266.0	2,589.1	2,691.9	2,818.5	2,894.0	17.4	17.8	21.3	30.7	32.1	32.6	33.4	33.8
Black	512.7	590.6	699.2	971.9	1,121.6	1,177.8	1,233.8	1,257.8	11.3	10.8	10.6	13.2	13.9	14.3	14.6	14.7
Hispanic	161.2	221.8	397.6	768.4	884.1	922.9	976.3	1,015.0	3.6	4.1	6.0	10.4	11.0	11.2	11.6	11.9
Asian/Pacific Islander	78.2	120.2	246.0	443.6	492.0	494.8	510.8	523.2	1.7	2.2	3.7	6.0	6.1	6.0	6.1	6.1
American Indian/Alaska Native	34.9	43.1	55.5	82.1	91.4	96.3	97.6	98.0	0.8	0.8	0.8	1.1	1.1	1.2	1.2	1.1
Nonresident alien	46.8	70.1	92.6	137.8	156.3	157.1	160.7	162.9	1.0	1.3	1.4	1.9	1.9	1.9	1.9	1.9
Graduate, total	**1,322.5**	**1,340.9**	**1,586.2**	**1,850.3**	**2,035.7**	**2,097.5**	**2,156.9**	**2,186.5**	**100.0**	**100.0**	**100.0**	**100.0**	**100.0**	**100.0**	**100.0**	**100.0**
White	1,115.6	1,104.7	1,228.4	1,258.5	1,348.0	1,378.6	1,413.3	1,428.7	84.4	82.4	77.4	68.0	66.2	65.7	65.5	65.3
Total minority	134.5	144.0	190.5	359.4	421.0	448.5	475.4	495.7	10.2	10.7	12.0	19.4	20.7	21.4	22.0	22.7
Black	78.5	75.1	83.9	157.9	189.6	204.9	220.4	233.2	5.9	5.6	5.3	8.5	9.3	9.8	10.2	10.7
Hispanic	26.4	32.1	47.2	95.4	112.3	119.5	125.8	130.7	2.0	2.4	3.0	5.2	5.5	5.7	5.8	6.0
Asian/Pacific Islander	24.5	31.6	53.2	95.8	107.1	111.7	115.9	118.4	1.9	2.4	3.4	5.2	5.3	5.3	5.4	5.4
American Indian/Alaska Native	5.1	5.2	6.2	10.3	11.9	12.5	13.4	13.4	0.4	0.4	0.4	0.6	0.6	0.6	0.6	0.6
Nonresident alien	72.4	92.2	167.3	232.3	266.6	270.4	268.1	262.1	5.5	6.9	10.5	12.6	13.1	12.9	12.4	12.0
Male	707.9	672.2	737.4	779.6	846.8	864.9	878.8	877.2	100.0	100.0	100.0	100.0	100.0	100.0	100.0	100.0
White	589.1	538.5	538.8	502.6	531.6	542.4	552.9	551.2	83.2	80.1	73.1	64.5	62.8	62.7	62.9	62.8
Total minority	63.7	65.0	82.1	135.1	152.7	160.5	168.0	172.7	9.0	9.7	11.1	17.3	18.0	18.6	19.1	19.7
Black	32.0	28.2	29.3	48.9	56.7	60.4	63.9	66.7	4.5	4.2	4.0	6.3	6.7	7.0	7.3	7.6
Hispanic	14.6	15.7	20.6	36.5	41.7	44.2	46.2	47.5	2.1	2.3	2.8	4.7	4.9	5.1	5.3	5.4
Asian/Pacific Islander	14.4	18.6	29.7	45.8	50.0	51.4	53.1	53.8	2.0	2.8	4.0	5.9	5.9	5.9	6.0	6.1
American Indian/Alaska Native	2.7	2.5	2.6	3.8	4.3	4.5	4.7	4.7	0.4	0.4	0.3	0.5	0.5	0.5	0.5	0.5
Nonresident alien	55.1	68.7	116.4	142.0	162.5	162.1	157.9	153.3	7.8	10.2	15.8	18.2	19.2	18.7	18.0	17.5
Female	614.6	668.7	848.8	1,070.7	1,188.8	1,232.6	1,278.1	1,309.3	100.0	100.0	100.0	100.0	100.0	100.0	100.0	100.0
White	526.5	566.2	689.5	756.0	816.4	836.2	860.4	877.5	85.7	84.7	81.2	70.6	68.7	67.8	67.3	67.0
Total minority	70.8	79.0	108.3	224.4	268.3	288.0	307.5	323.0	11.5	11.8	12.8	21.0	22.6	23.4	24.1	24.7
Black	46.5	46.9	54.6	109.0	132.9	144.4	156.4	166.4	7.6	7.0	6.4	10.2	11.2	11.7	12.2	12.7
Hispanic	11.8	16.4	26.6	58.8	70.6	75.2	79.5	83.2	1.9	2.4	3.1	5.5	5.9	6.1	6.2	6.4
Asian/Pacific Islander	10.1	13.0	23.6	50.0	57.1	60.3	62.8	64.6	1.6	1.9	2.8	4.7	4.8	4.9	4.9	4.9
American Indian/Alaska Native	2.4	2.7	3.6	6.5	7.7	8.1	8.7	8.7	0.4	0.4	0.4	0.6	0.6	0.7	0.7	0.7
Nonresident alien	17.3	23.5	50.9	90.3	104.1	108.4	110.2	108.8	2.8	3.5	6.0	8.4	8.8	8.8	8.6	8.3

See notes at end of table.

Table 210. Total fall enrollment in degree-granting institutions, by race/ethnicity, sex, attendance status, and level of student: Selected years,1976 through 2005—Continued

Race/ethnicity, sex, attendance status, and level of student	Fall enrollment (in thousands)								Percentage distribution of students							
	1976	1980	1990	2000	2002	2003	2004	2005	1976	1980	1990	2000	2002	2003	2004	2005
1	2	3	4	5	6	7	8	9	10	11	12	13	14	15	16	17
First-professional, total	244.1	276.8	273.4	306.6	319.0	329.1	334.5	337.0	100.0	100.0	100.0	100.0	100.0	100.0	100.0	100.0
White	220.0	247.7	221.5	220.1	227.4	234.3	238.2	238.1	90.1	89.5	81.0	71.8	71.3	71.2	71.2	70.7
Total minority	21.1	26.3	46.5	78.1	83.3	86.3	88.1	90.8	8.6	9.5	17.0	25.5	26.1	26.2	26.3	27.0
Black	11.2	12.8	15.9	23.5	25.3	25.8	25.9	26.0	4.6	4.6	5.8	7.7	7.9	7.8	7.7	7.7
Hispanic	4.5	6.5	10.7	15.4	16.1	16.9	17.0	17.7	1.9	2.4	3.9	5.0	5.1	5.1	5.1	5.3
Asian/Pacific Islander	4.1	6.1	18.7	36.8	39.6	41.3	42.9	44.6	1.7	2.2	6.8	12.0	12.4	12.6	12.8	13.2
American Indian/Alaska Native	1.3	0.8	1.1	2.3	2.2	2.3	2.4	2.5	0.5	0.3	0.4	0.8	0.7	0.7	0.7	0.7
Nonresident alien	3.1	2.9	5.4	8.4	8.3	8.4	8.2	8.1	1.3	1.0	2.0	2.7	2.6	2.5	2.5	2.4
Male	189.6	198.5	166.8	163.9	162.9	166.2	168.4	169.8	100.0	100.0	100.0	100.0	100.0	100.0	100.0	100.0
White	172.4	179.5	137.8	122.0	120.7	123.5	125.2	125.6	90.9	90.5	82.6	74.4	74.1	74.3	74.3	74.0
Total minority	14.7	16.7	25.3	36.8	37.4	38.0	38.7	39.8	7.7	8.4	15.1	22.4	22.9	22.8	23.0	23.4
Black	7.2	7.4	7.4	9.5	9.7	9.8	9.8	9.9	3.8	3.7	4.4	5.8	6.0	5.9	5.8	5.8
Hispanic	3.5	4.6	6.4	8.0	8.1	8.2	8.3	8.6	1.8	2.3	3.8	4.9	5.0	5.0	4.9	5.1
Asian/Pacific Islander	2.9	4.1	10.8	18.1	18.5	18.8	19.4	20.1	1.5	2.1	6.5	11.1	11.3	11.3	11.5	11.9
American Indian/Alaska Native	1.0	0.5	0.6	1.2	1.1	1.1	1.2	1.2	0.5	0.3	0.4	0.7	0.7	0.7	0.7	0.7
Nonresident alien	2.5	2.3	3.8	5.1	4.8	4.7	4.5	4.4	1.3	1.1	2.3	3.1	2.9	2.8	2.7	2.6
Female	54.5	78.4	106.6	142.7	156.1	162.8	166.1	167.2	100.0	100.0	100.0	100.0	100.0	100.0	100.0	100.0
White	47.6	68.1	83.7	98.1	106.6	110.8	113.0	112.5	87.3	86.9	78.5	68.7	68.3	68.1	68.0	67.3
Total minority	6.4	9.6	21.3	41.3	46.0	48.4	49.4	51.0	11.7	12.3	20.0	28.9	29.4	29.7	29.8	30.5
Black	3.9	5.5	8.5	14.0	15.6	16.0	16.1	16.2	7.2	7.0	8.0	9.8	10.0	9.8	9.7	9.7
Hispanic	1.0	1.9	4.3	7.4	8.0	8.7	8.6	9.1	1.9	2.4	4.0	5.2	5.2	5.3	5.2	5.5
Asian/Pacific Islander	1.1	2.0	7.9	18.7	21.2	22.5	23.5	24.5	2.1	2.6	7.4	13.1	13.5	13.8	14.1	14.6
American Indian/Alaska Native	0.2	0.3	0.5	1.1	1.2	1.2	1.2	1.3	0.4	0.3	0.5	0.8	0.7	0.7	0.7	0.8
Nonresident alien	0.5	0.6	1.6	3.3	3.5	3.7	3.7	3.7	1.0	0.8	1.5	2.3	2.3	2.2	2.2	2.2

NOTE: Race categories exclude persons of Hispanic origin. Because of underreporting and nonreporting of racial/ethnic data, some figures are slightly lower than corresponding data in other tables. Data through 1990 are for institutions of higher education, while later data are for degree-granting institutions. Degree-granting institutions grant associate's or higher degrees and participate in Title IV federal financial aid programs. The degree-granting classification is very similar to the earlier higher education classification, but it includes more 2-year colleges and excludes a few higher education institutions that did not grant degrees. (See Guide to Sources for details.) Detail may not sum to totals because of rounding.

SOURCE: U.S. Department of Education, National Center for Education Statistics, Higher Education General Information Survey (HEGIS), "Fall Enrollment in Colleges and Universities" surveys, 1976 and 1980; and 1990 through 2005 Integrated Postsecondary Education Data System (IPEDS), "Fall Enrollment Survey" (IPEDS-EF:90), and Spring 2001 through Spring 2006. (This table was prepared August 2006.)

Table 211. Total fall enrollment in degree-granting institutions, by race/ethnicity of student and type and control of institution: Selected years, 1976 through 2005

Race/ethnicity of student and type and control of institution	Fall enrollment (in thousands)								Percentage distribution of students							
	1976	1980	1990	2000	2002	2003	2004	2005	1976	1980	1990	2000	2002	2003	2004	2005
1	2	3	4	5	6	7	8	9	10	11	12	13	14	15	16	17
All students, total	**10,985.6**	**12,086.8**	**13,818.6**	**15,312.3**	**16,611.7**	**16,900.5**	**17,272.0**	**17,487.5**	**100.0**	**100.0**	**100.0**	**100.0**	**100.0**	**100.0**	**100.0**	**100.0**
White	9,076.1	9,833.0	10,722.5	10,462.1	11,140.2	11,275.4	11,422.8	11,495.4	82.6	81.4	77.6	68.3	67.1	66.7	66.1	65.7
Total minority	1,690.8	1,948.8	2,704.7	4,321.5	4,880.5	5,033.2	5,259.1	5,407.2	15.4	16.1	19.6	28.2	29.4	29.8	30.4	30.9
Black	1,033.0	1,106.8	1,247.0	1,730.3	1,978.7	2,068.9	2,164.7	2,214.6	9.4	9.2	9.0	11.3	11.9	12.2	12.5	12.7
Hispanic	383.8	471.7	782.4	1,461.8	1,661.7	1,716.0	1,809.6	1,882.0	3.5	3.9	5.7	9.5	10.0	10.2	10.5	10.8
Asian/Pacific Islander	197.9	286.4	572.4	978.2	1,074.2	1,075.7	1,108.7	1,134.4	1.8	2.4	4.1	6.4	6.5	6.4	6.5	6.5
American Indian/Alaska Native	76.1	83.9	102.8	151.2	165.9	172.7	176.1	176.3	0.7	0.7	0.7	1.0	1.0	1.0	1.0	1.0
Nonresident alien	218.7	305.0	391.5	528.7	590.9	591.8	590.2	584.8	2.0	2.5	2.8	3.5	3.6	3.5	3.4	3.3
Public	**8,641.0**	**9,456.4**	**10,844.7**	**11,752.8**	**12,752.0**	**12,857.1**	**12,980.1**	**13,021.8**	**100.0**	**100.0**	**100.0**	**100.0**	**100.0**	**100.0**	**100.0**	**100.0**
White	7,094.5	7,656.1	8,385.4	7,963.4	8,490.5	8,531.4	8,546.3	8,518.2	82.1	81.0	77.3	67.8	66.6	66.4	65.8	65.4
Total minority	1,401.2	1,596.2	2,199.2	3,446.3	3,867.4	3,937.7	4,062.4	4,130.8	16.2	16.9	20.3	29.3	30.3	30.6	31.3	31.7
Black	831.2	876.1	976.4	1,319.2	1,487.2	1,533.5	1,574.6	1,580.4	9.6	9.3	9.0	11.2	11.7	11.9	12.1	12.1
Hispanic	336.8	406.2	671.4	1,229.3	1,388.7	1,414.6	1,477.4	1,525.6	3.9	4.3	6.2	10.5	10.9	11.0	11.4	11.7
Asian/Pacific Islander	165.7	239.7	461.0	770.5	851.6	845.2	866.1	881.9	1.9	2.5	4.3	6.6	6.7	6.6	6.7	6.8
American Indian/Alaska Native	67.5	74.2	90.4	127.3	140.0	144.3	144.4	143.0	0.8	0.8	0.8	1.1	1.1	1.1	1.1	1.1
Nonresident alien	145.3	204.2	260.0	343.1	394.1	388.0	371.4	372.8	1.7	2.2	2.4	2.9	3.1	3.0	2.9	2.9
Private	**2,344.6**	**2,630.4**	**2,973.9**	**3,559.5**	**3,859.7**	**4,043.4**	**4,291.9**	**4,465.6**	**100.0**	**100.0**	**100.0**	**100.0**	**100.0**	**100.0**	**100.0**	**100.0**
White	1,981.6	2,176.9	2,337.0	2,498.7	2,649.8	2,744.1	2,876.5	2,977.3	84.5	82.8	78.6	70.2	68.7	67.9	67.0	66.7
Total minority	289.6	352.7	505.5	875.2	1,013.2	1,095.5	1,196.7	1,276.4	12.4	13.4	17.0	24.6	26.3	27.1	27.9	28.6
Black	201.8	230.7	270.6	411.1	491.6	535.3	590.1	634.2	8.6	8.8	9.1	11.5	12.7	13.2	13.7	14.2
Hispanic	47.0	65.6	111.0	232.5	273.1	301.4	332.2	356.4	2.0	2.5	3.7	6.5	7.0	7.5	7.7	8.0
Asian/Pacific Islander	32.2	46.7	111.5	207.7	222.6	230.5	242.6	252.4	1.4	1.8	3.7	5.8	5.8	5.7	5.7	5.7
American Indian/Alaska Native	8.6	9.7	12.4	23.9	25.9	28.3	31.8	33.3	0.4	0.4	0.4	0.7	0.7	0.7	0.7	0.7
Nonresident alien	73.4	100.8	131.4	185.6	196.8	203.9	218.8	212.0	3.1	3.8	4.4	5.2	5.1	5.0	5.1	4.7
4-year, total	**7,106.5**	**7,565.4**	**8,578.6**	**9,363.9**	**10,082.3**	**10,407.6**	**10,726.2**	**10,999.4**	**100.0**	**100.0**	**100.0**	**100.0**	**100.0**	**100.0**	**100.0**	**100.0**
White	5,999.0	6,274.5	6,768.1	6,658.0	7,053.8	7,198.7	7,359.0	7,496.0	84.4	82.9	78.9	71.1	70.0	69.2	68.6	68.2
Total minority	931.0	1,049.9	1,486.1	2,266.1	2,540.3	2,713.2	2,868.0	3,009.5	13.1	13.9	17.3	24.2	25.2	26.1	26.7	27.4
Black	603.7	634.3	722.8	995.4	1,119.7	1,189.0	1,258.9	1,313.4	8.5	8.4	8.4	10.6	11.1	11.4	11.7	11.9
Hispanic	173.6	216.6	358.2	617.9	702.9	783.4	837.2	900.5	2.4	2.9	4.2	6.6	7.0	7.5	7.8	8.2
Asian/Pacific Islander	118.7	162.1	357.2	576.3	633.1	650.4	678.0	700.0	1.7	2.1	4.2	6.2	6.3	6.2	6.3	6.4
American Indian/Alaska Native	35.0	36.9	47.9	76.5	84.6	90.4	93.9	95.6	0.5	0.5	0.6	0.8	0.8	0.9	0.9	0.9
Nonresident alien	176.5	240.9	324.3	439.7	488.3	495.6	499.2	493.1	2.5	3.2	3.8	4.7	4.8	4.8	4.7	4.5
Public	**4,892.9**	**5,127.6**	**5,848.2**	**6,055.4**	**6,481.6**	**6,649.4**	**6,736.5**	**6,837.6**	**100.0**	**100.0**	**100.0**	**100.0**	**100.0**	**100.0**	**100.0**	**100.0**
White	4,120.2	4,243.0	4,605.6	4,311.2	4,551.7	4,609.9	4,642.9	4,678.1	84.2	82.7	78.8	71.2	70.2	69.3	68.9	68.4
Total minority	666.7	740.8	1,046.2	1,486.4	1,636.2	1,745.8	1,811.5	1,876.9	13.6	14.4	17.9	24.5	25.2	26.3	26.9	27.5
Black	421.8	438.2	495.1	627.8	682.5	718.7	741.2	754.0	8.6	8.5	8.5	10.4	10.5	10.8	11.0	11.0
Hispanic	129.3	156.4	262.5	420.0	468.1	528.3	555.8	595.6	2.6	3.1	4.5	6.9	7.0	7.9	8.3	8.7
Asian/Pacific Islander	87.5	117.2	250.6	381.3	422.8	432.2	447.4	460.1	1.8	2.3	4.3	6.3	6.5	6.5	6.6	6.7
American Indian/Alaska Native	28.2	29.0	38.0	57.2	62.7	66.5	67.0	67.2	0.6	0.6	0.7	0.9	1.0	1.0	1.0	1.0
Nonresident alien	106.0	143.8	196.4	257.8	293.7	293.8	282.2	282.6	2.2	2.8	3.4	4.3	4.5	4.4	4.2	4.1
Private	**2,213.6**	**2,437.8**	**2,730.3**	**3,308.5**	**3,600.7**	**3,758.1**	**3,989.6**	**4,161.8**	**100.0**	**100.0**	**100.0**	**100.0**	**100.0**	**100.0**	**100.0**	**100.0**
White	1,878.8	2,031.5	2,162.5	2,346.9	2,502.1	2,588.8	2,716.1	2,818.8	84.9	83.3	79.2	70.9	69.5	68.9	68.1	67.7
Total minority	264.3	309.2	439.8	779.7	904.1	967.4	1,056.5	1,132.5	11.9	12.7	16.1	23.6	25.1	25.7	26.5	27.2
Black	182.0	196.1	227.7	367.6	437.2	470.3	517.7	559.4	8.2	8.0	8.3	11.1	12.1	12.5	13.0	13.4
Hispanic	44.3	60.2	95.7	197.9	234.7	255.1	281.3	304.9	2.0	2.5	3.5	6.0	6.5	6.8	7.1	7.3
Asian/Pacific Islander	31.2	44.9	106.6	195.0	210.3	218.2	230.6	239.8	1.4	1.8	3.9	5.9	5.8	5.8	5.8	5.8
American Indian/Alaska Native	6.8	7.9	9.9	19.3	21.9	23.9	26.9	28.4	0.3	0.3	0.4	0.6	0.6	0.6	0.7	0.7
Nonresident alien	70.5	97.1	127.9	181.9	194.5	201.8	217.0	210.4	3.2	4.0	4.7	5.5	5.4	5.4	4.2	5.1
2-year, total	**3,879.1**	**4,521.4**	**5,240.1**	**5,948.4**	**6,529.4**	**6,492.9**	**6,545.9**	**6,488.1**	**100.0**	**100.0**	**100.0**	**100.0**	**100.0**	**100.0**	**100.0**	**100.0**
White	3,077.1	3,558.5	3,954.3	3,804.1	4,086.5	4,076.7	4,063.8	3,998.6	79.3	78.7	75.5	64.0	62.6	62.8	62.1	61.6
Total minority	759.8	898.9	1,218.6	2,055.4	2,340.3	2,320.0	2,391.2	2,397.7	19.6	19.9	23.3	34.6	35.8	35.7	36.5	37.0
Black	429.3	472.5	524.3	734.9	859.1	879.9	905.8	901.1	11.1	10.4	10.0	12.4	13.2	13.6	13.8	13.9

See notes at end of table.

Table 211. Total fall enrollment in degree-granting institutions, by race/ethnicity of student and type and control of institution: Selected years, 1976 through 2005—Continued

Race/ethnicity of student and type and control of institution	Fall enrollment (in thousands)								Percentage distribution of students							
	1976	1980	1990	2000	2002	2003	2004	2005	1976	1980	1990	2000	2002	2003	2004	2005
1	2	3	4	5	6	7	8	9	10	11	12	13	14	15	16	17
Hispanic	210.2	255.1	424.2	843.9	958.9	932.6	972.4	981.5	5.4	5.6	8.1	14.2	14.7	14.4	14.9	15.1
Asian/Pacific Islander	79.2	124.3	215.2	401.9	441.0	425.3	430.7	434.4	2.0	2.8	4.1	6.8	6.8	6.6	6.6	6.7
American Indian/Alaska Native	41.2	47.0	54.9	74.7	81.3	82.2	82.2	80.7	1.1	1.0	1.0	1.3	1.2	1.3	1.3	1.2
Nonresident alien	42.2	64.1	67.1	89.0	102.6	96.2	90.9	91.8	1.1	1.4	1.3	1.5	1.6	1.5	1.4	1.4
Public	3,748.1	4,328.8	4,996.5	5,697.4	6,270.4	6,207.6	6,243.6	6,184.2	100.0	100.0	100.0	100.0	100.0	100.0	100.0	100.0
White	2,974.3	3,413.1	3,779.8	3,652.2	3,938.8	3,921.5	3,903.4	3,840.1	79.4	78.8	75.7	64.1	62.8	63.2	62.5	62.1
Total minority	734.5	855.4	1,153.0	1,959.9	2,231.2	2,191.9	2,251.0	2,253.9	19.6	19.8	23.1	34.4	35.6	35.3	36.1	36.4
Black	409.5	437.9	481.4	691.4	804.7	814.8	833.4	826.3	10.9	10.1	9.6	12.1	12.8	13.1	13.3	13.4
Hispanic	207.5	249.8	408.9	809.2	920.5	886.3	921.6	930.0	5.5	5.8	8.2	14.2	14.7	14.3	14.8	15.0
Asian/Pacific Islander	78.2	122.5	210.3	389.2	428.7	413.0	418.6	421.8	2.1	2.8	4.2	6.8	6.8	6.7	6.7	6.8
American Indian/Alaska Native	39.3	45.2	52.4	70.1	77.2	77.8	77.4	75.7	1.0	1.0	1.0	1.2	1.2	1.3	1.2	1.2
Nonresident alien	39.2	60.3	63.6	85.2	100.4	94.2	89.2	90.2	1.0	1.4	1.3	1.5	1.6	1.5	1.4	1.5
Private	131.0	192.6	243.6	251.0	259.0	285.3	302.3	303.8	100.0	100.0	100.0	100.0	100.0	100.0	100.0	100.0
White	102.8	145.4	174.5	151.8	147.7	155.2	160.4	158.4	78.5	75.5	71.6	60.5	57.0	54.4	53.1	52.1
Total minority	25.3	43.5	65.6	95.5	109.1	128.1	140.2	143.8	19.3	22.6	26.9	38.0	42.1	44.9	46.4	47.3
Black	19.8	34.6	42.9	43.5	54.4	65.1	72.5	74.8	15.1	17.9	17.6	17.3	21.0	22.8	24.0	24.6
Hispanic	2.6	5.3	15.3	34.7	38.3	46.2	50.8	51.4	2.0	2.8	6.3	13.8	14.8	16.2	16.8	16.9
Asian/Pacific Islander	0.9	1.8	4.9	12.7	12.3	12.3	12.1	12.6	0.7	0.9	2.0	5.1	4.7	4.3	4.0	4.2
American Indian/Alaska Native	1.8	1.8	2.5	4.5	4.1	4.4	4.9	5.0	1.4	0.9	1.0	1.8	1.6	1.6	1.6	1.6
Nonresident alien	3.0	3.7	3.5	3.8	2.2	2.0	1.7	1.6	2.3	1.9	1.4	1.5	0.9	0.7	0.6	0.5

NOTE: Race categories exclude persons of Hispanic origin. Because of underreporting and nonreporting of racial/ethnic data, some figures are slightly lower than corresponding data in other tables. Data through 1990 are for institutions of higher education, while later data are for degree-granting institutions. Degree-granting institutions grant associate's or higher degrees and participate in Title IV federal financial aid programs. The degree-granting classification is very similar to the earlier higher education classification, but it includes more 2-year colleges and excludes a few higher education institutions that did not grant degrees. (See Guide to Sources for details.) Detail may not sum to totals because of rounding.

SOURCE: U.S. Department of Education, National Center for Education Statistics, Higher Education General Information Survey (HEGIS), "Fall Enrollment in Colleges and Universities" surveys, 1976 and 1980; and 1990 through 2005 Integrated Postsecondary Education Data System (IPEDS), "Fall Enrollment Survey" (IPEDS-EF:90), and Spring 2001 through Spring 2006. (This table was prepared August 2006.)

Table 212. Fall enrollment in degree-granting institutions, by race/ethnicity of student and by state or jurisdiction: 2005

State or jurisdiction	Total	White	Minority					Non-resident alien	Percentage distribution							
			Total	Black	Hispanic	Asian/ Pacific Islander	American Indian/ Alaska Native		Total	White	Minority					Non-resident alien
											Total	Black	Hispanic	Asian/ Pacific Islander	American Indian/ Alaska Native	
1	2	3	4	5	6	7	8	9	10	11	12	13	14	15	16	17
United States	**17,487,475**	**11,495,440**	**5,407,221**	**2,214,561**	**1,881,975**	**1,134,382**	**176,303**	**584,814**	**100.0**	**65.7**	**30.9**	**12.7**	**10.8**	**6.5**	**1.0**	**3.3**
Alabama	256,389	166,394	84,157	74,968	3,717	3,577	1,895	5,838	100.0	64.9	32.8	29.2	1.4	1.4	0.7	2.3
Alaska	30,231	21,653	7,641	1,016	1,071	1,476	4,078	937	100.0	71.6	25.3	3.4	3.5	4.9	13.5	3.1
Arizona	545,597	347,468	171,818	48,521	85,654	19,763	17,880	26,311	100.0	63.7	31.5	8.9	15.7	3.6	3.3	4.8
Arkansas	143,272	107,865	32,790	26,242	2,913	2,059	1,576	2,617	100.0	75.3	22.9	18.3	2.0	1.4	1.1	1.8
California	2,399,833	1,034,430	1,291,478	185,659	632,358	451,454	22,007	73,925	100.0	43.1	53.8	7.7	26.4	18.8	0.9	3.1
Colorado	302,672	231,165	65,464	15,528	33,856	11,710	4,370	6,043	100.0	76.4	21.6	5.1	11.2	3.9	1.4	2.0
Connecticut	174,675	126,904	41,362	18,528	14,285	7,877	672	6,409	100.0	72.7	23.7	10.6	8.2	4.5	0.4	3.7
Delaware	51,612	36,537	13,641	10,169	1,818	1,500	154	1,434	100.0	70.8	26.4	19.7	3.5	2.9	0.3	2.8
District of Columbia	104,897	50,078	48,008	36,007	4,922	6,643	436	6,811	100.0	47.7	45.8	34.3	4.7	6.3	0.4	6.5
Florida	872,662	493,385	348,232	155,357	159,572	29,827	3,476	31,045	100.0	56.5	39.9	17.8	18.3	3.4	0.4	3.6
Georgia	426,650	255,587	158,614	131,040	10,597	15,790	1,187	12,449	100.0	59.9	37.2	30.7	2.5	3.7	0.3	2.9
Hawaii	67,083	17,817	44,305	1,534	2,040	40,352	379	4,961	100.0	26.6	66.0	2.3	3.0	60.2	0.6	7.4
Idaho	77,708	68,692	6,739	651	3,594	1,472	1,022	2,277	100.0	88.4	8.7	0.8	4.6	1.9	1.3	2.9
Illinois	832,967	543,072	265,892	118,905	95,542	48,336	3,109	24,003	100.0	65.2	31.9	14.3	11.5	5.8	0.4	2.9
Indiana	361,253	298,997	49,467	30,315	10,366	7,443	1,343	12,789	100.0	82.8	13.7	8.4	2.9	2.1	0.4	3.5
Iowa	227,722	196,992	23,932	11,660	6,423	4,804	1,045	6,798	100.0	86.5	10.5	5.1	2.8	2.1	0.5	3.0
Kansas	191,752	155,703	30,321	11,230	8,618	7,279	3,194	5,728	100.0	81.2	15.8	5.9	4.5	3.8	1.7	3.0
Kentucky	244,969	212,887	27,899	21,322	2,834	2,995	748	4,183	100.0	86.9	11.4	8.7	1.2	1.2	0.3	1.7
Louisiana	197,713	123,371	68,440	59,974	3,589	3,657	1,220	5,902	100.0	62.4	34.6	30.3	1.8	1.8	0.6	3.0
Maine	65,551	60,093	4,187	1,279	832	1,101	975	1,271	100.0	91.7	6.4	2.0	1.3	1.7	1.5	1.9
Maryland	314,151	181,270	120,524	86,984	12,063	20,185	1,292	12,357	100.0	57.7	38.4	27.7	3.8	6.4	0.4	3.9
Massachusetts	443,316	320,791	96,106	34,986	27,174	32,061	1,885	26,419	100.0	72.4	21.7	7.9	6.1	7.2	0.4	6.0
Michigan	626,751	477,811	126,617	83,007	17,520	20,819	5,271	22,323	100.0	76.2	20.2	13.2	2.8	3.3	0.8	3.6
Minnesota	361,701	299,792	52,743	24,452	8,368	15,670	4,253	9,166	100.0	82.9	14.6	6.8	2.3	4.3	1.2	2.5
Mississippi	150,457	86,626	61,861	58,758	1,203	1,252	648	1,970	100.0	57.6	41.1	39.1	0.8	0.8	0.4	1.3
Missouri	374,445	296,174	69,015	46,582	10,624	9,516	2,293	9,256	100.0	79.1	18.4	12.4	2.8	2.5	0.6	2.5
Montana	47,850	40,775	6,185	270	791	536	4,588	890	100.0	85.2	12.9	0.6	1.7	1.1	9.6	1.9
Nebraska	121,236	104,861	13,053	5,094	4,224	2,827	908	3,322	100.0	86.5	10.8	4.2	3.5	2.3	0.7	2.7
Nevada	110,705	70,454	37,701	8,651	15,515	11,877	1,658	2,550	100.0	63.6	34.1	7.8	14.0	10.7	1.5	2.3
New Hampshire	69,893	62,925	5,317	1,418	1,742	1,775	382	1,651	100.0	90.0	7.6	2.0	2.5	2.5	0.5	2.4
New Jersey	379,758	226,762	138,052	53,971	50,502	32,409	1,170	14,944	100.0	59.7	36.4	14.2	13.3	8.5	0.3	3.9
New Mexico	131,337	56,581	71,989	3,844	54,271	2,602	11,272	2,767	100.0	43.1	54.8	2.9	41.3	2.0	8.6	2.1
New York	1,152,081	699,226	384,276	160,007	130,198	89,927	4,144	68,579	100.0	60.7	33.4	13.9	11.3	7.8	0.4	6.0
North Carolina	484,392	325,552	146,674	116,786	12,052	11,740	6,096	12,166	100.0	67.2	30.3	24.1	2.5	2.4	1.3	2.5
North Dakota	49,389	43,037	4,776	682	489	530	3,075	1,576	100.0	87.1	9.7	1.4	1.0	1.1	6.2	3.2
Ohio	616,350	496,461	102,398	74,590	12,361	13,008	2,439	17,491	100.0	80.5	16.6	12.1	2.0	2.1	0.4	2.8
Oklahoma	208,053	146,358	52,211	19,039	7,272	4,742	21,158	9,484	100.0	70.3	25.1	9.2	3.5	2.3	10.2	4.6
Oregon	200,033	162,662	31,812	4,788	11,103	12,591	3,330	5,559	100.0	81.3	15.9	2.4	5.6	6.3	1.7	2.8
Pennsylvania	692,340	546,328	123,329	71,463	20,824	29,203	1,839	22,683	100.0	78.9	17.8	10.3	3.0	4.2	0.3	3.3
Rhode Island	81,382	64,726	13,962	4,897	5,246	3,468	351	2,694	100.0	79.5	17.2	6.0	6.4	4.3	0.4	3.3

See notes at end of table.

Table 212. Fall enrollment in degree-granting institutions, by race/ethnicity of student and by state or jurisdiction: 2005—Continued

State or jurisdiction	Total	White	Minority					Non-resident alien	Percentage distribution							
			Total	Black	Hispanic	Asian/ Pacific Islander	American Indian/ Alaska Native		Total	White	Minority					Non-resident alien
											Total	Black	Hispanic	Asian/ Pacific Islander	American Indian/ Alaska Native	
1	2	3	4	5	6	7	8	9	10	11	12	13	14	15	16	17
South Carolina	210,444	141,590	65,455	57,941	3,374	3,272	868	3,399	100.0	67.3	31.1	27.5	1.6	1.6	0.4	1.6
South Dakota	48,768	42,727	4,948	642	518	592	3,196	1,093	100.0	87.6	10.1	1.3	1.1	1.2	6.6	2.2
Tennessee	283,070	210,640	66,899	55,288	5,142	5,277	1,192	5,531	100.0	74.4	23.6	19.5	1.8	1.9	0.4	2.0
Texas	1,240,707	645,009	547,308	153,416	324,803	62,688	6,401	48,390	100.0	52.0	44.1	12.4	26.2	5.1	0.5	3.9
Utah	200,691	174,746	20,296	2,298	9,680	6,049	2,269	5,649	100.0	87.1	10.1	1.1	4.8	3.0	1.1	2.8
Vermont	39,915	36,445	2,663	725	827	857	254	807	100.0	91.3	6.7	1.8	2.1	2.1	0.6	2.0
Virginia	439,166	300,192	128,293	85,096	16,615	24,429	2,153	10,681	100.0	68.4	29.2	19.4	3.8	5.6	0.5	2.4
Washington	348,482	264,285	74,496	15,461	19,530	33,269	6,236	9,701	100.0	75.8	21.4	4.4	5.6	9.5	1.8	2.8
West Virginia	99,547	89,306	7,850	5,220	1,108	1,151	371	2,391	100.0	89.7	7.9	5.2	1.1	1.2	0.4	2.4
Wisconsin	335,258	288,185	40,209	17,185	9,605	9,691	3,728	6,864	100.0	86.0	12.0	5.1	2.9	2.9	1.1	2.0
Wyoming	35,334	31,888	2,881	336	1,612	322	611	565	100.0	90.2	8.2	1.0	4.6	0.9	1.7	1.6
U.S. Service Schools	15,265	12,165	2,935	779	1,018	932	206	165	100.0	79.7	19.2	5.1	6.7	6.1	1.3	1.1
Other jurisdictions	**223,165**	**652**	**221,792**	**2,040**	**208,442**	**11,292**	**18**	**721**	**100.0**	**0.3**	**99.4**	**0.9**	**93.4**	**5.1**	**#**	**0.3**
American Samoa	1,579	6	1,405	0	4	1,401	0	168	100.0	0.4	89.0	0.0	0.3	88.7	0.0	10.6
Federated States of Micronesia	2,283	6	2,277	0	0	2,277	0	0	100.0	0.3	99.7	0.0	0.0	99.7	0.0	0.0
Guam	6,064	328	5,658	56	38	5,559	5	78	100.0	5.4	93.3	0.9	0.6	91.7	0.1	1.3
Marshall Islands	604	0	604	0	0	604	0	0	100.0	0.0	100.0	0.0	0.0	100.0	0.0	0.0
Northern Marianas	967	38	754	1	1	751	1	175	100.0	3.9	78.0	0.1	0.1	77.7	0.1	18.1
Palau	651	0	651	0	0	651	0	0	100.0	0.0	100.0	0.0	0.0	100.0	0.0	0.0
Puerto Rico	208,625	127	208,323	38	208,249	32	4	175	100.0	0.1	99.9	#	99.8	#	#	0.1
Virgin Islands	2,392	147	2,120	1,945	150	17	8	125	100.0	6.1	88.6	81.3	6.3	0.7	0.3	5.2

#Rounds to zero.
NOTE: Race categories exclude persons of Hispanic origin. Degree-granting institutions grant associate's or higher degrees and participate in Title IV federal financial aid programs. Detail may not sum to totals because of rounding.

SOURCE: U.S. Department of Education, National Center for Education Statistics, 2005 Integrated Postsecondary Education Data System (IPEDS), Spring 2006. (This table was prepared August 2006.)

Table 213. Fall enrollment in degree-granting institutions, by race/ethnicity of student and by state or jurisdiction: 2004

State or jurisdiction	Total	White	Minority					Nonresident alien	Percentage distribution							Nonresident alien
			Total	Black	Hispanic	Asian/ Pacific Islander	American Indian/ Alaska Native		Total	White	Minority					
											Total	Black	Hispanic	Asian/ Pacific Islander	American Indian/ Alaska Native	
1	2	3	4	5	6	7	8	9	10	11	12	13	14	15	16	17
United States	**17,272,044**	**11,422,770**	**5,259,107**	**2,164,683**	**1,809,593**	**1,108,693**	**176,138**	**590,167**	**100.0**	**66.1**	**30.4**	**12.5**	**10.5**	**6.4**	**1.0**	**3.4**
Alabama	255,826	166,656	83,180	74,412	3,568	3,342	1,858	5,990	100.0	65.1	32.5	29.1	1.4	1.3	0.7	2.3
Alaska	30,869	22,316	7,637	1,094	1,044	1,344	4,155	916	100.0	72.3	24.7	3.5	3.4	4.4	13.5	3.0
Arizona	490,925	315,925	148,215	34,908	78,300	17,588	17,419	26,785	100.0	64.4	30.2	7.1	15.9	3.6	3.5	5.5
Arkansas	138,399	104,737	31,174	25,271	2,375	1,996	1,532	2,488	100.0	75.7	22.5	18.3	1.7	1.4	1.1	1.8
California	2,374,045	1,040,123	1,259,027	182,775	609,600	444,352	22,300	74,895	100.0	43.8	53.0	7.7	25.7	18.7	0.9	3.2
Colorado	300,914	231,068	63,150	14,002	33,308	11,490	4,350	6,696	100.0	76.8	21.0	4.7	11.1	3.8	1.4	2.2
Connecticut	172,775	126,513	39,738	17,903	13,673	7,440	722	6,524	100.0	73.2	23.0	10.4	7.9	4.3	0.4	3.8
Delaware	49,804	35,935	12,485	9,255	1,679	1,371	180	1,384	100.0	72.2	25.1	18.6	3.4	2.8	0.4	2.8
District of Columbia	99,988	48,634	44,654	33,207	4,444	6,627	376	6,700	100.0	48.6	44.7	33.2	4.4	6.6	0.4	6.7
Florida	866,665	492,832	343,545	156,587	154,246	29,044	3,668	30,288	100.0	56.9	39.6	18.1	17.8	3.4	0.4	3.5
Georgia	434,283	262,308	159,462	131,236	11,168	15,616	1,442	12,513	100.0	60.4	36.7	30.2	2.6	3.6	0.3	2.9
Hawaii	67,225	17,952	44,218	1,523	1,954	40,412	329	5,055	100.0	26.7	65.8	2.3	2.9	60.1	0.5	7.5
Idaho	76,311	67,429	6,263	596	3,202	1,397	1,068	2,619	100.0	88.4	8.2	0.8	4.2	1.8	1.4	3.4
Illinois	801,401	524,866	252,406	110,995	91,517	47,237	2,657	24,129	100.0	65.5	31.5	13.9	11.4	5.9	0.3	3.0
Indiana	356,801	295,973	47,495	29,117	9,947	7,115	1,316	13,333	100.0	83.0	13.3	8.2	2.8	2.0	0.4	3.7
Iowa	217,646	189,641	20,621	9,598	5,442	4,466	1,115	7,384	100.0	87.1	9.5	4.4	2.5	2.1	0.5	3.4
Kansas	191,590	156,552	29,079	11,177	8,082	6,737	3,083	5,959	100.0	81.7	15.2	5.8	4.2	3.5	1.6	3.1
Kentucky	240,097	208,553	27,200	21,041	2,661	2,799	699	4,344	100.0	86.9	11.3	8.8	1.1	1.2	0.3	1.8
Louisiana	246,301	150,456	88,085	75,586	5,919	5,037	1,543	7,760	100.0	61.1	35.8	30.7	2.4	2.0	0.6	3.2
Maine	65,415	60,277	3,753	1,106	772	1,013	862	1,385	100.0	92.1	5.7	1.7	1.2	1.5	1.3	2.1
Maryland	312,493	182,062	117,357	84,638	11,594	19,868	1,257	13,074	100.0	58.3	37.6	27.1	3.7	6.4	0.4	4.2
Massachusetts	439,245	319,010	93,579	33,961	26,054	31,650	1,914	26,656	100.0	72.6	21.3	7.7	5.9	7.2	0.4	6.1
Michigan	620,980	475,409	122,438	80,171	16,644	20,515	5,108	23,133	100.0	76.6	19.7	12.9	2.7	3.3	0.8	3.7
Minnesota	349,021	292,323	47,417	21,732	6,687	14,877	4,121	9,281	100.0	83.8	13.6	6.2	1.9	4.3	1.2	2.7
Mississippi	152,115	88,612	61,481	58,345	1,128	1,254	754	2,022	100.0	58.3	40.4	38.4	0.7	0.8	0.5	1.3
Missouri	365,204	290,291	65,107	43,938	9,939	8,993	2,237	9,806	100.0	79.5	17.8	12.0	2.7	2.5	0.6	2.7
Montana	47,173	40,219	6,109	287	717	503	4,602	845	100.0	85.3	13.0	0.6	1.5	1.1	9.8	1.8
Nebraska	121,053	104,754	12,814	5,076	3,949	2,790	999	3,485	100.0	86.5	10.6	4.2	3.3	2.3	0.8	2.9
Nevada	105,961	69,004	34,307	8,044	13,963	10,777	1,523	2,650	100.0	65.1	32.4	7.6	13.2	10.2	1.4	2.5
New Hampshire	70,163	63,040	5,450	1,552	1,734	1,784	380	1,673	100.0	89.8	7.8	2.2	2.5	2.5	0.5	2.4
New Jersey	380,374	228,670	136,474	53,986	49,132	32,232	1,124	15,230	100.0	60.1	35.9	14.2	12.9	8.5	0.3	4.0
New Mexico	131,577	57,086	71,423	3,721	53,672	2,527	11,503	3,068	100.0	43.4	54.3	2.8	40.8	1.9	8.7	2.3
New York	1,141,525	698,133	380,889	160,941	127,658	88,274	4,016	62,503	100.0	61.2	33.4	14.1	11.2	7.7	0.4	5.5
North Carolina	472,709	320,135	140,844	112,820	10,878	11,252	5,894	11,730	100.0	67.7	29.8	23.9	2.3	2.4	1.2	2.5
North Dakota	49,533	42,560	5,236	743	611	488	3,394	1,737	100.0	85.9	10.6	1.5	1.2	1.0	6.9	3.5

See notes at end of table.

Table 213. Fall enrollment in degree-granting institutions, by race/ethnicity of student and by state or jurisdiction: 2004—Continued

State or jurisdiction	Total	Minority						Non-resident alien	Percentage distribution							Non-resident alien
		White	Total	Black	Hispanic	Asian/ Pacific Islander	American Indian/ Alaska Native		Total	White	Minority Total	Black	Hispanic	Asian/ Pacific Islander	American Indian/ Alaska Native	
1	2	3	4	5	6	7	8	9	10	11	12	13	14	15	16	17
Ohio	614,234	497,895	98,273	71,307	11,649	12,994	2,323	18,066	100.0	81.1	16.0	11.6	1.9	2.1	0.4	2.9
Oklahoma	207,625	146,224	51,294	18,771	6,834	4,674	21,015	10,107	100.0	70.4	24.7	9.0	3.3	2.3	10.1	4.9
Oregon	199,985	163,889	30,616	4,509	10,230	12,606	3,271	5,480	100.0	82.0	15.3	2.3	5.1	6.3	1.6	2.7
Pennsylvania	688,780	546,202	119,657	69,837	19,496	28,457	1,867	22,921	100.0	79.3	17.4	10.1	2.8	4.1	0.3	3.3
Rhode Island	80,377	64,546	13,219	4,596	4,866	3,420	337	2,612	100.0	80.3	16.4	5.7	6.1	4.3	0.4	3.2
South Carolina	208,910	140,288	65,134	58,099	3,115	3,088	832	3,488	100.0	67.2	31.2	27.8	1.5	1.5	0.4	1.7
South Dakota	48,708	42,049	5,509	672	515	396	3,926	1,150	100.0	86.3	11.3	1.4	1.1	0.8	8.1	2.4
Tennessee	278,055	207,872	64,758	53,992	4,652	5,143	971	5,425	100.0	74.8	23.3	19.4	1.7	1.8	0.3	2.0
Texas	1,229,197	645,856	533,491	150,899	315,988	60,221	6,383	49,850	100.0	52.5	43.4	12.3	25.7	4.9	0.5	4.1
Utah	194,324	170,333	18,408	1,865	8,590	5,643	2,310	5,583	100.0	87.7	9.5	1.0	4.4	2.9	1.2	2.9
Vermont	38,639	35,301	2,550	706	772	828	244	788	100.0	91.4	6.6	1.8	2.0	2.1	0.6	2.0
Virginia	425,181	293,131	121,185	80,684	14,946	23,322	2,233	10,865	100.0	68.9	28.5	19.0	3.5	5.5	0.5	2.6
Washington	343,524	262,771	71,161	14,507	18,084	32,297	6,273	9,592	100.0	76.5	20.7	4.2	5.3	9.4	1.8	2.8
West Virginia	97,884	88,168	7,379	5,006	946	1,072	355	2,337	100.0	90.1	7.5	5.1	1.0	1.1	0.4	2.4
Wisconsin	331,506	285,736	38,577	16,759	9,126	9,191	3,501	7,193	100.0	86.2	11.6	5.1	2.8	2.8	1.1	2.2
Wyoming	33,955	30,700	2,753	329	1,509	298	617	502	100.0	90.4	8.1	1.0	4.4	0.9	1.8	1.5
U.S. Service Schools	14,754	11,755	2,831	801	1,014	836	180	168	100.0	79.7	19.2	5.4	6.9	5.7	1.2	1.1
Other jurisdictions	**220,920**	**529**	**219,674**	**2,145**	**207,064**	**10,448**	**17**	**717**	**100.0**	**0.2**	**99.4**	**1.0**	**93.7**	**4.7**	**#**	**0.3**
American Samoa	1,550	7	1,370	0	2	1,368	0	173	100.0	0.5	88.4	0.0	0.1	88.3	0.0	11.2
Federated States of Micronesia	2,608	4	2,604	0	0	2,604	0	0	100.0	0.2	99.8	0.0	0.0	99.8	0.0	0.0
Guam	4,642	222	4,356	40	35	4,274	7	64	100.0	4.8	93.8	0.9	0.8	92.1	0.2	1.4
Marshall Islands	623	0	623	0	0	623	0	0	100.0	0.0	100.0	0.0	0.0	100.0	0.0	0.0
Northern Marianas	1,101	48	890	2	2	884	2	163	100.0	4.4	80.8	0.2	0.2	80.3	0.2	14.8
Palau	651	0	645	0	0	645	0	6	100.0	0.0	99.1	0.0	0.0	99.1	0.0	0.9
Puerto Rico	207,180	113	206,930	34	206,864	28	4	137	100.0	0.1	99.9	#	99.8	#	#	0.1
Virgin Islands	2,565	135	2,256	2,069	161	22	4	174	100.0	5.3	88.0	80.7	6.3	0.9	0.2	6.8

#Rounds to zero.
NOTE: Race categories exclude persons of Hispanic origin. Degree-granting institutions grant associate's or higher degrees and participate in Title IV federal financial aid programs. Detail may not sum to totals because of rounding.

SOURCE: U.S. Department of Education, National Center for Education Statistics, 2004 Integrated Postsecondary Education Data System (IPEDS), Spring 2005. (This table was prepared September 2005.)

Table 214. Total number of institutions and fall enrollment in degree-granting institutions, by type and control of institution and percentage of minority enrollment: 2005

Minority percentage of total enrollment	Total, all institution types	Public institutions							Not-for-profit institutions							For-profit institutions		
		Total	Doctoral, extensive[1]	Doctoral, intensive[2]	Master's[3]	Baccalaureate[4]	Specialized[5]	2-year	Total	Doctoral, extensive[1]	Doctoral, intensive[2]	Master's[3]	Baccalaureate[4]	Specialized[5]	2-year	Total	4-year	2-year
1	2	3	4	5	6	7	8	9	10	11	12	13	14	15	16	17	18	19
All institutions																		
Number of institutions	4,253	1,675	102	63	273	104	97	1,036	1,645	48	42	326	490	626	113	933	408	525
Total enrollment	17,487,475	13,021,834	2,735,547	915,694	2,471,344	356,342	358,678	6,184,229	3,454,692	690,379	333,613	1,197,426	753,336	436,416	43,522	1,010,949	750,645	260,304
U.S. citizens[6]	16,902,661	12,649,023	2,568,662	879,645	2,408,138	347,906	350,649	6,094,023	3,282,303	613,355	313,736	1,163,337	732,259	416,915	42,701	971,335	711,765	259,570
White	11,495,440	8,518,181	1,912,950	642,718	1,661,522	252,937	207,936	3,840,118	2,431,320	435,404	212,455	880,849	568,177	309,346	25,089	545,939	412,588	133,351
Minority	5,407,221	4,130,842	655,712	236,927	746,616	94,969	142,713	2,253,905	850,983	177,951	101,281	282,488	164,082	107,569	17,612	425,396	299,177	126,219
Black	2,214,561	1,580,352	208,196	115,647	338,477	53,065	38,619	826,348	397,329	52,117	41,110	141,119	106,793	48,654	7,536	236,880	169,620	67,260
Hispanic	1,881,975	1,525,588	184,827	65,723	243,662	23,834	77,505	930,037	221,660	43,248	30,314	86,412	31,099	25,631	4,956	134,727	88,238	46,489
Asian/Pacific Islander	1,134,382	881,937	240,976	46,486	139,112	14,011	19,556	421,796	209,078	79,479	28,227	48,344	22,027	28,044	2,957	43,367	33,695	9,672
American Indian/Alaska Native	176,303	142,965	21,713	9,071	25,365	4,059	7,033	75,724	22,916	3,107	1,630	6,613	4,163	5,240	2,163	10,422	7,624	2,798
Nonresident alien	584,814	372,811	166,885	36,049	63,206	8,436	8,029	90,206	172,389	77,024	19,877	34,089	21,077	19,501	821	39,614	38,880	734
90.0 percent or more minority enrollment																		
Number of institutions	163	58	0	3	21	4	3	27	72	0	1	3	40	18	10	33	12	21
Total enrollment	393,445	288,258		24,765	125,784	8,930	18,453	110,326	75,868		4,469	12,280	46,426	9,401	3,292	29,319	10,476	18,843
U.S. citizens[6]	388,289	284,237		24,139	123,360	8,876	18,392	109,470	74,831		4,469	12,118	45,654	9,298	3,292	29,221	10,446	18,775
Minority	370,664	269,991		23,360	116,920	8,534	17,710	103,467	72,820		4,456	11,332	44,899	8,951	3,182	27,853	9,944	17,909
75.0 to 89.9 percent minority enrollment																		
Number of institutions	195	71	0	3	8	6	5	49	32	0	0	5	6	10	11	92	29	63
Total enrollment	698,755	603,928		34,330	81,937	34,930	58,427	394,304	31,172			14,812	6,707	4,894	4,759	63,655	24,642	39,013
U.S. citizens[6]	678,043	584,630		31,836	79,297	32,075	56,779	384,643	30,478			14,621	6,318	4,829	4,710	62,935	24,081	38,854
Minority	572,445	494,425		27,217	68,010	28,198	50,953	320,047	25,566			12,093	5,624	3,943	3,906	52,454	20,122	32,332
50.0 to 74.9 percent minority enrollment																		
Number of institutions	458	164	10	2	19	5	6	122	83	1	2	14	9	42	15	211	97	114
Total enrollment	2,174,957	1,811,093	273,293	16,908	314,982	25,374	19,716	1,160,820	143,994	10,930	34,483	54,478	8,297	30,613	5,193	219,870	154,777	65,093
U.S. citizens[6]	2,096,169	1,746,451	255,345	15,766	297,936	24,388	19,052	1,133,964	138,464	9,957	33,238	52,508	8,115	29,500	5,146	211,254	146,426	64,828
Minority	1,320,890	1,098,045	160,881	10,160	183,311	16,449	12,748	714,496	88,395	9,843	17,738	33,794	4,959	18,588	3,473	134,450	93,737	40,713
25.0 to 49.9 percent minority enrollment																		
Number of institutions	1,116	441	25	16	61	11	23	305	360	24	20	79	72	138	27	315	156	159
Total enrollment	5,449,254	3,757,236	714,559	265,365	530,364	63,580	86,850	2,096,508	1,165,927	366,030	172,146	356,481	127,849	130,707	12,714	526,091	453,155	72,936
U.S. citizens[6]	5,230,995	3,648,269	668,695	251,887	517,927	62,334	84,357	2,063,069	1,083,559	317,357	160,701	345,503	122,703	124,771	12,524	499,167	426,391	72,776
Minority	1,907,707	1,342,779	234,879	89,445	194,916	19,977	34,726	768,836	381,547	109,632	58,512	123,787	43,160	41,518	4,938	183,381	156,112	27,269
10.0 to 24.9 percent minority enrollment																		
Number of institutions	1,324	542	53	27	94	30	43	295	603	22	15	139	191	211	25	179	88	91
Total enrollment	6,177,871	4,659,946	1,472,645	432,392	864,274	83,492	140,469	1,666,674	1,385,310	279,352	98,087	519,419	304,526	173,682	10,244	132,615	92,694	39,921
U.S. citizens[6]	5,967,403	4,518,626	1,383,484	417,985	846,332	82,712	137,714	1,650,399	1,318,328	252,981	91,746	503,623	295,565	164,420	9,993	130,449	90,586	39,863
Minority	1,060,829	797,386	238,968	77,176	145,057	13,072	24,494	298,619	238,824	55,481	18,689	84,214	48,375	30,391	1,674	24,619	18,117	6,502
Less than 10.0 percent minority enrollment																		
Number of institutions	997	399	14	12	70	48	17	238	495	1	4	86	172	207	25	103	26	77
Total enrollment	2,593,193	1,901,373	275,050	141,934	554,003	140,026	34,763	755,597	652,421	34,067	24,428	239,956	259,531	87,119	7,320	39,399	14,901	24,498
U.S. citizens[6]	2,541,762	1,866,810	261,138	138,032	543,286	137,521	34,355	752,478	636,643	33,060	23,582	234,964	253,904	84,097	7,036	38,309	13,835	24,474
Minority	174,686	128,216	20,984	9,569	38,402	8,739	2,082	48,440	43,831	2,995	1,886	17,268	17,065	4,178	439	2,309	1,145	1,494

[1] Doctoral, extensive institutions are committed to graduate education through the doctorate, and award 50 or more doctor's degrees per year across at least 15 disciplines.

[2] Doctoral, intensive institutions are committed to education through the doctorate, and award at least 10 doctor's degrees per year across 3 or more disciplines or at least 20 doctor's degrees overall.

[3] Master's institutions offer a full range of baccalaureate programs and are committed to education through the master's degree. They award at least 20 master's degrees per year.

[4] Baccalaureate institutions primarily emphasize undergraduate education.

[5] Specialized 4-year institutions award degrees primarily in single fields of study, such as medicine, business, fine arts, theology, or engineering. Also, includes some institutions that have 4-year programs, but have not reported sufficient data to identify program category.

[6] Includes resident aliens.

NOTE: Degree-granting institutions grant associate's or higher degrees and participate in Title IV federal financial aid programs. Some institutions do not report separate enrollment data for each branch campus. For this reason, counts of institutions in this table are somewhat lower than the figures appearing in some other tables. Race categories exclude persons of Hispanic origin.

SOURCE: U.S. Department of Education, National Center for Education Statistics, 2005 Integrated Postsecondary Education Data System (IPEDS), Spring 2006. (This table was prepared August 2006.)

Table 215. Number and percentage of students enrolled in postsecondary institutions, by level, disability status, and selected student characteristics: 2003–04

Selected student characteristic	Undergraduate						Graduate and first-professional[1]					
	All students		Students with disabilities[2]		Nondisabled students		All students		Students with disabilities[2]		Nondisabled students	
1	2		3		4		5		6		7	
Number of students (in thousands)	19,054	(0.0)	2,156	(36.7)	16,897	(36.7)	2,826	(19.9)	189	(14.0)	2,637	(21.1)
Sex (percent)	100.0	(†)	100.0	(†)	100.0	(†)	100.0	(†)	100.0	(†)	100.0	(†)
Male	42.4	(0.39)	42.1	(0.84)	42.4	(0.39)	41.9	(1.23)	38.0	(3.50)	42.2	(1.29)
Female	57.6	(0.39)	57.9	(0.84)	57.6	(0.39)	58.1	(1.23)	62.0	(3.50)	57.8	(1.29)
Race/ethnicity of student (percent)	100.0	(†)	100.0	(†)	100.0	(†)	100.0	(†)	100.0	(†)	100.0	(†)
White	63.1	(0.76)	65.1	(0.99)	62.9	(0.76)	68.3	(1.05)	67.0	(3.39)	68.4	(1.09)
Black	14.0	(0.62)	13.2	(0.78)	14.1	(0.62)	9.6	(0.68)	12.5	(2.99)	9.3	(0.69)
Hispanic	12.7	(0.43)	12.3	(0.62)	12.8	(0.44)	7.7	(0.73)	7.9	(1.85)	7.6	(0.74)
Asian/Pacific Islander	5.9	(0.22)	3.8	(0.37)	6.2	(0.23)	11.0	(0.53)	5.9	(1.36)	11.3	(0.56)
American Indian/Alaska Native	0.9	(0.11)	1.2	(0.22)	0.9	(0.10)	0.6	(0.11)	0.4	(0.24)	0.6	(0.11)
Other	3.3	(0.11)	4.4	(0.31)	3.2	(0.11)	2.9	(0.30)	6.3	(1.59)	2.7	(0.31)
Age (percent)	100.0	(†)	100.0	(†)	100.0	(†)	100.0	(†)	100.0	(†)	100.0	(†)
15 to 23	56.8	(0.52)	45.8	(1.07)	58.2	(0.49)	11.2	(0.44)	8.5	(1.46)	11.4	(0.46)
24 to 29	17.3	(0.28)	15.5	(0.59)	17.5	(0.28)	39.6	(0.93)	33.9	(2.69)	40.0	(1.00)
30 or older	25.9	(0.42)	38.7	(1.06)	24.3	(0.39)	49.2	(1.03)	57.6	(2.72)	48.6	(1.08)
Attendance status (percent)	100.0	(†)	100.0	(†)	100.0	(†)	100.0	(†)	100.0	(†)	100.0	(†)
Full-time, full-year	38.6	(0.45)	33.5	(0.72)	39.2	(0.45)	32.7	(1.01)	28.9	(2.76)	32.9	(1.03)
Part-time or part-year	61.4	(0.45)	66.5	(0.72)	60.8	(0.45)	67.3	(1.01)	71.1	(2.76)	67.1	(1.03)
Student housing status (percent)	100.0	(†)	100.0	(†)	100.0	(†)	—	(†)	—	(†)	—	(†)
On-campus	13.8	(0.36)	10.7	(0.46)	14.2	(0.38)	—	(†)	—	(†)	—	(†)
Off-campus	55.2	(0.47)	61.5	(0.81)	54.4	(0.47)	—	(†)	—	(†)	—	(†)
With parents or relatives	31.0	(0.41)	27.7	(0.73)	31.4	(0.40)	—	(†)	—	(†)	—	(†)
Dependency status (percent)	100.0	(†)	100.0	(†)	100.0	(†)	100.0	(†)	100.0	(†)	100.0	(†)
Dependent	49.7	(0.56)	39.4	(0.95)	51.0	(0.55)	‡	(†)	‡	(†)	‡	(†)
Independent, unmarried	15.2	(0.25)	19.5	(0.72)	14.7	(0.25)	47.5	(1.01)	48.1	(3.03)	47.5	(1.03)
Independent, married	7.9	(0.18)	9.1	(0.50)	7.8	(0.17)	18.8	(0.81)	15.7	(2.45)	19.0	(0.82)
Independent with dependents	27.1	(0.42)	32.0	(0.78)	26.5	(0.42)	33.7	(1.11)	36.2	(3.64)	33.6	(1.11)
Veteran status (percent)	100.0	(†)	100.0	(†)	100.0	(†)	100.0	(†)	100.0	(†)	100.0	(†)
Veteran	3.4	(0.16)	6.2	(0.52)	3.0	(0.14)	3.8	(0.46)	2.7	(0.66)	3.9	(0.48)
Not veteran	96.6	(0.16)	93.8	(0.52)	97.0	(0.14)	96.2	(0.46)	97.3	(0.66)	96.1	(0.48)
Field of study (percent)	100.0	(†)	100.0	(†)	100.0	(†)	100.0	(†)	100.0	(†)	100.0	(†)
Business/management	15.6	(0.33)	14.6	(0.66)	15.7	(0.33)	16.1	(1.02)	12.7	(3.46)	16.4	(1.05)
Education	6.7	(0.23)	6.3	(0.42)	6.8	(0.23)	23.7	(1.53)	29.7	(3.09)	23.3	(1.64)
Engineering/computer science	4.7	(0.25)	3.8	(0.35)	4.8	(0.26)	8.1	(0.59)	4.3	(1.02)	8.4	(0.62)
Health	12.9	(0.37)	12.2	(0.59)	13.0	(0.37)	13.2	(0.87)	9.9	(1.76)	13.4	(0.90)
Humanities	10.3	(0.26)	10.8	(0.52)	10.3	(0.25)	7.3	(0.72)	6.3	(1.04)	7.4	(0.75)
Law	‡	(†)	‡	(†)	‡	(†)	5.5	(0.35)	5.6	(1.13)	5.5	(0.36)
Life/physical sciences	4.5	(0.12)	4.2	(0.29)	4.5	(0.12)	3.5	(0.23)	3.6	(0.92)	3.5	(0.23)
Social/behavioral sciences	7.0	(0.17)	7.3	(0.34)	7.0	(0.18)	5.5	(0.35)	7.8	(1.84)	5.3	(0.33)
Vocational/technical	2.4	(0.14)	2.9	(0.24)	2.3	(0.15)	‡	(†)	‡	(†)	‡	(†)
Undeclared	21.3	(0.51)	22.0	(0.79)	21.2	(0.52)	9.5	(1.02)	9.4	(1.71)	9.5	(1.06)
Other	14.6	(0.34)	15.9	(0.68)	14.4	(0.34)	7.6	(0.58)	10.6	(2.21)	7.4	(0.56)

—Not available.
†Not applicable.
‡Reporting standards not met.
[1]First-professional includes chiropractic medicine, medicine, dentistry, optometry, osteopathic medicine, pharmacy, podiatry, veterinary medicine, law, and theology.
[2]Disabled students are those who reported that they had one or more of the following conditions: a specific learning disability, a visual handicap, hard of hearing, deafness, a speech disability, an orthopedic handicap, or a health impairment.

NOTE: Data include Puerto Rico. Detail may not sum to totals because of survey item non-response and rounding. Race categories exclude persons of Hispanic origin. Standard errors appear in parentheses.
SOURCE: U.S. Department of Education, National Center for Education Statistics, 2003–04 National Postsecondary Student Aid Study (NPSAS:04). (This table was prepared August 2005.)

Table 216. Enrollment in postsecondary education, by student level, type of institution, age, and major field of study: 2003–04

Field of study	All students Total (in thousands)	All students Percentage distribution, by age Under 25	25 to 35	Over 35	Undergraduate Total (in thousands)	2-year institutions Percentage distribution, by age Under 25	25 to 35	Over 35	Total (in thousands)	4-year institutions Percentage distribution, by age Under 25	25 to 35	Over 35	Graduate and first-professional Total (in thousands)
1	2	3	4	5	6	7	8	9	10	11	12	13	14
Total	21,880 (19.9)	55.7 (0.47)	25.8 (0.36)	18.4 (0.32)	9,588 (23.7)	51.7 (0.70)	26.1 (0.49)	22.3 (0.49)	9,466 (23.7)	70.7 (0.76)	18.2 (0.44)	11.1 (0.44)	2,826 (19.9)
Agriculture and related sciences	95 (8.5)	72.0 (3.40)	19.2 (3.08)	8.8 (2.59)	36 (5.4)	62.0 (6.50)	23.2 (5.90)	14.8 (5.69)	52 (4.7)	82.7 (3.35)	13.4 (2.93)	3.9 (2.14)	8 (2.5)
Architecture and related services	126 (10.6)	68.0 (2.59)	24.8 (2.32)	7.2 (1.37)	46 (5.1)	57.2 (5.52)	28.7 (4.85)	14.0 (3.41)	68 (8.9)	80.4 (3.03)	16.8 (3.04)	2.8 (1.22)	12 (1.6)
Area, ethnic, and gender studies	44 (4.3)	63.2 (4.41)	21.2 (3.81)	15.6 (3.58)	‡ (†)	‡ (†)	‡ (†)	‡ (†)	30 (3.5)	80.7 (4.26)	12.3 (3.98)	7.0 (2.88)	8 (1.4)
Biological and biomedical sciences	500 (16.0)	77.6 (1.22)	18.2 (1.14)	4.2 (0.52)	94 (7.8)	70.8 (3.89)	21.1 (3.25)	8.1 (1.92)	350 (13.0)	87.4 (1.11)	10.4 (0.95)	2.1 (0.40)	56 (3.8)
Business, management, and marketing	3,431 (72.1)	51.1 (1.14)	28.3 (0.87)	20.5 (0.81)	1,170 (30.0)	51.7 (1.11)	25.7 (0.97)	22.7 (0.96)	1,805 (53.6)	60.7 (1.88)	23.2 (1.16)	16.1 (1.23)	456 (29.6)
Communication and journalism	433 (18.8)	82.3 (1.14)	12.8 (1.07)	4.9 (0.89)	72 (7.0)	81.1 (3.43)	13.2 (2.70)	5.6 (1.73)	334 (15.8)	86.9 (1.33)	10.3 (1.16)	2.8 (0.88)	27 (5.9)
Communications technologies/technicians	112 (9.9)	65.4 (3.54)	19.5 (2.76)	15.1 (2.88)	45 (5.9)	64.3 (6.32)	16.0 (3.85)	19.7 (5.14)	63 (7.6)	69.8 (4.82)	19.2 (3.86)	10.9 (3.37)	‡ (†)
Computer and information sciences	998 (36.7)	49.3 (1.33)	29.2 (1.15)	21.5 (1.18)	436 (21.6)	45.6 (2.00)	28.7 (1.95)	25.7 (1.68)	494 (23.6)	56 (2.15)	27 (1.50)	17 (1.59)	69 (9.2)
Construction trades	95 (12.9)	46.4 (5.16)	29.9 (3.67)	23.7 (3.82)	75 (12.4)	38.4 (5.63)	34.5 (4.17)	27.0 (4.78)	20 (2.7)	77.7 (5.53)	12.0 (5.22)	10.3 (4.73)	‡ (†)
Criminal justice	452 (21.0)	59.5 (1.96)	28.5 (1.73)	12.0 (1.18)	210 (14.2)	56.4 (2.96)	31.0 (2.50)	12.5 (1.72)	231 (16.9)	64.1 (2.73)	24.0 (2.06)	11.9 (1.88)	11 (3.1)
Economics	89 (7.0)	82.2 (2.53)	15.9 (2.26)	1.9 (0.80)	8 (2.0)	90.4 (6.26)	7.7 (6.28)	1.9 (0.98)	70 (6.7)	90.3 (2.29)	8.2 (1.93)	1.5 (0.94)	11 (1.4)
Education	1,951 (65.3)	48.0 (1.45)	30.2 (2.00)	21.8 (1.24)	491 (19.1)	55.9 (2.61)	22.6 (1.91)	21.5 (1.87)	790 (37.5)	73.5 (1.53)	16.3 (1.27)	10.2 (0.89)	670 (42.9)
Engineering	683 (51.6)	68.7 (1.87)	22.2 (1.18)	9.1 (1.56)	140 (9.6)	64.4 (3.62)	21.0 (2.46)	14.7 (2.41)	416 (42.3)	82.9 (1.80)	13.3 (1.68)	3.8 (0.62)	127 (13.8)
Engineering technologies/technicians	252 (15.1)	51.8 (2.80)	26.7 (2.45)	21.4 (2.45)	131 (10.5)	43.9 (3.81)	29.8 (3.76)	26.2 (3.64)	109 (9.6)	64.3 (3.77)	21.9 (3.28)	13.8 (2.42)	12 (2.8)
English language and literature/letters	273 (12.4)	72.4 (1.65)	19.3 (1.44)	8.4 (0.99)	48 (5.6)	74.7 (3.84)	17.8 (2.94)	7.4 (2.86)	192 (9.4)	79.9 (1.70)	13.1 (1.48)	7.0 (1.14)	33 (4.0)
Family and consumer/human sciences	104 (8.4)	54.7 (3.41)	22.8 (3.11)	22.5 (2.82)	44 (6.1)	37.2 (5.07)	32.5 (4.51)	30.3 (4.71)	52 (5.6)	73.8 (4.07)	12.8 (2.86)	13.4 (4.42)	‡ (†)
Foreign languages and literatures	104 (7.0)	55.0 (2.93)	24.3 (2.42)	20.7 (2.71)	28 (4.6)	38.7 (5.75)	22.8 (4.36)	38.5 (6.46)	59 (4.3)	73.6 (3.36)	16.9 (3.06)	9.5 (2.51)	16 (2.4)
Geography	37 (6.0)	59.4 (7.32)	21.8 (4.30)	18.8 (8.13)	‡ (†)	‡ (†)	‡ (†)	‡ (†)	25 (4.3)	72.9 (6.19)	16.0 (5.06)	11.1 (3.86)	5 (1.0)
Health professions and related sciences	2,672 (72.4)	45.6 (0.78)	32.9 (0.70)	21.5 (0.77)	1,646 (48.9)	41.8 (1.01)	34.1 (0.92)	24.1 (0.82)	692 (36.8)	60.8 (1.77)	23.2 (1.32)	16.0 (1.17)	334 (24.9)
History	220 (11.2)	70.8 (2.29)	18.9 (2.01)	10.3 (1.77)	36 (4.5)	60.2 (7.09)	18.7 (5.12)	21.1 (7.11)	159 (9.6)	81.6 (1.82)	13.2 (1.63)	5.2 (1.40)	26 (3.9)
International relations and affairs	41 (4.1)	76.3 (4.19)	17.1 (3.78)	6.6 (2.81)	‡ (†)	‡ (†)	‡ (†)	‡ (†)	29 (3.0)	88.6 (2.52)	10.6 (2.64)	0.8 (0.73)	‡ (†)
Legal professions and studies	273 (13.9)	39.7 (2.13)	43.2 (1.93)	17.1 (2.12)	78 (9.9)	41.3 (3.67)	32.4 (3.62)	26.3 (4.31)	41 (5.3)	53.9 (5.25)	27.0 (4.56)	19.1 (4.57)	153 (9.9)
Liberal arts, sciences and humanities	900 (40.5)	62.0 (1.71)	21.0 (1.16)	17.0 (1.36)	616 (38.1)	61.3 (2.36)	21.1 (1.66)	17.6 (1.74)	260 (15.8)	67.5 (1.62)	18.8 (1.26)	13.8 (1.35)	24 (3.6)
Library science	22 (5.5)	13.3 (4.65)	50.4 (8.62)	36.4 (8.32)	‡ (†)	‡ (†)	‡ (†)	‡ (†)	‡ (†)	‡ (†)	‡ (†)	‡ (†)	17 (4.7)
Mathematics and statistics	114 (7.1)	65.3 (3.28)	25.2 (2.49)	9.6 (1.79)	28 (4.1)	57.7 (7.71)	33.0 (6.20)	9.4 (4.13)	63 (5.0)	81.1 (3.39)	12.3 (2.57)	6.7 (2.10)	23 (2.8)
Mechanic and repair technologies	195 (14.8)	51.2 (2.56)	29.5 (1.89)	19.3 (1.97)	173 (14.0)	49.9 (2.71)	28.9 (1.86)	21.1 (2.19)	22 (4.4)	61.1 (7.36)	33.9 (6.80)	5.1 (3.51)	‡ (†)
Military technologies	‡ (†)	‡ (†)	‡ (†)	‡ (†)	‡ (†)	‡ (†)	‡ (†)	‡ (†)	‡ (†)	‡ (†)	‡ (†)	‡ (†)	‡ (†)
Multi/interdisciplinary studies	71 (7.0)	55.7 (4.17)	30.3 (3.26)	14.1 (2.51)	26 (3.0)	50.8 (6.76)	33.8 (6.25)	15.4 (3.13)	38 (6.2)	67.6 (6.16)	22.8 (4.74)	9.7 (3.79)	24 (3.6)
Natural resources and conservation	58 (6.8)	69.4 (5.72)	24.1 (5.61)	6.5 (2.20)	12 (2.2)	73.5 (7.90)	13.6 (5.97)	12.9 (6.91)	35 (5.7)	87.7 (4.13)	12.1 (4.05)	0.2 (0.23)	11 (2.6)
Natural sciences, other	59 (6.3)	66.5 (4.74)	26.3 (4.86)	7.2 (2.01)	12 (2.3)	72.0 (8.58)	16.1 (6.59)	11.9 (6.15)	34 (5.0)	76.8 (5.59)	20.3 (5.48)	2.9 (1.44)	13 (3.3)
Parks, recreation, and fitness studies	109 (8.4)	79.7 (2.56)	17.2 (2.24)	3.1 (1.23)	23 (4.0)	78.6 (5.92)	14.2 (4.45)	7.2 (4.33)	80 (7.2)	82.5 (3.18)	15.7 (2.89)	1.9 (1.25)	‡ (†)
Personal and culinary services	283 (39.4)	60.2 (2.83)	26.0 (1.62)	13.8 (1.97)	224 (29.7)	58.2 (2.32)	26.7 (1.49)	15.1 (1.73)	59 (30.4)	68.3 (8.13)	22.9 (5.22)	8.8 (5.46)	‡ (†)
Philosophy and religious studies	75 (6.7)	62.7 (3.76)	21.3 (2.42)	16.0 (3.18)	7 (1.7)	44.9 (12.50)	17.5 (9.13)	37.6 (13.01)	53 (5.6)	78.1 (3.39)	15.5 (2.78)	6.3 (1.87)	15 (3.0)
Physical sciences	153 (8.1)	66.0 (2.64)	27.2 (2.40)	6.8 (1.19)	24 (4.1)	75.8 (6.10)	15.9 (5.97)	8.3 (4.48)	95 (5.7)	78.9 (3.43)	15.8 (2.94)	5.3 (1.67)	34 (2.7)
Political science and government	209 (9.3)	80.3 (1.87)	14.7 (1.58)	5.1 (1.09)	27 (3.9)	66.4 (6.79)	25.6 (5.67)	8.0 (4.26)	167 (8.2)	87.6 (1.67)	9.7 (1.44)	2.7 (0.83)	15 (2.3)

See notes at end of table.

Table 216. Enrollment in postsecondary education, by student level, type of institution, age, and major field of study: 2003–04—Continued

Field of study	All students				Undergraduate								Graduate and first-professional
	Total (in thousands)	Percentage distribution, by age			2-year institutions[1]				4-year institutions				Total (in thousands)
		Under 25	25 to 35	Over 35	Total (in thousands)	Under 25	25 to 35	Over 35	Total (in thousands)	Under 25	25 to 35	Over 35	
1	2	3	4	5	6	7	8	9	10	11	12	13	14
Precision production	10 (2.1)	47.1 (10.35)	15.9 (5.84)	37.0 (11.06)	8 (2.0)	45.6 (11.79)	14.1 (6.18)	40.3 (12.10)	‡ (†)	‡ (†)	‡ (†)	‡ (†)	‡ (†)
Psychology	617 (20.8)	67.7 (1.57)	22.2 (1.14)	10.2 (0.98)	147 (11.4)	65.3 (3.61)	22.4 (2.92)	12.3 (2.46)	400 (15.2)	76.4 (1.49)	16.3 (1.21)	7.3 (0.80)	69 (7.0)
Public administration and social services	278 (27.0)	34.6 (3.09)	34.1 (2.77)	31.3 (3.04)	62 (7.6)	42.0 (4.76)	26.6 (4.41)	31.4 (4.61)	126 (19.5)	44.6 (6.29)	25.3 (3.69)	30.1 (4.59)	90 (10.7)
Residency programs	153 (9.0)	60.7 (2.63)	32.3 (2.45)	7.1 (1.20)	73 (7.2)	61.7 (4.25)	28.2 (3.56)	10.2 (2.11)	42 (4.1)	76.6 (4.99)	18.8 (3.82)	4.6 (2.46)	39 (3.1)
Science technologies/technicians	38 (5.9)	47.1 (5.77)	32.2 (5.21)	20.7 (4.29)	14 (2.8)	33.7 (9.00)	41.6 (9.19)	24.7 (8.35)	22 (5.0)	58.2 (8.99)	22.3 (7.96)	19.5 (5.89)	‡ (†)
Security and criminal justice	78 (7.9)	62.3 (5.22)	24.2 (3.60)	13.5 (3.25)	55 (7.6)	63.4 (6.25)	28.4 (4.96)	8.2 (2.62)	19 (3.3)	62.1 (9.36)	9.4 (3.27)	28.5 (9.27)	‡ (†)
Social sciences, other	116 (8.2)	55.3 (3.70)	26.0 (3.03)	18.7 (2.58)	32 (4.8)	57.4 (5.99)	23.8 (5.50)	18.9 (4.12)	66 (5.7)	64.8 (4.67)	20.7 (3.68)	14.5 (3.45)	18 (2.6)
Sociology	198 (12.0)	62.5 (2.96)	25.1 (2.43)	12.4 (2.31)	48 (6.9)	46.8 (6.33)	29.5 (6.14)	23.8 (7.41)	139 (8.8)	72.2 (3.12)	20.5 (2.62)	7.3 (1.68)	11 (1.6)
Theology and religious vocations	118 (20.2)	31.8 (4.58)	29.0 (4.99)	39.2 (4.02)	‡ (†)	‡ (†)	‡ (†)	‡ (†)	46 (10.7)	57.8 (4.51)	16.4 (3.81)	25.8 (5.18)	65 (14.9)
Transportation and materials moving	49 (7.3)	64.3 (7.30)	19.0 (3.95)	16.7 (5.23)	26 (4.2)	48.7 (7.74)	28.2 (6.05)	23.1 (4.62)	22 (5.6)	85.2 (13.25)	5.3 (3.46)	9.5 (10.49)	‡ (†)
Visual and performing arts	664 (27.0)	73.9 (1.27)	17.2 (1.27)	8.9 (0.80)	197 (11.6)	69.2 (2.90)	18.7 (2.39)	12.0 (2.02)	422 (23.6)	81.4 (1.81)	13.3 (1.64)	5.3 (0.71)	45 (6.3)
Undeclared or not in a degree program	4,328 (103.0)	53.7 (0.81)	22.2 (0.51)	24.1 (0.76)	2,890 (87.5)	50.3 (1.04)	23.5 (0.69)	26.1 (1.02)	1,169 (35.1)	71.8 (1.07)	15.6 (0.86)	12.5 (0.73)	268 (29.2)

†Not applicable.
‡Reporting standards not met.
[1]Includes less-than-2-year schools and schools not identified by level.

NOTE: Because of different survey editing and processing procedures, enrollment data in this table may differ from those appearing in other tables. Includes students who enrolled at any time during the 2003–04 academic year. Data include Puerto Rico. Detail may not sum to totals because of rounding. Standard errors appear in parentheses.
SOURCE: U.S. Department of Education, National Center for Education Statistics, 2003–04 National Postsecondary Student Aid Study (NPSAS:04), unpublished tabulations. (This table was prepared September 2005.)

Table 217. Graduate enrollment in science and engineering programs in degree-granting institutions, by field of study: Fall 1991 through fall 2003

Field of engineering or science	1991	1992	1993	1994	1995	1996	1997	1998	1999	2000	2001	2002	2003	Percent change, 1991 to 2003
1	2	3	4	5	6	7	8	9	10	11	12	13	14	15
Total, all sciences and engineering	**471,262**	**493,624**	**504,409**	**504,399**	**499,640**	**494,079**	**487,208**	**485,627**	**493,256**	**493,311**	**509,620**	**540,513**	**566,835**	**20.3**
Engineering	113,576	118,003	116,872	113,024	107,201	103,224	101,148	100,038	101,691	104,112	109,493	119,668	127,375	12.1
Aerospace	4,120	4,036	3,940	3,715	3,343	3,208	3,083	3,137	3,349	3,407	3,451	3,685	4,048	-1.7
Agricultural	983	1,008	1,018	1,061	1,037	1,012	941	925	934	899	907	912	1,012	3.0
Biomedical	2,239	2,537	2,675	2,750	2,732	2,732	2,847	2,905	3,121	3,241	3,639	4,378	5,347	138.8
Chemical	7,127	7,397	7,554	7,639	7,452	7,408	7,288	7,093	6,883	7,056	6,913	7,414	7,516	5.5
Civil	17,398	19,572	19,583	19,925	19,218	18,528	17,193	16,517	16,226	16,451	16,665	17,713	18,838	8.3
Electrical	35,182	36,428	35,290	33,020	30,861	29,941	30,787	31,384	31,822	33,611	36,100	39,948	41,745	18.7
Engineering science	2,154	2,218	2,180	2,089	1,955	1,751	1,647	1,701	1,627	1,632	1,798	2,121	2,240	4.0
Industrial/manufacturing	12,676	13,525	13,905	13,992	13,475	12,675	11,957	11,221	11,803	12,119	12,940	14,033	14,295	12.8
Mechanical	17,730	18,637	18,477	17,761	16,363	15,509	15,045	14,696	14,956	15,235	15,852	17,139	18,440	4.0
Metallurgical/materials	5,160	5,512	5,410	5,228	4,956	4,747	4,688	4,680	4,481	4,377	4,721	4,992	5,154	-0.1
Mining	489	437	427	424	373	371	348	304	328	287	240	267	278	-43.1
Nuclear	1,282	1,286	1,306	1,246	1,154	980	868	821	830	792	801	795	885	-31.0
Petroleum	705	737	725	624	610	562	561	571	642	627	656	766	849	20.4
Other engineering	6,331	4,673	4,382	3,550	3,672	3,800	3,895	4,083	4,689	4,378	4,810	5,505	6,728	6.3
All sciences	357,686	375,621	387,537	391,375	392,439	390,855	386,060	385,589	391,565	389,199	400,127	420,845	439,460	22.9
Physical sciences	34,710	35,348	35,328	34,466	33,399	32,333	31,105	30,575	30,691	30,385	31,038	32,341	34,298	-1.2
Astronomy	829	869	880	973	912	874	778	820	832	888	916	990	1,080	30.3
Chemistry	19,407	19,929	20,131	19,803	19,570	19,334	18,774	18,482	18,416	18,105	18,366	19,045	20,049	3.3
Physics	14,081	14,122	13,841	13,162	12,425	11,728	11,147	10,809	10,869	10,841	11,248	11,701	12,555	-10.8
Other physical sciences	393	428	476	528	492	397	406	464	574	551	508	605	614	56.2
Earth, atmospheric, and ocean sciences	14,480	15,333	15,721	15,957	15,716	15,183	14,548	14,258	14,083	13,941	13,841	14,240	14,655	1.2
Atmospheric sciences	968	1,089	1,112	1,109	1,072	1,086	1,092	965	913	963	924	1,036	1,150	18.8
Geosciences	7,567	7,744	7,759	7,713	7,582	7,304	6,959	6,687	6,637	6,596	6,544	6,712	6,889	-9.0
Oceanography	2,386	2,530	2,627	2,870	2,723	2,615	2,479	2,562	2,624	2,668	2,585	2,618	2,695	13.0
Other environmental sciences	3,559	3,970	4,223	4,265	4,339	4,178	4,018	4,044	3,909	3,714	3,788	3,874	3,921	10.2
Mathematical sciences	19,952	20,355	20,000	19,573	18,504	18,008	16,719	16,485	16,257	15,650	16,651	18,163	19,465	-2.4
Mathematics and applied mathematics	17,206	17,404	16,945	16,457	15,386	14,948	14,027	13,827	13,521	12,823	13,569	14,702	15,569	-9.5
Statistics	2,746	2,951	3,055	3,116	3,118	3,060	2,692	2,658	2,736	2,827	3,082	3,461	3,896	41.9
Computer sciences	34,610	36,325	36,213	34,158	33,458	34,626	35,991	38,027	42,478	47,350	52,196	55,269	53,678	55.1
Life sciences	121,849	129,010	136,948	143,560	148,286	148,948	148,486	149,634	151,345	148,080	150,252	159,452	170,513	39.9
Agricultural sciences	11,506	11,841	11,950	12,242	12,768	12,301	12,203	12,168	12,312	12,023	12,235	12,698	13,197	14.7
Biological sciences	51,778	54,180	56,292	58,033	58,344	57,749	56,705	56,695	56,959	56,282	57,639	61,133	64,684	24.9
Anatomy	1,051	991	961	1,018	850	878	856	785	749	795	735	951	908	-13.6
Biochemistry	5,201	5,376	5,489	5,615	5,562	5,275	5,102	5,148	5,101	4,966	4,917	5,190	5,552	6.7
Biology	13,292	13,874	14,330	14,208	14,280	14,611	14,646	14,277	13,989	13,407	13,352	13,822	14,720	10.7
Biometry/epidemiology	2,032	2,365	2,658	2,710	2,810	3,005	2,896	3,514	3,704	3,615	3,817	4,071	4,439	118.5
Biophysics	697	751	780	794	845	833	748	737	710	751	877	953	1,032	48.1
Botany	2,694	2,689	2,714	2,748	2,295	2,213	2,082	2,042	1,974	1,904	1,921	1,973	1,901	-29.4
Cell biology	2,809	3,132	3,440	3,829	4,174	4,207	4,300	4,379	4,637	4,820	4,911	5,375	5,722	103.7
Ecology	1,180	1,301	1,410	1,566	1,702	1,632	1,640	1,670	1,704	1,762	1,888	1,967	2,230	89.0
Entomology/parasitology	1,171	1,193	1,247	1,263	1,241	1,234	1,161	1,168	1,145	1,104	1,170	1,191	1,206	3.0
Genetics	1,520	1,639	1,785	1,699	1,712	1,741	1,776	1,727	1,783	1,712	1,841	1,909	2,073	36.4
Microbiology, immunology, and virology	4,928	4,972	5,021	5,094	5,026	4,912	4,805	4,773	4,815	4,814	4,798	5,208	5,256	6.7
Nutrition	4,164	4,159	4,388	4,791	5,071	4,918	4,604	4,486	4,508	4,413	4,429	4,539	4,695	12.8
Pathology	1,449	1,456	1,575	1,707	1,670	1,656	1,674	1,580	1,580	1,531	1,637	1,613	1,541	6.3
Pharmacology	2,432	2,532	2,651	2,839	2,710	2,663	2,597	2,730	2,757	2,963	3,140	3,234	3,357	38.0
Physiology	2,332	2,317	2,372	2,378	2,540	2,377	2,298	2,151	2,083	2,015	1,967	2,076	2,328	-0.2
Zoology	2,191	2,139	2,042	2,028	1,958	1,808	1,627	1,586	1,523	1,445	1,411	1,349	1,301	-40.6
Other biosciences	2,635	3,294	3,429	3,746	3,898	3,786	3,893	3,942	4,197	4,265	4,828	5,712	6,423	143.8
Health fields	58,565	62,989	68,706	73,285	77,174	78,898	79,578	80,771	82,074	79,775	80,378	85,621	92,632	58.2
Medical fields	11,707	12,594	14,233	15,065	15,538	15,363	15,470	16,643	17,276	16,407	17,363	19,246	20,773	77.4
Other health fields	46,858	50,395	54,473	58,220	61,636	63,535	64,108	64,128	64,798	63,368	63,015	66,375	71,859	53.4
Dentistry	1,016	1,121	1,228	1,298	1,338	1,388	1,491	1,518	1,467	1,430	1,494	1,446	1,654	62.8
Nursing	22,012	23,213	24,781	26,997	28,405	27,388	26,861	25,591	25,074	23,457	23,609	24,715	26,648	21.1
Pharmaceutical sciences	2,968	2,792	2,859	2,887	2,808	2,846	2,710	2,882	3,422	3,611	3,679	4,538	5,448	83.6
Speech pathology/audiology	8,945	9,791	10,740	11,356	11,982	12,857	13,212	13,198	13,600	13,636	13,193	13,368	13,694	53.1
Veterinary sciences	894	942	924	922	975	997	1,224	1,288	1,314	1,367	1,476	1,691	2,069	131.4
Other health related	11,023	12,536	13,941	14,760	16,128	18,059	18,610	19,651	19,921	19,867	19,564	20,617	22,346	102.7

See notes at end of table.

Table 217. Graduate enrollment in science and engineering programs in degree-granting institutions, by field of study: Fall 1991 through fall 2003—Continued

Field of engineering or science	1991	1992	1993	1994	1995	1996	1997	1998	1999	2000	2001	2002	2003	Percent change, 1991 to 2003
1	2	3	4	5	6	7	8	9	10	11	12	13	14	15
Psychology..	51,343	53,484	54,557	54,554	53,641	53,122	53,126	52,557	51,727	50,466	50,467	51,165	52,025	1.3
Psychology, general	19,555	18,802	18,962	18,356	12,519	12,787	13,098	12,733	12,798	12,488	12,488	12,609	13,203	-32.5
Clinical psychology.......................	10,834	12,090	12,526	12,684	17,647	16,833	17,249	17,098	16,238	15,624	15,837	15,159	15,562	43.6
Other psychology	20,954	22,592	23,069	23,514	23,475	23,502	22,779	22,726	22,691	22,354	22,142	23,397	23,260	11.0
Social sciences..................................	80,742	85,766	88,770	89,107	89,435	88,635	86,085	84,053	84,984	83,327	85,682	90,215	94,826	17.4
Agricultural economics..................	2,364	2,522	2,415	2,289	2,338	2,117	2,043	1,995	2,014	2,079	2,161	2,187	2,296	-2.9
Anthropology.................................	6,731	7,123	7,361	7,665	7,693	7,773	7,560	7,577	7,633	7,626	7,491	7,481	7,806	16.0
Economics (except agricultural)....	12,707	13,252	13,214	12,913	12,673	12,080	11,097	10,701	10,562	10,748	11,408	12,009	12,307	-3.1
Geography.....................................	3,760	4,102	4,378	4,502	4,371	4,331	4,287	4,326	4,250	4,036	4,304	4,383	4,654	23.8
History and philosophy of science.	337	360	369	387	401	409	443	508	557	532	571	663	677	100.9
Linguistics	3,425	3,277	3,321	3,279	3,194	3,156	3,068	2,935	2,799	2,674	2,744	2,875	3,028	-11.6
Political science............................	31,707	33,797	35,076	34,317	34,298	33,252	32,083	30,828	31,372	31,131	31,805	34,934	36,855	16.2
Sociology......................................	8,393	9,011	9,425	9,498	9,564	9,425	9,413	9,058	8,966	8,652	8,812	8,946	9,127	8.7
Sociology/anthropology................	899	979	935	987	941	923	948	857	741	745	808	719	773	-14.0
Other social sciences...................	10,419	11,343	12,276	13,270	13,962	15,169	15,143	15,268	16,090	15,104	15,578	16,018	17,303	66.1

NOTE: The survey on which this table is based includes institutions in other jurisdictions. Some data have been revised from previously published figures. Detail may not sum to totals because of rounding.

SOURCE: National Science Foundation, Division of Science Resources Studies, Survey of Graduate Students and Postdoctorates in Science and Engineering, 1991 through 2003. (This table was prepared April 2006.)

Table 218. Number of institutions and enrollment in degree-granting institutions, by size, type, and control of institution: Fall 2005

Type and control of institution	Total	Under 200	200 to 499	500 to 999	1,000 to 2,499	2,500 to 4,999	5,000 to 9,999	10,000 to 19,999	20,000 to 29,999	30,000 or more
1	2	3	4	5	6	7	8	9	10	11
Number of institutions										
Total	4,253	483	616	605	916	657	484	311	126	55
Doctoral, extensive[1]	150	0	0	0	2	1	12	48	52	35
Doctoral, intensive[2]	107	0	1	1	4	15	31	38	15	2
Master's[3]	635	1	6	24	140	187	171	84	16	6
Baccalaureate[4]	629	18	42	138	307	99	18	5	2	0
Specialized institutions[5]	1,058	280	287	209	183	71	17	7	2	2
2-year	1,674	184	280	233	280	284	235	129	39	10
Public	1,675	14	52	91	328	382	384	263	113	48
Doctoral, extensive[1]	102	0	0	0	0	1	0	23	47	31
Doctoral, intensive[2]	63	0	0	0	2	2	14	32	11	2
Master's[3]	273	0	0	2	19	49	114	73	13	3
Baccalaureate[4]	104	0	1	13	40	30	14	4	2	0
Specialized institutions[5]	97	3	10	10	37	25	7	2	1	2
Art, music, or design	2	0	0	1	1	0	0	0	0	0
Engineering or technology	8	0	1	0	3	4	0	0	0	0
Medical or other health	30	2	5	2	15	5	1	0	0	0
Other specialized	57	1	4	7	18	16	6	2	1	2
2-year	1,036	11	41	66	230	275	235	129	39	10
Private	2,578	469	564	514	588	275	100	48	13	7
Doctoral, extensive[1]	48	0	0	0	2	0	12	25	5	4
Doctoral, intensive[2]	44	0	1	1	2	13	17	6	4	0
Master's[3]	362	1	6	22	121	138	57	11	3	3
Baccalaureate[4]	525	18	41	125	267	69	4	1	0	0
Specialized institutions[5]	961	277	277	199	146	46	10	5	1	0
Art, music, or design	88	14	25	12	26	9	2	0	0	0
Business and management	123	26	35	27	21	9	4	1	0	0
Engineering or technology	66	9	8	28	13	5	1	2	0	0
Medical or other health	134	39	43	26	22	4	0	0	0	0
Theological	295	156	89	35	12	3	0	0	0	0
Other specialized	255	33	77	71	52	16	3	2	1	0
2-year	638	173	239	167	50	9	0	0	0	0
Enrollment of institutions										
Total	17,487,475	54,855	210,061	435,812	1,521,898	2,347,306	3,397,028	4,292,326	3,057,138	2,171,051
Doctoral, extensive[1]	3,425,926	0	0	0	4,212	4,554	83,966	699,528	1,284,277	1,349,389
Doctoral, intensive[2]	1,273,432	0	302	898	8,388	56,415	233,165	533,251	364,355	76,658
Master's[3]	3,996,517	61	2,183	18,994	261,932	670,811	1,207,060	1,132,207	399,587	303,682
Baccalaureate[4]	1,153,615	2,219	15,374	106,772	497,210	323,834	106,898	56,118	45,190	0
Specialized institutions[5]	1,149,930	30,696	97,866	148,239	279,598	242,338	119,063	98,986	44,424	88,720
2-year	6,488,055	21,879	94,336	160,909	470,558	1,049,354	1,646,876	1,772,236	919,305	352,602
Public	13,021,834	1,969	18,643	70,296	580,302	1,411,669	2,713,601	3,641,208	2,751,811	1,832,335
Doctoral, extensive[1]	2,735,547	0	0	0	0	4,554	0	352,598	1,166,870	1,211,525
Doctoral, intensive[2]	915,694	0	0	0	4,045	7,309	102,788	452,533	272,361	76,658
Master's[3]	2,471,344	0	0	1,608	38,094	186,125	829,997	988,987	323,703	102,830
Baccalaureate[4]	356,342	0	490	10,957	66,778	104,126	84,475	44,326	45,190	0
Specialized institutions[5]	358,678	239	3,864	7,895	65,159	88,426	49,465	30,528	24,382	88,720
Art, music, or design	2,956	0	0	829	2,127	0	0	0	0	0
Engineering or technology	22,200	0	382	0	5,482	16,336	0	0	0	0
Medical or other health	52,219	126	2,042	1,482	27,408	15,587	5,574	0	0	0
Other specialized	281,303	113	1,440	5,584	30,142	56,503	43,891	30,528	24,382	88,720
2-year	6,184,229	1,730	14,289	49,836	406,226	1,021,129	1,646,876	1,772,236	919,305	352,602
Private	4,465,641	52,886	191,418	365,516	941,596	935,637	683,427	651,118	305,327	338,716
Doctoral, extensive[1]	690,379	0	0	0	4,212	0	83,966	346,930	117,407	137,864
Doctoral, intensive[2]	357,738	0	302	898	4,343	49,106	130,377	80,718	91,994	0
Master's[3]	1,525,173	61	2,183	17,386	223,838	484,686	377,063	143,220	75,884	200,852
Baccalaureate[4]	797,273	2,219	14,884	95,815	430,432	219,708	22,423	11,792	0	0
Specialized institutions[5]	791,252	30,457	94,002	140,344	214,439	153,912	69,598	68,458	20,042	0
Art, music, or design	103,180	1,801	8,772	8,520	39,046	29,163	15,878	0	0	0
Business and management	137,560	3,314	12,457	18,163	31,605	31,148	28,050	12,823	0	0
Engineering or technology	95,649	681	2,871	19,358	18,440	18,884	6,734	28,681	0	0
Medical or other health	81,687	4,272	14,396	18,989	32,738	11,292	0	0	0	0
Theological	94,407	16,422	26,674	24,748	16,242	10,321	0	0	0	0
Other specialized	278,769	3,967	28,832	50,566	76,368	53,104	18,936	26,954	20,042	0
2-year	303,826	20,149	80,047	111,073	64,332	28,225	0	0	0	0

[1]Doctoral, extensive institutions are committed to graduate education through the doctorate, and award 50 or more doctor's degrees per year across at least 15 disciplines.
[2]Doctoral, intensive institutions are committed to education through the doctorate, and award at least 10 doctor's degrees per year across 3 or more disciplines or at least 20 doctor's degrees overall.
[3]Master's institutions offer a full range of baccalaureate programs and are committed to education through the master's degree. They award at least 20 master's degrees per year.

[4]Baccalaureate institutions primarily emphasize undergraduate education.
[5]Specialized 4-year institutions award degrees primarily in single fields of study, such as medicine, business, fine arts, theology, or engineering. Also, includes some institutions that have 4-year programs, but have not reported sufficient data to identify program category.
SOURCE: U.S. Department of Education, National Center for Education Statistics, 2005 Integrated Postsecondary Education Data System (IPEDS), Spring 2006. (This table was prepared August 2006.)

Table 219. Enrollment of the 120 largest degree-granting college and university campuses, by selected characteristics and institution: Fall 2005

Institution	State	Rank[1]	Control[2]	Type[3]	Total enrollment, fall 2005	Institution	State	Rank[1]	Control[2]	Type[3]	Total enrollment, fall 2005
1	2	3	4	5	6	1	2	3	4	5	6
University of Phoenix, Online Campus	AZ	1	3	1	117,309	Riverside Community College	CA	61	1	2	29,160
Miami-Dade College	FL	2	1	1	54,169	San Francisco State University	CA	62	1	1	28,950
Arizona State University at the Tempe Campus	AZ	3	1	1	51,612	Santa Monica College	CA	63	1	2	28,908
University of Minnesota, Twin Cities	MN	4	1	1	51,175	University of California, Davis	CA	64	1	1	28,815
Western International University	AZ	5	3	1	50,663	University of Tennessee	TN	65	1	1	28,512
Ohio State University, Main Campus	OH	6	1	1	50,504	University of Iowa	IA	66	1	1	28,426
University of Texas at Austin	TX	7	1	1	49,696	University of Nevada, Las Vegas	NV	67	1	1	28,134
University of Florida	FL	8	1	1	49,693	Texas Tech University	TX	68	1	1	28,001
Michigan State University	MI	9	1	1	45,166	Virginia Polytechnic Institute and State U.	VA	69	1	1	27,979
Texas A & M University	TX	10	1	1	44,910	California State University, Sacramento	CA	70	1	1	27,932
University of Central Florida	FL	11	1	1	44,856	University of Cincinnati, Main Campus	OH	71	1	1	27,932
City College of San Francisco	CA	12	1	2	43,255	University of Missouri, Columbia	MO	72	1	1	27,930
University of South Florida	FL	13	1	1	42,660	Colorado State University	CO	73	1	1	27,780
University of Illinois at Urbana, Champaign	IL	14	1	1	41,938	University of Wisconsin, Milwaukee	WI	74	1	1	27,502
University of Wisconsin, Madison	WI	15	1	1	40,793	University of Maryland, University College	MD	75	1	1	27,429
Pennsylvania State University, Main Campus	PA	16	1	1	40,709	University of Texas at San Antonio	TX	76	1	1	27,337
Purdue University, Main Campus	IN	17	1	1	40,151	Strayer University, Washington Campus	DC	77	3	1	27,309
New York University	NY	18	2	1	40,004	University of North Carolina at Chapel Hill	NC	78	1	1	27,276
University of Michigan, Ann Arbor	MI	19	1	1	39,993	Central Michigan University	MI	79	1	1	27,221
North Harris Montgomery Community Col. District	TX	20	1	2	39,949	SUNY at Buffalo	NY	80	1	1	27,220
Houston Community College System	TX	21	1	2	39,516	Pasadena City College	CA	81	1	2	27,199
University of Washington, Seattle Campus	WA	22	1	1	39,251	Mount San Antonio College	CA	82	1	2	27,195
Florida State University	FL	23	1	1	39,146	Texas State University, San Marcos	TX	83	1	1	27,129
Indiana University, Bloomington	IN	24	1	1	37,958	College of DuPage	IL	84	1	2	27,117
Northern Virginia Community College	VA	25	1	2	37,740	University of South Carolina at Columbia	SC	85	1	1	27,065
University of Arizona	AZ	26	1	1	37,036	University of Kansas, Main Campus	KS	86	1	1	26,934
Florida International University	FL	27	1	1	36,904	Troy State University	AL	87	1	1	26,880
University of California, Los Angeles	CA	28	1	1	35,625	El Paso Community College	TX	88	1	2	26,667
University of Maryland, College Park	MD	29	1	1	35,369	University of Pittsburgh, Main Campus	PA	89	1	1	26,559
University of Houston	TX	30	1	1	35,344	Mesa Community College	AZ	90	1	2	26,528
California State University, Fullerton	CA	31	1	1	35,040	University of Oklahoma, Norman Campus	OK	91	1	1	26,506
Tarrant County College District	TX	32	1	2	34,892	Nova Southeastern University	FL	92	2	1	26,335
Community College of Southern Nevada	NV	33	1	1	34,551	Western Michigan University	MI	93	1	1	26,239
California State University, Long Beach	CA	34	1	1	34,547	University of New Mexico, Main Campus	NM	94	1	1	26,172
Rutgers University, New Brunswick	NJ	35	1	1	34,449	West Virginia University	WV	95	1	1	26,051
Louisiana State U. & A&M & Hebert Laws Center	LA	36	1	1	34,128	National University	CA	96	2	1	26,035
Brigham Young University	UT	37	2	1	34,067	Georgia State University	GA	97	1	1	25,967
Temple University	PA	38	1	1	33,695	Iowa State University	IA	98	1	1	25,741
University of Georgia	GA	39	1	1	33,660	University of Kentucky	KY	99	1	1	25,672
University of California, Berkeley	CA	40	1	1	33,547	Florida Atlantic University	FL	100	1	1	25,645
California State University, Northridge	CA	41	1	1	33,243	University of Texas at Arlington	TX	101	1	1	25,432
American Intercontinental University Online	IL	42	3	1	32,880	University of California, San Diego	CA	102	1	1	25,320
University of Southern California	CA	43	2	1	32,836	Northern Illinois University	IL	103	1	1	25,208
Wayne State University	MI	44	1	1	32,160	Palomar College	CA	104	1	2	25,146
Santa Ana College	CA	45	1	2	32,096	University of Massachusetts, Amherst	MA	105	1	1	25,093
University of North Texas	TX	46	1	1	31,958	Harvard University	MA	106	2	1	25,017
Austin Community College	TX	47	1	2	31,908	University of Illinois at Chicago	IL	107	1	1	24,812
Broward Community College	FL	48	1	2	31,835	Cuyahoga Community College District	OH	108	1	2	24,788
San Diego State University	CA	49	1	1	31,802	University of California, Irvine	CA	109	1	1	24,400
University of Colorado at Boulder	CO	50	1	1	31,589	Saint Petersburg College	FL	110	1	1	24,382
Boston University	MA	51	2	1	30,957	San Jacinto College, Central Campus	TX	111	1	2	24,322
Pima Community College	AZ	52	1	2	30,884	Santa Rosa Junior College	CA	112	1	2	24,293
University of Utah	UT	53	1	1	30,558	Oakland Community College	MI	113	1	2	24,287
American River College	CA	54	1	2	30,527	Utah Valley State College	UT	114	1	1	24,180
North Carolina State University at Raleigh	NC	55	1	1	30,148	Salt Lake Community College	UT	115	1	2	24,111
San Jose State University	CA	56	1	1	29,975	George Washington University	DC	116	2	1	24,099
Indiana University-Purdue U., Indianapolis	IN	57	1	1	29,933	Portland Community College	OR	117	1	2	23,955
George Mason University	VA	58	1	1	29,728	Portland State University	OR	118	1	1	23,929
Valencia Community College	FL	59	1	2	29,544	El Camino College	CA	119	1	2	23,895
Virginia Commonwealth University	VA	60	1	1	29,168	University of Virginia, Main Campus	VA	120	1	1	23,765

[1]Colleges and university campuses ranked by fall 2005 enrollment data.
[2]Publicly controlled institutions are identified by a "1"; private, not-for-profit, by a "2"; and private, for-profit, by a "3."
[3]The types of institutions are identified as follows: "1" for 4-year institutions; and "2" for 2-year institutions.

NOTE: Degree-granting institutions grant associate's or higher degrees and participate in Title IV federal financial aid programs.
SOURCE: U.S. Department of Education, National Center for Education Statistics, 2005 Integrated Postsecondary Education Data System (IPEDS), Spring 2006. (This table was prepared September 2006.)

Table 220. Selected statistics for degree-granting institutions enrolling more than 15,000 students in 2005: Selected years, 1990 through 2005

Line number	Institution	State	Control[1]	Type[2]	Total fall enrollment					Fall enrollment, 2005		
					Fall 1990	Fall 2000	Fall 2002	Fall 2003	Fall 2004	Total	Sex	
											Males	Females
1	2	3	4	5	6	7	8	9	10	11	12	13
i	**United States, all institutions[5]**	†	†	†	**13,818,637**	**15,312,289**	**16,611,711**	**16,900,471**	**17,272,044**	**17,487,475**	**7,455,925**	**10,031,550**
ii	Colleges with enrollment over 15,000	†	†	†	5,554,800	5,995,686	6,554,724	6,623,043	6,764,125	6,933,523	3,096,591	3,836,932
1	Auburn University, Main Campus	AL	1	1	21,537	21,860	23,276	23,152	22,928	23,333	11,878	11,455
2	Troy State University	AL	1	1	5,024	12,541	16,513	17,613	20,855	26,880	11,221	15,659
3	University of Alabama	AL	1	1	19,794	19,277	19,584	20,290	20,929	21,793	10,086	11,707
4	University of Alabama at Birmingham	AL	1	1	15,356	14,951	15,579	16,357	16,693	16,572	6,573	9,999
5	University of Alaska, Anchorage	AK	1	1	17,490	14,794	15,843	16,607	16,261	16,412	6,339	10,073
6	Arizona State University at the Tempe Campus	AZ	1	1	42,936	44,126	47,359	48,901	49,171	51,612	24,992	26,620
7	Glendale Community College	AZ	1	2	18,512	20,091	20,399	20,692	20,649	20,070	8,805	11,265
8	Mesa Community College	AZ	1	2	19,818	22,821	25,005	26,138	27,332	26,528	12,243	14,285
9	Northern Arizona University	AZ	1	1	16,992	19,964	19,907	18,820	19,137	18,773	6,889	11,884
10	Pima Community College	AZ	1	2	28,766	28,078	31,135	31,216	31,545	30,884	13,294	17,590
11	Rio Salado College	AZ	1	2	10,480	11,275	14,572	14,527	16,092	17,415	6,460	10,955
12	University of Arizona	AZ	1	1	35,729	34,488	36,847	37,083	36,932	37,036	17,355	19,681
13	University of Phoenix, Online Campus	AZ	3	1	†	14,783	48,085	71,052	115,794	117,309	45,981	71,328
14	Western International University	AZ	3	1	1,245	1,520	1,811	2,138	2,610	50,663	14,355	36,308
15	University of Arkansas, Main Campus	AR	1	1	14,732	15,346	15,995	16,405	17,269	17,821	9,069	8,752
16	American River College	CA	1	2	18,716	28,420	31,743	26,513	30,055	30,527	15,094	15,433
17	California Polytechnic State U., San Luis Obispo	CA	1	1	17,751	16,877	18,453	18,303	17,582	18,475	10,365	8,110
18	California State Polytechnic U., Pomona	CA	1	1	19,468	18,424	19,821	19,804	19,003	19,885	11,109	8,776
19	California State University, Chico	CA	1	1	16,633	15,912	16,246	15,516	15,734	15,919	7,302	8,617
20	California State University, Fresno	CA	1	1	19,960	19,056	21,272	22,342	19,781	20,371	8,219	12,152
21	California State University, Fullerton	CA	1	1	25,592	28,381	32,143	32,592	32,744	35,040	14,335	20,705
22	California State University, Long Beach	CA	1	1	33,987	30,918	34,566	34,715	33,479	34,547	13,531	21,016
23	California State University, Los Angeles	CA	1	1	21,597	19,593	21,099	20,637	20,307	20,034	7,547	12,487
24	California State University, Northridge	CA	1	1	31,167	29,066	33,579	33,426	31,341	33,243	13,309	19,934
25	California State University, Sacramento	CA	1	1	26,336	25,714	28,558	28,375	27,972	27,932	11,367	16,565
26	California State University, San Bernardino	CA	1	1	11,923	14,909	16,341	16,927	16,194	16,431	5,627	10,804
27	Cerritos College	CA	1	2	15,886	24,536	24,081	23,129	22,155	22,349	9,919	12,430
28	Chaffey College	CA	1	2	10,985	15,220	18,480	17,435	17,963	17,188	6,666	10,522
29	City College of San Francisco	CA	1	2	24,408	39,386	42,975	42,043	42,438	43,255	18,135	25,120
30	College of the Canyons	CA	1	2	4,815	10,528	13,213	14,553	13,953	15,947	9,314	6,633
31	Cypress College	CA	1	2	11,917	21,361	15,928	12,681	13,299	21,965	9,273	12,692
32	De Anza College	CA	1	2	21,948	22,770	24,372	25,081	22,792	22,694	10,891	11,803
33	Diablo Valley College	CA	1	2	20,255	21,581	22,141	21,116	20,287	19,851	9,379	10,472
34	East Los Angeles College	CA	1	2	12,447	27,199	27,372	22,284	23,969	23,632	9,759	13,873
35	El Camino College	CA	1	2	25,789	24,067	27,876	25,563	24,732	23,895	10,785	13,110
36	Foothill College	CA	1	2	12,811	14,193	16,515	18,006	16,609	17,123	8,339	8,784
37	Fresno City College	CA	1	2	14,710	19,351	22,812	21,755	21,540	21,917	10,158	11,759
38	Fullerton College	CA	1	2	17,548	19,993	20,923	18,720	19,774	19,611	9,151	10,460
39	Glendale Community College	CA	1	2	12,072	15,596	17,321	14,377	15,872	15,480	6,294	9,186
40	Grossmont College	CA	1	2	15,357	16,309	18,379	17,827	17,288	16,381	6,913	9,468
41	Long Beach City College	CA	1	2	18,378	20,926	25,142	23,877	23,177	22,641	10,084	12,557
42	Los Angeles City College	CA	1	2	14,479	15,174	25,744	15,877	15,958	16,283	6,767	9,516
43	Los Angeles Pierce College	CA	1	2	16,970	16,111	18,483	17,720	17,381	17,859	7,639	10,220
44	Los Angeles Valley College	CA	1	2	16,457	17,393	18,761	17,027	16,688	16,130	6,459	9,671
45	Modesto Junior College	CA	1	2	11,300	15,158	18,483	17,291	17,177	17,810	7,124	10,686
46	Mount San Antonio College	CA	1	2	20,563	28,329	30,974	26,440	27,927	27,195	12,225	14,970
47	National University	CA	2	1	8,836	16,848	17,865	17,064	25,684	26,035	10,195	15,840
48	Orange Coast College	CA	1	2	22,365	23,315	25,628	22,520	23,194	22,412	11,174	11,238
49	Palomar College	CA	1	2	16,707	21,062	25,566	23,691	25,040	25,146	12,733	12,413
50	Pasadena City College	CA	1	2	19,581	22,948	25,798	27,876	27,584	27,199	12,039	15,160
51	Rio Hondo College	CA	1	2	12,048	19,506	18,529	16,795	16,748	19,012	11,154	7,858
52	Riverside Community College	CA	1	2	15,683	22,107	33,792	29,664	30,101	29,160	12,726	16,434
53	Sacramento City College	CA	1	2	14,474	20,878	23,682	19,232	21,409	21,784	8,779	13,005
54	Saddleback College	CA	1	2	14,527	18,563	19,888	13,735	18,621	18,351	8,077	10,274
55	San Diego City College	CA	1	2	13,737	27,165	15,925	15,120	15,036	15,204	6,978	8,226
56	San Diego Mesa College	CA	1	2	23,410	21,233	24,148	22,548	22,467	21,066	9,746	11,320
57	San Diego State University	CA	1	1	35,493	31,609	34,304	32,803	32,043	31,802	12,967	18,835
58	San Francisco State University	CA	1	1	29,343	26,826	28,378	29,686	28,804	28,950	11,365	17,585
59	San Joaquin Delta College	CA	1	2	14,792	16,973	17,800	17,131	17,011	16,949	6,952	9,997
60	San Jose State University	CA	1	1	30,334	26,698	30,350	28,932	29,044	29,975	13,762	16,213
61	Santa Ana College	CA	1	2	20,532	27,571	30,346	23,329	26,496	32,096	18,585	13,511
62	Santa Barbara City College	CA	1	2	11,031	13,834	19,719	15,206	15,735	15,811	7,476	8,335
63	Santa Monica College	CA	1	2	18,108	27,868	29,691	23,401	27,459	28,908	12,471	16,437
64	Santa Rosa Junior College	CA	1	2	20,475	27,020	27,227	25,137	24,176	24,293	10,402	13,891
65	Sierra College	CA	1	2	11,637	17,517	19,380	18,105	18,248	18,444	8,001	10,443
66	Southwestern College	CA	1	2	13,010	17,994	19,405	18,716	18,342	19,324	8,462	10,862
67	Stanford University	CA	2	1	14,724	18,549	18,297	17,824	18,836	19,042	10,933	8,109

See notes at end of table.

Table 220. Selected statistics for degree-granting institutions enrolling more than 15,000 students in 2005: Selected years, 1990 through 2005—Continued

Fall enrollment, 2005					Earned degrees conferred, 2004–05					Total expenses and deductions, 2003–04 (in thousands)[4]	Full-time-equivalent enrollment		Line number
Attendance status		Percent minority[3]	Student level		Associate's	Bachelor's	Master's	First professional	Doctor's		Fall 2004	Fall 2005	
Full-time	Part-time		Under-graduate	Postbacca-laureate									
14	15	16	17	18	19	20	21	22	23	24	25	26	27
10,797,011	**6,690,464**	**30.9**	**14,963,964**	**2,523,511**	**696,660**	**1,439,264**	**574,618**	**87,289**	**52,631**	**$316,750,382**	**13,000,994**	**13,200,790**	i
4,401,318	2,532,205	33.9	5,710,610	1,222,913	162,371	663,680	276,055	34,275	34,270	136,384,782	5,147,484	5,315,947	ii
20,035	3,298	11.7	19,254	4,079	†	3,917	791	189	174	545,764	20,980	21,318	1
11,520	15,360	45.6	18,778	8,102	454	1,995	3,078	†	†	107,023	15,451	17,510	2
18,541	3,252	14.8	17,550	4,243	†	2,931	1,283	183	154	393,588	18,768	19,789	3
11,326	5,246	32.3	11,470	5,102	†	1,622	1,223	258	138	1,561,356	13,331	13,366	4
7,150	9,262	23.0	15,611	801	512	778	263	†	†	180,817	10,811	10,864	5
39,571	12,041	24.1	41,256	10,356	†	7,498	2,198	164	314	806,045	42,189	44,279	6
6,108	13,962	35.3	20,070	†	980	†	†	†	†	59,599	11,064	10,796	7
8,176	18,352	28.0	26,528	†	1,631	†	†	†	†	81,968	14,959	14,337	8
13,150	5,623	23.1	13,249	5,524	†	2,829	1,890	†	111	267,495	15,440	15,275	9
9,187	21,697	41.2	30,884	†	1,835	†	†	†	†	126,405	16,944	16,471	10
1,621	15,794	25.5	17,415	†	245	†	†	†	†	49,327	6,384	6,924	11
30,776	6,260	25.5	28,462	8,574		5,741	1,454	310	386	1,114,990	32,983	33,197	12
117,309	0	28.5	70,845	46,464	847	6,462	10,128	†	62	410,549	115,794	117,309	13
50,470	193	33.3	49,886	777	21	232	97	†	†	14,727	2,306	50,544	14
13,372	4,449	12.3	14,281	3,540	†	2,197	909	160	145	438,301	14,606	15,088	15
8,388	22,139	40.0	30,527	†	1,516	†	†	†	†	(⁶)	15,591	15,821	16
17,226	1,249	25.9	17,509	966	†	3,374	273	†	†	227,894	16,893	17,716	17
15,568	4,317	66.6	18,010	1,875	†	3,207	355	†	†	251,481	16,443	17,257	18
14,011	1,908	22.0	14,525	1,394	†	2,724	344	†	†	164,697	14,581	14,762	19
16,448	3,923	53.4	17,557	2,814	†	3,069	795	†	9	211,503	17,487	17,980	20
23,492	11,548	57.1	29,580	5,460	†	5,761	1,222	†	†	267,666	26,151	28,018	21
25,216	9,331	57.4	28,719	5,828	†	5,790	1,433	†	†	288,955	27,657	28,845	22
13,023	7,011	80.8	14,991	5,043	†	2,220	735	†	†	195,082	15,906	15,730	23
22,865	10,378	56.2	27,039	6,204	†	5,488	1,218	†	†	268,234	25,139	26,883	24
20,437	7,495	46.2	23,256	4,676	†	4,659	1,202	†	†	274,029	23,210	23,370	25
11,939	4,492	57.6	12,686	3,745	†	2,684	693	†	†	152,437	13,472	13,658	26
6,360	15,989	82.2	22,349	†	1,232	†	†	†	†	89,336	11,381	11,728	27
5,709	11,479	67.6	17,188	†	1,110	†	†	†	†	70,698	9,856	9,563	28
8,474	34,781	72.3	43,255	†	1,215	†	†	†	†	205,946	19,737	20,151	29
4,486	11,461	44.2	15,947	†	853	†	†	†	†	57,251	7,784	8,334	30
4,933	17,032	64.7	21,965	†	679	†	†	†	†	(⁶)	7,914	10,651	31
8,976	13,718	65.4	22,694	†	1,135	†	†	†	†	(⁶)	13,484	13,582	32
7,379	12,472	40.4	19,851	†	764	†	†	†	†	93,676	11,630	11,566	33
6,084	17,548	92.8	23,632	†	1,254	†	†	†	†	71,059	11,911	11,976	34
7,489	16,406	73.5	23,895	†	1,377	†	†	†	†	104,436	13,194	12,997	35
4,099	13,024	49.8	17,123	†	644	†	†	†	†	81,903	8,352	8,472	36
7,845	14,072	66.2	21,917	†	1,468	†	†	†	†	82,777	12,336	12,569	37
8,101	11,510	57.8	19,611	†	1,104	†	†	†	†	(⁶)	12,005	11,965	38
4,831	10,649	43.0	15,480	†	829	†	†	†	†	89,218	8,649	8,406	39
6,749	9,632	39.0	16,381	†	1,085	†	†	†	†	(⁶)	10,485	9,983	40
7,201	15,440	68.4	22,641	†	873	†	†	†	†	135,176	12,370	12,385	41
5,595	10,688	72.6	16,283	†	658	†	†	†	†	110,699	8,735	9,183	42
5,245	12,614	56.9	17,859	†	1,075	†	†	†	†	57,437	9,300	9,480	43
4,405	11,725	62.7	16,130	†	893	†	†	†	†	62,708	8,668	8,342	44
6,595	11,215	47.2	17,810	†	1,129	†	†	†	†	(⁶)	10,025	10,360	45
8,567	18,628	76.0	27,195	†	1,264	†	†	†	†	116,154	15,103	14,821	46
8,253	17,782	38.7	6,521	19,514	18	992	3,360	†	†	112,453	15,112	15,100	47
9,296	13,116	49.1	22,412	†	1,348	†	†	†	†	(⁶)	14,108	13,700	48
7,979	17,167	38.5	25,146	†	1,183	†	†	†	†	96,595	13,953	13,743	49
8,022	19,177	77.8	27,199	†	1,844	†	†	†	†	118,573	14,697	14,460	50
4,748	14,264	82.2	19,012	†	736	†	†	†	†	65,281	8,763	9,537	51
8,659	20,501	59.7	29,160	†	2,133	†	†	†	†	118,192	15,921	15,542	52
6,892	14,892	62.0	21,784	†	897	†	†	†	†	(⁶)	11,546	11,892	53
6,337	12,014	29.4	18,351	†	717	†	†	†	†	(⁶)	10,290	10,371	54
2,986	12,218	63.7	15,204	†	605	†	†	†	†	(⁶)	7,007	7,088	55
5,756	15,310	52.1	21,066	†	1,117	†	†	†	†	(⁶)	11,645	10,896	56
24,462	7,340	43.4	26,271	5,531	†	6,109	1,662	†	44	352,968	27,201	27,317	57
21,020	7,930	56.8	23,575	5,375	†	4,865	1,615	†	†	329,203	23,808	24,114	58
6,725	10,224	62.7	16,949	†	1,466	†	†	†	†	89,425	10,214	10,158	59
20,074	9,901	60.8	22,733	7,242	†	4,259	2,189	†	†	274,077	23,029	23,897	60
4,439	27,657	65.7	32,096	†	1,373	†	†	†	†	(⁶)	12,001	13,724	61
6,261	9,550	34.7	15,811	†	1,186	†	†	†	†	81,174	9,379	9,467	62
9,649	19,259	57.0	28,908	†	1,409	†	†	†	†	134,488	15,591	16,115	63
7,787	16,506	25.5	24,293	†	1,128	†	†	†	†	118,616	13,275	13,329	64
6,709	11,735	18.8	18,444	†	2,424	†	†	†	†	68,429	10,427	10,649	65
6,724	12,600	85.0	19,324	†	1,064	†	†	†	†	85,813	10,443	10,954	66
12,993	6,049	32.0	6,576	12,466	†	1,790	2,014	233	671	2,365,894	15,183	15,325	67

See notes at end of table.

Table 220. Selected statistics for degree-granting institutions enrolling more than 15,000 students in 2005: Selected years, 1990 through 2005—Continued

Line number	Institution	State	Control[1]	Type[2]	Total fall enrollment					Fall enrollment, 2005		
											Sex	
					Fall 1990	Fall 2000	Fall 2002	Fall 2003	Fall 2004	Total	Males	Females
1	2	3	4	5	6	7	8	9	10	11	12	13
68	University of California, Berkeley	CA	1	1	30,634	31,277	33,145	33,065	32,803	33,547	16,273	17,274
69	University of California, Davis	CA	1	1	23,890	26,094	29,087	29,402	29,210	28,815	13,015	15,800
70	University of California, Irvine	CA	1	1	16,808	20,211	23,779	24,273	24,344	24,400	12,390	12,010
71	University of California, Los Angeles	CA	1	1	36,420	36,890	37,599	37,055	35,966	35,625	16,324	19,301
72	University of California, Riverside	CA	1	1	8,708	13,015	15,934	17,296	17,104	16,622	7,920	8,702
73	University of California, San Diego	CA	1	1	17,790	20,197	23,528	24,105	24,663	25,320	12,531	12,789
74	University of California, Santa Barbara	CA	1	1	18,385	19,962	20,559	20,847	21,026	21,016	9,721	11,295
75	University of California, Santa Cruz	CA	1	1	10,054	12,144	14,139	14,997	15,036	15,012	6,973	8,039
76	University of Phoenix, Southern California	CA	3	1	†	18,075	12,161	12,368	15,913	16,135	6,064	10,071
77	University of Southern California	CA	2	1	28,374	29,194	30,682	31,606	32,160	32,836	16,862	15,974
78	Colorado State University	CO	1	1	26,828	26,807	29,255	28,186	27,973	27,780	13,231	14,549
79	Metropolitan State College of Denver	CO	1	1	17,400	17,688	19,413	20,261	20,761	21,010	9,360	11,650
80	University of Colorado at Boulder	CO	1	1	28,600	29,352	31,415	32,423	32,362	31,589	16,752	14,837
81	U. of Colorado at Denver and Health Sciences Center	CO	1	1	11,512	13,737	15,596	15,746	16,610	19,766	7,900	11,866
82	University of Connecticut	CT	1	1	25,497	19,393	21,427	22,053	22,694	23,185	11,009	12,176
83	University of Delaware	DE	1	1	20,818	19,072	21,289	21,121	21,238	20,982	9,141	11,841
84	George Washington University	DC	2	1	19,103	20,527	23,019	23,417	24,092	24,099	10,846	13,253
85	Strayer University, Washington Campus	DC	3	1	2,916	1,425	16,456	20,138	23,667	27,309	10,278	17,031
86	Broward Community College	FL	1	2	24,365	27,389	30,496	32,030	32,948	31,835	12,106	19,729
87	Florida Atlantic University	FL	1	1	12,767	21,046	23,705	24,932	25,319	25,645	10,034	15,611
88	Florida Community College at Jacksonville	FL	1	2	20,974	20,838	23,611	25,692	24,769	23,627	8,846	14,781
89	Florida International University	FL	1	1	22,466	31,945	33,349	33,228	34,865	36,904	15,953	20,951
90	Florida State University	FL	1	1	28,170	33,971	36,210	36,884	38,431	39,146	16,971	22,175
91	Hillsborough Community College	FL	1	2	19,134	18,497	20,654	22,006	22,123	21,377	8,283	13,094
92	Miami-Dade College	FL	1	1	50,078	46,834	54,926	58,490	57,026	54,169	20,829	33,340
93	Nova Southeastern University	FL	2	1	9,562	18,587	21,619	23,522	25,430	26,335	7,730	18,605
94	Palm Beach Community College	FL	1	2	18,392	17,326	22,163	22,660	22,554	21,686	8,250	13,436
95	Saint Petersburg College	FL	1	1	20,012	19,900	22,824	23,859	24,102	24,382	8,949	15,433
96	University of Central Florida	FL	1	1	21,541	33,713	38,501	41,535	42,465	44,856	19,889	24,967
97	University of Florida	FL	1	1	35,477	45,114	47,373	47,858	47,993	49,693	23,325	26,368
98	University of Miami	FL	2	1	13,841	13,963	14,978	15,235	15,250	15,674	7,130	8,544
99	University of North Florida	FL	1	1	8,021	12,550	13,470	13,966	14,533	15,234	6,245	8,989
100	University of South Florida	FL	1	1	32,326	35,561	38,854	40,945	42,238	42,660	17,028	25,632
101	Valencia Community College	FL	1	2	18,438	27,565	29,515	29,269	29,556	29,544	12,518	17,026
102	Georgia Institute of Technology, Main Campus	GA	1	1	12,241	14,805	16,481	16,643	16,841	17,135	12,408	4,727
103	Georgia Perimeter College	GA	1	2	13,944	13,708	17,573	18,986	20,316	20,461	7,805	12,656
104	Georgia Southern University	GA	1	1	12,249	14,184	15,075	15,704	16,100	16,646	8,000	8,646
105	Georgia State University	GA	1	1	23,336	23,625	27,462	28,042	27,261	25,967	10,349	15,618
106	Kennesaw State University	GA	1	1	10,018	13,360	15,650	17,477	17,955	18,551	7,137	11,414
107	University of Georgia	GA	1	1	28,395	31,288	32,941	33,878	33,405	33,660	14,293	19,367
108	University of Hawaii at Manoa	HI	1	1	18,799	17,263	18,696	19,862	20,549	20,644	9,002	11,642
109	Boise State University	ID	1	1	13,367	16,287	17,637	18,332	18,332	18,385	8,398	9,987
110	American Intercontinental University Online	IL	3	1	†	†	†	†	†	32,880	12,713	20,167
111	College of DuPage	IL	1	2	29,185	28,862	30,235	30,378	29,854	27,117	12,165	14,952
112	College of Lake County	IL	1	2	13,526	14,441	15,457	15,822	15,868	15,745	6,743	9,002
113	DePaul University	IL	2	1	15,711	20,548	23,227	23,610	23,570	23,145	10,496	12,649
114	Illinois State University	IL	1	1	22,662	20,755	21,183	20,860	20,757	20,653	8,571	12,082
115	Moraine Valley Community College	IL	1	2	13,601	12,972	14,480	15,780	16,077	15,929	6,698	9,231
116	Northern Illinois University	IL	1	1	24,509	23,248	24,948	25,260	24,820	25,208	11,565	13,643
117	Northwestern University	IL	2	1	17,041	16,952	17,528	17,625	17,747	18,065	9,338	8,727
118	Southern Illinois University, Carbondale	IL	1	1	24,078	22,552	21,873	21,387	21,589	21,441	11,845	9,596
119	Triton College	IL	1	2	16,759	16,927	14,864	15,023	15,597	15,845	6,929	8,916
120	University of Illinois at Chicago	IL	1	1	24,959	24,942	26,138	25,764	24,865	24,812	11,073	13,739
121	University of Illinois at Urbana, Champaign	IL	1	1	38,163	38,465	39,999	40,458	40,687	41,938	22,314	19,624
122	William Rainey Harper College	IL	1	2	16,509	15,021	14,482	14,991	15,265	15,026	6,495	8,531
123	Ball State University	IN	1	1	20,343	19,004	19,411	20,490	20,507	20,351	9,491	10,860
124	Indiana University, Bloomington	IN	1	1	35,451	37,076	38,903	38,589	37,821	37,958	18,312	19,646
125	Indiana University-Purdue U., Indianapolis	IN	1	1	27,517	27,525	29,025	29,860	29,953	29,933	12,570	17,363
126	Purdue University, Main Campus	IN	1	1	37,588	39,667	40,117	40,376	40,108	40,151	23,910	16,241
127	Des Moines Area Community College	IA	1	2	10,553	10,998	13,206	13,719	15,256	16,046	7,128	8,918
128	Iowa State University	IA	1	1	25,737	26,845	27,898	27,380	26,380	25,741	14,499	11,242
129	Kaplan University	IA	3	1	641	376	3,334	9,195	10,881	20,042	5,126	14,916

See notes at end of table.

Table 220.   Selected statistics for degree-granting institutions enrolling more than 15,000 students in 2005: Selected years, 1990 through 2005—Continued

Fall enrollment, 2005					Earned degrees conferred, 2004–05					Total expenses and deductions, 2003–04 (in thousands)[4]	Full-time-equivalent enrollment		Line number
Attendance status			Student level										
Full-time	Part-time	Percent minority[3]	Under-graduate	Postbacca-laureate	Associate's	Bachelor's	Master's	First professional	Doctor's		Fall 2004	Fall 2005	
14	15	16	17	18	19	20	21	22	23	24	25	26	27
30,875	2,672	52.8	23,482	10,065	†	6,767	2,040	348	803	1,447,803	31,244	31,893	68
26,242	2,573	51.5	22,714	6,101	†	5,735	873	402	389	2,078,953	27,568	27,260	69
23,301	1,099	62.5	19,930	4,470	†	5,242	943	87	211	1,236,539	23,586	23,724	70
34,439	1,186	53.8	24,811	10,814	†	7,336	2,545	568	657	3,192,685	35,179	34,909	71
15,735	887	71.3	14,571	2,051	†	3,080	393	†	159	423,732	16,412	16,090	72
24,045	1,275	55.6	20,679	4,641	†	5,042	797	117	303	1,825,500	23,995	24,553	73
20,275	741	38.6	18,077	2,939	†	4,658	627	†	287	557,650	20,588	20,570	74
14,443	569	39.8	13,625	1,387	†	2,991	258	†	105	386,067	14,556	14,669	75
16,135	0	57.6	12,476	3,659	3	2,092	804	†	†	73,901	15,913	16,135	76
28,823	4,013	40.2	16,897	15,939	†	4,139	3,892	704	657	1,515,410	29,809	30,365	77
21,750	6,030	12.5	21,605	6,175	†	4,281	1,045	138	187	593,805	24,295	24,031	78
12,607	8,403	25.7	21,010	†	†	2,280	†	†	†	91,306	15,772	15,998	79
25,677	5,912	15.2	26,210	5,379	†	5,525	1,106	165	272	708,030	28,526	27,919	80
9,013	10,753	21.0	10,387	9,379	†	1,551	1,834	314	115	113,900	10,708	13,164	81
19,370	3,815	17.7	16,112	7,073	29	3,816	1,470	293	261	708,558	20,294	20,834	82
17,956	3,026	13.7	17,548	3,434	14	3,602	697	†	189	540,045	19,350	19,138	83
15,579	8,520	25.2	10,761	13,338	134	2,421	3,151	634	245	671,814	18,890	18,899	84
6,172	21,137	60.8	20,363	6,946	101	931	888	†	†	113,238	6,025	14,437	85
10,080	21,755	57.6	31,835	†	3,043	†	†	†	†	131,278	17,784	17,384	86
13,393	12,252	37.3	21,366	4,279	172	4,022	1,128	†	57	329,571	17,758	18,220	87
7,154	16,473	34.5	23,627	†	2,792	†	†	†	†	125,728	13,195	12,685	88
21,853	15,051	73.4	30,705	6,199	3	4,861	1,777	47	80	419,749	25,723	27,800	89
32,481	6,665	24.7	30,783	8,363	127	6,856	1,681	301	276	664,163	34,269	35,043	90
6,835	14,542	42.6	21,377	†	1,937	†	†	†	†	81,053	12,043	11,717	91
18,836	35,333	87.5	54,169	†	6,649	4	†	†	†	306,773	35,010	33,094	92
12,518	13,817	50.7	5,453	20,882	5	1,173	3,799	852	777	355,483	16,843	17,842	93
6,724	14,962	41.2	21,686	†	2,322	†	†	†	†	92,965	12,299	11,747	94
7,922	16,460	20.1	24,382	†	2,517	223	†	†	†	119,732	14,505	14,564	95
31,559	13,297	27.0	37,909	6,947	223	7,259	1,903	†	154	461,924	34,806	36,757	96
43,419	6,274	26.1	34,612	15,081	447	8,417	2,877	963	702	1,457,494	44,371	45,946	97
14,167	1,507	38.1	10,537	5,137	†	2,392	1,014	529	156	1,259,376	14,313	14,766	98
10,155	5,079	21.8	13,409	1,825	750	2,262	622	†	12	131,625	11,598	12,154	99
27,786	14,874	28.0	33,705	8,955	248	5,705	2,174	98	194	732,155	32,880	33,575	100
11,857	17,687	45.6	29,544	†	3,996	†	†	†	†	124,202	17,864	17,795	101
15,380	1,755	22.4	11,841	5,294	†	2,512	1,400	†	355	788,188	15,789	16,051	102
9,151	11,310	49.6	20,461	†	1,395	†	†	†	†	89,401	12,897	12,948	103
13,735	2,911	25.0	14,650	1,996	†	2,172	407	†	22	149,721	14,374	14,852	104
17,557	8,410	41.5	18,966	7,001	†	3,339	1,952	195	123	385,078	21,438	20,860	105
11,964	6,587	16.0	16,734	1,817	†	1,908	761	†	†	120,661	13,854	14,569	106
28,674	4,986	13.0	25,204	8,456	†	6,160	1,592	394	424	933,596	30,388	30,596	107
15,037	5,607	64.1	14,352	6,292	†	2,647	1,140	154	156	631,620	17,104	17,175	108
11,173	7,212	11.3	16,900	1,485	258	1,642	396	†	1	186,882	13,923	14,038	109
32,880	0	42.3	28,864	4,016	4,875	3,935	2,801	†	†	—	†	32,880	110
8,784	18,333	32.2	27,117	†	1,996	†	†	†	†	136,436	17,102	14,939	111
4,514	11,231	37.4	15,745	†	910	†	†	†	†	98,809	8,224	8,285	112
15,968	7,177	30.2	14,740	8,405	†	2,683	2,140	279	16	354,129	19,014	18,786	113
17,789	2,864	11.7	17,858	2,795	†	4,274	715	†	49	361,894	18,895	18,877	114
6,654	9,275	22.2	15,929	†	1,168	†	†	†	†	77,780	9,733	9,768	115
19,002	6,206	23.5	18,467	6,741	†	3,626	1,567	102	80	444,158	20,875	21,328	116
15,013	3,052	25.1	9,084	8,981	†	2,083	2,504	432	366	1,063,589	15,826	16,191	117
17,297	4,144	21.8	16,697	4,744	87	4,373	844	186	145	586,144	18,981	18,870	118
3,831	12,014	47.2	15,845	†	751	†	†	†	†	64,700	7,767	7,865	119
20,214	4,598	44.0	15,150	9,662	†	3,149	1,785	503	286	1,803,617	22,039	21,946	120
38,631	3,307	23.5	30,909	11,029	†	6,752	2,622	335	636	1,795,817	38,733	39,876	121
6,174	8,852	33.4	15,026	†	1,122	†	†	†	†	117,063	9,087	9,146	122
17,102	3,249	8.7	17,426	2,925	359	3,238	957	†	65	307,984	18,496	18,334	123
33,472	4,486	10.5	29,562	8,396	55	6,069	1,783	286	397	869,043	34,913	35,170	124
17,478	12,455	15.3	21,438	8,495	603	2,713	1,469	609	46	831,591	22,215	22,369	125
35,485	4,666	11.1	32,311	7,840	690	6,270	1,548	239	524	1,080,139	37,150	37,283	126
6,380	9,666	11.3	16,046	†	1,420	†	†	†	†	76,106	9,280	9,625	127
22,465	3,276	8.8	20,732	5,009	†	4,679	858	93	246	756,285	24,340	23,705	128
5,306	14,736	24.7	19,960	82	731	165	†	†	†	48,286	1,932	11,095	129

See notes at end of table.

Table 220. Selected statistics for degree-granting institutions enrolling more than 15,000 students in 2005: Selected years, 1990 through 2005—Continued

					Total fall enrollment					Fall enrollment, 2005		
											Sex	
Line number	Institution	State	Con-trol[1]	Type[2]	Fall 1990	Fall 2000	Fall 2002	Fall 2003	Fall 2004	Total	Males	Females
1	2	3	4	5	6	7	8	9	10	11	12	13
130	Kirkwood Community College	IA	1	2	8,623	11,645	13,949	15,030	15,432	15,110	6,969	8,141
131	University of Iowa	IA	1	1	28,785	28,311	29,697	29,745	28,442	28,426	13,341	15,085
132	Johnson County Community College	KS	1	2	13,740	16,383	18,011	18,432	18,612	18,673	8,497	10,176
133	Kansas State University	KS	1	1	21,137	21,929	22,762	23,050	23,151	23,182	11,350	11,832
134	University of Kansas, Main Campus	KS	1	1	26,434	25,920	26,458	26,814	26,980	26,934	13,226	13,708
135	Eastern Kentucky University	KY	1	1	15,290	13,285	14,695	15,951	16,183	16,219	6,135	10,084
136	University of Kentucky	KY	1	1	22,538	23,114	24,985	25,397	25,686	25,672	12,069	13,603
137	University of Louisville	KY	1	1	22,979	19,771	20,416	20,605	20,729	20,726	9,624	11,102
138	Western Kentucky University	KY	1	1	15,170	15,481	17,811	18,380	18,485	18,634	7,497	11,137
139	Louisiana State U. & A&M & Hebert Laws Center	LA	1	1	26,112	31,527	32,228	31,934	32,241	34,128	16,355	17,773
140	Southeastern Louisiana University	LA	1	1	10,262	14,525	15,175	15,656	15,465	16,054	5,875	10,179
141	University of Louisiana at Lafayette	LA	1	1	15,764	15,742	16,006	16,208	16,561	17,075	7,078	9,997
142	Community College of Baltimore County	MD	1	2	—	18,168	19,676	20,025	19,968	19,622	7,277	12,345
143	Johns Hopkins University	MD	2	1	13,363	17,774	17,989	18,820	18,626	19,225	9,402	9,823
144	Montgomery College	MD	1	2	14,361	20,923	21,805	21,671	22,256	22,263	9,940	12,323
145	Towson University	MD	1	1	15,035	16,729	17,481	17,188	17,667	18,011	6,525	11,486
146	University of Maryland, College Park	MD	1	1	34,829	33,189	34,801	35,329	34,933	35,369	18,036	17,333
147	University of Maryland, University College	MD	1	1	14,476	18,276	24,030	25,857	28,374	27,429	11,662	15,767
148	Boston University	MA	2	1	27,996	28,318	28,982	29,049	29,596	30,957	13,427	17,530
149	Harvard University	MA	2	1	22,851	24,279	24,969	24,851	24,648	25,017	12,727	12,290
150	Northeastern University	MA	2	1	30,510	23,897	23,357	22,944	22,932	22,604	10,845	11,759
151	University of Massachusetts, Amherst	MA	1	1	26,025	24,416	24,062	24,310	24,646	25,093	12,474	12,619
152	Central Michigan University	MI	1	1	18,286	26,845	27,919	27,758	27,683	27,221	11,163	16,058
153	Eastern Michigan University	MI	1	1	25,011	23,561	24,532	24,419	23,862	23,486	9,211	14,275
154	Grand Valley State University	MI	1	1	11,725	18,569	20,407	21,429	22,063	22,565	8,576	13,989
155	Lansing Community College	MI	1	2	22,343	16,011	18,302	18,575	19,471	20,057	8,945	11,112
156	Macomb Community College	MI	1	2	31,538	22,001	22,142	22,245	20,471	20,596	9,953	10,643
157	Michigan State University	MI	1	1	44,307	43,366	44,937	44,542	44,836	45,166	20,577	24,589
158	Oakland Community College	MI	1	2	28,069	23,188	23,713	24,145	24,296	24,287	10,207	14,080
159	Oakland University	MI	1	1	12,400	15,235	16,059	16,575	16,902	17,339	6,513	10,826
160	University of Michigan, Ann Arbor	MI	1	1	36,391	38,103	38,972	39,031	39,533	39,993	20,685	19,308
161	Wayne State University	MI	1	1	33,872	30,408	31,167	32,208	32,386	32,160	13,128	19,032
162	Western Michigan University	MI	1	1	26,989	28,657	29,732	29,178	27,829	26,239	12,504	13,735
163	Saint Cloud State University	MN	1	1	17,075	15,181	16,224	16,133	16,077	15,954	7,126	8,828
164	University of Minnesota, Twin Cities	MN	1	1	57,168	45,481	48,677	49,474	50,954	51,175	24,073	27,102
165	Walden University	MN	3	1	422	1,544	4,565	8,227	13,553	22,168	5,213	16,955
166	Mississippi State University	MS	1	1	14,391	16,561	16,610	16,173	15,934	16,101	8,290	7,811
167	University of Southern Mississippi	MS	1	1	13,490	14,509	15,267	15,050	15,253	15,030	5,866	9,164
168	Missouri State University	MO	1	1	19,480	17,703	18,718	18,930	19,114	18,928	8,148	10,780
169	University of Missouri, Columbia	MO	1	1	25,058	23,309	26,124	26,805	27,003	27,930	13,143	14,787
170	University of Missouri, St Louis	MO	1	1	15,393	15,397	15,658	15,599	15,498	15,548	5,988	9,560
171	Webster University	MO	2	1	8,745	13,783	17,249	18,740	19,038	18,407	7,579	10,828
172	University of Nebraska at Lincoln	NE	1	1	24,453	22,268	22,988	22,559	21,792	21,675	11,335	10,340
173	Community College of Southern Nevada	NV	1	1	14,161	29,905	32,136	34,204	33,627	34,551	15,694	18,857
174	University of Nevada, Las Vegas	NV	1	1	17,937	22,041	24,679	26,161	27,339	28,134	12,239	15,895
175	University of Nevada, Reno	NV	1	1	11,487	13,149	15,093	15,534	15,950	16,336	7,328	9,008
176	Montclair State University	NJ	1	1	13,067	13,502	14,673	15,204	15,637	16,063	5,791	10,272
177	Rutgers University, New Brunswick	NJ	1	1	33,016	35,236	35,886	35,318	34,696	34,449	15,891	18,558
178	Albuquerque Technical Vocational Institute	NM	1	2	9,739	17,265	20,018	22,077	22,927	23,107	9,374	13,733
179	New Mexico State University, Main Campus	NM	1	1	14,812	14,958	15,243	16,174	16,428	16,072	7,031	9,041
180	University of New Mexico, Main Campus	NM	1	1	23,950	23,670	24,593	25,686	26,242	26,172	10,970	15,202
181	CUNY, Bernard M. Baruch College	NY	1	1	15,849	15,698	15,361	15,126	15,537	15,756	7,267	8,489
182	CUNY, Borough of Manhattan Community College	NY	1	2	14,819	15,875	17,635	18,465	18,854	18,776	6,974	11,802
183	CUNY, Brooklyn College	NY	1	1	16,605	15,039	15,635	15,513	15,384	15,281	5,786	9,495
184	CUNY, Hunter College	NY	1	1	19,639	20,011	20,607	20,797	20,243	20,843	6,107	14,736
185	CUNY, Kingsborough College	NY	1	2	13,809	14,801	15,132	14,943	15,356	15,265	6,262	9,003
186	CUNY, Queens College	NY	1	1	18,072	15,061	16,604	16,993	17,395	17,638	6,302	11,336
187	Columbia University in the City of New York	NY	2	1	18,242	19,639	20,583	21,322	21,648	21,983	10,973	11,010
188	Cornell University	NY	2	1	11,533	12,043	12,566	19,620	19,518	19,642	10,331	9,311
189	Monroe Community College	NY	1	2	13,545	15,315	16,052	16,596	17,502	17,294	7,844	9,450

See notes at end of table.

Table 220. Selected statistics for degree-granting institutions enrolling more than 15,000 students in 2005: Selected years, 1990 through 2005—Continued

Fall enrollment, 2005					Earned degrees conferred, 2004–05					Total expenses and deductions, 2003–04 (in thousands)[4]	Full-time-equivalent enrollment		Line number
Attendance status			Student level										
Full-time	Part-time	Percent minority[3]	Under-graduate	Postbacca-laureate	Associate's	Bachelor's	Master's	First professional	Doctor's		Fall 2004	Fall 2005	
14	15	16	17	18	19	20	21	22	23	24	25	26	27
8,492	6,618	9.5	15,110	†	1,908	†	†	†	†	81,630	10,682	10,714	130
23,008	5,418	9.5	20,300	8,126	†	4,041	1,412	583	341	1,648,968	24,946	25,081	131
6,797	11,876	15.0	18,673	†	1,157	†	†	†	†	110,388	10,485	10,784	132
18,167	5,015	7.9	18,838	4,344	92	3,612	755	107	138	440,498	20,232	20,080	133
21,531	5,403	12.2	20,908	6,026	†	3,647	1,292	339	223	549,988	23,528	23,595	134
11,506	4,713	6.2	13,942	2,277	241	1,787	648	†	†	177,590	13,221	13,337	135
21,485	4,187	8.5	18,702	6,970	†	3,285	1,337	394	276	1,367,526	22,840	23,073	136
14,733	5,993	16.8	14,933	5,793	48	2,148	1,237	333	112	550,282	16,922	17,065	137
13,868	4,766	10.9	15,967	2,667	299	2,166	791	†	†	177,550	15,636	15,714	138
30,157	3,971	17.6	28,092	6,036	†	4,449	1,204	276	222	702,047	30,035	31,711	139
12,090	3,964	20.7	14,355	1,699	92	1,601	381	†	†	130,881	13,125	13,637	140
13,780	3,295	22.3	15,564	1,511	3	1,964	385	†	34	145,063	14,476	15,083	141
7,049	12,573	37.9	19,622	†	1,422	†	†	†	†	123,752	11,416	11,270	142
10,795	8,430	22.1	5,631	13,594	†	1,412	3,692	123	387	2,712,507	13,498	14,021	143
8,389	13,874	52.7	22,263	†	1,491	†	†	†	†	160,573	12,811	13,047	144
13,631	4,380	18.6	14,495	3,516	†	2,984	827	†	5	207,260	14,900	15,286	145
29,905	5,464	30.8	25,442	9,927	†	6,263	1,929	25	516	1,083,247	31,423	31,972	146
2,977	24,452	48.9	19,000	8,429	107	2,677	1,656	†	8	179,352	12,890	12,500	147
25,396	5,561	23.2	18,694	12,263	0	3,551	3,155	635	320	1,128,165	26,303	27,540	148
19,263	5,754	28.4	9,725	15,292	20	1,807	3,355	786	560	2,560,919	21,193	21,492	149
17,611	4,993	21.2	17,793	4,811	130	2,898	1,213	266	79	478,898	19,570	19,551	150
20,197	4,896	15.5	19,394	5,699	54	4,262	1,144	†	267	591,508	21,550	22,024	151
19,561	7,660	17.5	19,997	7,224	†	3,549	2,548	†	78	281,357	22,595	22,431	152
14,051	9,435	22.9	18,666	4,820	†	2,923	1,135	†	12	257,207	17,859	17,694	153
17,206	5,359	10.7	18,903	3,662	†	2,938	920	†	†	219,917	18,652	19,247	154
6,154	13,903	18.7	20,057	†	1,278	†	†	†	†	107,808	10,658	10,822	155
7,520	13,076	11.8	20,596	†	2,109	†	†	†	†	104,437	11,435	11,910	156
39,140	6,026	17.0	35,678	9,488	†	7,733	2,004	349	425	1,285,283	40,989	41,470	157
7,705	16,582	20.5	24,287	†	1,908	†	†	†	†	138,774	12,913	13,272	158
11,018	6,321	14.7	13,448	3,891	†	2,012	886	†	20	158,239	12,931	13,458	159
37,068	2,925	25.1	25,467	14,526	†	5,880	3,563	681	725	3,739,280	37,676	38,169	160
17,840	14,320	38.2	20,737	11,423	†	2,293	2,347	509	173	686,643	23,347	23,436	161
19,725	6,514	9.8	21,434	4,805	†	4,291	1,424	†	95	404,775	23,272	22,193	162
12,006	3,948	6.1	14,496	1,458	109	2,312	347	†	†	133,942	13,811	13,558	163
35,963	15,212	15.4	32,817	18,358	†	6,088	2,798	777	678	1,921,465	41,521	41,726	164
16,031	6,137	26.3	1,229	20,939	†	33	3,440	†	123	32,894	13,093	18,388	165
12,825	3,276	22.1	12,555	3,546	†	2,636	843	48	111	432,648	13,950	14,072	166
12,057	2,973	28.8	12,468	2,562	†	2,318	691	†	136	245,875	13,331	13,206	167
13,758	5,170	6.2	16,157	2,771	†	2,546	810	†	†	179,966	15,906	15,775	168
23,691	4,239	10.7	21,335	6,595	†	4,259	1,195	288	274	1,175,595	24,555	25,285	169
6,711	8,837	19.4	12,606	2,942	†	1,902	786	46	51	158,225	9,912	10,188	170
6,553	11,854	41.2	3,849	14,558	†	1,221	5,630	†	12	140,053	11,581	11,095	171
18,433	3,242	8.2	17,037	4,638	4	3,267	794	138	234	589,395	19,549	19,660	172
8,344	26,207	46.0	34,551	†	1,333	†	†	†	†	114,982	18,150	18,920	173
18,031	10,103	35.9	22,112	6,022	†	3,103	895	127	37	350,721	21,487	21,988	174
11,573	4,763	17.9	12,937	3,399	†	1,816	667	53	89	401,280	13,039	13,407	175
10,737	5,326	32.9	12,174	3,889	†	2,211	717	†	2	160,672	12,370	12,758	176
28,225	6,224	37.3	26,713	7,736	†	5,948	1,576	190	332	(6)	30,787	30,577	177
6,925	16,182	58.1	23,107	†	1,079	†	†	†	†	90,674	12,276	12,358	178
11,925	4,147	56.1	12,656	3,416	26	2,122	799	†	96	346,341	13,869	13,526	179
18,092	8,080	44.9	18,725	7,447	11	2,818	1,197	250	205	1,078,993	21,075	21,190	180
10,582	5,174	53.6	12,844	2,912	†	2,639	1,010	†	†	128,341	12,263	12,582	181
10,809	7,967	76.0	18,776	†	2,207	†	†	†	†	99,877	13,623	13,484	182
8,515	6,766	48.2	11,364	3,917	†	1,688	1,050	†	†	135,391	11,032	11,099	183
11,417	9,426	47.6	15,631	5,212	†	2,295	1,285	†	†	176,629	14,749	15,046	184
7,968	7,297	54.0	15,265	†	1,772	†	†	†	†	77,838	10,433	10,418	185
9,185	8,453	39.9	13,018	4,620	†	2,151	1,171	†	†	153,826	12,152	12,419	186
18,904	3,079	28.6	7,319	14,664	†	1,705	4,799	628	603	2,190,773	19,713	20,090	187
19,599	43	26.6	13,684	5,958	†	3,474	1,544	288	452	1,333,276	19,489	19,616	188
10,213	7,081	26.0	17,294	†	2,517	†	†	†	†	93,141	12,725	12,590	189

See notes at end of table.

Table 220. Selected statistics for degree-granting institutions enrolling more than 15,000 students in 2005: Selected years, 1990 through 2005—Continued

Line number	Institution	State	Control[1]	Type[2]	Total fall enrollment					Fall enrollment, 2005		
											Sex	
					Fall 1990	Fall 2000	Fall 2002	Fall 2003	Fall 2004	Total	Males	Females
1	2	3	4	5	6	7	8	9	10	11	12	13
190	Nassau Community College	NY	1	2	21,537	19,621	21,239	20,984	21,446	20,979	9,800	11,179
191	New York University	NY	2	1	32,813	37,150	38,096	38,188	39,408	40,004	16,414	23,590
192	Saint John's University, New York	NY	2	1	19,105	18,621	19,288	19,777	19,813	20,346	8,129	12,217
193	SUNY at Albany	NY	1	1	17,400	16,751	17,426	16,998	16,293	17,040	7,879	9,161
194	SUNY at Buffalo	NY	1	1	27,638	24,830	26,168	27,255	27,276	27,220	14,037	13,183
195	Stony Brook University	NY	1	1	17,624	19,924	21,989	22,344	21,685	22,011	10,523	11,488
196	Suffolk County Community College	NY	1	2	†	†	20,280	20,980	21,117	21,180	8,906	12,274
197	Syracuse University	NY	2	1	21,900	18,186	18,604	18,639	18,247	18,734	8,376	10,358
198	Touro College	NY	2	1	4,456	8,092	15,941	18,174	19,618	22,540	8,986	13,554
199	Central Piedmont Community College	NC	1	2	16,311	14,908	15,899	16,245	16,400	16,636	6,924	9,712
200	East Carolina University	NC	1	1	17,564	18,750	20,577	21,756	22,767	23,164	8,861	14,303
201	North Carolina State University at Raleigh	NC	1	1	27,199	28,619	29,637	29,854	29,957	30,148	17,024	13,124
202	University of North Carolina at Chapel Hill	NC	1	1	23,878	24,892	26,028	26,359	26,878	27,276	11,403	15,873
203	University of North Carolina at Charlotte	NC	1	1	14,699	17,241	18,916	19,605	19,846	20,772	9,289	11,483
204	University of North Carolina at Greensboro	NC	1	1	12,882	13,125	14,453	14,870	15,329	16,147	5,167	10,980
205	Bowling Green State University, Main Campus	OH	1	1	18,657	18,096	18,773	18,534	18,989	19,016	8,336	10,680
206	Cleveland State University	OH	1	1	19,214	15,294	15,971	16,014	15,664	15,482	6,604	8,878
207	Columbus State Community College	OH	1	2	13,290	18,094	22,222	23,297	21,941	22,014	9,126	12,888
208	Cuyahoga Community College District	OH	1	2	23,157	19,518	22,615	23,231	24,664	24,788	9,013	15,775
209	Kent State University, Main Campus	OH	1	1	24,434	21,924	23,504	24,242	24,347	23,622	9,056	14,566
210	Miami University, Oxford	OH	1	1	15,835	16,757	16,730	16,863	17,161	16,722	7,654	9,068
211	Ohio State University, Main Campus	OH	1	1	54,087	47,952	49,676	50,731	50,995	50,504	25,660	24,844
212	Ohio University, Main Campus	OH	1	1	18,505	19,920	20,548	20,452	20,143	20,461	9,776	10,685
213	Owens Community College	OH	1	2	6,857	15,845	17,921	19,341	19,671	20,595	11,393	9,202
214	Sinclair Community College	OH	1	2	16,367	19,026	19,381	19,860	19,622	18,937	8,196	10,741
215	University of Akron, Main Campus	OH	1	1	28,801	21,363	22,605	21,452	21,598	21,049	9,795	11,254
216	University of Cincinnati, Main Campus	OH	1	1	31,013	27,327	26,552	26,817	27,178	27,932	13,636	14,296
217	University of Toledo	OH	1	1	24,691	19,491	20,889	20,594	19,480	19,201	9,462	9,739
218	Wright State University, Main Campus	OH	1	1	16,393	13,964	14,397	14,648	15,985	16,207	7,006	9,201
219	Oklahoma State University, Main Campus	OK	1	1	19,827	18,676	23,220	23,844	23,819	23,692	12,203	11,489
220	Tulsa Community College	OK	1	2	17,955	16,270	17,227	16,931	17,143	16,770	6,229	10,541
221	University of Central Oklahoma	OK	1	1	14,232	14,099	15,239	15,044	14,598	15,859	6,435	9,424
222	University of Oklahoma, Norman Campus	OK	1	1	20,774	24,205	26,263	27,146	27,483	26,506	13,389	13,117
223	Oregon State University	OR	1	1	16,361	16,758	18,764	18,958	19,153	19,224	9,965	9,259
224	Portland Community College	OR	1	2	21,888	24,209	26,746	24,135	24,505	23,955	10,563	13,392
225	Portland State University	OR	1	1	16,921	18,889	21,672	23,081	23,444	23,929	10,741	13,188
226	University of Oregon	OR	1	1	18,840	17,801	19,997	19,992	20,296	20,347	9,609	10,738
227	Community College of Allegheny County	PA	1	2	20,553	15,556	17,989	19,103	19,292	18,404	7,900	10,504
228	Community College of Philadelphia	PA	1	2	15,151	15,953	19,395	20,615	20,606	17,102	5,631	11,471
229	Drexel University	PA	2	1	11,926	13,128	16,345	17,000	17,656	18,466	9,895	8,571
230	Pennsylvania State University, Main Campus	PA	1	1	38,864	40,571	41,445	41,795	41,289	40,709	22,182	18,527
231	Temple University	PA	1	1	29,714	28,355	32,359	32,877	33,551	33,695	14,671	19,024
232	University of Pennsylvania	PA	2	1	21,868	21,853	22,769	23,243	23,305	23,704	11,547	12,157
233	University of Pittsburgh, Main Campus	PA	1	1	28,120	26,329	27,190	26,795	26,731	26,559	12,320	14,239
234	Community College of Rhode Island	RI	1	2	16,620	15,583	15,929	16,223	16,293	16,042	5,916	10,126
235	University of Rhode Island	RI	1	1	16,047	14,362	14,180	14,791	14,749	15,095	6,227	8,868
236	Clemson University	SC	1	1	15,714	17,465	16,876	17,016	17,110	17,165	9,354	7,811
237	University of South Carolina at Columbia	SC	1	1	25,613	23,728	25,140	25,288	25,596	27,065	11,428	15,637
238	Middle Tennessee State University	TN	1	1	14,865	19,121	21,163	21,744	22,322	22,554	10,418	12,136
239	University of Memphis	TN	1	1	20,681	19,986	19,797	19,911	20,668	20,465	8,005	12,460
240	University of Tennessee	TN	1	1	26,055	25,890	27,971	27,281	27,792	28,512	13,651	14,861
241	Austin Community College	TX	1	2	24,251	25,735	35,576	30,638	35,622	31,908	13,831	18,077
242	Central Texas College	TX	1	2	4,815	14,636	17,992	17,255	18,351	17,792	10,050	7,742
243	Collin County Community College District	TX	1	2	9,059	12,996	15,970	16,574	17,702	18,457	8,031	10,426
244	El Paso Community College	TX	1	2	17,081	18,001	21,317	24,569	26,078	26,667	10,367	16,300
245	Houston Community College System	TX	1	2	36,437	40,929	39,528	37,846	39,715	39,516	16,417	23,099
246	North Harris Montgomery Community Col. District	TX	1	2	15,653	24,554	31,692	34,471	35,788	39,949	15,820	24,129
247	Sam Houston State University	TX	1	1	12,753	12,358	13,091	13,460	14,371	15,357	6,255	9,102
248	San Antonio College	TX	1	2	20,083	19,253	20,402	20,831	20,563	19,933	7,894	12,039
249	San Jacinto College, Central Campus	TX	1	2	9,424	10,507	11,283	22,747	24,519	24,322	10,175	14,147
250	South Texas College	TX	1	1	†	11,319	13,695	15,334	17,130	16,233	6,610	9,623
251	Tarrant County College District	TX	1	2	28,161	26,868	31,250	32,667	34,136	34,892	14,688	20,204
252	Texas A & M University	TX	1	1	41,171	44,026	45,083	44,813	44,435	44,910	23,473	21,437
253	Texas State University, San Marcos	TX	1	1	20,940	22,423	25,041	26,306	26,783	27,129	11,834	15,295

See notes at end of table.

Table 220. Selected statistics for degree-granting institutions enrolling more than 15,000 students in 2005: Selected years, 1990 through 2005—Continued

Fall enrollment, 2005					Earned degrees conferred, 2004–05					Total expenses and deductions, 2003–04 (in thousands)[4]	Full-time-equivalent enrollment		Line number
Attendance status		Percent minority[3]	Student level		Associate's	Bachelor's	Master's	First professional	Doctor's		Fall 2004	Fall 2005	
Full-time	Part-time		Under-graduate	Postbacca-laureate									
14	15	16	17	18	19	20	21	22	23	24	25	26	27
13,528	7,451	40.0	20,979	†	2,817	†	†	†	†	158,043	16,359	16,030	190
30,157	9,847	32.4	20,566	19,438	676	4,696	5,573	962	423	2,049,478	33,492	33,938	191
13,820	6,526	43.7	15,092	5,254	91	2,165	963	484	61	301,520	16,147	16,391	192
13,455	3,585	22.0	12,013	5,027	†	2,674	1,523	†	159	414,226	13,990	14,786	193
22,618	4,602	19.1	18,165	9,055	4	3,674	2,094	553	380	714,722	24,266	24,338	194
16,629	5,382	39.7	14,287	7,724	†	2,941	1,665	152	317	1,204,981	18,084	18,622	195
11,766	9,414	24.3	21,180	†	2,504	†	†	†	†	137,261	14,868	14,927	196
16,044	2,690	17.5	12,905	5,829	8	2,403	1,614	228	116	534,831	16,557	17,080	197
12,594	9,946	30.8	12,180	10,360	659	1,750	2,408	310	73	126,665	14,874	16,459	198
6,115	10,521	34.2	16,636	†	903	†	†	†	†	78,463	9,455	9,647	199
18,056	5,108	19.9	17,728	5,436	†	3,065	1,190	72	35	463,625	19,765	19,983	200
23,120	7,028	16.8	22,767	7,381	193	4,620	1,332	73	343	835,553	25,494	25,811	201
22,441	4,835	20.2	16,764	10,512	†	3,888	1,847	610	459	1,623,720	23,965	24,250	202
14,796	5,976	21.8	16,555	4,217	†	2,843	799	†	40	218,399	16,090	17,079	203
11,900	4,247	24.4	12,388	3,759	†	1,973	921	†	89	229,997	12,704	13,512	204
16,604	2,412	11.9	16,079	2,937	†	2,960	1,074	†	90	295,428	17,398	17,521	205
8,263	7,219	25.8	9,558	5,924	†	1,690	1,381	196	35	216,561	11,349	11,075	206
9,097	12,917	26.9	22,014	†	1,450	†	†	†	†	106,756	12,968	13,434	207
10,323	14,465	36.6	24,788	†	1,541	†	†	†	†	194,458	15,034	15,179	208
18,206	5,416	10.6	18,745	4,877	†	3,739	1,197	†	160	340,306	20,613	20,287	209
15,698	1,024	8.7	14,951	1,771	279	3,759	510	†	44	385,869	15,929	16,083	210
43,844	6,660	15.5	37,411	13,093	†	8,124	2,685	842	590	2,701,662	46,579	46,417	211
18,736	1,725	6.4	17,207	3,254	47	4,222	980	97	147	389,426	19,133	19,406	212
6,247	14,348	17.5	20,595	†	1,085	†	†	†	†	67,095	11,099	11,064	213
7,400	11,537	20.3	18,937	†	1,326	†	†	†	†	120,535	11,636	11,273	214
14,817	6,232	17.0	17,140	3,909	460	2,271	1,012	189	114	306,247	17,526	17,265	215
21,152	6,780	18.0	19,512	8,420	202	2,938	1,381	334	239	767,944	23,283	23,749	216
14,974	4,227	17.4	16,058	3,143	240	2,595	742	191	67	300,721	16,702	16,637	217
12,705	3,502	16.1	12,268	3,939	0	2,034	1,180	85	41	271,073	13,893	14,050	218
18,568	5,124	15.9	19,114	4,578	0	3,549	1,073	69	173	493,734	20,653	20,522	219
6,079	10,691	20.3	16,770	†	1,957	†	†	†	†	85,778	10,005	9,668	220
10,609	5,250	20.3	14,349	1,510	0	2,118	465	†	†	87,197	11,792	12,685	221
20,017	6,489	21.2	20,104	6,402	†	3,637	1,629	174	160	481,316	23,295	22,467	222
16,188	3,036	15.1	15,740	3,484	†	3,177	778	99	159	498,301	17,419	17,381	223
8,336	15,619	22.7	23,955	†	1,719	†	†	†	†	153,962	13,505	13,580	224
13,281	10,648	19.4	17,801	6,128	†	2,931	1,510	†	55	226,953	17,017	17,423	225
17,984	2,363	12.8	16,473	3,874	†	3,570	968	168	126	419,528	18,835	18,902	226
7,580	10,824	18.2	18,404	†	1,679	†	†	†	†	100,079	11,775	11,214	227
5,188	11,914	66.2	17,102	†	1,452	†	†	†	†	94,547	11,264	9,188	228
13,627	4,839	25.5	12,357	6,109	7	2,231	1,263	237	122	535,518	14,578	15,500	229
38,262	2,447	12.5	34,637	6,072	90	9,840	1,191	†	571	2,611,892	39,630	39,207	230
25,634	8,061	31.7	24,194	9,501	8	4,263	1,601	797	322	1,645,339	28,299	28,746	231
19,771	3,933	27.3	12,092	11,612	2	2,854	2,674	707	463	3,716,145	20,832	21,293	232
21,776	4,783	14.3	17,024	9,535	†	3,989	1,855	564	372	1,214,277	23,542	23,587	233
5,765	10,277	24.8	16,042	†	1,107	†	†	†	†	77,361	9,277	9,215	234
11,337	3,758	12.4	11,546	3,549	†	1,889	544	80	74	321,593	12,618	12,771	235
15,319	1,846	10.4	14,096	3,069	†	3,005	938	†	131	477,805	15,923	16,022	236
21,227	5,838	19.6	18,362	8,703	4	3,260	1,662	383	253	552,468	22,312	23,422	237
17,981	4,573	16.9	20,389	2,165	2	3,476	607	†	14	206,087	19,558	19,765	238
13,693	6,772	39.4	15,765	4,700	†	2,293	889	160	109	277,811	16,535	16,319	239
24,638	3,874	13.1	20,286	8,226	†	3,844	1,649	509	281	1,155,490	25,432	26,132	240
8,829	23,079	37.1	31,908	†	906	†	†	†	†	129,531	15,757	16,577	241
2,899	14,893	50.6	17,792	†	1,930	†	†	†	†	75,531	8,145	7,899	242
7,226	11,231	27.6	18,457	†	958	†	†	†	†	70,988	10,634	10,997	243
10,758	15,909	88.7	26,667	†	1,705	†	†	†	†	88,383	15,922	16,099	244
12,198	27,318	67.3	39,516	†	1,923	†	†	†	†	222,019	21,454	21,370	245
7,204	32,745	37.9	39,949	†	1,841	†	†	†	†	169,194	16,409	18,198	246
11,925	3,432	24.2	13,271	2,086	†	2,197	555	†	29	121,838	12,234	13,245	247
7,641	12,292	52.4	19,933	†	932	†	†	†	†	69,886	12,226	11,768	248
10,047	14,275	48.1	24,322	†	1,680	†	†	†	†	123,214	14,738	14,840	249
6,201	10,032	96.1	16,233	†	1,232	†	†	†	†	64,752	10,763	10,249	250
12,259	22,633	36.6	34,892	†	1,870	†	†	†	†	151,633	19,315	19,858	251
39,607	5,303	16.9	36,368	8,542	†	7,711	1,949	123	528	1,401,624	41,065	41,663	252
20,113	7,016	27.6	22,986	4,143	†	4,314	1,134	†	8	267,132	22,466	22,840	253

See notes at end of table.

Table 220. Selected statistics for degree-granting institutions enrolling more than 15,000 students in 2005: Selected years, 1990 through 2005—Continued

Line number	Institution	State	Con-trol[1]	Type[2]	Total fall enrollment					Fall enrollment, 2005		
					Fall 1990	Fall 2000	Fall 2002	Fall 2003	Fall 2004	Total	Sex	
											Males	Females
1	2	3	4	5	6	7	8	9	10	11	12	13
254	Texas Tech University	TX	1	1	25,363	24,558	27,569	28,549	28,325	28,001	15,213	12,788
255	University of Houston	TX	1	1	33,115	32,123	34,443	35,066	35,180	35,344	16,789	18,555
256	University of North Texas	TX	1	1	27,160	27,054	30,183	31,065	31,155	31,958	13,645	18,313
257	University of Texas at Arlington	TX	1	1	24,782	20,424	23,821	24,979	25,297	25,432	11,960	13,472
258	University of Texas at Austin	TX	1	1	49,617	49,996	52,261	51,426	50,377	49,696	24,385	25,311
259	University of Texas at El Paso	TX	1	1	16,524	15,224	17,232	18,542	18,918	19,268	8,596	10,672
260	University of Texas at San Antonio	TX	1	1	15,489	18,830	22,016	24,665	26,175	27,337	12,666	14,671
261	University of Texas, Pan American	TX	1	1	12,337	12,759	14,392	15,914	17,030	17,048	6,954	10,094
262	Brigham Young University	UT	2	1	31,662	32,554	32,408	33,008	34,347	34,067	17,548	16,519
263	Salt Lake Community College	UT	1	2	13,344	21,596	23,347	24,056	24,725	24,111	12,218	11,893
264	University of Utah	UT	1	1	24,922	24,948	28,369	28,436	28,933	30,558	16,636	13,922
265	Utah Valley State College	UT	1	1	7,879	20,946	23,609	23,803	24,149	24,180	13,955	10,225
266	Weber State University	UT	1	1	13,449	16,050	18,059	18,821	18,498	18,142	9,065	9,077
267	George Mason University	VA	1	1	20,308	23,408	26,796	28,246	28,874	29,728	13,659	16,069
268	James Madison University	VA	1	1	11,251	15,326	15,965	16,203	16,108	16,938	6,620	10,318
269	Northern Virginia Community College	VA	1	2	35,194	37,073	39,129	38,097	37,392	37,740	17,210	20,530
270	Old Dominion University	VA	1	1	16,729	18,969	20,105	20,802	20,595	21,274	8,684	12,590
271	Tidewater Community College	VA	1	2	17,726	20,184	21,698	23,088	22,691	23,718	9,284	14,434
272	University of Virginia, Main Campus	VA	1	1	21,110	22,411	23,144	23,077	23,341	23,765	10,641	13,124
273	Virginia Commonwealth University	VA	1	1	21,764	24,066	26,009	26,631	28,303	29,168	11,447	17,721
274	Virginia Polytechnic Institute and State U.	VA	1	1	25,568	27,869	28,027	27,755	27,619	27,979	16,367	11,612
275	University of Washington, Seattle Campus	WA	1	1	33,854	36,139	39,882	39,135	39,199	39,251	18,750	20,501
276	Washington State University	WA	1	1	18,412	20,492	21,880	22,712	23,241	23,544	11,096	12,448
277	West Virginia University	WV	1	1	20,854	21,987	23,492	24,260	25,255	26,051	13,335	12,716
278	Milwaukee Area Technical College	WI	1	2	21,600	14,296	17,715	17,767	18,524	18,545	7,721	10,824
279	University of Wisconsin, Madison	WI	1	1	43,209	40,658	40,884	40,879	40,455	40,793	19,210	21,583
280	University of Wisconsin, Milwaukee	WI	1	1	26,020	23,578	24,587	25,440	26,832	27,502	12,419	15,083

—Not available.
†Not applicable.
[1]Publicly controlled institutions are identified by a "1"; private, not-for-profit, by a "2"; and private, for-profit, by a "3"
[2]The types of institutions are identified as follows: "1" for 4-year institutions; and "2" for 2-year institutions.

[3]Minority students who are U.S. citizens or resident aliens as a percentage of total enroll-ment, including nonresident aliens.
[4]Includes private and some public institutions reporting total expenses and deductions under Financial Accounting Standards Board (FASB) reporting standards and public institu-tions reporting total expenses and deductions under Governmental Accounting Standards Board (GASB) 34/35 reporting standards.

Table 220. Selected statistics for degree-granting institutions enrolling more than 15,000 students in 2005: Selected years, 1990 through 2005—Continued

Fall enrollment, 2005					Earned degrees conferred, 2004–05					Total expenses and deductions, 2003–04 (in thousands)[4]	Full-time-equivalent enrollment		Line number
Attendance status			Student level										
Full-time	Part-time	Percent minority[3]	Under-graduate	Postbacca-laureate	Associate's	Bachelor's	Master's	First professional	Doctor's		Fall 2004	Fall 2005	
14	15	16	17	18	19	20	21	22	23	24	25	26	27
24,318	3,683	17.4	23,002	4,999	†	4,264	1,100	226	175	438,320	25,880	25,742	254
24,500	10,844	52.7	28,187	7,157	†	4,528	1,428	613	211	581,749	28,381	28,828	255
22,137	9,821	26.9	25,378	6,580	†	4,360	1,524	†	146	323,984	25,229	25,923	256
16,556	8,876	37.5	19,649	5,783	†	3,378	1,807	†	86	232,062	19,944	20,003	257
45,171	4,525	32.9	36,878	12,818	†	8,836	2,900	685	719	1,481,119	47,490	46,946	258
11,954	7,314	77.0	16,037	3,231	†	1,552	671	†	30	205,964	14,668	14,812	259
18,827	8,510	57.5	23,431	3,906	†	3,258	855	†	12	218,595	22,586	22,151	260
11,154	5,894	89.7	14,942	2,106	0	1,937	572	†	9	139,775	13,464	13,467	261
29,400	4,667	8.8	30,798	3,269	†	6,951	1,052	156	75	769,646	30,038	31,223	262
8,165	15,946	15.1	24,111	†	2,786	†	†	†	†	110,119	13,928	13,519	263
20,335	10,223	10.5	24,155	6,403	†	5,198	1,303	267	229	1,693,124	23,526	24,396	264
11,555	12,625	8.0	24,180	†	2,072	1,189	†	†	†	128,806	17,039	16,650	265
10,348	7,794	9.6	17,738	404	1,542	2,070	165	†	†	129,506	13,882	13,481	266
15,833	13,895	31.3	18,091	11,637	†	3,415	2,262	219	167	351,762	20,444	21,120	267
15,574	1,364	10.7	15,618	1,320	†	3,329	398	†	19	233,778	15,362	16,098	268
12,740	25,000	41.8	37,740	†	2,699	†	†	†	†	127,268	20,702	21,133	269
12,117	9,157	29.5	15,275	5,999	†	2,352	1,293	†	82	194,590	15,048	15,616	270
7,850	15,868	40.6	23,718	†	1,550	†	†	†	†	72,749	12,598	13,177	271
19,383	4,382	19.9	14,213	9,552	†	3,353	1,632	485	341	1,599,619	20,766	21,002	272
20,105	9,063	28.8	20,327	8,841	†	2,659	1,328	353	201	507,095	22,563	23,594	273
25,178	2,801	15.0	21,627	6,352	51	4,835	1,452	86	329	699,868	25,803	26,214	274
32,915	6,336	32.0	27,375	11,876	†	7,287	2,560	475	528	2,544,218	35,369	35,407	275
19,469	4,075	14.6	19,585	3,959	†	4,133	730	174	180	629,014	20,840	21,061	276
22,768	3,283	7.1	19,510	6,541	†	3,157	1,499	337	159	537,966	23,145	24,003	277
5,801	12,744	37.5	18,545	†	1,503	†	†	†	†	197,817	10,075	10,080	278
36,391	4,402	10.9	29,438	11,355	†	6,316	1,996	648	666	1,787,249	37,768	38,129	279
20,910	6,592	15.4	22,916	4,586	†	3,181	1,236	†	90	338,920	22,628	23,464	280

[5]Data for total enrollment in 1990 are for institutions of higher education, rather than degree-granting institutions.
[6]Data included with parent institution or central office.
NOTE: Degree-granting institutions grant associateís or higher degrees and participate in Title IV federal financial aid programs.

SOURCE: U.S. Department of Education, National Center for Education Statistics, 1990 through 2005 Integrated Postsecondary Education Data System, "Fall Enrollment Survey" (IPEDS-EF:90), Spring 2001 through Spring 2006, and Fall 2005. (This table was prepared September 2006.)

Table 221. Enrollment and degrees conferred in degree-granting women's colleges, by selected characteristics and institution: Fall 2005 and 2004–05

Institution[1]	State	Type and control[2]	Enrollment, fall 2005							Degrees awarded to females, 2004–05			
			Total	Females	Percent female	Males, full-time	Females, full-time	Males, part-time	Females, part-time	Associate's	Bachelor's	Master's	Doctor's
1	2	3	4	5	6	7	8	9	10	11	12	13	14
Total.............................	†	†	90,402	84,977	94.0	1,909	60,074	3,516	24,903	858	13,439	4,134	109
Judson College....................	AL	3	331	317	95.8	4	253	10	64	0	70	†	†
Mills College......................	CA	3	1,372	1,277	93.1	88	1,186	7	91	0	183	99	2
Mount Saint Mary's College...	CA	3	2,480	2,263	91.3	105	1,651	112	612	118	284	53	†
Scripps College	CA	3	908	904	99.6	1	890	3	14	0	181	†	†
Saint Joseph College.............	CT	3	1,858	1,771	95.3	15	999	72	772	0	226	153	†
Trinity Washington University....	DC	3	1,621	1,451	89.5	37	719	133	732	0	145	221	†
Agnes Scott College	GA	3	1,016	1,004	98.8	4	885	8	119	0	184	14	†
Brenau University	GA	3	2,168	1,882	86.8	113	1,136	173	746	0	374	207	†
Spelman College	GA	3	2,318	2,300	99.2	18	2,205	0	95	0	498	†	†
Wesleyan College.................	GA	3	640	613	95.8	16	416	11	197	0	131	32	†
Lexington College..................	IL	3	56	56	100.0	0	45	0	11	3	4	†	†
Saint Mary-of-the-Woods College...........	IN	3	1,757	1,718	97.8	1	509	38	1,209	5	138	16	†
Saint Mary's College.............	IN	3	1,397	1,396	99.9	0	1,366	1	30	0	376	†	†
Midway College	KY	3	1,279	1,105	86.4	87	789	87	316	61	179	†	†
College of Notre Dame of Maryland...........	MD	3	3,358	2,932	87.3	12	647	414	2,285	0	246	252	†
Bay Path College..................	MA	3	1,456	1,434	98.5	14	1,185	8	249	126	197	35	†
Mount Holyoke College..........	MA	3	2,127	2,122	99.8	0	2,056	5	66	0	553	2	†
Pine Manor College	MA	3	455	454	99.8	0	447	1	7	3	89	†	†
Regis College	MA	3	1,303	1,248	95.8	16	765	39	483	88	223	59	†
Simmons College	MA	3	4,805	4,358	90.7	78	2,251	369	2,107	0	381	707	66
Smith College......................	MA	3	3,093	3,035	98.1	56	2,977	2	58	0	734	154	9
Wellesley College	MA	3	2,331	2,283	97.9	1	2,215	47	68	0	576	†	†
College of Saint Benedict	MN	3	2,045	2,045	100.0	0	1,993	0	52	0	504	†	†
College of St. Catherine	MN	3	4,907	4,653	94.8	93	2,976	161	1,677	194	518	244	†
Cottey College	MO	4	314	314	100.0	0	306	0	8	97	†	†	†
Stephens College..................	MO	3	826	795	96.2	19	602	12	193	1	102	15	†
College of Saint Mary	NE	3	955	955	100.0	0	655	0	300	97	111	†	†
College of Saint Elizabeth	NJ	3	1,858	1,685	90.7	39	781	134	904	0	252	155	†
Georgian Court College.........	NJ	3	3,153	2,765	87.7	107	1,461	281	1,304	0	354	177	†
Barnard College....................	NY	3	2,356	2,356	100.0	0	2,296	0	60	0	585	†	†
College of New Rochelle..........	NY	3	6,891	6,165	89.5	439	4,426	287	1,739	0	923	310	†
Marymount College of Fordham U......	NY	3	949	921	97.0	14	830	14	91	0	238	†	†
Wells College	NY	3	416	380	91.3	35	370	1	10	0	88	†	†
Bennett College for Women...	NC	3	572	572	100.0	0	566	0	6	0	68	†	†
Meredith College	NC	3	2,168	2,137	98.6	0	1,665	31	472	0	423	38	†
Peace College	NC	3	668	668	100.0	0	647	0	21	37	92	†	†
Salem College	NC	3	1,109	1,074	96.8	8	715	27	359	0	181	23	†
Ursuline College	OH	3	1,494	1,351	90.4	57	782	86	569	0	217	86	†
Bryn Mawr College	PA	3	1,799	1,687	93.8	78	1,493	34	194	0	320	111	14
Carlow College	PA	3	2,123	1,978	93.2	78	1,202	67	776	0	273	87	†
Cedar Crest College..............	PA	3	1,911	1,810	94.7	15	937	86	873	0	295	11	†
Chatham College	PA	3	1,440	1,282	89.0	56	794	102	488	0	103	149	18
Moore College of Art and Design	PA	3	493	489	99.2	0	423	4	66	0	112	†	†
Rosemont College	PA	3	1,048	922	88.0	7	484	119	438	0	113	110	†
Wilson College.....................	PA	3	732	648	88.5	14	334	70	314	13	86	†	†
Columbia College	SC	3	1,493	1,444	96.7	29	1,181	20	263	0	214	242	†
Converse College	SC	3	2,170	1,935	89.2	26	792	209	1,143	0	153	157	†
Hollins University	VA	3	1,123	1,062	94.6	16	851	45	211	0	178	64	†
Mary Baldwin College...........	VA	3	1,740	1,570	90.2	64	1,042	106	528	0	285	53	†
Randolph-Macon Woman's College...........	VA	3	712	712	100.0	0	685	0	27	0	155	†	†
Sweet Briar College	VA	3	752	716	95.2	31	681	5	35	0	126	†	†
Alverno College	WI	3	2,372	2,330	98.2	2	1,529	40	801	15	226	40	†
Mount Mary College	WI	3	1,684	1,633	97.0	16	983	35	650	0	172	58	†

†Not applicable.
[1]Data are for colleges and universities identified by the Women's College Coalition as women's colleges in 2006. Excludes women's colleges whose IPEDS data are reported together with a coed institution or coordinate men's college. The following institutions were excluded for this reason: The Women's College of the University of Denver; Newcomb College of Tulane University; Douglass College of Rutgers University; and Russell Sage College of the Sage Colleges.

[2]3 = private not-for-profit, 4-year; and 4 = private, not-for-profit, 2-year.
NOTE: Degree-granting institutions grant associate's or higher degrees and participate in Title IV federal financial aid programs.
SOURCE: U.S. Department of Education, National Center for Education Statistics, 2005 and 2004–05 Integrated Postsecondary Education Data System (IPEDS), Spring 2006 and Fall 2005. (This table was prepared September 2006.)

Table 222. Enrollment and degrees conferred in degree-granting institutions that serve large proportions of Hispanic students, by selected characteristics and institution: Fall 2005 and 2004–05

Institution	Type and control[1]	Enrollment, fall 2005					Degrees awarded to Hispanics, 2004–05				
		Total	Hispanic	Percent Hispanic[2]	Hispanic under-graduate	Hispanic postbacca-laureate	Associate's	Bachelor's	Master's	First-professional	Doctor's
1	2	3	4	5	6	7	8	9	10	11	12
Total, 50 states and District of Columbia[3]	†	2,173,034	915,027	42.1	872,358	42,669	42,585	30,618	7,895	474	211
Total, 50 states, District of Columbia, and Puerto Rico[3].....	†	2,379,875	1,121,514	47.1	1,051,840	69,674	46,855	47,229	11,936	1,023	413
Arizona											
Apollo College Inc., Phoenix....................	6	2,598	1,032	39.7	1,032	†	27	†	†	†	†
Arizona Automotive Institute	6	737	262	35.5	262	†	†	†	†	†	†
Arizona Western College	2	6,761	3,670	54.3	3,670	†	277	†	†	†	†
Art Center Design College-Tucson	5	321	99	30.8	99	†	2	5	†	†	†
Bryman School	6	1,429	542	37.9	542	†	204	†	†	†	†
Central Arizona College...........................	2	6,388	2,118	33.2	2,118	†	62	†	†	†	†
Chaparral College...................................	5	385	155	40.3	155	0	32	16	†	†	†
Cochise College	2	4,610	1,590	34.5	1,590	†	138	†	†	†	†
Estrella Mountain Community College	2	5,978	2,223	37.2	2,223	†	61	†	†	†	†
Everest College	5	804	272	33.8	272	†	36	†	†	†	†
Gateway Community College	2	7,846	2,162	27.6	2,162	†	56	†	†	†	†
International Institute of the Americas, Mesa...	3	319	96	30.1	96	†	13	2	†	†	†
International Institute of the Americas, Phoenix, N. 75th Ave.	3	378	139	36.8	139	†	6	1	†	†	†
International Institute of the Americas, Phoenix, E. 22nd St..........................	3	376	168	44.7	168	†	14	3	†	†	†
International Institute of the Americas, Tucson..	3	470	241	51.3	241	†	37	2	†	†	†
ITT Technical Institute.............................	5	469	173	36.9	173	†	26	4	†	†	†
Phoenix College	2	12,549	4,896	39.0	4,896	†	227	†	†	†	†
Pima Community College	2	30,884	9,638	31.2	9,638	†	473	†	†	†	†
Pima Medical Institute	6	690	335	48.6	335	†	25	†	†	†	†
Refrigeration School Inc.	6	307	102	33.2	102	†	11	†	†	†	†
Remington College	5	297	120	40.4	120	†	0	0	†	†	†
South Mountain Community College	2	4,561	1,931	42.3	1,931	†	114	†	†	†	†
Tucson Design College	5	101	32	31.7	32	†	3	†	†	†	†
University of Phoenix, Southern Arizona Campus	5	3,394	947	27.9	753	194	1	105	56	†	†
Arkansas											
Ecclesia College	3	234	126	53.8	126	†	†	0	†	†	†
California											
Allan Hancock College............................	2	12,252	4,320	35.3	4,320	†	349	†	†	†	†
American Intercontinental University	5	1,591	673	42.3	666	7	4	44	8	†	†
Antelope Valley College	2	11,638	3,288	28.3	3,288	†	175	†	†	†	†
Argosy University, Orange Campus..........	5	853	153	17.9	61	92	†	10	17	†	4
Art Institute of California, Los Angeles	5	2,103	787	37.4	787	†	56	29	†	†	†
Art Institute of California, Orange County.	5	1,757	465	26.5	465	†	11	26	†	†	†
Art Institute of California, San Diego	5	1,912	541	28.3	541	†	20	37	†	†	†
Bakersfield College.................................	2	14,725	6,642	45.1	6,642	†	325	†	†	†	†
Barstow Community College	2	2,957	796	26.9	796	†	104	†	†	†	†
Brooks College, Long Beach	6	826	297	36.0	297	†	194	†	†	†	†
Brooks College, Sunnyvale.....................	6	370	123	33.2	123	†	34	†	†	†	†
Brown Mackie College, Los Angeles	6	42	19	45.2	19	†	0	†	†	†	†
Brown Mackie College, Orange County....	6	54	33	61.1	33	†	0	†	†	†	†
Brown Mackie College, San Diego	6	58	32	55.2	32	†	0	†	†	†	†
Bryman College.......................................	6	696	416	59.8	416	†	†	†	†	†	†
Bryman College, City of Industry..............	6	797	692	86.8	692	†	1	†	†	†	†
Bryman College, West Los Angeles	6	430	188	43.7	188	†	1	†	†	†	†
Cabrillo College.......................................	2	14,369	3,740	26.0	3,740	†	162	†	†	†	†
California College, San Diego..................	5	409	119	29.1	119	†	17	0	†	†	†
California Design College	5	520	189	36.3	189	†	27	0	†	†	†
California School of Culinary Arts.............	6	1,726	735	42.6	735	†	58	†	†	†	†
California State Polytechnic University, Pomona	1	19,885	5,759	29.0	5,286	473	†	681	56	†	†
California State University, Bakersfield	1	7,549	2,771	36.7	2,328	443	†	355	81	†	†

See notes at end of table.

Table 222. Enrollment and degrees conferred in degree-granting institutions that serve large proportions of Hispanic students, by selected characteristics and institution: Fall 2005 and 2004–05—Continued

Institution	Type and control[1]	Enrollment, fall 2005					Degrees awarded to Hispanics, 2004–05				
		Total	Hispanic	Percent Hispanic[2]	Hispanic under-graduate	Hispanic postbacca-laureate	Associate's	Bachelor's	Master's	First-professional	Doctor's
1	2	3	4	5	6	7	8	9	10	11	12
California State University, Channel Islands	1	2,575	682	26.5	645	37	†	79	†	†	†
California State University, Dominguez Hills	1	12,357	4,663	37.7	3,698	965	†	537	207	†	†
California State University, Fresno	1	20,371	6,664	32.7	5,828	836	†	776	158	†	1
California State University, Fullerton	1	35,040	10,015	28.6	8,957	1,058	†	1,380	143	†	†
California State University, Long Beach	1	34,547	9,344	27.0	8,024	1,320	†	1,301	224	†	†
California State University, Los Angeles	1	20,034	9,812	49.0	7,733	2,079	†	1,003	241	†	†
California State University, Monterey Bay	1	3,773	1,195	31.7	1,111	84	†	169	5	†	†
California State University, Northridge	1	33,243	10,551	31.7	9,001	1,550	†	1,310	196	†	†
California State University, San Bernardino	1	16,431	5,850	35.6	4,820	1,030	†	749	119	†	†
California State University, Stanislaus	1	8,137	2,494	30.7	2,106	388	†	334	28	†	†
Canada College	2	5,551	2,223	40.0	2,223	†	53	†	†	†	†
Cerritos College	2	22,349	12,996	58.2	12,996	†	588	†	†	†	†
Chaffey College	2	17,188	7,798	45.4	7,798	†	418	†	†	†	†
Citrus College	2	11,937	5,375	45.0	5,375	†	252	†	†	†	†
College of the Canyons	2	15,947	4,333	27.2	4,333	†	144	†	†	†	†
College of the Desert	2	8,341	4,254	51.0	4,254	†	171	†	†	†	†
College of the Sequoias	2	10,317	4,874	47.2	4,874	†	284	†	†	†	†
Compton Community College	2	4,574	1,968	43.0	1,968	†	90	†	†	†	†
Concorde Career College, Garden Grove	6	527	156	29.6	156	†	0	†	†	†	†
Concorde Career College, North Hollywood	6	487	244	50.1	244	†	18	†	†	†	†
Concorde Career College, San Bernardino	6	717	328	45.7	328	†	0	†	†	†	†
Contra Costa College	2	6,670	1,743	26.1	1,743	†	68	†	†	†	†
Crafton Hills College	2	4,862	1,242	25.5	1,242	†	49	†	†	†	†
Cypress College	2	21,965	7,033	32.0	7,033	†	151	†	†	†	†
DeVry University, California	5	6,043	1,912	31.6	1,795	117	53	345	36	†	†
Don Bosco Technical Institute	4	310	185	59.7	185	†	65	†	†	†	†
East Los Angeles College	2	23,632	16,983	71.9	16,983	†	873	†	†	†	†
East San Gabriel Valley Regional Occupational Program	2	737	255	34.6	255	†	7	†	†	†	†
El Camino College	2	23,895	8,095	33.9	8,095	†	399	†	†	†	†
Everest College	6	1,031	576	55.9	576	†	46	†	†	†	†
Evergreen Valley College	2	9,699	3,089	31.8	3,089	†	103	†	†	†	†
Fashion Careers College	6	101	32	31.7	32	†	10	†	†	†	†
Fresno City College	2	21,917	10,058	45.9	10,058	†	428	†	†	†	†
Fresno Pacific University	3	1,996	498	24.9	311	187	0	87	19	†	†
Fullerton College	2	19,611	6,788	34.6	6,788	†	304	†	†	†	†
Gavilan College	2	4,854	2,204	45.4	2,204	†	97	†	†	†	†
Hartnell College	2	9,685	5,564	57.4	5,564	†	296	†	†	†	†
Heald College, Concord	4	639	164	25.7	164	†	47	†	†	†	†
Heald College, Fresno	4	729	352	48.3	352	†	100	†	†	†	†
Heald College, Hayward	4	864	288	33.3	288	†	77	†	†	†	†
Heald College, Salinas	4	414	301	72.7	301	†	91	†	†	†	†
Heald College, San Francisco	4	389	115	29.6	115	†	30	†	†	†	†
Heald College, San Jose	4	639	284	44.4	284	†	74	†	†	†	†
Heald College, Stockton	4	530	234	44.2	234	†	33	†	†	†	†
Humphreys College, Stockton	3	991	338	34.1	319	19	10	10	†	2	†
ITT Technical Institute, Anaheim	5	714	383	53.6	383	†	71	22	†	†	†
ITT Technical Institute, Lathrop	5	633	235	37.1	235	†	39	8	†	†	†
ITT Technical Institute, Oxnard	5	509	260	51.1	260	†	75	12	†	†	†
ITT Technical Institute, San Bernardino	5	1,084	599	55.3	599	†	119	25	†	†	†
ITT Technical Institute, San Diego	5	1,045	370	35.4	370	†	88	10	†	†	†
ITT Technical Institute, Sylmar	5	933	543	58.2	543	†	112	27	†	†	†
ITT Technical Institute, Torrance	5	681	387	56.8	387	†	106	20	†	†	†
ITT Technical Institute, West Covina	5	919	631	68.7	631	†	81	15	†	†	†
Imperial Valley College	2	7,796	6,929	88.9	6,929	†	285	†	†	†	†
Institute of Computer Technology	5	167	86	51.5	86	†	20	3	†	†	†
Interamerican College	3	40	38	95.0	27	11	†	6	†	†	†
La Sierra University	3	1,941	519	26.7	477	42	†	42	13	†	2

See notes at end of table.

Table 222. Enrollment and degrees conferred in degree-granting institutions that serve large proportions of Hispanic students, by selected characteristics and institution: Fall 2005 and 2004–05—Continued

Institution	Type and control[1]	Enrollment, fall 2005					Degrees awarded to Hispanics, 2004–05				
		Total	Hispanic	Percent Hispanic[2]	Hispanic under-graduate	Hispanic postbacca-laureate	Associate's	Bachelor's	Master's	First-professional	Doctor's
1	2	3	4	5	6	7	8	9	10	11	12
Long Beach City College	2	22,641	7,649	33.8	7,649	†	231	†	†	†	†
Los Angeles City College	2	16,283	6,583	40.4	6,583	†	250	†	†	†	†
Los Angeles County College of Nursing and Allied Health	2	272	76	27.9	76	†	40	†	†	†	†
Los Angeles Harbor College	2	8,761	3,889	44.4	3,889	†	206	†	†	†	†
Los Angeles Mission College	2	7,347	5,267	71.7	5,267	†	262	†	†	†	†
Los Angeles Pierce College	2	17,859	5,398	30.2	5,398	†	195	†	†	†	†
Los Angeles Trade Technical College	2	13,377	7,362	55.0	7,362	†	249	†	†	†	†
Los Angeles Valley College	2	16,130	6,726	41.7	6,726	†	298	†	†	†	†
Los Medanos College	2	8,073	2,006	24.8	2,006	†	57	†	†	†	†
Maric College, Anaheim	6	123	39	31.7	39	†	9	†	†	†	†
Maric College, Fresno	6	112	64	57.1	64	†	0	†	†	†	†
Maric College, Modesto Campus	6	624	295	47.3	295	†	7	†	†	†	†
Maric College, Palm Springs	6	143	73	51.0	73	†	0	†	†	†	†
Maric College, Panorama City	6	529	349	66.0	349	†	30	†	†	†	†
Maric College, Sacramento Campus	6	323	87	26.9	87	†	9	†	†	†	†
Maric College, San Diego	6	585	154	26.3	154	†	21	†	†	†	†
Maric College, Vista	6	373	133	35.7	133	†	1	†	†	†	†
Merced College	2	8,463	3,513	41.5	3,513	†	162	†	†	†	†
Modesto Junior College	2	17,810	5,727	32.2	5,727	†	267	†	†	†	†
Mount Saint Mary's College	3	2,480	1,126	45.4	958	168	69	127	15	†	†
Mount San Antonio College	2	27,195	11,902	43.8	11,902	†	485	†	†	†	†
Mount San Jacinto College	2	11,518	3,142	27.3	3,142	†	210	†	†	†	†
Mount Sierra College	5	715	298	41.7	298	†	†	36	†	†	†
National Hispanic University	3	549	458	83.4	389	69	†	7	†	†	†
National Institute of Technology	6	1,144	683	59.7	683	†	2	†	†	†	†
New School of Architecture and Design	5	365	71	19.5	55	16	0	0	5	†	†
Notre Dame de Namur University	3	1,588	315	19.8	217	98	†	32	23	†	†
Oxnard College	2	6,140	3,922	63.9	3,922	†	311	†	†	†	†
Pacific Oaks College	3	978	303	31.0	86	217	†	34	37	†	†
Palo Verde College	2	4,214	1,136	27.0	1,136	†	54	†	†	†	†
Pasadena City College	2	27,199	10,179	37.4	10,179	†	478	†	†	†	†
Pima Medical Institute	6	582	275	47.3	275	†	10	†	†	†	†
Platt College	6	109	46	42.2	46	†	36	†	†	†	†
Platt College, Los Angeles	5	225	139	61.8	139	†	51	4	†	†	†
Platt College, Ontario	5	426	235	55.2	235	†	87	12	†	†	†
Platt College, San Diego	5	253	68	26.9	68	†	24	20	†	†	†
Porterville College	2	3,814	2,002	52.5	2,002	†	122	†	†	†	†
Reedley College	2	11,374	5,722	50.3	5,722	†	314	†	†	†	†
Remington College, San Diego Campus	5	242	104	43.0	104	†	22	0	0	†	†
Rio Hondo College	2	19,012	12,544	66.0	12,544	†	505	†	†	†	†
Riverside Community College	2	29,160	10,928	37.5	10,928	†	598	†	†	†	†
Sage College	6	387	130	33.6	130	†	0	†	†	†	†
San Bernardino Valley College	2	12,390	5,266	42.5	5,266	†	288	†	†	†	†
San Diego City College	2	15,204	5,004	32.9	5,004	†	139	†	†	†	†
San Diego State University, Imperial Valley Campus	1	911	803	88.1	597	206	†	180	6	†	†
San Joaquin Delta College	2	16,949	4,784	28.2	4,784	†	336	†	†	†	†
San Joaquin Valley College	6	876	512	58.4	512	†	174	†	†	†	†
San Joaquin Valley College, Bakersfield	6	708	366	51.7	366	†	102	†	†	†	†
San Joaquin Valley College, Fresno	6	651	349	53.6	349	†	178	†	†	†	†
San Joaquin Valley College, Modesto Campus	6	184	76	41.3	76	†	0	†	†	†	†
San Joaquin Valley College, Rancho Cucamonga	6	613	382	62.3	382	†	43	†	†	†	†
San Jose City College	2	9,073	3,098	34.1	3,098	†	71	†	†	†	†
Santa Ana College	2	32,096	15,705	48.9	15,705	†	680	†	†	†	†
Santa Barbara Business College, Bakersfield	6	501	248	49.5	248	†	10	†	†	†	†
Santa Barbara Business College, Santa Barbara	6	412	256	62.1	256	†	16	†	†	†	†
Santa Barbara Business College, Santa Maria Branch	6	394	181	45.9	181	†	8	†	†	†	†

See notes at end of table.

Table 222. Enrollment and degrees conferred in degree-granting institutions that serve large proportions of Hispanic students, by selected characteristics and institution: Fall 2005 and 2004–05—Continued

Institution	Type and control[1]	Enrollment, fall 2005					Degrees awarded to Hispanics, 2004–05				
		Total	Hispanic	Percent Hispanic[2]	Hispanic undergraduate	Hispanic postbacca-laureate	Associate's	Bachelor's	Master's	First-professional	Doctor's
1	2	3	4	5	6	7	8	9	10	11	12
Santa Monica College	2	28,908	8,389	29.0	8,389	†	350	†	†	†	†
Santiago Canyon College	2	12,152	4,971	40.9	4,971	†	150	†	†	†	†
Silicon Valley College, Fremont	5	264	68	25.8	68	†	28	9	†	†	†
Silicon Valley College, San Jose	5	422	175	41.5	175	†	†	†	†	†	†
South Coast College	6	368	120	32.6	120	†	4	†	†	†	†
Southern California Institute of Technology	5	319	85	26.6	85	†	28	29	†	†	†
Southwestern College	2	19,324	11,852	61.3	11,852	†	586	†	†	†	†
Taft College	2	8,466	3,721	44.0	3,721	†	44	†	†	†	†
Trinity Life Bible College	3	185	43	23.2	43	†	1	0	†	†	†
University of California, Merced	1	878	222	25.3	213	9	†	0	†	†	†
University of California, Riverside	1	16,622	3,942	23.7	3,712	230	†	685	43	†	9
University of La Verne	3	8,148	2,880	35.3	1,812	1,068	0	264	177	12	1
University of Phoenix, Central Valley Campus	5	1,889	661	35.0	579	82	†	39	8	†	†
University of Phoenix, Southern California Campus	5	16,135	4,646	28.8	3,871	775	0	308	83	†	†
Ventura College	2	11,261	4,373	38.8	4,373	†	305	†	†	†	†
Victor Valley Community College	2	10,486	2,977	28.4	2,977	†	219	†	†	†	†
West Coast University	5	157	57	36.3	57	†	11	4	†	†	†
West Hills Community College	2	4,842	2,208	45.6	2,208	†	184	†	†	†	†
West Los Angeles College	2	8,772	2,389	27.2	2,389	†	100	†	†	†	†
Westwood College, Anaheim	5	1,024	540	52.7	540	†	40	23	†	†	†
Westwood College, Inland Empire	5	1,374	819	59.6	819	†	36	35	†	†	†
Westwood College, Long Beach	5	554	355	64.1	355	†	44	0	†	†	†
Westwood College, Los Angeles	5	1,065	728	68.4	728	†	36	24	†	†	†
Whittier College	3	2,299	586	25.5	392	194	†	60	10	27	†
Woodbury University	3	1,436	466	32.5	438	28	†	88	17	†	†
WyoTech, Fremont	6	1,704	619	36.3	619	†	80	†	†	†	†
WyoTech, West Sacramento	6	709	186	26.2	186	†	36	†	†	†	†
Yuba College	2	8,799	2,334	26.5	2,334	†	173	†	†	†	†
Colorado											
Adams State College	1	9,157	1,337	14.6	808	529	5	58	34	†	†
College America, Denver	5	444	128	28.8	128	†	37	1	†	†	†
Colorado State University, Pueblo	1	5,870	1,459	24.9	1,308	151	†	182	7	†	†
Community College of Denver	2	8,909	2,362	26.5	2,362	†	75	†	†	†	†
Denver Automotive and Diesel College	6	1,100	293	26.6	293	†	86	†	†	†	†
Denver Career College	6	320	138	43.1	138	†	9	†	†	†	†
Heritage College	6	496	126	25.4	126	†	42	†	†	†	†
Intellitec College, Grand Junction	6	486	135	27.8	135	†	9	†	†	†	†
Otero Junior College	2	1,636	496	30.3	496	†	50	†	†	†	†
Parks College	6	964	333	34.5	333	†	27	†	†	†	†
Pima Medical Institute	6	661	169	25.6	169	†	6	†	†	†	†
Pueblo Community College	2	5,395	1,871	34.7	1,871	†	145	†	†	†	†
Remington College	5	155	78	50.3	78	†	13	†	†	†	†
Trinidad State Junior College	2	1,831	782	42.7	782	†	81	†	†	†	†
Connecticut											
Capital Community College	2	3,573	960	26.9	960	†	57	†	†	†	†
Gibbs College	6	950	250	26.3	250	†	85	†	†	†	†
Florida											
ATI College of Health	6	498	140	28.1	140	†	9	†	†	†	†
Acupuncture and Massage College	5	228	122	53.5	111	11	†	†	†	†	†
Ai Miami International University of Art and Design	5	1,486	1,023	68.8	986	37	52	43	4	†	†
American Intercontinental University	5	1,164	394	33.8	366	28	1	30	33	†	†
Americare School of Nursing	6	241	64	26.6	64	†	0	†	†	†	†
Argosy University, Tampa Campus	5	594	63	10.6	11	52	†	3	2	†	1
Art Institute of Fort Lauderdale Inc.	5	3,261	1,155	35.4	1,155	†	100	108	†	†	†
Barry University	3	9,324	3,047	32.7	2,220	827	†	556	181	21	4
Carlos Albizu University, Miami Campus	3	1,013	818	80.8	332	486	†	91	77	†	13

See notes at end of table.

Table 222. Enrollment and degrees conferred in degree-granting institutions that serve large proportions of Hispanic students, by selected characteristics and institution: Fall 2005 and 2004–05—Continued

Institution	Type and control[1]	Enrollment, fall 2005					Degrees awarded to Hispanics, 2004–05				
		Total	Hispanic	Percent Hispanic[2]	Hispanic under-graduate	Hispanic postbacca-laureate	Associate's	Bachelor's	Master's	First-professional	Doctor's
1	2	3	4	5	6	7	8	9	10	11	12
City College, Casselberry	4	187	51	27.3	51	†	28	†	†	†	†
City College, Miami	3	291	195	67.0	195	†	65	3	†	†	†
College of Business and Technology	6	119	102	85.7	102	†	3	†	†	†	†
DeVry University, Florida	5	2,832	809	28.6	709	100	31	55	21	†	†
Florida Career College	6	2,881	1,332	46.2	1,332	†	166	†	†	†	†
Florida College of Natural Health	6	166	106	63.9	106	†	35	†	†	†	†
Florida International University	1	36,904	20,869	56.5	18,381	2,488	3	2,677	715	23	20
Florida Metropolitan University, South Orlando	5	2,671	687	25.7	687	0	166	37	20	†	†
Florida Metropolitan University, Tampa.....	5	1,436	436	30.4	428	8	77	11	9	†	†
Florida National College	6	1,822	1,703	93.5	1,703	†	200	†	†	†	†
Herzing College	5	171	50	29.2	50	†	3	0	†	†	†
High-Tech Institute, Orlando	6	1,066	293	27.5	293	†	105	†	†	†	†
ITT Technical Institute, Fort Lauderdale ...	5	542	169	31.2	169	†	24	4	†	†	†
ITT Technical Institute, Miami	5	527	416	78.9	416	†	119	35	†	†	†
International Academy of Design and Technology	5	1,041	301	28.9	301	†	52	6	†	†	†
Jones College, Miami Campus.................	3	111	57	51.4	57	†	†	†	†	†	†
Le Cordon Bleu College of Culinary Arts, Miami	6	636	308	48.4	308	†	0	†	†	†	†
Medvance Institute, Miami	6	221	116	52.5	116	†	†	†	†	†	†
Miami Ad School.....................................	5	187	47	25.1	45	2	†	†	†	†	†
Miami Dade College	1	54,169	35,414	65.4	35,414	†	4,073	2	†	†	†
National School of Technology Inc., Hialeah	6	801	656	81.9	656	†	†	†	†	†	†
National School of Technology Inc., Miami	6	749	516	68.9	516	†	†	†	†	†	†
Nova Southeastern University	3	26,335	4,563	17.3	1,465	3,098	0	297	573	154	70
Saint John Vianney College Seminary	3	50	12	24.0	10	2	†	4	†	†	†
Saint Thomas University..........................	3	2,692	1,000	37.1	524	476	†	142	79	63	†
Trinity International University..................	3	312	117	37.5	91	26	†	32	4	†	†
Illinois											
City Colleges of Chicago, Harry S Truman College	2	12,518	6,399	51.1	6,399	†	39	†	†	†	†
City Colleges of Chicago, Malcolm X College	2	7,149	2,090	29.2	2,090	†	37	†	†	†	†
City Colleges of Chicago, Richard J. Daley College	2	9,977	6,577	65.9	6,577	†	149	†	†	†	†
City Colleges of Chicago, Wilbur Wright College	2	11,122	5,405	48.6	5,405	†	155	†	†	†	†
Fox College Inc.	6	202	114	56.4	114	†	61	†	†	†	†
ITT Technical Institute, Burr Ridge...........	5	328	109	33.2	109	†	37	0	†	†	†
ITT Technical Institute, Mount Prospect.....	5	547	157	28.7	157	†	26	6	†	†	†
Lexington College	3	56	17	30.4	17	†	0	1	†	†	†
Morton College	2	4,744	3,520	74.2	3,520	†	167	†	†	†	†
Northeastern Illinois University................	1	12,227	3,135	25.6	2,799	336	†	277	47	†	†
Northwestern Business College	6	1,126	354	31.4	354	†	38	†	†	†	†
Northwestern Business College, Southwestern Campus	6	1,060	335	31.6	335	†	34	†	†	†	†
Saint Augustine College	3	1,542	1,280	83.0	1,280	†	203	16	†	†	†
Westwood College, Chicago Loop...........	5	623	238	38.2	238	†	1	0	†	†	†
Westwood College, O'Hare Airport..........	5	604	237	39.2	237	†	28	5	†	†	†
Indiana											
Sawyer College, Hammond	6	552	158	28.6	158	†	13	†	†	†	†
Kansas											
Donnelly College	4	474	168	35.4	168	†	15	†	†	†	†
Seward County Community College.........	2	1,705	397	23.3	397	†	34	†	†	†	†
Massachusetts											
Cambridge College................................	3	4,480	674	15.0	247	427	†	13	102	†	†
Urban College of Boston	4	789	445	56.4	445	†	17	†	†	†	†

See notes at end of table.

Table 222. Enrollment and degrees conferred in degree-granting institutions that serve large proportions of Hispanic students, by selected characteristics and institution: Fall 2005 and 2004–05—Continued

Institution	Type and control[1]	Enrollment, fall 2005					Degrees awarded to Hispanics, 2004–05				
		Total	Hispanic	Percent Hispanic[2]	Hispanic under-graduate	Hispanic postbacca-laureate	Associate's	Bachelor's	Master's	First-professional	Doctor's
1	2	3	4	5	6	7	8	9	10	11	12
Minnesota											
Walden University....................................	5	22,168	2,016	9.1	1,011	1,005	†	0	116	†	4
Nevada											
Heritage College....................................	6	227	60	26.4	60	†	5	†	†	†	†
International Academy of Design and Technology....................................	5	378	93	24.6	93	†	0	0	†	†	†
Las Vegas College, Henderson, 170 N. Stephaine, St. Suite 145....................	6	243	80	32.9	80	†	1	†	†	†	†
Las Vegas College, Henderson, 170 N. Stephanie St....................................	6	245	94	38.4	94	†	0	†	†	†	†
New Jersey											
Berkeley College....................................	5	2,422	845	34.9	845	†	102	66	†	†	†
Hudson County Community College	2	6,447	3,021	46.9	3,021	†	165	†	†	†	†
New Jersey City University	1	8,464	2,627	31.0	2,167	460	†	250	82	†	†
Passaic County Community College	2	7,169	3,500	48.8	3,500	†	127	†	†	†	†
Saint Peters College	3	2,931	779	26.6	650	129	10	74	57	†	†
Union County College....................	2	10,976	3,074	28.0	3,074	†	88	†	†	†	†
University of Phoenix, Jersey City Campus	5	383	101	26.4	101	†	†	0	†	†	†
New Mexico											
Albuquerque Technical Vocational Institute	2	23,107	10,269	44.4	10,269	†	393	†	†	†	†
Art Center Design College, Albuquerque .	5	257	110	42.8	110	†	2	2	†	†	†
Clovis Community College....................	2	3,937	1,142	29.0	1,142	†	68	†	†	†	†
College of the Southwest....................	3	627	196	31.3	178	18	†	34	7	†	†
Eastern New Mexico University, Main Campus	1	4,033	1,128	28.0	979	149	1	109	20	†	†
Eastern New Mexico University, Roswell Campus	2	4,242	1,813	42.7	1,813	†	97	†	†	†	†
ITT Technical Institute....................	5	643	292	45.4	292	†	75	11	†	†	†
International Institute of the Americas	3	388	258	66.5	258	†	12	0	†	†	†
Luna Community College....................	2	2,175	1,838	84.5	1,838	†	72	†	†	†	†
Mesalands Community College................	2	533	194	36.4	194	†	6	†	†	†	†
Metropolitan College....................	3	134	65	48.5	65	†	28	2	†	†	†
National American University, Albuquerque	5	315	115	36.5	115	†	7	14	†	†	†
National American University, Rio Rancho	5	231	93	40.3	93	†	3	24	†	†	†
New Mexico Highlands University.............	1	3,595	1,896	52.7	1,171	725	1	179	84	†	†
New Mexico Junior College	2	2,510	1,047	41.7	1,047	†	74	†	†	†	†
New Mexico State University, Alamogordo	2	1,915	635	33.2	635	†	42	†	†	†	†
New Mexico State University, Carlsbad	2	1,226	550	44.9	550	†	40	†	†	†	†
New Mexico State University, Dona Ana...	2	6,570	4,649	70.8	4,649	†	283	†	†	†	†
New Mexico State University, Grants........	2	608	219	36.0	219	†	19	†	†	†	†
New Mexico State University, Main Campus	1	16,072	7,715	48.0	6,416	1,299	16	890	218	†	14
Northern New Mexico College.................	1	2,196	1,577	71.8	1,577	†	80	0	†	†	†
Pima Medical Institute	6	521	270	51.8	270	†	8	†	†	†	†
Santa Fe Community College.................	2	3,894	1,643	42.2	1,643	†	86	†	†	†	†
University of New Mexico, Los Alamos Campus	2	749	332	44.3	332	†	35	†	†	†	†
University of New Mexico, Main Campus..	1	26,172	8,433	32.2	6,832	1,601	6	933	240	63	25
University of New Mexico, Taos Branch	2	1,186	683	57.6	683	†	31	†	†	†	†
University of New Mexico, Valencia County Branch	2	1,582	949	60.0	949	†	50	†	†	†	†
University of Phoenix, New Mexico Campus	5	4,724	2,892	61.2	2,312	580	1	301	124	†	†
Western New Mexico University	1	2,753	1,250	45.4	1,104	146	56	48	29	†	†
New York											
Art Institute of New York City	6	1,477	517	35.0	517	†	78	†	†	†	†

See notes at end of table.

Table 222. Enrollment and degrees conferred in degree-granting institutions that serve large proportions of Hispanic students, by selected characteristics and institution: Fall 2005 and 2004–05—Continued

Institution	Type and control[1]	Total	Hispanic	Percent Hispanic[2]	Hispanic under-graduate	Hispanic postbacca-laureate	Associate's	Bachelor's	Master's	First-professional	Doctor's
1	2	3	4	5	6	7	8	9	10	11	12
ASA Institute of Business and Computer Technology	6	2,977	1,103	37.1	1,103	†	319	†	†	†	†
Berkeley College	5	2,931	803	27.4	803	†	71	128	†	†	†
Boricua College	3	1,142	1,005	88.0	965	40	151	117	3	†	†
CUNY, Borough of Manhattan Community College	2	18,776	5,530	29.5	5,530	†	532	†	†	†	†
CUNY, Bronx Community College	2	8,470	4,005	47.3	4,005	†	364	†	†	†	†
CUNY, City College	1	12,360	3,473	28.1	2,836	637	†	343	120	†	†
CUNY, Hostos Community College	2	4,477	2,538	56.7	2,538	†	244	†	†	†	†
CUNY, John Jay College Criminal Justice	1	14,295	5,058	35.4	4,772	286	31	452	51	†	†
CUNY, La Guardia Community College	2	13,489	4,654	34.5	4,654	†	471	†	†	†	†
CUNY, Lehman College	1	10,615	4,511	42.5	3,906	605	†	452	122	†	†
CUNY, New York City College of Technology	1	12,439	3,045	24.5	3,045	†	212	112	†	†	†
College of Mount Saint Vincent	3	1,855	512	27.6	450	62	1	68	25	†	†
DeVry Institute of Technology & Keller Graduate School	5	1,515	421	27.8	378	43	31	58	6	†	†
Interboro Institute	6	4,326	2,218	51.3	2,218	†	171	†	†	†	†
Katharine Gibbs School, New York City	6	2,039	796	39.0	796	†	362	†	†	†	†
Mercy College, Main Campus	3	9,539	2,658	27.9	1,853	805	48	378	318	†	†
Monroe College, Main Campus	5	4,285	2,348	54.8	2,348	†	528	231	†	†	†
Plaza College	6	736	236	32.1	236	†	78	†	†	†	†
Professional Business College	4	564	204	36.2	204	†	5	†	†	†	†
Taylor Business Institute	6	631	227	36.0	227	†	63	†	†	†	†
Technical Career Institutes	6	2,994	1,436	48.0	1,436	†	359	†	†	†	†
The College of Westchester	6	1,039	326	31.4	326	†	88	†	†	†	†
Vaughn College of Aeronautics and Technology	3	1,126	464	41.2	464	†	35	38	†	†	†
Wood Tobe, Coburn School	6	269	149	55.4	149	†	49	†	†	†	†
Oregon											
DeVry University, Oregon	5	167	46	27.5	44	2	†	0	0	†	†
Mount Angel Seminary	3	206	45	21.8	37	8	†	4	2	2	†
Pennsylvania											
Pace Institute	6	192	64	33.3	64	†	10	†	†	†	†
Pennsylvania School of Business	6	77	43	55.8	43	†	3	†	†	†	†
Texas											
Academy of Health Care Professions	6	357	126	35.3	126	†	4	†	†	†	†
ATI Career Training Center	6	689	178	25.8	178	†	4	†	†	†	†
American Intercontinental University	5	468	169	36.1	164	5	0	2	0	†	†
Art Institute of Houston	5	1,657	478	28.8	478	†	101	6	†	†	†
Austin Business College	6	342	192	56.1	192	†	20	†	†	†	†
Baptist University of the Americas	3	208	155	74.5	155	†	†	23	†	†	†
Bradford School of Business	6	134	86	64.2	86	†	0	†	†	†	†
Center for Advanced Legal Studies	5	74	20	27.0	17	3	12	†	†	†	†
Coastal Bend College	2	3,366	2,177	64.7	2,177	†	138	†	†	0	†
Computer Career Center	6	269	235	87.4	235	†	0	†	†	†	†
Del Mar College	2	12,006	7,002	58.3	7,002	†	389	†	†	†	†
El Centro College	2	6,166	1,760	28.5	1,760	†	87	†	†	†	†
El Paso Community College	2	26,667	22,690	85.1	22,690	†	1,443	†	†	†	†
Everest College	6	838	319	38.1	319	†	14	†	†	†	†
Hallmark Institute of Technology	6	771	476	61.7	476	†	231	†	†	†	†
Houston Community College System	2	39,516	11,296	28.6	11,296	†	470	†	†	†	†
Howard College	2	2,721	861	31.6	861	†	62	†	†	†	†
ITT Technical Institute, Arlington	6	666	193	29.0	193	†	35	†	†	†	†
ITT Technical Institute, Austin	6	758	266	35.1	266	†	81	†	†	†	†
ITT Technical Institute, Houston, S. Gessner	6	405	166	41.0	166	†	77	†	†	†	†
ITT Technical Institute, Houston, Blue Ash Dr.	6	380	150	39.5	150	†	71	†	†	†	†
ITT Technical Institute, Houston, Bay Area Blvd.	6	353	131	37.1	131	†	75	†	†	†	†

See notes at end of table.

Table 222. Enrollment and degrees conferred in degree-granting institutions that serve large proportions of Hispanic students, by selected characteristics and institution: Fall 2005 and 2004–05—Continued

Institution	Type and control[1]	Enrollment, fall 2005					Degrees awarded to Hispanics, 2004–05				
		Total	Hispanic	Percent Hispanic[2]	Hispanic under-graduate	Hispanic postbacca-laureate	Associate's	Bachelor's	Master's	First-professional	Doctor's
1	2	3	4	5	6	7	8	9	10	11	12
ITT Technical Institute, Richardson...........	6	696	212	30.5	212	†	72	†	†	†	†
ITT Technical Institute, San Antonio	6	750	421	56.1	421	†	132	†	†	†	†
International Business College	6	658	598	90.9	598	†	†	†	†	†	†
Laredo Community College	2	8,298	7,808	94.1	7,808	†	754	†	†	†	†
MTI College of Business and Technology, Houston, Regency Sq......................	6	348	166	47.7	166	†	86	†	†	†	†
MTI College of Business and Technology, Houston, Space Park........................	6	136	61	44.9	61	†	47	†	†	†	†
Midland College....................................	1	5,589	1,731	31.0	1,731	†	256	†	†	†	†
Mountain View College...........................	2	6,494	2,926	45.1	2,926	†	139	†	†	†	†
Northwest Vista College.........................	2	8,870	3,808	42.9	3,808	†	154	†	†	†	†
Odessa College	2	4,849	2,171	44.8	2,171	†	154	†	†	†	†
Our Lady of the Lake University, San Antonio	3	2,872	1,894	65.9	1,345	549	†	237	166	†	4
Palo Alto College	2	7,714	4,760	61.7	4,760	†	262	†	†	†	†
Remington College, Dallas Campus.........	6	861	256	29.7	256	†	18	†	†	†	†
Remington College, Houston Campus	6	962	350	36.4	350	†	16	†	†	†	†
Remington College, North Houston Campus	6	201	65	32.3	65	†	0	†	†	†	†
Saint Edward's University	3	4,947	1,407	28.4	1,241	166	†	208	39	†	†
Saint Mary's University	3	3,925	2,172	55.3	1,669	503	†	334	85	59	2
Saint Philip's College	2	9,792	4,673	47.7	4,673	†	297	†	†	†	†
San Antonio College................................	2	19,933	9,019	45.2	9,019	†	394	†	†	†	†
San Jacinto College, Central Campus......	2	24,322	7,938	32.6	7,938	†	418	†	†	†	†
South Plains College	2	9,273	2,366	25.5	2,366	†	67	†	†	†	†
South Texas College	1	16,233	15,409	94.9	15,409	†	1,135	†	†	†	†
Southwest Institute of Technology	6	48	21	43.8	21	†	7	†	†	†	†
Southwest Texas Junior College..............	2	5,067	4,118	81.3	4,118	†	366	†	†	†	†
Sul Ross State University	1	2,927	1,751	59.8	1,322	429	1	236	98	†	†
Texas A & M International University	1	4,298	3,845	89.5	3,061	784	†	601	132	†	†
Texas A & M University, Corpus Christi	1	8,365	3,148	37.6	2,538	610	†	442	158	†	5
Texas A & M University, Kingsville	1	6,662	4,041	60.7	3,404	637	†	646	157	†	11
Texas Culinary Academy	6	894	256	28.6	256	†	121	†	†	†	†
Texas State Technical College, Harlingen.	2	4,209	3,745	89.0	3,745	†	242	†	†	†	†
University of Texas Health Science, San Antonio	1	2,781	713	25.6	261	452	†	122	34	47	4
University of Texas at Brownsville............	1	13,316	12,070	90.6	11,449	621	†	640	128	†	†
University of Texas at El Paso.................	1	19,268	14,061	73.0	12,220	1,841	†	1,169	384	†	5
University of Texas at San Antonio	1	27,337	12,337	45.1	10,842	1,495	†	1,514	304	†	3
University of Texas of the Permian Basin..	1	3,406	1,176	34.5	981	195	†	184	22	†	†
University of Texas, Pan American	1	17,048	15,037	88.2	13,326	1,711	0	1,666	451	†	7
University of Houston, Downtown.............	1	11,484	4,176	36.4	4,154	22	†	458	10	†	†
University of Phoenix, San Antonio Campus	5	356	181	50.8	148	33	†	0	†	†	†
University of Saint Thomas......................	3	3,705	1,002	27.0	593	409	†	92	49	1	0
University of the Incarnate Word	3	5,046	2,837	56.2	2,501	336	2	353	83	†	2
Victoria College	2	4,006	1,295	32.3	1,295	†	65	†	†	†	†
Virginia College at Austin.......................	6	769	285	37.1	285	†	44	†	†	†	†
Western Technical College, El Paso, Diana Dr...	6	413	287	69.5	287	†	111	†	†	†	†
Western Technical College, El Paso, Texas St.	6	568	500	88.0	500	†	200	†	†	†	†
Westwood College, Dallas......................	6	702	179	25.5	179	†	52	†	†	†	†
Westwood College, Ft. Worth	6	515	166	32.2	166	†	33	†	†	†	†
Westwood College, Houston South	6	343	129	37.6	129	†	2	†	†	†	†
Utah											
Eagle Gate College	6	166	92	55.4	92	†	0	†	†	†	†
Neumont University	5	67	44	65.7	44	†	†	0	†	†	†
Washington											
Heritage University	3	1,311	520	39.7	428	92	9	54	32	†	†
Yakima Valley Community College...........	2	4,433	1,284	29.0	1,284	†	148	†	†	†	†

See notes at end of table.

Table 222. Enrollment and degrees conferred in degree-granting institutions that serve large proportions of Hispanic students, by selected characteristics and institution: Fall 2005 and 2004–05—Continued

Institution	Type and control[1]	Total	Hispanic	Percent Hispanic[2]	Hispanic undergraduate	Hispanic postbacca-laureate	Associate's	Bachelor's	Master's	First-professional	Doctor's
1	2	3	4	5	6	7	8	9	10	11	12
Puerto Rico											
American University of Puerto Rico, Bayamon	3	1,775	1,769	99.7	1,743	26	22	139	5	†	†
American University of Puerto Rico, Manati	3	1,609	1,609	100.0	1,609	†	19	111	0	†	†
Atlantic College	3	783	783	100.0	725	58	20	98	22	†	†
Bayamon Central University	3	2,913	2,913	100.0	2,446	467	18	284	140	†	†
Caguas Institute of Mechanical Technology	6	2,568	2,568	100.0	2,568	†	†	†	†	†	†
Caribbean University, Bayamon	3	1,603	1,603	100.0	1,358	245	30	98	77	†	†
Caribbean University, Carolina	3	930	930	100.0	544	386	40	31	71	†	†
Caribbean University, Ponce	3	1,338	1,338	100.0	917	421	10	30	126	†	†
Caribbean University, Vega Baja	3	1,217	1,217	100.0	648	569	20	44	112	†	†
Carlos Albizu University	3	857	857	100.0	166	691	†	58	74	†	82
Centro de Estudios Multidisciplinarios, Humacao	4	412	412	100.0	412	†	0	†	†	†	†
Centro de Estudios Multidisciplinarios, San Juan	4	1,687	1,687	100.0	1,687	†	152	†	†	†	†
Colegio Biblico Pentecostal de Puerto Rico	3	227	212	93.4	212	†	†	24	†	†	†
Colegio Pentecostal Mizpa	3	240	240	100.0	240	†	12	10	†	†	†
Colegio Universitario de San Juan	1	961	961	100.0	961	†	139	30	†	†	†
Colegio de las Ciencias Arte y Television.	6	381	381	100.0	381	†	0	†	†	†	†
Columbia College, Caguas	5	836	836	100.0	787	49	91	100	†	†	†
Columbia College, Yauco	5	388	388	100.0	388	†	69	6	†	†	†
EDIC College	6	376	376	100.0	376	†	0	†	†	†	†
EDP College of Puerto Rico Inc., San Sebastian	5	687	687	100.0	687	†	85	40	†	†	†
Electronic Data Processing College of Puerto Rico	5	911	911	100.0	835	76	45	40	9	†	†
Escuela de Artes Plasticas de Puerto Rico	1	459	459	100.0	459	†	†	38	†	†	†
Huertas Junior College	6	1,541	1,541	100.0	1,541	†	357	†	†	†	†
Humacao Community College	4	512	512	100.0	512	†	109	†	†	†	†
ICPR Junior College, Arecibo	6	395	395	100.0	395	†	74	†	†	†	†
ICPR Junior College, General Institutional	6	371	370	99.7	370	†	85	†	†	†	†
ICPR Junior College, Mayaguez	6	458	458	100.0	458	†	148	†	†	†	†
Instituto Tecnologico de Puerto Rico, Recinto de Guayama	2	669	669	100.0	669	†	161	†	†	†	†
Instituto Tecnologico de Puerto Rico, Recinto de Ponce	2	898	898	100.0	898	†	193	†	†	†	†
Instituto Tecnologico de Puerto Rico, Recinto de San Juan	2	690	690	100.0	690	†	142	†	†	†	†
Inter American University of Puerto Rico, Aguadilla	3	4,183	4,183	100.0	4,104	79	45	320	†	†	†
Inter American University of Puerto Rico, Arecibo	3	4,761	4,761	100.0	4,487	274	42	390	40	†	†
Inter American University of Puerto Rico, Barranqui	3	2,373	2,373	100.0	2,343	30	18	230	†	†	†
Inter American University of Puerto Rico, Bayamon	3	5,255	5,255	100.0	5,202	53	31	477	†	†	†
Inter American University of Puerto Rico, Fajardo	3	2,239	2,239	100.0	2,238	1	28	190	†	†	†
Inter American University of Puerto Rico, Guayama	3	2,270	2,270	100.0	2,221	49	59	255	12	†	†
Inter American University of Puerto Rico, Metro	3	10,474	10,474	100.0	6,756	3,718	37	855	740	†	23
Inter American University of Puerto Rico, Ponce	3	5,415	5,415	100.0	5,204	211	71	437	†	†	†
Inter American University of Puerto Rico, San Germa	3	6,134	6,134	100.0	4,965	1,169	51	551	225	†	12
International Junior College	6	207	207	100.0	207	†	20	†	†	†	†
John Dewey College, University Division	3	958	958	100.0	958	†	41	8	†	†	†
National College of Business and Technology, Arecibo	5	1,439	1,439	100.0	1,439	†	199	79	†	†	†

See notes at end of table.

Table 222. Enrollment and degrees conferred in degree-granting institutions that serve large proportions of Hispanic students, by selected characteristics and institution: Fall 2005 and 2004–05—Continued

Institution	Type and control[1]	Enrollment, fall 2005					Degrees awarded to Hispanics, 2004–05				
		Total	Hispanic	Percent Hispanic[2]	Hispanic under-graduate	Hispanic postbacca-laureate	Associate's	Bachelor's	Master's	First-professional	Doctor's
1	2	3	4	5	6	7	8	9	10	11	12
National College of Business and Technology, Bayamon	5	2,102	2,102	100.0	2,102	†	437	35	†	†	†
National College of Business and Technology, Rio Grande	6	873	873	100.0	873	†	58	†	†	†	†
Ponce Paramedical College Inc	6	2,465	2,465	100.0	2,465	†	61	†	†	†	†
Pontifical Catholic University of Puerto Rico, Arecibo	3	851	851	100.0	630	221	1	55	†	†	†
Pontifical Catholic University of Puerto Rico, Mayaguez	3	1,782	1,782	100.0	1,548	234	4	183	14	†	†
Pontifical Catholic University of Puerto Rico, Ponce	3	7,474	7,474	100.0	5,363	2,111	12	725	159	145	13
Puerto Rico Conservatory of Music	1	340	340	100.0	304	36	†	44	0	†	†
Puerto Rico Technical Junior College Inc.	6	137	137	100.0	137	†	33	†	†	†	†
Ramirez College of Business and Technology	6	406	406	100.0	406	†	92	†	†	†	†
Universal Technology College of Puerto Rico	4	1,342	1,342	100.0	1,342	†	83	†	†	†	†
Universidad Adventista de las Antillas	3	831	763	91.8	693	70	13	86	4	†	†
Universidad Central Del Caribe	3	366	350	95.6	81	269	20	†	12	56	†
Universidad Del Este	3	10,366	10,366	100.0	10,136	230	89	775	19	†	†
Universidad Del Turabo	3	14,769	14,769	100.0	11,921	2,848	63	740	617	†	†
Universidad Metropolitana	3	10,566	10,566	100.0	8,428	2,138	67	577	447	†	†
Universidad Politecnica de Puerto Rico	3	5,738	5,738	100.0	5,037	701	†	477	108	†	†
University of Phoenix, Puerto Rico Campus	5	2,715	2,550	93.9	780	1,770	†	37	266	†	†
University of Puerto Rico, Aguadilla	1	3,231	3,231	100.0	3,231	†	53	371	†	†	†
University of Puerto Rico, Arecibo	1	4,146	4,146	100.0	4,146	†	85	581	†	†	†
University of Puerto Rico, Bayamon	1	4,638	4,638	100.0	4,638	†	53	464	†	†	†
University of Puerto Rico, Carolina	1	3,879	3,879	100.0	3,879	†	105	496	†	†	†
University of Puerto Rico, Cayey University College	1	3,634	3,634	100.0	3,634	†	1	509	†	†	†
University of Puerto Rico, Humacao	1	4,282	4,268	99.7	4,268	†	91	564	†	†	†
University of Puerto Rico, Mayaguez	1	12,338	12,338	100.0	11,258	1,080	†	1,385	172	†	7
University of Puerto Rico, Medical Sciences Campus	1	2,289	2,258	98.6	441	1,817	19	160	223	169	3
University of Puerto Rico, Ponce	1	3,485	3,485	100.0	3,485	†	94	425	†	†	†
University of Puerto Rico, Rio Piedras Campus	1	20,528	20,490	99.8	16,436	4,054	†	2,332	300	179	62
University of Puerto Rico, Utuado	1	1,523	1,523	100.0	1,523		48	96	†	†	†
University of Sacred Heart	3	5,345	5,345	100.0	4,491	854	5	521	47	†	†

†Not applicable.
[1] 1 = public, 4-year; 2 = public, 2-year; 3 = private, not-for-profit, 4-year; 4 = private, not-for-profit, 2-year; 5 = private, for-profit, 4-year; and 6 = private, for-profit, 2-year.
[2] Hispanic students who are U.S. citizens or resident aliens as a percentage of total enrollment, including nonresident aliens.
[3] This table includes institutions that serve large proportions of Hispanic students, defined as institutions with a full-time-equivalent undergraduate enrollment of Hispanic students at 25 percent or more of full-time-equivalent undergraduate enrollment of U.S. citizens. The percentage appearing in column 5 is the Hispanic total headcount enrollment as a percentage of total headcount enrollment, including both resident and nonresident students, as well as undergraduate and graduate students.
NOTE: Degree-granting institutions grant associate's or higher degrees and participate in Title IV federal financial aid programs.
SOURCE: U.S. Department of Education, National Center for Education Statistics, 2005 and 2004–05 Integrated Postsecondary Education Data System (IPEDS), Spring 2006 and Fall 2005. (This table was prepared October 2006.)

Table 223. Enrollment and degrees conferred in degree-granting tribally controlled institutions, by institution: Fall 2000 through fall 2005, and 2003–04 and 2004–05

Institution	Type and control[1]	Fall 2000	Fall 2001	Fall 2002	Fall 2003	Fall 2004	Fall 2005 Total	Fall 2005 American Indian/ Alaska Native	Fall 2005 Percent American Indian/ Alaska Native	Fall 2005 American Indian/ Alaska Native, under-graduate	Associate's 2003–04	Associate's 2004–05	Bachelor's 2003–04	Bachelor's 2004–05
1	2	3	4	5	6	7	8	9	10	11	12	13	14	15
Tribally controlled institutions	†	13,358	13,796	15,152	17,359	17,391	16,889	13,168	78.0	13,019	1,290	1,234	148	137
Arizona														
Diné College	2	1,712	1,685	1,822	1,878	1,935	1,825	1,791	98.1	1,791	226	208	†	†
Tohono O'odham Community College	4	—	—	—	181	169	270	254	94.1	254	5	2	†	†
Kansas														
Haskell Indian Nations University	1	918	967	887	918	928	918	918	100.0	918	122	94	74	67
Michigan														
Bay Mills Community College	2	360	368	430	386	401	406	274	67.5	274	13	11	†	†
Saginaw Chippewa Tribal College	2	—	—	41	66	109	123	105	85.4	105	6	11	†	†
Minnesota														
Fond du Lac Tribal and Community College	1	999	1,023	1,315	1,735	1,775	1,981	301	15.2	301	22	40	†	†
Leech Lake Tribal College	2	240	174	244	162	195	189	178	94.2	178	15	7	†	†
White Earth Tribal and Community College	4	—	79	99	81	67	61	49	80.3	49	2	2	†	†
Montana														
Blackfeet Community College	4	299	341	418	546	561	485	465	95.9	465	68	73	†	†
Chief Dull Knife College	2	461	442	268	442	356	554	460	83.0	460	24	18	†	†
Fort Belknap College	2	295	170	158	215	257	175	160	91.4	160	27	8	†	†
Fort Peck Community College	2	400	419	443	419	504	408	327	80.1	327	33	32	†	†
Little Big Horn College	2	320	203	275	394	291	259	249	96.1	249	23	15	†	†
Salish Kootenai College	3	1,042	976	1,109	1,100	1,130	1,142	926	81.1	926	49	71	11	14
Stone Child College	2	38	242	83	434	347	344	293	85.2	293	23	26	†	†
Nebraska														
Little Priest Tribal College	4	141	88	146	130	154	109	95	87.2	95	5	5	†	†
Nebraska Indian Community College	2	170	191	118	190	190	107	88	82.2	88	15	5	†	†
New Mexico														
Crownpoint Institute of Technology	2	841	299	283	300	306	333	330	99.1	330	22	43	†	†
Institute of American Indian and Alaska Native Culture	1	139	44	155	154	176	113	96	85.0	96	21	15	9	11
Southwestern Indian Polytechnic Institute	2	304	723	777	936	772	614	614	100.0	614	65	79	†	†
North Dakota														
Candeska Cikana Community College	2	9	169	160	190	197	198	187	94.4	187	19	31	†	†
Fort Berthold Community College	2	50	50	249	274	285	241	219	90.9	219	36	28	†	†
Sitting Bull College	1	22	194	214	317	289	287	230	80.1	230	34	28	†	†
Turtle Mountain Community College	3	686	684	897	959	787	615	568	92.4	568	78	48	7	1
United Tribes Technical College	4	204	302	463	466	536	885	660	74.6	660	80	101	†	†
South Dakota														
Oglala Lakota College	1	1,174	1,270	1,279	1,441	1,501	1,302	1,030	79.1	941	73	65	34	34
Sinte Gleska University	3	900	895	787	1,055	1,400	1,123	838	74.6	778	51	29	13	10
Sisseton-Wahpeton College	2	250	275	285	287	287	290	242	83.4	242	18	22	†	†
Washington														
Northwest Indian College	2	524	600	667	643	519	495	395	79.8	395	27	63	†	†
Wisconsin														
College of the Menominee Nation	4	371	407	530	499	507	532	436	82.0	436	41	27	†	†
Lac Courte Oreilles Ojibwa Community College	2	489	516	550	561	460	505	390	77.2	390	47	27	†	†

—Not available.
†Not applicable.
[1] 1 = public, 4-year; 2 = public, 2-year; 3 = private not-for-profit, 4-year; and 4 = private not-for-profit, 2-year.
NOTE: These colleges are, with few exceptions, tribally controlled and located on reserva-tions. They are all members of the American Indian Higher Education Consortium. Degree-granting institutions grant associate's or higher degrees and participate in Title IV federal financial aid programs. Some data have been revised from previously published figures.
SOURCE: U.S. Department of Education, National Center for Education Statistics, 2000 through 2005, 2003–04, and 2004–05 Integrated Postsecondary Education Data System, Spring 2001 through Spring 2006, Fall 2004, and Fall 2005. (This table was prepared September 2006.)

Table 224. Fall enrollment, degrees conferred, and expenditures in degree-granting historically Black colleges and universities, by institution: 2003, 2003–04, 2004, and 2004–05

Institution	State	Type and control[1]	Enrollment, fall 2003	Enrollment, fall 2004		Degrees conferred, 2004–05					Total expenditures, 2003–04 (in thousands)
				Total	Black enrollment	Associate's	Bachelor's	Master's	First-professional	Doctor's	
1	2	3	4	5	6	7	8	9	10	11	12
Total........................	†	†	306,727 [2]	308,939	257,545	3,673	30,287	6,929	1,661	434	$5,457,142
Alabama A&M University[3]........................	AL	1	6,588	6,323	5,518	0	600	312	†	8	100,869
Alabama State University........................	AL	1	6,024	5,653	5,268	0	520	284	†	5	71,833
Bishop State Community College........................	AL	2	5,222	4,650	2,878	344	†	†	†	†	23,260
Concordia College........................	AL	3	851	905	845	54	47	†	†	†	5,257
Gadsden State Community College........................	AL	2	5,859	5,549	1,079	489	†	†	†	†	35,360
H. Councill Trenholm State Technical College, Trenholm.......	AL	2	672	1,522	969	164	†	†	†	†	16,065
J. F. Drake Technical College........................	AL	2	795	782	451	58	†	†	†	†	5,184
Lawson State Community College........................	AL	2	2,433	2,322	2,262	127	†	†	†	†	14,728
Miles College........................	AL	3	1,660	1,715	1,704	†	183	†	†	†	17,764
Oakwood College........................	AL	3	1,787	1,753	1,589	5	369	†	†	†	35,135
Shelton State Community College, C. A. Fredd campus.......	AL	2	300	320	164	0	†	†	†	†	4,694
Stillman College........................	AL	3	1,200	1,116	1,088	†	170	†	†	†	21,519
Talladega College........................	AL	3	468	362	360	†	68	†	†	†	11,117
Tuskegee University[3]........................	AL	3	2,763	2,869	2,726	†	397	41	53	1	101,318
Arkansas Baptist College........................	AR	3	375	245	245	†	29	†	†	†	4,850
Philander Smith College........................	AR	3	887	949	920	†	111	†	†	†	19,420
University of Arkansas, Pine Bluff[3]........................	AR	1	3,251	3,303	3,140	0	420	29	†	†	53,529
Delaware State University[3]........................	DE	1	3,178	3,270	2,688	†	368	81	†	†	63,907
Howard University........................	DC	3	10,658	10,623	9,283	†	1,395	415	525	114	716,631
University of the District of Columbia[3]........................	DC	1	5,241	5,168	4,423	166	281	37	†	†	86,728
University of the District of Columbia, David A. Clark, School of Law........................	DC	1	183	220	71	†	†	†	53	†	5,471
Bethune-Cookman College........................	FL	3	2,794	2,895	2,661	†	322	†	†	†	48,260
Edward Waters College........................	FL	3	1,301	1,206	1,166	†	141	†	†	†	21,567
Florida A&M University[3]........................	FL	1	13,013	13,067	11,953	83	1,317	293	169	21	246,645
Florida Memorial College........................	FL	3	2,176	2,219	2,142	†	317	34	†	†	35,178
Albany State College........................	GA	1	3,681	3,668	3,293	†	546	136	†	†	47,999
Clark Atlanta University........................	GA	3	4,915	4,588	4,562	†	592	251	†	26	98,417
Fort Valley State University[3]........................	GA	1	2,537	2,558	2,381	13	229	37	†	†	45,620
Interdenominational Theological Center........................	GA	3	406	479	446	†	†	2	87	5	9,118
Morehouse College........................	GA	3	2,859	2,891	2,787	†	434	†	†	†	66,885
Morehouse School of Medicine........................	GA	3	236	253	191	†	†	11	44	3	111,747
Morris Brown College[4]........................	GA	3	†	†	†	†	†	†	†	†	†
Paine College........................	GA	3	972	882	867	†	98	†	†	†	17,982
Savannah State College........................	GA	1	2,752	2,800	2,618	†	286	57	†	†	37,264
Spelman College........................	GA	3	2,063	2,186	2,144	†	498	†	†	†	61,333
Kentucky State University[3]........................	KY	1	2,306	2,335	1,436	48	224	52	†	†	52,506
Dillard University........................	LA	3	2,312	2,155	2,140	†	340	†	†	†	52,613
Grambling State University........................	LA	1	4,673	5,039	4,729	51	512	130	†	6	62,568
Southern University and A&M College, Baton Rouge[3]........	LA	1	8,884	9,438	8,961	5	923	303	†	14	126,398
Southern University at New Orleans........................	LA	1	3,500	3,647	3,504	31	440	166	†	†	31,241
Southern University at Shreveport........................	LA	2	2,208	2,331	2,027	239	0	†	†	†	12,965
Xavier University of Louisiana........................	LA	3	3,913	4,121	3,556	†	441	80	96	†	90,263
Bowie State University........................	MD	1	5,454	5,415	4,723	†	580	285	†	15	63,172
Coppin State College........................	MD	1	3,749	3,875	3,637	†	315	75	†	†	42,315
Morgan State University........................	MD	1	6,621	6,891	6,427	†	833	95	†	26	125,625
University of Maryland, Eastern Shore[3]........................	MD	1	3,762	3,775	2,902	†	389	62	†	5	70,785
Lewis College of Business........................	MI	4	285	345	337	38	†	†	†	†	3,092
Alcorn State University[3]........................	MS	1	3,309	3,443	3,058	28	397	169	†	†	54,393
Coahoma Community College........................	MS	2	1,842	1,961	1,904	237	†	†	†	†	18,268
Hinds Community College, Utica Campus........................	MS	2	1,734	1,345	1,247	60	†	†	†	†	†
Jackson State University........................	MS	1	7,815	8,351	7,756	†	812	314	†	31	151,260
Mary Holmes College[5]........................	MS	4	†	†	†	†	†	†	†	†	†
Mississippi Valley State University........................	MS	1	3,505	3,621	3,505	†	346	77	†	†	44,514
Rust College........................	MS	3	988	1,001	927	13	89	†	†	†	14,118
Tougaloo College........................	MS	3	940	971	964	3	106	†	†	†	24,744

See notes at end of table.

Table 224. Fall enrollment, degrees conferred, and expenditures in degree-granting historically Black colleges and universities, by institution: 2003, 2003–04, 2004, and 2004–05—Continued

Institution	State	Type and control[1]	Enrollment, fall 2003	Enrollment, fall 2004		Degrees conferred, 2004–05					Total expenditures, 2003–04 (in thousands)
				Total	Black enrollment	Associate's	Bachelor's	Master's	First-profes-sional	Doctor's	
1	2	3	4	5	6	7	8	9	10	11	12
Harris-Stowe State College	MO	1	1,911	1,605	1,355	†	133	†	†	†	16,756
Lincoln University[3]	MO	1	3,128	3,275	1,176	103	304	61	†	†	35,011
Barber-Scotia College[6]	NC	3	742	†	†	†	†	†	†	†	†
Bennett College	NC	3	429	505	488	†	68	†	0	†	16,810
Elizabeth City State University	NC	1	2,308	2,470	1,946	†	296	9	†	†	41,973
Fayetteville State University	NC	1	5,329	5,441	4,108	†	698	123	†	11	64,996
Johnson C. Smith University	NC	3	1,474	1,415	1,408	†	248	†	†	†	30,230
Livingstone College	NC	3	1,005	1,016	977	†	118	†	†	†	21,566
North Carolina Agricultural and Technical State University[3]	NC	1	10,030	10,383	9,301	†	998	306	†	7	160,494
North Carolina Central University	NC	1	7,191	7,727	6,345	†	732	317	109	†	112,962
St Augustine's College	NC	3	1,629	1,395	1,278	†	169	†	†	†	27,238
Shaw University	NC	3	2,616	2,709	2,598	7	411	2	25	†	38,942
Winston-Salem State University	NC	1	4,102	4,805	3,921	†	543	73	†	†	69,077
Central State University	OH	1	1,621	1,820	1,762	†	144	1	†	†	42,911
Wilberforce University	OH	3	1,180	998	909	†	259	†	†	†	17,005
Langston University[3]	OK	1	2,968	3,049	2,351	9	351	39	†	†	41,144
Cheyney University of Pennsylvania	PA	1	1,536	1,545	1,479	†	139	50	†	†	31,218
Lincoln University	PA	1	1,938	2,012	1,819	†	240	128	†	†	38,614
Allen University	SC	3	565	567	548	†	85	†	†	†	8,673
Benedict College	SC	3	2,850	2,769	2,749	†	312	†	†	†	55,524
Claflin College	SC	3	1,627	1,807	1,705	†	284	21	†	†	30,580
Clinton Junior College	SC	4	97	89	89	14	†	†	†	†	1,700
Denmark Technical College	SC	2	1,464	1,423	1,365	142	†	†	†	†	8,279
Morris College	SC	3	1,007	897	895	†	163	†	†	†	18,490
South Carolina State University[3]	SC	1	4,466	4,294	4,113	†	499	144	†	27	74,327
Voorhees College	SC	3	876	902	901	†	154	†	†	†	17,574
Fisk University	TN	3	881	842	797	†	140	8	†	†	23,409
Lane College	TN	3	952	1,045	1,041	†	116	†	†	†	13,125
Le Moyne-Owen College	TN	3	796	852	837	†	98	†	†	†	12,426
Meharry Medical College	TN	3	723	687	558	†	†	13	104	13	106,980
Tennessee State University[3]	TN	1	9,090	9,100	7,220	132	982	398	†	58	139,045
Huston-Tillotson College	TX	3	666	685	525	†	69	†	†	†	13,978
Jarvis Christian College	TX	3	654	538	524	†	59	†	†	†	12,772
Paul Quinn College	TX	3	858	966	876	†	146	†	†	†	12,220
Prairie View A&M University[3]	TX	1	7,808	8,350	7,506	†	778	671	†	2	111,338
Saint Philip's College	TX	2	9,490	10,164	1,743	631	†	†	†	†	44,739
Southwestern Christian College	TX	3	220	241	219	37	8	†	†	†	4,872
Texas College	TX	3	1,035	757	732	†	100	†	†	†	14,111
Texas Southern University	TX	1	10,888	11,635	10,041	†	538	209	245	11	127,038
Wiley College	TX	3	707	791	717	0	125	†	†	†	16,040
Hampton University	VA	3	5,797	6,154	5,491	5	790	97	38	4	148,402
Norfolk State University	VA	1	6,846	6,165	5,485	62	722	218	†	4	101,488
Saint Paul's College	VA	3	475	627	599	†	101	†	†	†	9,744
Virginia State University[3]	VA	1	4,933	4,859	4,570	†	727	156	†	†	74,029
Virginia Union University	VA	3	1,961	1,777	1,726	†	160	†	113	17	25,947
Bluefield State College	WV	1	3,511	3,506	336	182	185	†	†	†	20,561
West Virginia State College	WV	1	4,966	3,344	524	†	438	0	†	†	42,682
University of the Virgin Islands, St. Thomas Campus[3]	VI	1	1,481	1,565	1,270	93	172	57	†	†	56,612

†Not applicable.

[1] 1 = public, 4-year; 2 = public, 2-year; 3 = private, 4-year; and 4 = private, 2-year.

[2] Includes enrollment for institutions that are no longer Title IV participants.

[3] Land-grant institution.

[4] Not participating in Title IV programs after 2002.

[5] School closed in 2003.

[6] Not participating in Title IV programs after 2003.

NOTE: Excludes historically Black colleges and universities that are not participating in Title IV programs. Historically Black colleges and universities are degree-granting institutions established prior to 1964 with the principal mission of educating Black Americans. Federal regulations, 20 U.S. Code, Section 1061 (2), allow for certain exceptions to the founding date. Detail may not sum to totals due to rounding.

SOURCE: U.S. Department of Education, National Center for Education Statistics, 2003 through 2005 Integrated Postsecondary Education Data System (IPEDS), Fall 2004, Fall 2005, and Spring 2005. (This table was prepared July 2006.)

Table 225. Selected statistics on degree-granting historically Black colleges and universities: Selected years, 1980 through 2005

Enrollment, degrees, type of revenues, and type of expenditures	Total	Public			Private		
		Total	4-year	2-year	Total	4-year	2-year
1	2	3	4	5	6	7	8
Number of institutions, fall 2005	100	52	41	11	48	46	2
Fall enrollment							
Total enrollment, fall 1980	233,557	168,217	155,085	13,132	65,340	62,924	2,416
Males	106,387	76,994	70,236	6,758	29,393	28,352	1,041
Males, Black	81,818	56,435	53,654	2,781	25,383	24,412	971
Females	127,170	91,223	84,849	6,374	35,947	34,572	1,375
Females, Black	109,171	75,226	70,582	4,644	33,945	32,589	1,356
Total enrollment, fall 1990	257,152	187,046	171,969	15,077	70,106	68,528	1,578
Males	105,157	76,541	70,220	6,321	28,616	28,054	562
Males, Black	82,897	57,255	54,041	3,214	25,642	25,198	444
Females	151,995	110,505	101,749	8,756	41,490	40,474	1,016
Females, Black	125,785	86,949	80,883	6,066	38,836	38,115	721
Total enrollment, fall 2004	308,939	231,179	198,810	32,369	77,760	77,326	434
Males	118,129	87,983	75,690	12,293	30,146	30,005	141
Males, Black	96,750	68,943	63,715	5,228	27,807	27,671	136
Females	190,810	143,196	123,120	20,076	47,614	47,321	293
Females, Black	160,795	115,765	104,904	10,861	45,030	44,740	290
Full-time enrollment, fall 2004	245,200	173,909	155,313	18,596	71,291	70,962	329
Males	96,700	69,107	61,968	7,139	27,593	27,486	107
Females	148,500	104,802	93,345	11,457	43,698	43,476	222
Part-time enrollment, fall 2004	63,739	57,270	43,497	13,773	6,469	6,364	105
Males	21,429	18,876	13,722	5,154	2,553	2,519	34
Females	42,310	38,394	29,775	8,619	3,916	3,845	71
Earned degrees conferred, 2004–05							
Associate's	3,673	3,497	1,006	2,491	176	124	52
Males	1,135	1,102	262	840	33	23	10
Males, Black	476	450	154	296	26	16	10
Females	2,538	2,395	744	1,651	143	101	42
Females, Black	1,518	1,383	366	1,017	135	93	42
Bachelor's	30,287	19,957	19,957	†	10,330	10,330	†
Males	10,239	6,822	6,822	†	3,417	3,417	†
Males, Black	8,710	5,691	5,691	†	3,019	3,019	†
Females	20,048	13,135	13,135	†	6,913	6,913	†
Females, Black	17,733	11,315	11,315	†	6,418	6,418	†
Master's	6,929	5,954	5,954	†	975	975	†
Males	1,993	1,707	1,707	†	286	286	†
Males, Black	1,291	1,091	1,091	†	200	200	†
Females	4,936	4,247	4,247	†	689	689	†
Females, Black	3,736	3,134	3,134	†	602	602	†
First-professional	1,661	576	576	†	1,085	1,085	†
Males	636	221	221	†	415	415	†
Males, Black	394	95	95	†	299	299	†
Females	1,025	355	355	†	670	670	†
Females, Black	745	229	229	†	516	516	†
Doctor's	434	251	251	†	183	183	†
Males	163	92	92	†	71	71	†
Males, Black	106	53	53	†	53	53	†
Females	271	159	159	†	112	112	†
Females, Black	191	100	100	†	91	91	†
Financial statistics, 2003–04	In thousands of dollars						
Total revenue	—	—	—	—	$2,491,029	$2,486,285	$4,744
Student tuition and fees	—	—	—	—	633,113	630,854	2,259
Federal government[1]	—	—	—	—	742,818	741,732	1,086
State governments	—	—	—	—	64,026	63,853	173
Local governments	—	—	—	—	8,598	8,594	3
Private gifts and grants[2]	—	—	—	—	241,246	240,730	516
Investment return (gain or loss)	—	—	—	—	207,889	207,880	9
Educational activities	—	—	—	—	10,187	10,154	33
Auxiliary enterprises	—	—	—	—	246,955	246,910	44
Hospitals and other sources	—	—	—	—	336,196	335,576	621
Total expenditures	$5,457,142	$3,170,455	$2,986,915	$183,541	2,286,687	2,281,895	4,792
Instruction	—	—	—	—	609,199	608,034	1,165
Research	—	—	—	—	153,904	153,853	50
Academic support	—	—	—	—	142,673	142,177	496
Institutional support	—	—	—	—	456,099	455,465	634
Auxiliary enterprises	—	—	—	—	240,333	240,319	13
Other expenditures	—	—	—	—	684,479	682,047	2,432

—Not available.
†Not applicable.
[1]Includes independent operations.
[2]Includes contributions from affiliated entities.
NOTE: Historically Black colleges and universities are degree-granting institutions established prior to 1964 with the principal mission of educating Black Americans. Federal regulations, 20 U.S. Code, Section 1061 (2), allow for certain exceptions to the founding date.

Federal, state, and local governments revenue includes appropriations, grants, contracts, and independent operations. Detail may not sum to totals because of rounding.
SOURCE: U.S. Department of Education, National Center for Education Statistics, Higher Education General Information Survey (HEGIS), "Fall Enrollment in Institutions of Higher Education," 1980; and 1990 through 2005 Integrated Postsecondary Education Data System, "Fall Enrollment Survey" (IPEDS-EF:90), Spring 2005, and Fall 2005. (This table was prepared July 2006.)

Table 226. Fall enrollment in degree-granting historically Black colleges and universities, by type and control of institution: 1976 through 2004

Year	Total enrollment	4-year	2-year	Public			Private		
				Total	4-year	2-year	Total	4-year	2-year
1	2	3	4	5	6	7	8	9	10
1976	222,613	206,676	15,937	156,836	143,528	13,308	65,777	63,148	2,629
1977	226,062	209,898	16,164	158,823	145,450	13,373	67,239	64,448	2,791
1978	227,797	211,651	16,146	163,237	150,168	13,069	64,560	61,483	3,077
1979	230,124	214,147	15,977	166,315	153,139	13,176	63,809	61,008	2,801
1980	233,557	218,009	15,548	168,217	155,085	13,132	65,340	62,924	2,416
1981	232,460	217,152	15,308	166,991	154,269	12,722	65,469	62,883	2,586
1982	228,371	212,017	16,354	165,871	151,472	14,399	62,500	60,545	1,955
1983	234,446	217,909	16,537	170,051	155,665	14,386	64,395	62,244	2,151
1984	227,519	212,844	14,675	164,116	151,289	12,827	63,403	61,555	1,848
1985	225,801	210,648	15,153	163,677	150,002	13,675	62,124	60,646	1,478
1986	223,275	207,231	16,044	162,048	147,631	14,417	61,227	59,600	1,627
1987	227,994	211,654	16,340	165,486	150,560	14,926	62,508	61,094	1,414
1988	239,755	223,250	16,505	173,672	158,606	15,066	66,083	64,644	1,439
1989	249,096	232,890	16,206	181,151	166,481	14,670	67,945	66,409	1,536
1990	257,152	240,497	16,655	187,046	171,969	15,077	70,106	68,528	1,578
1991	269,335	252,093	17,242	197,847	182,204	15,643	71,488	69,889	1,599
1992	279,541	261,089	18,452	204,966	188,143	16,823	74,575	72,946	1,629
1993	282,856	262,430	20,426	208,197	189,032	19,165	74,659	73,398	1,261
1994	280,071	259,997	20,074	206,520	187,735	18,785	73,551	72,262	1,289
1995	278,725	259,409	19,316	204,726	186,278	18,448	73,999	73,131	868
1996	273,018	253,654	19,364	200,569	182,063	18,506	72,449	71,591	858
1997	269,167	248,860	20,307	194,674	175,297	19,377	74,493	73,563	930
1998	273,472	248,931	24,541	198,603	174,776	23,827	74,869	74,155	714
1999	274,212	249,169	25,043	199,704	175,364	24,340	74,508	73,805	703
2000	275,680	250,710	24,970	199,725	175,404	24,321	75,955	75,306	649
2001	289,985	260,547	29,438	210,083	181,346	28,737	79,902	79,201	701
2002	299,041	269,020	30,021	218,433	189,183	29,250	80,608	79,837	771
2003	306,727	274,326	32,401	228,096	196,077	32,019	78,631	78,249	382
2004	308,939	231,179	77,760	276,136	198,810	77,326	32,803	32,369	434

NOTE: Data through 1995 are for institutions of higher education, while later data are for degree-granting institutions. Degree-granting institutions grant associate's or higher degrees and participate in Title IV federal financial aid programs. The degree-granting classification is very similar to the earlier higher education classification, but it includes more 2-year colleges and excludes a few higher education institutions that did not grant degrees. (See Guide to Sources for details.)

SOURCE: U.S. Department of Education, National Center for Education Statistics, Higher Education General Information Survey (HEGIS), "Fall Enrollment in Colleges and Universities," 1976 through 1985 surveys; and 1986 through 2004 Integrated Postsecondary Education Data System "Fall Enrollment Survey" (IPEDS-EF:86–99), and Spring 2001 through Spring 2005. (This table was prepared July 2006.)

Table 227. Total and full-time-equivalent staff in degree-granting institutions, by employment status, control of institution, and occupation: Fall 1976, fall 1995, and fall 2005

Control of institution and primary occupation	Fall 1976					Fall 1995				Fall 2005			
	Total			Full-time equivalent (FTE)		Total		Full-time equivalent (FTE)		Total		Full-time equivalent (FTE)	
	Total	Percent	Full-time	Total	FTE students per FTE staff	Total	Percent	Total	FTE students per FTE staff	Number	Percent	Total	FTE students per FTE staff
1	2	3	4	5	6	7	8	9	10	11	12	13	14
All institutions	**1,863,790**	**100.0**	**1,339,911**	**1,541,339**	**5.4**	**2,662,075**	**100.0**	**2,129,260**	**4.9**	**3,379,087**	**100.0**	**2,630,636**	**5.0**
Professional staff	1,073,119	57.6	709,400	845,456	9.8	1,744,867	65.5	1,319,947	7.8	2,459,885	72.8	1,812,925	7.3
Executive/administrative/ managerial	101,263	5.4	97,003	98,972	84.0	147,445	5.5	143,965	71.8	196,324	5.8	192,963	68.4
Faculty (instruction and research)	633,210	34.0	434,071	500,533	16.6	931,706	35.0	677,736	15.2	1,290,426	38.2	881,306	15.0
Instruction and research assistants	160,086	8.6	28,007	82,684	100.5	215,909	8.1	89,238	115.8	317,141	9.4	131,415	100.5
Other professionals	178,560	9.6	150,319	163,267	50.9	449,807	16.9	409,008	25.3	655,994	19.4	607,240	21.7
Nonprofessional staff	790,671	42.4	630,511	695,883	11.9	917,208	34.5	809,313	12.8	919,202	27.2	817,712	16.1
Public	**1,329,122**	**100.0**	**946,354**	**1,092,558**	**5.8**	**1,865,930**	**100.0**	**1,469,140**	**5.3**	**2,267,687**	**100.0**	**1,743,382**	**5.4**
Professional staff	769,836	57.9	502,325	601,942	10.5	1,230,006	65.9	910,408	8.5	1,640,704	72.4	1,190,902	7.9
Executive/administrative/ managerial	60,733	4.6	58,649	59,579	106.6	82,396	4.4	80,504	96.3	101,011	4.5	99,292	94.6
Faculty (instruction and research)	448,733	33.8	313,367	357,761	17.7	656,833	35.2	475,208	16.3	841,188	37.1	578,693	16.2
Instruction and research assistants	127,925	9.6	19,076	63,420	100.1	181,743	9.7	74,040	104.7	257,952	11.4	105,087	89.4
Other professionals	132,445	10.0	111,233	121,182	52.4	309,034	16.6	280,655	27.6	440,553	19.4	407,831	23.0
Nonprofessional staff	559,286	42.1	444,029	490,616	12.9	635,924	34.1	558,732	13.9	626,983	27.6	552,480	17.0
Private	**534,668**	**100.0**	**393,557**	**448,781**	**4.4**	**796,145**	**100.0**	**660,119**	**3.9**	**1,111,400**	**100.0**	**887,254**	**4.3**
Professional staff	303,283	56.7	207,075	243,514	8.1	514,861	64.7	409,539	6.3	819,181	73.7	622,023	6.1
Executive/administrative/ managerial	40,530	7.6	38,354	39,393	49.8	65,049	8.2	63,461	40.7	95,313	8.6	93,672	40.7
Faculty (instruction and research)	184,477	34.5	120,704	142,772	13.7	274,873	34.5	202,527	12.8	449,238	40.4	302,614	12.6
Instruction and research assistants	32,161	6.0	8,931	19,264	101.9	34,166	4.3	15,197	170.0	59,189	5.3	26,328	144.7
Other professionals	46,115	8.6	39,086	42,085	46.6	140,773	17.7	128,353	20.1	215,441	19.4	199,409	19.1
Nonprofessional staff	231,385	43.3	186,482	205,267	9.6	281,284	35.3	250,580	10.3	292,219	26.3	265,231	14.4

NOTE: Data for 1976 and 1995 are for institutions of higher education, while later data are for degree-granting institutions. Degree-granting institutions grant associate's or higher degrees and participate in Title IV federal financial aid programs. The degree-granting classification is very similar to the earlier higher education classification, but it includes more 2-year colleges and excludes a few higher education institutions that did not grant degrees. (See Guide to Sources for details.) Detail may not sum to totals because of rounding.

SOURCE: U.S. Department of Education, National Center for Education Statistics, Higher Education General Information Survey (HEGIS), "Staff Survey," 1976; and 1995 and 2005 Integrated Postsecondary Education Data System, "Fall Staff Survey" (IPEDS-S:95), and Winter 2005–06. (This table was prepared August 2006.)

Table 228. Employees in degree-granting institutions, by employment status, sex, control and type of institution, and primary occupation: Fall 2005

Control and type of institution and primary occupation	Full-time and part-time					Full-time				Part-time		
	Total		Males	Females		Total		Males	Females	Total	Males	Females
	Number	Percentage distribution		Number	Percent of all employees	Number	Percent of all employees					
1	2	3	4	5	6	7	8	9	10	11	12	13
All institutions	3,379,087	100.0	1,581,498	1,797,589	53.2	2,179,864	64.5	1,006,846	1,173,018	1,199,223	574,652	624,571
Professional staff	2,459,885	72.8	1,240,030	1,219,855	49.6	1,432,107	58.2	725,798	706,309	1,027,778	514,232	513,546
Executive/administrative/managerial	196,324	5.8	95,223	101,101	51.5	190,078	96.8	92,854	97,224	6,246	2,369	3,877
Faculty (instruction and research)	1,290,426	38.2	714,453	575,973	44.6	675,624	52.4	401,507	274,117	614,802	312,946	301,856
Instruction and research assistants	317,141	9.4	167,529	149,612	47.2	†	†	†	†	317,141	167,529	149,612
Other professional	655,994	19.4	262,825	393,169	59.9	566,405	86.3	231,437	334,968	89,589	31,388	58,201
Nonprofessional staff	919,202	27.2	341,468	577,734	62.9	747,757	81.3	281,048	466,709	171,445	60,420	111,025
Technical and paraprofessionals	193,505	5.7	79,747	113,758	58.8	154,577	79.9	64,828	89,749	38,928	14,919	24,009
Clerical and secretarial	439,546	13.0	63,531	376,015	85.5	346,714	78.9	40,344	306,370	92,832	23,187	69,645
Skilled crafts	61,366	1.8	57,407	3,959	6.5	58,859	95.9	55,762	3,097	2,507	1,645	862
Service and maintenance	224,785	6.7	140,783	84,002	37.4	187,607	83.5	120,114	67,493	37,178	20,669	16,509
Public 4-year	1,656,709	100.0	789,988	866,721	52.3	1,133,735	68.4	539,391	594,344	522,974	250,597	272,377
Professional staff	1,200,168	72.4	614,380	585,788	48.8	745,279	62.1	388,008	357,271	454,889	226,372	228,517
Executive/administrative/managerial	74,241	4.5	38,451	35,790	48.2	72,102	97.1	37,547	34,555	2,139	904	1,235
Faculty (instruction and research)	486,691	29.4	284,565	202,126	41.5	339,058	69.7	210,163	128,895	147,633	74,402	73,231
Instruction and research assistants	257,578	15.5	135,267	122,311	47.5	†	†	†	†	257,578	135,267	122,311
Other professional	381,658	23.0	156,097	225,561	59.1	334,119	87.5	140,298	193,821	47,539	15,799	31,740
Nonprofessional staff	456,541	27.6	175,608	280,933	61.5	388,456	85.1	151,383	237,073	68,085	24,225	43,860
Technical and paraprofessionals	98,957	6.0	41,157	57,800	58.4	82,751	83.6	35,032	47,719	16,206	6,125	10,081
Clerical and secretarial	201,503	12.2	27,514	173,989	86.3	165,637	82.2	17,795	147,842	35,866	9,719	26,147
Skilled crafts	40,462	2.4	38,112	2,350	5.8	39,286	97.1	37,354	1,932	1,176	758	418
Service and maintenance	115,619	7.0	68,825	46,794	40.5	100,782	87.2	61,202	39,580	14,837	7,623	7,214
Public 2-year	610,978	100.0	263,995	346,983	56.8	295,629	48.4	121,465	174,164	315,349	142,530	172,819
Professional staff	440,536	72.1	203,641	236,895	53.8	182,149	41.3	81,415	100,734	258,387	122,226	136,161
Executive/administrative/managerial	26,770	4.4	12,646	14,124	52.8	25,804	96.4	12,224	13,580	966	422	544
Faculty (instruction and research)	354,497	58.0	169,715	184,782	52.1	111,538	31.5	53,213	58,325	242,959	116,502	126,457
Instruction and research assistants	374	0.1	202	172	46.0	†	†	†	†	374	202	172
Other professional	58,895	9.6	21,078	37,817	64.2	44,807	76.1	15,978	28,829	14,088	5,100	8,988
Nonprofessional staff	170,442	27.9	60,354	110,088	64.6	113,480	66.6	40,050	73,430	56,962	20,304	36,658
Technical and paraprofessionals	42,656	7.0	16,835	25,821	60.5	28,052	65.8	11,061	16,991	14,604	5,774	8,830
Clerical and secretarial	86,649	14.2	13,192	73,457	84.8	53,970	62.3	4,665	49,305	32,679	8,527	24,152
Skilled crafts	5,836	1.0	5,167	669	11.5	5,180	88.8	4,725	455	656	442	214
Service and maintenance	35,301	5.8	25,160	10,141	28.7	26,278	74.4	19,599	6,679	9,023	5,561	3,462
Private 4-year[1]	1,073,764	100.0	512,064	561,700	52.3	724,586	67.5	335,447	389,139	349,178	176,617	172,561
Professional staff	789,179	73.5	409,036	380,143	48.2	484,835	61.4	247,748	237,087	304,344	161,288	143,056
Executive/administrative/managerial	90,415	8.4	42,120	48,295	53.4	87,365	96.6	41,108	46,257	3,050	1,012	2,038
Faculty (instruction and research)	430,305	40.1	251,149	179,156	41.6	215,385	50.1	133,163	82,222	214,920	117,986	96,934
Instruction and research assistants	59,147	5.5	32,027	27,120	45.9	†	†	†	†	59,147	32,027	27,120
Other professional	209,312	19.5	83,740	125,572	60.0	182,085	87.0	73,477	108,608	27,227	10,263	16,964
Nonprofessional staff	284,585	26.5	103,028	181,557	63.8	239,751	84.2	87,699	152,052	44,834	15,329	29,505
Technical and paraprofessionals	50,896	4.7	21,318	29,578	58.1	43,004	84.5	18,369	24,635	7,892	2,949	4,943
Clerical and secretarial	146,284	13.6	21,823	124,461	85.1	122,866	84.0	17,079	105,787	23,418	4,744	18,674
Skilled crafts	14,950	1.4	14,057	893	6.0	14,298	95.6	13,626	672	652	431	221
Service and maintenance	72,455	6.7	45,830	26,625	36.7	59,583	82.2	38,625	20,958	12,872	7,205	5,667
Private 2-year[1]	37,636	100.0	15,451	22,185	58.9	25,914	68.9	10,543	15,371	11,722	4,908	6,814
Professional staff	30,002	79.7	12,973	17,029	56.8	19,844	66.1	8,627	11,217	10,158	4,346	5,812
Executive/administrative/managerial	4,898	13.0	2,006	2,892	59.0	4,807	98.1	1,975	2,832	91	31	60
Faculty (instruction and research)	18,933	50.3	9,024	9,909	52.3	9,643	50.9	4,968	4,675	9,290	4,056	5,234

See notes at end of table.

Table 228. Employees in degree-granting institutions, by employment status, sex, control and type of institution, and primary occupation: Fall 2005—Continued

| Control and type of institution and primary occupation | Full-time and part-time | | | | | Full-time | | | | Part-time | | |
| | Total | | | Females | | Total | | | | | | |
	Number	Percentage distribution	Males	Number	Percent of all employees	Number	Percent of all employees	Males	Females	Total	Males	Females
1	2	3	4	5	6	7	8	9	10	11	12	13
Instruction and research assistants	42	0.1	33	9	21.4	†	†	†	†	42	33	9
Other professional	6,129	16.3	1,910	4,219	68.8	5,394	88.0	1,684	3,710	735	226	509
Nonprofessional staff	7,634	20.3	2,478	5,156	67.5	6,070	79.5	1,916	4,154	1,564	562	1,002
Technical and paraprofessionals	996	2.6	437	559	56.1	770	77.3	366	404	226	71	155
Clerical and secretarial	5,110	13.6	1,002	4,108	80.4	4,241	83.0	805	3,436	869	197	672
Skilled crafts	118	0.3	71	47	39.8	95	80.5	57	38	23	14	9
Service and maintenance	1,410	3.7	968	442	31.3	964	68.4	688	276	446	280	166
Private not-for-profit 4-year	**964,068**	**100.0**	**453,267**	**510,801**	**53.0**	**679,742**	**70.5**	**314,760**	**364,982**	**284,326**	**138,507**	**145,819**
Professional staff	694,362	72.0	355,980	338,382	48.7	453,056	65.2	232,055	221,001	241,306	123,925	117,381
Executive/administrative/ managerial	84,270	8.7	39,097	45,173	53.6	81,279	96.5	38,102	43,177	2,991	995	1,996
Faculty (instruction and research)	357,913	37.1	207,770	150,143	41.9	205,046	57.3	126,730	78,316	152,867	81,040	71,827
Instruction and research assistants	59,054	6.1	31,984	27,070	45.8	†	†	†	†	59,054	31,984	27,070
Other professional	193,125	20.0	77,129	115,996	60.1	166,731	86.3	67,223	99,508	26,394	9,906	16,488
Nonprofessional staff	269,706	28.0	97,287	172,419	63.9	226,686	84.0	82,705	143,981	43,020	14,582	28,438
Technical and paraprofessionals	48,290	5.0	19,771	28,519	59.1	40,831	84.6	17,059	23,772	7,459	2,712	4,747
Clerical and secretarial	135,317	14.0	18,642	116,675	86.2	112,913	83.4	14,148	98,765	22,404	4,494	17,910
Skilled crafts	14,892	1.5	14,008	884	5.9	14,257	95.7	13,589	668	635	419	216
Service and maintenance	71,207	7.4	44,866	26,341	37.0	58,685	82.4	37,909	20,776	12,522	6,957	5,565

†Not applicable.
[1]Includes not-for-profit and for-profit private institutions.
NOTE: Degree-granting institutions grant associate's or higher degrees and participate in Title IV federal financial aid programs. The survey did not permit respondents to report instruction and research assistants as full-time staff. Detail may not sum to totals because of rounding.
SOURCE: U.S. Department of Education, National Center for Education Statistics, 2005 Integrated Postsecondary Education Data System (IPEDS), Winter 2005–06. (This table was prepared August 2006.)

Table 229. Employees in degree-granting institutions, by race/ethnicity and residency status, sex, employment status, control and type of institution, and primary occupation: Fall 2005

Sex, employment status, control and type of institution, and primary occupation	Total	White	Minority		Black	Hispanic	Asian/Pacific Islander	American Indian/ Alaska Native	Race/ ethnicity unknown	Nonresident alien[2]
			Number	Percent[1]						
1	2	3	4	5	6	7	8	9	10	11
All institutions	**3,379,087**	**2,393,428**	**711,834**	**21.9**	**328,715**	**184,952**	**178,194**	**19,973**	**121,312**	**152,513**
Professional staff	2,459,885	1,790,962	422,389	17.9	170,263	97,763	141,927	12,436	102,784	143,750
Executive/administrative/managerial	196,324	159,494	33,386	17.2	18,353	8,420	5,493	1,120	2,560	884
Faculty (instruction and research)	1,290,426	987,778	200,447	16.4	76,445	46,660	70,999	6,343	67,092	35,109
Instruction and research assistants	317,141	163,385	48,364	16.2	12,405	11,049	23,681	1,229	18,608	86,784
Other professional	655,994	480,305	140,192	21.9	63,060	31,634	41,754	3,744	14,524	20,973
Nonprofessional staff	919,202	602,466	289,445	32.1	158,452	87,189	36,267	7,537	18,528	8,763
Males	**1,581,498**	**1,123,365**	**303,257**	**19.9**	**124,746**	**79,854**	**90,146**	**8,511**	**61,184**	**93,692**
Professional staff	1,240,030	902,791	193,785	16.3	67,099	45,076	75,990	5,620	53,641	89,813
Executive/administrative/managerial	95,223	79,200	14,188	15.1	7,331	3,693	2,645	519	1,294	541
Faculty (instruction and research)	714,453	548,692	106,348	15.7	34,670	24,673	43,788	3,217	36,343	23,070
Instruction and research assistants	167,529	81,665	22,508	14.2	4,666	4,811	12,491	540	9,479	53,877
Other professional	262,825	193,234	50,741	19.8	20,432	11,899	17,066	1,344	6,525	12,325
Nonprofessional staff	341,468	220,574	109,472	32.8	57,647	34,778	14,156	2,891	7,543	3,879
Females	**1,797,589**	**1,270,063**	**408,577**	**23.5**	**203,969**	**105,098**	**88,048**	**11,462**	**60,128**	**58,821**
Professional staff	1,219,855	888,171	228,604	19.5	103,164	52,687	65,937	6,816	49,143	53,937
Executive/administrative/managerial	101,101	80,294	19,198	19.2	11,022	4,727	2,848	601	1,266	343
Faculty (instruction and research)	575,973	439,086	94,099	17.3	41,775	21,987	27,211	3,126	30,749	12,039
Instruction and research assistants	149,612	81,720	25,856	18.4	7,739	6,238	11,190	689	9,129	32,907
Other professional	393,169	287,071	89,451	23.2	42,628	19,735	24,688	2,400	7,999	8,648
Nonprofessional staff	577,734	381,892	179,973	31.8	100,805	52,411	22,111	4,646	10,985	4,884
Full-time	**2,179,864**	**1,586,274**	**509,397**	**23.7**	**244,083**	**130,684**	**120,804**	**13,826**	**30,901**	**53,292**
Professional staff	1,432,107	1,095,408	268,145	19.0	110,047	58,919	91,536	7,643	20,802	47,752
Executive/administrative/managerial	190,078	154,254	32,587	17.4	17,968	8,208	5,324	1,087	2,403	834
Faculty (instruction and research)	675,624	527,900	109,964	16.5	35,458	22,818	48,457	3,231	9,703	28,057
Other professional	566,405	413,254	125,594	22.5	56,621	27,893	37,755	3,325	8,696	18,861
Nonprofessional staff	747,757	490,866	241,252	32.7	134,036	71,765	29,268	6,183	10,099	5,540
Part-time	**1,199,223**	**807,154**	**202,437**	**18.3**	**84,632**	**54,268**	**57,390**	**6,147**	**90,411**	**99,221**
Professional staff	1,027,778	695,554	154,244	16.3	60,216	38,844	50,391	4,793	81,982	95,998
Executive/administrative/managerial	6,246	5,240	799	13.1	385	212	169	33	157	50
Faculty (instruction and research)	614,802	459,878	90,483	16.2	40,987	23,842	22,542	3,112	57,389	7,052
Instruction and research assistants	317,141	163,385	48,364	16.2	12,405	11,049	23,681	1,229	18,608	86,784
Other professional	89,589	67,051	14,598	17.4	6,439	3,741	3,999	419	5,828	2,112
Nonprofessional staff	171,445	111,600	48,193	29.6	24,416	15,424	6,999	1,354	8,429	3,223
Public 4-year	**1,656,709**	**1,146,857**	**363,976**	**22.5**	**157,692**	**91,594**	**104,105**	**10,585**	**39,238**	**106,638**
Professional staff	1,200,168	845,384	218,642	18.7	77,057	49,133	85,906	6,546	33,598	102,544
Executive/administrative/managerial	74,241	60,236	13,010	17.7	7,443	2,972	2,146	449	654	341
Faculty (instruction and research)	486,691	372,215	81,345	17.2	24,875	17,953	35,952	2,565	12,718	20,413
Instruction and research assistants	257,578	135,646	40,542	16.6	10,276	9,276	19,891	1,099	12,741	68,649
Other professional	381,658	277,287	83,745	22.4	34,463	18,932	27,917	2,433	7,485	13,141
Nonprofessional staff	456,541	301,473	145,334	32.2	80,635	42,461	18,199	4,039	5,640	4,094
Private 4-year	**1,073,764**	**767,184**	**213,736**	**20.9**	**106,109**	**50,836**	**53,092**	**3,699**	**50,691**	**42,153**
Professional staff	789,179	581,987	125,059	16.8	54,501	26,172	41,932	2,454	43,221	38,912
Executive/administrative/managerial	90,415	74,318	14,078	15.8	7,611	3,564	2,618	285	1,530	489
Faculty (instruction and research)	430,305	325,283	61,655	15.4	24,431	12,190	23,650	1,384	30,683	12,684
Instruction and research assistants	59,147	27,459	7,701	14.5	2,057	1,751	3,767	126	5,856	18,131
Other professional	209,312	154,927	41,625	20.4	20,402	8,667	11,897	659	5,152	7,608
Nonprofessional staff	284,585	185,197	88,677	32.0	51,608	24,664	11,160	1,245	7,470	3,241
Public 2-year	**610,978**	**452,254**	**124,831**	**21.5**	**60,209**	**39,626**	**19,860**	**5,136**	**30,196**	**3,697**
Professional staff	440,536	341,114	72,140	17.4	35,175	20,582	13,256	3,127	25,008	2,274
Executive/administrative/managerial	26,770	21,293	5,137	19.4	2,713	1,488	622	314	292	48
Faculty (instruction and research)	354,497	275,596	53,747	16.2	25,063	15,577	10,845	2,262	23,154	2,000
Instruction and research assistants	374	256	106	29.0	70	13	22	1	8	4
Other professional	58,895	43,969	13,150	22.9	7,329	3,504	1,767	550	1,554	222
Nonprofessional staff	170,442	111,140	52,691	31.9	25,034	19,044	6,604	2,009	5,188	1,423
Private 2-year	**37,636**	**27,133**	**9,291**	**25.5**	**4,705**	**2,896**	**1,137**	**553**	**1,187**	**25**
Professional staff	30,002	22,477	6,548	22.5	3,530	1,876	833	309	957	20
Executive/administrative/managerial	4,898	3,647	1,161	24.1	586	396	107	72	84	6
Faculty (instruction and research)	18,933	14,684	3,700	20.1	2,076	940	552	132	537	12
Instruction and research assistants	42	24	15	38.5	2	9	1	3	3	0
Other professional	6,129	4,122	1,672	28.8	866	531	173	102	333	2
Nonprofessional staff	7,634	4,656	2,743	37.0	1,175	1,020	304	244	230	5

[1]Minority staff as a percentage of total staff, excluding race/ethnicity unknown.
[2]Race/ethnicity not collected.
NOTE: Degree-granting institutions grant associate's or higher degrees and participate in Title IV federal financial aid programs. Race categories exclude persons of Hispanic origin.

The survey did not permit respondents to report instruction and research assistants as full-time staff.
SOURCE: U.S. Department of Education, National Center for Education Statistics, 2005 Integrated Postsecondary Education Data System (IPEDS), Winter 2005–06. (This table was prepared August 2006.)

Table 230. Number of full-time-equivalent staff and faculty, and full-time-equivalent staff and faculty/student ratios in degree-granting institutions, by control and type of institution and state or jurisdiction: Fall 2005

State or jurisdiction	Full-time-equivalent (FTE) staff				Full-time-equivalent (FTE) faculty				Full-time-equivalent faculty as a percent of FTE staff				Full-time-equivalent students per FTE staff				Full-time-equivalent students per FTE faculty			
	Public		Private		Public		Private		Public		Private		Public		Private		Public		Private	
	4-year	2-year	4-year	2-year	4-year	2-year	4-year	2-year	4-year	2-year	4-year	2-year	4-year	2-year	4-year	2-year	4-year	2-year	4-year	2-year
1	2	3	4	5	6	7	8	9	10	11	12	13	14	15	16	17	18	19	20	21
United States	1,337,858	405,524	857,095	30,159	387,475	191,218	289,756	12,858	29.0	47.2	33.8	42.6	4.3	9.0	4.1	9.2	14.8	19.2	12.2	21.6
Alabama	29,738	5,857	4,597	208	7,948	2,761	1,704	53	26.7	47.1	37.1	25.4	4.1	9.2	5.4	3.3	15.4	19.6	14.5	12.9
Alaska	4,972	140	278	†	1,588	31	97	†	31.9	22.4	34.8	†	3.7	3.3	3.3	†	11.6	14.8	9.8	†
Arizona	23,427	10,702	14,699	1,035	5,593	4,958	6,132	476	23.9	46.3	41.7	46.0	4.3	9.5	13.9	11.9	18.2	20.4	33.4	25.9
Arkansas	15,459	3,957	2,549	72	4,270	1,788	837	26	27.6	45.2	32.8	36.5	4.4	7.8	5.1	8.1	15.8	17.2	15.4	22.2
California	126,789	58,480	73,072	3,793	35,941	31,196	27,098	1,632	28.3	53.3	37.1	43.0	4.2	12.9	4.1	9.5	14.9	24.2	11.1	22.1
Colorado	24,434	5,538	8,186	670	10,358	2,554	3,109	310	42.4	46.1	38.0	46.3	5.1	7.9	5.9	13.0	11.9	17.2	15.5	28.0
Connecticut	13,005	2,976	20,025	239	3,522	1,518	6,634	104	27.1	51.0	33.1	43.8	4.1	8.9	2.6	6.2	15.3	17.4	7.9	14.1
Delaware	5,133	1,302	994	27	1,270	545	435	13	24.7	41.9	43.7	47.2	4.4	6.3	9.1	6.0	17.7	15.0	20.8	12.8
District of Columbia	1,038	†	20,201	†	398	†	6,120	†	38.3	†	30.3	†	3.5	†	3.7	†	9.1	†	12.3	†
Florida	52,063	19,482	30,603	1,851	18,289	7,837	11,443	715	35.1	40.2	37.4	38.6	5.5	8.3	5.4	11.0	15.8	20.6	14.4	28.3
Georgia	38,197	12,163	19,087	553	10,160	5,792	7,020	206	26.6	47.6	36.8	37.2	4.3	7.7	3.7	8.8	16.3	16.1	10.2	23.8
Hawaii	6,044	1,519	1,987	84	2,169	775	1,039	41	35.9	51.0	52.3	48.7	3.7	8.8	6.5	12.1	10.4	17.2	12.4	24.8
Idaho	6,853	1,095	1,773	67	2,326	438	851	34	33.9	40.0	48.0	50.1	5.6	7.2	8.8	7.6	16.5	17.9	18.4	15.2
Illinois	49,092	19,804	53,627	655	11,369	8,683	17,699	250	23.2	43.8	33.0	38.2	3.5	10.2	4.3	6.6	15.3	23.3	12.9	17.2
Indiana	40,415	3,747	16,541	832	10,691	2,060	5,427	360	26.5	55.0	32.8	43.2	4.3	9.3	4.5	11.9	16.2	16.9	13.7	27.6
Iowa	18,769	6,026	11,491	170	5,115	2,452	4,003	67	27.3	40.7	34.8	39.7	3.2	9.0	5.4	7.8	11.7	22.1	15.5	19.7
Kansas	17,834	6,174	2,948	254	5,642	2,584	1,087	104	31.6	41.8	36.9	40.7	4.5	7.2	5.4	6.0	14.1	17.1	14.7	14.7
Kentucky	25,927	5,546	5,802	391	7,096	2,741	2,146	177	27.4	49.4	37.0	45.1	3.8	9.2	5.6	10.2	13.9	18.6	15.1	22.7
Louisiana	23,344	3,282	6,161	344	7,215	1,760	2,051	155	30.9	53.6	33.3	45.2	5.5	7.1	1.8	10.9	17.7	13.2	5.5	24.0
Maine	6,201	991	3,631	109	1,848	558	1,040	55	29.8	56.3	28.6	50.6	4.3	8.1	3.9	8.3	14.6	14.5	13.7	16.4
Maryland	27,142	10,508	21,736	262	9,498	4,642	5,626	137	35.0	44.2	25.9	52.4	4.0	6.5	1.9	12.5	11.4	14.8	7.4	23.8
Massachusetts	20,604	6,892	72,655	284	6,024	2,912	24,273	140	29.2	42.3	33.4	49.6	4.1	7.5	3.0	7.9	13.9	17.8	9.0	15.9
Michigan	53,963	12,496	12,251	191	16,186	6,058	4,972	73	30.0	48.5	40.6	38.0	4.5	9.9	7.3	12.6	15.1	20.3	18.0	33.2
Minnesota	24,612	7,338	14,046	606	5,957	3,610	5,363	244	24.2	49.2	38.2	40.3	4.4	10.0	6.5	7.7	18.1	20.3	17.1	19.1
Mississippi	21,257	6,171	1,887	179	4,404	2,914	680	92	20.7	47.2	36.0	51.3	2.9	8.7	6.0	9.6	13.9	18.4	16.6	18.7
Missouri	29,048	7,037	27,764	1,025	8,625	3,024	10,118	443	29.7	43.0	36.4	43.2	3.7	7.8	4.0	7.8	12.5	18.2	10.9	18.1
Montana	6,376	889	814	101	1,974	345	325	36	31.0	38.8	39.9	35.4	4.7	7.0	4.6	4.4	15.1	18.0	11.6	12.5
Nebraska	12,677	2,851	5,362	88	3,635	1,355	1,888	38	28.7	47.5	35.2	43.3	3.6	8.7	4.5	6.4	12.5	18.3	12.7	14.9
Nevada	8,862	1,083	819	282	2,987	506	548	112	33.7	46.8	66.9	39.8	6.4	7.5	9.1	10.1	19.1	15.9	13.6	25.3
New Hampshire	5,249	1,243	7,310	161	1,437	723	1,898	56	27.4	58.2	26.0	35.0	4.5	5.9	3.2	7.3	16.5	10.2	12.4	20.9
New Jersey	35,075	9,844	14,195	148	9,849	4,244	4,867	49	28.1	43.1	34.3	32.9	3.5	10.2	4.2	7.9	12.4	23.6	12.3	24.1
New Mexico	14,685	5,274	1,129	35	3,383	2,013	637	19	23.0	38.2	56.4	54.7	3.1	6.9	7.8	14.7	13.4	18.0	13.8	26.9
New York	48,911	21,034	124,176	3,359	18,066	9,613	39,831	1,367	36.9	45.7	32.1	40.7	6.0	9.2	3.4	8.7	16.1	20.1	10.6	21.3
North Carolina	42,161	20,486	31,229	214	10,972	11,245	8,338	75	26.0	54.9	26.7	34.9	4.0	5.9	2.5	7.2	15.5	10.8	9.4	20.6
North Dakota	6,255	1,094	694	346	2,020	439	317	68	32.3	40.2	45.7	19.7	4.7	6.2	6.4	4.0	14.5	15.4	14.1	20.3
Ohio	53,405	11,845	26,934	1,774	15,381	5,749	9,558	778	28.8	48.5	35.5	43.8	4.5	9.1	4.5	10.9	15.7	18.7	12.6	24.9
Oklahoma	21,386	4,628	4,621	211	5,910	1,810	1,706	106	27.6	39.1	36.9	50.1	4.4	8.8	5.1	12.4	16.1	22.5	13.7	24.8
Oregon	20,873	7,896	5,786	288	6,149	3,276	2,441	105	29.5	41.5	42.2	36.4	3.3	6.1	5.1	8.9	11.3	14.6	12.0	24.4
Pennsylvania	52,782	8,413	64,639	4,174	17,965	4,143	21,319	1,917	34.0	49.2	33.0	45.9	4.4	9.0	3.6	7.6	12.8	18.3	11.0	16.6
Rhode Island	3,410	859	9,203	65	1,029	436	2,687	26	30.2	50.7	29.2	39.4	5.8	10.7	4.1	8.4	19.1	21.1	14.0	21.3

See notes at end of table.

Table 230. Number of full-time-equivalent staff and faculty, and full-time-equivalent staff and faculty/student ratios in degree-granting institutions, by control and type of institution and state or jurisdiction: Fall 2005—Continued

State or jurisdiction	Full-time-equivalent (FTE) staff				Full-time-equivalent (FTE) faculty				Full-time-equivalent faculty as a percent of FTE staff				Full-time-equivalent students per FTE staff				Full-time-equivalent students per FTE faculty			
	Public		Private		Public		Private		Public		Private		Public		Private		Public		Private	
	4-year	2-year	4-year	2-year	4-year	2-year	4-year	2-year	4-year	2-year	4-year	2-year	4-year	2-year	4-year	2-year	4-year	2-year	4-year	2-year
1	2	3	4	5	6	7	8	9	10	11	12	13	14	15	16	17	18	19	20	21
South Carolina	19,621	6,219	5,323	163	5,649	2,899	1,840	54	28.8	46.6	34.6	32.9	4.3	8.1	5.7	11.0	14.9	17.4	16.4	33.3
South Dakota	4,848	622	1,504	52	1,565	313	560	27	32.3	50.3	37.2	51.9	5.3	7.8	5.5	5.4	16.3	15.6	14.8	10.3
Tennessee	25,766	5,481	27,866	922	7,322	2,556	6,584	405	28.4	46.6	23.6	43.9	4.2	9.1	2.3	11.1	14.8	19.4	9.8	25.2
Texas	119,326	38,131	28,734	1,843	27,622	16,795	9,744	767	23.1	44.0	33.9	41.6	3.7	8.2	4.1	9.8	15.9	18.7	12.0	23.4
Utah	16,335	2,765	6,340	340	5,398	1,171	2,265	151	33.0	42.3	35.7	44.5	5.1	7.4	7.0	8.6	15.6	17.6	19.6	19.2
Vermont	4,685	363	3,800	366	1,549	193	1,185	136	33.1	53.1	31.2	37.1	3.4	6.9	3.6	1.6	10.4	12.9	11.6	4.4
Virginia	38,492	7,654	15,192	705	12,097	4,240	5,130	345	31.4	55.4	33.8	49.0	4.3	11.0	4.8	10.1	13.6	19.9	14.1	20.6
Washington	53	8,140	5,899	3,514	20	3,574	2,625	1,318	29.5	43.9	44.5	37.5	3.5	9.0	5.7	13.1	11.8	20.5	12.7	35.0
West Virginia	10,414	992	1,967	112	3,740	609	679	50	35.9	61.4	34.5	44.8	5.6	12.0	5.5	19.0	15.7	19.6	16.0	42.3
Wisconsin	28,711	11,263	12,963	101	8,373	5,644	4,892	28	29.2	50.1	37.7	28.3	4.8	5.8	4.2	4.8	16.5	11.5	11.0	17.0
Wyoming	2,981	1,935	†	358	994	811	†	216	33.3	41.9	†	60.4	3.5	6.2	†	7.3	10.6	14.7	†	12.1
U.S. Service Schools	1,647	†	†	†	767	†	†	†	46.6	†	†	†	9.3	†	†	†	19.9	†	†	†
Other jurisdictions	15,794	1,276	10,322	1,004	4,941	506	4,178	479	31.3	39.7	40.5	47.7	4.0	5.7	10.3	13.1	12.9	14.3	25.4	27.4
American Samoa	†	210	†	†	†	86	†	†	†	41.0	†	†	†	4.9	†	†	†	12.0	†	†
Federated States of Micronesia	†	340	†	†	†	105	†	†	†	30.9	†	†	†	5.3	†	†	†	17.1	†	†
Guam	610	227	21	†	187	89	5	†	30.6	39.2	23.8	†	4.0	5.7	7.4	†	13.2	14.5	31.0	†
Marshall Islands	†	130	†	†	†	51	†	†	†	39.2	†	†	†	4.0	†	†	†	10.1	†	†
Northern Marianas	190	†	†	†	78	†	†	†	41.1	†	†	†	4.4	†	†	†	10.7	†	†	†
Palau	†	140	†	†	†	42	†	†	†	29.7	†	†	†	3.6	†	†	†	12.2	†	†
Puerto Rico	14,329	228	10,301	1,004	4,511	133	4,173	479	31.5	58.4	40.5	47.7	4.1	9.2	10.3	13.1	13.0	15.8	25.3	27.4
Virgin Islands	665	†	†	†	165	†	†	†	24.8	†	†	†	2.6	†	†	†	10.4	†	†	†

†Not applicable.

NOTE: Degree-granting institutions grant associate's or higher degrees and participate in Title IV federal financial aid programs.

SOURCE: U.S. Department of Education, National Center for Education Statistics, 2005 Integrated Postsecondary Education Data System (IPEDS), Winter 2005–06 and Spring 2006. (This table was prepared August 2006.)

Table 231. Number of instructional faculty in degree-granting institutions, by employment status and control and type of institution: Selected years, fall 1970 through fall 2005

[In thousands]

Year	Total	Employment status			Control				Type	
		Full-time	Part-time	Percent full-time	Public	Private			4-year	2-year
						Total	Not-for-profit	For-profit		
1	2	3	4	5	6	7	8	9	10	11
1970	474	369	104	77.9	314	160	—	—	382	92
1971[1]	492	379	113	77.0	333	159	—	—	387	105
1972	500	380	120	76.0	343	157	—	—	384	116
1973[1]	527	389	138	73.8	365	162	—	—	401	126
1974[1]	567	406	161	71.6	397	170	—	—	427	140
1975[1]	628	440	188	70.1	443	185	—	—	467	161
1976	633	434	199	68.6	449	184	—	—	467	166
1977	678	448	230	66.1	492	186	—	—	485	193
1979[1]	675	445	230	65.9	488	187	—	—	494	182
1980[1]	686	450	236	65.6	495	191	—	—	494	192
1981	705	461	244	65.4	509	196	—	—	493	212
1982[1]	710	462	248	65.1	506	204	—	—	493	217
1983	724	471	254	65.0	512	212	—	—	504	220
1984[1]	717	462	255	64.4	505	212	—	—	504	213
1985[1]	715	459	256	64.2	503	212	—	—	504	211
1986[1]	722	459	263	63.6	510	212	—	—	506	216
1987[2]	793	523	270	66.0	553	240	—	—	548	246
1989[2]	824	524	300	63.6	577	247	—	—	584	241
1991[2]	826	536	291	64.8	581	245	—	—	591	235
1993[2]	915	546	370	59.6	650	265	254	11	626	290
1995[2]	932	551	381	59.1	657	275	261	14	647	285
1997[2]	990	569	421	57.5	695	295	271	24	683	307
1999[2]	1,028	591	437	57.5	713	315	285	30	714	314
2001[2]	1,113	618	495	55.5	771	342	306	36	764	349
2003[2]	1,175	632	543	53.8	793	382	331	52	816	359
2005[2]	1,290	676	615	52.4	841	449	362	88	917	373

—Not available.

[1]Estimated on the basis of enrollment. For methodological details on estimates, see National Center for Education Statistics, *Projections of Education Statistics to 2000*.

[2]Because of revised survey methods, data are not directly comparable with figures for years prior to 1987.

NOTE: Includes faculty members with the title of professor, associate professor, assistant professor, instructor, lecturer, assisting professor, adjunct professor, or interim professor (or the equivalent). Excluded are graduate students with titles such as graduate or teaching fellow who assist senior faculty. Data through 1995 are for institutions of higher education, while later data are for degree-granting institutions. Degree-granting institutions grant associate's or higher degrees and participate in Title IV federal financial aid programs. The degree-granting classification is very similar to the earlier higher education classification, but it includes more 2-year colleges and excludes a few higher education institutions that did not grant degrees. (See Guide to Sources for details.) Detail may not sum to totals because of rounding.

SOURCE: U.S. Department of Education, National Center for Education Statistics, Higher Education General Information Survey (HEGIS), *Employees in Institutions of Higher Education*, 1970 and 1972, and "Staff Survey" 1976; *Projections of Education Statistics to 2000*; 1987 through 2005 Integrated Postsecondary Education Data System (IPEDS), "Fall Staff Survey" (IPEDS-S:87–99), and Winter 2001–02 through Winter 2005–06; and U.S. Equal Employment Opportunity Commission, Higher Education Staff Information Survey (EEO-6), 1977, 1981, and 1983. (This table was prepared August 2006.)

Table 232. Full-time instructional faculty in degree-granting institutions, by race/ethnicity and residency status, sex, and academic rank: Fall 2003 and fall 2005

| Sex and academic rank | Total | White | Minority | | | | | | Race/ ethnicity unknown | Nonresident alien[2] |
			Number	Percent[1]	Black	Hispanic	Asian/Pacific Islander	American Indian/Alaska Native		
1	2	3	4	5	6	7	8	9	10	11
2003										
Total	631,596	506,466	97,327	15.6	33,137	20,079	41,133	2,978	6,603	21,200
Professors	166,415	144,924	19,481	11.8	5,343	3,429	10,202	507	821	1,189
Associate professors	132,961	109,313	20,777	15.7	7,204	3,861	9,183	529	904	1,967
Assistant professors	153,064	112,920	28,662	19.0	9,464	5,321	13,216	661	2,017	9,465
Instructors	93,023	73,254	16,660	18.2	6,751	4,780	4,299	830	1,351	1,758
Lecturers	23,448	18,473	3,589	15.5	1,199	1,084	1,206	100	314	1,072
Other faculty	62,685	47,582	8,158	13.3	3,176	1,604	3,027	351	1,196	5,749
Males	382,808	307,104	56,951	15.0	16,270	11,245	27,815	1,621	3,825	14,928
Professors	127,049	110,561	14,843	11.7	3,427	2,472	8,591	353	622	1,023
Associate professors	82,758	67,497	13,131	16.0	3,863	2,338	6,643	287	585	1,545
Assistant professors	83,564	60,166	15,576	18.9	4,276	2,812	8,167	321	1,150	6,672
Instructors	44,984	35,474	7,785	17.6	2,809	2,372	2,165	439	706	1,019
Lecturers	11,175	8,778	1,605	14.6	570	466	525	44	169	623
Other faculty	33,278	24,628	4,011	12.3	1,325	785	1,724	177	593	4,046
Females	248,788	199,362	40,376	16.4	16,867	8,834	13,318	1,357	2,778	6,272
Professors	39,366	34,363	4,638	11.8	1,916	957	1,611	154	199	166
Associate professors	50,203	41,816	7,646	15.3	3,341	1,523	2,540	242	319	422
Assistant professors	69,500	52,754	13,086	19.1	5,188	2,509	5,049	340	867	2,793
Instructors	48,039	37,780	8,875	18.7	3,942	2,408	2,134	391	645	739
Lecturers	12,273	9,695	1,984	16.4	629	618	681	56	145	449
Other faculty	29,407	22,954	4,147	14.4	1,851	819	1,303	174	603	1,703
2005										
Total	675,624	527,900	109,964	16.5	35,458	22,818	48,457	3,231	9,703	28,057
Professors	169,192	145,936	20,856	12.4	5,484	3,793	11,060	519	1,014	1,386
Associate professors	138,444	112,507	22,429	16.4	7,402	4,319	10,144	564	1,296	2,212
Assistant professors	159,689	114,470	31,253	19.9	9,897	5,728	14,922	706	2,809	11,157
Instructors	98,555	76,359	18,368	19.0	7,462	5,261	4,740	905	1,853	1,975
Lecturers	27,215	20,982	4,342	16.2	1,286	1,233	1,714	109	480	1,411
Other faculty	82,529	57,646	12,716	15.8	3,927	2,484	5,877	428	2,251	9,916
Males	401,507	313,685	62,923	15.9	17,029	12,486	31,711	1,697	5,668	19,231
Professors	126,788	109,128	15,706	12.5	3,498	2,680	9,180	348	764	1,190
Associate professors	84,783	68,383	13,893	16.5	3,947	2,551	7,099	296	835	1,672
Assistant professors	86,182	60,244	16,671	19.7	4,459	3,003	8,903	306	1,601	7,666
Instructors	46,481	36,034	8,360	18.4	2,987	2,581	2,320	472	978	1,109
Lecturers	12,976	9,898	1,980	15.6	595	495	839	51	264	834
Other faculty	44,297	29,998	6,313	14.7	1,543	1,176	3,370	224	1,226	6,760
Females	274,117	214,215	47,041	17.4	18,429	10,332	16,746	1,534	4,035	8,826
Professors	42,404	36,808	5,150	12.2	1,986	1,113	1,880	171	250	196
Associate professors	53,661	44,124	8,536	16.0	3,455	1,768	3,045	268	461	540
Assistant professors	73,507	54,226	14,582	20.2	5,438	2,725	6,019	400	1,208	3,491
Instructors	52,074	40,325	10,008	19.5	4,475	2,680	2,420	433	875	866
Lecturers	14,239	11,084	2,362	16.8	691	738	875	58	216	577
Other faculty	38,232	27,648	6,403	17.2	2,384	1,308	2,507	204	1,025	3,156

[1]Minority faculty as a percentage of total faculty, excluding race/ethnicity unknown.
[2]Race/ethnicity not collected.
NOTE: Degree-granting institutions grant associate's or higher degrees and participate in Title IV federal financial aid programs. Race categories exclude persons of Hispanic origin. Totals may differ from figures reported in other tables because of varying survey methodologies.

SOURCE: U.S. Department of Education, National Center for Education Statistics, 2003 and 2005 Integrated Postsecondary Education Data System (IPEDS), Winter 2003–04 and Winter 2005–06. (This table was prepared August 2006.)

Table 233. Percentage distribution of full-time instructional faculty and staff in degree-granting institutions, by type and control of institution, selected instruction activities, and number of classes taught for credit: Fall 2003

Instruction activity and number of classes	All institutions	Research		Doctoral		Comprehensive		Private liberal arts	Public 2-year	Other
		Public	Private	Public	Private	Public	Private			
1	2	3	4	5	6	7	8	9	10	11
Number of full-time instructional faculty and staff (in thousands)	681.8 (0.05)	162.1 (0.85)	63.5 (1.58)	51.3 (0.76)	21.7 (0.79)	107.3 (2.98)	41.4 (1.59)	49.6 (1.80)	138.3 (2.53)	46.6 (2.78)
Percentage distribution	100.0 (†)	23.8 (0.12)	9.3 (0.23)	7.5 (0.11)	3.2 (0.12)	15.7 (0.44)	6.1 (0.23)	7.3 (0.26)	20.3 (0.37)	6.8 (0.41)
Average hours worked per week	53.3 (0.13)	55.6 (0.21)	55.8 (0.42)	54.0 (0.38)	52.4 (0.59)	53.2 (0.31)	51.8 (0.53)	54.0 (0.39)	50.0 (0.28)	52.4 (0.67)
Paid activities within institution	45.4 (0.12)	48.8 (0.19)	47.8 (0.36)	45.9 (0.31)	44.7 (0.47)	44.4 (0.27)	42.9 (0.55)	45.6 (0.39)	42.1 (0.23)	43.7 (0.72)
Unpaid activities within institution	3.8 (0.04)	3.1 (0.08)	3.3 (0.15)	3.9 (0.14)	3.8 (0.20)	4.4 (0.13)	4.4 (0.15)	4.4 (0.11)	4.0 (0.11)	3.9 (0.31)
Paid activities outside institution	2.2 (0.05)	1.8 (0.08)	2.7 (0.21)	2.1 (0.13)	2.3 (0.25)	2.3 (0.12)	2.2 (0.17)	2.0 (0.13)	2.3 (0.12)	3.1 (0.34)
Unpaid activities outside institution	1.9 (0.03)	1.9 (0.05)	2.0 (0.09)	2.1 (0.11)	1.7 (0.11)	2.1 (0.09)	2.3 (0.12)	2.0 (0.14)	1.6 (0.07)	1.8 (0.14)
Work time distribution (percent)	100.0 (†)	100.0 (†)	100.0 (†)	100.0 (2.08)	100.0 (†)	100.0 (†)	100.0 (†)	100.0 (†)	100.0 (†)	100.0 (†)
Teaching	58.2 (0.27)	43.5 (0.43)	43.1 (0.76)	55.5 (0.72)	55.0 (1.15)	64.7 (0.70)	67.5 (0.78)	65.9 (0.80)	72.3 (0.57)	61.2 (2.14)
Research/scholarship	20.0 (0.44)	33.2 (0.42)	34.0 (0.84)	22.3 (0.72)	24.6 (0.84)	15.0 (0.49)	11.2 (0.57)	12.7 (0.67)	7.9 (0.32)	13.8 (1.29)
Other	21.7 (0.17)	23.2 (0.45)	22.8 (0.67)	22.2 (0.64)	20.4 (1.21)	20.4 (0.66)	21.3 (0.75)	21.3 (0.73)	19.8 (0.52)	25.0 (1.75)
Faculty/staff distribution by instruction activity (percent)										
Distribution by hours taught per week	100.0 (†)	100.0 (†)	100.0 (†)	100.0 (†)	100.0 (†)	100.0 (†)	100.0 (†)	100.0 (†)	100.0 (†)	100.0 (†)
Less than 4.0	30.3 (0.44)	48.9 (0.83)	52.2 (1.31)	30.0 (1.70)	26.5 (1.74)	16.3 (1.08)	14.9 (1.06)	15.5 (1.15)	20.3 (0.88)	29.5 (2.74)
4.0 to 5.9	5.8 (0.21)	8.4 (0.50)	8.8 (0.77)	6.0 (0.58)	8.4 (1.37)	4.1 (0.53)	4.1 (0.57)	4.1 (0.57)	3.7 (0.52)	5.3 (0.89)
6.0 to 7.9	13.8 (0.37)	20.0 (0.80)	15.2 (1.20)	22.2 (1.14)	22.0 (1.77)	12.0 (0.78)	11.0 (1.43)	13.3 (1.48)	5.0 (0.57)	9.6 (1.19)
8.0 to 9.9	12.5 (0.30)	9.0 (0.49)	9.3 (0.87)	16.9 (1.20)	19.3 (1.76)	21.5 (0.93)	18.7 (1.78)	19.5 (1.83)	6.1 (0.60)	6.9 (1.23)
10.0 to 14.9	18.2 (0.39)	7.9 (0.55)	8.8 (0.88)	15.1 (1.13)	15.0 (1.53)	31.5 (1.24)	32.7 (2.15)	33.5 (1.93)	14.7 (1.12)	22.1 (2.01)
15.0 or more	19.4 (0.40)	5.8 (0.43)	5.7 (0.67)	9.7 (0.92)	8.7 (1.34)	14.6 (0.93)	18.5 (1.92)	14.1 (1.39)	50.2 (1.49)	26.5 (2.54)
Distribution by number of students taught	100.0 (†)	100.0 (†)	100.0 (†)	100.0 (†)	100.0 (†)	100.0 (†)	100.0 (†)	100.0 (†)	100.0 (†)	100.0 (†)
Less than 25	30.6 (0.46)	46.0 (0.84)	51.5 (1.56)	29.7 (1.53)	31.9 (1.88)	16.8 (1.25)	16.5 (1.23)	20.8 (1.44)	21.8 (0.96)	29.7 (2.19)
25 to 49	17.0 (0.34)	17.0 (0.83)	16.9 (1.06)	17.1 (0.99)	18.8 (1.74)	17.9 (0.96)	22.7 (1.57)	25.4 (1.62)	11.6 (0.77)	15.4 (1.41)
50 to 74	16.2 (0.33)	11.9 (0.69)	10.0 (0.99)	16.3 (1.29)	20.9 (1.64)	18.7 (0.77)	26.5 (1.32)	24.4 (1.40)	14.8 (0.70)	17.8 (1.53)
75 to 99	13.0 (0.30)	7.6 (0.51)	6.2 (0.57)	13.9 (0.91)	11.2 (0.95)	17.5 (0.86)	17.6 (1.15)	15.8 (1.09)	16.4 (0.70)	13.3 (1.39)
100 to 149	14.2 (0.39)	7.6 (0.54)	7.0 (0.78)	13.2 (0.87)	9.9 (1.21)	19.4 (1.22)	13.1 (1.61)	10.6 (0.96)	23.7 (1.05)	15.4 (1.46)
150 or more	9.0 (0.27)	9.8 (0.59)	8.4 (0.73)	9.8 (0.87)	7.4 (1.04)	9.7 (0.85)	3.6 (0.72)	3.0 (0.62)	11.8 (0.66)	8.4 (0.83)
Distribution by student classroom contact hours per week[1]	100.0 (†)	100.0 (†)	100.0 (†)	100.0 (†)	100.0 (†)	100.0 (†)	100.0 (†)	100.0 (†)	100.0 (†)	100.0 (†)
Less than 50	24.2 (0.40)	38.3 (0.83)	42.7 (1.33)	23.2 (1.52)	22.0 (1.53)	11.9 (1.04)	12.6 (1.02)	12.2 (1.05)	17.3 (0.79)	24.1 (1.97)
50 to 99	5.3 (0.23)	7.7 (0.56)	7.0 (0.82)	6.4 (0.68)	7.0 (1.20)	4.3 (0.52)	2.7 (0.55)	4.9 (0.48)	3.0 (0.40)	5.1 (1.20)
100 to 199	7.1 (0.20)	9.4 (0.54)	10.7 (0.87)	8.0 (0.88)	8.6 (1.38)	6.2 (0.62)	4.5 (0.66)	7.2 (1.02)	3.8 (0.49)	6.2 (1.14)
200 to 349	9.0 (0.28)	10.9 (0.52)	10.4 (0.83)	10.4 (0.88)	12.8 (1.74)	8.6 (0.71)	10.9 (1.38)	11.9 (1.27)	4.0 (0.53)	7.4 (0.84)
350 to 499	7.7 (0.24)	8.0 (0.44)	8.1 (0.83)	10.6 (1.03)	11.5 (1.03)	7.9 (0.91)	10.2 (0.79)	12.4 (0.93)	3.7 (0.39)	4.4 (0.84)
500 or more	46.8 (0.44)	25.6 (0.74)	21.2 (1.21)	41.4 (1.36)	38.0 (1.81)	61.1 (1.46)	59.1 (1.75)	51.4 (2.13)	68.1 (1.03)	52.7 (2.88)
Distribution by total classroom credit hours	100.0 (†)	100.0 (†)	100.0 (†)	100.0 (†)	100.0 (†)	100.0 (†)	100.0 (†)	100.0 (†)	100.0 (†)	100.0 (†)
Less than 4.0	31.8 (0.54)	48.9 (0.82)	52.1 (1.55)	30.1 (1.46)	29.0 (1.75)	18.0 (1.03)	17.5 (1.44)	23.7 (2.18)	21.6 (0.88)	31.2 (2.66)
4.0 to 5.9	6.6 (0.22)	9.4 (0.54)	10.2 (0.63)	6.8 (0.67)	10.5 (1.53)	3.5 (0.35)	4.5 (0.61)	5.6 (0.67)	4.5 (0.43)	6.3 (1.17)
6.0 to 7.9	15.0 (0.37)	21.6 (0.66)	14.0 (1.04)	25.1 (1.29)	21.3 (1.71)	14.2 (0.94)	12.2 (1.04)	11.4 (1.15)	7.3 (0.70)	10.0 (1.30)
8.0 to 9.9	14.8 (0.33)	10.4 (0.60)	10.7 (0.84)	19.9 (1.28)	20.8 (1.47)	25.3 (1.15)	23.4 (1.73)	19.1 (1.16)	8.4 (0.58)	10.2 (1.59)
10.0 to 14.9	20.2 (0.38)	7.7 (0.51)	9.7 (0.99)	14.8 (1.17)	13.2 (1.40)	32.0 (1.20)	35.4 (1.94)	32.5 (2.20)	22.5 (1.10)	26.9 (1.89)
15.0 or more	11.6 (0.31)	1.9 (0.24)	3.2 (0.52)	3.3 (0.64)	5.2 (0.99)	7.0 (0.88)	6.9 (0.71)	7.7 (1.28)	35.8 (1.31)	15.5 (1.43)

See notes at end of table.

Table 233. Percentage distribution of full-time instructional faculty and staff in degree-granting institutions, by type and control of institution, selected instruction activities, and number of classes taught for credit: Fall 2003—Continued

Instruction activity and number of classes	All institutions	Research		Doctoral		Comprehensive		Private liberal arts	Public 2-year	Other
		Public	Private	Public	Private	Public	Private			
1	2	3	4	5	6	7	8	9	10	11
Faculty/staff distribution by number of classes taught for credit (percent)										
Faculty/staff with undergraduate classes only, by total for-credit courses	100.0 (†)	100.0 (†)	100.0 (†)	100.0 (†)	100.0 (†)	100.0 (†)	100.0 (†)	100.0 (†)	100.0 (†)	100.0 (†)
1	11.0 (0.43)	24.2 (2.40)	20.2 (2.97)	14.1 (2.91)	10.0 (2.52)	10.5 (1.31)	9.3 (1.13)	9.9 (0.98)	8.7 (0.74)	11.4 (1.89)
2	17.4 (0.62)	38.0 (2.80)	31.2 (3.96)	24.2 (3.05)	38.6 (5.05)	14.6 (1.51)	18.5 (2.14)	22.7 (2.32)	11.0 (0.77)	13.2 (2.34)
3	23.7 (0.65)	22.6 (2.21)	30.8 (3.42)	31.1 (2.98)	37.3 (3.60)	28.6 (1.89)	30.3 (2.48)	34.3 (2.57)	15.9 (0.94)	18.0 (2.99)
4	21.9 (0.73)	10.8 (1.43)	11.7 (2.99)	20.4 (1.92)	10.9 (2.75)	33.3 (1.87)	30.7 (2.77)	21.1 (2.22)	17.5 (1.02)	27.7 (2.67)
5 or more	26.1 (0.70)	4.4 (0.86)	6.1 (1.74)	10.1 (1.97)	3.2 (1.15)	13.0 (1.56)	11.2 (1.53)	12.0 (1.44)	46.9 (1.44)	29.7 (2.23)
Faculty/staff with graduate classes only, by total for-credit courses	100.0 (†)	100.0 (†)	100.0 (†)	100.0 (†)	100.0 (†)	100.0 (†)	100.0 (†)	100.0 (†)	100.0 (†)	100.0 (†)
1	40.1 (1.21)	50.4 (2.17)	48.0 (3.69)	34.3 (3.04)	25.9 (4.02)	23.6 (3.86)	13.0 (3.72)	15.8 (6.35)	41.0 (3.91)	32.8 (6.12)
2	31.0 (1.07)	26.3 (1.81)	27.9 (2.93)	39.1 (3.32)	50.7 (4.02)	33.6 (5.32)	28.7 (4.00)	31.6 (12.42)	30.4 (3.57)	37.1 (5.14)
3	16.7 (0.88)	14.3 (1.38)	13.3 (2.60)	16.3 (2.76)	14.1 (3.52)	29.6 (4.35)	36.3 (4.99)	22.7 (9.79)	13.3 (2.20)	13.0 (4.26)
4	7.1 (0.80)	4.5 (1.24)	7.4 (2.07)	7.4 (2.04)	3.7 (1.44)	10.1 (3.39)	16.5 (3.92)	16.7 (8.04)	6.7 (2.53)	8.6 (3.70)
5 or more	5.1 (0.52)	4.4 (0.69)	3.4 (1.33)	2.9 (1.62)	5.7 (2.80)	3.1 (1.52)	5.5 (2.85)	13.1 (6.95)	8.6 (2.21)	8.5 (2.95)
Faculty/staff with both undergraduate and graduate classes, by total for-credit courses	100.0 (†)	100.0 (†)	100.0 (†)	100.0 (†)	100.0 (†)	100.0 (†)	100.0 (†)	100.0 (†)	100.0 (†)	100.0 (†)
1	23.3 (0.68)	32.5 (1.37)	38.4 (1.89)	21.1 (2.17)	20.2 (2.37)	9.0 (1.04)	10.3 (2.14)	9.4 (2.00)	30.0 (6.42)	20.5 (4.49)
2	33.4 (0.83)	44.3 (1.36)	42.8 (2.33)	37.1 (2.15)	37.8 (2.58)	19.6 (1.30)	19.0 (2.78)	18.3 (2.62)	20.9 (5.73)	17.6 (4.17)
3	24.3 (0.70)	15.5 (0.99)	12.4 (1.37)	26.5 (1.75)	32.0 (3.01)	38.1 (1.91)	34.8 (2.85)	29.5 (3.77)	26.8 (3.63)	20.6 (4.69)
4	12.2 (0.54)	4.5 (0.64)	3.7 (1.06)	10.1 (1.37)	6.6 (2.02)	23.4 (1.69)	24.4 (3.39)	27.5 (3.74)	13.6 (6.37)	17.5 (3.31)
5 or more	6.7 (0.43)	3.1 (0.45)	2.8 (0.78)	5.2 (0.75)	3.2 (1.74)	9.9 (1.01)	11.4 (2.07)	15.2 (3.65)	8.7 (2.23)	23.9 (4.51)

†Not applicable.

[1]Distribution by student classroom contact hours per week is based on the number of contact hours that faculty and instructional staff spend each week with students during classroom instruction multiplied by the number of students taught.

NOTE: Totals may differ from figures reported in other tables because of varying survey methodologies. Detail may not sum to totals because of rounding. Standard errors appear in parentheses.
SOURCE: U.S. Department of Education, National Center for Education Statistics, 2004 National Study of Postsecondary Faculty (NSOPF:04). (This table was prepared September 2005.)

Table 234. Percentage distribution of part-time instructional faculty and staff in degree-granting institutions, by type and control of institution, selected instruction activities, and number of classes taught for credit: Fall 2003

Instruction activity and number of classes	All institutions	Research		Doctoral		Comprehensive		Private liberal arts	Public 2-year	Other
		Public	Private	Public	Private	Public	Private			
1	2	3	4	5	6	7	8	9	10	11
Number of part-time instructional faculty and staff (in thousands)	530.0 (0.02)	39.7 (0.78)	23.2 (0.96)	20.8 (0.82)	15.4 (0.83)	60.3 (2.49)	53.5 (2.17)	28.4 (2.19)	240.4 (2.90)	48.3 (2.42)
Percentage distribution	100.0 (†)	7.5 (0.15)	4.4 (0.18)	3.9 (0.15)	2.9 (0.16)	11.4 (0.47)	10.1 (0.41)	5.4 (0.41)	45.4 (0.55)	9.1 (0.46)
Average hours worked per week	39.9 (0.30)	41.1 (0.85)	42.6 (1.24)	43.5 (1.37)	42.1 (1.29)	38.8 (1.01)	42.7 (1.14)	39.6 (1.23)	38.2 (0.46)	41.7 (1.31)
Paid activities within institution	13.7 (0.13)	19.0 (0.61)	14.0 (0.65)	16.4 (0.76)	13.5 (0.97)	14.9 (0.48)	12.1 (0.56)	13.5 (0.73)	12.8 (0.20)	13.2 (0.47)
Unpaid activities within institution	1.7 (0.06)	1.8 (0.25)	2.5 (0.25)	2.3 (0.28)	2.8 (0.37)	2.3 (0.19)	2.7 (0.12)	2.6 (0.17)	2.2 (0.08)	2.4 (0.17)
Paid activities outside institution	22.1 (0.28)	18.3 (0.98)	23.9 (1.34)	23.3 (1.55)	24.1 (1.40)	19.9 (1.00)	26.6 (1.38)	21.9 (0.98)	21.5 (0.42)	24.4 (1.17)
Unpaid activities outside institution	2.3 (0.06)	2.0 (0.25)	2.2 (0.25)	1.6 (0.28)	1.7 (0.37)	1.8 (0.19)	1.3 (0.12)	1.6 (0.17)	1.7 (0.08)	1.7 (0.17)
Work time distribution (percent)	100.0 (†)	100.0 (†)	100.0 (†)	100.0 (†)	100.0 (†)	100.0 (†)	100.0 (†)	100.0 (†)	100.0 (†)	100.0 (†)
Teaching	88.3 (0.32)	74.1 (1.79)	80.6 (1.89)	84.9 (1.71)	87.2 (1.87)	90.8 (0.83)	90.4 (0.70)	90.2 (1.20)	90.8 (0.45)	86.8 (1.22)
Research/scholarship	3.9 (0.80)	13.3 (1.62)	7.0 (0.97)	7.4 (1.35)	5.2 (1.42)	3.2 (0.46)	2.4 (0.49)	2.6 (0.54)	2.3 (0.22)	3.7 (0.55)
Other	7.8 (0.20)	12.6 (1.04)	12.4 (1.75)	7.6 (1.03)	7.6 (1.22)	6.0 (0.63)	7.2 (0.81)	7.2 (0.92)	6.9 (0.40)	9.5 (1.00)
Faculty/staff distribution by instruction activity (percent)										
Distribution by hours taught per week	100.0 (†)	100.0 (†)	100.0 (†)	100.0 (†)	100.0 (†)	100.0 (†)	100.0 (†)	100.0 (†)	100.0 (†)	100.0 (†)
Less than 4.0	45.3 (0.80)	58.1 (2.25)	62.4 (3.87)	53.3 (2.71)	48.0 (2.67)	45.5 (1.68)	39.8 (2.34)	44.8 (2.96)	42.1 (1.29)	43.8 (2.72)
4.0 to 5.9	12.2 (0.48)	9.3 (1.25)	12.9 (2.46)	12.5 (1.49)	15.0 (1.57)	9.7 (1.25)	17.7 (2.07)	13.2 (1.73)	11.6 (0.72)	13.2 (1.67)
6.0 to 7.9	14.3 (0.57)	12.5 (1.50)	10.1 (1.69)	14.5 (1.76)	14.3 (2.01)	19.4 (1.68)	12.9 (2.14)	13.8 (1.98)	14.1 (1.02)	14.4 (1.66)
8.0 to 9.9	10.4 (0.47)	8.9 (1.22)	5.6 (1.46)	8.3 (1.82)	7.8 (1.58)	10.8 (1.11)	11.7 (1.93)	10.7 (1.54)	10.9 (0.72)	11.1 (1.64)
10.0 to 14.9	9.4 (0.47)	7.5 (1.27)	3.0 (1.16)	5.5 (1.29)	7.3 (2.03)	8.0 (1.27)	7.7 (1.29)	8.3 (1.55)	11.6 (0.94)	10.0 (1.45)
15.0 or more	8.3 (0.43)	3.6 (0.90)	6.0 (1.94)	5.9 (1.50)	7.6 (1.26)	6.5 (1.05)	10.3 (1.61)	9.1 (2.38)	9.7 (0.65)	7.5 (1.27)
Distribution by number of students taught	100.0 (†)	100.0 (†)	100.0 (†)	100.0 (†)	100.0 (†)	100.0 (†)	100.0 (†)	100.0 (†)	100.0 (†)	100.0 (†)
Less than 25	52.0 (0.82)	55.6 (2.16)	68.9 (3.98)	44.6 (2.68)	56.9 (3.29)	41.6 (2.07)	57.9 (2.45)	60.5 (2.34)	50.0 (1.35)	53.5 (3.60)
25 to 49	24.9 (0.58)	17.4 (1.54)	16.9 (2.13)	27.4 (2.51)	20.7 (2.48)	24.5 (2.10)	29.4 (1.90)	24.1 (1.76)	26.4 (0.94)	23.3 (2.51)
50 to 74	12.1 (0.54)	11.6 (1.23)	3.7 (1.15)	12.5 (1.71)	9.8 (2.48)	17.5 (1.52)	8.5 (0.77)	10.0 (1.65)	12.6 (0.93)	13.1 (1.76)
75 to 99	5.8 (0.30)	5.4 (0.89)	4.1 (1.57)	7.6 (1.52)	6.8 (1.62)	6.7 (1.22)	2.0 (0.44)	3.7 (0.97)	6.3 (0.45)	7.3 (1.42)
100 to 149	3.4 (0.23)	4.8 (1.07)	2.0 (0.72)	4.2 (1.46)	2.9 (0.89)	7.2 (1.14)	1.8 (0.55)	1.2 (0.66)	3.3 (0.41)	1.6 (0.70)
150 or more	1.9 (0.19)	5.2 (0.96)	4.5 (1.35)	3.7 (0.94)	2.8 (1.12)	2.6 (0.59)	0.4 (0.30)	0.4 (0.34)	1.3 (0.33)	1.2 (0.37)
Distribution by student classroom contact hours per week[1]	100.0 (†)	100.0 (†)	100.0 (†)	100.0 (†)	100.0 (†)	100.0 (†)	100.0 (†)	100.0 (†)	100.0 (†)	100.0 (†)
Less than 50	33.9 (0.80)	41.6 (2.52)	53.4 (3.98)	27.7 (2.98)	40.2 (2.67)	25.4 (1.88)	36.0 (2.52)	38.2 (2.66)	32.1 (1.35)	33.5 (3.71)
50 to 99	17.0 (0.54)	13.1 (1.46)	17.5 (2.13)	23.0 (3.38)	17.0 (2.30)	18.9 (1.40)	19.5 (1.53)	17.4 (1.97)	16.2 (0.96)	16.5 (1.79)
100 to 199	13.2 (0.49)	13.3 (1.51)	8.5 (1.44)	14.2 (2.34)	7.5 (1.56)	14.8 (1.72)	13.3 (1.65)	14.1 (2.01)	13.2 (0.74)	14.2 (1.95)
200 to 349	11.2 (0.46)	10.8 (1.29)	5.6 (1.42)	10.9 (1.97)	12.3 (1.88)	10.3 (1.80)	13.5 (0.93)	10.1 (1.26)	11.2 (0.67)	13.1 (1.63)
350 to 499	7.2 (0.34)	6.1 (0.98)	3.0 (0.96)	7.7 (1.74)	8.5 (1.74)	10.2 (1.00)	4.5 (0.64)	5.5 (0.95)	7.7 (0.66)	6.9 (1.06)
500 or more	17.5 (0.58)	15.1 (1.89)	12.1 (2.50)	16.5 (2.29)	14.5 (2.58)	20.3 (1.97)	13.3 (1.53)	14.6 (2.85)	19.5 (0.96)	15.8 (2.15)
Distribution by total classroom credit hours	100.0 (†)	100.0 (†)	100.0 (†)	100.0 (†)	100.0 (†)	100.0 (†)	100.0 (†)	100.0 (†)	100.0 (†)	100.0 (†)
Less than 4.0	53.3 (0.89)	59.8 (2.39)	67.5 (2.34)	62.2 (2.96)	55.4 (2.34)	52.0 (2.05)	51.3 (2.05)	58.9 (2.14)	50.5 (1.47)	51.1 (2.91)
4.0 to 5.9	11.7 (0.52)	12.2 (1.52)	11.8 (2.12)	10.8 (1.63)	10.6 (1.81)	9.3 (1.09)	14.1 (1.77)	10.3 (1.68)	12.3 (0.77)	10.9 (1.69)
6.0 to 7.9	16.9 (0.55)	12.8 (1.61)	10.2 (2.20)	14.9 (1.96)	18.7 (2.12)	23.1 (2.10)	18.1 (1.22)	15.4 (1.81)	16.2 (0.94)	19.1 (1.86)
8.0 to 9.9	9.4 (0.42)	8.2 (0.92)	6.2 (1.22)	8.5 (1.64)	8.3 (2.03)	9.5 (0.99)	9.0 (1.08)	8.3 (1.34)	10.6 (0.85)	7.3 (1.05)
10.0 to 14.9	6.6 (0.35)	5.6 (1.48)	1.8 (0.75)	3.6 (0.97)	4.8 (1.22)	3.8 (0.81)	5.2 (0.82)	5.1 (1.57)	8.2 (0.58)	9.4 (1.81)
15.0 or more	2.1 (0.21)	1.4 (0.58)	2.5 (0.91)	‡ (†)	2.2 (0.78)	2.2 (0.57)	2.3 (0.64)	2.0 (0.80)	2.2 (0.30)	2.2 (0.69)

See notes at end of table.

Table 234. Percentage distribution of part-time instructional faculty and staff in degree-granting institutions, by type and control of institution, selected instruction activities, and number of classes taught for credit: Fall 2003—Continued

Instruction activity and number of classes	All institutions	Research		Doctoral		Comprehensive		Private liberal arts	Public 2-year	Other
		Public	Private	Public	Private	Public	Private			
1	2	3	4	5	6	7	8	9	10	11
Faculty/staff distribution by number of classes taught for credit (percent)										
Faculty/staff with undergraduate classes only, by total for-credit courses	100.0 (†)	100.0 (†)	100.0 (†)	100.0 (†)	100.0 (†)	100.0 (†)	100.0 (†)	100.0 (†)	100.0 (†)	100.0 (†)
1	49.2 (0.90)	53.1 (3.85)	62.3 (5.20)	58.8 (4.27)	45.4 (4.58)	48.4 (2.43)	54.1 (2.78)	53.7 (3.42)	47.9 (1.24)	42.5 (2.88)
2	29.7 (0.86)	31.2 (3.04)	28.5 (5.51)	26.9 (3.12)	39.8 (4.33)	33.1 (2.35)	29.2 (2.27)	25.0 (2.20)	29.1 (1.24)	31.4 (2.69)
3	12.5 (0.47)	9.4 (1.83)	6.9 (2.33)	11.5 (2.36)	13.1 (3.15)	10.8 (1.26)	9.4 (1.35)	10.2 (1.62)	13.6 (0.81)	15.3 (2.04)
4	5.3 (0.41)	4.6 (1.41)	‡ (†)	‡ (†)	‡ (†)	4.0 (1.06)	5.4 (1.08)	5.6 (1.95)	6.1 (0.65)	5.3 (1.56)
5 or more	3.3 (0.32)	1.7 (1.03)	‡ (†)	2.6 (1.27)	1.3 (1.11)	3.7 (0.95)	1.8 (0.77)	5.5 (1.69)	3.3 (0.47)	5.5 (1.67)
Faculty/staff with graduate classes only, by total for-credit courses	100.0 (†)	100.0 (†)	100.0 (†)	100.0 (†)	100.0 (†)	100.0 (†)	100.0 (†)	100.0 (†)	100.0 (†)	100.0 (†)
1	72.6 (1.73)	71.7 (5.24)	81.7 (4.89)	81.8 (4.93)	72.2 (5.28)	74.8 (5.62)	62.2 (3.67)	69.9 (6.67)	69.8 (13.95)	76.9 (5.47)
2	16.6 (1.30)	20.6 (4.61)	7.4 (3.23)	10.8 (4.07)	16.2 (4.50)	12.9 (4.45)	23.3 (2.37)	18.8 (5.77)	26.4 (13.58)	14.5 (3.18)
3	5.3 (0.93)	4.0 (2.25)	5.7 (2.74)	7.4 (4.52)	5.7 (3.51)	3.7 (2.40)	7.6 (2.41)	2.9 (2.09)	‡ (†)	4.4 (2.87)
4	3.1 (0.81)	‡ (†)	5.2 (3.18)	‡ (†)	4.0 (1.41)	5.2 (3.55)	3.9 (1.32)	6.6 (4.24)	‡ (†)	‡ (†)
5 or more	2.4 (0.53)	3.7 (2.05)	‡ (†)	‡ (†)	‡ (†)	‡ (†)	2.9 (1.38)	‡ (†)	‡ (†)	2.8 (1.53)
Faculty/staff with both undergraduate and graduate classes, by total for-credit courses	100.0 (†)	100.0 (†)	100.0 (†)	100.0 (†)	100.0 (†)	100.0 (†)	100.0 (†)	100.0 (†)	‡ (†)	100.0 (†)
1	46.5 (2.05)	51.3 (5.19)	46.4 (10.59)	59.3 (5.24)	63.7 (8.93)	38.0 (6.03)	38.9 (4.23)	44.1 (8.69)	‡ (†)	47.2 (7.15)
2	28.7 (1.96)	29.6 (4.47)	36.3 (8.39)	18.5 (6.24)	18.1 (5.75)	30.7 (3.91)	32.7 (5.11)	35.1 (9.57)	‡ (†)	25.0 (6.53)
3	13.5 (1.78)	11.3 (3.25)	11.4 (5.72)	16.9 (6.27)	‡ (†)	17.8 (4.04)	16.6 (3.72)	12.3 (4.69)	‡ (†)	9.7 (5.61)
4	5.9 (1.19)	3.3 (1.63)	‡ (†)	‡ (†)	7.8 (5.97)	7.9 (3.54)	5.4 (3.06)	5.8 (2.25)	‡ (†)	7.7 (3.80)
5 or more	5.4 (1.18)	4.4 (2.08)	‡ (†)	5.0 (2.36)	‡ (†)	5.7 (2.75)	6.4 (2.36)	2.7 (2.30)	‡ (†)	10.3 (5.13)

†Not applicable.

‡Reporting standards not met.

[1]Distribution by student classroom contact hours per week is based on the number of contact hours that faculty and instructional staff spend each week with students during classroom instruction multiplied by the number of students taught.

NOTE: Totals may differ from figures reported in other tables because of varying survey methodologies. Detail may not sum to totals because of rounding. Standard errors appear in parentheses.
SOURCE: U.S. Department of Education, National Center for Education Statistics, 2004 National Study of Postsecondary Faculty (NSOPF:04). (This table was prepared September 2005.)

Table 235. Full-time and part-time instructional faculty and staff in degree-granting institutions, by type and control of institution and selected characteristics: Fall 1992, fall 1998, and fall 2003

Selected characteristic	Number (in thousands) 1992	1998	2003	Fall 2003 Total	Research Public	Research Private	Doctoral Public	Doctoral Private	Comprehensive Public	Comprehensive Private	Private liberal arts	Public 2-year	Other
1	2	3	4	5	6	7	8	9	10	11	12	13	14
Full-time instructional faculty and staff													
Number (in thousands)	528.3	560.4	681.8	681.8 (0.05)	162.1 (0.85)	63.5 (1.58)	51.3 (0.76)	21.7 (0.79)	107.3 (2.98)	41.4 (1.59)	49.6 (1.80)	138.3 (2.53)	46.6 (2.78)
Percentage distribution	†	†	†	100.0 (†)	23.8 (0.12)	9.3 (0.23)	7.5 (0.11)	3.2 (0.12)	15.7 (0.44)	6.1 (0.23)	7.3 (0.26)	20.3 (0.37)	6.8 (0.41)
				Percentage distribution of full-time instructional faculty and staff									
Total	†	†	†	100.0 (†)	100.0 (†)	100.0 (†)	100.0 (†)	100.0 (†)	100.0 (†)	100.0 (†)	100.0 (†)	100.0 (†)	100.0 (†)
Sex													
Male	352.7	356.9	420.4	61.7 (0.35)	69.9 (0.62)	68.8 (0.90)	62.8 (1.29)	66.7 (2.04)	58.8 (0.84)	57.6 (2.03)	59.7 (1.14)	52.3 (0.99)	59.8 (1.71)
Female	175.5	203.5	261.4	38.3 (0.35)	30.1 (0.62)	31.2 (0.90)	37.2 (1.29)	33.3 (2.04)	41.2 (0.84)	42.4 (2.03)	40.3 (1.14)	47.7 (0.99)	40.2 (1.71)
Race/ethnicity													
White	456.7	477.0	547.7	80.3 (0.27)	79.0 (0.50)	77.6 (0.73)	81.3 (1.33)	82.7 (1.55)	78.0 (1.12)	85.6 (1.02)	86.0 (0.81)	80.3 (0.82)	81.1 (1.64)
Black	27.4	28.4	38.1	5.6 (0.17)	3.7 (0.26)	4.9 (0.49)	4.1 (0.50)	5.1 (0.79)	8.7 (0.73)	4.8 (0.65)	6.3 (0.69)	6.3 (0.49)	5.4 (1.05)
Hispanic	13.9	18.5	23.8	3.5 (0.10)	2.9 (0.18)	3.5 (0.36)	2.9 (0.37)	2.2 (0.59)	3.6 (0.23)	2.4 (0.36)	2.3 (0.26)	5.3 (0.37)	3.1 (0.54)
Asian/Pacific Islander	27.7	32.5	62.3	9.1 (0.16)	13.2 (0.45)	12.8 (0.63)	10.1 (1.17)	9.3 (1.40)	7.9 (0.34)	5.9 (0.74)	3.8 (0.33)	6.2 (0.39)	9.2 (1.22)
American Indian/Alaska Native	2.6	4.0	10.0	1.5 (0.11)	1.1 (0.17)	1.2 (0.40)	1.6 (0.35)	0.7 (0.36)	1.8 (0.50)	1.2 (0.38)	1.6 (0.31)	1.9 (0.30)	1.2 (0.50)
Age													
29 or younger	7.6	8.8	17.5	2.6 (0.16)	2.5 (0.33)	3.0 (0.56)	2.5 (0.36)	2.0 (0.60)	2.2 (0.38)	2.7 (0.57)	3.1 (0.53)	2.6 (0.39)	2.4 (0.89)
30 to 34	35.4	32.2	54.8	8.0 (0.26)	8.9 (0.49)	9.2 (1.06)	8.5 (0.80)	6.9 (0.92)	7.7 (0.73)	8.6 (0.96)	9.7 (0.86)	5.8 (0.46)	8.6 (1.12)
35 to 39	66.8	60.1	83.1	12.2 (0.30)	13.7 (0.62)	15.5 (1.26)	11.8 (1.08)	10.4 (1.60)	10.7 (0.84)	10.1 (0.79)	13.5 (1.09)	11.2 (0.80)	10.2 (1.27)
40 to 44	90.2	81.9	92.9	13.6 (0.34)	15.0 (0.74)	14.4 (0.78)	12.9 (0.95)	11.4 (1.32)	12.0 (0.82)	14.2 (1.00)	12.8 (0.89)	13.1 (0.90)	15.4 (1.84)
45 to 49	97.7	96.8	108.5	15.9 (0.36)	16.3 (0.53)	15.0 (1.08)	17.0 (1.16)	15.8 (1.80)	16.2 (0.87)	13.6 (1.31)	14.9 (0.99)	15.4 (0.70)	18.9 (1.88)
50 to 54	94.9	104.7	114.1	16.7 (0.38)	15.9 (0.77)	14.5 (0.87)	15.6 (1.09)	16.1 (1.54)	16.6 (0.98)	17.3 (1.48)	16.2 (0.92)	19.3 (0.91)	16.9 (1.43)
55 to 59	67.3	90.2	107.8	15.8 (0.38)	13.7 (0.74)	11.3 (0.86)	15.4 (1.00)	15.6 (1.89)	17.1 (0.88)	17.0 (1.22)	14.6 (0.88)	19.8 (1.04)	15.3 (1.67)
60 to 64	44.6	55.0	69.5	10.2 (0.27)	9.4 (0.48)	9.6 (0.79)	11.7 (0.90)	12.7 (1.58)	12.5 (0.75)	11.0 (1.26)	11.3 (1.01)	8.7 (0.69)	8.2 (1.09)
65 or older	23.8	30.6	33.5	4.9 (0.20)	4.6 (0.35)	7.5 (0.70)	4.5 (0.62)	9.5 (1.34)	4.9 (0.55)	5.5 (0.66)	3.8 (0.59)	4.0 (0.55)	4.0 (0.77)
Highest degree													
Less than bachelor's	6.3	6.7	10.0	1.5 (0.12)	0.2 (0.09)	0.2 (0.14)	0.2 (0.09)	0.5 (0.37)	0.1 (0.07)	# (†)	0.8 (0.26)	5.1 (0.49)	3.6 (0.96)
Bachelor's	20.9	22.5	29.4	4.3 (0.24)	2.0 (0.27)	2.0 (0.41)	2.9 (0.51)	1.6 (0.46)	3.1 (0.63)	2.8 (0.58)	2.1 (0.53)	9.7 (0.81)	8.8 (1.23)
Master's	155.8	156.0	179.8	26.4 (0.39)	12.3 (0.49)	9.9 (0.93)	20.3 (1.19)	12.9 (1.17)	22.7 (1.08)	28.7 (2.10)	27.2 (1.71)	54.5 (1.16)	32.7 (2.71)
First-professional	58.3	51.7	56.1	8.2 (0.30)	11.8 (0.53)	18.4 (1.19)	4.7 (0.49)	9.7 (1.47)	2.0 (0.30)	3.5 (0.89)	0.9 (0.18)	7.3 (0.65)	14.4 (2.39)
Doctoral	283.8	323.5	406.6	59.6 (0.48)	73.7 (0.61)	69.4 (1.45)	71.9 (1.30)	75.4 (2.03)	72.1 (1.34)	65.0 (2.47)	69.1 (1.92)	23.4 (1.31)	40.4 (2.85)
Academic rank													
Professor	160.6	172.2	194.4	28.5 (0.54)	33.8 (0.95)	34.0 (1.15)	27.3 (1.34)	30.3 (2.37)	29.8 (1.23)	24.8 (1.61)	28.5 (1.79)	21.7 (1.57)	23.3 (2.04)
Associate professor	123.7	132.0	149.6	21.9 (0.37)	23.3 (0.63)	22.0 (1.12)	25.9 (1.54)	31.6 (1.73)	23.2 (1.30)	27.0 (1.41)	24.6 (1.27)	15.1 (1.04)	18.6 (1.85)
Assistant professor	124.3	125.0	158.1	23.2 (0.41)	22.5 (0.68)	26.6 (1.38)	23.5 (1.36)	21.6 (1.63)	28.3 (1.08)	31.8 (2.00)	30.3 (1.14)	14.4 (1.01)	20.8 (1.97)
Instructor	73.9	74.9	82.7	12.1 (0.42)	4.3 (0.27)	5.0 (0.79)	9.0 (0.94)	4.5 (0.89)	7.6 (0.81)	6.8 (1.02)	6.6 (0.91)	32.6 (1.88)	16.4 (1.74)
Lecturer	11.1	14.1	21.9	3.2 (0.22)	4.6 (0.34)	4.9 (0.59)	5.4 (0.80)	2.5 (0.40)	5.4 (0.99)	1.9 (0.67)	1.0 (0.23)	0.3 (0.07)	1.3 (0.42)
Other	17.1	26.3	56.5	8.3 (0.32)	10.6 (0.64)	7.1 (0.54)	8.5 (0.59)	8.9 (1.23)	5.7 (0.94)	7.3 (1.12)	8.8 (1.11)	7.8 (0.70)	9.1 (1.15)
No rank	16.9	15.8	18.6	2.7 (0.19)	0.8 (0.14)	0.4 (0.20)	0.5 (0.25)	0.6 (0.45)	0.1 (0.05)	0.5 (0.10)	0.2 (0.10)	8.2 (0.73)	10.6 (1.76)
Base salary													
Under $10,000	13.8	9.7	4.9	0.7 (0.07)	0.9 (0.17)	0.9 (0.32)	0.8 (0.26)	0.1 (0.08)	0.5 (0.20)	0.4 (0.23)	0.6 (0.19)	0.6 (0.13)	1.3 (0.56)
$10,000 to 24,999	29.4	19.3	18.6	2.7 (0.15)	2.4 (0.27)	2.8 (0.40)	3.8 (0.55)	1.7 (0.74)	3.1 (0.36)	2.8 (0.41)	2.6 (0.58)	2.7 (0.40)	2.5 (0.79)
$25,000 to 39,999	181.8	123.7	79.7	11.7 (0.42)	8.0 (0.49)	5.6 (0.66)	13.0 (0.65)	6.6 (1.03)	12.2 (1.12)	12.8 (1.85)	15.2 (1.38)	16.0 (1.18)	14.9 (1.76)
$40,000 to 54,999	163.8	171.1	192.4	28.2 (0.45)	19.2 (0.78)	15.5 (1.13)	27.4 (1.10)	21.3 (2.12)	34.0 (1.40)	38.8 (1.63)	39.6 (1.64)	33.7 (1.39)	29.8 (1.88)
$55,000 to 69,999	76.7	106.2	147.7	21.7 (0.52)	18.9 (0.58)	16.0 (0.99)	22.3 (1.05)	26.4 (2.02)	24.1 (1.26)	24.9 (1.78)	23.1 (1.34)	23.0 (1.36)	23.1 (1.95)
$70,000 to 84,999	32.1	57.9	94.8	13.9 (0.32)	15.3 (0.64)	16.0 (1.01)	14.7 (1.03)	15.6 (1.52)	14.7 (1.21)	10.5 (1.18)	11.2 (1.46)	13.5 (1.00)	9.8 (1.57)
$85,000 to 99,999	11.1	28.1	50.7	7.4 (0.29)	11.1 (0.54)	9.8 (0.80)	7.8 (0.79)	10.1 (1.32)	8.1 (0.78)	4.0 (1.15)	3.7 (0.56)	4.1 (0.52)	5.1 (0.74)
$100,000 or more	19.6	44.4	93.1	13.7 (0.34)	24.1 (0.76)	34.0 (1.20)	10.2 (0.82)	18.2 (1.63)	3.3 (0.46)	5.8 (0.90)	4.0 (0.57)	6.4 (0.50)	13.6 (2.72)

See notes at end of table.

Table 235. Full-time and part-time instructional faculty and staff in degree-granting institutions, by type and control of institution and selected characteristics: Fall 1992, fall 1998, and fall 2003—Continued

Selected characteristic	Number (in thousands) 1992	1998	2003	Fall 2003 Total	Research Public	Research Private	Doctoral Public	Doctoral Private	Comprehensive Public	Comprehensive Private	Private liberal arts	Public 2-year	Other
	2	3	4	5	6	7	8	9	10	11	12	13	14
Part-time instructional faculty and staff													
Number (in thousands)	376.7	416.0	530.0	530.0 (0.02)	39.7 (0.78)	23.2 (0.96)	20.8 (0.82)	15.4 (0.83)	60.3 (2.49)	53.5 (2.17)	28.4 (2.19)	240.4 (2.90)	48.3 (2.42)
Percentage distribution	†	†	†	100.0 (†)	7.5 (0.15)	4.4 (0.18)	3.9 (0.15)	2.9 (0.16)	11.4 (0.47)	10.1 (0.41)	5.4 (0.41)	45.4 (0.55)	9.1 (0.46)
Percentage distribution of part-time instructional faculty and staff													
Total	†	†	†	100.0 (†)	100.0 (†)	100.0 (†)	100.0 (†)	100.0 (†)	100.0 (†)	100.0 (†)	100.0 (†)	100.0 (†)	100.0 (†)
Sex													
Male	208.7	217.0	275.9	52.1 (0.45)	50.4 (1.97)	60.2 (1.92)	50.2 (2.26)	58.4 (3.34)	50.0 (1.59)	53.9 (1.53)	50.3 (1.95)	50.9 (0.63)	55.4 (1.85)
Female	168.0	199.1	254.1	47.9 (0.45)	49.6 (1.97)	39.8 (1.92)	49.8 (2.26)	41.6 (3.34)	50.0 (1.59)	46.1 (1.53)	49.7 (1.95)	49.1 (0.63)	44.6 (1.85)
Race/ethnicity													
White	332.8	364.4	451.6	85.2 (0.38)	82.4 (1.63)	85.8 (1.78)	87.9 (2.19)	88.9 (1.99)	87.2 (1.89)	91.0 (0.85)	86.2 (1.59)	83.5 (0.53)	84.1 (1.75)
Black	18.3	18.9	29.7	5.6 (0.20)	2.7 (0.72)	4.1 (1.14)	2.4 (1.01)	2.8 (0.99)	4.7 (1.20)	2.8 (0.40)	8.1 (1.27)	7.0 (0.24)	6.8 (1.10)
Hispanic	11.2	15.5	18.7	3.5 (0.13)	3.2 (0.56)	2.5 (0.78)	4.1 (0.81)	2.8 (0.66)	3.1 (0.39)	2.4 (0.30)	2.1 (0.48)	4.4 (0.21)	2.8 (0.60)
Asian/Pacific Islander	12.2	13.2	20.3	3.8 (0.22)	9.9 (1.39)	6.4 (1.05)	4.5 (1.14)	4.9 (1.79)	3.3 (0.59)	1.9 (0.61)	2.7 (0.63)	3.1 (0.30)	4.0 (0.95)
American Indian/Alaska Native	2.3	4.0	9.7	1.8 (0.22)	1.8 (0.68)	1.2 (0.74)	1.1 (0.69)	0.6 (0.35)	1.7 (0.61)	1.9 (0.42)	0.9 (0.35)	2.1 (0.36)	2.3 (0.85)
Age													
29 or younger	20.5	15.1	30.0	5.7 (0.32)	7.2 (1.02)	4.4 (1.40)	9.0 (1.78)	5.7 (1.86)	7.9 (1.18)	3.0 (0.60)	5.3 (0.84)	5.6 (0.54)	4.4 (1.02)
30 to 34	35.9	37.1	46.2	8.7 (0.33)	9.9 (1.37)	11.6 (1.47)	7.6 (1.30)	7.9 (1.96)	8.2 (0.91)	7.8 (0.94)	9.4 (1.38)	8.8 (0.58)	7.9 (1.04)
35 to 39	58.9	47.2	57.4	10.8 (0.44)	11.3 (1.43)	7.1 (1.35)	10.5 (1.93)	14.7 (2.41)	11.4 (1.46)	10.2 (1.01)	10.5 (1.76)	10.5 (0.76)	13.1 (1.47)
40 to 44	70.0	60.4	59.7	11.3 (0.46)	11.4 (1.43)	11.1 (1.94)	13.7 (2.32)	7.7 (1.71)	10.8 (1.37)	10.9 (1.24)	12.8 (1.87)	11.3 (0.72)	11.0 (1.59)
45 to 49	68.0	72.1	82.4	15.5 (0.51)	16.3 (1.52)	17.3 (1.70)	15.6 (2.56)	10.1 (1.90)	13.0 (1.28)	15.5 (1.06)	14.1 (1.96)	16.0 (0.80)	17.6 (2.15)
50 to 54	45.1	69.8	80.5	15.2 (0.52)	14.5 (1.56)	12.6 (2.33)	15.4 (2.34)	14.8 (2.52)	13.2 (1.34)	17.4 (1.28)	15.8 (1.63)	15.6 (0.90)	14.8 (1.31)
55 to 59	28.8	47.1	74.5	14.1 (0.44)	10.8 (1.46)	13.3 (2.99)	13.0 (2.08)	16.2 (2.51)	13.9 (1.08)	14.2 (1.36)	13.4 (1.93)	14.4 (0.70)	15.5 (1.68)
60 to 64	22.9	28.8	46.4	8.8 (0.43)	7.4 (1.42)	8.1 (1.80)	8.7 (1.65)	9.9 (2.91)	10.3 (1.37)	9.6 (1.37)	8.1 (1.32)	8.7 (0.77)	7.5 (1.28)
65 or older	26.6	38.4	52.9	10.0 (0.45)	11.2 (1.46)	14.4 (1.83)	6.4 (1.25)	13.0 (2.70)	11.2 (1.21)	11.4 (1.60)	10.6 (1.74)	9.1 (0.87)	8.1 (1.31)
Highest degree													
Less than bachelor's	17.2	20.3	41.1	7.8 (0.59)	2.2 (0.59)	2.5 (1.27)	0.5 (0.28)	2.1 (0.76)	2.1 (0.61)	0.7 (0.28)	0.9 (0.38)	14.1 (1.17)	7.1 (1.48)
Bachelor's	62.7	58.8	83.8	15.8 (0.55)	9.9 (1.32)	10.9 (1.94)	13.9 (2.09)	7.6 (2.48)	13.1 (1.84)	7.5 (1.08)	8.6 (1.52)	21.1 (1.13)	16.9 (1.98)
Master's	190.2	225.1	273.1	51.5 (0.80)	35.6 (2.39)	36.6 (3.36)	53.8 (3.16)	41.7 (3.47)	57.8 (2.32)	64.4 (2.33)	61.0 (2.21)	51.4 (1.59)	46.8 (3.82)
First-professional	39.6	36.0	38.5	7.3 (0.39)	16.7 (1.98)	21.3 (2.68)	7.7 (1.52)	13.6 (2.41)	4.2 (0.79)	4.8 (0.90)	7.2 (1.50)	4.2 (0.50)	12.6 (1.92)
Doctor's	58.9	75.8	93.5	17.6 (0.60)	35.6 (2.56)	28.7 (3.88)	24.1 (3.30)	35.0 (2.65)	22.7 (1.83)	22.6 (1.88)	22.2 (2.09)	9.2 (0.66)	16.7 (2.21)
Academic rank													
Professor	32.3	30.2	23.3	4.4 (0.30)	8.1 (1.54)	5.6 (1.18)	4.6 (1.43)	5.7 (1.40)	5.7 (1.01)	2.4 (0.55)	4.4 (0.85)	3.3 (0.49)	6.3 (1.12)
Associate professor	22.5	19.4	14.6	2.8 (0.22)	4.3 (0.94)	6.0 (1.45)	2.6 (1.14)	2.9 (1.03)	2.1 (0.69)	3.1 (0.79)	4.7 (1.11)	1.8 (0.31)	3.7 (1.12)
Assistant professor	24.2	23.1	19.8	3.7 (0.29)	11.0 (1.49)	11.9 (3.02)	3.3 (0.80)	7.0 (1.73)	2.0 (0.49)	3.0 (0.86)	5.1 (1.81)	1.5 (0.25)	6.5 (1.30)
Instructor	215.4	205.4	187.7	35.4 (0.83)	20.8 (1.72)	18.2 (1.92)	28.7 (2.27)	20.1 (3.25)	25.4 (2.41)	21.9 (1.64)	24.5 (2.13)	48.3 (1.57)	33.4 (2.27)
Lecturer	45.3	46.3	40.9	7.7 (0.41)	21.5 (1.67)	18.6 (2.30)	13.2 (2.07)	9.6 (1.72)	15.8 (2.18)	8.6 (2.32)	6.7 (1.72)	2.7 (0.41)	2.9 (0.95)
Other	27.6	75.2	230.9	43.6 (0.85)	33.3 (2.17)	38.2 (2.49)	45.4 (2.50)	53.4 (3.25)	47.7 (3.01)	59.7 (3.84)	52.2 (3.03)	39.7 (1.43)	41.6 (3.60)
No rank	9.3	16.5	12.8	2.4 (0.20)	1.0 (0.30)	1.6 (1.20)	2.3 (0.80)	1.4 (0.81)	1.2 (0.39)	1.2 (0.32)	2.3 (0.70)	2.7 (0.37)	5.5 (1.36)
Base salary													
Under $10,000	280.5	256.2	366.5	69.1 (0.65)	46.7 (2.34)	58.1 (2.98)	70.1 (3.01)	68.1 (3.50)	71.3 (2.39)	76.6 (2.71)	75.6 (3.02)	71.1 (1.03)	68.5 (2.14)
$10,000 to $24,999	68.1	112.4	114.8	21.7 (0.63)	26.3 (2.33)	24.1 (2.81)	19.7 (2.36)	21.5 (3.63)	21.0 (1.97)	16.5 (2.06)	15.3 (1.98)	23.0 (1.01)	21.3 (1.74)
$25,000 to $39,999	15.8	26.3	27.5	5.2 (0.32)	12.2 (1.38)	7.7 (1.76)	5.7 (1.48)	4.8 (1.72)	4.9 (1.09)	4.4 (1.15)	5.3 (1.24)	4.3 (0.43)	3.8 (0.89)
$40,000 to $54,999	5.3	11.8	9.6	1.8 (0.14)	5.8 (1.05)	5.0 (1.18)	1.9 (0.70)	3.0 (1.00)	1.6 (0.44)	0.9 (0.31)	1.1 (0.55)	0.6 (0.16)	4.2 (0.91)
$55,000 to $69,999	2.2	4.2	4.7	0.9 (0.15)	3.0 (0.65)	2.0 (1.00)	1.4 (0.71)	1.0 (0.65)	0.9 (0.59)	0.8 (0.21)	1.6 (0.65)	0.4 (0.14)	0.4 (0.31)
$70,000 to $84,999	1.1	2.4	1.9	0.4 (0.07)	2.2 (0.57)	0.9 (0.55)	0.2 (0.21)	0.4 (0.39)	0.0 (0.00)	0.3 (0.21)	0.1 (0.14)	0.1 (0.06)	0.5 (0.26)
$85,000 to $99,999	0.9	#	1.5	0.3 (0.07)	1.0 (0.46)	1.0 (0.51)	0.4 (0.30)	0.0 (0.05)	0.3 (0.23)	0.3 (0.04)	0.2 (0.22)	0.2 (0.09)	0.2 (0.13)
$100,000 or more	2.7	#	3.5	0.7 (0.10)	2.9 (0.63)	1.3 (0.72)	0.5 (0.52)	1.2 (0.75)	0.4 (0.00)	0.4 (0.27)	0.8 (0.46)	0.3 (0.08)	1.2 (0.58)

†Not applicable.
#Rounds to zero.
NOTE: Totals may differ from figures reported in other tables because of varying survey methodologies. Race categories exclude persons of Hispanic origin. Detail may not sum to totals because of rounding. Standard errors appear in parentheses.

SOURCE: U.S. Department of Education, National Center for Education Statistics, 1993, 1999, and 2004 National Study of Postsecondary Faculty (NSOPF:93;99;04). (This table was prepared September 2005.)

Table 236. Full-time and part-time instructional faculty and staff in degree-granting institutions, by race/ethnicity, sex, and selected characteristics: Fall 2003

Selected characteristic	Number (in thousands)	Percent	White Male	White Female	Black Male	Black Female	Hispanic Male	Hispanic Female	Asian/Pacific Islander Male	Asian/Pacific Islander Female	American Indian/Alaska Native Male	American Indian/Alaska Native Female
1	2	3	4	5	6	7	8	9	10	11	12	13
Full-time instructional faculty and staff												
Number (in thousands)	682 (#)	†	338 (2.6)	209 (2.4)	20 (1.0)	19 (0.9)	13 (0.6)	10 (0.6)	43 (1.0)	19 (1.0)	6 (0.6)	4 (0.5)
Percentage distribution	† (†)	100.0	49.6 (0.39)	30.7 (0.36)	2.9 (0.15)	2.7 (0.13)	2.0 (0.09)	1.5 (0.08)	6.3 (0.15)	2.8 (0.15)	0.8 (0.08)	0.6 (0.07)
Type and control												
Public research	162 (0.8)	100.0	55.4 (0.67)	23.6 (0.59)	2.1 (0.27)	1.7 (0.19)	1.8 (0.16)	1.1 (0.15)	10.0 (0.47)	3.2 (0.35)	0.6 (0.14)	0.6 (0.11)
Private research	64 (1.2)	100.0	54.7 (1.00)	22.9 (0.80)	2.2 (0.30)	2.7 (0.37)	2.1 (0.30)	1.4 (0.31)	8.9 (0.66)	3.9 (0.48)	0.8 (0.39)	0.4 (0.23)
Public doctoral	51 (0.9)	100.0	50.2 (1.48)	31.1 (1.22)	2.1 (0.44)	2.0 (0.30)	1.6 (0.20)	1.3 (0.27)	7.9 (1.27)	2.2 (0.56)	1.0 (0.32)	0.6 (0.22)
Private doctoral	22 (0.4)	100.0	56.0 (2.39)	26.7 (1.94)	3.0 (0.70)	2.1 (0.42)	1.4 (0.49)	0.8 (0.38)	5.8 (1.06)	3.5 (0.93)	0.6 (0.34)	‡ (†)
Public comprehensive	107 (0.3)	100.0	45.9 (1.03)	32.1 (0.98)	4.7 (0.64)	4.0 (0.42)	2.1 (0.20)	1.6 (0.19)	5.3 (0.40)	2.6 (0.28)	0.8 (0.23)	1.0 (0.33)
Private comprehensive	41 (0.3)	100.0	48.9 (2.00)	36.7 (1.93)	2.3 (0.53)	2.4 (0.44)	1.6 (0.31)	0.8 (0.22)	4.1 (0.65)	1.9 (0.53)	0.6 (0.26)	0.6 (0.30)
Private liberal arts	50 (0.2)	100.0	51.9 (1.20)	34.1 (0.99)	2.8 (0.56)	2.8 (0.36)	1.0 (0.20)	1.3 (0.27)	2.2 (0.28)	1.5 (0.29)	1.0 (0.24)	0.6 (0.18)
Public 2-year	138 (0.8)	100.0	42.2 (1.01)	38.1 (0.80)	2.8 (0.25)	3.5 (0.44)	2.8 (0.33)	2.5 (0.30)	3.3 (0.37)	2.8 (0.45)	1.2 (0.25)	0.7 (0.17)
Other	47 (0.2)	100.0	48.1 (2.17)	32.9 (1.66)	2.9 (0.80)	2.5 (0.55)	1.6 (0.40)	1.5 (0.39)	6.3 (1.01)	2.9 (0.73)	0.9 (0.51)	0.3 (0.18)
Academic rank												
Professor	194 (3.7)	100.0	65.5 (0.74)	20.3 (0.61)	2.6 (0.27)	1.1 (0.21)	1.8 (0.13)	0.8 (0.13)	5.7 (0.42)	1.1 (0.21)	0.8 (0.14)	0.4 (0.12)
Associate professor	150 (2.6)	100.0	51.6 (0.98)	28.4 (0.78)	3.1 (0.42)	2.4 (0.26)	1.7 (0.19)	1.3 (0.15)	7.0 (0.52)	2.9 (0.36)	1.0 (0.21)	0.5 (0.11)
Assistant professor	158 (2.8)	100.0	41.0 (0.83)	33.6 (0.81)	3.1 (0.37)	3.8 (0.38)	2.3 (0.22)	1.9 (0.15)	8.7 (0.49)	4.3 (0.35)	0.7 (0.16)	0.6 (0.15)
Instructor	83 (2.8)	100.0	38.2 (1.23)	41.2 (1.09)	3.2 (0.56)	4.4 (0.57)	2.5 (0.37)	2.3 (0.31)	3.1 (0.44)	3.1 (0.48)	0.9 (0.26)	1.1 (0.31)
Lecturer	22 (1.5)	100.0	36.7 (2.59)	43.9 (2.21)	2.9 (0.91)	3.0 (0.91)	1.3 (0.38)	3.8 (0.77)	2.4 (0.89)	4.0 (0.99)	1.3 (0.52)	0.7 (0.30)
Other	57 (2.2)	100.0	38.8 (1.51)	39.8 (1.37)	2.5 (0.54)	3.9 (0.56)	1.7 (0.22)	2.2 (0.35)	7.0 (0.98)	2.8 (0.56)	0.8 (0.39)	0.6 (0.18)
No rank	19 (1.3)	100.0	40.2 (2.37)	43.0 (2.45)	1.5 (0.52)	2.0 (0.83)	2.3 (0.75)	0.7 (0.24)	4.5 (1.17)	3.8 (1.39)	1.1 (0.74)	0.8 (0.46)
Age												
Under 35	72 (2.2)	100.0	39.4 (1.19)	33.5 (1.31)	2.9 (0.48)	4.6 (0.58)	2.6 (0.39)	2.7 (0.36)	8.9 (0.85)	4.3 (0.67)	0.6 (0.19)	0.5 (0.15)
35 to 44	176 (2.8)	100.0	44.4 (0.87)	30.1 (0.72)	2.7 (0.35)	3.2 (0.34)	2.6 (0.24)	1.9 (0.18)	9.0 (0.43)	4.8 (0.42)	0.8 (0.17)	0.6 (0.16)
45 to 54	223 (3.2)	100.0	46.9 (0.77)	34.6 (0.75)	3.0 (0.27)	2.6 (0.20)	1.8 (0.16)	1.5 (0.18)	5.9 (0.38)	2.1 (0.26)	1.0 (0.17)	0.6 (0.12)
55 to 64	177 (3.1)	100.0	58.6 (0.84)	27.8 (0.65)	2.8 (0.28)	1.8 (0.19)	1.4 (0.14)	0.9 (0.12)	3.8 (0.37)	1.4 (0.23)	0.9 (0.18)	0.7 (0.13)
65 to 69	25 (1.2)	100.0	69.6 (2.16)	18.6 (1.79)	2.8 (0.79)	1.9 (0.67)	1.8 (0.48)	0.3 (0.17)	3.3 (0.75)	1.1 (0.48)	0.4 (0.25)	‡ (†)
70 or older	9 (0.6)	100.0	71.4 (3.37)	12.5 (3.14)	3.8 (1.42)	2.0 (1.21)	0.8 (0.52)	‡ (†)	5.0 (1.92)	‡ (†)	1.7 (1.09)	‡ (†)
Base salary												
Under $10,000	5 (0.5)	100.0	40.3 (5.67)	32.5 (4.71)	5.2 (0.79)	4.1 (2.13)	0.5 (0.43)	4.0 (1.74)	7.1 (3.01)	6.1 (2.76)	‡ (†)	‡ (†)
$10,000 to 24,999	19 (1.0)	100.0	43.1 (2.69)	35.3 (2.59)	1.3 (0.38)	3.2 (0.91)	2.1 (0.63)	2.5 (0.61)	6.7 (1.26)	3.8 (0.94)	0.9 (0.52)	1.1 (0.50)
$25,000 to 39,999	80 (2.9)	100.0	36.0 (1.21)	44.5 (1.25)	2.9 (0.55)	3.7 (0.46)	1.8 (0.29)	2.1 (0.28)	3.8 (0.68)	3.6 (0.48)	0.7 (0.26)	0.8 (0.23)
$40,000 to 54,999	192 (3.1)	100.0	42.2 (0.95)	38.2 (0.79)	2.7 (0.27)	3.7 (0.37)	1.9 (0.18)	1.8 (0.14)	5.0 (0.43)	2.6 (0.27)	1.0 (0.15)	0.9 (0.14)
$55,000 to 69,999	148 (3.5)	100.0	48.7 (0.88)	31.9 (0.80)	3.1 (0.35)	2.5 (0.28)	2.0 (0.25)	1.6 (0.21)	6.0 (0.43)	2.6 (0.31)	1.0 (0.23)	0.6 (0.15)
$70,000 to 84,999	95 (2.2)	100.0	55.8 (1.29)	24.2 (1.14)	2.9 (0.39)	1.7 (0.40)	2.4 (0.34)	1.0 (0.20)	8.1 (0.67)	2.6 (0.41)	0.9 (0.23)	0.5 (0.19)
$85,000 to 99,999	51 (2.0)	100.0	61.9 (1.58)	18.5 (1.03)	3.8 (0.69)	1.5 (0.38)	1.5 (0.41)	1.0 (0.28)	8.3 (1.06)	2.5 (0.57)	0.8 (0.24)	0.2 (0.12)
$100,000 or more	93 (2.3)	100.0	66.9 (0.99)	13.7 (0.74)	2.4 (0.38)	1.6 (0.33)	2.1 (0.29)	0.8 (0.17)	9.0 (0.80)	2.8 (0.50)	0.6 (0.20)	0.1 (0.09)
Total household income												
Under $10,000	† (†)	100.0	† (†)	† (†)	† (†)	† (†)	† (†)	† (†)	† (†)	† (†)	‡ (†)	‡ (†)
$10,000 to 24,999	3 (0.3)	100.0	42.0 (6.54)	29.3 (6.12)	1.4 (1.13)	2.5 (1.38)	1.3 (1.47)	2.7 (1.60)	9.8 (3.74)	8.7 (3.59)	‡ (†)	‡ (†)
$25,000 to 39,999	20 (1.1)	100.0	36.5 (2.68)	39.0 (2.28)	3.3 (1.56)	4.5 (0.97)	1.5 (0.43)	2.5 (0.62)	7.3 (1.56)	3.8 (0.95)	0.6 (0.39)	0.9 (0.29)
$40,000 to 54,999	55 (1.8)	100.0	39.8 (1.66)	38.4 (1.42)	2.9 (0.59)	4.2 (0.59)	2.5 (0.35)	1.9 (0.29)	6.2 (0.80)	2.5 (0.51)	0.4 (0.18)	1.2 (0.31)
$55,000 to 69,999	86 (1.6)	100.0	43.1 (1.23)	34.2 (1.21)	4.1 (0.50)	4.4 (0.42)	2.1 (0.29)	1.9 (0.29)	5.6 (0.56)	2.5 (0.37)	1.1 (0.26)	1.0 (0.29)
$70,000 to 84,999	75 (2.2)	100.0	50.6 (1.20)	31.2 (1.11)	2.4 (0.40)	2.8 (0.45)	1.9 (0.26)	1.3 (0.17)	6.3 (0.59)	2.1 (0.40)	0.9 (0.30)	0.5 (0.17)
$85,000 to 99,999	95 (2.2)	100.0	46.7 (1.15)	32.5 (0.83)	2.8 (0.39)	3.0 (0.58)	2.7 (0.32)	1.6 (0.24)	7.0 (0.81)	2.5 (0.50)	0.6 (0.18)	0.5 (0.14)
$100,000 or more	347 (3.6)	100.0	50.9 (0.52)	27.5 (0.52)	2.6 (0.18)	1.9 (0.16)	1.7 (0.14)	1.3 (0.11)	6.3 (0.29)	3.0 (0.24)	0.9 (0.11)	0.4 (0.07)

See notes at end of table.

Table 236. Full-time and part-time instructional faculty and staff in degree-granting institutions, by race/ethnicity, sex, and selected characteristics: Fall 2003—Continued

Selected characteristic	Number (in thousands)	Percent	White Male	White Female	Black Male	Black Female	Hispanic Male	Hispanic Female	Asian/Pacific Islander Male	Asian/Pacific Islander Female	American Indian/Alaska Native Male	American Indian/Alaska Native Female
1	2	3	4	5	6	7	8	9	10	11	12	13
Part-time instructional faculty and staff												
Number (in thousands)	530 (#)	† (†)	236 (2.4)	216 (2.9)	14 (0.9)	16 (0.8)	10 (0.6)	9 (0.6)	11 (0.8)	9 (1.0)	6 (0.8)	4 (0.8)
Percentage distribution	† (†)	100.0	44.4 (0.5)	40.8 (0.5)	2.6 (0.2)	3.0 (0.1)	1.9 (0.1)	1.6 (0.1)	2.1 (0.2)	1.8 (0.2)	1.0 (0.1)	0.8 (0.1)
Type and control												
Public research	40 (0.8)	100.0	41.7 (1.93)	40.7 (2.12)	1.1 (0.37)	1.6 (0.60)	1.5 (0.40)	1.7 (0.43)	4.5 (1.03)	5.4 (0.90)	1.6 (0.67)	‡ (†)
Private research	23 (0.9)	100.0	51.1 (2.51)	34.7 (2.29)	2.7 (1.00)	1.4 (0.57)	1.5 (0.62)	0.9 (0.51)	3.6 (1.07)	2.8 (0.77)	‡ (†)	‡ (†)
Public doctoral	21 (0.8)	100.0	44.3 (2.27)	43.6 (2.39)	1.4 (0.85)	1.0 (0.47)	1.9 (0.68)	2.2 (0.61)	2.6 (0.86)	1.9 (0.83)	‡ (†)	1.1 (0.68)
Private doctoral	15 (0.1)	100.0	51.7 (3.99)	37.3 (3.60)	1.7 (0.77)	1.1 (0.55)	1.6 (0.64)	1.2 (0.36)	3.4 (1.06)	1.4 (0.90)	‡ (†)	0.6 (0.35)
Public comprehensive	60 (0.2)	100.0	43.1 (1.34)	44.1 (2.18)	2.3 (0.74)	2.4 (0.79)	1.6 (0.31)	1.5 (0.32)	2.0 (0.38)	1.3 (0.43)	1.0 (0.43)	0.7 (0.34)
Private comprehensive	53 (0.2)	100.0	49.1 (1.43)	41.9 (1.56)	1.7 (0.34)	1.1 (0.21)	1.0 (0.19)	1.4 (0.26)	1.1 (0.54)	0.8 (0.35)	1.0 (0.30)	0.9 (0.32)
Private liberal arts	28 (0.2)	100.0	44.2 (1.98)	42.0 (2.14)	2.5 (0.85)	5.6 (1.24)	1.1 (0.42)	1.0 (0.35)	1.7 (0.61)	1.1 (0.49)	0.9 (0.35)	‡ (†)
Public 2-year	240 (0.4)	100.0	42.7 (0.80)	40.8 (0.75)	3.0 (0.22)	3.9 (0.19)	2.5 (0.19)	1.9 (0.19)	1.6 (0.20)	1.5 (0.24)	1.1 (0.22)	1.0 (0.24)
Other	48 (0.1)	100.0	46.6 (2.15)	37.5 (2.18)	3.9 (0.85)	3.0 (0.80)	1.9 (0.56)	0.9 (0.25)	2.0 (0.73)	2.0 (0.57)	1.0 (0.45)	1.2 (0.60)
Academic rank												
Professor	23 (1.6)	100.0	59.3 (2.83)	25.0 (2.60)	4.0 (1.17)	2.6 (0.84)	0.6 (0.35)	1.0 (0.41)	3.6 (0.96)	‡ (†)	2.0 (1.08)	1.2 (0.85)
Associate professor	15 (1.2)	100.0	43.7 (4.03)	39.5 (3.88)	2.8 (0.84)	2.0 (1.02)	1.8 (0.92)	1.4 (0.49)	6.3 (2.27)	1.6 (0.85)	0.6 (0.44)	0.1 (0.13)
Assistant professor	20 (1.5)	100.0	38.8 (3.39)	42.7 (3.37)	2.8 (1.19)	2.5 (1.23)	1.3 (0.68)	1.0 (0.42)	4.8 (1.65)	6.0 (1.62)	‡ (†)	‡ (†)
Instructor	188 (4.4)	100.0	41.5 (1.09)	43.9 (1.11)	2.5 (0.30)	3.4 (0.25)	2.2 (0.24)	1.7 (0.22)	1.6 (0.25)	1.6 (0.28)	1.1 (0.26)	0.6 (0.18)
Lecturer	41 (2.1)	100.0	41.4 (2.05)	40.1 (1.96)	2.7 (0.63)	2.1 (0.77)	2.1 (0.45)	1.7 (0.42)	3.7 (0.80)	4.2 (0.93)	1.6 (0.56)	0.4 (0.25)
Other	231 (4.5)	100.0	46.5 (1.01)	39.9 (1.04)	2.5 (0.29)	3.1 (0.28)	1.8 (0.23)	1.5 (0.17)	1.5 (0.22)	1.3 (0.31)	0.9 (0.22)	1.0 (0.22)
No rank	13 (1.1)	100.0	43.8 (3.52)	39.8 (4.63)	2.4 (1.26)	0.9 (0.43)	2.8 (1.31)	3.5 (1.34)	2.0 (0.94)	1.8 (1.15)	‡ (†)	‡ (†)
Age												
Under 35	76 (2.4)	100.0	35.5 (1.72)	43.2 (1.95)	3.1 (0.57)	4.3 (0.47)	2.9 (0.46)	3.0 (0.32)	2.8 (0.56)	3.5 (0.82)	1.4 (0.59)	0.4 (0.20)
35 to 44	117 (2.8)	100.0	41.0 (1.45)	40.8 (1.42)	2.5 (0.40)	3.3 (0.38)	2.3 (0.31)	2.6 (0.34)	2.5 (0.36)	2.8 (0.42)	0.9 (0.26)	1.4 (0.32)
45 to 54	163 (3.2)	100.0	42.7 (1.20)	43.9 (1.21)	2.9 (0.34)	3.0 (0.32)	1.5 (0.23)	1.3 (0.18)	2.0 (0.36)	1.2 (0.24)	0.9 (0.24)	0.6 (0.23)
55 to 64	121 (3.2)	100.0	48.1 (1.09)	40.8 (1.02)	2.0 (0.39)	2.7 (0.34)	1.3 (0.32)	0.6 (0.11)	1.4 (0.32)	1.0 (0.24)	1.1 (0.33)	0.9 (0.27)
65 to 69	31 (1.9)	100.0	64.3 (2.77)	26.3 (2.75)	2.1 (0.85)	0.9 (0.31)	2.0 (0.65)	1.2 (0.60)	1.7 (0.64)	‡ (†)	1.2 (0.65)	‡ (†)
70 or older	22 (1.6)	100.0	59.2 (3.58)	29.4 (3.83)	2.8 (0.92)	1.8 (0.76)	2.4 (0.85)	‡ (†)	1.9 (0.76)	0.9 (0.51)	‡ (†)	‡ (†)
Base salary												
Under $10,000	366 (3.5)	100.0	44.9 (0.64)	40.4 (0.75)	2.7 (0.22)	3.4 (0.22)	1.9 (0.16)	1.6 (0.12)	1.7 (0.17)	1.4 (0.25)	1.1 (0.19)	1.0 (0.19)
$10,000 to 24,999	115 (3.3)	100.0	42.1 (1.52)	43.1 (1.61)	2.6 (0.39)	2.4 (0.29)	2.1 (0.31)	1.8 (0.26)	2.2 (0.43)	2.4 (0.48)	0.9 (0.28)	0.5 (0.20)
$25,000 to 39,999	28 (1.7)	100.0	47.3 (3.06)	38.8 (2.72)	3.3 (0.83)	1.6 (0.98)	1.2 (0.58)	1.6 (0.55)	3.2 (1.02)	1.9 (0.61)	0.8 (0.51)	‡ (†)
$40,000 to 54,999	10 (0.7)	100.0	48.2 (4.55)	34.0 (4.33)	0.7 (0.40)	1.4 (0.68)	3.2 (1.19)	0.7 (0.59)	6.2 (2.60)	3.8 (1.70)	‡ (†)	‡ (†)
$55,000 to 69,999	5 (0.8)	100.0	45.5 (6.46)	40.4 (6.35)	1.2 (0.72)	3.8 (2.18)	‡ (†)	2.2 (1.08)	‡ (†)	5.1 (2.57)	‡ (†)	‡ (†)
$70,000 to 84,999	2 (0.3)	100.0	39.0 (11.51)	43.0 (10.25)	‡ (†)	‡ (†)	‡ (†)	‡ (†)	‡ (†)	5.6 (4.00)	‡ (†)	‡ (†)
$85,000 to 99,999	1 (0.4)	100.0	33.4 (13.01)	51.7 (13.73)	‡ (†)	‡ (†)	‡ (†)	‡ (†)	‡ (†)	‡ (†)	‡ (†)	‡ (†)
$100,000 or more	4 (0.5)	100.0	47.4 (7.01)	37.1 (5.35)	‡ (†)	‡ (†)	‡ (†)	‡ (†)	10.8 (5.15)	‡ (†)	‡ (†)	‡ (†)
Total household income												
Under $10,000	2 (0.5)	100.0	43.0 (12.59)	34.5 (9.93)	‡ (†)	‡ (†)	4.0 (3.51)	‡ (†)	‡ (†)	‡ (†)	‡ (†)	‡ (†)
$10,000 to 24,999	28 (1.9)	100.0	35.5 (3.39)	43.3 (3.46)	2.0 (0.72)	4.1 (0.82)	1.7 (0.54)	2.4 (0.56)	1.6 (0.78)	3.3 (1.77)	3.8 (1.38)	2.3 (1.03)
$25,000 to 39,999	48 (1.9)	100.0	35.5 (2.27)	46.5 (2.32)	3.4 (0.58)	3.9 (0.66)	2.2 (0.44)	1.8 (0.47)	1.7 (0.55)	2.9 (0.92)	1.1 (0.46)	1.0 (0.43)
$40,000 to 54,999	56 (2.5)	100.0	38.1 (2.05)	46.2 (2.35)	3.2 (0.71)	3.4 (0.52)	3.1 (0.67)	2.5 (0.60)	1.1 (0.40)	1.1 (0.35)	0.8 (0.54)	0.5 (0.21)
$55,000 to 69,999	87 (2.9)	100.0	41.1 (1.50)	43.0 (1.48)	1.9 (0.38)	4.1 (0.38)	1.7 (0.37)	2.5 (0.35)	2.1 (0.42)	1.6 (0.45)	0.8 (0.27)	1.0 (0.37)
$70,000 to 84,999	58 (2.7)	100.0	44.7 (2.15)	41.2 (2.38)	2.3 (0.44)	2.3 (0.57)	2.3 (0.41)	1.3 (0.34)	1.4 (0.41)	2.0 (0.58)	1.1 (0.41)	1.1 (0.37)
$85,000 to 99,999	66 (2.4)	100.0	48.6 (1.85)	38.4 (1.81)	2.4 (0.59)	3.1 (0.52)	1.8 (0.37)	1.2 (0.34)	1.9 (0.49)	1.3 (0.41)	0.6 (0.29)	0.7 (0.25)
$100,000 or more	185 (3.6)	100.0	34.9 (0.68)	37.0 (0.91)	2.8 (0.32)	2.1 (0.26)	1.5 (0.21)	1.0 (0.17)	2.8 (0.34)	1.6 (0.25)	0.8 (0.22)	0.4 (0.17)

†Not applicable.
#Rounds to zero.
‡Reporting standards not met.

NOTE: Totals may differ from figures reported in other tables because of varying survey methodologies. Race categories exclude persons of Hispanic origin. Detail may not sum to totals because of rounding. Standard errors appear in parentheses.

SOURCE: U.S. Department of Education, National Center for Education Statistics, 2003 National Study of Postsecondary Faculty (NSOPF:04). (This table was prepared September 2005.)

Table 237. Full-time and part-time instructional faculty and staff in degree-granting institutions, by field and faculty characteristics: Fall 1992, fall 1998, and fall 2003

Selected characteristic	Number (in thousands) 1992	1998	2003	Fall 2003 All fields	Agriculture and home economics	Business	Education	Engineering	Fine arts	Health	Humanities[1]	Natural sciences[2]	Social sciences[3]	Other[4]
1	2	3	4	5	6	7	8	9	10	11	12	13	14	15
Full-time instructional faculty and staff														
Number (in thousands)	528	560	682	681.8 (0.05)	16.9 (0.80)	43.2 (1.40)	50.9 (1.89)	33.4 (1.32)	43.3 (1.68)	93.9 (2.67)	58.8 (1.82)	127.2 (2.19)	88.7 (2.07)	125.5 (2.36)
Percentage distribution	†	†	†	100.0 (†)	2.5 (0.12)	6.3 (0.21)	7.5 (0.28)	4.9 (0.19)	6.3 (0.25)	13.8 (0.39)	8.6 (0.27)	18.7 (0.32)	13.0 (0.30)	18.4 (0.35)
				Percentage distribution of full-time instructional faculty and staff										
Total	528	560	682	100.0 (†)	100.0 (†)	100.0 (†)	100.0 (†)	100.0 (†)	100.0 (†)	100.0 (†)	100.0 (†)	100.0 (†)	100.0 (†)	100.0 (†)
Sex														
Male	353	357	420	61.7 (0.35)	64.6 (2.88)	68.5 (1.61)	39.3 (1.57)	91.5 (1.06)	61.9 (1.38)	46.7 (1.32)	45.3 (1.47)	74.5 (0.88)	64.3 (1.13)	64.0 (0.94)
Female	176	203	261	38.3 (0.35)	35.4 (2.88)	31.5 (1.61)	60.7 (1.57)	8.5 (1.06)	38.1 (1.38)	53.3 (1.32)	54.7 (1.47)	25.5 (0.88)	35.7 (1.13)	36.0 (0.94)
Race/ethnicity														
White	457	477	548	80.3 (0.27)	87.8 (1.61)	79.5 (1.51)	80.5 (1.26)	70.9 (1.85)	86.4 (1.24)	79.7 (0.84)	80.7 (1.31)	77.8 (0.75)	81.4 (1.09)	82.0 (0.69)
Black	27	28	38	5.6 (0.17)	2.3 (0.76)	4.5 (0.79)	7.8 (1.01)	5.4 (0.99)	6.0 (0.88)	5.0 (0.50)	5.6 (0.58)	4.1 (0.48)	7.3 (0.72)	6.1 (0.44)
Hispanic	14	19	24	3.5 (0.10)	2.5 (0.76)	2.3 (0.51)	4.7 (0.63)	2.6 (0.47)	3.3 (0.75)	3.0 (0.32)	6.7 (0.53)	2.9 (0.30)	4.0 (0.47)	2.9 (0.33)
Asian/Pacific Islander	28	33	62	9.1 (0.16)	6.4 (1.34)	12.2 (1.22)	4.8 (0.70)	20.1 (1.64)	2.9 (0.74)	10.7 (0.79)	5.2 (0.94)	14.3 (0.69)	5.9 (0.71)	7.1 (0.49)
American Indian/Alaska Native	3	4	10	1.5 (0.11)	1.0 (0.49)	1.6 (0.37)	2.2 (0.40)	1.0 (0.57)	1.4 (0.38)	1.6 (0.33)	1.8 (0.35)	0.8 (0.17)	1.4 (0.22)	1.8 (0.32)
Age														
Under 30	8	9	18	2.6 (0.16)	2.9 (0.83)	1.2 (0.38)	3.3 (0.77)	2.1 (0.64)	3.0 (0.54)	1.6 (0.37)	2.9 (0.45)	2.3 (0.28)	2.2 (0.33)	3.8 (0.48)
30 to 34	35	32	55	8.0 (0.26)	5.8 (1.27)	4.6 (0.78)	7.9 (0.98)	8.4 (1.01)	5.8 (0.79)	8.4 (0.72)	8.4 (0.66)	7.9 (0.51)	9.9 (0.58)	8.6 (0.63)
35 to 39	67	60	83	12.2 (0.30)	8.6 (1.25)	12.5 (1.20)	7.8 (0.83)	13.2 (1.54)	11.9 (1.17)	14.0 (0.82)	12.5 (0.82)	12.7 (0.72)	12.7 (0.94)	11.8 (0.81)
40 to 44	90	82	93	13.6 (0.34)	12.3 (1.69)	11.3 (1.41)	10.3 (0.99)	13.3 (1.22)	14.2 (1.88)	14.6 (0.87)	13.6 (1.08)	15.7 (0.87)	13.8 (0.82)	12.9 (0.68)
45 to 49	98	97	109	15.9 (0.36)	19.8 (2.03)	18.9 (1.49)	13.6 (1.05)	17.3 (1.76)	17.4 (1.80)	18.5 (1.12)	15.2 (1.07)	15.6 (0.83)	12.8 (0.82)	15.4 (0.69)
50 to 54	95	105	114	16.7 (0.38)	23.3 (2.11)	18.8 (1.15)	19.7 (1.57)	16.2 (1.78)	18.7 (1.26)	19.1 (0.95)	13.8 (1.02)	14.2 (0.59)	15.0 (1.02)	16.8 (0.88)
55 to 59	67	90	108	15.8 (0.38)	16.3 (1.81)	19.0 (1.38)	20.4 (1.39)	14.3 (2.18)	15.9 (1.32)	13.7 (0.86)	16.0 (0.93)	13.4 (0.81)	15.4 (0.87)	17.3 (0.84)
60 to 64	45	55	70	10.2 (0.27)	7.7 (1.15)	9.1 (1.08)	11.5 (1.21)	9.6 (1.28)	10.2 (1.05)	6.8 (0.55)	11.7 (1.16)	11.7 (0.63)	13.0 (0.87)	8.9 (0.69)
65 or older	24	31	33	4.9 (0.20)	3.2 (1.09)	4.5 (0.67)	5.5 (0.66)	5.7 (0.93)	3.0 (0.66)	3.2 (0.46)	5.8 (0.74)	6.6 (0.45)	5.2 (0.51)	4.4 (0.41)
Highest degree														
Less than bachelor's	6	7	10	1.5 (0.12)	1.0 (0.68)	0.2 (0.12)	1.7 (0.74)	2.6 (0.77)	1.4 (0.46)	1.7 (0.31)	0.2 (0.12)	0.1 (0.09)	† (†)	4.4 (0.54)
Bachelor's	21	23	29	4.3 (0.24)	6.4 (1.71)	4.0 (0.80)	4.0 (0.64)	6.5 (1.22)	9.1 (1.10)	5.5 (0.69)	1.1 (0.31)	1.4 (0.23)	1.0 (0.26)	7.9 (0.67)
Master's	156	156	180	26.4 (0.39)	29.2 (2.18)	31.8 (1.69)	35.5 (1.37)	13.2 (1.64)	53.9 (1.82)	22.9 (1.16)	35.1 (1.42)	14.9 (0.72)	12.5 (0.72)	34.4 (1.24)
First-professional	58	52	56	8.2 (0.30)	0.3 (0.31)	2.1 (0.45)	1.1 (0.35)	0.5 (0.30)	1.1 (0.41)	41.1 (1.32)	0.4 (0.18)	3.0 (0.35)	0.5 (0.19)	8.7 (0.76)
Doctor's	284	324	407	59.6 (0.48)	63.0 (2.74)	61.9 (1.73)	57.7 (1.53)	77.1 (2.08)	34.6 (1.96)	28.9 (1.06)	63.2 (1.43)	80.6 (0.67)	86.0 (0.74)	44.6 (1.23)
Academic rank														
Professor	161	172	194	28.5 (0.54)	33.0 (2.71)	29.1 (1.66)	21.9 (1.41)	37.6 (1.69)	28.4 (1.85)	20.1 (0.93)	26.2 (1.46)	35.5 (0.87)	35.4 (1.20)	23.5 (1.09)
Associate professor	124	132	150	21.9 (0.37)	21.0 (2.55)	22.6 (1.32)	17.6 (1.07)	25.3 (1.77)	23.7 (1.64)	23.5 (0.96)	20.0 (1.27)	23.4 (0.93)	22.8 (0.97)	19.9 (1.08)
Assistant professor	124	125	158	23.2 (0.41)	19.2 (1.79)	23.4 (1.51)	23.8 (1.56)	19.6 (1.67)	23.2 (1.75)	32.2 (1.12)	21.7 (1.30)	21.1 (0.82)	24.8 (1.22)	19.2 (0.73)
Instructor	74	75	83	12.1 (0.42)	9.9 (1.60)	13.4 (1.37)	12.6 (1.18)	9.1 (1.39)	9.7 (1.01)	15.3 (0.90)	14.9 (1.17)	7.7 (0.56)	5.7 (0.53)	18.7 (1.02)
Lecturer	12	14	22	3.2 (0.22)	3.4 (1.50)	3.6 (0.68)	3.0 (0.60)	2.0 (0.52)	4.3 (0.64)	1.9 (0.37)	7.9 (0.78)	2.1 (0.25)	2.3 (0.42)	3.6 (0.57)
Other	17	26	57	8.3 (0.32)	11.8 (2.16)	4.9 (0.64)	18.2 (1.57)	5.4 (0.82)	7.1 (1.03)	5.5 (0.50)	5.7 (0.69)	6.7 (0.48)	6.4 (0.67)	12.4 (0.76)
No rank	17	16	19	2.7 (0.19)	1.8 (1.37)	3.0 (0.68)	2.9 (1.05)	0.9 (0.38)	3.6 (1.24)	1.5 (0.27)	3.6 (0.67)	3.5 (0.48)	2.6 (0.47)	2.7 (0.36)

See notes at end of table.

Table 237. Full-time and part-time instructional faculty and staff in degree-granting institutions, by field and faculty characteristics: Fall 1992, fall 1998, and fall 2003—Continued

Selected characteristic	Number (in thousands)			Fall 2003										
	1992	1998	2003	All fields	Agriculture and home economics	Business	Education	Engineering	Fine arts	Health	Humanities[1]	Natural sciences[2]	Social sciences[3]	Other[4]
1	2	3	4	5	6	7	8	9	10	11	12	13	14	15
Part-time instructional faculty and staff														
Number (in thousands)	377	416	530	530.0 (0.02)	7.3 (0.97)	44.9 (2.98)	63.5 (2.57)	14.0 (1.49)	47.8 (3.65)	57.8 (3.06)	58.9 (2.05)	63.7 (2.46)	53.0 (2.39)	119.2 (3.48)
Percentage distribution	†	†	†	100.0 (†)	1.4 (0.18)	8.5 (0.56)	12.0 (0.48)	2.7 (0.28)	9.0 (0.69)	10.9 (0.58)	11.1 (0.39)	12.0 (0.46)	10.0 (0.45)	22.5 (0.66)
			Percentage distribution of part-time instructional faculty and staff											
Total	377	416	530	100.0 (†)	100.0 (†)	100.0 (†)	100.0 (†)	100.0 (†)	100.0 (†)	100.0 (†)	100.0 (†)	100.0 (†)	100.0 (†)	100.0 (†)
Sex														
Male	209	217	276	52.1 (0.45)	32.0 (6.05)	69.6 (1.89)	29.1 (1.71)	90.8 (2.68)	51.4 (2.26)	34.5 (1.60)	31.6 (1.86)	58.2 (2.22)	60.5 (1.90)	66.2 (1.41)
Female	168	199	254	47.9 (0.45)	68.0 (6.05)	30.4 (1.89)	70.9 (1.71)	9.2 (2.68)	48.6 (2.26)	65.5 (1.60)	68.4 (1.86)	41.8 (2.22)	39.5 (1.90)	33.8 (1.41)
Race/ethnicity														
White	333	364	452	85.2 (0.38)	91.4 (3.66)	86.8 (1.54)	85.1 (1.34)	85.4 (2.89)	88.7 (1.22)	85.0 (1.14)	83.0 (1.14)	83.4 (1.35)	84.2 (1.62)	85.5 (0.80)
Black	18	19	30	5.6 (0.20)	2.7 (1.61)	6.7 (0.96)	6.6 (0.98)	2.0 (1.26)	3.0 (0.70)	5.2 (0.68)	5.0 (0.71)	6.0 (0.66)	5.8 (0.75)	6.5 (0.57)
Hispanic	11	16	19	3.5 (0.13)	0.4 (0.38)	2.2 (0.79)	5.1 (0.71)	2.6 (0.64)	2.7 (0.52)	2.2 (0.47)	6.5 (0.81)	2.2 (0.40)	3.7 (0.61)	3.6 (0.39)
Asian/Pacific Islander	12	13	20	3.8 (0.22)	2.7 (1.99)	3.0 (0.80)	1.6 (0.43)	8.4 (2.11)	2.9 (0.70)	6.5 (1.17)	4.2 (0.71)	7.1 (0.89)	2.7 (1.04)	2.5 (0.34)
American Indian/Alaska Native	2	4	10	1.8 (0.22)	2.9 (2.62)	1.4 (0.54)	1.5 (0.37)	1.6 (1.03)	2.8 (0.84)	1.0 (0.35)	1.3 (0.38)	1.4 (0.60)	3.6 (0.91)	1.9 (0.36)
Age														
Under 30	20	15	30	5.7 (0.32)	8.0 (2.66)	3.0 (0.87)	3.5 (0.66)	2.8 (1.78)	6.2 (1.05)	5.3 (0.85)	7.4 (1.02)	8.6 (1.14)	5.5 (0.82)	5.6 (0.71)
30 to 34	36	37	46	8.7 (0.33)	10.3 (3.24)	7.6 (1.25)	7.9 (0.97)	2.0 (1.04)	10.2 (1.32)	9.4 (1.13)	9.8 (0.97)	8.0 (1.21)	10.2 (1.20)	8.5 (0.76)
35 to 39	59	47	57	10.8 (0.44)	2.5 (1.58)	9.8 (1.48)	9.0 (1.20)	13.8 (3.89)	11.2 (1.47)	11.5 (1.31)	8.4 (1.12)	10.9 (1.20)	10.8 (1.35)	13.1 (1.18)
40 to 44	70	60	60	11.3 (0.46)	9.6 (3.92)	10.5 (1.45)	7.7 (0.96)	15.7 (3.25)	12.7 (1.39)	13.0 (1.64)	10.3 (1.00)	9.2 (1.10)	10.9 (1.05)	13.4 (0.97)
45 to 49	68	72	82	15.5 (0.51)	14.6 (5.03)	15.7 (1.83)	12.9 (1.22)	13.5 (3.13)	18.2 (1.78)	21.9 (1.67)	14.6 (1.76)	10.4 (1.33)	12.6 (1.10)	17.6 (1.17)
50 to 54	45	70	80	15.2 (0.52)	19.7 (5.36)	14.5 (1.48)	16.3 (1.46)	19.1 (4.00)	16.9 (1.60)	14.4 (1.67)	13.8 (1.25)	12.3 (1.30)	13.5 (1.43)	16.7 (1.14)
55 to 59	29	47	75	14.1 (0.44)	23.1 (5.83)	18.8 (2.12)	17.6 (1.52)	11.8 (2.71)	12.0 (1.62)	10.2 (1.23)	14.9 (1.33)	15.1 (1.46)	15.1 (1.48)	11.3 (0.88)
60 to 64	23	29	46	8.8 (0.43)	7.6 (3.82)	8.7 (1.08)	11.5 (1.30)	6.0 (2.00)	6.7 (0.93)	5.7 (1.05)	10.6 (1.23)	12.8 (1.67)	11.1 (1.45)	5.9 (0.71)
65 or older	27	38	53	10.0 (0.45)	4.7 (2.09)	11.4 (1.64)	13.6 (1.24)	15.4 (3.16)	5.9 (1.21)	8.5 (1.16)	10.2 (1.51)	12.7 (1.82)	10.4 (1.33)	7.8 (0.80)
Highest degree														
Less than bachelor's	17	20	41	7.8 (0.59)	5.5 (2.53)	1.8 (0.79)	3.7 (0.96)	17.1 (4.44)	9.1 (1.42)	17.3 (1.86)	1.1 (0.57)	0.9 (0.47)	0.5 (0.25)	16.2 (1.31)
Bachelor's	63	59	84	15.8 (0.55)	26.7 (5.80)	13.9 (1.84)	12.0 (1.25)	17.9 (3.50)	28.2 (2.09)	16.2 (1.61)	12.9 (1.65)	16.1 (1.46)	3.2 (0.82)	19.4 (1.11)
Master's	190	225	273	51.5 (0.80)	50.3 (6.09)	66.5 (2.34)	63.0 (1.84)	32.3 (4.61)	54.7 (2.95)	30.2 (1.86)	70.2 (2.33)	49.0 (1.94)	55.5 (1.83)	41.6 (1.56)
First-professional	40	36	39	7.3 (0.39)	2.0 (1.63)	6.3 (1.10)	1.9 (0.45)	1.5 (0.98)	0.9 (0.39)	25.2 (2.12)	2.3 (0.55)	4.3 (0.85)	3.1 (0.62)	11.2 (1.00)
Doctor's	59	76	94	17.6 (0.60)	15.5 (4.57)	11.5 (1.48)	19.4 (1.61)	31.2 (4.13)	7.1 (1.39)	11.1 (1.28)	13.4 (1.80)	29.7 (1.72)	37.7 (1.90)	11.7 (0.94)
Academic rank														
Professor	32	30	23	4.4 (0.30)	8.9 (4.03)	4.6 (1.06)	3.4 (0.55)	5.9 (2.27)	3.9 (1.05)	5.4 (0.84)	3.5 (0.75)	4.8 (0.82)	4.7 (1.01)	4.1 (0.63)
Associate professor	23	19	15	2.8 (0.22)	1.9 (1.37)	2.3 (0.74)	1.9 (0.47)	5.7 (2.24)	3.7 (0.92)	5.4 (0.89)	1.6 (0.35)	3.3 (0.63)	2.9 (0.60)	1.6 (0.30)
Assistant professor	24	23	20	3.7 (0.29)	2.8 (1.76)	1.5 (0.55)	2.0 (0.50)	3.3 (1.97)	3.6 (0.86)	15.1 (1.64)	1.7 (0.64)	2.8 (0.66)	3.7 (0.89)	1.7 (0.34)
Instructor	215	205	188	35.4 (0.83)	39.9 (5.70)	29.2 (2.00)	37.0 (2.11)	25.3 (4.10)	33.6 (2.12)	36.5 (2.40)	42.9 (2.29)	32.4 (2.05)	30.4 (1.85)	38.2 (1.54)
Lecturer	45	46	41	7.7 (0.41)	14.8 (4.39)	7.6 (1.52)	6.8 (0.97)	9.3 (2.49)	9.7 (1.16)	4.7 (0.93)	11.2 (1.10)	7.8 (1.02)	9.5 (1.20)	5.8 (0.67)
Other	28	75	231	43.6 (0.85)	30.8 (5.98)	51.8 (2.46)	46.6 (1.78)	49.4 (5.02)	42.4 (3.00)	30.5 (1.88)	37.4 (2.23)	45.8 (2.02)	46.0 (2.22)	46.6 (1.47)
No rank	9	16	13	2.4 (0.20)	1.1 (0.87)	3.0 (0.75)	2.1 (0.59)	1.2 (1.26)	3.2 (1.10)	2.4 (0.68)	1.7 (0.49)	3.1 (0.79)	2.8 (0.71)	2.1 (0.40)

†Not applicable.
‡Reporting standards not met.
[1]Excludes history and philosophy.
[2]Excludes computer sciences.
[3]Includes history.
[4]Includes philosophy, law, occupationally specific programs, computer sciences, and other.

NOTE: Totals may differ from figures reported in other tables because of varying survey methodologies. Race categories exclude persons of Hispanic origin. Detail may not sum to totals because of survey item nonresponse and rounding. Standard errors appear in parentheses.
SOURCE: U.S. Department of Education, National Center for Education Statistics, 1993, 1999, and 2004 National Study of Postsecondary Faculty (NSOPF:93;99;04). (This table was prepared September 2005.)

Table 238. Full-time and part-time instructional faculty and staff in degree-granting institutions, by race/ethnicity, sex, and program area: Fall 1998 and fall 2003

	Number (in thousands)		Percentage distribution, fall 2003										
	1998	2003	Total	White		Black		Hispanic		Asian/Pacific Islander		American Indian/Alaska Native	
				Male	Female	Male	Female	Male	Female	Male	Female	Male	Female
Program area	2	3	4	5	6	7	8	9	10	11	12	13	14
1	(#)	(#)											
Full-time instructional faculty and staff	560 (4.8)	682 (#)	100.0	49.6 (0.39)	30.7 (0.36)	2.9 (0.15)	2.7 (0.13)	2.0 (0.09)	1.5 (0.08)	6.3 (0.15)	2.8 (0.15)	0.8 (0.08)	0.6 (0.07)
Agriculture and home economics	10 (0.4)	17 (0.8)	100.0	58.9 (3.03)	28.9 (2.72)	0.5 (0.42)	1.8 (0.73)	1.2 (0.46)	1.3 (0.52)	3.6 (1.13)	2.8 (0.86)	0.4 (0.30)	0.6 (0.35)
Business	39 (1.1)	43 (1.4)	100.0	53.2 (1.49)	26.2 (1.71)	2.5 (0.73)	2.0 (0.44)	1.8 (0.48)	0.5 (0.16)	9.7 (1.06)	2.5 (0.46)	1.3 (0.35)	0.4 (0.17)
Communications	10 (1.0)	16 (1.4)	100.0	48.1 (3.39)	38.7 (3.30)	2.0 (0.73)	3.3 (0.94)	1.9 (0.58)	1.5 (0.59)	1.9 (0.87)	0.6 (0.39)	1.1 (0.77)	0.9 (0.64)
Education	40 (1.4)	51 (1.9)	100.0	32.5 (1.49)	48.0 (1.64)	3.0 (0.60)	4.9 (0.64)	1.5 (0.34)	3.2 (0.52)	1.3 (0.43)	3.5 (0.59)	0.9 (0.25)	1.3 (0.34)
Teacher education	14 (0.6)	18 (1.0)	100.0	31.1 (2.31)	54.4 (2.54)	2.1 (0.86)	5.2 (1.10)	0.4 (0.24)	3.1 (0.89)	0.3 (0.22)	2.1 (0.87)	0.5 (0.25)	0.9 (0.44)
Other education	26 (1.3)	33 (1.5)	100.0	33.3 (2.09)	44.4 (2.46)	3.4 (0.84)	4.7 (0.75)	2.2 (0.51)	3.2 (0.57)	1.9 (0.64)	4.2 (0.81)	1.1 (0.40)	1.5 (0.45)
Engineering	25 (0.9)	33 (1.3)	100.0	65.6 (1.93)	5.3 (0.90)	4.9 (0.84)	0.5 (0.26)	2.2 (0.42)	0.4 (0.17)	17.9 (1.61)	2.2 (0.63)	0.8 (0.53)	0.2 (0.16)
Fine arts	33 (1.4)	43 (1.7)	100.0	52.8 (1.68)	33.6 (1.36)	4.4 (0.83)	1.6 (0.34)	2.0 (0.59)	1.3 (0.44)	1.5 (0.42)	1.4 (0.59)	1.2 (0.36)	0.3 (0.18)
Health sciences	84 (2.0)	94 (2.7)	100.0	36.2 (1.23)	43.5 (1.15)	1.6 (0.26)	3.4 (0.44)	1.6 (0.25)	1.4 (0.19)	6.6 (0.60)	4.1 (0.57)	0.7 (0.22)	1.0 (0.28)
First-professional	40 (1.6)	45 (1.7)	100.0	53.9 (1.58)	20.1 (1.42)	2.2 (0.49)	2.5 (0.58)	2.2 (0.40)	1.3 (0.30)	10.6 (1.08)	5.3 (0.89)	1.1 (0.37)	0.8 (0.39)
Nursing	20 (0.6)	20 (1.2)	100.0	3.5 (0.86)	84.6 (2.21)	0.2 (0.22)	5.3 (1.29)	0.1 (0.09)	0.7 (0.27)	0.1 (0.07)	3.4 (1.10)	0.3 (0.31)	1.8 (0.85)
Other health sciences	24 (1.0)	29 (1.4)	100.0	31.0 (1.98)	52.0 (2.05)	1.5 (0.50)	3.6 (0.84)	1.6 (0.44)	1.9 (0.48)	4.8 (1.02)	2.6 (0.71)	0.3 (0.24)	0.7 (0.31)
Humanities	81 (1.8)	90 (2.4)	100.0	47.3 (1.40)	35.0 (1.33)	2.4 (0.43)	2.6 (0.39)	2.2 (0.24)	2.9 (0.31)	2.9 (0.48)	2.9 (0.54)	0.9 (0.23)	0.9 (0.25)
English and literature	40 (1.2)	39 (1.5)	100.0	38.8 (1.90)	46.0 (2.10)	2.1 (0.45)	4.5 (0.70)	1.3 (0.27)	1.9 (0.50)	0.8 (0.34)	2.7 (0.87)	0.5 (0.18)	1.4 (0.39)
Foreign languages	15 (0.8)	20 (1.0)	100.0	36.2 (1.86)	36.7 (2.07)	2.7 (0.89)	0.9 (0.46)	5.1 (0.75)	8.3 (1.07)	4.0 (1.11)	4.5 (1.01)	0.7 (0.43)	0.8 (0.44)
History	14 (0.6)	18 (1.0)	100.0	59.4 (2.90)	23.0 (2.12)	2.7 (0.80)	2.4 (0.94)	1.9 (0.71)	1.2 (0.52)	5.0 (1.49)	3.2 (0.91)	1.0 (0.45)	‡ (1.03)
Philosophy	12 (0.8)	13 (1.0)	100.0	72.3 (3.55)	16.6 (2.33)	2.3 (1.11)	0.1 (0.12)	1.0 (0.35)	1.0 (0.22)	4.0 (1.49)	0.6 (0.45)	2.0 (1.20)	0.7 (0.31)
Law	8 (0.6)	10 (1.0)	100.0	54.5 (3.56)	29.9 (3.63)	3.3 (1.10)	4.0 (2.03)	0.9 (0.68)	2.4 (1.15)	2.8 (1.36)	2.0 (1.12)	‡ (†)	0.2 (0.25)
Natural sciences	111 (2.1)	151 (2.5)	100.0	57.3 (1.12)	20.3 (0.80)	2.5 (0.31)	1.5 (0.22)	2.0 (0.20)	0.9 (0.15)	11.2 (0.65)	3.3 (0.35)	0.6 (0.16)	0.3 (0.09)
Biological sciences	40 (1.3)	59 (1.7)	100.0	55.4 (1.69)	21.6 (1.30)	2.2 (0.48)	1.2 (0.28)	1.9 (0.39)	1.2 (0.31)	11.1 (1.13)	4.8 (0.67)	0.3 (0.17)	0.3 (0.12)
Physical sciences	27 (0.8)	36 (1.3)	100.0	68.9 (2.03)	12.8 (1.50)	2.6 (0.59)	0.7 (0.31)	1.4 (0.29)	0.6 (0.19)	9.4 (1.05)	3.0 (0.64)	0.4 (0.33)	0.1 (0.10)
Mathematics	26 (1.0)	32 (1.3)	100.0	52.2 (2.15)	22.7 (1.84)	3.8 (0.67)	2.6 (0.67)	2.8 (0.67)	0.7 (0.28)	11.7 (1.41)	1.8 (0.67)	1.2 (0.56)	0.3 (0.18)
Computer sciences	17 (0.9)	24 (1.2)	100.0	51.0 (2.74)	25.1 (2.15)	1.5 (0.59)	2.0 (0.58)	2.3 (0.52)	0.9 (0.31)	13.5 (1.69)	2.0 (0.66)	1.1 (0.48)	0.6 (0.36)
Social sciences	58 (1.3)	70 (1.8)	100.0	52.2 (1.46)	29.0 (1.23)	3.7 (0.45)	4.1 (0.81)	2.6 (0.36)	1.7 (0.35)	3.4 (0.58)	1.9 (0.48)	0.9 (0.25)	0.6 (0.15)
Economics	9 (0.6)	12 (0.7)	100.0	62.3 (3.46)	18.0 (3.09)	3.5 (0.92)	0.1 (0.09)	3.1 (1.13)	0.0 (0.00)	8.9 (2.18)	3.2 (2.24)	0.6 (0.39)	0.3 (0.33)
Political science	8 (0.5)	10 (0.7)	100.0	67.1 (3.74)	16.8 (2.59)	2.8 (1.19)	3.2 (1.62)	5.1 (1.57)	0.2 (0.21)	2.9 (1.31)	0.3 (0.27)	0.3 (0.27)	1.1 (0.26)
Psychology	20 (0.7)	25 (1.1)	100.0	46.3 (2.33)	37.8 (2.16)	3.4 (1.01)	5.0 (1.99)	1.6 (0.42)	2.7 (0.70)	1.2 (0.49)	1.2 (0.39)	0.6 (0.34)	0.2 (0.19)
Sociology	9 (0.4)	9 (0.6)	100.0	49.9 (3.72)	30.1 (3.42)	3.9 (1.69)	8.0 (2.43)	3.0 (0.97)	1.4 (0.92)	1.3 (0.75)	1.3 (0.75)	1.0 (0.52)	0.3 (0.26)
Other social sciences	13 (0.6)	14 (0.9)	100.0	45.2 (3.59)	30.5 (3.09)	4.8 (1.33)	3.9 (1.28)	1.9 (0.80)	2.4 (0.71)	4.7 (1.50)	3.7 (1.22)	1.9 (0.75)	1.1 (0.54)
Occupationally specific programs	16 (0.8)	27 (1.1)	100.0	60.7 (2.47)	24.2 (2.16)	4.2 (1.16)	1.9 (0.55)	2.5 (0.63)	0.8 (0.26)	2.0 (0.92)	1.4 (0.46)	1.9 (0.62)	0.5 (0.36)
All other programs	44 (1.2)	36 (1.4)	100.0	41.6 (1.84)	37.1 (1.65)	3.8 (0.84)	5.3 (0.87)	1.5 (0.36)	1.4 (0.44)	5.3 (1.03)	2.6 (0.69)	0.7 (0.29)	0.6 (0.23)
Part-time instructional faculty and staff	416 (5.9)	530 (#)	100.0	44.4 (0.46)	40.8 (0.54)	2.6 (0.17)	3.0 (0.14)	1.9 (0.12)	1.6 (0.10)	2.1 (0.15)	1.8 (0.18)	1.0 (0.15)	0.8 (0.15)
Agriculture and home economics	3 (0.2)	7 (1.0)	100.0	30.8 (6.24)	60.6 (6.30)	0.5 (0.48)	2.1 (1.46)	‡ (†)	0.4 (0.38)	0.7 (0.78)	1.9 (1.69)	‡ (†)	2.9 (2.62)
Business	32 (1.8)	45 (3.0)	100.0	60.6 (1.96)	26.2 (1.73)	4.3 (0.70)	2.3 (0.54)	1.7 (0.77)	0.5 (0.28)	2.0 (0.69)	1.0 (0.50)	1.0 (0.52)	0.4 (0.23)
Communications	10 (1.0)	14 (1.2)	100.0	47.7 (3.71)	39.3 (3.89)	2.1 (0.97)	2.8 (0.95)	0.5 (0.36)	1.5 (0.99)	0.5 (0.48)	0.8 (0.52)	3.5 (1.82)	1.1 (0.86)

See notes at end of table.

Table 238. Full-time and part-time instructional faculty and staff in degree-granting institutions, by race/ethnicity, sex, and program area: Fall 1998 and fall 2003—Continued

Program area	Number (in thousands)		Percentage distribution, fall 2003											
	1998	2003	Total	White		Black		Hispanic		Asian/Pacific Islander		American Indian/Alaska Native	
				Male	Female	Male	Female	Male	Female	Male	Female	Male	Female
1	2	3	4	5	6	7	8	9	10	11	12	13	14
Education	34 (1.6)	64 (2.6)	100.0	25.3 (1.65)	59.8 (2.11)	1.4 (0.41)	5.2 (0.90)	1.7 (0.37)	3.4 (0.49)	0.4 (0.19)	1.3 (0.38)	0.3 (0.15)	1.2 (0.36)
Teacher education	13 (1.0)	29 (1.8)	100.0	22.2 (2.41)	63.9 (2.84)	0.9 (0.35)	6.4 (1.17)	1.3 (0.41)	2.2 (0.52)	0.3 (0.19)	0.9 (0.52)	0.4 (0.29)	1.6 (0.69)
Other education	20 (1.2)	34 (1.8)	100.0	27.9 (2.53)	56.4 (2.98)	1.9 (0.66)	4.1 (1.17)	2.0 (0.57)	4.5 (0.77)	0.5 (0.24)	1.6 (0.60)	0.3 (0.21)	0.8 (0.37)
Engineering	9 (0.8)	14 (1.5)	100.0	78.6 (3.70)	6.8 (2.77)	1.4 (1.22)	0.5 (0.43)	1.7 (0.46)	0.9 (0.46)	8.0 (2.13)	0.5 (0.46)	1.1 (0.92)	0.6 (0.59)
Fine arts	38 (1.5)	48 (3.6)	100.0	44.8 (2.06)	43.9 (2.44)	1.7 (0.54)	1.3 (0.34)	1.8 (0.49)	0.9 (0.25)	1.0 (0.36)	1.9 (0.58)	2.1 (0.84)	0.7 (0.30)
Health sciences	49 (2.2)	58 (3.1)	100.0	27.9 (1.65)	57.1 (1.74)	1.2 (0.41)	4.0 (0.52)	0.8 (0.26)	1.4 (0.38)	4.0 (0.87)	2.4 (0.72)	0.5 (0.32)	0.5 (0.23)
First-professional	15 (1.3)	17 (1.2)	100.0	47.2 (3.33)	34.7 (3.64)	2.0 (1.03)	2.1 (0.92)	1.2 (0.72)	0.9 (0.45)	6.4 (2.10)	5.1 (2.41)	0.4 (0.39)	‡ (†)
Nursing	12 (0.8)	13 (1.3)	100.0	0.7 (0.59)	86.3 (2.04)	0.4 (0.45)	8.0 (1.30)	0.4 (0.26)	1.4 (0.56)	0.5 (0.51)	1.3 (1.03)	‡ (†)	0.9 (0.47)
Other health sciences	21 (1.7)	28 (2.0)	100.0	29.4 (2.86)	56.4 (3.07)	1.2 (0.66)	3.2 (0.76)	0.8 (0.32)	1.7 (0.70)	4.3 (1.23)	1.4 (0.56)	0.8 (0.68)	0.7 (0.40)
Humanities	74 (2.1)	80 (2.5)	100.0	35.9 (1.52)	49.2 (1.61)	1.6 (0.35)	2.9 (0.45)	2.3 (0.35)	2.9 (0.44)	0.9 (0.30)	2.7 (0.55)	1.0 (0.33)	0.6 (0.22)
English and literature	43 (1.4)	44 (1.9)	100.0	29.5 (2.31)	58.5 (2.47)	1.2 (0.33)	4.3 (0.78)	1.0 (0.35)	1.3 (0.37)	1.0 (0.41)	1.6 (0.46)	0.8 (0.34)	0.8 (0.29)
Foreign languages	12 (1.2)	15 (1.2)	100.0	16.6 (3.57)	52.0 (3.38)	1.4 (0.83)	2.0 (0.80)	7.2 (1.50)	11.4 (1.97)	0.9 (0.67)	7.9 (2.18)	‡ (†)	0.6 (0.84)
History	11 (0.7)	11 (1.0)	100.0	61.1 (4.58)	28.9 (4.15)	1.5 (0.89)	0.5 (0.38)	2.5 (1.05)	0.2 (0.23)	‡ (†)	1.0 (0.63)	3.7 (1.99)	0.5 (0.44)
Philosophy	9 (0.6)	10 (1.2)	100.0	65.7 (4.20)	26.0 (4.60)	3.5 (1.71)	0.5 (0.28)	0.6 (0.46)	# (†)	1.8 (1.18)	1.5 (1.10)	0.4 (0.29)	‡ (†)
Law	11 (0.8)	11 (1.2)	100.0	52.6 (4.43)	32.8 (4.18)	4.4 (1.41)	2.0 (0.82)	2.2 (1.05)	0.4 (0.32)	3.5 (1.89)	‡ (†)	1.0 (0.86)	1.0 (0.89)
Natural sciences	65 (2.2)	90 (2.9)	100.0	50.5 (1.72)	32.4 (1.73)	3.8 (0.44)	2.7 (0.36)	1.9 (0.41)	0.7 (0.16)	4.2 (0.61)	2.3 (0.46)	1.0 (0.34)	0.5 (0.26)
Biological sciences	11 (0.9)	16 (1.0)	100.0	41.7 (3.76)	40.1 (3.78)	2.2 (0.67)	2.1 (0.90)	1.0 (0.39)	1.0 (0.40)	5.6 (2.32)	5.3 (1.63)	0.5 (0.44)	0.5 (0.48)
Physical sciences	11 (0.8)	16 (1.1)	100.0	57.8 (3.30)	28.7 (3.42)	3.9 (1.37)	0.9 (0.52)	1.9 (1.05)	0.9 (0.41)	3.1 (1.06)	2.6 (0.99)	‡ (†)	0.2 (0.23)
Mathematics	24 (1.4)	32 (2.3)	100.0	46.6 (3.20)	36.0 (3.04)	4.4 (0.78)	3.1 (0.83)	1.4 (0.48)	0.5 (0.24)	3.9 (0.85)	1.8 (0.64)	1.3 (0.85)	0.9 (0.59)
Computer sciences	19 (1.2)	26 (1.7)	100.0	56.4 (2.98)	25.3 (2.64)	4.1 (1.03)	3.7 (0.60)	3.0 (0.93)	0.7 (0.39)	4.2 (1.10)	0.9 (0.45)	1.4 (0.63)	0.3 (0.31)
Social sciences	41 (2.4)	42 (2.0)	100.0	49.8 (1.85)	32.9 (2.09)	3.7 (0.68)	3.0 (0.66)	2.5 (0.65)	1.5 (0.31)	0.9 (0.48)	2.3 (1.23)	1.5 (0.65)	2.0 (0.62)
Economics	4 (0.5)	5 (0.8)	100.0	68.6 (7.36)	9.3 (4.08)	7.2 (3.52)	0.8 (0.64)	7.0 (4.24)	0.3 (0.38)	0.3 (0.29)	3.9 (3.33)	2.7 (3.02)	‡ (†)
Political science	4 (0.4)	5 (0.8)	100.0	71.1 (5.32)	11.9 (3.93)	5.7 (2.79)	1.7 (1.32)	3.9 (2.30)	1.0 (0.67)	3.4 (2.98)	1.3 (1.06)	0.1 (0.12)	‡ (†)
Psychology	18 (2.1)	18 (1.2)	100.0	42.2 (3.36)	44.4 (3.12)	2.0 (0.76)	3.0 (0.91)	1.4 (0.64)	1.7 (0.58)	0.6 (0.39)	0.6 (0.52)	1.9 (1.11)	2.2 (0.93)
Sociology	6 (0.5)	7 (0.9)	100.0	44.6 (6.09)	30.7 (6.03)	4.0 (1.61)	4.1 (1.54)	1.7 (0.98)	1.6 (0.76)	‡ (†)	6.0 (6.26)	1.7 (1.52)	5.7 (3.43)
Other social sciences	10 (0.9)	8 (0.8)	100.0	46.2 (4.24)	36.4 (4.19)	3.8 (2.28)	4.5 (1.85)	1.8 (1.04)	1.9 (0.83)	1.2 (1.21)	2.8 (1.29)	0.3 (0.33)	1.1 (1.00)
Occupationally specific programs	17 (1.1)	37 (2.4)	100.0	68.2 (2.51)	18.6 (2.19)	4.5 (1.03)	1.8 (0.63)	4.0 (0.92)	0.6 (0.23)	0.6 (0.32)	0.3 (0.19)	1.1 (0.50)	0.4 (0.25)
All other programs	35 (1.6)	21 (1.3)	100.0	41.5 (3.08)	42.4 (2.96)	2.3 (0.75)	5.2 (1.37)	1.8 (0.55)	3.1 (0.98)	1.1 (0.73)	1.1 (0.59)	0.7 (0.53)	0.7 (0.62)

†Not applicable.
#Rounds to zero.
‡Reporting standards not met.

NOTE: Totals may differ from figures reported in other tables because of varying survey methodologies. Race categories exclude persons of Hispanic origin. Detail may not sum to totals because of rounding and nonresponse to program area question. Standard errors appear in parentheses.
SOURCE: U.S. Department of Education, National Center for Education Statistics, 1999 and 2004 National Study of Postsecondary Faculty (NSOPF:99;04). (This table was prepared August 2005.)

Table 239. Average base salary of full-time instructional faculty and staff in degree-granting institutions, by type and control of institution and field of instruction: Selected years, 1987–88 through 2003–04

[In 2005–06 dollars]

Program area	Institutions All	Institutions Public	Institutions Private	Research Public	Research Private	Doctoral Public	Doctoral Private	Comprehensive Public	Comprehensive Private	Private liberal arts	Public 2-year	Other
1	2	3	4	5	6	7	8	9	10	11	12	13
1987–88 salaries	**$67,549** (—)	**$68,171** (—)	**$66,160** (—)	**$81,143** (—)	**$88,893** (—)	**$75,433** (—)	**$79,883** (—)	**$63,306** (—)	**$55,239** (—)	**$49,512** (—)	**$55,634** (—)	**$52,634** (—)
Agriculture and home economics	67,648	68,012	(†)	75,997	(†)	60,736	(†)	65,529	(†)	(†)	(†)	(†)
Business	63,168	63,925	61,541	81,284	‡	68,639	‡	60,613	‡	41,048	56,835	49,274
Education	56,543	59,361	46,813	64,031	‡	60,476	‡	58,313	‡	‡	57,429	‡
Engineering	72,899	71,781	76,923	85,675	‡	74,184	‡	71,877	‡	‡	51,371	‡
Fine arts	52,832	55,215	47,985	56,263	‡	53,272	‡	46,311	‡	48,147	56,149	‡
Health	90,557	89,980	91,714	102,555	107,708	99,220	93,932	79,756	‡	‡	51,683	‡
Humanities	59,226	61,561	55,662	64,680	68,397	54,909	64,662	62,271	54,120	53,232	60,680	48,563
Natural sciences	66,753	67,574	64,916	80,905	86,188	69,693	65,498	65,179	52,720	52,720	55,418	52,356
Social sciences	64,551	64,931	63,848	73,778	85,227	66,931	‡	62,735	53,911	49,883	57,316	(—)
Other	62,426	61,766	63,993	73,504	(—)	63,425	(†)	58,434	49,890	50,872	52,723	61,895
1992–93 salaries	**65,388** (—)	**65,296** (—)	**65,611** (—)	**78,805** (—)	**89,309** (—)	**71,900** (—)	**78,202** (—)	**60,393** (—)	‡	**52,528** (—)	**54,941** (—)	**56,487** (—)
Agriculture and home economics	66,750	67,699	(†)	76,421	(†)	62,103	(†)	75,096	(†)	(†)	(†)	(†)
Business	68,724	69,747	66,065	82,107	‡	82,107	‡	66,652	‡	45,128	58,664	46,894
Education	58,704	60,398	52,522	69,561	‡	58,922	‡	53,001	‡	45,264	57,556	‡
Engineering	77,585	78,079	75,659	93,239	‡	74,803	‡	64,022	‡	‡	53,959	78,237
Fine arts	56,649	54,850	59,374	57,714	85,285	54,981	52,879	50,000	‡	52,725	52,390	47,610
Health	77,661	75,530	83,381	102,574	120,380	89,132	92,317	63,775	‡	59,146	49,969	58,501
Humanities	57,204	58,082	55,336	61,458	102,034	55,374	59,936	57,304	‡	52,590	57,499	51,027
Natural sciences	67,285	66,318	69,716	77,393	62,403	72,171	79,115	64,116	‡	52,405	55,360	58,840
Social sciences	64,169	64,369	63,760	74,192	93,782	68,007	69,119	55,155	‡	56,534	56,284	61,976
Other	62,261	60,638	65,663	71,215	91,708	61,121	86,360	58,252	‡	50,872	52,592	54,729
1998–99 salaries	**68,754** (459.3)	**67,798** (504.8)	**71,503** (1,050.8)	**80,301** (987.4)	**98,654** (3,032.1)	**79,172** (2,239.0)	**84,946** (2,400.2)	**59,712** (696.7)	**52,729** (1,356.5)	**52,729** (859.7)	**53,981** (512.2)	**57,115** (1,933.6)
Agriculture and home economics	70,668 (2,861.4)	73,406 (2,134.8)	(†)	81,434 (2,845.6)	(†)	‡	(†)	71,649 (1,895.6)	(†)	(†)	(†)	(†)
Business	67,528 (1,216.7)	66,031 (1,387.7)	71,060 (2,410.3)	83,738 (4,058.6)	97,897 (9,573.3)	66,802 (5,846.4)	83,874 (6,900.5)	52,822 (2,170.9)	51,649 (2,250.5)	51,190 (3,539.4)	53,487 (2,524.4)	51,325 (5,950.8)
Education	57,795 (1,093.5)	58,368 (1,257.9)	55,865 (2,209.8)	64,595 (2,138.3)	‡	56,096 (3,449.2)	‡	63,643 (6,037.4)	52,822 (2,319.4)	49,411 (2,456.7)	52,394 (1,573.9)	50,109 (4,491.8)
Engineering	76,675 (1,574.7)	75,302 (1,722.8)	81,835 (3,613.9)	84,495 (2,902.5)	92,002 (6,025.4)	77,817 (2,898.2)	‡	60,260 (8,373.5)	60,033 (7,065.6)	‡	54,545 (2,044.7)	‡
Fine arts	55,213 (1,404.1)	54,553 (1,390.7)	56,914 (3,389.2)	59,673 (3,413.1)	‡	50,681 (1,543.3)	‡	57,295 (4,922.5)	‡	52,573 (2,028.4)	55,579 (2,796.2)	44,254 (3,872.9)
Health	90,990 (1,832.9)	86,778 (1,875.0)	102,647 (4,480.9)	103,422 (3,357.1)	121,019 (9,158.0)	103,815 (5,319.0)	112,475 (5,996.6)	56,191 (2,149.2)	57,295 (1,777.3)	53,923 (4,443.7)	52,749 (1,381.6)	64,560 (4,093.6)
Humanities	57,684 (781.8)	57,886 (926.7)	57,191 (1,454.1)	65,220 (2,400.7)	68,974 (5,140.8)	56,885 (3,081.9)	59,665 (3,156.7)	57,765 (2,404.9)	56,191 (2,404.9)	52,243 (1,914.0)	54,477 (1,452.4)	52,248 (2,284.5)
Natural sciences	69,334 (869.6)	68,848 (940.1)	70,806 (2,021.4)	79,759 (1,669.9)	96,489 (4,814.7)	77,935 (2,242.9)	74,646 (3,696.4)	56,156 (1,354.9)	56,156 (2,169.9)	51,562 (1,610.1)	53,365 (1,061.8)	67,199 (6,295.8)
Social sciences	71,006 (2,149.8)	71,898 (2,726.8)	68,674 (2,962.9)	83,536 (3,775.8)	94,984 (8,074.7)	84,159 (16,521.1)	71,259 (3,728.1)	63,877 (3,638.8)	57,224 (2,886.6)	57,224 (2,856.6)	57,071 (1,919.7)	59,539 (4,706.5)
Other	63,069 (1,061.3)	60,978 (1,109.7)	69,655 (2,524.2)	72,437 (2,463.2)	97,530 (7,893.6)	68,266 (2,907.2)	78,761 (4,336.0)	‡	58,252	52,176 (2,271.1)	52,804 (1,233.6)	56,420 (4,672.4)
2003–04 salaries	**72,074** (404.3)	**75,684** (952.0)	**70,501** (379.3)	**84,233** (688.5)	**96,070** (1,438.3)	**67,346** (839.1)	**78,626** (2,034.5)	**62,065** (876.2)	**61,931** (1,653.4)	**58,703** (1,113.0)	**63,682** (760.0)	**70,423** (3,288.0)
Agriculture and home economics	69,009 (1,666.5)	70,202 (1,786.7)	(†)	75,240 (2,133.0)	(†)	‡	(†)	73,065 (3,314.6)	(†)	(†)	(†)	(†)
Business	79,119 (1,325.4)	76,743 (1,373.1)	84,977 (2,892.9)	97,140 (3,958.6)	118,544 (8,160.5)	93,635 (6,226.7)	‡	57,689 (2,496.8)	76,038 (1,690.1)	64,778 (2,885.2)	59,498 (1,669.3)	66,749 (6,213.5)
Education	61,040 (922.3)	61,791 (1,173.6)	59,021 (1,819.9)	69,889 (2,282.5)	78,199 (9,490.0)	60,672 (2,546.8)	‡	60,312 (2,398.6)	57,689 (2,260.5)	58,054 (2,851.9)	58,316 (2,039.8)	53,064 (2,917.2)
Engineering	81,974 (1,550.9)	77,957 (1,388.3)	95,394 (3,924.7)	89,678 (2,580.1)	105,142 (4,561.1)	78,295 (3,412.1)	‡	81,319 (3,154.9)	81,319 (1,574.9)	‡	57,056 (1,609.1)	‡
Fine arts	57,191 (776.8)	57,835 (799.6)	56,277 (1,398.9)	62,532 (1,588.7)	62,652 (3,887.4)	56,641 (1,713.4)	‡	54,031 (1,491.5)	54,031 (1,810.4)	52,661 (1,633.0)	56,629 (2,307.7)	59,302 (3,123.0)
Health	95,993 (1,691.7)	93,312 (1,621.7)	101,816 (3,997.2)	115,250 (2,123.7)	113,264 (3,604.3)	82,437 (6,334.5)	98,701 (14,914.7)	65,625 (5,043.0)	58,695 (1,491.5)	53,602 (4,681.9)	84,304 (3,329.6)	100,455 (8,475.8)
Humanities	58,458 (793.9)	56,960 (917.5)	61,556 (1,476.3)	60,282 (1,829.0)	67,917 (3,661.5)	53,847 (2,229.5)	72,556 (2,229.7)	56,702 (2,108.8)	58,723 (1,941.2)	59,257 (2,085.8)	54,630 (1,546.1)	52,728 (3,020.7)
Natural sciences	75,589 (923.6)	72,418 (871.7)	83,167 (2,044.3)	84,884 (1,324.3)	97,348 (3,703.6)	87,151 (1,317.4)	‡	61,637 (1,941.2)	61,637 (1,317.4)	59,612 (1,987.6)	54,224 (1,613.4)	82,577 (7,647.3)
Social sciences	69,066 (652.1)	67,531 (663.9)	72,173 (1,436.7)	77,324 (1,563.5)	93,916 (3,000.6)	67,883 (1,445.7)	‡	64,517 (1,317.4)	64,517 (1,445.7)	63,140 (2,341.0)	58,257 (1,551.7)	63,396 (2,797.1)
Other	64,085 (708.1)	62,966 (802.2)	66,661 (1,365.8)	73,213 (1,993.1)	88,774 (2,771.2)	70,816 (1,367.2)	70,816 (2,960.8)	59,589 (1,471.8)	60,764 (1,803.7)	55,430 (1,425.2)	58,456 (1,231.1)	60,668 (2,724.8)

—Not available.
†Not applicable.
‡Reporting standards not met.

NOTE: Constant dollars based on the Consumer Price Index, prepared by the Bureau of Labor Statistics, U.S. Department of Labor, adjusted to an academic-year basis. Totals may differ from figures reported in other tables because of varying survey methodologies. Standard errors appear in parentheses.
SOURCE: U.S. Department of Education, National Center for Education Statistics, 1988, 1993, 1999, and 2004 National Study of Postsecondary Faculty (NSOPF:88;93;99;04). (This table was prepared August 2006.)

Table 240. Average salary of full-time instructional faculty on 9-month contracts in degree-granting institutions, by academic rank, control and type of institution, and sex: Selected years, 1970–71 through 2005–06

Sex and academic year	All faculty	Academic rank						Public institutions			Private institutions		
		Professor	Associate professor	Assistant professor	Instructor	Lecturer	No rank	Total	4-year	2-year	Total	4-year	2-year
1	2	3	4	5	6	7	8	9	10	11	12	13	14
							Current dollars						
Total													
1970–71..........................	$12,710	$17,958	$13,563	$11,176	$9,360	$11,196	$12,333	$12,953	$13,121	$12,644	$11,619	$11,824	$8,664
1972–73..........................	13,856	19,191	14,580	12,032	10,737	11,637	12,676	14,016	14,417	12,919	13,452	13,622	9,288
1974–75..........................	15,622	21,277	16,146	13,295	12,691	12,575	13,532	15,879	16,271	14,897	14,912	15,092	10,242
1975–76..........................	16,659	22,649	17,065	13,986	13,672	12,906	15,196	16,942	17,400	15,820	15,921	16,116	10,901
1978–79..........................	19,820	26,470	20,047	16,374	13,193	15,281	18,725	20,179	20,722	18,844	18,807	19,010	12,496
1979–80..........................	21,348	28,388	21,451	17,465	14,023	16,122	20,262	21,798	22,349	20,429	20,105	20,318	13,250
1980–81..........................	23,302	30,753	23,214	18,901	15,178	17,301	22,334	23,745	24,373	22,177	22,093	22,325	15,065
1981–82..........................	25,449	33,437	25,278	20,608	16,450	18,756	24,331	25,886	26,591	24,193	24,255	24,509	15,926
1982–83..........................	27,196	35,540	26,921	22,056	17,601	20,072	25,557	27,488	28,293	25,567	26,393	26,691	16,595
1984–85..........................	30,447	39,743	29,945	24,668	20,230	22,334	27,683	30,646	31,764	27,864	29,910	30,247	18,510
1985–86..........................	32,392	42,268	31,787	26,277	20,918	23,770	29,088	32,750	34,033	29,590	31,402	31,732	19,436
1987–88..........................	35,897	47,040	35,231	29,110	22,728	25,977	31,532	36,231	37,840	32,209	35,049	35,346	21,867
1989–90..........................	40,133	52,810	39,392	32,689	25,030	28,990	34,559	40,416	42,365	35,516	39,464	39,817	24,601
1990–91..........................	42,165	55,540	41,414	34,434	26,332	30,097	36,395	42,317	44,510	37,055	41,788	42,224	24,088
1991–92..........................	43,851	57,433	42,929	35,745	30,916	30,456	37,783	43,641	45,638	38,959	44,376	44,793	25,673
1992–93..........................	44,714	58,788	43,945	36,625	28,499	30,543	37,771	44,197	46,515	38,935	45,985	46,427	26,105
1993–94..........................	46,364	60,649	45,278	37,630	28,828	32,729	40,584	45,920	48,019	41,040	47,465	47,880	28,435
1994–95..........................	47,811	62,709	46,713	38,756	29,665	33,198	41,227	47,432	49,738	42,101	48,741	49,379	25,613
1995–96..........................	49,309	64,540	47,966	39,696	30,344	34,136	42,996	48,837	51,172	43,295	50,466	50,819	31,915
1996–97..........................	50,829	66,659	49,307	40,687	31,193	34,962	44,200	50,303	52,718	44,584	52,112	52,443	32,628
1997–98..........................	52,335	68,731	50,828	41,830	32,449	35,484	45,268	51,638	54,114	45,919	54,039	54,379	33,592
1998–99..........................	54,097	71,322	52,576	43,348	33,819	36,819	46,250	53,319	55,948	47,285	55,981	56,284	34,821
1999–2000......................	55,888	74,410	54,524	44,978	34,918	38,194	47,389	55,011	57,950	48,240	58,013	58,323	35,925
2001–02..........................	59,742	80,792	58,724	48,796	46,959	41,798	46,569	58,524	62,013	50,837	62,818	63,088	33,139
2002–03..........................	61,330	83,466	60,471	50,552	48,304	42,622	46,338	60,014	63,486	52,330	64,533	64,814	34,826
2003–04..........................	62,615	85,352	61,744	51,808	49,076	43,689	47,746	60,912	64,398	53,080	66,693	66,953	36,429
2004–05..........................	64,234	88,158	63,558	53,308	49,730	44,514	48,942	62,346	66,053	53,932	68,755	68,995	37,329
2005–06..........................	66,172	91,208	65,714	55,106	50,883	45,896	50,425	64,158	67,951	55,405	71,016	71,263	38,549
Males													
1972–73..........................	14,422	19,414	14,723	12,193	11,147	12,106	13,047	14,545	14,944	13,268	14,116	14,253	9,571
1974–75..........................	16,303	21,532	16,282	13,458	13,350	13,232	14,008	16,522	16,918	15,350	15,709	15,852	10,633
1975–76..........................	17,414	22,902	17,209	14,174	14,430	13,579	15,761	17,661	18,121	16,339	16,784	16,946	11,378
1978–79..........................	20,777	26,727	20,221	16,602	13,441	15,927	19,400	21,080	21,628	19,475	19,935	20,086	13,048
1979–80..........................	22,394	28,672	21,651	17,720	14,323	16,932	20,901	22,789	23,350	21,131	21,317	21,472	13,938
1980–81..........................	24,499	31,082	23,451	19,227	15,545	18,281	23,170	24,873	25,509	22,965	23,493	23,669	16,075
1981–82..........................	26,796	33,799	25,553	21,025	16,906	19,721	25,276	27,149	27,864	25,085	25,849	26,037	16,834
1982–83..........................	28,664	35,956	27,262	22,586	18,160	21,225	26,541	28,851	29,661	26,524	28,159	28,380	17,346
1984–85..........................	32,182	40,269	30,392	25,330	21,159	23,557	28,670	32,240	33,344	28,891	32,028	32,278	19,460
1985–86..........................	34,294	42,833	32,273	27,094	21,693	25,238	30,267	34,528	35,786	30,758	33,656	33,900	20,412
1987–88..........................	38,112	47,735	35,823	30,086	23,645	27,652	32,747	38,314	39,898	33,477	37,603	37,817	22,641
1989–90..........................	42,763	53,650	40,131	33,781	25,933	31,162	35,980	42,959	44,834	37,081	42,312	42,595	25,218
1990–91..........................	45,065	56,549	42,239	35,636	27,388	32,398	38,036	45,084	47,168	38,787	45,019	45,319	25,937
1991–92..........................	46,848	58,494	43,814	36,969	33,359	32,843	39,422	46,483	48,401	40,811	47,733	48,042	26,825
1992–93..........................	47,866	59,972	44,855	37,842	29,583	32,512	39,365	47,175	49,392	40,725	49,518	49,837	27,402
1993–94..........................	49,579	61,857	46,229	38,794	29,815	34,796	42,251	48,956	50,989	42,938	51,076	51,397	30,783
1994–95..........................	51,228	64,046	47,705	39,923	30,528	35,082	43,103	50,629	52,874	44,020	52,653	53,036	29,639
1995–96..........................	52,814	65,949	49,037	40,858	30,940	36,135	44,624	52,163	54,448	45,209	54,364	54,649	33,301
1996–97..........................	54,465	68,214	50,457	41,864	31,738	36,932	45,688	53,737	56,162	46,393	56,185	56,453	34,736
1997–98..........................	56,115	70,468	52,041	43,017	33,070	37,481	46,822	55,191	57,744	47,690	58,293	58,576	36,157
1998–99..........................	58,048	73,260	53,830	44,650	34,741	38,976	47,610	57,038	59,805	48,961	60,392	60,641	38,040
1999–2000......................	60,084	76,478	55,939	46,414	35,854	40,202	48,788	58,984	62,030	50,033	62,631	62,905	38,636
2001–02..........................	64,320	83,356	60,300	50,518	48,844	44,519	48,049	62,835	66,577	52,360	67,871	68,100	33,395
2002–03..........................	66,126	86,191	62,226	52,441	50,272	45,469	47,412	64,564	68,322	53,962	69,726	69,976	34,291
2003–04..........................	67,509	88,254	63,465	53,660	50,997	46,273	48,977	65,508	69,290	54,630	72,026	72,248	35,734
2004–05..........................	69,337	91,290	65,394	55,215	51,380	46,929	50,102	67,130	71,145	55,398	74,318	74,540	34,970
2005–06..........................	71,569	94,733	67,654	57,099	52,519	48,256	51,811	69,191	73,353	56,858	76,941	77,143	38,215

See notes at end of table.

Table 240. Average salary of full-time instructional faculty on 9-month contracts in degree-granting institutions, by academic rank, control and type of institution, and sex: Selected years, 1970–71 through 2005–06—Continued

Sex and academic year	All faculty	Academic rank						Public institutions			Private institutions		
		Professor	Associate professor	Assistant professor	Instructor	Lecturer	No rank	Total	4-year	2-year	Total	4-year	2-year
1	2	3	4	5	6	7	8	9	10	11	12	13	14
Females													
1972–73	11,925	17,123	13,827	11,510	10,098	10,775	11,913	12,250	12,300	12,165	11,044	11,219	8,888
1974–75	13,471	19,012	15,481	12,858	11,740	11,543	12,619	13,892	13,831	13,987	12,233	12,423	9,735
1975–76	14,308	20,308	16,364	13,522	12,572	11,901	14,094	14,762	14,758	14,769	13,030	13,231	10,201
1978–79	17,080	24,143	19,300	15,914	12,966	14,465	17,482	17,646	17,627	17,676	15,388	15,611	11,898
1979–80	18,396	25,910	20,642	16,974	13,750	15,142	19,069	19,042	18,985	19,134	16,539	16,787	12,541
1980–81	19,996	27,959	22,295	18,302	14,854	16,168	20,843	20,673	20,608	20,778	18,073	18,326	13,892
1981–82	21,802	30,438	24,271	19,866	16,054	17,676	22,672	22,524	22,454	22,632	19,743	20,024	14,984
1982–83	23,261	32,221	25,738	21,130	17,102	18,830	23,855	23,892	23,876	23,917	21,451	21,785	15,845
1984–85	25,941	35,824	28,517	23,575	19,362	21,004	26,050	26,566	26,813	26,172	24,186	24,560	17,575
1985–86	27,576	38,252	30,300	24,966	20,237	22,273	27,171	28,299	28,680	27,693	25,523	25,889	18,504
1987–88	30,499	42,371	33,528	27,600	21,962	24,370	29,605	31,215	31,820	30,228	28,621	28,946	21,215
1989–90	34,183	47,663	37,469	31,090	24,320	26,995	32,528	34,796	35,704	33,307	32,650	33,010	24,002
1990–91	35,881	49,728	39,329	32,724	25,534	28,111	34,179	36,459	37,573	34,720	34,359	34,898	22,585
1991–92	37,534	51,621	40,766	34,063	28,873	28,550	35,622	37,800	38,634	36,517	36,828	37,309	24,683
1992–93	38,385	52,755	41,861	35,032	27,700	28,922	35,792	38,356	39,470	36,710	38,460	38,987	25,068
1993–94	40,058	54,746	43,178	36,169	28,136	31,048	38,474	40,118	41,031	38,707	39,902	40,378	26,142
1994–95	41,369	56,555	44,626	37,352	29,072	31,677	38,967	41,548	42,663	39,812	40,908	41,815	22,851
1995–96	42,871	58,318	45,803	38,345	29,940	32,584	41,085	42,871	43,986	41,086	42,871	43,236	30,671
1996–97	44,325	60,160	47,101	39,350	30,819	33,415	42,474	44,306	45,402	42,531	44,374	44,726	30,661
1997–98	45,775	61,965	48,597	40,504	32,011	33,918	43,491	45,648	46,709	43,943	46,106	46,466	30,995
1998–99	47,421	64,236	50,347	41,894	33,152	35,115	44,723	47,247	48,355	45,457	47,874	48,204	31,524
1999–2000	48,997	67,079	52,091	43,367	34,228	36,607	45,865	48,714	50,168	46,340	49,737	50,052	32,951
2001–02	52,662	72,542	56,186	46,824	45,262	39,538	45,003	52,123	53,895	49,290	54,149	54,434	32,921
2002–03	54,105	75,028	57,716	48,380	46,573	40,265	45,251	53,435	55,121	50,717	55,881	56,158	35,296
2003–04	55,425	76,749	59,093	49,696	47,414	41,562	46,555	54,445	56,183	51,592	57,989	58,255	36,980
2004–05	56,926	79,160	60,809	51,154	48,351	42,455	47,860	55,780	57,714	52,566	59,919	60,143	39,291
2005–06	58,665	81,514	62,860	52,901	49,533	43,934	49,172	57,462	59,437	54,082	61,830	62,092	38,786
					Constant 2005–06 dollars[1]								
Total													
1970–71	63,665	89,954	67,942	55,983	46,885	56,084	61,780	64,887	65,729	63,337	58,200	59,230	43,400
1972–73	64,410	89,207	67,776	55,929	49,909	54,092	58,924	65,152	67,016	60,052	62,532	63,320	43,177
1974–75	60,021	81,749	62,036	51,080	48,759	48,317	51,992	61,009	62,517	57,238	57,292	57,985	39,350
1975–76	59,774	81,269	61,233	50,184	49,059	46,308	54,526	60,791	62,434	56,764	57,126	57,828	39,113
1978–79	57,578	76,896	58,238	47,568	38,325	44,390	54,395	58,620	60,197	54,741	54,635	55,223	36,301
1979–80	54,720	72,766	54,984	44,767	35,943	41,323	51,935	55,874	57,285	52,365	51,533	52,079	33,963
1980–81	53,529	70,645	53,326	43,419	34,866	39,743	51,305	54,546	55,989	50,944	50,751	51,284	34,607
1981–82	53,812	70,703	53,451	43,576	34,784	39,660	51,448	54,736	56,227	51,156	51,288	51,825	33,675
1982–83	55,138	72,055	54,580	44,717	35,685	40,695	51,815	55,730	57,362	51,835	53,510	54,114	33,645
1984–85	57,284	74,773	56,339	46,411	38,061	42,020	52,083	57,658	59,761	52,424	56,273	56,907	34,825
1985–86	59,235	77,295	58,128	48,052	38,252	43,468	53,193	59,889	62,236	54,111	57,424	58,028	35,542
1987–88	61,664	80,805	60,519	50,005	39,041	44,622	54,166	62,237	65,001	55,328	60,207	60,717	37,563
1989–90	62,895	82,762	61,734	51,229	39,226	45,433	54,159	63,339	66,393	55,660	61,847	62,401	38,554
1990–91	62,655	82,529	61,538	51,167	39,127	44,723	54,081	62,881	66,139	55,061	62,094	62,743	35,793
1991–92	63,137	82,692	61,809	51,466	44,513	43,850	54,400	62,835	65,709	56,094	63,892	64,493	36,964
1992–93	62,429	82,079	61,355	51,135	39,790	42,643	52,735	61,707	64,944	54,361	64,204	64,821	36,448
1993–94	63,099	82,540	61,620	51,212	39,233	44,541	55,232	62,495	65,351	55,852	64,597	65,161	38,698
1994–95	63,255	82,964	61,802	51,275	39,247	43,921	54,544	62,753	65,804	55,700	64,484	65,329	33,886
1995–96	63,509	83,126	61,779	51,128	39,083	43,966	55,377	62,901	65,909	55,763	64,999	65,454	41,106
1996–97	63,651	83,474	61,745	50,950	39,062	43,781	55,350	62,992	66,015	55,830	65,257	65,672	40,859
1997–98	64,388	84,561	62,534	51,464	39,922	43,656	55,693	63,530	66,577	56,495	66,485	66,903	41,328
1998–99	65,423	86,255	63,583	52,424	40,899	44,527	55,934	64,482	67,661	57,185	67,702	68,068	42,111
1999–2000	65,693	87,465	64,089	52,869	41,044	44,895	55,703	64,662	68,116	56,704	68,190	68,555	42,227
2001–02	66,715	90,223	65,579	54,492	52,440	46,677	52,005	65,355	69,252	56,771	70,150	70,453	37,007
2002–03	67,016	91,205	66,077	55,239	52,783	46,574	50,635	65,578	69,372	57,182	70,516	70,823	38,054
2003–04	66,956	91,268	66,024	55,399	52,478	46,717	51,056	65,134	68,863	56,759	71,317	71,594	38,955
2004–05	66,680	91,515	65,978	55,338	51,624	46,209	50,806	64,720	68,568	55,986	71,373	71,623	38,751
2005–06	66,172	91,208	65,714	55,106	50,883	45,896	50,425	64,158	67,951	55,405	71,016	71,263	38,549

See notes at end of table.

Table 240. Average salary of full-time instructional faculty on 9-month contracts in degree-granting institutions, by academic rank, control and type of institution, and sex: Selected years, 1970–71 through 2005–06—Continued

Sex and academic year	All faculty	Academic rank						Public institutions			Private institutions		
		Professor	Associate professor	Assistant professor	Instructor	Lecturer	No rank	Total	4-year	2-year	Total	4-year	2-year
1	2	3	4	5	6	7	8	9	10	11	12	13	14
Males													
1972–73	67,041	90,246	68,440	56,679	51,817	56,272	60,649	67,614	69,466	61,676	65,617	66,255	44,490
1974–75	62,637	82,728	62,557	51,709	51,291	50,838	53,820	63,480	65,001	58,977	60,357	60,904	40,853
1975–76	62,483	82,176	61,747	50,860	51,777	48,723	56,552	63,371	65,020	58,628	60,225	60,804	40,825
1978–79	60,356	77,643	58,741	48,228	39,045	46,269	56,356	61,238	62,830	56,575	57,910	58,350	37,904
1979–80	57,401	73,493	55,496	45,420	36,714	43,400	53,574	58,414	59,852	54,163	54,642	55,038	35,727
1980–81	56,278	71,401	53,871	44,168	35,709	41,994	53,225	57,137	58,598	52,754	53,967	54,372	36,927
1981–82	56,660	71,468	54,032	44,458	35,748	41,700	53,446	57,406	58,918	53,042	54,658	55,055	35,596
1982–83	58,114	72,898	55,272	45,791	36,818	43,032	53,810	58,493	60,136	53,775	57,090	57,538	35,168
1984–85	60,548	75,763	57,180	47,656	39,809	44,321	53,940	60,657	62,734	54,356	60,258	60,728	36,612
1985–86	62,713	78,328	59,017	49,546	39,670	46,152	55,349	63,141	65,441	56,247	61,546	61,992	37,327
1987–88	65,468	81,998	61,536	51,682	40,617	47,501	56,252	65,815	68,536	57,506	64,594	64,962	38,892
1989–90	67,018	84,079	62,892	52,940	40,641	48,836	56,387	67,324	70,263	58,113	66,311	66,753	39,522
1990–91	66,964	84,028	62,764	52,952	40,697	48,141	56,519	66,992	70,088	57,635	66,896	67,342	38,540
1991–92	67,452	84,219	63,084	53,227	48,030	47,288	56,760	66,926	69,688	58,760	68,726	69,171	38,622
1992–93	66,829	83,732	62,627	52,834	41,304	45,393	54,961	65,865	68,961	56,859	69,137	69,582	38,258
1993–94	67,473	84,183	62,915	52,796	40,577	47,355	57,501	66,626	69,393	58,436	69,512	69,948	41,894
1994–95	67,776	84,734	63,115	52,818	40,389	46,414	57,026	66,983	69,953	58,239	69,661	70,168	39,213
1995–96	68,023	84,941	63,159	52,624	39,850	46,541	57,475	67,185	70,128	58,228	70,019	70,387	42,891
1996–97	68,203	85,421	63,184	52,424	39,744	46,248	57,213	67,292	70,329	58,095	70,358	70,693	43,498
1997–98	69,039	86,697	64,026	52,924	40,687	46,113	57,605	67,902	71,043	58,673	71,719	72,067	44,484
1998–99	70,201	88,599	65,100	53,998	42,015	47,136	57,579	68,980	72,327	59,212	73,036	73,337	46,005
1999–2000	70,625	89,895	65,752	54,556	42,144	47,255	57,347	69,332	72,912	58,811	73,619	73,941	45,414
2001–02	71,828	93,086	67,338	56,415	54,545	49,716	53,658	70,169	74,348	58,472	75,793	76,049	37,293
2002–03	72,257	94,182	67,995	57,303	54,933	49,684	51,808	70,550	74,656	58,965	76,190	76,464	37,470
2003–04	72,188	94,372	67,865	57,380	54,532	49,481	52,372	70,049	74,093	58,418	77,019	77,256	38,211
2004–05	71,978	94,766	67,884	57,318	53,337	48,716	52,010	69,686	73,854	57,508	77,148	77,379	36,302
2005–06	71,569	94,733	67,654	57,099	52,519	48,256	51,811	69,191	73,353	56,858	76,941	77,143	38,215
Females													
1972–73	55,431	79,594	64,273	53,503	46,941	50,086	55,379	56,946	57,177	56,547	51,338	52,150	41,314
1974–75	51,757	73,046	59,482	49,401	45,108	44,349	48,483	53,373	53,141	53,740	47,002	47,731	37,403
1975–76	51,338	72,868	58,716	48,519	45,110	42,701	50,571	52,970	52,956	52,993	46,755	47,474	36,601
1978–79	49,618	70,135	56,067	46,229	37,666	42,020	50,786	51,261	51,207	51,347	44,702	45,351	34,563
1979–80	47,154	66,415	52,910	43,508	35,246	38,814	48,880	48,809	48,663	49,046	42,393	43,029	32,144
1980–81	45,934	64,226	51,215	42,043	34,122	37,141	47,880	47,489	47,340	47,731	41,517	42,098	31,912
1981–82	46,100	64,361	51,321	42,007	33,946	37,376	47,940	47,626	47,479	47,856	41,746	42,340	31,684
1982–83	47,160	65,326	52,182	42,840	34,673	38,176	48,364	48,439	48,407	48,490	43,490	44,168	32,125
1984–85	48,806	67,400	53,652	44,354	36,428	39,517	49,011	49,982	50,446	49,240	45,504	46,208	33,066
1985–86	50,428	69,951	55,409	45,655	37,007	40,730	49,687	51,750	52,447	50,642	46,674	47,343	33,838
1987–88	52,391	72,784	57,594	47,411	37,726	41,862	50,855	53,621	54,660	51,925	49,165	49,723	36,443
1989–90	53,571	74,696	58,720	48,723	38,113	42,306	50,977	54,532	55,955	52,197	51,168	51,733	37,615
1990–91	53,316	73,893	58,441	48,626	37,942	41,772	50,787	54,176	55,831	51,592	51,055	51,856	33,560
1991–92	54,041	74,324	58,695	49,044	41,572	41,106	51,289	54,425	55,625	52,577	53,025	53,717	35,539
1992–93	53,592	73,657	58,445	48,912	38,675	40,381	49,972	53,552	55,107	51,255	53,697	54,433	34,999
1993–94	54,517	74,506	58,762	49,223	38,291	42,254	52,360	54,598	55,840	52,678	54,305	54,951	35,578
1994–95	54,732	74,823	59,041	49,417	38,463	41,908	51,554	54,968	56,443	52,671	54,122	55,322	30,233
1995–96	55,217	75,112	58,993	49,388	38,562	41,967	52,916	55,217	56,652	52,918	55,217	55,687	39,504
1996–97	55,505	75,335	58,982	49,276	38,593	41,844	53,188	55,482	56,854	53,259	55,567	56,008	38,395
1997–98	56,317	76,236	59,790	49,832	39,384	41,730	53,507	56,161	57,466	54,064	56,725	57,168	38,134
1998–99	57,349	77,685	60,889	50,665	40,093	42,467	54,086	57,139	58,478	54,974	57,898	58,297	38,124
1999–2000	57,593	78,847	61,229	50,976	40,232	43,029	53,911	57,260	58,969	54,470	58,463	58,833	38,732
2001–02	58,809	81,009	62,745	52,290	50,545	44,153	50,256	58,207	60,187	55,043	60,470	60,788	36,764
2002–03	59,121	81,984	63,068	52,865	50,891	43,998	49,446	58,389	60,231	55,420	61,062	61,365	38,569
2003–04	59,267	82,069	63,190	53,141	50,701	44,443	49,782	58,220	60,077	55,168	62,009	62,293	39,544
2004–05	59,094	82,174	63,125	53,102	50,192	44,072	49,682	57,904	59,912	54,568	62,201	62,433	40,787
2005–06	58,665	81,514	62,860	52,901	49,533	43,934	49,172	57,462	59,437	54,082	61,830	62,092	38,786

[1]Constant dollars based on the Consumer Price Index, prepared by the Bureau of Labor Statistics, U.S. Department of Labor, adjusted to an academic-year basis.
NOTE: Data through 1995–96 are for institutions of higher education, while later data are for degree-granting institutions. Degree-granting institutions grant associate's or higher degrees and participate in Title IV federal financial aid programs. The degree-granting classification is very similar to the earlier higher education classification, but it includes more 2-year colleges and excludes a few higher education institutions that did not grant degrees. (See Guide to Sources for details.) Data for 1987–88 and later years include imputations for nonrespondent institutions.

SOURCE: U.S. Department of Education, National Center for Education Statistics, Higher Education General Information Survey (HEGIS), "Faculty Salaries, Tenure, and Fringe Benefits" surveys, 1970–71 through 1985–86; and 1987–88 through 2005–06 Integrated Postsecondary Education Data System, "Salaries, Tenure, and Fringe Benefits of Full-Time Instructional Faculty Survey" (IPEDS-SA:87–99), and Winter 2001 through Winter 2005. (This table was prepared August 2006.)

Table 241. Average salary of full-time instructional faculty on 9-month contracts in degree-granting institutions, by academic rank, sex, and control and type of institution: Selected years, 1980–81 through 2005–06

[In current dollars]

Academic year, control and type of institution	All faculty	Academic rank						Sex	
		Professor	Associate professor	Assistant professor	Instructor	Lecturer	No academic rank	Males	Females
1	2	3	4	5	6	7	8	9	10
1980–81									
All institutions	$23,302	$30,753	$23,214	$18,901	$15,178	$17,301	$22,334	$24,499	$19,996
4-year	23,693	31,016	23,265	18,867	15,056	17,375	17,380	24,909	19,809
University	25,949	33,622	24,392	19,684	15,530	17,327	17,856	27,206	20,736
Other 4-year	22,230	28,798	22,558	18,398	14,887	17,425	17,334	23,271	19,372
2-year	21,898	26,528	22,750	19,166	15,621	16,222	22,615	22,736	20,434
Public institutions	23,745	31,077	23,772	19,431	15,613	17,620	22,820	24,873	20,673
4-year	24,373	31,442	23,898	19,442	15,486	17,712	19,240	25,509	20,608
University	25,571	32,945	24,268	19,637	15,305	17,426	17,358	26,788	20,564
Other 4-year	23,500	30,097	23,639	19,315	15,567	17,997	19,798	24,499	20,633
2-year	22,177	26,880	22,947	19,370	15,928	16,458	22,875	22,965	20,778
Private institutions	22,093	29,994	21,833	17,767	14,192	15,899	15,946	23,493	18,073
4-year	22,325	30,089	21,887	17,816	14,316	15,971	16,706	23,669	18,326
University	26,897	35,227	24,730	19,792	16,197	16,956	18,933	28,251	21,176
Other 4-year	19,996	26,173	20,502	16,939	13,905	14,741	16,617	21,040	17,342
2-year	15,065	18,645	17,685	14,663	12,155	12,441	14,993	16,075	13,892
1990–91									
All institutions	42,165	55,540	41,414	34,434	26,332	30,097	36,395	45,065	35,881
4-year	43,693	56,485	41,811	34,657	25,772	30,209	31,494	46,519	36,574
University	49,430	63,437	44,877	37,838	27,105	31,748	31,533	52,426	39,788
Other 4-year	40,313	51,467	39,994	33,020	25,370	29,009	31,488	42,660	35,135
2-year	36,642	44,916	37,650	32,253	27,933	28,048	36,752	38,465	34,224
Public institutions	42,317	55,371	42,101	35,137	26,907	29,881	36,990	45,084	36,459
4-year	44,510	56,668	42,742	35,520	26,134	29,956	32,349	47,168	37,573
University	47,499	60,536	43,851	36,889	25,647	30,429	30,412	50,405	38,363
Other 4-year	42,499	53,704	41,969	34,680	26,316	29,664	33,507	44,804	37,147
2-year	37,055	45,411	38,051	32,673	28,389	28,780	37,096	38,787	34,720
Private institutions	41,788	55,911	39,983	33,116	24,928	30,864	28,523	45,019	34,359
4-year	42,224	56,127	40,122	33,235	25,159	31,053	31,122	45,319	34,898
University	53,875	69,732	47,405	40,013	31,239	34,444	36,211	56,989	43,273
Other 4-year	36,888	47,405	36,965	30,688	23,973	25,416	30,915	39,162	32,251
2-year	24,088	29,520	26,353	24,587	20,911	—	23,187	25,937	22,585
1999–2000									
All institutions	55,888	74,410	54,524	44,978	34,918	38,194	47,389	60,084	48,997
4-year	58,087	76,419	55,198	45,312	33,950	38,124	40,452	62,348	50,124
University	67,507	88,079	59,996	50,678	35,465	40,306	44,591	72,363	56,060
Other 4-year	52,716	67,985	52,404	42,902	33,479	36,295	39,851	55,908	47,454
2-year	48,012	57,677	47,844	41,730	37,433	39,928	48,012	49,819	46,096
Public institutions	55,011	72,475	54,641	45,285	35,007	37,403	47,990	58,984	48,714
4-year	57,950	75,204	55,681	45,822	33,528	37,261	40,579	62,030	50,168
University	63,595	82,344	57,984	48,671	33,230	38,576	41,147	68,135	53,216
Other 4-year	54,255	69,641	54,062	44,293	33,641	36,351	40,430	57,618	48,527
2-year	48,240	57,806	48,056	41,984	37,634	40,061	48,233	50,033	46,340
Private institutions	58,013	78,490	54,295	44,410	34,641	40,652	39,630	62,631	49,737
4-year	58,323	78,582	54,384	44,494	34,809	40,674	40,381	62,905	50,052
University	76,132	99,634	64,782	55,232	43,456	43,822	49,454	81,418	62,787
Other 4-year	50,415	65,277	50,087	40,971	33,197	36,056	39,572	53,271	45,926
2-year	35,925	39,454	36,349	31,499	27,178	25,965	37,532	38,636	32,951
2005–06									
All institutions	66,172	91,208	65,714	55,106	50,883	45,896	50,425	71,569	58,665
4-year	69,182	94,142	66,830	55,865	40,434	45,911	50,456	74,758	60,427
University	81,807	111,399	74,465	63,429	41,141	48,127	52,941	88,634	68,534
Other 4-year	62,033	81,576	62,598	52,394	40,222	44,102	49,265	65,857	56,690
2-year	55,232	65,590	54,669	48,208	57,026	45,381	50,415	56,690	53,907
Public institutions	64,158	87,599	65,107	55,029	52,297	44,628	50,096	69,191	57,462
4-year	67,951	91,600	66,745	56,181	40,044	44,598	47,107	73,353	59,437
University	76,388	102,580	71,282	60,764	39,730	46,000	50,576	82,575	64,716
Other 4-year	62,511	82,724	63,661	53,653	40,159	43,707	45,639	66,709	56,596
2-year	55,405	65,740	54,870	48,425	57,224	45,427	50,513	56,858	54,082
Private institutions	71,016	98,175	66,864	55,252	41,023	49,777	52,627	76,941	61,830
4-year	71,263	98,300	66,969	55,347	41,253	49,786	53,337	77,143	62,092
University	93,400	128,400	82,076	69,704	46,488	52,001	54,682	101,184	77,239
Other 4-year	61,322	79,903	61,161	50,627	40,337	46,024	52,622	64,577	56,828
2-year	38,549	47,174	42,347	34,970	36,435	38,908	38,280	38,215	38,786

—Not available.

NOTE: Data for 1980–81 and 1990–91 are for institutions of higher education, while later data are for degree-granting institutions. Degree-granting institutions grant associate's or higher degrees and participate in Title IV federal financial aid programs. The degree-granting classification is very similar to the earlier higher education classification, but it includes more 2-year colleges and excludes a few higher education institutions that did not grant degrees. (See Guide to Sources for details.)

SOURCE: U.S. Department of Education, National Center for Education Statistics, Higher Education General Information Survey (HEGIS), "Faculty Salaries, Tenure, and Fringe Benefits," 1980–81; and 1990–91 through 2005–06 Integrated Postsecondary Education Data System, "Salaries, Tenure, and Fringe Benefits of Full-Time Instructional Faculty Survey" (IPEDS-SA:90–99), and Winter 2005–06. (This table was prepared August 2006.)

Table 242. Average salary of full-time instructional faculty on 9-month contracts in degree-granting institutions, by control and type of institution and state or jurisdiction: 2005–06

[In current dollars]

State or jurisdiction	All institutions	Public institutions					Private institutions				
		Total	4-year institutions			2-year	Total	4-year institutions			2-year
			Total	University	Other 4-year			Total	University	Other 4-year	
1	2	3	4	5	6	7	8	9	10	11	12
United States	$66,172	$64,158	$67,951	$76,388	$62,511	$55,405	$71,016	$71,263	$93,400	$61,322	$38,549
Alabama	56,542	57,677	61,908	70,997	56,309	47,094	50,515	50,708	†	50,708	31,315
Alaska	59,309	60,029	59,966	62,188	58,439	69,531	47,154	47,154	†	47,154	†
Arizona	69,344	69,893	74,324	78,879	60,215	62,495	56,170	56,170	†	56,170	†
Arkansas	50,398	50,655	55,027	68,187	51,343	40,094	48,978	49,216	†	49,216	26,560
California	78,292	76,730	80,576	104,391	76,143	72,402	84,595	84,784	104,763	74,172	53,780
Colorado	61,734	60,715	64,440	75,782	55,839	44,013	68,612	68,710	73,338	63,431	28,496
Connecticut	80,368	75,255	79,452	89,268	69,711	62,198	85,546	85,546	114,129	72,112	†
Delaware	76,668	77,123	80,529	82,710	62,494	61,199	72,557	72,557	†	72,557	†
District of Columbia	79,713	68,037	68,037	†	68,037	†	80,116	80,116	82,414	64,516	†
Florida	62,485	62,375	67,730	76,911	64,186	49,933	62,856	62,887	79,475	58,199	27,167
Georgia	61,093	60,111	63,242	76,942	60,363	42,991	63,821	63,974	105,755	53,059	51,470
Hawaii	64,403	64,869	69,127	72,846	55,501	55,318	62,541	62,541	†	62,541	†
Idaho	51,057	51,596	52,633	59,151	50,314	46,269	45,324	45,324	†	45,324	†
Illinois	68,314	64,623	67,029	73,710	61,397	60,270	74,044	74,238	95,021	59,371	33,168
Indiana	63,341	63,187	66,223	72,000	56,132	41,809	63,668	63,829	90,331	55,150	37,640
Iowa	58,504	61,896	70,701	73,669	61,382	44,943	53,078	53,117	67,234	51,579	45,057
Kansas	56,527	58,781	64,701	69,719	53,920	45,215	41,771	42,344	†	42,344	33,873
Kentucky	55,386	56,760	60,891	71,458	55,038	46,462	49,509	49,509	†	49,509	†
Louisiana	55,146	53,315	55,259	67,042	51,834	41,040	66,574	66,574	70,517	49,749	†
Maine	60,601	55,810	57,862	63,119	55,032	49,412	67,883	68,105	†	68,105	47,393
Maryland	66,871	65,237	68,649	86,055	61,511	59,168	72,101	72,101	91,401	61,834	†
Massachusetts	81,355	66,515	71,938	83,657	67,222	52,737	88,033	88,174	102,208	72,949	42,881
Michigan	70,308	72,473	73,103	86,674	62,598	69,814	58,048	58,132	63,275	57,602	32,233
Minnesota	64,140	66,104	71,604	90,410	61,958	57,718	59,604	59,673	†	59,673	39,946
Mississippi	49,182	49,472	54,085	58,663	50,631	43,596	46,557	46,557	†	46,557	†
Missouri	58,962	57,029	59,327	69,399	56,966	49,650	62,787	63,184	83,397	49,125	40,199
Montana	51,192	52,588	54,597	57,448	47,538	39,199	42,117	43,808	†	43,808	29,128
Nebraska	58,204	60,446	65,152	75,506	57,098	44,472	52,001	52,052	62,715	47,111	30,072
Nevada	69,790	69,868	71,063	77,908	68,439	60,872	61,679	61,679	†	61,679	†
New Hampshire	68,522	66,901	73,406	79,727	63,645	44,249	70,484	70,484	†	70,484	†
New Jersey	78,502	76,587	81,181	89,741	78,219	65,320	83,108	83,161	104,949	68,279	45,607
New Mexico	56,415	56,141	60,957	65,618	50,156	43,945	62,199	62,199	†	62,199	†
New York	73,760	67,098	70,043	81,754	68,309	61,314	79,945	80,183	95,878	68,636	41,118
North Carolina	57,638	55,024	66,324	80,784	60,833	40,989	65,967	66,139	92,670	50,484	36,808
North Dakota	47,422	48,671	51,140	54,446	43,780	38,853	40,072	41,993	†	41,993	31,881
Ohio	63,592	65,071	68,547	70,900	61,272	53,139	60,307	60,518	90,084	57,366	41,057
Oklahoma	54,515	54,741	58,002	66,219	50,227	43,243	53,579	53,579	72,252	45,872	†
Oregon	57,589	56,604	58,828	64,158	53,038	53,636	60,945	60,945	†	60,945	†
Pennsylvania	70,936	69,305	71,745	81,912	65,443	55,508	72,754	73,264	100,993	64,488	39,464
Rhode Island	75,146	66,547	70,076	75,570	60,173	55,184	80,879	80,879	†	80,879	†
South Carolina	56,472	57,702	64,592	72,900	56,001	43,594	50,850	51,156	†	51,156	37,313
South Dakota	50,822	52,266	54,513	55,484	53,261	41,164	45,053	45,053	†	45,053	†
Tennessee	57,891	56,700	60,053	70,359	56,701	45,379	60,433	60,683	91,628	49,208	26,510
Texas	62,273	61,397	67,077	76,550	59,208	49,278	66,377	66,582	78,525	56,749	31,923
Utah	64,644	58,299	61,790	67,372	51,416	43,899	79,637	79,938	82,410	57,733	50,323
Vermont	61,644	59,831	59,831	65,630	47,920	†	63,249	67,112	†	67,112	31,948
Virginia	64,272	66,439	71,601	80,432	66,658	48,659	57,673	57,682	†	57,682	31,200
Washington	64,563	65,403	78,485	90,807	59,646	48,739	61,239	61,239	†	61,239	†
West Virginia	51,456	53,008	54,657	63,444	50,253	42,004	43,196	43,196	†	43,196	†
Wisconsin	62,866	64,352	64,198	85,082	56,977	64,609	56,888	56,974	72,622	52,008	44,677
Wyoming	56,149	56,149	64,563	64,563	†	46,630	†	†	†	†	†
U.S. Service Schools	104,134	104,134	104,134	†	104,134	†	†	†	†	†	†
Other jurisdictions	50,399	50,711	54,076	†	54,076	30,024	29,829	29,829	†	29,829	†
American Samoa	28,052	28,052	†	†	†	28,052	†	†	†	†	†
Federated States of Micronesia	20,925	20,925	†	†	†	20,925	†	†	†	†	†
Guam	51,463	51,463	54,366	†	54,366	46,175	†	†	†	†	†
Marshall Islands	25,926	25,926	†	†	†	25,926	†	†	†	†	†
Northern Marianas	41,137	41,137	41,137	†	41,137	†	†	†	†	†	†
Palau	†	†	†	†	†	†	†	†	†	†	†
Puerto Rico	54,091	54,614	54,614	†	54,614	†	29,829	29,829	†	29,829	†
Virgin Islands	52,871	52,871	52,871	†	52,871	†	†	†	†	†	†

†Not applicable.
NOTE: Degree-granting institutions grant associate's or higher degrees and participate in Title IV federal financial aid programs. Data include imputations for nonrespondent institutions.

SOURCE: U.S. Department of Education, National Center for Education Statistics, 2005–06 Integrated Postsecondary Education Data System (IPEDS), Winter 2005–06. (This table was prepared August 2006.)

Table 243. Average salary of full-time instructional faculty on 9-month contracts in degree-granting institutions, by control and type of institution and state or jurisdiction: 2004–05

[In current dollars]

State or jurisdiction	All institutions	Public institutions					Private institutions				
		Total	4-year institutions			2-year	Total	4-year institutions			2-year
			Total	University	Other 4-year			Total	University	Other 4-year	
1	2	3	4	5	6	7	8	9	10	11	12
United States	$64,234	$62,346	$66,053	$73,913	$60,986	$53,932	$68,755	$68,995	$90,108	$59,451	$37,329
Alabama	54,269	55,321	59,999	69,203	54,054	44,135	48,803	49,112	†	49,112	30,422
Alaska	57,492	58,130	58,114	59,828	56,915	60,494	46,346	46,346	†	46,346	†
Arizona	67,271	68,058	72,085	76,925	59,209	61,231	51,948	51,948	†	51,948	†
Arkansas	48,668	48,872	52,907	65,221	49,523	38,833	47,553	47,697	†	47,697	24,245
California	76,119	74,856	78,488	100,865	74,161	70,751	81,182	81,416	100,014	71,606	47,356
Colorado	60,256	59,600	63,379	73,524	55,337	43,045	64,411	64,411	71,357	57,736	†
Connecticut	77,311	71,940	75,871	85,960	66,452	60,045	82,631	82,631	108,512	70,419	†
Delaware	75,312	76,093	79,664	82,578	59,327	57,895	68,249	69,153	†	69,153	41,476
District of Columbia	78,303	69,396	69,396	†	69,396	†	78,596	78,596	80,820	62,094	†
Florida	59,786	59,548	64,409	74,797	60,516	48,790	60,577	60,577	75,447	56,144	†
Georgia	59,453	58,481	61,155	73,734	58,514	42,801	62,165	62,363	102,165	52,035	48,126
Hawaii	63,045	63,468	68,550	71,066	55,937	54,216	61,287	61,287	†	61,287	†
Idaho	49,954	50,347	51,858	57,719	49,815	42,705	45,673	45,673	†	45,673	†
Illinois	66,464	62,899	65,220	71,268	60,168	58,665	72,193	72,386	94,865	57,368	30,056
Indiana	62,033	61,525	64,863	69,798	55,407	43,218	63,169	63,312	94,675	53,797	37,939
Iowa	58,186	62,279	71,291	74,329	60,982	43,675	51,519	51,531	63,740	50,147	49,052
Kansas	54,735	56,814	62,255	66,622	53,065	44,077	40,651	41,214	†	41,214	32,035
Kentucky	53,382	54,782	58,692	68,972	52,968	44,974	47,632	47,632	†	47,632	†
Louisiana	53,652	52,929	54,830	67,108	51,366	40,666	56,799	56,799	61,126	49,451	†
Maine	58,899	55,175	57,673	61,920	55,451	46,391	64,945	65,073	†	65,073	52,153
Maryland	65,231	63,829	67,555	82,996	60,853	57,320	69,748	69,748	89,761	58,680	†
Massachusetts	79,186	66,330	71,826	82,956	67,364	52,896	85,068	85,256	98,788	70,971	41,559
Michigan	68,342	70,449	70,959	83,701	61,048	68,296	56,535	56,610	61,606	56,073	33,965
Minnesota	62,114	64,001	69,382	87,064	60,051	55,657	57,741	57,826	†	57,826	39,508
Mississippi	48,500	48,900	53,922	58,803	50,236	42,591	44,974	44,974	†	44,974	†
Missouri	57,825	55,934	58,185	67,905	55,938	48,554	61,567	61,974	81,846	47,697	39,323
Montana	49,359	50,574	52,524	54,917	46,962	38,046	41,474	42,610	†	42,610	31,395
Nebraska	56,427	59,026	63,498	74,463	55,577	42,720	50,029	50,153	60,269	45,880	34,143
Nevada	67,796	67,845	68,860	75,649	66,190	60,057	61,618	61,618	†	61,618	†
New Hampshire	65,435	64,317	70,443	76,147	61,139	42,993	66,867	67,124	†	67,124	30,571
New Jersey	76,266	74,678	79,394	87,591	76,505	63,218	80,142	80,180	102,517	64,780	45,000
New Mexico	54,906	54,852	59,914	64,649	48,965	42,555	55,916	55,916	†	55,916	†
New York	71,944	66,120	69,007	79,358	67,494	60,413	77,328	77,625	91,586	67,038	38,592
North Carolina	56,214	53,601	65,391	79,568	59,815	39,359	64,420	64,640	90,770	49,368	35,329
North Dakota	46,340	47,912	50,889	55,681	42,073	37,779	38,557	41,378	†	41,378	30,971
Ohio	62,549	64,088	68,111	70,160	61,197	51,439	59,155	59,304	88,371	55,993	37,254
Oklahoma	52,848	52,881	55,993	63,501	48,751	41,759	52,712	52,712	69,544	45,672	†
Oregon	56,289	55,358	57,425	61,269	53,114	52,699	59,473	59,473	†	59,473	†
Pennsylvania	69,148	67,944	70,236	80,708	63,883	54,977	70,508	70,902	96,829	62,448	38,348
Rhode Island	72,047	62,343	65,374	69,548	57,461	52,581	78,467	78,467	†	78,467	†
South Carolina	54,342	55,426	62,207	71,350	53,330	41,960	49,337	49,606	†	49,606	37,275
South Dakota	48,941	50,070	51,977	53,201	50,455	40,284	43,880	43,880	†	43,880	†
Tennessee	56,613	55,729	59,705	68,505	56,726	43,481	58,507	58,748	91,091	47,186	26,882
Texas	60,105	59,189	65,185	73,598	57,873	47,627	64,350	64,552	76,063	55,053	31,853
Utah	61,184	55,319	58,179	64,400	50,378	41,467	76,549	76,844	78,973	56,803	47,893
Vermont	59,565	57,032	57,032	62,965	45,030	†	61,951	64,642	†	64,642	33,141
Virginia	61,854	63,604	68,569	76,049	64,323	46,309	56,523	56,523	†	56,523	†
Washington	57,646	57,370	64,982	71,556	55,155	47,880	58,679	58,679	†	58,679	†
West Virginia	50,034	51,469	53,009	61,338	48,968	41,269	42,574	42,574	†	42,574	†
Wisconsin	61,632	63,234	63,247	84,113	56,150	63,214	55,040	55,152	68,313	50,826	39,508
Wyoming	55,290	55,290	64,981	64,981	†	44,840	†	†	†	†	†
U.S. Service Schools	79,058	79,058	79,058	†	79,058	†	†	†	†	†	†
Other jurisdictions	48,612	48,866	52,163	†	52,163	29,526	27,437	27,437	†	27,437	†
American Samoa	27,388	27,388	†	†	†	27,388	†	†	†	†	†
Federated States of Micronesia	21,348	21,348	†	†	†	21,348	†	†	†	†	†
Guam	51,880	51,880	56,439	†	56,439	44,671	†	†	†	†	†
Marshall Islands	28,077	28,077	†	†	†	28,077	†	†	†	†	†
Northern Marianas	41,276	41,276	41,276	†	41,276	†	†	†	†	†	†
Palau	17,733	17,733	†	†	†	17,733	†	†	†	†	†
Puerto Rico	51,848	52,263	52,263	†	52,263	†	27,437	27,437	†	27,437	†
Virgin Islands	51,580	51,580	51,580	†	51,580	†	†	†	†	†	†

†Not applicable.
NOTE: Degree-granting institutions grant associate's or higher degrees and participate in Title IV federal financial aid programs. Data include imputations for nonrespondent institutions.

SOURCE: U.S. Department of Education, National Center for Education Statistics, 2004–05 Integrated Postsecondary Education Data System (IPEDS), Winter 2004–05. (This table was prepared September 2005.)

Table 244. Average salary of full-time instructional faculty on 9-month contracts in 4-year degree-granting institutions, by type and control of institution, rank of faculty, and state or jurisdiction: 2005–06

[In current dollars]

State or jurisdiction	Public university			Public other 4-year			Private university			Private other 4-year		
	Professor	Associate professor	Assistant professor	Professor	Associate professor	Assistant professor	Professor	Associate professor	Assistant professor	Professor	Associate professor	Assistant professor
1	2	3	4	5	6	7	8	9	10	11	12	13
United States	$102,580	$71,282	$60,764	$82,724	$63,661	$53,653	$128,400	$82,076	$69,704	$79,903	$61,161	$50,627
Alabama	96,362	69,188	49,705	75,161	60,226	49,926	†	†	†	66,210	52,478	43,218
Alaska	81,356	61,602	54,567	75,950	61,834	52,435	†	†	†	63,829	51,013	42,251
Arizona	104,306	71,484	63,409	78,954	60,898	52,434	†	†	†	59,023	65,949	52,563
Arkansas	90,632	68,072	53,964	67,757	56,693	48,271	†	†	†	59,745	49,561	43,066
California	127,045	82,614	72,352	95,293	69,548	60,113	136,983	89,814	77,324	93,466	70,706	58,723
Colorado	98,042	72,388	62,074	74,810	58,475	48,089	96,280	71,945	60,199	87,925	60,980	52,123
Connecticut	116,731	82,299	65,753	84,582	66,245	54,949	152,131	87,311	73,583	94,654	70,651	56,747
Delaware	112,945	78,661	64,003	77,265	65,066	59,403	†	†	†	100,234	73,422	54,159
District of Columbia	†	†	†	81,378	60,502	54,775	117,905	78,646	63,894	94,433	71,112	53,759
Florida	98,907	68,773	61,078	86,844	66,358	56,754	113,656	75,814	65,833	77,793	58,669	49,517
Georgia	99,412	67,152	61,874	86,416	62,344	52,687	138,429	84,876	78,168	62,474	54,094	45,462
Hawaii	92,243	68,434	60,475	69,237	58,252	51,146	†	†	†	81,848	69,792	57,534
Idaho	74,349	58,592	50,856	64,353	53,539	47,103	†	†	†	52,260	44,760	40,427
Illinois	105,508	70,602	61,490	84,363	64,799	54,436	136,783	84,269	70,264	73,971	60,032	49,844
Indiana	97,780	68,795	58,162	73,850	60,224	51,072	121,152	80,644	70,578	68,767	54,616	47,209
Iowa	98,494	70,898	61,041	79,014	62,688	52,979	87,608	64,724	51,679	63,829	52,605	44,896
Kansas	91,131	66,506	56,843	73,388	56,831	47,276	†	†	†	50,434	43,534	39,166
Kentucky	93,838	67,541	56,867	75,575	58,862	51,398	†	†	†	59,942	49,213	42,477
Louisiana	94,369	66,500	59,860	70,267	55,732	47,799	97,166	67,891	59,055	59,482	52,171	45,818
Maine	74,979	63,521	51,084	68,560	54,835	43,054	†	†	†	91,201	65,744	53,671
Maryland	112,817	78,275	74,239	86,735	66,644	55,716	119,306	84,960	68,919	79,106	62,534	51,818
Massachusetts	103,946	85,408	62,300	81,067	65,669	55,121	137,030	85,038	75,103	96,412	70,420	58,124
Michigan	114,536	79,180	66,634	81,270	63,830	53,017	83,500	62,098	52,863	69,620	57,110	47,831
Minnesota	112,643	74,890	64,839	77,307	61,602	52,607	†	†	†	76,682	58,957	49,866
Mississippi	82,303	62,359	54,744	67,030	53,844	47,779	†	†	†	60,917	47,478	42,573
Missouri	95,305	67,063	55,580	74,915	57,722	49,436	118,661	75,346	63,592	60,648	52,234	43,999
Montana	71,914	56,814	50,200	58,501	48,996	44,115	†	†	†	52,809	44,023	38,193
Nebraska	99,458	70,332	61,072	71,152	60,334	49,871	87,630	64,425	50,355	58,736	48,216	42,093
Nevada	105,962	77,917	58,482	79,461	76,398	60,274	†	†	†	70,535	54,415	44,588
New Hampshire	99,402	73,464	61,705	76,350	62,730	51,856	†	†	†	95,775	66,395	52,139
New Jersey	116,266	80,242	64,962	102,135	78,744	60,549	146,619	79,430	68,735	88,339	70,498	55,719
New Mexico	83,734	62,820	54,350	57,675	52,344	47,914	†	†	†	68,552	57,344	49,028
New York	107,763	74,390	62,358	88,519	67,118	55,864	128,921	85,454	72,271	93,666	69,561	55,853
North Carolina	108,127	73,600	66,114	81,169	63,718	56,078	129,431	85,633	66,622	63,504	52,572	43,965
North Dakota	72,859	60,476	53,725	57,102	48,365	42,890	†	†	†	51,394	44,612	39,748
Ohio	96,667	68,056	55,820	82,649	63,197	50,482	117,188	84,015	65,959	73,199	57,361	48,037
Oklahoma	88,822	64,555	55,144	63,820	54,858	47,426	96,942	68,247	54,014	59,321	47,557	39,814
Oregon	85,455	63,151	58,268	67,883	54,251	45,376	†	†	†	79,515	59,555	48,166
Pennsylvania	113,465	78,449	66,482	88,190	69,416	56,156	133,111	87,505	75,529	85,495	65,173	53,846
Rhode Island	93,008	67,604	59,702	68,717	59,707	49,388	†	†	†	108,081	72,870	61,766
South Carolina	96,766	69,430	61,763	69,976	59,085	49,373	†	†	†	65,461	51,301	43,591
South Dakota	72,242	58,409	50,757	71,102	56,951	48,200	†	†	†	55,728	48,495	42,554
Tennessee	94,789	71,040	58,143	71,908	57,414	48,519	128,255	80,701	65,589	60,061	51,398	43,399
Texas	104,378	69,713	62,999	79,806	63,992	56,384	107,787	75,252	67,674	72,691	56,435	46,755
Utah	87,373	64,348	57,755	65,014	52,158	45,806	105,000	76,626	67,769	67,639	59,287	52,358
Vermont	89,943	66,966	57,152	56,711	45,562	36,366	†	†	†	87,532	64,335	54,021
Virginia	109,000	78,029	63,816	88,867	67,780	54,861	†	†	†	75,079	58,146	47,973
Washington	118,054	83,920	76,203	72,656	61,377	55,478	†	†	†	75,700	61,709	51,760
West Virginia	80,062	61,759	51,126	61,315	51,345	43,001	†	†	†	52,531	45,843	37,829
Wisconsin	100,234	74,534	63,350	71,176	58,347	50,807	99,216	72,710	60,336	63,802	53,059	45,269
Wyoming	84,189	65,326	57,458	†	†	†	†	†	†	†	†	†
U.S. Service Schools	†	†	†	125,185	102,815	78,585	†	†	†	†	†	†
Other jurisdictions	†	†	†	65,099	55,000	45,870	†	†	†	†	†	34,771
American Samoa	†	†	†	†	†	†	†	†	†	†	†	†
Federated States of Micronesia	†	†	†	†	†	†	†	†	†	†	†	†
Guam	†	†	†	70,593	57,448	45,495	†	†	†	†	†	†
Marshall Islands	†	†	†	†	†	†	†	†	†	†	†	†
Northern Marianas	†	†	†	†	†	†	†	†	†	†	†	†
Palau	†	†	†	†	†	†	†	†	†	†	†	†
Puerto Rico	†	†	†	64,730	54,766	46,016	†	†	†	†	†	34,771
Virgin Islands	†	†	†	67,123	53,781	45,165	†	†	†	†	†	†

†Not applicable.
NOTE: Degree-granting institutions grant associate's or higher degrees and participate in Title IV federal financial aid programs. Data include imputations for nonrespondent institutions.

SOURCE: U.S. Department of Education, National Center for Education Statistics, 2005–06 Integrated Postsecondary Education Data System (IPEDS), Winter 2005–06. (This table was prepared August 2006.)

Table 245. Average salary of full-time instructional faculty on 9-month contracts in 4-year degree-granting institutions, by type and control of institution, rank of faculty, and state or jurisdiction: 2004–05

[In current dollars]

State or jurisdiction	Public university Professor	Associate professor	Assistant professor	Public other 4-year Professor	Associate professor	Assistant professor	Private university Professor	Associate professor	Assistant professor	Private other 4-year Professor	Associate professor	Assistant professor
1	2	3	4	5	6	7	8	9	10	11	12	13
United States	**$98,398**	**$68,315**	**$58,522**	**$80,463**	**$61,817**	**$51,983**	**$122,461**	**$78,841**	**$67,156**	**$77,305**	**$59,205**	**$48,953**
Alabama	91,411	65,146	54,498	70,680	57,289	48,367	†	†	†	63,745	50,161	41,895
Alaska	79,171	60,321	52,252	74,091	58,202	50,918	†	†	†	64,254	52,806	41,892
Arizona	99,179	68,468	60,970	76,459	60,588	49,917	†	†	†	52,900	67,054	49,102
Arkansas	86,126	64,892	55,208	64,501	55,443	46,597	†	†	†	57,620	48,946	41,492
California	122,458	78,596	69,678	92,316	68,148	57,709	130,792	85,512	74,829	90,818	68,236	56,740
Colorado	94,809	69,526	59,796	72,941	56,547	48,506	93,233	69,570	57,998	79,676	53,711	49,144
Connecticut	110,922	78,961	63,824	81,645	63,298	52,598	146,414	83,138	69,874	91,967	68,506	55,329
Delaware	111,112	76,580	62,807	68,339	62,640	55,189	†	†	†	96,271	69,420	52,795
District of Columbia	†	†	†	81,706	64,579	52,056	108,466	75,968	60,895	89,802	67,449	52,169
Florida	94,567	65,638	58,970	81,629	62,212	53,735	108,960	72,918	63,485	74,843	56,438	48,353
Georgia	95,755	64,635	57,970	83,294	60,447	50,802	132,809	83,007	76,589	61,811	52,739	44,219
Hawaii	89,394	67,574	58,756	68,807	57,924	50,371	†	†	†	80,331	67,700	55,725
Idaho	70,922	58,182	48,921	63,567	53,279	45,451	†	†	†	52,127	45,045	38,910
Illinois	100,705	68,026	58,590	81,128	62,700	52,428	131,671	81,685	67,853	71,397	58,446	47,713
Indiana	94,510	66,852	56,398	77,213	59,729	49,981	118,670	78,750	67,677	66,893	53,053	46,169
Iowa	97,061	68,969	60,262	77,770	61,522	52,920	84,564	59,511	48,836	61,919	50,689	43,351
Kansas	86,441	63,468	53,910	70,842	55,104	47,071	†	†	†	46,811	42,830	37,718
Kentucky	89,538	63,747	54,445	72,109	56,371	49,462	†	†	†	58,781	47,535	41,209
Louisiana	93,662	67,574	59,359	69,257	54,727	46,866	87,874	64,634	53,323	62,323	53,364	45,272
Maine	74,166	63,102	49,034	67,419	55,335	45,069	†	†	†	89,933	62,659	50,302
Maryland	108,149	73,990	73,781	84,820	64,715	54,219	115,074	76,178	66,840	76,049	60,286	50,557
Massachusetts	103,371	82,128	62,544	81,258	66,184	54,187	131,702	81,463	71,817	92,741	68,337	56,262
Michigan	110,538	77,056	64,668	78,703	61,859	51,493	80,632	61,357	50,404	67,425	56,215	46,869
Minnesota	107,484	71,900	62,475	74,475	59,820	50,036	†	†	†	73,266	57,958	48,425
Mississippi	81,811	63,368	54,035	65,850	54,210	47,391	†	†	†	58,723	47,834	41,735
Missouri	93,644	66,159	53,335	73,697	56,654	48,495	114,105	72,874	62,663	57,496	49,857	43,076
Montana	69,251	54,303	47,621	57,801	47,760	43,296	†	†	†	52,063	43,126	36,955
Nebraska	96,673	69,110	58,579	68,563	57,753	49,127	87,563	59,241	46,740	56,815	47,862	40,890
Nevada	101,691	75,685	57,230	76,727	73,317	60,361	†	†	†	75,231	52,305	53,020
New Hampshire	95,319	70,396	59,611	73,710	60,474	49,863	†	†	†	91,121	64,258	49,061
New Jersey	113,068	77,074	62,426	99,863	76,273	59,610	141,826	77,413	67,243	85,046	67,727	50,535
New Mexico	82,819	61,061	53,424	57,252	51,565	44,291	†	†	†	62,298	49,570	44,392
New York	103,736	72,964	60,392	87,633	66,517	54,962	122,313	81,803	69,486	90,442	67,112	54,354
North Carolina	105,772	72,618	64,817	79,631	62,090	54,730	125,022	83,107	65,525	61,667	51,016	43,279
North Dakota	72,270	58,452	51,751	53,254	46,346	41,684	†	†	†	50,352	43,381	39,241
Ohio	94,658	66,400	54,780	81,672	62,495	50,461	109,619	85,440	78,053	70,916	55,866	47,000
Oklahoma	84,691	61,480	52,809	61,590	53,059	45,537	92,758	64,763	55,150	58,582	46,323	40,362
Oregon	81,514	60,573	55,001	67,290	53,228	44,989	†	†	†	76,529	56,988	47,571
Pennsylvania	110,206	75,276	64,600	86,006	68,050	55,264	127,650	83,829	71,830	82,905	63,008	51,900
Rhode Island	85,757	62,451	56,070	65,061	54,925	48,143	†	†	†	104,125	70,601	60,285
South Carolina	92,215	66,392	59,783	66,006	56,636	46,735	†	†	†	64,795	49,556	42,909
South Dakota	69,087	56,660	48,362	69,208	50,021	46,097	†	†	†	54,517	48,409	39,912
Tennessee	91,365	68,309	57,192	71,926	57,134	48,353	124,263	79,040	64,990	58,201	48,939	41,540
Texas	99,797	66,899	59,352	78,519	61,740	53,449	104,504	72,236	65,410	70,966	53,776	45,105
Utah	84,366	60,775	55,044	60,779	51,519	46,550	100,373	74,673	65,390	66,842	58,699	50,544
Vermont	86,359	64,657	54,908	52,587	42,945	34,586	†	†	†	87,653	61,543	51,336
Virginia	102,757	72,166	59,696	85,322	64,357	52,577	†	†	†	73,707	55,937	46,120
Washington	90,744	65,438	60,997	68,125	56,209	49,086	†	†	†	73,145	58,933	49,481
West Virginia	76,966	59,619	48,818	59,989	49,994	42,042	†	†	†	52,014	45,415	36,938
Wisconsin	99,017	73,990	62,753	70,212	57,638	49,657	92,973	68,752	56,862	62,261	51,688	44,282
Wyoming	83,955	63,230	59,081	†	†	†	†	†	†	†	†	†
U.S. Service Schools	†	†	†	103,698	82,767	67,789	†	†	†	†	†	†
Other jurisdictions	†	†	†	62,807	53,013	43,832	†	†	†	†	27,600	31,110
American Samoa	†	†	†	†	†	†	†	†	†	†	†	†
Federated States of Micronesia	†	†	†	†	†	†	†	†	†	†	†	†
Guam	†	†	†	56,439	74,550	55,998	†	†	†	†	†	†
Marshall Islands	†	†	†	†	†	†	†	†	†	†	†	†
Northern Marianas	†	†	†	†	†	†	†	†	†	†	†	†
Palau	†	†	†	†	†	†	†	†	†	†	†	†
Puerto Rico	†	†	†	62,078	52,469	43,776	†	†	†	†	27,600	31,110
Virgin Islands	†	†	†	65,318	53,379	44,008	†	†	†	†	†	†

†Not applicable.
NOTE: Degree-granting institutions grant associate's or higher degrees and participate in Title IV federal financial aid programs. Data include imputations for nonrespondent institutions.

SOURCE: U.S. Department of Education, National Center for Education Statistics, 2004–05 Integrated Postsecondary Education Data System (IPEDS), Winter 2004–05. (This table was prepared September 2005.)

Table 246. Average benefit expenditure for full-time instructional faculty on 9-month contracts in degree-granting institutions, by type of benefit and control of institution: Selected years, 1977–78 through 2005–06

Control and year	Average total benefit per full-time faculty member	Retirement plans Total	Vested within 5 years	Vested after 5 years	Medical/ dental plans	Guaranteed disability income protection	Tuition plan for dependents	Housing plan	Social Security taxes	Unemploy- ment compen- sation	Group life insurance	Work- men's compen- sation	Other benefits
1	2	3	4	5	6	7	8	9	10	11	12	13	14
Current dollars													
Total													
1977–78	$3,203	$1,725	$1,739	$1,691	$521	$96	$1,410	$886	$899	$109	$105	$80	$288
1982–83	5,799	2,731	2,741	2,703	1,111	151	1,993	1,639	1,712	146	138	114	915
1987–88	7,227	3,677	3,494	4,028	1,682	132	1,585	2,004	2,379	134	178	190	716
1989–90	8,241	4,048	3,974	4,192	2,339	147	2,070	2,643	2,764	121	182	49	637
1992–93	10,473	4,397	4,391	4,410	3,266	179	2,196	2,574	3,168	143	237	344	874
1997–98	12,263	5,289	5,195	5,498	3,535	218	2,765	4,100	3,562	158	195	340	1,274
1998–99	12,580	5,256	5,268	5,228	3,726	213	3,012	3,698	3,668	152	190	347	1,093
1999–2000	13,227	5,292	5,365	5,125	3,989	237	3,362	4,187	3,793	146	190	343	1,415
2002–03	15,552	5,781	6,039	5,208	5,396	264	3,308	4,329	4,158	170	211	411	1,032
2003–04	16,423	5,907	6,178	5,280	5,915	262	3,504	6,101	4,240	192	215	438	1,188
2004–05	17,269	6,211	6,429	5,682	6,314	272	4,072	4,176	4,354	225	199	481	1,229
2005–06	18,082	6,402	6,571	6,010	6,863	280	4,511	5,599	4,451	228	210	473	1,262
Public													
1977–78	3,252	1,791	1,833	1,724	560	99	430	846	911	99	105	88	94
1982–83	5,920	2,846	2,880	2,776	1,189	153	576	1,027	1,741	139	140	115	980
1987–88	7,146	3,815	3,602	4,086	1,757	140	404	1,172	2,399	109	180	192	611
1989–90	8,361	4,186	4,128	4,259	2,425	154	605	1,767	2,771	97	182	60	602
1992–93	10,280	4,467	4,469	4,464	3,352	188	693	1,135	3,122	117	250	318	827
1997–98	12,114	5,432	5,302	5,617	3,646	219	830	2,614	3,482	133	187	340	1,442
1998–99	12,192	5,249	5,230	5,276	3,830	202	828	1,826	3,553	127	183	348	1,065
1999–2000	12,756	5,258	5,297	5,200	4,131	237	962	2,283	3,660	121	176	347	1,463
2002–03	15,097	5,703	5,968	5,323	5,565	274	978	2,415	4,005	142	198	402	1,058
2003–04	15,890	5,767	6,062	5,329	6,121	263	1,022	4,589	4,043	174	206	429	1,080
2004–05	16,769	6,104	6,321	5,760	6,498	274	1,280	3,655	4,161	202	189	479	1,227
2005–06	17,594	6,308	6,458	6,078	7,126	279	1,483	4,418	4,237	210	202	446	1,247
Private													
1977–78	3,071	1,509	1,542	905	404	89	2,025	890	873	131	103	60	838
1982–83	5,462	2,340	2,404	1,295	886	146	3,403	1,798	1,648	170	134	113	212
1987–88	7,438	3,280	3,306	2,906	1,488	120	3,666	2,303	2,337	197	175	184	977
1989–90	7,954	3,657	3,718	2,478	2,112	134	4,259	3,032	2,750	188	182	25	712
1992–93	10,958	4,206	4,259	2,877	3,039	163	4,523	2,956	3,267	212	207	402	957
1997–98	12,629	4,915	5,023	2,531	3,255	216	5,513	4,228	3,735	222	209	339	1,024
1998–99	13,519	5,274	5,327	3,879	3,468	231	6,722	3,936	3,915	219	205	345	1,151
1999–2000	14,366	5,380	5,471	3,354	3,638	237	6,951	4,349	4,074	213	215	335	1,337
2002–03	16,660	5,981	6,153	2,983	4,964	249	6,943	4,348	4,490	247	236	429	988
2003–04	17,701	6,262	6,363	4,225	5,395	259	7,477	6,104	4,668	240	231	457	1,354
2004–05	18,465	6,483	6,603	4,092	5,849	269	7,600	4,455	4,775	284	217	484	1,231
2005–06	19,258	6,637	6,756	5,037	6,195	281	8,594	6,001	4,914	275	223	528	1,287
Constant 2005-06 dollars[1]													
Total													
1977–78	10,177	5,479	5,526	5,373	1,655	304	4,479	2,816	2,857	345	332	253	914
1982–83	11,757	5,537	5,557	5,480	2,253	305	4,041	3,322	3,471	297	281	232	1,854
1987–88	12,414	6,316	6,002	6,919	2,890	227	2,722	3,443	4,086	230	306	326	1,229
1989–90	12,915	6,344	6,228	6,570	3,665	230	3,245	4,143	4,332	190	286	77	998
1992–93	14,622	6,139	6,131	6,158	4,560	249	3,067	3,594	4,423	200	331	480	1,221
1997–98	15,088	6,507	6,391	6,764	4,350	268	3,402	5,044	4,383	194	239	418	1,568
1998–99	15,214	6,356	6,371	6,322	4,506	258	3,643	4,472	4,435	184	230	420	1,322
1999–2000	15,547	6,221	6,306	6,024	4,688	279	3,952	4,921	4,459	172	223	404	1,663
2002–03	16,994	6,317	6,599	5,691	5,897	288	3,615	4,730	4,543	186	231	449	1,128
2003–04	17,562	6,317	6,606	5,646	6,325	280	3,747	6,524	4,534	205	230	468	1,270
2004–05	17,926	6,448	6,674	5,899	6,554	283	4,227	4,335	4,520	234	207	499	1,275
2005–06	18,082	6,402	6,571	6,010	6,863	280	4,511	5,599	4,451	228	210	473	1,262
Public													
1977–78	10,331	5,690	5,823	5,477	1,780	316	1,366	2,689	2,895	314	334	280	297
1982–83	12,003	5,770	5,839	5,628	2,410	310	1,168	2,082	3,530	281	284	233	1,988
1987–88	12,276	6,553	6,188	7,019	3,019	241	695	2,013	4,120	188	309	330	1,050
1989–90	13,103	6,560	6,469	6,675	3,801	242	949	2,769	4,342	151	286	93	943
1992–93	14,353	6,237	6,240	6,232	4,680	262	967	1,585	4,359	163	350	445	1,155
1997–98	14,904	6,683	6,523	6,911	4,486	270	1,021	3,216	4,284	164	230	419	1,774
1998–99	14,745	6,347	6,325	6,380	4,632	244	1,002	2,208	4,296	153	221	421	1,288
1999–2000	14,994	6,180	6,226	6,112	4,856	279	1,131	2,683	4,302	142	207	408	1,720
2002–03	16,497	6,232	6,522	5,816	6,081	300	1,069	2,639	4,377	155	217	439	1,156
2003–04	16,991	6,167	6,482	5,699	6,545	282	1,092	4,907	4,323	186	221	458	1,155
2004–05	17,407	6,336	6,562	5,980	6,745	285	1,329	3,794	4,320	210	196	497	1,274
2005–06	17,594	6,308	6,458	6,078	7,126	279	1,483	4,418	4,237	210	202	446	1,247

See notes at end of table.

Table 246. Average benefit expenditure for full-time instructional faculty on 9-month contracts in degree-granting institutions, by type of benefit and control of institution: Selected years, 1977–78 through 2005–06—Continued

Control and year	Average total benefit per full-time faculty member	Average benefit expenditure per full-time faculty member receiving benefit											
		Retirement plans			Medical/ dental plans	Guaranteed disability income protection	Tuition plan for dependents	Housing plan	Social Security taxes	Unemployment compensation	Group life insurance	Workmen's compensation	Other benefits
		Total	Vested within 5 years	Vested after 5 years									
1	2	3	4	5	6	7	8	9	10	11	12	13	14
Private													
1977–78.....................	9,758	4,793	4,899	2,876	1,285	283	6,435	2,826	2,772	415	329	191	2,662
1982–83.....................	11,074	4,745	4,874	2,626	1,797	296	6,899	3,645	3,341	345	272	229	431
1987–88.....................	12,777	5,635	5,680	4,992	2,556	205	6,298	3,957	4,015	339	301	316	1,678
1989–90.....................	12,466	5,732	5,826	3,883	3,310	210	6,674	4,752	4,310	295	286	39	1,116
1992–93.....................	15,299	5,873	5,946	4,017	4,243	228	6,315	4,127	4,562	296	289	561	1,336
1997–98.....................	15,537	6,048	6,180	3,113	4,004	266	6,782	5,202	4,596	274	257	417	1,260
1998–99.....................	16,349	6,379	6,443	4,691	4,194	279	8,129	4,759	4,734	265	248	417	1,392
1999–2000.................	16,887	6,324	6,431	3,942	4,276	279	8,170	5,112	4,789	250	253	393	1,571
2002–03.....................	18,205	6,536	6,723	3,260	5,424	272	7,587	4,752	4,906	269	258	469	1,079
2003–04.....................	18,928	6,696	6,804	4,518	5,769	277	7,996	6,528	4,992	257	247	489	1,448
2004–05.....................	19,168	6,730	6,855	4,248	6,072	279	7,889	4,625	4,957	295	225	502	1,278
2005–06.....................	19,258	6,637	6,756	5,037	6,195	281	8,594	6,001	4,914	275	223	528	1,287

[1]Constant dollars based on the Consumer Price Index, prepared by the Bureau of Labor Statistics, U.S. Department of Labor, adjusted to an academic-year basis.
NOTE: Data through 1992–93 are for institutions of higher education, while later data are for degree-granting institutions. Degree-granting institutions grant associate's or higher degrees and participate in Title IV federal financial aid programs. The degree-granting classification is very similar to the earlier higher education classification, but it includes more 2-year colleges and excludes a few higher education institutions that did not grant degrees. (See Guide to Sources for details.)

SOURCE: U.S. Department of Education, National Center for Education Statistics, Higher Education General Information Survey (HEGIS), "Faculty Salaries, Tenure, and Fringe Benefits" surveys, 1977–78 and 1982–83; and 1987–88 through 2005–06 Integrated Postsecondary Education Data System, "Salaries, Tenure, and Fringe Benefits of Full-Time Instructional Faculty Survey" (IPEDS-SA:87–99), and Winter 2002–03 through Winter 2005–06. (This table was prepared August 2006.)

Table 247. Full-time instructional staff with tenure for degree-granting institutions with a tenure system, by academic rank, sex, and control and type of institution: Selected years, 1993–94 through 2005–06

Academic year, control and type of institution	All ranks Total	Male	Female	Professor Total	Male	Female	Associate professor Total	Male	Female	Assistant professor Total	Male	Female	Instructor	Lecturer	No academic rank
1	2	3	4	5	6	7	8	9	10	11	12	13	14	15	16
1993–94															
All institutions	56.2	62.6	42.7	91.9	92.8	87.7	76.8	77.5	75.1	14.4	13.6	15.5	38.3	10.8	26.0
4-year	54.0	61.0	38.0	93.0	93.5	90.6	76.2	77.0	74.3	12.1	11.5	12.9	4.8	9.6	9.4
University	54.3	61.0	35.8	94.1	94.5	91.3	78.0	78.6	76.4	6.6	6.2	7.3	5.7	10.5	9.9
Other	53.8	61.1	39.4	92.1	92.5	90.2	74.9	75.7	73.1	15.7	15.4	16.0	4.4	8.3	8.7
2-year	69.3	74.7	62.4	80.8	83.7	75.7	83.8	86.1	81.1	46.6	50.5	43.2	67.9	41.2	65.6
Public institutions	58.9	65.4	45.6	92.6	93.6	87.5	80.8	81.6	78.9	17.1	16.1	18.5	45.5	7.2	28.6
4-year	56.3	63.5	39.3	94.3	94.7	92.0	80.4	81.2	78.4	13.8	13.0	14.8	4.4	5.4	6.1
University	57.0	64.2	37.2	95.6	96.0	92.5	83.9	84.4	82.6	7.6	7.0	8.6	3.1	1.0	7.0
Other	55.7	62.9	40.8	93.2	93.5	91.7	77.5	78.3	75.5	18.1	17.6	18.7	5.1	9.8	4.9
2-year	69.9	75.4	63.0	80.7	83.7	75.5	84.2	86.4	81.5	47.7	51.1	44.6	68.9	39.9	65.7
Private institutions	49.5	56.0	35.4	90.3	90.8	88.1	67.6	68.1	66.5	9.0	8.7	9.4	6.8	21.9	18.8
4-year	49.5	56.0	35.4	90.3	90.8	88.0	67.6	68.1	66.5	9.0	8.7	9.4	5.5	21.6	15.7
University	48.4	54.1	32.9	90.8	91.1	89.1	63.2	64.1	60.6	4.7	4.8	4.7	10.4	30.0	15.4
Other	50.3	57.5	36.8	89.9	90.5	87.4	70.2	70.7	69.1	11.6	11.5	11.7	3.1	1.4	16.3
2-year	45.4	51.9	36.8	89.8	86.8	95.0	62.9	64.1	61.8	12.0	11.8	12.0	25.8	—	64.8
1999–2000															
All institutions	53.6	59.6	43.1	92.8	93.2	91.2	76.8	76.8	76.7	11.7	10.9	12.8	34.1	3.4	18.4
4-year	51.5	58.3	38.5	92.9	93.2	91.5	76.3	76.5	76.0	9.1	8.6	9.7	3.6	2.5	4.9
University	50.1	57.1	34.5	92.5	92.9	90.3	77.1	77.4	76.6	4.1	3.9	4.5	1.7	0.9	1.3
Other	52.6	59.4	41.1	93.2	93.5	92.2	75.7	75.8	75.7	12.4	12.1	12.8	4.7	4.4	11.6
2-year	67.7	70.6	64.6	91.3	92.3	89.9	83.2	83.3	83.1	53.5	55.9	51.6	60.9	21.1	64.5
Public institutions	55.9	61.9	45.5	93.9	94.4	91.9	81.0	81.2	80.7	14.0	13.0	15.2	39.9	4.1	21.2
4-year	53.1	60.3	39.3	94.2	94.6	92.5	80.8	81.0	80.3	10.0	9.6	10.6	3.9	3.0	4.0
University	53.0	60.4	36.7	94.2	94.7	91.4	83.0	83.2	82.7	4.6	4.3	5.1	2.3	0.7	1.7
Other	53.2	60.2	41.2	94.1	94.4	93.1	78.9	79.0	78.5	13.8	13.5	14.1	4.8	5.2	7.5
2-year	67.8	70.7	64.6	91.3	92.3	89.8	83.4	83.5	83.4	53.7	56.0	51.8	61.0	21.2	64.4
Private institutions	48.3	54.3	37.0	90.3	90.5	89.7	68.1	67.9	68.5	7.5	6.9	8.2	4.1	1.2	8.6
4-year	48.2	54.3	36.8	90.3	90.5	89.7	68.1	67.9	68.5	7.4	6.8	8.2	3.1	1.2	7.2
University	44.1	50.3	29.8	88.9	89.1	87.9	64.1	64.6	62.8	3.2	3.1	3.3	0.4	1.3	0.4
Other	51.4	57.7	41.1	91.4	91.7	90.6	70.6	70.2	71.3	10.1	9.6	10.6	4.6	1.0	28.3
2-year	59.9	60.3	59.6	95.9	92.0	100.0	60.0	66.7	55.8	33.8	40.0	30.0	50.5	—	68.8
2003–04															
All institutions	50.4	56.0	41.5	91.8	92.0	91.1	74.6	74.2	75.3	9.0	8.2	9.9	30.7	2.1	22.5
4-year	48.2	54.6	37.2	91.9	92.1	91.3	74.2	73.8	74.8	6.6	6.1	7.3	3.2	1.5	3.9
University	47.4	54.0	34.0	91.7	91.9	90.5	75.0	74.8	75.4	3.1	3.0	3.2	1.1	0.4	1.7
Other	48.8	55.1	39.4	92.1	92.2	91.8	73.6	73.0	74.5	9.0	8.3	9.7	4.3	2.6	9.6
2-year	65.2	68.2	62.2	90.6	91.3	89.7	81.2	82.0	80.5	45.6	48.4	43.2	57.2	22.1	69.8
Public institutions	53.0	58.6	44.2	93.6	93.8	92.9	78.9	78.7	79.4	11.1	10.2	12.1	35.7	2.6	28.6
4-year	50.2	56.9	38.5	93.9	94.0	93.7	78.7	78.4	79.2	7.5	7.0	8.2	2.4	1.7	4.4
University	51.1	58.0	37.2	93.8	94.0	92.9	81.2	81.2	81.3	3.7	3.6	3.9	1.5	0.4	2.6
Other	49.4	56.0	39.4	94.0	94.0	94.2	76.6	76.0	77.6	10.1	9.4	10.8	2.8	2.7	8.3
2-year	65.2	68.3	62.2	90.5	91.3	89.6	81.3	82.1	80.6	45.9	48.8	43.5	57.2	22.0	69.8
Private institutions	44.7	50.3	35.0	88.2	88.4	87.2	66.2	65.5	67.3	5.2	4.6	5.9	6.7	0.7	3.7
4-year	44.6	50.3	34.9	88.2	88.4	87.1	66.2	65.5	67.3	5.2	4.6	5.9	4.9	0.7	2.8
University	40.5	46.6	27.9	87.5	87.8	85.6	62.1	61.9	62.6	2.0	2.0	2.0	0.4	0.2	0.3
Other	47.9	53.6	39.3	88.7	89.0	88.0	68.7	68.1	69.7	7.2	6.5	8.0	7.2	1.8	14.0
2-year	61.5	60.2	62.7	94.9	91.7	97.7	65.4	61.9	67.7	15.6	14.3	16.7	63.0	37.5	68.1
2005–06															
All institutions	49.6	55.2	41.0	91.3	91.6	90.5	73.6	73.0	74.5	8.0	7.4	8.6	28.4	1.8	26.1
4-year	47.5	53.9	37.0	91.4	91.6	90.9	73.3	72.8	74.2	5.6	5.2	6.0	1.7	1.3	5.3
University	46.7	53.3	33.9	90.8	91.1	89.2	72.5	72.1	73.2	2.1	2.1	2.1	1.0	0.7	1.9
Other	48.1	54.4	39.0	92.0	92.1	91.9	73.9	73.3	74.7	7.9	7.6	8.2	2.1	2.0	12.7
2-year	64.0	67.1	61.2	89.5	90.7	88.1	77.9	77.9	77.8	43.9	46.5	41.7	56.4	22.5	70.2
Public institutions	51.5	57.1	43.3	92.8	93.1	91.8	77.7	77.3	78.4	9.8	9.1	10.6	33.8	2.3	29.9
4-year	48.7	55.4	37.8	93.1	93.3	92.7	77.7	77.3	78.5	6.1	5.8	6.6	2.1	1.6	3.8
University	49.5	56.1	36.5	92.8	93.1	91.4	78.9	78.8	79.1	2.2	2.2	2.3	1.3	0.9	2.0
Other	48.1	54.7	38.7	93.4	93.4	93.6	76.8	76.0	78.0	8.8	8.4	9.3	2.5	2.2	7.5
2-year	64.1	67.2	61.2	89.5	90.7	88.2	77.9	77.8	77.9	44.1	46.8	41.8	56.2	22.4	70.3
Private institutions	45.2	51.1	35.5	88.3	88.5	87.6	65.4	64.7	66.6	4.6	4.3	4.9	2.7	0.5	9.8
4-year	45.1	51.1	35.5	88.3	88.5	87.6	65.4	64.6	66.6	4.6	4.3	4.9	0.9	0.5	9.4
University	41.5	47.9	28.8	86.8	87.2	85.0	59.4	58.9	60.5	2.0	2.0	1.9	0.3	0.3	1.6
Other	48.0	53.9	39.7	89.5	89.7	89.1	69.2	68.8	69.7	6.3	6.1	6.6	1.3	0.9	30.0
2-year	59.7	61.5	57.7	86.3	91.7	81.5	69.7	92.9	52.6	15.4	8.6	20.9	68.0	50.0	50.0

—Not available.
NOTE: The coverage of this table differs from similar tables published in editions of the *Digest* prior to 2003. Previous tenure tabulations included only instructional staff classified as full-time faculty; this table includes all staff with full-time instructional duties, including faculty and other instructional staff. Data for 1993–94 are for institutions of higher education, while later data are for degree-granting institutions. Degree-granting institutions grant associate's or higher degrees and participate in Title IV federal financial aid programs. The degree-granting classification is very similar to the earlier higher education classification, but it includes more 2-year colleges and excludes a few higher education institutions that did not grant degrees. (See Guide to Sources for details.)
SOURCE: U.S. Department of Education, National Center for Education Statistics, 1993–94 through 2005–06 Integrated Postsecondary Education Data System, "Fall Staff Survey" (IPEDS-S:93–99), Winter 2003–04, and Winter 2005–06. (This table was prepared September 2006.)

Table 248. Degree-granting institutions, by control and type of institution: Selected years, 1949–50 through 2005–06

Year	All institutions			Public			Private		
	Total	4-year	2-year	Total	4-year	2-year	Total	4-year	2-year
1	2	3	4	5	6	7	8	9	10
Excluding branch campuses									
1949–50	1,851	1,327	524	641	344	297	1,210	983	227
1959–60	2,004	1,422	582	695	367	328	1,309	1,055	254
1969–70	2,525	1,639	886	1,060	426	634	1,465	1,213	252
1970–71	2,556	1,665	891	1,089	435	654	1,467	1,230	237
1971–72	2,606	1,675	931	1,137	440	697	1,469	1,235	234
1972–73	2,665	1,701	964	1,182	449	733	1,483	1,252	231
1973–74	2,720	1,717	1,003	1,200	440	760	1,520	1,277	243
1974–75	2,747	1,744	1,003	1,214	447	767	1,533	1,297	236
1975–76	2,765	1,767	998	1,219	447	772	1,546	1,320	226
1976–77	2,785	1,783	1,002	1,231	452	779	1,554	1,331	223
1977–78	2,826	1,808	1,018	1,241	454	787	1,585	1,354	231
1978–79	2,954	1,843	1,111	1,308	463	845	1,646	1,380	266
1979–80	2,975	1,863	1,112	1,310	464	846	1,665	1,399	266
1980–81	3,056	1,861	1,195	1,334	465	869	1,722	1,396	326 [1]
1981–82	3,083	1,883	1,200	1,340	471	869	1,743	1,412	331 [1]
1982–83	3,111	1,887	1,224	1,336	472	864	1,775	1,415	360 [1]
1983–84	3,117	1,914	1,203	1,325	474	851	1,792	1,440	352
1984–85	3,146	1,911	1,235	1,329	461	868	1,817	1,450	367
1985–86	3,155	1,915	1,240	1,326	461	865	1,829	1,454	375
Including branch campuses									
1974–75	3,004	1,866	1,138	1,433	537	896	1,571	1,329	242
1975–76	3,026	1,898	1,128	1,442	545	897	1,584	1,353	231
1976–77	3,046	1,913	1,133	1,455	550	905	1,591	1,363	228
1977–78	3,095	1,938	1,157	1,473	552	921	1,622	1,386	236
1978–79	3,134	1,941	1,193	1,474	550	924	1,660	1,391	269
1979–80	3,152	1,957	1,195	1,475	549	926	1,677	1,408	269
1980–81	3,231	1,957	1,274	1,497	552	945	1,734	1,405	329 [1]
1981–82	3,253	1,979	1,274	1,498	558	940	1,755	1,421	334 [1]
1982–83	3,280	1,984	1,296	1,493	560	933	1,787	1,424	363 [1]
1983–84	3,284	2,013	1,271	1,481	565	916	1,803	1,448	355
1984–85	3,331	2,025	1,306	1,501	566	935	1,830	1,459	371
1985–86	3,340	2,029	1,311	1,498	566	932	1,842	1,463	379
1986–87	3,406	2,070	1,336	1,533	573	960	1,873	1,497	376
1987–88	3,587	2,135	1,452	1,591	599	992	1,996	1,536	460
1988–89	3,565	2,129	1,436	1,582	598	984	1,983	1,531	452
1989–90	3,535	2,127	1,408	1,563	595	968	1,972	1,532	440
1990–91	3,559	2,141	1,418	1,567	595	972	1,992	1,546	446
1991–92	3,601	2,157	1,444	1,598	599	999	2,003	1,558	445
1992–93	3,638	2,169	1,469	1,624	600	1,024	2,014	1,569	445
1993–94	3,632	2,190	1,442	1,625	604	1,021	2,007	1,586	421
1994–95	3,688	2,215	1,473	1,641	605	1,036	2,047	1,610	437
1995–96	3,706	2,244	1,462	1,655	608	1,047	2,051	1,636	415
1996–97	4,009	2,267	1,742	1,702	614	1,088	2,307	1,653	654
1997–98	4,064	2,309	1,755	1,707	615	1,092	2,357	1,694	663
1998–99	4,048	2,335	1,713	1,681	612	1,069	2,367	1,723	644
1999–2000	4,084	2,363	1,721	1,682	614	1,068	2,402	1,749	653
2000–01	4,182	2,450	1,732	1,698	622	1,076	2,484	1,828	656
2001–02	4,197	2,487	1,710	1,713	628	1,085	2,484	1,859	625
2002–03	4,168	2,466	1,702	1,712	631	1,081	2,456	1,835	621
2003–04	4,236	2,530	1,706	1,720	634	1,086	2,516	1,896	620
2004–05	4,216	2,533	1,683	1,700	639	1,061	2,516	1,894	622
2005–06	4,276	2,582	1,694	1,693	640	1,053	2,583	1,942	641

[1]Large increases are due to the addition of schools accredited by the Accrediting Commission of Career Schools and Colleges of Technology.
NOTE: Data through 1995–96 are for institutions of higher education, while later data are for degree-granting institutions. Degree-granting institutions grant associate's or higher degrees and participate in Title IV federal financial aid programs. The degree-granting classification is very similar to the earlier higher education classification, but it includes more 2-year colleges and excludes a few higher education institutions that did not grant degrees. (See Guide to Sources

for details.) Changes in counts of institutions over time are partly affected by increasing or decreasing numbers of institutions submitting separate data for branch campuses.
SOURCE: U.S. Department of Education, National Center for Education Statistics, *Education Directory, Colleges and Universities*, 1949–50 through 1965–66; Higher Education General Information Survey (HEGIS), "Institutional Characteristics of Colleges and Universities" surveys, 1966–67 through 1985–86; and 1986–87 through 2005–06 Integrated Postsecondary Education Data System, "Institutional Characteristics Survey" (IPEDS-IC:86–99), and Fall 2000 through Fall 2005. (This table was prepared September 2006.)

Table 249. Degree-granting institutions and branches, by type and control of institution and state or jurisdiction: 2005–06

State or jurisdiction	Total	All public institutions	Public 4-year institutions						Public 2-year	All private institutions	Private 4-year institutions						Private 2-year
			Total	Doctoral, extensive[1]	Doctoral, intensive[2]	Master's[3]	Baccalaureate[4]	Other 4-year[6]			Total	Doctoral, extensive[1]	Doctoral, intensive[2]	Master's[3]	Baccalaureate[4]	Other 4-year[6]	
1	2	3	4	5	6	7	8	9	10	11	12	13	14	15	16	17	18
United States	**4,276**	**1,693**	**640**	**102**	**63**	**275**	**103**	**97**	**1,053**	**2,583**	**1,942**	**49**	**44**	**363**	**534**	**952**	**641**
Alabama	66	39	14	3	3	7	1	0	25	27	23	0	0	4	9	10	4
Alaska	8	5	3	0	1	2	0	0	2	3	3	0	0	1	1	1	0
Arizona	76	25	5	2	1	1	0	1	20	51	35	0	0	6	1	28	16
Arkansas	48	33	11	1	1	5	2	2	22	15	13	0	0	1	8	4	2
California	408	146	35	8	2	21	2	2	111	262	195	4	7	30	26	128	67
Colorado	78	27	12	2	2	3	4	1	15	51	32	1	0	6	3	22	19
Connecticut	44	22	10	1	0	7	1	1	12	22	19	1	3	5	4	6	3
Delaware	10	5	2	1	0	1	0	0	3	5	4	0	1	0	1	2	1
District of Columbia	15	2	2	0	0	1	0	1	0	13	13	5	0	4	1	3	0
Florida	169	40	16	4	2	4	1	5	24	129	95	1	3	20	26	45	34
Georgia	132	74	21	3	0	13	1	4	53	58	46	1	1	4	15	25	12
Hawaii	23	10	4	1	0	0	2	1	6	13	9	0	0	3	1	5	4
Idaho	14	7	4	1	1	1	1	0	3	6	6	0	0	1	1	4	1
Illinois	172	60	12	4	1	7	0	0	48	112	100	3	3	16	19	59	12
Indiana	100	29	15	2	3	6	3	1	14	71	47	1	0	8	20	18	24
Iowa	65	19	3	2	0	1	0	0	16	46	42	0	0	4	22	16	4
Kansas	62	35	9	2	1	4	0	2	26	27	23	0	0	8	10	5	4
Kentucky	76	31	8	2	0	6	0	0	23	45	32	1	0	4	16	12	13
Louisiana	90	58	17	1	3	9	0	4	41	32	13	0	0	4	3	5	19
Maine	30	15	8	1	0	1	5	1	7	15	12	0	0	3	5	4	3
Maryland	58	29	13	2	1	9	1	0	16	29	25	1	0	5	6	13	4
Massachusetts	121	31	15	1	2	7	1	4	16	90	82	7	2	15	21	37	8
Michigan	104	45	15	4	3	8	0	0	30	59	54	0	1	9	16	28	5
Minnesota	109	42	12	1	0	7	3	1	30	67	55	0	1	6	13	33	12
Mississippi	41	26	9	3	1	3	1	1	17	15	11	0	0	2	5	4	4
Missouri	128	33	13	1	3	6	2	1	20	95	71	2	0	11	14	44	24
Montana	23	18	6	0	2	2	1	1	12	5	4	0	0	1	2	1	1
Nebraska	39	15	7	0	5	5	0	1	8	24	20	0	0	4	8	8	8
Nevada	23	7	5	2	1	0	1	2	2	16	8	0	0	1	5	2	4
New Hampshire	26	9	5	1	0	2	2	0	4	17	15	0	2	2	5	6	2
New Jersey	59	33	14	1	2	8	2	1	19	26	24	1	2	6	6	9	2
New Mexico	42	28	8	2	1	3	0	2	20	14	13	0	0	3	4	6	1
New York	308	78	43	5	1	20	7	10	35	230	179	9	7	33	34	96	51
North Carolina	128	75	16	2	1	8	3	1	59	53	50	1	1	7	25	16	3
North Dakota	22	14	7	0	0	1	3	3	7	8	5	0	0	1	1	3	3
Ohio	200	61	29	5	5	1	6	12	32	139	78	1	2	15	25	35	61
Oklahoma	57	29	16	2	0	7	3	4	13	28	22	0	1	5	7	9	6
Oregon	60	26	9	2	1	3	1	2	17	34	30	0	0	6	9	15	4
Pennsylvania	259	65	44	3	1	17	20	3	21	194	105	3	3	28	35	36	89
Rhode Island	14	3	2	1	0	1	0	0	1	11	10	1	0	4	1	4	1
South Carolina	64	33	13	2	1	5	3	1	20	31	26	0	0	3	15	8	5
South Dakota	24	12	7	0	2	1	2	0	5	12	11	1	0	2	5	4	1
Tennessee	98	22	9	2	3	4	0	0	13	76	57	1	2	11	16	29	19
Texas	213	109	45	6	6	20	2	11	64	104	65	2	2	14	20	27	39
Utah	31	13	7	2	0	2	2	1	6	18	10	1	0	2	1	6	8
Vermont	25	6	5	1	0	2	1	1	1	19	17	0	0	6	7	4	2
Virginia	107	39	15	4	2	6	3	0	24	68	54	0	0	8	18	28	14
Washington	80	43	8	2	0	5	1	0	35	37	33	0	0	11	4	18	4

See notes at end of table.

Table 249. Degree-granting institutions and branches, by type and control of institution and state or jurisdiction: 2005–06—Continued

State or jurisdiction	Total	All public institutions	Public 4-year institutions						Public 2-year	All private institutions	Private 4-year institutions						Private 2-year
			Total	Doctoral, extensive[1]	Doctoral, intensive[2]	Master's[3]	Baccalaureate[4]	Other 4-year[5]			Total	Doctoral, extensive[1]	Doctoral, intensive[2]	Master's[3]	Baccalaureate[4]	Other 4-year[5]	
1	2	3	4	5	6	7	8	9	10	11	12	13	14	15	16	17	18
West Virginia	44	23	13	1	0	1	9	2	10	21	10	0	0	2	7	1	11
Wisconsin	68	31	13	2	0	11	0	0	18	37	35	1	0	8	10	16	2
Wyoming	10	8	1	1	0	0	0	0	7	2	1	0	0	0	0	1	1
U.S. Service Schools	5	5	5	0	0	0	0	5	0	†	†	†	†	†	†	†	†
Other jurisdictions	**85**	**25**	**17**	**0**	**1**	**3**	**7**	**6**	**8**	**60**	**44**	**0**	**0**	**7**	**19**	**18**	**16**
American Samoa	1	1	0	0	0	0	0	0	1	0	0	0	0	0	0	0	0
Federated States of Micronesia	1	1	0	0	0	0	0	0	1	0	0	0	0	0	0	0	0
Guam	3	2	1	0	0	1	0	0	1	1	1	0	0	0	0	1	0
Marshall Islands	1	1	0	0	0	0	0	0	1	0	0	0	0	0	0	0	0
Northern Marianas	1	1	1	0	0	0	0	1	0	0	0	0	0	0	0	0	0
Palau	1	1	0	0	0	0	0	0	1	0	0	0	0	0	0	0	0
Puerto Rico	76	17	14	0	1	1	7	5	3	59	43	0	0	7	19	17	16
Virgin Islands	1	1	1	0	0	1	0	0	0	0	0	0	0	0	0	0	0

†Not applicable.

[1]Doctoral, extensive institutions are committed to graduate education through the doctorate, and award 50 or more doctor's degrees per year across at least 15 disciplines.

[2]Doctoral, intensive institutions are committed to education through the doctorate and award at least 10 doctor's degrees per year across 3 or more disciplines or at least 20 doctor's degrees overall.

[3]Master's institutions offer a full range of baccalaureate programs and are committed to education through the master's degree. They award at least 20 master's degrees per year.

[4]Baccalaureate institutions primarily emphasize undergraduate education.

[5]Other specialized 4-year institutions award degrees primarily in single fields of study, such as medicine, business, fine arts, theology, and engineering. Includes some institutions that have 4-year programs, but have not reported sufficient data to iden- tify program category. Also, includes institutions classified as 4-year under the IPEDS system, which had been classified as 2-year in the Carnegie classification system because they primarily award associate's degrees.

NOTE: Degree-granting institutions grant associate's or higher degrees and participate in Title IV federal financial aid programs. New institutions that do not have sufficient data to report by detailed level are included under "other 4-year" or 2-year, depending on the level reported by the institution. Count of institutions includes 13 institutions which were unable to respond to the Fall 2005 survey due to natural disaster.

SOURCE: U.S. Department of Education, National Center for Education Statistics, 2005–06 Integrated Postsecondary Education Data System (IPEDS), Fall 2005. (This table was prepared September 2006.)

Table 250. Degree-granting institutions that have closed their doors, by control and type of institution: 1969–70 through 2005–06

Year	All institutions			Public			Private		
	Total	4-year	2-year	Total	4-year	2-year	Total	4-year	2-year
1	2	3	4	5	6	7	8	9	10
Excluding branch campuses									
1969–70	18	8	10	3	0	3	15	8	7
1970–71	32	9	23	9	0	9	23	9	14
1971–72	12	3	9	3	0	3	9	3	6
1972–73	19	12	7	2	0	2	17	12	5
1973–74	18	11	7	0	0	0	18	11	7
1974–75	17	13	4	3	0	3	14	13	1
1975–76	8	6	2	2	1	1	6	5	1
1976–77	8	5	3	0	0	0	8	5	3
1977–78	12	9	3	0	0	0	12	9	3
1978–79	9	4	5	0	0	0	9	4	5
1979–80	6	5	1	0	0	0	6	5	1
1980–81	4	3	1	0	0	0	4	3	1
1981–82	7	6	1	0	0	0	7	6	1
1982–83	7	4	3	0	0	0	7	4	3
1983–84	4	4	0	0	0	0	4	4	0
1984–85	4	4	0	0	0	0	4	4	0
1985–86	10	6	4	1	0	1	9	6	3
1986–87 and 1987–88	25	19	6	1	0	1	24	19	5
1988–89	14	6	8	0	0	0	14	6	8
1989–90	12	6	6	0	0	0	12	6	6
1990–91	10	4	6	0	0	0	10	4	6
1991–92	10	7	3	0	0	0	10	7	3
Including branch campuses									
1969–70	24	10	14	5	1	4	19	9	10
1970–71	35	10	25	11	0	11	24	10	14
1971–72	14	5	9	3	0	3	11	5	6
1972–73	21	12	9	4	0	4	17	12	5
1973–74	20	12	8	1	0	1	19	12	7
1974–75	18	13	5	4	0	4	14	13	1
1975–76	9	7	2	2	1	1	7	6	1
1976–77	9	6	3	0	0	0	9	6	3
1977–78	12	9	3	0	0	0	12	9	3
1978–79	9	4	5	0	0	0	9	4	5
1979–80	6	5	1	0	0	0	6	5	1
1980–81	4	3	1	0	0	0	4	3	1
1981–82	7	6	1	0	0	0	7	6	1
1982–83	7	4	3	0	0	0	7	4	3
1983–84	5	5	0	1	1	0	4	4	0
1984–85	4	4	0	0	0	0	4	4	0
1985–86	12	8	4	1	1	0	11	7	4
1986–87 and 1987–88	26	19	7	1	0	1	25	19	6
1988–89	14	6	8	0	0	0	14	6	8
1989–90	19	8	11	0	0	0	19	8	11
1990–91	18	6	12	0	0	0	18	6	12
1991–92	26	8	18	1	0	1	25	8	17
1992–93	24	6	18	0	0	0	24	6	18
1993–94	38	10	28	1	0	1	37	10	27
1994–95	15	8	7	2	0	2	13	8	5
1995–96	21	8	13	1	1	0	20	7	13
1996–97	36	13	23	2	0	2	34	13	21
1997–98	5	0	5	0	0	0	5	0	5
1998–99	7	1	6	1	0	1	6	1	5
1999–2000	16	3	13	3	0	3	13	3	10
2000–01	14	9	5	0	0	0	14	9	5
2001–02	15	2	13	0	0	0	15	2	13
2002–03	13	7	6	0	0	0	13	7	6
2003–04	13	6	7	0	0	0	13	6	7
2004–05	3	1	2	0	0	0	3	1	2
2005–06	11	6	5	1	1	0	10	5	5

NOTE: This table indicates the year in which the institution closed. Some data have been revised from previously published figures. Data through 1995–96 are for institutions of higher education, while later data are for degree-granting institutions. Degree-granting institutions grant associate's or higher degrees and participate in Title IV federal financial aid programs. The degree-granting classification is very similar to the earlier higher education classification, but it includes more 2-year colleges and excludes a few higher education institutions that did not grant degrees. (See Guide to Sources for details.)

SOURCE: U.S. Department of Education, National Center for Education Statistics, *Education Directory, Higher Education,* 1969–70 through 1974–75; *Education Directory, Colleges and Universities,* 1975–76 through 1983–84; *1982–83 Supplement to the Education Directory, Colleges and Universities,* 1983; and 1986–87 through 2005–06 Integrated Postsecondary Education Data System, "Institutional Characteristics Survey" (IPEDS-IC:86–99), and Spring 2000 through Spring 2006. (This table was prepared June 2006.)

Table 251. Degrees conferred by degree-granting institutions, by level of degree and sex of student: Selected years, 1869–70 through 2015–16

Year	Associate's degrees			Bachelor's degrees			Master's degrees			First-professional degrees			Doctor's degrees[1]		
	Total	Males	Females	Total	Males	Females	Total	Males	Females	Total	Males	Females	Total	Males	Females
1	2	3	4	5	6	7	8	9	10	11	12	13	14	15	16
1869–70	—	—	—	9,371 [2]	7,993 [2]	1,378 [2]	0	0	0	(3)	(3)	(3)	1	1	0
1879–80	—	—	—	12,896 [2]	10,411 [2]	2,485 [2]	879	868	11	(3)	(3)	(3)	54	51	3
1889–90	—	—	—	15,539 [2]	12,857 [2]	2,682 [2]	1,015	821	194	(3)	(3)	(3)	149	147	2
1899–1900	—	—	—	27,410 [2]	22,173 [2]	5,237 [2]	1,583	1,280	303	(3)	(3)	(3)	382	359	23
1909–10	—	—	—	37,199 [2]	28,762 [2]	8,437 [2]	2,113	1,555	558	(3)	(3)	(3)	443	399	44
1919–20	—	—	—	48,622 [2]	31,980 [2]	16,642 [2]	4,279	2,985	1,294	(3)	(3)	(3)	615	522	93
1929–30	—	—	—	122,484 [2]	73,615 [2]	48,869 [2]	14,969	8,925	6,044	(3)	(3)	(3)	2,299	1,946	353
1939–40	—	—	—	186,500 [2]	109,546 [2]	76,954 [2]	26,731	16,508	10,223	(3)	(3)	(3)	3,290	2,861	429
1949–50	—	—	—	432,058 [2]	328,841 [2]	103,217 [2]	58,183	41,220	16,963	(3)	(3)	(3)	6,420	5,804	616
1959–60	—	—	—	392,440 [2]	254,063 [2]	138,377 [2]	74,435	50,898	23,537	(3)	(3)	(3)	9,829	8,801	1,028
1969–70	206,023	117,432	88,591	792,316	451,097	341,219	208,291	125,624	82,667	34,918	33,077	1,841	29,866	25,890	3,976
1970–71	252,311	144,144	108,167	839,730	475,594	364,136	230,509	138,146	92,363	37,946	35,544	2,402	32,107	27,530	4,577
1971–72	292,014	166,227	125,787	887,273	500,590	386,683	251,633	149,550	102,083	43,411	40,723	2,688	33,363	28,090	5,273
1972–73	316,174	175,413	140,761	922,362	518,191	404,171	263,371	154,468	108,903	50,018	46,489	3,529	34,777	28,571	6,206
1973–74	343,924	188,591	155,333	945,776	527,313	418,463	277,033	157,842	119,191	53,816	48,530	5,286	33,816	27,365	6,451
1974–75	360,171	191,017	169,154	922,933	504,841	418,092	292,450	161,570	130,880	55,916	48,956	6,960	34,083	26,817	7,266
1975–76	391,454	209,996	181,458	925,746	504,925	420,821	311,771	167,248	144,523	62,649	52,892	9,757	34,064	26,267	7,797
1976–77	406,377	210,842	195,535	919,549	495,545	424,004	317,164	167,783	149,381	64,359	52,374	11,985	33,232	25,142	8,090
1977–78	412,246	204,718	207,528	921,204	487,347	433,857	311,620	161,212	150,408	66,581	52,270	14,311	32,131	23,658	8,473
1978–79	402,702	192,091	210,611	921,390	477,344	444,046	301,079	153,370	147,709	68,848	52,652	16,196	32,730	23,541	9,189
1979–80	400,910	183,737	217,173	929,417	473,611	455,806	298,081	150,749	147,332	70,131	52,716	17,415	32,615	22,943	9,672
1980–81	416,377	188,638	227,739	935,140	469,883	465,257	295,739	147,043	148,696	71,956	52,792	19,164	32,958	22,711	10,247
1981–82	434,526	196,944	237,582	952,998	473,364	479,634	295,546	145,532	150,014	72,032	52,223	19,809	32,707	22,224	10,483
1982–83	449,620	203,991	245,629	969,510	479,140	490,370	289,921	144,697	145,224	73,054	51,250	21,804	32,775	21,902	10,873
1983–84	452,240	202,704	249,536	974,309	482,319	491,990	284,263	143,595	140,668	74,468	51,378	23,090	33,209	22,064	11,145
1984–85	454,712	202,932	251,780	979,477	482,528	496,949	286,251	143,390	142,861	75,063	50,455	24,608	32,943	21,700	11,243
1985–86	446,047	196,166	249,881	987,823	485,923	501,900	288,567	143,508	145,059	73,910	49,261	24,649	33,653	21,819	11,834
1986–87	436,304	190,839	245,465	991,264	480,782	510,482	289,349	141,269	148,080	71,617	46,523	25,094	34,041	22,061	11,980
1987–88	435,085	190,047	245,038	994,829	477,203	517,626	299,317	145,163	154,154	70,735	45,484	25,251	34,870	22,615	12,255
1988–89	436,764	186,316	250,448	1,018,755	483,346	535,409	310,621	149,354	161,267	70,856	45,046	25,810	35,720	22,648	13,072
1989–90	455,102	191,195	263,907	1,051,344	491,696	559,648	324,301	153,653	170,648	70,988	43,961	27,027	38,371	24,401	13,970
1990–91	481,720	198,634	283,086	1,094,538	504,045	590,493	337,168	156,482	180,686	71,948	43,846	28,102	39,294	24,756	14,538
1991–92	504,231	207,481	296,750	1,136,553	520,811	615,742	352,838	161,842	190,996	74,146	45,071	29,075	40,659	25,557	15,102
1992–93	514,756	211,964	302,792	1,165,178	532,881	632,297	369,585	169,258	200,327	75,387	45,153	30,234	42,132	26,073	16,059
1993–94	530,632	215,261	315,371	1,169,275	532,422	636,853	387,070	176,085	210,985	75,418	44,707	30,711	43,185	26,552	16,633
1994–95	539,691	218,352	321,339	1,160,134	526,131	634,003	397,629	178,598	219,031	75,800	44,853	30,947	44,446	26,916	17,530
1995–96	555,216	219,514	335,702	1,164,792	522,454	642,338	406,301	179,081	227,220	76,734	44,748	31,986	44,652	26,841	17,811
1996–97	571,226	223,948	347,278	1,172,879	520,515	652,364	419,401	180,947	238,454	78,730	45,564	33,166	45,876	27,146	18,730
1997–98	558,555	217,613	340,942	1,184,406	519,956	664,450	430,164	184,375	245,789	78,598	44,911	33,687	46,010	26,664	19,346
1998–99	559,954	218,417	341,537	1,200,303	518,746	681,557	439,986	186,148	253,838	78,439	44,339	34,100	44,077	25,146	18,931
1999–2000	564,933	224,721	340,212	1,237,875	530,367	707,508	457,056	191,792	265,264	80,057	44,239	35,818	44,808	25,028	19,780
2000–01	578,865	231,645	347,220	1,244,171	531,840	712,331	468,476	194,351	274,125	79,707	42,862	36,845	44,904	24,728	20,176
2001–02	595,133	238,109	357,024	1,291,900	549,816	742,084	482,118	199,120	282,998	80,698	42,507	38,191	44,160	23,708	20,452
2002–03	632,912	253,060	379,852	1,348,503	573,079	775,424	512,645	211,381	301,264	80,810	41,834	38,976	46,024	24,341	21,683
2003–04	665,301	260,033	405,268	1,399,542	595,425	804,117	558,940	229,545	329,395	83,041	42,169	40,872	48,378	25,323	23,055
2004–05	696,660	267,536	429,124	1,439,264	613,000	826,264	574,618	233,590	341,028	87,289	43,849	43,440	52,631	26,973	25,658
2005–06[4]	682,000	262,000	420,000	1,456,000	608,000	849,000	584,000	228,000	356,000	85,100	41,600	43,500	49,500	25,700	23,800
2006–07[4]	686,000	263,000	423,000	1,488,000	618,000	870,000	603,000	234,000	369,000	87,400	42,200	45,200	50,500	26,100	24,400
2007–08[4]	694,000	264,000	430,000	1,523,000	629,000	894,000	619,000	239,000	380,000	89,700	42,800	46,900	50,900	26,200	24,700
2008–09[4]	704,000	264,000	440,000	1,561,000	640,000	921,000	635,000	245,000	390,000	91,900	43,500	48,400	51,100	26,100	24,900
2009–10[4]	714,000	268,000	447,000	1,596,000	651,000	945,000	647,000	251,000	397,000	93,400	44,000	49,300	51,200	26,100	25,100
2010–11[4]	721,000	270,000	451,000	1,622,000	658,000	964,000	657,000	255,000	402,000	94,500	44,500	50,000	51,700	26,300	25,500
2011–12[4]	726,000	271,000	455,000	1,645,000	664,000	980,000	670,000	260,000	409,000	95,900	45,000	50,900	52,600	26,600	26,100
2012–13[4]	730,000	272,000	458,000	1,665,000	670,000	995,000	685,000	267,000	418,000	97,300	45,500	51,800	53,800	27,000	26,800
2013–14[4]	735,000	273,000	462,000	1,682,000	674,000	1,007,000	705,000	275,000	431,000	99,200	46,100	53,100	55,300	27,500	27,800
2014–15[4]	740,000	273,000	467,000	1,697,000	677,000	1,019,000	731,000	284,000	447,000	101,400	46,700	54,700	56,900	28,000	28,900
2015–16[4]	744,000	272,000	472,000	1,705,000	677,000	1,028,000	757,000	293,000	464,000	103,800	47,200	56,500	58,500	28,400	30,100

—Not available.

[1]Includes Ph.D., Ed.D., and comparable degrees at the doctoral level. Excludes first-professional, such as M.D., D.D.S., and law degrees.
[2]Includes first-professional degrees.
[3]First-professional degrees are included with bachelor's degrees.
[4]Projected.
NOTE: Data through 1994–95 are for institutions of higher education, while later data are for degree-granting institutions. Degree-granting institutions grant associate's or higher degrees and participate in Title IV federal financial aid programs. The degree-granting classification is very similar to the earlier higher education classification, but it includes more 2-year colleges and excludes a few higher education institutions that did not grant degrees. (See Guide to Sources for details.) Some data have been revised from previously published figures. Detail may not sum to totals because of rounding.
SOURCE: U.S. Department of Education, National Center for Education Statistics, *Earned Degrees Conferred*, 1869–70 through 1964–65; *Projections of Education Statistics to 2015*; Higher Education General Information Survey (HEGIS), "Degrees and Other Formal Awards Conferred" surveys, 1965–66 through 1985–86; and 1986–87 through 2004–05 Integrated Postsecondary Education Data System, "Completions Survey" (IPEDS-C:87–99), and Fall 2000 through Fall 2005. (This table was prepared July 2006.)

Table 252. Associate's degrees conferred by degree-granting institutions, by field of study: 1993–94 through 2004–05

Field of study	1993–94	1994–95	1995–96	1996–97	1997–98	1998–99	1999–2000	2000–01	2001–02	2002–03	2003–04	2004–05
1	2	3	4	5	6	7	8	9	10	11	12	13
Total	530,632	539,691	555,216	571,226	558,555	559,954	564,933	578,865	595,133	632,912	665,301	696,660
Agriculture and natural resources, total	5,625	5,730	6,182	6,463	6,673	6,632	6,666	6,649	6,494	6,208	6,283	6,404
Agriculture, agriculture operations, and related sciences	4,294	4,393	4,723	5,021	5,206	5,220	5,292	5,200	5,125	4,890	4,959	5,137
Natural resources and conservation	1,331	1,337	1,459	1,442	1,467	1,412	1,374	1,449	1,369	1,318	1,324	1,267
Architecture and related services	353	277	256	316	265	405	392	417	443	440	492	583
Area, ethnic, cultural, and gender studies	75	68	110	82	97	85	113	73	94	126	105	115
Biological and biomedical sciences	1,789	1,861	2,049	2,133	2,113	2,213	1,448	1,443	1,534	1,496	1,456	1,709
Business, management, and marketing	91,612	89,162	90,945	92,228	87,672	86,964	86,106	87,059	86,713	89,564	92,065	96,067
Accounting	15,307	14,970	15,926	16,017	14,807	14,325	13,562	13,158	12,315	13,234	14,506	13,988
Business, general	11,452	11,622	11,397	11,385	11,311	11,514	12,283	12,621	12,936	13,010	13,387	12,050
Business administration and management	29,691	28,967	28,901	29,804	28,793	28,615	28,486	28,947	30,268	33,024	33,652	42,979
Business and management, other	18,310	11,232	15,910	15,197	14,148	14,027	13,398	13,122	13,269	13,352	14,909	13,042
Management information systems	3,094	3,884	4,539	4,936	4,261	4,526	5,394	6,016	6,417	5,602	4,214	2,812
Secretarial and related programs	13,758	18,487	14,272	14,889	14,352	13,957	12,983	13,195	11,508	11,342	11,397	11,196
Communications	2,052	3,160	2,187	2,030	2,368	2,639	2,754	2,949	2,819	2,602	2,444	2,545
Communications technologies	3,420	3,035	2,807	2,863	2,642	2,528	2,625	3,038	3,006	3,300	3,401	3,516
Computer and information sciences	12,630	12,230	12,500	14,607	18,185	22,445	28,185	34,356	40,127	46,089	41,845	36,173
Construction trades	1,695	1,728	2,141	1,928	2,172	2,137	2,337	2,682	2,639	3,001	3,560	3,512
Education	9,301	9,691	9,809	10,587	9,461	10,165	8,510	9,533	9,611	11,199	12,465	13,329
Engineering	2,381	2,191	2,158	1,921	2,118	2,012	1,722	1,795	1,691	2,176	2,737	2,441
Engineering-related technologies	42,453	41,438	40,447	41,349	40,784	42,362	43,732	42,366	40,217	39,957	36,915	33,548
English language and literature/letters	697	895	813	892	1,035	1,032	947	877	864	896	828	995
Family and consumer sciences	6,960	7,234	7,651	7,998	7,811	8,063	8,031	8,329	9,208	9,471	9,478	9,707
Foreign languages and literatures	1,447	1,694	1,612	1,768	1,674	1,705	1,059	1,100	1,085	1,050	1,047	1,234
Health professions and related sciences	96,597	100,714	104,775	102,077	94,940	93,218	86,676	84,656	82,361	90,536	106,208	122,520
Dental assisting	3,989	4,312	4,564	4,866	4,904	6,628	5,569	5,193	5,223	5,466	5,652	5,813
Emergency medical technician-ambulance and paramedic	510	771	889	1,048	975	918	1,152	1,134	1,203	1,398	1,617	1,825
Medical lab technician	2,570	2,769	2,982	2,641	2,370	2,033	1,644	1,502	1,384	1,494	1,678	1,932
Medical assisting	2,785	3,544	4,941	5,019	5,102	5,358	5,414	5,863	4,748	5,846	8,499	10,411
Nursing assisting	6	2	7	13	23	12	7	2	0	8	4	38
Practical nursing	740	772	605	429	499	447	575	619	814	916	1,049	1,388
Nursing, R.N. and other	57,397	57,456	56,469	52,983	47,329	43,029	40,767	40,278	40,800	45,044	51,552	58,007
Health sciences, other	28,600	31,088	34,318	35,078	33,738	34,793	31,548	30,065	28,189	30,364	36,157	43,106
Legal professions and studies	10,905	11,147	11,916	11,242	9,890	9,133	8,842	8,119	7,815	8,390	9,466	9,885
Liberal arts and sciences, general studies, and humanities	165,106	170,817	174,970	181,341	186,248	181,977	187,454	196,843	207,163	216,814	227,650	240,131
Library science	118	101	94	126	96	86	98	103	96	87	114	108
Mathematics	704	782	758	792	844	823	675	695	685	732	801	807
Mechanics and repairers	11,348	11,503	12,519	12,126	10,576	10,781	11,678	12,689	12,063	11,994	12,553	13,619
Military technologies	265	364	556	556	22	42	65	120	62	85	293	355
Multi/interdisciplinary studies	8,450	8,719	8,619	9,182	9,402	8,661	11,784	10,439	13,205	14,067	14,794	13,888
Parks, recreation, leisure, and fitness studies	731	829	897	885	840	819	819	790	764	811	923	966
Personal and culinary services	5,177	5,627	7,720	8,172	7,648	8,933	9,203	9,786	9,325	12,593	14,239	16,311
Philosophy and religion	82	81	84	91	101	297	209	299	359	379	404	422
Physical sciences and science technologies	2,546	2,456	2,612	2,526	2,286	2,399	2,460	2,337	2,308	2,190	2,676	2,814
Physical sciences	1,567	1,645	1,749	1,728	1,584	1,679	1,350	1,207	1,346	1,141	1,588	1,626
Science technologies	979	811	863	798	702	720	1,110	1,130	962	1,049	1,088	1,188
Precision production trades	1,611	1,601	1,727	1,773	1,929	2,201	2,308	2,256	2,260	2,279	1,968	2,039
Psychology	1,377	1,600	1,583	1,612	1,765	1,625	1,455	1,554	1,705	1,784	1,887	1,942
Public administration and social services	3,696	3,882	4,218	4,270	4,156	3,881	3,656	3,333	3,323	3,533	3,728	4,027
Security and protective services	18,199	19,709	19,196	19,889	19,002	17,430	16,298	16,425	16,689	18,571	20,573	23,749
Criminal justice and corrections	15,262	16,584	15,990	16,644	15,915	14,448	13,487	13,589	13,603	15,136	17,040	19,942
Fire control and safety	2,243	2,447	2,523	2,638	2,480	2,395	2,364	2,346	2,619	2,917	3,012	3,366
Security and protective services, other	694	678	683	607	607	587	447	490	467	518	521	441
Social sciences and history	3,936	3,634	4,021	4,056	4,196	4,550	5,136	5,132	5,593	5,738	6,245	6,533
Social sciences	3,635	3,349	3,727	3,741	3,910	4,254	4,812	4,877	5,304	5,422	5,875	6,233
History	301	285	294	315	286	296	324	255	289	316	370	300
Theology and religious vocations	641	607	608	574	570	476	636	576	414	425	492	581
Transportation and material moving workers	1,900	1,434	1,551	1,572	977	1,101	956	1,028	1,122	1,202	1,217	1,435
Visual and performing arts	13,227	12,544	13,534	13,593	14,980	17,640	17,100	18,435	20,911	23,127	23,949	22,650
Fine arts, general	1,473	1,420	1,515	1,516	1,281	3,029	1,314	1,435	1,521	1,763	1,326	1,623
Design and music	10,173	9,805	10,579	10,459	11,591	12,026	12,780	14,410	16,388	18,503	18,836	17,482
Visual and performing arts, other	1,581	1,319	1,440	1,618	2,108	2,585	3,006	2,590	3,002	2,861	3,787	3,545
Not classified by field of study	1,526	1,146	1,591	7,606	3,017	2,494	2,798	584	365	0	0	0

SOURCE: U.S. Department of Education, National Center for Education Statistics, 1993–94 through 2004–05 Integrated Postsecondary Education Data System, "Completions Survey" (IPEDS-C:93–99), and Fall 2000 through Fall 2005. (This table was prepared July 2006.)

Table 253. Associate's degrees and other subbaccalaureate awards conferred by degree-granting institutions, by length of curriculum, sex of student, and field of study: 2004–05

Field of study	Less-than-1-year awards			1- to less-than-4-year awards			Associate's degrees		
	Total	Males	Females	Total	Males	Females	Total	Males	Females
1	2	3	4	5	6	7	8	9	10
Total	220,502	96,344	124,158	181,212	71,158	110,054	696,660	267,536	429,124
Agriculture and natural resources, total	3,044	2,137	907	1,759	1,090	669	6,404	4,009	2,395
Agriculture, agriculture operations and related sciences	2,259	1,408	851	1,679	1,030	649	5,137	3,020	2,117
Natural resources and conservation	785	729	56	80	60	20	1,267	989	278
Architecture and related services	162	88	74	171	55	116	583	237	346
Area, ethnic, cultural, and gender studies	352	95	257	105	28	77	115	38	77
Biological and biomedical sciences	36	4	32	20	4	16	1,709	548	1,161
Business, management, and marketing	25,827	8,198	17,629	17,573	4,119	13,454	96,067	30,262	65,805
Accounting	3,662	685	2,977	3,491	654	2,837	13,988	2,879	11,109
Business, general	876	535	341	1,013	391	622	12,050	4,526	7,524
Business administration and management	5,906	2,185	3,721	3,741	1,496	2,245	42,979	16,808	26,171
Business and management, other	7,325	2,922	4,403	2,577	896	1,681	13,042	3,532	9,510
Management information systems	453	295	158	514	272	242	2,812	1,606	1,206
Secretarial and related programs	7,605	1,576	6,029	6,237	410	5,827	11,196	911	10,285
Communications	463	186	277	393	223	170	2,545	1,254	1,291
Communications technologies	657	348	309	856	493	363	3,516	2,039	1,477
Computer and information sciences	10,865	6,709	4,156	7,665	4,722	2,943	36,173	25,552	10,621
Construction trades	5,691	5,370	321	7,711	7,421	290	3,512	3,308	204
Education	2,976	329	2,647	1,882	147	1,735	13,329	2,188	11,141
Engineering	94	69	25	69	60	9	2,441	2,078	363
Engineering-related technologies	7,583	6,372	1,211	7,072	6,148	924	33,548	28,675	4,873
English language and literature/letters	572	180	392	106	38	68	995	313	682
Family and consumer sciences	10,636	1,722	8,914	3,586	670	2,916	9,707	446	9,261
Foreign languages and literatures	687	149	538	391	47	344	1,234	197	1,037
Health professions and related sciences	86,875	17,503	69,372	77,688	9,952	67,736	122,520	17,097	105,423
Dental assisting	2,309	156	2,153	5,210	236	4,974	5,813	190	5,623
Emergency medical technician-ambulance and paramedic	12,318	8,401	3,917	2,534	1,876	658	1,825	1,242	583
Medical lab technician	153	12	141	373	164	209	1,932	414	1,518
Medical assisting	11,471	830	10,641	12,170	598	11,572	10,411	564	9,847
Nursing assisting	23,200	2,379	20,821	267	19	248	38	3	35
Practical nursing	1,747	159	1,588	26,905	2,664	24,241	1,388	143	1,245
Nursing, R.N. and other	2,827	247	2,580	3,151	368	2,783	58,007	6,553	51,454
Health sciences, other	32,850	5,319	27,531	27,078	4,027	23,051	43,106	7,988	35,118
Legal professions and studies	1,799	236	1,563	2,793	391	2,402	9,885	955	8,930
Liberal arts and sciences, general studies, and humanities	322	95	227	2,799	931	1,868	240,131	87,845	152,286
Library science	196	17	179	53	12	41	108	11	97
Mathematics	14	7	7	6	4	2	807	529	278
Mechanics and repairers	14,305	13,221	1,084	21,842	20,983	859	13,619	12,901	718
Military technologies	190	130	60	0	0	0	355	303	52
Multi/interdisciplinary studies	513	219	294	412	96	316	13,888	5,878	8,010
Parks, recreation, leisure, and fitness studies	391	208	183	193	92	101	966	581	385
Personal and culinary services	6,172	1,562	4,610	9,934	2,016	7,918	16,311	8,903	7,408
Philosophy and religion	18	6	12	85	42	43	422	122	300
Physical sciences and science technologies	221	126	95	300	149	151	2,814	1,647	1,167
Physical sciences	26	15	11	9	5	4	1,626	974	652
Science technologies	195	111	84	291	144	147	1,188	673	515
Precision production trades	5,071	4,811	260	4,888	4,664	224	2,039	1,877	162
Psychology	134	26	108	36	4	32	1,942	445	1,497
Public administration and social services	769	114	655	478	87	391	4,027	571	3,456
Security and protective services	19,675	14,958	4,717	5,575	4,001	1,574	23,749	13,360	10,389
Criminal justice and corrections	14,397	10,057	4,340	4,193	2,746	1,447	19,942	10,044	9,898
Fire control and safety	5,098	4,792	306	1,238	1,173	65	3,366	3,099	267
Security and protective services, other	180	109	71	144	82	62	441	217	224
Social sciences and history	263	125	138	180	107	73	6,533	2,191	4,342
Social sciences	263	125	138	178	107	71	6,233	2,017	4,216
History	0	0	0	2	0	2	300	174	126
Theology and religious vocations	59	24	35	438	198	240	581	270	311
Transportation and material moving workers	11,918	10,034	1,884	790	706	84	1,435	1,241	194
Visual and performing arts	1,952	966	986	3,363	1,458	1,905	22,650	9,665	12,985
Fine arts, general	63	20	43	113	41	72	1,623	538	1,085
Design and music	1,443	740	703	2,868	1,218	1,650	17,482	7,263	10,219
Visual and performing arts, other	446	206	240	382	199	183	3,545	1,864	1,681

SOURCE: U.S. Department of Education, National Center for Education Statistics, Integrated Postsecondary Education Data System (IPEDS), Fall 2005. (This table was prepared July 2006.)

Table 254. Bachelor's degrees conferred by degree-granting institutions, by discipline division: Selected years, 1970–71 through 2004–05

Discipline division	1970–71	1975–76	1980–81	1985–86	1990–91	1993–94	1994–95	1995–96	1997–98	1998–99	1999–2000	2000–01	2001–02	2002–03	2003–04	2004–05
1	2	3	4	5	6	7	8	9	10	11	12	13	14	15	16	17
Total	**839,730**	**925,746**	**935,140**	**987,823**	**1,094,538**	**1,169,275**	**1,160,134**	**1,164,792**	**1,184,406**	**1,200,303**	**1,237,875**	**1,244,171**	**1,291,900**	**1,348,503**	**1,399,542**	**1,439,264**
Agriculture and natural resources	12,672	19,402	21,886	16,823	13,124	18,056	19,832	21,425	23,276	23,916	24,238	23,370	23,331	23,294	22,835	23,002
Architecture and related services	5,570	9,146	9,455	9,119	9,781	8,975	8,756	8,352	7,652	8,246	8,462	8,480	8,808	9,054	8,838	9,237
Area, ethnic, cultural, and gender studies	2,579	3,577	2,887	3,021	4,776	5,435	5,511	5,633	5,976	6,009	6,212	6,160	6,390	6,629	7,181	7,569
Biological and biomedical sciences	35,683	54,085	43,003	38,320	39,377	51,157	55,790	60,750	65,583	64,608	63,005	59,865	59,415	60,072	61,509	64,611
Business	115,396	143,171	200,521	236,700	249,165	246,265	233,895	226,623	232,079	240,947	256,070	263,515	278,217	293,545	307,149	311,574
Communication, journalism, and related programs	10,324	20,045	29,428	41,666	51,650	51,164	48,104	47,320	49,385	51,384	55,760	58,013	62,791	67,859	70,968	72,715
Communications technologies	478	1,237	1,854	1,479	1,397	869	865	853	878	1,076	1,298	1,178	1,245	1,933	2,034	2,523
Computer and information sciences	2,388	5,652	15,121	42,337	25,159	24,527	24,737	24,506	27,829	30,574	37,788	44,142	50,365	57,439	59,488	54,111
Education	176,307	154,437	108,074	87,147	110,807	107,440	105,929	105,384	105,833	107,086	108,034	105,458	106,295	105,790	106,278	105,451
Engineering	45,034	38,733	63,642	77,391	62,448	62,247	62,331	62,257	60,252	58,260	58,822	58,315	59,627	62,611	63,558	64,906
Engineering technologies	5,148	7,943	11,713	19,731	17,303	16,415	16,238	15,829	14,397	14,405	14,597	14,660	15,052	14,656	14,669	14,837
English language and literature/letters	63,914	41,452	31,922	34,083	51,064	53,150	51,170	49,928	49,016	49,800	50,106	50,569	52,375	53,670	53,984	54,379
Family and consumer sciences/human sciences	11,167	17,409	18,370	13,847	13,920	14,432	14,081	14,353	15,654	16,059	16,321	16,421	16,938	18,166	19,172	20,074
Foreign languages, literatures, and linguistics	20,988	17,068	11,638	11,550	13,937	15,242	14,558	14,832	15,279	15,821	15,886	16,128	16,258	16,901	17,754	18,386
Health professions and related clinical sciences	25,223	53,885	63,665	65,309	59,875	75,890	81,596	86,087	86,843	85,214	80,863	75,933	72,887	71,223	73,934	80,685
Legal professions and studies	545	531	776	1,223	1,827	2,233	2,127	2,123	2,079	1,960	1,969	1,991	2,003	2,466	2,841	3,161
Liberal arts and sciences, general studies, and humanities	7,481	18,855	21,643	21,336	30,526	33,397	33,356	33,997	33,202	34,772	36,104	37,962	39,333	40,221	42,106	43,751
Library science	1,013	843	375	155	90	62	50	58	73	78	154	52	74	99	72	76
Mathematics and statistics	24,801	15,984	11,078	16,122	14,393	14,171	13,494	12,713	11,795	11,966	11,418	11,171	11,950	12,493	13,327	14,351
Military technologies	357	952	42	255	183	19	27	7	3	2	7	21	3	6	10	40
Multi/interdisciplinary studies	6,346	13,778	13,061	13,829	17,879	25,652	26,598	27,149	26,960	27,545	28,561	27,189	28,943	28,757	29,162	30,243
Parks, recreation, leisure and fitness studies	1,621	5,182	5,729	4,623	4,315	10,821	12,037	12,974	15,422	16,532	17,571	17,948	18,885	21,428	22,164	22,888
Philosophy and religious studies	8,149	8,447	6,776	6,396	7,423	7,684	7,471	7,541	8,384	8,506	8,535	8,717	9,473	10,344	11,152	11,584
Physical sciences and science technologies	21,410	21,458	23,936	21,711	16,334	18,392	19,161	19,627	19,362	18,285	18,331	17,919	17,799	17,940	17,983	18,905
Precision production	0	0	0	2	2	2	1	12	52	43	33	31	47	42	61	64
Psychology	38,187	50,278	41,068	40,628	58,655	69,419	72,233	73,416	74,107	73,636	74,194	73,645	76,775	78,613	82,098	85,614
Public administration and social services	5,466	15,440	16,707	11,887	14,350	17,815	18,586	19,849	20,408	20,287	20,185	19,447	19,392	19,878	20,552	21,769
Security and protective services	2,045	12,507	13,707	12,704	16,806	23,009	24,157	24,810	25,076	24,601	24,877	25,211	25,536	26,189	28,175	30,723
Social sciences and history	155,324	126,396	100,513	93,840	125,107	133,680	128,154	126,479	125,040	124,658	127,101	128,036	132,874	143,218	150,357	156,892
Theology and religious vocations	3,720	5,490	5,808	5,510	4,799	5,377	5,555	5,292	5,855	6,235	6,789	6,945	7,762	7,926	8,126	9,284
Transportation and materials moving	0	225	263	1,838	2,622	3,923	3,698	3,561	3,206	3,383	3,395	3,748	4,020	4,567	4,824	4,904
Visual and performing arts	30,394	42,138	40,479	37,241	42,186	49,053	48,690	49,296	52,077	54,404	58,791	61,148	66,773	71,474	77,181	80,955
Not classified by field of study	0	0	0	0	13,258	3,302	1,346	1,756	1,373	5	2,398	783	264	0	0	0

NOTE: The new Classification of Instructional Programs was initiated in 2002–03. The figures for earlier years have been reclassified when necessary to make them conform to the new taxonomy. To facilitate trend comparisons, certain aggregations have been made of the degree fields as reported in the IPEDS "Completions Survey": "Agriculture and natural resources" includes Agriculture, agriculture operations, and related sciences and Natural resources and conservation; "Business" includes Business, management, marketing, and related support services and Personal and culinary services; and "Engineering technologies" includes Engineering technologies/technicians, Construction trades, and Mechanic and repair technologies/technicians.

SOURCE: U.S. Department of Education, National Center for Education Statistics, Higher Education General Information Survey (HEGIS), "Degrees and Other Formal Awards Conferred" surveys, 1970–71 through 1985–86; and 1990–91 through 2004–05 Integrated Postsecondary Education Data System, "Completions Survey" (IPEDS-C:91–99), and Fall 2000 through Fall 2005. (This table was prepared July 2006.)

Table 255. Master's degrees conferred by degree-granting institutions, by discipline division: Selected years, 1970–71 through 2004–05

Discipline division	1970–71	1975–76	1980–81	1985–86	1990–91	1993–94	1994–95	1995–96	1997–98	1998–99	1999–2000	2000–01	2001–02	2002–03	2003–04	2004–05
1	2	3	4	5	6	7	8	9	10	11	12	13	14	15	16	17
Total	**230,509**	**311,771**	**295,739**	**288,567**	**337,168**	**387,070**	**397,629**	**406,301**	**430,164**	**439,986**	**457,056**	**468,476**	**482,118**	**512,645**	**558,940**	**574,618**
Agriculture and natural resources	2,457	3,340	4,003	3,801	3,295	4,110	4,234	4,551	4,464	4,404	4,360	4,272	4,503	4,492	4,783	4,746
Architecture and related services	1,705	3,215	3,153	3,260	3,490	3,943	3,923	3,993	4,347	4,172	4,268	4,302	4,566	4,925	5,424	5,674
Area, ethnic, cultural, and gender studies	1,032	993	802	915	1,233	1,573	1,585	1,652	1,528	1,438	1,544	1,555	1,541	1,509	1,683	1,755
Biological and biomedical sciences	5,623	6,453	5,759	5,043	4,796	5,390	5,824	6,544	6,788	6,913	6,781	6,955	6,937	6,990	7,657	8,199
Business	26,490	42,592	57,888	66,676	78,255	93,285	93,540	93,554	101,652	107,477	111,532	115,602	119,725	127,545	139,347	142,617
Communication, journalism, and related programs	1,770	2,961	2,896	3,500	4,123	5,005	5,142	5,080	5,611	5,293	5,169	5,218	5,510	6,053	6,535	6,762
Communications technologies	86	165	209	308	204	383	417	481	486	263	356	427	470	442	365	433
Computer and information sciences	1,588	2,603	4,218	8,070	9,324	10,568	10,595	10,579	11,765	12,858	14,990	16,911	17,173	19,503	20,143	18,416
Education	87,666	126,061	96,713	74,816	87,352	97,427	99,835	104,936	113,374	118,048	123,045	127,829	135,189	147,448	162,345	167,490
Engineering	16,813	16,472	16,893	21,529	24,454	28,293	28,137	26,892	25,146	24,734	24,850	25,259	24,908	32,337	32,698	32,633
Engineering technologies	134	328	323	617	996	1,879	1,894	2,054	2,181	2,004	1,876	2,013	2,149	2,332	2,499	2,500
English language and literature/letters	10,441	8,599	5,742	5,335	6,784	7,611	7,612	7,657	7,587	7,288	7,022	6,763	7,097	7,413	7,956	8,468
Family and consumer sciences/human sciences	1,452	2,179	2,570	2,011	1,541	1,559	1,702	1,712	1,838	1,736	1,882	1,838	1,683	1,610	1,794	1,827
Foreign languages, literatures, and linguistics	5,480	4,432	2,934	2,690	3,049	3,612	3,439	3,443	3,181	3,106	3,037	3,035	3,075	3,049	3,124	3,407
Health professions and related clinical sciences	5,330	12,164	16,176	18,603	21,354	28,442	31,770	33,920	39,567	40,707	42,593	43,623	43,560	42,715	44,939	46,703
Legal professions and studies	955	1,442	1,832	1,924	2,057	2,432	2,511	2,751	3,228	3,308	3,750	3,829	4,053	4,126	4,243	4,170
Liberal arts and sciences, general studies, and humanities	885	2,633	2,375	1,586	2,213	2,496	2,565	2,778	2,801	3,101	3,256	3,193	2,754	3,312	3,697	3,680
Library science	7,001	8,037	4,859	3,564	4,763	5,116	5,057	5,099	4,871	4,752	4,577	4,727	5,113	5,314	6,015	6,213
Mathematics and statistics	5,191	3,857	2,567	3,131	3,549	3,682	3,820	3,651	3,409	3,286	3,208	3,209	3,350	3,626	4,191	4,477
Military technologies	2	0	43	83	0	124	124	136	0	0	0	0	0	0	0	0
Multi/interdisciplinary studies	926	1,287	2,363	2,890	2,117	2,821	2,787	2,762	3,067	3,073	3,487	3,475	3,708	3,780	4,047	4,252
Parks, recreation, leisure, and fitness studies	218	571	643	570	483	1,559	1,684	1,684	1,917	2,011	2,322	2,354	2,580	2,978	3,199	3,740
Philosophy and religious studies	1,326	1,358	1,231	1,193	1,471	1,410	1,434	1,363	1,396	1,357	1,376	1,386	1,371	1,578	1,578	1,647
Physical sciences and science technologies	6,336	5,428	5,246	5,860	5,281	5,648	5,716	5,807	5,328	5,124	4,810	5,049	5,012	5,109	5,570	5,678
Precision production	0	0	0	0	0	2	5	8	10	7	5	2	2	3	13	6
Psychology	5,717	10,167	10,223	9,845	11,349	13,723	15,378	15,152	15,142	15,688	15,740	16,539	16,357	17,123	17,898	18,830
Public administration and social services	7,785	15,209	17,803	15,692	17,905	21,833	23,501	24,229	25,144	24,925	25,594	25,268	25,448	25,894	28,250	29,552
Security and protective services	194	1,197	1,538	1,074	1,108	1,437	1,706	1,812	2,000	2,249	2,609	2,514	2,935	2,955	3,717	3,991
Social sciences and history	16,539	15,953	11,945	10,564	12,233	14,561	14,845	15,012	14,938	14,431	14,066	13,791	14,112	14,634	16,110	16,952
Theology and religious vocations	2,692	3,258	4,163	4,543	4,803	4,906	5,170	5,030	4,649	4,679	5,534	4,850	4,909	5,099	5,486	5,815
Transportation and materials moving	0	0	0	454	406	664	823	919	736	713	697	756	709	765	728	802
Visual and performing arts	6,675	8,817	8,629	8,420	8,657	9,925	10,277	10,280	11,145	10,753	10,918	11,404	11,595	11,986	12,906	13,183
Not classified by field of study	0	0	0	0	8,523	1,651	577	780	868	88	1,802	528	24	0	0	0

NOTE: The new Classification of Instructional Programs was initiated in 2002–03. The figures for earlier years have been reclassified when necessary to make them conform to the new taxonomy. To facilitate trend comparisons, certain aggregations have been made of the degree fields as reported in the IPEDS "Completions Survey": "Agriculture and natural resources" includes Agriculture, agriculture operations, and related sciences and Natural resources and conservation; "Business" includes Business, management, marketing, and related support services and Personal and culinary services; and

"Engineering technologies" includes Engineering technologies/technicians, Construction trades, and Mechanic and repair technologies/technicians.
SOURCE: U.S. Department of Education, National Center for Education Statistics, Higher Education General Information Survey (HEGIS), "Degrees and Other Formal Awards Conferred" surveys, 1970–71 through 1985–86; and 1990–91 through 2004–05 Integrated Postsecondary Education Data System, "Completions Survey" (IPEDS-C:91–99), and Fall 2000 through Fall 2005. (This table was prepared July 2006.)

Table 256. Doctor's degrees conferred by degree-granting institutions, by discipline division: Selected years, 1970–71 through 2004–05

Discipline division	1970–71	1975–76	1980–81	1985–86	1990–91	1993–94	1994–95	1995–96	1997–98	1998–99	1999–2000	2000–01	2001–02	2002–03	2003–04	2004–05
1	2	3	4	5	6	7	8	9	10	11	12	13	14	15	16	17
Total	**32,107**	**34,064**	**32,958**	**33,653**	**39,294**	**43,185**	**44,446**	**44,652**	**46,010**	**44,077**	**44,808**	**44,904**	**44,160**	**46,024**	**48,378**	**52,631**
Agriculture and natural resources	1,086	928	1,067	1,158	1,185	1,262	1,256	1,259	1,290	1,231	1,168	1,127	1,148	1,229	1,185	1,173
Architecture and related services	36	82	93	73	135	161	141	141	131	123	129	153	183	152	173	179
Area, ethnic, cultural, and gender studies	143	186	161	156	159	149	185	183	176	187	205	216	212	186	209	189
Biological and biomedical sciences	3,595	3,313	3,591	3,352	4,034	4,724	4,881	5,035	5,236	5,024	5,180	4,953	4,823	5,003	5,242	5,578
Business	774	906	808	923	1,185	1,364	1,391	1,366	1,290	1,201	1,194	1,180	1,156	1,251	1,481	1,498
Communication, journalism, and related programs	145	196	171	212	259	337	320	338	354	347	347	368	374	394	418	465
Communications technologies	0	8	11	6	13	8	1	7	5	5	10	2	9	4	8	3
Computer and information sciences	128	244	252	344	676	810	887	869	858	801	779	768	752	816	909	1,119
Education	6,041	7,202	7,279	6,610	6,189	6,450	6,475	6,246	6,261	6,394	6,409	6,284	6,549	6,835	7,088	7,681
Engineering	3,687	2,872	2,598	3,444	5,316	5,968	6,122	6,381	5,996	5,432	5,390	5,542	5,187	5,276	5,923	6,547
Engineering technologies	1	2	10	12	14	43	51	50	42	29	31	62	58	57	58	54
English language and literature/letters	1,554	1,514	1,040	895	1,056	1,205	1,393	1,395	1,489	1,407	1,470	1,330	1,291	1,246	1,207	1,212
Family and consumer sciences/human sciences	123	178	247	307	229	318	346	375	386	323	327	354	311	372	329	331
Foreign languages, literatures, and linguistics	1,084	1,245	931	768	889	1,033	1,081	1,020	1,118	1,049	1,086	1,078	1,003	1,042	1,031	1,027
Health professions and related clinical sciences	518	617	868	1,139	1,534	1,552	1,653	1,651	1,975	1,920	2,053	2,242	2,913	3,328	4,361	5,868
Legal professions and studies	20	76	60	54	90	79	88	91	66	58	74	286	79	105	119	98
Liberal arts and sciences, general studies, and humanities	32	162	121	90	70	80	90	75	87	78	83	102	113	78	95	109
Library science	39	71	71	62	56	45	55	53	48	55	68	58	45	62	47	42
Mathematics and statistics	1,199	856	728	742	978	1,125	1,181	1,158	1,215	1,090	1,075	997	923	1,007	1,060	1,176
Multi/interdisciplinary studies	109	190	285	405	424	505	530	764	843	754	792	784	765	899	876	983
Parks, recreation, leisure, and fitness studies	2	15	42	39	28	116	149	104	129	137	134	177	151	199	222	207
Philosophy and religious studies	555	556	411	480	464	534	508	550	590	584	598	600	610	662	595	586
Physical sciences and science technologies	4,324	3,388	3,105	3,521	4,248	4,595	4,421	4,512	4,520	4,142	3,963	3,911	3,760	3,858	3,815	4,114
Psychology	2,144	3,157	3,576	3,593	3,932	4,021	4,252	4,141	4,541	4,695	4,731	5,091	4,759	4,831	4,827	5,106
Public administration and social services	174	292	362	382	430	519	556	499	499	532	537	574	571	596	649	673
Security and protective services	1	9	21	21	28	25	26	38	39	48	52	44	49	72	54	94
Social sciences and history	3,660	4,157	3,122	2,955	3,012	3,627	3,725	3,760	4,127	3,855	4,095	3,930	3,902	3,850	3,811	3,819
Theology and religious vocations	312	1,022	1,273	1,185	1,076	1,440	1,583	1,517	1,451	1,440	1,630	1,461	1,350	1,321	1,304	1,422
Transportation and materials moving	0	0	0	3	0	0	0	0	0	0	0	0	0	0	0	0
Visual and performing arts	621	620	654	722	838	1,054	1,080	1,067	1,163	1,130	1,127	1,167	1,114	1,293	1,282	1,278
Not classified by field of study	0	0	0	0	747	36	19	7	85	6	71	63	0	0	0	0

NOTE: Includes Ph.D., Ed.D., and comparable degrees at the doctoral level. Excludes first-professional degrees such as M.D., D.D.S., and law degrees. The new Classification of Instructional Programs was initiated in 2002–03. The figures for earlier years have been reclassified when necessary to make them conform to the new taxonomy. To facilitate trend comparisons, certain aggregations have been made of the degree fields as reported in the IPEDS "Completions Survey." "Agriculture and natural resources" includes Agriculture, agriculture operations, and related sciences and Natural resources and conservation; "Business" includes Business, management, marketing, and related support services and Personal and culinary services; and "Engineering technologies" includes Engineering technologies/technicians, Construction trades, and Mechanic and repair technologies/technicians.

SOURCE: U.S. Department of Education, National Center for Education Statistics, Higher Education General Information Survey (HEGIS) "Degrees and Other Formal Awards Conferred" surveys, 1970–71 through 1985–86; and 1990–91 through 2004–05 Integrated Postsecondary Education Data System, "Completions Survey" (IPEDS-C:91–99), and Fall 2000 through Fall 2005. (This table was prepared April 2006.)

Table 257. Bachelor's, master's, and doctor's degrees conferred by degree-granting institutions, by field of study and year: Selected years, 1970–71 through 2004–05

	Number of degrees conferred								Percentage distribution of degrees conferred							
Degree and school year	Total degrees	Humanities[1]	Social and behavioral sciences[2]	Natural sciences[3]	Computer sciences and engineering[4]	Education	Business	Other fields[5]	Total degrees	Humanities[1]	Social and behavioral sciences[2]	Natural sciences[3]	Computer sciences and engineering[4]	Education	Business	Other fields[5]
1	2	3	4	5	6	7	8	9	10	11	12	13	14	15	16	17
Bachelor's degrees																
1970–71	839,730	143,571	193,511	81,894	52,570	176,307	115,396	76,481	100.0	17.1	23.0	9.8	6.3	21.0	13.7	9.1
1975–76	925,746	150,805	176,674	91,527	52,328	154,437	143,171	156,804	100.0	16.3	19.1	9.9	5.7	16.7	15.5	16.9
1980–81	935,140	134,214	141,581	78,017	90,476	108,074	200,521	182,257	100.0	14.4	15.1	8.3	9.7	11.6	21.4	19.5
1985–86	987,823	132,966	134,468	76,153	139,459	87,147	236,700	180,930	100.0	13.5	13.6	7.7	14.1	8.8	24.0	18.3
1990–91	1,094,538	172,590	183,762	70,104	104,910	110,807	249,165	203,200	100.0	15.8	16.8	6.4	9.6	10.1	22.8	18.6
1995–96	1,164,792	193,668	199,895	93,090	102,592	105,384	226,623	243,540	100.0	16.6	17.2	8.0	8.8	9.0	19.5	20.9
2000–01	1,244,171	214,818	201,681	88,955	117,117	105,458	263,515	252,627	100.0	17.3	16.2	7.1	9.4	8.5	21.2	20.3
2001–02	1,291,900	227,307	209,649	89,164	125,044	106,295	278,217	256,224	100.0	17.6	16.2	6.9	9.7	8.2	21.5	19.8
2002–03	1,348,503	235,922	221,831	90,505	134,706	105,790	293,545	266,204	100.0	17.5	16.5	6.7	10.0	7.8	21.8	19.7
2003–04	1,399,542	246,646	232,455	92,819	137,715	106,278	307,149	276,480	100.0	17.6	16.6	6.6	9.8	7.6	21.9	19.8
2004–05	1,439,264	256,151	242,506	97,867	133,854	105,451	311,574	291,861	100.0	17.8	16.8	6.8	9.3	7.3	21.6	20.3
Master's degrees																
1970–71	230,509	29,457	22,256	17,150	18,535	87,666	26,490	28,955	100.0	12.8	9.7	7.4	8.0	38.0	11.5	12.6
1975–76	311,771	31,377	26,120	15,738	19,403	126,061	42,592	50,480	100.0	10.1	8.4	5.0	6.2	40.4	13.7	16.2
1980–81	295,739	28,239	22,168	13,572	21,434	96,713	57,888	55,725	100.0	9.5	7.5	4.6	7.2	32.7	19.6	18.8
1985–86	288,567	27,572	20,409	14,034	30,216	74,816	66,676	54,844	100.0	9.6	7.1	4.9	10.5	25.9	23.1	19.0
1990–91	337,168	30,327	23,582	13,626	34,774	87,352	78,255	69,252	100.0	9.0	7.0	4.0	10.3	25.9	23.2	20.5
1995–96	406,301	34,965	30,164	16,002	39,525	104,936	93,554	87,155	100.0	8.6	7.4	3.9	9.7	25.8	23.0	21.5
2000–01	468,476	35,661	30,330	15,213	44,183	127,829	115,602	99,658	100.0	7.6	6.5	3.2	9.4	27.3	24.7	21.3
2001–02	482,118	36,050	30,469	15,299	44,230	135,189	119,725	101,156	100.0	7.5	6.3	3.2	9.2	28.0	24.8	21.0
2002–03	512,645	37,726	31,757	15,725	50,172	147,448	127,545	102,272	100.0	7.4	6.2	3.1	9.8	28.8	24.9	19.9
2003–04	558,940	40,477	34,008	17,418	55,340	162,345	139,347	110,005	100.0	7.2	6.1	3.1	9.9	29.0	24.9	19.7
2004–05	574,618	42,207	35,782	18,354	53,549	167,490	142,617	114,619	100.0	7.3	6.2	3.2	9.3	29.1	24.8	19.9
Doctor's degrees																
1970–71	32,107	4,410	5,804	9,118	3,816	6,041	774	2,144	100.0	13.7	18.1	28.4	11.9	18.8	2.4	6.7
1975–76	34,064	5,495	7,314	7,557	3,118	7,202	906	2,472	100.0	16.1	21.5	22.2	9.2	21.1	2.7	7.3
1980–81	32,958	4,876	6,698	7,424	2,860	7,279	808	3,013	100.0	14.8	20.3	22.5	8.7	22.1	2.5	9.1
1985–86	33,653	4,701	6,548	7,615	3,800	6,610	923	3,456	100.0	14.0	19.5	22.6	11.3	19.6	2.7	10.3
1990–91	39,294	4,976	6,944	9,260	6,006	6,189	1,185	4,734	100.0	12.7	17.7	23.6	15.3	15.8	3.0	12.0
1995–96	44,652	6,571	7,901	10,705	7,300	6,246	1,366	4,563	100.0	14.7	17.7	24.0	16.3	14.0	3.1	10.2
2000–01	44,904	6,738	9,021	9,861	6,372	6,284	1,180	5,448	100.0	15.0	20.1	22.0	14.2	14.0	2.6	12.1
2001–02	44,160	6,458	8,661	9,506	5,997	6,549	1,156	5,833	100.0	14.6	19.6	21.5	13.6	14.8	2.6	13.2
2002–03	46,024	6,727	8,681	9,868	6,149	6,835	1,251	6,513	100.0	14.6	18.9	21.4	13.4	14.9	2.7	14.2
2003–04	48,378	6,599	8,638	10,117	6,890	7,088	1,481	7,565	100.0	13.6	17.9	20.9	14.2	14.7	3.1	15.6
2004–05	52,631	6,806	8,925	10,868	7,720	7,681	1,498	9,133	100.0	12.9	17.0	20.6	14.7	14.6	2.8	17.4

[1]Includes degrees in area, ethnic, cultural, and gender studies; English language and literature/letters; foreign languages, literatures, and linguistics; liberal arts and sciences, general studies and humanities; multi/interdisciplinary studies; philosophy and religious studies; theology and religious vocations; and visual and performing arts.
[2]Includes psychology; and social sciences and history.
[3]Includes biological and biomedical sciences; mathematics and statistics; and physical sciences and science technologies.
[4]Includes computer and information sciences; engineering; and engineering technologies.
[5]Includes agriculture and natural resources; architecture and related services; communication, journalism, and related programs; communications technologies; family and consumer sciences/human sciences; health professions and related clinical

sciences; legal professions and studies; library science; military technologies; parks, recreation, leisure, and fitness studies; precision production; public administration and social services; security and protective services; transportation and materials moving; and not classified by field of study.
SOURCE: U.S. Department of Education, National Center for Education Statistics, Higher Education General Information Survey (HEGIS), "Degrees and Other Formal Awards Conferred" surveys, 1970–71 through 1985–86; and 1990–91 through 2004–05 Integrated Postsecondary Education Data System, "Completions Survey" (IPEDS-C:91–99), and Fall 2000 through Fall 2005. (This table was prepared August 2006.)

Table 258. Bachelor's, master's, and doctor's degrees conferred by degree-granting institutions, by sex of student and field of study: 2004–05

Field of study	Bachelor's degrees requiring 4 or 5 years			Master's degrees			Doctor's degrees (Ph.D., Ed.D., etc.)		
	Total	Males	Females	Total	Males	Females	Total	Males	Females
1	2	3	4	5	6	7	8	9	10
All fields, total	1,439,264	613,000	826,264	574,618	233,590	341,028	52,631	26,973	25,658
Agriculture and natural resources	23,002	11,987	11,015	4,746	2,288	2,458	1,173	763	410
Agriculture, agriculture operations, and related sciences	14,453	7,366	7,087	2,229	1,111	1,118	743	491	252
Agriculture, general	1,482	877	605	259	120	139	8	5	3
Agricultural business and management, general	984	622	362	70	43	27	0	0	0
Agribusiness/agricultural business operations	1,539	1,007	532	39	26	13	0	0	0
Agricultural economics	892	628	264	406	224	182	138	96	42
Farm/farm and ranch management	112	86	26	4	2	2	0	0	0
Agricultural/farm supplies retailing and wholesaling	86	53	33	0	0	0	0	0	0
Agricultural business technology	0	0	0	2	0	2	0	0	0
Agricultural business and management, other	424	250	174	0	0	0	0	0	0
Agricultural mechanization, general	274	259	15	2	2	0	0	0	0
Agricultural power machinery operation	0	0	0	0	0	0	0	0	0
Agricultural mechanics and equipment/machine technology	0	0	0	1	1	0	0	0	0
Agricultural mechanization, other	12	12	0	0	0	0	0	0	0
Agricultural production operations, general	52	38	14	18	13	5	0	0	0
Animal/livestock husbandry and production	161	63	98	0	0	0	0	0	0
Aquaculture	49	34	15	39	26	13	7	7	0
Crop production	30	24	6	14	7	7	3	3	0
Horse husbandry/equine science and management	0	0	0	0	0	0	0	0	0
Agricultural and food products processing	130	90	40	8	4	4	4	4	0
Equestrian/equine studies	616	47	569	1	0	1	0	0	0
Applied horticulture/horticultural operations, general	172	106	66	14	7	7	4	2	2
Ornamental horticulture	159	106	53	7	2	5	3	3	0
Landscaping and groundskeeping	166	102	64	1	0	1	0	0	0
Turf and turfgrass management	119	113	6	0	0	0	0	0	0
Floriculture/floristry operations and management	0	0	0	0	0	0	0	0	0
Applied horticulture/horicultural business services, other	11	10	1	0	0	0	0	0	0
International agriculture	9	2	7	14	6	8	0	0	0
Agricultural and extension education services	31	18	13	32	17	15	6	3	3
Agricultural communication/journalism	202	51	151	15	4	11	0	0	0
Agricultural public services, other	34	15	19	0	0	0	0	0	0
Animal sciences, general	3,504	952	2,552	342	150	192	136	89	47
Agricultural animal breeding	45	29	16	12	5	7	8	5	3
Animal health	0	0	0	9	2	7	0	0	0
Animal nutrition	0	0	0	3	1	2	5	5	0
Dairy science	105	57	48	13	5	8	5	5	0
Livestock management	8	2	6	0	0	0	0	0	0
Poultry science	105	65	40	18	7	11	8	6	2
Animal sciences, other	155	30	125	9	4	5	6	3	3
Food science	630	185	445	234	76	158	111	57	54
Food technology and processing	4	3	1	2	1	1	0	0	0
Food science and technology, other	7	4	3	15	5	10	7	2	5
Plant sciences, general	345	228	117	94	56	38	31	23	8
Agronomy and crop science	432	347	85	165	113	52	84	62	22
Horticultural science	817	488	329	92	32	60	52	33	19
Agricultural and horticultural plant breeding	0	0	0	13	10	3	8	7	1
Plant protection and integrated pest management	18	14	4	14	7	7	2	2	0
Range science and management	110	65	45	41	24	17	16	10	6
Plant sciences, other	59	37	22	48	24	24	18	9	9
Soil science and agronomy, general	116	87	29	120	63	57	60	41	19
Soil sciences, other	8	5	3	9	3	6	2	2	0
Agriculture, agriculture operations, and related sciences, other	239	155	84	30	19	11	11	7	4
Natural resources and conservation	8,459	4,621	3,928	2,517	1,777	1,340	430	272	158
Natural resources/conservation, general	1,033	562	471	300	135	165	56	39	17
Environmental studies	2,719	1,204	1,515	493	183	310	40	23	17
Environmental science	1,813	884	929	611	290	321	99	56	43
Environmental science/studies	0	0	0	0	0	0	0	0	0
Natural resources conservation and research, other	0	0	0	0	0	0	1	1	0
Natural resources management and policy	322	185	137	283	124	159	26	16	10
Natural resource economics	16	8	8	2	1	1	3	2	1
Water, wetlands, and marine resources management	31	15	16	26	9	17	0	0	0
Land use planning and management/development	33	17	16	36	14	22	6	5	1
Natural resources management and policy, other	79	52	27	5	3	2	0	0	0
Fishing and fisheries sciences and management	233	145	88	75	35	40	28	16	12
Forestry, general	629	476	153	305	153	152	72	45	27
Forest sciences and biology	157	129	28	85	56	29	28	21	7
Forest management/forest resources management	128	114	14	21	16	5	1	1	0
Urban forestry	48	28	20	17	8	9	0	0	0
Wood science and wood products/pulp and paper technology	115	98	17	19	17	2	5	5	0
Forest resources production and management	5	4	1	16	11	5	5	4	1
Forest technology/technician	9	9	0	0	0	0	10	6	4
Forestry, other	46	35	11	14	11	3	1	1	0
Wildlife and wildlands science and management	943	555	388	167	93	74	43	25	18
Natural resources and conservation, other	190	101	89	42	18	24	6	6	0

See notes at end of table.

Table 258. Bachelor's, master's, and doctor's degrees conferred by degree-granting institutions, by sex of student and field of study: 2004–05—Continued

Field of study	Bachelor's degrees requiring 4 or 5 years			Master's degrees			Doctor's degrees (Ph.D., Ed.D., etc.)		
	Total	Males	Females	Total	Males	Females	Total	Males	Females
1	2	3	4	5	6	7	8	9	10
Architecture and related services	9,237	5,222	4,015	5,674	3,180	2,494	179	110	69
Architecture	5,543	3,393	2,150	3,056	1,889	1,167	88	61	27
City/urban, community and regional planning	587	370	217	1,988	1,028	960	73	43	30
Environmental design/architecture	825	488	337	13	5	8	14	4	10
Interior architecture	785	70	715	26	3	23	0	0	0
Landscape architecture	1,026	622	404	464	198	266	0	0	0
Architectural history and criticism, general	40	20	20	17	4	13	3	1	2
Architectural technology/technician	8	6	2	0	0	0	0	0	0
Architecture and related services, other	423	253	170	110	53	57	1	1	0
Area, ethnic, cultural, and gender studies	7,569	2,307	5,262	1,755	669	1,086	189	81	108
African studies	35	11	24	31	13	18	2	0	2
American/United States studies/civilization	1,671	595	1,076	269	106	163	87	38	49
Asian studies/civilization	532	238	294	95	45	50	0	0	0
East Asian studies	326	151	175	106	50	56	9	7	2
Central/Middle and Eastern European studies	9	2	7	12	5	7	0	0	0
European studies/civilization	118	26	92	22	7	15	0	0	0
Latin American studies	550	153	397	247	95	152	4	1	3
Near and Middle Eastern studies	178	76	102	102	55	47	37	19	18
Pacific Area/Pacific rim studies	16	5	11	10	2	8	0	0	0
Russian studies	83	33	50	62	28	34	0	0	0
Scandinavian studies	18	6	12	6	5	1	0	0	0
South Asian studies	11	4	7	18	8	10	4	3	1
Southeast Asian studies	2	1	1	16	8	8	0	0	0
Western European studies	11	1	10	47	19	28	2	1	1
Canadian studies	2	0	2	0	0	0	0	0	0
Slavic studies	3	0	3	0	0	0	0	0	0
Ural-Altaic and Central Asian studies	0	0	0	9	4	5	2	1	1
Regional studies (U.S., Canadian, foreign)	4	1	3	1	0	1	1	0	1
Chinese studies	11	4	7	11	6	5	0	0	0
French studies	39	5	34	2	1	1	4	1	3
German studies	35	12	23	0	0	0	0	0	0
Italian studies	31	8	23	4	1	3	0	0	0
Japanese studies	37	19	18	7	3	4	0	0	0
Korean studies	0	0	0	4	0	4	0	0	0
Spanish and Iberian studies	13	5	8	0	0	0	0	0	0
Area studies, other	504	178	326	75	37	38	0	0	0
African-American/Black studies	738	247	491	99	34	65	13	5	8
American Indian/Native American studies	156	58	98	34	12	22	4	1	3
Hispanic-American, Puerto Rican, and Mexican-American/Chicano studies	282	93	189	43	20	23	4	1	3
Asian-American studies	164	69	95	7	4	3	0	0	0
Women's studies	1,079	26	1,053	154	1	153	5	0	5
Gay/lesbian studies	3	0	3	0	0	0	0	0	0
Ethnic, cultural minority, and gender studies, other	455	130	325	72	24	48	7	2	5
Area, ethnic, cultural, and gender studies, other	453	150	303	190	76	114	4	1	3
Biological and biomedical sciences	64,611	24,617	39,994	8,199	3,318	4,881	5,578	2,845	2,733
Biology/biological sciences, general	45,540	16,707	28,833	2,564	1,009	1,555	712	356	356
Biomedical sciences, general	1,143	450	693	154	62	92	151	64	87
Biochemistry	3,957	1,861	2,096	249	115	134	456	258	198
Biophysics	71	41	30	46	30	16	103	64	39
Molecular biology	475	210	265	144	69	75	212	101	111
Molecular biochemistry	226	103	123	21	6	15	55	31	24
Molecular biophysics	0	0	0	0	0	0	9	3	6
Structural biology	0	0	0	9	4	5	1	1	0
Radiation biology/radiobiology	7	0	7	16	14	2	4	0	4
Biochemistry/biophysics and molecular biology	414	192	222	96	58	38	92	49	43
Biochemistry, biophysics, and molecular biology, other	58	22	36	2	1	1	7	2	5
Botany/plant biology	207	81	126	86	33	53	120	68	52
Plant pathology/phytopathology	9	2	7	54	27	27	76	39	37
Plant physiology	0	0	0	7	4	3	17	9	8
Plant molecular biology	0	0	0	2	0	2	9	2	7
Botany/plant biology, other	22	11	11	6	4	2	7	3	4
Cell/cellular biology and histology	453	212	241	36	12	24	129	69	60
Anatomy	99	54	45	95	52	43	52	27	25
Developmental biology and embryology	0	0	0	11	6	5	25	11	14
Neuroanatomy	0	0	0	3	1	2	3	2	1
Cell/cellular and molecular biology	1,572	672	900	110	42	68	303	174	129
Cell biology and anatomy	2	0	2	8	4	4	18	10	8
Cell/cellular biology and anatomical sciences, other	272	124	148	110	42	68	100	50	50
Microbiology, general	1,553	621	932	212	77	135	166	86	80
Medical microbiology and bacteriology	638	267	371	96	36	60	206	96	110
Virology	0	0	0	6	3	3	20	10	10
Parasitology	0	0	0	1	0	1	1	1	0
Immunology	0	0	0	29	11	18	108	54	54
Microbiological sciences and immunology, other	127	46	81	46	15	31	109	41	68
Zoology/animal biology	1,797	652	1,145	123	42	81	101	53	48
Entomology	62	24	38	170	83	87	101	59	42
Animal physiology	170	58	112	73	27	46	62	36	26
Animal behavior and ethology	28	7	21	5	0	5	3	2	1

See notes at end of table.

Table 258. Bachelor's, master's, and doctor's degrees conferred by degree-granting institutions, by sex of student and field of study: 2004–05—Continued

Field of study	Bachelor's degrees requiring 4 or 5 years			Master's degrees			Doctor's degrees (Ph.D., Ed.D., etc.)		
	Total	Males	Females	Total	Males	Females	Total	Males	Females
1	2	3	4	5	6	7	8	9	10
Wildlife biology	95	62	33	11	5	6	1	0	1
Physiology, human and animal	0	0	0	0	0	0	0	0	0
Zoology/animal biology, other	7	1	6	2	1	1	0	0	0
Genetics, general	275	102	173	46	14	32	106	53	53
Molecular genetics	38	16	22	18	8	10	64	29	35
Animal genetics	87	42	45	41	10	31	58	28	30
Plant genetics	3	1	2	10	6	4	17	13	4
Human/medical genetics	0	0	0	99	15	84	71	40	31
Genetics, plant and animal	0	0	0	0	0	0	0	0	0
Genetics, other	0	0	0	3	1	2	2	1	1
Physiology, general	556	214	342	298	152	146	120	66	54
Molecular physiology	0	0	0	3	3	0	25	14	11
Cell physiology	0	0	0	7	3	4	16	7	9
Endocrinology	0	0	0	5	2	3	3	1	2
Reproductive biology	0	0	0	3	1	2	3	1	2
Neurobiology and neurophysiology	264	96	168	16	8	8	78	46	32
Cardiovascular science	0	0	0	0	0	0	3	2	1
Exercise physiology	227	89	138	49	21	28	1	1	0
Vision science/physiological optics	29	12	17	8	0	8	16	7	9
Pathology/experimental pathology	19	4	15	114	37	77	154	86	68
Oncology and cancer biology	0	0	0	10	2	8	59	24	35
Medical physiology	0	0	0	0	0	0	0	0	0
Physiology, pathology, and related sciences, other	30	17	13	9	3	6	15	10	5
Pharmacology	45	19	26	111	46	65	228	104	124
Molecular pharmacology	28	16	12	4	4	0	27	14	13
Neuropharmacology	0	0	0	3	2	1	0	0	0
Toxicology	30	15	15	60	25	35	80	38	42
Molecular toxicology	0	0	0	1	1	0	6	2	4
Environmental toxicology	15	5	10	11	2	9	28	14	14
Pharmacology and toxicology	28	13	15	34	14	20	26	10	16
Biometry/biometrics	16	8	8	21	9	12	18	13	5
Biostatistics	19	9	10	248	89	159	102	52	50
Bioinformatics	66	39	27	182	110	72	16	13	3
Biomathematics and bioinformatics, other	3	1	2	6	5	1	1	1	0
Biotechnology	369	167	202	442	176	266	4	3	1
Ecology	617	243	374	181	73	108	149	76	73
Marine biology and biological oceanography	819	252	567	128	44	84	35	16	19
Evolutionary biology	0	0	0	22	9	13	25	11	14
Aquatic biology/limnology	56	20	36	9	4	5	1	1	0
Environmental biology	251	111	140	32	19	13	11	7	4
Population biology	0	0	0	4	2	2	14	7	7
Conservation biology	102	48	54	24	8	16	0	0	0
Epidemiology	0	0	0	622	190	432	161	51	110
Ecology, evolution, systematics and population biology, other	312	128	184	38	16	22	43	20	23
Biological and biomedical sciences, other	1,303	450	853	674	289	385	253	132	121
Business, management, marketing, and personal and culinary services	311,574	155,940	155,634	142,617	82,151	60,466	1,498	901	597
Business, management, marketing, and related support services	310,987	155,637	155,350	142,617	82,151	60,466	1,498	901	597
Business/commerce, general	22,575	11,886	10,689	9,912	6,025	3,887	206	120	86
Business administration and management, general	119,467	58,840	60,627	82,165	49,977	32,188	666	434	232
Purchasing, procurement/acquisitions and contracts management	279	150	129	220	131	89	0	0	0
Logistics and materials management	1,197	842	355	237	163	74	0	0	0
Office management and supervision	479	188	291	13	5	8	0	0	0
Operations management and supervision	2,119	1,380	739	872	528	344	7	5	2
Nonprofit/public/organizational management	684	277	407	405	113	292	3	1	2
Customer service management	30	12	18	1	0	1	0	0	0
E-commerce/electronic commerce	351	236	115	655	394	261	4	3	1
Transportation/transportation management	61	43	18	19	15	4	0	0	0
Business administration, management and operations, other	5,961	3,158	2,803	2,847	1,688	1,159	28	18	10
Accounting	37,722	15,192	22,530	9,085	4,041	5,044	52	28	24
Accounting technology/technician and bookkeeping	79	43	36	2	1	1	0	0	0
Auditing	0	0	0	43	22	21	0	0	0
Accounting and finance	190	58	132	365	141	224	0	0	0
Accounting and business/management	397	137	260	56	24	32	0	0	0
Accounting and related services, other	342	170	172	244	146	98	2	0	2
Administrative assistant and secretarial science, general	48	6	42	0	0	0	0	0	0
Executive assistant/executive secretary	4	0	4	0	0	0	0	0	0
Business/office automation/technology/data entry	149	68	81	0	0	0	0	0	0
General office occupations and clerical services	0	0	0	0	0	0	0	0	0
Business operations support and secretarial services, other	63	34	29	62	31	31	0	0	0
Business/corporate communications	351	112	239	98	35	63	0	0	0
Business/managerial economics	4,065	2,600	1,465	289	165	124	57	40	17
Entrepreneurship/entrepreneurial studies	1,186	695	491	1,170	431	739	0	0	0
Small business administration/management	163	77	86	97	52	45	0	0	0
Entrepreneurial and small business operations, other	25	21	4	15	9	6	0	0	0
Finance, general	27,998	18,119	9,879	4,744	3,243	1,501	42	37	5
Banking and financial support services	467	268	199	148	116	32	1	1	0
Financial planning and services	245	181	64	214	131	83	0	0	0
International finance	13	5	8	95	45	50	0	0	0
Investments and securities	637	313	324	178	115	63	0	0	0

See notes at end of table.

Table 258. Bachelor's, master's, and doctor's degrees conferred by degree-granting institutions, by sex of student and field of study: 2004–05—Continued

Field of study	Bachelor's degrees requiring 4 or 5 years			Master's degrees			Doctor's degrees (Ph.D., Ed.D., etc.)		
	Total	Males	Females	Total	Males	Females	Total	Males	Females
1	2	3	4	5	6	7	8	9	10
Public finance	0	0	0	0	0	0	0	0	0
Finance and financial management services, other	255	142	113	419	288	131	0	0	0
Hospitality administration/management, general	3,593	1,431	2,162	250	95	155	9	3	6
Tourism and travel services management	422	173	249	139	64	75	0	0	0
Hotel/motel administration/management	1,565	615	950	111	46	65	12	5	7
Restaurant/food services management	301	164	137	2	0	2	0	0	0
Resort management	29	12	17	0	0	0	0	0	0
Hotel/motel and restaurant management	0	0	0	0	0	0	0	0	0
Hospitality administration/management, other	638	297	341	12	4	8	1	1	0
Human resources management/personnel administration, general	5,002	1,604	3,398	3,764	1,071	2,693	42	13	29
Labor and industrial relations	864	428	436	549	199	350	10	6	4
Organizational behavior studies	2,793	1,100	1,693	3,318	1,178	2,140	198	95	103
Labor studies	121	95	26	1	0	1	1	1	0
Human resources development	246	55	191	230	45	185	2	2	0
Human resources management and services, other	703	323	380	879	329	550	2	1	1
International business/trade/commerce	5,346	2,366	2,980	3,144	1,856	1,288	30	22	8
Management information systems, general	12,935	8,926	4,009	7,107	4,758	2,349	9	5	4
Information resources management/CIO training	105	77	28	178	132	46	6	4	2
Knowledge management	5	3	2	41	24	17	3	1	2
Management information systems and services, other	396	289	107	48	26	22	0	0	0
Management science, general	4,512	2,449	2,063	1,077	604	473	9	6	3
Business statistics	51	32	19	28	9	19	4	1	3
Actuarial science	369	216	153	82	47	35	0	0	0
Management sciences and quantitative methods, other	430	272	158	267	116	151	4	4	0
Marketing/marketing management, general	31,572	14,191	17,381	2,102	913	1,189	36	13	23
Marketing research	28	12	16	112	43	69	0	0	0
International marketing	26	7	19	93	33	60	0	0	0
Marketing, other	1,357	639	718	80	36	44	1	0	1
Real estate	788	545	243	398	315	83	1	1	0
Taxation	0	0	0	1,251	575	676	0	0	0
Insurance	622	379	243	104	71	33	1	0	1
Sales, distribution, and marketing operations, general	1,589	728	861	303	166	137	0	0	0
Merchandising and buying operations	149	36	113	7	1	6	0	0	0
Retailing and retail operations	209	56	153	6	0	6	0	0	0
Selling skills and sales operations	330	196	134	0	0	0	0	0	0
General merchandising/sales/related marketing operations, other	382	106	276	0	0	0	0	0	0
Fashion merchandising	1,580	55	1,525	43	4	39	0	0	0
Apparel and accessories marketing operations	98	7	91	6	2	4	0	0	0
Tourism and travel services marketing operations	41	13	28	0	0	0	0	0	0
Tourism promotion operations	69	14	55	0	0	0	0	0	0
Vehicle and vehicle parts and accessories marketing operations	105	81	24	0	0	0	0	0	0
Business and personal/financial services marketing operations	10	8	2	0	0	0	0	0	0
Special products marketing operations	99	45	54	18	10	8	0	0	0
Hospitality and recreation marketing operations	72	59	13	0	0	0	0	0	0
Specialized merchandising/sales/related marketing operations, other	144	30	114	25	11	14	0	0	0
Construction management	1,124	1,037	87	93	74	19	0	0	0
Business/management/marketing/related support services, other	2,565	1,213	1,352	2,079	1,219	860	49	30	19
Personal and culinary services	587	303	284	0	0	0	0	0	0
Funeral service and mortuary science, general	161	88	73	0	0	0	0	0	0
Cosmetology/cosmetologist, general	0	0	0	0	0	0	0	0	0
Baking and pastry arts/baker/pastry chef	48	8	40	0	0	0	0	0	0
Culinary arts/chef training	297	175	122	0	0	0	0	0	0
Restaurant, culinary, and catering management/manager	50	20	30	0	0	0	0	0	0
Meat cutting/meat cutter	1	1	0	0	0	0	0	0	0
Food service, waiter/waitress, and dining room management/manager	0	0	0	0	0	0	0	0	0
Institutional food workers	0	0	0	0	0	0	0	0	0
Institutional food workers and administrators, general	0	0	0	0	0	0	0	0	0
Culinary arts and related services, other	30	11	19	0	0	0	0	0	0
Communication and communications technologies	75,238	26,926	48,312	7,195	2,535	4,660	468	195	273
Communication, journalism, and related programs	72,715	25,324	47,391	6,762	2,262	4,500	465	194	271
Communication studies/speech communication and rhetoric	32,055	10,775	21,280	2,202	627	1,575	283	113	170
Mass communication/media studies	7,482	2,662	4,820	652	244	408	97	40	57
Communication and media studies, other	1,152	408	744	316	124	192	14	5	9
Journalism	11,664	3,650	8,014	1,477	543	934	17	9	8
Broadcast journalism	874	364	510	78	16	62	10	5	5
Photojournalism	159	47	112	0	0	0	0	0	0
Journalism, other	673	222	451	114	39	75	0	0	0
Radio and television	6,060	3,270	2,790	319	159	160	12	8	4
Digital communication and media/multimedia	707	430	277	158	82	76	16	8	8
Radio, television, and digital communication, other	190	108	82	5	2	3	0	0	0
Organizational communication, general	835	239	596	130	30	100	2	0	2
Public relations/image management	3,879	801	3,078	203	55	148	0	0	0
Advertising	4,148	1,213	2,935	183	49	134	8	6	2
Political communication	63	23	40	0	0	0	0	0	0
Health communication	7	0	7	16	0	16	0	0	0
Public relations, advertising and applied communication, other	287	77	210	45	11	34	0	0	0
Publishing	0	0	0	70	7	63	0	0	0
Communication, journalism, and related programs, other	2,480	1,035	1,445	794	274	520	6	0	6

See notes at end of table.

Table 258. Bachelor's, master's, and doctor's degrees conferred by degree-granting institutions, by sex of student and field of study: 2004–05—Continued

Field of study	Bachelor's degrees requiring 4 or 5 years			Master's degrees			Doctor's degrees (Ph.D., Ed.D., etc.)		
	Total	Males	Females	Total	Males	Females	Total	Males	Females
1	2	3	4	5	6	7	8	9	10
Communications technologies/technicians and support services	2,523	1,602	921	433	273	160	3	1	2
Communications technology/technician	82	42	40	19	10	9	0	0	0
Photographic and film/video technology/technician and assistant	18	12	6	0	0	0	0	0	0
Radio and television broadcasting technology/technician	602	318	284	143	70	73	3	1	2
Recording arts technology/technician	157	130	27	0	0	0	0	0	0
Audiovisual communications technologies/technicians, other	137	89	48	0	0	0	0	0	0
Graphic communications, general	97	43	54	0	0	0	0	0	0
Printing management	102	45	57	16	9	7	0	0	0
Prepress/desktop publishing and digital imaging design	34	18	16	0	0	0	0	0	0
Animation/interactive technology/video graphics/special effects	828	610	218	111	75	36	0	0	0
Graphic and printing equipment operator, general production	85	55	30	0	0	0	0	0	0
Printing press operator	12	5	7	0	0	0	0	0	0
Graphic communications, other	60	38	22	0	0	0	0	0	0
Communications technologies/technicians and support services, other	309	197	112	144	109	35	0	0	0
Computer and information sciences and support services	54,111	42,125	11,986	18,416	13,136	5,280	1,119	905	214
Computer and information sciences, general	18,986	15,136	3,850	7,371	5,489	1,882	541	437	104
Artificial intelligence and robotics	0	0	0	35	23	12	12	10	2
Information technology	6,051	4,571	1,480	672	442	230	7	5	2
Computer and information sciences, other	117	98	19	19	17	2	0	0	0
Computer programming/programmer, general	607	491	116	86	61	25	0	0	0
Computer programming, specific applications	38	26	12	28	17	11	0	0	0
Computer programming, other	65	53	12	0	0	0	0	0	0
Data processing and data processing technology/technician	335	249	86	9	5	4	0	0	0
Information science/studies	6,900	4,825	2,075	2,593	1,630	963	73	46	27
Computer systems analysis/analyst	2,273	1,634	639	276	175	101	10	7	3
Computer science	11,281	9,383	1,898	4,664	3,393	1,271	429	368	61
Web page, digital/multimedia, and information resources design	573	354	219	36	19	17	0	0	0
Data modeling/warehousing and database administration	49	33	16	0	0	0	0	0	0
Computer graphics	390	270	120	115	74	41	0	0	0
Computer software and media applications, other	95	71	24	46	29	17	0	0	0
Computer systems networking and telecommunications	3,234	2,608	626	749	560	189	1	1	0
System administration/administrator	71	61	10	12	7	5	0	0	0
System, networking, and LAN/WAN management/manager	95	81	14	0	0	0	0	0	0
Computer and information systems security	526	451	75	95	73	22	0	0	0
Web/multimedia management and webmaster	128	81	47	10	5	5	0	0	0
Computer/information tech. services admin. and management, other	669	503	166	512	348	164	0	0	0
Computer and information sciences and support services, other	1,628	1,146	482	1,088	769	319	46	31	15
Education	105,451	22,513	82,938	167,490	38,863	128,627	7,681	2,557	5,124
Education, general	2,363	410	1,953	25,837	6,018	19,819	1,437	462	975
Bilingual and multilingual	151	13	138	810	165	645	14	4	10
Multicultural education	0	0	0	99	8	91	23	8	15
Indian/Native American education	0	0	0	0	0	0	0	0	0
Bilingual, multilingual, and multicultural education, other	0	0	0	34	3	31	0	0	0
Curriculum and instruction	5	1	4	15,126	2,956	12,170	989	243	746
Educational leadership and administration, general	7	0	7	17,215	6,521	10,694	2,505	911	1,594
Administration of special education	0	0	0	28	4	24	3	0	3
Adult and continuing education administration	8	7	1	223	43	180	53	25	28
Educational, instructional, and curriculum supervision	75	23	52	1,135	384	751	18	5	13
Higher education/higher education administration	0	0	0	786	233	553	319	126	193
Community college education	0	0	0	14	3	11	2	2	0
Elementary and middle school administration/principalship	0	0	0	1,331	522	809	33	13	20
Secondary school administration/principalship	0	0	0	386	189	197	16	4	12
Urban education and leadership	53	13	40	355	104	251	19	4	15
Superintendency and educational system administration	0	0	0	72	35	37	17	6	11
Elementary, middle, and secondary education/administration	0	0	0	0	0	0	0	0	0
Educational administration and supervision, other	3	0	3	1,200	489	711	268	115	153
Educational/instructional media design	46	28	18	4,614	1,324	3,290	90	36	54
Educational evaluation and research	0	0	0	53	8	45	37	20	17
Educational statistics and research methods	0	0	0	25	11	14	17	4	13
Educational assessment, testing, and measurement	0	0	0	59	6	53	8	2	6
Educational assessment, evaluation, and research, other	0	0	0	29	7	22	1	1	0
International and comparative education	0	0	0	105	24	81	16	7	9
Social and philosophical foundations of education	2	0	2	1,433	313	1,120	108	35	73
Special education and teaching, general	6,315	729	5,586	10,651	1,718	8,933	150	26	124
Education/teaching of individuals with hearing impairments/deafness	166	4	162	170	13	157	3	2	1
Education/teaching of the gifted and talented	2	0	2	220	28	192	3	0	3
Education/teaching of individuals with emotional disturbances	98	12	86	125	24	101	26	2	24
Education/teaching of individuals with mental retardation	230	17	213	108	14	94	2	0	2
Education/teaching of individuals with multiple disabilities	77	7	70	308	34	274	0	0	0
Educ./teach. of individuals with orthopedic/physical health impair.	25	2	23	31	3	28	4	0	4
Education/teaching of individuals with vision impairments/blindness	34	2	32	77	9	68	0	0	0
Educ./teach. of individuals with specific learning disabilities	334	33	301	704	95	609	3	1	2
Education/teaching of individuals with speech/language impairments	289	11	278	178	5	173	0	0	0
Education/teaching of individuals with autism	0	0	0	3	0	3	0	0	0
Education/teaching of individuals who are developmentally delayed	0	0	0	3	0	3	0	0	0
Educ./teach. of individuals in early childhood spec. educ. programs	47	3	44	350	87	263	1	0	1
Special education and teaching, other	343	26	317	579	80	499	7	1	6
Counselor education/school counseling and guidance services	21	7	14	12,470	2,207	10,263	304	79	225

See notes at end of table.

Table 258. Bachelor's, master's, and doctor's degrees conferred by degree-granting institutions, by sex of student and field of study: 2004–05—Continued

Field of study	Bachelor's degrees requiring 4 or 5 years			Master's degrees			Doctor's degrees (Ph.D., Ed.D., etc.)		
	Total	Males	Females	Total	Males	Females	Total	Males	Females
1	2	3	4	5	6	7	8	9	10
College student counseling and personnel services	0	0	0	727	197	530	7	6	1
Student counseling and personnel services, other	3	0	3	171	30	141	3	0	3
Adult and continuing education and teaching	25	13	12	1,655	504	1,151	136	39	97
Elementary education and teaching	43,915	4,242	39,673	18,963	2,331	16,632	49	3	46
Junior high/intermediate/middle school education and teaching	2,402	540	1,862	1,235	287	948	0	0	0
Secondary education and teaching	4,255	1,717	2,538	7,478	2,764	4,714	32	6	26
Teacher education, multiple levels	995	131	864	3,834	820	3,014	22	5	17
Montessori teacher education	4	0	4	109	5	104	0	0	0
Waldorf/Steiner teacher education	2	0	2	0	0	0	0	0	0
Kindergarten/preschool education and teaching	2,187	66	2,121	1,008	86	922	2	1	1
Early childhood education and teaching	8,166	322	7,844	1,872	93	1,779	11	1	10
Pre-elementary/early childhood/kindergarten teacher education	0	0	0	0	0	0	0	0	0
Teacher educ. and prof. dev., specific levels and methods, other	318	44	274	4,376	879	3,497	70	23	47
Agricultural teacher education	610	283	327	378	140	238	54	28	26
Art teacher education	1,689	312	1,377	918	154	764	28	6	22
Business teacher education	640	252	388	337	96	241	2	2	0
Driver and safety teacher education	0	0	0	24	6	18	0	0	0
English/language arts teacher education	2,678	511	2,167	1,163	259	904	13	2	11
Foreign language teacher education	153	22	131	216	34	182	21	7	14
Health teacher education	1,615	448	1,167	558	149	409	51	7	44
Family and consumer sciences/home economics teacher education	366	10	356	82	3	79	5	0	5
Technology teacher education/industrial arts teacher education	795	638	157	435	286	149	9	7	2
Sales and marketing operations/marketing and dist. teacher educ.	59	21	38	119	59	60	0	0	0
Mathematics teacher education	1,741	600	1,141	1,174	415	759	45	17	28
Music teacher education	3,151	1,232	1,919	955	362	593	57	21	36
Physical education teaching and coaching	8,679	4,990	3,689	2,405	1,292	1,113	102	56	46
Reading teacher education	122	11	111	6,505	333	6,172	45	7	38
Science teacher education/general science teacher education	854	310	544	852	290	562	42	18	24
Social science teacher education	730	379	351	254	112	142	2	1	1
Social studies teacher education	2,148	1,238	910	782	408	374	0	0	0
Technical teacher education	285	173	112	188	73	115	45	16	29
Trade and industrial teacher education	1,313	841	472	372	142	230	45	21	24
Computer teacher education	56	41	15	1,258	373	885	1	1	0
Biology teacher education	367	134	233	232	83	149	0	0	0
Chemistry teacher education	74	34	40	38	13	25	0	0	0
Drama and dance teacher education	112	20	92	40	9	31	0	0	0
French language teacher education	67	14	53	38	5	33	0	0	0
German language teacher education	21	4	17	0	0	0	0	0	0
Health occupations teacher education	8	0	8	28	10	18	1	1	0
History teacher education	783	425	358	53	33	20	0	0	0
Physics teacher education	44	28	16	29	22	7	0	0	0
Spanish language teacher education	387	74	313	91	24	67	0	0	0
Speech teacher education	236	115	121	5	2	3	0	0	0
Geography teacher education	7	5	2	4	2	2	0	0	0
Latin teacher education	2	0	2	3	2	1	0	0	0
School librarian/library media specialist	6	2	4	161	16	145	0	0	0
Psychology teacher education	14	4	10	32	5	27	7	1	6
Teacher educ. and prof. dev., specific subject areas, other	553	183	370	1,403	318	1,085	43	16	27
Teaching Eng. as a second/foreign language/ESL language instructor	122	20	102	1,905	390	1,515	11	2	9
Teaching French as a second or foreign language	0	0	0	0	0	0	0	0	0
Teacher assistant/aide	0	0	0	0	0	0	0	0	0
Adult literacy tutor/instructor	0	0	0	162	13	149	1	0	1
Education, other	1,998	716	1,282	5,917	1,247	4,670	223	92	131
Engineering and engineering technologies	79,743	65,164	14,579	35,133	27,161	7,972	6,601	5,368	1,233
Engineering	64,906	52,020	12,886	32,633	25,351	7,282	6,547	5,329	1,218
Engineering, general	1,989	1,573	416	1,539	1,178	361	258	216	42
Aerospace, aeronautical and astronautical engineering	2,384	1,980	404	935	771	164	205	178	27
Agricultural/biological engineering and bioengineering	652	446	206	204	133	71	77	62	15
Architectural engineering	622	437	185	115	72	43	6	5	1
Biomedical/medical engineering	2,418	1,393	1,025	1,027	584	443	340	247	93
Ceramic sciences and engineering	48	37	11	21	17	4	12	9	3
Chemical engineering	4,397	2,747	1,650	1,183	815	368	773	591	182
Civil engineering, general	8,030	6,187	1,843	3,534	2,624	910	676	522	154
Geotechnical engineering	0	0	0	6	4	2	0	0	0
Structural engineering	101	79	22	81	65	16	4	3	1
Transportation and highway engineering	0	0	0	100	68	32	6	4	2
Water resources engineering	7	6	1	39	20	19	18	16	2
Civil engineering, other	48	37	11	74	61	13	9	7	2
Computer engineering, general	6,521	5,785	736	1,739	1,309	430	171	145	26
Computer software engineering	214	186	28	607	394	213	0	0	0
Computer engineering, other	196	153	43	181	151	30	42	35	7
Electrical, electronics and communications engineering	14,171	12,201	1,970	9,054	7,257	1,797	1,566	1,347	219
Engineering mechanics	69	60	9	92	77	15	48	45	3
Engineering physics	344	277	67	77	56	21	22	19	3
Engineering science	277	180	97	321	232	89	64	50	14
Environmental/environmental health engineering	447	263	184	642	368	274	111	73	38
Materials engineering	535	365	170	559	408	151	337	254	83
Mechanical engineering	14,609	12,717	1,892	4,637	4,055	582	915	802	113
Metallurgical engineering	100	72	28	65	49	16	31	24	7
Mining and mineral engineering	105	87	18	38	32	6	8	8	0

See notes at end of table.

Table 258. Bachelor's, master's, and doctor's degrees conferred by degree-granting institutions, by sex of student and field of study: 2004–05—Continued

Field of study	Bachelor's degrees requiring 4 or 5 years			Master's degrees			Doctor's degrees (Ph.D., Ed.D., etc.)		
	Total	Males	Females	Total	Males	Females	Total	Males	Females
1	2	3	4	5	6	7	8	9	10
Naval architecture and marine engineering	302	269	33	29	25	4	6	4	2
Nuclear engineering	264	218	46	160	132	28	78	67	11
Ocean engineering	145	116	29	107	94	13	21	17	4
Petroleum engineering	322	263	59	248	213	35	49	36	13
Systems engineering	507	397	110	864	691	173	52	45	7
Textile sciences and engineering	142	52	90	40	24	16	20	10	10
Materials science	199	131	68	145	112	33	134	105	29
Polymer/plastics engineering	80	69	11	70	53	17	49	40	9
Construction engineering	252	233	19	11	7	4	0	0	0
Forest engineering	12	10	2	5	3	2	3	2	1
Industrial engineering	3,054	2,005	1,049	2,208	1,715	493	238	186	52
Industrial/manufacturing engineering	0	0	0	0	0	0	0	0	0
Manufacturing engineering	313	269	44	290	253	37	6	3	3
Operations research	387	247	140	267	181	86	42	35	7
Surveying engineering	23	21	2	5	1	4	3	3	0
Geological/geophysical engineering	93	49	44	39	26	13	7	4	3
Engineering, other	527	403	124	1,275	1,021	254	140	110	30
Engineering technologies/construction trades/mechanics and repairers	14,837	13,144	1,693	2,500	1,810	690	54	39	15
Engineering technologies/technicians	14,482	12,812	1,670	2,500	1,810	690	54	39	15
Engineering technology, general	1,163	1,039	124	177	140	37	0	0	0
Architectural engineering technology/technician	503	425	78	0	0	0	0	0	0
Civil engineering technology/technician	480	419	61	2	2	0	0	0	0
Electrical/electronic/communications eng. technology/technician	2,194	1,993	201	12	9	3	0	0	0
Laser and optical technology/technician	2	2	0	0	0	0	0	0	0
Telecommunications technology/technician	58	52	6	32	24	8	0	0	0
Electrical/electronic eng. technologies/technicians, other	333	307	26	0	0	0	0	0	0
Biomedical technology/technician	3	1	2	4	3	1	5	1	4
Electromechanical technology/electromechanical eng. technology	77	74	3	0	0	0	0	0	0
Instrumentation technology/technician	4	4	0	0	0	0	0	0	0
Robotics technology/technician	25	24	1	0	0	0	0	0	0
Electromechanical/instrumentation and maintenance technol./tech.	11	9	2	0	0	0	0	0	0
Heating, air conditioning, and refrigeration technology/technician	11	11	0	0	0	0	0	0	0
Energy management and systems technology/technician	31	31	0	19	16	3	0	0	0
Water quality/wastewater treatment manage./recycling technol./tech.	31	20	11	0	0	0	0	0	0
Environmental engineering technology/environmental technology	77	49	28	77	48	29	0	0	0
Hazardous materials management and waste technology/technician	3	3	0	7	3	4	0	0	0
Environmental control technologies/technicians, other	2	1	1	50	30	20	0	0	0
Plastics engineering technology/technician	90	81	9	5	4	1	0	0	0
Metallurgical technology/technician	1	1	0	0	0	0	0	0	0
Industrial technology/technician	1,903	1,652	251	289	216	73	3	2	1
Manufacturing technology/technician	594	537	57	43	35	8	0	0	0
Industrial/manufacturing technology/technician	0	0	0	0	0	0	0	0	0
Industrial production technologies/technicians, other	363	283	80	16	15	1	0	0	0
Occupational safety and health technology/technician	394	311	83	81	52	29	0	0	0
Quality control technology/technician	4	3	1	90	51	39	0	0	0
Industrial safety technology/technician	37	33	4	8	7	1	0	0	0
Quality control and safety technologies/technicians, other	22	19	3	3	3	0	0	0	0
Aeronautical/aerospace engineering technology/technician	102	94	8	0	0	0	0	0	0
Automotive engineering technology/technician	326	304	22	0	0	0	0	0	0
Mechanical engineering/mechanical technology/technician	1,106	1,041	65	0	0	0	0	0	0
Mechanical engineering-related technologies/technicians, other	292	269	23	0	0	0	0	0	0
Mining technology/technician	0	0	0	0	0	0	0	0	0
Petroleum technology/technician	10	10	0	0	0	0	0	0	0
Mining and petroleum technologies/technicians, other	2	2	0	1	1	0	0	0	0
Construction engineering technology/technician	1,361	1,245	116	63	39	24	0	0	0
Surveying technology/surveying	162	148	14	11	9	2	4	4	0
Engineering-related technologies, other	2	2	0	0	0	0	0	0	0
Computer engineering technology/technician	1,017	883	134	7	7	0	0	0	0
Computer technology/computer systems technology	72	64	8	0	0	0	0	0	0
Computer software technology/technician	57	50	7	0	0	0	0	0	0
Computer engineering technologies/technicians, other	0	0	0	0	0	0	0	0	0
Drafting/design engineering technologies/technicians, general	53	41	12	0	0	0	0	0	0
CAD/CADD drafting and/or design technology/technician	87	74	13	7	6	1	0	0	0
Electrical/electronics drafting and electrical/electronics	0	0	0	0	0	0	0	0	0
Mechanical drafting and mechanical drafting CAD/CADD	147	114	33	0	0	0	0	0	0
Drafting/design engineering technologies/technicians, other	4	4	0	0	0	0	0	0	0
Engineering/industrial management	441	347	94	1,366	1,006	360	42	32	10
Engineering technologies/technicians, other	825	736	89	130	84	46	0	0	0
Construction trades	117	107	10	0	0	0	0	0	0
Mason/masonry	0	0	0	0	0	0	0	0	0
Carpentry/carpenter	0	0	0	0	0	0	0	0	0
Electrician	0	0	0	0	0	0	0	0	0
Building/home/construction inspection/inspector	4	4	0	0	0	0	0	0	0
Building/construction finishing, management, and inspection, other	59	55	4	0	0	0	0	0	0
Plumber and pipefitter	0	0	0	0	0	0	0	0	0
Construction trades, other	54	48	6	0	0	0	0	0	0
Mechanic and repair technologies/technicians	238	225	13	0	0	0	0	0	0
Mechanics and repairers, general	0	0	0	0	0	0	0	0	0
Business machine repair	0	0	0	0	0	0	0	0	0

See notes at end of table.

Table 258. Bachelor's, master's, and doctor's degrees conferred by degree-granting institutions, by sex of student and field of study: 2004–05—Continued

Field of study	Bachelor's degrees requiring 4 or 5 years			Master's degrees			Doctor's degrees (Ph.D., Ed.D., etc.)		
	Total	Males	Females	Total	Males	Females	Total	Males	Females
1	2	3	4	5	6	7	8	9	10
Communications systems installation and repair technology	31	30	1	0	0	0	0	0	0
Industrial electronics technology/technician	0	0	0	0	0	0	0	0	0
Heavy equipment maintenance technology/technician	9	9	0	0	0	0	0	0	0
Industrial mechanics and maintenance technology	3	2	1	0	0	0	0	0	0
Auto body/collision and repair technology/technician	0	0	0	0	0	0	0	0	0
Automobile/automotive mechanics technology/technician	13	13	0	0	0	0	0	0	0
Diesel mechanics technology/technician	22	22	0	0	0	0	0	0	0
Airframe mechanics and aircraft maintenance technology/technician	90	82	8	0	0	0	0	0	0
Aircraft powerplant technology/technician	0	0	0	0	0	0	0	0	0
Avionics maintenance technology/technician	70	67	3	0	0	0	0	0	0
English language and literature/letters	54,379	17,154	37,225	8,468	2,615	5,853	1,212	494	718
English language and literature, general	41,125	12,623	28,502	5,233	1,600	3,633	1,038	416	622
English composition	501	171	330	108	33	75	5	3	2
Creative writing	1,841	691	1,150	2,015	713	1,302	14	7	7
American literature (United States)	113	30	83	14	2	12	4	0	4
English literature (British and Commonwealth)	959	273	686	122	37	85	23	12	11
Speech and rhetorical studies	8,369	2,864	5,505	570	124	446	84	44	40
Technical and business writing	459	176	283	250	63	187	3	2	1
English language and literature/letters, other	1,012	326	686	156	43	113	41	10	31
Family and consumer sciences/human sciences	20,074	2,435	17,639	1,827	229	1,598	331	68	263
Work and family studies	52	26	26	29	13	16	0	0	0
Family and consumer sciences/human sciences, general	4,163	415	3,748	401	53	348	65	19	46
Business family and consumer sciences/human sciences	105	30	75	5	1	4	0	0	0
Family and consumer sciences/human sciences communication	49	4	45	1	0	1	0	0	0
Consumer merchandising/retailing management	35	5	30	7	1	6	0	0	0
Family and consumer sciences/human sciences business serv., other	0	0	0	0	0	0	0	0	0
Family resource management studies, general	569	268	301	37	2	35	9	2	7
Consumer economics	599	247	352	6	0	6	0	0	0
Consumer services and advocacy	3	0	3	0	0	0	0	0	0
Family and consumer economics and related services, other	281	23	258	1	0	1	6	3	3
Foods, nutrition, and wellness studies, general	1,559	218	1,341	331	38	293	19	3	16
Human nutrition	250	22	228	127	22	105	8	2	6
Foodservice systems administration/management	474	253	221	8	0	8	0	0	0
Foods, nutrition, and related services, other	22	1	21	30	1	29	0	0	0
Housing and human environments, general	389	63	326	31	11	20	4	1	3
Facilities planning and management	7	4	3	0	0	0	0	0	0
Housing and human environments, other	10	1	9	0	0	0	0	0	0
Human development and family studies, general	6,189	504	5,685	470	56	414	101	22	79
Adult development and aging	29	2	27	33	4	29	0	0	0
Family systems	515	53	462	31	9	22	8	0	8
Child development	1,331	66	1,265	119	3	116	73	11	62
Family and community services	636	55	581	59	4	55	7	0	7
Child care and support services management	66	4	62	17	0	17	0	0	0
Child care provider/assistant	5	0	5	0	0	0	0	0	0
Human development, family studies, and related services, other	216	8	208	14	1	13	8	2	6
Apparel and textiles, general	2,130	139	1,991	57	8	49	15	1	14
Apparel and textile manufacture	28	3	25	0	0	0	0	0	0
Textile science	0	0	0	0	0	0	2	2	0
Apparel and textile marketing management	264	9	255	3	0	3	0	0	0
Family and consumer sciences/human sciences, other	98	12	86	10	2	8	6	0	6
Foreign languages, literatures, and linguistics	18,386	5,370	13,016	3,407	1,056	2,351	1,027	410	617
Foreign languages and literatures, general	1,351	354	997	229	59	170	27	7	20
Linguistics	1,020	317	703	603	176	427	168	57	111
Language interpretation and translation	36	15	21	107	22	85	0	0	0
Comparative literature	823	246	577	207	72	135	150	60	90
Linguistic/comparative/related language studies and serv., other	33	7	26	5	1	4	4	3	1
African languages, literatures, and linguistics	4	1	3	2	1	1	3	2	1
East Asian languages, literatures, and linguistics, general	80	42	38	82	34	48	25	17	8
Chinese language and literature	208	97	111	21	8	13	8	5	3
Japanese language and literature	429	237	192	24	2	22	8	4	4
Korean language and literature	8	7	1	0	0	0	0	0	0
East Asian languages, literatures, and linguistics, other	88	41	47	23	5	18	11	5	6
Slavic languages, literatures, and linguistics, general	46	18	28	52	17	35	37	14	23
Russian language and literature	298	138	160	18	5	13	0	0	0
Czech language and literature	2	1	1	0	0	0	0	0	0
Polish language and literature	1	0	1	0	0	0	0	0	0
Slavic/Baltic/Albanian languages, lit., and linguistics, other	2	0	2	1	0	1	1	0	1
Germanic languages, literatures, and linguistics, general	100	39	61	48	17	31	20	5	15
German language and literature	1,103	452	651	180	73	107	56	27	29
Scandinavian languages, literatures, and linguistics	8	2	6	6	3	3	5	2	3
Danish language and literature	2	1	1	0	0	0	0	0	0
Norwegian language and literature	3	0	3	0	0	0	0	0	0
Swedish language and literature	4	1	3	0	0	0	0	0	0
Germanic languages, literatures, and linguistics, other	0	0	0	0	0	0	0	0	0
Modern Greek language and literature	0	0	0	0	0	0	0	0	0
South Asian languages, literatures, and linguistics, general	3	0	3	3	2	1	5	0	5
Sanskrit and classical Indian languages, lit., and linguistics	0	0	0	1	1	0	1	1	0
Iranian and Persian languages, lit., and linguistics	0	0	0	0	0	0	1	0	1
Romance languages, literatures, and linguistics, general	61	14	47	52	23	29	40	15	25

See notes at end of table.

Table 258. Bachelor's, master's, and doctor's degrees conferred by degree-granting institutions, by sex of student and field of study: 2004–05—Continued

Field of study	Bachelor's degrees requiring 4 or 5 years			Master's degrees			Doctor's degrees (Ph.D., Ed.D., etc.)		
	Total	Males	Females	Total	Males	Females	Total	Males	Females
1	2	3	4	5	6	7	8	9	10
French language and literature	2,394	463	1,931	356	83	273	80	21	59
Italian language and literature	277	77	200	70	30	40	12	6	6
Portuguese language and literature	38	16	22	11	4	7	0	0	0
Spanish language and literature	8,304	2,139	6,165	919	246	673	190	68	122
Romanian language and literature	2	0	2	0	0	0	0	0	0
Romance languages, literatures, and linguistics, other	99	15	84	66	19	47	49	20	29
American Indian/Native American languages, literatures, and linguistics	0	0	0	0	0	0	0	0	0
Semitic languages, literatures, and linguistics, general	0	0	0	4	1	3	3	2	1
Arabic language and literature	21	8	13	5	2	3	1	0	1
Hebrew language and literature	24	14	10	5	1	4	6	4	2
Ancient Near Eastern and biblical languages, lit., and linguistics	28	20	8	10	9	1	5	5	0
Middle/Near Eastern and Semitic languages, lit., and ling., other	34	17	17	43	22	21	26	21	5
Classics and classical languages, lit., and linguistics, general	927	427	500	176	86	90	61	29	32
Ancient/classical Greek language and literature	39	23	16	5	4	1	1	1	0
Latin language and literature	90	48	42	14	7	7	0	0	0
Classics and classical languages, lit, and linguistics, other	22	10	12	26	14	12	1	0	1
Celtic languages, literatures, and linguistics	7	2	5	1	1	0	1	1	0
Filipino/Tagalog language and literature	2	1	1	0	0	0	0	0	0
American sign language (ASL)	44	3	41	0	0	0	0	0	0
Sign language interpretation and translation	174	11	163	9	1	8	0	0	0
Foreign languages, literatures, and linguistics, other	147	46	101	23	5	18	22	8	14
Health professions and related clinical sciences	80,685	10,858	69,827	46,703	9,816	36,887	5,868	1,710	4,158
Health services/allied health/health sciences, general	2,027	426	1,601	180	47	133	25	10	15
Communication disorders, general	1,660	79	1,581	1,153	49	1,104	17	5	12
Audiology/audiologist and hearing sciences	110	5	105	101	9	92	714	111	603
Speech-language pathology/pathologist	745	19	726	1,456	34	1,422	31	6	25
Audiology/audiologist and speech-language pathology/pathologist	3,317	132	3,185	2,414	109	2,305	71	13	58
Communication disorders sciences and services, other	86	3	83	71	3	68	7	2	5
Dental clinical sciences, general	0	0	0	254	166	88	14	6	8
Advanced general dentistry	0	0	0	12	9	3	0	0	0
Oral biology and oral pathology	0	0	0	37	22	15	21	10	11
Dental public health and education	0	0	0	6	0	6	0	0	0
Dental materials (M.S., Ph.D.)	0	0	0	2	1	1	0	0	0
Endodontics/endodontology	0	0	0	14	14	0	0	0	0
Oral/maxillofacial surgery	0	0	0	2	2	0	1	1	0
Orthodontics/orthodontology	0	0	0	62	42	20	0	0	0
Pediatric dentistry/pedodontics	0	0	0	15	7	8	0	0	0
Periodontics/periodontology	0	0	0	27	18	9	0	0	0
Prosthodontics/prosthodontology	0	0	0	14	11	3	0	0	0
Advanced/graduate dentistry and oral sciences, other	0	0	0	39	25	14	21	14	7
Dental assisting/assistant	0	0	0	0	0	0	0	0	0
Dental hygiene/hygienist	1,251	26	1,225	10	2	8	0	0	0
Dental laboratory technology/technician	9	3	6	6	5	1	0	0	0
Dental services and allied professions, other	9	0	9	5	3	2	0	0	0
Health/health care administration/management	2,496	608	1,888	3,402	1,098	2,304	40	17	23
Hospital and health care facilities administration/management	396	63	333	666	207	459	2	0	2
Health unit manager/ward supervisor	0	0	0	7	4	3	0	0	0
Medical office management/administration	3	0	3	2	0	2	0	0	0
Health information/medical records administration/administrator	521	63	458	8	2	6	0	0	0
Health information/medical records technology/technician	1	0	1	6	4	2	3	2	1
Medical/health management and clinical assistant/specialist	20	2	18	0	0	0	0	0	0
Health/medical claims examiner	0	0	0	0	0	0	0	0	0
Medical administrative/executive assistant and medical secretary	0	0	0	0	0	0	0	0	0
Health and medical administrative services, other	340	68	272	320	60	260	7	3	4
Medical/clinical assistant	8	1	7	0	0	0	0	0	0
Clinical/medical laboratory assistant	0	0	0	0	0	0	0	0	0
Occupational therapist assistant	0	0	0	0	0	0	0	0	0
Pharmacy technician/assistant	0	0	0	0	0	0	0	0	0
Physical therapist assistant	35	9	26	0	0	0	0	0	0
Veterinary/animal health technology/technician and vet. assistant	211	18	193	2	1	1	0	0	0
Anesthesiologist assistant	0	0	0	27	8	19	0	0	0
Pathology/pathologist assistant	1	0	1	0	0	0	0	0	0
Respiratory therapy technician/assistant	0	0	0	0	0	0	0	0	0
Allied health and medical assisting services, other	44	9	35	44	18	26	0	0	0
Cardiovascular technology/technologist	51	22	29	0	0	0	0	0	0
Electrocardiograph technology/technician	0	0	0	0	0	0	0	0	0
Electroneurodiagnostic/electroencephalographic tech./technologist	0	0	0	0	0	0	0	0	0
Emergency medical technology/technician (EMT paramedic)	94	56	38	16	12	4	0	0	0
Nuclear medical technology/technologist	266	88	178	0	0	0	0	0	0
Perfusion technology/perfusionist	22	13	9	28	15	13	0	0	0
Medical radiologic technology/science radiation therapist	743	174	569	7	7	0	0	0	0
Respiratory care therapy/therapist	395	117	278	0	0	0	0	0	0
Diagnostic medical sonography/sonographer and ultrasound technician	261	31	230	0	0	0	0	0	0
Radiologic technology/science radiographer	397	110	287	10	4	6	2	2	0
Physician assistant	1,312	455	857	3,152	941	2,211	0	0	0
Athletic training/trainer	1,746	631	1,115	122	57	65	0	0	0
Gene/genetic therapy	12	1	11	0	0	0	0	0	0
Radiation protection/health physics technician	13	1	12	7	2	5	0	0	0
Allied health diagnostic/intervention/treatment professions, other	149	62	87	16	5	11	0	0	0
Cytotechnology/cytotechnologist	87	18	69	0	0	0	0	0	0
Hematology technology/technician	0	0	0	4	3	1	0	0	0

See notes at end of table.

Table 258. Bachelor's, master's, and doctor's degrees conferred by degree-granting institutions, by sex of student and field of study: 2004–05—Continued

Field of study	Bachelor's degrees requiring 4 or 5 years			Master's degrees			Doctor's degrees (Ph.D., Ed.D., etc.)		
	Total	Males	Females	Total	Males	Females	Total	Males	Females
1	2	3	4	5	6	7	8	9	10
Clinical/medical laboratory technician	52	14	38	0	0	0	0	0	0
Clinical laboratory science/medical technology/technologist	1,713	409	1,304	87	33	54	0	0	0
Histologic technology/histotechnologist	1	0	1	0	0	0	0	0	0
Cytogenetics/genetics/clinical genetics technology/technologist	5	3	2	0	0	0	0	0	0
Clinical/medical laboratory science and allied professions, other	77	22	55	47	16	31	6	2	4
Predentistry studies	53	28	25	0	0	0	0	0	0
Premedicine/premedical studies	454	194	260	0	0	0	0	0	0
Prepharmacy studies	99	33	66	0	0	0	0	0	0
Preveterinary studies	167	32	135	0	0	0	0	0	0
Prenursing studies	4	2	2	0	0	0	0	0	0
Health/medical preparatory programs, other	559	145	414	14	5	9	0	0	0
Medical scientist (M.S., Ph.D.)	0	0	0	179	104	75	32	16	16
Substance abuse/addiction counseling	133	35	98	105	28	77	0	0	0
Psychiatric/mental health services technician	84	10	74	18	2	16	0	0	0
Clinical/medical social work	139	16	123	262	31	231	5	2	3
Community health services/liaison/counseling	846	151	695	155	34	121	2	0	2
Marriage and family therapy/counseling	5	3	2	1,353	277	1,076	60	23	37
Clinical pastoral counseling/patient counseling	0	0	0	38	14	24	6	3	3
Psychoanalysis and psychotherapy	0	0	0	4	1	3	5	0	5
Mental health counseling/counselor	0	0	0	242	38	204	3	0	3
Genetic counseling/counselor	0	0	0	46	2	44	0	0	0
Mental and social health services and allied professions, other	377	44	333	388	61	327	3	0	3
Nursing - registered nurse training (RN, ASN, BSN, MSN)	44,068	4,013	40,055	5,242	503	4,739	213	17	196
Nursing administration	278	24	254	750	58	692	19	2	17
Adult health nurse/nursing	69	10	59	281	26	255	0	0	0
Nurse anesthetist	0	0	0	1,017	411	606	0	0	0
Family practice nurse/nurse practitioner	25	1	24	1,285	131	1,154	0	0	0
Maternal/child health and neonatal nurse/nursing	0	0	0	185	6	179	0	0	0
Nurse midwife/nursing midwifery	0	0	0	75	0	75	0	0	0
Nursing science	662	56	606	1,943	145	1,798	186	13	173
Pediatric nurse/nursing	0	0	0	124	6	118	0	0	0
Psychiatric/mental health nurse/nursing	0	0	0	109	12	97	0	0	0
Public health/community nurse/nursing	0	0	0	164	14	150	0	0	0
Perioperative/operating room and surgical nurse/nursing	0	0	0	25	2	23	0	0	0
Licensed practical/voc. nurse training (LPN, LVN, cert. dipl. AAS)	6	1	5	0	0	0	0	0	0
Clinical nurse specialist	0	0	0	105	15	90	0	0	0
Critical care nursing	0	0	0	71	12	59	0	0	0
Occupational and environmental health nursing	0	0	0	0	0	0	0	0	0
Nursing, other	1,325	93	1,232	1,620	124	1,496	85	8	77
Opthalmic technician/technologist	5	0	5	4	2	2	0	0	0
Ophthalmic/optometric support services/allied professions, other	11	5	6	25	21	4	3	0	3
Pharmacy (PharmD, BS/BPharm)	301	115	186	0	0	0	0	0	0
Pharmacy admin. and pharmacy policy and regulatory affairs	0	0	0	148	61	87	26	11	15
Pharmaceutics and drug design	211	66	145	94	47	47	165	90	75
Medicinal and pharmaceutical chemistry	8	4	4	15	7	8	71	36	35
Natural products chemistry and pharmacognosy	0	0	0	1	0	1	6	1	5
Clinical and industrial drug development (M.S., Ph.D.)	5	1	4	18	5	13	0	0	0
Pharmacoeconomics/pharmaceutical economics	0	0	0	8	3	5	0	0	0
Clinical, hospital, and managed care pharmacy	0	0	0	4	1	3	0	0	0
Industrial and physical pharmacy and cosmetic sciences	0	0	0	2	1	1	1	0	1
Pharmacy, pharmaceutical sciences, and administration, other	210	79	131	253	76	177	85	40	45
Public health, general	385	69	316	4,142	1,278	2,864	230	85	145
Environmental health	214	113	101	312	132	180	50	21	29
Health/medical physics	14	9	5	25	19	6	1	1	0
Occupational health and industrial hygiene	45	28	17	76	50	26	11	4	7
Public health education and promotion	498	96	402	434	54	380	47	11	36
Community health and preventive medicine	189	35	154	77	15	62	33	10	23
Maternal and child health	0	0	0	59	5	54	5	1	4
International public health/international health	0	0	0	78	17	61	0	0	0
Health services administration	115	12	103	343	99	244	10	4	6
Public health, other	274	96	178	749	220	529	98	29	69
Art therapy/therapist	98	8	90	238	10	228	1	1	0
Dance therapy/therapist	0	0	0	11	1	10	0	0	0
Music therapy/therapist	214	25	189	51	7	44	1	1	0
Occupational therapy/therapist	1,357	111	1,246	2,001	151	1,850	72	9	63
Orthotist/prosthetist	24	16	8	8	4	4	0	0	0
Physical therapy/therapist	548	141	407	3,429	967	2,462	2,987	891	2,096
Therapeutic recreation/recreational therapy	380	78	302	17	2	15	3	1	2
Vocational rehabilitation counseling/counselor	212	26	186	867	202	665	9	1	8
Kinesiotherapy/kinesiotherapist	27	4	23	3	0	3	1	1	0
Assistive/augmentative technology and rehabilitation engineering	0	0	0	0	0	0	1	0	1
Rehabilitation and therapeutic professions, other	735	158	577	355	76	279	32	12	20
Veterinary sciences/veterinary clinical sciences, general	26	6	20	178	64	114	107	51	56
Veterinary anatomy	0	0	0	1	1	0	0	0	0
Veterinary physiology	0	0	0	0	0	0	3	2	1
Veterinary microbiology and immunobiology	0	0	0	9	4	5	7	7	0
Veterinary pathology and pathobiology	0	0	0	0	0	0	10	5	5
Veterinary toxicology and pharmacology (cert., M.S., Ph.D.)	0	0	0	1	1	0	1	1	0
Large animal/food animal/equine surgery and medicine	0	0	0	4	0	4	3	2	1
Small/companion animal surgery and medicine	0	0	0	1	1	0	0	0	0
Comparative and laboratory animal medicine	0	0	0	8	2	6	0	0	0
Veterinary preventive medicine epidemiology/public health	0	0	0	5	3	2	0	0	0

See notes at end of table.

Table 258. Bachelor's, master's, and doctor's degrees conferred by degree-granting institutions, by sex of student and field of study: 2004–05—Continued

Field of study	Bachelor's degrees requiring 4 or 5 years			Master's degrees			Doctor's degrees (Ph.D., Ed.D., etc.)		
	Total	Males	Females	Total	Males	Females	Total	Males	Females
1	2	3	4	5	6	7	8	9	10
Veterinary infectious diseases	0	0	0	2	0	2	2	0	2
Veterinary biomedical and clinical sciences, other	0	0	0	1	1	0	1	1	0
Health aide	1	0	1	0	0	0	0	0	0
Medical illustration/medical illustrator	27	9	18	26	7	19	0	0	0
Medical informatics	6	1	5	96	42	54	8	5	3
Dietetics/dietitian (RD)	1,449	119	1,330	185	17	168	5	3	2
Clinical nutrition/nutritionist	10	0	10	57	1	56	4	1	3
Dietetics/human nutritional services	0	0	0	0	0	0	0	0	0
Dietetics and clinical nutrition services, other	47	4	43	1	1	0	0	0	0
Bioethics/medical ethics	0	0	0	93	45	48	10	4	6
Acupuncture	40	20	20	1,165	492	673	0	0	0
Traditional Chinese/Asian medicine and Chinese herbology	69	19	50	517	165	352	0	0	0
Naturopathic medicine/naturopathy (ND)	0	0	0	0	0	0	19	4	15
Ayurvedic medicine/ayurveda	0	0	0	0	0	0	0	0	0
Acupuncture and oriental medicine	0	0	0	0	0	0	0	0	0
Alternative and complementary medicine and medical systems, other	10	2	8	34	1	33	0	0	0
Direct entry midwifery (LM, CPM)	2	0	2	0	0	0	0	0	0
Alternative and complementary medical support services, other	8	1	7	0	0	0	0	0	0
Massage therapy/therapeutic massage	1	1	0	0	0	0	0	0	0
Movement therapy and movement education	11	3	8	19	0	19	2	1	1
Movement and mind-body therapies and education, other	5	0	5	0	0	0	0	0	0
Herbalism/herbalist	23	12	11	0	0	0	0	0	0
Health professions and related clinical sciences, other	2,831	714	2,117	793	298	495	136	74	62
Legal professions and studies	3,161	918	2,243	4,170	2,304	1,866	98	58	40
Legal studies, general	1,041	380	661	29	12	17	0	0	0
Prelaw studies	291	152	139	0	0	0	0	0	0
Advanced legal research/studies, general (M.C.L., M.L.I., M.S.L.)[1]	0	0	0	602	338	264	71	49	22
Programs for foreign lawyers (LL.M., M.C.L.)	0	0	0	513	304	209	0	0	0
American/U.S. law/legal studies/jurisprudence (M.C.J.)[1]	38	15	23	179	94	85	3	0	3
Banking, corporate, finance, and securities law[1]	0	0	0	123	68	55	0	0	0
Comparative law (LL.M., M.C.L., J.S.D./S.J.D.)	0	0	0	57	32	25	0	0	0
Energy, environment, and natural resources law (M.S.)[1]	0	0	0	24	16	8	0	0	0
Health law (L.LM., M.J., J.S.D./S.J.D.)	0	0	0	65	15	50	0	0	0
International law and legal studies[1]	0	0	0	225	109	116	1	0	1
International business, trade, and tax law[1]	0	0	0	73	47	26	0	0	0
Tax law/taxation[1]	0	0	0	453	291	162	0	0	0
Legal research and advanced professional studies, other	0	0	0	933	530	403	8	5	3
Legal administrative assistant/secretary	14	1	13	0	0	0	0	0	0
Legal assistant/paralegal	1,345	235	1,110	38	3	35	0	0	0
Court reporting/court reporter	32	0	32	0	0	0	0	0	0
Legal professions and studies, other	400	135	265	856	445	411	15	4	11
Liberal arts and sciences, general studies, and humanities	43,751	13,732	30,019	3,680	1,381	2,299	109	38	71
Liberal arts and sciences/liberal studies	27,620	7,642	19,978	2,515	969	1,546	14	9	5
General studies	10,375	4,179	6,196	69	26	43	3	1	2
Humanities/humanistic studies	3,045	970	2,075	754	282	472	74	19	55
Liberal arts and sciences, general studies, and humanities, other	2,711	941	1,770	342	104	238	18	9	9
Library science	76	15	61	6,213	1,241	4,972	42	14	28
Library science/librarianship	76	15	61	6,064	1,210	4,854	36	14	22
Library assistant/technician	0	0	0	0	0	0	0	0	0
Library science, other	0	0	0	149	31	118	6	0	6
Mathematics and statistics	14,351	7,937	6,414	4,477	2,525	1,952	1,176	841	335
Mathematics, general	12,386	6,718	5,668	2,462	1,431	1,031	746	567	179
Mathematics, other	167	80	87	0	0	0	4	2	2
Applied mathematics	999	636	363	510	307	203	142	100	42
Computational mathematics	77	66	11	13	10	3	7	7	0
Applied mathematics, other	94	68	26	79	64	15	3	2	1
Statistics, general	479	280	199	1,285	627	658	259	155	104
Mathematical statistics and probability	6	2	4	9	6	3	4	2	2
Statistics, other	7	5	2	0	0	0	5	1	4
Mathematics and statistics, other	136	82	54	119	80	39	6	5	1
Military technologies	40	33	7	0	0	0	0	0	0
Military technologies	40	33	7	0	0	0	0	0	0
Multi/interdisciplinary studies	30,243	9,645	20,598	4,252	1,440	2,812	983	440	543
Biological and physical sciences	1,561	678	883	215	83	132	42	25	17
Peace studies and conflict resolution	181	62	119	288	120	168	11	2	9
Systems science and theory	127	98	29	195	93	102	21	15	6
Mathematics and computer science	305	236	69	44	27	17	17	16	1
Biopsychology	129	22	107	0	0	0	4	3	1
Gerontology	172	22	150	218	29	189	12	2	10
Historic preservation and conservation	82	16	66	143	36	107	0	0	0
Cultural resource management and policy analysis	0	0	0	13	7	6	0	0	0
Historic preservation and conservation, other	0	0	0	1	0	1	0	0	0
Medieval and Renaissance studies	50	14	36	24	11	13	7	4	3
Museology/museum studies	21	1	20	171	27	144	0	0	0
Science, technology, and society	356	208	148	105	37	68	12	8	4
Accounting and computer science	8	2	6	0	0	0	0	0	0

See notes at end of table.

Table 258. Bachelor's, master's, and doctor's degrees conferred by degree-granting institutions, by sex of student and field of study: 2004–05—Continued

Field of study	Bachelor's degrees requiring 4 or 5 years			Master's degrees			Doctor's degrees (Ph.D., Ed.D., etc.)		
	Total	Males	Females	Total	Males	Females	Total	Males	Females
1	2	3	4	5	6	7	8	9	10
Behavioral sciences	1,026	277	749	126	36	90	14	3	11
Natural sciences	335	134	201	108	39	69	0	0	0
Nutrition sciences	547	70	477	405	49	356	126	28	98
International/global studies	1,962	729	1,233	122	73	49	0	0	0
Holocaust and related studies	0	0	0	12	3	9	0	0	0
Ancient studies/civilization	95	26	69	3	2	1	3	2	1
Classical, ancient Mediterranean/Near Eastern studies/archaeology	92	28	64	7	4	3	2	0	2
Intercultural/multicultural and diversity studies	118	64	54	60	18	42	0	0	0
Neuroscience	1,304	487	817	85	43	42	357	180	177
Cognitive science	413	229	184	11	3	8	9	6	3
Multi/interdisciplinary studies, other	21,359	6,242	15,117	1,896	700	1,196	346	146	200
Parks, recreation, leisure and fitness studies	22,888	11,702	11,186	3,740	1,935	1,805	207	119	88
Parks, recreation and leisure studies	2,476	1,183	1,293	303	136	167	21	13	8
Parks, recreation and leisure facilities management	2,679	1,395	1,284	269	118	151	11	5	6
Health and physical education, general	7,586	3,949	3,637	1,109	551	558	28	13	15
Sport and fitness administration/management	3,426	2,349	1,077	996	631	365	14	11	3
Kinesiology and exercise science	5,804	2,419	3,385	946	448	498	112	69	43
Health and physical education/fitness, other	773	333	440	103	44	59	15	4	11
Parks, recreation, leisure and fitness studies, other	144	74	70	14	7	7	6	4	2
Philosophy and religious studies	11,584	7,225	4,359	1,647	995	652	586	418	168
Philosophy	6,567	4,618	1,949	695	496	199	349	265	84
Logic	4	1	3	6	5	1	2	2	0
Ethics	35	26	9	10	2	8	0	0	0
Philosophy, other	135	94	41	0	0	0	0	0	0
Religion/religious studies	3,971	2,028	1,943	523	298	225	197	123	74
Christian studies	202	128	74	45	24	21	0	0	0
Islamic studies	1	0	1	3	1	2	1	1	0
Jewish/Judaic studies	237	66	171	119	39	80	5	2	3
Religion/religious studies, other	31	19	12	9	8	1	0	0	0
Philosophy and religious studies, other	401	245	156	237	122	115	32	25	7
Physical sciences and science technologies	18,905	10,934	7,971	5,678	3,457	2,221	4,114	2,966	1,148
Physical sciences	18,677	10,790	7,887	5,654	3,444	2,210	4,114	2,966	1,148
Physical sciences	279	163	116	55	32	23	14	13	1
Astronomy	184	109	75	110	63	47	71	48	23
Astrophysics	125	72	53	31	23	8	36	23	13
Planetary astronomy and science	3	0	3	4	1	3	0	0	0
Astronomy and astrophysics, other	19	7	12	14	10	4	8	6	2
Atmospheric physics and dynamics	527	346	181	188	128	60	83	57	26
Atmospheric sciences and meteorology, general	3	2	1	0	0	0	0	0	0
Meteorology	139	87	52	24	15	9	13	10	3
Atmospheric sciences and meteorology, other	8	1	7	0	0	0	0	0	0
Chemistry, general	9,311	4,545	4,766	1,817	924	893	2,055	1,354	701
Analytical chemistry	12	2	10	13	8	5	11	7	4
Inorganic chemistry	0	0	0	5	1	4	6	5	1
Organic chemistry	0	0	0	3	1	2	4	4	0
Physical and theoretical chemistry	1	1	0	0	0	0	8	3	5
Polymer chemistry	7	5	2	14	10	4	46	34	12
Chemical physics	10	8	2	0	0	0	3	2	1
Chemistry, other	323	139	184	27	13	14	15	10	5
Geology/earth science, general	2,759	1,565	1,194	1,090	608	482	264	178	86
Geochemistry	4	3	1	6	4	2	3	2	1
Geophysics and seismology	60	36	24	85	49	36	58	39	19
Paleontology	2	2	0	10	4	6	0	0	0
Hydrology and water resources science	20	13	7	18	9	9	13	9	4
Oceanography, chemical and physical	136	68	68	111	47	64	97	52	45
Geological and earth sciences/geosciences, other	295	174	121	100	62	38	41	28	13
Physics, general	3,963	3,109	854	1,583	1,212	371	1,116	963	153
Atomic/molecular physics	16	9	7	10	7	3	3	3	0
Elementary particle physics	0	0	0	0	0	0	0	0	0
Nuclear physics	0	0	0	3	2	1	6	6	0
Optics/optical sciences	50	40	10	72	55	17	37	29	8
Acoustics	12	9	3	16	14	2	10	8	2
Theoretical and mathematical physics	14	10	4	0	0	0	0	0	0
Physics, other	127	108	19	101	76	25	82	63	19
Physical sciences, other	268	157	111	144	66	78	11	10	1
Science technologies/technicians	228	144	84	24	13	11	0	0	0
Biology technician/biotechnology laboratory technician	26	14	12	0	0	0	0	0	0
Nuclear/nuclear power technology/technician	14	14	0	3	1	2	0	0	0
Chemical technology/technician	7	2	5	0	0	0	0	0	0
Physical science technologies/technicians, other	3	2	1	0	0	0	0	0	0
Science technologies/technicians, other	178	112	66	21	12	9	0	0	0
Precision production	64	45	19	6	1	5	0	0	0
Machine tool technology/machinist	0	0	0	0	0	0	0	0	0
Tool and die technology/technician	0	0	0	0	0	0	0	0	0
Welding technology/welder	19	19	0	0	0	0	0	0	0
Precision metal working, other	0	0	0	0	0	0	0	0	0
Furniture design and manufacturing	45	26	19	6	1	5	0	0	0

See notes at end of table.

Table 258. Bachelor's, master's, and doctor's degrees conferred by degree-granting institutions, by sex of student and field of study: 2004–05—Continued

Field of study	Bachelor's degrees requiring 4 or 5 years			Master's degrees			Doctor's degrees (Ph.D., Ed.D., etc.)		
	Total	Males	Females	Total	Males	Females	Total	Males	Females
1	2	3	4	5	6	7	8	9	10
Psychology	85,614	19,000	66,614	18,830	3,900	14,930	5,106	1,466	3,640
Psychology, general	80,822	17,971	62,851	4,790	1,161	3,629	1,447	512	935
Clinical psychology	120	24	96	2,099	446	1,653	2,221	524	1,697
Cognitive psychology and psycholinguistics	110	37	73	42	11	31	12	7	5
Community psychology	177	14	163	294	60	234	0	0	0
Counseling psychology	426	81	345	6,372	1,206	5,166	355	125	230
Developmental and child psychology	441	38	403	86	6	80	57	11	46
Experimental psychology	297	60	237	66	17	49	56	21	35
Industrial and organizational psychology	307	105	202	1,067	312	755	90	32	58
Personality psychology	36	8	28	0	0	0	0	0	0
Physiological psychology/psychobiology	480	139	341	2	0	2	19	8	11
Social psychology	976	242	734	79	17	62	53	13	40
School psychology	0	0	0	1,198	155	1,043	192	44	148
Educational psychology	203	27	176	1,324	223	1,101	370	105	265
Psychometrics and quantitative psychology	1	0	1	73	14	59	2	0	2
Clinical child psychology	0	0	0	10	2	8	13	4	9
Environmental psychology	23	13	10	9	5	4	0	0	0
Health/medical psychology	13	2	11	30	3	27	10	2	8
Psychopharmacology	0	0	0	54	32	22	0	0	0
Family psychology	15	1	14	31	6	25	9	3	6
Forensic psychology	35	2	33	176	33	143	19	6	13
Psychology, other	1,132	236	896	1,028	191	837	181	49	132
Public administration and social service professions	21,769	4,209	17,560	29,552	7,370	22,182	673	272	401
Human services, general	2,019	439	1,580	170	44	126	17	8	9
Community organization and advocacy	2,115	460	1,655	742	201	541	8	2	6
Public administration	2,630	1,304	1,326	8,982	3,903	5,079	169	93	76
Public policy analysis	799	368	431	1,865	764	1,101	136	73	63
Social work	13,242	1,456	11,786	16,841	2,158	14,683	325	86	239
Youth services/administration	11	2	9	23	4	19	0	0	0
Social work, other	15	2	13	39	5	34	0	0	0
Public administration and social service professions, other	938	178	760	890	291	599	18	10	8
Security and protective services	30,723	15,354	15,369	3,991	1,974	2,017	94	55	39
Corrections	505	199	306	26	13	13	0	0	0
Criminal justice/law enforcement administration	7,771	4,011	3,760	1,582	910	672	13	6	7
Criminal justice/safety studies	18,867	9,097	9,770	1,562	719	843	75	44	31
Forensic science and technology	304	80	224	450	97	353	0	0	0
Criminal justice/police science	1,468	917	551	29	12	17	2	2	0
Security and loss prevention services	67	51	16	36	22	14	0	0	0
Juvenile corrections	2	0	2	0	0	0	0	0	0
Criminalistics and criminal science	41	12	29	0	0	0	0	0	0
Securities services administration/management	0	0	0	10	7	3	0	0	0
Corrections administration	66	30	36	6	2	4	0	0	0
Corrections and criminal justice, other	1,197	572	625	134	67	67	2	2	0
Fire protection and safety technology/technician	130	117	13	9	6	3	0	0	0
Fire services administration	176	165	11	5	4	1	0	0	0
Fire science/firefighting	48	47	1	22	22	0	0	0	0
Fire protection, other	35	27	8	17	14	3	2	1	1
Security and protective services, other	46	29	17	103	79	24	0	0	0
Social sciences and history	156,892	77,702	79,190	16,952	8,256	8,696	3,819	2,184	1,635
Social sciences	125,494	59,225	66,269	14,059	6,640	7,419	3,000	1,699	1,301
Social sciences, general	7,772	2,959	4,813	583	227	356	14	9	5
Anthropology	7,524	2,295	5,229	1,069	358	711	444	195	249
Physical anthropology	0	0	0	16	3	13	0	0	0
Anthropology, other	26	7	19	1	1	0	1	0	1
Archeology	175	53	122	21	8	13	14	3	11
Criminology	5,046	2,448	2,598	365	167	198	18	8	10
Demography and population studies	0	0	0	18	8	10	7	3	4
Economics, general	23,132	15,751	7,381	2,465	1,563	902	939	654	285
Applied economics	270	159	111	149	92	57	14	13	1
Econometrics and quantitative economics	131	96	35	2	2	0	0	0	0
Development economics and international development	112	32	80	256	113	143	6	3	3
International economics	188	91	97	170	91	79	11	5	6
Economics, other	384	233	151	50	25	25	3	1	2
Geography	4,150	2,668	1,482	895	515	380	210	137	73
Cartography	112	90	22	23	18	5	0	0	0
Geography, other	95	56	39	26	17	9	0	0	0
International relations and affairs	6,853	2,648	4,205	3,452	1,591	1,861	73	40	33
Political science and government, general	37,198	19,633	17,565	1,890	945	945	634	385	249
American government and politics (United States)	114	51	63	70	42	28	0	0	0
Canadian government and politics	0	0	0	0	0	0	0	0	0
Political science and government, other	795	422	373	23	11	12	2	0	2
Sociology	28,473	8,412	20,061	1,499	476	1,023	527	202	325
Urban studies/affairs	843	366	477	373	134	239	53	30	23
Social sciences, other	2,101	755	1,346	643	233	410	30	11	19
History	31,398	18,477	12,921	2,893	1,616	1,277	819	485	334
History, general	30,858	18,221	12,637	2,767	1,558	1,209	764	456	308
American history (United States)	40	24	16	14	6	8	6	4	2

See notes at end of table.

Table 258. Bachelor's, master's, and doctor's degrees conferred by degree-granting institutions, by sex of student and field of study: 2004–05—Continued

Field of study	Bachelor's degrees requiring 4 or 5 years			Master's degrees			Doctor's degrees (Ph.D., Ed.D., etc.)		
	Total	Males	Females	Total	Males	Females	Total	Males	Females
1	2	3	4	5	6	7	8	9	10
European history	16	7	9	5	4	1	2	0	2
History and philosophy of science and technology	117	53	64	29	17	12	28	17	11
Public/applied history and archival administration	16	5	11	36	10	26	0	0	0
Asian history	0	0	0	0	0	0	2	0	2
History, other	351	167	184	42	21	21	17	8	9
Theology and religious vocations	9,284	6,253	3,031	5,815	3,469	2,346	1,422	1,101	321
Bible/biblical studies	2,653	1,630	1,023	422	294	128	31	26	5
Missions/missionary studies and missiology	383	154	229	201	115	86	46	37	9
Religious education	1,065	528	537	575	246	329	23	12	11
Religious/sacred music	208	114	94	75	35	40	1	0	1
Theology/theological studies	1,200	813	387	2,634	1,616	1,018	657	513	144
Pre-theology/preministerial studies	174	141	33	0	0	0	0	0	0
Talmudic studies	1,606	1,592	14	362	362	0	63	63	0
Theological and ministerial studies, other	444	299	145	411	268	143	267	216	51
Pastoral studies/counseling	374	226	148	616	234	382	145	107	38
Youth ministry	497	341	156	30	15	15	0	0	0
Pastoral counseling and specialized ministries, other	124	59	65	73	34	39	16	12	4
Theology and religious vocations, other	556	356	200	416	250	166	173	115	58
Transportation and materials moving	4,904	4,323	581	802	679	123	0	0	0
Aeronautics/aviation/aerospace science and technology, general	2,607	2,323	284	11	8	3	0	0	0
Airline/commercial/professional pilot and flight crew	1,011	918	93	682	595	87	0	0	0
Aviation/airway management and operations	834	707	127	49	40	9	0	0	0
Air traffic controller	147	119	28	0	0	0	0	0	0
Air transportation, other	2	1	1	46	31	15	0	0	0
Marine science/merchant marine officer	284	241	43	0	0	0	0	0	0
Marine transportation, other	0	0	0	0	0	0	0	0	0
Transportation and materials moving, other	19	14	5	14	5	9	0	0	0
Visual and performing arts	80,955	31,355	49,600	13,183	5,646	7,537	1,278	594	684
Visual and performing arts, general	2,095	823	1,272	115	46	69	6	4	2
Crafts/craft design, folk art, and artisanry	147	35	112	6	2	4	0	0	0
Dance, general	1,665	161	1,504	187	27	160	8	0	8
Ballet	38	4	34	6	0	6	0	0	0
Dance, other	22	1	21	1	0	1	6	1	5
Design and visual communications, general	3,293	1,447	1,846	196	75	121	5	2	3
Commercial and advertising art	2,931	1,334	1,597	210	116	94	0	0	0
Industrial design	1,258	801	457	111	54	57	0	0	0
Commercial photography	1	0	1	12	7	5	0	0	0
Fashion/apparel design	1,410	87	1,323	19	2	17	0	0	0
Interior design	2,951	231	2,720	188	24	164	0	0	0
Graphic design	3,380	1,399	1,981	119	55	64	0	0	0
Illustration	976	499	477	34	9	25	0	0	0
Design and applied arts, other	776	403	373	245	92	153	1	0	1
Drama and dramatics/theatre arts, general	8,555	3,152	5,403	1,168	503	665	70	31	39
Technical theatre/theatre design and technology	263	109	154	73	32	41	0	0	0
Playwriting and screenwriting	98	56	42	93	58	35	0	0	0
Theatre literature, history, and criticism	18	11	7	4	3	1	2	1	1
Acting	329	133	196	133	61	72	0	0	0
Directing and theatrical production	38	13	25	35	18	17	0	0	0
Theatre/theatre arts management	72	17	55	2	1	1	0	0	0
Acting and directing	0	0	0	0	0	0	0	0	0
Dramatic/theatre arts and stagecraft, other	207	81	126	39	21	18	0	0	0
Film/cinema studies	1,976	1,253	723	295	160	135	13	5	8
Cinematography and film/video production	2,409	1,652	757	541	322	219	9	5	4
Photography	1,679	520	1,159	184	79	105	0	0	0
Film/video and photographic arts, other	897	543	354	48	28	20	0	0	0
Art/art studies, general	13,422	4,372	9,050	809	324	485	13	2	11
Fine/studio arts, general	8,237	2,959	5,278	1,269	556	713	3	1	2
Art history, criticism, and conservation	3,085	451	2,634	618	97	521	182	45	137
Arts management	434	92	342	301	53	248	3	1	2
Drawing	280	89	191	20	4	16	0	0	0
Intermedia/multimedia	856	513	343	75	43	32	0	0	0
Painting	777	323	454	217	95	122	0	0	0
Sculpture	320	153	167	59	37	22	0	0	0
Printmaking	150	54	96	51	22	29	0	0	0
Ceramic arts and ceramics	246	82	164	49	22	27	0	0	0
Fiber, textile, and weaving arts	136	7	129	35	4	31	4	2	2
Metal and jewelry arts	122	16	106	27	11	16	0	0	0
Fine arts and art studies, other	1,662	574	1,088	257	105	152	1	1	0
Music, general	6,775	3,306	3,469	1,579	752	827	404	225	179
Music history, literature, and theory	92	38	54	55	22	33	13	4	9
Music performance, general	3,580	1,702	1,878	2,126	992	1,134	322	147	175
Music theory and composition	430	3120	118	179	139	40	60	47	13
Musicology and ethnomusicology	36	25	11	57	20	37	30	13	17
Conducting	3	0	3	97	70	23	25	17	8
Piano and organ	114	30	84	151	42	109	26	13	15
Voice and opera	263	79	184	177	45	132	11	4	7
Music management and merchandising	954	575	379	8	3	5	0	0	0

See notes at end of table.

Table 258. Bachelor's, master's, and doctor's degrees conferred by degree-granting institutions, by sex of student and field of study: 2004–05—Continued

Field of study	Bachelor's degrees requiring 4 or 5 years			Master's degrees			Doctor's degrees (Ph.D., Ed.D., etc.)		
	Total	Males	Females	Total	Males	Females	Total	Males	Females
1	2	3	4	5	6	7	8	9	10
Jazz/jazz studies...	202	164	38	85	73	12	8	6	2
Violin, viola, guitar and other stringed instruments............................	131	51	80	104	27	77	8	1	7
Music pedagogy...	46	18	28	29	8	21	0	0	0
Music, other	703	444	259	226	118	108	25	13	12
Visual and performing arts, other..	415	161	254	459	163	296	20	5	15

[1]Includes LL.M. and J.S.D./S.J.D.
NOTE: Aggregations by field of study derived from the Classification of Instructional Programs developed by the National Center for Education Statistics.

SOURCE: U.S. Department of Education, National Center for Education Statistics, 2004–05 Integrated Postsecondary Education Data System (IPEDS), Fall 2005. (This table was prepared July 2006.)

Table 259. Degrees conferred by degree-granting institutions, by control of institution and level of degree: 1969–70 through 2004–05

Year	Public institutions					Private institutions				
	Associate's degrees	Bachelor's degrees	Master's degrees	First-professional degrees[1]	Doctor's degrees[2]	Associate's degrees	Bachelor's degrees	Master's degrees	First-professional degrees[1]	Doctor's degrees[2]
1	2	3	4	5	6	7	8	9	10	11
1969–70	170,966	519,550	134,545	14,542	19,183	35,057	272,766	73,746	20,376	10,683
1970–71	215,645	557,996	151,603	16,139	20,788	36,666	281,734	78,906	21,807	11,319
1971–72	255,218	599,615	167,075	18,521	21,776	36,796	287,658	84,558	24,890	11,587
1972–73	278,132	630,899	174,405	21,872	22,357	38,042	291,463	88,966	28,146	12,420
1973–74	303,188	651,544	184,632	23,208	21,810	40,736	294,232	92,401	30,608	12,006
1974–75	318,474	634,785	193,804	23,612	22,176	41,697	288,148	98,646	32,304	11,907
1975–76	345,006	635,161	206,298	25,766	21,751	46,448	290,585	105,473	36,883	12,313
1976–77	355,650	630,463	208,901	26,344	21,229	50,727	289,086	108,263	38,015	12,003
1977–78	358,874	627,903	202,099	27,097	20,456	53,372	293,301	109,521	39,484	11,675
1978–79	346,808	621,666	192,016	27,785	20,817	55,894	299,724	109,063	41,063	11,913
1979–80	344,536	624,084	187,499	27,942	20,608	56,374	305,333	110,582	42,189	12,007
1980–81	352,391	626,452	184,384	29,128	20,895	63,986	308,688	111,355	42,828	12,063
1981–82	366,732 [3]	636,475	182,295	29,611	20,889	67,794 [3]	316,523	113,251	42,421	11,818
1982–83	377,817	646,317	176,246	29,757	21,186	71,803	323,193	113,675	43,297	11,589
1983–84	379,249 [3]	646,013	170,693	29,586	21,141	72,991 [3]	328,296	113,570	44,882	12,068
1984–85	377,625	652,246	170,000	30,152	21,337	77,087	327,231	116,251	44,911	11,606
1985–86	369,052	658,586	169,903	29,568	21,433	76,995	329,237	118,664	44,342	12,220
1986–87	358,811	659,260	167,797	29,346	21,870	77,493	332,004	121,552	42,271	12,171
1987–88	354,180	658,491	173,778	29,153	22,488	80,905	336,338	125,539	41,582	12,382
1988–89	357,001	675,675	179,109	28,993	22,970	79,763	343,080	131,512	41,863	12,750
1989–90	375,635	700,015	186,104	28,810	24,641	79,467	351,329	138,197	42,178	13,730
1990–91	398,055	724,062	193,057	29,554	25,681	83,665	370,476	144,111	42,394	13,613
1991–92	420,265	759,475	203,398	29,366	26,820	83,966	377,078	149,440	44,780	13,839
1992–93	430,321	785,112	213,843	29,628	27,392	84,435	380,066	155,742	45,759	14,740
1993–94	444,373	789,148	221,428	29,842	28,524	86,259	380,127	165,642	45,576	14,661
1994–95	451,539	776,670	224,152	29,871	28,917	88,152	383,464	173,477	45,929	15,529
1995–96	454,291	774,070	227,179	29,882	29,516	100,925	390,722	179,122	46,852	15,136
1996–97	465,494	776,677	233,237	31,243	29,838	105,732	396,202	186,164	47,487	16,038
1997–98	455,084	784,296	235,922	31,233	29,715	103,471	400,110	194,242	47,365	16,295
1998–99	448,334	790,287	238,501	31,693	28,134	111,620	410,016	201,485	46,746	15,943
1999–2000	448,446	810,855	243,157	32,247	28,408	116,487	427,020	213,899	47,810	16,400
2000–01	456,487	812,438	246,054	32,633	28,187	122,378	431,733	222,422	47,074	16,717
2001–02	471,660	841,512	249,828	33,439	27,622	123,473	450,388	232,290	47,259	16,538
2002–03	497,132	875,420	265,695	33,549	28,069	135,780	473,083	246,950	47,261	17,955
2003–04	524,875	905,718	285,138	34,499	29,706	140,426	493,824	273,802	48,542	18,672
2004–05	547,519	932,443	291,505	35,768	31,743	149,141	506,821	283,113	51,521	20,888

[1]Includes degrees that require at least 6 years of college work for completion (including at least 2 years of preprofessional training).
[2]Doctor's degrees include Ph.D., Ed.D., and comparable degrees at the doctoral level. Excludes first-professional degrees such as M.D., D.D.S., and law degrees.
[3]Data are approximations.

SOURCE: U.S. Department of Education, National Center for Education Statistics, Higher Education General Information Survey (HEGIS), "Degrees and Other Formal Awards Conferred" surveys, 1969–70 through 1985–86; and 1986–87 through 2004–05 Integrated Postsecondary Education Data System, "Completions Survey" (IPEDS-C:87–99), and Fall 2000 through Fall 2005. (This table was prepared July 2006.)

Table 260. Degrees conferred by degree-granting institutions, by control of institution, level of degree, and discipline division: 2004–05

Discipline division	Public institutions				Private institutions			
	Associate's degrees	Bachelor's degrees	Master's degrees	Doctor's degrees[1]	Associate's degrees	Bachelor's degrees	Master's degrees	Doctor's degrees[1]
1	2	3	4	5	6	7	8	9
All fields, total	**547,519**	**932,443**	**291,505**	**31,743**	**149,141**	**506,821**	**283,113**	**20,888**
Agriculture and natural resources	6,121	19,862	4,045	1,106	283	3,140	701	67
Architecture and related services	491	7,000	3,511	110	92	2,237	2,163	69
Area, ethnic, cultural, and gender studies	110	4,738	1,006	117	5	2,831	749	72
Biological and biomedical sciences	1,651	43,732	5,073	3,771	58	20,879	3,126	1,807
Business	68,116	178,811	52,478	715	44,262	132,763	90,139	783
Communications, journalism, and related programs	1,977	50,495	3,461	367	568	22,220	3,301	98
Communications technologies	2,487	1,048	73	0	1,029	1,475	360	3
Computer and information sciences	18,447	27,563	9,278	729	17,726	26,548	9,138	390
Construction trades	2,842	113	0	0	670	4	0	0
Education	12,142	74,678	86,587	4,700	1,187	30,773	80,903	2,981
Engineering	1,806	49,677	23,573	4,725	635	15,229	9,060	1,822
Engineering technologies[2]	21,059	11,048	1,519	10	12,489	3,434	981	44
English language and literature/letters	989	37,626	5,880	912	6	16,753	2,588	300
Family and consumer sciences	8,994	17,172	1,348	244	713	2,902	479	87
Foreign languages, literatures, and linguistics	1,187	12,580	2,562	680	47	5,806	845	347
Health professions and related clinical sciences	92,427	52,492	24,758	2,866	30,093	28,193	21,945	3,002
Legal professions and studies	5,129	1,796	947	16	4,756	1,365	3,223	82
Liberal arts and sciences, general studies, and humanities	230,584	30,814	1,791	35	9,547	12,937	1,889	74
Library science	108	75	5,035	39	0	1	1,178	3
Mathematics and statistics	788	9,503	3,452	848	19	4,848	1,025	328
Mechanics and repair technologies	8,792	131	0	0	4,827	107	0	0
Military technologies	355	40	0	0	0	0	0	0
Multi/interdisciplinary studies	13,662	22,123	2,741	529	226	8,120	1,511	454
Parks, recreation, leisure and fitness studies	790	17,362	2,939	186	176	5,526	801	21
Philosophy and religious studies	98	5,114	515	208	324	6,470	1,132	378
Physical sciences and science technologies	2,768	12,720	4,247	2,845	46	6,185	1,431	1,269
Precision production	1,877	23	0	0	162	41	6	0
Psychology	1,842	57,274	7,547	2,145	100	28,340	11,283	2,961
Public administration and social service professions	3,675	13,923	18,424	425	352	7,846	11,128	248
Security and protective services	19,277	21,995	1,955	89	4,472	8,728	2,036	5
Social sciences and history	6,412	104,761	10,058	2,462	121	52,131	6,894	1,357
Social sciences	6,128	84,384	7,798	1,918	105	41,110	6,261	1,082
History	284	20,377	2,260	544	16	11,021	633	275
Theology and religious vocations	0	2	0	0	581	9,282	5,815	1,422
Transportation and materials moving	969	2,180	91	0	466	2,724	711	0
Visual and performing arts	9,547	43,972	6,611	864	13,103	36,983	6,572	414

[1]Includes Ph.D., Ed.D., and comparable degrees at the doctoral level. Excludes first-professional degrees, such as M.D., D.D.S., and law degrees.
[2]Excludes "Construction trades" and "Mechanics and repair technologies," which are listed separately.
NOTE: To facilitate trend comparisons, certain aggregations have been made of the degree fields as reported in the IPEDS Fall survey: "Agriculture and natural resources" includes Agriculture, agriculture operations, and related sciences and Natural resources and conservation; and "Business" includes Business management, marketing, and related support services and Personal and culinary services.
SOURCE: U.S. Department of Education, National Center for Education Statistics, 2004–05 Integrated Postsecondary Education Data System (IPEDS), Fall 2005. (This table was prepared July 2006.)

Table 261. Number of degree-granting institutions conferring degrees, by control, level of degree, and discipline division: 2004–05

Discipline division	Total number of institutions				Public institutions				Private institutions			
	Associate's degrees	Bachelor's degrees	Master's degrees	Doctor's degrees[1]	Associate's degrees	Bachelor's degrees	Master's degrees	Doctor's degrees[1]	Associate's degrees	Bachelor's degrees	Master's degrees	Doctor's degrees[1]
1	2	3	4	5	6	7	8	9	10	11	12	13
Total	**2,691**	**2,194**	**1,617**	**596**	**1,309**	**600**	**506**	**244**	**1,382**	**1,594**	**1,111**	**352**
Agriculture and natural resources	469	570	198	87	446	267	156	80	23	303	42	7
Architecture and related services	67	182	136	30	61	114	96	22	6	68	40	8
Area, ethnic, cultural, and gender studies	41	424	122	43	39	202	77	26	2	222	45	17
Biological and biomedical sciences	203	1,290	453	241	188	493	327	166	15	797	126	75
Business	1,867	1,673	978	146	1,155	550	377	89	712	1,123	601	57
Communications, journalism, and related programs	249	1,039	277	59	207	413	183	46	42	626	94	13
Communications technologies	261	100	15	1	225	38	4	0	36	62	11	1
Computer and information sciences	1,466	1,401	436	148	916	497	259	98	550	904	177	50
Construction trades	256	8	0	0	237	7	0	0	19	1	0	0
Education	599	1,183	1,029	281	516	434	444	175	83	749	585	106
Engineering	291	444	301	195	249	247	198	143	42	197	103	52
Engineering technologies[2]	1,176	340	133	9	879	214	90	4	297	126	43	5
English language and literature/letters	149	1,292	447	143	146	500	305	97	3	792	142	46
Family and consumer sciences	626	326	138	43	577	203	103	33	49	123	35	10
Foreign languages, literatures, and linguistics	172	898	210	93	159	397	151	60	13	501	59	33
Health professions and related clinical sciences	1,596	1,096	773	229	1,052	464	347	135	544	632	426	94
Legal professions and studies	680	172	103	21	424	53	40	5	256	119	63	16
Liberal arts and sciences, general studies, and humanities	1,403	868	180	16	1,075	365	91	5	328	503	89	11
Library science	25	10	69	12	25	9	55	11	0	1	14	1
Mathematics and statistics	152	1,131	325	153	146	481	252	110	6	650	73	43
Mechanics and repair technologies	644	19	0	0	591	10	0	0	53	9	0	0
Military technologies	4	3	0	0	4	3	0	0	0	0	0	0
Multi/interdisciplinary studies	282	786	281	129	255	316	180	83	27	470	101	46
Parks, recreation, leisure and fitness studies	170	690	206	43	149	305	163	39	21	385	43	4
Philosophy and religious studies	51	890	202	105	32	292	85	52	19	598	117	53
Physical sciences and science technologies	315	1,058	330	205	303	464	243	136	12	594	87	69
Precision production	314	7	2	0	301	3	0	0	13	4	2	0
Psychology	173	1,345	623	283	151	497	320	142	22	848	303	141
Public administration and social service professions	304	721	404	104	272	312	267	66	32	409	137	38
Security and protective services	992	641	188	18	826	293	124	15	166	348	64	3
Social sciences and history	233	1,325	427	176	210	508	303	118	23	817	124	58
Social sciences	223	1,246	355	160	202	492	251	107	21	754	104	53
History	71	1,186	336	127	65	473	258	88	6	713	78	39
Theology and religious vocations	83	396	300	125	0	1	0	0	83	395	300	125
Transportation and materials moving	99	79	13	0	87	46	4	0	12	33	9	0
Visual and performing arts	728	1,348	400	100	519	468	249	67	209	880	151	33

[1]Includes Ph.D., Ed.D., and comparable degrees at the doctoral level. Excludes first-professional degrees, such as M.D., D.D.S., and law degrees.
[2]Excludes "Construction trades" and "Mechanics and repair technologies," which are listed separately.

SOURCE: U.S. Department of Education, National Center for Education Statistics, 2004–05 Integrated Postsecondary Education Data System (IPEDS), Fall 2005. (This table was prepared July 2006.)

Table 262. First-professional degrees conferred by degree-granting institutions in dentistry, medicine, and law, by number of institutions conferring degrees and sex of student: Selected years, 1949–50 through 2004–05

	Dentistry (D.D.S. or D.M.D.)				Medicine (M.D.)				Law (LL.B. or J.D.)			
	Number of institutions conferring degrees	Degrees conferred			Number of institutions conferring degrees	Degrees conferred			Number of institutions conferring degrees	Degrees conferred		
Year		Total	Males	Females		Total	Males	Females		Total	Males	Females
1	2	3	4	5	6	7	8	9	10	11	12	13
1949–50	40	2,579	2,561	18	72	5,612	5,028	584	—	—	—	—
1951–52	41	2,918	2,895	23	72	6,201	5,871	330	—	—	—	—
1953–54	42	3,102	3,063	39	73	6,712	6,377	335	—	—	—	—
1955–56	42	3,009	2,975	34	73	6,810	6,464	346	131	8,262	7,974	288
1957–58	43	3,065	3,031	34	75	6,816	6,469	347	131	9,394	9,122	272
1959–60	45	3,247	3,221	26	79	7,032	6,645	387	134	9,240	9,010	230
1961–62	46	3,183	3,166	17	81	7,138	6,749	389	134	9,364	9,091	273
1963–64	46	3,180	3,168	12	82	7,303	6,878	425	133	10,679	10,372	307
1964–65	46	3,108	3,086	22	81	7,304	6,832	472	137	11,583	11,216	367
1965–66	47	3,178	3,146	32	84	7,673	7,170	503	136	13,246	12,776	470
1967–68	48	3,422	3,375	47	85	7,944	7,318	626	138	16,454	15,805	649
1968–69	—	3,408	3,376	32	—	8,025	7,415	610	—	17,053	16,373	680
1969–70	48	3,718	3,684	34	86	8,314	7,615	699	145	14,916	14,115	801
1970–71	48	3,745	3,703	42	89	8,919	8,110	809	147	17,421	16,181	1,240
1971–72	48	3,862	3,819	43	92	9,253	8,423	830	147	21,764	20,266	1,498
1972–73	51	4,047	3,992	55	97	10,307	9,388	919	152	27,205	25,037	2,168
1973–74	52	4,440	4,355	85	99	11,356	10,093	1,263	151	29,326	25,986	3,340
1974–75	52	4,773	4,627	146	104	12,447	10,818	1,629	154	29,296	24,881	4,415
1975–76	56	5,425	5,187	238	107	13,426	11,252	2,174	166	32,293	26,085	6,208
1976–77	57	5,138	4,764	374	109	13,461	10,891	2,570	169	34,104	26,447	7,657
1977–78	57	5,189	4,623	566	109	14,279	11,210	3,069	169	34,402	25,457	8,945
1978–79	58	5,434	4,794	640	109	14,786	11,381	3,405	175	35,206	25,180	10,026
1979–80	58	5,258	4,558	700	112	14,902	11,416	3,486	179	35,647	24,893	10,754
1980–81	58	5,460	4,672	788	116	15,505	11,672	3,833	176	36,331	24,563	11,768
1981–82	59	5,282	4,467	815	119	15,814	11,867	3,947	180	35,991	23,965	12,026
1982–83	59	5,585	4,631	954	118	15,484	11,350	4,134	177	36,853	23,550	13,303
1983–84	60	5,353	4,302	1,051	119	15,813	11,359	4,454	179	37,012	23,382	13,630
1984–85	59	5,339	4,233	1,106	120	16,041	11,167	4,874	181	37,491	23,070	14,421
1985–86	59	5,046	3,907	1,139	120	15,938	11,022	4,916	181	35,844	21,874	13,970
1986–87	58	4,741	3,603	1,138	121	15,428	10,431	4,997	179	36,056	21,561	14,495
1987–88	57	4,477	3,300	1,177	122	15,358	10,278	5,080	180	35,397	21,067	14,330
1988–89	58	4,265	3,124	1,141	124	15,460	10,310	5,150	182	35,634	21,069	14,565
1989–90	57	4,100	2,834	1,266	124	15,075	9,923	5,152	182	36,485	21,079	15,406
1990–91	55	3,699	2,510	1,189	121	15,043	9,629	5,414	179	37,945	21,643	16,302
1991–92	52	3,593	2,431	1,162	120	15,243	9,796	5,447	177	38,848	22,260	16,588
1992–93	55	3,605	2,383	1,222	122	15,531	9,679	5,852	184	40,302	23,182	17,120
1993–94	53	3,787	2,330	1,457	121	15,368	9,544	5,824	185	40,044	22,826	17,218
1994–95	53	3,897	2,480	1,417	119	15,537	9,507	6,030	183	39,349	22,592	16,757
1995–96	53	3,697	2,374	1,323	119	15,341	9,061	6,280	183	39,828	22,508	17,320
1996–97	52	3,784	2,387	1,397	118	15,571	9,121	6,450	184	40,079	22,548	17,531
1997–98	53	4,032	2,490	1,542	117	15,424	9,006	6,418	185	39,331	21,876	17,455
1998–99	53	4,144	2,674	1,470	118	15,562	8,954	6,608	188	39,167	21,628	17,539
1999–2000	54	4,250	2,547	1,703	118	15,286	8,761	6,525	190	38,152	20,638	17,514
2000–01	54	4,391	2,696	1,695	118	15,403	8,728	6,675	192	37,904	19,981	17,923
2001–02	53	4,239	2,608	1,631	118	15,237	8,469	6,768	192	38,981	20,254	18,727
2002–03	53	4,344	2,653	1,691	118	15,034	8,221	6,813	194	39,067	19,916	19,151
2003–04	53	4,335	2,532	1,803	118	15,442	8,273	7,169	195	40,209	20,332	19,877
2004–05	53	4,454	2,505	1,949	120	15,461	8,151	7,310	198	43,423	22,297	21,126

—Not available.
SOURCE: U.S. Department of Education, National Center for Education Statistics, *Earned Degrees Conferred*, 1949–50 through 1964–65; Higher Education General Information Survey (HEGIS), "Degrees and Other Formal Awards Conferred" surveys, 1965–66 through 1985–86; and 1986–87 through 2004–05 Integrated Postsecondary Education Data System (IPEDS), "Completions Survey" (IPEDS-C:87–99), and Fall 2000 through Fall 2005. (This table was prepared July 2006.)

Table 263. First-professional degrees conferred by degree-granting institutions, by sex of student, control of institution, and field of study: Selected years, 1985–86 through 2004–05

Control of institution and field of study	1985-86	1990-91	1993-94	1994-95	1995-96	1996-97	1997-98	1998-99	1999-2000	2000-01	2001-02	2002-03	2003-04			2004-05		
													Total	Males	Females	Total	Males	Females
1	2	3	4	5	6	7	8	9	10	11	12	13	14	15	16	17	18	19
Total, all institutions	73,910	71,948	75,418	75,800	76,734	78,730	78,598	78,439	80,057	79,707	80,698	80,810	83,041	42,169	40,872	87,289	43,849	43,440
Dentistry (D.D.S. or D.M.D.)	5,046	3,699	3,787	3,897	3,697	3,784	4,032	4,144	4,250	4,391	4,239	4,344	4,335	2,532	1,803	4,454	2,505	1,949
Medicine (M.D.)	15,938	15,043	15,368	15,537	15,341	15,571	15,424	15,562	15,286	15,403	15,237	15,034	15,442	8,273	7,169	15,461	8,151	7,310
Optometry (O.D.)	1,029	1,115	1,103	1,185	1,231	1,264	1,274	1,285	1,293	1,289	1,280	1,281	1,275	543	732	1,252	482	770
Osteopathic medicine (D.O.)	1,547	1,459	1,798	1,854	1,895	2,011	2,110	2,135	2,236	2,450	2,416	2,529	2,722	1,567	1,155	2,762	1,482	1,280
Pharmacy (Pharm.D.)	903	1,244	1,936	2,264	2,555	2,708	3,660	3,992	5,669	6,324	7,076	7,465	8,221	2,711	5,510	8,885	2,889	5,996
Podiatry (Pod.D. or D.P) or podiatric medicine (D.P.M.)	612	589	465	545	650	614	594	578	569	528	474	438	382	221	161	343	195	148
Veterinary medicine (D.V.M.)	2,270	2,032	2,089	2,148	2,109	2,188	2,193	2,226	2,251	2,248	2,289	2,354	2,228	569	1,659	2,354	574	1,780
Chiropractic (D.C. or D.C.M.)	3,395	2,640	2,806	2,968	3,379	3,654	3,735	3,639	3,809	3,796	3,284	2,718	2,730	1,868	862	2,560	1,665	895
Law (LL.B. or J.D.)	35,844	37,945	40,044	39,349	39,828	40,079	39,331	39,167	38,152	37,904	38,981	39,067	40,209	20,332	19,877	43,423	22,297	21,126
Theology (M.Div, M.H.L., B.D., or Ord. and M.H.L./Rav.)	7,283	5,695	5,967	5,978	5,879	5,859	5,873	5,558	6,129	5,026	5,195	5,351	5,332	3,511	1,821	5,533	3,565	1,968
Other	43	487	55	75	170	998	372	153	413	348	227	229	165	42	123	262	44	218
Total, public institutions	29,568	29,554	29,842	29,871	29,882	31,243	31,233	31,693	32,247	32,633	33,439	33,549	34,499	16,881	17,618	35,768	17,175	18,593
Dentistry (D.D.S. or D.M.D.)	2,827	2,308	2,189	2,236	2,198	2,350	2,468	2,479	2,512	2,477	2,525	2,493	2,498	1,509	989	2,577	1,488	1,089
Medicine (M.D.)	9,991	9,364	9,506	9,599	9,370	9,773	9,474	9,515	9,389	9,408	9,390	9,276	9,418	5,084	4,334	9,536	5,069	4,467
Optometry (O.D.)	441	477	471	461	499	498	537	488	493	497	503	481	476	191	285	477	159	318
Osteopathic medicine (D.O.)	486	493	531	492	528	527	568	548	535	562	538	571	586	335	251	568	285	283
Pharmacy (Pharm.D.)	473	808	1,185	1,344	1,557	1,765	2,212	2,503	3,485	3,876	4,382	4,558	4,930	1,671	3,259	5,352	1,768	3,584
Podiatry (Pod.D. or D.P) or podiatric medicine (D.P.M.)	0	0	0	0	0	0	103	97	84	84	75	81	64	34	30	64	40	24
Veterinary medicine (D.V.M.)	1,931	1,814	1,895	1,927	1,889	1,950	1,971	1,989	2,021	2,017	2,052	2,023	1,912	492	1,420	2,033	473	1,560
Chiropractic (D.C. or D.C.M.)	0	0	0	0	0	0	0	0	0	0	0	0	0	0	0	0	0	0
Law (LL.B. or J.D.)	13,419	14,290	14,065	13,812	13,841	14,380	13,900	14,074	13,728	13,712	13,974	14,066	14,615	7,565	7,050	15,161	7,893	7,268
Theology (M.Div, M.H.L., B.D., or Ord. and M.H.L./Rav.)	0	0	0	0	0	0	0	0	0	0	0	0	0	0	0	0	0	0
Other	0	0	0	0	0	0	0	0	0	0	0	0	0	0	0	0	0	0
Total, private institutions	44,342	42,394	45,576	45,929	46,852	47,487	47,365	46,746	47,810	47,074	47,259	47,261	48,542	25,288	23,254	51,521	26,674	24,847
Dentistry (D.D.S. or D.M.D.)	2,219	1,391	1,598	1,661	1,499	1,434	1,564	1,665	1,738	1,914	1,714	1,851	1,837	1,023	814	1,877	1,017	860
Medicine (M.D.)	5,947	5,679	5,862	5,938	5,971	5,798	5,950	6,047	5,897	5,995	5,847	5,758	6,024	3,189	2,835	5,925	3,082	2,843
Optometry (O.D.)	588	638	632	724	732	766	737	797	800	792	777	800	799	352	447	775	323	452
Osteopathic medicine (D.O.)	1,061	966	1,267	1,362	1,367	1,484	1,542	1,587	1,701	1,888	1,878	1,958	2,136	1,232	904	2,194	1,197	997
Pharmacy (Pharm.D.)	430	436	751	920	998	943	1,448	1,489	2,184	2,448	2,694	2,907	3,291	1,040	2,251	3,533	1,121	2,412
Podiatry (Pod.D. or D.P) or podiatric medicine (D.P.M.)	612	589	465	545	650	614	491	481	485	444	399	357	318	187	131	279	155	124
Veterinary medicine (D.V.M.)	339	218	194	221	220	238	222	237	230	231	237	331	316	77	239	321	101	220
Chiropractic (D.C. or D.C.M.)	3,395	2,640	2,806	2,968	3,379	3,654	3,735	3,639	3,809	3,796	3,284	2,718	2,730	1,868	862	2,560	1,665	895
Law (LL.B. or J.D.)	22,425	23,655	25,979	25,537	25,987	25,699	25,431	25,093	24,424	24,192	25,007	25,001	25,594	12,767	12,827	28,262	14,404	13,858
Theology (M.Div, M.H.L., B.D., or Ord. and M.H.L./Rav.)	7,283	5,695	5,967	5,978	5,879	5,859	5,873	5,558	6,129	5,026	5,195	5,351	5,332	3,511	1,821	5,533	3,565	1,968
Other	43	487	55	75	170	998	372	153	413	348	227	229	165	42	123	262	44	218

NOTE: Includes degrees that require at least 6 years of college work for completion (including at least 2 years of preprofessional training).
SOURCE: U.S. Department of Education, National Center for Education Statistics, Higher Education General Information Survey (HEGIS), "Degrees and Other Formal Awards Conferred," 1985–86; and 1990–91 through 2004–05 through Fall 2005 Integrated Post-secondary Education Data System, "Completions Survey" (IPEDS-C:91–99), and Fall 2000 through Fall 2005. (This table was prepared July 2006.)

Table 264. Associate's degrees conferred by degree-granting institutions, by race/ethnicity and sex of student: Selected years, 1976–77 through 2004–05

Year and sex	Number of degrees conferred							Percentage distribution of degrees conferred						
	Total	White	Black	Hispanic	Asian/ Pacific Islander	American Indian/ Alaska Native	Non-resident alien	Total	White	Black	Hispanic	Asian/ Pacific Islander	American Indian/ Alaska Native	Non-resident alien
1	2	3	4	5	6	7	8	9	10	11	12	13	14	15
Total														
1976–77[1]	404,956	342,290	33,159	16,636	7,044	2,498	3,329	100.0	84.5	8.2	4.1	1.7	0.6	0.8
1980–81[2]	410,174	339,167	35,330	17,800	8,650	2,584	6,643	100.0	82.7	8.6	4.3	2.1	0.6	1.6
1989–90	455,102	376,816	34,326	21,504	13,066	3,430	5,960	100.0	82.8	7.5	4.7	2.9	0.8	1.3
1990–91	481,720	391,264	38,835	25,540	15,257	3,871	6,953	100.0	81.2	8.1	5.3	3.2	0.8	1.4
1991–92	504,231	408,871	40,228	27,262	15,821	4,060	7,989	100.0	81.1	8.0	5.4	3.1	0.8	1.6
1992–93	514,756	411,435	42,886	30,283	16,763	4,408	8,981	100.0	79.9	8.3	5.9	3.3	0.9	1.7
1993–94	530,632	419,694	45,523	32,118	18,444	4,876	9,977	100.0	79.1	8.6	6.1	3.5	0.9	1.9
1994–95	539,691	420,656	47,067	35,962	20,677	5,482	9,847	100.0	77.9	8.7	6.7	3.8	1.0	1.8
1995–96	555,216	426,106	52,014	38,254	23,138	5,573	10,131	100.0	76.7	9.4	6.9	4.2	1.0	1.8
1996–97	571,226	429,464	56,306	43,549	25,159	5,984	10,764	100.0	75.2	9.9	7.6	4.4	1.0	1.9
1997–98	558,555	413,561	55,314	45,876	25,196	6,246	12,362	100.0	74.0	9.9	8.2	4.5	1.1	2.2
1998–99	559,954	409,086	57,439	48,670	27,586	6,424	10,749	100.0	73.1	10.3	8.7	4.9	1.1	1.9
1999–2000	564,933	408,772	60,221	51,573	27,782	6,497	10,088	100.0	72.4	10.7	9.1	4.9	1.2	1.8
2000–01	578,865	411,075	63,855	57,288	28,463	6,623	11,561	100.0	71.0	11.0	9.9	4.9	1.1	2.0
2001–02	595,133	417,733	67,343	60,003	30,945	6,832	12,277	100.0	70.2	11.3	10.1	5.2	1.1	2.1
2002–03	632,912	437,794	75,430	66,175	32,610	7,462	13,441	100.0	69.2	11.9	10.5	5.2	1.2	2.1
2003–04	665,301	456,047	81,183	72,270	33,149	8,119	14,533	100.0	68.5	12.2	10.9	5.0	1.2	2.2
2004–05	696,660	475,513	86,402	78,557	33,669	8,435	14,084	100.0	68.3	12.4	11.3	4.8	1.2	2.0
Males														
1976–77[1]	209,672	178,236	15,330	9,105	3,630	1,216	2,155	100.0	85.0	7.3	4.3	1.7	0.6	1.0
1980–81[2]	183,819	151,242	14,290	8,327	4,557	1,108	4,295	100.0	82.3	7.8	4.5	2.5	0.6	2.3
1989–90	191,195	158,954	12,502	9,370	6,170	1,364	2,835	100.0	83.1	6.5	4.9	3.2	0.7	1.5
1990–91	198,634	161,858	14,143	10,738	7,164	1,439	3,292	100.0	81.5	7.1	5.4	3.6	0.7	1.7
1991–92	207,481	168,976	14,529	11,664	7,349	1,545	3,418	100.0	81.4	7.0	5.6	3.5	0.7	1.6
1992–93	211,964	169,841	15,689	13,014	7,937	1,680	3,803	100.0	80.1	7.4	6.1	3.7	0.8	1.8
1993–94	215,261	170,905	16,931	13,214	8,289	1,837	4,085	100.0	79.4	7.9	6.1	3.9	0.9	1.9
1994–95	218,352	170,251	16,727	15,670	9,252	2,098	4,354	100.0	78.0	7.7	7.2	4.2	1.0	2.0
1995–96	219,514	169,230	17,941	15,740	10,229	1,993	4,381	100.0	77.1	8.2	7.2	4.7	0.9	2.0
1996–97	223,948	168,882	19,394	17,990	10,937	2,068	4,677	100.0	75.4	8.7	8.0	4.9	0.9	2.1
1997–98	217,613	161,212	18,686	19,108	10,953	2,252	5,402	100.0	74.1	8.6	8.8	5.0	1.0	2.5
1998–99	218,417	160,794	19,402	19,379	11,671	2,241	4,930	100.0	73.6	8.9	8.9	5.3	1.0	2.3
1999–2000	224,721	164,315	20,967	20,946	12,010	2,225	4,258	100.0	73.1	9.3	9.3	5.3	1.0	1.9
2000–01	231,645	166,322	22,147	23,350	12,339	2,294	5,193	100.0	71.8	9.6	10.1	5.3	1.0	2.2
2001–02	238,109	170,622	22,806	23,963	13,256	2,308	5,154	100.0	71.7	9.6	10.1	5.6	1.0	2.2
2002–03	253,060	178,959	25,518	26,300	14,048	2,619	5,616	100.0	70.7	10.1	10.4	5.6	1.0	2.2
2003–04	260,033	183,819	25,961	27,828	13,907	2,740	5,778	100.0	70.7	10.0	10.7	5.3	1.1	2.2
2004–05	267,536	188,569	27,151	29,658	13,802	2,774	5,582	100.0	70.5	10.1	11.1	5.2	1.0	2.1
Females														
1976–77[1]	195,284	164,054	17,829	7,531	3,414	1,282	1,174	100.0	84.0	9.1	3.9	1.7	0.7	0.6
1980–81[2]	226,355	187,925	21,040	9,473	4,093	1,476	2,348	100.0	83.0	9.3	4.2	1.8	0.7	1.0
1989–90	263,907	217,862	21,824	12,134	6,896	2,066	3,125	100.0	82.6	8.3	4.6	2.6	0.8	1.2
1990–91	283,086	229,406	24,692	14,802	8,093	2,432	3,661	100.0	81.0	8.7	5.2	2.9	0.9	1.3
1991–92	296,750	239,895	25,699	15,598	8,472	2,515	4,571	100.0	80.8	8.7	5.3	2.9	0.8	1.5
1992–93	302,792	241,594	27,197	17,269	8,826	2,728	5,178	100.0	79.8	9.0	5.7	2.9	0.9	1.7
1993–94	315,371	248,789	28,592	18,904	10,155	3,039	5,892	100.0	78.9	9.1	6.0	3.2	1.0	1.9
1994–95	321,339	250,405	30,340	20,292	11,425	3,384	5,493	100.0	77.9	9.4	6.3	3.6	1.1	1.7
1995–96	335,702	256,876	34,073	22,514	12,909	3,580	5,750	100.0	76.5	10.1	6.7	3.8	1.1	1.7
1996–97	347,278	260,582	36,912	25,559	14,222	3,916	6,087	100.0	75.0	10.6	7.4	4.1	1.1	1.8
1997–98	340,942	252,349	36,628	26,768	14,243	3,994	6,960	100.0	74.0	10.7	7.9	4.2	1.2	2.0
1998–99	341,537	248,292	38,037	29,291	15,915	4,183	5,819	100.0	72.7	11.1	8.6	4.7	1.2	1.7
1999–2000	340,212	244,457	39,254	30,627	15,772	4,272	5,830	100.0	71.9	11.5	9.0	4.6	1.3	1.7
2000–01	347,220	244,753	41,708	33,938	16,124	4,329	6,368	100.0	70.5	12.0	9.8	4.6	1.2	1.8
2001–02	357,024	247,111	44,537	36,040	17,689	4,524	7,123	100.0	69.2	12.5	10.1	5.0	1.3	2.0
2002–03	379,852	258,835	49,912	39,875	18,562	4,843	7,825	100.0	68.1	13.1	10.5	4.9	1.3	2.1
2003–04	405,268	272,228	55,222	44,442	19,242	5,379	8,755	100.0	67.2	13.6	11.0	4.7	1.3	2.2
2004–05	429,124	286,944	59,251	48,899	19,867	5,661	8,502	100.0	66.9	13.8	11.4	4.6	1.3	2.0

[1]Excludes 1,170 males and 251 females whose racial/ethnic group was not available.
[2]Excludes 4,819 males and 1,384 females whose racial/ethnic group was not available.
NOTE: Race categories exclude persons of Hispanic origin. For years 1989–90 to 2004–05, reported racial/ethnic distributions of students by level of degree, field of degree, and sex were used to estimate race/ethnicity for students whose race/ethnicity was not reported. (See Guide to Sources for details.) Detail may not sum to totals because of rounding.

SOURCE: U.S. Department of Education, National Center for Education Statistics, Higher Education General Information Survey (HEGIS), "Degrees and Other Formal Awards Conferred" surveys, 1976–77 and 1980–81; and 1988–89 through 2004–05 Integrated Postsecondary Education Data System, "Completions Survey" (IPEDS-C:89–99), and Fall 2000 through Fall 2005. (This table was prepared July 2006.)

Table 265. Associate's degrees conferred by degree-granting institutions, by sex, race/ethnicity, and major field of study: 2004–05

Major field of study	Total							Males							Females						
	Total	White	Black	Hispanic	Asian/ Pacific Islander	American Indian/ Alaska Native	Non-resident alien	Total	White	Black	Hispanic	Asian/ Pacific Islander	American Indian/ Alaska Native	Non-resident alien	Total	White	Black	Hispanic	Asian/ Pacific Islander	American Indian/ Alaska Native	Non-resident alien
1	2	3	4	5	6	7	8	9	10	11	12	13	14	15	16	17	18	19	20	21	22
All fields, total	696,660	475,513	86,402	78,557	33,669	8,435	14,084	267,536	188,569	27,151	29,658	13,802	2,774	5,582	429,124	286,944	59,251	48,899	19,867	5,661	8,502
Agriculture and natural resources	6,404	6,042	38	124	36	101	63	4,009	3,819	24	63	9	58	36	2,395	2,223	14	61	27	43	27
Architecture and related services	583	380	37	107	35	4	20	237	142	18	50	19	0	8	346	238	19	57	16	4	12
Area, ethnic, cultural, and gender studies	115	25	25	21	6	32	3	38	8	11	10	1	10	0	77	19	14	11	6	22	3
Biological and biomedical sciences	1,709	1,050	132	232	197	46	52	548	343	36	83	51	17	18	1,161	707	96	149	146	29	34
Business	112,378	72,333	17,842	11,913	5,986	1,310	2,994	39,165	26,558	4,881	4,104	2,124	360	1,138	73,213	45,775	12,961	7,809	3,862	950	1,856
Communications, journalism, and related programs	2,545	1,862	263	225	88	27	80	1,254	949	108	118	33	10	36	1,291	913	155	107	55	17	44
Communications technologies	3,516	2,496	411	362	142	29	76	2,039	1,394	259	247	85	16	38	1,477	1,102	152	115	57	13	38
Computer and information sciences	36,173	23,572	5,554	3,882	1,997	385	783	25,552	17,532	3,138	2,790	1,379	212	501	10,621	6,040	2,416	1,092	618	173	282
Construction trades	3,512	3,011	243	140	53	60	5	3,308	2,857	217	129	51	50	4	204	154	26	11	2	10	1
Education	13,329	8,462	2,250	1,857	178	461	121	2,188	1,487	332	251	22	79	17	11,141	6,975	1,918	1,606	156	382	104
Engineering	2,441	1,496	300	336	153	35	121	2,078	1,327	244	263	116	26	102	363	169	56	73	37	9	19
Engineering technologies[1]	33,548	24,118	3,691	3,701	1,362	346	330	28,675	20,824	2,933	3,222	1,164	280	252	4,873	3,294	758	479	198	66	78
English language and literature/letters	995	610	91	191	57	17	29	313	202	26	60	12	7	6	682	408	65	131	45	10	23
Family and consumer sciences	9,707	5,337	2,036	1,726	334	150	124	446	260	84	69	23	2	8	9,261	5,077	1,952	1,657	311	148	116
Foreign languages, literatures, and linguistics	1,234	871	80	203	28	18	34	197	110	13	49	13	2	10	1,037	761	67	154	15	16	24
Health professions and related clinical sciences	122,520	90,192	15,578	9,512	4,673	1,298	1,267	17,097	12,008	1,987	1,612	1,083	170	237	105,423	78,184	13,591	7,900	3,590	1,128	1,030
Legal professions and studies	9,885	6,690	1,673	1,188	179	108	47	955	577	196	135	30	14	3	8,930	6,113	1,477	1,053	149	94	44
Liberal arts and sciences, general studies, and humanities	240,131	161,795	25,669	30,748	13,109	2,690	6,120	87,845	60,870	8,215	10,389	5,112	847	2,412	152,286	100,925	17,454	20,359	7,997	1,843	3,708
Library science	108	86	9	8	3	1	1	11	8	2	0	0	1	0	97	78	7	8	3	0	1
Mathematics and statistics	807	433	37	162	102	13	60	529	285	25	108	62	7	42	278	148	12	54	40	6	18
Mechanics and repair technologies	13,619	10,267	966	1,451	673	179	83	12,901	9,782	884	1,372	628	162	73	718	485	82	79	45	17	10
Military technologies	355	215	87	39	9	5	0	303	186	74	30	8	5	0	52	29	13	9	1	0	0
Multi/interdisciplinary studies	13,888	8,627	1,561	1,761	1,466	110	363	5,878	3,723	683	702	572	44	154	8,010	4,904	878	1,059	894	66	209
Parks, recreation, leisure and fitness studies	966	734	116	67	7	20	22	581	448	71	37	5	10	10	385	286	45	30	2	10	12
Philosophy and religious studies	422	364	17	29	9	2	1	122	94	7	14	5	2	0	300	270	10	15	4	0	1
Physical sciences and science technologies	2,814	1,917	217	264	243	36	137	1,647	1,140	115	168	123	16	85	1,167	777	102	96	120	20	52
Precision production	2,039	1,735	88	110	67	36	3	1,877	1,614	79	101	49	31	3	162	121	9	9	18	5	0
Psychology	1,942	1,184	181	402	78	59	38	445	271	39	98	15	13	9	1,497	913	142	304	63	46	29
Public administration and social service professions	4,027	2,171	1,070	567	99	84	36	571	306	122	108	16	14	5	3,456	1,865	948	459	83	70	31
Security and protective services	23,749	16,684	3,221	2,918	521	326	79	13,360	10,357	1,043	1,424	348	147	41	10,389	6,327	2,178	1,494	173	179	38
Social sciences and history	6,533	3,685	735	1,270	483	201	159	2,191	1,302	196	401	183	53	56	4,342	2,383	539	869	300	148	103
Social sciences	6,233	3,480	719	1,212	471	192	159	2,017	1,181	184	369	178	49	56	4,216	2,299	535	843	293	143	103
History	300	205	16	58	12	9	0	174	121	12	32	5	4	0	126	84	4	26	7	5	3
Theology and religious vocations	581	421	107	21	8	8	16	270	192	50	12	3	3	10	311	229	57	9	5	5	6
Transportation and materials moving	1,435	1,095	91	142	43	21	43	1,241	969	78	111	37	16	30	194	126	13	31	6	5	13
Visual and performing arts	22,650	15,553	1,986	2,878	1,242	217	774	9,665	6,627	961	1,328	421	90	238	12,985	8,926	1,025	1,550	821	127	536

[1]Excludes "Construction trades" and "Mechanics and repair technologies," which are listed separately.

NOTE: Race categories exclude persons of Hispanic origin. Reported racial/ethnic distributions of students by level of degree, field of degree, and sex were used to estimate race/ethnicity for students whose race/ethnicity was not reported. To facilitate trend comparisons, certain aggregations have been made of the degree fields as reported in the IPEDS Fall survey: "Agriculture and natural resources" includes Agriculture, agriculture operations, and related sciences and Natural resources and conservation; and "Business" includes Business management, marketing, and related support services and Personal and culinary services.

SOURCE: U.S. Department of Education, National Center for Education Statistics, 2004–05 Integrated Postsecondary Education Data System (IPEDS), Fall 2005. (This table was prepared July 2006.)

Table 266. Associate's degrees conferred by degree-granting institutions, by sex, race/ethnicity, and major field of study: 2003–04

Major field of study	Total							Males							Females						
	Total	White	Black	Hispanic	Asian/Pacific Islander	American Indian/Alaska Native	Non-resident alien	Total	White	Black	Hispanic	Asian/Pacific Islander	American Indian/Alaska Native	Non-resident alien	Total	White	Black	Hispanic	Asian/Pacific Islander	American Indian/Alaska Native	Non-resident alien
1	2	3	4	5	6	7	8	9	10	11	12	13	14	15	16	17	18	19	20	21	22
All fields, total	665,301	456,047	81,183	72,270	33,149	8,119	14,533	260,033	183,819	25,961	27,828	13,907	2,740	5,778	405,268	272,228	55,222	44,442	19,242	5,379	8,755
Agriculture and natural resources	6,283	5,887	61	117	45	92	81	3,928	3,696	42	69	24	56	41	2,355	2,191	19	48	21	36	40
Architecture and related services	492	330	35	85	12	2	28	180	98	22	44	7	1	8	312	232	13	41	5	1	20
Area, ethnic, cultural, and gender studies	105	20	21	13	2	46	3	40	9	7	6	0	18	0	65	11	14	7	2	28	3
Biological and biomedical sciences	1,456	912	115	185	147	48	49	471	316	34	55	42	9	15	985	596	81	130	105	39	34
Business	106,304	68,615	16,359	10,764	5,963	1,304	3,299	35,720	24,526	4,247	3,427	1,972	371	1,177	70,584	44,089	12,112	7,337	3,991	933	2,122
Communications, journalism, and related programs	2,444	1,779	266	204	81	28	86	1,188	902	106	105	30	19	26	1,256	877	160	99	51	9	60
Communications technologies	3,401	2,506	294	322	124	58	97	1,926	1,409	166	210	65	34	42	1,475	1,097	128	112	59	24	55
Computer and information sciences	41,845	27,160	6,485	4,084	2,666	412	1,038	28,717	19,540	3,706	2,839	1,774	242	616	13,128	7,620	2,779	1,245	892	170	422
Construction trades	3,560	3,095	186	150	70	54	5	3,360	2,940	177	137	63	41	2	200	155	9	13	7	13	3
Education	12,465	7,931	2,066	1,689	199	457	123	2,198	1,452	287	298	49	87	25	10,267	6,479	1,779	1,391	150	370	98
Engineering	2,737	1,573	298	530	175	43	118	2,160	1,277	227	396	138	25	97	577	296	71	134	37	18	21
Engineering technologies[1]	36,915	26,158	4,033	3,983	1,848	429	464	31,452	22,569	3,176	3,442	1,563	328	374	5,463	3,589	857	541	285	101	90
English language and literature/letters	828	531	73	140	52	10	22	266	158	21	50	29	3	5	562	373	52	90	23	7	17
Family and consumer sciences	9,478	4,991	2,153	1,677	330	171	156	394	229	63	63	18	9	12	9,084	4,762	2,090	1,614	312	162	144
Foreign languages, literatures, and linguistics	1,047	723	51	192	24	18	39	180	114	6	43	11	3	3	867	609	45	149	13	15	36
Health professions and related clinical sciences	106,208	78,649	13,617	8,219	3,771	1,088	864	13,837	9,660	1,584	1,454	802	154	183	92,371	68,989	12,033	6,765	2,969	934	681
Legal professions and studies	9,466	6,410	1,702	1,030	161	120	43	939	580	201	116	21	14	7	8,527	5,830	1,501	914	140	106	36
Liberal arts and sciences, general studies, and humanities	227,650	154,929	23,837	27,705	12,650	2,547	5,982	83,216	57,967	7,674	9,462	4,935	789	2,389	144,434	96,962	16,163	18,243	7,715	1,758	3,593
Library science	114	97	1	5	7	3	1	13	11	0	2	0	0	0	101	86	1	3	7	3	1
Mathematics and statistics	801	461	38	138	106	11	47	502	294	23	87	60	5	33	299	167	15	51	46	6	14
Mechanics and repair technologies	12,553	9,705	829	1,165	607	147	100	11,825	9,240	735	1,083	543	134	90	728	465	94	82	64	13	10
Military technologies	293	176	73	32	9	3	0	240	152	52	26	8	2	0	53	24	21	6	1	1	0
Multi/interdisciplinary studies	14,794	9,863	1,463	1,673	1,311	124	360	6,404	4,329	670	671	542	45	147	8,390	5,534	793	1,002	769	79	213
Parks, recreation, leisure and fitness studies	923	717	98	48	21	13	26	540	408	67	28	15	7	15	383	309	31	20	6	6	11
Philosophy and religious studies	404	335	14	29	18	0	8	104	72	7	16	8	0	1	300	263	7	13	10	0	7
Physical sciences and science technologies	2,676	1,817	223	252	244	32	108	1,540	1,078	113	157	124	16	52	1,136	739	110	95	120	16	56
Precision production	1,968	1,733	63	88	45	34	5	1,828	1,615	59	82	42	25	5	140	118	4	6	3	9	0
Psychology	1,887	1,206	166	354	80	37	44	434	272	39	80	22	9	12	1,453	934	127	274	58	28	32
Public administration and social service professions	3,728	1,957	966	558	112	90	45	444	195	130	85	15	14	5	3,284	1,762	836	473	97	76	40
Security and protective services	20,573	14,784	2,494	2,491	484	267	53	12,002	9,397	861	1,298	312	111	23	8,571	5,387	1,633	1,193	172	156	30
Social sciences and history	6,245	3,580	749	1,155	429	157	175	2,088	1,244	214	377	151	43	59	4,157	2,336	535	778	278	114	116
Social sciences	5,875	3,304	735	1,094	417	152	173	1,883	1,090	205	340	148	42	58	3,992	2,214	530	754	269	110	115
History	370	276	14	61	12	5	2	205	154	9	37	3	1	1	165	122	5	24	9	4	1
Theology and religious vocations	492	338	112	11	8	7	16	220	134	61	8	4	2	11	272	204	51	3	4	5	5
Transportation and materials moving	1,217	921	69	135	45	12	35	1,035	802	52	109	42	8	22	182	119	17	26	3	4	13
Visual and performing arts	23,949	16,158	2,173	3,047	1,303	255	1,013	10,642	7,134	1,132	1,503	476	116	281	13,307	9,024	1,041	1,544	827	139	732

[1]Excludes "Construction trades" and "Mechanics and repair technologies," which are listed separately.
NOTE: Race categories exclude persons of Hispanic origin. Reported racial/ethnic distributions of students by level of degree, field of degree, and sex were used to estimate race/ethnicity for students whose race/ethnicity was not reported. To facilitate trend comparisons, certain aggregations have been made of the degree fields as reported in the IPEDS Fall survey: "Agriculture and natural resources" includes Agriculture, agriculture operations, and related sciences and Natural resources and conservation; and "Business" includes Business management, marketing, and related support services and Personal and culinary services.
SOURCE: U.S. Department of Education, National Center for Education Statistics, 2003–04 Integrated Postsecondary Education Data System (IPEDS), Fall 2004. (This table was prepared July 2005.)

Table 267. Bachelor's degrees conferred by degree-granting institutions, by race/ethnicity and sex of student: Selected years, 1976–77 through 2004–05

Year and sex	Number of degrees conferred							Percentage distribution of degrees conferred						
	Total	White	Black	Hispanic	Asian/ Pacific Islander	American Indian/ Alaska Native	Non-resident alien	Total	White	Black	Hispanic	Asian/ Pacific Islander	American Indian/ Alaska Native	Non-resident alien
1	2	3	4	5	6	7	8	9	10	11	12	13	14	15
Total														
1976–77[1]	917,900	807,688	58,636	18,743	13,793	3,326	15,714	100.0	88.0	6.4	2.0	1.5	0.4	1.7
1980–81[2]	934,800	807,319	60,673	21,832	18,794	3,593	22,589	100.0	86.4	6.5	2.3	2.0	0.4	2.4
1989–90	1,051,344	887,151	61,046	32,829	39,230	4,390	26,698	100.0	84.4	5.8	3.1	3.7	0.4	2.5
1990–91	1,094,538	914,093	66,375	37,342	42,529	4,583	29,616	100.0	83.5	6.1	3.4	3.9	0.4	2.7
1991–92	1,136,553	941,663	72,680	41,087	47,428	5,228	28,467	100.0	82.9	6.4	3.6	4.2	0.5	2.5
1992–93	1,165,178	952,194	78,099	45,417	51,481	5,683	32,304	100.0	81.7	6.7	3.9	4.4	0.5	2.8
1993–94	1,169,275	939,008	83,909	50,299	55,689	6,192	34,178	100.0	80.3	7.2	4.3	4.8	0.5	2.9
1994–95	1,160,134	914,610	87,236	54,230	60,502	6,610	36,946	100.0	78.8	7.5	4.7	5.2	0.6	3.2
1995–96	1,164,792	905,846	91,496	58,351	64,433	6,976	37,690	100.0	77.8	7.9	5.0	5.5	0.6	3.2
1996–97	1,172,879	900,809	94,349	62,509	68,859	7,425	38,928	100.0	76.8	8.0	5.3	5.9	0.6	3.3
1997–98	1,184,406	901,344	98,251	66,005	71,678	7,903	39,225	100.0	76.1	8.3	5.6	6.1	0.7	3.3
1998–99	1,200,303	907,245	102,214	70,085	74,197	8,423	38,139	100.0	75.6	8.5	5.8	6.2	0.7	3.2
1999–2000	1,237,875	929,106	108,013	75,059	77,912	8,719	39,066	100.0	75.1	8.7	6.1	6.3	0.7	3.2
2000–01	1,244,171	927,357	111,307	77,745	78,902	9,049	39,811	100.0	74.5	8.9	6.2	6.3	0.7	3.2
2001–02	1,291,900	958,597	116,623	82,966	83,093	9,165	41,456	100.0	74.2	9.0	6.4	6.4	0.7	3.2
2002–03	1,348,503	994,234	124,241	89,030	87,943	9,816	43,239	100.0	73.7	9.2	6.6	6.5	0.7	3.2
2003–04	1,399,542	1,026,114	131,241	94,644	92,073	10,638	44,832	100.0	73.3	9.4	6.8	6.6	0.8	3.2
2004–05	1,439,264	1,049,141	136,122	101,124	97,209	10,307	45,361	100.0	72.9	9.5	7.0	6.8	0.7	3.2
Males														
1976–77[1]	494,424	438,161	25,147	10,318	7,638	1,804	11,356	100.0	88.6	5.1	2.1	1.5	0.4	2.3
1980–81[2]	469,625	406,173	24,511	10,810	10,107	1,700	16,324	100.0	86.5	5.2	2.3	2.2	0.4	3.5
1989–90	491,696	414,982	23,257	14,932	19,711	1,860	16,954	100.0	84.4	4.7	3.0	4.0	0.4	3.4
1990–91	504,045	421,290	24,800	16,598	21,203	1,938	18,216	100.0	83.6	4.9	3.3	4.2	0.4	3.6
1991–92	520,811	432,635	27,092	18,167	23,652	2,195	17,070	100.0	83.1	5.2	3.5	4.5	0.4	3.3
1992–93	532,881	437,262	28,962	19,883	25,303	2,450	19,021	100.0	82.1	5.4	3.7	4.7	0.5	3.6
1993–94	532,422	430,526	30,766	21,834	26,952	2,620	19,724	100.0	80.9	5.8	4.1	5.1	0.5	3.7
1994–95	526,131	417,878	31,793	23,626	28,992	2,739	21,103	100.0	79.4	6.0	4.5	5.5	0.5	4.0
1995–96	522,454	409,565	32,974	25,029	30,669	2,885	21,332	100.0	78.4	6.3	4.8	5.9	0.6	4.1
1996–97	520,515	403,366	33,616	26,318	32,521	2,996	21,698	100.0	77.5	6.5	5.1	6.2	0.6	4.2
1997–98	519,956	399,553	34,510	27,677	33,445	3,151	21,620	100.0	76.8	6.6	5.3	6.4	0.6	4.2
1998–99	518,746	396,996	34,876	28,662	34,225	3,323	20,664	100.0	76.5	6.7	5.5	6.6	0.6	4.0
1999–2000	530,367	402,961	37,024	30,301	35,853	3,464	20,764	100.0	76.0	7.0	5.7	6.8	0.7	3.9
2000–01	531,840	401,780	38,103	31,368	35,865	3,700	21,024	100.0	75.5	7.2	5.9	6.7	0.7	4.0
2001–02	549,816	414,892	39,196	32,951	37,660	3,624	21,493	100.0	75.5	7.1	6.0	6.8	0.7	3.9
2002–03	573,079	430,024	41,472	35,080	40,210	3,853	22,440	100.0	75.0	7.2	6.1	7.0	0.7	3.9
2003–04	595,425	445,483	43,851	37,288	41,360	4,244	23,199	100.0	74.8	7.4	6.3	6.9	0.7	3.9
2004–05	613,000	456,592	45,810	39,490	43,711	4,143	23,254	100.0	74.5	7.5	6.4	7.1	0.7	3.8
Females														
1976–77[1]	423,476	369,527	33,489	8,425	6,155	1,522	4,358	100.0	87.3	7.9	2.0	1.5	0.4	1.0
1980–81[2]	465,175	401,146	36,162	11,022	8,687	1,893	6,265	100.0	86.2	7.8	2.4	1.9	0.4	1.3
1989–90	559,648	472,169	37,789	17,897	19,519	2,530	9,744	100.0	84.4	6.8	3.2	3.5	0.5	1.7
1990–91	590,493	492,803	41,575	20,744	21,326	2,645	11,400	100.0	83.5	7.0	3.5	3.6	0.4	1.9
1991–92	615,742	509,028	45,588	22,920	23,776	3,033	11,397	100.0	82.7	7.4	3.7	3.9	0.5	1.9
1992–93	632,297	514,932	49,137	25,534	26,178	3,233	13,283	100.0	81.4	7.8	4.0	4.1	0.5	2.1
1993–94	636,853	508,482	53,143	28,465	28,737	3,572	14,454	100.0	79.8	8.3	4.5	4.5	0.6	2.3
1994–95	634,003	496,732	55,443	30,604	31,510	3,871	15,843	100.0	78.3	8.7	4.8	5.0	0.6	2.5
1995–96	642,338	496,281	58,522	33,322	33,764	4,091	16,358	100.0	77.3	9.1	5.2	5.3	0.6	2.5
1996–97	652,364	497,443	60,733	36,191	36,338	4,429	17,230	100.0	76.3	9.3	5.5	5.6	0.7	2.6
1997–98	664,450	501,791	63,741	38,328	38,233	4,752	17,605	100.0	75.5	9.6	5.8	5.8	0.7	2.6
1998–99	681,557	510,249	67,338	41,423	39,972	5,100	17,475	100.0	74.9	9.9	6.1	5.9	0.7	2.6
1999–2000	707,508	526,145	70,989	44,758	42,059	5,255	18,302	100.0	74.4	10.0	6.3	5.9	0.7	2.6
2000–01	712,331	525,577	73,204	46,377	43,037	5,349	18,787	100.0	73.8	10.3	6.5	6.0	0.8	2.6
2001–02	742,084	543,705	77,427	50,015	45,433	5,541	19,963	100.0	73.3	10.4	6.7	6.1	0.7	2.7
2002–03	775,424	564,210	82,769	53,950	47,733	5,963	20,799	100.0	72.8	10.7	7.0	6.2	0.8	2.7
2003–04	804,117	580,631	87,390	57,356	50,713	6,394	21,633	100.0	72.2	10.9	7.1	6.3	0.8	2.7
2004–05	826,264	592,549	90,312	61,634	53,498	6,164	22,107	100.0	71.7	10.9	7.5	6.5	0.7	2.7

[1]Excludes 1,121 males and 528 females whose racial/ethnic group was not available.
[2]Excludes 258 males and 82 females whose racial/ethnic group was not available.
NOTE: Race categories exclude persons of Hispanic origin. For years 1989–90 to 2004–05, reported racial/ethnic distributions of students by level of degree, field of degree, and sex were used to estimate race/ethnicity for students whose race/ethnicity was not reported. (See Guide to Sources for details.) Detail may not sum to totals because of rounding.

SOURCE: U.S. Department of Education, National Center for Education Statistics, Higher Education General Information Survey (HEGIS), "Degrees and Other Formal Awards Conferred" surveys, 1976–77 and 1980–81; and 1988–89 through 2004–05 Integrated Postsecondary Education Data System, "Completions Survey" (IPEDS-C:89–99), and Fall 2000 through Fall 2005. (This table was prepared July 2006.)

Table 268. Bachelor's degrees conferred by degree-granting institutions, by sex, race/ethnicity, and major field of study: 2004–05

Major field of study	Total							Males							Females						
	Total	White	Black	Hispanic	Asian/Pacific Islander	American Indian/Alaska Native	Non-resident alien	Total	White	Black	Hispanic	Asian/Pacific Islander	American Indian/Alaska Native	Non-resident alien	Total	White	Black	Hispanic	Asian/Pacific Islander	American Indian/Alaska Native	Non-resident alien
1	2	3	4	5	6	7	8	9	10	11	12	13	14	15	16	17	18	19	20	21	22
All fields, total	1,439,264	1,049,141	136,122	101,124	97,209	10,307	45,361	613,000	456,592	45,810	39,490	43,711	4,143	23,254	826,264	592,549	90,312	61,634	53,498	6,164	22,107
Agriculture and natural resources	23,002	20,292	654	806	682	200	368	11,987	10,808	278	356	269	103	173	11,015	9,484	376	450	413	97	195
Architecture and related services	9,237	6,764	426	783	762	39	463	5,222	3,941	251	445	316	24	245	4,015	2,823	175	338	446	15	218
Area, ethnic, cultural, and gender studies	7,569	4,218	1,051	989	996	148	167	2,307	1,265	328	288	317	53	56	5,262	2,953	723	701	679	95	111
Biological and biomedical sciences	64,611	44,143	5,146	3,993	8,907	514	1,908	24,617	17,551	1,315	1,448	3,410	195	698	39,994	26,592	3,831	2,545	5,497	319	1,210
Business	311,574	214,361	34,464	21,955	23,429	1,952	15,413	155,940	114,502	12,477	9,665	10,523	899	7,874	155,634	99,859	21,987	12,290	12,906	1,053	7,539
Communications, journalism, and related programs	72,715	56,142	7,048	4,477	3,073	386	1,589	25,324	19,872	2,354	1,487	928	129	554	47,391	36,270	4,694	2,990	2,145	257	1,035
Communications technologies	2,523	1,841	262	177	140	8	95	1,602	1,220	126	111	85	2	58	921	621	136	66	55	6	37
Computer and information sciences	54,111	32,948	6,438	3,402	7,023	311	3,989	42,125	27,340	3,796	2,555	5,205	216	3,013	11,986	5,608	2,642	847	1,818	95	976
Construction trades	117	98	8	5	3	0	3	107	93	6	4	2	0	2	10	5	2	1	0	0	1
Education	105,451	90,645	6,434	4,845	1,747	933	847	22,513	19,167	1,622	930	340	220	234	82,938	71,478	4,812	3,915	1,407	713	613
Engineering	64,906	44,012	3,386	3,703	8,687	355	4,763	52,020	36,360	2,239	2,855	6,504	274	3,788	12,886	7,652	1,147	848	2,183	81	975
Engineering technologies[1]	14,482	10,657	1,537	891	799	109	489	12,812	9,638	1,211	757	689	96	421	1,670	1,019	326	134	110	13	68
English language and literature/letters	54,379	43,680	4,200	3,311	2,376	296	516	17,154	14,216	1,012	993	676	105	152	37,225	29,464	3,188	2,318	1,700	191	364
Family and consumer sciences	20,074	15,796	2,057	1,012	785	179	245	2,435	1,832	287	126	123	19	48	17,639	13,964	1,770	886	662	160	197
Foreign languages, literatures, and linguistics	18,386	13,169	753	2,964	961	104	435	5,370	3,982	196	772	265	40	115	13,016	9,187	557	2,192	696	64	320
Health professions and related clinical sciences	80,685	61,240	8,989	4,547	4,194	570	1,145	10,858	7,848	1,150	793	773	83	211	69,827	53,392	7,839	3,754	3,421	487	934
Legal professions and studies	3,161	2,042	618	248	215	16	22	918	622	128	79	79	8	2	2,243	1,420	490	169	136	8	20
Liberal arts and sciences, general studies, and humanities	43,751	30,042	5,657	4,715	2,039	479	819	13,732	9,966	1,610	1,089	613	151	303	30,019	20,076	4,047	3,626	1,426	328	516
Library science	76	72	3	1	0	0	0	15	14	1	0	0	0	0	61	58	2	1	0	0	0
Mathematics and statistics	14,351	10,399	885	816	1,457	80	714	7,937	5,733	433	478	818	51	424	6,414	4,666	452	338	639	29	290
Mechanics and repair technologies	238	164	15	24	18	7	10	225	157	15	21	17	6	9	13	7	0	3	1	1	1
Military technologies	40	35	1	3	1	0	0	33	29	1	3	0	0	0	7	6	0	0	1	0	0
Multi/interdisciplinary studies	30,243	21,458	2,674	3,115	2,086	223	687	9,645	7,005	834	683	756	69	298	20,598	14,453	1,840	2,432	1,330	154	389
Parks, recreation, leisure and fitness studies	22,888	18,227	2,042	1,424	610	207	378	11,702	9,132	1,171	803	292	97	207	11,186	9,095	871	621	318	110	171
Philosophy and religious studies	11,584	9,522	604	606	600	107	145	7,225	6,008	331	390	332	70	94	4,359	3,514	273	216	268	37	51
Physical sciences and science technologies	18,905	14,541	1,105	873	1,488	139	753	10,934	8,817	436	466	712	77	426	7,971	5,730	669	407	776	62	327
Precision production	64	56	0	4	3	0	1	45	41	0	3	0	0	1	19	15	0	1	3	0	0
Psychology	85,614	61,293	9,703	7,486	5,044	585	1,503	19,000	13,869	1,738	1,679	1,259	139	316	66,614	47,424	7,965	5,807	3,785	446	1,187
Public administration and social service professions	21,769	13,206	4,946	2,409	755	242	211	4,209	2,598	793	510	216	48	44	17,560	10,608	4,153	1,899	539	194	167
Security and protective services	30,723	20,355	5,545	3,435	883	311	194	15,354	11,051	2,013	1,585	477	152	76	15,369	9,304	3,532	1,850	406	159	118
Social sciences and history	156,892	112,777	14,323	12,339	11,967	1,185	4,301	77,702	58,905	5,202	5,286	5,618	530	2,161	79,190	53,872	9,121	7,053	6,349	655	2,140
Social sciences	125,494	86,500	12,733	10,401	10,801	978	4,081	59,225	43,124	4,452	4,204	5,004	399	2,042	66,269	43,376	8,281	6,197	5,797	579	2,039
History	31,398	26,277	1,590	1,938	1,166	207	220	18,477	15,781	750	1,082	614	131	119	12,921	10,496	840	856	552	76	101
Theology and religious vocations	9,284	8,048	538	309	184	38	167	6,253	5,527	303	197	107	19	100	3,031	2,521	235	112	77	19	67
Transportation and materials moving	4,904	4,015	291	266	148	37	147	4,323	3,538	253	231	139	33	129	581	477	38	35	9	4	18
Visual and performing arts	80,955	62,877	4,319	5,191	5,147	547	2,874	31,355	23,945	1,900	2,402	1,851	235	1,022	49,600	38,932	2,419	2,789	3,296	312	1,852

[1]Excludes "Construction trades" and "Mechanics and repair technologies," which are listed separately.
NOTE: Race categories exclude persons of Hispanic origin. Reported racial/ethnic distributions of students by level of degree, field of degree, and sex were used to estimate race/ethnicity for students whose race/ethnicity was not reported. To facilitate trend comparisons, certain aggregations have been made of the degree fields as reported in the IPEDS Fall survey: "Agriculture and natural resources" includes Agriculture, agriculture operations, and related sciences and Natural resources and conservation; and "Business" includes Business management, marketing, and related support services and Personal and culinary services.
SOURCE: U.S. Department of Education, National Center for Education Statistics, 2004–05 Integrated Postsecondary Education Data System (IPEDS), Fall 2005. (This table was prepared July 2006.)

Table 269. Bachelor's degrees conferred by degree-granting institutions, by sex, race/ethnicity, and major field of study: 2003–04

Major field of study	Total							Males							Females						
	Total	White	Black	Hispanic	Asian/ Pacific Islander	American Indian/ Alaska Native	Non-resident alien	Total	White	Black	Hispanic	Asian/ Pacific Islander	American Indian/ Alaska Native	Non-resident alien	Total	White	Black	Hispanic	Asian/ Pacific Islander	American Indian/ Alaska Native	Non-resident alien
1	2	3	4	5	6	7	8	9	10	11	12	13	14	15	16	17	18	19	20	21	22
All fields, total	1,399,542	1,026,114	131,241	94,644	92,073	10,638	44,832	595,425	445,483	43,851	37,288	41,360	4,244	23,199	804,117	580,631	87,390	57,356	50,713	6,394	21,633
Agriculture and natural resources	22,835	20,216	657	760	653	224	325	11,889	10,753	272	344	250	118	152	10,946	9,463	385	416	403	106	173
Architecture and related services	8,838	6,604	390	674	698	43	429	5,059	3,896	214	384	324	23	218	3,779	2,708	176	290	374	20	211
Area, ethnic, cultural, and gender studies	7,181	4,143	960	870	873	167	168	2,162	1,247	280	248	277	61	49	5,019	2,896	680	622	596	106	119
Biological and biomedical sciences	61,509	42,926	5,081	3,641	7,838	424	1,599	23,248	16,838	1,321	1,331	2,978	156	624	38,261	26,088	3,760	2,310	4,860	268	975
Business	307,149	213,892	33,404	20,942	22,185	2,048	14,678	152,513	112,686	11,959	9,489	9,764	917	7,698	154,636	101,206	21,445	11,453	12,421	1,131	6,980
Communications, journalism, and related programs	70,968	55,423	6,572	4,174	2,866	378	1,555	24,591	19,654	2,088	1,299	869	141	540	46,377	35,769	4,484	2,875	1,997	237	1,015
Communications technologies	2,034	1,547	201	117	110	20	39	1,222	923	100	82	82	15	20	812	624	101	35	28	5	19
Computer and information sciences	59,488	34,836	6,945	3,658	8,496	494	5,059	44,585	28,206	3,858	2,654	5,919	378	3,570	14,903	6,630	3,087	1,004	2,577	116	1,489
Construction trades	119	103	10	5	1	0	0	107	99	2	5	1	0	0	12	4	8	0	0	0	0
Education	106,278	91,279	6,457	4,792	1,759	990	1,001	22,802	19,463	1,571	945	333	241	249	83,476	71,816	4,886	3,847	1,426	749	752
Engineering	63,558	43,615	3,402	3,568	8,046	350	4,577	50,557	35,764	2,239	2,727	5,917	256	3,654	13,001	7,851	1,163	841	2,129	94	923
Engineering technologies[1]	14,391	10,444	1,557	946	732	201	511	12,689	9,405	1,217	839	624	171	433	1,702	1,039	340	107	108	30	78
English language and literature/letters	53,984	43,656	4,168	3,067	2,175	371	547	16,792	13,902	1,007	992	611	129	151	37,192	29,754	3,161	2,075	1,564	242	396
Family and consumer sciences	19,172	15,066	2,058	874	775	161	238	2,298	1,719	297	114	102	19	47	16,874	13,347	1,761	760	673	142	191
Foreign languages, literatures, and linguistics	17,754	12,692	761	2,843	935	97	426	5,215	3,836	176	786	277	35	105	12,539	8,856	585	2,057	658	62	321
Health professions and related clinical sciences	73,934	56,033	8,527	4,129	3,758	577	910	10,017	7,247	1,037	739	734	86	174	63,917	48,786	7,490	3,390	3,024	491	736
Legal professions and studies	2,841	1,931	435	241	182	31	21	896	617	115	76	73	8	7	1,945	1,314	320	165	109	23	14
Liberal arts and sciences, general studies, and humanities	42,106	29,164	5,255	4,593	1,875	509	710	13,336	9,903	1,504	983	529	161	256	28,770	19,261	3,751	3,610	1,346	348	454
Library science	72	69	3	0	0	0	0	4	4	0	0	0	0	0	68	65	3	0	0	0	0
Mathematics and statistics	13,327	9,861	805	676	1,283	62	640	7,203	5,394	344	367	697	39	362	6,124	4,467	461	309	586	23	278
Mechanics and repair technologies	159	131	5	4	3	6	10	149	121	5	4	3	6	10	10	10	0	0	0	0	0
Military technologies	10	10	0	0	0	0	0	9	9	0	0	0	0	0	1	1	0	0	0	0	1
Multi/interdisciplinary studies	29,162	20,743	2,651	2,872	2,047	247	602	9,537	6,915	800	668	821	73	260	19,625	13,828	1,851	2,204	1,226	174	342
Parks, recreation, leisure and fitness studies	22,164	17,621	1,996	1,463	569	165	350	11,289	8,761	1,161	808	282	86	191	10,875	8,860	835	655	287	79	159
Philosophy and religious studies	11,152	9,234	564	540	574	68	172	7,046	5,887	321	345	352	37	104	4,106	3,347	243	195	222	31	68
Physical sciences and science technologies	17,983	13,973	1,097	773	1,384	113	643	10,476	8,476	419	441	710	61	369	7,507	5,497	678	332	674	52	274
Precision production	61	58	0	0	1	0	2	38	36	0	0	1	0	1	23	22	0	0	0	0	1
Psychology	82,098	59,480	8,985	6,975	4,555	628	1,475	18,193	13,436	1,671	1,541	1,105	135	305	63,905	46,044	7,314	5,434	3,450	493	1,170
Public administration and social service professions	20,552	12,845	4,642	2,002	642	220	201	3,793	2,409	752	403	150	36	43	16,759	10,436	3,890	1,599	492	184	158
Security and protective services	28,175	18,964	5,080	2,960	731	266	174	14,195	10,434	1,866	1,327	382	114	72	13,980	8,530	3,214	1,633	349	152	102
Social sciences and history	150,357	108,775	13,723	11,190	11,197	1,158	4,314	73,834	56,266	4,985	4,816	5,141	483	2,143	76,523	52,509	8,738	6,374	6,056	675	2,171
Social sciences	120,549	83,663	12,163	9,538	10,130	936	4,119	56,431	41,275	4,229	3,867	4,653	365	2,042	64,118	42,388	7,934	5,671	5,477	571	2,077
History	29,808	25,112	1,560	1,652	1,067	222	195	17,403	14,991	756	949	488	118	101	12,405	10,121	804	703	579	104	94
Theology and religious vocations	8,126	6,882	466	342	182	47	207	5,381	4,627	277	201	117	23	136	2,745	2,255	189	141	65	24	71
Transportation and materials moving	4,824	3,995	249	242	153	33	152	4,263	3,524	216	218	141	28	136	561	471	33	24	12	5	16
Visual and performing arts	77,181	59,903	4,135	4,711	4,795	540	3,097	30,037	23,026	1,777	2,112	1,794	208	1,120	47,144	36,877	2,358	2,599	3,001	332	1,977

[1]Excludes "Construction trades" and "Mechanics and repair technologies," which are listed separately.

NOTE: Race categories exclude persons of Hispanic origin. Reported racial/ethnic distributions of students by level of degree, field of degree, and sex were used to estimate race/ethnicity for students whose race/ethnicity was not reported. To facilitate trend comparisons, certain aggregations have been made of the degree fields as reported in the IPEDS Fall survey: "Agriculture and natural resources" includes Agriculture, agriculture operations, and related sciences and Natural resources and conservation; and "Business" includes Business management, marketing, and related support services and Personal and culinary services.

SOURCE: U.S. Department of Education, National Center for Education Statistics, 2003–04 Integrated Postsecondary Education Data System (IPEDS), Fall 2004. (This table was prepared July 2005.)

Table 270. Master's degrees conferred by degree-granting institutions, by race/ethnicity and sex of student: Selected years, 1976–77 through 2004–05

Year and sex	Number of degrees conferred							Percentage distribution of degrees conferred						
	Total	White	Black	Hispanic	Asian/ Pacific Islander	American Indian/ Alaska Native	Non-resident alien	Total	White	Black	Hispanic	Asian/ Pacific Islander	American Indian/ Alaska Native	Non-resident alien
1	2	3	4	5	6	7	8	9	10	11	12	13	14	15
Total														
1976–77[1]	316,602	266,061	21,037	6,071	5,122	967	17,344	100.0	84.0	6.6	1.9	1.6	0.3	5.5
1980–81[2]	294,183	241,216	17,133	6,461	6,282	1,034	22,057	100.0	82.0	5.8	2.2	2.1	0.4	7.5
1989–90	324,301	254,299	15,336	7,892	10,439	1,090	35,245	100.0	78.4	4.7	2.4	3.2	0.3	10.9
1990–91	337,168	261,232	16,616	8,887	11,650	1,178	37,605	100.0	77.5	4.9	2.6	3.5	0.3	11.2
1991–92	352,838	271,177	18,256	9,521	12,960	1,280	39,644	100.0	76.9	5.2	2.7	3.7	0.4	11.2
1992–93	369,585	279,827	19,744	10,638	13,863	1,405	44,108	100.0	75.7	5.3	2.9	3.8	0.4	11.9
1993–94	387,070	289,536	21,986	11,933	15,411	1,699	46,505	100.0	74.8	5.7	3.1	4.0	0.4	12.0
1994–95	397,629	293,345	24,166	12,905	16,847	1,621	48,745	100.0	73.8	6.1	3.2	4.2	0.4	12.3
1995–96	406,301	298,133	25,822	14,442	18,216	1,778	47,910	100.0	73.4	6.4	3.6	4.5	0.4	11.8
1996–97	419,401	305,005	28,403	15,440	19,061	1,940	49,552	100.0	72.7	6.8	3.7	4.5	0.5	11.8
1997–98	430,164	308,196	30,155	16,248	21,133	2,053	52,379	100.0	71.6	7.0	3.8	4.9	0.5	12.2
1998–99	439,986	313,487	32,541	17,838	22,072	2,016	52,032	100.0	71.2	7.4	4.1	5.0	0.5	11.8
1999–2000	457,056	320,485	35,874	19,253	23,218	2,246	55,980	100.0	70.1	7.8	4.2	5.1	0.5	12.2
2000–01	468,476	320,480	38,265	21,543	24,283	2,481	61,424	100.0	68.4	8.2	4.6	5.2	0.5	13.1
2001–02	482,118	327,645	40,370	22,385	25,411	2,624	63,683	100.0	68.0	8.4	4.6	5.3	0.5	13.2
2002–03	512,645	341,735	44,272	24,974	27,245	2,837	71,582	100.0	66.7	8.6	4.9	5.3	0.6	14.0
2003–04	558,940	369,582	50,657	29,666	30,952	3,192	74,891	100.0	66.1	9.1	5.3	5.5	0.6	13.4
2004–05	574,618	379,350	54,482	31,485	32,783	3,295	73,223	100.0	66.0	9.5	5.5	5.7	0.6	12.7
Males														
1976–77[1]	167,396	139,210	7,781	3,268	3,123	521	13,493	100.0	83.2	4.6	2.0	1.9	0.3	8.1
1980–81[2]	145,666	115,562	6,158	3,085	3,773	501	16,587	100.0	79.3	4.2	2.1	2.6	0.3	11.4
1989–90	153,653	114,203	5,474	3,548	5,896	455	24,077	100.0	74.3	3.6	2.3	3.8	0.3	15.7
1990–91	156,482	114,419	5,916	3,936	6,575	488	25,148	100.0	73.1	3.8	2.5	4.2	0.3	16.1
1991–92	161,842	117,512	6,112	4,220	7,234	529	26,235	100.0	72.6	3.8	2.6	4.5	0.3	16.2
1992–93	169,258	120,783	6,803	4,722	7,545	584	28,821	100.0	71.4	4.0	2.8	4.5	0.3	17.0
1993–94	176,085	124,409	7,424	5,122	8,298	692	30,140	100.0	70.7	4.2	2.9	4.7	0.4	17.1
1994–95	178,598	124,277	8,097	5,487	8,923	659	31,155	100.0	69.6	4.5	3.1	5.0	0.4	17.4
1995–96	179,081	124,847	8,445	5,843	9,400	705	29,841	100.0	69.7	4.7	3.3	5.2	0.4	16.7
1996–97	180,947	125,552	8,960	6,246	9,218	734	30,237	100.0	69.4	5.0	3.5	5.1	0.4	16.7
1997–98	184,375	125,605	9,652	6,512	10,262	782	31,562	100.0	68.1	5.2	3.5	5.6	0.4	17.1
1998–99	186,148	126,674	10,058	7,032	10,491	771	31,122	100.0	68.1	5.4	3.8	5.6	0.4	16.7
1999–2000	191,792	128,046	11,212	7,635	11,047	836	33,016	100.0	66.8	5.8	4.0	5.8	0.4	17.2
2000–01	194,351	125,993	11,568	8,271	11,349	917	36,253	100.0	64.8	6.0	4.3	5.8	0.5	18.7
2001–02	199,120	128,776	11,795	8,430	11,746	993	37,380	100.0	64.7	5.9	4.2	5.9	0.5	18.8
2002–03	211,381	133,220	12,805	9,251	12,500	1,022	42,583	100.0	63.0	6.1	4.4	5.9	0.5	20.1
2003–04	229,545	143,827	14,653	10,813	14,347	1,127	44,778	100.0	62.7	6.4	4.7	6.3	0.5	19.5
2004–05	233,590	147,546	15,733	11,385	15,031	1,160	42,735	100.0	63.2	6.7	4.9	6.4	0.5	18.3
Females														
1976–77[1]	149,206	126,851	13,256	2,803	1,999	446	3,851	100.0	85.0	8.9	1.9	1.3	0.3	2.6
1980–81[2]	148,517	125,654	10,975	3,376	2,509	533	5,470	100.0	84.6	7.4	2.3	1.7	0.4	3.7
1989–90	170,648	140,096	9,862	4,344	4,543	635	11,168	100.0	82.1	5.8	2.5	2.7	0.4	6.5
1990–91	180,686	146,813	10,700	4,951	5,075	690	12,457	100.0	81.3	5.9	2.7	2.8	0.4	6.9
1991–92	190,996	153,665	12,144	5,301	5,726	751	13,409	100.0	80.5	6.4	2.8	3.0	0.4	7.0
1992–93	200,327	159,044	12,941	5,916	6,318	821	15,287	100.0	79.4	6.5	3.0	3.2	0.4	7.6
1993–94	210,985	165,127	14,562	6,811	7,113	1,007	16,365	100.0	78.3	6.9	3.2	3.4	0.5	7.8
1994–95	219,031	169,068	16,069	7,418	7,924	962	17,590	100.0	77.2	7.3	3.4	3.6	0.4	8.0
1995–96	227,220	173,286	17,377	8,599	8,816	1,073	18,069	100.0	76.3	7.6	3.8	3.9	0.5	8.0
1996–97	238,454	179,453	19,443	9,194	9,843	1,206	19,315	100.0	75.3	8.2	3.9	4.1	0.5	8.1
1997–98	245,789	182,591	20,503	9,736	10,871	1,271	20,817	100.0	74.3	8.3	4.0	4.4	0.5	8.5
1998–99	253,838	186,813	22,483	10,806	11,581	1,245	20,910	100.0	73.6	8.9	4.3	4.6	0.5	8.2
1999–2000	265,264	192,439	24,662	11,618	12,171	1,410	22,964	100.0	72.5	9.3	4.4	4.6	0.5	8.7
2000–01	274,125	194,487	26,697	13,272	12,934	1,564	25,171	100.0	70.9	9.7	4.8	4.7	0.6	9.2
2001–02	282,998	198,869	28,575	13,955	13,665	1,631	26,303	100.0	70.3	10.1	4.9	4.8	0.6	9.3
2002–03	301,264	208,515	31,467	15,723	14,745	1,815	28,999	100.0	69.2	10.4	5.2	4.9	0.6	9.6
2003–04	329,395	225,755	36,004	18,853	16,605	2,065	30,113	100.0	68.5	10.9	5.7	5.0	0.6	9.1
2004–05	341,028	231,804	38,749	20,100	17,752	2,135	30,488	100.0	68.0	11.4	5.9	5.2	0.6	8.9

[1]Excludes 387 men and 175 women whose racial/ethnic group was not available.
[2]Excludes 1,377 men and 179 women whose racial/ethnic group was not available.
NOTE: Race categories exclude persons of Hispanic origin. For years 1989–90 to 2004–05, reported racial/ethnic distributions of students by level of degree, field of degree, and sex were used to estimate race/ethnicity for students whose race/ethnicity was not reported. (See Guide to Sources for details.) Detail may not sum to totals because of rounding.

SOURCE: U.S. Department of Education, National Center for Education Statistics, Higher Education General Information Survey (HEGIS), "Degrees and Other Formal Awards Conferred" surveys, 1976–77 and 1980–81; and 1988–89 through 2004–05 Integrated Postsecondary Education Data System, "Completions Survey" (IPEDS-C:89–99), and Fall 2000 through Fall 2005. (This table was prepared July 2006.)

Table 271. Master's degrees conferred by degree-granting institutions, by sex, race/ethnicity, and major field of study: 2004–05

Major field of study	Total							Males							Females						
	Total	White	Black	Hispanic	Asian/Pacific Islander	American Indian/Alaska Native	Non-resident alien	Total	White	Black	Hispanic	Asian/Pacific Islander	American Indian/Alaska Native	Non-resident alien	Total	White	Black	Hispanic	Asian/Pacific Islander	American Indian/Alaska Native	Non-resident alien
1	2	3	4	5	6	7	8	9	10	11	12	13	14	15	16	17	18	19	20	21	22
All fields, total	574,618	379,350	54,482	31,485	32,783	3,295	73,223	233,590	147,546	15,733	11,385	15,031	1,160	42,735	341,028	231,804	38,749	20,100	17,752	2,135	30,488
Agriculture and natural resources	4,746	3,535	112	140	130	32	797	2,288	1,714	34	63	45	14	418	2,458	1,821	78	77	85	18	379
Architecture and related services	5,674	3,873	268	278	350	25	1,080	3,180	2,152	115	156	158	19	580	2,494	1,521	153	122	192	6	500
Area, ethnic, cultural, and gender studies	1,755	1,029	168	154	126	32	246	669	417	57	68	33	14	80	1,086	612	111	86	93	18	166
Biological and biomedical sciences	8,199	5,296	426	343	879	31	1,224	3,318	2,186	109	129	389	12	493	4,881	3,110	317	214	490	19	731
Business	142,617	85,714	16,025	7,013	11,294	770	21,801	82,151	52,074	6,042	4,005	6,336	397	13,297	60,466	33,640	9,983	3,008	4,958	373	8,504
Communications, journalism, and related programs	6,762	4,318	678	331	356	37	1,042	2,262	1,518	182	93	111	14	344	4,500	2,800	496	238	245	23	698
Communications technologies	433	222	48	21	27	2	113	273	163	26	3	12	1	68	160	59	22	18	15	1	45
Computer and information sciences	18,416	6,738	1,024	492	2,593	55	7,514	13,136	5,234	608	370	1,624	33	5,267	5,280	1,504	416	122	969	22	2,247
Construction trades	0	0	0	0	0	0	0	0	0	0	0	0	0	0	0	0	0	0	0	0	0
Education	167,490	129,176	16,977	11,194	4,195	993	4,955	38,863	30,359	3,614	2,479	889	214	1,308	128,627	98,817	13,363	8,715	3,306	779	3,647
Engineering	32,633	12,718	885	1,048	3,257	79	14,646	25,351	10,236	602	771	2,298	54	11,390	7,282	2,482	283	277	959	25	3,256
Engineering technologies[1]	2,500	1,351	203	106	212	15	613	1,810	1,016	125	71	143	12	443	690	335	78	35	69	3	170
English language and literature/letters	8,468	6,949	366	339	353	57	404	2,615	2,249	87	100	73	18	88	5,853	4,700	279	239	280	39	316
Family and consumer sciences	1,827	1,306	196	83	60	6	176	229	153	21	8	12	0	35	1,598	1,153	175	75	48	6	141
Foreign languages, literatures, and linguistics	3,407	1,887	81	485	137	12	805	1,056	641	28	109	30	1	247	2,351	1,246	53	376	107	11	558
Health professions and related clinical sciences	46,703	33,605	4,386	2,471	3,440	301	2,500	9,816	6,575	679	557	973	67	965	36,887	27,030	3,707	1,914	2,467	234	1,535
Legal professions and studies	4,170	1,450	201	139	205	20	2,155	2,304	839	76	58	109	8	1,214	1,866	611	125	81	96	12	941
Liberal arts and sciences, general studies, and humanities	3,680	2,974	306	159	96	22	123	1,381	1,142	87	50	42	11	49	2,299	1,832	219	109	54	11	74
Library science	6,213	5,168	288	328	211	47	171	1,241	1,002	53	66	50	9	61	4,972	4,166	235	262	161	38	110
Mathematics and statistics	4,477	2,150	143	131	336	9	1,708	2,525	1,262	79	72	161	3	948	1,952	888	64	59	175	6	760
Mechanics and repair technologies	0	0	0	0	0	0	0	0	0	0	0	0	0	0	0	0	0	0	0	0	0
Military technologies	0	0	0	0	0	0	0	0	0	0	0	0	0	0	0	0	0	0	0	0	0
Multi/interdisciplinary studies	4,252	2,910	322	199	213	36	572	1,440	938	76	62	70	14	280	2,812	1,972	246	137	143	22	292
Parks, recreation, leisure and fitness studies	3,740	2,906	318	175	102	23	216	1,935	1,516	149	106	42	13	109	1,805	1,390	169	69	60	10	107
Philosophy and religious studies	1,647	1,260	80	81	74	9	143	995	753	45	56	49	6	86	652	507	35	25	25	3	57
Physical sciences and science technologies	5,678	3,463	127	168	296	24	1,600	3,457	2,087	62	97	165	0	1,034	2,221	1,376	65	71	131	12	566
Precision production	6	3	0	2	0	0	1	5	1	0	0	0	0	0	1	0	0	0	0	0	1
Psychology	18,830	13,422	2,493	1,310	731	136	738	3,900	2,836	435	271	160	33	165	14,930	10,586	2,058	1,039	571	103	573
Public administration and social service professions	29,552	18,817	5,374	2,303	1,181	301	1,576	7,370	4,585	1,117	551	315	66	736	22,182	14,232	4,257	1,752	866	235	840
Security and protective services	3,991	2,811	663	298	95	40	84	1,974	1,468	256	150	40	18	42	2,017	1,343	407	148	55	22	42
Social sciences and history	16,952	10,458	1,206	890	859	92	3,447	8,256	5,224	440	427	326	49	1,790	8,696	5,234	766	463	533	43	1,657
Social sciences	14,059	8,022	1,085	768	804	62	3,318	6,640	3,855	382	344	300	34	1,725	7,419	4,167	703	424	504	28	1,593
History	2,893	2,436	121	122	55	30	129	1,616	1,369	58	83	26	15	65	1,277	1,067	63	39	29	15	64
Theology and religious vocations	5,815	4,221	489	210	251	7	637	3,469	2,566	232	124	124	3	420	2,346	1,655	257	86	127	4	217
Transportation and materials moving	802	668	48	36	23	3	24	679	562	41	34	21	2	19	123	106	7	2	7	1	5
Visual and performing arts	13,183	9,152	581	558	701	79	2,112	5,646	4,078	256	279	231	43	759	7,537	5,074	325	279	470	36	1,353

[1]Excludes "Construction trades" and "Mechanics and repair technologies," which are listed separately.

NOTE: Race categories exclude persons of Hispanic origin. Reported racial/ethnic distributions of students by level of degree, field of degree, and sex were used to estimate race/ethnicity for students whose race/ethnicity was not reported. To facilitate trend comparisons, certain aggregations have been made of the degree fields as reported in the IPEDS Fall survey: "Agriculture and natural resources" includes Agriculture, agriculture operations, and related sciences and Natural resources and conservation; and "Business" includes Business management, marketing, and related support services and Personal and culinary services.

SOURCE: U.S. Department of Education, National Center for Education Statistics, 2004–05 Integrated Postsecondary Education Data System (IPEDS), Fall 2005. (This table was prepared July 2006.)

Table 272. Master's degrees conferred by degree-granting institutions, by sex, race/ethnicity, and major field of study: 2003–04

Major field of study	Total							Males							Females						
	Total	White	Black	Hispanic	Asian/Pacific Islander	American Indian/Alaska Native	Nonresident alien	Total	White	Black	Hispanic	Asian/Pacific Islander	American Indian/Alaska Native	Nonresident alien	Total	White	Black	Hispanic	Asian/Pacific Islander	American Indian/Alaska Native	Nonresident alien
1	2	3	4	5	6	7	8	9	10	11	12	13	14	15	16	17	18	19	20	21	22
All fields, total	558,940	369,582	50,657	29,666	30,952	3,192	74,891	229,545	143,827	14,653	10,813	14,347	1,127	44,778	329,395	225,755	36,004	18,853	16,605	2,065	30,113
Agriculture and natural resources	4,783	3,516	140	114	135	26	852	2,306	1,693	56	55	53	11	438	2,477	1,823	84	59	82	15	414
Architecture and related services	5,424	3,330	220	307	301	21	1,245	3,049	1,966	88	165	129	15	686	2,375	1,364	132	142	172	6	559
Area, ethnic, cultural, and gender studies	1,683	998	149	130	112	31	263	642	394	50	48	34	14	102	1,041	604	99	82	78	17	161
Biological and biomedical sciences	7,657	4,907	431	320	835	35	1,129	3,227	2,080	130	153	364	11	489	4,430	2,827	301	167	471	24	640
Business	139,347	85,082	14,574	6,429	10,488	654	22,120	80,858	51,743	5,526	3,635	5,941	327	13,686	58,489	33,339	9,048	2,794	4,547	327	8,434
Communications, journalism, and related programs	6,535	4,162	646	341	315	28	1,043	2,127	1,370	166	122	84	14	371	4,408	2,792	480	219	231	14	672
Communications technologies	365	177	54	15	37	0	82	202	115	25	9	16	0	37	163	62	29	6	21	0	45
Computer and information sciences	20,143	6,696	1,086	638	2,760	67	8,896	13,868	5,034	598	415	1,647	40	6,134	6,275	1,662	488	223	1,113	27	2,762
Construction trades	0	0	0	0	0	0	0	0	0	0	0	0	0	0	0	0	0	0	0	0	0
Education	162,345	126,634	15,784	10,926	3,967	1,056	3,978	37,843	29,917	3,288	2,475	839	292	1,032	124,502	96,717	12,496	8,451	3,128	764	2,946
Engineering	32,698	12,131	856	1,019	3,151	83	15,458	25,824	9,797	577	755	2,306	57	12,332	6,874	2,334	279	264	845	26	3,126
Engineering technologies[1]	2,499	1,385	174	83	217	14	626	1,843	1,055	101	62	152	10	463	656	330	73	21	65	4	163
English language and literature/letters	7,956	6,491	393	302	267	61	442	2,459	2,074	102	87	74	16	106	5,497	4,417	291	215	193	45	336
Family and consumer sciences	1,794	1,281	195	85	53	15	165	239	166	24	9	7	3	30	1,555	1,115	171	76	46	12	135
Foreign languages, literatures, and linguistics	3,124	1,783	54	383	123	18	763	957	595	20	106	30	3	203	2,167	1,188	34	277	93	15	560
Health professions and related clinical sciences	44,939	32,735	3,994	2,210	3,269	288	2,443	9,670	6,471	647	532	949	60	1,011	35,269	26,264	3,347	1,678	2,320	228	1,432
Legal professions and studies	4,243	1,414	231	153	243	23	2,179	2,394	809	91	84	126	7	1,277	1,849	605	140	69	117	16	902
Liberal arts and sciences, general studies, and humanities	3,697	2,988	266	156	89	28	170	1,370	1,119	86	50	38	10	67	2,327	1,869	180	106	51	18	103
Library science	6,015	5,011	279	315	174	35	201	1,151	965	41	57	35	7	46	4,864	4,046	238	258	139	28	155
Mathematics and statistics	4,191	1,937	122	114	295	7	1,716	2,302	1,113	67	66	139	4	913	1,889	824	55	48	156	3	803
Mechanics and repair technologies	0	0	0	0	0	0	0	0	0	0	0	0	0	0	0	0	0	0	0	0	0
Military technologies	0	0	0	0	0	0	0	0	0	0	0	0	0	0	0	0	0	0	0	0	0
Multi/interdisciplinary studies	4,047	2,741	328	214	186	41	537	1,378	910	85	75	50	10	248	2,669	1,831	243	139	136	31	289
Parks, recreation, leisure and fitness studies	3,199	2,503	261	132	88	15	200	1,573	1,207	133	68	48	7	110	1,626	1,296	128	64	40	8	90
Philosophy and religious studies	1,578	1,222	73	71	73	4	135	972	762	41	48	39	2	80	606	460	32	23	34	2	55
Physical sciences and science technologies	5,570	3,397	154	139	249	16	1,615	3,364	2,045	68	78	136	6	1,031	2,206	1,352	86	61	113	10	584
Precision production	13	10	0	1	0	0	2	9	7	0	1	0	0	1	4	3	0	0	0	0	1
Psychology	17,898	12,951	2,294	1,097	715	140	701	3,789	2,814	413	210	153	34	165	14,109	10,137	1,881	887	562	106	536
Public administration and social service professions	28,250	18,183	5,087	2,124	1,037	274	1,545	7,001	4,392	1,073	522	256	77	681	21,249	13,791	4,014	1,602	781	197	864
Security and protective services	3,717	2,672	565	270	86	21	103	1,940	1,488	204	144	43	8	53	1,777	1,184	361	126	43	13	50
Social sciences and history	16,110	9,903	1,221	796	720	89	3,381	7,810	4,954	457	371	283	29	1,716	8,300	4,949	764	425	437	60	1,665
Social sciences	13,588	7,747	1,129	674	681	79	3,278	6,429	3,752	414	293	270	28	1,672	7,159	3,995	715	381	411	51	1,606
History	2,522	2,156	92	122	39	10	103	1,381	1,202	43	78	13	1	44	1,141	954	49	44	26	9	59
Theology and religious vocations	5,486	3,973	450	180	265	15	603	3,238	2,346	221	100	146	8	417	2,248	1,627	229	80	119	7	186
Transportation and materials moving	728	589	44	32	22	4	37	609	493	38	26	20	4	28	119	96	6	6	2	0	9
Visual and performing arts	12,906	8,780	532	570	680	83	2,261	5,531	3,933	237	285	210	41	825	7,375	4,847	295	285	470	42	1,436

[1]Excludes "Construction trades" and "Mechanics and repair technologies," which are listed separately.
NOTE: Race categories exclude persons of Hispanic origin. Reported racial/ethnic distributions of students by level of degree, field of degree, and sex were used to estimate race/ethnicity for students whose race/ethnicity was not reported. To facilitate trend comparisons, certain aggregations have been made of the degree fields as reported in the IPEDS Fall survey: "Agriculture and natural resources" includes Agriculture, agriculture operations, and related sciences and Natural resources

and conservation; and "Business" includes Business management, marketing, and related support services and Personal and culinary services.
SOURCE: U.S. Department of Education, National Center for Education Statistics, 2003–04 Integrated Postsecondary Education Data System (IPEDS), Fall 2004. (This table was prepared July 2005.)

Table 273. Doctor's degrees conferred by degree-granting institutions, by race/ethnicity and sex of student: Selected years, 1976–77 through 2004–05

Year and sex	Number of degrees conferred[1]							Percentage distribution of degrees conferred[1]						
	Total	White	Black	Hispanic	Asian/ Pacific Islander	American Indian/ Alaska Native	Non-resident alien	Total	White	Black	Hispanic	Asian/ Pacific Islander	American Indian/ Alaska Native	Non-resident alien
1	2	3	4	5	6	7	8	9	10	11	12	13	14	15
Total														
1976–77[2]	33,126	26,851	1,253	522	658	95	3,747	100.0	81.1	3.8	1.6	2.0	0.3	11.3
1980–81[3]	32,839	25,908	1,265	456	877	130	4,203	100.0	78.9	3.9	1.4	2.7	0.4	12.8
1989–90	38,371	26,221	1,149	780	1,225	98	8,898	100.0	68.3	3.0	2.0	3.2	0.3	23.2
1990–91	39,294	25,855	1,248	757	1,504	106	9,824	100.0	65.8	3.2	1.9	3.8	0.3	25.0
1991–92	40,659	26,229	1,239	824	1,598	120	10,649	100.0	64.5	3.0	2.0	3.9	0.3	26.2
1992–93	42,132	26,816	1,350	824	1,578	107	11,457	100.0	63.6	3.2	2.0	3.7	0.3	27.2
1993–94	43,185	27,212	1,385	900	2,024	134	11,530	100.0	63.0	3.2	2.1	4.7	0.3	26.7
1994–95	44,446	27,846	1,667	984	2,689	130	11,130	100.0	62.7	3.8	2.2	6.1	0.3	25.0
1995–96	44,652	27,773	1,632	997	2,641	159	11,450	100.0	62.2	3.7	2.2	5.9	0.4	25.6
1996–97	45,876	28,596	1,865	1,120	2,667	175	11,453	100.0	62.3	4.1	2.4	5.8	0.4	25.0
1997–98	46,010	28,803	2,067	1,275	2,339	186	11,340	100.0	62.6	4.5	2.8	5.1	0.4	24.6
1998–99	44,077	27,838	2,136	1,302	2,299	194	10,308	100.0	63.2	4.8	3.0	5.2	0.4	23.4
1999–2000	44,808	27,843	2,246	1,305	2,420	160	10,834	100.0	62.1	5.0	2.9	5.4	0.4	24.2
2000–01	44,904	27,454	2,207	1,516	2,587	177	10,963	100.0	61.1	4.9	3.4	5.8	0.4	24.4
2001–02	44,160	26,903	2,395	1,434	2,319	180	10,929	100.0	60.9	5.4	3.2	5.3	0.4	24.7
2002–03	46,024	27,698	2,517	1,561	2,426	196	11,626	100.0	60.2	5.5	3.4	5.3	0.4	25.3
2003–04	48,378	28,214	2,900	1,662	2,632	217	12,753	100.0	58.3	6.0	3.4	5.4	0.4	26.4
2004–05	52,631	30,261	3,056	1,824	2,911	237	14,342	100.0	57.5	5.8	3.5	5.5	0.5	27.3
Males														
1976–77[2]	25,036	20,032	766	383	540	67	3,248	100.0	80.0	3.1	1.5	2.2	0.3	13.0
1980–81[3]	22,595	17,310	694	277	655	95	3,564	100.0	76.6	3.1	1.2	2.9	0.4	15.8
1989–90	24,401	15,314	531	419	865	49	7,223	100.0	62.8	2.2	1.7	3.5	0.2	29.6
1990–91	24,756	14,853	597	399	1,017	59	7,831	100.0	60.0	2.4	1.6	4.1	0.2	31.6
1991–92	25,557	14,956	584	465	1,088	66	8,398	100.0	58.5	2.3	1.8	4.3	0.3	32.9
1992–93	26,073	14,991	617	437	1,040	52	8,936	100.0	57.5	2.4	1.7	4.0	0.2	34.3
1993–94	26,552	15,159	627	463	1,373	66	8,864	100.0	57.1	2.4	1.7	5.2	0.2	33.4
1994–95	26,916	15,375	730	488	1,756	58	8,509	100.0	57.1	2.7	1.8	6.5	0.2	31.6
1995–96	26,841	15,112	727	514	1,692	80	8,716	100.0	56.3	2.7	1.9	6.3	0.3	32.5
1996–97	27,146	15,499	795	585	1,645	87	8,535	100.0	57.1	2.9	2.2	6.1	0.3	31.4
1997–98	26,664	15,399	824	652	1,392	83	8,314	100.0	57.8	3.1	2.4	5.2	0.3	31.2
1998–99	25,146	14,726	873	625	1,337	92	7,493	100.0	58.6	3.5	2.5	5.3	0.4	29.8
1999–2000	25,028	14,472	876	611	1,356	57	7,656	100.0	57.8	3.5	2.4	5.4	0.2	30.6
2000–01	24,728	13,937	855	687	1,453	76	7,720	100.0	56.4	3.5	2.8	5.9	0.3	31.2
2001–02	23,708	13,330	922	650	1,242	67	7,497	100.0	56.2	3.9	2.7	5.2	0.3	31.6
2002–03	24,341	13,470	913	742	1,243	76	7,897	100.0	55.3	3.8	3.0	5.1	0.3	32.4
2003–04	25,323	13,567	1,015	766	1,293	90	8,592	100.0	53.6	4.0	3.0	5.1	0.4	33.9
2004–05	26,973	14,023	1,049	764	1,403	87	9,647	100.0	52.0	3.9	2.8	5.2	0.3	35.8
Females														
1976–77	8,090	6,819	487	139	118	28	499	100.0	84.3	6.0	1.7	1.5	0.3	6.2
1980–81[3]	10,244	8,598	571	179	222	35	639	100.0	83.9	5.6	1.7	2.2	0.3	6.2
1989–90	13,970	10,907	618	361	360	49	1,675	100.0	78.1	4.4	2.6	2.6	0.4	12.0
1990–91	14,538	11,002	651	358	487	47	1,993	100.0	75.7	4.5	2.5	3.3	0.3	13.7
1991–92	15,102	11,273	655	359	510	54	2,251	100.0	74.6	4.3	2.4	3.4	0.4	14.9
1992–93	16,059	11,825	733	387	538	55	2,521	100.0	73.6	4.6	2.4	3.4	0.3	15.7
1993–94	16,633	12,053	758	437	651	68	2,666	100.0	72.5	4.6	2.6	3.9	0.4	16.0
1994–95	17,530	12,471	937	496	933	72	2,621	100.0	71.1	5.3	2.8	5.3	0.4	15.0
1995–96	17,811	12,661	905	483	949	79	2,734	100.0	71.1	5.1	2.7	5.3	0.4	15.4
1996–97	18,730	13,097	1,070	535	1,022	88	2,918	100.0	69.9	5.7	2.9	5.5	0.5	15.6
1997–98	19,346	13,404	1,243	623	947	103	3,026	100.0	69.3	6.4	3.2	4.9	0.5	15.6
1998–99	18,931	13,112	1,263	677	962	102	2,815	100.0	69.3	6.7	3.6	5.1	0.5	14.9
1999–2000	19,780	13,371	1,370	694	1,064	103	3,178	100.0	67.6	6.9	3.5	5.4	0.5	16.1
2000–01	20,176	13,517	1,352	829	1,134	101	3,243	100.0	67.0	6.7	4.1	5.6	0.5	16.1
2001–02	20,452	13,573	1,473	784	1,077	113	3,432	100.0	66.4	7.2	3.8	5.3	0.6	16.8
2002–03	21,683	14,228	1,604	819	1,183	120	3,729	100.0	65.6	7.4	3.8	5.5	0.6	17.2
2003–04	23,055	14,647	1,885	896	1,339	127	4,161	100.0	63.5	8.2	3.9	5.8	0.6	18.0
2004–05	25,658	16,238	2,007	1,060	1,508	150	4,695	100.0	63.3	7.8	4.1	5.9	0.6	18.3

[1]Includes Ph.D., Ed.D, and comparable degrees at the doctoral level. Excludes first-professional degrees, such as M.D., D.D.S., and law degrees.
[2]Excludes 106 men whose racial/ethnic group was not available.
[3]Excludes 116 men and 3 women whose racial/ethnic group was not available.
NOTE: Race categories exclude persons of Hispanic origin. For years 1989–90 to 2004–05, reported racial/ethnic distributions of students by level of degree, field of degree, and sex were used to estimate race/ethnicity for students whose race/ethnicity

was not reported. (See Guide to Sources for details.) Detail may not sum to totals because of rounding.
SOURCE: U.S. Department of Education, National Center for Education Statistics, Higher Education General Information Survey (HEGIS), "Degrees and Other Formal Awards Conferred" surveys, 1976–77 and 1980–81; and 1988–89 through 2004–05 Integrated Postsecondary Education Data System, "Completions Survey" (IPEDS-C:89–99), and Fall 2000 through Fall 2005. (This table was prepared July 2006.)

Table 274. Doctor's degrees conferred by degree-granting institutions, by sex, race/ethnicity, and major field of study: 2004–05

Major field of study	Total							Males							Females						
	Total	White	Black	Hispanic	Asian/Pacific Islander	American Indian/Alaska Native	Non-resident alien	Total	White	Black	Hispanic	Asian/Pacific Islander	American Indian/Alaska Native	Non-resident alien	Total	White	Black	Hispanic	Asian/Pacific Islander	American Indian/Alaska Native	Non-resident alien
1	2	3	4	5	6	7	8	9	10	11	12	13	14	15	16	17	18	19	20	21	22
All fields, total	52,631	30,261	3,056	1,824	2,911	237	14,342	26,973	14,023	1,049	764	1,403	87	9,647	25,658	16,238	2,007	1,060	1,508	150	4,695
Agriculture and natural resources	1,173	597	23	20	28	4	501	763	384	9	12	13	2	343	410	213	14	8	15	2	158
Architecture and related services	179	68	5	6	21	0	79	110	36	4	4	10	0	56	69	32	1	2	11	0	23
Area, ethnic, cultural, and gender studies	189	100	24	14	15	4	32	81	49	8	2	5	1	16	108	51	16	12	10	3	16
Biological and biomedical sciences	5,578	3,186	155	194	514	18	1,511	2,845	1,643	49	99	247	8	799	2,733	1,543	106	95	267	10	712
Business	1,498	709	123	49	79	6	532	901	433	48	28	41	5	346	597	276	75	21	38	1	186
Communications, journalism, and related programs	465	270	25	13	17	2	138	194	107	9	6	5	0	67	271	163	16	7	12	2	71
Communications technologies	3	1	0	1	0	0	1	1	1	0	0	0	0	0	2	0	0	1	0	0	1
Computer and information sciences	1,119	356	22	18	102	0	621	905	287	13	12	83	0	510	214	69	9	6	19	0	111
Construction trades	0	0	0	0	0	0	0	0	0	0	0	0	0	0	0	0	0	0	0	0	0
Education	7,681	5,159	1,206	388	210	67	651	2,557	1,741	339	118	59	21	279	5,124	3,418	867	270	151	46	372
Engineering	6,547	1,822	111	104	399	6	4,105	5,329	1,474	79	75	303	6	3,392	1,218	348	32	29	96	0	713
Engineering technologies[1]	54	23	0	0	4	0	27	39	13	0	0	2	0	24	15	10	0	0	2	0	3
English language and literature/letters	1,212	899	80	39	60	15	119	494	389	23	13	13	5	51	718	510	57	26	47	10	68
Family and consumer sciences	331	208	37	8	5	1	72	68	45	5	0	0	0	18	263	163	32	8	5	1	54
Foreign languages, literatures, and linguistics	1,027	515	11	105	53	3	340	410	222	3	39	12	1	133	617	293	8	66	41	2	207
Health professions and related clinical sciences	5,868	4,348	257	160	453	26	624	1,710	1,154	71	47	161	10	267	4,158	3,194	186	113	292	16	357
Legal professions and studies	98	18	1	0	5	0	74	58	7	0	0	2	0	49	40	11	1	0	3	0	25
Liberal arts and sciences, general studies, and humanities	109	83	2	6	2	1	15	38	28	1	0	0	0	9	71	55	1	6	2	1	6
Library science	42	26	0	0	1	0	15	14	8	0	0	0	0	6	28	18	0	0	1	0	9
Mathematics and statistics	1,176	438	20	23	58	0	637	841	330	10	17	31	0	453	335	108	10	6	27	0	184
Mechanics and repair technologies	0	0	0	0	0	0	0	0	0	0	0	0	0	0	0	0	0	0	0	0	0
Military technologies	0	0	0	0	0	0	0	0	0	0	0	0	0	0	0	0	0	0	0	0	0
Multi/interdisciplinary studies	983	610	64	32	61	5	211	440	280	23	10	27	1	99	543	330	41	22	34	4	112
Parks, recreation, leisure and fitness studies	207	139	8	9	9	0	42	119	73	2	6	7	0	31	88	66	6	3	2	0	11
Philosophy and religious studies	586	426	25	12	23	0	100	418	303	17	8	17	0	73	168	123	8	4	6	0	27
Physical sciences and science technologies	4,114	1,962	60	88	232	10	1,762	2,966	1,385	41	51	155	6	1,328	1,148	577	19	37	77	4	434
Precision production	0	0	0	0	0	0	0	0	0	0	0	0	0	0	0	0	0	0	0	0	0
Psychology	5,106	3,911	323	302	250	36	284	1,466	1,134	67	98	66	10	91	3,640	2,777	256	204	184	26	193
Public administration and social service professions	673	410	92	28	21	7	115	272	152	27	12	13	1	67	401	258	65	16	8	6	48
Security and protective services	94	71	6	5	5	1	6	55	38	5	3	4	1	4	39	33	1	2	1	0	2
Social sciences and history	3,819	2,161	195	141	148	20	1,154	2,184	1,176	82	71	56	7	792	1,635	985	113	70	92	13	362
Social sciences	3,000	1,534	145	113	129	13	1,066	1,699	798	59	59	46	3	734	1,301	736	86	54	83	10	332
History	819	627	50	28	19	7	88	485	378	23	12	10	4	58	334	249	27	16	9	3	30
Theology and religious vocations	1,422	895	153	21	75	1	277	1,101	699	95	16	53	1	237	321	196	58	5	22	0	40
Transportation and materials moving	0	0	0	0	0	0	0	0	0	0	0	0	0	0	0	0	0	0	0	0	0
Visual and performing arts	1,278	850	28	38	61	4	297	594	432	19	17	18	1	107	684	418	9	21	43	3	190

[1]Excludes "Construction trades" and "Mechanics and repair technologies," which are listed separately.

NOTE: Race categories exclude persons of Hispanic origin. Reported racial/ethnic distributions of students by level of degree, field of degree, and sex were used to estimate race/ethnicity for students whose race/ethnicity was not reported. To facilitate trend comparisons, certain aggregations have been made of the degree fields as reported in the IPEDS Fall survey: "Agriculture and natural resources" includes Agriculture, agriculture operations, and related sciences and Natural resources and conservation; and "Business" includes Business management, marketing, and related support services and Personal and culinary services.

SOURCE: U.S. Department of Education, National Center for Education Statistics, 2004–05 Integrated Postsecondary Education Data System (IPEDS), Fall 2005. (This table was prepared July 2006.)

Table 275. Doctor's degrees conferred by degree-granting institutions, by sex, race/ethnicity, and major field of study: 2003–04

Major field of study	Total							Males							Females						
	Total	White	Black	Hispanic	Asian/ Pacific Islander	American Indian/ Alaska Native	Non-resident alien	Total	White	Black	Hispanic	Asian/ Pacific Islander	American Indian/ Alaska Native	Non-resident alien	Total	White	Black	Hispanic	Asian/ Pacific Islander	American Indian/ Alaska Native	Non-resident alien
1	2	3	4	5	6	7	8	9	10	11	12	13	14	15	16	17	18	19	20	21	22
All fields, total	48,378	28,214	2,900	1,662	2,632	217	12,753	25,323	13,567	1,015	766	1,293	90	8,592	23,055	14,647	1,885	896	1,339	127	4,161
Agriculture and natural resources	1,185	587	24	18	33	7	516	758	376	15	9	15	4	339	427	211	9	9	18	3	177
Architecture and related services	173	69	7	3	13	0	81	94	34	4	2	8	0	46	79	35	3	1	5	0	35
Area, ethnic, cultural, and gender studies	209	109	24	15	20	3	38	97	53	10	9	7	1	17	112	56	14	6	13	2	21
Biological and biomedical sciences	5,242	3,072	163	173	496	16	1,322	2,804	1,649	71	79	252	9	744	2,438	1,423	92	94	244	7	578
Business	1,481	673	112	51	67	9	569	960	434	56	36	39	8	387	521	239	56	15	28	1	182
Communications, journalism, and related programs	418	250	29	8	19	2	110	181	116	4	4	3	0	54	237	134	25	4	16	2	56
Communications technologies	8	5	0	0	0	0	3	5	3	0	0	0	0	2	3	2	0	0	0	0	1
Computer and information sciences	909	344	21	19	69	1	455	709	265	16	10	53	1	364	200	79	5	9	16	0	91
Construction trades	0	0	0	0	0	0	0	0	0	0	0	0	0	0	0	0	0	0	0	0	0
Education	7,088	4,746	1,111	307	203	56	665	2,403	1,647	314	109	56	12	265	4,685	3,099	797	198	147	44	400
Engineering	5,923	1,751	104	104	368	8	3,588	4,872	1,395	70	81	290	4	3,032	1,051	356	34	23	78	4	556
Engineering technologies[1]	58	20	6	1	4	0	27	51	19	4	2	2	0	25	7	2	2	0	2	0	2
English language and literature/letters	1,207	939	64	30	49	6	119	479	382	18	15	13	2	49	728	557	46	15	36	4	70
Family and consumer sciences	329	198	43	8	7	2	71	94	63	8	1	1	1	20	235	135	35	7	6	1	51
Foreign languages, literatures, and linguistics	1,031	567	26	89	39	1	309	410	240	9	42	7	0	112	621	327	17	47	32	1	197
Health professions and related clinical sciences	4,361	3,144	209	148	286	19	555	1,261	828	44	49	78	5	257	3,100	2,316	165	99	208	14	298
Legal professions and studies	119	17	8	0	3	0	91	80	11	3	0	1	0	65	39	6	5	0	2	0	26
Liberal arts and sciences, general studies, and humanities	95	76	4	6	1	0	8	39	29	1	2	1	0	6	56	47	3	4	0	0	2
Library science	47	24	5	2	3	0	13	16	8	2	0	1	0	5	31	16	3	2	2	0	8
Mathematics and statistics	1,060	419	9	25	50	0	557	762	290	8	19	36	0	409	298	129	1	6	14	0	148
Mechanics and repair technologies	0	0	0	0	0	0	0	0	0	0	0	0	0	0	0	0	0	0	0	0	0
Military technologies	0	0	0	0	0	0	0	0	0	0	0	0	0	0	0	0	0	0	0	0	0
Multi/interdisciplinary studies	876	575	50	32	61	5	153	410	281	16	19	25	2	67	466	294	34	13	36	3	86
Parks, recreation, leisure and fitness studies	222	146	9	9	8	5	49	118	67	5	5	8	0	33	104	79	4	4	1	0	16
Philosophy and religious studies	595	454	17	10	26	2	86	391	293	12	7	20	1	58	204	161	5	3	6	1	28
Physical sciences and science technologies	3,815	1,929	72	76	192	16	1,530	2,753	1,394	40	45	125	13	1,136	1,062	535	32	31	67	3	394
Precision production	0	0	0	0	0	0	0	0	0	0	0	0	0	0	0	0	0	0	0	0	0
Psychology	4,827	3,684	341	276	247	40	239	1,496	1,199	67	83	52	12	83	3,331	2,485	274	193	195	28	156
Public administration and social service professions	649	407	92	28	23	4	95	275	167	32	12	3	2	59	374	240	60	16	20	2	36
Security and protective services	54	46	3	0	0	0	5	21	18	0	0	0	0	3	33	28	3	0	0	0	2
Social sciences and history	3,811	2,354	188	153	152	16	948	2,188	1,312	78	80	75	10	633	1,623	1,042	110	73	77	6	315
Social sciences	2,956	1,678	139	124	124	13	878	1,687	910	59	66	60	8	584	1,269	768	80	58	64	5	294
History	855	676	49	29	28	3	70	501	402	19	14	15	2	49	354	274	30	15	13	1	21
Theology and religious vocations	1,304	762	130	39	116	2	255	1,024	595	95	28	94	1	211	280	167	35	11	22	1	44
Transportation and materials moving	0	0	0	0	0	0	0	0	0	0	0	0	0	0	0	0	0	0	0	0	0
Visual and performing arts	1,282	847	29	32	76	2	296	572	399	13	19	28	2	111	710	448	16	13	48	0	185

[1]Excludes "Construction trades" and "Mechanics and repair technologies," which are listed separately.

NOTE: Race categories exclude persons of Hispanic origin. Reported racial/ethnic distributions of students by level of degree, field of degree, and sex were used to estimate race/ethnicity for students whose race/ethnicity was not reported. To facilitate trend comparisons, certain aggregations have been made of the degree fields as reported in the IPEDS Fall survey: "Agriculture and natural resources" includes Agriculture, agriculture operations, and related sciences and Natural resources and conservation; and "Business" includes Business management, marketing, and related support services and Personal and culinary services.
SOURCE: U.S. Department of Education, National Center for Education Statistics, 2003–04 Integrated Postsecondary Education Data System (IPEDS), Fall 2004. (This table was prepared July 2005.)

Table 276. First-professional degrees conferred by degree-granting institutions, by race/ethnicity and sex of student: Selected years, 1976–77 through 2004–05

	Number of degrees conferred							Percentage distribution of degrees conferred						
Year and sex	Total	White	Black	Hispanic	Asian/ Pacific Islander	American Indian/ Alaska Native	Non-resident alien	Total	White	Black	Hispanic	Asian/ Pacific Islander	American Indian/ Alaska Native	Non-resident alien
1	2	3	4	5	6	7	8	9	10	11	12	13	14	15
Total														
1976–77[1]	63,953	58,422	2,537	1,076	1,021	196	701	100.0	91.4	4.0	1.7	1.6	0.3	1.1
1980–81[2]	71,340	64,551	2,931	1,541	1,456	192	669	100.0	90.5	4.1	2.2	2.0	0.3	0.9
1989–90	70,988	60,487	3,409	2,425	3,362	257	1,048	100.0	85.2	4.8	3.4	4.7	0.4	1.5
1990–91	71,948	60,631	3,588	2,547	3,835	261	1,086	100.0	84.3	5.0	3.5	5.3	0.4	1.5
1991–92	74,146	61,170	3,628	2,867	4,841	298	1,342	100.0	82.5	4.9	3.9	6.5	0.4	1.8
1992–93	75,387	61,165	4,132	2,996	5,176	370	1,548	100.0	81.1	5.5	4.0	6.9	0.5	2.1
1993–94	75,418	60,143	4,444	3,131	5,892	371	1,437	100.0	79.7	5.9	4.2	7.8	0.5	1.9
1994–95	75,800	59,402	4,747	3,231	6,396	413	1,611	100.0	78.4	6.3	4.3	8.4	0.5	2.1
1995–96	76,734	59,525	5,022	3,475	6,627	463	1,622	100.0	77.6	6.5	4.5	8.6	0.6	2.1
1996–97	78,730	60,280	5,301	3,615	7,374	514	1,646	100.0	76.6	6.7	4.6	9.4	0.7	2.1
1997–98	78,598	59,443	5,499	3,552	7,757	561	1,786	100.0	75.6	7.0	4.5	9.9	0.7	2.3
1998–99	78,439	58,720	5,333	3,864	8,152	612	1,758	100.0	74.9	6.8	4.9	10.4	0.8	2.2
1999–2000	80,057	59,637	5,555	3,865	8,584	564	1,852	100.0	74.5	6.9	4.8	10.7	0.7	2.3
2000–01	79,707	58,598	5,416	3,806	9,261	543	2,083	100.0	73.5	6.8	4.8	11.6	0.7	2.6
2001–02	80,698	58,874	5,811	3,965	9,584	581	1,883	100.0	73.0	7.2	4.9	11.9	0.7	2.3
2002–03	80,810	58,678	5,715	4,086	9,790	586	1,955	100.0	72.6	7.1	5.1	12.1	0.7	2.4
2003–04	83,041	60,379	5,930	4,273	9,964	565	1,930	100.0	72.7	7.1	5.1	12.0	0.7	2.3
2004–05	87,289	63,429	6,313	4,445	10,501	564	2,037	100.0	72.7	7.2	5.1	12.0	0.6	2.3
Males														
1976–77[1]	51,980	47,777	1,761	893	776	159	614	100.0	91.9	3.4	1.7	1.5	0.3	1.2
1980–81[2]	52,194	47,629	1,772	1,131	991	134	537	100.0	91.3	3.4	2.2	1.9	0.3	1.0
1989–90	43,961	38,036	1,671	1,449	1,962	135	708	100.0	86.5	3.8	3.3	4.5	0.3	1.6
1990–91	43,846	37,533	1,679	1,517	2,211	144	762	100.0	85.6	3.8	3.5	5.0	0.3	1.7
1991–92	45,071	37,849	1,645	1,695	2,775	159	948	100.0	84.0	3.6	3.8	6.2	0.4	2.1
1992–93	45,153	37,415	1,801	1,771	2,871	192	1,103	100.0	82.9	4.0	3.9	6.4	0.4	2.4
1993–94	44,707	36,574	1,902	1,780	3,214	222	1,015	100.0	81.8	4.3	4.0	7.2	0.5	2.3
1994–95	44,853	36,147	2,077	1,835	3,490	223	1,081	100.0	80.6	4.6	4.1	7.8	0.5	2.4
1995–96	44,748	35,786	2,112	1,947	3,539	256	1,108	100.0	80.0	4.7	4.4	7.9	0.6	2.5
1996–97	45,564	36,008	2,201	1,985	3,959	290	1,121	100.0	79.0	4.8	4.4	8.7	0.6	2.5
1997–98	44,911	35,172	2,310	1,973	4,017	291	1,148	100.0	78.3	5.1	4.4	8.9	0.6	2.6
1998–99	44,339	34,271	2,197	2,064	4,333	333	1,141	100.0	77.3	5.0	4.7	9.8	0.8	2.6
1999–2000	44,239	34,004	2,313	2,095	4,372	285	1,170	100.0	76.9	5.2	4.7	9.9	0.6	2.6
2000–01	42,862	32,717	2,110	1,977	4,518	278	1,262	100.0	76.3	4.9	4.6	10.5	0.6	2.9
2001–02	42,507	32,224	2,223	2,045	4,613	292	1,110	100.0	75.8	5.2	4.8	10.9	0.7	2.6
2002–03	41,834	31,596	2,172	2,047	4,618	296	1,105	100.0	75.5	5.2	4.9	11.0	0.7	2.6
2003–04	42,169	31,994	2,248	2,080	4,528	275	1,044	100.0	75.9	5.3	4.9	10.7	0.7	2.5
2004–05	43,849	33,268	2,257	2,214	4,709	288	1,113	100.0	75.9	5.1	5.0	10.7	0.7	2.5
Females														
1976–77[1]	11,973	10,645	776	183	245	37	87	100.0	88.9	6.5	1.5	2.0	0.3	0.7
1980–81[2]	19,146	16,922	1,159	410	465	58	132	100.0	88.4	6.1	2.1	2.4	0.3	0.7
1989–90	27,027	22,451	1,738	976	1,400	122	340	100.0	83.1	6.4	3.6	5.2	0.5	1.3
1990–91	28,102	23,098	1,909	1,030	1,624	117	324	100.0	82.2	6.8	3.7	5.8	0.4	1.2
1991–92	29,075	23,321	1,983	1,172	2,066	139	394	100.0	80.2	6.8	4.0	7.1	0.5	1.4
1992–93	30,234	23,750	2,331	1,225	2,305	178	445	100.0	78.6	7.7	4.1	7.6	0.6	1.5
1993–94	30,711	23,569	2,542	1,351	2,678	149	422	100.0	76.7	8.3	4.4	8.7	0.5	1.4
1994–95	30,947	23,255	2,670	1,396	2,906	190	530	100.0	75.1	8.6	4.5	9.4	0.6	1.7
1995–96	31,986	23,739	2,910	1,528	3,088	207	514	100.0	74.2	9.1	4.8	9.7	0.6	1.6
1996–97	33,166	24,272	3,100	1,630	3,415	224	525	100.0	73.2	9.3	4.9	10.3	0.7	1.6
1997–98	33,687	24,271	3,189	1,579	3,740	270	638	100.0	72.0	9.5	4.7	11.1	0.8	1.9
1998–99	34,100	24,449	3,136	1,800	3,819	279	617	100.0	71.7	9.2	5.3	11.2	0.8	1.8
1999–2000	35,818	25,633	3,242	1,770	4,212	279	682	100.0	71.6	9.1	4.9	11.8	0.8	1.9
2000–01	36,845	25,881	3,306	1,829	4,743	265	821	100.0	70.2	9.0	5.0	12.9	0.7	2.2
2001–02	38,191	26,650	3,588	1,920	4,971	289	773	100.0	69.8	9.4	5.0	13.0	0.8	2.0
2002–03	38,976	27,082	3,543	2,039	5,172	290	850	100.0	69.5	9.1	5.2	13.3	0.7	2.2
2003–04	40,872	28,385	3,682	2,193	5,436	290	886	100.0	69.4	9.0	5.4	13.3	0.7	2.2
2004–05	43,440	30,161	4,056	2,231	5,792	276	924	100.0	69.4	9.3	5.1	13.3	0.6	2.1

[1]Excludes 394 men and 12 women whose racial/ethnic group was not available.
[2]Excludes 598 men and 18 women whose racial/ethnic group was not available.
NOTE: Race categories exclude persons of Hispanic origin. For years 1989–90 to 2004–05, reported racial/ethnic distributions of students by level of degree, field of degree, and sex were used to estimate race/ethnicity for students whose race/ethnicity was not reported. (See Guide to Sources for details.) Detail may not sum to totals because of rounding.

SOURCE: U.S. Department of Education, National Center for Education Statistics, Higher Education General Information Survey (HEGIS), "Degrees and Other Formal Awards Conferred" surveys, 1976–77 and 1980–81; and 1988–89 through 2004–05 Integrated Postsecondary Education Data System, "Completions Survey" (IPEDS-C:89–99), and Fall 2000 through Fall 2005. (This table was prepared July 2006.)

Table 277. First-professional degrees conferred by degree-granting institutions, by sex, race/ethnicity, and major field of study: 2004–05

Major field of study	Total							Males							Females						
	Total	White	Black	Hispanic	Asian/Pacific Islander	American Indian/Alaska Native	Non-resident alien	Total	White	Black	Hispanic	Asian/Pacific Islander	American Indian/Alaska Native	Non-resident alien	Total	White	Black	Hispanic	Asian/Pacific Islander	American Indian/Alaska Native	Non-resident alien
1	2	3	4	5	6	7	8	9	10	11	12	13	14	15	16	17	18	19	20	21	22
All fields, total	87,289	63,429	6,313	4,445	10,501	564	2,037	43,849	33,268	2,257	2,214	4,709	288	1,113	43,440	30,161	4,056	2,231	5,792	276	924
Dentistry (D.D.S. or D.M.D.)	4,454	2,770	192	227	879	16	370	2,505	1,685	76	112	443	11	178	1,949	1,085	116	115	436	5	192
Medicine (M.D.)	15,461	10,269	1,083	748	3,084	96	181	8,151	5,586	370	412	1,628	52	103	7,310	4,683	713	336	1,456	44	78
Optometry (O.D.)	1,252	769	36	52	320	8	67	482	358	14	22	60	3	25	770	411	22	30	260	5	42
Osteopathic medicine (D.O.)	2,762	2,122	88	108	426	14	4	1,482	1,160	34	57	217	10	4	1,280	962	54	51	209	4	0
Pharmacy (Pharm.D.)	8,885	5,600	791	353	1,872	52	217	2,889	1,893	216	115	559	25	81	5,996	3,707	575	238	1,313	27	136
Podiatry (Pod.D. or D.P.) or podiatric medicine (D.P.M.)	343	229	34	28	43	1	8	195	134	14	15	25	1	6	148	95	20	13	18	0	2
Veterinary medicine (D.V.M.)	2,354	2,125	43	79	75	21	11	574	509	21	22	14	5	3	1,780	1,616	22	57	61	16	8
Chiropractic medicine (D.C. or D.C.M.)	2,560	1,943	135	129	204	19	130	1,665	1,269	67	82	143	10	94	895	674	68	47	61	9	36
Naturopathic medicine	262	212	13	13	14	2	8	44	39	3	2	0	0	0	218	173	10	11	14	2	8
Law (LL.B. or J.D.)	43,423	33,492	3,052	2,553	3,326	320	680	22,297	18,103	1,040	1,259	1,414	164	317	21,126	15,389	2,012	1,294	1,912	156	363
Theology (M.Div, M.H.L., B.D., or Ord.)	5,533	3,898	846	155	258	15	361	3,565	2,532	402	116	206	7	302	1,968	1,366	444	39	52	8	59

NOTE: Race categories exclude persons of Hispanic origin. Reported racial/ethnic distributions of students by level of degree, field of study, and sex were used to estimate race/ethnicity for students whose race/ethnicity was not reported.

SOURCE: U.S. Department of Education, National Center for Education Statistics, 2004–05 Integrated Postsecondary Education Data System (IPEDS), Fall 2005. (This table was prepared July 2006.)

Table 278. First-professional degrees conferred by degree-granting institutions, by sex, race/ethnicity, and major field of study: 2003–04

Major field of study	Total							Males							Females						
	Total	White	Black	Hispanic	Asian/Pacific Islander	American Indian/Alaska Native	Non-resident alien	Total	White	Black	Hispanic	Asian/Pacific Islander	American Indian/Alaska Native	Non-resident alien	Total	White	Black	Hispanic	Asian/Pacific Islander	American Indian/Alaska Native	Non-resident alien
1	2	3	4	5	6	7	8	9	10	11	12	13	14	15	16	17	18	19	20	21	22
All fields, total	83,041	60,379	5,930	4,273	9,964	565	1,930	42,169	31,994	2,248	2,080	4,528	275	1,044	40,872	28,385	3,682	2,193	5,436	290	886
Dentistry (D.D.S. or D.M.D.)	4,335	2,703	194	202	896	17	323	2,532	1,732	72	98	466	7	157	1,803	971	122	104	430	10	166
Medicine (M.D.)	15,442	10,255	1,051	792	3,034	111	199	8,273	5,697	388	397	1,631	58	102	7,169	4,558	663	395	1,403	53	97
Optometry (O.D.)	1,275	815	29	49	326	2	54	543	379	15	15	101	2	31	732	436	14	34	225	0	23
Osteopathic medicine (D.O.)	2,722	2,064	96	93	447	17	5	1,567	1,210	36	50	256	12	3	1,155	854	60	43	191	5	2
Pharmacy (Pharm.D.)	8,221	5,076	684	319	1,910	43	189	2,711	1,752	217	111	572	12	47	5,510	3,324	467	208	1,338	31	142
Podiatry (Pod.D. or D.P.) or podiatric medicine (D.P.M.)	382	237	46	31	52	6	10	221	148	18	15	28	5	7	161	89	28	16	24	1	3
Veterinary medicine (D.V.M.)	2,228	2,003	53	86	60	18	8	569	520	13	23	8	4	1	1,659	1,483	40	63	52	14	7
Chiropractic medicine (D.C. or D.C.M.)	2,730	2,129	97	125	211	15	153	1,868	1,475	50	95	146	11	91	862	654	47	30	65	4	62
Naturopathic medicine	165	141	3	6	9	1	5	42	35	0	0	3	0	4	123	106	3	6	6	0	2
Law (LL.B. or J.D.)	40,209	31,087	2,935	2,430	2,768	322	667	20,332	16,503	1,065	1,161	1,112	154	337	19,877	14,584	1,870	1,269	1,656	168	330
Theology (M.Div, M.H.L., B.D., or Ord.)	5,332	3,869	742	140	251	13	317	3,511	2,543	374	115	205	9	265	1,821	1,326	368	25	46	4	52

NOTE: Race categories exclude persons of Hispanic origin. Reported racial/ethnic distributions of students by level of degree, field of study, and sex were used to estimate race/ethnicity for students whose race/ethnicity was not reported.

SOURCE: U.S. Department of Education, National Center for Education Statistics, 2003–04 Integrated Postsecondary Education Data System (IPEDS), Fall 2004. (This table was prepared July 2005.)

Table 279. Degrees in agriculture and natural resources conferred by degree-granting institutions, by level of degree and sex of student: 1970–71 through 2004–05

Year	Bachelor's degrees			Master's degrees			Doctor's degrees		
	Total	Males	Females	Total	Males	Females	Total	Males	Females
1	2	3	4	5	6	7	8	9	10
1970–71	12,672	12,136	536	2,457	2,313	144	1,086	1,055	31
1971–72	13,516	12,779	737	2,680	2,490	190	971	945	26
1972–73	14,756	13,661	1,095	2,807	2,588	219	1,059	1,031	28
1973–74	16,253	14,684	1,569	2,928	2,640	288	930	897	33
1974–75	17,528	15,061	2,467	3,067	2,703	364	991	958	33
1975–76	19,402	15,845	3,557	3,340	2,862	478	928	867	61
1976–77	21,467	16,690	4,777	3,724	3,177	547	893	831	62
1977–78	22,650	17,069	5,581	4,023	3,268	755	971	909	62
1978–79	23,134	16,854	6,280	3,994	3,187	807	950	877	73
1979–80	22,802	16,045	6,757	3,976	3,082	894	991	879	112
1980–81	21,886	15,154	6,732	4,003	3,061	942	1,067	940	127
1981–82	21,029	14,443	6,586	4,163	3,114	1,049	1,079	925	154
1982–83	20,909	14,085	6,824	4,254	3,129	1,125	1,149	1,004	145
1983–84	19,317	13,206	6,111	4,178	2,989	1,189	1,172	1,001	171
1984–85	18,107	12,477	5,630	3,928	2,846	1,082	1,213	1,036	177
1985–86	16,823	11,544	5,279	3,801	2,701	1,100	1,158	966	192
1986–87	14,991	10,314	4,677	3,522	2,460	1,062	1,049	871	178
1987–88	14,222	9,744	4,478	3,479	2,427	1,052	1,142	926	216
1988–89	13,492	9,298	4,194	3,245	2,231	1,014	1,183	950	233
1989–90	12,900	8,822	4,078	3,382	2,239	1,143	1,295	1,038	257
1990–91	13,124	8,832	4,292	3,295	2,160	1,135	1,185	953	232
1991–92	15,113	9,867	5,246	3,730	2,409	1,321	1,205	955	250
1992–93	16,769	11,079	5,690	3,959	2,474	1,485	1,159	869	290
1993–94	18,056	11,746	6,310	4,110	2,512	1,598	1,262	969	293
1994–95	19,832	12,686	7,146	4,234	2,541	1,693	1,256	955	301
1995–96	21,425	13,531	7,894	4,551	2,642	1,909	1,259	926	333
1996–97	22,597	13,791	8,806	4,505	2,601	1,904	1,202	875	327
1997–98	23,276	13,806	9,470	4,464	2,545	1,919	1,290	924	366
1998–99	23,916	13,864	10,052	4,404	2,377	2,027	1,231	855	376
1999–2000	24,238	13,843	10,395	4,360	2,356	2,004	1,168	803	365
2000–01	23,370	12,840	10,530	4,272	2,251	2,021	1,127	741	386
2001–02	23,331	12,630	10,701	4,503	2,340	2,163	1,148	760	388
2002–03	23,294	12,327	10,967	4,492	2,232	2,260	1,229	790	439
2003–04	22,835	11,889	10,946	4,783	2,306	2,477	1,185	758	427
2004–05	23,002	11,987	11,015	4,746	2,288	2,458	1,173	763	410

NOTE: Includes degrees in agriculture, agriculture operations, and related sciences and in natural resources and conservation.
SOURCE: U.S. Department of Education, National Center for Education Statistics, Higher Education General Information Survey (HEGIS), "Degrees and Other Formal Awards Con- ferred" surveys, 1970–71 through 1985–86; and 1986–87 through 2004–05 Integrated Postsecondary Education Data System, "Completions Survey" (IPEDS-C:87–99), and Fall 2000 through Fall 2005. (This table was prepared April 2006.)

Table 280. Degrees in architecture and related services conferred by degree-granting institutions, by level of degree and sex of student: Selected years, 1949–50 through 2004–05

Year	Bachelor's degrees			Master's degrees			Doctor's degrees		
	Total	Males	Females	Total	Males	Females	Total	Males	Females
1	2	3	4	5	6	7	8	9	10
1949–50	2,563	2,441	122	166	159	7	1	1	0
1959–60	1,801	1,744	57	319	305	14	17	17	0
1967–68	3,057	2,931	126	1,021	953	68	15	15	0
1969–70	4,105	3,888	217	1,427	1,260	167	35	33	2
1970–71	5,570	4,906	664	1,705	1,469	236	36	33	3
1971–72	6,440	5,667	773	1,899	1,626	273	50	43	7
1972–73	6,962	6,042	920	2,307	1,943	364	58	54	4
1973–74	7,822	6,665	1,157	2,702	2,208	494	69	65	4
1974–75	8,226	6,791	1,435	2,938	2,343	595	69	58	11
1975–76	9,146	7,396	1,750	3,215	2,545	670	82	69	13
1976–77	9,222	7,249	1,973	3,213	2,489	724	73	62	11
1977–78	9,250	7,054	2,196	3,115	2,304	811	73	57	16
1978–79	9,273	6,876	2,397	3,113	2,226	887	96	74	22
1979–80	9,132	6,596	2,536	3,139	2,245	894	79	66	13
1980–81	9,455	6,800	2,655	3,153	2,234	919	93	73	20
1981–82	9,728	6,825	2,903	3,327	2,242	1,085	80	58	22
1982–83	9,823	6,403	3,420	3,357	2,224	1,133	97	74	23
1983–84	9,186	5,895	3,291	3,223	2,197	1,026	84	62	22
1984–85	9,325	6,019	3,306	3,275	2,148	1,127	89	66	23
1985–86	9,119	5,824	3,295	3,260	2,129	1,131	73	56	17
1986–87	8,950	5,617	3,333	3,163	2,086	1,077	92	66	26
1987–88	8,603	5,271	3,332	3,159	2,042	1,117	98	66	32
1988–89	9,150	5,545	3,605	3,383	2,192	1,191	86	63	23
1989–90	9,364	5,703	3,661	3,499	2,228	1,271	103	73	30
1990–91	9,781	5,788	3,993	3,490	2,244	1,246	135	101	34
1991–92	8,753	5,805	2,948	3,640	2,271	1,369	132	93	39
1992–93	9,167	5,940	3,227	3,808	2,376	1,432	148	105	43
1993–94	8,975	5,764	3,211	3,943	2,428	1,515	161	111	50
1994–95	8,756	5,741	3,015	3,923	2,310	1,613	141	95	46
1995–96	8,352	5,340	3,012	3,993	2,361	1,632	141	96	45
1996–97	7,944	5,090	2,854	4,034	2,336	1,698	135	93	42
1997–98	7,652	4,966	2,686	4,347	2,537	1,810	131	80	51
1998–99	8,246	5,157	3,089	4,172	2,394	1,778	123	80	43
1999–2000	8,462	5,193	3,269	4,268	2,508	1,760	129	85	44
2000–01	8,480	5,086	3,394	4,302	2,515	1,787	153	83	70
2001–02	8,808	5,224	3,584	4,566	2,606	1,960	183	117	66
2002–03	9,054	5,329	3,725	4,925	2,832	2,093	152	83	69
2003–04	8,838	5,059	3,779	5,424	3,049	2,375	173	94	79
2004–05	9,237	5,222	4,015	5,674	3,180	2,494	179	110	69

SOURCE: U.S. Department of Education, National Center for Education Statistics, *Earned Degrees Conferred*, 1949–50 and 1959–60; Higher Education General Information Survey (HEGIS), "Degrees and Other Formal Awards Conferred" surveys, 1967–68 through 1985–86; and 1986–87 through 2004–05 Integrated Postsecondary Education Data System, "Completions Survey" (IPEDS-C:87–99), and Fall 2000 through Fall 2005. (This table was prepared April 2006.)

Table 281. Degrees in the biological and biomedical sciences conferred by degree-granting institutions, by level of degree and sex of student: Selected years, 1951–52 through 2004–05

Year	Bachelor's degrees			Master's degrees			Doctor's degrees		
	Total	Males	Females	Total	Males	Females	Total	Males	Females
1	2	3	4	5	6	7	8	9	10
1951–52	11,094	8,212	2,882	2,307	1,908	399	764	680	84
1953–54	9,279	6,710	2,569	1,610	1,287	323	1,077	977	100
1955–56	12,423	9,515	2,908	1,759	1,379	380	1,025	908	117
1957–58	14,308	11,159	3,149	1,852	1,448	404	1,125	987	138
1959–60	15,576	11,654	3,922	2,154	1,668	486	1,205	1,086	119
1961–62	16,915	12,136	4,779	2,642	1,982	660	1,338	1,179	159
1963–64	22,723	16,321	6,402	3,296	2,348	948	1,625	1,432	193
1965–66	26,916	19,368	7,548	4,232	3,085	1,147	2,097	1,792	305
1967–68	31,826	22,986	8,840	5,506	3,959	1,547	2,784	2,345	439
1969–70	34,034	23,919	10,115	5,800	3,975	1,825	3,289	2,820	469
1970–71	35,683	25,303	10,380	5,623	3,780	1,843	3,595	3,011	584
1971–72	37,269	26,314	10,955	5,983	4,050	1,933	3,566	2,963	603
1972–73	42,205	29,624	12,581	6,153	4,314	1,839	3,569	2,880	689
1973–74	48,224	33,205	15,019	6,405	4,510	1,895	3,342	2,670	672
1974–75	51,576	34,559	17,017	6,422	4,551	1,871	3,315	2,598	717
1975–76	54,085	35,449	18,636	6,453	4,463	1,990	3,313	2,606	707
1976–77	53,420	34,150	19,270	6,948	4,666	2,282	3,299	2,601	698
1977–78	51,326	31,654	19,672	6,644	4,351	2,293	3,218	2,447	771
1978–79	48,668	29,146	19,522	6,631	4,194	2,437	3,410	2,560	850
1979–80	46,190	26,757	19,433	6,322	4,032	2,290	3,527	2,626	901
1980–81	43,003	24,069	18,934	5,759	3,597	2,162	3,591	2,581	1,010
1981–82	41,425	22,687	18,738	5,667	3,375	2,292	3,611	2,579	1,032
1982–83	39,767	21,483	18,284	5,693	3,284	2,409	3,331	2,268	1,063
1983–84	38,445	20,499	17,946	5,468	3,108	2,360	3,435	2,367	1,068
1984–85	38,229	20,017	18,212	5,100	2,770	2,330	3,408	2,302	1,106
1985–86	38,320	19,950	18,370	5,043	2,719	2,324	3,352	2,236	1,116
1986–87	37,977	19,626	18,351	4,980	2,637	2,343	3,397	2,216	1,181
1987–88	36,576	18,202	18,374	4,857	2,520	2,337	3,606	2,338	1,268
1988–89	35,957	17,935	18,022	5,009	2,583	2,426	3,535	2,245	1,290
1989–90	37,204	18,305	18,899	4,906	2,492	2,414	3,837	2,425	1,412
1990–91	39,377	19,358	20,019	4,796	2,396	2,400	4,034	2,547	1,487
1991–92	42,781	20,748	22,033	4,816	2,411	2,405	4,323	2,676	1,647
1992–93	46,868	22,795	24,073	4,974	2,505	2,469	4,595	2,767	1,828
1993–94	51,157	25,002	26,155	5,390	2,644	2,746	4,724	2,809	1,915
1994–95	55,790	26,628	29,162	5,824	2,885	2,939	4,881	2,901	1,980
1995–96	60,750	28,782	31,968	6,544	3,180	3,364	5,035	2,929	2,106
1996–97	63,679	29,432	34,247	6,925	3,389	3,536	5,094	2,890	2,204
1997–98	65,583	29,511	36,072	6,788	3,301	3,487	5,236	2,970	2,266
1998–99	64,608	28,175	36,433	6,913	3,247	3,666	5,024	2,875	2,149
1999–2000	63,005	26,310	36,695	6,781	3,131	3,650	5,180	2,887	2,293
2000–01	59,865	24,293	35,572	6,955	3,043	3,912	4,953	2,757	2,196
2001–02	59,415	23,346	36,069	6,937	2,996	3,941	4,823	2,667	2,156
2002–03	60,072	22,899	37,173	6,990	2,982	4,008	5,003	2,714	2,289
2003–04	61,509	23,248	38,261	7,657	3,227	4,430	5,242	2,804	2,438
2004–05	64,611	24,617	39,994	8,199	3,318	4,881	5,578	2,845	2,733

SOURCE: U.S. Department of Education, National Center for Education Statistics, *Earned Degrees Conferred*, 1951–52 through 1963–64; Higher Education General Information Survey (HEGIS), "Degrees and Other Formal Awards Conferred" surveys, 1965–66 through 1985–86; and 1986–87 through 2004–05 Integrated Postsecondary Education Data System, "Completions Survey" (IPEDS-C:87–99), and Fall 2000 through Fall 2005. (This table was prepared July 2006.)

Table 282. Degrees in biology, microbiology, and zoology conferred by degree-granting institutions, by level of degree: 1970–71 through 2004–05

Year	Biology, general			Microbiology			Zoology		
	Bachelor's	Master's	Doctor's	Bachelor's	Master's	Doctor's	Bachelor's	Master's	Doctor's
1	2	3	4	5	6	7	8	9	10
1970–71	26,294	2,665	536	1,475	456	365	5,721	1,027	878
1971–72	27,473	2,943	580	1,548	470	351	5,518	1,040	836
1972–73	31,185	2,959	627	1,940	517	344	5,763	1,042	803
1973–74	36,188	3,186	657	2,311	505	384	6,128	1,091	677
1974–75	38,748	3,109	637	2,767	552	345	6,110	1,039	697
1975–76	40,163	3,177	624	2,927	585	364	6,077	976	645
1976–77	39,530	3,322	608	2,884	659	325	5,574	985	696
1977–78	37,598	3,094	664	2,695	615	353	5,096	958	624
1978–79	35,962	3,093	663	2,670	597	395	4,738	946	669
1979–80	33,523	2,911	718	2,631	596	376	4,301	922	639
1980–81	31,323	2,598	734	2,414	482	370	3,873	881	613
1981–82	29,651	2,579	678	2,377	470	350	3,615	868	625
1982–83	28,022	2,354	521	2,324	499	358	3,407	738	533
1983–84	27,379	2,313	617	2,349	505	388	3,231	700	521
1984–85	27,593	2,130	658	2,207	471	319	3,069	664	508
1985–86	27,618	2,173	574	2,257	392	362	2,894	618	548
1986–87	27,465	2,022	537	2,159	451	380	2,791	623	464
1987–88	26,838	1,981	576	2,061	404	442	2,537	629	492
1988–89	26,229	2,097	527	1,833	449	423	2,549	634	466
1989–90	27,213	1,998	551	1,973	403	441	2,473	548	545
1990–91	29,285	1,956	632	1,788	343	443	2,641	551	516
1991–92	31,909	1,995	657	1,750	372	532	2,811	530	494
1992–93	34,932	2,000	671	1,798	367	621	3,036	559	465
1993–94	38,103	2,178	665	1,872	359	591	3,162	658	503
1994–95	41,658	2,350	729	1,992	326	572	3,149	586	487
1995–96	44,818	2,606	768	2,220	364	606	3,463	677	501
1996–97	46,632	2,742	693	2,530	363	612	3,438	720	474
1997–98	47,054	2,617	809	2,926	401	585	3,653	685	465
1998–99	46,078	2,608	711	2,871	410	547	3,426	604	461
1999–2000	44,982	2,599	727	3,049	383	551	3,226	616	481
2000–01	42,310	2,582	780	2,779	334	553	3,045	560	380
2001–02	42,281	2,424	689	2,622	325	538	2,979	578	413
2002–03	42,668	2,341	680	2,455	297	507	2,488	385	360
2003–04	43,465	2,529	681	2,365	350	599	2,454	367	245
2004–05	45,540	2,564	712	2,318	390	610	2,159	384	268

SOURCE: U.S. Department of Education, National Center for Education Statistics, Higher Education General Information Survey (HEGIS), "Degrees and Other Formal Awards Conferred" surveys, 1970–71 through 1985–86; and 1986–87 through 2004–05 Integrated Postsecondary Education Data System, "Completions Survey" (IPEDS-C:87–99), and Fall 2000 through Fall 2005. (This table was prepared July 2006.)

Table 283. Degrees in business conferred by degree-granting institutions, by level of degree and sex of student: Selected years, 1955–56 through 2004–05

Year	Bachelor's degrees			Master's degrees			Doctor's degrees		
	Total	Males	Females	Total	Males	Females	Total	Males	Females
1	2	3	4	5	6	7	8	9	10
1955–56	42,813	38,706	4,107	3,280	3,118	162	129	127	2
1957–58	51,991	48,063	3,928	4,223	4,072	151	110	105	5
1959–60	51,076	47,262	3,814	4,643	4,476	167	135	133	2
1961–62	49,017	45,184	3,833	7,691	7,484	207	226	221	5
1963–64	55,474	51,056	4,418	9,251	9,008	243	275	268	7
1965–66	62,721	57,516	5,205	12,959	12,628	331	387	370	17
1967–68	79,074	72,126	6,948	17,795	17,186	609	441	427	14
1969–70	105,580	96,346	9,234	21,561	20,792	769	620	610	10
1970–71	115,396	104,936	10,460	26,490	25,458	1,032	774	753	21
1971–72	121,917	110,331	11,586	30,509	29,317	1,192	876	857	19
1972–73	126,717	113,337	13,380	31,208	29,689	1,519	917	864	53
1973–74	132,304	115,363	16,941	32,691	30,557	2,134	922	873	49
1974–75	133,639	111,983	21,656	36,315	33,274	3,041	939	900	39
1975–76	143,171	114,986	28,185	42,592	37,654	4,938	906	856	50
1976–77	152,010	116,394	35,616	46,505	39,852	6,653	839	785	54
1977–78	160,775	117,103	43,672	48,347	40,224	8,123	834	760	74
1978–79	172,392	119,765	52,627	50,397	40,766	9,631	852	752	100
1979–80	186,264	123,639	62,625	55,008	42,744	12,264	767	650	117
1980–81	200,521	126,798	73,723	57,888	43,411	14,477	808	686	122
1981–82	215,190	130,693	84,497	61,251	44,230	17,021	826	676	150
1982–83	226,442	131,451	94,991	64,741	45,987	18,754	770	638	132
1983–84	229,013	129,296	99,717	66,129	46,167	19,962	926	727	199
1984–85	232,282	127,467	104,815	66,981	46,199	20,782	827	685	142
1985–86	236,700	128,415	108,285	66,676	45,927	20,749	923	720	203
1986–87	240,346	128,506	111,840	67,093	44,913	22,180	1,062	808	254
1987–88	242,859	129,467	113,392	69,230	45,980	23,250	1,063	810	253
1988–89	246,262	131,098	115,164	73,065	48,540	24,525	1,100	800	300
1989–90	248,568	132,284	116,284	76,676	50,585	26,091	1,093	818	275
1990–91	249,165	131,557	117,608	78,255	50,883	27,372	1,185	876	309
1991–92	256,298	135,263	121,035	84,517	54,609	29,908	1,242	953	289
1992–93	256,473	135,368	121,105	89,425	57,504	31,921	1,346	969	377
1993–94	246,265	128,946	117,319	93,285	59,223	34,062	1,364	980	384
1994–95	233,895	121,663	112,232	93,540	58,931	34,609	1,391	1,011	380
1995–96	226,623	116,545	110,078	93,554	58,400	35,154	1,366	972	394
1996–97	225,934	116,023	109,911	97,204	59,333	37,871	1,336	947	389
1997–98	232,079	119,379	112,700	101,652	62,357	39,295	1,290	885	405
1998–99	240,947	122,250	118,697	107,477	64,700	42,777	1,201	843	358
1999–2000	256,070	128,521	127,549	111,532	67,078	44,454	1,194	812	382
2000–01	263,515	132,275	131,240	115,602	68,471	47,131	1,180	783	397
2001–02	278,217	138,343	139,874	119,725	70,463	49,262	1,156	746	410
2002–03	293,545	145,151	148,394	127,545	75,184	52,361	1,251	820	431
2003–04	307,149	152,513	154,636	139,347	80,858	58,489	1,481	960	521
2004–05	311,574	155,940	155,634	142,617	82,151	60,466	1,498	901	597

NOTE: Includes degrees in business, management, marketing, and related support services and in personal and culinary services.
SOURCE: U.S. Department of Education, National Center for Education Statistics, *Earned Degrees Conferred*, 1955–56 through 1963–64; Higher Education General Information Survey (HEGIS), "Degrees and Other Formal Awards Conferred" surveys, 1965–66 through 1985–86; and 1986–87 through 2004–05 Integrated Postsecondary Education Data System, "Completions Survey" (IPEDS-C:87–99), and Fall 2000 through Fall 2005. (This table was prepared July 2006.)

Table 284. Degrees in communication, journalism, and related programs and in communications technologies conferred by degree-granting institutions, by level of degree and sex of student: 1970–71 through 2004–05

Year	Bachelor's degrees			Master's degrees			Doctor's degrees		
	Total	Males	Females	Total	Males	Females	Total	Males	Females
1	2	3	4	5	6	7	8	9	10
1970–71	10,802	6,989	3,813	1,856	1,214	642	145	126	19
1971–72	12,340	7,964	4,376	2,200	1,443	757	111	96	15
1972–73	14,317	9,074	5,243	2,406	1,546	860	139	114	25
1973–74	17,096	10,536	6,560	2,640	1,668	972	175	146	29
1974–75	19,248	11,455	7,793	2,794	1,618	1,176	165	119	46
1975–76	21,282	12,458	8,824	3,126	1,818	1,308	204	154	50
1976–77	23,214	12,932	10,282	3,091	1,719	1,372	171	130	41
1977–78	25,400	13,480	11,920	3,296	1,673	1,623	191	138	53
1978–79	26,457	13,266	13,191	2,882	1,483	1,399	192	138	54
1979–80	28,616	13,656	14,960	3,082	1,527	1,555	193	121	72
1980–81	31,282	14,179	17,103	3,105	1,448	1,657	182	107	75
1981–82	34,222	14,917	19,305	3,327	1,578	1,749	200	136	64
1982–83	38,647	16,213	22,434	3,600	1,660	1,940	208	123	85
1983–84	40,203	16,662	23,541	3,620	1,578	2,042	216	129	87
1984–85	42,102	17,233	24,869	3,657	1,574	2,083	232	141	91
1985–86	43,145	17,681	25,464	3,808	1,603	2,205	218	116	102
1986–87	45,521	18,201	27,320	3,881	1,584	2,297	275	158	117
1987–88	46,916	18,672	28,244	3,916	1,568	2,348	233	133	100
1988–89	48,889	19,357	29,532	4,249	1,734	2,515	248	137	111
1989–90	51,572	20,374	31,198	4,353	1,705	2,648	272	145	127
1990–91	53,047	20,806	32,241	4,327	1,711	2,616	272	150	122
1991–92	55,144	21,601	33,543	4,463	1,692	2,771	255	132	123
1992–93	54,907	22,154	32,753	5,179	1,969	3,210	301	146	155
1993–94	52,033	21,484	30,549	5,388	2,088	3,300	345	174	171
1994–95	48,969	20,501	28,468	5,559	2,086	3,473	321	162	159
1995–96	48,173	19,868	28,305	5,561	2,153	3,408	345	190	155
1996–97	47,894	19,771	28,123	5,552	1,989	3,563	300	155	145
1997–98	50,263	20,103	30,160	6,097	2,369	3,728	359	171	188
1998–99	52,460	20,950	31,510	5,556	2,001	3,555	352	183	169
1999–2000	57,058	22,152	34,906	5,525	2,030	3,495	357	168	189
2000–01	59,191	22,542	36,649	5,645	1,964	3,681	370	190	180
2001–02	64,036	23,692	40,344	5,980	2,169	3,811	383	168	215
2002–03	69,792	25,325	44,467	6,495	2,301	4,194	398	179	219
2003–04	73,002	25,813	47,189	6,900	2,329	4,571	426	186	240
2004–05	75,238	26,926	48,312	7,195	2,535	4,660	468	195	273

SOURCE: U.S. Department of Education, National Center for Education Statistics, Higher Education General Information Survey (HEGIS), "Degrees and Other Formal Awards Conferred" surveys, 1970–71 through 1985–86; and 1986–87 through 2004–05 Integrated Postsecondary Education Data System, "Completions Survey" (IPEDS-C:87–99), and Fall 2000 through Fall 2005. (This table was prepared July 2006.)

Table 285. Degrees in computer and information sciences conferred by degree-granting institutions, by level of degree and sex of student: 1970–71 through 2004–05

Year	Bachelor's degrees			Master's degrees			Doctor's degrees		
	Total	Males	Females	Total	Males	Females	Total	Males	Females
1	2	3	4	5	6	7	8	9	10
1970–71	2,388	2,064	324	1,588	1,424	164	128	125	3
1971–72	3,402	2,941	461	1,977	1,752	225	167	155	12
1972–73	4,304	3,664	640	2,113	1,888	225	196	181	15
1973–74	4,756	3,976	780	2,276	1,983	293	198	189	9
1974–75	5,033	4,080	953	2,299	1,961	338	213	199	14
1975–76	5,652	4,534	1,118	2,603	2,226	377	244	221	23
1976–77	6,407	4,876	1,531	2,798	2,332	466	216	197	19
1977–78	7,201	5,349	1,852	3,038	2,471	567	196	181	15
1978–79	8,719	6,272	2,447	3,055	2,480	575	236	206	30
1979–80	11,154	7,782	3,372	3,647	2,883	764	240	213	27
1980–81	15,121	10,202	4,919	4,218	3,247	971	252	227	25
1981–82	20,267	13,218	7,049	4,935	3,625	1,310	251	230	21
1982–83	24,565	15,641	8,924	5,321	3,813	1,508	262	228	34
1983–84	32,439	20,416	12,023	6,190	4,379	1,811	251	225	26
1984–85	39,121	24,737	14,384	7,101	5,064	2,037	248	223	25
1985–86	42,337	27,208	15,129	8,070	5,658	2,412	344	299	45
1986–87	39,767	25,962	13,805	8,481	5,985	2,496	374	322	52
1987–88	34,651	23,414	11,237	9,197	6,726	2,471	428	380	48
1988–89	30,560	21,143	9,417	9,414	6,775	2,639	551	466	85
1989–90	27,347	19,159	8,188	9,677	6,960	2,717	627	534	93
1990–91	25,159	17,771	7,388	9,324	6,563	2,761	676	584	92
1991–92	24,821	17,685	7,136	9,655	6,980	2,675	772	669	103
1992–93	24,519	17,606	6,913	10,353	7,557	2,796	805	689	116
1993–94	24,527	17,528	6,999	10,568	7,836	2,732	810	685	125
1994–95	24,737	17,684	7,053	10,595	7,805	2,790	887	726	161
1995–96	24,506	17,757	6,749	10,579	7,729	2,850	869	743	126
1996–97	25,422	18,527	6,895	10,513	7,526	2,987	857	721	136
1997–98	27,829	20,372	7,457	11,765	8,343	3,422	858	718	140
1998–99	30,574	22,298	8,276	12,858	8,871	3,987	801	650	151
1999–2000	37,788	27,185	10,603	14,990	9,978	5,012	779	648	131
2000–01	44,142	31,923	12,219	16,911	11,195	5,716	768	632	136
2001–02	50,365	36,462	13,903	17,173	11,447	5,726	752	581	171
2002–03	57,439	41,950	15,489	19,503	13,265	6,238	816	648	168
2003–04	59,488	44,585	14,903	20,143	13,868	6,275	909	709	200
2004–05	54,111	42,125	11,986	18,416	13,136	5,280	1,119	905	214

SOURCE: U.S. Department of Education, National Center for Education Statistics, Higher Education General Information Survey (HEGIS), "Degrees and Other Formal Awards Conferred" surveys, 1970–71 through 1985–86; and 1986–87 through 2004–05 Integrated Postsecondary Education Data System, "Completions Survey" (IPEDS-C:87–99), and Fall 2000 through Fall 2005. (This table was prepared July 2006.)

Table 286. Degrees in education conferred by degree-granting institutions, by level of degree and sex of student: Selected years, 1949–50 through 2004–05

Year	Bachelor's degrees			Master's degrees			Doctor's degrees		
	Total	Males	Females	Total	Males	Females	Total	Males	Females
1	2	3	4	5	6	7	8	9	10
1949–50	61,472	31,398	30,074	20,069	12,025	8,044	953	797	156
1959–60	89,002	25,556	63,446	33,433	18,057	15,376	1,591	1,279	312
1967–68	133,965	31,926	102,039	63,399	30,672	32,727	4,078	3,250	828
1969–70	163,964	40,420	123,544	78,020	34,832	43,188	5,588	4,479	1,109
1970–71	176,307	44,896	131,411	87,666	38,365	49,301	6,041	4,771	1,270
1971–72	190,880	49,344	141,536	96,668	41,141	55,527	6,648	5,104	1,544
1972–73	193,984	51,300	142,684	103,777	43,298	60,479	6,857	5,191	1,666
1973–74	184,907	48,997	135,910	110,402	44,112	66,290	6,757	4,974	1,783
1974–75	166,758	44,463	122,295	117,841	44,430	73,411	6,975	4,856	2,119
1975–76	154,437	42,004	112,433	126,061	44,831	81,230	7,202	4,826	2,376
1976–77	143,234	39,867	103,367	124,267	42,308	81,959	7,338	4,832	2,506
1977–78	135,821	37,410	98,411	116,916	37,662	79,254	7,018	4,281	2,737
1978–79	125,873	33,743	92,130	109,866	34,410	75,456	7,170	4,174	2,996
1979–80	118,038	30,901	87,137	101,819	30,300	71,519	7,314	4,100	3,214
1980–81	108,074	27,039	81,035	96,713	27,548	69,165	7,279	3,843	3,436
1981–82	100,932	24,380	76,552	91,601	25,339	66,262	6,999	3,612	3,387
1982–83	97,908	23,651	74,257	83,254	22,824	60,430	7,063	3,550	3,513
1983–84	92,310	22,200	70,110	75,700	21,164	54,536	6,914	3,448	3,466
1984–85	88,078	21,254	66,824	74,667	20,539	54,128	6,614	3,174	3,440
1985–86	87,147	20,982	66,165	74,816	20,302	54,514	6,610	3,088	3,522
1986–87	86,788	20,705	66,083	72,619	18,955	53,664	5,905	2,745	3,160
1987–88	90,928	20,947	69,981	75,270	18,777	56,493	5,568	2,530	3,038
1988–89	96,740	21,643	75,097	79,793	19,616	60,177	5,884	2,522	3,362
1989–90	105,112	23,007	82,105	84,890	20,469	64,421	6,503	2,776	3,727
1990–91	110,807	23,417	87,390	87,352	20,448	66,904	6,189	2,614	3,575
1991–92	107,836	22,655	85,181	91,225	20,897	70,328	6,423	2,652	3,771
1992–93	107,578	23,199	84,379	94,497	21,857	72,640	6,581	2,712	3,869
1993–94	107,440	24,424	83,016	97,427	22,656	74,771	6,450	2,555	3,895
1994–95	105,929	25,619	80,310	99,835	23,511	76,324	6,475	2,490	3,985
1995–96	105,384	26,214	79,170	104,936	24,955	79,981	6,246	2,404	3,842
1996–97	105,116	26,242	78,874	108,720	25,518	83,202	6,297	2,367	3,930
1997–98	105,833	26,285	79,548	113,374	26,814	86,560	6,261	2,334	3,927
1998–99	107,086	26,224	80,862	118,048	27,997	90,051	6,394	2,298	4,096
1999–2000	108,034	26,103	81,931	123,045	29,081	93,964	6,409	2,295	4,114
2000–01	105,458	24,580	80,878	127,829	29,997	97,832	6,284	2,237	4,047
2001–02	106,295	24,049	82,246	135,189	31,907	103,282	6,549	2,211	4,338
2002–03	105,790	22,602	83,188	147,448	33,871	113,577	6,835	2,315	4,520
2003–04	106,278	22,802	83,476	162,345	37,843	124,502	7,088	2,403	4,685
2004–05	105,451	22,513	82,938	167,490	38,863	128,627	7,681	2,557	5,124

SOURCE: U.S. Department of Education, National Center for Education Statistics, *Earned Degrees Conferred*, 1949–50 and 1959–60; Higher Education General Information Survey (HEGIS), "Degrees and Other Formal Awards Conferred" surveys, 1967–68 through 1985–86; and 1986–87 through 2004–05 Integrated Postsecondary Education Data System, "Completions Survey" (IPEDS-C:87–99), and Fall 2000 through Fall 2005. (This table was prepared July 2006.)

Table 287. Degrees in engineering and engineering technologies conferred by degree-granting institutions, by level of degree and sex of student: Selected years, 1949–50 through 2004–05

Year	Bachelor's degrees			Master's degrees			Doctor's degrees		
	Total	Males	Females	Total	Males	Females	Total	Males	Females
1	2	3	4	5	6	7	8	9	10
1949–50..........................	52,246	52,071	175	4,496	4,481	15	417	416	1
1959–60..........................	37,679	37,537	142	7,159	7,133	26	786	783	3
1969–70..........................	44,479	44,149	330	15,593	15,421	172	3,681	3,657	24
1970–71..........................	50,182	49,775	407	16,947	16,734	213	3,688	3,663	25
1971–72..........................	51,258	50,726	532	17,299	17,009	290	3,708	3,685	23
1972–73..........................	51,384	50,766	618	16,988	16,694	294	3,513	3,459	54
1973–74..........................	50,412	49,611	801	15,851	15,470	381	3,374	3,318	56
1974–75..........................	47,131	46,105	1,026	15,837	15,426	411	3,181	3,113	68
1975–76..........................	46,676	45,184	1,492	16,800	16,174	626	2,874	2,805	69
1976–77..........................	49,482	47,238	2,244	16,659	15,891	768	2,622	2,547	75
1977–78..........................	56,150	52,353	3,797	16,887	15,940	947	2,483	2,424	59
1978–79..........................	62,898	57,603	5,295	16,012	14,971	1,041	2,545	2,459	86
1979–80..........................	69,387	62,877	6,510	16,765	15,535	1,230	2,546	2,447	99
1980–81..........................	75,355	67,573	7,782	17,216	15,761	1,455	2,608	2,499	109
1981–82..........................	80,632	71,305	9,327	18,475	16,747	1,728	2,676	2,532	144
1982–83..........................	89,811	78,673	11,138	19,949	18,038	1,911	2,871	2,742	129
1983–84..........................	95,295	82,841	12,454	21,197	18,916	2,281	3,032	2,864	168
1984–85..........................	97,099	83,991	13,108	22,124	19,688	2,436	3,269	3,055	214
1985–86..........................	97,122	84,050	13,072	22,146	19,545	2,601	3,456	3,220	236
1986–87..........................	93,560	80,543	13,017	23,101	20,137	2,964	3,854	3,585	269
1987–88..........................	89,406	76,886	12,520	23,839	20,815	3,024	4,237	3,941	296
1988–89..........................	85,982	74,020	11,962	25,066	21,731	3,335	4,572	4,160	412
1989–90..........................	82,480	70,859	11,621	25,294	21,753	3,541	5,030	4,576	454
1990–91..........................	79,751	68,482	11,269	25,450	21,780	3,670	5,330	4,834	496
1991–92..........................	78,058	67,104	10,954	26,430	22,444	3,986	5,533	4,998	535
1992–93..........................	78,662	67,248	11,414	29,149	24,758	4,391	5,894	5,322	572
1993–94..........................	78,662	66,920	11,742	30,172	25,453	4,719	6,011	5,339	672
1994–95..........................	78,569	66,223	12,346	30,031	25,090	4,941	6,173	5,435	738
1995–96..........................	78,086	65,430	12,656	28,946	23,928	5,018	6,431	5,623	808
1996–97..........................	75,757	63,066	12,691	27,106	22,114	4,992	6,250	5,476	774
1997–98..........................	74,649	61,955	12,694	27,327	21,867	5,460	6,038	5,294	744
1998–99..........................	72,665	59,703	12,962	26,738	21,394	5,344	5,461	4,676	785
1999–2000......................	73,419	59,741	13,678	26,726	21,100	5,626	5,421	4,582	839
2000–01..........................	72,975	59,564	13,411	27,272	21,405	5,867	5,604	4,669	935
2001–02..........................	74,679	60,474	14,205	27,057	21,263	5,794	5,245	4,332	913
2002–03..........................	77,267	62,837	14,430	30,669	24,169	6,500	5,333	4,415	918
2003–04..........................	78,227	63,502	14,725	35,197	27,667	7,530	5,981	4,923	1,058
2004–05..........................	79,743	65,164	14,579	35,133	27,161	7,972	6,601	5,368	1,233

NOTE: Includes degrees in engineering, engineering-related technologies, mechanic and repair technologies, and construction trades from 1969–70 through 2004–05.
SOURCE: U.S. Department of Education, National Center for Education Statistics, *Earned Degrees Conferred*, 1949–50 and 1959–60; Higher Education General Information Survey (HEGIS), "Degrees and Other Formal Awards Conferred" surveys, 1969–70 through 1985–86; and 1986–87 through 2004–05 Integrated Postsecondary Education Data System, "Completions Survey" (IPEDS-C:87–99), and Fall 2000 through Fall 2005. (This table was prepared July 2006.)

Table 288. Degrees in chemical, civil, electrical, and mechanical engineering conferred by degree-granting institutions, by level of degree: 1970–71 through 2004–05

Year	Chemical engineering			Civil engineering			Electrical, electronics, and communications engineering			Mechanical engineering		
	Bachelor's	Master's	Doctor's	Bachelor's	Master's	Doctor's	Bachelor's	Master's	Doctor's	Bachelor's	Master's	Doctor's
1	2	3	4	5	6	7	8	9	10	11	12	13
1970–71	3,579	1,100	406	6,526	2,425	446	12,198	4,282	879	8,858	2,237	438
1971–72	3,625	1,154	394	6,803	2,487	415	12,101	4,206	824	8,530	2,282	411
1972–73	3,578	1,051	397	7,390	2,627	397	12,313	3,895	791	8,523	2,141	370
1973–74	3,399	1,044	400	8,017	2,652	368	11,316	3,499	705	7,677	1,843	385
1974–75	3,070	990	346	7,651	2,769	356	10,161	3,469	701	6,890	1,858	340
1975–76	3,140	1,031	308	7,923	2,999	370	9,791	3,774	649	6,800	1,907	305
1976–77	3,524	1,086	291	8,228	2,964	309	9,936	3,788	566	7,703	1,952	283
1977–78	4,569	1,235	259	9,135	2,685	277	11,133	3,740	503	8,875	1,942	279
1978–79	5,568	1,149	304	9,809	2,646	253	12,338	3,591	586	10,107	1,877	271
1979–80	6,320	1,270	284	10,326	2,683	270	13,821	3,836	525	11,808	2,060	281
1980–81	6,527	1,267	300	10,678	2,891	325	14,938	3,901	535	13,329	2,291	276
1981–82	6,740	1,285	311	10,524	2,995	329	16,455	4,462	526	13,922	2,399	333
1982–83	7,185	1,368	319	9,989	3,074	340	18,049	4,531	550	15,675	2,511	299
1983–84	7,475	1,514	330	9,693	3,146	369	19,943	5,078	585	16,629	2,797	319
1984–85	7,146	1,544	418	9,162	3,172	377	21,691	5,153	660	16,794	3,053	409
1985–86	5,877	1,361	446	8,679	2,926	395	23,742	5,534	722	16,194	3,075	426
1986–87	4,991	1,184	497	8,147	2,901	451	24,547	6,183	724	15,450	3,198	528
1987–88	3,917	1,088	579	7,488	2,836	481	23,597	6,688	860	14,900	3,329	596
1988–89	3,663	1,093	602	7,312	2,903	505	21,908	7,028	998	14,843	3,498	633
1989–90	3,430	1,035	562	7,252	2,812	516	20,711	7,225	1,162	14,336	3,424	742
1990–91	3,444	903	611	7,314	2,927	536	19,320	7,095	1,220	13,977	3,516	757
1991–92	3,754	956	590	8,034	3,113	540	17,958	7,360	1,282	14,067	3,653	851
1992–93	4,459	990	595	8,868	3,610	577	17,281	7,870	1,413	14,464	3,982	871
1993–94	5,163	1,032	604	9,479	3,873	651	15,823	7,791	1,470	15,030	4,099	887
1994–95	5,901	1,085	571	9,927	4,077	625	14,929	7,693	1,543	14,794	4,213	890
1995–96	6,319	1,176	670	10,607	3,905	616	13,900	7,103	1,591	14,177	3,881	940
1996–97	6,564	1,131	650	10,437	3,833	640	13,336	6,393	1,512	13,493	3,608	913
1997–98	6,319	1,128	652	9,926	3,795	610	12,995	6,737	1,458	13,071	3,441	933
1998–99	6,033	1,130	572	9,121	3,648	543	12,531	6,690	1,303	12,705	3,258	774
1999–2000	5,807	1,078	590	8,136	3,433	543	12,930	6,926	1,392	12,807	3,273	776
2000–01	5,611	1,083	610	7,588	3,310	571	13,091	6,815	1,417	12,817	3,371	849
2001–02	5,462	973	605	7,665	3,295	574	13,056	6,587	1,235	13,058	3,391	772
2002–03	5,109	1,065	542	7,835	3,596	599	13,627	7,621	1,256	13,693	3,695	747
2003–04	4,742	1,165	623	7,827	3,790	636	14,123	9,511	1,440	14,050	4,420	787
2004–05	4,397	1,183	773	8,186	3,834	713	14,171	9,054	1,566	14,609	4,637	915

NOTE: From 1970–71 through 1981–82, civil engineering includes construction and transportation engineering. For later years, civil engineering includes geotechnical, structural, transportation, and water resources engineering. Degrees in engineering technologies are not included in this table.

SOURCE: U.S. Department of Education, National Center for Education Statistics, Higher Education General Information Survey (HEGIS), "Degrees and Other Formal Awards Conferred" surveys, 1970–71 through 1985–86; and 1986–87 through 2004–05 Integrated Postsecondary Education Data System, "Completions Survey" (IPEDS-C:87–99), and Fall 2000 through Fall 2005. (This table was prepared July 2006.)

Table 289. Degrees in English language and literature/letters conferred by degree-granting institutions, by level of degree and sex of student: Selected years, 1949–50 through 2004–05

Year	Bachelor's degrees			Master's degrees			Doctor's degrees		
	Total	Males	Females	Total	Males	Females	Total	Males	Females
1	2	3	4	5	6	7	8	9	10
1949–50	17,240	8,221	9,019	2,259	1,320	939	230	181	49
1959–60	20,128	7,580	12,548	2,931	1,458	1,473	397	314	83
1967–68	47,977	15,700	32,277	7,916	3,434	4,482	977	717	260
1969–70	56,410	18,650	37,760	8,517	3,326	5,191	1,213	837	376
1970–71	63,914	22,005	41,909	10,441	4,126	6,315	1,554	1,107	447
1971–72	63,707	22,580	41,127	10,412	4,066	6,346	1,734	1,173	561
1972–73	60,607	22,022	38,585	10,035	3,988	6,047	1,817	1,189	628
1973–74	54,190	20,082	34,108	9,573	3,824	5,749	1,755	1,142	613
1974–75	47,062	17,689	29,373	9,178	3,463	5,715	1,595	974	621
1975–76	41,452	15,898	25,554	8,599	3,290	5,309	1,514	895	619
1976–77	37,343	14,135	23,208	7,824	2,907	4,917	1,373	768	605
1977–78	34,799	12,972	21,827	7,444	2,623	4,821	1,272	698	574
1978–79	33,218	12,085	21,133	6,503	2,307	4,196	1,186	639	547
1979–80	32,187	11,237	20,950	6,026	2,181	3,845	1,196	635	561
1980–81	31,922	11,082	20,840	5,742	2,026	3,716	1,040	497	543
1981–82	33,078	11,300	21,778	5,593	1,916	3,677	986	467	519
1982–83	31,327	10,699	20,628	4,866	1,653	3,213	877	419	458
1983–84	32,296	11,007	21,289	4,814	1,681	3,133	899	413	486
1984–85	32,686	11,195	21,491	4,987	1,723	3,264	915	414	501
1985–86	34,083	11,657	22,426	5,335	1,811	3,524	895	390	505
1986–87	35,667	12,133	23,534	5,298	1,819	3,479	853	367	486
1987–88	38,106	12,687	25,419	5,366	1,796	3,570	858	380	478
1988–89	41,786	13,729	28,057	5,716	1,930	3,786	929	405	524
1989–90	46,803	15,437	31,366	6,317	2,125	4,192	986	444	542
1990–91	51,064	16,891	34,173	6,784	2,203	4,581	1,056	469	587
1991–92	54,250	18,314	35,936	7,215	2,441	4,774	1,142	484	658
1992–93	55,289	19,007	36,282	7,537	2,570	4,967	1,201	495	706
1993–94	53,150	18,214	34,936	7,611	2,620	4,991	1,205	512	693
1994–95	51,170	17,581	33,589	7,612	2,672	4,940	1,393	589	804
1995–96	49,928	17,007	32,921	7,657	2,727	4,930	1,395	535	860
1996–97	48,641	16,325	32,316	7,487	2,650	4,837	1,431	610	821
1997–98	49,016	16,280	32,736	7,587	2,568	5,019	1,489	611	878
1998–99	49,800	16,285	33,515	7,288	2,442	4,846	1,407	560	847
1999–2000	50,106	16,124	33,982	7,022	2,315	4,707	1,470	611	859
2000–01	50,569	15,997	34,572	6,763	2,160	4,603	1,330	533	797
2001–02	52,375	16,457	35,918	7,097	2,270	4,827	1,291	532	759
2002–03	53,670	16,725	36,945	7,413	2,426	4,987	1,246	492	754
2003–04	53,984	16,792	37,192	7,956	2,459	5,497	1,207	479	728
2004–05	54,379	17,154	37,225	8,468	2,615	5,853	1,212	494	718

SOURCE: U.S. Department of Education, National Center for Education Statistics, *Earned Degrees Conferred*, 1949–50 and 1959–60; Higher Education General Information Survey (HEGIS), "Degrees and Other Formal Awards Conferred" surveys, 1967–68 through 1985–86; and 1986–87 through 2004–05 Integrated Postsecondary Education Data System, "Completions Survey" (IPEDS-C:87–99), and Fall 2000 through Fall 2005. (This table was prepared April 2006.)

Table 290. Degrees in modern foreign languages and literatures conferred by degree-granting institutions, by level of degree and sex of student: Selected years, 1949–50 through 2004–05

Year	Bachelor's degrees			Master's degrees			Doctor's degrees		
	Total	Males	Females	Total	Males	Females	Total	Males	Females
1	2	3	4	5	6	7	8	9	10
1949–50	4,477	1,746	2,731	919	456	463	168	135	33
1959–60	4,527	1,548	2,979	832	392	440	150	100	50
1967–68	17,499	4,450	13,049	3,911	1,555	2,356	491	336	155
1969–70	19,457	4,921	14,536	4,154	1,476	2,678	590	369	221
1970–71	19,806	4,994	14,812	4,847	1,668	3,179	854	536	318
1971–72	18,673	4,635	14,038	4,692	1,633	3,059	911	575	336
1972–73	18,989	4,589	14,400	4,422	1,578	2,844	1,092	650	442
1973–74	18,807	4,486	14,321	4,105	1,399	2,706	1,035	575	460
1974–75	17,842	4,174	13,668	4,004	1,330	2,674	969	504	465
1975–76	15,731	3,718	12,013	3,670	1,235	2,435	1,010	514	496
1976–77	14,162	3,416	10,746	3,293	1,019	2,274	875	430	445
1977–78	13,037	3,127	9,910	2,913	870	2,043	768	351	417
1978–79	11,957	2,845	9,112	2,563	771	1,792	765	363	402
1979–80	11,315	2,783	8,532	2,376	704	1,672	639	278	361
1980–81	10,464	2,542	7,922	2,255	739	1,516	708	328	380
1981–82	10,014	2,426	7,588	2,170	671	1,499	646	281	365
1982–83	10,026	2,560	7,466	1,891	633	1,258	594	254	340
1983–84	9,829	2,611	7,218	1,929	602	1,327	565	242	323
1984–85	10,357	2,719	7,638	1,879	597	1,282	558	236	322
1985–86	10,407	2,884	7,523	1,870	562	1,308	523	206	317
1986–87	10,740	2,988	7,752	1,918	586	1,332	545	230	315
1987–88	10,513	2,839	7,674	2,028	665	1,363	534	228	306
1988–89	11,376	3,037	8,339	2,110	654	1,456	512	216	296
1989–90	11,991	3,185	8,806	2,225	674	1,551	599	239	360
1990–91	12,704	3,526	9,178	2,282	710	1,572	647	274	373
1991–92	13,300	3,679	9,621	2,400	738	1,662	706	284	422
1992–93	13,904	3,848	10,056	2,683	857	1,826	717	287	430
1993–94	13,761	3,960	9,801	2,699	830	1,869	747	273	474
1994–95	13,196	3,949	9,247	2,578	790	1,788	814	335	479
1995–96	13,337	3,881	9,456	2,562	792	1,770	746	292	454
1996–97	13,053	3,792	9,261	2,470	753	1,717	793	316	477
1997–98	13,618	3,926	9,692	2,367	715	1,652	819	327	492
1998–99	14,163	4,084	10,079	2,267	657	1,610	757	294	463
1999–2000	14,186	3,939	10,247	2,228	669	1,559	804	311	493
2000–01	14,292	3,966	10,326	2,244	664	1,580	818	294	524
2001–02	14,236	3,945	10,291	2,284	648	1,636	780	313	467
2002–03	14,843	4,202	10,641	2,256	600	1,656	749	282	467
2003–04	15,408	4,362	11,046	2,307	662	1,645	743	278	465
2004–05	16,008	4,494	11,514	2,517	736	1,781	762	295	467

NOTE: Includes degrees conferred in a single language or a combination of modern foreign languages. Excludes degrees in linguistics, Latin, classics, ancient and Middle/Near Eastern biblical and Semitic languages, ancient/classical Greek, Sanskrit and classical Indian languages, and sign language and sign language interpretation.
SOURCE: U.S. Department of Education, National Center for Education Statistics, *Earned Degrees Conferred*, 1949–50 and 1959–60; Higher Education General Information Survey (HEGIS), "Degrees and Other Formal Awards Conferred" surveys, 1967–68 through 1985–86; and 1986–87 through 2004–05 Integrated Postsecondary Education Data System, "Completions Survey" (IPEDS-C:87–99), and Fall 2000 through Fall 2005. (This table was prepared July 2006.)

Table 291. Degrees in French, German, and Spanish conferred by degree-granting institutions, by level of degree: Selected years, 1949–50 through 2004–05

Year	French			German			Spanish		
	Bachelor's	Master's	Doctor's	Bachelor's	Master's	Doctor's	Bachelor's	Master's	Doctor's
1	2	3	4	5	6	7	8	9	10
1949–50	1,471	299	53	540	121	40	2,122	373	34
1959–60	1,927	316	58	659	126	21	1,610	261	31
1967–68	7,068	1,301	152	2,368	771	117	6,381	1,188	123
1969–70	7,624	1,409	181	2,652	669	118	7,226	1,372	139
1970–71	7,306	1,437	192	2,601	690	144	7,068	1,456	168
1971–72	6,822	1,421	193	2,477	608	167	6,847	1,421	152
1972–73	6,705	1,277	203	2,520	598	176	7,209	1,298	206
1973–74	6,263	1,195	213	2,425	550	149	7,250	1,217	203
1974–75	5,745	1,077	200	2,289	480	147	6,719	1,228	202
1975–76	4,783	914	190	1,983	471	164	5,984	1,080	176
1976–77	4,228	875	177	1,820	394	126	5,359	930	153
1977–78	3,708	692	155	1,647	357	101	4,832	822	113
1978–79	3,558	576	143	1,524	344	106	4,563	720	118
1979–80	3,285	513	128	1,466	309	94	4,331	685	103
1980–81	3,178	460	115	1,286	294	79	3,870	592	131
1981–82	3,054	485	92	1,327	324	76	3,633	568	140
1982–83	2,871	360	106	1,367	281	68	3,349	506	129
1983–84	2,876	418	86	1,292	241	63	3,254	537	102
1984–85	2,991	385	74	1,411	240	58	3,415	505	115
1985–86	3,015	409	86	1,396	249	73	3,385	521	95
1986–87	3,062	421	85	1,366	234	70	3,450	504	104
1987–88	3,082	437	89	1,350	244	71	3,416	553	93
1988–89	3,297	444	83	1,428	263	59	3,748	552	101
1989–90	3,259	478	115	1,437	253	67	4,176	573	108
1990–91	3,355	480	98	1,543	242	58	4,480	609	125
1991–92	3,371	465	112	1,616	273	85	4,768	647	143
1992–93	3,280	513	98	1,572	317	86	5,233	667	145
1993–94	3,094	479	104	1,580	298	61	5,505	691	160
1994–95	2,764	470	118	1,352	278	83	5,602	709	161
1995–96	2,655	446	113	1,290	305	75	5,995	769	151
1996–97	2,468	414	119	1,214	281	80	6,161	677	175
1997–98	2,530	389	104	1,181	209	94	6,595	781	160
1998–99	2,555	357	116	1,246	238	77	6,964	694	152
1999–2000	2,514	343	129	1,125	184	76	7,031	718	175
2000–01	2,371	376	115	1,143	242	73	7,164	716	185
2001–02	2,396	356	89	1,092	208	64	7,243	792	193
2002–03	2,291	348	75	1,097	188	77	7,613	791	190
2003–04	2,362	361	85	1,031	153	30	7,991	833	199
2004–05	2,394	356	80	1,103	180	56	8,304	919	190

SOURCE: U.S. Department of Education, National Center for Education Statistics, *Earned Degrees Conferred*, 1949–50 and 1959–60; Higher Education General Information Survey (HEGIS), "Degrees and Other Formal Awards Conferred" surveys, 1967–68 through 1985–86; and 1986–87 through 2004–05 Integrated Postsecondary Education Data System, "Completions Survey" (IPEDS-C:87–99), and Fall 2000 through Fall 2005. (This table was prepared April 2006.)

Table 292. Degrees in the health professions and related sciences conferred by degree-granting institutions, by level of degree and sex of student: 1970–71 through 2004–05

Year	Bachelor's degrees			Master's degrees			Doctor's degrees		
	Total	Males	Females	Total	Males	Females	Total	Males	Females
1	2	3	4	5	6	7	8	9	10
1970–71	25,223	5,785	19,438	5,330	2,165	3,165	518	437	81
1971–72	28,611	7,005	21,606	6,811	2,749	4,062	459	376	83
1972–73	33,562	7,752	25,810	7,978	3,189	4,789	685	519	166
1973–74	41,421	9,347	32,074	9,232	3,444	5,788	645	507	138
1974–75	49,002	10,844	38,158	10,277	3,686	6,591	666	481	185
1975–76	53,885	11,386	42,499	12,164	3,837	8,327	617	444	173
1976–77	57,222	11,896	45,326	12,627	3,865	8,762	578	402	176
1977–78	59,445	11,600	47,845	14,027	3,972	10,055	704	454	250
1978–79	62,095	11,214	50,881	15,110	4,155	10,955	731	463	268
1979–80	63,848	11,330	52,518	15,374	4,060	11,314	821	467	354
1980–81	63,665	10,531	53,134	16,176	4,024	12,152	868	499	369
1981–82	63,660	10,110	53,550	16,212	3,743	12,469	956	527	429
1982–83	65,642	10,247	55,395	16,941	4,138	12,803	1,093	615	478
1983–84	65,305	10,068	55,237	17,351	4,124	13,227	1,077	528	549
1984–85	65,331	9,741	55,590	17,442	4,046	13,396	1,142	546	596
1985–86	65,309	9,629	55,680	18,603	4,355	14,248	1,139	547	592
1986–87	63,963	9,137	54,826	18,442	3,818	14,624	1,120	518	602
1987–88	61,614	8,955	52,659	18,774	4,004	14,770	1,188	516	672
1988–89	59,850	8,878	50,972	19,493	4,197	15,296	1,329	555	774
1989–90	58,983	9,075	49,908	20,406	4,486	15,920	1,449	635	814
1990–91	59,875	9,619	50,256	21,354	4,423	16,931	1,534	649	885
1991–92	62,779	10,330	52,449	23,671	4,794	18,877	1,432	576	856
1992–93	68,434	11,605	56,829	26,190	5,249	20,941	1,451	571	880
1993–94	75,890	13,377	62,513	28,442	5,813	22,629	1,552	593	959
1994–95	81,596	14,812	66,784	31,770	6,718	25,052	1,653	647	1,006
1995–96	86,087	15,942	70,145	33,920	7,017	26,903	1,651	655	996
1996–97	87,997	16,440	71,557	36,162	7,536	28,626	2,179	926	1,253
1997–98	86,843	15,700	71,143	39,567	8,644	30,923	1,975	678	1,297
1998–99	85,214	15,187	70,027	40,707	9,202	31,505	1,920	721	1,199
1999–2000	80,863	13,342	67,521	42,593	9,500	33,093	2,053	720	1,333
2000–01	75,933	12,514	63,419	43,623	9,711	33,912	2,242	798	1,444
2001–02	72,887	10,869	62,018	43,560	9,588	33,972	2,913	991	1,922
2002–03	71,223	10,091	61,132	42,715	9,269	33,446	3,328	1,030	2,298
2003–04	73,934	10,017	63,917	44,939	9,670	35,269	4,361	1,261	3,100
2004–05	80,685	10,858	69,827	46,703	9,816	36,887	5,868	1,710	4,158

SOURCE: U.S. Department of Education, National Center for Education Statistics, Higher Education General Information Survey (HEGIS), "Degrees and Other Formal Awards Conferred" surveys, 1970–71 through 1985–86; and 1986–87 through 2004–05 Integrated Postsecondary Education Data System, "Completions Survey" (IPEDS-C:87–99), and Fall 2000 through Fall 2005. (This table was prepared July 2006.)

Table 293. Degrees in mathematics and statistics conferred by degree-granting institutions, by level of degree and sex of student: Selected years, 1949–50 through 2004–05

Year	Bachelor's degrees			Master's degrees			Doctor's degrees		
	Total	Males	Females	Total	Males	Females	Total	Males	Females
1	2	3	4	5	6	7	8	9	10
1949–50...........	6,382	4,942	1,440	974	784	190	160	151	9
1959–60...........	11,399	8,293	3,106	1,757	1,422	335	303	285	18
1967–68...........	23,513	14,782	8,731	5,527	4,199	1,328	947	895	52
1969–70...........	27,442	17,177	10,265	5,636	3,966	1,670	1,236	1,140	96
1970–71...........	24,801	15,369	9,432	5,191	3,673	1,518	1,199	1,106	93
1971–72...........	23,713	14,454	9,259	5,198	3,655	1,543	1,128	1,039	89
1972–73...........	23,067	13,796	9,271	5,028	3,525	1,503	1,068	966	102
1973–74...........	21,635	12,791	8,844	4,834	3,337	1,497	1,031	931	100
1974–75...........	18,181	10,586	7,595	4,327	2,905	1,422	975	865	110
1975–76...........	15,984	9,475	6,509	3,857	2,547	1,310	856	762	94
1976–77...........	14,196	8,303	5,893	3,695	2,396	1,299	823	714	109
1977–78...........	12,569	7,398	5,171	3,373	2,228	1,145	805	681	124
1978–79...........	11,806	6,899	4,907	3,036	1,985	1,051	730	608	122
1979–80...........	11,378	6,562	4,816	2,860	1,828	1,032	724	624	100
1980–81...........	11,078	6,342	4,736	2,567	1,692	875	728	614	114
1981–82...........	11,599	6,593	5,006	2,727	1,821	906	681	587	94
1982–83...........	12,294	6,888	5,406	2,810	1,838	972	697	581	116
1983–84...........	13,087	7,290	5,797	2,723	1,773	950	695	569	126
1984–85...........	15,009	8,080	6,929	2,859	1,858	1,001	699	590	109
1985–86...........	16,122	8,623	7,499	3,131	2,028	1,103	742	618	124
1986–87...........	16,257	8,673	7,584	3,283	1,995	1,288	723	598	125
1987–88...........	15,712	8,408	7,304	3,413	2,052	1,361	750	625	125
1988–89...........	15,017	8,081	6,936	3,405	2,061	1,344	866	700	166
1989–90...........	14,276	7,674	6,602	3,624	2,172	1,452	917	754	163
1990–91...........	14,393	7,580	6,813	3,549	2,096	1,453	978	790	188
1991–92...........	14,468	7,668	6,800	3,558	2,151	1,407	1,048	825	223
1992–93...........	14,384	7,566	6,818	3,644	2,151	1,493	1,138	867	271
1993–94...........	14,171	7,594	6,577	3,682	2,237	1,445	1,125	880	245
1994–95...........	13,494	7,154	6,340	3,820	2,289	1,531	1,181	919	262
1995–96...........	12,713	6,847	5,866	3,651	2,178	1,473	1,158	919	239
1996–97...........	12,401	6,649	5,752	3,504	2,055	1,449	1,134	861	273
1997–98...........	11,795	6,247	5,548	3,409	1,985	1,424	1,215	903	312
1998–99...........	11,966	6,181	5,785	3,286	1,901	1,385	1,090	803	287
1999–2000........	11,418	5,955	5,463	3,208	1,749	1,459	1,075	803	272
2000–01...........	11,171	5,791	5,380	3,209	1,857	1,352	997	715	282
2001–02...........	11,950	6,333	5,617	3,350	1,913	1,437	923	658	265
2002–03...........	12,493	6,776	5,717	3,626	2,000	1,626	1,007	734	273
2003–04...........	13,327	7,203	6,124	4,191	2,302	1,889	1,060	762	298
2004–05...........	14,351	7,937	6,414	4,477	2,525	1,952	1,176	841	335

SOURCE: U.S. Department of Education, National Center for Education Statistics, *Earned Degrees Conferred*, 1949–50 and 1959–60; Higher Education General Information Survey (HEGIS), "Degrees and Other Formal Awards Conferred" surveys, 1967–68 through 1985–86; and 1986–87 through 2004–05 Integrated Postsecondary Education Data System, "Completions Survey" (IPEDS-C:87–99), and Fall 2000 through Fall 2005. (This table was prepared April 2006.)

Table 294. Degrees in the physical sciences and science technologies conferred by degree-granting institutions, by level of degree and sex of student: Selected years, 1959–60 through 2004–05

Year	Bachelor's degrees			Master's degrees			Doctor's degrees		
	Total	Males	Females	Total	Males	Females	Total	Males	Females
1	2	3	4	5	6	7	8	9	10
1959–60	16,007	14,013	1,994	3,376	3,049	327	1,838	1,776	62
1967–68	19,380	16,739	2,641	5,499	4,869	630	3,593	3,405	188
1969–70	21,439	18,522	2,917	5,908	5,069	839	4,271	4,038	233
1970–71	21,410	18,457	2,953	6,336	5,495	841	4,324	4,082	242
1971–72	20,743	17,661	3,082	6,268	5,390	878	4,075	3,805	270
1972–73	20,692	17,622	3,070	6,230	5,388	842	3,961	3,698	263
1973–74	21,170	17,669	3,501	6,019	5,157	862	3,558	3,312	246
1974–75	20,770	16,986	3,784	5,782	4,949	833	3,577	3,284	293
1975–76	21,458	17,349	4,109	5,428	4,622	806	3,388	3,097	291
1976–77	22,482	17,985	4,497	5,281	4,411	870	3,295	2,981	314
1977–78	22,975	18,083	4,892	5,507	4,583	924	3,073	2,763	310
1978–79	23,197	17,976	5,221	5,418	4,438	980	3,061	2,717	344
1979–80	23,407	17,861	5,546	5,167	4,210	957	3,044	2,669	375
1980–81	23,936	18,052	5,884	5,246	4,172	1,074	3,105	2,733	372
1981–82	24,045	17,861	6,184	5,446	4,274	1,172	3,246	2,804	442
1982–83	23,374	16,988	6,386	5,250	4,131	1,119	3,214	2,767	447
1983–84	23,645	17,112	6,533	5,541	4,249	1,292	3,269	2,789	480
1984–85	23,694	17,065	6,629	5,752	4,425	1,327	3,349	2,808	541
1985–86	21,711	15,750	5,961	5,860	4,443	1,417	3,521	2,946	575
1986–87	20,060	14,365	5,695	5,586	4,193	1,393	3,629	3,004	625
1987–88	17,797	12,385	5,412	5,696	4,300	1,396	3,758	3,085	673
1988–89	17,179	12,071	5,108	5,691	4,180	1,511	3,795	3,046	749
1989–90	16,056	11,026	5,030	5,410	3,996	1,414	4,116	3,328	788
1990–91	16,334	11,170	5,164	5,281	3,823	1,458	4,248	3,417	831
1991–92	16,948	11,425	5,523	5,340	3,888	1,452	4,344	3,402	942
1992–93	17,534	11,819	5,715	5,346	3,803	1,543	4,348	3,404	944
1993–94	18,392	12,218	6,174	5,648	4,010	1,638	4,595	3,606	989
1994–95	19,161	12,490	6,671	5,716	3,996	1,720	4,421	3,386	1,035
1995–96	19,627	12,566	7,061	5,807	3,943	1,864	4,512	3,479	1,033
1996–97	19,496	12,213	7,283	5,526	3,732	1,794	4,417	3,411	1,006
1997–98	19,362	11,924	7,438	5,328	3,417	1,911	4,520	3,387	1,133
1998–99	18,285	11,003	7,282	5,124	3,366	1,758	4,142	3,144	998
1999–2000	18,331	10,946	7,385	4,810	3,114	1,696	3,963	2,959	1,004
2000–01	17,919	10,553	7,366	5,049	3,212	1,837	3,911	2,875	1,036
2001–02	17,799	10,292	7,507	5,012	3,135	1,877	3,760	2,719	1,041
2002–03	17,940	10,556	7,384	5,109	3,211	1,898	3,858	2,792	1,066
2003–04	17,983	10,476	7,507	5,570	3,364	2,206	3,815	2,753	1,062
2004–05	18,905	10,934	7,971	5,678	3,457	2,221	4,114	2,966	1,148

SOURCE: U.S. Department of Education, National Center for Education Statistics, *Earned Degrees Conferred*, 1959–60; Higher Education General Information Survey (HEGIS), "Degrees and Other Formal Awards Conferred" surveys, 1967–68 through 1985–86; and 1986–87 through 2004–05 Integrated Postsecondary Education Data System, "Completions Survey" (IPEDS-C:87–99), and Fall 2000 through Fall 2005. (This table was prepared April 2006.)

Table 295. Degrees in chemistry, geology, and physics conferred by degree-granting institutions, by level of degree: 1970–71 through 2004–05

Year	Chemistry			Geology and earth science[1]			Physics[2]		
	Bachelor's	Master's	Doctor's	Bachelor's	Master's	Doctor's	Bachelor's	Master's	Doctor's
1	2	3	4	5	6	7	8	9	10
1970–71	11,061	2,244	2,093	3,312	1,074	408	5,071	2,188	1,482
1971–72	10,588	2,229	1,943	3,766	1,233	433	4,634	2,033	1,344
1972–73	10,124	2,198	1,827	4,117	1,296	430	4,259	1,747	1,328
1973–74	10,430	2,082	1,755	4,526	1,479	416	3,952	1,655	1,115
1974–75	10,541	1,961	1,773	4,566	1,340	433	3,706	1,574	1,080
1975–76	11,015	1,745	1,578	4,677	1,384	445	3,544	1,700	997
1976–77	11,200	1,717	1,522	5,280	1,446	480	3,420	1,319	945
1977–78	11,304	1,832	1,461	5,648	1,633	419	3,330	1,294	873
1978–79	11,499	1,724	1,475	5,753	1,616	414	3,337	1,319	918
1979–80	11,229	1,671	1,500	5,785	1,623	440	3,396	1,192	830
1980–81	12,682	1,862	1,649	6,332	1,702	404	3,441	1,294	866
1981–82	11,058	1,683	1,682	6,650	1,865	452	3,503	1,318	878
1982–83	10,789	1,582	1,691	6,981	1,784	406	3,793	1,369	873
1983–84	10,698	1,632	1,707	7,524	1,747	408	3,907	1,532	953
1984–85	10,472	1,675	1,735	7,194	1,927	401	4,097	1,523	951
1985–86	10,110	1,712	1,878	5,760	2,036	395	4,180	1,501	1,010
1986–87	9,660	1,695	1,932	3,943	1,835	399	4,318	1,543	1,074
1987–88	9,043	1,671	1,944	3,204	1,722	462	4,100	1,675	1,093
1988–89	8,618	1,742	1,974	2,847	1,609	492	4,352	1,736	1,112
1989–90	8,122	1,643	2,135	2,372	1,399	562	4,155	1,831	1,192
1990–91	8,311	1,637	2,196	2,367	1,336	600	4,236	1,725	1,209
1991–92	8,629	1,746	2,233	2,784	1,245	549	4,098	1,834	1,337
1992–93	8,903	1,822	2,216	3,123	1,195	626	4,063	1,777	1,277
1993–94	9,417	1,968	2,298	3,456	1,221	577	4,001	1,945	1,465
1994–95	9,706	2,062	2,211	4,032	1,280	539	3,823	1,817	1,424
1995–96	10,395	2,214	2,228	4,019	1,288	555	3,679	1,678	1,462
1996–97	10,609	2,203	2,202	4,023	1,258	564	3,376	1,496	1,410
1997–98	10,528	2,108	2,291	3,866	1,227	588	3,441	1,371	1,393
1998–99	10,068	2,002	2,143	3,544	1,200	533	3,213	1,309	1,252
1999–2000	9,989	1,857	2,028	3,516	1,186	492	3,342	1,232	1,208
2000–01	9,466	1,952	2,056	3,495	1,220	472	3,418	1,365	1,169
2001–02	9,084	1,823	1,984	3,449	1,174	494	3,627	1,344	1,096
2002–03	9,006	1,777	2,092	3,381	1,323	466	3,898	1,438	1,089
2003–04	9,016	2,009	2,033	3,312	1,389	463	4,118	1,625	1,119
2004–05	9,664	1,879	2,148	3,276	1,420	476	4,182	1,785	1,254

[1]Includes geology/earth science, general; geochemistry; geophysics; paleontology; hydrology; oceanography; and geological and earth sciences, other.
[2]Includes physics, general; atomic/molecular physics; elementary particle physics; nuclear physics; optics; acoustics; theoretical physics; and physics, other.

SOURCE: U.S. Department of Education, National Center for Education Statistics, Higher Education General Information Survey (HEGIS), "Degrees and Other Formal Awards Conferred" surveys, 1970–71 through 1985–86; and 1986–87 through 2004–05 Integrated Postsecondary Education Data System, "Completions Survey" (IPEDS-C:87–99), and Fall 2000 through Fall 2005. (This table was prepared April 2006.)

Table 296. Degrees in psychology conferred by degree-granting institutions, by level of degree and sex of student: Selected years, 1949–50 through 2004–05

Year	Bachelor's degrees			Master's degrees			Doctor's degrees		
	Total	Males	Females	Total	Males	Females	Total	Males	Females
1	2	3	4	5	6	7	8	9	10
1949–50	9,569	6,055	3,514	1,316	948	368	283	241	42
1959–60	8,061	4,773	3,288	1,406	981	425	641	544	97
1967–68	23,819	13,792	10,027	3,479	2,321	1,158	1,268	982	286
1969–70	33,679	19,077	14,602	5,158	2,975	2,183	1,962	1,505	457
1970–71	38,187	21,227	16,960	5,717	3,395	2,322	2,144	1,629	515
1971–72	43,433	23,352	20,081	6,764	3,934	2,830	2,277	1,694	583
1972–73	47,940	25,117	22,823	7,619	4,325	3,294	2,550	1,797	753
1973–74	52,139	25,868	26,271	8,796	4,983	3,813	2,872	1,987	885
1974–75	51,245	24,284	26,961	9,394	5,035	4,359	2,913	1,979	934
1975–76	50,278	22,898	27,380	10,167	5,136	5,031	3,157	2,115	1,042
1976–77	47,861	20,627	27,234	10,859	5,293	5,566	3,386	2,127	1,259
1977–78	44,879	18,422	26,457	10,282	4,670	5,612	3,164	1,974	1,190
1978–79	42,697	16,540	26,157	10,132	4,405	5,727	3,228	1,895	1,333
1979–80	42,093	15,440	26,653	9,938	4,096	5,842	3,395	1,921	1,474
1980–81	41,068	14,332	26,736	10,223	4,066	6,157	3,576	2,002	1,574
1981–82	41,212	13,645	27,567	9,947	3,823	6,124	3,461	1,856	1,605
1982–83	40,460	13,131	27,329	9,981	3,647	6,334	3,602	1,838	1,764
1983–84	39,955	12,812	27,143	9,525	3,400	6,125	3,535	1,774	1,761
1984–85	39,900	12,706	27,194	9,891	3,452	6,439	3,447	1,739	1,708
1985–86	40,628	12,605	28,023	9,845	3,347	6,498	3,593	1,724	1,869
1986–87	43,152	13,395	29,757	11,000	3,516	7,484	4,062	1,801	2,261
1987–88	45,371	13,579	31,792	10,488	3,256	7,232	3,973	1,783	2,190
1988–89	49,083	14,265	34,818	11,329	3,465	7,864	4,143	1,773	2,370
1989–90	53,952	15,336	38,616	10,730	3,377	7,353	3,811	1,566	2,245
1990–91	58,655	16,067	42,588	11,349	3,329	8,020	3,932	1,520	2,412
1991–92	63,683	17,062	46,621	11,659	3,335	8,324	3,814	1,490	2,324
1992–93	66,931	17,942	48,989	12,518	3,380	9,138	4,100	1,570	2,530
1993–94	69,419	18,668	50,751	13,723	3,763	9,960	4,021	1,497	2,524
1994–95	72,233	19,570	52,663	15,378	4,210	11,168	4,252	1,562	2,690
1995–96	73,416	19,836	53,580	15,152	4,090	11,062	4,141	1,380	2,761
1996–97	74,308	19,408	54,900	15,769	4,155	11,614	4,507	1,495	3,012
1997–98	74,107	18,976	55,131	15,142	3,978	11,164	4,541	1,470	3,071
1998–99	73,636	18,304	55,332	15,688	3,990	11,698	4,695	1,510	3,185
1999–2000	74,194	17,451	56,743	15,740	3,821	11,919	4,731	1,529	3,202
2000–01	73,645	16,585	57,060	16,539	3,892	12,647	5,091	1,598	3,493
2001–02	76,775	17,284	59,491	16,357	3,814	12,543	4,759	1,503	3,256
2002–03	78,613	17,504	61,109	17,123	3,827	13,296	4,831	1,481	3,350
2003–04	82,098	18,193	63,905	17,898	3,789	14,109	4,827	1,496	3,331
2004–05	85,614	19,000	66,614	18,830	3,900	14,930	5,106	1,466	3,640

SOURCE: U.S. Department of Education, National Center for Education Statistics, *Earned Degrees Conferred*, 1949–50 and 1959–60; Higher Education General Information Survey (HEGIS), "Degrees and Other Formal Awards Conferred" surveys, 1967–68 through 1985–86; and 1986–87 through 2004–05 Integrated Postsecondary Education Data System, "Completions Survey" (IPEDS-C:87–99), and Fall 2000 through Fall 2005. (This table was prepared July 2006.)

Table 297. Degrees in public administration and social services conferred by degree-granting institutions, by level of degree and sex of student: 1970–71 through 2004–05

Year	Bachelor's degrees			Master's degrees			Doctor's degrees		
	Total	Males	Females	Total	Males	Females	Total	Males	Females
1	2	3	4	5	6	7	8	9	10
1970–71	5,466	1,726	3,740	7,785	3,893	3,892	174	132	42
1971–72	7,508	2,588	4,920	8,756	4,537	4,219	193	150	43
1972–73	10,690	3,998	6,692	10,068	5,271	4,797	198	160	38
1973–74	11,966	4,266	7,700	11,415	6,028	5,387	201	154	47
1974–75	13,661	4,630	9,031	13,617	7,200	6,417	257	192	65
1975–76	15,440	5,706	9,734	15,209	7,969	7,240	292	192	100
1976–77	16,136	5,544	10,592	17,026	8,810	8,216	292	197	95
1977–78	16,607	5,096	11,511	17,337	8,513	8,824	357	237	120
1978–79	17,328	4,938	12,390	17,306	8,051	9,255	315	215	100
1979–80	16,644	4,451	12,193	17,560	7,866	9,694	342	216	126
1980–81	16,707	4,248	12,459	17,803	7,460	10,343	362	212	150
1981–82	16,495	4,176	12,319	17,416	6,975	10,441	372	205	167
1982–83	14,414	3,343	11,071	16,046	5,961	10,085	347	184	163
1983–84	12,570	2,998	9,572	15,060	5,634	9,426	420	230	190
1984–85	11,754	2,829	8,925	15,575	5,573	10,002	431	213	218
1985–86	11,887	2,966	8,921	15,692	5,594	10,098	382	171	211
1986–87	12,328	2,993	9,335	16,432	5,673	10,759	398	216	182
1987–88	12,385	2,923	9,462	16,424	5,631	10,793	470	238	232
1988–89	13,162	3,214	9,948	17,020	5,615	11,405	428	210	218
1989–90	13,908	3,334	10,574	17,399	5,634	11,765	508	235	273
1990–91	14,350	3,215	11,135	17,905	5,679	12,226	430	190	240
1991–92	15,987	3,479	12,508	19,243	5,769	13,474	432	204	228
1992–93	16,775	3,801	12,974	20,634	6,105	14,529	459	215	244
1993–94	17,815	3,919	13,896	21,833	6,406	15,427	519	238	281
1994–95	18,586	3,935	14,651	23,501	6,870	16,631	556	274	282
1995–96	19,849	4,205	15,644	24,229	6,927	17,302	499	220	279
1996–97	20,649	4,177	16,472	24,781	6,957	17,824	518	243	275
1997–98	20,408	3,881	16,527	25,144	7,025	18,119	499	223	276
1998–99	20,287	3,791	16,496	24,925	6,556	18,369	532	239	293
1999–2000	20,185	3,816	16,369	25,594	6,808	18,786	537	227	310
2000–01	19,447	3,670	15,777	25,268	6,544	18,724	574	263	311
2001–02	19,392	3,706	15,686	25,448	6,505	18,943	571	250	321
2002–03	19,878	3,724	16,154	25,894	6,391	19,503	596	262	334
2003–04	20,552	3,793	16,759	28,250	7,001	21,249	649	275	374
2004–05	21,769	4,209	17,560	29,552	7,370	22,182	673	272	401

SOURCE: U.S. Department of Education, National Center for Education Statistics, Higher Education General Information Survey (HEGIS), "Degrees and Other Formal Awards Conferred" surveys, 1970–71 through 1985–86; and 1986–87 through 2004–05 Integrated Postsecondary Education Data System, "Completions Survey" (IPEDS-C:87–99), and Fall 2000 through Fall 2005. (This table was prepared July 2006.)

Table 298. Degrees in the social sciences and history conferred by degree-granting institutions, by level of degree and sex of student: 1970–71 through 2004–05

Year	Bachelor's degrees			Master's degrees			Doctor's degrees		
	Total	Males	Females	Total	Males	Females	Total	Males	Females
1	2	3	4	5	6	7	8	9	10
1970–71	155,324	98,173	57,151	16,539	11,833	4,706	3,660	3,153	507
1971–72	158,060	100,895	57,165	17,445	12,540	4,905	4,081	3,483	598
1972–73	155,970	99,735	56,235	17,477	12,605	4,872	4,234	3,573	661
1973–74	150,320	95,650	54,670	17,293	12,321	4,972	4,124	3,383	741
1974–75	135,190	84,826	50,364	16,977	11,875	5,102	4,212	3,334	878
1975–76	126,396	78,691	47,705	15,953	10,918	5,035	4,157	3,262	895
1976–77	117,040	71,128	45,912	15,533	10,413	5,120	3,802	2,957	845
1977–78	112,952	67,217	45,735	14,718	9,845	4,873	3,594	2,722	872
1978–79	108,059	62,852	45,207	12,963	8,395	4,568	3,371	2,501	870
1979–80	103,662	58,511	45,151	12,176	7,794	4,382	3,230	2,357	873
1980–81	100,513	56,131	44,382	11,945	7,457	4,488	3,122	2,274	848
1981–82	99,705	55,196	44,509	12,002	7,468	4,534	3,061	2,237	824
1982–83	95,228	52,771	42,457	11,205	6,974	4,231	2,931	2,042	889
1983–84	93,323	52,154	41,169	10,577	6,551	4,026	2,911	2,030	881
1984–85	91,570	51,226	40,344	10,503	6,475	4,028	2,851	1,933	918
1985–86	93,840	52,724	41,116	10,564	6,419	4,145	2,955	1,970	985
1986–87	96,342	53,949	42,393	10,506	6,373	4,133	2,916	2,026	890
1987–88	100,460	56,377	44,083	10,412	6,310	4,102	2,781	1,849	932
1988–89	108,151	60,121	48,030	11,023	6,599	4,424	2,885	1,949	936
1989–90	118,083	65,887	52,196	11,634	6,898	4,736	3,010	2,019	991
1990–91	125,107	68,701	56,406	12,233	7,016	5,217	3,012	1,956	1,056
1991–92	133,974	73,001	60,973	12,702	7,237	5,465	3,218	2,126	1,092
1992–93	135,703	73,589	62,114	13,471	7,671	5,800	3,460	2,203	1,257
1993–94	133,680	72,006	61,674	14,561	8,152	6,409	3,627	2,317	1,310
1994–95	128,154	68,139	60,015	14,845	8,207	6,638	3,725	2,319	1,406
1995–96	126,479	65,872	60,607	15,012	8,093	6,919	3,760	2,339	1,421
1996–97	124,891	64,115	60,776	14,787	7,830	6,957	3,989	2,479	1,510
1997–98	125,040	63,537	61,503	14,938	7,960	6,978	4,127	2,445	1,682
1998–99	124,658	61,736	62,922	14,431	7,456	6,975	3,855	2,270	1,585
1999–2000	127,101	62,062	65,039	14,066	7,024	7,042	4,095	2,407	1,688
2000–01	128,036	61,749	66,287	13,791	6,816	6,975	3,930	2,302	1,628
2001–02	132,874	64,170	68,704	14,112	6,941	7,171	3,902	2,219	1,683
2002–03	143,218	69,498	73,720	14,634	7,202	7,432	3,850	2,196	1,654
2003–04	150,357	73,834	76,523	16,110	7,810	8,300	3,811	2,188	1,623
2004–05	156,892	77,702	79,190	16,952	8,256	8,696	3,819	2,184	1,635

SOURCE: U.S. Department of Education, National Center for Education Statistics, Higher Education General Information Survey (HEGIS), "Degrees and Other Formal Awards Conferred" surveys, 1970–71 through 1985–86; and 1986–87 through 2004–05 Integrated Postsecondary Education Data System, "Completions Survey" (IPEDS-C:87–99), and Fall 2000 through Fall 2005. (This table was prepared April 2006.)

Table 299. Degrees in economics, history, political science and government, and sociology conferred by degree-granting institutions, by level of degree: Selected years, 1949–50 through 2004–05

Year	Economics			History			Political science and government			Sociology		
	Bachelor's	Master's	Doctor's	Bachelor's	Master's	Doctor's	Bachelor's	Master's	Doctor's	Bachelor's	Master's	Doctor's
1	2	3	4	5	6	7	8	9	10	11	12	13
1949–50	14,568	921	200	13,542	1,801	275	6,336	710	127	7,870	552	98
1951–52	8,593	695	239	10,187	1,445	317	4,911	525	147	6,648	517	141
1953–54	6,719	609	245	9,363	1,220	355	5,314	534	153	5,692	440	184
1955–56	6,555	581	232	10,510	1,114	259	5,633	509	203	5,878	402	170
1957–58	7,457	669	239	12,840	1,397	297	6,116	665	170	6,568	397	150
1959–60	7,453	708	237	14,737	1,794	342	6,596	722	201	7,147	440	161
1961–62	8,366	853	268	17,340	2,163	343	8,326	839	214	8,120	578	173
1963–64	10,583	1,104	385	23,668	2,705	507	12,126	1,163	263	10,943	646	198
1965–66	11,555	1,522	458	28,612	3,883	599	15,242	1,429	336	15,038	981	244
1967–68	15,193	1,916	600	35,291	4,845	688	20,387	1,937	457	21,710	1,193	367
1969–70	17,197	1,988	794	43,386	5,049	1,038	25,713	2,105	525	30,436	1,813	534
1970–71	15,758	1,995	721	44,663	5,157	991	27,482	2,318	700	33,263	1,808	574
1971–72	15,231	2,224	794	43,695	5,217	1,133	28,135	2,451	758	35,216	1,944	636
1972–73	14,770	2,225	845	40,943	5,030	1,140	30,100	2,398	747	35,436	1,923	583
1973–74	14,285	2,141	788	37,049	4,533	1,114	30,744	2,448	766	35,491	2,196	632
1974–75	14,046	2,127	815	31,470	4,226	1,117	29,126	2,333	680	31,488	2,112	693
1975–76	14,741	2,087	763	28,400	3,658	1,014	28,302	2,191	723	27,634	2,009	729
1976–77	15,296	2,158	758	25,433	3,393	921	26,411	2,222	641	24,713	1,830	714
1977–78	15,661	1,995	706	23,004	3,033	813	26,069	2,069	636	22,750	1,611	599
1978–79	16,409	1,955	712	21,019	2,536	756	25,628	2,037	563	20,285	1,415	612
1979–80	17,863	1,821	677	19,301	2,367	712	25,457	1,938	535	18,881	1,341	583
1980–81	18,753	1,911	727	18,301	2,237	643	24,977	1,875	484	17,272	1,240	610
1981–82	19,876	1,964	677	17,146	2,210	636	25,658	1,954	513	16,042	1,145	558
1982–83	20,517	1,972	734	16,467	2,041	575	25,791	1,829	435	14,105	1,112	522
1983–84	20,719	1,891	729	16,643	1,940	561	25,719	1,769	457	13,145	1,008	520
1984–85	20,711	1,992	749	16,049	1,921	468	25,834	1,500	441	11,968	1,022	480
1985–86	21,602	1,937	789	16,415	1,961	497	26,439	1,704	439	12,271	965	504
1986–87	22,378	1,855	750	16,997	2,021	534	26,817	1,618	435	12,239	950	451
1987–88	22,911	1,847	770	18,207	2,093	517	27,207	1,579	391	13,024	984	452
1988–89	23,454	1,886	827	20,159	2,121	487	30,450	1,598	452	14,435	1,135	451
1989–90	23,923	1,950	806	22,476	2,369	570	33,560	1,580	480	16,035	1,198	432
1990–91	23,488	1,951	802	24,541	2,591	606	35,737	1,772	468	17,550	1,260	465
1991–92	23,423	2,106	866	26,966	2,754	644	37,805	1,908	535	19,568	1,347	501
1992–93	21,321	2,292	879	27,774	2,952	690	37,931	1,943	529	20,896	1,521	536
1993–94	19,496	2,521	869	27,503	3,009	752	36,097	2,147	616	22,368	1,639	530
1994–95	17,673	2,400	910	26,598	3,091	816	33,013	2,019	637	22,886	1,748	546
1995–96	16,674	2,533	916	26,005	2,898	805	30,775	2,024	634	24,071	1,772	527
1996–97	16,539	2,433	968	25,214	2,901	873	28,969	1,909	686	24,672	1,731	591
1997–98	17,074	2,435	928	25,726	2,895	937	28,044	1,957	705	24,806	1,737	596
1998–99	17,611	2,323	810	24,794	2,633	921	27,418	1,681	696	24,933	1,943	515
1999–2000	18,441	2,168	851	25,247	2,573	984	27,635	1,627	693	25,598	1,996	595
2000–01	19,437	2,139	851	25,090	2,365	931	27,792	1,596	688	25,268	1,845	546
2001–02	20,927	2,330	826	26,001	2,420	924	29,354	1,641	625	25,202	1,928	534
2002–03	23,007	2,582	836	27,730	2,525	861	33,204	1,664	671	26,089	1,897	591
2003–04	24,069	2,824	849	29,808	2,522	855	35,581	1,869	618	26,939	2,009	558
2004–05	24,217	3,092	973	31,398	2,893	819	38,107	1,983	636	28,473	1,499	527

SOURCE: U.S. Department of Education, National Center for Education Statistics, *Earned Degrees Conferred*, 1949–50 through 1963–64; Higher Education General Information Survey (HEGIS), "Degrees and Other Formal Awards Conferred" surveys, 1965–66 through 1985–86; and 1986–87 through 2004–05 Integrated Postsecondary Education Data System, "Completions Survey" (IPEDS-C:87–99), and Fall 2000 through Fall 2005. (This table was prepared April 2006.)

Table 300. Degrees in visual and performing arts conferred by degree-granting institutions, by level of degree and sex of student: 1970–71 through 2004–05

Year	Bachelor's degrees			Master's degrees			Doctor's degrees		
	Total	Males	Females	Total	Males	Females	Total	Males	Females
1	2	3	4	5	6	7	8	9	10
1970–71	30,394	12,256	18,138	6,675	3,510	3,165	621	483	138
1971–72	33,831	13,580	20,251	7,537	4,049	3,488	572	428	144
1972–73	36,017	14,267	21,750	7,254	4,005	3,249	616	449	167
1973–74	39,730	15,821	23,909	8,001	4,325	3,676	585	440	145
1974–75	40,782	15,532	25,250	8,362	4,448	3,914	649	446	203
1975–76	42,138	16,491	25,647	8,817	4,507	4,310	620	447	173
1976–77	41,793	16,166	25,627	8,636	4,211	4,425	662	447	215
1977–78	40,951	15,572	25,379	9,036	4,327	4,709	708	448	260
1978–79	40,969	15,380	25,589	8,524	3,933	4,591	700	454	246
1979–80	40,892	15,065	25,827	8,708	4,067	4,641	655	413	242
1980–81	40,479	14,798	25,681	8,629	4,056	4,573	654	396	258
1981–82	40,422	14,819	25,603	8,746	3,866	4,880	670	380	290
1982–83	39,804	14,695	25,109	8,763	4,013	4,750	692	404	288
1983–84	40,131	15,089	25,042	8,526	3,897	4,629	730	406	324
1984–85	38,285	14,518	23,767	8,720	3,896	4,824	696	407	289
1985–86	37,241	14,236	23,005	8,420	3,775	4,645	722	396	326
1986–87	36,873	13,980	22,893	8,508	3,756	4,752	793	447	346
1987–88	37,150	14,225	22,925	7,939	3,442	4,497	727	424	303
1988–89	38,420	14,698	23,722	8,267	3,611	4,656	753	446	307
1989–90	39,934	15,189	24,745	8,481	3,706	4,775	849	472	377
1990–91	42,186	15,761	26,425	8,657	3,830	4,827	838	466	372
1991–92	46,522	17,616	28,906	9,353	4,078	5,275	906	504	402
1992–93	47,761	18,610	29,151	9,440	4,099	5,341	882	478	404
1993–94	49,053	19,538	29,515	9,925	4,229	5,696	1,054	585	469
1994–95	48,690	19,781	28,909	10,277	4,374	5,903	1,080	545	535
1995–96	49,296	20,126	29,170	10,280	4,361	5,919	1,067	524	543
1996–97	50,083	20,729	29,354	10,627	4,470	6,157	1,060	525	535
1997–98	52,077	21,483	30,594	11,145	4,596	6,549	1,163	566	597
1998–99	54,404	22,281	32,123	10,753	4,543	6,210	1,130	574	556
1999–2000	58,791	24,003	34,788	10,918	4,672	6,246	1,127	537	590
2000–01	61,148	24,967	36,181	11,404	4,788	6,616	1,167	568	599
2001–02	66,773	27,130	39,643	11,595	4,912	6,683	1,114	490	624
2002–03	71,474	27,916	43,558	11,986	4,975	7,011	1,293	613	680
2003–04	77,181	30,037	47,144	12,906	5,531	7,375	1,282	572	710
2004–05	80,955	31,355	49,600	13,183	5,646	7,537	1,278	594	684

SOURCE: U.S. Department of Education, National Center for Education Statistics, Higher Education General Information Survey (HEGIS), "Degrees and Other Formal Awards Conferred" surveys, 1970–71 through 1985–86; and 1986–87 through 2004–05 Integrated Postsecondary Education Data System, "Completions Survey" (IPEDS-C:87–99), and Fall 2000 through Fall 2005. (This table was prepared April 2006.)

Table 301. Statistical profile of persons receiving doctor's degrees, by field of study and selected characteristics: 2003–04

Selected characteristic	All fields	Education	Engineering	Humanities	Life sciences	Physical sciences[1] Total	Mathematics	Business and management	Social sciences and psychology	Other professional fields
1	2	3	4	5	6	7	8	9	10	11
Number of doctor's degrees conferred	42,155	6,635	5,776	5,467	8,819	6,049	1,075	1,264	6,795	1,347
Sex (percent)										
Male	54.6	34.2	82.4	48.1	50.5	73.5	71.6	63.9	44.8	44.8
Female	45.4	65.8	17.6	51.9	49.5	26.5	28.4	36.1	55.2	55.2
Racial/ethnic group (percent)[2]										
White	79.7	76.1	74.0	84.4	79.9	83.3	81.6	74.1	80.6	74.7
Black	7.3	14.9	4.5	4.4	4.8	3.0	2.0	11.3	7.3	14.0
Hispanic	4.8	5.1	4.2	5.5	4.4	3.6	5.3	4.8	5.7	4.1
Asian[3]	7.7	2.9	17.0	5.4	10.6	9.7	11.1	9.0	6.0	6.8
American Indian/Alaska Native	0.5	0.9	0.3	0.4	0.4	0.4	0.0	0.8	0.4	0.5
Citizenship (percent)										
United States	62.7	80.0	33.6	74.8	64.8	49.7	42.3	47.6	71.8	65.8
Non-U.S., permanent visa	3.6	1.7	4.2	5.0	3.9	4.0	5.1	4.0	3.1	3.8
Non-U.S., temporary visa	27.5	9.4	57.2	15.4	26.1	42.2	48.9	37.3	17.5	22.4
Unknown	6.2	8.9	5.1	4.8	5.2	4.1	3.6	11.0	7.6	8.0
Median age at doctorate (years)	33.3	43.1	31.4	35.0	31.7	30.6	30.4	35.8	33.1	38.0
Percent with bachelor's degree in same field as doctorate	52.5	31.2	75.6	53.4	48.4	65.9	70.7	33.0	54.6	30.4
Median time lapse (years) to doctorate										
Since bachelor's degree completion	10.0	17.7	8.4	11.7	8.7	7.8	7.8	12.1	9.8	13.9
Since starting graduate school	8.0	12.7	7.2	9.7	7.0	6.7	6.7	9.7	7.9	10.4
Definite postdoctoral plans (percent)										
Definite postdoctoral study[4]	35.3	6.0	36.3	11.6	67.0	56.2	47.1	3.3	30.7	7.3
Fellowship	18.7	2.2	12.4	8.2	37.9	26.6	27.5	1.4	21.4	2.6
Research associateship	13.0	2.1	21.8	1.6	20.5	27.6	17.5	1.3	5.6	3.2
Traineeship	0.7	0.4	0.8	0.3	1.1	0.5	1.0	‡	0.8	‡
Intern, clinical residency	1.1	0.3	0.2	0.2	3.1	0.4	‡	‡	1.7	‡
Other	1.8	1.1	1.1	1.3	4.4	1.1	‡	‡	1.2	1.4
Definite postdoctoral employment[5]	64.7	94.0	63.7	88.4	33.0	43.8	52.9	96.7	69.3	92.7
Educational institution[6]	43.4	81.2	17.0	77.3	18.3	20.7	39.6	79.1	44.5	67.5
Industry, business	11.7	3.6	35.8	3.5	7.0	17.5	9.9	11.3	8.8	6.4
Government	5.1	4.0	7.4	2.1	4.9	3.5	2.5	4.6	8.4	6.9
Nonprofit organization	3.6	3.8	2.6	4.7	2.2	1.6	‡	‡	6.1	9.6
Other and unknown	0.9	1.4	0.9	0.8	0.5	0.4	‡	‡	1.5	2.2
Primary work activity after doctorate (percent)[7]										
Research and development	31.2	7.7	70.3	10.5	41.5	58.1	42.6	41.2	32.2	18.2
Teaching	41.4	41.2	14.2	76.2	33.2	29.6	50.3	43.6	36.6	53.5
Administration	15.7	41.0	5.8	6.2	10.3	4.5	2.1	10.5	9.4	15.5
Professional services	9.8	8.8	8.7	4.0	12.7	5.6	3.9	3.7	19.8	10.4
Other	1.9	1.3	1.0	3.1	2.2	2.2	1.1	1.1	2.1	2.3
Region of employment after doctorate (percent)										
New England	5.9	4.4	6.0	6.9	6.3	7.0	4.7	6.9	6.2	3.7
Middle Atlantic	13.4	11.3	10.5	16.0	11.7	17.6	19.7	11.0	14.6	14.0
East North Central	12.8	13.6	11.3	14.3	12.7	10.0	14.5	13.0	12.8	13.7
West North Central	6.3	8.6	2.6	6.9	6.4	4.2	5.2	5.0	6.0	8.9
South Atlantic	18.0	22.3	13.0	16.3	17.3	16.5	18.1	16.5	19.2	18.9
East South Central	4.8	6.7	2.9	4.8	5.0	3.9	4.1	4.7	3.7	5.9
West South Central	8.5	9.7	8.6	8.4	8.8	7.1	5.7	10.8	6.6	9.1
Mountain	5.7	7.0	6.3	4.9	5.3	5.9	4.4	3.7	5.3	3.9
Pacific and insular	13.5	10.8	21.3	12.7	11.8	17.2	13.2	11.3	12.8	9.2
Foreign	11.1	5.5	17.4	8.6	14.7	10.4	10.4	17.0	12.7	12.7
Region unknown	0.1	0.1	0.2	#	0.1	0.1	#	0.1	0.1	#

#Rounds to zero.
‡Reporting standards not met.
[1]Includes mathematics, computer science, physics and astronomy, chemistry, and earth, atmospheric, and marine sciences.
[2]Distribution by race/ethnicity based on U.S. citizens and those with permanent visas only.
[3]Does not include Native Hawaiians or other Pacific Islanders.
[4]Percentages are based on only those doctorate recipients who indicated definite postdoctoral plans for study and who indicated the type of study.
[5]Percentages are based on only those doctorate recipients who indicated definite postdoctoral plans for employment and who indicated the sector of employment.
[6]Includes 2-year, 4-year, and foreign colleges and universities, medical schools, and elementary/secondary schools.
[7]Percentages are based on only those doctorate recipients who indicated definite postdoctoral plans for employment and who indicated their primary work activity.

NOTE: The above classification of degrees by field differs somewhat from that in most publications of the National Center for Education Statistics (NCES). The major differences are that history is included under humanities rather than social sciences and that psychology is included under social sciences. Includes Ph.D., Ed.D., and comparable degrees at the doctoral level. Excludes first-professional degrees, such as M.D., D.D.S., and D.V.M. The number of degrees also differs slightly from that reported in the NCES Integrated Postsecondary Education Data System (IPEDS). The above tabulation excludes some nonresearch doctoral degrees such as doctor's degrees in theology. Race categories exclude persons of Hispanic origin. Detail may not sum to totals because of rounding.
SOURCE: *Doctorate Recipients From United States Universities, 2004,* Survey of Earned Doctorates, National Science Foundation, National Institutes of Health, U.S. Department of Education, National Endowment for the Humanities, U.S. Department of Agriculture, and the National Aeronautics and Space Administration. (This table was prepared April 2006.)

Table 302. Statistical profile of persons receiving doctor's degrees in education: Selected years, 1979–80 through 2003–04

Selected characteristic	1979–80	1989–90	1990–91	1992–93	1993–94	1994–95	1995–96	1996–97	1997–98	1998–99	1999–2000	2000–01	2001–02	2002–03	2003–04
1	2	3	4	5	6	7	8	9	10	11	12	13	14	15	16
Number of degrees.......................	7,576	6,510	6,454	6,689	6,708	6,649	6,772	6,497	6,559	6,557	6,420	6,324	6,488	6,627	6.635
Sex (percent)															
Male..	55.5	42.4	41.9	41.3	39.1	38.4	38.3	36.7	37.0	35.8	35.1	35.4	33.8	33.9	34.2
Female......................................	44.5	57.6	58.1	58.7	60.9	61.6	61.7	63.3	63.0	64.2	64.9	64.6	66.2	66.1	65.8
Racial/ethnic group (percent)[1]															
White...	86.3	86.0	85.6	83.7	83.9	81.6	82.2	81.1	79.1	79.3	78.3	78.8	77.2	76.3	76.1
Black..	9.1	8.2	7.9	9.4	8.6	10.4	10.1	10.2	11.6	11.7	12.6	12.6	13.0	14.0	14.9
Hispanic..................................	2.4	3.3	3.3	3.7	4.0	4.4	3.6	4.6	5.1	4.8	5.1	5.1	6.2	6.2	5.1
Asian[2]......................................	1.3	1.8	2.2	2.4	2.9	3.0	3.1	3.2	3.2	3.1	3.1	2.7	2.6	2.8	2.9
American Indian/Alaska Native..	0.8	0.6	1.0	0.8	0.6	0.7	1.0	0.9	0.9	1.1	0.9	0.8	0.9	0.7	0.9
Citizenship (percent)															
United States............................	88.7	84.4	84.8	86.4	87.4	86.8	86.6	82.6	84.3	82.8	86.2	84.0	81.2	83.0	80.0
Foreign.....................................	8.2	9.7	10.2	10.8	11.0	11.0	9.9	8.2	9.1	10.6	10.3	9.7	9.0	10.8	11.1
Unknown..................................	3.1	5.8	5.0	2.7	1.6	2.3	3.4	9.3	6.6	6.5	3.5	6.2	9.8	6.2	8.9
Median age at doctorate (years)....	37.0	41.6	42.1	43.0	43.6	43.8	44.3	44.0	44.3	44.3	44.4	43.8	44.2	43.5	43.1
Percent with bachelor's degree in same field as doctorate	39.0	37.5	39.3	37.4	36.9	37.0	36.1	34.1	35.0	34.8	33.7	33.2	30.6	31.0	31.2
Median time lapse (years) to doctorate															
Since bachelor's degree completion	13.1	17.9	18.4	19.2	19.7	19.9	20.2	20.0	20.0	19.9	19.4	19.0	19.0	18.2	17.7
Since starting graduate school ..	6.9	8.1	8.1	8.2	8.1	8.2	8.2	8.4	8.4	8.2	8.1	8.3	8.5	8.3	12.7

[1]Distribution by race/ethnicity based on U.S. citizens and those with permanent visas only.
[2]Does not include Native Hawaiians or other Pacific Islanders.
NOTE: Longitudinal comparisons by race/ethnicity should be done with extreme care, due to periodic changes in the survey. In particular, large numbers of Asians converted from temporary visas to permanent visas in the mid-1990s. The classification of degrees by field used in this survey differs somewhat from that in most publications of the National Center for Education Statistics (NCES). The total number of degrees also differs slightly from that reported in the NCES Integrated Postsecondary Education Data System (IPEDS) "Completions Survey." Race categories exclude persons of Hispanic origin. Detail may not sum to totals because of rounding.
SOURCE: *Doctorate Recipients From United States Universities, 2004*, Survey of Earned Doctorates, National Science Foundation, National Institutes of Health, U.S. Department of Education, National Endowment for the Humanities, U.S. Department of Agriculture, and the National Aeronautics and Space Administration. (This table was prepared May 2006.)

Table 303. Statistical profile of persons receiving doctor's degrees in engineering: Selected years, 1979–80 through 2003–04

Selected characteristic	1979–80	1989–90	1990–91	1992–93	1993–94	1994–95	1995–96	1996–97	1997–98	1998–99	1999–2000	2000–01	2001–02	2002–03	2003–04
1	2	3	4	5	6	7	8	9	10	11	12	13	14	15	16
Number of degrees........................	2,479	4,894	5,214	5,698	5,822	6,008	6,305	6,052	5,919	5,337	5,330	5,502	5,073	5,265	5,776
Sex (percent)															
Male...	96.4	91.5	91.3	90.9	89.1	88.4	87.7	87.6	86.9	85.1	84.2	83.1	82.5	82.9	82.4
Female.......................................	3.6	8.5	8.7	9.1	10.9	11.6	12.3	12.4	13.1	14.9	15.8	16.9	17.5	17.1	17.6
Racial/ethnic group (percent)[1]															
White...	77.8	80.4	77.4	75.9	67.0	63.7	67.6	71.5	73.9	74.9	75.2	74.2	71.1	74.7	74.0
Black...	1.2	1.8	2.4	1.9	1.8	2.2	2.2	3.1	2.9	3.4	3.3	3.9	4.2	3.6	4.5
Hispanic.....................................	1.9	2.4	2.6	2.4	2.2	2.4	2.9	2.8	3.8	2.9	3.2	3.9	4.6	4.9	4.2
Asian[2].......................................	18.9	15.3	17.4	19.7	28.8	31.5	26.8	22.3	19.0	18.4	17.9	17.7	19.7	16.3	17.0
American Indian/Alaska Native..	0.2	0.2	0.3	0.1	0.2	0.3	0.4	0.4	0.4	0.4	0.3	0.3	0.3	0.5	0.3
Citizenship (percent)															
United States............................	50.6	39.4	37.9	39.1	38.0	39.7	41.1	44.3	43.0	46.4	41.4	38.9	37.3	36.0	33.6
Foreign.......................................	46.3	52.5	54.7	57.1	60.0	57.9	55.7	49.5	48.5	48.6	52.5	55.8	57.4	60.3	61.4
Unknown.....................................	3.1	8.1	7.3	3.9	2.1	2.5	3.3	6.2	8.5	5.1	6.2	5.4	5.3	3.7	5.1
Median age at doctorate (years)....	30.3	31.2	31.4	31.6	31.7	31.7	31.7	31.3	31.6	31.4	31.4	31.2	31.4	31.4	31.4
Percent with bachelor's degree in same field as doctorate	75.2	76.9	79.0	80.1	80.4	79.1	80.2	75.9	71.0	71.2	74.0	74.6	74.1	74.4	75.6
Median time lapse (years) to doctorate															
Since bachelor's degree completion	7.6	8.2	8.5	8.8	9.0	9.1	9.0	8.7	8.9	8.7	8.7	8.4	8.6	8.6	8.4
Since starting graduate school ..	5.6	6.0	6.1	6.3	6.4	6.4	6.4	6.5	6.7	6.6	6.8	6.7	6.7	6.9	7.2

[1]Distribution by race/ethnicity based on U.S. citizens and those with permanent visas only.
[2]Does not include Native Hawaiians or other Pacific Islanders.
NOTE: Longitudinal comparisons by race/ethnicity should be done with extreme care, due to periodic changes in the survey. In particular, large numbers of Asians converted from temporary visas to permanent visas in the mid-1990s. The classification of degrees by field used in this survey differs somewhat from that in most publications of the National Center for Education Statistics (NCES). The total number of degrees also differs slightly from that reported in the NCES Integrated Postsecondary Education Data System (IPEDS) "Completions Survey." Race categories exclude persons of Hispanic origin. Detail may not sum to totals because of rounding.
SOURCE: *Doctorate Recipients From United States Universities, 2004*, Survey of Earned Doctorates, National Science Foundation, National Institutes of Health, U.S. Department of Education, National Endowment for the Humanities, U.S. Department of Agriculture, and the National Aeronautics and Space Administration. (This table was prepared May 2006.)

Table 304. Statistical profile of persons receiving doctor's degrees in the humanities: Selected years, 1979–80 through 2003–04

Selected characteristic	1979–80	1989–90	1990–91	1992–93	1993–94	1994–95	1995–96	1996–97	1997–98	1998–99	1999–2000	2000–01	2001–02	2002–03	2003–04
1	2	3	4	5	6	7	8	9	10	11	12	13	14	15	16
Number of degrees........................	3,863	3,822	4,099	4,482	4,744	5,061	5,116	5,387	5,499	5,468	5,634	5,589	5,373	5,412	5.467
Sex (percent)															
Male..	60.4	54.4	53.5	52.5	52.3	51.7	50.3	51.9	51.3	51.1	49.7	49.4	49.6	49.2	48.1
Female......................................	39.6	45.6	46.5	47.5	47.7	48.3	49.7	48.1	48.7	48.9	50.3	50.6	50.4	50.8	51.9
Racial/ethnic group (percent)[1]															
White..	91.6	90.9	89.9	88.9	87.5	87.8	87.0	86.4	0.0	85.8	86.5	85.6	85.0	84.6	84.4
Black	3.0	2.3	3.0	3.0	2.9	2.9	3.1	3.6	0.0	4.2	3.8	4.2	4.1	3.9	4.4
Hispanic	3.0	4.2	4.3	4.2	4.4	3.8	4.3	4.5	0.0	4.7	4.8	5.3	6.0	6.3	5.5
Asian[2]......................................	2.0	2.4	2.5	3.6	4.6	5.1	5.1	4.9	0.0	4.8	4.4	4.4	4.3	4.7	5.4
American Indian/Alaska Native..	0.3	0.3	0.3	0.3	0.6	0.4	0.5	0.5	0.0	0.6	0.5	0.5	0.5	0.4	0.4
Citizenship (percent)															
United States	87.3	78.3	77.0	78.3	78.3	78.6	77.4	76.5	77.1	78.0	78.5	78.4	77.0	76.3	74.8
Foreign.....................................	8.8	15.2	18.3	18.7	19.9	19.4	19.6	16.1	15.9	17.4	17.6	17.1	17.8	19.2	20.4
Unknown...................................	3.9	6.5	4.7	3.0	1.8	1.9	3.0	7.4	7.0	4.6	3.9	4.5	5.2	4.5	4.8
Median age at doctorate (years)....	33.4	35.7	35.8	35.6	35.7	35.4	35.2	35.2	35.1	35.1	34.8	35.0	34.7	34.6	35.0
Percent with bachelor's degree in same field as doctorate	64.2	57.1	57.7	56.4	57.4	56.6	55.8	46.1	46.9	48.2	47.9	55.1	61.2	60.2	53.4
Median time lapse (years) to doctorate															
Since bachelor's degree completion	10.6	12.2	12.3	11.9	12.0	12.0	11.8	11.7	11.6	11.7	11.4	11.5	11.5	11.3	11.7
Since starting graduate school ..	7.7	8.3	8.4	8.3	8.5	8.4	8.3	8.6	8.7	8.9	8.8	9.0	9.0	9.0	9.7

[1]Distribution by race/ethnicity based on U.S. citizens and those with permanent visas only.
[2]Does not include Native Hawaiians or other Pacific Islanders.
NOTE: Longitudinal comparisons by race/ethnicity should be done with extreme care, due to periodic changes in the survey. In particular, large numbers of Asians converted from temporary visas to permanent visas in the mid-1990s. The classification of degrees by field used in this survey differs somewhat from that in most publications of the National Center for Education Statistics (NCES). The major differences are that history is included under humanities rather than social sciences and that psychology is included under social sciences. Includes American studies, archeology, art history, classics, comparative literature,

history, English language and literature, foreign languages and literatures, letters, linguistics, music, philosophy, religion, speech and rhetorical studies, and theatre. The total number of degrees also differs slightly from that reported in the NCES Integrated Postsecondary Education Data System (IPEDS) "Completions Survey." Race categories exclude persons of Hispanic origin. Detail may not sum to totals because of rounding.
SOURCE: *Doctorate Recipients From United States Universities, 2004,* Survey of Earned Doctorates, National Science Foundation, National Institutes of Health, U.S. Department of Education, National Endowment for the Humanities, U.S. Department of Agriculture, and the National Aeronautics and Space Administration. (This table was prepared May 2006.)

Table 305. Statistical profile of persons receiving doctor's degrees in the life sciences: Selected years, 1979–80 through 2003–04

Selected characteristic	1979–80	1989–90	1990–91	1992–93	1993–94	1994–95	1995–96	1996–97	1997–98	1998–99	1999–2000	2000–01	2001–02	2002–03	2003–04
1	2	3	4	5	6	7	8	9	10	11	12	13	14	15	16
Number of degrees	5,325	6,605	6,933	7,395	7,739	7,918	8,255	8,213	8,540	8,126	8,529	8,296	8,350	8,369	8,819
Sex (percent)															
Male	74.8	62.6	61.4	58.3	58.4	57.9	56.5	55.0	54.5	55.3	53.1	52.8	52.3	51.7	50.5
Female	25.2	37.4	41.7	41.7	41.6	42.1	43.5	45.0	45.5	44.7	46.9	47.2	47.7	48.3	49.5
Racial/ethnic group (percent)[1]															
White	91.8	89.6	88.0	85.1	78.2	74.9	75.5	77.5	78.5	78.5	80.1	80.4	79.8	80.1	79.9
Black	1.6	1.9	2.4	2.9	2.6	3.1	2.9	3.4	3.3	3.6	3.8	3.8	3.7	3.7	4.8
Hispanic	1.1	2.7	2.6	3.0	3.2	3.0	3.1	3.5	4.1	4.0	4.0	3.7	4.1	4.4	4.4
Asian[2]	5.3	5.6	6.6	8.7	15.7	18.5	17.9	15.3	13.6	13.4	11.7	11.7	12.1	11.4	10.6
American Indian/Alaska Native	0.2	0.2	0.4	0.3	0.4	0.5	0.5	0.3	0.4	0.5	0.4	0.4	0.3	0.3	0.4
Citizenship (percent)															
United States	80.4	68.0	66.8	65.3	64.0	63.1	60.7	62.0	61.9	63.0	64.6	65.0	63.8	64.9	64.8
Foreign	17.6	26.3	29.1	32.6	34.9	35.2	37.0	31.7	31.4	33.4	31.6	29.6	29.9	30.6	30.0
Unknown	2.0	5.6	4.0	2.2	1.1	1.7	2.2	6.3	6.7	3.6	3.9	5.4	6.3	4.6	5.2
Median age at doctorate (years)	30.0	32.3	32.4	32.5	32.7	32.4	32.5	32.3	32.3	32.1	32.1	31.8	31.9	31.8	31.7
Percent with bachelor's degree in same field as doctorate	40.9	53.8	54.1	51.9	51.0	50.8	49.2	46.9	48.9	47.0	49.3	47.3	47.4	47.8	48.4
Median time lapse (years) to doctorate															
Since bachelor's degree completion	7.3	9.1	9.1	9.4	9.5	9.5	9.6	9.2	9.1	9.0	9.0	9.0	8.9	8.8	8.7
Since starting graduate school	5.8	6.7	6.7	6.8	7.0	7.0	7.0	7.0	7.0	7.0	7.0	7.0	7.0	7.0	7.0

[1]Distribution by race/ethnicity based on U.S. citizens and those with permanent visas only.
[2]Does not include Native Hawaiians or other Pacific Islanders.
NOTE: Longitudinal comparisons by race/ethnicity should be done with extreme care, due to periodic changes in the survey. In particular, large numbers of Asians converted from temporary visas to permanent visas in the mid-1990s. The classification of degrees by field used in this survey differs somewhat from that in most publications of the National Center for Education Statistics (NCES). Includes agricultural, biological, and health sciences. The total number of degrees also differs slightly from that reported in the NCES Integrated Postsecondary Education Data System (IPEDS) "Completions Survey." Race categories exclude persons of Hispanic origin. Detail may not sum to totals because of rounding.
SOURCE: *Doctorate Recipients From United States Universities, 2004*, Survey of Earned Doctorates, National Science Foundation, National Institutes of Health, U.S. Department of Education, National Endowment for the Humanities, U.S. Department of Agriculture, and the National Aeronautics and Space Administration. (This table was prepared May 2006.)

Table 306. Statistical profile of persons receiving doctor's degrees in the physical sciences: Selected years, 1979–80 through 2003–04

Selected characteristic	1979–80	1989–90	1990–91	1992–93	1993–94	1994–95	1995–96	1996–97	1997–98	1998–99	1999–2000	2000–01	2001–02	2002–03	2003–04
1	2	3	4	5	6	7	8	9	10	11	12	13	14	15	16
Number of degrees[1]	3,151	4,262	4,441	4,470	4,799	4,618	4,632	4,573	4,639	4,389	4,168	4,138	3,987	4,103	4,025
Sex (percent)															
Male	87.7	81.2	81.0	78.9	79.0	77.3	78.1	77.2	75.2	76.2	74.4	74.1	71.9	71.9	72.7
Female	12.3	18.8	19.0	21.1	21.0	22.7	21.9	22.8	22.8	23.8	25.6	25.9	28.1	28.1	27.3
Racial/ethnic group (percent)[2]															
White	90.0	89.3	88.8	84.5	74.8	70.6	76.0	78.9	81.8	82.8	83.8	84.2	83.7	84.1	85.2
Black	1.0	1.0	1.2	1.6	1.6	1.4	2.1	2.0	2.2	2.9	2.7	2.4	3.0	3.1	3.0
Hispanic	1.1	3.1	2.9	3.4	2.6	2.5	2.8	2.6	2.4	2.8	3.8	3.3	3.4	3.8	3.4
Asian[3]	7.7	6.6	6.6	10.2	20.8	25.3	18.9	16.1	13.2	10.8	9.2	9.5	9.6	8.7	8.0
American Indian/Alaska Native	0.2	0.1	0.5	0.3	0.2	0.3	0.3	0.4	0.4	0.6	0.6	0.5	0.3	0.2	0.4
Citizenship (percent)															
United States	75.9	61.0	59.3	57.1	56.3	56.7	54.7	57.5	56.5	56.8	56.5	55.3	56.0	55.8	53.5
Foreign	21.6	32.4	35.9	39.7	41.7	41.7	41.8	36.3	36.4	37.9	38.2	40.7	39.1	39.1	42.3
Unknown	2.4	6.7	4.8	3.2	2.1	1.8	3.5	6.2	7.1	5.3	5.2	3.9	4.9	4.2	4.2
Median age at doctorate (years)	29.1	30.7	30.2	30.6	30.7	30.7	30.8	30.4	30.2	30.6	30.3	30.3	30.2	30.3	30.3
Percent with bachelor's degree in same field as doctorate	76.5	80.0	76.9	72.9	73.0	70.8	69.6	65.4	66.8	66.7	66.2	68.2	66.9	68.8	69.8
Median time lapse (years) to doctorate															
Since bachelor's degree completion	6.8	7.8	7.5	8.0	8.2	8.1	8.0	7.5	7.5	7.6	7.7	7.4	8.7	7.5	7.4
Since starting graduate school	5.7	6.3	6.2	6.4	6.6	6.8	6.6	6.6	6.5	6.6	6.7	6.6	6.5	6.6	6.4

[1]Excludes mathematics and computer science.
[2]Distribution by race/ethnicity based on U.S. citizens and those with permanent visas only.
[3]Does not include Native Hawaiians or other Pacific Islanders.
NOTE: Longitudinal comparisons by race/ethnicity should be done with extreme care, due to periodic changes in the survey. In particular, large numbers of Asians converted from temporary visas to permanent visas in the mid-1990s. The classification of degrees by field used in this survey differs somewhat from that in most publications of the National Center for Education Statistics (NCES). Includes physics; astronomy; chemistry; and earth, atmospheric, and marine sciences. The total number of degrees also differs slightly from that reported in the NCES Integrated Postsecondary Education Data System (IPEDS) "Completions Survey." Race categories exclude persons of Hispanic origin. Detail may not sum to totals because of rounding.
SOURCE: *Doctorate Recipients From United States Universities, 2004*, Survey of Earned Doctorates, National Science Foundation, National Institutes of Health, U.S. Department of Education, National Endowment for the Humanities, U.S. Department of Agriculture, and the National Aeronautics and Space Administration. (This table was prepared May 2006.)

Table 307. Statistical profile of persons receiving doctor's degrees in the social sciences and psychology: Selected years, 1979–80 through 2003–04

Selected characteristic	1979–80	1989–90	1990–91	1992–93	1993–94	1994–95	1995–96	1996–97	1997–98	1998–99	1999–2000	2000–01	2001–02	2002–03	2003–04
1	2	3	4	5	6	7	8	9	10	11	12	13	14	15	16
Number of degrees	6,253	6,093	6,152	6,545	6,613	6,635	6,814	6,917	7,075	7,036	7,115	6,825	6,611	6,777	6,795
Sex (percent)															
Male	65.4	53.7	50.6	50.7	50.6	49.2	48.4	47.3	45.5	45.5	45.4	45.6	44.7	44.6	44.8
Female	34.6	46.3	49.4	49.3	49.4	50.8	51.6	52.7	54.5	54.5	54.6	54.4	55.3	55.4	55.2
Racial/ethnic group (percent)[1]															
White	90.7	88.2	87.2	86.9	85.0	82.8	83.3	82.9	82.4	82.0	82.0	82.4	81.1	81.4	80.6
Black	4.2	4.4	4.9	4.7	4.7	5.2	5.0	5.5	5.6	6.0	6.6	6.3	6.7	6.6	7.3
Hispanic	2.0	3.9	4.2	4.1	3.6	4.2	4.6	4.8	5.8	5.4	5.1	5.4	6.1	6.0	5.7
Asian[2]	2.8	3.0	3.3	4.0	6.1	7.3	6.4	6.2	5.5	5.4	5.5	5.2	5.3	5.3	6.0
American Indian/Alaska Native	0.3	0.5	0.4	0.4	0.5	0.5	0.7	0.5	0.8	1.1	0.7	0.7	0.7	0.7	0.4
Citizenship (percent)															
United States	84.7	73.8	73.4	75.5	75.5	76.0	76.2	72.5	75.1	76.1	76.4	74.1	74.1	73.0	71.8
Foreign	11.6	18.0	19.8	21.3	21.7	21.4	20.7	17.8	17.1	17.5	18.1	19.3	18.9	20.8	20.6
Unknown	3.7	8.2	6.8	3.1	2.8	2.6	3.1	9.7	7.8	6.5	5.5	6.6	7.0	6.2	7.6
Median age at doctorate (years)	31.6	34.2	34.1	34.3	34.1	34.1	33.7	33.4	33.2	33.2	33.0	32.9	33.0	33.1	33.1
Percent with bachelor's degree in same field as doctorate	58.6	55.4	54.2	53.7	53.2	52.2	53.4	55.2	56.2	55.8	58.3	58.2	53.6	52.2	54.6
Median time lapse (years) to doctorate															
Since bachelor's degree completion	8.7	10.6	10.5	10.4	10.5	10.5	10.3	10.0	9.9	9.9	9.8	9.7	10.0	10.0	9.8
Since starting graduate school	6.4	7.5	7.5	7.5	7.5	7.5	7.4	7.5	7.5	7.5	7.5	7.6	7.8	7.8	7.9

[1]Distribution by race/ethnicity based on U.S. citizens and those with permanent visas only.
[2]Does not include Native Hawaiians or other Pacific Islanders.
NOTE: Longitudinal comparisons by race/ethnicity should be done with extreme care, due to periodic changes in the survey. In particular, large numbers of Asians converted from temporary visas to permanent visas in the mid-1990s. The classification of degrees by field used in this survey differs somewhat from that in most publications of the National Center for Education Statistics (NCES). The major differences are that history is included under humanities rather than social sciences and that psychology is included under social sciences. Includes anthropology, area studies, criminology, demographic/population studies,

economics, econometrics, geography, international relations/affairs, political science, public policy, psychology, sociology, statistics, and urban affairs/studies. The total number of degrees also differs slightly from that reported in the NCES Integrated Postsecondary Education Data System (IPEDS) "Completions Survey." Race categories exclude persons of Hispanic origin. Detail may not sum to totals because of rounding.
SOURCE: *Doctorate Recipients From United States Universities, 2004,* Survey of Earned Doctorates, National Science Foundation, National Institutes of Health, U.S. Department of Education, National Endowment for the Humanities, U.S. Department of Agriculture, and the National Aeronautics and Space Administration. (This table was prepared May 2006.)

Table 308. Degrees conferred by degree-granting institutions, by control, level of degree, and state or jurisdiction: 2004–05

State or jurisdiction	Public					Private				
	Associate's degrees	Bachelor's degrees	Master's degrees	First-professional degrees[1]	Doctor's degrees (Ph.D., Ed.D., etc.)	Associate's degrees	Bachelor's degrees	Master's degrees	First-professional degrees[1]	Doctor's degrees (Ph.D., Ed.D., etc.)
1	2	3	4	5	6	7	8	9	10	11
United States	**547,519**	**932,443**	**291,505**	**35,768**	**31,743**	**149,141**	**506,821**	**283,113**	**51,521**	**20,888**
Alabama	8,040	17,810	9,363	689	529	1,234	3,806	630	411	42
Alaska	816	1,304	571	0	25	63	123	84	0	0
Arizona	10,490	18,299	5,958	474	811	5,428	10,834	13,924	314	95
Arkansas	4,970	8,843	2,545	505	249	196	2,348	306	0	0
California	77,855	107,630	25,886	2,309	3,069	14,832	39,329	28,368	6,879	3,134
Colorado	6,151	20,064	5,771	617	707	3,637	5,166	5,150	437	355
Connecticut	3,795	8,506	3,303	402	261	1,227	8,111	5,548	612	414
Delaware	1,045	3,970	778	0	189	217	1,277	1,253	335	45
District of Columbia	166	281	37	53	0	281	8,918	8,499	2,897	613
Florida	44,961	43,481	13,128	1,578	1,518	15,480	22,358	10,886	2,138	1,546
Georgia	10,359	24,894	9,054	815	950	2,346	10,621	4,057	1,214	275
Hawaii	2,346	3,294	1,143	154	156	1,077	2,006	882	1	16
Idaho	1,963	4,939	1,431	163	139	1,226	2,356	192	0	0
Illinois	25,194	31,775	11,601	1,168	1,197	9,521	32,138	24,391	3,405	1,555
Indiana	9,637	24,774	7,332	1,134	1,096	4,199	11,881	3,755	630	210
Iowa	10,185	11,389	2,767	676	597	2,014	9,397	1,549	1,007	75
Kansas	7,356	12,856	4,186	759	413	598	3,365	1,482	8	0
Kentucky	6,759	13,549	5,379	864	388	2,250	4,313	1,185	247	123
Louisiana	4,384	17,537	5,092	792	425	1,350	3,957	1,782	859	137
Maine	1,889	3,908	917	95	40	485	2,592	731	122	0
Maryland	9,200	19,405	6,722	910	816	634	5,613	6,441	170	412
Massachusetts	8,915	13,754	4,663	104	424	2,680	31,960	23,000	4,201	2,252
Michigan	19,273	38,901	16,654	1,688	1,572	4,236	12,306	6,180	1,254	62
Minnesota	11,879	17,648	4,514	777	678	3,590	10,627	8,538	982	561
Mississippi	8,327	9,767	2,971	461	373	303	1,914	906	146	0
Missouri	8,768	17,998	5,032	711	439	4,683	16,354	12,148	1,914	924
Montana	1,584	4,607	1,089	129	117	198	570	33	0	0
Nebraska	3,828	7,352	2,714	353	391	802	4,647	1,222	511	101
Nevada	2,365	5,010	1,562	180	126	871	598	480	0	0
New Hampshire	1,795	4,263	968	0	63	1,703	3,844	1,783	183	104
New Jersey	13,284	23,110	6,923	1,145	623	1,442	8,877	5,463	672	519
New Mexico	4,302	6,052	2,553	250	313	288	1,290	666	0	0
New York	40,598	46,363	17,039	1,271	1,293	16,279	63,489	43,466	7,461	3,057
North Carolina	17,229	27,000	8,410	864	990	1,231	12,303	3,124	1,061	365
North Dakota	1,924	4,382	762	178	189	289	779	342	0	0
Ohio	17,446	36,749	12,605	2,160	1,541	5,228	20,220	7,755	1,238	477
Oklahoma	8,184	14,649	4,436	711	359	1,059	3,617	1,283	383	54
Oregon	6,964	12,426	4,133	439	378	1,542	4,441	2,015	708	99
Pennsylvania	13,613	39,219	9,474	1,715	1,376	12,006	38,546	16,976	3,175	1,583
Rhode Island	1,107	3,031	844	80	78	2,466	6,441	1,379	238	165
South Carolina	6,826	13,614	3,903	628	450	1,297	5,181	1,104	229	16
South Dakota	1,713	3,265	973	189	81	512	1,506	244	21	8
Tennessee	6,992	16,441	5,171	723	534	2,715	9,591	3,359	679	357
Texas	35,904	69,172	25,307	3,305	2,514	5,874	19,585	7,084	2,093	460
Utah	8,649	12,502	2,379	267	298	1,266	8,297	1,831	156	75
Vermont	834	2,560	523	88	59	437	2,332	1,161	171	3
Virginia	11,133	27,739	9,872	1,324	1,195	3,791	9,231	2,864	1,172	309
Washington	21,186	20,692	4,768	649	737	1,152	7,573	4,005	708	56
West Virginia	2,707	7,783	2,405	449	169	1,031	1,791	330	0	44
Wisconsin	10,690	22,742	5,439	648	756	1,015	8,402	3,277	479	190
Wyoming	1,939	1,695	455	125	52	860	0	0	0	0
U.S. Service Schools[2]	0	3,449	0	0	0	†	†	†	†	†
Other jurisdictions	**1,986**	**7,984**	**800**	**348**	**72**	**3,088**	**9,153**	**3,546**	**535**	**152**
American Samoa	191	0	0	0	0	0	0	0	0	0
Federated States of Micronesia	201	0	0	0	0	0	0	0	0	0
Guam	94	289	48	0	0	2	3	0	0	0
Marshall Islands	80	0	0	0	0	0	0	0	0	0
Northern Marianas	92	27	0	0	0	0	0	0	0	0
Palau	51	0	0	0	0	0	0	0	0	0
Puerto Rico	1,184	7,496	695	348	72	3,086	9,150	3,546	535	152
Virgin Islands	93	172	57	0	0	0	0	0	0	0

†Not applicable.
[1]Includes degrees that require at least 6 years of college work for completion (including at least 2 years of preprofessional training). See Definitions for details.
[2]Excludes Uniformed Services University of the Health Sciences, National Defense University, Air Force Institute of Technology, Community College of the Air Force, Naval Post-graduate School, Joint Military Intelligence College, and the U.S. Army Command and General Staff College.

SOURCE: U.S. Department of Education, National Center for Education Statistics, 2004–05 Integrated Postsecondary Education Data System (IPEDS), Fall 2005. (This table was prepared July 2006.)

Table 309. Bachelor's and master's degrees conferred by degree-granting institutions, by field of study and state or jurisdiction: 2004–05

State or jurisdiction	Total degrees		Humanities[1]		Social and behavioral sciences[2]		Natural sciences[3]		Computer sciences and engineering[4]		Education		Business/management		Other fields[5]	
	Bachelor's degrees	Master's degrees	Bachelor's degrees	Master's degrees	Bachelor's degrees	Master's degrees	Bachelor's degrees	Master's degrees	Bachelor's degrees	Master's degrees	Bachelor's degrees	Master's degrees	Bachelor's degrees	Master's degrees	Bachelor's degrees	Master's degrees
1	2	3	4	5	6	7	8	9	10	11	12	13	14	15	16	17
United States	1,439,264	574,618	256,151	42,207	242,506	35,782	97,867	18,354	133,854	53,549	105,451	167,490	311,574	142,617	291,861	114,619
Alabama	21,616	9,993	2,343	296	2,545	590	1,352	198	1,978	728	2,578	3,763	5,858	2,256	4,962	2,162
Alaska	1,427	655	236	64	240	39	115	47	125	77	61	221	285	100	365	107
Arizona	29,133	19,882	3,455	467	2,684	366	1,438	255	3,779	692	2,709	6,531	9,130	9,395	5,938	2,176
Arkansas	11,191	2,851	1,326	161	1,334	113	818	110	764	137	1,299	1,058	2,695	566	2,955	706
California	146,959	54,254	35,788	5,492	31,289	4,986	11,833	1,766	13,894	6,748	2,754	13,469	28,239	11,749	23,162	10,044
Colorado	25,230	10,921	5,131	653	4,798	828	2,127	340	2,662	1,365	151	2,404	5,367	3,568	4,994	1,763
Connecticut	16,617	8,851	3,758	736	4,163	504	1,065	414	933	681	650	2,575	2,954	2,055	3,094	1,886
Delaware	5,247	2,031	781	102	949	127	245	61	313	128	576	799	1,295	515	1,088	299
District of Columbia	9,199	8,536	1,485	836	2,895	1,135	506	304	793	775	83	796	1,960	2,149	1,477	2,541
Florida	65,839	24,014	8,218	963	10,512	1,236	3,031	664	5,916	2,072	4,644	5,919	18,000	7,398	15,518	5,762
Georgia	35,515	13,111	5,369	702	5,581	740	2,257	379	3,990	1,412	3,525	3,868	8,428	3,605	6,365	2,405
Hawaii	5,300	2,025	847	154	1,018	172	315	58	343	139	289	531	1,378	539	1,110	432
Idaho	7,295	1,623	1,067	118	840	71	439	76	579	144	1,069	635	1,321	197	1,980	382
Illinois	63,913	35,992	11,996	2,288	8,824	2,034	3,863	889	7,458	3,149	6,271	11,082	13,836	10,614	11,665	5,936
Indiana	36,655	11,087	5,551	869	4,603	532	2,069	434	4,334	844	4,329	2,679	7,673	3,535	8,096	2,194
Iowa	20,786	4,316	3,275	439	3,027	154	1,313	239	1,711	412	2,322	924	4,857	1,143	4,281	1,005
Kansas	16,221	5,668	2,514	371	2,092	271	1,082	158	1,464	575	1,669	1,772	3,434	1,280	3,966	1,241
Kentucky	17,862	6,564	2,524	394	2,562	416	1,186	237	1,052	554	2,205	2,656	3,650	805	4,683	1,502
Louisiana	21,494	6,874	3,613	594	2,808	357	1,633	387	1,887	617	1,865	1,614	4,977	1,465	4,711	1,840
Maine	6,500	1,648	1,227	119	1,289	26	562	33	410	47	746	724	726	168	1,540	531
Maryland	25,018	13,163	4,297	1,042	5,249	1,120	1,935	609	3,267	2,032	1,324	2,760	4,305	3,468	4,641	2,132
Massachusetts	45,714	27,663	9,115	2,020	10,738	1,978	3,487	910	4,042	2,476	1,288	7,767	8,758	6,132	8,286	6,380
Michigan	51,207	22,834	6,716	1,021	6,877	751	3,236	685	6,138	2,807	5,257	7,067	11,984	6,333	10,999	4,170
Minnesota	28,275	13,052	5,141	739	4,675	687	2,398	217	2,278	897	3,064	6,384	5,378	2,139	5,341	1,989
Mississippi	11,681	3,877	1,281	151	1,435	162	843	225	836	260	1,630	1,620	2,738	748	2,918	711
Missouri	34,352	17,180	4,607	892	4,558	1,406	2,088	334	3,265	903	3,312	4,384	9,259	6,392	7,263	2,869
Montana	5,177	1,122	777	101	815	97	455	70	543	90	646	299	865	117	1,076	348
Nebraska	11,999	3,936	1,188	167	1,491	156	772	115	786	292	1,516	1,201	3,154	679	3,092	1,326
Nevada	5,608	2,042	708	105	724	160	262	53	419	165	641	921	1,570	365	1,284	273
New Hampshire	8,107	2,751	1,498	126	1,762	142	453	68	563	175	451	788	1,826	978	1,554	474
New Jersey	31,987	12,386	6,302	980	7,158	674	2,284	401	3,066	1,599	2,267	3,722	5,679	2,617	5,231	2,393
New Mexico	7,342	3,219	1,177	301	815	154	505	137	863	322	918	1,061	1,649	622	1,415	622
New York	109,852	60,505	23,928	6,377	21,962	3,972	6,595	1,723	9,687	4,617	7,209	20,227	21,551	10,346	18,920	13,243
North Carolina	39,303	11,534	5,302	855	7,122	534	3,350	485	3,463	1,061	3,045	2,540	8,050	3,297	8,971	2,762
North Dakota	5,161	1,104	491	27	403	38	336	54	531	81	638	250	994	361	1,768	293
Ohio	56,969	20,360	8,505	1,892	8,053	1,086	3,323	804	5,071	1,718	6,687	6,560	12,598	4,714	12,732	3,586
Oklahoma	18,266	5,719	2,629	488	2,080	265	1,135	166	1,483	786	2,096	1,134	4,507	1,790	4,336	1,090
Oregon	16,867	6,148	4,055	455	3,499	362	1,238	183	1,249	507	676	2,629	2,816	895	3,334	1,117
Pennsylvania	77,765	26,450	12,930	1,825	12,155	1,433	5,335	980	7,947	2,557	6,835	7,087	16,564	6,680	15,999	5,888
Rhode Island	9,472	2,223	1,570	215	1,405	200	556	107	751	129	651	601	2,559	513	1,980	458
South Carolina	18,795	5,007	2,756	262	3,106	181	1,669	196	1,295	409	1,803	1,944	4,652	922	3,514	1,093
South Dakota	4,771	1,217	403	65	516	110	339	52	618	180	580	355	1,011	214	1,304	241
Tennessee	26,032	8,530	5,655	580	3,973	452	1,469	206	1,850	574	1,516	3,160	5,581	1,751	5,988	1,807
Texas	88,757	32,391	18,487	2,689	12,413	2,007	6,541	1,132	7,044	3,980	2,308	7,132	21,593	9,019	20,371	6,432
Utah	20,799	4,210	3,223	239	3,642	208	1,163	185	2,007	508	2,135	799	3,911	1,353	4,718	918

See notes at end of table.

Table 309. Bachelor's and master's degrees conferred by degree-granting institutions, by field of study and state or jurisdiction: 2004-05—Continued

State or jurisdiction	Total degrees		Humanities[1]		Social and behavioral sciences[2]		Natural sciences[3]		Computer sciences and engineering[4]		Education		Business/management		Other fields[5]	
	Bachelor's degrees	Master's degrees	Bachelor's degrees	Master's degrees	Bachelor's degrees	Master's degrees	Bachelor's degrees	Master's degrees	Bachelor's degrees	Master's degrees	Bachelor's degrees	Master's degrees	Bachelor's degrees	Master's degrees	Bachelor's degrees	Master's degrees
1	2	3	4	5	6	7	8	9	10	11	12	13	14	15	16	17
Vermont	4,892	1,684	1,251	284	1,159	267	318	35	266	149	328	534	622	181	948	234
Virginia	36,970	12,736	8,091	1,283	8,120	1,189	2,754	414	3,269	1,407	825	3,960	7,162	2,289	6,749	2,194
Washington	28,265	8,773	6,646	538	5,424	559	2,151	289	2,290	536	1,613	2,770	5,048	1,878	5,093	2,203
West Virginia	9,574	2,735	1,851	150	1,140	120	561	99	662	270	1,217	951	1,840	518	2,303	627
Wisconsin	31,144	8,716	4,487	481	4,882	573	2,585	316	2,491	728	2,888	2,781	6,729	2,136	7,082	1,701
Wyoming	1,695	455	121	39	206	42	119	55	187	38	292	82	285	68	485	131
U.S. Service Schools	3,449	0	459	0	896	0	363	0	1,242	0	0	0	273	0	216	0
Other jurisdictions	**17,137**	**4,346**	**936**	**93**	**1,215**	**214**	**1,235**	**84**	**1,890**	**224**	**2,975**	**1,594**	**5,373**	**1,398**	**3,513**	**739**
Guam	292	48	22	1	20	0	11	4	12	0	67	28	69	1	91	14
Northern Marianas	27	0	0	0	0	0	0	0	0	0	27	0	0	0	0	0
Puerto Rico	16,646	4,241	901	92	1,185	214	1,196	80	1,870	224	2,859	1,529	5,225	1,385	3,410	717
Virgin Islands	172	57	13	0	10	0	28	0	8	0	22	37	79	12	12	8

[1]Includes degrees in area, ethnic, cultural, and gender studies; English language and literature/letters; foreign languages, literatures, and linguistics; liberal arts and sciences, general studies and humanities; mult/interdisciplinary studies; philosophy and religious studies; theology and religious vocations; and visual and performing arts.
[2]Includes psychology; social sciences; and history.
[3]Includes biological and biomedical sciences; physical sciences; science technologies/technicians; and mathematics and statistics.
[4]Includes computer and information sciences and support services; engineering; engineering technologies/technicians; mechanic and repairer technologies/technicians; and construction trades.

[5]Includes agriculture, agricultural operations, and related sciences; natural resources and conservation; architecture and related services; communication, journalism, and related programs; communications technologies/technicians and support services; health professions and related clinical sciences; family and consumer services/human sciences; legal professions and studies; library science; military technologies; parks, recreation, leisure, and fitness studies; security and protective services; public administration and social service professions; transportation and materials moving; and not classified by field of study.
SOURCE: U.S. Department of Education, National Center for Education Statistics, 2004–05 Integrated Postsecondary Education Data System (IPEDS), Fall 2005. (This table was prepared July 2006.)

Table 310. Degrees conferred by degree-granting institutions, by level of degree and state or jurisdiction: 2003–04 and 2004–05

State or jurisdiction	2003–04					2004–05				
	Associate's degrees	Bachelor's degrees	Master's degrees	First-professional degrees[1]	Doctor's degrees (Ph.D., Ed.D., etc.)	Associate's degrees	Bachelor's degrees	Master's degrees	First-professional degrees[1]	Doctor's degrees (Ph.D., Ed.D., etc.)
1	2	3	4	5	6	7	8	9	10	11
United States	665,301	1,399,542	558,940	83,041	48,378	696,660	1,439,264	574,618	87,289	52,631
Alabama	8,914	21,386	9,059	1,016	521	9,274	21,616	9,993	1,100	571
Alaska	986	1,405	585	0	20	879	1,427	655	0	25
Arizona	14,018	26,225	17,464	770	931	15,918	29,133	19,882	788	906
Arkansas	4,887	10,784	2,597	465	219	5,166	11,191	2,851	505	249
California	89,534	142,418	53,293	8,703	5,913	92,687	146,959	54,254	9,188	6,203
Colorado	9,827	24,107	10,027	947	780	9,788	25,230	10,921	1,054	1,062
Connecticut	4,737	16,643	8,381	949	680	5,022	16,617	8,851	1,014	675
Delaware	1,159	5,101	1,940	243	201	1,262	5,247	2,031	335	234
District of Columbia	816	9,435	8,468	2,655	576	447	9,199	8,536	2,950	613
Florida	57,926	63,811	23,175	3,469	2,908	60,441	65,839	24,014	3,716	3,064
Georgia	12,927	36,162	14,442	2,118	1,134	12,705	35,515	13,111	2,029	1,225
Hawaii	3,654	5,499	1,897	145	127	3,423	5,300	2,025	155	172
Idaho	3,273	6,042	1,116	161	105	3,189	7,295	1,623	163	139
Illinois	28,738	59,537	32,732	4,422	2,498	34,715	63,913	35,992	4,573	2,752
Indiana	13,253	36,388	10,836	1,664	1,124	13,836	36,655	11,087	1,764	1,306
Iowa	11,076	20,174	3,967	1,526	606	12,199	20,786	4,316	1,683	672
Kansas	7,732	16,022	5,989	741	433	7,954	16,221	5,668	767	413
Kentucky	8,660	17,243	6,190	1,040	424	9,009	17,862	6,564	1,111	511
Louisiana	5,841	21,336	6,414	1,710	571	5,734	21,494	6,874	1,651	562
Maine	2,252	6,059	1,542	202	43	2,374	6,500	1,648	217	40
Maryland	9,023	23,999	12,999	1,140	1,063	9,834	25,018	13,163	1,080	1,228
Massachusetts	11,373	45,583	27,768	4,228	2,484	11,595	45,714	27,663	4,305	2,676
Michigan	21,836	51,166	24,204	2,716	1,559	23,509	51,207	22,834	2,942	1,634
Minnesota	14,189	27,324	11,433	1,659	1,032	15,469	28,275	13,052	1,759	1,239
Mississippi	8,224	11,663	3,668	528	357	8,630	11,681	3,877	607	373
Missouri	12,396	34,006	16,285	2,557	1,233	13,451	34,352	17,180	2,625	1,363
Montana	1,811	5,369	1,087	134	80	1,782	5,177	1,122	129	117
Nebraska	4,295	11,439	3,630	813	382	4,630	11,999	3,936	864	492
Nevada	2,872	5,136	1,796	169	121	3,236	5,608	2,042	180	126
New Hampshire	3,289	7,908	2,839	158	127	3,498	8,107	2,751	183	167
New Jersey	14,206	30,564	12,035	1,662	1,182	14,726	31,987	12,386	1,817	1,142
New Mexico	4,271	7,217	2,983	243	283	4,590	7,342	3,219	250	313
New York	55,634	106,995	63,270	8,373	3,990	56,877	109,852	60,505	8,732	4,350
North Carolina	17,517	38,774	11,378	1,888	1,248	18,460	39,303	11,534	1,925	1,355
North Dakota	2,172	5,033	1,054	181	90	2,213	5,161	1,104	178	189
Ohio	22,310	56,256	19,246	3,212	1,850	22,674	56,969	20,360	3,398	2,018
Oklahoma	8,701	17,424	5,607	1,098	402	9,243	18,266	5,719	1,094	413
Oregon	8,301	16,664	5,877	1,070	504	8,506	16,867	6,148	1,147	477
Pennsylvania	24,576	75,343	26,288	4,548	2,799	25,619	77,765	26,450	4,890	2,959
Rhode Island	3,540	9,251	2,171	321	249	3,573	9,472	2,223	318	243
South Carolina	8,039	17,891	4,765	820	432	8,123	18,795	5,007	857	466
South Dakota	2,508	4,752	1,116	204	91	2,225	4,771	1,217	210	89
Tennessee	8,733	24,983	8,304	1,431	846	9,707	26,032	8,530	1,402	891
Texas	39,302	85,539	30,549	5,082	2,752	41,778	88,757	32,391	5,398	2,974
Utah	9,401	19,909	4,167	416	362	9,915	20,799	4,210	423	373
Vermont	1,390	4,648	1,474	247	55	1,271	4,892	1,684	259	62
Virginia	14,034	35,660	11,948	2,407	1,249	14,924	36,970	12,736	2,496	1,504
Washington	23,676	27,240	8,481	1,170	729	22,338	28,265	8,773	1,357	793
West Virginia	3,323	9,101	2,829	453	169	3,738	9,574	2,735	449	213
Wisconsin	11,340	31,759	9,155	1,036	802	11,705	31,144	8,716	1,127	946
Wyoming	2,809	1,670	420	131	42	2,799	1,695	455	125	52
U.S. Service Schools[2]	0	3,499	0	0	0	0	3,449	0	0	0
Other jurisdictions	5,034	17,879	3,922	874	182	5,074	17,137	4,346	883	224
American Samoa	149	0	0	0	0	191	0	0	0	0
Federated States of Micronesia	171	0	0	0	0	201	0	0	0	0
Guam	90	287	100	0	0	96	292	48	0	0
Marshall Islands	80	0	0	0	0	80	0	0	0	0
Northern Marianas	98	32	0	0	0	92	27	0	0	0
Palau	69	0	0	0	0	51	0	0	0	0
Puerto Rico	4,300	17,370	3,750	874	182	4,270	16,646	4,241	883	224
Virgin Islands	77	190	72	0	0	93	172	57	0	0

[1]Includes degrees that require at least 6 years of college work for completion (including at least 2 years of preprofessional training). See Definitions for details.
[2]Excludes Uniformed Services University of the Health Sciences, National Defense University, Air Force Institute of Technology, Community College of the Air Force, Naval Postgraduate School, Joint Military Intelligence College, and the U.S. Army Command and General Staff College.

SOURCE: U.S. Department of Education, National Center for Education Statistics, 2003–04 and 2004–05 Integrated Postsecondary Education Data System (IPEDS), Fall 2004 and Fall 2005. (This table was prepared July 2006.)

Table 311. Doctor's degrees conferred by the 60 institutions conferring the most doctor's degrees: 1995–96 through 2004–05

Institution	Rank order[1]	Total, 1995–96 to 2004–05	1995–96	1996–97	1997–98	1998–99	1999–2000	2000–01	2001–02	2002–03	2003–04	2004–05
1	2	3	4	5	6	7	8	9	10	11	12	13
United States, all institutions	†	461,520	44,652	45,876	46,010	44,077	44,808	44,904	44,160	46,024	48,378	52,631
Total, 60 large institutions	†	243,454	24,856	24,992	25,280	23,710	23,907	23,639	22,860	23,505	24,696	26,009
University of California, Berkeley	1	7,675	770	759	756	720	756	759	805	772	775	803
University of Texas at Austin	2	7,246	744	786	836	754	659	733	639	674	702	719
University of Wisconsin, Madison	3	6,971	753	782	757	687	729	663	650	656	628	666
University of Minnesota, Twin Cities	4	6,480	763	704	729	658	604	632	560	560	592	678
University of Illinois at Urbana-Champaign	5	6,478	698	735	706	646	597	667	602	617	574	636
University of Michigan, Ann Arbor	6	6,474	691	635	690	650	629	568	610	616	660	725
Ohio State University, Main Campus	7	6,230	717	721	636	561	620	633	617	575	560	590
University of California, Los Angeles	8	6,153	611	616	607	589	606	612	593	596	666	657
Stanford University	9	5,989	585	607	606	574	589	573	548	611	625	671
Nova Southeastern University	10	5,933	447	534	540	537	587	519	555	732	705	777
Harvard University	11	5,914	528	623	803	615	602	520	543	548	572	560
University of Florida	12	5,448	434	429	456	445	516	574	607	591	694	702
Pennsylvania State University, Main Campus	13	5,335	510	523	571	560	513	526	519	503	539	571
University of Southern California	14	5,326	539	448	515	536	481	522	496	559	573	657
Texas A & M University	15	5,129	574	541	525	501	490	509	504	442	515	528
Massachusetts Institute of Technology	16	5,030	554	514	520	486	475	492	501	440	467	581
University of Washington, Seattle	17	4,968	495	526	479	520	486	486	452	493	503	528
Purdue University, Main Campus	18	4,752	508	478	496	496	468	464	409	463	446	524
University of Maryland, College Park	19	4,683	466	505	474	501	461	430	430	418	482	516
Columbia University in the City of New York	20	4,678	404	482	469	414	461	465	452	433	495	603
Cornell University[2]	21	4,481	516	485	474	485	441	423	382	411	412	452
Michigan State University	22	4,333	484	411	451	404	444	414	428	442	430	425
University of Pennsylvania	23	4,146	447	440	436	380	427	376	380	384	413	463
University of North Carolina at Chapel Hill	24	4,031	365	387	382	374	425	398	390	412	439	459
University of Arizona	25	3,947	384	445	411	411	405	359	370	378	398	386
New York University	26	3,920	356	392	446	300	402	368	415	411	407	423
Rutgers University, New Brunswick/Piscataway	27	3,801	416	410	402	375	371	392	363	358	382	332
Indiana University, Bloomington	28	3,779	374	366	361	363	409	420	347	367	375	397
University of Georgia	29	3,743	343	328	369	365	352	351	393	414	404	424
University of Pittsburgh, Main Campus	30	3,599	358	387	380	360	316	360	336	348	382	372
Johns Hopkins University	31	3,597	321	329	360	366	351	384	373	364	362	387
University of Chicago	32	3,582	381	364	368	384	391	371	333	332	331	327
University of California, Davis	33	3,572	397	351	337	310	357	337	346	373	375	389
Northwestern University	34	3,525	359	357	377	309	321	350	349	370	367	366
Yale University	35	3,318	367	329	365	322	334	313	310	317	332	329
University of Virginia, Main Campus	36	3,313	325	368	302	302	343	316	321	337	358	341
Virginia Polytechnic Institute and State U.	37	3,280	378	410	349	349	309	268	326	272	290	329
North Carolina State University at Raleigh	38	3,244	325	314	322	358	316	306	300	322	338	343
University of Iowa	39	3,239	377	364	327	310	317	334	320	249	300	341
State University of New York at Buffalo	40	3,002	346	314	295	271	303	294	231	269	299	380
Arizona State University at the Tempe Campus	41	2,994	315	274	287	273	286	277	313	300	355	314
University of California, San Diego	42	2,919	259	281	310	303	294	285	278	279	327	303
University of Colorado at Boulder	43	2,918	297	328	309	307	266	292	258	303	286	272
City University of New York, Graduate School and University Center	44	2,891	302	310	333	277	280	250	271	272	298	298
Boston University	45	2,860	309	276	307	287	274	304	246	270	267	320
University of Massachusetts, Amherst	46	2,767	338	282	299	270	276	261	287	213	274	267
Florida State University	47	2,757	273	306	305	273	263	252	248	290	271	276
University of Tennessee	48	2,709	281	295	254	255	286	239	276	262	280	281
Princeton University	49	2,681	286	296	263	250	279	268	230	260	276	273
Temple University	50	2,664	281	306	285	248	263	238	226	161	334	322
University of Missouri, Columbia	51	2,604	248	264	277	230	256	278	252	274	251	274
Georgia Institute of Technology, Main Campus	52	2,600	252	224	263	228	230	255	257	225	311	355
Iowa State University	53	2,521	287	255	300	257	238	243	239	228	228	246
University of South Carolina, Columbia	54	2,515	267	274	243	268	246	235	253	235	241	253
Duke University	55	2,499	230	258	238	249	230	259	246	253	259	277
University of Nebraska at Lincoln	56	2,493	261	276	282	251	251	235	213	254	236	234
University of Connecticut	57	2,458	239	254	253	227	275	234	221	237	257	261
Stony Brook University	58	2,423	261	275	265	227	244	231	20	298	285	317
University of California, Santa Barbara	59	2,420	222	225	264	229	232	258	199	251	253	287
Louisiana State University & A&M College	60	2,417	238	234	258	253	275	264	222	211	240	222

†Not applicable.
[1]Institutions are ranked by the total number of doctor's degrees conferred during the 10-year period ending June 30, 2005.
[2]Includes degrees conferred by the Endowed and Statutory Colleges.

SOURCE: U.S. Department of Education, National Center for Education Statistics, 1995–96 through 2004–05 Integrated Postsecondary Education Data System, "Completions Survey" (IPEDS-C:96-99), and Fall 2000 through Fall 2005. (This table was prepared July 2006.)

Table 312. Percentage distribution of 1990 high school sophomores, by highest level of education completed through 2000 and selected student characteristics: 1990, 1992, and 2000

Student characteristic	Total		Less than high school completion		High school completion		Some post-secondary		Certificate		Associate's degree		Bachelor's or higher degree Total		Bachelor's degree		Master's degree		Professional and doctor's degrees	
1	2		3		4		5		6		7		8		9		10		11	
Total...............................	100.0	(†)	8.8	(0.73)	17.8	(0.73)	30.2	(0.90)	7.9	(0.44)	6.6	(0.37)	28.7	(0.89)	25.5	(0.81)	2.8	(0.23)	0.4	(0.06)
Sex																				
Male.............................	100.0	(†)	8.5	(1.02)	19.7	(1.06)	32.6	(1.27)	6.8	(0.60)	6.6	(0.56)	25.8	(1.16)	23.2	(1.08)	2.2	(0.31)	0.4	(0.09)
Female..........................	100.0	(†)	9.1	(1.00)	15.9	(0.99)	27.9	(1.12)	8.9	(0.67)	6.6	(0.46)	31.5	(1.12)	27.8	(1.03)	3.3	(0.31)	0.4	(0.09)
Race/ethnicity																				
White............................	100.0	(†)	6.8	(0.75)	17.8	(0.75)	27.6	(0.85)	7.2	(0.44)	7.2	(0.46)	33.3	(0.98)	29.4	(0.91)	3.5	(0.30)	0.5	(0.08)
Black.............................	100.0	(†)	11.1	(2.14)	17.9	(2.29)	38.5	(3.51)	12.0	(1.91)	4.1	(0.66)	16.4	(1.68)	15.4	(1.64)	0.8	(0.25)	0.2	(0.08)
Hispanic........................	100.0	(†)	16.3	(3.23)	18.5	(2.63)	37.8	(2.93)	8.5	(1.43)	7.3	(1.12)	11.6	(1.16)	10.7	(1.10)	0.8	(0.20)	0.1	(0.07)
Asian/Pacific Islander..................	100.0	(†)	6.5	(3.14)	6.2	(1.33)	32.2	(4.09)	5.7	(1.62)	3.5	(1.37)	46.1	(4.63)	41.0	(4.45)	3.6	(0.91)	1.5	(0.41)
American Indian/Alaska Native......	100.0	(†)	21.6	(3.81)	40.1	(8.24)	23.0	(7.29)	6.4	(4.00)	3.0	(0.97)	5.9	(2.35)	5.3	(2.25)	‡	(†)	‡	(†)
Socioeconomic status[1] (1990)																				
Low quartile.................	100.0	(†)	19.9	(1.97)	31.7	(1.84)	25.4	(1.71)	10.6	(1.12)	5.4	(0.69)	6.9	(0.60)	6.5	(0.59)	0.3	(0.10)	#	(†)
Middle two quartiles.....................	100.0	(†)	6.1	(0.79)	17.0	(0.90)	34.4	(1.16)	8.2	(0.61)	8.5	(0.60)	25.7	(1.02)	23.6	(1.00)	1.9	(0.26)	0.2	(0.06)
High quartile	100.0	(†)	0.3	(0.10)	5.2	(0.81)	25.5	(1.47)	4.5	(0.79)	4.6	(0.56)	59.8	(1.58)	51.2	(1.48)	7.3	(0.68)	1.4	(0.23)
Test score composite[2] (1990)																				
Low quartile.................	100.0	(†)	19.3	(1.99)	31.8	(2.00)	28.1	(1.93)	11.2	(1.27)	4.9	(0.76)	4.7	(0.50)	4.5	(0.50)	0.2	(0.08)	0.1	(0.05)
Middle two quartiles.....................	100.0	(†)	4.9	(1.00)	17.0	(0.98)	34.4	(1.29)	8.9	(0.62)	9.2	(0.61)	25.5	(1.08)	23.6	(1.05)	1.8	(0.20)	0.1	(0.03)
High quartile	100.0	(†)	0.7	(0.09)	5.3	(0.72)	23.4	(1.23)	2.7	(0.59)	4.7	(0.57)	63.2	(1.44)	53.9	(1.43)	7.7	(0.75)	1.5	(0.24)
Locus of control[3] (1990)																				
Low quartile.................	100.0	(†)	13.6	(1.91)	26.2	(1.85)	29.9	(1.82)	7.6	(0.93)	6.4	(0.84)	16.2	(1.29)	14.9	(1.26)	1.2	(0.24)	0.1	(0.05)
Middle two quartiles.....................	100.0	(†)	6.8	(0.97)	15.6	(0.98)	30.6	(1.21)	8.0	(0.59)	7.2	(0.51)	31.8	(1.16)	28.5	(1.08)	2.7	(0.33)	0.5	(0.10)
High quartile	100.0	(†)	2.3	(0.60)	12.4	(1.24)	30.6	(1.73)	7.1	(1.05)	6.7	(0.76)	40.9	(1.74)	35.2	(1.60)	5.0	(0.62)	0.7	(0.17)
Self-concept[4] (1990)																				
Low quartile.................	100.0	(†)	8.7	(1.08)	20.6	(1.26)	31.9	(1.51)	7.1	(0.62)	6.9	(0.72)	24.8	(1.32)	22.2	(1.26)	2.5	(0.44)	0.2	(0.08)
Middle two quartiles.....................	100.0	(†)	7.9	(1.20)	18.3	(1.16)	28.6	(1.12)	7.6	(0.59)	7.7	(0.58)	29.9	(1.19)	26.5	(1.12)	2.9	(0.30)	0.5	(0.10)
High quartile	100.0	(†)	5.3	(1.20)	13.3	(1.39)	32.4	(2.26)	8.3	(1.16)	5.2	(0.66)	35.5	(1.81)	31.4	(1.66)	3.4	(0.54)	0.7	(0.15)
High school completion timing																				
Dropout (never completed)...........	100.0	(†)	100.0	(†)	‡	(†)	‡	(†)	‡	(†)	‡	(†)	‡	(†)	‡	(†)	‡	(†)	‡	(†)
Early (before January 1992).........	100.0	(†)	1.3	(0.71)	38.2	(5.06)	29.1	(3.87)	11.9	(2.68)	12.1	(4.28)	7.3	(1.78)	6.0	(1.43)	‡	(†)	‡	(†)
Normal (from January 1992 through August 1992)..............	100.0	(†)	#	(†)	16.2	(0.80)	32.7	(0.99)	7.9	(0.47)	7.4	(0.41)	35.7	(1.00)	31.7	(0.92)	3.4	(0.28)	0.5	(0.08)
Late (after August 1992)................	100.0	(†)	0.1	(0.08)	42.0	(3.00)	39.2	(3.14)	13.0	(2.35)	4.0	(0.95)	1.9	(0.52)	1.9	(0.52)	‡	(†)	‡	(†)
Control of school attended in 1992																				
Public............................	100.0	(†)	7.9	(0.70)	19.0	(0.78)	31.0	(1.00)	8.0	(0.48)	7.0	(0.40)	27.2	(0.91)	24.2	(0.83)	2.6	(0.24)	0.4	(0.07)
Private...........................	100.0	(†)	3.3	(0.99)	3.2	(0.56)	25.3	(2.37)	4.2	(1.10)	4.1	(0.77)	60.0	(2.69)	52.4	(2.64)	6.5	(0.99)	1.1	(0.28)
Postsecondary expectations in 1992																				
None	100.0	(†)	11.7	(5.67)	52.6	(5.00)	23.3	(4.45)	7.4	(1.43)	1.7	(0.60)	3.3	(0.79)	3.3	(0.79)	‡	(†)	‡	(†)
Some postsecondary	100.0	(†)	3.9	(1.14)	31.1	(1.82)	34.2	(1.89)	15.2	(1.26)	10.7	(0.98)	4.9	(0.71)	4.5	(0.69)	0.3	(0.18)	‡	(†)
Bachelor's degree	100.0	(†)	0.6	(0.33)	6.7	(0.71)	36.5	(1.47)	6.5	(0.92)	7.6	(0.62)	42.1	(1.48)	38.9	(1.42)	3.0	(0.44)	0.2	(0.08)
Master's degree	100.0	(†)	0.2	(0.09)	5.9	(0.93)	26.6	(1.64)	3.0	(0.51)	6.1	(1.01)	58.2	(1.87)	50.8	(1.86)	6.7	(0.67)	0.8	(0.23)
First-professional or doctor's degree..............................	100.0	(†)	0.9	(0.42)	2.2	(0.44)	28.2	(2.51)	4.7	(0.91)	5.6	(0.96)	58.4	(2.44)	48.4	(2.29)	7.8	(1.19)	2.2	(0.40)
Type of start in postsecondary education																				
Fall 1992 full-time 4-year...............	100.0	(†)	‡	(†)	0.6	(0.13)	22.7	(1.11)	2.2	(0.30)	3.7	(0.43)	70.7	(1.20)	61.4	(1.22)	8.0	(0.64)	1.3	(0.19)
Fall 1992 full-time public 2-year	100.0	(†)	‡	(†)	2.1	(0.60)	41.7	(2.34)	13.4	(1.61)	19.3	(1.54)	23.4	(1.79)	22.1	(1.75)	1.2	(0.36)	‡	(†)
Fall 1992 part-time 4-year...............	100.0	(†)	‡	(†)	‡	(†)	57.1	(7.33)	3.3	(1.70)	3.1	(1.91)	31.9	(6.33)	29.5	(6.17)	2.4	(1.80)	‡	(†)
Fall 1992 part-time public 2-year ...	100.0	(†)	2.7	(2.04)	2.8	(2.24)	57.6	(4.97)	15.1	(3.78)	9.7	(2.47)	12.2	(3.16)	12.0	(3.15)	‡	(†)	‡	(†)
Other enrollment..........................	100.0	(†)	2.2	(1.36)	12.4	(3.60)	35.3	(4.82)	15.3	(4.64)	8.2	(1.67)	26.5	(4.43)	24.6	(4.39)	1.6	(0.62)	‡	(†)
Never enrolled.............................	100.0	(†)	18.0	(1.39)	35.4	(1.34)	28.8	(1.37)	8.8	(0.66)	4.5	(0.48)	4.5	(0.47)	4.3	(0.46)	0.1	(0.06)	‡	(†)
Parents' educational attainment in 1990																				
No high school diploma	100.0	(†)	25.9	(3.46)	26.7	(2.51)	26.8	(2.81)	11.0	(1.77)	3.7	(0.64)	5.9	(0.99)	5.5	(0.97)	0.4	(0.17)	‡	(†)
High school graduate	100.0	(†)	12.7	(1.75)	30.6	(2.12)	26.1	(1.60)	8.3	(0.83)	9.0	(1.10)	13.3	(1.01)	12.1	(1.01)	1.0	(0.20)	0.1	(0.06)
Vocational/some college	100.0	(†)	4.6	(0.53)	17.3	(0.94)	35.1	(1.20)	9.1	(0.81)	8.1	(0.60)	25.7	(1.09)	23.7	(1.08)	1.9	(0.24)	0.2	(0.06)
Bachelor's degree	100.0	(†)	2.9	(1.35)	7.4	(1.24)	29.7	(2.15)	5.6	(0.91)	5.1	(0.64)	49.4	(2.10)	43.6	(2.02)	5.0	(0.74)	0.7	(0.22)
Master's degree	100.0	(†)	0.8	(0.46)	2.5	(0.74)	23.3	(2.49)	4.6	(1.18)	3.4	(0.62)	65.4	(2.50)	55.3	(2.46)	8.6	(1.39)	1.5	(0.39)
First-professional or doctor's degree..............................	100.0	(†)	0.6	(0.38)	1.8	(0.70)	18.3	(4.50)	2.0	(1.20)	4.1	(2.00)	73.3	(4.66)	61.1	(4.47)	9.3	(2.24)	2.9	(0.78)

†Not applicable.
#Rounds to zero.
‡Reporting standards not met.
[1]Socioeconomic status (SES) was measured by a composite score on parental education and occupations, and family income.
[2]Standardized quartile of composite of student assessments in mathematics and reading.
[3]Locus of control measures whether students attribute the events that happened to them, such as performing well on a test, to being under their own control (i.e., internal locus of control) or to being under the control of others or the environment (external locus of con-

trol). Higher scores (highest quartile) means greater internal control and lower scores (lowest quartile) means greater external control.
[4]Self-concept measures the degree to which students like and feel positively about themselves and perceive themselves as a person of worth. The NELS:88 variable is the general self-concept scale from Herbert Marsh's Self-Description Questionnaire (SDQ) II (Marsh 1990).
NOTE: Race categories exclude persons of Hispanic origin. Detail may not sum to totals because of rounding. Standard errors appear in parentheses.
SOURCE: National Center for Education Statistics, National Education Longitudinal Study of 1988 (NELS:88/2000), "Fourth Follow-up, Student Survey, 2000." (This table was prepared December 2005.)

Table 313. Mean number of semester credits completed by bachelor's degree recipients, by course area and major: 1976, 1984, and 1992–93

Selected college major	Course areas									
	Total	Business	Computer science	Education	Engineering	Mathematics	Biological sciences	Physical sciences	Social sciences and psychology	Other
1	2	3	4	5	6	7	8	9	10	11
1972 high school seniors who completed bachelor's degrees by 1976										
Mean, all majors	**124.0**	**7.8**	**1.0**	**9.7**	**2.3**	**7.4**	**7.6**	**9.0**	**30.3**	**48.8**
Business and management	124.4	41.2	2.3	0.5	0.4	10.2	2.5	4.8	30.4	32.0
Computer science................................	133.3	6.6	33.5	0.4	5.3	22.4	1.9	7.8	20.6	34.8
Education...	126.4	0.9	0.3	40.2	—	5.0	5.5	4.3	23.9	46.4
Engineering	134.8	1.6	2.0	0.1	50.0	18.2	1.3	20.5	14.0	27.1
English...	117.8	0.5	0.1	7.8	0.1	3.2	3.4	3.4	24.2	75.2
Fine arts	124.9	0.3	0.1	6.6	—	1.3	2.5	2.1	13.6	98.4
Life sciences	122.2	0.4	0.8	1.7	—	8.4	35.6	26.2	17.8	31.3
Physical sciences	122.7	0.8	1.4	0.9	1.9	16.2	9.6	49.5	13.1	29.2
Psychology	119.1	2.0	0.5	5.9	0.3	5.5	6.2	5.9	56.0	36.9
Social sciences...................................	120.6	3.4	0.4	3.3	0.4	5.3	3.2	4.3	60.3	40.1
1980 high school seniors who completed bachelor's degrees by 1984										
Mean, all majors	**123.5**	**12.8**	**3.3**	**6.2**	**4.6**	**8.4**	**5.3**	**8.1**	**27.5**	**47.2**
Business and management	122.8	41.2	4.5	0.6	1.1	8.9	2.2	3.9	27.5	32.7
Computer science................................	129.3	11.8	27.9	0.3	4.7	21.3	1.8	8.5	19.0	33.9
Education...	127.4	0.7	0.3	45.5	0.1	4.4	4.4	3.8	20.8	47.3
Engineering	132.3	1.0	2.3	0.8	52.5	16.2	1.1	20.2	12.3	25.9
English...	114.8	1.7	1.5	6.9	—	2.2	2.1	4.7	21.4	74.4
Fine arts	120.5	1.7	0.6	5.1	—	1.7	2.7	1.5	14.1	93.1
Life sciences	121.9	0.7	1.5	1.9	0.2	10.1	33.5	22.6	18.1	33.3
Physical sciences	124.3	0.2	4.9	0.1	2.0	14.1	12.9	48.7	11.6	30.0
Psychology	120.7	3.0	2.7	2.1	—	6.5	5.8	4.2	55.2	41.2
Social sciences...................................	119.2	6.0	1.4	1.0	0.5	5.4	4.4	5.1	52.0	43.3
1988–89 high school graduates who completed bachelor's degrees by 1992–93										
Mean, all majors	**126.5**	**12.8**	**3.0**	**5.7**	**3.2**	**7.3**	**6.0**	**7.6**	**29.5**	**51.7**
Business and management	123.9	44.4	3.9	0.9	0.1	7.6	2.6	3.3	23.1	37.9
Computer science................................	127.6	15.7	34.3	0.4	2.4	15.7	1.7	6.4	17.6	33.5
Education...	126.8	1.6	1.5	32.6	—	5.9	4.7	4.4	24.5	51.6
Engineering	136.9	1.4	7.0	0.6	57.9	16.7	1.4	19.0	12.2	20.8
English...	127.5	1.8	1.0	3.0	0.1	4.0	3.5	3.8	22.7	87.5
Fine arts	129.6	1.8	1.3	2.2	0.8	3.1	2.4	2.6	19.8	95.7
Life sciences	128.9	1.1	1.4	2.1	1.0	8.0	33.8	23.3	20.7	37.5
Physical sciences	129.1	1.1	2.7	1.1	2.3	15.0	7.5	49.3	16.9	33.2
Psychology	125.3	3.8	1.2	3.6	0.1	5.0	4.9	4.5	53.6	48.6
Social sciences...................................	125.5	6.2	1.2	1.8	0.1	4.8	2.9	5.1	55.7	47.6
All bachelor's degree recipients of 1992–93										
Mean, all majors	**132.2**	**14.6**	**3.7**	**7.2**	**5.4**	**8.3**	**6.0**	**7.8**	**27.3**	**52.0**
Business and management	129.5	46.8	4.7	0.9	0.7	8.8	2.8	3.6	23.6	37.6
Computer science................................	137.0	17.4	37.1	0.4	5.0	16.7	2.5	7.5	17.3	33.0
Education...	135.9	2.2	1.5	40.1	0.3	6.3	5.4	5.0	24.7	50.5
Engineering	142.1	2.1	7.1	0.3	61.3	17.8	1.3	18.1	11.4	22.8
English...	128.8	2.9	1.4	4.6	0.1	4.3	3.5	4.2	23.2	84.5
Fine arts	133.4	2.7	2.0	3.2	0.9	3.7	2.5	4.2	19.3	94.7
Life sciences	132.5	1.7	1.6	2.9	0.9	8.7	34.8	22.3	21.3	38.2
Physical sciences	137.8	2.6	2.9	1.9	4.0	15.5	8.2	50.6	18.2	33.9
Psychology	129.0	4.0	1.4	4.2	0.3	5.5	5.1	4.2	52.4	52.0
Social sciences...................................	127.9	6.2	1.4	2.3	0.3	5.6	3.3	5.4	54.8	48.6

—Not available.
NOTE: All majors total includes fields not shown separately. Detail may not sum to totals because of rounding.

SOURCE: U.S. Department of Education, National Center for Education Statistics, National Longitudinal Study of 1972, "Third Follow-up" (NLS:72/76); High School and Beyond Longitudinal Study (HS&B-Sr:80/84); and Baccalaureate and Beyond Longitudinal Study (B&B:93). (This table was prepared January 1999.)

Table 314. Number and percentage of degree-granting institutions with first-year undergraduates using various selection criteria for admission, by type and control of institution: Selected years, 2000–01 through 2005–06

Selection criteria	All institutions			Public institutions			Private institutions			Not-for-profit			For-profit		
	Total	4-year	2-year	Total	4-year	2-year	Total	4-year	2-year	Total	4-year	2-year	Total	4-year	2-year
1	2	3	4	5	6	7	8	9	10	11	12	13	14	15	16
Number of institutions with first-year undergraduates															
2000–01	3,717	2,034	1,683	1,647	580	1,067	2,070	1,454	616	1,383	1,247	136	687	207	480
2003–04	3,861	2,158	1,703	1,665	580	1,085	2,196	1,578	618	1,383	1,265	118	813	313	500
2004–05	3,835	2,158	1,677	1,644	584	1,060	2,191	1,574	617	1,355	1,245	110	836	329	507
2005–06	3,880	2,198	1,682	1,638	588	1,050	2,242	1,610	632	1,351	1,240	111	891	370	521
Percent of institutions															
Open admissions															
2000–01	40.2	12.9	73.2	63.8	12.1	91.9	21.4	13.3	40.7	14.0	11.7	34.6	36.5	22.7	42.5
2003–04	43.6	16.9	77.3	66.5	12.9	95.2	26.1	18.4	46.0	14.5	12.6	33.9	46.0	41.5	48.8
2004–05	44.0	17.1	78.1	65.2	13.3	93.0	27.9	18.4	51.9	14.7	12.6	37.3	50.3	42.2	55.4
2005–06	44.7	18.3	79.3	66.1	13.6	95.4	29.2	20.1	52.4	15.3	13.1	40.5	50.2	43.5	54.9
Some admission requirements[1]															
2000–01	58.4	85.8	25.1	35.4	87.4	7.1	76.6	85.2	56.3	84.5	86.8	63.2	60.7	75.4	54.4
2003–04	55.2	82.1	21.1	33.1	86.6	4.5	72.0	80.5	50.3	84.5	86.4	64.4	50.7	56.5	47.0
2004–05	54.2	82.3	18.7	33.3	87.2	4.5	70.1	80.5	43.5	82.8	85.5	54.2	48.5	60.4	41.0
2005–06	53.4	80.5	18.0	33.6	86.1	4.3	67.9	78.5	40.8	84.2	86.5	57.7	43.2	51.6	37.2
Secondary grades															
2000–01	34.6	58.7	5.5	23.9	63.4	2.4	43.0	56.7	10.7	60.1	64.1	23.5	8.7	12.6	7.1
2003–04	33.9	57.0	4.5	24.6	66.6	2.1	40.9	53.5	8.6	61.5	64.7	27.1	5.9	8.6	4.2
2004–05	34.2	57.7	4.3	25.1	68.3	2.0	41.0	53.9	8.3	61.0	64.5	23.7	7.0	10.9	4.6
2005–06	34.1	57.1	4.2	25.9	68.4	2.2	40.1	53.0	7.4	62.8	66.2	25.2	5.7	8.6	3.6
Secondary class rank															
2000–01	13.7	24.3	1.0	10.9	30.3	0.3	16.0	21.9	2.3	23.2	25.1	5.9	1.6	2.4	1.3
2003–04	11.8	20.5	0.7	10.3	29.3	0.2	12.8	17.2	1.6	19.8	21.1	5.9	1.0	1.6	0.6
2004–05	11.6	20.2	0.7	10.5	29.8	0.2	12.4	16.7	1.6	19.2	20.4	5.9	1.0	1.6	0.6
2005–06	11.3	19.4	0.7	10.4	28.7	0.2	11.9	16.0	1.6	19.3	20.5	6.3	0.7	0.8	0.6
Secondary school record															
2000–01	45.8	70.3	16.2	29.4	72.9	5.8	58.7	69.2	34.1	73.2	75.5	52.2	29.5	30.9	29.0
2003–04	48.6	73.4	17.3	29.5	77.1	4.1	63.1	72.1	40.3	77.2	78.9	59.3	39.1	44.4	35.8
2004–05	48.3	74.3	15.3	30.0	78.3	4.2	62.1	72.8	34.6	76.4	78.8	50.8	37.6	48.6	30.8
2005–06	48.5	73.3	15.9	30.8	78.2	4.2	61.4	71.6	35.4	77.6	79.7	55.0	36.7	44.3	31.3
College preparatory program															
2000–01	15.5	27.3	1.2	16.2	44.0	1.1	14.9	20.7	1.3	22.1	24.1	4.4	0.4	0.5	0.4
2003–04	15.5	27.2	0.8	17.5	48.4	0.9	14.0	19.3	0.5	22.2	24.0	2.5	0.1	0.3	0.0
2004–05	15.6	27.4	0.6	17.3	48.1	0.8	14.3	19.8	0.3	22.6	24.6	1.7	0.2	0.6	0.0
2005–06	15.2	26.4	0.6	17.4	47.1	0.8	13.6	18.8	0.3	22.4	24.3	1.8	0.2	0.5	0.0
Recommendations															
2000–01	20.4	34.4	3.5	2.7	7.4	0.2	34.4	45.1	9.3	46.6	49.2	22.8	10.0	20.8	5.4
2003–04	19.7	33.0	2.8	2.8	7.6	0.3	32.5	42.4	7.1	49.2	51.8	22.0	3.9	4.5	3.6
2004–05	19.2	32.5	2.3	2.9	7.9	0.2	31.6	41.6	6.1	47.9	50.7	18.6	3.8	4.8	3.2
2005–06	19.2	31.9	2.5	2.9	7.7	0.2	31.1	40.8	6.3	49.1	51.5	23.4	3.7	5.1	2.7
Demonstration of competencies[2]															
2000–01	8.0	12.1	3.0	2.2	5.0	0.7	12.7	15.0	7.1	12.1	12.7	7.4	13.7	29.0	7.1
2003–04	7.1	9.5	4.1	2.2	5.7	0.3	10.9	11.0	10.7	10.1	10.3	8.5	12.2	13.7	11.2
2004–05	6.9	9.5	3.5	2.2	5.9	0.3	10.4	10.9	9.1	9.7	9.9	7.6	11.6	15.0	9.4
2005–06	7.0	9.8	3.3	2.3	6.1	0.2	10.3	11.1	8.4	10.2	10.3	9.0	10.5	13.8	8.3
Test scores[3]															
2000–01	47.2	72.5	16.7	33.2	83.4	5.8	58.5	68.2	35.6	70.3	73.4	41.9	34.6	36.7	33.8
2003–04	43.3	68.5	11.4	31.3	83.1	3.6	52.4	63.1	25.1	68.4	71.5	34.7	25.2	29.1	22.8
2004–05	39.7	65.0	7.7	31.4	83.4	3.6	46.0	58.2	14.9	66.5	70.3	26.3	11.2	9.6	12.2
2005–06	36.5	62.5	2.6	31.1	82.3	2.4	40.5	55.2	3.0	65.7	70.5	12.6	2.2	4.1	1.0
TOEFL[4]															
2000–01	43.4	71.2	9.9	30.2	77.4	4.6	54.0	68.7	19.2	66.2	70.1	30.9	29.3	60.4	15.8
2003–04	42.5	69.3	8.5	30.2	79.5	3.9	51.8	65.6	16.7	67.3	70.8	29.7	25.5	44.4	13.6
2004–05	42.0	69.3	7.4	30.5	80.0	4.0	50.8	65.4	13.4	66.4	70.2	26.3	24.1	46.0	10.4
2005–06	41.5	67.9	7.1	31.0	79.3	3.9	49.3	63.8	12.3	67.0	70.6	27.0	22.4	41.1	9.2
No admission requirements, only recommendations															
2000–01	1.4	1.2	1.7	0.8	0.5	0.9	1.9	1.5	2.9	1.5	1.4	2.2	2.8	1.9	3.1
2003–04	1.2	1.0	1.5	0.4	0.5	0.3	1.9	1.1	3.7	1.0	0.9	1.7	3.3	1.9	4.2
2004–05	1.1	0.6	1.7	0.2	0.2	0.2	1.8	0.8	4.4	0.5	0.4	1.7	4.1	2.6	5.0
2005–06	1.8	1.1	2.7	0.3	0.3	0.3	2.9	1.4	6.8	0.5	0.4	1.8	6.6	4.9	7.9

[1]Many institutions have more than one admission requirement.
[2]Formal demonstration of competencies (e.g., portfolios, certificates of mastery, assessment instruments).
[3]Includes SAT, ACT, or other admission tests.
[4]Test of English as a Foreign Language.

NOTE: Some data have been revised from previously published figures. Detail may not sum to totals because of rounding.
SOURCE: U.S. Department of Education, National Center for Education Statistics, 2000–01 through 2005–06 Integrated Postsecondary Education Data System, Fall 2000 through Fall 2005. (This table was prepared September 2006.)

Table 315. Number of applications, admissions, and enrollees; their distribution across institutions accepting various percentages of applications; and SAT and ACT scores of applicants, by type and control of institution: 2004–05

Applications, admissions, enrollees, and SAT and ACT scores	All institutions			Public institutions			Private institutions								
							Total			Not-for-profit			For-profit		
	Total	4-year	2-year	Total	4-year	2-year	Total	4-year	2-year	Total	4-year	2-year	Total	4-year	2-year
1	2	3	4	5	6	7	8	9	10	11	12	13	14	15	16
Number of undergraduate institutions reporting application data[1]	3,821	2,145	1,676	1,643	583	1,060	2,178	1,562	616	1,349	1,239	110	829	323	506
Percentage distribution of institutions by their acceptance of applications	100.0	100.0	100.0	100.0	100.0	100.0	100.0	100.0	100.0	100.0	100.0	100.0	100.0	100.0	100.0
No application criteria	44.4	17.2	79.4	66.1	13.2	95.2	28.1	18.6	52.1	15.0	12.8	40.0	49.3	40.9	54.7
More than 90 percent accepted	9.2	10.7	7.3	4.9	10.3	2.0	12.4	10.9	16.4	11.1	11.1	10.9	14.6	9.9	17.6
75.0 to 89.9 percent accepted	16.1	25.2	4.5	11.2	29.3	1.2	19.9	23.7	10.2	25.5	27.0	9.1	10.7	11.1	10.5
50.0 to 74.9 percent accepted	20.6	33.0	4.9	13.1	35.2	1.0	26.3	32.1	11.5	33.7	34.8	21.8	14.2	22.0	9.3
25.0 to 49.9 percent accepted	8.2	11.8	3.6	0.8	9.8	0.6	11.5	12.5	8.8	11.7	11.6	12.7	11.1	16.1	7.9
10.0 to 24.9 percent accepted	1.3	2.0	0.3	0.0	2.2	0.0	1.6	1.9	0.8	2.6	2.4	4.5	0.0	0.0	0.0
Less than 10 percent accepted	0.1	0.1	0.1	0.0	0.0	0.0	0.2	0.2	0.2	0.3	0.2	0.9	0.0	0.0	0.0
Number of applications (in thousands)	5,765	5,580	185	3,244	3,149	95	2,521	2,431	90	2,335	2,318	17	186	113	73
Percentage distribution of applications by institutions' acceptance of applications	100.0	100.0	100.0	100.0	100.0	100.0	100.0	100.0	100.0	100.0	100.0	100.0	100.0	100.0	100.0
No application criteria	†	†	†	†	†	†	†	†	†	†	†	†	†	†	†
More than 90 percent accepted	4.8	4.0	30.4	5.7	4.8	34.7	3.7	2.9	25.8	2.6	2.5	16.4	17.2	10.3	28.0
75.0 to 89.9 percent accepted	24.7	24.9	17.8	27.9	28.3	15.1	20.6	20.6	20.6	20.8	20.9	14.9	17.9	15.3	22.0
50.0 to 74.9 percent accepted	42.2	42.7	25.7	45.7	46.3	24.0	37.6	38.0	27.6	37.6	37.6	47.8	37.5	46.9	22.8
25.0 to 49.9 percent accepted	21.0	20.8	25.9	15.8	15.5	26.2	27.7	27.7	25.5	27.7	27.7	18.2	27.3	27.4	27.2
10.0 to 24.9 percent accepted	7.2	7.5	0.2	4.9	5.1	0.0	10.2	10.5	0.4	11.0	11.1	2.0	0.0	0.0	0.0
Less than 10 percent accepted	0.1	0.1	0.1	0.0	0.0	0.0	0.2	0.2	0.2	0.2	0.2	0.8	0.0	0.0	0.0
Number of admissions (in thousands)	3,514	3,382	133	2,082	2,013	69	1,433	1,369	64	1,309	1,298	11	123	71	52
Percentage distribution of admissions by institutions acceptance of applications	100.0	100.0	100.0	100.0	100.0	100.0	100.0	100.0	100.0	100.0	100.0	100.0	100.0	100.0	100.0
No application criteria	†	†	†	†	†	†	†	†	†	†	†	†	†	†	†
More than 90 percent accepted	7.5	6.2	41.6	8.4	7.1	47.1	6.3	4.9	35.7	4.4	4.3	23.9	25.6	16.2	38.3
75.0 to 89.9 percent accepted	33.0	33.4	20.8	35.4	36.0	17.7	29.4	29.6	24.2	30.1	30.2	18.4	22.1	19.6	25.5
50.0 to 74.9 percent accepted	43.7	44.5	22.6	44.5	45.4	20.5	42.5	43.3	25.0	43.2	43.2	47.0	34.9	45.7	20.2
25.0 to 49.9 percent accepted	13.7	13.6	14.8	10.0	10.0	14.7	18.7	18.9	15.0	18.9	18.9	10.2	17.4	18.5	16.0
10.0 to 24.9 percent accepted	2.1	2.2	0.0	1.5	1.5	0.0	3.1	3.2	0.1	3.4	3.4	0.4	0.0	0.0	0.0
Less than 10 percent accepted	0.0	0.0	0.1	0.0	0.0	0.0	0.1	0.0	0.0	0.0	0.0	0.1	0.0	0.0	0.0
Number of enrollees (in thousands)	1,446	1,340	106	898	843	55	548	497	51	453	445	8	95	51	44
Percentage distribution of enrollees by institutions' acceptance of applications	100.0	100.0	100.0	100.0	100.0	100.0	100.0	100.0	100.0	100.0	100.0	100.0	100.0	100.0	100.0
No application criteria	†	†	†	†	†	†	†	†	†	†	†	†	†	†	†
More than 90 percent accepted	10.0	7.6	39.5	10.6	8.5	42.4	9.0	6.2	36.5	5.4	5.0	26.1	26.3	16.0	38.3
75.0 to 89.9 percent accepted	32.7	33.8	19.0	35.3	36.5	17.0	28.5	29.3	21.1	30.2	30.4	18.9	20.7	20.1	21.4
50.0 to 74.9 percent accepted	40.9	42.2	24.0	42.3	43.6	23.0	38.5	39.9	25.2	40.0	39.9	42.4	31.7	39.7	22.1
25.0 to 49.9 percent accepted	13.6	13.3	17.4	9.9	9.4	17.6	19.6	19.9	17.2	19.3	19.4	12.0	21.4	24.2	18.1
10.0 to 24.9 percent accepted	2.8	3.0	0.0	1.9	2.0	0.0	4.2	4.7	0.1	5.1	5.2	0.5	0.0	0.0	0.0
Less than 10 percent accepted	0.0	0.0	0.0	0.0	0.0	0.0	0.1	0.1	0.0	0.1	0.1	0.2	0.0	0.0	0.0
Mean SAT scores of applicants															
Critical reading, 25th percentile[2]	478	480	405	462	466	410	486	488	398	486	488	391	483	475	‡
Critical reading, 75th percentile[2]	589	591	530	570	573	516	599	600	554	600	600	554	570	570	‡
Mathematics, 25th percentile[2]	479	482	399	468	472	400	485	487	399	485	487	392	474	468	‡
Mathematics, 75th percentile[2]	590	592	523	577	581	513	597	598	538	597	598	538	560	560	‡
Mean ACT scores of applicants															
Composite, 25th percentile[2]	19.7	19.9	15.8	19.0	19.3	15.7	20.1	20.1	16.1	20.1	20.1	17.0	18.5	20.4	‡
Composite, 75th percentile[2]	24.8	25.0	20.5	23.9	24.3	20.1	25.2	25.3	21.6	25.3	25.3	21.6	24.3	24.3	‡
English, 25th percentile[2]	18.7	18.8	14.6	17.9	18.2	14.7	19.1	19.2	14.4	19.1	19.2	15.4	17.3	20.0	‡
English, 75th percentile[2]	25.0	25.2	20.8	24.0	24.3	20.5	25.6	25.6	21.5	25.6	25.6	21.5	24.4	24.4	‡
Mathematics, 25th percentile[2]	18.5	18.7	15.2	18.1	18.4	15.3	18.8	18.9	15.0	18.8	18.9	16.3	16.8	20.0	‡
Mathematics, 75th percentile[2]	24.3	24.6	19.7	23.7	24.2	19.3	24.7	24.8	21.1	24.7	24.8	21.1	24.2	24.2	‡

†Not applicable.
‡Reporting standards not met.
[1]Excludes institutions not enrolling freshmen. The total on this table differs slightly from other counts of undergraduate institutions because approximately 0.4 percent of undergraduate institutions did not report application information.
[2]Data are only for institutions that require test scores for admission. Relatively few 2-year institutions require test scores for admissions.

NOTE: Excludes information for the 0.4 percent of institutions that did not respond to survey questions. Detail may not sum to totals because of rounding.
SOURCE: U.S. Department of Education, National Center for Education Statistics, 2004–05 Integrated Postsecondary Education Data System, Fall 2004. (This table was prepared April 2006.)

Table 316. Percentage of degree-granting institutions offering remedial services, by type and control of institution: 1989–90 through 2005–06

Type and control of institution	1989–90	1990–91	1991–92	1992–93	1993–94	1994–95	1995–96	1996–97	1997–98	1998–99	1999–2000	2000–01	2001–02	2002–03	2003–04	2004–05	2005–06	Change in percentage points 1989–90 to 1996–97	1997–98 to 2005–06
1	2	3	4	5	6	7	8	9	10	11	12	13	14	15	16	17	18	19	20
All institutions	**76.6**	**77.7**	**78.6**	**78.5**	**79.0**	**79.8**	**79.5**	**80.0**	**76.7**	**76.1**	**76.1**	**75.1**	**73.3**	**72.5**	**72.1**	**72.6**	**72.2**	**3.4**	**-4.5**
All 4-year colleges	69.6	70.6	71.4	71.5	72.2	73.6	73.0	73.1	72.5	72.0	71.6	71.4	69.0	67.6	67.1	67.4	66.9	3.5	-5.5
All 2-year colleges	87.2	88.4	89.2	88.8	89.5	89.1	89.4	91.0	82.2	81.5	82.2	80.4	79.5	79.5	79.7	80.3	80.2	3.8	-2.0
Public institutions	92.4	93.0	93.9	93.5	93.5	93.7	93.7	94.0	93.8	93.6	93.5	93.1	92.3	91.7	91.3	90.6	90.2	1.6	-3.7
4-year colleges	82.9	83.5	84.5	84.5	84.6	85.3	85.4	85.1	85.2	84.2	83.6	81.7	79.9	78.4	77.3	75.6	75.2	2.2	-10.0
2-year colleges	98.2	98.9	99.6	98.8	98.7	98.6	98.6	99.2	98.7	99.0	99.2	99.7	99.4	99.4	99.5	99.6	99.3	1.0	0.6
Private institutions	64.1	65.6	66.3	66.4	67.4	68.6	68.0	68.6	64.2	63.6	63.9	62.8	60.2	59.0	59.0	60.4	60.4	4.4	-3.9
4-year colleges	64.5	65.6	66.4	66.5	67.5	69.2	68.4	68.6	67.8	67.7	67.4	67.9	65.3	63.9	63.7	64.7	64.2	4.1	-3.6
2-year colleges	63.0	65.5	65.8	65.8	67.0	66.6	66.3	68.4	55.1	52.8	54.4	48.8	45.0	44.8	44.8	47.4	48.8	5.4	-6.2
Not-for-profit	65.0	65.6	66.2	66.7	67.7	69.3	68.9	69.2	69.0	68.6	69.2	67.6	66.1	65.4	65.0	63.1	62.2	4.2	-6.8
4-year colleges	64.2	64.9	65.8	66.2	67.0	68.7	68.3	68.3	68.3	68.3	68.5	67.0	65.5	64.7	64.0	62.5	61.3	4.1	-6.9
2-year colleges	71.8	71.3	69.9	71.5	73.5	74.0	73.3	77.3	75.4	71.6	76.7	73.6	72.6	74.0	77.1	71.4	74.3	5.6	-1.1
For-profit	59.5	65.6	66.6	64.6	65.6	65.2	63.5	65.2	51.7	51.1	51.5	52.7	48.0	45.6	47.4	55.4	57.2	5.7	5.5
4-year colleges	71.7	81.3	79.2	73.7	76.3	76.0	69.2	72.7	63.9	63.4	60.1	72.9	64.5	59.6	62.0	73.7	75.0	1.0	11.1
2-year colleges	57.0	62.0	63.2	62.0	62.1	60.8	60.5	60.8	47.5	46.2	47.7	41.8	37.3	37.2	37.3	42.2	43.4	3.8	-4.1

NOTE: Data through 1995–96 are for institutions of higher education, while later data are for degree-granting institutions. Degree-granting institutions grant associate's or higher degrees and participate in Title IV federal financial aid programs. The degree-granting classification is very similar to the earlier higher education classification, but it includes more 2-year colleges and excludes a few higher education institutions that did not grant degrees. (See Guide to Sources for details.)

SOURCE: U.S. Department of Education, National Center for Education Statistics, 1989–90 through 2005–06 Integrated Postsecondary Education Data System, "Institutional Characteristics Survey" (IPEDS-IC:89–99), and Fall 2000 through Fall 2005. (This table was prepared September 2006.)

Table 317. Percentage distribution of enrollment and completion status of first-time postsecondary students starting during the 1995–96 academic year, by type of institution and other student characteristics: 2001

Student and institution characteristic	Students starting in 2-year institutions						Students starting in 4-year institutions					
	Highest degree attained				No degree, still enrolled	No degree, not enrolled	Highest degree attained				No degree, still enrolled	No degree, not enrolled
	Total, any degree[1]	Certificate	Associate's	Bachelor's[2]			Total, any degree[1]	Certificate	Associate's	Bachelor's[2]		
1	2	3	4	5	6	7	8	9	10	11	12	13
Total	**38.4** (1.7)	**11.5** (1.2)	**17.3** (1.3)	**9.7** (1.1)	**16.4** (1.4)	**45.2** (1.6)	**65.1** (1.0)	**2.7** (0.3)	**4.0** (0.4)	**58.4** (1.2)	**14.4** (0.6)	**20.5** (0.8)
Male	39.2 (2.4)	10.8 (1.6)	18.7 (1.9)	9.7 (1.5)	18.0 (2.2)	42.8 (2.4)	60.6 (1.4)	2.5 (0.4)	3.6 (0.6)	54.6 (1.5)	16.2 (0.9)	23.2 (1.1)
Female	37.7 (2.2)	12.0 (1.6)	15.9 (1.7)	9.8 (1.4)	14.9 (1.7)	47.4 (2.2)	68.7 (1.3)	2.9 (0.3)	4.3 (0.5)	61.6 (1.4)	12.9 (0.8)	18.4 (1.0)
Age when first enrolled												
18 years or younger	43.8 (2.3)	7.3 (1.2)	19.4 (2.0)	17.0 (1.9)	17.8 (2.1)	38.4 (2.1)	70.0 (1.0)	1.8 (0.2)	3.4 (0.4)	64.7 (1.1)	13.4 (0.6)	16.6 (0.7)
19 years	38.2 (4.1)	8.2 (2.0)	24.3 (4.0)	5.7 (2.2)	20.9 (3.6)	40.9 (4.0)	57.1 (2.8)	3.3 (0.9)	6.0 (1.3)	47.9 (2.9)	16.4 (2.0)	26.6 (2.3)
20 to 23 years	29.9 (4.2)	13.1 (3.0)	13.0 (3.4)	3.7 (1.6)	20.1 (4.2)	50.0 (4.8)	37.7 (3.8)	8.7 (2.1)	6.7 (2.1)	22.3 (3.0)	20.9 (3.0)	41.4 (3.6)
24 to 29 years	36.5 (4.8)	25.6 (4.6)	8.4 (2.2)	2.5 (1.5)	11.0 (3.5)	52.6 (5.1)	34.4 (5.5)	4.3 (1.8)	7.2 (3.5)	23.0 (4.7)	22.7 (5.8)	42.9 (6.3)
30 years or over	30.6 (5.5)	14.1 (3.8)	14.5 (3.3)	2.0 (1.5)	8.7 (2.4)	60.7 (5.8)	26.1 (4.3)	11.5 (3.5)	4.3 (1.6)	10.3 (2.8)	17.0 (4.2)	56.9 (5.1)
Race/ethnicity												
White	40.5 (2.0)	10.9 (1.3)	18.2 (1.5)	11.4 (1.6)	16.5 (1.7)	43.0 (2.0)	68.1 (1.1)	2.4 (0.3)	3.8 (0.4)	61.9 (1.3)	12.5 (0.7)	19.4 (0.9)
Black	28.4 (4.2)	16.7 (4.0)	8.5 (2.3)	3.2 (1.3)	13.3 (2.9)	58.3 (4.3)	51.3 (2.6)	4.6 (1.0)	3.2 (0.8)	43.4 (2.8)	20.6 (2.3)	28.2 (2.2)
Hispanic	34.3 (4.8)	11.1 (3.2)	17.8 (3.2)	5.5 (2.3)	18.1 (3.3)	47.6 (4.8)	53.9 (2.3)	3.1 (0.7)	6.8 (1.7)	44.0 (2.4)	20.4 (1.8)	25.7 (2.1)
Asian/Pacific Islander	41.9 (9.2)	11.6 (6.4)	23.0 (8.2)	7.4 (3.7)	21.2 (7.7)	36.9 (8.7)	71.3 (3.1)	0.2 (0.2)	2.0 (0.8)	69.1 (3.1)	13.9 (2.3)	14.8 (2.4)
American Indian/Alaska Native	‡ (†)	‡ (†)	‡ (†)	‡ (†)	‡ (†)	‡ (†)	55.4 (10.6)	‡ (†)	3.7 (3.7)	51.7 (10.7)	26.1 (8.4)	18.5 (6.8)
Highest education level of parents												
High school diploma or less	36.5 (2.3)	13.5 (1.8)	17.0 (1.9)	6.0 (1.2)	12.4 (1.6)	51.1 (2.4)	52.0 (1.6)	4.1 (0.6)	4.8 (0.6)	43.1 (1.6)	16.5 (1.3)	31.5 (1.5)
Some postsecondary	32.8 (3.3)	10.1 (2.1)	14.3 (2.6)	8.4 (2.0)	19.0 (2.8)	48.2 (2.9)	59.5 (1.9)	3.1 (0.7)	5.4 (1.1)	50.9 (2.1)	16.4 (1.4)	24.2 (1.6)
Bachelor's degree	47.7 (4.2)	9.1 (2.3)	22.4 (3.7)	16.2 (3.2)	18.8 (3.5)	33.5 (4.0)	72.1 (1.5)	1.8 (0.4)	4.0 (0.6)	66.3 (1.5)	13.4 (1.1)	14.5 (1.1)
Advanced degree	45.4 (6.0)	3.1 (2.0)	17.2 (4.4)	25.2 (5.5)	25.2 (5.4)	29.4 (6.0)	76.5 (1.7)	1.2 (0.3)	1.4 (0.3)	73.9 (1.7)	11.7 (1.2)	11.8 (1.2)
Dependency status when first enrolled												
Dependent	42.1 (2.2)	8.2 (1.2)	20.1 (1.8)	13.8 (1.7)	18.3 (1.9)	39.6 (2.1)	68.0 (1.0)	2.1 (0.2)	3.6 (0.4)	62.1 (1.2)	14.0 (0.6)	18.1 (0.7)
Independent	32.9 (3.1)	17.6 (2.4)	12.3 (2.4)	3.0 (0.9)	13.8 (2.4)	53.4 (3.5)	35.9 (2.9)	8.8 (1.7)	6.4 (1.6)	20.6 (2.3)	19.1 (2.5)	45.0 (3.2)
Dependent student family income in 1994												
Less than $25,000	43.0 (3.8)	10.9 (2.6)	24.5 (3.4)	7.6 (2.1)	14.3 (2.6)	42.7 (3.5)	58.8 (1.8)	3.4 (0.7)	5.1 (1.0)	50.3 (2.1)	18.6 (1.5)	22.6 (1.5)
$25,000 to $44,999	41.2 (4.5)	10.5 (2.3)	16.4 (2.9)	14.3 (2.7)	19.1 (3.0)	39.6 (4.6)	61.7 (1.7)	2.3 (0.4)	4.4 (0.8)	55.0 (1.7)	15.1 (1.3)	23.1 (1.4)
$45,000 to $69,999	40.2 (3.8)	5.3 (1.7)	22.1 (3.2)	12.8 (2.5)	19.3 (3.5)	40.5 (4.0)	69.1 (1.6)	1.7 (0.4)	3.7 (0.7)	63.6 (1.7)	13.2 (1.0)	17.7 (1.3)
$70,000 or more	44.7 (5.5)	4.5 (1.8)	15.8 (3.6)	24.4 (4.5)	22.1 (4.2)	33.2 (4.8)	77.4 (1.3)	1.6 (0.4)	2.0 (0.4)	73.8 (1.5)	10.7 (1.0)	11.9 (0.9)
Timing of postsecondary enrollment												
Did not delay[3]	43.9 (2.3)	7.0 (1.1)	20.9 (2.0)	15.9 (1.8)	18.4 (2.0)	37.7 (2.1)	69.2 (1.0)	1.9 (0.2)	3.3 (0.4)	64.0 (1.1)	13.7 (0.6)	17.1 (0.7)
Delayed entry	32.8 (2.7)	15.6 (2.0)	13.7 (1.8)	3.5 (1.0)	14.9 (2.0)	52.3 (2.8)	45.0 (2.2)	6.6 (1.0)	7.0 (1.3)	31.4 (2.1)	18.0 (1.6)	37.0 (2.2)
Attendance status when first enrolled												
Full-time	47.3 (2.4)	10.2 (1.4)	21.3 (1.9)	15.8 (2.1)	15.9 (2.0)	36.8 (2.3)	69.3 (1.0)	1.9 (0.2)	4.0 (0.4)	63.3 (1.2)	12.7 (0.6)	18.0 (0.8)
Part-time	29.5 (3.2)	13.9 (2.7)	12.2 (2.3)	3.4 (1.0)	15.6 (2.4)	54.9 (3.4)	33.4 (3.2)	7.3 (2.0)	2.1 (0.8)	23.9 (3.3)	27.3 (3.0)	39.3 (3.4)
Intensity of enrollment through 2001												
Always part-time	13.2 (2.9)	11.5 (2.8)	1.7 (0.8)	# (†)	13.3 (3.0)	73.4 (3.8)	10.3 (2.9)	9.7 (2.9)	0.6 (0.6)	# (†)	12.9 (3.8)	76.8 (4.1)
Mixed	42.3 (2.5)	12.6 (1.7)	20.8 (2.0)	8.9 (1.3)	21.7 (2.1)	36.0 (2.2)	51.7 (1.5)	4.4 (0.6)	5.5 (0.6)	41.8 (1.6)	26.6 (1.3)	21.7 (1.1)
Always full-time	49.5 (3.2)	9.3 (1.4)	22.0 (2.8)	18.1 (3.1)	9.1 (1.8)	41.4 (3.1)	74.2 (1.1)	1.5 (0.2)	3.3 (0.5)	69.4 (1.2)	8.1 (0.6)	17.8 (0.9)
Degree goal at first institution												
Certificate	45.2 (5.1)	38.4 (5.3)	6.2 (2.3)	0.7 (0.4)	6.8 (2.5)	48.0 (4.8)	37.7 (7.0)	16.1 (6.2)	14.2 (7.5)	7.5 (3.0)	19.4 (6.5)	42.8 (6.7)
Associate's degree	40.9 (2.3)	8.7 (1.3)	24.7 (2.1)	7.5 (1.4)	15.6 (2.0)	43.5 (2.3)	52.6 (4.2)	7.3 (2.4)	24.7 (3.7)	20.7 (3.3)	8.9 (2.3)	38.5 (4.2)
Bachelor's degree	40.3[4] (3.7)	6.0[4] (1.9)	11.7[4] (2.4)	22.6[4] (3.3)	21.9[4] (3.5)	37.8[4] (3.4)	67.6 (1.0)	2.1 (0.3)	2.7 (0.3)	62.9 (1.1)	14.2 (0.7)	18.2 (0.7)

See notes at end of table.

Table 317. Percentage distribution of enrollment and completion status of first-time postsecondary students starting during the 1995–96 academic year, by type of institution and other student characteristics: 2001—Continued

	Students starting in 2-year institutions						Students starting in 4-year institutions					
	Highest degree attained				No degree, still enrolled	No degree, not enrolled	Highest degree attained				No degree, still enrolled	No degree, not enrolled
Student and institution characteristic	Total, any degree[1]	Certificate	Associate's	Bachelor's[2]			Total, any degree[1]	Certificate	Associate's	Bachelor's[2]		
1	2	3	4	5	6	7	8	9	10	11	12	13
Worked while enrolled, 1995–96												
Did not work	43.0 (3.0)	13.9 (2.3)	21.5 (2.8)	7.6 (1.9)	10.4 (2.5)	46.6 (3.1)	71.1 (1.3)	2.0 (0.4)	3.7 (0.7)	65.3 (1.6)	11.9 (0.8)	17.0 (1.1)
Worked part time	44.7 (2.6)	8.5 (1.5)	20.9 (2.1)	15.2 (2.0)	18.4 (2.4)	36.9 (2.3)	65.0 (1.3)	2.3 (0.4)	4.0 (0.4)	58.6 (1.4)	14.7 (0.8)	20.3 (1.0)
Worked full time	27.2 (2.6)	14.3 (2.2)	9.6 (1.5)	3.4 (0.9)	17.0 (2.5)	55.8 (2.9)	41.7 (2.6)	7.1 (1.3)	4.2 (1.1)	30.5 (2.5)	21.7 (2.2)	36.6 (2.5)
Control of first institution												
Public	36.7 (1.8)	10.1 (1.3)	16.4 (1.4)	10.3 (1.3)	17.4 (1.6)	45.9 (1.7)	60.5 (1.2)	2.8 (0.3)	4.4 (0.6)	53.3 (1.4)	17.4 (0.8)	22.2 (1.0)
Private, not for profit	58.9 (5.4)	19.3 (4.6)	27.8 (3.9)	11.8 (3.3)	8.4 (2.4)	32.7 (4.6)	73.6 (1.7)	1.8 (0.3)	2.8 (0.5)	68.9 (2.0)	9.3 (0.8)	17.1 (1.3)
Private, for profit	55.6 (3.2)	27.8 (3.9)	25.8 (3.9)	2.0 (0.8)	4.3 (1.2)	40.0 (3.4)	52.8 (10.5)	17.9 (7.2)	14.9 (6.0)	20.0 (5.1)	11.1 (3.1)	36.1 (8.6)
Socioeconomic status in 1995–96[5]												
Not disadvantaged	41.7 (2.8)	8.9 (1.8)	18.1 (2.1)	14.6 (2.0)	20.4 (2.7)	38.0 (2.7)	71.4 (1.1)	2.0 (0.3)	3.3 (0.4)	66.1 (1.3)	12.3 (0.7)	16.3 (0.8)
Minimally disadvantaged	33.9 (2.4)	12.8 (1.7)	14.9 (1.8)	6.2 (1.4)	13.1 (1.6)	53.0 (2.7)	59.8 (1.6)	3.7 (0.6)	5.4 (0.7)	50.8 (1.7)	16.4 (1.2)	23.8 (1.3)
Moderately or highly disadvantaged	43.7 (3.6)	14.6 (3.0)	21.6 (3.4)	7.5 (1.9)	14.5 (2.7)	41.8 (3.7)	47.1 (2.0)	3.7 (0.8)	3.8 (0.8)	39.6 (2.1)	19.5 (1.9)	33.4 (2.1)

†Not applicable.
#Rounds to zero.
‡Reporting standards not met.
[1]Includes a small percentage of students who had attained a degree and were still enrolled. Includes recipients of degrees not shown separately.
[2]Includes a small percentage of students who had attained an advanced degree.
[3]Includes students with a standard high school diploma who enrolled in postsecondary education in the same year as their graduation.
[4]Includes students whose goal was to transfer to a 4-year institution.

[5]Determined by a socioeconomic diversity index that includes parental income as a percentage of the 1994 federal poverty level, parental education, and the proportion of the student body at the student's high school that was eligible for free or reduced-price lunch.
NOTE: Data reflect completion and enrollment status by spring 2001 of first-time postsecondary students starting in academic year 1995–96. Race categories exclude persons of Hispanic origin. Detail may not sum to totals because of rounding. Standard errors appear in parentheses.
SOURCE: U.S. Department of Education, National Center for Education Statistics, 1996/01 Beginning Postsecondary Students Longitudinal Study (BPS:96/01). (This table was prepared August 2003.)

Table 318. Scores on Graduate Record Examination (GRE) general and subject tests: 1965 through 2005

			General test sections				Subject tests									
Academic year ending	Number of GRE takers	GRE takers as a percent of bachelor's degrees[1]	Verbal	Quantitative	Analytical reasoning	Analytical writing	Biochemistry, cell and molecular biology	Biology	Chemistry	Computer science	Education	Engineering	Literature	Mathematics	Physics	Psychology
1	2	3	4	5	6	7	8	9	10	11	12	13	14	15	16	17
1965	93,792	18.7	530 (124)	533 (137)	† (†)	† (†)	†	617 (117)	628 (114)	†	481 (86)	618 (108)	591 (95)	—	— (†)	556 (91)
1966	123,960	23.8	520 (124)	528 (133)	† (†)	† (†)	†	610 (115)	618 (110)	†	474 (87)	609 (106)	588 (94)	—	— (†)	552 (91)
1967	151,134	27.0	519 (125)	528 (134)	† (†)	† (†)	†	613 (114)	615 (104)	†	476 (90)	603 (104)	582 (91)	—	— (†)	553 (93)
1968	182,432	28.8	520 (124)	527 (135)	† (†)	† (†)	†	614 (114)	617 (104)	†	478 (87)	601 (105)	572 (91)	—	— (†)	547 (93)
1969	206,113	28.3	515 (124)	524 (132)	† (†)	† (†)	†	613 (112)	613 (104)	†	477 (88)	591 (103)	569 (89)	—	— (†)	543 (89)
1970	265,359	33.5	503 (123)	516 (132)	† (†)	† (†)	†	603 (111)	613 (113)	†	462 (92)	586 (110)	556 (90)	—	— (†)	532 (91)
1971	293,600	35.0	497 (125)	512 (134)	† (†)	† (†)	†	603 (114)	618 (117)	†	457 (95)	587 (115)	546 (91)	—	— (†)	530 (92)
1972	293,506	33.1	494 (126)	508 (136)	† (†)	† (†)	†	606 (115)	624 (124)	†	446 (93)	594 (119)	544 (96)	—	— (†)	528 (92)
1973	290,104	31.5	497 (125)	512 (135)	† (†)	† (†)	†	619 (110)	630 (114)	†	459 (96)	593 (114)	545 (96)	—	— (†)	529 (92)
1974	301,070	31.8	492 (126)	509 (137)	† (†)	† (†)	†	624 (110)	634 (115)	†	452 (93)	591 (121)	547 (99)	—	— (†)	530 (95)
1975	298,335	32.3	493 (125)	508 (137)	† (†)	† (†)	†	— (†)	— (†)	—	— (†)	— (†)	— (†)	—	— (†)	— (†)
1976	299,292	32.3	492 (127)	510 (138)	† (†)	† (†)	†	627 (112)	627 (107)	—	454 (93)	594 (119)	539 (101)	—	— (†)	531 (93)
1977	287,715	31.3	490 (129)	514 (139)	498 (126)	† (†)	†	625 (113)	630 (109)	—	453 (93)	592 (115)	532 (101)	—	— (†)	532 (95)
1978	286,383	31.1	484 (128)	518 (135)	504 (128)	† (†)	†	622 (113)	624 (108)	—	452 (91)	594 (114)	530 (102)	—	— (†)	529 (97)
1979	282,482	30.7	476 (130)	517 (135)	512 (129)	† (†)	†	621 (117)	623 (104)	—	451 (89)	592 (115)	525 (102)	—	— (†)	530 (97)
1980	272,281	29.3	474 (131)	522 (136)	516 (129)	† (†)	†	619 (115)	618 (105)	—	449 (90)	590 (116)	521 (105)	—	— (†)	534 (98)
1981	262,855	28.1	473 (128)	523 (136)	520 (129)	† (†)	†	617 (115)	615 (103)	—	453 (90)	590 (116)	520 (99)	—	— (†)	532 (97)
1982	256,381	26.9	469 (130)	533 (137)	521 (128)	† (†)	†	616 (114)	616 (105)	—	456 (89)	593 (115)	521 (100)	—	— (†)	532 (97)
1983	263,674	27.2	473 (131)	541 (138)	528 (128)	† (†)	†	623 (115)	620 (105)	—	459 (90)	599 (114)	527 (98)	—	— (†)	542 (95)
1984	265,221	27.2	475 (130)	541 (139)	530 (129)	† (†)	†	622 (115)	619 (102)	—	461 (90)	604 (114)	530 (97)	—	— (†)	543 (96)
1985	271,972	27.8	474 (126)	545 (140)	534 (128)	† (†)	—	619 (114)	621 (101)	—	459 (89)	615 (120)	531 (95)	—	— (†)	541 (95)
1986	279,428	28.3	475 (126)	552 (140)	536 (129)	† (†)	—	612 (114)	628 (106)	—	464 (87)	616 (119)	527 (96)	—	— (†)	542 (97)
1987	293,560	29.6	477 (126)	550 (140)	537 (129)	† (†)	—	616 (116)	629 (104)	—	465 (86)	619 (119)	526 (95)	—	— (†)	536 (95)
1988	303,703	30.5	483 (123)	557 (140)	541 (129)	† (†)	—	615 (114)	631 (108)	—	467 (85)	622 (120)	525 (94)	—	— (†)	537 (94)
1989	326,096	32.0	484 (125)	560 (142)	545 (129)	† (†)	—	612 (114)	642 (117)	—	465 (87)	626 (116)	528 (91)	—	— (†)	538 (95)
1990	344,572	32.8	486 (123)	562 (143)	544 (131)	† (†)	—	612 (114)	662 (123)	—	461 (84)	617 (111)	523 (92)	—	— (†)	537 (95)
1991	379,882	34.7	485 (122)	562 (141)	549 (131)	† (†)	—	609 (113)	660 (123)	—	457 (85)	611 (111)	523 (93)	—	— (†)	535 (95)
1992	411,528	36.2	483 (120)	561 (140)	548 (129)	† (†)	—	605 (113)	654 (128)	—	462 (82)	610 (117)	525 (92)	—	— (†)	536 (95)
1993	400,246	34.4	481 (117)	557 (140)	543 (133)	† (†)	—	606 (114)	662 (133)	—	462 (80)	602 (115)	516 (94)	—	— (†)	536 (97)
1994	399,395[2]	34.2	479 (116)	553 (139)	542 (133)	† (†)	—	620 (116)	627 (113)	—	493[3] (104)	601 (115)	517 (95)	—	— (†)	538 (96)
1995	389,539[2]	33.6	477 (115)	553 (140)	† (†)	† (†)	—	622 (116)	675 (138)	—	488[3] (102)	596 (113)	513 (96)	—	— (†)	544 (98)
1996	376,013[2]	32.3	473 (114)	558 (139)	† (†)	† (†)	—	614 (114)	678 (135)	—	489[3] (104)	604 (119)	512 (97)	—	— (†)	547 (99)
1997	376,062[2]	32.1	472 (113)	562 (139)	† (†)	† (†)	—	620 (115)	684 (143)	—	487[3] (103)	602 (114)	525 (100)	—	— (†)	554 (99)
1998	364,554[2]	30.8	471 (113)	569 (141)	† (†)	† (†)	—	628 (113)	686 (137)	—	477[3] (100)	609 (118)	530 (100)	—	— (†)	563 (100)
1999[4]	396,330	33.0	468 (114)	565 (143)	† (†)	† (†)	—	626 (114)	684 (137)	—	† (†)	604 (115)	527 (100)	—	— (†)	559 (99)

See notes at end of table.

Table 318. Scores on Graduate Record Examination (GRE) general and subject tests: 1965 through 2005—Continued

Academic year ending	Number of GRE takers	GRE takers as a percent of bachelor's degrees[1]	General test sections				Subject tests									
			Verbal	Quantitative	Analytical reasoning	Analytical writing	Biochemistry, cell and molecular biology	Biology	Chemistry	Computer science	Education	Engineering	Literature	Mathematics	Physics	Psychology
1	2	3	4	5	6	7	8	9	10	11	12	13	14	15	16	17
2000[4]	397,489	32.1	465 (116)	578 (147)	562 (141)	† (†)	— (†)	629 (114)	686 (133)	— (†)	†	— (†)	530 (99)	— (†)	— (†)	563 (98)
2001	432,667	—	— (†)	— (†)	— (†)	† (†)	— (†)	— (†)	— (†)	— (†)	†	— (†)	— (†)	— (†)	— (†)	— (†)
2002	520,547	40.3	473 (123)	597 (151)	571 (139)	† (†)	— (†)	— (†)	— (†)	— (†)	†	† (†)	— (†)	— (†)	— (†)	— (†)
2003[5]	571,606	42.4	470 (120)	593 (147)	†	4.2 (0.96)	517 (100)	635 (114)	682 (125)	712 (97)	†	† (†)	538 (98)	620 (131)	669 (151)	580 (101)
2004[5,6]	418,463	29.9	469 (120)	597 (148)	†	4.2 (1.00)	517 (101)	643 (115)	675 (120)	715 (93)	†	† (†)	537 (97)	621 (130)	665 (148)	586 (101)
2005[5,6]	431,776	30.0	467 (118)	591 (148)	†	4.2 (0.90)	518 (100)	647 (117)	675 (117)	715 (91)	†	† (†)	540 (97)	623 (130)	672 (151)	592 (101)

—Not available.
†Not applicable.
[1]GRE takers include examinees from inside and outside of the United States, while the bachelor's degree recipients include U.S. institutions only.
[2]Total includes examinees who received no score on one or more general test measures.
[3]Data reported for 1994 through 1998 are from the revised education test.
[4]Subject test score data reflect the three-year average for all examinees who tested between October 1 three years prior to the reported test year and September 30 of the reported test year. These data are not directly comparable with data for most other years.
[5]Subject test score data reflect the three-year average for all examinees who tested between July 1 three years prior to the reported test year and June 30 of the reported test year. These data are not directly comparable with previous years, except for 1999 and 2000.
[6]Verbal and quantitative test score data reflect the three-year average for all examinees who tested between July 1 three years prior to the reported test year and June 30 of the reported test year. Analytical writing test score data reflect the average for all examinees who tested between October 1, 2002, and June 30 of the reported test year. These data are not directly comparable with previous years.

NOTE: GRE data include test takers from both within and outside of the United States. GRE scores for the verbal, quantitative, and analytical reasoning sections range from 200 to 800. Scores for the analytical writing section range from 0 to 6, in half-point increments. The range of scores is different for the various subject tests, from as low as 200 to as high as 990. The analytical reasoning section of the GRE, a multiple-choice test, was discontinued in September 2002, and replaced by the analytical writing section, an essay-based test. The education subject test was administered for the final time in April 1998. The engineering subject test was administered for the final time in April 2001. Some data have been revised from previously published figures. Standard deviations appear in parentheses.
SOURCE: Graduate Record Examination Board, *Examinee and Score Trends for the GRE General Test, 1964–65 through 1985–86; A Summary of Data Collected From Graduate Record Examinations Test-Takers During 1986–87; Guide to the Use of Scores, 1987–88 through 2001–02; Sex, Race, Ethnicity, and Performance on the GRE General Test, 2000–01 through 2001–02; Factors That Can Influence Performance on the GRE General Test, 2003–2004; GRE Volumes by Country, 2000–05;* and *Interpreting Your GRE Scores: 2006–07.* U.S. Department of Education, National Center for Education Statistics, Higher Education General Information Survey (HEGIS), "Degrees and Other Formal Awards Conferred" surveys, 1964–65 through 1985–86; and 1986–87 through 2004–05 Integrated Postsecondary Education Data System (IPEDS), "Completions Survey" (IPEDS-C:87–99), and Fall 2000 through Fall 2005. (This table was prepared August 2006.)

Table 319. Average undergraduate tuition and fees and room and board rates charged for full-time students in degree-granting institutions, by type and control of institution: 1964–65 through 2005–06

Year and control of institution	Total tuition, room, and board					Tuition and required fees (in-state)					Dormitory rooms					Board (7-day basis)[1]				
	All institutions	4-year institutions			2-year	All institutions	4-year institutions			2-year	All institutions	4-year institutions			2-year	All institutions	4-year institutions			2-year
		All 4-year	Universities	Other 4-year			All 4-year	Universities	Other 4-year			All 4-year	Universities	Other 4-year			All 4-year	Universities	Other 4-year	
1	2	3	4	5	6	7	8	9	10	11	12	13	14	15	16	17	18	19	20	21
All institutions																				
1976–77	$2,275	$2,577	$2,647	$2,527	$1,598	$924	$1,218	$1,210	$1,223	$346	$603	$611	$649	$584	$503	$748	$748	$788	$719	$750
1977–78	2,411	2,725	2,777	2,685	1,703	984	1,291	1,269	1,305	378	645	654	691	628	525	781	780	818	752	801
1978–79	2,587	2,917	2,967	2,879	1,828	1,073	1,397	1,370	1,413	411	688	696	737	667	575	826	825	860	800	842
1979–80	2,809	3,167	3,223	3,124	1,979	1,163	1,513	1,484	1,530	451	751	759	803	729	628	895	895	936	865	900
1980–81	3,101	3,499	3,535	3,469	2,230	1,289	1,679	1,634	1,705	526	836	846	881	821	705	976	975	1,020	943	1,000
1981–82	3,489	3,951	4,005	3,908	2,476	1,457	1,907	1,860	1,935	590	950	961	1,023	919	793	1,083	1,082	1,121	1,055	1,094
1982–83	3,877	4,406	4,466	4,356	2,713	1,626	2,139	2,081	2,173	675	1,064	1,078	1,150	1,028	873	1,187	1,189	1,235	1,155	1,165
1983–84	4,167	4,747	4,793	4,712	2,854	1,783	2,344	2,300	2,368	730	1,145	1,162	1,211	1,130	916	1,239	1,242	1,282	1,214	1,208
1984–85	4,563	5,160	5,236	5,107	3,179	1,985	2,567	2,539	2,583	821	1,267	1,282	1,343	1,242	1,058	1,310	1,311	1,353	1,282	1,301
1985–86[2]	4,885	5,504	5,597	5,441	3,367	2,181	2,784	2,770	2,793	888	1,338	1,355	1,424	1,309	1,107	1,365	1,365	1,403	1,339	1,372
1986–87	5,206	5,964	6,124	5,857	3,295	2,312	3,042	3,042	3,042	897	1,405	1,427	1,501	1,376	1,034	1,489	1,495	1,581	1,439	1,364
1987–88	5,494	6,272	6,339	6,226	3,263	2,458	3,201	3,168	3,220	809	1,488	1,516	1,576	1,478	1,017	1,549	1,555	1,596	1,529	1,437
1988–89	5,869	6,725	6,801	6,673	3,573	2,658	3,472	3,422	3,499	979	1,575	1,609	1,665	1,573	1,085	1,636	1,644	1,715	1,601	1,509
1989–90	6,207	7,212	7,347	7,120	3,705	2,839	3,800	3,765	3,819	978	1,638	1,675	1,732	1,638	1,105	1,730	1,737	1,850	1,663	1,622
1990–91	6,562	7,602	7,709	7,528	3,930	3,016	4,009	3,958	4,036	1,087	1,743	1,782	1,848	1,740	1,182	1,802	1,811	1,903	1,751	1,660
1991–92	7,077	8,238	8,390	8,142	4,092	3,286	4,385	4,368	4,394	1,189	1,874	1,921	1,996	1,875	1,210	1,918	1,931	2,026	1,872	1,692
1992–93	7,452	8,758	8,934	8,648	4,207	3,517	4,752	4,665	4,795	1,276	1,939	1,991	2,104	1,926	1,240	1,996	2,015	2,165	1,927	1,692
1993–94	7,931	9,296	9,495	9,186	4,449	3,827	5,119	5,104	5,127	1,399	2,057	2,111	2,190	2,068	1,332	2,047	2,067	2,201	1,992	1,718
1994–95	8,306	9,728	9,863	9,646	4,633	4,044	5,391	5,287	5,441	1,488	2,145	2,200	2,281	2,155	1,396	2,116	2,138	2,295	2,049	1,750
1995–96	8,800	10,330	10,560	10,195	4,725	4,338	5,786	5,733	5,812	1,522	2,264	2,318	2,423	2,260	1,473	2,199	2,226	2,404	2,123	1,730
1996–97	9,206	10,841	11,033	10,726	4,895	4,564	6,118	6,055	6,150	1,543	2,365	2,422	2,518	2,368	1,522	2,276	2,301	2,460	2,208	1,830
1997–98	9,588	11,277	11,382	11,205	5,192	4,755	6,351	6,232	6,408	1,695	2,444	2,507	2,575	2,469	1,598	2,389	2,419	2,576	2,327	1,900
1998–99	10,076	11,888	12,123	11,752	5,291	5,013	6,723	6,713	6,728	1,725	2,557	2,626	2,710	2,578	1,616	2,506	2,540	2,700	2,446	1,950
1999–2000	10,444	12,352	12,613	12,198	5,408	5,238	7,044	7,026	7,052	1,721	2,682	2,749	2,845	2,695	1,733	2,524	2,559	2,741	2,451	1,954
2000–01	10,818	12,922	13,177	12,775	5,460	5,377	7,372	7,360	7,377	1,698	2,819	2,893	2,999	2,833	1,744	2,622	2,658	2,818	2,565	2,017
2001–02	11,380	13,639	13,942	13,468	5,718	5,646	7,786	7,788	7,785	1,800	2,981	3,060	3,184	2,992	1,848	2,753	2,793	2,970	2,692	2,070
2002–03	12,014	14,439	14,827	14,233	6,252	6,002	8,309	8,406	8,264	1,903	3,179	3,263	3,377	3,201	2,077	2,832	2,867	3,044	2,767	2,272
2003–04	12,955	15,504	16,096	15,203	6,716	6,608	9,027	9,267	8,922	2,175	3,360	3,448	3,599	3,368	2,206	2,987	3,028	3,230	2,914	2,335
2004–05	13,792	16,509	17,219	16,164	7,086	7,122	9,706	10,051	9,559	2,338	3,569	3,661	3,813	3,582	2,336	3,100	3,142	3,355	3,023	2,413
2005–06	14,629	17,447	18,229	17,075	7,231	7,601	10,279	10,666	10,119	2,417	3,804	3,899	4,050	3,821	2,396	3,224	3,269	3,513	3,153	2,418
Public institutions																				
1964–65	950	—	1,051	867	638	243	—	298	224	99	271	—	291	241	178	436	—	462	402	361
1965–66	983	—	1,105	904	670	257	—	327	241	109	281	—	304	255	194	445	—	474	408	367
1966–67	1,026	—	1,171	947	710	275	—	360	259	121	294	—	321	271	213	457	—	490	417	376
1967–68	1,064	—	1,199	997	789	283	—	366	268	144	313	—	337	292	243	468	—	496	437	402
1968–69	1,117	—	1,245	1,063	883	295	—	377	281	170	337	—	359	318	278	485	—	509	464	435
1969–70	1,203	—	1,362	1,135	951	323	—	427	306	178	369	—	395	346	308	511	—	540	483	465
1970–71	1,287	—	1,477	1,206	998	351	—	478	332	187	401	—	431	375	338	535	—	568	499	473
1971–72	1,357	—	1,579	1,263	1,073	376	—	526	354	192	430	—	463	400	366	551	—	590	509	515
1972–73	1,458	—	1,668	1,460	1,197	407	—	566	455	233	476	—	500	455	398	575	—	602	550	566
1973–74	1,517	—	1,707	1,506	1,274	438	—	581	463	274	480	—	505	464	409	599	—	621	579	591

See notes at end of table.

Table 319. Average undergraduate tuition and fees and room and board rates charged for full-time students in degree-granting institutions, by type and control of institution: 1964–65 through 2005–06—Continued

Year and control of institution	Total tuition, room, and board					Tuition and required fees (in-state)					Dormitory rooms					Board (7-day basis)[1]				
	All insti-tutions	4-year institutions			2-year	All insti-tutions	4-year institutions			2-year	All insti-tutions	4-year institutions			2-year	All insti-tutions	4-year institutions			2-year
		All 4-year	Univer-sities	Other 4-year			All 4-year	Univer-sities	Other 4-year			All 4-year	Univer-sities	Other 4-year			All 4-year	Univer-sities	Other 4-year	
1	2	3	4	5	6	7	8	9	10	11	12	13	14	15	16	17	18	19	20	21
1974–75	1,563	—	1,760	1,558	1,339	432	—	599	448	277	506	—	527	497	424	625	—	634	613	638
1975–76	1,666	—	1,935	1,657	1,386	433	—	642	469	245	544	—	573	533	442	689	—	720	655	699
1976–77	1,789	1,935	2,067	1,827	1,491	479	617	689	564	283	582	592	614	572	465	728	727	763	692	742
1977–78	1,888	2,038	2,170	1,931	1,590	512	655	736	596	306	621	631	649	616	486	755	752	785	720	797
1978–79	1,994	2,145	2,289	2,027	1,691	543	688	777	622	327	655	664	689	641	527	796	793	823	764	837
1979–80	2,165	2,327	2,487	2,198	1,822	583	738	840	662	355	715	725	750	703	574	867	865	898	833	893
1980–81	2,373	2,550	2,712	2,421	2,027	635	804	915	722	391	799	811	827	796	642	940	936	969	904	994
1981–82	2,663	2,871	3,079	2,705	2,224	714	909	1,042	813	434	909	925	970	885	703	1,039	1,036	1,067	1,006	1,086
1982–83	2,945	3,196	3,403	3,032	2,390	798	1,031	1,164	936	473	1,010	1,030	1,072	993	755	1,136	1,134	1,167	1,103	1,162
1983–84	3,156	3,433	3,628	3,285	2,534	891	1,148	1,284	1,052	528	1,087	1,110	1,131	1,092	801	1,178	1,175	1,213	1,141	1,205
1984–85	3,408	3,682	3,899	3,518	2,807	971	1,228	1,386	1,117	584	1,196	1,217	1,237	1,200	921	1,241	1,237	1,276	1,201	1,302
1985–86[2]	3,571	3,859	4,146	3,637	2,981	1,045	1,318	1,536	1,157	641	1,242	1,263	1,290	1,240	960	1,285	1,278	1,320	1,240	1,380
1986–87	3,805	4,138	4,469	3,891	2,989	1,106	1,414	1,651	1,248	660	1,301	1,323	1,355	1,295	979	1,398	1,401	1,464	1,348	1,349
1987–88	4,050	4,403	4,619	4,250	3,066	1,218	1,537	1,726	1,407	706	1,378	1,410	1,410	1,409	943	1,454	1,456	1,482	1,434	1,417
1988–89	4,274	4,678	4,905	4,526	3,183	1,285	1,646	1,846	1,515	730	1,457	1,496	1,483	1,506	965	1,533	1,536	1,576	1,504	1,488
1989–90	4,504	4,975	5,324	4,723	3,299	1,356	1,780	2,035	1,608	756	1,513	1,557	1,561	1,554	962	1,635	1,638	1,728	1,561	1,581
1990–91	4,757	5,243	5,585	5,004	3,467	1,454	1,888	2,159	1,707	824	1,612	1,657	1,658	1,655	1,050	1,691	1,698	1,767	1,641	1,594
1991–92	5,138	5,693	6,050	5,458	3,623	1,628	2,117	2,409	1,931	936	1,731	1,785	1,789	1,782	1,074	1,780	1,792	1,852	1,745	1,612
1992–93	5,379	6,020	6,442	5,740	3,799	1,782	2,349	2,604	2,192	1,025	1,756	1,816	1,856	1,787	1,106	1,841	1,854	1,982	1,761	1,668
1993–94	5,694	6,365	6,710	6,146	3,996	1,942	2,537	2,820	2,360	1,125	1,873	1,934	1,897	1,958	1,190	1,880	1,895	1,993	1,828	1,681
1994–95	5,965	6,670	7,077	6,409	4,137	2,057	2,681	2,977	2,499	1,192	1,959	2,023	1,992	2,044	1,232	1,949	1,967	2,108	1,866	1,712
1995–96	6,256	7,014	7,448	6,730	4,217	2,179	2,848	3,151	2,660	1,239	2,057	2,121	2,104	2,133	1,297	2,020	2,045	2,192	1,937	1,681
1996–97	6,530	7,334	7,792	7,035	4,404	2,271	2,987	3,323	2,778	1,276	2,148	2,214	2,187	2,232	1,339	2,111	2,133	2,282	2,025	1,789
1997–98	6,813	7,673	8,210	7,318	4,509	2,360	3,110	3,486	2,877	1,314	2,225	2,301	2,285	2,312	1,401	2,228	2,263	2,438	2,130	1,795
1998–99	7,107	8,027	8,625	7,631	4,604	2,430	3,229	3,640	2,974	1,327	2,330	2,409	2,408	2,410	1,450	2,347	2,389	2,576	2,247	1,828
1999–2000	7,310	8,275	8,912	7,852	4,720	2,506	3,349	3,768	3,091	1,338	2,440	2,519	2,516	2,521	1,549	2,364	2,406	2,628	2,239	1,834
2000–01	7,586	8,653	9,321	8,218	4,839	2,562	3,501	3,979	3,208	1,333	2,569	2,654	2,657	2,652	1,600	2,455	2,499	2,686	2,358	1,906
2001–02	8,022	9,196	9,948	8,715	5,137	2,700	3,735	4,273	3,409	1,380	2,723	2,816	2,838	2,801	1,722	2,598	2,645	2,837	2,504	2,036
2002–03	8,502	9,787	10,604	9,280	5,601	2,903	4,046	4,686	3,668	1,483	2,930	3,029	3,023	3,032	1,954	2,669	2,712	2,895	2,580	2,164
2003–04	9,249	10,674	11,679	10,063	6,020	3,319	4,587	5,363	4,141	1,702	3,107	3,212	3,232	3,198	2,086	2,823	2,875	3,084	2,724	2,233
2004–05	9,864	11,426	12,588	10,734	6,375	3,629	5,027	5,939	4,512	1,849	3,304	3,418	3,427	3,413	2,174	2,931	2,981	3,222	2,809	2,353
2005–06	10,454	12,108	13,424	11,335	6,492	3,874	5,351	6,399	4,765	1,935	3,545	3,664	3,654	3,672	2,251	3,035	3,093	3,372	2,899	2,306
Private institutions																				
1964–65	1,907	—	2,202	1,810	1,455	1,088	—	1,297	1,023	702	331	—	390	308	289	488	—	515	479	464
1965–66	2,005	—	2,316	1,899	1,557	1,154	—	1,369	1,086	768	356	—	418	330	316	495	—	529	483	473
1966–67	2,124	—	2,456	2,007	1,679	1,233	—	1,456	1,162	845	385	—	452	355	347	506	—	548	490	487
1967–68	2,205	—	2,545	2,104	1,762	1,297	—	1,534	1,237	892	392	—	455	366	366	516	—	556	501	504
1968–69	2,321	—	2,673	2,237	1,876	1,383	—	1,638	1,335	956	404	—	463	382	391	534	—	572	520	529
1969–70	2,530	—	2,920	2,420	1,993	1,533	—	1,809	1,468	1,034	436	—	503	409	413	561	—	608	543	546
1970–71	2,738	—	3,163	2,599	2,103	1,684	—	1,980	1,603	1,109	468	—	542	434	434	586	—	641	562	560
1971–72	2,917	—	3,375	2,748	2,186	1,820	—	2,133	1,721	1,172	494	—	576	454	449	603	—	666	573	565

See notes at end of table.

Table 319. Average undergraduate tuition and fees and room and board rates charged for full-time students in degree-granting institutions, by type and control of institution: 1964–65 through 2005–06—Continued

Year and control of institution	Total tuition, room, and board					Tuition and required fees (in-state)					Dormitory rooms					Board (7-day basis)[1]				
	All insti-tutions	4-year institutions			2-year	All insti-tutions	4-year institutions			2-year	All insti-tutions	4-year institutions			2-year	All insti-tutions	4-year institutions			2-year
		All 4-year	Univer-sities	Other 4-year			All 4-year	Univer-sities	Other 4-year			All 4-year	Univer-sities	Other 4-year			All 4-year	Univer-sities	Other 4-year	
1	2	3	4	5	6	7	8	9	10	11	12	13	14	15	16	17	18	19	20	21
1972–73	3,038	—	3,512	2,934	2,273	1,898	—	2,226	1,846	1,221	524	—	622	490	457	616	—	664	598	595
1973–74	3,164	—	3,717	3,040	2,410	1,989	—	2,375	1,925	1,303	533	—	622	502	483	642	—	720	613	624
1974–75	3,403	—	4,076	3,156	2,591	2,117	—	2,614	1,954	1,367	586	—	691	536	564	700	—	771	666	660
1975–76	3,663	—	4,467	3,385	2,711	2,272	—	2,881	2,084	1,427	636	—	753	583	572	755	—	833	718	712
1976–77	3,906	3,977	4,715	3,714	2,971	2,467	2,534	3,051	2,351	1,592	649	651	783	604	607	790	791	882	759	772
1977–78	4,158	4,240	5,033	3,967	3,148	2,624	2,700	3,240	2,520	1,706	698	702	850	648	631	836	838	943	800	811
1978–79	4,514	4,609	5,403	4,327	3,389	2,867	2,958	3,487	2,771	1,831	758	761	916	704	700	889	890	1,000	851	858
1979–80	4,912	5,013	5,891	4,700	3,751	3,130	3,225	3,811	3,020	2,062	827	831	1,001	768	766	955	957	1,078	912	923
1980–81	5,470	5,594	6,569	5,249	4,303	3,498	3,617	4,275	3,390	2,413	918	921	1,086	859	871	1,054	1,056	1,209	1,000	1,019
1981–82	6,166	6,330	7,443	5,947	4,746	3,953	4,113	4,887	3,853	2,605	1,038	1,039	1,229	970	1,022	1,175	1,178	1,327	1,124	1,119
1982–83	6,920	7,126	8,536	6,646	5,364	4,439	4,639	5,583	4,329	3,008	1,181	1,181	1,453	1,083	1,177	1,300	1,306	1,501	1,234	1,179
1983–84	7,508	7,759	9,308	7,244	5,571	4,851	5,093	6,217	4,726	3,099	1,278	1,279	1,531	1,191	1,253	1,380	1,387	1,559	1,327	1,219
1984–85	8,202	8,451	10,243	7,849	6,203	5,315	5,556	6,843	5,135	3,485	1,426	1,426	1,753	1,309	1,424	1,462	1,469	1,647	1,405	1,294
1985–86[2]	8,885	9,228	11,034	8,551	6,512	5,789	6,121	7,374	5,641	3,672	1,553	1,557	1,940	1,420	1,500	1,542	1,551	1,720	1,490	1,340
1986–87[2]	9,676	10,039	12,278	9,276	6,384	6,316	6,658	8,118	6,171	3,684	1,658	1,673	2,097	1,518	1,266	1,702	1,708	2,063	1,587	1,434
1987–88	10,512	10,659	13,075	9,854	7,078	6,988	7,116	8,771	6,574	4,161	1,748	1,760	2,244	1,593	1,380	1,775	1,783	2,060	1,687	1,537
1988–89	11,189	11,474	14,073	10,620	7,967	7,461	7,722	9,451	7,172	4,817	1,849	1,863	2,353	1,686	1,540	1,880	1,889	2,269	1,762	1,609
1989–90	12,018	12,284	15,098	11,374	8,670	8,147	8,396	10,348	7,778	5,196	1,923	1,935	2,411	1,774	1,663	1,948	1,953	2,339	1,823	1,811
1990–91	12,910	13,237	16,503	12,220	9,302	8,772	9,083	11,379	8,389	5,570	2,063	2,077	2,654	1,889	1,744	2,074	2,077	2,470	1,943	1,989
1991–92	13,892	14,258	17,572	13,201	9,632	9,419	9,759	12,037	9,060	5,754	2,221	2,241	2,825	2,042	1,788	2,252	2,257	2,709	2,098	2,090
1992–93	14,634	15,009	18,898	13,882	9,903	9,942	10,294	13,055	9,533	6,059	2,348	2,362	3,018	2,151	1,970	2,344	2,354	2,825	2,197	1,875
1993–94	15,496	15,904	20,097	14,640	10,406	10,572	10,952	13,874	10,100	6,370	2,490	2,506	3,277	2,261	2,067	2,434	2,445	2,946	2,278	1,970
1994–95	16,207	16,602	21,041	15,363	11,170	11,111	11,481	14,537	10,653	6,914	2,587	2,601	3,469	2,347	2,233	2,509	2,520	3,035	2,362	2,023
1995–96	17,208	17,612	22,502	16,198	11,563	11,864	12,243	15,605	11,297	7,094	2,738	2,751	3,680	2,473	2,371	2,606	2,617	3,218	2,429	2,098
1996–97	18,039	18,442	23,520	16,994	11,954	12,498	12,881	16,552	11,871	7,236	2,878	2,889	3,826	2,602	2,537	2,663	2,672	3,142	2,520	2,181
1997–98	18,516	19,070	24,116	17,717	12,921	12,801	13,344	17,229	12,338	7,464	2,954	2,964	3,756	2,731	2,672	2,762	2,761	3,132	2,648	2,785
1998–99	19,368	19,929	25,443	18,430	13,319	13,428	13,973	18,340	12,815	7,854	3,075	3,091	3,914	2,850	2,581	2,865	2,865	3,188	2,765	2,884
1999–2000	20,186	20,706	26,534	19,127	13,965	14,081	14,588	19,307	13,361	8,235	3,224	3,237	4,070	2,976	2,808	2,882	2,881	3,157	2,790	2,922
2000–01	21,368	21,856	27,676	20,247	14,788	15,000	15,470	20,106	14,233	9,067	3,374	3,392	4,270	3,121	2,722	2,993	2,993	3,300	2,893	3,000
2001–02	22,413	22,896	29,115	21,220	15,825	15,742	16,211	21,176	14,923	10,076	3,567	3,576	4,478	3,301	3,116	3,104	3,109	3,462	2,996	2,633
2002–03	23,340	23,787	31,043	21,965	17,753	16,383	16,826	22,716	15,416	10,651	3,752	3,764	4,724	3,478	3,232	3,206	3,197	3,602	3,071	3,870
2003–04	24,636	25,083	32,886	23,166	19,559	17,327	17,777	24,128	16,298	11,546	3,945	3,952	4,979	3,647	3,581	3,364	3,354	3,778	3,222	4,432
2004–05	25,810	26,257	34,761	24,274	20,093	18,154	18,604	25,643	17,050	12,122	4,171	4,170	5,263	3,854	4,243	3,485	3,483	3,855	3,370	3,728
2005–06	26,889	27,317	36,510	25,282	21,170	18,862	19,292	26,954	17,702	12,450	4,380	4,386	5,517	4,063	3,994	3,647	3,639	4,039	3,517	4,726

—Not available.
[1]Data for 1986–87 and later years reflect a basis of 20 meals per week rather than meals 7 days per week. Because of this revision in data collection and tabulation procedures, data are not entirely comparable with figures for previous years. In particular, data on board rates are somewhat higher than earlier years because they reflect the basis of 20 meals per week rather than meals served 7 days per week. Since many institutions serve fewer than 3 meals each day, the 1986–87 and later data reflect a more accurate accounting of total board costs.
[2]Room and board data are estimated.
NOTE: Data are for the entire academic year and are average total charges for full-time attendance. Tuition and fees were weighted by the number of full-time-equivalent undergraduates, but were not adjusted to reflect student residency. Room and board were based on full-time students. The data have not been adjusted for changes in the purchasing power of the dollar over time. Data through 1995–96 are for institutions of higher education, while later data are for degree-granting institutions. Degree-granting institu-

tions grant associate's or higher degrees and participate in Title IV federal financial aid programs. The degree-granting classification is very similar to the earlier higher education classification, but it includes more 2-year colleges and excludes a few higher education institutions that did not grant degrees. (See Guide to Sources for details.) Because of their low response rate, data for private 2-year colleges must be interpreted with caution. Some data have been revised from previously published figures. Detail may not sum to totals because of rounding.
SOURCE: U.S. Department of Education, National Center for Education Statistics, Higher Education General Information Survey (HEGIS), "Institutional Characteristics of Colleges and Universities" surveys, 1965–66 through 1985–86; "Fall Enrollment in Institutions of Higher Education" surveys, 1965–66 through 1985–86; and 1986–87 through 2005–06 Integrated Postsecondary Education Data System, "Fall Enrollment Survey" (IPEDS-EF:86–99), "Institutional Characteristics Survey" (IPEDS-C:86–99), Spring 2001 through Spring 2006, and Fall 2000 through Fall 2005. (This table was prepared September 2006.)

Table 320. Average undergraduate tuition and fees and room and board rates charged for full-time students in degree-granting institutions, by type and control of institution and state or jurisdiction: 2004–05 and 2005–06

State or jurisdiction	Public 4-year						Private 4-year						Public 2-year, tuition and required fees (in-state)	
	2004–05		2005–06				2004–05		2005–06					
	Total	Tuition and required fees (in-state)	Total	Tuition and required fees (in-state)	Room	Board	Total	Tuition and required fees	Total	Tuition and required fees	Room	Board	2004-05	2005-06
1	2	3	4	5	6	7	8	9	10	11	12	13	14	15
United States	$11,426	$5,027	$12,108	$5,351	$3,664	$3,093	$26,257	$18,604	$27,317	$19,292	$4,386	$3,639	$1,849	$1,935
Alabama	9,813	4,376	9,625	4,578	2,757	2,290	17,586	11,724	18,520	12,426	3,034	3,060	2,736	2,764
Alaska..................	9,944	3,779	10,620	4,054	3,723	2,843	21,631	14,300	21,651	14,891	3,055	3,705	2,285	2,353
Arizona	10,857	4,075	11,480	4,426	4,032	3,022	19,370	13,093	18,734	11,397	3,925	3,411	1,225	1,344
Arkansas...............	8,739	4,294	9,192	4,643	2,496	2,053	17,070	11,839	18,122	12,691	2,623	2,808	1,717	1,780
California	13,354	4,322	13,685	4,408	4,850	4,427	29,971	20,795	31,266	21,691	5,409	4,166	721	718
Colorado	10,241	3,520	11,569	4,465	3,447	3,657	26,645	17,857	27,779	18,493	4,873	4,413	1,847	1,991
Connecticut............	13,827	6,388	14,658	6,709	4,273	3,676	33,937	24,641	36,026	26,183	5,388	4,455	2,404	2,536
Delaware...............	13,351	6,669	14,326	7,074	4,177	3,076	16,968	10,114	18,176	10,819	3,694	3,663	2,088	2,240
District of Columbia	†	2,070	†	2,070	†	†	31,501	22,134	32,556	22,748	6,314	3,494	†	†
Florida..................	9,357	2,648	10,141	2,941	4,054	3,146	23,457	16,285	24,985	17,503	4,011	3,471	1,743	1,844
Georgia.................	9,430	3,377	10,062	3,632	3,980	2,450	24,532	16,938	26,081	18,120	4,558	3,403	1,475	1,645
Hawaii..................	9,141	3,353	9,042	3,226	3,103	2,713	18,156	9,756	19,437	10,334	4,000	5,103	1,175	1,226
Idaho...................	9,061	3,588	8,982	3,919	2,304	2,759	11,394	5,505	11,614	5,490	2,501	3,624	1,817	1,891
Illinois..................	12,789	6,491	13,976	7,158	3,411	3,407	26,925	18,930	27,875	19,406	5,044	3,425	1,949	2,104
Indiana.................	12,232	5,654	12,388	5,892	3,126	3,371	26,262	19,911	27,582	20,851	3,446	3,285	29,512	2,589
Iowa	11,539	5,406	12,329	5,619	3,101	3,609	22,896	17,218	23,444	17,513	2,789	3,143	2,880	3,032
Kansas.................	9,392	4,174	9,980	4,560	2,604	2,817	19,724	14,238	20,741	15,044	2,603	3,094	1,883	1,938
Kentucky	9,401	4,505	10,663	5,136	2,918	2,609	19,221	13,524	20,674	13,764	3,879	3,031	2,545	2,404
Louisiana	7,968	3,524	8,506	3,679	2,666	2,161	26,347	19,071	17,207	11,264	2,858	3,086	1,438	1,469
Maine...................	11,838	5,574	12,568	6,027	3,348	3,193	28,040	20,417	29,550	21,508	3,985	4,057	2,803	3,039
Maryland...............	14,086	6,614	14,793	7,045	4,381	3,366	31,017	22,642	32,617	23,934	5,179	3,503	2,829	2,833
Massachusetts..........	13,686	7,000	14,651	7,290	4,128	3,233	35,410	25,863	37,282	27,335	5,582	4,365	2,835	2,925
Michigan................	12,659	6,189	13,693	6,938	3,494	3,262	18,772	12,728	19,732	13,303	3,325	3,104	1,934	2,076
Minnesota..............	11,971	6,485	12,777	6,912	3,301	2,564	25,819	19,360	27,314	20,519	3,631	3,164	3,869	4,085
Mississippi	8,997	3,984	9,461	4,177	2,794	2,490	16,437	11,435	17,112	11,839	2,702	2,571	1,512	1,660
Missouri	11,368	5,843	11,861	5,831	3,627	2,403	21,250	14,871	22,441	15,718	3,467	3,255	2,125	2,247
Montana................	9,870	4,510	10,613	4,952	2,580	3,081	17,754	12,009	18,093	12,937	2,480	2,676	2,575	2,721
Nebraska...............	10,702	4,671	11,286	4,880	3,106	3,300	19,471	14,182	21,017	15,234	2,915	2,867	1,772	1,899
Nevada.................	10,526	2,511	10,865	2,671	4,754	3,440	20,504	11,789	20,691	12,622	4,369	3,700	1,498	1,635
New Hampshire	14,538	7,981	15,479	8,458	4,306	2,715	29,675	21,409	31,154	22,534	4,988	3,632	5,342	5,720
New Jersey	16,344	7,981	17,708	8,649	5,853	3,206	29,723	20,901	31,335	22,114	5,038	4,183	2,566	2,712
New Mexico	8,683	3,396	9,579	3,701	3,231	2,647	18,833	12,542	20,006	13,256	3,256	3,494	1,073	1,179
New York.......................	12,442	4,917	13,275	4,987	4,610	3,678	30,901	21,640	32,478	22,900	5,587	3,992	3,072	3,181
North Carolina	9,421	3,551	9,675	3,631	3,317	2,727	24,666	18,145	26,411	19,166	3,520	3,725	1,246	1,295
North Dakota	9,018	4,554	9,829	5,038	1,963	2,828	12,679	8,735	13,553	9,376	1,774	2,403	2,845	3,084
Ohio.....................	15,251	8,032	16,032	8,457	4,312	3,264	25,390	18,748	26,906	19,901	3,570	3,436	3,001	3,127
Oklahoma..............	8,448	3,504	9,404	3,806	2,890	2,708	19,104	13,400	20,113	14,033	2,891	3,189	1,710	2,111
Oregon.................	12,201	5,163	12,720	5,348	3,657	3,716	27,286	20,370	27,945	20,844	3,627	3,474	2,557	2,635
Pennsylvania..........	14,759	8,330	15,464	8,710	3,812	2,942	30,550	22,211	31,963	23,450	4,606	3,908	2,752	2,976
Rhode Island	13,550	5,873	14,315	6,316	4,310	3,688	30,916	22,385	33,101	24,140	4,938	4,022	2,310	2,470
South Carolina...............	12,158	6,746	13,145	7,337	3,470	2,338	21,057	15,298	22,170	16,165	2,948	3,057	2,818	2,932
South Dakota	8,965	4,728	9,493	4,908	2,114	2,471	17,813	12,893	18,930	13,686	2,491	2,754	2,826	3,154
Tennessee	9,443	4,260	9,956	4,765	2,811	2,379	21,902	15,761	23,039	16,552	3,526	2,962	2,209	2,395
Texas	10,218	4,400	10,973	4,666	3,393	2,914	22,078	15,800	23,440	16,809	3,462	3,168	1,234	1,273
Utah....................	8,344	3,174	8,745	3,445	2,180	3,120	10,700	4,940	11,275	5,249	3,014	3,012	2,089	2,224
Vermont................	15,656	8,769	16,571	9,279	4,640	2,652	27,384	19,951	29,072	21,273	4,171	3,628	3,796	4,012
Virginia.................	11,621	5,554	12,279	5,912	3,406	2,961	22,773	16,555	23,823	17,185	3,340	3,297	1,927	2,049
Washington.............	11,884	4,924	12,384	5,250	3,443	3,692	25,884	18,915	27,280	20,110	3,862	3,308	2,391	2,554
West Virginia............	9,508	3,584	9,992	3,816	3,157	3,019	18,913	13,146	20,002	13,856	2,984	3,163	2,983	2,509
Wisconsin	9,867	5,291	10,560	5,672	2,907	1,981	24,442	18,249	25,656	19,083	3,339	3,235	2,793	2,965
Wyoming................	8,514	2,721	8,946	2,874	2,709	3,363	†	†	†	9,450	†	†	1,684	1,772

†Not applicable.
NOTE: Data are for the entire academic year and are average charges. Tuition and fees were weighted by the number of full-time-equivalent undergraduates, but were not adjusted to reflect student residency. Room and board are based on full-time students. (See Guide to Sources for details.) Degree-granting institutions grant associate's or higher degrees and participate in Title IV federal financial aid programs. Some data have been revised from previously published figures. Detail may not sum to totals because of rounding.
SOURCE: U.S. Department of Education, National Center for Education Statistics, 2004–05 and 2005–06 Integrated Postsecondary Education Data System (IPEDS), Fall 2004, Fall 2005, Spring 2005, and Spring 2006. (This table was prepared September 2006.)

Table 321. Average undergraduate tuition and fees and room and board rates of degree-granting institutions, by control and type of institution and percentile of students: 2004–05 and 2005–06

Type of student charge and percentile of students	Public institutions						Private institutions					
	Total		4-year		2-year		Total		4-year		2-year	
	2004–05	2005–06	2004–05	2005–06	2004–05	2005–06	2004–05	2005–06	2004–05	2005–06	2004–05	2005–06
1	2	3	4	5	6	7	8	9	10	11	12	13
Tuition, room, and board												
10th percentile	$7,265	$7,700	$8,380	$8,863	$4,097	$4,380	$17,144	$18,243	$17,156	$18,350	$13,807	$11,560
25th percentile	9,081	9,623	9,574	10,219	4,889	4,822	21,746	23,044	21,808	23,238	15,486	15,680
Median (50th percentile)	10,797	11,348	11,022	11,596	6,021	6,234	27,872	29,279	27,925	29,294	19,844	18,410
75th percentile	12,842	13,543	13,031	13,830	7,420	7,567	34,342	35,783	34,468	35,912	27,276	22,809
90th percentile	15,401	16,264	15,622	16,443	9,015	8,993	39,565	41,707	39,565	41,707	34,385	43,425
Tuition and required fees only												
10th percentile	900	990	2,880	3,094	710	691	9,184	9,285	9,570	9,675	7,008	7,560
25th percentile	1,920	2,070	3,582	3,822	1,048	1,109	12,750	12,840	13,200	12,956	8,813	9,285
Median (50th percentile)	3,152	3,329	4,665	5,084	1,803	1,920	17,590	18,120	18,170	18,900	10,629	11,180
75th percentile	4,977	5,322	6,081	6,458	2,459	2,589	22,712	24,030	23,386	24,366	13,548	14,196
90th percentile	6,752	6,972	7,542	8,097	3,033	3,100	29,786	31,444	29,910	31,452	18,025	17,995

NOTE: Data are for the entire academic year and are average rates for full-time students. Student charges were weighted by the number of full-time-equivalent undergraduates, but were not adjusted to reflect student residency. The data have not been adjusted for changes in the purchasing power of the dollar. Degree-granting institutions grant associ- ate's or higher degrees and participate in Title IV federal financial aid programs. Some data have been revised from previously published figures.
SOURCE: U.S. Department of Education, National Center for Education Statistics, 2004-05 and 2005-06 Integrated Postsecondary Education Data System (IPEDS), Fall 2004, Fall 2005, Spring 2005, and Spring 2006. (This table was prepared September 2006.)

Table 322. Average graduate and first-professional tuition and required fees in degree-granting institutions, by first-professional discipline and control of institution: 1987–88 through 2005–06

Year and control	Average full-time graduate tuition	Average full-time first-professional tuition									
		Chiropractic	Dentistry	Medicine	Optometry	Osteopathic medicine	Pharmacy	Podiatry	Veterinary medicine	Law	Theology
1	2	3	4	5	6	7	8	9	10	11	12
All institutions											
1987–88........................	$3,599	$6,996	$9,399	$9,034	$7,926	$10,674	$5,201	$12,736	$4,503	$6,636	$3,572
1988–89........................	3,728	7,972	9,324	9,439	8,503	11,462	4,952	13,232	4,856	7,099	3,911
1989–90........................	4,135	8,315	10,515	10,597	9,469	11,888	5,890	14,611	5,470	8,059	4,079
1990–91........................	4,488	9,108	10,270	10,571	9,512	12,830	5,889	15,143	5,396	8,708	4,569
1991–92........................	5,116	10,226	12,049	11,646	9,610	13,004	6,731	16,257	6,367	9,469	4,876
1992–93........................	5,475	11,117	12,710	12,265	10,858	14,297	6,635	17,426	6,771	10,463	5,331
1993–94........................	5,973	11,503	14,403	13,074	10,385	15,038	7,960	17,621	7,159	11,552	5,253
1994–95........................	6,247	12,324	15,164	13,834	11,053	15,913	8,315	18,138	7,741	12,374	5,648
1995–96........................	6,741	12,507	15,647	14,860	11,544	16,785	8,602	18,434	8,208	13,278	5,991
1996–97........................	7,111	12,721	16,585	15,481	12,250	17,888	9,207	19,056	8,668	14,081	6,558
1997–98........................	7,246	13,131	17,393	16,075	12,685	18,654	9,544	19,355	9,013	14,877	6,761
1998–99........................	7,685	13,582	18,800	17,110	14,066	19,718	9,636	19,547	9,392	15,590	7,147
1999–2000....................	8,071	14,256	19,314	17,775	14,389	20,817	10,601	20,102	9,865	16,399	7,425
2000–01........................	8,429	15,092	21,696	18,935	15,360	21,685	11,175	20,313	10,365	17,659	10,100
2001–02........................	8,857	15,605	22,643	19,973	16,066	22,753	12,008	21,115	10,940	18,577	8,543
2002–03........................	9,226	—	—	—	—	—	—	—	—	—	—
2003–04........................	10,308	—	—	—	—	—	—	—	—	—	—
2004–05........................	11,004	—	—	—	—	—	—	—	—	—	—
2005–06........................	11,621	—	—	—	—	—	—	—	—	—	—
Public[1]											
1987–88........................	1,827	†	4,614	5,245	2,789	5,125	2,462	†	3,523	2,810	†
1988–89........................	1,913	†	5,286	5,669	3,455	6,269	2,218	†	3,889	2,766	†
1989–90........................	1,999	†	5,728	6,259	3,569	6,521	2,816	†	4,505	3,196	†
1990–91........................	2,206	†	5,927	6,437	3,821	7,188	2,697	†	4,840	3,430	†
1991–92........................	2,524	†	6,595	7,106	4,161	7,699	2,871	†	5,231	3,933	†
1992–93........................	2,791	†	7,006	7,867	5,106	8,404	2,987	†	5,553	4,261	†
1993–94........................	3,050	†	7,525	8,329	5,325	8,640	3,567	†	6,107	4,835	†
1994–95........................	3,250	†	8,125	8,812	5,643	8,954	3,793	†	6,571	5,307	†
1995–96........................	3,449	†	8,806	9,585	6,130	9,448	4,100	†	6,907	5,821	†
1996–97........................	3,607	†	9,434	10,057	6,561	9,932	4,884	†	7,343	6,565	†
1997–98........................	3,744	†	9,657	10,501	7,366	10,358	5,065	19,541	7,742	7,004	†
1998–99........................	3,897	†	10,277	11,141	7,890	10,802	5,482	19,818	7,975	7,425	†
1999–2000....................	4,043	†	10,615	11,569	8,021	11,211	5,897	19,578	8,601	7,740	†
2000–01........................	4,243	†	11,574	12,074	8,302	11,516	6,245	20,228	8,964	8,326	†
2001–02........................	4,496	†	12,446	13,264	9,060	12,587	7,020	21,254	9,524	9,043	†
2002–03........................	4,842	†	—	—	—	—	—	—	—	—	†
2003–04........................	5,544	†	—	—	—	—	—	—	—	—	†
2004–05........................	6,080	†	—	—	—	—	—	—	—	—	†
2005–06........................	6,493	†	—	—	—	—	—	—	—	—	†
Private											
1987–88........................	6,769	6,996	16,201	14,945	11,635	13,311	8,834	12,736	12,544	9,048	3,572
1988–89........................	6,945	7,972	16,127	15,610	12,050	13,536	9,692	13,232	13,285	9,892	3,911
1989–90........................	7,881	8,315	16,800	16,826	13,640	14,117	10,656	14,611	14,184	10,901	4,079
1990–91........................	8,507	9,108	18,270	17,899	13,767	15,009	11,546	15,143	14,159	12,247	4,569
1991–92........................	9,592	10,226	20,318	19,225	14,366	16,098	12,937	16,257	15,816	12,946	4,876
1992–93........................	10,008	11,117	21,309	19,585	14,459	17,098	13,373	17,426	17,103	13,975	5,331
1993–94........................	10,790	11,503	23,824	20,769	14,156	17,720	14,838	17,621	17,433	15,193	5,253
1994–95........................	11,338	12,324	24,641	21,819	14,497	18,422	14,894	18,138	17,940	16,201	5,648
1995–96........................	12,083	12,507	25,678	23,001	15,235	19,619	15,618	18,434	19,380	17,251	5,991
1996–97........................	12,537	12,721	26,618	24,242	15,949	20,714	15,934	19,056	19,526	18,276	6,558
1997–98........................	12,774	13,151	29,923	25,189	16,415	21,710	16,307	19,316	20,299	19,171	6,761
1998–99........................	13,299	13,582	31,659	26,502	17,848	22,796	16,905	19,492	21,286	20,154	7,147
1999–2000....................	13,782	14,256	32,268	27,694	18,087	23,838	18,091	20,193	21,772	21,081	7,425
2000–01........................	14,420	15,092	35,234	29,863	19,592	24,712	19,031	20,329	22,600	22,775	10,100
2001–02........................	15,165	15,605	36,207	30,485	20,463	25,779	20,459	21,089	23,303	23,911	8,543
2002–03........................	14,983	—	—	—	—	—	—	—	—	—	—
2003–04........................	16,241	—	—	—	—	—	—	—	—	—	—
2004–05........................	16,751	—	—	—	—	—	—	—	—	—	—
2005–06........................	17,244	—	—	—	—	—	—	—	—	—	—

—Not available.
†Not applicable.
[1]Data are based on in-state tuition only.
NOTE: Average graduate student tuition weighted by fall full-time-equivalent graduate enrollment. Average first-professional tuition weighted by number of degrees conferred during the academic year. Some year-to-year fluctuations in tuition data may reflect nonreporting by individual institutions. Excludes institutions not reporting degrees conferred and institutions not reporting tuition. Data through 1995–96 are for institutions of higher education, while later data are for degree-granting institutions. Degree-granting institutions grant associate's or higher degrees and participate in Title IV federal financial aid programs. The degree-granting classification is very similar to the earlier higher education classification, but it includes more 2-year colleges and excludes a few higher education institutions that did not grant degrees. (See Guide to Sources for details.) Some data have been revised from previously published figures. Detail may not sum to totals because of rounding.
SOURCE: U.S. Department of Education, National Center for Education Statistics, 1987–88 through 2005–06 Integrated Postsecondary Education Data System, "Fall Enrollment Survey" (IPEDS-EF:87–99); "Completions Survey," (IPEDS-C:88–99); "Institutional Characteristics Survey" (IPEDS-IC:87–99); Fall 2000 through Fall 2005; and Spring 2001 through Spring 2006. (This table was prepared September 2006.)

Table 323. Percentage of undergraduates receiving aid, by type and source of aid and selected student characteristics: 2003–04

Selected student characteristic	Enrollment of undergraduates,[1] in thousands	Any aid Total[2]	Any aid Federal	Any aid Nonfederal	Grants Total	Grants Federal	Grants Nonfederal	Loans Total	Loans Federal[3]	Loans Nonfederal	Work study Total[4]	Other Total	Other Federal	Other Nonfederal
1	2	3	4	5	6	7	8	9	10	11	12	13	14	15
All undergraduates	19,054 (#)	63.2 (0.36)	48.0 (0.28)	40.9 (0.48)	50.7 (0.41)	27.6 (0.17)	36.8 (0.46)	35.2 (0.23)	34.0 (0.22)	5.9 (0.19)	7.5 (0.22)	3.6 (0.16)	2.9 (0.13)	0.8 (0.09)
Sex														
Male	8,073 (73.8)	60.6 (0.54)	44.8 (0.50)	40.1 (0.58)	46.5 (0.55)	22.8 (0.36)	35.6 (0.57)	33.7 (0.45)	32.3 (0.43)	6.3 (0.29)	7.4 (0.24)	5.3 (0.22)	4.7 (0.21)	0.7 (0.09)
Female	10,980 (73.8)	65.2 (0.41)	50.4 (0.36)	41.4 (0.54)	53.7 (0.47)	31.1 (0.28)	37.7 (0.51)	36.4 (0.34)	35.2 (0.34)	5.6 (0.17)	7.6 (0.25)	2.3 (0.17)	1.5 (0.11)	0.8 (0.11)
Race/ethnicity[5]														
White	12,025 (144.6)	61.5 (0.56)	44.4 (0.53)	41.7 (0.54)	47.8 (0.58)	21.3 (0.39)	37.7 (0.54)	35.5 (0.48)	34.2 (0.48)	6.2 (0.22)	7.3 (0.27)	3.5 (0.18)	2.6 (0.14)	0.9 (0.13)
Black	2,666 (117.6)	75.8 (0.88)	64.6 (1.11)	41.6 (1.07)	64.3 (0.98)	47.7 (1.03)	37.2 (1.01)	43.2 (1.63)	42.0 (1.65)	5.1 (0.46)	8.5 (0.45)	5.1 (0.38)	4.4 (0.34)	0.8 (0.15)
Hispanic	2,426 (81.3)	63.2 (0.82)	51.9 (0.87)	37.4 (1.02)	53.4 (0.84)	37.7 (0.80)	33.3 (1.04)	29.9 (0.96)	28.7 (0.95)	5.4 (0.42)	6.8 (0.52)	3.1 (0.19)	2.5 (0.17)	0.5 (0.09)
Asian/Pacific Islander	1,127 (41.7)	51.5 (1.51)	38.1 (1.18)	37.0 (1.35)	41.2 (1.38)	22.7 (0.87)	33.7 (1.26)	25.3 (0.97)	23.6 (0.87)	5.3 (0.57)	9.1 (0.55)	2.1 (0.32)	1.8 (0.32)	0.3 (0.07)
American Indian/Alaska Native	176 (20.5)	67.4 (3.84)	50.4 (3.94)	46.1 (3.35)	59.1 (3.69)	35.8 (3.44)	41.8 (3.41)	32.5 (2.99)	31.4 (2.98)	5.0 (1.08)	5.1 (1.27)	3.3 (0.98)	2.4 (0.77)	1.0 (0.41)
Age														
Younger than 24	10,820 (98.6)	64.2 (0.49)	49.4 (0.42)	44.7 (0.54)	51.4 (0.47)	25.7 (0.24)	40.5 (0.51)	37.9 (0.42)	36.3 (0.42)	7.5 (0.24)	10.6 (0.31)	2.0 (0.10)	1.6 (0.08)	0.4 (0.05)
24 to 29 years old	3,299 (53.0)	66.8 (0.74)	55.0 (0.76)	35.2 (0.72)	52.7 (0.72)	36.9 (0.55)	30.7 (0.64)	39.5 (0.66)	38.3 (0.68)	5.0 (0.34)	4.1 (0.23)	5.7 (0.42)	5.1 (0.41)	0.6 (0.07)
30 years old or over	4,935 (79.6)	58.8 (0.78)	40.3 (0.72)	36.2 (0.75)	47.6 (0.75)	25.4 (0.49)	32.7 (0.79)	26.7 (0.60)	25.8 (0.60)	3.0 (0.19)	3.0 (0.18)	5.7 (0.35)	4.0 (0.28)	1.7 (0.24)
Marital status														
Not married[6]	14,613 (78.1)	64.4 (0.44)	50.2 (0.32)	42.5 (0.51)	52.0 (0.47)	28.6 (0.19)	38.3 (0.50)	37.6 (0.30)	36.3 (0.30)	6.7 (0.21)	8.9 (0.26)	2.8 (0.13)	2.2 (0.11)	0.6 (0.06)
Married	4,056 (76.4)	57.5 (0.78)	38.1 (0.84)	35.2 (0.76)	44.2 (0.76)	21.1 (0.66)	31.6 (0.70)	26.0 (0.64)	25.1 (0.65)	3.1 (0.22)	2.9 (0.18)	6.3 (0.41)	5.1 (0.35)	1.3 (0.22)
Separated	385 (14.3)	78.5 (1.96)	67.7 (2.43)	37.9 (1.98)	69.8 (2.10)	58.1 (2.22)	33.1 (1.94)	41.8 (2.32)	40.4 (2.39)	4.5 (0.75)	4.0 (0.52)	5.4 (0.73)	4.2 (0.66)	1.2 (0.35)
Attendance status														
Full-time, full-year	7,824 (93.5)	76.1 (0.40)	61.7 (0.42)	54.3 (0.52)	62.2 (0.48)	33.2 (0.32)	49.3 (0.51)	49.9 (0.44)	48.5 (0.43)	9.0 (0.31)	13.5 (0.41)	3.2 (0.17)	2.4 (0.12)	0.8 (0.09)
Part-time or part-year	11,230 (93.5)	54.3 (0.56)	38.5 (0.44)	31.5 (0.59)	42.7 (0.57)	23.6 (0.35)	28.1 (0.57)	25.0 (0.30)	23.8 (0.30)	3.7 (0.16)	3.4 (0.14)	3.9 (0.20)	3.2 (0.19)	0.8 (0.10)
Dependency status and family income														
Dependent	9,476 (106.4)	63.8 (0.53)	48.5 (0.44)	45.9 (0.58)	50.4 (0.51)	22.8 (0.25)	41.7 (0.56)	38.6 (0.46)	37.0 (0.46)	7.9 (0.26)	11.2 (0.32)	1.6 (0.10)	1.3 (0.08)	0.3 (0.04)
Less than $20,000	1,241 (29.1)	62.7 (0.49)	47.5 (0.49)	35.9 (0.57)	51.0 (0.50)	32.3 (0.33)	31.9 (0.56)	32.0 (0.43)	31.0 (0.43)	3.9 (0.19)	4.0 (0.15)	5.6 (0.27)	4.4 (0.24)	1.2 (0.15)
$20,000–$39,999	1,827 (27.3)	77.8 (0.87)	67.2 (0.95)	50.9 (1.13)	75.3 (0.96)	63.7 (0.96)	48.0 (1.12)	36.2 (1.01)	34.9 (1.07)	5.6 (0.45)	14.2 (0.77)	1.6 (0.25)	1.3 (0.23)	0.5 (0.06)
$40,000–$59,999	1,710 (27.5)	76.2 (0.78)	65.2 (0.73)	54.0 (0.92)	69.6 (0.83)	53.6 (0.81)	49.9 (0.86)	43.1 (0.70)	41.8 (0.73)	7.7 (0.45)	15.0 (0.61)	1.7 (0.18)	1.4 (0.17)	0.4 (0.06)
$60,000–$79,999	1,596 (32.7)	63.2 (0.83)	48.0 (0.79)	46.8 (0.83)	48.4 (0.77)	18.0 (0.51)	42.6 (0.81)	41.4 (0.82)	39.9 (0.79)	8.8 (0.36)	12.1 (0.54)	1.8 (0.23)	1.4 (0.20)	0.4 (0.11)
$80,000–$99,999	1,124 (27.5)	58.7 (1.09)	40.9 (1.00)	44.3 (0.94)	40.6 (0.90)	3.3 (0.25)	39.7 (0.91)	39.6 (0.98)	37.7 (0.97)	8.9 (0.42)	10.2 (0.47)	1.6 (0.15)	1.1 (0.13)	0.5 (0.10)
$100,000 or more	1,978 (43.6)	60.5 (1.30)	41.6 (1.05)	44.3 (1.24)	39.9 (1.24)	0.9 (0.15)	39.6 (1.25)	41.1 (1.08)	39.0 (1.03)	9.9 (0.48)	9.6 (0.64)	1.5 (0.32)	1.3 (0.31)	0.1 (0.05)
Independent	9,578 (106.4)	62.7 (0.49)	47.5 (0.49)	35.9 (0.57)	51.0 (0.50)	32.3 (0.33)	31.9 (0.56)	32.0 (0.43)	31.0 (0.43)	3.9 (0.19)	4.0 (0.15)	5.6 (0.27)	4.4 (0.24)	1.2 (0.15)
Less than $9,999	2,157 (36.5)	70.5 (0.79)	61.6 (0.85)	38.5 (0.86)	65.7 (0.76)	56.2 (0.77)	34.0 (0.84)	37.8 (0.85)	36.6 (0.86)	4.7 (0.39)	8.0 (0.46)	4.2 (0.36)	3.0 (0.31)	1.3 (0.17)
$10,000–$19,999	1,745 (43.2)	73.3 (0.86)	62.7 (0.84)	38.6 (0.92)	63.4 (1.05)	49.3 (0.84)	33.9 (0.89)	40.7 (0.97)	39.5 (0.99)	4.9 (0.34)	5.2 (0.34)	5.9 (0.39)	4.6 (0.37)	1.3 (0.21)
$20,000–$29,999	1,512 (35.6)	68.4 (1.05)	55.9 (1.18)	35.0 (0.94)	53.8 (0.96)	37.2 (0.89)	30.5 (0.91)	38.1 (1.09)	37.2 (1.09)	3.8 (0.35)	3.2 (0.28)	6.1 (0.47)	4.4 (0.33)	1.7 (0.30)
$30,000–$49,999	1,809 (44.1)	60.6 (0.89)	42.3 (0.95)	36.1 (0.83)	46.3 (0.77)	23.2 (0.82)	32.4 (0.82)	29.6 (0.84)	28.7 (0.83)	3.8 (0.31)	2.6 (0.27)	6.4 (0.47)	5.5 (0.42)	1.0 (0.17)
$50,000 or more	2,356 (50.8)	45.6 (0.97)	22.0 (0.74)	31.9 (0.92)	30.1 (0.97)	1.8 (0.18)	29.2 (0.95)	18.1 (0.64)	17.2 (0.61)	2.5 (0.22)	0.9 (0.14)	5.7 (0.50)	4.9 (0.49)	0.9 (0.16)
Housing status														
School-owned	2,632 (69.3)	79.2 (0.60)	62.3 (0.78)	64.9 (0.77)	66.3 (0.70)	25.7 (0.59)	60.3 (0.79)	57.2 (0.82)	55.5 (0.83)	12.9 (0.66)	22.6 (0.72)	1.8 (0.16)	1.3 (0.14)	0.4 (0.09)
Off-campus, not with parents	10,524 (89.4)	62.9 (0.50)	47.4 (0.47)	37.9 (0.58)	49.9 (0.56)	28.8 (0.36)	33.7 (0.55)	33.7 (0.40)	32.5 (0.39)	4.8 (0.20)	5.1 (0.19)	4.6 (0.22)	3.7 (0.19)	1.0 (0.13)
With parents	5,899 (77.7)	56.7 (0.69)	42.7 (0.54)	35.5 (0.66)	45.1 (0.65)	26.2 (0.41)	31.8 (0.63)	28.2 (0.55)	26.9 (0.53)	4.7 (0.19)	5.2 (0.23)	2.6 (0.16)	2.1 (0.14)	0.5 (0.07)

#Rounds to zero.
[1]Numbers of undergraduates may not equal figures reported in other tables, since these data are based on a sample survey of students who enrolled at any time during the school year. Includes all postsecondary institutions.
[2]Includes students who reported they were awarded aid, but did not specify the source or type of aid.
[3]Includes Parent Loans for Undergraduate Students (PLUS).
[4]Details on federal and nonfederal work study participants are not available.
[5]Excludes persons not reported by race/ethnicity and persons reporting more than one race.
[6]Includes students who were single, divorced, or widowed.
NOTE: Rows may not sum to totals because of rounding and/or the fact that some students receive aid from multiple sources. Data include undergraduates in degree-granting and non-degree-granting institutions. Estimates for loans include PLUS loans and may differ from previously published figures. Race categories exclude persons of Hispanic origin. Standard errors appear in parentheses. Data include Puerto Rico.
SOURCE: U.S. Department of Education, National Center for Education Statistics, 2003–04 National Postsecondary Student Aid Study (NPSAS:04). (This table was prepared September 2005.)

Table 324. Average amount of financial aid awarded to full-time, full-year undergraduates, by type and source of aid and selected student characteristics: 2003–04

Selected student characteristic	Any aid — Total[1]	Any aid — Federal	Any aid — Nonfederal	Grants — Total	Grants — Federal	Grants — Nonfederal	Loans — Total	Loans — Federal[2]	Loans — Nonfederal	Work study — Total[3]	Other — Total	Other — Federal	Other — Nonfederal
1	2	3	4	5	6	7	8	9	10	11	12	13	14
All full-time, full-year undergraduates	$9,899 (106.7)	$7,304 (50.5)	$5,586 (109.1)	$5,565 (92.6)	$3,247 (24.2)	$4,828 (103.3)	$7,336 (80.9)	$6,426 (53.2)	$6,089 (158.5)	$1,942 (41.6)	$4,777 (170.1)	$5,283 (197.0)	$3,008 (180.3)
Sex													
Male	9,989 (148.0)	7,416 (76.3)	5,669 (129.5)	5,517 (105.2)	3,160 (27.6)	4,840 (117.0)	7,577 (103.1)	6,522 (66.6)	6,442 (194.6)	2,022 (46.6)	5,215 (240.2)	5,560 (265.3)	3,060 (273.4)
Female	9,831 (114.9)	7,223 (57.0)	5,524 (128.9)	5,600 (106.8)	3,303 (31.3)	4,819 (122.6)	7,159 (85.1)	6,356 (62.7)	5,783 (179.5)	1,886 (49.4)	4,087 (220.1)	4,705 (295.9)	2,969 (214.6)
Race/ethnicity[4]													
White	9,917 (131.5)	7,318 (61.2)	5,733 (122.8)	5,479 (105.1)	3,075 (30.3)	4,887 (111.1)	7,443 (90.2)	6,450 (57.3)	6,222 (174.7)	1,917 (42.5)	4,942 (215.1)	5,669 (264.7)	2,868 (196.9)
Black	10,520 (250.9)	7,901 (162.9)	5,256 (202.5)	5,694 (185.5)	3,442 (41.9)	4,754 (210.2)	7,111 (205.3)	6,510 (154.4)	5,401 (298.1)	1,959 (88.6)	4,338 (303.8)	4,485 (327.7)	2,991 (458.5)
Hispanic	9,006 (199.9)	6,670 (134.9)	4,838 (163.3)	5,399 (146.6)	3,431 (57.7)	4,251 (150.0)	6,990 (221.3)	6,193 (161.0)	5,500 (375.6)	1,985 (99.8)	4,808 (648.2)	5,170 (734.5)	3,401 (866.8)
Asian/Pacific Islander	10,039 (228.5)	6,745 (168.8)	6,180 (244.3)	6,700 (219.9)	3,411 (57.3)	5,545 (236.8)	7,079 (280.3)	6,136 (200.6)	6,728 (584.3)	2,027 (91.0)	4,390 (805.2)	4,321 (856.1)	‡ (†)
American Indian/Alaska Native	9,513 (689.1)	7,463 (430.5)	4,271 (605.1)	5,366 (558.4)	3,545 (378.7)	3,859 (568.1)	6,922 (441.8)	6,387 (329.5)	‡ (†)	‡ (†)	‡ (†)	‡	‡
Age													
23 years old or younger	9,984 (127.5)	6,881 (61.9)	6,102 (121.1)	5,958 (109.4)	3,174 (26.6)	5,288 (117.5)	7,224 (86.6)	6,166 (62.7)	6,261 (152.2)	1,895 (42.1)	4,630 (281.1)	5,117 (329.8)	2,794 (269.3)
24 to 29 years old	10,184 (136.4)	8,710 (97.5)	3,809 (136.0)	4,605 (90.2)	3,375 (42.5)	3,161 (106.3)	7,616 (125.4)	7,093 (93.7)	5,320 (393.8)	2,148 (93.0)	5,497 (342.4)	5,762 (364.2)	3,395 (544.4)
30 years old or over	9,086 (154.8)	8,100 (125.7)	3,240 (133.9)	4,114 (84.7)	3,381 (57.5)	2,577 (101.7)	7,688 (140.2)	7,187 (88.9)	5,269 (442.6)	2,372 (143.8)	4,350 (245.2)	4,975 (291.2)	3,080 (222.2)
Marital status[5]													
Not married	10,037 (115.2)	7,215 (53.5)	5,813 (112.6)	5,755 (98.6)	3,256 (24.7)	5,022 (110.0)	7,312 (84.3)	6,337 (56.4)	6,185 (160.6)	1,927 (42.8)	4,758 (201.7)	5,269 (228.0)	3,008 (220.1)
Married	8,785 (160.9)	7,845 (121.0)	3,502 (123.2)	4,013 (100.2)	3,078 (54.3)	2,930 (116.7)	7,671 (125.2)	7,213 (97.8)	5,074 (385.3)	2,243 (124.1)	4,808 (311.2)	5,279 (393.6)	3,043 (268.3)
Separated	9,554 (409.7)	8,315 (330.7)	3,122 (262.7)	4,758 (230.7)	3,719 (114.5)	2,801 (261.4)	6,532 (260.9)	6,318 (250.0)	3,895 (837.8)	1,846 (208.2)	4,939 (710.6)	‡ (†)	‡ (†)
Dependency status and family income													
Dependent	10,053 (136.5)	6,799 (61.5)	6,256 (126.7)	6,048 (117.8)	3,099 (27.2)	5,412 (123.3)	7,266 (89.3)	6,157 (63.8)	6,333 (153.0)	1,897 (44.1)	4,689 (341.1)	5,145 (403.2)	2,981 (254.6)
Less than $20,000	10,350 (237.7)	7,374 (135.3)	5,401 (172.5)	6,936 (169.8)	4,027 (30.8)	4,975 (174.4)	5,808 (150.1)	5,276 (124.8)	4,661 (307.8)	1,904 (72.9)	4,235 (604.8)	4,484 (689.6)	2,902 (641.4)
$20,000–$39,999	10,551 (194.1)	6,816 (105.9)	5,817 (166.8)	6,445 (130.8)	2,937 (31.8)	5,249 (149.9)	6,280 (130.2)	5,498 (93.8)	5,135 (253.9)	1,948 (72.6)	4,550 (679.1)	4,975 (848.8)	2,725 (618.1)
$40,000–$59,999	9,678 (211.8)	6,083 (127.0)	6,179 (176.6)	5,471 (158.8)	1,749 (47.0)	5,306 (166.0)	6,935 (156.4)	5,765 (123.7)	5,722 (254.8)	1,872 (67.9)	4,622 (542.8)	4,852 (659.3)	‡ (†)
$60,000–$79,999	9,755 (219.5)	6,503 (107.5)	6,473 (179.6)	5,461 (162.9)	1,477 (90.6)	5,447 (165.4)	7,617 (144.5)	6,371 (157.1)	6,700 (313.1)	1,820 (69.0)	3,755 (608.4)	4,145 (708.9)	‡ (†)
$80,000–$99,999	10,093 (263.8)	6,791 (157.7)	6,897 (248.3)	5,722 (215.3)	2,264 (616.9)	5,709 (211.0)	8,067 (199.1)	6,674 (199.7)	6,959 (321.3)	1,745 (60.3)	6,164 (1,623.3)	6,486 (1,771.4)	‡ (†)
$100,000 or more	9,850 (201.3)	7,263 (133.1)	6,868 (180.8)	5,854 (171.4)	1,659 (449.7)	5,849 (169.5)	8,719 (162.6)	7,296 (129.7)	7,971 (343.3)	2,059 (86.0)	5,235 (1,142.2)	6,614 (1,607.4)	‡ (†)
Independent	9,552 (96.2)	8,283 (77.5)	3,603 (89.6)	4,515 (63.9)	3,419 (36.8)	3,006 (69.4)	7,486 (100.7)	6,992 (65.4)	5,204 (300.0)	2,143 (68.8)	4,820 (190.8)	5,352 (225.9)	3,020 (206.7)
Less than $10,000	10,450 (139.1)	8,723 (123.3)	3,709 (112.1)	5,411 (79.3)	3,875 (36.9)	3,208 (106.2)	7,014 (113.2)	6,610 (102.7)	5,006 (349.9)	1,975 (84.2)	4,654 (376.2)	5,434 (471.0)	2,901 (393.7)
$10,000–$19,999	9,674 (208.8)	8,215 (139.9)	3,578 (195.9)	4,366 (99.7)	3,244 (54.2)	2,852 (130.2)	7,301 (121.5)	6,746 (121.5)	5,826 (764.2)	2,380 (129.1)	5,139 (359.7)	5,735 (717.9)	2,964 (386.8)
$20,000–$29,999	9,494 (172.2)	8,262 (138.3)	3,528 (205.1)	4,342 (106.7)	3,365 (65.2)	2,978 (147.5)	7,697 (181.9)	7,236 (144.7)	5,520 (813.8)	2,044 (236.9)	4,859 (514.5)	5,575 (406.7)	2,901 (296.9)
$30,000–$49,999	8,700 (256.4)	7,554 (194.3)	3,690 (191.8)	3,387 (136.9)	2,229 (79.0)	2,973 (181.2)	7,977 (187.9)	7,292 (151.3)	5,009 (437.7)	2,351 (215.7)	3,976 (431.7)	4,085 (529.6)	3,233 (503.0)
$50,000 or more	7,799 (232.5)	7,910 (228.1)	3,321 (184.9)	2,765 (166.0)	1,339 (171.6)	2,773 (167.1)	8,391 (223.9)	7,992 (149.4)	4,503 (497.5)	‡ (†)	5,445 (571.1)	5,857 (650.1)	3,276 (395.8)
Housing status													
School-owned	13,204 (219.3)	7,856 (82.6)	8,258 (210.4)	7,827 (185.3)	3,273 (51.4)	7,092 (191.2)	8,064 (131.0)	6,628 (85.7)	7,104 (231.6)	1,801 (49.9)	5,391 (565.2)	5,971 (664.9)	3,696 (409.9)
Off-campus, not with parents	9,391 (114.3)	7,735 (83.7)	4,392 (99.5)	4,741 (88.8)	3,307 (33.0)	3,713 (99.1)	7,356 (108.9)	6,659 (75.8)	5,661 (248.7)	2,203 (63.1)	4,826 (216.0)	5,407 (255.3)	2,953 (220.0)
With parents	7,420 (117.8)	6,054 (85.8)	4,032 (97.0)	4,461 (88.5)	3,134 (30.7)	3,534 (104.1)	6,338 (98.8)	5,713 (89.8)	5,045 (148.1)	1,888 (70.5)	4,219 (214.6)	4,531 (234.7)	2,592 (324.3)

†Not applicable.
‡Reporting standards not met.
[1]Includes students who reported they were awarded aid, but did not specify the source or type of aid.
[2]Includes Parent Loans for Undergraduate Students (PLUS).
[3]Details on federal and nonfederal work study participants are not available.
[4]Excludes persons not reported by race/ethnicity and persons reporting more than one race.
[5]Includes students who were single, divorced, or widowed.
NOTE: Rows may not sum to totals because of rounding, survey item nonresponse, and/or the fact that some students receive aid from multiple sources. Data include undergraduates in degree-granting and non-degree-granting institutions. Race categories exclude persons of Hispanic origin. Data include Puerto Rico.
SOURCE: U.S. Department of Education, National Center for Education Statistics, 2003–04 National Postsecondary Student Aid Study (NPSAS:04). (This table was prepared September 2005.)

Table 325. Average amount of financial aid awarded to part-time or part-year undergraduates, by type and source of aid and selected student characteristics: 2003–04

Selected student characteristic	Any aid			Grants			Loans			Work study	Other		
	Total¹	Federal	Nonfederal	Total	Federal	Nonfederal	Total	Federal²	Nonfederal	Total³	Total	Federal	Nonfederal
1	2	3	4	5	6	7	8	9	10	11	12	13	14
All part-time or part-year undergraduates	$4,860 (67.1)	$4,765 (51.3)	$2,549 (66.7)	$2,449 (35.3)	$1,983 (18.4)	$2,054 (45.7)	$5,642 (89.2)	$5,145 (64.6)	$4,958 (243.0)	$2,012 (62.7)	$2,891 (119.8)	$2,995 (126.6)	$2,373 (155.8)
Sex													
Male	5,042 (117.0)	4,991 (92.3)	2,783 (103.4)	2,504 (51.7)	1,975 (31.9)	2,208 (63.9)	5,989 (146.4)	5,359 (98.0)	5,268 (401.4)	2,046 (78.8)	3,067 (138.5)	3,112 (143.9)	2,572 (227.5)
Female	4,746 (64.6)	4,634 (56.3)	2,396 (65.9)	2,418 (39.3)	1,986 (20.7)	1,954 (56.2)	5,433 (78.6)	5,017 (71.8)	4,714 (185.4)	1,987 (85.7)	2,569 (134.9)	2,723 (172.1)	2,270 (163.0)
Race/ethnicity⁴													
White	4,837 (100.9)	4,901 (83.0)	2,620 (89.9)	2,370 (48.2)	1,872 (23.6)	2,105 (59.9)	5,764 (123.9)	5,214 (88.4)	5,235 (275.4)	1,963 (85.3)	2,940 (144.6)	3,219 (156.1)	1,952 (175.0)
Black	4,908 (149.4)	4,735 (115.6)	2,187 (94.1)	2,476 (73.3)	2,045 (35.7)	1,901 (97.1)	5,214 (113.7)	5,009 (114.4)	3,669 (196.1)	1,978 (132.7)	2,758 (249.5)	2,826 (267.4)	2,138 (249.8)
Hispanic	4,622 (121.6)	4,306 (105.8)	2,355 (109.2)	2,487 (56.0)	2,089 (26.8)	1,843 (94.0)	5,466 (160.6)	4,927 (120.9)	4,562 (327.4)	1,975 (154.2)	2,795 (261.8)	2,505 (294.9)	4,126 (520.9)
Asian/Pacific Islander	5,316 (253.5)	4,833 (169.9)	3,158 (236.5)	3,046 (161.0)	2,284 (90.1)	2,438 (182.2)	6,313 (358.0)	5,609 (235.5)	4,901 (753.2)	2,496 (181.0)	3,294 (741.3)	‡ (†)	‡ (†)
American Indian/Alaska Native	4,246 (422.6)	4,289 (373.3)	2,090 (282.6)	2,384 (236.4)	2,284 (246.5)	1,697 (212.6)	5,130 (577.6)	4,479 (419.3)	‡ (†)	‡ (†)	‡ (†)	‡ (†)	‡ (†)
Age													
23 years old or younger	5,273 (128.2)	4,439 (83.7)	3,288 (117.0)	2,952 (63.8)	2,055 (22.1)	2,646 (84.6)	5,369 (139.7)	4,652 (97.0)	5,248 (294.7)	1,943 (75.9)	2,644 (167.4)	2,708 (203.7)	2,229 (331.6)
24 to 29 years old	5,059 (80.3)	5,125 (67.9)	2,168 (82.0)	2,195 (44.2)	1,957 (29.9)	1,629 (61.3)	5,855 (97.1)	5,436 (74.5)	4,902 (339.1)	2,076 (156.7)	3,231 (223.1)	3,296 (246.8)	2,629 (283.4)
30 years old or over	4,260 (86.6)	4,913 (84.4)	1,975 (61.2)	2,069 (40.1)	1,907 (29.8)	1,677 (49.0)	5,852 (110.2)	5,590 (98.4)	4,279 (315.3)	2,160 (142.6)	2,824 (165.9)	2,962 (170.1)	2,359 (200.3)
Marital status													
Not married⁵	5,153 (89.2)	4,729 (59.8)	2,813 (87.8)	2,634 (45.0)	2,028 (20.5)	2,225 (61.4)	5,596 (104.2)	5,005 (70.0)	5,188 (272.6)	1,963 (59.5)	2,952 (137.5)	3,094 (158.1)	2,285 (197.1)
Married	4,142 (86.9)	4,868 (86.5)	2,020 (63.9)	1,984 (42.6)	1,764 (29.6)	1,724 (50.9)	5,837 (115.4)	5,588 (103.9)	4,157 (285.0)	2,318 (208.9)	2,784 (175.2)	2,808 (187.6)	2,569 (267.9)
Separated	4,872 (225.6)	4,826 (210.5)	1,918 (167.7)	2,460 (96.4)	2,155 (70.8)	1,591 (143.2)	5,315 (214.0)	5,089 (185.2)	3,711 (459.0)	‡ (†)	3,226 (627.4)	‡ (†)	‡ (†)
Dependency status and family income													
Dependent	5,458 (151.5)	4,454 (97.5)	3,549 (131.2)	3,111 (79.0)	2,043 (27.1)	2,846 (95.0)	5,481 (166.2)	4,672 (114.7)	5,485 (318.9)	1,919 (71.4)	2,405 (182.5)	2,405 (235.4)	2,402 (422.6)
Less than $20,000	5,075 (180.1)	4,205 (111.9)	2,821 (201.0)	3,334 (113.9)	2,483 (37.6)	2,432 (196.4)	4,567 (214.3)	3,998 (173.3)	4,430 (479.1)	1,773 (170.6)	2,540 (534.8)	‡ (†)	‡ (†)
$20,000–$39,999	5,224 (152.0)	4,105 (99.0)	3,171 (160.1)	3,050 (97.5)	1,963 (39.0)	2,654 (128.0)	4,912 (260.8)	4,203 (184.9)	4,830 (484.7)	1,849 (88.9)	2,187 (322.4)	2,469 (396.7)	‡ (†)
$40,000–$59,999	5,370 (293.3)	4,392 (190.6)	3,528 (269.8)	2,740 (175.1)	1,249 (58.8)	2,801 (205.0)	5,308 (260.8)	4,590 (184.9)	5,878 (820.3)	1,868 (116.8)	1,970 (322.2)	2,145 (393.3)	‡ (†)
$60,000–$79,999	5,454 (249.0)	4,526 (206.0)	3,772 (221.7)	3,071 (221.6)	1,301 (129.3)	3,039 (224.1)	5,363 (258.8)	4,595 (217.4)	4,805 (371.6)	2,033 (158.1)	3,230 (464.3)	3,202 (700.0)	‡ (†)
$80,000–$99,999	5,716 (305.5)	4,989 (284.1)	4,060 (307.5)	3,014 (264.5)	776 (300.7)	3,032 (268.9)	6,127 (328.9)	5,103 (300.7)	5,994 (473.4)	2,296 (283.2)	‡ (†)	‡ (†)	‡ (†)
$100,000 or more	6,530 (346.1)	5,697 (314.3)	4,639 (345.6)	3,523 (235.9)	922 (303.9)	3,523 (246.0)	7,394 (393.7)	6,186 (319.1)	7,172 (742.2)	2,014 (160.0)	2,220 (476.3)	2,113 (496.3)	‡ (†)
Independent	4,586 (54.5)	4,917 (50.3)	2,055 (54.8)	2,165 (28.0)	1,959 (19.7)	1,669 (37.7)	5,731 (81.8)	5,399 (66.4)	4,486 (280.0)	2,109 (94.6)	2,981 (132.7)	3,105 (138.7)	2,368 (161.1)
Less than $10,000	5,130 (128.2)	4,876 (100.9)	2,171 (125.3)	2,599 (56.5)	2,255 (30.3)	1,626 (82.1)	5,391 (164.2)	4,935 (112.3)	4,654 (503.2)	1,971 (123.8)	3,248 (288.9)	3,662 (384.1)	2,213 (276.3)
$10,000–$19,999	4,816 (109.4)	4,718 (100.9)	1,947 (98.4)	2,142 (52.0)	1,868 (30.8)	1,483 (86.9)	5,529 (118.4)	5,224 (110.1)	4,198 (316.3)	2,339 (158.3)	3,091 (241.3)	3,350 (308.0)	2,082 (251.0)
$20,000–$29,999	4,789 (102.9)	4,961 (78.1)	1,844 (73.9)	2,196 (48.2)	2,065 (33.6)	1,480 (63.3)	5,472 (117.1)	5,234 (111.4)	4,000 (239.9)	1,664 (246.7)	3,104 (265.3)	3,453 (323.8)	2,042 (196.8)
$30,000–$49,999	4,307 (113.1)	4,773 (122.2)	2,051 (88.9)	1,835 (50.0)	1,381 (32.7)	1,689 (69.4)	5,931 (163.8)	5,580 (139.1)	4,798 (593.7)	2,401 (304.3)	2,954 (228.6)	2,988 (244.9)	2,572 (333.6)
$50,000 or more	3,889 (121.8)	5,508 (169.5)	2,171 (83.8)	1,910 (71.0)	1,152 (227.2)	1,906 (73.5)	6,570 (176.4)	6,280 (158.6)	4,752 (479.6)	2,410 (450.7)	2,726 (194.5)	2,658 (213.2)	3,060 (370.5)
Housing status													
School-owned	8,776 (400.3)	5,858 (201.2)	6,066 (350.0)	4,967 (226.5)	2,208 (78.9)	4,867 (238.4)	6,422 (387.3)	5,146 (203.0)	6,962 (795.5)	1,883 (118.2)	3,237 (383.1)	3,394 (489.3)	‡ (†)
Off-campus, not with parents	4,596 (59.6)	4,775 (55.3)	2,222 (53.8)	2,216 (29.9)	1,943 (21.4)	1,775 (36.2)	5,670 (85.6)	5,242 (70.3)	4,856 (225.5)	2,063 (75.7)	2,891 (148.4)	3,000 (161.0)	2,344 (155.5)
With parents	4,554 (85.8)	4,460 (81.8)	2,283 (77.1)	2,406 (47.5)	2,032 (24.1)	1,871 (67.5)	5,283 (109.0)	4,901 (97.0)	4,134 (206.5)	2,000 (135.3)	2,847 (143.6)	2,931 (148.8)	2,450 (338.0)

†Not applicable.
‡Reporting standards not met.
¹Includes students who reported they were awarded aid, but did not specify the source or type of aid.
²Includes Parent Loans for Undergraduate Students (PLUS).
³Details on federal and nonfederal work study participants are not available.
⁴Excludes persons not reported by race/ethnicity and persons reporting more than one race.
⁵Includes students who were single, divorced, or widowed.
NOTE: Rows may not sum to totals because of rounding, survey item nonresponse, and/or the fact that some students receive aid from multiple sources. Data include undergraduates in degree-granting and non-degree-granting institutions. Race categories exclude persons of Hispanic origin. Standard errors appear in parentheses. Data include Puerto Rico.
SOURCE: U.S. Department of Education, National Center for Education Statistics, 2003–04 National Postsecondary Student Aid Study (NPSAS:04). (This table was prepared September 2005.)

Table 326. Amount borrowed, aid status, and sources of aid for full-time and part-time undergraduates, by control and type of institution: 2003–04

Control and type of institution	Number of undergraduates[1] (in thousands)		Cumulative amount borrowed for undergraduate education[2]		Aid status (percent of students)										
					Nonaided		Receiving aid, by source									
							Any aid[3]		Federal		State		Institutional		Other[3]	
1		2		3		4		5		6		7		8		9
Full-time, full-year students																
All institutions.................	7,824	(93.5)	$12,750	(130.4)	23.9	(0.40)	76.1	(0.40)	61.7	(0.42)	22.6	(0.48)	31.4	(0.66)	22.6	(0.35)
Public............................	5,662	(78.1)	11,260	(125.7)	28.9	(0.49)	71.1	(0.49)	56.1	(0.47)	21.7	(0.52)	23.6	(0.63)	19.0	(0.38)
4-year doctoral.....................	2,411	(33.2)	12,707	(136.8)	24.5	(0.64)	75.5	(0.64)	58.2	(0.71)	22.9	(0.47)	31.7	(0.72)	21.7	(0.46)
Other 4-year......................	1,198	(42.8)	11,500	(313.3)	23.0	(1.12)	77.0	(1.12)	64.0	(1.20)	26.7	(1.68)	23.6	(1.58)	20.0	(0.86)
2-year.............................	2,026	(59.1)	8,294	(263.5)	37.7	(1.22)	62.3	(1.22)	48.9	(1.15)	17.5	(0.84)	14.2	(0.99)	14.9	(0.73)
Less than 2-year..................	27	(2.1)	6,870	(362.3)	33.3	(2.51)	66.7	(2.51)	48.7	(2.75)	4.7	(1.08)	6.4	(1.39)	29.8	(2.76)
Private, not-for-profit..............	1,635	(38.9)	15,458	(287.8)	11.4	(0.78)	88.6	(0.78)	73.1	(0.81)	28.5	(1.50)	64.9	(1.77)	33.7	(0.96)
4-year doctoral.....................	668	(27.5)	16,033	(568.0)	15.9	(1.16)	84.1	(1.16)	66.2	(1.69)	23.1	(1.93)	63.6	(2.55)	34.3	(1.66)
Other 4-year......................	921	(36.8)	15,268	(453.4)	8.2	(1.08)	91.8	(1.08)	77.9	(1.25)	32.4	(2.41)	67.2	(3.44)	33.8	(1.88)
Less than 4-year..................	47	(4.4)	11,436	(1,847.7)	11.2	(2.63)	88.8	(2.63)	76.8	(4.76)	30.3	(5.45)	37.7	(6.84)	23.5	(3.81)
Private, for-profit....................	527	(21.6)	15,100	(500.8)	7.9	(0.72)	92.1	(0.72)	86.9	(0.92)	13.3	(1.80)	11.1	(1.42)	27.9	(1.66)
2-year and above.................	393	(21.0)	16,950	(596.3)	5.2	(0.89)	94.8	(0.89)	90.6	(1.14)	16.5	(2.49)	11.0	(1.95)	30.2	(2.12)
Less than 2-year..................	134	(3.0)	8,044	(368.5)	15.7	(1.13)	84.3	(1.13)	76.0	(1.31)	3.9	(0.49)	11.4	(0.97)	20.9	(1.22)
Part-time or part-year students																
All institutions..................	11,230	(93.5)	$8,363	(138.1)	45.7	(0.56)	54.3	(0.56)	38.5	(0.44)	9.2	(0.41)	10.1	(0.42)	17.6	(0.35)
Public............................	9,015	(74.6)	7,340	(136.5)	52.4	(0.69)	47.6	(0.69)	32.0	(0.52)	9.1	(0.44)	7.8	(0.37)	15.0	(0.39)
4-year doctoral.....................	1,516	(33.3)	13,524	(329.0)	41.0	(1.12)	59.0	(1.12)	42.9	(0.92)	9.8	(0.47)	14.6	(0.80)	17.8	(0.74)
Other 4-year......................	984	(47.7)	10,243	(520.6)	43.9	(2.33)	56.1	(2.33)	42.0	(2.03)	9.9	(1.21)	8.9	(1.07)	16.7	(0.99)
2-year.............................	6,449	(59.1)	4,831	(128.4)	56.4	(0.92)	43.6	(0.92)	28.0	(0.66)	8.8	(0.56)	6.1	(0.48)	14.0	(0.51)
Less than 2-year..................	66	(2.1)	4,584	(1,507.7)	57.6	(4.11)	42.4	(4.11)	19.6	(1.80)	3.6	(1.81)	4.1	(1.23)	24.0	(3.02)
Private, not-for-profit..............	1,204	(37.4)	11,341	(502.2)	23.7	(1.07)	76.3	(1.07)	52.4	(1.42)	13.0	(1.11)	29.8	(2.24)	30.9	(1.37)
4-year doctoral.....................	356	(17.6)	12,537	(678.9)	26.9	(1.48)	73.1	(1.48)	45.8	(2.20)	11.5	(1.28)	38.5	(3.12)	30.5	(1.63)
Other 4-year......................	786	(37.2)	11,153	(733.0)	22.6	(1.45)	77.4	(1.45)	54.2	(2.21)	13.5	(1.61)	26.4	(3.32)	31.8	(2.19)
Less than 4-year..................	62	(4.4)	7,391	(1,168.4)	19.3	(3.62)	80.7	(3.62)	66.9	(3.72)	14.7	(3.12)	22.7	(4.44)	21.3	(3.10)
Private, for-profit....................	1,011	(19.5)	10,233	(349.2)	12.4	(0.54)	87.6	(0.54)	79.8	(0.85)	5.4	(0.84)	6.6	(0.80)	24.6	(1.41)
2-year and above.................	636	(19.2)	12,418	(497.4)	9.3	(0.72)	90.7	(0.72)	83.3	(1.26)	7.5	(1.33)	6.5	(1.23)	27.3	(2.27)
Less than 2-year..................	375	(3.0)	6,145	(159.3)	17.7	(0.97)	82.3	(0.97)	73.8	(0.91)	1.9	(0.18)	6.7	(0.93)	19.9	(0.73)

[1]Numbers of undergraduates may not equal figures reported in other tables, since these data are based on a sample survey of students who enrolled at any time during the academic year.
[2]Includes only those students who borrowed to finance their undergraduate education. Excludes loans from family sources.
[3]Includes students who reported that they were awarded aid, but did not specify the source of the aid.

NOTE: Excludes students whose attendance status was not reported. Detail may not sum to totals because of rounding and because some students receive multiple types of aid and aid from different sources. Standard errors appear in parentheses. The numbers in column 2 may not add to totals because of rounding. Data include Puerto Rico.
SOURCE: U.S. Department of Education, National Center for Education Statistics, 2003–04 National Postsecondary Student Aid Study (NPSAS:04). (This table was prepared August 2005.)

Table 327. Percentage of full-time, full-year undergraduates receiving aid, by type and source of aid received and control and type of institution: Selected years, 1992–93 through 2003–04

Control and type of institution	Any aid			Grants			Loans			Work study[1]		Other		
	Total[2]	Federal	Nonfederal	Total	Federal	Nonfederal	Total	Federal	Nonfederal	Total	Federal	Total	Federal	Nonfederal
1	2	3	4	5	6	7	8	9	10	11	12	13	14	15
1992–93, all institutions	**58.7 (0.81)**	**45.6 (0.80)**	**37.9 (0.76)**	**48.9 (0.75)**	**29.4 (0.76)**	**34.0 (0.71)**	**32.3 (0.78)**	**31.3 (0.77)**	**2.7 (0.20)**	**10.2 (0.48)**	**6.8 (0.39)**	**9.5 (0.40)**	**5.2 (0.28)**	**4.6 (0.32)**
Public	52.6 (1.03)	40.0 (0.98)	33.0 (0.88)	43.1 (0.94)	27.8 (0.83)	29.1 (0.79)	25.5 (0.89)	24.8 (0.88)	2.0 (0.22)	6.8 (0.43)	4.2 (0.30)	7.9 (0.40)	3.7 (0.27)	4.4 (0.33)
4-year doctoral	54.1 (1.18)	39.3 (1.17)	34.8 (0.81)	42.4 (1.02)	23.8 (0.96)	30.8 (0.74)	31.2 (1.05)	30.4 (1.04)	2.4 (0.26)	7.1 (0.55)	4.3 (0.37)	8.6 (0.43)	5.0 (0.37)	3.9 (0.27)
Other 4-year	57.1 (1.56)	46.1 (1.61)	37.4 (1.69)	46.1 (1.65)	32.1 (1.63)	32.4 (1.55)	32.2 (1.38)	31.1 (1.34)	2.8 (0.59)	9.5 (0.76)	5.4 (0.57)	7.9 (0.63)	4.2 (0.42)	3.8 (0.55)
2-year	47.2 (2.35)	36.0 (2.09)	27.0 (1.96)	41.9 (2.19)	29.9 (1.81)	24.3 (1.87)	12.1 (1.40)	11.7 (1.38)	0.7 (0.24)	4.1 (0.75)	3.0 (0.58)	7.0 (0.94)	1.3 (0.47)	5.7 (0.84)
Less than 2-year	35.4 (7.28)	31.6 (7.27)	15.7 (6.50)	30.3 (5.52)	26.6 (5.70)	12.8 (5.75)	3.0 (1.63)	3.0 (1.63)	0.6 (0.51)	1.5 (0.98)	1.4 (0.95)	5.1 (2.59)	0.8 (0.62)	4.4 (2.49)
Private, not-for-profit	70.2 (1.52)	53.4 (1.43)	58.0 (1.60)	62.9 (1.50)	27.7 (1.78)	54.1 (1.64)	45.4 (1.33)	43.6 (1.31)	5.0 (0.48)	22.2 (1.11)	15.9 (0.99)	12.1 (0.98)	7.7 (0.54)	5.0 (0.90)
4-year doctoral	63.6 (1.80)	44.5 (1.57)	54.8 (1.78)	56.1 (1.79)	17.3 (1.29)	51.8 (1.70)	40.5 (1.37)	38.5 (1.31)	6.1 (0.65)	18.9 (1.24)	13.2 (1.38)	11.6 (0.96)	7.4 (0.70)	4.5 (0.67)
Other 4-year	76.2 (2.07)	60.8 (2.07)	62.7 (2.66)	69.4 (2.07)	35.6 (2.77)	58.1 (2.81)	50.6 (2.17)	49.0 (2.20)	4.1 (0.77)	27.0 (1.61)	19.7 (1.47)	12.2 (1.80)	7.9 (0.85)	5.3 (1.71)
Less than 4-year	73.9 (4.01)	63.9 (5.69)	42.0 (5.38)	61.3 (4.73)	47.3 (7.16)	35.4 (6.71)	39.7 (5.73)	38.1 (5.51)	2.5 (0.97)	4.6 (1.36)	3.0 (1.01)	17.2 (3.97)	9.4 (4.28)	7.8 (3.07)
Private, for-profit	77.3 (2.53)	72.4 (2.76)	16.4 (2.97)	57.0 (2.67)	50.9 (2.69)	11.4 (2.75)	52.9 (3.87)	52.4 (3.87)	2.1 (0.66)	1.9 (1.18)	0.8 (0.36)	15.6 (2.42)	11.3 (2.29)	4.5 (1.02)
2-year and above	82.7 (3.43)	77.4 (4.27)	22.7 (5.67)	52.5 (4.19)	43.4 (4.13)	16.4 (5.15)	63.3 (4.16)	63.0 (4.18)	3.0 (1.41)	3.5 (2.55)	1.4 (0.78)	24.6 (4.64)	18.8 (4.48)	6.5 (2.11)
Less than 2-year	73.2 (3.27)	68.6 (3.26)	11.5 (2.43)	60.4 (3.57)	56.7 (3.75)	7.5 (2.47)	45.0 (5.12)	44.3 (5.09)	1.5 (0.40)	0.7 (0.43)	0.2 (0.09)	8.7 (1.48)	5.6 (1.21)	3.1 (0.86)
1995–96, all institutions	**68.4 (0.76)**	**55.6 (0.79)**	**45.7 (0.85)**	**54.1 (0.80)**	**30.6 (0.79)**	**41.0 (0.82)**	**43.7 (0.80)**	**43.2 (0.80)**	**1.7 (0.24)**	**11.0 (0.55)**	**9.0 (0.46)**	**10.9 (0.43)**	**5.0 (0.27)**	**5.9 (0.36)**
Public	62.8 (0.97)	50.8 (0.97)	39.0 (0.97)	47.5 (0.99)	29.6 (0.99)	34.2 (0.89)	37.2 (0.93)	36.9 (0.92)	0.8 (0.19)	7.0 (0.52)	5.4 (0.42)	9.3 (0.52)	3.7 (0.30)	5.5 (0.42)
4-year doctoral	65.4 (1.16)	51.9 (1.12)	42.2 (1.18)	47.6 (1.20)	26.1 (1.13)	37.2 (1.19)	44.5 (1.10)	44.1 (1.10)	1.4 (0.34)	7.4 (0.74)	5.3 (0.46)	11.0 (0.75)	5.6 (0.58)	5.4 (0.54)
Other 4-year	69.3 (1.38)	59.8 (1.34)	44.5 (1.58)	52.3 (1.48)	34.4 (1.53)	40.0 (1.45)	47.4 (1.60)	47.2 (1.60)	0.4 (0.14)	9.2 (0.86)	6.7 (0.63)	8.6 (0.66)	3.7 (0.45)	4.8 (0.48)
2-year	55.9 (2.29)	44.5 (2.33)	31.3 (2.25)	44.6 (2.36)	31.1 (2.43)	26.9 (1.93)	21.8 (1.85)	21.3 (1.83)	0.4 (0.39)	5.1 (1.16)	4.7 (1.07)	7.4 (1.17)	1.3 (0.35)	6.0 (1.04)
Less than 2-year	39.5 (9.87)	20.6 (6.51)	27.5 (7.17)	30.9 (7.49)	18.5 (5.86)	16.0 (5.29)	4.4 (2.28)	4.4 (2.28)	# (†)	0.1 (0.14)	0.1 (0.14)	12.6 (4.52)	0.1 (0.06)	12.0 (4.36)
Private, not-for-profit	80.3 (1.12)	64.0 (1.43)	67.6 (1.58)	71.3 (1.34)	28.6 (1.37)	64.8 (1.64)	56.9 (1.41)	56.2 (1.42)	3.4 (0.64)	24.7 (1.45)	21.0 (1.26)	14.0 (0.86)	8.2 (0.61)	6.1 (0.74)
4-year doctoral	70.6 (1.56)	55.4 (1.77)	61.2 (1.84)	61.6 (1.69)	19.3 (0.93)	58.7 (1.92)	50.9 (1.80)	49.9 (1.88)	3.9 (0.84)	22.6 (1.66)	20.2 (1.62)	13.3 (0.86)	8.6 (0.77)	4.9 (0.52)
Other 4-year	85.6 (1.43)	68.3 (1.99)	72.5 (2.19)	77.3 (1.83)	32.5 (2.10)	70.1 (2.27)	60.4 (1.94)	60.0 (1.95)	2.6 (0.59)	27.6 (2.10)	23.0 (1.80)	14.6 (1.29)	8.2 (0.90)	6.7 (1.15)
Less than 4-year	79.2 (5.71)	67.5 (6.37)	52.0 (8.29)	61.9 (4.87)	40.0 (4.69)	42.0 (6.10)	52.9 (7.57)	51.7 (7.28)	9.3 (7.17)	5.3 (2.22)	4.6 (2.00)	11.4 (3.30)	5.0 (1.43)	6.3 (2.16)
Private, for-profit	86.2 (1.73)	79.7 (2.05)	32.8 (3.11)	61.3 (2.40)	53.9 (2.53)	20.2 (2.64)	67.7 (3.40)	65.5 (3.67)	5.1 (1.89)	0.5 (0.16)	0.5 (0.15)	17.2 (1.74)	7.6 (1.09)	8.9 (1.32)
2-year and above	85.8 (1.85)	80.3 (2.58)	33.0 (3.41)	60.0 (3.02)	49.1 (3.23)	26.0 (3.83)	70.9 (3.50)	70.9 (3.51)	1.4 (0.74)	0.7 (0.26)	0.7 (0.26)	15.3 (1.86)	7.8 (1.36)	6.9 (1.19)
Less than 2-year	86.6 (2.92)	79.1 (3.16)	32.5 (5.18)	62.5 (3.72)	58.6 (3.83)	14.5 (3.61)	64.6 (5.75)	60.3 (6.32)	8.7 (3.61)	0.3 (0.18)	0.2 (0.15)	19.1 (2.92)	7.4 (1.69)	10.9 (2.33)
1999–2000, all institutions	**72.5 (0.51)**	**57.7 (0.56)**	**51.8 (0.64)**	**58.7 (0.59)**	**30.3 (0.59)**	**48.3 (0.65)**	**45.4 (0.62)**	**44.3 (0.63)**	**6.8 (0.25)**	**11.2 (0.38)**	**8.5 (0.31)**	**9.6 (0.31)**	**5.6 (0.22)**	**1.9 (0.17)**
Public	67.5 (0.64)	52.6 (0.68)	46.0 (0.72)	53.0 (0.70)	29.8 (0.69)	42.5 (0.72)	38.9 (0.74)	37.9 (0.75)	4.4 (0.24)	7.2 (0.36)	5.4 (0.30)	8.2 (0.35)	3.9 (0.22)	1.9 (0.19)
4-year doctoral	71.0 (0.65)	54.7 (0.70)	48.7 (0.74)	53.1 (0.70)	25.7 (0.72)	44.6 (0.71)	48.3 (0.76)	47.2 (0.78)	5.5 (0.36)	8.3 (0.46)	5.8 (0.38)	9.6 (0.45)	6.1 (0.37)	1.6 (0.15)
Other 4-year	75.0 (1.24)	62.2 (1.48)	50.0 (1.61)	57.7 (1.74)	34.5 (2.11)	46.2 (1.60)	49.1 (1.75)	48.2 (1.78)	4.5 (0.46)	10.4 (1.05)	7.7 (0.83)	7.8 (0.69)	3.9 (0.58)	1.7 (0.36)
2-year	58.2 (1.34)	43.8 (1.28)	40.0 (1.56)	49.9 (1.42)	32.1 (1.17)	37.7 (1.60)	20.5 (1.26)	19.6 (1.24)	3.1 (0.47)	3.8 (0.53)	3.4 (0.50)	6.5 (0.74)	1.1 (0.19)	2.4 (0.49)
Less than 2-year	60.7 (5.94)	48.1 (6.42)	33.6 (4.81)	49.2 (6.35)	40.8 (6.85)	25.0 (5.05)	11.0 (4.14)	11.0 (4.14)	0.3 (0.31)	0.8 (0.77)	# (†)	17.2 (2.19)	0.1 (0.10)	11.7 (2.02)
Private, not-for-profit	84.0 (0.77)	67.6 (1.02)	71.6 (1.27)	74.7 (1.12)	27.7 (1.23)	68.9 (1.36)	59.3 (1.14)	57.7 (1.18)	13.4 (0.65)	24.4 (1.07)	18.8 (0.82)	12.8 (0.67)	9.7 (0.56)	1.5 (0.40)
4-year doctoral	78.8 (1.13)	62.3 (1.41)	69.4 (1.29)	69.7 (1.24)	22.4 (0.95)	66.4 (1.36)	57.3 (1.42)	55.5 (1.43)	15.1 (0.86)	24.7 (1.17)	20.9 (1.06)	12.0 (0.74)	9.9 (0.66)	1.1 (0.20)
Other 4-year	88.3 (1.12)	72.2 (1.53)	74.1 (2.12)	78.7 (1.81)	30.9 (2.13)	71.6 (2.27)	62.2 (1.79)	60.6 (1.87)	12.8 (1.01)	24.8 (1.75)	17.7 (1.26)	13.2 (1.09)	9.6 (0.90)	1.8 (0.73)
Less than 4-year	81.1 (3.64)	62.6 (3.94)	61.5 (4.76)	73.9 (3.59)	40.0 (3.66)	59.4 (5.18)	40.3 (5.18)	40.2 (5.19)	5.0 (0.80)	15.1 (2.91)	10.9 (2.54)	14.6 (1.94)	8.8 (0.95)	2.0 (0.81)
Private, for-profit	89.2 (1.25)	86.0 (1.50)	35.3 (3.45)	61.8 (2.49)	52.0 (2.95)	28.8 (3.14)	75.0 (2.87)	74.1 (2.93)	7.3 (1.69)	2.3 (0.84)	2.0 (0.83)	16.1 (1.55)	10.9 (1.42)	2.3 (0.50)
2-year and above	88.3 (1.60)	85.3 (1.90)	38.3 (4.46)	58.5 (2.99)	46.3 (3.47)	33.1 (4.01)	79.5 (2.77)	78.7 (2.80)	6.8 (2.15)	2.6 (1.03)	2.1 (1.00)	17.1 (1.91)	12.3 (1.80)	1.8 (0.47)
Less than 2-year	91.7 (1.27)	88.3 (1.92)	26.1 (3.49)	71.9 (3.47)	69.9 (3.52)	15.6 (3.83)	61.0 (7.08)	59.9 (7.28)	8.9 (1.89)	1.6 (1.41)	1.6 (1.41)	12.9 (2.42)	6.7 (1.87)	3.8 (1.40)
2003–04, all institutions	**76.1 (0.40)**	**61.7 (0.42)**	**54.3 (0.52)**	**62.2 (0.48)**	**33.2 (0.32)**	**49.3 (0.51)**	**49.9 (0.44)**	**48.5 (0.43)**	**9.0 (0.31)**	**13.5 (0.41)**	**10.3 (0.36)**	**3.2 (0.17)**	**2.4 (0.12)**	**0.8 (0.09)**
Public	71.1 (0.49)	56.1 (0.47)	48.3 (0.56)	56.0 (0.58)	31.6 (0.33)	43.7 (0.54)	42.6 (0.46)	41.1 (0.47)	6.0 (0.16)	9.9 (0.34)	7.3 (0.31)	3.3 (0.19)	2.5 (0.13)	0.9 (0.11)
4-year doctoral	75.5 (0.64)	58.2 (0.71)	54.4 (0.55)	58.5 (0.61)	27.8 (0.79)	49.7 (0.57)	51.6 (0.74)	50.1 (0.74)	7.3 (0.31)	10.8 (0.41)	9.9 (0.87)	2.5 (0.20)	2.1 (0.16)	0.4 (0.11)
Other 4-year	77.0 (1.12)	64.0 (1.20)	53.4 (1.36)	58.8 (1.78)	34.6 (1.38)	48.1 (1.33)	52.2 (1.34)	50.5 (1.38)	7.3 (0.49)	12.9 (0.96)	5.3 (0.50)	3.5 (0.44)	2.6 (0.31)	1.0 (0.30)
2-year	62.3 (1.22)	48.9 (1.15)	38.1 (1.22)	51.5 (1.20)	34.5 (0.88)	34.2 (1.17)	26.4 (1.03)	25.1 (1.02)	3.7 (0.26)	7.1 (0.54)	1.1 (0.57)	3.9 (0.38)	2.8 (0.26)	1.2 (0.23)
Less than 2-year	66.7 (2.51)	48.7 (2.75)	36.5 (2.39)	49.7 (2.87)	36.0 (1.79)	23.1 (2.58)	24.8 (2.52)	24.2 (2.54)	4.1 (0.89)	2.0 (0.76)	22.5 (1.53)	15.0 (2.50)	1.9 (1.00)	13.2 (2.30)
Private, not-for-profit	88.6 (0.78)	73.1 (0.81)	78.3 (1.28)	81.0 (0.97)	31.9 (0.72)	74.5 (1.34)	66.0 (1.03)	64.4 (1.05)	17.0 (0.96)	29.2 (1.26)	23.0 (1.17)	2.1 (0.19)	1.7 (0.18)	0.4 (0.10)
4-year doctoral	84.1 (1.16)	66.2 (1.69)	76.0 (1.74)	75.9 (1.34)	24.3 (3.06)	72.1 (1.54)	60.8 (2.07)	59.0 (2.02)	17.7 (1.85)	27.7 (1.50)	24.2 (1.93)	1.6 (0.26)	1.4 (0.23)	0.3 (0.11)
Other 4-year	91.8 (1.08)	77.9 (1.25)	80.7 (2.77)	85.0 (1.36)	36.5 (2.12)	77.2 (2.75)	70.3 (2.35)	68.8 (2.34)	16.9 (1.64)	31.3 (2.29)	8.6 (2.71)	2.2 (0.29)	2.0 (0.28)	0.3 (0.12)
Less than 4-year	88.8 (2.63)	76.8 (4.76)	63.4 (5.93)	76.3 (3.71)	49.6 (3.98)	57.4 (6.16)	56.4 (5.05)	54.3 (5.04)	10.1 (2.42)	10.1 (3.38)	3.7 (0.82)	5.0 (1.68)	1.6 (1.02)	3.4 (1.39)
Private, for-profit	92.1 (0.72)	86.9 (0.92)	44.3 (1.90)	69.7 (1.68)	54.8 (1.69)	31.3 (1.88)	79.4 (1.18)	78.2 (1.17)	16.6 (1.45)	3.6 (0.70)	3.1 (0.62)	5.2 (0.69)	4.0 (0.57)	1.2 (0.30)
2-year and above	94.8 (0.89)	90.6 (1.14)	48.0 (2.45)	70.1 (2.17)	53.6 (2.21)	35.0 (2.50)	86.8 (1.43)	86.1 (1.44)	18.1 (1.91)	4.2 (0.93)	1.5 (0.22)	5.5 (0.90)	4.7 (0.76)	0.8 (0.39)
Less than 2-year	84.3 (1.13)	76.0 (1.31)	33.3 (1.59)	68.4 (1.44)	58.2 (1.61)	20.2 (1.87)	57.7 (1.62)	55.2 (1.59)	12.2 (1.18)	1.7 (0.21)	10.8 (0.41)	4.2 (0.45)	1.9 (0.28)	2.4 (0.30)

†Not applicable.
#Rounds to zero.
[1]Details on nonfederal work study participants are not available.
[2]Includes students who reported they were awarded aid, but did not specify the source of aid.
NOTE: Excludes students whose attendance status was not reported. Detail may not sum to totals because of rounding and because some students receive multiple types of aid and aid from different sources. Standard errors appear in parentheses. The 2003–04 loan estimates include Parent Loans for Undergraduate Students (PLUS) and may differ from previously published figures. Data include Puerto Rico.
SOURCE: U.S. Department of Education, National Center for Education Statistics, 1992–93, 1995–96, 1999–2000, and 2003–04 National Postsecondary Student Aid Studies (NPSAS:93, NPSAS:96, NPSAS:2000, and NPSAS:04). (This table was prepared August 2005.)

Table 328. Percentage of part-time or part-year undergraduates receiving aid, by type and source of aid received and control and type of institution: Selected years, 1992–93 through 2003–04

Control and type of institution	Any aid			Grants			Loans			Work study[1]		Other		
	Total[2]	Federal	Nonfederal	Total	Federal	Nonfederal	Total	Federal	Nonfederal	Total	Federal	Total	Federal	Nonfederal
1	2	3	4	5	6	7	8	9	10	11	12	13	14	15
1992–93, all institutions	**37.6 (0.80)**	**25.0 (0.83)**	**16.5 (0.44)**	**32.4 (0.76)**	**18.8 (0.77)**	**14.5 (0.39)**	**13.5 (0.50)**	**13.1 (0.49)**	**0.8 (0.09)**	**2.1 (0.13)**	**1.2 (0.09)**	**4.0 (0.26)**	**13.5 (0.49)**	**2.7 (0.24)**
Public	31.7 (0.71)	19.8 (0.67)	14.5 (0.46)	27.6 (0.66)	15.3 (0.60)	12.6 (0.40)	9.3 (0.41)	8.9 (0.39)	0.6 (0.09)	1.7 (0.12)	0.9 (0.09)	3.5 (0.30)	9.3 (0.40)	2.6 (0.29)
4-year doctoral	40.5 (1.02)	27.5 (0.95)	19.5 (0.66)	31.3 (0.85)	17.1 (0.68)	16.6 (0.61)	20.9 (0.83)	20.4 (0.82)	1.1 (0.18)	3.6 (0.32)	2.1 (0.24)	6.2 (0.43)	21.4 (0.84)	3.4 (0.33)
Other 4-year	39.5 (1.24)	28.4 (1.25)	19.2 (1.00)	33.8 (1.17)	22.0 (1.17)	16.1 (0.88)	16.2 (0.99)	15.6 (0.93)	1.3 (0.32)	3.1 (0.42)	1.6 (0.26)	4.1 (0.46)	16.3 (0.98)	2.6 (0.41)
2-year	28.6 (0.91)	16.5 (0.83)	12.7 (0.61)	25.9 (0.87)	13.7 (0.76)	11.2 (0.52)	5.6 (0.44)	5.3 (0.43)	0.4 (0.11)	1.1 (0.11)	0.6 (0.10)	2.9 (0.42)	5.5 (0.43)	2.5 (0.41)
Less than 2-year	21.2 (3.11)	15.1 (3.55)	6.9 (1.47)	19.4 (3.43)	13.8 (3.90)	6.0 (1.41)	0.7 (0.32)	0.7 (0.32)	# (†)	0.6 (0.36)	0.4 (0.34)	1.7 (0.70)	0.7 (0.32)	1.3 (0.57)
Private, not-for-profit	56.4 (1.96)	35.1 (2.65)	33.7 (1.54)	50.2 (2.12)	23.2 (2.96)	31.7 (1.49)	23.7 (1.38)	23.2 (1.34)	1.8 (0.23)	5.9 (0.71)	3.8 (0.42)	5.3 (0.48)	23.6 (1.36)	2.9 (0.49)
4-year doctoral	51.4 (1.91)	28.3 (1.49)	33.0 (1.91)	44.4 (1.90)	12.8 (0.98)	31.7 (1.91)	24.2 (1.42)	23.3 (1.39)	2.7 (0.47)	5.4 (0.88)	3.1 (0.58)	4.2 (0.48)	23.8 (1.45)	1.5 (0.29)
Other 4-year	59.4 (2.83)	38.1 (4.18)	35.6 (2.25)	53.8 (3.14)	26.8 (4.73)	33.6 (2.19)	24.4 (2.08)	23.9 (2.02)	1.5 (0.32)	7.3 (1.14)	4.8 (0.65)	5.7 (0.62)	24.4 (2.04)	3.4 (0.65)
Less than 4-year	53.9 (5.17)	35.8 (4.98)	28.4 (4.07)	47.3 (4.83)	28.3 (4.56)	24.4 (4.05)	20.7 (3.59)	20.3 (3.58)	1.2 (0.44)	1.2 (0.66)	1.2 (0.66)	5.8 (1.88)	20.6 (3.55)	3.6 (1.85)
Private, for-profit	71.0 (3.08)	64.4 (3.44)	11.8 (1.58)	55.3 (3.30)	48.8 (3.61)	8.6 (1.34)	42.3 (3.54)	41.9 (3.51)	1.5 (0.46)	0.9 (0.29)	0.4 (0.11)	6.8 (0.95)	42.2 (3.54)	2.5 (0.65)
2-year and above	64.4 (5.75)	54.9 (5.93)	14.3 (2.75)	46.2 (4.25)	35.0 (4.19)	12.1 (2.45)	45.7 (5.59)	45.5 (5.58)	0.9 (0.63)	1.4 (0.58)	0.6 (0.24)	8.0 (1.52)	45.9 (5.61)	2.1 (0.57)
Less than 2-year	75.5 (2.78)	70.8 (3.36)	10.2 (1.74)	61.5 (4.15)	58.1 (4.52)	6.3 (1.27)	40.0 (4.50)	39.4 (4.42)	1.8 (0.63)	0.5 (0.27)	0.3 (0.08)	5.9 (1.22)	39.7 (4.46)	2.7 (1.03)
1995–96, all institutions	**38.3 (0.84)**	**24.8 (0.73)**	**24.0 (0.71)**	**29.9 (0.76)**	**16.6 (0.62)**	**19.7 (0.62)**	**14.4 (0.49)**	**14.1 (0.48)**	**0.7 (0.16)**	**1.4 (0.12)**	**1.1 (0.11)**	**5.4 (0.36)**	**0.8 (0.07)**	**4.3 (0.35)**
Public	33.7 (0.93)	20.8 (0.77)	21.8 (0.80)	26.6 (0.84)	14.4 (0.66)	17.9 (0.69)	10.5 (0.47)	10.3 (0.46)	0.3 (0.15)	1.2 (0.13)	0.9 (0.12)	4.7 (0.40)	0.5 (0.06)	3.9 (0.39)
4-year doctoral	41.8 (1.25)	31.2 (1.14)	23.7 (1.19)	28.9 (1.13)	16.9 (0.95)	19.0 (1.02)	25.9 (1.09)	25.6 (1.09)	0.7 (0.22)	2.4 (0.37)	1.4 (0.23)	5.8 (0.65)	1.7 (0.34)	3.9 (0.56)
Other 4-year	41.9 (1.54)	30.9 (1.53)	22.8 (1.11)	30.2 (1.23)	18.2 (1.13)	19.3 (1.05)	22.3 (1.39)	22.1 (1.39)	0.4 (0.14)	2.3 (0.41)	2.0 (0.37)	4.8 (0.55)	0.8 (0.18)	3.7 (0.51)
2-year	30.7 (1.23)	17.2 (0.99)	21.1 (1.06)	25.4 (1.11)	13.4 (0.87)	17.5 (0.90)	5.7 (0.57)	5.5 (0.54)	0.3 (0.20)	0.8 (0.15)	0.7 (0.14)	4.4 (0.53)	0.2 (0.05)	3.9 (0.52)
Less than 2-year	34.3 (6.35)	13.9 (3.57)	26.0 (5.95)	27.8 (6.70)	12.3 (2.89)	17.4 (6.64)	2.2 (1.32)	2.2 (1.32)	# (†)	# (†)	# (†)	8.6 (2.67)	# (†)	8.3 (2.65)
Private, not-for-profit	55.6 (1.64)	34.9 (1.73)	41.5 (1.66)	44.1 (1.68)	17.9 (1.41)	36.1 (1.63)	26.4 (1.44)	26.1 (1.43)	1.4 (0.53)	4.0 (0.50)	3.1 (0.39)	8.6 (1.09)	2.0 (0.28)	6.6 (1.07)
4-year doctoral	51.0 (1.80)	27.7 (1.60)	39.7 (2.08)	39.3 (1.89)	12.0 (1.36)	34.3 (1.97)	24.4 (1.33)	23.6 (1.33)	1.4 (0.63)	4.6 (0.71)	3.7 (0.67)	8.4 (0.86)	2.1 (0.36)	5.9 (0.80)
Other 4-year	58.4 (2.25)	37.0 (2.49)	44.6 (2.25)	47.5 (2.41)	19.1 (2.07)	39.7 (2.28)	27.3 (2.04)	27.2 (2.03)	0.8 (0.28)	4.5 (0.75)	3.3 (0.56)	8.9 (1.65)	1.7 (0.36)	7.1 (1.64)
Less than 4-year	50.8 (6.21)	39.7 (5.91)	28.3 (5.56)	36.8 (4.69)	24.6 (4.01)	20.5 (3.57)	26.2 (5.37)	25.9 (5.26)	4.3 (3.90)	0.4 (0.19)	0.3 (0.18)	7.8 (2.41)	2.9 (0.97)	5.1 (1.93)
Private, for-profit	74.1 (2.94)	66.5 (3.33)	24.3 (2.58)	53.4 (3.08)	46.4 (3.13)	15.3 (2.37)	50.3 (3.58)	49.3 (3.53)	4.6 (1.50)	0.4 (0.14)	0.4 (0.14)	10.4 (1.15)	4.2 (0.76)	5.8 (0.86)
2-year and above	74.5 (2.80)	66.9 (3.16)	25.5 (2.74)	53.4 (3.30)	44.8 (3.42)	17.9 (2.73)	50.2 (3.77)	49.8 (3.72)	1.7 (1.06)	0.8 (0.27)	0.7 (0.27)	12.2 (1.81)	4.9 (1.07)	6.9 (1.29)
Less than 2-year	73.8 (4.99)	66.1 (5.67)	23.2 (4.24)	53.5 (5.06)	47.9 (5.14)	13.0 (3.82)	50.5 (5.89)	48.8 (5.83)	7.2 (2.68)	0.1 (0.08)	0.1 (0.08)	8.7 (1.45)	3.5 (1.07)	4.7 (1.12)
1999–2000, all institutions	**44.6 (0.81)**	**29.8 (0.64)**	**27.4 (0.75)**	**35.4 (0.70)**	**18.6 (0.52)**	**25.0 (0.73)**	**18.4 (0.56)**	**17.7 (0.55)**	**2.1 (0.12)**	**1.9 (0.11)**	**1.4 (0.10)**	**5.2 (0.36)**	**1.2 (0.07)**	**1.5 (0.29)**
Public	39.7 (0.85)	24.8 (0.57)	25.3 (0.86)	31.7 (0.78)	15.9 (0.48)	23.3 (0.83)	13.5 (0.41)	13.0 (0.39)	1.3 (0.11)	1.5 (0.11)	1.1 (0.10)	4.5 (0.38)	0.7 (0.06)	1.4 (0.33)
4-year doctoral	51.0 (0.93)	36.8 (0.93)	30.0 (0.83)	35.7 (0.79)	17.9 (0.70)	26.7 (0.70)	31.5 (0.96)	30.3 (0.87)	3.3 (0.42)	3.0 (0.28)	1.9 (0.25)	5.2 (0.35)	2.3 (0.22)	0.8 (0.12)
Other 4-year	51.2 (1.33)	37.0 (1.36)	29.9 (1.10)	39.1 (1.24)	21.5 (1.33)	27.9 (1.10)	27.4 (1.04)	26.6 (1.02)	2.4 (0.34)	3.1 (0.48)	2.5 (0.44)	4.7 (0.43)	0.9 (0.20)	1.0 (0.19)
2-year	34.9 (1.14)	19.8 (0.69)	23.5 (1.20)	29.5 (1.08)	14.4 (0.62)	21.9 (1.16)	6.9 (0.42)	6.5 (0.40)	0.6 (0.10)	0.8 (0.12)	0.7 (0.11)	4.1 (0.52)	0.3 (0.05)	1.5 (0.47)
Less than 2-year	38.6 (3.11)	21.9 (3.93)	22.2 (1.77)	29.6 (3.16)	18.2 (3.53)	14.4 (2.46)	5.0 (3.12)	4.7 (3.10)	0.4 (0.27)	1.6 (0.47)	0.9 (0.33)	11.1 (2.44)	0.4 (0.26)	7.9 (2.10)
Private, not-for-profit	64.8 (1.02)	44.5 (1.56)	47.2 (1.32)	53.9 (1.15)	22.1 (1.33)	44.8 (1.44)	34.8 (1.48)	33.4 (1.39)	6.0 (0.50)	5.9 (0.52)	4.0 (0.41)	8.2 (0.81)	3.4 (0.36)	1.2 (0.28)
4-year doctoral	60.2 (1.59)	40.9 (1.74)	46.8 (1.64)	49.9 (1.54)	17.0 (1.15)	44.2 (1.48)	35.1 (1.76)	34.1 (1.74)	7.6 (1.01)	6.5 (0.93)	4.7 (0.80)	7.5 (1.12)	3.7 (0.61)	1.7 (0.70)
Other 4-year	66.2 (1.33)	44.6 (2.23)	48.5 (1.78)	54.9 (1.58)	22.2 (1.94)	46.3 (2.02)	34.4 (2.11)	32.8 (1.95)	5.7 (0.63)	5.8 (0.68)	3.7 (0.52)	8.5 (1.15)	2.9 (0.46)	0.9 (0.28)
Less than 4-year	71.2 (4.24)	57.3 (5.11)	37.2 (6.39)	61.0 (4.36)	41.7 (4.22)	34.4 (6.66)	36.4 (5.14)	35.9 (5.04)	2.9 (0.62)	4.6 (1.49)	3.5 (1.12)	8.6 (1.69)	5.6 (1.40)	2.0 (0.91)
Private, for-profit	83.1 (1.78)	78.5 (1.53)	22.3 (1.82)	58.9 (2.03)	53.3 (2.19)	14.6 (1.69)	62.7 (3.06)	61.2 (3.07)	6.1 (0.86)	0.3 (0.16)	0.3 (0.15)	11.4 (1.84)	4.6 (0.49)	3.9 (1.22)
2-year and above	81.8 (2.03)	77.9 (2.24)	25.4 (2.77)	54.0 (2.92)	45.6 (2.94)	19.3 (2.16)	69.5 (3.09)	68.5 (3.12)	6.0 (1.28)	0.3 (0.24)	0.3 (0.24)	11.1 (1.36)	5.9 (0.80)	2.5 (0.76)
Less than 2-year	84.7 (2.75)	79.1 (1.97)	18.7 (2.41)	64.5 (2.44)	62.2 (2.45)	9.1 (1.83)	54.8 (6.25)	52.9 (6.32)	6.3 (1.11)	0.4 (0.19)	0.3 (0.18)	11.8 (3.55)	3.1 (0.60)	5.5 (2.15)
2003–04, all institutions	**54.3 (0.56)**	**38.5 (0.44)**	**31.5 (0.59)**	**42.7 (0.57)**	**23.6 (0.35)**	**28.1 (0.57)**	**25.0 (0.30)**	**23.8 (0.30)**	**3.7 (0.16)**	**3.4 (0.14)**	**2.2 (0.09)**	**3.9 (0.20)**	**3.2 (0.19)**	**0.8 (0.10)**
Public	47.6 (0.69)	32.0 (0.52)	28.2 (0.67)	37.6 (0.65)	20.3 (0.38)	25.6 (0.63)	17.5 (0.35)	16.5 (0.35)	2.1 (0.11)	2.9 (0.15)	1.9 (0.10)	3.6 (0.19)	2.9 (0.17)	0.7 (0.12)
4-year doctoral	59.0 (1.12)	42.9 (0.92)	34.9 (1.06)	41.7 (1.10)	20.5 (0.71)	30.7 (1.07)	37.4 (0.88)	35.5 (0.83)	4.8 (0.33)	4.2 (0.37)	2.1 (0.41)	2.9 (0.26)	2.4 (0.27)	0.5 (0.18)
Other 4-year	56.1 (2.33)	42.0 (2.03)	30.6 (2.08)	40.2 (2.56)	22.7 (1.78)	27.6 (1.87)	31.1 (1.58)	30.0 (1.48)	3.3 (0.52)	3.2 (0.58)	1.7 (0.12)	3.2 (0.56)	2.8 (0.53)	0.5 (0.20)
2-year	43.6 (0.92)	28.0 (0.66)	26.2 (0.87)	36.3 (0.88)	20.0 (0.51)	24.2 (0.82)	10.8 (0.37)	10.1 (0.37)	1.3 (0.11)	2.6 (0.18)	1.0 (0.56)	3.8 (0.27)	3.1 (0.22)	0.7 (0.16)
Less than 2-year	42.4 (4.11)	19.6 (1.80)	30.0 (3.95)	32.4 (3.52)	15.4 (1.63)	20.2 (3.13)	7.5 (1.90)	5.8 (1.26)	2.0 (1.02)	3.3 (1.06)	8.4 (1.16)	9.3 (2.12)	1.4 (0.45)	7.9 (2.10)
Private, not-for-profit	76.3 (1.07)	52.4 (1.42)	55.3 (1.97)	62.6 (1.67)	24.6 (1.04)	52.1 (2.16)	43.5 (1.30)	41.2 (1.25)	8.6 (0.78)	8.4 (0.71)	5.9 (0.64)	4.7 (0.87)	4.3 (0.89)	0.4 (0.12)
4-year doctoral	73.1 (1.48)	45.8 (2.20)	60.1 (2.23)	62.2 (1.70)	19.0 (2.07)	56.4 (2.25)	41.7 (2.06)	38.6 (2.16)	11.0 (1.14)	12.7 (1.40)	5.0 (0.78)	1.2 (0.40)	1.1 (0.41)	‡ (†)
Other 4-year	77.4 (1.45)	54.2 (2.21)	53.8 (3.05)	62.4 (2.43)	25.3 (1.85)	51.0 (3.26)	44.2 (2.09)	42.5 (2.06)	7.5 (1.14)	6.8 (0.86)	2.9 (0.83)	6.3 (1.33)	6.0 (1.39)	0.3 (0.17)
Less than 4-year	80.7 (3.62)	66.9 (3.72)	47.1 (4.44)	67.1 (3.26)	48.4 (3.52)	40.1 (4.20)	44.0 (5.58)	39.8 (4.53)	8.5 (2.78)	3.8 (1.06)	1.0 (0.31)	4.6 (1.52)	1.4 (0.86)	3.3 (1.36)
Private, for-profit	87.6 (0.54)	79.8 (0.85)	32.8 (1.44)	63.7 (1.20)	51.9 (1.36)	21.2 (1.10)	70.3 (1.03)	68.5 (1.01)	12.2 (1.12)	1.6 (0.23)	1.1 (0.21)	5.4 (0.78)	3.9 (0.77)	1.5 (0.19)
2-year and above	90.7 (0.72)	83.3 (1.26)	36.5 (2.28)	64.5 (1.85)	50.5 (2.15)	24.9 (1.77)	77.9 (1.44)	76.4 (1.40)	13.6 (1.75)	1.3 (0.34)	1.2 (0.15)	5.6 (1.26)	5.1 (1.24)	0.5 (0.18)
Less than 2-year	82.3 (0.97)	73.8 (0.91)	26.5 (1.13)	62.4 (0.96)	54.2 (0.73)	14.9 (0.91)	57.6 (0.76)	55.0 (0.84)	9.8 (0.53)	2.1 (0.19)	4.2 (0.37)	5.0 (0.46)	1.9 (0.20)	3.2 (0.38)

†Not applicable.
#Rounds to zero.
‡Reporting standards not met.
[1]Details on nonfederal work study participants are not available.
[2]Includes students who reported they were awarded aid, but did not specify the source of aid.
NOTE: Excludes students whose attendance status was not reported. Detail may not sum to totals because of rounding and because some students receive multiple types of aid and aid from different sources. The 2003–04 loan estimates include Parent Loans for Undergraduate Students (PLUS) and may differ from previously published figures. Standard errors appear in parentheses. Data include Puerto Rico.
SOURCE: U.S. Department of Education, National Center for Education Statistics, 1992–93, 1995–96, 1999–2000, and 2003–04 National Postsecondary Student Aid Studies (NPSAS:93, NPSAS:96, NPSAS:2000, and NPSAS:04). (This table was prepared August 2005.)

Table 329. Percentage of full-time and part-time undergraduates receiving federal aid, by aid program and control and type of institution: 2003–04

Control and type of institution	Number of undergraduates[1] (in thousands)	Percent receiving federal aid in 2003–04, by type							
		Any federal aid	Selected Title IV programs[2]						
			Any Title IV aid	Pell	SEOG[3]	CWS[4]	Perkins[5]	Stafford[6]	PLUS[7]
1	2	3	4	5	6	7	8	9	10
Full-time, full-year students									
All institutions	7,824 (93.5)	61.7 (0.42)	60.6 (0.44)	32.1 (0.34)	10.0 (0.37)	10.3 (0.36)	7.0 (0.31)	47.1 (0.44)	6.3 (0.22)
Public	5,662 (78.1)	56.1 (0.47)	54.9 (0.49)	30.6 (0.33)	7.9 (0.33)	7.3 (0.31)	5.3 (0.25)	39.9 (0.46)	4.9 (0.23)
4-year doctoral	2,411 (33.2)	58.2 (0.71)	57.1 (0.75)	26.5 (0.77)	8.0 (0.49)	7.9 (0.34)	8.5 (0.34)	48.2 (0.77)	7.7 (0.33)
Other 4-year	1,198 (42.8)	64.0 (1.20)	63.2 (1.22)	34.0 (1.40)	8.1 (0.67)	9.9 (0.87)	6.3 (0.98)	49.6 (1.37)	5.7 (0.82)
2-year	2,026 (59.1)	48.9 (1.15)	47.4 (1.16)	33.5 (0.88)	7.7 (0.51)	5.3 (0.50)	1.1 (0.16)	24.4 (1.03)	1.2 (0.15)
Less than 2-year	27 (2.1)	48.7 (2.75)	47.8 (2.70)	35.9 (1.73)	2.3 (0.88)	1.1 (0.57)	‡ (†)	24.1 (2.56)	0.3 (0.28)
Private, not-for-profit	1,635 (38.9)	73.1 (0.81)	72.5 (0.82)	30.4 (0.77)	14.6 (0.92)	23.0 (1.17)	14.0 (0.95)	62.2 (1.05)	11.0 (0.51)
4-year doctoral	668 (27.5)	66.2 (1.69)	65.3 (1.72)	22.9 (3.07)	11.7 (1.78)	22.5 (1.53)	18.1 (1.24)	55.6 (2.22)	11.5 (0.87)
Other 4-year	921 (36.8)	77.9 (1.25)	77.5 (1.26)	35.0 (2.30)	16.9 (1.31)	24.2 (1.93)	11.6 (1.57)	67.4 (2.38)	10.8 (0.90)
Less than 4-year	47 (4.4)	76.8 (4.76)	75.5 (4.30)	48.0 (3.70)	12.2 (3.24)	8.6 (2.71)	1.3 (0.88)	53.5 (5.17)	8.1 (2.92)
Private, for-profit	527 (21.6)	86.9 (0.92)	86.1 (0.98)	53.2 (1.74)	17.5 (2.05)	3.1 (0.62)	2.6 (0.79)	78.0 (1.17)	6.7 (0.88)
2-year and above	393 (21.0)	90.6 (1.14)	89.6 (1.24)	52.7 (2.24)	16.2 (2.63)	3.7 (0.82)	3.3 (1.07)	85.8 (1.46)	6.8 (1.10)
Less than 2-year	134 (3.0)	76.0 (1.31)	75.8 (1.33)	54.7 (1.59)	21.4 (2.14)	1.5 (0.22)	0.8 (0.63)	55.0 (1.55)	6.5 (0.89)
Part-time or part-year students									
All institutions	11,230 (93.5)	38.5 (0.44)	36.3 (0.43)	23.0 (0.34)	4.4 (0.20)	2.2 (0.09)	1.2 (0.08)	23.5 (0.31)	1.2 (0.07)
Public	9,015 (74.6)	32.0 (0.52)	29.8 (0.51)	19.9 (0.38)	2.9 (0.19)	1.9 (0.10)	1.0 (0.08)	16.2 (0.36)	0.7 (0.05)
4-year doctoral	1,516 (33.3)	42.9 (0.92)	41.6 (0.91)	19.8 (0.70)	3.4 (0.36)	2.8 (0.27)	3.3 (0.31)	34.7 (0.84)	2.5 (0.22)
Other 4-year	984 (47.7)	42.0 (2.03)	40.2 (2.07)	22.5 (1.77)	3.4 (0.42)	2.1 (0.41)	2.0 (0.41)	29.3 (1.48)	0.7 (0.18)
2-year	6,449 (59.1)	28.0 (0.66)	25.5 (0.63)	19.6 (0.52)	2.8 (0.22)	1.7 (0.12)	0.3 (0.05)	9.9 (0.37)	0.3 (0.04)
Less than 2-year	66 (2.1)	19.6 (1.80)	18.4 (1.75)	14.9 (1.61)	2.1 (0.70)	1.0 (0.56)	0.2 (0.24)	5.6 (1.21)	# (†)
Private, not-for-profit	1,204 (37.4)	52.4 (1.42)	49.2 (1.37)	24.0 (0.99)	6.3 (0.44)	5.9 (0.64)	3.4 (0.45)	40.5 (1.28)	3.2 (0.44)
4-year doctoral	356 (17.6)	45.8 (2.20)	44.8 (2.24)	18.3 (2.01)	6.2 (0.84)	8.4 (1.16)	4.9 (0.67)	37.7 (2.30)	3.4 (0.64)
Other 4-year	786 (37.2)	54.2 (2.21)	49.8 (2.18)	24.8 (1.83)	6.0 (0.66)	5.0 (0.78)	3.0 (0.60)	41.9 (2.08)	3.0 (0.64)
Less than 4-year	62 (4.4)	66.9 (3.72)	66.3 (3.79)	45.9 (3.05)	9.9 (2.31)	2.9 (0.83)	0.6 (0.62)	39.2 (4.40)	3.6 (1.35)
Private, for-profit	1,011 (19.5)	79.8 (0.85)	78.6 (0.96)	49.8 (1.34)	14.7 (1.37)	1.1 (0.21)	0.9 (0.26)	68.2 (1.02)	4.0 (0.35)
2-year and above	636 (19.2)	83.3 (1.26)	81.9 (1.40)	49.3 (2.10)	14.3 (2.17)	1.0 (0.31)	1.3 (0.41)	76.1 (1.43)	2.8 (0.50)
Less than 2-year	375 (3.0)	73.8 (0.91)	73.0 (0.90)	50.7 (0.58)	15.5 (0.77)	1.2 (0.15)	0.2 (0.03)	54.7 (0.81)	5.9 (0.38)

†Not applicable.
#Rounds to zero.
‡Reporting standards not met.
[1]Numbers of undergraduates may not equal figures reported in other tables, since these data are based on a sample survey of students who enrolled at any point during the year.
[2]Title IV of the Higher Education Act.
[3]Supplemental Educational Opportunity Grants.
[4]College Work Study. Prior to October 17, 1986, private, for-profit institutions were prohibited by law from spending CWS funds for on-campus work. Includes persons who participated in the program, but had no earnings.

[5]Formerly National Direct Student Loans (NDSL).
[6]Formerly Guaranteed Student Loans (GSL).
[7]Parent Loans for Undergraduate Students.
NOTE: Excludes students whose attendance status was not reported. Detail may not sum to totals because of rounding and because some students receive multiple types of aid and aid from different sources. The numbers in column 2 may not add to totals because of rounding. Standard errors appear in parentheses. Data include Puerto Rico.
SOURCE: U.S. Department of Education, National Center for Education Statistics, 2003–04 National Postsecondary Student Aid Study (NPSAS:04). (This table was prepared August 2005.)

Table 330. Amount borrowed, aid status, and sources of aid for full-time, full-year postbaccalaureate students, by level of study and control and type of institution: Selected years, 1992–93 through 2003–04

Level of study, control and type of institution	Cumulative amount borrowed for post-baccalaureate education		Aid status (percent of students)										
			Nonaided		Receiving aid, by source								
					Any aid[1]		Federal		State		Institutional		Employer	
1	2		3		4		5		6		7		8	
1992–93, all institutions	$18,572	(706.5)	31.9	(1.03)	68.1	(1.03)	44.4	(1.47)	7.0	(0.66)	40.6	(1.73)	5.3	(0.52)
Master's degree	11,109	(467.1)	37.5	(2.13)	62.5	(2.13)	33.8	(2.01)	5.8	(0.79)	42.4	(2.70)	8.3	(0.87)
Public	9,335	(543.5)	34.6	(1.98)	65.4	(1.98)	33.9	(1.93)	7.8	(1.07)	44.0	(2.31)	7.6	(1.02)
4-year doctoral	9,597	(648.5)	34.3	(2.14)	65.7	(2.14)	32.4	(2.02)	6.7	(1.18)	46.3	(2.52)	7.7	(1.09)
Other 4-year	7,970	(401.3)	36.1	(4.12)	63.9	(4.12)	42.5	(4.41)	14.4	(2.90)	30.4	(4.28)	6.8	(2.59)
Private	13,628	(807.2)	41.6	(4.05)	58.4	(4.05)	33.7	(3.69)	3.2	(1.04)	40.2	(5.27)	9.4	(1.56)
4-year doctoral	13,879	(905.0)	39.3	(4.44)	60.7	(4.44)	34.2	(4.37)	2.9	(1.20)	42.9	(5.75)	8.9	(1.84)
Other 4-year	‡	(†)	56.5	(3.79)	43.5	(3.79)	30.5	(3.17)	5.1	(2.58)	22.8	(2.27)	12.1	(2.27)
Doctor's degree	16,895	(1,432.1)	30.4	(2.28)	69.6	(2.28)	28.3	(2.45)	4.4	(0.71)	51.6	(2.32)	3.0	(0.85)
Public	12,758	(1,004.8)	30.3	(2.77)	69.7	(2.77)	22.3	(2.44)	6.5	(1.02)	55.5	(2.70)	3.9	(1.23)
Private	21,742	(2,707.7)	30.4	(4.11)	69.6	(4.11)	37.8	(4.48)	1.1	(0.73)	45.5	(4.00)	1.7	(0.96)
First-professional	30,045	(1,237.1)	23.0	(1.17)	77.0	(1.17)	68.2	(1.82)	10.0	(1.54)	37.0	(1.89)	2.3	(0.47)
Public	24,469	(1,354.3)	20.7	(1.30)	79.3	(1.30)	72.5	(1.78)	13.4	(2.13)	37.7	(2.04)	2.3	(0.70)
Private	35,301	(2,055.6)	25.1	(1.71)	74.9	(1.71)	64.3	(2.29)	6.8	(1.32)	36.4	(3.10)	2.3	(0.62)
Other graduate	13,102	(2,268.0)	39.3	(5.42)	60.7	(5.42)	42.4	(4.39)	6.7	(1.44)	22.9	(3.01)	6.0	(1.91)
1995–96, all institutions	$27,122	(1,029.4)	23.9	(1.39)	76.1	(1.39)	49.3	(1.80)	4.1	(0.84)	43.4	(2.03)	5.0	(0.61)
Master's degree	18,807	(774.6)	27.4	(2.16)	72.6	(2.16)	43.6	(2.14)	2.4	(0.61)	42.8	(2.49)	6.6	(1.02)
Public	15,905	(749.5)	25.3	(2.63)	74.7	(2.63)	40.7	(2.37)	3.0	(0.89)	45.7	(3.12)	7.1	(1.36)
4-year doctoral	16,910	(865.1)	23.5	(2.96)	76.5	(2.96)	40.5	(2.64)	2.6	(0.78)	47.9	(3.68)	7.6	(1.55)
Other 4-year	11,417	(1,296.4)	34.0	(5.20)	66.0	(5.20)	41.4	(5.45)	5.1	(3.44)	35.0	(3.96)	4.5	(2.55)
Private	22,568	(1,326.4)	30.6	(3.73)	69.4	(3.73)	48.2	(3.98)	1.4	(0.70)	38.3	(4.23)	5.9	(1.50)
4-year doctoral	23,816	(1,530.2)	28.8	(4.56)	71.2	(4.56)	44.6	(4.45)	1.5	(0.97)	42.2	(4.98)	7.1	(2.07)
Other 4-year	20,299	(2,777.3)	34.6	(6.60)	65.4	(6.60)	56.1	(6.87)	1.3	(0.65)	29.7	(7.95)	3.2	(1.39)
Doctor's degree	24,380	(2,127.9)	17.1	(2.70)	82.9	(2.70)	27.6	(2.87)	0.6	(0.35)	75.7	(3.08)	5.5	(1.55)
Public	22,687	(2,716.2)	14.1	(3.31)	85.9	(3.31)	27.6	(3.51)	1.0	(0.54)	77.8	(3.90)	5.9	(1.99)
Private	28,083	(3,178.4)	22.5	(4.39)	77.5	(4.39)	27.6	(4.94)	#	(†)	72.0	(4.88)	4.9	(2.44)
First-professional	37,540	(1,429.1)	16.8	(1.46)	83.2	(1.46)	73.9	(2.31)	9.4	(2.34)	31.6	(3.10)	1.3	(0.48)
Public	34,463	(2,685.1)	14.3	(1.88)	85.7	(1.88)	79.5	(2.30)	9.7	(4.20)	33.5	(5.41)	1.5	(0.82)
Private	40,350	(1,564.7)	19.0	(2.04)	81.0	(2.04)	69.3	(3.50)	9.2	(2.46)	30.0	(3.53)	1.2	(0.56)
Other graduate	13,557	(1,609.5)	43.5	(5.11)	56.5	(5.11)	34.0	(4.61)	2.2	(1.13)	31.4	(4.90)	6.1	(2.67)
Public 4-year doctoral	‡	(†)	36.9	(8.67)	63.1	(8.67)	32.2	(7.80)	4.0	(2.86)	35.2	(9.43)	1.8	(1.71)
Public other 4-year	12,057	(1,706.8)	46.8	(6.29)	53.2	(6.29)	35.0	(5.67)	1.2	(0.88)	29.4	(5.58)	8.3	(3.89)
1999–2000, all institutions	$38,428	(1,233.2)	17.8	(0.73)	82.2	(0.73)	54.0	(1.05)	6.2	(0.53)	48.7	(1.17)	5.8	(0.45)
Master's degree	24,751	(721.5)	20.6	(1.09)	79.4	(1.09)	50.4	(1.33)	5.4	(0.72)	46.2	(1.38)	8.4	(0.88)
Public	20,219	(704.1)	21.5	(1.49)	78.5	(1.49)	45.8	(1.62)	7.7	(1.17)	49.6	(1.74)	6.8	(0.88)
4-year doctoral	19,850	(826.4)	19.8	(1.60)	80.2	(1.60)	43.9	(1.74)	7.2	(1.34)	54.3	(1.93)	7.1	(1.03)
Other 4-year	21,815	(1,104.6)	29.8	(3.69)	70.2	(3.69)	54.9	(4.45)	10.4	(2.31)	26.8	(3.17)	5.3	(1.30)
Private	29,290	(1,160.7)	19.4	(1.59)	80.6	(1.59)	56.3	(2.16)	2.5	(0.60)	41.9	(2.22)	10.4	(1.66)
4-year doctoral	31,307	(1,436.9)	17.5	(1.82)	82.5	(1.82)	57.7	(2.32)	3.0	(0.79)	49.4	(2.56)	8.3	(1.06)
Other 4-year	23,032	(1,217.1)	24.8	(3.30)	75.2	(3.30)	52.4	(5.10)	1.1	(0.36)	20.9	(4.74)	16.3	(5.55)
Doctor's degree	37,234	(4,065.7)	11.5	(1.39)	88.6	(1.39)	30.2	(2.85)	2.6	(0.63)	77.5	(1.73)	5.4	(0.65)
Public	29,929	(1,750.0)	10.7	(1.23)	89.4	(1.23)	26.5	(1.60)	3.2	(0.88)	80.6	(1.71)	7.4	(0.97)
Private	47,129	(7,597.7)	12.7	(2.94)	87.3	(2.94)	35.9	(6.36)	1.6	(0.79)	72.9	(3.44)	2.3	(0.54)
First-professional	57,556	(2,062.5)	11.5	(1.06)	88.5	(1.06)	80.1	(1.48)	9.8	(1.43)	40.2	(2.65)	1.6	(0.44)
Public	48,328	(1,993.7)	11.4	(1.57)	88.6	(1.57)	81.7	(1.81)	13.1	(2.18)	39.5	(2.87)	1.6	(0.64)
Private	65,299	(3,141.0)	11.6	(1.45)	88.4	(1.45)	78.8	(2.29)	7.1	(1.84)	40.8	(4.22)	1.5	(0.60)
Other graduate	21,238	(1,419.4)	37.3	(3.60)	62.7	(3.60)	44.4	(3.70)	6.3	(1.44)	23.3	(3.35)	7.3	(1.82)
2003–04, all institutions	$44,623	(1,391.0)	13.0	(0.95)	87.0	(0.95)	62.4	(1.39)	3.7	(0.81)	40.0	(1.19)	9.2	(1.00)
Master's degree	28,662	(1,600.4)	19.0	(1.84)	81.0	(1.84)	55.8	(2.35)	2.5	(0.65)	35.5	(2.28)	10.4	(1.80)
Public	22,418	(1,008.8)	20.8	(2.36)	79.2	(2.36)	47.4	(2.76)	2.5	(0.68)	44.0	(2.61)	6.7	(1.06)
4-year doctoral	23,084	(1,088.0)	18.3	(1.76)	81.7	(1.76)	47.7	(2.80)	2.7	(0.77)	47.0	(2.73)	7.5	(1.26)
Other 4-year	17,862	(2,130.9)	36.7	(11.02)	63.3	(11.02)	45.7	(11.86)	‡	(†)	24.3	(7.15)	1.2	(0.77)
Private	33,505	(2,641.5)	17.1	(3.35)	82.9	(3.35)	64.5	(4.01)	2.6	(1.19)	20.8	(2.36)	14.4	(3.57)
4-year doctoral	38,458	(3,903.1)	13.5	(2.49)	86.5	(2.49)	63.2	(4.04)	2.3	(1.66)	36.3	(3.47)	12.3	(4.73)
Other 4-year	24,624	(2,107.0)	23.3	(6.71)	76.7	(6.71)	66.7	(7.54)	3.2	(2.29)	9.5	(4.03)	18.0	(6.09)
Doctor's degree	48,039	(3,078.6)	7.1	(0.69)	92.9	(0.69)	39.8	(2.52)	2.9	(0.78)	69.0	(2.65)	8.7	(1.59)
Public	38,138	(1,921.7)	6.3	(0.68)	93.7	(0.68)	36.6	(2.18)	2.6	(0.60)	76.7	(1.91)	8.8	(1.46)
Private	58,821	(5,481.6)	8.3	(1.43)	91.7	(1.43)	44.0	(4.54)	3.3	(1.82)	58.8	(5.01)	8.5	(3.07)
First-professional	63,323	(1,937.1)	7.9	(0.79)	92.1	(0.79)	83.3	(1.19)	6.0	(2.00)	32.5	(1.87)	4.5	(0.67)
Public	54,706	(1,303.7)	7.8	(1.06)	92.2	(1.06)	83.0	(1.58)	4.7	(0.91)	36.7	(1.61)	4.5	(0.88)
Private	70,761	(3,387.0)	8.1	(1.12)	91.9	(1.12)	83.6	(1.82)	7.2	(3.39)	28.9	(2.94)	4.5	(1.06)
Other graduate	25,368	(3,096.7)	17.1	(5.58)	82.9	(5.58)	75.9	(6.54)	3.4	(1.77)	16.2	(4.66)	21.3	(9.96)

†Not applicable.
#Rounds to zero.
‡Reporting standards not met.
[1]Includes students who reported they were awarded aid, but did not specify the source of aid.

NOTE: Total includes some students whose level of study was unknown. Detail may not sum to totals because of rounding and because some students receive multiple types of aid and aid from different sources. Standard errors appear in parentheses. Data include Puerto Rico.
SOURCE: U.S. Department of Education, National Center for Education Statistics, 1992–93, 1995–96, 1999–2000, and 2003–04 National Postsecondary Student Aid Studies (NPSAS:93, NPSAS:96, NPSAS:2000, and NPSAS:2004). (This table was prepared September 2005.)

Table 331. Amount borrowed, aid status, and sources of aid for part-time or part-year postbaccalaureate students, by level of study and control and type of institution: Selected years, 1992–93 through 2003–04

Level of study, control and type of institution	Cumulative amount borrowed for post-baccalaureate education		Aid status (percent of students)									
			Nonaided		Receiving aid, by source							
					Any aid[1]		Federal		State		Institutional		Employer	
1	2		3		4		5		6		7		8	
1992–93, all institutions	$9,577	(476.4)	71.3	(0.84)	28.7	(0.84)	10.8	(0.48)	1.9	(0.19)	12.7	(0.65)	16.7	(0.69)
Master's degree	8,003	(477.5)	71.7	(0.93)	28.3	(0.93)	10.5	(0.56)	1.6	(0.21)	11.1	(0.67)	18.7	(0.85)
Public	7,246	(376.4)	73.9	(0.99)	26.1	(0.99)	10.1	(0.64)	2.5	(0.36)	11.7	(0.79)	14.6	(0.90)
4-year doctoral	8,058	(499.3)	69.6	(1.28)	30.4	(1.28)	11.9	(0.80)	2.5	(0.43)	15.3	(1.03)	14.6	(1.06)
Other 4-year	5,396	(512.1)	81.2	(1.59)	18.8	(1.59)	6.9	(0.99)	2.4	(0.56)	5.5	(1.01)	14.4	(1.30)
Private	8,958	(801.9)	68.6	(1.73)	31.4	(1.73)	11.1	(0.95)	0.4	(0.14)	10.3	(1.02)	24.4	(1.25)
4-year doctoral	9,794	(1,208.0)	66.9	(1.96)	33.1	(1.96)	12.1	(1.30)	0.4	(0.16)	12.1	(1.43)	25.1	(1.65)
Other 4-year	7,313	(534.0)	71.7	(2.92)	28.3	(2.92)	9.3	(1.25)	0.6	(0.27)	6.9	(1.13)	23.1	(2.32)
Doctor's degree	12,858	(1,369.8)	56.2	(2.41)	43.8	(2.41)	8.6	(1.07)	3.5	(0.83)	33.1	(2.18)	12.0	(1.53)
Public	9,628	(1,227.0)	56.1	(2.58)	43.9	(2.58)	8.5	(1.19)	4.4	(1.23)	33.3	(2.48)	12.9	(1.63)
Private	17,048	(2,506.1)	56.4	(4.85)	43.6	(4.85)	8.9	(2.03)	1.6	(0.69)	32.6	(4.21)	10.2	(3.19)
First-professional	26,158	(2,269.0)	42.6	(3.20)	57.4	(3.20)	44.9	(3.10)	3.3	(0.70)	25.7	(2.26)	6.1	(1.16)
Public	21,931	(3,100.7)	50.8	(5.23)	49.2	(5.23)	42.9	(4.44)	3.6	(1.19)	22.2	(3.54)	5.1	(1.87)
Private	27,842	(2,711.4)	37.8	(3.98)	62.2	(3.98)	46.1	(4.24)	3.2	(0.88)	27.8	(2.91)	6.7	(1.50)
Other graduate	7,223	(895.5)	79.7	(1.50)	20.3	(1.50)	7.7	(0.83)	1.7	(0.45)	8.4	(0.97)	13.4	(1.17)
1995–96, all institutions	$16,193	(651.8)	59.3	(1.23)	40.7	(1.23)	13.8	(0.63)	1.4	(0.31)	16.7	(1.20)	16.1	(0.89)
Master's degree	14,635	(739.4)	56.3	(1.53)	43.7	(1.53)	15.1	(0.78)	1.2	(0.23)	16.5	(1.35)	18.4	(1.20)
Public	12,971	(915.3)	57.3	(2.04)	42.7	(2.04)	13.6	(0.91)	1.7	(0.38)	18.5	(1.87)	16.0	(1.35)
4-year doctoral	14,443	(1,152.0)	52.8	(2.74)	47.2	(2.74)	14.8	(1.23)	1.2	(0.41)	22.6	(2.69)	16.6	(1.79)
Other 4-year	9,273	(756.3)	66.4	(2.83)	33.6	(2.83)	11.1	(1.21)	2.8	(0.78)	10.3	(1.59)	14.8	(1.93)
Private	16,904	(1,246.0)	54.9	(2.28)	45.1	(2.28)	17.2	(1.36)	0.5	(0.16)	13.7	(1.92)	21.8	(2.11)
4-year doctoral	19,948	(1,966.7)	55.3	(3.03)	44.7	(3.03)	17.7	(1.70)	0.6	(0.28)	17.2	(2.99)	18.3	(2.33)
Other 4-year	13,006	(1,023.9)	54.5	(3.50)	45.5	(3.50)	16.6	(2.17)	0.3	(0.15)	9.6	(2.10)	25.9	(3.49)
Doctor's degree	19,530	(1,758.5)	48.6	(3.55)	51.4	(3.55)	12.1	(1.72)	0.6	(0.30)	39.3	(3.48)	9.0	(2.03)
Public	16,288	(1,357.9)	46.1	(4.67)	53.9	(4.67)	9.5	(1.92)	0.9	(0.46)	42.5	(4.57)	9.2	(2.44)
Private	24,882	(2,957.7)	53.3	(4.88)	46.7	(4.88)	17.2	(2.84)	#	(†)	33.3	(4.77)	8.6	(3.59)
First-professional	32,803	(2,151.7)	32.2	(5.02)	67.8	(5.02)	47.4	(5.87)	4.3	(1.49)	27.0	(8.08)	7.0	(1.78)
Public	31,882	(2,069.9)	29.6	(5.44)	70.4	(5.44)	59.6	(4.96)	4.0	(1.96)	25.7	(4.64)	7.5	(3.25)
Private	33,160	(2,893.6)	33.1	(6.46)	66.9	(6.46)	43.5	(7.17)	4.3	(1.87)	27.4	(10.53)	6.8	(2.13)
Other graduate	13,008	(1,214.6)	74.0	(1.69)	26.0	(1.69)	7.0	(0.81)	1.9	(0.94)	8.4	(1.25)	13.3	(1.25)
Public 4-year doctoral	15,473	(2,279.8)	67.8	(2.61)	32.2	(2.61)	9.8	(1.57)	0.5	(0.26)	12.4	(2.54)	14.9	(2.07)
Public other 4-year	11,166	(1,313.0)	77.3	(2.20)	22.7	(2.20)	5.5	(0.90)	2.6	(1.42)	6.3	(1.32)	12.4	(1.58)
1999–2000, all institutions	$20,929	(554.5)	52.1	(0.77)	47.9	(0.77)	18.1	(0.60)	1.6	(0.19)	15.9	(0.55)	20.3	(0.67)
Master's degree	17,489	(517.1)	50.3	(0.92)	49.7	(0.92)	18.6	(0.73)	1.4	(0.21)	14.2	(0.68)	23.2	(0.84)
Public	14,420	(613.8)	53.7	(1.30)	46.3	(1.30)	15.9	(0.92)	2.0	(0.33)	15.3	(0.95)	20.6	(1.15)
4-year doctoral	15,891	(781.1)	50.3	(1.61)	49.7	(1.61)	17.1	(1.12)	2.0	(0.43)	17.9	(1.22)	21.5	(1.40)
Other 4-year	10,593	(651.1)	61.5	(2.03)	38.5	(2.03)	13.3	(1.54)	2.0	(0.49)	9.5	(1.43)	18.6	(2.04)
Private	20,692	(801.0)	45.9	(1.28)	54.1	(1.28)	22.0	(1.14)	0.6	(0.22)	12.7	(0.95)	26.5	(1.20)
4-year doctoral	23,434	(1,090.2)	43.6	(1.48)	56.4	(1.48)	23.1	(1.40)	0.8	(0.32)	14.7	(1.16)	25.9	(1.33)
Other 4-year	14,910	(1,092.3)	50.6	(2.47)	49.4	(2.47)	19.7	(1.97)	0.3	(0.18)	8.4	(1.53)	27.7	(2.41)
Doctor's degree	28,829	(1,883.3)	45.5	(1.68)	54.5	(1.68)	14.5	(1.30)	1.0	(0.33)	37.8	(1.69)	13.9	(1.30)
Public	25,423	(1,444.3)	46.4	(2.13)	53.6	(2.13)	12.8	(1.14)	1.5	(0.48)	40.8	(2.01)	12.2	(1.30)
Private	34,511	(3,883.0)	43.4	(2.66)	56.6	(2.66)	18.1	(3.18)	#	(†)	31.4	(2.97)	17.5	(2.96)
First-professional	46,159	(2,527.3)	22.2	(2.29)	77.8	(2.29)	58.1	(4.76)	5.2	(1.35)	28.3	(2.81)	10.1	(1.90)
Public	36,078	(3,271.1)	20.6	(4.87)	79.4	(4.87)	60.7	(6.96)	6.6	(3.17)	23.9	(5.65)	6.5	(3.62)
Private	50,469	(3,018.2)	22.8	(2.56)	77.2	(2.56)	57.0	(6.00)	4.6	(1.40)	30.1	(3.19)	11.5	(2.22)
Other graduate	18,175	(1,363.8)	58.9	(2.85)	41.1	(2.85)	16.8	(2.46)	1.5	(0.74)	9.1	(1.52)	18.6	(2.40)
2003–04, all institutions	$25,776	(27,528.1)	34.5	(1.29)	65.5	(1.29)	31.4	(1.44)	1.7	(0.43)	19.0	(1.13)	26.0	(1.23)
Master's degree	22,959	(754.4)	32.5	(1.61)	67.5	(1.61)	34.5	(1.60)	1.7	(0.49)	17.0	(1.49)	27.6	(1.47)
Public	18,759	(563.8)	36.7	(1.49)	63.3	(1.49)	28.4	(1.36)	2.0	(0.41)	22.1	(1.37)	24.6	(1.38)
4-year doctoral	19,795	(626.1)	36.1	(1.30)	63.9	(1.30)	27.5	(1.21)	1.8	(0.37)	24.2	(1.47)	24.8	(1.37)
Other 4-year	16,263	(1,102.0)	38.2	(4.02)	61.8	(4.02)	30.7	(3.74)	2.6	(1.22)	16.5	(2.64)	24.1	(3.82)
Private	26,387	(1,553.3)	27.8	(2.78)	72.2	(2.78)	41.1	(3.03)	1.3	(0.83)	11.4	(2.12)	30.9	(2.69)
4-year doctoral	26,953	(1,644.4)	31.2	(2.41)	68.8	(2.41)	38.0	(2.86)	1.6	(1.71)	14.8	(2.28)	28.1	(2.93)
Other 4-year	25,880	(2,512.1)	24.6	(5.15)	75.4	(5.15)	44.0	(4.85)	0.9	(0.46)	8.1	(3.12)	33.7	(4.41)
Doctor's degree	40,223	(1,847.5)	27.8	(1.28)	72.2	(1.28)	22.2	(1.38)	1.7	(0.31)	45.8	(1.91)	19.9	(1.64)
Public	31,510	(1,507.1)	25.6	(1.17)	74.4	(1.17)	18.2	(1.28)	2.4	(0.44)	55.8	(1.21)	17.3	(1.02)
Private	50,278	(4,508.8)	31.7	(3.35)	68.3	(3.35)	29.1	(3.39)	0.7	(0.54)	28.2	(2.86)	24.3	(4.13)
First-professional	49,170	(5,227.6)	24.6	(3.94)	75.4	(3.94)	54.2	(5.50)	6.8	(3.18)	23.6	(4.34)	13.2	(2.65)
Public	56,475	(6,550.3)	20.8	(5.05)	79.2	(5.05)	63.4	(6.24)	3.0	(2.16)	31.2	(5.74)	9.4	(3.26)
Private	46,862	(6,795.8)	25.6	(4.81)	74.4	(4.81)	51.9	(6.84)	7.7	(4.04)	21.7	(5.47)	14.1	(3.24)
Other graduate	19,975	(1,493.9)	48.8	(2.31)	51.2	(2.31)	19.5	(2.61)	1.0	(0.42)	10.3	(1.38)	25.7	(2.55)

†Not applicable.
#Rounds to zero.
[1]Includes students who reported they were awarded aid, but did not specify the source of aid.
NOTE: Total includes some students whose level of study was unknown. Detail may not sum to totals because of rounding and because some students receive multiple types of aid and aid from different sources. Standard errors appear in parentheses. Data include Puerto Rico.

SOURCE: U.S. Department of Education, National Center for Education Statistics, 1992–93, 1995–96, 1999–2000, and 2003–04 National Postsecondary Student Aid Studies (NPSAS:93, NPSAS:96, NPSAS:2000, and NPSAS:2004). (This table was prepared September 2005.)

Table 332. Percentage of full-time, full-year postbaccalaureate students receiving aid, by type of aid, level of study, and control and type of institution: Selected years, 1992–93 through 2003–04

Level of study, control and type of institution	Number of students[1] (in thousands)	Any aid[2]	Fellowship grants	Tuition waivers	Assistantships[3]	Employer	Any loans	Stafford[4]	Perkins[5]
1	2	3	4	5	6	7	8	9	10
1992–93, all institutions	673 (—)	68.1 (1.03)	[6] (6)	12.4 (1.00)	14.3 (1.21)	3.3 (0.39)	43.5 (1.49)	41.1 (1.50)	9.0 (0.97)
Master's degree	281 (—)	62.5 (2.13)	[6] (6)	15.7 (1.32)	18.1 (1.92)	5.1 (0.66)	32.5 (2.01)	30.5 (1.99)	5.0 (0.80)
Public	163 (—)	65.4 (1.98)	[6] (6)	20.5 (1.80)	22.4 (1.85)	4.8 (0.76)	32.2 (1.96)	30.8 (1.86)	4.0 (0.74)
4-year doctoral	139 (—)	65.7 (2.14)	[6] (6)	23.3 (1.99)	23.5 (2.09)	4.7 (0.78)	30.6 (2.06)	29.6 (1.94)	3.3 (0.69)
Other 4-year	24 (—)	63.9 (4.12)	[6] (6)	4.4 (2.00)	15.8 (3.34)	5.3 (2.44)	41.5 (4.87)	38.4 (4.64)	8.3 (3.11)
Private	118 (—)	58.4 (4.05)	[6] (6)	8.9 (1.67)	12.2 (3.95)	5.6 (1.08)	32.9 (3.56)	30.0 (3.60)	6.4 (1.66)
4-year doctoral	102 (—)	60.7 (4.44)	[6] (6)	9.5 (1.92)	13.6 (4.50)	5.7 (1.26)	33.6 (4.23)	30.8 (4.32)	6.8 (1.92)
Other 4-year	16 (—)	43.5 (3.79)	[6] (6)	5.4 (0.64)	3.0 (1.45)	4.7 (0.37)	28.7 (2.47)	24.6 (2.50)	4.4 (0.35)
Doctor's degree	120 (—)	69.6 (2.28)	[6] (6)	19.5 (1.95)	27.1 (2.06)	2.2 (0.74)	25.8 (2.44)	23.9 (2.40)	3.5 (0.62)
Public	73 (—)	69.7 (2.77)	[6] (6)	23.1 (2.70)	31.6 (2.63)	3.1 (1.12)	20.6 (2.38)	18.9 (2.30)	2.9 (0.73)
Private	46 (—)	69.6 (4.11)	[6] (6)	13.6 (2.80)	19.9 (3.42)	0.9 (0.59)	34.1 (4.62)	31.9 (4.57)	4.3 (1.15)
First-professional	211 (—)	77.0 (1.17)	[6] (6)	5.6 (0.99)	4.4 (0.66)	1.2 (0.40)	67.8 (1.77)	65.6 (1.72)	19.3 (1.95)
Public	101 (—)	79.3 (1.30)	[6] (6)	5.4 (1.41)	4.3 (0.57)	1.3 (0.60)	71.8 (1.82)	69.9 (1.58)	23.2 (2.73)
Private	110 (—)	74.9 (1.71)	[6] (6)	5.8 (1.25)	4.5 (1.17)	1.2 (0.54)	64.1 (2.21)	61.6 (2.26)	15.7 (1.80)
Other graduate	61 (—)	60.7 (5.42)	[6] (6)	7.5 (1.78)	6.2 (1.93)	3.7 (1.05)	44.4 (4.16)	39.6 (4.30)	2.7 (0.75)
1995–96, all institutions	861 (—)	76.1 (1.39)	[6] (6)	11.7 (1.34)	19.5 (1.42)	5.0 (0.61)	48.7 (1.77)	48.0 (1.79)	8.1 (0.87)
Master's degree	387 (—)	72.6 (2.16)	[6] (6)	13.5 (1.94)	20.2 (1.85)	6.6 (1.02)	43.1 (2.14)	42.5 (2.13)	5.1 (0.75)
Public	236 (—)	74.7 (2.63)	[6] (6)	17.8 (2.85)	28.9 (2.69)	7.1 (1.36)	39.5 (2.39)	38.8 (2.34)	3.5 (0.85)
4-year doctoral	195 (—)	76.5 (2.96)	[6] (6)	19.5 (3.31)	31.1 (3.18)	7.6 (1.55)	39.2 (2.67)	38.6 (2.60)	4.0 (1.00)
Other 4-year	41 (—)	66.0 (5.20)	[6] (6)	9.9 (4.21)	18.1 (3.30)	4.5 (2.55)	40.8 (5.40)	39.8 (5.39)	1.5 (1.11)
Private	151 (—)	69.4 (3.73)	[6] (6)	6.7 (1.91)	6.6 (1.60)	5.9 (1.50)	48.6 (3.96)	48.2 (3.98)	7.6 (1.35)
4-year doctoral	104 (—)	71.2 (4.56)	[6] (6)	6.4 (2.13)	8.8 (2.32)	7.1 (2.07)	44.6 (4.45)	44.6 (4.45)	9.6 (1.75)
Other 4-year	47 (—)	65.4 (6.60)	[6] (6)	7.4 (3.93)	1.9 (0.99)	3.2 (1.39)	57.4 (6.62)	56.1 (6.87)	3.3 (1.68)
Doctor's degree	147 (—)	82.9 (2.70)	[6] (6)	24.3 (3.37)	51.8 (4.06)	5.5 (1.55)	25.2 (2.62)	25.2 (2.62)	1.5 (0.61)
Public	94 (—)	85.9 (3.31)	[6] (6)	30.9 (4.55)	59.9 (4.62)	5.9 (1.99)	26.7 (3.32)	26.7 (3.32)	1.4 (0.69)
Private	53 (—)	77.5 (4.39)	[6] (6)	12.4 (4.38)	37.3 (6.51)	4.9 (2.44)	22.6 (4.28)	22.6 (4.28)	1.7 (1.16)
First-professional	253 (—)	83.2 (1.46)	[6] (6)	3.0 (0.66)	4.0 (0.74)	1.3 (0.48)	74.4 (2.30)	73.0 (2.46)	18.4 (1.86)
Public	115 (—)	85.7 (1.88)	[6] (6)	3.8 (1.03)	4.1 (1.08)	1.5 (0.82)	79.0 (2.37)	78.6 (2.39)	20.7 (2.49)
Private	138 (—)	81.0 (2.04)	[6] (6)	2.4 (0.90)	3.8 (1.03)	1.2 (0.56)	70.6 (3.53)	68.3 (3.76)	16.4 (2.55)
Other graduate	54 (—)	56.5 (5.11)	[6] (6)	9.8 (3.84)	6.4 (2.08)	6.1 (2.67)	31.3 (4.19)	30.9 (4.17)	2.6 (1.09)
Public 4-year doctoral	18 (—)	63.1 (8.67)	[6] (6)	9.2 (8.59)	6.2 (3.12)	1.8 (1.71)	30.2 (7.40)	30.2 (7.40)	0.7 (0.71)
Public other 4-year	36 (—)	53.2 (6.29)	[6] (6)	10.1 (3.83)	6.6 (2.70)	8.3 (3.89)	31.8 (5.05)	31.2 (5.02)	3.6 (1.59)
1999–2000, all institutions	918 (—)	82.2 (0.73)	20.0 (1.02)	11.5 (0.54)	23.2 (0.80)	5.8 (0.45)	53.7 (1.08)	52.0 (1.08)	8.7 (0.87)
Master's degree	395 (—)	79.4 (1.09)	17.2 (1.03)	12.0 (0.88)	22.6 (1.17)	8.4 (0.88)	50.2 (1.36)	48.7 (1.34)	5.9 (0.64)
Public	222 (—)	78.5 (1.49)	15.5 (1.43)	18.5 (1.41)	30.5 (1.67)	6.8 (0.88)	44.4 (1.62)	43.6 (1.62)	3.0 (0.64)
4-year doctoral	184 (—)	80.2 (1.60)	16.6 (1.60)	19.4 (1.65)	34.0 (1.95)	7.1 (1.03)	42.2 (1.74)	41.6 (1.74)	3.1 (0.74)
Other 4-year	38 (—)	70.2 (3.69)	10.7 (3.06)	14.0 (1.99)	13.7 (2.05)	5.3 (1.30)	54.7 (4.48)	53.3 (4.41)	2.2 (1.14)
Private	172 (—)	80.6 (1.59)	19.2 (1.49)	3.6 (0.75)	12.3 (1.55)	10.4 (1.66)	57.7 (2.24)	55.3 (2.18)	9.8 (1.19)
4-year doctoral	127 (—)	82.5 (1.82)	23.4 (1.89)	4.2 (0.98)	14.0 (1.54)	8.3 (1.06)	60.1 (2.48)	56.7 (2.35)	11.5 (1.50)
Other 4-year	46 (—)	75.2 (3.31)	7.7 (2.01)	1.9 (0.67)	7.8 (4.20)	16.3 (5.55)	51.2 (5.08)	51.2 (5.08)	4.9 (1.86)
Doctor's degree	184 (—)	88.6 (1.39)	37.8 (2.28)	23.3 (1.50)	55.0 (2.55)	5.4 (0.65)	29.5 (2.90)	27.9 (2.90)	4.7 (2.89)
Public	111 (—)	89.4 (1.23)	30.1 (1.54)	35.5 (1.79)	63.5 (1.88)	7.4 (0.97)	26.2 (1.67)	24.4 (1.51)	1.1 (0.37)
Private	73 (—)	87.3 (2.94)	49.5 (4.61)	4.9 (1.03)	41.9 (4.98)	2.3 (0.54)	34.4 (6.49)	33.1 (6.55)	10.2 (6.83)
First-professional	253 (—)	88.5 (1.06)	16.4 (2.18)	4.1 (0.79)	6.5 (0.99)	1.6 (0.44)	80.8 (1.41)	78.7 (1.60)	18.0 (1.83)
Public	113 (—)	88.6 (1.57)	12.3 (1.98)	7.3 (1.55)	6.5 (1.55)	1.6 (0.64)	81.8 (1.83)	80.6 (1.82)	20.1 (2.46)
Private	140 (—)	88.4 (1.45)	19.8 (3.62)	1.5 (0.55)	6.5 (1.28)	1.5 (0.60)	79.9 (2.11)	77.2 (2.55)	16.3 (2.69)
Other graduate	86 (—)	62.7 (3.60)	5.3 (1.48)	6.0 (1.68)	7.4 (1.86)	7.3 (1.82)	42.2 (4.08)	40.6 (4.08)	3.1 (1.13)
2003–04, all institutions	923 (27.8)	87.0 (0.95)	38.2 (1.22)	12.8 (0.71)	21.6 (0.93)	9.2 (1.00)	63.6 (1.31)	56.6 (1.44)	11.8 (1.34)
Master's degree	373 (23.4)	81.0 (1.84)	32.3 (2.22)	11.7 (1.20)	21.4 (1.66)	10.4 (1.80)	58.4 (2.14)	50.5 (2.27)	5.5 (0.85)
Public	190 (11.3)	79.2 (2.36)	37.5 (2.30)	18.4 (1.75)	32.9 (2.49)	6.7 (1.06)	48.5 (2.75)	41.0 (2.37)	4.1 (0.87)
4-year doctoral	165 (10.4)	81.7 (1.76)	38.8 (2.42)	19.5 (1.84)	36.1 (2.58)	7.5 (1.26)	48.8 (2.97)	40.4 (2.60)	4.8 (0.98)
Other 4-year	25 (5.1)	63.3 (11.02)	28.8 (8.09)	11.4 (6.20)	11.9 (6.94)	1.2 (0.77)	46.1 (11.92)	44.8 (11.78)	‡ (†)
Private	182 (19.9)	82.9 (3.35)	26.9 (3.54)	4.7 (1.13)	9.5 (1.46)	14.4 (3.57)	68.7 (3.54)	60.4 (4.04)	6.8 (1.42)
4-year doctoral	116 (8.3)	86.5 (2.49)	36.2 (4.29)	6.9 (1.62)	12.0 (1.96)	12.3 (4.73)	69.3 (3.56)	59.1 (4.23)	9.9 (2.21)
Other 4-year	66 (17.3)	76.7 (6.71)	10.5 (3.79)	1.0 (1.03)	5.1 (2.71)	18.0 (6.09)	67.8 (7.01)	62.5 (7.61)	1.6 (1.14)
Doctor's degree	195 (11.3)	92.9 (0.69)	59.6 (2.36)	30.2 (1.66)	48.9 (2.39)	8.7 (1.59)	38.4 (2.58)	33.2 (2.14)	8.7 (1.65)
Public	111 (5.4)	93.7 (0.68)	65.3 (1.77)	41.7 (1.76)	56.7 (1.93)	8.8 (1.46)	34.1 (2.18)	29.8 (2.24)	6.7 (1.43)
Private	83 (8.8)	91.7 (1.43)	51.9 (4.88)	14.7 (1.63)	38.6 (4.06)	8.5 (3.07)	44.2 (4.44)	37.6 (3.67)	11.5 (3.50)
First-professional	280 (7.3)	92.1 (0.79)	37.5 (2.55)	4.3 (1.25)	7.0 (0.83)	4.5 (0.67)	84.7 (1.06)	78.3 (1.45)	24.7 (3.20)
Public	128 (7.0)	92.2 (1.06)	40.3 (2.20)	5.2 (0.63)	9.5 (1.57)	4.5 (0.88)	84.1 (1.59)	77.8 (1.68)	24.9 (1.98)
Private	152 (9.2)	91.9 (1.12)	35.1 (3.69)	3.5 (2.16)	4.9 (0.95)	4.5 (1.06)	85.1 (1.59)	78.8 (2.44)	24.6 (5.71)
Other graduate	76 (14.4)	82.9 (5.58)	15.6 (4.38)	5.4 (2.65)	5.8 (2.33)	21.3 (9.96)	76.3 (6.53)	66.5 (7.83)	3.3 (1.54)

—Not available.
†Not applicable.
‡Reporting standards not met.
[1]Numbers of full-time, full-year postbaccalaureate students may not equal figures reported in other tables, since these data are based on a sample survey of all postbaccalaureate students who enrolled at any time during the school year.
[2]Includes students who reported they were awarded aid, but did not specify the source of aid.
[3]Includes students who received teaching or research assistantships and/or participated in work-study programs.
[4]Formerly Guaranteed Student Loans (GSL).
[5]Formerly National Direct Student Loans (NDSL).

[6]Fellowship estimates for 1992–93 and 1995–96 were based primarily on information provided by institutions and are not comparable to data for 1999–2000 or 2003–04, which were based on information provided by both students and institutions.
NOTE: Excludes students whose attendance status was not reported. Total includes some students whose level of study or control of institution was unknown. Detail may not sum to totals because of rounding and because some students receive aid from multiple sources. Standard errors appear in parentheses. Data include Puerto Rico.
SOURCE: U.S. Department of Education, National Center for Education Statistics, 1992–93, 1995–96, 1999–2000, and 2003–04 National Postsecondary Student Aid Studies (NPSAS:93, NPSAS:96, NPSAS:2000, and NPSAS:04). (This table was prepared September 2005.)

Table 333. Percentage of part-time or part-year postbaccalaureate students receiving aid, by type of aid, level of study, and control and type of institution: Selected years, 1992–93 through 2003–04

Level of study, control and type of institution	Number of students[1] (in thousands)	Percent receiving aid, by type					Loans		
		Any aid[2]	Fellowship grants	Tuition waivers	Assistantships[3]	Employer	Any loans	Stafford[4]	Perkins[5]
1	2	3	4	5	6	7	8	9	10
1992–93, all institutions	1,950 (—)	28.7 (0.84)	[6] ([6])	5.1 (0.34)	4.3 (0.30)	7.9 (0.43)	10.5 (0.46)	9.4 (0.43)	1.0 (0.10)
Master's degree	1,322 (—)	28.3 (0.93)	[6] ([6])	4.6 (0.35)	3.8 (0.32)	8.8 (0.52)	10.3 (0.54)	9.3 (0.52)	0.9 (0.12)
Public	773 (—)	26.1 (0.99)	[6] ([6])	4.9 (0.47)	5.2 (0.43)	6.7 (0.50)	9.9 (0.62)	9.0 (0.60)	1.2 (0.16)
4-year doctoral	489 (—)	30.4 (1.28)	[6] ([6])	6.5 (0.64)	6.7 (0.60)	6.7 (0.69)	11.8 (0.76)	10.7 (0.74)	1.5 (0.21)
Other 4-year	284 (—)	18.8 (1.59)	[6] ([6])	2.3 (0.53)	2.6 (0.63)	6.5 (0.77)	6.5 (0.92)	6.0 (0.87)	0.6 (0.24)
Private	549 (—)	31.4 (1.73)	[6] ([6])	4.2 (0.51)	1.8 (0.43)	11.8 (0.91)	11.0 (0.95)	9.7 (0.89)	0.5 (0.17)
4-year doctoral	357 (—)	33.1 (1.96)	[6] ([6])	4.4 (0.67)	2.5 (0.65)	12.1 (1.17)	11.9 (1.27)	10.5 (1.19)	0.6 (0.25)
Other 4-year	192 (—)	28.3 (2.92)	[6] ([6])	3.8 (0.87)	0.7 (0.25)	11.2 (1.48)	9.3 (1.15)	8.1 (1.10)	0.3 (0.17)
Doctor's degree	149 (—)	43.8 (2.41)	[6] ([6])	12.7 (1.70)	17.0 (1.87)	5.5 (1.18)	7.3 (0.98)	6.9 (0.97)	0.8 (0.13)
Public	97 (—)	43.9 (2.58)	[6] ([6])	15.0 (2.09)	17.0 (1.90)	6.4 (1.16)	7.1 (1.00)	6.5 (0.95)	0.7 (0.10)
Private	51 (—)	43.6 (4.85)	[6] ([6])	8.3 (2.62)	17.0 (3.97)	3.7 (2.67)	7.7 (2.04)	7.5 (2.06)	1.2 (0.35)
First-professional	64 (—)	57.4 (3.20)	[6] ([6])	5.9 (1.06)	3.1 (0.84)	3.4 (0.92)	45.6 (3.13)	42.0 (2.89)	6.2 (0.98)
Public	24 (—)	49.2 (5.23)	[6] ([6])	6.8 (1.62)	6.1 (2.09)	2.5 (1.21)	42.4 (4.37)	41.4 (4.27)	8.5 (1.99)
Private	40 (—)	62.2 (3.98)	[6] ([6])	5.4 (1.40)	1.4 (0.52)	3.9 (1.32)	47.5 (4.29)	42.3 (3.95)	4.9 (1.07)
Other graduate	415 (—)	20.3 (1.50)	[6] ([6])	3.4 (0.61)	1.6 (0.36)	6.4 (0.91)	7.1 (0.81)	6.0 (0.70)	0.5 (0.27)
1995–96, all institutions	1,842 (—)	40.7 (1.23)	[6] ([6])	6.1 (0.64)	7.4 (0.85)	16.1 (0.89)	13.4 (0.63)	13.1 (0.62)	0.9 (0.14)
Master's degree	1,118 (—)	43.7 (1.53)	[6] ([6])	5.6 (0.69)	7.4 (1.06)	18.4 (1.20)	14.5 (0.77)	14.3 (0.76)	0.7 (0.15)
Public	649 (—)	42.7 (2.04)	[6] ([6])	6.0 (0.96)	10.7 (1.74)	16.0 (1.35)	13.2 (0.89)	12.9 (0.87)	0.9 (0.22)
4-year doctoral	432 (—)	47.2 (2.74)	[6] ([6])	7.1 (1.36)	13.7 (2.54)	16.6 (1.79)	14.3 (1.19)	14.2 (1.19)	1.0 (0.31)
Other 4-year	217 (—)	33.6 (2.83)	[6] ([6])	3.9 (0.95)	4.9 (1.08)	14.8 (1.93)	11.0 (1.22)	10.5 (1.19)	0.6 (0.25)
Private	470 (—)	45.1 (2.28)	[6] ([6])	5.1 (0.97)	2.7 (0.57)	21.8 (2.11)	16.4 (1.35)	16.1 (1.33)	0.5 (0.20)
4-year doctoral	255 (—)	44.7 (3.03)	[6] ([6])	4.3 (1.11)	4.0 (0.97)	18.3 (2.33)	17.6 (1.78)	17.0 (1.70)	0.8 (0.36)
Other 4-year	215 (—)	45.5 (3.50)	[6] ([6])	5.9 (1.67)	1.2 (0.45)	25.9 (3.49)	15.0 (2.10)	14.9 (2.10)	0.1 (0.08)
Doctor's degree	181 (—)	51.4 (3.55)	[6] ([6])	12.7 (2.80)	26.0 (3.52)	9.0 (2.03)	12.0 (1.73)	12.0 (1.73)	0.4 (0.24)
Public	119 (—)	53.9 (4.67)	[6] ([6])	15.6 (3.57)	31.9 (4.55)	9.2 (2.44)	9.2 (1.93)	9.2 (1.93)	0.3 (0.27)
Private	62 (—)	46.7 (4.88)	[6] ([6])	7.4 (3.82)	14.7 (4.03)	8.6 (3.59)	17.2 (2.84)	17.2 (2.84)	0.7 (0.45)
First-professional	60 (—)	67.8 (5.02)	[6] ([6])	3.8 (1.16)	3.1 (1.03)	7.0 (1.78)	47.8 (5.75)	45.7 (5.90)	9.5 (2.29)
Public	15 (—)	70.4 (5.44)	[6] ([6])	4.8 (2.47)	7.9 (3.23)	7.5 (3.25)	58.1 (4.96)	57.4 (4.99)	12.2 (2.72)
Private	46 (—)	66.9 (6.46)	[6] ([6])	3.5 (1.33)	1.6 (0.75)	6.8 (2.13)	44.5 (7.10)	41.9 (7.23)	8.6 (2.87)
Other graduate	483 (—)	26.0 (1.69)	[6] ([6])	5.5 (1.07)	1.5 (0.50)	13.3 (1.25)	6.7 (0.81)	6.6 (0.80)	0.5 (0.18)
Public 4-year doctoral	166 (—)	32.2 (2.61)	[6] ([6])	8.6 (2.19)	0.4 (0.22)	14.9 (2.07)	9.7 (1.60)	9.6 (1.57)	0.4 (0.31)
Public other 4-year	317 (—)	22.7 (2.20)	[6] ([6])	3.8 (1.16)	2.1 (0.76)	12.4 (1.58)	5.2 (0.89)	5.0 (0.88)	0.6 (0.23)
1999–2000, all institutions	1,740 (—)	47.9 (0.77)	4.8 (0.32)	5.8 (0.32)	5.4 (0.30)	20.3 (0.67)	18.0 (0.61)	16.9 (0.59)	1.0 (0.17)
Master's degree	1,103 (—)	49.7 (0.92)	4.5 (0.40)	5.1 (0.38)	4.8 (0.38)	23.2 (0.84)	18.4 (0.73)	17.2 (0.71)	0.7 (0.14)
Public	625 (—)	46.3 (1.30)	3.9 (0.56)	6.4 (0.57)	6.3 (0.56)	20.6 (1.15)	15.7 (0.88)	14.7 (0.89)	0.7 (0.17)
4-year doctoral	434 (—)	49.7 (1.61)	4.2 (0.63)	7.4 (0.72)	8.0 (0.78)	21.5 (1.40)	16.7 (1.07)	15.6 (1.08)	0.5 (0.17)
Other 4-year	191 (—)	38.5 (2.03)	3.2 (1.15)	4.1 (0.90)	2.3 (0.55)	18.6 (2.04)	13.5 (1.53)	12.7 (1.52)	1.2 (0.39)
Private	478 (—)	54.1 (1.28)	5.3 (0.58)	3.3 (0.43)	2.8 (0.47)	26.5 (1.20)	21.8 (1.20)	20.5 (1.14)	0.7 (0.24)
4-year doctoral	323 (—)	56.4 (1.48)	6.3 (0.77)	3.6 (0.53)	3.3 (0.57)	25.9 (1.33)	22.7 (1.47)	21.4 (1.39)	0.8 (0.29)
Other 4-year	156 (—)	49.4 (2.47)	3.1 (0.77)	2.7 (0.74)	1.7 (0.86)	27.7 (2.41)	20.0 (2.07)	18.6 (1.96)	0.6 (0.43)
Doctor's degree	153 (—)	54.5 (1.68)	11.2 (1.17)	14.9 (1.21)	21.3 (1.46)	13.9 (1.30)	14.1 (1.27)	13.5 (1.29)	1.3 (0.91)
Public	104 (—)	53.6 (2.13)	9.1 (1.02)	19.4 (1.48)	25.9 (1.74)	12.2 (1.30)	12.3 (1.11)	11.7 (1.11)	0.3 (0.17)
Private	49 (—)	56.6 (2.66)	15.6 (2.81)	5.3 (1.56)	11.4 (1.80)	17.5 (2.96)	18.0 (3.13)	17.3 (3.20)	3.3 (2.74)
First-professional	72 (—)	77.8 (2.29)	10.1 (2.35)	5.3 (1.35)	4.0 (1.67)	10.1 (1.90)	60.7 (4.03)	57.4 (4.83)	7.2 (2.53)
Public	21 (—)	79.4 (4.87)	9.5 (3.72)	4.3 (2.24)	6.6 (4.99)	6.5 (3.62)	65.1 (6.77)	60.7 (6.96)	6.0 (2.12)
Private	52 (—)	77.2 (2.56)	10.3 (2.93)	5.7 (1.69)	2.9 (1.08)	11.5 (2.22)	59.0 (4.88)	56.1 (6.10)	7.6 (3.42)
Other graduate	412 (—)	41.1 (2.85)	2.5 (0.42)	4.4 (0.78)	1.5 (0.34)	16.8 (1.47)	11.1 (1.26)	10.3 (1.23)	0.4 (0.18)
2003–04, all institutions	1,903 (33.7)	65.5 (1.29)	14.3 (1.11)	5.9 (0.62)	11.5 (0.73)	26.0 (1.23)	31.5 (1.39)	27.4 (1.50)	1.7 (0.21)
Master's degree	1,320 (37.8)	67.5 (1.61)	12.9 (1.48)	5.4 (0.87)	10.2 (0.93)	27.6 (1.47)	34.5 (1.56)	30.2 (1.76)	1.6 (0.27)
Public	689 (27.5)	63.3 (1.49)	13.2 (1.08)	7.4 (0.90)	16.0 (1.08)	24.6 (1.38)	29.0 (1.30)	24.6 (1.37)	2.2 (0.41)
4-year doctoral	499 (18.6)	63.9 (1.30)	14.8 (1.23)	8.3 (1.06)	17.9 (1.04)	24.8 (1.37)	28.0 (1.24)	23.4 (1.24)	2.6 (0.43)
Other 4-year	190 (15.0)	61.8 (4.02)	9.0 (2.11)	5.0 (1.38)	11.2 (2.46)	24.1 (3.82)	31.5 (3.63)	27.8 (3.65)	1.2 (0.91)
Private	631 (45.2)	72.2 (2.78)	12.5 (2.63)	3.3 (1.18)	3.8 (0.81)	30.9 (2.69)	40.5 (2.96)	36.2 (3.44)	0.9 (0.35)
4-year doctoral	313 (26.0)	68.8 (2.41)	15.4 (2.80)	2.9 (0.61)	6.0 (1.20)	28.1 (2.93)	37.4 (2.67)	31.5 (3.14)	1.7 (0.72)
Other 4-year	318 (43.1)	75.4 (5.15)	9.6 (4.26)	3.6 (2.25)	1.8 (0.87)	33.7 (4.41)	43.5 (4.90)	40.9 (5.47)	0.1 (0.15)
Doctor's degree	192 (11.1)	72.2 (1.28)	29.0 (1.60)	15.2 (1.11)	33.4 (1.66)	19.9 (1.64)	22.5 (1.46)	18.0 (1.36)	1.5 (0.29)
Public	122 (5.5)	74.4 (1.17)	34.5 (1.49)	21.0 (1.32)	42.2 (1.32)	17.3 (1.02)	18.2 (1.22)	13.5 (1.15)	1.9 (0.40)
Private	70 (8.7)	68.3 (3.35)	19.2 (2.35)	4.9 (1.10)	17.9 (2.37)	24.3 (4.13)	30.0 (3.57)	25.9 (3.35)	0.8 (0.37)
First-professional	69 (12.1)	75.4 (3.94)	34.6 (6.42)	3.5 (1.70)	6.5 (1.67)	13.2 (2.65)	52.8 (6.17)	46.6 (5.74)	6.1 (1.83)
Public	14 (1.8)	79.2 (5.05)	28.9 (6.70)	7.2 (3.25)	8.3 (3.65)	9.4 (3.26)	64.4 (5.91)	49.6 (6.77)	20.5 (3.71)
Private	56 (12.1)	74.4 (4.81)	36.0 (7.90)	2.5 (1.89)	6.1 (1.98)	14.1 (3.24)	49.9 (7.56)	45.8 (7.07)	2.6 (1.42)
Other graduate	321 (28.6)	51.2 (2.31)	7.2 (1.38)	3.0 (0.63)	5.1 (0.87)	25.7 (2.55)	20.0 (2.69)	17.3 (2.59)	1.0 (0.39)

—Not available.
[1]Numbers of part-time or part-year postbaccalaureate students may not equal figures reported in other tables, since these data are based on a sample survey of all postbaccalaureate students enrolled at any time during the school year.
[2]Includes students who reported they were awarded aid, but did not specify the source of aid.
[3]Includes students who received teaching or research assistantships and/or participated in work-study programs.
[4]Formerly Guaranteed Student Loans (GSL).
[5]Formerly National Direct Student Loans (NDSL).

[6]Fellowship estimates for 1992–93 and 1995–96 were based primarily on information provided by institutions and are not comparable to data for 1999–2000 or 2003–04, which were based on information provided by both students and institutions.
NOTE: Excludes students whose attendance status was not reported. Totals include some students whose level of study or control of institution was unknown. Data include Puerto Rico. Detail may not sum to totals because of rounding and because some students receive aid from multiple sources. Standard errors appear in parentheses.
SOURCE: U.S. Department of Education, National Center for Education Statistics, 1992–93, 1995–96, 1999–2000, and 2003–04 National Postsecondary Student Aid Studies (NPSAS:93, NPSAS:96, NPSAS:2000, and NPSAS:04). (This table was prepared September 2005.)

Table 334. State awards for need-based undergraduate scholarship and grant programs, by state: Selected years, 1989–90 through 2004–05

[In thousands]

State	1989–90	1990–91	1993–94[1]	1994–95[1]	1995–96[1]	1996–97[1]	1997–98[1]	1998–99[1]	1999–2000[1]	2000–01[1]	2001–02[1]	2002–03	2003–04	2004–05	Percent change, 1994–95 to 2004–05[2]
1	2	3	4	5	6	7	8	9	10	11	12	13	14	15	16
Need-based undergraduate aid as a percent of all need-based and non-need-based aid[3]	76.8	77.4	75.7	77.5	84.4	83.5	81.5	79.9	76.7	75.1	74.4	76.7	74.4	73.0	†
Need-based aid	$1,529,421	$1,658,221	$2,195,993	$2,421,952	$2,435,687	$2,555,667	$2,735,670	$2,927,206	$3,102,348	$3,475,500	$3,790,435	$3,930,714	$4,226,378	$4,644,599	92.9
Alabama	2,984	2,878	2,283	2,281	2,142	1,950	2,270	2,046	1,831	1,820	1,841	1,646	3,260	1,167	-48.8
Alaska	228	464	454	444	430	213	240	0	0	0	0	—	—	—	†
Arizona	3,420	3,318	3,476	3,482	2,291	2,748	3,160	2,731	2,727	2,990	2,812	2,790	2,865	2,954	-15.2
Arkansas	3,946	3,885	7,701	8,907	10,765	12,569	13,160	15,922	25,010	30,887	29,006	20,981	19,931	17,420	95.6
California	153,045	161,642	207,969	232,067	235,582	257,544	284,410	331,636	369,785	461,914	514,348	544,893	654,549	723,165	211.6
Colorado	10,349	11,276	16,480	18,252	21,076	28,236	31,670	41,884	41,884[4]	41,884[4]	46,700	43,178	47,834	45,731	150.6
Connecticut	19,915	20,580	20,641	20,690	20,372	20,297	26,360	33,113	37,001	44,364	44,820	15,938[5]	36,434	36,434	76.1
Delaware	956	1,066	1,270	1,033	1,188	959	1,290	1,409	967	1,057	1,211	1,713	11,553	8,513	724.1
District of Columbia	1,069	947	1,022	1,022	939	939[6]	940	728	743	781	1,321	—	27,572	2,778	171.8
Florida	20,134	24,729	31,277	36,824	34,822	33,854	35,680	36,659	44,892	66,193	75,656	88,731	88,496	93,816	154.8
Georgia	4,607	5,070	26,853	5,147	4,757	2,165	1,060	472	0	0	1,540	1,501	1,460	1,516	-70.5
Hawaii	726	612	748	732	499	379	590	493	490	535	531	408	408	418	-42.9
Idaho	346	350	634	779	763	714	710	756	830	700	814	874	823	976	25.3
Illinois	171,361	183,508	214,809	244,352	256,872	272,898	288,870	315,657	337,003	359,932	384,477	343,262	339,624	338,192	38.4
Indiana	41,874	46,756	55,814	67,742	68,340	77,834	85,040	99,490	104,737	110,147	114,708	135,892	150,706	160,813	137.4
Iowa	32,467	35,586	34,718	35,642	38,953	41,938	44,900	48,242	51,351	52,632	51,191	49,620	48,838	50,847	42.7
Kansas	6,478	6,462	9,060	9,802	9,526	10,171	10,310	11,669	12,265	12,692	12,974	—	14,073	15,061	53.7
Kentucky	12,605	19,866	20,619	25,517	26,215	28,902	27,200	38,441	40,118	45,327	48,322	51,742	68,433	75,385	195.4
Louisiana	2,786	3,827	6,374	6,429	6,580	7,172	8,190	1,393	1,388	1,463	1,452	1,452	1,452	1,485	-76.9
Maine	1,877	4,802	5,170	5,787	6,988	6,636	7,700	7,700[4]	10,360	11,961	12,021	12,547	12,561	12,608	117.9
Maryland	14,800	15,607	23,713	24,571	30,350	36,264	37,190	38,515	39,592	43,665	45,535	39,512	46,503	52,736	114.6
Massachusetts	50,844	46,000	45,059	61,850	54,565	57,413	74,340	92,127	102,056	114,058	110,711	83,177	79,714	79,503	28.5
Michigan	70,721	68,918	79,735	81,340	84,154	85,872	90,480	92,299	91,109	102,164	106,244	95,719	91,782	91,972	13.1
Minnesota	58,136	74,656	102,920	97,920	92,069	92,707	96,400	113,381	113,714	120,426	130,370	133,586	119,583	130,986	33.8
Mississippi	1,243	1,136	1,255	1,248	1,175	540	1,070	859	1,563	1,563[4]	1,489	1,340	17,226	2,081	66.7
Missouri	10,796	11,078	11,124	11,913	12,233	13,681	14,690	20,003	24,100	28,058	27,847	25,603	25,111	24,294	103.9
Montana	415	383	401	419	393	314	460	474	1,990	2,204	2,810	2,824	2,541	3,018	620.3
Nebraska	1,276	2,192	2,686	2,726	3,114	3,211	4,090	4,692	5,645	5,975	7,380	2,458	8,742	8,337	205.8
Nevada	352[6]	321	342	342	2,595	3,180	5,900	5,900[4]	6,083	6,529	6,545	—	7,755	9,999	2,823.7
New Hampshire	918	770	840	1,425	765	669	1,330	1,744	1,497	1,488	3,066	3,170	3,647	3,643	155.6
New Jersey	84,347	87,054	135,251	159,683	132,383	152,458	153,420	160,859	170,015	174,554	187,756	191,913	198,722	217,806	36.4
New Mexico	5,601	6,479	9,266	13,886	14,629	14,289	14,510	16,229	15,745	17,469	15,950	12,906	2,424	14,267	2.7
New York	382,655	428,358	618,849	636,704	625,711	629,940	636,760	619,065	599,435	645,940	684,342	737,075	856,143	886,018	39.2
North Carolina	3,046	2,519	14,436	13,774	16,659	17,435	37,090	41,579	50,572	58,769	71,897	76,344	107,211	105,586	666.6
North Dakota	1,242	1,177	2,036	1,996	1,898	2,202	2,070	2,016	2,076	779	1,402	1,397	1,346	1,407	-29.5

See notes at end of table.

Table 334. State awards for need-based undergraduate scholarship and grant programs, by state: Selected years, 1989–90 through 2004–05—Continued

[In thousands]

State	1989–90	1990–91	1993–94[1]	1994–95[1]	1995–96[1]	1996–97[1]	1997–98[1]	1998–99[1]	1999–2000[1]	2000–01[1]	2001–02[1]	2002–03	2003–04	2004–05	Percent change, 1994–95 to 2004–05[2]
1	2	3	4	5	6	7	8	9	10	11	12	13	14	15	16
Ohio	53,848	54,600	77,940	91,225	86,053	86,770	92,950	93,122	95,482	98,607	112,264	132,293	144,777	159,549	74.9
Oklahoma	11,591	11,871	13,405	13,325	13,642	14,558	16,920	17,387	17,579	19,608	22,091	22,272	28,027	37,273	179.7
Oregon	10,092	11,809	12,903	13,761	13,651	16,241	15,800	16,027	17,891	19,711	19,866	17,290	21,782	23,137	68.1
Pennsylvania	132,344	142,389	188,751	218,604	232,020	240,459	251,550	270,724	280,402	325,234	337,014	348,788	360,816	365,712	67.3
Rhode Island	9,917	9,522	6,500	6,340	5,741	5,699	6,010	5,717	6,098	6,164	6,077	6,310	12,297	13,821	118.0
South Carolina	18,150	17,901	16,795	17,297	18,622	21,540	21,920	22,853	33,198	39,098	34,971	26,127[5]	41,181	45,848	165.1
South Dakota	504	468	589	589	562	346	0	0	0	0	0	—	—	—	†
Tennessee	12,977	13,487	16,755	18,313	18,811	18,652	20,440	20,648	21,383	29,304	37,320	45,806	41,833	121,987	566.1
Texas	24,784	24,135	29,102	29,102	40,768	42,761	60,670	61,728	93,814	106,382	197,252	318,784	156,529	336,433	1,056.0
Utah	1,091	1,001	1,132	1,129	1,197	2,170	1,960	1,957	2,656	2,511	4,069	3,779	3,713	6,705	493.9
Vermont	11,137	10,184	11,167	11,788	11,865	11,309	12,330	12,760	13,739	14,327	15,545	16,225	16,858	15,690	33.1
Virginia	7,966	7,351	6,408	53,885	59,568	59,025	59,260	62,972	66,641	70,260	70,289	69,138	77,346	82,872	53.8
Washington	13,925	21,095	46,617	53,369	56,573	58,149	69,430	74,159	76,581	90,651	101,247	113,345	126,096	138,943	160.3
West Virginia	5,217	5,559	5,802	6,761	8,132	10,527	12,140	13,103	16,135	18,217	21,054	19,175	22,863	23,966	254.5
Wisconsin	38,072	42,365	46,592	49,511	46,470	49,008	50,540	53,711	52,020	65,356	62,124	67,029	72,775	79,118	59.8
Wyoming	241[6]	212[6]	250	225	219	160	200	155	155	0	163	161	163	167	-25.8

—Not available.
†Not applicable.
[1]Estimated.
[2]Changes may reflect introduction of new programs or discontinuation of existing programs.
[3]Includes aid for graduate education and data for Puerto Rico. Participation requirements vary from state to state.
[4]Prior-year data used for nonreporting states.

[5]May include 2001–02 data.
[6]Data are estimated based on prior year's report.
NOTE: Detail may not sum to totals because of rounding.
SOURCE: National Association of State Student Grant and Aid Programs, *Annual Survey Report,* 1989–90 through 2004–05. Retrieved on August 9, 2006, from http://www.nassgap.org/viewrepository.aspx?categoryID=3#. (This table was prepared August 2006.)

Table 335. Current-fund revenue of degree-granting institutions, by source of funds: Selected years, 1919–20 through 1995–96

[In thousands of current dollars]

Year	Current-fund revenue	Student tuition and fees[1]	Federal government[2]	State governments[3]	Local governments	Endowment earnings	Private gifts and grants[4]	Sales and services of educational activities	Auxiliary enterprises	Hospitals[5]	Other current income
1	2	3	4	5	6	7	8	9	10	11	12
Institutions of higher education[6]											
1919–20	$199,922	$42,255	$12,783	$61,690	(7)	$26,482	$7,584	—	$26,993	—	$22,135
1929–30	554,511	144,126	20,658	150,847	(7)	68,605	26,172	—	60,419	—	83,684
1939–40	715,211	200,897	38,860	151,222	$24,392	71,304	40,453	$32,777	143,923	—	11,383
1949–50	2,374,645	394,610	524,319	491,636	61,700	96,341	118,627	111,987	511,265	—	64,160
1959–60	5,785,537	1,157,482	1,036,990	1,374,476	151,715	206,619	382,569	102,525	1,004,283	$187,769	181,110
1969–70	21,515,242	4,419,845	4,130,066	5,873,626	778,162	516,038	1,129,438	612,777	2,900,390	619,578	535,323
1975–76	39,703,166	8,171,942	6,477,178	12,260,885	1,616,975	687,470	1,917,036	645,420	4,547,622	2,494,340	884,298
1976–77	43,436,827	9,024,932	7,169,031	13,285,684	1,626,908	764,788	2,105,070	779,058	4,919,602	2,859,376	902,377
1977–78	47,034,032	9,855,270	6,968,501	14,746,166	1,744,230	832,286	2,320,368	882,715	5,327,821	3,268,956	1,087,719
1978–79	51,837,789	10,704,171	7,851,326	16,363,784	1,573,018	985,242	2,489,366	1,037,130	5,741,309	3,763,453	1,328,991
1979–80	58,519,982	11,930,340	8,902,844	18,378,299	1,587,552	1,176,627	2,808,075	1,239,439	6,481,458	4,373,384	1,641,965
1980–81	65,584,789	13,773,259	9,747,586	20,106,222	1,790,740	1,364,443	3,176,670	1,409,730	7,287,290	4,980,346	1,948,503
1981–82	72,190,856	15,774,038	9,591,805	21,848,791	1,937,669	1,596,813	3,563,558	1,582,922	8,121,611	5,838,565	2,335,084
1982–83	77,595,726	17,776,041	9,631,097	23,065,636	2,031,353	1,720,677	4,052,649	1,723,484	8,769,521	6,531,562	2,293,706
1983–84	84,417,287	19,714,884	10,406,166	24,706,990	2,192,275	1,873,945	4,415,275	1,970,747	9,456,369	7,040,662	2,639,973
1984–85	92,472,694	21,283,329	11,509,125	27,583,011	2,387,212	2,096,298	4,896,325	2,126,927	10,100,410	7,474,575	3,015,483
1985–86	100,437,616	23,116,605	12,704,750	29,911,500	2,544,506	2,275,898	5,410,905	2,373,494	10,674,136	8,226,635	3,199,186
1986–87	108,809,827	25,705,827	13,904,049	31,309,303	2,799,321	2,377,958	5,952,682	2,641,906	11,364,188	9,277,834	3,476,760
1987–88	117,340,109	27,836,781	14,771,954	33,517,166	3,006,263	2,586,441	6,359,282	2,918,090	11,947,778	10,626,566	3,769,787
1988–89	128,501,638	30,806,566	15,893,978	36,031,208	3,363,676	2,914,396	7,060,730	3,315,620	12,855,580	11,991,265	4,268,618
1989–90	139,635,477	33,926,060	17,254,874	38,349,239	3,639,902	3,143,696	7,781,422	3,632,100	13,938,469	13,216,664	4,753,051
1990–91	149,766,051	37,434,462	18,236,082	39,480,874	3,931,239	3,268,629	8,361,265	4,054,703	14,903,127	15,149,672	4,945,998
1991–92	161,395,896	41,559,037	19,833,317	40,586,907	4,159,876	3,442,009	8,977,271	4,520,890	15,758,599	17,240,338	5,317,651
1992–93	170,880,503	45,346,071	21,014,564	41,247,955	4,444,875	3,627,773	9,659,977	5,037,901	16,662,850	18,124,015	5,714,523
1993–94	179,226,601	48,646,538	22,076,385	41,910,288	4,998,306	3,669,536	10,203,062	5,294,030	17,537,514	18,959,776	5,931,167
1994–95	189,120,570	51,506,876	23,243,172	44,343,012	5,165,961	3,988,217	10,866,749	5,603,251	18,336,094	19,100,217	6,967,023
1995–96	197,414,848	54,725,982	23,879,098	45,621,627	5,589,988	4,570,933	11,942,987	5,552,907	18,861,585	18,672,680	7,997,061
Degree-granting institutions											
1995–96	197,973,236	55,260,293	23,939,075	45,692,673	5,607,909	4,562,171	11,903,126	5,530,763	18,867,540	18,611,570	7,998,116

—Not available.

[1]Tuition and fees received from veterans under Public Law 550 are reported under student fees and are not under income from the federal government.

[2]Federally supported student aid that is received through students is included under tuition and auxiliary enterprises.

[3]Includes federal aid received through state channels and regional compacts, through 1959–60.

[4]Beginning in 1969–70, the private grants represent nongovernmental revenue for sponsored research, student aid, and other sponsored programs.

[5]Prior to 1959–60, data for hospitals are included under sales and services of educational activities.

[6]Institutions that were accredited by an agency or association that was recognized by the U.S. Department of Education, or recognized directly by the Secretary of Education.

[7]Income from state and local governments tabulated under "State governments."

NOTE: Degree-granting institutions grant associate's or higher degrees and participate in Title IV federal financial aid programs. The degree-granting classification is very similar to the earlier higher education classification, but it includes more 2-year colleges and excludes a few higher education institutions that did not grant degrees. (See Guide to Sources for details.) Data for years prior to 1969–70 are not entirely comparable with data for later years. Also, some details for 1969–70 are not directly comparable with data for later years. Detail may not sum to totals because of rounding.

SOURCE: U.S. Department of Education, National Center for Education Statistics, *Annual Report of the Commissioner of Education*, 1919–20; *Biennial Survey of Education in the United States*, 1929–30 through 1959–60; Higher Education General Information Survey (HEGIS), "Financial Statistics of Institutions of Higher Education," 1969–70 through 1985–86; and 1986–87 through 1995–96 Integrated Postsecondary Education Data System, "Finance Survey" (IPEDS-F:FY86–96). (This table was prepared October 1998.)

Table 336. Current-fund revenue of public degree-granting institutions, by source of funds: Selected years, 1980–81 through 2000–01

Source	1980–81	1985–86	1990–91	1995–96	1996–97	1997–98	1998–99[1]	1999–2000	2000–01
1	2	3	4	5	6	7	8	9	10
	In thousands of current dollars								
Total current-fund revenue....	$43,195,617	$65,004,632	$94,904,506	$123,501,152	$129,504,834	$137,570,935	$144,969,708	$157,313,664	$176,645,215
Tuition and fees..............	5,570,404	9,439,177	15,258,024	23,257,454	24,631,120	26,058,092	27,427,984	29,125,603	31,919,611
Federal government............	5,540,101	6,852,370	9,763,427	13,672,467	14,189,358	14,544,027	15,554,372	16,952,116	19,744,966
Appropriations...............	1,128,101	1,401,367	1,604,548	1,826,738	1,830,604	1,570,329	1,679,660	1,583,132	1,719,963
Unrestricted grants and contracts	529,424	816,364	1,319,035	1,996,861	1,912,736	2,049,105	2,254,726	(2)	(2)
Restricted grants and contracts[3]..	3,812,197	4,481,723	6,629,484	9,598,340	10,173,113	10,586,439	11,287,950	14,819,488	17,088,332
Independent operations (FFRDC)[4]..	70,379	152,916	210,360	250,529	272,906	338,154	332,037	549,496	936,671
State governments	19,675,968	29,220,586	38,239,978	44,242,546	46,113,543	49,114,782	52,132,474	56,369,564	62,895,892
Appropriations...............	19,006,716	28,071,070	35,898,653	40,081,437	42,026,368	44,737,656	47,369,188	50,818,832	56,268,990
Unrestricted grants and contracts	45,390	88,779	250,168	924,837	690,665	498,485	497,396	(2)	(2)
Restricted grants and contracts ...	623,863	1,060,737	2,091,157	3,236,272	3,396,510	3,878,641	4,265,889	5,550,732	6,626,902
Local governments	1,622,938	2,325,844	3,531,714	5,074,511	5,019,600	5,279,349	5,546,546	6,039,978	7,052,431
Appropriations...............	1,478,001	2,150,459	3,159,789	4,397,098	4,348,960	4,594,289	4,792,860	5,217,976	5,582,287
Unrestricted grants and contracts	9,915	27,852	73,281	184,597	193,262	226,024	275,326	(2)	(2)
Restricted grants and contracts ...	135,022	147,533	298,644	492,815	477,377	459,036	478,360	822,003	1,470,144
Private gifts, grants, and contracts...	1,100,084	2,109,782	3,651,107	5,089,344	5,584,198	6,123,038	6,752,392	7,488,781	8,948,322
Unrestricted	110,462	279,381	529,496	784,979	900,449	993,528	1,127,013	—	—
Restricted.............................	989,622	1,830,401	3,121,611	4,304,365	4,683,749	5,129,511	5,625,378	—	—
Endowment income	214,561	398,603	431,235	721,079	784,695	887,093	958,363	1,170,163	1,351,989
Unrestricted	102,888	181,624	147,368	304,860	299,237	330,570	331,074	—	—
Restricted.............................	111,673	216,979	283,867	416,219	485,458	556,523	627,288	—	—
Sales and services	8,455,449	12,990,670	21,546,202	27,399,796	28,851,838	30,491,654	31,595,145	33,982,146	38,250,128
Educational activities	943,737	1,596,946	2,700,185	3,528,610	3,888,767	4,142,825	4,559,546	4,817,258	4,988,373
Auxiliary enterprises	4,614,561	6,684,794	9,058,745	11,595,408	12,280,517	13,070,055	13,775,599	15,174,301	16,501,834
Hospitals	2,897,151	4,708,930	9,787,271	12,275,778	12,682,554	13,278,773	13,260,000	13,990,587	16,759,921
Other sources	1,016,110	1,667,600	2,482,819	4,043,955	4,330,483	5,072,901	5,002,432	6,185,313	6,481,876
	Percentage distribution								
Total current-fund revenue....	100.0	100.0	100.0	100.0	100.0	100.0	100.0	100.0	100.0
Tuition and fees..............	12.9	14.5	16.1	18.8	19.0	18.9	18.9	18.5	18.1
Federal government............	12.8	10.5	10.3	11.1	11.0	10.6	10.7	10.8	11.2
Appropriations...............	2.6	2.2	1.7	1.5	1.4	1.1	1.2	1.0	1.0
Unrestricted grants and contracts	1.2	1.3	1.4	1.6	1.5	1.5	1.6	(2)	(2)
Restricted grants and contracts[3]..	8.8	6.9	7.0	7.8	7.9	7.7	7.8	9.4	9.7
Independent operations (FFRDC)[4]............	0.2	0.2	0.2	0.2	0.2	0.2	0.2	0.3	0.5
State governments	45.6	45.0	40.3	35.8	35.6	35.7	36.0	35.8	35.6
Appropriations...............	44.0	43.2	37.8	32.5	32.5	32.5	32.7	32.3	31.9
Unrestricted grants and contracts	0.1	0.1	0.3	0.7	0.5	0.4	0.3	(2)	(2)
Restricted grants and contracts ...	1.4	1.6	2.2	2.6	2.6	2.8	2.9	3.5	3.8
Local governments	3.8	3.6	3.7	4.1	3.9	3.8	3.8	3.8	4.0
Appropriations...............	3.4	3.3	3.3	3.6	3.4	3.3	3.3	3.3	3.2
Unrestricted grants and contracts	#	#	0.1	0.1	0.1	0.2	0.2	(2)	(2)
Restricted grants and contracts ...	0.3	0.2	0.3	0.4	0.4	0.3	0.3	0.5	0.8
Private gifts, grants, and contracts...	2.5	3.2	3.8	4.1	4.3	4.5	4.7	4.8	5.1
Unrestricted	0.3	0.4	0.6	0.6	0.7	0.7	0.8	—	—
Restricted.............................	2.3	2.8	3.3	3.5	3.6	3.7	3.9	—	—
Endowment income	0.5	0.6	0.5	0.6	0.6	0.6	0.7	0.7	0.8
Unrestricted	0.2	0.3	0.2	0.2	0.2	0.2	0.2	—	—
Restricted.............................	0.3	0.3	0.3	0.3	0.3	0.4	0.4	—	—
Sales and services	19.6	20.0	22.7	22.2	22.3	22.2	21.8	21.6	21.7
Educational activities	2.2	2.5	2.8	2.9	3.0	3.0	3.1	3.1	2.8
Auxiliary enterprises	10.7	10.3	9.5	9.4	9.5	9.5	9.5	9.6	9.3
Hospitals	6.7	7.2	10.3	9.9	9.8	9.7	9.1	8.9	9.5
Other sources	2.4	2.6	2.6	3.3	3.3	3.7	3.5	3.9	3.7

—Not available.
#Rounds to zero.
[1]Data were imputed using alternative procedures. (See Guide to Sources for details.)
[2]Included under restricted grants and contracts.
[3]Excludes Pell Grants. Federally supported student aid that is received through students is included under tuition and auxiliary enterprises.
[4]Generally includes only those revenues associated with major federally funded research and development centers (FFRDC).
NOTE: Data through 1990–91 are for institutions of higher education, while later data are for degree-granting institutions. Degree-granting institutions grant associate's or higher degrees and participate in Title IV federal financial aid programs. The degree-granting classification is very similar to the earlier higher education classification, but it includes more 2-year colleges and excludes a few higher education institutions that did not grant degrees. (See Guide to Sources for details.) Detail may not sum to totals because of rounding.
SOURCE: U.S. Department of Education, National Center for Education Statistics, Higher Education General Information Survey (HEGIS), "Financial Statistics of Institutions of Higher Education," 1980–81 and 1985–86 surveys; and 1990–91 through 2000–01 Integrated Postsecondary Education Data System, "Finance Survey" (IPEDS-F:FY91–00), and Spring 2001 and Spring 2002. (This table was prepared October 2003.)

Table 337. Revenues of public degree-granting institutions, by type of institution and source of revenue: 2003–04

Source of revenue	Revenues (in thousands)			Percentage distribution of revenues			Revenue per full-time-equivalent student		
	Total	4-year	2-year	Total	4-year	2-year	Total	4-year	2-year
1	2	3	4	5	6	7	8	9	10
Total revenues	$221,921,288	$182,008,588	$39,912,699	100.0	100.0	100.0	$24,026	$32,750	$10,849
Operating revenues	128,677,712	112,574,089	16,103,622	58.0	61.9	40.3	13,931	20,256	4,377
Tuition and fees[1]	35,150,615	28,739,354	6,411,261	15.8	15.8	16.1	3,806	5,171	1,743
Grants and contracts	42,553,845	35,501,531	7,052,314	19.2	19.5	17.7	4,607	6,388	1,917
Federal (excludes FDSL loans)	28,881,888	24,154,274	4,727,614	13.0	13.3	11.8	3,127	4,346	1,285
State	6,585,978	4,838,356	1,747,622	3.0	2.7	4.4	713	871	475
Local	7,085,979	6,508,901	577,078	3.2	3.6	1.4	767	1,171	157
Sales and services of auxiliary enterprises[2]	16,989,172	15,196,430	1,792,742	7.7	8.3	4.5	1,839	2,734	487
Sales and services of hospitals	19,587,282	19,587,282	0	8.8	10.8	0.0	2,121	3,524	0
Independent operations	918,775	914,221	4,554	0.4	0.5	#	99	164	1
Other operating revenues	13,478,024	12,635,272	842,752	6.1	6.9	2.1	1,459	2,274	229
Nonoperating revenues	81,211,146	59,401,324	21,809,823	36.6	32.6	54.6	8,792	10,688	5,928
Federal appropriations	1,605,958	1,473,410	132,548	0.7	0.8	0.3	174	265	36
State appropriations	53,888,233	42,504,491	11,383,743	24.3	23.4	28.5	5,834	7,648	3,094
Local appropriations	7,707,966	230,203	7,477,762	3.5	0.1	18.7	835	41	2,033
Nonoperating grants	3,603,243	1,586,149	2,017,094	1.6	0.9	5.1	390	285	548
Federal	2,565,883	1,245,113	1,320,769	1.2	0.7	3.3	278	224	359
State	942,960	313,215	629,745	0.4	0.2	1.6	102	56	171
Local	94,400	27,821	66,579	#	#	0.2	10	5	18
Gifts	4,191,696	3,956,515	235,181	1.9	2.2	0.6	454	712	64
Investment income	7,164,011	6,936,235	227,777	3.2	3.8	0.6	776	1,248	62
Other nonoperating revenues	3,050,039	2,714,320	335,719	1.4	1.5	0.8	330	488	91
Other revenues and additions	12,032,429	10,033,175	1,999,254	5.4	5.5	5.0	1,303	1,805	543
Capital appropriations	4,808,048	3,438,251	1,369,797	2.2	1.9	3.4	521	619	372
Capital grants and gifts	3,149,016	2,672,009	477,008	1.4	1.5	1.2	341	481	130
Additions to permanent endowments	995,144	987,743	7,401	0.4	0.5	#	108	178	2
Other revenues and additions	3,080,221	2,935,172	145,049	1.4	1.6	0.4	333	528	39

#Rounds to zero.
[1]Net of allowances and discounts.
[2]After deducting discounts and allowances.
NOTE: Degree-granting institutions grant associate's or higher degrees and participate in Title IV federal financial aid programs. Includes data for public institutions reporting data according to the Financial Accounting Standards Board (FASB) questionnaire. Detail may not sum to totals because of rounding.
SOURCE: U.S. Department of Education, National Center for Education Statistics, 2003–04 Integrated Postsecondary Education Data System, Spring 2004 and Spring 2005. (This table was prepared October 2006.)

Table 338. Revenues of public degree-granting institutions, by source of revenue and state or jurisdiction: 2003–04

[In thousands of current dollars]

| State or jurisdiction | Total revenues | Operating revenue | | | | | | | Nonoperating revenue[1] | | | Other revenues and additions |
| | | Total | Tuition and fees[2] | Federal grants and contracts | State and local grants and contracts | Sales and services of auxiliary enterprises[3] | Sales and services of hospitals | Independent operations and other | Total | State appropriations | Local appropriations | |
1	2	3	4	5	6	7	8	9	10	11	12	13
United States	$221,921,288	$128,677,712	$35,150,615	$28,881,888	$13,671,956	$16,989,172	$19,587,282	$14,396,799	$81,211,146	$53,888,233	$7,707,966	$12,032,429
Alabama	4,619,801	3,085,667	691,668	803,804	156,381	247,378	861,719	324,717	1,422,874	1,095,040	712	111,260
Alaska......................	633,218	303,684	61,653	139,820	51,178	35,283	0	15,751	242,933	217,745	5,800	86,601
Arizona	3,372,212	1,730,565	650,258	615,232	131,456	260,112	0	73,507	1,591,083	888,236	476,381	50,565
Arkansas..................	2,278,709	1,407,112	236,690	206,813	127,159	149,516	535,148	151,787	814,479	585,078	20,238	57,118
California	32,988,724	19,385,995	2,885,793	3,775,844	2,158,310	2,285,643	3,679,835	4,600,571	11,685,880	7,405,508	2,402,519	1,916,848
Colorado	3,414,694	2,546,327	767,886	833,894	206,457	419,621	200,218	118,251	751,770	494,764	42,052	116,597
Connecticut..............	2,265,773	1,290,087	355,695	193,196	64,929	157,242	186,910	332,114	819,669	718,291	0	156,018
Delaware..................	887,508	450,433	226,889	107,164	23,557	79,105	0	13,717	425,541	193,911	0	11,533
District of Columbia ...	110,522	42,480	14,038	15,512	8,498	2,863	0	1,569	58,470	4,139	50,861	9,572
Florida.....................	7,302,566	3,435,799	1,139,144	952,812	724,306	448,960	0	170,577	3,209,772	2,800,829	0	656,994
Georgia....................	4,955,055	2,582,380	772,975	769,498	535,791	378,806	0	125,310	1,909,127	1,751,732	5,541	463,548
Hawaii......................	1,112,058	510,816	111,365	272,498	39,788	79,466	0	7,700	570,488	459,620	0	30,754
Idaho.......................	840,056	465,385	141,633	152,399	60,811	74,978	0	35,565	350,839	317,794	5,635	23,833
Illinois.....................	8,982,680	4,069,494	1,222,368	742,629	317,580	667,922	336,946	782,049	4,599,760	1,822,869	680,732	313,425
Indiana.....................	4,655,031	2,962,508	1,179,058	562,192	307,338	630,893	0	283,027	1,603,452	1,294,406	6,600	89,070
Iowa	3,340,524	2,292,923	500,542	526,000	108,057	311,336	609,438	237,551	958,020	750,111	65,217	89,581
Kansas.....................	2,377,235	1,307,072	414,234	345,826	107,208	213,965	0	225,838	992,252	662,320	192,994	77,912
Kentucky	3,418,774	2,092,032	441,616	439,515	274,831	192,870	634,273	108,926	1,235,487	984,564	10,084	91,255
Louisiana	3,266,033	1,972,420	499,039	486,604	360,079	242,776	299,013	84,908	1,174,155	1,081,957	0	119,458
Maine.......................	710,322	399,951	137,433	71,021	59,827	78,312	0	53,359	275,012	216,910	0	35,358
Maryland...................	4,240,132	2,524,588	959,547	580,944	374,638	430,004	0	179,454	1,425,739	993,743	216,456	289,805
Massachusetts..........	2,785,585	1,810,923	666,102	390,367	177,187	224,916	0	352,352	898,215	820,888	0	76,447
Michigan	10,458,353	6,695,550	2,054,136	1,312,007	453,101	795,098	1,712,285	368,924	3,417,629	1,731,675	503,319	345,174
Minnesota	3,809,567	2,173,982	872,150	535,769	287,466	329,781	0	148,816	1,456,064	1,120,554	0	179,521
Mississippi	2,735,438	1,642,160	302,674	510,182	161,698	193,711	390,015	83,880	945,474	757,385	55,899	147,805
Missouri	3,443,094	2,062,307	642,157	282,492	127,139	437,676	409,557	163,286	1,249,846	850,139	119,597	130,942
Montana....................	737,297	506,832	170,283	169,386	30,696	81,230	0	55,237	214,536	148,593	5,404	15,929
Nebraska	1,616,070	847,799	220,106	173,620	108,627	186,096	109,067	50,283	728,561	486,098	68,594	39,710
Nevada	1,170,378	513,081	166,107	142,613	62,723	80,610	0	61,028	545,742	453,144	0	111,555
New Hampshire	671,597	467,507	203,102	92,076	26,845	122,756	0	22,729	138,777	106,405	0	65,313
New Jersey	5,258,294	3,327,215	1,087,480	566,276	402,236	365,909	624,625	280,690	1,789,129	1,410,600	185,689	141,950
New Mexico	2,261,815	1,300,035	147,529	447,966	151,336	97,939	348,898	106,368	884,575	606,600	75,811	77,204
New York...................	9,970,865	5,793,545	1,599,537	1,032,482	1,059,660	574,399	1,373,510	153,956	3,853,676	2,894,535	518,520	323,644
North Carolina	6,950,981	3,023,732	827,660	874,460	265,931	974,533	0	81,148	3,090,710	2,334,186	130,037	836,539
North Dakota	698,620	464,259	152,091	162,051	31,013	73,570	0	45,535	218,669	173,578	0	15,692
Ohio.........................	8,710,377	5,580,661	2,044,662	846,367	447,815	721,578	1,224,326	295,913	2,766,468	1,821,109	121,944	363,248
Oklahoma.................	2,701,140	1,654,197	364,981	372,754	205,186	301,012	0	410,265	894,033	707,140	38,114	152,910
Oregon.....................	3,522,318	2,431,995	609,830	597,100	258,378	229,643	590,114	146,929	1,009,173	628,220	138,313	81,151
Pennsylvania.............	8,471,720	6,107,891	2,209,069	1,043,202	277,186	643,725	1,549,143	385,567	2,308,850	1,282,991	107,355	54,978
Rhode Island	527,868	327,662	146,173	74,314	17,904	68,836	0	20,436	177,761	166,289	0	22,445
South Carolina..........	2,695,888	1,765,406	635,439	486,440	236,051	240,180	0	167,297	837,254	656,585	43,568	93,228
South Dakota............	482,318	312,623	117,016	98,813	28,115	40,391	0	28,287	155,234	142,532	0	14,461
Tennessee	2,928,646	1,468,316	594,370	258,057	296,523	193,240	0	126,127	1,371,979	1,002,907	0	88,351
Texas	21,126,371	10,342,044	2,314,850	2,566,067	1,224,767	815,553	1,924,244	1,496,563	8,023,861	4,248,841	824,392	2,760,466
Utah........................	3,023,058	2,085,192	340,566	430,681	115,124	139,005	510,700	549,115	744,262	600,043	0	193,604
Vermont	566,066	423,910	188,830	111,387	42,334	59,866	0	21,494	130,014	59,606	0	12,142
Virginia....................	5,560,538	3,578,573	1,127,398	802,130	171,974	652,068	701,206	123,777	1,684,812	1,189,861	1,872	297,153
Washington...............	5,705,168	3,538,499	856,336	947,859	414,529	385,141	688,521	246,114	1,751,846	1,162,885	0	414,822
West Virginia.............	1,123,491	728,446	262,085	194,530	103,447	129,093	0	39,290	375,503	361,838	310	19,542
Wisconsin	4,480,447	2,416,008	770,753	630,549	264,841	338,362	0	411,503	1,932,489	1,027,362	565,152	131,950
Wyoming...................	470,157	187,842	46,505	52,218	22,919	38,557	0	27,644	254,866	196,077	22,253	27,449
U.S. Service Schools	1,486,136	241,802	1,113	84,456	1,033	67,649	87,550	0	1,244,335	0	0	0
Other jurisdictions	1,394,562	389,975	69,415	181,428	42,784	15,501	50,664	30,183	993,183	786,856	42,679	11,403
American Samoa	8,526	1,293	1,247	0	0	46	0	0	6,977	0	3,462	257
Federated States of Micronesia	28,985	17,940	2,571	12,866	928	849	0	726	11,045	112	0	0
Guam.......................	88,626	40,192	9,690	20,435	2,628	2,399	0	5,040	48,236	27,654	12,422	199
Marshall Islands........	5,984	3,570	0	3,180	26	364	0	0	2,215	0	2,200	200
Northern Marianas	18,236	8,952	927	5,397	0	561	0	2,068	9,284	9,054	0	0
Palau.......................	9,456	9,016	1,296	4,226	2,415	652	0	427	440	299	0	0
Puerto Rico...............	1,170,036	278,025	44,478	120,367	34,365	6,698	50,664	21,452	884,455	749,737	0	7,556
Virgin Islands............	64,712	30,988	9,205	14,959	2,422	3,933	0	470	30,532	0	24,596	3,192

[1]Includes other categories not separately shown.
[2]Net of allowances and discounts.
[3]After deducting discounts and allowances.
NOTE: Degree-granting institutions grant associate's or higher degrees and participate in Title IV federal financial aid programs. Includes data for public institutions reporting data according to the Financial Accounting Standards Board (FASB) questionnaire. Detail may not sum to totals because of rounding.
SOURCE: U.S. Department of Education, National Center for Education Statistics, 2003–04 Integrated Postsecondary Education Data System, Spring 2005. (This table was prepared October 2006.)

Table 339. Appropriations from state and local governments for public degree-granting institutions, by state or jurisdiction: Selected years, 1990–91 through 2003–04

[In thousands of current dollars]

State or jurisdiction	State appropriations						Local appropriations					
	1990–91	1995–96	1999–2000	2000–01	2002–03	2003–04	1990–91	1995–96	1999–2000	2000–01	2002–03	2003–04
1	2	3	4	5	6	7	8	9	10	11	12	13
United States	$35,898,653	$40,081,437	$50,818,832	$56,268,990	$54,760,010	$53,888,233	$3,159,789	$4,397,098	$5,217,976	$5,582,287	$7,174,422	$7,707,966
Alabama	708,191	879,680	999,252	991,302	1,086,580	1,095,040	6,796	4,736	4,632	4,829	0	712
Alaska.....................	168,395	171,580	178,353	190,650	211,152	217,745	260	693	10,581	10,340	5,800	5,800
Arizona	591,656	691,335	869,878	903,196	891,255	888,236	149,337	217,426	288,758	310,762	442,032	476,381
Arkansas................	315,372	437,257	581,735	583,794	585,788	585,078	216	2,524	7,214	9,496	17,182	20,238
California	5,313,052	4,811,297	6,753,849	7,891,669	7,919,246	7,405,508	771,160	1,353,630	1,631,164	1,764,717	2,162,154	2,402,519
Colorado	423,710	497,663	621,766	655,037	564,451	494,764	22,400	28,786	26,794	36,840	42,503	42,052
Connecticut............	363,427	462,183	672,824	664,356	715,304	718,291	0	0	0	0	0	0
Delaware................	115,729	107,968	173,819	193,695	190,335	193,911	0	12,379	0	0	0	0
District of Columbia ...	0	0	0	3,019	4,154	4,139	73,495	68,257	43,259	46,933	50,544	50,861
Florida.....................	1,638,218	1,898,618	2,497,632	2,656,376	2,755,551	2,800,829	1,850	116	0	2	0	0
Georgia....................	915,303	1,254,216	1,710,769	1,826,961	1,785,986	1,751,732	25,705	17,371	19,594	21,615	9,518	5,541
Hawaii.....................	304,131	280,503	279,745	395,884	462,453	459,620	0	0	0	0	0	0
Idaho.......................	177,918	223,108	275,415	290,746	302,898	317,794	6,161	10,435	10,615	11,148	5,340	5,635
Illinois.....................	1,296,895	1,161,833	1,659,027	1,760,300	1,703,137	1,822,869	284,635	418,269	494,611	520,136	651,532	680,732
Indiana....................	886,124	977,517	1,212,921	1,257,919	1,267,690	1,294,406	1,507	2,831	6,420	6,190	6,539	6,600
Iowa	544,945	649,901	787,783	813,805	780,047	750,111	21,624	29,098	34,393	36,129	65,771	65,217
Kansas....................	437,413	528,243	634,217	664,201	662,822	662,320	87,026	117,684	152,910	160,873	187,451	192,994
Kentucky.................	617,915	690,328	891,949	939,047	943,876	984,564	4,682	6,041	7,176	14,930	9,800	10,084
Louisiana	566,798	603,825	812,042	834,643	1,037,543	1,081,957	1,462	8,061	478	517	0	0
Maine	174,737	158,044	200,638	212,144	218,528	216,910	0	27	0	0	0	0
Maryland..................	724,223	717,377	893,175	999,723	1,024,608	993,743	117,913	136,661	174,854	185,034	194,127	216,456
Massachusetts..........	471,368	669,102	910,366	1,038,998	917,956	820,888	0	1,779	0	0	0	0
Michigan..................	1,326,884	1,572,241	1,872,214	1,991,098	1,931,256	1,731,675	159,202	215,733	275,186	288,112	483,305	503,319
Minnesota................	744,381	901,114	1,121,315	1,174,797	1,212,946	1,120,554	2,040	0	0	0	0	0
Mississippi...............	365,574	570,035	794,196	758,242	731,047	757,385	25,670	31,725	37,844	38,167	53,126	55,899
Missouri...................	563,430	669,832	887,533	945,746	854,915	850,139	38,097	72,895	92,705	101,562	114,098	119,597
Montana...................	110,199	121,730	129,663	137,341	145,727	148,593	3,310	3,526	3,868	4,069	4,685	5,404
Nebraska	318,482	382,465	487,148	514,235	512,976	486,098	36,569	53,004	24,949	19,892	60,242	68,594
Nevada	161,581	223,413	311,649	333,117	397,539	453,144	0	0	0	0	3,311	0
New Hampshire	71,226	79,376	92,403	96,157	104,728	106,405	6	0	140	0	0	0
New Jersey	854,989	1,045,117	1,180,754	1,246,554	1,374,123	1,410,600	145,010	156,011	165,640	172,667	181,996	185,689
New Mexico	307,083	413,344	524,859	538,822	577,647	606,600	34,364	42,363	57,282	60,183	73,117	75,811
New York..................	2,313,128	2,202,186	2,582,286	4,461,671	2,995,208	2,894,535	372,650	405,160	422,712	431,415	490,841	518,520
North Carolina	1,351,111	1,686,718	2,095,190	2,221,600	2,208,058	2,334,186	62,785	79,490	106,933	113,448	121,914	130,037
North Dakota	129,986	138,785	166,945	188,047	194,719	173,578	9	170	21	21	1,549	0
Ohio.........................	1,360,141	1,488,806	1,829,799	1,922,571	1,812,533	1,821,109	63,899	120,161	104,247	101,647	108,492	121,944
Oklahoma.................	473,898	536,307	701,735	754,540	724,840	707,140	12,822	18,578	21,942	28,367	36,909	38,114
Oregon.....................	377,476	442,603	591,047	640,347	547,268	628,220	118,499	82,282	101,786	106,436	132,680	138,313
Pennsylvania............	962,121	1,110,896	1,251,589	1,331,544	1,330,460	1,282,991	62,794	78,912	97,904	94,338	105,163	107,355
Rhode Island	113,614	121,153	150,114	157,137	165,060	166,289	0	0	0	0	0	0
South Carolina	578,794	647,111	833,464	853,139	737,934	656,585	18,670	25,737	32,693	36,060	42,400	43,568
South Dakota	81,859	105,090	128,989	129,680	140,096	142,532	0	957	0	0	143	0
Tennessee	663,536	850,110	920,988	969,316	1,007,059	1,002,907	1,779	2,113	3,758	3,824	3,889	0
Texas	2,627,916	3,302,958	4,025,328	4,236,852	4,220,459	4,248,841	210,934	280,141	383,443	439,342	736,280	824,392
Utah	304,738	414,407	499,301	531,975	578,426	600,043	0	0	507	0	0	0
Vermont	40,997	42,400	50,478	53,605	58,482	59,606	4	62	0	0	0	0
Virginia....................	886,208	839,587	1,281,545	1,395,308	1,285,924	1,189,861	973	1,282	1,492	1,570	1,807	1,872
Washington...............	828,700	914,200	1,110,049	1,200,392	1,208,061	1,162,885	2,470	100	0	0	0	0
West Virginia.............	263,269	320,198	359,956	382,269	389,532	361,838	574	693	603	503	0	310
Wisconsin	841,192	937,513	1,084,212	1,186,415	1,093,719	1,027,362	197,712	275,712	349,917	379,648	540,600	565,152
Wyoming..................	120,623	130,162	136,925	149,009	187,907	196,077	12,721	13,489	18,955	20,525	27,582	22,253
U.S. Service Schools	0	0	0	0	0	0	0	0	0	0	0	0
Other jurisdictions	337,393	551,957	641,333	709,473	740,240	786,856	12,724	22,579	21,244	20,612	47,093	42,679
American Samoa.......	0	0	0	0	0	0	0	9,443	2,800	0	2,139	3,462
Federated States of Micronesia	0	11	0	40	5,420	112	0	2,978	2,637	3,327	0	0
Guam.......................	28,283	29,975	29,163	29,122	28,572	27,654	10,028	10,118	10,495	12,826	12,704	12,422
Marshall Islands........	0	324	461	1,924	0	0	0	0	0	0	2,668	2,200
Northern Marianas	0	8,164	7,958	9,055	8,551	9,054	0	0	0	0	0	0
Palau.......................	644	2,040	2,345	2,345	2,345	299	0	0	0	0	0	0
Puerto Rico..............	277,295	493,833	581,107	647,623	695,352	749,737	2,375	40	5,312	4,459	4,872	0
Virgin Islands............	31,170	17,610	20,299	19,365	0	0	320	0	0	0	24,710	24,596

NOTE: Data for 1990–91 are for institutions of higher education, while later data are for degree-granting institutions. Degree-granting institutions grant associate's or higher degrees and participate in Title IV federal financial aid programs. The degree-granting classification is very similar to the earlier higher education classification, but it includes more 2-year colleges and excludes a few higher education institutions that did not grant degrees. (See Guide to Sources for details.) Includes data for public institutions reporting data according to the Financial Accounting Standards Board (FASB) questionnaire. Detail may not sum to totals because of rounding.
SOURCE: U.S. Department of Education, National Center for Education Statistics, 1990–91 through 2003–04 Integrated Postsecondary Education Data System, "Finance Survey" (IPEDS-F:FY91-99), and Spring 2001 through Spring 2005. (This table was prepared October 2006.)

Table 340. Total revenue of private not-for-profit degree-granting institutions, by source of funds and type of institution: 1996–97 through 2003–04

Type of institution and year	Total revenue and investment return	Student tuition and fees (net of allowances)	Federal appropriations, grants, and contracts[1]	State appropriations, grants, and contracts	Local appropriations, grants, and contracts	Private gifts, grants, and contracts[2]	Investment return (gain or loss)	Educational activities	Auxiliary enterprises	Hospitals	Other
1	2	3	4	5	6	7	8	9	10	11	12
						In thousands of current dollars					
All institutions											
1996–97	$91,319,861	$25,375,721	(3)	$930,976	$510,189	$11,239,080	$22,378,196	$2,179,010	$7,213,906	(3)	$21,492,785
1997–98[4]	95,240,891	26,499,174	$11,156,948	953,624	520,115	13,245,613	22,311,899	2,656,621	7,655,732	$6,278,828	3,962,337
1998–99[4]	95,680,731	28,044,077	11,622,152	1,044,815	545,600	14,253,692	18,735,718	2,703,488	8,028,235	6,784,998	3,917,956
1999–2000	120,625,806	29,651,812	12,191,827	1,117,742	580,237	16,488,984	37,763,518	2,865,606	8,317,607	7,208,600	4,439,874
2000–01	82,174,492	31,318,106	13,378,019	1,176,060	508,365	15,859,313	-3,602,326	3,468,680	8,742,610	7,126,343	4,199,323
2001–02	84,346,652	33,499,121	14,790,235	1,303,772	493,158	15,394,353	-6,545,330	3,220,868	9,317,922	8,083,935	4,788,618
2002–03	105,683,294	36,024,148	16,633,951	1,518,494	476,147	14,374,926	9,340,251	3,056,259	9,833,972	8,942,047	5,483,099
2003–04	134,230,762	38,505,631	18,335,784	1,455,556	485,717	15,847,571	30,896,917	3,290,420	10,325,606	9,657,753	5,429,805
4–year											
1996–97	90,478,094	25,006,562	(3)	909,041	509,210	11,113,821	22,303,001	2,165,166	7,139,963	(3)	21,331,329
1997–98[4]	94,529,717	26,158,716	11,109,406	938,004	519,025	13,120,588	22,244,963	2,641,456	7,584,913	6,278,278	3,934,367
1998–99[4]	94,812,541	27,695,568	11,572,739	1,026,270	543,561	14,044,604	18,705,741	2,684,664	7,965,778	6,784,463	3,789,154
1999–2000	119,708,625	29,257,523	12,133,829	1,098,961	574,746	16,346,616	37,698,219	2,837,784	8,261,507	7,208,600	4,290,841
2000–01	81,568,928	30,996,381	13,318,572	1,156,503	503,002	15,788,869	-3,623,323	3,452,731	8,703,316	7,125,648	4,147,227
2001–02	83,764,907	33,165,965	14,708,582	1,280,787	490,596	15,328,974	-6,547,915	3,206,440	9,263,171	8,083,935	4,784,371
2002–03	105,074,698	35,681,617	16,524,734	1,492,010	471,383	14,314,197	9,338,535	3,041,307	9,779,275	8,942,047	5,489,594
2003–04	133,594,668	38,181,648	18,236,313	1,423,269	480,104	15,789,672	30,854,091	3,277,767	10,287,215	9,657,753	5,406,836
2–year											
1996–97	841,767	369,159	(3)	21,934	978	125,259	75,195	13,844	73,942	(3)	161,456
1997–98[4]	711,175	340,459	47,541	15,620	1,090	125,024	66,937	15,165	70,818	550	27,970
1998–99[4]	868,190	348,508	49,414	18,545	2,039	209,088	29,977	18,824	62,457	535	128,803
1999–2000	917,181	394,289	57,998	18,781	5,491	142,368	65,299	27,822	56,100	0	149,033
2000–01	605,564	321,724	59,446	19,557	5,363	70,444	20,996	15,949	39,294	694	52,096
2001–02	581,745	333,156	81,653	22,985	2,562	65,379	2,585	14,429	54,750	0	4,246
2002–03	608,596	342,531	109,217	26,483	4,764	60,729	1,716	14,953	54,697	0	-6,495
2003–04	636,094	323,983	99,471	32,287	5,613	57,900	42,826	12,653	38,391	0	22,969
						Percentage distribution					
All institutions											
1996–97	100.00	27.79	(3)	1.02	0.56	12.31	24.51	2.39	7.90	(3)	23.54
1997–98[4]	100.00	27.82	11.71	1.00	0.55	13.91	23.43	2.79	8.04	6.59	4.16
1998–99[4]	100.00	29.31	12.15	1.09	0.57	14.90	19.58	2.83	8.39	7.09	4.09
1999–2000	100.00	24.58	10.11	0.93	0.48	13.67	31.31	2.38	6.90	5.98	3.68
2000–01	100.00	38.11	16.28	1.43	0.62	19.30	-4.38	4.22	10.64	8.67	5.11
2001–02	100.00	39.72	17.54	1.55	0.58	18.25	-7.76	3.82	11.05	9.58	5.68
2002–03	100.00	34.09	15.74	1.44	0.45	13.60	8.84	2.89	9.31	8.46	5.19
2003–04	100.00	28.69	13.66	1.08	0.36	11.81	23.02	2.45	7.69	7.19	4.05
4–year											
1996–97	100.00	27.64	(3)	1.00	0.56	12.28	24.65	2.39	7.89	(3)	23.58
1997–98[4]	100.00	27.67	11.75	0.99	0.55	13.88	23.53	2.79	8.02	6.64	4.16
1998–99[4]	100.00	29.21	12.21	1.08	0.57	14.81	19.73	2.83	8.40	7.16	4.00
1999–2000	100.00	24.44	10.14	0.92	0.48	13.66	31.49	2.37	6.90	6.02	3.58
2000–01	100.00	38.00	16.33	1.42	0.62	19.36	-4.44	4.23	10.67	8.74	5.08
2001–02	100.00	39.59	17.56	1.53	0.59	18.30	-7.82	3.83	11.06	9.65	5.71
2002–03	100.00	33.96	15.73	1.42	0.45	13.62	8.89	2.89	9.31	8.51	5.22
2003–04	100.00	28.58	13.65	1.07	0.36	11.82	23.10	2.45	7.70	7.23	4.05
2–year											
1996–97	100.00	43.86	(3)	2.61	0.12	14.88	8.93	1.64	8.78	(3)	19.18
1997–98[4]	100.00	47.87	6.68	2.20	0.15	17.58	9.41	2.13	9.96	0.08	3.93
1998–99[4]	100.00	40.14	5.69	2.14	0.23	24.08	3.45	2.17	7.19	0.06	14.84
1999–2000	100.00	42.99	6.32	2.05	0.60	15.52	7.12	3.03	6.12	0.00	16.25
2000–01	100.00	53.13	9.82	3.23	0.89	11.63	3.47	2.63	6.49	0.11	8.60
2001–02	100.00	57.27	14.04	3.95	0.44	11.24	0.44	2.48	9.41	0.00	0.73
2002–03	100.00	56.28	17.95	4.35	0.78	9.98	0.28	2.46	8.99	0.00	-1.07
2003–04	100.00	50.93	15.64	5.08	0.88	9.10	6.73	1.99	6.04	0.00	3.61
						Revenue per full-time-equivalent student in constant 2005–06 dollars[5]					
All institutions											
1996–97	$47,285	$13,139	(3)	$482	$264	$5,820	$11,587	$1,128	$3,735	(3)	$11,129
1997–98[4]	47,782	13,294	$5,597	478	261	6,645	11,194	1,333	3,841	$3,150	1,988
1998–99[4]	46,397	13,599	5,636	507	265	6,912	9,085	1,311	3,893	3,290	1,900
1999–2000	55,825	13,723	5,642	517	269	7,631	17,477	1,326	3,849	3,336	2,055
2000–01	36,055	13,741	5,870	516	223	6,958	-1,581	1,522	3,836	3,127	1,843
2001–02	35,584	14,132	6,240	550	208	6,494	-2,761	1,359	3,931	3,410	2,020
2002–03	42,217	14,390	6,645	607	190	5,742	3,731	1,221	3,928	3,572	2,190
2003–04	51,221	14,693	6,997	555	185	6,047	11,790	1,256	3,940	3,685	2,072

See notes at end of table.

Table 340. Total revenue of private not-for-profit degree-granting institutions, by source of funds and type of institution: 1996–97 through 2003–04—Continued

Type of institution and year	Total revenue and investment return	Student tuition and fees (net of allowances)	Federal appropriations, grants, and contracts[1]	State appropriations, grants, and contracts	Local appropriations, grants, and contracts	Private gifts, grants, and contracts[2]	Investment return (gain or loss)	Educational activities	Auxiliary enterprises	Hospitals	Other
1	2	3	4	5	6	7	8	9	10	11	12
4–year											
1996–97........................	48,122	13,300	(3)	483	271	5,911	11,862	1,152	3,797	(3)	11,345
1997–98........................	48,651	13,463	5,718	483	267	6,753	11,449	1,359	3,904	3,231	2,025
1998–99[4].....................	47,049	13,743	5,743	509	270	6,969	9,282	1,332	3,953	3,367	1,880
1999–2000.....................	56,587	13,830	5,736	519	272	7,727	17,820	1,341	3,905	3,408	2,028
2000–01........................	36,348	13,812	5,935	515	224	7,036	-1,615	1,539	3,878	3,175	1,848
2001–02........................	35,866	14,201	6,298	548	210	6,563	-2,804	1,373	3,966	3,461	2,049
2002–03........................	42,538	14,445	6,690	604	191	5,795	3,781	1,231	3,959	3,620	2,222
2003–04........................	51,629	14,756	7,048	550	186	6,102	11,924	1,267	3,976	3,732	2,090
2–year											
1996–97........................	16,476	7,226	(3)	429	19	2,452	1,472	271	1,447	(3)	3,160
1997–98........................	14,162	6,780	947	311	22	2,490	1,333	302	1,410	11	557
1998–99[4].....................	18,467	7,413	1,051	394	43	4,448	638	400	1,329	11	2,740
1999–2000.....................	20,233	8,698	1,279	414	121	3,141	1,441	614	1,238	0	3,288
2000–01........................	17,284	9,183	1,697	558	153	2,011	599	455	1,122	20	1,487
2001–02........................	16,673	9,548	2,340	659	73	1,874	74	414	1,569	0	122
2002–03........................	18,333	10,318	3,290	798	144	1,829	52	450	1,648	0	-196
2003–04........................	19,261	9,810	3,012	978	170	1,753	1,297	383	1,162	0	695

[1]Includes independent operations.
[2]Includes contributions from affiliated entities.
[3]Included under "Other."
[4]Data imputed using alternative procedures. (See Guide to Sources for details.)
[5]Constant dollars based on the Consumer Price Index, prepared by the Bureau of Labor Statistics, U.S. Department of Labor, adjusted to a school-year basis.

NOTE: Detail may not sum to totals because of rounding.
SOURCE: U.S. Department of Education, National Center for Education Statistics, 1996–97 through 2003–04 Integrated Postsecondary Education Data System, "Fall Enrollment Survey" (IPEDS-EF:96–99) and "Finance Survey" (IPEDS-F:FY97–99), and Spring 2001 through Spring 2005. (This table was prepared May 2006.)

Table 341. Total revenue of private not-for-profit degree-granting institutions, by source of funds and type of institution: 2003–04

Type of institution	Total revenue and investment return	Student tuition and fees (net of allowances)	Federal appro-priations, grants, and contracts[1]	State appro-priations, grants, and contracts	Local appro-priations, grants, and contracts	Private gifts, grants, and contracts[2]	Investment return (gain or loss)	Educational activities	Auxiliary enterprises	Hospitals	Other
1	2	3	4	5	6	7	8	9	10	11	12
					In thousands						
Total	$134,230,762	$38,505,631	$18,335,784	$1,455,556	$485,717	$15,847,571	$30,896,917	$3,290,420	$10,325,606	$9,657,753	$5,429,805
4-year	133,594,668	38,181,648	18,236,313	1,423,269	480,104	15,789,672	30,854,091	3,277,767	10,287,215	9,657,753	5,406,836
Doctoral, extensive[3]	70,197,335	11,011,516	14,274,307	632,536	273,673	7,642,266	20,363,566	2,060,449	3,637,107	8,024,425	2,277,491
Doctoral, intensive[4]	9,239,196	4,270,343	687,482	144,260	22,975	860,965	1,564,946	582,573	851,717	0	253,935
Master's[5]	19,245,022	11,158,416	943,571	255,737	7,152	1,871,599	1,891,001	115,898	2,393,863	122,876	484,908
Baccalaureate[6]	20,641,752	7,650,903	630,104	176,147	5,586	3,103,045	5,580,709	112,925	2,743,878	0	638,454
Specialized institutions[7]	14,271,364	4,090,470	1,700,850	214,590	170,717	2,311,796	1,453,869	405,922	660,649	1,510,453	1,752,049
Art, music, or design	1,574,591	835,513	19,120	12,873	1,949	205,392	217,114	17,752	117,696	0	147,183
Business and management	797,275	588,572	10,688	11,673	684	37,343	51,317	4,595	82,432	0	9,971
Engineering or technology	362,955	168,588	32,265	18,006	0	40,846	64,799	324	35,788	0	2,341
Medical or other health	7,240,553	1,089,544	1,491,484	147,079	165,018	1,127,029	470,765	335,709	141,825	1,509,720	762,380
Theological	1,979,685	441,683	52,878	5,335	382	663,447	511,029	16,472	178,282	0	110,178
Tribal[8]	48,089	894	35,148	1,145	0	4,263	77	478	1,161	0	4,923
Other specialized	2,268,216	965,677	59,266	18,480	2,683	233,477	138,770	30,592	103,465	732	715,074
2-year	636,094	323,983	99,471	32,287	5,613	57,900	42,826	12,653	38,391	0	22,969
Associate's of arts	590,187	319,937	70,857	31,307	2,469	55,043	42,625	12,477	37,071	0	18,402
Tribal[8]	45,906	4,046	28,615	980	3,144	2,857	201	176	1,321	0	4,567
					Percentage distribution						
Total	100.00	28.69	13.66	1.08	0.36	11.81	23.02	2.45	7.69	7.19	4.05
4-year	100.00	28.58	13.65	1.07	0.36	11.82	23.10	2.45	7.70	7.23	4.05
Doctoral, extensive[3]	100.00	15.69	20.33	0.90	0.39	10.89	29.01	2.94	5.18	11.43	3.24
Doctoral, intensive[4]	100.00	46.22	7.44	1.56	0.25	9.32	16.94	6.31	9.22	0.00	2.75
Master's[5]	100.00	57.98	4.90	1.33	0.04	9.73	9.83	0.60	12.44	0.64	2.52
Baccalaureate[6]	100.00	37.07	3.05	0.85	0.03	15.03	27.04	0.55	13.29	0.00	3.09
Specialized institutions[7]	100.00	28.66	11.92	1.50	1.20	16.20	10.19	2.84	4.63	10.58	12.28
Art, music, or design	100.00	53.06	1.21	0.82	0.12	13.04	13.79	1.13	7.47	0.00	9.35
Business and management	100.00	73.82	1.34	1.46	0.09	4.68	6.44	0.58	10.34	0.00	1.25
Engineering or technology	100.00	46.45	8.89	4.96	0.00	11.25	17.85	0.09	9.86	0.00	0.64
Medical or other health	100.00	15.05	20.60	2.03	2.28	15.57	6.50	4.64	1.96	20.85	10.53
Theological	100.00	22.31	2.67	0.27	0.02	33.51	25.81	0.83	9.01	0.00	5.57
Tribal[8]	100.00	1.86	73.09	2.38	0.00	8.87	0.16	0.99	2.41	0.00	10.24
Other specialized	100.00	42.57	2.61	0.81	0.12	10.29	6.12	1.35	4.56	0.03	31.53
2-year	100.00	50.93	15.64	5.08	0.88	9.10	6.73	1.99	6.04	0.00	3.61
Associate's of arts	100.00	54.21	12.01	5.30	0.42	9.33	7.22	2.11	6.28	0.00	3.12
Tribal[8]	100.00	8.81	62.33	2.13	6.85	6.22	0.44	0.38	2.88	0.00	9.95
					Revenue per full-time-equivalent student						
Total	$47,918	$13,746	$6,546	$520	$173	$5,657	$11,030	$1,175	$3,686	$3,448	$1,938
4-year	48,300	13,804	6,593	515	174	5,709	11,155	1,185	3,719	3,492	1,955
Doctoral, extensive[3]	115,943	18,187	23,577	1,045	452	12,623	33,634	3,403	6,007	13,254	3,762
Doctoral, intensive[4]	34,884	16,123	2,596	545	87	3,251	5,909	2,200	3,216	0	959
Master's[5]	21,189	12,286	1,039	282	8	2,061	2,082	128	2,636	135	534
Baccalaureate[6]	31,247	11,582	954	267	8	4,697	8,448	171	4,154	0	966
Specialized institutions[7]	43,671	12,517	5,205	657	522	7,074	4,449	1,242	2,022	4,622	5,361
Art, music, or design	33,734	17,900	410	276	42	4,400	4,652	380	2,522	0	3,153
Business and management	18,439	13,612	247	270	16	864	1,187	106	1,906	0	231
Engineering or technology	21,602	10,034	1,920	1,072	0	2,431	3,857	19	2,130	0	139
Medical or other health	120,145	18,079	24,749	2,441	2,738	18,701	7,812	5,571	2,353	25,051	12,650
Theological	26,791	5,977	716	72	5	8,978	6,916	223	2,413	0	1,491
Tribal[8]	22,419	417	16,386	534	0	1,988	36	223	541	0	2,295
Other specialized	27,075	11,527	707	221	32	2,787	1,656	365	1,235	9	8,536
2-year	18,019	9,178	2,818	915	159	1,640	1,213	358	1,088	0	651
Associate's of arts	17,496	9,485	2,101	928	73	1,632	1,264	370	1,099	0	546
Tribal[8]	29,258	2,579	18,237	625	2,004	1,821	128	112	842	0	2,911

[1]Includes independent operations.
[2]Includes contributions from affiliated entities.
[3]Doctoral, extensive institutions are committed to graduate education through the doctorate, and award 50 or more doctor's degrees per year across at least 15 disciplines.
[4]Doctoral, intensive institutions are committed to education through the doctorate and award at least 10 doctor's degrees per year across 3 or more disciplines or at least 20 doctor's degrees overall.
[5]Master's institutions offer a full range of baccalaureate programs and are committed to education through the master's degree. They award at least 20 master's degrees per year.
[6]Baccalaureate institutions primarily emphasize undergraduate education.
[7]Specialized 4-year institutions award degrees primarily in single fields of study, such as medicine, business, fine arts, theology, and engineering. Includes some institutions that

have 4-year programs, but have not reported sufficient data to identify program category. Also includes institutions classified as 4-year under the IPEDS system, which had been classified as 2-year in the Carnegie system because they primarily award associate's degrees.
[8]Tribally controlled colleges are located on reservations and are members of the American Indian Higher Education Consortium.
NOTE: Detail may not sum to totals because of rounding.
SOURCE: U.S. Department of Education, National Center for Education Statistics, 2003–04 Integrated Postsecondary Education Data System (IPEDS), Spring 2004 and Spring 2005. (This table was prepared May 2006.)

Table 342. Total revenue of private for-profit degree-granting institutions, by source of funds and type of institution: 1997–98 through 2003–04

Type of institution and year	Total revenue and investment return	Student tuition and fees (net of allowances)	Federal appropriations, grants, and contracts	State and local appropriations, grants, and contracts	Private gifts, grants, and contracts	Investment return	Educational activities	Auxiliary enterprises	Other
1	2	3	4	5	6	7	8	9	10
In thousands of current dollars									
All institutions									
1997–98	$2,790,362	$2,320,594	$200,454	$55,647	$3,691	$11,334	$32,063	$87,502	$79,077
1998–99[1]	3,791,729	3,185,304	263,665	60,991	3,741	14,275	34,956	139,533	89,264
1999–2000	4,321,985	3,721,032	198,923	71,904	2,151	18,537	70,672	156,613	82,153
2000–01	4,967,700	4,340,478	187,353	87,348	2,848	19,737	63,392	172,987	93,557
2001–02	6,181,906	5,423,949	211,372	47,486	5,690	17,127	73,085	216,284	186,914
2002–03	7,499,808	6,715,662	282,521	50,265	5,545	15,035	92,380	250,964	87,436
2003–04	8,989,815	8,049,205	397,828	59,112	7,079	16,813	139,125	238,735	81,918
4-year									
1997–98	1,371,764	1,192,755	66,825	16,356	719	7,569	15,926	44,496	27,118
1998–99[1]	1,874,874	1,603,889	99,215	27,565	1,264	7,441	16,355	84,749	34,398
1999–2000	2,381,042	2,050,136	103,865	39,460	1,109	10,340	33,764	102,103	40,266
2000–01	2,952,254	2,583,644	81,879	59,922	1,659	12,574	40,081	106,327	66,168
2001–02	3,775,017	3,382,888	64,761	13,137	2,809	10,691	46,676	132,401	121,655
2002–03	4,756,640	4,356,876	108,806	9,757	3,064	5,875	58,281	173,280	40,703
2003–04	6,016,415	5,489,245	196,945	15,076	3,696	10,931	104,314	164,260	31,948
2-year									
1997–98	1,418,598	1,127,839	133,629	39,291	2,972	3,765	16,137	43,006	51,959
1998–99[1]	1,916,855	1,581,415	164,450	33,426	2,478	6,834	18,601	54,784	54,867
1999–2000	1,940,943	1,670,896	95,058	32,444	1,042	8,197	36,908	54,510	41,888
2000–01	2,015,446	1,756,833	105,474	27,426	1,189	7,163	23,311	66,660	27,389
2001–02	2,406,889	2,041,061	146,611	34,349	2,881	6,436	26,409	83,883	65,259
2002–03	2,743,168	2,358,786	173,715	40,508	2,482	9,160	34,099	77,685	46,733
2003–04	2,973,400	2,559,960	200,883	44,036	3,383	5,882	34,811	74,475	49,970
Percentage distribution									
All institutions									
1997–98	100.00	83.16	7.18	1.99	0.13	0.41	1.15	3.14	2.83
1998–99[1]	100.00	84.01	6.95	1.61	0.10	0.38	0.92	3.68	2.35
1999–2000	100.00	86.10	4.60	1.66	0.05	0.43	1.64	3.62	1.90
2000–01	100.00	87.37	3.77	1.76	0.06	0.40	1.28	3.48	1.88
2001–02	100.00	87.74	3.42	0.77	0.09	0.28	1.18	3.50	3.02
2002–03	100.00	89.54	3.77	0.67	0.07	0.20	1.23	3.35	1.17
2003–04	100.00	89.54	4.43	0.66	0.08	0.19	1.55	2.66	0.91
4-year									
1997–98	100.00	86.95	4.87	1.19	0.05	0.55	1.16	3.24	1.98
1998–99[1]	100.00	85.55	5.29	1.47	0.07	0.40	0.87	4.52	1.83
1999–2000	100.00	86.10	4.36	1.66	0.05	0.43	1.42	4.29	1.69
2000–01	100.00	87.51	2.77	2.03	0.06	0.43	1.36	3.60	2.24
2001–02	100.00	89.61	1.72	0.35	0.07	0.28	1.24	3.51	3.22
2002–03	100.00	91.60	2.29	0.21	0.06	0.12	1.23	3.64	0.86
2003–04	100.00	91.24	3.27	0.25	0.06	0.18	1.73	2.73	0.53
2-year									
1997–98	100.00	79.50	9.42	2.77	0.21	0.27	1.14	3.03	3.66
1998–99[1]	100.00	82.50	8.58	1.74	0.13	0.36	0.97	2.86	2.86
1999–2000	100.00	86.09	4.90	1.67	0.05	0.42	1.90	2.81	2.16
2000–01	100.00	87.17	5.23	1.36	0.06	0.36	1.16	3.31	1.36
2001–02	100.00	84.80	6.09	1.43	0.12	0.27	1.10	3.49	2.71
2002–03	100.00	85.99	6.33	1.48	0.09	0.33	1.24	2.83	1.70
2003–04	100.00	86.10	6.76	1.48	0.11	0.20	1.17	2.50	1.68
Revenue per full-time-equivalent student in constant 2005–06 dollars[2]									
All institutions									
1997–98	$11,677	$9,711	$839	$233	$15	$47	$134	$366	$331
1998–99[1]	14,077	11,826	979	226	14	53	130	518	331
1999–2000	13,204	11,368	608	220	7	57	216	478	251
2000–01	12,362	10,802	466	217	7	49	158	430	233
2001–02	15,116	13,263	517	116	14	42	179	529	457
2002–03	15,152	13,567	571	102	11	30	187	507	177
2003–04	15,063	13,487	667	99	12	28	233	400	137
4-year									
1997–98	12,467	10,840	607	149	7	69	145	404	246
1998–99[1]	13,924	11,911	737	205	9	55	121	629	255
1999–2000	13,401	11,539	585	222	6	58	190	575	227
2000–01	14,707	12,871	408	299	8	63	200	530	330
2001–02	15,242	13,659	261	53	11	43	188	535	491
2002–03	15,030	13,767	344	31	10	19	184	548	129
2003–04	15,399	14,050	504	39	9	28	267	420	82
2-year									
1997–98	11,003	8,748	1,036	305	23	29	125	334	403
1998–99[1]	14,231	11,741	1,221	248	18	51	138	407	407
1999–2000	12,969	11,165	635	217	7	55	247	364	280
2000–01	13,891	12,109	727	189	8	49	161	459	189
2001–02	14,923	12,655	909	213	18	40	164	520	405
2002–03	15,367	13,213	973	227	14	51	191	435	262
2003–04	14,426	12,420	975	214	16	29	169	361	242

[1]Data imputed using alternative procedures. (See Guide to Sources for details.)
[2]Constant dollars based on the Consumer Price Index, prepared by the Bureau of Labor Statistics, U.S. Department of Labor, adjusted to a school-year basis.
NOTE: Detail may not sum to totals because of rounding.

SOURCE: U.S. Department of Education, National Center for Education Statistics, 1997–98 through 2003–04 Integrated Postsecondary Education Data System, "Fall Enrollment Survey" (IPEDS-EF:97–99) and "Finance Survey" (IPEDS-F:FY98–99), and Spring 2001 through Spring 2005. (This table was prepared May 2006.)

Table 343. Total revenue of private for-profit degree-granting institutions, by source of funds and type of institution: 2002–03 and 2003–04

Year and type of institution	Total revenue and investment return	Student tuition and fees (net of allowances)	Federal appropriations, grants, and contracts	State and local appropriations, grants, and contracts	Private gifts, grants, and contracts	Investment return (gain or loss)	Educational activities	Auxiliary enterprises	Other
1	2	3	4	5	6	7	8	9	10
	In thousands of current dollars								
2002–03									
Total	$7,499,808	$6,715,662	$282,521	$50,265	$5,545	$15,035	$92,380	$250,964	$87,436
4-year	4,756,640	4,356,876	108,806	9,757	3,064	5,875	58,281	173,280	40,703
Doctoral, intensive[1]	47,687	47,687	0	0	0	0	0	0	0
Master's[2]	1,356,234	1,324,251	673	0	0	45	17,648	9,817	3,800
Baccalaureate[3]	417,314	382,783	2,546	2,034	46	4,254	1,903	21,581	2,166
Specialized institutions[4]	2,935,405	2,602,155	105,587	7,723	3,017	1,575	38,730	141,881	34,737
Art, music, or design	744,498	673,156	19,574	1,003	0	-766	-133	50,469	1,195
Business and management	224,360	210,444	1,050	5	0	-5	2,317	4,057	6,492
Engineering or technology	607,456	584,060	2,950	405	1,599	89	2,808	15,457	88
Medical or other health	40,177	30,537	0	0	224	13	4,014	918	4,471
Other specialized	1,318,914	1,103,957	82,013	6,310	1,194	2,244	29,724	70,981	22,491
2-year	2,743,168	2,358,786	173,715	40,508	2,482	9,160	34,099	77,685	46,733
2003–04									
Total	8,989,815	8,049,205	397,828	59,112	7,079	16,813	139,125	238,735	81,918
4-year	6,016,415	5,489,245	196,945	15,076	3,696	10,931	104,314	164,260	31,948
Doctoral, intensive[1]	52,594	52,594	0	0	0	-197	0	0	197
Master's[2]	1,799,726	1,738,389	2,038	0	1,630	226	43,977	7,671	5,794
Baccalaureate[3]	443,992	411,215	2,552	2,050	43	3,815	4,097	19,730	490
Specialized institutions[4]	3,720,104	3,287,048	192,355	13,027	2,023	7,087	56,239	136,858	25,466
Art, music, or design	800,129	722,880	22,905	645	25	1,326	4,842	42,469	5,037
Business and management	364,451	344,272	3,275	22	0	-46	7,884	4,812	4,232
Engineering or technology	739,318	714,573	2,253	276	139	83	5,968	9,553	6,474
Medical or other health	55,484	44,907	1,406	465	210	36	5,452	845	2,164
Other specialized	1,760,722	1,460,417	162,516	11,619	1,649	5,688	32,093	79,180	7,560
2-year	2,973,400	2,559,960	200,883	44,036	3,383	5,882	34,811	74,475	49,970
	Percentage distribution								
2003–04									
Total	100.00	89.54	4.43	0.66	0.08	0.19	1.55	2.66	0.91
4-year	100.00	91.24	3.27	0.25	0.06	0.18	1.73	2.73	0.53
Doctoral, intensive[1]	100.00	100.00	0.00	0.00	0.00	-0.38	0.00	0.00	0.38
Master's[2]	100.00	96.59	0.11	0.00	0.09	0.01	2.44	0.43	0.32
Baccalaureate[3]	100.00	92.62	0.57	0.46	0.01	0.86	0.92	4.44	0.11
Specialized institutions[4]	100.00	88.36	5.17	0.35	0.05	0.19	1.51	3.68	0.68
Art, music, or design	100.00	90.35	2.86	0.08	#	0.17	0.61	5.31	0.63
Business and management	100.00	94.46	0.90	0.01	0.00	-0.01	2.16	1.32	1.16
Engineering or technology	100.00	96.65	0.30	0.04	0.02	0.01	0.81	1.29	0.88
Medical or other health	100.00	80.94	2.53	0.84	0.38	0.06	9.83	1.52	3.90
Other specialized	100.00	82.94	9.23	0.66	0.09	0.32	1.82	4.50	0.43
2-year	100.00	86.10	6.76	1.48	0.11	0.20	1.17	2.50	1.68
	Revenue per full-time-equivalent student								
2003–04									
Total	$14,092	$12,617	$624	$93	$11	$26	$218	$374	$128
4-year	14,406	13,144	472	36	9	26	250	393	76
Doctoral, intensive[1]	5,496	5,496	0	0	0	-21	0	0	21
Master's[2]	11,480	11,089	13	0	10	1	281	49	37
Baccalaureate[3]	13,212	12,237	76	61	1	114	122	587	15
Specialized institutions[4]	17,089	15,100	884	60	9	33	258	629	117
Art, music, or design	18,981	17,149	543	15	1	31	115	1,007	119
Business and management	13,240	12,507	119	1	0	-2	286	175	154
Engineering or technology	17,783	17,188	54	7	3	2	144	230	156
Medical or other health	13,389	10,837	339	112	51	9	1,316	204	522
Other specialized	17,213	14,277	1,589	114	16	56	314	774	74
2-year	13,496	11,619	912	200	15	27	158	338	227

#Rounds to zero.
[1]Doctoral, intensive institutions are committed to education through the doctorate and award at least 10 doctor's degrees per year across 3 or more disciplines or at least 20 doctor's degrees overall.
[2]Master's institutions offer a full range of baccalaureate programs and are committed to education through the master's degree. They award at least 20 master's degrees per year.
[3]Baccalaureate institutions primarily emphasize undergraduate education.
[4]Specialized 4-year institutions award degrees primarily in single fields of study, such as medicine, business, fine arts, theology, and engineering. Includes some institutions that

have 4-year programs, but have not reported sufficient data to identify program category. Also includes institutions classified as 4-year under the IPEDS system, which had been classified as 2-year in the Carnegie system because they primarily award associate's degrees.
NOTE: Detail may not sum to totals because of rounding.
SOURCE: U.S. Department of Education, National Center for Education Statistics, 2002–03 and 2003–04 Integrated Postsecondary Education Data System (IPEDS), Spring 2004 and Spring 2005. (This table was prepared May 2006.)

Table 344. Current-fund revenue received from the federal government by the 120 degree-granting institutions receiving the largest amounts, by control and rank order: 2003–04

Institution	Control[1]	Rank order	Revenue from the federal govern- ment[2] (in thousands)	Institution	Control[1]	Rank order	Revenue from the federal govern- ment[2] (in thousands)
1	2	3	4	1	2	3	4
United States (all institutions)	†	†	$52,706,116				
120 institutions receiving the largest amounts	†	†	33,987,956				
California Institute of Technology	2	1	1,840,251	University of Cincinnati, Main Campus	1	61	203,962
Johns Hopkins University (MD)	2	2	1,460,879	Rutgers, the State University, Central Office (NJ)	1	62	203,464
Massachusetts Institute of Technology	2	3	914,733	University of New Mexico, Main Campus	1	63	189,379
Columbia University in the City of New York	2	4	842,200	Georgetown University (DC)	2	64	184,500
University of Chicago (IL)	2	5	830,054	Purdue University, Main Campus (IN)	1	65	183,241
Stanford University (CA)	2	6	796,034	University of California, Irvine	1	66	183,153
University of Washington, Seattle	1	7	755,689	Princeton University (NJ)	2	67	181,673
University of Michigan, Ann Arbor	1	8	639,564	University of Tennessee	1	68	181,632
University of Pennsylvania	2	9	603,035	U. of Massachusetts Medical School, Worcester	1	69	179,459
University of California, Los Angeles	1	10	574,534	George Washington University (DC)	2	70	175,000
University of California, San Diego	1	11	525,908	University of Kentucky	1	71	172,838
University of Southern California	2	12	475,476	Colorado State University	1	72	167,997
University of Pittsburgh, Main Campus (PA)	1	13	473,609	Iowa State University	1	73	160,078
Harvard University (MA)	2	14	473,500	University of Texas Anderson Cancer Center	1	74	156,901
University of California, San Francisco	1	15	464,176	Yeshiva University (NY)	2	75	156,295
Weill Cornell Medical College (NY)	2	16	462,729	University of South Florida	1	76	156,285
University of Wisconsin, Madison	1	17	461,236	University of Maryland, Baltimore	1	77	152,191
United States Air Force Academy (CO)	1	18	447,034	University of Medicine and Dentistry of New Jersey	1	78	150,151
University of Utah	1	19	439,917	Utah State University	1	79	149,044
University of North Carolina at Chapel Hill	1	20	433,454	Indiana University, Purdue University, Indianapolis	1	80	147,014
New York University	2	21	429,901	SUNY at Stony Brook (NY)	1	81	146,246
Washington University in St Louis (MO)	2	22	426,858	University of Georgia	1	82	139,084
University of Miami (FL)	2	23	426,632	Wayne State University (MI)	1	83	136,264
United States Military Academy (NY)	1	24	415,765	Virginia Commonwealth University	1	84	135,400
Yale University (CT)	2	25	403,799	Florida State University	1	85	135,097
University of Minnesota, Twin Cities	1	26	385,591	University of Texas Health Science Center	1	86	133,822
Duke University (NC)	2	27	385,073	Oregon State University	1	87	132,878
Pennsylvania State University, Main Campus	1	28	358,103	Arizona State University at the Tempe Campus	1	88	132,400
University of Alabama at Birmingham	1	29	356,108	Mount Sinai School of Medicine (NY)	2	89	132,028
University of Oklahoma Health Sciences Center	1	30	352,013	SUNY at Buffalo (NY)	1	90	128,928
University of Arizona	1	31	346,282	Mississippi State University	1	91	127,636
Baylor College of Medicine (TX)	2	32	342,226	Wake Forest University (NC)	2	92	126,847
University of California, Berkeley	1	33	336,659	Dartmouth College (NH)	2	93	126,390
Texas A & M University	1	34	330,861	Tulane University of Louisiana	2	94	126,305
University of Illinois at Urbana-Champaign	1	35	322,235	North Carolina State University at Raleigh	1	95	123,443
United States Naval Academy (MD)	1	36	316,880	Louisiana State U. & Ag. & Mech. & Hebert Laws Ctr.	1	96	118,030
Vanderbilt University (TN)	2	37	313,661	Virginia Polytechnic Institute and State U.	1	97	117,519
Cornell University, Endowed Colleges (NY)	2	38	301,409	Medical University of South Carolina	1	98	115,469
Ohio State University, Main Campus	1	39	290,945	Washington State University	1	99	113,093
University of Texas at Austin	1	40	287,971	Miami Dade College (FL)	1	100	113,020
Emory University (GA)	2	41	287,095	University of Missouri, Columbia	1	101	112,411
University of Florida	1	42	271,582	University of California, Santa Barbara	1	102	110,961
University of Virginia, Main Campus	1	43	270,996	University of Nebraska at Lincoln	1	103	110,633
Case Western Reserve University (OH)	2	44	267,688	Rockhurst University (MO)	2	104	107,819
Georgia Institute of Technology, Main Campus	1	45	266,015	New Mexico State University, Main Campus	1	105	107,174
University of Iowa	1	46	261,594	University of Texas Medical Branch	1	106	106,847
Howard University (DC)	2	47	261,589	University of South Carolina, Columbia	1	107	106,717
University of California, Davis	1	48	260,980	University of Texas Health Science, San Antonio	1	108	106,042
University of Illinois at Chicago	1	49	254,012	Brown University (RI)	2	109	105,768
University of Colorado at Boulder	1	50	242,511	Tufts University (MA)	2	110	104,775
Carnegie Mellon University (PA)	2	51	236,770	Medical College of Wisconsin	2	111	104,353
University of Maryland, College Park	1	52	235,499	University of Alaska, Fairbanks	1	112	104,006
Northwestern University (IL)	2	53	235,312	SUNY, System Office (NY)	1	113	103,919
Oregon Health & Science University	1	54	234,136	Thomas Jefferson University (PA)	2	114	100,994
University of Colorado Health Sciences Center	1	55	232,582	University of Massachusetts, Amherst	1	115	98,990
University of Rochester (NY)	2	56	226,296	Kentucky Community and Technical College System	1	116	98,163
Boston University (MA)	2	57	218,259	University of Vermont and State Agricultural College	1	117	96,946
University of Hawaii at Manoa	1	58	213,820	Kansas State University	1	118	91,698
Michigan State University	1	59	211,727	Indiana University, Bloomington	1	119	88,817
U. of Texas Southwestern Medical Center at Dallas	1	60	207,747	University of Arkansas for Medical Sciences	1	120	87,573

†Not applicable.
[1]Publicly controlled institutions are identified by a "1," and private, not-for-profit, by a "2."
[2]Includes federal appropriations, unrestricted and restricted federal contracts and grants, and revenue for independent operations. Independent operations generally include only the revenues associated with major federally funded research and development centers. Federally supported student aid that is received through students is excluded. Data for

public and private institutions are only roughly comparable because they were collected using different survey instruments.
NOTE: Degree-granting institutions grant associate's or higher degrees and participate in Title IV federal financial aid programs.
SOURCE: U.S. Department of Education, National Center for Education Statistics, 2003–04 Integrated Postsecondary Education Data System (IPEDS), Spring 2005. (This table was prepared October 2006.)

Table 345. Current-fund expenditures and current-fund expenditures per full-time-equivalent student in degree-granting institutions, by type and control of institution: Selected years, 1970–71 through 2000–01

Control of institution and year	All institutions			4-year institutions			2-year institutions		
	Current-fund expenditures (in millions)		Current-fund expenditures per student, in constant 2005–06 dollars[1]	Current-fund expenditures (in millions)		Current-fund expenditures per student, in constant 2005–06 dollars[1]	Current-fund expenditures (in millions)		Current-fund expenditures per student, in constant 2005–06 dollars[1]
	Unadjusted dollars	Constant 2005–06 dollars[1]		Unadjusted dollars	Constant 2005–06 dollars[1]		Unadjusted dollars	Constant 2005–06 dollars[1]	
1	2	3	4	5	6	7	8	9	10
All institutions									
1970–71	$23,375	$117,092	$17,378	$21,049	$105,437	$20,491	$2,327	$11,655	$7,319
1975–76	38,903	139,591	16,462	33,811	121,320	20,561	5,092	18,271	7,084
1977–78	45,971	146,054	17,356	39,899	126,762	21,358	6,072	19,292	7,778
1978–79	50,721	147,344	17,649	44,163	128,293	21,626	6,558	19,051	7,885
1979–80	56,914	145,883	17,188	49,661	127,292	21,159	7,253	18,591	7,523
1980–81	64,053	147,140	16,684	55,840	128,275	20,819	8,212	18,865	7,099
1981–82	70,339	148,733	16,499	61,333	129,690	20,751	9,006	19,043	6,888
1982–83	75,936	153,954	16,934	66,238	134,293	21,491	9,697	19,661	6,916
1983–84	81,993	160,302	17,488	71,680	140,138	22,155	10,314	20,164	7,097
1984–85	89,951	169,236	18,905	78,744	148,150	23,543	11,207	21,086	7,930
1985–86	97,536	178,362	19,943	85,560	156,463	24,858	11,976	21,900	8,267
1986–87	105,764	189,207	20,874	92,985	166,346	26,154	12,779	22,861	8,455
1987–88	113,786	195,461	21,177	100,143	172,024	26,520	13,644	23,437	8,544
1988–89	123,867	203,385	21,490	109,141	179,205	26,891	14,726	24,180	8,635
1989–90	134,656	211,029	21,576	118,578	185,833	27,274	16,077	25,196	8,491
1990–91	146,088	217,077	21,744	128,594	191,083	27,423	17,494	25,995	8,621
1991–92	156,189	224,881	21,705	137,375	197,793	27,931	18,814	27,088	8,261
1992–93	165,241	230,708	22,105	145,300	202,866	28,455	19,941	27,842	8,418
1993–94	173,351	235,919	22,791	152,164	207,085	29,081	21,187	28,834	8,926
1994–95	182,969	242,070	23,393	160,891	212,861	29,824	22,078	29,209	9,097
1995–96	190,476	245,328	23,738	166,954	215,032	29,979	23,522	30,296	9,581
1996–97	—	—	—	—	—	—	—	—	—
1997–98	—	—	—	—	—	—	—	—	—
1998–99	—	—	—	—	—	—	—	—	—
1999–2000	—	—	—	—	—	—	—	—	—
2000–01	—	—	—	—	—	—	—	—	—
Public institutions									
1970–71	14,996	75,119	15,166	12,899	64,614	18,628	2,097	10,505	7,076
1975–76	26,184	93,952	14,405	21,392	76,757	18,922	4,792	17,195	6,973
1977–78	30,725	97,617	15,261	25,013	79,469	19,675	5,712	18,148	7,698
1978–79	33,733	97,994	15,606	27,600	80,179	20,064	6,132	17,815	7,803
1979–80	37,768	96,808	15,144	30,979	79,406	19,562	6,789	17,402	7,458
1980–81	42,280	97,124	14,622	34,677	79,660	19,157	7,602	17,464	7,030
1981–82	46,219	97,731	14,412	37,890	80,118	19,037	8,330	17,613	6,846
1982–83	49,573	100,505	14,671	40,616	82,345	19,510	8,957	18,160	6,905
1983–84	53,087	103,788	15,082	43,588	85,217	19,977	9,499	18,570	7,100
1984–85	58,315	109,714	16,413	48,017	90,340	21,317	10,298	19,374	7,918
1985–86	63,194	115,562	17,331	52,184	95,429	22,509	11,010	20,133	8,292
1986–87	67,654	121,030	17,856	56,003	100,187	23,324	11,651	20,844	8,396
1987–88	72,641	124,782	17,986	60,137	103,302	23,501	12,505	21,480	8,450
1988–89	78,946	129,625	18,265	65,349	107,300	23,814	13,597	22,325	8,616
1989–90	85,771	134,417	18,235	70,865	111,058	24,039	14,906	23,360	8,489
1990–91	92,961	138,134	18,277	76,722	114,004	24,051	16,239	24,130	8,563
1991–92	98,847	142,320	18,100	81,334	117,105	24,419	17,513	25,215	8,221
1992–93	104,570	146,000	18,454	86,065	120,163	25,045	18,505	25,837	8,298
1993–94	109,310	148,763	19,042	89,697	122,072	25,613	19,612	26,691	8,761
1994–95	115,465	152,762	19,624	94,895	125,547	26,434	20,570	27,215	8,967
1995–96	119,525	153,944	19,859	97,905	126,099	26,507	21,620	27,846	9,299
1996–97	125,429	157,068	20,150	103,069	129,068	27,075	22,360	28,000	9,248
1997–98	132,846	163,441	20,768	109,190	134,337	27,906	23,656	29,104	9,524
1998–99	140,539	169,963	21,569	115,158	139,268	28,604	25,381	30,695	10,193
1999–2000	152,325	179,048	22,325	124,878	146,786	29,686	27,447	32,263	10,490
2000–01	170,345	193,597	23,418	140,578	159,767	31,791	29,766	33,830	10,437
Private institutions									
1970–71	8,379	41,973	23,519	8,150	40,823	24,345	230	1,150	10,664
1975–76	12,719	45,639	23,316	12,419	44,563	24,168	300	1,076	9,482
1979–80	19,146	49,075	23,428	18,682	47,886	24,472	464	1,189	8,619
1980–81	21,773	50,016	22,978	21,163	48,615	24,270	610	1,401	8,072
1981–82	24,120	51,003	22,838	23,444	49,572	24,284	676	1,430	7,453

See notes at end of table.

Table 345. Current-fund expenditures and current-fund expenditures per full-time-equivalent student in degree-granting institutions, by type and control of institution: Selected years, 1970–71 through 2000–01—Continued

	All institutions			4-year institutions			2-year institutions		
	Current-fund expenditures (in millions)		Current-fund expenditures per student, in constant 2005–06 dollars[1]	Current-fund expenditures (in millions)		Current-fund expenditures per student, in constant 2005–06 dollars[1]	Current-fund expenditures (in millions)		Current-fund expenditures per student, in constant 2005–06 dollars[1]
Control of institution and year	Unadjusted dollars	Constant 2005–06 dollars[1]		Unadjusted dollars	Constant 2005–06 dollars[1]		Unadjusted dollars	Constant 2005–06 dollars[1]	
1	2	3	4	5	6	7	8	9	10
1982–83	26,363	53,449	23,850	25,623	51,948	25,612	740	1,501	7,053
1983–84	28,907	56,514	24,734	28,092	54,921	26,668	815	1,593	7,065
1984–85	31,637	59,522	26,255	30,727	57,810	28,134	910	1,712	8,065
1985–86	34,342	62,800	27,597	33,376	61,034	29,704	966	1,766	7,995
1986–87	38,110	68,177	29,822	36,982	66,159	32,041	1,128	2,018	9,117
1987–88	41,145	70,679	30,837	40,006	68,722	32,869	1,139	1,957	9,723
1988–89	44,922	73,759	31,157	43,792	71,905	33,314	1,130	1,855	8,874
1989–90	48,885	76,611	31,798	47,713	74,775	34,085	1,172	1,836	8,519
1990–91	53,127	78,943	32,548	51,872	77,079	34,596	1,255	1,864	9,439
1991–92	57,342	82,561	33,054	56,041	80,688	35,300	1,301	1,873	8,835
1992–93	60,671	84,708	33,547	59,235	82,703	35,472	1,436	2,005	10,356
1993–94	64,041	87,156	34,327	62,466	85,013	36,100	1,575	2,143	11,641
1994–95	67,504	89,308	34,836	65,996	87,314	36,566	1,508	1,995	11,342
1995–96	70,952	91,384	35,377	69,050	88,934	36,816	1,902	2,450	14,625
1996–97	—	—	—	—	—	—	—	—	—
1997–98	—	—	—	—	—	—	—	—	—
1998–99	—	—	—	—	—	—	—	—	—
1999–2000	—	—	—	—	—	—	—	—	—
2000–01	—	—	—	—	—	—	—	—	—

—Not available.
[1]Constant dollars based on the Consumer Price Index, prepared by the Bureau of Labor Statistics, U.S. Department of Labor, adjusted to a school-year basis.
NOTE: Data through 1995–96 are for institutions of higher education, while later data are for degree-granting institutions. Degree-granting institutions grant associate's or higher degrees and participate in Title IV federal financial aid programs. The degree-granting classification is very similar to the earlier higher education classification, but it includes more 2-year colleges and excludes a few higher education institutions that did not grant degrees. (See Guide to Sources for details.) Private college data not collected on a basis

consistent with public institutions after 1995–96. Detail may not sum to totals because of rounding.
SOURCE: U.S. Department of Education, National Center for Education Statistics, Higher Education General Information Survey (HEGIS), "Financial Statistics of Institutions of Higher Education," 1970–71 through 1985–86, "Fall Enrollment in Institutions of Higher Education," 1970 through 1985; 1986–87 through 2000–01 Integrated Postsecondary Education Data System, "Finance Survey" (IPEDS-F:FY86–99), "Fall Enrollment Survey" (IPEDS-F:FY86–99), and Spring 2001 and Spring 2002. (This table was prepared October 2006.)

Table 346. Current-fund expenditures and educational and general expenditures of degree-granting institutions, by purpose and per student: Selected years, 1929–30 through 1995–96

Year	Current-fund expenditures (in thousands)	Total	Administration and general expense	Instruction and departmental research	Organized research	Libraries	Plant operation and maintenance	Organized activities related to instructional departments[1]	Other sponsored programs[2]	Extension and public service	Scholarships and fellowships	Other general expenditures	Auxiliary enterprises (in thousands)	Independent operations[3] (in thousands)	Hospitals (in thousands)	Other current expenditures (in thousands)	Current dollars	Constant 2005–06 dollars[5]
1	2	3	4	5	6	7	8	9	10	11	12	13	14	15	16	17	18	19
Institutions of higher education																		
1929–30	$507,142	$377,903	$42,633	$221,598	$18,007 [6]	$9,622	$61,061	(7)	—	$24,982	(7)	—	$3,127	(6)	(8)	$126,112	$343	$3,991
1931–32	536,523	420,633	47,232	232,645	21,978 [6]	11,379	56,797	21,297 [8]	—	24,066	(7)	$5,239	90,897	(6)	(8)	24,993	364	5,031
1933–34	469,329	369,661	43,155	203,332	17,064 [6]	13,387	51,046	14,155 [8]	—	20,020	(7)	7,502	78,730	(6)	(8)	20,938	350	5,264
1935–36	541,391	419,883	48,069	225,143	22,091 [6]	15,531	56,802	20,241 [8]	—	29,426	(7)	2,580	95,332	(6)	(8)	26,176	348	5,032
1937–38	614,385	475,191	56,406	253,006	25,213 [6]	17,588	62,738	24,031 [8]	—	34,189	(7)	2,020	115,620	(6)	(8)	23,574	352	4,886
1939–40	674,688	521,990	62,827	280,248	27,266 [6]	19,487	69,612	27,225 [8]	—	35,325	(7)	—	124,184	(6)	(8)	28,514	349	4,974
1941–42	738,169	572,465	66,968	298,558	34,287 [6]	19,763	72,594	37,771 [8]	—	42,525	(7)	—	137,328	(6)	(8)	28,375	408	5,204
1943–44	974,118	753,846	69,668	334,189	58,456 [6]	20,452	81,201	48,415 [8]	$97,044 [9]	44,421	(7)	—	199,344	(6)	(8)	20,928	653	7,452
1945–46	1,088,422	820,326	104,808	375,122	86,812 [6]	26,560	110,947	60,604 [8]	—	55,473	(7)	—	242,028	(6)	(8)	26,068	489	5,336
1947–48	1,883,269	1,391,594	171,829	657,945	159,090 [6]	44,208	201,996	85,346 [8]	—	71,180	(7)	—	438,988	(6)	(8)	52,687	595	5,083
1949–50	2,245,661	1,706,444	213,070	780,994	225,341 [6]	56,147	225,110	119,108 [8]	—	86,674	(7)	—	476,401	(6)	(8)	62,816	698	5,864
1951–52	2,471,008	1,960,481	233,844	823,117	317,928 [6]	60,612	240,446	177,854 [8]	—	97,408	$39,272	—	477,672	(6)	(8)	32,855	933	7,062
1953–54	2,882,864	2,345,331	288,147	960,556	372,643 [6]	72,944	277,874	186,905 [8]	—	112,227	74,035	—	537,533	(6)	(8)	—	1,051	7,779
1955–56	3,499,463	2,861,858	355,207	1,140,655	500,793 [6]	85,563	324,229	222,007 [8]	—	137,914	95,490	—	637,605	(6)	(8)	—	1,079	7,985
1957–58	4,509,666	3,734,350	473,945	1,465,603	727,776 [6]	109,715	406,226	238,455 [8]	—	175,256	129,935	7,439	775,316	(6)	(8)	—	1,124	7,829
1959–60	5,601,376	4,685,258	583,224	1,793,320	1,022,353 [6]	135,384	469,943	294,255 [8]	—	205,595	172,050	9,134	916,117	(6)	(8)	—	1,287	8,717
1961–62	7,154,526	5,997,007	730,429	2,202,443	1,474,406 [6]	177,362	564,225	375,040 [8]	—	244,337	228,765	—	1,157,517	(6)	(8)	—	1,447	9,578
1963–64	9,177,677	7,725,433	957,512	2,801,707	1,973,383 [6]	236,718	686,054	458,507 [8]	—	297,350	300,370	13,832	1,452,244	(6)	(8)	—	1,616	10,429
1965–66	12,509,489	10,376,630	1,251,107	3,756,175	2,448,300 [6]	346,248	844,506	558,170 [8]	155,202	438,385	425,524	153,013	1,887,744	(6)	(8)	245,115 [10]	1,753	10,930
1966–67	14,230,341	10,724,974	1,445,074	4,356,413	1,565,102	415,903	969,275	591,848	350,950	226,566	583,390	220,453	2,060,130	$951,668	$253,790	239,780 [10]	1,678	10,147
1967–68	16,480,786	12,847,350	1,738,946	5,139,179	1,933,473	493,266	1,127,290	350,711	514,294	597,544	712,425	240,222	2,302,419	765,495	290,000	275,523 [10]	1,859	10,876
1968–69	18,481,583	14,718,140	2,277,585	5,941,972	2,034,074	571,572	1,337,903	535,269	668,483	536,527	814,755	—	2,539,183	697,317	526,943	—	1,959	10,930
1969–70	21,043,113	16,845,212	2,627,993	6,883,844	2,144,076	652,596	1,541,698	648,089	769,253	593,067	984,594	—	2,769,276	757,388	671,236	—	2,104	11,086
1970–71	23,375,197	18,714,642	2,983,911	7,804,410	2,209,338	716,212	1,730,664	693,011	890,507	588,390	1,098,198	—	2,988,407	829,596	842,552	—	2,181	10,925
1971–72	25,559,560	20,441,878	3,344,215	8,443,261	2,265,282	764,481	1,927,553	779,728	1,059,989	615,997	1,241,372	—	3,178,272	940,825	998,585	—	2,284	11,047
1972–73	27,955,624	22,400,379	3,713,068	9,243,641	2,394,261	840,727	2,141,162	791,290	1,284,085	669,735	1,322,411	—	3,337,789	1,033,746	1,183,709	—	2,431	11,300
1973–74	30,713,581	24,653,849	4,200,955	10,219,118	2,480,450	939,023	2,494,057	838,170	1,355,027	730,560	1,396,488	—	3,613,256	1,014,872	1,431,604	—	2,568	10,958
1974–75	35,057,563	27,547,620	4,495,391	11,797,823	3,132,132	1,001,868	2,786,768	1,253,824	—	1,097,788	1,449,542	532,485	4,073,590	1,085,590	2,350,763	—	2,694	10,353
1975–76	38,903,177	30,598,685	5,240,066	13,094,943	3,287,364	1,223,723	3,082,959	1,248,670	—	1,238,603	1,635,859	546,498	4,476,841	1,132,016	2,695,635	—	2,736	9,816
1976–77	42,599,816	33,151,681	5,590,669	14,031,145	3,600,067	1,250,314	3,436,705	1,544,646	—	1,343,404	1,770,214	584,515	4,858,328	1,434,738	3,155,069	—	3,010	10,207
1977–78	45,970,790	36,256,604	6,177,029	15,336,229	3,919,830	1,348,747	3,795,043	1,781,160	—	1,425,294	1,839,298	633,973	5,261,477	855,054	3,597,655	—	3,213	10,207
1978–79	50,720,984	39,833,116	6,832,004	16,662,820	4,447,760	1,426,614	4,178,574	2,044,386	—	1,593,097	1,944,599	703,262	5,749,974	1,007,119	4,130,775	—	3,538	10,277
1979–80	56,913,588	44,542,843	7,621,143	18,496,717	5,099,151	1,623,811	4,700,070	2,252,577	—	1,816,521	2,200,468	732,385	6,485,608	1,127,728	4,757,409	—	3,850	9,868
1980–81	64,052,938	50,073,805	8,681,513	20,733,166	5,657,719	1,759,784	5,350,310	2,513,502	—	2,057,770	2,504,525	815,516	7,288,089	1,257,934	5,433,111	—	4,139	9,509
1981–82	70,339,448	54,848,752	9,648,069	22,962,527	5,929,894	1,922,416	5,979,281	2,734,038	—	2,203,726	2,684,945	783,854	7,997,632	1,258,777	6,234,287	—	4,433	9,374
1982–83	75,935,749	58,929,218	10,412,233	24,673,293	6,265,280	2,039,671	6,391,596	3,047,220	—	2,320,478	2,922,897	856,548	8,614,316	1,406,126	6,986,089	—	4,742	9,615

See notes at end of table.

Table 346. Current-fund expenditures and educational and general expenditures of degree-granting institutions, by purpose and per student: Selected years, 1929–30 through 1995–96—Continued

Year	Current-fund expenditures (in thousands)	Educational and general expenditures (in thousands of current dollars)											Auxiliary enterprises (in thousands)	Independent operations[3] (in thousands)	Hospitals (in thousands)	Other current expenditures (in thousands)	Educational and general expenditures per student in fall enrollment[4]	
		Total	Administration and general expense	Instruction and departmental research	Organized research	Libraries	Plant operation and maintenance	Organized activities related to instructional departments[1]	Other sponsored programs[2]	Extension and public service	Scholarships and fellowships	Other general expenditures					Current dollars	Constant 2005–06 dollars[5]
1	2	3	4	5	6	7	8	9	10	11	12	13	14	15	16	17	18	19
1983–84	81,993,360	63,741,276	11,561,260	26,436,308	6,723,534	2,231,149	6,729,825	3,300,003	—	2,499,203	3,301,673	958,321	9,250,196	1,622,233	7,379,654	—	5,114	9,998
1984–85	89,951,263	70,061,324	12,765,452	28,777,183	7,551,892	2,361,793	7,345,482	3,712,460	—	2,861,095	3,670,355	1,015,613	10,012,248	1,867,550	8,010,141	—	5,723	10,767
1985–86	97,535,742	76,127,965	13,913,724	31,032,099	8,437,367	2,551,331	7,605,226	4,116,061	—	3,119,533	4,160,174	1,192,449	10,528,303	2,187,361	8,692,113	—	6,216	11,367
1986–87	105,763,557	82,955,555	15,060,576	33,711,146	9,352,309	2,441,184	7,819,032	5,134,267	—	3,448,453	4,776,100	1,212,488	11,037,333	2,597,655	9,173,014	—	6,635	11,869
1987–88	113,786,476	89,157,430	16,171,015	35,833,563	10,350,931	2,836,498	8,230,986	5,305,083	—	3,786,362	5,325,358	1,317,633	11,399,953	2,822,632	10,406,461	—	6,984	11,996
1988–89	123,867,184	96,803,377	17,309,956	38,812,690	11,432,170	3,009,870	8,739,895	5,894,409	—	4,227,323	5,918,666	1,458,397	12,280,063	2,958,962	11,824,782	—	7,415	12,175
1989–90	134,655,571	105,585,076	19,062,179	42,145,987	12,505,961	3,254,239	9,458,262	6,183,405	—	4,689,758	6,655,544	1,629,742	13,203,984	3,187,224	12,679,286	—	7,799	12,222
1990–91	146,087,836	114,139,901	20,751,966	45,496,117	13,444,040	3,343,892	10,062,581	6,706,881	—	5,076,177	7,551,184	1,707,063	14,272,247	3,349,824	14,325,865	—	8,260	12,274
1991–92	156,189,161	121,567,157	21,984,118	47,997,196	14,261,554	3,595,834	10,346,580	6,981,184	—	5,489,298	9,060,000	1,851,393	14,966,100	3,551,592	16,104,313	—	8,466	12,190
1992–93	165,241,040	128,977,968	23,414,977	50,340,914	15,291,309	3,684,852	10,783,727	7,388,118	—	5,935,095	10,148,373	1,990,603	15,561,508	3,651,891	17,049,672	—	8,903	12,430
1993–94	173,350,617	136,024,350	24,489,022	52,775,599	16,117,610	3,908,412	11,368,496	7,769,499	—	6,242,414	11,238,010	2,115,288	16,429,341	3,387,323	17,509,603	—	9,509	12,941
1994–95	182,968,610	144,158,002	25,904,821	55,719,707	17,109,541	4,165,761	11,745,905	8,112,930	—	6,691,485	12,285,328	2,422,524	17,204,917	3,534,332	18,071,359	—	10,096	13,357
1995–96	189,986,238	150,927,324	27,683,381	57,572,851	17,519,665	4,299,177	12,257,540	9,010,262	—	7,045,145	13,138,965	2,400,338	17,569,276	3,492,548	17,997,090	—	10,583	13,630
Degree-granting institutions																		
1995–96	190,476,163	151,445,605	27,886,345	57,810,033	17,517,887	4,293,363	12,330,885	9,003,700	—	7,007,413	13,195,102	2,400,876	17,599,061	3,490,511	17,940,986	—	—	—

—Not available.
[1]Academic support excluding expenditures for libraries.
[2]Includes all separately budgeted programs, other than research, which are supported by sponsors outside the institution. Examples are training programs, workshops, and training and instructional institutes. For years not shown, most expenditures for these programs are included under "Extension and public service."
[3]Generally includes only those expenditures associated with federally funded research and development centers (FFRDCs).
[4]Data for 1929–30 to 1945–46 are based on school-year enrollment.
[5]Constant dollars based on the Consumer Price Index, prepared by the Bureau of Labor Statistics, U.S. Department of Labor, adjusted to a school-year basis.
[6]Expenditures for federally funded research and development centers are included under "Organized research."
[7]Included under "Other current expenditures."
[8]Expenditures for hospitals included under "Organized activities related to instructional departments."
[9]Expenditures were for federal contract courses.
[10]Includes current expenditures for physical plant assets. In later years, the educational and general expenditures for physical plant assets are included under "Other general expenditures."

NOTE: Institutions of higher education were accredited by an agency or association that was recognized by the U.S. Department of Education, or recognized directly by the Secretary of Education. The degree-granting classification is very similar to the earlier higher education classification, except that it includes some additional institutions, primarily 2-year colleges, and excludes a few higher education institutions that did not award associate's or higher degrees. (See Guide to Sources for details.) The data in this table reflect limitations of data availability and comparability. Major changes in data collection forms in 1965–66 and 1974–75 cause significant data comparability problems among the three mostly consistent time periods, 1929–30 to 1963–64, 1965–66 to 1973–74, and 1974–75 to 1995–96. The largest problems affect Hospitals, Independent operations, Organized research, Other sponsored programs, Extension and public service, and Scholarships and fellowships. Detail may not sum to totals because of rounding.
SOURCE: U.S. Department of Education, National Center for Education Statistics, Biennial Survey of Education in the United States, 1929–30 through 1963–64; Higher Education General Information Survey (HEGIS), "Financial Statistics of Institutions of Higher Education," 1965–66 through 1985–86; and 1986–87 through 1995–96 Integrated Postsecondary Education Data System, "Finance Survey" (IPEDS-F:FY87–96). (This table was prepared February 2006.)

Table 347. Expenses of public degree-granting institutions, by type of expense and type of institution: 2003–04

Type of expense	Expenses (in thousands)			Percentage distribution of expenses			Expense per full-time-equivalent student		
	Total	4-year	2-year	Total	4-year	2-year	Total	4-year	2-year
1	2	3	4	5	6	7	8	9	10
Total expenses................	$205,068,500	$167,654,408	$37,414,092	100.0	100.0	100.0	$22,202	$30,167	$10,170
Operating expenses	198,321,711	161,575,599	36,746,112	96.7	96.4	98.2	21,471	29,073	9,988
Instruction	56,767,947	42,287,792	14,480,155	27.7	25.2	38.7	6,146	7,609	3,936
Salaries and wages................	39,431,881	29,290,396	10,141,485	19.2	17.5	27.1	4,269	5,270	2,757
Research	21,408,497	21,394,125	14,371	10.4	12.8	#	2,318	3,850	4
Public service................	8,981,907	8,293,533	688,374	4.4	4.9	1.8	972	1,492	187
Academic support................	13,613,774	10,904,235	2,709,539	6.6	6.5	7.2	1,474	1,962	736
Student services	9,426,787	6,062,776	3,364,011	4.6	3.6	9.0	1,021	1,091	914
Institutional support	16,849,813	11,691,429	5,158,384	8.2	7.0	13.8	1,824	2,104	1,402
Operation and maintenance of plant........	12,611,040	9,469,470	3,141,570	6.1	5.6	8.4	1,365	1,704	854
Depreciation................	8,999,651	7,586,394	1,413,258	4.4	4.5	3.8	974	1,365	384
Scholarships and fellowships[1]................	8,172,682	5,123,190	3,049,492	4.0	3.1	8.2	885	922	829
Auxiliary enterprises	15,705,951	13,680,554	2,025,397	7.7	8.2	5.4	1,700	2,462	551
Hospitals	18,471,970	18,471,970	0	9.0	11.0	0.0	2,000	3,324	0
Independent operations................	736,799	711,188	25,612	0.4	0.4	0.1	80	128	7
Other operating expenses and deductions	6,574,893	5,898,943	675,949	3.2	3.5	1.8	712	1,061	184
Nonoperating expenses................	6,746,790	6,078,810	667,980	3.3	3.6	1.8	730	1,094	182
Interest................	2,679,502	2,240,096	439,406	1.3	1.3	1.2	290	403	119
Other nonoperating expenses and deductions	4,067,287	3,838,714	228,574	2.0	2.3	0.6	440	691	62

#Rounds to zero.
[1]Excludes discounts and allowances.
NOTE: Degree-granting institutions grant associate's or higher degrees and participate in Title IV federal financial aid programs. Includes data for public institutions reporting data according to the Financial Accounting Standards Board (FASB) questionnaire. Detail may not sum to totals because of rounding.
SOURCE: U.S. Department of Education, National Center for Education Statistics, 2003–04 Integrated Postsecondary Education Data System, Spring 2004 and Spring 2005. (This table was prepared October 2006.)

Table 348. Current-fund expenditures of public degree-granting institutions, by purpose: Selected years, 1980–81 through 2000–01

Purpose	1980–81	1985–86	1990–91	1995–96	1996–97	1997–98	1998–99[1]	1999–2000	2000–01
1	2	3	4	5	6	7	8	9	10
	In thousands of current dollars								
Total current-fund expenditures.................	$42,279,806	$63,193,853	$92,961,093	$119,524,500	$125,428,736	$132,846,205	$140,538,586	$152,324,948	$170,344,840
Educational and general expenditures..........................	34,173,013	50,872,962	74,395,428	96,085,623	101,026,553	106,740,858	113,594,381	122,708,551	136,612,739
Instruction...............................	14,849,822	21,880,782	31,371,394	38,653,245	40,272,894	42,149,852	44,300,187	47,215,750	51,824,409
Research..................................	3,813,350	5,705,144	9,364,213	12,076,357	12,708,360	13,415,392	14,308,155	15,999,142	18,031,825
Public service	1,718,924	2,515,734	3,990,232	5,321,014	5,697,527	6,111,046	6,764,341	7,421,841	8,381,261
Academic support.........................	3,029,284	4,693,543	6,933,847	9,004,113	9,587,779	10,280,536	11,188,644	12,087,782	13,328,044
Libraries.............................	1,187,116	1,685,052	2,167,161	2,690,547	2,836,286	2,929,549	3,098,540	—	—
Student services........................	1,950,566	2,921,758	4,398,365	5,810,403	6,177,234	6,611,180	7,053,197	7,636,530	8,377,026
Institutional support	3,563,194	5,667,144	8,030,642	10,710,279	11,213,870	11,842,815	12,730,698	13,768,079	15,344,522
Operation and maintenance of plant	3,681,921	5,177,254	6,655,605	8,005,101	8,265,279	8,572,699	8,953,015	9,710,370	10,973,589
Scholarships and fellowships...........	1,064,864	1,575,909	2,688,532	5,084,653	5,554,360	5,947,587	6,417,812	6,785,423	7,766,208
From unrestricted funds	367,476	696,973	1,270,158	2,457,139	2,734,268	2,944,138	3,168,528	—	—
From restricted funds[2].................	697,388	878,935	1,418,374	2,627,514	2,820,091	3,003,449	3,249,284	—	—
Mandatory transfers.................	501,087	735,695	962,598	1,420,459	1,549,250	1,809,751	1,878,331	2,083,634	2,585,857
Other expenditures......................	8,106,793	12,320,891	18,565,665	23,438,877	24,402,183	26,105,347	26,944,205	29,616,397	33,732,101
Auxiliary enterprises	4,658,140	6,830,235	9,049,935	11,309,031	12,031,612	12,819,009	13,566,912	14,448,423	16,377,079
Mandatory transfers....................	344,043	410,777	623,146	793,125	842,635	844,478	862,449	—	—
Hospitals.....................................	3,377,972	5,358,699	9,315,902	11,878,939	12,111,616	12,964,071	13,058,104	14,057,107	16,146,401
Mandatory transfers....................	26,613	75,569	195,961	213,387	293,030	285,820	251,306	—	—
Independent operations (FFRDC)[3]..	70,681	131,956	199,827	250,906	258,955	322,267	319,188	533,868	779,242
Mandatory transfers....................	322	846	1,201	1,343	1,172	1,379	#	—	—
Other current expenditures.............	†	†	†	†	†	†	†	576,999	429,379
	Percentage distribution								
Total current-fund expenditures....................	100.0	100.0	100.0	100.0	100.0	100.0	100.0	100.0	100.0
Educational and general expenditures..........................	80.8	80.5	80.0	80.4	80.5	80.3	80.8	80.6	80.2
Instruction.....................................	35.1	34.6	33.7	32.3	32.1	31.7	31.5	31.0	30.4
Research...	9.0	9.0	10.1	10.1	10.1	10.1	10.2	10.5	10.6
Public service	4.1	4.0	4.3	4.5	4.5	4.6	4.8	4.9	4.9
Academic support.........................	7.2	7.4	7.5	7.5	7.6	7.7	8.0	7.9	7.8
Libraries.....................................	2.8	2.7	2.3	2.3	2.3	2.2	2.2	—	—
Student services...........................	4.6	4.6	4.7	4.9	4.9	5.0	5.0	5.0	4.9
Institutional support	8.4	9.0	8.6	9.0	8.9	8.9	9.1	9.0	9.0
Operation and maintenance of plant	8.7	8.2	7.2	6.7	6.6	6.5	6.4	6.4	6.4
Scholarships and fellowships...........	2.5	2.5	2.9	4.3	4.4	4.5	4.6	4.5	4.6
From unrestricted funds	0.9	1.1	1.4	2.1	2.2	2.2	2.3	—	—
From restricted funds[2].................	1.6	1.4	1.5	2.2	2.2	2.3	2.3	—	—
Mandatory transfers......................	1.2	1.2	1.0	1.2	1.2	1.4	1.3	1.4	1.5
Other expenditures......................	19.2	19.5	20.0	19.6	19.5	19.7	19.2	19.4	19.8
Auxiliary enterprises	11.0	10.8	9.7	9.5	9.6	9.6	9.7	9.5	9.6
Mandatory transfers....................	0.8	0.7	0.7	0.7	0.7	0.6	0.6	—	—
Hospitals.....................................	8.0	8.5	10.0	9.9	9.7	9.8	9.3	9.2	9.5
Mandatory transfers....................	0.1	0.1	0.2	0.2	0.2	0.2	0.2	—	—
Independent operations (FFRDC)[3]..	0.2	0.2	0.2	0.2	0.2	0.2	0.2	0.4	0.5
Mandatory transfers....................	#	#	#	#	#	#	#	—	—
Other current expenditures.............	†	†	†	†	†	†	†	0.4	0.3

—Not available.
†Not applicable.
#Rounds to zero.
[1]Data imputed using alternative procedures.
[2]Excludes Pell Grants.
[3]Generally includes only those expenditures associated with major federally funded research and development centers (FFRDC).
NOTE: Data through 1990–91 are for institutions of higher education, while later data are for degree-granting institutions. Degree-granting institutions grant associate's or higher degrees and participate in Title IV federal financial aid programs. The degree-granting classification is very similar to the earlier higher education classification, but it includes more 2-year colleges and excludes a few higher education institutions that did not grant degrees. (See Guide to Sources for details.) Detail may not sum to totals because of rounding.
SOURCE: U.S. Department of Education, National Center for Education Statistics, Higher Education General Information Survey (HEGIS), "Financial Statistics of Institutions of Higher Education" surveys, 1980–81 and 1985–86; and 1990–91 through 2000–01 Integrated Postsecondary Education Data System, "Finance Survey" (IPEDS-F:FY90–99), and Spring 2001 and Spring 2002. (This table was prepared October 2003.)

Table 349. Current-fund expenditures of public degree-granting institutions, by state or jurisdiction: Selected years, 1980–81 through 2000–01

[In thousands of current dollars]

State or jurisdiction	1980–81	1985–86	1990–91	1994–95	1995–96	1996–97	1997–98	1998–99[1]	1999–2000	2000–01	Percent change, 1995–96 to 2000–01
1	2	3	4	5	6	7	8	9	10	11	12
United States	$42,279,806	$63,193,853	$92,961,093	$115,464,975	$119,524,500	$125,428,736	$132,846,205	$140,538,586	$152,324,948	$170,344,840	42.5
Alabama	839,366	1,324,774	2,054,798	2,648,077	2,715,643	2,840,619	3,013,873	3,202,503	3,337,958	3,508,298	29.2
Alaska	158,700	224,042	289,606	336,584	352,811	344,723	349,939	361,140	385,553	432,793	22.7
Arizona	691,481	1,017,203	1,586,891	1,854,180	1,976,169	2,070,170	2,232,166	2,350,274	2,508,136	2,677,742	35.5
Arkansas	340,621	528,831	797,291	1,070,668	1,181,083	1,247,987	1,318,057	1,430,166	1,528,643	1,636,672	38.6
California	5,775,482	8,515,440	12,023,304	13,899,338	14,284,348	15,489,455	16,349,033	17,894,180	20,204,478	22,674,570	58.7
Colorado	738,363	1,057,558	1,452,137	1,862,438	1,974,306	2,077,034	2,257,920	2,358,290	2,440,045	2,630,166	33.2
Connecticut	367,850	562,696	886,846	1,134,014	1,168,038	1,193,722	1,301,238	1,419,257	1,568,490	1,621,083	38.8
Delaware	158,332	229,377	367,012	469,085	491,597	510,290	542,429	578,210	606,042	625,737	27.3
District of Columbia	71,791	80,764	97,556	99,351	103,072	92,985	69,345	83,575	81,990	91,938	-10.8
Florida	1,170,305	1,782,180	2,896,046	3,549,470	3,714,984	3,968,197	4,235,932	4,634,378	4,947,847	5,442,666	46.5
Georgia	754,060	1,255,964	1,929,993	2,728,682	2,835,505	3,043,813	3,337,172	3,506,991	3,955,764	4,049,036	42.8
Hawaii	222,718	312,248	498,307	653,303	634,970	638,096	684,248	688,307	679,287	737,605	16.2
Idaho	166,844	238,438	353,561	473,733	510,601	530,013	556,349	603,889	626,644	685,758	34.3
Illinois	1,780,403	2,571,409	3,528,967	4,293,437	4,498,142	4,712,347	4,942,580	5,217,493	5,525,410	5,932,860	31.9
Indiana	1,064,395	1,602,203	2,391,173	2,967,184	2,783,027	3,021,556	3,298,268	3,429,404	3,633,100	3,852,626	38.4
Iowa	767,590	1,092,542	1,734,476	2,051,631	2,163,536	2,233,470	2,368,381	2,478,128	2,612,023	2,603,053	20.3
Kansas	579,857	848,602	1,190,573	1,495,926	1,547,154	1,587,212	1,692,700	1,687,445	1,734,127	1,830,606	18.3
Kentucky	673,775	898,718	1,400,529	1,663,738	1,779,945	1,994,760	2,061,525	2,235,257	2,442,117	2,589,557	45.5
Louisiana	716,702	1,039,177	1,439,415	1,909,675	1,970,177	2,056,770	2,890,392	3,051,898	3,236,605	3,293,683	67.2
Maine	153,658	216,737	355,074	391,269	407,819	431,850	442,573	475,783	507,930	549,851	34.8
Maryland	795,100	1,064,430	1,684,341	1,997,636	2,136,898	2,309,739	2,490,326	2,567,437	2,920,899	3,141,491	47.0
Massachusetts	553,019	980,585	1,435,063	1,557,225	1,647,254	1,739,959	1,915,680	1,992,772	2,149,182	2,337,046	41.9
Michigan	2,053,795	2,946,336	4,416,914	5,395,757	5,653,791	5,980,104	6,293,933	6,658,103	7,329,879	7,966,990	40.9
Minnesota	876,632	1,324,691	2,012,225	2,624,464	2,694,395	2,583,477	2,607,348	2,763,990	2,898,495	3,076,832	14.2
Mississippi	539,222	706,380	978,366	1,358,795	1,440,692	1,490,260	1,636,580	1,816,580	2,008,628	2,111,975	46.6
Missouri	687,643	999,869	1,453,608	1,836,878	1,994,150	2,117,072	2,257,626	2,402,362	2,617,736	2,836,688	42.3
Montana	121,894	182,102	254,175	376,618	402,792	443,314	450,665	474,278	507,851	552,708	37.2
Nebraska	378,928	537,858	848,778	1,076,670	1,143,547	1,218,519	1,089,700	1,158,111	1,225,449	1,259,443	10.1
Nevada	111,347	180,107	330,592	447,901	505,518	547,065	597,026	648,485	701,413	757,424	49.8
New Hampshire	134,391	183,959	281,542	371,554	390,816	405,304	424,077	439,768	469,642	500,329	28.0
New Jersey	903,169	1,406,490	2,309,968	2,982,535	3,064,901	3,147,805	3,276,738	3,479,536	3,853,074	4,127,205	34.7
New Mexico	325,960	456,600	896,299	1,278,741	1,329,422	1,372,587	1,439,205	1,502,684	1,609,904	1,727,683	30.0
New York	2,519,104	3,802,602	5,605,621	6,922,118	6,728,593	6,872,196	7,180,732	7,170,827	7,798,717	13,541,832	101.3
North Carolina	1,128,383	1,799,173	2,581,156	3,406,215	3,538,606	3,791,447	4,057,906	4,335,879	4,665,386	5,062,536	43.1
North Dakota	192,046	288,214	367,959	456,730	440,332	450,580	472,760	481,388	487,364	516,617	17.3
Ohio	1,784,754	2,718,408	4,084,840	4,907,686	4,818,930	4,880,235	5,248,688	5,521,383	6,010,509	6,433,761	33.5
Oklahoma	583,174	844,829	1,057,248	1,263,002	1,329,938	1,458,358	1,592,465	1,698,453	1,904,467	2,129,124	60.1
Oregon	642,411	880,696	1,329,794	1,756,424	1,815,638	1,984,619	2,107,519	2,270,364	2,503,013	2,699,552	48.7
Pennsylvania	1,544,586	2,392,145	3,602,685	4,506,833	4,781,347	4,919,829	4,961,929	5,303,351	5,678,716	6,454,947	35.0
Rhode Island	158,365	213,253	292,199	344,457	353,270	368,598	376,190	401,526	421,252	451,179	27.7
South Carolina	617,963	951,848	1,475,074	1,817,631	1,903,952	2,020,736	2,192,724	2,311,108	2,515,415	2,194,033	15.2
South Dakota	124,103	149,092	197,853	252,443	290,868	294,514	319,705	335,243	350,211	382,250	31.4
Tennessee	665,885	1,081,052	1,585,614	2,042,171	2,062,547	2,126,871	2,185,603	2,286,000	2,258,072	2,430,880	17.9
Texas	2,736,276	4,375,082	5,959,584	7,817,433	8,300,915	8,758,306	9,313,169	9,843,327	10,820,078	12,744,081	53.5
Utah	405,314	669,714	993,625	1,354,017	1,442,592	1,536,120	1,654,048	1,867,303	1,978,429	2,085,409	44.6
Vermont	122,708	188,112	274,746	316,455	329,457	347,605	355,673	374,752	411,271	426,370	29.4
Virginia	1,143,755	1,825,156	2,812,109	3,414,167	3,515,201	3,804,552	3,608,285	3,832,003	4,085,736	4,415,701	25.6
Washington	993,171	1,399,780	2,157,074	2,807,168	2,945,074	3,102,644	3,599,004	3,521,717	3,807,514	4,205,962	42.8
West Virginia	317,482	376,293	548,802	674,664	718,596	741,058	755,252	799,193	847,145	916,466	27.5
Wisconsin	1,208,396	1,754,395	2,469,260	2,941,034	3,024,877	2,827,128	3,088,341	3,255,308	3,512,443	3,814,064	26.1
Wyoming	126,082	203,307	240,216	294,334	291,864	296,393	305,567	314,762	333,127	354,195	21.4
U.S. Service Schools	592,454	912,393	1,150,209	1,313,438	1,394,800	1,406,676	1,047,619	1,024,025	1,081,740	1,223,770	-12.3
Other jurisdictions	268,310	451,370	516,958	727,524	809,779	864,454	924,241	940,891	975,025	1,048,185	29.4
American Samoa	1,609	1,092	3,187	3,483	15,486	6,462	7,532	7,103	7,289	3,994	-74.2
Federated States of Micronesia	†	†	3,777	5,056	8,442	7,381	6,949	7,288	9,111	11,031	30.7
Guam	16,100	31,310	57,645	81,148	68,230	69,168	73,311	73,140	73,052	74,747	9.6
Marshall Islands	†	†	†	1,237	1,282	1,566	1,781	3,143	3,453	1,478	15.2
Northern Marianas	†	1,350	2,798	12,366	15,029	16,393	16,536	13,557	14,759	342	-97.7
Palau	†	†	3,837	3,667	5,942	3,940	4,032	4,567	4,127	4,494	-24.4
Puerto Rico	237,319	394,046	385,511	586,910	659,617	724,397	780,586	793,069	825,102	902,747	36.9
Trust Territory of the Pacific	1,447	5,992	†	†	†	†	†	†	†	†	†
Virgin Islands	11,835	17,580	60,202	33,656	35,750	35,149	33,513	39,023	38,131	49,352	38.0

[1]Data were imputed using alternative procedures. (See Guide to Sources for details.)
NOTE: Data through 1994–95 are for institutions of higher education, while later data are for degree-granting institutions. Degree-granting institutions grant associate's or higher degrees and participate in Title IV federal financial aid programs. The degree-granting classification is very similar to the earlier higher education classification, but it includes more 2-year colleges and excludes a few higher education institutions that did not grant degrees. (See Guide to Sources for details.) Detail may not sum to totals because of rounding.

SOURCE: U.S. Department of Education, National Center for Education Statistics, Higher Education General Information Survey (HEGIS), "Financial Statistics of Institutions of Higher Education" surveys, 1980–81 and 1985–86; and 1990–91 through 2000–01 Integrated Postsecondary Education Data System, "Finance Survey" (IPEDS-F:FY91–99), and Spring 2001 and Spring 2002. (This table was prepared October 2003.)

Table 350. Educational and general expenditures of public degree-granting institutions, by state or jurisdiction: Selected years, 1980–81 through 2000–01

[In thousands of dollars]

State or jurisdiction	1980–81	1985–86	1990–91	1994–95	1995–96	1996–97	1997–98	1998–99[1]	1999–2000	2000–01
1	2	3	4	5	6	7	8	9	10	11
United States	$34,173,013	$50,872,962	$74,395,428	$92,173,768	$96,085,623	$101,026,553	$106,740,858	$113,594,381	$122,708,551	$136,612,739
Alabama	611,409	979,770	1,415,440	1,834,533	1,880,788	1,925,722	2,006,575	2,143,719	2,277,004	2,411,292
Alaska	150,421	210,894	273,577	316,397	331,723	323,377	325,345	332,095	353,349	396,775
Arizona	554,120	862,816	1,364,060	1,653,840	1,759,850	1,844,250	1,997,271	2,107,384	2,250,444	2,400,827
Arkansas	266,522	415,800	633,194	746,129	843,906	891,912	943,747	1,022,299	1,118,485	1,209,522
California	4,847,879	7,049,635	9,615,356	11,280,758	11,719,821	12,617,059	13,524,973	14,950,202	16,549,206	18,305,943
Colorado	561,552	809,621	1,258,356	1,604,656	1,705,832	1,786,774	1,945,537	2,022,100	2,098,281	2,280,930
Connecticut	281,581	439,397	673,182	883,759	911,255	928,747	995,683	1,061,353	1,198,363	1,218,821
Delaware	135,164	202,331	325,838	413,692	429,293	455,194	487,107	520,014	544,439	545,645
District of Columbia	71,245	79,922	96,411	98,041	101,839	91,957	68,669	82,721	81,390	91,099
Florida	1,071,754	1,638,227	2,657,553	3,234,938	3,390,561	3,638,284	3,895,763	4,244,904	4,545,842	4,992,475
Georgia	628,939	1,046,341	1,617,020	2,277,756	2,366,561	2,558,514	2,771,965	2,911,113	3,307,923	3,615,137
Hawaii	202,154	282,058	454,880	590,389	569,448	580,744	621,595	619,690	623,915	679,041
Idaho	141,296	202,736	303,224	395,733	428,068	445,369	467,873	513,240	535,078	587,247
Illinois	1,487,123	2,152,955	2,979,768	3,583,012	3,794,018	3,974,499	4,174,159	4,426,248	4,691,497	5,040,293
Indiana	771,564	1,183,098	1,842,610	2,196,013	2,300,841	2,444,413	2,566,025	2,692,360	2,856,862	3,032,769
Iowa	512,205	736,894	1,172,328	1,392,753	1,459,013	1,518,118	1,615,935	1,693,895	1,789,004	1,909,848
Kansas	461,979	660,995	928,772	1,196,211	1,244,531	1,281,762	1,367,841	1,473,238	1,579,598	1,659,330
Kentucky	527,235	737,101	1,112,190	1,321,523	1,419,040	1,551,033	1,630,119	1,788,799	1,974,482	2,123,064
Louisiana	557,825	810,479	1,135,955	1,449,305	1,570,429	1,651,304	1,731,835	1,854,505	1,953,126	2,043,645
Maine	127,983	183,349	308,699	343,665	360,331	380,156	390,584	420,791	449,117	485,566
Maryland	604,419	911,562	1,443,669	1,737,204	1,878,053	2,017,888	2,179,292	2,251,347	2,596,770	2,781,822
Massachusetts	441,068	779,341	1,122,629	1,400,824	1,476,589	1,562,825	1,719,631	1,777,119	1,922,321	2,119,517
Michigan	1,610,016	2,278,217	3,325,625	4,042,460	4,306,553	4,502,657	4,724,680	4,992,712	5,343,081	5,746,572
Minnesota	667,119	1,023,324	1,563,054	2,068,280	2,076,375	2,183,151	2,368,748	2,516,599	2,637,556	2,802,651
Mississippi	409,942	542,022	756,492	1,049,356	1,111,120	1,136,217	1,248,177	1,379,388	1,536,840	1,588,438
Missouri	553,793	802,936	1,155,531	1,456,516	1,566,489	1,691,270	1,818,890	1,938,643	2,038,897	2,225,375
Montana	99,990	148,099	210,813	322,880	350,086	386,562	391,181	408,078	438,668	479,071
Nebraska	286,122	397,523	600,224	727,977	753,703	788,822	826,605	895,091	930,495	994,155
Nevada	105,177	163,714	301,487	402,097	459,599	488,685	526,507	572,423	622,883	677,192
New Hampshire	104,285	143,191	229,360	304,474	316,456	324,076	340,758	354,291	380,788	406,806
New Jersey	735,097	1,140,310	1,875,481	2,363,439	2,461,249	2,533,747	2,627,961	2,795,026	2,996,834	3,192,725
New Mexico	278,960	393,151	671,206	899,545	953,396	985,558	1,027,034	1,093,374	1,155,772	1,263,713
New York	2,249,821	3,238,773	4,680,376	5,799,931	5,630,108	5,713,257	5,950,196	5,908,907	6,371,063	10,686,388
North Carolina	971,928	1,527,535	2,227,060	2,849,310	2,881,827	3,080,391	3,289,339	3,542,330	3,787,462	4,129,879
North Dakota	151,372	228,609	292,978	361,276	372,051	381,349	397,021	408,849	414,035	441,745
Ohio	1,327,483	2,019,351	3,046,603	3,616,901	3,774,974	3,873,433	4,109,766	4,328,462	4,603,159	4,941,079
Oklahoma	404,178	594,561	830,929	996,963	1,037,701	1,139,724	1,236,772	1,335,929	1,433,937	1,538,080
Oregon	497,593	672,175	996,887	1,281,381	1,351,507	1,486,678	1,565,280	1,675,772	1,826,458	1,962,882
Pennsylvania	1,231,502	1,814,384	2,737,817	3,439,340	3,562,793	3,646,801	3,863,724	4,107,792	4,400,378	4,699,431
Rhode Island	138,965	185,215	251,992	297,597	306,825	318,710	327,202	350,697	368,113	390,828
South Carolina	481,737	741,740	1,065,867	1,310,645	1,369,352	1,462,262	1,580,666	1,680,470	1,869,656	1,949,359
South Dakota	108,632	130,825	173,396	222,811	258,488	261,558	283,557	299,020	316,193	336,906
Tennessee	515,578	865,946	1,231,619	1,581,929	1,627,212	1,671,134	1,714,071	1,861,231	1,955,029	2,098,364
Texas	2,278,337	3,674,109	5,105,246	6,643,734	7,026,170	7,394,605	7,757,269	8,191,952	9,055,432	10,099,991
Utah	320,278	503,557	730,496	991,014	1,073,017	1,146,939	1,231,532	1,404,696	1,484,168	1,575,810
Vermont	101,539	157,266	238,512	279,882	292,072	308,235	316,435	333,975	370,007	376,869
Virginia	796,616	1,241,534	1,852,416	2,248,402	2,282,078	2,472,071	2,611,639	2,773,374	2,998,532	3,223,168
Washington	837,281	1,143,285	1,757,053	2,211,588	2,308,241	2,437,310	2,550,318	2,721,736	2,954,648	3,259,061
West Virginia	228,755	310,142	459,984	579,349	622,712	642,896	647,584	688,008	732,479	781,737
Wisconsin	998,862	1,438,918	2,057,786	2,437,859	2,513,244	2,585,549	2,830,557	2,980,108	3,217,057	3,498,903
Wyoming	111,170	171,335	204,028	254,469	251,339	253,867	260,114	271,901	287,765	307,712
U.S. Service Schools	555,447	805,892	1,030,399	1,181,234	1,247,093	1,259,138	889,749	874,411	884,669	1,007,248
Other jurisdictions .	253,820	421,500	498,958	700,528	777,274	832,461	876,605	890,343	922,802	993,234
American Samoa	1,609	1,092	3,187	3,483	14,909	6,237	7,385	6,996	6,725	3,408
Federated States of Micronesia	†	†	3,302	4,589	7,965	6,844	6,418	6,716	8,473	10,275
Guam	15,582	29,916	55,641	77,783	65,258	65,965	70,448	70,356	70,409	72,398
Marshall Islands	†	†	†	1,183	1,226	1,497	1,701	3,041	3,327	1,425
Northern Marianas	†	1,328	2,472	12,305	14,989	16,393	16,536	13,557	14,759	342
Palau	†	†	3,277	3,156	3,332	3,377	3,518	4,037	3,558	3,910
Puerto Rico	224,988	367,523	378,352	567,140	637,571	701,227	740,982	750,522	781,325	856,197
Trust Territory of the Pacific	1,320	5,992	†	†	†	†	†	†	†	†
Virgin Islands	10,322	15,649	52,726	30,889	32,024	30,922	29,616	35,118	34,226	45,279

†Not applicable.
[1]Data were imputed using alternative procedures. (See Guide to Sources for details.)
NOTE: Data through 1994–95 are for institutions of higher education, while later data are for degree-granting institutions. Degree-granting institutions grant associate's or higher degrees and participate in Title IV federal financial aid programs. The degree-granting classification is very similar to the earlier higher education classification, but it includes more 2-year colleges and excludes a few higher education institutions that did not grant degrees. (See Guide to Sources for details.) Detail may not sum to totals because of rounding.
SOURCE: U.S. Department of Education, National Center for Education Statistics, Higher Education General Information Survey (HEGIS), "Financial Statistics of Institutions of Higher Education" surveys, 1980–81 and 1985–86; and 1990–91 through 2000–01 Integrated Postsecondary Education Data System, "Finance Survey" (IPEDS-F:FY90–99), and Spring 2001 and Spring 2002. (This table was prepared October 2003.)

Table 351. Voluntary support for degree-granting institutions, by source and purpose of support: Selected years, 1959–60 through 2004–05

[In millions of current dollars]

Year	Total voluntary support[1]	Sources						Purpose		Voluntary support as a percent of total expenditures[2]
		Alumni	Nonalumni individuals	Corporations	Foundations	Religious organizations	Other	Current operations	Capital purposes	
1	2	3	4	5	6	7	8	9	10	11
1959–60	$815	$191	$194	$130	$163	$80	$57	$385	$430	14.6
1965–66	1,440	310	350	230	357	108	85	675	765	11.5
1970–71	1,860	458	495	259	418	104	126	1,050	810	8.0
1975–76	2,410	588	569	379	549	130	195	1,480	930	6.2
1980–81	4,230	1,049	1,007	778	922	140	334	2,590	1,640	6.6
1985–86	7,400	1,825	1,781	1,702	1,363	211	518	4,022	3,378	7.6
1990–91	10,200	2,680	2,310	2,230	2,030	240	710	5,830	4,370	7.0
1994–95	12,750	3,600	2,940	2,560	2,460	250	940	7,230	5,520	7.0
1995–96	14,250	4,040	3,400	2,800	2,815	255	940	7,850	6,400	7.5
1996–97	16,000	4,650	3,850	3,050	3,200	250	1,000	8,500	7,500	8.0
1997–98	18,400	5,500	4,500	3,250	3,800	300	1,050	9,000	9,400	8.8
1998–99	20,400	5,930	4,810	3,610	4,530	330	1,190	9,900	10,500	9.3
1999–2000	23,200	6,800	5,420	4,150	5,080	370	1,380	11,270	11,930	9.8
2000–01	24,200	6,830	5,200	4,350	6,000	370	1,450	12,200	12,000	9.3
2001–02	23,900	5,900	5,400	4,370	6,300	360	1,570	12,400	11,500	8.5
2002–03	23,600	6,570	4,280	4,250	6,600	360	1,540	12,900	10,700	7.8
2003–04	24,400	6,700	5,200	4,400	6,200	350	1,550	13,600	10,800	7.7
2004–05	25,600	7,100	5,000	4,400	7,000	370	1,730	14,200	11,400	7.5

[1]Data are based on sample surveys of colleges and universities.
[2]Total expenditures include current-fund expenditures and additions to plant value through 1995–96.
NOTE: Some data have been revised from previously published figures.
SOURCE: Council for Aid to Education, "Voluntary Support of Education," selected years, 1959–60 through 2004–05. U.S. Department of Education, National Center for Education Statistics, Higher Education General Information Survey (HEGIS), 1965–66 through 1985–86; *Financial Statistics of Institutions of Higher Education, 1959–60*; 1986–87 through 2004–05 Integrated Postsecondary Education Data System, "Finance Survey" (IPEDS-F:FY87–99), and Spring 2001 through Spring 2005; and unpublished tabulations. (This table was prepared October 2006.)

Table 352. Total expenditures of private not-for-profit degree-granting institutions, by purpose and type of institution: 1996–97 through 2003–04

Type of institution and year	Total expenditures	Instruction	Research	Public service	Academic support	Student services	Institutional support	Auxiliary enterprises[1]	Net grant aid to students[2]	Hospitals	Independent operations	Other
1	2	3	4	5	6	7	8	9	10	11	12	13
					In thousands of current dollars							
All institutions												
1996–97	$67,399,563	$21,126,357	$6,702,520	$1,621,583	$4,942,411	$4,430,241	$8,226,648	$7,079,116	$1,529,456	—	—	$11,741,232
1997–98	69,300,699	23,404,428	7,267,877	1,672,991	5,738,254	4,903,988	9,138,895	7,698,614	1,297,749	$6,395,808	$1,782,095	—
1998–99[3]	75,516,696	25,181,848	7,779,001	1,521,440	6,349,076	5,295,059	9,901,658	8,027,492	1,222,565	7,258,939	2,979,619	—
1999–2000	80,613,037	26,012,599	8,381,926	1,446,958	6,510,951	5,688,499	10,585,850	8,300,021	1,180,882	7,355,110	2,753,679	2,396,563
2000–01	85,625,016	27,607,324	9,025,739	1,473,292	7,368,263	6,117,195	11,434,074	9,010,853	1,176,160	7,255,376	3,134,609	2,022,132
2001–02	92,192,297	29,689,041	10,035,480	1,665,884	7,802,637	6,573,185	12,068,120	9,515,829	1,188,690	7,633,043	3,397,979	2,622,409
2002–03	99,757,733	32,062,218	11,079,532	1,878,380	8,156,688	7,096,223	13,158,794	9,938,658	1,187,285	7,586,208	3,879,736	3,734,011
2003–04	104,317,870	33,909,179	12,039,531	1,972,351	8,759,743	7,544,021	13,951,408	10,508,719	1,101,738	8,374,128	4,222,980	1,934,070
4-year												
1996–97	66,668,808	20,922,069	6,701,053	1,616,019	4,902,188	4,294,812	8,095,791	7,011,791	1,502,866	—	—	11,622,219
1997–98	68,677,274	23,164,693	7,267,228	1,669,650	5,704,216	4,817,585	8,988,203	7,621,887	1,276,848	6,395,610	1,771,355	—
1998–99[3]	74,805,484	24,823,398	7,778,900	1,513,641	6,308,251	5,224,455	9,766,020	7,957,265	1,198,516	7,257,021	2,978,017	—
1999–2000	79,699,659	25,744,199	8,376,568	1,438,544	6,476,338	5,590,978	10,398,914	8,228,409	1,162,570	7,355,110	2,752,019	2,176,011
2000–01	85,048,123	27,413,897	9,019,966	1,467,325	7,333,851	6,036,478	11,292,310	8,957,973	1,160,660	7,253,479	3,133,099	1,979,086
2001–02	91,612,337	29,492,583	10,035,394	1,658,781	7,768,870	6,497,127	11,914,149	9,470,557	1,173,725	7,632,942	3,396,831	2,571,376
2002–03	99,146,893	31,866,310	11,079,332	1,871,274	8,122,181	7,014,149	12,997,886	9,879,117	1,174,881	7,586,208	3,854,471	3,701,085
2003–04	103,733,257	33,712,542	12,039,080	1,964,898	8,726,505	7,466,472	13,774,084	10,464,984	1,084,880	8,374,128	4,221,611	1,904,075
2-year												
1996–97	730,755	204,288	1,467	5,564	40,223	135,429	130,857	67,324	26,590	—	—	119,013
1997–98	623,424	239,735	649	3,341	34,038	86,403	150,692	76,726	20,901	198	10,740	—
1998–99[3]	711,212	358,450	101	7,799	40,826	70,603	135,638	70,226	24,049	1,917	1,602	—
1999–2000	913,378	268,400	5,358	8,415	34,612	97,521	186,936	71,612	18,311	0	1,660	220,553
2000–01	576,893	193,428	5,772	5,967	34,412	80,717	141,764	52,880	15,500	1,896	1,510	43,046
2001–02	579,960	196,459	86	7,102	33,767	76,058	153,971	45,271	14,965	100	1,147	51,033
2002–03	610,840	195,909	200	7,106	34,506	82,074	160,908	59,541	12,404	0	25,265	32,926
2003–04	584,612	196,637	451	7,453	33,238	77,549	177,324	43,735	16,859	0	1,369	29,995
					Percentage distribution							
All institutions												
1996–97	100.00	31.34	9.94	2.41	7.33	6.57	12.21	10.50	2.27	—	—	17.42
1997–98	100.00	33.77	10.49	2.41	8.28	7.08	13.19	11.11	1.87	9.23	2.57	—
1998–99[3]	100.00	33.35	10.30	2.01	8.41	7.01	13.11	10.63	1.62	9.61	3.95	—
1999–2000	100.00	32.27	10.40	1.79	8.08	7.06	13.13	10.30	1.46	9.12	3.42	2.97
2000–01	100.00	32.24	10.54	1.72	8.61	7.14	13.35	10.52	1.37	8.47	3.66	2.36
2001–02	100.00	32.20	10.89	1.81	8.46	7.13	13.09	10.32	1.29	8.28	3.69	2.84
2002–03	100.00	32.14	11.11	1.88	8.18	7.11	13.19	9.96	1.19	7.60	3.89	3.74
2003–04	100.00	32.51	11.54	1.89	8.40	7.23	13.37	10.07	1.06	8.03	4.05	1.85
4-year												
1996–97	100.00	31.38	10.05	2.42	7.35	6.44	12.14	10.52	2.25	—	—	17.43
1997–98	100.00	33.73	10.58	2.43	8.31	7.01	13.09	11.10	1.86	9.31	2.58	—
1998–99[3]	100.00	33.18	10.40	2.02	8.43	6.98	13.06	10.64	1.60	9.70	3.98	—
1999–2000	100.00	32.30	10.51	1.80	8.13	7.02	13.05	10.32	1.46	9.23	3.45	2.73
2000–01	100.00	32.23	10.61	1.73	8.62	7.10	13.28	10.53	1.36	8.53	3.68	2.33
2001–02	100.00	32.19	10.95	1.81	8.48	7.09	13.00	10.34	1.28	8.33	3.71	2.81
2002–03	100.00	32.14	11.17	1.89	8.19	7.07	13.11	9.96	1.18	7.65	3.89	3.73
2003–04	100.00	32.50	11.61	1.89	8.41	7.20	13.28	10.09	1.05	8.07	4.07	1.84
2-year												
1996–97	100.00	27.96	0.20	0.76	5.50	18.53	17.91	9.21	3.64	—	—	16.29
1997–98	100.00	38.45	0.10	0.54	5.46	13.86	24.17	12.31	3.35	0.03	1.72	—
1998–99[3]	100.00	50.40	0.01	1.10	5.74	9.93	19.07	9.87	3.38	0.27	0.23	—
1999–2000	100.00	29.39	0.59	0.92	3.79	10.68	20.47	7.84	2.00	0.00	0.18	24.15
2000–01	100.00	33.53	1.00	1.03	5.96	13.99	24.57	9.17	2.69	0.33	0.26	7.46
2001–02	100.00	33.87	0.01	1.22	5.82	13.11	26.55	7.81	2.58	0.02	0.20	8.80
2002–03	100.00	32.07	0.03	1.16	5.65	13.44	26.34	9.75	2.03	0.00	4.14	5.39
2003–04	100.00	33.64	0.08	1.27	5.69	13.27	30.33	7.48	2.88	0.00	0.23	5.13

See notes at end of table.

Table 352. Total expenditures of private not-for-profit degree-granting institutions, by purpose and type of institution: 1996–97 through 2003–04—Continued

Type of institution and year	Total expenditures	Instruction	Research	Public service	Academic support	Student services	Institutional support	Auxiliary enterprises[1]	Net grant aid to students[2]	Hospitals	Independent operations	Other
1	2	3	4	5	6	7	8	9	10	11	12	13
	Expenditure per full-time-equivalent student in current dollars											
All institutions												
1996–97	$27,880	$8,739	$2,772	$671	$2,044	$1,833	$3,403	$2,928	$633	—	—	$4,857
1997–98	28,270	9,547	2,965	682	2,341	2,000	3,728	3,141	529	$2,609	$727	—
1998–99[3]	30,291	10,101	3,120	610	2,547	2,124	3,972	3,220	490	2,912	1,195	—
1999–2000	31,751	10,246	3,301	570	2,564	2,241	4,169	3,269	465	2,897	1,085	944
2000–01	33,069	10,662	3,486	569	2,846	2,363	4,416	3,480	454	2,802	1,211	781
2001–02	34,841	11,220	3,793	630	2,949	2,484	4,561	3,596	449	2,885	1,284	991
2002–03	36,482	11,725	4,052	687	2,983	2,595	4,812	3,635	434	2,774	1,419	1,366
2003–04	37,240	12,105	4,298	704	3,127	2,693	4,980	3,751	393	2,989	1,508	690
4-year												
1996–97	28,327	8,890	2,847	687	2,083	1,825	3,440	2,979	639	—	—	4,938
1997–98	28,740	9,694	3,041	699	2,387	2,016	3,761	3,190	534	2,676	741	—
1998–99[3]	30,706	10,189	3,193	621	2,589	2,145	4,009	3,266	492	2,979	1,222	—
1999–2000	32,064	10,357	3,370	579	2,605	2,249	4,184	3,310	468	2,959	1,107	875
2000–01	33,359	10,753	3,538	576	2,877	2,368	4,429	3,514	455	2,845	1,229	776
2001–02	35,139	11,312	3,849	636	2,980	2,492	4,570	3,633	450	2,928	1,303	986
2002–03	36,746	11,810	4,106	694	3,010	2,600	4,817	3,661	435	2,812	1,429	1,372
2003–04	37,504	12,188	4,353	710	3,155	2,699	4,980	3,784	392	3,028	1,526	688
2-year												
1996–97	11,426	3,194	23	87	629	2,118	2,046	1,053	416	—	—	1,861
1997–98	10,094	3,882	11	54	551	1,399	2,440	1,242	338	3	174	—
1998–99[3]	12,514	6,307	2	137	718	1,242	2,387	1,236	423	34	28	—
1999–2000	17,148	5,039	101	158	650	1,831	3,510	1,345	344	0	31	4,141
2000–01	14,494	4,860	145	150	865	2,028	3,562	1,329	389	48	38	1,081
2001–02	14,890	5,044	2	182	867	1,953	3,953	1,162	384	3	29	1,310
2002–03	16,846	5,403	6	196	952	2,263	4,438	1,642	342	0	697	908
2003–04	16,561	5,570	13	211	942	2,197	5,023	1,239	478	0	39	850
	Expenditure per full-time-equivalent student in constant 2005–06 dollars[4]											
All institutions												
1996–97	$34,899	$10,939	$3,471	$840	$2,559	$2,294	$4,260	$3,666	$792	—	—	$6,080
1997–98	34,768	11,742	3,646	839	2,879	2,460	4,585	3,862	651	$3,209	$894	—
1998–99[3]	36,619	12,211	3,772	738	3,079	2,568	4,801	3,893	593	3,520	1,445	—
1999–2000	37,307	12,038	3,879	670	3,013	2,633	4,899	3,841	547	3,404	1,274	1,109
2000–01	37,569	12,113	3,960	646	3,233	2,684	5,017	3,954	516	3,183	1,375	887
2001–02	38,893	12,525	4,234	703	3,292	2,773	5,091	4,014	501	3,220	1,434	1,106
2002–03	39,850	12,808	4,426	750	3,258	2,835	5,256	3,970	474	3,030	1,550	1,492
2003–04	39,806	12,939	4,594	753	3,343	2,879	5,324	4,010	420	3,195	1,611	738
4-year												
1996–97	35,459	11,128	3,564	860	2,607	2,284	4,306	3,729	799	—	—	6,181
1997–98	35,345	11,922	3,740	859	2,936	2,479	4,626	3,923	657	3,292	912	—
1998–99[3]	37,121	12,318	3,860	751	3,130	2,593	4,846	3,949	595	3,601	1,478	—
1999–2000	37,675	12,170	3,960	680	3,061	2,643	4,916	3,890	550	3,477	1,301	1,029
2000–01	37,899	12,216	4,019	654	3,268	2,690	5,032	3,992	517	3,232	1,396	882
2001–02	39,226	12,628	4,297	710	3,326	2,782	5,101	4,055	503	3,268	1,454	1,101
2002–03	40,138	12,900	4,485	758	3,288	2,840	5,262	3,999	476	3,071	1,560	1,498
2003–04	40,089	13,028	4,653	759	3,372	2,885	5,323	4,044	419	3,236	1,631	736
2-year												
1996–97	14,303	3,999	29	109	787	2,651	2,561	1,318	520	—	—	2,329
1997–98	12,414	4,774	13	67	678	1,721	3,001	1,528	416	4	214	—
1998–99[3]	15,128	7,625	2	166	868	1,502	2,885	1,494	512	41	34	—
1999–2000	20,149	5,921	118	186	764	2,151	4,124	1,580	404	0	37	4,865
2000–01	16,466	5,521	165	170	982	2,304	4,046	1,509	442	54	43	1,229
2001–02	16,622	5,631	2	204	968	2,180	4,413	1,297	429	3	33	1,463
2002–03	18,401	5,901	6	214	1,039	2,472	4,847	1,794	374	0	761	992
2003–04	17,702	5,954	14	226	1,006	2,348	5,369	1,324	510	0	41	908

—Not available.

[1]Essentially self-supporting operations of institutions that furnish a service to students, faculty, or staff, such as residence halls and food services.

[2]Excludes tuition and fee allowances and agency transactions, such as student awards made from contributed funds or grant funds.

[3]Data were imputed using alternative procedures. (See Guide to Sources for details.)

[4]Constant dollars based on the Consumer Price Index, prepared by the Bureau of Labor Statistics, U.S. Department of Labor, adjusted to a school-year basis.

NOTE: Detail may not sum to totals because of rounding.

SOURCE: U.S. Department of Education, National Center for Education Statistics, 1996–97 through 2003–04 Integrated Postsecondary Education Data System, "Fall Enrollment Survey" (IPEDS-EF:96–99) and "Finance Survey" (IPEDS-F:FY97–99), and Spring 2001 through Spring 2005. (This table was prepared May 2006.)

Table 353. Total expenditures of private not-for-profit degree-granting institutions, by purpose and type of institution: 2003–04

Type of institution	Total expenditures	Instruction	Research	Public service	Academic support	Student services	Institutional support	Auxiliary enterprises[1]	Net grant aid to students[2]	Hospitals	Independent operations	Other
1	2	3	4	5	6	7	8	9	10	11	12	13
	In thousands of current dollars											
Total	$104,317,870	$33,909,179	$12,039,531	$1,972,351	$8,759,743	$7,544,021	$13,951,408	$10,508,719	$1,101,738	$8,374,128	$4,222,980	$1,934,070
4-year	103,733,257	33,712,542	12,039,080	1,964,898	8,726,505	7,466,472	13,774,084	10,464,984	1,084,880	8,374,128	4,221,611	1,904,075
Doctoral, extensive[3]	51,823,284	15,658,838	9,813,832	741,393	3,724,702	1,870,012	4,657,056	4,188,485	337,394	6,518,450	3,818,964	494,158
Doctoral, intensive[4]	7,765,979	3,024,249	646,398	233,654	1,062,049	599,008	1,198,294	865,206	74,781	0	36,334	26,007
Master's[5]	16,611,897	6,460,170	249,278	208,975	1,620,673	2,112,407	3,106,998	2,264,568	199,795	87,402	131,580	170,049
Baccalaureate[6]	15,252,042	5,341,683	145,646	156,598	1,376,744	2,182,571	2,894,353	2,521,677	323,244	0	60,294	249,233
Specialized institutions[7]	12,280,055	3,227,602	1,183,927	624,278	942,337	702,474	1,917,383	625,047	149,666	1,768,276	174,438	964,628
Art, music, or design	1,297,648	496,044	720	21,092	123,665	115,718	246,615	121,101	21,141	0	21,825	129,727
Business and management	736,308	238,563	5,021	1,861	100,267	127,235	153,068	78,810	17,134	0	9,100	5,248
Engineering or technology	339,785	127,073	9,794	2,539	27,653	35,436	65,014	34,664	4,672	0	15,713	17,226
Medical or other health	6,396,477	1,337,238	1,156,377	552,597	400,368	130,610	693,167	121,056	26,283	1,767,777	112,774	98,229
Theological	1,474,863	454,032	5,047	23,380	136,933	128,260	398,355	170,504	61,259	0	13,259	83,833
Tribal[8]	45,073	13,142	97	5,039	1,997	3,294	12,006	1,587	3,355	0	0	4,556
Other specialized	1,989,900	561,510	6,871	17,769	151,453	161,919	349,158	97,325	15,822	498	1,766	625,810
2-year	584,612	196,637	451	7,453	33,238	77,549	177,324	43,735	16,859	0	1,369	29,995
Associate's of arts	540,840	187,912	150	4,149	30,501	69,192	165,423	42,039	14,724	0	1,369	25,382
Tribal[8]	43,772	8,725	302	3,304	2,738	8,357	11,901	1,697	2,135	0	0	4,614
	Percentage distribution											
Total	100.00	32.51	11.54	1.89	8.40	7.23	13.37	10.07	1.06	8.03	4.05	1.85
4-year	100.00	32.50	11.61	1.89	8.41	7.20	13.28	10.09	1.05	8.07	4.07	1.84
Doctoral, extensive[3]	100.00	30.22	18.94	1.43	7.19	3.61	8.99	8.08	0.65	12.58	7.37	0.95
Doctoral, intensive[4]	100.00	38.94	8.32	3.01	13.68	7.71	15.43	11.14	0.96	0.00	0.47	0.33
Master's[5]	100.00	38.89	1.50	1.26	9.76	12.72	18.70	13.63	1.20	0.53	0.79	1.02
Baccalaureate[6]	100.00	35.02	0.95	1.03	9.03	14.31	18.98	16.53	2.12	0.00	0.40	1.63
Specialized institutions[7]	100.00	26.28	9.64	5.08	7.67	5.72	15.61	5.09	1.22	14.40	1.42	7.86
Art, music, or design	100.00	38.23	0.06	1.63	9.53	8.92	19.00	9.33	1.63	0.00	1.68	10.00
Business and management	100.00	32.40	0.68	0.25	13.62	17.28	20.79	10.70	2.33	0.00	1.24	0.71
Engineering or technology	100.00	37.40	2.88	0.75	8.14	10.43	19.13	10.20	1.38	0.00	4.62	5.07
Medical or other health	100.00	20.91	18.08	8.64	6.26	2.04	10.84	1.89	0.41	27.64	1.76	1.54
Theological	100.00	30.78	0.34	1.59	9.28	8.70	27.01	11.56	4.15	0.00	0.90	5.68
Tribal[8]	100.00	29.16	0.22	11.18	4.43	7.31	26.64	3.52	7.44	0.00	0.00	10.11
Other specialized	100.00	28.22	0.35	0.89	7.61	8.14	17.55	4.89	0.80	0.03	0.09	31.45
2-year	100.00	33.64	0.08	1.27	5.69	13.27	30.33	7.48	2.88	0.00	0.23	5.13
Associate's of arts	100.00	34.74	0.03	0.77	5.64	12.79	30.59	7.77	2.72	0.00	0.25	4.69
Tribal[8]	100.00	19.93	0.69	7.55	6.25	19.09	27.19	3.88	4.88	0.00	0.00	10.54
	Expenditure per full-time-equivalent student											
Total	$37,240	$12,105	$4,298	$704	$3,127	$2,693	$4,980	$3,751	$393	$2,989	$1,508	$690
4-year	37,504	12,188	4,353	710	3,155	2,699	4,980	3,784	392	3,028	1,526	688
Doctoral, extensive[3]	85,595	25,863	16,209	1,225	6,152	3,089	7,692	6,918	557	10,766	6,308	816
Doctoral, intensive[4]	29,322	11,419	2,441	882	4,010	2,262	4,524	3,267	282	0	137	98
Master's[5]	18,290	7,113	274	230	1,784	2,326	3,421	2,493	220	96	145	187
Baccalaureate[6]	23,088	8,086	220	237	2,084	3,304	4,381	3,817	489	0	91	377
Specialized institutions[7]	37,577	9,877	3,623	1,910	2,884	2,150	5,867	1,913	458	5,411	534	2,952
Art, music, or design	27,801	10,627	15	452	2,649	2,479	5,284	2,595	453	0	468	2,779
Business and management	17,029	5,517	116	43	2,319	2,943	3,540	1,823	396	0	210	121
Engineering or technology	20,223	7,563	583	151	1,646	2,109	3,869	2,063	278	0	935	1,025
Medical or other health	106,139	22,189	19,188	9,169	6,643	2,167	11,502	2,009	436	29,333	1,871	1,630
Theological	19,959	6,144	68	316	1,853	1,736	5,391	2,307	829	0	179	1,135
Tribal[8]	21,013	6,127	45	2,349	931	1,536	5,597	740	1,564	0	0	2,124
Other specialized	23,753	6,703	82	212	1,808	1,933	4,168	1,162	189	6	21	7,470
2-year	16,561	5,570	13	211	942	2,197	5,023	1,239	478	0	39	850
Associate's of arts	16,033	5,571	4	123	904	2,051	4,904	1,246	436	0	41	752
Tribal[8]	27,898	5,561	192	2,106	1,745	5,327	7,585	1,081	1,361	0	0	2,941

[1]Essentially self-supporting operations of institutions that furnish a service to students, faculty, or staff, such as residence halls and food services.
[2]Excludes tuition and fee allowances and agency transactions, such as student awards made from contributed funds or grant funds.
[3]Doctoral, extensive institutions are committed to graduate education through the doctorate, and award 50 or more doctor's degrees per year across at least 15 disciplines.
[4]Doctoral, intensive institutions are committed to education through the doctorate and award at least 10 doctor's degrees per year across 3 or more disciplines or at least 20 doctor's degrees overall.
[5]Master's institutions offer a full range of baccalaureate programs and are committed to education through the master's degree. They award at least 20 master's degrees per year.
[6]Baccalaureate institutions primarily emphasize undergraduate education.

[7]Specialized 4-year institutions award degrees primarily in single fields of study, such as medicine, business, fine arts, theology, and engineering. Includes some institutions that have 4-year programs, but have not reported sufficient data to identify program category. Also includes institutions classified as 4-year under the IPEDS system, which had been classified as 2-year in the Carnegie system because they primarily award associate's degrees.
[8]Tribally controlled colleges are located on reservations and are members of the American Indian Higher Education Consortium.
NOTE: Detail may not sum to totals because of rounding.
SOURCE: U.S. Department of Education, National Center for Education Statistics, 2003–04 Integrated Postsecondary Education Data System (IPEDS), Spring 2004 and Spring 2005. (This table was prepared May 2006.)

Table 354. Total expenditures of private for-profit degree-granting institutions, by purpose and type of institution: 2002–03 and 2003–04

Year and type of institution	Total expenditures	Instruction	Research and public service	Student services, academic and institutional support	Auxiliary enterprises[1]	Net grant aid to students[2]	Other
1	2	3	4	5	6	7	8
	In thousands of current dollars						
2002–03							
Total	$6,112,791	$1,748,254	$17,987	$3,671,541	$240,598	$36,031	$398,380
4–year	3,757,141	1,030,999	5,339	2,338,711	153,746	14,813	213,534
Doctoral, intensive[3]	40,223	15,455	0	24,767	0	0	0
Master's[4]	806,712	252,245	0	525,138	8,019	198	21,113
Baccalaureate[5]	345,908	87,113	0	239,179	16,959	0	2,658
Specialized institutions[6]	2,564,298	676,186	5,339	1,549,627	128,768	14,615	189,763
Art, music, or design	647,383	149,318	2,218	357,050	43,650	5,538	89,609
Business and management	197,333	51,397	177	138,888	4,271	277	2,323
Engineering or technology	537,187	162,729	215	354,609	10,541	147	8,947
Medical or other health	36,742	11,630	186	14,349	539	1,054	8,984
Other specialized	1,145,653	301,113	2,543	684,730	69,768	7,599	79,901
2–year	2,355,650	717,255	12,648	1,332,830	86,853	21,218	184,846
2003–04							
Total	$7,364,012	$1,883,733	$8,606	$4,592,730	$249,472	$56,467	$573,004
4–year	4,821,864	1,143,050	3,705	3,108,697	168,069	32,603	365,740
Doctoral, intensive[3]	46,025	17,258	0	28,284	0	0	483
Master's[4]	1,236,904	218,128	0	780,281	6,067	6,466	225,961
Baccalaureate[5]	387,191	82,571	141	288,373	15,359	0	747
Specialized institutions[6]	3,151,744	825,092	3,564	2,011,760	146,642	26,136	138,549
Art, music, or design	653,656	162,586	190	384,543	53,675	9,616	43,045
Business and management	308,455	70,083	235	225,920	4,358	487	7,373
Engineering or technology	674,908	185,103	71	463,071	9,333	162	17,167
Medical or other health	53,114	16,856	254	24,584	773	1,139	9,507
Other specialized	1,461,612	390,464	2,814	913,642	78,503	14,732	61,457
2–year	2,542,148	740,683	4,901	1,484,033	81,403	23,864	207,264
	Percentage distribution						
2003–04							
Total	100.00	25.58	0.12	62.37	3.39	0.77	7.78
4–year	100.00	23.71	0.08	64.47	3.49	0.68	7.59
Doctoral, intensive[3]	100.00	37.50	0.00	61.45	0.00	0.00	1.05
Master's[4]	100.00	17.64	0.00	63.08	0.49	0.52	18.27
Baccalaureate[5]	100.00	21.33	0.04	74.48	3.97	0.00	0.19
Specialized institutions[6]	100.00	26.18	0.11	63.83	4.65	0.83	4.40
Art, music, or design	100.00	24.87	0.03	58.83	8.21	1.47	6.59
Business and management	100.00	22.72	0.08	73.24	1.41	0.16	2.39
Engineering or technology	100.00	27.43	0.01	68.61	1.38	0.02	2.54
Medical or other health	100.00	31.74	0.48	46.29	1.46	2.14	17.90
Other specialized	100.00	26.71	0.19	62.51	5.37	1.01	4.20
2–year	100.00	29.14	0.19	58.38	3.20	0.94	8.15
	Expenditure per full-time-equivalent student in current dollars						
2003–04							
Total	$11,543	$2,953	$13	$7,199	$391	$89	$898
4–year	11,546	2,737	9	7,444	402	78	876
Doctoral, intensive[3]	4,810	1,804	0	2,956	0	0	50
Master's[4]	7,890	1,391	0	4,977	39	41	1,441
Baccalaureate[5]	11,522	2,457	4	8,581	457	0	22
Specialized institutions[6]	14,478	3,790	16	9,241	674	120	636
Art, music, or design	15,506	3,857	5	9,122	1,273	228	1,021
Business and management	11,206	2,546	9	8,207	158	18	268
Engineering or technology	16,234	4,452	2	11,138	224	4	413
Medical or other health	12,817	4,068	61	5,933	187	275	2,294
Other specialized	14,289	3,817	28	8,932	767	144	601
2–year	11,538	3,362	22	6,736	369	108	941

[1]Essentially self-supporting operations of institutions that furnish a service to students, faculty, or staff, such as residence halls and food services.
[2]Excludes tuition and fee allowances and agency transactions, such as student awards made from contributed funds or grant funds.
[3]Doctoral, intensive institutions are committed to education through the doctorate and award at least 10 doctor's degrees per year across 3 or more disciplines or at least 20 doctor's degrees overall.
[4]Master's institutions offer a full range of baccalaureate programs and are committed to education through the master's degree. They award at least 20 master's degrees per year.
[5]Baccalaureate institutions primarily emphasize undergraduate education.

[6]Specialized 4-year institutions award degrees primarily in single fields of study, such as medicine, business, fine arts, theology, and engineering. Includes some institutions that have 4-year programs, but have not reported sufficient data to identify program category. Also includes institutions classified as 4-year under the IPEDS system, which had been classified as 2-year in the Carnegie system because they primarily award associate's degrees.
NOTE: Detail may not sum to totals because of rounding.
SOURCE: U.S. Department of Education, National Center for Education Statistics, 2002–03 and 2003–04 Integrated Postsecondary Education Data System (IPEDS), Spring 2004 and Spring 2005. (This table was prepared May 2006.)

Table 355. Total expenditures of private not-for-profit and for-profit degree-granting institutions, by level and state or jurisdiction: 1997–98 through 2003–04

[In thousands of current dollars]

State or jurisdiction	Not–for–profit institutions						2003–04			For–profit institutions	
	1997–98	1998–99	1999–2000	2000–01	2001–02	2002–03	Total	4–year	2–year	2002–03	2003–04
1	2	3	4	5	6	7	8	9	10	11	12
United States	$69,300,699	$75,516,696	$80,613,037	$85,625,016	$92,192,297	$99,757,733	$104,317,870	$103,733,257	$584,612	$6,112,791	$7,364,012
Alabama	351,948	366,326	393,465	400,987	419,872	435,190	440,158	434,184	5,974	40,885	51,435
Alaska	10,202	16,663	19,042	19,106	19,823	20,561	20,916	20,916	†	3,975	3,975
Arizona	117,603	129,980	143,698	160,787	162,471	182,548	141,307	137,268	4,039	606,684	811,709
Arkansas	160,182	164,307	230,860	197,313	213,645	216,809	224,969	223,633	1,336	8,815	10,544
California	5,740,704	7,417,634	7,871,651	8,682,192	9,588,524	10,268,563	10,838,473	10,711,139	127,334	970,021	1,061,082
Colorado	303,769	335,298	376,887	399,613	430,242	450,245	486,523	483,133	3,390	202,309	250,744
Connecticut	1,792,100	1,894,898	2,094,981	2,193,752	2,343,067	2,517,664	2,684,855	2,679,916	4,939	24,930	23,325
Delaware	37,647	43,320	52,533	56,670	62,625	70,783	80,634	78,168	2,466	†	†
District of Columbia	2,492,285	2,641,207	2,267,409	2,230,368	2,387,245	2,530,695	2,673,493	2,673,493	†	96,971	115,876
Florida	1,776,443	1,905,829	2,031,623	2,247,374	2,472,362	2,695,985	2,908,264	2,888,622	19,642	555,859	847,890
Georgia	2,289,149	2,508,080	2,635,438	2,795,105	2,946,777	3,188,042	3,266,674	3,243,370	23,304	270,926	266,573
Hawaii	111,103	122,340	209,135	138,660	146,050	152,348	173,261	173,261	†	16,924	17,941
Idaho	104,558	110,393	118,150	130,256	139,029	147,022	152,512	152,512	†	8,369	9,716
Illinois	4,720,747	5,130,189	5,668,566	5,910,538	6,188,489	6,304,076	6,666,469	6,656,659	9,810	322,046	364,853
Indiana	1,125,545	1,246,522	1,343,315	1,425,665	1,525,312	1,612,609	1,702,487	1,696,526	5,961	136,851	195,155
Iowa	673,346	689,698	740,760	767,891	800,428	847,857	875,162	863,937	11,225	30,287	59,742
Kansas	187,707	196,897	208,729	222,036	232,720	237,781	252,050	238,958	13,092	7,356	8,402
Kentucky	347,011	375,598	400,513	406,358	437,092	458,584	457,484	457,484	†	78,431	104,940
Louisiana	673,645	692,914	746,629	773,107	828,300	876,419	909,744	909,744	†	52,983	62,234
Maine	271,228	290,439	316,114	341,350	373,835	384,085	399,609	398,275	1,334	5,171	5,253
Maryland	1,994,345	2,113,725	2,205,880	2,410,284	2,725,616	3,019,626	3,271,571	3,271,571	†	25,306	36,659
Massachusetts	6,845,932	7,218,867	7,591,344	8,187,834	8,831,619	9,506,793	10,037,913	10,025,556	12,357	44,673	60,609
Michigan	901,576	936,454	995,384	1,065,100	1,134,361	1,206,723	1,259,243	1,256,151	3,092	37,532	47,021
Minnesota	874,507	930,959	1,004,427	1,093,937	1,164,763	1,157,173	1,222,082	1,199,303	22,779	216,771	260,327
Mississippi	130,497	136,859	150,123	156,292	158,464	167,822	170,290	170,290	†	5,363	6,443
Missouri	1,988,750	2,019,795	2,144,299	2,380,876	2,561,036	3,355,385	2,961,937	2,941,125	20,811	126,696	157,178
Montana	57,049	64,772	69,426	74,446	72,297	78,561	86,364	78,002	8,362	†	†
Nebraska	338,473	355,512	387,569	422,879	445,634	840,326	510,418	508,082	2,336	14,444	15,773
Nevada	7,440	7,679	7,006	9,130	10,919	9,657	8,677	8,677	†	43,598	65,642
New Hampshire	523,575	572,609	589,823	654,213	719,549	786,283	837,504	836,506	998	37,787	39,577
New Jersey	1,160,843	1,252,181	1,362,090	1,479,492	1,588,295	1,641,561	1,765,956	1,764,159	1,797	74,683	79,531
New Mexico	51,204	47,256	54,280	63,824	60,571	59,119	52,502	52,502	†	32,449	33,962
New York	10,525,903	11,511,493	12,519,671	13,099,910	14,177,942	15,801,483	16,557,418	16,498,070	59,349	540,167	560,525
North Carolina	2,761,327	3,292,928	3,530,337	3,845,125	3,978,481	4,224,812	4,439,832	4,428,393	11,439	24,574	31,080
North Dakota	45,200	51,613	56,000	59,677	63,207	68,513	83,942	61,422	22,520	2,012	2,962
Ohio	1,912,254	2,017,835	2,211,035	2,368,824	2,530,980	2,637,737	2,843,939	2,830,333	13,606	167,023	200,456
Oklahoma	323,212	319,214	338,276	360,772	363,611	370,604	367,119	367,119	†	49,721	47,722
Oregon	398,742	424,420	456,683	447,516	473,270	487,996	512,749	512,749	†	57,669	65,534
Pennsylvania	6,952,322	7,219,858	7,590,629	7,841,530	8,397,080	8,894,900	9,386,083	9,283,974	102,109	401,065	462,037
Rhode Island	696,398	737,297	828,715	897,056	978,710	1,062,719	1,141,689	1,141,689	†	†	8,735
South Carolina	366,727	392,369	408,127	432,035	483,551	507,157	532,950	521,539	11,411	13,949	16,845
South Dakota	59,837	64,155	69,555	75,488	90,290	94,117	93,352	90,104	3,248	17,721	18,468
Tennessee	1,804,783	1,842,893	1,971,564	2,131,732	2,367,380	2,609,840	2,819,415	2,812,195	7,220	91,545	114,385
Texas	2,080,235	2,249,979	2,490,597	2,662,275	2,921,130	3,142,104	3,266,787	3,252,795	13,992	247,302	287,165
Utah	553,754	610,830	648,035	694,025	741,519	785,441	824,774	819,060	5,714	49,031	51,788
Vermont	306,150	333,738	347,293	369,832	382,794	400,154	426,338	407,833	18,506	24,224	23,972
Virginia	833,774	891,622	944,905	1,000,236	1,057,465	1,109,551	1,224,687	1,221,025	3,662	158,870	197,747
Washington	492,504	544,781	600,315	594,393	639,129	674,622	737,957	737,957	†	84,366	102,174
West Virginia	160,681	162,994	170,653	185,101	194,652	201,085	197,437	197,437	†	19,713	21,921
Wisconsin	865,782	913,475	999,502	1,062,053	1,160,074	1,258,006	1,321,899	1,316,443	5,457	28,456	33,595
Wyoming	†	†	†	†	†	†	†	†	†	36,289	42,792
Other jurisdictions	372,019	413,323	431,216	456,532	494,476	680,257	578,021	566,739	11,282	58,180	69,613
Guam	†	†	†	†	1,160	1,161	999	999	†	†	†
Puerto Rico	372,019	413,323	431,216	456,532	493,316	679,096	577,023	565,741	11,282	58,180	69,613

†Not applicable.
NOTE: Detail may not sum to totals because of rounding.

SOURCE: U.S. Department of Education, National Center for Education Statistics, 1997–98 through 2003–04 Integrated Postsecondary Education Data System, "Finance Survey" (IPEDS-F:FY98–99), and Spring 2001 through Spring 2005. (This table was prepared May 2006.)

Table 356. Value of property and liabilities of degree-granting institutions: Selected years, 1899–1900 through 1995–96
[In thousands of current dollars]

Year	Property value at end of year					Endowment (end of year book value)[1]	Endowment (end of year market value)[1]	Liabilities of plant funds
	Total	Physical plant value						
		Total	Land	Buildings	Equipment			
1	2	3	4	5	6	7	8	9
Institutions of higher education[2]								
1899–1900	$448,597	$253,599	—	—	—	$194,998 [3]	—	—
1909–10	781,255	457,594	$92,359	$297,153	$68,082	323,661 [3]	—	—
1919–20	1,316,404	747,333	128,922	495,920	122,491	569,071 [3]	—	—
1929–30	3,437,117	2,065,049	304,114	1,490,014	270,921	1,372,068 [3]	—	—
1935–36	3,913,028	2,359,418	334,085	1,636,722	388,611	1,553,610 [3]	—	—
1937–38	4,208,695	2,556,075	313,665	1,811,309	431,101	1,652,620	—	—
1939–40	4,440,063	2,753,780	—	—	—	1,686,283	—	—
1941–42	4,525,925	2,759,261	—	—	—	1,766,664 [3]	—	—
1947–48	6,076,212	3,691,725	—	—	—	2,384,487	—	—
1949–50	4,799,964	4,799,964	—	—	—	2,601,223 [3]	—	—
1951–52	9,241,725	6,373,195	—	—	—	2,868,530	—	—
1953–54	10,717,082	7,523,193	—	—	—	3,193,889	—	—
1955–56	12,561,046	8,858,907	624,467	6,697,648 [4]	1,536,792	3,702,139	—	$894,383
1957–58	15,770,197	11,124,489	733,182	8,540,429 [4]	1,850,878	4,645,708	—	1,444,602
1959–60	18,870,628	13,548,548	842,664	10,472,478 [4]	2,233,407	5,322,080	—	1,964,306
1961–62	22,761,193	16,681,844	1,009,294	12,900,093 [4]	2,772,457	6,079,349	—	2,806,868
1963–64	28,232,362	21,279,346	1,292,691	16,460,867 [4]	3,525,788	6,953,016	—	4,190,189
1965–66	35,274,597	26,851,273	1,758,901	20,653,028 [4]	4,439,344	8,423,324	$11,126,831	6,071,750
1967–68	—	34,506,348	2,062,545	26,673,826 [4]	5,769,977	—	—	—
1969–70	52,930,923	42,093,580	3,076,751	31,865,179	7,151,649	10,837,343	11,206,632	9,384,731
1970–71	57,394,951	46,053,585	3,117,895	35,042,590	7,893,100	11,341,366	13,714,330	9,786,240
1971–72	62,136,459	50,153,251	3,287,326	38,131,339	8,734,586	11,983,208	15,180,934	10,291,095
1972–73	66,814,103	53,814,596	3,492,611	40,808,481	9,513,503	12,999,507	15,099,840	10,823,595
1973–74	71,305,817	58,002,777	3,888,372	43,701,491	10,412,914	13,303,040	13,168,076	11,400,916
1974–75	75,585,674	62,183,078	4,210,901	46,453,642	11,518,536	13,402,596	14,364,545	12,413,420
1975–76	80,300,595	66,348,304	4,345,232	49,349,224	12,653,847	13,952,291	15,488,265	12,687,015
1976–77	85,486,550	70,739,427	4,444,927	52,384,393	13,910,107	14,747,123	16,304,553	13,068,341
1977–78	90,337,044	74,770,804	4,621,071	55,188,603	14,961,131	15,566,240	16,840,129	13,437,861
1978–79	95,442,468	78,637,991	4,824,250	57,563,005	16,250,737	16,804,477	18,158,634	13,712,648
1979–80	102,294,859	83,733,387	5,037,172	60,847,097	17,849,119	18,561,472	20,743,045	14,181,991
1980–81	109,701,242	88,760,567	5,212,453	64,158,017	19,390,097	20,940,675	23,465,001	14,794,669
1981–82	117,601,954	94,516,512	5,402,339	67,794,877	21,319,297	23,085,442	24,415,245	15,487,618
1982–83	127,345,302	100,992,841	5,889,080	71,519,718	23,584,042	26,352,461	32,691,133	16,749,900
1983–84	137,141,741	107,640,113	6,109,746	75,220,765	26,309,602	29,501,629	32,975,610	18,277,315
1984–85	148,163,096	114,763,986	6,236,159	79,133,998	29,393,829	33,399,110	39,916,361	22,105,712
1985–86	160,959,517	122,261,355	6,573,923	82,886,012	32,801,419	38,698,162	50,280,775	25,699,408
1986–87	—	126,426,171	7,165,445	84,838,657	34,422,069	—	56,585,153	—
1987–88	—	139,456,342	8,307,789	92,428,615	38,719,937	—	57,391,814	—
1988–89	—	158,693,085	9,462,095	104,743,145	44,487,845	—	64,155,247	—
1989–90	—	164,635,000	9,968,000	108,609,000	46,058,000	—	67,978,726	—
1990–91	—	178,084,000	10,028,000	117,683,000	50,373,000	—	72,048,579	—
1991–92	—	184,813,238	10,528,395	122,422,566	51,862,277	—	82,534,026	—
1992–93	—	192,760,817	11,006,451	128,436,599	53,317,767	—	92,239,311	—
1993–94	—	199,463,715	11,197,662	133,124,680	55,141,373	—	96,012,591	—
1994–95	—	212,201,113	11,710,436	142,553,837	57,936,840	—	109,706,704	—
Degree–granting institutions								
1995–96	—	220,400,104	11,407,020	150,458,886	58,534,198	—	128,837,030	—

—Not available.
[1]Includes funds functioning as endowment.
[2]Institutions that were accredited by an agency or association that was recognized by the U.S. Department of Education, or recognized directly by the Secretary of Education.
[3]Includes annuity funds.
[4]Includes improvements to land and equipment. These funds are included under appropriate categories after 1967–68.
NOTE: Degree-granting institutions grant associate's or higher degrees and participate in Title IV federal financial aid programs. The degree-granting classification is very similar to the earlier higher education classification, but it includes more 2-year colleges and excludes a few higher education institutions that did not grant degrees. (See Guide to Sources for details.) Detail may not sum to totals because of rounding.
SOURCE: U.S. Department of Education, National Center for Education Statistics, *Annual Report of the Commissioner of Education*, 1899–1900 and 1909–10; *Biennial Survey of Education in the United States*, 1919–20 through 1963–64; Higher Education General Information Survey (HEGIS), "Financial Statistics of Institutions of Higher Education" surveys, 1965–66 through 1985–86; and 1986–87 through 1995–96 Integrated Postsecondary Education Data System, "Finance Survey" (IPEDS-F:FY87–96). (This table was prepared November 1998.)

Table 357. Endowment funds of the 120 colleges and universities with the largest amounts, by rank order: 2004 and 2005

Institution	Rank order[1]	Market value of endowment, as of June 30 (in thousands of dollars)		1-year percent change[2]	Institution	Rank order[1]	Market value of endowment, as of June 30 (in thousands of dollars)		1-year percent change[2]
		2004	2005				2004	2005	
1	2	3	4	5	1	2	3	4	5
120 institutions with the largest amounts in 2005		**$208,425,902**	**$235,109,739**	**12.8**					
Harvard University (MA)	1	22,143,649	25,473,721	15.0	Princeton Theological Seminary (NJ)	61	801,193	863,653	7.8
Yale University (CT)	2	12,747,150	15,224,900	19.4	Berea College (KY)	62	794,963	861,679	8.4
Stanford University (CA)	3	9,922,000	12,205,000	23.0	University of Missouri System	63	762,248	848,612	11.3
University of Texas System	4	10,336,687	11,610,997	12.3	Tufts University (MA)	64	752,428	845,389	12.4
Princeton University (NJ)	5	9,928,200	11,206,500	12.9	Lehigh University (PA)	65	796,946	844,672	6.0
Massachusetts Institute of Technology	6	5,865,212	6,712,436	14.4	Carnegie Mellon University (PA)	66	768,990	837,459	8.9
University of California	7	4,767,466	5,221,916	9.5	University of Florida (FL)	67	738,299	835,698	13.2
Columbia University (NY)	8	4,493,085	5,190,564	15.5	George Washington University (DC)	68	733,801	823,129	12.2
Texas A&M University System[3]	9	4,373,047	4,963,879	13.5	Syracuse University (NY)	69	770,167	818,258	6.2
University of Michigan	10	4,163,382	4,931,338	18.4	University of Iowa[3]	70	737,704	786,100	6.6
Emory University (GA)	11	4,535,587	4,376,272	-3.5	Tulane University (LA)	71	692,665	780,200	12.6
University of Pennsylvania	12	4,018,660	4,369,782	8.7	University of Oklahoma[3]	72	631,376	777,514	23.1
Washington University (MO)	13	4,000,823	4,268,415	6.7	Boston University (MA)	73	694,051	776,900	11.9
Northwestern University (IL)	14	3,668,405	4,215,275	14.9	University of Tulsa (OK)	74	701,948	769,551	9.6
University of Chicago (IL)	15	3,620,728	4,137,494	14.3	University of Alabama System	75	699,200	764,882	9.4
Duke University (NC)	16	3,313,859	3,826,153	15.5	Baylor University (TX)	76	672,341	750,237	11.6
Cornell University (NY)	17	3,238,350	3,777,092	16.6	Georgetown University (DC)	77	680,611	741,063	8.9
University of Notre Dame (IN)	18	3,095,703	3,650,224	17.9	Trinity University (TX)	78	673,572	733,261	8.9
Rice University (TX)	19	3,302,455	3,611,127	9.3	Middlebury College (VT)	79	664,781	721,839	8.6
University of Virginia	20	2,793,225	3,219,098	15.2	University of Tennessee System	80	666,085	714,968	7.3
University of Southern California	21	2,399,960	2,746,051	14.4	Oberlin College (OH)	81	593,742	704,329	18.6
Dartmouth College (NH)	22	2,454,293	2,714,300	10.6	University of Arkansas[3]	82	626,446	691,524	10.4
Vanderbilt University (TN)	23	2,296,262	2,628,437	14.5	Vassar College (NY)	83	608,261	672,010	10.5
Johns Hopkins University (MD)	24	2,055,542	2,176,909	5.9	University of California, Los Angeles[3]	84	586,839	668,338	13.9
University of Minnesota[3]	25	1,730,063	1,968,930	13.8	Rensselaer Polytechnic Institute (NY)	85	570,175	624,279	9.5
Brown University (RI)	26	1,647,295	1,843,904	11.9	University of Louisville (KY)[3]	86	554,840	607,636	9.5
Ohio State University[3]	27	1,541,175	1,726,007	12.0	University of Maryland System[3]	87	533,059	595,000	11.6
Rockefeller University (NY)	28	1,394,736	1,556,945	11.6	Lafayette College (PA)	88	544,317	587,418	7.9
New York University	29	1,449,500	1,548,000	6.8	Bowdoin College (ME)	89	514,243	578,206	12.4
University of Pittsburgh (PA)	30	1,364,882	1,529,884	12.1	University of Kentucky	90	526,589	576,721	9.5
Case Western Reserve University (OH)	31	1,441,819	1,516,481	5.2	Wesleyan University (CT)	91	517,631	564,879	9.1
University of Washington	32	1,315,894	1,489,924	13.2	Washington State University	92	515,571	553,287	7.3
University of NC, Chapel Hill[3]	33	1,317,211	1,486,147	12.8	Northeastern University (MA)	93	498,481	543,174	9.0
California Institute of Technology	34	1,261,122	1,417,931	12.4	Carleton College (MN)	94	511,200	540,039	5.6
Grinnell College (IA)	35	1,291,781	1,390,545	7.6	Washington and Lee University (VA)	95	477,504	531,992	11.4
University of Rochester (NY)	36	1,261,562	1,369,969	8.6	Hamilton College (NY)	96	486,477	529,708	8.9
Williams College (MA)	37	1,229,516	1,348,374	9.7	Macalester College (MN)	97	487,010	524,067	7.6
Purdue University (IN)	38	1,207,131	1,340,536	11.1	University of Miami (FL)	98	472,262	523,706	10.9
Pomona College (CA)	39	1,149,720	1,298,629	13.0	Brandeis University (MA)	99	467,727	519,538	11.1
Wellesley College (MA)	40	1,179,988	1,275,529	8.1	University of Georgia[3]	100	474,596	517,170	9.0
Boston College (MA)	41	1,150,148	1,270,303	10.4	Berry College (GA)	101	581,725	516,135	-11.3
University of Richmond (VA)	42	1,103,465	1,207,573	9.4	University of Colorado[3]	102	468,744	512,371	9.3
Pennsylvania State University	43	1,056,078	1,174,828	11.2	Santa Clara University (CA)	103	449,543	509,149	13.3
Swarthmore College (PA)	44	1,080,026	1,164,069	7.8	Colgate University (NY)	104	463,436	508,665	9.8
Amherst College (MA)	45	993,417	1,154,570	16.2	Bryn Mawr College (PA)	105	477,444	505,861	6.0
Yeshiva University (NY)	46	1,003,024	1,148,687	14.5	Louisiana State University System	106	460,365	504,841	9.7
University of Illinois[3]	47	1,058,167	1,147,517	8.4	Rochester Institute of Technology (NY)	107	472,363	498,990	5.6
University of Wisconsin[3]	48	994,172	1,124,855	13.1	Drexel University (PA)	108	424,346	497,918	17.3
Indiana University[3]	49	1,012,707	1,107,498	9.4	Rutgers University (NJ)	109	449,889	496,292	10.3
University of Delaware	50	995,889	1,077,102	8.2	Pepperdine University (CA)	110	434,457	475,841	9.5
University of Nebraska[3]	51	959,861	1,042,290	8.6	Denison University (OH)	111	441,365	475,466	7.7
Smith College (MA)	52	924,464	1,035,542	12.0	Bucknell University (PA)	112	429,402	472,070	9.9
University of Cincinnati (OH)	53	987,785	1,032,124	4.5	College of the Holy Cross (MA)	113	419,222	465,304	11.0
Southern Methodist University (TX)	54	914,527	1,013,703	10.8	State University of New York, Buffalo[3]	114	428,072	463,214	8.2
Baylor College of Medicine (TX)	55	972,351	1,008,261	3.7	Texas Tech University	115	392,595	461,903	17.7
Kansas University Endowment Association	56	849,255	954,943	12.4	Florida State University[3]	116	412,020	459,959	11.6
Texas Christian University	57	868,907	941,798	8.4	University of Utah (UT)	117	394,461	458,531	16.2
Georgia Institute of Technology[3]	58	814,963	937,410	15.0	Iowa State University (IA)[3]	118	400,621	456,627	14.0
Wake Forest University (NC)	59	812,192	906,803	11.6	DePauw University (IN)	119	410,001	451,576	10.1
Michigan State University	60	749,365	906,342	20.9	Mount Holyoke College (MA)	120	397,464	449,108	13.0

[1]Institutions ranked by size of endowment in 2005.
[2]Change in market value of endowment. Includes growth from gifts and returns on investments, as well as reductions from expenditures and withdrawals.
[3]Includes foundations.

NOTE: Data include institutions participating in the comparative-performance study by the National Association of College and University Business Officers. Some data have been revised from previously published figures.
SOURCE: National Association of College and University Business Officers, *NACUBO Endowment Study, 2005.* (This table was prepared April 2006.)

Table 358. Participants in adult basic and secondary education programs, by type of program and state or jurisdiction: Selected fiscal years, 1990 through 2005

State or jurisdiction	1990	2000	2003	2004 Total	2004 Adult basic education	2004 English literacy	2004 Adult secondary education	2005 Total	2005 Adult basic education	2005 English literacy	2005 Adult secondary education
1	2	3	4	5	6	7	8	9	10	11	12
United States	3,535,970	3,306,687	2,679,927	2,627,618	1,044,111	1,168,897	414,610	2,543,953	1,009,706	1,139,965	394,282
Alabama	40,177	22,430	22,019	21,555	17,423	1,576	2,556	19,827	15,691	1,626	2,510
Alaska	5,067	5,396	4,723	3,588	2,206	502	880	3,791	2,434	600	757
Arizona	33,805	55,274	32,492	27,699	10,340	16,140	1,219	26,881	11,205	14,544	1,132
Arkansas	29,065	39,102	38,336	35,512	22,425	5,149	7,938	37,102	22,570	5,868	8,664
California	1,021,227	456,125	565,311	591,574	89,320	435,777	66,477	591,893	96,986	429,024	65,883
Colorado	12,183	13,743	15,137	15,097	4,406	9,295	1,396	15,011	4,244	9,427	1,340
Connecticut	46,434	27,698	33,062	32,878	5,576	14,675	12,627	31,958	4,852	13,891	13,215
Delaware	2,662	3,278	5,953	6,119	3,549	1,698	872	6,329	3,221	1,968	1,140
District of Columbia	19,586	2,828	3,226	3,170	1,165	1,502	503	3,646	1,382	1,845	419
Florida	419,429	399,772	387,710	370,985	145,141	125,891	99,953	348,119	130,805	114,310	103,004
Georgia	69,580	107,980	114,008	118,458	64,728	41,598	12,132	95,434	54,240	31,659	9,535
Hawaii	52,012	16,176	10,687	9,089	1,296	3,919	3,874	7,461	1,895	3,061	2,505
Idaho	11,171	10,542	8,780	7,261	3,795	2,400	1,066	7,744	4,250	2,475	1,019
Illinois	87,121	120,752	130,492	124,404	40,592	68,253	15,559	118,296	30,897	72,311	15,088
Indiana	44,166	41,760	41,397	41,148	21,678	8,315	11,155	43,498	24,181	8,197	11,120
Iowa	41,507	31,757	16,338	12,242	6,053	3,844	2,345	11,989	5,482	3,915	2,592
Kansas	10,274	11,410	10,386	9,788	4,906	3,873	1,009	9,475	4,567	3,830	1,078
Kentucky	28,090	37,061	34,700	32,235	23,030	3,113	6,092	30,931	22,488	2,768	5,675
Louisiana	40,039	38,873	31,998	32,502	24,856	1,910	5,736	29,367	22,621	1,917	4,829
Maine	14,964	9,807	10,485	8,814	3,758	1,469	3,587	8,151	3,645	1,765	2,741
Maryland	41,230	27,556	30,082	30,304	12,712	12,020	5,572	27,055	11,414	10,347	5,294
Massachusetts	34,220	24,565	21,337	21,578	7,471	11,888	2,219	21,448	7,317	12,013	2,118
Michigan	194,178	86,218	70,893	48,273	24,281	13,301	10,691	34,768	20,560	10,843	3,365
Minnesota	45,648	517,693	43,864	44,220	12,196	25,729	6,295	47,174	13,081	27,507	6,586
Mississippi	18,957	40,370	36,614	26,467	21,304	834	4,329	25,675	21,437	781	3,457
Missouri	31,815	38,773	41,928	37,729	24,186	8,036	5,507	37,052	23,518	7,955	5,579
Montana	6,071	4,995	4,437	3,864	2,641	198	1,025	3,291	2,266	199	826
Nebraska	6,158	9,095	10,200	10,267	4,842	4,237	1,188	10,226	4,795	4,217	1,214
Nevada	17,262	22,346	7,601	8,732	1,148	7,015	569	9,981	1,400	8,163	418
New Hampshire	7,198	5,519	6,444	5,866	1,833	1,866	2,167	5,804	1,916	1,925	1,963
New Jersey	64,080	44,712	42,465	41,803	12,918	24,497	4,388	40,889	12,235	25,265	3,389
New Mexico	30,236	29,197	21,587	22,842	12,383	8,466	1,993	24,132	13,409	8,299	2,424
New York	156,611	194,028	138,184	165,618	63,755	90,305	11,558	157,486	59,929	86,111	11,446
North Carolina	109,740	154,786	108,431	110,185	60,695	29,646	19,844	109,047	60,673	29,711	18,663
North Dakota	3,587	1,964	2,145	2,154	1,321	263	570	2,063	1,225	273	565
Ohio	95,476	81,010	59,761	56,607	37,335	9,040	10,232	50,869	33,893	8,031	8,945
Oklahoma	24,307	20,534	21,620	21,164	13,699	4,580	2,885	20,447	13,338	4,480	2,629
Oregon	37,075	27,981	24,863	21,701	9,404	11,023	1,274	21,668	9,753	10,436	1,479
Pennsylvania	52,444	46,836	52,823	53,706	26,222	15,912	11,572	54,274	27,652	16,195	10,427
Rhode Island	7,347	7,950	4,567	5,166	1,995	1,950	1,221	6,697	2,442	3,138	1,117
South Carolina	81,200	132,497	69,284	67,408	44,713	7,524	15,171	65,901	45,497	7,534	12,870
South Dakota	3,184	5,431	3,446	3,607	2,356	598	653	3,517	2,218	545	754
Tennessee	41,721	49,386	46,166	47,755	34,564	6,600	6,591	48,924	35,770	6,738	6,416
Texas	218,747	106,516	128,363	122,773	49,283	66,667	6,823	119,867	49,237	64,726	5,904
Utah	24,841	28,987	32,883	31,429	13,213	11,690	6,526	29,320	14,170	10,218	4,932
Vermont	4,808	4,436	1,937	2,283	1,289	254	740	2,015	1,099	273	643
Virginia	31,649	31,211	31,574	28,037	12,462	12,068	3,507	29,222	12,260	13,020	3,942
Washington	31,776	57,999	55,363	40,193	14,157	23,495	2,541	50,386	18,488	28,296	3,602
West Virginia	21,186	22,403	10,717	10,213	8,048	275	1,890	9,444	7,049	287	2,108
Wisconsin	61,081	27,297	30,437	29,132	13,986	7,618	7,528	26,029	12,748	7,034	6,247
Wyoming	3,578	2,632	2,671	2,424	1,456	403	565	2,379	1,261	404	714
Other jurisdictions	31,400	53,799	54,259	49,410	17,661	3,672	28,077	37,328	7,525	2,784	27,019
American Samoa	—	—	824	833	373	380	80	838	343	410	85
Federated States of Micronesia	—	—	—	—	—	—	—	—	—	—	—
Guam	1,311	902	989	900	572	71	257	1062	552	132	378
Marshall Islands	—	2,963	302	311	112	129	70	—	—	—	—
Northern Marianas	—	527	475	436	27	189	220	740	59	274	407
Palau	—	—	89	—	—	—	—	206	66	56	84
Puerto Rico	28,436	47,974	50,301	45,796	16,079	2,674	27,043	33,463	6,186	1,482	25,795
Virgin Islands	1,653	1,433	1,279	1,134	498	229	407	1,019	319	430	270

—Not available.
NOTE: Adult basic education provides instruction in basic skills for adults 16 and over functioning at literacy levels below the secondary level. Adult secondary education provides instruction at the high school level for adults who are seeking to pass the GED or obtain an adult high school credential. English literacy instruction is for adults who lack proficiency in English and who seek to improve their literacy and competence in English.

SOURCE: U.S. Department of Education, Office of Vocational and Adult Education, Division of Adult Education and Literacy, "Adult Education Program Facts, Program Year 1990–1991," *Enrollment and Participation in the State-Administered Adult Education Program,* selected years, 2000 through 2005, retrieved on August 11, 2005, from http://www.ed.gov/about/offices/list/ovae/pi/AdultEd/aedatatables.html, and unpublished tabulations. (This table was prepared September 2006.)

Table 359. Participation of employed persons, 17 years old and over, in career-related adult education during the previous 12 months, by selected characteristics of participants: Various years, 1995 through 2005

Characteristic of employed person	1995 — Percent of adults participating in career or job-related courses	1995 — Number of career or job-related courses taken, per employee	1999 — Percent of adults participating in career or job-related courses	1999 — Number of career or job-related courses taken, per employee	2003 — Percent of adults participating in career or job-related courses[1]	2003 — Number of career or job-related courses taken, per employee[1]	2005 — Employed persons, in thousands	2005 — Percent participating in career or job-related courses	2005 — Percent participating in apprentice programs	2005 — Percent participating in personal interest courses	2005 — Percent in informal learning activities for personal interest	2005 — Number of career or job-related courses taken (in thousands)	2005 — Number of career or job-related courses taken, per employee
1	2	3	4	5	6	7	8	9	10	11	12	13	14
Total	31.1	0.8	30.5 (1.14)	0.7 (0.03)	46.0 (0.70)	0.9 (0.02)	133,386 (1,508.1)	38.8 (0.83)	1.4 (0.24)	21.8 (0.94)	73.5 (1.01)	108,443	0.8 (0.03)
Sex													
Male	29.0	0.7	28.3 (1.15)	0.6 (0.03)	42.7 (1.15)	0.8 (0.03)	71,754 (934.7)	31.7 (1.22)	2.0 (0.37)	18.5 (1.30)	73.4 (1.52)	44,512	0.6 (0.03)
Female	33.4	0.9	32.9 (1.14)	0.8 (0.03)	49.4 (0.99)	1.0 (0.03)	61,632 (1,219.3)	47.1 (1.43)	0.8 (0.23)	25.8 (1.23)	73.6 (1.37)	63,931	1.0 (0.05)
Age													
17 through 24 years	18.6	0.4	19.1 (1.91)	0.4 (0.06)	33.9 (2.31)	0.5 (0.06)	15,027 (1,030.4)	26.4 (3.01)	3.0 (1.03)	25.2 (3.37)	71.4 (3.15)	8,024	0.5 (0.09)
25 through 29 years	31.2	0.8	34.3 (2.44)	0.8 (0.08)	49.7 (2.62)	0.9 (0.05)	14,555 (918.4)	36.1 (2.94)	3.1 (1.12)	24.5 (3.66)	70.9 (4.49)	9,493	0.7 (0.06)
30 through 34 years	31.6	0.8	34.4 (2.50)	0.8 (0.08)	48.4 (2.50)	0.9 (0.06)	15,250 (977.2)	41.0 (3.06)	2.7 (1.10)	23.7 (2.63)	74.0 (2.54)	12,681	0.8 (0.07)
35 through 39 years	35.1	0.7	29.2 (2.15)	0.7 (0.07)	48.8 (2.32)	1.0 (0.06)	15,286 (922.4)	41.7 (4.16)	1.0 (0.46)	21.6 (3.15)	77.7 (3.00)	13,807	0.9 (0.14)
40 through 44 years	36.6	0.9	36.4 (2.44)	0.8 (0.07)	46.1 (2.23)	0.9 (0.06)	18,141 (946.3)	39.8 (2.73)	0.9 (0.48)	23.3 (2.60)	71.2 (3.15)	15,586	0.9 (0.07)
45 through 49 years	39.6	1.0	30.4 (2.42)	0.7 (0.06)	50.8 (2.15)	1.1 (0.06)	18,149 (842.5)	45.0 (2.15)	0.7 (0.29)	19.0 (2.09)	73.5 (2.68)	16,809	0.9 (0.06)
50 through 54 years	34.4	0.9	34.7 (2.57)	0.8 (0.07)	52.5 (2.21)	1.2 (0.08)	14,624 (732.1)	42.6 (2.49)	0.7 (0.32)	19.5 (1.92)	76.3 (2.27)	14,881	1.0 (0.10)
55 through 59 years	26.7	0.7	30.3 (2.83)	0.6 (0.08)	46.3 (2.49)	1.0 (0.06)	10,522 (676.0)	44.7 (2.98)	0.2 (0.12)	18.3 (1.93)	73.0 (2.95)	9,901	0.9 (0.09)
60 through 64 years	21.1	0.5	27.2 (3.80)	0.7 (0.15)	37.8 (2.63)	0.8 (0.08)	6,021 (498.8)	38.9 (3.97)	0.6 (0.43)	23.4 (3.52)	73.0 (4.22)	4,919	0.8 (0.10)
65 and over	13.7	0.4	20.3 (4.21)	0.4 (0.08)	—	—	5,812 (493.3)	21.6 (3.48)	# (†)	17.4 (3.13)	74.2 (3.75)	2,343	0.4 (0.07)
65 through 69 years	—	—	— (†)	— (†)	33.5 (3.42)	0.7 (0.08)	3,385 (415.5)	19.1 (4.05)	# (†)	20.9 (4.88)	75.4 (5.18)	1,102	0.3 (0.08)
70 years and over	—	—	— (†)	— (†)	22.3 (3.35)	0.5 (0.09)	2,427 (282.3)	25.1 (5.81)	# (†)	12.6 (2.93)	72.6 (6.11)	1,241	0.5 (0.14)
Race/ethnicity													
White	33.2	0.8	32.8 (0.98)	0.6 (0.03)	48.5 (0.85)	1.0 (0.02)	94,881 (1,538.6)	41.3 (0.93)	1.2 (0.25)	22.2 (1.11)	75.3 (1.17)	82,511	0.9 (0.03)
Black	26.2	0.7	28.1 (2.34)	1.0 (0.07)	43.4 (2.19)	0.9 (0.06)	13,773 (533.2)	39.2 (3.82)	1.7 (0.83)	23.5 (3.04)	66.9 (3.02)	10,311	0.7 (0.11)
Hispanic	18.1	0.4	16.4 (1.83)	0.5 (0.05)	31.8 (2.32)	0.6 (0.06)	15,741 (681.1)	25.0 (2.66)	2.9 (0.85)	16.2 (2.31)	65.8 (3.39)	8,786	0.6 (0.11)
Asian	—	—	— (†)	— (†)	— (†)	— (†)	3,770 (520.7)	36.9 (7.00)	0.9 (0.90)	32.3 (7.26)	81.1 (5.88)	2,207	0.6 (0.12)
Pacific Islander	—	—	— (†)	— (†)	— (†)	— (†)	‡ (†)	‡ (†)	‡ (†)	‡ (†)	‡ (†)	‡	‡ (†)
Asian/Pacific Islander	25.5	0.6	32.8 (4.84)	0.4 (0.15)	50.4 (4.77)	0.8 (0.09)	— (†)	— (†)	— (†)	— (†)	— (†)	—	— (†)
American Indian/Alaska Native	34.0	0.9	29.5 (11.52)	0.7 (0.52)	40.0 (15.14)	0.7 (0.25)	‡ (†)	‡ (†)	‡ (†)	‡ (†)	‡ (†)	‡	‡ (†)
More than one race	—	—	— (†)	— (†)	— (†)	— (†)	3,786 (562.7)	39.1 (6.85)	1.4 (0.85)	22.6 (6.34)	77.6 (8.40)	3,083	0.8 (0.15)
Other races	—	—	— (†)	— (†)	— (†)	— (†)	‡ (†)	‡ (†)	‡ (†)	‡ (†)	‡ (†)	‡	‡ (†)
Highest level of education completed													
Less than high school completion	8.8	0.1	7.9 (2.29)	0.4 (0.05)	— (†)	— (†)	16,627 (838.2)	10.4 (2.11)	2.4 (0.90)	11.0 (2.06)	57.0 (3.76)	2,592	0.2 (0.03)
Eighth grade or less	—	—	— (†)	— (†)	—	—	5,016 (599.7)	2.7 (1.12)	4.4 (2.43)	3.8 (1.71)	46.7 (7.11)	197	# (†)
9th through 12th grade, no completion	—	—	— (†)	— (†)	9.9 (3.11)	0.1 (0.05)	11,610 (792.8)	13.7 (2.99)	1.5 (0.78)	17.1 (1.89)	61.5 (4.05)	2,396	0.2 (0.04)
High school completion	20.9	0.4	21.4 (1.45)	0.8 (0.03)	16.3 (2.32)	0.2 (0.04)	34,121 (1,147.2)	24.7 (1.76)	1.3 (0.46)	25.5 (4.61)	63.4 (2.55)	16,640	0.5 (0.05)
Some vocational/technical	32.3	0.8	28.7 (5.76)	0.9 (0.17)	33.2 (1.39)	0.6 (0.03)	3,744 (393.1)	48.2 (5.92)	2.0 (1.56)	25.2 (5.54)	74.0 (5.54)	3,802	1.0 (0.17)
Some college	29.9	0.7	29.0 (1.78)	0.7 (0.06)	41.7 (3.26)	1.0 (0.11)	24,479 (1,067.7)	39.9 (2.36)	1.9 (0.69)	19.1 (2.50)	79.8 (2.04)	18,437	0.8 (0.05)
Associate's degree	39.2	1.0	39.7 (3.07)	0.9 (0.09)	45.6 (1.83)	0.9 (0.05)	9,943 (730.7)	53.1 (1.88)	2.3 (0.84)	29.0 (2.86)	78.4 (3.88)	14,224	1.4 (0.21)
Bachelor's degree	44.6	1.2	43.8 (2.01)	1.0 (0.06)	54.5 (2.74)	1.1 (0.07)	26,475 (902.7)	61.1 (2.16)	0.2 (0.12)	28.6 (1.77)	78.7 (1.94)	28,099	1.1 (0.06)
Some graduate work (or study)	50.2	1.4	46.8 (4.17)	1.2 (0.14)	64.2 (1.42)	1.3 (0.05)	17,998 (735.4)	61.1 (2.16)	1.5 (0.80)	39.3 (6.05)	88.8 (1.16)	24,649	1.4 (0.07)
No degree	44.3	1.2	54.2 (4.94)	1.2 (0.14)	71.5 (1.87)	1.7 (0.07)	2,125 (227.9)	53.8 (5.79)	‡ (†)	28.2 (2.27)	75.0 (5.64)	2,412	1.1 (0.16)
Master's	50.5	1.4	45.3 (2.97)	1.1 (0.11)	68.3 (4.90)	1.6 (0.15)	11,330 (614.7)	62.7 (2.98)	‡ (†)	28.2 (2.27)	90.5 (1.40)	15,394	1.4 (0.09)
Doctor's	40.4	1.0	34.4 (4.79)	0.7 (0.12)	73.4 (2.44)	1.7 (0.09)	1,600 (227.2)	49.0 (5.80)	‡ (†)	28.8 (4.76)	87.8 (4.35)	2,204	1.4 (0.36)
Professional	67.6	2.0	67.6 (6.98)	1.9 (0.31)	58.9 (6.15)	1.4 (0.25)	2,943 (382.7)	66.5 (6.39)	‡ (†)	22.1 (5.05)	92.9 (2.21)	4,639	1.6 (0.21)

See notes at end of table.

Table 359. Participation of employed persons, 17 years old and over, in career-related adult education during the previous 12 months, by selected characteristics of participants: Various years, 1995 through 2005—Continued

Characteristic of employed person	1995		1999		2003		2005						
	Percent of adults participating in career or job-related courses	Number of career or job-related courses taken, per employee	Percent of adults participating in career or job-related courses	Number of career or job-related courses taken per employee	Percent of adults participating in career or job-related courses[1]	Number of career or job-related courses taken, per employee[1]	Employed persons, in thousands	Percent of adults participating				Number of career or job-related courses taken (in thousands)	Number of career or job-related courses taken, per employee
								In career or job-related courses	In apprentice programs	In personal interest courses	In informal learning activities for personal interest		
1	2	3	4	5	6	7	8	9	10	11	12	13	14
Urbanicity													
Urban	32.4	0.8	31.5 (1.67)	0.7 (0.05)	48.0 (0.75)	1.0 (0.02)	105,542 (1,279.1)	39.8 (1.06)	1.4 (0.27)	22.6 (0.94)	74.0 (1.13)	88,140	0.8 (0.03)
Urban, inside urbanized area	33.3	0.8	31.2 (0.99)	0.7 (0.03)	47.7 (0.88)	1.0 (0.02)	— (†)	— (†)	— (†)	— (†)	— (†)	—	— (†)
Urban, outside urbanized area	27.9	0.7	32.9 (2.48)	0.8 (0.08)	49.5 (2.19)	1.0 (0.06)	— (†)	— (†)	— (†)	— (†)	— (†)	—	— (†)
Rural	26.9	0.7	27.1 (1.74)	0.6 (0.05)	38.2 (2.08)	0.8 (0.05)	27,845 (849.4)	34.9 (2.18)	1.4 (0.58)	19.1 (2.17)	71.7 (2.30)	20,303	0.7 (0.06)
Occupation													
Executive, administrative, or managerial occupations	42.9	1.2	40.6 (2.06)	1.0 (0.07)	61.7 (2.13)	1.3 (0.06)	14,596 (707.6)	53.6 (2.79)	0.4 (0.25)	29.5 (2.89)	77.7 (2.87)	16,567	1.1 (0.09)
Engineers, surveyors, and architects	44.2	1.1	52.1 (6.96)	1.0 (0.16)	66.8 (4.60)	1.3 (0.13)	1,987 (244.9)	56.3 (5.68)	‡ (†)	30.5 (6.36)	81.0 (4.73)	2,323	1.2 (0.16)
Natural scientists and mathematicians	59.7	1.7	46.0 (6.61)	0.8 (0.14)	60.7 (5.89)	1.2 (0.13)	4,130 (445.4)	51.5 (5.64)	2.1 (1.55)	31.2 (4.83)	85.3 (5.44)	3,693	0.9 (0.11)
Social scientists and workers, religious workers, and lawyers	59.5	1.8	56.9 (5.66)	1.7 (0.24)	77.7 (3.90)	1.9 (0.15)	4,697 (480.9)	66.8 (4.48)	‡ (†)	28.3 (3.81)	88.6 (2.95)	7,822	1.7 (0.29)
Teachers, elementary/secondary	53.9	1.5	52.1 (3.53)	1.2 (0.11)	76.5 (2.43)	1.5 (0.19)	7,085 (568.5)	67.7 (4.16)	0.6 (0.37)	31.5 (3.93)	83.0 (2.79)	12,233	1.7 (0.13)
Teachers, postsecondary and counselors, librarians, and archivists	41.6	1.0	35.6 (5.85)	0.7 (0.14)	65.7 (5.63)	1.8 (0.09)	2,393 (420.9)	53.1 (8.63)	‡ (†)	17.7 (4.91)	90.9 (3.97)	2,122	0.9 (0.09)
Health diagnosing and treating practitioners	68.6	2.0	65.2 (11.99)	1.5 (0.50)	88.5 (4.11)	2.0 (0.24)	978 (208.8)	78.9 (7.10)	‡ (†)	27.4 (9.60)	86.6 (5.37)	1,951	2.0 (0.25)
Registered nurses, pharmacists, dieticians, therapists, and physician's assistants	72.8	2.2	72.2 (5.04)	1.8 (0.21)	84.9 (2.80)	1.9 (0.11)	2,794 (238.8)	79.7 (4.60)	‡ (†)	29.4 (4.17)	84.3 (3.70)	4,984	1.8 (0.15)
Writers, artists, entertainers, and athletes	23.4	0.5	30.6 (6.21)	0.6 (0.18)	35.1 (4.84)	0.6 (0.11)	2,969 (405.2)	29.9 (5.69)	‡ (†)	31.8 (6.15)	88.9 (4.39)	1,865	0.6 (0.15)
Health technologists and technicians	50.0	1.4	41.8 (6.00)	1.0 (0.19)	59.4 (6.12)	1.4 (0.21)	3,060 (436.7)	70.6 (7.31)	2.0 (1.50)	27.8 (6.48)	77.5 (6.40)	4,473	1.5 (0.18)
Technologists and technicians, except health	43.8	1.1	37.6 (4.87)	1.0 (0.15)	51.9 (3.47)	1.2 (0.14)	1,774 (336.5)	29.4 (8.10)	‡ (†)	5.3 (2.02)	75.2 (8.98)	1,015	0.6 (0.17)
Marketing and sales occupations	25.2	0.6	21.1 (2.27)	0.4 (0.06)	38.7 (2.36)	0.6 (0.05)	14,845 (971.9)	32.3 (3.17)	1.3 (0.92)	20.8 (2.64)	70.5 (3.53)	7,724	0.5 (0.05)
Administrative support occupations, including clerical	30.8	0.7	27.4 (2.02)	0.6 (0.05)	45.1 (2.20)	0.8 (0.04)	21,167 (1,179.4)	36.1 (2.95)	0.8 (0.40)	28.2 (2.28)	72.9 (2.37)	15,443	0.7 (0.10)
Service occupations	22.6	0.6	21.0 (2.15)	0.5 (0.07)	37.2 (2.04)	0.8 (0.06)	17,180 (1,033.7)	33.7 (3.13)	1.1 (0.36)	16.2 (2.31)	69.0 (2.74)	13,029	0.8 (0.10)

See notes at end of table.

Table 359. Participation of employed persons, 17 years old and over, in career-related adult education during the previous 12 months, by selected characteristics of participants: Various years, 1995 through 2005—Continued

Characteristic of employed person	1995 — Percent of adults participating in career or job-related courses	1995 — Number of career or job-related courses taken, per employee	1999 — Percent of adults participating in career or job-related courses	1999 — Number of career or job-related courses taken, per employee	2003 — Percent of adults participating in career or job-related courses[1]	2003 — Number of career or job-related courses taken, per employee[1]	2005 — Employed persons, in thousands	2005 — Percent of adults participating: In career or job-related courses	2005 — In apprentice programs	2005 — In personal interest courses	2005 — In informal learning activities for personal interest	2005 — Number of career or job-related courses taken (in thousands)	2005 — Number of career or job-related courses taken, per employee
1	2	3	4	5	6	7	8	9	10	11	12	13	14
Agriculture, forestry, and fishing occupations	12.4	0.3	12.2 (4.09)	0.2 (0.07)	33.9 (6.19)	0.5 (0.09)	2,522 (423.8)	22.4 (7.61)	2.4 (1.69)	23.0 (11.03)	62.9 (11.04)	960	0.4 (0.12)
Mechanics and repairers	29.1	0.7	15.0 (3.40)	0.3 (0.09)	32.1 (3.84)	0.7 (0.11)	5,241 (521.6)	28.3 (4.47)	4.0 (1.44)	12.6 (3.24)	69.3 (4.36)	2,669	0.5 (0.09)
Construction and extractive occupations	18.6	0.3	13.2 (3.16)	0.2 (0.06)	22.1 (2.87)	0.4 (0.06)	6,827 (647.1)	12.4 (3.04)	5.3 (2.26)	7.8 (1.88)	69.0 (5.25)	2,323	0.3 (0.13)
Precision production[2]	25.6	0.6	18.3 (6.52)	0.4 (0.12)	22.5 (6.15)	0.5 (0.13)	10,483 (839.3)	23.5 (3.79)	1.6 (0.90)	14.0 (3.34)	64.9 (3.74)	4,904	0.5 (0.07)
Production workers	14.8	0.3	23.0 (3.17)	0.5 (0.08)	27.6 (3.04)	0.5 (0.07)	— (†)	— (†)	— (†)	— (†)	— (†)	—	— (†)
Transportation and material moving	15.8	0.3	18.4 (3.62)	0.3 (0.06)	25.8 (3.39)	0.4 (0.05)	7,858 (742.5)	15.2 (2.81)	3.4 (1.77)	10.5 (3.10)	62.5 (5.32)	1,935	0.2 (0.05)
Handlers, equipment cleaners, helpers, and laborers	11.7	0.2	6.8 (3.45)	0.2 (0.12)	15.9 (4.27)	0.3 (0.11)	— (†)	— (†)	—	—	—	—	—
Miscellaneous occupations	38.8	1.0	14.2 (4.62)	0.3 (0.08)	63.0 (21.53)	1.5 (0.61)	801 (189.4)	17.2 (6.87)	— (†)	8.7 (4.31)	48.3 (13.96)	409	0.5 (0.28)
Annual household income													
$10,000 or less	12.6	0.2	9.5 (3.09)	0.2 (0.05)	—	—	4,425 (444.8)	16.7 (4.35)	0.6 (0.48)	26.1 (7.96)	69.7 (5.72)	1,556	0.4 (0.12)
$5,000 or less	—	—	— (†)	— (†)	19.4 (4.50)	0.3 (0.09)	1,635 (252.7)	19.1 (6.52)	‡ (†)	22.9 (7.91)	60.9 (8.84)	850	0.5 (0.26)
$5,001 to $10,000	—	—	— (†)	— (†)	17.5 (2.85)	0.3 (0.04)	2,791 (454.1)	15.3 (5.68)	‡ (†)	28.1 (12.27)	74.8 (6.88)	706	0.3 (0.10)
$10,001 to $15,000	15.1	0.4	8.3 (1.88)	0.1 (0.03)	20.1 (3.00)	0.3 (0.05)	4,814 (633.4)	22.2 (5.77)	— (†)	17.3 (5.25)	64.5 (7.57)	2,189	0.5 (0.12)
$15,001 to $20,000	20.1	0.4	16.3 (2.75)	0.3 (0.05)	22.7 (3.44)	0.4 (0.07)	4,515 (398.8)	18.2 (3.09)	5.7 (2.71)	11.5 (1.96)	60.4 (5.11)	1,322	0.3 (0.05)
$20,001 to $25,000	20.4	0.5	18.8 (2.79)	0.4 (0.08)	29.4 (2.73)	0.5 (0.07)	5,593 (490.2)	23.8 (4.02)	1.1 (0.51)	13.3 (3.21)	71.5 (4.11)	2,817	0.5 (0.10)
$25,001 to $30,000	24.7	0.5	22.2 (2.73)	0.5 (0.07)	27.7 (2.60)	0.5 (0.07)	7,444 (680.4)	31.4 (4.88)	0.7 (0.44)	16.7 (3.77)	73.5 (3.91)	4,322	0.6 (0.11)
$30,001 to $40,000	30.2	0.8	26.6 (2.82)	0.6 (0.07)	40.4 (2.43)	0.8 (0.06)	13,123 (928.5)	35.1 (3.45)	1.5 (0.65)	21.7 (3.71)	69.1 (3.55)	8,224	0.6 (0.06)
$40,001 to $50,000	34.7	0.8	32.3 (2.34)	0.7 (0.07)	47.9 (2.50)	1.0 (0.07)	13,647 (1,058.4)	31.5 (3.01)	1.8 (0.72)	20.1 (3.32)	73.5 (2.78)	10,072	0.7 (0.10)
$50,001 to $75,000	40.0	1.0	36.6 (1.86)	0.9 (0.06)	49.3 (1.57)	1.0 (0.04)	33,665 (1,430.4)	42.7 (1.80)	1.2 (0.51)	20.9 (2.10)	71.3 (2.55)	28,991	0.9 (0.06)
More than $75,000	45.2	1.3	42.5 (1.79)	1.0 (0.06)	60.5 (1.36)	1.3 (0.04)	46,160 (1,263.3)	48.1 (1.57)	1.3 (0.39)	26.0 (1.37)	79.2 (1.55)	48,951	1.1 (0.05)

—Not available.
†Not applicable.
#Rounds to zero.
‡Reporting standards not met.
[1]Estimates are not directly comparable to 1995, 1999, or 2005 estimates due to wording in questionnaire.
[2]For 2005, figures include "Production workers" occupations data.

NOTE: Data do not include persons enrolled in high school or below. Race categories exclude persons of Hispanic origin. Detail may not sum to totals because of rounding. Standard errors appear in parentheses.
SOURCE: U.S. Department of Education, National Center for Education Statistics, Adult Education Survey (AE-NHES:1995, AE-NHES:1999, and AE-NHES:2005) and Adult Education for Work-Related Reasons Survey (AEWR-NHES:2003) of the National Household Education Surveys Program. (This table was prepared August 2006.)

Table 360. Participation of persons, 17 years old and over, in adult education during the previous 12 months, by selected characteristics of participants: Selected years, 1991 through 2005

Characteristic of participant	Percent participating in any program				Percent participating, 2005							
	1991	1995	1999	2001	In any program	In basic education[1]	In English as a second language	In part-time postsecondary education[2]	In career or job-related courses	In apprentice programs	In personal-interest courses	In informal learning activities for personal interest
1	2	3	4	5	6	7	8	9	10	11	12	13
Total	33.0	40.2	44.5 (0.77)	46.4 (0.55)	44.4 (0.74)	0.7 (0.21)	0.9 (0.17)	4.0 (0.25)	27.0 (0.63)	1.2 (0.18)	21.4 (0.71)	70.5 (0.79)
Sex												
Male	32.6	38.2	41.7 (1.15)	43.1 (0.83)	41.0 (1.20)	0.7 (0.38)	0.9 (0.29)	3.7 (0.42)	24.5 (0.99)	1.7 (0.31)	18.3 (1.08)	70.8 (1.10)
Female	33.2	42.1	47.1 (1.02)	49.5 (0.78)	47.5 (1.01)	0.8 (0.16)	0.9 (0.15)	4.3 (0.34)	29.2 (0.95)	0.7 (0.15)	24.2 (0.88)	70.2 (1.03)
Age												
17 to 24 years	37.8	47.0	49.9 (2.34)	52.8 (2.04)	52.8 (2.79)	3.1 (1.39)	1.7 (0.61)	9.4 (1.28)	21.3 (2.22)	2.7 (0.76)	26.3 (2.60)	69.2 (2.54)
25 to 29 years	40.0	49.6	56.5 (2.53)	52.9 (2.60)	51.6 (3.82)	0.8 (0.30)	3.3 (1.48)	8.0 (1.36)	29.5 (2.48)	3.2 (1.06)	20.9 (2.78)	66.8 (3.75)
30 to 34 years	37.6	47.3	56.2 (2.57)	53.7 (2.18)	52.7 (2.52)	1.4 (0.60)	1.6 (0.64)	6.3 (1.11)	33.8 (2.71)	2.5 (0.89)	23.2 (2.23)	73.8 (2.22)
35 to 39 years	42.1	47.7	50.1 (2.43)	54.0 (1.71)	54.0 (3.21)	0.3 (0.15)	0.7 (0.26)	5.3 (0.86)	32.6 (3.29)	0.9 (0.36)	20.7 (2.67)	75.5 (2.69)
40 to 44 years	49.2	50.9	50.5 (2.43)	53.5 (1.88)	48.9 (2.43)	0.3 (0.12)	0.6 (0.23)	3.2 (0.59)	34.8 (2.30)	0.9 (0.42)	23.4 (2.29)	71.5 (2.62)
45 to 49 years	40.0	48.7	49.8 (2.69)	55.4 (2.02)	49.0 (2.09)	0.4 (0.20)	0.6 (0.25)	2.2 (0.36)	37.7 (1.83)	0.5 (0.23)	19.3 (1.88)	71.6 (2.52)
50 to 54 years	26.8	42.5	47.2 (2.51)	51.1 (2.22)	46.6 (2.36)	0.2 (0.10)	0.3 (0.15)	3.4 (0.70)	35.2 (2.25)	0.6 (0.28)	20.3 (1.64)	75.6 (1.89)
55 to 59 years	29.0	32.2	38.0 (2.60)	44.1 (1.98)	42.2 (2.78)	0.3 (0.29)	0.4 (0.26)	1.4 (0.35)	31.9 (2.39)	0.3 (0.17)	18.0 (1.63)	69.5 (2.56)
60 to 64 years	17.4	23.7	31.4 (2.83)	30.8 (2.18)	37.9 (3.00)	† (†)	0.4 (0.29)	0.8 (0.34)	20.9 (2.07)	0.3 (0.20)	24.1 (2.40)	71.4 (3.04)
65 to 69 years	14.2	18.1	25.4 (2.54)	20.5 (1.74)	26.2 (2.67)	† (†)	† (†)	0.2 (0.13)	8.1 (1.36)	‡ (†)	20.9 (2.41)	67.6 (2.52)
70 years and over	8.6	13.8	15.0 (1.38)	21.7 (1.37)	21.5 (1.44)	0.1 (0.06)	† (†)	‡ (†)	4.0 (0.78)	‡ (†)	17.9 (1.33)	62.9 (1.82)
Racial/ethnic group												
White	34.1	41.5	44.4 (0.89)	47.4 (0.59)	45.6 (0.84)	0.4 (0.21)	0.2 (0.08)	3.9 (0.29)	29.1 (0.70)	0.9 (0.17)	22.1 (0.87)	73.0 (0.92)
Black	25.9	37.0	46.3 (2.30)	43.3 (1.50)	46.4 (2.81)	1.1 (0.42)	‡ (†)	4.0 (0.72)	27.0 (2.53)	1.5 (0.73)	23.7 (2.11)	65.3 (2.02)
Hispanic	31.4	33.7	41.3 (2.51)	41.7 (2.28)	37.8 (2.43)	2.2 (0.65)	5.6 (1.22)	4.0 (1.02)	16.9 (1.72)	2.2 (0.63)	15.4 (1.75)	57.5 (2.86)
Asian	—	—	— (†)	— (†)	48.3 (5.39)	0.8 (0.55)	2.6 (1.03)	7.3 (2.67)	27.2 (4.70)	† (†)	26.5 (5.06)	81.1 (4.10)
Pacific Islander	—	—	— (†)	— (†)	‡ (†)	‡ (†)	‡ (†)	‡ (†)	‡ (†)	‡ (†)	‡ (†)	‡ (†)
Asian/Pacific Islander	35.9	39.7	51.1 (4.63)	49.5 (3.81)	— (†)	— (†)	— (†)	— (†)	— (†)	— (†)	— (†)	— (†)
American Indian/Alaska Native	29.3	38.8	36.3 (9.16)	50.2 (8.28)	36.3 (10.17)	† (†)	‡ (†)	‡ (†)	23.0 (8.51)	† (†)	13.0 (6.16)	70.6 (9.18)
More than one race	—	—	— (†)	—	39.4 (4.94)	0.5 (0.35)	‡ (†)	3.9 (2.20)	23.8 (4.06)	1.3 (0.59)	21.0 (4.13)	77.6 (5.28)
Highest level of education completed												
8th grade or less	7.7	10.0	14.7 (2.92)	19.7 (2.84)	15.5 (2.47)	1.3 (0.47)	4.3 (1.70)	† (†)	1.7 (0.55)	1.7 (0.91)	7.3 (1.24)	38.1 (3.27)
9th through 12th grade, no completion	15.8	20.2	25.6 (2.55)	25.5 (1.53)	27.2 (2.40)	4.2 (1.67)	1.1 (0.41)	0.8 (0.29)	7.6 (1.44)	1.5 (0.61)	12.5 (1.53)	55.7 (2.52)
High school completion	24.1	30.7	34.8 (1.37)	33.9 (1.07)	33.0 (1.62)	0.2 (0.12)	0.7 (0.24)	1.6 (0.31)	17.2 (1.18)	1.1 (0.35)	16.8 (1.27)	63.6 (1.93)
Some vocational/technical	34.2	41.9	41.1 (3.97)	50.7 (3.51)	43.3 (4.30)	‡ (†)	‡ (†)	1.1 (0.54)	28.3 (3.71)	† (†)	23.2 (3.09)	77.6 (3.98)
Some college	41.4	49.3	51.1 (1.76)	57.4 (1.29)	51.1 (1.79)	0.3 (0.18)	0.8 (0.52)	7.2 (0.99)	28.8 (1.54)	1.4 (0.47)	26.8 (1.80)	79.8 (1.52)
Associate's degree	49.2	56.1	56.6 (2.93)	62.5 (2.15)	56.5 (3.64)	‡ (†)	1.1 (0.51)	5.5 (1.36)	40.8 (3.27)	1.9 (0.66)	20.1 (2.48)	75.9 (3.70)
Bachelor's degree	51.1	56.9	60.3 (1.84)	64.5 (1.39)	59.8 (1.56)	‡ (†)	0.4 (0.17)	5.4 (0.78)	44.1 (1.61)	0.4 (0.17)	28.6 (1.55)	79.3 (1.72)
Some graduate work (or study)	55.1	59.9	63.6 (1.96)	68.9 (1.64)	66.3 (1.99)	‡ (†)	0.5 (0.32)	8.1 (0.84)	49.3 (2.15)	1.2 (0.61)	30.7 (1.77)	88.0 (1.06)
No degree	—	62.2	64.7 (4.39)	64.2 (3.54)	65.3 (4.84)	‡ (†)	0.9 (0.52)	13.7 (2.49)	40.5 (4.68)	1.4 (0.97)	38.7 (4.81)	78.2 (4.34)
Master's	—	59.1	65.7 (2.64)	70.7 (2.10)	67.5 (2.59)	‡ (†)	‡ (†)	8.4 (1.28)	51.4 (2.81)	† (†)	30.6 (2.04)	88.8 (1.33)
Doctor's	—	54.0	53.1 (4.73)	63.7 (3.98)	58.0 (4.94)	‡ (†)	‡ (†)	9.0 (3.06)	34.0 (4.53)	‡ (†)	31.4 (3.95)	90.3 (3.26)
Professional	—	65.9	72.5 (5.75)	72.8 (3.79)	68.2 (5.77)	‡ (†)	‡ (†)	1.2 (0.78)	59.0 (6.35)	‡ (†)	23.9 (4.35)	91.6 (2.15)
Urbanicity												
Urban	34.5	41.8	46.0 (0.88)	48.0 (0.70)	45.7 (0.87)	0.8 (0.27)	1.1 (0.21)	4.4 (0.31)	27.8 (0.79)	1.2 (0.20)	22.2 (0.72)	71.4 (0.86)
Urban, inside urbanized area	—	42.3	46.5 (0.95)	49.3 (0.78)	— (†)	— (†)	— (†)	— (†)	— (†)	— (†)	— (†)	— (†)
Urban, outside urbanized area	—	39.5	43.4 (2.23)	41.6 (1.70)	— (†)	— (†)	— (†)	— (†)	— (†)	— (†)	— (†)	— (†)
Rural	28.3	35.4	39.9 (1.58)	41.6 (1.17)	39.2 (2.06)	0.3 (0.13)	0.3 (0.15)	2.5 (0.50)	23.7 (1.39)	1.1 (0.40)	18.5 (1.76)	67.2 (1.77)
Labor force status												
In labor force	40.7	49.8	52.1 (0.94)	(†)	52.3 (0.93)	0.7 (0.30)	0.8 (0.19)	5.0 (0.34)	37.1 (0.83)	1.5 (0.24)	21.9 (0.91)	73.0 (0.94)
Employed	42.0	50.7	52.5 (0.96)	(†)	53.4 (0.94)	0.5 (0.29)	0.7 (0.20)	5.1 (0.35)	38.8 (0.83)	1.4 (0.24)	21.8 (0.94)	73.5 (1.01)
Unemployed	26.0	36.6	44.9 (4.60)	(†)	37.8 (4.26)	3.4 (1.24)	1.9 (0.79)	3.4 (0.99)	13.5 (2.16)	2.1 (1.23)	22.1 (3.99)	66.7 (3.80)
Not in labor force	15.7	21.3	24.9 (1.17)	(†)	27.6 (1.18)	0.7 (0.21)	1.3 (0.36)	1.8 (0.39)	5.7 (0.55)	0.6 (0.22)	20.5 (0.97)	65.2 (1.27)
Occupation												
Executive, administrative, or managerial occupations	49.3	55.8	57.0 (2.11)	66.2 (1.61)	64.1 (2.73)	‡ (†)	‡ (†)	4.9 (0.98)	51.8 (2.82)	0.4 (0.24)	28.8 (2.89)	78.6 (2.71)
Engineers, surveyors, and architects	62.6	65.5	79.8 (6.01)	68.1 (4.46)	71.2 (5.68)	‡ (†)	‡ (†)	9.3 (3.21)	55.6 (5.60)	‡ (†)	31.4 (6.19)	81.1 (4.63)

See notes at end of table.

Table 360. Participation of persons, 17 years old and over, in adult education during the previous 12 months, by selected characteristics of participants: Selected years, 1991 through 2005—Continued

Columns 2–6: Percent participating in any program. Columns 7–13: Percent participating, 2005. (Standard errors appear in parentheses.)

Characteristic of participant	1991	1995	1999	2001	In any program	In basic education[1]	In English as a second language	In part-time postsecondary education[2]	In career or job-related courses	In apprentice programs	In personal-interest courses	In informal learning activities for personal interest
1	2	3	4	5	6	7	8	9	10	11	12	13
Natural scientists and mathematicians......	48.2	72.3	60.5 (6.74)	74.0 (4.46)	69.1 (4.63)	‡ (†)	‡ (†)	7.3 (2.13)	49.6 (5.27)	2.0 (1.47)	30.2 (4.53)	85.5 (5.16)
Social scientists and workers, religious workers, and lawyers......	55.6	76.6	79.3 (4.35)	83.5 (3.05)	77.7 (4.11)	‡ (†)	‡ (†)	11.7 (3.11)	64.3 (4.42)	‡ (†)	29.2 (3.52)	89.4 (2.78)
Teachers, elementary/secondary......	55.0	54.8	66.5 (5.61)	79.9 (2.95)	79.7 (2.59)	‡ (†)	1.6 (1.00)	14.6 (2.49)	65.0 (3.99)	0.6 (0.34)	31.7 (3.78)	83.8 (2.62)
Teachers, postsecondary and counselors, librarians, and archivists......	45.5	76.7	78.4 (3.11)	69.4 (4.60)	61.3 (6.96)	‡ (†)	‡ (†)	8.3 (3.16)	49.0 (8.50)	‡ (†)	19.5 (4.98)	91.7 (3.58)
Health diagnosing and treating practitioners......	67.1	71.1	79.8 (9.02)	78.5 (6.38)	88.8 (5.59)	‡ (†)	‡ (†)	‡ (†)	79.5 (6.59)	‡ (†)	31.9 (9.15)	84.5 (5.63)
Registered nurses, pharmacists, dieticians, therapists, and physician's assistants......	59.6	86.7	85.4 (4.10)	82.7 (3.83)	85.4 (4.05)	‡ (†)	‡ (†)	7.6 (2.15)	78.2 (4.89)	‡ (†)	27.4 (3.73)	83.1 (3.92)
Writers, artists, entertainers, and athletes......	42.9	49.9	50.0 (6.93)	46.8 (6.03)	52.5 (6.59)	‡ (†)	‡ (†)	4.7 (2.13)	27.8 (5.02)	2.2 (1.53)	35.3 (6.42)	88.2 (3.89)
Health technologists and technicians......	68.6	74.8	66.9 (6.16)	85.6 (3.25)	72.1 (8.37)	‡ (†)	‡ (†)	6.0 (2.08)	63.2 (8.67)	1.7 (1.23)	24.6 (5.91)	75.6 (7.26)
Technologists and technicians, except health......	55.4	64.3	59.6 (5.07)	70.2 (3.32)	33.8 (8.53)	‡ (†)	‡ (†)	2.3 (1.76)	29.1 (7.68)	1.4 (0.80)	6.2 (2.14)	76.0 (8.80)
Marketing and sales occupations......	34.4	44.2	44.4 (2.73)	51.1 (2.10)	45.7 (3.00)	1.0 (0.45)	0.4 (0.26)	3.7 (0.76)	30.2 (2.77)	‡ (†)	21.5 (2.43)	68.9 (3.37)
Administrative support occupations, including clerical......	29.9	51.7	50.1 (2.29)	58.7 (1.72)	54.6 (2.70)	‡ (†)	‡ (†)	4.9 (0.84)	33.5 (2.70)	1.3 (0.63)	27.7 (2.18)	73.8 (2.33)
Service occupations......	25.2	46.5	50.9 (2.74)	49.3 (2.24)	44.7 (2.47)	0.6 (0.19)	1.9 (0.88)	5.8 (1.38)	28.5 (2.64)	1.4 (0.57)	17.5 (2.10)	65.4 (2.71)
Agriculture, forestry, and fishing occupations......	14.3	26.4	34.3 (7.16)	46.4 (6.80)	44.4 (9.02)	‡ (†)	5.7 (4.02)	‡ (†)	20.3 (6.92)	2.3 (1.53)	21.6 (10.05)	64.0 (10.03)
Mechanics and repairers......	32.1	47.6	42.2 (5.44)	35.1 (3.40)	40.1 (5.10)	‡ (†)	‡ (†)	1.4 (0.74)	27.4 (4.26)	3.8 (1.38)	12.7 (3.18)	69.3 (4.27)
Construction and extractive occupations......	21.9	38.0	34.5 (4.78)	32.3 (3.19)	27.6 (3.73)	0.6 (0.33)	1.1 (0.49)	1.6 (0.87)	12.3 (2.54)	5.2 (1.89)	11.4 (2.72)	72.3 (4.48)
Precision production[3]......	31.2	43.0	38.3 (8.48)	35.1 (6.19)	33.0 (3.98)	‡ (†)	0.4 (0.16)	2.8 (1.29)	22.2 (3.41)	1.5 (0.81)	13.3 (2.99)	63.9 (3.46)
Production workers......	21.1	30.7	38.0 (3.47)	39.4 (2.82)	— (†)	— (†)	— (†)	— (†)	— (†)	— (†)	— (†)	— (†)
Transportation, material moving......	20.7	28.4	33.3 (4.25)	30.4 (3.29)	34.6 (5.27)	3.6 (3.31)	3.3 (2.35)	1.2 (0.70)	14.7 (2.63)	3.2 (1.57)	11.2 (2.85)	60.8 (4.98)
Handler, equipment, cleaners, helpers, and laborers......	20.8	25.1	19.6 (4.56)	18.2 (3.20)	— (†)	— (†)	— (†)	— (†)	— (†)	— (†)	— (†)	— (†)
Miscellaneous occupations......	—	56.6	43.0 (7.98)	64.9 (7.07)	39.2 (11.25)	‡ (†)	‡ (†)	‡ (†)	15.7 (5.81)	‡ (†)	7.8 (3.63)	52.2 (12.32)
Annual household income												
$5,000 or less......	13.6	21.3	21.0 (3.22)	25.1 (2.92)	35.9 (4.83)	0.5 (0.29)	1.8 (1.04)	2.3 (1.38)	13.7 (4.00)	2.3 (1.89)	17.2 (3.59)	52.9 (4.97)
$5,001 to $10,000......	17.5	23.9	24.5 (3.39)	28.0 (2.74)	29.6 (4.49)	0.9 (0.39)	1.5 (0.71)	1.2 (0.52)	8.4 (2.11)	‡ (†)	21.8 (4.75)	61.0 (3.75)
$10,001 to $15,000......	22.8	26.7	22.8 (2.45)	28.6 (2.30)	25.0 (3.41)	0.8 (0.31)	0.8 (0.33)	3.0 (1.17)	11.3 (2.52)	0.9 (0.66)	15.5 (3.14)	58.6 (4.43)
$15,001 to $20,000......	21.9	31.8	31.4 (2.75)	30.2 (2.48)	24.3 (2.54)	‡ (†)	0.5 (0.30)	3.0 (1.18)	10.1 (1.37)	2.6 (1.20)	12.9 (2.00)	61.1 (3.17)
$20,001 to $25,000......	26.7	31.4	35.8 (2.81)	28.2 (2.27)	28.2 (2.51)	1.6 (0.77)	1.9 (0.62)	3.3 (1.13)	12.8 (2.04)	1.1 (0.50)	13.6 (1.88)	63.2 (3.11)
$25,001 to $30,000......	32.1	37.9	36.7 (2.61)	38.3 (2.43)	38.6 (3.63)	0.9 (0.54)	1.3 (0.61)	5.3 (2.03)	20.2 (3.37)	0.7 (0.38)	18.4 (2.52)	71.0 (3.38)
$30,001 to $40,000......	35.6	42.7	45.2 (2.05)	44.6 (1.54)	42.7 (2.65)	1.4 (0.54)	1.0 (0.49)	2.8 (0.64)	22.8 (2.27)	1.1 (0.39)	23.0 (2.49)	68.7 (2.36)
$40,001 to $50,000......	44.8	46.8	47.9 (2.31)	49.1 (1.93)	41.4 (2.92)	0.7 (0.35)	2.4 (1.25)	2.0 (0.43)	22.4 (2.00)	1.5 (0.56)	20.5 (2.47)	71.9 (2.62)
$50,001 to $75,000......	46.6	52.0	55.1 (1.80)	55.7 (1.48)	47.7 (1.74)	0.3 (0.15)	0.3 (0.17)	5.0 (0.63)	33.0 (1.37)	0.9 (0.36)	20.5 (1.67)	70.6 (2.15)
More than $75,000......	48.7	58.0	56.9 (1.66)	59.5 (1.29)	57.5 (1.49)	0.7 (0.50)	0.5 (0.23)	5.0 (0.53)	39.1 (1.35)	1.3 (0.38)	26.9 (1.13)	78.5 (1.34)

—Not available.
†Not applicable.
‡Reporting standards not met.
[1]The estimates of participation in basic education include only those participating in courses to improve "reading, writing, and math skills," and do not count participation in GED or other high-school equivalency courses.
[2]Includes college and university degree and post-degree certificate programs.
[3]For 2005, figures include "Production workers" occupations data.

NOTE: Adult education is defined as all education activities, except full-time enrollment in higher education credential programs. Data do not include persons enrolled in high school or below. Race categories exclude persons of Hispanic origin. Standard errors appear in parentheses.
SOURCE: U.S. Department of Education, National Center for Education Statistics, Adult Education Survey (AE-NHES:1991, AE-NHES:1995, AE-NHES:1999, and AE-NHES:2005) and Adult Education and Lifelong Learning Survey (AELL-NHES:2001) of the National Household Education Surveys Program. (This table was prepared October 2006.)

Table 361. Number of non-degree-granting Title IV institutions offering postsecondary education, by control and state or jurisdiction: Selected years, 2000–01 through 2005–06

State or jurisdiction	2000–01, total	2003–04 Total	Public	Private Total	Not-for-profit	For-profit	2004–05 Total	Public	Private Total	Not-for-profit	For-profit	2005–06 Total	Public	Private Total	Not-for-profit	For-profit
1	2	3	4	5	6	7	8	9	10	11	12	13	14	15	16	17
United States	2,297	2,176	327	1,849	249	1,600	2,167	327	1,840	238	1,602	2,187	320	1,867	219	1,648
Alabama	10	8	0	8	2	6	8	0	8	2	6	9	0	9	2	7
Alaska	3	2	1	1	0	1	2	1	1	0	1	2	1	1	0	1
Arizona	33	32	3	29	0	29	32	3	29	0	29	34	3	31	0	31
Arkansas	36	32	4	28	3	25	31	3	28	3	25	32	3	29	3	26
California	230	233	11	222	31	191	229	9	220	29	191	235	8	227	28	199
Colorado	21	24	4	20	2	18	25	4	21	2	19	26	4	22	2	20
Connecticut	37	35	0	35	5	30	33	0	33	5	28	36	0	36	5	31
Delaware	4	5	0	5	1	4	6	0	6	1	5	6	0	6	1	5
District of Columbia	5	5	0	5	2	3	6	0	6	2	4	6	0	6	2	4
Florida	124	121	37	84	6	78	119	37	82	7	75	126	37	89	4	85
Georgia	38	45	1	44	1	43	46	1	45	1	44	44	1	43	2	41
Hawaii	6	5	0	5	0	5	6	0	6	1	5	5	0	5	0	5
Idaho	11	12	0	12	0	12	12	0	12	0	12	13	0	13	0	13
Illinois	88	86	2	84	16	68	89	3	86	15	71	94	2	92	13	79
Indiana	34	33	4	29	1	28	29	3	26	1	25	28	3	25	1	24
Iowa	27	26	0	26	2	24	26	0	26	2	24	26	0	26	2	24
Kansas	23	23	4	19	2	17	23	4	19	2	17	25	4	21	2	19
Kentucky	52	29	0	29	1	28	30	0	30	1	29	32	0	32	2	30
Louisiana	57	53	3	50	2	48	54	7	47	2	45	57	9	48	2	46
Maine	11	12	0	12	3	9	10	0	10	4	6	9	0	9	3	6
Maryland	34	24	0	24	0	24	26	0	26	0	26	27	0	27	0	27
Massachusetts	60	55	5	50	5	45	57	5	52	3	49	61	5	56	3	53
Michigan	72	64	2	62	5	57	64	2	62	4	58	65	2	63	3	60
Minnesota	20	19	0	19	5	14	20	1	19	4	15	21	0	21	4	17
Mississippi	16	18	0	18	0	18	17	0	17	0	17	20	0	20	0	20
Missouri	69	61	25	36	5	31	61	25	36	5	31	61	25	36	4	32
Montana	10	7	0	7	2	5	8	0	8	1	7	8	0	8	1	7
Nebraska	12	9	0	9	3	6	9	0	9	3	6	10	0	10	3	7
Nevada	10	7	0	7	1	6	7	0	7	1	6	9	0	9	2	7
New Hampshire	11	12	0	12	3	9	13	0	13	3	10	14	0	14	3	11
New Jersey	89	90	5	85	11	74	90	5	85	11	74	91	4	87	10	77
New Mexico	6	9	0	9	0	9	7	0	7	0	7	7	0	7	0	7
New York	152	138	30	108	44	64	138	32	106	37	69	133	32	101	33	68
North Carolina	36	31	1	30	3	27	30	1	29	3	26	29	1	28	2	26
North Dakota	5	5	0	5	0	5	5	0	5	0	5	5	0	5	0	5
Ohio	130	127	51	76	12	64	125	50	75	13	62	119	50	69	12	57
Oklahoma	84	83	46	37	1	36	79	46	33	0	33	78	45	33	0	33
Oregon	28	27	0	27	0	27	29	0	29	0	29	27	0	27	0	27
Pennsylvania	167	151	33	118	31	87	140	31	109	30	79	131	29	102	27	75
Rhode Island	12	10	0	10	1	9	10	0	10	2	8	10	0	10	2	8
South Carolina	14	15	1	14	0	14	18	1	17	0	17	21	0	21	0	21
South Dakota	5	5	0	5	3	2	6	0	6	3	3	6	0	6	3	3
Tennessee	54	53	26	27	2	25	54	26	28	2	26	58	26	32	2	30
Texas	161	162	3	159	4	155	169	4	165	4	161	169	0	169	4	165
Utah	26	24	3	21	0	21	23	2	21	0	21	24	2	22	0	22
Vermont	3	3	0	3	1	2	4	1	3	1	2	4	1	3	1	2
Virginia	56	51	8	43	8	35	46	6	40	9	31	42	7	35	7	28
Washington	42	43	1	42	4	38	44	1	43	4	39	37	1	36	4	32
West Virginia	36	30	12	18	8	10	30	12	18	8	10	31	14	17	7	10
Wisconsin	24	20	0	20	7	13	20	0	20	7	13	22	0	22	8	14
Wyoming	3	2	1	1	0	1	2	1	1	0	1	2	1	1	0	1
Other jurisdictions	74	69	0	69	8	61	75	0	75	9	66	74	0	74	9	65
American Samoa	0	0	0	0	0	0	0	0	0	0	0	0	0	0	0	0
Guam	0	0	0	0	0	0	0	0	0	0	0	0	0	0	0	0
Northern Marianas	0	0	0	0	0	0	0	0	0	0	0	0	0	0	0	0
Palau	0	0	0	0	0	0	0	0	0	0	0	0	0	0	0	0
Puerto Rico	74	69	0	69	8	61	75	0	75	9	66	74	0	74	9	65
Virgin Islands	0	0	0	0	0	0	0	0	0	0	0	0	0	0	0	0

NOTE: Includes all Title IV institutions that did not grant degrees at the associate's or higher level.

SOURCE: U.S. Department of Education, National Center for Education Statistics, 2000–01 through 2005–06 Integrated Postsecondary Education Data System (IPEDS), Fall 2000 through Fall 2005. (This table was prepared August 2006.)

CHAPTER 4
Federal Programs for Education and Related Activities

This chapter provides a summary of federal legislation and funds for education to describe the scope and variety of federal education programs. Data in this chapter reflect outlays and obligations of federal agencies. These tabulations differ from federal receipts reported in other chapters because of numerous variations in the data collection systems. Federal dollars are not necessarily spent by recipient institutions in the same year they are appropriated. In some cases, institutions cannot identify the source of federal revenues because they flow through state agencies. Some types of revenues, such as tuition and fees, are reported as revenues from students even though they may be supported by federal student aid programs. Some institutions that receive federal education funds are not included in regular surveys conducted by the National Center for Education Statistics (NCES). Thus, the federal programs data tabulated in this chapter are not comparable with figures reported in other chapters. Readers should be careful about comparing data on obligations shown in some tables with data on outlays and appropriations appearing in others.

Federal on-budget funding for education showed sizable growth between fiscal years (FYs) 1965 and 2006, after adjustment for inflation (table 362). Large increases occurred between 1965 and 1975. After a slight decrease from 1975 to 1980, there was a further decrease from 1980 to 1985 (16 percent). Thereafter, federal on-budget funding for education generally increased. After adjustment for inflation, federal on-budget funding for education increased by 14 percent from 1985 to 1990, by 20 percent from 1990 to 1995, by 9 percent from 1995 to 2000, and by 65 percent from 2000 to 2006.

Between 1990 and 1995, after adjustment for inflation, federal funds increased for each of the four major categories reported: elementary and secondary education (by 32 percent), postsecondary education (by 12 percent), other education (by 21 percent), and research at educational institutions (by 7 percent) (table 362 and figure 18). During the 1995 to 2000 period, federal funding increased for three of these categories: elementary and secondary education (by 19 percent), other education (by 6 percent), and research at educational institutions (by 26 percent). During the same period, however, funding for postsecondary education decreased by 22 percent. From 2000 to 2006, funding once again increased across all four categories, with a 38 percent increase for elementary and secondary education, a 226 percent increase for postsecond-

ary education, a 12 percent increase for other education, and a 21 percent increase for research at educational institutions.

Off-budget support (federal support for education not tied to appropriations) and nonfederal funds generated by federal legislation (e.g., private loans, grants, and aid) showed an increase in constant dollars between FY 1980 and FY 2006 (441 percent), but there were fluctuations throughout the period (table 362). Changes in interest rates and program legislation, which affect the number and volume of student loans, may play a role in these fluctuations. Between FY 1990 and FY 2006, these same funds showed an increase of 268 percent.

According to FY 2006 estimates, $93.9 billion (about 57 percent of the $166.1 billion spent by the federal government on education) came from the U.S. Department of Education (figure 19 and table 363). Large amounts of money also came from the U.S. Department of Health and Human Services ($25.8 billion), the U.S. Department of Agriculture ($14.5 billion), the U.S. Department of Defense ($6.2 billion), the U.S. Department of Veterans Affairs ($4.5 billion), the U.S. Department of Labor ($4.2 billion), the National Science Foundation ($4.1 billion), and the U.S. Department of Energy ($4.0 billion).

For FY 2006, estimates show federal program funds for elementary and secondary education at $70.7 billion, for postsecondary education at $57.4 billion, for research at universities and related institutions at $30.8 billion, and for other programs at $7.2 billion (table 364).

In 2006, educational institutions (including local education agencies, state education agencies, and degree-granting institutions) received 64 percent of federal program funds for education (table 365). Another 18 percent was used for postsecondary student support. Multiple recipients (including libraries and museums) received 10 percent, banks and other lending agencies received 5 percent, and federal institutions received 3 percent.

Of the $93.9 billion spent by the U.S. Department of Education in FY 2006, about 33 percent ($30.6 billion) went to local education agencies (school districts) and 9 percent ($8.5 billion) to state education agencies (table 366 and figure 20). About 23 percent ($21.3 billion) went to postsecondary institutions and another 24 percent ($22.7 billion) to postsecondary students. Smaller percentages (totaling $10.8 billion) went to federal agencies, multiple recipients, and other recipients.

Chronology of Federal Education Legislation

A capsule view of the history of federal education activities is provided in the following list of selected legislation:

1787 *Northwest Ordinance* authorized land grants for the establishment of educational institutions.

1802 *An Act Fixing the Military Peace Establishment of the United States* established the U.S. Military Academy. (The U.S. Naval Academy was established in 1845 by the Secretary of the Navy.)

1862 *First Morrill Act* authorized public land grants to the states for the establishment and maintenance of agricultural and mechanical colleges.

1867 *Department of Education Act* authorized the establishment of the U.S. Department of Education.[1]

1876 *Appropriation Act*, U.S. Department of the Treasury, established the U.S. Coast Guard Academy.

1890 *Second Morrill Act* provided for money grants for support of instruction in the agricultural and mechanical colleges.

1911 *State Marine School Act* authorized federal funds to be used for the benefit of any nautical school in any of 11 specified state seaport cities.

1917 *Smith-Hughes Act* provided for grants to states for support of vocational education.

1918 *Vocational Rehabilitation Act* provided for grants for rehabilitation through training of World War I veterans.

1920 *Smith-Bankhead Act* authorized grants to states for vocational rehabilitation programs.

1935 *Bankhead-Jones Act* (Public Law 74-182) authorized grants to states for agricultural experiment stations.

Agricultural Adjustment Act (Public Law 74-320) authorized 30 percent of the annual customs receipts to be used to encourage the exportation and domestic consumption of agricultural commodities. Commodities purchased under this authorization began to be used in school lunch programs in 1936. The National School Lunch Act of 1946 continued and expanded this assistance.

1936 *An Act to Further the Development and Maintenance of an Adequate and Well-Balanced American Merchant Marine* (Public Law 74-415) established the U.S. Merchant Marine Academy.

1937 *National Cancer Institute Act* established the Public Health Service fellowship program.

---

[1] The U.S. Department of Education as established in 1867 was later known as the Office of Education. In 1980, under Public Law 96-88, it became a cabinet-level department. Therefore, for purposes of consistency, it is referred to as the "U.S. Department of Education" even in those tables covering years when it was officially the Office of Education.

1941 *Amendment to Lanham Act of 1940* authorized federal aid for construction, maintenance, and operation of schools in federally impacted areas. Such assistance was continued under Public Law 815 and Public Law 874, 81st Congress, in 1950.

1943 *Vocational Rehabilitation Act* (Public Law 78-16) provided assistance to disabled veterans.

School Lunch Indemnity Plan (Public Law 78-129) provided funds for local lunch food purchases.

1944 *Servicemen's Readjustment Act* (Public Law 78-346), known as the GI Bill, provided assistance for the education of veterans.

Surplus Property Act (Public Law 78-457) authorized transfer of surplus property to educational institutions.

1946 *National School Lunch Act* (Public Law 79-396) authorized assistance through grants-in-aid and other means to states to assist in providing adequate foods and facilities for the establishment, maintenance, operation, and expansion of nonprofit school lunch programs.

George-Barden Act (Public Law 80-402) expanded federal support of vocational education.

1948 *United States Information and Educational Exchange Act* (Public Law 80-402) provided for the interchange of persons, knowledge, and skills between the United States and other countries.

1949 *Federal Property and Administrative Services Act* (Public Law 81-152) provided for donation of surplus property to educational institutions and for other public purposes.

1950 *Financial Assistance for Local Educational Agencies Affected by Federal Activities* (Public Law 81-815 and Public Law 81-874) provided assistance for construction (Public Law 815) and operation (Public Law 874) of schools in federally affected areas.

Housing Act (Public Law 81-475) authorized loans for construction of college housing facilities.

1954 *An Act for the Establishment of the United States Air Force Academy and Other Purposes* (Public Law 83-325) established the U.S. Air Force Academy.

Educational Research Act (Public Law 83-531) authorized cooperative arrangements with universities, colleges, and state educational agencies for educational research.

School Milk Program Act (Public Law 83-597) provided funds for purchase of milk for school lunch programs.

1956 *Library Services Act* (Public Law 84-597) provided grants to states for extension and improvement of rural public library services.

1957 *Practical Nurse Training Act* (Public Law 84-911) provided grants to states for practical nurse training.

1958 *National Defense Education Act* (Public Law 85-864) provided assistance to state and local school systems for strengthening instruction in science, mathematics, modern foreign languages, and other critical subjects; improvement of state statistical services; guidance, counseling, and testing services and training institutes; higher education student loans and fellowships; foreign language study and training provided by colleges and universities; experimentation and dissemination of information on more effective utilization of television, motion pictures, and related media for educational purposes; and vocational education for technical occupations necessary to the national defense.

Education of Mentally Retarded Children Act (Public Law 85-926) authorized federal assistance for training teachers of the handicapped.

Captioned Films for the Deaf Act (Public Law 85-905) authorized a loan service of captioned films for the deaf.

1961 *Area Redevelopment Act* (Public Law 87-27) included provisions for training or retraining of persons in redevelopment areas.

1962 *Manpower Development and Training Act* (Public Law 87-415) provided training in new and improved skills for the unemployed and underemployed.

Migration and Refugee Assistance Act of 1962 (Public Law 87-510) authorized loans, advances, and grants for education and training of refugees.

1963 *Health Professions Educational Assistance Act of 1963* (Public Law 88-129) provided funds to expand teaching facilities and for loans to students in the health professions.

Vocational Education Act of 1963 (Part of Public Law 88-210) increased federal support of vocational education schools; vocational work-study programs; and research, training, and demonstrations in vocational education.

Higher Education Facilities Act of 1963 (Public Law 88-204) authorized grants and loans for classrooms, libraries, and laboratories in public community colleges and technical institutes, as well as undergraduate and graduate facilities in other institutions of higher education.

1964 *Civil Rights Act of 1964* (Public Law 88-352) authorized the Commissioner of Education to arrange for support for institutions of higher education and school districts to provide inservice programs for assisting instructional staff in dealing with problems caused by desegregation.

Economic Opportunity Act of 1964 (Public Law 88-452) authorized grants for college work-study programs for students from low-income families; established a Job Corps program and authorized support for work-training programs to provide education and vocational training and work experience opportunities in welfare programs; authorized support of education and training activities and of community action programs, including Head Start, Follow Through, and Upward Bound; and authorized the establishment of Volunteers in Service to America (VISTA).

1965 *Elementary and Secondary Education Act of 1965* (Public Law 89-10) authorized grants for elementary and secondary school programs for children of low-income families; school library resources, textbooks, and other instructional materials for school children; supplementary educational centers and services; strengthening state education agencies; and educational research and research training.

Health Professions Educational Assistance Amendments of 1965 (Public Law 89-290) authorized scholarships to aid needy students in the health professions.

Higher Education Act of 1965 (Public Law 89-329) provided grants for university community service programs, college library assistance, library training and research, strengthening developing institutions, teacher training programs, and undergraduate instructional equipment. Authorized insured student loans, established a National Teacher Corps, and provided for graduate teacher training fellowships.

National Foundation on the Arts and the Humanities Act (Public Law 89-209) authorized grants and loans for projects in the creative and performing arts and for research, training, and scholarly publications in the humanities.

National Technical Institute for the Deaf Act (Public Law 89-36) provided for the establishment, construction, equipping, and operation of a residential school for postsecondary education and technical training of the deaf.

School Assistance in Disaster Areas Act (Public Law 89-313) provided for assistance to local education agencies to help meet exceptional costs resulting from a major disaster.

1966 *International Education Act* (Public Law 89-698) provided grants to institutions of higher education for the establishment, strengthening, and operation of centers for research and training in international studies and the international aspects of other fields of study.

National Sea Grant College and Program Act (Public Law 89-688) authorized the establishment and operation of Sea Grant Colleges and programs by initiating and supporting programs of education and research in the various fields relating to the development of marine resources.

Adult Education Act (Public Law 89-750) authorized grants to states for the encouragement and expansion of educational programs for adults, including training of teachers of adults and demonstrations in adult education (previously part of Economic Opportunity Act of 1964).

Model Secondary School for the Deaf Act (Public Law 89-694) authorized the establishment and operation, by Gallaudet College, of a model secondary school for the deaf.

1967 *Education Professions Development Act* (Public Law 90-35) amended the Higher Education Act of 1965 for the purpose of improving the quality of teaching and to help meet critical shortages of adequately trained educational personnel.

Public Broadcasting Act of 1967 (Public Law 90-129) established a Corporation for Public Broadcasting to assume major responsibility in channeling federal funds to noncommercial radio and television stations, program production groups, and ETV networks; conduct research, demonstration, or training in matters related to noncommercial broadcasting; and award grants for construction of educational radio and television facilities.

1968 *Elementary and Secondary Education Amendments of 1968* (Public Law 90-247) modified existing programs, authorized support of regional centers for education of handicapped children, model centers and services for deaf-blind children, recruitment of personnel and dissemination of information on education of the handicapped; technical assistance in education to rural areas; support of dropout prevention projects; and support of bilingual education programs.

Handicapped Children's Early Education Assistance Act (Public Law 90-538) authorized preschool and early education programs for handicapped children.

Vocational Education Amendments of 1968 (Public Law 90-576) modified existing programs and provided for a National Advisory Council on Vocational Education and collection and dissemination of information for programs administered by the Commissioner of Education.

1970 *Elementary and Secondary Education Assistance Programs, Extension* (Public Law 91-230) authorized comprehensive planning and evaluation grants to state and local education agencies; provided for the establishment of a National Commission on School Finance.

National Commission on Libraries and Information Services Act (Public Law 91-345) established a National Commission on Libraries and Information Science to effectively utilize the nation's educational resources.

Office of Education Appropriation Act (Public Law 91-380) provided emergency school assistance to desegregating local education agencies.

Environmental Education Act (Public Law 91-516) established an Office of Environmental Education to develop curriculum and initiate and maintain environmental education programs at the elementary-secondary levels; disseminate information; provide training programs for teachers and other educational, public, community, labor, and industrial leaders and employees; provide community education programs; and distribute material dealing with the environment and ecology.

Drug Abuse Education Act of 1970 (Public Law 91-527) provided for development, demonstration, and evaluation of curricula on the problems of drug abuse.

1971 *Comprehensive Health Manpower Training Act of 1971* (Public Law 92-257) amended Title VII of the Public Health Service Act, increasing and expanding provisions for health manpower training and training facilities.

1972 *Drug Abuse Office and Treatment Act of 1972* (Public Law 92-255) established a Special Action Office for Drug Abuse Prevention to provide overall planning and policy for all federal drug-abuse prevention functions; a National Advisory Council for Drug Abuse Prevention; community assistance grants for community mental health centers for treatment and rehabilitation of persons with drug-abuse problems; and, in December 1974, a National Institute on Drug Abuse.

Education Amendments of 1972 (Public Law 92-318) established the Education Division in the U.S. Department of Health, Education, and Welfare and the National Institute of Education; general aid for institutions of higher education; federal matching grants for state Student Incentive Grants; a National Commission on Financing Postsecondary Education; State Advisory Councils on Community Colleges; a Bureau of Occupational and Adult Education and State Grants for the design, establishment, and conduct of postsecondary occupational education; and a bureau-level Office of Indian Education. Amended current U.S. Department of Education programs to increase their effectiveness and better meet special needs. Prohibited sex bias in admission to vocational, professional, and graduate schools, and public institutions of undergraduate higher education.

1973 *Older Americans Comprehensive Services Amendment of 1973* (Public Law 93-29) made available to older citizens comprehensive programs of health, education, and social services.

Comprehensive Employment and Training Act of 1973 (Public Law 93-203) provided for opportunities for employment and training to unemployed and underemployed persons. Extended and expanded provisions in the Manpower Development and Training Act of 1962, Title I of the Economic Opportunity Act of 1962, Title I of the Economic Opportunity Act of 1964, and the Emergency Employment Act of 1971 as in effect prior to June 30, 1973.

1974 *Education Amendments of 1974* (Public Law 93-380) provided for the consolidation of certain programs;

and established a National Center for Education Statistics.

Juvenile Justice and Delinquency Prevention Act of 1974 (Public Law 93-415) provided for technical assistance, staff training, centralized research, and resources to develop and implement programs to keep students in elementary and secondary schools; and established, in the U.S. Department of Justice, a National Institute for Juvenile Justice and Delinquency Prevention.

1975 *Indian Self-Determination and Education Assistance Act* (Public Law 93-638) provided for increased participation of Indians in the establishment and conduct of their education programs and services.

Harry S Truman Memorial Scholarship Act (Public Law 93-642) established the Harry S Truman Scholarship Foundation and created a perpetual education scholarship fund for young Americans to prepare and pursue careers in public service.

Indochina Migration and Refugee Assistance Act of 1975 (Public Law 94-23) authorized funds to be used for education and training of aliens who have fled from Cambodia or Vietnam.

Education for All Handicapped Children Act (Public Law 94-142) provided that all handicapped children have available to them a free appropriate education designed to meet their unique needs.

1976 *Educational Broadcasting Facilities and Telecommunications Demonstration Act of 1976* (Public Law 94-309) established a telecommunications demonstration program to promote the development of nonbroadcast telecommunications facilities and services for the transmission, distribution, and delivery of health, education, and public or social service information.

1977 *Youth Employment and Demonstration Projects Act of 1977* (Public Law 95-93) established a youth employment training program that includes, among other activities, promoting education-to-work transition, literacy training and bilingual training, and attainment of certificates of high school equivalency.

Career Education Incentive Act (Public Law 95-207) authorized the establishment of a career education program for elementary and secondary schools.

1978 *Tribally Controlled Community College Assistance Act of 1978* (Public Law 95-471) provided federal funds for the operation and improvement of tribally controlled community colleges for Indian students.

Education Amendments of 1978 (Public Law 95-561) established a comprehensive basic skills program aimed at improving pupil achievement (replaced the existing National Reading Improvement program); and established a community schools program to provide for the use of public buildings.

Middle Income Student Assistance Act (Public Law 95-566) modified the provisions for student financial assistance programs to allow middle-income as well as low-income students attending college or other postsecondary institutions to qualify for federal education assistance.

1979 *Department of Education Organization Act* (Public Law 96-88) established a U.S. Department of Education containing functions from the Education Division of the U.S. Department of Health, Education, and Welfare along with other selected education programs from HEW, the U.S. Department of Justice, U.S. Department of Labor, and the National Science Foundation.

1980 *Asbestos School Hazard Detection and Control Act of 1980* (Public Law 96-270) established a program for inspection of schools for detection of hazardous asbestos materials and provided loans to assist educational agencies to contain or remove and replace such materials.

1981 *Education Consolidation and Improvement Act of 1981* (Part of Public Law 97-35) consolidated 42 programs into 7 programs to be funded under the elementary and secondary block grant authority.

1983 *Student Loan Consolidation and Technical Amendments Act of 1983* (Public Law 98-79) established an 8 percent interest rate for Guaranteed Student Loans and an extended Family Contribution Schedule.

Challenge Grant Amendments of 1983 (Public Law 98-95) amended Title III, Higher Education Act, and added authorization of Challenge Grant program. The Challenge Grant program provides funds to eligible institutions on a matching basis as an incentive to seek alternative sources of funding.

Education of the Handicapped Act Amendments of 1983 (Public Law 98-199) added the Architectural Barrier amendment and clarified participation of handicapped children in private schools.

1984 *Education for Economic Security Act* (Public Law 98-377) added new science and mathematics programs for elementary, secondary, and postsecondary education. The new programs included magnet schools, excellence in education, and equal access.

Carl D. Perkins Vocational Education Act (Public Law 98-524) continued federal assistance for vocational education through FY 1989. The act replaced the Vocational Education Act of 1963. It provided aid to the states to make vocational education programs accessible to all persons, including handicapped and disadvantaged, single parents and homemakers, and the incarcerated.

Human Services Reauthorization Act (Public Law 98-558) created a Carl D. Perkins scholarship program, a National Talented Teachers Fellowship program, a

Federal Merit Scholarships program, and a Leadership in Educational Administration program.

1985 *Montgomery GI Bill—Active Duty* (Public Law 98-525), brought about a new GI Bill for individuals who initially entered active military duty on or after July 1, 1985.

Montgomery GI Bill—Selected Reserve (Public Law 98-525), established an education program for members of the Selected Reserve (which includes the National Guard) who enlist, reenlist, or extend an enlistment after June 30, 1985, for a 6-year period.

1986 *Handicapped Children's Protection Act of 1986* (Public Law 99-372) allowed parents of handicapped children to collect attorneys' fees in cases brought under the Education of the Handicapped Act and provided that the Education of the Handicapped Act does not preempt other laws, such as Section 504 of the Rehabilitation Act.

Drug-Free Schools and Communities Act of 1986 (Part of Public Law 99-570), part of the Anti-Drug Abuse Act of 1986, authorized funding for FYs 1987–89. Established programs for drug abuse education and prevention, coordinated with related community efforts and resources, through the use of federal financial assistance.

1988 *Augustus F. Hawkins-Robert T. Stafford Elementary and Secondary School Improvement Amendments of 1988* (Public Law 100-297) reauthorized through 1993 major elementary and secondary education programs including: Chapter 1, Chapter 2, Bilingual Education, Math-Science Education, Magnet Schools, Impact Aid, Indian Education, Adult Education, and other smaller education programs.

Technology-Related Assistance for Individuals with Disabilities Act of 1988 (Public Law 100-407) provided financial assistance to states to develop and implement consumer-responsive statewide programs of technology-related assistance for persons of all ages with disabilities.

Stewart B. McKinney Homeless Assistance Amendments Act of 1988 (Public Law 100-628) extended for 2 additional years programs providing assistance to the homeless, including literacy training for homeless adults and education for homeless youths.

Tax Reform Technical Amendments (Public Law 100-647) authorized an Education Savings Bond for the purpose of postsecondary educational expenses. The bill grants tax exclusion for interest earned on regular series EE savings bonds.

1989 *Children with Disabilities Temporary Care Reauthorization Act of 1989* (Public Law 101-127) revised and extended the programs established in the Temporary Child Care for Handicapped Children and Crises Nurseries Act of 1986.

Childhood Education and Development Act of 1989 (Part of Public Law 101-239) authorized the appropriations to expand Head Start Programs and programs carried out under the Elementary and Secondary Education Act of 1965 to include child care services.

1990 *Excellence in Mathematics, Science and Engineering Education Act of 1990* (Public Law 101-589) was established to promote excellence in American mathematics, science, and engineering education by creating a national mathematics and science clearinghouse, and creating several other mathematics, science, and engineering education programs.

Student Right-To-Know and Campus Security Act (Public Law 101-542) required institutions of higher education receiving federal financial assistance to provide certain information with respect to the graduation rates of student-athletes at such institutions. The act also requires the institution to certify that it has a campus security policy and will annually submit a uniform crime report to the Federal Bureau of Investigation (FBI).

Americans with Disabilities Act of 1990 (Public Law 101-336) prohibited discrimination against persons with disabilities.

National and Community Service Act of 1990 (Public Law 101-610) increased school and college-based community service opportunities and authorized the President's Points of Light Foundation.

1991 *National Literacy Act of 1991* (Public Law 102-73) established the National Institute for Literacy, the National Institute Board, and the Interagency Task Force on Literacy. Amended various federal laws to establish and extend various literacy programs.

High-Performance Computing Act of 1991 (Public Law 102-194) directed the President to implement a National High-Performance Computing Program. Provided for: (1) establishment of a National Research and Education Network; (2) standards and guidelines for high performance networks; and (3) the responsibility of certain federal departments and agencies with regard to the Network.

Veterans' Educational Assistance Amendments of 1991 (Public Law 102-127) restored certain educational benefits available to reserve and active-duty personnel under the Montgomery GI Bill to students whose course of studies were interrupted by the Persian Gulf War.

Civil Rights Act of 1991 (Public Law 102-166) amended the Civil Rights Act of 1964, the Age Discrimination in Employment Act of 1967, and the Americans with Disabilities Act of 1990, with regard to employment discrimination. Established the Technical Assistance Training Institute.

1992 *Ready-To-Learn Act* (Public Law 102-545) amended the General Education Provisions Act to establish Ready-To-Learn Television programs to support educational programming and support materials for preschool and elementary school children and their parents, child care providers, and educators.

1993 *Student Loan Reform Act* (Public Law 103-66) reformed the student aid process by phasing in a system of direct lending designed to provide savings for taxpayers and students. Allows students to choose among a variety of repayment options, including income contingency.

National Service Trust Act (Public Law 103-82) amended the National and Community Service Act of 1990 to establish a Corporation for National Service and enhance opportunities for national service. In addition, the Act provided education grants up to $4,725 per year for 2 years to people age 17 years or older who perform community service before, during, or after postsecondary education.

NAEP Assessment Authorization (Public Law 103-33) authorized the use of NAEP for state-by-state comparisons.

1994 *Goals 2000: Educate America Act* (Public Law 103-227) established a new federal partnership through a system of grants to states and local communities to reform the nation's education system. The Act formalized the national education goals and established the National Education Goals Panel. It also created a National Education Standards and Improvement Council (NESIC) to provide voluntary national certification of state and local education standards and assessments and established the National Skill Standards Board to develop voluntary national skill standards.

School-To-Work Opportunities Act of 1994 (Public Law 103-239) established a national framework within which states and communities can develop School-To-Work Opportunities systems to prepare young people for first jobs and continuing education. The Act also provided money to states and communities to develop a system of programs that include work-based learning, school-based learning, and connecting activities components. School-To-Work programs will provide students with a high school diploma (or its equivalent), a nationally recognized skill certificate, or an associate degree (if appropriate) and may lead to a first job or further education.

Safe Schools Act of 1994 (Part of Public Law 103-227) authorized the award of competitive grants to local educational agencies with serious crime to implement violence prevention activities such as conflict resolution and peer mediation.

1996 *Contract With America: Unfunded Mandates* (Public Law 104-4) curbed the practice of imposing unfunded federal mandates on states and local governments; strengthened the partnership between the federal government and state, local, and tribal governments; ended the imposition, in the absence of full consideration by Congress, of federal mandates on state, local, and tribal governments without adequate funding, in a manner that may displace other essential governmental priorities; and ensured that the federal government

pays the costs incurred by those governments in complying with certain requirements under federal statutes and regulations.

Human Rights, Refugee, and Other Foreign Relations Provisions Act of 1996 (Public Law 104-319) made certain provisions with respect to internationally recognized human rights, refugees, and foreign relations to revise U.S. human rights policy.

1997 *The Taxpayer Relief Act of 1997* (Public Law 105-34) enacted the Hope Scholarship and Life-Long Learning Tax Credit provisions into law.

Emergency Student Loan Consolidation Act of 1997 (Public Law 105-78) amended the Higher Education Act to provide for improved student loan consolidation services.

1998 *Workforce Investment Act of 1998* (Public Law 105-220) enacted the Adult Education and Family Literacy Act, and substantially revised and extended, through FY 2003, the Rehabilitation Act of 1973.

Omnibus Consolidated and Emergency Supplemental Appropriations Act, 1999 (Public Law 105-277) enacted the Reading Excellence Act, to promote the ability of children to read independently by the third grade; and earmarked funds to help states and school districts reduce class sizes in the early grades.

Charter School Expansion Act (Public Law 105-278) amended the charter school program, enacted in 1994 as Title X, Part C of the Elementary and Secondary Education Act of 1965.

Carl D. Perkins Vocational and Applied Technology Education Amendments of 1998 (Public Law 105-332) revised, in its entirety, the Carl D. Perkins Vocational and Applied Technology Education Act, and reauthorized the Act through FY 2003.

Assistive Technology Act of 1998 (Public Law 105-394) replaced the Technology-Related Assistance for Individuals with Disabilities Act of 1988 with a new Act, authorized through FY 2004, to address the assistive-technology needs of individuals with disabilities.

1999 *Education Flexibility Partnership Act of 1999* (Public Law 106-25) authorized the Secretary of Education to allow all states to participate in the Education Flexibility Partnership program.

District of Columbia College Access Act of 1999 (Public Law 106-98) established a program to afford high school graduates from the District of Columbia the benefits of in-state tuition at state colleges and universities outside the District of Columbia.

2000 *The National Defense Authorization Act for Fiscal Year 2001* (Public Law 106-398) included, as Title XVIII, the Impact Aid Reauthorization Act of 2000, which extended the Impact Aid programs through FY 2003.

College Scholarship Fraud Prevention Act of 2000 (Public Law 106-420) enhanced federal penalties for offenses involving scholarship fraud; required an annual scholarship fraud report by the Attorney General, the Secretary of Education, and the Federal Trade Commission (FTC); and required the Secretary of

Education, in conjunction with the FTC, to maintain a scholarship fraud awareness website.

Consolidated Appropriations Act 2001 (Public Law 106-554) created a new program of assistance for school repair and renovation, and amended the Elementary and Secondary Education Act of 1965 to authorize credit enhancement initiatives to help charter schools obtain, construct, or repair facilities; reauthorized the Even Start program; and enacted the "Children's Internet Protection Act."

2001 *50th Anniversary of Brown v. the Board of Education* (Public Law 107-41) established a commission for the purpose of encouraging and providing for the commemoration of the 50th anniversary of the 1954 Supreme Court decision Brown v. Board of Education.

2002 *No Child Left Behind Act of 2001* (Public Law 107-110) provided for the comprehensive reauthorization of the Elementary and Secondary Education Act of 1965, incorporating specific proposals in such areas as testing, accountability, parental choice, and early reading.

Reauthorization of the National Center for Education Statistics and the Creating of the Institute of Education Sciences of 2002 (Public Law 107-279) established the Institute of Education Sciences within the U.S. Department of Education to carry out a coordinated, focused agenda of high-quality research, statistics, and evaluation that is relevant to the educational challenges of the nation. The Institute is administered by a Director, appointed by the President, and is comprised of three National Education Centers, each headed by a Commissioner.

The Higher Education Relief Opportunities for Students Act of 2001 (Public Law 107-122) provided the Secretary of Education with waiver authority under student financial aid programs under Title IV of the Higher Education Act of 1965, to deal with student and family situations resulting from the September 11, 2001, terrorist attacks.

Established fixed interest rates for student and parent borrowers (Public Law 107-139) under Title IV of the Higher Education Act of 1965.

2003 *The Higher Education Relief Opportunities for Students Act of 2003* (Public Law 108-76) provided the Secretary of Education with waiver authority under student financial aid programs under Title IV of the Higher Education Act of 1965, to deal with student and family situations resulting from wars or national emergencies.

2004 *Assistive Technology Act of 2004* (Public Law 108-364) reauthorized the Assistive Technology program, administered by the Department of Education.

Higher Education Extension Act of 2004 (Public Law 108-366) provided a 1-year extension of the Higher Education Act of 1965.

Taxpayer-Teacher Protection Act of 2004 (Public Law 108-409) temporarily stopped excessive special allowance payments to certain lenders under the Federal Family Education Loan (FFEL) Program and increases the amount of loans that can be forgiven for certain borrowers who are highly qualified mathematics, science, and special education teachers who serve in high-poverty schools for 5 years.

Individuals with Disabilities Education Improvement Act of 2004 (Public Law 108-446) provided a comprehensive reauthorization of the Individuals with Disabilities Education Act.

2005 *Student Grant Hurricane and Disaster Relief Act* (Public Law 109-67) authorized the Secretary of Education to waive certain repayment requirements for students receiving campus-based federal grant assistance if they were residing in, employed in, or attending an institution of higher education located in a major disaster area, or their attendance was interrupted because of the disaster.

Natural Disaster Student Aid Fairness Act (Public Law 109-86) authorized the Secretary of Education during FY 2006 to reallocate campus-based student aid funds to institutions of higher learning in Louisiana, Mississippi, Alabama, and Texas, or institutions that have accepted students displaced by Hurricane Katrina or Rita. The law also waived requirements for matching funds that are normally imposed on institutions and students.

Hurricane Education Recovery Act (HERA) (Public Law 109-148, provision in the Defense Department Appropriations Act for FY 2006) provided funds for states affected by Hurricane Katrina to restart school operations, provide temporary emergency aid for displaced students, and assist homeless youth. The law also permitted the Secretary of Education to extend deadlines under the Individuals with Disabilities Education Act for those affected by Katrina or Rita.

2006 *Higher Education Reconciliation Act of 2005* (Public Law 109-171) made various amendments to programs of student financial assistance under Title IV of the Higher Education Act of 1965.

Public Law 109-211 reauthorized the "ED-FLEX" program (under the Education Flexibility Partnership Act of 1999), under which the Secretary permits states to waive certain requirements of federal statutes and regulations if they meet certain conditions.

Carl D. Perkins Career and Technical Education Improvement Act of 2006 (Public Law 109-270) reauthorized the vocational and technical education programs under the Perkins Act through 2012.

Third Higher Education Extension Act of 2006 (Public Law 109-292) extended the Higher Education Act through June 30, 2007, to afford Congress additional time to complete work on a comprehensive reauthorization.

Public Law 109-323 extended, for an additional year (through September 30, 2007), the period for which the Secretary may waive certain fiscal requirements for states in which the President declared disaster areas as a result of Hurricanes Katrina and Rita.

Figure 18. Federal on-budget funds for education, by level or other educational purpose: Selected years, 1965 through 2006

In billions of constant FY 2006 dollars

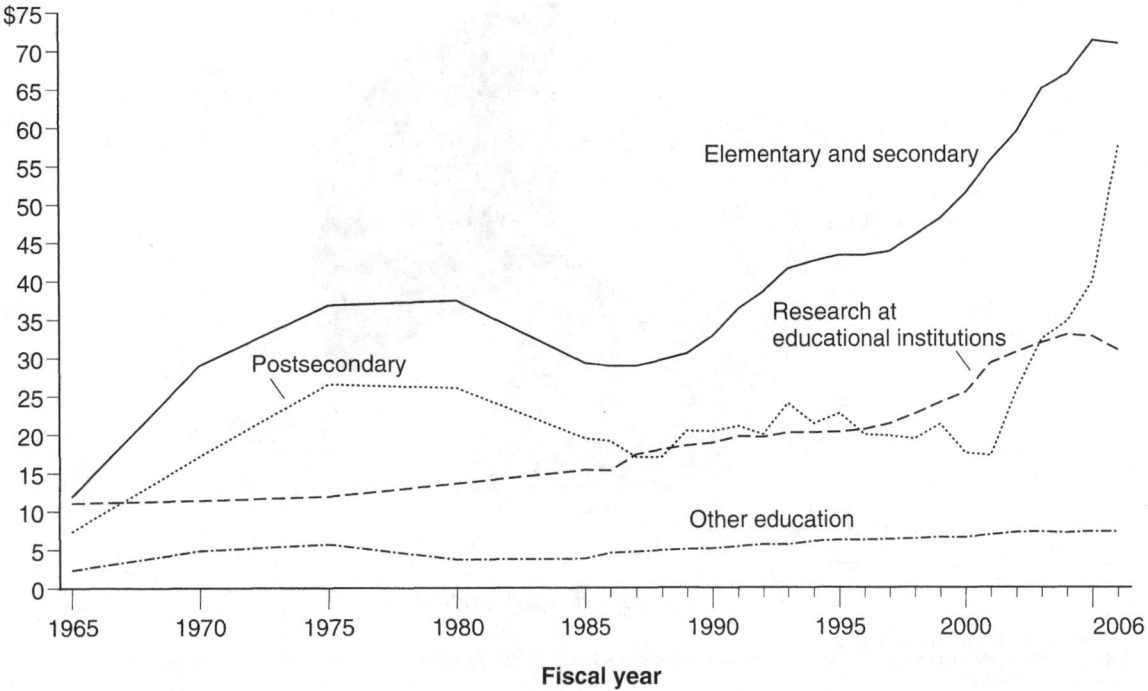

Fiscal year

SOURCE: U.S. Department of Education, Budget Service, unpublished tabulations. U.S. Department of Education, National Center for Education Statistics, unpublished tabulations. U.S. Office of Management and Budget, *Budget of the U.S. Government, Appendix,* fiscal years 1967 through 2007. National Science Foundation, *Federal Funds for Research and Development,* fiscal years 1965 through 2006.

Figure 19. Percentage of federal on-budget funds for education, by agency: Fiscal year 2006

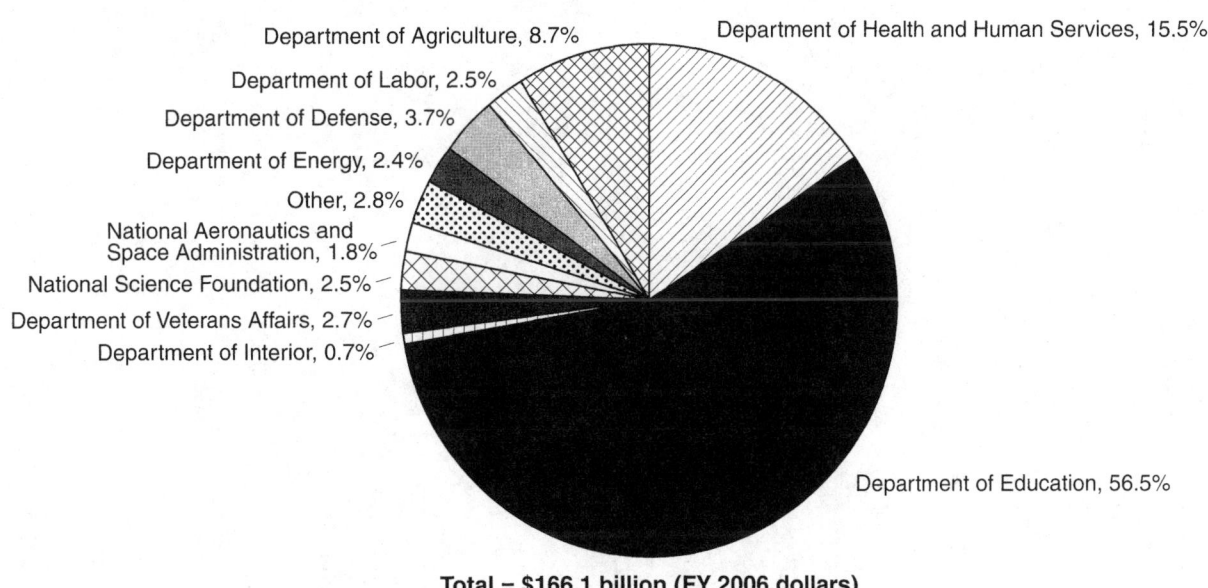

Total = $166.1 billion (FY 2006 dollars)

NOTE: Detail may not sum to totals because of rounding.
SOURCE: U.S. Department of Education, National Center for Education Statistics, unpublished tabulations. U.S. Office of Management and Budget, *Budget of the U.S. Government, Appendix, Fiscal Year 2007.* National Science Foundation, *Federal Funds for Research and Development, Fiscal Year 2006.*

Figure 20. Department of Education outlays, by type of recipient: Fiscal year 2006

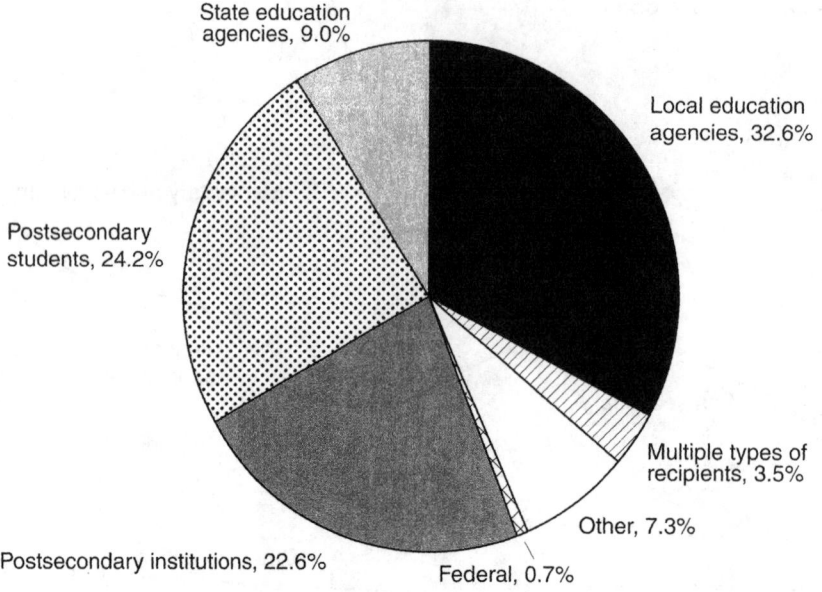

Total outlays = $93.9 billion

NOTE: Detail may not sum to totals because of rounding.
SOURCE: U.S. Office of Management and Budget, *Budget of the U.S. Government, Fiscal Year 2007.* U.S. Department of Education, Office of the Deputy Secretary, Budget Office, unpublished tabulations.

Table 362. Federal support and estimated federal tax expenditures for education, by category: Selected fiscal years, 1965 through 2006

[In millions of dollars]

Fiscal year	Total on-budget support, off-budget support, and nonfederal funds generated by federal legislation	On-budget support[1]					Off-budget support and nonfederal funds generated by federal legislation	Off-budget support	Nonfederal funds						Estimated federal tax expenditures for education[2]
		Total	Elementary and secondary	Post-secondary	Other education[3]	Research at educational institutions	Total	Direct Loan Program[4]	Federal Family Education Loan Program[5]	Perkins Loans[6]	Income Contingent Loans[7]	Leveraging Educational Assistance Partnerships[8]	Supplemental Educational Opportunity Grants[9]	Work-Study Aid[10]	
1	2	3	4	5	6	7	8	9	10	11	12	13	14	15	16
							Current dollars								
1965	$5,354.7	$5,331.0	$1,942.6	$1,197.5	$374.7	$1,816.3	$23.7	†	†	$16.1	†	†	†	$7.6	—
1970	13,359.1	12,526.5	5,830.4	3,447.7	964.7	2,283.6	832.6	†	$770.0	21.0	†	†	†	41.6	—
1975	24,691.5	23,288.1	10,617.2	7,644.0	1,608.5	3,418.4	1,403.4	†	1,233.0	35.7	†	$20.0	†	114.7	$8,605.0
1980	39,349.5	34,493.5	16,027.7	11,115.9	1,548.7	5,801.2	4,856.0	†	4,598.0	31.8	†	76.8	†	149.4	13,320.0
1985	47,753.4	39,027.9	16,901.3	11,174.4	2,107.6	8,844.6	8,725.5	†	8,467.0	21.4	†	76.0	†	161.1	19,105.0
1986	48,357.3	39,962.9	17,049.9	11,283.6	2,620.0	9,009.4	8,394.4	†	8,142.0	20.2	$0.6	72.7	†	159.5	20,425.0
1987	50,724.6	41,194.7	17,535.7	10,300.0	2,820.4	10,538.6	9,529.8	†	9,272.0	20.9	0.5	76.0	†	160.4	20,830.0
1988	54,078.7	43,454.4	18,564.9	10,657.5	2,981.6	11,250.5	10,624.3	†	10,380.0	20.6	0.5	72.8	$22.0	150.4	17,025.0
1989	59,537.4	48,269.6	19,809.5	13,269.9	3,180.3	12,009.8	11,267.8	†	10,938.0	20.4	0.5	71.9		215.0	17,755.0
1990	62,811.5	51,624.3	21,984.4	13,650.9	3,383.0	12,606.0	11,187.2	†	10,826.0	15.0	0.5	59.2	48.8	237.7	19,040.0
1991	70,375.6	57,599.5	25,418.0	14,707.4	3,698.6	13,775.4	12,776.1	†	12,372.0	17.3	0.5	63.5	87.7	235.0	18,995.0
1992	74,481.1	60,483.1	27,926.9	14,387.4	3,992.0	14,176.9	13,998.0	†	13,568.0	17.3	0.5	72.0	97.2	242.9	19,950.0
1993	84,741.5	67,740.6	30,834.3	17,844.0	4,107.2	14,955.1	17,000.8	†	16,524.0	29.3	†	72.4	184.6	190.5	21,010.0
1994	92,781.5	68,254.2	32,304.4	16,177.1	4,483.7	15,289.1	24,527.3	$813.0	23,214.0	52.7	†	72.4	184.6	190.5	22,630.0
1995	95,810.8	71,639.5	33,623.8	17,618.1	4,719.7	15,677.9	24,171.2	5,161.0	18,519.0	52.7	†	63.4	184.6	190.5	24,600.0
1996	96,842.8	71,337.2	34,401.3	15,775.5	4,828.0	16,332.3	25,505.6	8,357.0	16,711.0	31.1	†	31.4	184.6	190.5	26,340.0
1997	103,259.8	73,731.8	35,478.9	15,959.4	5,021.2	17,272.4	29,528.0	9,838.0	19,163.0	52.7	†	50.0	184.6	239.7	28,125.0
1998	107,810.5	76,909.2	37,486.2	15,799.6	5,148.5	18,475.0	30,901.3	10,400.1	20,002.5	45.0	†	25.0	194.3	234.4	29,540.0
1999	113,417.2	82,863.6	39,937.9	17,651.2	5,318.0	19,956.5	30,553.6	9,953.0	20,107.0	33.3	†	25.0	195.9	239.4	37,360.0
2000	119,541.6	85,944.2	43,790.8	15,008.7	5,484.6	21,660.1	33,597.4	10,347.0	22,711.0	33.3	†	50.0	199.7	256.4	39,475.0
2001	130,668.5	94,846.5	48,846.5	14,938.3	5,880.0	25,498.1	35,822.0	10,635.0	24,694.0	25.0	†	80.0	184.0	204.0	41,460.0
2002	150,034.5	109,211.5	52,754.1	22,964.2	6,297.7	27,195.5	40,823.0	11,689.0	28,606.0	25.0	†	104.0	192.0	207.0	—
2003	170,671.5	124,374.5	59,274.2	29,499.7	6,532.5	29,068.1	46,297.0	11,969.0	33,791.0	33.0	†	103.0	202.0	199.0	—
2004	185,176.7	132,420.7	62,653.2	32,433.0	6,576.8	30,757.7	52,756.0	12,840.0	39,266.0	33.0	†	102.0	244.0	271.0	—
2005	202,818.2	145,989.2	68,957.7	38,587.3	6,908.5	31,535.7 [11]	56,829.0	12,930.0	43,284.0	0.0	†	101.0	246.0	268.0	—
2006[11]	227,320.5	166,134.5	70,748.6	57,381.5	7,186.7	30,817.8	61,186.0	13,874.0	46,703.0	0.0	†	100.0	244.0	265.0	—
							Constant fiscal year 2006 dollars[12]								
1965	$32,533.9	$32,389.8	$11,802.6	$7,275.7	$2,276.3	$11,035.2	$144.1	†	†	$97.9	†	†	†	$46.2	—
1970	66,224.4	62,097.1	28,903.0	17,091.1	4,782.4	11,320.6	4,127.3	†	$3,817.1	104.0	†	†	†	206.2	—
1975	85,471.7	80,613.8	36,752.3	26,460.5	5,567.9	11,833.1	4,857.9	†	4,268.1	123.5	†	$69.2	†	397.0	$29,786.9
1980	91,656.4	80,345.4	37,333.1	25,892.1	3,607.4	13,512.7	11,311.0	†	10,710.1	74.0	†	178.9	†	348.0	31,026.1
1985	82,492.7	67,419.6	29,196.6	19,303.4	3,640.8	15,278.8	15,073.1	†	14,626.5	36.9	†	131.3	†	278.3	33,003.4
1986	81,539.9	67,385.3	28,749.5	19,026.3	4,417.9	15,191.5	14,154.6	†	13,729.0	34.1	$0.9	122.6	†	268.9	34,440.5
1987	83,184.6	67,556.3	28,757.3	16,891.2	4,625.3	17,282.5	15,628.3	†	15,205.4	34.3	0.8	124.6	†	263.0	34,159.7
1988	86,082.1	69,170.4	29,551.4	16,964.6	4,746.0	17,908.4	16,911.7	†	16,522.8	32.8	0.8	115.9	$33.8	239.4	27,100.3
1989	91,393.2	74,096.4	30,408.7	20,370.0	4,882.0	18,435.7	17,296.7	†	16,790.4	31.3	0.8	110.4		330.0	27,254.9
1990	93,348.7	76,722.6	32,672.5	20,287.6	5,027.8	18,734.7	16,626.1	†	16,089.3	22.3	0.7	88.0	72.5	353.3	28,296.7
1991	100,216.3	82,022.9	36,195.8	20,943.7	5,266.9	19,616.5	18,193.4	†	17,618.0	24.7	0.7	90.5	124.9	334.6	27,049.3
1992	102,547.3	83,274.4	38,450.3	19,808.9	5,496.2	19,519.0	19,272.8	†	18,680.7	23.9	0.7	99.1	133.9	334.5	27,467.6
1993	113,772.1	90,947.1	41,397.5	23,957.0	5,514.2	20,078.4	22,825.0	†	22,184.8	39.3	†	97.2	247.9	255.8	28,207.6
1994	122,089.7	89,814.6	42,508.8	21,287.1	5,900.0	20,118.7	32,275.0	$1,069.8	30,546.9	69.3	†	95.3	242.9	250.7	29,778.5

See notes at end of table.

Table 362. Federal support and estimated federal tax expenditures for education, by category: Selected fiscal years, 1965 through 2006—Continued

[In millions of dollars]

Fiscal year	Total on-budget support, off-budget support, and nonfederal funds generated by federal legislation	On-budget support[1]					Off-budget support and nonfederal funds generated by federal legislation								Estimated federal tax expenditures for education[2]
		Total	Elementary and secondary	Post-secondary	Other education[3]	Research at educational institutions	Off-budget support			Nonfederal funds					
							Total	Direct Loan Program[4]	Federal Family Education Loan Program[5]	Perkins Loans[6]	Income Contingent Loans[7]	Leveraging Educational Assistance Partnerships[8]	Supplemental Educational Opportunity Grants[9]	Work-Study Aid[10]	
1	2	3	4	5	6	7	8	9	10	11	12	13	14	15	16
1995	123,062.2	92,015.9	43,187.4	22,629.3	6,062.1	20,137.2	31,046.3	6,628.9	23,786.4	67.6	†	81.4	237.1	244.7	31,597.0
1996	121,614.1	89,584.5	43,200.8	19,810.7	6,063.0	20,509.9	32,029.7	10,494.6	20,985.5	39.1	†	39.4	231.8	239.2	33,077.5
1997	127,217.7	90,838.8	43,710.5	19,662.3	6,186.1	21,279.8	36,378.9	12,120.6	23,609.1	64.9	†	61.6	227.4	295.3	34,650.4
1998	131,510.2	93,816.0	45,726.6	19,272.7	6,280.3	22,536.3	37,694.2	12,686.3	24,399.6	54.9	†	30.5	237.0	285.9	36,033.7
1999	136,291.4	99,575.7	47,992.7	21,211.1	6,390.6	23,981.3	36,715.7	11,960.3	24,162.2	40.0	†	30.0	235.4	287.7	44,894.9
2000	140,031.0	100,675.0	51,296.5	17,581.2	6,424.6	25,372.7	39,356.0	12,120.5	26,603.7	39.0	†	58.6	233.9	300.3	46,241.0
2001	149,579.8	108,573.4	55,553.7	17,100.3	6,731.0	29,188.4	41,006.4	12,174.2	28,267.9	28.6	†	91.6	210.6	233.5	47,460.4
2002	168,585.5	122,714.9	59,276.9	25,803.6	7,076.4	30,558.1	45,870.6	13,134.3	32,143.0	28.1	†	116.9	215.7	232.6	—
2003	186,967.7	136,250.1	64,933.9	32,316.4	7,156.2	31,843.6	50,717.6	13,111.8	37,017.5	36.2	†	112.8	221.3	218.0	—
2004	197,555.5	141,272.9	66,841.5	34,601.1	7,016.5	32,813.8	56,282.7	13,698.3	41,890.9	35.2	†	108.8	260.3	289.1	—
2005	209,396.5	150,724.3	71,194.3	39,838.8	7,132.6	32,558.5 [11]	58,672.2	13,349.4	44,687.9	0.0	†	104.3	254.0	276.7	—
2006[11]	227,320.5	166,134.5	70,748.6	57,381.5	7,186.7	30,817.8	61,186.0	13,874.0	46,703.0	0.0	†	100.0	244.0	265.0	—

—Not available.
†Not applicable.
[1]On-budget support includes federal funds for education programs tied to appropriations.
[2]Losses of tax revenue attributable to provisions of the federal income tax laws that allow a special exclusion, exemption, or deduction from gross income or provide a special credit, preferential rate of tax, or a deferral of tax liability affecting individual or corporate income tax liabilities.
[3]Other education includes libraries, museums, cultural activities, and miscellaneous research.
[4]The William D. Ford Direct Program (commonly referred to as the Direct Loan Program) provides students with the same benefits they are currently eligible to receive under the Federal Family Education Loan (FFEL) program, but provides loans to students through federal capital rather than through private lenders.
[5]Formerly the Guaranteed Student Loan program. New student loans guaranteed by the federal government and disbursed to borrowers.
[6]Student loans created from institutional matching funds (since 1993 one-third of federal capital contributions). Excludes repayments of outstanding loans.
[7]Student loans created from institutional matching funds (one-ninth of the federal contribution). This was a demonstration project that involved only 10 institutions and had unsubsidized interest rates. Program repealed in fiscal year 1992.

[8]Formerly the State Student Incentive Grant program. Starting in fiscal year 2000, amounts under $30.0 million have required dollar-for-dollar state matching contributions, while amounts over $30.0 million have required two-to-one state matching contributions.
[9]Institutions award grants to undergraduate students, and the federal share of such grants may not exceed 75 percent of the total grant.
[10]Employer contributions to student earnings are generally one-third of federal allocation.
[11]Estimated.
[12]Data adjusted by the federal funds composite deflator reported in the U.S. Office of Management and Budget, *Budget of the U.S. Government, Historical Tables, Fiscal Year 2007.*
NOTE: To the extent possible, federal education funds data represent outlays rather than obligations. Some data have been revised from previously published figures. Detail may not sum to totals because of rounding.
SOURCE: U.S. Department of Education, Budget Service, unpublished tabulations. U.S. Department of Education, National Center for Education Statistics, unpublished tabulations. U.S. Office of Management and Budget, *Budget of the U.S. Government, Appendix,* fiscal years 1967 through 2007. National Science Foundation, *Federal Funds for Research and Development,* fiscal years 1967 through 2006. (This table was prepared November 2006.)

Table 363. Federal on-budget funds for education and related programs, by agency: Selected fiscal years, 1970 through 2006

[In thousands of current dollars]

Agency	1970	1975	1980	1985	1990	1995	2000	2004	2005	2006[1]
1	2	3	4	5	6	7	8	9	10	11
Total..............................	$12,526,499	$23,288,120	$34,493,502	$39,027,876	$51,624,342	$71,639,520	$85,944,203	$132,420,703	$145,989,203	$166,134,544
Department of Education................	4,625,224	7,350,355	13,137,785	16,701,065	23,198,575	31,403,000	34,106,697	62,903,421	72,893,301	93,928,361
Department of Agriculture	960,910	2,219,352	4,562,467	4,782,274	6,260,843	9,092,089	11,080,031	12,934,115	13,927,753	14,528,386
Department of Commerce	13,990	38,967	135,561	55,114	53,835	88,929	114,575	228,940	219,248	185,248
Department of Defense	821,388	1,009,229	1,560,301	3,119,213	3,605,509	3,879,002	4,525,080	5,935,924	6,525,355	6,170,826
Department of Energy	551,527	764,676	1,605,558	2,247,822	2,561,950	2,692,314	3,577,004	4,331,482	4,216,467	4,024,439
Department of Health and Human Services..................................	1,796,854	3,675,225	5,613,930	5,322,356	7,956,011	12,469,563	17,670,867	25,410,694	25,871,526	25,818,014
Department of Homeland Security ...	†	†	†	†	†	†	†	334,804	450,329	493,570
Department of Housing and Urban Development.................................	114,709	-52,768	5,314	438	118	1,613	1,400	2,200	2,200	1,800
Department of the Interior	190,975	300,191	440,547	549,479	630,537	702,796	959,802	1,288,744	1,244,933	1,183,527
Department of Justice....................	15,728	61,542	60,721	66,802	99,775	172,350	278,927	529,270	599,948	646,721
Department of Labor	424,494	1,103,935	1,862,738	1,948,685	2,511,380	3,967,914	4,696,100	5,686,800	5,667,300	4,216,200
Department of State	59,742	89,433	25,188	23,820	51,225	54,671	388,349	490,017	533,309	525,254
Department of Transportation...........	27,534	52,290	54,712	82,035	76,186	135,816	117,054	120,490	140,900	140,921
Department of the Treasury.............	18	1,118,840	1,247,463	290,276	41,715	49,496	83,000	0	0	0
Department of Veterans Affairs........	1,032,918	4,402,212	2,351,233	1,289,849	757,476	1,324,382	1,577,374	2,844,965	4,293,624	4,526,508
Other agencies and programs										
ACTION...	†	7,081	2,833	1,761	8,472	†	†	†	†	†
Agency for International Development...............................	88,034	78,896	176,770	198,807	249,786	290,580	332,500	567,600	603,500	583,500
Appalachian Regional Commission..	37,838	45,786	19,032	4,745	93	10,623	7,243	8,237	8,542	8,500
Barry Goldwater Scholarship and Excellence in Education Foundation..................................	†	†	†	†	1,033	3,000	3,000	3,000	3,000	4,000
Corporation for National and Community Service	†	†	†	†	†	214,600	386,000	493,000	472,000	467,000
Environmental Protection Agency.....	19,446	33,875	41,083	60,521	87,481	125,721	98,900	94,200	81,400	80,900
Estimated education share of federal aid to the District of Columbia.....	33,019	55,487	81,847	107,340	104,940	78,796	127,127	184,749	154,962	216,801
Federal Emergency Management Agency.......................................	290	290	1,946	1,828	215	170,400	14,894	†	†	†
General Services Administration	14,775	22,532	34,800	†	†	†	†	†	†	†
Harry S Truman Scholarship fund.....	†	†	-1,895	1,332	2,883	3,000	3,000	4,000	3,000	3,000
Institute of American Indian and Alaska Native Culture and Arts Development................................	†	†	†	†	4,305	13,000	2,000	6,000	6,000	6,000
Institute of Museum and Library Services.......................................	†	†	†	†	†	†	166,000	207,000	250,000	324,000
James Madison Memorial Fellowship Foundation...................................	†	†	†	†	191	2,000	7,000	2,000	2,000	2,000
Japanese-United States Friendship Commission.................................	†	†	2,294	2,236	2,299	2,000	3,000	3,000	3,000	3,000
Library of Congress	29,478	63,766	151,871	169,310	189,827	241,000	299,000	402,000	430,000	424,000
National Aeronautics and Space Administration.............................	258,366	197,901	255,511	487,624	1,093,303	1,757,900	2,077,830	2,758,564	2,867,179	3,010,619
National Archives and Records Administration.............................	†	†	†	52,118	77,397	105,172	121,879	244,000	276,000	272,000
National Commission on Libraries and Information Science............	†	449	2,090	723	3,281	1,000	2,000	1,000	1,000	1,000
National Endowment for the Arts......	340	4,754	5,220	5,536	5,577	9,421	10,048	10,531	10,976	10,664
National Endowment for the Humanities..................................	8,459	63,955	142,586	125,671	141,048	151,727	100,014	125,071	117,825	117,500
National Science Foundation...........	295,628	535,294	808,392	1,147,115	1,588,891	2,086,195	2,955,244	4,183,035	4,011,737	4,106,928
Nuclear Regulatory Commission......	†	7,093	32,590	30,261	42,328	22,188	12,200	15,400	12,000	8,000
Office of Economic Opportunity........	1,092,410	16,619	†	†	†	†	†	†	†	†
Smithsonian Institution	2,461	5,509	5,153	7,886	5,779	9,961	25,764	41,850	45,890	48,910
United States Arms Control Agency.	100	0	661	395	25	†	†	†	†	†
United States Information Agency	8,423	9,405	66,210	143,007	201,547	294,800	†	†	†	†
United States Institute of Peace	†	†	†	†	7,621	12,000	13,000	16,000	28,000	31,000
Other agencies..............................	1,421	5,949	990	432	885	500	300	8,600	15,000	15,447

†Not applicable.

[1]Estimated except U.S. Department of Education, which are actual budget reports.

NOTE: To the extent possible, amounts reported represent outlays, rather than obligations. Some data have been revised from previously published figures. Detail may not sum to totals because of rounding. Negative amounts occur when program receipts exceed outlays.

SOURCE: U.S. Department of Education, National Center for Education Statistics, unpublished tabulations. U.S. Office of Management and Budget, *Budget of the U.S. Government, Appendix*, fiscal years 1972 through 2007. National Science Foundation, *Federal Funds for Research and Development*, fiscal years 1970 to 2006. (This table was prepared November 2006.)

Table 364.   Federal on-budget funds for education, by level/educational purpose, agency, and program: Selected fiscal years, 1970 through 2006

[In thousands of current dollars]

Level/educational purpose, agency, and program	1970	1975	1980	1985	1990[1]	1995[1]	2000[1]	2004[1]	2005[1]	2006[1,2]
1	2	3	4	5	6	7	8	9	10	11
Total..	$12,526,499	$23,288,120	$34,493,502	$39,027,876	$51,624,342	$71,639,520	$85,944,203	$132,420,703	$145,989,203	$166,134,544
Elementary/secondary education	5,830,442	10,617,195	16,027,686	16,901,334	21,984,361	33,623,809	43,790,783	62,653,231	68,957,711	70,748,551
Department of Education[3]............	2,719,204	4,132,742	6,629,095	7,296,702	9,681,313	14,029,000	20,039,563	33,689,396	37,477,594	39,770,475
Education for the disadvantaged	1,339,014	1,874,353	3,204,664	4,206,754	4,494,111	6,808,000	8,529,111	12,486,303	14,635,566	14,655,315
Impact aid program[4]...............	656,372	618,711	690,170	647,402	816,366	808,000	877,101	1,238,536	1,262,174	1,253,466
School improvement programs[5]	288,304	700,470	788,918	526,401	1,189,158	1,397,000	2,549,971	7,459,849	7,918,091	8,154,465
Indian education.......................	†	40,036	93,365	82,328	69,451	71,000	65,285	114,434	121,911	126,132
English Language Acquisition...	21,250	92,693	169,540	157,539	188,919	225,000	362,662	644,956	667,485	641,289
Special education	79,090	151,244	821,777	1,017,964	1,616,623	3,177,000	4,948,977	9,749,398	10,940,312	11,462,573
Vocational and adult education	335,174	655,235	860,661	658,314	1,306,685	1,482,000	1,462,977	1,945,155	1,967,086	2,069,929
Education Reform—Goals 2000[6]	†	†	†	†	†	61,000	1,243,479	50,765	-35,031	-64,194
Hurricane Education Recovery	†	†	†	†	†	†	†	†	†	1,471,500
Department of Agriculture............	760,477	1,884,345	4,064,497	4,134,906	5,528,950	8,201,294	10,051,278	11,725,259	12,577,265	13,419,758
Child nutrition programs[7]..........	299,131	1,452,267	3,377,056	3,664,561	4,977,075	7,644,789	9,554,028	11,206,422	11,901,943	12,660,758
McGovern-Dole International Food for Education and Child Nutrition Program[8]	†	†	†	†	†	†	†	150,000	86,000	99,000
Agricultural Marketing Service—commodities[9]......................	341,597	248,839	388,000	336,502	350,441	400,000	400,000	171,000	399,322	465,000
Special milk program.................	83,800	122,858	159,293	15,993	18,707	(7)	(7)	(7)	(7)	(7)
Estimated education share of Forest Service permanent appropriations	35,949	60,381	140,148	117,850	182,727	156,505	97,250	197,837	190,000	195,000
Department of Commerce	†	†	54,816	†	†	†	†	†	†	†
Local public works program—school facilities[10]	†	†	54,816	†	†	†	†	†	†	†
Department of Defense................	143,100	264,500	370,846	831,625	1,097,876	1,295,547	1,485,611	1,642,139	1,786,253	1,932,772
Junior ROTC	12,100	12,500	32,000	55,600	39,300	155,600	210,432	292,737	315,122	319,470
Overseas dependents schools..	131,000	252,000	338,846	613,437	864,958	855,772	904,829	959,296	1,060,920	1,212,012
Domestic schools[4]....................	†	†	†	162,588	193,618	284,175	370,350	390,106	410,211	401,290
Department of Energy..................	200	300	77,633	23,031	15,563	12,646	†	†	†	†
Energy conservation for school buildings[11]	†	†	77,240	22,731	15,213	10,746	†	†	†	†
Pre-engineering program	200	300	393	300	350	1,900	†	†	†	†
Department of Health and Human Services................................	167,333	683,885	1,077,000	1,531,059	2,396,793	5,116,559	6,011,036	7,727,454	8,003,348	8,007,071
Head Start[12]...........................	†	403,900	735,000	1,075,059	1,447,758	3,534,000	5,267,000	6,774,420	6,842,348	6,875,771
Payments to states for AFDC work programs[13].................	†	†	†	†	459,221	953,000	15,000	—	—	—
Social Security student benefits[14].............................	167,333	279,985	342,000	456,000	489,814	629,559	729,036	953,034	1,161,000	1,131,300
Department of Homeland Security	†	†	†	†	†	†	†	500	500	562
Tuition assistance for educational accreditation—Coast Guard personnel[15]	†	†	†	†	†	†	†	500	500	562
Department of the Interior............	140,705	220,392	318,170	389,810	445,267	493,124	725,423	983,290	938,506	881,231
Mineral Leasing Act and other funds Payments to states—estimated education share	12,294	27,389	62,636	127,369	123,811	18,750	24,610	65,090	60,290	59,168
Payments to counties—estimated education share	16,359	29,494	48,953	59,016	102,522	37,490	53,500	85,000	79,686	74,232
Indian Education Bureau of Indian Affairs schools	95,850	141,056	178,112	177,265	192,841	411,524	466,905	520,611	517,647	523,673
Johnson-O'Malley assistance[16]......................	16,080	22,251	28,081	25,675	25,556	24,359	17,387	16,666	16,510	16,371
Education construction..........	†	†	†	†	†	†	161,021	294,923	263,373	206,787
Education expenses for children of employees, Yellowstone National Park.....................	122	202	388	485	538	1,000	2,000	1,000	1,000	1,000
Department of Justice..................	8,237	9,822	23,890	36,117	65,997	128,850	224,800	482,500	554,500	600,600
Vocational training expenses for prisoners in federal prisons	2,720	3,039	4,966	8,292	2,066	3,000	1,000	4,000	—	—
Inmate programs[17]	5,517	6,783	18,924	27,825	63,931	125,850	223,800	478,500	554,500	600,600
Department of Labor....................	420,927	1,097,811	1,849,800	1,945,268	2,505,487	3,957,800	4,683,200	5,675,000	5,654,000	4,203,000
Job Corps..............................	†	175,000	469,800	604,748	739,376	1,029,000	1,256,000	1,438,000	1,521,000	—
Training programs—estimated funds for education programs[18].........................	420,927	922,811	1,380,000	1,340,520	1,766,111	2,928,800	3,427,200	4,237,000	4,133,000	4,203,000

See notes at end of table.

Table 364. Federal on-budget funds for education, by level/educational purpose, agency, and program: Selected fiscal years, 1970 through 2006—Continued

[In thousands of current dollars]

Level/educational purpose, agency, and program	1970	1975	1980	1985	1990[1]	1995[1]	2000[1]	2004[1]	2005[1]	2006[1,2]
1	2	3	4	5	6	7	8	9	10	11
Department of Transportation	45	50	60	60	46	62	188	†	†	†
Tuition assistance for educational accreditation— Coast Guard personnel[15]	45	50	60	60	46	62	188	†	†	†
Department of the Treasury	†	847,139	935,903	273,728	†	†	†	†	†	†
Estimated education share of general revenue sharing[19] State[20]	†	475,224	525,019	†	†	†	†	†	†	†
Local	†	371,915	410,884	273,728	†	†	†	†	†	†
Department of Veterans Affairs...	338,910	1,371,500	545,786	344,758	155,351	311,768	445,052	551,000	1,815,000	1,725,000
Noncollegiate and job training programs[21]	281,640	1,249,410	439,993	224,035	12,848	†	†	†	†	†
Vocational rehabilitation for disabled veterans[22]	41,700	73,100	87,980	107,480	136,780	298,132	438,635	551,000	1,815,000	1,725,000
Dependents' education[23]	15,570	48,990	17,813	13,243	5,723	5,961	6,417	—	—	—
Service members occupational conversion training act of 1992	†	†	†	†	†	7,675	†	†	†	†
Other agencies Appalachian Regional Commission	33,161	41,667	9,157	4,632	93	2,173	2,588	2,495	2,962	3,000
National Endowment for the Arts	†	3,686	4,989	4,399	4,641	7,117	6,002	8,951	8,470	8,164
Arts in education	†	3,686	4,989	4,399	4,641	7,117	6,002	8,951	8,470	8,164
National Endowment for the Humanities	20	149	330	321	404	997	812	326	603	500
Office of Economic Opportunity	1,072,375	16,619	†	†	†	†	†	†	†	†
Head Start[24]	325,700	†	†	†	†	†	†	†	†	†
Other elementary and secondary programs[25]	42,809	16,612	†	†	†	†	†	†	†	†
Job Corps[26]	144,000	†	†	†	†	†	†	†	†	†
Youth Corps and other training programs[26]	553,368	7	†	†	†	†	†	†	†	†
Volunteers in Service to America (VISTA)[27]	6,498	†	†	†	†	†	†	†	†	†
Other programs Estimated education share of federal aid to the District of Columbia	25,748	42,588	65,714	84,918	86,579	66,871	115,230	164,921	138,710	196,417
Postsecondary education	**$3,447,697**	**$7,644,037**	**$11,115,882**	**$11,174,379**	**$13,650,915**	**$17,618,137**	**$15,008,715**	**$32,432,975**	**$38,587,287**	**$57,381,474**
Department of Education[3]	1,187,962	2,089,184	5,682,242	8,202,499	11,175,978	14,234,000	10,727,315	25,340,999	31,420,023	49,953,501
Student financial assistance	†	†	3,682,789	4,162,695	5,920,328	7,047,000	9,060,317	14,968,595	15,209,515	14,092,970
Federal Direct Student Loan Program	†	†	†	†	†	840,000	-2,862,240	3,246,326	3,020,992	6,885,774
Federal Family Education Loan Program	2,323	111,087	1,407,977	3,534,795	4,372,446	5,190,000	2,707,473	4,661,638	10,777,470	26,296,971
Higher education	1,029,131	1,838,066	399,787	404,511	659,492	871,000	1,530,779	2,041,113	2,053,288	2,066,870
Facilities—loans and insurance	114,199	16,292	-19,031	5,307	19,219	-6,000	-2,174	-4,859	-1,464	-937
College housing loans[28]	†	†	14,082	-164,061	-57,167	-46,000	-41,886	31,691	-33,521	-22,221
Educational activities overseas	774	1,881	3,561	1,838	82	†	†	†	†	†
Historically Black Colleges and Universities Capital Financing, Program Account	†	†	†	†	†	†	150	151	169	222
Gallaudet College and Howard University	38,559	111,971	176,829	229,938	230,327	292,000	291,060	342,593	339,823	330,377
National Technical Institute for the Deaf	2,976	9,887	16,248	27,476	31,251	46,000	43,836	53,751	53,751	53,475
Hurricane Katrina, aid to institutions	†	†	†	†	†	†	†	†	†	250,000
Department of Agriculture	†	6,450	10,453	17,741	31,273	33,373	30,676	93,831	61,957	82,933
Agriculture Extension Service, Second Morrill Act payments to agricultural and mechanical colleges and Tuskegee Institute	†	6,450	10,453	17,741	31,273	33,373	30,676	93,831	61,957	82,933
Department of Commerce	8,277	14,973	29,971	2,163	3,312	3,487	3,800	4,000	0	0
Sea Grant Program[29]	†	1,886	3,123	2,163	3,312	3,487	3,800	4,000	—	—
Merchant Marine Academy[30].....	6,160	10,152	14,809	†	†	†	†	†	†	†
State marine schools[30]	2,117	2,935	12,039	†	†	†	†	†	†	†
Department of Defense	322,100	379,800	545,000	1,041,700	635,769	729,500	1,147,759	1,780,339	1,858,301	1,925,353
Tuition assistance for military personnel	57,500	86,800	—	77,100	95,300	127,000	263,303	594,350	608,109	636,551
Service academies...................	78,700	86,200	106,100	196,400	120,613	163,300	212,678	286,222	300,760	293,607
Senior R.O.T.C.	108,100	116,500	—	354,000	193,056	219,400	363,461	525,239	537,525	566,733
Professional development education[31]	77,800	90,300	—	414,200	226,800	219,800	308,317	374,528	411,907	428,462

See notes at end of table.

Table 364. Federal on-budget funds for education, by level/educational purpose, agency, and program: Selected fiscal years, 1970 through 2006—Continued

[In thousands of current dollars]

Level/educational purpose, agency, and program	1970	1975	1980	1985	1990[1]	1995[1]	2000[1]	2004[1]	2005[1]	2006[1,2]
1	2	3	4	5	6	7	8	9	10	11
Department of Energy	3,000	3,000	57,701	19,475	25,502	28,027	†	†	†	†
University laboratory cooperative program	3,000	3,000	2,800	6,500	9,402	8,552	†	†	†	†
Teacher development projects	†	†	1,400	†	†	†	†	†	†	†
Energy conservation for buildings—higher education[11]	†	†	53,501	12,705	7,459	7,381	†	†	†	†
Minority honors vocational training	†	†	†	150	†	†	†	†	†	†
Honors research program	†	†	†	120	6,472	2,221	†	†	†	†
Students and teachers	†	†	†	†	2,169	9,873	†	†	†	†
Department of Health and Human Services	981,483	1,686,650	2,412,058	516,088	578,542	796,035	954,190	1,535,283	1,433,516	1,275,808
Health professions training programs[32]	353,029	599,350	460,736	212,200	230,600	298,302	340,361	698,256	581,661	420,405
Indian health manpower	†	†	7,187	5,577	9,508	27,000	16,000	29,000	27,000	31,000
National Health Service Corps scholarships	†	1,206	70,667	2,268	4,759	78,206	33,300	45,000	45,000	40,000
National Institutes of Health training grants[33]	†	154,875	176,388	217,927	241,356	380,502	550,220	740,506	756,014	760,830
National Institute of Occupational Safety and Health training grants	8,088	7,182	12,899	8,760	10,461	11,660	14,198	22,521	23,841	23,573
Alcohol, drug abuse, and mental health training programs[34]	118,366	83,727	122,103	43,617	81,353	†	†	†	†	†
Health teaching facilities[35]	†	353	3,078	739	505	365	110	†	†	†
Social Security postsecondary students' benefits[36]	502,000	839,957	1,559,000	25,000	†	†	†	†	†	†
Department of Homeland Security	†	†	†	†	†	†	†	41,100	36,400	41,500
Coast Guard Academy[15]	†	†	†	†	†	†	†	22,300	16,400	18,000
Postgraduate training for Coast Guard officers[37]	†	†	†	†	†	†	†	8,300	8,700	11,500
Tuition assistance to Coast Guard military personnel[15]	†	†	†	†	†	†	†	10,500	11,300	12,000
Department of Housing and Urban Development[28]	114,199	-55,418	†	†	†	†	†	†	†	†
College housing loans[28]	114,199	-55,418	†	†	†	†	†	†	†	†
Department of the Interior	31,749	50,844	80,202	125,247	135,480	159,054	187,179	246,154	249,227	255,596
Shared revenues, Mineral Leasing Act and other receipts—estimated education share	6,949	15,480	35,403	71,991	69,980	82,810	98,740	142,300	146,235	149,862
Indian programs Continuing education	9,380	13,311	16,909	24,338	34,911	43,907	57,576	76,212	76,271	79,610
Higher education scholarships	15,420	22,053	27,890	28,918	30,589	32,337	30,863	27,642	26,721	26,124
Department of State	30,850	50,347	†	†	2,167	3,000	319,000	399,600	424,000	411,000
Educational exchange[38]	30,850	50,347	†	†	—		319,000	399,600	424,000	411,000
Mutual educational and cultural exchange activities	30,454	50,300	†	†	—	†	303,000	381,600	402,000	392,000
International educational exchange activities	396	47	†	†	—	†	16,000	18,000	22,000	19,000
Russian, Eurasian, and East European Research and Training	†	†	†	†	2,167	3,000	†	†	†	†
Department of Transportation	11,197	11,885	12,530	55,569	46,025	59,257	60,300	66,000	73,000	72,000
Merchant Marine Academy[30]	†	†	†	19,898	20,926	30,850	34,000	56,000	61,000	61,000
State marine schools[30]	†	†	†	19,777	8,269	8,980	7,000	10,000	12,000	11,000
Coast Guard Academy[15]	9,342	9,780	10,000	11,857	12,074	13,500	15,500	†	†	†
Postgraduate training for Coast Guard officers[37]	1,655	1,855	2,230	3,499	4,173	5,513	2,500	†	†	†
Tuition assistance to Coast Guard military personnel[15]	200	250	300	538	582	414	1,300	†	†	†
Department of the Treasury	†	268,605	296,750	†	†	†	†	†	†	†
General revenue sharing—estimated state share to higher education[19,20]	†	268,605	296,750	†	†	†	†	†	†	†

See notes at end of table.

Table 364. Federal on-budget funds for education, by level/educational purpose, agency, and program: Selected fiscal years, 1970 through 2006—Continued

[In thousands of current dollars]

Level/educational purpose, agency, and program	1970	1975	1980	1985	1990[1]	1995[1]	2000[1]	2004[1]	2005[1]	2006[1,2]
1	2	3	4	5	6	7	8	9	10	11
Department of Veterans Affairs.....	693,490	3,029,600	1,803,847	944,091	599,825	1,010,114	1,132,322	2,293,965	2,478,624	2,801,508
Vietnam-era veterans................	638,260	2,840,600	1,579,974	694,217	46,998	†	†	†	†	†
College student support........	†	†	1,560,081	679,953	39,458	†	†	†	†	†
Work-study	†	†	19,893	14,264	7,540	†	†	†	†	†
Service persons college support	18,900	74,690	46,617	35,630	8,911	†	†	†	†	†
Post-Vietnam veterans	†	†	922	82,554	161,475	33,596	3,958	1,044	1,136	905
All-volunteer-force educational assistance..........................	†	†	†	196	269,947	868,394	984,068	1,942,781	2,070,996	2,351,263
Veterans	†	†	†	†	183,765	760,390	876,434	1,768,253	1,887,239	2,173,310
Reservists	†	†	†	196	86,182	108,004	107,634	174,528	183,757	177,953
Veteran dependents' education	36,330	114,310	176,334	131,494	100,494	95,124	131,296	332,140	388,719	430,340
Payments to state education agencies.............................	†	†	†	†	12,000	13,000	13,000	18,000	17,773	19,000
Other agencies										
Appalachian Regional Commission	4,105	2,545	1,751	—	—	2,741	2,286	2,500	4,407	3,500
National Endowment for the Humanities...........................	3,349	25,320	56,451	49,098	50,938	56,481	28,395	29,824	29,253	29,000
National Science Foundation	42,000	60,283	64,583	60,069	161,884	211,800	389,000	566,000	490,000	496,000
Science and engineering education programs...........	37,000	60,283	64,583	60,069	161,884	211,800	389,000	566,000	490,000	496,000
Sea Grant Program[29]..............	5,000	†	†	†	†	†	†	†	†	†
United States Information Agency[39]	8,423	9,405	51,095	124,041	181,172	260,800	†	†	†	†
Educational and cultural affairs[38]	†	†	49,546	21,079	35,862	13,600	†	†	†	†
Educational and cultural exchange programs[40]	†	†	†	101,529	145,307	247,200	†	†	†	†
Educational exchange activities, international	†	†	1,549	1,433	3	†	†	†	†	†
Information center and library activities..........................	8,423	9,405	†	†	†	†	†	†	†	†
Other programs										
Barry Goldwater Scholarship and Excellence in Education Foundation	†	†	†	—	1,033	3,000	3,000	3,000	3,000	4,000
Estimated education share of federal aid to the District of Columbia...........................	5,513	10,564	13,143	15,266	14,637	9,468	11,493	18,380	14,578	18,775
Harry S Truman Scholarship fund	†	†	-1,895	1,332	2,883	3,000	3,000	4,000	3,000	3,000
Institute of American Indian and Alaska Native Culture and Arts Development...............	†	†	†	—	4,305	13,000	2,000	6,000	6,000	6,000
James Madison Memorial Fellowship Foundation	†	†	†	—	191	2,000	7,000	2,000	2,000	2,000
Other education	**$964,719**	**$1,608,478**	**$1,548,730**	**$2,107,588**	**$3,383,031**	**$4,719,655**	**$5,484,571**	**$6,576,820**	**$6,908,504**	**$7,186,744**
Department of Education[3]............	630,235	1,045,659	747,706	1,173,055	2,251,801	2,861,000	3,223,355	3,437,807	3,538,862	3,721,334
Administration	47,456	108,372	187,317	284,900	328,293	404,000	458,054	525,188	548,842	531,064
Libraries[41].................................	108,284	225,810	129,127	85,650	137,264	117,000	†	†	†	†
Rehabilitative services and disability research	473,091	709,483	426,886	798,298	1,780,360	2,333,000	2,755,468	2,893,992	2,973,346	3,168,675
American Printing House for the Blind	1,404	1,994	4,349	4,230	5,736	7,000	9,368	18,627	16,538	21,595
Trust funds and contributions	0	0	0	27	-23	148	0	465	0	136	0
Department of Agriculture............	135,637	220,395	271,112	336,375	352,511	422,878	444,477	462,125	468,631	473,395
Extension Service	131,734	215,523	263,584	325,986	337,907	405,371	424,174	439,125	445,631	451,395
National Agricultural Library......	3,903	4,872	7,528	10,389	14,604	17,507	20,303	23,000	23,000	22,000
Department of Commerce	1,226	2,317	2,479	†	†	†	†	†	†	†
Maritime Administration Training for private sector employees[30]	1,226	2,317	2,479	†	†	†	†	†	†	†
Department of Health and Human Services................................	24,273	31,653	37,819	47,195	77,962	138,000	214,000	310,000	313,000	315,000
National Library of Medicine	24,273	31,653	37,819	47,195	77,962	138,000	214,000	310,000	313,000	315,000
Department of Homeland Security	†	†	†	†	†	†	†	205,370	278,243	316,000
Federal Law Enforcement Training Center[42]	†	†	†	†	†	†	†	147,000	159,000	196,000
Estimated disaster relief[43].........	†	†	†	†	†	†	†	58,370	119,243	120,000
Department of Justice.................	5,546	42,818	27,642	25,517	26,920	36,296	34,727	25,170	26,148	26,721
Federal Bureau of Investigation National Academy..............	2,066	5,100	7,234	4,189	6,028	12,831	22,479	15,072	15,619	15,931
Federal Bureau of Investigation Field Police Academy..........	2,500	5,254	7,715	10,220	10,548	11,140	11,962	10,051	10,456	10,770
Narcotics and dangerous drug training	980	1,152	2,416	83	850	325	286	47	73	20
National Institute of Corrections	†	31,312	10,277	11,025	9,494	12,000	†	†	†	†

See notes at end of table.

Table 364. Federal on-budget funds for education, by level/educational purpose, agency, and program: Selected fiscal years, 1970 through 2006—Continued

[In thousands of current dollars]

Level/educational purpose, agency, and program	1970	1975	1980	1985	1990[1]	1995[1]	2000[1]	2004[1]	2005[1]	2006[1,2]
1	2	3	4	5	6	7	8	9	10	11
Department of State	20,672	28,113	25,000	23,791	47,539	51,648	69,349	90,417	109,309	114,254
Foreign Service Institute	15,857	20,750	25,000	23,791	47,539	51,648	69,349	90,417	109,309	114,254
Center for Cultural and Technical Interchange[38]	4,815	7,363	†	†	†	†	†	†	†	†
Department of Transportation	3,964	11,877	10,212	3,785	1,507	650	700	890	1,100	1,021
Highways training and education grants	2,418	3,250	3,412	1,500	—	—	—	—	—	—
Maritime Administration Training for private sector employees[30]	†	†	†	1,135	1,507	650	700	890	1,100	1,021
Urban mass transportation—managerial training grants	1,546	2,627	500	1,150	†	†	†	†	†	†
Federal Aviation Administration Air traffic controllers second career program	—	6,000	6,300	—	—	—	—	—	—	—
Department of the Treasury	18	3,096	14,584	16,160	41,488	48,000	83,000	†	†	†
Federal Law Enforcement Training Center[42]	18	3,096	14,584	16,160	41,488	48,000	83,000	†	†	†
Other agencies ACTION[44]	†	7,045	2,833	1,761	8,472	†	†	†	†	†
Estimated education funds	†	7,045	2,833	1,761	8,472	†	†	†	†	†
Agency for International Development	88,034	78,896	99,707	141,847	170,371	260,408	299,000	536,000	574,000	554,000
Education and human resources	61,570	58,349	80,518	115,104	142,801	248,408	299,000	536,000	574,000	554,000
American schools and hospitals abroad	26,464	20,547	19,189	26,743	27,570	12,000	†	†	†	†
Appalachian Regional Commission	572	1,574	8,124	113	†	5,709	2,369	3,242	1,173	2,000
Corporation for National and Community Service[44]	†	†	†	†	†	214,600	386,000	493,000	472,000	467,000
Estimated education funds	†	†	†	†	†	214,600	386,000	493,000	472,000	467,000
Federal Emergency Management Agency[45]	290	290	281	405	215	170,400	14,894	†	†	†
Estimated architect/engineer student development program	40	40	31	155	200	—	—	†	†	†
Estimated other training programs[46]	250	250	250	250	15	—	—	†	†	†
Estimated disaster relief[43]	—	—	—	—	—	170,400	14,894	†	†	†
General Services Administration Libraries and other archival activities[47]	14,775	22,532	34,800	†	†	†	†	†	†	†
Institute of Museum and Library Services[41]	†	†	†	†	†	†	166,000	207,000	250,000	324,000
Japanese-United States Friendship Commission	†	†	2,294	2,236	2,299	2,000	3,000	3,000	3,000	3,000
Library of Congress	29,478	63,766	151,871	169,310	189,827	241,000	299,000	402,000	430,000	424,000
Salaries and expenses	20,700	48,798	102,364	130,354	148,985	198,000	247,000	352,000	383,000	371,000
Books for the blind and the physically handicapped	6,195	11,908	31,436	32,954	37,473	39,000	46,000	49,000	47,000	53,000
Special foreign currency program	2,273	2,333	3,492	4,621	10	†	†	†	†	†
Furniture and furnishings	310	727	14,579	1,381	3,359	4,000	6,000	1,000	—	—
National Aeronautics and Space Administration Aerospace education services project	350	600	882	1,800	3,300	5,923	6,800	—	—	—
National Archives and Records Administration Libraries and other archival activities	†	†	†	52,118	77,397	105,172	121,879	244,000	276,000	272,000
National Commission on Libraries and Information Science	†	449	2,090	723	3,281	1,000	2,000	1,000	1,000	1,000
National Endowment for the Arts	340	1,068	231	1,137	936	2,304	4,046	1,580	2,506	2,500
National Endowment for the Humanities	5,090	38,486	85,805	76,252	89,706	94,249	70,807	94,920	87,969	88,000

See notes at end of table.

Table 364. Federal on-budget funds for education, by level/educational purpose, agency, and program: Selected fiscal years, 1970 through 2006—Continued

[In thousands of current dollars]

Level/educational purpose, agency, and program	1970	1975	1980	1985	1990[1]	1995[1]	2000[1]	2004[1]	2005[1]	2006[1,2]
1	2	3	4	5	6	7	8	9	10	11
Smithsonian Institution	2,461	5,509	5,153	7,886	5,779	9,961	25,764	41,850	45,890	48,910
Museum programs and related research	2,261	4,203	3,254	4,665	690	3,190	18,000	34,000	32,000	39,000
National Gallery of Art extension service	200	300	426	675	474	771	764	850	890	910
Woodrow Wilson International Center for Scholars	†	1,006	1,473	2,546	4,615	6,000	7,000	7,000	13,000	9,000
U.S. Information Agency— Center for Cultural and Technical Interchange[38]	†	†	15,115	18,966	20,375	34,000	†	†	†	†
U.S. Institute of Peace	†	†	†	—	7,621	12,000	13,000	16,000	28,000	31,000
Other programs Estimated education share of federal aid for the District of Columbia	1,758	2,335	2,990	7,156	3,724	2,457	404	1,449	1,674	1,609
Research programs at universities and related institutions[48]	**$2,283,641**	**$3,418,410**	**$5,801,204**	**$8,844,575**	**$12,606,035**	**$15,677,919**	**$21,660,134**	**$30,757,677**	**$31,535,702**	**$30,817,776**
Department of Education[49]	87,823	82,770	78,742	28,809	89,483	279,000	116,464	435,219	456,822	483,051
Department of Agriculture	64,796	108,162	216,405	293,252	348,109	434,544	553,600	652,900	819,900	552,300
Department of Commerce	4,487	21,677	48,295	52,951	50,523	85,442	110,775	224,940	219,248	185,248
Department of Defense	356,188	364,929	644,455	1,245,888	1,871,864	1,853,955	1,891,710	2,513,446	2,880,801	2,312,701
Department of Energy	548,327	761,376	1,470,224	2,205,316	2,520,885	2,651,641	3,577,004	4,331,482	4,216,467	4,024,439
Department of Health and Human Services	623,765	1,273,037	2,087,053	3,228,014	4,902,714	6,418,969	10,491,641	15,837,957	16,121,662	16,220,135
Department of Homeland Security	†	†	†	†	†	†	†	87,834	135,186	135,508
Department of Housing and Urban Development	510	2,650	5,314	438	118	1,613	1,400	2,200	2,200	1,800
Department of the Interior	18,521	28,955	42,175	34,422	49,790	50,618	47,200	59,300	57,200	46,700
Department of Justice	1,945	8,902	9,189	5,168	6,858	7,204	19,400	21,600	19,300	19,400
Department of Labor	3,567	6,124	12,938	3,417	5,893	10,114	12,900	11,800	13,300	13,200
Department of State	8,220	10,973	188	29	1,519	23	†	†	†	†
Department of Transportation	12,328	28,478	31,910	22,621	28,608	75,847	55,866	53,600	66,800	67,900
Department of the Treasury	†	†	226	388	227	1,496	†	†	†	†
Department of Veterans Affairs	518	1,112	1,600	1,000	2,300	2,500	†	†	†	†
ACTION	†	36	†	†	†	†	†	†	†	†
Agency for International Development	†	†	77,063	56,960	79,415	30,172	33,500	31,600	29,500	29,500
Environmental Protection Agency	19,446	33,875	41,083	60,521	87,481	125,721	98,900	94,200	81,400	80,900
Federal Emergency Management Agency	†	†	1,665	1,423	†	†	†	†	†	†
National Aeronautics and Space Administration	258,016	197,301	254,629	485,824	1,090,003	1,751,977	2,071,030	2,758,564	2,867,179	3,010,619
National Science Foundation	253,628	475,011	743,809	1,087,046	1,427,007	1,874,395	2,566,244	3,617,035	3,521,737	3,610,928
Nuclear Regulatory Commission	†	7,093	32,590	30,261	42,328	22,188	12,200	15,400	12,000	8,000
Office of Economic Opportunity	20,035	†	†	†	†	†	†	†	†	†
U.S. Arms Control and Disarmament Agency	100	†	661	395	25	†	†	†	†	†
Other agencies	1,421	5,949	990	432	885	500	300	8,600	15,000	15,447

—Not available.

†Not applicable.

[1]Excludes federal support for medical education benefits under Medicare in the U.S. Department of Health and Human Services. Benefits excluded from total because data before fiscal year (FY) 1990 are not available. This program existed since Medicare began, but was not available as a separate budget item until FY 1990. Excluded amounts are as follows: $4,440,000,000 in FY 1990, $7,510,000,000 in FY 1995, $8,020,000,000 in FY 2000, $7,700,000,000 in FY 2004, $8,400,000,000 in 2005, and an estimated $8,500,000,000 in FY 2006.

[2]Estimated, except the U.S. Department of Education, which are actual numbers.

[3]The U.S. Department of Education was created in May 1980. It formerly was the Office of Education in the U.S. Department of Health, Education, and Welfare.

[4]Arranges for the education of children who reside on federal property when no suitable local school district can or will provide for the education of these children.

[5]Includes many programs, such as No Child Left Behind, 21st Century Community Learning Centers, Class Size Reduction, Charter Schools, Safe and Drug-Free Schools, and Innovative programs.

[6]Included the School-To-Work Opportunities program, which initiated a national system to be administered jointly by the U.S. Departments of Education and Labor. Programs in the Education Reform program were transferred to the School Improvement program or discontinued in FY 2002. Amounts after FY 2002 reflect balances that are spending out from prior-year appropriations.

[7]Starting in FY 1994, the Special Milk program was included in the Child Nutrition program.

[8]The Farm Security and Rural Investment Act of 2002 (Public Law 107-171) carries out preschool and school feeding programs in foreign countries to help reduce the incidence of hunger and malnutrition, and improve literacy and primary education.

[9]These commodities are purchased under Section 32 of the Act of August 24, 1935, for use in the child nutrition programs.

[10]Assisted in the construction of public facilities, such as vocational schools, through grants or loans. No funds have been appropriated for this program since FY 1977, and it was completely phased out in FY 1984.

[11]Established in 1979, with funds first appropriated in FY 1980.

[12]Formerly in the Office of Economic Opportunity. Beginning in FY 1972, funds have been appropriated to the U.S. Department of Health, Education, and Welfare, Office of Child Development.

[13]Created by the Family Support Act of 1988 to provide funds for the Job Opportunities and Basic Skills Training program. Replaced by Temporary Assistance for Needy Families program.

[14]After age 18, benefits terminate at the end of the school term or in 3 months, whichever comes first.

[15]Transferred from the U.S. Department of Transportation to the U.S. Department of Homeland Security in March of 2003.

[16]Provides funding for supplemental programs for eligible American Indian students in public schools.

[17]Finances the cost of academic, social, and occupational education courses for inmates in federal prisons.

[18]Some of the work and training programs were in the Office of Economic Opportunity and were transferred to the U.S. Department of Labor in FYs 1971 and 1972. Beginning in FY 1994, includes the School-to-Work Opportunities program, which is administered jointly by the U.S. Departments of Education and Labor.

[19]Established in FY 1972 and closed in FY 1986.

[20]The states' share of revenue-sharing funds could not be spent on education in FYs 1981 through 1986.

[21]Provides educational assistance allowances in order to restore lost educational opportunities to those individuals whose careers were interrupted or impeded by reason of active military service between January 31, 1955, and January 1, 1977.

[22]This program is in "Readjustment Benefits" program, Chapter 31, and covers the costs of subsistence, tuition, books, supplies, and equipment for disabled veterans requiring vocational rehabilitation.

[23]This program is in "Readjustment Benefits" program, Chapter 35, and provides benefits to children and spouses of veterans.

[24]Head Start program funds were transferred to the U.S. Department of Health, Education, and Welfare, Office of Child Development, in FY 1972.

[25]Most of these programs were transferred to the U.S. Department of Health, Education, and Welfare, Office of Education, in FY 1972.

[26]Transferred to the U.S. Department of Labor in FYs 1971 and 1972.

[27]Transferred to the ACTION Agency in FY 1972.

[28]Transferred from the U.S. Department of Housing and Urban Development to the U.S. Department of Health, Education, and Welfare, Office of Education, in FY 1979.

[29]Transferred from the National Science Foundation to the U.S. Department of Commerce in October 1970.

[30]Transferred from the U.S. Department of Commerce to the U.S. Department of Transportation in FY 1981.

[31]Includes special education programs (military and civilian); legal education program; flight training; advanced degree program; college degree program (officers); and "Armed Forces Health Professions Scholarship" program.

[32]Does not include higher education assistance loans.

[33]Alcohol, drug abuse, and mental health training programs are included starting in FY 1992.

[34]Beginning in FY 1992, data were included in the National Institutes of Health training grants program.

[35]This program closed in FY 2004.

[36]Postsecondary student benefits were ended by the Omnibus Budget Reconciliation Act of 1981 (Public Law 97-35) and were completely phased out by August 1985.

[37]Includes flight training. Transferred to the U.S. Department of Homeland Security in March of 2003.

[38]Transferred from the U.S. Department of State to the International Communication Agency (I.C.A.) in 1977, then transferred back to the U.S. Department of State in FY 1998.

[39]Transferred from the U.S. Department of State to the International Communication Agency (I.C.A.) in 1977.

[40]Included in the "Educational and Cultural Affairs" program in FYs 1980 through 1983, and became an independent program in FY 1984.

[41]Transferred from U.S. Department of Education to the Institute of Museum and Library Services in FY 1997.

[42]Transferred to the U.S. Department of Homeland Security in FY 2003.

[43]The disaster relief program repairs and replaces damaged and destroyed school buildings. In FY 1995, funds were for repairs due to the Northridge Earthquake in California. In FY 1995, $74.4 million was spent on school districts, $8.4 million on community colleges, and $87.6 million on colleges and universities. This program was transferred from the Federal Emergency Management Agency to the U.S. Department of Homeland Security in FY 2003.

[44]The National Service Trust Act of 1993 established the Corporation for National and Community Service. In 1993, ACTION became part of this agency.

[45]The Federal Emergency Management Agency was created in 1979, representing a combination of five existing agencies. The funds for the Federal Emergency Management Agency in FY 1970 to FY 1975 were in other agencies. This agency was transferred to the U.S. Department of Homeland Security in March of 2003.

[46]These programs include the Fall-Out Shelter Analysis, Blast Protection Design through FY 1992. Starting in FY 1993, earthquake training and safety for teachers and administrators for grades 1 through 12 are included.

[47]Transferred from the General Services Administration to the National Archives and Records Administration in April 1985.

[48]Includes federal obligations for research and development centers and R&D plant administered by colleges and universities. FY 2005 and FY 2006 are estimated.

[49]FY 1970 includes outlays for the "Research and Training" program. FY 1975 includes the "National Institute of Education" program. FYs 1990 through 2006 include outlays for the Office of Educational Research and Improvement and Institute for Education Sciences.

NOTE: Some data have been revised from previously published figures. To the extent possible, amounts reported represent outlays rather than obligations. Detail may not sum to totals because of rounding. Negative amounts occur when program receipts exceed outlays.

SOURCE: U.S. Department of Education, Budget Service, unpublished tabulations. U.S. Office of Management and Budget, *Budget of the U.S. Government, Appendix*, fiscal years 1972 through 2007. National Science Foundation, *Federal Funds for Research and Development*, fiscal years 1970 through 2006. (This table was prepared November 2006.)

Table 365. Estimated federal support for education, by type of ultimate recipient and agency: Fiscal year 2006

[In millions of dollars]

Agency	Total	Local education agencies	State education agencies	Post-secondary students	Degree-granting institutions	Federal	Multiple types of recipients	Other[1]
1	2	3	4	5	6	7	8	9
Total[2]	$227,320.1	$44,230.0	$11,031.4	$53,789.1	$78,848.0	$5,181.5	$16,550.7	$17,690.0
Total program funds—on-budget	166,134.5	44,230.0	9,195.8	29,926.5	53,149.8	5,181.5	16,550.7	7,900.2
Department of Education	93,928.4	30,592.2	8,484.6	22,744.7	21,271.3	700.5	3,252.3	6,882.8
Department of Agriculture	14,528.4	12,222.7	633.0	†	635.2	22.0	564.0	451.4
Department of Commerce	185.2	†	†	†	185.2	†	†	†
Department of Defense	6,170.8	319.5	†	685.9	2,830.1	1,906.9	428.5	†
Department of Energy	4,024.4	†	†	†	4,024.4	†	†	†
Department of Health and Human Services	25,818.0	687.6	†	1,665.6	16,768.1	315.0	6,381.7	†
Department of Homeland Security	493.6	120.0	†	14.0	145.6	214.0	†	†
Department of Housing and Urban Development	1.8	†	†	†	1.8	†	†	†
Department of the Interior	1,183.5	91.6	59.2	26.1	196.6	523.7	286.4	†
Department of Justice	646.7	†	†	†	19.4	627.3	†	†
Department of Labor	4,216.2	†	†	†	13.2	†	4,203.0	†
Department of State	525.3	†	†	†	†	114.3	411.0	†
Department of Transportation	140.9	†	†	†	67.9	61.0	1.0	11.0
Department of Veterans Affairs	4,526.5	†	19.0	4,507.5	†	†	†	†
Other agencies and programs								
Agency for International Development	583.5	†	†	†	29.5	†	†	554.0
Appalachian Regional Commission	8.5	†	†	†	3.5	†	5.0	†
Barry Goldwater Scholarship and Excellence in Education Foundation	4.0	†	†	†	†	†	4.0	†
Corporation for National and Community Service	467.0	†	†	†	†	†	467.0	†
Environmental Protection Agency	80.9	†	†	†	80.9	†	†	†
Estimated education share of federal aid to the District of Columbia	216.8	196.4	†	†	18.8	†	1.6	†
Harry S Truman scholarship fund	3.0	†	†	†	†	†	3.0	†
Institute of American Indian and Alaska Native Culture and Arts Development	6.0	†	†	†	†	†	6.0	†
Institute of Library and Museum Services	324.0	†	†	†	†	†	324.0	†
James Madison Memorial Fellowship Foundation	2.0	†	†	†	†	†	2.0	†
Japanese-United States Friendship Commission	3.0	†	†	†	†	†	3.0	†
Library of Congress	424.0	†	†	†	†	424.0	†	†
National Aeronautics and Space Administration	3,010.6	†	†	†	3,010.6	†	†	†
National Archives and Records Administration	272.0	†	†	†	†	272.0	†	†
National Commission on Libraries and Information Science	1.0	†	†	†	†	†	†	1.0
National Endowment for the Arts	10.7	†	†	†	†	†	10.7	†
National Endowment for the Humanities	117.5	†	†	†	†	†	117.5	†
National Science Foundation	4,106.9	†	†	282.7	3,824.2	†	†	†
Nuclear Regulatory Commission	8.0	†	†	†	8.0	†	†	†
Smithsonian Institution	48.9	†	†	†	†	0.9	48.0	†
U.S. Institute of Peace	31.0	†	†	†	†	†	31.0	†
Other agencies	15.4	†	†	†	15.4	†	†	†
Off-budget support and nonfederal funds generated by federal legislation	61,186.0	†	1,835.6	23,862.5	25,698.1	†	†	9,789.8

†Not applicable.

[1]Other recipients include American Indian tribes, private nonprofit agencies, and banks.

[2]Includes on-budget funds, off-budget support, and nonfederal funds generated by federal legislation. Excludes federal tax expenditures.

NOTE: Outlays by type of recipient are estimated based on obligation data. Detail may not sum to totals because of rounding.

SOURCE: U.S. Department of Education, Budget Service, unpublished tabulations. U.S. Department of Education, National Center for Education Statistics, unpublished tabulations. U.S. Office of Management and Budget, *Budget of the U.S. Government, Appendix*, fiscal year 2007. National Science Foundation, *Federal Funds for Research and Development*, fiscal years 2004, 2005, and 2006. (This table was prepared November 2006.)

Table 366. U.S. Department of Education outlays, by type of recipient and level of education: Selected fiscal years, 1980 to 2006

[In millions of current dollars]

Year and level of education	Total	Local education agencies	State education agencies	Postsecondary students	Postsecondary institutions	Federal	Multiple types of recipients	Other[1]
1	2	3	4	5	6	7	8	9
1980 total	**$13,137.8**	**$5,313.7**	**$1,103.2**	**$2,137.4**	**$2,267.2**	**$249.8**	**$693.8**	**$1,372.7**
Elementary/secondary	6,629.1	5,309.4	662.2	34.2	22.0	62.5	513.4	25.5
Postsecondary	5,682.2	†	99.5	2,103.2	2,166.5	†	†	1,313.0
Other programs	747.7	4.3	341.5	†	†	187.3	180.4	34.2
Education research and statistics	78.7	†	†	†	78.7	†	†	†
1984 total	**15,534.7**	**5,256.5**	**1,879.0**	**2,193.4**	**2,167.4**	**330.2**	**516.7**	**3,191.4**
Elementary/secondary	6,220.8	5,252.4	536.0	55.5	35.3	22.9	259.9	58.8
Postsecondary	7,341.2	†	211.5	2,137.9	1,972.5	†	†	3,019.3
Other programs	1,813.1	4.1	1,131.5	†	†	307.3	256.8	113.3
Education research and statistics	159.6	†	†	†	159.6	†	†	†
1988 total	**18,326.9**	**6,614.8**	**2,234.6**	**3,103.4**	**2,519.5**	**319.4**	**838.8**	**2,696.3**
Elementary/secondary	8,098.4	6,606.3	717.9	66.2	39.5	23.8	616.7	28.0
Postsecondary	8,247.1	†	184.6	3,037.2	2,437.6	†	†	2,587.7
Other programs	1,939.0	8.5	1,332.1	†	†	295.6	222.1	80.6
Education research and statistics	42.4	†	†	†	42.4	†	†	†
1990 total	**23,198.6**	**8,000.7**	**2,490.3**	**3,859.6**	**3,649.8**	**441.4**	**912.2**	**3,844.4**
Elementary/secondary	9,681.3	7,995.0	700.3	80.5	85.4	113.1	650.7	56.3
Postsecondary	11,176.0	†	261.6	3,779.1	3,475.0	†	†	3,660.4
Other programs	2,251.8	5.7	1,528.5	†	†	328.3	261.5	127.8
Education research and statistics	89.5	†	†	†	89.5	†	†	†
1994 total	**29,713.4**	**10,935.6**	**3,264.8**	**4,800.5**	**4,831.3**	**504.5**	**1,258.2**	**4,118.5**
Elementary/secondary	13,769.2	10,929.2	1,354.0	159.9	275.2	60.9	902.1	87.9
Postsecondary	12,871.4	†	53.0	4,640.6	4,279.3	†	†	3,898.5
Other programs	2,796.0	6.4	1,857.8	†	†	443.6	356.1	132.1
Education research and statistics	276.8	†	†	†	276.8	†	†	†
1995 total	**31,403.0**	**11,210.7**	**3,584.0**	**4,964.7**	**5,016.1**	**485.4**	**1,349.2**	**4,792.9**
Elementary/secondary	14,029.0	11,203.3	1,410.0	190.5	170.1	70.3	946.9	37.9
Postsecondary	14,234.0	†	250.8	4,774.2	4,567.0	†	†	4,642.0
Other programs	2,861.0	7.4	1,923.2	†	†	415.1	402.3	113.0
Education research and statistics	279.0	†	†	†	279.0	†	†	†
1996 total	**29,977.8**	**11,077.8**	**3,669.6**	**5,129.8**	**5,053.4**	**562.1**	**1,682.3**	**2,802.9**
Elementary/secondary	14,323.8	11,073.1	1,650.7	161.1	141.5	59.2	1,201.4	36.8
Postsecondary	12,257.6	†	90.7	4,968.7	4,601.0	†	†	2,597.2
Other programs	3,085.6	4.7	1,928.2	†	†	502.9	480.9	168.9
Education research and statistics	310.9	†	†	†	310.9	†	†	†
1998 total	**31,559.0**	**12,094.5**	**3,978.2**	**5,362.0**	**5,910.2**	**465.8**	**1,769.0**	**1,979.3**
Elementary/secondary	16,001.8	12,086.7	1,920.5	265.5	162.4	52.7	1,454.7	59.3
Postsecondary	12,122.3	†	57.8	5,096.5	5,206.6	†	†	1,761.4
Other programs	2,893.7	7.8	1,999.9	†	†	413.1	314.3	158.6
Education research and statistics	541.2	†	†	†	541.2	†	†	†
2000 total	**34,106.7**	**16,016.0**	**4,316.5**	**4,711.7**	**5,005.7**	**506.6**	**1,820.2**	**1,730.1**
Elementary/secondary	20,039.6	16,003.5	1,989.6	260.5	198.9	48.5	1,461.8	76.8
Postsecondary	10,727.3	†	55.2	4,451.2	4,690.3	†	†	1,530.6
Other programs	3,223.4	12.5	2,271.7	†	†	458.1	358.4	122.7
Education research and statistics	116.5	†	†	†	116.5	†	†	†
2002 total	**46,324.4**	**19,742.1**	**4,967.8**	**8,306.0**	**8,668.2**	**608.9**	**2,200.3**	**1,831.3**
Elementary/secondary	25,246.2	19,729.2	2,429.8	490.0	454.9	77.6	1,829.5	235.3
Postsecondary	17,056.2	†	199.2	7,816.0	7,588.1	†	†	1,452.9
Other programs	3,396.8	12.9	2,338.8	†	†	531.3	370.8	143.1
Education research and statistics	625.2	†	†	†	625.2	†	†	†
2004 total	**62,903.4**	**26,012.4**	**6,334.5**	**12,005.0**	**10,977.0**	**648.9**	**2,730.1**	**4,195.4**
Elementary/secondary	33,689.4	25,990.0	3,611.7	606.2	642.5	126.4	2,300.0	412.6
Postsecondary	25,341.0	†	420.9	11,398.8	9,899.3	†	†	3,621.9
Other programs	3,437.8	22.4	2,301.9	†	†	522.5	430.1	160.9
Education research and statistics	435.2	†	†	†	435.2	†	†	†
2005 total	**72,893.3**	**28,900.2**	**7,126.3**	**14,708.2**	**13,362.4**	**669.8**	**3,023.0**	**5,103.4**
Elementary/secondary	37,477.6	28,878.6	3,971.6	698.1	790.0	145.9	2,578.4	415.0
Postsecondary	31,420.0	†	777.1	14,010.1	12,115.6	†	†	4,517.2
Other programs	3,538.9	21.6	2,377.6	†	†	523.9	444.6	171.2
Education research and statistics	456.8	†	†	†	456.8	†	†	†
2006 total	**93,928.4**	**30,592.2**	**8,484.6**	**22,744.7**	**21,271.3**	**700.5**	**3,252.3**	**6,882.8**
Elementary/secondary	39,770.5	30,570.6	4,258.7	749.9	797.1	170.6	2,805.5	418.1
Postsecondary	49,953.5	†	1,674.0	21,994.8	19,991.1	†	†	6,293.6
Other programs	3,721.3	21.6	2,551.9	†	†	529.9	446.8	171.1
Education research and statistics	483.1	†	†	†	483.1	†	†	†

†Not applicable.

[1]Other recipients include American Indian tribes, private nonprofit agencies, and banks.

NOTE: Outlays by type of recipient are estimated based on obligation data. Some data have been revised from previously published figures. Detail may not sum to totals because of rounding.

SOURCE: U.S. Office of Management and Budget, *Budget of the U.S. Government,* fiscal years 1982 through 2007. U.S. Department of Education, Office of the Deputy Secretary, Budget Office, unpublished tabulations. (This table was prepared November 2006.)

Table 367. U.S. Department of Education appropriations for major programs, by state or jurisdiction: Fiscal year 2005
[In thousands]

State or jurisdiction	Total	Grants for the disadvantaged[1]	Block grants to states for school improvement[2]	School assistance in federally affected areas[3]	Vocational and adult education[4]	Education for the handicapped[5]	Language assistance[6]	American Indian education	Degree-granting institutions[7]	Student financial assistance[8]	Rehabilitation services[9]
1	2	3	4	5	6	7	8	9	10	11	12
Total, 50 states and D.C.[10]	$54,459,729	$13,907,514	$5,569,424	$1,080,611	$1,819,899	$11,165,171	$576,269	$95,165	$2,010,442	$15,561,488	$2,673,746
Total, 50 states, D.C., other activities, and other jurisdictions	56,815,011	14,641,638	5,862,823	1,173,528	1,891,639	11,415,151	675,765	95,165	2,060,926	16,215,878	2,782,497
Alabama	965,478	223,383	93,502	3,019	32,257	179,683	2,969	1,701	71,949	299,458	57,556
Alaska	264,113	44,770	29,058	103,063	5,705	35,936	835	9,136	12,601	12,802	10,208
Arizona	1,303,625	288,014	102,726	158,533	36,798	177,181	16,054	10,635	27,130	443,111	43,444
Arkansas	575,095	146,110	60,868	475	19,781	112,833	1,986	1,071	32,328	164,252	35,391
California	6,704,728	2,108,649	693,513	67,856	224,109	1,225,429	149,566	6,349	187,128	1,779,951	262,178
Colorado	673,903	146,142	65,264	16,327	23,936	149,610	9,948	669	25,982	205,762	30,265
Connecticut	467,519	121,781	53,633	5,712	17,224	131,970	4,440	0	11,913	100,389	20,455
Delaware	150,759	38,421	29,102	84	7,020	33,215	876	0	7,600	24,247	10,193
District of Columbia	441,936	55,280	28,741	2,129	6,168	17,388	922	0	258,665	59,183	13,460
Florida	2,761,887	705,169	265,474	11,408	103,899	622,053	38,999	60	53,857	814,421	146,546
Georgia	1,633,419	461,069	164,598	20,697	56,193	309,693	13,282	0	61,850	464,573	81,464
Hawaii	241,227	53,366	29,328	42,630	8,785	40,031	1,645	0	17,663	35,791	11,987
Idaho	263,764	52,716	30,304	7,252	9,798	54,475	2,107	444	6,704	84,238	15,725
Illinois	2,235,602	597,237	232,349	20,188	73,711	503,926	24,732	83	71,450	611,660	100,268
Indiana	958,596	200,651	90,611	165	39,474	253,821	7,644	0	24,761	277,318	64,150
Iowa	509,741	74,153	45,287	577	18,585	120,475	2,907	199	25,394	190,860	31,305
Kansas	485,877	101,305	47,082	23,348	17,059	106,947	2,418	968	24,380	135,419	26,950
Kentucky	819,572	216,825	89,219	598	29,270	161,631	2,404	0	34,939	234,410	50,275
Louisiana	1,062,465	313,643	125,381	9,679	34,580	188,156	3,317	774	50,647	278,074	58,214
Maine	242,222	54,640	33,201	2,579	8,457	55,204	500	125	11,337	60,116	16,063
Maryland	766,047	189,192	81,448	7,204	28,247	199,183	6,654	159	35,573	178,042	40,347
Massachusetts	1,029,356	255,304	101,177	655	31,026	280,354	11,259	41	32,100	271,025	46,415
Michigan	1,755,174	485,208	200,709	3,921	60,595	395,717	11,540	3,223	36,763	463,995	93,503
Minnesota	767,470	123,428	70,287	13,729	27,501	189,474	6,595	3,244	33,181	257,448	42,583
Mississippi	734,899	191,125	83,193	3,768	22,376	118,561	1,017	352	36,879	229,635	47,992
Missouri	1,034,801	222,291	101,024	21,192	36,447	223,516	4,538	105	30,569	335,667	59,452
Montana	260,664	47,413	34,487	42,144	7,520	37,286	500	2,964	18,165	58,212	11,975
Nebraska	394,794	62,691	38,027	20,593	10,886	73,746	2,143	693	9,160	158,805	18,050
Nevada	272,200	78,366	32,917	3,583	13,140	66,802	6,865	685	8,861	45,897	15,083
New Hampshire	192,772	36,787	31,101	10	8,305	47,537	1,056	0	5,737	50,911	11,329
New Jersey	1,232,015	302,799	127,319	14,945	44,448	356,902	20,187	54	26,274	283,116	55,972
New Mexico	539,478	123,964	50,124	87,069	13,999	90,109	5,347	7,905	21,915	115,873	23,174
New York	4,161,991	1,349,563	456,260	16,316	108,689	760,395	53,923	1,564	69,177	1,202,402	143,702
North Carolina	1,415,547	331,988	134,339	15,364	53,690	312,581	9,979	3,370	71,133	397,401	85,703
North Dakota	197,067	36,451	29,547	28,193	5,823	27,175	500	1,587	9,235	48,407	10,149
Ohio	1,878,028	432,595	193,650	3,023	69,891	432,079	6,567	0	41,998	581,879	116,346
Oklahoma	771,265	160,197	77,222	38,246	24,536	145,369	4,869	22,413	37,437	220,098	40,876
Oregon	589,338	153,608	59,414	2,574	21,527	127,528	5,300	2,393	14,087	169,246	33,659
Pennsylvania	2,013,124	535,670	210,016	1,251	72,008	422,921	8,983	0	39,592	602,140	120,543
Rhode Island	226,027	53,519	29,288	1,843	8,735	44,212	2,375	0	4,707	69,989	11,359
South Carolina	800,040	200,101	76,929	3,352	29,218	174,652	2,588	0	41,676	224,616	46,908
South Dakota	474,753	41,245	29,862	43,284	6,312	32,449	516	3,235	9,545	298,109	10,195
Tennessee	1,011,541	229,493	99,233	2,809	38,143	230,238	4,547	0	45,094	298,763	63,221
Texas	4,657,523	1,374,254	485,019	82,864	152,738	951,227	82,422	278	141,369	1,182,916	204,434
Utah	450,345	65,563	37,168	8,196	17,325	106,919	2,888	1,127	14,542	170,558	26,059
Vermont	155,846	34,100	28,777	8	5,633	26,359	500	134	9,289	40,859	10,187
Virginia	1,574,042	243,096	103,927	37,929	42,260	279,487	9,223	10	43,510	752,886	61,714
Washington	956,759	214,604	92,312	56,943	34,134	220,556	8,547	4,431	35,940	241,726	47,566
West Virginia	408,900	114,682	49,071	29	13,327	75,776	611	0	23,733	105,977	25,696
Wisconsin	824,032	180,305	87,636	12,173	33,163	208,708	6,172	2,463	36,501	202,486	54,426
Wyoming	152,361	34,591	28,699	11,081	5,448	27,697	500	522	8,426	26,369	9,029
Other activities/jurisdictions											
Indian Tribe (Set-Aside)	277,138	102,599	33,522	0	14,929	88,988	5,000	0	0	0	32,099
Other	330,445	70,221	48,481	91,222	21,065	10,000	88,222	0	0	0	1,234
American Samoa	95,936	10,554	7,283	0	408	6,723	1,153	0	500	2,652	66,665
Guam	50,707	9,411	10,655	51	874	15,044	1,190	0	4,682	7,547	1,253
Marshall Islands	1,931	0	0	0	0	0	0	0	1,931	0	0
Federated States of Micronesia	7,914	0	0	0	48	6,579	0	0	1,287	0	0
Northern Mariana Islands	19,568	4,453	4,194	0	479	5,113	905	0	1,612	1,473	1,338
Palau	14,570	0	0	0	0	0	0	0	1,844	12,726	0
Puerto Rico	1,516,012	523,445	179,928	1,531	32,830	108,121	2,896	0	36,260	627,085	3,916
Virgin Islands	41,061	13,441	9,336	113	1,106	9,412	131	0	2,368	2,907	2,246

[1]Title I includes Grants to Local Education Agencies (Basic, Concentration, Targeted, and Education Finance Incentive Grants); Reading First State Grants; Even Start; Migrant Education Grants; Neglected and Delinquent Children Grants; and Comprehensive School Reform Grants.

[2]Title VI includes Teacher Quality State Grants; 21st Century Community Learning Centers; Educational Technology State Grants; State Grants for Innovative Programs; state assessments, including No Child Left Behind; Education for the Homeless Children and Youth; Rural and Low-Income Schools Program; Small, Rural School Achievement Program; Safe and Drug Free Schools and Communities State Grants; and Mathematics and Science Partnerships.

[3]Includes Impact Aid—Basic Support Payments; Impact Aid—Payments for Children with Disabilities; and Impact Aid—Construction.

[4]Includes Vocational Education State Grants; English Literacy and Civics Education State Grants; Tech-Prep Education; State Grants for Incarcerated Youth Offenders; and Adult Basic and Literacy Education State Grants.

[5]Includes Special Education—Grants to States; Preschool Grants; and Grants for Infants and Families.

[6]Includes Language Acquisition State Grants.

[7]Includes Institutional Aid to Strengthen Higher Education Institutions serving significant numbers of low-income students; Other Special Programs for the Disadvantaged; Cooperative Education; Fund for the Improvement of Postsecondary Education; Fellowships and Scholarships; and annual interest subsidy grants for facilities construction.

[8]Includes Pell Grants; Leveraging Educational Assistance Partnership; Federal Supplemental Educational Opportunity Grants; Federal Work-Study; and Guaranteed Student Loan interest subsidies.

[9]Includes Vocational Rehabilitation State Grants; Supported Employment State Grants; Client Assistance State Grants; Independent Living State Grants; Services for Older Blind Individuals; Protection and Advocacy for Assistive Technology; Assistive Technology State Grant Program; and Protection and Advocacy of Individual Rights.

[10]Total excludes other activities and other jurisdictions.

NOTE: Data reflect revisions to figures in the Budget of the United States Government, Fiscal Year 2007. Detail may not sum to totals because of rounding.

SOURCE: U.S. Department of Education, Budget Service, unpublished tabulations. (This table was prepared May 2006.)

Table 368. Appropriations for Title I, No Child Left Behind Act of 2001, by program and state or jurisdiction: Fiscal years 2005 and 2006
[In thousands of dollars]

State or jurisdiction	Total, fiscal year 2005	Fiscal year 2006							
		Total	Grants to local education agencies[1]	State agency programs		Even Start	Reading First State Grants	State Grants for Innovative Programs	State Assessments
				Neglected and Delinquent	Migrant				
1	2	3	4	5	6	7	8	9	10
Total, 50 states and D.C.[2]	$13,906,260	$13,590,608	$12,142,590	$47,727	$366,063	$86,165	$948,063	$96,928	$389,537
Total, 50 states, D.C., other activities, and other jurisdictions	14,651,638	14,277,680	12,713,125	49,797	386,524	99,000	1,029,234	99,000	407,563
Alabama	223,002	221,922	198,974	1,007	2,053	1,372	18,515	1,413	6,550
Alaska	44,767	43,116	33,198	260	6,749	445	2,463	492	3,616
Arizona	287,362	295,653	261,504	1,998	6,362	1,801	23,987	1,942	7,878
Arkansas	145,535	143,505	125,428	363	5,103	857	11,753	869	5,183
California	2,115,160	2,015,638	1,730,433	2,836	125,572	11,911	144,887	12,322	33,953
Colorado	146,309	148,772	129,180	508	7,400	886	10,798	1,486	6,733
Connecticut	121,985	111,392	100,418	1,105	2,942	655	6,272	1,107	5,782
Delaware	38,414	37,411	33,814	390	298	445	2,463	492	3,621
District of Columbia	54,866	52,027	48,910	208	0	445	2,463	492	3,331
Florida	707,175	733,090	647,491	1,275	22,571	4,526	57,227	5,154	15,946
Georgia	455,777	455,429	410,369	1,286	8,278	2,849	32,648	2,926	10,351
Hawaii	53,414	50,529	46,179	167	734	445	3,005	492	3,933
Idaho	52,558	51,204	42,446	226	4,047	445	4,038	492	4,196
Illinois	597,357	584,574	540,228	1,368	1,904	3,733	37,341	4,155	13,437
Indiana	198,259	206,023	184,239	923	5,072	1,276	14,513	2,070	8,200
Iowa	73,979	73,112	65,012	413	1,656	445	5,585	884	5,221
Kansas	101,097	100,373	81,754	391	11,461	556	6,211	876	5,199
Kentucky	215,023	208,614	183,956	836	7,106	1,266	15,451	1,263	6,172
Louisiana	313,969	312,952	283,842	1,500	2,389	1,945	23,277	1,488	6,739
Maine	55,920	50,024	45,553	171	1,048	445	2,806	492	3,954
Maryland	190,256	185,851	171,874	944	520	1,196	11,316	1,806	7,536
Massachusetts	255,654	225,073	207,610	1,859	1,611	1,342	12,652	1,891	7,750
Michigan	485,184	466,710	426,535	652	8,482	2,919	28,122	3,334	11,374
Minnesota	123,757	120,681	109,437	201	1,670	740	8,633	1,607	7,038
Mississippi	190,685	189,980	170,466	1,453	1,316	1,138	15,608	958	5,406
Missouri	222,339	207,765	187,238	1,331	1,514	1,279	16,403	1,793	7,504
Montana	47,378	45,425	41,020	119	946	445	2,896	492	3,692
Nebraska	62,092	60,165	50,696	287	5,094	445	3,642	553	4,389
Nevada	76,563	84,710	76,918	377	223	538	6,655	769	4,932
New Hampshire	36,742	34,520	30,974	496	141	445	2,463	492	4,033
New Jersey	302,752	289,231	265,252	2,842	1,997	1,784	17,356	2,787	10,000
New Mexico	123,757	124,159	112,602	353	859	779	9,566	635	4,596
New York	1,355,345	1,299,035	1,206,244	3,441	9,382	8,359	71,609	5,887	17,788
North Carolina	331,745	329,132	292,402	1,022	5,893	2,035	27,779	2,687	9,750
North Dakota	36,395	33,311	30,110	73	219	445	2,463	492	3,459
Ohio	432,138	446,221	410,372	1,592	2,447	2,846	28,964	3,627	12,110
Oklahoma	160,319	157,041	140,632	375	1,974	962	13,098	1,093	5,746
Oregon	152,461	154,925	130,800	1,033	11,749	907	10,437	1,108	5,784
Pennsylvania	534,771	528,506	484,370	972	9,046	3,357	30,761	3,748	12,415
Rhode Island	53,522	51,373	47,231	561	68	445	3,068	492	3,810
South Carolina	201,109	195,908	177,378	1,275	532	1,238	15,485	1,317	6,309
South Dakota	41,226	40,399	36,431	250	809	445	2,463	492	3,619
Tennessee	230,018	226,239	204,530	542	527	1,430	19,211	1,781	7,475
Texas	1,370,937	1,358,261	1,188,392	3,634	56,948	8,179	101,109	7,829	22,667
Utah	65,480	62,787	54,383	689	1,723	445	5,546	898	5,255
Vermont	34,080	32,389	28,332	544	604	445	2,463	492	3,461
Virginia	242,750	227,389	207,717	771	779	1,426	16,695	2,312	8,808
Washington	213,876	209,167	176,459	650	15,338	1,212	15,508	1,944	7,884
West Virginia	114,096	107,761	99,331	545	82	683	7,120	502	4,260
Wisconsin	181,537	168,582	155,101	1,015	609	1,054	10,802	1,716	7,311
Wyoming	35,366	32,549	28,824	600	216	445	2,463	492	3,383
Other activities/jurisdictions									
Indian Tribe Set-Aside	102,599	95,055	88,423	0	0	1,485	5,146	0	2,000
Other nonstate allocations	80,221	71,657	8,437	1,245	20,461	7,940	33,573	0	7,563
American Samoa	10,554	10,253	8,494	0	0	126	1,633	131	379
Guam	9,411	11,900	10,290	0	0	153	1,456	282	815
Northern Marianas	4,453	4,116	3,477	0	0	46	593	89	256
Puerto Rico	524,699	481,046	440,001	825	0	2,915	37,305	1,379	6,463
Virgin Islands	13,441	13,046	11,413	0	0	170	1,463	191	551

[1]Includes Basic, Concentration, Targeted, and Education Finance Incentive Grants.
[2]Total excludes other activities and other jurisdictions.
NOTE: Detail may not sum to totals because of rounding. These are preliminary estimates for fiscal year 2006. Comprehensive School Reform has no allocations for fiscal year 2006.

SOURCE: U.S. Department of Education, Budget Service, Elementary, Secondary, and Vocational Education Analysis Division, unpublished tabulations. (This table was prepared July 2006.)

Table 369. U.S. Department of Agriculture obligations for child nutrition programs, by state or jurisdiction: Fiscal years 2004 and 2005

[In thousands of dollars]

State or jurisdiction	Total, fiscal year 2004	Fiscal year 2005							
		Total	Special milk	School lunch[1]	School breakfast	State administrative expenses	Commodities and cash in lieu of commodities[2]	Child and adult care	Summer food service
1	2	3	4	5	6	7	8	9	10
United States[3]	$11,545,006	$12,103,170	$16,471	$6,890,355	$1,885,645	$122,316	$1,016,130	$1,918,403	$253,849
Alabama	216,062	229,348	63	134,787	37,153	1,714	18,130	33,102	4,398
Alaska	31,145	34,150	9	19,883	3,967	573	2,090	7,283	344
Arizona	242,291	263,064	141	155,099	39,763	2,785	20,015	44,097	1,164
Arkansas	135,003	151,671	24	82,294	26,908	1,583	12,381	26,405	2,074
California	1,493,347	1,554,521	748	938,538	241,835	14,952	103,246	241,324	13,878
Colorado	109,780	116,644	140	69,284	14,721	1,339	10,082	19,804	1,274
Connecticut	89,000	92,407	418	57,336	12,272	878	10,663	10,033	806
Delaware	30,731	33,448	47	15,349	4,388	552	2,527	9,230	1,354
District of Columbia	38,099	27,687	12	15,133	3,952	421	1,710	3,323	3,135
Florida	655,189	719,258	110	415,135	118,893	6,982	54,638	107,809	15,690
Georgia	482,052	510,059	36	281,878	91,886	4,490	44,275	76,915	10,579
Hawaii	43,172	39,765	10	27,974	6,540	504	3,927	49	762
Idaho	48,530	53,878	220	32,429	9,111	620	4,197	4,787	2,513
Illinois	446,795	384,648	3,295	275,770	47,348	4,497	39,560	4,705	9,473
Indiana	205,058	215,234	347	125,964	29,606	1,913	23,869	29,152	4,382
Iowa	99,363	104,898	99	58,528	12,329	1,600	11,440	19,733	1,169
Kansas	110,506	116,803	162	59,847	14,668	1,204	9,590	29,864	1,468
Kentucky	200,009	210,092	94	116,788	40,056	1,343	18,775	25,027	8,009
Louisiana	290,600	290,397	51	154,746	49,616	3,533	22,700	52,130	7,622
Maine	39,258	40,760	76	21,083	5,582	678	3,376	9,177	787
Maryland	155,757	168,835	470	90,348	22,828	2,200	14,663	33,573	4,752
Massachusetts	182,209	190,580	497	96,675	25,448	2,197	18,592	43,140	4,029
Michigan	294,187	310,390	843	179,314	46,468	3,310	26,083	50,280	4,091
Minnesota	183,696	188,555	1,022	88,925	19,761	2,068	18,565	55,451	2,763
Mississippi	197,519	195,086	5	112,324	38,563	1,502	13,677	25,064	3,953
Missouri	219,698	238,494	523	129,621	37,993	2,354	23,654	36,786	7,563
Montana	38,599	32,962	37	16,183	4,057	576	2,479	8,817	812
Nebraska	76,049	79,279	86	38,145	7,949	890	8,533	22,813	864
Nevada	57,731	66,515	120	44,884	11,081	701	5,126	3,833	770
New Hampshire	24,862	24,718	212	14,267	2,748	465	3,714	2,723	589
New Jersey	229,955	257,820	1,063	139,282	32,949	2,652	26,794	47,865	7,214
New Mexico	124,640	134,178	28	61,754	20,243	1,688	10,071	35,637	4,756
New York	770,045	827,036	1,071	456,276	111,087	8,229	67,043	146,616	36,714
North Carolina	382,468	387,373	194	207,768	64,404	4,002	31,993	73,753	5,258
North Dakota	26,006	26,972	89	11,706	2,586	474	2,803	8,870	445
Ohio	349,495	360,014	841	203,843	50,724	4,140	36,926	57,555	5,986
Oklahoma	189,681	203,357	56	99,840	35,215	2,302	14,585	48,912	2,447
Oregon	120,755	128,441	158	68,891	24,644	1,108	8,597	22,405	2,639
Pennsylvania	347,428	368,863	738	213,753	47,416	3,566	38,515	52,857	12,017
Rhode Island	34,112	36,738	90	20,067	5,025	873	3,165	6,424	1,093
South Carolina	206,122	216,137	10	124,966	42,661	1,919	17,540	22,937	6,103
South Dakota	32,811	33,797	45	18,128	4,474	530	3,570	6,311	740
Tennessee	246,625	263,635	35	150,573	44,114	2,945	22,275	39,729	3,964
Texas	1,270,382	1,353,600	79	784,132	261,784	11,057	100,024	168,742	27,781
Utah	95,540	99,376	79	55,301	10,341	1,108	10,996	19,537	2,015
Vermont	18,005	18,917	106	9,249	2,963	451	1,807	3,931	411
Virginia	211,645	226,176	281	133,381	35,616	1,264	21,856	28,329	5,449
Washington	195,938	206,173	290	115,403	29,681	2,497	18,018	37,743	2,542
West Virginia	80,472	84,759	46	44,807	15,982	1,111	6,143	14,926	1,745
Wisconsin	159,232	167,419	1,230	93,623	14,109	1,636	19,490	34,149	3,182
Wyoming	17,352	18,242	25	9,080	2,131	340	1,642	4,744	279
Other activities/jurisdictions									
Administrative and other costs	9,576	0	0	0	0	0	0	0	0
Department of Defense dependents schools	5,341	5,430	0	5,399	21	0	9	0	0
American Samoa	0	0	0	0	0	0	0	0	0
Guam	5,945	6,592	0	4,753	1,619	0	171	49	0
Northern Marianas	0	0	0	0	0	0	0	0	0
Puerto Rico	181,784	185,171	0	108,322	27,782	2,028	17,337	20,565	9,137
Virgin Islands	6,801	7,124	1	4,353	796	304	359	625	685
Undistributed[4]	185,323	285,423	163	10,647	21,553	21,062	27,691	194,777	9,530

[1]Includes the Special Meal Assistance program.
[2]Commodities are based on preliminary food orders for fiscal year 2005.
[3]Excludes other activities, other jurisdictions, and undistributed.
[4]Undistributed amount reflects the difference between preliminary state earnings reports and federal obligations as of September 30, 2005. Undistributed amount under school lunch includes obligations of American Samoa and the Northern Mariana Islands.

NOTE: Data are based on obligations as reported September 30, 2005. Detail may not sum to totals because of rounding.
SOURCE: U.S. Department of Agriculture, Food and Nutrition Service, Budget Division, unpublished tabulations. (This table was prepared May 2006.)

Table 370. U.S. Department of Health and Human Services allocations for Head Start and enrollment in Head Start, by state or jurisdiction: Fiscal years 2002 through 2005

State or jurisdiction	2002 Allocations in thousands	2002 Enrollment[1]	2003 Allocations in thousands	2003 Enrollment[2]	2004 Allocations in thousands	2004 Enrollment[3]	2005 Allocations in thousands	2005 Enrollment[4]
1	2	3	4	5	6	7	8	9
United States[5]	$5,627,581	810,472	$5,739,294	808,140	$5,828,994	807,147	$5,872,705	807,528
Alabama	100,154	16,529	103,588	16,509	105,500	16,374	106,345	16,374
Alaska	12,104	1,839	12,126	1,817	12,353	1,725	12,439	1,634
Arizona	96,913	13,297	100,174	13,215	102,023	13,215	103,225	13,215
Arkansas	61,024	10,930	62,645	10,915	63,808	10,942	64,355	10,879
California	801,430	98,687	811,487	98,767	823,694	98,432	829,440	98,933
Colorado	65,716	9,872	66,428	9,843	67,676	9,820	68,157	9,820
Connecticut	49,985	7,224	50,604	7,129	51,401	7,126	51,760	7,148
Delaware	12,286	2,231	12,537	2,214	12,771	2,197	13,201	2,197
District of Columbia	24,091	3,403	24,408	3,403	24,865	3,403	25,041	3,403
Florida	252,370	35,610	255,501	35,350	260,307	35,530	262,433	35,574
Georgia	161,740	23,414	163,757	23,400	166,837	23,508	168,059	23,450
Hawaii	21,977	3,073	22,248	3,063	22,665	3,049	22,825	3,063
Idaho	21,663	3,347	21,820	2,939	22,411	2,640	22,753	2,957
Illinois	259,780	39,619	263,047	39,640	267,111	39,640	270,041	39,672
Indiana	88,667	14,145	93,523	14,148	95,093	14,231	95,943	14,234
Iowa	49,495	7,620	50,109	7,717	51,050	7,735	51,412	7,775
Kansas	47,909	8,013	49,503	7,924	50,433	7,931	50,791	7,949
Kentucky	103,473	16,190	104,829	16,091	106,799	16,071	107,558	16,071
Louisiana	135,048	22,136	141,892	22,108	144,497	21,982	145,513	21,982
Maine	26,661	4,002	26,991	3,970	27,344	3,955	27,537	3,979
Maryland	74,929	10,527	75,851	10,235	77,277	10,347	77,826	10,344
Massachusetts	104,182	13,040	105,476	12,981	107,299	12,846	108,061	13,011
Michigan	225,290	35,269	228,045	35,099	232,215	35,069	233,924	35,124
Minnesota	69,643	10,331	70,369	10,332	71,119	10,332	71,811	10,339
Mississippi	155,259	26,742	157,165	26,762	160,121	26,657	161,258	26,754
Missouri	113,256	17,646	115,663	17,573	117,837	17,451	118,674	17,473
Montana	20,117	2,982	20,365	2,952	20,747	2,939	20,893	2,945
Nebraska	34,580	5,252	35,008	5,203	35,709	5,080	35,962	5,080
Nevada	19,786	2,754	23,315	2,754	23,698	2,754	24,215	2,754
New Hampshire	12,861	1,632	13,018	1,632	13,257	1,632	13,350	1,632
New Jersey	125,176	15,262	126,711	15,099	127,761	14,717	128,669	15,130
New Mexico	49,185	7,749	50,852	7,651	51,790	7,451	52,160	7,451
New York	418,239	49,493	422,350	49,473	430,086	49,127	432,036	49,300
North Carolina	132,667	19,202	137,403	19,125	139,360	19,003	140,898	19,098
North Dakota	16,036	2,307	16,697	2,357	17,009	2,353	17,129	2,353
Ohio	236,999	38,081	239,770	38,017	244,102	38,021	246,237	38,029
Oklahoma	76,910	13,460	78,784	13,474	80,249	13,915	80,833	13,474
Oregon	57,105	9,199	57,704	9,052	58,893	8,792	59,311	8,716
Pennsylvania	219,115	30,986	222,603	30,908	226,002	32,282	227,563	30,868
Rhode Island	21,184	3,150	21,446	3,150	21,802	3,150	21,956	3,150
South Carolina	78,507	12,248	80,223	12,248	81,718	12,248	82,282	12,248
South Dakota	18,079	2,827	18,301	2,827	18,644	2,827	18,775	2,827
Tennessee	112,344	16,507	116,072	16,473	118,217	16,445	119,022	16,437
Texas	454,292	67,664	475,422	67,764	474,092	67,327	477,433	67,785
Utah	36,270	5,527	36,709	5,527	37,399	5,518	37,664	5,518
Vermont	13,023	1,573	13,183	1,573	13,429	1,569	13,523	1,569
Virginia	95,366	13,772	96,214	13,768	98,142	13,696	98,833	13,768
Washington	97,247	11,167	98,022	11,001	100,193	11,118	100,094	11,102
West Virginia	48,625	7,650	49,227	7,650	50,152	7,650	50,508	7,610
Wisconsin	86,941	13,489	88,082	13,515	89,784	13,532	90,635	13,538
Wyoming	11,882	1,803	12,028	1,803	12,252	1,793	12,338	1,792
Other activities								
Migrant programs	257,815	33,850	260,201	33,609	264,621	33,154	285,729	35,461
Support activities	210,255	†	†	†	†	†	†	†
American Indian/Alaska Native programs	181,794	23,837	183,412	23,802	186,704	23,737	186,937	23,592

See notes at end of table.

Table 370. U.S. Department of Health and Human Services allocations for Head Start and enrollment in Head Start, by state or jurisdiction: Fiscal years 2002 through 2005—Continued

State or jurisdiction	2002		2003		2004		2005	
	Allocations in thousands	Enrollment[1]	Allocations in thousands	Enrollment[2]	Allocations in thousands	Enrollment[3]	Allocations in thousands	Enrollment[4]
1	2	3	4	5	6	7	8	9
Training and other assistance	—	†	169,688	†	174,078	†	174,078	†
Research, etc.; monitoring program review......................................	—	†	46,051	†	59,746	†	58,980	†
Other jurisdictions								
Puerto Rico....................................	234,304	36,920	243,016	36,687	246,792	37,498	248,652	36,842
Pacific jurisdictions.........................	14,943	6,209	15,128	6,209	7,262	3,060	7,292	3,060
Virgin Islands	9,878	1,161	9,992	1,161	7,919	942	7,976	942

—Not available.

†Not applicable.

[1]Distribution of enrollment by age: 5 years old and over, 5 percent; 4 years old, 52 percent; 3 years old, 36 percent; and under 3 years old, 7 percent. Disabled children as percentage of total enrollment: 13 percent. Racial/ethnic composition: American Indian/Alaska Native, 3 percent; Hispanic, 30 percent; Black, 33 percent; White, 28 percent; Asian, 2 percent; and Hawaiian/Pacific Islander, 1 percent.

[2]Distribution of enrollment by age: 5 years old and over, 5 percent; 4 years old, 53 percent; 3 years old, 34 percent; and under 3 years old, 7 percent. Disabled children as percentage of total enrollment: 13 percent. Racial/ethnic composition: American Indian/Alaska Native, 3 percent; Hispanic, 31 percent; Black, 32 percent; White, 28 percent; Asian, 2 percent; and Hawaiian/Pacific Islander, 1 percent.

[3]Distribution of enrollment by age: 5 years old and over, 5 percent; 4 years old, 52 percent; 3 years old, 34 percent; and under 3 years old, 9 percent. Disabled children as percentage of total enrollment: 13 percent. Racial/ethnic composition: American Indian/Alaska Native, 3 percent; Hispanic, 31 percent; Black, 31 percent; White, 27 percent; Asian, 2 percent; Hawaiian/Pacific Islander, 1 percent; and multiracial/other, 5 percent.

[4]Distribution of enrollment by age: 5 years old and over, 4 percent; 4 years old, 52 percent; 3 years old, 34 percent; and under 3 years old, 10 percent. Disabled children as percentage of total enrollment: 13 percent. Racial/ethnic composition: American Indian/Alaska Native, 5 percent; Hispanic, 33 percent; Black, 31 percent; White, 35 percent; Asian, 2 percent; Hawaiian/Pacific Islander, 1 percent; and multiracial/other, 7 percent.

[5]Excludes other activities and other jurisdictions.

NOTE: Detail may not sum to totals because of rounding.

SOURCE: U.S. Department of Health and Human Services, Office of Human Development Services, unpublished tabulations. (This table was prepared May 2006.)

Table 371. Federal science and engineering obligations to colleges and universities, by agency and state or jurisdiction: Fiscal year 2004
[In thousands of dollars]

State or jurisdiction	Total	Department of Agriculture	Department of Defense	Department of Education	Department of Energy	Environmental Protection Agency	Department of Health and Human Services	National Aeronautics and Space Administration	National Science Foundation	Other[1]
1	2	3	4	5	6	7	8	9	10	11
United States[2]	$27,217,616	$1,131,001	$2,468,046	$230,111	$802,870	$132,015	$16,434,354	$1,165,863	$4,171,597	$681,759
Alabama	410,187	28,756	24,186	3,302	6,896	2,575	257,478	33,165	47,222	6,607
Alaska	87,292	10,858	9,499	0	4,052	678	8,159	10,755	28,466	14,825
Arizona	345,254	12,216	26,207	2,183	8,315	2,241	148,299	37,231	101,183	7,379
Arkansas	101,188	27,177	4,104	220	595	213	55,822	1,742	9,546	1,769
California	3,772,923	46,507	318,402	28,404	104,138	11,917	2,334,064	251,616	639,822	38,053
Colorado	669,043	15,984	25,070	411	17,424	2,697	286,430	65,714	211,427	43,886
Connecticut	499,549	8,994	17,530	4,069	11,433	1,003	409,394	3,710	39,363	4,053
Delaware	69,555	8,700	10,777	0	3,685	1,039	23,309	1,320	17,280	3,445
District of Columbia	218,810	2,168	18,777	1,485	1,497	793	155,136	7,530	23,040	8,384
Florida	638,557	32,250	69,201	12,214	17,875	5,277	312,192	29,987	130,616	28,945
Georgia	596,611	34,075	56,275	1,493	13,403	4,297	373,894	8,533	95,321	9,320
Hawaii	198,720	15,299	51,331	3,229	4,891	1,664	51,397	15,767	31,071	24,071
Idaho	51,465	12,160	4,479	1,856	1,247	39	13,409	2,366	10,288	5,621
Illinois	1,009,067	30,740	44,069	16,779	40,545	5,538	626,317	14,850	216,401	13,828
Indiana	375,738	25,308	28,280	2,505	21,144	2,462	197,247	6,824	87,832	4,136
Iowa	316,638	36,216	11,553	3,012	9,995	2,107	197,326	8,853	37,829	9,747
Kansas	157,267	19,364	9,114	1,944	6,408	427	75,871	6,358	29,090	8,691
Kentucky	228,656	29,277	5,905	1,119	4,374	1,026	149,525	2,066	28,413	6,951
Louisiana	268,180	21,497	20,887	3,928	6,100	1,706	165,773	5,588	34,936	7,765
Maine	35,169	6,936	5,070	519	358	423	4,274	674	12,759	4,156
Maryland	1,662,914	18,068	457,513	5,170	13,923	2,775	820,063	213,248	94,398	37,756
Massachusetts	1,496,390	10,884	112,533	5,216	89,104	4,781	924,169	38,484	287,991	23,228
Michigan	819,046	34,070	71,868	5,055	30,710	5,587	501,295	17,922	134,664	17,875
Minnesota	378,680	29,755	15,196	11,691	7,307	641	236,236	5,675	66,783	5,396
Mississippi	201,382	47,728	41,562	2,276	8,868	1,839	45,321	15,064	24,329	14,395
Missouri	599,185	33,345	18,074	3,620	5,141	649	483,862	9,108	40,864	4,522
Montana	85,592	17,878	4,791	2,983	2,206	0	28,293	5,368	19,024	5,049
Nebraska	142,578	22,984	14,193	1,368	2,231	0	69,500	2,290	27,180	2,832
Nevada	79,774	4,307	8,486	0	32,350	0	19,109	3,009	10,047	2,466
New Hampshire	165,170	5,150	1,659	248	1,293	1,924	96,185	14,392	15,850	28,469
New Jersey	347,567	10,965	36,547	2,833	11,924	3,633	167,228	12,983	92,852	8,602
New Mexico	204,772	12,148	53,665	1,139	8,077	2,119	66,598	25,042	32,128	3,856
New York	2,223,117	41,304	85,623	13,619	109,636	12,643	1,482,064	34,523	354,934	88,771
North Carolina	1,076,923	45,363	60,591	7,548	15,992	6,685	803,759	11,444	106,596	18,945
North Dakota	74,224	17,204	12,112	546	9,552	1,257	19,659	2,098	9,274	2,522
Ohio	758,414	31,432	75,595	7,624	13,328	1,069	500,548	25,411	81,720	21,687
Oklahoma	136,045	20,441	9,337	2,265	3,901	75	59,602	9,998	25,388	5,038
Oregon	332,207	16,857	11,019	3,639	6,764	5,482	216,868	7,872	54,646	9,060
Pennsylvania	1,634,436	25,037	225,283	21,121	30,718	2,573	1,084,108	31,337	207,232	7,027
Rhode Island	127,220	5,183	12,542	397	2,809	523	63,112	5,345	30,796	6,513
South Carolina	208,975	19,091	9,383	1,170	4,275	159	122,815	5,265	24,186	22,631
South Dakota	46,529	11,055	6,544	2,445	125	0	13,109	2,160	9,552	1,539
Tennessee	491,315	28,146	21,013	5,892	10,063	2,026	361,522	8,854	49,980	3,819
Texas	1,558,383	63,945	193,182	10,226	30,295	6,616	1,053,133	32,027	149,088	19,871
Utah	260,433	15,115	29,198	1,097	7,516	2,818	145,073	18,044	38,083	3,489
Vermont	90,913	11,931	566	794	1,037	990	66,403	1,188	7,255	749
Virginia	519,435	24,934	47,466	8,460	9,523	846	260,166	54,659	91,136	22,245
Washington	736,150	25,127	46,591	1,315	21,348	12,171	489,648	9,545	106,689	23,716
West Virginia	69,736	14,694	1,727	1,515	1,437	2,981	22,663	14,389	3,947	6,383
Wisconsin	613,194	37,186	22,621	9,994	25,798	1,031	359,129	12,833	133,533	11,069
Wyoming	27,048	5,192	850	173	1,244	0	7,798	1,637	9,547	607
Other jurisdictions	120,277	22,606	2,305	2,375	703	0	64,158	10,121	16,404	1,605
American Samoa	1,630	1,615	0	0	0	0	0	0	0	15
Guam	4,239	2,832	0	0	0	0	1,247	0	0	160
Puerto Rico	105,879	12,869	2,305	2,375	703	0	61,412	9,971	14,922	1,322
Trust Territory of the Pacific	3,249	3,249	0	0	0	0	0	0	0	0
Virgin Islands	5,280	2,041	0	0	0	0	1,499	150	1,482	108

[1]Includes U.S. Department of Commerce, U.S. Department of Housing and Urban Development, U.S. Department of the Interior, Agency for International Development, U.S. Department of Labor, U.S. Department of State, U.S. Department of Transportation, Bureau of Engraving and Printing, General Services Administration, Office of Justice Programs, Social Security Administration, and Nuclear Regulatory Commission.
[2]Excludes other jurisdictions.
NOTE: Dollars reflect actual obligations during the fiscal year regardless of when the funds were actually spent by a recipient institution. Data are not comparable with *Digest of Edu-*

cation Statistics tables for previous years because prior to fiscal year 1999, data include obligations to federally funded research and development centers administered by colleges and universities. Detail may not sum to totals because of rounding.
SOURCE: National Science Foundation, Division of Science Resources Statistics, *Survey of Federal Science and Engineering Support to Universities, Colleges, and Nonprofit Institutions, Fiscal Year 2004.* (This table was prepared November 2006.)

Table 372. Federal obligations for research, development, and R&D plant, by performers, fields of science, and category of obligation: Fiscal years 1998 through 2006

[In millions of current dollars]

Performers, fields of science, and category of obligation	Actual							Estimated		Percent change, 2005 to 2006
	1998	1999	2000	2001	2002	2003	2004	2005	2006	
1	2	3	4	5	6	7	8	9	10	11
Total obligations for research, development, and R&D plant.............	$73,743.5	$77,386.6	$77,356.1	$84,003.0	$90,157.7	$97,927.9	$109,717.2	$118,996.3	$116,100.0	-2.4
Research and development obligations.....................	71,903.3	75,340.8	72,863.2	79,933.2	85,853.0	93,661.3	105,723.1	115,072.2	112,418.2	-2.3
Performers										
Federal intramural[1]..........................	17,114.0	18,084.7	17,149.8	20,219.8	21,044.8	22,861.6	26,769.8	30,785.9	28,275.4	-8.2
Industrial firms..........................	31,839.7	31,901.6	27,735.5	27,006.2	29,538.2	33,852.7	39,214.6	43,518.4	44,314.8	1.8
FFRDCs[2] administered by										
industrial firms......................	1,188.8	1,328.1	1,100.9	1,186.6	1,351.1	1,507.6	1,543.1	1,619.3	1,502.9	-7.2
Universities and colleges..............	13,365.9	14,959.1	16,815.1	19,587.9	21,290.1	22,693.5	24,169.7	24,870.4	24,277.1	-2.4
FFRDCs[2] administered by										
universities and colleges........	3,890.2	3,896.5	4,053.2	4,617.7	4,641.2	4,754.2	5,400.9	5,530.9	5,431.6	-1.8
Other nonprofit institutions............	3,155.1	3,608.8	4,216.6	5,138.8	5,739.1	5,706.7	5,623.7	5,813.4	5,724.3	-1.5
FFRDCs[2] administered by										
nonprofit institutions...............	603.0	913.3	1,231.5	1,269.1	1,404.8	1,352.8	1,443.2	1,468.8	1,465.4	-0.2
State and local governments........	447.5	357.5	224.0	450.6	452.2	400.0	880.1	883.3	878.4	-0.6
Foreign....................................	299.1	291.3	336.7	456.5	391.6	532.4	677.9	581.7	548.3	-5.7
Research obligations	30,922.3	33,527.5	38,470.5	44,713.7	48,006.7	51,071.8	53,357.8	55,546.3	54,979.1	-1.0
Performers										
Federal intramural[1]....................	7,964.7	8,685.8	9,449.6	11,130.9	11,857.4	12,419.6	12,085.2	12,810.4	12,734.2	-0.6
Industrial firms.....................	4,635.1	4,579.8	4,801.2	5,262.3	5,786.8	6,042.4	6,782.7	7,418.7	7,385.6	-0.4
FFRDCs[2] administered by										
industrial firms.....................	844.1	879.3	700.3	822.3	937.3	1,103.5	1,131.6	1,122.6	1,081.3	-3.7
Universities and colleges	11,741.0	13,203.8	16,015.9	18,657.1	20,285.4	21,676.5	22,699.1	23,244.9	22,915.1	-1.4
FFRDCs[2] administered by										
universities and colleges.....	2,743.0	2,554.1	2,773.2	3,096.3	3,219.4	3,272.6	3,687.3	3,767.4	3,673.3	-2.5
Other nonprofit institutions	2,425.2	2,806.7	3,719.8	4,577.9	4,723.0	5,196.3	5,216.4	5,329.9	5,336.2	0.1
FFRDCs[2] administered by										
nonprofit institutions............	214.5	469.5	696.1	739.4	749.6	779.0	795.5	865.3	862.2	-0.4
State and local governments.....	240.1	232.4	162.5	308.7	275.5	305.8	532.9	549.6	549.3	-0.1
Foreign...................................	114.5	116.1	152.0	118.9	172.3	276.1	427.0	437.5	441.9	1.0
Fields of science										
Life sciences...........................	13,557.6	15,422.5	17,964.7	23,057.3	25,476.8	27,772.2	27,728.5	28,543.2	28,207.2	-1.2
Psychology.............................	591.0	632.6	1,626.7	741.9	905.9	1,104.4	1,854.9	1,916.0	1,934.2	1.0
Physical sciences	4,209.7	4,066.2	4,787.9	4,600.8	4,983.2	5,021.6	5,211.1	5,473.3	5,393.6	-1.5
Environmental sciences	3,062.0	3,095.3	3,328.8	3,251.7	3,418.3	3,740.9	3,741.6	3,876.0	3,754.4	-3.1
Mathematics and computer										
sciences............................	1,836.8	1,980.6	2,205.6	2,610.6	2,630.7	1,104.4	2,949.4	3,115.2	3,080.7	-1.1
Engineering.............................	5,895.4	6,263.4	6,346.4	8,197.0	8,274.9	8,405.1	8,866.4	9,480.8	9,396.9	-0.9
Social sciences	806.1	854.9	1,050.3	1,008.6	1,038.5	1,025.8	1,089.6	1,131.5	1,177.8	4.1
Other sciences	963.7	1,212.1	1,160.2	1,245.8	1,278.4	1,329.3	1,916.3	2,010.3	2,034.2	1.2
Basic research obligations	15,613.0	17,443.7	19,569.8	21,958.1	23,668.3	24,751.4	26,120.7	26,919.4	26,938.1	0.1
Performers										
Federal intramural[1]	2,917.8	3,255.2	3,621.8	4,193.8	4,460.0	4,662.1	4,671.6	4,923.0	4,915.1	-0.2
Industrial firms....................	1,119.7	1,082.8	1,356.5	917.1	1,231.9	1,279.6	1,969.4	2,166.6	2,204.5	1.7
FFRDCs[2] administered by										
industrial firms.....................	326.4	313.4	171.3	175.1	239.6	312.8	292.2	299.1	295.0	-1.4
Universities and colleges.......	7,952.2	9,107.1	10,056.7	11,792.2	12,668.2	13,151.8	13,398.5	13,559.9	13,483.5	-0.6
FFRDCs[2] administered by										
universities and colleges ...	1,642.3	1,565.5	1,674.0	1,762.1	1,805.2	1,827.8	2,005.8	2,108.0	2,170.2	3.0
Other nonprofit institutions	1,397.6	1,650.0	1,985.3	2,441.7	2,531.7	2,703.9	2,746.1	2,756.3	2,754.7	-0.1
FFRDCs[2] administered by										
nonprofit institutions...........	121.8	354.9	521.6	540.5	563.4	582.1	606.8	666.4	666.4	0.0
State and local governments.	84.9	61.4	75.7	71.5	71.5	85.4	197.9	204.7	209.3	2.2
Foreign	50.4	53.4	106.9	64.0	96.8	146.1	232.3	235.3	239.4	1.7
Fields of science										
Life sciences..........................	7,853.4	9,197.1	10,049.0	12,835.5	14,024.1	14,765.3	14,490.0	14,815.5	14,684.7	-0.9
Psychology.............................	312.0	347.3	817.8	292.9	464.6	543.8	979.2	1,014.9	1,027.6	1.3
Physical sciences	2,941.4	3,089.8	3,470.6	3,327.1	3,405.9	3,454.0	3,662.6	3,815.8	3,794.2	-0.6
Environmental sciences	1,528.7	1,615.7	1,838.4	1,663.0	1,833.3	1,899.5	2,022.9	2,060.4	2,081.6	1.0
Mathematics and computer										
sciences............................	705.5	734.9	798.3	957.8	998.7	1,120.2	1,239.1	1,278.9	1,253.7	-2.0
Engineering.............................	1,594.4	1,639.7	1,764.2	1,911.5	1,864.9	1,913.1	2,271.7	2,424.1	2,564.4	5.8
Social sciences.....................	224.8	246.5	308.0	278.4	361.7	352.8	419.3	429.6	444.6	3.5
Other sciences	452.7	572.5	523.6	691.7	715.2	702.7	1,035.9	1,080.3	1,087.4	0.7
Applied research obligations.....	15,309.3	16,083.7	18,900.7	22,755.6	24,338.4	26,320.4	27,237.1	28,626.9	28,041.0	-2.0
Performers										
Federal intramural[1]	5,046.9	5,430.6	5,827.8	6,937.2	7,397.4	7,757.5	7,413.6	7,887.4	7,819.1	-0.9
Industrial firms....................	3,515.4	3,497.0	3,444.6	4,345.2	4,554.9	4,762.8	4,813.3	5,252.1	5,181.1	-1.4
FFRDCs[2] administered by										
industrial firms	517.7	565.8	528.9	647.2	697.7	790.7	839.3	823.5	786.3	-4.5
Universities and colleges.......	3,788.9	4,096.7	5,959.2	6,864.9	7,617.2	8,524.7	9,300.6	9,685.0	9,431.6	-2.6
FFRDCs[2] administered by										
universities and colleges ...	1,100.7	988.6	1,099.2	1,334.2	1,414.1	1,444.8	1,681.6	1,659.4	1,503.1	-9.4
Other nonprofit institutions	1,027.7	1,156.7	1,734.5	2,136.2	2,191.3	2,492.5	2,470.3	2,573.6	2,581.5	0.3
FFRDCs[2] administered by										
nonprofit institutions...........	92.6	114.6	174.5	198.9	186.2	197.0	188.7	198.9	195.8	-1.6
State and local governments.	155.2	171.0	86.9	237.1	204.0	220.4	335.0	344.9	340.0	-1.4
Foreign	64.1	62.8	45.1	54.9	75.6	130.0	194.7	202.1	202.5	0.2

See notes at end of table.

Table 372. Federal obligations for research, development, and R&D plant, by performers, fields of science, and category of obligation: Fiscal years 1998 through 2006—Continued

[In millions of current dollars]

Performers, fields of science, and category of obligation	Actual							Estimated		Percent change, 2005 to 2006
	1998	1999	2000	2001	2002	2003	2004	2005	2006	
1	2	3	4	5	6	7	8	9	10	11
Fields of science										
Life sciences	5,704.1	6,225.3	7,915.7	10,221.8	11,452.7	13,007.0	13,238.5	13,727.7	13,522.5	-1.5
Psychology	279.0	285.3	808.9	449.0	441.3	560.6	875.6	901.1	906.6	0.6
Physical sciences	1,268.3	976.4	1,317.3	1,273.6	1,577.4	1,567.6	1,548.6	1,657.5	1,599.5	-3.5
Environmental sciences	1,533.2	1,479.5	1,490.3	1,588.6	1,585.0	1,841.4	1,718.7	1,815.6	1,672.9	-7.9
Mathematics and computer sciences	1,131.4	1,245.7	1,407.3	1,652.8	1,632.0	1,552.2	1,710.3	1,836.3	1,827.0	-0.5
Engineering	4,301.0	4,623.7	4,582.2	6,285.5	6,410.0	6,492.0	6,594.7	7,056.8	6,832.5	-3.2
Social sciences	581.3	608.3	742.3	730.2	676.9	673.0	670.3	701.9	733.2	4.5
Other sciences	510.9	639.6	636.6	554.1	563.3	626.6	880.5	930.0	946.8	1.8
Development obligations	**40,981.0**	**41,813.1**	**34,392.7**	**35,219.5**	**37,846.3**	**42,589.5**	**52,365.3**	**59,525.9**	**57,439.1**	**-3.5**
Performers										
Federal intramural[1]	9,149.3	9,398.9	7,700.2	9,088.9	9,187.4	10,442.0	14,684.6	17,975.4	15,541.1	-13.5
Industrial firms	27,204.6	27,321.8	22,934.4	21,744.0	23,751.4	27,810.3	32,431.8	36,099.8	36,929.2	2.3
FFRDCs[2] administered by industrial firms	344.7	448.8	400.6	364.3	413.7	404.1	411.6	496.7	421.6	-15.1
Universities and colleges	1,624.8	1,755.3	799.3	930.8	1,004.7	1,017.0	1,470.6	1,625.5	1,362.0	-16.2
FFRDCs[2] administered by universities and colleges	1,147.2	1,342.3	1,279.9	1,521.4	1,421.8	1,481.6	1,713.5	1,763.5	1,758.4	-0.3
Other nonprofit institutions	729.9	802.0	496.8	560.8	1,016.1	510.3	407.4	483.5	388.1	-19.7
FFRDCs[2] administered by nonprofit institutions	388.5	443.7	535.4	529.7	655.2	573.7	647.7	603.5	603.2	0.0
State and local governments	207.4	125.1	61.5	141.9	176.7	94.1	347.2	333.7	329.1	-1.4
Foreign	184.6	175.2	184.7	337.6	219.2	256.3	250.9	144.3	106.4	-26.2
R&D plant obligations	**1,840.2**	**2,045.8**	**4,492.8**	**4,069.8**	**4,304.7**	**4,266.5**	**3,994.2**	**3,924.1**	**3,681.9**	**-6.2**
Performers										
Federal intramural[1]	475.3	483.3	573.3	520.4	414.8	609.7	961.3	938.1	859.5	-8.4
Industrial firms	487.7	544.7	2,814.6	2,179.8	2,524.9	1,817.0	1,442.0	1,573.6	1,486.8	-5.5
FFRDCs[2] administered by industrial firms	45.6	172.8	27.6	41.8	109.1	145.7	188.3	127.7	89.1	-30.3
Universities and colleges	139.5	141.2	213.5	284.7	241.1	686.9	354.3	295.8	280.6	-5.1
FFRDCs[2] administered by universities and colleges	663.6	615.5	613.8	615.9	583.3	578.4	603.9	563.9	566.7	0.5
Other nonprofit institutions	10.9	12.2	55.5	27.9	29.1	70.7	164.5	163.5	169.7	3.8
FFRDCs[2] administered by nonprofit institutions	12.1	70.7	193.5	357.5	388.8	333.9	252.4	232.6	199.1	-14.4
State and local governments	—	5.3	0.9	1.4	2.0	0.8	15.8	16.6	17.5	5.1
Foreign	5.5	—	0.1	40.4	11.7	23.4	11.7	12.3	12.9	5.0

—Not available.

[1]Includes costs associated with the administration of intramural and extramural programs by federal personnel as well as actual intramural performance.

[2]Federally funded research and development centers.

NOTE: Some data have been revised from previously published figures. Detail may not sum to totals because of rounding. Totals do not include the U.S. Department of Homeland Security.

SOURCE: National Science Foundation, *Federal Funds for Research and Development*, 1997 through 2006. (This table was prepared November 2006.)

Table 373. Federal obligations for research and development and R&D plant, by agency and state or jurisdiction: Fiscal year 2004

[In thousands of dollars]

State or jurisdiction	Total	Department of Agriculture	Department of Commerce	Department of Defense	Department of Energy	Department of Homeland Security	Department of Health and Human Services	Department of the Interior	Department of Transportation	Environmental Protection Agency	National Aeronautics and Space Administration	National Science Foundation
1	2	3	4	5	6	7	8	9	10	11	12	13
United States[1]	$107,159,014	$2,257,392	$1,146,135	$51,356,669	$8,557,009	$1,062,765	$28,136,384	$608,830	$646,416	$660,076	$8,595,908	$4,131,430
Alabama	3,101,656	22,405	1,187	2,365,203	9,238	30,230	328,294	2,252	7,143	3,373	309,553	22,778
Alaska	387,774	19,070	27,902	236,973	10,131	882	21,138	23,173	2,925	808	15,076	29,696
Arizona	2,459,204	47,663	1,990	1,979,295	8,680	18,426	165,251	9,454	5,698	187	94,418	128,142
Arkansas	148,973	35,636	0	9,410	535	0	87,989	1,516	2,050	268	1,852	9,717
California	19,921,786	134,733	117,818	10,404,912	1,839,026	190,365	3,163,210	82,037	25,380	12,812	3,296,801	654,692
Colorado	1,889,115	41,228	140,178	564,057	147,157	1,484	346,079	87,877	22,364	10,542	303,200	224,949
Connecticut	2,274,984	9,496	5,818	1,662,292	34,349	21,626	430,984	1,452	2,711	958	66,507	38,791
Delaware	86,022	5,256	2,492	17,794	4,216	203	28,782	779	974	1,451	7,492	16,583
District of Columbia	3,355,839	235,035	4,503	1,934,151	290,470	86,723	245,869	2,038	175,275	70,079	187,364	124,332
Florida	3,151,357	63,896	32,854	2,345,882	14,773	13,199	360,961	33,737	10,663	21,845	141,845	111,702
Georgia	1,738,946	67,975	1,887	956,329	39,357	20,869	517,696	5,405	6,711	12,447	29,014	81,256
Hawaii	399,654	50,002	17,244	199,394	2,631	8	75,319	7,649	816	204	23,307	23,080
Idaho	282,414	24,994	1,742	18,100	182,750	21,240	14,365	4,436	4,281	193	3,322	6,991
Illinois	1,959,416	65,166	11,692	240,584	673,444	38,673	687,534	1,473	9,302	4,349	23,766	203,433
Indiana	548,819	18,455	1,767	205,127	19,228	478	203,127	2,189	4,217	1,733	11,224	81,274
Iowa	584,888	167,671	476	78,144	85,246	255	194,578	2,100	9,885	1,690	11,164	33,679
Kansas	211,310	19,386	30	61,180	11,650	0	76,065	2,372	7,526	0	5,681	27,420
Kentucky	244,709	15,649	4	37,728	5,500	6,363	148,101	1,076	2,964	658	7,884	18,782
Louisiana	436,657	47,413	1,074	158,867	5,822	3	168,141	14,883	2,874	1,635	6,794	29,151
Maine	193,205	10,129	2,747	81,939	832	379	74,715	2,733	1,003	102	5,535	13,091
Maryland	13,060,703	158,448	422,363	3,836,604	31,704	119,762	7,098,006	18,957	19,977	7,485	1,248,233	99,164
Massachusetts	5,653,019	23,788	32,551	2,714,976	115,566	21,638	2,219,291	10,605	53,228	10,027	176,330	275,019
Michigan	1,080,923	28,489	22,594	287,138	32,919	689	541,462	6,255	13,638	9,480	22,109	116,150
Minnesota	832,089	36,103	4,807	231,068	11,615	3,785	442,861	3,032	2,420	23,087	10,715	62,596
Mississippi	1,604,698	108,047	13,992	1,388,674	2,862	83	44,420	4,379	3,251	1,782	24,707	12,501
Missouri	2,984,020	33,323	1,146	2,383,063	5,465	516	486,798	9,153	7,596	95	21,005	35,860
Montana	190,621	31,397	113	47,199	2,937	0	74,483	7,715	1,537	70	9,095	16,075
Nebraska	156,780	37,557	907	13,715	1,740	0	74,608	2,700	2,629	0	5,622	17,302
Nevada	517,789	3,176	1,236	50,118	368,147	2,811	22,744	3,040	3,836	23,876	26,255	12,550
New Hampshire	360,615	9,628	23,192	143,621	2,588	42,607	98,821	712	2,752	1,046	20,320	15,328
New Jersey	2,191,448	6,860	28,164	1,528,864	99,844	30,063	275,899	2,842	44,389	7,445	78,788	88,290
New Mexico	3,338,517	12,778	5,914	815,876	2,213,083	86,346	111,488	14,195	7,532	3,799	41,748	25,758
New York	4,105,429	42,360	25,731	992,267	657,170	32,017	1,928,930	4,561	14,981	13,016	77,046	317,350
North Carolina	1,698,066	41,540	18,295	175,615	20,907	3,408	1,128,737	3,589	4,697	191,926	22,267	87,085
North Dakota	102,998	34,799	1,326	20,380	10,009	0	20,553	3,578	1,995	1,209	2,203	6,946
Ohio	2,723,962	27,980	9,099	1,342,520	36,716	33,548	713,027	2,598	21,402	132,503	329,139	75,430
Oklahoma	321,615	22,040	20,796	101,924	9,195	600	91,495	1,860	17,161	14,161	22,685	19,698
Oregon	455,870	51,201	6,975	30,097	22,639	5	259,470	10,857	5,025	15,867	12,620	41,114
Pennsylvania	3,438,353	57,890	8,859	1,294,929	421,355	3,909	1,391,008	3,608	9,539	1,888	48,749	196,619
Rhode Island	507,209	2,477	1,933	315,386	2,918	35	131,975	1,672	960	15,686	5,846	28,321
South Carolina	381,866	23,952	9,005	154,179	23,102	1,838	125,940	2,325	3,203	1,143	11,081	26,098
South Dakota	80,834	20,103	17	7,888	123	0	16,507	13,248	3,419	714	12,565	6,250
Tennessee	1,263,071	23,950	3,571	122,664	567,364	21,070	398,124	2,632	4,846	912	78,266	39,672
Texas	5,761,395	97,645	18,218	3,338,870	47,870	2,620	1,148,047	9,498	21,013	4,645	958,540	114,429
Utah	683,264	28,675	763	426,117	11,770	1,492	154,759	3,335	1,802	666	21,651	32,234
Vermont	212,229	10,410	1,139	115,701	1,453	371	72,135	1,027	705	993	1,935	6,360
Virginia	6,924,887	15,530	12,983	5,005,843	111,770	175,456	467,456	142,261	49,284	14,376	676,350	253,578
Washington	2,103,233	51,690	63,290	777,989	204,584	26,146	816,742	7,749	8,007	12,599	37,074	97,363
West Virginia	300,012	36,443	3,054	77,141	103,193	543	42,842	5,241	3,681	1,518	19,830	6,523
Wisconsin	700,809	68,301	10,344	55,977	26,082	1	389,531	14,956	3,432	2,621	19,480	110,084
Wyoming	45,962	9,554	353	2,902	5,284	0	10,027	2,019	3,717	107	1,855	10,144
Other jurisdictions	130,379	14,635	2,047	15,918	795	0	62,546	1,100	0	0	10,275	23,063
Puerto Rico	102,495	9,810	537	442	795	0	58,503	628	0	0	10,125	21,655
Other areas	27,884	4,825	1,510	15,476	0	0	4,043	472	0	0	150	1,408
Offices abroad	99,368	5,474	0	77,596	0	0	16,280	18	0	0	0	0

[1]Excludes other jurisdictions and offices abroad.
NOTE: Only the agencies shown are required to report on this section of the survey. The obligations of the 11 major R&D supporting agencies included in this table represent approximately 98 percent of total federal R&D and R&D plant obligations in fiscal year 2004. Geographic distribution of Department of Defense development funding to industry reflects location of only prime contractors and not numerous subcontractors who perform much of the R&D. Detail may not sum to totals because of rounding.
SOURCE: National Science Foundation, *Federal Funds for Research and Development*, fiscal years 2004, 2005, and 2006. (This table was prepared November 2006.)

CHAPTER 5
Outcomes of Education

This chapter contains tables comparing educational attainment and workforce characteristics. The data show labor force participation and income levels of high school dropouts and high school and college graduates. Population characteristics are provided for many of the measures to help provide comparisons among various demographic groups. Tables 374 to 376 contain data from the U.S. Census Bureau on educational attainment of the labor force and data from the Bureau of Labor Statistics on employment and unemployment. These tables provide information on the educational attainment of the labor force, by occupation, sex, race/ethnicity, and unemployment rates. Tables 377 and 378 provide an income comparison by education level and sex.

Tables 381 and 382, compiled from Bureau of Labor Statistics data on high school completers and dropouts, show the labor force participation and college enrollment of high school students within the year after they leave school. The tabulations also provide comparative labor force participation and unemployment rates for high school completers and dropouts. Additional information on college enrollment rates by race/ethnicity and sex has been included to help form a more complete picture of high school outcomes. Tables 384 to 387 were prepared from the Recent College Graduates and Baccalaureate and Beyond surveys by the National Center for Education Statistics (NCES). These tables provide data on employment outcomes and salaries for college graduates 1 year after graduation. The last tables in this chapter deal with community service, drug use, and life values of high school seniors and young adults.

Statistics related to outcomes of education appear in other sections of the *Digest*. For example, statistics on educational attainment of the entire population are in chapter 1. More detailed data on the numbers of high school and college graduates are contained in chapters 2 and 3. Chapter 3 contains trend data on the proportion of high school completers going to college. Additional data on the income of persons by educational attainment may be obtained from the U.S. Census Bureau in the *Current Population Reports*, Series P-60. The Bureau of Labor Statistics has a series of publications dealing with the educational characteristics of the labor force. Further information on survey methodologies is in Appendix A: Guide to Sources and in the publications cited in the table source notes.

Labor Force

Adults with higher levels of education were generally more likely to participate in the labor force than adults with less education (table 374 and figure 21). (Persons participating in the labor force are those employed or actively seeking employment.) Among persons 25 to 64 years old, about 86 percent of those with a bachelor's or higher degree participated in the labor force in 2005, compared with 76 percent of those who had completed only high school. In comparison, 63 percent of those 25 to 64 who had not completed high school were in the labor force. The 2005 labor force participation rate for those ages 25 to 64 who completed only high school was higher for Hispanics (79 percent) than for Blacks (75 percent), but neither the Hispanic nor Black rate was substantially different from the White rate (77 percent) (table 374). Whites, Blacks, and Hispanics ages 25 to 64 with a bachelor's or higher degree had labor force participation rates that were about the same (86 to 87 percent).

Persons with lower levels of educational attainment were generally more likely to be unemployed than those with higher levels of educational attainment (table 375). The 2005 unemployment rate for adults (25 years old and over) who had not completed high school was 7.6 percent, compared with 4.7 percent for those who had completed high school and 2.3 percent for those with a bachelor's or higher degree (figure 22). Younger people who completed only high school tended to have higher unemployment rates than persons 25 years old and over who completed only high school (table 375).

The relative difficulties dropouts have in entering the job market are highlighted by comparing their labor force participation and unemployment rates to those of other youth. Of the 2005 high school completers who were not in college in October 2005, 78 percent were in the labor force (employed or looking for work), and 21 percent of those in the labor force were looking for work (table 381). In comparison, about 57 percent of 2004–05 dropouts were in the labor force in October 2005, and 33 percent of those in the labor force were looking for work (table 382 and figure 23).

One year after graduating from college in 1999–2000, 87 percent of individuals receiving bachelor's degrees were employed (77 percent full time and 11 percent part time), 6 percent were unemployed, and 6 percent were not in the labor force (table 385).

Income

The median annual income of male full-time year-round workers, when adjusted for inflation, increased between 1995 and 1999, but decreased between 1999 and 2005 (table 377). Income for females rose between 1995 and 2001, but then declined between 2001 and 2005, for a net increase of 4 percent for the entire period. Women's incomes remained lower than men's incomes overall, as well as by education level. For example, the average 2005 income for full-time year-round workers with a bachelor's degree was $60,020 for men and $42,172 for women.

Figure 21. Labor force participation rate of persons 20 to 64 years old, by age group and highest level of education: 2005

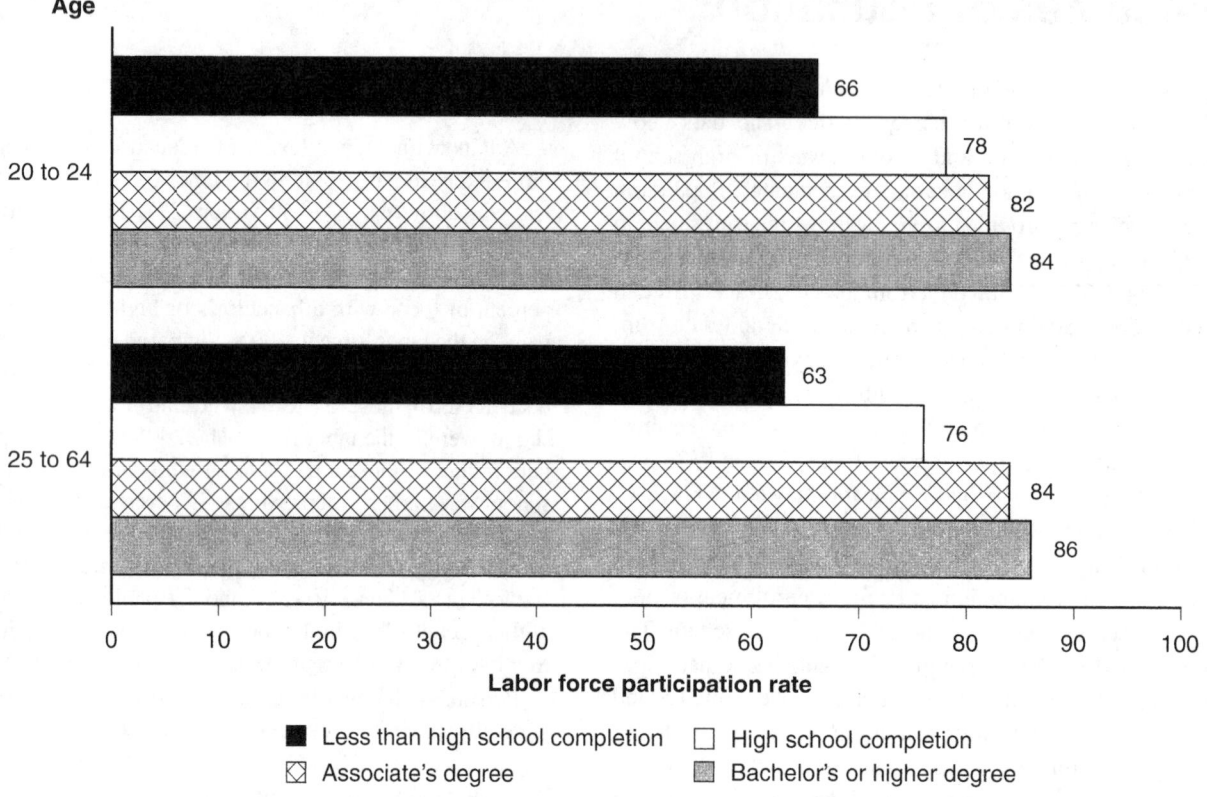

SOURCE: U.S. Department of Labor, Bureau of Labor Statistics, Office of Employment and Unemployment Statistics, Current Population Survey (CPS), 2005.

Figure 22. Unemployment rates of persons 25 years old and over, by highest level of education: 2005

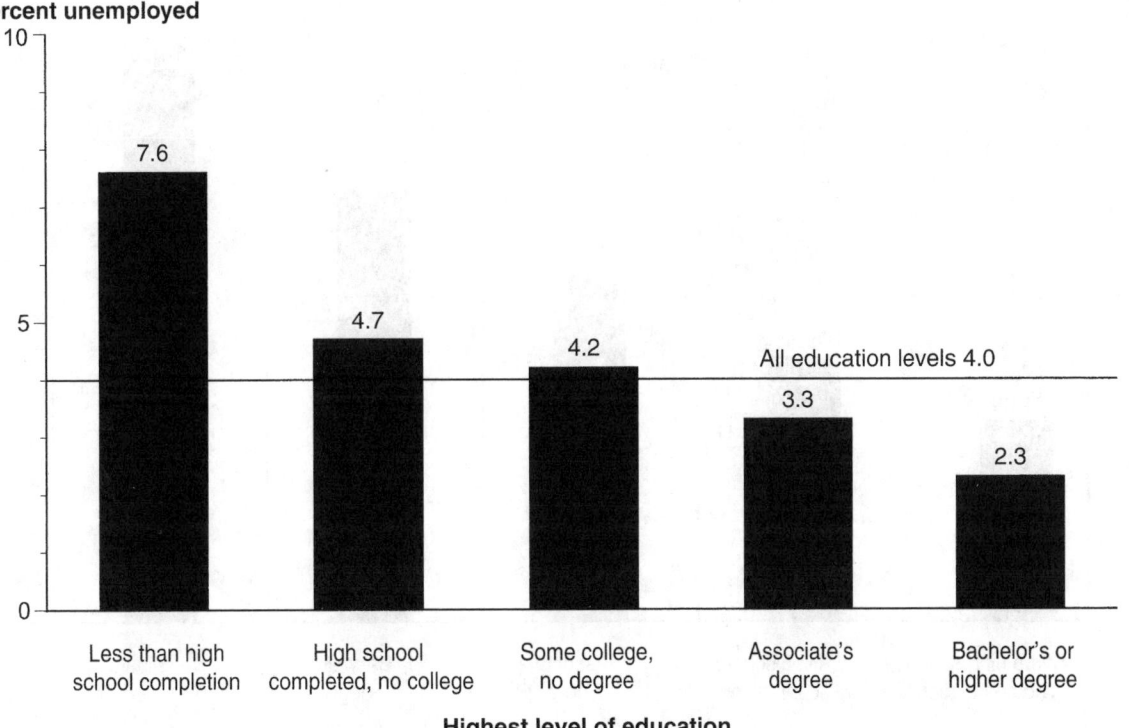

SOURCE: U.S. Department of Labor, Bureau of Labor Statistics, Office of Employment and Unemployment Statistics, Current Population Survey (CPS), 2005.

Figure 23. Labor force status of 2004–05 high school dropouts and completers not enrolled in college: October 2005

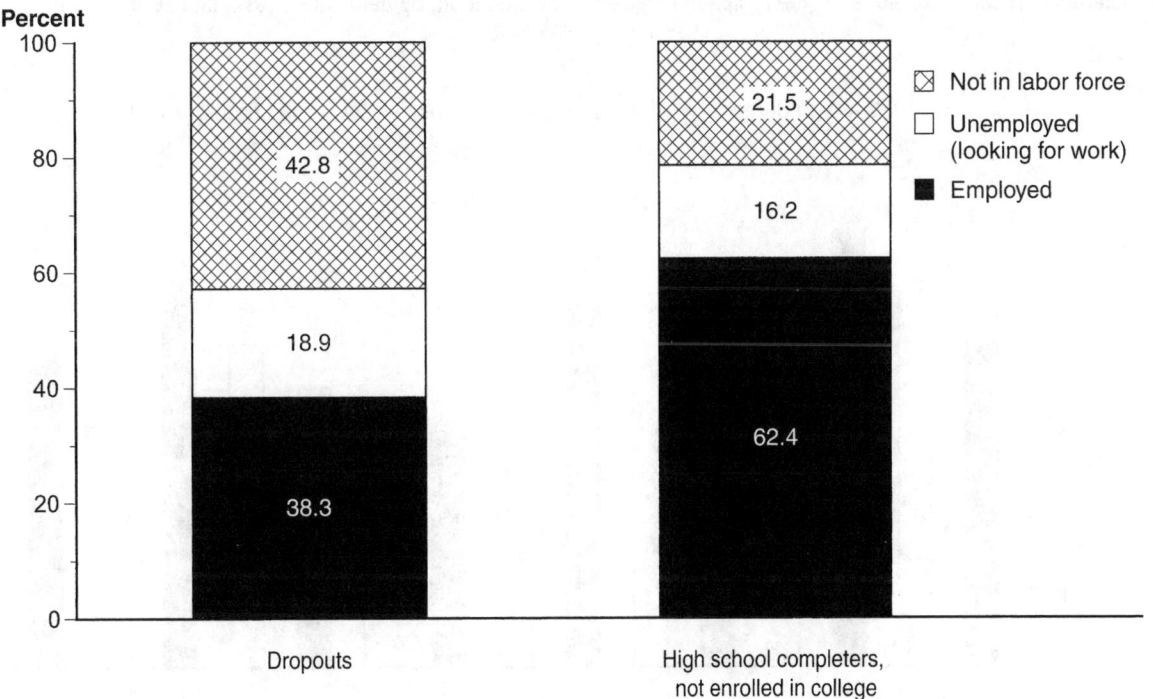

NOTE: Dropouts are persons who have not completed high school, and are not enrolled in school. Detail may not sum to totals because of rounding.
SOURCE: U.S. Department of Labor, Bureau of Labor Statistics, "College Enrollment and Work Activity of 2005 High School Graduates."

Figure 24. Median annual earnings of persons 25 years old and over, by highest level of education and sex: 2005

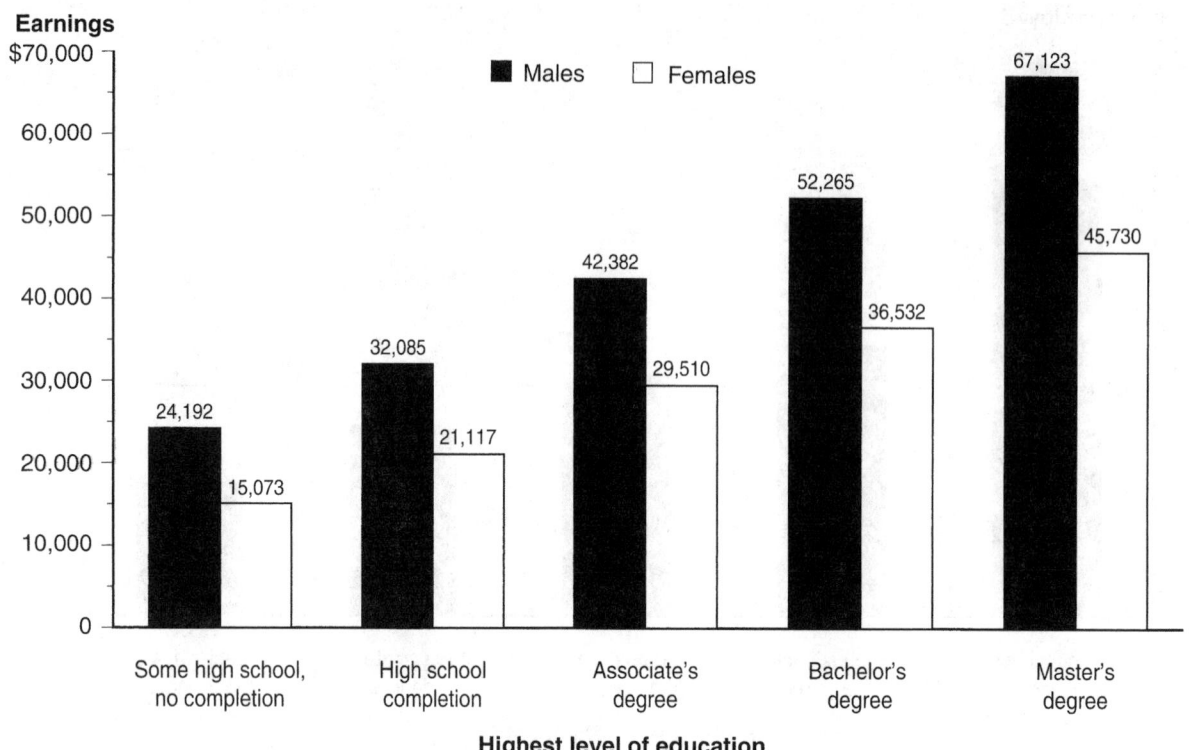

NOTE: Excludes persons without earnings.
SOURCE: U.S. Department of Commerce, Census Bureau, Current Population Survey (CPS), March 2005.

Figure 25. Salaries of recent bachelor's degree recipients 1 year after graduation, by field: 1991, 1994, and 2001
(in constant 2005 dollars)

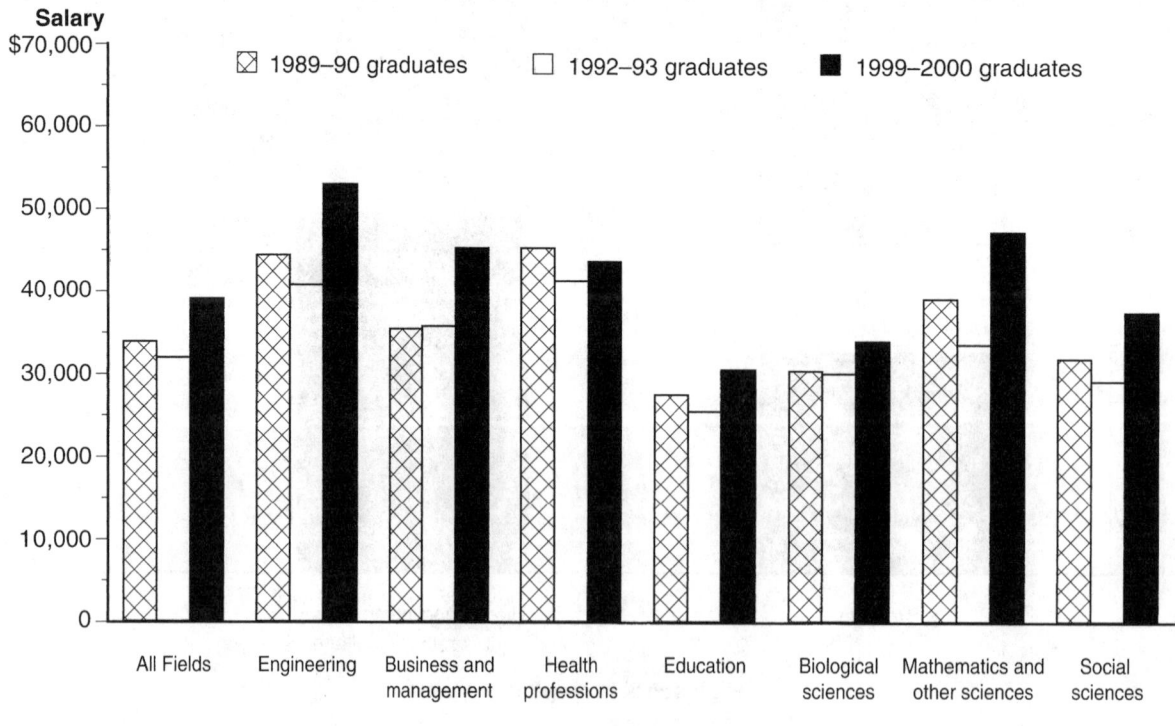

SOURCE: U.S. Department of Education, National Center for Education Statistics, Recent College Graduates Study (RCG), 1991; and 1993/94 and 2000/01 Baccalaureate and Beyond Longitudinal Study (B&B:93/94) and (B&B:2000/01).

Table 374. Labor force participation rates and employment to population ratios of persons 16 to 64 years old, by highest level of education, age, sex, and race/ethnicity: 2005

Age, sex, and race/ethnicity	Labor force participation rate[1]						Employment/population ratio[2]					
	Total	Less than high school completion[3]	High school completion	College			Total	Less than high school completion[3]	High school completion	College		
				Some college, no degree	Associate's degree	Bachelor's or higher degree				Some college, no degree	Associate's degree	Bachelor's or higher degree
1	2	3	4	5	6	7	8	9	10	11	12	13
16 to 19 years old[4]	43.7 (0.39)	35.4 (0.45)	63.6 (0.89)	58.2 (1.04)	‡ (†)	‡ (†)	36.5 (0.38)	28.5 (0.43)	53.6 (0.93)	52.9 (1.05)	‡ (†)	‡ (†)
Male	43.2 (0.54)	35.2 (0.62)	65.9 (1.26)	57.1 (1.57)	‡ (†)	‡ (†)	35.1 (0.52)	27.5 (0.58)	54.7 (1.33)	51.3 (1.59)	‡ (†)	‡ (†)
Female	44.2 (0.55)	35.7 (0.66)	61.3 (1.26)	59.1 (1.39)	‡ (†)	‡ (†)	37.8 (0.54)	29.5 (0.63)	52.6 (1.30)	54.2 (1.41)	‡ (†)	‡ (†)
White	48.7 (0.50)	40.6 (0.60)	67.0 (1.10)	61.8 (1.23)	‡ (†)	‡ (†)	42.2 (0.49)	34.1 (0.58)	58.4 (1.15)	57.2 (1.26)	‡ (†)	‡ (†)
Black	32.3 (0.95)	24.3 (1.03)	53.6 (2.37)	49.4 (3.21)	‡ (†)	‡ (†)	21.3 (0.83)	14.5 (0.84)	37.5 (2.30)	39.0 (3.13)	‡ (†)	‡ (†)
Hispanic	38.6 (0.87)	29.9 (0.96)	63.2 (2.10)	57.8 (2.76)	‡ (†)	‡ (†)	31.5 (0.83)	23.4 (0.89)	52.8 (2.18)	51.9 (2.79)	‡ (†)	‡ (†)
20 to 24 years old[4]	74.6 (0.35)	66.2 (1.02)	78.4 (0.60)	70.4 (0.61)	82.1 (1.22)	83.8 (0.87)	68.0 (0.38)	55.4 (1.08)	70.0 (0.67)	65.8 (0.63)	77.1 (1.33)	79.6 (0.95)
Male	79.1 (0.46)	79.3 (1.15)	85.3 (0.69)	70.5 (0.86)	85.1 (1.67)	85.4 (1.29)	71.5 (0.51)	67.8 (1.33)	75.9 (0.83)	65.2 (0.90)	79.9 (1.88)	80.5 (1.44)
Female	70.1 (0.50)	49.2 (1.56)	69.9 (0.96)	70.3 (0.81)	79.8 (1.62)	82.8 (1.10)	64.5 (0.52)	39.5 (1.53)	62.8 (1.01)	66.4 (0.83)	74.8 (1.75)	79.1 (1.18)
White	77.3 (0.43)	67.2 (1.69)	80.8 (0.75)	72.4 (0.73)	84.6 (1.37)	85.9 (0.94)	71.9 (0.46)	56.0 (1.79)	73.8 (0.84)	68.5 (0.75)	80.7 (1.50)	82.0 (1.03)
Black	68.9 (1.09)	56.6 (2.81)	73.0 (1.74)	67.2 (1.85)	74.5 (4.60)	84.0 (3.35)	56.1 (1.17)	36.5 (2.73)	57.2 (1.94)	59.7 (1.94)	63.4 (5.09)	76.8 (3.86)
Hispanic	72.7 (0.88)	69.7 (1.56)	76.3 (1.45)	70.0 (1.84)	77.7 (3.79)	77.1 (4.18)	66.4 (0.93)	63.0 (1.63)	69.8 (1.56)	64.3 (1.93)	71.6 (4.10)	74.1 (4.36)
25 to 64 years old	78.9 (0.12)	63.0 (0.41)	76.4 (0.22)	79.8 (0.28)	84.0 (0.35)	85.7 (0.19)	75.7 (0.13)	58.1 (0.42)	72.8 (0.24)	76.5 (0.30)	81.3 (0.37)	83.8 (0.20)
Male	86.4 (0.14)	75.8 (0.49)	84.7 (0.26)	86.9 (0.34)	89.4 (0.44)	91.8 (0.21)	83.1 (0.15)	70.9 (0.52)	80.7 (0.29)	83.5 (0.38)	86.5 (0.48)	89.7 (0.23)
Female	71.6 (0.18)	48.7 (0.58)	68.1 (0.33)	73.5 (0.41)	79.8 (0.49)	79.9 (0.29)	68.6 (0.18)	43.8 (0.58)	64.8 (0.34)	70.2 (0.42)	77.1 (0.51)	78.0 (0.30)
White	79.9 (0.14)	58.3 (0.66)	76.7 (0.27)	79.9 (0.33)	84.5 (0.40)	86.0 (0.21)	77.3 (0.15)	53.9 (0.67)	73.6 (0.28)	77.1 (0.35)	82.0 (0.42)	84.2 (0.22)
Black	75.9 (0.39)	55.3 (1.22)	74.6 (0.66)	78.9 (0.84)	82.8 (1.17)	87.2 (0.70)	70.2 (0.42)	47.0 (1.23)	68.1 (0.70)	72.8 (0.91)	78.6 (1.27)	84.3 (0.76)
Hispanic	77.0 (0.35)	70.2 (0.61)	78.6 (0.63)	82.0 (0.86)	83.1 (1.27)	85.8 (0.81)	73.3 (0.37)	65.8 (0.63)	75.0 (0.67)	78.7 (0.92)	79.8 (1.36)	83.4 (0.87)

†Not applicable.

‡Reporting standards not met.

[1]Percent of the civilian population who are employed or seeking employment.

[2]Number of persons employed as a percent of civilian population.

[3]Includes persons reporting no school years completed.

[4]Excludes persons enrolled in school.

NOTE: Race categories exclude persons of Hispanic origin. Standard errors appear in parentheses.

SOURCE: U.S. Department of Labor, Bureau of Labor Statistics, Office of Employment and Unemployment Statistics, unpublished 2005 annual average data from the Current Population Survey (CPS). (This table was prepared July 2006.)

Table 375. Unemployment rate of persons 16 years old and over, by age, sex, race/ethnicity, and educational attainment: 2003, 2004, and 2005

Sex, race/ethnicity, and educational attainment	Unemployment rate, 2003				Unemployment rate, 2004				Unemployment rate, 2005			
	16- to 24-year-olds[1]			25 years old and over	16- to 24-year-olds[1]			25 years old and over	16- to 24-year-olds[1]			25 years old and over
	Total	16 to 19 years	20 to 24 years		Total	16 to 19 years	20 to 24 years		Total	16 to 19 years	20 to 24 years	
1	2	3	4	5	6	7	8	9	10	11	12	13
All persons, all education levels	12.4 (0.16)	17.4 (0.33)	10.0 (0.18)	4.8 (0.04)	11.9 (0.17)	17.0 (0.34)	9.4 (0.18)	4.4 (0.04)	11.3 (0.16)	16.6 (0.34)	8.8 (0.18)	4.0 (0.04)
Less than high school completion	19.1 (0.37)	19.6 (0.45)	18.2 (0.64)	8.8 (0.18)	18.8 (0.39)	20.0 (0.49)	16.4 (0.65)	8.5 (0.19)	18.5 (0.39)	19.6 (0.49)	16.2 (0.66)	7.6 (0.18)
High school completion, no college	13.4 (0.30)	17.4 (0.65)	12.0 (0.34)	5.5 (0.08)	12.4 (0.31)	15.8 (0.65)	11.1 (0.35)	5.0 (0.09)	12.1 (0.31)	15.6 (0.65)	10.7 (0.34)	4.7 (0.08)
Some college, no degree	7.8 (0.25)	10.3 (0.64)	7.3 (0.26)	5.2 (0.11)	7.8 (0.26)	9.1 (0.64)	7.5 (0.28)	4.5 (0.11)	7.0 (0.24)	9.1 (0.61)	6.5 (0.26)	4.2 (0.10)
Associate's degree	6.8 (0.58)	‡ (†)	6.6 (0.58)	4.0 (0.13)	6.1 (0.57)	‡ (†)	5.9 (0.57)	3.7 (0.13)	6.2 (0.56)	‡ (†)	6.1 (0.56)	3.3 (0.12)
Bachelor's or higher degree	6.1 (0.39)	‡ (†)	6.1 (0.39)	3.1 (0.06)	5.6 (0.39)	‡ (†)	5.6 (0.39)	2.7 (0.06)	5.0 (0.37)	‡ (†)	5.0 (0.38)	2.3 (0.06)
Male, all education levels	13.4 (0.23)	19.3 (0.48)	10.6 (0.26)	5.0 (0.06)	12.6 (0.23)	18.4 (0.49)	10.1 (0.25)	4.4 (0.06)	12.4 (0.23)	18.6 (0.49)	9.6 (0.25)	3.8 (0.06)
Less than high school completion	19.3 (0.49)	21.1 (0.64)	16.3 (0.75)	8.2 (0.23)	18.8 (0.51)	21.4 (0.68)	14.7 (0.74)	7.6 (0.23)	19.0 (0.51)	21.7 (0.69)	14.5 (0.75)	6.4 (0.21)
High school completion, no college	14.0 (0.41)	19.6 (0.95)	12.1 (0.45)	5.7 (0.12)	12.7 (0.41)	16.4 (0.90)	11.4 (0.45)	5.1 (0.12)	12.5 (0.40)	17.1 (0.93)	11.0 (0.44)	4.6 (0.11)
Some college, no degree	8.3 (0.37)	11.0 (1.05)	7.7 (0.39)	5.4 (0.16)	8.7 (0.39)	10.2 (1.01)	8.4 (0.42)	4.4 (0.15)	8.0 (0.37)	10.2 (0.96)	7.5 (0.40)	3.9 (0.14)
Associate's degree	7.8 (0.93)	‡ (†)	7.6 (0.93)	4.4 (0.20)	5.7 (0.83)	‡ (†)	5.6 (0.83)	4.0 (0.20)	6.0 (0.79)	‡ (†)	6.0 (0.81)	3.3 (0.18)
Bachelor's or higher degree	6.7 (0.64)	‡ (†)	6.8 (0.64)	3.2 (0.09)	5.9 (0.60)	‡ (†)	5.9 (0.60)	2.7 (0.08)	5.7 (0.61)	‡ (†)	5.8 (0.61)	2.3 (0.08)
Female, all education levels	11.4 (0.21)	15.6 (0.41)	9.3 (0.23)	4.6 (0.06)	11.0 (0.22)	15.5 (0.45)	8.7 (0.25)	4.4 (0.06)	10.1 (0.21)	14.5 (0.43)	7.9 (0.24)	4.2 (0.06)
Less than high school completion	18.9 (0.52)	17.9 (0.58)	22.1 (1.11)	9.8 (0.29)	18.9 (0.57)	18.4 (0.66)	20.1 (1.17)	10.0 (0.33)	17.9 (0.56)	17.2 (0.64)	19.8 (1.18)	9.7 (0.32)
High school completion, no college	12.7 (0.42)	15.1 (0.81)	11.7 (0.48)	5.2 (0.11)	12.1 (0.45)	15.2 (0.87)	10.6 (0.51)	4.9 (0.12)	11.5 (0.44)	14.2 (0.85)	10.2 (0.50)	4.8 (0.12)
Some college, no degree	7.5 (0.30)	9.8 (0.75)	6.8 (0.33)	4.9 (0.14)	7.1 (0.32)	8.4 (0.77)	6.8 (0.35)	4.7 (0.15)	6.0 (0.30)	8.2 (0.74)	5.5 (0.32)	4.5 (0.15)
Associate's degree	6.1 (0.68)	‡ (†)	5.9 (0.68)	3.7 (0.16)	6.3 (0.74)	‡ (†)	6.2 (0.74)	3.4 (0.17)	6.4 (0.72)	‡ (†)	6.2 (0.73)	3.3 (0.16)
Bachelor's or higher degree	5.5 (0.45)	‡ (†)	5.6 (0.45)	2.9 (0.08)	5.3 (0.47)	‡ (†)	5.3 (0.47)	2.7 (0.09)	4.5 (0.44)	‡ (†)	4.5 (0.44)	2.4 (0.08)
White, all education levels	10.2 (0.18)	14.4 (0.36)	8.0 (0.20)	4.0 (0.05)	9.8 (0.19)	14.1 (0.38)	7.6 (0.21)	3.6 (0.05)	9.2 (0.18)	13.5 (0.37)	7.0 (0.20)	3.3 (0.05)
Less than high school completion	16.7 (0.45)	16.4 (0.50)	18.1 (1.04)	7.6 (0.27)	16.2 (0.48)	16.3 (0.54)	15.7 (1.05)	7.7 (0.30)	16.1 (0.48)	16.0 (0.54)	16.7 (1.10)	7.1 (0.29)
High school completion, no college	10.9 (0.35)	13.8 (0.71)	9.7 (0.39)	4.6 (0.09)	10.6 (0.36)	13.5 (0.73)	9.3 (0.41)	4.3 (0.10)	10.0 (0.36)	12.9 (0.74)	8.7 (0.40)	4.0 (0.09)
Some college, no degree	6.7 (0.27)	8.9 (0.70)	6.2 (0.29)	4.3 (0.12)	6.7 (0.29)	8.2 (0.70)	6.4 (0.31)	3.7 (0.12)	5.7 (0.26)	7.4 (0.65)	5.3 (0.29)	3.5 (0.11)
Associate's degree	5.1 (0.59)	‡ (†)	4.8 (0.58)	3.5 (0.14)	4.9 (0.61)	‡ (†)	4.8 (0.61)	3.3 (0.14)	4.6 (0.57)	‡ (†)	4.6 (0.58)	3.0 (0.13)
Bachelor's or higher degree	5.5 (0.42)	‡ (†)	5.5 (0.42)	2.8 (0.07)	5.0 (0.42)	‡ (†)	4.9 (0.42)	2.5 (0.07)	4.5 (0.40)	‡ (†)	4.5 (0.40)	2.1 (0.06)
Black, all education levels	23.8 (0.66)	33.2 (1.34)	19.9 (0.73)	8.3 (0.19)	22.4 (0.67)	32.0 (1.41)	18.6 (0.74)	8.1 (0.19)	23.0 (0.67)	34.0 (1.40)	18.6 (0.73)	7.6 (0.18)
Less than high school completion	36.8 (1.43)	35.9 (1.81)	38.2 (2.32)	13.9 (0.70)	37.1 (1.51)	38.7 (1.99)	34.9 (2.33)	15.5 (0.78)	38.4 (1.53)	40.4 (1.98)	35.3 (2.40)	14.5 (0.74)
High school completion, no college	24.7 (1.11)	34.0 (2.54)	22.0 (1.21)	9.4 (0.33)	21.9 (1.12)	28.0 (2.49)	19.9 (1.24)	8.7 (0.33)	23.7 (1.13)	30.1 (2.48)	21.6 (1.26)	8.7 (0.32)
Some college, no degree	14.6 (1.03)	21.1 (3.05)	13.5 (1.08)	8.6 (0.40)	14.2 (1.06)	16.2 (2.94)	13.9 (1.13)	8.4 (0.42)	12.7 (0.98)	21.4 (3.10)	11.1 (1.01)	7.7 (0.41)
Associate's degree	13.6 (2.86)	‡ (†)	12.8 (2.81)	6.1 (0.53)	6.9 (2.22)	‡ (†)	7.2 (2.32)	5.9 (0.55)	14.4 (2.82)	‡ (†)	15.0 (2.92)	5.2 (0.50)
Bachelor's or higher degree	6.8 (1.70)	‡ (†)	6.8 (1.70)	4.3 (0.29)	8.8 (1.83)	‡ (†)	8.8 (1.84)	4.2 (0.30)	8.4 (1.83)	‡ (†)	8.6 (1.87)	3.4 (0.27)
Hispanic origin,[2] all education levels	12.8 (0.42)	20.0 (0.98)	10.2 (0.45)	6.4 (0.15)	12.3 (0.44)	20.4 (1.04)	9.3 (0.46)	5.7 (0.15)	11.3 (0.43)	18.4 (0.98)	8.6 (0.44)	4.8 (0.14)
Less than high school completion	16.1 (0.73)	23.0 (1.33)	11.5 (0.81)	8.2 (0.28)	16.2 (0.78)	24.0 (1.43)	10.9 (0.85)	7.5 (0.29)	14.5 (0.76)	21.7 (1.40)	9.6 (0.82)	6.2 (0.26)
High school completion, no college	12.4 (0.73)	18.3 (1.86)	10.8 (0.77)	5.9 (0.27)	11.6 (0.76)	17.2 (1.91)	10.0 (0.80)	5.2 (0.27)	10.3 (0.71)	16.4 (1.79)	8.4 (0.52)	4.5 (0.25)
Some college, no degree	7.7 (0.74)	9.7 (2.02)	7.3 (0.80)	5.8 (0.38)	8.0 (0.79)	10.6 (2.19)	7.4 (0.84)	5.1 (0.38)	8.6 (0.82)	10.0 (1.94)	8.2 (0.91)	4.1 (0.34)
Associate's degree	10.0 (2.18)	‡ (†)	10.2 (2.22)	5.3 (0.56)	8.0 (1.89)	‡ (†)	8.1 (1.93)	4.2 (0.53)	7.9 (1.86)	‡ (†)	7.5 (1.87)	4.0 (0.50)
Bachelor's or higher degree	11.1 (2.31)	‡ (†)	11.1 (2.31)	4.1 (0.33)	5.0 (1.61)	‡ (†)	5.0 (1.61)	3.5 (0.32)	3.5 (1.42)	‡ (†)	3.6 (1.46)	2.9 (0.28)

†Not applicable.
‡Reporting standards not met.
[1]Excludes persons enrolled in school.
[2]Persons of Hispanic origin may be of any race.
NOTE: The unemployment rate is the percentage of individuals in the labor force who are not working and who made specific efforts to find employment sometime during the prior 4 weeks. The labor force includes both employed and unemployed persons.

Race categories exclude persons of Hispanic origin. Some data have been revised from previously published figures. Standard errors appear in parentheses.
SOURCE: U.S. Department of Labor, Bureau of Labor Statistics, Office of Employment and Unemployment Statistics, unpublished 2003, 2004, and 2005 annual average data from the Current Population Survey (CPS). (This table was prepared July 2006.)

Table 376. Occupation of employed persons 25 years old and over, by educational attainment and sex: 2005

Occupation and sex	Total employed, in thousands	Total	Percentage distribution, by highest level of educational attainment						
			High school				College		
			Less than 1 year of high school	1–4 years of high school, no completion	High school completion	Some college, no degree	Associate's degree	Bachelor's degree	Master's or higher degree
1	2	3	4	5	6	7	8	9	10
All persons	**121,960** (234.04)	**100.0**	**3.6** (0.06)	**6.1** (0.08)	**29.8** (0.15)	**17.5** (0.13)	**10.0** (0.10)	**21.3** (0.14)	**11.6** (0.11)
Management, professional, and related	46,303 (215.13)	100.0	0.5 (0.04)	1.2 (0.06)	12.6 (0.18)	13.1 (0.18)	10.6 (0.17)	35.4 (0.26)	26.7 (0.24)
Management, business, and financial operations	19,617 (153.02)	100.0	0.8 (0.07)	1.9 (0.11)	18.2 (0.32)	16.9 (0.31)	9.1 (0.24)	35.8 (0.40)	17.4 (0.31)
Professional and related	26,686 (174.59)	100.0	0.2 (0.03)	0.6 (0.06)	8.4 (0.20)	10.3 (0.22)	11.7 (0.23)	35.1 (0.34)	33.5 (0.33)
Education, training, and library	7,429 (97.60)	100.0	0.2 (0.06)	0.4 (0.09)	8.0 (0.36)	7.7 (0.36)	5.2 (0.30)	36.6 (0.65)	41.9 (0.66)
Preschool and kindergarten teachers	610 (28.50)	100.0	0.3 (0.27)	1.0 (0.46)	14.6 (1.65)	14.9 (1.67)	13.4 (1.60)	39.2 (2.28)	16.9 (1.75)
Elementary and middle school teachers	2,485 (57.23)	100.0	# (†)	0.1 (0.08)	1.9 (0.31)	2.4 (0.36)	2.1 (0.33)	50.3 (1.16)	43.2 (1.15)
Secondary school teachers	1,091 (38.07)	100.0	# (†)	# (†)	1.4 (0.41)	1.7 (0.46)	1.9 (0.48)	42.8 (1.73)	52.2 (1.75)
Special education teachers	396 (22.98)	100.0	—	0.3 (0.29)	2.3 (0.87)	2.8 (0.95)	1.3 (0.65)	44.2 (2.88)	49.2 (2.90)
Postsecondary teachers	1,093 (38.10)	100.0	# (†)	0.1 (0.11)	1.2 (0.38)	3.2 (0.62)	3.0 (0.60)	14.8 (1.24)	77.7 (1.46)
Other education, training, and library workers	1,755 (48.20)	100.0	0.6 (0.21)	1.2 (0.30)	24.0 (1.18)	20.1 (1.11)	11.2 (0.87)	24.2 (1.18)	18.6 (1.07)
Service occupations	17,448 (145.26)	100.0	7.7 (0.23)	11.4 (0.28)	39.9 (0.43)	18.8 (0.34)	9.9 (0.26)	10.2 (0.27)	2.1 (0.12)
Sales and office occupations	29,322 (181.46)	100.0	1.2 (0.07)	4.1 (0.13)	34.8 (0.32)	24.7 (0.29)	10.8 (0.21)	20.5 (0.27)	3.9 (0.13)
Natural resources, construction, and maintenance	13,173 (127.83)	100.0	9.4 (0.29)	12.7 (0.33)	43.5 (0.50)	16.6 (0.37)	10.4 (0.31)	6.4 (0.25)	1.1 (0.10)
Production, transportation, and material moving	15,714 (138.57)	100.0	7.5 (0.24)	12.6 (0.31)	48.8 (0.46)	16.6 (0.34)	6.9 (0.23)	6.3 (0.22)	1.3 (0.10)
Male	**65,772** (156.90)	**100.0**	**4.5** (0.09)	**6.9** (0.36)	**30.6** (0.20)	**16.7** (0.17)	**8.7** (0.13)	**20.8** (0.18)	**11.8** (0.14)
Management, professional, and related	23,111 (149.79)	100.0	0.6 (0.06)	1.3 (0.27)	12.4 (0.25)	12.8 (0.25)	8.1 (0.20)	35.8 (0.36)	28.9 (0.34)
Management, business, and financial operations	11,369 (113.60)	100.0	1.0 (0.11)	2.2 (0.49)	17.8 (0.41)	15.9 (0.39)	7.7 (0.28)	37.0 (0.52)	18.4 (0.41)
Professional and related	11,742 (115.18)	100.0	0.2 (0.05)	0.6 (0.25)	7.2 (0.27)	9.9 (0.31)	8.5 (0.29)	34.7 (0.50)	39.0 (0.51)
Education, training, and library	1,946 (49.65)	100.0	0.2 (0.12)	0.2 (0.32)	3.9 (0.50)	5.0 (0.56)	3.3 (0.46)	31.7 (1.20)	55.7 (1.28)
Service occupations	7,334 (93.48)	100.0	8.9 (0.38)	10.0 (1.26)	37.0 (0.64)	19.4 (0.53)	9.4 (0.39)	12.6 (0.44)	2.7 (0.21)
Sales and office occupations	10,734 (110.81)	100.0	1.7 (0.14)	4.0 (0.68)	29.6 (0.50)	22.8 (0.46)	9.3 (0.32)	27.1 (0.49)	5.5 (0.25)
Natural resources, construction, and maintenance	12,563 (118.53)	100.0	9.3 (0.29)	12.8 (1.07)	43.8 (0.50)	16.4 (0.38)	10.4 (0.31)	6.3 (0.25)	1.0 (0.10)
Production, transportation, and material moving	12,030 (116.37)	100.0	6.8 (0.26)	12.0 (1.07)	48.7 (0.52)	17.4 (0.39)	7.3 (0.27)	6.5 (0.26)	1.3 (0.12)
Female	**56,188** (162.16)	**100.0**	**2.5** (0.07)	**5.1** (0.10)	**29.0** (0.21)	**18.5** (0.18)	**11.6** (0.15)	**22.0** (0.19)	**11.5** (0.15)
Management, professional, and related	23,192 (144.87)	100.0	0.3 (0.04)	1.0 (0.07)	12.8 (0.24)	13.4 (0.25)	13.1 (0.24)	35.0 (0.34)	24.5 (0.31)
Management, business, and financial operations	8,248 (95.37)	100.0	0.5 (0.08)	1.5 (0.15)	18.9 (0.47)	18.3 (0.47)	10.9 (0.38)	34.0 (0.57)	15.9 (0.44)
Professional and related	14,944 (123.11)	100.0	0.2 (0.04)	0.7 (0.08)	9.4 (0.26)	10.6 (0.28)	14.3 (0.32)	35.5 (0.43)	29.2 (0.41)
Education, training, and library	5,483 (79.04)	100.0	0.2 (0.06)	0.5 (0.11)	9.4 (0.43)	8.6 (0.42)	5.9 (0.35)	38.3 (0.72)	37.1 (0.72)
Service occupations	10,114 (104.42)	100.0	6.8 (0.28)	12.5 (0.36)	42.0 (0.54)	18.3 (0.42)	10.3 (0.33)	8.6 (0.31)	1.6 (0.14)
Sales and office occupations	18,589 (133.99)	100.0	1.0 (0.08)	4.1 (0.16)	37.9 (0.39)	25.8 (0.35)	11.6 (0.26)	16.7 (0.30)	3.0 (0.14)
Natural resources, construction, and maintenance	609 (27.08)	100.0	11.0 (1.40)	9.2 (1.29)	36.8 (2.15)	19.7 (1.77)	10.7 (1.38)	10.0 (1.34)	2.6 (0.71)
Production, transportation, and material moving	3,684 (65.46)	100.0	10.1 (0.55)	14.7 (0.64)	48.9 (0.91)	14.1 (0.63)	5.6 (0.42)	5.5 (0.41)	1.2 (0.19)

—Not available.
†Not applicable.
#Rounds to zero.

NOTE: Detail may not sum to totals because of rounding. Standard errors appear in parentheses.
SOURCE: U.S. Department of Labor, Bureau of Labor Statistics, Office of Employment and Unemployment Statistics, unpublished 2005 annual average data from the Current Population Survey (CPS). (This table was prepared July 2006.)

Table 377. Median annual income of year-round, full-time workers 25 years old and over, by highest level of educational attainment and sex: 1990 through 2005

		Elementary/secondary				College						
							Bachelor's or higher degree[5]				
Sex and year	Total	Less than 9th grade	Some high school, no completion[1]	High school completion (includes equivalency)[2]	Some college, no degree[3]	Associate's degree[4]	Total	Bachelor's degree[6]	Master's degree[4]	Professional degree[4]	Doctor's degree[4]
1	2	3	4	5	6	7	8	9	10	11	12
						Current dollars					
Males											
1990	$30,733 (—)	$17,394 (—)	$20,902 (—)	$26,653 (—)	$31,734 (—)	— (†)	$42,671 (—)	$39,238 (—)	— (†)	— (†)	— (†)
1991	31,613 (—)	17,623 (—)	21,402 (—)	26,779 (—)	31,663 (—)	$33,817 (—)	45,138 (—)	40,906 (—)	$49,734 (—)	$73,996 (—)	$57,187 (—)
1992	32,057 (120)	17,294 (120)	21,274 (175)	27,280 (175)	32,103 (304)	33,433 (—)	45,802 (—)	41,355 (304)	49,973 (—)	76,220 (—)	57,418 (—)
1993	32,359 (124)	16,863 (124)	21,752 (204)	27,370 (204)	32,077 (536)	33,690 (—)	47,740 (—)	42,757 (536)	51,867 (854)	80,549 (3,040)	63,149 (1,619)
1994	33,440 (246)	17,532 (453)	22,048 (319)	28,037 (322)	32,279 (300)	35,794 (430)	49,228 (707)	43,663 (633)	53,500 (854)	75,009 (3,040)	61,921 (2,188)
1995	34,551 (275)	18,354 (545)	22,185 (342)	29,510 (358)	33,883 (517)	35,201 (535)	50,481 (312)	45,266 (510)	55,216 (973)	79,667 (2,582)	65,336 (3,362)
1996	35,622 (150)	17,962 (594)	22,717 (414)	30,709 (184)	34,845 (456)	37,131 (435)	51,436 (303)	45,846 (458)	60,508 (945)	85,963 (3,317)	71,227 (3,611)
1997	36,678 (149)	19,291 (629)	24,726 (466)	31,215 (171)	35,945 (293)	38,022 (774)	53,450 (755)	48,616 (851)	61,690 (771)	85,011 (4,253)	76,234 (2,507)
1998	37,906 (291)	19,380 (600)	23,958 (547)	31,477 (169)	36,934 (291)	40,274 (539)	56,524 (421)	51,405 (349)	62,244 (847)	94,737 (12,105)	75,078 (3,953)
1999	40,333 (144)	20,429 (444)	25,035 (535)	33,184 (388)	39,221 (581)	41,638 (459)	60,201 (439)	52,985 (722)	66,243 (690)	100,000 (37,836)	81,687 (2,446)
2000	41,059 (156)	20,789 (376)	25,095 (436)	34,303 (457)	40,337 (312)	41,952 (460)	61,868 (303)	56,334 (573)	68,322 (1,506)	99,411 (20,832)	80,250 (3,013)
2001	41,617 (104)	21,361 (235)	26,209 (251)	34,723 (299)	41,045 (214)	42,776 (561)	62,223 (279)	55,929 (335)	70,899 (687)	100,000 (†)	86,965 (2,076)
2002	41,152 (100)	20,919 (213)	25,903 (207)	33,206 (311)	40,851 (195)	42,856 (673)	61,700 (201)	56,077 (385)	67,281 (1,294)	100,000 (†)	83,305 (2,528)
2003	41,939 (90)	21,217 (227)	26,468 (280)	35,412 (168)	41,348 (182)	42,871 (719)	62,075 (187)	56,502 (365)	70,640 (562)	100,000 (†)	87,131 (2,423)
2004	42,085 (89)	21,659 (191)	26,277 (234)	35,725 (148)	41,895 (175)	44,404 (931)	62,797 (798)	57,220 (393)	71,530 (490)	100,000 (†)	82,401 (3,061)
2005	43,317 (367)	22,330 (220)	27,189 (237)	36,302 (141)	42,418 (323)	47,180 (367)	66,166 (356)	60,020 (653)	75,025 (1,229)	100,000 (†)	85,864 (2,490)
Females											
1990	21,372 (—)	12,251 (—)	14,429 (—)	18,319 (—)	22,227 (—)	— (†)	30,377 (—)	28,017 (—)	— (†)	— (†)	— (†)
1991	22,043 (—)	12,066 (—)	14,455 (—)	18,836 (—)	22,143 (—)	25,000 (—)	31,310 (—)	29,079 (—)	34,949 (—)	46,742 (—)	43,303 (—)
1992	23,139 (159)	12,958 (159)	14,559 (176)	19,427 (176)	23,157 (294)	25,624 (—)	32,304 (—)	30,326 (294)	36,037 (—)	46,257 (—)	45,790 (—)
1993	23,629 (166)	12,415 (166)	15,386 (173)	19,963 (173)	23,056 (310)	25,883 (—)	34,307 (—)	31,197 (310)	38,612 (606)	50,211 (2,154)	47,248 (2,888)
1994	24,399 (165)	12,430 (427)	15,133 (328)	20,373 (158)	23,514 (327)	25,940 (295)	35,378 (280)	31,741 (314)	39,457 (556)	50,615 (2,532)	51,119 (2,373)
1995	24,875 (160)	13,577 (490)	15,825 (293)	20,463 (162)	23,997 (274)	27,311 (428)	35,259 (313)	32,051 (273)	40,263 (564)	50,000 (3,635)	48,141 (3,300)
1996	25,808 (131)	14,414 (559)	16,953 (333)	21,175 (143)	25,167 (267)	28,083 (526)	36,461 (296)	33,525 (437)	41,901 (837)	57,624 (4,737)	56,267 (3,626)
1997	26,974 (134)	14,161 (492)	16,697 (335)	22,067 (148)	26,335 (291)	28,812 (660)	38,038 (481)	35,379 (295)	44,949 (760)	61,051 (1,705)	53,038 (1,881)
1998	27,956 (199)	14,467 (429)	16,482 (322)	22,780 (254)	27,420 (271)	29,924 (513)	39,786 (408)	36,559 (305)	45,283 (862)	57,565 (4,479)	57,796 (3,130)
1999	28,844 (216)	15,098 (492)	17,015 (298)	23,061 (279)	27,757 (369)	30,919 (318)	41,747 (275)	37,993 (614)	48,097 (735)	59,904 (3,552)	60,079 (2,999)
2000	30,327 (138)	15,798 (327)	17,919 (434)	24,970 (236)	28,697 (364)	31,071 (307)	42,706 (439)	40,415 (284)	50,139 (328)	58,957 (3,976)	57,081 (2,228)
2001	31,356 (91)	16,691 (255)	19,156 (359)	25,303 (132)	30,418 (186)	32,153 (231)	44,776 (367)	40,994 (231)	50,669 (595)	61,748 (2,421)	62,123 (2,268)
2002	31,010 (83)	16,510 (297)	19,307 (360)	25,182 (121)	29,400 (299)	31,625 (211)	43,245 (568)	40,853 (173)	48,890 (454)	57,018 (3,469)	65,715 (2,462)
2003	31,565 (85)	16,907 (256)	18,938 (327)	26,074 (118)	30,142 (176)	32,253 (241)	45,116 (291)	41,327 (204)	50,163 (263)	66,491 (2,436)	67,214 (2,450)
2004	31,990 (80)	17,023 (241)	19,162 (319)	26,029 (116)	30,816 (135)	33,481 (489)	45,911 (229)	41,681 (172)	51,316 (283)	75,036 (2,774)	68,875 (2,450)
2005	33,075 (242)	16,142 (250)	20,125 (274)	26,289 (134)	31,399 (165)	33,939 (497)	46,948 (232)	42,172 (179)	51,412 (†)	80,458 (†)	66,852 (2,490)

See notes at end of table.

Table 377. Median annual income of year-round, full-time workers 25 years old and over, by highest level of educational attainment and sex: 1990 through 2005—Continued

Constant 2005 dollars[7]

Sex and year	Elementary/secondary					College			Bachelor's or higher degree[5]		
	Total	Less than 9th grade	Some high school, no completion[1]	High school completion (includes equivalency)[2]	Some college, no degree[3]	Associate's degree[4]	Total	Bachelor's degree[6]	Master's degree[4]	Professional degree[4]	Doctor's degree[4]
1	2	3	4	5	6	7	8	9	10	11	12
Males											
1990	$45,923 (—)	$25,991 (—)	$31,233 (—)	$39,827 (—)	$47,419 (—)	— (†)	$63,762 (—)	$58,632 (—)	$71,315 (†)	— (†)	— (†)
1991	45,331 (—)	25,270 (—)	30,689 (—)	38,399 (—)	45,402 (—)	$48,491 (—)	64,724 (—)	58,656 (—)	69,563 (—)	$106,104 (—)	$82,002 (—)
1992	44,624 (167)	24,074 (167)	29,614 (244)	37,974 (244)	44,688 (—)	46,539 (—)	63,757 (—)	57,567 (423)	70,101 (—)	106,100 (—)	79,927 (—)
1993	43,735 (168)	22,791 (168)	29,399 (276)	36,992 (276)	43,354 (395)	45,534 (—)	64,523 (932)	57,789 (724)	70,503 (1,125)	108,867 (4,006)	85,349 (—)
1994	44,068 (324)	23,104 (597)	29,055 (420)	36,948 (424)	42,538 (663)	47,170 (567)	64,873 (400)	57,540 (834)	70,759 (1,247)	98,848 (3,309)	81,600 (2,134)
1995	44,277 (352)	23,521 (698)	28,430 (438)	37,817 (459)	43,421 (568)	45,110 (686)	64,691 (377)	58,008 (654)	75,317 (1,176)	102,093 (4,129)	83,728 (2,804)
1996	44,340 (187)	22,358 (739)	28,277 (515)	38,225 (229)	43,373 (357)	46,219 (541)	64,025 (919)	57,066 (570)	75,066 (938)	107,002 (5,175)	88,659 (4,185)
1997	44,631 (181)	23,474 (765)	30,087 (567)	37,983 (208)	43,739 (349)	46,266 (942)	65,039 (504)	59,157 (1,036)	74,578 (1,015)	103,443 (14,504)	92,763 (4,394)
1998	45,417 (349)	23,220 (719)	28,706 (655)	37,714 (202)	44,253 (681)	48,255 (646)	67,725 (515)	61,591 (418)	77,655 (809)	113,510 (44,354)	89,955 (3,004)
1999	47,281 (169)	23,948 (520)	29,348 (627)	38,901 (455)	45,978 (354)	48,811 (538)	70,572 (344)	62,113 (846)	77,487 (1,708)	117,227 (23,627)	95,759 (4,634)
2000	46,567 (177)	23,578 (426)	28,461 (494)	38,905 (518)	45,748 (236)	47,580 (522)	70,167 (308)	63,891 (650)	78,185 (758)	112,747 (†)	91,015 (2,774)
2001	45,894 (115)	23,556 (259)	28,902 (277)	38,291 (330)	45,263 (212)	47,172 (619)	68,617 (218)	61,677 (369)	73,040 (1,405)	110,277 (†)	95,902 (3,323)
2002	44,675 (109)	22,710 (231)	28,120 (225)	36,049 (338)	44,348 (193)	46,525 (731)	66,982 (198)	60,877 (418)	74,978 (597)	108,560 (†)	90,436 (2,254)
2003	44,515 (96)	22,520 (241)	28,093 (297)	37,587 (178)	43,887 (181)	45,504 (763)	65,887 (825)	59,972 (387)	73,953 (507)	106,141 (†)	92,482 (2,683)
2004	43,511 (92)	22,393 (197)	27,167 (242)	36,935 (153)	43,314 (323)	45,908 (963)	64,925 (356)	59,159 (406)	75,025 (1,229)	103,388 (†)	85,193 (2,505)
2005	43,317 (367)	22,330 (220)	27,189 (237)	36,302 (141)	42,418 (—)	47,180 (367)	66,166 (—)	60,020 (653)	—	100,000 (†)	85,864 (3,061)
Females											
1990	31,935 (—)	18,306 (—)	21,561 (—)	27,373 (—)	33,213 (—)	— (†)	45,391 (—)	41,865 (—)	— (†)	— (†)	— (†)
1991	31,608 (—)	17,302 (—)	20,727 (—)	27,009 (—)	31,751 (—)	$35,848 (—)	44,896 (—)	41,697 (—)	$50,114 (—)	$67,024 (—)	$62,093 (—)
1992	32,210 (221)	18,038 (221)	20,266 (245)	27,043 (245)	32,235 (—)	35,669 (—)	44,968 (—)	42,214 (409)	50,164 (—)	64,391 (—)	63,740 (—)
1993	31,936 (224)	16,780 (224)	20,795 (234)	26,981 (234)	31,162 (431)	34,982 (389)	46,368 (369)	42,165 (419)	52,186 (799)	67,863 (2,839)	63,858 (3,806)
1994	32,153 (217)	16,380 (563)	19,942 (432)	26,848 (208)	30,987 (351)	34,184 (548)	46,622 (401)	41,829 (414)	51,997 (713)	66,701 (3,245)	67,365 (3,041)
1995	31,877 (205)	17,399 (628)	20,280 (375)	26,223 (208)	30,752 (332)	34,999 (655)	45,184 (368)	41,073 (350)	51,597 (702)	64,075 (4,525)	61,693 (4,108)
1996	32,124 (163)	17,942 (696)	21,102 (414)	26,357 (178)	31,326 (354)	34,956 (803)	45,385 (585)	41,730 (544)	52,156 (1,018)	71,727 (5,764)	70,038 (4,412)
1997	32,823 (163)	17,231 (599)	20,317 (408)	26,852 (180)	32,045 (325)	35,059 (615)	46,285 (489)	43,050 (359)	54,695 (911)	74,288 (2,043)	64,538 (2,254)
1998	33,496 (238)	17,334 (514)	19,748 (386)	27,294 (304)	32,854 (433)	35,854 (373)	47,670 (322)	43,804 (365)	54,256 (1,010)	68,972 (5,251)	69,249 (3,669)
1999	33,813 (253)	17,699 (577)	19,946 (349)	27,034 (327)	32,539 (498)	36,245 (348)	48,939 (498)	44,538 (720)	56,383 (834)	70,224 (4,028)	70,429 (3,401)
2000	34,395 (157)	17,917 (371)	20,323 (492)	28,320 (268)	32,547 (405)	35,239 (255)	48,435 (405)	45,837 (322)	56,865 (362)	66,866 (4,385)	64,738 (2,457)
2001	34,578 (100)	18,406 (281)	21,125 (396)	27,903 (146)	33,544 (617)	35,457 (229)	49,377 (617)	45,207 (255)	55,876 (646)	68,094 (2,628)	68,507 (2,462)
2002	33,665 (90)	17,923 (322)	20,960 (391)	27,338 (131)	31,917 (309)	34,332 (256)	46,947 (309)	44,350 (188)	53,075 (482)	61,899 (3,682)	71,340 (2,613)
2003	33,504 (90)	17,945 (272)	20,101 (347)	27,675 (125)	31,993 (237)	34,234 (506)	47,887 (237)	43,865 (217)	53,244 (272)	70,574 (2,519)	71,342 (2,533)
2004	33,074 (83)	17,600 (249)	19,811 (330)	26,911 (120)	31,860 (140)	34,615 (497)	47,466 (232)	43,093 (178)	53,055 (283)	77,578 (2,774)	71,209 (2,490)
2005	33,075 (242)	16,142 (250)	20,125 (274)	26,289 (134)	31,399 (165)	33,939 (—)	46,948 (—)	42,172 (179)	51,412 (—)	80,458 (—)	66,852 (—)

See notes at end of table.

Table 377. Median annual income of year-round, full-time workers 25 years old and over, by highest level of educational attainment and sex: 1990 through 2005—Continued

Sex and year	Elementary/secondary						College				
							Bachelor's or higher degree[5]				
	Total	Less than 9th grade	Some high school, no completion[1]	High school completion (includes equivalency)[2]	Some college, no degree[3]	Associate's degree[4]	Total	Bachelor's degree[6]	Master's degree[4]	Professional degree[4]	Doctor's degree[4]
1	2	3	4	5	6	7	8	9	10	11	12
Males						Number of persons with income (in thousands)					
1990	44,406 (268.6)	2,250 (73.9)	3,315 (89.3)	16,394 (188.0)	9,113 (144.6)	— (†)	13,334 (171.8)	7,569 (132.6)	— (†)	— (†)	— (†)
1991	44,199 (268.3)	1,807 (66.3)	3,083 (86.2)	15,025 (181.1)	8,034 (136.4)	2,899 (83.6)	13,350 (171.9)	8,456 (139.7)	3,073 (86.1)	1,147 (53.0)	674 (40.7)
1992	44,752 (269.1)	1,815 (66.5)	3,009 (85.2)	14,722 (179.5)	8,067 (136.6)	3,203 (87.8)	13,937 (175.2)	8,719 (141.7)	3,178 (87.5)	1,295 (56.3)	745 (42.8)
1993	45,873 (270.6)	1,790 (66.0)	3,083 (86.2)	14,604 (178.9)	8,493 (140.0)	3,557 (92.4)	14,346 (177.5)	9,178 (145.1)	3,131 (86.8)	1,231 (54.9)	808 (44.5)
1994	47,566 (272.8)	1,895 (67.9)	3,057 (85.8)	15,109 (181.5)	8,783 (142.2)	3,735 (94.6)	14,987 (180.9)	9,636 (148.4)	3,225 (88.1)	1,258 (55.4)	868 (46.1)
1995	48,500 (324.3)	1,946 (71.6)	3,335 (93.5)	15,331 (195.8)	8,908 (151.1)	3,926 (101.3)	15,054 (194.1)	9,597 (156.7)	3,395 (94.3)	1,208 (56.5)	853 (47.5)
1996	49,764 (339.9)	2,041 (76.2)	3,441 (98.7)	15,840 (206.6)	9,173 (159.3)	3,931 (105.4)	15,339 (203.5)	9,898 (165.3)	3,272 (96.3)	1,277 (60.4)	893 (50.5)
1997	50,807 (342.6)	1,914 (73.8)	3,548 (100.2)	16,225 (208.9)	9,170 (159.3)	4,086 (107.4)	15,864 (206.7)	10,349 (168.9)	3,228 (95.6)	1,321 (61.4)	966 (52.5)
1998	52,381 (346.6)	1,870 (73.0)	3,613 (101.1)	16,442 (210.2)	9,375 (161.0)	4,347 (110.7)	16,733 (212.0)	11,058 (174.3)	3,414 (98.3)	1,264 (60.1)	998 (53.4)
1999	53,062 (348.2)	1,993 (75.3)	3,295 (96.6)	16,589 (211.1)	9,684 (163.6)	4,359 (110.9)	17,142 (214.4)	11,142 (174.9)	3,725 (102.6)	1,267 (60.1)	1,008 (53.7)
2000	54,065 (350.7)	1,968 (74.9)	3,354 (97.5)	16,834 (212.6)	9,792 (164.4)	4,729 (115.4)	17,387 (215.8)	11,395 (176.8)	3,680 (102.0)	1,274 (60.3)	1,038 (54.5)
2001	54,013 (350.5)	2,207 (79.2)	3,503 (99.6)	16,314 (209.5)	9,494 (162.0)	4,714 (115.2)	17,780 (218.0)	11,479 (177.4)	3,961 (105.8)	1,298 (60.9)	1,041 (54.5)
2002	54,108 (225.0)	2,154 (50.7)	3,680 (66.1)	16,005 (134.2)	9,603 (105.5)	4,399 (72.2)	18,267 (142.7)	11,829 (116.5)	4,065 (69.4)	1,308 (39.6)	1,065 (35.8)
2003	54,253 (225.2)	2,209 (51.4)	3,369 (63.3)	16,285 (135.3)	9,340 (104.1)	4,696 (74.5)	18,354 (143.0)	11,846 (116.6)	4,124 (69.9)	1,348 (40.2)	1,037 (35.3)
2004	55,469 (227.0)	2,427 (53.8)	3,468 (64.2)	17,067 (135.3)	9,257 (103.6)	4,913 (76.2)	18,338 (142.9)	11,701 (115.9)	4,243 (70.9)	1,305 (39.6)	1,088 (36.1)
2005	56,717 (228.7)	2,425 (53.8)	3,652 (65.9)	17,266 (139.0)	9,532 (105.1)	5,022 (77.0)	18,820 (144.7)	12,032 (117.4)	4,275 (71.2)	1,369 (40.5)	1,144 (37.1)
Females											
1990	28,636 (234.7)	847 (45.6)	1,861 (67.3)	11,810 (162.8)	6,462 (123.1)	— (†)	7,655 (133.3)	4,704 (105.8)	— (†)	— (†)	— (†)
1991	29,474 (237.1)	733 (42.4)	1,819 (66.5)	10,959 (157.9)	5,633 (115.3)	2,523 (78.1)	7,807 (134.6)	5,263 (111.6)	2,025 (70.1)	312 (27.7)	206 (22.5)
1992	30,346 (239.6)	734 (42.4)	1,659 (63.6)	11,039 (157.9)	5,904 (117.9)	2,655 (80.1)	8,355 (138.9)	5,604 (115.0)	2,192 (72.9)	334 (28.7)	225 (23.5)
1993	30,683 (240.5)	765 (43.3)	1,576 (62.0)	10,513 (154.4)	6,279 (121.4)	3,067 (86.0)	8,483 (139.9)	5,735 (116.3)	2,166 (72.5)	323 (28.2)	260 (25.3)
1994	31,379 (242.4)	696 (41.3)	1,675 (63.9)	10,785 (156.2)	6,256 (121.2)	3,210 (87.9)	8,756 (142.0)	5,901 (117.9)	2,174 (72.6)	398 (31.3)	283 (26.4)
1995	32,673 (275.7)	774 (45.2)	1,763 (68.2)	11,064 (167.7)	6,329 (128.0)	3,336 (93.5)	9,406 (155.1)	6,434 (129.1)	2,268 (77.2)	421 (33.4)	283 (27.4)
1996	33,549 (289.6)	750 (46.3)	1,751 (70.6)	11,363 (176.6)	6,582 (135.7)	3,468 (99.1)	9,636 (163.2)	6,689 (136.7)	2,213 (79.3)	413 (34.4)	322 (30.4)
1997	34,624 (293.5)	791 (47.6)	1,765 (70.9)	11,475 (177.4)	6,628 (136.1)	3,538 (100.1)	10,427 (169.5)	7,173 (141.5)	2,448 (83.4)	488 (37.4)	318 (30.2)
1998	35,628 (297.1)	814 (48.3)	1,878 (73.1)	11,613 (178.4)	7,070 (140.5)	3,527 (99.9)	10,725 (171.8)	7,288 (142.6)	2,639 (86.6)	468 (36.6)	329 (30.7)
1999	37,091 (302.1)	886 (50.3)	1,883 (73.2)	11,824 (180.0)	7,453 (144.1)	3,804 (103.7)	11,242 (175.7)	7,607 (145.6)	2,818 (89.4)	470 (36.7)	346 (31.5)
2000	37,762 (304.4)	930 (51.6)	1,950 (74.5)	11,789 (179.7)	7,391 (143.5)	4,118 (107.8)	11,584 (178.2)	7,899 (148.2)	2,823 (89.5)	509 (38.2)	353 (31.8)
2001	38,228 (305.9)	927 (51.5)	1,869 (73.0)	11,690 (179.0)	7,283 (142.5)	4,190 (108.8)	12,269 (183.2)	8,257 (151.5)	3,089 (93.6)	531 (39.0)	392 (33.5)
2002	38,510 (197.6)	858 (32.1)	1,841 (46.9)	11,687 (115.8)	7,354 (92.7)	4,285 (71.2)	12,484 (119.5)	8,229 (97.9)	3,281 (62.5)	572 (26.2)	402 (22.0)
2003	38,681 (197.9)	882 (32.6)	1,739 (45.6)	11,587 (115.3)	7,341 (92.6)	4,397 (72.2)	12,735 (120.6)	8,330 (98.5)	3,376 (63.4)	567 (26.1)	462 (23.6)
2004	39,072 (198.7)	917 (33.2)	1,797 (46.4)	11,392 (114.4)	7,330 (92.6)	4,505 (73.0)	13,131 (122.4)	8,664 (100.4)	3,451 (64.0)	564 (26.0)	452 (23.3)
2005	40,021 (200.6)	902 (32.9)	1,740 (45.6)	11,419 (114.5)	7,452 (93.3)	4,751 (74.9)	13,758 (125.1)	9,074 (102.6)	3,591 (65.3)	657 (28.1)	437 (22.9)

—Not available.
†Not applicable.
[1]Includes 1 to 3 years of high school for 1990.
[2]Includes 4 years of high school for 1990.
[3]Includes 1 to 3 years of college and associate's degrees for 1990.
[4]Not reported separately for 1990.
[5]Includes 4 or more years of college for 1990.
[6]Includes 4 years of college for 1990.
[7]Constant dollars based on the Consumer Price Index, prepared by the Bureau of Labor Statistics, U.S. Department of Labor.

NOTE: Data for 1992 and later years are based on 1990 census counts; prior years are based on 1980 counts. Total standard errors for bachelor's or higher degrees are not available for 1992 and 1993 from the source document. Detail may not sum to totals because of rounding. Standard errors appear in parentheses.
SOURCE: U.S. Department of Commerce, Census Bureau, Current Population Reports, Series P-60, Money Income of Households, Families, and Persons in the United States and Income, Poverty, and Valuation of Noncash Benefits, selected years, 1990 through 1994; Series P-60, Money Income in the United States, selected years, 1995 through 2002; and Detailed Income Tabulations from the CPS, 2003 through 2006. Retrieved August 31, 2006, from http://www.census.gov/hhes/www/income/dinctabs.html. (This table was prepared August 2006.)

Table 378. Distribution of earnings and median earnings of persons 25 years old and over, by highest level of educational attainment and sex: 2005

Sex and earnings	Total	Less than 9th grade	Some high school (no completion)	High school completion (includes equivalency)	Some college, no degree	Associate's degree	College — Bachelor's or higher degree: Total	Bachelor's degree	Master's degree	Professional degree	Doctor's degree
1	2	3	4	5	6	7	8	9	10	11	12
Males and females (in thousands)	**191,884** (136.9)	**11,742** (117.6)	**16,154** (136.4)	**60,898** (232.0)	**32,611** (185.3)	**16,760** (138.7)	**53,720** (223.1)	**35,153** (191.0)	**13,053** (123.6)	**3,050** (61.3)	**2,464** (55.1)
With earnings	131,915 (245.7)	4,870 (77.1)	8,130 (98.8)	39,254 (199.5)	23,651 (161.8)	13,155 (124.1)	42,856 (206.2)	27,832 (173.5)	10,429 (111.2)	2,558 (56.2)	2,037 (50.2)
Distribution of males and females with earnings, by total annual earnings	100.0 (t)	100.0 (t)	100.1 (t)	100.0 (t)	100.0 (t)	100.0 (t)	100.0 (t)	100.0 (t)	100.0 (t)	100.0 (t)	100.0 (t)
$1 to $4,999 or loss	6.0 (0.30)	9.3 (1.53)	10.0 (1.18)	6.6 (0.55)	6.6 (0.70)	5.1 (0.95)	4.3 (0.53)	4.6 (0.65)	4.2 (1.07)	3.3 (2.17)	2.7 (2.44)
$5,000 to $9,999	5.6 (0.30)	10.6 (1.51)	9.8 (1.18)	6.8 (0.54)	5.9 (0.70)	4.4 (0.95)	3.3 (0.53)	3.7 (0.66)	2.8 (1.08)	1.7 (2.19)	2.2 (2.45)
$10,000 to $14,999	7.5 (0.30)	19.7 (1.44)	13.9 (1.15)	9.4 (0.54)	7.6 (0.70)	6.1 (0.94)	3.6 (0.53)	3.9 (0.66)	3.3 (1.08)	2.3 (2.18)	2.6 (2.44)
$15,000 to $19,999	8.1 (0.29)	17.7 (1.45)	15.1 (1.14)	11.0 (0.53)	7.9 (0.69)	6.6 (0.94)	3.6 (0.53)	4.2 (0.66)	2.8 (1.08)	2.2 (2.18)	2.1 (2.45)
$20,000 to $24,999	9.2 (0.29)	15.5 (1.47)	13.5 (1.15)	12.0 (0.53)	9.5 (0.69)	8.7 (0.93)	5.0 (0.53)	6.0 (0.65)	3.5 (1.07)	2.3 (2.18)	1.7 (2.46)
$25,000 to $29,999	8.0 (0.30)	8.2 (1.53)	9.3 (1.18)	10.0 (0.54)	9.6 (0.69)	9.1 (0.93)	4.8 (0.53)	5.9 (0.65)	3.1 (1.08)	1.8 (2.19)	1.6 (2.46)
$30,000 to $34,999	8.5 (0.29)	6.8 (1.55)	9.1 (1.18)	9.6 (0.54)	9.1 (0.69)	10.0 (0.92)	6.6 (0.52)	7.8 (0.64)	4.9 (1.07)	3.1 (2.17)	3.2 (2.44)
$35,000 to $39,999	7.2 (0.30)	4.1 (1.57)	5.5 (1.21)	7.7 (0.54)	7.8 (0.70)	7.8 (0.94)	6.7 (0.52)	7.3 (0.64)	6.5 (1.06)	3.0 (2.18)	3.5 (2.43)
$40,000 to $49,999	11.5 (0.29)	4.4 (1.57)	6.7 (1.20)	10.5 (0.53)	12.7 (0.68)	14.5 (0.90)	12.5 (0.50)	13.0 (0.62)	13.4 (1.02)	6.0 (2.14)	9.1 (2.36)
$50,000 to $74,999	15.8 (0.28)	2.5 (1.58)	5.4 (1.21)	11.7 (0.53)	15.2 (0.67)	19.3 (0.88)	22.4 (0.48)	21.6 (0.59)	25.3 (0.95)	17.0 (2.01)	24.8 (2.15)
$75,000 to $99,999	5.8 (0.30)	0.6 (1.60)	1.0 (1.23)	2.7 (0.56)	4.6 (0.71)	5.2 (0.95)	11.2 (0.51)	10.2 (0.63)	12.5 (1.02)	14.0 (2.05)	14.4 (2.29)
$100,000 or more	6.8 (0.30)	0.7 (1.60)	0.8 (1.23)	1.9 (0.56)	3.4 (0.71)	3.2 (0.96)	16.0 (0.49)	11.7 (0.63)	17.7 (0.99)	43.2 (1.66)	32.1 (2.04)
Median earnings[1]	$32,140 (60)	$17,422 (215)	$20,321 (165)	$26,505 (102)	$31,054 (133)	$35,009 (327)	$49,303 (381)	$43,143 (560)	$52,390 (420)	$82,473 (2,162)	$70,853 (821)
Males (in thousands)	**90,896** (252.9)	**5,912** (84.7)	**7,789** (96.8)	**29,173** (177.0)	**14,869** (131.3)	**6,925** (91.4)	**26,228** (169.2)	**16,628** (138.2)	**6,123** (86.2)	**1,994** (48.4)	**1,584** (44.3)
With earnings	70,630 (241.4)	3,277 (63.5)	4,944 (77.6)	21,717 (155.9)	11,913 (118.4)	6,088 (85.9)	22,691 (158.9)	14,497 (129.8)	5,172 (79.4)	1,635 (45.0)	1,388 (41.5)
Distribution of males with earnings, by total annual earnings	100.0 (t)	100.0 (t)	100.0 (t)	100.0 (t)	100.0 (t)	100.0 (t)	100.0 (t)	100.0 (t)	100.0 (t)	100.0 (t)	100.0 (t)
$1 to $4,999 or loss	4.2 (0.41)	6.2 (1.89)	6.9 (1.53)	4.7 (0.74)	3.9 (1.00)	3.1 (1.41)	3.2 (0.73)	3.3 (0.91)	3.4 (1.53)	2.6 (2.73)	1.6 (2.98)
$5,000 to $9,999	3.7 (0.41)	7.4 (1.88)	6.9 (1.53)	4.4 (0.74)	3.6 (1.01)	2.7 (1.41)	2.0 (0.73)	2.2 (0.92)	1.9 (1.54)	1.1 (2.75)	1.6 (2.98)
$10,000 to $14,999	5.6 (0.41)	16.4 (1.79)	9.6 (1.51)	6.6 (0.73)	5.7 (0.99)	3.8 (1.40)	2.5 (0.73)	2.7 (0.92)	2.3 (1.54)	2.3 (2.73)	1.8 (2.97)
$15,000 to $19,999	6.4 (0.41)	17.5 (1.77)	13.6 (1.48)	8.3 (0.73)	5.2 (1.00)	3.8 (1.40)	2.6 (0.73)	3.0 (0.91)	2.2 (1.54)	1.8 (2.74)	1.7 (2.97)
$20,000 to $24,999	8.0 (0.40)	17.9 (1.77)	14.5 (1.47)	10.1 (0.72)	7.5 (0.98)	6.8 (1.38)	3.8 (0.73)	4.7 (0.91)	2.7 (1.53)	1.5 (2.74)	1.0 (2.98)
$25,000 to $29,999	7.3 (0.40)	10.5 (1.85)	10.2 (1.51)	9.4 (0.72)	7.9 (0.98)	7.3 (1.38)	3.8 (0.73)	4.8 (0.91)	2.3 (1.54)	1.2 (2.75)	1.9 (2.97)
$30,000 to $34,999	8.2 (0.40)	8.8 (1.86)	11.9 (1.49)	10.2 (0.72)	8.8 (0.98)	8.0 (1.37)	5.1 (0.72)	6.1 (0.90)	3.8 (1.52)	2.3 (2.73)	3.0 (2.96)
$35,000 to $39,999	7.2 (0.41)	5.1 (1.90)	6.9 (1.53)	9.0 (0.72)	8.2 (0.98)	7.5 (1.38)	5.3 (0.72)	6.2 (0.90)	4.4 (1.52)	2.3 (2.73)	2.6 (2.96)
$40,000 to $49,999	12.5 (0.39)	5.4 (1.90)	9.1 (1.52)	13.6 (0.70)	15.4 (0.94)	17.2 (1.30)	10.3 (0.70)	11.7 (0.87)	9.1 (1.48)	4.6 (2.70)	7.5 (2.89)
$50,000 to $74,999	19.1 (0.38)	3.2 (1.92)	7.6 (1.53)	16.8 (0.69)	21.3 (0.91)	26.1 (1.23)	23.1 (0.65)	23.6 (0.81)	23.9 (1.36)	15.8 (2.54)	23.0 (2.63)
$75,000 to $99,999	7.8 (0.40)	0.7 (1.95)	1.6 (1.58)	4.0 (0.74)	7.0 (0.99)	8.4 (1.37)	14.2 (0.69)	13.4 (0.86)	15.9 (1.42)	14.3 (2.56)	16.2 (2.75)
$100,000 or more	10.1 (0.40)	0.9 (1.94)	1.2 (1.58)	2.9 (0.75)	5.5 (1.00)	5.4 (1.39)	23.9 (0.65)	18.2 (0.84)	28.0 (1.32)	50.3 (1.95)	38.1 (2.36)
Median earnings[1]	$39,403 (261)	$20,542 (209)	$24,192 (429)	$32,085 (122)	$39,150 (611)	$42,382 (448)	$60,493 (209)	$52,265 (202)	$67,123 (951)	$100,000 (t)	$78,324 (1,914)

See notes at end of table.

Table 378. Distribution of earnings and median earnings of persons 25 years old and over, by highest level of educational attainment and sex: 2005—Continued

							College				
								Bachelor's or higher degree			
Sex and earnings	Total	Less than 9th grade	Some high school (no completion)	High school completion (includes equivalency)	Some college, no degree	Associate's degree	Total	Bachelor's degree	Master's degree	Professional degree	Doctor's degree
1	2	3	4	5	6	7	8	9	10	11	12
Females (in thousands)	**98,465** (254.6)	**6,026** (85.5)	**8,314** (99.8)	**31,743** (183.3)	**16,929** (139.4)	**9,379** (105.8)	**26,074** (168.8)	**17,591** (141.8)	**6,693** (89.9)	**1,031** (35.8)	**759** (30.7)
With earnings	61,287 (232.4)	1,593 (44.4)	3,186 (62.6)	17,537 (141.6)	11,738 (117.6)	7,066 (92.3)	20,165 (150.8)	13,336 (124.9)	5,257 (80.0)	923 (33.9)	649 (28.4)
Distribution of females with earnings, by total annual earnings	100.0 (†)	100.0 (†)	100.0 (†)	100.0 (†)	100.0 (†)	100.0 (†)	100.0 (†)	100.0 (†)	100.0 (†)	100.0 (†)	100.0 (†)
$1 to $4,999 or loss	8.2 (0.43)	15.6 (2.57)	14.8 (1.83)	9.0 (0.81)	9.4 (0.98)	6.8 (1.28)	5.6 (0.76)	6.0 (0.94)	4.9 (1.50)	4.6 (3.59)	5.1 (4.27)
$5,000 to $9,999	7.8 (0.43)	17.1 (2.55)	14.3 (1.83)	9.8 (0.80)	8.2 (0.99)	5.9 (1.29)	4.7 (0.77)	5.3 (0.94)	3.7 (1.51)	2.8 (3.63)	3.4 (4.31)
$10,000 to $14,999	9.8 (0.43)	26.6 (2.40)	20.6 (1.76)	12.9 (0.79)	9.6 (0.98)	8.1 (1.27)	4.8 (0.77)	5.2 (0.94)	4.3 (1.51)	2.4 (3.63)	4.2 (4.29)
$15,000 to $19,999	10.1 (0.43)	18.4 (2.53)	17.4 (1.80)	14.2 (0.78)	10.6 (0.98)	8.9 (1.27)	4.8 (0.77)	5.6 (0.94)	3.4 (1.52)	3.0 (3.62)	2.9 (4.32)
$20,000 to $24,999	10.5 (0.43)	10.5 (2.65)	11.9 (1.86)	14.3 (0.78)	11.6 (0.97)	10.3 (1.26)	6.3 (0.76)	7.4 (0.93)	4.3 (1.51)	3.8 (3.61)	2.9 (4.32)
$25,000 to $29,999	8.9 (0.43)	3.5 (2.75)	7.8 (1.90)	10.9 (0.80)	11.3 (0.97)	10.6 (1.26)	5.9 (0.76)	7.2 (0.93)	3.9 (1.51)	2.8 (3.63)	0.9 (4.37)
$30,000 to $34,999	8.8 (0.43)	2.5 (2.76)	4.6 (1.93)	8.9 (0.81)	9.5 (0.98)	11.8 (1.25)	8.3 (0.75)	9.7 (0.92)	6.0 (1.49)	4.4 (3.60)	3.9 (4.30)
$35,000 to $39,999	7.1 (0.44)	2.1 (2.77)	3.2 (1.95)	6.2 (0.82)	7.5 (0.99)	8.1 (1.27)	8.2 (0.75)	8.6 (0.93)	8.4 (1.48)	4.3 (3.60)	5.4 (4.27)
$40,000 to $49,999	10.3 (0.43)	2.4 (2.77)	2.9 (1.95)	6.6 (0.82)	10.0 (0.98)	12.1 (1.25)	15.0 (0.73)	14.5 (0.89)	17.7 (1.40)	8.2 (3.52)	12.6 (4.10)
$50,000 to $74,999	12.0 (0.42)	1.1 (2.78)	2.0 (1.96)	5.4 (0.82)	8.9 (0.98)	13.6 (1.24)	21.6 (0.70)	19.4 (0.87)	26.8 (1.32)	19.1 (3.31)	28.7 (3.71)
$75,000 to $99,999	3.6 (0.44)	0.3 (2.80)	0.1 (1.98)	1.1 (0.84)	2.1 (1.02)	2.5 (1.31)	7.7 (0.76)	6.6 (0.94)	9.1 (1.47)	13.9 (3.41)	10.8 (4.14)
$100,000 or more	2.9 (0.44)	0.1 (2.80)	0.3 (1.98)	0.7 (0.84)	1.3 (1.02)	1.2 (1.32)	7.0 (0.76)	4.6 (0.95)	7.5 (1.48)	30.8 (3.06)	19.3 (3.94)
Median earnings[1]	$26,507 (94)	$12,532 (297)	$15,073 (260)	$21,117 (116)	$25,185 (166)	$29,510 (457)	$40,483 (144)	$36,532 (201)	$45,730 (337)	$66,055 (2,431)	$54,666 (2,029)

†Not applicable.
[1]Excludes persons without earnings.
NOTE: Detail may not sum to totals because of rounding. Standard errors appear in parentheses.

SOURCE: U.S. Department of Commerce, Census Bureau, Current Population Survey, March 2005. Retrieved August 31, 2006, from http://pubdb3.census.gov/macro/032006/perinc/new03_253.htm. (This table was prepared August 2006.)

Table 379. Literacy skills of adults, by type of literacy, proficiency levels, and selected characteristics: 1992 and 2003

Selected characteristic	Prose literacy[1] — Average score 1992	Average score 2003	Percent Below Basic 2003	Basic	Intermediate	Proficient	Document literacy[2] — Average score 1992	Average score 2003	Percent Below Basic 2003	Basic	Intermediate	Proficient	Quantitative literacy[3] — Average score 1992	Average score 2003	Percent Below Basic 2003	Basic	Intermediate	Proficient
1	2	3	4	5	6	7	8	9	10	11	12	13	14	15	16	17	18	19
Total	276 (1.1)	275 (1.3)	14 (0.6)	29 (0.6)	44 (0.7)	13 (0.5)	271 (1.1)	271 (1.2)	12 (0.5)	22 (0.5)	53 (0.7)	13 (0.6)	275 (1.1)	283 (1.2)	22 (0.6)	33 (0.5)	33 (0.5)	13 (0.5)
Sex																		
Male	276 (1.2)	272 (1.5)	15 (0.6)	29 (0.7)	43 (0.7)	13 (0.6)	274 (1.2)	269 (1.5)	14 (0.6)	23 (0.5)	51 (0.8)	13 (0.6)	283 (1.4)	286 (1.3)	21 (0.6)	31 (0.5)	33 (0.5)	16 (0.6)
Female	277 (1.3)	277 (1.4)	12 (0.6)	29 (0.6)	46 (0.8)	14 (0.6)	268 (1.2)	272 (1.2)	11 (0.6)	22 (0.6)	54 (0.8)	13 (0.6)	269 (1.2)	279 (1.3)	22 (0.8)	35 (0.7)	32 (0.7)	11 (0.6)
Age																		
16 to 18 years old	270 (2.3)	267 (2.8)	11 (1.7)	37 (2.5)	48 (2.7)	5 (1.4)	270 (2.2)	268 (2.9)	11 (1.4)	24 (1.8)	56 (2.4)	9 (1.7)	264 (2.5)	267 (3.1)	28 (2.3)	38 (2.1)	28 (2.1)	6 (1.3)
19 to 24 years old	280 (2.0)	276 (2.4)	11 (1.1)	29 (1.3)	48 (1.5)	12 (1.2)	282 (2.2)	277 (2.5)	9 (1.1)	20 (1.2)	58 (1.7)	13 (1.5)	277 (2.0)	279 (2.3)	21 (1.4)	36 (1.3)	33 (1.4)	10 (1.1)
25 to 39 years old	288 (1.3)	283 (1.7)	12 (1.2)	25 (0.7)	45 (0.7)	17 (1.1)	286 (1.3)	282 (1.8)	8 (0.7)	19 (0.7)	56 (1.1)	17 (1.1)	286 (1.8)	292 (1.8)	17 (0.8)	32 (0.8)	35 (0.8)	17 (0.9)
40 to 54 years old	293 (2.0)	282 (2.3)	11 (0.9)	27 (1.1)	47 (1.2)	15 (1.1)	284 (1.9)	277 (1.8)	10 (0.7)	20 (0.8)	54 (1.1)	15 (1.1)	292 (1.8)	289 (1.9)	19 (0.9)	30 (0.8)	34 (0.8)	16 (0.9)
55 to 64 years old	269 (1.4)	278 (1.9)	13 (0.8)	27 (0.9)	44 (1.1)	15 (0.8)	258 (1.4)	270 (2.1)	12 (0.9)	23 (0.9)	54 (1.2)	12 (1.1)	272 (1.8)	289 (1.9)	19 (1.0)	30 (1.0)	34 (0.9)	17 (0.8)
65 years old and older	235 (1.7)	248 (2.0)	23 (1.3)	38 (1.2)	34 (1.4)	4 (0.6)	221 (2.2)	235 (2.0)	27 (1.5)	33 (1.0)	38 (1.4)	3 (0.4)	235 (2.7)	257 (2.2)	34 (1.6)	37 (1.2)	24 (1.2)	5 (0.6)
Race/ethnicity																		
White	287 (1.2)	288 (1.5)	7 (0.5)	25 (0.8)	51 (0.9)	17 (0.9)	281 (1.2)	282 (1.5)	8 (0.5)	19 (0.7)	58 (1.0)	15 (1.0)	288 (1.1)	297 (1.3)	13 (0.7)	32 (0.7)	39 (0.8)	17 (0.8)
Black	237 (1.4)	243 (1.8)	24 (1.4)	43 (1.4)	31 (1.4)	2 (0.4)	230 (1.4)	238 (1.5)	24 (1.7)	35 (1.4)	40 (1.9)	2 (0.5)	222 (1.6)	238 (1.8)	47 (1.8)	36 (1.3)	15 (1.1)	2 (0.4)
Hispanic	234 (2.3)	216 (3.1)	44 (1.8)	30 (1.0)	23 (1.1)	4 (0.4)	238 (2.2)	224 (3.6)	36 (1.6)	26 (0.8)	33 (1.2)	5 (0.5)	233 (3.2)	233 (3.2)	50 (1.7)	29 (0.9)	17 (1.1)	4 (0.5)
Asian/Pacific Islander	255 (6.1)	271 (4.0)	14 (2.0)	32 (2.2)	42 (2.5)	12 (1.8)	259 (6.1)	272 (5.0)	11 (2.2)	22 (2.1)	54 (3.0)	13 (2.3)	268 (7.8)	285 (5.1)	19 (3.0)	34 (2.9)	35 (2.8)	12 (2.5)
Highest level of education																		
Still in high school	268 (2.5)	262 (3.7)	14 (2.5)	37 (2.8)	45 (3.1)	4 (1.5)	270 (2.4)	265 (4.3)	13 (2.3)	24 (2.2)	54 (3.0)	9 (1.9)	263 (3.2)	261 (4.2)	31 (2.9)	38 (2.5)	25 (2.3)	5 (1.4)
Less than high school completion	216 (1.4)	207 (2.4)	50 (1.4)	33 (1.0)	16 (0.9)	1 (0.2)	211 (1.5)	208 (2.6)	45 (1.4)	29 (0.7)	25 (1.0)	2 (0.3)	209 (2.1)	211 (2.2)	64 (1.3)	25 (0.8)	10 (0.7)	1 (0.2)
GED/high school equivalency	265 (2.2)	260 (2.1)	10 (1.8)	45 (2.9)	43 (3.0)	3 (1.1)	259 (2.3)	257 (2.5)	13 (1.9)	30 (2.3)	53 (2.8)	4 (1.2)	265 (2.3)	265 (3.1)	26 (3.1)	43 (3.1)	28 (2.9)	3 (1.2)
High school graduate	268 (1.0)	262 (1.3)	13 (1.0)	39 (1.0)	44 (1.3)	4 (0.6)	261 (1.4)	258 (1.5)	13 (1.5)	29 (1.1)	52 (1.4)	5 (0.7)	267 (1.4)	269 (1.6)	24 (1.4)	42 (1.3)	29 (1.3)	5 (0.7)
Vocational/trade/business	278 (2.1)	268 (3.0)	10 (1.8)	36 (2.6)	49 (2.7)	5 (1.5)	273 (2.1)	267 (2.3)	10 (1.5)	26 (2.3)	57 (2.7)	7 (1.5)	280 (2.2)	279 (2.3)	18 (2.1)	41 (2.3)	35 (2.3)	6 (1.4)
Some college	292 (1.4)	287 (1.6)	5 (0.7)	25 (1.4)	59 (1.7)	11 (1.4)	288 (1.6)	280 (1.7)	5 (0.8)	19 (1.3)	65 (1.8)	10 (1.5)	295 (1.7)	294 (1.7)	10 (1.2)	36 (1.8)	43 (1.8)	11 (1.5)
Associate's degree	306 (1.9)	298 (2.4)	4 (0.5)	20 (1.5)	56 (1.9)	19 (2.0)	301 (1.9)	291 (2.0)	3 (0.7)	15 (1.5)	66 (2.3)	16 (2.2)	305 (1.8)	305 (2.1)	7 (1.1)	30 (1.9)	45 (2.1)	18 (2.1)
Bachelor's degree	325 (1.9)	314 (2.1)	3 (0.5)	14 (1.0)	53 (1.7)	31 (1.8)	317 (1.9)	303 (2.0)	2 (0.6)	15 (1.5)	62 (2.5)	25 (2.2)	324 (1.8)	323 (1.9)	7 (0.6)	18 (1.2)	43 (2.1)	31 (1.9)
Graduate studies/degree	340 (2.0)	327 (2.8)	1 (0.4)	10 (1.2)	48 (2.3)	41 (2.6)	328 (1.9)	311 (2.2)	1 (0.4)	9 (1.1)	59 (2.6)	31 (2.8)	336 (2.1)	332 (2.1)	3 (0.6)	18 (1.5)	43 (2.1)	36 (2.6)
Employment																		
Full-time	290 (1.3)	285 (1.5)	— (†)	— (†)	— (†)	— (†)	286 (1.2)	281 (1.2)	— (†)	— (†)	— (†)	— (†)	292 (1.3)	296 (1.1)	— (†)	— (†)	— (†)	— (†)
Part-time	285 (1.7)	281 (2.2)	— (†)	— (†)	— (†)	— (†)	279 (1.8)	277 (1.8)	— (†)	— (†)	— (†)	— (†)	281 (1.7)	287 (2.2)	— (†)	— (†)	— (†)	— (†)
Unemployed	263 (2.3)	269 (2.8)	— (†)	— (†)	— (†)	— (†)	261 (2.2)	265 (0.3)	— (†)	— (†)	— (†)	— (†)	261 (3.2)	270 (3.6)	— (†)	— (†)	— (†)	— (†)
Not in labor force	252 (1.4)	255 (1.7)	— (†)	— (†)	— (†)	— (†)	244 (1.5)	250 (1.9)	— (†)	— (†)	— (†)	— (†)	247 (1.9)	261 (1.8)	— (†)	— (†)	— (†)	— (†)
Language spoken before starting school																		
English only	282 (1.2)	283 (1.4)	9 (0.5)	27 (0.7)	49 (0.8)	15 (0.7)	275 (1.2)	276 (1.3)	9 (0.5)	21 (0.6)	56 (0.8)	13 (0.7)	280 (1.2)	289 (1.2)	18 (0.6)	33 (0.6)	35 (0.6)	15 (0.6)
English and Spanish	255 (2.9)	262 (3.1)	14 (2.1)	38 (2.2)	42 (2.4)	6 (2.1)	253 (3.6)	259 (3.4)	12 (2.5)	29 (3.0)	54 (3.8)	5 (1.8)	247 (4.6)	261 (3.8)	31 (3.3)	39 (2.6)	26 (2.8)	4 (1.3)
English and other language	273 (4.0)	278 (3.1)	7 (1.5)	33 (2.8)	51 (3.1)	9 (2.1)	271 (4.5)	268 (3.2)	10 (2.0)	25 (2.3)	57 (2.9)	8 (2.0)	271 (5.6)	289 (4.1)	15 (2.7)	38 (2.7)	34 (3.0)	14 (2.6)
Spanish	205 (2.9)	188 (3.8)	61 (1.8)	25 (1.1)	13 (0.9)	1 (0.3)	216 (2.8)	199 (4.6)	49 (2.0)	25 (1.0)	23 (1.3)	3 (0.4)	212 (3.3)	211 (4.6)	62 (2.3)	25 (1.2)	11 (1.1)	2 (0.5)
Other language	239 (3.4)	249 (4.6)	26 (2.2)	33 (2.0)	34 (2.3)	7 (1.3)	241 (3.7)	257 (4.2)	20 (1.9)	24 (1.3)	46 (2.0)	10 (2.0)	246 (4.3)	270 (4.3)	28 (2.3)	33 (1.7)	29 (1.9)	10 (1.5)

—Not available.

†Not applicable.

[1]Prose literacy refers to the knowledge and skills needed to search, comprehend, and use information from continuous texts. Adults at the Below Basic level, rated 0 to 209, range from being nonliterate in English to being able to locate easily identifiable information in short, commonplace prose texts. At the Basic level, rated 210 to 264, adults are able to read and understand moderately dense, less commonplace prose texts. At the Intermediate level, rated 265 to 339, adults are able to read and understand moderately dense, less commonplace prose texts as well as summarize, make simple inferences, determine cause and effect, and recognize the author's purpose. At the Proficient level, rated 340 to 500, adults are able to read lengthy, complex, abstract prose texts as well as synthesize information and make complex inferences.

[2]Document literacy refers to the knowledge and skills needed to search, comprehend, and use information from noncontinuous texts in various formats. Adults at the Below Basic level, rated 0 to 204, range from being nonliterate in English to being able to locate easily identifiable information and follow instructions in simple documents (e.g., charts or forms). At the Basic level, rated 205 to 249, adults are able to read and understand information in simple documents. At the Intermediate level, rated 250 to 334, adults are able to locate information located in complex documents.

[3]Quantitative literacy refers to the knowledge and skills required to identify and perform computations, either alone or sequentially, using numbers embedded in printed materials. Adults at the Below Basic level, rated 0 to 234, range from being nonliterate in English to being able to locate numbers and use them to perform simple quantitative operations (primarily addition) when the mathematical information is very concrete and familiar. At the Basic level, rated 235 to 289, adults are able to locate easily identifiable quantitative information and use it to solve simple, one-step problems when the arithmetic operation is specified or easily inferred. At the Intermediate level, rated 290 to 349, adults are able to locate less familiar quantitative information and use it to solve problems when the arithmetic operation is not specified or easily inferred. At the Proficient level, rated 350 to 500, adults are able to locate more abstract quantitative information and use it to solve multistep problems when the arithmetic operations are not easily inferred and the problems are more complex.

NOTE: Adults are defined as people age 16 and older living in households or prisons. Adults who could not be interviewed due to language spoken or cognitive or mental disabilities (3 percent in 2003 and 4 percent in 1992) are excluded from this table. Race categories exclude persons of Hispanic origin. Detail may not sum to totals because of rounding. Standard errors appear in parentheses.

SOURCE: U.S. Department of Education, National Center for Education Statistics, 1992 National Adult Literacy Survey (NALS) and 2003 National Assessment of Adult Literacy (NAAL), A First Look at the Literacy of America's Adults in the 21st Century, and supplemental data retrieved July 6, 2006, from http://nces.ed.gov/naal/Excel/2006470_DataTable.xls. (This table was prepared July 2006.)

Table 380. Percentage of 12th-graders working different numbers of hours per week, by selected student characteristics and school locale type: 1992 and 2004

Percentage distribution of students by average hours worked per week during senior year

Selected student characteristic and school locale type	Total	Did not work during year	1 to 5	6 to 10	11 to 15	16 to 20	More than 20: Total	21 to 25	26 to 30	31 to 35	36 to 40	More than 40
1	2	3	4	5	6	7	8	9	10	11	12	13
1992, total	100.0 (†)	31.8 (—)	6.8 (—)	9.8 (—)	12.7 (—)	16.1 (—)	22.7 (—)	9.8 (—)	5.6 (—)	2.5 (—)	3.3 (—)	1.5 (—)
Sex												
Male	100.0 (†)	33.0 (—)	6.0 (—)	8.9 (—)	11.1 (—)	15.0 (—)	26.0 (—)	10.2 (—)	6.5 (—)	3.1 (—)	4.2 (—)	2.0 (—)
Female	100.0 (†)	30.7 (—)	7.6 (—)	10.7 (—)	14.4 (—)	17.2 (—)	19.5 (—)	9.5 (—)	4.8 (—)	1.9 (—)	2.4 (—)	1.0 (—)
Race/ethnicity												
White	100.0 (†)	27.6 (—)	7.0 (—)	11.2 (—)	14.1 (—)	17.3 (—)	22.8 (—)	10.0 (—)	5.5 (—)	2.6 (—)	3.3 (—)	1.5 (—)
Black	100.0 (†)	47.4 (—)	4.9 (—)	6.5 (—)	7.2 (—)	11.9 (—)	22.1 (—)	8.8 (—)	6.4 (—)	2.4 (—)	2.9 (—)	1.7 (—)
Hispanic	100.0 (†)	38.9 (—)	6.0 (—)	5.3 (—)	11.3 (—)	13.3 (—)	25.2 (—)	10.7 (—)	6.6 (—)	2.4 (—)	4.1 (—)	1.4 (—)
Asian/Pacific Islander	100.0 (†)	43.3 (—)	9.5 (—)	6.7 (—)	9.3 (—)	13.5 (—)	17.7 (—)	8.1 (—)	4.4 (—)	0.8 (—)	3.7 (—)	0.8 (—)
American Indian/Alaska Native	100.0 (†)	45.0 (—)	8.5 (—)	5.6 (—)	6.2 (—)	12.5 (—)	22.3 (—)	12.0 (—)	3.8 (—)	5.0 (—)	0.9 (—)	0.7 (—)
Socioeconomic status[1]												
Low	100.0 (†)	38.2 (—)	5.2 (—)	6.7 (—)	9.5 (—)	13.4 (—)	27.1 (—)	10.2 (—)	6.8 (—)	3.6 (—)	4.3 (—)	2.2 (—)
Middle low	100.0 (†)	29.8 (—)	5.5 (—)	8.3 (—)	11.9 (—)	18.6 (—)	25.9 (—)	10.9 (—)	6.4 (—)	3.2 (—)	4.2 (—)	1.4 (—)
Middle high	100.0 (†)	28.2 (—)	5.8 (—)	10.6 (—)	13.7 (—)	18.4 (—)	23.3 (—)	10.8 (—)	5.9 (—)	2.4 (—)	2.7 (—)	1.6 (—)
High	100.0 (†)	32.5 (—)	10.1 (—)	12.6 (—)	15.0 (—)	14.0 (—)	15.8 (—)	8.0 (—)	3.4 (—)	1.3 (—)	2.1 (—)	1.0 (—)
Locale type of school attended												
Urban	100.0 (†)	35.6 (—)	6.7 (—)	9.4 (—)	12.2 (—)	14.3 (—)	21.7 (—)	9.5 (—)	5.3 (—)	2.3 (—)	3.3 (—)	1.3 (—)
Suburban	100.0 (†)	29.4 (—)	6.6 (—)	9.6 (—)	13.6 (—)	18.3 (—)	22.5 (—)	10.6 (—)	5.7 (—)	2.5 (—)	2.4 (—)	1.4 (—)
Rural	100.0 (†)	31.6 (—)	7.2 (—)	10.6 (—)	12.1 (—)	14.9 (—)	23.7 (—)	9.1 (—)	5.8 (—)	2.7 (—)	4.3 (—)	1.8 (—)
2004, total	100.0 (†)	11.8 (0.38)	8.7 (0.38)	12.2 (0.42)	15.0 (0.39)	18.7 (0.50)	33.5 (0.63)	12.9 (0.40)	8.9 (0.35)	4.4 (0.24)	5.0 (0.26)	2.4 (0.17)
Sex												
Male	100.0 (†)	12.1 (0.55)	8.2 (0.51)	11.2 (0.53)	13.3 (0.54)	18.4 (0.67)	36.9 (0.89)	12.9 (0.56)	9.4 (0.52)	4.9 (0.35)	6.3 (0.44)	3.3 (0.28)
Female	100.0 (†)	11.6 (0.54)	9.3 (0.50)	13.1 (0.58)	16.7 (0.58)	19.0 (0.74)	30.2 (0.80)	13.0 (0.54)	8.3 (0.46)	4.0 (0.33)	3.6 (0.30)	1.4 (0.20)
Race/ethnicity												
White	100.0 (†)	10.9 (0.47)	8.5 (0.48)	13.2 (0.57)	16.3 (0.53)	19.1 (0.60)	31.9 (0.77)	13.1 (0.52)	8.1 (0.40)	4.0 (0.29)	4.5 (0.30)	2.2 (0.21)
Black	100.0 (†)	11.9 (0.94)	8.2 (0.85)	9.1 (0.86)	11.4 (0.94)	18.6 (1.30)	40.7 (1.59)	13.6 (1.11)	11.2 (1.16)	6.5 (0.83)	6.7 (0.86)	2.8 (0.53)
Hispanic	100.0 (†)	13.4 (1.04)	8.4 (0.99)	9.3 (1.00)	12.4 (1.01)	17.6 (1.31)	39.0 (1.59)	12.3 (1.12)	11.6 (1.17)	6.4 (0.75)	6.0 (0.80)	2.7 (0.48)
Asian/Pacific Islander	100.0 (†)	17.1 (1.90)	14.8 (1.87)	12.6 (1.28)	14.9 (1.68)	18.6 (2.06)	21.9 (1.86)	9.2 (1.17)	5.4 (1.01)	2.1 (0.64)	3.9 (0.94)	1.3 (0.45)
American Indian/Alaska Native	100.0 (†)	21.3 (6.29)	14.0 (5.43)	10.8 (4.64)	13.3 (4.01)	18.0 (4.48)	22.6 (5.99)	12.3 (5.22)	3.7 (2.36)	# (†)	3.0 (1.38)	3.5 (1.82)
Socioeconomic status[1]												
Low	100.0 (†)	11.1 (0.78)	7.5 (0.65)	9.5 (0.74)	11.2 (0.78)	18.1 (0.98)	42.6 (1.19)	14.3 (0.88)	11.9 (0.84)	6.3 (0.61)	7.0 (0.59)	3.1 (0.44)
Middle low	100.0 (†)	10.2 (0.72)	7.0 (0.62)	10.8 (0.82)	13.7 (0.80)	19.7 (0.92)	38.5 (1.18)	14.5 (0.90)	9.6 (0.67)	5.2 (0.52)	6.2 (0.59)	3.0 (0.42)
Middle high	100.0 (†)	10.2 (0.69)	8.0 (0.64)	11.7 (0.75)	15.7 (0.78)	19.8 (0.87)	34.5 (1.09)	14.0 (0.85)	9.4 (0.68)	4.5 (0.53)	4.6 (0.48)	2.2 (0.33)
High	100.0 (†)	15.3 (0.80)	11.8 (0.89)	15.7 (0.86)	18.2 (0.91)	17.3 (0.89)	21.7 (0.97)	9.7 (0.60)	5.5 (0.54)	2.3 (0.32)	2.8 (0.34)	1.3 (0.23)
Locale type of school attended												
Urban	100.0 (†)	13.6 (0.69)	10.2 (0.82)	12.7 (0.87)	14.2 (0.89)	16.6 (0.89)	32.8 (1.38)	12.2 (0.80)	9.7 (0.85)	4.7 (0.55)	4.1 (0.50)	2.2 (0.36)
Suburban	100.0 (†)	10.4 (0.55)	8.8 (0.58)	12.5 (0.61)	16.2 (0.57)	19.6 (0.76)	32.5 (0.89)	13.7 (0.62)	8.4 (0.43)	3.9 (0.34)	4.4 (0.35)	2.1 (0.24)
Rural	100.0 (†)	10.9 (0.78)	8.0 (0.73)	12.8 (1.06)	15.4 (0.81)	19.6 (1.10)	33.2 (1.27)	13.2 (0.90)	8.2 (0.71)	4.0 (0.51)	5.3 (0.62)	2.5 (0.39)

—Not available.
†Not applicable.
#Rounds to zero.
[1]Socioeconomic status (SES) was measured by a composite score of parental education and occupations, and family income.

NOTE: Race categories exclude persons of Hispanic origin. Detail may not sum to totals because of rounding.
SOURCE: U.S. Department of Education, National Center for Education Statistics, National Education Longitudinal Study of 1988 (NELS:88/92), "Second Follow-up, Student Survey, 1992"; and Education Longitudinal Study of 2002 (ELS:2002/04), "First Follow-up, Student Survey, 2004." (This table was prepared December 2006.)

Table 381. College enrollment and labor force status of 2003, 2004, and 2005 high school completers, by sex and race/ethnicity: 2003, 2004, and 2005

Selected characteristic	Civilian noninstitutional population			Civilian labor force[1]		Employed		Unemployed		Not in labor force (in thousands)
	Number (in thousands)	Percent	Percent of high school completers	Number (in thousands)	Labor force participation rate	Number (in thousands)	Percent of population	Number (in thousands)	Unemployment rate	
1	2	3	4	5	6	7	8	9	10	11
2003 high school completers[2]										
Total	2,677 (107.7)	100.0 (†)	100.0 (†)	1,470 (48.1)	54.8 (1.21)	1,190 (43.3)	44.5 (1.21)	280 (29.0)	19.0 (1.78)	1,208 (43.6)
Male	1,306 (75.3)	48.8 (2.09)	48.8 (2.09)	748 (46.6)	57.3 (2.34)	591 (41.4)	45.3 (2.36)	157 (21.4)	20.9 (2.54)	558 (40.3)
Female	1,372 (77.0)	51.3 (2.09)	51.3 (2.09)	722 (43.9)	52.6 (2.21)	599 (40.0)	43.7 (2.20)	123 (18.2)	16.9 (2.29)	650 (41.7)
White[3]	2,106 (95.5)	78.7 (1.71)	78.7 (1.71)	1,181 (43.1)	56.1 (1.36)	1,020 (40.1)	48.4 (1.37)	161 (22.0)	13.7 (1.74)	925 (38.2)
Black[3]	333 (45.8)	12.4 (1.66)	12.4 (1.66)	163 (23.1)	48.9 (4.97)	80 (16.2)	24.0 (4.25)	83 (16.5)	51.0 (7.11)	170 (23.6)
Hispanic[4]	314 (58.1)	11.7 (2.09)	11.7 (2.09)	162 (23.0)	51.7 (5.12)	135 (21.0)	43.2 (5.08)	27 (9.4)	16.6 (5.30)	152 (22.3)
Enrolled in college, 2003	1,711 (58.9)	100.0 (†)	63.9 (1.35)	713 (33.6)	41.7 (1.50)	631 (31.6)	36.9 (1.47)	82 (15.7)	11.5 (2.07)	998 (39.7)
Male	799 (40.3)	46.7 (1.76)	29.8 (1.29)	339 (31.4)	42.4 (2.99)	294 (29.3)	36.7 (2.92)	45 (11.5)	13.3 (3.15)	459 (36.6)
Female	913 (43.0)	53.4 (1.76)	34.1 (1.34)	374 (31.7)	41.0 (2.67)	338 (30.1)	37.1 (2.62)	36 (9.8)	9.5 (2.49)	539 (38.0)
2-year	574 (34.7)	33.5 (1.67)	21.4 (1.16)	332 (22.9)	57.8 (2.60)	311 (22.2)	54.2 (2.62)	21 (7.9)	6.3 (2.32)	243 (19.6)
4-year	1,137 (48.4)	66.5 (1.67)	42.5 (1.39)	381 (24.6)	33.5 (1.76)	320 (22.5)	28.1 (1.68)	61 (13.5)	16.0 (3.26)	756 (34.6)
Full-time students	1,580 (56.7)	92.3 (0.94)	59.0 (1.39)	631 (31.6)	39.9 (1.55)	559 (29.7)	35.4 (1.51)	72 (14.7)	11.4 (2.19)	949 (38.7)
Part-time students	131 (16.7)	7.7 (0.94)	4.9 (0.61)	81 (11.3)	61.9 (5.34)	72 (10.7)	54.9 (5.48)	10 (5.5)	12.5 (6.38)	49 (8.8)
White[3]	1,368 (52.7)	80.0 (1.41)	51.1 (1.41)	586 (30.4)	42.8 (1.68)	525 (28.8)	38.4 (1.66)	60 (13.4)	10.2 (2.17)	782 (35.1)
Black[3]	194 (21.2)	11.3 (1.19)	7.2 (0.78)	55 (13.4)	28.4 (5.87)	42 (11.8)	21.7 (5.38)	13 (6.5)	— (†)	139 (21.3)
Hispanic[4]	184 (22.1)	10.8 (1.24)	6.9 (0.81)	67 (14.8)	36.3 (6.44)	60 (14.0)	32.7 (6.28)	7 (4.8)	— (†)	117 (19.6)
Not enrolled in college, 2003	966 (44.8)	100.0 (†)	36.1 (1.35)	757 (34.6)	78.4 (1.67)	558 (29.7)	57.8 (2.00)	198 (24.4)	26.2 (2.77)	209 (18.2)
Male	507 (32.4)	52.5 (2.35)	18.9 (1.11)	409 (34.5)	80.8 (2.99)	297 (29.4)	58.7 (3.74)	111 (18.0)	27.2 (3.77)	98 (16.9)
Female	459 (30.9)	47.5 (2.35)	17.1 (1.06)	348 (30.5)	75.9 (3.28)	261 (26.5)	56.9 (3.79)	87 (15.3)	25.1 (3.81)	111 (17.3)
White[3]	738 (39.1)	76.4 (1.99)	27.6 (1.26)	595 (30.7)	80.6 (1.83)	494 (28.0)	66.8 (2.18)	101 (17.4)	16.9 (2.66)	143 (15.1)
Black[3]	139 (18.1)	14.4 (1.75)	5.2 (0.67)	108 (18.8)	77.8 (6.40)	38 (11.2)	27.2 (6.86)	70 (15.2)	65.1 (8.33)	30 (9.9)
Hispanic[4]	130 (18.7)	13.5 (1.82)	4.9 (0.69)	95 (17.6)	73.3 (7.05)	75 (15.7)	57.9 (7.86)	20 (8.1)	21.1 (7.59)	35 (10.7)
2004 high school completers[5]										
Total	2,752 (109.2)	100.0 (†)	100.0 (†)	1,533 (68.3)	55.7 (1.66)	1,282 (62.5)	46.6 (1.67)	251 (27.9)	16.4 (1.66)	1,219 (47.1)
Male	1,327 (76.0)	48.2 (2.06)	48.2 (2.06)	764 (47.4)	57.6 (2.34)	645 (43.6)	48.6 (2.36)	119 (18.8)	15.6 (2.26)	562 (40.7)
Female	1,425 (78.4)	51.8 (2.06)	51.8 (2.06)	768 (46.0)	53.9 (2.20)	636 (41.9)	44.6 (2.20)	132 (19.1)	17.2 (2.27)	657 (42.6)
White[3]	2,111 (95.7)	76.7 (1.74)	76.7 (1.74)	1,211 (60.8)	57.4 (1.89)	1,037 (56.3)	49.1 (1.91)	174 (23.2)	14.4 (1.77)	900 (40.5)
Black[3]	416 (50.8)	15.1 (1.77)	15.1 (1.77)	204 (26.4)	48.9 (4.56)	152 (22.8)	36.6 (4.39)	51 (13.3)	25.1 (5.64)	213 (27.0)
Hispanic[4]	286 (55.6)	10.4 (1.96)	10.4 (1.96)	153 (22.9)	53.5 (5.48)	129 (21.1)	45.3 (5.47)	23 (8.9)	15.3 (5.41)	133 (21.4)
Enrolled in college, 2004	1,835 (60.9)	100.0 (†)	66.7 (1.31)	821 (50.1)	44.8 (2.03)	712 (46.7)	38.8 (1.99)	109 (18.4)	13.3 (2.08)	1,013 (43.0)
Male	815 (40.7)	44.4 (1.69)	29.6 (1.27)	347 (32.0)	42.6 (2.99)	293 (29.5)	35.9 (2.90)	54 (12.7)	15.6 (3.35)	468 (37.2)
Female	1,020 (45.3)	55.6 (1.69)	37.1 (1.34)	475 (36.3)	46.6 (2.61)	420 (34.1)	41.1 (2.57)	55 (12.4)	11.6 (2.45)	545 (38.8)
2-year	618 (36.0)	33.7 (1.61)	22.5 (1.16)	378 (34.0)	61.1 (3.44)	321 (31.4)	51.9 (3.52)	57 (13.3)	15.0 (3.23)	240 (21.0)
4-year	1,217 (50.1)	66.3 (1.61)	44.2 (1.38)	444 (36.9)	36.5 (2.42)	392 (34.6)	32.2 (2.35)	52 (12.7)	11.8 (2.70)	773 (37.6)
Full-time students	1,711 (58.9)	93.2 (0.86)	62.2 (1.35)	720 (46.9)	42.1 (2.09)	624 (43.7)	36.5 (2.04)	95 (17.1)	13.3 (2.23)	991 (42.5)
Part-time students	124 (16.2)	6.8 (0.86)	4.5 (0.58)	102 (17.7)	82.4 (6.00)	88 (16.4)	71.3 (7.12)	14 (6.6)	13.5 (5.96)	22 (6.3)
White[3]	1,444 (54.0)	78.7 (1.40)	52.5 (1.39)	685 (45.8)	47.5 (2.30)	602 (42.9)	41.7 (2.27)	84 (16.1)	12.2 (2.20)	759 (37.2)
Black[3]	254 (24.1)	13.8 (1.25)	9.2 (0.86)	91 (17.7)	35.9 (5.60)	72 (15.7)	28.2 (5.25)	19 (8.1)	21.3 (7.97)	163 (23.6)
Hispanic[4]	177 (21.7)	9.6 (1.14)	6.4 (0.77)	74 (16.0)	41.8 (6.89)	67 (15.2)	37.8 (6.77)	7 (4.9)	— (†)	103 (18.8)
Not enrolled in college, 2004	918 (43.7)	100.0 (†)	33.4 (1.31)	711 (46.6)	77.5 (2.42)	569 (41.7)	62.1 (2.80)	142 (21.0)	20.0 (2.64)	206 (19.4)
Male	512 (32.6)	55.8 (2.39)	18.6 (1.08)	418 (35.2)	81.6 (2.95)	353 (32.3)	68.9 (3.52)	65 (13.9)	15.6 (3.06)	94 (16.7)
Female	406 (29.1)	44.2 (2.39)	14.8 (0.99)	294 (28.6)	72.4 (3.70)	217 (24.5)	53.5 (4.13)	77 (14.6)	26.2 (4.28)	112 (17.6)
White[3]	667 (37.3)	72.7 (2.15)	24.2 (1.19)	526 (40.1)	78.8 (2.77)	435 (36.5)	65.2 (3.23)	91 (16.8)	17.3 (2.90)	141 (16.1)
Black[3]	162 (19.5)	17.6 (1.95)	5.9 (0.70)	112 (19.6)	69.4 (6.73)	81 (16.7)	49.8 (7.30)	32 (10.5)	28.2 (7.90)	49 (13.0)
Hispanic[4]	109 (17.1)	11.9 (1.77)	4.0 (0.62)	79 (17.6)	72.1 (7.99)	63 (14.7)	57.3 (8.81)	16 (7.4)	20.4 (8.42)	31 (10.3)

See notes at end of table.

Table 381. College enrollment and labor force status of 2003, 2004, and 2005 high school completers, by sex and race/ethnicity: 2003, 2004, and 2005—Continued

Selected characteristic	Civilian noninstitutional population			Civilian labor force[1]						Not in labor force (in thousands)
	Number (in thousands)	Percent	Percent of high school completers	Number (in thousands)	Labor force participation rate	Employed		Unemployed		
						Number (in thousands)	Percent of population	Number (in thousands)	Unemployment rate	
1	2	3	4	5	6	7	8	9	10	11
2005 high school completers[6]										
Total	2,675 (107.8)	100.0 (†)	100.0 (†)	1,529 (68.2)	57.2 (1.68)	1,320 (63.4)	49.3 (1.69)	209 (25.4)	13.7 (1.55)	1,146 (45.7)
Male	1,262 (74.2)	47.2 (2.09)	47.2 (2.09)	751 (47.0)	59.5 (2.38)	652 (43.9)	51.7 (2.42)	99 (17.1)	13.1 (2.12)	511 (38.9)
Female	1,414 (78.2)	52.9 (2.09)	52.9 (2.09)	778 (46.3)	55.0 (2.21)	668 (42.9)	47.2 (2.21)	110 (17.5)	14.2 (2.09)	635 (41.9)
White[3]	2,147 (96.5)	80.3 (1.67)	80.3 (1.67)	1,256 (61.9)	58.5 (1.86)	1,106 (58.1)	51.5 (1.89)	149 (21.5)	11.9 (1.61)	891 (40.3)
Black[3]	354 (47.2)	13.2 (1.70)	13.2 (1.70)	196 (25.9)	55.3 (4.91)	146 (22.4)	41.1 (4.86)	50 (13.1)	25.5 (5.79)	159 (23.4)
Hispanic[4]	390 (64.4)	14.6 (2.30)	14.6 (2.30)	237 (28.4)	60.6 (4.60)	193 (25.7)	49.4 (4.71)	44 (12.3)	18.5 (4.68)	154 (23.0)
Enrolled in college, 2005	1,834 (60.9)	100.0 (†)	68.6 (1.31)	869 (51.5)	47.4 (2.04)	795 (49.3)	43.4 (2.03)	73 (15.0)	8.4 (1.66)	965 (42.0)
Male	839 (41.3)	45.7 (1.70)	31.4 (1.31)	406 (34.7)	48.4 (2.97)	364 (32.8)	43.4 (2.95)	42 (11.2)	10.3 (2.61)	433 (35.8)
Female	995 (44.8)	54.3 (1.70)	37.2 (1.36)	463 (35.8)	46.5 (2.64)	431 (34.5)	43.3 (2.62)	31 (9.3)	6.8 (1.95)	533 (38.4)
2-year	642 (36.7)	35.0 (1.63)	24.0 (1.21)	393 (34.7)	61.3 (3.37)	350 (32.7)	54.5 (3.44)	43 (11.5)	11.0 (2.78)	249 (21.4)
4-year	1,192 (49.6)	65.0 (1.63)	44.6 (1.40)	475 (38.1)	39.9 (2.48)	445 (36.9)	37.4 (2.46)	30 (9.6)	6.3 (1.96)	717 (36.2)
Full-time students	1,672 (58.3)	91.2 (0.97)	62.5 (1.37)	741 (47.6)	44.3 (2.13)	676 (45.5)	40.4 (2.10)	65 (14.2)	8.7 (1.82)	931 (41.2)
Part-time students	162 (18.5)	8.8 (0.97)	6.1 (0.67)	128 (19.8)	79.0 (5.60)	120 (19.2)	73.8 (6.05)	8 (5.0)	6.6 (3.85)	34 (7.9)
White[3]	1,490 (54.9)	81.2 (1.33)	55.7 (1.40)	728 (47.2)	48.8 (2.27)	674 (45.4)	45.2 (2.26)	54 (12.9)	7.4 (1.71)	762 (37.3)
Black[3]	201 (21.6)	11.0 (1.13)	7.5 (0.79)	82 (16.8)	40.7 (6.44)	68 (15.3)	33.9 (6.21)	14 (7.0)	16.8 (7.67)	119 (20.2)
Hispanic[4]	211 (23.7)	11.5 (1.23)	7.9 (0.86)	96 (18.2)	45.7 (6.37)	91 (17.7)	43.1 (6.34)	6 (4.6)	5.8 (4.42)	114 (19.8)
Not enrolled in college, 2005	841 (41.8)	100.0 (†)	31.4 (1.31)	660 (44.9)	78.5 (2.48)	525 (40.1)	62.4 (2.93)	136 (20.5)	20.6 (2.77)	181 (18.2)
Male	423 (29.7)	50.3 (2.52)	15.8 (1.03)	345 (32.0)	81.6 (3.25)	288 (29.2)	68.2 (3.90)	57 (13.0)	16.4 (3.44)	78 (15.2)
Female	418 (29.5)	49.7 (2.52)	15.6 (1.02)	315 (29.6)	75.4 (3.52)	236 (25.6)	56.5 (4.04)	79 (14.8)	25.1 (4.07)	103 (16.9)
White[3]	656 (37.0)	78.0 (2.09)	24.5 (1.21)	528 (40.2)	80.4 (2.72)	432 (36.4)	65.9 (3.24)	96 (17.2)	18.1 (2.95)	129 (15.4)
Black[3]	153 (18.9)	18.2 (2.07)	5.7 (0.70)	114 (19.8)	74.4 (6.56)	78 (16.4)	50.7 (7.51)	36 (11.1)	31.9 (8.11)	39 (11.6)
Hispanic[4]	179 (21.8)	21.3 (2.34)	6.7 (0.80)	140 (21.9)	78.2 (5.74)	102 (18.7)	56.9 (6.88)	38 (11.4)	27.3 (7.00)	39 (11.6)

—Not available.
†Not applicable.
[1]The labor force includes all employed persons plus those seeking employment. The labor force participation rate is the percentage of persons either employed or seeking employment. The unemployment rate is the percentage of persons in the labor force who are seeking employment.
[2]Includes 16- to 24-year-olds who completed high school between January and October 2003.
[3]Includes persons of Hispanic origin.
[4]Persons of Hispanic origin may be of any race.
[5]Includes 16- to 24-year-olds who completed high school between January and October 2004.

[6]Includes 16- to 24-year-olds who completed high school between January and October 2005.
NOTE: Enrollment data are for October of given year. Data are based on sample surveys of the civilian noninstitutional population. Percents are only shown when the base is 75,000 or greater. Even though the standard errors are large, smaller estimates are shown to permit users to combine categories in various ways. Detail for the above race and Hispanic-origin groups does not sum to totals because data for the other racial groups are not presented and Hispanics are included in both the White and Black population groups. Standard errors have been revised from previous years. Detail may not sum to totals because of rounding. Standard errors appear in parentheses.
SOURCE: U.S. Department of Labor, Bureau of Labor Statistics, *College Enrollment and Work Activity of High School Graduates*, 2003, 2004, and 2005. (This table was prepared May 2006.)

Table 382. Labor force status of high school dropouts, by sex and race/ethnicity: Selected years, 1980 through 2005

Year, sex, and race or ethnicity	Dropouts Number (in thousands)	Percent of total	Dropouts in civilian labor force[1] Number (in thousands)	Labor force participation rate	Unemployed Number (in thousands)	Unemployment rate	Dropouts not in labor force Number (in thousands)	Percent of population
1	2	3	4	5	6	7	8	9
All dropouts[2]								
1980	739 (44.1)	100.0 (†)	471 (35.2)	63.7 (2.87)	149 (19.9)	31.6 (3.50)	268 (26.6)	36.3 (2.87)
1985	612 (42.4)	100.0 (†)	413 (34.8)	67.5 (3.25)	147 (20.9)	35.6 (4.06)	199 (24.2)	32.5 (3.25)
1990	405 (35.7)	100.0 (†)	280 (29.7)	69.0 (4.08)	90 (16.9)	32.3 (4.99)	125 (19.9)	31.0 (4.08)
1995	604 (43.6)	100.0 (†)	409 (35.9)	67.7 (3.38)	121 (19.6)	29.6 (4.03)	195 (24.8)	32.3 (3.38)
2000	515 (28.5)	100.0 (†)	350 (23.5)	68.0 (2.59)	99 (17.2)	28.1 (4.16)	165 (16.2)	32.0 (2.59)
2001	506 (28.3)	100.0 (†)	324 (22.7)	64.0 (2.69)	116 (18.7)	35.9 (4.62)	182 (17.0)	36.0 (2.69)
2002	401 (25.2)	100.0 (†)	271 (20.7)	67.7 (2.94)	81 (15.6)	29.8 (4.82)	129 (14.3)	32.3 (2.94)
2003	457 (26.9)	100.0 (†)	271 (20.7)	59.3 (2.89)	84 (15.9)	30.8 (4.86)	186 (17.2)	40.7 (2.89)
2004	496 (39.0)	100.0 (†)	267 (28.6)	53.7 (3.92)	106 (18.1)	39.9 (5.27)	229 (20.5)	46.3 (3.03)
2005	407 (35.3)	100.0 (†)	233 (26.7)	57.2 (4.30)	77 (15.4)	32.9 (5.42)	174 (17.9)	42.8 (3.32)
Male								
1980	422 (32.8)	57.1 (2.91)	305 (27.9)	72.3 (3.48)	93 (15.4)	30.5 (4.21)	117 (17.3)	27.7 (3.48)
1985	321 (30.2)	52.5 (3.41)	261 (27.2)	81.3 (3.67)	98 (16.7)	37.5 (5.06)	60 (13.1)	18.7 (3.67)
1990	215 (25.6)	53.1 (4.34)	173 (23.0)	80.2 (4.76)	63 (13.9)	36.2 (6.39)	42 (11.3)	19.8 (4.76)
1995	339 (32.1)	56.1 (3.53)	251 (27.7)	74.0 (4.17)	72 (14.8)	28.7 (4.99)	88 (16.4)	26.0 (4.17)
2000	295 (29.3)	57.3 (3.73)	220 (25.3)	74.4 (4.35)	54 (12.6)	24.5 (4.96)	76 (14.9)	25.6 (4.35)
2001	298 (29.5)	58.9 (3.74)	198 (24.0)	66.5 (4.68)	68 (14.1)	34.2 (5.77)	100 (17.1)	33.5 (4.68)
2002	214 (25.0)	53.4 (4.26)	149 (20.9)	69.5 (5.38)	35 (10.1)	23.4 (5.93)	65 (13.8)	30.5 (5.38)
2003	242 (26.6)	53.0 (3.99)	159 (21.6)	65.6 (5.22)	53 (12.5)	33.2 (6.39)	83 (15.6)	34.4 (5.22)
2004	278 (28.7)	56.0 (3.84)	166 (22.2)	59.9 (5.07)	67 (14.1)	40.4 (6.56)	112 (18.2)	40.1 (5.07)
2005	227 (25.9)	55.8 (4.24)	136 (20.1)	59.7 (5.61)	49 (12.1)	35.9 (7.09)	91 (16.4)	40.3 (5.61)
Female								
1980	317 (27.5)	42.9 (2.82)	166 (19.9)	52.4 (4.34)	56 (11.6)	33.7 (5.68)	151 (19.0)	47.6 (4.34)
1985	291 (27.8)	47.5 (3.30)	152 (20.1)	52.2 (4.79)	49 (11.4)	32.2 (6.20)	139 (19.3)	47.8 (4.79)
1990	190 (23.3)	46.9 (4.20)	107 (17.5)	56.3 (6.09)	28 (9.0)	26.1 (7.18)	83 (15.4)	43.7 (6.09)
1995	265 (27.5)	43.9 (3.42)	157 (21.2)	59.5 (5.10)	49 (11.8)	30.9 (6.24)	107 (17.5)	40.5 (5.10)
2000	220 (24.3)	42.7 (3.58)	131 (18.8)	59.4 (5.43)	45 (11.0)	34.2 (6.80)	90 (15.6)	40.6 (5.43)
2001	207 (23.6)	40.9 (3.59)	126 (18.4)	60.6 (5.57)	48 (11.4)	38.6 (7.12)	82 (14.9)	39.4 (5.57)
2002	187 (22.4)	46.6 (4.09)	122 (18.1)	65.6 (5.70)	46 (11.1)	37.6 (7.20)	64 (13.1)	34.4 (5.70)
2003	215 (24.0)	47.0 (3.83)	112 (17.4)	52.1 (5.59)	31 (9.1)	27.6 (6.93)	103 (16.6)	47.9 (5.59)
2004	218 (24.6)	44.0 (3.72)	100 (16.7)	45.9 (5.63)	39 (10.4)	38.9 (8.13)	118 (18.1)	54.1 (5.63)
2005	180 (22.4)	44.2 (4.11)	97 (16.4)	54.0 (6.20)	28 (8.8)	28.8 (7.67)	83 (15.2)	46.0 (6.20)
White[3]								
1980	580 (39.1)	78.5 (2.46)	392 (32.1)	67.6 (3.16)	106 (16.8)	27.0 (3.66)	188 (22.3)	32.4 (3.16)
1985	458 (36.7)	74.8 (3.01)	330 (31.1)	72.1 (3.60)	116 (18.6)	35.2 (4.53)	128 (19.4)	27.9 (3.60)
1990	303 (30.9)	74.8 (3.83)	211 (25.8)	69.8 (4.69)	56 (13.4)	26.3 (5.42)	92 (17.0)	30.2 (4.69)
1995	448 (37.6)	74.2 (3.17)	312 (31.4)	69.8 (3.85)	85 (16.5)	27.2 (4.50)	135 (20.6)	30.2 (3.85)
2000	384 (24.7)	74.6 (2.42)	280 (21.1)	73.0 (2.85)	70 (14.5)	24.9 (4.48)	104 (12.8)	27.0 (2.85)
2001	401 (25.2)	79.2 (2.27)	273 (20.8)	68.1 (2.93)	89 (16.3)	32.4 (4.91)	128 (14.2)	31.9 (2.93)
2002	281 (21.1)	70.1 (2.88)	188 (17.3)	67.0 (3.53)	48 (12.0)	25.6 (5.52)	93 (12.1)	33.0 (3.53)
2003	336 (23.1)	73.5 (2.60)	215 (18.5)	64.0 (3.30)	58 (13.2)	27.1 (5.25)	121 (13.8)	36.0 (3.30)
2004	370 (33.7)	74.6 (3.42)	196 (24.5)	53.0 (4.54)	56 (13.2)	28.8 (5.69)	174 (17.9)	47.0 (3.51)
2005	273 (28.9)	67.1 (4.08)	166 (22.6)	61.1 (5.17)	52 (12.7)	31.4 (6.34)	106 (13.9)	38.9 (3.99)
Black[3]								
1980	146 (20.7)	19.8 (2.52)	73 (14.7)	50.0 (7.13)	40 (10.9)	‡ (†)	73 (14.7)	50.0 (7.13)
1985	132 (20.9)	21.6 (3.03)	69 (15.1)	52.3 (7.92)	30 (10.0)	‡ (†)	63 (14.4)	47.7 (7.92)
1990	86 (17.5)	21.2 (3.83)	56 (14.1)	65.3 (9.68)	30 (10.3)	‡ (†)	30 (10.3)	34.7 (9.68)
1995	109 (19.6)	18.0 (2.95)	66 (15.3)	61.0 (8.82)	27 (9.8)	‡ (†)	42 (12.2)	39.0 (8.82)
2000	111 (19.1)	21.5 (3.28)	58 (13.8)	51.9 (8.61)	27 (9.4)	‡ (†)	53 (13.2)	48.1 (8.61)
2001	85 (16.7)	16.8 (3.02)	42 (11.8)	49.9 (9.85)	21 (8.3)	‡ (†)	43 (11.9)	50.1 (9.85)
2002	79 (16.1)	19.7 (3.61)	55 (13.4)	69.8 (9.38)	27 (9.4)	‡ (†)	24 (8.9)	30.2 (9.38)
2003	88 (17.0)	19.3 (3.35)	42 (11.8)	47.8 (9.67)	19 (7.9)	‡ (†)	46 (12.0)	52.2 (9.67)
2004	91 (17.7)	18.3 (3.23)	50 (13.1)	54.4 (9.70)	39 (11.6)	‡ (†)	42 (12.0)	45.6 (9.70)
2005	114 (19.8)	28.0 (4.14)	52 (13.4)	45.4 (8.67)	20 (8.3)	‡ (†)	62 (14.6)	54.6 (8.67)
Hispanic[4]								
1980	91 (19.4)	12.3 (2.46)	60 (15.8)	65.9 (10.12)	17 (8.4)	‡ (†)	31 (11.3)	34.1 (10.12)
1985	106 (18.7)	17.3 (2.79)	73 (15.5)	68.9 (8.19)	33 (10.5)	‡ (†)	33 (10.5)	31.1 (8.19)
1990	67 (15.4)	16.5 (3.48)	32 (10.7)	‡ (†)	10 (6.0)	‡ (†)	35 (11.2)	‡ (†)
1995	174 (24.8)	28.8 (3.48)	119 (20.5)	68.6 (6.64)	35 (11.2)	29.3 (7.87)	55 (14.0)	31.4 (6.64)
2000	101 (18.2)	19.6 (3.18)	62 (14.3)	61.1 (8.81)	22 (8.5)	‡ (†)	39 (11.3)	38.9 (8.81)
2001	119 (19.7)	23.5 (3.42)	84 (16.6)	70.6 (7.58)	27 (9.4)	32.6 (9.29)	35 (10.7)	29.4 (7.58)
2002	94 (17.6)	23.4 (3.84)	62 (14.3)	66.5 (8.84)	23 (8.7)	‡ (†)	31 (10.1)	33.5 (8.84)
2003	124 (20.1)	27.1 (3.78)	68 (14.9)	54.5 (8.12)	17 (7.5)	‡ (†)	57 (13.7)	45.5 (8.12)
2004	154 (23.0)	31.0 (3.86)	87 (17.3)	56.8 (7.42)	27 (9.7)	30.7 (9.19)	67 (15.2)	43.2 (7.42)
2005	86 (17.2)	21.1 (3.76)	55 (13.8)	64.3 (9.61)	17 (7.7)	‡ (†)	31 (10.3)	35.7 (9.61)

†Not applicable.

‡Reporting standards not met.

[1]The labor force includes all employed persons plus those seeking employment. The labor force participation rate is the percentage of persons either employed or seeking employment. The unemployment rate is the percentage of persons in the labor force who are seeking employment.

[2]Persons 16 to 24 years old who dropped out of school in the 12-month period ending in October of years shown.

[3]Includes persons of Hispanic origin.

[4]Persons of Hispanic origin may be of any race.

NOTE: Data are based on sample surveys of the civilian noninstitutional population. Includes dropouts from any grade, including a small number from elementary and middle schools. Even though the standard errors are large, smaller estimates are shown to permit users to combine categories in various ways. Detail for the above race and Hispanic-origin groups does not sum to totals because data for the other racial groups are not presented and Hispanics are included in both the White and Black population groups. Some data have been revised from previously published figures. Detail may not sum to totals because of rounding. Standard errors appear in parentheses.

SOURCE: U.S. Department of Labor, Bureau of Labor Statistics, *College Enrollment and Work Activity of High School Graduates,* selected years, 1980 through 2005, and unpublished tabulations. (This table was prepared September 2006.)

Table 383. Current postsecondary education and employment status, wages earned, and living arrangements of special education students out of secondary school up to 4 years, by type of disability: 2005

Type of disability	Percentage attending postsecondary institutions										Percentage competitively employed[2]		Mean hourly wage at current job[3]		Percentage living independently[4]	
	Any post-secondary[1]		4-year		2-year		Vocational/technical									
1	2		3		4		5				6		7		8	
All disabilities[5]	23.4	(2.62)	7.8	(1.66)	12.9	(2.08)	6.3	(1.51)			69.5	(3.51)	$8.30	(0.32)	28.1	(2.94)
Specific learning disability	25.0	(3.99)	8.8	(2.61)	13.1	(3.12)	6.3 !	(2.24)			77.2	(4.85)	8.30	(0.38)	31.8	(4.53)
Mental retardation	12.0	(3.44)	1.4 !	(1.24)	7.8 !	(2.85)	5.3 !	(2.38)			36.3	(6.04)	7.40	(0.65)	13.7	(3.82)
Emotional disturbance	11.8	(2.95)	2.1 !	(1.31)	8.2 !	(2.54)	4.3 !	(1.86)			64.5	(5.56)	8.90	(0.75)	25.2	(4.21)
Speech or language impairment	36.0	(4.80)	19.6	(3.98)	19.6	(3.98)	6.7 !	(2.51)			71.0	(5.37)	8.00	(0.53)	31.4	(4.85)
Multiple disabilities	25.7	(6.64)	6.7 !	(3.82)	12.5 !	(5.07)	6.7 !	(3.81)			39.8	(8.76)	8.80	(1.17)	6.6 !	(3.91)
Other health impairment	33.3	(4.54)	8.8 !	(2.74)	23.1	(4.09)	11.9	(3.14)			76.2	(4.80)	8.10	(0.38)	20.4	(4.08)
Hearing impairment[6]	50.7	(5.88)	21.2	(4.89)	26.0	(5.22)	12.9 !	(3.99)			56.3	(6.95)	7.70	(0.55)	29.4	(5.66)
Orthopedic impairment	35.8	(5.37)	12.6	(3.72)	22.9	(4.75)	7.5 !	(2.96)			32.0	(6.13)	7.80	(0.97)	25.4	(5.15)
Visual impairment	63.9	(7.60)	34.4	(7.52)	31.7	(7.47)	5.2 !	(3.52)			59.5	(8.79)	9.60	(1.95)	39.9	(8.21)
Autism	35.8	(8.23)	16.1 !	(6.36)	19.0 !	(6.76)	5.1 !	(3.80)			56.0	(9.64)	6.90	(0.69)	17.1 !	(6.51)
Deaf-blindness	24.6 !	(8.26)	12.2 !	(6.42)	8.5 !	(5.47)	8.2 !	(5.26)			37.0	(9.96)	‡	(†)	24.4 !	(8.64)
Traumatic brain injury	17.0 !	(7.57)	4.5 !	(4.20)	11.1 !	(6.33)	5.3 !	(4.54)			50.2	(11.68)	7.80	(0.78)	28.0 !	(9.64)

†Not applicable.
!Interpret data with caution.
‡Reporting standards not met.
[1]Includes 2- and 4-year colleges, and vocational\technical schools.
[2]Competitively employed refers to those receiving more than minimum wage and working in an environment where the majority of workers are not disabled.
[3]Includes wages from noncompetitive jobs.
[4]Living independently includes living alone, with a spouse or roommate, in a college dormitory, in Job Corps housing, or in military housing as a service member.

[5]Includes disability categories with less than 30 youths in the sample, which are not shown separately.
[6]Includes deaf and hard of hearing.
NOTE: Data based on students who had been out of secondary school up to 4 years and had attended special or regular schools in the 1999–2000 or 2000–01 school year. Standard errors appear in parentheses.
SOURCE: U.S. Department of Education, Institute of Education Sciences, National Center for Special Education Research, National Longitudinal Transition Study-2 (NLTS2), Wave 3 parent/youth telephone interview/mail survey, 2005. (This table was prepared August 2006.)

Table 384. Full-time employment status of bachelor's degree recipients 1 year after graduation, by field of study: Selected years, 1976 through 2001

Field of study	Percent employed full time						Percent employed full time in a job closely related to field of study					
	1974–75 graduates in May 1976	1979–80 graduates in May 1981	1983–84 graduates in June 1985	1985–86 graduates in June 1987	1989–90 graduates in June 1991	1999–2000 graduates in July 2001	1974–75 graduates in May 1976	1979–80 graduates in May 1981	1983–84 graduates in June 1985	1985–86 graduates in June 1987	1989–90 graduates in June 1991	1999–2000 graduates in July 2001
1	2	3	4	5	6	7	8	9	10	11	12	13
Total	67	71	73	74	74	84 (0.6)	35	38	38	38	39	52 (0.8)
Professional/technical fields	77	80	82	81	80	88 (0.8)	51	51	47	47	48	63 (1.3)
Arts and sciences fields	56	56	56	62	64	77 (1.1)	18	17	15	25	26	39 (1.3)
Other	65	74	75	74	73	88 (1.2)	36	43	47	36	38	45 (2.2)
Newly qualified to teach	66	75	73	68	74	82 (1.0)	43	56	54	47	58	44 (1.3)
Not newly qualified to teach	67	71	73	74	73	86 (0.7)	33	36	36	37	36	56 (1.1)
Professional/technical fields	80	81	82	82	83	89 (0.9)	52	49	47	47	48	66 (1.5)
Engineering	79	84	84	83	84	87 (2.3)	57	55	53	46	50	71 (3.3)
Business and management	84	83	85	85	83	93 (1.2)	49	44	41	40	42	62 (2.3)
Health	75	77	75	76	86	84 (1.7)	71	66	70	65	83	81 (2.3)
Education[1]	66	67	63	73	67	81 (6.9)	22	29	24	57	39	30 (9.2)
Public affairs and services	—	77	74	72	66	87 (2.8)	—	46	31	37	49	58 (4.6)
Arts and sciences fields	57	56	56	63	64	77 (1.5)	17	16	15	25	23	42 (1.8)
Biological sciences	56	45	43	42	50	66 (3.9)	26	18	17	15	26	47 (5.0)
Physical sciences and mathematics[2]	50	58	51	76	72	89 (2.3)	19	29	20	48	48	66 (3.4)
Psychology	61	56	57	66	59	80 (3.2)	22	17	12	22	22	37 (4.5)
Social sciences	59	61	61	61	68	76 (2.8)	12	10	13	12	16	25 (3.1)
Humanities	56	55	59	59	59	72 (3.5)	12	14	17	19	11	41 (3.9)
Other	68	75	77	75	73	89 (1.5)	36	43	42	36	37	48 (2.8)
Communications	—	71	76	77	75	— (†)	—	31	31	33	29	— (†)
Miscellaneous	66	76	77	74	73	— (†)	35	46	46	38	38	— (†)

—Not available.
†Not applicable.
[1]Includes those who have not finished all requirements for teaching certification or were previously qualified to teach.
[2]Includes computer sciences.
NOTE: Data are from sample surveys of recent college graduates. Notes on methodology are included in the Guide to Sources. Data exclude bachelor's recipients from U.S.

Service Schools, deceased graduates, and graduates living at foreign addresses at the time of the survey. Standard errors appear in parentheses. Standard error values are not available for all years.
SOURCE: U.S. Department of Education, National Center for Education Statistics, "Recent College Graduates" surveys, 1976 through 1991; and 2000/01 Baccalaureate and Beyond Longitudinal Study (B&B:2000/01). (This table was prepared September 2003.)

Table 385. Percentage distribution of 1999–2000 bachelor's degree recipients 1 year after graduation, by field of study, time to completion, enrollment status, employment status, occupational area, job characteristics, and annual salaries: 2001

| Status | All fields of study | | Professional/technical fields | | | | | | | | | | Arts and sciences | | | | | | | | | | | | | |
| | | | Business and management | | Education | | Engineering | | Health professions | | Public affairs and social services | | Biological sciences | | Mathematics and physical sciences | | Social sciences | | History | | Humanities | | Psychology | | Other fields | |
1	2	(†)	3	(†)	4	(†)	5	(†)	6	(†)	7	(†)	8	(†)	9	(†)	10	(†)	11	(†)	12	(†)	13	(†)	14	(†)
Total 1999–2000 graduates	100.0	(†)	100.0	(†)	100.0	(†)	100.0	(†)	100.0	(†)	100.0	(†)	100.0	(†)	100.0	(†)	100.0	(†)	100.0	(†)	100.0	(†)	100.0	(†)	100.0	(†)
Time between high school graduation and degree completion																										
4 years or less	32.7	(0.79)	28.2	(1.72)	25.6	(1.80)	23.0	(2.26)	26.2	(2.05)	27.6	(2.58)	44.5	(2.40)	32.5	(2.42)	44.7	(2.37)	42.5	(4.42)	38.1	(2.07)	42.8	(2.37)	31.3	(1.55)
More than 4, up to 5 years	22.9	(0.59)	19.7	(1.40)	25.8	(1.67)	32.4	(2.49)	21.5	(1.75)	23.1	(2.70)	24.6	(2.27)	22.2	(2.00)	22.1	(1.98)	18.3	(2.95)	20.2	(1.50)	18.4	(1.86)	26.3	(1.38)
More than 5, up to 6 years	10.8	(0.48)	10.0	(1.14)	14.2	(1.14)	15.3	(1.14)	11.1	(1.14)	9.1	(1.14)	6.5	(1.14)	11.8	(1.14)	9.5	(1.14)	7.4	(1.14)	11.6	(1.14)	8.5	(1.14)	11.2	(1.14)
More than 6, up to 10 years	14.8	(0.56)	15.3	(1.49)	15.7	(1.66)	15.4	(2.13)	14.9	(1.59)	15.7	(2.93)	16.6	(2.18)	15.0	(2.06)	11.5	(1.43)	12.3	(2.74)	15.4	(1.55)	14.0	(1.78)	14.3	(1.40)
More than 10 years	18.9	(0.62)	26.8	(1.78)	18.6	(1.79)	13.9	(1.81)	26.3	(1.77)	24.6	(2.71)	7.8	(1.44)	18.4	(2.13)	12.2	(1.52)	19.5	(3.47)	14.8	(1.45)	16.4	(1.92)	17.0	(1.45)
Enrollment status																										
Enrolled full time	14.2	(0.49)	7.0	(0.91)	6.8	(1.00)	9.7	(1.47)	16.4	(1.35)	11.5	(1.86)	41.5	(2.79)	17.2	(2.00)	23.9	(2.00)	16.7	(2.48)	14.7	(1.24)	23.3	(2.02)	11.1	(0.97)
Enrolled part time	6.5	(0.31)	5.4	(0.80)	11.2	(1.15)	8.9	(1.55)	5.6	(1.00)	7.6	(1.76)	4.0	(0.92)	7.2	(1.40)	4.7	(0.90)	12.2	(3.20)	6.5	(0.94)	7.7	(1.15)	5.0	(0.72)
Not enrolled	79.4	(0.54)	87.6	(1.09)	82.0	(1.45)	81.4	(2.03)	78.1	(1.62)	80.9	(2.34)	54.6	(2.73)	75.6	(2.38)	71.5	(2.14)	71.1	(3.67)	78.9	(1.53)	69.0	(2.13)	83.9	(1.18)
Employment status																										
Employed	87.4	(0.44)	91.8	(1.05)	93.9	(0.91)	93.0	(1.39)	88.5	(1.25)	90.9	(1.90)	70.2	(2.49)	88.4	(1.59)	81.2	(1.70)	88.7	(2.27)	85.2	(1.49)	80.8	(1.97)	87.0	(1.02)
Full time	76.5	(0.54)	85.5	(1.29)	84.0	(1.44)	86.0	(1.78)	74.8	(1.67)	85.1	(2.21)	52.6	(2.78)	80.7	(2.02)	66.0	(2.18)	76.8	(2.99)	67.5	(1.83)	64.0	(2.50)	78.6	(1.27)
Part time	10.9	(0.42)	6.2	(0.90)	9.8	(1.15)	6.9	(1.23)	13.7	(1.29)	5.8	(1.23)	17.6	(1.88)	7.7	(1.23)	15.2	(1.71)	11.9	(2.11)	17.7	(1.55)	16.8	(1.92)	8.4	(0.86)
Unemployed[1]	6.2	(0.33)	5.4	(0.90)	2.2	(0.49)	4.4	(1.06)	4.9	(0.90)	4.9	(1.32)	6.7	(1.31)	4.4	(1.06)	7.8	(1.08)	5.5	(1.80)	8.1	(1.07)	9.8	(1.58)	7.8	(0.78)
Not in labor force[2]	6.4	(0.32)	2.9	(0.59)	4.0	(0.74)	2.7	(0.83)	6.6	(0.89)	4.2	(1.04)	23.2	(2.26)	7.3	(1.26)	11.0	(1.40)	5.8	(1.47)	6.7	(0.93)	9.5	(1.38)	5.2	(0.74)
Unemployment rate[3]	4.0	(0.33)	2.9	(0.65)	2.6	(1.38)	2.9	(0.86)	3.1	(0.78)	3.5	(1.01)	8.6	(2.08)	2.8	(1.09)	6.1	(1.25)	7.2	(2.06)	4.9	(1.02)	3.9	(0.92)	3.9	(0.69)
Total employed	100.0	(†)	100.0	(†)	100.0	(†)	100.0	(†)	100.0	(†)	100.0	(†)	100.0	(†)	100.0	(†)	100.0	(†)	100.0	(†)	100.0	(†)	100.0	(†)	100.0	(†)
Occupation																										
Business management	25.3	(0.57)	55.4	(1.78)	4.2	(0.83)	11.1	(1.85)	10.8	(1.37)	19.0	(2.68)	15.2	(2.12)	14.6	(2.17)	33.7	(2.07)	22.5	(4.14)	18.1	(1.65)	19.8	(2.24)	22.9	(1.51)
Education	18.1	(0.56)	3.2	(0.65)	81.9	(1.67)	3.0	(1.01)	7.6	(1.08)	11.0	(2.69)	12.6	(1.91)	11.7	(1.90)	13.5	(1.69)	24.0	(3.90)	24.5	(1.72)	21.9	(2.36)	14.2	(1.26)
Engineering	4.8	(0.31)	1.2	(0.33)	#	(†)	53.0	(3.11)	#	(†)	0.7	(0.47)	1.2	(0.81)	9.2	(1.40)	0.5	(0.24)	#	(†)	0.5	(0.37)	#	(†)	3.9	(0.76)
Health professions	7.8	(0.38)	1.0	(0.36)	1.6	(0.51)	0.4	(0.30)	61.8	(2.27)	4.3	(1.15)	15.6	(1.96)	2.0	(0.77)	3.4	(0.96)	2.0	(1.97)	1.5	(0.42)	7.9	(1.28)	3.6	(0.67)
Other profession[4]	11.2	(0.42)	2.3	(0.51)	1.5	(0.37)	13.5	(1.93)	5.7	(1.06)	26.7	(2.78)	32.7	(2.82)	16.7	(1.82)	15.2	(1.78)	9.1	(2.34)	10.8	(1.28)	21.2	(2.09)	14.7	(1.19)
Computer science/programming	6.8	(0.37)	9.0	(1.05)	1.2	(0.41)	10.1	(1.93)	0.8	(0.33)	2.3	(1.00)	2.3	(0.70)	35.9	(2.42)	4.9	(1.22)	1.8	(0.97)	5.4	(0.99)	2.1	(0.73)	4.8	(0.94)
Administrative/clerical/support	5.4	(0.33)	5.7	(0.91)	3.5	(0.74)	1.6	(0.60)	2.8	(0.70)	5.1	(1.30)	5.0	(1.40)	3.0	(0.82)	8.8	(1.27)	7.6	(2.15)	8.6	(1.05)	5.9	(1.39)	5.1	(0.73)
Mechanic/operator/laborer	3.3	(0.27)	3.8	(0.78)	1.1	(0.41)	3.6	(1.08)	2.0	(0.74)	2.0	(0.96)	6.1	(1.72)	1.8	(0.68)	1.2	(0.57)	8.3	(2.47)	4.7	(0.85)	2.0	(1.01)	4.8	(0.75)
Sales	6.8	(0.38)	12.2	(1.21)	1.0	(0.45)	1.3	(0.53)	2.9	(0.69)	2.2	(0.79)	3.3	(1.08)	2.0	(0.96)	4.0	(0.91)	11.1	(2.44)	6.8	(1.07)	4.3	(0.93)	12.3	(1.13)
Service	8.1	(0.41)	5.1	(0.83)	3.3	(0.86)	1.7	(0.57)	4.4	(1.05)	5.4	(1.61)	5.0	(1.09)	1.5	(0.54)	11.1	(1.75)	12.2	(2.84)	18.5	(1.60)	11.3	(1.74)	10.7	(1.15)
Military/protective service	2.4	(0.24)	1.2	(0.41)	0.8	(0.47)	0.6	(0.36)	1.2	(0.47)	21.5	(2.89)	1.0	(0.47)	1.7	(0.62)	3.6	(0.81)	1.5	(0.88)	0.6	(0.29)	3.5	(1.02)	2.9	(0.64)
Job characteristics																										
Job is start of career	71.4	(0.67)	75.7	(1.60)	86.6	(1.41)	89.1	(1.61)	73.4	(1.88)	75.8	(2.62)	60.0	(3.28)	76.3	(2.37)	62.4	(2.54)	58.9	(4.08)	61.7	(1.98)	56.6	(2.84)	68.1	(1.62)
Job closely related to bachelor's degree	54.0	(0.72)	55.8	(1.66)	82.7	(1.48)	69.3	(2.85)	74.6	(1.95)	59.3	(2.93)	47.1	(3.06)	66.3	(2.62)	29.0	(2.09)	24.8	(3.78)	41.3	(1.95)	35.8	(2.82)	47.0	(2.14)
Annual salaries[5]																										
Less than $10,000	1.4	(0.16)	0.4	(0.20)	1.8	(0.57)	0.8	(0.74)	0.6	(0.22)	1.1	(0.58)	1.8	(0.69)	0.8	(0.64)	2.2	(0.70)	3.3	(2.14)	1.8	(0.42)	5.5	(1.48)	1.3	(0.45)
$10,000 to $14,999	2.6	(0.24)	1.0	(0.41)	1.6	(0.42)	0.5	(0.37)	1.3	(0.50)	2.7	(1.44)	4.7	(1.43)	0.7	(0.33)	2.9	(0.79)	2.0	(0.85)	5.4	(0.98)	4.1	(1.24)	3.0	(0.60)
$15,000 to $19,999	5.4	(0.34)	1.8	(0.57)	7.3	(1.14)	1.4	(0.58)	2.8	(0.76)	8.0	(2.16)	9.7	(2.04)	4.2	(1.06)	4.3	(1.03)	8.1	(3.02)	9.1	(1.10)	7.8	(1.85)	7.4	(1.01)
$20,000 to $24,999	11.2	(0.47)	5.7	(0.92)	16.4	(1.76)	1.5	(0.64)	6.4	(1.20)	18.2	(2.74)	13.7	(2.24)	6.6	(1.41)	13.6	(1.79)	11.2	(2.63)	14.7	(1.43)	18.9	(1.99)	15.0	(1.36)
$25,000 to $34,999	36.4	(0.81)	29.3	(1.96)	62.0	(2.18)	5.7	(1.54)	30.2	(2.07)	46.2	(3.38)	37.1	(3.43)	24.7	(2.87)	39.0	(2.77)	47.2	(4.85)	43.3	(2.25)	41.1	(3.12)	37.3	(2.03)
$35,000 to $49,999	28.0	(0.77)	41.1	(2.01)	9.5	(1.24)	44.0	(3.20)	40.3	(2.23)	16.3	(2.39)	25.5	(3.27)	28.3	(2.83)	26.7	(2.41)	26.9	(4.48)	20.2	(1.86)	16.1	(2.38)	24.4	(1.73)
$50,000 to $74,999	12.3	(0.54)	15.9	(1.48)	1.4	(0.59)	43.1	(3.19)	14.7	(1.73)	4.5	(1.38)	5.8	(1.73)	29.5	(2.94)	8.4	(1.58)	1.3	(1.08)	4.9	(1.05)	4.8	(1.22)	9.5	(1.25)
$75,000 or more	2.9	(0.29)	4.9	(0.90)	#	(†)	3.0	(0.93)	3.8	(0.99)	2.9	(1.44)	1.7	(1.10)	5.2	(1.13)	2.8	(0.86)	#	(†)	0.7	(0.32)	1.8	(1.13)	2.2	(0.60)
Average annual salary[6]	$35,408	(316.0)	$41,008	(941.2)	$27,634	(345.7)	$47,931	(790.0)	$39,441	(1,089.6)	$30,400	(1,054.7)	$30,749	(978.4)	$42,755	(981.0)	$33,892	(916.0)	$29,984	(1,053.2)	$30,102	(846.5)	$28,835	(905.7)	$32,780	(627.5)

†Not applicable.
#Rounds to zero.
[1]Percent of all persons (including those not in the labor force) who are not working, but are looking for work.
[2]Percent not working and not looking for work.
[3]Percent of persons in the labor force (excluding those not in the labor force) who are not working, but are looking for work.
[4]All other professional occupations excluding business, teaching, engineering, and health.
[5]Salaries for those employed full time.
[6]Respondents reporting salaries less than $1,000 or more than $500,000 were excluded.
NOTE: Detail may not sum to totals because of rounding. Standard errors appear in parentheses.
SOURCE: U.S. Department of Education, National Center for Education Statistics, 2000/01 Baccalaureate and Beyond Longitudinal Study (B&B:2000/01). (This table was prepared September 2003.)

Table 386. Enrollment in postbaccalaureate certificate or advanced degree programs and highest degree attained by 1992–93 bachelor's degree recipients, by education characteristics: 2003

Education characteristic	Percent				Distribution by highest degree attained				
		Of those ever enrolled[1]			Bachelor's degree or post-baccalaureate certificate	Advanced degree			
	Ever enrolled	Ever completed[2]	Never completed, no longer enrolled	Currently enrolled		Total	Master's degree	First-professional degree	Doctor's degree
1	2	3	4	5	6	7	8	9	10
Total...	**42.5**	**63.4**	**23.5**	**17.2**	**74.4**	**25.6**	**19.7**	**4.0**	**1.9**
Undergraduate major									
Professional fields............................	37.4	60.7	24.8	18.3	78.7	21.3	19.0	1.8	0.5
Business and management	27.5	65.0	22.5	15.9	83.3	16.7	14.7	1.8	0.2
Education...	54.6	56.5	27.1	20.4	71.1	28.9	26.3	1.5	1.1
Health..	38.0	61.8	24.1	18.4	77.9	22.1	19.4	2.1	0.6
Arts and sciences	49.3	64.8	22.4	17.3	69.4	30.7	20.8	6.3	3.6
Arts and humanities	46.6	62.7	24.2	18.6	73.0	27.1	21.5	4.3	1.2
Social and behavioral sciences.........	49.3	62.2	22.5	19.9	70.8	29.2	21.1	6.1	2.0
Science/math/engineering	51.1	68.4	21.2	14.0	65.7	34.3	20.1	7.7	6.6
Other...	36.1	65.7	24.4	13.4	77.6	22.4	18.0	3.4	1.0
Cumulative undergraduate GPA									
Less than 2.75....................................	63.5	59.5	25.4	18.5	79.7	20.4	16.8	2.2	1.3
2.75 to 3.74..	51.5	66.1	21.5	17.0	69.4	30.6	21.3	7.1	2.3
3.75 or higher.....................................	43.7	70.0	22.0	13.1	61.6	38.4	30.1	4.3	4.1
Institution granting bachelor's degree									
Public 4-year.......................................	40.6	61.2	24.6	18.0	76.6	23.4	18.1	3.5	1.9
Private not-for-profit 4-year	47.1	66.3	22.5	16.0	70.0	30.0	22.7	5.3	2.0
Other...	33.7	75.3	11.3	14.3	74.6	25.4	22.5	1.6	1.3
Highest degree attained as of 2003									
Bachelor's degree or postbaccalaureate certificate	77.3	7.9	59.1	33.9	100.0	†	†	†	†
Master's degree	100.0	100.0	†	7.1	†	100.0	100.0	†	†
Doctor's/first-professional degree	100.0	100.0	†	2.9	†	100.0	†	67.5	32.5
Field of advanced degree[3]									
Business and management	100.0	100.0	†	3.4	†	100.0	98.4	#	1.6
Education...	100.0	100.0	†	7.4	†	100.0	98.3	0.3	1.4
Health..	100.0	100.0	†	4.3	†	100.0	48.7	48.1	3.2
Arts and humanities	100.0	100.0	†	7.1	†	100.0	86.6	3.6	9.9
Social and behavioral sciences.........	100.0	100.0	†	9.2	†	100.0	89.4	#	10.6
Science/math/engineering	100.0	100.0	†	10.7	†	100.0	76.3	#	23.7
Other...	100.0	100.0	†	4.5	†	100.0	43.5	5.1	11.4

†Not applicable.
#Rounds to zero.
[1]Columns are not mutually exclusive; bachelor's degree recipients who are currently enrolled could have completed a prior graduate program.
[2]Includes completion of postbaccalaureate certificates.

[3]Only includes respondents who completed a master's, doctor's, or first-professional degree. These graduates could also have left another graduate program without completing or be currently enrolled in another graduate program.
NOTE: Detail may not sum to totals because of rounding.
SOURCE: U.S. Department of Education, National Center for Education Statistics, 1993/03 Baccalaureate and Beyond Longitudinal Study (B&B:93/03). (This table was prepared August 2006.)

Table 387. Average annual salary of bachelor's degree recipients employed full time 1 year after graduation, by field of study: Selected years, 1976 through 2001

Average salary of degree recipients	Total	Engineering	Business and management	Health professions	Education[1]	Public affairs and social services	Biological sciences	Mathematics and other sciences	Psychology	Social sciences	History	Humanities	Communications	Miscellaneous
1	2	3	4	5	6	7	8	9	10	11	12	13	14	15
Current dollars														
1974–75 recipients—salary in February 1976[2]	$7,600 (—)	$12,200 (—)	$10,200 (—)	$8,600 (—)	$6,300 (—)	— (†)	$6,500 (—)	$7,000 (—)	— (†)	$6,700 (—)	— (†)	$5,800 (—)	— (†)	$6,800 (—)
1979–80 recipients—salary in May 1981[2]	15,200 (—)	22,400 (—)	16,300 (—)	17,300 (—)	11,500 (—)	$13,700 (—)	14,500 (—)	16,300 (—)	$12,500 (—)	14,000 (—)	— (†)	12,600 (—)	— (†)	15,100 (—)
1983–84 recipients—salary in June 1985[2]	17,700 (—)	24,100 (—)	18,700 (—)	20,800 (—)	13,800 (—)	15,100 (—)	15,100 (—)	17,500 (—)	14,600 (—)	15,800 (—)	— (†)	14,000 (—)	$16,200 (—)	18,600 (—)
1985–86 recipients—salary in June 1987	20,400 (—)	26,600 (—)	21,100 (—)	22,600 (—)	15,800 (—)	17,700 (—)	16,400 (—)	22,500 (—)	17,300 (—)	20,300 (—)	— (†)	16,200 (—)	— (†)	17,600 (—)
1989–90 recipients—salary in June 1991	23,600 (—)	30,900 (—)	24,700 (—)	31,500 (—)	19,100 (—)	20,800 (—)	21,100 (—)	27,200 (—)	19,200 (—)	22,200 (—)	— (†)	19,100 (—)	— (†)	20,800 (—)
1992–93 recipients—salary in April 1994[2]	24,200 (—)	30,900 (—)	27,100 (—)	31,300 (—)	19,300 (—)	22,000 (—)	22,800 (—)	25,400 (—)	19,500 (—)	22,100 (—)	$21,000 (—)	21,300 (—)	— (†)	21,600 (—)
1999–2000 recipients—salary in 2001[2]	35,400 (320)	47,900 (790)	41,000 (940)	39,400 (1,090)	27,600 (350)	30,400 (1,050)	30,700 (980)	42,800 (940)	28,800 (910)	33,900 (920)	30,000 (1,050)	30,100 (850)	— (†)	32,800 (630)
Constant 2005 dollars														
1974–75 recipients—salary in February 1976[2]	$26,100 (—)	$41,900 (—)	$35,000 (—)	$29,500 (—)	$21,600 (—)	— (†)	$22,300 (—)	$24,000 (—)	— (†)	$23,000 (—)	— (†)	$19,900 (—)	— (†)	$23,300 (—)
1979–80 recipients—salary in May 1981[2]	32,700 (—)	48,100 (—)	35,000 (—)	37,200 (—)	24,700 (—)	$29,400 (—)	31,200 (—)	35,000 (—)	$26,900 (—)	30,100 (—)	— (†)	27,100 (—)	— (†)	32,400 (—)
1983–84 recipients—salary in June 1985[2]	32,100 (—)	43,700 (—)	33,900 (—)	37,800 (—)	25,000 (—)	27,400 (—)	27,400 (—)	31,800 (—)	26,500 (—)	28,700 (—)	— (†)	25,400 (—)	$29,400 (—)	33,800 (—)
1985–86 recipients—salary in June 1987	35,100 (—)	45,700 (—)	36,300 (—)	38,900 (—)	27,200 (—)	30,400 (—)	28,200 (—)	38,700 (—)	29,700 (—)	34,900 (—)	— (†)	27,900 (—)	— (†)	30,300 (—)
1989–90 recipients—salary in June 1991	33,800 (—)	44,300 (—)	35,400 (—)	45,200 (—)	27,400 (—)	29,800 (—)	30,300 (—)	39,000 (—)	27,500 (—)	31,800 (—)	— (†)	27,400 (—)	— (†)	29,800 (—)
1992–93 recipients—salary in April 1994[2]	31,900 (—)	40,700 (—)	35,700 (—)	41,200 (—)	25,400 (—)	29,000 (—)	30,000 (—)	33,500 (—)	25,700 (—)	29,100 (—)	$27,700 (—)	28,100 (—)	— (†)	28,500 (—)
1999–2000 recipients—salary in 2001[2]	39,000 (350)	52,900 (870)	45,200 (1,040)	43,500 (1,200)	30,500 (380)	33,500 (1,160)	33,900 (1,080)	47,100 (1,080)	31,800 (1,000)	37,400 (1,010)	33,100 (1,160)	33,200 (930)	— (†)	36,100 (690)
Percent change, in constant 2005 dollars														
1976 to 2001	49.7	26.2	29.2	47.3	40.9	— (†)	52.0	96.2	— (†)	62.5	— (†)	66.7	— (†)	54.9
1991 to 2001	15.4	19.3	27.5	-3.6	11.2	12.4	12.3	21.1	15.8	17.3	— (†)	21.5	— (†)	21.4

—Not available.
†Not applicable.
[1] Most educators work 9- to 10-month contracts.
[2] Reported salaries of full-time workers under $2,600 in 1976, $4,200 in 1981, $5,000 in 1985, and $1,000 in 1994 and 2001 were excluded from the tabulations. Also, those with salaries over $500,000 in 1994 and 2001 were excluded.

NOTE: Data exclude bachelor's recipients from U.S. Service Schools, deceased graduates, and graduates living at foreign addresses at the time of the survey. Constant dollars based on the Consumer Price Index, prepared by the Bureau of Labor Statistics, U.S. Department of Labor. Standard errors appear in parentheses.
SOURCE: U.S. Department of Education, National Center for Education Statistics, "Recent College Graduates" surveys, 1976 through 1991; and 1993/94 and 2000/01 Baccalaureate and Beyond Longitudinal Study (B&B:93/94 and B&B:2000/01). (This table was prepared August 2006.)

Table 388. Percentage of 1988 8th-graders who volunteered in various capacities in a 12-month period ending in 2000, by selected young adult characteristics: 2000

Young adult characteristic	Percent participating in voluntary or community service activity					
	Volunteered in a youth organization		Volunteered in a civic or community organization		Participated in a political campaign	
1	2		3		4	
Total	19.0	(0.67)	21.5	(0.99)	3.9	(0.43)
Sex						
Male	17.4	(0.95)	20.2	(1.68)	3.8	(0.45)
Female	20.7	(0.93)	22.9	(1.09)	4.0	(0.71)
Race/ethnicity						
White	18.8	(0.70)	21.2	(0.73)	3.7	(0.38)
Black	19.5	(2.72)	25.9	(6.09)	2.4	(0.90)
Hispanic	20.4	(2.48)	19.0	(3.02)	6.7	(2.68)
Asian/Pacific Islander	19.4	(2.73)	19.7	(2.62)	3.5	(1.09)
American Indian/Alaska Native	20.5	(5.89)	18.1	(7.85)	2.9	(1.43)
8th-grade socioeconomic status						
Lowest quartile	14.5	(1.19)	12.7	(1.04)	2.4	(0.42)
Middle two quartiles	18.8	(1.00)	22.4	(1.76)	4.0	(0.79)
Highest quartile	23.6	(1.29)	27.8	(1.21)	5.0	(0.52)
Mathematics achievement in 8th grade						
Low	16.1	(1.58)	21.0	(3.66)	2.4	(0.42)
Middle two quartiles	18.8	(0.89)	18.5	(0.84)	3.5	(0.44)
High	23.3	(1.26)	28.0	(1.24)	4.2	(0.55)
Method of high school completion by 2000						
High school diploma	20.6	(0.75)	23.7	(1.11)	4.1	(0.49)
GED certificate	14.9	(2.27)	12.3	(1.76)	4.1	(1.39)
No diploma or equivalent	7.9	(1.47)	9.5	(1.80)	1.8	(0.88)
Postsecondary attainment by 2000						
None	12.4	(1.29)	12.0	(1.26)	2.3	(0.62)
Less than bachelor's degree	18.7	(1.07)	21.3	(1.87)	4.1	(0.77)
Bachelor's degree	24.6	(1.11)	29.3	(1.16)	5.1	(0.68)
Master's or higher degree	27.2	(3.48)	32.2	(3.69)	3.5	(1.02)

NOTE: Race categories exclude persons of Hispanic origin. Standard errors appear in parentheses.
SOURCE: U.S. Department of Education, National Center for Education Statistics, *Coming of Age in the 1990s: The Eighth-Grade Class of 1988 12 Years Later*, National Education Longitudinal Study of 1988 (NELS:88/2000), "Fourth Follow-up, 2000." (This table was prepared April 2005.)

Table 389. Percentage of 18- to 25-year-olds reporting drug use during the past 30 days and the past year, by drug used: Selected years, 1982 through 2005

Year	Percent reporting drug use during the past 30 days					Percent reporting drug use during past year				
	Illicit drug use			Alcohol	Cigarettes	Illicit drug use			Alcohol	Cigarettes
	Any[1]	Marijuana	Cocaine			Any[1]	Marijuana	Cocaine		
1	2	3	4	5	6	7	8	9	10	11
1982	— (†)	27.2 (—)	7.0 (—)	66.6 (—)	— (†)	— (†)	37.4 (—)	15.9 (—)	80.6 (—)	— (†)
1985	25.3 (—)	21.7 (—)	8.1 (—)	70.1 (—)	47.4 (—)	37.4 (—)	34.0 (—)	13.6 (—)	84.2 (—)	49.9 (—)
1988	17.9 (—)	15.3 (—)	4.8 (—)	64.7 (—)	45.6 (—)	29.1 (—)	26.1 (—)	10.5 (—)	79.6 (—)	50.9 (—)
1990	15.0 (—)	12.7 (—)	2.3 (—)	62.8 (—)	40.9 (—)	26.1 (—)	23.0 (—)	6.5 (—)	78.1 (—)	45.1 (—)
1991	15.4 (—)	12.9 (—)	2.2 (—)	63.1 (—)	41.7 (—)	26.6 (—)	22.9 (—)	6.7 (—)	80.7 (—)	46.9 (—)
1992	13.1 (—)	10.9 (—)	2.0 (—)	58.6 (—)	41.5 (—)	24.1 (—)	21.2 (—)	5.5 (—)	75.6 (—)	46.8 (—)
1993	13.6 (—)	11.1 (—)	1.6 (—)	58.7 (—)	37.9 (—)	24.2 (—)	21.4 (—)	4.4 (—)	76.9 (—)	43.7 (—)
1994	13.3 (—)	12.1 (—)	1.2 (—)	63.1 (—)	34.6 (—)	24.6 (—)	21.8 (—)	3.6 (—)	78.5 (—)	41.1 (—)
1995	14.2 (—)	12.0 (—)	1.3 (—)	61.3 (—)	35.3 (—)	25.5 (—)	21.8 (—)	4.3 (—)	76.5 (—)	42.5 (—)
1996	15.6 (—)	13.2 (—)	2.0 (—)	60.0 (—)	38.3 (—)	26.8 (—)	23.8 (—)	4.7 (—)	75.3 (—)	44.7 (—)
1997	14.7 (—)	12.8 (—)	1.2 (—)	58.4 (—)	40.6 (—)	25.3 (—)	22.3 (—)	3.9 (—)	75.1 (—)	45.9 (—)
1998	16.1 (—)	13.8 (—)	2.0 (—)	60.0 (—)	41.6 (—)	27.4 (—)	24.1 (—)	4.7 (—)	74.2 (—)	47.1 (—)
1999	16.4 (0.40)	14.2 (0.38)	1.7 (0.12)	57.2 (0.54)	39.7 (0.47)	29.1 (0.48)	24.5 (0.46)	5.2 (0.21)	74.8 (0.48)	47.5 (0.52)
2000	15.9 (0.36)	13.6 (0.34)	1.4 (0.11)	56.8 (0.51)	38.3 (0.48)	27.9 (0.46)	23.7 (0.43)	4.4 (0.18)	74.5 (0.46)	45.8 (0.49)
2001	18.8 (0.41)	16.0 (0.39)	1.9 (0.13)	58.8 (0.50)	39.1 (0.47)	31.9 (0.48)	26.7 (0.48)	5.7 (0.23)	75.4 (0.41)	46.8 (0.48)
2002	20.2 (0.37)	17.3 (0.36)	2.0 (0.12)	60.5 (0.53)	40.8 (0.48)	35.5 (0.46)	29.8 (0.43)	6.7 (0.24)	77.9 (0.41)	49.0 (0.50)
2003	20.3 (0.40)	17.0 (0.37)	2.2 (0.13)	61.4 (0.50)	40.2 (0.47)	34.6 (0.48)	28.5 (0.46)	6.6 (0.23)	78.1 (0.41)	47.6 (0.46)
2004	19.4 (0.40)	16.1 (0.37)	2.1 (0.13)	60.5 (0.51)	39.5 (0.49)	33.9 (0.48)	27.8 (0.47)	6.6 (0.25)	78.0 (0.44)	47.5 (0.52)
2005	20.1 (0.40)	16.6 (0.37)	2.6 (0.15)	60.9 (0.51)	39.0 (0.47)	34.2 (0.47)	28.0 (0.45)	6.9 (0.23)	77.9 (0.43)	47.2 (0.48)

—Not available.
†Not applicable.
[1]Includes other illegal drug use not shown separately.
NOTE: Marijuana includes hashish usage for 1996 and later years. Due to changes in the survey instrument and administration and to improve comparability with new data, estimates for 1982 through 1993 have been adjusted and may differ from those reported in previous years. Data for 1999 have been revised from previously published figures. Data for 1999 and later years were gathered using Computer Assisted Interviewing (CAI) and may not be directly comparable to previous years. Standard errors appear in parentheses.
SOURCE: U.S. Department of Health and Human Services, Substance Abuse and Mental Health Services Administration, *National Household Survey on Drug Abuse: Main Findings,* selected years, 1982 through 2001; and National Survey on Drug Use and Health, 2002 through 2005. (This table was prepared September 2006.)

Table 390. Percentage of 1972 high school seniors, 1992 high school seniors, and 2004 high school seniors who felt that certain life values were "very important," by sex: Selected years, 1972 through 2004

Life value	Percent of 1972 seniors						Percent of 1992 seniors						Percent of 2004 seniors					
	1972		1974 (2 years after high school)		1976 (4 years after high school)		1992			1994 (2 years after high school)			Total		Male		Female	
	Male	Female	Male	Female	Male	Female	Male	Female	Total	Male	Female							
1	2	3	4	5	6	7	8	9	10	11	12		13		14		15	
Being successful in work	86.5	83.0	81.2	74.9	80.3	69.7	89.0	89.6	90.1	89.9	90.3		91.3	(0.33)	89.7	(0.49)	92.9	(0.40)
Finding steady work.................................	82.3	73.7	74.7	59.9	79.3	62.1	87.1	88.6	89.7	88.7	90.7		87.3	(0.40)	85.6	(0.55)	89.0	(0.49)
Having lots of money	26.0	9.8	17.8	9.1	17.7	9.4	45.3	29.4	35.2	39.5	30.9		35.1	(0.58)	42.7	(0.80)	27.6	(0.69)
Being a leader in the community	14.9	8.0	8.5	4.4	9.2	4.2	—	—	—	—	—		—	(†)	—	(†)	—	(†)
Importance of helping others in the community..	—	—	—	—	—	—	—	—	—	—	—		41.7	(0.57)	35.2	(0.77)	48.1	(0.74)
Correcting inequalities.............................	22.5	31.1	16.6	18.2	16.2	17.1	17.0	23.6	—	—	—		19.7	(0.46)	18.1	(0.60)	21.2	(0.67)
Having children..	—	—	—	—	—	—	39.0	49.2	—	—	—		49.3	(0.55)	45.4	(0.75)	53.2	(0.78)
Having a happy family life	78.6	85.7	83.1	86.7	84.2	86.4	—	—	—	—	—		81.0	(0.46)	80.1	(0.63)	81.9	(0.64)
Providing better opportunities for my children	66.6	66.2	59.5	61.6	59.8	58.8	74.5	76.5	90.5	90.3	90.8		82.5	(0.45)	82.1	(0.64)	82.9	(0.58)
Living closer to parents or relatives	6.8	8.2	8.3	12.4	7.7	11.9	15.2	18.7	—	—	—		—	(†)	—	(†)	—	(†)
Moving from area.....................................	14.3	14.6	8.3	7.4	6.7	6.4	20.7	20.1	—	—	—		—	(†)	—	(†)	—	(†)
Having strong friendships	81.2	78.7	76.5	74.7	76.1	72.1	79.8	80.0	87.6	88.1	87.0		85.5	(0.41)	84.9	(0.56)	86.1	(0.57)
Having leisure time	—	—	60.9	55.1	65.4	60.1	65.3	62.0	—	—	—		69.0	(0.55)	70.2	(0.69)	67.8	(0.74)

—Not available.
†Not applicable.
NOTE: Standard errors appear in parentheses.
SOURCE: U.S. Department of Education, National Center for Education Statistics, National Longitudinal Study of the High School Class of 1972, "Base Year" (NLS:72), "Second Fol-low-up" (NLS:72/74), and "Third Follow-up" (NLS:72/76); National Education Longitudinal Study of 1988, "Second Follow-up, Student Survey, 1992" (NELS:88/92) and "Third Follow-up, 1994" (NELS:88/94); and Education Longitudinal Study of 2002, "First Follow-up" (ELS:02/04). (This table was prepared November 2005.)

Table 391. Percentage of employed 1988 8th-graders satisfied with various aspects of their job, by educational attainment: 2000

Educational attainment	Percentage who were satisfied with															
	Fringe benefits		Further training		Use of past training		Promotion opportunity		Job security		Work importance		Pay		Job overall	
1	2		3		4		5		6		7		8		9	
Method of high school completion by 2000																
High school diploma	79.2	(0.84)	79.0	(0.89)	80.3	(1.24)	71.5	(1.19)	89.9	(0.59)	83.7	(0.78)	73.0	(0.95)	86.8	(0.69)
GED certificate	69.1	(4.47)	74.4	(4.22)	74.9	(4.46)	73.1	(4.35)	90.3	(2.48)	80.4	(4.26)	75.6	(4.13)	83.7	(4.01)
No diploma or equivalent	48.2	(6.61)	68.9	(6.38)	72.5	(6.29)	62.5	(6.68)	72.8	(6.21)	85.3	(5.14)	65.0	(6.90)	74.0	(6.44)
Postsecondary attainment by 2000																
None	69.4	(2.80)	71.7	(2.73)	77.1	(2.68)	69.1	(2.65)	85.6	(2.18)	84.0	(2.48)	74.5	(2.45)	83.3	(2.53)
Less than bachelor's degree	74.7	(1.62)	77.0	(1.36)	76.0	(2.06)	68.1	(1.98)	89.3	(0.93)	81.2	(1.18)	71.3	(1.65)	84.0	(1.19)
Bachelor's degree	83.0	(1.15)	83.2	(1.18)	84.7	(1.02)	75.8	(1.21)	90.2	(0.99)	85.9	(1.00)	73.0	(1.30)	89.3	(0.91)
Master's or higher degree	87.0	(2.19)	89.3	(1.91)	92.8	(1.32)	82.1	(2.31)	92.0	(1.70)	93.1	(1.38)	75.1	(3.64)	94.5	(1.18)

NOTE: Standard errors appear in parentheses.
SOURCE: U.S. Department of Education, National Center for Education Statistics, *Coming of Age in the 1990s: The Eighth-Grade Class of 1988 12 Years Later*, National Education Longitudinal Study of 1988 (NELS:88/2000), "Fourth Follow-up, 2000." (This table was prepared April 2005.)

CHAPTER 6
International Comparisons of Education

This chapter offers a broad perspective on education across the nations of the world. It also provides an international context for examining the condition of education in the United States. Insights into the educational practices and outcomes of the United States are obtained by comparing them with those of other countries. The National Center for Education Statistics (NCES) carries out a variety of these activities to provide statistical data for international comparisons of education.

This chapter presents data drawn from materials prepared by the United Nations Educational, Scientific, and Cultural Organization (UNESCO), the Institute of International Education, the Organization for Economic Cooperation and Development (OECD), and the International Association for the Evaluation of Educational Achievement (IEA). The basic summary data on enrollments, teachers, enrollment ratios, and finances were synthesized from information appearing in *Education at a Glance*, published by OECD. Even though OECD tabulations are very carefully prepared, international data users should be cautioned about the many problems of definition and reporting involved in the collection of data about the educational systems in the world (see the OECD entry in Appendix A: Guide to Sources).

This chapter also presents data from the Trends in International Mathematics and Science Study (TIMSS) carried out under the aegis of the IEA and supported by NCES and the National Science Foundation. This survey was formerly known as the Third International Mathematics and Science Study. TIMSS, conducted every 4 years, is an assessment of fourth- and eighth-graders in mathematics and science. In 1995, TIMSS collected data for fourth and eighth grades. In 1999, TIMSS collected data for eighth grade only. With the 2003 data collection, TIMSS offers the first international trend comparisons in mathematics and science at grades 4 and 8. In 2003, the United States and a number of other countries participated in data collection at two grade levels: 25 nations collected data on fourth-graders, and 45 nations collected data on eighth-graders. For 15 of these nations, including the United States, TIMSS offers comparisons of fourth-grade student achievement between 1995 and 2003. For 34 of these nations, including the United States, TIMSS also offers comparisons of eighth-grade student achievement between 2003 and at least one prior data collection year, either 1995 or 1999.

This chapter includes additional information on performance scores of 15-year-olds in the areas of reading, mathematics, and science literacy from the Program for International Student Assessment (PISA). PISA also measures general, or cross-curricular, competencies such as learning strategies. While this study focuses on OECD countries, data from some non-OECD countries are also provided.

The role that the United States plays in the world of higher education is illuminated by data on foreign students enrolled in U.S. institutions of higher education. The Institute of International Education provides estimates of the number of foreign students and their countries of origin.

Further information on survey methodologies is in Appendix A: Guide to Sources and in the publications cited in the table source notes.

Population

Among the reporting OECD countries, Iceland had the largest percentage of young people ages 5 to 14 (16 percent in 2002) (table 394), followed by New Zealand (15 percent) and the United States (15 percent). Countries with relatively small proportions of persons these ages included Greece, Spain, Japan, and Italy (all at 10 percent). Turkey had the largest percentage of young people ages 5 to 14 (21 percent) among reporting OECD countries in 1999 (2002 data were not available for Turkey).

Enrollments

In 2004, about 1.3 billion students were enrolled in schools around the world (table 392). Of these students, 685 million were in elementary-level programs, 503 million were in secondary programs, and 132 million were in higher education programs. Between 1990 and 2004, enrollment changes varied from region to region. Changes in elementary enrollment ranged from increases of 56 percent in Africa, 23 percent in Oceania, 16 percent in Asia, and 9 percent in Northern America (defined in UNESCO tabulations as including the United States, Canada, Greenland, Bermuda, St. Pierre, and Miquelon) to a 21 percent decrease in Europe and an 8 percent decrease in Central and South America (figure 26). Over the same period, enrollment increases at the secondary level outpaced increases at the primary (elementary) level. At the secondary level, enrollments increased by 158 percent in Central and South America, 99 percent in Africa, 85 percent in Oceania, 66 percent in Asia, 25 percent in Northern America, and 5 percent in Europe.

At the postsecondary level, developing areas of the world also had substantial increases in enrollment between 1990 and 2004 (table 392 and figure 26). Postsecondary enrollment rose by 173 percent in Africa, 154 percent in Asia, 103 percent in Oceania, 101 percent in Central and South America, 64 percent in Europe, and 16 percent in Northern America (figure 26). These increases are due to both growth in the proportion of the people attending postsecondary institutions and increases in the populations.

Postsecondary enrollment varied among countries due partially to differences in how postsecondary education is defined and the age at which postsecondary education is thought to begin. In 2002, the OECD countries with the highest proportion of 22- to 25-year-olds enrolled in postsecondary education were Finland (39 percent), followed by the Republic of Korea (32 percent), Denmark (29 percent), Sweden (28 percent), Norway (27 percent), and Poland (26 percent) (table 395). The United States' proportion was 25 percent.

In 2004–05, there were about 565,000 foreign students studying at U.S. colleges and universities (table 414). Fifty-eight percent of these students were from Asian countries. Between 1990 and 2005, the proportion of students at U.S. colleges who were nonresident aliens rose from 2.8 to 3.3 percent (table 210).

Achievement

On the 2003 TIMSS assessment, U.S. fourth-grade students scored 518, on average, in mathematics, exceeding the international average of 495 for the 25 participating countries (table 399). (Average scale scores from the TIMSS assessment are based on a range of possible scores from 1 to 1,000.) U.S. fourth-graders were outperformed by their peers in 11 countries, including four Asian countries (Chinese Taipei, Hong Kong SAR, Japan, and Singapore) and seven European countries (Flemish Belgium, England, Hungary, Latvia, Lithuania, the Netherlands, and the Russian Federation). On the other hand, U.S. fourth-graders outscored students in 13 countries. In 2003, U.S. eighth-grade students scored 504 in mathematics, on average, exceeding the international average of 467 for the 45 participating countries (table 400). U.S. eighth-graders were outperformed by their peers in nine countries, including five Asian countries (Chinese Taipei, Hong Kong SAR, Japan, Korea, and Singapore) and four European countries (Flemish Belgium, Estonia, Hungary, and the Netherlands). On the other hand, U.S. eighth-graders outscored students in 25 countries.

In 2003, U.S. performance in mathematics literacy among 15-year-old students on the PISA assessment was lower than the average performance for 20 of the other 28 OECD countries for which comparable PISA results were reported (table 397). In problem solving, U.S. performance on PISA was lower than 22 of the other 28 OECD countries. The U.S. average score in reading literacy was not measurably different from the OECD average, and the U.S. average score in science literacy was below the OECD average.

Degrees

Ratios of bachelor's degrees conferred per 100 persons at the typical age of graduation in 2004 ranged from 14 in Mexico and 19 in Belgium to 51 in Iceland and New Zealand and 55 in Finland (table 409 and figure 27). The ratio for the United States was 33. In 2004, women had higher bachelor's degree ratios than men in 21 out of 23 countries reporting data.

The percentages of undergraduate degrees awarded in science fields (including natural sciences, mathematics and computer science, and engineering) reported by OECD countries ranged from 11 percent in Denmark to 38 percent in Korea for 2003 (table 410). Germany, the Czech Republic, the United Kingdom, and Korea all awarded at least 30 percent of their undergraduate degrees in science fields. Denmark, Norway, Poland, Iceland, the United States, Japan, Portugal, and New Zealand awarded 20 percent or less of their undergraduate degrees in science fields. The proportion of graduate degrees awarded in science fields also ranged widely across countries in 2003 (table 411). Among the countries with the highest proportions of their graduate degrees in science were Korea (46 percent), Japan (39 percent), Germany (36 percent), and Spain (36 percent). Among the countries with the lowest proportions were Poland (4 percent), Hungary (8 percent), the Czech Republic (12 percent), Italy (13 percent), and the United States (14 percent).

Finances

In 2003, per student expenditures at the elementary level of education were at least $7,500 in six OECD countries (table 412). Specifically, Luxembourg spent approximately $11,500 per student at the elementary level, the United States approximately $8,300, Switzerland approximately $8,100, Norway approximately $8,000, and Denmark and Iceland each approximately $7,800. At the secondary level, four countries had expenditures of over $9,000 per student: Luxembourg (approximately $17,100), Switzerland (approximately $12,200), Norway (approximately $10,900), and the United States (approximately $9,600). At the higher education level, the following five countries had expenditures of at least $14,000 per student in 2003: Switzerland ($25,900), the United States (approximately $24,100), Canada ($19,992 in 2002), Sweden (approximately $16,100), and Denmark (approximately $14,000). These expenditures were adjusted to U.S. dollars using the purchasing-power-parity (PPP) index. This index is considered more stable and comparable than indexes using currency exchange rates.

A comparison of public direct expenditures on education as a percentage of gross domestic product (GDP) in OECD countries shows that national investment in education in 2003 ranged from 3.5 percent in Japan and 3.6 percent in Turkey to 6.7 percent in Denmark and 7.5 percent in Iceland (table 413 and figure 28). Among reporting countries, the average public investment in education in 2003 was 5.1 percent of GDP. In the United States, the public expenditure on education as a percentage of GDP was 5.4 percent. The percentage of expenditures on education in the Russian Federation, a non-OECD country, was 3.7 percent.

Figure 26. Percentage change in enrollment, by selected areas of the world and level of education: 1990 to 2004

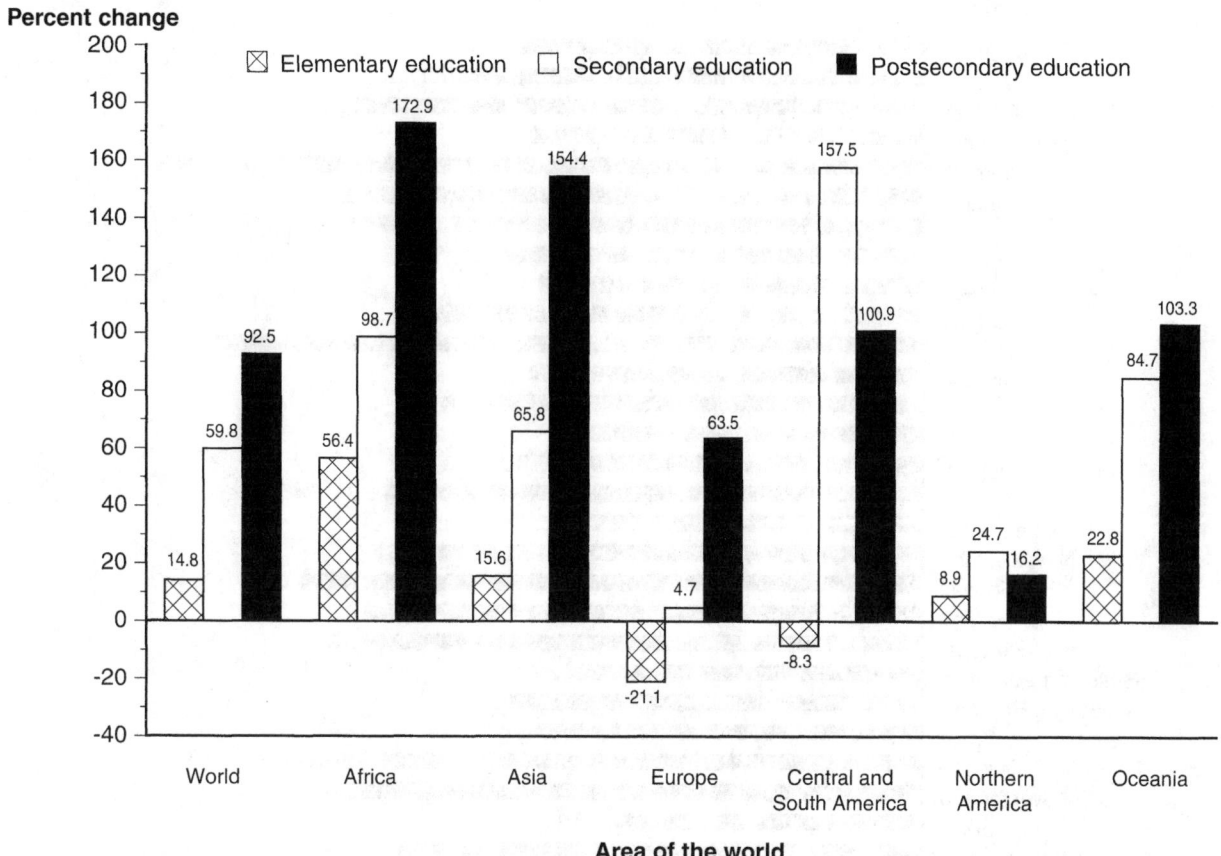

SOURCE: United Nations Educational, Scientific, and Cultural Organization (UNESCO), *Statistical Yearbook, 1999*, and unpublished tabulations.

Figure 27. Bachelor's degree recipients as a percentage of the population of the typical ages of graduation, by country: 2004

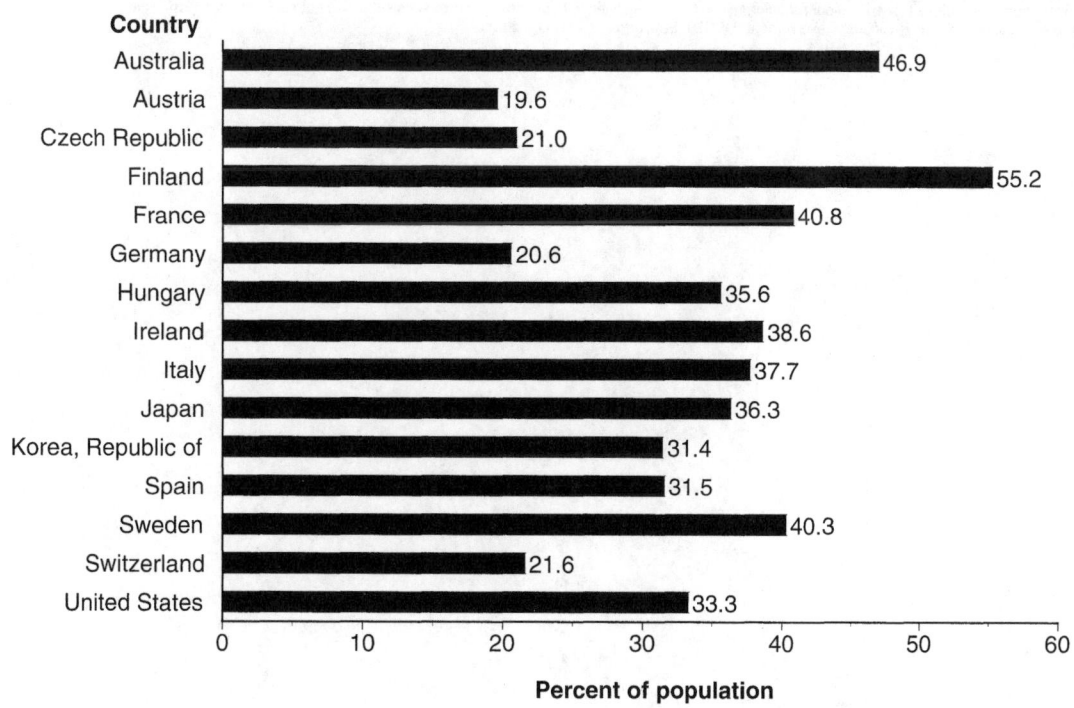

NOTE: Includes graduates of any age.
SOURCE: Organization for Economic Cooperation and Development (OECD), Education Online Database.

Figure 28. Public direct expenditures for education as a percentage of the gross domestic product (GDP), by country: 2003

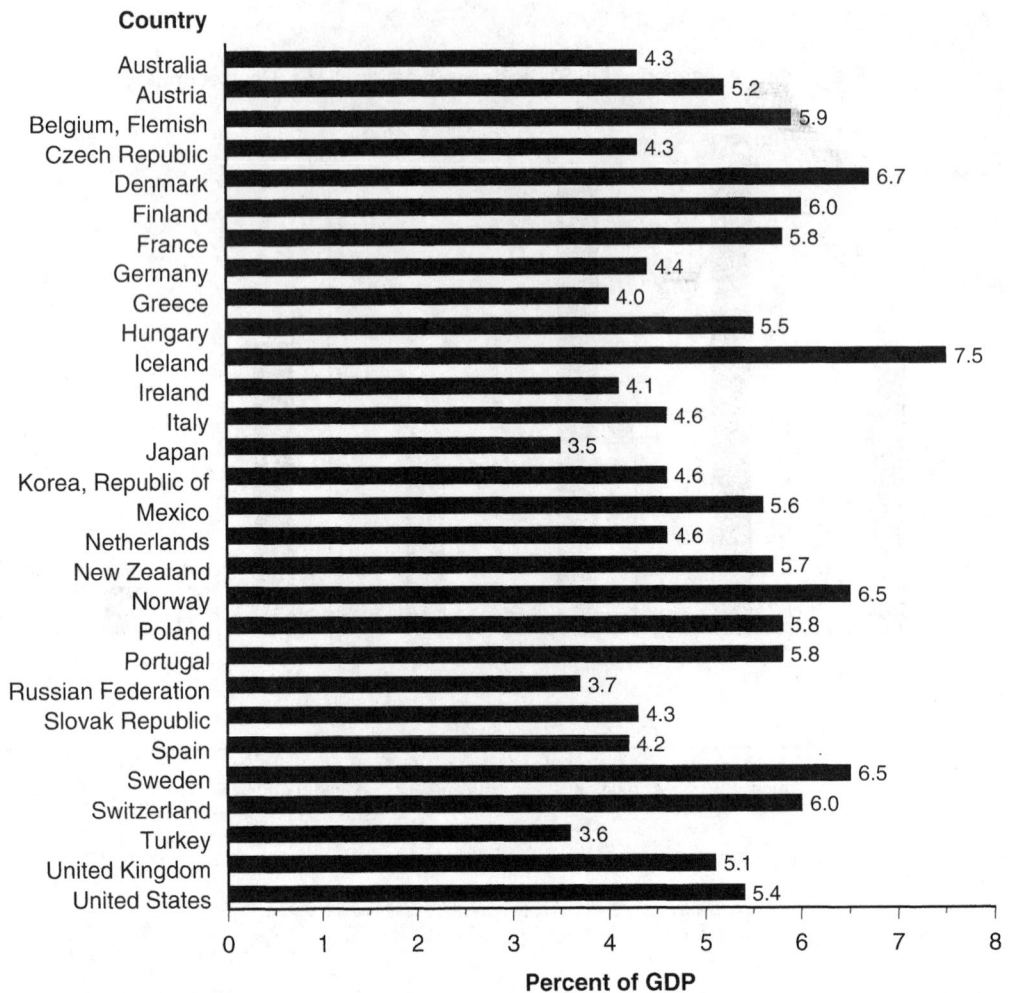

NOTE: Includes all government expenditures for education institutions, plus public subsidies to households for living costs that are not spent at education institutions.
SOURCE: Organization for Economic Cooperation and Development (OECD), *Education at a Glance, 2006.*

Table 392. Selected population and finance statistics, school enrollment, and teachers, by major areas of the world: Selected years, 1980 through 2004

Selected characteristic	World total[1]	Major areas of the world					
		Africa[2]	Asia[3]	Europe[4]	Central and South America[5]	Northern America[5]	Oceania[6]
1	2	3	4	5	6	7	8
1980							
Population, all ages[7] (in thousands)	4,447,090	475,714	2,641,312	693,075	359,307	255,109	22,573
Enrollment, all levels (in thousands)	856,971	78,036	495,155	131,633	87,291	60,041	4,815
First (primary) level[8]	541,556	62,134	336,174	52,471	65,414	22,611	2,752
Second level[9]	264,379	14,360	144,755	62,734	16,969	23,913	1,647
Third level[10]	51,037	1,542	14,227	16,428	4,908	13,516	416
Teachers, all levels (in thousands)	38,285	2,338	19,641	8,225	3,730	4,079	272
First (primary) level[8]	19,044	1,661	10,874	2,541	2,260	1,580	129
Second level[9]	15,398	584	7,554	4,387	1,083	1,679	112
Third level[10]	3,843	94	1,213	1,297	387	820	31
Public expenditures on education							
In millions of U.S. dollars	516,400	22,900	93,800	200,600	33,500	155,100	10,400
As a percent of gross national product	4.8	5.3	4.0	5.1 [11]	3.8	5.2	5.6
1990							
Population, all ages[7] (in thousands)	5,281,986	629,389	3,184,342	722,109	437,822	282,020	26,304
Enrollment, all levels (in thousands)	980,474	107,871	569,179	131,255	104,968	62,007	5,194
First (primary) level[8]	596,853	80,640	364,213	48,968	75,505	24,810	2,717
Second level[9]	315,008	24,378	181,652	63,366	22,194	21,569	1,849
Third level[10]	68,613	2,853	23,314	18,922	7,269	15,628	628
Teachers, all levels (in thousands)	47,105	3,791	24,455	9,398	5,131	4,000	330
First (primary) level[8]	22,626	2,390	12,692	2,812	3,006	1,582	143
Second level[9]	19,380	1,241	9,947	5,076	1,520	1,449	146
Third level[10]	5,100	160	1,816	1,509	605	969	41
Public expenditures on education							
In millions of U.S. dollars	986,500	25,700	199,800	367,500	44,600	330,300	18,600
As a percent of gross national product	4.8	5.6	3.7	5.1 [11]	4.1	5.4	5.6
1995							
Population, all ages[7] (in thousands)	5,686,775	719,497	3,437,791	728,034	476,641	296,644	28,168
Enrollment, all levels (in thousands)	1,103,756	130,794	644,609	137,839	116,821	66,510	7,183
First (primary) level[8]	649,480	95,928	394,304	47,344	82,279	26,501	3,124
Second level[9]	372,724	30,899	219,415	69,448	26,087	23,984	2,891
Third level[10]	81,552	3,966	30,890	21,047	8,455	16,026	1,167
Teachers, all levels (in thousands)	52,047	4,486	26,955	10,113	5,784	4,269	439
First (primary) level[8]	24,356	2,811	13,499	2,863	3,374	1,649	161
Second level[9]	21,746	1,471	11,273	5,561	1,696	1,528	217
Third level[10]	5,945	205	2,183	1,689	714	1,092	61
2000							
Enrollment, all levels (in thousands)	1,202,702	151,466	702,941	137,235	136,462	66,943	7,655
First (primary) level[8]	651,866	106,073	403,765 [12]	41,464	69,936	27,408	3,222
Second level[9]	452,828	39,027 [12]	259,692	70,397	55,213	25,110	3,390
Third level[10]	98,008	6,366 [12]	39,485	25,375 [12]	11,314	14,425	1,043 [12]
Teachers, all levels (in thousands)	57,211 [13]	5,177	30,137	10,360	6,443	4,648	‡
First (primary) level[8]	25,713 [12]	2,929	15,342	2,745	2,735	1,805	157 [12]
Second level[9]	24,780	1,891 [12]	12,371	5,746 [12]	2,850	1,686	236 [12]
Third level[10]	6,718 [13]	357 [12]	2,424	1,869 [12]	858	1,157	‡
2004							
Enrollment, all levels (in thousands)	1,320,808	182,388	781,369	135,935	141,007	72,082	8,027
First (primary) level[8]	685,275	126,157	420,861 [12]	38,640	69,256 [12]	27,025	3,335 [12]
Second level[9]	503,455	48,444 [12]	301,190	66,357	57,150 [12]	26,900	3,415 [12]
Third level[10]	132,077	7,787 [12]	59,318	30,937	14,600 [12]	18,157	1,276
Teachers, all levels (in thousands)	62,349	5,784	33,373	10,487	7,219	4,991	‡
First (primary) level[8]	26,474	3,332	15,542	2,638	2,891 [12]	1,896	‡
Second level[9]	27,398	2,149 [12]	14,364	5,669	3,181 [12]	1,787	‡
Third level[10]	8,477 [12,13]	303 [12]	3,468 [12]	2,180	1,148 [12]	1,307	‡

‡Reporting standards not met.

[1]Enrollment and teacher data exclude the Democratic People's Republic of Korea.

[2]Excludes Rodrigues and other small islands.

[3]Includes five countries of the former Union of Soviet Socialist Republics (U.S.S.R.), Arab states, and both the Asian and the European portions of Turkey.

[4]Includes all countries of the former U.S.S.R. except Kazakhstan, Uzbekistan, Kyrgyzstan, Tajikistan, and Turkmenistan.

[5]Northern America includes Bermuda, Canada, Greenland, St. Pierre and Miquelon, and the United States of America. Hawaii is included in Northern America rather than Oceania. Central and South America includes Latin America and the Caribbean.

[6]Includes American Samoa, Australia, Cook Islands, Fiji, French Polynesia, Guam, Kiribati, Marshall Islands, Nauru, New Caledonia, New Zealand, Niue, Norfolk Island, Pacific Islands, Papua New Guinea, Samoa, Solomon Islands, Tokelau, Tonga, Tuvalu, and the Republic of Vanuatu.

[7]Estimate of midyear population.

[8]First-level enrollment generally consists of elementary school, grades 1–6.

[9]Second-level enrollment includes general education, teacher training (at the second level), and technical and vocational education. This level generally corresponds to secondary education in the United States, grades 7–12.

[10]Third-level enrollment includes college and university enrollment, and technical and vocational education beyond the high school level. There is considerable variation in reporting from country to country.

[11]This figure is for Europe, not including the former U.S.S.R.

[12]Includes relatively high proportion of imputed values for nonrespondent countries.

[13]Includes estimates for Oceania not separately shown.

NOTE: Detail may not sum to totals because of rounding. Public expenditure data not available for 1995, 2000, and 2004.

SOURCE: United Nations Educational, Scientific, and Cultural Organization (UNESCO), *Statistical Yearbook, 1999,* and unpublished tabulations. (This table was prepared October 2006.)

Table 393. Selected population and enrollment statistics for countries with populations over 10 million, by continent: Selected years, 1980 through 2004

Country[1]	Midyear population (in millions)				Persons per square kilometer, 2004	First level[2] Enrollment (in thousands)				First level Gross enrollment ratio[5]			
	1980	1990	2000	2004		1980	1990	2000	2004[6]	1980	1990	2000	2004[6]
1	2	3	4	5	6	7	8	9	10	11	12	13	14
World total[7]	4,447	5,282	6,054	6,345	49	541,556	596,853	651,866	685,275	96	99.2	—	106
Africa													
Algeria[8]	19	25	30	32	14	3,119	4,189	4,721	4,508	94	100	112	112
Angola	7	9	13	14	11	1,301	990 [9]	1,178 [10]	—	175	92	74 [10]	—
Burkina Faso	7	9	11	12	45	202	504	901	1,140	17	33	44	53
Cameroon	9	11	15	16	35	1,379	1,964	2,689 [12]	2,979	98	101	108 [12]	117
Cote d'Ivoire	8	12	16	17	54	1,025	1,415	2,047	2,046 [11,13]	75	67	79	72 [11,13]
Democratic Rep. of the Congo	27	37	51	55	24	4,196	4,562	—	—	92	70	—	—
Egypt[8,16]	44	56	64	69	69	4,663	6,964	7,856 [10]	7,874 [10,11]	73	94	100 [10]	100 [10,11]
Ethiopia	36	48	64	70	70	2,131	2,466	6,651	8,019 [19]	37	33	64	93 [19]
Ghana[8]	11	15	19	21	93	1,378 [17]	1,945	2,478	2,930 [19]	79	75	80	88 [19]
Kenya[8]	17	23	30	32	57	3,927	5,392	5,700 [10]	5,926	115	95	94 [10]	111
Madagascar	9	13	16	17	30	1,724	1,571	2,308	3,366	130	103	103	134
Malawi	6	9	11	11	119	810	1,401	—	2,842	60	68	—	125
Mali	7	8	11	12	10	291	395	1,127	1,397	26	26	61	64
Morocco[8]	19	24	29	31	69	2,172	2,484	3,842	4,070	83	67	94	106
Mozambique[8]	12	14	18	19	24	1,387 [24]	1,260	2,316	3,569	—	67	92	95
Niger	6	8	11	12	10	229	369	657	980	25	29	35	45
Nigeria[8]	72	96	127	140	154	12,117	13,607	—	21,111	109	91	—	99
Senegal	6	8	10	11	54	420	708	1,160	1,383	46	59	75	76
South Africa	29	37	43	46	38	4,353 [25]	6,952	7,445	7,470 [11]	90	122	111	105 [11]
Sudan[8]	19	24	—	34	14	1,464	2,043	2,800	3,208	50	53	59	60
Tunisia[16]	6	8	10	10	64	1,054	1,406	1,374	1,277 [11]	102	113	117	111 [11]
Uganda	13	17	22	26	132	1,292 [29]	2,470 [25,29]	6,559	7,152 [19]	50	74	136	118 [19]
United Republic of Tanzania	19	25	34	37	41	3,368	3,379	4,280 [10]	7,541 [19]	93	70	63 [10]	106 [19]
Zambia	6	8	10	11	14	1,042	1,461	1,590	2,251	90	99	78	99
Zimbabwe[16]	7	10	12	13	34	1,235	2,116	2,461	2,362 [11]	85	116	95	96 [11]
Asia													
Afghanistan[8]	16	15	—	—	—	1,116	623	500	4,430	34	27	15	93
Bangladesh	88	110	130	141	1,079	8,240	11,940	17,668	17,953	61	72	100	109
Cambodia	6	9	12	14	77	1,328	1,330	2,431 [12]	2,763	—	121	110	137
China[16]	999	1,155	1,261	1,297	139	146,270	122,414	125,757	120,999	113	125	114	118
India	689	851	1,016	1,080	363	73,873	99,118	—	125,569 [11]	83	97	—	107 [11]
Indonesia[16]	151	183	210	218	120	25,537	29,754	28,690	29,051 [11]	107	115	110	116 [11]
Iran, Islamic Republic of	39	59	64	67	41	4,799	9,370	7,968	7,307	98 [30]	112	86	103
Iraq	13	18	—	—	—	2,616	3,328	—	4,335	113	111	—	98
Japan[16]	117	124	127	128	351	11,827	9,373	7,395	7,269 [11]	101	100	101	100 [11]
Kazakhstan	15	17	15	15	6	1,064	1,197	1,190	1,080	84	87	99	109
Korea, North (DPR)	18	20	—	—	—	—	—	—	—	—	—	—	—
Korea, South (Republic of)[16]	38	43	47	48	488	5,658	4,869	4,030	4,185	110	105	101	105
Malaysia[16]	14	18	23	25	77	2,009	2,456	3,018	3,009 [14]	93	94	98	93 [14]
Myanmar	34	41	46	—	—	4,148	5,385	4,782	4,948 [19]	91	106	89	97 [19]
Nepal[8]	14	19	24	25	176	1,068	2,789	3,623	4,030 [19]	86	108	118	113 [19]
Pakistan[16]	85	119	138	152	197	5,474 [31]	11,451 [31]	14,562 [13]	16,207	40	61	75 [13]	82
Philippines[16]	48	61	76	83	278	8,034 [17]	10,427	12,760	12,971 [11]	112	111	113	113 [11]
Saudi Arabia	10	16	21	23	11	927	1,877	2,308	2,386	61	73	68	67
Sri Lanka[8,16]	15	17	19	19	301	2,081	2,112	—	1,702 [10,11]	103	106	—	102 [10,11]
Syrian Arab Republic	9	12	16	18	97	1,556	2,452	2,835	2,193	100	108	109	123
Thailand[16]	47	56	61	62	122	7,393	6,957	6,179	6,113	99	99	95	99
Turkey[16]	44	56	65	72	93	5,656	6,862	8,015 [10]	7,904 [10,11]	96	99	101 [10]	95 [10,11]
Uzbekistan	16	21	25	26	63	1,391	1,778	—	2,441 [10]	81	81	—	100 [10]
Vietnam	54	67	79	82	252	7,887	8,862	9,751	8,350	109	103	106	98
Yemen	8	12	18	20	37	—	2,679 [27]	2,644 [10]	3,108	—	79 [27]	79 [10]	87
Europe													
Belarus[8]	10	10	10	10	47	750	615	551 [10]	404	104	95	109 [10]	101
Belgium[16]	10	10	10	10	344	842	719	772	762 [11]	104	101	105	105 [11]
Czech Republic[16]	10	10	10	10	132	647	546	631	567 [11]	96	96	104	105 [11]
France[16]	54	57	59	60	109	4,610	4,149	3,838	3,792 [11]	111	108	105	105 [11]
Germany[16,34]	78	79	82	83	237	3,636	3,431	3,519	3,304 [11]	—	101	104	99 [11]
Greece[16]	10	10	11	11	86	901	813	636	652 [11]	103	98	99	100 [11]
Hungary[8,16]	11	10	10	10	109	1,162	1,131	490	464 [11]	96	95	102	99 [11]
Italy[8,16]	56	57	58	58	196	4,423	3,056	2,810	2,779 [11]	100	103	101	101 [11]
Netherlands[8,16]	14	15	16	16	480	1,333	1,082	1,282	1,291 [11]	100	102	108	108 [11]
Poland[8,16]	36	38	39	38	125	4,167	5,189	3,221	2,983 [11]	100	98	100	100 [11]
Portugal[16]	10	10	10	10	114	1,240	1,020	802	768 [11]	123	123	121	118 [11]
Romania[8]	22	23	22	22	95	3,308	1,253	1,090	991 [11]	104	91	99	100 [11]
Russian Federation[16]	139	148	146	143	8	6,009	7,596	5,702	5,417 [11]	102	109	109	118 [11]
Spain[8,16]	38	39	39	41	83	3,610	2,820	2,505	2,488 [11]	109	109	105	107 [11]
Ukraine[8]	50	52	50	48	83	3,592	3,991	1,851	—	102	89	—	95
United Kingdom[8,16]	56	58	60	59	247	4,911	4,533	4,596	4,488 [11]	103	104	99	101 [11]
North America													
Canada[16]	25	28	31	32	3	2,185	2,376	2,456	2,482 [10,14]	99	103	100	101 [10,14]
Cuba	10	11	—	—	—	1,469	888	1,007	906	106	98	102	100
Guatemala	7	9	11	13	116	803	1,165	1,909	2,281	71	78	102	113
Mexico[16]	68	83	98	104	54	14,666	14,402	14,793	14,857 [11]	120	114	113	109 [11]
United States[16]	230	254	282	294	32	20,420	22,429	25,298	24,849 [11]	99	102	101	100 [11]
South America													
Argentina[16]	28	33	37	38	14	3,917	4,965	4,898	4,914 [14]	106	106	120	118 [14]
Brazil[16]	122	148	170	179	21	22,598	28,944	20,212	19,380 [14]	98	106	155	145 [14]
Chile[16]	11	13	15	16	21	2,185	1,991	1,799	1,714 [11]	109	100	103	99 [11]
Colombia	27	33	42	45	44	4,168	4,247	5,221	5,259	112	102	112	111
Ecuador	8	10	13	13	48	1,534	1,846	1,955	1,990	117	116	115	117
Peru[16]	17	22	26	28	22	3,161	3,855	4,338	4,283 [14]	114	118	127	118 [14]
Venezuela	15	20	24	26	30	3,158	4,053	3,347	3,453	93	96	102	105
Oceania													
Australia[8,16]	15	17	19	20	3	1,718	1,583	1,906	1,932 [11]	112	108	102	102 [11]

—Not available.

#Rounds to zero.

[1]Selection based on total population for midyear 2004.

[2]First-level enrollment generally consists of elementary school, grades 1–6.

[3]Second-level enrollment includes general education, teacher training (at the second level), and technical and vocational education. This level generally corresponds to secondary education in the United States, grades 7–12.

[4]Third-level enrollment includes college and university enrollment, and technical and vocational education beyond the high school level. There is considerable variation in reporting from country to country.

[5]Data represent the total enrollment of all ages in the school level divided by the population of the specific age groups that correspond to the school level. For 1980, 1990, and 2000, the year shown in this column is the one in which the school or academic year starts. Adjustments have been made for the varying lengths of first- and second-level programs. Ratios may exceed 100 because some countries have many students from outside the normal age range.

[6]In 2006, the UNESCO Institute for Statistics changed its naming convention for citing the reference year of education data from the calendar year to the ending year of the academic or fiscal year cited.

[7]Enrollment totals and ratios exclude Democratic People's Republic of Korea. Data do not include adult education or special education provided outside regular schools.

[8]Classification or data coverage of levels has been revised. Data by level may not be comparable over time.

[9]Data for 1994–95.

[10]Estimated by the UNESCO Institute for Statistics.

[11]Data for 2002–03.

[12]Policy change in 2000–01: introduction of free universal primary education.

[13]National estimation.

[14]Data for 2001–02.

[15]Data for 1991–92.

[16]Data in the 2004 enrollment columns are provisional.

Table 393. Selected population and enrollment statistics for countries with populations over 10 million, by continent: Selected years, 1980 through 2004—Continued

Second level[3]								Third level[4]							
Enrollment (in thousands)				Gross enrollment ratio[5]				Enrollment (in thousands)				Gross enrollment ratio[5]			
1980	1990	2000	2004[6]	1980	1990	2000	2004[6]	1980	1990	2000	2004[6]	1980	1990	2000	2004[6]
15	16	17	18	19	20	21	22	23	24	25	26	27	28	29	30
264,379	315,008	452,828	503,455	47	52	—	65	51,037	68,613	98,008	132,077	12	14	—	24
1,029	2,176	2,991	3,677	33	61	71	81	79	286	—	716	6	11	—	20
191	186	400 [10]	—	21	12	18 [10]	—	2	7	—	13 [10,11]	#	1	—	1 [10,11]
28	99	199	246 [10]	3	7	10	12 [10]	2	5	—	19 [10]	#	1	—	2 [10]
234	500		1,161	18	28	—	44	12	33	68	84 [13]	2	3	5	5 [13]
198	361	664 [10]	737 [10,14]	19	22	23 [10]	25 [10,14]	20	30 [11]	—	—	3	—	—	—
862	1,097 [15]			24	21 [15]			28	80	—	—	1	2	—	—
2,929	5,507	8,324 [10]	8,384 [10,11]	50	76	86 [10]	87 [10,11]	716	628 [17,18]	—	2,154 [11]	16	16	—	29 [11]
426	866	1,495 [10]	4,506 [19]	9	14	18 [10]	31 [19]	14	34	87	172	#	1	2	2
693		1,031	1,350 [10,19]	41	36	36	44 [10,19]	8	10 [20]	64	70	2	1	3	3
428	618 [21]	1,251 [10]	2,420 [10]	20	24	31 [10]	48 [10]	13	35 [20]	99	108	2	2	3	3
	323 [21]				18	—	—	23	36	31	42	1	3	2	3
26	61	488 [10]	505	5	8	36 [10]	29	3	5	—	5	1	1	—	#
	84	—	398	8	7	—	22	4 [22]	5	—	26	1	1	—	2
797 [23]	1,194		1,851	26 [23]	35	—	47	112	256	310	344	6	11	10	11
90 [21]	160	352	243	5	8	12	11	1 [25]	5 [26]	10 [10]	22	#	#	1 [10]	1
39	77	108 [10]	158	5	7	6 [10]	8	1		13	9	#	1	1	1
1,865	2,908		6,316	18	25	—	35	150	208 [20,27]	—	1,290	3	4 [26,27]	—	10
96		263 [10]	360	11	16	18 [10]	19	14	19	—[8]	52	3	3	—	5
	2,742	4,142	4,447 [11]		74	—	90 [11]	—	439 [28]	645	718 [11]		13	15	15 [11]
384	732		1,293	16	24	—	33	29	60 [17]	—	—	2	3	—	—
293	565 [21,29]	1,143 [10]	1,149 [10,19]	27	45	78	77 [11]	32	69	207	263 [11]	5	9	22	26 [11]
73 [21,29]	245 [21,29]		651 [10,19]	5	13	—	16 [10,19]	6	18	63	88	1	1	3	3
79	167	279 [10]	—	3	5	6 [10]	—	—	7 [15]	22	43	0	0	—	1
102	190	283 [10]	364	16	24	24 [10]	26	—	15	25 [10]	—	1	2	2 [10]	3
75	661	844	758 [11]	8	50	44	36 [11]	8	49	49 [10]	56 [10,11]	1	5	4 [10]	4 [10,11]
137	182	—	594	10	9	—	16		24	20	28	—	2	1	1
2,659	3,593	10,329	11,051 [11]	18	19	46	51 [11]	240	434	879	877 [11]	3	4	7	7 [11]
18 [21]	264	397	632 [10]	—	32	19	29 [10]	1	7	25	45	—	1	3	3
56,778	52,386	90,723	98,763	46	49	68	73	1,663	3,822	12,144	19,417	2	3	13	19
32,748	54,180 [21]		81,050 [11]	30	44	—	52 [11]	3,545	4,951	—	11,295 [11]	5	6	—	11 [11]
5,722	10,965	14,828	15,873 [11]	29	44	57	62 [11]	543	1,773 [15]	3,018	3,441 [11]	4	9	15	16 [11]
2,718	5,085	9,091	10,313	45 [30]	55	78	82	184 [17,30]	312 [17]	734	1,955	5 [30]	10	10	22
1,033	1,024 [21]		1,706	57	47	—	45	107	170 [30]	—	413	9	12 [30]	—	15
9,558	11,026	8,606	8,131 [11]	93	97	102	102 [11]	2,412	2,899 [15]	3,972	4,032	31	30	48	54
1,996	2,144	2,032	2,090	93	98	88	98	525	537	446 [10]	664	34	40	31 [10]	48
4,286	4,560	3,959	3,646	78	90	94	91	648	1,691	3,003	3,223	15	39	78	89
1,084	1,456	2,205	2,300 [14]	48	56	70	70 [14]	58	121	549	632 [14]	4	7	28	29 [14]
1,066	1,281	2,318 [10]	2,589 [19]	22	23	39 [10]	41 [19]	163	196 [15]	553	555 [10,14]	5	4	12	11 [10,14]
512	709	1,350 [10]	2,054 [19]	22	33	51 [10]	46 [19]	34 [17]	94	103	147	3	5	5	6
2,166	4,345	5,772 [13]	7,272	14	23	25 [13]	27	268 [30]	—	—	521	2 [30]	3	—	3
2,929	4,034	5,386	6,069 [11]	64	73	77	84 [11]	1,276	1,709	2,432	2,427 [11]	24	28	31	29 [11]
349	893	1,914	2,037	29	44	68	68	62	154	—	574	7	12	—	28
1,267	2,082		2,320 [10,11]	55	74	—	81 [10,11]	59 [30]	55 [15,32]	—	—	3	5	—	—
604	914	1,125	2,249	46	52	43	63	140	222	—	—	17	18	—	—
1,920	2,230	5,577	5,010	29	30	82	77	911 [22]	1,156 [26]	2,096	2,251	15	19 [26]	35	41
2,218	3,808		5,742 [10,11]	35	47	—	85 [10,11]	246	750	1,607	1,918 [11]	5	13	24	28 [11]
2,879	3,295	—	4,235 [10]	105	99	—	95 [10]	516	603	—	408 [10]	28	30	—	15 [10]
3,847 [21]	3,236	8,321	9,589	42	32	67	73	115	130	750	845 [10]	2	2	10	10 [10]
	212 [27]		1,446	—	23 [27]	—	48	—	53 [15]	—	192	—	4 [15]	—	9
760	968	981 [10]	970	98	93	84 [10]	93	340	335	438	507	39	48	56	61
836	769		181 [11]	91	103	—	160 [11]	196	276	359	386	26	40	58	63
1,161 [30]	1,268	1,004	1,000 [11]	99	91	95	97 [11]	118 [33]	118 [33]	260	287 [11]	17	16	30	37 [11]
5,014	5,522	5,876	5,859 [11]	85	99	108	110 [11]	1,077	1,699	2,032	2,160	25	40	54	56
8,457	7,398	8,388	8,447 [11]	—	98	99	100 [11]	1,624	2,049	—	—	27	34	—	—
740	851	743	714 [11]	81	93	98	96 [11]	121	283	478	561 [11]	17	36	63	72 [11]
357	514		1,030 [11]	70	79	—	103 [11]	101	102	331	390 [11]	14	14	40	52 [11]
5,308	5,118	4,473	4,528 [11]	72	83	96	99 [11]	1,118	1,452	1,812	1,986	27	32	50	63
1,391	1,402	1,403	1,415 [11]	93	120	124	122 [11]	360	479	504	527 [11]	29	40	55	58 [11]
1,674	1,888	3,974	3,895 [11]	77	81	101	105 [11]	589	545	1,775	1,983 [11]	18	22	56	59 [11]
398	670	813	766 [11]	37	67	114	109 [11]	92	186	388	401 [11]	11	23	50	56 [11]
1,148	2,838	2,249	2,218 [11]	94	92	82	85 [11]	193	193	533	644 [11]	12	10	27	36 [11]
12,991	13,956	13,858	14,522 [11]	96	93	83	93 [11]	5,700	5,100	7,224	8,622 [10]	46	52	64	68 [10]
3,977	4,755	3,183	3,053 [11]	87	104	116	117 [11]	698	1,222	1,834	1,840	23	37	59	66
3,406	3,408		4,446	94	93	—	93	1,684	1,652	—	2,465	42	47	—	66
5,342	4,336	8,374	9,219 [11]	83	85	156	170 [11]	827	1,258	2,067	2,247	19	30	60	60
2,323	2,292	2,621	2,622 [10,14]	88	101	106	105 [10,14]	1,173 [35]	1,917	1,212	1,193 [10,14]	57	95	59	57 [10,14]
1,146	1,002	837	932	81	89	85	93	152	242	178	236 [11]	17	21	25	33 [11]
172	295 [15]	504	699	19	23 [15]	37	49	51	70 [26]	—	115 [10,11]	8	8 [26]	—	10 [10,11]
4,742	6,704	9,357	10,188 [11]	49	53	75	79 [11]	930	1,311	2,048	2,237 [11]	14	15	21	22 [11]
21,585	19,270	23,087	23,854 [11]	91	93	95	95 [11]	12,097	13,710	13,596	16,900	56	75	73	82
1,327	2,160	3,832	3,976 [14]	56	71	97	99 [14]	491	1,008 [15]	—	2,027 [14]	22	38 [15]	—	61 [14]
2,819	3,499	26,097	26,789 [14]	33	38	108	110 [14]	1,409	1,540 [36]	2,781	3,582 [14]	11	11	17	20 [14]
538	720	1,391	1,557 [11]	53	73	85	88 [11]	145	262 [15]	452	567 [11]	12	21 [15]	38	43 [11]
1,733	2,378 [15]	3,569	4,051	39	50	70	75	272	487	934	1,113	9	13	23	27
592	786 [21,37]	936	997	53	55	57	61	270	207	—	—	35	20	—	—
1,203	1,698	2,376 [10]	2,540 [14]	59	67	86 [10]	90 [14]	306	678	—	831 [10,14]	17	30	—	32 [10,14]
222	281	1,544 [10]	1,954	21	35	59	72	307	550	681 [10]	983 [10,11]	21	29	29 [10]	39 [10,11]
1,100	1,278	2,589	2,569 [11]	71	82	161	154 [11]	324 [38]	485 [38]	845	1,003	25	36	63	72

[17] Excludes private institutions.
[18] Data refer to universities and exclude Al Azhar.
[19] Data for 2004–05.
[20] Excludes nonuniversity institutions (such as teacher training colleges and technical colleges) and excludes distance-learning universities.
[21] General education enrollment only. Excludes teacher training and vocational education enrollments.
[22] Data for 1981–82.
[23] Does not include professional schools.
[24] Includes initiation classes where students learn Portuguese.
[25] Estimated.
[26] Data for 1992–93.
[27] Data for 1993–94.
[28] Not including the former Independent States of Transke, Bophuthatswana, Venda, and Ciskei.
[29] Data refer to government aided and maintained schools only.
[30] Data for 1985–86.

[31] Includes preprimary education.
[32] Excludes some nonuniversity institutions.
[33] Includes full-time students only.
[34] Data include both former East and West Germany.
[35] Not including part-time students at community colleges.
[36] Not including former ISCED level 7.
[37] Including vocational education.
[38] Data do not include Vocational Education and Training Institutes (VETS).
NOTE: Some data have been revised from previously published figures. Detail may not sum to totals because of rounding.
SOURCE: United Nations Educational, Scientific, and Cultural Organization (UNESCO), *Statistical Yearbook, 1999* and *Global Education Digest*, 2003, 2005, and 2006, and unpublished tabulations. World Bank, *World Development Indicators, 2000* and *World Development Report*, 2002, 2004, and 2006. U.S. Department of Commerce, Census Bureau, International Data Base, retrieved May 6, 2005, from http://www.census.gov/ipc/ www/idbnew.html. (This table was prepared August 2006.)

Table 394. School-age populations as a percentage of total population, by age group and country: Selected years,1985 through 2002

Country	5- to 14-year-olds as a percent of total population							15- to 19-year-olds as a percent of total population						
	1985[1]	1990[1]	1995[1]	1996	1998	1999	2002	1985[2]	1990[2]	1995[2]	1996	1998	1999	2002
1	2	3	4	5	6	7	8	9	10	11	12	13	14	15
Australia............................	14	13	13	14	14	14	14	7	6	6	7	7	7	7
Belgium..............................	11	11	11	12	12	12	12	6	5	5	6	6	6	6
Canada...............................	13	12	12	13	14	14	—	6	5	5	7	7	7	—
Czech Republic..................	—	—	12	13	13	12	12	—	—	6	8	8	7	7
Denmark.............................	12	10	10	11	11	12	12	6	6	5	6	6	5	5
Finland...............................	11	12	11	13	13	13	12	6	5	5	6	6	6	6
France................................	13	12	12	13	13	13	12	6	6	5	7	7	7	7
Germany[3]	9	9	10	11	11	11	11	6	4	4	5	6	6	6
Greece................................	—	—	11	12	11	11	10	—	5	6	7	7	7	6
Iceland...............................	16	15	14	16	16	16	16	7	7	6	8	8	8	7
Ireland...............................	18	18	15	17	16	15	14	8	8	8	9	9	9	8
Italy...................................	13	10	9	10	10	10	10	6	6	5	6	6	5	5
Japan.................................	14	12	10	11	11	10	10	6	7	5	7	6	6	6
Korea, Republic of	—	—	14	15	14	14	14	—	—	7	9	9	8	7
Luxembourg........................	10	10	11	12	12	12	13	5	4	4	5	6	6	6
Netherlands........................	12	11	11	12	12	12	12	7	5	5	6	6	6	6
New Zealand.......................	15	13	13	15	15	15	15	7	7	6	7	7	7	7
Norway...............................	13	11	11	13	13	13	13	6	6	5	6	6	6	6
Russian Federation..............	—	—	14	16	—	14	12	—	—	6	7	—	8	8
Spain	15	13	10	11	11	10	10	7	7	6	8	7	7	6
Sweden...............................	11	10	11	12	13	13	13	5	5	5	6	6	6	6
Switzerland.........................	11	10	10	12	12	12	12	6	5	5	6	6	6	6
Turkey	21	21	20	20	21	21	—	9	9	9	11	11	11	—
United Kingdom	11	11	12	13	13	13	13	6	5	5	6	6	6	6
United States......................	13	13	13	15	14	15	15	6	5	6	7	7	7	7

—Not available.

[1]Data are for the 5- to 13-year-old population.
[2]Data are for the 14- to 17-year-old population.

[3]Data for 1985 are for the former West Germany.
SOURCE: Organization for Economic Cooperation and Development (OECD), *Education at a Glance*, selected years, 1987 through 2004. (This table was prepared April 2005.)

Table 395. Percentage of population enrolled in secondary and postsecondary institutions, by age group and country: Selected years, 1985 through 2003

Country	Secondary schools, 16 years old, 2003	Secondary schools, 17 years old, 2003	Postsecondary education											
			18 to 21 years old				22 to 25 years old				26 to 29 years old			
			1985	1990	1999	2002	1985	1990	1999	2002	1985	1990	1999	2002
1	2	3	4	5	6	7	8	9	10	11	12	13	14	15
Australia	93	80	—	—	31	35	—	—	15	20	—	—	8	10
Austria	90	77	—	—	15	14	—	—	20	17	—	—	12	8
Belgium[1]	102	104	25	—	42	42	7	—	15	18	2	—	3	5
Canada	—	—	—	—	27	—	—	—	18	—	—	—	7	—
Czech Republic	100	98	—	—	17	20	—	—	12	16	—	—	4	5
Denmark	93	86	7	7	8	10	16	18	27	29	8	9	15	16
Finland	96	95	9	14	23	21	17	21	35	39	8	10	18	19
France	96	89	19	25	35	35	10	12	20	20	4	4	5	5
Germany[2]	97	91	9	9	11	12	—	16	19	20	9	10	11	12
Greece	97	68	—	—	54	46	—	—	7	24	—	—	2	11
Hungary	94	89	—	—	20	24	—	—	14	18	—	—	5	7
Iceland	93	83	—	—	7	10	—	—	21	23	—	—	9	11
Ireland	96	76	—	21	33	—	—	—	11	—	—	—	3	—
Italy	88	81	—	—	22	24	—	—	21	21	—	—	7	8
Japan	97	95	—	—	—	—	—	—	—	—	—	—	—	—
Korea, Republic of	98	93	—	—	51	56	—	—	26	32	—	—	6	7
Mexico	50	38	—	—	12	15	—	—	8	7	—	—	1	3
Netherlands	97	81	14	18	26	28	12	13	20	22	6	5	5	6
New Zealand	85	67	—	21	29	30	—	15	14	17	—	—	8	8
Norway	94	93	9	14	19	17	14	17	28	27	6	8	12	13
Poland	97	94	—	—	21	26	—	—	21	26	—	—	5	7
Portugal	79	74	6	—	25	25	5	—	17	20	2	—	6	8
Spain	92	81	15	21	32	35	11	14	24	24	4	5	8	8
Sweden	97	97	8	9	16	17	11	11	25	28	7	6	12	13
Switzerland	90	86	6	6	10	10	11	12	17	18	5	6	9	9
Turkey	53	31	—	7	14	—	—	4	9	—	—	2	4	—
United Kingdom	94	81	15	16	29	30	7	11	12	12	—	—	6	6
United States	94	82	37	41	44	46	15	17	18	25	8	9	11	11

—Not available.

[1]Data for Flemish Belgium only.

[2]Data for 1985 are for the former West Germany.

NOTE: Data in this table refer to programs classified by the Organization for Economic Cooperation and Development (OECD) as International Standard Classification of Education (ISCED) level 3, level 5A (first and second award), level 5B, and level 6. The table includes both full-time and part-time students. ISCED 3 corresponds to secondary education in the United States. ISCED 5A (first and second award), ISCED 5B, and ISCED 6 correspond to 2-year and 4-year college undergraduate and graduate programs in the United States. Some increases in enrollment rates may be due to more complete reporting by countries. Enrollment figures may not be directly comparable due to differing definitions of postsecondary education and the age at which postsecondary education begins. Differences in reference dates between enrollment and population data can result in enrollment rates that exceed 100 percent.

SOURCE: Organization for Economic Cooperation and Development (OECD), *Education at a Glance*, selected years, 1987 through 2004; and Education Online Database, 2003, retrieved March 20, 2006, from http://stats.oecd.org/WBOS/Default/aspx. U.S. Department of Commerce, Census Bureau, Current Population Survey (CPS), October 2000 through October 2003. (This table was prepared March 2006.)

Table 396. Pupils per teacher in public and private elementary and secondary schools, by level of education and country: Selected years, 1985 through 2004

Country	Elementary								Junior high school (lower secondary)								Senior high school (upper secondary)							
	1985	1990	1996	2000	2001	2002	2003	2004	1985	1990	1996	2000	2001	2002	2003	2004	1985	1990	1996	2000	2001	2002	2003	2004
	2	3	4	5	6	7	8	9	10	11	12	13	14	15	16	17	18	19	20	21	22	23	24	25
Australia	13.8[1]	—	18.1	17.3	17.0	16.9	16.6	16.4	—	—	—	—	—	12.5[2,3]	12.4[2,3]	12.3[2,3]	3.2	—	—	—	—	12.5[2,3]	12.4[2,3]	12.3[2,3]
Austria	11.3	11.6	12.7	—	14.3	14.4	14.4	15.1	9.2	7.7	9.2	—	9.8	9.8	10.0	10.4	15.2	12.4	8.5	—	9.9	10.3	10.2	11.0
Belgium	—	—	—	15.0	13.4	13.1	13.1	12.9	—	—	—	9.7[2]	9.8[2]	9.3[2]	10.6	10.6	—	—	—	9.7[2]	9.8[2]	9.3[2]	9.6	9.2
Canada	18.1	17.1	17.0	18.1	18.3	—	—	—	16.0	15.5	20.0	18.1	18.4	—	—	—	16.0	15.3	19.5	19.5	17.2	—	—	—
Denmark	12.7	11.2	11.2	10.4	10.0	10.9[4]	10.8[4]	11.3[4]	10.2	9.3	10.1	11.4	11.1	10.9[4]	10.8[4]	11.3[4]	14.8	13.3	12.1	14.4	13.9	14.2	13.4	—
France	—	—	19.5	19.8	19.5	19.4	19.4	19.4	—	—	—	14.7	13.5	13.7	13.7	14.1	—	—	—	10.4	11.2	10.6	10.6	10.3
Germany[5]	20.7	20.3	20.9	19.8	19.4	18.9	18.7	18.8	16.9	14.6	16.0	15.7	15.7	15.7	15.6	15.6	23.7	21.0	13.1	13.9	13.7	13.6	13.7	13.9
Ireland	—	—	22.6	21.5	20.3	19.5	18.7	18.3	—	—	—	15.9[2]	15.2[2]	14.3[2]	13.7[2]	14.3[2]	7.2	8.3	9.8	15.9[2]	15.2[2]	14.3[2]	13.7[2]	14.3[2]
Italy	12.8	10.7	11.2	11.0	10.8	10.6	10.9	10.7	9.6	8.5	10.8	10.4	9.9	9.9	10.3	10.3	10.8	10.7	9.8	10.2	10.4	10.3	10.8	11.5
Japan	—	20.8[1]	19.7	20.9	20.6	20.3	19.9	19.6	—	18.6	16.2	16.8	16.6	16.2	15.7	15.3	—	16.2	15.6	14.0	14.0	13.7	13.5	13.2
Netherlands	20.2	19.2	20.0	16.8	17.2	17.0	16.0	15.9	12.7	12.4	18.1	17.1[2]	17.1[2]	15.9[2]	15.7[2]	15.8[2]	—	—	—	17.1[2]	17.1[2]	15.9[2]	15.7[2]	15.8[2]
New Zealand	20.1	19.1	22.0	20.6	19.6	19.6	19.9	16.7	—	—	—	19.9	18.7	19.4	18.8	17.3	—	—	14.1	13.1	12.8	13.8	10.9	12.5
Norway	—	—	—	12.4	11.6	11.5	11.7[1]	11.9[1]	—	—	—	9.9	9.3	10.3	10.4[1]	10.5[1]	—	—	—	9.7	9.2	9.2	9.2[1]	9.6[1]
Portugal	—	—	—	12.1	11.6	11.0	—	11.1	—	—	—	10.4	9.9	9.3	—	10.0	—	—	—	7.9	8.0	7.5	—	7.3
Spain	26.8	21.2	18.0	14.9	14.7	14.6	14.3	14.3	21.4	18.8	17.8	11.9[2]	11.0[2]	13.7	13.3	12.9	15.3	14.8	14.2	11.9[2]	11.0[2]	8.3	7.9	8.0
Sweden	11.6	10.6	12.7	12.8	12.4	12.5	12.3	12.1	10.8	10.2	12.2	12.8	12.4	12.2	12.1	11.9	13.1	11.9	15.2	15.2	16.6	14.1	14.1	14.0
Turkey	31.1	30.6	—	30.5	29.8	27.5	25.9	26.5	41.3	48.4	—	—	†	†	†	†	11.0	12.1	—	14.0	17.2	17.7	18.0	16.9
United Kingdom	19.7	22.0	21.3	21.2	20.5	19.9	20.0[3]	21.1	18.5	18.5	16.0	17.6[3]	17.3[3]	17.6[3]	17.4[3]	17.1[3]	11.1	13.9	15.3	12.5[3]	12.3[3]	12.5[3]	12.6[3]	12.3[3]
United States	17.0	15.6	16.9	15.8	16.3	15.5	15.5	15.0	16.5	15.9	17.5	16.3	17.0	15.5	15.5	15.2	16.2	15.8	14.7	14.1	14.8	15.6	15.6	16.0

—Not available.

†Not applicable.

[1]Public schools only.

[2]Junior high school and senior high school data are combined.

[3]Includes only general programs in junior high school and senior high school.

[4]Elementary school data and junior high school data are combined.

[5]Data for 1985 are for the former West Germany.

NOTE: In the U.S. data in this table, elementary corresponds to grades 1 through 6, junior high school corresponds to grades 7 through 9, and senior high school corresponds to grades 10 through 12.

SOURCE: Organization for Economic Cooperation and Development (OECD), Education Online Database; *Annual National Accounts, Vol. 1, 1997*, and *Education at a Glance*, 2002 through 2006. (This table was prepared September 2006.)

Table 397. Average mathematics literacy, reading literacy, science literacy, and problem-solving scores of 15-year-olds, by sex and country: 2003

Country	Mathematics literacy Total	Mathematics literacy Male	Mathematics literacy Female	Reading literacy Total	Reading literacy Male	Reading literacy Female	Science literacy Total	Science literacy Male	Science literacy Female	Problem solving Total	Problem solving Male	Problem solving Female
1	2	3	4	5	6	7	8	9	10	11	12	13
OECD total[1]	489 (1.1)	494 (1.3)	484 (1.3)	488 (1.2)	472 (1.4)	503 (1.3)	496 (1.1)	499 (1.3)	493 (1.3)	490 (1.2)	489 (1.4)	490 (1.3)
OECD average[2]	500 (0.6)	506 (0.8)	494 (0.8)	494 (0.6)	477 (0.7)	511 (0.7)	500 (0.6)	503 (0.7)	497 (0.8)	500 (0.6)	499 (0.8)	501 (0.8)
Australia	524 (2.1)	527 (3.0)	522 (2.7)	525 (2.1)	506 (2.8)	545 (2.6)	525 (2.1)	525 (2.9)	525 (2.8)	530 (2.0)	527 (2.7)	533 (2.5)
Austria	506 (3.3)	509 (4.0)	502 (4.0)	491 (3.8)	467 (4.5)	514 (4.2)	491 (3.4)	490 (4.3)	492 (4.2)	506 (3.2)	505 (3.9)	508 (3.8)
Belgium	529 (2.3)	533 (3.4)	525 (3.2)	507 (2.6)	489 (3.8)	526 (3.8)	509 (2.5)	509 (3.6)	509 (3.5)	525 (2.2)	524 (3.1)	527 (3.2)
Canada	532 (1.8)	541 (2.1)	530 (1.9)	528 (1.7)	514 (2.0)	546 (1.8)	519 (2.0)	527 (2.3)	516 (2.2)	529 (1.7)	533 (2.0)	532 (1.8)
Czech Republic	516 (3.5)	524 (4.3)	509 (4.4)	489 (3.5)	473 (4.1)	504 (4.4)	523 (3.4)	526 (4.3)	520 (4.1)	516 (3.4)	520 (4.1)	513 (4.3)
Denmark	514 (2.7)	523 (3.4)	506 (3.0)	492 (2.8)	479 (3.3)	505 (3.0)	475 (3.0)	484 (3.6)	467 (3.2)	517 (2.5)	519 (3.1)	514 (2.9)
Finland	544 (1.9)	548 (2.5)	541 (2.1)	543 (1.6)	521 (2.2)	565 (2.0)	548 (1.9)	545 (2.6)	551 (2.2)	548 (1.9)	543 (2.5)	553 (2.2)
France	511 (2.5)	515 (3.6)	507 (2.9)	496 (2.7)	476 (3.8)	514 (3.2)	511 (3.0)	511 (4.1)	511 (3.5)	519 (2.7)	519 (3.8)	520 (2.9)
Germany	503 (3.3)	508 (4.0)	499 (3.9)	491 (3.4)	471 (4.2)	513 (3.9)	502 (3.6)	506 (4.5)	500 (4.2)	513 (3.2)	511 (3.9)	517 (3.7)
Greece	445 (3.9)	455 (4.8)	436 (3.8)	472 (4.1)	453 (5.1)	490 (4.0)	481 (3.8)	487 (4.8)	475 (3.9)	449 (4.0)	449 (4.9)	448 (4.1)
Hungary	490 (2.8)	494 (3.3)	486 (3.3)	482 (2.5)	467 (3.2)	498 (3.0)	503 (2.8)	503 (3.3)	504 (3.3)	501 (2.9)	499 (3.4)	503 (3.4)
Iceland	515 (1.4)	508 (2.3)	523 (2.2)	492 (1.6)	464 (2.3)	522 (2.2)	495 (1.5)	490 (2.4)	500 (2.4)	505 (1.4)	490 (2.2)	520 (2.5)
Ireland	503 (2.4)	510 (3.0)	495 (3.4)	515 (2.6)	501 (3.3)	530 (3.7)	505 (2.7)	506 (3.1)	504 (3.9)	498 (2.3)	499 (2.8)	498 (3.5)
Italy	466 (3.1)	475 (4.6)	457 (3.8)	476 (3.0)	455 (5.1)	495 (3.4)	486 (3.1)	490 (5.2)	484 (3.6)	470 (3.1)	467 (5.0)	471 (3.5)
Japan	534 (4.0)	539 (5.8)	530 (4.0)	498 (3.9)	487 (5.5)	509 (4.1)	548 (4.1)	550 (6.0)	546 (4.1)	547 (4.1)	546 (5.7)	548 (4.1)
Korea, Republic of	542 (3.2)	552 (4.4)	528 (5.3)	534 (3.1)	525 (3.7)	547 (4.3)	538 (3.5)	546 (4.7)	527 (5.5)	550 (3.1)	554 (4.0)	546 (4.8)
Luxembourg	493 (1.0)	502 (1.9)	485 (1.5)	479 (1.5)	463 (2.6)	496 (1.8)	483 (1.5)	489 (2.5)	477 (1.9)	494 (1.4)	495 (2.4)	492 (1.9)
Mexico	385 (3.6)	391 (4.3)	380 (4.1)	400 (4.1)	389 (4.6)	410 (4.6)	405 (3.5)	410 (3.9)	400 (4.2)	384 (4.3)	387 (5.0)	382 (4.7)
Netherlands	538 (3.1)	540 (4.1)	535 (3.5)	513 (2.9)	503 (3.7)	524 (3.2)	524 (3.1)	527 (4.2)	522 (3.6)	520 (3.0)	522 (3.6)	518 (3.6)
New Zealand	523 (2.3)	531 (2.8)	516 (3.2)	522 (2.5)	508 (3.1)	535 (3.3)	521 (2.4)	529 (3.0)	513 (3.4)	533 (2.2)	531 (2.6)	534 (3.1)
Norway	495 (2.4)	498 (2.8)	492 (2.9)	500 (2.8)	475 (3.4)	525 (3.4)	484 (2.9)	485 (3.5)	483 (3.3)	490 (2.6)	486 (3.1)	494 (3.2)
Poland	490 (2.5)	493 (3.0)	487 (2.9)	497 (2.9)	477 (3.6)	516 (3.2)	498 (2.9)	501 (3.2)	494 (3.4)	487 (2.8)	486 (3.4)	487 (3.4)
Portugal	466 (3.4)	472 (4.2)	460 (3.4)	478 (3.7)	459 (4.3)	495 (3.7)	468 (3.5)	471 (4.0)	465 (3.6)	470 (3.9)	470 (4.6)	470 (3.9)
Slovak Republic	498 (3.3)	507 (3.9)	489 (3.9)	469 (3.1)	453 (3.8)	486 (3.3)	495 (3.7)	502 (4.3)	487 (3.9)	492 (3.4)	495 (4.1)	488 (3.6)
Spain	485 (2.4)	490 (3.4)	481 (2.2)	481 (2.6)	461 (3.8)	500 (2.5)	487 (2.6)	489 (3.9)	485 (2.6)	482 (2.7)	479 (3.6)	485 (2.6)
Sweden	509 (2.6)	512 (3.0)	506 (3.1)	514 (2.4)	496 (2.8)	533 (2.9)	506 (2.7)	509 (3.1)	504 (3.5)	509 (2.4)	504 (3.0)	514 (2.8)
Switzerland	527 (3.4)	535 (4.7)	518 (3.6)	499 (3.3)	482 (4.4)	517 (3.1)	513 (3.7)	518 (5.0)	508 (3.9)	521 (3.0)	520 (4.0)	523 (3.8)
Turkey	423 (6.7)	430 (7.9)	415 (6.7)	441 (5.8)	426 (6.8)	459 (6.1)	434 (5.9)	434 (6.7)	434 (6.4)	408 (6.0)	408 (7.3)	406 (5.8)
United Kingdom[3]	508 (2.4)	512 (2.9)	505 (2.9)	507 (2.5)	492 (3.1)	520 (3.6)	518 (2.5)	520 (3.1)	517 (4.0)	510 (2.4)	506 (3.0)	514 (3.5)
United States	483 (2.9)	486 (3.3)	480 (3.2)	495 (3.2)	479 (3.7)	511 (3.5)	491 (3.1)	494 (3.5)	489 (3.5)	477 (3.1)	477 (3.4)	478 (3.5)
Non-OECD countries												
Brazil	356 (4.8)	365 (6.1)	348 (4.4)	403 (4.6)	384 (5.8)	419 (4.1)	390 (4.3)	393 (5.3)	387 (4.3)	371 (4.8)	374 (6.0)	368 (4.3)
Hong Kong-China	550 (4.5)	552 (6.5)	548 (4.6)	510 (3.7)	494 (5.3)	525 (3.5)	539 (4.3)	538 (6.1)	541 (4.2)	548 (4.2)	545 (6.2)	550 (4.0)
Indonesia	360 (3.9)	362 (3.9)	358 (4.6)	382 (3.4)	369 (3.4)	394 (3.9)	395 (3.2)	396 (3.1)	394 (3.8)	361 (3.3)	358 (3.1)	365 (4.0)
Latvia	483 (3.7)	485 (4.8)	482 (3.6)	491 (3.7)	470 (4.5)	509 (3.7)	489 (3.9)	487 (5.1)	491 (3.9)	483 (3.9)	481 (5.1)	484 (4.0)
Liechtenstein	536 (4.1)	550 (7.2)	521 (6.3)	525 (3.6)	517 (7.2)	534 (6.5)	525 (4.3)	538 (7.7)	512 (7.3)	529 (3.9)	535 (6.6)	524 (5.9)
Macao-China	527 (2.9)	538 (4.8)	517 (3.3)	498 (2.2)	491 (3.6)	504 (2.8)	525 (3.0)	529 (5.0)	521 (4.0)	532 (2.5)	538 (4.3)	527 (3.2)
Russian Federation	468 (4.2)	473 (5.3)	463 (4.2)	442 (3.9)	428 (4.7)	456 (3.7)	489 (4.1)	494 (5.3)	485 (4.0)	479 (4.6)	480 (5.9)	477 (4.4)
Serbia and Montenegro	437 (3.8)	437 (4.2)	436 (4.5)	412 (3.6)	390 (3.7)	433 (3.9)	436 (3.5)	434 (3.7)	439 (4.2)	420 (3.3)	416 (3.8)	424 (3.9)
Thailand	417 (3.0)	415 (4.0)	419 (3.4)	420 (2.8)	396 (3.7)	439 (3.0)	429 (2.7)	425 (3.7)	433 (3.1)	425 (2.7)	418 (3.9)	431 (3.1)
Tunisia	359 (2.5)	365 (2.7)	353 (2.9)	375 (2.8)	362 (3.3)	387 (3.3)	385 (2.6)	380 (2.7)	390 (3.0)	345 (2.1)	346 (2.5)	343 (2.5)
Uruguay	422 (3.3)	428 (4.0)	416 (3.8)	434 (3.4)	414 (4.5)	453 (3.7)	438 (2.9)	441 (3.7)	436 (3.6)	411 (3.7)	412 (4.6)	409 (4.2)

[1]Illustrates how a country compares with the OECD area as a whole. Computed taking the OECD countries as a single entity, to which each country contributes in proportion to the number of 15-year-olds enrolled in its schools.

[2]Refers to the mean of the data values for all OECD countries, to which each country contributes equally, regardless of the absolute size of the student population of each country.

[3]Response rate is too low to ensure comparability with other countries.

NOTE: Scales were designed to have an average score of 500 points and standard deviation of 100. Possible scores range from 0 to 1000. Standard errors appear in parentheses.
SOURCE: Organization for Economic Cooperation and Development (OECD), Program for International Student Assessment (PISA), 2003, Learning for Tomorrow's World, 2003, and Problem Solving for Tomorrow's World, 2003. U.S. Department of Education, National Center for Education Statistics, PISA, 2003, International Outcomes of Learning in Mathematics Literacy and Problem Solving, 2003. (This table was prepared March 2005.)

Table 398. Mean scores and percentage distribution of 15-year-olds scoring at each mathematics literacy proficiency level, by country: 2003

Country	Mean score	Below level 1[1]		Level 1[2]		Level 2[3]		Level 3[4]		Level 4[5]		Level 5[6]		Level 6[7]	
1	2	3		4		5		6		7		8		9	
OECD total[8]	489 (1.07)	11.0	(0.32)	14.6	(0.32)	21.2	(0.28)	22.4	(0.32)	17.6	(0.25)	9.6	(0.19)	3.5	(0.19)
OECD average[9]	500 (0.63)	8.2	(0.17)	13.2	(0.16)	21.1	(0.15)	23.7	(0.18)	19.1	(0.17)	10.6	(0.13)	4.0	(0.10)
Australia	524 (2.15)	4.3	(0.45)	10.0	(0.51)	18.6	(0.62)	24.0	(0.71)	23.3	(0.64)	14.0	(0.53)	5.8	(0.45)
Austria	506 (3.27)	5.6	(0.70)	13.2	(0.84)	21.6	(0.90)	24.9	(1.14)	20.5	(0.84)	10.5	(0.85)	3.7	(0.52)
Belgium	529 (2.29)	7.2	(0.56)	9.3	(0.49)	15.9	(0.65)	20.1	(0.71)	21.0	(0.62)	17.5	(0.69)	9.0	(0.48)
Canada	532 (1.82)	2.4	(0.26)	7.7	(0.36)	18.3	(0.61)	26.2	(0.67)	25.1	(0.60)	14.8	(0.55)	5.5	(0.45)
Czech Republic	516 (3.55)	5.0	(0.69)	11.6	(0.90)	20.1	(0.96)	24.3	(0.95)	20.8	(0.87)	12.9	(0.80)	5.3	(0.53)
Denmark	514 (2.74)	4.7	(0.50)	10.7	(0.62)	20.6	(0.89)	26.2	(0.88)	21.9	(0.83)	11.8	(0.86)	4.1	(0.50)
Finland	544 (1.87)	1.5	(0.23)	5.3	(0.38)	16.0	(0.57)	27.7	(0.65)	26.1	(0.89)	16.7	(0.64)	6.7	(0.46)
France	511 (2.50)	5.6	(0.68)	11.0	(0.77)	20.2	(0.82)	25.9	(0.99)	22.1	(0.97)	11.6	(0.72)	3.5	(0.40)
Germany	503 (3.32)	9.2	(0.84)	12.4	(0.81)	19.0	(1.05)	22.6	(0.82)	20.6	(1.02)	12.2	(0.87)	4.1	(0.48)
Greece	445 (3.90)	17.8	(1.21)	21.2	(1.15)	26.3	(1.04)	20.2	(1.01)	10.6	(0.87)	3.4	(0.53)	0.6	(0.17)
Hungary	490 (2.84)	7.8	(0.80)	15.2	(0.81)	23.8	(1.05)	24.3	(0.93)	18.2	(0.90)	8.2	(0.73)	2.5	(0.42)
Iceland	515 (1.42)	4.5	(0.40)	10.5	(0.55)	20.2	(1.02)	26.1	(0.88)	23.2	(0.81)	11.7	(0.61)	3.7	(0.36)
Ireland	503 (2.45)	4.7	(0.57)	12.1	(0.84)	23.6	(0.83)	28.0	(0.82)	20.2	(1.06)	9.1	(0.76)	2.2	(0.33)
Italy	466 (3.08)	13.2	(1.19)	18.7	(0.93)	24.7	(1.03)	22.9	(0.84)	13.4	(0.73)	5.5	(0.43)	1.5	(0.19)
Japan	534 (4.02)	4.7	(0.65)	8.6	(0.72)	16.3	(0.80)	22.4	(1.02)	23.6	(1.24)	16.1	(0.96)	8.2	(1.14)
Korea, Republic of	542 (3.24)	2.5	(0.32)	7.1	(0.65)	16.6	(0.80)	24.1	(0.98)	25.0	(1.08)	16.7	(0.81)	8.1	(0.93)
Luxembourg	493 (0.97)	7.4	(0.41)	14.3	(0.65)	22.9	(0.87)	25.9	(0.79)	18.7	(0.85)	8.5	(0.59)	2.4	(0.31)
Mexico	385 (3.64)	38.1	(1.71)	27.9	(1.02)	20.8	(0.87)	10.1	(0.84)	2.7	(0.39)	0.4	(0.10)	#	(†)
Netherlands	538 (3.13)	2.6	(0.65)	8.4	(0.95)	18.0	(1.11)	23.0	(1.14)	22.6	(1.34)	18.2	(1.09)	7.3	(0.58)
New Zealand	523 (2.26)	4.9	(0.44)	10.1	(0.63)	19.2	(0.71)	23.2	(0.90)	21.9	(0.80)	14.1	(0.60)	6.6	(0.44)
Norway	495 (2.38)	6.9	(0.50)	13.9	(0.82)	23.7	(1.16)	25.2	(1.01)	18.9	(1.00)	8.7	(0.57)	2.7	(0.35)
Poland	490 (2.50)	6.8	(0.61)	15.2	(0.76)	24.8	(0.75)	25.3	(0.94)	17.7	(0.89)	7.8	(0.49)	2.3	(0.31)
Portugal	466 (3.40)	11.3	(1.11)	18.8	(0.99)	27.1	(0.99)	24.0	(1.03)	13.4	(0.94)	4.6	(0.47)	0.8	(0.16)
Slovak Republic	498 (3.35)	6.7	(0.85)	13.2	(0.86)	23.5	(0.88)	24.9	(1.08)	18.9	(0.82)	9.8	(0.68)	2.9	(0.38)
Spain	485 (2.41)	8.1	(0.66)	14.9	(0.87)	24.7	(0.78)	26.7	(1.02)	17.7	(0.65)	6.5	(0.62)	1.4	(0.25)
Sweden	509 (2.56)	5.6	(0.52)	11.7	(0.60)	21.7	(0.84)	25.5	(0.95)	19.8	(0.81)	11.6	(0.57)	4.1	(0.49)
Switzerland	527 (3.38)	4.9	(0.45)	9.6	(0.57)	17.5	(0.80)	24.3	(0.98)	22.5	(0.72)	14.2	(1.05)	7.0	(0.90)
Turkey	423 (6.74)	27.7	(2.01)	24.6	(1.33)	22.1	(1.12)	13.5	(1.27)	6.8	(1.05)	3.1	(0.82)	2.4	(1.02)
United Kingdom[10]	508 (2.43)	5.2	(0.54)	12.5	(0.67)	21.2	(1.20)	25.6	(0.88)	20.6	(0.73)	11.0	(0.73)	3.9	(0.43)
United States	483 (2.95)	10.2	(0.80)	15.5	(0.81)	23.9	(0.80)	23.8	(0.79)	16.6	(0.73)	8.0	(0.53)	2.0	(0.36)
Non-OECD countries															
Brazil	356 (4.83)	53.3	(1.94)	21.9	(1.09)	14.1	(0.86)	6.8	(0.78)	2.7	(0.47)	0.9	(0.36)	0.3	(0.16)
Hong Kong-China	550 (4.54)	3.9	(0.72)	6.5	(0.64)	13.9	(1.00)	20.0	(1.25)	25.0	(1.17)	20.2	(1.00)	10.5	(0.94)
Indonesia	360 (3.91)	50.5	(2.08)	27.6	(1.05)	14.8	(1.07)	5.5	(0.71)	1.4	(0.39)	0.2	(0.09)	#	(†)
Latvia	483 (3.69)	7.6	(0.86)	16.1	(1.08)	25.5	(1.17)	26.3	(1.15)	16.6	(1.17)	6.3	(0.70)	1.6	(0.36)
Liechtenstein	536 (4.12)	4.8	(1.33)	7.5	(1.66)	17.3	(2.78)	21.6	(2.54)	23.2	(3.09)	18.3	(3.22)	7.3	(1.73)
Macao-China	527 (2.89)	2.3	(0.60)	8.8	(1.34)	19.6	(1.40)	26.8	(1.77)	23.7	(1.71)	13.8	(1.55)	4.8	(0.96)
Russian Federation	468 (4.20)	11.4	(1.03)	18.8	(1.09)	26.4	(1.13)	23.1	(1.02)	13.2	(0.92)	5.4	(0.58)	1.6	(0.38)
Serbia and Montenegro	437 (3.75)	17.6	(1.35)	24.5	(1.08)	28.6	(1.16)	18.9	(1.11)	8.1	(0.88)	2.1	(0.41)	0.2	(0.10)
Thailand	417 (3.00)	23.8	(1.28)	30.2	(1.25)	25.4	(1.12)	13.7	(0.85)	5.3	(0.53)	1.5	(0.31)	0.2	(0.10)
Tunisia	359 (2.54)	51.1	(1.37)	26.9	(0.95)	14.7	(0.75)	5.7	(0.61)	1.4	(0.30)	0.2	(0.12)	#	(†)
Uruguay	422 (3.29)	26.3	(1.30)	21.8	(0.80)	24.2	(0.89)	16.8	(0.68)	8.2	(0.65)	2.3	(0.33)	0.5	(0.17)

†Not applicable.

#Rounds to zero.

[1]Less than or equal to 357.77 score points. Does not meet the requirements for proficiency at level 1.

[2]A score greater than 357.77 and less than or equal to 420.07. Indicates an ability to answer questions involving familiar contexts where all relevant information is present and the questions are clearly defined.

[3]A score greater than 420.07 and less than or equal to 482.38. Indicates an ability to interpret and recognize situations in contexts that require no more than direct inference, extract relevant information from a single source, and employ direct reasoning for literal interpretations of results.

[4]A score greater than 482.38 and less than or equal to 544.68. Indicates an ability to execute clearly described procedures, interpret and use representations based on different information sources, and develop short communications reporting their interpretations, results, and reasoning.

[5]A score greater than 544.68 and less than or equal to 606.99. Indicates an ability to work effectively with explicit models for complex concrete situations that may involve constraints or call for making assumptions, select and integrate different representations, reason with some insight, and construct and communicate explanations and arguments based on their interpretations and actions.

[6]A score greater than 606.99 and less than or equal to 669.3. Indicates an ability to develop and work with models for complex situations, work strategically using broad, well-developed thinking and reasoning skills, and communicate their interpretations and reasoning.

[7]A score greater than 669.3. Indicates an ability to conceptualize, generalize, and utilize information, link different information sources and representations, and formulate and precisely communicate actions and reflections regarding findings and interpretations.

[8]Illustrates how a country compares with the OECD area as a whole. Computed by taking the OECD countries as a single entity to which each country contributes in proportion to the number of 15-year-olds enrolled in its schools.

[9]Refers to the mean of the data values for all OECD countries, to which each country contributes equally, regardless of the absolute size of the student population of each country.

[10]Response rate was too low to ensure comparability with other countries.

NOTE: Mean score was designed to have an average of 500 points, and a standard deviation of 100. Standard errors appear in parentheses. Possible scores range from 0 to 1000. Detail may not sum to totals because of rounding.

SOURCE: Organization for Economic Cooperation and Development (OECD), Program for International Student Assessment (PISA), 2003, Learning for Tomorrow's World, 2003. U.S. Department of Education, National Center for Education Statistics, PISA, 2003, International Outcomes of Learning in Mathematics Literacy and Problem Solving, 2003. (This table was prepared March 2005.)

Table 399. Average fourth-grade mathematics scores, by content areas, index of time students spend doing mathematics homework in a normal school week, and country: 2003

Country	Average score by content area						Index of time students spend doing mathematics homework (TMH) in a normal school week					
	Mathematics overall	Number[1]	Patterns and relationships[2]	Measurement[3]	Geometry[4]	Data[5]	High TMH[6]		Medium TMH[7]		Low TMH[8]	
							Percent	Mean score	Percent	Mean score	Percent	Mean score
1	2	3	4	5	6	7	8	9	10	11	12	13
International average	**495** (0.8)	**495** (0.7)	**495** (0.7)	**495** (0.7)	**495** (0.7)	**495** (0.6)	**18** (0.2)	**489** (1.3)	**56** (0.3)	**500** (0.9)	**26** (0.3)	**494** (1.6)
Armenia[9]	456 (3.5)	473 (3.0)	461 (4.1)	465 (3.1)	431 (3.8)	417 (3.6)	33 (1.3)	467 (5.1)	65 (1.3)	465 (3.5)	2 (0.3)	‡ (†)
Australia[10]	499 (3.9)	479 (4.3)	495 (3.7)	514 (3.7)	524 (3.7)	525 (3.6)	7 (0.8)	486 (13.0)	43 (2.1)	500 (4.6)	50 (2.1)	505 (4.4)
Belgium (Flemish)	551 (1.8)	549 (1.9)	542 (1.9)	550 (1.4)	533 (1.8)	548 (2.2)	9 (0.7)	538 (3.9)	48 (1.7)	549 (2.7)	43 (2.0)	557 (2.0)
Chinese Taipei	564 (1.8)	568 (1.8)	555 (2.4)	557 (1.6)	553 (2.5)	564 (2.3)	11 (0.6)	546 (3.5)	62 (1.1)	569 (2.0)	27 (1.2)	561 (2.7)
Cyprus	510 (2.4)	514 (2.7)	519 (2.4)	506 (2.3)	505 (2.3)	509 (2.3)	14 (0.6)	494 (4.6)	76 (0.9)	521 (2.4)	10 (0.6)	497 (5.3)
England[10]	531 (3.7)	519 (4.1)	523 (3.9)	535 (3.3)	542 (3.7)	552 (3.4)	4 (0.6)	489 (14.3)	37 (1.8)	531 (4.8)	59 (1.9)	540 (4.2)
Hong Kong, SAR[10,11]	575 (3.2)	574 (3.3)	568 (3.5)	563 (2.7)	557 (2.9)	562 (2.3)	24 (1.0)	575 (3.8)	71 (0.9)	580 (3.2)	5 (0.5)	530 (5.6)
Hungary	529 (3.1)	524 (2.9)	545 (3.7)	532 (2.7)	514 (3.3)	513 (3.2)	17 (0.9)	515 (4.9)	78 (1.1)	538 (3.1)	5 (0.9)	535 (10.6)
Iran, Islamic Republic of	389 (4.2)	410 (3.7)	394 (3.9)	398 (3.2)	416 (3.9)	356 (4.4)	31 (2.3)	404 (5.1)	52 (1.8)	391 (5.0)	17 (2.3)	376 (8.1)
Italy	503 (3.7)	502 (3.6)	496 (4.3)	504 (3.4)	522 (3.5)	497 (3.0)	24 (1.1)	496 (5.2)	52 (1.1)	504 (4.5)	24 (1.6)	512 (3.6)
Japan	565 (1.6)	556 (2.0)	554 (1.4)	568 (1.6)	559 (1.9)	593 (1.6)	8 (0.6)	543 (4.6)	57 (1.8)	568 (2.3)	35 (2.1)	565 (2.7)
Latvia[12]	536 (2.8)	531 (2.6)	532 (3.4)	545 (2.6)	523 (2.2)	526 (2.7)	25 (1.1)	525 (4.1)	71 (1.1)	546 (2.7)	4 (0.6)	517 (9.1)
Lithuania[12]	534 (2.8)	535 (2.9)	531 (3.0)	540 (2.7)	524 (2.2)	517 (2.5)	29 (1.2)	527 (3.8)	66 (1.3)	545 (3.1)	5 (0.6)	510 (10.7)
Moldova, Republic of	504 (4.9)	507 (4.7)	521 (5.1)	505 (4.0)	501 (4.9)	477 (4.3)	31 (2.0)	518 (6.3)	66 (1.9)	504 (5.4)	3 (0.6)	494 (10.9)
Morocco[13]	347 (5.1)	359 (4.7)	360 (4.7)	345 (5.5)	362 (4.9)	355 (5.0)	22 (1.3)	362 (5.9)	58 (1.9)	365 (4.8)	20 (2.1)	353 (12.3)
Netherlands[10]	540 (2.1)	536 (2.2)	527 (2.4)	545 (2.2)	521 (3.2)	553 (2.4)	1 (0.2)	‡ (†)	10 (0.8)	508 (6.6)	89 (0.9)	546 (1.8)
New Zealand	493 (2.2)	475 (2.3)	495 (2.9)	503 (2.0)	517 (1.8)	522 (2.0)	7 (0.4)	489 (6.7)	41 (1.1)	491 (3.3)	52 (1.3)	504 (3.1)
Norway[14]	451 (2.3)	440 (2.2)	439 (2.7)	475 (2.2)	478 (2.2)	479 (2.3)	12 (1.0)	447 (4.7)	56 (1.8)	462 (3.2)	32 (2.1)	467 (4.0)
Philippines	358 (7.9)	380 (7.4)	382 (7.0)	330 (7.8)	335 (8.8)	384 (7.5)	17 (0.8)	349 (7.0)	52 (1.7)	362 (6.7)	31 (1.9)	372 (15.7)
Russian Federation	532 (4.7)	532 (4.6)	531 (5.0)	538 (3.8)	528 (4.8)	505 (4.1)	38 (1.3)	531 (5.3)	59 (1.2)	537 (4.7)	2 (0.4)	‡ (†)
Scotland[10]	490 (3.3)	475 (3.3)	495 (2.9)	499 (3.1)	511 (2.5)	516 (2.7)	6 (0.8)	477 (6.8)	40 (2.0)	488 (4.2)	54 (2.2)	498 (3.4)
Singapore	594 (5.6)	612 (6.0)	579 (5.4)	566 (4.6)	570 (5.5)	575 (3.9)	40 (1.5)	604 (6.0)	49 (1.3)	595 (5.8)	11 (0.6)	575 (7.2)
Slovenia[10]	479 (2.6)	461 (2.7)	490 (2.7)	497 (2.8)	498 (2.2)	486 (2.7)	14 (0.9)	466 (6.7)	76 (1.2)	490 (2.6)	10 (0.9)	455 (8.6)
Tunisia[13]	339 (4.7)	360 (4.1)	330 (4.7)	308 (5.5)	346 (5.1)	308 (4.7)	22 (2.2)	373 (8.6)	50 (2.8)	365 (6.3)	28 (3.0)	365 (8.0)
United States[10]	518 (2.4)	516 (2.6)	524 (2.7)	500 (2.1)	518 (2.2)	549 (2.0)	12 (0.6)	504 (4.0)	63 (1.3)	524 (2.7)	25 (1.5)	520 (3.5)

†Not applicable.
‡Reporting standards not met.
[1]Topic includes whole numbers; fractions and decimals; integers; and ratio, proportion, and percent.
[2]Topic includes patterns, equations and formulas, and relationships.
[3]Topic includes attributes and units and tools, techniques, and formulas.
[4]Topic includes lines and angles, two- and three-dimensional shapes, congruence and similarity, locations and spatial relationships, and symmetry and transformations.
[5]Topic includes data collection and organization, data representation, and data interpretation.
[6]High level indicates more than 30 minutes of mathematics homework assigned 3-4 times a week.
[7]Medium level indicates more than 30 minutes of mathematics homework assigned no more than twice a week.
[8]Low level indicates no more than 30 minutes of mathematics homework assigned no more than twice a week.

[9]Response rate for the TMH index was at least 70 but less than 85 percent of the students, with missing data having not been explicitly accounted for in the analysis.
[10]Met international guidelines for participation rates only after replacement schools were included.
[11]SAR = Special Administrative Region.
[12]National Desired Population does not cover all of the International Desired Population.
[13]Response rate for the TMH index was at least 50 but less than 70 percent of the students, with missing data having not been explicitly accounted for in the analysis.
[14]Students had received 4 years of formal schooling, but first grade is called "First grade/preschool."
NOTE: TMH index data are provided by students. Data are for fourth-grade students or equivalent in most countries. Possible scores range from 1 to 1,000. Detail may not sum to totals because of rounding. Standard errors appear in parentheses.
SOURCE: International Association for the Evaluation of Educational Achievement (IEA), Trends in International Mathematics and Science Study (TIMSS), 2003, TIMSS 2003 International Mathematics Report, by Ina V.S. Mullis et al. (This table was prepared March 2005.)

Table 400. Average eighth-grade mathematics scores, by content areas, index of time students spend doing mathematics homework in a normal school week, and country: 2003

Country	Average score by content area						Index of time students spend doing mathematics homework (TMH) in a normal school week					
	Mathematics overall	Number[1]	Algebra[2]	Measurement[3]	Geometry[4]	Data[5]	High TMH[6]		Medium TMH[7]		Low TMH[8]	
							Percent	Mean score	Percent	Mean score	Percent	Mean score
1	2	3	4	5	6	7	8	9	10	11	12	13
International average[9]	467 (0.5)	467 (0.5)	467 (0.5)	467 (0.5)	467 (0.5)	467 (0.5)	26 (0.2)	468 (0.8)	54 (0.2)	471 (0.6)	19 (0.2)	456 (1.0)
Armenia	478 (3.0)	473 (3.1)	489 (2.6)	488 (3.3)	481 (3.1)	419 (2.7)	35 (1.3)	490 (3.9)	60 (1.2)	478 (3.7)	4 (0.4)	475 (7.5)
Australia	505 (4.6)	498 (4.6)	499 (4.4)	511 (4.3)	491 (4.8)	531 (3.8)	19 (1.6)	520 (6.0)	50 (1.5)	509 (5.4)	31 (2.0)	497 (5.5)
Bahrain	401 (1.7)	380 (1.9)	411 (2.5)	388 (2.1)	438 (2.1)	414 (2.1)	18 (0.8)	387 (3.3)	69 (1.2)	409 (2.0)	13 (1.1)	398 (4.9)
Belgium (Flemish)	537 (2.8)	539 (2.7)	523 (2.8)	535 (2.5)	527 (3.1)	546 (2.9)	13 (1.1)	542 (4.5)	42 (1.4)	546 (3.2)	44 (2.0)	532 (3.7)
Botswana	366 (2.6)	382 (2.2)	377 (2.7)	377 (2.0)	335 (3.9)	375 (2.7)	25 (0.8)	385 (3.9)	53 (0.8)	368 (2.6)	22 (0.9)	355 (3.0)
Bulgaria	476 (4.3)	477 (4.1)	481 (4.0)	473 (4.6)	484 (4.5)	458 (3.9)	33 (1.8)	482 (6.4)	54 (1.5)	478 (4.6)	14 (1.5)	469 (5.4)
Chile	387 (3.3)	390 (3.1)	384 (3.1)	404 (2.9)	378 (3.3)	412 (3.4)	10 (0.7)	387 (6.9)	43 (1.0)	389 (3.8)	47 (1.4)	388 (3.7)
Chinese Taipei	585 (4.6)	585 (4.6)	585 (4.9)	574 (4.4)	588 (5.1)	568 (3.4)	18 (1.5)	611 (6.0)	45 (1.2)	594 (4.4)	37 (2.0)	563 (5.6)
Cyprus	459 (1.7)	464 (1.5)	455 (1.7)	459 (2.2)	457 (2.4)	458 (1.7)	21 (0.8)	459 (2.8)	70 (0.7)	469 (1.8)	9 (0.6)	438 (5.3)
Egypt	406 (3.5)	421 (3.0)	408 (3.9)	401 (3.3)	408 (3.6)	393 (3.2)	26 (0.8)	402 (4.3)	60 (1.0)	418 (3.6)	14 (0.7)	419 (4.7)
England[10]	‡ (†)	‡ (†)	‡ (†)	‡ (†)	‡ (†)	‡ (†)	‡ (†)	‡ (†)	‡ (†)	‡ (†)	‡ (†)	‡ (†)
Estonia	531 (3.0)	523 (3.1)	528 (2.6)	528 (3.0)	540 (2.6)	535 (2.8)	28 (1.3)	519 (4.0)	66 (1.3)	538 (3.2)	7 (1.2)	523 (10.3)
Ghana	276 (4.7)	289 (5.1)	288 (4.8)	262 (3.7)	278 (4.3)	293 (4.1)	24 (0.9)	288 (5.8)	56 (0.9)	280 (4.5)	20 (1.0)	275 (7.5)
Hong Kong, SAR[11,12]	586 (3.3)	586 (3.2)	580 (3.2)	584 (3.3)	588 (3.6)	566 (3.0)	32 (1.4)	600 (3.5)	49 (1.5)	587 (3.6)	19 (1.5)	566 (7.6)
Hungary	529 (3.2)	529 (3.6)	534 (3.1)	525 (3.1)	515 (3.1)	526 (2.9)	20 (1.2)	516 (5.8)	77 (1.2)	537 (3.1)	3 (0.5)	501 (14.1)
Indonesia[13]	411 (4.8)	421 (4.6)	418 (4.5)	394 (4.9)	413 (4.6)	418 (4.0)	37 (1.1)	435 (4.3)	48 (0.8)	406 (5.3)	15 (0.8)	391 (7.3)
Iran, Islamic Republic of	411 (2.4)	416 (2.3)	412 (3.1)	399 (2.6)	437 (3.1)	404 (2.6)	24 (1.2)	420 (3.8)	52 (0.9)	414 (2.8)	25 (1.1)	403 (3.4)
Israel[14]	496 (3.4)	504 (3.3)	498 (3.2)	480 (3.4)	488 (3.7)	492 (3.3)	33 (1.4)	498 (3.9)	55 (1.3)	505 (4.1)	12 (0.9)	479 (6.3)
Italy	484 (3.2)	480 (3.2)	477 (3.4)	500 (3.2)	469 (3.5)	490 (3.0)	54 (1.4)	484 (3.8)	40 (1.1)	487 (3.6)	7 (0.7)	471 (8.0)
Japan	570 (2.1)	557 (2.3)	568 (2.0)	559 (2.0)	587 (2.1)	573 (1.9)	6 (0.7)	565 (10.1)	36 (1.5)	566 (2.8)	58 (1.9)	576 (2.1)
Jordan	424 (4.1)	413 (4.4)	434 (4.4)	418 (4.4)	446 (4.0)	430 (3.5)	25 (0.8)	425 (4.7)	64 (1.1)	437 (4.1)	11 (0.9)	411 (4.9)
Korea, Republic of[15]	589 (2.2)	586 (2.1)	597 (2.2)	577 (2.0)	598 (2.6)	569 (2.0)	11 (1.0)	582 (4.3)	46 (1.6)	592 (2.6)	43 (2.0)	590 (2.8)
Latvia	508 (3.2)	507 (3.2)	508 (3.2)	500 (3.0)	515 (3.3)	506 (3.8)	33 (1.3)	502 (4.7)	61 (1.3)	516 (3.0)	6 (0.7)	508 (9.3)
Lebanon	433 (3.1)	430 (3.3)	448 (3.1)	430 (3.7)	459 (3.0)	394 (4.0)	42 (1.7)	436 (3.5)	52 (1.7)	437 (3.5)	5 (0.6)	412 (7.6)
Lithuania[13]	502 (2.5)	500 (2.7)	501 (2.4)	492 (3.0)	506 (2.5)	502 (2.5)	32 (1.4)	493 (3.1)	63 (1.3)	509 (3.0)	5 (0.8)	490 (8.7)
Macedonia, Republic of[14]	435 (3.5)	438 (3.5)	442 (3.6)	434 (3.6)	442 (3.7)	419 (3.6)	26 (1.1)	440 (4.5)	61 (1.3)	444 (3.9)	13 (1.3)	439 (6.0)
Malaysia	508 (4.1)	524 (4.0)	495 (3.9)	504 (4.5)	495 (4.8)	505 (3.2)	33 (1.3)	515 (4.4)	56 (1.1)	510 (4.5)	11 (0.8)	485 (5.9)
Moldova	460 (4.0)	463 (3.8)	464 (4.2)	468 (4.0)	463 (4.7)	428 (3.4)	38 (1.4)	472 (4.3)	57 (1.3)	458 (4.6)	5 (0.5)	437 (8.3)
Morocco[13,16,17]	387 (2.5)	384 (2.7)	400 (2.8)	376 (3.4)	415 (2.3)	374 (2.5)	34 (1.5)	390 (4.5)	52 (1.1)	392 (3.2)	14 (1.0)	380 (4.8)
Netherlands[11]	536 (3.8)	539 (3.6)	514 (4.0)	549 (3.7)	513 (4.1)	560 (3.1)	19 (1.3)	540 (5.2)	62 (1.4)	542 (4.4)	19 (1.7)	518 (6.5)
New Zealand	494 (5.3)	481 (6.0)	490 (5.2)	500 (4.8)	488 (4.6)	526 (5.1)	14 (1.1)	488 (5.1)	49 (1.8)	505 (6.0)	37 (2.1)	492 (7.2)
Norway	461 (2.5)	456 (2.3)	428 (2.7)	481 (2.9)	461 (2.8)	498 (2.5)	26 (1.3)	454 (4.0)	52 (1.3)	466 (2.5)	22 (1.3)	472 (3.5)
Palestinian National Authority	390 (3.1)	385 (3.6)	392 (3.5)	386 (2.8)	423 (3.1)	390 (2.8)	27 (1.1)	393 (3.5)	65 (1.1)	398 (3.5)	8 (0.6)	371 (6.6)
Philippines	378 (5.2)	393 (5.1)	400 (5.2)	372 (4.8)	344 (5.3)	390 (4.5)	24 (0.9)	390 (5.4)	54 (1.0)	382 (5.5)	22 (1.2)	361 (6.6)
Romania	475 (4.8)	474 (4.9)	480 (4.7)	485 (4.7)	476 (4.9)	445 (4.6)	68 (1.6)	492 (4.5)	28 (1.4)	451 (6.4)	3 (0.4)	437 (13.0)

See notes at end of table.

Table 400. Average eighth-grade mathematics scores, by content areas, index of time students spend doing mathematics homework in a normal school week, and country: 2003—Continued

Country	Average score by content area						Index of time students spend doing mathematics homework (TMH) in a normal school week					
	Mathematics overall	Number[1]	Algebra[2]	Measurement[3]	Geometry[4]	Data[5]	High TMH[6]		Medium TMH[7]		Low TMH[8]	
							Percent	Mean score	Percent	Mean score	Percent	Mean score
1	2	3	4	5	6	7	8	9	10	11	12	13
Russian Federation	508 (3.7)	505 (4.0)	516 (3.2)	507 (3.9)	515 (4.2)	484 (3.2)	53 (1.2)	509 (4.4)	45 (1.2)	511 (3.4)	2 (0.2)	‡ (†)
Saudi Arabia	332 (4.6)	307 (5.3)	331 (4.7)	338 (3.4)	382 (4.3)	339 (3.8)	15 (1.0)	315 (8.1)	62 (1.6)	335 (4.6)	23 (1.6)	345 (5.7)
Scotland[11]	498 (3.7)	484 (4.2)	488 (3.9)	508 (3.6)	491 (3.3)	531 (3.7)	8 (0.8)	493 (5.8)	46 (2.1)	507 (4.5)	46 (2.5)	496 (4.1)
Serbia[13]	477 (2.6)	477 (2.8)	488 (2.5)	475 (2.5)	471 (3.0)	456 (2.6)	25 (1.3)	466 (4.1)	54 (1.2)	481 (3.5)	20 (1.7)	497 (3.5)
Singapore	605 (3.6)	618 (3.5)	590 (3.5)	611 (3.6)	580 (3.7)	579 (3.2)	38 (1.1)	621 (3.1)	51 (0.9)	604 (3.8)	11 (0.8)	566 (7.8)
Slovak Republic	508 (3.3)	514 (3.3)	505 (3.3)	508 (3.7)	501 (3.6)	495 (2.9)	11 (0.9)	495 (6.4)	81 (1.4)	511 (3.4)	8 (1.3)	500 (7.7)
Slovenia	493 (2.2)	498 (2.0)	487 (2.3)	496 (2.3)	483 (2.5)	494 (2.3)	25 (1.1)	482 (2.9)	71 (1.2)	500 (2.5)	4 (0.8)	463 (8.8)
South Africa	264 (5.5)	274 (5.4)	275 (5.1)	298 (4.7)	247 (5.4)	296 (5.3)	21 (0.8)	275 (8.1)	58 (0.8)	270 (6.3)	20 (1.0)	260 (5.4)
Sweden	499 (2.6)	496 (2.6)	480 (3.0)	512 (2.6)	467 (3.4)	539 (3.0)	4 (0.5)	453 (7.0)	38 (1.4)	494 (3.5)	58 (1.5)	509 (2.7)
Tunisia	410 (2.2)	419 (2.3)	405 (2.4)	407 (2.2)	427 (2.0)	387 (2.2)	39 (1.1)	410 (2.7)	50 (1.1)	414 (2.2)	11 (0.9)	414 (4.3)
United States[16]	504 (3.3)	508 (3.4)	510 (3.1)	495 (3.2)	472 (3.1)	527 (3.2)	31 (1.0)	518 (4.1)	60 (0.9)	506 (3.2)	9 (0.9)	461 (6.3)

†Not applicable.

‡Reporting standards not met.

[1]Topic includes whole numbers; fractions and decimals; integers; and ratio, proportion, and percent.

[2]Topic includes patterns, algebraic expressions, equations and formulas, and relationships.

[3]Topic includes attributes and units and tools, techniques, and formulas.

[4]Topic includes lines and angles, two- and three-dimensional shapes, congruence and similarity, locations and spatial relationships, and symmetry and transformations.

[5]Topic includes data collection and organization, data representation, data interpretation, and uncertainty and probability.

[6]High level indicates more than 30 minutes of mathematics homework assigned 3–4 times a week.

[7]Medium level includes all possible combinations of responses not included in the high or low level categories (see below for details on the low level).

[8]Low level indicates no more than 30 minutes of mathematics homework assigned no more than twice a week.

[9]The international average of 467 may sometimes appear as 466. In that case, the TIMSS 2003 average for eighth-graders published in the National Center for Education Statistics report reflects the deletion of England from the average.

[10]Did not satisfy guidelines for sample participation rates.

[11]Met guidelines for sample participation rates only after replacement schools were included.

[12]SAR = Special Administrative Region.

[13]National Desired Population does not cover all of International Desired Population.

[14]National Defined Population covers less than 90 percent of National Desired Population.

[15]Korea tested the same cohort of students as other countries, but later in 2003, at the beginning of the next school year.

[16]Nearly satisfied guidelines for sample participation rates only after replacement schools were included.

[17]Response rate for the TMH index was at least 70 but less than 85 percent of the students, with missing data having not been explicitly accounted for in the analysis.

NOTE: TMH index data are provided by students. Data are for eighth grade or equivalent in most countries. Possible scores range from 1 to 1,000. Standard errors appear in parentheses. Detail may not sum to totals because of rounding.

SOURCE: International Association for the Evaluation of Educational Achievement (IEA), Trends in International Mathematics and Science Study (TIMSS), 2003, *TIMSS 2003 International Mathematics Report*, by Ina V.S. Mullis et al. (This table was prepared April 2005.)

Table 401. Percentage of lesson time spent on various mathematics activities, yearly mathematics instructional time, and mathematics instructional time as a percentage of total instructional time in eighth grade, by country: 2003

Country	Reviewing homework	Listening to lecture-style presentations	Working problems with teacher's guidance	Working problems on their own without teacher's guidance	Listening to teachers reteach and clarify content/procedures	Taking tests and quizzes	Participating in classroom management tasks not related to the lesson's content/purpose	Other student activities	Students' average yearly mathematics instructional time, in hours	Mathematics instructional time as a percent of total instructional time
1	2	3	4	5	6	7	8	9	10	11
International average	11 (0.1)	19 (0.1)	22 (0.2)	18 (0.2)	11 (0.1)	10 (0.1)	5 (0.1)	4 (0.1)	123 (0.4)	12 (#)
Armenia	10[1] (0.5)	14[1] (0.8)	26[1] (1.1)	19[1] (0.9)	13[1] (0.6)	11[1] (0.6)	4[1] (0.3)	4[1] (0.3)	‡ (†)	‡ (†)
Australia	8 (0.5)	15 (0.8)	23 (1.2)	28 (1.2)	9 (0.4)	7 (0.4)	7 (0.6)	3 (0.4)	136[1] (2.9)	13[1] (0.3)
Bahrain	13 (0.5)	24 (0.9)	17 (0.5)	12 (0.5)	12 (0.3)	13 (0.5)	6 (0.5)	6 (0.3)	142 (0.8)	16 (0.1)
Belgium (Flemish)	7 (0.4)	14 (1.0)	26 (1.0)	20 (0.9)	16 (0.8)	11 (0.4)	4 (0.3)	2 (0.2)	123[2] (2.2)	13 (0.3)
Botswana	13[1] (0.9)	16[1] (1.1)	19[1] (1.1)	21[1] (1.2)	11[1] (0.8)	10[1] (0.7)	6[1] (0.5)	5[1] (0.4)	‡ (†)	‡ (†)
Bulgaria	10 (0.6)	18 (1.3)	26 (1.0)	16 (0.8)	17 (0.9)	8 (0.5)	3 (0.4)	2 (0.3)	96[1] (1.7)	11[1] (0.2)
Chile	10 (0.4)	18 (0.8)	21 (0.9)	18 (0.8)	14 (0.7)	11 (0.5)	6 (0.4)	3 (0.3)	160[1] (4.1)	14[1] (0.4)
Chinese Taipei	12 (0.5)	42 (1.3)	13 (1.3)	7 (0.5)	9 (0.4)	10 (0.4)	4 (0.3)	3 (0.3)	141 (2.0)	13 (0.2)
Cyprus	22[1] (0.4)	16[1] (0.5)	20[1] (0.6)	14[1] (0.4)	12[1] (0.4)	10[1] (0.5)	5[1] (0.2)	2[1] (0.2)	75[2] (0.4)	8 (0.1)
Egypt	11 (0.4)	18 (1.0)	17 (0.8)	15 (0.7)	15 (0.8)	11 (0.4)	6 (0.3)	7 (0.4)	‡ (†)	‡ (†)
England[3]	‡[2] (†)	‡[2] (†)	‡[2] (†)	‡[2] (†)	‡[2] (†)	‡[2] (†)	‡[2] (†)	‡[2] (†)	‡ (†)	‡ (†)
Estonia	10 (0.4)	12 (0.6)	25 (1.0)	25 (0.8)	11 (0.5)	13 (0.6)	3 (0.3)	2 (0.3)	125 (1.2)	12 (0.2)
Ghana	11[1] (0.4)	16[1] (0.9)	20[1] (0.8)	18[1] (0.7)	12[1] (0.7)	12[1] (0.4)	7[1] (0.4)	6[1] (0.3)	‡ (†)	‡ (†)
Hong Kong, SAR[4,5]	8 (0.4)	36 (1.5)	18 (0.7)	16 (0.8)	9 (0.7)	6 (0.3)	4 (0.5)	4 (0.4)	145[2] (5.2)	15 (0.5)
Hungary	12 (0.4)	13 (0.7)	25 (0.9)	25 (1.0)	10 (0.4)	10 (0.4)	3 (0.3)	3 (0.3)	112[2] (2.0)	11 (0.2)
Indonesia[6]	12[1] (0.5)	25[1] (1.1)	20[1] (0.9)	14[1] (0.9)	12[1] (0.5)	12[1] (0.7)	3[1] (0.4)	3[1] (0.5)	169[2] (4.4)	13 (0.4)
Iran, Islamic Republic of	12 (0.6)	17 (0.8)	18 (0.7)	14 (0.7)	15 (0.7)	11 (0.5)	6 (0.3)	6 (0.6)	115[2] (3.5)	12 (0.4)
Israel[7]	14[1] (0.6)	15[1] (0.8)	22[1] (0.7)	21[1] (0.8)	11[1] (0.4)	10[1] (0.5)	5[1] (0.5)	3[1] (0.3)	‡ (†)	‡ (†)
Italy	15 (0.6)	22 (0.6)	19 (0.6)	13 (0.6)	13 (0.4)	11 (0.5)	4 (0.3)	2 (0.3)	132[1] (1.7)	13[1] (0.2)
Japan	7 (0.6)	29 (1.3)	28 (1.1)	11 (1.0)	15 (0.9)	6 (0.4)	2 (0.2)	2 (0.4)	107 (2.6)	10 (0.2)
Jordan	15 (0.7)	23 (1.0)	17 (0.8)	13 (0.8)	11 (0.5)	9 (0.4)	6 (0.4)	6 (0.5)	110 (0.9)	12 (0.2)
Korea, Republic of[8]	6[2] (0.3)	30[2] (1.2)	19[2] (0.6)	20[2] (0.7)	9[2] (0.4)	8[2] (0.4)	5[2] (0.3)	3[2] (0.5)	109[2] (1.2)	9 (0.1)
Latvia	8[1] (0.6)	12[1] (0.7)	25[1] (1.1)	22[1] (0.9)	11[1] (0.6)	15[1] (0.7)	2[1] (0.2)	4[1] (0.4)	122[2] (1.4)	13 (0.3)
Lebanon	24[2] (1.6)	17[2] (0.9)	23[2] (1.1)	8[2] (0.8)	10[2] (0.6)	11[2] (0.6)	4[2] (0.4)	4[2] (0.4)	‡ (†)	‡ (†)
Lithuania[6]	9 (0.5)	7 (0.6)	30 (1.2)	26 (0.9)	11 (0.7)	14 (0.6)	1 (0.2)	2 (0.2)	121[1] (0.9)	11[1] (0.2)
Macedonia, Republic of[7]	7 (0.3)	37 (1.1)	19 (0.7)	15 (0.7)	6 (0.4)	8 (0.3)	3 (0.3)	4 (0.3)	80[1] (1.2)	9[1] (0.1)
Malaysia	13 (0.7)	21 (1.0)	21 (0.9)	16 (0.8)	9 (0.5)	8 (0.4)	6 (0.4)	6 (0.4)	120 (1.4)	12 (0.1)
Moldova	9[2] (0.6)	15[2] (1.0)	23[2] (1.0)	18[2] (0.9)	11[2] (0.8)	14[2] (0.8)	4[2] (0.7)	5[2] (0.6)	‡ (†)	‡ (†)
Morocco[6,9]	‡ (†)	‡ (†)	‡ (†)	‡ (†)	‡ (†)	‡ (†)	‡ (†)	‡ (†)	‡ (†)	‡ (†)
Netherlands[4]	15 (1.1)	13 (0.7)	21 (2.0)	28 (2.5)	7 (0.5)	8 (0.5)	5 (0.5)	4 (0.4)	94[2] (1.4)	9 (0.1)
New Zealand	7 (0.4)	17 (0.8)	24 (1.1)	23 (1.3)	9 (0.4)	8 (0.4)	7 (0.5)	4 (0.5)	136 (1.7)	14 (0.2)
Norway	8 (0.4)	19 (0.6)	26 (1.2)	25 (1.5)	10 (0.4)	6 (0.3)	4 (0.3)	3 (0.4)	114 (2.3)	13 (0.3)
Palestinian National Authority	13[1] (0.6)	23[1] (1.0)	18[1] (0.8)	16[1] (0.9)	11[1] (0.5)	9[1] (0.3)	6[1] (0.3)	6[1] (0.4)	127[1] (2.3)	14 (0.3)
Philippines	9[1] (0.4)	20[1] (0.9)	16[1] (0.8)	15[1] (1.0)	11[1] (0.5)	16[1] (0.7)	7[1] (0.3)	6[1] (0.4)	193 (3.6)	17 (0.4)
Romania	9 (0.4)	24 (0.8)	29 (1.0)	15 (0.7)	10 (0.4)	9 (0.5)	3 (0.3)	2 (0.2)	120[1] (2.1)	13[1] (0.3)
Russian Federation	11 (0.2)	20 (0.7)	20 (0.7)	18 (0.7)	8 (0.4)	18 (0.5)	1 (0.2)	3 (0.3)	128[1] (2.1)	15[1] (0.3)
Saudi Arabia	15[1] (1.0)	16[1] (1.6)	13[1] (1.0)	8[1] (0.7)	23[1] (2.2)	12[1] (1.0)	6[1] (0.4)	7[1] (0.8)	110[2] (1.0)	11 (0.2)
Scotland[4]	8[1] (0.3)	22[1] (0.7)	26[1] (1.3)	22[1] (1.5)	8[1] (0.5)	4[1] (0.3)	6[1] (0.5)	3[1] (0.5)	142[2] (2.2)	14 (0.2)
Serbia[6]	7 (0.4)	25 (1.4)	23 (1.2)	20 (1.2)	9 (0.5)	7 (0.4)	3 (0.3)	5 (0.5)	107[2] (1.5)	13 (0.2)
Singapore	11 (0.4)	27 (0.7)	19 (0.6)	15 (0.5)	9 (0.3)	8 (0.3)	6 (0.4)	4 (0.4)	114 (1.6)	13 (0.2)

See notes at end of table.

Table 401. Percentage of lesson time spent on various mathematics activities, yearly mathematics instructional time, and mathematics instructional time as a percentage of total instructional time in eighth grade, by country: 2003—Continued

Country	Percentage of time in mathematics lessons students spend on various activities in a typical week								Students' average yearly mathematics instructional time, in hours	Mathematics instructional time as a percent of total instructional time
	Reviewing homework	Listening to lecture-style presentations	Working problems with teacher's guidance	Working problems on their own without teacher's guidance	Listening to teachers reteach and clarify content/procedures	Taking tests and quizzes	Participating in classroom management tasks not related to the lesson's content/purpose	Other student activities		
1	2	3	4	5	6	7	8	9	10	11
Slovak Republic..........	8 (0.3)	17 (0.7)	27 (0.9)	17 (0.7)	13 (0.5)	12 (0.4)	3 (0.3)	3 (0.3)	126[1] (1.9)	14[1] (0.3)
Slovenia..........	11 (0.4)	21 (0.8)	24 (0.7)	22 (0.9)	10 (0.6)	6 (0.3)	2 (0.2)	4 (0.4)	116 (1.3)	11 (0.1)
South Africa..........	15[2] (0.9)	13[2] (0.7)	19[2] (0.9)	18[2] (0.9)	11[2] (0.6)	12[2] (0.6)	7[2] (0.4)	5[2] (0.4)	‡ (†)	‡ (†)
Sweden..........	4 (0.4)	11 (0.6)	37 (1.8)	28 (1.8)	9 (0.3)	6 (0.3)	3 (0.3)	3 (0.4)	91[1] (1.6)	10[1] (0.2)
Tunisia..........	18[1] (0.9)	14[1] (1.0)	17[1] (0.9)	18[1] (0.9)	14[1] (0.8)	13[1] (0.7)	4[1] (0.4)	4[1] (0.5)	‡ (†)	‡ (†)
United States[5]..........	13 (0.5)	18 (0.7)	21 (0.6)	18 (0.6)	11 (0.3)	11 (0.4)	5 (0.3)	4 (0.4)	135[2] (2.2)	13 (0.2)

†Not applicable.

#Rounds to zero.

‡Reporting standards not met.

[1]Data available for at least 70 but less than 85 percent of students, with missing data having not been explicitly accounted for in the analysis.

[2]Data available for at least 50 but less than 70 percent of students, with missing data having not been explicitly accounted for in the analysis.

[3]Did not satisfy guidelines for sample participation rates.

[4]Met guidelines for sample participation rates only after replacement schools were included.

[5]SAR = Special Administrative Region.

[6]National Desired Population does not cover all of International Desired Population.

[7]National Defined Population covers less than 90 percent of National Desired Population.

[8]Korea tested the same cohort of students as other countries, but later in 2003, at the beginning of the next school year.

[9]Nearly satisfied guidelines for sample participation rates only after replacement schools were included.

NOTE: Percentage of time in mathematics lessons students spend on various activities in a typical week provided by teachers. Mathematics instructional time provided by teachers and total instructional time provided by schools. Data are for eighth grade or equivalent in most countries. Detail may not sum to totals because of rounding. Standard errors appear in parentheses.

SOURCE: International Association for the Evaluation of Educational Achievement (IEA), Trends in International Mathematics and Science Study (TIMSS), 2003, *TIMSS 2003 International Mathematics Report*, by Ina V.S. Mullis et al. (This table was prepared April 2005.)

Table 402. Average size and scores of eighth-grade mathematics classes and Index of Teachers' Emphasis on Mathematics Homework (EMH), by country: 2003

Country	Overall average class size	Percentage distribution and mean scores of mathematics classes, by average class size								Index of Teachers' Emphasis on Mathematics Homework (EMH)[1]					
		1 to 24 students		25 to 32 students		33 to 40 students		41 or more students		High EMH[2]		Medium EMH[3]		Low EMH[4]	
		Percent	Mean score	Percent	Mean score	Percent	Mean score	Percent	Mean score	Percent	Mean score	Percent	Mean score	Percent	Mean score
1	2	3	4	5	6	7	8	9	10	11	12	13	14	15	16
International average	30 (0.1)	29 (0.5)	461 (1.9)	35 (0.5)	473 (1.4)	24 (0.5)	470 (2.1)	13 (0.3)	448 (1.7)	30 (0.5)	473 (1.4)	51 (0.6)	469 (0.9)	19 (0.4)	453 (1.7)
Armenia	27[5] (†)	39 (4.4)	474 (5.6)	43 (4.3)	485 (5.0)	7 (1.8)	460 (9.9)	11 (2.8)	462 (8.4)	65[6] (4.6)	481 (4.2)	31 (4.7)	474 (6.6)	4 (2.1)	467 (11.5)
Australia	26 (0.5)	31 (4.2)	482 (9.4)	65 (4.7)	518 (5.9)	4 (2.2)	492 (14.2)	# (#)	‡ (†)	10 (3.0)	544 (19.7)	56 (4.1)	518 (5.9)	34 (3.8)	475 (9.5)
Bahrain	32 (0.1)	6 (0.7)	451 (5.8)	52 (2.7)	402 (2.1)	40 (2.6)	395 (3.5)	3 (#)	412 (3.8)	15 (2.5)	389 (6.1)	72 (3.7)	404 (2.3)	14 (3.1)	396 (8.7)
Belgium (Flemish)	20 (0.3)	90 (2.3)	538 (3.3)	10 (2.3)	553 (10.5)	# (†)	‡ (†)	# (†)	‡ (†)	9 (2.5)	555 (6.5)	30 (3.8)	555 (5.8)	60 (3.9)	529 (5.6)
Botswana	37 (0.4)	1 (0.7)	‡ (†)	14 (2.6)	392 (9.1)	60 (4.3)	360 (3.7)	25 (4.1)	362 (4.1)	44 (4.6)	364 (4.0)	49 (4.5)	368 (4.0)	7 (2.5)	379 (7.0)
Bulgaria	22 (0.5)	64 (4.2)	468 (4.9)	32 (3.9)	503 (8.0)	3 (2.4)	423 (5.0)	1 (#)	‡ (†)	53 (4.2)	483 (6.1)	38 (4.2)	467 (7.7)	9 (2.5)	469 (15.6)
Chile	35 (0.4)	9 (1.5)	385 (17.0)	22 (2.6)	384 (8.1)	47 (3.6)	390 (5.7)	23 (3.6)	389 (6.9)	10 (2.2)	401 (14.9)	49 (3.6)	388 (5.1)	40 (3.3)	383 (5.5)
Chinese Taipei	37 (0.4)	4 (1.5)	598 (28.9)	14 (2.8)	567 (11.5)	65 (4.0)	575 (4.7)	17 (3.2)	636 (8.7)	29 (3.9)	602 (8.6)	39 (3.9)	588 (6.3)	32 (3.9)	570 (7.6)
Cyprus	26 (0.1)	21 (1.9)	463 (3.2)	79 (1.9)	460 (2.0)	# (†)	‡ (†)	# (†)	‡ (†)	35 (3.1)	455 (3.2)	65 (3.1)	462 (2.3)	# (†)	‡ (†)
Egypt	38 (0.6)	3 (1.2)	422 (13.8)	9 (2.1)	428 (11.3)	61 (4.1)	403 (4.3)	27 (3.7)	407 (7.5)	23 (3.3)	401 (8.6)	57 (3.8)	409 (4.8)	20 (3.2)	406 (8.1)
England[7]	‡[8] (†)	‡ (†)	‡ (†)	‡ (†)	‡ (†)	‡ (†)	‡ (†)	‡ (†)	‡ (†)	‡[6] (†)	‡ (†)	‡ (†)	‡ (†)	‡ (†)	‡ (†)
Estonia	27 (0.5)	32 (3.4)	523 (5.1)	41 (4.2)	530 (4.3)	27 (3.8)	550 (5.4)	# (†)	‡ (†)	12 (2.3)	540 (9.9)	78 (3.2)	532 (3.3)	9 (2.5)	518 (14.1)
Ghana	37[5] (1.0)	16 (2.7)	232 (7.4)	18 (3.1)	249 (8.9)	29 (4.0)	292 (9.0)	37 (4.7)	289 (9.1)	48 (5.0)	271 (7.9)	37 (5.0)	275 (7.1)	15 (3.0)	284 (10.2)
Hong Kong, SAR[9,10]	39 (0.3)	3 (1.1)	504 (28.1)	6 (1.6)	513 (21.3)	49 (4.1)	575 (5.7)	43 (4.1)	612 (4.7)	26 (3.7)	598 (6.0)	50 (4.6)	593 (6.0)	24 (4.0)	566 (10.0)
Hungary	22 (0.4)	64 (3.9)	522 (4.2)	35 (4.0)	540 (6.5)	2 (0.9)	‡ (†)	# (†)	‡ (†)	8 (2.0)	532 (8.9)	90 (2.2)	530 (3.5)	2 (0.9)	‡ (†)
Indonesia[11]	40 (0.5)	3 (1.7)	413 (8.6)	10 (2.8)	366 (20.0)	38 (4.1)	413 (8.3)	48 (4.3)	421 (6.7)	45 (3.9)	421 (7.4)	45 (4.4)	402 (9.4)	10 (2.6)	412 (15.3)
Iran, Islamic Republic of	29 (0.4)	23 (2.9)	397 (5.7)	50 (4.0)	413 (4.5)	25 (3.3)	420 (6.0)	3 (1.4)	431 (13.7)	63 (4.4)	417 (3.2)	26 (4.0)	406 (7.2)	12 (2.8)	399 (9.3)
Israel[12]	34[5] (0.4)	9 (2.2)	512 (18.3)	23 (3.7)	500 (9.2)	64 (4.5)	490 (4.9)	4 (1.7)	531 (4.5)	50 (3.8)	501 (5.4)	44 (4.1)	500 (6.1)	6 (1.7)	438 (17.8)
Italy	22 (0.3)	78 (3.1)	483 (3.4)	22 (3.1)	488 (8.3)	# (†)	‡ (†)	# (†)	‡ (†)	71 (3.6)	482 (3.2)	25 (3.2)	489 (8.4)	4 (1.5)	480 (11.2)
Japan	35 (0.3)	3 (1.2)	561 (6.1)	18 (2.6)	557 (4.5)	78 (2.6)	571 (2.7)	1 (1.0)	‡ (†)	7 (2.2)	583 (23.4)	29 (3.8)	573 (6.9)	64 (3.9)	567 (2.5)
Jordan	35 (0.7)	14 (2.8)	430 (9.4)	26 (3.6)	424 (13.3)	32 (4.4)	417 (5.9)	28 (3.8)	428 (7.4)	30 (3.8)	422 (5.5)	55 (4.4)	430 (6.3)	14 (2.8)	410 (8.6)
Korea, Republic of[13]	37[8] (0.4)	1 (0.9)	‡ (†)	20 (3.0)	569 (4.6)	57 (4.6)	594 (2.9)	22 (3.5)	600 (7.0)	9[14] (2.1)	582 (10.8)	31 (3.6)	589 (4.7)	60 (3.5)	591 (3.5)
Latvia	24 (0.7)	52 (3.5)	497 (4.4)	42 (3.4)	519 (5.5)	3 (1.0)	527 (20.3)	3 (1.7)	506 (12.6)	17 (2.9)	523 (8.8)	75 (3.8)	505 (3.5)	9 (2.6)	500 (11.7)
Lebanon	29 (0.9)	32 (3.9)	429 (6.0)	44 (4.8)	429 (5.1)	16 (3.1)	443 (10.4)	8 (3.1)	464 (8.7)	49 (4.6)	433 (4.6)	45 (4.4)	436 (5.8)	6 (1.9)	401 (13.1)
Lithuania[12]	25 (0.3)	39 (3.2)	486 (4.2)	61 (3.2)	510 (3.0)	# (†)	‡ (†)	# (†)	‡ (†)	13 (2.7)	512 (7.7)	76 (3.6)	501 (3.4)	11 (2.6)	477 (11.3)
Macedonia, Republic of[12]	28 (0.4)	24 (3.5)	439 (9.2)	58 (4.3)	435 (5.9)	17 (3.6)	429 (13.7)	1 (1.0)	‡ (†)	22 (3.3)	450 (8.1)	66 (3.9)	428 (5.2)	12 (2.6)	432 (13.8)
Malaysia	37 (0.3)	1 (0.7)	‡ (†)	18 (3.3)	514 (11.0)	56 (4.4)	503 (5.1)	25 (3.5)	515 (8.8)	60 (4.5)	508 (5.0)	34 (4.2)	515 (8.5)	5 (1.9)	466 (10.1)
Moldova[11,15]	24[5] (0.5)	56 (4.5)	449 (6.0)	38 (4.6)	460 (7.0)	5 (2.5)	485 (25.2)	1 (0.6)	‡ (†)	43[6] (4.8)	451 (6.1)	52 (5.0)	463 (7.9)	5 (1.9)	468 (10.1)
Morocco[11,15]	‡ (†)	‡ (†)	‡ (†)	‡ (†)	‡ (†)	‡ (†)	‡ (†)	‡ (†)	‡ (†)	54[14] (6.2)	391 (5.9)	37 (6.4)	383 (5.2)	9 (4.1)	389 (11.1)
Netherlands[9]	26 (0.3)	33 (3.9)	514 (9.4)	66 (4.1)	546 (5.8)	1 (1.0)	534 (34.7)	# (†)	‡ (†)	7 (2.4)	550 (15.3)	82 (3.7)	541 (4.9)	11 (3.1)	495 (14.1)
New Zealand	27 (0.4)	22 (3.0)	469 (8.9)	72 (4.1)	500 (5.7)	6 (3.2)	538 (17.8)	# (†)	‡ (†)	7 (2.1)	479 (15.6)	67 (4.1)	510 (6.6)	25 (4.2)	471 (5.3)
Norway	25 (0.3)	34 (3.8)	467 (4.3)	65 (3.6)	460 (3.5)	1 (0.7)	‡ (†)	1 (0.7)	‡ (†)	25 (3.4)	460 (6.5)	46 (4.3)	465 (3.8)	29 (4.3)	455 (5.0)
Palestinian National Authority	39 (0.6)	6 (2.0)	398 (20.0)	17 (2.8)	393 (7.4)	27 (3.9)	394 (8.9)	50 (3.7)	385 (4.2)	30 (4.0)	389 (6.4)	58 (4.3)	391 (4.6)	12 (2.5)	388 (14.9)
Philippines	54 (0.7)	1 (0.6)	‡ (†)	1 (0.7)	‡ (†)	7 (2.0)	448 (23.4)	91 (2.1)	372 (5.4)	24 (4.0)	358 (10.9)	61 (4.8)	384 (7.1)	15 (3.7)	377 (19.1)
Romania	24 (0.5)	51 (4.5)	469 (6.7)	46 (4.5)	480 (7.4)	3 (1.4)	534 (34.7)	1 (#)	‡ (†)	78 (3.3)	478 (5.5)	21 (3.3)	463 (10.1)	1 (0.7)	‡ (†)
Russian Federation	24 (0.6)	47 (4.2)	500 (5.1)	47 (3.6)	515 (5.0)	6 (3.4)	533 (11.0)	# (†)	‡ (†)	56 (3.5)	514 (4.3)	43 (3.5)	499 (4.7)	1 (0.5)	‡ (†)
Saudi Arabia	28 (0.9)	36 (5.3)	333 (7.5)	26 (4.8)	340 (8.1)	29 (5.8)	330 (10.1)	8 (3.0)	325 (4.1)	14 (3.0)	331 (8.9)	69 (3.9)	332 (4.6)	17 (3.0)	346 (15.0)
Scotland[9]	27[5] (0.5)	33 (3.9)	457 (7.2)	56 (4.4)	520 (6.2)	11 (3.4)	548 (10.1)	1 (0.7)	‡ (†)	3 (1.7)	549 (10.6)	45 (4.6)	527 (5.7)	51 (4.5)	477 (6.2)
Serbia[11]	26 (0.4)	38 (3.7)	464 (4.4)	51 (4.0)	483 (3.8)	11 (2.9)	489 (8.2)	# (†)	‡ (†)	34 (4.1)	474 (4.9)	45 (4.3)	481 (4.5)	22 (3.7)	470 (5.6)
Singapore	38 (0.2)	2 (0.6)	‡ (†)	8 (1.6)	613 (18.0)	63 (2.7)	606 (5.0)	26 (2.5)	607 (5.7)	59 (2.4)	620 (4.2)	33 (2.5)	592 (6.6)	8 (1.3)	563 (13.1)

See notes at end of table.

Table 402. Average size and scores of eighth-grade mathematics classes and Index of Teachers' Emphasis on Mathematics Homework (EMH), by country: 2003—Continued

Country	Overall average class size		Percentage distribution and mean scores of mathematics classes, by average class size								Index of Teachers' Emphasis on Mathematics Homework (EMH)[1]					
			1 to 24 students		25 to 32 students		33 to 40 students		41 or more students		High EMH[2]		Medium EMH[3]		Low EMH[4]	
			Percent	Mean score	Percent	Mean score	Percent	Mean score	Percent	Mean score	Percent	Mean score	Percent	Mean score	Percent	Mean score
1	2		3	4	5	6	7	8	9	10	11	12	13	14	15	16
Slovak Republic	25	(0.4)	42 (4.6)	498 (4.7)	53 (4.7)	512 (5.4)	5 (1.8)	543 (19.7)	# (†)	‡ (†)	5 (1.5)	510 (12.4)	79 (2.9)	511 (4.0)	16 (2.7)	492 (6.3)
Slovenia	22	(0.3)	70 (4.1)	491 (3.0)	30 (4.1)	500 (4.1)	# (†)	‡ (†)	# (†)	‡ (†)	13 (2.9)	490 (9.2)	85 (3.1)	495 (2.5)	3 (1.0)	473 (9.7)
South Africa	45 [8]	(1.3)	4 (1.2)	309 (35.8)	14 (3.0)	290 (23.8)	30 (3.7)	265 (11.7)	52 (4.1)	249 (8.7)	26 [6] (3.4)	266 (9.2)	54 (3.9)	267 (9.6)	20 (3.3)	250 (9.1)
Sweden	21	(0.4)	71 (3.6)	491 (3.3)	27 (3.7)	522 (5.5)	1 (1.0)	‡ (†)	# (†)	‡ (†)	17 (2.8)	503 (7.0)	25 (3.2)	506 (6.0)	59 (3.7)	494 (4.0)
Tunisia	34	(0.3)	1 (1.0)	‡ (†)	26 (3.3)	404 (3.6)	71 (3.5)	412 (3.2)	2 (1.1)	‡ (†)	12 (2.5)	423 (9.1)	84 (3.0)	407 (2.2)	4 (1.6)	442 (11.3)
United States[15]	24 [5]	(0.4)	56 (2.9)	504 (3.9)	39 (2.7)	510 (5.1)	4 (1.2)	531 (16.4)	1 (0.7)	‡ (†)	27 (2.5)	531 (8.0)	62 (2.9)	504 (3.8)	11 (2.2)	471 (9.5)

†Not applicable.

#Rounds to zero.

‡Reporting standards not met.

[1]Index based on teachers' responses to two questions about how often they usually assign mathematics homework and how many minutes of mathematics homework they usually assign.

[2]High EMH indicates the assignment of more than 30 minutes of homework in about half of the lessons or more.

[3]Medium level includes all possible combinations of responses not included in the high or low level categories (see below for details on the low level).

[4]Low level indicates no assignment or the assignment of less than 30 minutes of homework in about half the lessons or less.

[5]Class size data available for at least 70 but less than 85 percent of students, with missing data having not been explicitly accounted for in the analysis.

[6]EMH data available for at least 70 but less than 85 percent of students, with missing data having not been explicitly accounted for in the analysis.

[7]Did not satisfy guidelines for sample participation rates.

[8]Class size data available for at least 50 but less than 70 percent of students, with missing data having not been explicitly accounted for in the analysis.

[9]Met guidelines for sample participation rates only after replacement schools were included.

[10]SAR = Special Administrative Region.

[11]National Desired Population does not cover all of International Desired Population.

[12]National Defined Population covers less than 90 percent of National Desired Population.

[13]Korea tested the same cohort of students as other countries, but later in 2003, at the beginning of the next school year.

[14]EMH data available for at least 50 but less than 70 percent of students, with missing data having not been explicitly accounted for in the analysis.

[15]Nearly satisfied guidelines for sample participation rates only after replacement schools were included.

NOTE: Background data provided by teachers. Data are for 8th grade or equivalent in most countries. Possible scores range from 0 to 1000. Detail may not sum to totals because of rounding. Standard errors appear in parentheses.

SOURCE: International Association for the Evaluation of Educational Achievement (IEA), Trends in International Mathematics and Science Study (TIMSS), 2003, *TIMSS 2003 International Mathematics Report*, by Ina V. S. Mullis et al. (This table was prepared April 2005.)

Table 403. Eighth-grade students' perceptions about mathematics and hours spent on leisure activities, by country: 2003

Country	Index of students' self-confidence in learning mathematics (SCM)[1]						Average hours spent each day[2]							
	High SCM		Medium SCM		Low SCM		Watching TV or videos	Playing computer games	Playing or talking with friends	Doing jobs at home	Playing sports	Reading for enjoyment	Using the Internet	Working at a paid job
	Percent	Mean score	Percent	Mean score	Percent	Mean score								
1	2	3	4	5	6	7	8	9	10	11	12	13	14	15
Armenia	41 (1.1)	505 (4.0)	40 (1.0)	468 (3.7)	19 (0.9)	462 (4.1)	1.8 (0.03)	‡ (†)	‡ (†)	‡ (†)	‡ (†)	‡ (†)	‡ (†)	‡ (†)
Australia	50 (1.7)	542 (4.5)	31 (1.1)	483 (3.7)	19 (1.2)	451 (6.4)	2.0 (0.03)	0.9 (0.02)	1.7 (0.04)	1.0 (0.02)	1.6 (0.03)	0.7 (0.02)	1.3 (0.03)	0.4 (0.03)
Bahrain	44 (0.9)	437 (2.0)	38 (0.9)	379 (2.4)	18 (0.6)	366 (3.2)	2.0 (0.03)	1.2 (0.02)	1.6 (0.04)	1.2 (0.02)	1.5 (0.03)	0.9 (0.02)	1.4 (0.03)	0.6 (0.02)
Belgium (Flemish)	45 (0.9)	556 (3.2)	30 (0.7)	526 (3.0)	25 (0.8)	518 (3.5)	2.1 (0.03)	1.0 (0.02)	1.9 (0.03)	0.9 (0.02)	1.6 (0.02)	0.5 (0.01)	1.3 (0.03)	0.2 (0.02)
Botswana	38 (0.9)	390 (2.8)	45 (0.8)	361 (2.5)	17 (0.8)	352 (3.4)	1.4 (0.03)	0.5 (0.02)	2.1 (0.04)	2.3 (0.03)	1.5 (0.02)	1.8 (0.03)	0.7 (0.02)	0.6 (0.03)
Bulgaria	33 (1.3)	519 (5.5)	39 (1.4)	467 (4.2)	28 (1.2)	445 (4.8)	2.5 (0.04)	1.1 (0.04)	2.6 (0.05)	1.5 (0.03)	1.2 (0.04)	0.7 (0.03)	1.0 (0.04)	0.3 (0.02)
Chile	35 (0.9)	427 (3.9)	42 (0.7)	369 (3.4)	23 (0.7)	361 (3.9)	2.2 (0.02)	0.7 (0.04)	2.3 (0.02)	1.5 (0.02)	1.8 (0.03)	0.6 (0.01)	0.7 (0.02)	0.3 (0.01)
Chinese Taipei	26 (1.0)	661 (4.1)	30 (0.7)	593 (5.1)	44 (1.1)	534 (4.0)	1.7 (0.03)	1.4 (0.04)	1.4 (0.03)	0.7 (0.01)	1.0 (0.02)	1.0 (0.02)	1.4 (0.04)	0.2 (0.01)
Cyprus	46 (0.8)	503 (2.0)	32 (0.8)	437 (2.2)	22 (0.7)	407 (3.6)	2.1 (0.03)	1.3 (0.02)	2.1 (0.03)	1.0 (0.03)	1.7 (0.03)	0.9 (0.02)	1.2 (0.02)	0.6 (0.02)
Egypt	58 (1.0)	437 (3.3)	35 (0.9)	383 (3.7)	7 (0.4)	374 (5.3)	0.8 (0.02)	0.7 (0.02)	0.8 (0.02)	1.3 (0.03)	1.1 (0.03)	1.0 (0.02)	0.6 (0.02)	0.6 (0.02)
England[3]	41 (0.9)	569 (3.2)	32 (0.7)	520 (3.1)	28 (0.8)	489 (3.5)	‡ (†)	‡ (†)	‡ (†)	‡ (†)	‡ (†)	‡ (†)	‡ (†)	‡ (†)
Estonia	— (†)	— (†)	— (†)	— (†)	— (†)	— (†)	2.3 (0.03)	1.1 (0.03)	2.8 (0.03)	1.1 (0.02)	1.4 (0.03)	1.7 (0.02)	1.5 (0.04)	0.4 (0.02)
Ghana	30 (0.9)	627 (2.9)	38 (0.7)	581 (4.1)	33 (0.9)	556 (4.0)	0.7 (0.02)	0.6 (0.02)	1.2 (0.03)	1.5 (0.03)	1.3 (0.02)	1.7 (0.03)	0.8 (0.03)	0.8 (0.03)
Hong Kong, SAR[4]	44 (1.0)	574 (3.3)	32 (1.0)	507 (3.9)	24 (0.8)	479 (3.9)	2.3 (0.03)	2.0 (0.04)	1.6 (0.03)	0.7 (0.01)	1.0 (0.03)	2.0 (0.03)	2.0 (0.03)	0.1 (0.01)
Hungary	44 (1.0)	574 (3.3)	32 (1.0)	507 (3.9)	24 (0.8)	479 (3.9)	2.1 (0.03)	1.1 (0.02)	2.2 (0.03)	1.1 (0.02)	1.5 (0.03)	0.8 (0.02)	0.6 (0.03)	0.2 (0.02)
Indonesia	27 (1.1)	420 (6.6)	59 (0.8)	408 (4.5)	15 (0.9)	416 (4.7)	1.5 (0.03)	0.5 (0.02)	1.3 (0.03)	2.2 (0.03)	1.1 (0.02)	1.1 (0.02)	0.3 (0.02)	0.8 (0.03)
Iran, Islamic Republic of	35 (0.9)	447 (3.5)	49 (0.8)	399 (2.6)	16 (0.7)	377 (3.4)	1.6 (0.03)	0.4 (0.02)	1.4 (0.03)	1.5 (0.03)	1.4 (0.04)	1.0 (0.02)	0.2 (0.02)	0.7 (0.05)
Israel	59 (1.2)	526 (3.5)	30 (0.9)	461 (3.8)	11 (0.7)	451 (5.7)	2.5 (0.03)	1.9 (0.03)	2.3 (0.03)	1.4 (0.03)	1.6 (0.03)	0.9 (0.04)	1.8 (0.04)	0.6 (0.02)
Italy	46 (0.9)	521 (3.3)	29 (0.8)	466 (3.6)	25 (1.0)	439 (3.4)	1.8 (0.03)	1.0 (0.02)	2.6 (0.03)	1.1 (0.03)	1.8 (0.03)	0.7 (0.02)	0.6 (0.02)	0.9 (0.03)
Japan	17 (0.6)	634 (3.1)	38 (0.7)	580 (2.7)	45 (0.8)	538 (2.3)	2.7 (0.03)	0.9 (0.02)	1.6 (0.04)	0.6 (0.01)	1.3 (0.03)	0.9 (0.02)	0.6 (0.02)	0.1 (0.01)
Jordan	49 (1.2)	463 (4.7)	38 (1.0)	400 (3.7)	13 (0.7)	390 (4.4)	1.5 (0.03)	0.9 (0.03)	1.2 (0.03)	1.3 (0.03)	1.2 (0.03)	0.9 (0.02)	0.6 (0.03)	0.6 (0.03)
Korea, Republic of[5]	30 (0.7)	650 (2.8)	36 (0.6)	592 (2.5)	34 (0.8)	534 (2.3)	1.7 (0.03)	1.5 (0.03)	1.8 (0.03)	0.7 (0.01)	0.7 (0.02)	0.6 (0.01)	1.7 (0.03)	0.6 (0.01)
Latvia	34 (1.0)	555 (3.4)	33 (0.9)	499 (3.2)	33 (1.0)	473 (3.4)	2.4 (0.03)	1.0 (0.02)	2.8 (0.03)	1.6 (0.03)	1.3 (0.02)	0.8 (0.03)	0.8 (0.03)	0.5 (0.02)
Lebanon	43 (1.4)	462 (3.6)	44 (1.1)	416 (3.1)	13 (0.7)	403 (4.4)	1.8 (0.04)	1.3 (0.02)	1.6 (0.04)	1.3 (0.03)	1.6 (0.03)	1.0 (0.02)	0.7 (0.03)	0.3 (0.02)
Lithuania	36 (1.0)	552 (3.1)	37 (0.9)	486 (2.8)	26 (0.9)	456 (2.7)	2.1 (0.03)	1.1 (0.03)	2.6 (0.04)	1.6 (0.04)	1.1 (0.03)	0.6 (0.02)	0.7 (0.03)	0.3 (0.02)
Macedonia, Republic of	33 (1.0)	482 (4.0)	37 (1.0)	418 (4.7)	31 (1.0)	424 (3.9)	2.3 (0.04)	1.3 (0.03)	2.2 (0.03)	1.6 (0.03)	1.8 (0.03)	1.0 (0.02)	0.9 (0.03)	0.7 (0.03)
Malaysia	39 (1.2)	546 (4.2)	45 (1.0)	490 (3.7)	16 (0.7)	471 (4.4)	2.1 (0.04)	0.8 (0.03)	1.5 (0.03)	1.7 (0.04)	1.1 (0.03)	1.2 (0.02)	0.6 (0.02)	0.3 (0.02)
Moldova, Republic of	30 (1.2)	494 (5.0)	50 (0.9)	451 (4.5)	20 (1.1)	441 (5.3)	1.9 (0.04)	0.7 (0.03)	2.0 (0.04)	2.2 (0.06)	1.3 (0.03)	1.1 (0.03)	0.7 (0.03)	0.5 (0.03)
Morocco	‡ (†)	‡ (†)	‡ (†)	‡ (†)	‡ (†)	‡ (†)	1.3 (0.04)	2.3 (0.06)	1.3 (0.03)	1.8 (0.03)	1.5 (0.03)	0.7 (0.03)	0.7 (0.03)	0.8 (0.03)
Netherlands	45 (1.4)	557 (4.4)	33 (1.0)	527 (4.7)	23 (1.0)	511 (4.8)	2.1 (0.05)	1.2 (0.04)	2.0 (0.05)	0.8 (0.02)	1.7 (0.04)	0.5 (0.02)	1.5 (0.04)	0.8 (0.05)
New Zealand	43 (1.4)	534 (6.4)	36 (1.1)	475 (5.4)	21 (0.9)	452 (4.1)	2.1 (0.04)	1.0 (0.04)	1.8 (0.05)	1.0 (0.02)	1.5 (0.03)	0.7 (0.03)	1.3 (0.04)	0.7 (0.03)
Norway	46 (1.1)	502 (2.0)	32 (0.8)	445 (2.9)	21 (0.8)	405 (3.4)	2.2 (0.03)	1.2 (0.03)	2.7 (0.03)	1.0 (0.03)	1.8 (0.03)	0.6 (0.02)	1.2 (0.03)	0.7 (0.02)
Palestinian National Authority	43 (1.0)	428 (3.9)	41 (0.9)	370 (2.9)	16 (0.6)	355 (3.6)	1.2 (0.02)	0.7 (0.02)	1.3 (0.03)	1.5 (0.03)	1.1 (0.03)	1.0 (0.03)	0.5 (0.02)	0.6 (0.03)
Philippines	29 (0.7)	405 (6.1)	59 (0.7)	369 (4.8)	12 (0.5)	366 (6.5)	1.6 (0.04)	0.6 (0.03)	1.7 (0.03)	1.9 (0.03)	1.4 (0.02)	1.0 (0.03)	0.5 (0.03)	0.5 (0.04)
Romania	30 (1.2)	533 (4.6)	45 (1.1)	465 (4.5)	25 (0.9)	442 (5.4)	2.0 (0.04)	0.9 (0.03)	2.1 (0.03)	1.7 (0.05)	1.3 (0.03)	1.0 (0.02)	0.8 (0.04)	0.5 (0.04)
Russian Federation	43 (1.1)	548 (3.0)	30 (0.8)	492 (4.1)	27 (0.8)	466 (4.6)	2.0 (0.03)	1.0 (0.03)	2.5 (0.04)	1.6 (0.03)	1.3 (0.03)	1.1 (0.02)	0.4 (0.02)	0.2 (0.02)
Saudi Arabia	41 (1.4)	361 (4.8)	43 (1.1)	321 (5.4)	16 (0.9)	303 (5.8)	1.6 (0.05)	1.1 (0.04)	1.3 (0.04)	1.5 (0.04)	1.2 (0.04)	0.9 (0.02)	0.8 (0.05)	0.8 (0.03)
Scotland	52 (1.5)	524 (3.9)	32 (1.0)	477 (3.8)	15 (0.9)	456 (5.0)	2.2 (0.03)	1.4 (0.03)	2.7 (0.03)	0.8 (0.03)	1.7 (0.04)	0.6 (0.03)	1.4 (0.03)	0.6 (0.03)
Serbia	44 (1.1)	530 (2.8)	26 (0.7)	458 (3.2)	30 (1.1)	422 (3.4)	2.1 (0.03)	1.0 (0.03)	2.1 (0.03)	1.3 (0.03)	1.7 (0.03)	0.8 (0.03)	0.6 (0.03)	0.3 (0.03)
Singapore	39 (0.8)	639 (3.0)	34 (0.7)	594 (3.9)	27 (0.7)	571 (4.6)	2.3 (0.02)	1.4 (0.03)	1.7 (0.03)	0.7 (0.02)	1.4 (0.03)	0.9 (0.02)	1.6 (0.03)	0.2 (0.02)
Slovak Republic	40 (1.1)	556 (3.7)	35 (1.0)	487 (3.9)	25 (1.0)	462 (4.1)	2.5 (0.03)	1.1 (0.03)	2.8 (0.03)	1.5 (0.03)	1.9 (0.04)	0.7 (0.02)	0.6 (0.03)	0.4 (0.02)
Slovenia	40 (0.9)	533 (3.2)	39 (1.0)	474 (2.5)	20 (0.9)	453 (2.8)	2.2 (0.03)	1.3 (0.03)	2.0 (0.03)	1.2 (0.03)	1.7 (0.03)	0.8 (0.02)	1.1 (0.03)	0.4 (0.02)
South Africa	37 (0.9)	300 (8.3)	48 (0.9)	242 (3.9)	15 (0.8)	255 (9.9)	1.5 (0.03)	0.7 (0.03)	2.7 (0.03)	1.8 (0.03)	1.6 (0.03)	1.6 (0.03)	0.8 (0.03)	0.8 (0.02)
Sweden	49 (1.3)	534 (2.6)	36 (0.9)	477 (3.1)	16 (0.9)	446 (3.4)	2.1 (0.03)	1.1 (0.03)	2.1 (0.03)	1.0 (0.02)	1.5 (0.03)	0.6 (0.02)	1.7 (0.04)	0.4 (0.02)
Tunisia	44 (1.0)	436 (2.7)	36 (0.8)	399 (2.5)	20 (0.9)	384 (2.2)	1.4 (0.02)	0.8 (0.03)	1.5 (0.02)	1.9 (0.03)	1.5 (0.02)	1.3 (0.02)	0.7 (0.02)	0.6 (0.02)
United States	51 (0.8)	534 (3.3)	29 (0.6)	483 (3.5)	20 (0.6)	461 (3.6)	2.2 (0.03)	1.1 (0.02)	2.4 (0.03)	1.2 (0.02)	1.8 (0.02)	0.7 (0.01)	1.8 (0.03)	0.6 (0.02)

—Not available.

†Not applicable.

‡Reporting standards not met.

[1]Index based on students' responses to four statements about mathematics: 1) I usually do well in mathematics; 2) Mathematics is more difficult for me than for many of my classmates; 3) Mathematics is not one of my strengths; 4) I learn things quickly in mathematics. Average is computed across the four items based on a 4-point scale: 1. Agree a lot; 2. Agree a little; 3. Disagree a little; 4. Disagree a lot. Students showing positive attitudes a little or a lot of the time across the four statements were assigned to the high level. Students showing negative attitudes a little or a lot of the time across the four statements were assigned to the low level. Students showing mixed attitudes across the four statements were assigned to the middle level.

[2]Number of hours based on: No time = 0; Less than 1 hour = 0.5; 1–2 hours = 1.5; More than 2, but less than 4 hours = 3; 4 or more hours = 4.5. Activities are not necessarily exclusive; students may have reported engaging in more than one activity at the same time.

[3]Did not satisfy guidelines for sample participation rates.

[4]SAR = Special Administrative Region.

[5]Korea tested the same cohort of students as other countries, but later in 2003, at the beginning of the next school year.

NOTE: Data are for eighth grade or equivalent in most countries. Possible scores range from 0 to 1000. Detail may not sum to totals because of rounding. Standard errors appear in parentheses.

SOURCE: International Association for the Evaluation of Educational Achievement (IEA), Trends in International Mathematics and Science Study (TIMSS), 2003, *TIMSS 2003 International Mathematics and Science Report*, by Ina V. S. Mullis et al. (This table was prepared April 2005.)

Table 404. Average mathematics scores at the end of secondary school, by sex, average time spent studying mathematics out of school, and country: 1995

Country	Average score in mathematics						Amount of daily out-of-school study time in mathematics									
	Total		Males		Females		Less than 1 hour				1 to 2 hours				3 or more hours				Average hours[1]	
							Percent		Mean score		Percent		Mean score		Percent		Mean score			
1	2		3		4		5		6		7		8		9		10		11	
Australia[2]	522	(9.3)	540	(10.3)	510	(9.3)	59	(2.2)	521	(8.3)	36	(2.2)	557	(10.2)	5	(0.8)	534	(13.4)	1.0	(0.04)
Austria[2]	518	(5.3)	545	(7.2)	503	(5.5)	77	(1.7)	526	(5.8)	19	(1.6)	533	(9.4)	4	(0.8)	502	(13.7)	0.6	(0.04)
Canada[2]	519	(2.8)	537	(3.8)	504	(3.5)	56	(2.1)	539	(5.1)	38	(1.9)	547	(5.0)	7	(1.0)	526	(14.6)	1.1	(0.05)
Cyprus[2]	446	(2.5)	454	(4.9)	439	(3.7)	63	(2.1)	435	(4.3)	29	(1.8)	471	(4.8)	8	(1.3)	451	(9.0)	1.0	(0.05)
Czech Republic	466	(12.3)	488	(11.3)	443	(16.8)	92	(1.5)	464	(13.8)	8	(1.4)	482	(17.8)	#	(†)	—	(†)	0.4	(0.03)
Denmark[2]	547	(3.3)	575	(4.0)	523	(4.0)	68	(2.0)	571	(4.9)	28	(1.6)	563	(4.7)	4	(0.7)	562	(11.9)	0.9	(0.04)
France[2]	523	(5.1)	544	(5.6)	506	(5.3)	59	(2.3)	517	(5.1)	35	(2.3)	539	(6.7)	5	(0.7)	505	(14.7)	1.0	(0.04)
Germany[2]	495	(5.9)	509	(8.7)	480	(8.8)	—	(†)	—	(†)	—	(†)	—	(†)	—	(†)	—	(†)	—	(†)
Hungary	483	(3.2)	485	(4.9)	481	(4.8)	74	(0.9)	480	(3.2)	24	(0.8)	496	(5.5)	2	(0.2)	—	(†)	0.7	(0.02)
Iceland[2]	534	(2.0)	558	(3.4)	514	(2.2)	79	(1.1)	553	(3.2)	19	(1.1)	542	(7.0)	2	(0.4)	—	(†)	0.7	(0.02)
Italy[2]	476	(5.5)	490	(7.4)	464	(6.0)	55	(2.6)	479	(6.3)	40	(2.2)	486	(7.2)	5	(0.9)	477	(11.2)	1.0	(0.05)
Lithuania[2]	469	(6.1)	485	(7.3)	461	(7.7)	67	(1.8)	472	(5.8)	29	(1.7)	480	(5.2)	4	(0.5)	484	(11.5)	0.8	(0.03)
Netherlands[2]	560	(4.7)	585	(5.6)	533	(5.9)	82	(1.7)	606	(6.2)	16	(1.6)	581	(11.1)	1	(0.3)	—	(†)	0.7	(0.03)
New Zealand	522	(4.5)	536	(4.9)	507	(6.2)	75	(1.4)	544	(6.1)	23	(1.4)	552	(5.9)	2	(0.3)	—	(†)	0.7	(0.03)
Norway[2]	528	(4.1)	555	(5.3)	501	(4.8)	85	(1.4)	541	(5.1)	14	(1.3)	558	(9.5)	1	(0.3)	—	(†)	0.5	(0.03)
Russian Federation[2]	471	(6.2)	488	(6.5)	460	(6.6)	56	(2.0)	463	(5.9)	33	(1.4)	484	(7.5)	11	(1.2)	494	(8.1)	1.2	(0.06)
Slovenia[2]	512	(8.3)	535	(12.7)	490	(8.0)	72	(2.7)	521	(9.4)	25	(2.6)	518	(9.5)	2	(0.6)	—	(†)	0.7	(0.05)
South Africa[2]	356	(8.3)	365	(9.3)	348	(10.8)	33	(1.8)	394	(17.1)	51	(1.8)	375	(10.9)	17	(1.2)	344	(7.2)	1.7	(0.05)
Sweden	552	(4.3)	573	(5.9)	531	(3.9)	90	(0.9)	579	(5.4)	9	(0.9)	580	(7.8)	1	(0.2)	—	(†)	0.4	(0.02)
Switzerland	540	(5.8)	555	(6.4)	522	(7.4)	67	(1.6)	569	(4.9)	28	(1.3)	550	(5.6)	5	(0.9)	522	(10.6)	0.9	(0.04)
United States[2]	461	(3.2)	466	(4.1)	456	(3.6)	76	(1.5)	475	(3.8)	22	(1.5)	486	(5.9)	2	(0.2)	—	(†)	0.7	(0.02)

—Not available.
†Not applicable.
#Rounds to zero.
[1]Average hours based on: No time = 0; Less than 1 hour = .5; 1–2 hours = 1.5; 3–5 hours = 4; More than 5 hours = 7.
[2]Countries did not meet all International Association for the Evaluation of Educational Achievement sampling specifications.

NOTE: End of secondary school is equivalent to 12th grade in the United States and a few other countries, but ranges from 9th to 14th grades among the survey countries. Possible scores range from 1 to 1000. Detail may not sum to totals because of rounding. Standard errors appear in parentheses.
SOURCE: International Association for the Evaluation of Educational Achievement (IEA), Trends in International Mathematics and Science Study, 1995, *Mathematics and Science Achievement in the Final Year of Secondary School*, by Ina V. S. Mullis et al. (This table was prepared October 1998.)

Table 405. Average fourth-grade science scores in content areas and average time spent teaching science in school, by country: 2003

Country	Average score by content area								Average yearly science instructional time in hours		Science instructional time as a percent of total instructional time[1]	
	Science overall		Life science		Physical science		Earth science					
1	2		3		4		5		6		7	
Armenia	437	(4.3)	435	(4.4)	429	(4.3)	450	(3.6)	‡	(†)	‡	(†)
Australia	521 [2]	(4.2)	523 [2]	(3.8)	518 [2]	(3.9)	518 [2]	(4.1)	45 [3]	(2.6)	5	(0.3)
Austria	—	(†)	—	(†)	—	(†)	—	(†)	—	(†)	—	(†)
Belgium (Flemish)	518	(1.8)	524	(1.7)	507	(2.3)	522	(1.7)	‡	(†)	‡	(†)
Canada	—	(†)	—	(†)	—	(†)	—	(†)	—	(†)	—	(†)
Chinese Taipei	551	(1.7)	540	(1.6)	554	(2.0)	559	(2.6)	84	(1.0)	11	(0.2)
Cyprus	480	(2.4)	482	(2.1)	479	(2.3)	487	(2.5)	46 [3]	(1.4)	5	(0.2)
Czech Republic	—	(†)	—	(†)	—	(†)	—	(†)	—	(†)	—	(†)
England	540 [2]	(3.6)	532 [2]	(3.1)	546 [2]	(3.2)	535 [2]	(3.5)	‡	(†)	‡	(†)
Greece	—	(†)	—	(†)	—	(†)	—	(†)	—	(†)	—	(†)
Hong Kong, SAR[4]	542 [2]	(3.1)	535 [2]	(2.6)	548 [2]	(2.7)	536 [2]	(2.7)	77 [3]	(5.4)	8	(0.5)
Hungary	530	(3.0)	536	(2.5)	526	(2.7)	526	(3.7)	54 [3]	(1.0)	6	(0.1)
Iceland	—	(†)	—	(†)	—	(†)	—	(†)	—	(†)	—	(†)
Iran, Islamic Republic of	414	(4.1)	424	(4.6)	419	(4.5)	428	(3.0)	‡	(†)	‡	(†)
Ireland	—	(†)	—	(†)	—	(†)	—	(†)	—	(†)	—	(†)
Israel	—	(†)	—	(†)	—	(†)	—	(†)	—	(†)	—	(†)
Italy	516	(3.8)	521	(3.5)	512	(3.5)	519	(3.7)	73 [5]	(2.3)	8 [5]	(0.3)
Japan	543	(1.5)	530	(1.3)	557	(1.7)	535	(1.9)	81	(1.2)	8	(0.2)
Korea, Republic of[6]	—	(†)	—	(†)	—	(†)	—	(†)	—	(†)	—	(†)
Kuwait	—	(†)	—	(†)	—	(†)	—	(†)	—	(†)	—	(†)
Latvia	532	(2.5)	531	(2.3)	532	(2.6)	534	(2.9)	‡	(†)	‡	(†)
Lithuania	512	(2.6)	516 [2,7]	(2.0)	512 [2,7]	(2.5)	503 [2,7]	(3.2)	53	(1.6)	6	(0.2)
Netherlands	525 [2]	(2.0)	547 [2]	(1.8)	505 [2]	(1.9)	503 [2]	(2.3)	33 [3]	(1.8)	3	(0.2)
New Zealand	520	(2.5)	520	(2.3)	516	(2.3)	522	(2.3)	65 [3]	(3.5)	7	(0.4)
Norway	466	(2.6)	480	(2.2)	456	(2.3)	473	(2.8)	38 [5]	(1.8)	4 [5]	(0.2)
Philippines	332	(9.4)	330	(9.0)	343	(9.6)	324	(9.2)	176 [5]	(3.2)	16 [5]	(0.4)
Portugal	—	(†)	—	(†)	—	(†)	—	(†)	—	(†)	—	(†)
Russian Federation	526	(5.2)	526	(4.7)	527	(5.2)	527	(6.0)	33 [3]	(1.2)	5	(0.2)
Scotland	502 [2]	(2.9)	506 [2]	(3.1)	503 [2]	(2.6)	498 [2]	(2.6)	‡	(†)	‡	(†)
Singapore	565	(5.5)	506	(3.1)	503	(2.6)	498	(2.6)	64	(0.6)	7	(0.1)
Slovenia	490	(2.5)	489	(2.9)	497	(2.3)	490	(2.7)	75 [5]	(2.2)	9 [5]	(0.3)
Thailand	—	(†)	—	(†)	—	(†)	—	(†)	—	(†)	—	(†)
Tunisia	314	(5.7)	290	(5.9)	324	(5.3)	336	(4.8)	‡	(†)	‡	(†)
United States	536 [2]	(2.5)	537 [2]	(2.2)	531 [2]	(2.3)	535 [2]	(2.5)	83 [5]	(3.0)	8 [5]	(0.3)

—Not available.
†Not applicable.
‡Reporting standards not met.
[1]Computed as the ratio of science instructional time to the total instructional time averaged across students.
[2]Met guidelines for participation rates only after replacement schools were included.
[3]Data are available for at least 50 but less than 70 percent of the students.
[4]SAR = Special Administrative Region.
[5]Data are available for at least 70 but less than 85 percent of the students.

[6]Korea tested the same cohort of students as other countries, but later in 2003, at the beginning of the next school year.
[7]National Desired Population does not cover all of International Desired Population.
NOTE: Data are for fourth grade or equivalent in most countries. Detail may not sum to totals because of rounding. Standard errors appear in parentheses.
SOURCE: International Association for the Evaluation of Educational Achievement (IEA), Trends in International Mathematics and Science Study (TIMSS), 2003, *TIMSS 2003 International Science Report*, by Michael O. Martin et al. (This table was prepared October 2005.)

Table 406. Average eighth-grade science scores in content areas and average time spent studying out of school, by country: 2003

Country	Science overall	Average score by content area — Life science	Chemistry	Physics	Earth science	Environmental science	Index of time students spend doing science homework (TSH) in a normal school week[1] — High TSH Percent	High TSH Mean score	Medium TSH Percent	Medium TSH Mean score	Low TSH Percent	Low TSH Mean score
1	2	3	4	5	6	7	8	9	10	11	12	13
International average	**473 (0.5)**	**474 (0.5)**	**474 (0.5)**	**474 (0.5)**	**474 (0.5)**	**474 (0.5)**	**13 (0.2)**	**458 (1.3)**	**44 (0.2)**	**466 (0.9)**	**43 (0.3)**	**467 (0.9)**
Armenia	461 (3.5)	453[2] (3.3)	466[2] (4.2)	479 (3.2)	460[2] (3.7)	417[2] (4.4)	— (†)	— (†)	— (†)	— (†)	— (†)	— (†)
Australia	527 (3.8)	532[3] (3.8)	506[3] (3.8)	521[3] (3.7)	531[3] (4.2)	536[3] (3.4)	9 (0.8)	520 (6.4)	35 (1.6)	530 (3.3)	56 (2.0)	530 (4.4)
Bahrain	438 (1.8)	445[2] (1.9)	441[2] (2.6)	443[2] (2.0)	440[2] (2.4)	439[2] (3.1)	13 (0.7)	426 (4.1)	56 (1.3)	441 (2.5)	31 (1.4)	445 (2.6)
Belgium (Flemish)	516 (2.5)	526[3] (2.4)	503[3] (2.0)	514[3] (2.5)	508[3] (2.5)	523[3] (2.7)	— (†)	— (†)	— (†)	— (†)	— (†)	— (†)
Botswana	365 (2.8)	370[2] (2.7)	348[2] (3.1)	371[2] (3.2)	361[2] (3.1)	381[2] (3.3)	14 (0.7)	378 (6.1)	45 (1.0)	368 (3.2)	40 (1.2)	366 (3.6)
Bulgaria	479 (5.2)	474 (5.2)	482 (5.7)	485[3] (5.0)	491[3] (4.9)	464[3] (5.0)	— (†)	— (†)	— (†)	— (†)	— (†)	— (†)
Chile	413 (2.9)	427[2] (2.7)	405[2] (3.3)	401[2] (3.1)	435[2] (3.1)	436[2] (2.9)	— (†)	— (†)	— (†)	— (†)	— (†)	— (†)
Chinese Taipei	571 (3.5)	563[3] (3.1)	584[3] (4.0)	569[3] (3.3)	548[3] (3.1)	560[3] (3.1)	12[4] (1.2)	588[4] (4.6)	37[4] (1.3)	581[4] (4.0)	51[4] (2.1)	561[4] (3.5)
Cyprus	441 (2.0)	437[2] (2.2)	443[2] (2.6)	450[2] (1.7)	447[2] (2.1)	441[2] (2.3)	— (†)	— (†)	— (†)	— (†)	— (†)	— (†)
England[5]	‡ (†)	‡ (†)	‡ (†)	‡ (†)	‡ (†)	‡ (†)	‡ (†)	‡ (†)	‡ (†)	‡ (†)	‡ (†)	‡ (†)
Egypt	421 (3.9)	425[2] (3.7)	442[2] (3.8)	414[2] (4.1)	403[2] (4.4)	430[2] (4.0)	23 (0.7)	416 (4.4)	64 (0.8)	436 (4.0)	13 (0.6)	430 (6.6)
Estonia	552 (2.5)	547[3] (2.4)	552[3] (2.1)	544[3] (2.4)	558[3] (2.9)	540[3] (2.2)	— (†)	— (†)	— (†)	— (†)	— (†)	— (†)
Ghana	255 (5.9)	256[2] (5.6)	276[2] (6.6)	239[2] (5.4)	254[2] (5.6)	267[2] (6.2)	25 (1.2)	267 (8.5)	54 (1.0)	262 (6.0)	22 (1.0)	258 (8.1)
Hong Kong, SAR[6,7]	556 (3.0)	551[3] (2.9)	542[3] (2.6)	555[3] (2.8)	549[3] (2.9)	555[3] (2.6)	6 (0.5)	548 (4.6)	43 (1.4)	563 (2.9)	50 (1.4)	554 (3.9)
Hungary	543 (2.8)	536[3] (2.7)	560[3] (3.1)	536[3] (2.7)	537[3] (3.1)	528[3] (2.9)	— (†)	— (†)	— (†)	— (†)	— (†)	— (†)
Indonesia[8]	420 (4.1)	424[2] (3.9)	391[2] (3.8)	430[2] (4.0)	431[2] (3.8)	454[2] (3.4)	— (†)	— (†)	— (†)	— (†)	— (†)	— (†)
Iran, Islamic Republic of	453 (2.3)	447[2] (2.6)	445[2] (2.7)	445[2] (3.0)	468[2] (2.9)	487[3] (2.1)	8 (0.7)	451 (5.6)	42 (1.4)	457 (2.9)	49 (1.7)	452 (2.7)
Israel[9]	488[10] (3.1)	491[3] (3.0)	499[3] (3.4)	484[3] (2.9)	485[3] (3.0)	486[3] (2.9)	13 (0.9)	480 (4.7)	43 (1.6)	485 (4.3)	44 (2.0)	505 (3.4)
Italy	491 (3.1)	498[3] (3.2)	487[3] (3.3)	470 (3.2)	513[3] (3.2)	497[3] (3.0)	14 (1.0)	489 (5.9)	41 (1.1)	487 (3.7)	45 (1.4)	496 (3.7)
Japan	552 (1.7)	549[3] (2.0)	552[3] (2.1)	564[3] (1.9)	530[3] (2.1)	537[3] (2.0)	— (†)	— (†)	— (†)	— (†)	— (†)	— (†)
Jordan	475 (3.8)	475 (4.0)	478 (4.4)	465[2] (3.8)	472 (4.0)	492[3] (3.2)	19 (0.9)	466 (4.2)	52 (1.2)	478 (3.9)	29 (1.5)	499 (5.0)
Korea, Republic of[11]	558 (1.6)	558[3] (1.6)	529[3] (2.5)	579[3] (1.6)	540[3] (1.9)	544[3] (1.4)	4 (0.4)	549 (6.3)	26 (1.7)	562 (2.4)	70 (2.0)	559 (1.9)
Latvia	513 (2.9)	511[3] (2.5)	514[3] (3.2)	512[3] (2.4)	514[3] (2.8)	508[3] (3.3)	— (†)	— (†)	— (†)	— (†)	— (†)	— (†)
Lebanon	393 (4.3)	360[2] (5.0)	433[2] (4.9)	419[2] (4.0)	395[2] (4.0)	374[2] (5.1)	— (†)	— (†)	— (†)	— (†)	— (†)	— (†)
Lithuania[8]	519 (2.1)	517 (2.4)	534[3] (2.3)	519[3] (2.7)	512[3] (2.7)	507[3] (2.0)	— (†)	— (†)	— (†)	— (†)	— (†)	— (†)
Macedonia[8]	449 (3.6)	448[2] (3.8)	467[2] (3.9)	458[2] (3.1)	440[2] (4.3)	442[2] (3.7)	— (†)	— (†)	— (†)	— (†)	— (†)	— (†)
Malaysia	510 (3.7)	504[3] (3.7)	514[3] (3.8)	519[3] (3.6)	502[3] (3.8)	513[3] (3.2)	20 (1.0)	513 (4.4)	49 (0.9)	510 (3.6)	31 (1.3)	510 (4.6)
Moldova	472 (3.4)	466[2] (3.7)	479 (3.9)	479 (3.7)	454[2] (4.0)	454[2] (3.8)	— (†)	— (†)	— (†)	— (†)	— (†)	— (†)
Morocco[7,8]	396[10] (2.5)	390[2] (2.6)	402[2] (2.7)	410[2] (2.7)	397[2] (3.4)	396[2] (3.3)	14[12] (0.7)	391[12] (5.3)	47[12] (1.1)	396[12] (3.4)	39[12] (1.3)	408[12] (3.5)
Netherlands[7]	536 (3.1)	536[3] (3.3)	514[3] (2.6)	538[3] (3.4)	534[3] (3.2)	539[3] (2.8)	— (†)	— (†)	— (†)	— (†)	— (†)	— (†)
New Zealand	520 (5.0)	523[3] (5.1)	501[3] (5.6)	515[3] (4.7)	525[3] (4.8)	525[3] (3.9)	10 (1.3)	519 (6.2)	41 (1.6)	531 (6.9)	48 (2.0)	518 (5.1)
Norway	494 (2.2)	496[3] (2.5)	485[3] (3.0)	488[3] (2.6)	517[3] (2.7)	496[3] (2.2)	13 (0.8)	485 (3.7)	44 (1.2)	493 (3.1)	43 (1.7)	503 (2.3)
Palestinian National Authority	435 (3.2)	435[2] (3.6)	444[2] (3.9)	432[2] (3.6)	439[2] (3.0)	444[2] (3.7)	21 (1.1)	433 (4.4)	56 (1.3)	442 (3.4)	23 (1.3)	441 (4.8)
Philippines[13]	377 (5.8)	387[2] (5.8)	342[2] (6.1)	380[2] (4.7)	377[2] (5.7)	403[2] (5.4)	17 (0.7)	381 (7.5)	50 (0.8)	379 (5.7)	33 (1.2)	381 (7.2)
Romania	470 (4.9)	471 (4.8)	474 (4.9)	473 (4.1)	469 (5.2)	472 (4.7)	— (†)	— (†)	— (†)	— (†)	— (†)	— (†)
Russian Federation	514 (3.7)	514[3] (3.3)	527[3] (4.0)	511[3] (3.4)	518[3] (3.3)	491[3] (3.2)	8 (0.7)	382 (6.0)	61 (1.5)	402 (4.6)	31 (1.7)	403 (4.6)
Saudi Arabia	398 (4.0)	412[2] (3.9)	382[2] (4.8)	394[2] (3.9)	394[2] (4.0)	410[2] (3.8)	— (†)	— (†)	— (†)	— (†)	— (†)	— (†)
Scotland[7]	512 (3.4)	512[3] (3.3)	499[3] (3.2)	515[3] (3.0)	515[3] (3.8)	511[3] (3.5)	3 (0.4)	487 (14.2)	27 (1.4)	508 (5.0)	71 (1.5)	517 (3.4)
Serbia[8]	468 (2.5)	468[2] (2.6)	474 (3.2)	471 (2.6)	471 (3.0)	457[2] (2.4)	— (†)	— (†)	— (†)	— (†)	— (†)	— (†)
Singapore	578 (4.3)	569[3] (4.0)	582[3] (4.2)	579[3] (3.4)	549[3] (3.9)	568[3] (3.8)	18 (0.7)	595 (4.1)	48 (0.7)	585 (4.4)	34 (0.9)	564 (5.5)

See notes at end of table.

Table 406. Average eighth-grade science scores in content areas and average time spent studying out of school, by country: 2003—Continued

Country	Average score by content area						Index of time students spend doing science homework (TSH) in a normal school week [1]					
	Science overall	Life science	Chemistry	Physics	Earth science	Environmental science	High TSH		Medium TSH		Low TSH	
							Percent	Mean score	Percent	Mean score	Percent	Mean score
1	2	3	4	5	6	7	8	9	10	11	12	13
Slovak Republic............	517 (3.2)	514 [3] (2.9)	519 [3] (3.6)	519 [3] (2.9)	523 [3] (3.3)	509 [3] (2.8)	—	(†)	—	(†)	—	(†)
Slovenia.......................	520 (1.8)	521 [3] (2.2)	532 [3] (2.6)	509 [3] (1.8)	523 [3] (2.2)	515 [3] (2.2)	—	(†)	—	(†)	—	(†)
South Africa..................	244 (6.7)	250 [2] (6.0)	285 [2] (5.9)	244 [2] (6.2)	247 [2] (6.3)	261 [2] (6.6)	17	234 (9.6)	52	246 (7.9)	32	263 (7.4)
Sweden..........................	524 (2.7)	528 [3] (2.7)	526 [3] (2.6)	525 [3] (2.9)	532 [3] (3.3)	499 [3] (2.6)	—	(†)	—	(†)	—	(†)
Tunisia..........................	404 (2.1)	417 [2] (2.0)	413 [2] (2.5)	386 [2] (2.5)	408 [2] (2.0)	436 [2] (2.2)	9	398 (4.0)	35	400 (2.8)	56	411 (2.6)
United States [9]............	527 [10] (3.1)	537 [3] (3.0)	513 [3] (3.2)	515 [3] (2.9)	532 [3] (2.9)	533 [3] (2.9)	13	519 (4.3)	43	530 (3.4)	45	531 (3.7)

—Not available.

†Not applicable.

‡Reporting standards not met.

[1] Index based on students' reports on the frequency and amount of science homework they are given. High level indicates more than 30 minutes of science homework assigned 3–4 times a week. Low level indicates no more than 30 minutes of science homework no more than twice a week. Medium level includes all other possible combinations of responses.

[2] Country average significantly lower than international average.

[3] Country average significantly higher than international average.

[4] Students were asked about natural science; data pertain to grade 8 physics/chemistry course.

[5] Did not satisfy guidelines for sample participation rates.

[6] SAR = Special Administrative Region.

[7] Met guidelines for sample participation rates only after replacement schools were included.

[8] National Desired Population does not cover all of International Desired Population.

[9] National Defined Population covers less than 90 percent of National Desired Population.

[10] Did not meet international sampling or other guidelines.

[11] Korea tested the same cohort of students as other countries, but later in 2003, at the beginning of the next school year.

[12] Met guidelines for sample participation rates only after replacement schools were included.

[13] Students study only biology at grade 8.

NOTE: Data are for eighth grade or equivalent in most countries. Possible scores range from 0 to 1000. Detail may not sum to totals because of rounding. Standard errors appear in parentheses.

SOURCE: International Association for the Evaluation of Educational Achievement (IEA), Trends in International Mathematics and Science Study (TIMSS), 2003, TIMSS 2003 International Science Report, by Michael O. Martin et al. (This table was prepared October 2005.)

Table 407. Instructional practices and time spent teaching science in eighth grade, by country: 2003

Country	Percent of students who reported doing activity about half the lessons or more						Students' average yearly instructional time in hours				
	Watch the teacher demonstrate an experiment or investigation	Design or plan an experiment or investigation	Conduct an experiment or investigation	Work in small groups on an experiment or investigation	Write explanations about what was observed and why it happened	Relate what is being learned in science to our daily lives	General integrated science	Earth science	Chemistry	Biology	Physics
1	2	3	4	5	6	7	8	9	10	11	12
International average	64 (0.2)	49 (0.2)	57 (0.3)	59 (0.3)	66 (0.2)	57 (0.2)	117 (0.7)	55 (0.6)	61 (0.8)	61 (0.8)	68 (0.6)
Australia	54 (1.6)	49 (1.7)	60 (2.2)	68 (2.1)	75 (1.5)	42 (1.1)	132[1] (3.6)	— (†)	— (†)	— (†)	— (†)
Bahrain	83 (0.8)	63 (0.8)	64 (0.8)	66 (1.1)	68 (0.9)	64 (0.9)	119 (1.1)	— (†)	— (†)	— (†)	— (†)
Belgium (Flemish)	— (†)	— (†)	— (†)	— (†)	— (†)	— (†)	— (†)	52[1] (3.2)	— (†)	55[1] (3.3)	58[1] (2.7)
Botswana	61 (0.9)	45 (0.8)	48 (1.0)	50 (1.1)	61 (0.9)	71 (0.8)	‡ (†)	— (†)	— (†)	— (†)	— (†)
Bulgaria	— (†)	— (†)	— (†)	— (†)	— (†)	— (†)	— (†)	53[2] (2.2)	63[2] (2.9)	65[1] (3.2)	64[2] (3.3)
Chile	57 (1.3)	56 (1.4)	54 (1.5)	61 (1.4)	69 (1.0)	62 (0.7)	118[2] (2.2)	— (†)	— (†)	— (†)	— (†)
Chinese Taipei	48[3] (1.1)	24[3] (0.9)	36[3] (1.3)	37[3] (1.5)	37[3] (1.1)	40[3] (1.0)	— (†)	— (†)	—[4] (†)	— (†)	134[4] (2.0)
Cyprus	— (†)	— (†)	— (†)	— (†)	— (†)	— (†)	— (†)	53[1] (0.7)	34[1] (1.6)	— (†)	52[1] (0.8)
England	‡ (†)	‡ (†)	‡ (†)	‡ (†)	‡ (†)	‡ (†)	‡ (†)	— (†)	— (†)	— (†)	— (†)
Egypt	80 (0.7)	61 (1.0)	62 (1.0)	60 (0.8)	71 (0.7)	73 (0.7)	‡ (†)	— (†)	— (†)	— (†)	— (†)
Estonia	— (†)	— (†)	— (†)	— (†)	— (†)	— (†)	‡ (†)	55 (2.9)	65 (3.9)	80 (4.8)	59 (1.8)
Ghana	73 (1.2)	54 (1.3)	55 (1.3)	54 (1.5)	64 (1.5)	75 (1.0)	‡ (†)	— (†)	— (†)	— (†)	— (†)
Hong Kong, SAR[5]	66 (1.2)	35 (1.0)	71 (1.5)	75 (1.2)	67 (1.2)	61 (0.8)	103[1] (4.0)	— (†)	— (†)	— (†)	— (†)
Hungary	— (†)	— (†)	— (†)	— (†)	— (†)	— (†)	— (†)	58[1] (2.5)	59[1] (2.1)	61[1] (2.8)	57[1] (2.5)
Indonesia	— (†)	— (†)	— (†)	— (†)	— (†)	— (†)	— (†)	— (†)	— (†)	93[1] (3.6)	93[1] (3.3)
Iran, Islamic Republic of	87 (1.0)	66 (1.4)	77 (1.2)	73 (1.5)	78 (1.0)	70 (1.0)	106[1] (3.7)	— (†)	— (†)	— (†)	— (†)
Israel	73 (1.6)	56 (1.4)	63 (1.6)	52 (1.8)	76 (1.3)	56 (1.0)	— (†)	— (†)	— (†)	— (†)	— (†)
Italy	26 (1.3)	16 (0.9)	13 (0.8)	12 (0.8)	32 (1.4)	35 (1.1)	69[1] (1.1)	— (†)	— (†)	— (†)	— (†)
Japan	66 (1.5)	51 (1.7)	75 (1.7)	79 (1.6)	69 (1.5)	27 (1.1)	99[2] (1.5)	— (†)	— (†)	— (†)	— (†)
Jordan	67 (1.5)	56 (1.4)	55 (1.7)	53 (1.6)	66 (1.3)	70 (1.1)	135 (0.8)	— (†)	— (†)	— (†)	— (†)
Korea, Republic of	31 (1.0)	14 (0.8)	20 (1.1)	39 (1.3)	44 (1.3)	36 (0.9)	103[1] (2.7)	— (†)	— (†)	— (†)	— (†)
Latvia	— (†)	— (†)	— (†)	— (†)	— (†)	— (†)	— (†)	— (†)	‡ (†)	64[1] (4.2)	56[1] (4.1)
Lebanon	— (†)	— (†)	— (†)	— (†)	— (†)	— (†)	‡ (†)	— (†)	— (†)	— (†)	— (†)
Lithuania	— (†)	— (†)	— (†)	— (†)	— (†)	— (†)	— (†)	59[2] (0.4)	65[2] (1.2)	46[2] (3.5)	60[2] (0.8)
Macedonia	— (†)	— (†)	— (†)	— (†)	— (†)	— (†)	— (†)	53[2] (1.4)	64[2] (2.5)	59[2] (2.0)	79[2] (1.5)
Malaysia	83 (1.1)	46 (1.3)	71 (1.7)	77 (1.3)	73 (1.3)	72 (1.0)	119 (1.8)	— (†)	— (†)	— (†)	— (†)
Moldova	— (†)	— (†)	— (†)	— (†)	— (†)	— (†)	‡ (†)	—[6] (†)	— (†)	‡[6] (†)	— (†)
Morocco	82 (1.2)	62 (1.3)	61[2] (1.2)	50 (1.3)	74 (1.0)	65[2] (1.2)	— (†)	— (†)	—[4] (†)	— (†)	‡[4] (†)
Netherlands	— (†)	— (†)	— (†)	— (†)	— (†)	— (†)	— (†)	54[1] (1.7)	—[4] (†)	58[1] (1.8)	68[2,4] (2.4)
New Zealand	60 (2.0)	50 (2.1)	56 (2.5)	66 (2.3)	73 (1.8)	45 (1.3)	132 (2.4)	— (†)	— (†)	— (†)	— (†)
Norway	40 (1.5)	34 (1.6)	49 (2.2)	49 (2.2)	56 (1.9)	31 (0.9)	92 (2.5)	— (†)	— (†)	— (†)	— (†)
Palestinian National Authority	70 (1.2)	56 (1.2)	57 (1.0)	54 (1.5)	66 (1.2)	69 (0.9)	101[1] (1.8)	— (†)	— (†)	— (†)	— (†)
Philippines[7]	74 (0.9)	58 (1.2)	57 (1.0)	62 (1.1)	72 (1.0)	76 (0.8)	202 (4.2)	— (†)	— (†)	— (†)	— (†)
Romania	— (†)	— (†)	— (†)	— (†)	— (†)	— (†)	— (†)	60[2] (1.1)	67[2] (2.4)	38[2] (2.6)	67[2] (2.4)
Russian Federation	— (†)	— (†)	— (†)	— (†)	— (†)	— (†)	— (†)	49[2] (0.7)	59[2] (1.2)	49[2] (0.8)	49[2] (0.9)

See notes at end of table.

Table 407. Instructional practices and time spent teaching science in eighth grade, by country: 2003—Continued

Country	Percent of students who reported doing activity about half the lessons or more						Students' average yearly instructional time in hours				
	Watch the teacher demonstrate an experiment or investigation	Design or plan an experiment or investigation	Conduct an experiment or investigation	Work in small groups on an experiment or investigation	Write explanations about what was observed and why it happened	Relate what is being learned in science to our daily lives	General integrated science	Earth science	Chemistry	Biology	Physics
1	2	3	4	5	6	7	8	9	10	11	12
Saudi Arabia	68 (1.3)	50 (1.3)	51 (1.4)	43 (1.4)	60 (1.3)	67 (1.0)	106[1] (1.6)	— (†)	— (†)	— (†)	— (†)
Scotland	69 (1.4)	54 (1.3)	74 (1.4)	81 (1.2)	83 (1.1)	47 (1.0)	‡ (†)	— (†)	— (†)	— (†)	— (†)
Serbia	— (†)	— (†)	— (†)	— (†)	— (†)	— (†)	— (†)	53[2] (2.2)	61[1] (3.7)	53[1] (1.0)	56[1] (2.5)
Singapore	49 (0.9)	31 (0.6)	55 (1.0)	57 (0.8)	68 (0.8)	58 (0.7)	107 (1.9)	— (†)	— (†)	— (†)	— (†)
Slovak Republic	— (†)	— (†)	— (†)	— (†)	— (†)	— (†)	— (†)	66[2] (3.9)	76[2] (3.8)	72[2] (5.2)	70[2] (4.5)
Slovenia	— (†)	— (†)	— (†)	— (†)	— (†)	— (†)	— (†)	— (†)	59 (1.1)	56 (0.7)	57[2] (0.5)
South Africa	72 (1.1)	64 (1.2)	63 (1.1)	70 (1.1)	73 (0.7)	77 (0.7)	‡ (†)	— (†)	— (†)	— (†)	— (†)
Sweden	— (†)	— (†)	— (†)	— (†)	— (†)	— (†)	131[2] (7.6)	— (†)	— (†)	— (†)	— (†)
Tunisia	79 (0.7)	65 (1.0)	69 (1.0)	55 (1.2)	73 (0.8)	54 (0.9)	‡ (†)	— (†)	— (†)	— (†)	— (†)
United States	57 (1.3)	48 (1.2)	55 (1.4)	65 (1.5)	65 (1.4)	51 (0.9)	135[1] (2.2)	— (†)	— (†)	— (†)	— (†)

—Not available.
†Not applicable.
‡Reporting standards not met.
[1]Data are available for at least 50 but less than 70 percent of the students.
[2]Data are available for at least 70 but less than 85 percent of the students.
[3]Students in Chinese Taipei were asked about natural science; data pertain to grade 8 physics/chemistry course.
[4]Data reported in physics column are for grade 8 physics/chemistry.
[5]SAR = Special Administrative Region.

[6]Data reported in biology column are for grade 8 biology/earth science.
[7]Students study only biology at grade 8.
NOTE: Data are for eighth grade or equivalent in most countries. Standard errors appear in parentheses. Detail may not sum to totals because of rounding.
SOURCE: International Association for the Evaluation of Educational Achievement (IEA), Trends in International Mathematics and Science Study (TIMSS) 2003, TIMSS 2003 International Science Report, by Michael O. Martin et al. (This table was prepared April 2005.)

Table 408. Average science scores at the end of secondary school, by sex, average time spent studying science out of school, and country: 1995

Country	Average score in science						Amount of daily out-of-school study time in science								Average hours[1]	
							Less than 1 hour				1 to 2 hours				3 or more hours	
	Total		Male		Female		Percent		Mean score		Percent		Mean score		Percent		Mean score		
1	2		3		4		5		6		7		8		9		10		11
Australia[2]	527	(9.8)	547	(11.5)	513	(9.4)	58	(1.8)	540	(9.5)	35	(1.7)	575	(6.9)	7	(1.0)	588	(33.0)	1.0	(0.04)
Austria[2]	520	(5.6)	554	(8.7)	501	(5.8)	87	(1.4)	529	(6.0)	11	(1.4)	526	(13.8)	1	(0.3)	—	(†)	0.4	(0.03)
Canada[2]	532	(2.6)	550	(3.6)	518	(3.8)	57	(2.1)	554	(4.2)	35	(1.8)	567	(6.8)	8	(0.9)	537	(18.0)	1.1	(0.05)
Cyprus[2]	448	(3.0)	459	(5.8)	439	(3.0)	80	(1.1)	436	(3.7)	16	(0.9)	483	(10.7)	4	(0.6)	552	(11.8)	0.5	(0.03)
Czech Republic	487	(8.8)	512	(8.8)	460	(11.0)	84	(2.6)	520	(11.6)	14	(2.3)	571	(11.5)	3	(0.5)	583	(13.6)	0.5	(0.05)
Denmark[2]	509	(3.6)	532	(5.4)	490	(4.1)	73	(1.8)	555	(4.7)	25	(1.6)	570	(6.1)	3	(0.6)	565	(15.0)	0.7	(0.03)
France[2]	487	(5.1)	508	(6.7)	468	(4.8)	59	(2.0)	497	(5.7)	35	(1.8)	525	(7.0)	6	(0.8)	515	(9.1)	1.0	(0.04)
Germany[2]	497	(5.1)	514	(7.9)	478	(8.5)	—	(†)	—	(†)	—	(†)	—	(†)	—	(†)	—	(†)	—	(†)
Hungary	471	(3.0)	484	(4.2)	455	(4.3)	67	(1.2)	475	(3.9)	27	(0.9)	486	(4.9)	6	(0.6)	497	(11.5)	0.9	(0.03)
Iceland[2]	549	(1.5)	572	(2.7)	530	(2.1)	87	(1.0)	566	(2.5)	12	(1.0)	575	(4.6)	1	(0.3)	—	(†)	0.4	(0.01)
Italy[2]	475	(5.3)	495	(6.7)	458	(5.6)	70	(2.8)	487	(6.3)	25	(2.5)	482	(9.7)	5	(1.2)	462	(13.9)	0.8	(0.06)
Lithuania[2]	461	(5.7)	481	(6.4)	450	(7.3)	69	(1.5)	465	(5.5)	26	(1.3)	469	(6.5)	5	(0.6)	470	(11.4)	0.8	(0.03)
Netherlands[2]	558	(5.3)	582	(5.7)	532	(6.2)	78	(2.8)	593	(6.4)	20	(2.9)	605	(16.9)	1	(0.4)	—	(†)	0.7	(0.03)
New Zealand	529	(5.2)	543	(7.1)	515	(5.2)	80	(1.1)	551	(6.3)	18	(1.1)	581	(6.6)	3	(0.5)	553	(15.3)	0.6	(0.02)
Norway[2]	544	(4.1)	574	(5.1)	513	(4.5)	74	(2.4)	592	(7.1)	23	(2.2)	598	(10.8)	3	(0.7)	583	(23.8)	0.7	(0.05)
Russian Federation[2]	481	(5.7)	510	(5.7)	463	(6.7)	61	(1.6)	478	(6.0)	30	(1.3)	488	(7.0)	10	(0.8)	501	(8.0)	1.1	(0.04)
Slovenia[2]	517	(8.2)	541	(12.7)	494	(6.4)	85	(2.0)	528	(8.1)	13	(1.9)	548	(8.9)	2	(0.6)	—	(†)	0.5	(0.04)
South Africa[2]	349	(10.5)	367	(11.5)	333	(13.0)	47	(1.6)	373	(15.5)	35	(1.3)	367	(12.2)	18	(1.4)	326	(7.3)	1.5	(0.05)
Sweden	559	(4.4)	585	(5.9)	534	(3.5)	81	(1.9)	599	(7.4)	17	(1.8)	632	(10.1)	2	(0.5)	—	(†)	0.6	(0.03)
Switzerland	523	(5.3)	540	(6.1)	500	(7.8)	76	(2.3)	564	(6.6)	21	(2.3)	564	(10.9)	3	(0.9)	508	(29.0)	0.7	(0.04)
United States[2]	480	(3.3)	492	(4.5)	469	(3.9)	76	(2.1)	505	(4.3)	21	(2.1)	517	(5.7)	2	(0.4)	—	(†)	0.7	(0.04)

—Not available.
†Not applicable.
[1]Average hours based on: No time = 0; Less than 1 hour = 5; 1–2 hours = 1.5; 3–5 hours = 4; More than 5 hours = 7.
[2]Country did not meet all International Association for the Evaluation of Educational Achievement sampling specifications.

NOTE: End of secondary school is equivalent to 12th grade in the United States and a few other countries, but ranges from 9th to 14th grade among the survey countries. Possible scores range from 1 to 1000. Detail may not sum to totals because of rounding. Standard errors appear in parentheses.
SOURCE: International Association for the Evaluation of Educational Achievement (IEA), Trends in International Mathematics and Science Study (TIMSS), 1995, *Mathematics and Science Achievement in the Final Year of Secondary School*, by Ina V. S. Mullis et al. (This table was prepared October 1998.)

Table 409. Number of bachelor's degree recipients per 100 persons of the typical age of graduation, by sex and country: 2002, 2003, and 2004

Country	Male and female			Male			Female		
	2002	2003	2004	2002	2003	2004	2002	2003	2004
1	2	3	4	5	6	7	8	9	10
Australia	50.7	54.8	46.9	43.0	46.7	37.4	58.8	63.4	57.0
Austria	18.0	19.0	19.6	17.9	18.7	19.0	18.1	19.4	20.3
Belgium[1]	19.2[1]	—	18.8	18.7	—	18.0	19.7	—	19.6
Canada	—	—	—	—	—	—	—	—	—
Czech Republic	15.4	17.3	21.0	14.3	15.9	18.8	16.6	18.8	23.4
Denmark	34.4	38.6	46.6	23.4	25.1	33.3	45.7	52.3	59.9
Finland	51.8	55.8	55.2	37.7	40.4	39.9	66.4	72.2	71.3
France	39.0	41.5	40.8	32.9	34.9	34.1	45.3	48.4	47.6
Germany	19.2	19.5	20.6	19.3	19.3	20.3	19.1	19.7	20.9
Hungary	31.1	33.6	35.6	23.2	24.6	25.4	39.3	43.2	46.3
Iceland	40.0	44.2	50.7	27.2	29.4	31.5	53.1	59.1	70.4
Ireland	30.9	36.8	38.6	25.6	29.7	31.9	36.2	44.0	45.3
Italy	22.4	27.8	37.7	19.2	24.0	31.4	25.6	31.6	44.3
Japan	34.1	34.4	36.3	40.2	40.1	41.4	27.6	28.5	31.0
Korea, Republic of	31.5	31.7	31.4	31.6	32.1	30.9	31.3	31.2	31.9
Mexico	16.5	14.3	14.0	15.6	13.3	13.3	17.4	15.3	14.6
Netherlands	38.6	42.5	42.0	34.4	36.4	36.4	42.9	48.7	47.8
New Zealand	41.6	39.0	50.9	31.8	29.1	37.8	51.3	49.1	64.4
Norway	41.1	42.0	42.9	29.7	30.0	30.9	52.8	54.2	55.2
Portugal	—	—	—	—	—	—	—	—	—
Spain	33.1	32.0	31.5	26.4	25.5	24.7	40.0	38.9	38.7
Sweden	35.2	38.4	40.3	26.5	28.6	30.1	44.1	48.5	50.9
Switzerland	20.8	20.9	21.6	23.3	23.5	23.3	18.3	18.4	19.9
Turkey	—	—	—	—	—	—	—	—	—
United Kingdom	—	—	39.2	—	—	34.2	—	—	44.3
United States	36.1	33.4	33.3	29.7	27.6	27.6	42.9	39.4	39.3

—Not available.
[1]Data for Flemish Belgium only.
NOTE: The recipients per 100 persons ratio relates the number of people of all ages earning bachelor's degrees in a particular year to the number of people in the population at the typical age of graduation. The typical age is based on full-time attendance and normal progression through the education system (without repeating a year, taking a year off, etc.); this age varies across countries because of differences in their education systems.
SOURCE: Organization for Economic Cooperation and Development (OECD), Education Online Database. Retrieved October 24, 2006, from http://stats.oecd.org/WBOS/Default.aspx. (This table was prepared October 2006.)

Table 410. Percentage of bachelor's degrees awarded in science, by field and country: Selected years, 1985 through 2003

Country	All science degrees[1]					Natural sciences[2]					Mathematics and computer science[3]					Engineering				
	1985	1990	1995	2000	2003	1985	1990	1995	2000	2003	1985	1990	1995	2000	2003	1985	1990	1995	2000	2003
1	2	3	4	5	6	7	8	9	10	11	12	13	14	15	16	17	18	19	20	21
Australia	—	—	19.3	21.1	23.7	—	—	9.9	7.6	5.5	—	—	3.8	5.1	10.2	—	—	5.6	8.5	8.0
Austria	16.8	19.6	21.1	25.7	26.5	5.0	5.3	6.0	5.0	5.3	4.1	5.2	5.3	3.4	3.4	7.7	9.0	9.9	17.3	17.8
Belgium[4]	—	—	—	—	24.6	4.6	—	—	—	7.0	1.7	—	—	—	2.8	—	—	—	—	14.9
Canada	17.1	16.4	16.7	20.0	—	4.9	6.0	6.5	8.1	—	4.5	4.2	3.8	4.3	—	7.7	6.2	6.4	7.6	—
Czech Republic	—	—	—	29.5	30.2	—	—	—	4.2	4.7	—	—	—	8.4	4.2	—	—	—	16.9	21.4
Denmark	—	—	—	10.5	11.4	6.3	4.4	2.5	6.8	3.2	—	—	—	3.1	1.1	16.2	21.7	17.0	0.6	7.1
Finland	39.3	33.5	37.2	32.2	28.8	7.7	4.1	4.0	3.9	2.6	6.3	5.9	6.9	3.3	4.5	25.3	23.4	26.3	24.9	21.8
France	—	—	—	30.1	27.1	—	—	—	12.2	9.0	—	—	—	5.5	4.7	—	—	—	12.5	13.4
Germany[5]	23.8	31.3	31.6	31.7	30.1	5.0	7.2	6.7	6.4	6.0	2.3	3.5	5.2	4.9	5.8	16.5	20.5	19.7	20.3	18.3
Hungary	—	—	—	12.6	—	—	—	—	1.1	—	—	—	—	1.2	—	—	—	—	10.4	—
Iceland	—	—	—	16.5	17.3	—	—	—	6.0	4.7	—	—	—	4.0	6.6	—	—	—	6.5	6.1
Ireland	28.8	34.1	32.3	29.3	27.0	12.8	14.1	16.9	11.5	8.4	4.0	6.3	4.7	7.2	9.6	12.0	13.7	10.7	10.6	8.9
Italy	19.5	19.7	19.5	27.5	25.6	8.1	7.6	6.8	5.9	5.1	3.1	3.9	3.8	3.2	2.9	8.3	8.3	8.9	18.4	17.6
Japan	22.7	23.5	22.8	—	—	2.4	2.4	3.4	—	—	—	—	—	—	—	20.3	21.0	19.3	18.9	18.2
Korea, Republic of	—	—	—	36.9	37.8	—	—	—	6.3	6.6	—	—	—	4.3	3.9	—	—	—	26.3	27.3
Mexico	—	—	—	23.0	28.1	—	—	—	2.2	2.5	—	—	—	6.7	8.9	—	—	—	14.1	16.8
Netherlands	21.8	21.1	—	16.2	—	8.5	7.1	—	3.2	—	1.2	1.6	1.6	1.9	—	12.1	12.4	—	11.1	—
New Zealand	20.5	19.5	—	17.8	20.4	11.7	8.2	—	11.2	5.8	5.5	5.5	—	1.9	8.7	3.3	5.8	3.2	4.7	5.8
Norway	—	12.9	16.8	11.6	16.5	2.5	2.1	3.1	0.7	0.4	1.8	0.6	0.5	3.4	6.5	—	10.2	13.2	7.5	9.7
Poland	—	—	—	16.7	17.0	—	—	—	2.7	2.6	—	—	—	2.0	3.0	—	—	—	12.0	11.4
Portugal	—	—	15.0	17.5	18.2	6.5	6.7	2.2	1.7	2.9	—	—	2.8	3.6	2.4	—	10.5	9.9	12.2	12.9
Spain	13.9	15.0	18.2	22.7	24.7	5.5	5.7	4.3	5.3	4.7	1.3	2.6	4.5	4.3	4.6	7.0	6.7	9.4	13.1	15.4
Sweden	15.4	24.0	26.4	27.7	—	2.6	4.1	3.9	3.7	—	1.6	4.7	5.5	3.7	—	11.3	15.2	17.0	20.3	—
Switzerland	20.2	23.0	22.3	25.1	23.9	10.3	11.2	10.4	6.0	5.6	2.1	3.7	3.7	1.8	3.6	7.9	8.1	8.3	17.3	14.7
Turkey	23.0	20.6	20.9	24.1	21.7	3.6	4.6	5.1	7.4	6.4	1.6	2.1	2.7	3.6	3.8	17.8	13.8	13.1	13.1	11.5
United Kingdom	—	—	—	28.5	31.2	—	—	—	12.5	13.0	—	—	—	5.8	8.5	—	—	—	10.2	9.7
United States	21.7	16.9	—	17.1	17.6	6.3	5.1	—	6.6	6.0	5.5	4.0	3.3	3.9	5.2	9.8	7.8	6.7	6.6	6.4

—Not available.

[1]Includes life sciences, physical sciences, mathematics/statistics, computer science, and engineering.
[2]Includes life sciences and physical sciences.
[3]Includes mathematics/statistics and computer science.
[4]Data for Flemish Belgium only.
[5]Data for 1985 are for the former West Germany.

NOTE: Data in this table refer to degrees classified by the Organization for Economic Cooperation and Development (OECD) as International Standard Classification of Education (ISCED), level 5A, first award. This level corresponds to the bachelor's degree in the United States.
SOURCE: Organization for Economic Cooperation and Development (OECD), Education Online Database. Retrieved October 31, 2005, from http://stats.oecd.org/WBOS/Default.aspx. (This table was prepared November 2005.)

Table 411. Percentage of graduate degrees awarded in science, by field and country: Selected years, 1985 through 2003

Country	All science degrees[1]						Natural sciences[2]						Mathematics and computer science[3]						Engineering					
	1985	1990	1996	1999	2000	2003	1985	1990	1996	1999	2000	2003	1985	1990	1996	1999	2000	2003	1985	1990	1996	1999	2000	2003
1	2	3	4	5	6	7	8	9	10	11	12	13	14	15	16	17	18	19	20	21	22	23	24	25
Australia	—	—	14.0	17.9	15.2	15.5	—	—	5.4	6.3	4.0	3.6	—	—	3.8	3.8	4.9	7.2	—	—	4.7	7.7	6.3	4.7
Austria	43.3	37.7	38.8	38.4	39.2	35.4	14.2	12.3	17.5	15.0	16.7	14.9	7.3	4.6	4.7	3.6	4.7	5.3	21.7	20.8	16.6	19.8	17.7	15.1
Belgium[4]	—	—	—	17.6	—	18.8	—	—	—	7.0	—	9.5	—	—	—	2.4	—	4.9	—	—	—	8.3	—	4.4
Canada	19.7	20.0	22.3	23.0	22.4	—	7.5	7.8	7.7	7.9	7.4	—	2.8	3.4	3.5	3.6	4.1	—	9.4	8.8	11.2	11.5	10.9	—
Czech Republic	—	—	—	21.3	21.0	12.4	—	—	—	5.6	5.3	3.5	—	—	—	6.3	7.9	2.2	—	—	—	9.3	7.7	6.7
Denmark	16.0	22.2	12.3	—	30.2	27.8	4.1	5.8	3.1	—	9.8	8.1	2.7	4.8	1.5	—	2.5	4.1	9.2	11.6	7.8	—	15.4	15.7
Finland	47.6	30.6	28.3	31.1	28.7	28.1	24.0	14.7	11.6	8.5	11.3	10.3	6.3	5.4	4.0	3.9	2.4	3.5	17.2	10.5	12.7	18.7	14.9	14.3
France	—	—	—	21.0	26.4	34.4	—	—	—	6.4	13.5	17.1	—	—	—	1.6	5.6	8.5	—	—	—	13.0	7.3	8.9
Germany[5]	27.7	33.2	38.6	38.9	38.1	36.0	18.7	23.5	25.5	25.2	24.9	22.2	1.8	2.3	3.5	4.0	3.7	4.2	7.2	7.4	9.5	9.8	9.5	9.6
Hungary	—	—	—	13.5	9.9	7.7	—	—	—	4.8	1.7	1.7	—	—	—	1.2	0.7	1.1	—	—	—	7.6	7.5	4.9
Iceland	31.4	34.5	23.1	30.7	35.9	20.5	18.9	19.5	10.9	20.0	19.4	10.3	2.6	5.8	3.0	—	—	1.0	9.9	9.3	9.2	10.7	16.5	9.2
Ireland	—	—	—	24.8	28.1	21.0	—	—	—	4.0	6.9	5.1	—	—	—	16.0	15.2	10.0	—	—	—	4.8	6.0	6.0
Italy	—	—	—	13.1	11.7	12.8	—	—	—	1.0	0.3	2.8	—	—	—	6.5	5.7	3.9	—	—	—	5.6	5.7	6.1
Japan	50.1	54.6	—	—	—	—	—	—	—	—	—	—	—	—	—	—	—	—	40.5	45.1	44.4	42.4	41.9	38.5
Korea, Republic of	—	—	—	48.3	51.7	45.6	—	—	—	8.8	8.5	10.2	—	—	—	4.1	5.7	3.1	—	—	—	35.4	34.3	32.3
Mexico	—	28.9	18.6	22.7	31.4	20.0	—	17.7	4.4	14.3	18.9	6.8	—	1.5	3.7	2.0	4.1	2.5	—	9.7	10.6	6.4	8.4	10.8
Netherlands	—	—	16.7	17.6	—	24.2	—	—	12.7	8.7	—	3.9	—	—	1.1	—	—	0.7	—	—	3.0	—	—	—
New Zealand	45.1	22.6	38.3	24.4	20.5	16.7	24.6	13.8	8.7	13.4	11.6	6.7	5.4	4.7	1.9	1.5	1.4	6.0	15.1	4.0	27.7	9.4	7.5	4.7
Norway	40.1	33.4	—	21.0	22.0	22.0	17.9	8.0	—	15.0	14.9	11.8	3.5	2.1	—	4.3	4.6	5.6	18.7	23.3	—	1.7	2.5	4.7
Poland	—	—	—	3.1	3.3	4.1	—	—	—	0.6	0.7	0.8	—	—	—	0.9	0.7	0.6	—	—	—	1.7	1.9	2.7
Portugal	—	—	—	—	39.3	—	—	—	—	—	11.7	—	—	—	—	—	9.4	—	—	—	—	—	18.2	—
Spain	35.6	26.9	36.0	40.1	36.1	35.8	28.6	19.7	24.8	24.8	23.9	22.7	1.8	1.4	4.1	4.2	5.4	5.7	5.1	5.7	7.1	11.1	6.8	7.3
Sweden	48.0	48.5	32.3	41.5	40.5	32.2	21.2	19.4	9.2	14.4	14.3	11.4	6.8	9.2	5.9	4.1	4.0	3.8	20.0	19.9	17.1	23.0	22.2	17.0
Switzerland	30.7	30.2	40.1	41.5	42.7	32.6	20.3	22.0	25.8	11.4	11.7	9.8	2.8	1.7	4.1	17.0	19.5	12.6	7.6	6.5	10.1	13.1	11.6	10.2
Turkey	35.8	24.0	—	29.8	25.7	22.9	6.6	7.6	—	8.0	7.6	6.9	2.8	3.3	—	3.0	3.0	3.2	26.3	13.2	—	18.7	15.2	12.7
United Kingdom	—	—	13.8	21.8	21.7	22.1	—	—	4.0	6.0	7.4	7.5	—	—	—	4.7	5.0	6.2	—	—	—	11.0	9.2	8.4
United States	13.5	14.5	13.8	13.7	13.0	13.7	4.5	4.2	4.0	3.8	3.4	3.4	2.8	3.4	3.2	3.1	3.4	4.0	6.3	6.9	6.7	6.8	6.2	6.4

—Not available.
[1] Includes life sciences, physical sciences, mathematics/statistics, computer science, and engineering.
[2] Includes life sciences and physical sciences.
[3] Includes mathematics/statistics and computer science.
[4] Data for Flemish Belgium only.
[5] Data for 1985 are for the former West Germany.

NOTE: Data in this table refer to degrees classified by the Organization for Economic Cooperation and Development (OECD) as International Standard Classification of Education (ISCED), level 5A, second award and ISCED 6. ISCED 5A, second award, corresponds to master's and first-professional degrees in the United States, and ISCED 6 corresponds to doctor's degrees.
SOURCE: Organization for Economic Cooperation and Development (OECD), Education Online Database. Retrieved October 31, 2005, from http://stats.oecd.org/WBOS/Default.aspx. (This table was prepared November 2005.)

Table 412. Public and private education expenditures per student, by level of education and country: 2000 through 2003

Country	Elementary				Secondary				Higher education			
	2000	2001	2002	2003	2000	2001	2002	2003	2000	2001	2002	2003
1	2	3	4	5	6	7	8	9	10	11	12	13
	Current dollars											
Australia.........................	$4,967	$5,052	$5,169	$5,494	$6,894	$7,239	$7,375	$7,788	$12,854	$12,688	$12,416	$12,406
Austria	6,560	6,571	7,015	7,139	8,578	8,562	8,887	8,943	10,851	11,274	12,448	12,344
Belgium.........................	4,310	5,321	5,665	6,180	6,889	7,912	8,272	7,708	10,771	11,589	12,019	11,824
Canada.........................	—	—	—	—	5,947 [1]	—	6,482	—	14,983	—	19,992	—
Czech Republic...............	1,827	1,871	2,077	2,273	3,239	3,448	3,628	4,088	5,431	5,555	6,236	6,774
Denmark.........................	7,074	7,572	7,727	7,814	7,726	8,113	8,003	8,183	11,981	14,280	15,183	14,014
Finland.........................	4,317	4,708	5,087	5,321	6,094	6,537	7,121	7,402	8,244	10,981	11,768	12,047
France.........................	4,486	4,777	5,033	4,939	7,636	8,107	8,472	8,653	8,373	8,837	9,276	10,704
Germany.........................	4,198	4,237	4,537	4,624	6,826	6,620	7,025	7,173	10,898	10,504	10,999	11,594
Greece.........................	3,318 [2]	3,299	3,803	4,218	3,859 [2]	3,768	4,058	4,954	3,402 [2]	4,280	4,731	4,924
Hungary[2].........................	2,245	2,592	3,016	3,286	2,446	2,633	3,184	3,948	7,024	7,122	8,205	8,576
Iceland.........................	5,854 [2]	6,373	7,171	7,752	6,518 [2]	7,265	7,229	6,898	7,994 [2]	7,674	8,251	8,023
Ireland.........................	3,385	3,743	4,180	4,760	4,638	5,245	5,725	6,374	11,083	10,003	9,809	9,341
Italy[2].........................	5,973	6,783	7,231	7,366	7,218	8,258	7,598	7,938	8,065	8,347	8,636	8,764
Japan.........................	5,507	5,771	6,117	6,350	6,266	6,534	6,952	7,283	10,914	11,164	11,716	11,556
Korea, Republic of	3,155	3,714	3,553	4,098	4,069	5,159	5,882	6,410	6,118	6,618	6,047	7,089
Luxembourg.........................	—	7,873	10,611	11,481	—	11,091	15,195	17,078	—	—	—	—
Mexico	1,291	1,357	1,467	1,656	1,615	1,915	1,768	1,918	4,688	4,341	6,074	5,774
Netherlands.........................	4,325	4,862	5,558	5,836	5,912	6,403	6,823	6,996	11,934	12,974	13,101	13,444
New Zealand.........................	—	—	4,536	4,841	—	—	5,698	5,693	—	—	—	8,832
Norway.........................	6,550 [2]	7,404	7,508	7,977	8,476 [2]	9,040	10,154	10,919	13,353 [2]	13,189	13,739	13,772
Poland[2].........................	2,105	2,322	2,585	2,859	—	—	—	2,951	3,222	3,579	4,834	4,589
Portugal	3,672	4,181	4,940 [2]	4,503 [2]	5,349	5,976	6,921 [2]	6,094 [2]	4,766	5,199	6,960	7,200[2]
Slovak Republic.........................	1,308	1,252	1,471	2,020	1,927	1,874	2,193	2,401	4,949	5,285	4,756	4,678
Spain	3,941	4,168	4,592	4,829	5,185	5,442	6,010	6,418	6,666	7,455	8,020	8,943
Sweden.........................	6,336	6,295	7,143	7,291	6,339	6,482	7,400	7,662	15,097	15,188	15,715	16,073
Switzerland[2].........................	6,631	6,889	7,776	8,131	9,780	10,916	11,900	12,209	18,450	20,230	23,714	25,900
Turkey[2].........................	—	—	—	869	—	—	—	1,428	4,121	—	—	—
United Kingdom.........................	3,877	4,415	5,150	5,851	5,991	5,933	6,505	7,290	9,657	10,753	11,822	11,866
United States.........................	6,995	7,560	8,049	8,305	8,855	8,779	9,098	9,590	20,358	22,234	20,545	24,074
	Constant 2005 dollars											
Australia.........................	$5,633	$5,571	$5,611	$5,831	$7,819	$7,983	$8,006	$8,266	$14,578	$13,992	$13,479	$13,168
Austria	7,440	7,246	7,616	7,577	9,729	9,442	9,648	9,492	12,307	12,433	13,514	13,102
Belgium.........................	4,888	5,868	6,150	6,560	7,813	8,725	8,980	8,181	12,216	12,780	13,048	12,550
Canada.........................	—	—	—	—	6,745 [1]	—	6,880	—	16,993	—	21,220	—
Czech Republic...............	2,072	2,063	2,255	2,413	3,674	3,802	3,939	4,339	6,160	6,126	6,770	7,190
Denmark.........................	8,023	8,350	8,388	8,294	8,762	8,947	8,688	8,686	13,588	15,748	16,483	14,875
Finland.........................	4,896	5,192	5,522	5,648	6,911	7,209	7,731	7,857	9,350	12,109	12,775	12,787
France.........................	5,088	5,268	5,464	5,242	8,660	8,940	9,197	9,184	9,496	9,745	10,070	11,361
Germany.........................	4,761	4,672	4,925	4,908	7,742	7,300	7,626	7,614	12,360	11,583	11,941	12,306
Greece.........................	3,763 [2]	3,638	4,129	4,477	4,377 [2]	4,155	4,405	5,258	3,858 [2]	4,720	5,136	5,226
Hungary[2].........................	2,546	2,858	3,274	3,488	2,774	2,904	3,457	4,190	7,966	7,854	8,907	9,103
Iceland.........................	6,639 [2]	7,028	7,785	8,228	7,392 [2]	8,012	7,848	7,322	9,066 [2]	8,463	8,957	8,516
Ireland.........................	3,839	4,128	4,538	5,052	5,260	5,784	6,215	6,765	12,570	11,031	10,649	9,915
Italy[2].........................	6,774	7,480	7,850	7,818	8,186	9,107	8,248	8,425	9,147	9,205	9,375	9,302
Japan.........................	6,246	6,364	6,641	6,740	7,107	7,205	7,547	7,730	12,378	12,311	12,719	12,266
Korea, Republic of	3,578	4,096	3,857	4,350	4,615	5,689	6,386	6,804	6,939	7,298	6,565	7,524
Luxembourg.........................	—	8,682	11,519	12,186	—	12,231	16,496	18,127	—	—	—	—
Mexico	1,464	1,496	1,593	1,758	1,832	2,112	1,919	2,036	5,317	4,787	6,594	6,129
Netherlands.........................	4,905	5,362	6,034	6,194	6,705	7,061	7,407	7,426	13,535	14,307	14,222	14,270
New Zealand.........................	—	—	4,924	5,138	—	—	6,186	6,043	—	—	—	9,374
Norway.........................	7,429 [2]	8,165	8,151	8,467	9,613 [2]	9,969	11,023	11,590	15,144 [2]	14,544	14,915	14,618
Poland[2].........................	2,387	2,561	2,806	3,035	—	—	—	3,132	3,654	3,947	5,248	4,871
Portugal	4,165	4,611	5,363 [2]	4,780 [2]	6,067	6,590	7,513 [2]	6,468 [2]	5,405	5,733	7,556	7,642[2]

See notes at end of table.

Table 412. Public and private education expenditures per student, by level of education and country: 2000 through 2003—Continued

Country	Elementary				Secondary				Higher education			
	2000	2001	2002	2003	2000	2001	2002	2003	2000	2001	2002	2003
1	2	3	4	5	6	7	8	9	10	11	12	13
Slovak Republic.............................	1,483	1,381	1,597	2,144	2,186	2,067	2,381	2,548	5,613	5,828	5,163	4,965
Spain	4,470	4,596	4,985	5,126	5,881	6,001	6,524	6,812	7,560	8,221	8,707	9,492
Sweden..	7,186	6,942	7,754	7,739	7,189	7,148	8,033	8,133	17,122	16,749	17,060	17,060
Switzerland[2].................................	7,521	7,597	8,442	8,630	11,092	12,038	12,919	12,959	20,925	22,309	25,744	27,491
Turkey[2]	—	—	—	922	—	—	—	1,516	4,674	—	—	—
United Kingdom.............................	4,397	4,869	5,591	6,210	6,795	6,543	7,062	7,738	10,952	11,858	12,834	12,595
United States.................................	7,933	8,337	8,738	8,815	10,043	9,681	9,877	10,179	23,089	24,519	22,304	25,552

—Not available.
[1]Includes elementary education.
[2]Public institutions only.

NOTE: Data adjusted to U.S. dollars using the purchasing-power-parity (PPP) index. Constant dollars based on the Consumer Price Index, prepared by the Bureau of Labor Statistics, U.S. Department of Labor.
SOURCE: Organization for Economic Cooperation and Development (OECD), *Education at a Glance*, 2002 through 2006. (This table was prepared September 2006.)

Table 413. Total public direct expenditures on education as a percentage of the gross domestic product, by level and country: Selected years, 1985 through 2003

Country	All institutions							Primary and secondary institutions							Higher education institutions						
	1985	1990	1995	2000	2001[1]	2002[1]	2003[1]	1985	1990	1995	2000	2001[1]	2002[1]	2003[1]	1985	1990	1995	2000	2001[1]	2002[1]	2003[1]
1	2	3	4	5	6	7	8	9	10	11	12	13	14	15	16	17	18	19	20	21	22
Average for year	5.3	4.9	4.9	5.1	4.9	5.0	5.1	3.7	3.5	3.5	3.5	3.6	3.5	3.6	1.1	1.0	0.9	1.2	1.0	1.0	1.0
Average for countries reporting data for all years	5.2	5.2	5.2	5.4	5.1	5.3	5.2	3.7	3.6	3.6	3.6	3.7	3.7	3.7	1.1	1.1	1.1	1.4	1.1	1.2	1.0
Australia	5.4	4.3	4.5	5.1	4.5	4.4	4.3	3.5	3.2	3.2	3.9	3.6	3.6	3.4	1.7	1.0	1.2	1.2	0.8	0.8	0.8
Austria	5.6	5.2	5.3	5.8	5.6	5.4	5.2	3.7	3.6	3.8	3.8[2]	3.8	3.7	3.7	1.0	1.0	0.9	1.4[2]	1.2	1.1	1.1
Belgium[3]	6.3	4.8	5.0	5.2	6.0	6.1	5.9	4.0	3.4	3.4	3.4[4]	4.0[4]	4.1[4]	4.0	1.0	0.8	0.9	1.3[4]	1.2[4]	1.2[4]	1.2
Canada	6.1	5.4	5.8	5.5	4.9	4.6	—	4.1	3.7	4.0	3.3[5]	3.1[5]	3.2[5,6]	—	2.0	1.5	1.5	2.0[5]	1.5[5]	1.3[5]	—
Czech Republic	—	—	4.8	4.4	4.2	4.2	4.3	—	—	3.4	3.0[4]	2.8[4]	2.8	2.9	—	—	0.7	0.8[4]	0.8	0.8	0.9
Denmark	6.2	6.2	6.5	8.4	6.8[2]	6.8[2]	6.7	4.7	4.4	4.2	4.8[2,7]	4.2[2,7]	4.1[2,7]	4.1[7]	1.2	1.3	1.3	2.5[2,7]	1.8[2,7]	1.9[2,7]	1.7[7]
Finland	5.8	6.4	6.6	6.0	5.7	5.9	6.0	—	4.3	4.2	3.6	3.7	3.8	3.9	1.2	1.2	1.7	2.0	1.7	1.7	1.7
France	—	5.1	5.8	5.8	5.6	5.7	5.8	2.8	3.7	4.1	4.1	4.0	4.0	4.0	—	0.8	1.0	1.0	1.0	1.0	1.1
Germany[8]	4.6	—	4.5	4.5	4.4	4.4	4.4	2.8	—	2.9	3.0	2.9	3.0	2.9	1.0	—	1.0	1.1	1.0	1.0	1.0
Greece	—	—	3.7	3.8	3.8[2]	3.9[2]	4.0	—	—	2.8	2.7[2]	2.4[2]	2.5[2]	2.6[6]	—	—	0.8	0.9[2]	1.1[2]	1.2[2]	1.2
Hungary	—	5.0	4.9	4.9	4.6	5.0	5.5	—	3.5	3.3	3.1	2.8	3.1	3.5	—	0.8	0.8	1.0	0.9	1.0	1.0
Iceland	—	4.3	4.5	6.0	6.1[2]	6.8[2]	7.5	—	3.3	3.4	4.7[2]	5.0[2]	5.4[2,7]	5.2[7]	—	0.6	0.7	1.1[2]	0.9[2]	1.0[2,7]	1.1[7]
Ireland	5.6	4.7	4.7	4.4	4.1	4.1	4.1	4.0	3.3	3.3	3.0[4]	2.9[4]	3.0[4]	3.1	0.9	0.9	0.9	1.3[4]	1.1[4]	1.1[4]	1.0
Italy	4.7	5.8	4.5	4.6	4.9	4.6	4.6	3.2	4.1	3.2	3.2	3.6	3.4	3.5	0.6	1.0	0.7	0.8	0.8	0.8	0.7
Japan	—	3.6	3.6	3.6	3.5	3.5	3.5	—	2.9	2.8	2.7[7]	2.7[7]	2.7[7]	2.7[7]	—	0.4	0.4	0.5[7]	0.5[7]	0.4[7]	0.5[7]
Korea, Republic of	—	—	3.6	4.3	4.8	4.2	4.6	—	—	3.0	3.3	3.5	3.3	3.5	—	—	0.3	0.7	0.4	0.3	0.6
Luxembourg	—	—	4.3	—	3.6[2]	3.9[2,7]	—	—	—	4.2	—	3.6[2]	3.9[2,7]	4.0[6]	—	—	0.1	—	—	—	—
Mexico	—	3.2	4.6	4.9	5.1	5.1	5.6	—	2.2	3.4	3.4	3.8	3.5	3.8	—	0.7	0.8	0.9	0.7	1.0	0.9
Netherlands	6.2	5.7	4.6	4.8	4.5	4.6	4.6	4.1	3.6	3.0	3.2	3.1	3.3	3.2	1.5	1.6	1.1	1.3	1.0	1.0	1.1
New Zealand	—	5.5	5.3	7.0	5.5	5.6	5.7	—	3.9	3.8	4.9	4.3	4.4	4.5	—	1.2	1.1	1.7	0.9	0.9	0.9
Norway	5.1	6.2	6.8	6.7	6.1	6.7	6.5	4.0	4.1	4.1	3.9	4.6	4.2	4.6	0.7	1.1	1.5	1.7	1.3	1.4	1.5
Poland	—	—	5.2	5.2	5.6[2]	5.5[2]	5.8	—	—	3.3	3.8[2]	4.0[2]	4.0[2]	4.2	—	—	0.8	0.8[2]	1.1[2]	1.1[2]	1.0
Portugal	—	—	5.4	5.7	5.8[2]	5.7[2]	5.8	—	—	4.1	4.2[2]	4.2[2]	4.2[2]	4.2	—	—	1.0	1.0[2]	1.0[2]	0.9[2]	1.0
Russian Federation	†	†	3.4	3.0	3.0	3.7[2]	3.7	†	†	1.9	1.7	1.7	2.2	2.1	†	†	0.7	0.5	0.5	0.6	0.7
Slovak Republic	†	4.8	4.6	4.2	4.0[2,4]	3.7[2,4]	4.3	†	—	—	2.7[2,4]	2.6[2,4]	2.7[2,4]	2.8[9,10]	†	—	—	0.7[2,4]	0.8[2,4]	0.7[2,4]	0.8[9,10]
Spain	3.6	4.2	4.8	4.4	4.3	4.3	4.2	2.9	3.2	3.5	3.1	3.0	2.9	2.8	0.4	0.7	0.8	1.0	1.0	1.0[4]	0.9
Sweden	—	5.3	6.6	7.4	6.3	6.7	6.5	—	4.4	4.4	4.9[4]	4.3[4]	4.6[4]	4.5	—	1.0	1.6	2.0[4]	1.5[4]	1.6[4]	1.6
Switzerland	4.9	5.0	5.5	5.4	5.4	5.7	6.0	4.0	3.7	4.1	3.9	3.9	4.0	4.0	0.9	1.0	1.1	1.2	1.3	1.4	1.6
Turkey	—	3.2	2.2	3.5	3.5[2]	3.4[2]	3.6	—	2.3	1.4	2.4[2]	2.5[2]	2.3[2]	2.5[2]	—	0.9	0.8	1.1[2]	1.0[2]	1.0[2]	1.1
United Kingdom	4.9	4.3	4.6	4.8	4.7	5.0	5.1	3.1	3.5	3.8	3.4	3.4	3.7	4.0	1.0	0.7	0.7	0.8	0.8	0.8	0.8
United States	4.7	5.3	5.0	5.0	5.1	5.3	5.4	3.2	3.8	3.5	3.5[5]	3.8[5]	3.8	3.9	1.3	1.4	1.1	1.1[5]	0.9[5]	1.2	1.2

—Not available.

†Not applicable. Country did not exist during this time period.

[1]Includes public subsidies to households attributable for educational institutions and direct expenditure on educational institutions from international sources, except where noted.

[2]Public subsidies to households not included in public expenditure.

[3]Data are for Flemish Belgium only.

[4]Direct expenditure on education institutions from international sources exceeds 1.5 percent of all public expenditure.

[5]Postsecondary non-higher-education included in higher education.

[6]Preprimary education (for children age 3 and older) is included in primary and secondary education.

[7]Postsecondary non-higher-education included in both secondary and higher education.

[8]Data for 1985 are for the former West Germany.

[9]Postsecondary non-higher-education included in primary and secondary education.

[10]Education at the associate's degree level is included in primary and secondary education.

NOTE: Direct public expenditure on educational services includes both amounts spent directly by governments to hire educational personnel and to procure other resources, and amounts provided by governments to public or private institutions, or households. Figures for 1985 also include transfers and payments to private entities, and thus are not strictly comparable with later figures. Some data have been revised from previously published figures.

SOURCE: Organization for Economic Cooperation and Development (OECD), Education Online Database; *Annual National Accounts, Vol. 1,* 1997; and *Education at a Glance,* 2002 through 2006. (This table was prepared September 2006.)

Table 414. Foreign students enrolled in institutions of higher education in the United States and other jurisdictions, by continent, region, and selected countries of origin: Selected years, 1980–81 through 2004–05

Continent, region, and country	1980–81 Number	Percent	1985–86 Number	Percent	1990–91 Number	Percent	1995–96 Number	Percent	2000–01 Number	Percent	2001–02 Number	Percent	2002–03 Number	Percent	2003–04 Number	Percent	2004–05 Number	Percent
1	2	3	4	5	6	7	8	9	10	11	12	13	14	15	16	17	18	19
Total	**311,880**	**100.0**	**343,780**	**100.0**	**407,530**	**100.0**	**453,787**	**100.00**	**547,867**	**100.0**	**582,996**	**100.0**	**586,323**	**100.0**	**572,509**	**100.0**	**565,039**	**100.0**
Africa	38,180	12.2	34,190	9.9	23,800	5.8	20,844	4.59	34,217	6.2	37,724	6.5	40,193	6.9	38,150	6.7	36,100	6.4
Eastern Africa	6,260	2.0	6,730	2.0	7,590	1.9	7,596	1.67	13,516	2.5	15,331	2.6	15,996	2.7	14,831	2.6	13,675	2.4
Central Africa	1,130	0.4	1,540	0.4	1,650	0.4	1,346	0.30	1,859	0.3	1,972	0.3	2,371	0.4	2,331	0.4	2,505	0.4
North Africa	7,310	2.3	5,980	1.7	4,540	1.1	3,422	0.75	5,184	0.9	5,593	1.0	5,218	0.9	4,487	0.8	3,898	0.7
Southern Africa	1,480	0.5	2,360	0.7	2,840	0.7	2,657	0.59	3,304	0.6	3,443	0.6	3,017	0.5	2,679	0.5	2,240	0.4
West Africa	22,000	7.1	17,580	5.1	7,180	1.8	5,818	1.28	10,346	1.9	11,385	2.0	13,590	2.3	13,821	2.4	13,782	2.4
Nigeria	17,350	5.6	13,710	4.0	3,710	0.9	2,093	0.46	3,820	0.7	4,499	0.8	5,816	1.0	6,140	1.1	6,335	1.1
Asia	94,640	30.3	156,830	45.6	229,830	56.4	259,893	57.27	302,058	55.1	324,812	55.7	332,298	56.7	324,006	56.6	325,112	57.5
East Asia	51,650	16.6	80,720	23.5	146,020	35.8	166,717	36.74	189,371	34.6	196,813	33.8	199,666	34.1	189,874	33.2	192,561	34.1
China	2,770	0.9	13,980	4.1	39,600	9.7	39,613	8.73	59,939	10.9	63,211	10.8	64,757	11.0	61,765	10.8	62,523	11.1
Hong Kong	9,660	3.1	10,710	3.1	12,630	3.1	12,018	2.65	7,627	1.4	7,757	1.3	8,076	1.4	7,353	1.3	7,180	1.3
Japan	13,500	4.3	13,360	3.9	36,610	9.0	45,531	10.03	46,497	8.5	46,810	8.0	45,960	7.8	40,835	7.1	42,215	7.5
Korea, Republic of	6,150	2.0	18,660	5.4	23,360	5.7	36,231	7.98	45,685	8.3	49,046	8.4	51,519	8.8	52,484	9.2	53,358	9.4
Taiwan	19,460	6.2	23,770	6.9	33,530	8.2	32,702	7.21	28,566	5.2	28,930	5.0	28,017	4.8	26,178	4.6	25,914	4.6
South and Central Asia	14,540	4.7	25,800	7.5	42,370	10.4	45,401	10.00	71,765	13.1	86,131	14.8	93,767	16.0	98,138	17.1	97,961	17.3
India	9,250	3.0	16,070	4.7	28,860	7.1	31,743	7.00	54,664	10.0	66,836	11.5	74,603	12.7	79,736	13.9	80,466	14.2
Pakistan	2,990	1.0	5,440	1.6	7,730	1.9	6,427	1.42	6,948	1.3	8,644	1.5	8,123	1.4	7,325	1.3	6,296	1.1
Southeast Asia	28,450	9.1	50,310	14.6	41,440	10.2	47,774	10.53	40,916	7.5	41,868	7.2	38,865	6.6	35,994	6.3	34,590	6.1
Indonesia	3,250	1.0	8,210	2.4	9,520	2.3	12,820	2.83	11,625	2.1	11,614	2.0	10,432	1.8	8,880	1.6	7,760	1.4
Malaysia	6,010	1.9	23,020	6.7	13,610	3.3	14,015	3.09	7,795	1.4	7,395	1.3	6,595	1.1	6,483	1.1	6,142	1.1
Philippines	—	—	3,920	1.1	4,270	1.0	3,127	0.69	3,139	0.6	3,295	0.6	3,576	0.6	3,467	0.6	3,531	0.6
Singapore	—	—	3,930	1.1	4,500	1.1	4,098	0.90	4,166	0.8	4,141	0.7	4,141	0.7	3,955	0.7	3,769	0.7
Thailand	6,550	2.1	6,940	2.0	7,090	1.7	12,165	2.68	11,187	2.0	11,606	2.0	9,982	1.7	8,937	1.6	8,637	1.5
Europe	25,330	8.1	34,310	10.0	49,640	12.2	67,358	14.84	80,584	14.7	81,579	14.0	78,001	13.3	74,134	12.9	71,609	12.7
Eastern Europe	1,670	0.5	1,770	0.5	4,780	1.2	18,032	3.97	27,674	5.1	29,591	5.1	29,167	5.0	27,710	4.8	26,553	4.7
Western Europe	23,660	7.6	32,540	9.5	44,860	11.0	49,326	10.87	52,910	9.7	51,988	8.9	48,834	8.3	46,424	8.1	45,056	8.0
France	—	—	3,680	1.1	5,630	1.4	5,710	1.26	7,273	1.3	7,401	1.3	7,223	1.2	6,818	1.2	6,555	1.2
Germany[1]	3,310	1.1	4,730	1.4	7,000	1.7	9,017	1.99	10,128	1.8	9,613	1.6	9,302	1.6	8,745	1.5	8,640	1.5
Greece	3,750	1.2	4,440	1.3	4,360	1.1	3,365	0.74	2,768	0.5	2,599	0.4	2,341	0.4	2,126	0.4	2,035	0.4
Spain	—	—	1,740	0.5	4,300	1.1	4,809	1.06	4,156	0.8	4,048	0.7	3,633	0.6	3,631	0.6	3,512	0.6
United Kingdom	4,440	1.4	5,940	1.7	7,300	1.8	7,799	1.72	8,139	1.5	8,414	1.4	8,326	1.4	8,439	1.5	8,236	1.5
Latin America	49,810	16.0	45,480	13.2	47,580	11.7	47,253	10.41	63,634	11.6	68,358	11.7	68,950	11.8	69,658	12.2	67,818	12.0
Caribbean	10,650	3.4	11,100	3.2	12,610	3.1	10,737	2.37	14,423	2.6	13,879	2.4	14,895	2.5	15,606	2.7	13,898	2.5
Central America	12,970	4.2	12,740	3.7	15,950	3.9	14,220	3.13	16,764	3.1	18,826	3.2	18,856	3.2	19,264	3.4	19,227	3.4
Mexico	6,730	2.2	5,460	1.6	6,740	1.7	8,687	1.91	10,670	1.9	12,518	2.1	12,801	2.2	13,329	2.3	13,063	2.3
South America	26,190	8.4	21,640	6.3	19,020	4.7	22,296	4.91	32,447	5.9	35,653	6.1	35,199	6.0	34,788	6.1	34,693	6.1
Brazil	—	—	2,840	0.8	3,900	1.0	5,497	1.21	8,846	1.6	8,972	1.5	8,388	1.4	7,799	1.4	7,244	1.3
Colombia	6,770	2.2	4,010	1.2	3,180	0.8	3,462	0.76	6,765	1.2	8,068	1.4	7,771	1.3	7,533	1.3	7,334	1.3
Venezuela	10,440	3.3	7,040	2.0	2,890	0.7	4,456	0.98	5,217	1.0	5,627	1.0	5,333	0.9	5,575	1.0	5,279	0.9
Middle East	84,710	27.2	52,720	15.3	33,420	8.2	30,563	6.74	36,858	6.7	38,545	6.6	34,803	5.9	31,852	5.6	31,248	5.5
Iran	47,550	15.2	14,210	4.1	6,260	1.5	2,628	0.58	1,844	0.3	2,216	0.4	2,258	0.4	2,321	0.4	2,251	0.4
Israel	—	—	—	—	—	—	—	—	—	—	3,458	0.6	3,521	0.6	3,474	0.6	3,323	0.6
Jordan	6,140	2.0	6,590	1.9	4,320	1.1	2,222	0.49	2,187	0.4	2,417	0.4	2,212	0.4	1,853	0.3	1,752	0.3
Kuwait	—	—	—	—	—	—	—	—	—	—	2,966	0.5	2,364	0.4	1,846	0.3	1,720	0.3
Lebanon	6,770	2.2	7,090	2.1	3,900	1.0	1,554	0.34	2,005	0.4	2,435	0.4	2,179	0.4	2,040	0.4	2,040	0.4
Saudi Arabia	10,440	3.3	6,900	2.0	3,500	0.9	4,191	0.92	5,273	1.0	5,579	1.0	4,175	0.7	3,521	0.7	3,035	0.5
Turkey	—	—	2,460	0.7	4,080	1.0	7,678	1.69	10,983	2.0	12,091	2.1	11,601	2.0	11,398	2.0	12,474	2.2
North America[2]	14,790	4.7	16,030	4.7	18,950	4.6	23,644	5.21	25,888	4.7	27,039	4.6	27,227	4.6	27,650	4.8	28,634	5.1
Canada	14,320	4.6	15,410	4.5	18,350	4.5	23,005	5.07	25,279	4.6	26,514	4.5	26,513	4.5	27,017	4.7	28,140	5.0
Oceania	4,180	1.3	4,030	1.2	4,230	1.0	4,202	0.93	4,624	0.8	4,852	0.8	4,811	0.8	4,534	0.8	4,534	0.8
Stateless[3]	240	0.1	190	0.1	80	#	30	#	10	#	87	#	33	#	19	#	37	#

—Not available.

#Rounds to zero.

[1]Data for 1980–81 and 1985–86 are for West Germany (Federal Republic of Germany before unification).

[2]Excludes Mexico and Central America, which are included with Latin America.

[3]Home country unknown or undeclared.

NOTE: Totals and subtotals include other countries not shown separately. Data are for "nonimmigrants" (i.e., students who have not migrated to this country). Detail may not sum to totals because of rounding.

SOURCE: Institute of International Education, *Open Doors: Report on International Educational Exchange,* 1981 through 2005 (selected years). (This table was prepared June 2006.)

CHAPTER 7
Libraries and Educational Technology

This chapter contains statistics on libraries and the use of information technologies. These data show the extent of America's public access to information technologies outside of formal classroom activities. The data also provide a capsule description of the magnitude and availability of library resources.

The first section of the chapter (tables 415 to 421) deals with public libraries, public and private school libraries, and college and university libraries. It contains data on collections, population served, staff, and expenditures. Table 419 provides institutional-level information for the 60 largest college libraries in the country.

The second part of the chapter (tables 422 to 427) provides information on the availability and use of technology at school, home, and work. For example, the proportion of children using computers at school is shown over time. Also included are data on the use of home computers and the Internet by adults and school children, with comparisons among various demographic groups.

Related data may be found in other chapters of the *Digest*. For example, statistics on the number of degrees conferred in computer and information sciences and library sciences are in chapter 3. Further information on survey methodologies is in Appendix A: Guide to Sources and the publications cited in the table source notes.

Libraries

The average number of library staff per school with a library was 1.8 at public schools in 2003–04 and 1.2 at private schools in 1999–2000 (table 415). On average, public school libraries had smaller numbers of books on a per student basis (1,803 per 100 students) than private school libraries (2,857 per 100 students) in 1999–2000. The number of books on a per student basis in public school libraries (1,891 per 100 students) in 2003–04 was not measurably different from the number in 1999–2000. In 2003–04, public elementary school libraries had larger holdings than public secondary school libraries on a per student basis (2,127 books per 100 students, compared to 1,376 books per 100 students).

Between 1991–92 and 1999–2000, the increase in college library resources was greater than the increase in enrollment; after adjustment for inflation, the library operating expenditure per student rose 6 percent during this period (table 418). Between 1999–2000 and 2001–02, library operating expendi-

tures per student dropped 5 percent. Overall, there was a net increase of 1 percent in library operating expenditures per student between 1991–92 and 2001–02. In 2001–02, the average library operating expenditure per student was $460.

In 2004, there were 9,207 public libraries in the United States with a total of 805 million books and serial volumes. The annual number of visits per capita was 4.7, and the annual reference transactions per capita were 1.1 (table 421).

Computers and Technology

There has been widespread introduction of computers into the schools in recent years. In 2003, the average public school contained 136 instructional computers (table 422). One important technological advance that has come to classrooms following the introduction of computers has been connections to the Internet. The proportion of instructional rooms with internet access increased from 51 percent in 1998 to 93 percent in 2003 (figure 29). Nearly all schools had access to the Internet in 2003 (table 422).

The increasing number of computers in schools has coincided with rising proportions of students using computers (table 426). The proportion of elementary and secondary school students using computers at school rose from 70 percent in 1997 to 83 percent in 2003. In 2003, the use of computers at school by elementary and secondary school students varied by age and family income. Students in elementary and secondary schools who were 10 years old or older were more likely to use computers at school than children younger than 10. In general, elementary and secondary school students from higher income families were more likely to use computers at school than students from lower income families. For example, in 2003, 80 percent of children from families with incomes of $20,000 to $24,999 used computers at school, compared to 86 percent of children from families with incomes of $75,000 or more.

Just as large proportions of elementary and secondary students used computers at school, so a majority of students in 2003 used computers at home (table 426). In 2003, 68 percent of elementary and secondary school students used computers at home, compared to 43 percent in 1997. Between 1997 and 2003, the proportion of students using computers at home for school work rose from 25 to 47 percent. In 2003, female students were slightly more likely to use computers at home for school work than males (49 vs. 46 percent). About 54 percent of

White elementary and secondary school students used computers at home for school work in 2003, compared to 35 percent of Black students and 34 percent of Hispanic students. Computer usage at home for school work was more likely among students from families with higher incomes than those from families with lower incomes. For instance, about 63 percent of students from families with an income of $75,000 or more used a computer at home for school work, compared to 32 percent of students from families with incomes of $20,000 to $24,999.

The proportion of college students using computers at school rose from 63 percent in 1997 to 85 percent in 2003. About 76 percent used computers at home for school work in 2003 (table 426).

Computers are widely used in the workplace. In 2003, 56 percent of all workers used computers at work (table 427). More frequent use of computers at work was associated with higher levels of education and higher incomes. For example, 16 percent of high school dropouts and 40 percent of high school graduates used computers at work, compared to 82 to 87 percent of workers with bachelor's, master's, first-professional, or doctor's degrees. Among the common computer applications used by all employees using computers on the job were Internet and e-mail (75 percent), word processing/desktop publishing (68 percent), spreadsheets/databases (64 percent), and calendar/schedule (57 percent).

Figure 29. Percentage of all public schools and instructional rooms with internet access: Fall 1994 through fall 2003

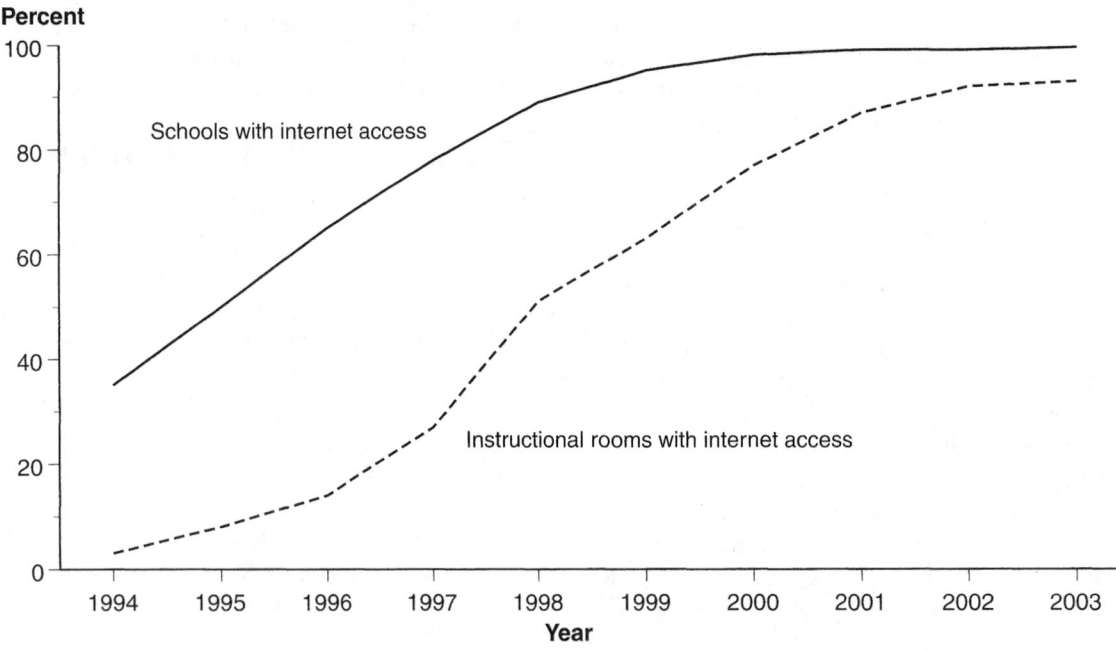

SOURCE: U.S. Department of Education, National Center for Education Statistics, *Internet Access in U.S. Public Schools and Classrooms: 1994–2003.*

Table 415. Selected statistics on school libraries/media centers, by control and level of school: 1999–2000 and 2003–04

Selected statistic	Public, 1999–2000	Public, 2003–04 Total	Elementary	Secondary	Combined elementary/ secondary	Private, 1999–2000 Total	Elementary	Secondary	Combined elementary/ secondary
	1	3	4	5	6	7	8	9	10
	2								
Number of schools with libraries	77,288 (420.6)	78,257 (548.2)	57,404 (439.8)	16,268 (313.4)	4,586 (201.4)	17,054 (323.2)	10,961 (251.4)	1,955 (91.2)	4,138 (173.8)
Average number of staff per library	1.89 (0.018)	1.76 (0.014)	1.66 (0.018)	2.09 (0.018)	1.74 (0.116)	1.18 (0.026)	1.01 (0.032)	1.80 (0.083)	1.33 (0.055)
Certified library/media specialists	0.81 (0.007)	0.79 (0.009)	0.73 (0.012)	1.03 (0.018)	0.73 (0.023)	0.23 (0.011)	0.13 (0.009)	0.55 (0.027)	0.35 (0.027)
Full-time	0.65 (0.007)	0.65 (0.009)	0.58 (0.010)	0.92 (0.018)	0.55 (0.027)	0.17 (0.009)	0.07 (0.007)	0.47 (0.025)	0.27 (0.022)
Part-time	0.16 (0.006)	0.14 (0.007)	0.15 (0.009)	0.11 (0.009)	0.18 (0.020)	0.06 (0.005)	0.06 (0.006)	0.07 (0.010)	0.08 (0.013)
Other professional staff	0.17 (0.007)	0.19 (0.008)	0.19 (0.011)	0.14 (0.010)	0.28 (0.036)	0.48 (0.014)	0.47 (0.020)	0.53 (0.039)	0.46 (0.024)
Full-time	0.12 (0.005)	0.13 (0.007)	0.14 (0.009)	0.11 (0.010)	0.16 (0.022)	0.22 (0.009)	0.19 (0.012)	0.33 (0.023)	0.27 (0.020)
Part-time	0.06 (0.004)	0.05 (0.005)	0.05 (0.006)	0.03 (0.004)	0.11 (0.031)	0.25 (0.012)	0.29 (0.017)	0.20 (0.029)	0.19 (0.017)
Other paid employees	0.91 (0.014)	0.78 (0.011)	0.75 (0.013)	0.93 (0.017)	0.73 (0.085)	0.48 (0.014)	0.41 (0.020)	0.72 (0.048)	0.52 (0.030)
Full-time	0.49 (0.008)	0.46 (0.009)	0.41 (0.011)	0.65 (0.017)	0.35 (0.028)	0.14 (0.009)	0.11 (0.011)	0.24 (0.024)	0.18 (0.015)
Part-time	0.41 (0.014)	0.33 (0.012)	0.34 (0.014)	0.28 (0.014)	0.38 (0.085)	0.34 (0.014)	0.31 (0.018)	0.48 (0.043)	0.34 (0.025)
Percentage of schools' library media centers with certain media equipment									
Telephone	84.8 (0.53)	90.5 (0.55)	89.9 (0.69)	95.3 (0.62)	82.1 (1.94)	53.2 (1.48)	45.3 (2.02)	78.2 (2.67)	62.3 (2.25)
Fax machine	11.5 (0.43)	10.9 (0.50)	6.9 (0.64)	23.1 (1.08)	17.0 (1.94)	6.7 (0.64)	4.8 (0.82)	13.6 (1.38)	8.7 (1.50)
Automated catalog	72.8 (0.69)	82.7 (0.66)	81.9 (0.89)	90.6 (0.76)	63.7 (2.59)	34.2 (1.25)	28.1 (1.54)	55.8 (2.61)	39.9 (2.25)
Automated circulation system	74.4 (0.65)	86.9 (0.61)	86.7 (0.82)	92.8 (0.80)	68.8 (2.45)	29.0 (1.17)	22.9 (1.31)	52.3 (2.48)	33.9 (2.33)
Video laser disc or DVD	43.0 (0.69)	44.1 (0.84)	39.3 (1.02)	52.3 (1.47)	43.2 (2.21)	12.7 (0.67)	10.4 (0.99)	21.2 (1.79)	15.0 (1.40)
Connection to Internet	90.1 (0.57)	95.1 (0.35)	94.1 (0.48)	99.2 (0.22)	92.6 (1.40)	60.6 (1.37)	55.1 (1.77)	81.6 (2.46)	65.2 (2.05)
Video cassette recorders (VCR)	— (†)	86.3 (0.65)	85.4 (0.77)	89.4 (1.21)	86.8 (1.69)	— (†)	— (†)	— (†)	— (†)
Disability assistance technologies, such as TDD	— (†)	11.9 (0.50)	10.2 (0.61)	18.0 (0.79)	11.7 (1.34)	— (†)	— (†)	— (†)	— (†)
Percentage of schools with certain services									
Students permitted to check out computer hardware	2.2 (0.14)	5.2 (0.37)	3.5 (0.45)	10.1 (0.77)	9.6 (1.34)	1.0 (0.17)	0.9 (0.25)	2.2 (0.41)	1.0 (0.29)
Students permitted to check out computer software	6.9 (0.31)	11.7 (0.44)	7.6 (0.56)	23.5 (1.05)	21.7 (2.22)	6.9 (0.57)	3.8 (0.50)	16.6 (1.53)	10.5 (1.59)
Number of library computer stations per 100 students	— (†)	2.3 (0.04)	2.2 (0.05)	2.5 (0.05)	2.7 (0.17)	— (†)	— (†)	— (†)	— (†)
Average holdings per 100 students at the end of the school year[1]									
Books (number of volumes)	1,803 (19.7)	1,891 (45.1)	2,127 (70.2)	1,376 (20.0)	2,407 (117.7)	2,857 (84.8)	2,801 (86.0)	2,737 (178.3)	3,043 (213.2)
Video materials (tape and disc)	51 (0.8)	68 (3.5)	70 (5.3)	61 (2.1)	87 (13.2)	71 (2.5)	66 (3.3)	72 (6.0)	81 (5.8)
CD-ROM titles	8 (0.3)	12 (0.9)	16 (1.4)	4 (0.3)	10 (1.7)	10 (0.6)	10 (0.8)	10 (1.3)	10 (1.0)
Average additions per 100 students during the school year[1]									
Books (number of volumes)	— (†)	99.3 (2.08)	118.4 (3.13)	61.2 (1.75)	109.2 (8.40)	— (†)	— (†)	— (†)	— (†)
Video materials (tape and disc)	— (†)	4.3 (0.17)	4.4 (0.23)	4.1 (0.19)	5.9 (0.75)	— (†)	— (†)	— (†)	— (†)
CD-ROM titles	— (†)	0.7 (0.09)	0.9 (0.14)	0.3 (0.03)	1.0 (0.23)	— (†)	— (†)	— (†)	— (†)
Total expenditures for library/media materials per pupil[1,2]	$23.37 (0.438)	$16.24 (0.322)	$16.00 (0.469)	$16.11 (0.320)	$21.24 (2.498)	$29.02 (1.050)	$23.60 (1.646)	$38.72 (1.582)	$33.40 (1.831)
Books	9.97 (0.153)	10.99 (0.299)	11.72 (0.452)	9.68 (0.275)	10.19 (0.631)	10.57 (0.625)	9.29 (1.115)	11.18 (0.472)	12.68 (0.834)
Video materials	1.07 (0.022)	0.97 (0.042)	0.91 (0.046)	1.01 (0.061)	1.76 (0.617)	1.34 (0.051)	1.04 (0.057)	1.51 (0.106)	1.83 (0.153)
CD-ROM titles	0.59 (0.020)	0.17 (0.016)	0.21 (0.031)	0.10 (0.011)	0.20 (0.040)	0.82 (0.056)	0.72 (0.081)	1.15 (0.109)	0.81 (0.081)
Current serial subscriptions	1.26 (0.016)	1.38 (0.025)	1.06 (0.031)	1.87 (0.049)	2.50 (0.148)	1.34 (0.035)	0.62 (0.030)	2.71 (0.120)	1.86 (0.098)
Electronic subscriptions	0.81 (0.018)	0.88 (0.033)	0.39 (0.042)	1.79 (0.061)	1.25 (0.249)	1.35 (0.056)	0.17 (0.036)	3.85 (0.213)	2.08 (0.124)
Value of donated computers, A/V equipment, and other items per student[1,3]	— (†)	$1.56 (0.083)	$1.64 (0.108)	$1.12 (0.074)	$3.88 (0.761)	— (†)	— (†)	— (†)	— (†)

—Not available.
†Not applicable.
[1] Data are for the prior school year.
[2] Includes other expenditures not separately shown.
[3] Includes grants and other contributions.

NOTE: Percentages are based on schools that have library/media centers. Detail may not sum to totals because of rounding. Standard errors appear in parentheses.
SOURCE: U.S. Department of Education, National Center for Education Statistics, Schools and Staffing Survey (SASS), "Public School Library Media Center Questionnaire," 1999–2000 and 2003–04; "Charter School Questionnaire," 1999–2000; and "Private School Library Media Center Questionnaire," 1999–2000, unpublished tabulations. (This table was prepared September 2006.)

Table 416. Selected statistics on public school libraries/media centers, by level and enrollment size of school: 2003–04

Selected statistic	All public school libraries/media centers	Elementary school libraries — Total	Less than 150	150 to 499	500 to 749	750 or more	Secondary school libraries — Total	Less than 500	500 to 749	750 to 1,499	1,500 or more
1	2	3	4	5	6	7	8	9	10	11	12
Number of schools with libraries	78,257 (548.2)	57,404 (439.8)	3,227 (273.1)	29,803 (594.0)	15,735 (540.8)	8,639 (343.4)	16,268 (313.4)	5,444 (243.4)	2,914 (148.8)	4,933 (190.9)	2,976 (155.6)
Average number of staff per library	1.76 (0.014)	1.66 (0.018)	1.21 (0.094)	1.62 (0.023)	1.71 (0.029)	1.91 (0.040)	2.09 (0.025)	1.56 (0.040)	1.83 (0.045)	2.25 (0.040)	3.06 (0.088)
Certified library/media specialists	0.79 (0.009)	0.73 (0.012)	0.51 (0.052)	0.70 (0.019)	0.76 (0.019)	0.83 (0.024)	1.03 (0.018)	0.78 (0.032)	0.96 (0.031)	1.12 (0.025)	1.38 (0.050)
Full-time	0.65 (0.009)	0.58 (0.010)	0.16 (0.027)	0.51 (0.016)	0.68 (0.019)	0.76 (0.023)	0.92 (0.018)	0.61 (0.029)	0.88 (0.027)	1.04 (0.025)	1.33 (0.047)
Part-time	0.14 (0.007)	0.15 (0.009)	0.36 (0.044)	0.19 (0.015)	0.08 (0.011)	0.07 (0.014)	0.11 (0.009)	0.17 (0.017)	0.08 (0.017)	0.08 (0.015)	0.06 (0.010)
Other professional staff	0.19 (0.008)	0.19 (0.011)	0.17 (0.048)	0.21 (0.017)	0.18 (0.016)	0.16 (0.018)	0.14 (0.010)	0.15 (0.019)	0.13 (0.020)	0.13 (0.016)	0.15 (0.024)
Full-time	0.13 (0.007)	0.14 (0.009)	0.08 (0.044)	0.15 (0.014)	0.14 (0.015)	0.13 (0.016)	0.11 (0.009)	0.11 (0.016)	0.11 (0.018)	0.11 (0.017)	0.12 (0.023)
Part-time	0.05 (0.005)	0.05 (0.006)	0.09 (0.024)	0.06 (0.008)	0.05 (0.010)	0.04 (0.010)	0.03 (0.004)	0.04 (0.008)	0.02 (0.008)	0.02 (0.004)	0.04 (0.016)
Other paid employees	0.78 (0.011)	0.75 (0.013)	0.53 (0.059)	0.72 (0.018)	0.76 (0.027)	0.91 (0.031)	0.93 (0.017)	0.63 (0.028)	0.74 (0.047)	1.00 (0.033)	1.53 (0.058)
Full-time	0.46 (0.009)	0.41 (0.011)	0.20 (0.036)	0.37 (0.017)	0.43 (0.024)	0.61 (0.028)	0.65 (0.017)	0.39 (0.028)	0.46 (0.031)	0.74 (0.032)	1.16 (0.053)
Part-time	0.33 (0.012)	0.34 (0.014)	0.33 (0.062)	0.35 (0.020)	0.33 (0.024)	0.31 (0.029)	0.28 (0.014)	0.24 (0.025)	0.28 (0.047)	0.26 (0.023)	0.36 (0.032)
Percentage of schools' library media centers with certain media equipment											
Telephone	90.5 (0.55)	89.9 (0.69)	76.4 (4.00)	87.5 (0.99)	93.6 (0.92)	96.2 (0.88)	95.3 (0.62)	88.3 (1.69)	96.6 (1.37)	99.7 (0.10)	99.5 (0.32)
Fax machine	10.9 (0.50)	6.9 (0.64)	12.2 (5.01)	4.9 (0.69)	8.1 (1.24)	9.6 (1.41)	23.1 (1.08)	15.0 (1.71)	17.8 (2.04)	27.4 (1.79)	36.2 (2.31)
Automated catalog	82.7 (0.66)	81.9 (0.89)	54.2 (4.94)	79.6 (1.37)	89.7 (1.08)	85.9 (2.00)	90.6 (0.76)	79.3 (1.89)	92.3 (1.41)	96.7 (0.64)	99.5 (0.20)
Automated circulation system	86.7 (0.61)	86.7 (0.82)	54.6 (4.74)	84.9 (1.18)	93.1 (0.92)	93.4 (1.17)	92.8 (0.80)	83.9 (1.89)	94.3 (1.65)	97.7 (0.48)	99.5 (0.23)
Video laser disc or DVD	44.1 (0.84)	39.3 (1.02)	17.7 (4.56)	38.3 (1.42)	39.6 (1.72)	50.5 (2.51)	61.3 (1.47)	53.4 (3.10)	65.6 (2.86)	63.2 (1.89)	68.7 (2.43)
Connection to Internet	95.1 (0.35)	94.1 (0.48)	81.3 (3.62)	94.4 (0.69)	96.3 (0.83)	94.0 (1.16)	99.2 (0.22)	97.7 (0.66)	99.9 (0.06)	100.0 (#)	98.8 (0.20)
Video cassette recorders (VCR)	86.3 (0.65)	85.4 (0.77)	76.1 (4.11)	84.8 (1.15)	87.7 (1.16)	87.1 (1.40)	89.4 (1.21)	88.4 (2.87)	88.6 (2.36)	91.2 (1.45)	89.0 (1.82)
Disability assistance technologies, such as TDD	11.9 (0.50)	10.2 (0.61)	5.5 (2.03)	8.6 (0.90)	11.5 (1.24)	14.9 (1.95)	18.0 (0.79)	14.1 (1.56)	16.5 (2.17)	18.9 (1.28)	25.0 (2.09)
Percentage of schools with certain services											
Students permitted to check out computer hardware	5.2 (0.37)	3.5 (0.45)	9.4 (4.01)	3.7 (0.69)	1.8 (0.54)	3.7 (1.06)	10.1 (0.77)	13.0 (1.70)	9.2 (1.85)	7.3 (0.86)	10.3 (1.60)
Students permitted to check out computer software	11.7 (0.44)	7.6 (0.56)	15.2 (5.09)	7.5 (0.79)	5.7 (0.85)	8.6 (1.54)	23.5 (1.05)	21.6 (1.86)	22.5 (2.30)	23.9 (1.73)	27.3 (2.33)
Number of library computer stations per 100 students	2.3 (0.04)	2.2 (0.05)	6.2 (0.69)	3.0 (0.11)	1.9 (0.07)	1.4 (0.05)	2.5 (0.05)	4.9 (0.25)	3.0 (0.12)	2.4 (0.06)	1.7 (0.06)
Average holdings per 100 students at the end of the school year[1]											
Books (number of volumes)	1,891 (45.1)	2,127 (70.2)	5,996 (404.4)	2,818 (188.7)	1,937 (46.1)	1,386 (42.3)	1,376 (20.0)	2,886 (97.1)	1,726 (43.4)	1,291 (22.0)	975 (25.5)
Video materials (tape and disc)	68 (3.5)	70 (5.3)	131 (20.0)	88 (13.8)	69 (4.9)	47 (2.8)	61 (2.1)	114 (10.6)	70 (4.8)	62 (3.3)	45 (3.4)
CD-ROM titles	12 (0.9)	16 (1.4)	34 (8.6)	18 (1.9)	19 (3.1)	10 (1.8)	4 (0.3)	13 (2.6)	5 (0.7)	3 (0.4)	2 (0.2)
Average additions per 100 students during the school year[1]											
Books (number of volumes)	118.4 (2.08)	118.4 (3.13)	264.7 (27.02)	144.1 (5.57)	114.5 (5.21)	87.4 (4.91)	61.2 (1.75)	125.7 (7.33)	68.6 (3.18)	60.4 (3.32)	43.8 (2.43)
Video materials (tape and disc)	4.4 (0.17)	4.4 (0.23)	11.7 (2.30)	5.4 (0.46)	4.0 (0.35)	3.3 (0.26)	4.1 (0.19)	7.5 (0.98)	4.8 (0.39)	4.4 (0.39)	2.8 (0.21)
CD-ROM titles	0.7 (0.09)	0.9 (0.14)	4.2 (1.92)	1.3 (0.31)	0.9 (0.20)	0.5 (0.17)	0.3 (0.03)	0.9 (0.16)	0.4 (0.10)	0.3 (0.04)	0.2 (0.03)
Total expenditures for library/media materials per pupil[1,2]	$16.24 (0.322)	$16.00 (0.469)	$37.51 (5.208)	$19.35 (0.825)	$15.45 (0.859)	$11.90 (0.558)	$16.11 (0.320)	$25.80 (1.109)	$18.09 (0.838)	$16.71 (0.675)	$12.64 (0.507)
Books	10.99 (0.299)	11.72 (0.452)	21.69 (3.274)	14.08 (0.745)	11.40 (0.898)	8.94 (0.491)	9.68 (0.275)	14.97 (0.732)	11.25 (0.685)	9.85 (0.523)	7.77 (0.457)
Video materials	0.97 (0.042)	0.91 (0.046)	1.25 (0.208)	0.99 (0.077)	0.91 (0.087)	0.79 (0.065)	1.01 (0.061)	1.58 (0.175)	1.10 (0.093)	1.02 (0.100)	0.84 (0.117)
CD-ROM titles	0.17 (0.016)	0.21 (0.026)	0.37 (0.121)	0.31 (0.061)	0.20 (0.046)	0.08 (0.012)	0.10 (0.011)	0.24 (0.051)	0.10 (0.022)	0.10 (0.011)	0.07 (0.017)
Current serial subscriptions	1.38 (0.025)	1.06 (0.031)	3.02 (0.409)	1.32 (0.064)	0.94 (0.032)	0.82 (0.067)	1.87 (0.049)	3.76 (0.198)	2.28 (0.120)	1.92 (0.076)	1.24 (0.063)
Electronic subscriptions	0.88 (0.033)	0.39 (0.042)	1.02 (0.362)	0.50 (0.096)	0.33 (0.057)	0.31 (0.048)	1.79 (0.061)	2.15 (0.197)	1.85 (0.202)	1.90 (0.108)	1.59 (0.107)
Value of donated computers, A/V equipment, and other items per student[1,3]	$1.56 (0.083)	$1.64 (0.108)	$7.47 (1.785)	$2.24 (0.167)	$1.56 (0.202)	$0.83 (0.118)	$1.12 (0.074)	$3.05 (0.328)	$1.68 (0.201)	$0.98 (0.115)	$0.60 (0.113)

#Rounds to zero.
[1]Data are for the prior school year.
[2]Includes other expenditures not separately shown.
[3]Includes grants and other contributions.

NOTE: Percentages are based on schools that have library/media centers. Detail may not sum to totals because of rounding. Standard errors appear in parentheses.
SOURCE: U.S. Department of Education, National Center for Education Statistics, Schools and Staffing Survey (SASS), "Public School Library Media Center Questionnaire," 2003–04. (This table was prepared September 2006.)

Table 417. Selected statistics on public school libraries/media centers, by state: 2003–04

State	Percent of centers offering selected services/equipment				Average number of staff per library[1]	Books held at end of year per 100 students[2]	Books acquired during year per 100 students[2]	Total expenditure for materials per student[2]	Value of donated computers, A/V equipment, and other items per student[2,3]
	Automated catalog	Automated circulation system	Connection to the Internet	Digital video disk (DVD)					
1	2	3	4	5	6	7	8	9	10
United States	**82.7** (0.66)	**86.9** (0.61)	**95.1** (0.35)	**44.1** (0.84)	**1.8** (0.01)	**1,891** (45.1)	**99** (2.1)	**$16.2** (0.32)	**$1.6** (0.08)
Alabama	87.6 (2.83)	95.9 (1.73)	100.0 (†)	44.0 (4.27)	1.7 (0.07)	1,713 (82.8)	99 (8.0)	15.2 (1.13)	2.6 (0.65)
Alaska	68.5 (4.60)	73.3 (5.55)	86.9 (4.69)	39.5 (5.90)	1.4 (0.08)	3,580 (230.9)	152 (24.2)	19.6 (2.30)	3.0 (1.03)
Arizona	81.5 (2.74)	90.5 (2.74)	93.3 (2.03)	38.8 (4.12)	1.8 (0.08)	2,298 (274.6)	121 (17.1)	15.3 (1.39)	0.9 (0.41)
Arkansas	86.7 (3.02)	93.0 (1.97)	97.0 (1.43)	44.0 (3.98)	1.7 (0.06)	1,931 (101.7)	89 (6.4)	18.1 (1.24)	2.3 (0.51)
California	81.6 (2.42)	87.9 (2.19)	88.7 (2.29)	31.4 (3.10)	1.4 (0.05)	1,488 (62.8)	108 (8.2)	16.5 (0.84)	1.1 (0.26)
Colorado	87.5 (3.96)	87.4 (3.44)	97.4 (1.77)	50.8 (5.03)	1.8 (0.09)	2,289 (423.3)	112 (13.4)	16.1 (1.30)	2.1 (0.64)
Connecticut	66.7 (5.42)	67.7 (5.41)	95.6 (2.46)	55.9 (5.08)	2.0 (0.10)	2,145 (105.2)	113 (17.5)	19.5 (2.16)	1.6 (0.43)
Delaware	97.3 (2.35)	97.8 (1.82)	97.3 (1.99)	29.9 (4.91)	1.6 (0.11)	1,702 (80.8)	75 (6.2)	12.9 (0.83)	1.9 (0.43)
District of Columbia	62.3 (7.68)	77.7 (5.90)	97.5 (2.20)	23.3 (6.71)	1.1 (0.04)	1,715 (307.5)	46 (8.8)	9.3 (2.17)	2.5 (0.74)
Florida	92.4 (2.27)	96.8 (1.72)	96.4 (2.01)	51.9 (4.84)	2.0 (0.08)	1,476 (79.3)	87 (8.6)	13.1 (0.97)	0.9 (0.18)
Georgia	96.4 (2.47)	97.7 (2.05)	98.6 (1.42)	50.8 (5.59)	2.2 (0.06)	1,653 (57.4)	76 (9.1)	14.2 (1.24)	1.4 (0.44)
Hawaii	94.6 (6.01)	95.5 (6.02)	98.1 (0.86)	42.9 (4.78)	1.5 (0.11)	2,029 (147.8)	71 (6.2)	11.5 (2.46)	1.2 (0.23)
Idaho	83.2 (3.01)	89.5 (2.75)	92.7 (2.20)	33.5 (3.84)	1.5 (0.06)	2,340 (102.7)	83 (9.9)	11.9 (1.16)	0.7 (0.18)
Illinois	66.4 (5.04)	70.8 (4.32)	89.2 (3.46)	38.0 (5.47)	2.1 (0.17)	1,703 (82.2)	118 (16.2)	13.7 (1.27)	1.8 (0.44)
Indiana	91.1 (2.83)	93.3 (2.52)	94.6 (2.97)	50.4 (5.76)	1.7 (0.07)	1,977 (95.4)	84 (9.1)	14.9 (0.97)	0.9 (0.30)
Iowa	74.9 (3.43)	78.0 (3.65)	90.6 (3.18)	51.9 (5.11)	2.0 (0.06)	2,605 (121.1)	100 (6.4)	13.9 (0.78)	1.6 (0.52)
Kansas	84.9 (3.50)	86.8 (3.70)	97.2 (1.48)	46.5 (4.24)	1.9 (0.07)	3,059 (142.5)	140 (12.0)	22.2 (2.14)	1.5 (0.35)
Kentucky	89.6 (2.82)	94.1 (2.40)	98.8 (1.02)	56.0 (4.88)	1.7 (0.07)	1,709 (77.6)	91 (8.8)	13.3 (0.65)	0.8 (0.25)
Louisiana	71.1 (4.00)	80.1 (3.26)	96.8 (1.64)	44.5 (4.61)	1.3 (0.05)	1,944 (131.2)	54 (4.6)	15.2 (3.54)	1.9 (0.42)
Maine	62.9 (4.83)	62.7 (4.41)	90.4 (3.73)	30.6 (4.03)	1.6 (0.10)	2,796 (260.5)	102 (8.7)	24.1 (2.68)	2.5 (0.98)
Maryland	82.8 (4.14)	91.0 (3.19)	98.7 (1.50)	46.9 (4.61)	1.6 (0.06)	1,507 (62.8)	125 (24.9)	17.3 (1.74)	1.3 (0.30)
Massachusetts	71.0 (6.43)	70.4 (6.35)	88.0 (5.02)	45.7 (5.69)	1.7 (0.12)	1,841 (126.0)	85 (14.8)	12.5 (1.33)	1.6 (0.44)
Michigan	83.8 (4.23)	82.8 (4.39)	100.0 (†)	48.8 (5.31)	1.8 (0.08)	3,010 (1,266.5)	88 (13.7)	12.8 (1.57)	1.1 (0.47)
Minnesota	92.0 (2.86)	94.6 (2.38)	97.2 (1.41)	59.7 (4.28)	2.1 (0.07)	2,509 (143.1)	111 (9.7)	15.2 (1.08)	2.1 (0.47)
Mississippi	73.2 (4.38)	86.5 (3.43)	95.5 (1.64)	35.6 (4.52)	1.6 (0.06)	1,476 (56.6)	102 (11.2)	14.9 (1.53)	1.4 (0.31)
Missouri	85.8 (3.59)	88.0 (3.33)	96.0 (1.67)	45.0 (4.73)	1.7 (0.06)	2,047 (62.0)	120 (9.0)	22.1 (1.01)	3.3 (0.96)
Montana	62.9 (3.53)	69.2 (3.32)	86.6 (3.56)	37.2 (3.37)	1.5 (0.08)	3,372 (214.8)	147 (17.7)	22.6 (1.40)	3.5 (0.75)
Nebraska	71.8 (4.35)	73.7 (4.27)	82.6 (3.89)	42.4 (5.55)	1.9 (0.09)	3,160 (228.1)	129 (10.4)	21.3 (1.38)	3.5 (0.71)
Nevada	92.2 (4.13)	88.6 (5.05)	93.9 (3.10)	44.2 (4.72)	1.5 (0.06)	1,616 (80.0)	114 (14.3)	13.5 (1.65)	1.4 (0.40)
New Hampshire	65.5 (4.11)	70.6 (4.04)	93.9 (3.02)	45.6 (5.04)	1.8 (0.07)	1,817 (78.5)	96 (11.2)	19.7 (1.28)	1.9 (0.68)
New Jersey	70.0 (6.08)	71.4 (6.08)	97.7 (2.04)	43.1 (6.13)	1.8 (0.08)	2,110 (142.1)	85 (13.6)	21.0 (2.72)	1.1 (0.30)
New Mexico	77.8 (3.58)	85.7 (3.12)	94.0 (1.81)	25.1 (2.74)	1.4 (0.06)	2,153 (105.1)	131 (10.7)	20.7 (1.66)	1.9 (0.43)
New York	76.0 (4.05)	83.9 (3.74)	94.9 (2.59)	47.7 (4.37)	2.2 (0.07)	1,626 (88.6)	95 (7.5)	19.8 (1.93)	2.2 (0.51)
North Carolina	93.3 (2.76)	97.0 (1.95)	96.3 (2.20)	53.0 (5.12)	1.9 (0.08)	1,622 (46.3)	110 (11.9)	18.3 (1.57)	1.1 (0.26)
North Dakota	51.8 (3.25)	53.4 (3.25)	90.1 (2.54)	30.1 (3.17)	1.6 (0.06)	3,710 (168.3)	146 (13.0)	26.1 (1.75)	1.3 (0.42)
Ohio	82.2 (3.47)	82.7 (3.40)	95.9 (2.10)	49.6 (4.89)	1.5 (0.08)	1,669 (78.4)	75 (9.4)	10.9 (0.78)	1.9 (0.46)
Oklahoma	75.5 (2.73)	89.8 (1.87)	95.6 (1.25)	35.0 (2.46)	1.8 (0.04)	2,159 (114.6)	99 (6.2)	15.5 (1.08)	2.5 (0.37)
Oregon	81.1 (4.49)	82.0 (4.69)	100.0 (†)	33.0 (4.61)	1.6 (0.08)	2,631 (221.4)	85 (10.5)	10.7 (0.96)	2.9 (1.11)
Pennsylvania	81.7 (3.59)	87.1 (4.16)	94.8 (3.09)	37.4 (3.87)	1.8 (0.08)	1,961 (83.9)	88 (10.0)	15.1 (0.91)	0.6 (0.16)
Rhode Island	72.3 (4.54)	83.5 (3.79)	98.9 (1.13)	26.4 (5.06)	1.8 (0.08)	1,538 (95.6)	84 (14.5)	16.9 (2.56)	1.5 (0.70)
South Carolina	98.2 (1.69)	99.9 (0.10)	100.0 (†)	46.6 (4.13)	2.1 (0.05)	1,674 (56.6)	94 (11.8)	15.7 (1.16)	2.0 (0.41)
South Dakota	53.6 (4.24)	53.6 (3.92)	89.5 (3.34)	42.6 (4.36)	1.5 (0.08)	3,105 (204.0)	173 (27.6)	22.3 (1.40)	2.1 (0.55)
Tennessee	81.2 (3.63)	89.3 (2.94)	98.6 (0.96)	47.1 (4.72)	1.6 (0.06)	1,652 (56.4)	94 (10.7)	13.0 (1.25)	1.8 (0.33)
Texas	93.7 (1.77)	98.3 (0.71)	99.0 (0.48)	42.4 (4.30)	1.7 (0.06)	1,779 (63.3)	106 (8.6)	18.8 (2.04)	1.6 (0.33)
Utah	87.2 (3.22)	94.8 (2.31)	86.2 (3.96)	51.0 (3.97)	1.4 (0.05)	1,651 (95.2)	84 (7.8)	9.8 (0.56)	1.4 (0.30)
Vermont	74.6 (5.33)	73.5 (5.29)	96.8 (2.06)	38.0 (4.20)	1.7 (0.10)	2,939 (127.9)	138 (10.3)	29.8 (1.27)	1.5 (0.69)
Virginia	95.2 (2.13)	99.5 (0.42)	95.5 (2.14)	52.6 (4.21)	1.9 (0.06)	1,717 (61.9)	88 (6.5)	16.2 (0.70)	1.3 (0.24)
Washington	92.9 (1.78)	96.0 (1.72)	98.9 (1.20)	46.5 (4.30)	2.0 (0.05)	2,060 (93.3)	92 (7.3)	15.7 (2.49)	1.8 (0.47)
West Virginia	42.7 (5.50)	54.6 (5.54)	86.8 (4.34)	33.4 (5.28)	0.9 (0.06)	1,594 (99.8)	74 (10.1)	8.9 (0.65)	1.6 (0.58)
Wisconsin	92.7 (3.07)	91.4 (3.67)	100.0 (†)	55.4 (4.43)	2.1 (0.06)	2,545 (141.8)	121 (8.5)	25.0 (1.26)	1.5 (0.59)
Wyoming	91.2 (3.40)	94.3 (2.92)	96.3 (2.72)	49.7 (5.02)	1.8 (0.07)	3,125 (142.3)	156 (22.4)	21.8 (1.59)	3.1 (0.87)

†Not applicable.
[1]Includes professional and nonprofessional staff.
[2]Data are for the prior school year.
[3]Includes grants and other contributions.

NOTE: Percentages are based on schools that have library/media centers. Standard errors appear in parentheses.
SOURCE: U.S. Department of Education, National Center for Education Statistics, Schools and Staffing Survey (SASS), "Public School Library Media Center Questionnaire," 2003–04. (This table was prepared September 2006.)

Table 418. Collections, staff, and operating expenditures of degree-granting institution libraries: Selected years, 1976–77 through 2001–02

Collections, staff, and operating expenditures	1976–77[1]	1978–79[1]	1981–82	1984–85	1987–88	1991–92	1994–95	1996–97	1997–98	1999–2000	2001–02
1	2	3	4	5	6	7	8	9	10	11	12
Number of libraries	3,058	3,122	3,104	3,322	3,438	3,274	3,303	3,408	3,658	3,527	3,568
Number of circulation transactions (in thousands)	—	—	—	—	—	—	231,503	230,733	216,067	193,948	189,248
Total enrollment (in thousands)[2]	11,121	11,392	12,372	12,242	12,767	14,359	14,279	14,300	14,502	14,791	15,928
Full-time-equivalent enrollment[2]	8,313	8,348	9,015	8,952	9,230	10,361	10,348	10,402	10,615	10,944	11,766
Collections (in thousands)											
Number of volumes at end of year[3]	481,442	519,895	567,826	631,727	718,504	749,429	776,447	806,717	878,906	913,547	954,030
Number of volumes added during year	22,367	21,608	19,507	20,658	21,907	20,982	21,544	21,346	24,551	24,436	24,574
Number of serial subscriptions at end of year	4,670	4,775	4,890	6,317	6,416	6,966	6,212	5,709	10,908 [4]	7,499	9,855
Microform units at end of year	—	—	—	—	—	—	—	—	1,062,082	1,111,389	1,143,678
Electronic units at end of year[5]	—	—	—	—	—	—	465	983	3,473	—	—
Full-time-equivalent (FTE) library staff											
Total staff in regular positions[6]	57,087	58,416	58,476	58,476	67,251	67,166	67,433	67,581	68,337	69,123	69,526
Librarians and professional staff	23,308	23,676	23,816	21,822	25,115	26,341	26,726	27,268	30,041	31,001	32,053
Other paid staff	33,779	34,740	34,660	38,026	40,733	40,421	40,381	40,022	38,026	37,893	37,473
Contributed services	—	—	—	—	1,403	404	326	291	270	229	—
Student assistants	—	—	—	—	33,821	29,075	28,411	27,998	28,373	26,518	25,305
FTE student enrollment per FTE staff member	146	143	154	153	137	154	153	154	155	158	169
Hours of student and other assistance (in thousands)	39,950	39,552	40,068	28,360	—	—	—	—	—	—	—
Library operating expenditures[7]											
Total operating expenditures (in thousands)	$1,259,637	$1,502,158	$1,943,769	$2,404,524	$2,770,075	$3,648,654	$4,013,333	$4,301,815	$4,592,657	$5,023,198	$5,416,716
Salaries[8]	698,090	824,438	1,081,894	1,156,138	1,451,551	1,889,368	2,021,233	2,147,842	2,314,380	2,430,541	2,753,404
Hourly wages	68,683	79,535	100,847	—	—	—	—	—	—	—	—
Fringe benefits	—	—	—	231,209	—	—	—	—	—	271,954	—
Preservation	22,521	25,274	30,351	32,939	34,144	43,126	46,554	45,610	42,919	43,832	46,499
Furniture/equipment	—	—	—	—	—	—	55,915	56,128	57,013	63,459	—
Computer hardware/software	—	—	—	—	—	—	128,128	157,949	164,379	160,294	155,791
Utilities/networks/consortia	—	—	—	—	—	—	81,106	85,113	89,618	90,264	92,242
Information resources	373,699	450,180	561,199	750,282	891,281	1,197,293	1,348,933	1,499,249	1,600,995	1,822,277	1,944,490
Books and serial backfiles—paper	—	—	—	—	—	—	—	—	514,048	552,100	563,007
Books and serial backfiles—electronic	—	—	—	—	—	—	—	—	28,061	33,888	44,792
Current serials—paper	—	—	—	—	—	—	—	—	849,399	945,958	926,105
Current serials—electronic	—	—	—	—	—	—	—	—	125,470	203,371	297,657
Audiovisual materials	—	—	—	—	—	23,879	28,753	28,879	30,623	32,039	37,041
Document delivery/interlibrary loan	—	—	—	—	—	—	12,238	17,645	19,309	20,540	22,913
Other collection expenditures	373,699	450,180	561,199	750,282	891,281	1,173,414	1,307,942	1,452,725	34,086	34,381	52,976
Other library operating expenditures	96,643	122,731	169,478	233,957	393,099	518,867	331,463	309,925	323,354	140,579	424,290
Operating expenditures per FTE student	152	180	216	269	300	352	388	414	433	459	460
Operating expenditures per FTE student in constant 2005–06 dollars[9]	514	523	456	505	516	507	513	518	532	540	514
Operating expenditures (percentage distribution)	100.0	100.0	100.0	100.0	100.0	100.0	100.0	100.0	100.0	100.0	100.0
Salaries[8]	55.4	54.9	55.7	48.1	52.4	51.8	50.4	49.9	50.4	48.4	50.8
Hourly wages	5.5	5.3	5.2	—	—	—	—	—	—	—	—
Fringe benefits	—	—	—	9.6	—	—	—	—	—	5.4	—
Preservation	1.8	1.7	1.6	1.4	1.2	1.2	1.2	1.1	0.9	0.9	0.9
Information resources	29.7	30.0	28.9	31.2	32.2	32.8	33.6	34.9	34.9	36.3	35.9
Other library operating expenditures[10]	7.7	8.2	8.7	9.7	14.2	14.2	14.9	14.2	13.8	9.0	12.4
Library operating expenditures as percent of total institutional expenditures for educational and general purposes	3.8	3.7	3.5	3.4	3.2	3.0	2.8	—	—	—	—

—Not available.
[1]Includes data for U.S. territories.
[2]Fall enrollment for the academic year specified.
[3]Includes data for schools newly added to the survey system, so end of year figure exceeds total of additions plus end of year value from previous year.
[4]Includes microform and electronic serials.
[5]Electronic files, formerly labeled "Computer files."
[6]Excludes student assistants.
[7]Excludes capital outlay.
[8]Includes expenditures for fringe benefits (except for 1984–85 and 1987–88), salary equivalents of contributed services staff, and hourly wages for 1996–97 and 1997–98.
[9]Constant dollars based on the Consumer Price Index, prepared by the Bureau of Labor Statistics, U.S. Department of Labor, adjusted to a school-year basis.

[10]Includes furniture/equipment, computer hardware/software, and utilities/networks/consortia as well as expenditures classified as "other library operating expenditures."
NOTE: Data through 1995 are for institutions of higher education, while later data are for degree-granting institutions. Degree-granting institutions grant associate's or higher degrees and participate in Title IV federal financial aid programs. The degree-granting classification is very similar to the earlier higher education classification, but it includes more 2-year colleges and excludes a few higher education institutions that did not grant degrees. (See Guide to Sources for details.) Detail may not sum to totals because of rounding.
SOURCE: U.S. Department of Education, National Center for Education Statistics, *Library Statistics of Colleges and Universities*, selected years, 1976–77 through 1984–85; 1987–88 through 2001–02 Integrated Postsecondary Education Data System, "Academic Libraries Survey" (IPEDS-L:88–98), "Fall Enrollment Survey" (IPEDS-EF:87–99), and Spring 2002; and Academic Libraries Survey (ALS), 2000 and 2002. (This table was prepared September 2006.)

Table 419. Collections, staff, and operating expenditures of the 60 largest college and university libraries: 2001–02

Institution	Rank order, by number of volumes	Number of volumes at end of year (in thousands)	Full-time-equivalent staff Total	Librarians	Operating expenditures (in thousands) Total	Salaries and wages	Public service hours per week	Gate count per week	Reference transactions per week
1	2	3	4	5	6	7	8	9	10
Harvard University (MA)	1	14,615	1,307	420	96,454	51,702	107	37,243	8,154
Yale University (CT)	2	10,707	632	163	54,518	22,388	111	13,961	2,559
University of Illinois, Urbana Campus	3	9,709	522	88	31,458	16,906	107	33,233	7,516
University of California, Berkeley	4	9,389	688	119	51,649	26,191	98	27,000	3,489
University of Texas, Austin	5	8,230	562	118	36,480	18,106	103	110,114	4,104
University of Michigan, Ann Arbor	6	7,643	643	167	43,358	19,307	168	63,202	4,194
Stanford University (CA)	7	7,616	629	114	54,785	21,915	98	24,438	2,084
Columbia University in the City of NY	8	7,557	535	140	39,114	18,628	106	69,000	5,000
University of California, Los Angeles	9	7,445	601	142	37,671	—	96	89,092	3,819
Cornell University (NY)	10	6,964	590	133	39,162	18,764	114	20,092	2,462
University of Chicago (IL)	11	6,833	344	71	25,416	10,677	146	41,100	1,154
Indiana University, Bloomington	12	6,512	458	95	30,067	13,075	115	75,546	7,573
University of Washington, Seattle	13	6,274	506	128	31,568	17,742	135	87,877	6,500
University of Wisconsin, Madison	14	6,216	513	190	33,614	18,491	131	83,419	4,718
University of Minnesota, Twin Cities	15	6,082	423	99	32,444	16,089	106	41,548	3,648
Princeton University (NJ)	16	5,990	371	100	31,006	14,297	110	13,642	970
Ohio State University, Main Campus	17	5,603	433	92	27,822	13,101	168	50,696	6,990
University of North Carolina, Chapel Hill	18	5,366	429	133	26,413	13,465	146	41,046	4,294
Duke University (NC)	19	5,234	343	109	30,589	12,166	122	56,872	2,516
University of Pennsylvania	20	5,153	403	119	30,651	13,702	111	36,000	6,254
University of Virginia, Main Campus	21	4,868	349	94	28,625	15,786	149	71,206	4,550
Rutgers University, New Brunswick (NJ)	22	4,832	316	69	20,619	12,263	108	57,909	1,879
New York University	23	4,645	427	120	33,054	15,703	119	38,000	3,419
University of Pittsburgh, Main Campus (PA)	24	4,553	344	75	25,177	9,864	123	23,971	5,326
Michigan State University	25	4,504	284	63	19,461	9,182	148	39,929	1,720
University of Kansas, Main Campus	26	4,447	269	65	16,022	7,878	140	32,914	2,673
University of Arizona	27	4,442	290	77	20,201	8,025	168	29,157	836
University of Iowa	28	4,303	308	70	20,165	10,421	123	50,145	6,603
Northwestern University (IL)	29	4,217	340	91	22,663	10,443	116	18,646	2,176
University of Oklahoma, Norman Campus	30	3,951	159	41	12,246	3,893	107	20,277	1,202
University of Florida	31	3,950	407	103	24,138	10,993	110	42,569	2,919
University of Georgia	32	3,873	364	87	21,546	9,655	101	26,206	2,428
University of Southern California	33	3,740	339	73	27,512	12,891	159	55,838	1,365
Washington University in St Louis (MO)	34	3,548	285	95	26,328	9,815	120	33,000	1,500
Johns Hopkins University (MD)	35	3,509	338	69	26,698	11,576	120	28,933	2,398
University of Hawaii, Manoa	36	3,421	238	63	15,299	7,251	94	31,379	2,980
Arizona State University, Main Campus	37	3,360	306	85	20,181	9,337	106	60,272	3,486
University of South Carolina at Columbia	38	3,334	292	78	17,003	7,216	111	25,000	3,700
Brigham Young University (UT)	39	3,305	350	87	20,294	9,549	101	70,000	2,400
Wayne State University (MI)	40	3,296	309	50	18,558	8,925	142	56,471	13,435
State University of New York, Buffalo	41	3,288	249	80	17,822	8,906	97	12,600	1,400
University of Rochester (NY)	42	3,277	208	66	13,918	6,272	117	4,000	1,252
University of California, Santa Barbara	43	3,207	236	45	16,245	8,113	103	33,381	1,956
State University of New York, Stony Brook	44	3,200	164	36	12,666	5,674	100	17,967	5,755
Brown University (RI)	45	3,192	217	60	16,318	7,565	101	17,762	54,032
Louisiana State U. & A&M & Hebert Laws Center	46	3,175	205	49	12,763	5,632	93	39,944	2,595
North Carolina State University at Raleigh	47	3,144	264	97	21,672	9,628	146	39,005	2,042
Pennsylvania State University, Main Campus	48	3,118	438	77	29,457	15,328	168	53,469	4,416
University of Missouri, Columbia	49	3,111	222	56	14,390	5,763	104	30,000	2,080
University of Massachusetts, Amherst	50	3,089	170	49	11,406	6,926	93	20,750	1,775
University of Oregon	51	3,030	215	39	14,066	6,780	96	15,553	2,826
Southern Illinois University, Carbondale	52	3,030	236	42	14,318	6,707	150	15,275	2,206
University of Colorado at Boulder	53	3,023	236	51	18,143	7,840	104	1,969	4,062
University of Kentucky	54	2,989	290	73	20,091	8,178	160	32,000	1,948
Kansas State University	55	2,979	117	37	10,564	4,496	105	13,714	611
University of Utah	56	2,978	365	69	21,783	10,648	115	39,686	7,584
University of Notre Dame (IN)	57	2,976	272	59	18,456	8,444	126	18,001	571
University of California, Davis	58	2,958	272	52	18,935	8,912	95	32,225	2,181
University of Maryland, College Park Campus	59	2,957	296	124	23,689	11,237	110	53,029	5,428
University of California, San Diego	60	2,938	341	52	24,272	12,606	112	40,514	2,022

—Not available.

SOURCE: U.S. Department of Education, National Center for Education Statistics, Academic Libraries Survey (ALS), 2002. (This table was prepared September 2006.)

Table 420. Selected statistics of public libraries, by population size of legal service area: Fiscal year 2004

Selected statistic	Total	Population of legal service area[1]										
		Less than 1,000	1,000 to 2,499	2,500 to 4,999	5,000 to 9,999	10,000 to 24,999	25,000 to 49,999	50,000 to 99,999	100,000 to 249,999	250,000 to 499,999	500,000 to 999,999	1,000,000 or more
1	2	3	4	5	6	7	8	9	10	11	12	13
Public library service outlets, total	17,393	1,031	1,642	1,396	1,678	2,398	1,843	1,793	2,181	1,159	1,204	1,068
Central libraries	9,047	1,023	1,613	1,336	1,468	1,752	908	516	292	79	42	18
Branch libraries	7,502	5	20	47	171	516	800	1,101	1,725	1,005	1,094	1,018
Bookmobiles	844	3	9	13	39	130	135	176	164	75	68	32
Collections, in thousands												
Books and serial volumes	804,943	8,961	21,849	28,028	47,377	98,875	96,685	95,662	117,016	84,097	106,612	99,780
Audio and video materials and films	74,737	549	1,505	2,117	4,020	8,911	9,186	9,240	11,256	7,700	9,940	10,313
Serial subscriptions	1,822	20	53	69	122	241	212	187	250	185	225	258
Public-use internet terminals, total	170,782	2,708	5,935	6,726	11,151	21,025	19,117	20,726	26,885	16,174	20,153	20,182
Average per stationary outlet	10.3	2.6	3.6	4.9	6.8	9.3	11.2	12.8	13.3	14.9	17.7	19.5
Per 5,000 population	3.0	23.0	11.3	7.0	5.3	3.8	3.0	2.8	2.6	2.4	2.6	2.3
Uses of electronic resources per year, in thousands	343,013	984	3,492	5,653	12,760	34,929	37,995	46,499	56,539	40,456	58,537	45,168
Per capita	1.2	1.7	1.3	1.2	1.2	1.3	1.2	1.2	1.1	1.2	1.5	1.0
Paid staff, in full-time equivalents												
Librarians	45,037	469	1,380	1,763	2,928	6,127	5,896	5,523	6,138	4,568	5,474	4,771
Librarians with ALA-MLS[2]	30,560	20	102	267	940	3,223	4,012	3,983	4,912	3,804	4,728	4,571
Other staff	90,977	150	563	1,236	3,556	9,543	11,436	12,361	16,529	10,692	13,332	11,579
Total operating income, in thousands	$9,129,588	$20,514	$80,543	$141,148	$338,645	$942,575	$1,117,968	$1,155,771	$1,491,431	$1,079,238	$1,378,322	$1,383,432
Percentage distribution of operating income, by source, total	100.0	100.0	100.0	100.0	100.0	100.0	100.0	100.0	100.0	100.0	100.0	100.0
Federal[3]	0.5	1.0	1.1	0.7	0.5	0.4	0.4	0.5	0.6	0.4	0.5	0.6
State	10.0	6.7	5.2	7.4	11.2	8.9	10.2	11.8	9.8	12.2	11.1	6.6
Local	81.5	72.4	74.4	76.8	77.7	81.8	82.4	81.3	83.0	81.2	81.9	80.9
Other and private	8.0	19.9	19.3	15.1	10.6	8.9	7.0	6.4	6.6	6.2	6.5	12.0

[1]The number of people in the geographic area for which a public library has been established to offer services and from which (or on behalf of which) the library derives income, plus any areas served under contract for which the library is the primary service provider.
[2]Librarians with a master's degree (MLS) from a graduate library education program accredited by the American Library Association (ALA).
[3]Excludes some federal funds received through state library agencies.

NOTE: Data include imputations for nonresponse. Detail may not sum to totals because of rounding.
SOURCE: U.S. Department of Education, National Center for Education Statistics, Public Libraries Survey (PLS), fiscal year 2004, *Public Libraries in the United States: Fiscal Year 2004*. (This table was prepared September 2006.)

Table 421. Public libraries, books and serial volumes, library visits, circulation, and reference transactions, by state: Fiscal year 2004

State	Number of public libraries	Number of books and serial volumes (in thousands)	Number of books and serial volumes per capita	Library visits per capita[1]	Circulation per capita	Public library reference transactions per capita[2]
1	2	3	4	5	6	7
United States	9,207 [3]	804,943	2.8	4.7	7.1	1.1
Alabama................................	208	9,125	2.0	3.2	4.1	0.8
Alaska...................................	88	2,236	3.4	5.2	6.3	0.5
Arizona.................................	91	9,512	1.8	4.0	7.5	0.9
Arkansas...............................	48	5,706	2.1	3.1	4.4	0.7
California..............................	179	77,776	2.2	4.2	5.5	1.0
Colorado...............................	115	11,546	2.6	6.7	10.6	1.3
Connecticut...........................	194	14,778	4.2	6.6	9.2	1.3
Delaware...............................	21	1,628	2.1	4.5	6.4	0.6
District of Columbia	1	2,436	4.4	3.5	1.9	2.0
Florida..................................	70	32,599	1.9	4.0	5.4	1.3
Georgia................................	58	15,027	1.8	3.7	4.7	0.9
Hawaii..................................	1	3,177	2.5	4.4	5.0	0.7
Idaho...................................	104	3,785	3.1	6.0	8.2	0.8
Illinois..................................	626	43,172	3.8	5.7	8.3	1.5
Indiana.................................	239	23,906	4.2	6.7	11.9	1.3
Iowa.....................................	540	12,066	4.1	5.5	9.1	0.6
Kansas.................................	325	10,818	4.7	6.2	10.7	1.2
Kentucky..............................	116	8,254	2.0	3.8	5.7	0.6
Louisiana..............................	66	11,581	2.6	3.1	4.3	1.2
Maine...................................	269	6,294	5.3	5.4	7.3	0.7
Maryland...............................	24	14,825	2.7	5.1	9.4	1.3
Massachusetts.......................	370	31,571	4.9	5.8	7.7	0.9
Michigan...............................	384	33,258	3.4	4.5	6.3	0.8
Minnesota.............................	140	16,160	3.2	5.0	9.9	0.9
Mississippi............................	49	5,728	2.0	2.8	3.2	0.5
Missouri................................	151	18,165	3.6	4.8	8.7	0.9
Montana................................	79	2,695	3.0	4.1	6.0	0.5
Nebraska..............................	276	6,446	4.6	5.4	8.8	0.8
Nevada.................................	22	4,037	1.7	4.1	6.2	0.7
New Hampshire	231	5,986	4.6	4.8	7.6	0.7
New Jersey............................	306	31,030	3.7	5.1	6.4	0.9
New Mexico	92	4,228	2.6	3.7	5.3	0.9
New York...............................	753	73,771	3.9	5.7	7.1	1.5
North Carolina	75	16,134	1.9	3.9	5.3	1.2
North Dakota	83	2,314	4.2	4.7	7.5	0.7
Ohio.....................................	250	48,610	4.2	7.2	14.8	1.6
Oklahoma..............................	112	6,830	2.4	4.6	6.4	0.7
Oregon.................................	125	9,005	2.8	6.2	14.5	0.9
Pennsylvania.........................	455	29,263	2.4	3.6	5.2	0.7
Rhode Island	48	4,212	3.9	5.8	6.7	0.9
South Carolina.......................	42	8,698	2.1	3.4	4.9	1.2
South Dakota.........................	125	3,199	5.5	6.4	9.0	0.9
Tennessee	184	11,038	1.9	3.2	4.1	0.8
Texas	555	39,749	2.0	3.2	4.8	1.1
Utah.....................................	72	6,391	2.7	6.7	12.5	1.6
Vermont................................	189	2,855	5.0	5.4	7.3	0.8
Virginia.................................	90	19,353	2.6	4.5	8.4	1.1
Washington...........................	66	17,274	2.9	5.9	10.8	1.0
West Virginia.........................	97	4,822	2.7	3.4	4.3	0.6
Wisconsin	380	19,462	3.5	6.0	10.2	1.0
Wyoming...............................	23	2,409	4.8	6.0	8.3	1.2

[1]The total number of persons entering the library for any purpose during the year.
[2]A reference transaction is an information contact that involves the knowledge, use, recommendations, interpretation, or instructions in the use of one or more information sources by a member of the library staff.
[3]Excludes branches that are associated with a central library. Consists of 7,441 single-outlet libraries and 1,766 multiple-outlet libraries. Some single-outlet libraries are bookmobiles, and some multiple-outlet libraries consist of or include bookmobiles.

NOTE: Data include imputations for nonresponse. Detail may not sum to totals because of rounding.
SOURCE: U.S. Department of Education, National Center for Education Statistics, Public Libraries Survey (PLS), fiscal year 2004, *Public Libraries in the United States: Fiscal Year 2004*. (This table was prepared September 2006.)

Table 422. Public schools and instructional rooms with access to the Internet, by selected school characteristics: 1994 through 2003

Schools, computers, instructional rooms, and access	All public schools	Instructional level[1]		Size of school enrollment			Metropolitan status				Percent of students eligible for free or reduced-price lunch[2]			
		Elementary	Secondary	Less than 300	300 to 999	1,000 or more	City	Urban fringe	Town	Rural	Less than 35 percent	35 to 49 percent	50 to 74 percent	75 percent or more
1	2	3	4	5	6	7	8	9	10	11	12	13	14	15
Estimated total number of schools														
1995	77,853	57,705	18,083	20,673	50,044	7,136	17,906	18,464	19,539	21,944	37,450	13,627	12,808	13,166
1997	79,125	59,695	19,430	20,540	51,169	7,416	21,071	23,419	12,637	21,998	37,525	12,250	16,302	12,864
1998	78,791	59,173	19,193	20,095	50,655	8,041	20,698	26,265	11,306	20,522	38,156	12,088	13,967	14,541
1999	78,399	59,575	17,110	20,018	50,389	7,992	21,034	26,245	11,235	19,885	35,653	13,908	16,099	11,993
2000	80,127	59,782	18,414	20,067	51,887	8,173	21,115	26,584	11,879	20,550	36,563	12,414	17,030	13,912
2001	81,066	61,640	17,627	20,665	51,968	8,433	17,997	26,260	10,180	26,628	34,928	14,753	16,627	14,710
2002	82,036	62,134	17,608	21,429	51,876	8,731	18,550	26,431	10,774	26,280	34,989	13,243	19,040	14,765
2003	82,232	62,298	17,889	21,623	51,952	8,657	18,803	26,485	10,597	26,347	32,501	14,869	18,577	16,285
1998 (standard error)	(333)	(293)	(220)	(479)	(467)	(165)	(88)	(98)	(182)	(273)	(1,530)	(1,185)	(991)	(1,263)
1999 (standard error)	(665)	(722)	(521)	(1,263)	(681)	(291)	(605)	(514)	(343)	(506)	(1,211)	(977)	(1,067)	(949)
2000 (standard error)	(650)	(569)	(359)	(697)	(206)	(217)	(1,380)	(1,746)	(1,323)	(1,478)	(1,215)	(792)	(1,071)	(923)
2001 (standard error)	(492)	(527)	(414)	(589)	(274)	(139)	(1,416)	(1,002)	(746)	(1,087)	(1,191)	(1,203)	(995)	(814)
2002 (standard error)	(780)	(647)	(371)	(761)	(253)	(145)	(963)	(922)	(1,080)	(1,289)	(1,194)	(1,050)	(1,134)	(862)
2003 (standard error)	(763)	(759)	(396)	(697)	(448)	(154)	(1,160)	(1,060)	(1,098)	(1,422)	(1,381)	(1,111)	(1,095)	(999)
Percent of schools having access to the Internet														
1994	35	30	49	30	35	58	40	38	29	35	39	35	32	18
1995	50	46	65	39	52	69	47	59	47	48	60	48	41	31
1996	65	61	77	57	66	80	64	75	61	60	74	59	53	53
1997	78	75	89	75	78	89	74	78	84	79	86	81	71	62
1998	89	88	94	87	89	95	92	85	90	92	92	93	88	79
1999	95	94	98	96	94	96	93	96	94	96	95	98	96	89
2000	98	97	98	96	98	99	96	98	98	99	99	99	97	94
2001	99	99	100³	99	99	100³	97	99	100³	100³	99	100³	99	97
2002	99	99	100³	99	100³	100³	99	100³	98	98	98	100³	100³	99
2003	100³	100³	100	100	100³	100	100	100	100	100	100	100	100	99
1998 (standard error)	(1.3)	(1.6)	(2.1)	(3.4)	(1.4)	(2)	(2)	(2.8)	(3.2)	(3.4)	(2.0)	(2.2)	(3.0)	(3.7)
1999 (standard error)	(0.8)	(1.0)	(0.8)	(1.5)	(1.0)	(2)	(2)	(1.2)	(2.5)	(1.4)	(1.1)	(0.9)	(1.7)	(3.1)
2000 (standard error)	(0.5)	(0.7)	(†)	(1.7)	(0.5)	(1)	(1)	(1.2)	(1.2)	(0.9)	(0.7)	(0.7)	(1.3)	(1.7)
2001 (standard error)	(0.3)	(0.4)	(†)	(1.0)	(0.4)	(†)	(1)	(0.5)	(†)	(†)	(0.6)	(†)	(0.5)	(1.1)
2002 (standard error)	(0.5)	(0.6)	(†)	(1.7)	(†)	(†)	(1)	(†)	(2.2)	(1.0)	(1.0)	(†)	(†)	(0.9)
2003 (standard error)	(†)	(†)	(†)	(†)	(†)	(†)	(†)	(†)	(†)	(†)	(†)	(†)	(†)	(0.8)
Number of computers for instructional purposes, in thousands														
1995[4]	5,621	3,453	2,021	850	3,600	1,171	1,497	1,526	1,404	1,195	2,905	806	950	882
1997	5,959	3,701	2,258	839	3,767	1,353	1,727	2,084	934	1,214	3,154	886	1,013	890
1998	7,111	4,519	2,549	952	4,414	1,744	2,148	2,606	1,047	1,311	3,630	1,105	1,127	1,235
1999	7,806	4,923	2,728	1,021	4,952	1,834	2,320	2,975	1,022	1,489	3,900	1,245	1,429	1,170
2000	8,776	5,296	3,271	1,135	5,524	2,117	2,537	3,396	1,155	1,689	4,394	1,373	1,606	1,384
2001	10,058	6,165	3,654	1,085	6,273	2,700	2,685	3,791	1,134	2,448	4,781	1,707	1,862	1,698
2002	10,711	6,775	3,705	1,347	6,533	2,831	2,662	4,043	1,320	2,686	4,982	1,673	2,265	1,792
2003	11,180	6,879	4,087	1,275	6,709	3,196	2,825	4,188	1,357	2,810	5,049	1,923	2,248	1,960
1998 (standard error)	(183)	(145)	(94)	(53)	(136)	(106)	(74)	(129)	(58)	(77)	(198)	(114)	(89)	(155)
1999 (standard error)	(147)	(114)	(103)	(76)	(127)	(101)	(113)	(121)	(50)	(75)	(152)	(115)	(116)	(98)
2000 (standard error)	(174)	(149)	(113)	(73)	(121)	(103)	(179)	(213)	(132)	(131)	(147)	(93)	(112)	(107)
2001 (standard error)	(180)	(165)	(98)	(57)	(140)	(85)	(192)	(168)	(78)	(142)	(206)	(120)	(132)	(117)
2002 (standard error)	(237)	(187)	(105)	(101)	(181)	(101)	(158)	(173)	(172)	(164)	(170)	(172)	(137)	(136)
2003 (standard error)	(265)	(234)	(115)	(77)	(179)	(118)	(163)	(177)	(139)	(220)	(252)	(165)	(139)	(110)

See notes at end of table.

Table 422. Public schools and instructional rooms with access to the Internet, by selected school characteristics: 1994 through 2003—Continued

Schools, computers, instructional rooms, and access	All public schools	Instructional level[1]		Size of school enrollment			Metropolitan status				Percent of students eligible for free or reduced-price lunch[2]			
		Elementary	Secondary	Less than 300	300 to 999	1,000 or more	City	Urban fringe	Town	Rural	Less than 35 percent	35 to 49 percent	50 to 74 percent	75 percent or more
1	2	3	4	5	6	7	8	9	10	11	12	13	14	15
Average number of instructional computers per school														
1995[4]	72	60	112	41	72	164	84	83	72	54	78	59	74	67
1997	75	62	116	41	74	183	82	89	74	55	84	72	62	69
1998	90	76	133	47	87	217	104	99	93	64	95	91	81	85
1999	100	83	159	51	98	229	110	113	91	75	109	90	89	98
2000	110	89	178	57	106	259	120	128	97	82	120	111	94	99
2001	124	100	207	52	121	320	149	144	111	92	137	116	112	115
2002	131	109	210	63	126	324	144	153	123	102	142	126	119	122
2003	136	110	228	59	129	369	150	158	128	107	155	129	121	120
1998 (standard error)	(2.3)	(2.4)	(4.9)	(2.6)	(2.5)	(13.0)	(3.6)	(4.9)	(5.2)	(3.6)	(3.7)	(6.1)	(4.5)	(7.7)
1999 (standard error)	(2.2)	(2.2)	(6.4)	(2.5)	(2.3)	(10.7)	(4.7)	(4.2)	(4.2)	(3.6)	(2.8)	(6.8)	(5.6)	(5.2)
2000 (standard error)	(2.0)	(2.4)	(5.3)	(3.1)	(2.3)	(9.0)	(4.9)	(4.3)	(5.6)	(3.6)	(3.4)	(5.9)	(5.7)	(5.5)
2001 (standard error)	(2.3)	(2.7)	(6.2)	(2.5)	(2.6)	(10.1)	(6.4)	(4.7)	(6.0)	(4.0)	(4.9)	(5.8)	(6.0)	(5.0)
2002 (standard error)	(2.8)	(2.9)	(6.4)	(4.1)	(3.5)	(10.8)	(6.4)	(5.2)	(9.3)	(4.5)	(4.7)	(8.5)	(5.3)	(5.9)
2003 (standard error)	(2.6)	(3.1)	(4.9)	(2.9)	(3.2)	(11.0)	(6.1)	(5.6)	(6.7)	(4.9)	(5.9)	(7.0)	(5.6)	(5.1)
Number of instructional computers with access to the Internet, in thousands														
1995[4]	447	232	187	59	315	73	96	131	126	94	286	46	57	36
1998	3,569	2,100	1,450	407	2,276	887	1,026	1,334	481	727	2,064	608	439	458
1999	4,809	2,773	1,945	663	2,988	1,158	1,265	1,887	691	966	2,762	778	810	428
2000	6,759	3,813	2,779	882	4,191	1,686	1,782	2,688	955	1,335	3,608	1,064	1,215	858
2001	8,500	4,936	3,357	874	5,229	2,396	2,175	3,178	1,008	2,139	4,225	1,447	1,529	1,289
2002	9,658	5,912	3,525	1,214	5,827	2,618	2,329	3,677	1,222	2,431	4,586	1,474	2,049	1,549
2003	10,361	6,225	3,935	1,156	6,169	3,036	2,593	3,887	1,264	2,616	4,751	1,724	2,121	1,726
1998 (standard error)	(173)	(148)	(79)	(38)	(140)	(73)	(87)	(105)	(46)	(73)	(151)	(79)	(48)	(78)
1999 (standard error)	(145)	(111)	(89)	(60)	(132)	(68)	(94)	(93)	(50)	(70)	(140)	(59)	(79)	(55)
2000 (standard error)	(174)	(136)	(113)	(69)	(114)	(97)	(148)	(178)	(111)	(91)	(139)	(80)	(93)	(87)
2001 (standard error)	(176)	(144)	(92)	(61)	(139)	(89)	(164)	(150)	(74)	(137)	(196)	(105)	(114)	(101)
2002 (standard error)	(236)	(183)	(105)	(97)	(183)	(102)	(145)	(160)	(162)	(148)	(167)	(158)	(129)	(122)
2003 (standard error)	(270)	(237)	(117)	(71)	(186)	(122)	(160)	(168)	(128)	(217)	(244)	(158)	(134)	(107)
Percent of instructional computers with access to the Internet														
1995[4]	8	7	9	7	9	6	6	9	9	8	10	6	6	4
1998	50	46	57	43	52	51	48	51	46	55	57	55	39	37
1999	62	56	71	65	60	63	55	63	68	65	71	62	57	37
2000	77	72	85	78	76	80	70	79	83	79	82	77	76	62
2001	85	80	92	81	83	89	81	84	89	87	88	85	82	76
2002	90	87	95	90	89	92	87	91	93	90	92	88	90	86
2003	93	90	96	91	92	95	92	93	93	93	95	90	94	88
1998 (standard error)	(1.7)	(2.5)	(2.1)	(3.4)	(2.2)	(3.4)	(3.0)	(2.8)	(4.1)	(3.4)	(2.0)	(4.2)	(2.9)	(4.6)
1999 (standard error)	(1.4)	(1.6)	(2.4)	(3.0)	(1.7)	(3.6)	(2.6)	(2.4)	(3.1)	(2.7)	(2.2)	(3.6)	(2.8)	(3.6)
2000 (standard error)	(1.1)	(1.5)	(1.2)	(2.6)	(1.3)	(1.8)	(2.1)	(1.7)	(2.5)	(2.1)	(1.2)	(2.9)	(2.6)	(3.1)
2001 (standard error)	(0.8)	(1.2)	(0.8)	(2.8)	(1.2)	(1.4)	(2.1)	(1.5)	(2.1)	(1.3)	(1.2)	(2.0)	(2.5)	(2.2)
2002 (standard error)	(0.8)	(1.1)	(0.6)	(1.8)	(0.9)	(1.3)	(1.6)	(1.2)	(1.9)	(1.4)	(1.1)	(2.0)	(1.5)	(1.6)
2003 (standard error)	(0.6)	(0.8)	(0.8)	(1.9)	(0.8)	(1.0)	(1.0)	(1.1)	(1.6)	(1.3)	(0.8)	(2.3)	(1.0)	(1.5)
Number of public school students per instructional computer with access to the Internet														
1998	12.1	13.6	9.9	9.1	12.3	13.0	14.1	12.4	12.2	8.6	10.6	10.9	15.8	16.8

See notes at end of table.

Table 422. Public schools and instructional rooms with access to the Internet, by selected school characteristics: 1994 through 2003—Continued

Schools, computers, instructional rooms, and access	All public schools	Instructional level[1]		Size of school enrollment			Metropolitan status				Percent of students eligible for free or reduced-price lunch[2]			
		Elementary	Secondary	Less than 300	300 to 999	1,000 or more	City	Urban fringe	Town	Rural	Less than 35 percent	35 to 49 percent	50 to 74 percent	75 percent or more
1	2	3	4	5	6	7	8	9	10	11	12	13	14	15
1999	9.1	10.6	7.0	5.7	9.4	10.0	11.4	9.1	8.2	6.6	7.6	9.0	10.0	16.8
2000	6.6	7.8	5.2	3.9	7.0	7.2	8.2	6.6	6.2	5.0	6.0	6.3	7.2	9.1
2001	5.4	6.1	4.3	4.1	5.6	5.4	5.9	5.7	5.0	4.6	4.9	5.2	5.6	6.8
2002	4.8	5.2	4.1	3.1	5.0	5.1	5.5	4.9	4.4	4.0	4.6	4.5	4.7	5.5
2003	4.4	4.9	3.8	3.2	4.7	4.3	5.0	4.6	4.1	3.8	4.2	4.4	4.4	5.1
1998 (standard error)	(0.6)	(0.9)	(0.4)	(0.7)	(0.7)	(1.0)	(1.2)	(0.9)	(1.2)	(0.8)	(0.6)	(1.2)	(1.4)	(2.5)
1999 (standard error)	(0.3)	(0.4)	(0.3)	(0.4)	(0.4)	(0.6)	(0.8)	(0.4)	(0.6)	(0.4)	(0.3)	(0.8)	(0.8)	(2.2)
2000 (standard error)	(0.1)	(0.2)	(0.2)	(0.3)	(0.2)	(0.3)	(0.4)	(0.2)	(0.3)	(0.3)	(0.2)	(0.4)	(0.4)	(0.7)
2001 (standard error)	(0.1)	(0.2)	(0.1)	(0.3)	(0.1)	(0.2)	(0.2)	(0.2)	(0.3)	(0.1)	(0.2)	(0.2)	(0.3)	(0.3)
2002 (standard error)	(0.1)	(0.2)	(0.1)	(0.2)	(0.2)	(0.2)	(0.2)	(0.2)	(0.4)	(0.2)	(0.1)	(0.3)	(0.2)	(0.3)
2003 (standard error)	(0.1)	(0.2)	(0.1)	(0.2)	(0.1)	(0.2)	(0.2)	(0.2)	(0.2)	(0.2)	(0.1)	(0.3)	(0.2)	(0.2)
Number of instructional rooms[5] in thousands														
1997	2,625	1,720	906	335	1,725	566	830	902	388	505	1,336	375	462	447
1998	2,709	1,772	916	349	1,740	620	839	981	390	498	1,372	413	451	471
1999	2,811	1,830	926	360	1,805	645	857	1,049	375	530	1,325	477	541	437
2000	2,905	1,864	972	377	1,871	657	866	1,086	413	541	1,380	465	570	482
2001	2,851	1,854	929	332	1,829	690	726	1,068	339	718	1,299	486	551	510
2002	2,988	2,006	919	396	1,896	696	748	1,101	378	761	1,368	451	648	520
2003	3,004	1,998	952	378	1,919	707	777	1,104	375	748	1,281	524	626	512
1998 (standard error)	(41)	(29)	(25)	(15)	(34)	(21)	(22)	(24)	(14)	(17)	(60)	(39)	(29)	(42)
1999 (standard error)	(36)	(33)	(29)	(26)	(39)	(30)	(29)	(33)	(16)	(23)	(46)	(34)	(42)	(34)
2000 (standard error)	(35)	(28)	(24)	(22)	(23)	(23)	(56)	(61)	(47)	(39)	(46)	(28)	(36)	(29)
2001 (standard error)	(31)	(30)	(18)	(17)	(23)	(15)	(49)	(46)	(24)	(36)	(48)	(34)	(35)	(29)
2002 (standard error)	(37)	(30)	(19)	(25)	(20)	(16)	(36)	(39)	(40)	(48)	(45)	(38)	(38)	(33)
2003 (standard error)	(47)	(44)	(20)	(18)	(33)	(16)	(45)	(51)	(38)	(54)	(51)	(39)	(38)	(34)
Percent of instructional rooms[5] with access to the Internet														
1994	3	3	4	3	3	3	4	4	3	3	3	2	4	2
1995	8	8	8	9	8	4	6	8	8	8	9	6	6	3
1996	14	13	16	15	13	16	12	16	14	14	17	12	11	5
1997	27	24	32	27	28	25	20	29	34	30	33	33	20	14
1998	51	51	52	54	53	45	47	50	55	57	57	60	41	38
1999	64	62	67	71	64	58	52	67	72	71	73	69	61	38
2000	77	76	79	83	78	70	66	78	87	85	82	81	77	60
2001	87	86	88	87	87	86	82	87	91	89	90	89	87	79
2002	92	92	91	91	93	89	88	92	96	93	93	90	91	89
2003	93	93	94	93	93	94	90	94	97	94	95	93	94	90
1998 (standard error)	(1.8)	(2.3)	(2.1)	(3.7)	(2.2)	(3.9)	(3.2)	(2.9)	(4.0)	(3.6)	(2.4)	(5.1)	(3.9)	(4.3)
1999 (standard error)	(1.6)	(1.8)	(2.6)	(3.2)	(1.9)	(3.0)	(2.6)	(2.5)	(3.4)	(3.0)	(2.3)	(3.4)	(3.1)	(4.4)
2000 (standard error)	(1.1)	(1.5)	(1.6)	(2.8)	(1.5)	(2.2)	(2.2)	(2.0)	(2.6)	(1.7)	(1.5)	(2.9)	(2.8)	(3.3)
2001 (standard error)	(0.9)	(1.1)	(1.2)	(2.1)	(1.1)	(1.7)	(2.1)	(1.3)	(2.2)	(1.3)	(1.2)	(2.2)	(2.4)	(2.4)
2002 (standard error)	(0.6)	(0.8)	(1.0)	(1.9)	(0.7)	(1.7)	(1.6)	(0.9)	(1.1)	(1.0)	(0.8)	(2.1)	(1.4)	(1.9)
2003 (standard error)	(0.5)	(0.7)	(0.9)	(1.6)	(0.7)	(1.1)	(1.0)	(0.9)	(0.9)	(1.2)	(1.0)	(1.4)	(1.1)	(1.5)

†Not applicable.
[1]Excludes combined elementary/secondary schools because of small sample size.
[2]Excludes schools with missing data for free and reduced-price lunch participation.
[3]This estimate fell between 99.5 percent and 100.0 percent and therefore was rounded to 100 percent.
[4]Includes computers used for instructional or administrative purposes.
[5]Includes all classrooms, computer labs, and library/media centers.
NOTE: Detail may not sum to totals because of rounding. Standard errors for some years were not available.
SOURCE: U.S. Department of Education, National Center for Education Statistics, Fast Response Survey System (FRSS), *Internet Access in U.S. Public Schools and Classrooms: 1994–2003*; and unpublished tabulations. (This table was prepared April 2005.)

Table 423. Use of the Internet by persons 3 years old and over, by type of use and selected characteristics of students and other users: 2003

Selected characteristic	Number of persons using the Internet (in thousands)	Percent using the Internet anywhere	Percent using the Internet at school	Percent of internet users using the Internet for various activities during the year[1] — School assignments	E-mail and messaging	Playing games	Online courses	Product purchases and information	News, weather, and sports	Health information[2]	Government information[3]	Conduct financial transactions[3,4]	Look for jobs[3]
1	2	3	4	5	6	7	8	9	10	11	12	13	14
Total, all persons	161,636 (309.1)	58.7 (0.14)	— (†)	— (†)	82.1 (0.15)	42.2 (0.19)	5.6 (0.09)	71.2 (0.17)	60.6 (0.19)	39.3 (0.20)	44.7 (0.21)	30.4 (0.19)	18.7 (0.16)
Sex													
Male	78,070 (343.4)	58.2 (0.21)	— (†)	— (†)	80.4 (0.22)	45.5 (0.27)	5.4 (0.12)	71.8 (0.25)	65.5 (0.26)	34.1 (0.28)	45.5 (0.30)	32.3 (0.28)	19.1 (0.24)
Female	83,567 (348.1)	59.2 (0.20)	— (†)	— (†)	83.7 (0.20)	39.2 (0.26)	5.7 (0.12)	70.6 (0.24)	55.9 (0.26)	44.1 (0.28)	44.0 (0.29)	28.6 (0.26)	18.3 (0.22)
Race/ethnicity													
White	122,243 (353.9)	65.1 (0.17)	— (†)	— (†)	84.8 (0.16)	41.4 (0.22)	5.5 (0.10)	74.4 (0.19)	62.9 (0.21)	41.1 (0.23)	45.9 (0.24)	31.3 (0.22)	17.4 (0.18)
Black	14,898 (131.5)	45.2 (0.45)	— (†)	— (†)	71.1 (0.61)	50.2 (0.67)	5.6 (0.31)	59.7 (0.66)	50.8 (0.67)	33.6 (0.67)	41.1 (0.73)	22.3 (0.62)	25.6 (0.65)
Hispanic	14,038 (132.7)	37.2 (0.43)	— (†)	— (†)	69.6 (0.68)	43.0 (0.73)	5.0 (0.32)	57.2 (0.73)	50.6 (0.74)	30.1 (0.73)	36.4 (0.81)	26.6 (0.74)	21.5 (0.69)
Other	10,457 (133.9)	61.6 (0.65)	— (†)	— (†)	83.3 (0.64)	39.5 (0.84)	7.1 (0.44)	68.4 (0.79)	60.7 (0.83)	37.6 (0.87)	45.4 (0.93)	35.2 (0.89)	21.5 (0.76)
Age													
3 and 4	1,662 (62.5)	19.9 (0.67)	— (†)	— (†)	26.5 (1.67)	64.6 (1.81)	0.6 (0.29)	15.4 (1.36)	11.3 (1.19)	— (†)	— (†)	— (†)	— (†)
5 to 9	8,259 (137.2)	42.0 (0.54)	— (†)	— (†)	33.5 (0.80)	64.8 (0.81)	1.0 (0.17)	17.3 (0.64)	16.6 (0.63)	— (†)	— (†)	— (†)	— (†)
10 to 14	14,570 (179.4)	68.9 (0.49)	— (†)	— (†)	62.4 (0.62)	66.1 (0.60)	1.1 (0.13)	34.4 (0.61)	35.7 (0.61)	6.2 (0.38)	— (†)	— (†)	— (†)
15 to 19	15,768 (186.1)	77.7 (0.45)	— (†)	— (†)	84.0 (0.45)	61.1 (0.60)	5.0 (0.27)	61.3 (0.60)	55.4 (0.61)	13.2 (0.42)	19.3 (0.48)	8.6 (0.34)	10.5 (0.38)
20 to 24	13,800 (174.9)	69.4 (0.50)	— (†)	— (†)	87.1 (0.44)	51.9 (0.65)	8.8 (0.37)	76.4 (0.56)	65.6 (0.62)	28.4 (0.59)	36.2 (0.63)	27.6 (0.59)	30.5 (0.60)
25 to 29	12,492 (167.0)	66.7 (0.53)	— (†)	— (†)	88.7 (0.44)	42.2 (0.68)	8.0 (0.37)	83.1 (0.52)	71.0 (0.62)	44.7 (0.68)	50.2 (0.69)	41.3 (0.68)	31.5 (0.64)
30 to 39	28,580 (242.3)	69.2 (0.35)	— (†)	— (†)	88.6 (0.29)	35.9 (0.44)	7.1 (0.23)	83.6 (0.34)	70.9 (0.41)	45.0 (0.45)	49.9 (0.46)	38.8 (0.44)	23.3 (0.38)
40 to 49	29,978 (247.3)	67.5 (0.34)	— (†)	— (†)	88.3 (0.29)	33.1 (0.42)	6.3 (0.22)	83.4 (0.33)	70.1 (0.41)	48.0 (0.44)	50.9 (0.44)	34.6 (0.42)	19.0 (0.35)
50 to 59	21,911 (215.9)	62.7 (0.40)	— (†)	— (†)	89.3 (0.32)	26.9 (0.46)	5.9 (0.24)	82.1 (0.40)	66.4 (0.49)	50.5 (0.52)	51.2 (0.52)	30.0 (0.48)	12.8 (0.35)
60 to 69	9,677 (148.0)	43.9 (0.51)	— (†)	— (†)	87.5 (0.52)	27.7 (0.70)	3.7 (0.30)	77.8 (0.65)	60.2 (0.77)	49.3 (0.78)	45.6 (0.78)	24.2 (0.67)	6.1 (0.37)
70 or older	4,940 (106.9)	20.1 (0.39)	— (†)	— (†)	86.7 (0.74)	27.9 (0.98)	2.9 (0.37)	67.6 (1.03)	56.8 (1.08)	47.6 (1.09)	37.8 (1.06)	19.0 (0.86)	2.4 (0.34)
Family income[5]													
Less than $10,000	5,290 (112.1)	31.5 (0.63)	— (†)	— (†)	69.3 (1.11)	48.0 (1.20)	6.4 (0.59)	60.6 (1.17)	53.3 (1.20)	33.8 (1.21)	40.4 (1.31)	22.9 (1.12)	34.5 (1.27)
$10,000 to $19,999	8,119 (195.6)	32.5 (0.66)	— (†)	— (†)	70.6 (1.12)	45.0 (1.22)	5.9 (0.58)	60.4 (1.20)	51.3 (1.23)	33.4 (1.23)	39.7 (1.34)	20.7 (1.11)	26.1 (1.20)
$20,000 to $29,999	12,830 (243.1)	43.8 (0.64)	— (†)	— (†)	75.5 (0.84)	46.1 (0.97)	5.4 (0.44)	64.3 (0.94)	54.9 (0.97)	35.8 (0.99)	39.3 (1.04)	24.8 (0.92)	23.6 (0.91)
$30,000 to $39,999	15,730 (267.2)	54.3 (0.65)	— (†)	— (†)	79.4 (0.71)	44.9 (0.88)	5.1 (0.39)	67.0 (0.83)	56.1 (0.88)	36.3 (0.90)	40.4 (0.95)	26.3 (0.85)	21.2 (0.79)
$40,000 to $49,999	13,596 (249.8)	64.8 (0.73)	— (†)	— (†)	80.2 (0.76)	43.7 (0.94)	4.8 (0.40)	70.6 (0.86)	58.0 (0.94)	37.6 (0.97)	41.9 (1.02)	27.3 (0.92)	18.5 (0.80)
$50,000 to $74,999	32,025 (365.2)	71.8 (0.47)	— (†)	— (†)	83.6 (0.46)	42.7 (0.61)	5.1 (0.27)	72.9 (0.55)	61.7 (0.60)	39.7 (0.63)	45.7 (0.67)	31.3 (0.62)	18.2 (0.52)
$75,000 or more	48,795 (429.4)	82.9 (0.34)	— (†)	— (†)	87.3 (0.33)	39.7 (0.49)	6.5 (0.25)	77.7 (0.42)	67.4 (0.47)	44.0 (0.52)	51.5 (0.54)	38.4 (0.53)	15.9 (0.40)
Total, all students	49,520 (300.6)	66.1 (0.27)	48.8 (0.28)	82.2 (0.26)	70.1 (0.32)	59.3 (0.34)	5.9 (0.16)	49.8 (0.35)	46.5 (0.35)	20.1 (0.33)	32.8 (0.45)	20.5 (0.39)	17.8 (0.37)
Elementary/secondary[6]	34,636 (262.4)	59.4 (0.31)	43.3 (0.32)	77.9 (0.34)	60.6 (0.40)	64.2 (0.40)	2.0 (0.12)	37.1 (0.40)	36.0 (0.40)	9.3 (0.31)	15.8 (0.53)	5.6 (0.34)	7.0 (0.37)
3 and 4 years old	1,063 (50.1)	23.2 (0.96)	7.6 (0.60)	29.4 (2.15)	25.1 (2.05)	63.5 (2.27)	‡ (†)	12.7 (1.57)	8.5 (1.32)	— (†)	— (†)	— (†)	— (†)
5 to 9 years old	8,116 (136.0)	42.7 (0.55)	26.1 (0.49)	51.6 (0.85)	33.3 (0.81)	64.9 (0.82)	1.0 (0.17)	17.3 (0.61)	16.5 (0.63)	— (†)	— (†)	— (†)	— (†)
10 to 14 years old	14,422 (178.5)	69.4 (0.49)	53.4 (0.53)	85.6 (0.45)	62.4 (0.62)	66.1 (0.61)	1.0 (0.13)	34.2 (0.61)	35.5 (0.61)	5.9 (0.38)	— (†)	— (†)	— (†)
15 years old and over	11,035 (157.5)	79.5 (0.53)	63.6 (0.63)	91.9 (0.40)	81.6 (0.57)	61.3 (0.71)	4.2 (0.29)	57.8 (0.72)	53.6 (0.73)	12.2 (0.48)	15.8 (0.53)	5.6 (0.34)	7.0 (0.37)
College	14,884 (181.2)	89.5 (0.37)	68.1 (0.56)	92.0 (0.34)	92.4 (0.34)	47.8 (0.63)	14.9 (0.45)	79.2 (0.51)	71.1 (0.57)	34.9 (0.60)	45.4 (0.63)	31.5 (0.59)	25.8 (0.55)
Sex													
Male	24,107 (225.2)	64.6 (0.38)	47.7 (0.40)	80.7 (0.39)	66.8 (0.47)	64.1 (0.48)	5.3 (0.22)	50.5 (0.50)	49.9 (0.50)	16.1 (0.44)	31.4 (0.65)	20.2 (0.56)	17.0 (0.52)
Elementary/secondary[6]	17,519 (195.3)	58.4 (0.44)	42.2 (0.44)	76.6 (0.49)	57.2 (0.58)	67.5 (0.54)	2.1 (0.17)	39.4 (0.57)	39.3 (0.57)	7.6 (0.40)	15.4 (0.74)	5.6 (0.47)	6.4 (0.50)
3 and 4 years old	591 (37.4)	24.2 (1.34)	7.2 (0.81)	26.9 (2.81)	23.7 (2.69)	66.4 (2.99)	‡ (†)	11.4 (2.01)	8.7 (1.79)	— (†)	— (†)	— (†)	— (†)
5 to 9 years old	4,051 (97.0)	41.8 (0.77)	25.1 (0.68)	50.4 (1.21)	30.2 (1.11)	66.8 (1.14)	1.2 (0.27)	18.9 (0.95)	17.8 (0.93)	— (†)	— (†)	— (†)	— (†)
10 to 14 years old	7,233 (128.7)	68.1 (0.70)	51.9 (0.75)	84.0 (0.66)	58.0 (0.89)	68.9 (0.84)	1.4 (0.21)	37.6 (0.88)	38.1 (0.88)	4.6 (0.48)	— (†)	— (†)	— (†)
15 years old and over	5,645 (114.1)	77.9 (0.75)	62.8 (0.87)	91.2 (0.58)	79.1 (0.83)	66.3 (0.97)	3.9 (0.40)	59.5 (1.01)	59.6 (1.01)	9.9 (0.61)	15.4 (0.74)	5.6 (0.47)	6.4 (0.50)
College	6,587 (123.0)	90.0 (0.54)	70.2 (0.82)	91.4 (0.53)	92.3 (0.51)	55.1 (0.94)	13.6 (0.65)	79.8 (0.76)	77.9 (0.79)	29.2 (0.86)	45.0 (0.94)	32.7 (0.89)	26.0 (0.83)

See notes at end of table.

Table 423. Use of the Internet by persons 3 years old and over, by type of use and selected characteristics of students and other users: 2003—Continued

Selected characteristic	Number of persons using the Internet (in thousands)	Percent using the Internet anywhere	Percent using the Internet at school	Percent of internet users using the Internet for various activities during the year[1]									
				School assignments	E-mail and messaging	Playing games	Online courses	Product purchases and information	News, weather, and sports	Health information[2]	Government information[2]	Conduct financial transactions[3,4]	Look for jobs[3]
1	2	3	4	5	6	7	8	9	10	11	12	13	14
Female	25,413 (230.4)	67.6 (0.37)	49.9 (0.40)	83.6 (0.36)	73.3 (0.43)	54.7 (0.48)	6.5 (0.24)	49.1 (0.48)	43.4 (0.48)	23.8 (0.48)	34.1 (0.62)	20.7 (0.53)	18.6 (0.51)
Elementary/secondary[6]	17,117 (193.2)	60.5 (0.45)	44.4 (0.45)	79.3 (0.48)	64.0 (0.56)	60.8 (0.57)	1.9 (0.16)	34.8 (0.56)	32.6 (0.55)	11.1 (0.48)	16.2 (0.77)	5.7 (0.48)	7.6 (0.56)
3 and 4 years old	472 (33.4)	21.9 (1.37)	8.0 (0.90)	32.5 (3.32)	26.8 (3.14)	60.0 (3.47)	‡ (†)	14.3 (2.48)	8.3 (1.95)	— (†)	— (†)	— (†)	— (†)
5 to 9 years old	4,065 (97.2)	43.7 (0.79)	27.1 (0.71)	52.9 (1.21)	36.3 (1.16)	62.9 (1.17)	0.7 (0.20)	15.7 (0.88)	15.1 (0.86)	— (†)	— (†)	— (†)	— (†)
10 to 14 years old	7,189 (128.3)	70.7 (0.69)	54.9 (0.76)	87.3 (0.60)	66.9 (0.85)	63.3 (0.87)	0.7 (0.15)	30.9 (0.84)	32.9 (0.85)	7.1 (0.57)	— (†)	— (†)	— (†)
15 years old and over	5,390 (111.6)	81.2 (0.74)	64.5 (0.90)	92.6 (0.55)	84.1 (0.77)	56.0 (1.04)	4.4 (0.43)	56.1 (1.04)	47.4 (1.05)	14.6 (0.74)	16.2 (0.77)	5.7 (0.48)	7.6 (0.56)
College	8,297 (137.5)	89.0 (0.50)	66.4 (0.75)	92.4 (0.45)	92.4 (0.45)	42.0 (0.83)	15.9 (0.62)	78.8 (0.69)	65.7 (0.80)	39.4 (0.83)	45.8 (0.84)	30.4 (0.78)	25.7 (0.74)
Race/ethnicity													
White	34,066 (260.6)	73.4 (0.32)	54.0 (0.36)	82.6 (0.32)	74.0 (0.37)	60.1 (0.41)	6.0 (0.20)	52.9 (0.42)	48.8 (0.42)	20.8 (0.40)	34.6 (0.55)	21.9 (0.48)	16.7 (0.43)
Elementary/secondary[6]	23,592 (223.1)	67.1 (0.39)	48.7 (0.41)	78.2 (0.41)	65.1 (0.48)	65.7 (0.48)	1.9 (0.14)	39.9 (0.49)	38.0 (0.49)	9.5 (0.38)	17.3 (0.68)	6.7 (0.45)	5.8 (0.42)
3 and 4 years old	769 (42.6)	26.8 (1.27)	7.2 (0.74)	23.9 (2.37)	24.1 (2.37)	63.5 (2.67)	‡ (†)	9.9 (1.66)	6.5 (1.37)	— (†)	— (†)	— (†)	— (†)
5 to 9 years old	5,557 (113.2)	49.6 (0.73)	30.4 (0.67)	49.7 (1.03)	35.4 (0.99)	65.5 (0.98)	0.9 (0.19)	17.4 (0.78)	17.2 (0.78)	— (†)	— (†)	— (†)	— (†)
10 to 14 years old	9,836 (149.1)	78.2 (0.57)	60.4 (0.67)	87.4 (0.52)	68.5 (0.72)	67.8 (0.72)	0.8 (0.14)	37.0 (0.75)	37.6 (0.75)	5.4 (0.44)	— (†)	— (†)	— (†)
15 years old and over	7,430 (130.4)	87.4 (0.55)	69.6 (0.77)	92.9 (0.46)	87.2 (0.60)	63.4 (0.86)	4.1 (0.36)	63.5 (0.86)	57.4 (0.88)	12.9 (0.60)	17.3 (0.68)	6.7 (0.45)	5.8 (0.42)
College	10,475 (153.6)	92.7 (0.38)	70.3 (0.66)	92.4 (0.40)	94.0 (0.36)	47.5 (0.75)	15.4 (0.54)	82.3 (0.57)	73.1 (0.67)	35.7 (0.72)	46.8 (0.75)	32.7 (0.71)	24.4 (0.65)
Black	5,810 (110.1)	53.0 (0.78)	40.8 (0.77)	82.6 (0.81)	57.4 (1.06)	61.5 (1.05)	5.9 (0.51)	41.9 (1.06)	39.3 (1.05)	18.8 (0.99)	28.2 (1.33)	12.7 (0.99)	22.8 (1.24)
Elementary/secondary[6]	4,137 (96.7)	46.6 (0.87)	36.2 (0.83)	79.1 (1.04)	46.8 (1.27)	64.9 (1.21)	2.0 (0.36)	31.0 (1.18)	31.2 (1.18)	8.7 (0.92)	11.7 (1.42)	1.6 (0.55)	11.5 (1.41)
3 and 4 years old	103 (16.6)	15.0 (2.24)	7.2 (1.62)	51.6 (8.06)	32.5 (7.55)	56.8 (7.99)	‡ (†)	35.3 (7.70)	20.0 (6.45)	— (†)	— (†)	— (†)	— (†)
5 to 9 years old	925 (48.9)	33.1 (1.46)	21.5 (1.27)	58.2 (2.65)	27.1 (2.39)	65.6 (2.56)	0.6 (0.40)	20.0 (2.15)	16.3 (1.99)	— (†)	— (†)	— (†)	— (†)
10 to 14 years old	1,732 (65.8)	53.6 (1.44)	42.7 (1.42)	83.8 (1.45)	45.5 (1.96)	68.6 (1.83)	2.1 (0.57)	29.0 (1.79)	31.6 (1.83)	8.2 (1.33)	— (†)	— (†)	— (†)
15 years old and over	1,377 (59.1)	63.6 (1.69)	54.5 (1.75)	89.2 (1.37)	62.7 (2.13)	60.4 (2.16)	3.1 (0.76)	40.5 (2.17)	41.6 (2.17)	9.2 (1.27)	11.7 (1.42)	1.6 (0.55)	11.5 (1.41)
College	1,673 (64.8)	80.0 (1.43)	60.7 (1.75)	91.4 (1.12)	83.5 (1.48)	53.0 (2.00)	15.4 (1.45)	68.9 (1.85)	59.4 (1.97)	33.9 (1.89)	41.9 (1.97)	21.8 (1.65)	32.2 (1.87)
Hispanic	5,862 (116.2)	49.1 (0.80)	34.9 (0.76)	77.6 (0.95)	58.0 (1.13)	53.3 (1.14)	4.9 (0.49)	38.7 (1.11)	38.1 (1.11)	16.2 (1.02)	27.3 (1.47)	15.9 (1.21)	18.6 (1.29)
Elementary/secondary[6]	4,517 (105.7)	44.2 (0.86)	31.2 (0.80)	74.5 (1.13)	49.1 (1.30)	56.1 (1.29)	2.8 (0.43)	29.1 (1.18)	30.3 (1.19)	8.6 (0.95)	13.9 (1.58)	3.7 (0.87)	9.0 (1.31)
3 and 4 years old	114 (18.6)	15.6 (2.35)	7.2 (1.67)	41.4 (8.08)	16.2 (6.04)	71.0 (7.44)	‡ (†)	7.0 (4.19)	10.6 (5.04)	— (†)	— (†)	— (†)	— (†)
5 to 9 years old	1,095 (56.5)	30.3 (1.33)	17.9 (1.11)	53.6 (2.63)	26.6 (2.33)	59.9 (2.59)	1.8 (0.70)	15.2 (1.89)	15.5 (1.91)	— (†)	— (†)	— (†)	— (†)
10 to 14 years old	1,855 (72.3)	51.9 (1.46)	38.7 (1.42)	78.5 (1.67)	48.2 (2.03)	54.9 (2.02)	1.4 (0.48)	25.5 (1.77)	28.1 (1.82)	6.5 (1.23)	— (†)	— (†)	— (†)
15 years old and over	1,454 (64.5)	63.2 (1.76)	47.9 (1.82)	87.6 (1.51)	69.8 (2.10)	53.7 (2.28)	5.3 (1.02)	45.8 (2.28)	45.8 (2.28)	10.3 (1.39)	13.9 (1.58)	3.7 (0.87)	9.0 (1.31)
College	1,344 (62.2)	78.4 (1.74)	56.9 (2.09)	88.2 (1.54)	88.1 (1.54)	43.9 (2.36)	12.0 (1.55)	71.2 (2.16)	64.2 (2.28)	31.5 (2.21)	41.8 (2.35)	29.0 (2.16)	29.0 (2.16)
Family income[5]													
Less than $10,000	2,642 (84.7)	51.9 (1.22)	41.1 (1.21)	81.4 (1.32)	64.0 (1.63)	56.0 (1.69)	7.9 (0.92)	51.9 (1.70)	50.3 (1.70)	27.1 (1.71)	39.2 (2.07)	25.4 (1.85)	32.9 (1.99)
$10,000 to $19,999	3,477 (95.2)	52.8 (1.07)	41.8 (1.06)	82.2 (1.13)	60.8 (1.45)	52.5 (1.48)	6.9 (0.75)	46.7 (1.48)	42.6 (1.46)	22.6 (1.44)	37.2 (1.90)	19.8 (1.57)	21.4 (1.62)
$20,000 to $29,999	4,226 (103.0)	55.8 (1.00)	42.8 (0.99)	79.7 (1.08)	64.5 (1.29)	56.5 (1.33)	6.8 (0.68)	47.3 (1.34)	43.4 (1.33)	22.8 (1.32)	35.4 (1.75)	19.3 (1.44)	21.7 (1.51)
$30,000 to $39,999	4,860 (108.7)	62.8 (0.96)	45.1 (0.99)	78.5 (1.03)	66.8 (1.18)	60.9 (1.22)	6.6 (0.62)	45.1 (1.25)	41.4 (1.23)	20.5 (1.23)	31.9 (1.68)	20.7 (1.46)	19.1 (1.41)
$40,000 to $49,999	3,812 (98.9)	69.0 (1.09)	49.7 (1.17)	80.2 (1.13)	65.5 (1.35)	60.1 (1.39)	5.5 (0.64)	48.2 (1.41)	41.2 (1.39)	18.7 (1.33)	28.2 (1.82)	17.4 (1.53)	14.8 (1.43)
$50,000 to $74,999	9,038 (130.9)	72.1 (0.70)	51.6 (0.78)	82.0 (0.71)	71.5 (0.83)	60.9 (0.90)	5.0 (0.40)	49.9 (0.92)	46.9 (0.92)	20.2 (0.88)	35.0 (1.23)	20.5 (1.04)	17.2 (0.98)
$75,000 or more	14,314 (132.1)	79.5 (0.53)	57.3 (0.64)	84.3 (0.53)	76.2 (0.62)	61.9 (0.71)	5.9 (0.34)	54.0 (0.73)	51.3 (0.73)	18.6 (0.69)	32.9 (0.97)	22.4 (0.86)	14.6 (0.73)

—Not available.
†Not applicable.
‡Reporting standards not met.
[1]Individuals may be counted in more than one internet activity.
[2]Data are for persons 12 years old and over.
[3]Data are for persons 15 years old and over.
[4]Includes online banking and stock and securities transactions.
[5]Excludes persons whose income data were not available.
[6]Includes prekindergarten through grade 12.

NOTE: Data are based on a sample survey of households and are subject to sampling and nonsampling error. Race categories exclude persons of Hispanic origin. Detail may not sum to totals because of rounding. Standard errors appear in parentheses.
SOURCE: U.S. Department of Commerce, Census Bureau, Current Population Survey (CPS), October 2003, unpublished tabulations. (This table was prepared May 2005.)

Table 424. Number and percentage of home computer users, by type of application and selected characteristics: 1997 and 2003

Selected characteristic	1997 Number of home computer users (in thousands)	1997 Percent of persons using computers at home	2003 Number of home computer users (in thousands)	2003 Percent of persons using computers at home	Word processing	Connect to Internet	E-mail	Spreadsheets/databases[2]	Graphics/design[2]	School assignments[3]	Household records/finances[2]	Games
1	2	3	4	5	6	7	8	9	10	11	12	13
Total, age 3 and over	81,013 (600.0)	31.7 (0.16)	156,744 (954.0)	56.9 (0.16)	53.1 (0.22)	82.7 (0.17)	72.7 (0.19)	32.0 (0.23)	37.6 (0.24)	75.9 (0.29)	30.8 (0.22)	58.5 (0.22)
Sex												
Male	41,260 (412.6)	33.1 (0.22)	76,777 (637.8)	57.2 (0.22)	49.5 (0.30)	82.4 (0.23)	70.5 (0.27)	33.7 (0.32)	39.5 (0.33)	73.9 (0.42)	31.6 (0.31)	61.5 (0.29)
Female	39,753 (384.7)	30.3 (0.20)	79,967 (627.8)	56.7 (0.21)	56.7 (0.28)	83.0 (0.21)	74.8 (0.24)	30.3 (0.29)	35.9 (0.30)	77.8 (0.39)	30.1 (0.29)	55.6 (0.28)
Race/ethnicity												
White	68,026 (543.7)	36.9 (0.19)	119,495 (801.4)	63.7 (0.19)	53.9 (0.25)	84.9 (0.18)	75.4 (0.22)	32.6 (0.26)	38.6 (0.27)	75.4 (0.34)	31.8 (0.26)	58.0 (0.25)
Black	4,943 (136.3)	15.6 (0.36)	13,457 (254.7)	40.8 (0.48)	50.5 (0.76)	74.4 (0.67)	62.5 (0.74)	26.8 (0.77)	33.4 (0.82)	79.3 (0.89)	26.9 (0.78)	64.8 (0.73)
Hispanic	4,081 (139.0)	14.5 (0.41)	13,497 (300.2)	35.8 (0.49)	46.6 (0.85)	72.4 (0.76)	59.4 (0.83)	27.8 (0.90)	31.4 (0.93)	74.9 (0.97)	25.1 (0.87)	59.5 (0.83)
Other	3,963 (136.6)	34.8 (0.88)	10,296 (248.9)	60.7 (0.74)	56.3 (0.96)	81.1 (0.76)	71.6 (0.88)	36.4 (1.06)	39.3 (1.07)	76.7 (1.14)	31.4 (1.02)	54.2 (0.97)
Age												
3 to 14	18,774 (249.8)	39.1 (0.39)	30,772 (330.0)	62.6 (0.38)	37.9 (0.48)	57.6 (0.49)	34.5 (0.47)	— (†)	— (†)	61.9 (0.44)	— (†)	86.0 (0.34)
15 and over	62,239 (505.5)	30.0 (0.17)	125,972 (813.4)	55.7 (0.18)	56.8 (0.24)	88.8 (0.15)	82.0 (0.19)	32.0 (0.23)	37.6 (0.24)	92.8 (0.29)	30.8 (0.22)	51.8 (0.24)
15 to 19	8,395 (162.3)	43.1 (0.61)	14,656 (218.2)	72.2 (0.54)	68.9 (0.66)	86.6 (0.49)	77.9 (0.59)	23.2 (0.60)	43.8 (0.71)	93.1 (0.34)	6.2 (0.34)	72.4 (0.64)
20 to 24	4,975 (123.7)	28.5 (0.59)	11,848 (194.7)	59.6 (0.60)	63.7 (0.76)	86.4 (0.54)	80.6 (0.63)	29.9 (0.73)	40.9 (0.78)	94.5 (0.53)	20.5 (0.64)	61.9 (0.77)
25 to 29	5,963 (135.8)	31.7 (0.59)	11,059 (187.7)	59.0 (0.62)	56.0 (0.82)	88.5 (0.52)	83.7 (0.61)	36.2 (0.79)	42.1 (0.81)	94.2 (0.96)	37.1 (0.79)	54.2 (0.82)
30 to 39	15,393 (224.1)	35.8 (0.40)	26,407 (302.3)	64.0 (0.41)	54.3 (0.53)	89.7 (0.32)	83.3 (0.40)	35.5 (0.51)	40.6 (0.52)	89.0 (1.26)	37.6 (0.52)	50.4 (0.53)
40 to 49	15,346 (223.7)	38.3 (0.42)	27,660 (310.4)	62.3 (0.40)	55.4 (0.52)	90.1 (0.31)	82.7 (0.39)	35.3 (0.50)	37.3 (0.50)	88.6 (1.67)	37.5 (0.50)	47.3 (0.52)
50 to 59	7,679 (154.9)	28.5 (0.48)	19,976 (258.5)	57.2 (0.46)	55.4 (0.61)	90.7 (0.35)	83.4 (0.45)	32.5 (0.57)	33.6 (0.58)	90.0 (2.49)	34.4 (0.58)	41.9 (0.60)
60 to 69	3,162 (98.1)	16.2 (0.46)	9,233 (170.6)	41.8 (0.57)	51.8 (0.90)	87.9 (0.59)	81.9 (0.69)	28.5 (0.81)	29.0 (0.82)	69.8 (9.14)	31.8 (0.84)	44.3 (0.89)
70 or older	1,327 (63.2)	5.9 (0.27)	5,134 (125.7)	20.9 (0.45)	43.9 (1.20)	84.5 (0.87)	78.1 (1.00)	20.5 (0.97)	20.6 (0.98)	‡ (†)	25.4 (1.05)	47.0 (1.20)
Family income[4]												
Under $20,000	7,374 (151.6)	11.0 (0.21)	11,951 (195.6)	28.6 (0.38)	48.5 (0.79)	70.1 (0.72)	59.9 (0.77)	23.2 (0.75)	31.5 (0.83)	78.5 (0.85)	22.5 (0.75)	64.4 (0.76)
$20,000 to $29,999	7,819 (156.3)	19.9 (0.35)	12,136 (197.2)	41.4 (0.50)	47.7 (0.78)	74.0 (0.69)	64.5 (0.75)	25.6 (0.77)	32.4 (0.82)	74.8 (1.02)	24.7 (0.76)	63.6 (0.75)
$30,000 to $39,999	10,370 (181.4)	28.5 (0.41)	15,176 (222.4)	52.4 (0.51)	45.6 (0.70)	78.9 (0.57)	68.7 (0.65)	24.9 (0.68)	31.8 (0.73)	72.8 (0.95)	27.1 (0.70)	62.8 (0.68)
$40,000 to $49,999	9,627 (174.4)	36.9 (0.52)	13,300 (207.1)	63.4 (0.57)	50.1 (0.75)	81.9 (0.58)	71.6 (0.68)	28.5 (0.75)	35.6 (0.80)	74.9 (1.03)	28.8 (0.76)	61.5 (0.73)
$50,000 to $74,999	21,685 (270.5)	46.5 (0.40)	31,581 (335.0)	70.8 (0.37)	51.9 (0.49)	85.6 (0.34)	74.8 (0.42)	30.8 (0.50)	37.4 (0.52)	74.9 (0.66)	30.5 (0.50)	59.3 (0.48)
$75,000 or more	24,138 (287.3)	60.3 (0.42)	48,583 (433.0)	82.5 (0.27)	61.3 (0.38)	89.7 (0.24)	79.8 (0.31)	41.2 (0.43)	45.1 (0.43)	77.0 (0.51)	37.8 (0.42)	55.0 (0.39)

Columns 6–13 fall under the span: **2003 — Percent of home computer users using specific applications[1]**

—Not available.
†Not applicable.
‡Reporting standards not met.
[1]Individuals may be counted in more than one computer activity.
[2]Data are for persons 15 years old and over.
[3]Data are for students only.
[4]Excludes persons whose income data were not available.
NOTE: Excludes persons under age 3. Race categories exclude persons of Hispanic origin. Detail may not sum to totals because of rounding. Standard errors appear in parentheses.
SOURCE: U.S. Department of Commerce, Census Bureau, Current Population Survey (CPS), October 1997 and October 2003, unpublished tabulations. (This table was prepared August 2004.)

Table 425. Number and percentage of student home computer users, by type of application and selected characteristics: 2003

Selected characteristic of students	Number (in thousands)	Number using computers at home (in thousands)	Percent using computers at home	Percent of home computer users using specific applications[1]							
				Games	Internet	School assignments	E-mail	Word processing	Graphics and design	Spreadsheets and databases	Personal finances
1	2	3	4	5	6	7	8	9	10	11	12
Total, all students	74,911 (312.9)	52,942 (286.3)	70.7 (0.24)	76.2 (0.27)	72.3 (0.28)	75.9 (0.27)	56.5 (0.31)	55.1 (0.32)	— (†)	— (†)	— (†)
Elementary/secondary	58,273 (324.9)	39,364 (282.0)	67.6 (0.30)	82.8 (0.30)	66.0 (0.37)	69.9 (0.36)	46.2 (0.39)	46.8 (0.39)	— (†)	— (†)	— (†)
Under age 5	4,590 (105.0)	2,291 (74.6)	49.9 (1.16)	84.3 (1.19)	29.2 (1.49)	15.1 (1.17)	8.9 (0.93)	9.4 (0.96)	— (†)	— (†)	— (†)
Ages 5 to 9	19,015 (206.6)	11,887 (166.1)	62.5 (0.55)	87.6 (0.47)	45.9 (0.72)	42.0 (0.71)	18.8 (0.56)	22.6 (0.60)	— (†)	— (†)	— (†)
Ages 10 to 14	20,788 (215.0)	14,875 (184.5)	71.6 (0.49)	85.3 (0.45)	74.1 (0.56)	85.1 (0.46)	53.0 (0.64)	56.5 (0.64)	— (†)	— (†)	— (†)
15 years old or over	13,880 (165.7)	10,311 (144.2)	74.3 (0.54)	73.4 (0.64)	85.8 (0.50)	92.4 (0.38)	76.3 (0.61)	69.1 (0.66)	43.1 (0.71)	21.1 (0.59)	4.5 (0.30)
White	8,500 (131.6)	7,186 (121.4)	84.5 (0.57)	75.3 (0.74)	90.2 (0.51)	93.3 (0.43)	81.5 (0.67)	72.1 (0.77)	46.3 (0.86)	22.1 (0.71)	4.7 (0.36)
Black	2,164 (68.8)	1,073 (49.7)	49.6 (1.67)	73.5 (2.09)	73.6 (2.09)	90.3 (1.40)	60.7 (2.31)	59.0 (2.33)	38.9 (2.31)	15.9 (1.73)	3.5 (0.88)
Hispanic	2,298 (75.0)	1,280 (57.5)	55.7 (1.72)	68.2 (2.16)	72.0 (2.08)	87.8 (1.51)	60.8 (2.26)	59.9 (2.27)	30.0 (2.12)	18.2 (1.78)	6.1 (1.11)
Other	918 (45.9)	771 (42.2)	83.9 (1.88)	64.5 (2.68)	83.7 (2.07)	94.3 (1.30)	75.3 (2.41)	69.9 (2.57)	41.4 (2.75)	24.2 (2.40)	2.2 (0.82)
Undergraduate	13,370 (162.9)	10,701 (146.8)	80.0 (0.50)	60.5 (0.69)	89.6 (0.43)	92.8 (0.37)	84.8 (0.51)	77.1 (0.59)	46.5 (0.70)	36.8 (0.68)	21.4 (0.58)
White	8,964 (135.0)	7,551 (124.4)	84.2 (0.56)	60.8 (0.82)	91.1 (0.48)	93.0 (0.43)	86.5 (0.57)	78.7 (0.69)	48.9 (0.84)	37.8 (0.81)	21.1 (0.69)
Black	1,766 (62.8)	1,151 (51.4)	65.2 (1.76)	62.1 (2.22)	83.2 (1.71)	91.1 (1.30)	77.0 (2.05)	72.4 (2.05)	37.7 (2.22)	32.0 (2.13)	23.0 (1.93)
Hispanic	1,544 (62.7)	1,102 (53.6)	71.4 (1.91)	56.8 (2.47)	86.7 (1.69)	92.1 (1.34)	80.5 (1.98)	68.6 (2.32)	38.8 (2.43)	33.4 (2.35)	19.8 (1.99)
Other	1,095 (49.9)	898 (45.4)	82.0 (1.80)	61.5 (2.52)	89.5 (1.59)	94.0 (1.23)	86.3 (1.78)	80.3 (2.06)	47.3 (2.59)	39.4 (2.53)	23.7 (2.20)
Graduate	3,268 (66.0)	2,876 (64.1)	88.0 (0.83)	43.6 (1.35)	93.7 (0.66)	94.6 (0.61)	91.7 (0.75)	86.1 (0.94)	52.2 (1.36)	56.2 (1.35)	45.4 (1.36)
Males	37,323 (253.4)	26,168 (219.6)	70.1 (0.35)	80.1 (0.36)	71.2 (0.41)	73.9 (0.40)	53.0 (0.45)	51.7 (0.45)	— (†)	— (†)	— (†)
Elementary/secondary	30,005 (252.4)	20,050 (211.6)	66.8 (0.43)	84.9 (0.40)	65.3 (0.53)	68.3 (0.51)	43.1 (0.55)	44.2 (0.55)	— (†)	— (†)	— (†)
Under age 5	2,437 (76.9)	1,222 (54.6)	50.2 (1.59)	85.3 (1.59)	30.3 (2.06)	14.9 (1.60)	10.7 (1.38)	9.1 (1.29)	— (†)	— (†)	— (†)
Ages 5 to 9	9,703 (150.9)	6,060 (120.3)	62.5 (0.77)	88.5 (0.64)	44.6 (1.00)	40.7 (0.99)	16.6 (0.75)	20.9 (0.82)	— (†)	— (†)	— (†)
Ages 10 to 14	10,622 (157.5)	7,453 (132.9)	70.2 (0.70)	87.5 (0.60)	73.9 (0.80)	83.3 (0.68)	48.0 (0.91)	53.0 (0.91)	— (†)	— (†)	— (†)
15 years old or over	7,243 (121.9)	5,313 (104.9)	73.4 (0.76)	77.1 (0.84)	84.8 (0.72)	90.9 (0.58)	73.8 (0.88)	66.4 (0.95)	43.3 (0.99)	21.0 (0.82)	4.2 (0.40)
Undergraduate	5,902 (110.4)	4,859 (100.5)	82.3 (0.72)	68.6 (0.97)	89.7 (0.64)	91.7 (0.58)	84.0 (0.77)	75.1 (0.91)	50.2 (1.05)	37.6 (1.01)	22.3 (0.87)
Graduate	1,416 (54.7)	1,259 (51.6)	88.9 (1.22)	48.9 (2.06)	93.8 (0.99)	94.1 (0.97)	91.6 (1.14)	81.2 (1.61)	53.0 (2.05)	58.3 (2.03)	46.9 (2.05)
Females	37,588 (254.1)	26,774 (221.7)	71.2 (0.34)	72.3 (0.40)	73.4 (0.39)	77.8 (0.37)	59.8 (0.44)	58.4 (0.44)	— (†)	— (†)	— (†)
Elementary/secondary	28,269 (246.1)	19,315 (208.0)	68.3 (0.43)	80.7 (0.45)	66.8 (0.53)	71.6 (0.51)	49.4 (0.56)	49.5 (0.56)	— (†)	— (†)	— (†)
Under age 5	2,154 (72.3)	1,069 (51.1)	49.6 (1.69)	83.2 (1.79)	28.0 (2.15)	15.3 (1.72)	6.8 (1.21)	9.8 (1.43)	— (†)	— (†)	— (†)
Ages 5 to 9	9,312 (147.9)	5,827 (118.0)	62.6 (0.79)	86.7 (0.70)	47.1 (1.02)	43.3 (1.02)	21.0 (0.84)	24.4 (0.88)	— (†)	— (†)	— (†)
Ages 10 to 14	10,166 (154.3)	7,422 (132.7)	73.0 (0.69)	83.1 (0.68)	74.4 (0.79)	86.8 (0.62)	57.9 (0.90)	60.0 (0.89)	— (†)	— (†)	— (†)
15 years old or over	6,637 (116.9)	4,997 (101.9)	75.3 (0.77)	69.6 (0.95)	86.7 (0.70)	94.0 (0.49)	78.9 (0.84)	71.8 (0.93)	42.9 (1.02)	21.3 (0.85)	4.9 (0.45)
Undergraduate	7,468 (123.7)	5,842 (109.9)	78.2 (0.70)	53.9 (0.95)	89.6 (0.58)	93.7 (0.47)	85.5 (0.67)	78.8 (0.78)	43.4 (0.95)	36.2 (0.92)	20.6 (0.77)
Graduate	1,852 (62.5)	1,617 (58.5)	87.3 (1.13)	39.5 (1.77)	93.5 (0.89)	95.1 (0.78)	91.8 (0.99)	90.0 (1.09)	51.5 (1.81)	54.5 (1.81)	44.3 (1.80)

—Not available.
†Not applicable.
[1]Individuals may be counted in more than one computer activity.

NOTE: Estimates are as of October 1. Race categories exclude persons of Hispanic origin. Detail may not sum to totals because of rounding. Standard errors appear in parentheses.
SOURCE: U.S. Department of Commerce, Census Bureau, Current Population Survey (CPS), October 2003, unpublished tabulations. (This table was prepared May 2005.)

Table 426. Student use of computers, by level of enrollment, age, and student and school characteristics: 1993, 1997, and 2003

Student and school characteristic	1993			1997			2003						
	Total	Elementary and secondary¹	College²	Total	Elementary and secondary¹	College²	Total	Elementary and secondary¹ Total	Under 5 years old	5 to 9 years old	10 to 14 years old	15 years old or over	College²
1	2	3	4	5	6	7	8	9	10	11	12	13	14
Percent of students using computers at school													
Total	59.0 (0.32)	60.1 (0.38)	54.7 (0.71)	68.8 (0.27)	70.4 (0.32)	62.9 (0.60)	83.8 (0.20)	83.5 (0.24)	42.6 (1.14)	80.1 (0.45)	90.3 (0.32)	91.2 (0.35)	84.9 (0.41)
Sex													
Male	59.4 (0.44)	59.9 (0.53)	57.4 (1.04)	70.1 (0.37)	71.0 (0.44)	66.3 (0.88)	83.7 (0.28)	83.4 (0.34)	43.5 (1.57)	79.7 (0.64)	90.1 (0.45)	91.8 (0.47)	85.3 (0.60)
Female	58.7 (0.45)	60.5 (0.54)	52.4 (0.96)	67.6 (0.38)	69.9 (0.46)	60.2 (0.81)	83.8 (0.28)	83.5 (0.35)	41.5 (1.66)	80.7 (0.64)	90.6 (0.45)	90.5 (0.53)	84.6 (0.55)
Race/ethnicity													
White	61.6 (0.37)	63.8 (0.45)	54.0 (0.81)	71.1 (0.32)	73.9 (0.38)	62.1 (0.70)	85.0 (0.24)	84.9 (0.30)	41.1 (1.44)	82.5 (0.56)	92.4 (0.37)	91.9 (0.43)	85.0 (0.49)
Black	51.5 (0.98)	50.6 (0.98)	57.0 (2.54)	66.3 (0.74)	66.1 (0.75)	66.8 (1.78)	82.7 (0.56)	82.5 (0.67)	49.4 (3.18)	78.5 (1.30)	88.0 (0.95)	89.9 (1.01)	83.8 (1.25)
Hispanic	52.3 (1.50)	52.3 (1.16)	52.1 (4.06)	61.5 (0.89)	61.3 (0.69)	62.6 (2.38)	80.3 (0.60)	79.8 (0.71)	39.5 (3.22)	75.6 (1.27)	86.8 (1.01)	88.5 (1.10)	83.0 (1.50)
Other	59.0 (2.24)	57.7 (2.50)	62.7 (4.20)	65.3 (1.32)	65.6 (1.45)	64.6 (2.56)	83.3 (0.77)	81.7 (1.01)	48.9 (4.78)	76.3 (1.89)	86.1 (1.54)	94.1 (1.20)	87.6 (1.30)
Family income³													
Less than $5,000	51.2 (1.32)	48.1 (1.50)	62.4 (2.73)	62.1 (1.21)	61.6 (1.41)	63.4 (2.36)	80.9 (1.87)	79.5 (2.31)	42.4 (9.47)	78.3 (3.82)	86.9 (3.39)	86.5 (4.37)	83.8 (3.12)
$5,000 to $9,999	53.3 (1.06)	53.1 (1.17)	54.3 (2.51)	63.5 (1.02)	61.9 (1.14)	70.4 (2.20)	84.4 (1.43)	82.4 (1.74)	49.2 (7.71)	77.8 (3.30)	91.3 (2.18)	88.3 (3.04)	90.1 (2.35)
$10,000 to $14,999	56.4 (1.03)	56.7 (1.13)	55.1 (2.50)	66.2 (0.96)	66.4 (1.06)	65.2 (2.26)	81.7 (1.37)	80.0 (1.61)	50.1 (7.20)	74.1 (3.11)	84.6 (2.41)	90.4 (2.40)	88.0 (2.48)
$15,000 to $19,999	58.1 (1.18)	59.4 (1.30)	52.3 (2.77)	65.9 (1.10)	66.5 (1.21)	63.2 (2.72)	81.3 (1.57)	79.8 (1.84)	26.6 (7.08)	77.0 (3.27)	89.1 (2.38)	89.2 (3.09)	86.7 (2.92)
$20,000 to $24,999	56.4 (1.07)	56.3 (1.18)	56.6 (2.58)	66.9 (0.99)	67.5 (1.10)	64.3 (2.24)	81.3 (1.41)	80.3 (1.61)	43.7 (7.03)	73.0 (3.00)	88.9 (2.16)	92.6 (2.31)	85.3 (2.81)
$25,000 to $29,999	60.0 (1.13)	61.9 (1.25)	52.4 (2.61)	68.5 (1.01)	70.4 (1.11)	61.2 (2.37)	81.9 (1.32)	81.3 (1.48)	35.6 (7.03)	78.0 (2.66)	87.0 (2.21)	90.8 (2.21)	84.4 (2.90)
$30,000 to $34,999	59.1 (1.08)	61.3 (1.20)	50.5 (2.46)	67.6 (0.97)	71.0 (1.05)	53.9 (2.31)	82.2 (1.33)	82.5 (1.46)	40.1 (7.16)	78.5 (2.67)	90.6 (1.86)	88.8 (2.59)	80.9 (3.17)
$35,000 to $39,999	60.7 (1.11)	63.3 (1.21)	49.0 (2.67)	69.0 (0.98)	71.1 (1.08)	60.4 (2.35)	87.1 (1.17)	87.5 (1.30)	54.8 (7.43)	85.2 (2.37)	94.0 (1.53)	90.4 (2.48)	85.7 (2.69)
$40,000 to $49,999	59.3 (0.94)	60.8 (1.04)	53.1 (2.12)	70.5 (0.79)	72.6 (0.85)	60.9 (1.99)	83.5 (1.08)	84.2 (1.18)	47.1 (6.20)	80.0 (2.29)	90.8 (1.56)	90.3 (1.94)	80.4 (2.63)
$50,000 to $74,999	62.6 (0.73)	64.9 (0.82)	55.0 (1.58)	71.7 (0.57)	74.2 (0.63)	63.2 (1.28)	83.8 (0.71)	84.0 (0.80)	35.7 (3.64)	80.5 (1.53)	92.6 (0.94)	92.4 (1.21)	83.1 (1.56)
$75,000 or more	64.6 (0.90)	67.0 (1.04)	58.2 (1.78)	72.1 (0.60)	75.1 (0.68)	63.9 (1.25)	85.6 (0.57)	85.6 (0.65)	39.2 (2.98)	85.3 (1.15)	92.7 (0.81)	93.2 (0.96)	85.8 (1.16)
Control of school													
Public	60.2 (0.34)	61.6 (0.40)	54.0 (0.80)	70.2 (0.28)	72.1 (0.33)	62.3 (0.68)	85.2 (0.21)	85.4 (0.25)	47.7 (1.61)	80.5 (0.48)	90.5 (0.34)	91.2 (0.36)	84.6 (0.46)
Private	52.1 (0.85)	49.8 (1.10)	57.3 (1.52)	60.7 (0.73)	58.6 (0.96)	65.2 (1.27)	75.4 (0.60)	70.5 (0.82)	37.1 (1.61)	77.5 (1.33)	89.1 (1.09)	90.5 (1.36)	86.1 (0.85)
Percent of students using computers at home													
Total	27.0 (0.28)	24.5 (0.33)	36.2 (0.65)	45.1 (0.29)	42.8 (0.34)	53.2 (0.62)	70.7 (0.24)	67.6 (0.30)	49.9 (1.16)	62.5 (0.55)	71.6 (0.49)	74.3 (0.54)	81.6 (0.44)
Sex													
Male	27.4 (0.39)	24.3 (0.45)	40.1 (0.99)	45.2 (0.40)	43.2 (0.48)	53.7 (0.93)	70.1 (0.35)	66.8 (0.43)	50.2 (1.59)	62.5 (0.77)	70.2 (0.70)	73.4 (0.76)	83.6 (0.63)
Female	26.6 (0.39)	24.7 (0.47)	33.0 (0.87)	44.9 (0.40)	42.5 (0.49)	52.8 (0.83)	71.2 (0.34)	68.3 (0.43)	49.6 (1.69)	62.6 (0.79)	73.0 (0.69)	75.3 (0.77)	80.0 (0.60)
Race/ethnicity													
White	32.8 (0.35)	30.8 (0.42)	39.2 (0.76)	54.9 (0.35)	53.9 (0.43)	58.2 (0.72)	80.1 (0.27)	78.3 (0.34)	59.6 (1.43)	74.6 (0.64)	81.8 (0.54)	84.5 (0.57)	85.4 (0.49)
Black	10.9 (0.59)	8.7 (0.54)	22.7 (2.01)	21.1 (0.64)	19.1 (0.62)	31.0 (1.75)	50.2 (0.74)	46.2 (0.88)	31.7 (2.96)	41.6 (1.55)	50.8 (1.46)	49.6 (1.67)	67.5 (1.59)
Hispanic	10.4 (0.90)	7.9 (0.62)	25.0 (3.31)	21.1 (0.74)	18.3 (0.54)	38.8 (2.40)	51.1 (0.76)	47.5 (0.88)	25.8 (2.88)	41.7 (1.46)	52.5 (1.48)	55.7 (1.72)	72.5 (1.79)
Other	28.7 (2.00)	25.8 (2.16)	36.0 (3.99)	49.1 (1.38)	46.5 (1.52)	56.3 (2.66)	74.6 (0.91)	71.3 (1.19)	57.5 (4.73)	61.6 (2.16)	75.7 (1.90)	83.9 (1.88)	83.1 (1.48)

See notes at end of table.

Table 426. Student use of computers, by level of enrollment, age, and student and school characteristics: 1993, 1997, and 2003—Continued

Student and school characteristic	1993			1997			2003						
	Total	Elementary and secondary[1]	College[2]	Total	Elementary and secondary[1]	College[2]	Total	Elementary and secondary[1] Total	Under 5 years old	5 to 9 years old	10 to 14 years old	15 years old or over	College[2]
1	2	3	4	5	6	7	8	9	10	11	12	13	14
Family income[3]													
Less than $5,000	9.7 (0.76)	4.3 (0.59)	28.3 (2.43)	22.6 (1.04)	15.2 (1.04)	43.7 (2.43)	44.1 (2.36)	29.8 (2.62)	20.5 (7.74)	29.9 (4.24)	29.5 (4.58)	34.2 (6.07)	75.2 (3.65)
$5,000 to $9,999	8.0 (0.56)	4.2 (0.46)	25.0 (2.08)	15.8 (0.77)	9.3 (0.68)	42.9 (2.39)	47.0 (1.97)	36.6 (2.20)	31.0 (7.14)	30.7 (3.66)	41.3 (3.82)	40.1 (4.65)	77.7 (3.27)
$10,000 to $14,999	11.4 (0.64)	6.7 (0.56)	33.4 (2.26)	18.4 (0.78)	13.6 (0.77)	39.7 (2.32)	47.0 (1.77)	39.3 (1.96)	36.4 (6.93)	32.8 (3.33)	43.2 (3.31)	42.9 (4.03)	75.2 (3.30)
$15,000 to $19,999	15.1 (0.84)	11.2 (0.82)	31.0 (2.44)	20.7 (0.94)	16.5 (0.95)	41.2 (2.77)	48.3 (2.02)	40.8 (2.25)	16.5 (5.95)	33.4 (3.67)	49.1 (3.82)	48.4 (4.97)	74.6 (3.73)
$20,000 to $24,999	16.8 (0.79)	13.6 (0.80)	31.0 (2.27)	30.5 (0.97)	26.2 (1.04)	47.5 (2.34)	53.1 (1.80)	46.6 (2.02)	27.1 (6.29)	41.1 (3.33)	52.5 (3.43)	53.9 (4.39)	77.8 (3.29)
$25,000 to $29,999	21.1 (0.92)	19.1 (0.99)	29.0 (2.28)	34.6 (1.03)	32.0 (1.13)	45.0 (2.42)	59.0 (1.69)	54.7 (1.89)	40.6 (7.21)	47.7 (3.21)	59.5 (3.22)	61.9 (3.72)	78.3 (3.30)
$30,000 to $34,999	24.1 (0.92)	22.6 (1.02)	29.7 (2.15)	38.7 (1.01)	36.1 (1.11)	49.2 (2.32)	64.2 (1.66)	61.5 (1.87)	41.4 (7.19)	54.7 (3.23)	64.9 (3.04)	72.9 (3.66)	76.1 (3.43)
$35,000 to $39,999	27.1 (0.99)	24.9 (1.08)	36.1 (2.44)	44.1 (1.06)	42.6 (1.17)	50.5 (2.40)	70.0 (1.60)	67.8 (1.83)	49.0 (7.46)	63.0 (3.23)	71.9 (2.91)	74.6 (3.66)	78.5 (3.16)
$40,000 to $49,999	32.2 (0.87)	31.6 (0.98)	34.4 (1.92)	50.6 (0.86)	50.4 (0.95)	51.7 (2.04)	75.9 (1.25)	73.4 (1.43)	54.6 (6.18)	68.9 (2.65)	77.5 (2.24)	78.2 (2.70)	86.6 (2.26)
$50,000 to $74,999	43.0 (0.74)	42.9 (0.84)	43.5 (1.52)	61.7 (0.62)	62.2 (0.70)	59.9 (1.30)	81.3 (0.75)	79.5 (0.88)	58.9 (3.74)	74.9 (1.67)	83.8 (1.33)	86.5 (1.56)	87.8 (1.36)
$75,000 or more	56.1 (0.92)	58.1 (1.08)	50.9 (1.74)	74.2 (0.59)	77.2 (0.66)	65.8 (1.23)	88.6 (0.51)	87.6 (0.61)	66.1 (2.89)	85.3 (1.15)	91.0 (0.89)	94.1 (0.90)	91.7 (0.92)
Control of school													
Public	25.3 (0.29)	23.0 (0.34)	34.5 (0.73)	43.2 (0.31)	40.9 (0.37)	52.4 (0.70)	69.3 (0.27)	66.3 (0.33)	41.1 (1.58)	60.4 (0.59)	70.1 (0.52)	73.1 (0.57)	80.9 (0.50)
Private	37.4 (0.80)	35.0 (1.03)	42.5 (1.45)	56.1 (0.75)	56.1 (0.97)	56.1 (1.32)	78.3 (0.57)	75.6 (0.77)	59.3 (1.63)	77.3 (1.34)	84.7 (1.26)	89.3 (1.43)	84.1 (0.90)
Total	**14.8 (0.22)**	**12.0 (0.25)**	**25.0 (0.59)**	**28.6 (0.26)**	**24.8 (0.30)**	**42.5 (0.61)**	**53.6 (0.27)**	**47.2 (0.32)**	**7.5 (0.61)**	**26.2 (0.50)**	**60.9 (0.53)**	**68.6 (0.57)**	**76.0 (0.48)**
Percent of students using computers at home for school work													
Sex													
Male	14.7 (0.31)	11.4 (0.34)	28.2 (0.91)	28.3 (0.37)	24.7 (0.42)	43.3 (0.92)	51.8 (0.38)	45.6 (0.45)	7.5 (0.83)	25.4 (0.69)	58.5 (0.75)	66.7 (0.81)	77.1 (0.72)
Female	14.8 (0.32)	12.5 (0.36)	22.4 (0.77)	28.9 (0.37)	24.9 (0.43)	41.9 (0.82)	55.4 (0.37)	48.9 (0.47)	7.6 (0.89)	27.1 (0.72)	63.4 (0.75)	70.8 (0.82)	75.2 (0.65)
Race													
White	18.0 (0.29)	15.1 (0.33)	27.4 (0.70)	35.0 (0.34)	31.3 (0.40)	47.0 (0.72)	60.4 (0.33)	54.1 (0.42)	7.3 (0.76)	29.1 (0.67)	70.5 (0.64)	78.9 (0.65)	79.8 (0.55)
Black	5.7 (0.44)	4.3 (0.39)	13.4 (1.64)	12.5 (0.51)	10.4 (0.48)	22.8 (1.59)	39.8 (0.73)	34.6 (0.84)	8.2 (1.75)	22.5 (1.32)	43.7 (1.45)	44.8 (1.66)	62.2 (1.65)
Hispanic	5.6 (0.68)	3.6 (0.42)	17.8 (2.92)	12.5 (0.60)	9.8 (0.42)	29.2 (2.24)	38.3 (0.74)	33.5 (0.83)	6.7 (1.65)	20.2 (1.19)	42.6 (1.47)	48.9 (1.73)	66.7 (1.89)
Other	15.8 (1.61)	12.4 (1.63)	24.5 (3.57)	33.6 (1.31)	29.3 (1.39)	45.3 (2.67)	57.2 (1.03)	49.4 (1.31)	10.3 (2.91)	26.8 (1.97)	60.9 (2.16)	79.1 (2.08)	77.8 (1.65)
Family income[3]													
Less than $5,000	6.6 (0.64)	2.4 (0.45)	21.1 (2.20)	15.1 (0.89)	8.0 (0.79)	35.5 (2.35)	36.5 (2.29)	19.4 (2.27)	4.2 (3.83)	14.4 (3.25)	22.7 (4.21)	30.4 (5.88)	73.8 (3.72)
$5,000 to $9,999	4.7 (0.44)	1.5 (0.28)	18.8 (1.88)	10.4 (0.65)	4.2 (0.47)	36.5 (2.32)	36.5 (1.90)	24.1 (1.96)	4.0 (3.01)	14.0 (2.75)	32.3 (3.62)	34.1 (4.49)	72.8 (3.49)
$10,000 to $14,999	7.2 (0.52)	3.0 (0.38)	27.1 (2.14)	11.4 (0.64)	6.7 (0.56)	32.4 (2.22)	36.9 (1.71)	27.1 (1.78)	14.3 (5.04)	14.4 (2.49)	34.6 (3.18)	36.8 (3.93)	72.2 (3.42)
$15,000 to $19,999	8.5 (0.65)	5.6 (0.60)	20.5 (2.12)	13.2 (0.79)	8.5 (0.72)	36.0 (2.70)	37.2 (1.95)	27.4 (2.04)	0.7 (1.36)	10.8 (2.42)	40.2 (3.75)	42.9 (4.92)	71.5 (3.87)
$20,000 to $24,999	9.7 (0.62)	6.3 (0.57)	24.5 (2.11)	19.4 (0.83)	15.0 (0.84)	37.1 (2.26)	40.5 (1.77)	31.9 (1.89)	8.2 (3.89)	18.9 (2.65)	40.7 (3.38)	48.8 (4.40)	73.4 (3.50)
$25,000 to $29,999	10.3 (0.69)	7.5 (0.66)	21.4 (2.06)	21.9 (0.90)	18.4 (0.94)	35.7 (2.33)	43.4 (1.70)	36.9 (1.84)	8.3 (4.05)	18.0 (2.47)	48.9 (3.28)	55.2 (3.81)	72.2 (3.58)
$30,000 to $34,999	12.9 (0.72)	10.8 (0.75)	20.8 (1.91)	24.4 (0.89)	20.3 (0.93)	40.5 (2.28)	46.8 (1.73)	41.8 (1.89)	8.8 (4.13)	20.4 (2.61)	55.4 (3.17)	64.1 (3.95)	69.0 (3.73)
$35,000 to $39,999	15.2 (0.80)	12.9 (0.83)	24.6 (2.20)	26.5 (0.94)	22.8 (0.99)	41.7 (2.37)	50.9 (1.96)	45.5 (1.89)	7.0 (3.82)	25.9 (2.93)	58.4 (3.19)	66.7 (3.96)	71.8 (3.46)
$40,000 to $49,999	17.1 (0.70)	15.4 (0.76)	23.3 (1.71)	30.1 (0.79)	28.3 (0.86)	38.5 (1.99)	56.9 (1.44)	51.6 (1.62)	12.9 (4.16)	26.3 (2.52)	67.6 (2.51)	71.4 (2.95)	79.0 (2.70)
$50,000 to $74,999	23.1 (0.63)	21.4 (0.70)	28.7 (1.38)	39.3 (0.62)	36.7 (0.70)	48.2 (1.32)	60.9 (0.94)	55.0 (1.09)	4.8 (1.63)	30.2 (1.77)	71.6 (1.62)	81.0 (1.79)	82.4 (1.58)
$75,000 or more	30.2 (0.85)	29.5 (1.00)	32.0 (1.63)	48.3 (0.67)	47.3 (0.78)	51.3 (1.30)	68.2 (0.75)	62.8 (0.89)	6.5 (1.51)	36.2 (1.56)	83.6 (1.15)	90.0 (1.14)	85.7 (1.16)
Control of school													
Public	14.1 (0.24)	11.7 (0.26)	24.1 (0.66)	27.9 (0.28)	24.5 (0.32)	41.9 (0.69)	53.4 (0.29)	47.8 (0.35)	8.0 (0.87)	25.4 (0.53)	59.2 (0.56)	67.5 (0.60)	75.1 (0.55)
Private	18.5 (0.65)	13.8 (0.75)	28.5 (1.33)	32.6 (0.70)	26.9 (0.87)	44.6 (1.32)	54.7 (0.69)	43.3 (0.89)	7.1 (0.85)	32.3 (1.50)	76.5 (1.48)	83.3 (1.73)	79.3 (1.00)

[1]Includes students enrolled in prekindergarten through grade 12, ages 3 and above.
[2]Includes students enrolled at the undergraduate and postbaccalaureate levels.
[3]Excludes persons whose income data were not available.

NOTE: Data are based on a sample survey of households and are subject to sampling and nonsampling error. Race categories exclude persons of Hispanic origin. Standard errors appear in parentheses.
SOURCE: U.S. Department of Commerce, Census Bureau, Current Population Survey (CPS), October 1993, October 1997, and October 2003, unpublished tabulations. (This table was prepared May 2005.)

Table 427. Percentage of workers, 18 years old and over, using computers on the job, by type of computer application and selected characteristics: 1993, 1997, and 2003

Selected characteristic	Percent using computers at work, 1993	Percent using computers at work, 1997	Percent using computers at work	Number using computers at work (in thousands)	Spreadsheets/ databases	Internet/e-mail	Calendar/ schedule	Graphics/design	Programming	Word processing/ desktop publishing	Other uses only	Using 4 or more categories
1	2	3	4	5	6	7	8	9	10	11	12	13
Total	**45.8**	**49.4** (0.24)	**56.1** (0.19)	**76,570**	**64.4** (0.30)	**75.4** (0.27)	**57.0** (0.31)	**29.7** (0.29)	**16.4** (0.23)	**67.8** (0.29)	**8.2** (0.17)	**45.3** (0.31)
Age												
18 to 24	34.4	37.1 (0.66)	38.5 (0.55)	6,575	56.0 (1.06)	62.1 (1.03)	48.9 (1.07)	21.7 (0.88)	12.4 (0.70)	57.9 (1.05)	14.2 (0.74)	33.0 (1.00)
25 to 29	48.3	52.5 (0.70)	56.9 (0.57)	8,203	66.2 (0.90)	75.6 (0.82)	58.3 (0.94)	30.3 (0.88)	18.8 (0.75)	67.8 (0.89)	8.5 (0.53)	47.2 (0.95)
30 to 39	50.7	53.3 (0.46)	59.0 (0.37)	19,225	68.0 (0.58)	78.3 (0.51)	61.8 (0.61)	31.7 (0.58)	18.0 (0.48)	69.8 (0.57)	6.8 (0.31)	49.6 (0.62)
40 to 49	51.3	54.9 (0.47)	60.8 (0.35)	21,772	66.9 (0.55)	77.1 (0.49)	59.0 (0.58)	31.8 (0.55)	17.7 (0.45)	69.7 (0.54)	7.1 (0.30)	48.4 (0.59)
50 to 59	43.9	50.7 (0.61)	60.1 (0.42)	15,423	62.5 (0.67)	76.5 (0.59)	54.6 (0.69)	29.7 (0.64)	15.1 (0.50)	68.1 (0.65)	8.0 (0.38)	43.7 (0.69)
60 or older	27.2	32.6 (0.88)	48.5 (0.67)	5,373	53.8 (1.18)	71.2 (1.07)	46.1 (1.18)	23.5 (1.00)	10.6 (0.72)	63.7 (1.13)	11.1 (0.74)	35.0 (1.12)
Educational attainment and sex												
Not high school completer	10.0	11.9 (0.48)	15.6 (0.50)	2,149	44.1 (1.85)	49.7 (1.86)	40.4 (1.83)	15.3 (1.34)	11.7 (1.20)	43.2 (1.85)	21.6 (1.53)	21.4 (1.53)
High school completer	34.2	36.4 (0.40)	40.4 (0.35)	16,914	53.3 (0.66)	61.4 (0.65)	47.7 (0.66)	18.5 (0.52)	11.8 (0.43)	52.4 (0.66)	14.6 (0.47)	29.3 (0.60)
Some college	50.4	53.6 (0.53)	55.7 (0.42)	15,060	61.5 (0.68)	70.2 (0.64)	53.6 (0.70)	25.3 (0.61)	14.5 (0.50)	62.5 (0.68)	10.0 (0.42)	39.6 (0.69)
Associate's degree	58.2	60.7 (0.81)	62.9 (0.59)	7,813	61.1 (0.95)	71.7 (0.88)	54.4 (0.97)	26.1 (0.86)	15.4 (0.71)	62.6 (0.95)	9.9 (0.58)	39.8 (0.96)
Bachelor's degree	68.8	73.9 (0.50)	82.0 (0.30)	22,540	73.3 (0.51)	85.6 (0.40)	64.2 (0.55)	37.4 (0.56)	20.1 (0.46)	78.0 (0.48)	3.7 (0.22)	57.3 (0.57)
Master's degree	71.2	78.7 (0.81)	87.2 (0.43)	8,292	73.8 (0.83)	90.0 (0.57)	64.9 (0.91)	43.3 (0.94)	20.4 (0.77)	85.6 (0.67)	1.8 (0.25)	62.2 (0.92)
Doctor's or professional degree	66.9	74.6 (1.24)	85.4 (0.67)	3,803	68.8 (1.30)	88.0 (0.91)	66.1 (1.33)	37.5 (1.36)	19.3 (1.11)	81.7 (1.08)	2.9 (0.47)	56.9 (1.39)
Male	40.3	44.1 (0.31)	50.5 (0.25)	36,976	67.2 (0.42)	77.7 (0.37)	58.6 (0.44)	33.8 (0.42)	21.4 (0.37)	65.6 (0.43)	7.8 (0.24)	48.8 (0.45)
Not high school completer	8.5	9.8 (0.53)	12.5 (0.55)	1,095	44.4 (2.59)	48.7 (2.61)	39.4 (2.55)	18.2 (2.01)	13.6 (1.79)	39.7 (2.56)	23.3 (2.21)	20.5 (2.11)
High school completer	24.2	27.1 (0.49)	31.9 (0.45)	7,305	52.1 (1.01)	60.1 (0.99)	45.0 (1.01)	21.6 (0.83)	14.9 (0.72)	45.0 (1.01)	16.1 (0.74)	28.3 (0.91)
Some college	42.8	46.0 (0.71)	49.2 (0.58)	6,718	62.0 (1.02)	71.4 (0.95)	53.0 (1.05)	29.3 (0.96)	18.7 (0.82)	58.2 (1.04)	10.6 (0.65)	40.8 (1.04)
Associate's degree	52.6	55.2 (1.16)	56.9 (0.86)	3,326	64.8 (1.43)	74.1 (1.31)	53.5 (1.49)	33.2 (1.41)	22.1 (1.24)	60.5 (1.46)	9.9 (0.90)	43.7 (1.49)
Bachelor's degree	69.8	74.3 (0.65)	82.5 (0.39)	11,787	77.6 (0.66)	88.4 (0.51)	68.0 (0.74)	40.4 (0.78)	25.6 (0.69)	76.9 (0.67)	2.6 (0.25)	61.7 (0.77)
Master's degree	75.4	79.8 (1.05)	88.0 (0.57)	4,186	78.7 (1.09)	92.1 (0.72)	69.0 (1.23)	44.9 (1.33)	26.8 (1.18)	83.5 (0.99)	1.3 (0.31)	66.2 (1.26)
Doctor's or professional degree	66.5	73.4 (1.43)	85.5 (0.78)	2,559	70.9 (1.55)	88.9 (1.08)	66.5 (1.61)	38.7 (1.66)	21.7 (1.41)	80.1 (1.36)	2.5 (0.53)	58.5 (1.68)
Female	52.4	56.5 (0.32)	62.5 (0.24)	39,594	61.7 (0.42)	73.3 (0.38)	55.5 (0.43)	26.0 (0.38)	11.8 (0.28)	69.8 (0.40)	8.6 (0.24)	42.2 (0.43)
Not high school completer	12.5	15.4 (0.80)	21.0 (0.83)	1,054	43.7 (2.64)	50.7 (2.66)	41.4 (2.62)	12.4 (1.75)	9.7 (1.58)	46.8 (2.66)	19.8 (2.12)	22.3 (2.21)
High school completer	45.2	46.9 (0.56)	50.7 (0.47)	9,609	54.2 (0.88)	62.4 (0.85)	49.7 (0.88)	16.2 (0.65)	9.5 (0.52)	58.0 (0.87)	13.4 (0.60)	30.1 (0.81)
Some college	58.6	61.5 (0.68)	62.4 (0.52)	8,341	61.2 (0.92)	69.3 (0.87)	54.2 (0.94)	22.2 (0.79)	11.1 (0.59)	66.0 (0.90)	9.6 (0.56)	38.5 (0.92)
Associate's degree	63.7	65.4 (0.99)	68.3 (0.70)	4,487	58.4 (1.27)	70.0 (1.18)	55.1 (1.28)	20.7 (1.05)	10.4 (0.79)	64.2 (1.24)	9.9 (0.77)	36.9 (1.24)
Bachelor's degree	67.6	73.5 (0.67)	81.5 (0.40)	10,752	68.7 (0.77)	82.6 (0.63)	60.1 (0.82)	34.1 (0.79)	14.0 (0.58)	79.2 (0.68)	4.9 (0.36)	52.5 (0.83)
Master's degree	66.5	77.5 (1.10)	86.3 (0.58)	4,106	68.9 (1.25)	87.7 (0.88)	60.7 (1.32)	41.7 (1.33)	13.9 (0.93)	87.7 (0.89)	2.3 (0.41)	58.0 (1.33)
Doctor's or professional degree	68.2	77.6 (2.06)	85.1 (1.09)	1,244	64.5 (2.34)	86.2 (1.69)	65.3 (2.33)	34.9 (2.34)	14.3 (1.72)	85.0 (1.75)	3.9 (0.95)	53.6 (2.44)
Race/ethnicity												
White	48.7	53.8 (0.28)	61.6 (0.21)	59,806	65.5 (0.34)	76.6 (0.30)	56.7 (0.35)	30.7 (0.33)	16.0 (0.26)	68.6 (0.33)	7.8 (0.19)	46.2 (0.35)
Black	36.2	40.0 (0.74)	46.5 (0.61)	6,556	55.4 (1.09)	67.8 (1.02)	56.8 (1.08)	24.2 (0.94)	16.7 (0.82)	61.7 (1.06)	11.6 (0.70)	38.0 (1.06)
Hispanic	29.3	30.2 (0.80)	31.2 (0.61)	5,421	58.9 (1.32)	68.1 (1.25)	56.5 (1.33)	24.8 (1.16)	15.6 (0.97)	63.0 (1.29)	10.4 (0.82)	39.6 (1.31)
Other	—	— (†)	59.4 (0.86)	4,786	68.7 (1.32)	79.2 (1.16)	60.9 (1.39)	31.3 (1.32)	22.9 (1.20)	71.1 (1.29)	6.6 (0.71)	51.0 (1.43)

See notes at end of table.

Table 427. Percentage of workers, 18 years old and over, using computers on the job, by type of computer application and selected characteristics: 1993, 1997, and 2003—Continued

| | | | | | 2003 | | | | | | | |
| | | | | | Percent of on-the-job computer users using specific computer applications[1] | | | | | | | |
Selected characteristic	Percent using computers at work, 1993	Percent using computers at work, 1997	Percent using computers at work	Number using computers at work (in thousands)	Spreadsheets/ databases	Internet/e-mail	Calendar/ schedule	Graphics/design	Programming	Word processing/ desktop publishing	Other uses only	Using 4 or more categories
1	2	3	4	5	6	7	8	9	10	11	12	13
Occupational group												
Management, business, and financial...	[2]	[2]	80.8 (0.36)	15,840	79.8 (0.55)	88.0 (0.45)	69.1 (0.63)	35.8 (0.66)	18.5 (0.53)	79.9 (0.55)	2.8 (0.23)	61.3 (0.67)
Professional and related occupations....	[2]	[2]	78.8 (0.31)	22,517	64.4 (0.55)	81.9 (0.44)	58.7 (0.57)	38.9 (0.56)	22.1 (0.48)	74.8 (0.50)	5.2 (0.25)	51.8 (0.58)
Service occupations....................	23.2	26.4 (0.51)	28.2 (0.48)	5,898	48.8 (1.12)	58.4 (1.11)	48.9 (1.12)	20.0 (0.90)	12.0 (0.73)	55.3 (1.12)	15.7 (0.82)	29.7 (1.03)
Sales and related occupations............	44.5	51.7 (0.68)	61.1 (0.53)	9,464	61.4 (0.86)	73.0 (0.79)	53.6 (0.89)	26.4 (0.78)	11.7 (0.57)	60.9 (0.87)	11.5 (0.57)	41.0 (0.87)
Office and administrative support..........	[2]	[2]	73.9 (0.41)	14,206	63.2 (0.70)	70.4 (0.66)	54.4 (0.72)	19.3 (0.57)	11.5 (0.46)	66.0 (0.69)	8.5 (0.40)	37.5 (0.70)
Farming, fishing, and forestry............	7.9	8.6 (0.80)	10.8 (1.46)	132	55.5 (7.49)	57.7 (7.44)	42.2 (7.44)	20.7 (6.10)	6.5 (3.71)	55.3 (7.49)	9.4 (4.39)	26.1 (6.61)
Construction and extraction..............	16.4	18.7 (0.73)	19.0 (0.68)	1,585	56.7 (2.15)	66.0 (2.06)	44.0 (2.15)	25.8 (1.90)	12.7 (1.44)	61.1 (2.12)	9.9 (1.30)	31.8 (2.02)
Installation, maintenance, and repair......	11.7	12.6 (0.79)	42.0 (0.98)	2,229	50.8 (1.83)	61.4 (1.78)	44.5 (1.82)	21.1 (1.49)	18.3 (1.41)	44.4 (1.82)	17.9 (1.40)	29.7 (1.67)
Production occupations..................	21.8	23.7 (0.60)	29.6 (0.70)	2,869	52.4 (1.61)	54.9 (1.61)	43.0 (1.60)	26.0 (1.41)	14.9 (1.15)	42.0 (1.59)	17.4 (1.22)	27.5 (1.44)
Transportation and material moving......	11.8	15.1 (0.80)	22.1 (0.71)	1,830	46.4 (2.01)	51.5 (2.02)	43.4 (2.00)	14.5 (1.42)	11.2 (1.27)	40.1 (1.98)	23.1 (1.70)	21.7 (1.66)
Family income[3]												
Less than $20,000...................	25.1	26.7 (0.51)	30.1 (0.62)	3,814	51.6 (1.40)	60.1 (1.37)	44.2 (1.39)	22.6 (1.17)	14.0 (0.97)	54.9 (1.39)	16.0 (1.03)	30.6 (1.29)
$20,000 to $29,999...................	38.4	38.4 (0.61)	38.8 (0.63)	4,944	56.6 (1.22)	63.2 (1.18)	46.8 (1.23)	21.4 (1.01)	12.9 (0.82)	59.4 (1.21)	12.8 (0.82)	32.0 (1.15)
$30,000 to $39,999...................	45.7	45.8 (0.62)	47.0 (0.59)	6,775	57.5 (1.04)	68.0 (0.98)	49.9 (1.05)	23.5 (0.89)	13.4 (0.72)	61.0 (1.02)	12.0 (0.68)	36.5 (1.01)
$40,000 to $49,999...................	51.9	52.3 (0.71)	54.3 (0.64)	6,290	61.6 (1.06)	70.9 (0.99)	52.9 (1.09)	26.6 (0.96)	14.4 (0.76)	63.9 (1.05)	9.8 (0.65)	39.3 (1.06)
$50,000 to $74,999...................	60.6	59.9 (0.50)	62.2 (0.41)	16,195	63.6 (0.65)	74.8 (0.59)	56.1 (0.67)	28.5 (0.61)	16.5 (0.50)	65.4 (0.65)	8.3 (0.38)	43.6 (0.67)
$75,000 or more.....................	65.9	69.7 (0.51)	75.0 (0.30)	26,732	72.4 (0.47)	84.3 (0.38)	64.3 (0.51)	36.4 (0.51)	19.2 (0.42)	76.4 (0.45)	4.5 (0.22)	56.3 (0.52)

—Not available.
†Not applicable.
[1]Individuals may be counted in more than one computer activity.
[2]Due to changes in occupational definitions, older data are not comparable to 2003 data.
[3]Excludes persons whose income data were not available.

NOTE: Data are based on a sample survey of households and are subject to sampling and nonsampling error. Race categories exclude persons of Hispanic origin. Standard errors appear in parentheses.
SOURCE: U.S. Department of Commerce, Census Bureau, Current Population Survey (CPS), October 1993, October 1997, and October 2003, unpublished tabulations. (This table was prepared May 2005.)

APPENDIX A
Guide to Sources

Sources and Comparability of Data

The information presented in this report was obtained from many sources, including federal and state agencies, private research organizations, and professional associations. The data were collected using many research methods, including surveys of a universe (such as all colleges) or of a sample, compilations of administrative records, and statistical projections. *Digest* users should take particular care when comparing data from different sources. Differences in sampling, data collection procedures, coverage of target population, timing, phrasing of questions, scope of nonresponse, interviewer training, and data processing and coding mean that results from different sources may not be strictly comparable. Following the general discussion of data accuracy below, descriptions of the information sources and data collection methods are presented, grouped by sponsoring organization. More extensive documentation of a particular survey's procedures does not imply more problems with the data, only that more information is available.

Accuracy of Data

The joint effects of "sampling" and "nonsampling" errors determine the accuracy of any statistic. Estimates based on a sample will differ somewhat from the figures that would have been obtained if a complete census had been taken using the same survey instruments, instructions, and procedures. In addition to such sampling errors, all surveys, both universe and sample, are subject to design, reporting, and processing errors and errors due to nonresponse. To the extent possible, these nonsampling errors are kept to a minimum by methods built into the survey procedures. In general, however, the effects of nonsampling errors are more difficult to gauge than those produced by sampling variability.

Sampling Errors

The samples used in surveys are selected from large numbers of possible samples of the same size that could have been selected using the same sample design. Estimates derived from the different samples would differ from each other. The difference between a sample estimate and the average of all possible samples is called the sampling deviation. The standard, or sampling, error of a survey estimate is a measure of the variation among the estimates from all possible samples and thus is a measure of the precision with which an estimate from a particular sample approximates the average result of all possible samples.

The sample estimate and an estimate of its standard error permit us to construct interval estimates with prescribed confidence that the interval includes the average result of all possible samples. If all possible samples were selected under essentially the same conditions and an estimate and its estimated standard error were calculated from each sample, then (1) approximately 66.7 percent of the intervals from one standard error below the estimate to one standard error above the estimate would include the average value of all possible samples; and (2) approximately 95.0 percent of the intervals from two standard errors below the estimate to two standard errors above the estimate would include the average value of all possible samples. We call an interval from two standard errors below the estimate to two standard errors above the estimate a 95 percent confidence interval.

To illustrate this concept, consider the data and standard errors appearing in table 104. For the 2005 estimate that 9.4 percent of 16- to 24-year-olds were high school dropouts, the table shows that the standard error is 0.22 percent. The sampling error above and below the stated figure is approximately double (1.96) the standard error, or about 0.44 percentage points. Therefore, we can create a 95 percent confidence interval, which is approximately 8.97 to 9.83 (9.4 percent ± 1.96 x 0.22 percent).

Analysis of standard errors can help assess how valid a comparison between two estimates might be. The **standard error of a difference** between two independent sample estimates is equal to the square root of the sum of the squared standard errors of the estimates. The standard error (*se*) of the difference between independent sample estimates *a* and *b* is

$$se_{a,b} = (se_a{}^2 + se_b{}^2)^{1/2}$$

It should be noted that most of the standard error estimates presented in the *Digest* and in the original documents are approximations. That is, to derive estimates of standard errors that would be applicable to a wide variety of items and could be prepared at a moderate cost, a number of approximations were required. As a result, the standard error estimates provide a general order of magnitude rather than the exact standard error for any specific item. The preceding discussion on sampling variability was directed toward a situation concerning one or two estimates. Determining the accuracy of statistical projections is more difficult. In general, the further away the projection date is from the date of the actual data being used for the projection, the greater the probable error in the projections. If, for instance, annual data from 1970 to 2004 are being used to project enrollment in institutions of higher education, the further beyond 2004 one projects, the more variability there is in the projection. One will be less sure of the 2015 enrollment projection than of the 2007 projection. A detailed discussion of the projections methodology is contained in *Projections of Education Statistics to 2015* (National Center for Education Statistics [NCES] 2006-084).

Nonsampling Errors

Universe and sample surveys are subject to nonsampling errors. Nonsampling errors may arise when respondents or interviewers interpret questions differently; when respondents must estimate values, or when coders, keyers, and other processors handle answers differently; when persons who should be included in the universe are not; or when persons fail to respond (completely or partially). Nonsampling errors usually, but not always, result in an underestimate of total survey error and thus an overestimate of the precision of survey estimates. Since estimating the magnitude of nonsampling errors often would require special experiments or access to independent data, these nonsampling errors are seldom measured.

To compensate for nonresponse, adjustments of the sample estimates are often made. For universe surveys, an adjustment made for either type of nonresponse, total or partial, is often referred to as an imputation, which is often a substitution of the "average" questionnaire response for the nonresponse. For universe surveys, imputations are usually made separately within various groups of sample members that have similar survey characteristics. For sample surveys, missing cases (i.e., total nonresponse) are handled through nonresponse adjustments to the sample weights. For sample surveys, imputation for item nonresponse is usually made by substituting for a missing item the response to that item of a respondent having characteristics that are similar to those of the nonrespondent. For more information, see the *NCES Statistical Standards* (NCES 2003-601).

Although the magnitude of nonsampling error in the data compiled in this *Digest* is frequently unknown, idiosyncrasies that have been identified are noted in the appropriate tables.

National Center for Education Statistics (NCES)

Baccalaureate and Beyond Longitudinal Study

The Baccalaureate and Beyond Longitudinal Study (B&B) is based on the National Postsecondary Student Aid Study (NPSAS) and provides information concerning education and work experience after completing the bachelor's degree. A special emphasis of B&B is on those entering teaching. B&B provides cross-sectional information 1 year after bachelor's degree completion (comparable to the information that was provided in the Recent College Graduates study), while at the same time providing longitudinal data concerning entry into and progress through graduate-level education and the workforce. This information has not been available through follow-ups involving high school cohorts or even college-entry cohorts, both of which are restricted in the number who actually complete a bachelor's degree and continue their education.

B&B followed NPSAS baccalaureate degree completers for a 10-year period after completion, beginning with NPSAS:93. About 11,000 students who completed their degrees in the 1992–93 academic year were included in the first B&B (B&B:93/94). In addition to the student data, B&B collected postsecondary transcripts covering the undergraduate period, which provided complete information on progress and persistence at the undergraduate level. The second B&B follow-up took place in spring 1997 (B&B:93/97) and gathered information on employment history, family formation, and enrollment in graduate programs. The third B&B follow-up occurred in 2003 (B&B:93/03) and provides information concerning graduate study and long-term employment experiences after degree completion.

The most recent B&B cohort, which was associated with NPSAS:2000, included 11,700 students who completed their degrees in the 1999–2000 academic year. The first and only planned follow-up survey of this cohort was conducted in 2001 (B&B:2000/01) and focused on time to degree completion, participation in postbaccalaureate education and employment, and the activities of newly qualified teachers.

Further information on B&B may be obtained from

Paula R. Knepper
Postsecondary Studies Division
National Center for Education Statistics
1990 K Street NW
Washington, DC 20006
paula.knepper@ed.gov
http://nces.ed.gov/surveys/b&b

Beginning Postsecondary Students Longitudinal Study

The Beginning Postsecondary Students Longitudinal Study (BPS) provides information on persistence, progress, and attainment from initial time of entry into postsecondary education through entering and leaving the workforce. BPS includes traditional and nontraditional (e.g., older) students and is representative of all beginning students in postsecondary education. BPS follows first-time, beginning students for at least 5 years at approximately 2-year intervals, collecting student data and financial aid reports. By starting with a cohort that has already entered postsecondary education and following it for 5 years, BPS can determine to what extent students who start postsecondary education at various ages differ in their progress, persistence, and attainment. The first BPS was conducted in 1989–90, with follow-ups in 1992 and 1994. The second BPS was conducted in 1995–96, with follow-ups in 1998 and 2001.

Further information on BPS may be obtained from

Aurora M. D'Amico
Postsecondary Cooperative System, Analysis, and
    Dissemination Program
National Center for Education Statistics
1990 K Street NW
Washington, DC 20006
aurora.d'amico@ed.gov
http://nces.ed.gov/surveys/bps

Common Core of Data

NCES uses the Common Core of Data (CCD) to acquire and maintain statistical data from each of the 50 states, the District of Columbia, the Bureau of Indian Affairs, Department of Defense dependents schools (overseas and domestic), and the other jurisdictions. Information about staff and students is reported annually at the school, local education agency (LEA) or school district, and state levels. Information about revenues and expenditures is also collected at the state and LEA levels.

Data are collected for a particular school year via an on-line reporting system open to state education agencies during the school year. Since the CCD is a universe collection, CCD data are not subject to sampling errors. However, nonsampling errors could come from two sources: nonresponse and inaccurate reporting. Almost all of the states submit the five CCD survey instruments each year, but submissions are sometimes incomplete.

Misreporting can occur when 58 education agencies compile and submit data for approximately 97,000 public schools and over 17,000 local education agencies. Typically, this results from varying interpretations of NCES definitions and differing record-keeping systems. NCES attempts to minimize these errors by working closely with the state education agencies through the National Forum on Education Statistics.

The state education agencies report data to NCES from data collected and edited in their regular reporting cycles. NCES encourages the agencies to incorporate into their own survey systems the NCES items they do not already collect so that these items will also be available for the subsequent CCD survey. Over time, this has meant fewer missing data cells in each state's response, reducing the need to impute data.

NCES subjects data from the state education agencies to a comprehensive edit. Where data are determined to be inconsistent, missing, or out of range, NCES contacts the agencies for verification. NCES-prepared state summary forms are returned to the agencies for verification. Each

year, states are also given an opportunity to revise their state-level aggregates from the previous survey cycle.

Further information on the nonfiscal CCD data may be obtained from

John Sietsema
Elementary/Secondary and Library Studies Division
Elementary/Secondary Cooperative System and Institutional
    Studies Program
National Center for Education Statistics
1990 K Street NW
Washington, DC 20006
john.sietsema@ed.gov
http://nces.ed.gov/ccd

Further information on the fiscal CCD data may be obtained from

Frank H. Johnson
Elementary/Secondary and Library Studies Division
Elementary/Secondary Cooperative System and Institutional
    Studies Program
National Center for Education Statistics
1990 K Street NW
Washington, DC 20006
frank.johnson@ed.gov
http://nces.ed.gov/ccd

Early Childhood Longitudinal Study, Birth Cohort 2001

The Early Childhood Longitudinal Study is designed to provide decisionmakers, researchers, child care providers, teachers, and parents with detailed information about children's early life experiences. The Early Childhood Longitudinal Study, Birth Cohort of 2001 (ECLS-B) looks at children's health, development, care, and education during the formative years from birth through kindergarten entry.

Data were collected from a sample of 10,688 children born in the year 2001, representing a population of approximately 4 million. The response rate for the survey was 74.1 percent. To be considered complete, the first three sections of the parent interview had to be completed.

The children participating in the study come from diverse socioeconomic and racial/ethnic backgrounds with oversamples of Chinese children, other Asian and Pacific Islander children, American Indian children, twins, and children with moderately low and very low birth weights. Children, their parents, their child care providers, and their teachers and school administrators provide information on children's cognitive, social, emotional, and physical development across multiple settings (e.g., home, child care, school).

At all waves of the study (at 9 months in 2001–02, 2 years in 2003–04, 4 years in 2005, and kindergarten in 2006 and 2007), parents are asked about themselves, their families, and their children; fathers are asked about themselves and the role they play in their children's lives; and children are observed and participate in assessment activities. In addition, when the children are 2 and 4 years old, child care and early education providers are asked to provide information about their own experience and training and the setting's learning environment. When the children are in kindergarten and first grade, teachers and schools are also asked to provide information about the children's early learning and the school and classroom environments.

Further information on ECLS-B may be obtained from

Jennifer Park
Early Childhood, International, and Crosscutting Studies Division
Early Childhood and Household Studies Program
National Center for Education Statistics
1990 K Street NW
Washington, DC 20006
jennifer.park@ed.gov
http://nces.ed.gov/ecls/Birth.asp

Early Childhood Longitudinal Study, Kindergarten Class of 1998–99

The Early Childhood Longitudinal Study, Kindergarten Class of 1998–99 (ECLS-K) was designed to provide detailed information on children's early school experiences. The study began in the fall of 1998. A nationally representative sample of 22,782 children enrolled in 1,277 kindergarten programs during the 1998–99 school year was selected to participate in the ECLS-K. The children attended both public and private kindergartens, and full-day and part-day programs. The sample included children from different racial/ethnic and socioeconomic backgrounds and oversamples of Asian and Pacific Islander children and private kindergartners. Base-year data were collected in the fall and spring of the kindergarten year. Data were collected again in the fall of first grade (from a 30 percent subsample) and the spring of first grade, and then in the spring of third grade in 2002 and the spring of fifth grade in 2004. The same children will be followed through the eighth grade.

The ECLS-K includes a direct child cognitive assessment that is administered one-on-one with each child in the study. The assessment uses a computer-assisted personal interview (CAPI) approach and a two-stage adaptive testing methodology. It includes three cognitive domains: reading, mathematics, and general knowledge at kindergarten and first grade. (General knowledge was replaced by science at third and fifth grade.) Children's height and weight are measured at each data collection point, and a direct measure of children's psychomotor development was administered in the fall of the kindergarten year only. In addition to these measures, the ECLS-K collects information about children's social skills and academic achievement through teacher reports.

A computer-assisted telephone interview with the children's parents/guardians is conducted at each data collection point. Parents/guardians are asked to provide key information

about their children on subjects such as family demographics (e.g., family members, age, relation to child, race/ethnicity), family structure (e.g., household members and composition), parent involvement, home educational activities (e.g., reading to the child), child health, parental education and employment status, and child's social skills and behaviors.

Data on the schools that children attend and their classrooms are collected by self-administered questionnaires completed by school administrators and classroom teachers. Administrators provide information about the school population, programs, and policies. At the classroom level, data are collected on the composition of the classroom, teaching practices, curriculum, and teacher qualifications and experience.

Further information on the ECLS-K may be obtained from

Elvira Germino Hausken
Early Childhood, International, and Crosscutting Studies Division
Early Childhood and Household Studies Program
National Center for Education Statistics
1990 K Street NW
Washington, DC 20006
ecls@ed.gov
http://nces.ed.gov/ecls

Education Longitudinal Study of 2002

The Education Longitudinal Study of 2002 (ELS:2002) is a longitudinal survey that is monitoring the transitions of a national probability sample of 10th-graders in public, Catholic, and other private schools. Survey waves follow both students and high school dropouts and monitor the transition of the cohort to postsecondary education, the labor force, and family formation.

In the base year of the study, of 1,221 eligible contacted schools, 752 participated, for an overall weighted school participation rate of approximately 68 percent (62 percent unweighted). Of 17,591 selected eligible students, 15,362 participated, for an overall weighted student response rate of approximately 87 percent. (School and student weighted response rates reflect use of the base weight [design weight] and do not include nonresponse adjustments.) Information for the study is obtained not just from students and their school records, but also from the students' parents, their teachers, their librarians, and the administrators of their schools.

The first follow-up was conducted in 2004, when most sample members were high school seniors. Base-year students who remained in their base schools were resurveyed and tested in mathematics, along with a freshening sample to make the study representative of spring 2004 high school seniors nationwide. Students who were not still at their base schools were administered a questionnaire.

The second follow-up, completed in 2006 (data not available at this writing), continued to follow the sample of students into postsecondary education or work, or both. The next follow-up is scheduled for 2012.

Further information on ELS:2002 may be obtained from

John Wirt
Elementary/Secondary and Libraries Studies Division
Elementary/Secondary Sample Survey Studies Program
National Center for Education Statistics
1990 K Street NW
Washington, DC 20006
john.wirt@ed.gov
http://nces.ed.gov/surveys/els2002

Fast Response Survey System

The Fast Response Survey System (FRSS) was established in 1975 to collect issue-oriented data quickly and with a minimal burden on respondents. The FRSS, whose surveys collect and report data on key education issues at the elementary and secondary levels, was designed to meet the data needs of Department of Education analysts, planners, and decision-makers when information could not be collected quickly through NCES's large recurring surveys. Findings from FRSS surveys have been included in congressional reports, testimony to congressional subcommittees, NCES reports, and other Department of Education reports. The findings are also often used by state and local education officials.

Data collected through FRSS surveys are representative at the national level, drawing from a universe that is appropriate for each study. The FRSS collects data from state education agencies and national samples of other educational organizations and participants, including local education agencies, public and private elementary and secondary schools, elementary and secondary school teachers and principals, and public libraries and school libraries. To ensure a minimal burden on respondents, the surveys are generally limited to three pages of questions, with a response burden of about 30 minutes per respondent. Sample sizes are relatively small (usually about 1,000 to 1,500 respondents per survey) so that data collection can be completed quickly.

Further information on the FRSS may be obtained from

Bernie Greene
Early Childhood, International, and Crosscutting Studies
    Division
Data Development Program
National Center for Education Statistics
1990 K Street NW
Washington, DC 20006
bernard.greene@ed.gov
http://nces.ed.gov/surveys/frss

Condition of America's Public School Facilities: 1999

This report (NCES 2000-032) provides national data about the condition of public schools in 1999 based on a survey conducted by NCES using its Fast Response Survey System (FRSS). Specifically, this report provides information about the condition of school facilities and the costs to bring them into good condition; school plans for repairs, ren-

ovations, and replacements; the age of public schools; and overcrowding and practices used to address overcrowding. The results presented in this report are based on questionnaire data for 903 public elementary and secondary schools in the United States. The responses were weighted to produce national estimates that represent all regular public schools in the United States.

Further information about the contents of this report may be obtained from

Bernie Greene
Early Childhood, International, and Crosscutting Studies
    Division
Data Development Program
National Center for Education Statistics
1990 K Street NW
Washington, DC 20006
bernard.greene@ed.gov
http://nces.ed.gov/surveys/frss

Internet Access in Public Schools and Classrooms

The Internet Access in U.S. Public Schools and Classrooms survey is part of the NCES Fast Response Survey System (FRSS). It is designed to assess the federal government's commitment to assist every school and classroom in connecting to the Internet by the year 2000. In 1994, NCES began surveying approximately 1,000 public schools each year about their access to the Internet, access in classrooms, and, since 1996, their type of internet connections. Recent administrations of this survey have been expanded to cover emerging issues. The 2003 survey was designed to update the questions in the 2002 survey and covered the following topics: school connectivity, student access to computers and the Internet, school websites, technologies and procedures to prevent student access to inappropriate websites, and teacher professional development on how to incorporate use of the Internet into the curriculum.

Further information on internet access in public schools and classrooms may be obtained from

Bernie Greene
Early Childhood, International, and Crosscutting Studies
    Division
Data Development Program
National Center for Education Statistics
1990 K Street NW
Washington, DC 20006
bernard.greene@ed.gov
http://nces.ed.gov/surveys/frss

Federal Support for Education

NCES prepares an annual compilation of federal funds for education for the *Digest*. Data for U.S. Department of Education programs come from the *Budget of the United States Government*. Budget offices of other federal agencies provide information for all other federal program support except for research funds, which are obligations reported by the National Science Foundation in *Federal Funds for Research and Development*. Some data are estimated, based on reports from the federal agencies contacted and the *Budget of the United States Government*.

Except for money spent on research, outlays are used to report program funds to the extent possible. Some *Digest* tables report program funds as obligations, as noted in the title of the table. Some federal program funds not commonly recognized as education assistance are also included in the totals reported. For example, portions of federal funds paid to some states and counties as shared revenues resulting from the sale of timber and minerals from public lands have been estimated as funds used for education purposes. Parts of the funds received by states (in 1980) and localities (in all years) under the General Revenue Sharing Program are also included, as are portions of federal funds received by the District of Columbia. The share of these funds allocated to education is assumed to be equal to the share of general funds expended for elementary and secondary education by states and localities in the same year as reported by the U.S. Census Bureau in its annual publication, *Government Finances*.

All state intergovernmental expenditures for education are assumed to be earmarked for elementary/secondary education. Contributions of parent governments of dependent school systems to their public schools amounted to approximately 9 percent of local government revenues and local government revenue sharing in each year. Therefore, 9 percent of local government revenue-sharing funds were assumed allocated each fiscal year to elementary and secondary education. Parent government contributions to public school systems were obtained from *Finances of Public School Systems*, published by the U.S. Census Bureau. The amount of state revenue-sharing funds allocated for postsecondary education in 1980 was assumed to be 13 percent, the proportion of direct state expenditures for institutions of higher education reported in *Government Finances* for that year.

The share of federal funds for the District of Columbia assigned to education is assumed to be equal to the share of the city's general fund expenditures for each level of education.

For the job training programs conducted by the Department of Labor, only estimated sums spent on classroom training have been reported as educational program support.

During the 1970s, the Office of Management and Budget (OMB) prepared an annual analysis of federal education program support. These were published in the *Budget of the United States Government, Special Analyses*. The information presented in this report is not, however, a continuation of the OMB series. A number of differences in the two series should be noted. OMB required all federal agencies to report outlays for education-related programs using a standardized form, thereby assuring agency compliance in reporting. The scope of education programs reported in the *Digest* differs from the scope of programs reported in the OMB reports. Off-budget items such as the annual volume of guaranteed student loans were not included in OMB's reports. Finally, while some mention is made of an annual estimate of federal tax expenditures,

OMB did not include them in its annual analysis of federal education support. Estimated federal tax expenditures for education are the difference between current federal tax receipts and what these receipts would be without existing education deductions to income allowed by federal tax provisions.

Recipients' data are estimated based on *Estimating Federal Funds for Education: A New Approach Applied to Fiscal Year 1980* (Miller, V., and Noell, J., 1982, Journal of Education Finance); *Federal Support for Education*, various years; and the *Catalog of Federal Domestic Assistance* (cfda.gov). The recipients' data are estimated and tend to undercount institutions of higher education, students, and local education agencies. This is because some of the federal programs have more than one recipient receiving funds. In these cases, the recipients were put into a "mixed recipients" category, because there was no way to disaggregate the amount each recipient received.

Further information on federal support for education may be obtained from

William Sonnenberg
Early Childhood, International, and Crosscutting Studies Division
Annual Reports Program
1990 K Street NW
Washington, DC 20006
william.sonnenberg@ed.gov
http://nces.ed.gov/surveys/AnnualReports/federal.asp

High School and Beyond Longitudinal Study

The High School and Beyond Longitudinal Study (HS&B) is a national longitudinal survey of individuals who were high school sophomores and seniors in 1980. The base-year survey (conducted in 1980) was a probability sample of 1,015 high schools with a target number of 36 sophomores and 36 seniors in each school. A total of 58,270 students participated in the base-year survey. Substitutions were made for nonparticipating schools—but not for students—in those strata where it was possible. Overall, 1,122 schools were selected in the original sample and 811 of these schools participated in the survey. An additional 204 schools were drawn in a replacement sample. Student refusals and absences resulted in an 82 percent completion rate for the survey.

Several small groups in the population were oversampled to allow for special study of certain types of schools and students. Students completed questionnaires and took a battery of cognitive tests. In addition, a sample of parents of sophomores and seniors (about 3,600 for each cohort) was surveyed.

HS&B first follow-up activities took place in the spring of 1982. The sample for the first follow-up survey included approximately 30,000 persons who were sophomores in 1980. The completion rate for sample members eligible for on-campus survey administration was about 96 percent. About 89 percent of the students who left school between the base-year and first follow-up surveys (e.g., dropouts, transfer students, and early graduates) completed the first follow-up sophomore questionnaire.

As part of the first follow-up survey of HS&B, transcripts were requested in fall 1982 for an 18,152-member subsample of the sophomore cohort. Of the 15,941 transcripts actually obtained, 1,969 were excluded because the students had dropped out of school before graduation, 799 were excluded because they were incomplete, and 1,057 were excluded because the student graduated before 1982 or the transcript indicated neither a dropout status nor graduation. Thus, 12,116 transcripts were utilized for the overall curriculum analysis presented in this publication. All courses in each transcript were assigned a 6-digit code based on the Classification of Secondary School Courses (a coding system developed to standardize course descriptions; see http://nces.ed.gov/surveys/hst/courses.asp). Credits earned in each course are expressed in Carnegie units. (The Carnegie unit is a standard of measurement that represents one credit for the completion of a 1-year course. To receive credit for a course, the student must have received a passing grade—"pass," "D," or higher.) Students who transferred from public to private schools or from private to public schools between their sophomore and senior years were eliminated from public/private analyses.

In designing the senior cohort first follow-up survey, one of the goals was to reduce the size of the retained sample, while still keeping sufficient numbers of minorities to allow important policy analyses. A total of 11,227 (94 percent) of the 11,995 persons subsampled completed the questionnaire. Information was obtained about the respondents' school and employment experiences, family status, and attitudes and plans.

The samples for the second follow-up, which took place in spring 1984, consisted of about 12,000 members of the senior cohort and about 15,000 members of the sophomore cohort. The completion rate for the senior cohort was 91 percent, and the completion rate for the sophomore cohort was 92 percent.

HS&B third follow-up data collection activities were performed in spring 1986. Both the sophomore and senior cohort samples for this round of data collection were the same as those used for the second follow-up survey. The completion rates for the sophomore and senior cohort samples were 91 percent and 88 percent, respectively.

HS&B fourth follow-up data collection activities were performed in 1992, but only surveyed the 1980 sophomore class. They examined aspects of these students' early adult years, such as enrollment in postsecondary education, experience in the labor market, marriage and child rearing, and voting behavior.

Appendix table A-1 contains the maximum number of HS&B cases that are available for tabulations of specific classification variables used throughout this publication.

The standard error (*se*) of an individual percentage (*p*) based on HS&B data can be approximated by the formula

$$se_p = \text{DEFT} \, [p(100 - p)/n]^{1/2}$$

where *n* is the sample size and DEFT, the square root of the design effect, is a factor used to adjust for the particular sample design used in HS&B. Appendix table A-2 provides the DEFT factors for different HS&B samples and subsamples.

In evaluating a difference between two independent percentages, the standard error of the difference may be conservatively approximated by taking the square root of the sum of the squared standard errors of the two percentages. For example, in the 1986 follow-up of 1980 sophomores, 84.0 percent of the men and 77.2 percent of the women felt that being successful in work was "very important," a difference of 6.8 percentage points. Using the formula and the sample sizes from table A-1 and the DEFT factors from table A-2, the standard errors of the two percentages being compared are calculated to be

$$1.43[(84.0)(16.0)/(5,391)]^{1/2} = .714$$
$$1.43[(77.2)(22.8)/(5,857)]^{1/2} = .784$$

The standard error of the difference is therefore

$$(.714^2 + .784^2)^{1/2} = (.510 + .615]^{1/2} = 1.06$$

The sampling error of the difference is approximately double the standard error, or approximately 2.1 percentage points, and the 95 percent confidence interval for the difference is 6.8 ± 2.1, or 4.7 to 8.9 percentage points.

The standard error estimation procedure outlined above does not compensate for survey item nonresponse, which is a source of nonsampling error. (Table A-1 reflects the maximum number of responses that could be tabulated by demographic characteristics.) For example, of the 10,925 respondents in the 1984 follow-up survey of 1980 high school graduates, 372, or 3.4 percent, did not respond to the particular question on whether they had ever used a pocket calculator. Item nonresponse varied considerably. A very low nonresponse rate of 0.1 percent was obtained for a question asking whether the respondent had attended a postsecondary institution. A much higher item nonresponse rate of 12.2 percent was obtained for a question asking if the respondent had used a micro- or minicomputer in high school. Typical item nonresponse rates ranged from 3 to 4 percent.

The Hispanic analyses presented in this publication rely on students' self-identification as members of one of four Hispanic subgroups: Mexican, Mexican-American, Chicano; Cuban; Puerto Rican, Puertorriqueño, Boricuan; or other Hispanic origins.

An NCES series of technical reports and data file user's manuals, available electronically, provides additional information on the survey methodology.

Further information on HS&B may be obtained from

Aurora M. D'Amico
Postsecondary Studies Division
Postsecondary Cooperative System, Analysis, and
    Dissemination Program
National Center for Education Statistics
1990 K Street NW
Washington, DC 20006
aurora.d'amico@ed.gov
http://nces.ed.gov/surveys/hsb

High School Transcript Study Tabulations

High school transcript studies have been conducted since 1982 and are associated with a major NCES data collection. The studies collect information that is contained in a student's high school record—courses taken while attending secondary school, information on credits earned, when specific courses were taken, and final grades.

A high school transcript study was conducted in 2004 as part of the Education Longitudinal Study of 2002 (ELS:2002/2004). A total of 1,549 schools participated in the request for transcripts, for an unweighted participation rate of approximately 79 percent. Transcript information was received on 14,920 members of the student sample (not just graduates), for an unweighted response rate of 91 percent.

Similar studies were conducted of the coursetaking patterns of 1982, 1987, 1990, 1992, 1994, 1998, and 2000 high school graduates. The 1982 data are based on approximately 12,000 transcripts collected by the High School and Beyond Longitudinal Study (HS&B). The 1987 data are based on approximately 22,799 transcripts from 433 schools obtained as part of the 1987 NAEP High School Transcript Study, a scope comparable to that of the NAEP transcript studies conducted in 1990, 1994, 1998, and 2000. The 1992 data are based on approximately 7,600 transcripts collected by the National Education Longitudinal Study of 1988 (NELS:88/92).

Because the 1982 HS&B transcript study used a different method for identifying handicapped students than was used in the 1987 and 1990 NAEP transcript studies, and in order to make the statistical summaries as comparable as possible, all the counts and percentages in this report are restricted to students whose records indicate that they had not participated in a special education program. This restriction lowers the number of 1990 graduates represented in the tables to 20,866.

Further information on high school transcript studies may be obtained from

Carl Schmitt
Elementary/Secondary and Library Studies Division
National Center for Education Statistics
1990 K Street NW
Washington, DC 20006
carl.schmitt@ed.gov
http://nces.ed.gov/surveys/hst

Integrated Postsecondary Education Data System

The Integrated Postsecondary Education Data System (IPEDS) surveys approximately 6,500 postsecondary institutions, including universities and colleges, as well as institutions offering technical and vocational education beyond the high school level. IPEDS, which began in 1986, replaced the Higher Education General Information Survey (HEGIS).

IPEDS consists of nine interrelated components that obtain information on who provides postsecondary education (institutions), who participates in it and completes it (students), what programs are offered and what programs are completed, and both the human and financial resources involved in the provision of institutionally based postsecondary education. Until 2000, these components included institutional characteristics, fall enrollment, completions, salaries, finance, and fall staff. Since 2000, data are collected in the fall for institutional characteristics and completions; in the winter for employees by assigned position (EAP), salaries, and fall staff; and in the spring for enrollment, student financial aid, finances, and graduation rates.

The degree-granting institutions portion of IPEDS is a census of colleges awarding associate's or higher degrees that are eligible to participate in Title IV financial aid programs. Prior to 1993, data from technical and vocational institutions were collected through a sample survey. Beginning in 1993, all data are gathered in a census of all postsecondary institutions. The tabulations on "institutional characteristics" developed for this edition of the *Digest* are based on lists of all institutions and are not subject to sampling errors.

The definition of institutions generally thought of as offering college and university education changed between FY 95 and FY 96. The old standard for higher education institutions included those institutions that had courses leading to an associate's or higher degree or that had courses accepted for credit toward those degrees. Higher education institutions were accredited by an agency or association that was recognized by the U.S. Department of Education or were recognized directly by the Secretary of Education. Tables, or portions of tables, that use only this standard are labeled "higher education" in the *Digest*. The newer standard includes institutions that award associate's or higher degrees and that are eligible to participate in Title IV federal financial aid programs. Tables that contain any data according to this standard are titled "degree-granting" institutions. Time-series tables may contain data from both series, and they are labeled accordingly. The impact of this change on data collected in 1996 was not large. For example, tables on faculty salaries and benefits were only affected to a very small extent. Also, degrees awarded at the bachelor's level or higher were not heavily affected. The largest impact was on private 2-year college enrollment. In contrast, most of the data on public 4-year colleges were affected to a minimal extent. The impact on enrollment in public 2-year colleges was noticeable in certain states, but was relatively small at the national level. Overall, total enrollment for all institutions was about one-half a percent higher in 1996 for degree-granting institutions than for higher education institutions.

Prior to the establishment of IPEDS in 1986, HEGIS acquired and maintained statistical data on the characteristics and operations of institutions of higher education. Implemented in 1966, HEGIS was an annual universe survey of institutions accredited at the college level by an agency recognized by the Secretary of the U.S. Department of Education. These institutions were listed in NCES's *Education Directory, Colleges and Universities*.

HEGIS surveys collected information on institutional characteristics, faculty salaries, finances, enrollment, and degrees.

Since these surveys, like IPEDS, were distributed to all higher education institutions, the data presented are not subject to sampling error. However, they are subject to nonsampling error, the sources of which varied with the survey instrument.

The NCES Taskforce for IPEDS Redesign recognized that there were issues related to the consistency of data definitions as well as the accuracy, reliability, and validity of other quality measures within and across surveys. The IPEDS redesign in 2000 provided institution-specific web-based data forms. While the new system shortened data processing time and provided better data consistency, it did not address the accuracy of the data provided by institutions.

Beginning in 2003–04 with the Prior Year Data Revision System, prior-year data have been available to institutions entering current data. This allows institutions to make changes to their prior-year entries either by adjusting the data or by providing missing data. These revisions allow the evaluation of the data's accuracy by looking at the changes made.

NCES conducted a study (NCES 2005-175) of the 2002–03 data that were revised in 2003–04 to determine the accuracy of the imputations, track the institutions that submitted revised data, and analyze the revised data they submitted. When institutions made changes to their data, it was assumed that the revised data were the "true" data. The data were analyzed for the number and type of institutions making changes, the type of changes, the magnitude of the changes, and the impact on published data.

Because NCES imputes missing data, imputation procedures were also addressed by the Redesign Taskforce. For the 2003–04 assessment, differences between revised values and values that were imputed in the original files were compared (i.e., revised value minus imputed value). These differences were then used to provide an assessment of the effectiveness of imputation procedures. The size of the differences also provides an indication of the accuracy of imputation procedures. To assess the overall impact of changes on aggregate IPEDS estimates, published tables for each component were reconstructed using the revised 2002–03 data. These reconstructed tables were then compared to the published tables to determine the magnitude of aggregate bias and the direction of this bias.

Though IPEDS provides the most comprehensive data system for postsecondary education, there are 100 or more entities that collect their own information from postsecondary institutions. This raises the issue of how valid IPEDS data are when compared to education data collected by non-IPEDS sources. In the Data Quality Study, Thomson Peterson data were chosen to assess the validity of IPEDS data, because Thomson Peterson is one of the largest and most comprehensive sources of postsecondary data available.

Not all IPEDS components could be compared to Thomson Peterson. Either Thomson Peterson did not collect data related to a particular IPEDS component, or the data items collected by Thomson Peterson were not comparable to the IPEDS items (i.e., the data items were defined differently). Comparisons were made for a selected number of data items in five areas—tuition and price, employees by assigned posi-

tion, enrollment, student financial aid, and finance. More details on the accuracy and reliability of IPEDS data can be found in the *Integrated Postsecondary Education Data System Data Quality Study* (NCES 2005-175).

Further information on IPEDS may be obtained from

Elise Miller
Postsecondary Studies Division
Postsecondary Institutional Studies Program
National Center for Education Statistics
1990 K Street NW
Washington, DC 20006
elise.miller@ed.gov
http://nces.ed.gov/ipeds

Fall (Completions)

This survey was part of the HEGIS series throughout its existence. However, the degree classification taxonomy was revised in 1970–71, 1982–83, 1991–92, and 2002–03. Collection of degree data has been maintained through IPEDS.

Degrees-conferred trend tables arranged by the 2002–03 classification are included in the *Digest* to provide consistent data from 1970–71 to the most recent year. Data in this edition on associate's and other formal awards below the baccalaureate degree, by field of study, cannot be made comparable with figures from prior to 1982–83. The nonresponse rate does not appear to be a significant source of nonsampling error for this survey. The response rate over the years has been high, with the degree-granting institution response rate for the 2004–05 survey at 99.9 percent. The overall response rate for non-degree-granting institutions was 99.6 percent in 2004–05. Because of the high response rate for degree-granting institutions, nonsampling error caused by imputation is also minimal. Imputation methods and the response bias analysis for the 2004–05 survey are discussed in *Postsecondary Institutions in the United States: Fall 2004 and Degrees and Other Awards Conferred: 2003–04* (NCES 2005-182).

The *Integrated Postsecondary Education Data System Data Quality Study* (NCES 2005-175) indicated that most Title IV institutions supplying revised data on completions in 2003–04 were able to supply missing data for the prior year. The small differences between imputed data for the prior year and the revised actual data supplied by the institution indicated that the imputed values produced by NCES were acceptable.

Further information on the IPEDS Completions survey may be obtained from

Andrew Mary
Postsecondary Studies Division
Postsecondary Institutional Studies Program
National Center for Education Statistics
1990 K Street NW
Washington, DC 20006
andrew.mary@ed.gov
http://nces.ed.gov/ipeds

Fall (Institutional Characteristics)

This survey collects the basic information necessary to classify institutions, including control, level, and types of programs offered, as well as information on tuition, fees, and room and board charges. Beginning in 2000, the survey collected institutional pricing data from institutions with first-time, full-time, degree/certificate-seeking undergraduate students. Unduplicated full-year enrollment counts and instructional activity are now collected in the Fall Enrollment survey. The overall response rate was 100.0 percent for Title IV degree-granting institutions for 2004 data.

The *Integrated Postsecondary Education Data System Data Quality Study* (NCES 2005-175) looked at tuition and price in Title IV institutions. Only 8 percent of institutions in 2002–03 and 2003–04 reported the same data to IPEDS and Thomson Peterson consistently across all selected data items. Differences in wordings or survey items may account for some of these inconsistencies.

Further information on the IPEDS Institutional Characteristics survey may be obtained from

Frank Morgan
Postsecondary Studies Division
Postsecondary Institutional Studies Program
National Center for Education Statistics
1990 K Street NW
Washington, DC 20006
frank.morgan@ed.gov
http://nces.ed.gov/ipeds

Winter (Fall Staff)

The fall staff data presented in this publication were collected by NCES through IPEDS, which collects data from postsecondary institutions, including all 2- and 4-year degree-granting education institutions. IPEDS collects staff data biennially, in odd numbered years.

Questionnaires for the 2003–04 Fall Staff survey were completed on the IPEDS data collection website between December 2003 and January 2004; respondents report employment statistics for their institution that cover the payroll period in the fall of the survey year. The 2003–04 survey had an overall response rate of 99.9 percent and a response rate of 99.9 percent for both degree-granting institutions and for non-degree-granting institutions. Imputation methods and the response bias analysis for the 2003–04 Fall Staff survey are discussed in *Staff in Postsecondary Institutions, Fall 2003, and Salaries of Full-Time Instructional Faculty, 2003–04* (NCES 2005-155).

The most recent data quality study, *Integrated Postsecondary Education Data System Data Quality Study* (NCES 2005-175), found that for 2003–04 employee data items, changes were made by 1.2 percent (77) of the institutions that responded. All who made changes made changes that resulted in different employee counts. For both institutional and aggregate differences, the changes had little impact on the original employee count submissions. A large number of institutions reported different staff data to IPEDS and Thomson Peterson; however, the magnitude of the differences was small—usually no more than 17 faculty members for any faculty variable.

Further information on the Fall Staff survey may be obtained from

Sabrina Ratchford
Postsecondary Studies Division
Postsecondary Institutional Studies Program
National Center for Education Statistics
1990 K Street NW
Washington, DC 20006
sabrina.ratchford@ed.gov
http://nces.ed.gov/ipeds

Winter (Salaries, Tenure, and Fringe Benefits of Full-Time Instructional Faculty)

This institutional survey was conducted for most years from 1966–67 to 1987–88; it has been conducted annually since 1989–90, except for 2000–01. Although the survey form has changed a number of times during these years, only comparable data are presented in this report.

Between 1966–67 and 1985–86, this survey differed from other HEGIS surveys in that imputations were not made for nonrespondents. Thus, there is some possibility that the salary averages presented in this report may differ from the results of a complete enumeration of all colleges and universities. Beginning with the surveys for 1987–88, the IPEDS data tabulation procedures included imputations for survey nonrespondents. The response rate for the 2004–05 survey was 99.8 percent for degree-granting institutions. Imputation methods and the response bias analysis for the 2004–05 survey are discussed in *Employees in Postsecondary Institutions, Fall 2004, and Salaries of Full-Time Instructional Faculty, 2004–05* (NCES 2006-187). Although data from these surveys are not subject to sampling error, sources of nonsampling error may include computational errors and misclassification in reporting and processing. The electronic reporting system does allow corrections to prior-year reported or missed data and this should help with these problems. Also, NCES reviews individual institutions' data for internal and longitudinal consistency and contacts institutions to check inconsistent data.

The *Integrated Postsecondary Education Data System Data Quality Study* (NCES 2005-175) found that only 1.3 percent of the responding Title IV institutions in 2003–04 made changes to their salaries data. The imputations made in the original publication proved to be acceptable when the revised data indicated small differences, and therefore had little impact on the published data.

Further information on the Salaries, Tenure, and Fringe Benefits survey may be obtained from

Sabrina Ratchford
Postsecondary Studies Division
Postsecondary Institutional Studies Program
National Center for Education Statistics
1990 K Street NW
Washington, DC 20006
sabrina.ratchford@ed.gov
http://nces.ed.gov/ipeds

Winter/Spring (Fall Enrollment)

This survey has been part of the HEGIS and IPEDS series since 1966. Response rates for this survey have been relatively high, generally exceeding 85 percent. Beginning in 2000, with web-based data collection, higher response rates were attained. In 2004–05, the overall response rates were 100.0 percent for degree-granting, 4-year public and not-for-profit institutions, and 99.9 and 99.6 percent, respectively, for 2-year public and not-for-profit institutions. Imputation methods and the response bias analysis for the 2004–05 survey are discussed in *Enrollment in Postsecondary Institutions, Fall 2004; Graduation Rates, 1998 & 2001 Cohorts; and Financial Statistics, Fiscal Year 2004* (NCES 2006-155).

Beginning with the fall 1986 survey and the introduction of IPEDS (see above), the survey was redesigned. The survey allows (in alternating years) for the collection of age and residence data. Beginning in 2000, the survey collected instructional activity and unduplicated headcount data, which are needed to compute a standardized, full-time-equivalent (FTE) enrollment statistic for the entire academic year.

The *Integrated Postsecondary Education Data System Data Quality Study* (NCES 2005-175) showed that public institutions made the majority of changes to enrollment data during the 2004 revision period. The majority of changes were made to unduplicated headcount data, with the net differences between the original data and the revised data at about 1 percent. Part-time students in general and enrollment in private not-for-profit institutions were often underestimated. The fewest changes by institutions were to Classification of Instructional Programs (CIP) code data. (The CIP is a taxonomic coding scheme that contains titles and descriptions of primarily postsecondary instructional programs.) More institutions provided enrollment data to IPEDS than to Thomson Peterson. A fairly high percentage of institutions that provided data to both provided the same data, and among those that did not, the difference in magnitude was less than 10 percent.

Further information on the IPEDS Fall Enrollment survey may be obtained from

Cathy Statham
Postsecondary Studies Division
Postsecondary Institutional Studies Program
National Center for Education Statistics
1990 K Street NW
Washington, DC 20006
cathy.statham@ed.gov
http://nces.ed.gov/ipeds

Spring (Finance)

This survey was part of the HEGIS series and has been continued under IPEDS. Substantial changes were made in the financial survey instruments in fiscal year (FY) 1976, FY 82, FY 87, FY 97, and FY 02. While these changes were significant, considerable effort has been made to present only comparable information on trends in this report and to note inconsistencies. The FY 76 survey instrument contained numerous revisions to earlier survey forms, which made direct comparisons of line items very difficult. Beginning in FY 82, Pell Grant data were collected in the categories of federal restricted grant and contract revenues and restricted scholarship and fellowship expenditures. Finance tables for this publication have been adjusted by subtracting the largely duplicative Pell Grant amounts from the later data to maintain comparability with pre-FY 82 data. The introduction of IPEDS in the FY 87 survey included several important changes to the survey instrument and data processing procedures. Beginning in FY 97, data for private institutions were collected using new financial concepts consistent with Financial Accounting Standards Board (FASB) reporting standards, which provide a more comprehensive view of college finance activities. The data for public institutions continued to be collected using the older survey form. The data for public and private institutions were no longer comparable and, as a result, no longer presented together in analysis tables. Beginning in FY 01, public institutions had the option of either continuing to report using Government Accounting Standards Board (GASB) standards or using the new FASB reporting standards. Beginning in FY 02, public institutions had three options: the original GASB standards, the FASB standards, or the new GASB Statement 35 standards (GASB35). Because of the complexity of the multiple forms used by public institutions, finance data for public institutions for some recent years are not presented in the *Digest*.

Possible sources of nonsampling error in the financial statistics include nonresponse, imputation, and misclassification. The response rate has been about 85 to 90 percent for most of the historic years presented in the *Digest*; however, in more recent years, response rates have been much higher because Title IV institutions are required to respond. The 2002 IPEDS data collection was a full-scale web-based collection, which offered features that improved the quality and timeliness of the data. The ability of IPEDS to tailor online data entry forms for each institution based on characteristics such as institutional control, level of institution, and calendar system, and the institutions' ability to submit their data online, were two such features that improved response. The response rate for the FY 04 Finance survey was 100.0 percent for degree-granting institutions. The response rates were 100.0 percent for public 4-year, 99.8 percent for public 2-year, 99.8 percent for not-for-profit 4-year, and 99.6 percent for not-for-profit 2-year institutions. Imputation methods and the response bias analysis for the FY 04 survey are discussed in *Enrollment in Postsecondary Institutions, Fall 2004; Graduation Rates, 1998 & 2001 Cohorts; and Financial Statistics, Fiscal Year 2004* (NCES 2006-155).

Two general methods of imputation were used in HEGIS. If prior-year data were available for a nonresponding institution, they were inflated using the Higher Education Price Index and adjusted according to changes in enrollments. If prior-year data were not available, current data were used from peer institutions selected for location (state or region), control, level, and enrollment size of institution. In most cases, estimates for nonreporting institutions in HEGIS were made using data from peer institutions.

Beginning with FY 87, IPEDS included all postsecondary institutions, but maintained comparability with earlier surveys by allowing 2- and 4-year institutions to be tabulated separately. For FY 87 through FY 91, in order to maintain comparability with the historical time series of HEGIS institutions, data were combined from two of the three different survey forms that make up IPEDS. The vast majority of the data were tabulated from form 1, which was used to collect information from public and private not-for-profit 2- and 4-year colleges. Form 2, a condensed form, was used to gather data for 2-year for-profit institutions. Because of the differences in the data requested on the two forms, several assumptions were made about the form 2 reports so that their figures could be included in the degree-granting institution totals.

In IPEDS, the form 2 institutions were not asked to separate appropriations from grants and contracts, nor were they asked to separate state from local sources of funding. For the form 2 institutions, all federal revenues were assumed to be federal grants and contracts, and all state and local revenues were assumed to be restricted state grants and contracts. All other form 2 sources of revenue, except for tuition and fees and sales and services of educational activities, were included under "other." Similar adjustments were made to the expenditure accounts. The form 2 institutions reported instruction and scholarship and fellowship expenditures only. All other educational and general expenditures were allocated to academic support.

The *Integrated Postsecondary Education Data System Data Quality Study* (NCES 2005-175) found that only a small percentage (2.9 percent, or 168) of postsecondary institutions either revised 2002–03 data or submitted data for items they previously left unreported. Though relatively few institutions made changes, the changes made were relatively large—greater than 10 percent of the original data. With a few exceptions, these changes, large as they were, did not greatly affect the aggregate totals.

Again, institutions were more likely to report data to IPEDS than to Thomson Peterson, and there was a higher percentage reporting different values among those reporting to both. The magnitude of the difference was generally greater for research expenditures. It is likely that the large differences are a function of the way institutions report these data to both entities.

Further information on the IPEDS Finance survey may be obtained from

Cathy Statham
Postsecondary Studies Division
Postsecondary Institutional Studies Program
National Center for Education Statistics

1990 K Street NW
Washington, DC 20006
cathy.statham@ed.gov
http://nces.ed.gov/ipeds

Library Statistics Program

Public library statistics are collected annually by NCES using the Public Libraries Survey (PLS) and disseminated annually through the Federal-State Cooperative System (FSCS) for Public Library Data. Descriptive statistics are produced for over 9,200 public libraries. The PLS includes information about staffing; operating income and expenditures; type of governance; type of administrative structure; size of collection; and service measures such as reference transactions, public service hours, interlibrary loans, circulation, and library visits. In FSCS, respondents supply the information electronically, and data are edited and tabulated in machine-readable form.

The respondents are 9,200 public libraries identified in the 50 states and the District of Columbia by state library agencies. At the state level, FSCS is administered by State Data Coordinators, appointed by the Chief Officer of each State Library Agency. The State Data Coordinator collects the requested data from local public libraries and submits these data to NCES. An annual training conference sponsored by NCES is provided for the State Data Coordinators. A steering committee representing State Data Coordinators and other public library constituents is active in the development of FSCS data elements and software. Technical assistance to states is provided by phone and in person by the FSCS steering committee and by NCES staff and contractors. All 50 states and the District of Columbia have submitted data for individual public libraries, which are also aggregated to state and national levels.

Since 1994, NCES has conducted the State Library Agencies (StLA) Survey for the 50 states and the District of Columbia. A state library agency is the official agency of a state that is charged by state law with the extension and development of public library services throughout the state and that has adequate authority under state law to administer state plans in accordance with the provisions of the Library Services and Technology Act (LSTA) of 2003. The StLA Survey collects data on services, collections, staffing, revenue, and expenditures.

Beginning on October 1, 2007, the PLS and the StLA Survey will be conducted by the Institute of Museum and Library Services (IMLS). The transfer of these surveys to IMLS is the result of President Bush's fiscal year 2007 budget request.

Under the Academic Libraries Survey (ALS), NCES surveyed academic libraries on a 3-year cycle between 1966 and 1988. From 1988 through 1999, ALS was a component of the Integrated Postsecondary Education Data System (IPEDS) and was on a 2-year cycle. Beginning with fiscal year (FY) 2000, ALS was no longer a component of IPEDS, but it remains on a 2-year cycle. ALS provides data on about

3,700 academic libraries. In aggregate, these data provide an overview of the status of academic libraries nationally and statewide. The survey collects data on the libraries in the entire universe of degree-granting institutions. Beginning with the collection of FY 2000 data, the ALS changed to web-based data collection. ALS produces descriptive statistics on academic libraries in postsecondary institutions in the 50 states, the District of Columbia, and the outlying areas.

School library data were collected on the School and Principal Surveys during the 1990–91 Schools and Staffing Survey (SASS). The School Library Media Centers (LMC) Survey became a component of SASS with the 1993–94 administration. Since then, the LMC Survey has been conducted during the 1999–2000 and 2003–04 school years. During the 2003–04 administration, only the public and Bureau of Indian Affairs (BIA) school library media centers were surveyed. School library questions focus on staff, collections, equipment, services, and expenditures.

Further information on the Library Statistics Program may be obtained from

Barbara Holton
Elementary/Secondary and Library Studies Division
Elementary/Secondary Sample Survey Studies Program
National Center for Education Statistics
1990 K Street NW
Washington, DC 20006
barbara.holton@ed.gov
http://nces.ed.gov/surveys/libraries

National Adult Literacy Survey

The National Adult Literacy Survey (NALS), funded by the U.S. Department of Education and 12 states, was created in 1992 as a new measure of literacy. The aim of the survey was to profile the English literacy of adults in the United States based on their performance across a wide array of tasks that reflect the types of materials and demands they encounter in their daily lives.

To gather information on adults' literacy skills, trained staff interviewed a nationally representative sample of nearly 13,600 individuals age 16 and older during the first 8 months of 1992. These participants had been randomly selected to represent the adult population in the country as a whole. Black and Hispanic households were oversampled to ensure reliable estimates of literacy proficiencies and to permit analyses of the performance of these subpopulations. In addition, some 1,100 inmates from 80 federal and state prisons were interviewed to gather information on the proficiencies of the prison population. In total, nearly 26,000 adults were surveyed.

Each survey participant was asked to spend approximately an hour responding to a series of diverse literacy tasks, as well as questions about his or her demographic characteristics, educational background, reading practices, and other areas related to literacy. Based on their responses to the survey tasks, adults received proficiency scores along three scales that reflect varying degrees of skill in prose, document, and quantitative literacy. The results of the 1992 survey were first published in a report, *Adult Literacy in America* (NCES 93-275), in September 1993.

Further information on NALS may be obtained from

Sheida White
Assessment Division
Assessment Design and Analysis Program
National Center for Education Statistics
1990 K Street NW
Washington, DC 20006
sheida.white@ed.gov

National Assessment of Adult Literacy

The 2003 National Assessment of Adult Literacy (NAAL) was conducted to measure both English literacy and health literacy. The assessment was administered to 19,000 adults (including 1,200 prison inmates) age 16 and over in all 50 states and the District of Columbia. Components of the assessment included a background questionnaire, a prison component, the State Assessment of Adult Literacy (SAAL), a health literacy component, the Fluency Addition to NAAL (FAN), and the Adult Literacy Supplemental Assessment (ALSA). The assessment measured literacy directly through the completion of tasks, and results were reported using the following achievement levels: *below basic, basic, intermediate*, and *proficient*.

By comparing the 1992 NALS and 2003 NAAL results, NAAL provides an indicator of the progress of adult literacy in the nation.

Further information on NAAL may be obtained from

Sheida White
Assessment Division
Assessment Design and Analysis Program
National Center for Education Statistics
1990 K Street NW
Washington, DC 20006
sheida.white@ed.gov
http://nces.ed.gov/naal

National Assessment of Educational Progress

The National Assessment of Educational Progress (NAEP) is a series of cross-sectional studies initially implemented in 1969 to gather information about selected levels of educational achievement across the country. At the national level, NAEP is divided into two assessments: main NAEP and long-term trend NAEP. NAEP has surveyed students at specific ages (9, 13, and 17) for the long-term trend NAEP and at grades 4, 8, and 11 or 12 for the main NAEP, state NAEP, and long-term writing NAEP. NAEP has also surveyed young adults (ages 25 to 35).

NAEP long-term trend assessments are designed to inform the nation of changes in the basic achievement of

America's youth. Nationally representative samples of students have been assessed in science, mathematics, and reading at ages 9, 13, and 17 since the early 1970s. Students were assessed in writing at grades 4, 8, and 11 between 1984 and 1996. To measure trends accurately, assessment items (mostly multiple choice) and procedures have remained unchanged since the first assessment in each subject. Recent trend assessments were conducted in 1994, 1996, 1999, and 2004. Nearly 33,000 students took part in the 2004 trend assessment. Results are reported as average scores for the nation, for regions, and for various subgroups of the population, such as racial and ethnic groups. Data from the trend assessments are available in the most recent report, *NAEP 2004 Trends in Academic Progress* (NCES 2005-464).

The 2004 NAEP long-term trend assessments marked the end of tests designed and administered from 1971, marked the beginning of a modified design that provides greater accommodations for students with disabilities and English language learners, and limited the assessments to reading and math. Science and writing are now assessed only in main NAEP.

To ensure that the assessment results can be reported on the same trend line, a "bridge" assessment was administered in addition to the modified assessment. Students were randomly assigned to take either the bridge assessment or the modified assessment. The bridge assessment replicated the instrument given in 1999 and used the same administrative techniques. The 2004 modified assessment provides the basis of comparison for all future assessments, and the bridge links its results to the results from the past 30 years.

In the main national NAEP, a nationally representative sample of students is assessed at grades 4, 8, and 12 in various academic subjects. The assessments change periodically and are based on frameworks developed by the National Assessment Governing Board (NAGB). Items include both multiple-choice and constructed-response (requiring written answers) items. Results are reported in two ways. Average scores are reported for the nation, for participating states and jurisdictions, and for subgroups of the population. In addition, the percentage of students at or above *basic, proficient*, and *advanced* achievement levels is reported for these same groups. The achievement levels are developed by NAGB.

From 1990 until 2001, main NAEP was conducted for states and other jurisdictions that chose to participate (e.g., 47 participated in 1996). Prior to 1992, the national NAEP samples were not designed to support the reporting of accurate and representative state-level results. Separate representative samples of students were selected for each participating jurisdiction. State data are usually available at grades 4 and/or 8, and may not include all subjects assessed in the national-level assessment. In 1994, for example, NAEP assessed reading, geography, and history at the national level at grades 4, 8, and 12; however, only reading at grade 4 was assessed at the state level. In 1996, mathematics and science were assessed nationally at grades 4, 8, and 12; at the state level, mathematics was assessed at grades 4 and 8, and science was assessed at grade 8 only. In 1997, the arts were assessed only at the national level, at grade 8. Reading and writing were assessed in 1998 at

the national level for grades 4, 8, and 12 and at the state level for grades 4 and 8; civics was also assessed in 1998 at the national level for grades 4, 8, and 12. These assessments generally involved about 130,000 students at the national and state levels.

In 2002, under the provisions of the No Child Left Behind Act of 2001, all states began to participate in main NAEP and a separate national sample was replaced with the aggregate of all state samples. In 2002, students were assessed in reading and writing at grades 4, 8, and 12 for the national assessment and at grades 4 and 8 for the state assessment. In 2003, reading and mathematics were assessed at grades 4 and 8 for both national and state assessments.

The NAEP national samples in 2003 and 2005 were obtained by aggregating the samples from each state, rather than by obtaining an independently selected national sample. As a consequence, the size of the national sample increased, and smaller differences between scores across years or types of students were found to be statistically significant than would have been detected in previous assessments.

The assessment data presented in this publication were derived from tests designed and conducted by the Education Commission of the States (from 1969–1983) and by the Educational Testing Service (ETS) (from 1983 to the present).

Sample sizes and overall participation rates in 2004 for the long-term trend reading assessment for the bridge group were 5,200 9-year-olds (81 percent), 5,700 13-year-olds (77 percent), and 3,800 17-year-olds (55 percent); for those taking the modified assessment, the sizes and rates for the bridge group were 7,300 9-year-olds (80 percent), 7,500 13-year-olds (76 percent), and 7,600 17-year-olds (56 percent). Sample sizes and overall participation rates for the math assessment for the bridge group were 4,600 9-year-olds (80 percent), 4,700 13-year-olds (76 percent), and 4,600 17-year-olds (57 percent); for those taking the modified assessment, the sizes and rates for the bridge group were 7,500 9-year-olds (80 percent), 8,300 13-year-olds (76 percent), and 8,300 17-year-olds (56 percent).

Sample sizes for the reading proficiency portion of the 1999 NAEP long-term trend study were 5,793 for 9-year-olds, 5,933 for 13-year-olds, and 5,288 for 17-year-olds. Overall participation rates were 78 percent, 73 percent, and 59 percent, respectively. Sample sizes for the math and science portions of the 1999 long-term trend study were 6,032 9-year-olds, 5,941 13-year-olds, and 3,795 17-year-olds.

The main NAEP assessments are conducted separately from the long-term assessments. The 2000 mathematics assessment was administered to 13,511 4th-graders, 15,694 8th-graders, and 13,432 12th-graders. The response rates were 96 percent for 4th-graders, 92 percent for 8th-graders, and 77 percent for 12th-graders. The 2003 mathematics assessment was administered to 190,147 4th-graders and 153,189 8th-graders.

In 2000, a reading assessment was administered to 77,914 4th-graders. The response rate was 96 percent. In 2002, a reading assessment was administered to 140,487 4th-graders, 115,176 8th-graders, and 14,724 12th-graders. The 2003 reading assessment was administered to 187,581 4th-graders and 155,183 8th-graders.

The 1997–98 writing assessment was administered to 19,816 4th-graders, 20,586 8th-graders, and 19,505 12th-graders. The response rates were 95 percent for the 4th-graders, 92 percent for the 8th-graders, and 80 percent for the 12th-graders. The 2002 writing assessment was administered to 139,200 4th-graders, 118,500 8th-graders, and 18,500 12th-graders.

In 1995–96, a science assessment was administered to 7,305 4th-graders, 7,774 8th-graders, and 7,537 12th-graders. The response rates were 94 percent for the 4th-graders, 94 percent for the 8th-graders, and 93 percent for the 12th-graders. In 2000, a science assessment was administered to 16,749 4th-graders, 16,837 8th-graders, and 15,879 12th-graders. The response rates were 96 percent for the 4th-graders, 92 percent for the 8th-graders, and 76 percent for the 12th-graders.

The 1993–94 geography assessment was administered to 5,507 4th-graders, 6,878 8th-graders, and 6,234 12th-graders. The response rates for the assessment were 93 percent for the 4th-graders, 93 percent for the 8th-graders, and 90 percent for the 12th-graders. The 2000–01 geography assessment was administered to 7,779 4th-graders, 10,037 8th-graders, and 9,660 12th-graders. The response rates were 95 percent for the 4th-graders, 93 percent for the 8th-graders, and 77 percent for the 12th-graders.

Information from NAEP is subject to both nonsampling and sampling errors. Two possible sources of nonsampling error are nonparticipation and instrumentation. Certain populations have been oversampled to ensure samples of sufficient size for analysis. Instrumentation nonsampling error could result from failure of the test instruments to measure what is being taught and, in turn, what the students are learning.

Further information on NAEP may be obtained from

Suzanne Triplett
State Support and Constituency Outreach
Assessment Division
National Center for Education Statistics
1990 K Street NW
Washington, DC 20006
suzanne.triplett@ed.gov
http://nces.ed.gov/nationsreportcard

National Education Longitudinal Study of 1988

The National Education Longitudinal Study of 1988 (NELS:88) was the third major secondary school student longitudinal study conducted by NCES. The two studies that preceded NELS:88, the National Longitudinal Study of the High School Class of 1972 (NLS:72) and the High School and Beyond Longitudinal Study (HS&B) in 1980, surveyed high school seniors (and sophomores in HS&B) through high school, postsecondary education, and work and family formation experiences. Unlike its predecessors, NELS:88

began with a cohort of 8th-grade students. In 1988, some 25,000 8th-graders, their parents, their teachers, and their school principals were surveyed. Follow-ups were conducted in 1990 and 1992, when a majority of these students were in the 10th and 12th grades, respectively, and then 2 years after their scheduled high school graduation, in 1994. A fourth follow-up was conducted in 2000.

NELS:88 was designed to provide trend data about critical transitions experienced by young people as they develop, attend school, and embark on their careers. It complements and strengthens state and local efforts by furnishing new information on how school policies, teacher practices, and family involvement affect student educational outcomes (i.e., academic achievement, persistence in school, and participation in postsecondary education). For the base year, NELS:88 included a multifaceted student questionnaire, four cognitive tests, a parent questionnaire, a teacher questionnaire, and a school questionnaire.

In 1990, when most of the students were in 10th grade, students, school dropouts, their teachers, and their school principals were surveyed. (Parents were not surveyed in the 1990 follow-up.) In 1992, when most of the students were in 12th grade, the second follow-up conducted surveys of students, dropouts, parents, teachers, and school principals. Also, information from the students' transcripts was collected. The 1994 survey data were collected when most sample members had completed high school. The primary goals of the 1994 survey were (1) to provide data for trend comparisons with NLS:72 and HS&B; (2) to address issues of employment and postsecondary access and choice; and (3) to ascertain how many dropouts had returned to school and by what route. The 2000 follow-up examined the educational and labor market outcomes of the 1988 cohort at a time of transition. Most had been out of high school 8 years; many had completed their postsecondary educations, were embarking on first or even second careers, and were starting families.

Further information on NELS:88 may be obtained from

Jeffrey Owings
Elementary/Secondary and Library Studies Division
National Center for Education Statistics
1990 K Street NW
Washington, DC 20006
jeffrey.owings@ed.gov
http://nces.ed.gov/surveys/nels88

National Household Education Surveys Program

The National Household Education Surveys Program (NHES) is a data collection system that is designed to address a wide range of education-related issues. Surveys have been conducted in 1991, 1993, 1995, 1996, 1999, 2001, 2003, and 2005. The next surveys are planned for 2007.

NHES targets specific populations for detailed data collection. It is intended to provide more detailed data on the topics and populations of interest than are collected through supplements to other household surveys.

The topics addressed by NHES:1991 were early childhood education and adult education. About 60,000 households were screened for NHES:1991. In the Early Childhood Education survey, about 14,000 parents/guardians of 3- to 8-year-olds completed interviews about their children's early educational experiences. Included in this component were participation in nonparental care/education; care arrangements and school; and family, household, and child characteristics. In the NHES:1991 Adult Education survey, about 9,800 persons 16 years of age and older, identified as having participated in an adult education activity in the previous 12 months, were questioned about their activities. Data were collected on programs and up to four courses, including the subject matter, duration, sponsorship, purpose, and cost. Information on the household and the adult's background and current employment was also collected.

In NHES:1993, nearly 64,000 households were screened. Approximately 11,000 parents of 3- to 7-year-olds completed interviews for the School Readiness survey. Topics included the developmental characteristics of preschoolers; school adjustment and teacher feedback to parents for kindergartners and primary students; center-based program participation; early school experiences; home activities with family members; and health status. In the School Safety and Discipline survey, about 12,700 parents of children in grades 3–12 and about 6,500 youth in grades 6–12 were interviewed about their school experiences. Topics included the school learning environment, discipline policy, safety at school, victimization, the availability and use of alcohol/drugs, and alcohol/drug education. Peer norms for behavior in school and substance use were also included in this topical component. Extensive family and household background information was collected, as well as characteristics of the school attended by the child.

In NHES:1995, the Early Childhood Program Participation survey and the Adult Education survey were similar to those in 1991. In the Early Childhood component, about 14,000 parents of children from birth to third grade were interviewed. In the Adult Education survey, 23,969 adults were sampled and 80 percent (19,722) completed the interview.

NHES:1996 covered parent and family involvement in education and civic involvement. For the Parent and Family Involvement survey, nearly 21,000 parents of children in grades 3 to 12 were interviewed. For the Civic Involvement survey, about 8,000 youth in grades 6 to 12, about 9,000 parents, and about 2,000 adults were interviewed. The 1996 survey also addressed public library use. Adults in almost 55,000 households were interviewed to support state-level estimates of household public library use.

NHES:1999 collected end-of-decade estimates of key indicators from the surveys conducted throughout the 1990s. Approximately 60,000 households were screened for a total of about 31,000 interviews with parents of children from birth through 12th grade and adults age 16 or older not enrolled in grade 12 or below. Key indicators included participation of children in nonparental care and early childhood programs, school experiences, parent/family involvement in education at home and at school, youth community service activities, plans for future education, and adult participation in educational activities and community service.

NHES:2001 included two surveys that were largely repeats of similar surveys included in earlier NHES collections. The Early Childhood Program Participation survey was similar in content to the Early Childhood Program Participation survey fielded as part of NHES:1995, and the Adult Education and Lifelong Learning survey was similar in content to the Adult Education survey of NHES:1995. The Before- and After-School Programs and Activities survey, while containing items fielded in earlier NHES collections, had a number of new items that collected information about what children were doing during the time spent in child care or in other activities, what parents were looking for in care arrangements and activities, and parent evaluations of care arrangements and activities. Parents of approximately 6,700 preschool children completed Early Childhood Program Participation survey interviews. Nearly 10,900 adults completed Adult Education and Lifelong Learning survey interviews, and parents of nearly 9,600 children in kindergarten though grade 8 completed Before- and After-School Programs and Activities survey interviews.

NHES:2003 included two surveys: Adult Education for Work-Related Reasons and Parent and Family Involvement in Education. The adult education survey allows for the analysis of change over time and provide in-depth information on participation in training and education that prepares adults for work or careers and maintains or improves their skills.

NHES:2005 included surveys that covered Adult Education, Early Childhood Program Participation, and After-School Programs and Activities. Data were collected from about 8,900 adults for the Adult Education survey, parents of about 7,200 children for the Early Childhood Program Participation survey, and parents of nearly 11,700 children for the After-School Programs and Activities survey. These surveys were substantially similar to the surveys conducted in 2001.

Further information on NHES may be obtained from

Gail Mulligan
Early Childhood, International, and Crosscutting Studies Division
Early Childhood and Household Studies Program
National Center for Education Statistics
1990 K Street NW
Washington, DC 20006
gail.mulligan@ed.gov
http://nces.ed.gov/nhes

National Longitudinal Study of the High School Class of 1972

The National Longitudinal Study of the High School Class of 1972 (NLS:72) began with the collection of base-year survey data from a sample of about 19,000 high school seniors in the spring of 1972. Five follow-up surveys of these students were conducted in 1973, 1974, 1976, 1979, and 1986. NLS:72 was designed to provide the education community with information on the transitions of young adults from high school through postsecondary education and the workplace.

In addition to the follow-ups, a number of supplemental data collection efforts were undertaken. For example, a Postsecondary Education Transcript Study (PETS) was undertaken in 1984; in 1986, the fifth follow-up included a supplement for those who became teachers.

The sample design for NLS:72 was a stratified, two-stage probability sample of 12th-grade students from all schools, public and private, in the 50 states and the District of Columbia during the 1971–72 school year. During the first stage of sampling, about 1,070 schools were selected for participation in the base-year survey. As many as 18 students were selected at random from each of the sample schools. The sizes of both the school and student samples were increased during the first follow-up survey. Beginning with the first follow-up and continuing through the fourth follow-up, about 1,300 schools participated in the survey and slightly fewer than 23,500 students were sampled. The response rates for each of the different rounds of data collection were 80 percent or higher.

Sample retention rates across the survey years were quite high. For example, of the individuals responding to the base-year questionnaire, the percentages who responded to the first, second, third, and fourth follow-up questionnaires were about 94, 93, 89, and 83 percent, respectively.

Further information on NLS:72 may be obtained from

Aurora D'Amico
Postsecondary Studies Division
Postsecondary Cooperative System, Analysis, and
    Dissemination Program
National Center for Education Statistics
1990 K Street NW
Washington, DC 20006
aurora.d'amico@ed.gov
http://nces.ed.gov/surveys/nls72

National Postsecondary Student Aid Study

The National Postsecondary Student Aid Study (NPSAS) is a comprehensive nationwide study of how students and their families pay for postsecondary education. It covers nationally representative samples of undergraduates, graduates, and first-professional students in the 50 states, the District of Columbia, and Puerto Rico, including students attending less-than-2-year institutions, community colleges, 4-year colleges, and major universities. Participants include students who do not receive aid and their parents, as well as students who do receive financial aid and their parents. Study results are used to help guide future federal policy regarding student financial aid. NPSAS was conducted every

3 years. Beginning with the 1999–2000 study, NPSAS is conducted every 4 years.

The first NPSAS was conducted during the 1986–87 school year. Data were gathered from about 1,074 colleges, universities, and other postsecondary institutions; 60,000 students; and 14,000 parents. These data provided information on the cost of postsecondary education, the distribution of financial aid, and the characteristics of both aided and nonaided students and their families.

As a part of NPSAS:93, information on 77,000 undergraduates and graduate students enrolled during the school year was collected at 1,000 postsecondary institutions. The sample included students enrolled at any time between July 1, 1992, and June 30, 1993. About 66,000 students and a subsample of their parents were interviewed by telephone. NPSAS:96 contained information on more than 48,000 undergraduate and graduate students from 973 postsecondary institutions enrolled at any time during the 1995–96 school year. NPSAS:2000 included nearly 62,000 students (49,930 undergraduates, 10,640 graduate students, and 1,200 first-professional students) from 999 postsecondary institutions. NPSAS:04 collected data on 69,100 undergraduates and 31,800 graduate students from 1,360 postsecondary institutions.

Further information on NPSAS may be obtained from

James Griffith
Postsecondary Studies Division
Postsecondary Longitudinal and Sample Studies Program
National Center for Education Statistics
1990 K Street NW
Washington, DC 20006
james.griffith@ed.gov
http://nces.ed.gov/npsas

National Study of Postsecondary Faculty

The National Study of Postsecondary Faculty (NSOPF) was designed to provide data about faculty to postsecondary researchers, planners, and policymakers. NSOPF is the most comprehensive study of faculty in postsecondary education institutions ever undertaken.

The first cycle of NSOPF (NSOPF:88) was conducted by NCES with support from the National Endowment for the Humanities (NEH) in 1987–88 with a sample of 480 colleges and universities, over 3,000 department chairpersons, and over 11,000 instructional faculty. The second cycle of NSOPF (NSOPF:93) was conducted by NCES with support from NEH and the National Science Foundation in 1992–93. NSOPF:93 was limited to surveys of institutions and faculty, but with a substantially expanded sample of 974 colleges and universities, and 31,354 faculty and instructional staff. The third cycle, NSPOF:99, included 960 degree-granting postsecondary institutions and approximately 18,000 faculty and instructional staff. The fourth cycle of NSOPF was conducted in 2003–04 and included 1,080 degree-granting postsecondary institutions and approximately 26,000 faculty and instructional staff. The fifth cycle is scheduled to take place in 2008–09.

Further information on NSOPF may be obtained from

Linda J. Zimbler
Postsecondary Studies Division
Postsecondary Longitudinal and Sample Studies Program
National Center for Education Statistics
1990 K Street NW
Washington, DC 20006
linda.zimbler@ed.gov
http://nces.ed.gov/surveys/nsopf

Private School Universe Survey

The purposes of the Private School Universe Survey (PSS) data collection activities are (1) to build an accurate and complete list of private schools to serve as a sampling frame for NCES sample surveys of private schools; and (2) to report data on the total number of private schools, teachers, and students in the survey universe. Begun in 1989, the PSS has been conducted every 2 years, and data for the 1989–90, 1991–92, 1993–94, 1995–96, 1997–98, 1999–2000, 2001–02, and 2003–04 school years have been released.

The PSS produces data similar to that of the CCD for public schools, and can be used for public-private comparisons. The data are useful for a variety of policy and research-relevant issues, such as the growth of religiously affiliated schools, the number of private high school graduates, the length of the school year for various private schools, and the number of private school students and teachers.

The target population for this universe survey is all private schools in the United States that meet the PSS criteria of a private school (i.e., the private school is an institution that provides instruction for any of grades K through 12, has one or more teachers to give instruction, is not administered by a public agency, and is not operated in a private home). The survey universe is composed of schools identified from a variety of sources. The main source is a list frame initially developed for the 1989–90 PSS. The list is updated regularly by matching it with lists provided by nationwide private school associations, state departments of education, and other national guides and sources that list private schools. The other source is an area frame search in approximately 124 geographic areas, conducted by the U.S. Census Bureau.

Further information on the PSS may be obtained from

Steve Broughman
Elementary/Secondary and Libraries Studies Division
Elementary/Secondary Sample Survey Studies Program
National Center for Education Statistics
1990 K Street NW
Washington, DC 20006
stephen.broughman@ed.gov
http://nces.ed.gov/surveys/pss

Projections of Education Statistics

Since 1964, NCES has published projections of key statistics for elementary and secondary schools and institutions of higher education. The latest report is titled *Projections of Education Statistics to 2015* (NCES 2006-084). These projections include statistics for enrollments, instructional staff, graduates, earned degrees, and expenditures. These reports include several alternative projection series and a methodology section describing the techniques and assumptions used to prepare them. Data in this edition of the *Digest* reflect the middle alternative projection series.

Differences between the reported and projected values are, of course, almost inevitable. An evaluation of past projections revealed that, at the elementary and secondary level, projections of enrollments have been quite accurate: mean absolute percentage differences for enrollment were less than 1 percent for projections from 1 to 5 years in the future, while those for teachers were less than 4 percent. At the higher education level, projections of enrollment have been fairly accurate: mean absolute percentage differences were 5 percent or less for projections from 1 to 5 years into the future.

Further information on *Projections of Education Statistics* may be obtained from

William Hussar
Early Childhood, International, and Crosscutting Studies Division
Annual Reports Program
National Center for Education Statistics
1990 K Street NW
Washington, DC 20006
william.hussar@ed.gov
http://nces.ed.gov/edstats

Recent College Graduates Survey

Between 1976 and 1991, NCES conducted periodic surveys of baccalaureate and master's degree recipients 1 year after graduation with the Recent College Graduates (RCG) Study. The RCG Study—which has been replaced by the Baccalaureate and Beyond Longitudinal Study (B&B) (see listing above)—concentrated on those graduates entering the teaching profession. The study linked respondents' major field of study with outcomes such as whether the respondent entered the labor force or was seeking additional education. Labor force data collected included employment status (unemployed, employed part time, or employed full time), occupation, salary, career potential, relation to major field of study, and need for a college degree. To obtain accurate results on teachers, graduates with a major in education were oversampled. The last two studies oversampled education majors and increased the sampling of graduates with majors in other fields.

For each of the selected institutions, a list of graduates by major field of study was obtained, and a sample of graduates was drawn by major field of study. Graduates in certain major fields of study (e.g., education, mathematics, physical sciences) were sampled at higher rates than were graduates in other fields. Roughly 1 year after graduation, the sample of graduates was located, contacted by mail or telephone, and asked to respond to the questionnaire.

The locating process was more detailed than that in most surveys. Nonresponse rates were directly related to the time, effort, and resources used in locating graduates, rather than to graduates' refusals to participate. Despite the difficulties in locating graduates, RCG response rates are comparable to studies that do not face problems locating their sample membership.

The 1976 study of 1974–75 college graduates was the first, and smallest, of the series. The sample consisted of 211 schools, of which 200 (96 percent) responded. Of the 5,854 graduates in the sample, 4,350 responded, for a response rate of 79 percent.

The 1981 study was somewhat larger, covering 297 institutions and 15,852 graduates. Responses were obtained from 283 institutions, for an institutional response rate of 95 percent, and from 9,312 graduates (716 others were determined to be out of scope), for a response rate of 74 percent.

The 1985 study sampled 404 colleges and 18,738 graduates, of whom 17,853 were found to be in scope. Responses were obtained from 13,200 graduates, for a response rate of 78 percent. The response rate for colleges was 98 percent. The 1987 study sampled 21,957 graduates. Responses were received from 16,878, for a response rate of nearly 80 percent.

The 1991 study sampled 18,135 graduates of 400 bachelor's and master's degree-granting institutions, including 16,172 bachelor's degrees recipients and 1,963 master's degree recipients receiving diplomas between July 1, 1989, and June 30, 1990. Random samples of graduates were selected from lists stratified by field of study. Graduates in education, mathematics, and the physical sciences were sampled at a higher rate, as were minority graduates, to provide a sufficient number of these graduates for analysis purposes. The graduates included in the sample were selected in proportion to the institution's number of graduates. The institutional response rate was 95 percent, and the graduate response rate was 83 percent.

Appendix table A-3 contains sample sizes for number of graduates, by field, for the 1976, 1981, 1985, 1987, and 1991 surveys.

Further information on the RCG Study may be obtained from

Aurora D'Amico
Postsecondary Studies Division
Postsecondary Cooperative System, Analysis, and
    Dissemination Program
National Center for Education Statistics
1990 K Street NW
Washington, DC 20006
aurora.d'amico@ed.gov
http://nces.ed.gov/surveys/b&b

School Survey on Crime and Safety (SSOCS)

The most recent School Survey on Crime and Safety (SSOCS) was conducted by NCES in spring/summer of the 2003–04 school year. SSOCS focuses on incidents of specific crimes/offenses and a variety of specific discipline issues in public schools. It also covers characteristics of school policies, school violence prevention programs and policies, and school characteristics that have been associated with school crime. The survey was conducted with a nationally representative sample of regular public elementary, middle, and high schools in the 50 states and the District of Columbia. Special education, alternative, and vocational schools; schools in the other jurisdictions; and schools that taught only prekindergarten, kindergarten, or adult education were not included in the sample.

The sampling frame for the 2004 SSOCS was constructed from the public school universe file created for the 2003–04 Schools and Staffing Survey from the 2001–02 NCES Common Core of Data public school universe file. The sample was stratified by instructional level, type of locale, and enrollment size. Within the primary strata, schools were also sorted by geographic region and by percentage of minority enrollment. The sample sizes were then allocated to the primary strata in rough proportion to the aggregate square root of the size of enrollment of schools in the stratum. A total of 3,743 schools were selected for the study. Of those schools, 2,270 completed the survey. In March 2004, questionnaires were mailed to school principals, who were asked to complete the survey or to have it completed by the person at the school most knowledgeable about discipline issues. The weighted overall response rate was 77.2 percent, and item nonresponse rates in the public-use data file ranged from 0 to 33.3 percent. A nonresponse bias analysis was conducted on the nine items with weighted item nonresponse rates above 15 percent, and minimal bias was detected. Weights were developed to adjust for the variable probabilities of selection and differential nonresponse and can be used to produce national estimates for regular public schools in the 2003–04 school year.

For more information about the SSOCS, contact

Kathryn Chandler
Elementary/Secondary and Libraries Studies Division
Elementary/Secondary Sample Survey Studies Program
National Center for Education Statistics
1990 K Street NW
Washington, DC 20006
kathryn.chandler@ed.gov
http://nces.ed.gov/surveys/ssocs

Schools and Staffing Survey

The Schools and Staffing Survey (SASS) is a set of linked questionnaires used to collect data on the nation's public and private elementary and secondary teaching force, characteristics of schools and school principals, demand for teachers, and school/school district policies. SASS data are collected through a mail questionnaire with telephone follow-up. SASS was first conducted for NCES by the Census Bureau during the 1987–88 school year. SASS subsequently was conducted in 1990–91, 1993–94, 1999–2000, and 2003–04. The 1990–91, 1993–94, 1999–2000, and 2003–04 SASS also obtained data on Bureau of Indian Affairs (BIA) schools (schools funded or operated by the BIA). Charter schools were included for the first time in the 1999–2000 SASS administration. The universe of charter schools in operation in 1998–99 was given the Charter School Questionnaire to complete. In the 2003–04 SASS administration, charter schools were not administered a separate questionnaire, but were included in the public school sample. Another change in the 2003–04 administration included a revised data collection methodology using a primary in-person contact with the school with the aim of reducing the field follow-up phase. Also, school library media centers were surveyed only in the public and BIA schools. (See discussion on the School Library Media Centers Survey in "Library Statistics Program," above.)

The 2003–04 SASS estimates are based upon a sample consisting of approximately 8,000 public schools, 2,500 private schools, and 145 BIA schools. The public school sample for the 2003–04 SASS was based on an adjusted public school universe file from the 2001–02 school year Common Core of Data (CCD), the compilation of all the nation's public school districts and public schools. The sampling frame includes regular public schools, Department of Defense-operated military base schools in the United States, and other schools, such as special education, vocational, and alternative schools. SASS is designed to provide national estimates for public and private school characteristics and state estimates for school districts, public schools, principals, and teachers. In addition, the teacher survey is designed to allow comparisons between new and experienced teachers and between bilingual/ESL teachers and other teachers.

The BIA sample consisted of all BIA schools that met the SASS definition of a school.

The private school sample for the 2003–04 SASS was selected from the 2001–02 Private School Universe Survey, supplemented with updates from state lists collected by the Census Bureau and lists by private school associations and religious denominations. Private school estimates are available at the national level and by private school affiliation.

In 2003–04, the weighted response rate for the School District Questionnaire was 82.9 percent. Weighted response rates for the Public School Principal Questionnaire, the Private School Principal Questionnaire, and the BIA-funded School Principal Questionnaire were 82.2 percent, 74.9 percent, and 90.7 percent, respectively.

Weighted response rates in 2003–04 for the Public School Questionnaire, the Private School Questionnaire, and the BIA-funded School Questionnaire were 80.8 percent, 75.9 percent, and 89.5 percent, respectively. The weighted overall response rates were 84.8 percent for public school teachers, 82.4 percent for private school teachers, and 92.0 percent for BIA-funded school teachers.

Public-use data files are available on CD-ROM. Summary data from the 2003–04 SASS can be found in *Characteristics of Schools, Districts, Teachers, Principals, and School Libraries in the United States, 2003–04* (NCES 2006-313 REVISED). There is also a methodology report on SASS, the *Quality Profile for SASS, Rounds 1–3: 1987–1995* (NCES 2000-308).

The most recent administration of SASS occurred during the 2005–06 school year. Further information on SASS may be obtained from

Kerry Gruber
Elementary/Secondary and Libraries Studies Division
Elementary/Secondary Sample Survey Studies Program
National Center for Education Statistics
1990 K Street NW
Washington, DC 20006
kerry.gruber@ed.gov
http://nces.ed.gov/surveys/sass

Other Department of Education Agencies

Office for Civil Rights

OCR Elementary and Secondary School Survey

The OCR Elementary and Secondary School (E&S) Survey has been used since 1968 by the U.S. Department of Education's Office for Civil Rights (OCR) to obtain trend data from the nation's public elementary and secondary schools. The E&S Survey provides information about the enrollment of students in public schools in every state and about some education services provided to those students. These data are reported by race/ethnicity, sex, and disability.

Data in the E&S Survey are collected pursuant to 34 C.F.R. Section 100.6(b) of the Department of Education regulation implementing Title VI of the Civil Rights Act of 1964. The requirements are also incorporated by reference in Department regulations implementing Title IX of the Education Amendments of 1972, Section 504 of the Rehabilitation Act of 1973, and the Age Discrimination Act of 1975. School, district, state, and national data are currently available. Data from individual public schools and districts are used to generate projected national and state data.

In recent surveys, the sample has been approximately 6,000 districts and 60,000 schools; however, in 2000, data were collected from all public school districts. In sample surveys, the following districts are sampled with certainty: districts having more than 25,000 students; all districts in states having 25 or fewer public school districts; and districts subject to federal court order and monitored by the U.S. Department of Justice. The survey is conducted biennially (with few exceptions); the most recent survey was conducted in 2004. Data currently are available from the 2002 survey.

Further information on the E&S Survey can be obtained from

Mary Schifferli
Office for Civil Rights
U.S. Department of Education
555 12th Street SW
Washington, DC 20202
mary.schifferli@ed.gov
http://www.ed.gov/about/offices/list/ocr/data.html?src=rt

Office of Special Education and Rehabilitative Services

Annual Report to Congress on the Implementation of the Individuals With Disabilities Education Act

The Individuals With Disabilities Education Act (IDEA), formerly the Education of the Handicapped Act (EHA), requires the Secretary of Education to transmit to Congress annually a report describing the progress made in serving the nation's disabled children. This annual report contains information on children served by public schools under the provisions of Part B of the IDEA and on children served in state-operated programs for the handicapped under Chapter I of the Elementary and Secondary Education Act.

Statistics on children receiving special education and related services in various settings and school personnel providing such services are reported in an annual submission of data to the Office of Special Education and Rehabilitative Services (OSERS) by the 50 states, the District of Columbia, and the outlying areas. The child count information is based on the number of disabled children receiving special education and related services on December 1 of each year. Count information is available from http://www.ideadata.org.

Since each participant in programs for the disabled is reported to OSERS, the data are not subject to sampling error. However, nonsampling error can arise from a variety of sources. Some states follow a noncategorical approach to the delivery of special education services, but produce counts by disabling condition because Part B of the EHA requires it. In those states that do categorize their disabled students, definitions and labeling practices vary.

Further information on this annual report to Congress may be obtained from

Office of Special Education Programs
Office of Special Education and Rehabilitative Services
U.S. Department of Education
550 12th Street SW
Washington, DC 20065
http://www.ed.gov/about/offices/list/osers/osep/index.html
http://www.ideadata.org

Office of Vocational and Adult Education

Division of Adult Education and Literacy

The Division of Adult Education and Literacy (DAEL) promotes programs that help American adults get the basic skills they need to be productive workers, family members, and citizens. The major areas of support are Adult Basic Education, Adult Secondary Education, and English Language Acquisition. These programs emphasize basic skills such as reading, writing, math, English language competency, and problem solving. Each year, DAEL reports enrollment numbers in state-administered adult education programs for these major areas of support for all 50 states, the District of Columbia, and the eight U.S. jurisdictions (American Samoa, the Federated States of Micronesia, Guam, the Marshall Islands, the Northern Marianas, Palau, Puerto Rico, and the U.S. Virgin Islands).

Further information on DAEL may be obtained from

Office of Vocational and Adult Education
Division of Adult Education and Literacy
U.S. Department of Education
400 Maryland Avenue SW
Washington, DC 20202
http://www.ed.gov/about/offices/list/ovae/pi/AdultEd/index.html

Other Governmental Agencies

Bureau of Labor Statistics

Consumer Price Indexes

The Consumer Price Index (CPI) represents changes in prices of all goods and services purchased for consumption by urban households. Indexes are available for two population groups: a CPI for All Urban Consumers (CPI-U) and a CPI for Urban Wage Earners and Clerical Workers (CPI-W). Unless otherwise specified, data in the *Digest* are adjusted for inflation using the CPI-U. These values are frequently adjusted to a school-year basis by averaging the July through June figures. Price indexes are available for the United States, the four Census regions, size of city, cross-classifications of regions and size classes, and 26 local areas. The major uses of the CPI include the CPI as an economic indicator, as a deflator of other economic series, and as a means of adjusting income payments.

Also available is the Consumer Price Index research series using current methods (CPI-U-RS), which presents an estimate of the CPI-U from 1978 to the present that incorporates most of the improvements that the Bureau of Labor Statistics has made over that time span into the entire series. The historical price index series of the CPI-U does not reflect these changes, though these changes do make the present and future CPI more accurate. The limitations of the

CPI-U-RS include considerable uncertainty surrounding the magnitude of the adjustments and the several improvements in the CPI that have not been incorporated into the CPI-U-RS for various reasons. Nonetheless, the CPI-U-RS can serve as a valuable proxy for researchers needing a historical estimate of inflation using current methods.

Further information on consumer price indexes may be obtained from

Consumer Price Indexes
Bureau of Labor Statistics
U.S. Department of Labor
2 Massachusetts Avenue NE
Washington, DC 20212
http://www.bls.gov/cpi

Unemployment Surveys

Statistics on the employment status of the population and related data are compiled by the Bureau of Labor Statistics (BLS) using data from the Current Population Survey (CPS) and other surveys. The monthly CPS of households is conducted for BLS by the U.S. Census Bureau through a scientifically selected sample designed to represent the civilian noninstitutional population. Respondents are interviewed to obtain information about the employment status of each member of the household 15 years of age and over, although only data on those 16 years of age and older are published. Each month, about 60,000 occupied household units are eligible for interview. Some 4,500 of these households are contacted, but interviews are not obtained because the occupants are not at home after repeated calls or are unavailable for other reasons. This represents a noninterview rate that ranges between 7 and 8 percent. In addition to the 60,000 occupied household units, about 12,000 sample units in an average month are visited but are found to be vacant or otherwise not eligible for enumeration.

The current sample design, introduced in July 2001, includes about 72,000 households from 754 sample areas and maintains a 1.9 percent coefficient of variation (c.v.) on national monthly estimates of unemployment level. This translates into a change of 0.2 percentage points in the unemployment rate being significant at a 90 percent confidence level. For each of the 50 states and the District of Columbia, the design maintains a c.v. of at most 8 percent on the annual average estimate of unemployment level, assuming a 6 percent unemployment rate.

Further information on unemployment surveys may be obtained from

Bureau of Labor Statistics
U.S. Department of Labor
2 Massachusetts Avenue NE
Washington, DC 20212
cpsinfo@bls.gov
http://www.bls.gov/bls/employment.htm

Census Bureau

Census of Population–Education in the United States

Some tables in this report are based on a part of the decennial census that consists of questions asked of a one-in-six sample of persons and housing units in the United States. This sample was asked more detailed questions about income, occupation, and housing costs, in addition to general demographic information.

School Enrollment Persons classified as enrolled in school reported attending a "regular" public or private school or college. They were asked whether the institution they attended was public or private and what level of school they were enrolled in.

Educational Attainment Data for educational attainment were tabulated for persons age 15 and older and classified according to the highest grade completed or the highest degree received. Instructions were also given to include the level of the previous grade attended or the highest degree received for persons currently enrolled in school.

Poverty Status To determine poverty status, answers to income questions were used to make comparisons to the appropriate poverty threshold. All persons except those who were institutionalized, persons in military group quarters and college dormitories, and unrelated persons under age 15 were considered. If the total income of each family or unrelated individual in the sample was below the corresponding cutoff, that family or individual was classified as "below the poverty level."

Further information on the 1990 and 2000 Census of Population may be obtained from

Population Division
Census Bureau
U.S. Department of Commerce
Washington, DC 20233
http://www.census.gov/prod/www/abs/decenial.html
http://www.census.gov/main/www/cen2000.html

Current Population Survey

Prior to July 2001, estimates of school enrollment rates, as well as social and economic characteristics of students, were based on data collected in the Census Bureau's monthly household survey of about 50,000 dwelling units. Beginning in July 2001, this sample was expanded to 60,000 dwelling units. The monthly Current Population Survey (CPS) sample consists of 754 areas comprising 2,007 geographic areas, independent cities, and minor civil divisions throughout the 50 states and the District of Columbia. The samples are initially selected based on the decennial census files and are periodically updated to reflect new housing construction.

The monthly CPS deals primarily with labor force data for the civilian noninstitutional population (i.e., excluding military personnel and their families living on bases and inmates of institutions). In addition, in October of each year, supplemental questions are asked about highest grade completed, level and grade of current enrollment, attendance status, number and type of courses, degree or certificate objective, and type of organization offering instruction for each member of the household. In March of each year, supplemental questions on income are asked. The responses to these questions are combined with answers to two questions on educational attainment: highest grade of school ever attended and whether that grade was completed.

The estimation procedure employed for monthly CPS data involves inflating weighted sample results to independent estimates of characteristics of the civilian noninstitutional population in the United States by age, sex, and race. These independent estimates are based on statistics from decennial censuses; statistics on births, deaths, immigration, and emigration; and statistics on the population in the armed services. Generalized standard error tables are provided in the *Current Population Reports*. The data are subject to both nonsampling and sampling errors.

Caution should also be used when comparing data from 1994 through 2001, which reflect 1990 census-based population controls, with data from March 1993 and earlier, which reflect 1980 or earlier census-based population controls, as well as with data from 2002 onward, which reflect 2000 census-based controls. Changes in population controls generally have relatively little impact on summary measures such as means, medians, and percentage distributions. They can have a significant impact on population counts. For example, use of the 1990 census-based population control resulted in about a 1 percent increase in the civilian noninstitutional population and in the number of families and households. Thus, estimates of levels for data collected in 1994 and later years will differ from those for earlier years by more than what could be attributed to actual changes in the population. These differences could be disproportionately greater for certain subpopulation groups than for the total population.

Further information on CPS may be obtained from

Education and Social Stratification Branch
Population Division
Census Bureau
U.S. Department of Commerce
Washington, DC 20233
http://www.census.gov/cps

Dropouts

Each October, the Current Population Survey (CPS) includes supplemental questions on the enrollment status of the population 3 years old and over as part of the monthly basic survey on labor force participation. In addition to gathering the information on school enrollment, with the limitations on accuracy as noted below under "School Enrollment," the survey data permit calculations of dropout rates. Both status and event dropout rates are tabulated from the October CPS. The *Digest* provides information using the status rate calculation. Event rates describe the proportion of students who leave school each year without completing a high school program. Status rates provide cumulative data on dropouts among all young adults within a specified age range. Status rates are higher than event rates because they include all dropouts ages 16 through 24, regardless of when they last attended school.

In addition to other survey limitations, dropout rates may be affected by survey coverage and exclusion of the institutionalized population. The incarcerated population has grown more rapidly and has a higher dropout rate than the general population. Dropout rates for the total population might be higher than those for the noninstitutionalized population if the prison and jail populations were included in the dropout rate calculations. On the other hand, if military personnel, who tend to be high school graduates, were included, it might offset some or all of the impact from the theoretical inclusion of the jail and prison population.

Another area of concern with tabulations involving young people in household surveys is the relatively low coverage ratio compared to older age groups. CPS undercoverage results from missed housing units and missed persons within sample households. Overall CPS undercoverage is estimated to be about 8 percent. CPS undercoverage varies with age, sex, and race. Generally, undercoverage is larger for males than for females and larger for Blacks and other races combined than for Whites. For example, the undercoverage ratio for Black 20- to 29-year-old males is 34 percent. Ratio estimation to independent age-sex-race-Hispanic population controls partially corrects for the bias due to undercoverage. However, biases exist in the estimates to the extent that missed persons in missed households or missed persons in interviewed households have different characteristics from those of interviewed persons in the same age-sex-race-origin-state group. Further information on CPS methodology may be obtained from http://www.census.gov/cps.

Further information on the calculation of dropouts and dropout rates may be obtained from *Dropout Rates in the United States: 2002 and 2003* at http://nces.ed.gov/pubs2006/2006062.pdf or by contacting

Chris Chapman
Early Childhood, International, and Crosscutting Studies Division
Early Childhood and Household Studies Program
National Center for Education Statistics
1990 K Street NW
Washington, DC 20006
chris.chapman@ed.gov

Educational Attainment

Data on years of school completed are derived from two questions on the Current Population Survey (CPS) instrument. Reports documenting educational attainment are produced by the Census Bureau using March CPS supplement (Annual Demographic Survey) results. The latest release is *Educational Attainment in the United States: 2005*, which may be downloaded at http://www.census.gov/population/www/socdemo/education/cps2005.html.

In addition to the general constraints of CPS, some data indicate that the respondents have a tendency to overestimate the educational level of members of their household. Some inaccuracy is due to a lack of the respondent's knowledge of the exact educational attainment of each household member and the hesitancy to acknowledge anything less than a high school education. Another cause of nonsampling variability is the change in the numbers in the armed services over the years.

The March 2004 basic CPS response rate was 91.5 percent and the educational attainment supplement response rate was 91.8 percent, for a total supplement response rate of 84.0 percent.

The March 2005 basic CPS response rate was 90.6 percent and the educational attainment supplement response rate was 91.2 percent, for a total supplement response rate of 82.3 percent. The variability in estimates for subgroups (region, household relationships, etc.) can be estimated using the tables presented in *Current Population Reports*. Further information on CPS and its supplements may be obtained from the CPS website at http://www.census.gov/cps.

Further information on CPS's educational attainment data may be obtained from

Education and Social Stratification Branch
Census Bureau
U.S. Department of Commerce
Washington, DC 20233
http://www.census.gov/population/www/socdemo/
    educ-attn.html

School Enrollment

Each October, the Current Population Survey (CPS) includes supplemental questions on the enrollment status of the population 3 years old and over, in addition to the monthly basic survey on labor force participation. Prior to 2001, the October supplement consisted of approximately 47,000 interviewed households. Beginning with the October 2001 supplement, the sample was expanded by 9,000 to a total of approximately 56,000 interviewed households. The main sources of nonsampling variability in the responses to the supplement are those inherent in the survey instrument. The question of current enrollment may not be answered accurately for various reasons. Some respondents may not know current grade information for every student in the household, a problem especially prevalent for households with members in college or in nursery school. Confusion over college credits or hours taken by a student may make it difficult to determine the year in which the student is enrolled. Problems may occur with the definition of nursery school (a group or class organized to provide educational

experiences for children), where respondents' interpretations of "educational experiences" vary.

The October 2004 basic CPS response rate was 92.3 percent and the school enrollment supplement response rate was 96.0 percent, for a combined supplement response rate of 88.6 percent.

The October 2005 basic CPS response rate was 92.6 percent and the school enrollment supplement response rate was 96.6 percent, for a combined supplement response rate of 89.5 percent.

Further information on CPS methodology may be obtained from http://www.census.gov/cps.

Further information on the CPS School Enrollment Supplement may be obtained from

Education and Social Stratification Branch
Census Bureau
U.S. Department of Commerce
Washington, DC 20233
http://www.census.gov/population/www/socdemo/
    school.html

Government Finances

The Census Bureau conducts an Annual Survey of Government Finances as authorized by law under Title 13, United States Code, Section 182. This survey covers the entire range of government finance activities: revenue, expenditure, debt, and assets. Revenues and expenditures comprise actual receipts and payments of a government and its agencies, including government-operated enterprises, utilities, and public trust funds. The expenditure-reporting categories comprise all amounts of money paid out by a government and its agencies, with the exception of amounts for debt retirement and for loan, investment, agency, and private trust transactions.

Most of the federal government statistics are based on figures that appear in *The Budget of the United States Government*. Since the classification used by the Census Bureau for reporting state and local government finance statistics differs in a number of important respects from the classification used in the U.S. budget, it was necessary to adjust the federal data. For this report, federal budget expenditures include interest accrued, but not paid, during the fiscal year; Census data on interest are on a disbursement basis.

State government finances are based primarily on the annual Census Bureau Survey of Government Finances. Census analysts compile figures from official records and reports of the state governments for most of the state financial data. States differ in the ways they administer activities; they may fund such activities directly, or they may disburse the money to a lower level government or government agency. Therefore, caution is advised when attempting to make a direct comparison between states on their state fiscal aid data.

The sample of local governments is drawn from the periodic Census of Governments and consists of certain local governments sampled with certainty plus a sample below the certainty level.

The statistics in *Government Finances* that are based wholly or partly on data from the sample are subject to sampling error. State government finance data are not subject to sampling error. Estimates of major U.S. totals for local governments are subject to a computed sampling variability of less than one-half of l percent. The estimates are also subject to the inaccuracies in classification, response, and processing that would occur if a complete census had been conducted under the same conditions as the sample.

Further information on government finances may be obtained from

Governments Division
Census Bureau
U.S. Department of Commerce
Washington, DC 20233
http://www.census.gov/govs/www/index.html

Survey of Income and Program Participation

The main objective of the Survey of Income and Program Participation (SIPP) is to provide accurate and comprehensive information about the income and program participation of individuals and households in the United States, and about the principal determinants of income and program participation. SIPP offers detailed information on cash and noncash income on a subannual basis. The survey also collects data on taxes, assets, liabilities, and participation in government transfer programs. SIPP data allow the government to evaluate the effectiveness of federal, state, and local programs.

The survey design is a continuous series of national panels, with sample size ranging from approximately 14,000 to 36,700 interviewed households. The duration of each panel ranges from 2 1/2 years to 4 years. The SIPP sample is a multistage-stratified sample of the U.S. civilian noninstitutionalized population. For the 1984–93 panels, a panel of households was introduced each year in February. A 4-year panel was introduced in April 1996. A 2000 panel was introduced in February 2000 for two waves. A 3-year 2001 panel was introduced in February 2001. All household members 15 years old and over are interviewed by self-response, if possible. Proxy response is permitted when household members are not available for interviewing.

The SIPP content is built around a "core" of labor force, program participation, and income questions designed to measure the economic situation of persons in the United States. These questions expand the data currently available on the distribution of cash and noncash income and are repeated at each interviewing wave. The survey uses a 4-month recall period, with approximately the same number of interviews being conducted in each month of the 4-month period for each wave. Interviews are conducted by personal visit and by decentralized telephone.

The survey has been designed to also provide a broader context for analysis by adding questions on a variety of topics not covered in the core section. These questions are labeled "topical modules" and are assigned to particular interviewing waves of the survey. Topics covered by the modules include personal history, child care, wealth, program eligibility, child support, disability, school enrollment, taxes, and annual income.

Further information on the SIPP may be obtained from

Economics and Statistics Administration
U.S. Census Bureau
U.S. Department of Commerce
Washington, DC 20233
http://www.census.gov/hhes/www/disability/sipp.html

National Institute on Drug Abuse

The National Institute on Drug Abuse of the U.S. Department of Health and Human Services is the primary supporter of the long-term study entitled "Monitoring the Future: A Continuing Study of the Lifestyles and Values of Youth," conducted by the University of Michigan Institute for Social Research. One component of the study deals with student drug abuse. Results of the national sample survey have been published annually since 1975. With the exception of 1975, when about 9,400 students participated in the survey, the annual senior samples comprise roughly 15,000 students in 133 schools. Students complete self-administered questionnaires given to them in their classrooms by University of Michigan personnel. Each year, 8th-, 10th-, and 12th-graders are surveyed (12th-graders since 1975, and 8th- and 10th-graders since 1991). The 8th- and 10th-grade surveys are anonymous, while the 12th-grade survey is confidential. The 10th-grade samples involve about 17,000 students in 140 schools each year, while the 8th-grade samples have approximately 18,000 students in 150 schools. In all, approximately 49,000 students from 402 public and private secondary schools are surveyed annually. Over the years, the response rate has varied from 77 to 87 percent.

Understandably, there is some reluctance to admit illegal activities. Also, students who are out of school on the day of the survey are nonrespondents, and the survey does not include high school dropouts. The inclusion of absentees and dropouts would tend to increase the proportion of individuals who had used drugs. A 1983 study found that the inclusion of absentees could increase some of the drug usage estimates by as much as 2.7 percentage points. (Details on that study and its methodology were published in *Drug Use Among American High School Students, College Students, and Other Young Adults*, by L.D. Johnston, P.M. O'Malley, and J.G. Bachman, available from the National Clearinghouse on Drug Abuse Information, 5600 Fishers Lane, Rockville, MD 20857.)

Further information on the Monitoring the Future drug abuse survey may be obtained from

National Institute on Drug Abuse
Division of Epidemiology and Statistical Analysis
5600 Fishers Lane
Rockville, MD 20857
http://www.monitoringthefuture.org

National Science Foundation

Survey of Federal Science and Engineering Support to Universities, Colleges, and Nonprofit Institutions

Each year, the National Science Foundation collects data on obligations to colleges and universities from federal agencies. Obligations differ from expenditures in that funds obligated during one fiscal year may be spent by the recipient in later years. Obligation amounts include direct federal support, so that amounts subcontracted to other institutions are included. Those funds received through subcontracts from prime contractors are excluded. Also excluded from the data are certain types of financial assistance, such as the U.S. Department of Education's Federal Family Education Loans and obligations to the U.S. service academies. For purposes of tabulations in this publication, university-administered federally funded research and development centers (FFRDCs) are now excluded from state totals.

The universe of academic institutions for this survey is based on the Integrated Postsecondary Education Data System, conducted by the National Center for Education Statistics (see above). Institutions without federal support are excluded and some systems are combined into single reporting units.

Further information on federal support obligations to universities, colleges, and nonprofit institutions may be obtained from

Science and Engineering Activities Program
Division of Science Resources Studies
National Science Foundation
4201 Wilson Boulevard
Arlington, VA 22230
http://www.nsf.gov/statistics/srvyfedsupport

Survey of Earned Doctorates

The Survey of Earned Doctorates has collected basic statistics from the universe of doctoral recipients in the United States each year since 1958. It has been supported by five federal agencies: the National Science Foundation, in conjunction with the U.S. Department of Education; the National Endowment for the Humanities; the U.S. Department of Agriculture; and the National Institutes of Health.

With the assistance of graduate deans, a survey form is distributed to each person completing the requirements for a doctorate. Of the 42,155 new research doctorates granted in 2004, the response rate was 91 percent. The questionnaire obtains information on sex, race/ethnicity, marital status, citizenship, disabilities, dependents, specialty field of doctorate, educational institutions attended, time spent in completion of doctorate, financial support, education debt, postgraduation plans, and educational attainment of parents.

Further information on the Survey of Earned Doctorates may be obtained from

Science and Engineering Education and Human Resources
    Program
Division of Science Resources Studies
National Science Foundation
4201 Wilson Boulevard
Arlington, VA 22230
http://www.nsf.gov/statistics/srvydoctorates
http://www.norc.uchicago.edu/issues/docdata.htm

Survey of Graduate Students and Postdoctorates in Science and Engineering

The Survey of Graduate Students and Postdoctorates in Science and Engineering, also known as the graduate student survey (GSS), is an annual survey at the academic department level of all U.S. institutions offering graduate programs in any science, engineering, or health field. It is an institution-based survey that provides data on the number and characteristics of graduate science and engineering students enrolled in approximately 600 U.S. academic institutions.

Data for the 2003 GSS were collected at the beginning of academic year 2003–04. This survey includes all branch campuses, affiliated research centers, and separately organized components—such as medical or dental schools, nursing schools, and schools of public health—from all academic institutions that offer doctor's and master's degree programs. Only those graduate students enrolled for credit in a master's or doctoral program in science or engineering in the fall of 2003 were included in the survey. M.D., D.O., D.V.M., or D.D.S. candidates, interns, and residents were counted if they were concurrently working on a master's or doctoral degree in science or engineering or were enrolled in a joint M.D./Ph.D. program.

The final 2003 survey universe consisted of 712 reporting units (schools) at 591 graduate institutions: 226 master's-granting institutions and 486 reporting units associated with 365 doctorate-granting institutions.

Further information on the Survey of Graduate Students and Postdoctorates in Science and Engineering may be obtained from

Julia Oliver
GSS Survey Manager
Division of Science Resources Statistics
National Science Foundation
4201 Wilson Boulevard, Suite 965
Arlington, VA 22230
http://www.nsf.gov/statistics/gradpostdoc

Substance Abuse and Mental Health Services Administration

National Survey on Drug Use and Health

Conducted by the federal government since 1971, the National Survey on Drug Use and Health (NSDUH) is an annual survey of the civilian, noninstitutionalized population of the United States age 12 or older. It is the primary source of information on the prevalence, patterns, and consequences of alcohol, tobacco, and illegal drug abuse. The survey collects data by administering questionnaires to a representative sample of the population (since 1999, the NSDUH interview has been carried out using computer-assisted interviewing). NSDUH collects information from residents of households, noninstitutional group quarters, and civilians living on military bases. The main results of the NSDUH present national estimates of rates of use, numbers of users, and other measures related to illicit drugs, alcohol, and tobacco products.

Prior to 2002, the survey was called the National Household Survey on Drug Abuse (NHSDA). Because of improvements to the survey in 2002, the data from 2002 through 2005 should not be compared with 2001 and earlier NHSDA data to assess changes in substance use over time. The 2005 NSDUH screened 134,055 addresses, and 68,308 completed interviews were obtained. The survey was conducted from January through December 2005. Weighted response rates were 91.3 percent for household screening and 76.2 percent for interviewing. The 2005 NSDUH is the first in a coordinated 5-year sample design providing estimates for all 50 states and the District of Columbia for the years 2005 through 2009. Because the 2005 design enables estimates to be developed by state, states may be viewed as the first level of stratification, as well as a reporting variable.

Further information on the 2005 NSDUH may be obtained from

SAMHSA, Office of Applied Studies
1 Choke Cherry Road, Room 7-1044
Rockville, MD 28057
http://www.oas.samhsa.gov/nsduh.htm

Other Organization Sources

American College Testing Program

The American College Testing (ACT) assessment is designed to measure educational development in the areas of English, mathematics, social studies, and natural sciences. The ACT assessment is taken by college-bound high school students and by all graduating seniors in Colorado and Illinois. The test results are used to predict how well students might perform in college.

Prior to the 1984–85 school year, national norms were based on a 10 percent sample of the students taking the test. Since then, national norms are based on the test scores of all

students taking the test. Beginning with 1984–85, these norms have been based on the most recent ACT scores available from students scheduled to graduate in the spring of the year. Duplicate test records are no longer used to produce national figures.

Separate ACT standard scores are computed for English, mathematics, science reasoning, and, as of October 1989, reading. ACT standard scores are reported for each subject area on a scale from 1 to 36. The four ACT standard scores have a mean (average) of 21.1 and a standard deviation of 4.8 for test-taking students nationally. A composite score is obtained by taking the simple average of the four standard scores and is an indication of a student's overall academic development across these subject areas.

It should be noted that graduating students who take the ACT assessment are not necessarily representative of graduating students nationally. Students who live in the Midwest, Rocky Mountains, Plains, and South are overrepresented among ACT-tested students as compared to graduating students nationally. These students more often attend public colleges and universities, which require the ACT assessment more often than the SAT test.

Further information on the ACT may be obtained from

The American College Testing Program
2201 North Dodge Street
P.O. Box 168
Iowa City, IA 52243
http://www.act.org/aboutact

American Council on Education

One of the American Council on Education's (ACE) programs and services is the General Educational Development Testing Service (GEDTS), which develops and distributes General Educational Development (GED) tests. A GED credential documents high school-level academic skills. ACE publishes *Who Passed the GED Tests?* This report looks not only at those who take the GED, but also at how each jurisdiction uses the GED as the basis for awarding high school credentials.

Further information on the GED may be obtained from

American Council on Education
One Dupont Circle NW
Washington, DC 20036
http://www.acenet.edu/

College Entrance Examination Board

The Admissions Testing Program of the College Board comprises a number of college admissions tests, including the Preliminary Scholastic Assessment Test (PSAT) and the Scholastic Assessment Test (SAT). High school students participate in the testing program as sophomores, juniors, or seniors—some more than once during these 3 years. If they have taken the tests more than once, only the most recent scores are tabulated. The PSAT and SAT report subscores in the areas of mathematics and verbal ability.

The SAT results are not representative of high school students or college-bound students nationally since the sample is self-selected, i.e., taken by students who need the results to apply to a particular college or university. Public colleges in many states, particularly in the Midwest, parts of the South, and the West, require ACT scores rather than SAT scores. The proportion of students taking the SAT in these states is very low and is inappropriate for comparison. In recent years, more than 1.4 million high school students have taken the SAT examination annually. The latest version of the SAT, which includes a writing component, was first administered in March 2005.

Further information on the SAT can be obtained from

College Entrance Examination Board
Educational Testing Service
Princeton, NJ 08541
http://www.collegeboard.org/

Commonfund Institute

Commonfund Institute took over management of the Higher Education Price Index (HEPI) in September 2004 from Research Associates of Washington, which originated the index in 1961. HEPI measures average changes in prices of goods and services purchased by colleges and universities through educational and general expenditures. Sponsored research and auxiliary enterprises are not priced by HEPI.

HEPI is based on the prices (or salaries) of faculty and of administrators and other professional service personnel; clerical, technical, service, and other nonprofessional personnel; and contracted services, such as data processing, communication, transportation, supplies and materials, equipment, books and periodicals, and utilities. These represent the items purchased for current operations by colleges and universities. Prices for these items are obtained from salary surveys conducted by various national higher education associations, the American Association of University Professors, the Bureau of Labor Statistics, and the National Center for Education Statistics; and from components of the Consumer Price Index (CPI) and the Producer Price Index (PPI) published by the U.S. Department of Labor, Bureau of Labor Statistics.

The quantities of these goods and services have been kept constant based on the 1971–72 buying pattern of colleges and universities. The weights assigned the various items, which represent their relative importance in the current-fund educational and general budget, are estimated national averages. Variance in spending patterns of individual institutions from these national averages reduces only slightly the applicability of HEPI to any given institutional situation. Modest differences in the weights attached to expenditure categories have little effect on overall index values. This is because HEPI is dominated by the trend in faculty salaries and similar salary trends for other personnel hired by institutions,

which minimizes the impact of price changes in other items purchased in relatively small quantities.

Further information on HEPI may be obtained from

Commonfund Institute
15 Old Danbury Road
P.O. Box 812
Wilton, CT 06897-0812
http://www.commonfund.org

Council for Aid to Education

The Council for Aid to Education, Inc. (CFAE) is a not-for-profit corporation funded by contributions from businesses. CFAE largely provides consulting and research services to corporations and information on voluntary support services to education institutions. Each year, CFAE conducts a survey of colleges and universities and private elementary and secondary schools to obtain information on the amounts, sources, and purposes of private gifts, grants, and bequests received during the academic year.

In the 2005 study, approximately 3,080 colleges and universities were invited to participate and 1,005 responded, for a response rate of 33 percent. CFAE estimates that about 85 percent of all voluntary support is reported in the survey because of the high participation of institutions receiving large amounts of funding.

Survey forms are reviewed by CFAE for internal consistency before preparing a computerized database. Institutional reports of voluntary support data from the CFAE Survey of Voluntary Support of Education are more comprehensive and detailed than the related data in the Integrated Postsecondary Education Data System (IPEDS) Finance survey conducted by NCES. The results from the Survey of Voluntary Support of Education are published in the annual *Voluntary Support of Education*, which may be purchased from CFAE.

Further information on voluntary support of education may be obtained from

Ann Kaplan
Council for Aid to Education, Inc.
215 Lexington Avenue
21st Floor
New York, NY 10016
vse@cae.org
http://www.cae.org/content/publications.htm

Council of Chief State School Officers

The Council of Chief State School Officers (CCSSO) is a nonprofit organization of the 57 public officials who head departments of public education in every state, the outlying areas, the District of Columbia, and the U.S. Department of Defense dependents schools. In 1985, the CCSSO founded the State Education Assessment Center to provide a locus of leadership to the states to improve the monitoring and assessment of education. This center has since combined with two other CCSSO centers to form the Division of State Services and Technical Assistance, which supports state education agencies in developing standards-based systems that enable all children to succeed. *Key State Education Policies on PK–12 Education* is one of the publications issued by the State Educators Project. Most of the data are obtained from a member questionnaire, and the remainder of the data are from federal government agencies.

Further information on CCSSO publications may be obtained from

Rolf Blank
State Education Indicators Program
Council of Chief State School Officers
One Massachusetts Avenue NW
7th Floor
Washington, DC 20001
http://www.ccsso.org

Education Commission of the States

The Education Commission of the States (ECS) Clearinghouse collects information on laws and standards in the field of education and reports them periodically in *Clearinghouse Notes*. ECS collects information about administrators, principals, and teachers. It also examines policy areas, such as assessment and testing, collective bargaining, early childhood issues, quality education, and school schedules. The information is collected by reading state newsletters, tracking state legislation, and surveying state education agencies. Data are verified by the individual states when necessary. Even though ECS monitors state activity on a continuous basis, it updates the reports only when there is significant change.

Further information on *Clearinghouse Notes* is available from

Kathy Christie
Education Commission of the States
700 Broadway, #1200
Denver, CO 80203-3460
kchristie@ecs.org
http://www.ecs.org

Graduate Record Examinations Board

Graduate Record Examinations (GRE) tests are taken by individuals applying to graduate or professional school. GRE offers two types of tests, the General Test and Subject Tests. The General Test, which is mainly offered on computer, measures verbal, quantitative, and analytical writing skills. The writing section consists of two analytical writing tasks and replaced the analytical reasoning section on the general GRE after December 31, 2002. The Subject Tests measure achievement in subject areas that include biochemistry, cell and molecular biology, biology, chemistry, computer science, literature in English, mathematics, physics, and psychology. Each graduate institution or division of the institution determines which GRE tests are required for admission.

Individuals may take GRE tests more than once. Score reports only reflect scores earned within the past 5-year period.

Further information on the GRE may be obtained from

Graduate Record Examinations Board
Educational Testing Service
Princeton, NJ 08541
http://www.gre.org

Institute of International Education

Each year, the Institute of International Education (IIE) conducts a survey of the number of foreign students studying in American colleges and universities and reports these data in the publication *Open Doors*. All of the regionally accredited institutions in NCES's Integrated Postsecondary Education Data System (IPEDS) are surveyed by IIE. The foreign student enrollment data presented in the *Digest* are drawn from IIE surveys, which ask institutions for information on enrollment of foreign students, as well as student characteristics, such as country of origin. For the 2004–05 survey, approximately 70.5 percent of the 2,042 institutions surveyed reported data.

Additional information can be obtained from the publication *Open Doors* or by contacting

Sharon Witherell
Institute of International Education–Public Affairs
809 United Nations Plaza
New York, NY 10017-3580
sharonwitherell@iie.org
http://opendoors.iienetwork.org

International Association for the Evaluation of Educational Achievement

The International Association for the Evaluation of Educational Achievement, known as the IEA, is composed of governmental research centers and national research institutions around the world whose aim is to investigate education problems common among countries. Since its inception in 1958, the IEA has conducted more than 23 research studies of cross-national achievement. The regular cycle of studies encompasses learning in basic school subjects. Examples are the Trends in Mathematics and Science Study (TIMSS) and the Progress in International Reading Literacy Study (PIRLS). IEA projects also include studies of particular interest to IEA members, such as the TIMSS-Repeat Video Study of Classroom Practices, the Civic Education Study (see below), and studies on information technology in education and preprimary education.

Civic Education Study

In 1994, the IEA General Assembly, composed of the research institutes participating in IEA projects, decided to undertake a two-phase study of civic knowledge called the Civic Education Study (CivEd). Phase I of CivEd, begun in 1996, was designed to collect extensive documentary evidence and expert opinion describing the circumstances, content, and process of civic education in 24 countries. Phase II, the assessment phase of the study, conducted in 1999, was designed to assess the civic knowledge of 14-year-old students across 28 countries. The assessment items in CivEd were designed to measure knowledge and understanding of key principles that are universal across democracies. Another key component of the Phase II study focuses on measuring the attitudes of students toward civic issues. Although the study was designed as an international comparison, the data collected allow individual countries to conduct in-depth, national-level comparisons and analyses.

Further information on the IEA Civic Education Study may be obtained from

Laurence Ogle
Early Childhood, International, and Crosscutting Studies
    Division
International Activities Program
National Center for Education Statistics
1990 K Street NW
Washington, DC 20006
laurence.ogle@ed.gov
http://www.nces.ed.gov/surveys/cived

Trends in International Mathematics and Science Study

The Trends in International Mathematics and Science Study (TIMSS, formerly known as the Third International Mathematics and Science Study) provides reliable and timely data on the mathematics and science achievement of U.S. students compared to that of students in other countries. TIMSS data has been collected in 1995, 1999, and 2003. TIMSS collects information through mathematics and science achievement tests and questionnaires. The questionnaires request information to help provide a context for the performance scores, focusing on such topics as students' attitudes and beliefs about learning, students' habits and homework, and their lives both in and outside of school; teachers' attitudes and beliefs about teaching and learning, teaching assignments, class size and organization, instructional practices, and participation in professional development activities; and principals' viewpoints on policy and budget responsibilities, curriculum and instruction issues, and student behavior, as well as descriptions of the organization of schools and courses. The assessments and questionnaires are designed to specifications in a guiding framework. The TIMSS framework describes the mathematics and science content to be assessed by providing grade-specific

objectives, an overview of the assessment design, and guidelines for item development.

Each participating country, like the United States, is required to draw random samples of schools. In the United States, a national probability sample drawn for each study has resulted in over 500 schools and approximately 33,000 students participating in 1995, 221 schools and 9,000 students participating in 1999, and 480 schools and almost 19,000 students participating in 2003. This sample design ensures the appropriate number of schools and students are participating to provide a representative sample of the students in a specific grade in the United States as a whole.

The 2003 U.S. fourth-grade sample achieved an initial school response rate of 70 percent (weighted), with a school response rate of 82 percent after replacement schools were added. From the schools that agreed to participate, students were sampled in intact classes. A total of 10,795 fourth-grade students were sampled for the assessment, and 9,829 participated, for a 95 percent student response rate. The resulting fourth-grade overall response rate, with replacements included, was 78 percent. The U.S. eighth-grade sample achieved an initial school response rate of 71 percent, with a school response rate of 78 percent after replacement schools were added. A total of 9,891 students were sampled for the eighth-grade assessment, and 8,912 completed the assessment, for a 94 percent student response rate. The resulting eighth-grade overall response rate, with replacements included, was 73 percent.

Further information on the study may be obtained from

Patrick Gonzales
Early Childhood, International, and Crosscutting Studies
    Division
International Activities Program
National Center for Education Statistics
1990 K Street NW
Washington, DC 20006
patrick.gonzales@ed.gov
http://nces.ed.gov/timss/index.asp

National Association of College and University Business Officers

The National Association of College and University Business Officers (NACUBO) is a nonprofit professional organization representing chief administrative and financial officers at more than 2,500 colleges and universities across the country. Over two-thirds of all institutions of higher learning in the United States are members of NACUBO. Each year, TIAA-CREF Trust Company, a pension system for educators and a manager of college endowments, conducts an in-depth study of college and university endowments for NACUBO, through its subsidiary, the Trust Company. Endowment assets for 2005 NACUBO Endowment Study participants are for the fiscal year ending June 30, 2005.

Endowments include stocks, bonds, cash, and real estate that colleges and universities receive as gifts. Colleges or universities receiving endowments may not spend the endowment principal, only investment income derived from the principal. Quasi-endowments (year-end surplus assets that institutions choose to treat as permanent capital) may also be included in an investment pool's endowment composition. Also, because donors frequently stipulate that their gifts support specific programs at colleges and universities, the overall size of the endowment can be misleading in terms of available income to support the education of undergraduate students. For example, the income from an endowment gift to a medical school or law school may only be spent on those schools. In such cases, the income would not be available to support undergraduate education. Thus, at some research universities with extensive graduate and professional schools, as little as one-third of the institution's endowment may actually be available to generate income to support undergraduate programs and students.

The 2005 study was administered entirely in a web-based format; there were 746 respondents.

Further information on the 2005 NACUBO Endowment Study may be obtained from

National Association of College and University Business Officers
2501 M Street NW, Suite 400
Washington, DC 20037
http://www.nacubo.org

National Association of State Directors of Teacher Education and Certification

The NASDTEC Manual on the Preparation & Certification of Educational Personnel

The National Association of State Directors of Teacher Education and Certification (NASDTEC) was organized in 1928 to represent professional standards boards and commissions and state departments of education that are responsible for the preparation, licensure, and discipline of educational personnel. Currently, NASDTEC's membership includes all 50 states, the District of Columbia, the U.S. Department of Defense Education Activity, U.S. jurisdictions, and Canadian provinces and territories.

The *NASDTEC Manual* was first printed in 1984 and is the most comprehensive printed source of state-by-state information pertaining to the certification requirements and preparation of teachers and other school personnel in the United States and Canada.

Further information on the *NASDTEC Manual* may be obtained from

Roy Einreinhofer, Executive Director
NASDTEC
1225 Providence Rd., PMB #116
Whitinsville, MA 01588
rje@nasdtec.com
http://www.nasdtec.org/about.tpl

National Association of State Student Grant and Aid Programs

The National Association of State Student Grant and Aid Programs (NASSGAP) is an association of states with general programs of scholarship or grant assistance for undergraduate study. Prior to 1995–96, NASSGAP was known as the National Association of State Scholarship and Grant Programs. Executive officers responsible for grant program administration represent each state in the association. The *36th Annual Survey Report: 2004–05 Academic Year* was produced by the Illinois Student Assistance Commission. This survey looks at state-funded expenditures for postsecondary student financial aid and contains data for all 50 states, the District of Columbia, and Puerto Rico.

Further information on the *36th Annual Survey Report: 2004–05 Academic Year* may be obtained from

Michael Solomon
Manager, Policy Analysis
Illinois Student Assistance Commission
msolomon@isac.org
nassgap@nassgap.org
http://www.nassgap.org/viewrepository.aspx?categoryID=3

National Catholic Educational Association

The National Catholic Educational Association (NCEA) has been providing leadership and service to Catholic education since 1904. NCEA began to publish *The United States Catholic Elementary and Secondary Schools: Annual Statistical Report on Schools, Enrollment and Staffing* in 1970 because of the lack of educational data on the private sector. The report is based on data gathered by each of the 176 archdiocesan and diocesan offices of education in the United States. These data enable NCEA to present information on school enrollment and staffing patterns for prekindergarten through grade 12. The first part of the report presents data concerning the context of American education, while the following segment focuses on statistical data of Catholic schools. Statistics include enrollment by grade level, ethnicity, and religious affiliation.

Further information on *The United States Catholic Elementary and Secondary Schools: Annual Statistical Report on Schools, Enrollment, and Staffing* may be obtained from

Sister Dale McDonald
National Catholic Educational Association
1077 30th Street NW, Suite 100
Washington, DC 20007-6232
mcdonald@ncea.org
http://www.ncea.org

National Education Association

Estimates of School Statistics

The National Education Association (NEA) produces *Estimates of School Statistics* annually. This report provides projections of public school enrollment, employment and personnel compensation, and finances, as reported by individual state departments of education. The state-level data in *Estimates of School Statistics* allow broad assessments of trends in the above areas. These data should be looked at with the understanding that the state-level data do not necessarily reflect the varying conditions within a state on education issues.

Data in this report are provided by state and District of Columbia departments of education and by other, mostly governmental, sources. Surveys are sent to the departments of education requesting estimated data for the current year and revisions to 4 years of historical data, as necessary. Twice a year, NEA submits current-year estimates on more than 35 education statistics to state departments of education for verification or revision. The estimates are generated using regression analyses and are used in the *Estimates* report only if the states do not provide current data.

Further information on Estimates of School Statistics may be obtained from

Editor—Research
1201 16th Street NW
Washington, DC 20036
http://www.nea.org/aboutnea/contact.html
http://www.nea.org /index.html

Status of the American Public School Teacher

The Status of the American Public School Teacher Survey is conducted every 5 years by the National Education Association (NEA). The survey was designed by the NEA Research Division and was initially administered in 1956. The intent of the survey is to solicit information covering various aspects of public school teachers' professional, family, and civic lives.

In the 2000–01 survey, 1,467 public school teachers responded and the response rate was 67.4 percent.

Possible sources of nonsampling errors are nonresponses, misinterpretation, and—when comparing data over years—changes in the sampling method and instrument. Misinterpretation of the survey items should be minimal, as the sample responding is not from the general population, but one knowledgeable about the area of concern. The sampling procedure changed after 1956 and some wording of items has changed over different administrations of the survey.

Since sampling is used, sampling variability is inherent in the data. An approximation to the maximum standard error for estimating the population percentages is 1.4 percent. Approximations for significance for other comparisons appear in appendix table A-6. To estimate the 95 percent confidence interval for population percentages, the maximum standard error of 1.4 percent is multiplied by 2 (1.4 x 2). The resulting percentage (2.8) is added and subtracted from the population estimate to establish upper and lower bounds for the confidence interval. For example, if a sample percentage is 60 percent, there is a 95 percent chance that the population percentage lies between 57.2 percent and 62.8 percent (60 percent ± 2.8 percent).

Further information on Status of the American Public School Teacher Survey may be obtained from

Brooke E. Whiting
National Education Association—Research
1201 16th Street NW
Washington, DC 20036
http://www.nea.org/aboutnea/contact.html
http://www.nea.org /index.html

Organization for Economic Cooperation and Development

Education at a Glance

The Organization for Economic Cooperation and Development (OECD) publishes analyses of national policies and survey data in education, training, and economics in about 30 countries. The countries surveyed are Australia, Austria, Belgium, Canada, the Czech Republic, Denmark, Finland, France, Germany, Greece, Hungary, Iceland, Ireland, Italy, Japan, Korea, Luxembourg, Mexico, the Netherlands, New Zealand, Norway, Poland, Portugal, the Slovak Republic, Spain, Sweden, Switzerland, Turkey, the United Kingdom, and the United States. In addition to these OECD countries, a number of other countries are participating in the related World Education Indicators (WEI), a joint project sponsored by the OECD and UNESCO. These countries include Argentina, Brazil, Chile, China, Egypt, India, Indonesia, Jamaica, Jordan, Malaysia, Paraguay, Peru, the Philippines, the Russian Federation, Thailand, Tunisia, Uruguay, and Zimbabwe.

To highlight current education issues and create a set of comparative education indicators that represent key features of education systems, OECD initiated the International Education Indicators Project (INES) and charged the Centre for Educational Research and Innovation (CERI) with developing the cross-national indicators for it. The development of these indicators involved representatives of the OECD countries and the OECD Secretariat. Improvements in data quality and comparability among OECD countries have resulted from the country-to-country interaction sponsored through the INES and WEI projects. The most recent publication in this series is *Education at a Glance, OECD Indicators, 2006*.

Documentation for the enrollment, degree, staff, and finance data appearing in *Education at a Glance, OECD Indicators* has been published in the *OECD Handbook for Internationally Comparative Education Statistics: Concepts, Standards, Definitions and Classifications*. This publication provides countries with specific guidance on how to prepare information for OECD education surveys. Chapter 6 of the *OECD Handbook for Internationally Comparative Education Statistics* contains a discussion of data quality issues.

Further information on INES may be obtained from

Andreas Schleicher
Indicators & Analysis Division
OECD Directorate for Education
2, rue Andre–Pascal
75775 Paris CEDEX 16
France
andreas.schleicher@oecd.org
http://www.oecd.org

Phi Delta Kappa/Gallup Poll

Public Attitudes Toward the Public Schools Survey

Each year, the Gallup Poll conducts the Public Attitudes Toward the Public Schools Survey, funded by the Phi Delta Kappa Educational Foundation. The survey includes interviews with adults representing the civilian noninstitutional population, age 18 and older.

Gallup uses an unclustered, directory-assisted, random-digit-dial telephone sample, based on a proportionate stratified sampling design. In 2000, the final sample was weighted so that the distribution corresponded with the U.S. Census Bureau's Current Population Survey (CPS) estimates for the adult population living in households with telephones in the continental United States. The sample used in the 38th (2006) annual survey was made up of a total of 1,007 adults age 18 and older. Field work for the survey was conducted between June 11 and July 5, 2006.

The survey is a sample survey and is subject to sampling error. The size of the error depends largely on the number of respondents providing data. Appendix table A-4 shows the approximate sampling errors associated with different percentages and sample sizes for the survey. Appendix table A-5 provides approximate sampling errors for comparisons of two sample percentages.

For example, an estimated percentage of about 10 percent based on the responses of 1,000 sample members maintains an approximate sampling error of 2 percent at the 95 percent confidence level. The sampling error for the difference in two percentages (50 percent versus 41 percent) based on two samples of 750 members and 400 members, respectively, is about 8 percent at the 95 percent confidence level.

Further information on the Public Attitudes Toward the Public Schools Survey may be obtained from

Delaine McCullough
Phi Delta Kappa
P.O. Box 789
Bloomington, IN 47402-0789
dmccullough@pdkintl.org
http://www.pdkintl.org

Program for International Student Assessment

The Program for International Student Assessment (PISA) is a system of international assessments that focus on 15-year-olds' capabilities in reading literacy, mathematics literacy, and science literacy. PISA also includes measures of general, or cross-curricular, competencies such as learning strategies. PISA emphasizes functional skills that students have acquired as they near the end of mandatory schooling. PISA is organized by the Organization for Economic Cooperation and Development (OECD), an intergovernmental organization of industrialized countries, and was administered for the first time in 2000, when 32 countries participated. In 2003, 42 countries took part in the assessment.

PISA is a 2-hour-long paper-and-pencil exam. Assessment items include a combination of multiple-choice and open-ended questions, which require students to come up with their own response. PISA scores are reported on a scale with a mean score of 500 and a standard deviation of 100.

PISA is implemented on a 3-year cycle that began in 2000. Each PISA assessment cycle focuses on one subject in particular, although all three subjects are assessed every 3 years. In the first cycle, PISA 2000, reading literacy was the major focus, occupying roughly two-thirds of assessment time. For 2003, PISA focused on mathematics literacy as well as the ability of students to solve problems in real-life settings. In 2006, PISA focused on science literacy.

The intent of PISA reporting is to provide an overall description of performance in reading literacy, mathematics literacy, and science literacy every 3 years, and to provide a more detailed look at each domain in the years when it is the major focus. These cycles will allow countries to compare changes in trends for each of the three subject areas over time.

To implement PISA, each of the participating countries selects a nationally representative sample of 15-year-olds, regardless of grade level. In the United States, nearly 5,500 students from public and nonpublic schools took the PISA 2003 assessment.

In each country, the assessment is translated into the primary language of instruction; in the United States, all materials are written in English.

Further information on PISA may be obtained from

Holly Xie
Early Childhood, International, and Crosscutting Studies Division
International Activities Program
National Center for Education Statistics
1990 K Street NW
Washington, DC 20006
IAP@ed.gov
http://nces.ed.gov/surveys/pisa

SRI International

The National Longitudinal Transition Study-2

The National Longitudinal Transition Study-2 (NLTS-2) is a follow-up of the original National Longitudinal Transition Study conducted from 1985 through 1993. NLTS-2 began in 2001 with a sample of special education students who were ages 13 through 16 and in at least 7th grade on December 1, 2000. The study will continue for 10 years and is designed to provide a national picture of these youths' experiences and achievements as they transition into adulthood. Data will be collected from parents, youth, and schools by survey, telephone interviews, student assessments, and transcripts.

NLTS-2 is designed to align with the original NLTS by including many of the same questions and data items, thus allowing comparisons between the NLTS and NLTS-2 youths' experiences. NLTS-2 also includes items that have been collected in other national databases to permit comparisons between NLTS-2 youth and the general youth population.

Further information on NLTS-2 may be obtained from

Lynn Newman
SRI International
333 Ravenswood Ave.
Menlo Park, CA 94025
lynn.newman@sri.com
http://www.sri.com

United Nations Educational, Scientific, and Cultural Organization

The United Nations Educational, Scientific, and Cultural Organization (UNESCO) conducts annual surveys of education statistics of its member countries. Data from official surveys are supplemented by information obtained by UNESCO through other publications and sources. Each year, more than 200 countries reply to the UNESCO surveys. In some cases, estimates are made by UNESCO for particular items, such as world and continent totals. While great efforts are made to make them as comparable as possible, the data still reflect the vast differences among the countries of the world in the structure of education. While there is some agreement about the reporting of primary and secondary data, tertiary-level data (i.e., postsecondary education data) present numerous substantive problems. Some countries report only university enrollment, while other countries report all postsecondary enrollment, including enrollment in vocational and technical schools and correspondence programs. A very high proportion of some countries' tertiary-level students attend institutions in other countries. The member countries that provide data to UNESCO are responsible for their validity. Thus, data for particular countries are subject to nonsampling error and perhaps sampling error as well. Users should examine footnotes carefully to recognize some of the data limitations.

Further information on the *Statistical Yearbook* and the *Global Education Digest* may be obtained from

UNESCO Institute for Statistics
Publications
C.P. 6128
Succursale Centre-Ville
Montreal, Quebec, H3C 3J7
Canada
http://www.uis.unesco.org

Table A-1. Respondent counts for selected High School and Beyond surveys: 1982, 1984, and 1986

Classification variable and subgroup	Follow-up survey of 1980 sophomores in 1982	Follow-up survey of 1980 seniors in 1982	Follow-up survey of 1980 sophomores in 1984	Follow-up survey of 1980 seniors in 1984	Follow-up survey of 1980 sophomores in 1986	Follow-up survey of 1980 seniors in 1986
Total respondents (unweighted)	**25,830**	**11,227**	**11,463**	**10,925**	**11,248**	**10,536**
Sex						
Male	12,717	5,213	5,514	5,058	5,391	4,832
Female	13,113	6,014	5,949	5,867	5,857	5,704
Race/ethnicity						
White, non-Hispanic	17,295	5,180	7,285	5,057	7,194	5,246
Black, non-Hispanic	3,338	2,724	1,651	2,625	1,585	2,726
Hispanic	4,439	2,749	1,795	2,654	1,745	1,950
Asian or Pacific Islander	413	367	425	355	413	356
American Indian or Alaska Native	248	191	253	185	246	200
Other or unclassified	97	16	54	49	65	58
Socioeconomic status composite (SES)[1]						
Low	6,752	3,940	2,831	3,857	2,751	3,668
Low-middle	6,234	2,390	2,624	2,314	2,559	2,289
High-middle	6,134	2,168	2,849	2,107	2,817	1,995
High	6,341	1,988	3,086	1,936	3,044	1,900
Unclassified	369	741	73	711	77	684
Father's highest level of education						
Less than high school	5,179	—	—	—	—	—
High school completion[2]	11,961	—	—	—	—	—
College graduate[3]	5,169	—	—	—	—	—
Don't know/missing	3,521	—	—	—	—	—
High school program (self-reported)						
Academic	10,152	4,145	6,547	4,007	—	3,899
General	8,789	3,829	3,468	3,764	—	3,602
Vocational	6,664	2,660	3,611	2,581	—	2,481
Unclassified	225	593	56	573	—	554
High school type						
Public	—	9,969	8,647	9,727	—	9,385
Catholic	—	964	2,479	911	—	876
Other private	—	294	337	287	—	275
Postsecondary education status[4]						
Full-time	—	—	4,466	—	—	—
Part-time	—	—	3,275	—	—	—
Never enrolled	—	—	3,678	—	—	—
Missing/unclassified	—	—	44	—	—	—
October 1980 postsecondary education attendance status						
Part-time 2-year public institution	—	—	—	—	—	352
Part-time 4-year public institution	—	—	—	—	—	152
Full-time 2-year public institution	—	—	—	—	—	1,312
Full-time 4-year public institution	—	—	—	—	—	1,986
Full-time 4-year private institution	—	—	—	—	—	1,015
Not a student	—	—	—	—	—	4,523
Other and missing	—	—	—	—	—	1,196
Postsecondary education plans						
No plans	—	—	—	—	—	1,623
Attend vocational/technical school	—	—	—	—	—	1,835
Attend college less than 4 years	—	—	—	—	—	1,528
Earn bachelor's degree	—	—	—	—	—	2,631
Earn advanced degree	—	—	—	—	—	2,265
Missing	—	—	—	—	—	654
Participation in high school extracurricular activities[5]						
Never participated	—	—	—	—	—	1,024
Participated as a member	—	—	—	—	—	4,104
Participated as a leader	—	—	—	—	—	4,457

—Not available.

[1]The SES index is a composite of five equally weighted measures: father's education, mother's education, family income, father's occupation, and presence of certain items in the respondent's household.

[2]Includes attendance at a vocational, trade, or business school, or 2-year college; or attendance at a 4-year college resulting in less than a bachelor's degree.

[3]Includes those with a bachelor's or higher level degree.

[4]Postsecondary education status was determined by students' enrollment in academic or vocational study during the four semesters—fall 1982, spring 1983, fall 1983, and spring 1984—following their scheduled high school graduation. Students who enrolled in full-time study in each of the four semesters were classified as full time. Students who were enrolled in part-time study in any of the four semesters and those who were enrolled in full-time study in fewer than four semesters were classified as part time. Students who had neither enrolled on a full-time nor part-time basis in each of the four semesters were classified as never enrolled.

[5]Responses to questions concerning participation in each of 15 different extracurricular activity areas (i.e., varsity sports, debate, band, subject-matter clubs, etc.) were used to classify students' overall level of participation in extracurricular activities. The difference between the sum of the three category respondent counts and the total sample size is due to missing data.

NOTE: Data from students who dropped out of school between the 10th and 12th grades were not used in analyses of sophomore samples.

SOURCE: U.S. Department of Education, National Center for Education Statistics, High School and Beyond Study of 1980 Sophomores (HS&B-So:80/82, HS&B-So:80/84, and HS&B-So:80/86); and High School and Beyond Study of 1980 Seniors (HS&B-Sr:80/82, HS&B-Sr:80/84, and HS&B-Sr:80/86).

Table A-2. Design effects (DEFF) and root design effects (DEFT) for selected High School and Beyond surveys and subsamples: 1984 and 1986

Subsample characteristic	Follow-up survey of 1980 sophomores in 1984		Follow-up survey of 1980 seniors in1984		Follow-up survey of 1980 sophomores in 1986		Follow-up survey of 1980 seniors in 1986	
Total sample	**2.40**	**(1.54)**	**2.87**	**(1.69)**	**2.19**	**(1.47)**	**2.28**	**(1.50)**
Sex								
Male	—	(†)	—	(†)	2.07	(1.43)	2.13	(1.45)
Female	—	(†)	—	(†)	2.06	(1.43)	2.26	(1.50)
Race/ethnicity								
White and other	2.06	(1.42)	2.09	(1.44)	1.92	(1.38)	1.70	(1.30)
Black	2.22	(1.47)	2.26	(1.50)	2.19	(1.47)	2.40	(1.54)
Hispanic	3.15	(1.73)	3.72	(1.92)	3.11	(1.76)	4.06	(2.01)
Socioeconomic status composite (SES)[1]								
Low	1.91	(1.37)	2.28	(1.50)	1.83	(1.35)	2.31	(1.51)
Middle	1.95	(1.39)	1.81	(1.34)	2.06	(1.42)	2.02	(1.42)
High	2.05	(1.42)	1.93	(1.38)	1.92	(1.38)	1.71	(1.30)

—Not available.

†Not applicable.

[1]The SES index is a composite of five equally weighted measures: father's education, mother's education, family income, father's occupation, and presence of certain items in the respondent's household.

NOTE: The average design effect for the 1980 sophomore cohort first follow-up (1982) survey is 3.6 (1.89) and the average design effect for the 1980 senior first follow-up (1982) survey is 2.6 (1.62). Standard errors appear in parentheses.

SOURCE: U.S. Department of Education, National Center for Education Statistics, High School and Beyond Study of 1980 Sophomores (HS&B-So:80/84 and HS&B-So:80/86); and High School and Beyond Study of 1980 Seniors (HS&B-Sr:80/84 and HS&B-Sr:80/86).

Table A-3. Respondent counts of full-time workers from the Recent College Graduates survey: Selected years, 1976 to 1991

Field of study	Number employed full time				
	1974–75 graduates in May 1976	1979–80 graduates in May 1981	1983–84 graduates in April 1985	1985–86 graduates in April 1987	1989–90 graduates in April 1991
Total respondents (unweighted)	**2,464**	**5,521**	**6,799**	**15,024**	**9,451**
Professions	1,840	4,260	3,730	8,987	3,825
Arts and sciences	514	811	2,586	4,869	2,256
Other	110	450	483	1,168	3,370
Newly qualified to teach	1,337	2,469	1,109	2,546	1,966
Not newly qualified to teach	1,127	3,052	5,690	12,478	7,485
Professions	601	1,841	2,809	7,043	2,549
Engineering	80	270	601	915	411
Business and management	290	749	1,532	2,407	1,598
Health	72	252	387	3,106	281
Education[1]	141	464	146	521	188
Public affairs and services	18	106	143	94	71
Arts and sciences	433	770	2,430	4,369	2,006
Biological sciences	83	116	243	380	179
Physical sciences and mathematics	40	103	1,062	1,782	466
Psychology	64	105	189	366	316
Social sciences	107	252	449	780	813
Humanities	139	194	487	1,061	232
Other	93	441	451	1,066	2,930
Communications	7	73	240	392	217
Miscellaneous	86	368	211	674	2,713

[1]Includes those who had not finished all requirements for teaching certification or were previously qualified to teach.

SOURCE: U.S. Department of Education, National Center for Education Statistics, Recent College Graduates (RCG) surveys, 1976, 1981, 1985, 1987, and 1991.

Table A-4. Sampling errors (95 percent confidence level) for percentages estimated from the Gallup Poll: 1992, 1993, and 1996 through 2006

Percent	Size of sample						
	1,500	1,000	750	600	400	200	100
Recommended allowance for sampling error of a percentage							
Percentages near 10 or 90	2	2	3	3	4	5	8
Percentages near 20 or 80	3	3	4	4	5	7	10
Percentages near 30 or 70	3	4	4	5	6	8	12
Percentages near 40 or 60	3	4	5	5	6	9	12
Percentages near 50	3	4	5	5	6	9	13

SOURCE: Phi Delta Kappa, *Phi Delta Kappan*, "The Annual Gallup Poll of the Public's Attitudes Toward the Public Schools," 1992, 1993, and 1996 through 2006.

Table A-5. Sampling errors (95 percent confidence level) for the difference in two percentages estimated from the Gallup Poll: 1992, 1993, and 1996 through 2006

Size of first sample	Size of second sample					
	1,500	1,000	750	600	400	200
Recommended allowance for sampling error of a difference in percentages (percentages near 80 or 20)						
1,500	4	4	5	5	6	8
1,000	4	5	5	5	6	8
750	5	5	5	6	6	8
600	5	5	6	6	7	8
400	6	6	6	7	7	9
200	8	8	8	8	9	10
Recommended allowance for sampling error of a difference in percentages (percentages near 50)						
1,500	5	5	6	6	7	10
1,000	5	6	6	7	8	10
750	6	6	7	7	8	10
600	6	7	7	7	8	10
400	7	8	8	8	9	11
200	10	10	10	10	11	13

SOURCE: Phi Delta Kappa, *Phi Delta Kappan*, "The Annual Gallup Poll of the Public's Attitudes Toward the Public Schools," 1992, 1993, and 1996 through 2006.

Table A-6. Maximum differences required for significance (90 percent confidence level) between sample subgroups from the "Status of the American Public School Teacher" survey: 2000–01

Size of first subgroup	Size of second subgroup						
	100	200	300	400	500	600	700
100	11.6	10.1	9.5	9.2	9.0	8.9	8.8
200	10.1	8.2	7.5	7.1	6.9	6.7	6.6
300	9.5	7.5	6.7	6.3	6.0	5.8	5.7
400	9.2	7.1	6.3	5.8	5.5	5.3	5.2
500	9.0	6.9	6.0	5.5	5.2	5.0	4.8
600	8.9	6.7	5.8	5.3	5.0	4.7	4.6
700	8.8	6.6	5.7	5.2	4.8	4.6	4.4

SOURCE: National Education Association, *Status of the American Public School Teacher*, 2000-01.

APPENDIX B
Definitions

Academic support This category of college expenditures includes expenditures for support services that are an integral part of the institution's primary missions of instruction, research, or public service. It also includes expenditures for libraries, galleries, audio/visual services, academic computing support, ancillary support, academic administration, personnel development, and course and curriculum development.

Achievement test An examination that measures the extent to which a person has acquired certain information or mastered certain skills, usually as a result of specific instruction.

Achievement levels, NAEP Specific achievement levels for each subject area and grade to provide a context for interesting student performance. At this time they are being used on a trial basis.

 Basic—denotes partial mastery of the knowledge and skills that are fundamental for proficient work at a given grade.

 Proficient—represents solid academic performance. Students reaching this level have demonstrated competency over challenging subject matter.

 Advanced—signifies superior performance.

Administrative support staff Includes personnel dealing with salary, benefits, supplies, and contractual fees for the office of the principal, full-time department chairpersons, and graduation expenses.

Agriculture Courses designed to improve competencies in agricultural occupations. Included is the study of agricultural production, supplies, mechanization and products, agricultural science, forestry, and related services.

ACT The ACT (formerly the American College Testing Program) assessment program measures educational development and readiness to pursue college-level coursework in English, mathematics, natural science, and social studies. Student performance on the tests does not reflect innate ability and is influenced by a student's educational preparedness.

Alternative schools Alternative schools serve students whose needs cannot be met in a regular, special education, or vocational school. They provide nontraditional education and may serve as an adjunct to a regular school. Although these schools fall outside the categories of regular, special education, and vocational education, they may provide similar services or curriculum. Some examples of alternative schools are schools for potential dropouts; residential treatment centers for substance abuse (if they provide elementary or secondary education); schools for chronic truants; and schools for students with behavioral problems.

Appropriation (federal funds) Budget authority provided through the congressional appropriation process that permits federal agencies to incur obligations and to make payments.

Appropriation (institutional revenues) An amount (other than a grant or contract) received from or made available to an institution through an act of a legislative body.

Associate's degree A degree granted for the successful completion of a sub-baccalaureate program of studies, usually requiring at least 2 years (or equivalent) of full-time college-level study. This includes degrees granted in a cooperative or work-study program.

Auxiliary enterprises This category includes those essentially self-supporting operations which exist to furnish a service to students, faculty, or staff, and which charge a fee that is directly related to, although not necessarily equal to, the cost of the service. Examples are residence halls, food services, college stores, and intercollegiate athletics.

Average daily attendance (ADA) The aggregate attendance of a school during a reporting period (normally a school year) divided by the number of days school is in session during this period. Only days on which the pupils are under the guidance and direction of teachers should be considered days in session.

Average daily membership (ADM) The aggregate membership of a school during a reporting period (normally a school year) divided by the number of days school is in session during this period. Only days on which the pupils are under the guidance and direction of teachers should be considered as days in session. The average daily membership for groups of schools having varying lengths of terms is the average of the average daily memberships obtained for the individual schools.

Bachelor's degree A degree granted for the successful completion of a baccalaureate program of studies, usually requiring at least 4 years (or equivalent) of full-time college-level study. This includes degrees granted in a cooperative or work-study program.

Books Non-periodical printed publications bound in hard or soft covers, or in loose-leaf format, of at least 49 pages, exclusive of the cover pages; juvenile nonperiodical publications of any length found in hard or soft covers.

Budget authority (BA) Authority provided by law to enter into obligations that will result in immediate or future outlays. It may be classified by the period of availability (1-year, multiple-year, no-year), by the timing of congressional action (current or permanent), or by the manner of determining the amount available (definite or indefinite).

Business Program of instruction that prepares individuals for a variety of activities in planning, organizing, directing, and controlling business office systems and procedures.

Capital outlay Funds for the acquisition of land and buildings; building construction, remodeling, and additions; the initial installation or extension of service systems and other built-in equipment; and site improvement. The category also encompasses architectural and engineering services including the development of blueprints.

Carnegie unit The number of credits a student received for a course taken every day, one period per day, for a full year; a factor used to standardize all credits indicated on transcripts across studies.

Catholic school A private school over which a Roman Catholic church group exercises some control or provides some form of subsidy. Catholic schools for the most part include those operated or supported by a parish, a group of parishes, a diocese, or a Catholic religious order.

Central cities The largest cities, with 50,000 or more inhabitants, in a Metropolitan Statistical Area (MSA). Additional cities within the metropolitan area can also be classified as "central cities" if they meet certain employment, population, and employment/residence ratio requirements.

City school See Locale codes.

Class size The membership of a class at a given date.

Classification of Instructional Programs (CIP) The CIP is a taxonomic coding scheme that contains titles and descriptions of primarily postsecondary instructional programs. It was developed to facilitate NCES's collection and reporting of postsecondary degree completions by major field of study using standard classifications that capture the majority of

reportable program activity. It was originally published in 1980 and was revised in 1985, 1990, and 2000.

Classification of Secondary School Courses (CSSC) A modification of the Classification of Instructional Programs used for classifying high school courses. The CSSC contains over 2,200 course codes that help compare the thousands of high school transcripts collected from different schools.

Classroom teacher A staff member assigned the professional activities of instructing pupils in self-contained classes or courses, or in classroom situations; usually expressed in full-time equivalents.

Cohort A group of individuals that have a statistical factor in common, for example, year of birth.

College A postsecondary school which offers general or liberal arts education, usually leading to an associate, bachelor's, master's, doctor's, or first-professional degree. Junior colleges and community colleges are included under this terminology.

Combined elementary and secondary school A school which encompasses instruction at both the elementary and the secondary levels; includes schools starting with grade 6 or below and ending with grade 9 or above.

Computer science A group of instructional programs that describes computer and information sciences, including computer programming, data processing, and information systems.

Constant dollars Dollar amounts that have been adjusted by means of price and cost indexes to eliminate inflationary factors and allow direct comparison across years.

Consumer Price Index (CPI) This price index measures the average change in the cost of a fixed market basket of goods and services purchased by consumers.

Consumption That portion of income which is spent on the purchase of goods and services rather than being saved.

Control of institutions A classification of institutions of elementary/secondary or higher education by whether the institution is operated by publicly elected or appointed officials and derives its primary support from public funds (public control) or by privately elected or appointed officials and derives its major source of funds from private sources (private control).

Credit The unit of value, awarded for the successful completion of certain courses, intended to indicate the quantity of course instruction in relation to the total requirements for a diploma, certificate, or degree. Credits are frequently expressed in terms such as "Carnegie units," "semester credit hours," and "quarter credit hours."

Current dollars Dollar amounts that have not been adjusted to compensate for inflation.

Current expenditures (elementary/secondary) The expenditures for operating local public schools, excluding capital outlay and interest on school debt. These expenditures include such items as salaries for school personnel, fixed charges, student transportation, school books and materials, and energy costs. Beginning in 1980–81, expenditures for state administration are excluded.

Current expenditures per pupil in average daily attendance Current expenditures for the regular school term divided by the average daily attendance of full-time pupils (or full-time equivalency of pupils) during the term. See also Current expenditures and Average daily attendance.

Current-fund expenditures (higher education) Money spent to meet current operating costs, including salaries, wages, utilities, student services, public services, research libraries, scholarships and fellowships, auxiliary enterprises, hospitals, and independent operations; excludes loans, capital expenditures, and investments.

Current-fund revenues (higher education) Money received during the current fiscal year from revenue which can be used to pay obligations currently due, and surpluses reappropriated for the current fiscal year.

Current Population Survey See Guide to Sources.

Degree-granting institutions Postsecondary institutions that are eligible for Title IV federal financial aid programs and grant an associate's or higher degree. For an institution to be eligible to participate in Title IV financial aid programs it must offer a program of at least 300 clock hours in length, have accreditation recognized by the U.S. Department of Education, have been in business for at least 2 years, and have signed a participation agreement with the Department.

Disabilities, children with Those children evaluated as having any of the following impairments and needing special education and related services because of these impairments. (These definitions apply specifically to data from the U.S. Office of Special Education and Rehabilitative Services presented in this publication.)

Deafness Having a hearing impairment which is so severe that the student is impaired in processing linguistic information through hearing (with or without amplification) and which adversely affects educational performance.

Deaf-blindness Having concomitant hearing and visual impairments which cause such severe communication and other developmental and educational problems that the student cannot be accommodated in special education programs solely for deaf or blind students.

Hearing impairment Having a hearing impairment, whether permanent or fluctuating, which adversely affects the student's educational performance, but which is not included under the definition of "deaf" in this section.

Mental retardation Having significantly subaverage general intellectual functioning, existing concurrently with defects in adaptive behavior and manifested during the developmental period, which adversely affects the child's educational performance.

Multiple disabilities Having concomitant impairments (such as mentally retarded-blind, mentally retarded-orthopedically impaired, etc.), the combination of which causes such severe educational problems that the student cannot be accommodated in special education programs solely for one of the impairments. Term does not include deaf-blind students.

Orthopedic impairment Having a severe orthopedic impairment which adversely affects a student's educational performance. The term includes impairment resulting from congenital anomaly, disease, or other causes.

Other health impairment Having limited strength, vitality, or alertness due to chronic or acute health problems, such as a heart condition, tuberculosis, rheumatic fever, nephritis, asthma, sickle cell anemia, hemophilia, epilepsy, lead poisoning, leukemia, or diabetes which adversely affects the student's educational performance.

Serious emotional disturbance Exhibiting one or more of the following characteristics over a long period of time, to a marked degree, and adversely affecting educational performance: an inability to learn which cannot be explained by intellectual, sensory, or health factors; an inability to build or maintain satisfactory interpersonal relationships with peers and teachers; inappropriate types of behavior or feelings under normal circumstances; a general pervasive mood of unhappiness or depression; or a tendency to develop physical symptoms or fears associated with personal or school problems. This term does not include children who are socially maladjusted, unless they also display one or more of the listed characteristics.

Specific learning disability Having a disorder in one or more of the basic psychological processes involved in understanding or in using spoken or written language, which may manifest itself in an imperfect ability to listen, think, speak, read, write, spell, or do mathematical calculations. The term includes such conditions as perceptual disabilities, brain injury, minimal brain dysfunction, dyslexia, and developmental aphasia. The term does not include children who have learning problems which are primarily the result of visual, hearing, or environmental, cultural, or economic disadvantage.

Speech/language impairment Having a communication disorder, such as stuttering, impaired articulation, language impairment, or voice impairment, which adversely affects the student's educational performance.

Visual impairment Having a visual impairment which, even with correction, adversely affects the student's educational performance. The term includes partially seeing and blind children.

Disposable personal income Current income received by persons less their contributions for social insurance, personal tax, and nontax payments. It is the income available to persons for spending and saving. Nontax payments include passport fees, fines and penalties, donations, and tuitions and fees paid to schools and hospitals operated mainly by the government. See also Personal income.

Doctor's degree An earned degree carrying the title of Doctor. The Doctor of Philosophy degree (Ph.D.) is the highest academic degree and requires mastery within a field of knowledge and demonstrated ability to perform scholarly research. Other doctorates are awarded for fulfilling specialized requirements in professional fields, such as education (Ed.D.), musical arts (D.M.A.), business administration (D.B.A.), and engineering (D.Eng. or D.E.S.). Many doctor's degrees in academic and professional fields require an earned master's degree as a prerequisite. First-professional degrees, such as M.D. and D.D.S., are not included under this heading.

Educational and general expenditures The sum of current funds expenditures on instruction, research, public service, academic support, student services, institutional support, operation and maintenance of plant, and awards from restricted and unrestricted funds.

Educational attainment The highest grade of regular school attended and completed.

Elementary education/programs Learning experiences concerned with the knowledge, skills, appreciations, attitudes, and behavioral characteristics which are considered to be needed by all pupils in terms of their awareness of life within our culture and the world of work, and which normally may be achieved during the elementary school years (usually kindergarten through grade 8 or kindergarten through grade 6), as defined by applicable state laws and regulations.

Elementary school A school classified as elementary by state and local practice and composed of any span of grades not above grade 8. A preschool or kindergarten school is included under this heading only if it is an integral part of an elementary school or a regularly established school system.

Elementary/secondary school As reported in this publication, includes only regular schools (i.e., schools that are part of state and local school systems, and also most not-for-profit private elementary/secondary schools, both religiously affiliated and nonsectarian). Schools not reported include sub-

collegiate departments of institutions of higher education, residential schools for exceptional children, federal schools for American Indians, and federal schools on military posts and other federal installations.

Employment Includes civilian, noninstitutional persons who: (1) worked during any part of the survey week as paid employees; worked in their own business, profession, or farm; or worked 15 hours or more as unpaid workers in a family-owned enterprise; or (2) were not working but had jobs or businesses from which they were temporarily absent due to illness, bad weather, vacation, labor-management dispute, or personal reasons whether or not they were seeking another job.

Endowment A trust fund set aside to provide a perpetual source of revenue from the proceeds of the endowment investments. Endowment funds are often created by donations from benefactors of an institution, who may designate the use of the endowment revenue. Normally, institutions or their representatives manage the investments, but they are not permitted to spend the endowment fund itself, only the proceeds from the investments. Typical uses of endowments would be an endowed chair for a particular department or for a scholarship fund. Endowment totals tabulated in this book also include funds functioning as endowments, such as funds left over from the previous year and placed with the endowment investments by the institution. These funds may be withdrawn by the institution and spent as current funds at any time. Endowments are evaluated by two different measures, book value and market value. Book value is the purchase price of the endowment investment. Market value is the current worth of the endowment investment. Thus, the book value of a stock held in an endowment fund would be the purchase price of the stock. The market value of the stock would be its selling price as of a given day.

Engineering Instructional programs that describe the mathematical and natural science knowledge gained by study, experience, and practice and applied with judgment to develop ways to utilize the materials and forces of nature economically for the benefit of mankind. Include programs that prepare individuals to support and assist engineers and similar professionals.

English A group of instructional programs that describes the English language arts, including composition, creative writing, and the study of literature.

Enrollment The total number of students registered in a given school unit at a given time, generally in the fall of a year.

Expenditures Charges incurred, whether paid or unpaid, which are presumed to benefit the current fiscal year. For elementary/secondary schools, these include all charges for current outlays plus capital outlays and interest on school debt. For institutions of higher education, these include current outlays plus capital outlays. For government, these include charges net of recoveries and other correcting transactions other than for retirement of debt, investment in securities, extension of credit, or as agency transactions. Government expenditures include only external transactions, such as the provision of perquisites or other payments in kind. Aggregates for groups of governments exclude intergovernmental transactions among the governments.

Expenditures per pupil Charges incurred for a particular period of time divided by a student unit of measure, such as average daily attendance or average daily membership.

Extracurricular activities Activities that are not part of the required curriculum and that take place outside of the regular course of study. As used here, they include both school-sponsored (e.g., varsity athletics, drama, and debate clubs) and community-sponsored (e.g., hobby clubs and youth organizations like the Junior Chamber of Commerce or Boy Scouts) activities.

Family A group of two persons or more (one of whom is the householder) related by birth, marriage, or adoption and residing together. All such persons (including related subfamily members) are considered as members of one family.

Federal funds Amounts collected and used by the federal government for the general purposes of the government. There are four types of federal fund accounts: the general fund, special funds, public enterprise funds, and intragovernmental funds. The major federal fund is the general fund, which is derived from general taxes and borrowing. Federal funds also include certain earmarked collections, such as those generated by and used to finance a continuing cycle of business-type operations.

Federal sources Includes federal appropriations, grants, and contracts, and federally-funded research and development centers (FFRDCs). Federally subsidized student loans and Pell Grants are not included.

First-professional degree A degree that signifies both completion of the academic requirements for beginning practice in a given profession and a level of professional skill beyond that normally required for a bachelor's degree. This degree usually is based on a program requiring at least 2 academic years of work prior to entrance and a total of at least 6 academic years of work to complete the degree program, including both prior-required college work and the professional program itself. By NCES definition, first-professional degrees are awarded in the fields of dentistry (D.D.S. or D.M.D.), medicine (M.D.), optometry (O.D.), osteopathic medicine (D.O.), pharmacy (D.Phar.), podiatric medicine (D.P.M.), veterinary medicine (D.V.M.), chiropractic (D.C. or D.C.M.), law (J.D.), and theological professions (M.Div. or M.H.L.).

First-professional enrollment The number of students enrolled in a professional school or program which requires at least 2

years of academic college work for entrance and a total of at least 6 years for a degree. By NCES definition, first-professional enrollment includes only students in certain programs. (See also First-professional degree for a list of programs.)

Fiscal year The yearly accounting period for the federal government, which begins on October 1 and ends on the following September 30. The fiscal year is designated by the calendar year in which it ends; e.g., fiscal year 1988 begins on October 1, 1987, and ends on September 30, 1988. (From fiscal year 1844 to fiscal year 1976, the fiscal year began on July 1 and ended on the following June 30.)

For-profit institution A private institution in which the individual(s) or agency in control receives compensation other than wages, rent, or other expenses for the assumption of risk.

Foreign languages A group of instructional programs that describes the structure and use of language that is common or indigenous to people of the same community or nation, the same geographical area, or the same cultural traditions. Programs cover such features as sound, literature, syntax, phonology, semantics, sentences, prose, and verse, as well as the development of skills and attitudes used in communicating and evaluating thoughts and feelings through oral and written language.

Full-time enrollment The number of students enrolled in higher education courses with total credit load equal to at least 75 percent of the normal full-time course load.

Full-time-equivalent (FTE) enrollment For institutions of higher education, enrollment of full-time students, plus the full-time equivalent of part-time students. The full-time equivalent of the part-time students is estimated using different factors depending on the type and control of institution and level of student.

Full-time instructional faculty Those members of the instruction/research staff who are employed full time as defined by the institution, including faculty with released time for research and faculty on sabbatical leave. Full time counts exclude faculty who are employed to teach less than two semesters, three quarters, two trimesters, or two 4-month sessions; replacements for faculty on sabbatical leave or those on leave without pay; faculty for preclinical and clinical medicine; faculty who are donating their services; faculty who are members of military organizations and paid on a different pay scale from civilian employees; academic officers, whose primary duties are administrative; and graduate students who assist in the instruction of courses.

Full-time worker In educational institutions, an employee whose position requires being on the job on school days throughout the school year at least the number of hours the schools are in session. For higher education, a member of an educational institution's staff who is employed full time.

General administration support services Includes salary, benefits, supplies, and contractual fees for boards of education staff and executive administration. Excludes state administration.

General Educational Development (GED) program Academic instruction to prepare persons to take the high school equivalency examination. See also GED recipient.

GED recipient A person who has obtained certification of high school equivalency by meeting state requirements and passing an approved exam, which is intended to provide an appraisal of the person's achievement or performance in the broad subject matter areas usually required for high school graduation.

General program A program of studies designed to prepare students for the common activities of a citizen, family member, and worker. A general program of studies may include instruction in both academic and vocational areas.

Government appropriation An amount (other than a grant or contract) received from or made available to an institution through an act of a legislative body.

Government grant or contract Revenues from a government agency for a specific research project or other program.

Graduate An individual who has received formal recognition for the successful completion of a prescribed program of studies.

Graduate enrollment The number of students who hold the bachelor's or first-professional degree, or the equivalent, and who are working towards a master's or doctor's degree. First-professional students are counted separately. These enrollment data measure those students who are registered at a particular time during the fall. At some institutions, graduate enrollment also includes students who are in postbaccalaureate classes, but not in degree programs. In specified tables, graduate enrollment includes all students in regular graduate programs and all students in postbaccalaureate classes, but not in degree programs (unclassified postbaccalaureate students).

Graduate Record Examination (GRE) Multiple-choice examinations administered by the Educational Testing Service and taken by college students who are intending to attend certain graduate schools. There are two types of testing available: (1) the general exam which measures critical thinking, analytical writing, verbal reasoning, and quantitative reasoning skills, and (2) the subject test which is offered in eight specific subjects and gauges undergraduate achievement in a specific field. The subject tests are intended for those who have majored in or have extensive background in that specific area.

Graduation Formal recognition given an individual for the successful completion of a prescribed program of studies.

Gross domestic product (GDP) The total national output of goods and services valued at market prices. GDP can be viewed in terms of expenditure categories which include purchases of goods and services by consumers and government, gross private domestic investment, and net exports of goods and services. The goods and services included are largely those bought for final use (excluding illegal transactions) in the market economy. A number of inclusions, however, represent imputed values, the most important of which is rental value of owner-occupied housing. GDP, in this broad context, measures the output attributable to the factors of production—labor and property—supplied by U.S. residents.

Handicapped See Disabled.

Higher education Study beyond secondary school at an institution that offers programs terminating in an associate, baccalaureate, or higher degree.

Higher education institutions (Carnegie classification)

Doctorate-granting Characterized by a significant level and breadth of activity in commitment to doctoral-level education as measured by the number of doctorate recipients and the diversity in doctoral-level program offerings.

Master's Characterized by diverse postbaccalaureate programs (including first-professional), but not engaged in significant doctoral-level education.

Baccalaureate Characterized by primary emphasis on general undergraduate, baccalaureate-level education. Not significantly engaged in postbaccalaureate education.

Special focus Baccalaureate or postbaccalaureate institution emphasizing one area (plus closely related specialties), such as business or engineering. The programmatic emphasis is measured by the percentage of degrees granted in the program area.

Associate's Conferring at least 90 percent of its degrees and awards for work below the bachelor's level.

Tribal Colleges and universities that are members of the American Indian Higher Education Consortium, as identified in IPEDS Institutional Characteristics.

Non-degree-granting Offering undergraduate or graduate study, but not conferring degrees or awards. In this volume, these institutions are included under Specialized.

Higher education institutions (basic classification)

4-year institution An institution legally authorized to offer and offering at least a 4-year program of college-level studies wholly or principally creditable toward a baccalaureate degree. In some tables, a further division between universities and other 4-year institutions is made. A "university" is a postsecondary institution which typically comprises one or more graduate professional schools (see also University). For purposes of trend comparisons in this volume, the selection of universities has been held constant for all tabulations after 1982. "Other 4-year institutions" would include the rest of the nonuniversity 4-year institutions.

2-year institution An institution legally authorized to offer and offering at least a 2-year program of college-level studies which terminates in an associate degree or is principally creditable toward a baccalaureate degree. Also includes some institutions that have a less than 2-year program, but were designated as institutions of higher education in the Higher Education General Information Survey.

Higher Education Price Index A price index which measures average changes in the prices of goods and services purchased by colleges and universities through current-fund education and general expenditures (excluding expenditures for sponsored research and auxiliary enterprises).

High school A secondary school offering the final years of high school work necessary for graduation, usually includes grades 10, 11, 12 (in a 6-3-3 plan) or grades 9, 10, 11, and 12 (in a 6-2-4 plan).

High school program A program of studies designed to prepare students for their postsecondary education and occupation. Three types of programs are usually distinguished—academic, vocational, and general. An academic program is designed to prepare students for continued study at a college or university. A vocational program is designed to prepare students for employment in one or more semiskilled, skilled, or technical occupations. A general program is designed to provide students with the understanding and competence to function effectively in a free society and usually represents a mixture of academic and vocational components.

Hispanic serving institutions pursuant to 302 (d) of Public Law 102-325 (20 U.S.C. 1059c), most recently amended December 20, 1993, in 2(a)(7) of Public Law 103-208, where Hispanic serving institutions are defined as those with full-time-equivalent undergraduate enrollment of Hispanic students at 25 percent or more.

Historically black colleges and universities Accredited institutions of higher education established prior to 1964 with the principal mission of educating black Americans. Federal regulations (20 USC 1061 (2)) allow for certain exceptions of the founding date.

Household All the persons who occupy a housing unit. A house, apartment, mobile home, or other group of rooms, or a single room, is regarded as a housing unit when it is occupied or intended for occupancy as separate living quarters, that is, when the occupants do not live and eat with any other persons in the structure, and there is direct access from the outside or through a common hall.

Housing unit A house, an apartment, a mobile home, a group of rooms, or a single room that is occupied as separate living quarters.

Income tax Taxes levied on net income, that is, on gross income less certain deductions permitted by law. These taxes can be levied on individuals or on corporations or unincorporated businesses where the income is taxed distinctly from individual income.

Independent operations A group of self-supporting activities under control of a college or university. For purposes of financial surveys conducted by the National Center for Education Statistics, this category is composed principally of federally funded research and development centers (FFRDC).

Institutional support The category of higher education expenditures that includes day-to-day operational support for colleges, excluding expenditures for physical plant operations. Examples of institutional support include general administrative services, executive direction and planning, legal and fiscal operations, and community relations.

Instruction (budgetary) That functional category including expenditures of the colleges, schools, departments, and other instructional divisions of higher education institutions and expenditures for departmental research and public service which are not separately budgeted; includes expenditures for both credit and noncredit activities. Excludes expenditures for academic administration where the primary function is administration (e.g., academic deans).

Instruction (elementary and secondary) Instruction encompasses all activities dealing directly with the interaction between teachers and students. Teaching may be provided for students in a school classroom, in another location such as a home or hospital, and in other learning situations such as those involving co-curricular activities. Instruction may be provided through some other approved medium, such as television, radio, telephone, and correspondence. Instruction expenditures include: salaries, employee benefits, purchased services, supplies, and tuition to private schools.

Instructional staff Full-time-equivalent number of positions, not the number of different individuals occupying the positions during the school year. In local schools, includes all public elementary and secondary (junior and senior high) day-school positions that are in the nature of teaching or in the improvement of the teaching-learning situation; includes consultants or supervisors of instruction, principals, teachers, guidance personnel, librarians, psychological personnel, and other instructional staff, and excludes administrative staff, attendance personnel, clerical personnel, and junior college staff.

Instructional support services Includes salary, benefits, supplies, and contractual fees for staff providing instructional improvement, educational media (library and audiovisual), and other instructional support services.

Junior high school A separately organized and administered secondary school intermediate between the elementary and senior high schools, usually includes grades 7, 8, and 9 (in a 6-3-3 plan) or grades 7 and 8 (in a 6-2-4 plan).

Labor force Persons employed as civilians, unemployed but looking for work, or in the armed services during the survey week. The "civilian labor force" comprises all civilians classified as employed or unemployed. See also Unemployed.

Land-grant colleges The First Morrill Act of 1862 facilitated the establishment of colleges through grants of land or funds in lieu of land. The Second Morrill Act in 1890 provided for money grants and for the establishment of black land-grant colleges and universities in those states with dual systems of higher education.

Local education agency (LEA) See School district.

Locale codes A classification system to describe a location. The "Metro-Centric" locale codes, developed in the 1980s, classified all schools an school districts based on their county's proximity to metro statistical areas (MSA) and their specific location's population size and density. In 2006, the "Urban-Centric" locale codes were introduced. These locale codes are based on an address's proximity to an urbanized area. For more information see http://nces.ed.gov/ccd/rural_locales.asp.

Pre-2006 Metro-Centric Locale Codes

Large City: A central city of a consolidated metropolitan statistical area (CMSA) or MSA, with the city having a population greater than or equal to 250,000.

Mid-size City: A central city of a CMSA or MSA, with the city having a population less than 250,000.

Urban Fringe of a Large City: Any territory within a CMSA or MSA of a Large City and defined as urban by the Census Bureau.

Urban Fringe of a Mid-size City: Any territory within a CMSA or MSA of a Mid-size City and defined as urban by the Census Bureau.

Large Town: An incorporated place or Census-designated place with a population greater than or equal to 25,000 and located outside a CMSA or MSA.

Small Town: An incorporated place or Census-designated place with a population less than 25,000 and greater than or equal to 2,500 and located outside a CMSA or MSA.

Rural, Outside MSA: Any territory designated as rural by the Census Bureau that is outside a CMSA or MSA of a Large or Mid-size City.

Rural, Inside MSA: Any territory designated as rural by the Census Bureau that is within a CMSA or MSA of a Large or Mid-size City.

2006 Urban-Centric Locale Codes

City, Large: Territory inside an urbanized area and inside a principal city with population of 250,000 or more.

City, Midsize: Territory inside an urbanized area and inside a principal city with population less than 250,000 and greater than or equal to 100,000.

City, Small: Territory inside an urbanized area and inside a principal city with population less than 100,000.

Suburb, Large: Territory outside a principal city and inside an urbanized area with population of 250,000 or more.

Suburb, Midsize: Territory outside a principal city and inside an urbanized area with population less than 250,000 and greater than or equal to 100,000.

Suburb, Small: Territory outside a principal city and inside an urbanized area with population less than 100,000.

Town, Fringe: Territory inside an urban cluster that is less than or equal to 10 miles from an urbanized area.

Town, Distant: Territory inside an urban cluster that is more than 10 miles and less than or equal to 35 miles from an urbanized area.

Town, Remote: Territory inside an urban cluster that is more than 35 miles from an urbanized area.

Rural, Fringe: Census-defined rural territory that is less than or equal to 5 miles from an urbanized area, as well as rural territory that is less than or equal to 2.5 miles from an urban cluster.

Rural, Distant: Census-defined rural territory that is more than 5 miles but less than or equal to 25 miles from an urbanized area, as well as rural territory that is more than 2.5 miles but less than or equal to 10 miles from an urban cluster.

Rural, Remote: Census-defined rural territory that is more than 25 miles from an urbanized area and is also more than 10 miles from an urban cluster.

Mandatory transfer A transfer of current funds that must be made in order to fulfill a binding legal obligation of the institution. Included under mandatory transfers are debt service provisions relating to academic and administrative buildings, including (1) amounts set aside for debt retirement and interest and (2) required provisions for renewal and replacement of buildings to the extent these are not financed from other funds.

Master's degree A degree awarded for successful completion of a program generally requiring 1 or 2 years of full-time college-level study beyond the bachelor's degree. One type of master's degree, including the Master of Arts degree, or M.A., and the Master of Science degree, or M.S., is awarded in the liberal arts and sciences for advanced scholarship in a subject field or discipline and demonstrated ability to perform scholarly research. A second type of master's degree is awarded for the completion of a professionally oriented program, for example, an M.Ed. in education, an M.B.A. in business administration, an M.F.A. in fine arts, an M.M. in music, an M.S.W. in social work, and an M.P.A. in public administration. A third type of master's degree is awarded in professional fields for study beyond the first-professional degree, for example, the Master of Laws (L.L.M.) and Master of Science in various medical specializations.

Mathematics A group of instructional programs that describes the science of numbers and their operations, inter-relations, combinations, generalizations, and abstractions and of space configurations and their structure, measurement, transformations, and generalizations.

Mean test score The score obtained by dividing the sum of the scores of all individuals in a group by the number of individuals in that group.

Metropolitan population The population residing in Metropolitan Statistical Areas (MSAs). See Metropolitan Statistical Area.

Metropolitan Statistical Area (MSA) A large population nucleus and the nearby communities which have a high degree of economic and social integration with that nucleus. Each MSA consists of one or more entire counties (or county equivalents) that meet specified standards pertaining to population, commuting ties, and metropolitan character. In New England, towns and cities, rather than counties, are the basic units. MSAs are designated by the Office of Management and Budget. An MSA includes a city and, generally, its entire urban area and the remainder of the county or counties in which the urban area is located. An MSA also includes such additional outlying counties which meet specified criteria relating to metropolitan character and level of commuting of workers into the central city or counties. Specified criteria governing the definition of MSAs recognized before 1980 are published in Standard Metropolitan Statistical Areas: 1975, issued by the Office of Management and Budget. New MSAs were designated when 1980 counts showed that they met one or both of the following criteria:

1. Included a city with a population of at least 50,000 within their corporate limits, or

2. Included a Census Bureau-defined urbanized area (which must have a population of at least 50,000) and a total MSA population of at least 100,000 (or, in New England, 75,000).

Migration Geographic mobility involving a change of usual residence between clearly defined geographic units, that is, between counties, states, or regions.

Minimum-competency testing Measuring the acquisition of competence or skills to or beyond a certain specified standard.

National Assessment of Educational Progress (NAEP) See Guide to Sources.

Newly qualified teacher Persons who: (1) first became eligible for a teaching license during the period of the study referenced or who were teaching at the time of survey, but were not certified or eligible for a teaching license; and (2) had never held full-time, regular teaching positions (as opposed to substitute) prior to completing the requirements for the degree which brought them into the survey.

Nonmetropolitan residence group The population residing outside Metropolitan Statistical Areas. See Metropolitan Statistical Area.

Nonresident alien A person who is not a citizen of the United States and who is in this country on a temporary basis and does not have the right to remain indefinitely.

Nonsupervisory instructional staff Persons such as curriculum specialists, counselors, librarians, remedial specialists, and others possessing education certification, but not responsible for day-to-day teaching of the same group of pupils.

Not-for-profit institution A private institution in which the individual(s) or agency in control receives no compensation other than wages, rent, or other expenses for the assumption of risk. Nonprofit institutions may be either independent nonprofit (i.e., having no religious affiliation) or religiously affiliated.

Obligations Amounts of orders placed, contracts awarded, services received, or similar legally binding commitments made by federal agencies during a given period that will require outlays during the same or some future period.

Occupational home economics Courses of instruction emphasizing the acquisition of competencies needed for getting and holding a job or preparing for advancement in an occupational area using home economics knowledge and skills.

Occupied housing unit Separate living quarters with occupants currently inhabiting the unit. See also Housing unit.

Off-budget federal entities Organizational entities, federally owned in whole or in part, whose transactions belong in the budget under current budget accounting concepts, but that have been excluded from the budget totals under provisions of law.

Operation and maintenance services Includes salary, benefits, supplies, and contractual fees for supervision of operations and maintenance, operating buildings (heating, lighting, ventilating, repair, and replacement), care and upkeep of grounds and equipment, vehicle operations and maintenance (other than student transportation), security, and other operations and maintenance services.

Other foreign languages and literatures Any instructional program in foreign languages and literatures not described in table 259, including language groups and individual languages, such as the non-Semitic African languages, Native American languages, the Celtic languages, Pacific language groups, the Ural-Altaic languages, Basque, and others.

Other support services Includes salary, benefits, supplies, and contractual fees for business support services, central support services, and other support services not otherwise classified.

Other support services staff All staff not reported in other categories. This group includes media personnel, social workers, bus drivers, security, cafeteria workers, and other staff.

Outlays The value of checks issued, interest accrued on the public debt, or other payments made, net of refunds and reimbursements.

Part-time enrollment The number of students enrolled in higher education courses with a total credit load less than 75 percent of the normal full-time credit load.

Personal income Current income received by persons from all sources, minus their personal contributions for social insurance. Classified as "persons" are individuals (including owners of unincorporated firms), nonprofit institutions serving individuals, private trust funds, and private noninsured welfare funds. Personal income includes transfers (payments not resulting from current production) from government and business such as social security benefits and military pensions, but excludes transfers among persons.

Physical plant assets Includes the values of land, buildings, and equipment owned, rented, or utilized by colleges. Does not include those plant values which are a part of endowment or other capital fund investments in real estate; excludes construction in progress.

Postbaccalaureate enrollment The number of graduate and first-professional students working towards advanced degrees and of students enrolled in graduate-level classes, but not enrolled in degree programs. See also Graduate enrollment and First-professional enrollment.

Postsecondary education The provision of formal instructional programs with a curriculum designed primarily for students who have completed the requirements for a high school diploma or equivalent. This includes programs of an academic, vocational, and continuing professional education purpose, and excludes avocational and adult basic education programs.

Private school or institution A school or institution which is controlled by an individual or agency other than a state, a subdivision of a state, or the federal government, which is usually supported primarily by other than public funds, and the operation of whose program rests with other than publicly elected or appointed officials. Private schools and institutions include both not-for-profit and for-profit institutions.

Property tax The sum of money collected from a tax levied against the value of property.

Proprietary (for profit) institution A private institution in which the individual(s) or agency in control receives compensation other than wages, rent, or other expenses for the assumption of risk.

Public school or institution A school or institution controlled and operated by publicly elected or appointed officials and deriving its primary support from public funds.

Pupil/teacher ratio The enrollment of pupils at a given period of time, divided by the full-time-equivalent number of classroom teachers serving these pupils during the same period.

Racial/ethnic group Classification indicating general racial or ethnic heritage based on self-identification, as in data collected by the Census Bureau or on observer identification, as in data collected by the Office for Civil Rights. These categories are in accordance with the Office of Management and Budget standard classification scheme presented below:

White A person having origins in any of the original peoples of Europe, North Africa, or the Middle East. Normally excludes persons of Hispanic origin except for tabulations produced by the Census Bureau, which are noted accordingly in this volume.

Black A person having origins in any of the black racial groups in Africa. Normally excludes persons of Hispanic origin except for tabulations produced by the Census Bureau, which are noted accordingly in this volume.

Hispanic A person of Mexican, Puerto Rican, Cuban, Central or South American, or other Spanish culture or origin, regardless of race.

Asian A person having origins in any of the original peoples of the Far East, Southeast Asia, or the Indian subcontinent, e.g., China, India, Japan, the Philippines, Vietnam, and Korea.

Native Hawaiian/Other Pacific Islander A person having origins in any of the original peoples of the Pacific Islands, e.g., Hawaii, Guam, and Samoa.

American Indian or Alaska Native A person having origins in any of the original peoples of North America and South America and maintains their cultural identification through tribal affiliation or community recognition.

Related children Related children in a family include own children and all other children in the household who are related to the householder by birth, marriage, or adoption.

Remedial education Instruction for a student lacking those reading, writing, or math skills necessary to perform college-level work at the level required by the attended institution.

Resident population Includes civilian population and armed forces personnel residing within the United States; excludes armed forces personnel residing overseas.

Revenue All funds received from external sources, net of refunds, and correcting transactions. Noncash transactions, such as receipt of services, commodities, or other receipts in kind are excluded, as are funds received from the issuance of debt, liquidation of investments, and nonroutine sale of property.

Rural school See Locale codes.

Salary The total amount regularly paid or stipulated to be paid to an individual, before deductions, for personal services rendered while on the payroll of a business or organization.

Sales and services Revenues derived from the sales of goods or services that are incidental to the conduct of instruction, research, or public service. Examples include film rentals, scientific and literary publications, testing services, university presses, and dairy products.

Sales tax Tax imposed upon the sale and consumption of goods and services. It can be imposed either as a general tax on the retail price of all goods and services sold or as a tax on the sale of selected goods and services.

Scholarships and fellowships This category of college expenditures applies only to money given in the form of outright grants and trainee stipends to individuals enrolled in formal coursework, either for credit or not. Aid to students in the form of tuition or fee remissions is included. College work-study funds are excluded and are reported under the program in which the student is working. In the tabulations in this volume, Pell Grants are not included in this expenditure category.

SAT An examination administered by the Educational Testing Service and used to predict the facility with which an individual will progress in learning college-level academic subjects. It was formerly called the Scholastic Assessment Test.

School A division of the school system consisting of students in one or more grades or other identifiable groups and organized to give instruction of a defined type. One school may share a building with another school or one school may be housed in several buildings.

School administration support services Includes salary, benefits, supplies, and contractual fees for the office of the principal, full-time department chairpersons, and graduation expenses.

School climate The social system and culture of the school, including the organizational structure of the school and values and expectations within it.

School district An education agency at the local level that exists primarily to operate public schools or to contract for public school services. Synonyms are "local basic administrative unit" and "local education agency."

Science The body of related courses concerned with knowledge of the physical and biological world and with the processes of discovering and validating this knowledge.

Secondary enrollment The total number of students registered in a school beginning with the next grade following an elementary or middle school (usually 7, 8, or 9) and ending with or below grade 12 at a given time.

Secondary instructional level The general level of instruction provided for pupils in secondary schools (generally covering grades 7 through 12 or 9 through 12) and any instruction of a comparable nature and difficulty provided for adults and youth beyond the age of compulsory school attendance.

Secondary school A school comprising any span of grades beginning with the next grade following an elementary or middle school (usually 7, 8, or 9) and ending with or below grade 12. Both junior high schools and senior high schools are included.

Senior high school A secondary school offering the final years of high school work necessary for graduation.

Serial volumes Publications issued in successive parts, usually at regular intervals, and as a rule, intended to be continued indefinitely. Serials include periodicals, newspapers, annuals, memoirs, proceedings, and transactions of societies.

Social studies A group of instructional programs that describes the substantive portions of behavior, past and present activities, interactions, and organizations of people associated together for religious, benevolent, cultural, scientific, political, patriotic, or other purposes.

Socioeconomic status (SES) For the High School and Beyond study and the National Longitudinal Study of the High School Class of 1972, the SES index is a composite of five equally weighted, standardized components: father's education, mother's education, family income, father's occupation, and household items. The terms high, middle, and low SES refer to the upper, middle two, and lower quartiles of the weighted SES composite index distribution.

Special education Direct instructional activities or special learning experiences designed primarily for students identified as having exceptionalities in one or more aspects of the cognitive process or as being underachievers in relation to general level or model of their overall abilities. Such services usually are directed at students with the following conditions: (1) physically handicapped; (2) emotionally disabled; (3) culturally different, including compensatory education; (4) mentally retarded; and (5) students with learning disabilities. Programs for the mentally gifted and talented are also included in some special education programs. See also Handicapped.

Standardized test A test composed of a systematic sampling of behavior, administered and scored according to specific instructions, capable of being interpreted in terms of adequate norms, and for which there are data on reliability and validity.

Standardized test performance The weighted distributions of composite scores from standardized tests used to group students according to performance.

Standard Metropolitan Statistical Area (SMSA) See Metropolitan Statistical Area (MSA).

Student An individual for whom instruction is provided in an educational program under the jurisdiction of a school, school system, or other education institution. No distinction is made between the terms "student" and "pupil," though "student" may refer to one receiving instruction at any level while "pupil" refers only to one attending school at the elementary or secondary level. A student may receive instruction in a school facility or in another location, such as at home or in a hospital. Instruction may be provided by direct student-teacher interaction or by some other approved medium such as television, radio, telephone, and correspondence.

Student support services Includes salary, benefits, supplies, and contractual fees for staff providing attendance and social work, guidance, health, psychological services, speech pathology, audiology, and other support to students.

Subject-matter club Organizations that are formed around a shared interest in a particular area of study and whose primary activities promote that interest. Examples of such organizations are math, science, business, and history clubs.

Supervisory staff Principals, assistant principals, and supervisors of instruction; does not include superintendents or assistant superintendents.

Tax base The collective value of objects, assets, and income components against which a tax is levied.

Tax expenditures Losses of tax revenue attributable to provisions of the federal income tax laws that allow a special exclusion, exemption, or deduction from gross income or provide a special credit, preferential rate of tax, or a deferral of tax liability affecting individual or corporate income tax liabilities.

Technical education A program of vocational instruction that ordinarily includes the study of the sciences and mathematics underlying a technology, as well as the methods, skills, and materials commonly used and the services performed in the technology. Technical education prepares individuals for positions—such as draftsman or lab technician—in the occupational area between the skilled craftsman and the professional person.

Title IV Refers to a section of the Higher Education Act of 1965 that covers the administration of the federal student financial aid program.

Title IV eligible institution A postsecondary institution that meets the criteria for participating in the federal student financial aid program. An eligible institution must be any of the following: (1) an institution of higher education (with public or private, non-profit control), (2) a proprietary institution (with private for-profit control), and (3) a postsecondary vocational institution (with public or private, non-profit control). In addition, it must have acceptable legal authorization, acceptable accreditation and admission stands, eligible academic program(s), administrative capability, and financial responsibility.

Total expenditure per pupil in average daily attendance Includes all expenditures allocable to per pupil costs divided by average daily attendance. These allocable expenditures include current expenditures for regular school programs, interest on school debt, and capital outlay. Beginning in 1980–81, expenditures for state administration are excluded and expenditures for other programs (summer schools, community colleges, and private schools) are included.

Town school See Locale codes.

Trade and industrial occupations The branch of vocational education which is concerned with preparing persons for initial employment or with updating or retraining workers in a wide range of trade and industrial occupations. Such occupations are skilled or semiskilled and are concerned with layout designing, producing, processing, assembling, testing, maintaining, servicing, or repairing any product or commodity.

Transcript An official list of all courses taken by a student at a school or college showing the final grade received for each course, with definitions of the various grades given at the institution.

Trust funds Amounts collected and used by the federal government for carrying out specific purposes and programs according to terms of a trust agreement or statute, such as the social security and unemployment trust funds. Trust fund receipts that are not anticipated to be used in the immediate future are generally invested in interest-bearing government securities and earn interest for the trust fund.

Tuition and fees A payment or charge for instruction or compensation for services, privileges, or the use of equipment, books, or other goods.

Unclassified students Students who are not candidates for a degree or other formal award, although they are taking higher education courses for credit in regular classes with other students.

Unadjusted dollars See Current dollars.

Undergraduate students Students registered at an institution of higher education who are working in a program leading to a baccalaureate degree or other formal award below the baccalaureate, such as an associate degree.

Unemployed Civilians who had no employment but were available for work and: (1) had engaged in any specific job seeking activity within the past 4 weeks; (2) were waiting to be called back to a job from which they had been laid off; or (3) were waiting to report to a new wage or salary job within 30 days.

U.S. Service Schools These institutions of higher education are controlled by the U.S. Department of Defense and the U.S. Department of Transportation. The 5 institutions counted in the NCES surveys of degree granting institutions include: the U.S. Air Force Academy, U.S. Coast Guard Academy, U.S. Merchant Marine Academy, U.S. Military Academy, and the U.S. Naval Academy.

University An institution of higher education consisting of a liberal arts college, a diverse graduate program, and usually two or more professional schools or faculties and empowered to confer degrees in various fields of study. For purposes of maintaining trend data in this publication, the selection of university institutions has not been revised since 1982.

Urban fringe school See Locale codes.

Visual and performing arts A group of instructional programs that generally describes the historic development, aesthetic qualities, and creative processes of the visual and performing arts.

Vocational education Organized educational programs, services, and activities which are directly related to the preparation of individuals for paid or unpaid employment, or for additional preparation for a career, requiring other than a baccalaureate or advanced degree.

APPENDIX C
Index of Table Numbers

Academic rank of faculty in postsecondary institutions, 232, 235, 236, 237
  salaries by, 240, 241, 244, 245
  tenure by, 247
Academic support, expenditures at postsecondary institutions, 348, 352, 353
Achievement levels. *See also under individual subjects*
  eighth-graders attaining, 115, 125
  fourth-graders attaining, 114, 124
  various ages and grades of students attaining, 113, 117, 118, 120, 122, 128
ACT scores, 135, 315
Administration/Administrative staff
  postsecondary institutions, expenditures for, 346
  in public elementary and secondary schools, 77, 78, 79
  public elementary and secondary schools, expenditures for, 161, 163, 164, 165
Admission requirements for postsecondary institutions, 314
Admissions to undergraduate institutions, 315
Adult education, 358, 359, 360
Advanced Placement courses in public secondary schools, 141
Affiliation of postsecondary institutions, 183
Age
  adult education participation by, 359, 360
  attendance status at postsecondary institutions and, 177
  child care arrangements by, 42, 43
  cognitive and motor skills by, 107
  computer usage by, 424, 425, 427
  educational attainment by, 8, 9
  enrollment in grades 9 to 12 compared to population, 52
  faculty in postsecondary institutions, 235, 236
  field of study in postsecondary institutions by, 216
  GED (General Educational Development) credentials issued by, 103
  international comparisons of bachelor's degree recipients, 409
  international comparisons of school-age population, 394
  internet usage by, 423
  labor force participation by, 374
  literacy skills of adults by, 379
  mathematics scores by, 121, 122, 123
  number of persons with bachelor's degrees by, 10
  percentage of population enrolled in school by, 7
  population by, 15, 16
  postsecondary enrollment by, 179
  preprimary education and, 41
  range for compulsory school attendance, 153
  reading scores by, 110, 111, 113
  school-age population, by state, 17
  student financial aid by, 323, 324, 325

  students exiting special education by, 106
  teachers in public schools by, 66
  unemployment rate by, 375
Agriculture
  associate's degrees in, 252, 253, 265, 266
  bachelor's degrees in, 10, 254, 268, 269
  degrees conferred in, 258, 260, 279
  doctor's degrees in, 256, 274, 275
  enrollment, postsecondary education, 216
  institutions conferring degrees in, 261
  master's degrees in, 255, 271, 272
Alcohol usage
  by high school seniors, 152
  by teenagers, 151
  on school property, 150
Algebra course work in high school, 139
  mathematics scores and, 123
Alumni, support for institutions by, 351
American Indians/Alaska Natives
  with associate's degrees, 264, 265, 266
  attendance patterns by tenth-graders, 145
  with bachelor's degrees, 10, 267, 268, 269
  course work by high school graduates in mathematics and science, 139
  distribution in public schools, 93
  with doctor's degrees, 273, 274, 275, 301–307
  educational attainment by state, 12
  employment of high school seniors, 380
  enrollment distribution in public schools by state, 40
  estimates of resident population by age, 16
  with first-professional degrees, 276, 277, 278
  high school graduates and dropouts, 102
  with master's degrees, 270, 271, 272
  mathematics scores by grade, 127
  postsecondary institutions
    employment in, 229
    enrollment in, 210, 211, 212, 213
    faculty in, 232, 236, 238
  in public charter and traditional public schools, 97
  reading scores of fourth- and eighth-graders, 116
  reading scores and achievement levels of fourth-graders, 114
  SAT scores for college-bound seniors, 131
  science scores and achievement levels by grade, 128
  science scores of eighth-graders in public schools by state, 129
  tribally controlled institutions, 223
Applications to undergraduate institutions, 315
Appropriations for public postsecondary institutions by state, 339
Architecture
  associate's degrees in, 252, 253, 265, 266

bachelor's degrees in, 10, 254, 268, 269
degrees conferred in, 258, 260, 280
doctor's degrees in, 256, 274, 275
enrollment, postsecondary education, 216
institutions conferring degrees in, 261
master's degrees in, 255, 271, 272
Area studies
associate's degrees in, 252, 253, 265, 266
bachelor's degrees in, 254, 268, 269
degrees conferred in, 258, 260
doctor's degrees in, 256, 274, 275
enrollment, postsecondary education, 216
institutions conferring degrees in, 261
master's degrees in, 255, 271, 272
Arts
associate's degrees in, 252, 253, 265, 266
bachelor's degrees in, 10, 254, 268, 269
Carnegie units earned by high school graduates, 137
Carnegie units required by state for high school graduation, 154
degrees conferred in, 258, 260, 300
doctor's degrees in, 256, 274, 275
eighth-graders, scores for, 130
enrollment, postsecondary education, 216
institutions conferring degrees in, 261
master's degrees in, 255, 271, 272
Asians/Pacific Islanders
with associate's degrees, 264, 265, 266
attendance patterns by tenth-graders, 145
with bachelor's degrees, 10, 267, 268, 269
course work by high school graduates in mathematics and
    science, 139
distribution in public schools, 93
with doctor's degrees, 273, 274, 275, 301–307
educational attainment by state, 12
employment of high school seniors, 380
enrollment distribution in public schools by state, 40
estimates of resident population by age, 16
with first-professional degrees, 276, 277, 278
high school graduates and dropouts, 102
with master's degrees, 270, 271, 272
mathematics scores by grade, 127
postsecondary institutions
    employment in, 229
    enrollment in, 210, 211, 212, 213
    faculty in, 232, 236, 238
poverty rates, 21
in public charter and traditional public schools, 97
reading scores of fourth- and eighth-graders, 116
reading scores and achievement levels of fourth-graders, 114
SAT scores for college-bound seniors, 131
science scores and achievement levels by grade, 128
science scores of eighth-graders in public schools by state, 129
Assessment, state
criterion-referenced assessments, 155
minimum-competency testing, 156
teacher certification testing, 157
Associate's degrees
by control of institution, 259, 260, 308
by field of study, 252, 253
by gender, 251
number of institutions conferring, 261
by race/ethnicity and gender, 264, 265, 266

by state, 310
Attendance, elementary/secondary schools
age range for compulsory, 153
average daily in public schools, 39, 172
patterns by tenth-graders, 145
Attendance status, postsecondary institutions, 175, 177, 182
by control and type of institution, 179
first-professional level, 192
of first-time freshmen, 184, 185
graduate level, 191
institutions with more than 15,000 students, 220
by level, 180, 181
in private institutions by state, 198, 199
in public institutions by state, 197
by race/ethnicity and gender, 210
by state, 196
student financial aid
    graduate level, 330, 331, 332, 333
    undergraduate level, 323, 324, 325, 326, 327, 328, 329
undergraduate level, 190
Attendance status, preprimary programs, 41
Attrition rate for teachers in public schools, 70
Auxiliary enterprises, postsecondary institutions
current-fund expenditures for, 348
current-fund revenues, 335, 336
expenditures for, 346, 347, 352, 353, 354
revenues, 337, 338
revenues to private institutions, 340, 341, 342, 343
Average daily attendance, public elementary and secondary
schools, 39
current expenditures per pupil, 171
transportation expenditures and, 172

Bachelor's degrees
by control of institution, 259, 260, 308
course work for, 313
by field of study, 254, 279–300, 385 (See also Field of study)
by gender, 251
international comparisons of, 409
international comparisons of science, 410
number of institutions conferring, 261
number of persons with, 10
by race/ethnicity and gender, 267, 268, 269
salaries of recipients, 387
salaries of teachers with, 73
by state, 309, 310
Benefit expenditures for faculty in postsecondary institutions, 246
Biology
associate's degrees in, 252, 253, 265, 266
bachelor's degrees in, 254, 268, 269
course work for bachelor's degrees, 313
course work in high school, 137, 139
degrees conferred in, 258, 260, 281, 282
doctor's degrees in, 256, 274, 275
enrollment, postsecondary education, 216
institutions conferring degrees in, 261
international comparisons of time spent on eighth-grade science,
    407
master's degrees in, 255, 271, 272
Blacks
with associate's degrees, 264, 265, 266
attendance patterns by tenth-graders, 145

with bachelor's degrees, 10, 267, 268, 269

child care arrangements by, 43

college enrollment and labor force status of high school graduates, 381

course work and mathematics scores of 17-year-olds, 123

course work by high school graduates in mathematics and science, 139

distribution in public schools, 93

with doctor's degrees, 273, 274, 275, 301–307

dropouts from high school, 104

educational attainment, 8, 9, 12

employment of high school seniors, 380

enrollment distribution in public schools by state, 40

estimates of resident population by age, 16

family characteristics of, 19

with first-professional degrees, 276, 277, 278

high school graduates and dropouts, 102

internet usage, 423

labor force status of high school dropouts, 382

leisure activities of high school seniors, 142

with master's degrees, 270, 271, 272

mathematics achievement levels by age, 122

mathematics scores by age, 121

mathematics scores by grade, 127

percentage of population enrolled in school, 6

postsecondary institutions

    employment in, 229

    enrollment in, 187, 189, 210, 211, 212, 213

    faculty in, 232, 235, 236, 237, 238

    historically black colleges and universities, 224, 225, 226

poverty rates, 21

in public charter and traditional public schools, 97

reading levels by age, 113

reading scores by age, 110

reading scores and achievement levels of fourth-graders, 114

reading scores of fourth- and eighth-graders, 116

SAT scores for college-bound seniors, 131

science scores and achievement levels by grade, 128

science scores of eighth-graders in public schools by state, 129

unemployment rate, 375

violence and drug use on school property, 150

Branch campuses, postsecondary institutions, 248, 250

Building deficiencies in public schools, 98

Business and management

associate's degrees in, 252, 253, 265, 266

bachelor's and master's degrees in, 309

bachelor's degrees in, 10, 254, 268, 269

course work for bachelor's degrees, 313

degrees conferred in, 257, 258, 260, 283

doctor's degrees in, 256, 274, 275, 301

enrollment, postsecondary education, 216

institutions conferring degrees in, 261

master's degrees in, 255, 271, 272

Calculus course work in high school, 139

mathematics scores and, 123

Careers and adult education participation, 359, 360. *See also* Occupation

Carnegie units earned in high school, 137

state requirements for graduation, 154

in vocational education, 138

Catholic schools. *See also* Private elementary and secondary schools

attendance patterns by tenth-graders, 145

enrollment, teachers, and characteristics, 55, 58

extracurricular activities of high school sophomores, 143

leisure activities of high school seniors, 142

staff-to-student ratios, 57

tuition for, 56

Center-based programs, 42. *See also* Preprimary education

Certification of teachers, states requiring test for, 157

Charter schools, 97

Chemical engineering, degrees in, 288. *See also* Engineering

Chemistry

course work in high school, 137, 139

degrees in, 295

international comparisons of eighth-grade science, 406, 407

Child care, 42, 43

Cigarettes, teenagers smoking, 150, 151

Citizenship, 301–307

Civil engineering, degrees in, 288. *See also* Engineering

Classroom teachers. *See* Teachers

Class size

international comparisons of mathematics, 402

by teacher characteristics, 64

Closing of postsecondary institutions, 250

Cognitive skills of young children, 107

Collections in college and university libraries, 418, 419

Collections in public libraries, 420, 421

Communications

associate's degrees in, 252, 253, 265, 266

bachelor's degrees in, 10, 254, 268, 269

degrees conferred in, 258, 260, 284

doctor's degrees in, 256, 274, 275

enrollment, postsecondary education, 216

institutions conferring degrees in, 261

master's degrees in, 255, 271, 272

Completion status in postsecondary education, 317

Computer and information sciences

associate's degrees in, 252, 253, 265, 266

bachelor's and master's degrees in, 309

bachelor's degrees in, 10, 254, 268, 269

course work for bachelor's degrees, 313

degrees conferred in, 257, 258, 260, 285

doctor's degrees in, 256, 274, 275

enrollment, postsecondary education, 216

institutions conferring degrees in, 261

master's degrees in, 255, 271, 272

Computers

home use, 424, 425

number used for instruction in public elementary and secondary schools, 422

usage by educational level, 426

work use, 427

Construction projects for public schools, 98

Construction trades

associate's degrees in, 252, 253, 265, 266

bachelor's degrees in, 254, 268, 269

degrees conferred in, 258, 260

doctor's degrees in, 256, 274, 275

enrollment, postsecondary education, 216

institutions conferring degrees in, 261

master's degrees in, 271, 272

Consumer Price Index, 31

Control of institutions. *See* Private elementary and secondary schools; Private postsecondary institutions; Public elementary and secondary schools; Public postsecondary institutions

Course work/Credits

  Advanced Placement, dual placement, and International Baccalaureate in public high schools, 141

  bachelor's-degree recipients, 313

  Carnegie units required by states for high school graduation, 154

  by public high school graduates

    in mathematics and science, 139

    in various courses, 137

    in vocational courses, 138

  mathematics scores of 17-year-olds and, 123

  minimum recommended for college-bound high school graduates, 140

Crime at public elementary and secondary schools, 147

Criminal justice enrollment in postsecondary education, 216. *See also* Security

Criterion-referenced assessments by state, 155

Current expenditures. *See also* Expenditures

  per pupil in public schools, 167–171

  in public elementary and secondary schools, 161–165

Current-fund expenditures. *See also* Expenditures

  postsecondary institutions, 345, 346

  public postsecondary institutions, 348, 349

Current-fund revenues. *See also* Revenues

  largest amounts from federal government to postsecondary institutions, 344

  by source for postsecondary institutions, 335, 336

Degree-granting institutions. *See* Postsecondary education

Degrees conferred. *See also under individual degree levels and fields*

  associate's degrees, 252, 253

  bachelor's degrees, 254

  by control of institution, 259, 260, 261

  doctor's degrees, 256

  by field of study, 257, 258

  first-professional degrees 262, 263

  at historically black colleges and universities, 224, 225

  at institutions with more than 15,000 students, 220

  at institutions serving large proportions of Hispanic students, 222

  by level and gender, 251

  master's degrees, 255

  by state, 308, 309, 310

  at Title IV postsecondary institutions, 173

  at tribally controlled institutions, 223

  at women's colleges, 221

Degrees earned. *See also* Educational attainment; *and under individual degree levels and fields*

  completions by type of institution, 317

  income by educational attainment, 377, 378

  by teachers, 64, 65, 71

Dentistry, first-professional degrees in, 262, 263, 277, 278

Department of Agriculture, 369. *See also* Federal government, expenditures for education

Department of Education, 366, 367. *See also* Federal government, expenditures for education

Department of Health and Human Services, 370. *See also* Federal government, expenditures for education

Dependency status and student financial aid, 323, 324, 325

Disabilities, students with

  3–21 years old, 48

    by state, 50

  6–21 years old, 49

  exiting special education, 106

  postsecondary education and employment status of, 383

  at postsecondary institutions, 215

Discipline division. *See* Field of study

Disposable personal income, 30. *See also* Income

Distance education, high school participation in, 54

Doctor's degrees

  by control of institution, 259, 260, 308

  by field of study, 256, 279–300

  by gender, 251

  by institutions conferring the most, 311

  number of institutions conferring, 261

  by race/ethnicity and gender, 273, 274, 275

  by state, 310

  statistical profile of persons receiving, 301–307

  student financial aid for, 330, 331, 332, 333

Dropouts from high school

  among persons 16–24 years old

    by gender and race/ethnicity, 104

    labor force status of, 105

    years of school completed, 105

  students dropping out

    in school districts of more than 15,000 students, 87

    by state and race/ethnicity, 102

  labor force status of persons dropping out in previous year, 382

Drug usage

  by high school seniors, 152

  by high school students, 150

  by teenagers, 151

  by young adults, 389

Dual credit courses in public secondary schools, 141

Economics

  degrees conferred in, 299

  enrollment, postsecondary education, 216

Education (as field of study)

  associate's degrees in, 252, 253, 265, 266

  bachelor's and master's degrees in, 309

  bachelor's degrees in, 10, 254, 268, 269

  course work for bachelor's degrees, 313

  degrees conferred in, 257, 258, 260, 286

  doctor's degrees in, 256, 274, 275, 301, 302

  enrollment, postsecondary education, 216

  institutions conferring degrees in, 261

  master's degrees in, 255, 271, 272

Education, federal support for, 362

  by agency, 363, 364, 365

  Department of Education appropriations, 367

  Department of Education outlays, 366

  Head Start, 370

  science and engineering obligations to postsecondary institutions, 371

  Title I, No Child Left Behind Act of 2001, 368

Education agencies (public), by state, 85

Educational attainment
    adult education participation, 359, 360
    bachelor's degrees, number of persons with, 10 (*See also*
        Bachelor's degrees)
    computer usage at work, 427
    high school sophomores of 1990, 312
    income by, 377, 378
    job satisfaction of 1988 eighth-graders, 391
    labor force participation by, 374
    by largest 25 states, 13
    by level of attainment, 8, 9
    literacy skills of adults, 379
    by metropolitan area, 14
    occupations by, 376
    of parents and their
        children's reading scores, 110, 116 (*See also* Parental level of
            education)
        participation in educational activities with children, 24
        participation in activities at children's school, 23
    by state, 11
    by state and race/ethnicity, 12
    of teachers in public schools, 64, 65
    unemployment rate, 375
    volunteer activity by eighth-graders, 388
Educational institutions, number of, 5
Eighth grade
    arts scores, 130
    geography achievement levels, 120
    geography and history scores, 119
    history achievement levels, 118
    international comparisons
        of mathematics instructional practices, 401
        of mathematics scores, 400, 402
        of science instructional practices, 407
        of science scores, 406
        of students' perceptions of mathematics, 403
    mathematics scores, 127
    mathematics scores and achievement levels in public schools by
        state, 125
    reading scores, 116
    reading scores and achievement levels in public schools, 115
    science scores and achievement levels, 128
    science scores in public schools by state, 129
    writing achievement levels, 117
Electrical engineering, degrees in, 288. *See also* Engineering
Elementary and secondary education, 32–172. *See also* Private
    elementary and secondary schools; Public elementary and
    secondary schools
    computer usage by students, 426
    enrollment overview, 2, 3
    expenditures of institutions related to gross domestic product,
        25
    expenditures of institutions, 26
    expenditures by state, 28
    federal support for, 362, 364
    number of institutions, 5
    participants in, 1
    per capita expenditures on, 29
    pupil-to-teacher ratios in public and private schools, 61
Elementary schools, 83. *See also* Private elementary and
    secondary schools; Public elementary and secondary schools
Employees in postsecondary institutions. *See* Staff

Employment
    bachelor's degree recipients' status, 384, 385
    computer usage on the job, 427
    high school dropouts' status, 382
    high school graduates' status, 381
    of high school seniors, 380
    ratio to population, 374
    special education students' status, 383
    of teachers outside of teaching, 72
Endowment funds, 356, 357
Engineering
    associate's degrees in, 252, 253, 265, 266
    bachelor's degrees in, 10, 254, 268, 269
    course work for bachelor's degrees, 313
    degrees conferred in, 258, 260, 287
    doctor's degrees in, 256, 274, 275, 301, 303
    enrollment, postsecondary education, 216
    federal support to postsecondary institutions for, 371
    graduate-level enrollment in, 217
    institutions conferring degrees in, 261
    international comparisons of bachelor's degrees in, 410
    international comparisons of graduate degrees in, 411
    master's degrees in, 255, 271, 272
English and literature
    associate's degrees in, 252, 253, 265, 266
    bachelor's degrees in, 10, 254, 268, 269
    Carnegie units earned by high school graduates, 137
    Carnegie units required by states for high school graduation,
        154
    degrees conferred in, 258, 260, 289
    doctor's degrees in, 256, 274, 275
    enrollment, postsecondary education, 216
    institutions conferring degrees in, 261
    master's degrees in, 255, 271, 272
English as a second language, 358
Enrollment
    at all levels of education, 2
    in Catholic elementary and secondary schools, 58
    in grades 9 to 12 compared to population, 52
    international comparisons, 392
    international comparisons at secondary and postsecondary
        levels, 395
    in 100 largest school districts, 89
    percentage of population enrolled, 6, 7
    postsecondary institutions, 173–226
        applications and admissions compared to, 315
        attendance status, 175, 177, 182, 196
        of bachelor's degree recipients 1 year after graduation, 385,
            386
        by control and affiliation, 183
        by control and type, 176, 179, 200, 218
        disabled students in, 215
        field of study, 216
        first-professional level, 192
        first-time freshmen, 184, 185
        full-time equivalent enrollment in, 204, 205
        by gender and race/ethnicity, 189, 210
        graduate level, 191
        historically black colleges and universities, 224, 225, 226
        institutions with large proportions of Hispanic students, 222
        institutions with more than 15,000 students, 220
        largest colleges and universities, 219

by level, 178, 180, 181, 201, 202, 203
private institutions, 195, 198, 199
public institutions by state, 194, 197
by race/ethnicity, 211, 212
by race/ethnicity and gender, 189, 210
by recent high school completers, 186, 187, 188
by state, 193–203
Title IV, 173
tribally controlled institutions, 223
undergraduate, 190, 381
women's colleges, 221
preprimary education, 41, 44
in private elementary and secondary schools, 55, 56, 58, 59
in public elementary and secondary schools
charter schools, 97
by grade, 36
historical statistics of, 32
pupil-to-staff ratios, 81
pupil-to-teacher ratios, 60, 63
racial/ethnic distribution of, 40, 93
size, distribution of schools by, 92
by state, 33, 34, 35, 40
by urbanicity, 86
in school districts, 84
by school districts of more than 15,000 students, 87
Environment in schools
building deficiencies in public schools, 98
violence and drug use, 150
Expenditures
current for public elementary and secondary schools by state, 162, 170, 171
of educational institutions, 25, 26
governmental by function, 27
international comparisons on education, 412, 413
postsecondary institutions
current-fund, 345, 346, 348, 349
libraries, 418, 419
private institutions, 352, 353, 354, 355
public institutions, 347, 350
public elementary and secondary schools
by function and subfunction, 165
historical statistics of, 32
for instruction, 166
by metropolitan status, 86
per pupil, 167, 168, 169
by purpose, 161, 162, 163, 164
in school districts of more than 15,000 students, 88
for school libraries and media centers, 415, 416, 417
of state and local governments, 28, 29, 30
Expulsions from public schools, 148
Extracurricular activities (school sponsored), 143

Faculty, postsecondary
benefit expenditures for, 246
by employment status, 228, 231
full-time-equivalent, 227, 230
by field of study, 237, 238
full-time by race/ethnicity, 232
historical statistics of degree-granting institutions, 174
instructional activities of, 233, 234
number of, 1, 4
by race/ethnicity and gender, 229, 236

salaries
by field of instruction, 239
by rank, 240, 241
by state, 242, 243, 244, 245
with tenure, 247
total and full-time-equivalent, 227
by type and control of institution, 235
Families
care of children in, 42, 43
characteristics of, 19
homeschooled children, 37
median income of, 30 (*See also* Income, family)
poverty rates by race/ethnicity, 21
preschool literacy activities at home, 45, 46
by status and presence of children, 18
Federal government, 362–373
budget composite deflator, 31
Department of Agriculture nutrition programs, 369
Department of Health and Human Services, 370
education agencies operated by, 85
expenditures for education, 362
by agency, 363, 364, 365
Department of Education appropriations, 367
Department of Education outlays, 366
by function, 27
research and development, 372, 373
science and engineering obligations to postsecondary institutions, 371
Title I allocations, 368
funds to largest school districts, 89
Head Start programs, 370
programs for students with disabilities, 48
revenues
for postsecondary institutions, 335, 336, 337, 338, 344
for private postsecondary institutions, 340, 341, 342, 343
for public elementary and secondary schools, 158, 159, 160
student financial aid, 323–331
Field of study. *See also under individual subjects*
associate's degrees by, 252, 253
bachelor's degree recipients, enrollment status by, 385, 386
bachelor's degrees by, 254
bachelor's degrees by course work completed, 313
degrees conferred by, 258, 279–300
doctor's degrees by, 256, 274, 275
faculty in postsecondary institutions, 237, 238
faculty salaries by, 239
first-professional degrees by, 262, 263
full-time employment by, 384
intended major and SAT scores for college-bound seniors, 133
by level and type of institution, 216
master's degrees by, 255, 271, 272
salaries of bachelor's degree recipients by, 387
Finances for postsecondary institutions, historical statistics, 174. *See also* Expenditures; Revenues
Financial aid to students
graduate level, 330, 331, 332, 333
undergraduates receiving, 323, 324, 325, 326, 327, 328, 329
First-professional degrees
by control of institution, 259
by field of study, 262, 263
by gender, 251
number of institutions conferring, 262

by race/ethnicity and gender, 276, 277, 278
by state, 308, 310
First-professional level
disabled students enrolled at, 215
enrollment at, 178, 180, 181
by attendance status, 192
by race/ethnicity and gender, 210
by state, 201, 202, 203
field of study, 216
student financial aid for, 330, 331, 332, 333
tuition and fees for, 322
Foreign languages
associate's degrees in, 252, 253, 265, 266
bachelor's degrees in, 10, 254, 268, 269
Carnegie units earned by high school graduates, 137
Carnegie units required by state for high school graduation, 154
degrees conferred in, 258, 260, 290
doctor's degrees in, 256, 274, 275
enrollment, postsecondary education, 216
enrollment in high school, 53
institutions conferring degrees in, 261
master's degrees in, 255, 271, 272
Foreign postsecondary students in United States, 414
Fourth grade
geography achievement levels, 120
geography and history scores, 119
history achievement levels, 118
international comparisons of mathematics, 399
international comparisons of science, 405
mathematics scores, 127
mathematics scores and achievement levels by state, 124
reading scores, 116
reading scores and achievement levels in public schools, 114
science scores and achievement levels, 128
time spent on homework and television, 144
writing achievement levels, 117
Four-year postsecondary institutions
admission requirements for, 314
applications, admissions, and enrollment comparisons, 315
attendance status at, 182
with branch campuses, 248
closing of institutions, 250
completion status for students, 317
enrollment in, 176, 179, 180, 181
by race/ethnicity, 211
by recent high school completers, 188
by state, 200, 202, 203
expenditures at private institutions, 352, 353, 354
expenditures of, 345, 347, 353, 354
faculty in, 231
salaries, 240, 241, 242, 243, 244, 245
tenure, 247
field of study at, 216
first-time freshmen at, 184
full-time-equivalent enrollment in, 204, 205
full-time-equivalent staff at, 230
historically black colleges and universities, 226
number of institutions, 214
number of institutions by state, 249
remedial coursework offered by, 316
residence and migration of freshmen in, 209
revenues of private institutions, 340, 341, 342, 343

revenues of public institutions, 337
staff in, 228, 229
student financial aid
graduate students, 330, 331, 332, 333
undergraduates, 326, 327, 328, 329
Title IV postsecondary institutions, 173
tuition, fees, and board rates for undergraduates, 319, 320, 321
Free school lunch program
building deficiencies in public schools, 98
crime incidents reported at public schools, 147
Department of Agriculture obligations for, 369
geography achievement levels by grade, 120
geography and history scores by grade, 119
history achievement levels by grade, 118
public elementary and secondary schools with internet access, 422
schools with security measures, 146
science scores and achievement levels by grade, 128
science scores of eighth-graders in public schools, 129
writing achievement levels by grade, 117
French
degrees conferred in, 291
enrollment in high school, 53
Freshmen (postsecondary institutions)
enrollment, 184
enrollment by state, 185
residence and migration of, 207, 208, 209
Full-day kindergarten, 153
mathematic and science skills for 1998 kindergarten cohort, 109
reading skills for 1998 kindergarten cohort, 108
Full-time attendance at postsecondary institutions, 175, 182
by age and gender, 177
by control and affiliation of institution, 183
by control and type of institution, 179
first-professional level enrollment at, 192
first-time freshmen, 184, 185
graduate enrollment, 191
graduate-level student financial aid, 330, 332
institutions with more than 15,000 students, 220
by level, 178, 180, 181
in private institutions by state, 198, 199
in public institutions by state, 197
by race/ethnicity and gender, 210
by state, 196
student financial aid, 324, 326, 327, 329
Full-time employment. See also Employment
bachelor's degree recipients and, 384
in postsecondary institutions, 228, 229, 231
Full-time-equivalent enrollment in postsecondary institutions, 204, 205, 206, 220
Full-time-equivalent staff in postsecondary institutions, 227, 230. See also Faculty, postsecondary; Staff
Full-time-equivalent students (postsecondary institutions), expenditures per, 345
Full-time faculty, 232, 233. See also Faculty, postsecondary
Funding for public elementary and secondary schools. See Revenues

GED (General Educational Development) test, 103
Gender
ACT scores, 135
adult education participation, 359, 360
art scores of eighth-graders, 130

associate's degrees by, 264, 265, 266
attendance status at postsecondary institutions, 177, 178, 180, 181, 182
bachelor's degrees by, 267, 268, 269
bachelor's degree holders by, 10
Carnegie units earned by high school graduates, 137, 138
college enrollment and labor force status of high school graduates by, 381
computer usage, 424, 425, 426, 427
course work and mathematics scores of 17-year-olds, 123
course work by high school graduates in mathematics and science, 139
degrees conferred by field of study, 258
doctor's degrees by, 273, 274, 275, 301–307
dropouts from high school by, 104
educational attainment, 8, 9
    of high school sophomores of 1990, 312
    in largest 25 states, 13
    by metropolitan area, 14
employment of high school seniors, 380
enrollment in postsecondary institutions, 175, 186, 189, 210
enrollment in Title IV postsecondary institutions, 173
extracurricular activities of high school sophomores, 143
first-professional degrees by, 262, 263, 276, 277, 278
geography achievement levels by grade, 120
geography and history scores by grade, 119
gifted and talented students by state, 51
grade point averages of elementary and secondary students, 136
high school graduates by control of school, 99
historical statistics of degree-granting institutions, 174
history achievement levels by grade, 118
income by educational attainment, 377, 378
international comparisons
    of bachelor's degree recipients, 409
    of mathematics, 404
    of mathematics, reading, science, and problem-solving skills, 397
    of science scores, 408
internet usage, 423
labor force participation by, 374
labor force status of high school dropouts, 382
leisure activities of high school seniors, 142
life values of high school students, 390
literacy skills of adults, 379
master's degrees by, 270, 271, 272
mathematics and science skills for 1998 kindergarten cohort, 109
mathematics scores by age, 121, 122
mathematics scores by grade, 127
minimum credits earned by high school graduates, 140
occupations by, 376
postsecondary institutions
    associate's degrees by field of study, 253
    attendance status and state, 196
    attendance status at private institutions by state, 198
    attendance status at public institutions by state, 197
    degrees conferred by, 251
    employment in, 228, 229
    enrollment in, 178, 180, 181, 189
    enrollment in private institutions, 198, 199
    faculty in, 232, 235, 236, 237, 238
    faculty salaries by, 240, 241
    faculty with tenure in, 247

first-professional level enrollment at, 192
first-time freshmen at, 184, 185
    graduate enrollment at, 191
    historically black colleges and universities, 225
    institutions with more than 15,000 students, 220
    undergraduate enrollment at, 190
    women's colleges, 221
reading achievement levels by, 113
reading scores by, 110
reading skills for 1998 kindergarten cohort, 108
science scores and achievement levels of eighth-graders in public schools, 129
science scores and achievement levels by grade, 128
SAT scores for college-bound seniors, 132
student financial aid, 323, 324, 325
suspensions and expulsions from public schools, 148–149
teachers' educational attainment in schools by, 65
teachers in public schools, 66
time spent on homework and television by fourth-graders, 144
unemployment rate, 375
violence and drug use on school property, 150
volunteer activity by eighth-graders, 388
writing achievement levels by grade, 117
General Educational Development (GED), 103
Geography
    achievement levels by grade, 120
    scores by grade, 119
    enrollment, postsecondary education, 216
Geology, degrees in, 295
Geometry course work in high school, 139
    mathematics scores and, 123
German
    degrees conferred in, 291
    enrollment in high school, 53
Gifted and talented students, 51
Goals for education for college-bound seniors, 133
Government. *See also* Federal government; Local governments; States
    expenditures by level and function, 27
    support for education by agency, 363–364, 373
Grade levels
    enrollment in public elementary and secondary schools by, 34, 35, 36
    geography achievement levels by, 120
    geography and history scores by, 119
    history achievement levels by, 118
    minimum-competency testing by, 156
    percentage of children by type of schooling, 38
    public elementary and secondary schools by, 90
    public elementary schools by, 95
    public secondary schools by, 96
    violence and drug use on school property, 150
    writing achievement levels by, 117
Grades, average
    distribution of elementary and secondary school children by, 136
    SAT scores by, 133
Graduate-level studies
    disabled students enrolled in, 215
    enrollment in, 178, 180, 181
        by attendance status, 191
        by race/ethnicity and gender, 210

by state, 201, 202, 203
faculty teaching at, 233
field of study, 216
at institutions with more than 15,000 students, 220
international comparisons of degrees in science, 411
part-time faculty teaching at, 234
in science and engineering postsecondary programs, 217
tuition and fees for, 322
Graduate Record Examination (GRE), 318
Graduation requirements for high school, 154
Grants to students
graduate students receiving, 332, 333
undergraduates receiving, 323, 324, 325, 327, 328, 329, 334
Gross domestic product
compared to state and local government expenditures and
personal income, 30
compared to expenditures of educational institutions, 25
international comparisons of education expenditures as a
percentage of, 413
price index, 31

Half-day kindergarten, 153
mathematic and science skills for 1998 kindergarten cohort, 109
reading skills for 1998 kindergarten cohort, 108
Head Start program
allocations and enrollment by state, 370
percentage of preschoolers enrolled in, 42
Health sciences
associate's degrees in, 252, 253, 265, 266
bachelor's degrees in, 10, 254, 268, 269
Carnegie units required by state for high school graduation, 154
degrees conferred in, 258, 260, 292
doctor's degrees in, 256, 274, 275
enrollment, postsecondary education, 216
institutions conferring degrees in, 261
master's degrees in, 255, 271, 272
Higher education. *See* Postsecondary education
High school graduates
Carnegie units earned by, 137
Carnegie units required by state, 154
college enrollment and labor force status, 381
educational attainment of high school sophomores of 1990, 312
enrollment in postsecondary institutions, 186, 187, 188
GED credentialed, 103
by gender and control of school, 99
job satisfaction of 1988 eighth-graders, 391
from private secondary schools, 59
by state, 100, 101
by state and race/ethnicity, 102
students with disabilities, 106
High schools, 83. *See also* Private elementary and secondary
schools; Public elementary and secondary schools
High school seniors
drug usage by, 152
employment of, 380
leisure activities of, 142
life values of, 390
mathematics scores, 127
science scores and achievement levels, 128
Hispanics
with associate's degrees, 264, 265, 266
attendance patterns by tenth-graders, 145

with bachelor's degrees, 10, 267, 268, 269
child care arrangements by, 43
college enrollment and labor force status of high school
graduates, 381
course work and mathematics scores of 17-year-olds, 123
course work by high school graduates in mathematics and
science, 139
distribution in public schools, 93
with doctor's degrees, 273, 274, 275, 301–307
dropouts from high school, 102, 104
educational attainment, 8, 9, 12
employment of high school seniors, 380
enrollment distribution in public schools by state, 40
estimates of resident population by age, 16
family characteristics of, 19
with first-professional degrees, 276, 277, 278
high school graduates and dropouts, 102
internet usage, 423
labor force status of high school dropouts, 382
leisure activities of high school seniors, 142
with master's degrees, 270, 271, 272
mathematics achievement levels by age, 122
mathematics scores by age, 121
mathematics scores by grade, 127
percentage of population enrolled in school, 6
postsecondary institutions
employment in, 229
enrollment in, 187, 189, 210, 211, 212, 213
faculty in, 232, 235, 236, 237, 238
serving large proportions of, 222
poverty rates, 21
in public charter and traditional public schools, 97
reading levels by age, 113
reading scores by age, 110
reading scores and achievement levels of fourth-graders, 114
reading scores of fourth- and eighth-graders, 116
SAT scores for college-bound seniors, 131
science scores and achievement levels by grade, 128
science scores of eighth-graders in public schools by state, 129
unemployment rate, 375
violence and drug use on school property, 150
Historically black colleges and universities, 224, 225, 226
Historical summary statistics
Catholic schools, 58
degree-granting institutions, 174
enrollment at all levels, 3
expenditures of educational institutions, 25, 26
level of education attained, 8
number of school districts and public and private schools, 83
public elementary and secondary schools, 32
History
associate's degrees in, 252, 253, 265, 266
bachelor's degrees in, 10, 254, 268, 269
Carnegie units earned by high school graduates, 137
degrees conferred in, 258, 260, 298, 299
doctor's degrees in, 256, 274, 275
elementary and secondary achievement
levels by grade, 118
scores by grade, 119
enrollment, postsecondary education, 216
institutions conferring degrees in, 261
master's degrees in, 255, 271, 272

Home activities
    computers, 424, 425
    preschool literacy activities, 45, 46
Homeschooled students, 37, 38
Homework
    international comparisons in mathematics, 399, 400, 402, 404
    international comparisons in science, 406, 408
    mathematics, 124
    reading scores by amount of time on, 112
    time fourth-graders spent on, 144
Hospitals
    current-fund expenditures for at postsecondary institutions, 348
    current-fund revenues for postsecondary institutions, 335, 336
    expenditures at postsecondary institutions for, 346, 347, 352, 353
    revenues for postsecondary institutions, 337
    revenues for private postsecondary institutions, 340, 341
Household income. *See also* Income, family
    adult education participation, 359, 360
    center-based preprimary programs and, 42
    enrollment in preprimary education, 44
    homeschooled children, 37
    percentage of children by type of schooling, 38
    by state, 20
Humanities
    bachelor's and master's degrees in, 309
    doctor's degrees in, 301, 304

Illicit drug usage. *See* Drug usage
Income
    compared to gross domestic product and state and local government expenditures, 30
    by educational attainment, 377, 378
    family
        computer usage, 424, 426, 427
        of dropouts from high school, 105
        educational goals for college-bound seniors, 133
        grades earned by elementary and secondary students, 136
        internet usage, 423
        parental participation in educational activities with children, 24
        parental participation in school activities, 23
        student financial aid, 323, 324, 325
    household by state, 20 (*See also* Household income)
    for public libraries, 420
    teacher salaries, 72 (*See also* Salaries)
Index of Teachers' Emphasis on Mathematics Homework (EMH), 402
Individuals with Disabilities Education Act, 50
Instructional levels. *See* Grade levels
Instructional methods in science, 407
Instructional time in mathematics, 124, 126. *See also* Time
Instruction/Instructional staff. *See also* Faculty, postsecondary; Teachers, elementary and secondary
    postsecondary institutions
        expenditures for, 346, 347, 354
        expenditures for at private institutions, 352, 353
        Title IV, 173
    in public elementary and secondary schools, 77, 78, 79
        expenditures for, 161, 162, 163, 164, 165, 166
Interdisciplinary studies
    associate's degrees in, 252, 253, 265, 266

bachelor's degrees in, 254, 268, 269
degrees conferred in, 258, 260
doctor's degrees in, 256, 274, 275
institutions conferring degrees in, 261
master's degrees in, 255, 271, 272
Interest on school debt, 168. *See also* Expenditures
International Baccalaureate programs in public secondary schools, 141
International comparisons, 392–414
    bachelor's degree recipients, 409
    bachelor's degrees in science, 410
    education expenditures per student, 412
    eighth-graders' perceptions of mathematics, 403
    foreign students enrolled in United States, 414
    graduate degrees in science, 411
    instructional activities in science, 407
    mathematics
        class size for, 402
        instruction time, 401
        scores, 398, 399, 400, 404
    mathematics, reading, science, and problem-solving skills, 397
    population and enrollment, 392, 393
    public direct expenditures on education, 413
    pupils per teacher in elementary and secondary schools, 396
    school age population, 394
    science scores, 405, 406, 408
    secondary and postsecondary enrollment, 395
International relations, enrollment in postsecondary education, 216
Internet access/usage, 423
    home activities, 424, 425
    public elementary and secondary schools with, 422
Italian, enrollment in high school in, 53

Japanese, enrollment in high school in, 53
Job satisfaction, 391
Journalism, 284
Junior high schools, 90. *See also* Public elementary and secondary schools

Kindergarten
    age range for compulsory school attendance, 153
    mathematics and science skills for 1998 cohort, 109
    preschool literacy activities at home, 46
    readiness for, 47
    reading skills for 1998 cohort, 108

Labor force. *See also* Employment
    dropouts from high school, 105, 382
    high school graduates in, 381
    participation rates, 374
Language initially learned
    literacy skills of adults, 379
Latin, enrollment in high school in, 53
Law, first-professional degrees in, 262, 263, 277, 278
Legal professions
    associate's degrees in, 252, 253, 265, 266
    bachelor's degrees in, 254, 268, 269
    degrees conferred in, 258, 260
    doctor's degrees in, 256, 274, 275
    enrollment, postsecondary education, 216
    institutions conferring degrees in, 261
    master's degrees in, 255, 271, 272

Leisure activities
    of high school seniors, 142
    international comparisons of eighth-graders' perceptions about, 403
    reading scores in school influenced by, 112
Liabilities of postsecondary institutions, 356
Liberal arts and humanities
    associate's degrees in, 252, 253, 265, 266
    bachelor's degrees in, 10, 254, 268, 269
    degrees conferred in, 257, 258, 260
    doctor's degrees in, 256, 274, 275
    enrollment, postsecondary education, 216
    institutions conferring degrees in, 261
    master's degrees in, 255, 271, 272
Libraries
    expenditures at postsecondary institutions for, 346, 347
    in postsecondary institutions, 418, 419
    public, 420, 421
    school, 415, 416, 417
Library science
    associate's degrees in, 252, 253, 265, 266
    bachelor's degrees in, 254, 268, 269
    degrees conferred in, 258, 260
    doctor's degrees in, 256, 274, 275
    enrollment, postsecondary education, 216
    institutions conferring degrees in, 261
    master's degrees in, 255, 271, 272
Life sciences
    doctor's degrees in, 301, 305
    international comparisons of eighth-graders' scores, 406
    international comparisons of fourth-graders' scores, 405
Life values of high school seniors, 390
Literacy skills of adults, 379
Loans to students
    graduate students receiving, 330, 331, 332, 333
    undergraduates receiving, 323, 324, 325, 327, 328, 329
Local communities, public opinion on condition of public schools, 22
Local governments
    expenditures by, 27, 28
    expenditures on education, 29
    postsecondary institutions
        appropriations for, 339
        revenues for, 335, 336, 337, 338
        revenues for private, 340, 341, 342, 343
        revenues for public elementary and secondary schools, 158, 159, 160

Marital status, 18
Master's degrees
    by control of institution, 259, 260, 308
    by field of study, 255, 279–300
    by gender, 251
    number of institutions conferring, 261
    by race/ethnicity and gender, 270, 271, 272
    salaries of teachers with, 74
    by state, 309, 310
    student financial aid for, 330, 331, 332, 333
Mathematics
    achievement in eighth grade and volunteer activity of young adults, 388

elementary and secondary education
    Carnegie units earned by high school graduates, 137
    Carnegie units required by states for high school graduation, 154
    course work and scores of 17-year-olds, 123
    course work by high school graduates, 139
    proficiency levels by age, 122
    scores and achievement levels of eighth-graders in public schools, 125
    scores and achievement levels of fourth-graders, 124
    scores by grade, 127
    scores by student and school characteristics, 121
    skill levels for 1998 kindergartners until 2004, 109
    statistics on public school education, 126
international comparisons, 397, 398, 399, 400, 404
    of bachelor's degrees in, 410
    of class size, 402
    of eighth-graders perceptions about, 403
    of graduate degrees in, 411
    of time spent in mathematics instruction, 401
postsecondary education
    associate's degrees in, 252, 253, 265, 266
    bachelor's degrees in, 10, 254, 268, 269
    course work for bachelor's degrees, 313
    degrees conferred in, 258, 260, 293
    doctor's degrees in, 256, 274, 275, 301
    enrollment, 216
    institutions conferring degrees in, 261
    master's degrees in, 255, 271, 272
Mechanical engineering, degrees in, 288. *See also* Engineering
Media centers in schools, 415, 416, 417
Medicine, first-professional degrees in, 262, 263, 277, 278. *See also* Health sciences
Metropolitan status
    adult education participation, 359, 360
    building deficiencies in public schools, 98
    center-based preprimary programs and, 42
    crime incidents reported at public schools, 147
    dual credit, Advanced Placement, and International Baccalaureate enrollment in public schools, 141
    educational attainment by, 14
    employment of high school seniors, 380
    high school graduates enrolled in postsecondary institutions by, 188
    homeschooled children, 37
    largest school districts, 89
    percentage of children by type of schooling, 38
    public elementary and secondary schools, 86
    public elementary and secondary schools with internet access, 422
    reading scores of eighth-graders by, 115
    school districts of more than 15,000 students, 87, 88
    schools with security measures, 146
    time spent on homework and television by fourth-graders, 144
Microbiology, degrees in, 282
Middle schools, 90. *See also* Public elementary and secondary schools
Military technologies
    associate's degrees in, 252, 253, 265, 266
    bachelor's degrees in, 254, 268, 269
    degrees conferred in, 258, 260
    doctor's degrees in, 256, 274, 275
    enrollment, postsecondary education, 216

institutions conferring degrees in, 261
   master's degrees in, 255, 271, 272
Minimum-competency testing by state, 156
Minority enrollment in postsecondary institutions, 212, 213, 214.
   See also Race/ethnicity
Mobility
   residence and migration of freshmen in postsecondary
      institutions, 207, 208, 209
   of teachers in public and private schools, 70
Mothers
   center-based preprimary programs and, 42
   level of education and literacy activities, 46 (*See also* Parents)
   preprimary education and, 44
Motor skills, 107
Music, scores for eighth-graders, 130

Natural sciences. *See also* Science
   enrollment, postsecondary education, 216
   international comparisons of graduate degrees in science, 411
Need-based student financial aid, 334. *See also* Financial aid to
   students
No Child Left Behind Act (2001). *See also* Title I allocations
   appropriations by states, 368
Non-degree-granting institutions, 173, 361
Nonsectarian private elementary and secondary schools, 55, 56
Not-for-profit private postsecondary institutions, 199. *See also*
   Private postsecondary institutions
   enrollment in, 179
   revenues to, 341
Nutrition programs, 369

Occupation
   adult education participation, 359, 360
   bachelor's degree recipients by, 385
   computer usage at work, 427
   by educational attainment, 376
One-parent households, 18, 21
One-teacher schools, 90, 94
Opinions on education
   public on condition of public schools, 22
   teachers on problems in schools, 68
   teachers on school conditions, 69
Organization of Economic Cooperation and Development (OECD)
   mathematics, reading, science and problem-solving skills, 397
   mathematics scores, 398

Parental level of education
   art scores of children, 130
   educational attainment of high school sophomores of 1990, 312
   educational goals for college-bound seniors, 133
   grades earned by elementary and secondary students, 136
   geography and history scores of children, 118, 119
   homeschooled children and, 37
   mathematics and science skills for 1998 kindergarten cohort,
     109
   mathematics scores of children, 121, 125, 127
   reading scores of children, 110, 116
   reading skills for 1998 kindergarten cohort, 108
   writing achievement levels of children, 117
Parents
   involvement in educational activities with children, 24
   preprimary education and characteristics of mothers, 44

readiness for kindergarten, 47
   school activities, participation in, 23
Part-time attendance at postsecondary institutions, 175, 182
   by age and gender, 177
   by control and type of institution, 179
   first-professional level enrollment at, 192
   first-time freshmen, 184, 185
   graduate enrollment, 191, 331
   graduate-level student financial aid, 333
   institutions with more than 15,000 students, 220
   by level, 178, 180, 181
   in private institutions by state, 198, 199
   in public institutions by state, 197
   by race/ethnicity and gender, 210
   by state, 196
   student financial aid, 325, 328, 329
Part-time employment in postsecondary institutions, 228, 229, 231
Part-time faculty, 234. *See also* Faculty
Performing arts
   associate's degrees in, 252, 253, 265, 266
   bachelor's degrees in, 254, 268, 269
   degrees conferred in, 258, 260, 300
   doctor's degrees in, 256, 274, 275
   eighth-graders, scores for, 130
   enrollment, postsecondary education, 216
   institutions conferring degrees in, 261
   master's degrees in, 255, 271, 272
Pharmacy, first-professional degrees in, 263, 277, 278
Philosophy, religion, and theology
   associate's degrees in, 252, 253, 265, 266
   bachelor's degrees in, 10, 254, 268, 269
   degrees conferred in, 258, 260
   doctor's degrees in, 256, 274, 275
   first-professional degrees in theology, 263, 277, 278
   enrollment, postsecondary education, 216
   institutions conferring degrees in, 261
   master's degrees in, 255, 271, 272
Physical education, state requirements for high school graduation,
   154
Physical plant value, postsecondary institutions, 356
Physical sciences
   associate's degrees in, 252, 253, 265, 266
   bachelor's degrees in, 254, 268, 269
   course work for bachelor's degrees, 313
   degrees conferred in, 257, 258, 260, 294
   doctor's degrees in, 256, 274, 275, 301, 306
   enrollment, postsecondary education, 216
   institutions conferring degrees in, 261
   international comparisons of eighth-graders' scores, 406
   international comparisons of fourth-graders' scores, 405
   master's degrees in, 255, 271, 272
Physics
   course work in high school, 137, 139
   degrees in, 295
   international comparisons of time spent on eighth-grade science,
    407
Podiatry, first-professional degrees in, 263, 277, 278
Political science and government
   degrees conferred in, 299
   enrollment, postsecondary education, 216
Population
   by age and race/ethnicity, 16

by age group, 15
gross domestic product and income, 30
historical statistics of, 32
international comparisons, 392, 393
international comparisons of secondary and postsecondary enrollment, 395
percentage enrolled in school, 6, 7
public libraries serving, 420
ratio to employment status, 374
school-age, by state, 17
Postbaccalaureate education, 386. *See also* Graduate-level studies
Postsecondary education, 173–361
admission requirements for institutions, 314
applications, admissions, and enrollment for undergraduates, 315
assets and liabilities of institutions, 356
closing of institutions, 250
computer usage by students, 426
course work in, 313
Department of Education outlays for, 366
doctor's degrees by institution, 311
endowment funds for institutions, 356, 357
enrollment at all levels, 2
enrollment status of bachelor's degree recipients, 386
expenditures on, 25, 26, 28, 346 (*See also under* Expenditures)
federal support for, 362, 364
high school graduates enrolling in, 381
institutions with more than 15,000 students, 220
largest colleges and universities, 219
libraries in institutions, 418, 419
non-degree-granting Title IV institutions, 361
number of institutions, 5, 214, 218, 248
number of institutions by state, 249
participants in, 1
per capita expenditures on, 29
special education students enrolled in, 383
Poverty rates
in largest 100 school districts, 89
by race/ethnicity, 21
in school districts of more than 15,000 students, 88
by state, 20
Poverty status
center-based preprimary programs and, 42
Preprimary education
center-based programs, 42
enrollment and characteristics of children, 44
enrollment in, 41
literacy activities at home, 45, 46
in public elementary schools, 95
Preschool programs, 41. *See also* Preprimary education
Price indexes, 31
Primary schools. *See* Private elementary and secondary schools; Public elementary and secondary schools
Principals
in private elementary and secondary schools, 57, 82
in public elementary and secondary schools, 82
Private elementary and secondary schools
attendance patterns by tenth-graders, 145
Catholic schools, 58 (*See also* Catholic schools)
course work by high school graduates in mathematics and science, 139
disabled students in, 49

enrollment in, 2, 55
enrollment in grades 9 to 12 compared to population, 52
expenditures of, 26
extracurricular activities of high school sophomores, 143
grade point averages, 136
graduates enrolled in postsecondary institutions, 188
high school graduates, 59, 99
historical and projected enrollment statistics, 3
international comparisons of expenditures on, 412
leisure activities of high school seniors, 142
mathematics and science skills for 1998 kindergarten cohort, 109
mathematics scores by grade, 127
minimum credits earned by high school graduates, 140
mobility of teachers, 70
number of, 5, 83
opinions of teachers on school conditions, 68, 69
parental participation in educational activities with children, 24
parental participation in school activities, 23
participants in, 1
percentage of children in, 38
preprimary education, 41
principals in, 82
reading scores of fourth- and eighth-graders in, 116
reading skills for 1998 kindergarten cohort, 108
salaries of teachers, 72
school libraries and media centers, 415
with security measures, 146
staff-to-student ratios, 57
teachers
characteristics of, 65
number of, 4, 55
time spent on homework and television by fourth-graders, 144
tuition for, 56
Private funding for public elementary and secondary schools, 159, 160
Private gifts and grants
postsecondary institutions, 335, 336, 337
revenues to private postsecondary institutions, 340, 341, 342, 343
by source, 351
Private postsecondary institutions
admission requirements for, 314
applications, admissions and enrollment comparisons, 315
attendance status of students at, 182, 198
with branch campuses, 248
closing of institutions, 250
by control and affiliation, 183
current-fund revenues, 344
degrees conferred at, 218, 259, 260, 261, 308
enrollment, 175, 176, 179, 180, 181
by race/ethnicity in, 211
by state, 195, 200, 202, 203
expenditures of, 26, 345, 352, 353, 355
faculty in, 4, 231, 233, 235, 236
benefit expenditures for, 246
salaries, 239, 240, 241, 242, 243, 244, 245
tenure, 247
first-professional level enrollment at, 192
first-time freshmen at, 184, 185
full-time-equivalent enrollment in, 204, 205, 206
full-time-equivalent staff at, 230

graduate enrollment, 191
historically black colleges and universities, 226
international comparisons of expenditures on, 412
non-degree-granting Title IV institutions, 361
not-for-profit institutions, 199
number of, 5, 214, 249
part-time faculty in, 234
remedial coursework offered by, 316
revenues for by source, 340, 341, 342, 343
staff in, 227, 228, 229
student financial aid
   graduate students receiving, 330, 331, 332, 333
   undergraduate students receiving, 326, 327, 328, 329
tuition, fees and board rates for undergraduates, 319, 320, 321
tuition and fees for graduate-level studies, 322
undergraduate enrollment at, 190
Problems in schools, opinions of teachers on, 68
Problem-solving skills of 15-year-olds by country, 397
Proficiency levels. *See* Achievement levels *and under individual subjects*
Projections of statistics, enrollment at all levels, 3
Psychology
   associate's degrees in, 252, 253, 265, 266
   bachelor's degrees in, 10, 254, 268, 269
   course work for bachelor's degrees, 313
   degrees conferred in, 258, 260, 296
   doctor's degrees in, 256, 274, 275, 301, 307
   enrollment, postsecondary education, 216
   institutions conferring degrees in, 261
   master's degrees in, 255, 271, 272
Public administration
   associate's degrees in, 252, 253, 265, 266
   bachelor's degrees in, 254, 268, 269
   degrees conferred in, 258, 260, 297
   doctor's degrees in, 256, 274, 275
   enrollment, postsecondary education, 216
   institutions conferring degrees in, 261
   master's degrees in, 255, 271, 272
Public elementary and secondary schools
   attendance patterns by tenth-graders, 145
   average daily attendance at, 39
   charter schools, 97
   course work by high school graduates in mathematics and science, 139
   crime incidents at, 147
   disabled students in, 49
   distance education participation, 54
   dual credit, Advanced Placement, and International Baccalaureate enrollment, 141
   education agencies, 85
   elementary schools by state and grade span, 95
   enrollment
      at all levels, 2
      distribution by state and race/ethnicity, 40
      by grade, 36
      in grades 9 to 12 compared to population, 52
      by size, 91
      by state, 33, 34, 35
   expenditures, 26
      by function, 163, 164, 165
      for instruction, 166
      per pupil, 167, 168, 169, 170, 171

by purpose, 161
by state, 162
for transportation to school, 172
extracurricular activities of high school sophomores, 143
foreign language enrollment, 53
grades earned by students, 136
by grade spans included, 90
graduates enrolled in postsecondary institutions, 188
high school graduates, 99, 100, 101
high school graduates and dropouts, 102
historical and projected enrollment statistics, 3
historical statistics for, 32
international comparisons of expenditures on, 412
internet access, 422
leisure activities of high school seniors, 142
mathematics and science skills for 1998 kindergarten cohort, 109
mathematics instruction in, 126
mathematics scores by grade, 127
mathematics scores and achievement levels of eighth-graders by state, 125
mathematics scores and achievement levels of fourth-graders by state, 124
minimum credits earned by high school graduates, 140
mobility of teachers, 70
number of, 5, 83
number of school districts, 83
opinions of teachers on problems in schools, 68
opinions of teachers on school conditions, 69
parental participation in educational activities with children, 24
parental participation in school activities, 23
participants in, 1
percentage of children in, 38
preprimary education, 41
principals in, 82
public opinion on condition of, 22
pupil-to-staff ratios in, 81
pupil-to-teacher ratios, 60, 63
race/ethnicity distribution in, 93
reading scores and achievement levels of eighth-graders in, 115
reading scores of fourth- and eighth-graders in, 116
reading scores and achievement levels of fourth-graders in, 114
   (*See also under* Reading)
reading skills for 1998 kindergarten cohort, 108
revenues by source of funds, 158, 159, 160
school libraries and media centers, 415, 416, 417
school size, 92
science scores of eighth-graders by state, 129
science scores and achievement levels by grade, 128
secondary schools by state and grade levels, 96
with security measures, 146
staff in, 77, 78, 79
by state and type of school, 94
subjects taught in high school, 67
suspensions and expulsions from, 148–149
teachers, 4, 62 (*See also* Teachers)
   characteristics of, 64, 65, 66
   as percentage of staff in, 80
   salaries, 71, 72, 73, 74, 75, 76
time spent on homework and television by fourth-graders, 144
transportation to school, 172
by urbanicity, 86

Public libraries, 420, 421
Public opinion. *See* Opinions on education
Public postsecondary institutions
    admission requirements for, 314
    affiliation of, 183
    applications, admissions and enrollment comparisons, 315
    appropriations for by state, 339
    attendance status at, 175, 182, 197
    with branch campuses, 248
    closing of institutions, 250
    current-fund expenditures at, 348, 349
    current-fund revenues, 344
    degrees conferred at, 218, 259, 260, 308
    educational and general expenditures at, 350
    enrollment, 176, 179, 180, 181
        by race/ethnicity in, 211
        by state, 194, 200, 202, 203
    expenditures of, 26, 345, 347
    faculty in, 4, 231, 233, 235, 236
        benefit expenditures for, 246
        salaries, 239, 240, 241, 242, 243, 244, 245
        tenure, 247
    first-professional level enrollment at, 192
    first-time freshmen at, 184, 185
    full-time-equivalent enrollment in, 204, 205, 206
    full-time-equivalent staff at, 230
    graduate enrollment, 191
    historically black colleges and universities, 226
    institutions conferring degrees in, 261
    international comparisons of expenditures on, 412
    non-degree-granting Title IV institutions, 361
    number of, 5, 214, 249
    part-time faculty in, 234
    remedial coursework offered by, 316
    revenues, 337
    staff in, 227, 228, 229
    student financial aid
        graduate students receiving, 330, 331, 332, 333
        undergraduate students receiving, 326, 327, 328, 329
    tuition, fees, and board rates for undergraduates, 319, 320, 321
    tuition and fees for graduate-level studies, 322
    undergraduate enrollment, 190
Pupils
    average number in public elementary schools, 95
    expenditures per in public schools, 167, 168, 169, 170, 171
    to-staff ratios in public elementary and secondary schools, 81
    to-teacher ratios, 60, 61
        international comparisons, 396
        by state in public schools, 63
        by urbanicity in public schools, 86

Race/ethnicity
    ACT scores, 135
    adult education participation, 359, 360
    art scores for eighth-graders, 130
    associate's degrees by, 264, 265, 266
    attendance patterns by tenth-graders, 145
    bachelor's degrees by, 267, 268, 269
    Carnegie units earned by high school graduates, 137
    Carnegie units earned by high school graduates in vocational education by, 138
    center-based programs and, 42
    child care arrangements by, 43
    college enrollment and labor force status of high school graduates by, 381
    computer usage, 424, 425, 426, 427
    course work and mathematics scores of 17-year-olds, 123
    course work by high school graduates in mathematics and science, 139
    distribution in public schools, 93
    doctor's degrees by, 273, 274, 275, 301–307
    dropouts from high school by, 104
    educational attainment, 8, 9, 12
    educational attainment of high school sophomores of 1990, 312
    employment of high school seniors, 380
    enrollment distribution in public schools by state, 40
    enrollment in postsecondary institutions, 187, 210, 211
    estimates of resident population by age, 16
    extracurricular activities of high school sophomores, 143
    family characteristics by, 19
    first-professional degrees by, 276, 277, 278
    geography scores and achievement levels by grade, 119, 120
    grades earned by elementary and secondary students, 136
    high school graduates and dropouts by, 102
    history scores and achievement levels by grade, 118, 119
    homeschooled children, 37
    internet usage, 423
    labor force participation by, 374
    labor force status of high school dropouts, 382
    leisure activities of high school seniors, 142
    literacy skills of adults, 379
    master's degrees by, 270, 271, 272
    mathematics and science skills for 1998 kindergarten cohort, 109
    mathematics scores and achievement levels by age, 121, 122
    mathematics scores by grade, 127
    minimum credits earned by high school graduates, 140
    number of persons with bachelor's degrees, 10
    parental participation in educational activities with children, 24
    parental participation in school activities, 23
    percentage of children by type of schooling, 38
    percentage of population enrolled in school, 6
    postsecondary institutions
        employment in, 229
        enrollment in, 189, 211, 212, 213
        faculty in, 232, 235, 236, 237, 238
    poverty rates by, 21
    preschool literacy activities at home, 46
    in public charter and traditional public schools, 97
    reading scores by age, 110
    reading levels by age, 113
    reading scores of fourth- and eighth-graders, 116
    reading scores and achievement levels of fourth-graders, 114
    reading skills for 1998 kindergarten cohort, 108
    SAT scores for college-bound seniors, 131
    school districts of more than 15,000 students, 87
    science scores and achievement levels by grade, 128
    science scores of eighth-graders in public schools by state, 129
    student financial aid, 323, 324, 325
    suspensions and expulsions from public schools, 148–149
    teachers' educational attainment in schools by, 65
    time spent on homework and television by fourth-graders, 144
    unemployment rate, 375
    violence and drug use on school property, 150
    volunteer activity by 1988 eighth-graders as young adults, 388

writing achievement levels by grade, 117

Reading
   levels by age, gender, and race/ethnicity, 113
   scores by age, 110
      and percentile, 111
      and time spent on reading and homework, 112
   eighth-graders, scores and achievement levels for, 115
   fourth- and eighth-graders, scores for, 116
   fourth-graders, scores and achievement levels for, 114
   international comparisons of 15-year-olds, 397
   preschool literacy activities at home, 45, 46
   skill levels for 1998 kindergarten students by age, 108

Regional distribution
   art scores for eighth-graders, 130
   doctoral recipients' anticipated employment, 301
   dual credit, Advanced Placement, and International
      Baccalaureate enrollment in public schools, 141
   extracurricular activities of high school sophomores, 143
   geography scores and achievement levels by grade, 119, 120
   history scores and achievement levels by grade, 118, 119
   homeschooled children, 37
   mathematics scores by age, 121
   reading scores by age, 110
   schooling type, percentage of children by, 38

Religious affiliation
   postsecondary institutions, 183
   private elementary and secondary schools, 55, 57

Remedial coursework, postsecondary institutions offering, 316

Renovations in public elementary and secondary schools, 98

Research
   expenditures at postsecondary institutions for, 346, 347, 352,
      353, 354
   federal support for, 362, 364, 372, 373

Residency of freshmen attending in-state postsecondary
   institutions, 207, 208, 209

Revenues
   postsecondary institutions
      current-fund by source, 335, 336
      from federal government, 344
      private institutions, 340, 341, 342, 343
      for public postsecondary institutions, 338
      by source, 337
      voluntary support, 351
   public elementary and secondary schools
      historical statistics, 32
      source of funds for, 158, 159, 160
      by urbanicity, 86
   in school districts of more than 15,000 students, 88

Risk factors for students
   mathematic and science skills for 1998 kindergarten cohort, 109
   reading skills for 1998 kindergarten cohort, 108

Room and board for undergraduates at postsecondary institutions,
   319, 320, 321

Rural areas, public elementary and secondary schools, 86

Russian, enrollment in high school in, 53

Salaries
   of recent bachelor's degree recipients, 385, 387
   of faculty in postsecondary institutions, 235, 236
      by academic rank, 240, 241
      by field of study, 239
      by state, 242, 243, 244, 245

   of principals in public and private schools, 82
   public school expenditures for, 165, 166
   of teachers in public schools, 71, 73, 74, 75, 76
   of teachers in public and private schools, 72

SAT scores
   of postsecondary applicants, by type and control of institution,
      315
   of college-bound seniors
      by student characteristics, 131, 132, 133
      by state, 134

Scholarships for college, 334. *See also* Financial aid to students

Scholastic Aptitude Test. *See* SAT scores

School activities, parental participation in, 23

School-age population
   international comparisons, 394
   by state, 17

School conditions
   building deficiencies in public schools, 98
   crime at public schools, 147
   teachers' opinions on, 69
   violence and drug use, 150

School districts, 85
   enrollment and poverty in 100 largest, 89
   by enrollment size, 84
   with more than 15,000 students, 87, 88
   number of, 83

School libraries, 415, 416, 417

School lunch program. *See* Free school lunch program

Science
   elementary and secondary education
      Carnegie units earned by high school graduates, 137
      Carnegie units required by states for high school graduation,
         154
      course work by high school graduates in, 139
      scores and achievement levels by grade, 128
      scores of eighth-graders in public schools, 129
      skill levels for 1998 kindergartners till 2004, 109
   international comparisons, 397
      of bachelor's degree recipients, 410
      of eighth-graders' scores, 406
      of fourth-graders' scores, 405
      of graduate degrees in, 411
      of instructional practices, 407
      of scores at the end of secondary school, 408
   postsecondary education
      associate's degrees in, 252, 253
      bachelor's and master's degrees in, 309
      bachelor's degrees in, 10, 254
      biology degrees, 281, 282
      course work for bachelor's degrees, 313
      degrees conferred in, 257, 258, 260
      doctor's degrees in, 256, 301, 305–306
      enrollment, 216
      federal support to institutions for, 371
      graduate-level enrollment in, 217
      institutions conferring degrees in, 261
      master's degrees in, 255
      physical sciences degrees, 294

Secondary education for adults, 358

Secondary schools. *See* Private elementary and secondary schools;
   Public elementary and secondary schools

Security
  associate's degrees in, 252, 253, 265, 266
  bachelor's degrees in, 254, 268, 269
  degrees conferred in, 258, 260
  doctor's degrees in, 256, 274, 275
  institutions conferring degrees in, 261
  master's degrees in, 255, 271, 272
  schools with measures for, 146
Self-confidence in learning mathematics (SCM), international comparisons of eighth-graders', 403. *See also* Mathematics
Sex. *See* Gender
Shutdowns of postsecondary institutions, 250
Skills. *See also under individual subjects*
  international comparisons of problem-solving for 15-year-olds, 397
  literacy skills of adults, 379
  in mathematics by age, 122
  readiness for kindergarten, 47
  specific mathematics skills of fifth-graders, 109
  specific reading skills of fifth-graders, 108
Social sciences
  associate's degrees in, 252, 253, 265, 266
  bachelor's and master's degrees in, 309
  bachelor's degrees in, 10, 254, 268, 269
  course work for bachelor's degrees, 313
  degrees conferred in, 257, 258, 260, 298
  doctor's degrees in, 256, 274, 275, 301, 307
  enrollment, postsecondary education, 216
  institutions conferring degrees in, 261
  master's degrees in, 255, 271, 272
Social services, degrees in, 297
Social studies, Carnegie units required by states for high school graduation, 154
Socioeconomic status
  attendance patterns by tenth-graders, 145
  educational attainment of high school sophomores of 1990, 312
  employment of high school seniors, 380
  extracurricular activities of high school sophomores, 143
  leisure activities of high school seniors, 142
  mathematics and science skills for 1998 kindergarten cohort, 109
  reading skills for 1998 kindergarten cohort, 108
  volunteer activity of young adults, 388
Sociology
  degrees conferred in, 299
  enrollment, postsecondary education, 216
Spanish
  degrees conferred in, 291
  enrollment in high school, 53
Special education
  age range for compulsory attendance, 153
  postsecondary education and employment status of students in, 383
  students exiting, 106
Staff. *See also* Teachers, elementary and secondary; Faculty, postsecondary
  in postsecondary institutions, 227–247
    by employment status, 228
    full-time-equivalent, 230
    in libraries, 418, 419
    by race/ethnicity and gender, 229
  in private elementary and secondary schools, 57

  in public elementary and secondary schools, 77, 78, 79, 80
  pupil-to-staff ratios in public schools, 81
States
  adult education participation, 358
  age range for compulsory school attendance, 153
  average daily attendance at public schools, 39
  Carnegie units required for high school graduation, 154
  certification test for teachers, 157
  child nutrition programs, Department of Agriculture obligations for, 369
  criterion-referenced assessments, 155
  degrees conferred in, 308, 309, 310
  Department of Education appropriations, 367
  education agencies in, 85
  educational attainment, 11, 12, 13
  enrollment in public elementary and secondary schools, 33, 34, 35
  enrollment by race/ethnicity in public schools, 40
  expenditures
    on education, 29
    by governments of, 27, 28
    in public elementary and secondary schools, 162, 163, 164, 166, 168, 169, 170, 171
    on research, 373
  first-time freshmen at postsecondary institutions, 185
  gifted and talented students, 51
  graduates from private schools, 59
  Head Start programs, allocations for, 370
  high school graduates and dropouts, 102
  high school graduates, 100, 101
  household income and poverty rates, 20
  Individuals with Disabilities Education Act, children served under, 50
  mathematics education in public schools, 126
  mathematics scores and achievement levels of eighth-graders in public schools, 125
  mathematics scores and achievement levels of fourth-graders in public schools, 124
  minimum-competency testing by, 156
  postsecondary institutions
    appropriations for, 339
    attendance status and gender, 196, 197
    current-fund expenditures at, 349
    employment in, 230
    enrollment in, 193, 200, 201, 202, 203, 212, 213
    enrollment in private institutions, 199
    expenditures for private institutions, 355
    expenditures for public institutions, 350
    faculty salaries, 242, 243, 244, 245
    full-time-equivalent enrollment, 205, 206
    institutions with more than 15,000 students, 220
    non-degree-granting Title IV institutions, 361
    number in, 249
    private institutions, 195, 198
    public institutions, 194
    residence and migration of freshmen, 207, 208, 209
    revenues for, 338
  public elementary and secondary schools by type of school, 94
  public elementary schools by grade span, 95
  public libraries in, 421
  public secondary schools by grade span, 96
  pupil-to-staff ratios in public schools, 81
  pupil-to-teacher ratios in public schools, 63

reading scores and achievement levels of eighth-graders in public schools, 115

reading scores and achievement levels of fourth-graders in public schools, 114

revenues for public elementary and secondary schools, 158, 159, 160

revenues to postsecondary institutions, 335, 336, 337

revenues to private postsecondary institutions, 340, 341, 342, 343

salaries of teachers in public schools, 73, 74, 76

SAT scores, 134

school-age population, 17

school districts of more than 15,000 students, 87, 88

school libraries and media centers, 417

science scores of eighth-graders in public schools, 129

staff in public elementary and secondary schools, 78, 79

student financial aid, 326, 330, 331, 334

suspensions and expulsions from public schools, 148–149

teachers as percentage of staff in public schools, 80

teachers in public elementary and secondary schools, 62, 64

Title I agency programs, appropriations for, 368

tuition, fees, and board rates for undergraduates, 320

Statistics and mathematics. *See also* Mathematics

bachelor's degrees in, 10

degrees conferred in, 293

enrollment, postsecondary education, 216

Status dropouts from high school, 104. *See also* Dropouts from high school

Student financial aid

graduate level, 330, 331, 332, 333

undergraduate level, 323, 324, 325, 326, 327, 328, 329

Students. *See* Graduate-level studies; Pupils; Undergraduate-level studies

Student-to-faculty ratios, 230

Subjects taught in public high schools, characteristics of teachers by, 67

Suburban areas, public elementary and secondary schools, 86

Suspensions from public schools, 149

Talented students, 51

Teachers, elementary and secondary

average class size for in public schools, 64

in Catholic schools, 58

characteristics of in public schools, 66

degrees and teaching experience at the elementary/secondary level, 65

historical statistics of public schools, 32

international comparisons, 392, 396

mobility of, 70

number of, 1, 4

opinions on readiness for kindergarten, 47

opinions on school conditions, 68, 69

in private elementary and secondary schools, 55, 57, 59

in public charter and traditional public schools, 97

in public elementary and secondary schools, 62, 63, 80

salaries in public schools, 71, 73, 74, 75, 76

salaries in public and private schools, 72

states requiring test for certification, 157

subjects taught in public high schools, 67

Teachers' Emphasis on Mathematics Homework (EMH), international comparisons of eighth-grade, 402

Teaching experience

salaries by, 71, 73, 74

teachers in public schools, 64

teachers in public and private schools, 65

Teenagers

drug usage by, 151

international comparisons of mathematics, 398

international comparisons of mathematics, reading, science, and problem-solving, 397

Television viewing by fourth-graders, 124, 144

Tenth grade

attendance patterns, 145

extracurricular activities of high school sophomores, 143

Tenure for faculty, 247

Testing, state

criterion-referenced assessments, 155

minimum-competency testing, 156

teacher certification testing, 157

Theatre, scores for eighth-graders, 130

Theology, first-professional degrees in, 263, 277, 278. *See also* Philosophy, religion, and theology

Time, use of

by fourth-graders on homework and television, 144

on homework and reading by age, 112

international comparisons

on mathematics homework and study outside of school, 399, 400, 404

in mathematics instruction, 401

on science homework and study outside of school, 406, 408

in science instruction, 405, 407

in mathematics instruction by state, 124, 126

Time-series studies

birth cohort of 2001, 107

eighth-graders of 1988, 388, 391

high school sophomores of 1990, 312

kindergartners of 1998, 47, 108, 109

Title I allocations

to largest school districts, 89

in school districts of more than 15,000 students, 88

by states, 368

Title IV postsecondary institutions, 173

non-degree-granting, 361

number of, 5, 361

Transportation to school, 172

Tribally controlled institutions, 223

Tuition

for private elementary and secondary schools, 56

as revenue to postsecondary institutions, 335, 336, 337, 338

as revenue to private institutions, 340, 341, 342, 343

for undergraduates, 319, 320, 321

Two-year postsecondary institutions

admission requirements for, 314

applications, admissions and enrollment comparisons, 315

attendance status at, 182

with branch campuses, 248

closing of institutions, 250

completion status for students, 317

current-fund revenues for postsecondary institutions, 337

enrollment in, 176, 179, 180, 181

by race/ethnicity, 211

by recent high school completers, 188

by state, 200, 202, 203

expenditures at private institutions, 352
expenditures of, 345, 347, 353, 354
faculty in, 231
    salaries, 241, 242, 243
    tenure, 247
field of study at, 216
first-time freshmen at, 184
full-time-equivalent enrollment in, 204, 205
full-time-equivalent staff at, 230
historically black colleges and universities, 226
number of institutions, 214, 249
remedial coursework offered by, 316
revenues of private institutions, 340, 341, 342, 343
revenues of public institutions, 337, 338
staff in, 228, 229
student financial aid, 326, 327, 328, 329
Title IV postsecondary institutions, 173
tuition, fees, and board rates, 319, 320, 321
undergraduate enrollment at, 190

Undergraduate-level studies
    admission requirements for institutions, 314
    applications, admissions, and enrollment comparisons, 315
    disabled students enrolled in, 215
    enrollment, 178, 180, 181
        by attendance status, 190
        by field of study, 216
        by race/ethnicity and gender, 210
        by state, 201, 202, 203
    faculty teaching at, 233
    at institutions with more than 15,000 students, 220
    part-time faculty teaching at, 234
    student financial aid, 323, 324, 325, 326, 327, 328, 329, 334
    tuition, fees, and board rates for, 319, 320, 321
Unemployment rate, 375
    for dropouts from high school, 105, 382
    of high school graduates, 381
United States Department of Education. *See* Department of Education
United States history, achievement levels and scores by grade, 118, 119. *See also* History
Universities, 176. *See also* Private postsecondary institutions; Public postsecondary institutions
Urbanicity. *See* Metropolitan status

Value of property, postsecondary institutions, 356
Values of high school senior, 390
Veterinary medicine, first-professional degrees in, 263, 277, 278
Violent crimes
    percentage of students experiencing, 150
    at public elementary and secondary schools, 147
Visual arts
    associate's degrees in, 252, 253, 265, 266
    bachelor's degrees in, 254, 268, 269
    degrees conferred in, 258, 260, 300
    doctor's degrees in, 256, 274, 275
    eighth-graders, scores for, 130
    enrollment, postsecondary education, 216
    institutions conferring degrees in, 261
    master's degrees in, 255, 271, 272

Vocational schools/education
    Carnegie units earned by high school graduates, 137, 138
    Carnegie units required by state for high school graduation, 154
    public secondary schools, vocational, 96
Voluntary support for postsecondary institutions, 351
Volunteering by young adults, 388

Whites
    with associate's degrees, 264, 265, 266
    attendance patterns by tenth-graders, 145
    with bachelor's degrees, 10, 267, 268, 269
    child care arrangements by, 43
    college enrollment and labor force status of high school graduates, 381
    course work and mathematics scores of 17-year-olds, 123
    course work by high school graduates in mathematics and science, 139
    distribution in public schools, 93
    with doctor's degrees, 273, 274, 275, 301–307
    dropouts from high school, 104
    educational attainment, 8, 9, 12
    employment of high school seniors, 380
    enrollment distribution in public schools by state, 40
    estimates of resident population by age, 16
    family characteristics of, 19
    with first-professional degrees, 276, 277, 278
    high school graduates and dropouts, 102
    internet usage, 423
    labor force status of high school dropouts, 382
    leisure activities of high school seniors, 142
    with master's degrees, 270, 271, 272
    mathematics achievement levels by age, 122
    mathematics scores by grade, 127
    percentage of population enrolled in school, 6
    postsecondary institutions
        employment in, 229
        enrollment in, 187, 189, 210, 211, 212, 213
        faculty in, 232, 236, 238
    poverty rates, 21
    in public charter and traditional public schools, 97
    reading levels by age, 113
    reading scores by age, 110
    reading scores and achievement levels of fourth-graders, 114
    reading scores of fourth- and eighth-graders, 116
    SAT scores for college-bound seniors, 131
    science scores and achievement levels by grade, 128
    science scores of eighth-graders in public schools, 129
    unemployment rate, 375
    violence and drug use on school property, 150
Women's colleges, 221
Work experience. *See also* Teaching experience
    computer usage, 427
    of principals, 82
Work load of faculty in postsecondary institutions, 233, 234
Writing achievement levels by grade, 117

Year-round schools, 153
Years of school completed and level of attainment, 8. *See also* Educational attainment

Zoology, degrees in, 282